M000250469

TLA
VIDEO & DVD
GUIDE

THE DISCERNING
FILM LOVER'S GUIDE
2005

DAVID BLEILER,
EDITOR

ST. MARTIN'S GRIFFIN
New York

TLA VIDEO & DVD GUIDE
THE DISCERNING FILM LOVER'S GUIDE
2005

Edited by David Bleiler

MANAGING EDITOR/DESIGNER
Eric Moore

ASSOCIATE EDITORS
David Gorgos
Ann M. Yarabinee

CONTRIBUTING EDITOR
Steven D. Segal

CONTRIBUTING WRITERS
Darren Chadwick
PJ Chaykin
Maurene Cooper
Scott Cranin
Tom Fischer
Dean C. Galanis
Dan Gasiewski
Claire Brown Kohler
Mekado Murphy
Raymond Murray
Bill Parker
Irv Slifkin
Geo. Stewart

CONTENTS

Introduction

This year marks the 25th year that VHS has been available to the public. It's been a great and prosperous quarter century for the format, but alas its time has come to go the route of the LP, the 8-track and Beta. This will be the last year in which we include VHS pricing in the TLA Video & DVD Guide. It's a move meant to reflect the overwhelming popularity of DVD, which for many video stores across the country is now the only format available for rental or sale.

Even with this hardware revolution that's afoot, don't get rid of your old, reliable VCR just yet. Even though you will be hard-pressed in 2005 to find new releases available on VHS, there are still thousands of titles that have yet to be made available on DVD, and some stores are still carrying a substantial VHS catalog. So if you can't find *Bringing Up Baby* on DVD, it's nice to know it's still available somewhere on VHS.

With the ever-changing video industry, we have attempted to keep pace with each and every development. Our DVD pricing information is more complete, and some of our reviews include DVD-specific information.

The TLA Video & DVD Guide is presented in an easy-to-read A–Z listing, and includes over 10,000 reviews, hundred of photos, and an exhaustive index and cross-reference system. We only include titles for review that are available on VHS or DVD, though many may not be available for sale.

We should point out that we are quite selective as to what we have chosen to review. It's not our goal to include every film ever made, but to bring attention to films that we feel have achieved artistic success, amassed some popularity, or made an impact — past or present — on the art form. So please be aware that there are thousands of films that would have received one- or two-star reviews that are not included here.

We've made a few changes just to spice things up a bit. Throughout the book you will find Favorite Line, a memorable quote from a film that can be from a classic — or not-so-classic.

In the last chapter of the book, you will find ETS — Estimated Ticket Sales. A form of inflation factoring, this list suggests the most popular films and stars of all time. Obviously no one could ever know every single ticket sold, but this equation serves as a barometer to compare films from various decades in an industry that only looks at gross income.

The history of TLA is important in understanding our commitment to film. TLA Video was established in 1985 as a subsidiary of the Theater of the Living Arts, one of the country's leading repertory cinemas. With the advent of video and the unfortunate demise of rep (which hopefully will make a welcome comeback), we concentrated our energies on the home–video market with the same vigor as we did our theater.

This enthusiasm also went into the production of this film guide. It is my hope that our love, regard and knowledge of film can be found on every page, and that in some small way we can help continue the great tradition of the cinema to the casual viewer looking for a good film to watch tonight, or to a generation or two unfamiliar with our glorious cinematic past. —*David Bleiler*

About the Editor

David Bleiler has been involved in the film and video industry since the 1970s. He has worked in theatrical exhibition as manager and programmer of the Roxy Screening Rooms; in publishing as Senior Editor of *Home Viewer Magazine* and *Video Extra*, Managing Editor of the *New York Metro Herald*, Editor of *Rewind* magazine; and is currently the buyer for TLA Video.

EXPLANATION OF TEXT

Alphabetization:

The guide is alphabetized in word order, not letter order; therefore *All That Jazz* would come before *Alligator*. Also, foreign titles adhere to the English rule concerning A, An and The beginning a sentence: whereas *The Godfather* would be listed under G, *La Cage aux Folles* would be listed under C, *Das Boot* under B, etc.

Foreign articles include:

French: *La, Le, Les, Un, Une*
German: *Das, Die*
Italian: *I, Il, La, Le*
Spanish: *El, La*

(American films beginning with *El* are listed under E)

With the exception of *Mrs.*, abbreviations are alphabetized under the word's full spelling:

Mr. Smith Goes to Washington is under *Mister*;
Dr. Strangelove is under *Doctor*;
The St. Valentine's Day Massacre is under *Saint*.

Pricing:

Prices listed are as of publication date.

VHS prices currently range from $20 to $100 for new releases, and $7 to $25 for catalog titles. With the decline of VHS, some studios are choosing to eliminate VHS after its initial release. VHS pricing therefore is subject to change.

DVD prices currently range from $25 to $40 for new releases, and $10 to $30 for catalog titles. Many new releases are reduced in price six to nine months after their initial release, so please call for updated information.

In a case when a title has no price, that title was unavailable for sale at publication date; but it's possible it could be reissued at a later date. Please call for updated information.

Index Listings:

There are several instances in which a film can be found in the indexes but lacks a corresponding review. This is to make the indexes more complete and therefore more useful. However, only films on video have been mentioned.

Ordering:

To order any title listed in the *TLA Video and DVD Guide 2005* please visit **www.tlavideo.com** or call 800-333-8521. TLA offers special rates to institutions and individuals placing large orders.

Anatomy of a Review

Title   (Year, Running Time, Country, Director)   *Cast*

Some Like It Hot

(1959, 122 min, US, Billy Wilder) *Jack Lemmon, Tony Curtis, Marilyn Monroe, Joe E. Brown, George Raft, Pat O'Brien.* Director Wilder's masterpiece rates as one of the funniest American comedies of all time, and it only gets better with age. Lemmon and Curtis, at their comic best, star as down-and-out musicians in 1920s Chicago who, upon witnessing the St. Valentine's Day Massacre, don wig and dress and join an all-female band to escape the murderous thugs looking for them. Marilyn is Sugar Kane, the band's beautiful blonde singer who the boys are enraptured by. Curtis romances MM (out of drag, of course) and Lemmon is courted by millionaire Brown ("Well, nobody's perfect"). They just don't come any better than this. ★★★★ VHS: $9.99; DVD: $14.99

Rating   Pricing Info
(If no price is listed, the film is currently not available for sale)

A.I. Artificial Intelligence

(2001, 145 min, US, Steven Spielberg) *Haley Joel Osment, Jude Law, Frances O'Connor, William Hurt, Brendan Gleeson, Sam Robards.* Stanley Kubrick is apparently alive and well, having directed about two thirds of the Steven Spielberg collaboration *A.I.* Or at least that's the impression one could take away from this companion piece to *2001* and *Close Encounters*, which also succeeds in being a visionary work all its own. In the future, the polar ice caps have melted, limiting land mass for humans. Lifelike robots have been created to take on tasks in the service industry (sex, housekeeping, etc). A corporation led by Hurt thinks it's broken the final frontier in creating a prototype robot named David, capable of understanding, giving and needing love. As David, Osment gives a nuanced and deeply affecting performance, conveying the complexity of a programmed being in conflict with its emotions. Chapter two sends this flesh-and-chip Pinocchio on a quest to find its Blue Fairy to make him human. The final part, which seems at first to be an epilog, surprises by going further, tying the first two acts together, and, in sentimental and sentient Spielberg fashion, exploring nothing less than the meaning of life. Spielberg juggles Kubrick's cool cynicism and his own optimism, and they clash in electrifying, fascinating and sometimes frustrating ways. Seamless special effects are handled subtly, as Spielberg lets the acting and story remain at the forefront. This is a singular, dazzling medley of two masters that resists weepy-eyed mysticism, opting instead for provocation of thought and the exhilaration of craft. ★★★½ DVD Letterbox 2-disc set: $14.99, DVD Pan & Scan 2-disc set: $14.99, VHS: $9.99

À la Mode

(1994, 90 min, France, Rémy Duchemin) *Jean Yanne, Ken Higelin, François Hautesserre.* Can you say "French fluff"? In some regards, this is too soft a term for this mildly enjoyable but ultimately wispy comedy. In keeping with the genre of "Sex and the French Teenager," *À la Mode* follows the ever eventful life of young Fausto — from the bicycle accident that leaves him orphaned to his apprenticeship with a Jewish tailor in Paris. It is not an exaggeration to say that practically nothing by way of significant story or character development comes Fausto's way, but he does, almost magically, find himself becoming a prestigious fashion designer — overnight! The standard stuff is on display here: the coy redhead with whom he gets his first lay, the good-hearted best friend with a talent for farting the tunes of Beethoven . . . beginning to get the picture? Still, the film is amiable, gooey fun for those in search of hollow entertainment. (aka: *Fausto*) (French with English subtitles) ★★½ DVD: $19.99

À Nos Amours (To Our Loves)

(1983, 102 min, France, Maurice Pialat) *Sandrine Bonnaire, Evelyne Ker, Dominique Besnehard, Maurice Pialat.* A beautifully rendered portrait of a sexually explosive young girl and her tumultuous home life. Sixteen-year-old Suzanne faces the wrath of a neurotic mother, a withdrawn father and an abusive brother because of her casually nubile air and promiscuous wanderings. In this fascinating study of a smoldering family climate, Bonnaire (*Vagabond*) charges the role of the troubled teenager with a powerfully erotic presence. (French with English subtitles) ★★★½

À Nous la Liberté

(1931, 97 min, France, René Clair) *Henri Marchand, Raymond Corby, Rolla France.* A surreal and satirical attack on automation and industrialization, this intoxicating, brilliantly executed romp follows the exploits of a bum who becomes a millionaire only to realize that he was happier poor. The central character and many comic scenes provided the inspiration for Charlie Chaplin's *Modern Times*. (French with English subtitles) ★★★★ DVD Criterion Collection: $29.99, VHS: $19.99

Aaron Loves Angela

(1975, 98 min, US, Gordon Parks, Jr.) *Kevin Hooks, Irene Cara, Ernestine Jackson, Moses Gunn, Robert Hooks.* In this pleasing, updated "Romeo and Juliet" set in Harlem, Aaron, a black youth, falls in love with a beautiful Puerto Rican girl, Angela. Surprisingly involving and thankfully devoid of clichés. Music by José Feliciano. ★★★

Abandon

(2002, 99 min, US, Stephen Gaghan) *Katie Holmes, Benjamin Bratt, Charlie Hunnam, Zooey Deschanel, Fred Ward, Gabrielle Union.* Holmes plays a promising business major who comes under the scrutiny of detective Bratt when he's assigned the missing persons case of Holmes' oddball ex-boyfriend. Most people (including Holmes) believe the wealthy eccentric just left for another country, until Holmes starts catching glimpses of him on campus. Marketed as a thriller, *Abandon* is really just a wan psychological drama with some intermittent suspense scenes. It never really engages, and the "shocking" revelation, coupled with a clichéd, silly denouement, renders the film pointless and empty. ★½ DVD Letterbox: $29.99, DVD Pan & Scan: $29.99, VHS: $9.99

Abandon Ship!

(1957, 97 min, GB, Richard Sale) *Tyrone Power, Mai Zetterling, Lloyd Nolan, Stephen Boyd.* When a luxury ocean liner hits a derelict mine in the waters of the Atlantic, the surviving passengers must cram into the only lifeboat, now commanded by second mate Power. As they fight the elements and each other, it soon becomes a struggle for survival. A sometimes rousing, tension-filled drama. (aka: *Seven Waves Away*) ★★★

Abbott and Costello Meet Dr. Jekyll and Mr. Hyde

(1953, 77 min, US, Charles Lamont) *Bud Abbott, Lou Costello, Boris Karloff, Reginald Denny.* After much success meeting Frankenstein and Captain Kidd, Abbott and Costello set their sights on Robert Louis Stevenson's famous doc and his alter ego. In Victorian London, Bud & Lou are policemen on the trail of Jekyll, or is it Hyde? Some good laughs though the film is not as consistently funny as their earlier efforts. ★★½

Abbott and Costello Meet Frankenstein

(1949, 83 min, US, Charles Barton) *Bud Abbott, Lou Costello, Bela Lugosi, Lon Chaney, Jr., Glenn Strange, Jane Randolph.* Bud and Lou found great success in this very funny horror spoof. The boys get involved with Frankenstein (Strange), Dracula (Lugosi) and the Wolf Man (Chaney) — even the Invisible Man makes an "appearance." There are plenty of snappy one-liners and silly shenanigans, and Bud and Lou's enjoyment is clearly infectious. ★★★½

Abe Lincoln in Illinois

(1940, 110 min, US, John Cromwell) *Raymond Massey, Gene Lockhart, Ruth Gordon, Mary Howard.* Featuring a career performance by Massey as our 16th president, this outstanding biography of Abraham Lincoln, based on Robert Sherwood's Pulitzer Prize-winning play, is American history on film at its finest. The story covers Lincoln's life from his young adult years (including his romances with Ann Rutledge and Mary Todd) to his election as president. The Lincoln-Douglas debate scene is a particular highlight. ★★★★ VHS: $14.99

Aberdeen

(2001, 113 min, GB/Norway/Sweden, Hans Petter Moland) *Stellan Skarsgård, Lena Headey, Ian Hart, Charlotte Rampling.* A promiscuous, coke-snorting, young corporate climber receives a last request from her dying mother: to come with her estranged, alcoholic father (whom she hasn't spoken to in years) to her deathbed to say good-bye. Certainly this premise has vast potential to be an emotionally rich, moving film, but Aberdeen squanders this promise to make way for a collection of awkward, uncomfortable scenes between characters who are, quite frankly, a pair of jerks. Nice photography, a moody score, some good acting (especially by Hart, who plays the only appealing character) and a handful of touching moments can't

À Nous la Liberté

Dermot Mulroney, Hope Davis and Jack Nicholson in *About Schmidt*

compensate for the surface-level pointlessness of it all. Even the predictably "heartwarming" ending is unsatisfying. ★★ DVD Letterbox: $29.99

Abigail's Party

(1977, 105 min, GB, Mike Leigh) *Alison Steadman, Tim Stern.* Steadman stars as an overwrought hostess of a small get-together with the neighbors. Clearly adapted from the stage, the action is filmed on video and never leaves the claustrophobic confines of her living room. As she and her guests top off with gin and tonic after gin and tonic, the sparks begin to fly and her highly strung husband becomes all the more agitated. While the piece is filled with several hilarious moments, the overall tenor becomes more and more nerve-wracking due to Steadman's almost fascistic insistence that her guests "drink up." ★★½ DVD: $29.99, VHS: $29.99

The Abominable Dr. Phibes

(1971, 94 min, GB, Robert Fuest) *Vincent Price, Joseph Cotten, Terry-Thomas, Peter Jeffrey, Hugh Griffith.* Price camps it up in one of the few horror films which successfully marries laughs and shivers. Cotten and Terry-Thomas are just two of the victims on whom Price seeks vengeance for his disfigurement and his wife's death. The Art Deco sets give the film a stylish look. (Sequel: *Dr. Phibes Rises Again*) ★★★ DVD: $14.99

About a Boy

(2002, 101 min, GB, Paul Weitz & Chris Weitz) *Hugh Grant, Nicholas Hoult, Rachel Weisz, Toni Collette, Victoria Smurfit.* Leaving behind his amusing mannerisms, Grant turns that rarefied corner from movie star to accomplished actor with a multilayered portrait that is funny, touching and quite poised. An enjoyable and very smart adaptation of Nick Hornby's novel, *About a Boy* allows Grant to be more grown-up on-screen than he's ever been before while portraying a character who is anything but mature. Grant plays Will, a rich ne'er-do-well who avoids work, relationships and responsibility. When he thinks he's found the perfect scam to meet women, he unwittingly enters the life of 12-year-old Marcus, a misfit whose friendship offers Will some much-needed stability in exchange for paternal guidance for the fatherless boy. The Weitz brothers wouldn't appear to be the first choice for a story that requires nuance and subtlety, but they, too, abandon some stock traits without forgetting how to wrestle a laugh. The sardonic, sharp screenplay allows the directors to display uncharacteristic sentiment and maintain an edgy, cheeky mindset. ★★★½ DVD Letterbox: $14.99, DVD Pan & Scan: $14.99, VHS: $9.99

About Adam

(2001, 97 min, US/Ireland, Gerard Stembridge) *Stuart Townsend, Frances O'Connor, Charlotte Bradley, Kate Hudson, Alan Maher.* Love 'em and leave 'em Lucy (Hudson, sporting a serviceable Irish accent) falls hard for charmer Adam (Townsend), and wedding bells seem to be in their future. It turns out, however, that Lucy isn't the only member of her family smitten with the lad — and he's more than willing to reciprocate their desire. Off-putting and clunky, *About Adam* is salvaged somewhat by its performances: Townsend, despite his secretive betrayals, remains likable throughout, and Hudson and O'Connor fare well with rather unappealing characters. A snappier pace, wittier script and a good half-hour lost, however, would have gone a long way in making this film more palatable. ★★ DVD Letterbox: $19.99, VHS: $9.99

About Last Night . . .

(1986, 113 min, US, Edward Zwick) *Rob Lowe, Demi Moore, James Belushi, Elizabeth Perkins, George DiCenzo.* David Mamet's play "Sexual Perversity in Chicago" comes to the screen in the form of this sluggish adaptation which fails to fully capture the play's hard edge. Lowe and Moore play Chicago singles who begin an affair, but their relationship suffers from Lowe's lack of commitment. Ditto the film. Belushi and Perkins costar in far more interesting roles as the leads' respective best friends. ★★ DVD: $9.99

About Schmidt

(2002, 124 min, US, Alexander Payne) *Jack Nicholson, Hope Davis, Kathy Bates, Dermot Mulroney, Len Cariou, Howard Hesseman, June Squibb.* The opening scene of director Payne's *About Schmidt*, an indelible portrait of loss and self-discovery, is able to say more about its leading character — without saying a word — than most films can with two hours of dialogue. And then it gets insightful. Warren Schmidt (Nicholson) lives a buttoned-down existence, partly to mask the ennui he's not even aware he feels. An insurance actuary who is retiring after 35 years, Warren is just another nondescript family man who must come to terms with spending his days around the house. But when his wife suddenly dies, Warren is thrust into the unfamiliar terrain of not only taking care of himself, but having to discover a little some-

thing about himself, as well. Based on the novel by Louis Begley, and adapted by Payne and Jim Taylor, *About Schmidt* is so relaxed it may give the impression of immobility, but Payne and his great cast make sure this subtle, often very funny film zings exactly when it should. Its characters are alive, the observations spot-on, and the comedy smart and scintillating. As good as the writing and direction are, however, it is Nicholson that is the heart of *About Schmidt*. The actor leaves no doubt that Warren Schmidt has led a life of quiet desperation, and his ability to embody this man with such integrity, dimension and ordinariness is nothing short of a revelation. It just may be the best performance of a long, illustrious career. ★★★★ DVD Letterbox: $19.99, VHS: $8.99

Above Suspicion

(1943, 90 min, US, Richard Thorpe) *Joan Crawford, Fred MacMurray, Conrad Veidt, Basil Rathbone.* Crawford takes on the Nazis in this standard but nevertheless compelling spy thriller set in 1939. Joan and Fred are newlyweds on a European honeymoon who are asked to do their part for British intelligence. Up against Crawford, who had the benefit of those shoulders, the Germans never had a chance. ★★★ VHS: $19.99

Above the Law

(1988, 99 min, US, Andrew Davis) *Steven Seagal, Pam Grier, Sharon Stone, Henry Silva.* The fact that martial arts macho guy Seagal was allowed to make more movies after this, his debut, must be proof of his being above the laws of common sense. Seagal's performance is robotic, and the story that he gets partial credit for is conventional, convoluted and, at times, preachy. On top of all that, the fight scenes here are surprisingly tame. Director Davis had previously made the half-decent Chuck Norris film *Code of Silence* and would go on to make *The Package* and *The Fugitive*, but here his talents seem to be in hibernation; there are few action sequences of note. ★★ DVD: $14.99, VHS: $9.99

Absence of Malice

(1981, 116 min, US, Sydney Pollack) *Paul Newman, Sally Field, Wilford Brimley, Melinda Dillon, Bob Balaban, Josef Sommer.* Newman's and Field's first-rate performances distinguish this absorbing social drama about Newman's efforts to clear his name after reporter Field is duped into printing an article falsely implicating him in the murder of a union leader. Dillon gives a touching performance as Newman's girlfriend also affected by the story. Screenwriter Kurt Luedtke (a former reporter) has fashioned an insightful and penetrating treatise on the responsibility of the press and of the manipulation of truth and the media. Brimley nearly steals the show as a no-nonsense prosecutor. ★★★ DVD: $19.99

Absence of the Good

(1999, 99 min, US, John Flynn) *Stephen Baldwin, Rob Knepper, Shawn Huff, Tyne Daly, Allen Garfield.* In this creepy little thriller, a Salt Lake City detective, Caleb Barnes (Baldwin), returns to work following the death of his six-year-old son. Taking on a brutal case involving a serial killer, Caleb pursues clues that show the murderer was abused as a child. A psychiatrist (Daly) assigned to the investigation helps Caleb personally and professionally, but the film passes on the chance to explore the duality of child abuse/loss of a child completely. Director Flynn has made a wholly servicable B-movie, with a nice twist among the predictable genre elements, but much of this low-budget film seems cheesy. ★★ VHS: $21.99

The Absent-Minded Professor

(1961, 97 min, US, Robert Stevenson) *Fred MacMurray, Nancy Olson, Keenan Wynn, Tommy Kirk, Ed Wynn, Leon Ames.* The quintessential '60s Disney comedy! MacMurray plays the title character, who invents a bouncy substance called flubber that can make cars fly and basketball players do amazing things. Problem is, no one will believe him, and the town's evil tycoon is out to steal the invention. A fun story with lively special effects and a breezy, gee-whiz attitude. (Sequel: *Son of Flubber*) (Remade in 1997 as *Flubber*) ★★★ DVD Colorized version: $19.99, DVD Black & White: $19.99, VHS: $9.99

Absolut Warhola

(2001, 80 min, Germany, Stanislaw Mucha) Located in the "Ruthenian Bermuda Triangle" (the land between Slovakia, Poland and Ukraine) is Europe's only Pop Art Museum. Mucha's lighthearted documentary traces the roots of America's Pop icon Andy Warhol, whose family heritage can be traced to the town of Medzilaborce and the neighboring village of Miková. His clan have always lived here, and they always will. Andrijku, alias Andy, inspires the imagination of his surviving relatives. Everyone has their own vision of the region's most famous son. Nobody knew him, but everybody talks about him. Warhol, the famous hometown boy, sent original works of art to his unsuspecting relatives back home, but they made them into toy trumpets for their children. With a gentle, humanistic touch, the film swings from the art of Warhol to his relatives – all characters in their own right – and their "art" of coming to grips with life despite poverty and hopelessness. Most memorable is Warhol's quite funny 90-year-old aunt. ★★★ DVD: $24.99, VHS: $24.99

Absolute Beginners

(1986, 107 min, GB, Julien Temple) *Eddie O'Connell, Patsy Kensit, David Bowie, James Fox, Ray Davies, Ege Ferret, Anita Morris, Sade, Slim Gaillard.* Temple's rousing musical is a journey into the heart of the swinging teenage scene of London in the late 1950s and the brutal racism which still afflicts that city today. O'Connell stars as a young photographer drawn into the music and fashion worlds; Kensit is the designer he's in love with. Bowie makes a neat cameo as a slick associate of the nefarious Fox, and he sings the title tune, too. The music, as orchestrated by jazz giant Gil Evans, is unbeatable and includes a truly seductive number by Sade. ★★★½ DVD: $14.99

Absolute Power

(1997, 120 min, US, Clint Eastwood) *Clint Eastwood, Gene Hackman, Ed Harris, Laura Linney, Judy Davis, Scott Glenn, Dennis Haysbert, E.G. Marshall.* There's more to worry about than campaign finances in President Alan Richmond's White House; the Secret Service just murdered his girlfriend, and hampering a cover-up is the witness who was hiding in the next room. In Eastwood's sleek, competent thriller, efficiently adapted by William Goldman (based on David Baldacci's novel), politics does indeed breed strange bedfellows. Eastwood plays Luther Whitney, a thief who is now on the run after witnessing the handiwork of President Richmond (played with great vigor and venom by Hackman) and his staff. All of Washington, D.C., becomes a board game of cat and mouse as Whitney tries to elude government agents and the police. Though the story isn't always plausi-

ble, *Absolute Power* is a wild ride up and down the Beltway all the same. ★★★ DVD: $14.99, VHS: $9.99, VHS Letterbox: $9.99

Absolution

(1978, 105 min, GB, Anthony Page) *Richard Burton, Dominic Guard, Dai Bradley, Billy Connelly.* Another wicked thriller from Anthony Shaffer, the author of *Sleuth*. Burton stars as a "holier-than-thou" priest whose teaching efforts at a Catholic boarding school are mocked by his mischievous star pupil, with tragic results. Though made in 1978, the film was not released in this country until 1988, four years after Burton's death. ★★★

Abuse

(1983, 85 min, US, Arthur Bressan, Jr.) *Richard Ryder, Raphael Sbarge.* This daring, powerful yet sensitive account of a battered adolescent's coming to grips with his abusive parents and his awakening homosexuality caused quite a stir in the gay community with its positive approach to man/boy love. While filming a documentary on child abuse for his master's thesis, 35-year-old Larry (Ryder) befriends 14-year-old Thomas (Sbarge), the victim of abuse from his violent mother and father. Their nurturing relationship, spurred by the advances of Thomas, eventually turns to love. A controversial film which isn't quite as incendiary as it may appear. ★★★ VHS: $39.99

The Abyss

(1989, 145 min, US, James Cameron) *Ed Harris, Mary Elizabeth Mastrantonio, Michael Biehn, Leo Burmester, Todd Graff.* Outstanding special effects and production design highlight this suspenseful underwater science-fiction adventure. Though Cameron combines the same excitement and tension he created in *Aliens* and *The Terminator*, he shifts the pace halfway through the film, and the result is a heart-pounding thriller which gradually becomes an under-the-sea *E.T.* Harris stars as the commander of an oil rigging outfit who makes contact with an alien being. Forget the similarly themed *Deep Star Six* and the silly *Leviathan* which came before it, for this is far superior entertainment. ★★★ DVD Letterbox 2-disc Special Edition: $26.99, DVD Pan & Scan Basic Edition: $14.99, DVD Basic Edition: $14.99, VHS: $9.99

Accattone

(1961, 120 min, Italy, Pier Paolo Pasolini) *Franco Citti, Franca Pasut, Silvana Corsini.* Pasolini's first feature film is a harrowing, realistic and unsentimental look inside the slums of Rome, where its denizens — the prostitutes, hustlers and petty thieves — attempt to eke out an existence any way they can. Within this underworld of corruption is Accattone (Citti), a young pimp who is torn between the easy pickings on the street and his efforts, motivated by love, to go straight. A brutal slice-of-life film that documents Pasolini's lifelong obsession with the outcasts of society. (Italian with English subtitles) ★★★½ DVD Letterbox: $29.99, VHS: $29.99

Accident

(1967, 105 min, GB, Joseph Losey) *Dirk Bogarde, Michael York, Jacqueline Sassard, Stanley Baker, Vivien Merchant.* Harold Pinter wrote the screenplay adaptation for this penetrating and thought-provoking examination of a love affair between a professor (Bogarde) and his student (Sassard). Bogarde and York both deliver sterling performances in this complex psychological drama. ★★★½

The Accidental Tourist

(1988, 121 min, US, Lawrence Kasdan) *William Hurt, Kathleen Turner, Geena Davis, Bill Pullman, Amy Wright, David Ogden Stiers.* Hurt stars in this Oscar-nominated adaptation of Anne Tyler's whimsical best-seller as an emotionally numb travel-guide writer who must begin life anew after the death of his young son and separation from his wife (Turner). As he sets out into the world, he becomes involved, almost unwittingly, with an eccentric dog trainer (Davis) who slowly reawakens his long-dormant feelings. The film, like its hero, is leisurely and a bit distant but also enormously endearing, thanks mostly to a refreshingly open and enchanting performance by Oscar-winner Davis. ★★★ DVD Letterbox: $14.99

The Accompanist

(1992, 111 min, France, Claude Miller) *Romane Bohringer, Elena Safonova, Richard Bohringer.* Sophie, a naïve, unworldly 20-year-old pianist in Nazi-occupied France, is hired as accompanist to a concert vocalist, a beautiful and talented woman who, with her industrialist husband, is viewed as a collaborator. Sophie is an accompanist not only in concerts and practice sessions: She views it as her life's role, and not even the devastation and upheaval of war shakes her position of observer and accomplice. The film's denouement is curiously anticlimactic, yet is an unnerving reflection of Sophie's suppressed affect and despondency. In the end, a disturbing character study of an isolated individual adrift in a world of turmoil. (French with English subtitles) ★★★

The Accused

(1988, 110 min, US, Jonathan Kaplan) *Jodie Foster, Kelly McGillis, Bernie Coulson, Leo Rossi, Ann Hearn, Steve Antin.* A harrowing and hard-hitting look at the emotional and moral consequences of rape. Foster won an Oscar for her stunning and gritty portrayal of a back room gang-rape victim who struggles to regain her self-respect while battling an insensitive legal system. McGillis is compelling as the prosecuting attorney who becomes entangled in her own moral sense of right and wrong. Based on an actual and highly publicized incident, this superbly acted and tightly focused film expertly examines the pain endured by the victims of rape long after the crime has been committed. ★★★ DVD: $14.99, VHS: $14.99

Ace Ventura, Pet Detective

(1994, 85 min, US, Tom Shadyac) *Jim Carrey, Courteney Cox, Sean Young, Tone Loc, Dan Marino.* This nauseating comedy became a surprise box-office success, sending Carrey to the unlikely ranks of stardom. To be fair, Carrey is an outstanding physical comedian, but his schtick needs the support of an intelligent script and that is what's most lacking here. The story follows the exploits of Carrey's Ace Ventura, who retrieves lost or stolen pets for their heartbroken owners. Hired by the Miami Dolphins to locate their kidnapped mascot, he finds himself doing battle with Miami's police chief, played by Young, who yawns her way through the film with the excitement of a tranquilized basset hound. ★½ DVD: $14.99, VHS: $9.99

Ace Ventura: When Nature Calls

(1995, 92 min, US, Steve Oedekerk) *Jim Carrey, Simon Callow, Ian McNeice, Bob Gunton, Tommy Davidson, Adewale Akinnuoye-Agbaje.* This annoying sequel starts off with a couple of funny and silly laughs with a way over-the-top Carrey shamelessly mugging and making idiotic faces. A couple good sight gags (and a William Shatner imitation) seem to get the film rolling. However, the ridiculous, boring plot takes over — about Ace tracking down the sacred bat of an African village — and no matter how much Carrey wiggles his ears or says, "All righty," this is a poor excuse for comedy and enough to insult the very memory of those broadly played Jerry Lewis comedies of the 1960s — for which Carrey obviously has an affection. No one expects high-brow from Ace, but Carrey is such a talented comedian we all have a right to expect better. ★½ DVD: $14.99, VHS: $9.99

Aclá

(1992, 86 min, Italy, Aurelio Grimaldi) *Luigi Maria Burruano, Francesco Cusimano, Lucia Sardo, Tony Sperandeo.* The inordinately harsh life of Sicilian peasant miners — and one blond, 11-year-old boy in particular — in 1930s Italy is the subject of this unrelentingly grim drama. Young Aclá, a handsome youth with a streak of independence, comes of age to accompany his father and two older brothers to the underground sulfur mines where they work six days a week for little pay and food. Only his dreams of the sea and escape enable Aclá to struggle against the surrounding inhumanity. Using poetic (pederastic?) license, the director displays all of the workers in the excessively hot mines laboring only in loincloths. (Italian with English subtitles) ★★½ VHS: $59.99

Across 110th Street

(1972, 102 min, US, Barry Shear) *Anthony Quinn, Yaphet Kotto, Anthony Franciosa, Richard Ward, Paul Benjamin, Ed Bernard, Antonio Fargas, Norma Donaldson.* Three black men hit a Mafia cash drop in Harlem for $300,000, killing family members, associates and two policemen, precipitating an intensive manhunt — one conducted by the police, the other by the mob. Racism is the permeating undercurrent, defining the tensions between the Mafia and their Harlem counterparts, and mirrored in the relationship between white, old-guard captain Quinn and black lieutenant Kotto. The film is harsh, rough-hewn and uncompromising, filled with raw anger and seething violence, and bolstered by on-target performances from the entire cast. ★★★ DVD Letterbox: $14.99

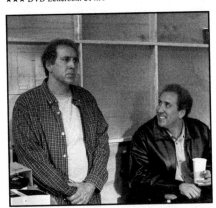

Nicolas Cage plays both Charlie and Donald Kaufman in *Adaptation*

Across the Pacific

(1942, 97 min, US, John Huston) *Humphrey Bogart, Mary Astor, Sydney Greenstreet, Sen Yung, Richard Loo.* Director Huston and his *Maltese Falcon* stars Bogart, Astor and Greenstreet reteamed for this involving spy thriller. Bogey goes undercover and sets sail for the Orient to get the goods on agent Greenstreet. Astor is the mysterious passenger romanced by Bogart. Suspenseful action, more humor than would be expected, and solid performances by all make this a winner. ★★★ VHS: $19.99

Acting on Impulse

(1993, 93 min, US, Sam Irvin) *Linda Fiorentino, C. Thomas Howell, Nancy Allen, Dick Sargent, Paul Bartel, Adam Ant, Mary Woronov, Isaac Hayes, Patrick Bauchau, Zelda Rubinstein.* Made for cable, this comic thriller has its tongue planted firmly in cheek, as with director Irvin's previous outing *Guilty as Charged.* The ravishing Fiorentino plays a "scream queen" goddess of B-horror films. After a fatal argument in which her producer is found dead, Fiorentino sets out for a little R&R, where she is stalked by "adoring" fans. Then the body count starts piling up. Featuring a little lesbian teasing between a playful Fiorentino and Allen, and a steamy Fiorentino-Howell sex scene, the film is leisurely paced, offers a few well-placed jabs at the horror film industry, and has an eclectic supporting line-up. ★★½

Action in the North Atlantic

(1943, 127 min, US, Lloyd Bacon) *Humphrey Bogart, Raymond Massey, Alan Hale, Ruth Gordon, Sam Levene.* Bogart heads a good cast in this stirring WWII actioner with Bogey and Massey as Merchant Marine officers leading their men in action against the Nazis in the North Atlantic. ★★★

Action Jackson

(1988, 95 min, US, Craig R. Baxley) *Carl Weathers, Craig T. Nelson, Vanity, Sharon Stone, Bill Duke.* Weathers stars as the title character in this stiffly acted but enjoyable panoply of car chases, explosions and fistfights. Weathers' Jackson is an ex-cop who is determined to uncover the evil doings of an unscrupulous businessman (Nelson) who had been the instrument of Jackson's fall from grace. Vanity is the token dame who accompanies Weathers on his vengeful rampage. A pyrotechnical juggernaut that is short on script and ideas, but combustible fun nonetheless. ★★½ DVD: $9.99, VHS: $9.99

An Actor's Revenge

(1963, 113 min, Japan, Kon Ichikawa) *Kazuo Hasegawa, Fujiko Yamamoto, Ayako Wakao.* With magnificently stylized sets, vibrant color and a spectacular performance by Kabuki actor Hasegawa, this tale of revenge and murder ranks as one of Japan's greatest films. Set in the early part of the 19th century, Hasegawa, an *onnagata* (female impersonator) of the Kabuki theatre, discovers the identity of the three nobles who forced the suicide of his parents many years before. In an elaborate scheme of revenge, our hero/heroine exacts a plot that does not have him simply kill them, but rather have the men turn against themselves or die at their own hands. A complex period melodrama that concerns itself with opposites: love/hate, illusion/reality, masculinity/femininity. (Japanese with English subtitles) ★★★★ VHS: $29.99

Adam Had Four Sons

(1941, 81 min, US, Gregory Ratoff) *Ingrid Bergman, Warner Baxter, Susan Hayward, Richard Denning, Fay Wray.* Bergman is in Bette Davis/*All This and Heaven, Too* territory as a governess looking after four children after their mother dies. Baxter is the father, and a young Hayward plays the "bad" girl who pits the family against each other. Warm dramatics and a pleasing performance by Bergman more than compensate for the sometimes predictable direction of the story line. ★★★ DVD: $24.99, VHS: $19.99

Adam Sandler's Eight Crazy Nights

(2002, 86 min, US, Seth Kearsley) *Voices of: Adam Sandler, Jackie Titone, Austin Stout, Kevin Nealon, Rob Schneider.* Having ever seen Adam Sandler in action, one would think that his exaggerated clowning would actually translate quite well in an animated film. And, at times, it does. Unfortunately, those moments are so few and far between that they are all but lost amid the excessive poop jokes and gratuitous product placement. Sandler handles the bulk of the vocal duties playing at least three of the main characters (four if you count the deer). The eight musical numbers (all written by Sandler) sprinkled sporadically throughout the film are barely worth mentioning. The worthless story involves a bitter alcoholic who learns the meaning of the holiday spirit from a couple of midgets. The whys and hows don't really seem to matter. Perhaps the biggest gag comes in the closing minutes; the "surprise" happy ending — that's neither surprising, happy or satisfying — is a cop-out. ★½ DVD 2-disc Special Edition: $26.99, VHS: $14.99

Adam's Rib

(1949, 101 min, US, George Cukor) *Katharine Hepburn, Spencer Tracy, Judy Holliday, David Wayne, Tom Ewell, Jean Hagen.* In their sixth film together, Hepburn and Tracy demonstrate such a magnificent rapport on-screen that they make (with the exception of *Woman of the Year*) their prior film appearances together look like blind dates by comparison. Kate and Spence play lawyers on opposite sides of an attempted murder case. He's the prosecutor, she's the defense attorney. In her first major role, Holliday is the defendant accused of trying to kill her philandering husband (Ewell). Garson Kanin and Ruth Gordon's wonderfully funny screenplay is full of sublime observations on romantic expectations and the roles men and women play (or are expected to play), and director Cukor deftly brings together slapstick, sophistication and romance to create a classic battle-of-the-sexes comedy. ★★★★ DVD: $19.99, VHS: $14.99

Favorite Line: "Lawyers should never marry other lawyers. This is called in-breeding; from this comes idiot children . . . and other lawyers." —*David Wayne as Kip Lurie*

Adam's Rib

(1992, 77 min, USSR, Vyacheslav Krishtofovich) *Inna Churikova, Yelena Bogdanova, Svetlana Ryabova.* Based on the novel "House of Young Women" by Anatole Kourtchatkine, *Adam's Rib* is a wonderfully endearing story revolving around three generations of Russian women (a grandmother, mother and her two daughters) all sharing the same apartment. The film slips in elements of coming-of-age and parental disputes with social commentary on the new elements of capitalism in Russia. Lida, the older daughter, is having an affair with a married man while the younger daughter is a rebel and a

A

savvy businessperson. Mother is trying to make ends meet, take care of her ailing mother and she just happens to be picked up by a farmer at her job. A poignant and quite remarkable film. (Russian with English subtitles) ★★★★

Adaptation.

(2002, 114 min, US, Spike Jonze) *Nicolas Cage, Meryl Streep, Chris Cooper, Tilda Swinton, Brian Cox, Maggie Gyllenhaal, Ron Livingston.* Adaptation of a species to a planet, adaptation of a book to a screenplay, adaptation of the individual to society . . . *Adaptation* considers it all, over millennia, between brothers, in the swamp primeval. Screenwriter Charlie Kaufman (Cage), a ghost on the set of his own movie (*Being John Malkovich*), is approached to write the adaptation of "The Orchid Thief," written by Susan Orlean (Streep), a *New Yorker* writer. The story moves between Kaufman's tortured existence, of which his writing experience is only one aspect, and Orlean's experience in the Everglades researching the book. As Kaufman struggles with an inability to commit and a massive writer's block, his (fictional) twin brother Donald (Cage delivers the best twins since Jeremy Irons in *Dead Ringers*) connects to others with easy glee and whips out a hackneyed potboiler that sells immediately. Episodic, nonlinear, straddling the gap between inner truths and outer presentation, *Adaptation* makes maximum use of its superlative cast, including the incomparable Streep; and Oscar winner Cooper, who as the orchid thief in question, impacts Orlean's ordered sanity with the gritty force of emotive spontaneity. ★★★★ DVD Letterbox Superbit Edition: $19.99, VHS: $14.99

The Addams Family

(1991, 102 min, US, Barry Sonnenfeld) *Raul Julia, Anjelica Huston, Christopher Lloyd, Christina Ricci, Dan Hedaya, Elizabeth Wilson, Dana Ivey.* Sonnenfeld's hilarious revival of the cult-TV series may be thin on plot but the action flies furiously and the laughs are abundant. Julia and Huston deliver inspired, macabre performances as Gomez and Morticia, the bizarre patriarch and matriarch of Charles Addams' ghoulish family (thankfully, they do justice to the characters created by John Astin and Carolyn Jones). Lloyd feasts on the role of Uncle Fester and young Ricci is devil-

ishly coy as the younger Addams, Wednesday, with a penchant for girl scout cookies made from *real* girl scouts. (Sequel: *Addams Family Values*) ★★★ DVD: $14.99, VHS: $9.99

Addams Family Values

(1993, 87 min, US, Barry Sonnenfeld) *Raul Julia, Anjelica Huston, Christopher Lloyd, Joan Cusack, Christina Ricci, Carol Kane, David Krumholtz.* Dripping with deliciously mordant one-liners, this outlandish sequel to *The Addams Family* is a possibly funnier outing than the original. Morticia (Huston) has a baby, Pubert, much to the delight of Gomez (Julia) and most of the family. The children, however, see the little nipper as nothing more than a usurper and respond to his arrival with murderous zeal. The kids are soon dragged off to summer camp by the baby's new nanny (Cusack), a golddigging black widow with designs on Fester (Lloyd). This broad plot outline is ripe with hilariously morbid jokes and is a sly fable on the revenge of the outcasts. Ricci is especially good as the death-obsessed, pale-faced Wednesday, who supplies the film with its best retorts. ★★★ DVD: $14.99, VHS: $9.99

Addicted to Love

(1997, 100 min, US, Griffin Dunne) *Meg Ryan, Matthew Broderick, Kelly Preston, Tcheky Karyo, Maureen Stapleton.* When his fiancée Linda leaves him for handsome Frenchman Anton, astronomer Sam (Broderick) begins spying on her. He's soon joined by Maggie (Ryan), Anton's former girlfriend, in his *Rear Window* vigil from the abandoned building across the street. Maggie and Sam then engage in a series of revenge schemes and sometimes hilarious bits of malicious "ex"-bashings. Though nasty as it wants to be, *Addicted to Love*'s shortcoming is that it aims for the jugular but often settles for the heart; the mean-spiritedness just isn't consistent. When *Love* loses its edge, it becomes just another dopey romantic comedy. Ryan and Broderick, both of whom can be cloyingly cute, have a wonderful chemistry. ★★½ DVD: $14.99

The Addiction

(1995, 84 min, US, Abel Ferrara) *Lili Taylor, Christopher Walken, Annabella Sciorra, Kathryn Erbe, Paul Calderon.* Needlessly dense, pretentious, and shot so amateurishly as to sometimes look like a student film, *The Addiction* is Ferrara's take on the vampire mythos, equating vampirism with a physical drug addiction and setting it among the angst-ridden, intellectual elite of New York's graduate student culture. Taylor plays a philosophy doctoral student who is bitten by a vampire (Sciorra). She spends the rest of the film trying to come to terms with her new existence. Light on narrative, the film's characters spend most of their time in philosophical discussions, which works completely against the purposes of the film. While the premise of the film is intriguing, *The Addiction* is ultimately a horror film without any scares, a philosophical meditation without any good ideas, and a vampire film without any blood. ★½

L'Addition (The Patsy)

(1984, 93 min, France, Denis Amar) *Richard Berry, Victoria Abril.* This incisive and compelling prison drama stars Berry as an out-of-work actor who gets himself imprisoned when he goes to the aid of a woman accused of shoplifting. From there it is an ever-deepening descent into hell as he becomes the twisted obsession of a sadistic prison guard who follows the rules only as a means to pervert them. (aka: *The Caged Heart*) ★★★

The Adjuster

(1992, 102 min, Canada, Atom Egoyan) *Elias Koteas, Maury Chaykin, Arsinée Khanjian.* Original and bizarre, director Egoyan's twisted tale follows Noah (Koteas), a predatory insurance adjuster who shows up at house fires to comfort the victims and process their claims. He keeps all of his clients in a run-down motel, where he visits them daily, often engaging them in sex (male and female alike). Meanwhile, his wife (Khanjian) is secretly videotaping the graphic sex she watches as part of her job as a government censor. Into the picture comes Bubba (Chaykin), an off-the-wall con artist who convinces the Renders that he wants to use their house. Egoyan uses this odd conglomeration of circumstances to plumb the depths of his characters' existential loneliness and to voyeuristically expose their sexual proclivities. ★★★½

Adoption

(1975, 89 min, Hungary, Márta Mészáros) *Kati Berek, László Szabó, Gyon Gyver Vigh.* Kari wants a child, but her married lover is insensitive to her desire. So it is up to Anna, her newfound friend, to help her fulfill her dream of motherhood and learn about love and survival. A warm and intimate drama exploring a love and friendship between two women. The winner of the Best Film Award at the Berlin Film Festival. (Hungarian with English subtitles) ★★★ VHS: $69.99

Adrenalin, Fear the Rush

(1996, 76 min, US/GB, Albert Pyun) *Christopher Lambert, Natasha Henstridge.* Loud, meandering and pointless, *Adrenalin* is set in the 21st century where plague carriers have been quarantined. Somehow, though it's never explained, the government has created among the secluded carriers a super killing machine. Lambert and Henstridge are the cops who set out to track him down. The film begins swiftly, but immediately lands itself in a prison basement, becoming one long boring chase where the superhuman appears and disappears without explanation. Pyun (*Cyborg*) gives the film a good futuristic look, but knows nothing about maintaining suspense or logic. ★ DVD: $14.99, VHS: $9.99

The Adventurers

(1970, 171 min, US, Lewis Gilbert) *Bekim Fehmiu, Candice Bergen, Ernest Borgnine, Olivia de Havilland, Leigh Taylor-Young, Thommy Berggren, Rossano Brazzi.* The epic, all-star melodrama suffered a blow in the 1970s and died a rather quick death — this bombastic, static adaptation of Harold Robbins' trashy novel may have had something to do with it. Set in a fictional South American country, the story follows a playboy and his romantic conquests, all acted out against political upheaval and hoary plot developments. Everyone seems embarrassed, though Bergen comes off best as an American heiress who suffers tragedy upon tragedy that only bad soap opera can produce. ★ VHS: $14.99

Adventures in Babysitting

(1987, 99 min, US, Chris Columbus) *Elisabeth Shue, Keith Coogan, Anthony Rapp, Vincent D'Onofrio, Penelope Ann Miller, Lolita Davidovich.* There's charm to spare in this entertaining teen comedy with Shue (long before her *Leaving Las Vegas* triumph) a delight as a baby-sitter whose journey into Chicago with her three charges turns into a comic nightmare. Directorial debut for writer Columbus, who would go on to helm such hits as *Home Alone* and *Mrs. Doubtfire*. ★★★ DVD: $14.99

A

The Adventures of Baron Munchausen

(1989, 126 min, GB, Terry Gilliam) *John Neville, Eric Idle, Sarah Polley, Oliver Reed, Jonathan Pryce, Valentina Cortese, Uma Thurman.* The third and final entry in director Gilliam's fantasy trilogy (*Time Bandits* and *Brazil* were before it) is a whimsical, outlandishly funny and visually stunning adventure film chronicling the amazing exploits of the infamous adventurer/explorer/soldier and man-about-town, Baron Munchausen. Set during the late 18th century, the film follows the odyssey taken by a now-older Baron who travels to the Moon, Heaven and numerous exotic locations in-between to help save a small city under siege. ★★★ DVD: $29.99, VHS: $14.99

The Adventures of Buckaroo Banzai

(1984, 103 min, US, W.D. Richter) *Peter Weller, John Lithgow, Ellen Barkin, Jeff Goldblum, Christopher Lloyd.* Renowned neurosurgeon, respected physicist and charismatic rock star . . . he's Buckaroo Banzai — savior of the universe and star of this gonzo sci-fi fantasy. Don't even bother to follow the pretzel-like plot twists; just remember: red lectoids dislike black lectoids, Rastafarians in silver lamé sports coats are on our side, Lord John Whorfin (alias Emilio Lizardo) is a dastardly sort and no matter where you go . . . there you are. ★★★ DVD Special Edition: $14.99

Adventures of Don Juan

(1948, 110 min, US, Vincent Sherman) *Errol Flynn, Viveca Lindfors, Alan Hale, Una O'Connor, Raymond Burr.* Flynn is in swashbuckling good form in this opulent costumer. He stars as the legendary Spanish lover who battles the evil Duke de Lorca and protects the royal crown. Much of the mood is tongue-in-cheek, and Flynn, though a decade past his great '30s epics, and resembling Ronald Colman, still cuts a fine figure. Max Steiner's score and the outstanding sets and costumes help immeasurably. ★★★

The Adventures of Eliza Fraser

(1976, 114 min, Australia, Tim Burstall) *Susannah York, Trevor Howard, John Castle.* In the mood for an Australian burlesque period romp starring British actress Susannah York? If that doesn't scare you off, read on. Reminiscent of the American West, 1830s Australia was a lawless and untamed land and definitely not a place for a beautiful, cultured woman. Eliza Fraser not only survived but flourished despite the chains of a jealous husband, being pursued and lusted after by penal colony escapees, captured by aboriginal savages and even hounded by the police. Though there's some moments of fun, this action stuff is best left to the Americans. ★★½

The Adventures of Felix

(2000, 95 min, France, Jacques Martineau & Olivier Ducastel) *Sami Bouajila, Patachou, Ariane Ascaride.* Armed with only a backpack, a rainbow flag and his HIV medications, young, carefree Felix (Bouajila), a handsome French-Arab gay man, leaves his adoring lover in their Normandy flat and sets out on the road in search of his biological father (whom he has never met). The adventures and people he meets on his way south to Marseilles form the core of this magical, gentle, endearing road movie. Hitchhiking those many miles, Felix meets a variety of engaging strangers who become his new, imagined family. This includes a "brother" who lusts after him, a "cousin" who turns out to be of the kissing

The Adventures of Priscilla, Queen of the Desert

kind, and a "grandmother" who offers sage advice. Writer-directors Ducastel and Martineau infuse the film with whimsy and sweetness, romance and sensuality, while not ignoring such realities such as racism and AIDS. As unpretentious and charming as its beguiling hero. (French with English subtitles) ★★★½ DVD: $24.99, VHS: $14.99

The Adventures of Ford Fairlane

(1990, 96 min, US, Renny Harlin) *Andrew Dice Clay, Wayne Newton, Priscilla Presley, Lauren Holly, Gilbert Gottfried, Ed O'Neill, Robert Englund.* Forget the controversy surrounding comic Clay and his treatment of women and minorities; his starring debut is just a bad film. Clay's arrogant, chauvinistic persona, here in the form of a detective, is the center of an unfunny comedy that is poorly scripted and directed, and whose rambling plot will keep one and all scratching their heads in disbelief and confusion. ★ DVD: $9.99, VHS: $9.99

The Adventures of Huck Finn

(1993, 106 min, US, Stephen Sommers) *Elijah Wood, Courtney B. Vance, Jason Robards, Robbie Coltrane, Ron Perlman, Dana Ivey, Anne Heche.* Disney's version of the Mark Twain classic is a highly entertaining adaptation which should more than entrance children of most ages, effortlessly transporting them to another time and place. Sparked by two engaging performances from young Wood and Vance as Huck and Jim, respectively, the film is actually better than most screen versions. Robards and Coltrane, both enjoying themselves overplaying their parts as greedy con men, add to the film's level of high-spiritedness and rustic charm, as does a good evocation of 19th-century America. ★★★ DVD: $19.99, VHS: $9.99

The Adventures of Huckleberry Finn

(1939, 90 min, US, Richard Thorpe) *Mickey Rooney, Walter Connelly, Rex Ingram, William Frawley.* Faithful film version of Mark Twain's family classic about the misadventures of Mississippi youths Huck Finn and Tom Sawyer, and of Huck's relationship with Jim, a runaway slave. Of all the many screen versions, this may well be the best. (aka: *Huckleberry Finn*) ★★★

The Adventures of Mark Twain

(1986, 90 min, US, Will Vinton) Outstanding claymation highlights this average children's film about Twain characters Huck Finn, Tom Sawyer and Becky Thatcher accompanying their literary creator on a balloon ride to Halley's Comet. ★★½

The Adventures of Milo and Otis

(1986, 76 min, Japan, Masanori Hata) *Narrated by: Dudley Moore.* Sort of like "Wild Kingdom" for the pet set, this lushly photographed nature story about the friendship and adventures of a kitten and dog has shown remarkable appeal with children. It's harmless, corny and just the change of pace from old "Lassie" reruns. ★★ DVD: $14.99, VHS: $9.99

The Adventures of Pinocchio

(1996, 94 min, US, Steve Barron) *Martin Landau, Jonathan Taylor Thomas, Geneviève Bujold, Rob Schneider, Udo Kier, Bebe Neuwirth.* Although this story has been filmed several times, most notably Disney's 1940 classic, this live action twist offers a good cast and strong production values, particularly with the special effects that animate the wooden Pinocchio. Thomas' voice adds warmth and character to the puppet who would be a boy, and Landau's Giuseppe is convincingly enraptured and befuddled by his little creation. Bujold, in a surprising addition as Giuseppe's love interest of sorts, adds another level of emotional depth. ★★★ DVD: $9.99, VHS: $9.99

The Adventures of Pluto Nash

(2002, 90 min, US, Ron Underwood) *Eddie Murphy, Randy Quaid, Rosario Dawson, Joe Pantoliano, Jay Mohr, Luis Guzman, Pam Grier.* Has it really been 20 years since Eddie Murphy made his film debut? In that time, the comedian with the amazing box-office record has more than demonstrated a superior comic ability (we still say he was robbed of an Oscar nomination for *The Nutty Professor*, but we digress). But nothing — nothing — he's ever done measures up to the sheer incompetence as this awful sci-fi comedy. He plays a nightclub owner (on the Moon) who is muscled out of the business and then must track down the man responsible. The idea of robots and spaceships and lunar travel probably sounded great on paper, but the execution is jaw-droppingly bad. ★ DVD Letterbox: $14.99, VHS: $22.99

The Adventures of Priscilla, Queen of the Desert

(1994, 102 min, Australia, Stephan Elliott) *Terence Stamp, Guy Pearce, Hugo Weaving, Bill Hunter, Sarah Chadwick.* 1960s international sex symbol Stamp is a transgendered marvel as the mature, demure but tough transsexual Bernadette who teams up with two transvestites on a cross-country trip through Australia's Outback in this rousingly fun cross-dressing musical comedy. On a ramshackle tour bus named Priscilla, muscular Felicia (Pearce), sad-sack Mitzi (Weaving) and the wisecracking Bernadette travel nearly a thousand miles to play a four-week casino engagement. Along the way, the fabulously attired threesome encounter their fair share of problems but through it all keep their spirits high, their feathers unruffled and their gravity-defying wigs straight (so to speak). There are moments of seriousness when homophobia and regret of roads not taken confront them, but they readily conquer all in this buoyant and infectiously good-natured tale. ★★★½ DVD: $19.99

The Adventures of Robin Hood

(1938, 106 min, US, Michael Curtiz) *Errol Flynn, Olivia de Havilland, Claude Rains, Basil Rathbone, Alan Hale, Patric Knowles, Eugene Pallette.* The quintessential swashbuckler as Flynn is a devilishly dashing Robin Hood, de Havilland as Maid Marion, Rains as a particularly villainous Prince John, and the great Rathbone, master swordsman and scene stealer, as Sir Guy. The film sports great action scenes, tongue-in-cheek humor, the very best in swordplay and glorious Technicolor cinematography. ★★★★ DVD 2-disc Special Edition: $26.99

The Adventures of Rocky & Bullwinkle

(2000, 88 min, US, Des McAnuff) *Robert De Niro, Jason Alexander, Rene Russo, Piper Perabo, Keith Scott, June Foray.* A misplacement of priorities by the filmmakers, so common to big-budget adaptations of TV shows, buries this live action/computer animation blend, but the charms of our heroes almost save the day. Whereas the plots of the episodes harkened to old-time cliffhangers, writer Kenneth Lonergan fashions a road movie, thrusting Moose and Squirrel out of syndication and into real life. Under this kiddie sheen is the old subversive humor, especially evident in a breathless, traditionally animated opening segment that gets the plot churning. Even the computer-animated duo get some good barbs (and wretchedly bad puns) that sustain interest and smiles throughout the brief running time. It just could have been a whole lot better by aiming a whole lot lower. ★★ DVD: $26.99, VHS: $14.99

The Adventures of Sebastian Cole

(1999, 100 min, US, Tod Williams) *Adrian Grenier, Margaret Colin, Clark Gregg, Gabriel Macht, John Shea.* This off-beat, independently produced comedy-drama set in a small New York town is a charming film undermined by trying to tackle too much. Is it a poignant coming-of-age tale about charismatic 17-year-old Sebastian? Or is it a story of the difficulties of a transgendered man-to-woman trying to cope with a rebellious stepson as well as a longing for love and understanding in a backwater town? Despite going in different directions, the film remains entertaining, thanks to the appealing characters, especially Grenier, who brings intensity and charm to the familiar tale of a teen stifled by life in a small town. A refreshing and at times original spin on the coming-of-age theme. ★★★ DVD: $29.99, VHS: $79.99

The Adventures of Sherlock Holmes

(1939, 85 min, US, Alfred L. Werker) *Basil Rathbone, Nigel Bruce, Ida Lupino.* One of the definitive Sherlock Holmes pictures, this exciting and atmospheric piece stars Rathbone and Bruce as the famous sleuth and his companion Dr. Watson. Holmes' archenemy, the evil Professor Moriarty, attempts to commit the "crime of the century" right beneath the detective's nose. ★★★ DVD: $19.99, VHS: $16.99

Advertising Rules!

(2001, 104 min, Germany, Lars Kraume) *Alexander Scheer, Chupan Khamatova, Götz George. Advertising Rules!* — like countless American films from the '80s starring people like Andrew McCarthy — provides a somewhat stale look at youthful ambition plotted against the all-too-familiar landscape of corporate lunacy. Viktor's boyish charm (read: obnoxiousness) makes an immediate splash with the firm's bigwigs and he's immediately pitching a brilliant idea.

Problem is, the idea isn't exactly his — it's part of an upcoming exhibition created by his new artist flame Rosa (Khamatova) — and now he must choose between love and career. Predictable, yes, but what's worse is that the performances are so gaudy that one doesn't really care what happens to any of these selfish buffoons. (aka: *Viktor Vogel: Commercial Man*) (German with English subtitles) ★★ DVD Letterbox: $29.99

Advise and Consent

(1962, 139 min, US, Otto Preminger) *Henry Fonda, Charles Laughton, Walter Pidgeon, Gene Tierney, Don Murray, Lew Ayres, Burgess Meredith, Franchot Tone, Peter Lawford, Inga Swenson.* A finely interwoven plot and exceptional ensemble acting highlight Preminger's treatment of the Allen Drury novel. The machinations of government, on the floor of the Senate and behind the scenes, are examined with an eye to formal procedure and individual idiosyncracy in this story of a controversial presidential nomination. Murray is full of idealistic vigor as the chairman of a House subcommittee investigating the Secretary of State nominee (played by Fonda). However, when he refuses to endorse Fonda, he is blackmailed for a homosexual encounter while in the service. In his final film, Laughton offers an excellent performance as a slick Southern senator. Mammoth in scope and engrossing in detail, this makes an interesting companion piece to *The Best Man*. ★★★½

The Advocate

(1994, 101 min, GB, Leslie Megahey) *Colin Firth, Amina Annabi, Ian Holm, Jim Carter, Donald Pleasence, Nicol Williamson.* Writer-director Megahey has taken what has to be a virtually unknown medieval law and with it fashioned a scintillating black comedy masquerading as a murder mystery. Firth plays a 15th-century Parisian lawyer who escapes the rigors and hardships of the city for a simpler life in the country. But a peaceful landscape and gentle countryfolk are not what he finds when he immediately becomes embroiled in the murder trial of a young boy — and his defendant is a pig! As Firth tries to uncover the facts, he comes face to face with political corruption, religious bureaucracy and a bevy of beautiful women all trying to bed him. The situation is ripe with satiric possibilities, and Megahey has wondrously exploited them with a light touch and marvelous wit. ★★★½ DVD: $19.99

Aelita: Queen of Mars

(1924, 113 min, USSR, Yakov Protazanov) *Julia Solntseva, Nikolai Batalov.* Definitely not your typical silent Soviet film, *Aelita* is a big-budget science-fiction spectacle boasting enormous, Cubist-inspired futuristic sets and wildly designed costumes. A Russian engineer, a soldier and a detective all travel to Mars where they become embroiled in a Martian proletarian uprising. Their situation gets even more complicated when the engineer falls madly in love with Queen Aelita. A huge popular success in its time, the film is an interesting precursor to Fritz Lang's similarly themed *Metropolis*. (Silent with piano accompaniment) ★★★ DVD: $24.99, VHS: $29.99

Aenigma

(1987, 85 min, Italy, Lucio Fulci) *Jared Martin, Lara Naszinsky.* A teenage girl ends up in a coma after a prank gone wrong, then possesses the new girl at school and exacts her revenge long-distance. An incredibly silly, oddball *Carrie*-ripoff, *Aenigma* has some nice, creepy moments, but for most horror viewers, this will be a disappointment. Not up to director Fulci's classics (*The Beyond, Zombie*), this still man-

ages to retain that special something Fulci-ites love. The goofy dubbing (of the ridiculous dialogue), bizarre motivations and corny music only enhance the unsettling atmosphere and nightmarish feel. No one would accuse *Aenigma* of being a "good" film, but for fans of this kind of thing, it sure is an entertaining one. And don't miss that heartfelt opening credits song! ★★ DVD: $24.99, VHS: $14.99

An Affair of Love

(2000, 78 min, France, Frédéric Fonteyne) *Nathalie Baye, Sergi Lopéz.* A sensuous, intelligent and passionate film about sex and love. Baye is radiant as a middle-aged Parisian woman who meets a younger man through a personal ad. They rendezvous to fulfill a secret sexual fantasy, vowing not to fall in love. Complications arise, however, when they do just that. The simple plot gives these two great characters room to breathe, in an exploration of desire that's both romantic and sexy. A wondrous film that has a warm intimate feel. (French wth English subtitles) ★★★ DVD: $24.99

The Affair of the Necklace

(2001, 117 min, US/GB, Charles Shyer) *Hilary Swank, Jonathan Pryce, Simon Baker, Adrien Brody, Brian Cox, Joely Richardson, Christopher Walken.* Victor Hugo, Charles Dickens et al. had it all wrong — it wasn't the victimization of the poor, or the disparity of wealth, or hunger, violence and corruption that brought about the French Revolution in the late 18th century. It was jewelry. A dazzling, sparkling necklace to be precise. At least that's what one could come away with from the muddled storytelling of director Shyer's opulent but lifeless costume epic. Playing her as neither cunning nor duplicitous, Swank is Jeanne St. Remy de Valois, a noblewoman who will stop at nothing to restore her disgraced family name. She concocts a plan that involves scamming Marie Antoinette, among a few other highly placed players. The film offers little of the era's climate other than dastardly court intrigue and Jeanne's manipulation, failing to properly lay the foundation for the story's big payoff. ★★ DVD Letterbox: $14.99, VHS: $9.99

An Affair to Remember

(1957, 115 min, US, Leo McCarey) *Cary Grant, Deborah Kerr, Cathleen Nesbitt.* Based on the 1939 classic *Love Affair*, this sentimental soap opera features Grant and Kerr in very appealing performances as two lovers separated by fate. Artist Grant and engaged Kerr enjoy a shipboard romance. In a famous cinematic rendezvous, they vow to meet six months later at the Empire State Building. One of them doesn't make it. Though the film is awash in hokey drama, the chemistry of the two stars, Grant's expert comic timing and a touching romance make this a semiclassic and fan fave. (Remade in 1994) ★★★ DVD: $14.99, VHS: $9.99

Affliction

(1998, 113 min, US, Paul Schrader) *Nick Nolte, Sissy Spacek, James Coburn, Willem Dafoe, Mary Beth Hurt.* Career performances by Nolte and Coburn (who won an Academy Award) accentuate this sobering, absorbing, rough-going psychological study of the precarious relationship between an abusive father and his two sons. Nolte is Wade Whitehouse, the middle-aged sheriff of a small New Hampshire town. When his aged mother dies, he attempts a reconciliation with his alcoholic father (Coburn), but painful memories of the past begin to resurface, and Wade finds his world crumbling around him. Adapted from the novel by Russell Banks ("The Sweet Hereafter"), the film shares the desperation and sadness that tinged Banks' other film adaptation, but Schrader's gloomy film doesn't have *Hereafter*'s storytelling agility. But what it may lack in cinematic expression is more than made up for by Nolte's and Coburn's brilliant portraits — this is very much an actor's vehicle. ★★★ DVD: $14.99

Afraid of the Dark
(1992, 91 min, GB, Mark Peploe) *James Fox, Fanny Ardant, Paul McGann, Ben Keyworth.* Screenwriter Peploe (*The Last Emperor*) turns his hand to directing with this psychological thriller in which nothing is as it seems. Fox stars as the father of a precocious kid who decides to track down a psychopath preying on the blind. To say more would be detrimental to the plot's essential twist, but the patient viewer will be rewarded. ★★½ VHS: $14.99

An African Dream
(1990, 94 min, GB, John Smallcombe) *John Kani, Kitty Aldridge.* When a young schoolteacher (Aldridge) moves to colonial South Africa with her husband, she is appalled by the racial hatred which pervades her new home. She develops a relationship with an educated African (Kani) who is teaching at a small school in the black area and is involuntarily sucked into the fray. ★★★ VHS: $79.99

The African Queen
(1951, 106 min, US/GB, John Huston) *Humphrey Bogart, Katharine Hepburn, Robert Morley, Peter Bull, Theodore Bikel.* One of the all-time greats, *The African Queen* stars Bogart (in his Oscar-winning role) and Hepburn as unlikely lovebirds who encounter the dangers of the rapids, the Germans and each other. In a quintessential performance, Hepburn plays Rose Sawyer, a missionary serving in the Congo. She is paired with boozy captain Charlie Alnut (Bogey in a wonderfully endearing performance) when she must flee her village from the enemy army via Bogey's dilapidated boat. Aided by two veteran performers at the peak of their talents and an excellent screenplay, director Huston has crafted a thrilling adventure both comic and exciting. ★★★★

Favorite Line: "Nature, Mr. Allnut, is what we are put in this world to rise above." —*Katharine Hepburn as Rose Sayer*

After Dark, My Sweet
(1990, 114 min, US, James Foley) *Jason Patric, Rachel Ward, Bruce Dern.* 1990 was a good year for gritty adaptations of the books of Jim Thompson. In addition to *The Grifters*, this disturbing yet highly entertaining melodrama represented a miniature revival for the novelist. Patric stars as Collie, a literally punch-drunk ex-boxer who is on the run from a mental institution. Dazed, Collie wanders into the seedier side of Palm Springs and becomes tragically entangled with an alcoholic widow (Ward) and a local con man (Dern) who are hatching a scheme to pick up some quick bucks. Patric's performance is strikingly complex and intense. Ward is equally good, and Dern has found his best role in years. *After Dark, My Sweet* is an excellent and claustrophobic study of three social misfits caught in a dangerous pas de trois. ★★★½ DVD: $14.99

After Hours
(1985, 97 min, US, Martin Scorsese) *Griffin Dunne, Rosanna Arquette, Teri Garr, John Heard, Linda Fiorentino, Tommy Chong, Cheech Marin, Catherine O'Hara, Dick Miller, Bronson Pinchot.* Ever had one of those days? Paul Hackett (Dunne) is about to have one of those nights. What begins as an innocent date with a kooky girl he meets at a coffee shop escalates into a night befitting a "Twilight Zone" episode. This exhilarating Scorsese black comedy follows Paul's misadventures in Greenwich Village (and vicinity) where each character confronted is crazier and more unpredictable than the one before. ★★★★

After Life
(1998, 118 min, Japan, Kore-eda Hirokazu) *Arata, Oda Erika, Susumu Terajima.* In Hirokazu's *After Life*, the recently departed are given three days to determine the most meaningful memory of their lives, which will be their only memory for eternity — thus creating their own Heaven or Hell. Each soul gets a caseworker to assist in the evaluation, prodding remembrance and reflection in examining what was truly valuable in their lives. The film is deceptively simple as it presents ordinary, unexceptional people who begin the recall process with momentous events. Inevitably, these memories lead to the small, special, seemingly insignificant moments, which in the end are the real substance of life. *After Life* is profound and moving and deeply affecting as it balances compassion with wry observation, watching the dead sift through their memories until they find the one that resonates for all eternity. (Japanese with English subtitles) ★★★½ DVD: $29.99, VHS: $29.99

After Sex
(1997, 97 min, France, Brigitte Roüan) *Brigitte Roüan, Patrick Chesnais, Boris Terral, Nils Tavernier, Jean-Louis Richard, Françoise Arnoul.* Passionate love scenes and emotional despair mark *After Sex*, an erotic-neurotic middle-age-crisis drama from France. Director Roüan stars as Diane Clovier, a forty-something publishing executive who begins an unexpected romance with Emilio (Terral), a shaggy-haired hydroelectric engineer twenty years her junior. Jeopardizing her career as well as her life with her husband and two sons, Diane becomes consumed with the intense sexual relationship. However, it ends abruptly. Roüan, who employs jump-cut editing to tell this fractured story, threatens to make *After Sex* a vanity production, but there are only a few really pretentious moments. (French with English subtitles) ★★★ VHS: $29.99

After the Fox
(1966, 103 min, GB, Vittorio De Sica) *Peter Sellers, Victor Mature, Britt Ekland, Akim Tamiroff, Martin Balsam.* Who would imagine Vittorio De Sica directing Peter Sellers in a film scripted by Neil Simon? Well, here it is — and not an unworthy effort, at that. Sellers is an ingenious convict who produces a film in order to cover up a big caper. As the movie star Sellers convinces to star in the "movie," Mature gets the most laughs just for being himself. ★★★ DVD Dual: $14.99

After the Rehearsal
(1984, 72 min, Sweden, Ingmar Bergman) *Erland Josephson, Lena Olin, Ingrid Thulin.* A provocative probing of the thoughts and fears of a renowned stage director (Josephson) poised between love and solitude, ambition and resignation, bitterness and longing. On the verge of a production, he is confronted by two actresses, who in distinctly different fashions, force him into a position of self-examination. Along with *Wild Strawberries*, this is one of Bergman's most personal reflections on the demands and delusions of the artist. (Swedish with English subtitles) ★★★½ VHS: $19.99

After the Thin Man
See: *The Thin Man Series*

Afterburn
(1992, 100 min, US, Robert Markowitz) *Laura Dern, Robert Loggia, Vincent Spano, Michael Rooker.* Dern is arresting as a fighter pilot's widow who takes on the U.S. military when her husband's crash in an F-16 in Korea is attributed to pilot error. Knowing that her husband (Spano) was one of the most highly rated pilots, her doubts and suspicions regarding the official story escalate in the face of increasing evidence of a cover-up. Loggia delivers a strong performance as Dern's lawyer. A compelling HBO treatment of a real-life incident. ★★★½ VHS: $9.99

Afterglow
(1998, 114 min, US/Canada, Alan Rudolph) *Nick Nolte, Julie Christie, Lara Flynn Boyle, Jonny Lee Miller, Jay Underwood.* Director Rudolph again casts his eye on contemporary relationships, intertwining and enmeshing two disparate couples in crisis. Lucky (Nolte), a high-ticket handyman who takes care of the plumbing in more ways than one, is married to Phyllis (Christie), a faded former film star. Marianne and Jeffrey, a younger, upper-strata corporate couple (Boyle and Miller), bicker in their expensive but sterile condo — a perfect reflection of their life together. While the older twosome have the depth of character provided by life experience, it affords them no greater ability to understand or communicate. Nolte and Christie are perfect complements; Christie providing subtle yet profound emotional depth to a character that would have been easy to overplay. The film is slightly choppy, but remains an adult exploration of the magnitude of a lie's impact and the saving grace of its forgiveness. ★★★ DVD: $19.99, VHS: $21.99

Against All Odds

(1984, 128 min, US, Taylor Hackford) *Jeff Bridges, Rachel Ward, James Woods, Jane Greer, Richard Widmark, Swoosie Kurtz, Saul Rubinek.* An interesting if not totally successful updating of the noir classic *Out of the Past.* Bridges stars as a down-and-out ex-football player who is hired by an ex-teammate-turned-gangster (Woods) to locate the woman (Ward) who he says tried to kill him. Hackford's remake relies on solid performances, star chemistry and a few plot twists to puff up what could have been a rather shopworn premise, and the film also benefits from an over-the-top performance by Woods. Greer, who plays Ward's mother, starred as the missing femme fatale in the original film. ★★½ DVD Special Edition: $9.99

Against the Ropes

(2004, 111 min, US, Charles S. Dutton) *Meg Ryan, Omar Epps, Tony Shalhoub, Tim Daly, Charles S. Dutton, Kerry Washington, Joe Cortese.* Meg Ryan draws the collar, going 0 for 3 in her recent attempts to flush *America's Sweetheart* image from her and the moviegoing public's system in this latest movie makeover. Meg stars as the real-life Jackie Kallen, a secretary who bucks the system and chauvinism in order to break into the male dominated boxing game. Wearing tight leather outfits and spouting as many obscenities as a PG-13 rating would allow her to, Ryan's Cleveland-based Kallen finds herself up against an assortment of male creeps and would-be thugs who stand in her way of getting a fair shake in the ring. She takes a talented but troubled boxer (Epps) under her wing and manages to lead him to middleweight champion contention. It's cliché city all the way, but some nifty in-the-ring segments and likable spunk by Ryan keep things floating — but certainly not like a butterfly — at a serviceable TV movie level. Ultimately, however, the female empowerment angle is dropped for some dopey beyond-the-rope plot complications. There's an edgier boxing film in here somewhere that coulda been a contender. ★★ DVD Letterbox: $29.99

Against the Wall

(1993, 111 min, US, John Frankenheimer) *Samuel L. Jackson, Clarence Williams III, Harry Dean Stanton, Frederic Forrest, Kyle MacLachlan.* This made-for-HBO docudrama chronicles the events that took place during the violent uprising at the Attica State Penitentiary in the early '70s. MacLachlan stars as the rookie guard who gets stuck in the middle and becomes a hostage for the inmates. Jackson gives a fine performance as the Islamic inmate who unofficially becomes the go-between for the media and the prisoners. Exciting and heart-pounding. ★★★★ VHS: $9.99

Agatha

(1978, 98 min, US/GB, Michael Apted) *Vanessa Redgrave, Dustin Hoffman, Timothy Dalton.* Director Apted (*Coal Miner's Daughter*) weaves this fictional account of the 1926 11-day disappearance of famed mystery writer Agatha Christie. Redgrave's sensitive portrayal lends touching insight into "the price of fame," while helping to offset Hoffman's grating turn as the American reporter who ultimately tracks her down. ★★½ VHS: $14.99

L'Âge d'Or

(1930, 60 min, France, Luis Buñuel) Following the success of their first collaboration, *Un Chien Andalou,* Buñuel and Salvador Dali further antagonized the Right, the Church and the powers that be with this wickedly funny, bizarre and scandalous masterpiece. Buñuel has said that this dreamlike tale of mad love unconsummated is "a romantic film performed in full surrealist frenzy." (French with English subtitles) ★★★½

The Age of Innocence

(1993, 133 min, US, Martin Scorsese) *Daniel Day-Lewis, Michelle Pfeiffer, Winona Ryder, Miriam Margolyes, Richard E. Grant, Alec McCowen, Geraldine Chaplin, Robert Sean Leonard.* Scorsese's period drama is visually dazzling and sumptuously produced, but it's ultimately a disappointing adaptation of Edith Wharton's novel. Set in 1870s New York City, the film stars Day-Lewis as Newland Archer, a young lawyer and rising member of the ruling elite. Smitten by the Countess Olenska (Pfeiffer), a former member of polite society who has returned home surrounded by scandal, Archer risks his future by falling in love with her despite his betrothal to Olenska's cousin (Ryder). The acting by all three principals is superbly nuanced and first-rate; special mention goes to Margolyes as a matronly aunt. While the film aptly captures the sense of social suffocation that Wharton no doubt intended, it lacks a much-needed passion. ★★½ DVD Letterbox: $19.99

Agnes Browne

(1999, 92 min, Ireland, Anjelica Huston) *Anjelica Huston, Marion O'Dwyer, Niall O'Shea, Ciaran Owens, Ray Winstone.* In 1967 Dublin, a poor widow (Huston) with seven children sets out to support her family and begin a new life for herself in the wake of social change. Culminating with a quest to see Tom Jones in concert, this is about as fun as a film about a newly widowed, dirt-poor mother can be. However, the mood is consistently spoiled by lackluster line readings, surprising being directed by such a fine actress. In spite of its flaws, *Agnes Browne* is an amiable slice-of-Irish-life. ★★½

Agnes of God

(1985, 98 min, US, Norman Jewison) *Jane Fonda, Anne Bancroft, Meg Tilly.* A trio of solid performances highlight this intriguing mystery based on the Broadway hit. Fonda plays a court-appointed psychiatrist who must determine the sanity of a novice accused of murdering her newborn baby. Oscar nominations went to Bancroft as the convent's worldly Mother Superior and Tilly as the troubled young woman. ★★★ DVD: $19.99, VHS: $9.99

The Agony and the Ecstasy

(1965, 140 min, US, Carol Reed) *Charlton Heston, Rex Harrison, Diane Cilento, Harry Andrews.* Not considered a Reed classic, this historical account follows Michelangelo's aesthetic battles with Pope Julius II as he toiled on the Sistine Chapel. Heston and Harrison provide worthy performances, but the film's slightly overblown production values and its considerable length overshadow their efforts. ★★½ VHS: $9.99

Aguirre, the Wrath of God

(1972, 94 min, Germany, Werner Herzog) *Klaus Kinski, Ruy Guerra, Helena Rojo.* A mesmerizing, adventurous tale of a Spanish expedition's search for El Dorado, the lost city of gold. Along the way, a power-hungry conquistador, Aguirre, takes control and leads them on an insane journey into the Amazon and the heart of darkness. Although Herzog's hyper-realistic style of direction makes for a few slow sequences, Kinski's intense performance as the traitorous title character is riveting. A compelling portrait of a mad and brilliant leader. (German with English subtitles) ★★★½ DVD: $29.99

Ah, Wilderness!

(1935, 98 min, US, Clarence Brown) *Lionel Barrymore, Wallace Beery, Spring Byington, Eric Linden, Mickey Rooney.* A very able cast brings Eugene O'Neill's stage comedy about a 1906 New England family merrily to life. The film's success is painting a heartwarming portrait of early 20th-century Americana while avoiding the bathetic trappings of so many films of the '30s — the *Andy Hardy* series, for example. Heading a fine ensemble is Barrymore as the patriarch of the Miller clan. He makes the most of the film's best lines; Beery gives a showy portrayal as an uncle prone to drink; Byington sparkles as the family's mother. ★★★½ VHS: $19.99

Aileen Wuornos: The Selling of a Serial Killer

(1993, 87 min, GB, Nick Broomfield) *Aileen Wuornos.* A chilling crime and justice documentary that would make the events in *The Thin Blue Line* seem like a paragon of legal competence, this mesmerizing and tenacious investigative film attempts to gather the facts in the case against convicted serial killer Aileen Wuornos. Wuornos, a lesbian and prostitute, was convicted of brutally killing seven men. Director Broomfield digs beyond the seemingly open-and-shut case and uncovers an elaborate web of deception and profiteering both on the part of law enforcement officers, her "friends" and her lover. Wuornos' story was also told in the Oscar-winning *Monster.* ★★★★ DVD: $14.99, VHS: $14.99

Aimee & Jaguar

(1999, 126 min, Germany, Max Farberbock) *Maria Schrader, Juliane Kohler, Johana Wokalek, Heike Makatsch.* *Aimee & Jaguar* is a rare film, it leaves the audience weeping about the dire consequences an intense love has wrought, but exhilarated over the existence of such love. From the first bars of the mournful lush score we know this story won't end well, but the journey takes us to a place

Aguirre, the Wrath of God

A

of love we have seldom seen in a film. *Aimee* tells the true story of Lilly (Kohler) and Felice (Schrader), lovers in WWII Germany. Lilly Wust is married to a Nazi officer away at the front and has many affairs while her handsome husband is gone. Felice works for the underground and is the leading light of her circle of lesbians, in love with Ilse but smitten with Lilly. Felice is not only a lesbian, but Jewish as well . . . prime target for the Nazis to ship off to the camps. The story is told through flashbacks when Lilly is an old woman being brought to a retirement home where she happens to meet another of their circle from the war. Director Farberbock brings a sincerity to the touching and intense film, and the performances by Schrader and Kohler are authentic and moving. (German with English subtitles) ★★★½ DVD Special Edition: $29.99, VHS: $24.99

Air America

(1990, 112 min, US, Roger Spottiswoode) *Mel Gibson, Robert Downey, Jr., Nancy Travis, David Marshall Grant.* Lumbering political satire with Gibson and Downey as off-the-wall pilots working for a covert government airline in Laos during the years of the Vietnam War. The film can't decide what it wants to be — left-wing, right-wing, comic romp, antiwar — and suffers as a result. The appealing chemistry of the two stars is wasted on this nonsense. ★ DVD: $9.99

Air Bud

(1997, 97 min, US, Charles Martin Smith) *Michael Jeter, Kevin Zegers, Wendy Makkena, Norm Snively.* After the death of his beloved father, 12-year-old Josh moves with his mother and sister to a new town where he has a tough time adjusting. He soon befriends a golden retriever named Buddy, who can play a mean game of basketball. While the plot development from here is fairly obvious — Josh finds the confidence to try out for the team, while Buddy becomes the team mascot who shoots hoops at halftime — it is nonetheless heartwarming. The ending is hokier than the rest of the film but kids should appreciate good winning out. (Followed by 4 sequels) ★★½ DVD: $14.99, VHS: $9.99

Un Air de Famille

(1996, 110 min, France, Cédric Klapisch) *Jean-Pierre Bacri, Jean-Pierre Darroussin, Catherine Frot, Agnès Jaoui, Claire Maurier.* A family's dinner gathering sets the stage for hilarious confrontations in this winning character piece. The plot is familiar, but the absence of melodrama and the subtly witty dialogue make it a winner. Maurier as the domineering mother is merely the best of a terrific ensemble cast. (French with English subtitles) ★★★½ DVD: $14.99, VHS: $9.99

Air Force

(1943, 124 min, US, Howard Hawks) *John Garfield, Gig Young, Arthur Kennedy, Charles Drake, George Tobias.* After years of supporting roles, Garfield takes center stage in this crisp WWII actioner about the aerial adventures of a B-17 bomber crew, both before and after Pearl Harbor. Hawks directs with his usual keen eye for adventure. Garfield is a commanding presence, and what Warner film would be complete without Tobias. ★★★ VHS: $14.99

Air Force One

(1997, 124 min, US, Wolfgang Petersen) *Harrison Ford, Gary Oldman, Glenn Close, William H. Macy, Wendy Crewson, Dean Stockwell, Diesel Matthews.* As if American presidents haven't suffered enough, along come a couple of slimy Russian terrorists to shake things up when they take over Air Force One. In Petersen's crisp thriller, action and suspense are neatly packaged to make for one exciting ride. And Ford proves that even as the Commander in Chief, he's ready to kick butt whenever necessary. That occurs when Oldman and his gang of revolutionaires commandeer the president's plane. Left on his own, Ford takes on the terrorists, who have threatened to start killing hostages. The scenario is ripe for swift action pieces, and Petersen, whose *Das Boot* created maximum suspense from an enclosed space, knows how and when to push just the right buttons. ★★★ DVD Letterbox Superbit Edition: $26.99, DVD: $19.99, VHS: $9.99

The Air Up There

(1994, 88 min, US, Paul M. Glaser) *Kevin Bacon, Charles Gitonga Maina, Yolanda Vasquez.* Bacon stars as an assistant college basketball coach who travels all the way to Kenya to recruit a nearly seven-foot tribesman (an engaging Maina) for his team. While there, he suffers culture shock, befriends the natives, and helps right the village's wrongs. The locale provides a nice travelogue backdrop, and the finale's basketball game is rather exciting despite its obvious outcome; but this formulaic sports film is only for those who think Hollywood doesn't make enough basketball flicks. Bacon has an easy-going, natural charm which all the more makes one wish the film was as noteworthy as its star. ★★

Airheads

(1994, 91 min, US, Michael Lehmann) *Brendan Fraser, Steve Buscemi, Adam Sandler, Joe Mantegna, Michael McKean, Michael Richards, Judd Nelson, Ernie Hudson.* Lehmann's self-consciously hip, one-joke comedy is about a rock band — The Lone Rangers — who hold a radio station hostage in order to get their demo played. The one joke? That a rock band holds a radio station hostage in order to get their demo played. As repetitious as it sounds, the film isn't helped by a tired script and one-dimensional performances. However, Sandler saves the day with an amusing portrayal of the band's dim-witted drummer. ★½ DVD: $9.99, VHS: $9.99

Airplane!

(1980, 86 min, US, David Zucker, Jerry Zucker, Jim Abrahams) *Robert Hays, Julie Hagerty, Robert Stack, Leslie Nielsen, Lloyd Bridges, Peter Graves, Stephen Stucker, Kareem Abdul-Jabbar.* A dash of Marx Brothers, a taste of Chaplin, a whole lot of Three Stooges slapstick and puns, puns and more puns are the ingredients for this send-up of every airplane disaster film from *Zero Hour* to *Airport.* This nonstop laugh fest relentlessly hits us over the head with jokes. There are so many jokes, in fact, that blinking is not advised. Besides the million or so laughs, this is the film that first introduced Nielsen as a comic actor — let's give thanks for that, too. Cameos include "Beaver"'s mom Barbara Billingsley and Ethel Merman. (Sequel: *Airplane II: The Sequel*) ★★★★ DVD: $14.99, VHS: $9.99

Favorite Line: "Chump don't want no hep, chump don't get de hep. Jive ass fool ain't got no brains anyhow." —*Barbara Billingsley as Jive Lady*

Airplane II: The Sequel

(1982, 85 min, US, Ken Finkleman) *Robert Hays, Julie Haggerty, William Shatner, Lloyd Bridges, Peter Graves, Chad Everett, Stephen Stucker, Raymond Burr, Rip Torn, Chuck Connors, John Vernon.* This sequel to the hit *Airplane!* doesn't pack the stomach-wrenching humor as did the first. Handed over to first-time director Finkleman, the film just can't match the pace of its predecessor. This time around, retired pilot Hays becomes the only man available to fly a Space Shuttle-like craft. Although the plot is predictable, there are still enough funny moments to satisfy fans of the first. ★★½ DVD: $14.99

Akermania Vol. 1

(1968-84, 89 min, Belgium, Chantal Akerman) *Chantal Akerman, Maria de Medeiros, Pascale Salkin.* Three short subjects from independent feminist filmmaker Akerman. *J'ai faim, J'ai froid (I'm Hungry, I'm Cold)* (1984): Two young girls run away to Paris from their native Brussels and learn very direct, immediate approaches to getting their needs met. *Salute ma ville (Blow Up My Town)* (1968): A young woman in a small flat with too much unchanneled energy races through the mundane activities of daily life until she's caught in the vortex of their execution. *Hotel Monterey* (1974): Without sound, the camera wanders through the lobby, into the elevator, hallways and various rooms to create a portrait of impersonal space. An eerie and disquieting experience. ★★★ VHS: $19.99

Akira

(1989, 124 min, Japan, Katsuhiro Otomo) A sometimes grim but entertaining look into a not-too-distant future. Taking place in neo-Tokyo, complete with bike gangs, mutants and corrupt government officials, this film pushes the boundaries of animation into a truly adult realm. Visually striking, *Akira* will especially appeal to those who grew up on a diet of "8th Man," "Astro Boy" and "Speed Racer" cartoons. A groundbreaking state-of-the-art Japanese animation classic which makes some earlier efforts (like *Laputa*) look like stick-figure drawings. ★★★★ DVD Letterbox: $24.99, DVD Letterbox DTS Edition: $24.99, DVD Special Edition: $39.99, VHS Letterbox Subtitled: $19.99, VHS Letterbox Dubbed: $19.99

Akira Kurosawa's Dreams

(1990, 120 min, Japan, Akira Kurosawa) *Mitsuko Baisho, Toshihiko Nakano, Mitsunori Isaki, Martin Scorsese.* In his most personal film, Kurosawa takes time to reflect on his innermost hopes, fears and joys. Through a series of eight vignettes, or "dreams," Kurosawa takes us through his childhood terrors, his horror at the state of the environment and the use of nuclear power, his love of art and, finally, his peaceful vision of a world where people live harmoniously with nature. Filmed in vivid, sometimes explosive colors, *Dreams* represents a thoughtful summing to the impressive filmography of this cinematic giant. (Japanese with English subtitles) ★★★★ DVD Letterbox: $19.99

Aladdin

(1992, 87 min, US, John Musker & Ron Clements) *Voices of: Robin Williams, Gilbert Gottfried, Scott Weinger, Linda Larkin, Lea Salonga.* A consistently entertaining and gloriously funny adventure, *Aladdin* features a nice musical score by Alan Menken, Tim Rice and Howard Ashman; delightful animation; and wonderful

An affair to forget: Patrick Wilson, Billy Bob Thornton and Jason Patric star in the uninspired big-budget retelling of *The Alamo*

laugh-out-loud jokes. This alone makes the film first-class. But it also has Robin Williams. As the voice of the genie whose iconoclastic references will split any side, Williams catapults the film to unimaginable comic. The third and possibly strongest of the Disney-Menken-Ashman trilogy, which also includes *The Little Mermaid* and *Beauty and the Beast*. A film adults will love even more than children. (Followed by 2 sequels) ★★★★ DVD 2-disc Platinum Series Special Edition: $29.99, DVD Collector's Gift Set: $49.99

The Alamo

(1960, 186 min, US, John Wayne) *John Wayne, Richard Widmark, Laurence Harvey, Richard Boone, Frankie Avalon, Chill Wills.* Wayne's dream project (writer, producer, director, star) is an epic of Texas-sized proportions. The story, of course, has to do with the heroic last stand made by Texas patriots in the face of the overwhelming Mexican army. Wayne stars as a larger-than-life Davy Crockett, Widmark plays Jim Bowie, and Harvey is Will Travis. The battle scenes are impressive and include great cavalry charges and hundreds of extras. The first half of the film is slow going, but Wayne creates an effective sense of impending doom throughout. The remastered, restored full-length version. (Remade in 2004) ★★★ DVD Special Edition: $14.99

The Alamo

(2004, 137 min, US, John Lee Hancock) *Dennis Quaid, Billy Bob Thornton, Jason Patric, Patrick Wilson, Jordi Moll, Emilio Echevarria.* Oh, for the excesses of John Wayne! This eighth screen version (4 silents, 1935, 1936, 1960) about the fight for Texas independence is a sincere but lackluster affair, devoid of truly inspiring dramatics, good characterizations or stirring action scenes. The 1960 Wayne version — over-the-top and all — remains the best to date. The film attempts to be "historically accurate," but loses most of its momentum in doing so. The story is a familiar one: a few stalwart Texans stand guard at the remote outpost against Santa Anna's army, ultimately facing crushing defeat. Director Hancock takes his time setting character and plot, which would have been fine if there were involving players at work here. Thornton gives the best performance as Davy Crockett, but for some

reason he's not as heroic as the myth — Fess Parker may want to get a lawyer. The siege on the Alamo itself is well-staged, but getting there is a chore, and by then the film has squandered what little passion and excitement it was able to produce. ★★ DVD Letterbox: $29.99

Alamo Bay

(1985, 98 min, US, Louis Malle) *Ed Harris, Amy Madigan, Ho Nguyen, Donald Moffat.* Harris stars as a fisherman and Vietnam vet who, like most of his small Texas community, feels a sense of resentment towards the Asian refugees who have settled in their town. Paradoxical complexity arrives when these ex-soldiers, who once fought to defend the Vietnamese, must now fight them for jobs and a way of life. Though the film retains a certain power, Malle creates little tension in this precarious moral dilemma, letting the conflict speak for itself instead of adding dimension for the camera. ★★

Alan and Naomi

(1992, 95 min, US, Sterling VanWagenen) *Lukas Haas, Vanessa Zaoui, Michael Gross.* Young Haas' sincere, heartfelt performance dominates this slowly paced but nevertheless touching WWII drama. Haas brings unexpected depth to the role of a 14-year-old Brooklyn youth who is forced by his family to befriend a traumatized French girl, whose father was murdered by Nazis right before her eyes. He slowly develops a relationship with the girl, allowing the tormented youngster to escape her protective shell, and present a glimmer of hope for recovery. Good evocation of wartime America. ★★½

The Alarmist

(1998, 93 min, US, Evan Dunsky) *David Arquette, Stanley Tucci, Mary McCormack, Kate Capshaw, Ryan Reynolds.* An alarmingly bad comedy, this dark tale of robbery, kidnapping and murder is based on a stage play, and adapted for the screen by director Dunsky. *The Alarmist* concerns Tommy (Arquette), a security systems salesman, who begins an affair with his first paying customer. Meanwhile, Tommy's boss breaks into clients' homes to help business, and becomes the chief suspect in a murder. Dunsky displays such a lack of focus that his film can't decide if it wants to be a deadpan black comedy or an edgy thriller. Arquette gives an energetic,

eager-to-please performance, and he is fun to watch, but Tucci looks like he would rather be anywhere else. Capshaw isn't bad, she's simply an enigma. (aka: *Life During Wartime*) ★ DVD: $29.99

Alberto Express

(1992, 90 min, Italy, Arthur Joffe) *Sergio Castellitto, Nino Manfredi.* With a wickedly farcical premise and the presence, however brief, of Italian funny man Manfredi, this frantic family comedy should be more entertaining than it is. Alberto, a frumpy 40-year-old man about to be a first-time father, is summoned to his father's attic for a meeting. Pop, observing a family tradition, calmly begins calculating every expense incurred in raising Alberto and presents him with a bill that must be repaid. From this, Alberto schemes and connives his way through the continent, in hopes of somehow coming up with the money. While his antics are at times quite hilarious, Castellitto as Alberto is somehow not quite right for the part — too much of a forlorn sad-sack with not enough comic inventiveness to carry a comedy of this type. (Italian with English subtitles) ★★½ VHS: $19.99

Albino Alligator

(1997, 105 min, US, Kevin Spacey) *Matt Dillon, Faye Dunaway, Gary Sinise, Viggo Mortensen, William Fichtner, Skeet Ulrich, Joe Mantegna, M. Emmet Walsh.* Demonstrating moments of great understanding of the gangster film, Spacey's directorial debut has terrific scenes but doesn't quite come together as a whole. The story concerns small-time New Orleans hoods Dillon, Sinise and Fichtner who, after bungling a burglary, hole up in a seedy bar. Taking customers and employees hostage, the little remaining remnants of rational thought these men have dissipate, eventually causing a crisis of morality for all concerned. Dillon ably walks the fine line between mug and thug, Dunaway is smashing as a bartender unafraid to talk back, and Fichtner makes a great impression as the hoodlums' loose cannon. Spacey captures the mood, but the screenplay lacks some of the necessary grit. ★★½ DVD: $19.99, VHS: $14.99

Alex & Emma

(2003, 98 min, US, Rob Reiner) *Kate Hudson, Luke Wilson, Sophie Marceau, David Paymer.* Reiner tries to fan the romantic flames of his *When Harry Met Sally* but comes up winded with this dull romantic comedy. Wilson plays Alex, an author who must write a book in 30 days to pay off a gambling debt. He hires Emma (Hudson) to help transcribe it. She also helps him through his writer's block and romance blossoms. The two stars also play the lead characters in the book, set in 1924 — a tutor torn between a rich French divorcée (Marceau) and her nanny (Hudson again). The stars demonstrate little chemistry, and the tired screenplay offers little for either to do but look awkward. Add to this Reiner's static direction and this becomes quite difficult to watch. ★½ DVD Letterbox: $27.99, DVD Pan & Scan: $27.99, VHS: $8.99

Alex in Wonderland

(1970, 109 min, US, Paul Mazursky) *Donald Sutherland, Ellen Burstyn, Jeanne Moreau.* What do you do when your filmmaking debut is a huge box-office success? Mazursky's response was this meandering trifle which poses the very same. Sutherland offers a nice portrayal of Mazursky's alter ego Alex, a hippie-dippie director whose initial triumph makes him a hot property at the studio, but whose conscience bristles at the thought of becoming another

A

Hollywood lapdog. Mazursky's loosely scattered narrative makes it clear that he yearns for the freedoms enjoyed by European directors. The result, sadly, is a jumble, but the subject is of enough interest to film enthusiasts to be worth a look. Burstyn is excellent as Sutherland's wife. ★★½ VHS: $19.99

Alexander Nevsky

(1938, 108 min, USSR, Sergei Eisenstein) *Nikolai Cherkassov, Nikolai Okhlopkov.* Eisenstein's first sound film is a grand epic of Prince Nevsky's heroic defense of Russia against the invading Teutonic Knights in 1242. The final battle sequence on the ice of Lake Piepus is magnificent in its visual splendor and in the use of a stirring Prokofiev score instead of natural sound. (Digitally remastered) (Russian with English subtitles) ★★★★ DVD: $24.99, VHS: $29.99

Alexander's Ragtime Band

(1938, 105 min, US, Henry King) *Tyrone Power, Alice Faye, Don Ameche, Ethel Merman, Jack Haley.* Corny but entertaining, this backstage musical features 26 Irving Berlin songs to chronicle the story of two friends, a socialite turned bandleader (Power) and his composer sidekick (Ameche), and of the singer (Faye) they both love. Faye is in good voice, Merman is better, and the three leads have a wonderful chemistry together to make you forget all about the sappy screenplay. ★★★

Alfie

(1966, 114 min, GB, Lewis Gilbert) *Michael Caine, Vivien Merchant, Shirley Anne Field, Millicent Martin, Shelley Winters, Denholm Elliott, Eleanor Bron.* Caine is flawless as an unscrupulous Cockney womanizer who can't decide whether his lustful life is really worth the effort. It's a quirky film which strips bare all the lecherous qualities nurtured within the male mystique. There's an excellent supporting cast, and this was the film that catapulted Caine into the realm of international stardom. ★★★★ DVD: $29.99, VHS: $14.99

Algiers

(1938, 95 min, US, John Cromwell) *Charles Boyer, Sigrid Gurie, Hedy Lamarr, Joseph Calleia, Alan Hale, Gene Lockhart.* Boyer exudes sinister charm as Pepe le Moko, the crown prince of thieves in the Casbah, a labyrinthine complex of dens and warrens in the heart of Algiers, whose inhabitants are dedicated to the procurement of ill-gotten gains. A police inspector newly arrived from France intends to capture the nefarious Pepe, much to the amusement of the local constabulary. While the pace is somewhat laborious by contemporary standards, the film evokes an inticing aura of menace. ★★★

Ali

(2001, 157 min, US, Michael Mann) *Will Smith, Jamie Foxx, Jon Voight, Mario Van Peebles, Ron Silver, Jeffrey Wright, Mykelti Williamson, Jada Pinkett Smith, Joe Morton.* Will Smith is faced with the challenge of portraying a living legend in *Ali,* director Mann's compelling but fractured biography of champion boxer Muhammad Ali. And, he gives quite an accomplished dramatic performance, giving this look at ten years in the life of Ali an energy and focus all his own. However fragmented and overlong the film may be, *Ali* paints an often powerful portrait of the heavyweight champ, who is followed from his first championship bout in 1964 through his historic 1974 "Rumble in the Jungle" match. The film traces his various romantic and personal relationships, including Malcolm X, Howard

Mario Van Peebles and Will Smith in *Ali*

Cosell (Voight is unrecognizable), his wives, trainers, managers, and his publicized battle with the U.S. Army. Mann too often allows the action to ramble, but the dramatics that unfold have an intensity that overcome the occasional slow stretch. *Ali* may not be totally befitting of the American icon, but it's certainly up to the challenge. ★★★ DVD Letterbox: $14.99, DVD Letterbox Director's Expanded Edition: $24.99, VHS: $9.99

Ali: Fear Eats the Soul

(1973, 94 min, Germany, Rainer Werner Fassbinder) *Brigitte Mira, El Hedi Ben Salem, Barbara Valentin, Irm Hermann.* Fassbinder's bittersweet love story about the affair between a lonely 60-year old German cleaning woman and a reticent Moroccan auto mechanic half her age is a raw, intense look at racial attitudes and unconventional relationships. Fassbinder's first film to play theatrically in the U.S., *Ali* is startling in its examination of xenophobia, and is an unflinching study of the passion between "societal misfits," one of the director's favorite themes. (German with English subtitles) ★★★½ DVD Criterion Collection: $39.99, VHS: $19.99

Alias Betty

(2001, 103 min, France, Claude Miller) *Sandrine Kiberlain, Nicole Garcia, Mathilde Seigner, Luck Mervil.* A completely engaging film, *Alias Betty* mixes elements of crime thriller, family drama, mystery, morality tale and, surprisingly, comedy. But aside from its ability to expertly handle multiple genres, the film has a passionate interest in its characters. Each one is written and directed with a human touch, thanks to Miller's intelligent adaptation of Ruth Rendell's novel "The Tree of Hands." When an internationally acclaimed novelist (Kiberlain) loses her young son in a freak accident, her mentally unstable mother tries to heal the wounds by kidnapping another boy as a replacement. This sets off a spectacular chain of events for all parties involved. The narrative is a bit pulpy, but the characters are crafted with the kind of sensitivity that prevents the film from steamrolling into melodramatic mayhem. (French with English subtitles) ★★★½ DVD Subtitled: $24.99, VHS: $14.99

Alice

(1987, 86 min, Czechoslovakia, Jan Svankmajer) Animator Svankmajer has taken Lewis Carroll's "Alice in Wonderland" and created a distinctly original and personal interpretation of the classic chil-

dren's story. Utilizing live-action with his trademark stop-motion animation, Svankmajer's *Alice* owes more to the surrealist techniques of Buñuel and Dali than to Disney. While the narration of the familiar tale unfolds, the filmmaker's interest lies less with the story's odd and fanciful characters and more with the underlying cruel, erotic and amoral ideas of an innocent girl lost during a wickedly bizarre journey. Not for children, obviously, and not even for many adults, this extraordinary work will amaze, baffle and delight fans of the surreal. (Dubbed in English) ★★★★ DVD: $29.99, VHS: $19.99

Alice

(1991, 106 min, US, Woody Allen) *Mia Farrow, Joe Mantegna, Keye Luke, Alec Baldwin, Blythe Danner, Judy Davis, William Hurt, Bernadette Peters, Cybill Shepherd, Gwen Verdon.* This is Allen's delightful paean to Lewis Carroll's "Alice in Wonderland" and Federico Fellini's *Juliet of the Spirits.* Farrow stars as Alice, a woman who has been married for 16 years to a highly successful businessman (Hurt). But something is missing for Alice; she has a calling, she's just not sure what. With the help of a strange herbalist/acupuncturist, and through the fantasy of having an affair with divorcé Mantegna, she experiences a series of whimsical, supernatural and often hilarious events which help guide her toward inner happiness. Farrow is superb as she presents the perfect female embodiment of Allen's nebbish, and veteran actor Luke steals the film as the beguiling and mysterious doctor. ★★★½ DVD: $19.99

Alice Adams

(1935, 99 min, US, George Stevens) *Katharine Hepburn, Fred MacMurray, Evelyn Venable.* In one of her best roles, Hepburn is a girl of the bourgeoisie trying to compete with the swells for the attentions of extremely eligible and quite well-heeled MacMurray in Stevens' adaptation of the Booth Tarkington novel. Throw in a little corporate skullduggery and some strikingly visualized evidences of class distinctions. ★★★★ DVD: $19.99, VHS: $19.99

Alice and Martin

(1999, 124 min, France, André Téchiné) *Juliette Binoche, Alexis Loret, Mathieu Amalric, Carmen Maura, Marthe Villonga.* In this enigmatic tapestry of a film, director Téchiné pays attention to the most extraordinary of details, and the film is chock full of them. Distressed by his father's death, Martin (Loret) travels from his rural home in France to live with his gay half-brother Benjamin (Amalric) in Paris. Alice (Binoche) is Benjamin's roomate, and they both lead a bohemian existence on a small amount of francs. Martin's presence soon causes friction when he begins to fall for Alice. . . and she for him. Their affair is tempestuous and Martin's mental problems make for an uncertain future with both Alice and Benjamin. Filled with beauty and sadness, *Alice and Martin* is a compelling look at relationships and the frailty of the mind, told in lush strokes of the sensuous and the chaotic. (French with English subtitles) ★★★

Alice Doesn't Live Here Anymore

(1974, 113 min, US, Martin Scorsese) *Ellen Burstyn, Kris Kristofferson, Diane Ladd, Jodie Foster, Alfred Lutter, Billy Green Bush, Vic Tayback.* Burstyn won an Oscar for her bravura performance in this touching, sometimes humorous and sensitive character study of one woman's personal liberation. After her husband dies and leaves her penniless, Alice, with her young son Tommy (Lutter), moves to Phoenix, Arizona, where she attempts to survive on her own, both emotionally and financially.

Wonderful supporting from Ladd as Flo, Tayback as Mel (both of whom would reprise their roles for the TV series based on the film), and Foster as Tommy's young friend. ★★★★ VHS: $14.99

Alice in the Cities

(1973, 110 min, West Germany, Wim Wenders) *Rudiger Vogler, Yella Rottlander, Lisa Kreuzer, Chuck Berry.* Wenders' German-made films usually share several recurring themes: man's alienation and his ensuing search for meaning in life, American cultural imperialism in Germany, and the exploration of personal relationships. In *Alice in the Cities*, a brooding, remarkable examination of the director's favorite themes, we follow a 31-year-old journalist who, when traveling in the United States, suddenly finds himself with a precocious nine-year-old girl abandoned by her mother. The two return to Germany in search of the girl's grandmother. (German with English subtitles) ★★★

Alice in Wonderland

(1950, 83 min, GB, Lou Bunin) Released a year before Disney's version of the story, this mixture of animation and live action virtually disappeared in the U.S. after threats of reprisal from the Disney studio. Closer to Lewis Carroll's original work in satirical tone than Disney's, this *Alice* is equally enjoyable by both adults and children, although aimed at the latter. The story begins at Oxford, where lonely lecturer Charles Dodgson spins fantastic tales for Alice Liddel and her two sisters. It then shifts to Wonderland, where the familiar characters are brought vividly to life through stop-motion animation. The animation is impressively intercut with the live Alice, creating a fantasy world of giant talking caterpillars, gryphons and mock turtles. ★★★ VHS: $24.99

Alice in Wonderland

(1951, 75 min, US, Clyde Geronimi, Hamilton Luske, Wilfred Jackson) *Voices of: Kathryn Beaumomt, Ed Wynn, Jerry Colonna, Sterling Holloway, Richard Haydn.* Disney's adaptation of Lewis Carroll's classic is a colorful, tune-filled excursion through Wonderland. More eccentric and slightly more surreal than Disney's usual, the film follows the familiar journey taken by Alice as she enters a wondrous dimension populated by the White Rabbit, talking caterpillars and where she's likely to be any size from one moment to the next. Of the songs, "I'm Late" is the most well-known, though "A Very Merry Un-Birthday" is kinda cute, too. ★★★½ DVD: $29.99, DVD The Masterpiece Edition 2-disc Set: $29.99, VHS: $22.99

Alice to Nowhere

(1986, 212 min, Australia, John Power) *Rosey Jones, John Waters.* An exceedingly long but at times rousing adventure yarn made for Aussie television. A woman, who doesn't know that in her possession is a cache of priceless jewels, finds herself pursued by thieves and just regular bad guys. Her adventures take her and her two guides through many perilous, grueling outback regions in this *Indiana Jones*-like epic. ★★★

Alice's Restaurant

(1969, 111 min, US, Arthur Penn) *Arlo Guthrie, Pat Quinn, James Broderick.* Penn's follow-up to *Bonnie and Clyde* was a film version of Guthrie's communal sing-along which accurately captures the cultural upheaval going on at the end of the 1960s. Quirky and entertaining, the film features a surprisingly downbeat ending proving to be more prophetic than the hyperbole of *Easy Rider.* ★★★ DVD: $19.99

Alien

(1979, 117 min, US, Ridley Scott) *Sigourney Weaver, Tom Skerritt, Yaphet Kotto, Harry Dean Stanton, Ian Holm, John Hurt, Veronica Cartwright.* Terror lurks in every corner in this frightening story of a completely hostile and virtually indestructible creature which sneaks aboard the spaceship *Nostromo*, via Hurt's navel, and brings an absolute nightmare to its crew. Director Scott masterfully blends pulse-pounding suspense and some gory, amazing F/X, and the film is greatly benefitted by H.R. Giger's outstanding production design. (Sequel: *Aliens*) ★★★½ DVD 2-disc Collector's Edition: $26.99, VHS: $14.99, VHS Letterbox: $14.99

Aliens

(1986, 137 min, US, James Cameron) *Sigourney Weaver, Michael Biehn, Bill Paxton, Lance Henriksen, Carrie Henn, Paul Reiser, Jenette Goldstein.* The blockbuster sequel to *Alien* does the original one better; dazzling special effects and nerve-wracking suspense make this definitely not for the weak of heart. Weaver reprises her role as Warrant Officer Ripley in an Oscar-nominated performance. Ripley is convinced to return to the planet where the deadly aliens were initially found when an Earth colony loses contact with its home base. Director Cameron assaults the senses in a unrelenting barrage of terror, and just when you thought it couldn't get any more suspenseful — it does! (Sequel: *Alien 3*) ★★★★ DVD 2-disc Collector's Edition: $26.99, VHS: $14.99

Alien³

(1992, 115 min, US, David Fincher) *Sigourney Weaver, Charles S. Dutton, Charles Dance, Pete Postlethwaite, Paul McCann, Lance Henriksen.* In the third chapter in the *Alien* series, first-time director Fincher had his work cut out for him — and though his film delivers some of the goods, there's no comparison to the first two films. Weaver, with shaved head, returns as Lt. Ripley, now the sole survivor of the escape made at the end of *Aliens*. And it seems she's brought an old friend along. Ripley has crash landed at a maximum security prison on some distant bleak planet. And there's not much for her to do but balance her time between the hostile inmates and one angry alien. Like the music videos Fincher cut his teeth on, *Alien³* has a great look but very little substance. (Sequel: *Alien Resurrection*) ★★½ DVD 2-disc Collector's Edition: $26.99, VHS: $14.99, VHS Letterbox: $14.99

Alien Resurrection

(1997, 120 min, US, Jean-Pierre Jeunet) *Sigourney Weaver, Winona Ryder, Dominique Pinon, Ron Perlman, Michael Wincott, Brad Dourif, Dan Hedaya, Raymond Cruz.* Weaver returns in this unsatisfying fourth *Alien* film as Ripley, who immolated herself in the previous film while "giving birth" to an alien queen. A couple of centuries later, scientists have succeeded in cloning her in order to extract the alien queen embryo from her womb for research and weapons purposes. Unfortunately for them, they also have the "meat by-product" of Ripley herself left over. Now, the genetically enhanced Ripley is thrust once again into the center of an alien war. The opening sequence opens beautifully, showing off director Jeunet's visual talents. But aside from a couple of exciting scenes, the film is a repeat of the clichés of its predecessors. The *Alien* series should have died with its heroine. ★★ DVD 2-disc Collector's Edition: $26.99, VHS: $14.99, VHS Letterbox: $19.99

Alien Nation

(1988, 94 min, US, Graham Baker) *James Caan, Mandy Patinkin, Terence Stamp.* Caan is well cast as a tough L.A. cop who is partnered with an alien — from outer space. It seems in the not-so-distant future, an alien race will arrive on Earth after the destruction of their own planet, though they are welcomed with not-so-open arms. The first half of the film is an intriguing sci-fi adventure, but the story disintegrates into a routine buddy film. Patinkin is oddly affecting as Caan's man-from-outer space partner. ★★½ DVD: $24.99, VHS: $9.99

Alien Visitor

(1995, 92 min, Australia, Rolf de Heer) *Ulli Birve, Syd Brisbane, Aletha McGrath.* A young woman from the planet Epsilon accidentally crash lands in the Australian Outback. She meets a lone surveyor and together they walk in circles trying to understand each other. They eventually fall in love in the process. Despite a few dead-on moments of clarity, *Alien Visitor* is a rather one-dimensional character study that tries to affirm its environmental and worldly messages, but winds up beating these points into the ground, culminating in a nice but predictable ending. (aka: *Epsilon*) ★★ DVD: $14.99, VHS: $9.99

Alive

(1993, 125 min, US, Frank Marshall) *Ethan Hawke, Vincent Spano, Josh Hamilton, Bruce Ramsay, David Kriegel, Illeana Douglas.* Despite containing some truly trite Hollywood contrivances, this high-altitude action film offers excellent thrills and a lot of food for thought. Recounting the harrowing two-month ordeal suffered by the surviving passengers of an Uruguayan airliner which crashed in the Chilean Andes, the film begins with a bang with an extremely well-staged crash sequence. The film bogs down a little towards the middle, occasionally straying into the haze of religious piety. Overall, however, the film is an exciting testament to the power of the human spirit to survive in absolutely untenable conditions. ★★★ DVD 30th Anniversary: $14.99, VHS: $9.99

Alive & Kicking

(1996, 98 min, GB, Nancy Meckler) *Anthony Higgins, Jason Flemyng, Dorothy Tutin, Antony Sher.* Tonio (Flemyng) is a young ballet dancer working with a dance troupe whose ranks have been decimated by AIDS. Flamboyant and narcissistic, the handsome Tonio uses his single-minded commitment to his career as a shield against others. Now sick himself, he continues to prepare for the ballet "Indian Summer." He also becomes attracted to Jack (Sher), a short, bald, middle-aged therapist. Despite their differences in age, they fall in love. Written for the screen by Martin Sherman ("Bent"), this moving tale of endurance, survival and the redemptive power of love is deeply affecting despite the pedestrian handling by the director. (aka: *Indian Summer*) ★★★ DVD: $9.99, VHS: $9.99

All about Eve

(1950, 138 min, US, Joseph L. Mankiewicz) *Bette Davis, Anne Baxter, George Sanders, Celeste Holm, Gary Merrill, Hugh Marlowe, Thelma Ritter, Marilyn Monroe.* The Bette Davis classic, which still remains the definitive Hollywood movie about theatre life. Bette, in what is possibly the quintessential Davis role, stars as Margo Channing, a first lady of the theatre whose professional and personal life is changed forever when a seemingly starstruck young woman (Baxter) enters her life. A brilliantly scathing, enor-

All about My Mother

mously witty look behind the masks of the players who strut and fret their hour upon the stage. Holm, Sanders and Ritter are all superb in supporting roles. ★★★★ DVD: $14.99, VHS: $9.99

All about My Mother

(1999, 101 min, Spain, Pedro Almodóvar) *Cecilia Roth, Marisa Paredes, Candela Peña, Antonia San Juan, Penélope Cruz.* A sweet, funny, big-hearted valentine of a film, dedicated to "actresses who have played actresses," Almodóvar's Academy Award-winning melodrama at once recalls the best of those '50s Douglas Sirk movies while at the same time examining — in quintessential Almodóvar style — lives of the disenfranchised. Roth is wondrous as a mother who, mourning the death of her teenaged son, journeys back to a forgotten past and searches for the boy's father — now a transvestite prostitute. Paredes brings sublime elegance to the role of a legendary stage actress whom Roth befriends. A joyous celebration of diversity, motherhood and the theatre. (Spanish with English subtitles) ★★★★ DVD Subtitled: $29.99

All about the Benjamins

(2002, 99 min, US, Kevin Bray) *Ice Cube, Mike Epps, Eva Mendes, Tommy Flanagan, Anthony Michael Hall.* Cube plays a bounty hunter who teams with small-time thief Epps to find a $60 million winning lottery ticket Epps lost while running from both Cube and some big-time diamond smugglers. Totally charmless, *All about the Benjamins* steals the premise of *Uptown Saturday Night*, and drains all the fun and humor (alas, Cube and Epps are certainly no Cosby and Poitier, and the pseudo-tough Eurovillain here can't hold a candle to Harry Belafonte's hysterical Godfather impression). There's a supremely ugly torture scene, and the two "heroes" are unlikable, greedy jerks. Aren't we supposed to hate the *villains* in this kind of action/comedy? A low point for the usually reliable Cube. ★ DVD Platinum Series: $19.99, VHS: $6.99

All Dogs Go to Heaven

(1989, 85 min, US, Don Bluth) *Voices of: Burt Reynolds, Loni Anderson, Dom DeLuise, Melba Moore, Charles Nelson Reilly.* Charming animated tale about a roguish German Shepherd who becomes the unlikely guardian to an orphaned girl named Anne Marie. Beautiful visuals from Don Bluth and company (*An American Tail*). (Followed by two sequels) ★★★ DVD: $14.99, VHS: $9.99

All Fall Down

(1962, 110 min, US, John Frankenheimer) *Warren Beatty, Karl Malden, Angela Lansbury, Eva Marie Saint, Brandon de Wilde, Barbara Baxley.* Adapted for the screen by William Inge, *All Fall Down* centers on a dysfunctional Cleveland family headed by alcoholic father Malden and domineering mother Lanbury. Beatty, looking impossibly young and handsome, is the eldest son Berry-berry, a louse of a drifter who returns home at the insistence of his idolizing brother de Wilde. Director Frankenheimer concentrates on the dark side of the American family, exploring a bruised familial psyche with numerous open wounds. And thanks to its perceptive direction and script, the film cuts deeper than the usual Gothic drama. It's Lansbury who walks away with the acting honors, though Baxley is fine in a small but potent role as one of Beatty's pickups. ★★★½ VHS: $19.99

All Night Long

(1981, 88 min, US, Jean-Claude Tramont) *Barbra Streisand, Gene Hackman, Diane Ladd, Dennis Quaid, William Daniels.* An offbeat and marvelous comic romp with Hackman in great form as an all-night drugstore manager who begins an affair with his neighbor's sexually frustrated wife (Streisand). She, in turn, is involved with Hackman's teenage son (Quaid). A small gem, and vastly underrated. ★★★½

All of Me

(1984, 93 min, US, Carl Reiner) *Steve Martin, Lily Tomlin, Victoria Tennant, Madolyn Smith, Richard Libertini.* Reincarnation, the hereafter, gurus and modern romance are all equally spoofed in director Reiner's splendidly funny romp which offered Martin his first real chance to prove his considerable comic abilities. Tomlin costars as a dying, rich invalid whose belief in returning from the dead prompts some hasty legal maneuvering. This sends lawyer Martin to her side. But in a strange turn of events, Tomlin's soul has now been transported into the body of Martin. Though the premise and its execution are engaging, it is really Martin's virtuoso performance which distinguishes the film. He literally gets in touch with both his masculine and feminine sides as he fights for control of his body, sending him on a hilarious, slapstick search for inner tranquility. ★★★½ DVD: $9.99

All or Nothing

(2002, 128 min, GB, Mike Leigh) *Timothy Spall, Lesley Manville, Alison Garland, James Corden.* Few filmmakers are able to get to the center of life better than Mike Leigh. His films ache with the harsh realities that working-class families experience. *All or Nothing*, Leigh's haunting, somber look at three families caught in the daily grind of "getting by, week in and week out," strips bare human emotion with profoundly moving exactness. Tracking the lives of several residents of a housing estate, the film pays the most attention to the Bassetts. The father, Phil (Spall), drives a cab to help support the family. He receives little respect or emotional support from his hardworking wife or distant children. It takes a tragedy to bring the family together and to analyze what truly matters in their world. As heartbreaking as it is powerful, *All or Nothing* understands the complexities of relationships and the ebb and flow of love. And though the characters' lives are sad ones, this tempered, quiet film ultimately becomes an unexpectedly uplifting experience. ★★★½ DVD Letterbox: $19.99

All over Me

(1997, 90 min, US, Alex Sichel) *Alison Folland, Tara Subkoff, Wilson Cruz, Cole Hauser, Leisha Haley.* This first feature film from the Sichel sisters (Alex directed, Sylvia wrote) is a painfully tender and knowing tale of one 15-year-old girl's emerging lesbian sexuality. Set in New York's Hell's Kitchen, the story follows Claude (Folland), a high schooler secretly in love with her straight best friend. How Claude deals with the emotional pain of unrequited first love as well as having to deal with coming out is the involving drama's central tale. *All over Me* is told with grit and real emotion. Cruz appears as Claude's friend who shares her same-sex feelings and urges for a first love. ★★★ VHS: $19.99

All over the Guy

(2000, 95 min, US, Julie Davis) *Dan Bucatinsky, Richard Ruccolo, Adam Goldberg, Sasha Alexander, Doris Roberts, Christina Ricci, Lisa Kudrow, Andrea Martin.* Opposites attract in this sweet romantic comedy about two very different gay men and their search for true love. Eli (Bucatinsky, who wrote the screenplay based on his stage production) is a cute neurotic whose favorite film is *Gone with the Wind*. When his straight best friend Brett (Goldberg) falls in love with Jackie (Alexander), Eli is set up with Jackie's best friend, Tom (Ruccolo), an unsentimental, pragmatic teacher. However, whereas Eli is commitment oriented, Tom claims to be only looking for a good time. From their disastrous first date, through a tentative romance, Tom and Eli try to get close but are often foiled by their own insecurities. The film amusingly flips back and forth between Eli and Tom recounting their relationship to strangers, each trying to believe that they are "all over the guy." Director Davis coaxes wonderful performances from her cast, and Bucatinsky's witty screenplay features some potent, fast-talking dialogue. ★★★ DVD: $14.99

All Quiet on the Western Front

(1930, 130 min, US, Lewis Milestone) *Lew Ayres, Louis Wolheim, Slim Summerville, Beryl Mercer.* Milestone won an Oscar as Best Director for this classic antiwar film based on the Erich Maria Remarque novel about the experiences of a group of young German soldiers in battle during WWI. The film won an Oscar for Best Picture, and Ayres became a star with his haunting portrayal of the young infantryman. In supporting roles, Summerville and especially Wolheim are terrific as Ayres' fellow soldiers. (Remade for TV in 1979) ★★★★ DVD: $14.99, VHS: $9.99

All Screwed Up

(1973, 105 min, Italy, Lina Wertmüller) *Luigi Diberti, Nino Bignamini.* Two young men, orphans from the countryside, come to the big city (here Milan) looking for fame and fortune. Upon their arrival, they get arrested, swindled and fall in love, eventually living in a commune with three women while all their romantic and professional aspirations experience ups and downs. Wertmüller's social comedy has its appealing moments, especially when the director allows her camera to sit still and concentrate on the characters' interpersonal relationships. But much of the film is static, and in an effort to demonstrate the frenzy of city life, the story becomes victim to what it is satirizing. (Italian with English subtitles) ★★

All That Heaven Allows

(1956, 89 min, US, Douglas Sirk) *Rock Hudson, Jane Wyman, Agnes Moorehead, Conrad Nagel, Virginia Grey.* Hudson, Wyman and director Sirk all reunited from their 1954 success *Magnificent Obsession* for this involving May-December melodrama. Wyman plays a middle-aged widow who begins a romance with younger gardener Hudson. True to 1950s form, the tongues start wagging. Good performances, a compelling story and typically lush direction from Sirk make this quite enjoyable. (Remade in 1974 as *Ali — Fear Eats the Soul* and in 2002 as *Far from Heaven*) ★★★ DVD Criterion Collection: $39.99

All That Jazz

(1979, 119 min, US, Bob Fosse) *Roy Scheider, Ann Reinking, Jessica Lange, Ben Vereen, Leland Palmer, Cliff Gorman, John Lithgow, Keith Gordon.* Fosse's dynamic and semiautobiographical tribute to the rigors and razzle-dazzle of showbiz. Scheider portrays Fosse's self-absorbed alter ego whose creativity is well matched by his destructive excesses. Lange is a most appealing Angel of Death. Film includes some brilliant, unparalleled dance sequences. ★★★½ DVD: $14.99

All That Money Can Buy

See: *The Devil and Daniel Webster*

All Quiet on the Western Front

All the King's Men

(1949, 109 min, US, Robert Rossen) *Broderick Crawford, Mercedes McCambridge, John Ireland, Joanne Dru, John Derek.* A Best Picture Oscar went to this searing adaptation of Robert Penn Warren's Pulitzer Prize-winning novel about the rise and fall of a Huey Long-like politician. Academy Award winner Crawford gives the performance of a lifetime as the power-crazed senator. McCambridge also won an Oscar for her rich portrayal of his devoted secretary. ★★★★ DVD: $24.99

All the Mornings of the World (Tous les Matins du Monde)

(1991, 114 min, France, Alain Corneau) *Jean-Pierre Marielle, Gérard Depardieu, Anne Brochet, Guillaume Depardieu.* An elaborately costumed and acted story of creativity, passion and betrayal between two composers in 17th-century France. Marin Marais (Depardieu), a successful composer at the Court of Versailles, painfully looks back into his youth and his volatile relationship with his taciturn music teacher, composer Sainte Colombe (Marielle). Told in flashbacks with Depardieu's son, Guillaume, playing the younger Marais, the story explores the contentious relationship between the prodigious student and his gifted teacher Sainte Colombe. Studied and intense, the film's greatest moments occur in the stirring chords of its passionate Baroque music. (French with English subtitles) ★★★½

All the President's Men

(1976, 138 min, US, Alan J. Pakula) *Robert Redford, Dustin Hoffman, Jason Robards, Jack Warden, Jane Alexander, Martin Balsam, Hal Holbrook, Ned Beatty, F. Murray Abraham.* The film that successfully captures the heady paranoia of the Watergate years. Journalism departments' enrollments skyrocketed after the Woodward-Bernstein team, who broke the Watergate story in *The Washington Post*, were portrayed in this film by Redford and Hoffman. Superlative support (including Oscar-winner Robards) and an Oscar-winning script by William Goldman and taut, incisive direction by Pakula are weaved together to produce an intelligent, blistering account of political chicanery and investigative prowess. Yes, this is the first time you asked the question, "What did the President know and when did he know it?" ★★★★ DVD: $19.99

All the Pretty Horses

(2000, 117 min, US, Billy Bob Thornton) *Matt Damon, Henry Thomas, Penélope Cruz, Lucas Black, Sam Shepard, Ruben Blades, Miriam Colon, Bruce Dern, Robert Patrick.* The wide-open vistas of Texas and Mexico set the tone for a picturesque tale of a West in transition, but the majestic scenery can't compensate for a thin story of romance, friendship and the search for adventure. Based on the novel by Cormac McCarthy, the film — set in 1949 — follows cowboys John Grady Cole (Damon) and Lacey Rawlins (Thomas) who leave their San Antonio birthplace for the unknown wilds of Mexico. It is there Cole soon begins a forbidden love affair with the beautiful daughter (Cruz) of his cattle-baron boss. Though the film features wondrous cinematography and an involving subplot of a jailed comrade, *All the Pretty Horses* offers little else for the eye or the heart. Damon and Cruz lack chemistry, and the pacing veers towards lethargic. ★★ DVD: $14.99, VHS: $14.99

All the Real Girls

(2003, 108 min, US, David Gordon Green) *Paul Schneider, Zooey Deschanel, Patricia Clarkson.* Love ain't easy. And neither is the path the characters wander in director Green's impressive second feature, *All the Real Girls.* Taking a few unconventional turns at chronicling a young relationship, Green gets to the heart of young love and all its highs and lows. Schneider stars as Paul, a Southern small-town dweller who has experienced many a girl, just not in any meaningful way until he falls for Noel (the spectacular Deschanel), a young woman who is also taking her first crack at love. Several vignettes in the midst of a golden leaf-drenched autumn show the excitement of a budding relationship and the two leads perform it with naturalistic simplicity. The film begins with the couple's relationship in progress and we are allowed to peek in on their journey, their joys and their mistakes. An appealing alternate to most superficial romantic stories, *All the Real Girls* doesn't pay dumb for its audience, nor does it supply all the answers to love's most difficult questions. ★★★ DVD: $24.99

All the Right Moves

(1983, 91 min, US, Michael Chapman) *Tom Cruise, Craig T. Nelson, Lea Thompson, Christopher Penn.* An earnest Cruise plays a Pennsylvania high school football star who sees an athletic scholarship as a way out of his small mining town. Nelson also stars as his hot-tempered coach himself looking for a ticket out. Predictable, uneventful but slickly directed and performed. ★★ DVD: $14.99

All the Vermeers in New York

(1990, 87 min, US, Jon Jost) *Stephen Lack, Emmanuelle Chaulet, Gracie Mansion, Gordon Joseph Weiss.* Radical independent filmmaker Jost presents an austere, amusing jab at wealthy New Yorkers and the commodification of art in this story of a lonely stockbroker (Lack) who becomes obsessed with a wispy, emotionally reserved French actress (Chaulet). With an almost cinema verité starkness, the film uncovers the hollow lives of Manhattan's power brokers and effectively unmasks their haughty pretenses. Exquisitely shot, the film features an excellent jazz score by The Bay Area Jazz Composers Orchestra. ★★★ DVD Letterbox: $29.99, VHS Letterboxed: $19.99

All This, and Heaven Too

(1940, 143 min, US, Anatole Litvak) *Bette Davis, Charles Boyer, Jeffrey Lynn, June Lockhart.* Handsomely produced tearjerker starring Davis and Boyer with Boyer as a 19th-century Paris aristocrat who murders his wife after falling in love with his children's governess (Davis). Great performances by the two leads. ★★★

All Through the Night

(1942, 107 min, US, Vincent Sherman) *Humphrey Bogart, William Demarest, Peter Lorre, Phil Silvers, Jackie Gleason, Frank McHugh, Judith Anderson.* Before he tangled with Nazis in *Casablanca,* Bogart took on German spies right here in the USA. Bogey plays Gloves Donahue, a hotshot Manhattan gambler whose investigation into the murder of an old family friend leads him hot on the trail of a Nazi spy ring. With its Runyon-esque characters, sparkling dialogue, snappy one-liners and detestable villains, this comic espionage thriller is a supremely enjoyable lark. ★★★½ VHS: $19.99

Allegro non Troppo

(1976, 75 min, Italy, Bruno Bozzetto) Italian animation artist Bozzetto offers his own answer to Walt Disney's *Fantasia*. This delightfully whimsical work features a variety of bizarre creatures cavorting to the music of Debussy, Dvorak, Ravel, Sibelius, Vivaldi and Stravinsky. ★★★½ DVD: $29.99, VHS: $29.99

The Alley Cats

(1966, 83 min, France, Radley Metzger) The swinging '60s have never looked so sexy, fun and erotic as in Metzger's second solo feature *The Alley Cats*. When Leslie, a member of Europe's wealthy swinging set, feels ignored by her philandering fiancée, she decides to do some swinging herself. Her first lover, the suave, debonair Christian, pleases her greatly. But soon Leslie responds to the advances of Irena, a beautiful lesbian socialite. She must then choose between her fiancée and her awakened lesbian feelings. This newly remastered video feature a scintillating, jazzy lounge music soundtrack. ★★★ VHS: $19.99

Alligator

(1980, 94 min, US, Lewis Teague) *Robert Forster, Robin Riker, Henry Silva, Michael Gazzo, Dean Jagger.* John Sayles wrote the screenplay for this tongue-in-cheek, very entertaining horror film about a giant alligator terrorizing the populace of Chicago. (Those stories about gators being flushed down the toilet are obviously true.) ★★★

The Alligator People

(1959, 74 min, US, Roy Del Ruth) *Beverly Garland, George Macready, Lon Chaney, Jr..* Cheesy horror semiclassic about a doctor who discovers a serum enabling humans to grow back amputated parts of their bodies — guess what the side effects are. ★★ VHS: $14.99

Allonsanfan

(1974, 100 min, Italy, Paolo & Vittorio Taviani) *Marcello Mastroianni, Lea Massari, Mimsy Farmer.* The year 1816 finds Europe settling into a conservative period after the upheavals of the Napoleonic era. This unusual time is the setting for the Taviani brothers' lavish yet intelligent political costume drama. Mastroianni is Giulio, a petite bourgeois who returns to the new European order after spending time in prison. Disillusioned by what he sees, he becomes torn between his comfortable upbringing and his revolutionary past. Mastroianni excels as the spineless aristocrat who must decide between loyalty to his old radical compatriots or betrayal of them for personal gain. (Italian with English subtitles) ★★★½

Almonds and Raisins

(1984, 85 min, US, Russ Karel) *Narrated by: Orson Welles.* Welles narrates this delightful account of the history of a once-flourishing segment of American movie making: the Yiddish cinema. From 1927 through 1939, some 300 Yiddish films — including musicals, gangster films, screwball comedies and even a Yiddish western — were produced. Few of these films exist in their entirety, but through film clips and interviews with surviving actors, directors and producers, filmmaker Karel has fashioned an enthralling image of this lost industry and culture. ★★★½ VHS: $79.99

Almost Famous

(2000, 123 min, US, Cameron Crowe) *Billy Crudup, Patrick Fugit, Kate Hudson, Frances McDormand, Jason Lee, Anna Paquin, Philip Seymour Hoffman, Fairuza Balk, Noah Taylor.* Writer-director Crowe turns to a page of his own youth with this warm and winning comic portrait of coming-of-age amid rock's golden age. Crowe's alter ego is William Miller (engagingly played by Fugit), a 15-year-old aspiring writer who — sight unseen — lands a freelance writing assignment with *Rolling Stone* to accompany the fictitious group Stillwater on tour (Crowe actually traveled with Led Zeppelin). This small-town boy gets a big-time lesson in the ways of the world when he befriends a fractured family unit of inner and outer circle members, including the sweet-natured "band-aid" Penny Lane (Hudson). Crowe has captured the cadence and minutiae of the early 1970s with remarkable precision, and his ensemble is first-rate: Hudson is nothing short of smashing as Penny; and possibly best of all is McDormand as William's overprotective mother. What a time to come of age, and what a splendid reminiscence this is — hail, hail rock 'n' roll. ★★★★ DVD Letterbox Untitled: The Bootleg Cut: $34.99, DVD Theatrical Cut: $14.99

Almost You

(1984, 96 min, US, Adam Brooks) *Brooke Adams, Griffin Dunne, Karen Young, Josh Mostel.* Mostel's wonderful supporting turn nearly makes this mediocre romantic comedy worth watching. Too bad the rest of the cast can't accomplish as much. Dunne plays a New York executive who begins an affair with his injured wife's nurse. ★★ VHS: $79.99

Along Came a Spider

(2001, 103 min, US, Lee Tamahori) *Morgan Freeman, Monica Potter, Michael Wincott, Mika Boorem, Dylan Baker, Penelope Ann Miller, Michael Moriarty, Jay O. Sanders.* Based on the first book in James Patterson's Alex Cross series, this convoluted prequel to 1997's *Kiss the Girls* brings back Freeman as the noted forensics detective, and the actor absolutely shines as the sleuthing shrink. Freeman endows the good doctor with such wisdom and humanity that his appearing in this tangled thriller is a crime almost worthy of an investigation by Cross himself. When the daughter of a U.S. senator is kidnapped, Cross teams with a Secret Service agent (Potter) to find her as the kidnapper engages them in cat-and-mouse games. Director Tamahori gives the film a polished look, and maintains a minimum of suspense throughout. But Marc Moss' screenplay adaptation relies too heavily on coincidence and illogical plot developments. ★★ DVD Letterbox: $14.99, VHS Special Edition: $9.99

Along Came Polly

(2004, 90 min, US, John Hamburg) *Ben Stiller, Jennifer Aniston, Philip Seymour Hoffman, Debra Messing, Alec Baldwin, Hank Azaria, Bryan Brown.* Overly silly and chemistry-free, *Along Came Polly* manages to produce a few laughs in spite of its dumbing down and formula romance. Stiller plays an extremely uptight insurance risk-assessor who's jilted on his honeymoon; he meets old high school acquaintance Aniston, his complete opposite, and is surprised to find himself attracted to her. Typical cutesy romantic comedy material clashes with (increasingly typical, these days) unfunny bathroom humor, resulting in a by-the-books comedy. Luckily, there are three great comic performers in support:

Almost Famous

Baldwin as Stiller's crass boss; Hoffman as a rather pathetic former child star; and especially Brown in a hilarious "crude Australian" parody. The typecast Stiller and Aniston are fine individually, but can't connect as a couple, making this — when the supporting players aren't on-screen — a tedious chore. ★★ DVD Letterbox: $26.99

Alphaville

(1965, 100 min, France/Italy, Jean-Luc Godard) *Eddie Constantine, Anna Karina, Akim Tamiroff, Howard Vernon.* This is quintessential Godard, complete with fragmented musical score, existential reflections, jump cuts, hyperbolic expostulation, disjointed conversations and unexpected silences. Positing the notion that a fabricated legend can communicate complex realities, Godard creates Lemmy Caution (Constantine), a chiseled-face man with a gun who's not hesitant to use it. He says he's been assigned by his newspaper to Alphaville, a sterile, joyless urban complex, where day is as dark as night and language has no meaning. Karina is Caution's official government tour guide, a woman of ethereal beauty and mechanical compliance, who becomes both savior and saved. (Remastered print) (French with English subtitles) ★★★½ DVD Criterion Collection: $29.99, VHS Subtitled: $29.99

Alpine Fire (Höhenfeuer)

(1985, 117 min, Switzerland, Fredi M. Murer) *Thomas Nock, Johanna Lier.* Visually stunning and scrupulously detailed, this sublime drama is about the life and traumas of a family of four who live in near isolation in a remote area of the Alps. The film focuses on the teenage son, a mildly retarded deaf-mute whose pangs of adolescent sexual and emotional turmoil are comforted by his understanding older sister — a close bind which inevitably leads to incest. (German with English subtitles) ★★★

Alsino and the Condor

(1982, 90 min, Nicaragua, Miguel Littin) *Dean Stockwell, Alan Esquivel.* The recipient of the Best Feature awards at the L.A. Filmex and the Moscow International Film Festival, this remarkably moving drama concerns the abrupt abduction of a young boy in a battle-scarred Nicaraguan village. Chilean director Littin strikes a rueful, poetic tone and the expressive face of Esquivel (as Alsino) captures the searing pain of a stolen childhood. (Spanish with English subtitles) ★★★½

A

Altered States

(1980, 120 min, US, Ken Russell) *William Hurt, Blair Brown, Bob Balaban, Charles Haid, Drew Barrymore.* This fantastic assault on the senses is one of Russell's best films. Hurt plays an inquisitive scientist who experiments with powerful mind-altering drugs in a quest for his primal self. Gradually, he undergoes a series of mental and physical transformations and experiences some spine-chilling hallucinations. Paddy Chayefsky's novel is brought to life with the help of some shocking, state-of-the-art special effects. And though Chayefsky disowned the film, this is nevertheless an unforgettable film experience. Haid is terrific as one of Hurt's disbelieving colleagues. ★★★★ DVD: $14.99, VHS: $9.99

Always

(1985, 105 min, US, Henry Jaglom) *Henry Jaglom, Patrice Townsend, Andre Gregory.* One of director Jaglom's most accomplished and accessible works, this funny, semiautobiographical comedy examines the interaction of three couples spending the July 4th holiday together. As usual, Jaglom unflinchingly bares his soul in front of the camera to present a discourse on the modern relationship. ★★★ DVD: $24.99, VHS: $19.99

Always

(1989, 121 min, US, Steven Spielberg) *Richard Dreyfuss, Holly Hunter, John Goodman, Audrey Hepburn, Brad Johnson.* A glossy, over-produced, technically superior remake of *A Guy Named Joe*. Dreyfuss stars in the Spencer Tracy role, stars as a dedicated Montana forest firefighter who dies in the line of duty, only to return to guide (spiritually) an apprentice firefighter — who happens to be romantically involved with the woman (Hunter) he left behind. Though the story lapses into sappy sentimentality, the strength of this Spielberg film is the conviction which a mostly talented cast brings to it. ★★½ DVD Letterboxed: $14.99

Amadeus

(1984, 158 min, US, Milos Forman) *Tom Hulce, F. Murray Abraham, Jeffrey Jones, Elizabeth Berridge, Simon Callow, Christine Ebersole, Roy Dotrice, Cynthia Nixon, Vincent Schiavelli.* Forman's masterful adaptation of Peter Shaffer's Broadway smash is a literate, humorous and visually stunning examination of the rivalry (albeit a fictional one) between musical genius Wolfgang Amadeus Mozart and court composer Antonio Salieri in 18th-century Vienna. Abraham is brilliant as the tortured Salieri, and Hulce is equally commanding as the childish Mozart. Winner of eight Academy Awards including Picture, Director and Actor (Abraham). ★★★★ DVD Letterbox: $19.99, DVD Director's Cut: $26.99, VHS Pan & Scan: $8.99, VHS Director's Cut: $19.99, VHS Letterbox: $8.99

Amarcord

(1974, 127 min, Italy, Federico Fellini) *Magali Noel, Bruno Zanin.* Fellini uses a gentle mixture of dreamlike fantasy and bittersweet cynicism in this autobiographical examination of a small Italian town. Young Zanin (the director's alter ego) hangs out with his friends, gets in trouble, obsesses over women, and attempts to figure out his life. On the surface, the film is a funny and warm coming-of-age story (Fellini's recollection of facing a father confessor as an adolescent boy is alone worth the price of rental). But the specter of impending fascism that looms throughout the picture raises complex and challenging questions. One of Fellini's most accessible and compelling films. (Italian with English subtitles) ★★★★ DVD Criterion Collection: $39.99, VHS: $29.99

Amateur

(1995, 105 min, US, Hal Hartley) *Isabelle Huppert, Martin Donovan, Elina Löwensohn, Damian Young.* Huppert stars in this quirky, appealing black comedy of errors about a wannabe-nymphomaniacal ex-nun who discovers an amnesiac (Donovan) left for dead on the streets of New York City. She becomes determined to unlock the mystery of his identity. Along the way, the two encounter various urban denizens (a porn star, corporate assassins) each holding a piece of the puzzle. Hartley's deliberately kinky examination of sex, love, identity and intimacy is more plot-driven than his earlier works, but still relies too much on having the characters speak their thoughts. ★★★ DVD: $24.99

The Amazing Colossal Man

(1957, 80 min, US, Bert I. Gordon) *Glenn Langan, Cathy Downs.* This above-average 1950s sci-fi schlockfest features better than usual F/X and employs documentary footage. Cold war nuclear paranoia combines with a cynicism uncharacteristic of the era in this story of an Army officer who grows 60-feet tall. ★★½

The Amazing Dr. Clitterhouse

(1938, 87 min, US, Anatole Litvak) *Edward G. Robinson, Humphrey Bogart, Claire Trevor, Allen Jenkins, Donald Crisp.* An amusing, nicely played gangster comedy/melodrama with Robinson doing a switch from his underworld roles playing a kindly professor who joins Bogart's gang to study criminal behavior. Much to his dismay, he becomes addicted to crime. Director Litvak smartly juggles comedy, suspense and drama, and coaxes splendid performances from the ensemble. ★★★ VHS: $14.99

Amazing Grace (Hessed Mufla)

(1992, 95 min, Israel, Amos Gutman) *Gal Hoyberger, Sharon Alexander.* Set in Tel Aviv, this intense, melancholy drama focuses on Jonathan, a gangly and romantic gay teenager who faces an early-life crisis when he finds himself abandoned by his lover. The youth's passions are rekindled after he befriends Thomas, the handsome, HIV-positive older son of his upstairs neighbor. Their budding yet tentative relationship provides the backdrop for this ambitious, thought-provoking social and sexual drama which touches upon such issues as AIDS, death, drug abuse, the gay milieu of Tel Aviv and family dysfunctionalism. (Hebrew with subtitles) ★★★ VHS: $39.99

Amazing Grace and Chuck

(1987, 115 min, US, Mike Newell) *Jamie Lee Curtis, Gregory Peck, Alex English, William L. Petersen.* Engaging Capra-esque drama about a 12-year-old little league champ who trades the athletic field for the political arena when he refuses to play in protest of nuclear arms. Soon, other athletes the world over follow his lead. ★★½

Amazon Women on the Moon

(1986, 85 min, US, John Landis) *Rosanna Arquette, Griffin Dunne, Paul Bartel, Michelle Pfeiffer, Arsenio Hall, David Alan Grier.* Inconsistent series of vignettes is meant to evoke the feeling of channel surfing through 57 channels of TV schlock. While some sequences are genuinely hysterical and feature interesting cameos (Russ Meyer as a video store clerk), the central joke of a hokey sci-fi movie drags on way too long. You'll be reaching for the fast-forward button. ★★ DVD Letterbox Collector's Edition: $14.99

Amélie

(2001, 122 min, France, Jean-Pierre Jeunet) *Audrey Tautou, Mathieu Kassovitz, Rufus, Lorella Cravotta.* Shot in saturated color evoking the heightened reality of dreams, *Amélie* celebrates the infinite variety of human idiosyncrasy in a world where everyday serendipity oils the wheels of chance. Amélie (an effervescent Tautou) tweaks the course of destiny with whimsical Rube Goldberg-esque stratagems and fanciful ploys (traveling gnomes, breaking and entering), aimed at righting wrongs, enlarging limited world views and aiding the progress of attraction and love. A quirk of fate (what else?) sends her on a quest involving the mystery of the man at the photo booths and the longings of her own precious heart. *Amélie* is a delightful lark, both sweet and subversive — intelligent, funny, insight-

Audrey Tautou sparkles in *Amélie*

A

ful; reminiscent of *Celine and Julie Go Boating* in its charm and fancy. Director Jeunet uses the medium to full effect, with invention and a warm humanism, and the supporting cast matches Tautou in capturing the essential, endearing peculiarities of their characters. (French with English subtitles) ★★★★ DVD 2-disc set: $19.99, VHS: $9.99

America, America

(1963, 168 min, US, Elia Kazan) *Stathis Giallelis, Frank Wolff, Elena Karam, Lou Antonio, John Marley, Paul Mann.* In his most personal film, director Kazan tells the often harrowing true tale of his uncle, a Greek living in Turkey who struggles to emigrate to the United States at the turn of the century. Based on Kazan's own book, the story follows 20-year-old Stavros (Giallelis), who leaves the political and social oppression of his small Turkish town and travels to Constantinople, where he will then set sail for America. Though the film's episodic structure reduces in a small degree the overpowering scenes of poverty and sacrifice, Kazan has given the film an extraordinary look (thanks in part to Haskell Wexler's glorious cinematography), and instills in almost every frame an urgency clearly from the heart. Newcomer Giallelis lacks the skill to bring emotional depth needed for the part, but he is ably supported by a terrific ensemble, especially Antonio as a crooked companion and Mann as a father-in-law to be. ★★★½

America's Sweethearts

(2001, 102 min, US, Joe Roth) *Julia Roberts, Billy Crystal, Catherine Zeta-Jones, John Cusack, Hank Azaria, Stanley Tucci, Christopher Walken, Seth Green, Alan Arkin.* A popular ex-husband-and-wife acting team reunite to publicize their last film together — but if their movie is as stifling as this romantic comedy, no amount of good will and smiles will save it. Cusack and Zeta-Jones are Eddie Thomas and Gwen Harrison, America's Sweethearts. They split more than a year ago, but have one final film together ready for release. It's up to agent Lee Phillips (Crystal) to bring them together for the film's press junket, with a little help from Gwen's sister/secretary Kiki (Roberts). Crystal must bear the brunt of much of this, for as cowriter and producer he's settled to use the cast's well-known screen images to suffice for characterization. And with uninspired direction, Roth has also seen to it there's no heart to the romance, little humor to the comedy, and plenty of clichés. ★★ DVD: $14.99, VHS: $9.99

American Beauty

(1999, 122 min, US, Sam Mendes) *Kevin Spacey, Annette Bening, Thora Birch, Chris Cooper, Wes Bentley, Peter Gallagher, Mena Suvari, Allison Janney, Scott Bakula, Sam Robards.* Satirizing the dark recesses, or at least, the banal conformity of suburbia has been a frequent target for American comedies. Few, however, have succeeded as potently as *American Beauty*, a scathing, acerbic, almost deadpan bit of hilarity. Like William Holden's Joe Gillis in *Sunset Boulevard*, Spacey's Lester Burnham narrates from the grave. Lester is a 42-year-old ad exec fighting a losing battle at work and home. His brittle wife Carolyn (Bening) is more concerned with her real estate business, and teenaged daughter Jane (Birch) is embarrassed by them both. After a midlife crisis reawakening, Lester's new attitude paves the way for the story's scintillating comedy, whether it be blackmailing his boss or lusting over his daughter's young girlfriend. Debuting director Mendes and writer Alan Ball have found fresh ingredients for this tale of

suburban unbliss, and an exceptional ensemble brings it to full bloom. Oscar winner Spacey is miraculous as a doormat who finds his voice, and Bening is just right as the wife who refuses to change. Winner of 5 Academy Awards including Best Picture and Director. ★★★★ DVD Awards Edition: $19.99

American Boyfriends

(1990, 90 min, Canada, Sandy Wilson) *Margaret Langrick, John Wildman.* A heartwarming though ordinary sequel to the successful *My American Cousin*. Set in 1965, this coming-of-age film opens with three young Canadian teenyboppers searching for American adventure, good times, and boys boys boys! What our three young thrill-seekers end up with is an unforgettable lesson about the meaning of friendship, love and understanding. Featuring an upbeat soundtrack of classic 1960s tunes. ★★½ VHS: $79.99

American Buffalo

(1996, 88 min, US, Michael Corrente) *Dustin Hoffman, Dennis Franz, Sean Nelson.* David Mamet's play receives mixed results courtesy of director Corrente. Franz plays Don, a pawn shop owner who enlists the aid of a troubled teen (Nelson) to help him steal from a scam-artist customer. Teach (Hoffman), Don's loser friend, convinces him to let him in on the deal. As is often the case with Mamet, loyalties shift, tempers flare, regrets are voiced and recriminations are answered all during the course of events until the inevitable conclusion. Franz gives a superb, subtle performance, Hoffman is terrific, and Nelson more than holds his own with these two vets. The acting more than compensates for Corrente's static direction, which lacks imagination and can't overcome an uncinematic, filmed-play feel. ★★½ DVD: $19.99

American Dream

(1989, 100 min, US, Barbara Kopple) In this stunning documentary, director Kopple brilliantly chronicles the long and bitter strike at the Hormel Meat Packing plant in Austin, Minnesota. Kopple spent a period of several months living with the townspeople, letting her camera roll until it almost faded into the background. Consequently, she is able to capture some incredibly poignant and uncensored moments in the lives of the people affected by

Kevin Spacey and Annette Bening become distant in *American Beauty*

the strike. She shows how the Union Local steered its members in the wrong direction, much to the consternation of the International, in pushing their demands beyond the breaking point. But of course, she doesn't let industry off the hook, either, as she documents the steady lifestyle decline of the American worker under laissez faire policies which put the bottom line and greed above people and community. ★★★★ DVD: $19.99

American Dreamer

(1984, 105 min, US, Rick Rosenthal) *JoBeth Williams, Giancarlo Giannini, Tom Conti.* Williams stars in this endearing action-comedy about a bored housewife who wins a trip to Paris via a creative writing contest — thanks to the adventures of a female superspy, "Rebecca Ryan." Once there, she's mugged, develops amnesia and begins to think she *is* Rebecca Ryan. Cutish romance and intrigue follow. Call this one *Romancing the Clone.* ★★½

American Flyers

(1985, 113 min, US, John Badham) *Kevin Costner, David Grant, Rae Dawn Chong, Robert Townsend, Jennifer Grey.* Steve Tisch (*Breaking Away*) wrote the screenplay for this involving story about two estranged brothers (Costner and Grant), each coming to terms with the death of their father, who enter a grueling three-day bicycle race in the Colorado Rockies. ★★½ DVD: $9.99, VHS: $7.99

The American Friend

(1977, 125 min, US/France/Germany, Wim Wenders) *Bruno Ganz, Dennis Hopper, Lisa Kreuzer, Sam Fuller, Nicholas Ray.* Complexities abound when a mysterious American go-between (Hopper) lures a dying man (Ganz) into a cunning game of murder and revenge. Director Wenders illustrates his favorite themes of anomie, mortality and cultural infiltration. Based on a "Ripley" novel by Patricia Highsmith. (In English and German with English subtitles) ★★★ DVD: $24.99

American Gigolo

(1980, 117 min, US, Paul Schrader) *Richard Gere, Lauren Hutton, Hector Elizondo, Bill Duke.* Gere plays Julian Kaye, a shallow, narcissistic, high-priced prostitute who becomes involved with a senator's wife (Hutton). As their affair gets steamy and serious, Gere is framed for the murder of one of his clients. And the only person who could help him — Hutton — can't. Writer-director Schrader seems to enjoy wallowing in the sleaze of Los Angeles' underbelly; though he unsuccessfully tries to masquerade his tale with a pretentious and artsy examination of one man's failure to find himself. Stylish and empty. ★★ DVD: $19.99, VHS: $9.99

American Graffiti

(1973, 110 min, US, George Lucas) *Richard Dreyfuss, Paul LeMat, Ron Howard, Cindy Williams, Charles Martin Smith, Mackenzie Phillips, Harrison Ford, Candy Clark.* This film turns back the clock to a summer night in 1962 — wait! This film isn't like the rest; it's the first and best of its kind. In this classic comedy, we spend the evening with a couple of teens who are getting together before leaving for college in the fall. Most of the cast is famous now, not to mention the director, who went on to do this minor space movie. Great performances, a great score and a great feel to it. ★★★★

American Heart

(1993, 117 min, US, Martin Bell) *Jeff Bridges, Edward Furlong, Lucinda Jenny.* Director Bell picks up where *Streetwise*, his gripping 1984 documentary about Seattle street kids, left off with this hard-edged, brutally honest depiction of an ex-convict father and his teenage son scrapping for both a living and reconciliation. In a startling performance, Bridges plays a recently paroled jewel thief who is reunited with his estranged son (Furlong). The two move into a sleazy Seattle apartment building living amongst the city's underbelly and forgotten classes. As Bridges attempts to go straight and, however improbably, act as head of this fragile family unit, Furlong takes up with a youthful street clique, slowly entangling him in a life of petty crime. *American Heart* is unflinching in its realistic portrayal of life on the edge, and only misses the mark at the very end with an unsatisfactory finale. Bridges' stinging portrayal is smartly complemented by Furlong's anguished dreamer. ★★★½ DVD: $14.99

American History X

(1998, 117 min, US, Tony Kaye) *Edward Norton, Edward Furlong, Beverly D'Angelo, Jennifer Lien, Fairuza Balk, Elliott Gould, Stacy Keach.* An uneven but powerful drama of racism, *American History X* was the focus of a post-production battle between director Kaye and New Line studio over the final cut. The studio won out. Norton plays a neo-Nazi skinhead who is a hero to his younger brother (Furlong). After finishing a prison term (for the murder of a young black man, a gruesome scene shown in flashback), Norton is a changed man, much to the chagrin of his sibling, girlfriend and fascist friends. It's difficult to tell if this studio version is improved or weakened, because it's so hot and cold. Norton's commanding, riveting performance, however, rescues potentially pretentious moments, making the stronger scenes much more powerful. While the screenplay doesn't quite convince us of Norton's transformation in prison, that segment remains engrossing. ★★★ DVD: $19.99

An American in Paris

(1951, 102 min, US, Vincente Minnelli) *Gene Kelly, Leslie Caron, Nina Foch, Oscar Levant.* The glorious music of George and Ira Gershwin and the incomparable dancing/choreography of Gene Kelly combine to make this one of the most accomplished musicals of all time. Gene plays an artist living in post-WWII Paris who is torn between waif Caron and patron Foch. Winner of 6 Academy Awards including Best Picture. ★★★★ DVD: $19.99

American Me

(1992, 125 min, US, Edward James Olmos) *Edward James Olmos, William Forsythe, Pepe Serna, Danny De La Paz.* Olmos makes a skilled directorial debut with this good-looking if heavily dramatic and clichéd prison/gang drama. Olmos stars as Santana Montoya, a Mexican youth who is incarcerated, and from his lengthy stay behind bars becomes the leader of the Mexican Mafia of Folsom Prison. On his release, however, he finds it difficult to go straight, and becomes another victim to injustice as he is unable to escape his past. Though anti-gang in theme, Olmos seems to relish in the violence he is protesting. A brutal, dark work that, at least, has something to say. ★★½ DVD Letterbox: $14.99, VHS: $9.99

American Movie

(1999, 107 min, US, Chris Smith) *Mark Borchardt, Mike Schank.* Mark Borchardt is a 30ish man from Menominee Falls, where every T-shirt tells a story. He tells documentarian Smith that it's no longer time to drink and dream, but to create and complete. His planned tribute to his hometown, *Northwestern*, has been in preproduction for six years, lacking a script, a cast and funding. This spiritual heir to Herschell Gordon Lewis sometimes works on the script in his car at the airport parking lot to avoid familial commitments and distractions. Whatever his failings, Mark is a trooper: scrabbling against a sea of mediocrity and despair, attempting to raise money from suspicious relatives, with grandiose plans in various nascent stages of actualization. Director Smith wisely lets Borchardt do the talking, constructing his life scene after scene. Smith has delivered a riveting glimpse into an R. Crumb world of muddled thinking, ill-formed beliefs and thwarted endeavors. ★★★½ DVD: $27.99

American Outlaws

(2001, 94 min, US, Les Mayfield) *Colin Farrell, Scott Caan, Ali Larter, Timothy Dalton, Kathy Bates, Gabriel Macht, Harris Yulin, Terry O'Quinn.* This repugnant swill shouldn't appeal to anyone except those looking for some cheap beefcake. A moronic retelling of the James/Younger Gang story, *American Outlaws* has little basis in historical fact (Jesse is a beacon of virtue in this rendition!) and seems to drag on forever, despite its short running time. The story has to do with Jesse and his gang protecting a group of farmers against corrupt railroad barons. But you've seen it all before. Dalton, Yulin and O'Quinn add some class to this mess, but Farrell (so good and charismatic in *Tigerland*) here seems bland and dull. ★ DVD Letterbox: $14.99, VHS: $9.99

American Pie

(1999, 95 min, US, Paul Weitz) *Jason Biggs, Chris Klein, Thomas Ian Nichols, Natasha Lyonne, Seann William Scott, Alyson Hannigan, Shannon Elizabeth, Eddie Kaye Thomas, Eugene Levy, Jennifer Coolidge.* Though it may forever be remembered for discovering new uses for apple pie, *American Pie* is a funny, often raunchy teen comedy that manages to capture the essence of coming-of-age while offering a succession of hilariously rude sex jokes and familiar teen shenanigans. Four friends make a vow to lose their virginity by the Senior Prom. Each goes about the task in amusing sketches of seduction, impersonation, voyeurism and public relations as the final hour draws near. Director Weitz and writer Adam Herz delight in their naughty concoction, tweaking the noses of good taste and cliché with just the right balance of travesty, cleverness and hormonal longing. Klein makes the best impression as a jock who infiltrates enemy territory: the choir! (Sequel: *American Pie 2*) ★★★ DVD Letterbox Beneath the Crust Unrated 2-DVD set: $26.99, DVD Unrated: $19.99

American Pie 2

(2001, 104 min, US, J.B. Rogers) *Jason Biggs, Shannon Elizabeth, Alyson Hannigan, Chris Klein, Natasha Lyonne, Thomas Ian Nicholas, Tara Reid, Seann William Scott, Mena Suvari, Eddie Kaye Thomas, Eugene Levy.* It's a case of déjà vu through and through as the gaggle of horny teenagers from *American Pie* is reassembled for another hasty helping of adolescent sexual prankishness. We follow the hormonal partiers to a lake house retreat and even get a peek at the hijinx going on at a certain notorious band camp. Alas, though *American Pie 2* reunites the entire original cast and was co-scripted by the original writer, there's a thick choking air of desperation to replicate and one-up each of the first movie's naughty, rowdy highlights. Expect more gross-out gags involving bodily fluids, a bit of misplaced homophobia and some outrageously embarrassing masturbation mishaps. (Sequel: *American Wedding*) ★★ DVD Letterbox Beneath the Crust Unrated 2-DVD set: $26.99, VHS Unrated: $9.99

American Pimp

(2000, 87 min, US, The Hughes Brothers) The Hughes Brothers have bucked the system once again with this unflinching and brutally honest "mackumentary" that examines a staple of many urban communities: the pimp. Comprised of skillfully conducted interviews with real-life pimps, and heavily peppered with film clips with blaxploitation movies from the '70s, *American Pimp* asserts that many stereotypes revolving around this segment of society are firmly grounded in truth. Opening with a montage of "the man" dissing pimp morality, the film jumps across several major U.S. cities to introduce some amazing characters with mesmerizing wardrobes and more gold than Fort Knox. One pimp, Bishop Don "Magic" Juan, gave up pimping for the ministry, another went into telemarketing. But all offer zero apologies for their choice of lifestyle. Sure to provoke, this is badder than a muhfuh. ★★★½ DVD: $14.99

American Pop

(1981, 96 min, US, Ralph Bakshi) After the success of *Fritz the Cat* and the failures of *Coonskin* and *Lord of the Rings*, renegade animator Bakshi decided to tackle the entire history of popular music, starting with Tin Pan Alley and ending in the bloated rock arena of the 1970s. Surprisingly, he makes quite a good job of it, too, cataloging the amorality that fuels this art form and so often destroys it. Bakshi's rotoscoping brings to life some of the best vocal characterizations ever to appear in any animated feature. And while the script must at times weld too broad a brush to render nuance, it does manage to capture eras in bold, vivid impressions. Featuring the music of Lou Reed, Jimi Hendrix, Janis Joplin, Helen Morgan and all stops in-between. ★★★½ DVD: $29.99, VHS: $14.99

The American President

(1995, 112 min, US, Rob Reiner) *Michael Douglas, Annette Bening, Martin Sheen, Michael J. Fox, Richard Dreyfuss, Anna Deavere Smith, David Paymer, John Mahoney, Joshua Malina.* "I'm trying to savor the Capra-esque quality" Bening's enthusiastic lobbyist says as she enters the White House. "Capra-esque" also ably describes Reiner's sweet-natured romantic comedy set against the drama of Washington, D.C.'s behind-the-scenes deals and presidential procedure. Douglas plays a Democratic president up for reelection. An idealistic widower, he meets Bening when she lashes out against his policies — and in true Capra fashion love is on the horizon. Reiner balances the film with equal parts joyful romantic comedy and bristling political observations. Written by Aaron Sorkin ("The West Wing"). ★★★ DVD Letterbox: $14.99, VHS Pan & Scan: $9.99, VHS Letterbox: $9.99

American Psycho

(2000, 101 min, US, Mary Harron) *Christian Bale, Willem Dafoe, Jared Leto, Reese Witherspoon, Samantha Mathis, Chloë Sevigny, Justin Theroux.* The self-congratulatory avarice of the '80s elegantly fused an antiseptic minimalism with a most conspicuous consumption. Patrick Bateman, played with obsessive splendor by Bale, skims with apparent effortlessness over the crest of the Reagan years' money tsunami. He's perfectly coifed and meticulously pampered, and the concentrated effort necessary to maintain the façade is starting to take its toll. Perhaps it's the curse of self-awareness that pushes him over the line into the ultimate release of mass murder; when he looks in the mirror, there's nobody there. But is he really that different from the people around him? His is a world of interchangable blondes on the arms of interchangable suits with interchangable sneering, vacant faces. Director Harron has taken a dreadful book and crafted a wry entertainment, with able assistance from a picture-perfect cast. (Sequel: *American Psycho 2*) ★★★ DVD: $14.99, VHS: $9.99

American Psycho 2

(2001, 88 min, US, Morgan J. Freeman) *Mila Kunis, William Shatner, Geraint Wyn Davies.* A horrible, clueless "sequel" to Mary Harron's admirable horror satire. Tenuously (to be charitable) linked to the first film in that the lead character is the lone survivor of Patrick Bateman's killing spree, *American Psycho 2* trots out another sexy psycho killer who'll kill anyone who gets in the way of her goal; in this case, to be assistant to professor . . . William Shatner! Kunis is truly bad in an admittedly awful role and the film's attempts at "humor" are so obvious that the whole thing becomes painful within minutes. ★ DVD: $14.99

An American Rhapsody

(2001, 106 min, Éva Gardos) *Nastassja Kinski, Scarlett Johansson, Tony Goldwyn, Mae Whitman, Lisa Jane Persky, Colleen Camp.* Abandonment and reunion — and one girl's crushing experience with both — forms the core of this moving if heavy-handed true story about identity, family and separation. Kinski and Goldwyn are a Hungarian couple who escape Communist rule in the 1950s. Their joy of leaving is countered by the devastation of having to leave their baby daughter behind to be raised by a peasant family. Years later, the now-teenage daughter (Johansson) is reunited with her parents in America, and is faced with clashes both cultural and familial. The conflict of the girl being torn between two sets of parents and two homelands makes for compelling dramatics, but director Gardos' storytelling favors bombastic outbursts when subtlety is required. ★★½ DVD Letterbox: $29.99, VHS: $14.99

The American Soldier

(1970, 80 min, Germany, Rainer Werner Fassbinder) *Ingrid Caven, Kurt Raab, Karl Scheydt.* Fassbinder pays homage to American film noir and the milieu of Samuel Fuller, Humphrey Bogart and Lemmy Caution in this atmospheric gangster pic. The story concerns the fatalistic prowlings of Rickey, a professional killer hired to bump off a few problem crooks (and then some) for the German police. (German with English subtitles) ★★★ DVD: $24.99, VHS: $19.99

Hope Davis and Paul Giamatti in *American Splendor*

American Splendor

(2003, 101 min, US, Robert Pulcini & Shari Springer Berman) *Paul Giamatti, Hope Davis, Earl Billings, Judah Friedlander, James Urbaniak, Harvey Pekar, Joyce Brabner.* Harvey Pekar, quintessential Everyman, boorish, slovenly, Cleveland civil servant, elevates the mundane to a universal sublime by making comic books out of his pedestrian life. Pekar can't draw, so he writes the script and myriad artists flesh out his words, with R. Crumb as the first. Interviews with Pekar and his third wife Joyce Brabner intertwine with dramatic reenactments from his life story. Giamatti as Pekar and Davis as Brabner capture their subjects, body and soul. As we follow Pekar from his first attempts at writing, his appearances on "Letterman" and his battle with cancer, the film takes on a mesmerizing, self-reflexive quality, becoming a meditation on identity and meaning. This seemingly pointless recounting of moments from the life of a negative, miserly, crude, curmudgeonly sad sack imparts in the end an improbable feeling of contentment and well-being. American splendor, indeed; it's clear that the entire cast and crew became as spellbound as the viewer during this inspired evocation of the sacred commonplace. The film is a haunting, wry tribute to life's ethereal flip side, hinting that the most base and ordinary is the only feasible representation of the transcendent. ★★★★ DVD: $27.99, VHS: $26.99

Favorite Line: "You might as well know right off the bat, I had a vasectomy." —*Paul Giamatti as Harvey Pekar*

An American Tail

(1986, 80 min, US, Don Bluth) *Voices of: Dom DeLuise, Christopher Plummer, Madeline Kahn.* A charming animated feature produced by Steven Spielberg about a young immigrant mouse who becomes separated from his family upon arrival in America, then finds all sorts of adventures with his new friends. The cute story, which is easy for little ones to follow, draws upon some serious subjects without heavy-handedness, and the animation is well done. (Followed by 3 sequels) ★★★ DVD Pan & Scan: $14.99

American Wedding

(2003, 96 min, US, Jesse Dylan) *Jason Biggs, Alyson Hannigan, January Jones, Thomas Ian Nicholas, Seann William Scott, Eddie Kaye Thomas, Eugene Levy, Fred Willard, Jennifer Coolidge.* This by-the-numbers third entry in the *American Pie* series sees many of the cast members converging around the nuptials for Jim (Biggs) and Michelle (Hannigan). Of course, the true purpose of the reunion is to show off a series of gross-out gags involving pubic hair and granny sex, while the film lumbers in between the set pieces as it struggles to set up each one. Thankfully, the presence of verbal diarrhetic Stifler (Scott) puts a lot of energy into the otherwise flagging proceedings; his dance-off in a gay bar is an unrestrained relief from Jim and Michelle's surprisingly sappy romance. As Michelle's dad, Willard reunites with Levy and Coolidge, a treat for fans of Christopher Guest's stock company. Yet all these talented performers also highlight just how disappointing the script is (Levy in particular has but one line that's funny). The unrated home video edition adds some marginal jokes while further deadening the pace. ★★ DVD Letterbox Extended Party Edition (Unrated): $19.99, DVD Letterbox Gift Set: $39.99, DVD Pan & Scan Extended Party Edition (Unrated): $19.99, VHS Extended Party Edition (Unrated): $14.99

An American Werewolf in London

(1981, 98 min, US, John Landis) *David Naughton, Griffin Dunne, Jenny Agutter, John Woodvine.* Two typical American lads on holiday in Europe find more adventure than they bargained for in this chilling and entertaining mirth-filled terror fest. Director Landis combines a great rock score, excellent F/X, an erotic love story and moments of inspired humor to tell the tale of a vacationing college student, David (Naughton), who is attacked by a werewolf on the moors of the English countryside. As his friend Jack (Dunne), who died in the same attack, haunts him from the grave in a gruesome series of deteriorating visits, a hallucinating David begins to doubt his own sanity until he eventually terrorizes London under the glow of the silvery full moon. Rick Baker was the first recipient for the newly created Oscar category of Makeup. ★★★½ DVD 20th Anniversary: $14.99, VHS: $9.99

An American Werewolf in Paris

(1997, 98 min, US, Anthony Waller) *Tom Everett Scott, Julie Delpy, Vince Vieluf.* A terrible rehash, *An American Werewolf in Paris* is so bad it could easily make one forget how good *An American Werewolf in London* is. Andy (Scott) and his buddies are traipsing around Europe trying to get laid when Andy saves Serafine (Delpy) from an attempted dive off the Eiffel Tower. It turns out she's a werewolf, and Andy soon finds himself bitten as well. He then must save his friends, save the girl, save Paris from other werewolves, and try not to eat everyone in the process. The horror sequences are adequate at best, but then it's hard to get scared when your heroes are being chased by the worst computer graphics this side of "Babylon 5." ★½ DVD: $9.99, VHS: $9.99

American Women

(2000, 92 min, Ireland, Aileen Ritchie) *Ian Hart, Sean McGinley, Niamh Cusack, Ewan Stewart, Ruth McCabe.* A handful of boys-will-be-boys, Guinness-swilling slackers in a remote Donegal coastal town in Ireland decide to spice up the lackluster local female selection by placing an ad in a Miami, Florida, newspaper calling for young, sexy women to come to their town. Obvious wackiness ensues. While the box art and poster present the film as a horny teens gross-out, *American Women* is actually a watered-down, quaintly dull *Full Monty*-like social comedy. Certainly not painful to sit through, *American Women* is still pretty thin stuff; it's the kind of comedy that hopes and prays its audience finds those Irish accents hysterically quirky. (aka: *The Closer You Get*) ★★ VHS: $9.99

The Americanization of Emily

(1964, 117 min, US, Arthur Hiller) *Julie Andrews, James Garner, James Coburn, Melvyn Douglas.* Biting military satire with Garner in top form as an American naval officer who is the unwitting dupe in an admiral's plan to turn a Normandy invasion casualty into a publicity stunt. Andrews (in her first film after *Mary Poppins*) plays a British war widow who falls in love with Garner. Exceptional script by Paddy Chayefsky (based on William Bradford Huie's novel). ★★★½ VHS: $19.99

Amistad

(1997, 155 min, US, Steven Spielberg) *Morgan Freeman, Anthony Hopkins, Djimon Hounsou, Matthew McConaughey, Nigel Hawthorne, David Paymer, Pete Postlethwaite, Stellan Skarsgård.* In the same waters as his Academy Award-winning *Schindler's List*, director Spielberg casts an unflinching and unsentimental eye towards prejudice and its ugly consequences with this startling glimpse into an unknown chapter in American history. Based on an actual incident in 1839, the story begins as the slave ship *Amistad* speeds towards America. Under the leadership of Cinque (an impressive Hounsou), the slaves break free and kill all but two of their captors. In America, they stand trial for mutiny, and are defended by former President John Quincy Adams (Hopkins) in the film's powerful, stirring finale. Spielberg doesn't compromise in the depiction of the horrors faced by the slaves. Whether showing them shackled together en masse in the bowels of the ship (much like the Jews on their way to the camps), or examining the moralistic attitudes of a fledgling nation, the film works on an artisitic level as well as an emotional one. Though an inconsistent narrative structure keeps this from being a classic story of injustice, the central theme and context of the film will linger in the mind for a very long time. ★★★½ DVD Letterbox: $14.99, DVD DTS sound: $14.99, VHS Letterbox: $9.99

The Amityville Horror

(1979, 117 min, US, Stuart Rosenberg) *Margot Kidder, Rod Steiger, Don Stroud, Michael Sacks, Murray Hamilton, James Brolin.* Mediocre film version of Jay Anson's popular novel detailing the supposedly true-life events which led the Lutz family to leave their Long Island dream home. The film offers little of the ghostly scares produced by the book. (Sequel: *Amityville II: The Possession*) ★½ DVD: $14.99, VHS: $7.99

Amityville II: The Possession

(1982, 104 min, US, Damiano Damiani) *Burt Young, Rutanya Alda, Moses Gunn.* An awful Freudian prequel to the 1979 haunted house shocker, this time focusing on the original tenants, an "average American family" whose run-of-the-mill existence is ripped asunder by demonic possession. Senseless and curiously lethargic. ★ VHS: $7.99

Among Giants

(1999, 92 min, GB, Sam Miller) *Rachel Griffiths, Pete Postlethwaite, James Thornton, Andy Serkis.* The sad romance between Ray (Postlethwaite), an older, down-on-his-luck foreman, and Gerry (Griffiths), a reckless younger woman who joins his crew, is only mildly diverting despite the engaging stars. Writer Simon Beaufoy (*The Full Monty*) allows his lovers to run around naked, and talk sincerely about their fears and dreams, but this intriguing character study falls short of being truly special. The characters practically work at being unlikable as if they have to prove how meaningful their relationship is. Thornton provides some needed comic relief, but, ultimately, the film's dreariness and clichés overwhelm its virtues. ★★ VHS: $102.99

Amongst Friends

(1993, 88 min, US, Rob Weiss) *Joseph Lindsey, Patrick McGraw, Steve Parlavecchio, Mira Sorvino, Brett Lambson.* Tightly structured, swiftly moving and surprisingly effective, this film from director Weiss begs comparison to Scorsese's gritty classics. Strong performances and a hyperkinetic script (by Weiss) highlight this story about the lives of three youths on the deceptively mean streets of Long Island. Childhood loyalties fall prey to the harsh realities of the adult world as young men with everything look for the one thing that can never be given but only earned — respect. The director appears as the thug at the post-holdup party who explains why he had to shoot that security guard in the ass. ★★★½ VHS: $14.99

Amor Bandido

(1980, 90 min, Brazil, Bruno Barreto) *Paulo Gracindo, Cristina Ache.* Told with melodramatic gusto and imbued with loads of nudity, this torrid and violent story of doomed love is played out amidst the backdrop of an alternately seedy, and yet beautiful, Rio de Janeiro. Thrown out by her detective father, a 17-year-old girl becomes an erotic dancer and hooker at a club in the tough Copacabana. It is here that Sandra meets Tony, a baby-faced teenager and cold-blooded killer. Fueled by loneliness and lust, the two fall passionately in love — all the while unaware that the noose of retribution is tightening around their necks. (Portuguese with English subtitles) ★★★ VHS: $14.99

El Amor Brujo

(1986, 100 min, Spain, Carlos Saura) *Antonio Gades, Laura del Sol.* Manuel de Falla's electrifying and passionate gypsy ballet is brought to the screen by the incomparable team of choreographer Antonio Gades and director Saura. Exuberant flamenco dance punctuates this steamy tale of a young widow (the undeniably sensual del Sol) who is tormented by her late husband's ghost. The strikingly handsome Gades plays her suitor, who desperately seeks to break the spell. (Spanish with English subtitles) ★★★

Amor de Hombre

(1997, 88 min, Spain, Yolanda Garcia Serrano & Juan Luis Iborra) *Loles León, Andrea Occhipinti, Pedro Mari Sánchez, Armando Del Río.* *Amor de Hombre* tells the emotionally complex story of the friendship between a gay man and a woman, long before — and with more emotional affect — than *Object of My Affection* or even *My Best Friend's Wedding*. Ramon is a sexually active gay man; his best friend Esperanza is a single woman who can't seem to connect to men unless they are gay. When Ramon meets handsome schoolteacher Roberto, they begin a relationship that endangers the precious bond he has with Esperanza. This colorful and somewhat hyperactive film is in the style of Almodóvar, and there's plenty of on-screen action, rapid-fire dialogue and intense color to keep viewers happy. (Spanish with English subtitles) ★★★½ DVD: $24.99, VHS: $24.99

Amore

(1948, 78 min, Italy, Roberto Rossellini) *Anna Magnani, Federico Fellini.* Two episodes, dedicated by Rossellini to "the art of Anna Magnani," comprise this indulgent drama about the illusion and pain of love. "The Miracle" stars Magnani as a slightly retarded farm girl who is seduced by a stranger (Fellini) whom she believes to be St. Joseph and her newborn son the child of God. "The Human Voice," based on a Jean Cocteau play, features Magnani as a woman distraught by the recent breakup with her lover. In a painfully personal monologue to her unseen and unheard lover on the telephone, she attempts to persuade him not to leave. Interestingly, the film was banned in New York for blasphemy. (Italian with English subtitles) (aka: *Ways of Love*) ★★½ VHS: $29.99

Amores Perros (Love's a Bitch)

(2000, 154 min, Mexico, Alejandro González Iñárritu) *Emilio Echevarria, Gael Garcia Bernal, Goya Toledo, Alvaro Guerrero, Marco Perez.* In a stunning feature-film debut, director Iñárritu finds himself in the realm of Tarantino and Altman, but adds his own distinctive flavor to a provocative story of crime, betrayal, murder, seduction and unlikely redemption set in the slums and high-rises of Mexico City. Using a car crash as a focal point, the director and writer Guillermo Arriaga have several stories intersect before and after the accident, making optimum use of flashbacks and other non-linear editing techniques. How these characters' lives crisscross, and what they must endure, forms the core of this demanding, intense, often spellbinding drama that is the cinematic equivalent of a knockout punch. (Spanish with English subtitles) ★★★★ DVD Letterbox Lions Gate Signature Series: $19.99

Gael Garcia Bernal in *Amores Perros*

Analyze This

Amos & Andrew

(1993, 95 min, US, E. Max Frye) *Samuel L. Jackson, Nicolas Cage, Dabney Coleman, Brad Dourif, Michael Lerner, Giancarlo Esposito, Loretta Devine.* When Andrew Sterling (Jackson), Pulitzer Prize-winning playwright and wealthy black man, arrives at his new home on an island in New England, his neighbors mistake him for a burglar and call in the local police and set in motion what was surely intended to be a comical farce, poking fun at racial attitudes. Instead, the result is non-stop inanity and annoying stereotypes. Cage and Jackson seem to sleepwalk their way through the anemic screenplay. ★ DVD: $9.99

Amsterdamned

(1988, 114 min, Netherlands, Dick Maas) *Huub Stapel, Monique Van De Ven.* The city of Amsterdam becomes an unwitting accomplice to a series of grisly murders when a sadistic killer uses the city's canals to amphibiously stalk his prey. This "Amsterdam Vice" police thriller proves that Hollywood does not have a lock on good action films. The story follows the frantic efforts of a good-looking detective with a five-day beard (shades of you-know-who) who is assigned to seek out the underwater killer. Great locales, wonderful camera work and a heart-throbbing chase scene through the canals help make this a memorable action drama. (Dutch with English subtitles) ★★★

Amy's O

(2002, 85 min, US, Julie Davis) *Julie Davis, Caroline Aaron, Nick Chinlund, Jeff Cesario.* Amy (Davis) is a successful, controversial author of self-help books dealing primarily with women's relationships. Her opinion of romance and the role of women in society can be found in her book "Why Love Doesn't Work," and she's quick to comment that "women don't need men to be complete." Too bad she didn't take her own advice. If she had, she wouldn't have started an improbable romance with the shock-jock DJ who invited her on his show, and we wouldn't have to suffer through some of the clichés that make up this breezy but pretentious comedy. Davis attempts to create a vibrant battle of the sexes, but, in spite of an engagingly light direc-

torial touch, comes up short. As such, *Amy's O* is never as smart as it pretends to be. ★★ DVD: $19.99, VHS: $79.99

Anaconda

(1997, 100 min, US, Luis Llosa) *Jon Voight, Jennifer Lopez, Ice Cube, Eric Stoltz, Kari Wuhrer.* Basically this story of a bunch of people lost in the jungle and who are chased and killed off by a giant snake (as if you couldn't guess) succeeds at being suspenseful and fun at the same time. Where it doesn't succeed is in originality and in successful execution of its special effects. The computer-generated anaconda looks terrible, but fortunately is on-screen so little (until the end) and moves so quickly, that its artificiality can be overlooked by an extra-generous suspension of disbelief. It may be brainless, but *Anaconda* manages to consistently entertain. ★★½ DVD Dual: $14.99, DVD Letterbox Superbit Edition: $27.99, VHS: $12.99

Analyze That

(2002, 95 min, US, Harold Ramis) *Robert De Niro, Billy Crystal, Lisa Kudrow, Joe Viterelli, Cathy Moriarty, Anthony LaPaglia.* De Niro and Crystal return for this inevitable sequel to their 1999 hit *Analyze This*, but as this mediocre comedy proves, the difference between *this* and *that* is significant, indeed. Picking up a few years after Paul Vitti's (De Niro) incarceration, the story brings the Mafia kingpin and his favorite shrink, Ben Sobel (Crystal), back together again after Paul has suffered a nervous breakdown (De Niro is quite funny here singing show tunes from "West Side Story"). When Paul is released from jail into Ben's care, both men become at odds in determining the direction of Paul's future — no surprise who wins. Sadly, the freshness and cleverness that made the first film so enjoyable is missing. There are a few laughs to be had, but most of them feel forced, and the story smacks of cliché. ★★ DVD Letterbox: $14.99, DVD Pan & Scan: $14.99, VHS: $6.99

Analyze This

(1999, 103 min, US, Harold Ramis) *Robert De Niro, Billy Crystal, Lisa Kudrow, Chazz Palminteri, Joe Viterelli, Pat Cooper, Leo Rossi, Max Casella.* What has to be the funniest gangster comedy since *Some Like It Hot, Analyze This* is non-stop hilarity and proves that De Niro can handle comedy with the

skill of his great, dramatic portrayals. Who knew? A very funny screenplay by Peter Tolan, Kenneth Lonergan and director Ramis sets up the clever, high-concept scenario: Mafia kingpin Paul Vitti (De Niro) is experiencing such stress as to cause him to seek out psychiatric help. And what doctor does he put the hit on? Ben Sobel (Crystal). Quicker than you can say "The Godfather," Sobel's professional and private lives are turned upside-down. The rapport between the two stars is priceless, and the consistently funny screenplay is an endless parade of sharp one-liners and sticky situations. In support, Kudrow and Palminteri are both shortchanged in their parts; but not Viterelli, who is perfect as Vitti's dense but loyal henchman. (Sequel: *Analyze That*) ★★★½ DVD: $14.99, VHS: $9.99

The Anarchist Cookbook

(2003, 101 min, US, Jordan Susman) *Devon Gummersall, Gina Phillips.* All the telltale signs of "indie garbage" are there right at the beginning: bad narration, trendy, unfunny humor, toothless satire and drab photography. Heed these warnings. Gummersall (Brian from TV's "My So-Called Life") plays a disaffected activist who squats with a group of like-minded folks at a Dallas bookstore who play at civil disobedience. Their routine is disrupted by the arrival of a "by any means necessary" anarchist who's all for violence to achieve social change. While borrowing from *Fight Club, Heathers* and other, better films (as well as the famous, titular book, which is only given passing mention), *The Anarchist Cookbook* learns nothing from them in terms of tone, style, or most importantly, a point. The film just drones on (along with that tiresome narration) until its ha-ha "humorous" twist ending, which means . . . nothing. ★ DVD: $26.99

Anastasia

(1956, 105 min, US, Anatole Litvak) *Ingrid Bergman, Yul Brynner, Helen Hayes, Akim Tamiroff.* In 1956, Bergman appeared in her first American production in six years since being exiled to Europe for her affair with the director Roberto Rossellini. Shot on location in Paris, *Anastasia* heralded her triumphant return, and she was justly rewarded an Oscar for her excellent performance. Bergman stars as a woman who, while in an asylum, claimed to be the youngest daughter of assassinated Russian Czar Nicholas. Brynner is an ex-Russian military leader searching for a look-alike of the princess to set up a swindle. Based on the hit play, the film is a captivating story of identity and remembrance, made all the more appealing by the virtuoso portrayal by Bergman. ★★★½ DVD: $14.99

Anastasia

(1997, 96 min, US, Don Bluth & Gary Goldman) *Voices of: Meg Ryan, John Cusack, Kelsey Grammer, Christopher Lloyd, Hank Azaria, Bernadette Peters, Kirsten Dunst, Angela Lansbury.* A sumptuous animated epic, with all the grace, beauty and spirit of the best Disney classics, *Anastasia* is all the more surprising because it's *not* a Disney movie. Okay, so it's historically inaccurate, but the filmmakers aren't telling history here, they're merely using it as a springboard for their own fairy-tale plot. The music isn't quite up to par, but the breathtaking artistry and the clever vocal casting elevate *Anastasia* far above other pretenders to the Disney throne. Appealing to kids and adults alike, the film may be missing that certain, unnameable Disney magic, but makes up for its lack of "pixie dust" with spirited ambition and enthralling spectacle. ★★★ DVD: $14.99, VHS Pan & Scan: $6.99

Anatomy

(2000, 100 min, Germany, Stefan Ruzowitzky) *Franka Potente, Benno Fürmann, Anna Loos, Holger Speckhahn.* A creepy, sick but atmospheric horror film, *Anatomy* tries to create suspense using disgusting effects to simulate realism but ends up just being disgusting. Potente is Paula, an ambitious medical student who is accepted into a prestigious anatomy class. What looks like a splendid opportunity soon becomes a nightmare when she uncovers a ruthless secret medical society whose prime goal is to learn more about medicine by dissecting bodies while they are still alive. Unable to sustain tension or believability, the filmmakers rely on horror clichés and gross-outs for its too few scares. (German with English subtitles) (Sequel: *Anatomy 2*) ★½ DVD: $24.99, VHS Dubbed: $14.99

Anatomy of a Murder

(1959, 160 min, US, Otto Preminger) *James Stewart, George C. Scott, Ben Gazzara, Lee Remick, Arthur O'Connell, Eve Arden, Joseph Welch.* This riveting courtroom drama, a groundbreaker when released, maintains its punch and relevance today. The tension-filled, complex plot — about small-town lawyer Stewart defending soldier Gazzara who murdered a bartender who allegedly raped his wife Remick — is sustained by tour de force ensemble acting from the star-studded cast; highlighted by Stewart's portrayal of the deceptively easy-going defense attorney. Strong direction by Preminger is punctuated by the throbbing Duke Ellington score. ★★★★ DVD: $24.99

Anchors Aweigh

(1945, 140 min, US, George Sidney) *Gene Kelly, Frank Sinatra, Kathryn Grayson, Dean Stockwell.* Kelly and Sinatra's first musical together is a sentimental though fun romp about two sailors on leave (a theme that would reoccur in *On the Town* and even indirectly in *It's Always Fair Weather*) in Tinseltown. This is the one where Gene dances with Jerry the Mouse. ★★½ DVD: $19.99

And a Nightingale Sang

(1989, 90 min, GB, Robert Knights) *Joan Plowright, Tom Watt, Phyllis Logan, John Woodvine.* Made for "Masterpiece Theatre," this delightfully charming little comedy-drama tells the tale of a working-class British family during WWII. The story revolves around Helen, the family's eldest daughter, a 31-year-old spinster who at long last finds love with a young soldier. Filled with mirth and a smattering of social commentary, the film exhibits the same kind of tenderness for the misbegotten that makes Mike Leigh's films so thoroughly enjoyable. ★★★ VHS: $19.99

And God Created Woman

(1956, 91 min, France, Roger Vadim) *Brigitte Bardot, Curt Jurgens, Jean-Louis Trintignant.* BB Mania (Brigitte Bardot that is) pulsated after the release of this sex comedy, which by today's standards is chastefully harmless. Bardot is a man-teasing 18-year-old whose lustful encounters with the irresistible opposite sex are enacted out amid the sun and splendor of St. Tropez. (Remade by Vadim in 1987) (French with English subtitles) ★★½ DVD Criterion Collection: $29.99, VHS: $19.99

And God Created Woman

(1987, 98 min, US, Roger Vadim) *Rebecca DeMornay, Vincent Spano, Frank Langella.* Vadim's tepid remake of his own 1957 cause célèbre stars DeMornay in the Brigitte Bardot role. The story's about a prison escapee who just wants to play rock 'n' roll. Spano plays the carpenter wrapped around her thumb, and Langella is her sexual plaything. ★½

And Hope to Die

(1972, 95 min, Canada/France, René Clément) *Robert Ryan, Jean-Louis Trintignant, Aldo Ray, Tisa Farrow.* From the director of such intriguing films as *Forbidden Games, Joy House* and *Rider on the Rain* comes this stylish but disappointing thriller made in Canada. Three criminals plan and execute an elaborate plot to kidnap the moll of an underworld chief and hold her for a million dollar ransom. (Filmed in English) ★★½

. . . And Justice for All

(1979, 117 min, US, Norman Jewison) *Al Pacino, Jack Warden, Christine Lahti, John Forsythe, Lee Strasberg, Joe Morton, Craig T. Nelson, Jeffrey Tambor.* Pacino received an Oscar nomination for his impassioned portrayal of an idealistic lawyer defending a judge accused of rape. Though dramatically uneven in its sometimes satirical portrait of the legal system, a good cast more than compensates for the occasional heavy-handedness. ★★½ DVD: $9.99

And Nothing But the Truth

(1982, 90 min, GB, Karl Francis) *Glenda Jackson, Jon Finch.* This earnest examination of the roles and responsibilities of the media stars Jackson and Finch as a documentary filmmaker and reporter. While covering a story, they find themselves passionately split on how to investigate the issue at hand. The film offers an intriguing look at how television news is selected, edited and finally seen by the viewer. (aka: *Giro City*) ★★★

And Now for Something Completely Different

(1972, 80 min, GB, Ian McNaughton) *Graham Chapman, John Cleese, Eric Idle, Terry Gilliam, Michael Palin, Terry Jones, Connie Booth.* Supreme silliness prevails in this, Monty Python's first movie. Essentially it's a collection of the best of their BBC television program and features dead parrots, transvestite lumberjacks, a killer joke, upper-class twits, and a lesson on how to defend yourself against a person who is armed with fresh fruit. Nod's as good as a wink to a blind bat, eh? Say no more! ★★★ DVD: $24.99, VHS: $19.99

And Now My Love (Toute une Vie)

(1974, 121 min, France, Claude Lelouch) *Marthe Keller, André Dussollier.* Director Lelouch has fashioned an intoxicating romantic fable with the twist that the lovers don't meet until the film's final seconds. The story begins during WWI, tracing the lives of three generations of Jewish women to introduce the story's young heroine, Sara, an heiress with Marxist leanings who is waiting for the right man. That man is Simon, a petty crook who after his imprisonment becomes a filmmaker despite his idealistic beliefs. Lelouch mixes romance, politics, religion and many of the 20th century's most momentous occasions in his masterful blender to serve a humorous, energetic and fascinating dis-

course on human emotions and the role of fate and passion in our lives. (French with English subtitles) ★★★½ DVD: $24.99

And the Band Played On

(1993, 140 min, US, Roger Spottiswoode) *Matthew Modine, Lily Tomlin, Alan Alda, Ian McKellen, Richard Gere, Steve Martin, Anjelica Huston, Tcheky Karyo, Swoosie Kurtz, Glenne Headly, Bud Cort, Donal Logue, Richard Masur, Saul Rubinek, Charles Martin Smith, Stephen Spinella, B.D. Wong.* Based on Randy Shilts' controversial book, this star-studded film adaptation is structured as an investigative medical thriller, and as such has an almost insurmountable problem in that the villain is a virus, its discoveries bring no joy, and there is no happy ending. Historically and scientifically comprehensive, the story centers on a government virologist, Don Francis (Modine), who almost single-handedly works on solving the mystery that was (is) HIV. The film indicts nearly everyone involved; and while powerful and engrossing, it does suffer in the depiction of gay characters and in the perception that straight men and women came to the rescue of the gay community. ★★★½ DVD: $14.99, VHS: $14.99

And the Ship Sails On

(1983, 138 min, Italy, Federico Fellini) *Freddie Jones, Barbara Jefford, Janet Suzman, Victor Poletti.* Fellini presents a deliberately artificial yet graceful spectacle aboard a luxury ocean liner in 1914. In his serious moments, Fellini concerns himself with the creative force of artistic expression and also portrays a world about to lose its innocence and plunge into WWI. The film's greatest rewards lie in its sweeping images, boldly stylized scenery, impromptu operatic turns and the usual circus of Fellini oddities. (Italian with English subtitles) ★★★ DVD Criterion Collection: $29.99, VHS Letterboxed: $29.99

The Anderson Platoon

(1967, 65 min, France, Pierre Schoendoerffer) With English narration by director Schoendoerffer himself, this harrowing documentary follows the very real battle conditions endured by a group of American soldiers stationed in Vietnam. Returning to a land where he himself was stationed for 13 years with the French Army, the director joined for six weeks an integrated platoon headed by a black West Point graduate, Lt. Joseph B. Anderson. Their involvement in actual combat creates real danger and fear. A fascinating film that finally produces an overwhelming sadness for the embattled young men. Winner of the Academy Award for Best Documentary. ★★★½ VHS: $19.99

The Anderson Tapes

(1972, 98 min, US, Sidney Lumet) *Sean Connery, Dyan Cannon, Martin Balsam, Christopher Walken, Alan King.* Connery stars as the mastermind of an elaborate scheme to rob every apartment in a large complex. Little does he know that, for one reason or another, each vault is under surveillance. The tension, along with the irony, is high in this entertaining action film from director Lumet. However, Balsam's gay caricature is offensive. ★★★

Andersonville

(1995, 168 min, US, John Frankenheimer) *Jarrod Emick, Frederic Forrest, Ted Marcoux, Cliff De Young, William H. Macy, Justin Henry.* The most notorious Confederate prisoner of war camp during the Civil War was Andersonville, located in Georgia; the

A

commandant was the only soldier tried for crimes against humanity after that conflict. Its squalor and misery are unflinchingly presented in this compelling made-for-cable drama. *Andersonville* begins when a small group of Union soldiers are captured and imprisoned. They are greeted by disease, brutality and death. At its best, which is much of the time, *Andersonville* conveys in a sometimes repulsive though gripping manner the hardships endured. An often moving, rarely maudlin testament to the moral heights — and depths — man can attain. ★★★ DVD: $14.99

Andre
(1994, 94 min, US, George Miller) *Keith Carradine, Tina Majorina, Keith Szarabajka, Chelsea Field.* A harbor master (Carradine) and his family befriend an orphaned seal and alienate many of the human inhabitants of their Maine fishing village. The father's eldest daughter and the fishermen are angered by the amount of time he spends with the seal and his youngest daughter (Majorino). Although this is based on a true story, the manipulative plot and overly dramatic ending will limit its appeal to fans of animal stories or, at least, seal lovers. ★★ DVD Letterbox: $14.99, VHS: $9.99

Andrei Rublev
(1965, 185 min, USSR, Andrei Tarkovsky) *Anatoli Solonitzine, Ivan Lapikov.* The life, times and art of early 15th-century icon painter Andrei Rublev are explored in this brilliant and visionary work. Told in eight imaginary episodes, the film follows the painter's journeys through Russia where the artist, numbed by the horrors he sees, gradually loses his faith in God, his ability to speak and his drive to create art. A powerful, slow and dense epic that probes into the role of the artist in society. (Russian with English subtitles) ★★★★ DVD Criterion Collection: $39.99

Androcles and the Lion
(1952, 98 min, US, Chester Erskine) *Jean Simmons, Victor Mature, Alan Young, Maurice Evans.* George Bernard Shaw's delicious satire makes a pleasant film comedy for this story about a young tailor in Imperial Rome who saves his fellow Christians from a lion he once befriended. ★★★ VHS: $29.99

Android
(1982, 80 min, US, Aaron Lipstadt) *Klaus Kinski, Don Opper.* A fun-filled futuristic adventure set on an isolated space station. Max 404 (Opper) is a capable, somewhat waifish android — with a penchant for Jimmy Stewart movies and rock 'n' roll — whose job is to assist his creator, a renegade scientist (Kinski). Unknown to Max, the good doctor is working on a female and prototype android destined to replace him. Part *Metropolis*, part *Frankenstein* and part *2001*, *Android* is genuinely inspired and thoroughly entertaining. ★★★

The Andromeda Strain
(1971, 131 min, US, Robert Wise) *Arthur Hill, James Olson, David Wayne, Kate Reid, Paula Kelly.* The first screen adaptation of a Michael Crichton novel is a pulse-pounding, extremely intelligent sci-fi thriller expertly directed by Wise, who summons both the suspense and style of his *The Haunting* and the imagination and enterprise of his *The Day the Earth Stood Still*. Crichton, who studied to be a doctor, makes efficient use of medical vocabulary and possibility to tell the story of a group of scientists investigating a space virus that has devastated a small New Mexico town. As they race against the clock, their only clues are two survivors: a screaming baby and an alcoholic. Reid is great as a glib doc. ★★★½ DVD: $19.99, VHS: $9.99

Andy Warhol's Bad
(1976, 100 min, US, Jed Johnson) *Carroll Baker, Perry King, Susan Tyrrell.* Andy Warhol lent his name to this slick, sick and subversive *Pink Flamingos*-like black comedy of extremely bad taste by former Warhol soundman and editor Johnson. A slumming-for-dollars Baker stars as the tough, nefarious head of a female kill-for-hire organization based in Queens which specializes in especially difficult cases. All is going well for her and her immoral ingenues until a stranger (King) enters the scene. *Bad* is gross, highly offensive and disgustingly enjoyable, though the infamous "baby splatter" scene" has been edited out. ★★★ VHS: $19.99

Andy Warhol's Dracula
(1974, 103 min, France/Italy, Paul Morrissey) *Udo Kier, Joe Dallesandro, Roman Polanski.* Spawned by the commercial success of *Flesh for Frankenstein*, this campy treatment of the well-worn Transylvanian tale features Kier as Dracula, the creepy vampire in search of ripe, succulent throats and virginal blood. Leaving Hungary for the purer pastures offered in Catholic Italy, the Count's toothy appetite for a fix of virgins proves elusive as the strapping Dallesandro makes sure that the Count's intended victims are no virgins — even if it means deflowering a 14-year-old. (aka: *Blood for Dracula*) ★★½

Andy Warhol's Frankenstein
(1974, 94 min, France/Germany/Italy, Paul Morrissey) *Joe Dallesandro, Monique Van Vooren, Udo Kier.* B-movie dialogue, over-the-top performances and buckets of gore abound in this campy retelling of the classic horror story, served up with a weird sexual twist. Kier is the mad baron who feverishly works on piecing together body parts from the recently dead to create a pair of perfect creatures — a beautiful female and a sex-crazed male. Dallesandro plays the horny stud to the baron's wife/sister. Originally shown in 3-D, and rated a tantalizing "X." As the baron says, "You haven't known life till you've fucked it in the gall bladder." (aka: *Flesh for Frankenstein*) ★★ DVD: $39.99, VHS: $19.99

Andy Warhol's Heat
(1972, 100 min, US, Paul Morrissey) *Sylvia Miles, Joe Dallesandro.* Kinky and funny, this many times vulgar takeoff of *Sunset Boulevard* stars Miles as the shrillish Sally Todd, a fading movie star (actually a has-been chorus girl) who shares her dreary home with her lesbian daughter and the latter's sadistic girlfriend. Their lives are briefly stimulated when Dallesandro enters the scene. All have the hots for Little Joe — prompting mom to complain her daughter "can't even make a good dyke." An insightful tale of unsatisfactory sex, elusive love and ever-present alienation masked as delightful camp. (aka: *Heat*) ★★★

Angel
(1937, 91 min, US, Ernst Lubitsch) *Marlene Dietrich, Melvyn Douglas, Herbert Marshall, Edward Everett Horton.* A minor Lubitsch melodrama that is nearly saved by three good lead performances and the director's usual sophisticated touch. Dietrich plays a neglected diplomat's wife who is tempted by an old friend of her husband's. They may not say much but they sure look good doing it. ★★ VHS: $14.99

Angel
(1982, 126 min, Greece, Yorgos Katakouzinos) *Michael Maniatis, Dionyssis Xanthos, Katerina Helmi.* A commercial and critical hit in Greece, this was that country's first film to deal with homosexuality. The uneven drama is a harrowing, tragic account

of a shy young man from a dysfunctional family who thinks he's found love after meeting a macho sailor. Their relationship soon becomes abusive, with the handsome Angel forced to become a transvestite prostitute in Athens. His helplessness and humiliation soon end in inevitable violence. (Greek with English subtitles) ★★½ DVD: $29.99, VHS: $39.99

An Angel at My Table
(1990, 150 min, New Zealand, Jane Campion) *Kerry Fox, Alexia Keogh, Karen Fergusson.* The story of New Zealand novelist and poet Janet Frame is lovingly rendered and subtly moving without ever employing cheap sentimental devices. Frame published various successful works while hospitalized for schizophrenia, but that's only one part of this sprawling portrait of self-discovery from *Sweetie* director Campion. A remarkable performance by Fox as the adult Frame. ★★★ VHS: $19.99

Angel Baby
(1995, 105 min, Australia, Michael Rymer) *John Lynch, Jacqueline McKenzie, Colin Friels.* Two magnificent performances enliven this otherwise ordinary drama about two mental patients in love. For Harry (Lynch), it is love at first sight when he meets Kate (McKenzie), a young woman who receives coded messages from "Wheel of Fortune." When the couple decide to move in together, have a baby, and stop taking their medication, things sour quickly. Director Rymer does achieve some lyrical moments, but all too often the film takes a heavy-handed approach to its sensitive subject matter. *Angel Baby*'s tone shifts dramatically from whimsical to serious, thereby making it difficult to watch Harry and Kate struggle without any payoff. ★★ VHS: $79.99

Angel Dust
(1994, 116 min, Japan, Sogo [Toshihiro] Ishii) *Kaho Minami, Takeshi Wakamatsu.* This ambitious effort falls short of the mark due to an unnecessarily dense, convoluted script. Relentlessly stylish, particularly during its excellent first half hour, the story centers around Setsuko, a police psychologist who has the bizarre ability to place herself into the mind of a killer. She begins investigating a series of murders which have been occurring at the same time on the Tokyo subway. Each of the victims is a young woman killed by an injection of poison while in the middle of a large crowd. Multiple viewings are probably required to pick up all of the film's clues and red herrings, but unfortunately the story is not involving enough to support such scrutiny. (Japanese with English subtitles) ★★½ VHS: $19.99

Angel Eyes
(2001, 110 min, US, Luis Mandoki) *Jennifer Lopez, Jim Caviezel, Sonia Braga, Shirley Knight, Terrence Howard, Jeremy Sisto.* Director Mandoki and writer Gerald DiPego reunite after their near-miss *Message in a Bottle* for an even murkier romantic drama that shares a little in common with DiPego's misfire *Phenomenon*. Slow moving and never sure exactly where it wants to go, *Angel Eyes* stars the alluring Lopez as a Chicago cop who, in the film's good opening moments, arrives on the scene to aid an accident victim. Cut to one year later. An enigmatic, trench-coated man known only as Catch (Caviezel) rescues her from a gunman's bullet, and these two lonely souls begin to see one another. The film tries to add some mystery through mood and plot development (Is this the same man in the film's opening? Is he a ghost? Is he crazy?), but the scattershot screenplay is unable to create tension or much sympathy. ★★ DVD Letterbox: $14.99, VHS Bonus Edition: $9.99

Emma Thompson in *Angels in America*

Angel Heart

(1986, 112 min, US, Alan Parker) *Mickey Rourke, Robert De Niro, Lisa Bonet, Charlotte Rampling, Kathleen Wilhoite, Pruitt Taylor Vince.* Yes, the film with the controversial nude scene with Bonet. That's all most people seem to remember from this story about a private eye (Rourke) and a case he is given by Mr. Louis Cypher (De Niro). Parker combines film noir and his penchant for stark, brutal realism to create a creepy, atmospheric film. Not for all tastes, due to its gore. This is the uncut version. ★★★ DVD Special Edition: $19.99

Angela

(1977, 91 min, Canada, Boris Sagal) *Sophia Loren, Steve Railsback, John Huston, John Vernon.* Loren stars in this curiously uninvolving drama as an older woman who begins an affair with a handsome young man (Railsback) who, unbeknowst to either of them, is her son — separated when he was a child. The stars ignite few sparks between them, and even the film's controversial story line is boring. ★

Angela's Ashes

(1999, 146 min, GB/Ireland, Alan Parker) *Emily Watson, Robert Carlyle, Michael Legge, Joe Breen, Ciaran Owens.* In adapting Frank McCourt's Pulitzer Prize-winning novel for the screen, director Parker has more than one obstacle in his way; but the biggest is the loss of the author's unique narrative voice that gave the book its humor amid the despair. The story of McCourt's impoverished childhood in Limerick, Ireland, during the 1930s and '40s remains a powerful memory piece of sacrifice, poverty and hope. But having lost that voice so essential to the novel only magnifies its few limitations as to make them appear greater than they are. A superb evocation of the era, the film in heartbreaking fashion details how the McCourt family moves back to Ireland where life becomes no easier than in America. The performances are uniformly good, the tone is reverent, and the family's loss significant, but the spirit of the novel seems to be slightly amiss. ★★½ DVD: $19.99, VHS: $14.99

Angèle

(1934, 130 min, France, Marcel Pagnol) *Fernandel, Orane Demazis.* Acknowledged by De Sica and Rossellini as a great inspiration in their careers, this innovative neorealist melodrama about a girl's seduction, betrayal and eventual redemption is considered by many to be Pagnol's finest work. In the naturalist setting of Provence, a naive peasant girl (Demazis) has a child. Abandoned by her lover and bullied by her domineering father (Fernandel, in his first dramatic role), she runs off to Marseilles where she is soon forced into prostitution. Her father, a simple-minded farmer, driven by love for his daughter, goes to the city to find Angèle and return her home. (French with English subtitles) ★★★★ VHS: $59.99

The Angelic Conversation

(1985, 78 min, GB, Derek Jarman) *Judi Dench.* Eschewing narrative form, with the only dialogue being Dench's offscreen reading of twelve Shakespeare sonnets, this cryptic assemblage of stop-action photography can be slow-going; but for those who watch, this allegorical mood piece can be a hypnotically beautiful film. Featuring several Bruce Weber beauties, Jarman's soul-searching mission celebrates life and captures his feelings on premature death caused by AIDS. An affirmation of life as well as an original and daring work. ★★★

Angelo, My Love

(1983, 115 min, US, Robert Duvall) *Angelo Evans, Michael Evans.* Duvall wrote and directed this charming film about an 11-year-old Gypsy boy in his quest to find a stolen ancestral ring. Evans plays himself in this loosely structured and somewhat improvisational film, full of wit, energy and passion. ★★★

Angels & Insects

(1995, 117 min, US/GB, Philip Haas) *Mark Rylance, Patsy Kensit, Kristin Scott Thomas, Jeremy Kemp, Douglas Henshall.* A marvelously twisted, psychosexual period piece that examines not only the class inequities, but the repressed sexual mores of Victorian society — as if *Sense and Sensibility* had been interpreted by Peter Greenaway. The story (based on A.S. Byatt's novella "Morpho Eugenia") revolves around William Adamson (Rylance), a low-born entomologist who lands a position at the manor of Sir Harold Alabaster (Kemp). He falls in love with Alabaster's emotion-ally reserved daughter Eugenia (Kensit) despite the obvious attraction between him and the family's outgoing and well-educated niece Matty (an engaging Scott Thomas). Dark family secrets lurk in the background, however, giving everything in the film an overriding sense of dread. Haas sustains a visually striking and emotionally haunting narrative that effectively uses its protaganist's fascination with insects as a metaphor for human interaction. ★★★½ DVD Letterbox: $19.99

Angels in America

(2003, 352 min, US, Mike Nichols) *Meryl Streep, Al Pacino, Emma Thompson, Justin Kirk, Jeffrey Wright, Mary-Louise Parker, Ben Shenkman, Patrick Wilson.* An unprecedented success, this superb, exhilarating HBO adaptation of Tony Kushner's two Tony Award-winning Broadway plays is one of the damndest things you'll ever see. Surreal, heartbreaking, hilarious, spiritual, insightful and powerful beyond words, *Angels in America* is told in two parts, three acts each, to examine an America in crisis, specifically an AIDS-ravaged New York City in the mid-1980s, a marriage in disrepair, heavenly angels in turmoil, and the death of a notorious figure. Prior (Kirk) and Louis (Shenkman) have been lovers for four years, and are about to embark on a path neither expected when Prior learns he has AIDS. Another person with AIDS, real-life conservative lawyer Roy Cohn (Pacino), is just beginning his decline without apology or repentance — not for being gay, but for being a bloody bastard. Displaced Mormon married couple Joe (Wilson) and Harper (Parker) are experiencing marital woes, to such an extent that his repressive mother (Streep) packs up and moves to New York. How these lives come together through sickness, romance and politics is what distinguishes and sets in motion this highly intelligent discourse on sexuality, health and religion. The cast is simply astonishing, with Streep, Thompson and Wright playing various roles. Streep as a rabbi has to be seen to be believed, and to watch her Mormom mother's maturation is to witness the most talented actress of her generation at her peak. Pacino is a revelation as Cohn, Wright is miraculous as a gay nurse and hallucinatory figure, and special mention must go to Kirk for being the glue holding the entire piece together as a man uncertain not only of his physical state but mental one as well. Director Nichols has taken an almost unfilmable project and with it fashioned a modern masterpiece. ★★★★ DVD 2-disc set: $39.99

Angels in the Outfield

(1951, 99 min, US, Clarence Brown) *Paul Douglas, Janet Leigh, Keenan Wynn, Spring Byington, Ellen Corby.* This funny, semiclassic baseball fantasy stars the always delightfully gruff Douglas as the manager of the Pittsburgh Pirates, whose season makes the 1994 San Diego Padres look like champions. With the help of a young orphan and some heavenly spirits, the team turns around and makes a drive towards the pennant. There's plenty of surprise cameos, and a very young Leigh looks ravishing. (Remade in 1994) ★★★½ VHS: $14.95

Angels in the Outfield

(1994, 105 min, US, William Dear) *Danny Glover, Tony Danza, Christopher Lloyd, Brenda Fricker, Ben Johnson, Joseph Gordon-Levitt, Dermot Mulroney, Matthew McConaughey, Adrien Brody.* Disney's remake of the wonderfully sweet 1951 baseball fantasy has been updated both technically and in story without capturing the charm and cheerfulness of the original. Glover plays the manager of the California Angels, a bunch of screw-ups and has-beens. They're soon aided by angel Lloyd and some heavenly friends whom only a foster child can see. While some of the baseball footage is genuinely amusing, it's surrounded by sappy, even depressing dramatics. ★★ DVD: $14.99, VHS: $9.99

Angels over Broadway

(1940, 80 min, US, Ben Hecht) *Rita Hayworth, Douglas Fairbanks, Jr., Thomas Mitchell, John Qualen.* One of the most offbeat and original film projects of the 1940s, *Angels over Broadway*, written and directed by noted author Hecht (in his only directing job), is a puzzling though irresistible black comedy set in the theatrical confines of New York City. A suicidal embezzler (Qualen) has his final act rewritten for him by three of life's lost souls: a failing, boozy playwright (Mitchell in a scintillating performance), a con man determined to do good (Fairbanks) and a call girl (the beautiful Hayworth in one of her first starring roles). ★★★ DVD: $19.99

Angels with Dirty Faces

(1938, 97 min, US, Michael Curtiz) *James Cagney, Pat O'Brien, Ann Sheridan, Humphrey Bogart, Dead End Kids.* This is the classic with Cagney and O'Brien as childhood friends; the former becoming a gangster, the latter a priest. When Jimmy returns to his old neighborhood, Pat has his hands full when the street kids "doing time" at the local parish come to idolize the criminal. *Angels* is fast-paced and well acted, and who could forget Cagney's walk to the chair? ★★★½ VHS: $14.99

Anger Management

(2003, 103 min, US, Peter Segal) *Jack Nicholson, Adam Sandler, Marisa Tomei, Luis Guzman, Lynne Thigpen, Woody Harrelson, John Turturro.* Jack and the jackass together for the first time! Introvert ad exec Sandler is mistaken for a hot-tempered bully, and is ordered by the court to spend time with therapist Nicholson. So, naturally, Jack moves in with him, and turns his life upside down. A comedy that fails to deliver laughs, or make sense much of the time, or even to take advantage of the odd pairing of its two stars. *Anger Management* amounts to nothing more than a screeching, audience-winking, lowbrow piece of high concept that suggests that the suits in Hollywood think that any by-committee project with the "right" stars can be made — and the movie-going public fell for it again. ★½ DVD Letterbox Special Edition: $19.99, DVD Pan & Scan: $19.99, VHS: $14.99

Angie

(1994, 108 min, US, Martha Coolidge) *Geena Davis, Stephen Rea, James Gandolfini, Philip Bosco.* A poor woman's *Moonstruck*, *Angie*, based on Avra Wing's novel "Angie, I Says," stars Davis as a Bensonhurst secretary who reexamines her life. Engaged to a likable, macho plumber, Angie learns she is pregnant. But instead of marrying the father, she dumps him and begins an affair with an affected Manhattan artist (Rea). The film begins on a congenial level — introducing affable characters and playful moments of schtick. Halfway through, however, the story takes a distressing turn and disintegrates into a depressing, yawn-producing soap opera. ★★ DVD: $9.99

Angry Harvest

(1985, 102 min, Poland, Agnieszka Holland) *Armin Mueller-Stahl, Elisabeth Trissenaar.* A powerful, sometimes brutal and always gripping view of the Holocaust. Rosa, a Viennese matron, jumps the

transport to Auschwitz; Leon, a sexually repressed farmer, reluctantly shelters and then guiltily lusts after her. Mueller-Stahl brilliantly portrays Leon, a bundle of contradictions: coarse and complicated, prissy and sadistic. He becomes infatuated with Rosa's helplessness and his own sense of control. *Angry Harvest* might be called a psychological action film in which the characters are inexorably drawn together by the forces of war. (German with English subtitles) ★★★½

The Angry Red Planet

(1959, 83 min, US, Ib Melchior) *Gerald Mohr, Nora Hayden, Les Tremayne, Jack Kruschen.* It's cheesy. It's silly. It's wonderful. This is an extremely schlocky tale of an expedition to Mars (the angry red planet) where astronauts encounter giant spider-like creatures and killer plants. The acting is stiff and the dialogue is so bad it's funny. Hilarious use of bogus scientific theories to explain what is going on is the staple in these B-flicks and you get plenty of it in this one. A perfect Saturday matinee film. ★★ DVD: $14.99

Angus

(1995, 90 min, US, Patrick Read Johnson) *George C. Scott, Charlie Talbert, Kathy Bates, Chris Owen, Ariana Richards.* Overweight and overly bright, Angus is the sworn enemy of his high school's most popular student, who makes his life a living hell. The story is taken to such lengths that it is literally painful to watch. The saving grace comes at the end in a stirring and inspired speech from Angus about being different — it should comfort many outcasts. A good cast (with Scott as the youth's grandfather) and soundtrack help distract from the very heavy-handedness of the plot. ★★ VHS: $14.99

The Animal

(2001, 83 min, US, Luke Greenfield) *Rob Schneider, Colleen Haskell, John C. McGinley, Ed Asner, Guy Torry.* Schneider plays Marvin, a nerdy clerk for the police department. His secret wish to become a police officer comes true when he begins to demonstrate superhuman powers. Could it have something to do with the mad scientist who rescued him from a near-fatal car accident? Surprisingly, what little comedy there is is of the tame variety. . . a sexual overture towards a goat is about as dicey as things get. Even considering its target audience of adolescents, *The Animal* is mild, unfunny tomfoolery. ★½ DVD Special Edition: $19.99, VHS: $9.99

Animal Behavior

(1989, 88 min, US, H. Anne Riley) *Karen Allen, Armande Assante, Holly Hunter, Josh Mostel.* A good cast is wasted in this mindless romantic comedy about a music teacher (Assante) who meets a psychologist (Allen) and her "subject": a chimp named Michael. ★ VHS: $19.99

Animal Crackers

(1930, 98 min, US, Victor Heerman) *Groucho Marx, Harpo Marx, Chico Marx, Zeppo Marx, Margaret Dumont, Lillian Roth.* The Marx Brothers' second film finds them still struggling to get a footing in their new medium. With blocking that exposes its stage origins, *Animal Crackers* finds the farcical foursome crashing a society party being held by Dumont (who else?). Groucho makes his grand entrance as the noted African explorer Jeffrey T. Spaulding ("The 'T' stands for Edgar") while Harpo follows close behind blowing chocolate smoke bubbles. Ultimately, Chico and Harpo get

Garbo Speaks: *Anna Christie*

roped into stealing a painting, which leads to one of their classic routines. Despite its flaws, though, the film is at times a riotous skewering of the upper class that will leave one resting assured that in "Alabama the tusks are loosa.'" ★★½

Animal Factory

(2000, 94 min, US, Steve Buscemi) *Willem Dafoe, Edward Furlong, Danny Trejo, John Heard, Mickey Rourke, Tom Arnold, Seymour Cassel, Steve Buscemi.* Nicely avoiding the usual prison drama clichés, this gritty, often compelling drama is based on the novel by Edward Bunker (*Reservoir Dogs*). Furlong plays Ron Decker, a sweet-faced young man of privilege who is sentenced to jail on a drug offense. The naïve youngster is befriended by Earl Copen (Dafoe), the powerful con who controls the prison's black market. Caught in a maelstrom of violence, sexual intimidation and corruption, Decker quickly adapts to his surroundings; exchanging innocence for guile, morality for a blind eye. An effective supporting cast includes Rourke's dentally impaired drag queen and Arnold's sexual predator. ★★★ DVD: $19.99

Animal Farm

(1955, 75 min, GB, John Halas & Joy Batchelor) George Orwell's famous satire on totalitarianism and fascism tells the story of a group of farm animals who band together to oust their oppressive farmer only to find that their chosen leader, the pig, is a ruthless dictator. A simplistic translation, *Animal Farm*'s animation is perfunctory, and though Orwell's allegory is a striking one, there's an overall haziness to the production. This is one animated feature that's not for kids. (Remade in 1999) ★★

Anita: Dances of Vice

(1987, 82 min, Germany, Rosa von Praunheim) *Lotti Huber, Ina Blum, Mikhael Honesseau.* Huber stars as an old woman who thinks that she is the reincarnation of Anita Berber, the infamous nude dancer in Weimar Berlin who flaunted her bisexuality, acknowledged taking drugs and generally scandalized the nation with her notorious behavior. Von Praunheim's splashy, provocative film intercuts black-and-white footage of the ragged old woman spouting her outrageous claims with colorful re-creations of the old woman living the life of her alter ego. (German with English subtitles) ★★★ VHS: $39.99

Anna

(1987, 100 min, US, Yurek Bogayevicz) *Sally Kirkland, Paulina Porizkova, Robert Fields.* Kirkland's riveting Oscar-nominated performance highlights this involving, offbeat version of *All About Eve,* about a middle-aged, once-famous Czech film actress, now struggling in New York, and the young immigrant who befriends her to learn the craft. ★★★ DVD: $14.99

Anna and the King

(1999, 147 min, US, Andy Tennant) *Jodie Foster, Chow Yun-Fat, Ling Bai, Tony Felton.* In its fourth film incarnation, the memoir of 19th-century schoolteacher Anna Leonowens and her momentous trip to Siam makes for a sumptuous if not totally fluid rendering of the popular story. The widowed Anna, accompanied by her young son, travels to Siam to tutor the king's many children. The headstrong Anna and the monarch at first clash, but in time come to respect and love one another. Director Tennant has an eye for period detail, but is less successful in creating a lasting dramatic tension. Foster, looking terrific in period costume, seems a bit out of sync with Anna; Yun-Fat is commanding but isn't able to exorcise the ghost of Yul Brynner hanging about. ★★½ DVD Pan & Scan: $19.99, DVD: $14.99, VHS: $9.99

Anna and the King of Siam

(1946, 128 min, US, John Cromwell) *Irene Dunne, Rex Harrison, Linda Darnell, Lee J. Cobb, Gale Sondergaard.* The inspiration for the 1956 musical *The King and I,* this usually overlooked classic is a perfect blend of Hollywood schmaltz and heart-tugging drama. In an effervescent performance, Dunne is Anna, a mid-19th-century English schoolteacher who travels to Bangkok to instruct the children of the King (an excellent Harrison). As the strong-willed teacher comes in conflict with the equally determined ruler, they fall in love, all the while aware neither is able to act on their feelings. (Also remade in 1999 . . . twice!) ★★★½ VHS: $14.99

Anna Christie

(1930, 89 min, US, Clarence Brown) *Greta Garbo, Charles Bickford, Marie Dressler.* "Gimme a whiskey, ginger ale on the side. And don't be stingy, baby." With these words, the immortal Garbo spoke her first words on film, evolving from silent star to full-fledged screen legend. Based on Eugene O'Neill's classic play, Garbo plays Anna, the disillusioned prostitute who returns home after 15 years to her sea captain father. Dressler is outstanding as Garbo's alcoholic confidant and drinking buddy, and a youthful Bickford portrays the gruff sailor who falls in love with and then rejects the embittered woman. Though the pace may be slow and the production less than technically savvy, O'Neill's earthy prose and Garbo's radiant performance contribute to make this a rewarding film experience. ★★★

Anna Karenina

(1935, 95 min, US, Clarence Brown) *Greta Garbo, Fredric March, Freddie Bartholomew, Basil Rathbone, Maureen O'Sullivan.* Tolstoy's tragic love story is immortalized by the outstanding performance of Garbo in the title role. Her fusion with the character of the doomed heroine is so complete that one might think that Tolstoy had her in mind when he penned the tale. Rathbone is superb as Karenin. ★★★½

Anne Frank

(2001, 160 min, US, Robert Dornhelm) *Hannah Taylor-Gordon, Ben Kingsley, Brenda Blethyn, Lili Taylor, Tatjana Blacher.* Young Taylor-Gordon brings nuance and sincerity to the role of Anne Frank, the Jewish teenager whose diaries and words of hope have inspired generations, in this moving made-for-TV drama. The story follows Anne and her family in the days before Hitler's occupation of Holland, during their years in hiding, and their imprisonment by the Nazis. In attempting to flesh out Anne and her family, the filmmakers have chosen to include Melissa Muller's biography "Anne Frank: A Biography" for their adaptation. Anne is now more of an average teen, an ordinary girl yearning to be extraordinary. Director Dornhelm's even-tempered pacing brings focus to the story. ★★★½ DVD: $19.99, VHS 2-tape set: $14.99

Anne Frank Remembered

(1995, 123 min, US/GB, Jon Blair) *Miep Gies, Narrated by: Kenneth Branagh, Glenn Close.* With 26 million copies of her diary sold around the world and various films made about her, there's not much more one could possibly think there would be to know about Anne Frank. Such is the beauty of *Anne Frank Remembered,* an illuminating documentary which not only presents heretofore unknown information on the courageous Jewish teen killed during WWII, but also pays tribute to Miep Gies, the heroic woman who hid the Frank family in Nazi-occupied Amsterdam for two years. All of the traditional components of the documentary are here, but director Blair and the film's participants make it seem so fresh. ★★★½ DVD: $24.99, VHS: $19.99

Anne of the 1,000 Days

(1969, 145 min, US, Charles Jarrott) *Richard Burton, Geneviève Bujold, Irene Papas, Anthony Quayle.* Henry VIII is at it again as he courts, weds and later beheads Anne Boleyn. Burton gives a larger-than-life performance befitting the monarch, and Bujold is excellent in her first starring role as the doomed queen. Terrific production values (art direction, costumes, cinematography, editing) and Bujold's lovely portrayal combine to make this a commendable historical epic. ★★★

Annie

(1982, 128 min, US, John Huston) *Carol Burnett, Aileen Quinn, Bernadette Peters, Tim Curry, Ann Reinking, Albert Finney.* One of the most popular and admittedly annoying songs ever to come from a Broadway musical, "Tomorrow," is given the red-carpet, zillion-piece orchestra, sing-it-till-you-drop treatment in this over-produced film. Quinn is Annie, who is whisked from her orphanage to spend time with Daddy Warbucks (Finney), the richest man in the world. Burnett, who gives the film's most spirited performance, is the head of the orphanage who sees a way to "Easy Street" thanks to Annie's rich new pal. The Tony Award-winning stage production had charm in abundance; this *Annie* is cloying and frivolous. (Remade in 1999) ★★ DVD Special Anniversary Edition: $19.99, VHS: $14.99

Annie

(1999, 102 min, US, Rob Marshall) *Alicia Morton, Alan Cumming, Kathy Bates, Victor Garber, Audra McDonald, Kristin Chenoweth, Andrea McArdle.* Superior to the over-produced 1982 movie version, this made-for-TV adaptation sticks closer to its stage origins — and is better for it. Morton makes an appealing Annie, and she is surrounded by a top-notch adult cast, including Bates as the nefarious Miss Hannigan; Garber as Daddy Warbucks; and show-stopper Cumming, who helps make "Easy Street" one for the books. (Director Marshall would go on to direct the Oscar-winning *Chicago*) ★★★ DVD: $14.99, VHS: $9.99

Annie Get Your Gun

(1950, 107 min, US, George Sidney) *Betty Hutton, Howard Keel, Louis Calhern, J. Carrol Naish, Edward Arnold, Keenan Wynn.* A colorful rendition of the classic Broadway musical. Hutton (filling in for an ailing Judy Garland) plays Annie Oakley, who challenges Keel's Frank Butler as the premier sharpshooter of the Wild West and ends up falling in love. Music by Irving Berlin, and songs include "There's No Business Like Show Business." ★★★ DVD: $19.99

Annie Hall

(1977, 94 min, US, Woody Allen) *Woody Allen, Diane Keaton, Tony Roberts, Paul Simon, Christopher Walken, Colleen Dewhurst, Shelley Duvall, Carol Kane.* Allen's masterpiece is still perhaps his sharpest and wittiest work to date. In this ultimate of crowd pleasers, Allen adroitly puts his finger on the social milieu of the '70s as he explores the ups and downs of modern relationships. Oscar winner Diane Keaton is at her best as Woody's star-crossed lover. A delightful blend of uproarious one-liners, delicious comic schtick, intuitive dialogue, smart performances and penetrating observations on today's mores, *Annie Hall* is pure enchantment. Winner of 4 Academy Awards including Picture and Director. ★★★★ DVD: $14.99

Annie Oakley

(1935, 88 min, US, George Stevens) *Barbara Stanwyck, Melvyn Douglas, Preston Foster, Moroni Olsen.* Stanwyck stars as that rootin'-tootin' markswoman Annie Oakley in this episodic but amiable western which follows her rise to fame in Buffalo Bill's Wild West Show in the 1880s. Giving a rather subdued portrayal considering the flamboyant characteristics usually associated with Oakley, Stanwyck plays Annie as a naive and rather feminine romantic who gets all gooey-eyed at the sight of an egocentric sharpshooter (Foster). The film is a little rough around the edges, but most scenes are well-staged and entertaining. ★★★

The Anniversary

(1968, 95 min, GB, Roy Ward Baker) *Bette Davis, Sheila Hancock, Jack Hedley.* Davis camps it up like a drunken drag queen (with an eye-patch) in this black comedy about a manipulative mother who uses the occasion of her wedding anniversary gathering to emotionally torture her three sons. ★★½ VHS: $19.99

A

A

The Anniversary Party

(2001, 115 min, US, Alan Cumming & Jennifer Jason Leigh) *Alan Cumming, Jennifer Jason Leigh, Gwyneth Paltrow, Kevin Kline, Phoebe Cates, Jane Adams, John C. Reilly, Parker Posey, Jennifer Beals.* What is unspoken by the guests attending the sixth anniversary party of Joe and Sally, a novelist and his actress wife who are newly reconciled, is as piercing as the truths and gossip verbalized by these Hollywood insiders who spend an evening drinking, eating, game-playing and drug-taking. Written and directed by Cumming and Leigh in their feature-film debuts, *The Anniversary Party* is an entertaining, often witty examination of Hollywood personalities and what makes them tick. Cumming and Leigh are Joe and Sally, who are hosting their first party since a recent split. They've tried to surround themselves with close friends, but as everyone attending this evening will discover, not all plans come to full term. Cumming and Leigh nicely avoid the usual clichés of movie folk, shading everyone with pleasing strokes of familiarity and dimension. ★★★ DVD: $24.99, VHS: $14.99

The Annunciation

(1990, 101 min, Hungary, András Jeles) Defying placement in any simple category, *The Annunciation* is a strange, poetic and almost surreal feature which — with a cast composed entirely of children from ages eight thru 12 — enacts nothing less than mankind's tragic and tumultuous tale of life on earth. A self-satisfied Satan, in the guise of a pretty blond cherub boy, decides to take Adam and Eve through time, to both witness and partake in the violence, sadness and struggle brought on by their disobedience to God's will. In what could have been a simple gimmick film, similar to what *Bugsy Malone* was to gangster flicks, *The Annunciation* soon develops into a hypnotic journey through history infused with melancholic religious and existential themes. (Hungarian with English subtitles) ★★★½ VHS: $59.95

Another Country

(1984, 90 min, GB, Marek Kanievska) *Rupert Everett, Colin Firth, Cary Elwes.* This marvelously acted and elegantly photographed film version of Julien Mitchell's hit London play speculates on the public school days of real-life traitor/defector Guy Burgess. Everett is the languid "innocent," denied entry to the school's ruling elite because of an indiscreet homosexual affair. Elwes is Everett's handsome lover. ★★★½

Another Day in Paradise

(1999, 101 min, US, Larry Clark) *James Woods, Melanie Griffith, Vincent Kartheiser, Natasha Gregson Wagner, Paul Hipp.* Clark's follow-up to his vile *Kids* fares slightly better, but is fairly negligible save for two good performances from Woods and Griffith. Two junkie teens, who support their habit by looting vending machines, are taken under the wing of a middle-aged junkie couple, who support their habit by robbing pharmacies and pulling other jobs. Things go swimmingly for a while, with the foursome forming a bizarre, ersatz family. That is until the inevitable "heist-gone-wrong" part of the story. The teens are uninteresting, the story barely watchable, and the direction is unremarkable. ★★ DVD: $9.99

Another 48 HRS.

(1990, 98 min, US, Walter Hill) *Nick Nolte, Eddie Murphy, Brion James, Bernie Casey.* A sequel — no, let's call it a Xerox — to Murphy's 1982 debut. Director Hill keeps the action moving at a brisk enough pace and the villains have been suitably modernized for the '90s; but it's all been done before and it was much better the first time. Murphy and Nolte are carbon copies of their former selves. ★★ DVD: $14.99, VHS: $9.99

Another Stakeout

(1993, 109 min, US, John Badham) *Richard Dreyfuss, Emilio Estevez, Rosie O'Donnell.* In this inferior, ill-timed sequel to *Stakeout*, Dreyfuss and Estevez, neither looking the worse for wear, repeat their roles as Seattle surveillance cops. Their new assignment is to lay in waiting for a government witness who has flown the coop. They are joined by Assistant D.A. O'Donnell, whose lack of both training and tact causes an immediate personality clash with our laid-back jokesters. Only a mistaken identity subplot elevates the film, as the policework is virtually nonexistent and the comedy hit-and-miss. ★★ DVD: $14.99, VHS: $9.99

Another Thin Man

See: *The Thin Man Series*

Another Time, Another Place

(1958, 98 min, US, Lewis Allen) *Lana Turner, Barry Sullivan, Sean Connery, Glynis Johns.* Turner chews the scenery in this ordinary soap opera with Turner as a correspondent based in England during WWII who suffers a nervous breakdown when her lover dies. ★★ VHS: $14.99

Another Time, Another Place

(1983, 104 min, GB/Scotland, Michael Radford) *Phyllis Logan, Giovanni Mauriello.* This poignant drama observes the effects of a group of Italian POWs on a remote Scottish village in 1944. Three of the Italians are housed next to Janie (Logan), who lives a tedious life with her taciturn husband. As they try to relieve each other's loneliness, a sexual attraction develops between Janie and one of the POWs which both frightens and entices her. An impressive debut for writer-director Radford. ★★★

Another Way

(1982, 102 min, Hungary, Karoly Makk) *Péter Andorai, Jadwiga Jankowska-Cieślak, Jozef Króner.* This courageous and intelligent lesbian love story is set in Hungary immediately after the 1956 uprising and concerns the mutual attraction and budding relationship between two female journalists. Livia, married to an army officer, shyly begins accepting the advances of Eva, an outspoken reporter with whom she shares an office. Director Makk juxtaposes this tender but doomed love affair with the high hopes and bitter suppression of the Budapest Spring. (Hungarian with English subtitles) ★★★

Another Woman

(1988, 81 min, US, Woody Allen) *Gena Rowlands, Mia Farrow, Gene Hackman, Blythe Danner, Ian Holm, John Houseman, Sandy Dennis.* After the disaster of *September*, Allen turns yet again to Ingmar Bergman territory with this complex examination of a woman (Rowlands) whose lifelong resistance to her passions is shattered when she accidentally overhears the confessions of a therapy patient (Farrow). Though not as subtle as *Interiors*, the film is a complete success thanks to Rowlands' remarkable performance and the efforts of a powerhouse cast. ★★★ DVD: $19.99

Another You

(1991, 98 min, US, Maurice Phillips) *Gene Wilder, Richard Pryor, Mercedes Ruehl, Stephen Lang, Vanessa L. Williams, Kevin Pollak.* In this fourth and final screen pairing of Pryor and Wilder, Gene plays a compulsive liar who leaves a sanitarium and is left in the custody of con man Richard, who's doing community service. They soon are on the run from crooked businessmen using Gene in a corporate scam. Sadly, the screenplay offers nothing for these comedians to do other than look bemused and their chemistry suffers as a result. Also, Pryor is beginning to show signs of his coming illness, making this all the more painful to watch. ★½ DVD Letterbox: $14.99

Antarctica

(1985, 112 min, Japan, Koreyoshi Kurahara) *Ken Takahura, Masako Natsume.* A harrowing adventure story about survival and companionship set in the harshest climate on earth. Based on a true incident, the film features breathtaking cinematography by Akira Shizaka and a haunting score by Vangelis. ★★★

Anthony Adverse

(1936, 137 min, US, Mervyn LeRoy) *Fredric March, Gale Sondergaard, Olivia de Havilland, Claude Rains, Edmund Gwenn.* An intermittently interesting adaptation of Hervey Allen's epic novel set during the Napoleonic era. March ably plays the title character, whose life is covered from his youthful world travels to his rise to power and his marriage to an opera star from poor beginnings. ★★ VHS: $14.99

Antigone

(1962, 93 min, Greece, George Tzavellas) *Irene Papas.* Sophocles' poetic parable is successfully translated to the screen in this eloquent drama. Papas gives a magnificent performance as Antigone, daughter of Oedipus who, following the dictates of her own conscience, is condemned to death for defying King Creon and burying her two dead brothers. Director Tzavellas, aware of the difficulties of filming Greek tragedies, substitutes the traditional chorus with an unobtrusive offscreen narrator and, coupled with Papas' excellent portrayal, brings this ancient tale to life. (Greek with English subtitles) ★★★ VHS: $29.99

Antitrust

(2001, 108 min, US, Peter Howitt) *Ryan Phillippe, Claire Forlani, Rachael Leigh Cook, Tim Robbins, Yee Jee Tso, Richard Roundtree.* It's difficult to create much suspense when characters spend most of their time typing at their computer keyboards. Unless the plot hinges on whether or not the hero makes a typo. Such is the case with *Antitrust*, a tame thriller that ruins a workable premise thanks to static direction and some silly plot developments. Phillippe stars as a hotshot computer whiz who is lured by software mogul Robbins to work on a highly sensitive computer program that would give the CEO unlimited power on a global scale. Phillippe then uncovers the truth. Robbins seems to be having fun as the charming megalomaniac, but everyone else looks like they'd rather be in *Traffic*. ★½ DVD: $14.99, VHS: $9.99

Antonia and Jane

(1991, 75 min, GB, Beeban Kidron) *Imelda Staunton, Saskia Reeves, Patricia Leventon.* This delightfully funny low-budget gem, an Anglicized, feminist homage to Woody Allen, explores the loving and tempestuous relationship between two decidedly different women. Antonia, the plain-looking, insecure but adventurous one narrates the film's opening, giving details of her hilarious obsession

Any Given Sunday

with Jane, her pretty, married and seemingly well-balanced childhood friend whom she is about to meet for their annual lunch. Midway through the film, Jane takes over the narration duties and gives us her side of the story. Pleasantly amusing and deceptively simple. ★★★½ VHS: $7.99

Antonia's Line

(1995, 93 min, Netherlands, Marleen Gorris) *Willeke van Ammelrooy, Els Dottermans, Veere Van Overloop.* A celebration of the love, unity and strength of women, this wonderfully endearing and touching family chronicle/fable centering on four generations of women playfully alternates between dramatic and magical realism. The story, set in a small Dutch village, spans decades and follows the fiercely independent-minded Antonia (Ammelrooy), who returns to her childhood farmhouse to till the soil and raise a family; all without the aid of the misogynist townsfolk, a hypocritical church and the often violence-prone men. Antonia is aided by her lesbian daughter, a granddaughter and great-grand-daughter and a group of social rejects who flock to her. This Oscar-winning Best Foreign Film is masterful storytelling that enthralls. (Dutch with English subtitles) ★★★★ DVD: $14.99, VHS: $9.99

Antonio das Mortes

(1969, 95 min, Brazil, Glauber Rocha) *Maurico Do Valle, Odete Lara.* Brazilian filmmaker Rocha, winner of the Best Director Award at Cannes in 1969, was forced into exile after the release of this impassioned protest against the oppression of workers by the landowning class. Set in the arid northeast of Brazil, the film, mixing suspenseful storytelling with the area's rich legacy of cultural mysticism and native folk art, follows the violent uprising of a group of peasants who draw strength and inspiration when the "warrior saint," Santo Antonio, aids their rebellion. A powerful drama as well as a stirring political allegory. (Portuguese with English subtitles) ★★★½

Antwone Fisher

(2002, 120 min, US, Denzel Washington) *Derek Luke, Denzel Washington, Joy Bryant, Salli Richardson, Vernee Watson Johnson, Earl Billings.* Choosing the affecting true-life story of a conflicted sailor unable to confront his childhood demons in which to make his directorial debut, Washington proves every bit as capable behind the camera as he is in front of it. Compelling, unsettling and ultimately heartwarming, *Antwone Fisher* — scripted by Fisher himself — recounts the troubled life of the young sailor. Unable to control his anger, he is sent to Navy psychiatrist Dr. Jerome Davenport

(Washington), whose attempt to discover the root of his hostility is initially met with reluctance. As Antwone's difficult life is recalled in a series of devastating flashbacks, he is able to come to terms with his past and put it to rest once and for all. In need of a little editing, Fisher's story can't quite escape some of the trappings of the genre, but thanks to newcomer Luke's ingratiating performance, Washington's sure hand, and a story that never loses focus, *Antwone Fisher* is a moving, even inspirational life story. ★★★ DVD Pan & Scan: $19.99, DVD Letterboxed: $19.99, VHS: $12.99

Antz

(1998, 83 min, US, Eric Darnell & Tim Johnson) *Voices of: Sharon Stone, Woody Allen, Christopher Walken, Gene Hackman, Sylvester Stallone, Danny Glover.* The all-computer-generated animated adventure comedy *Antz* is a joyous bonanza of clever sight gags and amazing three-dimensional visual effects. As with any great animated epic, the story is full of strange characters who exhibit human traits and emotions, all brought to vibrant life by one of the most prolific collections of vocal talent. Z (Allen) is a neurotic worker ant who strikes the ire of the stern General Mandible (Hackman), who is engaged to Princess Bala (Stone). Z is also smitten with Bala, and after a hair-brained scheme to impress her, inadvertently kidnaps the princess. That's when the real adventure and fun begins and a colony revolution is ignited. ★★★½ DVD: $19.99, VHS: $9.99

Any Given Sunday

(1999, 160 min, US, Oliver Stone) *Al Pacino, Cameron Diaz, Jamie Foxx, Dennis Quaid, James Woods, LL Cool J, Jim Brown, Matthew Modine, Ann-Margret, Lawrence Taylor, Aaron Eckhart, John C. McGinley, Lauren Holly, Lela Rochon, Elizabeth Berkley.* Stone is the perfect director to capture the visceral intensity of football, the game based on the strategies of armed conflict. This is one of the most successful attempts in taking the viewer inside the action on the field of battle; you can smell the sweat and get the wind knocked out of you with every tackle. The story line is tried and true: grizzled veteran (Quaid) playing through pain, rookie loose cannon (Foxx) rewriting the playbook. And in the center of it all, the coach (Pacino), negotiating between tradition and new blood, and steering through excesses on and off the field. Stone's trademark hyper-action is well served by the ensemble's most effective performances, especially Foxx's accomplished portrayal of hotshot Willie Beaman. The film is physically exhausting to watch and, while not completely successful in imparting a sense of the

game's history, serves as an intelligent entertainment. (Director's cut) ★★★½ DVD Letterbox Special Edition: $14.99, DVD: $24.99, VHS: $9.99

Any Wednesday

(1966, 109 min, US, Robert Ellis Miller) *Jane Fonda, Jason Robards, Dean Jones, Rosemary Murphy.* Fonda sparkles in this saucy bedroom farce based on the hit Broadway comedy about a married executive (Robards) who uses his mistress' apartment to entertain clients. ★★★ VHS: $19.99

Any Which Way You Can

(1980, 116 min, US, Clint Eastwood) *Clint Eastwood, Sondra Locke, Geoffrey Lewis, Ruth Gordon, William Smith, Anne Ramsey, Logan Ramsey.* Ever so slightly more appealing than the first film, this sequel to *Every Which Way But Loose* follows bare-knuckler Clint as he reluctantly takes on challenger Smith. Clyde is back, as are a slew of stupid pet tricks and low-down humor. ★★ DVD Letterbox: $19.99, VHS: $14.99

Anything Else

(2003, 108 min, US, Woody Allen) *Woody Allen, Jason Biggs, Christina Ricci, Stockard Channing, Danny DeVito, Jimmy Fallon.* Jerry Falk (Biggs) is an up-and-coming young comedy writer (with seemingly unlimited financial resources) caught in the throes of anxiety, romantic complications and professional crises — all handled with a little bit of pessimism, a dash of philosophy and a whole lot of one-liners. Sound like anyone we know? Writer-director Allen, thankfully abandoning the recently uncomfortable role of romantic lead, passes the torch to young Biggs in this funny comedy that borrows themes from a few of Woody's best works but nevertheless possesses an air of freshness. Sharing an apartment but not sexual relations with his actress girlfriend, Amanda (Ricci), Jerry is uncertain of many aspects of his life, especially Amanda's fidelity and his manager's (DeVito) competence. He comes to rely on the advice and extraneous comic musings of his new friend Dobel (Allen), a 60-ish schoolteacher testing the waters of comedy writing. As Jerry attempts to sort out his life, Woody sets right a few minor cinematic missteps, returning to the kind of romantic comedy that has served him best. The film moves at a breezy pace, the lines are funny and the characters are his most appealing in quite a few years. ★★★ DVD Letterbox: $14.99, VHS: $9.99

Anywhere but Here

(1999, 114 min, US, Wayne Wang) *Susan Sarandon, Natalie Portman, Hart Bochner, Bonnie Bedelia, Shawn Hatosy.* Two good lead performances by Sarandon and Portman can't totally save this overly familiar, alternately touching and maudlin story of a mother and daughter which plays like a low-rent *Tumbleweeds*. Based on the best-seller by Mona Simpson, the film follows Sarandon and Portman as they move from their small town in Wisconsin to Beverly Hills for a new start. Constantly at odds, each woman finds direction and, ultimately, respect for the other. The acting here is strong enough to counterbalance the film's sappiness and cliché. ★★ DVD: $19.99, VHS: $14.99

Anzio

(1968, 118 min, US, Edward Dmytryk) *Robert Mitchum, Peter Falk, Robert Ryan, Earl Holliman, Arthur Kennedy.* A few distinguished battle scenes add little to this all-star WWII actioner about the Allied invasion of Anzio. ★★ DVD: $19.99, VHS: $9.99

A

A

Aparajito

(1956, 113 min, India, Satyajit Ray) *Pinaki Sen Gupla, Karuna Banerjee.* Ray's second installment of the Apu Trilogy portrays Apu's life from the age of 10, when his father moves the family to the holy city of Benares, to his entrance to college years later. The family's struggles, including the father's death and Apu's efforts to win a scholarship, are vividly chronicled in this unbearably poignant, beautifully filmed cinematic treasure. (Bengali with English subtitles) ★★★★ DVD: $29.99, VHS: $19.99

Apart from Hugh

(1994, 87 min, US, Jon FitzGerald) *David Merwin, Steve Arnold.* This low-budget film, while affectionate and sincere, fails as either gay romance or character study. Living in rural domesticity, Collin and Hugh find their seemingly happy relationship undergoing a potential crisis when Collin contemplates leaving. The two young men's struggle to maintain their independence and commitment to each other is handed deadly blows with its laborious plot, slow pacing and a heavy-handed somberness. ★½ VHS: $39.99

The Apartment

(1960, 125 min, US, Billy Wilder) *Jack Lemmon, Shirley MacLaine, Fred MacMurray, Ray Walston, Jack Kruschen, Edie Adams.* This Oscar-winning Best Picture stars Lemmon and MacLaine in what may be their best screen performances. Lemmon plays a young executive on the go who gets more than he bargains for when he allows superiors to use his apartment for extramarital encounters and falls in love with his boss' mistress (MacLaine). Writer-director Wilder offers his customary sardonic wit and stinging commentary to lay bare the hypocrisies of the corporate world and the imperfections of love. A scintillating comedy-drama. MacMurray, Kruschen (an Oscar nominee) and Walston offer fine support. ★★★★ DVD: $14.99

Apartment Zero

(1989, 114 min, GB, Martin Donovan) *Colin Firth, Hart Bochner, Fabrizio Bentivoglio, Liz Smith.* A multi-layered, stylish thriller, *Apartment Zero* creates an atmosphere of wicked sexual tension through the subtle use of suggestion and innuendo. In an English-speaking community in Buenos Aires, a sexually repressed cinephile (Firth) with a penchant for the classics takes in a swaggering, handsome American boarder (Bochner) with many skeletons in his "closet." Suspicions abound as gruesome political murders haunt the Argentine city upon the arrival of the new roommate. Firth and Bochner bring a subtle suggestion of sexual manipulation and dormant passion to an already explosive scenario. Donovan uses stylish camerawork and extreme close-ups to seduce the viewer into his world of intrigue. ★★★ VHS: $14.99

Aphrodite

(1984, 90 min, France, Robert Fuest) *Valerie Kaprisky.* The meltingly beautiful Kaprisky stars in this sensuous staging of Pierre Louys' materpiece of erotic literature. Set in the Greek islands in 1914, the story is a sensual journey into a world of licentiousness, debauchery and unleashed sexual splendor. In other words, it's not *Mary Poppins*! The complete, unrated and unedited version. ★★

Apocalypse Now

(1979, 150 min, US, Francis Ford Coppola) *Marlon Brando, Robert Duvall, Martin Sheen, Frederic Forrest, Albert Hall, Sam Bottoms, Laurence Fishburne, Dennis Hopper, G.D. Spradlin, Harrison Ford, Scott Glenn.* A masterpiece of modern cinema, Coppola's epic reworking of Joseph Conrad's "Heart of Darkness" is a mind-blowing, semihallucinatory examination of not only the insanity of the Vietnam War, but of war itself. Sheen gives a career performance as a military assassin sent on a mission deep into enemy territory to hunt down a renegade colonel (Brando). Duvall, as an air cavalry commander, gets to utter the classic line, "I love the smell of napalm in the morning." Coppola, cast and crew made a real-life, two-year sojourn into the Philippine jungle to make the film. Along the way Sheen suffered a heart attack, sets were destroyed by typhoons, and the script was rewritten daily. The result, which could have easily been disastrous, is instead a remarkably coherent, superbly acted peek into human cruelty and frailty. ★★★★ DVD Letterbox Original Version: $29.99, DVD Letterbox Apocalypse Now Redux: $19.99, VHS Original Version: $14.99, VHS Letterbox Original Version: $24.99

Apollo 13

(1995, 135 min, US, Ron Howard) *Tom Hanks, Kevin Bacon, Bill Paxton, Gary Sinise, Ed Harris, Kathleen Quinlan, Brent Cullen.* Though comparisons to *The Right Stuff* are inevitable, director Howard's epic is an impressive, suspenseful telling of the near-disastrous 1970 attempted lunar landing. While lacking *The Right Stuff*'s determined style and hard edge, *Apollo 13* is nevertheless a well-crafted story of heroism in the face of insurmountable odds. History tells us of the flight of *Apollo 13*, whose mission to the moon was thwarted by a tank explosion and whose uncertain return home kept Americans spellbound for nearly a week. What Howard has created in his fascinating, straightforward adventure film — aided by excellent effects and a knowing mood of the times — is a hypnotic tale which follows almost to the letter the actual events. The cast is almost secondary to the action, but led by Hanks (as Jim Lovell), the entire ensemble lends credibility and conviction to their roles. ★★★★ VHS Letterbox: $14.99

The Apostle

(1997, 131 min, US, Robert Duvall) *Robert Duvall, Farrah Fawcett, Miranda Richardson, Billy Bob Thornton, John Beasley, June Carter Cash.* Euliss "Sonny" Dewey (Duvall) is a Texas Pentecostal minister with some damning characteristics of his own. He's powerful and charismatic, especially when preaching the word of God. But he's got a bad temper, and when wife Fawcett asks for a divorce, he goes ballistic on her new boyfriend with a baseball bat. With the police on his trail, Sonny takes to the road and lands in Louisiana, where he starts a new church. Although Duvall's Sonny is a flamboyant character, this is not a flamboyant movie. Its best moments are quiet ones, like those involving Sonny's relationship with his mother (well played by Cash) or the churchgoers in his newly established church. Duvall is galvanizing in the lead, painting an indelible picture of a complicated but flawed man on a mission. Praise should be heaped on him for delivering a compelling, challenging tale. And to that we add, hallelujah! ★★★½ DVD Letterbox: $14.99

The Appaloosa

(1966, 99 min, US, Sidney J. Furie) *Marlon Brando, John Saxon, Anjanette Comer.* A lushly photographed though sluggish western with Brando as a horse breeder who embarks on a south-of-the-border trek to retrieve his prized stallion, stolen by a Mexican outlaw. Saxon is the ruthless bandit. ★★ VHS: $14.99

Appointment with Death

(1988, 108 min, US, Michael Winner) *Peter Ustinov, Lauren Bacall, Carrie Fisher, John Gielgud, Piper Laurie, Hayley Mills.* Ustinov returns as Agatha Christie's Belgian detective Hercule Poirot, here investigating the murder of greedy widow Bacall. Disappointing thriller will leave you caring little about who done it. ★★ VHS: $14.99

Apprentice to Murder

(1988, 94 min, US, R.L. Thomas) *Donald Sutherland, Chad Lowe, Mia Sara.* In the late 1920s in rural Pennsylvania, a 16-year-old farm boy befriends a "powwow" doctor (a combination of a religious faith healer and an herbalist) who may or may not be crazy and a murderer. Lowe is the innocent teenager who comes under the influence of the creepy Sutherland, the two setting out to undermine a suspected demonic neighbor. Based on a true story. Note: The cover art on the box is very misleading. It is not the spooky, satanic horror film it suggests. Rather, the film is a slowly paced mystery about manipulation and religious hysteria. ★★

The Apprenticeship of Duddy Kravitz

(1974, 121 min, Canada, Ted Kotcheff) *Richard Dreyfuss, Denholm Elliott, Jack Warden, Randy Quaid, Joe Silver.* In a career-defining role, Dreyfuss stars as Duddy Kravitz, a likable young man from Montreal's Jewish ghetto who stops at nothing and for no one in his ambitious drive for success. Set in 1948, this seriocomedic film features many enjoyable scenes and characters, with the highlight being Elliott's hilarious performance as a drunken English film director hired by Duddy to "tastefully" film a Bar Mitzvah. ★★★½ VHS: $14.99

April Fool's Day

(1986, 88 min, US, Fred Walton) *Deborah Foreman, Griffin O'Neal, Thomas F. Wilson.* Friday the 13th horror and teen comedy don't mix in this attempted spoof about a group of teens staying at a friend's mansion, being bumped off one by one. ★½ DVD Letterbox: $14.99, VHS: $9.99

Apt Pupil

(1998, 111 min, US, Bryan Singer) *Ian McKellen, Brad Renfro, Bruce Davison, Elias Koteas, David Schwimmer.* The sophomore film from *Usual Suspects* director Singer, *Apt Pupil* is a disappointing adaptation of the well-crafted Stephen King novella. Singer displays little aptitude for the subject matter: the appeal and mystique of evil, and the question of whether evil is contagious. An inscrutable Renfo plays a Holocaust-obsessed high schooler who discovers his elderly German neighbor (McKellen) is actually a Nazi war criminal. The youth's fascination with the past drives him to blackmail the old man to regale him with tales of suffering and death from his concentration camp days. Full of clichés, *Apt Pupil* features none of the style or tension of his great debut, and the screenplay does nothing to illuminate or give psychological insight into the central charcter. McKellen, however, is terrific; he isn't as frightening as he should be, but he creates a detailed, compelling portrait of dormant evil reawakened. ★★ DVD: $9.99

Arabesque

(1966, 105 min, US, Stanley Donen) *Gregory Peck, Sophia Loren, George Coulouris.* Director Donen (*Charade*) is in familiar Hitchcock territory with this effective spy thriller about a college professor (Peck) who unwittingly becomes involved in a plot to assassinate an Arab prime minister. Though this doesn't deliver the thrills to the degree *Charade* did, Peck and costar Loren and a rather complex story compensate. ★★★ VHS: $14.99

Arabian Nights

(1974, 130 min, Italy, Pier Paolo Pasolini) *Ninetto Davoli, Franco Merli.* Pasolini's final film in his "Trilogy of Life" series — which includes *The Decameron* and *The Canterbury Tales* — is a bawdy and visually opulent fable of idyllic sexuality based on the classic Arabian tales. Told in dreamlike vignettes, the stories derive from three cultures — Persia, Egypt and India — and range from the ninth century to the Renaissance. A celebration of joyous sensuality rarely found in our present industrialized Western culture. (Italian and Arabic with English subtitles) ★★★½

Arachnophobia

(1990, 109 min, US, Frank Marshall) *Jeff Daniels, John Goodman, Julian Sands, Harley Jane Kozak, Brian McNamara.* Marshall, a product of the Spielberg farm system, made his directorial debut with this entertaining horror-laced comedy. A highly poisonous spider from the Amazon hitches a ride stateside and takes up residence in the home of a relocated big-city doctor (Daniels); it mates with a domestic female and thereby creates a whole new breed of creepy-crawlers. Goodman steals the show as a know-it-all, G.I. Joe exterminator. But, of course, the real stars are the spiders themselves, who provide many a nonoffensive scare. ★★★ DVD: $14.99

L'Argent

(1983, 90 min, France/Switzerland, Robert Bresson) *Christian Patey, Sylvie van den Elsen, Michel Briguet.* The corrupting power of money, the cancerous spread of evil resulting from its use, and man's eventual redemption from its sins are the themes in director Bresson's thoughtful Marxist fable. Based on a short story by Tolstoy, the film — shot in Bresson's unique style of ascetic realism — follows the tragic course of Yvon, a young truck driver accused of counterfeiting. Fired from his job as a result of a set-up, he is eventually sent to prison, where he is incarcerated for years. Losing his wife and child, Yvon finally rebels and purges himself of his rage. ★★★ VHS: $19.99

Aria

(1987, 85 min, GB, Bruce Beresford, Charles Sturridge, Derek Jarman, Franc Roddam, Jean-Luc Godard, Julien Temple, Ken Russell, Nicolas Roeg, Robert Altman, Bill Bryden) *Theresa Russell, Buck Henry, Beverly D'Angelo, John Hurt, Anita Morris, Bridget Fonda, Tilda Swinton.* A sensual explosion of sight and sound, Aria is a bold and adventurous collage of vignettes inspired by the greatest opera arias of all time. Ten of the finest and most innovative contemporary filmmakers (including Robert Altman, Bruce Beresford, Jean-Luc Godard, Derek Jarman, Nicolas Roeg, Ken Russell, Julien Temple) were asked to choose their favorite operatic arias and create a short interpretation of the music, independent of the original libretto. The result is a series of mini-masterpieces filled with tantalizing imagery exposing the raw emotional power and deeply erotic nature of opera. ★★★ DVD: $19.99

Ariel

(1988, 74 min, Finland, Aki Kaurismäki) *Susanna Haavisto, Turo Pajala.* Director Kaurismaki probes in his films the gritty, near-hopeless condition of his characters using a deadpan cinematic style graced with both insight and biting satire. This black-and-white comedy-drama of forgotten hopes and resilient love follows an alienated, down-on-his-heels drifter who, in his huge Cadillac convertible, embarks on a journey from Lapland to Helsinki that soon involves him in crime, a murder, a jailbreak, a marriage and eventually a chance to escape all his problems. An invigorating black comedy that will remind one of a European Jim Jarmusch or a quirkier Wim Wenders. (Finnish with English subtitles) ★★★ VHS: $79.99

The Aristocats

(1970, 78 min, US, Wolfgang Reitherman) *Voices of: Phil Harris, Eva Gabor, Sterling Holloway, Scatman Crothers.* This Disney animated feature isn't in the same league as some of their "classics," but is charming nonetheless. Duchess and her three kittens belong to a wealthy old lady who has willed them her fortune. The jealous butler kidnaps them and leaves them in the country. Enter the charming Thomas O'Malley, Alley Cat (Harris), who rescues them and returns them to their rightful home. The usual high Disney quality in addition to some adorable songs. ★★★½ DVD: $29.99, VHS: $22.99

Arizona Dream

(1994, 119 min, US, Emir Kusturica) *Johnny Depp, Faye Dunaway, Lili Taylor, Jerry Lewis.* Director Kusturica seemlessly blends together reality, fantasy and dreams to create this emotionally complex vision of a young man's journey into adulthood. Depp stars as a lyrical N.Y.C. government employee who travels to Arizona to attend the wedding of his car salesman uncle (a somewhat schticky Lewis). Both Dunaway and Taylor give appropriately bizarre but grounded performances as a mother and daughter who take turns seducing/torturing Depp with their weird and dangerous charms. Not for everyone and somewhat psychedelic in mood. ★★★

Arlington Road

(1999, 119 min, US, Mark Pellington) *Jeff Bridges, Tim Robbins, Joan Cusack, Hope Davis, Mason Gamble.* Reminiscent of *The Parallax View* in terms of suspense and smarts, this stylish, tense conspiracy thriller sets a taut pace for itself and rarely lets up. In a gripping performance, Bridges is Michael Farraday, a college professor who befriends the new next-door neighbors. Farraday slowly begins to suspect that this Ozzie and Harriet couple may be plotting terrorist bombings. As he digs deeper, he soon puts himself and those around him in harm's way. Director Pellington is equally adept with his action scenes and the more intimate, personal moments. He makes sure that you're never ahead of the game, and rattles you a little if you think you have it all figured out. ★★★ DVD: $9.99, VHS: $9.99

Armageddon

(1998, 150 min, US, Michael Bay) *Bruce Willis, Ben Affleck, Will Patton, Billy Bob Thornton, Liv Tyler, Steve Buscemi.* It's hard to totally dislike a film that boasts a world-ending meteor and a cast of top-drawer actors instructed to play this action sci-fi yarn to melodramatic excess. When a meteor the size of Manhattan takes aim, the world powers select a tough-talkin' oil rigger (Willis) and his colorful gang of misfit employees to save the day. This includes

Affleck as Willis' sidekick who, when not trying to save the world, keeps company with Tyler, the daughter of a mightily disapproving Willis. The scenes in which the riggers-cum-astronauts land on the meteor are rather good, though the story doesn't equal the effects. *Armageddon* can be mindless fun if not taken too seriously because it doesn't take itself too seriously. ★★ DVD Letterbox Criterion Collection: $39.99, DVD Letterboxed: $19.99, VHS: $9.99

Armed and Dangerous

(1986, 113 min, US, Mark L. Lester) *John Candy, Eugene Levy, Robert Loggia, Meg Ryan.* This bungling comedy stars the big guy as an ex-policeman who becomes a security guard and, through no skill of his own, exposes a crooked union official. ★½ VHS: $9.99

Bruce Campbell vs. *Army of Darkness*

Army of Darkness

(1993, 85 min, US, Sam Raimi) *Bruce Campbell, Embeth Davidtz, Bridget Fonda.* This wildly stylish and deliriously imaginative sequel to the cult classics *Evil Dead* and *Evil Dead 2* continues the misadventures of the reluctant hero, Ash (Campbell), as he, along with a chainsaw, a sawed-off shotgun and a 1970s Oldsmobile, are mysteriously sent back to medieval times to retrieve "The Book of the Dead," battle netherworld demons and more. Laced with director Raimi's trademark seizure-inducing camera work, hysterically gruesome special effects and black-humored violence, the film succeeds on all levels as we follow Ash's exploits as he attempts to get back to modern times and his job at S-Mart ("Shop smart — shop S-mart"). ★★★ DVD Letterbox: $14.99, DVD Bootleg Cut: $19.99, DVD 2-disc Boomstick Edition: $29.99, VHS: $9.99, VHS Letterbox Collector's Edition: $14.99

Around the World in 80 Days

(1956, 167 min, US, Michael Anderson) *David Niven, Cantinflas, Shirley MacLaine.* A mammoth and vastly entertaining version of Jules Verne's novel. Niven stars as Phineas Fogg, the globe-trotting British gentleman whose bet that he can circle the world in 80 days leads him and Cantinflas on a

Arsenic and Old Lace

succession of adventures, including meeting up with princess MacLaine. The film features 44 cameos and the location shootings are remarkable. Winner of 5 Academy Awards, including Best Picture. (Remade in 1989 and 2004) ★★★★ DVD Letterbox 2-disc Special Edition: $26.99, VHS: $19.99

Around the World in Eighty Ways

(1986, 90 min, Australia, Stephen MacLean) *Philip Quast, Alan Penney, Diana Davidson.* While it would help to have a Sydney audience cue an American in on the cultural humor and inside jokes, this energetically wacky Aussie comedy is still entertaining in an easygoing, nondemanding way. Quast is Wally, a resourceful and cash-poor tour guide who comes up with the zaniest of schemes: take dear old senile dad on an improvised and very fake tour around the world — staged in a neighbor's tacky suburban home — and pocket the money that would have paid for a real trip. Quickly paced and manic, the film has a sweet, gentle heart. Quast gives a fast, funny performance — impersonating everyone from Hawaiian hula dancers to Elvis to the Pope — in this infectious, spirited comedy. ★★★

Around the World with Orson Welles

(1955, 134 min, GB, Orson Welles) In 1955, long past his enfant terrible stage and in what arguably should have been the most productive period of his creative life, Orson Welles was making travel documentaries for the BBC. While the programs are charming and stimulating, you're left with the feeling that you've just watched Babe Ruth play bush league. There are five episodes. "St. Germain des Pres" explores the artistic life in one of Paris' oldest quarters, with an interview with expatriate American Raymond Duncan. In "Chelsea Pensioners," Welles interviews two sets of retirees in and near London. "Madrid Bullfight" enters the bloody arena and provides just enough explanation of technique and history. Two episodes on the Basque country, "Pays Basque I & II," are lyrical poems to this borderland between Spain and France. Well worth checking out, especially for Welles aficionados. ★★★ DVD: $29.99, VHS: $19.99

The Arrival

(1996, 109 min, US, David Twohy) *Charlie Sheen, Ron Silver, Lindsay Crouse, Teri Polo.* Sheen stars as a radio astronomer and all-around good guy who uncovers a secret government plot and intergalactic conspiracy. When he uncovers proof of alien contact, he is promptly demoted and those who know about it are quickly disappearing. Sheen soon follows a trail to Mexico where uncovers the truth: the temperature of the Earth is increasing, making it habitable for alien life — but deadly for humans! Pleasantly surprising, this medium-budgeted sci-fi thriller, though not entirely original (it is reminiscent of *They Live*), it is consistently engaging. (Sequel: *The Arrival II*) ★★★ DVD Double Feature: $14.99

Arrowsmith

(1931, 101 min, US, John Ford) *Ronald Colman, Helen Hayes, Myrna Loy.* Colman's stirring performance as a dedicated medical researcher highlights this sincere, classy adaptation of the Sinclair Lewis novel. ★★★★

Arsenic and Old Lace

(1944, 118 min, US, Frank Capra) *Cary Grant, Priscilla Lane, Josephine Hull, Raymond Massey, Jean Adair, Peter Lorre, Edward Everett Horton.* This Capra gem takes place in Brooklyn on Halloween. The skeletons aren't in the closet, they're in the basement. Grant's brother thinks he's Teddy Roosevelt, and his poison-happy aunts think of themselves as sane. Cary's other brother (played with panache by Massey) bears a striking resemblance to Boris Karloff and hangs out with Lorre. And the viewer has as much fun watching all this as the cast obviously had in making it. ★★★★ DVD: $19.99, VHS: $14.99

Favorite Line: "Insanity runs in my family . . . it practically gallops." —*Cary Grant as Mortimer Brewster*

The Art of War

(2000, 117 min, US, Christian Duguay) *Wesley Snipes, Anne Archer, Maury Chaykin, Donald Sutherland, Michael Biehn.* In this by-the-books thriller, Snipes plays a covert agent for the United Nations, using state-of-the-art technological gadgets and good old-fashioned blackmail to accomplish his goals. When a mission goes awry, Snipes is framed for murder and left on his own. What begins as a passable *Mission: Impossible*/James Bond puzzler becomes a formulaic chase and shoot-'em-up actioner. Too bad, because Snipes is in good form here. ★½ DVD: $19.99, VHS: $14.99

Artemisia

(1998, 102 min, France, Agnes Merlet) *Valentina Cervi, Michel Serrault, Miki Manojlovic, Luca Zingaretti.* Soft-core masquerading as an art film, *Artemisia* is a biopic about the first woman painter in 17th-century Italy. The film, which presents the life and times of Artemisia Gentileschi (Cervi) has some notable things going for it — a few ideas on perspective, and ample nudity — but the dramatic crux of the narrative is flimsy. Director Merlet, who cowrote the screenplay, focuses on Artemisia's relationship with her mentor, and a large segment of the film is devoted to a trial about whether or not he raped her. Very little in the film gives any insight into the title subject, and this is the main flaw with *Artemisia*. It tries to be an intelligent examination of the life of a female painter trying to overcome the prejudices of the time, and it ends up being artless. (French with English subtitles) ★★ DVD Letterbox: $19.99, VHS: $9.99

Arthur

(1981, 97 min, US, Steve Gordon) *Dudley Moore, Liza Minnelli, John Gielgud, Geraldine Fitzgerald, Barney Martin, Ted Ross.* Recalling the very best of the screwball comedies, first-time director Gordon's hilariously sweet tale is rich in both near-convulsive one-liners and high spirits. In a role that brought him an Oscar nomination, Moore is perfection as the title character, a drunken poor little rich man (net worth: $700 mil) who risks it all to woo the personable (but penniless) Minnelli. Moore's endearing clown is one of the screen's great comedic inebriates, but even he is upstaged by Gielgud, who won a much-deserved Academy Award as Arthur's acerbic valet and confidant. (Sequel: *Arthur 2: On the Rocks*) ★★★★ DVD: $19.99, VHS: $9.99

Arthur 2: On the Rocks

(1988, 110 min, US, Bud Yorkin) *Dudley Moore, Liza Minnelli, Geraldine Fitzgerald, Kathy Bates, Jack Gilford, John Gielgud.* The presence of the original's writer-director, Steve Gordon, is sorely missed in this uninspired sequel. Moore can probably do this bit in his sleep, and he manages to produce a few laughs despite the absence of a substantial script; but for the most part, this is tough going. You wanna see lovable Dudley and Liza again, rent the original. ★½ VHS: $14.99

Article 99

(1992, 99 min, US, Howard Deutch) *Kiefer Sutherland, Forest Whitaker, Ray Liotta, Lea Thompson, John Mahoney, Eli Wallach, Kathy Baker, John C. McGinley, Keith David.* A compelling if familiar comedy-drama in the *M*A*S*H* vein about a group of dedicated doctors working for the Veterans Administration. Liotta plays the chief surgeon who, along with new-cutter-on-the-block Sutherland, leads the fight against bureaucratic red tape and administrative corruption. ★★½ DVD Dual: $14.99

Artists and Models

(1955, 109 min, US, Frank Tashlin) *Dean Martin, Jerry Lewis, Shirley MacLaine, Dorothy Malone, Eva Gabor.* A crazy Martin-Lewis romp with artist Martin and writer Lewis trying to get ahead. Dean ultimately uses Jerry's nightly dreams as inspiration for a comic book. MacLaine plays Jerry's kooky, astrology-reading girlfriend. Jerry's antics are particularly funny. ★★★ VHS: $14.99

As Good as It Gets

(1997, 139 min, US, James L. Brooks) *Jack Nicholson, Helen Hunt, Greg Kinnear, Cuba Gooding, Jr., Shirley Knight, Skeet Ulrich.* With one of his richest characterizations, Nicholson (who won an Oscar) soars as a misanthropic, obsessive-compulsive writer who despite himself finds romance and friendship in this extremely well-acted, sweetly endearing and offbeat romantic comedy. Melvin (Nicholson) is the neighbor from hell to all the tenants of his New York apartment building. His personality is so off-putting that there's only one waitress at his favorite restaurant who will wait on him. That's Carol (the Oscar-winning Hunt), who's looking after her sick son. When Melvin's neighbor Simon (Kinnear), a gay artist, is seriously injured in a robbery, Melvin's life is turned around when he agrees to watch Simon's dog. Brooks and Mark Andrus' story doesn't really go very far plot wise, but it is their funny, intuitive dialogue which causes sparks, and the cast is wonderful in bringing these characters to life. ★★★½ DVD Letterbox: $14.99

As Is

(1986, 86 min, US, Michael Lindsay-Hogg) *Robert Carradine, Jonathan Hadary.* Based on the acclaimed Broadway production, this powerful, opened-up play stars Carradine and Hadary as ex-lovers who are brought together when the former is stricken with AIDS. Often humorous and never morose, author William Hoffman doesn't pull his punches with either his portrayal of a gay lifestyle or of the emotional toll the disease takes. ★★★ VHS: $19.99

As Summers Die

(1986, 88 min, US, Jean-Claude Tramont) *Bette Davis, Scott Glenn, Jamie Lee Curtis.* A small Southern town's richest family makes an attempt to take away farmland from an elderly black woman, believing that the land is rich with oil, in this tale of greed, racism and justice circa 1950. A pleasant if slender made-for-TV drama. ★★½

As You Desire Me

(1932, 71 min, US, George Fitzmaurice) *Greta Garbo, Melvyn Douglas, Erich Von Stroheim.* Garbo gives an earnest performance in this fair adaptation of Pirandello's play. Garbo stars as an amnesiac who is reunited with husband Douglas, only she doesn't remember him. Von Stroheim is appropriately slimy as an ex-lover who has other ideas about her true identity. ★★ VHS: $19.99

As You Like It

(1936, 96 min, GB, Paul Czinner) *Laurence Olivier, Elizabeth Bergner, Sophie Stewart.* Less cinematic than 1935's deliriously kitschy *A Midsummer Night's Dream*, this more earth-and-stagebound London production still manages to entertain. Fascinating performances from Olivier and Bergner almost compensate for Czinner's unsure direction and perverse penchant for shooting speakers from behind excessively large hats. Though distracting, Olivier's ardent nervous ticks add unusual depth to the exiled Orlando, though Bergner's thick Teutonic accent spitting Elizabethan iambs disallows easy listening. Uneven fun, with a William Walton score as airy as his *Hamlet* was crushing, and confusing editing credited to David Lean. ★★★ DVD: $29.99

As Young as You Feel

(1951, 77 min, US, Harmon Jones) *Monty Woolley, Thelma Ritter, David Wayne, Marilyn Monroe.* Woolley gives a spirited performance in this fetching comedy (based on a Paddy Chayefsky story) that takes a playful swipe at big business. Woolley plays an employee who is retired upon turning 65. In response, he impersonates the president of his firm's parent company to reverse the retirement policy. Things get out of hand when he is forced to continue the charade. ★★★ DVD: $14.99

Ashes and Diamonds

(1958, 104 min, Poland, Andrzej Wajda) *Zbigniew Cybulski, Eva Krzyzewska.* Wajda, initiator of the Polish Film Renaissance, creates a penetrating account of a young WWII Resistance fighter whose loyalty to his comrades conflicts with his internal desires. Cybulski ("the Polish Brando") is the ambivalent youth lost in the chaos of the post-war days. A serious, insightful and brilliantly structured examination of both wartime and peacetime allegiances and turmoil. Wajda's final film in his acclaimed "War Trilogy," which includes *A Generation* and *Kanal*. (Polish with English subtitles) ★★★★ DVD: $29.99, VHS: $24.99

Ashes of Time

(1994, 100 min, Hong Kong, Wong Kar-Wai) *Leslie Cheung, Tony Leung Ka Fai, Maggie Cheung, Brigitte Lin Ching Hsia.* From the director of *Chungking Express* comes this lyrical, haunting samurai tale set in a small desert village in ancient China. Ou-yang Feng (Cheung) is a swordsman who is hired to track down a band of horse thieves. But as he prepares for that hunt, he becomes stuck in the middle of a romantic entanglement between a jilted woman and her lover. (Cantonese with English subtitles) ★★★ DVD: $29.99, VHS: $14.99

Ashik Kerib

(1988, 75 min, USSR, Sergei Paradjanov) *Yiur Mgoyan, Veronika Metonidze.* Dedicated to the memory of Andrei Tarkovsky, Paradjanov's final film is an exotic and ebullient Georgian folktale based on a story by Mikhail Lermontov. Although pregnant with symbolism and oblique nationalist references to Georgia's ancient culture, the film remains accessible and even quite enjoyable essentially because of its age-old story of love conquering all. A handsome but poor minstrel must travel through the countryside to earn enough money to marry his young love. His fantastic adventures are spectacularly filmed in poetic, almost fantastic images. There is little dialogue, with the episodic story infused with striking visuals and hypnotic traditional music and dances. (Georgian with English subtitles) ★★★ DVD: $34.99, VHS: $29.99

Ask Any Girl

(1959, 101 min, US, Charles Walters) *Shirley MacLaine, David Niven, Gig Young, Rod Taylor.* MacLaine has one of her best early-career roles in this effervescent gender-gap comedy. She plays a small-town girl who moves to the big city, thus beginning an enchanting, laugh-filled sex farce. The story follows MacLaine's romantic trials and tribulations as she searches for the perfect mate. After a few false starts, MacLaine is employed by brothers Niven and Young. Thinking Young "the one," she cajoles Niven to help her trap his brother. MacLaine absolutely beguiles: she's sassy, daffy and smart. Niven is as debonair as ever. And Young is a good comic foil. One of the best of that era's sexual comedies. ★★★½ VHS: $19.99

The Asphalt Jungle

(1950, 112 min, US, John Huston) *Sterling Hayden, James Whitmore, Sam Jaffe, Louis Calhearn, Marilyn Monroe.* One of Huston's most memorable efforts, this taut drama is a brilliantly stylized crime story about a group of hoods plotting a major heist. Led by a curious, almost mystical German expatriate, the gang woos the local establishment for backing. An insightful tale of moral corruption, the film is a classic example of superb

ensemble acting featuring flawless characterizations by the cast. Filmed in a striking and moody black and white. ★★★★ DVD: $19.99

The Asphyx

(1972, 99 min, GB, Peter Newbrook) *Robert Stephens, Robert Powell, Jane Lapotaire.* Intriguing, highly original horror film about a 19th-century British scientist (Stephens) who uncovers one of the secrets of death and uses it to become immortal. ★★★ DVD: $24.99

The Assassination Bureau

(1969, 110 min, GB, Basil Dearden) *Diana Rigg, Oliver Reed, Telly Savalas, Curt Jurgens, Clive Revill.* Fans of the old "Avengers" series won't want to miss this lustrous black pearl of a comedy. The ex-"Mrs. Peel," Rigg, stars as a turn-of-the-century journalist who goes up against a secret society of self-appointed assassins charged with ridding the world of undesirables. Based on a story by Robert Louis Stevenson, the film recalls such cinematic treasures as *The Abominable Doctor Phibes* and *The Wrong Box*. ★★★ DVD: $14.99

The Assassination of Trotsky

(1972, 103 min, France/GB, Joseph Losey) *Richard Burton, Alain Delon, Romy Schneider.* Losey's uneven and unhistorical account of the last days of the exiled Trotsky is buoyed by an outstanding performance from Burton. Delon is effectively enigmatic as the Stalinist assassin sent to Mexico to hunt him down. ★★

Assassination Tango

(2003, 113 min, US, Robert Duvall) *Robert Duvall, Luciana Pedraza, Ruben Blades, Kathy Baker, Julio Oscar Mechoso.* John J. Anderson (Duvall) is an aging hit man for a Brooklyn gangster. Married with a much younger wife and a ten-year-old stepdaughter he adores, John seems to be aware that his best years are behind him, though you would never know it by the way he still carries himself in the neighborhood. When he is asked to do a job in Buenos Aires, his reality — for a short time, anyway — will change from one of casual violence to romantic expression upon meeting a beautiful tango dancer. As written and directed by Duvall, *Assassination Tango* is a mildly engaging affair, melancholy but passionate, quiescent though alert. The film moves at a temperate pace while John absorbs the colorful art, history and performance of the dance, but sometimes forgets the underworld tensions that brought him there in the first place. It's a sometimes uneasy balance dramatically, but Duvall is nothing less than a pleasure. ★★½ DVD Letterbox: $14.99, VHS: $49.99

Assassins

(1995, 132 min, US, Richard Donner) *Sylvester Stallone, Antonio Banderas, Julianne Moore.* Playing an aging professional killer, Stallone looks as though he can't wait to get to the phone to fire his agent. But it's too little, too late. In this brainless actioner, Sly finds himself dogged and pursued by new hit man-on-the-block Banderas. The inevitable chase begins, ending in a dusty Mexican town which gives way to too many clichés. Director Donner seems to be copying John Woo, down to slow-motion shots and protagonists leaping through the air, pistols blazing. What he produces, however, is a boring and confusing movie. Stallone comes off best — that should be warning enough. ★½ DVD: $14.99, VHS: $9.99

The Assault

(1986, 150 min, Netherlands, Fons Rademakers) *Derek De Lint, Marc Van Uchelen, Monique Van De Ven.* The moving and emotional story of a boy's traumatic wartime experiences and its aftereffects on him as an adult, won the 1986 Academy Award for Best Foreign-Language Film, yet oddly was released on video only in the dubbed version. The film is set in two time periods: a small town during World War II, where a young boy's family is killed by the Nazis; and in the adult years of the boy, as he struggles to reconcile his parents' death and begin a new life. ★★★½

Assault at West Point

(1993, 98 min, US, Harry Moses) *Al Freeman, Jr., Samuel L. Jackson, Sam Waterston, Seth Gilliam, John Glover, Eddie Bracken.* Told in flashback by a notably lighter-in-skin-tone Freeman, this real-life tale of racism focuses on a young African-American West Point cadet (Gilliam) who is accused and finally court-martialed for faking his own attack. With Waterston and Jackson as the defendant's lawyers, the film features zombie-esque performances, and this combined with Gilliam's even less-impressive thesping, help to reduce what should have been a thought-provoking, intense experience to a disappointment. ★½ VHS: $9.99

Assault of the Killer Bimbos

(1988, 85 min, US, Anita Rosenberg) *Patti Astor, Christina Whitaker, Griffin O'Neal, Nick Cassavetes, Eddie Deezen.* Sophomoric hijinks as three buxom beauties, planning their careers in the movie biz, head for Mexico. But not before they take on over-sexed surfers, jealous boyfriends and the police. ★½ DVD: $9.99

Assault on Precinct 13

(1976, 90 min, US, John Carpenter) *Austin Stoker, Darwin Joston, Nancy Loomis.* A novice Carpenter directed this intense, immensely satisfying thriller, a harbinger of things to come from the young filmmaker. A Los Angeles gang seizes control of an almost deserted police station, forcing the officers and civilians trapped inside to fight for their lives. Suggested by Howard Hawks' *Rio Bravo.* ★★★½ DVD Widescreen Edition: $19.99

The Assignment

(1997, 115 min, US, Christian Duguay) *Donald Sutherland, Ben Kingsley, Aidan Quinn.* Navy officer and family man Quinn is quite content to follow orders, toe the line, and lead a nice, quiet life. Unfortunately for him, he happens to be physically identical to the notorious terrorist, the Jackal, and he is forced by CIA operative Sutherland to accept an undercover mission to put an end to the Jackal's reign. The film never achieves that neat balance between probing psychodrama and slam-bang action. This is strictly comic book stuff, and as such, it can be rather entertaining. Good performances, especially by Sutherland, elevate this a notch, and the action scenes are suspenseful, if unremarkable. ★★½ DVD: $14.99, VHS: $9.99

The Associate (L'Associé)

(1979, 94 min, France, Rene Gainville) *Michel Serrault, Claudine Auger.* In this delightful French comedy, Serrault is Julien Pardot, a meek businessman who invents an imaginary English business partner. When his clients, wife and mistress all begin to prefer the imaginary "Ms. Davis" over him, Pardot devises a plot to kidnap and murder his creation. (American remake: *The Associate*) (French with English subtitles) ★★★ VHS: $29.99

The Associate

(1996, 114 min, US, Donald Petrie) *Whoopi Goldberg, Tim Daly, Dianne Wiest, Eli Wallach, Bebe Neuwirth, Austin Pendleton, Lainie Kazan, Kenny Kerr.* Based on the 1979 French comedy of the same name, *The Associate* is an enjoyable satire of Wall Street, sort of a low-keyed *Jerry Maguire* meets *Tootsie*. Whoopi plays a talented financial analyst who is passed over for a promotion at her firm for reasons of gender. Deciding to start her own agency, she invents a ficticious male partner. With the help of savvy secretary Wiest, Whoopi takes Wall Street by storm — even if it means a little male drag. *The Associate* doesn't go as far as it could have, but it does have good-natured barbs, humorous characterizations, and Whoopi in good form. ★★★ DVD: $9.99, VHS: $9.99

The Astronaut's Wife

(1999, 110 min, US, Rand Ravich) *Johnny Depp, Charlize Theron, Joe Morton, Clea DuVall.* Despite the presence of Depp, this is nearly a worthless sci-fi/horror film. Theron is the dippy wife of national hero Depp, whose latest mission was marred by a two-minute scare when communications with NASA were lost while he was floating in space. Now back on Earth, he seems . . . different somehow. This boring, predictable, choppy, uninvolving *Rosemary's Baby* ripoff features Depp and Morton's worst performances, moronic, obvious camerawork, and a crappy, would-be cynical, twist ending. ★ DVD: $9.99, VHS: $9.99

Asylum

(1972, 92 min, GB, Roy Ward Baker) *Peter Cushing, Herbert Lom, Charlotte Rampling.* A young psychiatrist arrives at his new job and must hear the personal stories of four inmates in this horror anthology film. Written by Robert Bloch (the creator of *Psycho*), the film is very interesting and effectively scary; some characters are better than others, but most films of this type are similarly uneven. Rampling's story is the weakest, probably because it is concerned more with psychology than with the supernatural. The first story in the quartet is the most frightening, involving the bizarre form a murdered wife's revenge takes. And just when you think the whole thing is over, one final terror awaits the unwary viewer. Fun, frightening and solidly enjoyable. ★★★

Asylum

(1996, 92 min, US, James Seale) *Robert Patrick, Malcolm McDowell, Sarah Douglas, Jason Schombing, Deborah Worthing, Henry Gibson.* A sleeper in the negative sense of the term, *Asylum*, a miscalculated thriller, stars Patrick as a suicidal P.I. who's also a patient of a childhood friend (now a psychiatrist), who works at a local asylum. When the chipper, optimistic doctor is found dead, Patrick gets himself admitted and begins his own investigation. This weak ripoff of *Shock Corridor* (and every other asylum movie) is a boring, obvious mystery. ★ VHS: $79.99

At Close Range

(1986, 115 min, US, James Foley) *Sean Penn, Christopher Walken, Mary Stuart Masterson, Chris Penn, Crispin Glover.* This intense drama examines the brittle relationship between a teenager and his estranged father, a small-time hood who introduces the youth to petty crime and murder. As the father and son, respectively, Walken and Penn offer stunning performances. Based on a true story. ★★★½ DVD: $14.99

At First Sight

(1999, 126 min, US, Irwin Winkler) *Val Kilmer, Mira Sorvino, Kelly McGillis, Nathan Lane, Steven Weber, Bruce Davison.* Adapted from the story by Dr. Oliver Sacks (*Awakenings*) comes another tale of a medically impaired man who temporarily beats the odds. Not as dramatically involving nor as nicely paced as *Awakenings*, the sincere though ordinary *At First Sight* stars Kilmer as Virgil, a blind masseur who works at a mountain resort in upstate New York. Sorvino is Amy, a workaholic NYC architect who vacations there and falls for the handsome Virgil. Their romance begins to fall apart when Virgil undergoes an operation and has his sight restored, undergoing difficulty in adjusting to a sighted world. As the sensitive Virgil, Kilmer is easygoing and nice to look at, but the part offers little for the actor to grab hold to. ★★ DVD: $14.99

At Home with the Webbers

(1993, 109 min, US, Brad Marlowe) *Jeffrey Tambor, Jennifer Tilly, David Arquette, Robby Benson, Luke Perry.* Could you imagine having your family broadcast live on television during its most intimate moments? The Webbers are chosen to be the stars of a new 24-hour cable show. They are moved into a house equipped with video cameras in almost every corner. Tilly plays the sex-hungry daughter who is willing to do anything to get plaster casts of male body parts. ★★½ VHS: $79.99

At Play in the Fields of the Lord

(1992, 186 min, US, Hector Babenco) *Tom Berenger, John Lithgow, Kathy Bates, Aidan Quinn, Daryl Hannah, Tom Waits.* An ambitious and sweeping epic about a group of fundamentalist missionaries who come in conflict with a tribe of Amazonian Indians. Berenger stars as a half-breed Native American who believes he's returned to his spiritual source. Those familiar with Peter Matthiessen's richly textured parable on faith and the soul might be disappointed by the film's lack of cohesive direction. However, the finely detailed work of the ensemble cast, coupled with the beautiful cinematography of the lush South American jungle, will carry the viewer easily through the long running time. ★★★

At the Circus

(1939, 87 min, US, Edward Buzzell) *Groucho Marx, Harpo Marx, Chico Marx, Margaret Dumont, Eve Arden.* Lydia, oh Lydia, say, have you met Lydia . . . Groucho walks on the ceiling with Arden; it's all in the line of duty, of course. He's after the $10,000 stolen from the disinherited nephew of Newport heiress Dumont, which is needed to keep the circus from being taken over by the nefarious scallywag who stole the money. Got that? Chico and Harpo are there to assist. Though not among the handful of Marx Brothers' classics, there are quite a few funny scenes to be had. (DVD only available in a seven-film pack for $59.99) ★★½ VHS: $19.99

L'Atalante

(1934, 89 min, France, Jean Vigo) *Dita Parlo, Jean Dasté, Michel Simon.* This lyrical, cinematic poem follows a honeymooning couple (Parlo and Dasté) as they blissfully float down the Seine on a barge accompanied by their first mate, the crusty Simon. Long considered one of the greatest romance stories in film history, *L'Atalante* was one of only two films made by director Vigo before his untimely death at age 29, but this classic was surrounded by controversy and innuendo from its inception. Having just recently finished *Zero for Conduct* (which had been banned in France), Vigo was a contentious choice to direct *L'Atalante* and indeed his original cut was rejected by the movie theatre owners and ultimately re-edited. Tragically, Vigo died just weeks after the film's unsuccessful run at the box office and a year later, the film was once again amended. This unhappy saga at long last came to an end in 1989 when archivists went into the vaults and resurrected Vigo's original version of the film, now available in a remastered print. (French with English subtitles) ★★★★ DVD: $29.99, VHS: $19.99

Atlantic City

(1981, 104 min, Canada, Louis Malle) *Burt Lancaster, Susan Sarandon, Kate Reid, Hollis McLaren, Robert Joy, Michel Piccoli.* In this fascinating, intelligent character study, director Malle captures the Atlantic City of the '80s, a city living with its faded past and a fragile optimism for the future. Lancaster, in what may be the performance of his career, brilliantly plays a small-time numbers runner with notions of grandeur who gets a chance at the big score when he crosses paths with casino employee Sarandon and her ex-husband and drug pusher Joy. The simplicity of the characters' lives and dreams belies the tumultuous events which follow when all are eventually tempted by the attainable usually just beyond their grasp. Reid is especially good as a former beauty contest winner living with the ghost of her gangster husband, and Sarandon, whose first great performance this was, demonstrates the eroticism of lemons in an unforgettable scene. Arguably Malle at his very best. ★★★★ DVD Letterbox: $14.99, VHS: $14.99

The Atomic Cafe

(1982, 90 min, US, Kevin Rafferty, Jayne Loader, Pierce Rafferty) A nervously funny juxtaposition of atomic propaganda films. The footage includes testament to the beauty of the blast, reassurances of the minimal cause for worry and other testing examples of governmental lunacy. ★★★ DVD 20th Anniversary: $24.99, VHS: $19.99

Attack Force Z

(1981, 84 min, Australia, Tim Burstall) *Mel Gibson, John Phillip Law, Sam Neill, Chris Haywood.* A young Gibson stars in this competent WWII adventure film about an elite group of commandos who are assigned to rescue a defecting Japanese official from an enemy-held island in the Pacific. Awaiting the men are unbearable heat, an uncharted jungle and thousands of Japanese soldiers. ★★½

Attack of the Killer Tomatoes

(1980, 87 min, US, John DeBello) *David Miller, Sharon Taylor, George Wilson, Jack Riley.* Unbelievably silly horror spoof about some ravenous, rampaging tomatoes ravaging San Diego and its poor, defenseless citizens. Is there no one but the San Diego chicken to help? Will the Secret Service outwit these gruesome garnishments from a chef's salad? Will Nixon end the war? ★★ DVD: $14.99, DVD Special Collector's Edition: $24.99

Attila 74: The Rape of Cyprus

(1975, 103 min, Greece, Michael Cacoyannis) Filmmaker Cacoyannis (*Zorba the Greek*) was in London at the time of the Turkish invasion of Cyprus in 1974. Returning immediately to his besieged homeland, he began making this part-documentary, part-personal journal. A deeply passionate and devastatingly powerful film that bears witness to the horrors of the invasion and mounts strong evidence on its accusations against the Turks, the Greek puppet leaders and international indifference. (Greek with English subtitles) ★★★½ DVD: $29.99, VHS: $19.99

Au Revoir les Enfants

(1987, 103 min, France, Louis Malle) *Gaspard Manesse, Raphael Fejto, Francine Racette, Irène Jacob.* Director Malle's acclaimed autobiographical tale of his early school days is a poignant reminiscence of childhood camaraderie, social responsibility and the human tragedy of war. Set in occupied France during WWII, the story centers on the friendship which blossoms between two young, gifted schoolboys — one Catholic and one Jewish — when the latter hides out in a private boarding school to escape the Nazis. The beauty and mastery of Malle's film lies in his precise eye for period detail, well-structured character development, and an insightful and accurate portrayal of adolescent behavior. (French with English subtitles) ★★★★

Audition

(2000, 115 min, Japan, Takashi Miike) *Ryo Ishibashi, Eihi Shiina, Tetsu Sawaki. Audition* begins disarmingly when Aoyama (Ishibashi), a widower of seven years, decides it's time to find a new wife. He holds auditions for potential mates under the guise they are auditioning for a film he'll produce. After settling on Asami (Shiina), a quiet, fetching young actress, he begins dating her. Their polite, timid courtship takes a 180-degree turn when Asami, trumping the stereotype of the submissive Asian woman, visits her revenge on Aoyama in the most nightmarish of ways. The film morphs from romance to psycho-thriller in the bat of a pierced eyelid. An intriguing premise is handled well by the uber-prolific Miike, with the leads giving excellent performances. *Audition* may be a bit too deliberately paced, but it's nevertheless a small gem of a movie, and contains some shocking moments you won't soon forget. (Japanese with English subtitles) ★★★ DVD Letterbox Unrated Director's Cut: $24.99, VHS Letterbox Unrated Director's Cut: $29.99

Audrey Rose

(1977, 114 min, US, Robert Wise) *Anthony Hopkins, Marsha Mason, John Beck, Susan Swift, Norman Lloyd.* This overlong, plodding thriller about reincarnation tries to be both scary and meaningful, but fails in both departments. Ivy is a precocious young girl living with her well-to-do parents in New York City. A mysterious stranger (Hopkins) soon begins following the family. He believes his daughter, Audrey Rose, killed in an auto accident, has been reincarnated as Ivy. Mason is Ivy's distraught mother, who initially refuses to believe the story. The weak script makes the film, alternately, a ghost story, a courtroom drama and a diatribe on Eastern religion. ★½ DVD Letterbox: $14.99

August

(1995, 99 min, Wales, Anthony Hopkins) *Anthony Hopkins, Leslie Phillips, Kate Burton, Rhian Morgan, Gawn Grainger.* Hopkins' directorial debut is a spry adaptation of Chekhov's "Uncle Vanya" set on the sun-drenched coast of Wales. Proficient in most regards, the film has the unfortunate honor of being held up to the mirror of Louis Malle and Andre Gregory's collaboration *Vanya on 42nd Street.* Here, Hopkins eschews the minute and intricate character study of *Vanya* for a more theatrical, composed variation. Hopkins provides his ample thespian talents in front of the camera as Ieuan (Vanya's Welsh doppelganger), a ne'er-do-well whose hopes of living high on his family's country estate are dashed by the presence of his ex-brother-in-law, an undistinguished retired college professor. This slightly comic take on Chekhov's classic tale should delight those who live on a diet of BBC period pieces and the like. ★★½

Auntie Mame

(1958, 144 min, US, Morton Da Costa) *Rosalind Russell, Forrest Tucker, Coral Browne, Roger Smith, Peggy Cass, Fred Clark, Patric Knowles, Jan Handzlik.* Russell shines in a career-topping performance as everybody's favorite relative: Auntie Mame. Based on the hit play by Patrick Dennis, this gloriously funny adaptation follows the comic antics of an orphaned nephew who moves in with his eccentric aunt. A classic instance in which role and performer were destined for each other. Cass is terrific in support as Mame's secretary and "sponge." ★★★★ DVD Letterbox: $19.99

Favorite Line: "Life's a banquet and most poor suckers are starving to death!" —*Rosalind Russell as Auntie Mame*

Austin Powers in Goldmember

(2002, 94 min, US, Jay Roach) *Mike Myers, Beyoncé Knowles, Seth Green, Michael Caine, Verne Troyer, Robert Wagner, Michael York, Mindy Sterling.* Mike Myers is now officially out of control. Whereas the first *Austin Powers* installment was a well-structured parody of '60s spy flicks, with occasional outbursts of manic Myersness, all semblance of structure is thrown to the four winds in *Goldmember.* The law of diminishing returns is in play as well, with Myers now playing *four* roles, each less funny than the previous. The creation here is a gold-flaky Hollander named (and possessing a) Goldmember, who is just as one-note as Fat Bastard (Myers #3). There are also plenty of guest stars, and they are all necessarily upstaged by Myers' ego, shoved offscreen to repeat jokes from earlier films. While *Goldmember* does have plenty of isolated laughs, one just wishes Myers could rediscover his first film's balance between out-there improv and semi-cohesive filmmaking. ★★ DVD Letterbox infinifilm Special Edition: $19.99, VHS: $6.99

Austin Powers: International Man of Mystery

(1997, 95 min, US, Jay Roach) *Mike Myers, Elizabeth Hurley, Mimi Rogers, Michael York, Robert Wagner, Seth Green, Mindy Sterling, Will Ferrell.* A hilariously goofy, off-the-wall and dead-on-target spoof of James Bond and other '60s spy movies. Myers sports a set of crooked dentures, thick horn-rimmed glasses and gets decked out in velvety '60s garb as Austin Powers, a "swingin'" 1960s English superspy. Myers also plays Powers' nemesis, the nefarious but insecure Dr. Evil. Both Powers and Dr. Evil are cryogenically frozen and thawed out in 1997, and they awake to a world that has long since surpassed them. The key to the film's very funny humor is the loving attention to detail and its no-holds-barred, un-PC naughtiness (instead of Pussy Galore, a luscious femme fatale named Alotta Fagina!). A few of the jokes fall flat, but *Austin Powers* nevertheless is witty, inspired lunacy from start to finish. (Sequel: *Austin Powers: The Spy Who Shagged Me*) ★★★½ DVD Letterbox Platinum Series: $19.99, VHS Pan & Scan: $9.99, VHS Letterbox: $9.99

Austin Powers: The Spy Who Shagged Me

(1999, 95 min, US, Jay Roach) *Mike Myers, Heather Graham, Seth Green, Robert Wagner, Rob Lowe, Verne Troyer, Michael York, Elizabeth Hurley.* Not as fresh or consistent as the original, this still very funny sequel provides many a laugh through potty jokes and expanded retreads in place of the first film's sharper wit and innocent naughtiness. Myers returns as delusionally sexy agent

Austin Powers as well as his bald-headed maniacal nemesis Dr. Evil (who gets more comic mileage this go-round). Dr. Evil escapes his space exile to travel back in time to 1969, where he incapacitates Powers by stealing his "mojo." Like Samson without his hair, Powers must also travel back to get his "mojo" rising once more. The jokes are frequent (and frequently tasteless), while the multitude of espionage movie parodies have been replaced with more '90s pop culture references. (Sequel: *Austin Powers in Goldmember*) ★★★ DVD Letterbox: $19.99, VHS Pan & Scan: $9.99, VHS Letterbox: $9.99

Author! Author!

(1982, 110 min, US, Arthur Hiller) *Al Pacino, Dyan Cannon, Tuesday Weld, Andre Gregory, Alan King.* Pacino stars in this heartwarming comedy as a struggling playwright who must contend with raising his children when his flaky wife leaves him. Hiller directs a fine cast who deliver endearing performances across the board. ★★½

Auto Focus

(2002, 107 min, US, Paul Schrader) *Greg Kinnear, Willem Dafoe, Rita Wilson, Maria Bello, Ron Liebman, Michael E. Rodgers.* Director Schrader, son of a Calvinist minister, again tackles his recurring theme of the conflict between man's higher nature and his base proclivities. Kinnear, in a brilliant performance, essentially morphs into Bob Crane, the churchgoing family man who, as his career breaks open when he lands the lead role in TV's *Hogan's Heroes*, finds himself able to realize the fantasies previously relegated to his secret stashes of girlie magazines. Dafoe is perfect as John Carpenter (*not* the director), Crane's buddy/hanger-on who provides him with the latest photography equipment and introduces him to the swinging scene. A sex addict before the phrase was coined, with no convenient psychobabble to talk away the guilt, Crane wanders through the years satisfying his carnal desires and watching his career reverse itself from hit TV series to movie bomb to dinner theater; and, in his personal life, goes through two marriages and more casual encounters than he can track. Sometimes wry and funny, *Auto Focus* — which cannily captures the look and feel of the "Donna Reed" times — ultimately conveys profound sadness and regret, an aching tale of a life lost to compelling obsession. ★★★½ DVD: $14.99, VHS: $14.99

Autobiography of a Princess

(1975, 59 min, GB, James Ivory) *James Mason, Madhur Jaffrey.* Produced by Ismail Merchant with a screenplay by Ruth Prawer Jhabvala, this delicate character study is of an imperious princess, self-exiled in London and long divorced, who invites her father's ex-tutor to a yearly tea. There they reminisce about a "happier" past only to find that their memories of the Royal India differ. ★★★ VHS: $29.99

An Autumn Afternoon

(1962, 115 min, Japan, Yasujiro Ozu) *Chishu Ryu, Shima Iwashita.* Master Japanese filmmaker Ozu's final film is a deceptively simple, contemplative and lyrical family drama. Continuing his theme from *Late Summer*, the story follows an aging widower who, against his wishes, arranges for a marriage for his only daughter; a move that leaves him lonely, with only his old drinking cronies for company. (Japanese with English subtitles) ★★★½

Autumn in New York

(2000, 104 min, US, Joan Chen) *Richard Gere, Winona Ryder, Anthony LaPaglia, Elaine Stritch, Sherry Stringfield, Mary Beth Hurt, J.K. Simmons.* Old-fashioned and sentimental, but not necessarily

Rita Wilson (l.) and Greg Kinnear in *Auto Focus*

in the best sense of those words, this romantic tearjerker is long on the sap but does manage to produce a few affecting moments. Gere plays a 40-ish restaurateur and womanizer (successful on both counts) who falls for the 22-year-old daughter (Ryder) of a former girlfriend. Complications arise when he learns she hasn't long to live. Gere and Ryder exhibit little chemistry together, though individually each is satisfactory. The best performance, however, comes from Stritch as Ryder's acerbic grandmother. ★★ DVD: $14.99

Autumn Leaves

(1956, 108 min, US, Robert Aldrich) *Joan Crawford, Cliff Robertson, Vera Miles, Lorne Greene.* Crawford is in long-suffering mode as a lonely, middle-aged secretary who weds a younger man (Robertson), only to learn he's not only married but has psychological problems as well. A tense, moody drama that occasionally gives in to the broad trappings of many a 1950s melodrama, but is involving all the same thanks to Crawford's solid performance. ★★★

Autumn Marathon

(1979, 100 min, USSR, Georgy Panelia) *Oleg Basilashvili, Natalia Gundareva.* Midlife crisis is the theme of this poignant and at times funny drama. Georgy, a mild-mannered Leningrad professor, finds himself dissatisfied and unfulfilled by his seemingly successful life. He becomes increasingly muddled in his relationships with his loving wife, his attractive but demanding mistress, his students and colleagues and even his jogging-buddy neighbor. (Russian with English subtitles) ★★★ VHS: $59.99

Autumn Sonata

(1978, 97 min, Sweden, Ingmar Bergman) *Ingrid Bergman, Liv Ullmann.* Director Bergman's emotionally shattering drama about the frail yet indestructible bond between a mother (Ingrid) and her daughter (Liv). Bergman and Ullmann give extraordinary portrayals. (Swedish with English subtitles). ★★★★ DVD Criterion Collection: $39.99, VHS: $29.99

Autumn Tale

(1998, 110 min, France, Eric Rohmer) *Béatrice Romand, Marie Rivière, Alain Libolt, Alexia Portal.* A delightful conclusion to Rohmer's cycle "Tales of the Four Seasons," *Autumn Tale* is not unlike many of the French director's films in that the gentle humor stems from characters saying one thing while really meaning another. Magali (Romand) is in her forties and single. Although she claims that she has no interest in a relationship — her winery and her children take up her time —Magali's friend Isabelle

(Riviere) and her son's girlfriend Rosine (Portal) conspire independently to jump-start her love life. The result is a party in which two suitors vie for Magali's affections. Rohmer's strength is his patented ability to make ordinary characters interesting even though the situations are somewhat contrived. Typical of the director's films, *Autumn Tale* is very talky, but it is beautifully photographed. (French with English subtitles) ★★★ VHS: $14.99

Avalon

(1990, 127 min, US, Barry Levinson) *Aidan Quinn, Armin Mueller-Stahl, Elizabeth Perkins, Joan Plowright, Kevin Pollack, Lou Jacobi, Elijah Wood.* Director Levinson continues his acclaimed Baltimore stories (*Diner* and *Tin Men*) with this heartfelt reminiscence — spanning five decades — about three generations of a Jewish immigrant family. Mueller-Stahl gives a towering performance as the Krichinsky family's proud patriarch, whose haunting stories of emigration to "a place called Avalon" are constantly echoing from his memory. Quinn ably plays his son, a salesman with Wanamaker-sized dreams of department store splendor. A superb evocation of postwar life, *Avalon* is a remarkable achievement: an intimate memory piece rich in atmosphere and flowing with good humor. Levinson's most personal film, and one of his best. ★★★★ DVD: $19.99

Avanti!

(1972, 144 min, US, Billy Wilder) *Jack Lemmon, Juliet Mills, Clive Revill, Edward Andrews, Gianfranco Barra.* Wilder is in Lubitsch territory with this witty black comedy that while retaining the director's cynical touch also manages to be sweetly romantic. Lemmon is in good form as a stuffy corporate exec who travels to Italy to retrieve the body of his father, killed while on vacation. When he arrives, he learns his father had a mistress (who was also killed). While trying to wade through red tape in getting the body back, he begins a relationship with the woman's daughter (Mills). Not quintessential Wilder, but very amusing and often charming. ★★★ DVD Letterbox: $19.99

The Avengers

(1998, 90 min, GB, Jeremiah Chechik) *Ralph Fiennes, Uma Thurman, Sean Connery, Jim Broadbent, Fiona Shaw.* Fiennes and Thurman are quite good in this otherwise underwhelming update of the classic '60s TV series. All the elements are here — the stiff-upper-lip nonchalance of the heroes, the *veddy* British costumes and production design, the tongue-in-cheek attitude. But the film never comes to life, despite some nice sequences (especially an absurd bit with a gang of criminals wearing fuzzy

teddy bear suits), some of which are cribbed from the original series. Uma and Ralph are both sexy, but have no spark between them. The real surprise, however, is Connery, a huge disappointment in his first major villain role. As such, there is *zero* threat or excitement, and the story and characters go nowhere and, as a result, the film grinds to a halt long before the end credits. A frustrating missed opportunity. ★½
DVD: $9.99, VHS: $9.99, VHS Letterbox: $9.99

L'Avventura (The Adventure)

(1960, 145 min, Italy, Michelangelo Antonioni) *Monica Vitti, Lea Massari.* Antonioni established his international reputation with this perceptive study of the alienation, ennui and despair suffered by a group of vacationing friends when faced with the disappearance of a young woman from the party. (Italian with English subtitles) ★★★ DVD Letterbox Criterion Collection: $39.99, VHS: $29.99

Awakenings

(1990, 121 min, US, Penny Marshall) *Robert De Niro, Robin Williams, Julie Kavner, Ruth Nelson, Penelope Ann Miller, Max von Sydow, John Heard, Anne Meara.* Based on Oliver Sachs' true story, this extremely moving and accomplished film stars Williams as a neurologist whose experiments in a 1960s Brooklyn hospital "awaken" patients who have been victims of a decades-long "sleeping sickness." De Niro gives an astonishing performance as Leonard, Williams' first patient to undergo the medical treatment. The story centers on the doctor's fight to use the experimental medicine, and the recovering and orienting process facing all the patients. Williams nicely underplays his part as the introverted physician; he and De Niro make a remarkable team. ★★★½ DVD: $14.99, VHS: $12.99

The Awful Truth

(1937, 94 min, US, Leo McCarey) *Cary Grant, Irene Dunne, Ralph Bellamy.* McCarey won a well-deserved Best Director Oscar for this hilarious screwball classic. At the peak of their comic abilities, Grant and Dunne play a divorcing couple waiting out their 90-day interlocutory period (and fighting a custody battle for their pet terrier). When they begin dating other people, each goes to great lengths to disrupt the other's newfound romance; each scheme being more outrageous than the one before it. *The Awful Truth* is screwball comedy at its best and, in addition to Grant's *Bringing Up Baby*, is the epitome of the genre. ★★★★ DVD: $24.99, VHS: $19.99

An Awfully Big Adventure

(1994, 113 min, GB, Mike Newell) *Hugh Grant, Alan Rickman, Peter Firth, Georgina Cates, Alan Cox.* A dingy 1947 Liverpool is the setting for this very British comedy-drama on life within a repertory theatre troupe. Fifteen-year-old orphan Stella (Cates) finds a family and many life lessons when she is hired as a starry-eyed apprentice and part-time actress. The troupe is headed by Meredith Potter (Grant), a maniacally egotistical gay director with a taste for using and abusing the younger male workers. Grant's Meredith is a wonderful creation — a pale, nervous, obviously vain chain-smoker with looks that suggest a prissy, upper-class Clark Kent. At its best, *Adventure* is an entertaining glimpse behind the curtain, but the film suffers from a disjointed story line and a menagerie of perpetually pitiful characters. ★★½

Ay, Carmela!

(1990, 107 min, Spain, Carlos Saura) *Carmen Maura, Andrés Pajares.* Maura, the perky star of so many Pedro Almodóvar films, teams with director Saura in this stirring look at the Spanish Civil War.

Carmela (Maura) and Paulino (Pajares) are Republican entertainers who contribute to the war effort by putting on shows for the troops. The film follows them as they travel to various war-torn areas of Spain, always fearful of being apprehended by the Fascists. Maura, in her first major role outside of the Almodóvar camp, delivers a sparkling, heartfelt performance as the vivacious vaudevillain whose political passions and love for the troops lead her to place her own life in danger. *Ay, Carmela!*, while clearly Republican in its sentiment, offers an even-handed and humantistic view of Spain's bloody past. (Spanish with English subtitles) ★★★

B. Monkey

(1999, 91 min, GB, Michael Radford) *Asia Argento, Rupert Everett, Jared Harris, Jonathan Rhys Meyers, Ian Hart.* B. Monkey, or *La Femme Nikita Sees the Errors of Her Ways, Marries and Settles Down in a Cottage in the Country,* is bursting with flashing style, over-the-top acting and some great action sequences. This thriller is great fun to watch, but don't try to make any sense out of the mindless plot or unbelievable characters. Argento is the sexy sly jewel thief B. Monkey who, after meeting a dorky jazz-loving school teacher, decides to retire from the biz. But that "one last job" done as a favor to her crime pal becomes her undoing when the heist goes awry. Not art, but fast-paced, classy and action-packed. And if the plot doesn't work for you, the attractive cast should. ★★½ DVD: $9.99, VHS: $9.99

Baadasssss!

(2004, 108 min, US, Mario Van Peebles) *Mario Van Peebles, Joy Bryant, T. K. Carter, Ossie Davis, David Alan Grier, Terry Crews, Nia Long, Paul Rodriguez, Saul Rubinek.* What do you do when your father defied Hollywood conventions and advice by following up a commercially successful

comedy with a radical, fiercely independent, seminal film that reflected the political realities of its revolutionary times, flew in the face of all accepted mores, and single-handedly created a new genre? Why, make a movie about the making of the movie, of course. Son Mario chronicles dad Melvin overcoming all obstacles to get *Sweet Sweetback's Baadasssss Song* made with no money, no studio backing and no unions. He finds a then-unknown band — Earth, Wind and Fire — to do the soundtrack, and wrote a song for the movie to get free advertising when it got radio play. *Sweetback's* odyssey plays against Melvin's, as Mario re-creates scenes from the original film and shows what went on behind the camera. The film takes on the feel of a documentary: *Baadasssss!* works as a dramatic reflection of the era, a fully realized independent film in its own right, and a loving tribute to a larger-than-life father. ★★★½

Babe

(1995, 91 min, Australia, Chris Noonan) *James Cromwell, Magda Szubanski, Voices of: Christine Cavanaugh, Hugo Weaving, Miriam Margolyes, Roscoe Lee Browne.* It's hard to believe, but it would take a while to find another children's film as thoroughly irresistible as this one about a talking pig. The story follows the misadventures of Babe, a piglet who is won by the kindly farmer Hoggett (Cromwell). On this farm, Hoggett's animals are able to communicate with each other, though each must obey the social structure the animals have set for themselves. That is until Babe works his magic and brings all the animals together. The film ingeniously interacts the animals and humans, and its clever screenplay and a splendid use of ground-level cinematography bring all the animals (some real, some Henson creations) to life. An Oscar nominee for Best Picture. (Sequel: *Babe: Pig in the City*) ★★★★ DVD Letterbox Special Edition: $19.99, DVD Pan & Scan Special Edition: $19.99

Babe: Pig in the City

(1998, 96 min, Australia, George Miller) *James Cromwell, Magda Szubanski, Mickey Rooney, Voices of: Elizabeth Daily, Steven Wright, Adam Goldberg.* Babe: Pig in the City shatters any expectations of what a kid's film should be, stranding the famous porker in a fan-

Plenty of cuddly animal folk populate *Babe: Pig in the City*

tasy city that is nowhere and everywhere. Mrs. Hoggett, far from the farm, misses her connection to take Babe to a big sheepherding show. They spend the rest of the movie enduring every calamity that can befall wide-eyed tourists. Naturally, their kind hearts eventually win over hardened cityfolk, but what a trip they have getting there! Particularly lovable are Wright's jaded chimp and Goldberg's handicapped Flealick. A ravishing odyssey that — though dark in tone and therefore maybe not for the tiniest ones — never ceases to enthrall and delight. ★★★★ DVD: $19.99, VHS: $14.99

The Babe

(1992, 115 min, US, Arthur Hiller) *John Goodman, Kelly McGillis, Trini Alvarado.* As old-fashioned as the period costumes its large cast wears, *The Babe* is a brash, sentimental and fairly entertaining look at the life of baseball legend Babe Ruth. Weighed down by some heavily dramatic scenes, the story follows Ruth's meteoric rise in the 1920s where, first as a Red Sox and then as a New York Yankee, he would make baseball history. Fans of the sport should find *The Babe* endearing; though nonfans may be at a loss as the film almost canonizes the Bambino. ★★½ DVD Letterbox: $14.99, VHS: $7.49

Babes in Arms

(1939, 91 min, US, Busby Berkeley) *Judy Garland, Mickey Rooney, Charles Winninger, Guy Kibbee, Margaret Hamilton.* Trimmed-down but delightfully entertaining version of the Rodgers and Hart Broadway musical. Garland and Rooney are terrific together as the children of vaudevillians who decide to "put on a show" to help their struggling parents. Though '30s schmaltz all the way, this is probably the best of the Judy-Mickey "Let's put on a show" musicals. ★★★ VHS: $14.99

Babette's Feast

(1987, 102 min, Denmark, Gabriel Axel) *Stéphane Audran, Bibi Andersson.* Director Axel's Oscar-winning adaptation of Isak Dinesen's ("Out of Africa") poignant novella is an inspired celebration of the triumph of art over puritanical zeal. Set in a tiny and bleak 19th-century Scandinavian village, the story follows the lives of two devoutly religious sisters who have retreated into the desolate, but safe, enclave of their pious upbringings. Into their lives comes Babette (Audran) — a maid who was forced to flee her native France and unbeknownst to the two women, was once a renowned and celebrated gourmet chef. After years of service, Babette one day receives word that she has won the lottery, and decides to lavish the household with the most extravagant dinner ever to be seen (or tasted) on the entire Jutland peninsula; a feast which kindles the fire of humanity in the deadened souls of the tiny hamlet. (Danish and French with English subtitles) ★★★★ DVD: $19.99

Baby Boom

(1987, 103 min, US, Charles Shyer) *Diane Keaton, Sam Shepard, Harold Ramis, James Spader.* One of the more enjoyable baby comedies which proliferated in the late 1980s. Keaton gives a charming performance as a successful executive whose life is turned upside down when she becomes guardian to a deceased relative's infant. Ramis does the aggressive yuppie thing again, and Shepard does the nice-guy thing again. ★★★ DVD: $14.99

Baby Boy

(2001, 129 min, US, John Singleton) *Tyrese Gibson, A.J. Johnson, Ving Rhames, Snoop Doggy Dogg, Tamara Bass, Omar Gooding.* Most urban dramas tend to deal with the consequences of adolescents being forced to grow up too soon, so it's an intriguing twist to find the main character of director Singleton's foray back into the 'hood to be an underachieving twenty-something with two small children who still lives at home with his mama. Gibson brings considerable charisma to the titular role of Jody, an unemployed poser trying to cut a living for himself and provide for his two kids. When mama's new ex-con boyfriend (Rhames) threatens Jody's cozy place in the nest, he's forced to become a man and finally cut the apron strings. Oedipal subtext notwithstanding, the plot trajectory leads to an overwrought boys-with-guns showdown that feels like a weak extrapolation of the filmmaker's earlier work. ★★ DVD Special Edition: $19.99, VHS: $14.99

Baby Doll

(1956, 114 min, US, Elia Kazan) *Carroll Baker, Karl Malden, Eli Wallach, Mildred Dunnock, Rip Torn.* The first motion picture from a major American studio ever to be publicly condemned by the Legion of Decency, this twisted piece of Southern Gothic is still quite effective some four decades after its initial release. Tennessee Williams wrote and Kazan directed this tale of "Baby Doll," a childlike bride who sleeps in a crib and endures the ever-lurking (and sexual pressures) of her "adult" husband, an over-the-top Malden. The film features excellent supporting performances, but the film belongs to Baker as Baby Doll; she is the embodiment of adolescent sexuality and manipulation. A decadent delight. ★★★½

Baby Face

(1933, 70 min, US, Alfred E. Green) *Barbara Stanwyck, George Brent, Donald Cook, John Wayne.* Stanwyck is in great form in a "bad girl" role in this provocative pre-Production Code melodrama. Stanwyck literally sleeps her way to the top when she leaves her Erie speakeasy to conquer a New York banking company, using and discarding men at her whim. A must see for Stanwyck fans, students of 1930s cinema, or anyone interested in an exorbitantly good time. ★★★ VHS: $19.99

Baby Geniuses

(1999, 95 min, US, Bob Clark) *Kathleen Turner, Christopher Lloyd, Kim Cattrall, Peter MacNicol, Dom DeLuise.* Lloyd and poor Turner are the twisted masterminds behind a scientific experiment that uses wizard babies for their own dastardly purposes, but the film is a clumsy, uneven, unfunny disaster from the first frame till the last. The only element worth noting is the clever "Babe"-like visual effects work that syncs-up the babies' mouths with their dialogue. ★ DVD: $9.99, VHS: $9.99

Baby, It's You

(1983, 105 min, US, John Sayles) *Vincent Spano, Rosanna Arquette, Matthew Modine, Robert Downey, Jr..* One of the most popular films ever to play at TLA, this is Sayles' endearing ode to adolescent yearning and awakening maturity. Arquette stars in a remarkably textured performance as a young woman whose horizons expand beyond the grasp of her volatile high school beau (Spano). A warm comic remembrance of faded affections, bygone youth and the golden age of rock 'n' roll. ★★★½ VHS: $9.99

Baby, the Rain Must Fall

(1965, 100 min, US, Robert Mulligan) *Steve McQueen, Lee Remick, Don Murray, Paul Fix.* Based on Horton Foote's play "The Traveling Lady," this involving, unsentimental drama features McQueen (in a particularly effective performance) as a rockabilly singer, just released from prison, who reunites with his estranged wife and daughter. His uncontrolled temper and restless spirit put their reunion in jeopardy. ★★★ DVD: $24.99, VHS: $19.99

Babyfever

(1994, 110 min, US, Henry Jaglom) *Matt Salinger, Frances Fisher, Victoria Foyt, Zack Norman, Eric Roberts.* Sometimes called the "West Coast Woody Allen," director Jaglom crafts films around topics of neurotic obsession and lets his actors run with it through a loosely structured narrative. This time around, the topic of white, middle-aged angst is reproduction: As biological clocks tick away, a collection of female friends explore their options from turkey basters to men more interested in having children than they are. The various protagonists balance the instinct to procreate with the many entanglements and obligations inherent in late 20th-century America. Often self-indulgent and sometimes unexpectedly touching, *Babyfever* — like the director's other films — is an acquired taste which may not be palatable for all. But if your own clock is ticking, or if you fantasize about father-son softball games, this might suit your fancy. ★★½ DVD: $24.99, VHS: $19.99

The Bachelor

(1991, 105 min, GB/Hungary/Italy, Roberto Faenza) *Keith Carradine, Miranda Richardson, Kristin Scott Thomas, Max von Sydow.* Richardson stars in a dual role in this sumptuous though somewhat confusing period piece about a turn-of-the-century doctor (Carradine) who is unexpectedly given a second chance at life and love when his spinster sister (Richardson) commits suicide. While cut from the same cloth as *Howards End* and *A Room with a View*, the unusual tale of a man's sexual awakening lacks the skillful tailoring of either and at times works better as a travelogue than as the character study it was meant to be. ★★ VHS: $79.99

The Bachelor

(1999, 102 min, US, Gary Sinyor) *Chris O'Donnell, Renée Zellweger, Artie Lange, James Cromwell, Ed Asner, Peter Ustinov.* Suggested by Buster Keaton's 1925 short *Seven Chances*, this tired comedy casts O'Donnell as a confirmed bachelor who must marry before his 30th birthday or forfeit a fortune. His problem is that his birthday is in one day and his fiancée has just walked out on him. O'Donnell is a likable personality, and Zellweger is as sweet as sweet can be, but there's hardly a laugh or a smile to be had in this one-note joke without a punchline. Even the sight gag of hundreds of eager brides chasing our hapless hero falls flat. ★½ DVD: $9.99, VHS: $9.99

The Bachelor and the Bobbysoxer

(1947, 95 min, US, Irving Reis) *Cary Grant, Shirley Temple, Myrna Loy, Rudy Vallee.* The usually dapper Grant gets a chance to let down his well-ordered hair by acting like a teenager in this delightful Oscar-winning comedy, one of Grant's biggest box-office hits. When "bobbysoxer" Temple becomes infatuated with playboy/artist Grant, little Shirley's sister, judge Loy, orders the bemused bachelor to date the adolescent adulator in the hopes she

The Bachelor and the Bobbysoxer

soon gets over him. In no time, Myrna and the born-again teenager are falling in love. Academy Award for Best Original Screenplay. ★★★½ DVD: $19.99

Bachelor Mother

(1939, 81 min, US, Garson Kanin) *Ginger Rogers, David Niven, Charles Coburn.* A charming romantic comedy with Rogers as a single working girl who finds an abandoned baby; everyone around her presumes it's hers, including boss Niven. Directed with style by Kanin, this is one of the better screwball romances popular at the time. ★★★ VHS: $14.99

Bachelor Party

(1984, 106 min, US, Neal Israel) *Tom Hanks, Tawny Kitaen, Adrian Zmed, George Grizzard, Wendie Jo Sperber, Michael Dudikoff.* In his first box-office hit, Hanks demonstrates little of the comic presence that would be tapped that same year in *Splash.* This goonish comedy casts Hanks as a groom-to-be celebrating his upcoming wedding. Predictable shenanigans happen as the party gets out of hand. Harmless but very silly. ★★ DVD: $19.99

Back Street

(1961, 107 min, US, David Miller) *Susan Hayward, John Gavin, Vera Miles.* Ross Hunter produced this third screen adaptation of Fannie Hurst's novel, giving it the same glossy treatment as his other late-1950s melodramas (*Imitation of Life, Magnificent Obsession,* etc). Hayward stars as the young woman entangled in a hopeless love affair with a married man (Gavin). Though the earlier two versions are dramatically superior, this is nevertheless an effective (if campily fantastic) soaper. ★★½

Back to Ararat

(1990, 100 min, US/Armenia, Pea Holmquist) The 1915 death march, the eventual genocide of 1.5 million Armenians and the ensuing annexation of parts of Armenia by Turkish forces are explored in this startling documentary. In addition to recounting the horrors of the genocide, the film focuses on three generations of Armenians scattered throughout the world, all of whom dream of the day when it will be possible to return to the lands surrounding the holy mountain of Ararat. ★★★

Back to School

(1986, 96 min, US, Alan Metter) *Rodney Dangerfield, Keith Gordon, Robert Downey, Jr., Sally Kellerman, Burt Young, Ned Beatty, Sam Kinison, M. Emmet Walsh.* Dangerfield had a big hit with this funny campus comedy. The Man-of-No-Respect shines as a crass but lovable millionaire who enrolls in his son's college, both getting an unexpected education. Gordon plays his son, and Downey is a fellow student. Good one-liners. ★★★ DVD: $14.99

Back to the Beach

(1987, 92 min, US, Lyndall Hobbs) *Frankie Avalon, Annette Funicello, Connie Stevens.* Frankie and Annette are back together again in this forced piece of baby boomer nostalgia. The sweethearts of the '60s, now parents living in the Midwest, travel to California to visit their daughter, and keep running into various '60s TV stars. Stevens, looking great as ever, is there, as well as cameos by Bob Denver, Alan Hale, Jr., Jerry Mathers, Tony Dow and Don Adams. ★★ DVD: $14.99, VHS: $14.99

Back to the Future

(1985, 116 min, US, Robert Zemeckis) *Michael J. Fox, Christopher Lloyd, Lea Thompson, Crispin Glover, Thomas F. Wilson, Marc McClure, Wendie Jo Sperber, Casey Siemaszko, Billy Zane, James Tolkan.* Classic time-travel comedy with Fox as a teenager who travels back in time to 1955. There he interferes with the meeting of his parents, and is forced to play Cupid to his beautiful mom and nerdish dad. Lloyd is terrific as Fox's "crazy scientist" pal, and Glover and Thompson are his parents. An inventive, very funny and well-structured screenplay, nice special effects and a genuinely charismatic cast all contribute to the enjoyment level of this box-office smash. (Followed by 2 sequels) ★★★★ Available in a DVD Letterboxed Trilogy-pack for $39.99

Back to the Future, Part II

(1989, 107 min, US, Robert Zemeckis) *Michael J. Fox, Christopher Lloyd, Thomas F. Wilson, Lea Thompson, Elisabeth Shue, Casey Siemaszko, Billy Zane, Charles Fleischer, James Tolkan.* Picking up where the original left off, Doc Brown whisks Marty and girlfriend Jennifer to the year 2015. In the future, however, the time machine is stolen by Biff, who uses it to alter the past. Doc and Marty must return to the past to save the present. If it sounds a bit confusing, it is. Fox and Lloyd return, and both are in fine form, though the screenwriters don't give either actor the opportunity for a comic tour de force as in the original. There are some truly impressive split-screen special effects, but the story is rambling and only occasionally funny. This *Future* is decidedly dark and inferior to its predecessor. ★★½ Available in a DVD Letterboxed Trilogy-pack for $39.99

Back to the Future, Part III

(1990, 119 min, US, Robert Zemeckis) *Michael J. Fox, Christopher Lloyd, Mary Steenburgen, Thomas F. Wilson, Lea Thompson, Elisabeth Shue, James Tolkan.* The exciting finale to Zemeckis' trilogy finds our hero Marty McFly (Fox) scrambling back in time to the Old West to track down his friend Dr. Emmett Brown (Lloyd). Unlike the second film, which jumped back and forth between eons and even took a hitch into an alternative dimension, the main part of the narrative here stays with the frontier setting and to great effect. Lloyd and Fox are both in their element as they get to ham up their respective roles and Steenburgen is a pleasing addition as a Victorian schoolteacher who romances Dr. Brown. ★★★ Available in a DVD Letterboxed Trilogy-pack for $39.99

Backbeat

(1994, 100 min, GB, Iain Softley) *Stephen Dorff, Ian Hart, Sheryl Lee, Gary Bakewell, Chris O'Neill.* With the high-octane energy of a Beatles song, *Backbeat* is the exhilarating story of artist and musician Stu Sutcliffe, who flirted with fame as the "fifth Beatle." It's 1960, and the struggling Beatles have accepted a gig at a dive bar in Hamburg. The story focuses on the friendship of best mates Sutcliffe (Dorff) and John Lennon (Hart), whose close relationship is put to the test when Sutcliffe falls in love with a bohemian German woman. Though the many musical sequences are thrilling, they are only a small part of the film's success, and these scenes are smartly complemented by bristling characterizations and finely tuned dramatics. Hart's extraordinary portrayal goes beyond mimicry in bringing Lennon's wit, sarcasm and genius to the surface. ★★★★ DVD Letterbox Special Edition: $19.99

Backdraft

(1991, 135 min, US, Ron Howard) *Kurt Russell, Robert De Niro, William Baldwin, Scott Glenn, Jennifer Jason Leigh, Donald Sutherland, Rebecca DeMornay, J.T. Walsh.* An impressively mounted if dramatically awkward homage to the bravery of our nation's firefighters. Russell and Baldwin stars as brothers and firemen, whose volatile relationship is as explosive as the fires they fight. The fine cast also includes the splendid De Niro as a fire inspector investigating a series of arsons, and Glenn as Russell's seasoned coworker. But the real star of the film is the spectacular fire-fighting scenes — director Howard has captured some awe-inspiring footage of firefighting in action. ★★★

Backfire

(1987, 93 min, US/Canada, Gilbert Cates) *Jeff Fahey, Karen Allen, Keith Carradine, Bernie Casey.* Another duplicitous housewife (Allen) plans to drive her wealthy shell-shocked husband (Fahey) to suicide and collect his fortune. The plan backfires when he is left an invalid in her care. Some nice twists punctuate this noirish thriller, which is short on development but contains some stylish flourishes. ★★½ VHS: $29.99

Background to Danger

(1943, 80 min, US, Raoul Walsh) *George Raft, Brenda Marshall, Sydney Greenstreet, Peter Lorre.* As a poor man's Humphrey Bogart, Raft finds himself up against the Nazis in this WWII espionage thriller that, while cheesy, is not without its fair share of twists and intrigue. Raft plays an American salesman traveling through Turkey who becomes involved with German, Russian and Turkish agents when he stumbles upon a Nazi plot trying to force the hand of Turkey to rescind its neutrality. Greenstreet is the iniquitous Nazi agent behind the set-up, and Lorre is a spy who may or may not be a Russian agent, but who definitely likes his vodka. ★★★ VHS: $19.99

The Bad and the Beautiful

(1952, 118 min, US, Vincente Minnelli) *Kirk Douglas, Lana Turner, Dick Powell, Gloria Graham, Barry Sullivan.* The film Minnelli directed in between his glorious Technicolor musicals *An American in Paris* and *The Band Wagon* is black-and-white melodrama of the highest studio order. It's a quintessential Hollywood story with Douglas as an ambitious (ruthless?) producer and his effect on an actress (Turner), a writer (Powell) and a director (Sullivan). Winner of five Oscars including Best Screenplay (Charles Schnee) and Best Supporting Actress (Graham). ★★★★ DVD: $19.99, VHS: $14.99

Bad Behavior

(1992, 103 min, GB, Les Blair) *Stephen Rea, Sinéad Cusack, Phil Daniels, Philip Jackson.* This mostly improvised domestic comedy skillfully hits its mark. Rea and Cusack are Gerry and Ellie McAllister: middle-aged, the parents of two sons, and owners of a North London row home in need of repairs. While he trudges off to work every day to the town planning commission, she plays host to a parade of locals who stop in to share their worries over a cup of tea. In the tradition of Mike Leigh, director Blair has molded a film where not much happens, but we are nonetheless drawn into the characters' lives on a wonderfully intimate and enjoyable level. ★★★½

Bad Boys

(1983, 105 min, US, Rick Rosenthal) *Sean Penn, Esai Morales, Reni Santoni, Ally Sheedy, Clancy Brown.* Sparks fly in this intense drama as Penn and Morales square off as adversaries in a juvenile prison. Tough and violent, the film packs quite a wallop in its presentation of youthful lives behind bars. ★★★ DVD Letterbox Uncut: $14.99, VHS Uncut: $9.99

Bad Boys

(1995, 118 min, US, Michael Bay) *Will Smith, Martin Lawrence, Téa Leoni, Joe Pantoliano, Tcheky Karyo, Theresa Randle, Marg Helgenberger.* Lawrence and Smith are used to good effect in this otherwise formulaic buddy movie/police actioner. The story begins when a friend is killed investigating murderous drug dealers. Teaming with an eyewitness (Leoni), they try to track down the killers while protecting their charge at the same time. Balancing comedy and action, the film is much more appealing when the two stars are snapping the one-liners rather than blasting the bullets. There are only two action sequences of note, but both are well-paced and very exciting. (Sequel: *Bad Boys 2*) ★★½ DVD Letterbox Special Edition: $19.99, VHS Special Edition: $9.99

Bad Boys II

(2003, 144 min, US, Michael Bay) *Will Smith, Martin Lawrence, Gabrielle Union, Joe Pantoliano, Jordi Moll, Peter Stormare.* The action/buddy/cop formula has long since worn thin, yet producer Jerry Bruckheimer and director Bay persist in flooring the pedal and over-revving their engine 'til it chokes. It's entertainment by velocity and bombardment as the Bad Boys tear up Miami while chasing down a vicious drug czar trafficking deadly ecstasy. Tossed into the mix are glossy panoramas of South Beach; a generic hip-hop soundtrack; loud shootouts; juvenile race- and gay-baiting jokes; a trite domestic squabble concerning Smith's romantic interest in Lawrence's sister (Union); the stock "I'm too old for this shit" lovers'/partners' spats that keep the two stars at odds for much of the (overlong) running time; a staggering body count and stock chase sequences, demonstrative of the witless pyrotechnical excess that has earned Bay a reputation as the Satan of modern-day cinema. ★½ DVD 2-disc Special Edition: $29.99

Bad Company

(1972, 93 min, US, Robert Benton) *Jeff Bridges, Barry Brown, John Savage, Jim Davis.* This lyrical, haunting western from director Benton stars Bridges and Brown as two drifters robbing their way West during the Civil War. Benton and David Newman, who worked together on *Bonnie and Clyde*, wrote the insightful and unexpectedly humorous screenplay, and the film is enhanced by beautiful cinematography (Gordon Willis). ★★★½ DVD Letterbox: $14.99, VHS: $9.99

Bad Company

(1995, 108 min, US, Damian Harris) *Ellen Barkin, Laurence Fishburne, Frank Langella, Michael Beach, Spalding Gray, David Ogden Stiers.* A simplistic yet thought-provoking spy thriller which gives a sardonic clue as to what some soldiers may do once the war is over. Fishburne plays a blacklisted ex-CIA agent enlisted by Barkin and Langella to join a mysterious company whose stock-in-trade is translating post-Cold War tactics (blackmail, bribery, murder) to the world of big business and high finance. This intriguing premise turns stale, however, as in high order Barkin lures Fishburne first into bed and then into a deadly hostile takeover. ★★½ DVD: $14.99

Bad Company

(2002, 117 min, US, Joel Schumacher) *Anthony Hopkins, Chris Rock, Gabriel Macht, Matthew Marsh, Peter Stormare.* Wouldn't it be hilarious to make a movie starring a serious actor (Hopkins) playing opposite a smart-alecky young comedian (Rock) about some spy games gone afoul? There could be chase scenes, explosions, Eastern Europeans, and to assure that audiences will be rolling in the aisles, how about the young comedian guy is African-American and has to learn the tricks of the trade from the stoic "old pro"? The comedian guy would be committing all kinds of faux pas; meanwhile, the actor guy could learn a thing or two about life on the street . . . and with the ladies! Hey, let's make it topical — it could be about blowing up New York, but the good guys prevail this time. We could even get Jerry Bruckheimer to produce it. Doesn't that sound like a great idea for a movie? ★ DVD: $19.99, VHS: $9.99

Bad Day at Black Rock

(1955, 81 min, US, John Sturges) *Spencer Tracy, Robert Ryan, Lee Marvin, Ernest Borgnine, Walter Brennan, Dean Jagger.* Tracy heads a first-rate cast in this suspenseful modern-day western. He gives a commanding performance as a one-armed visitor to a small town who unwittingly uncovers a local secret, which puts him in imminent danger. Director Sturges maintains high tension throughout, and the story is an invigorating study of mob mentality and the bravery to stand against it. ★★★★ VHS: $19.99

Bad Dreams

(1988, 84 min, US, Andrew Fleming) *Jennifer Rubin, Bruce Abbott, Harris Yulin.* Sickly, gory horror film about a young woman, waking up after a long coma — which she went into after escaping from a mass suicide — who is haunted by those who died those many years before. ★ VHS: $29.99

Bad Girls

(1994, 100 min, US, Jonathan Kaplan) *Madeleine Stowe, Mary Stuart Masterson, Andie MacDowell, Drew Barrymore, James Russo, James LeGros, Dermot Mulroney.* MacDowell, Barrymore and Masterson save fellow honky tonk harlot Stowe from the hangman's noose. The four newly minted outlaws hit the road, with hired Pinkerton detectives on their trail. This revisionist, feminist western is actually better than the bullets and bustiers, girls-with-guns expectations it generates. Although certainly not perfect, with an often meandering script and many hackneyed contrivances, it's hard not to appreciate women who shoot to kill when sufficiently provoked. Also appreciated is one particularly memorable line: "If your laws don't include me, then they just don't apply to me, either." Amen, sister. ★★½ VHS: $9.99

Bad Influence

(1990, 99 min, US, Curtis Hanson) *Rob Lowe, James Spader, Lisa Zane, Christian Clemenson.* This pulsating, gritty thriller stars Spader as a successful businessman who is befriended by mysterious ne'er-do-well Lowe. Taking the passive yuppie under his wing, Lowe introduces Spader to the seedier side of Los Angeles life. With hints of *Strangers on a Train* and writer David Koepp's own *Apartment Zero*, their seemingly innocent friendship becomes twisted and lethal, leading to blackmail and murder. ★★★ DVD Dual: $14.99

Bad Lieutenant

(1992, 96 min, US, Abel Ferrara) *Harvey Keitel, Frankie Thorn, Paul Calderone, Brian McElroy.* Erupting from the bowels of Hell comes this highly

Billy Bob Thornton is *Bad Santa*

original, raw and shocking slice of life. Beginning with a corrupt, money-stealing, gambling-addicted cop (Keitel) snorting coke off his dashboard after dropping his two sons off at school, we soon begin a slow, painful journey into a swirling abyss of heroin shooting, crack smoking, hooker humping and countless acts of self-degradation. Looking for redemption, our bad seed of a cop takes on a brutal rape case involving a nun, sending him further into a self-destructive Hades. The vividly realistic screenplay and the gutsy, riveting performance of Keitel combine to make this one of the sleaziest films ever made. (NC-17 version) ★★★½ DVD NC-17 version: $14.99

Bad Moon

(1996, 79 min, US, Eric Red) *Michael Paré, Mariel Hemingway, Mason Gamble.* It's dog versus werewolf in this poorly written attempt to teach an old genre some new tricks. Unfortunately, all *Bad Moon* can do is roll over and play dead. Paré is some sort of adventurer who is bitten by a werewolf. He relocates to the Pacific Northwest (the movie includes some fantastic scenery) to stay with his sister (Hemingway) and her child; they can't understand all the animal attacks which are plaguing the region. A cliché-ridden, lame-brained child-in-peril movie. ★½ DVD: $14.99, VHS: $14.99

The Bad News Bears

(1976, 102 min, US, Michael Ritchie) *Walter Matthau, Tatum O'Neal, Vic Morrow, Joyce Van Patten, Jackie Earle Haley.* Though two pallid sequels have soured the memory of the original, this is quite a delightful and funny baseball comedy. Matthau is especially good as a beer-guzzling, slobbish coach to a team of misfit Little Leaguers. O'Neal is charming as the team's last hope — a pitcher with a wicked fast ball. (Followed by 2 sequels: *The Bad News Bears in Breaking Training* and *The Bad News Bears Go to Japan*.) ★★★ DVD Letterbox: $14.99, VHS: $14.99

Bad Santa

(2003, 91 min, US, Terry Zwigoff) *Billy Bob Thornton, Tony Cox, Brett Kelly, Lauren Graham, Bernie Mac, John Ritter, Lauren Tom, Cloris Leachman.* Leave the PC Police at the door for this one, for *Bad Santa* is a low-down and crude black comedy with the potential to offend nearly everyone. It's also downright hilarious, a refreshingly un-PC laughfest that is guaranteed to make you cringe while you hold your sides. Making one of the great film creeps, Thornton is venom dipped in sleaze as Willie Stokes, a low-life, alcoholic con man who every year at the holidays teams with his dwarf partner-in-crime Marcus (Cox) to play Santa and his elf, and then rob the store where they're working on Christmas Eve. In Phoenix, they find the perfect store and store manager/patsy (Ritter in his final film role). What they didn't count on is a parentless eight-year-old (Kelly) who latches on to "Santa" and becomes the target of what has to be some of the most vitriolic verbal abuse ever heaped upon a child. It's hysterical, and one can't but wonder what series of tricks and tortures they had to conceive to make this kid react like he does. As Marcus, Cox is great as the foul-mouthed sidekick . . . just when you thought you heard it all out of Willie's mouth, then comes Marcus with a vulgar, hilarious barrage as to make Quentin Tarantino rethink free speech. Though the film could have been more tightly edited, the final result is laugh-out-loud funny . . . this is the most enjoyably "offensive" comedy since *South Park*. ★★★½ DVD Unrated: $29.99, VHS: $24.99

The Bad Seed

(1956, 129 min, US, Mervyn LeRoy) *Patty McCormack, Nancy Kelly, Eileen Heckart, Henry Jones.* This unsettling version of the Broadway hit about a psychopathic little girl is so effective it prompted the studio upon its release to add a closing introduction to the featured players — perhaps the birth of the tagline, "Remember, it's only a movie." McCormack and Kelly re-create their stage roles as, respectively, the amoral title character and her disbelieving mother. ★★★½ DVD: $19.99

The Bad Sleep Well

(1960, 151 min, Japan, Akira Kurosawa) *Toshiro Mifune, Takashi Shimura.* This chilling tale of corruption in the modern Japanese corporate world stars director Kurosawa's mainstay, Mifune, as an embittered, grieving son and rising executive whose father supposedly committed suicide. Not believing the official version of his death, and convinced that a large corporation and its officials were somehow involved, Mifune plots revenge. This stylish crime thriller, based on an Ed McBain story, provides a fascinating commentary on the twisted self-interests of big business. (Japanese with English subtitles) ★★★ VHS Letterboxed: $29.99

Bad Taste

(1987, 90 min, New Zealand, Peter Jackson) *Peter Jackson, Pete O'Herne.* This hysterical horror spoof from first-time director Jackson is about a group of paramilitary investigators who are the first line of defense against an attempted alien invasion of the Earth. The members of the team, including Jackson himself, must thwart an attempt by these "intergalactic wankers" to harvest the latest universal fast-food sensation: human flesh. Many horror and action clichés are sent up in the meantime and the body count and amount of gore make the film live up to its title in every way. It is as funny as it is gross. ★★★ DVD: $19.99, VHS: $9.99

Badlands

(1973, 95 min, US, Terrence Malick) *Martin Sheen, Sissy Spacek, Warren Oates.* As legend has it, Malick just decided that he wanted to give filmmaking a whirl. That whirl yielded a classic — a haunting, touching and often humorous piece of work. Based on the story of 1950s killer Charles Starkweather, *Badlands* boasts a richly textured screenplay, exquisite cinematography, wonderful use of music and, above all else, astonishing performances by Sheen and Spacek as young lovers on the run. In a film full of moody, funny, breathtaking sequences, the all-too-brief scene where Sheen and Spacek, hiding out in the woods, dance around while their radio plays Mickey and Sylvia singing "Love Is Strange" is a standout, a priceless moment of cinematic art. ★★★★ DVD: $19.99, VHS Pan & Scan: $14.99, VHS Letterboxed: $14.99

Bagdad Cafe

(1988, 91 min, US/West Germany, Percy Adlon) *Marianne Sagebrecht, CCH Pounder, Jack Palance.* This enchanting and affectionate fable unveils, in a series of wonderful vignettes, the developing friendship between several oddball characters. Sagebrecht is a corpulent Bavarian tourist who, stranded somewhere in the Mojave Desert, arrives one day at the near-comatose Bagdad Cafe, a dusty roadside cafe run by an irascible black woman (Pounder). Director Adlon takes his time in showing their dif-

ferences, as well as their blossoming friendship. A wonderful comedy-drama about misfits in tune with the world. ★★★½ DVD Letterbox: $19.99

Bail Jumper

(1989, 95 min, US, Christian Faber) *Eszter Balint, B.J. Spalding.* Unnatural natural calamities befall two Southern thieves in love in this strange, wacky comedy. Joe and Elaine, both petty criminals, decide to leave their home in Murky Springs, Missouri, for the more promising shores of Long Island. But along the way, they are visited by a swarm of locusts, hit with a tornado and, in their new home, greeted with a tidal wave. ★★½ VHS: $19.99

Bait

(2000, 119 min, US, Antoine Fuqua) *Jamie Foxx, David Morse, Doug Hutchison, Kimberly Elise, Robert Pastorelli.* Small-time crook Foxx is caught trying to steal a load of shrimp from a restaurant and is privy to the dying words of his cellmate in jail. Unbeknownst to Foxx, the dead man's cryptic words gave the location of a fortune in stolen booty; the feds surgically implant a tracer and recording device inside Foxx's shoulder, and upon his release from jail, use him as bait to bring out the mastermind behind the theft. A silly rip-off of *Enemy of the State*, this can be entertaining, but only in a stupid, derivative, flashy sort of way. *Bait* is harmless, popcorn-munching garbage. ★★ DVD: $19.99, VHS: $9.99

The Baker's Wife

(1938, 124 min, France, Marcel Pagnol) *Raimu, Ginette Leclerc.* The wonderfully enchanting comedic actor Raimu shines as a lovesick and inconsolable baker who goes on a baking strike after he discovers that his flighty wife has run off with a handsome shepherd. The breadless villagers, desperate to get him back to normal, take the situation in their own hands in an effort to get the two back together again. Infused with humor and casting a sympathetic eye toward the villagers and provincial life, Pagnol's charming tale is successful in dealing with the natural pleasures and sufferings of life. (French with English subtitles) ★★★★ VHS: $59.99

Le Bal

(1982, 110 min, France/Italy, Ettore Scola) Within the setting of a Parisian dance hall, director Scola ingeniously presents 50 years of European social and political history through a series of vignettes. With no dialogue, just the musical accompaniment of Charles Aznavour, Irving Berlin, Charele Trene and others, *Le Bal* sweeps us through the turbulent 20th century in a highly stylized yet poignant and absorbing way. ★★★ VHS: $79.99

La Balance

(1982, 102 min, France, Bob Swaim) *Nathalie Baye, Philippe Leotard, Richard Berry.* This gangster sensation swept the French César Awards and took the Best Feature, Actor and Actress honors. Baye stars as a tough, high-class hooker caught in a cat-and-mouse struggle between her boyfriend/pimp and a determined detective. A kind of Gallic *Dirty Harry*, *La Balance* is a taut and jolting journey through the Parisian underworld. ★★★ VHS Letterboxed: $29.99

The Balcony

(1963, 83 min, US/GB, Joseph Strick) *Shelley Winters, Peter Falk, Lee Grant, Ruby Dee, Leonard Nimoy.* Jean Genet's allegorical play set in a brothel comes to life in this vivid and boisterous low-budget film. Winters is the beleaguered lesbian madam

The Ballad of Narayama

of the bustling bordello. This "house of illusion," where people play out their dreams, is left undisturbed despite a ravaging rebellion outside its doors. An interesting and at times surreal find. ★★★ DVD: $29.99, VHS: $19.99

Balkan Express

(1984, 102 min, Yugoslavia, Branko Baletic) This offbeat and tragic comedy follows the manic adventures of the Balkan Express Band, a troupe of roving musicians whose music is just a cover for their real work: con men and thieves. Their easy and wild living is interrupted during the Nazi occupation as this motley group discover that they must overcome their petty self-interests and work to overcome the oppression. Outrageously madcap and full of dramatic twists set against the dark horror of war. ★★★

Ball of Fire

(1941, 111 min, US, Howard Hawks) *Gary Cooper, Barbara Stanwyck, Dana Andrews, S.Z. Sakall, Henry Travers.* Cooper stars as a professor of English researching slang for an encyclopedia — he's shy but he's a real solid sender anyway. Stanwyck is Sugarpuss O'Shea, a gangster's moll on the lam — now she's definitely rockin' with a solid eight. When Coop and his seven associates unwittingly give shelter to this killer diller, she turns their lives topsy-turvy, and when Cooper and Stanwyck hit the giggles, oh boy, it's hoi toi toi: root, zoot, cute, and solid to boot. This delightful, whimsical comedy gave Stanwyck her second Oscar nomination. (Give a ring on the Ameche if you liked it.) ★★★½

Ballad in Blue

(1966, 89 min, GB, Paul Henreid) *Ray Charles, Tom Bell.* Charles found the perfect showcase for his talents in this restrained melodrama about an American jazz musician who befriends a young blind boy. The story is overly maudlin and not too substantial, but the film provides ample footage of Charles at his piano belting out his favorites, including "I Got a Woman," "What'd I Say?" and "Cry." A pleasure for even the mildest of fans. ★★½

Ballad of a Soldier

(1959, 89 min, USSR, Grigori Chukhrai) *Vladimir Ivashov, Zhanna Prokhorenko.* A sensitive and romantic story about a 19-year-old soldier in WWII who sets out on leave to visit his mother. The trip is punctuated with scenes of the horrors of war but is highlighted by the hero falling in love with a beautiful young girl. A moving experience, this ten-

der love story will soften even the hardest of hearts. (Russian with English subtitles) ★★★½ DVD Criterion Collection: $29.99, VHS: $29.99

The Ballad of Cable Hogue

(1970, 121 min, US, Sam Peckinpah) *Jason Robards, Stella Stevens, David Warner, Strother Martin, Slim Pickens.* Peckinpah is in a notably lighter mood with this vigorously entertaining western. Though the Old West is still dusty and dangerous as in any of his other more volatile works, the wild in this Wild West is for unpredictable and strange antics. Robards heads a good cast as an eccentric prospector whose dream of an oasis in the middle of the desert may not be as crazy as everyone thinks. In her best screen role, Stevens is sharp as a needle as the good-hearted, feisty prostitute who takes up with Robards. ★★★½ VHS: $14.99

The Ballad of Gregorio Cortez

(1982, 99 min, US, Robert M. Young) *Edward James Olmos, James Gammon, Barry Corbin, Rosana De Soto, Pepe Serna.* Sincere telling of one of the most notorious manhunts in Texas history is a gritty and unsettling examination of bigotry. Olmos stars as a young Mexican who, in a miscommunication of language, kills a U.S. sheriff and becomes the object of a statewide hunt. ★★★

The Ballad of Little Jo

(1993, 120 min, US, Maggie Greenwald) *Suzy Amis, Ian McKellen, Bo Hopkins, Rene Auberjonois, David Chung, Carrie Snodgress, Heather Graham, Anthony Heald.* This profound little odyssey examines feminine oppression in the tale of a young woman who finds herself wandering the countryside at the end of the Civil War. Constantly at peril of being raped by marauding ex-soldiers, she decides to head west where she masquerades as a man in a shithole mining town. Based on a true story lifted from a newspaper headline of the day, Greenwald's film delivers a wonderfully satisfying, gritty look at the Old West that rivals *Unforgiven.* Amis, in the lead role, creates an excellent portrait of rugged and determined survival. McKellen gives great support as a grizzly miner, portrayed initially as a decent man but who eventually shows his true misogynist colors. ★★★★ DVD: $19.99

The Ballad of Narayama

(1983, 130 min, Japan, Shohei Imamura) *Ken Ogata, Sumiko Sakamota.* This exquisitely photographed film paints a sublime portrait of the harsh life endured in a secluded, 19th-century village high in the mountains of northern Japan. Reacting to their raw existence, the people have adopted several unusual customs, including one which dictates that the elderly, upon reaching the age of 70, are escorted to the top of Narayama Mountain to die in solitude. Director Imamura depicts a cruel and sometimes shocking world to the viewer but one which is based on simple survival. (Japanese with English subtitles) ★★★★ VHS Letterboxed: $29.99

The Ballad of the Sad Cafe

(1991, 108 min, US, Simon Callow) *Vanessa Redgrave, Keith Carradine, Rod Steiger, Cork Hubbert, Austin Pendleton.* The Deep South has played host to many a curious tale, but none more bewildering than this wildly uneven but nevertheless hypnotic adaptation of the Edward Albee play, itself based on the Carson McCullers novella. Redgrave gives a bold performance as Miss Amelia, the masculine town tycoon who sends fear into the local residents. All except Lymon (Hubbard), her hunchback dwarf cousin. Lymon convinces her to open a cafe, which becomes the pulse of the tiny town. However, things change drastically when Miss Amelia's estranged husband, Marvin (Carradine), returns from prison. The stage is set for a battle-of-the-sexes showdown. Not for all tastes, but for the more adventurous viewer. ★★½ VHS: $19.99

Ballistic: Ecks vs. Sever

(2002, 105 min, US, Kaos) *Antonio Banderas, Lucy Liu, Gregg Henry, Ray Park, Talisa Soto.* Yet another wretched video game turned into a wretched action film. Despite being directed by promising Thai action maestro Wych Kaosayananda (nee: "Kaos"), this may be the worst of its genre. Banderas sleepwalks through his role as a retired government hit man-cum-alcoholic bum who still hasn't gotten over his wife's death years ago. Turns out she didn't actually die, and only the nefarious Liu knows her whereabouts. Lots of poorly choreographed shoot-outs, tired dialogue, annoying acting (the main offender being Liu), and lurching plot kill any attempts at stylishness by Mr. Kaos. It's not even remotely diverting, and not inept enough to be so-bad-it's-good. ★ DVD Letterbox: $14.99, VHS: $14.99

Balto

(1995, 78 min, US, Simon Wells) *Voices of: Kevin Bacon, Bridget Fonda, Miriam Margolyes, Bob Hoskins, Phil Collins.* This charming piece of animation has a strong plot (based on a true story), good vocals and high production values. Balto is half-wolf, half-dog, and lives in Nome, Alaska, in the mid-1920s. Spurned by dog and man alike for his mixed heritage, he steps in to save the day when he leads a ragtag team through Arctic blizzards to deliver much-needed diphtheria medicine. *Balto* is an appealing package that offers an exciting story, and a few rather sophisticated innuendos should keep adults interested as well. (Sequel: *Balto II: Wolf Quest*) ★★★ DVD: $24.99, VHS: $14.99

La Bamba

(1986, 108 min, US, Luis Valdez) *Lou Diamond Phillips, Esai Morales, Rosana DeSoto, Elizabeth Peña, Joe Pantoliano.* An enthralling musical biopic of 1950s singing star Richie Valens. Phillips offers a strong portrayal of the teen idol, whose course is tracked from his high school days up until his fateful crash. Morales is vibrant as Richie's brother, and DeSoto is especially good as their hard-working and loving mother. ★★★½ DVD: $14.99

Bambi

(1942, 72 min, US, David Hand) One of the few films which can be said to have affected generations that have seen it, Walt Disney's classic animated feature follows the adventures of a forest deer, Bambi, and his little forest friends, including the lovable Thumper the rabbit. The animation is brilliant, and the story will captivate viewers of all ages. ★★★½

Bamboozled

(2000, 136 min, US, Spike Lee) *Damon Wayans, Savion Glover, Jada Pinkett-Smith, Tommy Davidson, Michael Rapaport.* Extremely disappointing effort from Lee, all the more lamentable because it could have been great. The premise is terrific: a black TV writer, deemed too "white" by his trendy boss, decides to get himself fired by writing a show that is a throwback to blackface minstrel shows. In true *Producers* fashion, the show becomes a surprise hit, and success goes to the celebrated writer's head. Sadly, this fertile ground for satire is botched, with murky (at best) character motivations and a lack of focus. The film is, shockingly, not edgy at all (save for two hysterically funny TV commercial parodies), rather monotonous, at times incoherent, and completely unconvincing, even for a broad satire. ★★ DVD: $24.99

Bananas

(1971, 81 min, US, Woody Allen) *Woody Allen, Louise Lasser, Carlos Montalban, Howard Cosell.* After the very funny escapades of *Take the Money and Run*, Allen sharpened both his comic skills and his filmmaking techniques to tell the riotous story of Fielding Melish, a meek and mild products tester in New York who finds himself the rebel leader of a group of South American guerrillas. The film is a non-stop barrage of sight gags and one-liners, most of which hit the bullseye. ★★★½ DVD: $19.99

Favorite Line: "I object, your honor! This trial is a travesty. It's a travesty of a mockery of a sham of a mockery of a travesty of two mockeries of a sham." *—Woody Allen as Fielding Mellish*

Band of Outsiders

(1964, 97 min, France, Jean-Luc Godard) *Anna Karina, Sami Frey.* Godard's fresh approach to the gangster musical follows the antics of three highly spirited but ineffectual crooks. Interesting aspect of the film is the inserts of Godard's personal philosophical observations and his thoughts on the action in the story. One of Godard's most interesting and accessible films. (French with English subtitles) ★★★½ DVD Criterion Collection: $29.99, VHS Subtitled: $19.99

The Band Wagon

(1953, 112 min, US, Vincente Minnelli) *Fred Astaire, Cyd Charisse, Nanette Fabray, Oscar Levant, Jack Buchanan.* One of Astaire's most captivating musicals, this glorious comedic look at the making of a Broadway show has Fred as a Hollywood actor who is persuaded to star on the Great White Way with a renowned ballerina (the beautiful Charisse). A fine score, sensational dance numbers and charming performances by all combine to make this a classic of the musical genre. ★★★★ VHS: $14.99

Bandit Queen

(1994, 119 min, GB/India, Shekhar Kapur) *Seema Biswas, Nirmal Pandey, Manoj Bajpai.* This film adaptation of the harrowing yet ultimately triumphant life of Indian folk hero Phoolan Devi is a blistering attack on her culture's horrifying treatment of women and its crushing caste system. After being raped by her new husband, Phoolan escapes and returns to her home village only to be kidnapped and brutally humiliated by a gang of bandits. She eventually rises within their ranks to become the leader of her own gang. Her bitter and ruthless quest for vengeance leads her to become regarded as a savior by throngs of lowborn Indians. With an unrelentingly hard-core depiction of Indian society, the film offers a fascinating peek into the intricate and complex social machinations of India's highly organized bandit armies. ★★★½

Bandits

(1987, 98 min, France, Claude Lelouch) *Jean Yanne, Marie-Sophie Lelouch.* Director Lelouch has fashioned a real gem about the relationship between an imprisoned jewel thief and his daughter. Yanne is charming as the father who hides his young daughter in a Swiss boarding school after a jewel heist ends in his wife's murder and his arrest. This is a near-perfect film with a great script, first-rate acting and plenty of plot twists. (French with English subtitles) ★★★★

Bandits

(1999, 110 min, Germany, Katja von Garnier) *Katja Riemann, Jasmin Tabatabai, Nicolette Krebitz, Jutta Hoffmann.* A group of female convicts, all musicians, are brought together to form a rock band under a new government rehabilitation program. They are scheduled to perform at a policemen's ball, but escape, and become huge celebrities while on the lam. This German *Thelma and Louise: The Musical* lacks that film's emotional involvement and resonance, as well as any memorable tunes. The cheesy VH1-esque music interludes stop the movie cold, and the drama is trite and clichéd. *Bandits* has one or two fun moments, but also has the prefab feel of a feature-length advert for a band that never was. (German with English subtitles) ★★

Bandits

(2001, 118 min, US, Barry Levinson) *Bruce Willis, Billy Bob Thornton, Cate Blanchett, Troy Garity.* Sporting a head of hair and a toothy grin, Willis has a glorious time in playing Joe Blake, an escaped convict who finds his 15 minutes of fame as a "gentleman bank robber." However, what his two costars, Thornton and Blanchett, are up to amounts to nothing less than grand larceny. A highly enjoyable caper comedy that's as smart as it is funny, *Bandits* follows the merry exploits of Blake and fellow escapee Terry Collins (Thornton), who when we first meet them are telling their story of a life of crime. Everything had been going swimmingly until they hooked up with unhappily married Kate (Blanchett), who after hitting Terry with her car becomes a hostage. She also sets both men's hearts aflutter, which sets the stage for some divine romantic sparring. Director Levinson keeps the pace brisk and the comedy tangy, though what really makes this work are the extraordinary performances from Thornton and Blanchett, who nearly bring modern screwball comedy/romance to a new level. ★★★ DVD Dual Special Edition: $19.99, VHS: $9.99

Bandolero

(1968, 106 min, US, Andrew V. McLaglen) *James Stewart, Dean Martin, Raquel Welch, George Kennedy.* Stewart and Martin play sibling outlaws who escape to Mexico with Welch as a hostage. Stewart and Martin are riding in familiar western territory here, though they play well together. ★★½ DVD: $14.99, VHS: $19.99

Bang the Drum Slowly

(1973, 97 min, US, John Hancock) *Robert De Niro, Michael Moriarty, Vincent Gardenia, Ann Wedgeworth, Danny Aiello.* Two stand-out performances by Moriarty and De Niro highlight this stirring drama, based on a 1956 TV drama (which starred a young Paul Newman) about the relationship between two big-league ball players: a star pitcher (Moriarty) and his catcher (De Niro), dying of Hodgkin's Disease. Gardenia is priceless as their colorful manager. ★★★½ DVD: $14.99, VHS: $14.99

The Banger Sisters

(2002, 94 min, US, Bob Dolman) *Goldie Hawn, Susan Sarandon, Geoffrey Rush, Erika Christensen, Robin Thomas, Eva Amurri.* In his directorial debut, writer Dolman goes against the Hollywood grain and gives two actresses in their 50s juicy roles they can sink their teeth into. For this alone it's possible to overlook the contrivances of a meager script and to instead enjoy the wonderful chemistry that Hawn and Sarandon produce. The high-concept screenplay has two former groupies reuniting after 20 years. Goldie is Suzette, still a free spirit. Susan is Vinnie, who has abandoned her former, carefree existence and is now a suburban wife and mother. It's not long till their reunion has a lasting effect on each other, one of the more obvious and sentimental ploys in the story. As predictable as most of *The Banger Sisters* is, however, there's a degree of fun in watching these two women strut their stuff, and they certainly make the most of a line and a situation — whether it's funny or not. ★★½ DVD Dual: $19.99, VHS: $12.99

Bangkok Dangerous

(2000, 105 min, Thailand, Danny Pang & Oxide Pang) *Powarit Mongkolpisit, Premsince Ratanasopha, Pisek Intarakanchit.* Entertaining if disposable Hong Kong-influenced actioner has Mongkolpisit as a deaf-mute assassin (yeah, that'd work) who falls in love with a cute pharmacist who thinks he's a gas station attendant. Meanwhile, his washed-up mentor and his mentor's girlfriend get into deep trouble, and it's up to our hero to do the vengeance thing. Overdirected by the Pang Brothers (who also collaborated on the solid shocker *The Eye*), *Bangkok Dangerous* gives Oliver Stone a run for his money by using every type of film stock available, utilizing countless edits, and piling up a considerable number of corpses. Of course, this isn't believable for a second. But it makes up for it with dazzling editing and an eye-popping visual style. It's a hyperventilating, hyperviolent piece of nihilistic fluff. (Thai with English subtitles) ★★½ DVD: $14.99, VHS: $9.99

The Bank Dick

(1940, 74 min, US, Eddie Cline) *W.C. Fields, Cora Witherspoon, Una Merkel, Franklin Pangborn, Shemp Howard.* Inept, bungling Fields gets a job as a guard in a bank, forcing him to deal with the stress of employment as well as the encumbrance of wife and family. But forget the plot. This is one of the true comedy classics. The only problem is, it's too short. ★★★½ DVD Criterion Collection: $29.99

B

43

Bank Robber

(1993, 94 min, US, Nick Mead) *Patrick Dempsey, Lisa Bonet, Forest Whitaker, Judge Reinhold.* Writer-director Mead combines the typical heist film with a story line inspired by Ionesco's Theatre of the Absurd to produce this entertainingly bizarre and challenging film. A pumped-up Dempsey plays a nice-guy bank robber who is forced to hide out in a creepy L.A. hotel until the heat blows over. His nightmare begins, however, as he is visited by a succession of characters who know his identity and exploit him at every turn. These include the pizza delivery boy, the hotel clerk and a gay motorcycle cop into S&M. ★★★

B*A*P*S

(1997, 90 min, US, Robert Townsend) *Halle Berry, Natalie Dessalle, Martin Landau, Bernie Mac, Rudy Ray Moore.* In Townsend's unfunny spoof, Berry and Dessalle star as Nisi and Mickey, two waitresses from the South who dream of opening a hair salon/soul food restaurant. However, in this homogenized *Pretty Woman* meets *Clueless* about wish fulfillment, clashing cultures and really tacky fashion choices, dreams prove fleeting as they head to El Lay for fame and fortune. Upon their arrival, they are offered exactly that if Nisi will masquerade as the granddaughter of the former sweetheart of a dying millionaire (Landau). Generic R&B tunes, an annoying dramatic score, and "so-what" spot-the-star cameos can't deflect the tame writing and directing. ★½ DVD: $19.99, VHS: $9.99

Bar Girls

(1995, 95 min, US, Marita Giovanni) *Nancy Allison Wolfe, Lisa Parker, Camila Griggs, Paula Sorge, Justine Slater.* The mating rites and the accompanying mind games of L.A. lesbians are uncovered in this knowing romantic comedy. Lauran Hoffman's script (based on her autobiographical play) centers most of the action at the West Hollywood Girl Bar. Loretta, a writer and one of the bar's bed-hopping regulars, meets and all-too-quickly falls for the self-assured Rachel, a bewitching aspiring actress. Their union is threatened, however, when J.R., an attractively butch cop, enters the scene. While the acting is unremarkable, the staging uninspired and the production values minimal, the film nevertheless is endowed with spunky charm that ultimately wins the viewer over. ★★★ DVD Letterbox: $19.99

Baraka

(1992, 96 min, US, Ron Fricke) "Baraka" is an ancient Sufi word meaning a blessing or the breath or essence of life from which the evolutionary process unfolds. An examination of the diversity of the world's life is the subject of the film, shot in 24 countries in Todd-AO 70mm format. Like the similar *Koyaanisqatsi*, it has no dialogue or narration and combines images and music to inform and entertain. Always an incredibly beautiful film, *Baraka* is relentlessly confusing, feeling sometimes like a harmless travelogue and other times like a manipulative, self-conscious political treatise. However, it's also terrific viewing — its scope and magnificence unfortunately diminished by the home viewing screen. ★★★ DVD Collector's Edition: $19.99, VHS: $19.99

Barb Wire

(1996, 90 min, US, David Hogan) *Pamela Anderson Lee, Temuera Morrison, Victoria Rowell, Udo Kier, Steve Railsback, Xander Berkeley.* Imagine a futuristic *Casablanca*, but with a silicone-enhanced Bogart packing automatic weapons, and you have, in a C-cup, the plot of this camp showcase for TV sex symbol Lee. In this adaptation of the comic, she plays a former soldier-now-nightclub proprietess who's content to wait out the ongoing Second American Civil War. Her peace is shattered when a freedom-fighting ex reenters her life. As a piece of kitsch, *Barb Wire* is somewhat enjoyable, but it's all just rather flat. The production values are of the "always raining because it looked cool in *Blade Runner*" variety, and the action scenes are competently done. ★★ DVD Unrated: $9.99, VHS Unrated: $9.99

Barbarella

(1967, 98 min, France, Roger Vadim) *Jane Fonda, John Phillip Law, Anita Pallenberg, Milo O'Shea.* There's something for everyone in this imaginative, sexually charged sci-fi camp classic. Featuring a young Fonda — before Vietnam, exercise videos, two Oscars and rich Southern media moguls — as a fetching, pre-liberated sex goddess, this wacky film shows off all of her best bodily talents. As the sexy 40th-century space traveler, Fonda, when not fighting off demonic, razor-teethed dolls or killer canaries, displays a wonderful assortment of the latest in revealing intergalactic fashion. ★★★ DVD: $19.99

The Barbarian Invasions

(2003, 99 min, Canada, Denys Arcand) *Rémy Girard, Stéphane Rousseau, Marie-Josée Croze, Dorothée Berryman.* The people we met in *The Decline of the American Empire* reunite as one of their group finds himself in the hands of a Canadian health care system so bureaucratized that old equipment is not replaced because the paperwork is insurmountable. Despite (and maybe because of) the toll his cancer has inflicted on him, Rémy is still an insatiable sensualist, checking the curve of a nurse's thigh as she checks his IV drip. One of his distant sons returns from London to care for his father; the Atlantic was easier to cross than the emotional chasm between them. Rémy is a left-wing, retired professor of history with an impressive personal library; his son makes tons of money and plays computer games. As Rémy's condition continues to deteriorate, recriminations and familial squabbling transmute into compassion and caring, and the son who crossed an ocean for escape becomes a tender caregiver. Old friends are gathered together to celebrate Rémy's life, as his son negotiates life's current realities to provide his father as much comfort as possible. Director Arcand once again offers intelligent and witty discussions of big issues by focusing on the minutia of daily living, presenting the universal in the details of a single person's life, evoking wildly divergent emotions and complex philosophic musings with apparent effortlessness. *The Barbarian Invasions* is a mature, engaging and most rewarding offering from an underappreciated auteur. Academy Award winner for Best Foreign Film. (French with English subtitles) ★★★★ DVD: $29.99

Barbarians at the Gate

(1993, 122 min, US, Glenn Jordan) *James Garner, Jonathan Pryce, Peter Riegert, Joanna Cassidy.* It's the 1980s and it's morning in America. Entire companies are bought, sold and discarded faster than pantyhose. Multimillion-dollar leveraged buyouts are routinely handled before lunch; the billion-dollar deals take a little more time. Sweeping across this frenetic landscape is one rich former Canadian who concocts a plan to purchase the leading baking corporation in the land. Fantastic parody, right? The truly fantastic element is that it's all true — well, not true in the sense of This Dialogue Guaranteed Verbatim. Garner is mesmerizing as F. Ross Johnson, CEO of RJR Nabisco, whose attempts to buy out the company are set forth in this humorous and extremely entertaining HBO production. ★★★½ DVD Letterbox: $9.99

Barbarosa

(1981, 90 min, Australia, Fred Schepisi) *Willie Nelson, Gary Busey, Gilbert Roland.* A thrilling western yarn that combines the charismatic acting of Nelson and the spectacular photography and sharp, tightly controlled direction of Schepisi. A farm boy (Busey) on the lam is rescued from the ravages of the desert by the outlaw Barbarosa (Nelson). A strong alliance and friendship develops as they roam the West battling thieves, the elements and angry in-laws. ★★★ VHS: $9.99

Barbary Coast

(1935, 90 min, US, Howard Hawks) *Edward G. Robinson, Miriam Hopkins, Joel McCrea, Walter Brennan, Brian Donlevy.* Hawks distinguished himself as a director par excellence in two film genres: the screwball comedy and the action-flavored drama. This story of 19th-century San Francisco during the

Father and son reconciliation in *The Barbarian Invasions*

California Gold Rush days falls into the latter category, and features the director in fine form. Robinson is perfectly cast as a gangster nightclub owner, Hopkins is the club's star attraction, and McCrea is the Easterner who comes between them. ★★★

Barbershop

(2002, 102 min, US, Tim Story) *Ice Cube, Anthony Anderson, Sean Patrick Thomas, Cedric the Entertainer, Eve, Troy Garity, Keith David.* Cedric the Entertainer lives up to his name and steals the show in this urban punchline-fest. He plays Eddie, a regular at an established black Chicago barbershop. Though he's rarely seen getting a haircut, he's often seen getting into hairy discussions. His riff on Rosa Parks, whom he claims "didn't do nothing but sit her black ass down" is a thought-provoking riot. While the hodge-podge of barbershop personalities are nothing new (thuggy barber here, token whitey there), the writing is still sharp and gives us a good feel for the tight-knit communities built in black haircutting establishments nationwide. *Barbershop* is a good-natured mixture of Hollywood sassiness and neighborhood substance. (Sequel: *Barbershop 2: Back in Business*) ★★★ DVD Letterbox Special Edition: $14.99, VHS: $9.99

Barcelona

(1994, 101 min, US, Whit Stillman) *Taylor Nichols, Chris Eigeman, Tushka Bergen, Mira Sorvino, Thomas Gibson.* The sophomore curse strikes again as Stillman's follow-up to his acclaimed *Metropolitan* fails to totally capture the freshness and ingenuity of his first film. Set in Spain during the last days of the Cold War, the story follows the romantic exploits of two Americans living in Barcelona. Nichols plays a dweeby salesman whose cousin (Eigeman), a Navy attaché, arrives unexpectedly. This gives way to the two aimlessly musing about life, death, romance, politics, and whatever else randomly enters their minds. Stillman's script occasionally offers amusing observations on the machinations of the modern relationship, though the women's roles are rather underwritten. ★★½ DVD: $19.99, VHS: $14.99

The Barefoot Contessa

(1954, 131 min, US, Joseph L Mankiewicz) *Humphrey Bogart, Ava Gardner, Edmond O'Brien, Marius Goring, Valentina Cortesa, Rossano Brazzi.* Another slick, savvy "showbiz of the '50's fairy tale" from the pen of writer-director Mankiewicz. Gardner is radiant in the title role, a "Cinderella" who refuses to wear the Hollywood glass slipper, while Bogart dons the mantle of world-weary cynic (a staple in Mankiewicz's screenplays) all too well and willingly. O'Brien's performance as a press agent earned him a well-deserved Oscar. Not as potent of a biting exposé as the director's earlier triumph, *All About Eve*; but nevertheless, it manages some well-aimed shots. ★★★ DVD: $14.99

Barefoot in the Park

(1967, 105 min, US, Gene Saks) *Robert Redford, Jane Fonda, Mildred Natwick, Charles Boyer, Herb Edelman.* Frothy Neil Simon comedy, based on his hit Broadway play, with Redford and Fonda as newlyweds living on top of a five-floor walk-up in New York City, experiencing big city life and marital woes. Though not one of Simon's classics, there's more than enough to entertain, and a good supporting cast adds sparkle. ★★★ DVD: $14.99, VHS: $14.99

Barbershop

Barfly

(1987, 97 min, US, Barbet Schroeder) *Mickey Rourke, Faye Dunaway, Alice Krige, Jack Nance.* Director Schroeder has perfectly captured the spirit of Charles Bukowski's autobiography about the resilience of the creative force. Rourke, in possibly his best performance, plays the alcoholic writer who begins an affair with fellow inebriate Dunaway (remarkable in a non-typecast role); the two enjoying the seedy Los Angeles bar scene in search of libation and unorthodox fulfillment. A brilliantly conceived and hilariously funny character study. ★★★★ DVD Letterbox: $19.99, VHS: $14.99

The Barkleys of Broadway

(1949, 109 min, US, Charles Walters) *Fred Astaire, Ginger Rogers, Oscar Levant.* The last Astaire-Rogers musical (made after a 10-year separation) is charming fluff about a theatrical couple who split when one wants to abandon the act for "serious" drama. Screenplay by Betty Comden and Adolph Green (*Singin' in the Rain*). ★★★ VHS: $14.99

Barnum

(1986, 113 min, GB, Terry Hughes) *Michael Crawford, Eileen Battye.* The London theatrical production of the smash musical extravaganza is brought to video in this rousing musical starring a leaping, spinning and singing Crawford. With music by Cy Coleman ("Sweet Charity") and lyrics by Michael Stewart, the story follows the famed showman's career from his beginnings as a sideshow promoter to his co-founding of the Barnum & Bailey Circus, "The Greatest Show on Earth!" ★★★ DVD: $29.99, VHS: $29.99

Barocco

(1976, 102 min, France, André Téchiné) *Gérard Depardieu, Isabelle Adjani, Marie-France Pisier.* Depardieu and Adjani star in this frustrating noir tale of blackmail and murder. Adjani plays a young woman who convinces her ex-boxer boyfriend (Depardieu) to accept a bribe to discredit a local politician. Then the boyfriend is murdered by a hit man (also played by Depardieu). Adjani, who witnesses the murder, remembers every detail about the killer with the exception that he's a look-alike of the deceased, a fact which escapes the police, as well. It's the old, annoying Superman/Clark Kent story. Eventually and predictably, the woman reinvents the hit man as her boyfriend and they escape together. If you can get past the forced plot device of identity, *Barocco* is an acceptable thriller. (French with English subtitles) ★★ VHS: $29.99

Barry Lyndon

(1975, 184 min, GB, Stanley Kubrick) *Ryan O'Neal, Marisa Berenson, John Alcott, Patrick Magee.* Almost all of Kubrick's films are masterpieces, and this is no exception to that rule. In *Barry Lyndon*, Kubrick goes beyond the bounds of normal cinematography and uses the camera as a paintbrush and the screen as a canvas with which to tell his story through still lifes and landscapes. Adapted from Thackeray's novel, the film follows Barry Lyndon on his search for success in 18th-century England. ★★★★ DVD: $19.99, VHS: $14.99

Barry Mackenzie Holds His Own

(1974, 93 min, Australia, Bruce Beresford) *Barry Crocker, Barry Humphries, Donald Pleasence.* This zany Aussie comedy is filled with Down Under in-jokes, raunchy humor and an always unpredictable plot. Australia's Everyman (before the advent of "Crocodile" Dundee), Barry Mackenzie (Crocker), with his Aunt Edna (drag superstar Humphries), gets into all sorts of adventures, including being kidnapped to Transylvania. Fans of lowbrow, off-the-wall humor will appreciate this romp. ★★★

Barton Fink

(1991, 112 min, US, Joel Coen) *John Turturro, John Goodman, Judy Davis, Michael Lerner, Steve Buscemi, John Mahoney, Tony Shalhoub.* The Coen brothers have manufactured a mesmerizing parable on the death of innocence and the perversion of artistic integrity in the face of gross crudity and greed. Turturro is terrific as the title character, Barton Fink, an acclaimed, socially conscious New York playwright (styled after Clifford Odets) who is lured by Hollywood's false hope. While being reduced to another cog in the studio machine, he develops a strained camaraderie with Goodman, the next-door neighbor in his steam-bath hotel — it's a relationship that comes to define his California experience. Turturro and Goodman bring total credibility to otherwise fantastical characters in an exaggerated, surreal world of peeling wallpaper and oddly threatening drainpipes. ★★★½ DVD: $19.99, VHS: $9.99

B

45

BASEketball

(1998, 103 min, US, David Zucker) *Trey Parker, Matt Stone, Dian Bachar, Yasmine Bleeth, Jenny McCarthy, Robert Vaughn, Ernest Borgnine.* Parker and Stone (creators of "South Park") make their feature debut in director Zucker's silly but humorous romp — they may not invigorate the "dumb comedy" genre, but they produce a high number of funny jokes which poke fun at sports, television, and those that make both tick. Parker and Stone play the inventors of the latest sports craze — BASEketball, a combination of basketball and Home-Run Derby. As the popularity of the sport soars, our heroes fight to keep their integrity and their friendship intact. *BASEketball* doesn't have the fluid comic style of Zucker's previous gems like *Airplane!* and *The Naked Gun*, but between the slapstick, lowbrow humor and celebrity guests, there's plenty of dumb, funny bits. ★★½ DVD: $14.99, VHS: $9.99

Basic

(2003, 98 min, US, John McTiernan) *John Travolta, Connie Nielsen, Samuel L. Jackson, Giovanni Ribisi, Brian Van Holt, Taye Diggs, Harry Connick, Jr..* Another *Rashomon*-inspired, multi-perspective mystery film, *Basic* is also another gimmick twist-ending movie — but alas, to little avail. Ex-Army Ranger (and currently disgraced DEA agent) Travolta is called in by an old military acquaintance to help question the only two survivors of a Ranger mission led by tyrannical sergeant Jackson. Of course, the stories vary wildly, and Travolta and fellow interrogator Nielsen must weed out the truth from the lies. What little suspense the film musters is for naught thanks mostly to the convoluted plot, many twists, and self-defeating twist ending. ★★ DVD Letterbox: $19.99, VHS: $102.99

Basic Instinct

(1992, 127 min, US, Paul Verhoeven) *Michael Douglas, Sharon Stone, Jeanne Tripplehorn, George Dzunda, Dorothy Malone, Denis Arndt, Wayne Knight, Stephen Tobolowsky.* When it opened at movie theatres, this ultra-chic, sexually explicit thriller was surrounded by controversy. Picketed in several cities, the film raised a red flag for gays, lesbians and feminists with its shockingly "retro" stereotypes of man-hating lesbians with a "basic instinct" for murder. Basically an adolescent sex fantasy disguised as a murder mystery, the film follows Douglas as a burned-out cop who inadvisably falls in "lust" with the prime suspect in a series of brutal icepick murders, lasciviously portrayed by Stone. Verhoeven, as always, directs with a sense of style and atmosphere, but at the heart of the film is Joe Eszterhas' misanthropic screenplay. Worthy of controversy? Perhaps, but basically this is just another thriller that really doesn't cover any new ground. (A "Director's Cut" with 40 additional minutes is available, but it doesn't make it any better.) ★★ DVD Unrated Special Edition: $14.99, VHS R-Rated: $9.99

Basil

(1998, 102 min, GB, Radha Bharadwaj) *Christian Slater, Derek Jacobi, Claire Forlani, David Ross, Jared Leto.* A weak costumer, *Basil* fails on almost every level. Leto plays the son of a well-to-do aristocrat (a slumming Jacobi) who's forced to forego friends and fun to pursue his studies and uphold the family name. After his life is saved by gentlemanly rogue Slater (sporting a hilarious British accent), Leto strikes up a friendship with him and soon his outlook changes. Flat and uninvolving from the

start, the film is full of betrayals, twists and Gothic trappings, but the execution is reminiscent of a high school Merchant-Ivory production. ★½ DVD: $9.99, VHS: $19.99

Basileus Quartet

(1982, 118 min, Italy, Fabio Capri) *Omero Antonutti, Pierre Malet, Hector Alterio, Michel Vitold.* When one of the elderly members of a staid classical quartet dies, he is replaced by a handsome young man. His effervescent approach to life and music proves to be both a tonic and a curse as he affects each member. A stylized drama of artistic expression, the film is sabotaged by an irresponsible portrayal of a gay quartet member. (Italian with English subtitles) ★★½

Basket Case

(1982, 91 min, US, Frank Henenlotter) *Kevin Van Hentenryck, Terri Susan Smith.* If John Waters ever makes a splatter movie, it won't be any better than this, one of independent horrordom's most cherished cult classics. A country bumpkin tries to make it in New York City while saddled with his mutant brother that he carries around Times Square in a wicker basket. Few serious filmmakers have captured the seamier side of the city better than this little gross-out gem. (Followed by two sequels) ★★★ DVD 20th Anniversary: $14.99

The Basketball Diaries

(1995, 102 min, US, Scott Kalvert) *Leonardo DiCaprio, Mark Wahlberg, Bruno Kirby, Lorraine Bracco, Ernie Hudson, Patrick McGaw, Juliette Lewis.* Jim Carroll's underground, autobiographical novel depicting his young adult years as a drug addict makes for powerful moments of anguish and alienation and gives DiCaprio solid ground to construct an impressive portrayal, but this screen adaptation falls short in its dramatic foundation. Whereas Carroll's book took place in the mid-1960s and defined a generational mindset, the story has been ill-advisedly updated to the 1990s, where counterculture ritual and spirit are at odds with MTV sensibilities. In examining the lives of streetwise teens living on the mean streets of New York, *The Basketball Diaries* covers little new ground; but Carroll's vivid perspective on camaraderie and his harrowing search for redemption are at the heart of a film whose voice is muted but aware. ★★½ DVD: $14.99

Basquiat

(1996, 108 min, US, Julian Schnabel) *Jeffrey Wright, Benicio del Toro, David Bowie, Michael Wincott, Claire Forlani, Gary Oldman, Dennis Hopper, Parker Posey, Christopher Walken, Willem Dafoe.* Wright is mesmerizing as Jean-Michael Basquiat, a poor Haitian-American graffiti artist who rapidly ascends New York's rarified art world only to lose it all to heroin addiction and an early death. While the premise of blind ambition and the price that is to be paid has been used in films many times before, this story is unusual in the depiction of the title character. For instead of a headstrong, "success or bust" personality, we see an innocent and emotionally fragile artist lured, seduced and used by others — to the point where self-destruction seems the only escape. The result is an indelible portrait of an artist as a doomed young man. ★★★½ DVD: $19.99, VHS: $9.99

Bastard Out of Carolina

(1996, 101 min, US, Anjelica Huston) *Jena Malone, Jennifer Jason Leigh, Ron Eldard, Glenne Headly, Micheal Rooker, Dermot Mulroney, Lyle*

Lovett, Grace Zabriskie. Huston delivers a solid directorial debut making optimum use of a uniformly talented cast through a story line that easily could have surrendered to bathos. Malone is a wonder as the illegitimate daughter of an illegitimate daughter growing up in 1950s South Carolina. From the casual cruelty of other children and uncaring bureaucracies to physical and sexual abuse at the hands of adults, the film delineates the financial and emotional dependence of single mothers struggling to support their families. Malone's character maintains a vibrant autonomy with the aid of a strong extended family and an unyielding if sometimes tragically misguided mother's love. Huston seems to have inherited her father's facility for revealing base human weaknesses as well as those occasional moments of triumph which elevate mundane existence and daily toil. ★★★ DVD: $24.99

Bat 21

(1988, 105 min, US, Peter Markle) *Gene Hackman, Danny Glover, Jerry Reed, David Marshall Grant.* America's awakening to the horrors of the Vietnam War is the theme of this rather routine action film elevated to prominence by Hackman's performance. Hackman stars as a desk officer, far removed from the war, who is literally plunged into a Viet Cong-infested jungle — and forced to fend for himself. Glover costars as the copter pilot assigned to rescue him. ★★½ DVD: $14.99

Batman

(1989, 126 min, US, Tim Burton) *Michael Keaton, Jack Nicholson, Kim Basinger, Robert Wuhl, Billy Dee Williams, Michael Gough, Pat Hingle, Jack Palance.* What can we say about this megahit? That it fell short of its potential; that Keaton's understated portrayal of the Caped Crusader — while challenging and daringly offbeat — was somehow flat; that Basinger's Vicky Vale plays far too great a role; that we couldn't understand why Williams was all but written out of the picture; and finally that the film's finale appears to have been scraped together in the midst of the writers' strike. We could say all that, but you probably wouldn't believe us anyway. Nicholson's Joker is astounding: Jack, we love ya, and you deserve every penny — it's your movie, babe. (Sequel: *Batman Returns*) ★★½ DVD: $19.99, VHS Pan & Scan: $9.99, VHS Letterbox: $9.99

Batman & Robin

(1997, 125 min, US, Joel Schumacher) *George Clooney, Chris O'Donnell, Arnold Schwarzenegger, Uma Thurman, Alicia Silverstone, Michael Gough, Pat Hingle, John Glover.* Clooney becomes the third actor to don the mask and cape in this star-filled, flashy, megabudget testament to Hollywood gloss. This time, Batman and his Boy Wonder Robin (O'Donnell) are up against a truly titanic villain: the blue-faced Mr. Freeze (Schwarzenegger). Thurman also headlines as Poison Ivy, a nebbishy chemist transformed into a maniacal supervillain through a scientific accident. While more substantial dramatically than its predecessor, it nevertheless succumbs to a problem that has plagued all the sequels: it focuses too little on its hero. Clooney is relegated to under ten minutes of screen time as Bruce Wayne, and his scenes as Batman almost all involve him playing second fiddle to the villains or to Robin and their new partner Batgirl. At least the extravagant sets and shiny costumes look good. (Sequel: *Batman Begins*) ★★½ DVD Letterbox: $19.99, VHS Pan & Scan: $9.99, VHS Letterbox: $9.99

B

Claws and hisses to Halle: Michelle Pfeiffer laps up her Catwoman role like a bowl of warm milk in Tim Burton's *Batman Returns*

Batman Forever

(1995, 121 min, US, Joel Schumacher) *Val Kilmer, Jim Carrey, Tommy Lee Jones, Chris O'Donnell, Nicole Kidman, Drew Barrymore, Michael Gough, Pat Hingle, Debi Mazar.* Kilmer replaces Michael Keaton in the title role and breathes some depth of character into a role made far too enigmatic by his predecessor. As in the previous two episodes, the plot is mostly incidental filler that sets up outrageous pyrotechnical action sequences. But hey, the name of the game here is Gothic atmosphere, special effects and action, action and more action; and in this arena *Batman Forever* does not disappoint. O'Donnell is an orphaned circus performer who transforms himself into Robin. As for the villains, Carrey offers a spectacularly rubber-faced and over-the-top interpretation of The Riddler which overshadows Jones' Two-Face. Kidman has a throwaway role as a criminal psychologist who tries to probe the depths of Bruce Wayne's psyche — as well as some parts of his anatomy. (Sequel: *Batman & Robin*) ★★★ DVD Letterbox: $19.99, VHS Pan & Scan: $9.99, VHS Letterbox: $9.99

Batman Returns

(1992, 126 min, US, Tim Burton) *Michael Keaton, Michelle Pfeiffer, Danny DeVito, Christopher Walken, Michael Murphy, Michael Gough, Pat Hingle, Paul Reubens, Jan Hooks.* Burton's follow-up to 1989's box-office megahit is a more entertaining foray into the shadowy world of Gotham City and the Caped Crusader. As in the original film, Keaton's brooding and gloomy Batman/Bruce Wayne character takes a back seat to the story's vivacious villains — here Pfeiffer as Catwoman and DeVito as The Penguin. Pfeiffer shines as the furtive feline antihero, and DeVito ably fills the shoes of Burgess Meredith with his demented Dickensian take on the grotesquely deformed Penguin. The screenplay, penned by *Heathers* writer Daniel Waters, provides a far more interesting spin than the original through its parable of urban decay and political corruption. (Sequel: *Batman Forever*) ★★★ DVD Letterbox: $19.99, VHS Pan & Scan: $9.99, VHS Letterbox: $9.99

Batman: The Movie

(1966, 105 min, US, Leslie Martinson) *Adam West, Burt Ward, Burgess Meredith, Cesar Romero, Frank Gorshin, Lee Meriwether, Alan Napier, Neil Hamilton.* Before Keaton and Nicholson came on the scene, there was West and Ward as the crime-fighting Dynamic Duo (you only get one crime fighter with Keaton). All-out camp. The Joker, The Penguin, Catwoman and The Riddler battle the Caped Crusader and the Boy Wonder. ★★½ DVD: $9.99, VHS: $9.99

Baton Rouge

(1988, 94 min, Spain, Rafael Moleon) *Antonio Banderas, Victoria Abril, Carmen Maura.* In this smarmy psychological thriller, a late-night encounter between prowling gigolo Banderas and monied neurotic Abril leads to double cross and murder. The socialite's recurring nightmares of rape by an unknown assailant lead her to seek help from psychologist Maura. Maura's ensuing involvement with Banderas and the lure of Abril's supposed wealth are the catalysts for plot and counterplot. (Spanish with English subtitles) ★★

Bats

(1999, 91 min, US, Louis Morneau) *Lou Diamond Phillips, Dina Meyer, Leon, Carlos Jacott, Bob Gunton.* Genetically altered bats have been unleashed by a deranged scientist and they're attacking a small Texas town. Phillips is the town sheriff and Meyer (who is about as convincing as Saffron Burrows in *Deep Blue Sea*) is the biologist who team to combat the little pesky critters. The dialogue is right out of a bad '50s sci-fi opus, though there's enough mayhem and blood to satisfy horror geeks with low expectations. ★★ DVD Special Edition: $9.99, VHS: $9.99

*batteries not included

(1987, 106 min, US, Matthew Robbins) *Jessica Tandy, Hume Cronyn, Frank McRae, Elizabeth Peña, Dennis Boutsikaris.* Sentimental sci-fi tale about tiny alien creatures who come to the aid of a group of tenants whose building is marked for demolition. Husband and wife Cronyn and Tandy give it more class than what's up on the screen. ★★½ DVD: $14.99, VHS: $7.49

Battle Angel

(1993, 70 min, Japan, Hiroshi Fukutomi) Based on the long-running *manga* by writer/illustrator Yukito Kishiro, this animated feature is a faithful adaptation of the artist's original work. Known as *Gunnm* in Japan, *Battle Angel* is actually two short episodic films: "Gunnm — Rusty Angel" and "Gunnm — Tears Sign." Tersely directed by Fukutomi, the story line follows the exploits of a female bounty hunter cyborg, Gally, and her numerous battles with the violent denizens of the futuristic Scrap Iron City. Fluid animation, memorable character designs, and an exciting science-fiction setting make this essential viewing for anime fans. (Japanese with English subtitles) ★★★½ VHS: $34.99

Battle Beyond the Stars

(1980, 102 min, US, Jimmy T. Murakami) *Richard Thomas, John Saxon, Robert Vaughn.* John Sayles wrote the script for this entertaining sci-fi quickie produced by Roger Corman about intergalactic soldiers of fortune coming to the rescue to save the planet Akira. ★★★ DVD: $19.99, VHS: $14.99

Battle Cry

(1955, 149 min, US, Raoul Walsh) *Van Heflin, Aldo Ray, Mona Freeman, Nancy Olson, James Whitmore, Raymond Massey, Tab Hunter, Dorothy Malone, Anne Francis.* Leon Uris adapted his mammoth best-seller about a group of Marines during WWII. Director Walsh brings an epic feel to this involving tale of Marines training for battle, finding love, and eventually seeing action overseas. Among a terrific cast, Ray stands out as a tough soldier. Though much of the book's violence and salty language was toned down by the censors, this still packs a punch. ★★★ DVD: $19.99

Battle for the Planet of the Apes

(1973, 89 min, US, J. Lee Thompson) *Roddy McDowall, Claude Akins, Natalie Trundy, Lew Ayres, Paul Williams, John Huston.* The fifth and final entry in the *Planet of the Apes* series finds the apes and man warring for control of the planet. The series long ago lost its charm, and this last episode is for die-hard fans only. ★★

Battle Hymn

(1957, 108 min, US, Douglas Sirk) *Rock Hudson, Martha Hyer, Anna Kashfi, Dan Duryea, Don DeFore.* Hudson offers a sensitive performance in this heartwarming true story of a minister/Air Force pilot who helps evacuate orphans during the Korean War. ★★★ DVD: $14.99

Battle of Algiers

(1965, 123 min, Algeria, Gillo Pontecorvo) *Yacef Saadi, Jean Martin.* Director Pontecorvo brilliantly re-creates the street riots and other events that led up to Algeria's independence from France in this astonishingly realistic movie masterpiece. Pontecorvo's triumph includes his sympathetic handling of both sides of the agonizing, brutal struggle for independence. The cast of superbly used nonprofessional actors and the director's technical ability to create newsreel-like authenticity combine to make this a legendary film. (French with English subtitles) ★★★★

The Battle of Austerlitz

(1960, 175 min, France/Italy, Abel Gance) *Orson Welles, Jack Palance, Claudia Cardinale, Jean-Louis Trintignant.* This is a recently restored, full-length version of Gance's grand re-creation of Napoleon's most important battle. An epic, lavish production that features an international cast. Unbelievably, the film was originally shown in a 73-minute version. (French with English subtitles) ★★★½

Battle of Britain

(1969, 132 min, GB, Guy Hamilton) *Michael Caine, Laurence Olivier, Trevor Howard, Christopher Plummer, Michael Redgrave, Ralph Richardson, Robert Shaw, Kenneth More, Susannah York.* One of those WWII epics that probably cost more than the actual war effort. The action follows a stalwart group of RAF pilots who battle an invading Nazi air unit. There's lots of air battles, and the film has a cast of thousands — well, hundreds and hundreds — headed up by half the known thespians in England. There's good special effects and extremely well-staged battle sequences, but the story treads on familiar war-movie ground. ★★

The Battle of Shaker Heights

(2003, 79 min, US, Efram Potelle & Kyle Rankin) *Shia LaBeouf, Amy Smart, Elden Henson.* A cynical, Holden Caulfield-esque high school student braves the raging battlefield of adolescence in the result of the second installment of HBO's Affleck-Damon produced "Project Greenlight" series. Kelly and his new friend Bart are polar opposites in most ways, excluding their passion for WWII reenactments. When a jock bully enrages Kelly to the point of retaliation, he and Bart execute a somewhat absurd attack upon the offender. Adding to the protagonist's woes are a troubled home life, an unattainable crush, and an uncertain future. *The Battle of Shaker Heights,* while worth watching for its wit and sensitivity to the struggles of a misfit youth, is true on most levels to its amateur roots. ★★½ DVD: $29.99, VHS: $102.99

Battle Royale

(2000, 114 min, Japan, Kinji Fukasaku) *Tatsuya Fujiwara, Aki Maeda, Taro Yamamoto, Takeshi Kitano.* A middle-school class is ostensibly taken on a field trip; unfortunately, when they arrive, they discover they're to fight each other to the death on an uninhabited island, until only one of them is left alive. The rules are laid out by their teacher (the frightening and funny Kitano): they each receive a weapon (ranging from rifles to pot lids!) and are each fitted with explosive necklaces that will detonate if they try to run, or if there is more than one student alive after 72 hours. This sick, incendiary satire would *never* have been made (or widely shown) in the U.S., especially after Columbine. But while there are some big (if very cynical) laughs, and the film is an exciting entertainment, this isn't exploitation; elder director Fukasaku (whose last complete feature this was) based the tone of the film on his WWII experiences as a child, and there's a real rage beneath the surface. Also, while *Battle Royale's* extreme violence is certainly over-the-top, the kids react in realistic ways; there are no mini-Rambos or La Femme Nikitas on hand. Fukasaku has made a minor masterpiece here. (Japanese with English subtitles) ★★★½

Battlefield Earth

(2000, 117 min, US, Roger Christian) *John Travolta, Barry Pepper, Forest Whitaker, Kim Coates, Richard Tyson, Kelly Preston.* Travolta conceived and produced this sci-fi dud, based on the thinly veiled Scientology manifesto by L. Ron Hubbard. Travolta also takes the vanity spot, starring as the arrogant leader of an alien race who've invaded Earth with the intent to strip-mine the planet dry. He's stunningly bad. Costar Pepper makes for a likable hero, the reluctant leader of a scraggly band of rebels living in the wasteland. Decent visual effects are undercut by a decrepit production design, arrhythmic editing and murky cinematography. This is disjointed, tedious and every bit as bad as its reputation. We saw it so you don't *have* to, but if you're up for a dare . . . .★ DVD: $14.99, VHS: $9.99

Battleground

(1949, 118 min, US, William Wellman) *Van Johnson, John Hodiak, Ricardo Montalban, George Murphy, James Whitmore.* Despite some of the clichés and stock characters, this well-produced, evocative WWII film about courageous American G.I.s caught up in the Battle of the Bulge still manages to be quite moving and often exciting. Suggested by screenwriter Robert Pirosh's (who won an Oscar for this script) own wartime experiences. Among the credible cast, Whitmore excels as a gruff sergeant. A Best Picture nominee. ★★★ DVD: $19.99

Battleship Potemkin

(1925, 74 min, USSR, Sergei Eisenstein) *Alexander Antonov, Vladimir Barsky.* This gripping account of the revolt by the crew of the *Potemkin* and their part in the Revolution of 1905 is a landmark film for its groundbreaking use of editing and montage. The rebellion, the support for it by the people of Odessa and the ensuing attack by Cossack troops still excite and overwhelm audiences today. (Silent with a musical soundtrack) ★★★★ DVD: $24.99, VHS: $19.99

The Bawdy Adventures of Tom Jones

(1976, 94 min, GB, Cliff Owen) *Trevor Howard, Joan Collins, Terry-Thomas.* Based on the London stage musical, this mildly amusing version of Henry Fielding's tale has its moments, but it can't hold a candle to Tony Richardson's classic. The cast fails to elevate the film above its mediocre status. ★★ VHS: $59.99

Baxter

(1989, 85 min, France, Jérôme Boivin) *Lise Delamare, Jean Mercure.* This maliciously dark French comedy is told primarily from the point of view of a misanthropic bull terrier who gets bounced around to a series of different masters. Starting in the kennel, he is originally given as a present to the dowdy old mother of the pound owner's wife. But fate (or is it?) intervenes and he winds up with the sex-obsessed couple next door, and then a sadistic young boy. Peppered with wry narration from the twisted mind of this pesky canine, the film points to the vicious behavior of humans and pets alike in this dog-eat-dog world. (French with English subtitles) ★★★

The Bay Boy

(1985, 107 min, Canada, Daniel Petrie) *Kiefer Sutherland, Liv Ullman.* A well-meaning but predictable coming-of-age drama set in 1930s Nova Scotia. Sutherland plays an awkward 16-year-old who is eager to be initiated into the rites of manhood, although opportunities are limited in the dismal mining town in which he and his mother (Ullmann) live. Attractively photographed, the film falls flat when dealing with the well-trodden theme of adolescent angst. ★★ VHS: $79.99

The Beach

(1999, 119 min, US, Danny Boyle) *Leonardo DiCaprio, Robert Carlyle, Tilda Swinton, Virginia Ledoyen, Guillaume Canet.* Beautiful tropical scenery and a back-to-nature theme aren't enough to sustain interest in this picturesque though water-logged parable of one young man's search for paradise. DiCaprio stars as an American traveling through Asia searching for adventure. He finds it when he learns of a lush and very private island. It has a gorgeous beach, perfect weather, bountiful forest, and is already inhabited not only by gun-toting natives, but a secretive commune as well. The moral of the evils of civilization is played with a heavy hand here, though it is conveyed under the most attractive circumstances. At least the cast takes this seriously, which is more than most viewers will be able to do. ★★ DVD: $14.99, VHS: $6.99

Beach Blanket Bingo

(1965, 96 min, US, William Asher) *Frankie Avalon, Annette Funicello, Paul Lynde, Don Rickles.* Though not exactly Preston Sturges or Billy Wilder, this playful '60s beach movie is probably the best of the series. Frankie Avalon and Annette Funicello and the rest of the gang get involved with mermaids and kidnappers. ★★½ DVD: $14.99, VHS: $7.99

Beaches

(1988, 123 min, US, Garry Marshall) *Bette Midler, Barbara Hershey, John Heard, Spalding Gray, Lainie Kazan, Mayim Bialik.* An effective though familiar tearjerker which follows the friendship — and its ups and downs — of two women through the years. Midler is dynamic, giving one of her patented larger-than-life performances as a singer/actress determined to make it in show business. Hershey, new lips and all, is slightly eclipsed in Midler's shadow, but nicely essays the role of an upper-class attorney beset by personal misfortunes. Get out the hankies for this one. ★★½ DVD: $19.99, VHS: $9.99

Bean

(1997, 90 min, GB, Mel Smith) *Rowan Atkinson, Peter MacNicol, Pamela Reed, Harris Yulin, Burt Reynolds, John Mills.* Atkinson's lovable mischief maker Mr. Bean makes a rather inauspicious theatrical debut. On the TV, Mr. Bean performs his hilarious and crazy antics in small set pieces, vignettes not really tied together by plot. This is possibly why they work so well. In a film stretched to 90 minutes and bound somewhat by narrative structure, only occasionally is Atkinson allowed to really let loose. The story has to do with Bean being sent by the British Museum as a guest speaker for a Los Angeles art museum. The writers seem content on snot and toilet humor, and these jokes fall flat. However, when not borrowing some TV gags (including the funny turkey bit), Atkinson does provide many a laugh when aiming his sights higher than the belt line. ★★½

Rowan Atkinson as Mr. *Bean*

The Bear

(1989, 95 min, France, Jean-Jacques Annaud) *Tchéky Karyo.* Some people steered clear of this wildlife adventure story about an orphaned bear cub on the assumption that it would be "too cute." On a certain level, they would have been right, but what a shame to miss this spectacularly photographed and brilliantly directed tale about the cruelty and the compassion of nature and man. Filmed in the dazzling peaks of the Dolomite Mountain range (a part of the Alps that stretches from Austria to northern Italy), the film tells the story of a young cub who, upon being orphaned, wanders aimlessly until one day he meets up with a massive male grizzly. Together they flee the sights of a group of tenacious hunters who have it out for the big bear. ★★★½ DVD: $9.99

The Beast

(1988, 109 min, US, Kevin Reynolds) *Jason Patric, George Dzundza, Steven Bauer, Stephen Baldwin.* Set in Afghanistan during the Soviet occupation, this suspenseful war adventure follows a Russian tank crew's fight for survival when a group of Afghan civilians seek vengeance for their small village's brutal destruction. As the citizens are able to demobilize the monster tank, its crew must battle their sadistic commander as well as the Afghans, while struggling with the moral dilemma of war. Patric plays an idealistic soldier, and Dzundza is very effective as the maniacal chief. ★★★½ DVD: $29.99

The Beast from 20,000 Fathoms

(1953, 80 min, US, Eugene Lourie) *Paul Christian, Paula Raymond, Cecil Kelloway.* Based on a short story by Ray Bradbury, this sci-fi favorite features nifty special effects by F/X master Ray Harryhausen. One of the first films to warn of the dangers of atomic bomb testings (the '50s tell us they would unleash some horrible monster or another), a giant beast (a prehistoric rhedosaurus to be exact) goes for a swim after its atomic wake-up call and decides to munch on the Big Apple. The Coney Island roller coaster proves to be too much for it, however. ★★★ DVD: $19.99, VHS: $14.99

The Beast with Five Fingers

(1947, 89 min, US, Robert Florey) *Robert Alda, Peter Lorre, J. Carrol Naish.* A heavily atmospheric chiller about the severed hand of a dead pianist that may be murdering the pianist's squabbling inheritors during their stay at his shadowy old mansion in Italy. Despite its lurid title, the film is actually a reasonably intelligent exploration of madness and superstition with smart performances. Fine special effects and a good musical score contribute to the film's success, but its real highlight is Florey's use of the camera. The only major problem with the film is a goofy coda tacked onto its end, that effectively ridicules any supernatural element it may have contained. ★★★ VHS: $19.99

The Beast Within

(1982, 90 min, US, Philippe Mora) *Ronny Cox, Meshach Taylor.* A woman is raped by a large demon-like creature with very hairy legs and gives birth to — you guessed it — a Jekyll and Hyde-like boy who transforms himself when he gets upset. This Hulk-like tale goes absolutely nowhere. Some interesting gore effects, including a sputtering decapitation scene, won't satisfy even die-hard slasher film fans. ★ DVD Letterbox: $14.99

Beat

(1999, 93 min, US, Gary Walkow) *Kiefer Sutherland, Courtney Love, Ron Livingston, Norman Reedus, Daniel Martinez, Kyle Secor.* The early years of the Beats is told in this stylish drama. The story focuses primarily on the tangled relationships between William S. Burroughs, his wife Joan, a young Allen Ginsberg and Lucien Carr, a handsome rogue and eventual muse for several of them. It's the early 1950s in Mexico City. While our beloved junkie Burroughs (wonderfully played by a sonorous, deep-voiced, suit-and-tie-wearing Sutherland) is off on holiday with an indifferent male love, his Benzedrine-addicted wife Joan (Love) decides to take off on her own. Soon she is on the road with Ginsberg (Livingston) and Carr (Reedus) to visit a dormant volcano – a journey filled with feelings of longing, jealousy, misplaced love and creative urges. Though the film is picturesque when it should be grimy, it's nevertheless jazzy and evocative, capturing a long-gone world. ★★★ DVD Letterbox: $24.99

Beat Girl

(1960, 90 min, GB, Edmond T. Greville) *Gillian Hills, David Farrar, Christopher Lee, Noelle Adam, Oliver Reed.* Hills plays Jennifer, a spoiled rich girl who hates her buxom French stepmother (the atrocious Adam) and spends the movie trying to get her egoistic father (Farrar) back all to herself. She escapes to be with the beatniks at the art school, and checks out the strip club to dig up some dirt on her new stepmom. Jennifer's severe unlikability, and some genuine sympathy for the woman she's smearing, work against the film's campy tendencies. Plenty of fun still exists, including Reed's poor singing/guitar-synching as the plaid shirt called "Plaid Shirt." The crisp b&w cinematography and John Barry's strong score lend a hint of class to this fabulous and fresh bad-girl movie. (aka: *Wild for Kicks*) ★★★ VHS: $19.99

Beat the Devil

(1954, 92 min, US, John Huston) *Humphrey Bogart, Gina Lollabrigida, Jennifer Jones, Peter Lorre, Robert Morley.* This offbeat black comedy left audiences in a daze when first released. Reportedly, the filming began without a finished script, forcing Huston and a young Truman Capote to collaborate daily before shooting and allowing the actors to ad-lib many scenes. The result is a zany spoof of spy thrillers dealing with a gang of international crooks concocting a uranium swindle. Not to be missed. ★★★½

Béatrice

(1987, 132 min, France, Bertrand Tavernier) *Julie Delpy, Berbard Pierre Donnadieu, Nils Tavernier.* Tavernier's somber exploration of medieval life abandons many of the traditional myths and instead concentrates on the dark side of human nature: infidelity, jealousy, humiliation, hatred, incest and murder. François, as a child, killed his mother's lover. He returns from war 25 years later, tormented by his hatred of women, only to be greeted at his castle by his loving and beautiful daughter, Béatrice. Having faithfully awaited her father's return, her love turns to defiance and repulsion as her increasingly demented father turns to incest. A compelling mood piece. (French with English subtitles) (aka: *The Passion of Béatrice*) ★★★

Beau Geste

(1939, 114 min, US, William Wellman) *Gary Cooper, Brian Donlevy, Susan Hayward, Robert Preston, Ray Milland.* Part of the 1939 wave of some of the greatest films in American history, this sweeping — and superlative — version of P.C. Wren's romantic novel is every bit as exciting and moving as you would think. A strong and courageous Cooper stars as the title character, with an Oscar-nominated Donlevy as the sadistic sergeant. In essence the story of a missing gem, a debt of honor and of savagery in the Foreign Legion, this beautifully shot epic still stirs the soul. Remake of the Ronald Colman 1926 silent classic; an inferior version followed in 1966. ★★★½

Le Beau Marriage (A Good Marriage)

(1982, 100 min, France, Eric Rohmer) *Béatrice Romand, André Dussollier, Féodor Atkine, Arielle Dombasle.* Rohmer continues his series of "Comedies and Proverbs" with this witty and engaging story of a young student's attempts to snare the perfect man and a "good marriage." An insightful comedy of logic and love in modern Paris. (French with English subtitles) ★★★ DVD: $29.99, VHS: $19.99

Le Beau Serge

(1958, 110 min, France, Claude Chabrol) *Jean-Claude Brialy, Gérard Blain.* Chabrol's first feature film is about a young man who leaves the city to go back to the village of his youth in an attempt to rehabilitate a childhood friend, now a drunkard living in squalor. A deeply felt drama that explores male friendship and commitment. (French with English subtitles) ★★★

Beau Travail

(1999, 90 min, France, Claire Denis) *Denis Lavant, Michel Subor, Grégoire Colin, Richard Courcet.* We have heard tales of the French Foreign Legion and their exploits in many a film, but none of them have been as sensuous as this homoerotic entry. A small troop of soldiers is stationed in the East African enclave of Djibouti. Sergeant Galoup (Lavant) rules the men with an iron fist. If one man steps out of line, he is punished by this fierce and unpleasant loner. When a charismatic new recruit (Colin) arrives, Galoup becomes consumed by jealousy, leading to tragic consequences. Though the story line is sparse, Denis' visuals are hypnotic, creating a cinematic poem to masculinity. Ultimately, *Beau Travail* is a journey into a world of male rituals, codes and an always simmering sexuality and anger. (French with English subtitles) ★★★ DVD: $29.99, VHS: $29.99

Beaumarchais, the Scoundrel

(1997, 100 min, France, Edouard Molinaro) *Fabrice Luchini, Sandrine Kiberlain, Michel Serrault, Michel Piccoli.* Depicting how the celebrated playwright of "The Barber of Seville" and "The Marriage of Figaro" ultimately prompted the French Revolution, *Beaumarchais, the Scoundrel*, set in 1773 France, is a lavishly mounted series of episodes of dangerous political and sexual liaisons. Director Molinaro has crafted a striking portrait of this notable and fascinating figure, but the film will appeal mostly to viewers fond of costume dramas, or the historic period in question. It is a well-made and well-acted drama, sprinkled with rapier wit, a bit of swashbuckling, and moments of international intrigue. (French with English subtitles) ★★★ VHS: $19.99

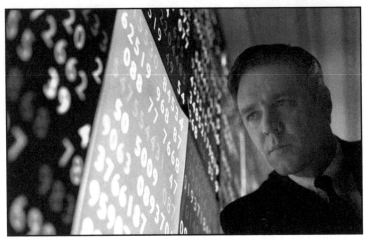

Russell Crowe in *A Beautiful Mind*

The Beautician and the Beast

(1997, 107 min, US, Ken Kwapis) *Fran Drescher, Timothy Dalton, Ian McNeice, Michael Lerner, Patrick Malahide.* Drescher stars as Joy Miller, a Brooklyn beautician who is mistakenly hired to be the teacher and nanny for the gaggle of children of a dictator (Dalton) of a ficticious Eastern block country. Before you can say Maria Von Trapp, the perky Joy whips the kids into shape, and soon her abrasive charm is taming the beastly ruler as well. Highly obvious take on *The King and I* is spotty but can be quite enjoyable, with Drescher in snappy comic form, even though she basically plays the same sort of grating, so-irritating-she's-adorable wench she played on TV's "The Nanny." ★★½ DVD: $14.99, VHS: $9.99

Beautiful

(2000, 112 min, US, Sally Field) *Minnie Driver, Hallie Kate Eisenberg, Joey Lauren Adams, Kathleen Turner.* Field makes an unimpressive directorial debut with this poorly written comedy about beauty pageant contestants and the lengths one of them will go to win. The foibles of back-stabbing entrants and behind-the-scenes tomfoolery have already been told with humor and style in the winning *Smile*, but here they're excruciating. The biggest offense is the main character, Mona (Driver). She's selfish, self-serving and mean; fine traits had this been a black comedy, but as written by Jon Bernstein, it's all meant to be heartwarming. Heartburning is more like it. Add a sorry subplot about Mona looking after a soccer-loving girl, and this is truly one huge mess of a film. ★ DVD: $14.99, VHS: $9.99

The Beautiful Blonde
from Bashful Bend

(1949, 77 min, US, Preston Sturges) *Betty Grable, Rudy Vallee, Cesar Romero.* Old West dance-hall chanteuse and eagle-eye sharpshooter Grable skips town after shooting a federal judge — Twice! Accidentally! — and poses as a schoolmarm. A minor though entertaining Sturges spoof. ★★½ VHS: $19.99

Beautiful Dreamers

(1990, 108 min, Canada, John Harrison) *Rip Torn, Colm Feore, Sheila McCarthy.* Torn stars as Walt Whitman in this touching drama in which he befriends the superintendent of a Canadian insane asylum. Their friendship results in the young doctor challenging the beliefs and practices of his profession as he tries to put a more human face on the psychiatry of the late 1800s. The film portrays the conflict between the Christian-based hierarchy of the day and the nascent humanism represented by Whitman — it's a struggle which, it could be argued, is still with us. Torn puts in another strong performance as the free-thinking poet. ★★★

Beautiful Girls

(1996, 114 min, US, Ted Demme) *Timothy Hutton, Matt Dillon, Mira Sorvino, Michael Rapaport, Natalie Portman, Rosie O'Donnell, Max Perlich, Lauren Holly, Martha Plimpton.* A good cast gives it their best shot in this rambling comedy-drama about young adults coming dangerously close to settling into the grooves that could carry them through the rest of their lives. The problem here is that, despite a rich portrayal of life in a small, blue-collar town, screenwriter Scott Rosenberg has no compelling narrative to offer. The film is a collection of subplots which feature a smattering of nice moments (the near romance of thirtysomething Hutton and 13-year-old Portman — who gives the film's best performance) and speeches (O'Donnell's "anatomy of a supermodel" speech) that are, for the most part, totally out of place in the movie and the characters. ★★ DVD: $14.99, VHS: $9.99

A Beautiful Mind

(2001, 136 min, US, Ron Howard) *Russell Crowe, Jennifer Connelly, Ed Harris, Paul Bettany, Christopher Plummer, Judd Hirsch, Adam Goldberg.* It is a difficult task to accurately portray mental illness on-screen, for the temptation to over-dramatize or simplify is inherent by the very nature of its subject. What an achievement, then, director Howard and actor Crowe have managed in *A Beautiful Mind*, the brilliantly realized true story of John Nash, Jr., a mathematical genius who suffered from paranoid schizophrenia but went on to win the Nobel Prize. Howard cleverly uses Nash's reality for narrative, and as the story progresses, it's soon clear that all is not what it appears to be. This unique perspective then becomes just another facet to a fascinating biographical tale, one that traces Nash's troubled life from his entrance to Princeton University to his graduate years to working as a code breaker for the CIA. Crowe is extraordinary as Nash, giving a multilayered portrait of a most intriguing, distinctive personality. Like Nash himself, *A Beautiful Mind* is a thrilling swirl of emotions and contradictions befitting a madman and genius, all at once compelling, defiant and unpredictable. Winner of 4 Academy Awards, including Best Picture. ★★★★ DVD Letterbox 2-disc set: $14.99, DVD Pan & Scan 2-disc set: $14.99, VHS Awards Edition: $9.99

Beautiful People

(2000, 100 min, GB, Jasmin Dizdar) *Rosalind Ayres, Charles Kay, Charlotte Coleman, Nicholas Farrell.* "If life works out even a tiny bit in your favor, it can be beautiful," says Dr. Mouldy (Farrell) at the end of director Dizdar's wonderful *Beautiful People*. This sentiment sums up just how moving this dark comedy about Bosnians living in London really is. Cross-cutting among a handful of characters, each dealing with various disappointments and struggles in life, Didzar has crafted a warmhearted, tender comedy-drama about how families are redefined and the horrors of war can affect people living far away from the battle lines. As a Serb and a Croat try to kill each other in a hospital ward, the daughter (Coleman) of a weathly family falls in love with a refugee looking for the meaning of "Life." The comic reversals may at times be contrived, but Didzar nevertheless manages to make them funny and touching at the same time. ★★★★ DVD: $24.99

Beautiful Thing

(1996, 90 min, GB, Hettie MacDonald) *Linda Henry, Glen Barry, Scott Neal, Tameka Empson.* This affectionate story of two teenagers' sexual coming out is an inspiring, tender, emotional tale that is sure to enthrall. Jamie (Berry) is a reserved 16-year-old, close to his pub manager mum (Henry), who prefers old Hollywood musicals to sports. His friendship with neighbor Ste (Neal), a fellow student who suffers through a troubled family life, soon develops into a sexual and eventually a loving relationship. How the two boys tentatively handle their nascent sexual drives is handled in both a fresh and surprisingly upbeat fashion. A wonderful comedy-drama and possibly the best gay coming-out film of the decade. ★★★½ DVD Widescreen: $29.99, VHS: $21.99

Beauty and the Beast

(1946, 90 min, France, Jean Cocteau) *Jean Marais, Josette Day.* This enchanting interpretation of the famous fairy tale is a sumptuous and beguiling adventure in surrealist cinema. Marais gives a moving performance as the love-stricken Beast and Day is the beautiful object of his amour. (French with English subtitles) ★★★★ DVD Criterion Collection: $39.99, VHS: $19.99

Beauty and the Beast

(1991, 85 min, US, Gary Trousdale & Kirk Wise) *Voices of: Robby Benson, Paige O'Hara, Angela Lansbury, Jerry Orbach.* The first animated film to be nominated for an Academy Award as Best Picture. Based on the classic fairy tale, Disney animators have created a masterpiece of color and scope, complete with refreshingly good humor and a captivating text. But what makes *Beauty* soar is the outstanding musical score by *Mermaid* and *Little Shop of Horrors* team Alan Menken and Howard Ashman, which has the style and brilliance of a classic Broadway musical (which it would become). A total delight for all ages. ★★★★ VHS Platinum Edition: $24.99

Beavis and Butt-head Do America

(1996, 80 min, US, Mike Judge) *Voices of: Mike Judge, Robert Stack, Cloris Leachman, Eric Bogosian, Richard Linklater.* MTV's lame-brained bad boys Beavis and Butt-head get the Hollywood feature film treatment — and while creator Judge's nasty wit is undiluted, he's unable to maintain the pace of the TV show for a feature-length film. The film begins — à la *Pee-wee's Big Adventure* — with the boys' most valuable possession (their TV, of course) being stolen. This leads them on a cross-country search, and their ever-present mission to "score." Much of the film is laugh-out-loud funny (much as you may try to stifle a giggle), with Cornholio, a dig at Congress and the terrific opening credits sequence among the highlights. But it's never quite as funny as you want it to be. Still, any film which ends with Englebert Humperdink singing "Lesbian Seagull" can't be all bad. ★★½ DVD: $14.99, VHS: $9.99

Bebe's Kids

(1992, 74 min, US, Bruce Smith) *Voices of: Jim Carrey, Robin Harris.* This adult-oriented, street-hip animated feature is based on popular characters created by Harris (*House Party*). His cartoon alter-ego is smitten with the beautiful Jamika. On their first date, she greets him with her soft-spoken son, Leon, and homegirl Bebe's hellraising spawn, who turn the couple's date at a theme park into a nightmare. Also included is the highly entertaining seven-minute animated short *Itsy Bitsy Spider*. ★★★ VHS: $14.99

Becket

(1964, 148 min, GB, Peter Glenville) *Peter O'Toole, Richard Burton, John Gielgud, Martita Hunt, Pamela Brown.* Burton and O'Toole deliver magnificent performances in this gritty adaptation of the Jean Anouilh play. Burton is the stoic and indomitable Thomas Becket, Archbishop of Canterbury, whose longstanding friendship with King Henry II (O'Toole) becomes irrevocably frayed as they stray down opposite political paths. A gripping and powerful historical exploration of the inhuman burdens of power. ★★★★ VHS: $19.99

Becky Sharp

(1935, 67 min, US, Rouben Mamoulian) *Miriam Hopkins, Frances Dee, Cedric Hardwicke.* The

Becket

first Technicolor (three-strip) film is a witty though stagey adaptation of Thackeray's "Vanity Fair" with Hopkins giving a notable Oscar-nominated performance as the social-climbing title character. (Note: This copy is in black and white, and runs 67 minutes as opposed to its original 83 minutes. It is, unfortunately, the only version available on video.) ★★★

Becoming Colette

(1992, 97 min, US/France, Danny Huston) *Klaus Maria Brandauer, Mathilda May, Virginia Madsen, Jean-Pierre Aumont.* While never quite overcoming its pedestrian handling of a potentially illuminating subject, this steamy drama is filmed in a lush, bombastic and romantic style. The story concerns the early years in the life of Sidone-Gabrielle Colette, one of France's greatest and most popular writers of the 20th century. Young Gabrielle (May) meets sweet-talking bon vivant Willy (Brandauer) and quickly sweeps him off his feet. But when Gabrielle shows him some of her writing, he publishes the work as his own. It's not until she begins a lesbain relationship with a friend that the increasingly sophisticated Gabrielle starts on her road to self-determination. Despite director Huston's heavy handling, the film is entertaining in telling the story of one woman's growth, accomplished on her own terms. ★★★ VHS: $19.99

Bed and Board

(1970, 100 min, France, François Truffaut) *Jean-Pierre Léaud, Claude Jade.* Antoine Doinel is all grown up and now married to Christine from *Stolen Kisses*. But his marriage, new child, and job selling dyed flowers is certainly no recipe for happiness, and his affair with a Japanese woman threatens to tear his life apart. Like the other Doinel films, *Bed and Board* takes the drama of love affairs and growing up and twists it into a bittersweet comedy; Léaud is, as always, incredibly charming and effective as Doinel. (French with English subtitles) ★★★ DVD: $19.99, VHS: $14.99

Bed of Roses

(1996, 87 min, US, Michael Goldenberg) *Christian Slater, Mary Stuart Masterson, Pamela Segall, Josh Brolin.* A pleasing if uneventful romantic comedy-drama, *Bed of Roses* casts Slater in another shy-boy role and Masterson as yet another neurotic romantic. Seeing her crying through her apartment window one night, Slater anonymously sends Masterson a bouquet of flowers. After much cuteness, they begin a relationship, but she's unable to fully commit. She then spends the rest of the film whining about her past and inability to love. The film sets a genuinely sweet tone as the two court and fall in love, though once they've moved in together and met the folks, the film has nowhere to go and idles till its inevitable climax. ★★½ DVD: $9.99, VHS: $9.99

Bedazzled

(1967, 107 min, GB, Stanley Donen) *Dudley Moore, Peter Cook, Eleanor Bron, Raquel Welch, Barry Humphries.* This hysterical adaptation of the Faust legend stars Cook as a mischievous Mephistopheles who grants the nebbishy Moore seven wishes in exchange for his soul. All of his wishes end in disaster for Moore who only wants his Whimpy Burger coworker (Bron) to love him. The humor is hurled about so unrelentingly and with such outrageous and inventive abandon that only the most mordant of viewers

Dudley Moore takes it all in in Bedazzled *(1967)*

won't find some cause for laughter. The screenplay by Cook provides an even better vehicle for himself and Moore than *The Wrong Box*. Welch appears as "Lust." (Remade in 2000) ★★★★ VHS: $9.99

Bedazzled

(2000, 93 min, US, Harold Ramis) *Brendan Fraser, Elizabeth Hurley, Frances O'Connor.* A lighthearted, occasionally funny remake of the 1967 Peter Cook-Dudley Moore classic comedy, with Fraser in good form as a clueless office nerd who sells his soul to the Devil (an attractive Hurley) for seven wishes. Assuming various disguises, Fraser is very appealing as the nebbishy Elliott, who — foiled by Satan at every turn — seems to never quite get what he wants. Though the script doesn't offer either Fraser or Hurley the kind of material for a knock-out comedy, Fraser's several impersonations and a breezy tempo sustained by director Ramis make this genial rather than bedazzling. ★★½ DVD Special Edition: $9.99, VHS: $9.99

The Bedford Incident

(1965, 102 min, US, James B. Harris) *Richard Widmark, Sidney Poitier, Martin Balsam, Donald Sutherland.* Widmark and Poitier give compelling performances in this exciting Cold War thriller. Widmark is a ship's captain and Poitier is a newspaper reporter who are at odds with each other when a Russian ship is discovered off the coast of Greenland. ★★★ DVD: $24.99

Bedknobs and Broomsticks

(1971, 139 min, US, Robert Stevenson) *Angela Lansbury, David Tomlinson, Roddy McDowall.* Charming live-action and animated musical fantasy from Disney. An apprentice witch (Lansbury), with the help of three children, repels Nazi invaders from her British countryside home. Music is by Richard and Robert Sherman (*Mary Poppins*), and an Oscar was won for Special Effects. ★★★ DVD: $22.99, VHS: $14.99

The Bedroom Window

(1987, 112 min, US, Curtis Hanson) *Steve Guttenberg, Elizabeth McGovern, Isabelle Huppert, Wallace Shawn.* Hitchcockian thriller, with more than a nod to *Rear Window*, stars Guttenberg as a young exec who admits to seeing an attempted murder to protect his mistress, who actually saw the crime. In doing so, he becomes the prime suspect. Clever plot twists and engaging performances elevate the sometimes obvious scenario. ★★½ DVD: $24.99, VHS: $9.99

Bedrooms & Hallways

(1998, 96 min, GB, Rose Troche) *Kevin McKidd, Tom Hollander, Hugo Weaving, James Purefoy, Simon Callow, Jennifer Ehle.* Troche's follow-up to *Go Fish* is an often hilarious comedy set in London about the tangled love affairs of a gay man. Failed romantic Leo (McKidd) is just hitting thirty. Alone and uncertain, Leo joins a men's group to bond with his fellow males and get his mind off romance. However, the latter notion didn't account for sexy straight Irishman Brendan (Purefoy). But wait . . . is Brendan straight? For that matter, is Leo? And life is never as black and white as it seems, especially after Leo and his group go on a drum-thumping, chest-banging camping retreat where a snarl of love triangles and jealousy explodes. Colorful production design, glossy production values and an energetic ensemble cast contribute to all this lightheartedness. ★★★ DVD: $29.99, VHS: $24.99

Bedtime for Bonzo

(1951, 83 min, US, Frederick de Cordova) *Ronald Reagan, Diana Lynn, Jesse White.* Reagan, later to be the leader of the Free World, plays daddy to a chimp in the interests of science. Is this where George Bush got the idea for a kinder, gentler nation? Did Ron think he was really once a scientist? We don't know. The film's kinda cute, though. ★★½

Bedtime Story

(1964, 99 min, US, Ralph Levy) *Marlon Brando, David Niven, Shirley Jones.* It's a race to the finish as con men Brando and Niven are out to outdo each other in their efforts to swindle American heiress Jones. Some good laughs, though the recent remake, *Dirty Rotten Scoundrels*, is funnier. ★★½ VHS: $14.99

Beethoven

(1936, 117 min, France, Abel Gance) *Harry Baur, Jean-Louis Barrault.* One of the pioneering masters of early French cinema, Gance had an unusually long filmmaking career that stretched over almost 60 years. His epic productions featured innovative techniques of editing and montage as well as the experimental use of music. In this symphonic epic, Baur portrays the towering musical genius as a successful but lonely and heartsick man. Restored to its full length, this melodramatic look at the life of one of history's little understood masters has been given a facelift and had its soundtrack restored. (French with English subtitles) ★★★ DVD: $24.99

Beethoven

(1992, 87 min, US, Brian Levant) *Charles Grodin, Bonnie Hunt, Dean Jones, Oliver Platt, Stanley Tucci, David Duchovny.* This congenial shaggy dog comedy holds few surprises. A runaway St. Bernard takes up residence at the middle-class home of Grodin and family. It's a comedy of errors as the big-as-life mutt creates havoc for Grodin and proves to be a canine Mary Poppins for the rest of the family. An unrecognizable Jones costars as a villainous vet, who looks suspiciously like a dastardly doc from *Marathon Man*. Preadolescent children should be entertained, though nonanimal lovers should probably avoid it. (Followed by four sequels) ★★½ VHS: $14.99

Beethoven's Nephew

(1985, 103 min, France/Germany, Paul Morrissey) *Wolfgang Reichmann, Ditmar Prinz, Jane Birkin, Nathalie Baye.* Morrissey sheds his well-deserved reputation as a sensationalistic chronicler of life on the fringe in this thoughtful and opulent story of the destructively possessive relationship between Ludwig Von Beethoven and his handsome nephew.

In a rewrite of history, Morrissey shows Beethoven in his later years as a furious and demanding "superstar" who, after winning a vicious court battle for the custody of his sister's son, becomes consumed with an insanely jealous love for the boy. The film elicits a deep sympathy for his torment without compromising the severity of his tyrannical grip on the boy's life. (Filmed in English) ★★★

Beetlejuice

(1988, 92 min, US, Tim Burton) *Michael Keaton, Geena Davis, Alec Baldwin, Winona Ryder, Catherine O'Hara, Jeffrey Jones, Sylvia Sidney, Dick Cavett, Glenn Shadix.* Dick Cavett's acting is just one of the lesser surprises in Burton's breakthrough comedy about a dead couple (Davis and Baldwin) learning how to haunt their house from mad ghoul Keaton. Similar in tone to his *Pee-wee's Big Adventure*, Burton's film sports a more comprehensive story, more outlandish special effects, another great score by Danny Elfman, plus a winning performance by Ryder. ★★★½ DVD: $19.99, VHS: $14.99

Before and After

(1996, 108 min, US, Barbet Schroeder) *Meryl Streep, Liam Neeson, Edward Furlong, Julia Weldon, Alfred Molina, John Heard, Ann Magnuson.* There's a fine sense of mystery to the opening moments of *Before and After*, an awkward drama that solemnly attempts to explore the boundaries of love and law. Parents Streep and Neeson learn their son's girlfriend is found murdered and he was the last one to be seen with her. As the father attempts to "cover up" the evidence he discovers in the garage, his mother puts her faith in her son and legal procedure. But as the story unfolds, the narrative becomes unfocused, undecided whether to be a hard-hitting exposé of community ostracism or a sappy drama of parents coming to terms with the possibility that their child has taken a life. ★★½ DVD: $19.99

Before Night Falls

(2000, 130 min, US, Julian Schnabel) *Javier Bardem, Olivier Martinez, Johnny Depp, Andrea Di Stefano, Sean Penn, Michael Wincott, Hector Babenco, Jerzy Skolimowski.* The fallout of the political oppression and institutionalized homophobia of Castro's Cuba makes for a disturbing but dazzling portrait of a writer's tragic life. Based on the

posthumously released memoir by gay Cuban poet Reinaldo Arenas, *Before Night Falls* details Arenas' life in his native country before emigrating to the United States. In a stunning performance, Bardem plays Arenas, who was born in poverty and at a young age joined Castro's revolution. In the 1960s, he attended college where he sharpened his writing skills and discovered his sexuality. Under Castro's regime, however, it became increasingly difficult for him to fully realize either, as the government began to crack down on gays and intellectuals — resulting in Arenas' imprisonment. Director Schnabel utilizes Arenas' writings through effective voiceovers to underscore the more significant times in the author's life. (In English and Spanish with English subtitles) ★★★★ DVD Letterbox: $24.99

Before Stonewall

(1985, 87 min, US, Greta Schiller) *Narrated by:, Rita Mae Brown, Harry Hay, Barbara Gittings.* This extraordinary recollection/documentary traces the evolution of the gay movement in the U.S. from the 1920s to the '60s and touches on the major milestones in the development of gay-lesbian consciousness. Aided by archival footage and memorable interviews, *Before Stonewall* vividly paints a picture of what it was like to be "in the life" during this period of repression. The pioneers of the liberation recall their experiences — from the lesbian bars in 1920s Harlem to the gay soldier's experiences in WWII to what it was like for gay blacks and Native Americans. ★★★½ DVD: $29.99, VHS: $24.99

Before Sunrise

(1995, 101 min, US, Richard Linklater) *Ethan Hawke, Julie Delpy.* A pleasant surprise about a chance encounter between two students traveling through Europe. This encounter develops into that rarest of occurrences — an enchanted commingling of mind and spirit, a gift of pure happenstance. Engaging characterizations by Hawke and Delpy and an intelligent, whimsical script capture that time of young adulthood when possibilities are unlimited and time retains the fluidity of childhood. The director makes good use of silence and empty spaces to explore how people get to know one another and, through that, themselves. Linklater has managed to create a confection which is sweet but not cloying, winsome but not silly, idealized but not artificial. ★★★ DVD: $14.99, VHS: $14.99

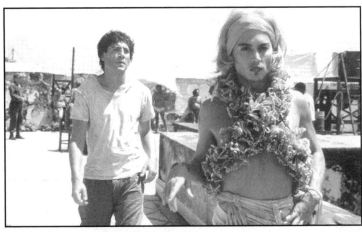

Javier Bardem and Johnny Depp in *Before Night Falls*

Before the Rain

(1994, 112 min, Macedonia, Milchio Manchevski) *Rade Serbedzija, Katrin Cartlidge.* Three interwoven stories about choices, fate and the inevitability of violence form a circle which "is not round" in this Oscar nominee for Best Foreign-Language Film. The stories focus on a young monk's relationship with an Albanian refugee; an Englishwoman's decision whether to leave her husband for a Macedonian photographer; and that photographer's return to his home village after 16 years. All of the stories converge, more or less, at the film's end, and drive home the belabored lesson that all violence is futile though inescapable. The final story, the best of the three, works on a deeper level because in it we watch the approaching storm of conflict in Macedonia through the eyes of an estranged native. Featuring gorgeous camerawork, *Before the Rain* is an interesting if obvious tale. (Macedonian with English subtitles) ★★½

Before the Revolution

(1964, 112 min, Italy, Bernardo Bertolucci) *Francesco Barilli, Adrianna Asti.* An absorbing polemic about European politics and Marxism. A young man flirts with Communism and incestuously lusts after his aunt. This potentially volatile mix of youthful idealism and unbridled desire leads him to a crisis of faith over his political ideals. (Italian with English subtitles) ★★★½

Begotten

(1989, 78 min, US, E. Elias Merhige) *Brian Salzberg, Donna Dempsey.* This disgusting nightmare vision of life as a wriggling, oozing, pus-encrusted torment is without a doubt for adventurous viewers only! The film's opening scene portrays a man (later identified as God) disemboweling himself in a river of blood; out of his corpse crawls a young maiden (later identified as Mother Earth) who proceeds to stroke the still-erect penis of the eviscerated deity and impregnate herself with his posthumous cum — get the picture? Filmed in high-contrast, grainy black and white reminiscent of the German Expressionist period, and without a scintilla of dialogue, the film is at the same time visually interesting and infuriatingly obscure. Its visceral thrills are akin to taking a peek at life in a leper colony. ★½ DVD: $29.99, VHS: $24.99

The Beguiled

(1971, 109 min, US, Don Siegel) *Clint Eastwood, Geraldine Page, Elizabeth Hartman.* Very effective and complex psychosexual Gothic chiller with Eastwood as a wounded Union soldier who is taken in by the women of a Southern girls' school, awakening the dormant sexual emotions of head mistress Page and teacher Hartman. An unusual though exceptional study of passion and jealousy, with Eastwood giving one of his best performances. ★★★½ DVD: $14.99

Behind Enemy Lines

(2001, 106 min, US, John Moore) *Gene Hackman, Owen Wilson, Gabriel Macht, Charles Malik Whitfield, David Keith.* A gung-ho (yet recently disillusioned) pilot (Wilson) is shot down in war-torn former Yugoslavia, after photographing illegal mass graves. He then spends the rest of the film running away a lot, while his paternal-yet-gruff commanding officer (Hackman) yells at his superiors and yaks into his radio, trying to save the lad. Badly shot and edited, this throwback to '80s jingoistic pap offers few thrills, and doesn't even make an attempt

Catherine Keener and John Cusack in *Being John Malkovich*

at characterization. Even with shoot-outs, jet plane action and cat-and-mouse soldiering, this isn't nearly as much fun as it could have been. Wilson looks lost throughout, and the majority of the film is sorta dull and cartoonish, with an egregiously idiotic climax that wouldn't convince the slowest five year old. ★½ DVD: $14.99, VHS: $12.99

Behind Locked Doors

(1948, 62 min, US, Budd Boetticher) *Richard Carlson, Lucille Bremer, Dickie Moore, Tor Johnson.* An obvious "inspiration" for Sam Fuller's *Shock Corridor*, this poverty-row gem is every bit as manic. When he is discovered for what he is, private detective Carlson comes to regret his latest undercover assignment: find the corrupt judge hiding in the mental hospital. Death lurks at the hands of *Plan Nine from Outer Space*'s Johnson, a crazed ex-boxer who can't forget the ring. As hard-edged as a tabloid headline, this 62-minute programmer recalls the glory days of Warner Brothers when films darted instead of moving, and hollered instead of talked. ★★★½ DVD: $29.99, VHS: $24.99

Behind the Sun

(2001, 92 min, Brazil/France/Switzerland, Walter Salles) *José Dumont, Rodrigo Santoro, Rita Assemany.* Director Salles (*Central Station*) provides a deft directorial touch to this haunting story of familial obligation, inevitable violence and the desire for something more. Salles' strong direction is complimented by Walter Carvalho's magical cinematography and fine performances by the entire cast. It is the year 1910 in the small Brazilian town of "Stream of Souls." The impoverished Breves family is locked in a blood feud with their neighbors over a land dispute in which their eldest son is murdered. Following tradition, the next eldest son (in this case, Tonho) must seek revenge. The possibility of escaping this futile cycle of inevitable violence for Tonho and his younger brother Pacu becomes possible, but not without a price. *Behind the Sun* is an uncompromising film that shows us the beauty of life and love even in the face of hardship and violence. (Portuguese with English subtitles) ★★★½ DVD: $19.99, VHS: $9.99

Being at Home with Claude

(1991, 90 min, Canada, Jean Beaudin) *Roy Dupuis, Jean-François Pichette, Gaston Lepage,* *Hugo Dubé.* Queer criminality meets romantic love in this riveting and unconventional murder mystery. Set in Montreal, this adaptation of Rene-Daniel Dubois' taut, claustrophobic play opens up the action and heightens its original dramatic force. Yves, a sexy male prostitute, is arrested for murder. Confessing to killing his lover Claude, Yves soon becomes embroiled in a harrowing interrogation which lays bare his tortured soul to the tough but strangely sympathetic cop. A fine drama that works both as a suspense thriller and an absorbing tale of gay passions and desperate love. (French with English subtitles) ★★★½

Being Human

(1994, 118 min, GB, Bill Forsyth) *Robin Williams, Kelly Hunter, John Turturro, Anna Galiena.* Williams plays a series of characters set in time periods ranging from the stone age to the new age and proves that no matter what age you live in, your life can be deathly boring — at least to those watching it on the screen. As Williams struggles dryly with daily dilemmas related to being a homo sapien, the film's unbelievably slow pace and poorly constructed episodes will give any viewer a struggle to stay awake. ★ VHS: $19.99

Being John Malkovich

(1999, 112 min, US, Spike Jonze) *John Cusack, Cameron Diaz, Catherine Keener, John Malkovich, Orson Bean, Mary Kay Place, Charlie Sheen.* Wild, dark, mysterious and, at times, uproariously funny, this profane little gem is one of the most unprecedented movies ever made. Cusack is the hapless Craig Schwartz, an immensely talented but morose puppeteer who lives in a shabby New York City apartment with his wife Lotte (an almost unrecognizable Diaz). Craig takes a menial job with a filing agency on the seventh-and-a-half floor (literally a half-floor!). While retrieving a lost file, he discovers a hidden doorway that when entered, transports people into the psyche (body?) of John Malkovich and then, after about 15 minutes, spits them out on the Jersey turnpike. Whatever twists and turns can be imagined from this odd setup cannot possibly compare with what director Jonze has in store. It's part comic romp, part fractured fairy tale and part existential howl. Special mention to Malkovich himself for being such a good sport about being "that guy in the jewel thief movie." ★★★★ DVD: $14.99, VHS: $9.99

Peter Sellers in *Being There*

Being There

(1979, 130 min, US, Hal Ashby) *Peter Sellers, Shirley MacLaine, Melvyn Douglas, Jack Warden, Richard Dysart.* A sublime satire of the TV age and American myth-making, *Being There* stars Sellers in a tour de force performance as Chance, a dim-witted gardener whose homelessness sets him on the road to the presidency. Wandering the streets of Washington, D.C., Sellers is struck by the limo of dying millionaire/power player Douglas (in a sterling Oscar-winning performance). When he's given shelter by the influential businessman, Chance's naiveté is mistaken for insight and wisdom, ultimately making him a media darling and political prospect. Jerzy Kosinski's literate and biting adaptation of his own story has been wonderfully complemented by director Ashby's marvelous pacing and his keen observations of cultural attitudes. ★★★★ DVD: $19.99, VHS: $14.99

Beirut: The Last Home Movie

(1988, 90 min, US, Jennifer Fox) This unusual documentary, set in war-torn Beirut, eschews the typical politics one would expect and instead focuses on one wealthy (and atypical) family who decide to remain in the battle-scarred city. Residing in an opulent 200-year-old palace, the Bustros family — seemingly oblivious to the dangers and destruction all around — continues their normal life undisturbed. Fiercely insular, their personal feelings, relationships and motivations in staying home become the focus of the film, the result being a humanistic approach to a subject all too accustomed to inhuman violence. Academy Award winner for Best Documentary. ★★★½

Believe

(1999, 97 min, US, Robert Tinnell) *Jan Rubes, Ricky Mabe, Elisha Cuthbert, Ben Gazzara, Andrea Martin.* Young Ben is carted from one private school to another, always getting in trouble. He has a knack for scaring his fellow students with elaborate stunts. He is finally sent to live with his rich grandfather, whom he has never met. It is there that Ben begins to see the ghostly spirit of a young woman. But is he crying wolf with more stunts, or is it real this time? This ghost story has a pleasant feel to it, and plays like a Hardy Boys-Nancy Drew tale of the supernatural. Sometimes clumsy, sometimes effective, this should definitely appeal to adolescents. ★★½ VHS: $89.99

The Believer

(2001, 99 min, US, Henry Bean) *Ryan Gosling, Summer Phoenix, Theresa Russell, Billy Zane, A.D. Miles, Joshua Harto.* With more to say about the intricacies and ironies of religion than a year's worth of sermons, *The Believer* — director Bean's jolting debut — has an astonishing energy that rarely lets up. In an impressive performance, Gosling plays Danny, a young neo-Nazi who looks to fellow skinheads and fascist groups to help him eradicate the influence of Jewish culture in the city. But Danny is actually Jewish, struggling with his identity and faith and the hatred he has developed toward those of his own religious upbringing. *The Believer* doesn't see the need to try to crack open Danny's dualistic mind to find resolution, but is more concerned with the questions of faith and their relationship to race and heritage in contemporary society. At once nomadic and staid, *The Believer* lives and breathes ideas to contemplate long after its compelling conclusion. ★★★½ DVD: $24.99

The Believers

(1987, 114 min, US, John Schlesinger) *Martin Sheen, Helen Shaver, Robert Loggia, Richard Masur, Jimmy Smits.* Suspenseful occult thriller with Sheen as a New York therapist whose counseling of a disturbed policeman leads him into a series of bizarre and gory ritual slayings. Director Schlesinger creates a chilling atmosphere as he juxtaposes a menacing New York City with the tribal rituals of the voodoo ceremony Santeria. ★★★ DVD Letterbox: $14.99

Bell, Book & Candle

(1958, 108 min, US, Richard Quine) *James Stewart, Kim Novak, Jack Lemmon, Ernie Kovacs, Hermione Gingold.* A lively cast brightens up this fun-filled adaptation of John Van Druten's Broadway comedy about an engaged publisher (Stewart) who becomes entangled with a coven of Greenwich Village witches — and lovely (and bewitching) Novak, in particular. Great support from Lemmon as a bongo-playing warlock, Gingold as a high priestess, and Kovacs as a skeptical author. ★★★ DVD: $24.99, VHS: $19.99

Belle de Jour

(1967, 100 min, France/Italy, Luis Buñuel) *Catherine Deneuve, Jean Sorel, Geneviéve Page.* Buñuel's kinky skewering of bourgeois pretensions stars a luminous Deneuve as a terminally bored doctor's wife who escapes her ennui in bizarre, masochistic sexual daydreams. These fantasies turn to reality when she lands an afternoon shift at a high-class Parisian brothel where she is given the titular alias. *Belle de Jour* is a mostly cerebral but masterful and at times giddy dialectic on sexual repression, the Church and the meaningless, philistine lives of the upper classes. As usual, Buñuel mixes fantasy, reality and flashback to the point where the viewer is pressed to wonder which is real. Deneuve is hypnotic as the wistful Belle, whose desire for sexual humiliation seems to be her only avenue for rebellion against the constraints of her social position. Page is in fine form as the Belle's madam, a lesbian who fancies the icy beauty of her newest protégé. (French with English subtitles) ★★★½ DVD Letterbox: $19.99, VHS: $14.99

Belle Epoque

(1993, 108 min, Spain, Fernando Trueba) *Fernando Fernan Gomez, Penélope Cruz, Jorge Sanz, Maribel Verdú, Ariadna Gil.* The winner of the 1993 Academy Award for Best Foreign-Language Film, *Belle Epoque* is a disarmingly gentle and comic tale of female seduction set in the Civil War-ravaged Spain of 1931. AWOL soldier Fernando (Sanz), a handsome rogue wannabe, finds brief solace, love, sex and emotional turmoil in the home of an elderly gentleman who has four beautiful and flirtatious daughters. Each woman, with a different reason for doing so, seduces the confused but eagerly accomodating young man, all under the blind eye of Papa. The sexual shenanigans continue when Mama, a traveling cabaret performer, returns with her lover in tow and, à la *Smiles of a Summer Night*, all the characters are thrown into romantic confusion. (Spanish with English subtitles) ★★★ DVD Letterbox: $29.99

La Belle Noiseuse

(1991, 240 min, France, Jacques Rivette) *Emmanuelle Béart, Michel Piccoli, Jane Birkin.* A renowned painter's ten-year hiatus comes to an end after becoming inspired by a young artist, and in particular the young artist's lover (Beart), who becomes the model for his return to the canvas. It's a slow, methodical exploration into the artistic process and the ensuing obsessions it brings for both artist and model. Rivette's brilliant direction makes this four-hour film a rich and rewarding experience. (French with English subtitles) ★★★½ DVD 2-disc set: $39.99

The Belle of Amherst

(1976, 90 min, US, Charles S. Dubin) *Julie Harris.* In 1976, Harris won a Tony Award for Best Actress for her tour-de-force performance as writer Emily Dickinson. This one-woman play on film captures the brilliance of Harris' portrayal and the lovely prose of the 19th-century poet. Set in two acts, the story covers through both imaginary conversation and bittersweet recollections the life of Dickinson. Author William Luce magically incorporates her writings into Emily's monologue to illustrate how her work commented on her life. Witty and touching, and Harris standing center stage and alone for 90 minutes is simply exhilarating. ★★★½ DVD: $29.99

The Belle of New York

(1952, 82 min, US, Charles Walters) *Fred Astaire, Vera-Ellen, Marjorie Main, Keenan Wynn, Alice Pearce.* Good dance sequences highlight this otherwise ordinary Astaire musical with Fred as a Gay '90s playboy who courts Salvation Army girl Vera-Ellen. ★★½ VHS: $19.99

Belle of the Nineties

(1934, 73 min, US, Leo McCarey) *Mae West, Roger Pryor, Johnny Mack Brown.* Only somewhat restricted by the Production Code, West is her usual bouncy, naughty self in this effervescent comedy. Mae, who also wrote the snappy screenplay, stars as a Gay '90s entertainer involved with an up-and-coming boxer (Pryor). There's treachery and deceit on their course of true love, and the boxer falls victim to a set-up. He leaves her, which sends her packing to New Orleans. But as luck has it, Pryor comes to town, but he's being set up again, unknown to Mae who is out for revenge — Mae West style. West gets to sing a couple songs, and her witty one-liners still manage to titillate. Duke Ellington and His Orchestra are featured, and wait till you see West dressed up as the Statue of Liberty. ★★★

Bellissima

(1951, 108 min, Italy, Luchino Visconti) *Anna Magnani, Tina Apicella.* With the fury of a hurricane, the magnificent Magnani plays a mother determined to get her seven-year-old daughter into the movies. When a casting call is announced for an unknown girl, hundreds of stage mothers storm the Cinecittá Studios in Rome. None, however, with the determination of the blustery Maddalena Cecconi (Magnani), a working-class wife from the tenements. When her daughter Maria (the wide-eyed Apicella) is chosen for a second call, Maddalena involves herself with a variety of show business hangers-on and con artists, all in the hopes of getting an edge. Visconti's neorealist glimpse into the absurdities of moviemaking is an intoxicating blend of observational comedy and human drama that bears the hallmarks of both Sturges and Wilder. (Italian with English subtitles) ★★★½

Bellissimo

(1987, 110 min, Italy, Gianfranco Mingozzi) This ambitious documentary sets out to encapsulate the important events, movements, stars and directors of Italy's filmmaking history during the past 40 years. Interspersing footage from many of the classics of Italian cinema with interviews from both behind and in front of the camera, the film attempts to reconstruct a detailed history of one of the world's great filmmaking centers. An invaluable aid to all students and fans of Italian filmmaking. (Italian with English subtitles) ★★★ VHS: $29.99

Bellman and True

(1988, 112 min, GB, Richard Loncraine) *Bernard Hill, Kieran O'Brien, Richard Hope.* An outstanding crime thriller that masterfully combines the exciting tale of a computer engineer caught up in an elaborate bank heist scheme and the very human drama of that man's battle for both the safety of his kidnapped son and his own personal redemption. Hill plays Hiller, who is coerced by a ruthless gang to plan and execute a daring robbery of one of England's largest banks. Director Loncraine weaves a hypnotic and rewarding tale rich in style, atmosphere and suspense. ★★★½

Bells Are Ringing

(1960, 127 min, US, Vincente Minnelli) *Judy Holliday, Dean Martin, Jean Stapleton, Eddie Foy, Jr.* A good-natured adaptation of Betty Comden and Adolph Green's hit Broadway musical with Holliday re-creating her acclaimed stage role as an answering service operator who falls in love with one of her clients (Martin). Judy is a delight in her final screen appearance. Songs include "The Party's Over" and "Just in Time." ★★★ VHS: $14.99

The Bells of St. Mary's

(1945, 126 min, US, Leo McCarey) *Ingrid Bergman, Bing Crosby, Henry Travers.* Heartwarming tale of Father O'Malley (Crosby) coming to a New York parish run by a strict Mother Superior (Bergman) where they come in conflict over how to run the school and to teach the children. Crosby repeats his Academy Award-winning role from *Going My Way.* ★★★ DVD: $14.99, VHS: $14.99

Belly

(1998, 95 min, US, Hype Williams) *Nas, DMX, Taral Hicks, Tionne "T-Boz" Watkins, Method Man.* MTV video director Williams makes an impressive debut with this brutally raw portrait of urban street life. Chart-topping rappers Nas and DMX star as best friends who soon begin to grow apart as they sink deeper into the dark and dangerous world of drug dealing. With the events unfolding in a dreamlike, trance-inducing style, *Belly* manages to actually allow the viewer to gain insight into the many characters. Some may be put off by the realistic violence, the negative portrayal of women, and the use of profanity, but these are necessary in making the characters believable. ★★★ DVD Special Edition DVD with Uncensored Music CD: $26.99, VHS: $9.99

The Belly of an Architect

(1987, 118 min, GB, Peter Greenaway) *Brian Dennehy, Chloe Webb, Lambert Wilson.* Dennehy stars as a rotund American architect who travels to Rome with wife Webb to oversee the mounting of a show honoring 18th-century French designer Boulée. As Dennehy becomes more and more obsessed with the project, his life begins to mirror that of the ill-fated Boulée, who died of a mysterious stomach ailment. For Greenaway's part, he's obsessed with Dennehy's portly midsection. The stocky actor puts in what can only be called an immense performance as Greenaway's camera explores his tummy from all angles. While visually stunning, the film is one of Greenaway's less-successful efforts. ★★½ DVD: $14.99

Beloved

(1998, 172 min, US, Jonathan Demme) *Oprah Winfrey, Danny Glover, Thandie Newton, Kimberly Elise, Beah Richards, Lisa Gay Hamilton, Irma P. Hall.* Toni Morrison's Pulitzer Prize-winning novel makes for riveting drama, but isn't as wholly successful as it could have been due to director Demme's sometimes fragmented filmmaking style. Winfrey is Sethe, an ex-slave raising her family in rural Ohio. However, their isolated tranquility is shattered when they are visited by the ghost of Sethe's long-dead child, Beloved. Her presence sets in motion the resurfacing of faded memories and buried secrets of the past, acts which were only performed to escape a life of slavery. Demme has true command over the scenes of the haunting, which are spellbinding. But the intricacies of the characters are often overshadowed by the film's stylized storytelling. He does, however, get superb performances from his cast, especially Elise as Sethe's surviving daughter Denver. ★★★ DVD: $14.99, VHS: $9.99

Below

(2002, 105 min, US, David Twohy) *Matthew Davis, Bruce Greenwood, Olivia Williams, Holt McCallany, Scott Foley, Jason Flemyng, Dexter Fletcher, Zach Galifianakis.* From the writer-director of *Pitch Black*, this sleeper should please fans of both suggestive, creepy ghost stories and WWII submarine films. A U.S. sub picks up the only three survivors of a British hospital ship that had been torpedoed by a German U-boat. When unexplained phenomena begin occurring on the sub at an alarming rate, more than a few of the crew begin to suspect they've also picked up something supernatural as well. A well-told "revenge from beyond the grave" tale is enhanced greatly by the unique (for a horror film) setting: the cold, watery, claustrophobic confines of a submarine. It all makes for an inspired variation on the haunted house genre. A deliberately paced, highly atmospheric chiller, *Below* is a cut above. ★★★ DVD: $19.99, VHS: $9.99

Ben Hur

(1926, 148 min, US, Fred Niblo) *Ramon Navarro, Francis X. Bushman, May McAvoy.* One of the great spectaculars of all times, with all the pluses and minuses inherent in the genre. The chariot race and the sea battle have rarely been equaled for sheer edge-of-your-seat excitement. A Brownlow & Gill reconstruction, with the original tinting and toning, plus the two-strip Technicolor sequence and another fabulous score by Carl Davis. ★★★½

Ben-Hur

(1959, 212 min, US, William Wyler) *Charlton Heston, Stephen Boyd, Jack Hawkins, Hugh Griffiths, Haya Harareet, Martha Scott, Sam Jaffe.* A biblical epic on a scale even the Caesars could appreciate. This tale of two friends (Heston, Boyd) who become enemies during the time of Jesus is bathed in sincerity and brimming with spectacle. Director Wyler uses all his skill with actors to even bring a human element to the production. This winner of 11 Oscars is better — and less corny — than anyone would have a right to expect. The famed chariot race remains a knockout. ★★★½ DVD Letterbox: $19.99, VHS Pan & Scan: $19.99, VHS Letterbox: $19.99

Bend It Like Beckham

(2003, 112 min, GB, Gurinder Chadha) *Parminder Nagra, Keira Knightley, Jonathan Rhys-Meyers,*

Bend It Like Beckham

Anupam Kher, Juliet Stevenson. Even for American audiences unacquainted with soccer or the absurdly popular player David Beckham (who is idolized by our heroine, along with about a billion others worldwide), this delightful coming-of-age comedy will be impossible to resist. Which is strange, since everything within is utterly familiar: overcoming obstacles on and off the field on the way to "the big game," growing pains and young loves. Nagra is absorbing in the lead, dreaming of playing soccer professionally while under the thumb of her traditional Indian parents. She's taken under the wing of the bubbly Knightley and her dreamy coach, Rhys-Meyers (chaste tension ensues). The charismatic performers weave quite a spell, while the novelty of a soccer film seemingly reinvents the clichés. The most remarkable asset is the refreshingly two-sided exploration of the conservative parents, rebellious kids and their cultural assimilation: Mom can be just as happy with her tradition as her daughter can be in English culture. Beckham appears in a cameo. ★★★ DVD Pan & Scan: $19.99, DVD: $19.99, VHS: $12.99

Bend of the River

(1952, 91 min, US, Anthony Mann) *James Stewart, Arthur Kennedy, Rock Hudson.* Robust western adventure with Stewart and Kennedy squaring off against each other during a wagon train's journey to Oregon in the mid-1800s. ★★★ DVD: $14.99, VHS: $14.99

Beneath the Planet of the Apes

(1970, 95 min, US, Ted Post) *James Franciscus, Charlton Heston, Kim Hunter, Maurice Evans.* The sequel to *Planet of the Apes* pits astronaut Franciscus against the simian inhabitants of a futuristic Earth in his search for Heston and crew. Not as satisfying as the original, but not without its entertaining moments. (Sequel: *Escape from the Planet of the Apes*) ★★½

Beneath the Valley of the Ultravixens

(1979, 93 min, US, Russ Meyer) *Kitten Natividad, Ken Kerr, Robert Pearson.* Meyer's last theatrical release once again features the hyperkinetic editing and absurdly large breasts that have been the trademarks of his singular vision. The plot, which concerns faith healing and sexual misadventures in a small California town, is really just an excuse for an endless parade of naked bodies and bad dialogue. The film is complete schlock, of course, but Meyer is in on the joke. Perverse fun. ★★½ DVD: $39.99

Benny & Joon

(1993, 98 min, US, Jeremiah Chechik) *Johnny Depp, Mary Stuart Masterson, Aidan Quinn, Julianne Moore, Oliver Platt, CCH Pounder, Dan Hedaya.* Not since *Harold and Maude* have two crazies endeared themselves so winningly as Depp and Masterson in this often hilarious, offbeat charmer. Quinn is Benny, a thoughtful garage mechanic who gallantly looks after his mentally ill sister Joon (Masterson). Into their lives steps Sam (Depp), a Buster Keaton clone whom Benny wins in a card game. Soon, Sam and Joon bring new definition to "crazy in love." The film works as comedy, romantic fable, hip character study, and even homage to the great silent clowns. As Sam, Depp is a marvel: his silent comedy schtick is uncanny, and Masterson ably captures the right mixture of waif and firebrand. ★★★½ DVD: $14.99

The Benny Goodman Story

(1955, 116 min, US, Valentine Davies) *Steve Allen, Donna Reed.* With the tremendous success of *The Glenn Miller Story*, this biography of another bigband giant was supposed to cash in on that film's popularity. Only problem — it didn't have James Stewart. Allen does his best in the title role in this Hollywood-ized look at the rise of the legendary Benny Goodman, and Reed plays the June Allyson role. A good score though. ★★½ DVD: $14.99

Bent

(1997, 104 min, GB, Sean Mathias) *Clive Owen, Lothaire Bluteau, Mick Jagger, Ian McKellen, Rupert Graves.* A striking adaptation of the stage play, *Bent* shifts its drama from the decadent gay German nightlife (which earned the film its NC-17 rating) to the horrors of a Nazi concentration camp. And yet, playwright Martin Sherman has created a moving love story out of the characters' despair. The intense passion that develops between Max (Owen) and Horst (Bluteau) is heartfelt especially considering their relationship is mental and emotional, rather than physical. However, in opening up the play for the screen, director Mathias (who directed the London stage version) cannot escape some of its theatrical trappings. Owen and Blutheau give gutsy performances, and they are ably supported by Jagger and McKellen. ★★★ DVD: $19.99

The Berlin Affair

(1986, 101 min, Italy/West Germany, Liliana Cavani) *Gudrun Landgrebe, Mio Takaki.* A searing and provocative tale of sexual obsession and domination set in 1938 where the dangerously seductive charms of a beautiful Japanese woman entraps more willing victims and takes them into the netherworld of blackmail, drugs and forbidden love. ★★★

Berlin Alexanderplatz

(1980, 940 min, West Germany, Rainer Werner Fassbinder) *Hanna Schygulla, Gunter Lamprecht, Rainer Werner Fassbinder, Barbara Sukowa.* Fassbinder's stunning 15½-hour epic is set in post-WWI Germany and continues through the birth and growth of Nazism. Simply told, it's the story of a slow-witted Berlin transit worker who, after accidentally killing his girlfriend and serving time, unwittingly becomes involved in the Berlin underworld. Originally produced for German TV, Fassbinder's masterpiece is one of the few films in our collection that probably works better on home video rather than at a theatre. (German with English subtitles) ★★★★

Berlin Express

(1948, 86 min, US, Jacques Tourneur) *Robert Ryan, Merle Oberon, Paul Lukas.* Authentic locations (filmed in the war-torn cities of Frankfurt and Berlin) heighten the realism of this taut and suspenseful spy thriller. Four train passengers, a crosssection of the Allied forces, band together with secretary Oberon to search for a German statesman — a key figure for German unification — who has been kidnapped by the Nazi underground. ★★★½

Berserk

(1967, 96 min, GB, Jim O'Connolly) *Joan Crawford, Diana Dors, Judy Geeson, Ty Hardin.* In this twisted, plodding shocker, Crawford is the owner of a British circus which is being haunted by brutal murders. Once the public gets wind of the performers' deaths, ticket sales begin to skyrocket. The police begin to investigate the strange circumstances and Joan herself. Crawford is typically overwrought in this late role. ★★

Bert Rigby, You're a Fool

(1989, 94 min, US, Carl Reiner) *Robert Lindsay, Anne Bancroft, Cathryn Bradshaw, Robbie Coltrane, Bruno Kirby.* For those who have ever uttered those infamous nine words, "They sure don't make 'em like they used to," comes this entertaining, sweetly old-fashioned though plodding musical comedy that is a 94-minute tribute to the musicals of the '50s. Lindsay gives an effervescent performance as an English coal miner who dreams of stardom and through a series of odd twists arrives in Hollywood for a chance at the brass ring. Sure, the film is too sentimental, and some scenes creak along, but it's Lindsay's performance that is the attraction here. ★★½ VHS: $14.99

Beshkempir: The Adopted Son

(1999, 81 min, Kyrgyzstan, Aktan Abdykalykov) *Mirlan Abdykalykov, Albina Imasheva, Adir Abilkassimov.* In a small village in Asiatic Russia, an infant is blessed and welcomed to Mother Earth with a ritual from the old religions. The inhabitants eke out a meager existence in what is essentially an agrarian, preindustrial society; it takes a while for the viewer to realize that the setting is present-day. Beshkempir is a young boy just at the threshold of adulthood, in his early teens, no longer a child and not yet a man . . . a tough time to find out that he is a foundling, an adopted son. The natural simplicity and unforced authenticity of the film is almost enhanced by the limited production values; the film is shot primarily in black and white, with the use of color film limited yet effective. (Kyrgyzstani with English subtitles) ★★½ DVD: $19.99, VHS: $14.99

Besieged

(1999, 95 min, Italy, Bernardo Bertolucci) *Thandie Newton, David Thewlis, Claudio Santamaria.* Shandurai (Newton), a young African woman who has just left work at a hospital ward filled with unending civilian casualties suffering war wounds, watches as her husband is dragged out of his classroom and loaded into military transport. We see her next in Rome, continuing her medical education while housekeeper for Jason (Thewlis), a reclusive pianist/composer. Believing her husband gone forever, she attempts to reestablish her life, battling the harsh memories that come to her in nightmares, and the unwelcome advances of the initially creepy, stalking Jason. Director Bertolucci seems to have added yet another wrinkle to his arsenal of cinematic tricks: a fluid camera jumps and glides; layerings of image and sound overlap, compressing and expanding time and space. A personal tale of erotic obsession, told against a backdrop of political madness. (In English and Italian with English subtitles) ★★★½ DVD: $24.99, VHS: $19.99

Best Boy

(1979, 111 min, US, Ira Wohl) This Academy Award winner follows the director's 52-year-old retarded cousin Philly as he comes to grips with his father's death, his mother's failing health and subsequent efforts to better integrate him into society. Moving yet unsentimental, Wohl has captured moments of epiphany for Philly as he realizes untapped skills and new joys such as a backstage duet with Zero Mostel singing "If I Were a Rich Man." (DVD includes sequel *Best Man*) ★★★★ DVD 2-disc set: $29.99

Best Friends

(1982, 116 min, US, Norman Jewison) *Burt Reynolds, Goldie Hawn, Jessica Tandy, Barnard Hughes, Audra Lindley, Keenan Wynn, Ron Silver.* Reynolds and Hawn star as married screenwriters

B

experiencing professional and personal ups and downs in this only sporadically amusing comedy written by Barry Levinson and Valerie Curtin. ★★ DVD Letterbox: $19.99, VHS: $19.99

Best in Show

(2000, 89 min, US, Christopher Guest) *Christopher Guest, Parker Posey, Eugene Levy, Fred Willard, Michael Hitchcock, Catherine O'Hara, John Michael Higgins, Bob Balaban, Michael McKean, Jennifer Coolidge.* In this very funny mockumentary, an eccentric group of dog owners come together for the annual Mayflower Dog Show. Director Guest nary misses a beat in capturing the absurdity of it all. Sure there are some easy targets (like Posey and Hitchcock's neurotic yuppie couple or McKean and Higgins' queeny lovers fussing over their shih tzu). And like *Guffman* not every bit works. But this is fun through and through, thanks to a plethora of laughs and wonderful characterizations. ★★★½ DVD Letterbox: $19.99, VHS Letterbox: $9.99

The Best Intentions

(1992, 183 min, Sweden, Bille August) *Pernilla August, Samuel Froler, Max von Sydow.* Ingmar Bergman wrote the screenplay for this moving epic about the lives of his parents. The story begins when a young Henrik Bergman, a poor seminarian, falls for Anna, a somewhat spoiled rich girl. Despite her mother's best efforts to derail their affections, the young lovers persist and eventually wed. Their class differences become apparent immediately, but in the end their devotion is true, and the film follows their life together for 20 years, right up to Ingmar's birth. A heartwarming love story, the film's charm is augmented by winning performances from Froler and August in the lead roles. (Swedish with English subtitles) ★★★ VHS: $49.99

The Best Little Whorehouse in Texas

(1982, 114 min, US, Colin Higgins) *Burt Reynolds, Dolly Parton, Charles Durning, Dom DeLuise, Jim Nabors.* Reynolds and Parton bring a degree of charm to this glossy but uneven adaptation of the hit Broadway musical about a Texas bordello — called the Chicken Ranch — run by Parton and under attack by a local televangelist. Burt is the sheriff caught in the middle. Durning received an Oscar nomination for his scene-stealing bit as the Governor. ★★½ DVD Letterbox: $14.99, VHS: $9.99

The Best Man

(1964, 102 min, US, Franklin J. Schaffner) *Henry Fonda, Cliff Robertson, Edie Adams, Margaret Leighton, Shelley Berman, Lee Tracy.* Outstanding adaptation of Gore Vidal's vitriolic play centering on two politicians campaigning for the presidential nomination, each trying to woo support of the party and the ailing ex-president. Robertson stars as a ruthless conservative nominee running against the idealistic Fonda. Through the course of their politicking, betrayal, blackmail and political chicanery will rear their ugly heads as Vidal rips open (years before it became fashionable) the sometimes corrupt facade of politics. Tracy is excellent as the former chief. ★★★½

The Best Man

(1999, 121 min, US, Malcolm D. Lee) *Taye Diggs, Nia Long, Morris Chestnut, Harold Perrineau, Terrence Howard. The Best Man* is an effective comedy-drama that boasts good ensemble performances and a smart script. Diggs plays an about-to-be-published author of a semiautobiographical novel that his old college friends have gotten ahold of. Through some loose lips and the thinly veiled situations in the novel, many skeletons are let out of

the closet during a weekend wedding/reunion. Though the end is a bit too pat, and things are never as intense or rich as they could be, *The Best Man* is nevertheless a solid, involving and entertaining film, with many universal dilemmas addressed. ★★★ DVD: $24.99, VHS: $9.99

Best Men

(1997, 89 min, US, Tamra Davis) *Dean Cain, Sean Patrick Flanery, Mitchell Whitfield, Luke Wilson, Fred Ward, Drew Barrymore, Andy Dick.* This offbeat comedy/crime drama — about an unlikely gang of bank robbers — falters a bit but nonetheless makes for an entertaining and quirky tale. The story revolves around five buddies who — while at one of the group's wedding — become involved in a bank robbery-turned hostage stand-off-turned media circus. The story has been seen before, but the actors and their off-center characters save the film from being just a stupid straight-to-video actioner. Cain is especially effective as a gay ex-Marine, Dick as the dorky dude who sees his macho side come out, and Ward as the frustrated sheriff. ★★½ DVD Dual: $9.99

The Best of Times

(1986, 104 min, US, Roger Spottiswoode) *Kurt Russell, Robin Williams, Pamela Reed, Holly Palance, Donald Moffat, Margaret Whitton, M. Emmet Walsh.* This disappointing comedy manages a few smiles, but considering the talent involved, there should have been more. Williams is a former high school football player who dropped the winning pass in a championship game. He stages a rematch 20 years later. Russell is his former teammate. ★★ DVD: $24.99

Best Seller

(1987, 110 min, US, John Flynn) *James Woods, Brian Dennehy, Victoria Tennant, Paul Shenar.* Woods stars as a retired hit man whose offer to collaborate with a cop-turned-author (Dennehy) on a tell-all autobiography ruffles the feathers of his wealthy ex-employer (Shenar). Powerhouse performances by Woods and Dennehy distinguish this intriguing and tightly focused thriller. ★★★ DVD Dual: $14.99

The Best Way

(1976, 85 min, France, Claude Miller) *Patrick Dewaere, Patrick Bouchitey.* A summer camp for boys is the setting for this absorbing study of the tensions and sexual attraction of two male counselors. Marc, the overly masculine sports director, discovers Philippe, the music teacher, dressed in women's clothing. His inability to deal with his repressed feeling causes him to humiliate and persecute Philippe to the point were he must deal with the truth of his actions. A fine drama on sexual identity and male friendships. (French with English subtitles) ★★★ VHS: $49.99

The Best Years of Our Lives

(1946, 172 min, US, William Wyler) *Fredric March, Myrna Loy, Dana Andrews, Teresa Wright, Virginia Mayo, Harold Russell.* A landmark war film, and immensely popular in its day, this Oscar-winning drama is a masterful examination into the lives of three WWII veterans returning home. March won the second of his two Oscars for his rich portrayal of a family man having difficulty reorienting himself to civilian life. A great cast includes Loy as his wife, Andrews in his best screen performance as a pilot haunted by his experiences, and Russell, a real-life amputee who also won an Oscar as a young soldier adjusting to life without hands. ★★★★ DVD: $14.99

La Bête Humaine

(1938, 99 min, France, Jean Renoir) *Jean Gabin, Simone Simon.* This atmospheric thriller follows the actions of a psychotic train engineer who falls for a married woman and plots to kill her husband. A dark, intense work from one of the masters of the French cinema. Based on the Emile Zola novel. (French with English subtitles) ★★★½ VHS: $19.99

Betrayal

(1988, 95 min, GB, David Jones) *Ben Kingsley, Jeremy Irons, Patricia Hodge.* Harold Pinter, in adapting his acclaimed stage production, has crafted a marvelous study of entwined lives, conflicting loyalties and emotional ambiguity that is both wickedly funny and endlessly intriguing. Kingsley and Irons are bound by their literary pursuits, their enduring friendship and their mutual involvement with Kingsley's wife (Hodge). Director Jones and writer Pinter effectively use the author's theatrical device of presenting the story's many acts backwards — thus beginning with the outcome of the characters' infidelity and then tracing the steps leading to that point. The three leads are uniformly good. ★★★★

Betrayed

(1988, 127 min, US, Constantin Costa-Gavras) *Debra Winger, Tom Berenger, John Mahoney, John Heard, Betsy Blair, Ted Levine.* Director Costa-Gavras turns his eyes on racial intolerance in this powerful but ultimately contrived thriller. Winger stars as an FBI agent who goes undercover to expose a white supremacist group responsible for a series of racially motivated murders. While its scenes of racial prejudice are all too real and emotionally devastating, the film itself is betrayed by an unbelievable romantic subplot between the agent and her prime suspect, a farmer played with chilling intensity by Berenger. ★★½ DVD: $14.99

The Betsy

(1978, 125 min, US, Daniel Petrie) *Robert Duvall, Laurence Olivier, Tommy Lee Jones, Katharine Ross, Jane Alexander, Edward Herrmann.* An all-star cast, headed by a slumming Olivier, gives varying degrees of over-the-top performances in this overwrought potboiler adapted from Harold Robbins' best-seller. With only occasional moments of interest, this heavy-handed melodrama charts the course of an auto manufacturing dynasty. Olivier plays the patriarch, and Duvall is the grandson now running the company. About as subtle as a . . . well, Harold Robbins novel, this is the usual cacophony of lurid melodramatic loves and familial treachery. ★★ DVD: $9.99, VHS: $19.99

Betsy's Wedding

(1990, 94 min, US, Alan Alda) *Alan Alda, Madeline Kahn, Molly Ringwald, Ally Sheedy, Anthony LaPaglia, Joe Pesci, Catherine O'Hara.* Alda is in *Father of the Bride* territory with this sitcomish tale of a family preparing their daughter's wedding. Ringwald is the bride-to-be, and surprise! — the wedding plans go awry. Though Alda does create some amusing scenarios for his characters, the story is remarkably familiar and the film's pacing is either too meandering or too over-the-top to achieve a comedic consistency. LaPaglia steals the show as a mobster with a touch of class. ★★ DVD: $9.99

Better off Dead

(1985, 97 min, US, Savage Steve Holland) *John Cusack, Curtis Armstrong, Diane Franklin, Kim Darby, David Ogden Stiers.* This wacky and hilarious — if underrated — comedy stars Cusack as a teenager who loses the girl of his dreams and thinks himself *Better Off Dead*. Not a satire on suicide (à la *Heathers*), but rather a collection of crazy sketches, the majority of which hit the comedic bull's-eye. ★★★ DVD Letterbox: $24.99, VHS: $9.99

Better than Chocolate

(1999, 98 min, Canada, Anne Wheeler) *Wendy Crewson, Karyn Dwyer, Christina Cox, Anne-Marie MacDonald, Peter Outerbridge.* This refreshingly sexy tale tells of lesbian love winning against all the odds. When 19-year-old Maggie's nutty mother calls and says she is moving in, Maggie, who quit law school and has been sleeping on the couch of the lesbian bookstore, must find a sublet apartment and fast. To complicate matters, she has just met the sultry Kim, an artistic road warrior who has just rolled into town. But Maggie hasn't come out to her mother yet so it's time to hide the sex toys and "straighten up." A boisterous and entertaining romantic comedy of errors and the frailty of the human heart. ★★★½ DVD: $14.99, VHS: $14.99

A Better Tomorrow

(1986, 95 min, Hong Kong, John Woo) *Chow Yun-Fat, Leslie Cheung, Ti Lung, Lee Tse Ho.* The film that started the hugely popular slate of "heroic bloodshed" films remains one of the very best. Offering a violent view of extreme gunplay and evincing the strong influence of Sam Peckinpah and Sergio Leone, the operatic gangster tale finds good-hearted criminal Lung at odds with his brother, a cop. Standard premise is given singular treatment by director Woo (this film put him on the map, and made Yun-Fat a superstar in Asia); over-the-top action and sentimental drama mix surprisingly well in this fast-paced, exhilarating film. The formula will be familiar to those who've seen Woo's subsequent work; that shouldn't deter them from catching this still-potent film (with a shocking ending). For those who aren't familiar with Woo's work, what on earth are you waiting for? (Sequel: *A Better Tomorrow II*) (Cantonese with English subtitles) ★★★½ DVD Letterboxed: $24.99, VHS Letterbox Dubbed: $9.99

A Better Tomorrow II

(1987, 104 min, Hong Kong, John Woo) *Chow Yun-Fat, Leslie Cheung, Ti Lung.* A truly goofy sequel, *A Better Tomorrow II* overcomes some huge obstacles and manages to be a solid action film. In this one, Lung is released from prison in order to go undercover to nab a former Triad kingpin; turns out, his brother is on the same case. Way too melodramatic at times (even for a Woo film), and contrived, to say the least (there is one plot device that is forgivable only because it allows Chow Yun-Fat to make an appearance), the film is almost undone by its flaws. It's the lightning pace, committed performances and terrific action (the climax is particularly thrilling) that save the film. Woo once called this "the worst film ever made," but in truth, it's unnecessary, yes, but quite entertaining. (Prequel: *A Better Tomorrow III*) (Cantonese with English subtitles) ★★★ DVD: $24.99, VHS: $9.99

A Better Tomorrow 3

(1990, 114 min, Hong Kong, Tsui Hark) *Chow Yun-Fat, Anita Mui.* This prequel finds Chow's Mark character in 1974 Vietnam, attempting to get his cousin and uncle back to Hong Kong before the fall of Saigon. Hark, producer of the first two films, had a falling-out with John Woo, so he took over the

director's reins. The result is an uneasy mix of ridiculous (if exciting) action scenes and the usual melodrama (a bit soapy this time out), against the too-real backdrop of the end of the Vietnam War. The characters come across as a bit selfish (despite their seeming allegiance to each other), and the overall tone is pretty tacky. It also gets bogged down for a while in a love triangle subplot, and it's just too long. Not especially bad, but not up to the first two. For a more powerful take on the same basic premise, check out Woo's superior *Bullet in the Head*. (Cantonese with English subtitles) ★★½ DVD: $29.99

Betty

(1993, 103 min, France, Claude Chabrol) *Marie Trintignant, Stéphane Audran, Jean-François Garreau.* Director Chabrol delivers another existential look at a French woman trying to find her place in life. Told in flashbacks, the film tells the story of Betty (Trintignant), a young alcoholic woman cast aside by her husband and desperately trying to keep her emotions and sanity in check. Betty is befriended by an older woman (Audran), and as the story unfolds, the viewer learns more about these two women's lives and how they got to where they are. *Betty* is highly emotional, tragic and ultimately satisfying. (French with English subtitles) ★★★★ VHS: $29.99

Betty Blue

(1986, 110 min, France, Jean-Jacques Beineix) *Beatrice Dalle, Jean-Hugues Anglade.* Beineix, director of the trendsetting *Diva* as well as the stilted *Moon in the Gutter*, has fashioned this humorous and engrossing tale of *amour fou*. The story follows the passionate and at times tempestuous relationship between Betty (Dalle), a vulnerable young beauty, and her boyfriend Zorg (Anglade), a young man hopelessly captivated by her enigmatic but beguiling charm. Wonderfully scripted and acted, this charmer should not be missed. (French with English subtitles) ★★★½

Between Heaven and Earth

(1992, 80 min, France, Marion Hansel) *Carmen Maura, Jean-Pierre Cassel.* Truly a bizarre French twist on *Look Who's Talking*, this odd little film stars Spanish leading lady Maura as a Parisian TV reporter whose developing fetus talks to her from in utero. As an epidemic of overdue babies and stillbirths occupy the headlines, Maura's talking zygote explains that the fetuses are essentially on strike and refuse to be born into such a miserable world. It's a slight premise on which to build a feature-length film, but certainly more could have been made of it. Maura, for her part, is always a pleasure, and performs in French with what looks to be relative ease. (French with English subtitles) ★★ VHS: $14.99

Between Heaven and Hell

(1956, 93 min, US, Richard Fleischer) *Robert Wagner, Broderick Crawford, Terry Moore, Buddy Ebsen.* An interesting if talky war drama with Wagner in his semisuccessful bid to become a full-fledged movie star. He plays an unscrupulous Southern landowner whose experiences in the Pacific during WWII help him recover his lost compassion and humanity. Crawford is the maniacal commanding officer at odds with the young soldier. ★★½ DVD: $19.99, VHS: $9.99

Between the Lines

(1977, 101 min, US, Joan Micklin Silver) *Jeff Goldblum, John Heard, Jill Eikenberry, Lindsay Crouse, Bruno Kirby, Stephen Collins, Joe Morton, Marilu Henner, Lane Smith.* The trials and tribulations of the staff of a Boston underground newspaper during the 1960s is at the heart of director Silver's quirky and highly spirited low-budget charmer. Full of counterculture sentiments and refreshingly original humor, the film boasts an endearing cast of eccentrics fighting the system and fulfilling their journalistic aspirations — until faced with the fateful decision to "sell out." A solid ensemble of then-unknowns are all first-rate in bringing the convictions and passions of a generation to life. ★★★½

The Beverly Hillbillies

(1993, 93 min, US, Penelope Spheeris) *Jim Varney, Cloris Leachman, Lily Tomlin, Dabney Coleman, Diedrich Bader, Erica Eleniak, Lea Thompson, Rob Schneider, Dolly Parton.* It's bad news for a comedy when its funniest moments stem from surprise "star" cameos and outtakes during the end credits. Such is the case for *The Beverly Hillbillies*, a sappy, big-screen rendition of the popular 1960s TV series. In an A-to-B plot line, Arkansas hillbilly patriarch Jed Clampett strikes it rich, moves to Beverly (Hills, that is), and becomes the target for con artists. The comedy is played even broader than the TV series, which seems subtle by comparison. ★★ VHS: $9.99

Beverly Hills Cop

(1984, 105 min, US, Martin Brest) *Eddie Murphy, Judge Reinhold, James Russo, Paul Reiser, Bronson Pinchot, Damon Wayans.* Murphy is Axel Foley, a Detroit cop who travels to Beverly Hills to avenge a friend's death . . . and make the biggest grossing comedy of the decade. Not nearly as memorable as *48 Hrs.*, but entertaining if you don't think about it too much. Reinhold steals the show as Rosewood, an unorthodox cop who helps the displaced detective. Good soundtrack, and a slam-bang opening scene. ★★★ DVD Letterbox Special Edition: $14.99, VHS Special Edition: $9.99

Beverly Hills Cop 2

(1987, 103 min, US, Tony Scott) *Eddie Murphy, Judge Reinhold, Jürgen Prochnow, Dean Stockwell, Paul Reiser.* This extremely disappointing sequel has none of the ingredients that made the first film the popular success it was. Murphy tries his best, but how many times can we watch him con his way into ritzy Beverly Hills establishments? There's some slick, polished direction by Scott, but it can't hide the formulaic script and forced performances. For die-hard Murphy fans only. ★★ DVD Letterbox: $14.99, VHS: $9.99

Beverly Hills Cop III

(1994, 103 min, US, John Landis) *Eddie Murphy, Judge Reinhold, Hector Elizondo, Bronson Pinchot, Theresa Randle, John Saxon, Alan Young.* Murphy dusts off the gun and jacket of Axel Foley for this third installment. Featuring uninspired direction by Landis, this occasionally amusing but incredibly formulaic film has Axel returning to California to investigate a lead in a carjack ring/murder case. The trail leads to a Disneyland-type park, which serves as a cover for the bad guys. Murphy gives an earnest try, though he's been through all this before, and it shows. ★★½ DVD Letterbox: $14.99, VHS: $14.99

Beverly Hills Ninja

(1997, 89 min, US, Dennis Dugan) *Chris Farley, Nicolette Sheridan, Chris Rock, Robin Shou, Nathaniel Parker.* What could have been a funny parody of martial arts movies instead turns out to be a series of "look at the fat guy fall down" jokes that fails even at the sophomoric level it sets for itself early on. Farley is Haru, a "gravity-challenged" inept white ninja who comes to the United States to help a con woman (Sheridan) he believes to be a damsel in distress. Lacking an original idea, the film has only a few funny sequences that go on much too long. ★½ DVD: $14.99, VHS: $9.99

Beware, My Lovely

(1952, 77 min, US, Harry Horner) *Robert Ryan, Ida Lupino.* This thrilling study of insanity and terror stars Ryan as a deranged handyman who holds captive his widowed employer, Lupino, inside her home. Haunted by the murder of his previous employer (whom he may or may not have killed), Ryan alternates between being a gentle if slightly dazed man and an angry, potentially violent loony. ★★★ VHS: $19.99

Beware of a Holy Whore

(1970, 103 min, Germany, Rainer Werner Fassbinder) *Lou Castel, Hanna Schygulla, Eddie Constantine, Rainer Werner Fassbinder, Ulli Lommel.* An autobiographical meditation on the turbulent interactions and shifting power relationships which make up the filmmaking process, this is RFW's *8½, Day for Night* and *Contempt.* Based in part on Fassbinder's own experiences making *Whity, Beware a Holy Whore* follows a film crew and a group of actors who anxiously lounge around an opulent Spanish hotel arguing, drinking and becoming involved in destructive sex and power games as they endlessly wait for the film's star (Constantine), production money and especially the director (played by Fassbinder) to bring them to life. (German with English subtitles) ★★★ DVD: $24.99, VHS: $19.99

Beyond a Reasonable Doubt

(1956, 80 min, US, Fritz Lang) *Dana Andrews, Joan Fontaine.* An anti-capital punishment newspaper publisher implicates himself in a murder by using circumstantial evidence, hoping to expose the weakness of the system. However, things go wrong when he plays it too convincingly, is found guilty and then sent to prison. Lang's final American film, while far-fetched, is an undeniably grim and gripping melodrama. ★★★

Beyond Borders

(2003, 126 min, GB, Martin Campbell) *Angelina Jolie, Clive Owen, Teri Polo, Linus Roache, Noah Emmerich.* Well-meaning but poorly executed, *Beyond Borders* follows well-heeled socialite wife turned hunger relief worker Jolie as she helps the helpless around the world after receiving a wake-up call in the form of handsome but righteously angry Owen. A dreadful opening scene gives way to about 40 minutes or so of mediocre drama, as Jolie is indoctrinated into the world of on-location charity work. The film becomes increasingly silly and pointless as it goes on, however, and Jolie becomes less sympathetic as she leaves her very young children at the drop of a hat to travel to extremely dangerous parts of the world. The last chunk of the film is actually embarrassing, as director Campbell allows the film to slip into exotic-locale action mode as Jolie fights to release Owen from some evil kidnappers. You will

have already become beyond bored at this point. Watch out for the creepy CGI starving baby! What were these people thinking? ★½ DVD: $29.99

Beyond Rangoon

(1995, 100 min, US, John Boorman) *Patricia Arquette, U Aung Ko, Frances McDormand, Spalding Gray.* Arquette plays an American tourist visiting Burma who becomes involved in that country's bloody struggle for democracy in this gripping and moving political drama. After the murder of her husband and son, Laura Bowman (Arquette) attempts to find solace in the peaceful landscapes of the Far East. She sets out with an "unofficial" tour guide, U Aung Ko, to see the country beyond the city. However, a military crackdown forces both of them to flee for their lives in an attempt to reach the border. A strong narrative and taut direction combine to tell a harrowing true-life tale of political oppression and heroism. Expatriate professor U Aung Ko, playing himself, gives a nurtured performance. ★★★½ VHS: $19.99

Beyond Reasonable Doubt

(1980, 117 min, New Zealand, John Laing) *David Hemmings, John Hargreaves.* A jolting, true-life drama that documents the stilted investigation and legislative practices responsible for the incarceration of a mild-mannered New Zealand farmer. Hemmings gives a powerful performance as the corrupt police inspector who makes it a personal quest to seal the fate of the accused man, a baffled witness to his own demise. This Hitchcockian tale of questionable guilt and justice is a fascinating and thoroughly engrossing motion picture. ★★★

Beyond Silence

(1997, 107 min, Germany, Caroline Link) *Sylvie Testud, Tatjana Trieb, Howie Seago, Emmanuelle Laibrot.* Courtesy of the New German Feel-Good Cinema, the light and bright *Beyond Silence* is pleasant and inoffensive; so what's the point? Well, mainly, it gives a window into the world of the deaf. Lara works overtime to translate between her deaf parents and the hearing world. The story focuses on Lara and her desire to become a clarinet player. Under the tutelage of her aunt, Lara travels to Berlin to study. A series of routine plot adornments — death, love — take us comfortably to the groaner of a Mentos commercial ending. (German with English subtitles) ★★ DVD: $19.99, VHS: $14.99

Beyond Suspicion

(2001, 109 min, US, Matthew Tabak) *Jeff Goldblum, Anne Heche, Timothy Olyphant, Nancy Travis, Richard T. Jones.* An intriguing character piece, the inappropriately titled *Beyond Suspicion* features two compelling performances by Goldblum and Heche, each making this low-keyed but effective drama probably more involving than it has any right to be. Goldblum plays John, a hotshot insurance salesman who witnesses the murder of a store clerk during a robbery. As he becomes obsessed to learn all he can about the dead man, Auggie Rose, John soon assumes Auggie's identity, including living in the ex-con's apartment and beginning a relationship with Auggie's pen pal Lucy (Heche). Writer-director Tabak gives his film a nice, easy-going tempo, one in which the actors can take their time discovering their characters and where events unfold unhurriedly and steadfastly. (aka: *Auggie Rose*) ★★★ DVD: $9.99, VHS: $9.99

Beyond the Forest

(1949, 96 min, US, King Vidor) *Bette Davis, Joseph Cotten, Ruth Roman.* Davis misses her mark as a murderous crack shot in this tepid melodrama about a woman who'll stop at nothing to rise above

her life as the wife of a country doctor (Cotten). Notable for Davis' immortal line, "What a dump." ★★ VHS: $19.99

Beyond the Poseidon Adventure

(1979, 115 min, US, Irwin Allen) *Michael Caine, Sally Field, Telly Savalas, Peter Boyle, Jack Warden, Shirley Knight, Shirley Jones, Karl Malden.* More upside-down adventure from producer Allen, who here directs. Judging from this disaster, he should have been at the back of his desk instead of in back of the camera. Caine, who at the time was zeroing in on a Guinness Record for film appearances, plays a salvager who enters the grounded *Poseidon* and finds more survivors. The original, with its good set design and silly story, was cheesy fun; this is just cheesy. ★ VHS: $9.99

Beyond the Valley of the Dolls

(1970, 109 min, US, Russ Meyer) *Edy Williams, Dolly Reed.* A classic late-nite cult title, this brilliantly raunchy, in-name-only sequel to *Valley of the Dolls* tells the torrid tale of a female rock band, The Carrie Nations, and their deliriously funny struggle to get to the top. Featuring director Meyer's trademark wit and camerawork, this ahead-of-its-time exploitation favorite remains one of the best of the genre. Coscripted by film critic Roger Ebert. ★★★★

Beyond the Walls

(1984, 103 min, Israel, Uri Barbash) *Arnon Zadok, Muhamad Bakri, Assi Dayan.* Inside the walls of an Israeli prison, Jews and Arabs are confined in a society that mirrors the pressures and tensions on the outside. Cruelty is commonplace and loyalty is fleeting. This already volatile situation is further exacerbated by the arrival of an Israeli army officer who is jailed for attempting to speak to the PLO. As the inmates struggle with ideological hatreds on the inside, they attempt to maintain contact with their families and communities on the outside, with decreasing effectiveness and increasing frustration. The cast delivers uniformly authentic portrayals, conveyed with raw intensity and unflinching emotion. (Hebrew with English subtitles) ★★★ VHS: $79.99

Beyond Therapy

(1987, 93 min, US, Robert Altman) *Glenda Jackson, Tom Conti, Jeff Goldblum, Julie Hagerty, Christopher Guest, Cris Campion.* Christopher Durang co-adapted his own hit off-Broadway play for the screen in this Altman comedy about the frantic goings-on of a group of sex-obsessed neurotics and their equally unbalanced psychologists. Goldblum is the bisexual Bruce, who lives with semi-swishy Bob (Guest) but who takes a liking to hopelessly frazzled Prudence (Hagerty). Conti and Jackson play two crazy therapists whose advice only makes everyone more crazy. Unpredictable, loony and wildly uneven, *Beyond Therapy* can also be quite charming in-between the out-of-control shenanigans. Though set in New York, Altman filmed in Paris. ★★½

Bhaji on the Beach

(1994, 100 min, GB, Gurinder Chadha) *Kim Vithana, Jimmi Harkishin, Sarita Khajuria, Mo Sesay.* This well-intentioned and somewhat lighthearted look at the lives of a group of Anglo-Indian/Pakistani women has its moments, but ultimately fails to captivate. The film follows three generations of women on an outing to the British seaside resort of Blackpool. Led by the self-assured feminist Simi, they land on the beach with a variety of issues at hand. Individually, all of the stories are interesting enough and the acting is strong throughout, but as the film wanders among its characters, it becomes diluted and ultimately comes off like a protracted episode of "EastEnders." ★★½

The Bible

(1966, 174 min, US, John Huston) *John Huston, Richard Harris, George C. Scott, Peter O'Toole, Ava Gardner, Franco Nero.* Dino De Laurentiis produced this megalithic and completely blundering attempt to bring the "number one best-seller" to the screen. Some projects are better left alone. Why Huston agreed to helm this ill-begotten ship is a mystery. Perhaps only so he himself could portray Noah in the film's only redeeming chapter. If you're really interested, read the book. ★½ DVD: $14.99, VHS: $6.99

Bicentennial Man

(1999, 132 min, US, Chris Columbus) *Robin Williams, Sam Neill, Embeth Davidtz, Wendy Crewson, Oliver Platt.* An affluent family in the not-so-distant future purchases the latest suburban trend: a robotic family servant. They dub him Andrew, and he goes about cooking, cleaning and the other sundry tasks expected of a robot housekeeper. But it soon becomes clear that Andrew is a little special: He soon shows signs of individuality and sets out to discover what it's like to be human. Data from "Star Trek: The Next Generation" may want to get a lawyer. Williams is understated, just like the rest of the cast; to such an extent that the film has no energy. Add a weird romantic twist, and *Bicentennial Man* leaves little hope for the future. ★½ DVD: $14.99, VHS: $9.99

Les Biches

(1968, 104 min, France/Italy, Claude Chabrol) *Stéphane Audran, Jean-Louis Trintignant.* Audran has never looked more elegantly decadent than in this twisted bisexual drama of sexual domination, obsession, despair and revenge, filmed in Chabrol's trademark cool, detached style. Audran is Frederique, a glamorous woman of lesbian leaning who, on a trip to Paris, meets then seduces a poor, enigmatic young woman named Why. She soon whisks her new love off to her home in St. Tropez to continue their affair, but the balance is changed when a man (Trintignant) enters the picture and, after a brief attraction to Why, takes up permanently with Frederique. The centerpiece of this explosive love triangle is Audran's wanton sexual appeal, a power that eventually leads to bitter consequences. (French with English subtitles) ★★★½ DVD: $19.99

The Bicycle Thief

(1948, 90 min, Italy, Vittorio De Sica) *Lamberto Maggiorani, Lianella Carelli, Enzo Staiola,*

The Bicycle Thief

Elena Altieri. One of the undisputed neorealist classics, *The Bicycle Thief* adeptly uses the post-war devastation of Italy as harsh backdrop for this poignant story of a marginal man whose simple existence depends on his bicycle, which he needs to earn his living. He is devastated by the bicycle's theft; his family's well-being is jeopardized and the police are indifferent. He is left to his own devices to scour the city with his young son, a victim without aid or support, alienated and isolated. Filmed with great caring and compassion, and yet without sympathetic gloss, by director De Sica, who can use a single human face to speak volumes about the human condition. (Italian with English subtitles) ★★★★ DVD: $24.99, VHS: $19.99

Il Bidone (The Swindlers)

(1955, 98 min, Italy, Federico Fellini) *Broderick Crawford, Guilietta Masina, Richard Basehart, Franco Fabrizi.* Crawford is memorable as the selfish ringleader of a trio of con men who impersonate priests in an elaborate scam that preys on the avarice of ignorant peasants. A satire that begins as a light comedy and concludes with tragedy, this pre-flamboyant Fellini forms part two of his trilogy (which includes *La Strada* and *Nights of Cabiria*) of outsiders eking out an existence on the road. (Italian with English subtitles) ★★★ DVD: $24.99, VHS: $19.99

Big

(1988, 102 min, US, Penny Marshall) *Tom Hanks, Elizabeth Perkins, John Heard, Robert Loggia, Jared Rushton, Jon Lovitz, Mercedes Ruehl.* Hanks gives a wonderfully complex and funny performance as the end result of a 12-year-old boy's wish to be "big." When his wish comes true, he is thrust into an adult world of big business, office politics and romance, all the while maintaining his refreshing child's-eye view of the world. Gary Ross' delightful script takes aim at corporate rivalry, consumerism and alienation while bringing a fresh perspective to the "fish out of water" scenario. Director Marshall exhibits a playful knack for comedy both physical and verbal, though she does somewhat bask in the sentimental. ★★★½ DVD Pan & Scan: $14.99, DVD: $14.99, VHS: $9.99

Big Bad Mama

(1974, 83 min, US, Steve Carver) *Angie Dickinson, William Shatner, Tom Skerritt, Susan Sennett, Robbie Lee, Noble Willingham, Dick Miller.* Dickinson stars in this enjoyably cheesy Roger Corman knock-off of *Bonnie and Clyde* as Mom and her daughters rob banks and share men — one of whom is con man Shatner (prepared to go where no man has gone before). ★★½ DVD: $14.99, VHS: $14.99

The Big Bang

(1989, 81 min, US, James Toback) Beginning with his theory that the creation of the universe was the result of an "orgasmic explosion of God," director Toback leaves the world of fiction to explore various other thoughts on existence in this rambling yet entertaining documentary. Interviewing a series of people from diverse backgrounds, Toback elicits their divergent thoughts on life, death, creativity, sex, love and the existence of God. Funny, touching and even a little enlightening. ★★★

The Big Blue

(1988, 119 min, France, Luc Besson) *Rosanna Arquette, Jean Reno, Jean-Marc Barr, Griffin Dunne.* Only Besson's most ardent fans, or those of you who fantasize about things aquatic, will be swayed by the stunning underwater photography in this waterlogged story about the rivalry between two deep-sea free divers (Reno and Barr). Arquette is a ditzy New York insurance salesperson who falls in love with one of them only to be rejected for a dolphin. (In English and French with English subtitles) ★★ DVD: $29.99, VHS: $14.99

The Big Brass Ring

(1999, 104 min, US, George Hickenlooper) *William Hurt, Nigel Hawthorne, Miranda Richardson, Iréne Jacob.* Based on an unfilmed screenplay by Orson Welles, this lackluster drama begs the question "What if Welles had . . . ?" As adapted and directed by Hickenlooper, *The Big Brass Ring* is tepid, tired hooey elevated by some good performances. It all starts off well, with politician Hurt confronted with some compromising photos from his youth. The possibilities of the premise are squandered for a quasi-mystery, which is subsequently solved about halfway through the film. Little of interest remains, and while the story may have been controversial at the time Welles wished to film it, in the age of Monica Lewinsky and Jerry Springer, this is last week's dishwater. ★★ DVD: $27.99, VHS: $14.99

The Big Brawl

(1980, 95 min, US, Robert Clouse) *Jackie Chan, Jose Ferrer.* This gangster film set in 1930s Chicago is more or less a showcase for the incredibly talented Chan. Lots of comedy and fighting keep the film interesting, but this is far from being one of Chan's best. Not much here for non-Jackie fans. ★★½

Big Business

(1988, 97 min, US, Jim Abrahams) *Bette Midler, Lily Tomlin, Fred Ward, Edward Herrmann, Michele Placido.* Lightning doesn't strike twice as *Ruthless People* star Midler and director Abrahams reunite in this rather tame though genial comedy. Midler and Tomlin star as two sets of twins switched at birth who run across each other's paths in the Big Apple. A good premise, a nice turn from the Divine Miss M and some nifty special effects can't save this lightweight comedy; though it does manage a few laughs, it is a disappointment considering the talent involved. ★★ DVD: $9.99, VHS: $9.99

The Big Chill

(1983, 105 min, US, Lawrence Kasdan) *William Hurt, Kevin Kline, Glenn Close, Tom Berenger, Jeff Goldblum, Meg Tilly, Mary Kay Place, JoBeth Williams.* Borrowing liberally from John Sayles' wonderful *Return of the Secaucus Seven*, director and coauthor Kasdan has fashioned an equally entertaining and smartly written ode to the lasting power of friendship. Utilizing a talented all-star cast, Kasdan's comedy-drama focuses on the reunion of a group of college friends from the '60s who have come together in the '80s for the funeral of one of their own. What distinguishes Kasdan's story are the personable characters and the remarkable relationships between them. *The Big Chill* is as comfortable as a longtime friend. ★★★½ DVD Letterbox: $14.99, VHS: $9.99

The Big Clock

(1948, 95 min, US, John Farrow) *Ray Milland, Charles Laughton, Maureen O'Sullivan, George Macready, Harry Morgan, Elsa Lanchester.* Nifty film noir thriller with Laughton as a seedy publisher who commits murder and tries to make it look as if his editor (Milland) did it. Nice characterizations and a good story complement the taut pacing and splendid cinematography. (Remade in 1987 as *No Way Out*) ★★★

The Big Combo

(1954, 89 min, US, Joseph H. Lewis) *Cornel Wilde, Richard Conte, Brian Donlevy, Jean Wallace, Earl Holliman, Lee Van Cleef.* A classic, if little acknowledged, film noir crime drama. The setting is the seedy crime underworld where a good cop (Wilde) attempts to take on a sadistic crime boss (Conte) with a luscious but oh-so-dangerous blonde bombshell (Wallace) in the middle. The cop becomes obsessed with bringing the thug to justice but Conte's ruthless clutch on power embroils Wilde in a violent and even savage struggle. ★★★½ DVD: $24.99, VHS: $19.99

The Big Country

(1958, 167 min, US, William Wyler) *Gregory Peck, Charlton Heston, Burl Ives, Jean Simmons, Carroll Baker.* Epic western adventure starring Peck as an ex-sea captain who returns home to marry and start a ranch, becoming caught in a feud over water rights. This mammoth production also features Ives in an Oscar-winning performance as the patriarch of one of the feuding families. ★★★ DVD: $14.99

Big Daddy

(1999, 93 min, US, Dennis Dugan) *Adam Sandler, Joey Lauren Adams, Jon Stewart, Rob Schneider, Joe Bologna, Kristy Swanson, Jackie Titone.* This box-office hit casts Sandler as an unlikely parental guardian to a cute five-year-old when he takes over responsibility of his vacationing roommate's son, who has been literally dropped off at his doorstep. This *One Moron and a Kid* follows the layabout's attempts to keep the kid under control. Stupid sight gags, lazy one-liners and boring toilet humor at which only a prepubescent would smirk accentuate how unfunny this really is. ★½ DVD: $19.99, VHS: $9.99

Big Deal on Madonna Street

(1956, 91 min, Italy, Mario Monticelli) *Marcello Mastroianni, Vittoria Gassman, Claudia Cardinale.* The wild misadventures of a group of bungling would-be crooks who attempt to rob a pawn shop and who make a complete mess of it is a classic example of *commedia all'italiana.* A hilarious parody of American caper films that many think to be one of the funniest Italian films to come out of the era. (Remade as *Crackers*) (Italian with English subtitles) ★★★½ DVD Criterion Collection: $29.99, VHS: $29.99

The Big Dis

(1988, 88 min, US, Gordon Eriksen & John O'Brien) This charming, black-and-white low-budget comedy-drama will remind one of Spike Lee's *She's Gotta Have It* in its often hilarious theme about the sexual attitudes and posturing of young middle-class blacks. J.D., a handsome but thoroughly sexist black soldier, returns to his family's suburban home on a weekend leave; his overwhelming ambition: to get laid. But everything seems to go wrong as he comes ever so close but never grabs the ring. ★★★ VHS: $19.99

The Big Doll House

(1971, 93 min, US, Jack Hill) *Pam Grier, Judy Brown.* Valley girls and Hollywood starlets trapped in a hellhole Filipino prison! One of the earliest and most commercially succesful of the "women-in-prison" films which were so popular in the 1970s, this is almost chaste compared to its cheesier successors. Filmed in a breezy, comedic fashion, the film features the requisite S&M beating, shower and claws-out fighting sequences to tell its tale of prisoners who revolt against their ruthless warden. ★★½ DVD: $14.99, VHS: $9.99

The Big Easy

(1987, 101 min, US, Jim McBride) *Ellen Barkin, John Goodman, Ned Beatty, Dennis Quaid, Ebbe Roe Smith, Charles Ludlam.* A glorious blend of screwball comedy and detective story, this scintillating thriller stars Quaid as a New Orleans detective who becomes involved with sexy district attorney Barkin, who is investigating local police corruption. Quaid and Barkin are about the most attractive duo on the screen in years, and their love scenes are among the steamiest, also. Great supporting cast includes Ludlam in a stand-out role as a Tennessee Williams-ish lawyer. ★★★½ DVD: $9.99

Big Eden

(2000, 117 min, US, Thomas Bezucha) *Arye Gross, Eric Schweig, George Coe, Louise Fletcher, Nan Martin.* A warm, cuddly film, *Big Eden* tells a traditional tale of the triangulated relationship with several new spins. There's the gay artist Henry Hart; he loves the waspishly handsome and sexually confused Dean Stewart; and then there's Pike who pines secretly for Henry. Twenty years ago a gay romance set in a small town would have been unthinkable — now it's celebrated (if somewhat far-fetched) in Bezucha's debut feature. When Henry is called back to his hometown, Big Eden, Montana, after his grandfather falls ill, he reunites with Dean, his high school crush. While this old crush flares again, the quiet, shy Native-American owner of Big Eden's general store, Pike Dexter, has his eyes on the big-city returnee. Rich, funny performances help gloss over the fact that this big-hearted film is really nothing more than a fairy tale. ★★★ DVD 2-disc set: $24.99, VHS: $39.99

Big Fat Liar

(2002, 87 min, US, Shawn Levy) *Frankie Muniz, Paul Giamatti, Amanda Bynes, Amanda Detmer, Lee Majors.* Fourteen-year-old Jason (Muniz) is nearly an artist when it comes to telling tales. When he writes one elaborate story down on paper, it falls into the hands of a seedy Hollywood producer who passes it off as his own. Jason and his girlfriend Kaylee (Bynes) then spend the rest of the film getting even with the . . . big fat liar. A teenaged revenge comedy combining *Home Alone's* nasty

Ewan McGregor in Tim Burton's fantasy *Big Fish*

pratfalls with dumb and dumber comedy, *Big Fat Liar* is a laborious affair that will only entertain Jason's peers wanting to see adults get theirs. ★½ DVD: $14.99, VHS: $9.99

Big Fish

(2003, 125 min, US, Tim Burton) *Ewan McGregor, Albert Finney, Jessica Lange, Billy Crudup, Helena Bonham Carter, Danny DeVito, Alison Lohman, Robert Guillaume, Matthew McGrory, Steve Buscemi.* After a couple of mammoth commercial undertakings like *Planet of the Apes,* director Burton successfully returns to a more personal (if no less ambitious) project. The central character, terminally ill Ed Bloom (Finney), is taken to telling fanciful tales when reminiscing about his youth, to the endless frustration of his son (Crudup, in a thanklessly overshadowed role). His legend (whether true or just in his mind) is so large that the bulk of the film is shown in flashback through the charming McGregor, who strikes an uncanny resemblance to *Tom Jones*-era Finney. It is here that Burton's flights of fancy soar: Ed's WWII paradrop into a USO show featuring conjoined twins; a run-in with a softhearted giant looking for a place to belong; and most hauntingly, his stumbling on a literal ghost town called Spectre that is a wistful mirror image of the perfectly manicured suburbia of *Edward Scissorhands.* These sequences are so whimsical, so inventive, so magically colorful, that the only quibble is that the more grounded present-day portion can't possibly measure up. Give thanks once again for the wonderful Finney, who animates his bedridden Bloom with a mischievous face and a baritone voice that's full of life. ★★★½ DVD Letterbox: $28.99

The Big Fix

(1978, 108 min, US, Jeremy Paul Kagan) *Richard Dreyfuss, Susan Anspach, Bonnie Bedelia, John Lithgow, F. Murray Abraham.* Roger L. Simon adapted his own novel about private eye Moses Wine, a former '60s campus radical, who is hired by an old college girlfriend to help locate a fugitive from their Berkeley days. An entertaining comedy-mystery with Dreyfuss in good form as Wine. ★★★ VHS: $59.99

Big Girls Don't Cry . . . They Get Even

(1992, 90 min, US, Joan Micklin Silver) *Hillary Wolf, Griffin Dunne, David Strathairn, Margaret Whitton, Adrienne Shelly.* If you are postpubescent, you might feel slightly silly watching this tale of the ultimate dysfunctional family. However, *Big Girls Don't Cry . . . They Get Even* is actually entertaining once you get over the embarrassment of watching something with such an inane title. Wolf stars as Lauren (a 14-year-old with a ready canister of one-liners), who runs away after she decides that her mother, stepfather and various step-siblings just don't care about her. The ensuing search to bring her home unites the various and eccentric members of her family. ★★½ VHS: $9.99

The Big Grab (Melodie en sous-sol)
(1963, 118 min, France, Henri Verneuil) *Jean Gabin, Alain Delon.* A young Delon is the punk assistant to master thief Gabin in this taut cops and robbers flick. Their attempt to pull off "the crime of the century" is intricately detailed as their plans become more and more complicated. A good, well-told story in the tradition of *Bob le Flambeur*. (French with English subtitles) ★★★

The Big Green
(1995, 100 min, US, Holly Goldberg Sloan) *Steve Guttenberg, Olivia d'Abo, Jay O. Sanders.* A young exchange teacher from England (d'Abo) decides to teach soccer to her students, a group of kids from a very small and depressed Texas town. Guttenberg is the local sheriff who, despite his dislike of kids, ends up as her assistant coach. Among the team of fairly likable kids is the inevitable ringer, a Mexican youth whose mother is reluctant to let him play because she is an illegal alien. Not as sappy as it could have been, the underdog theme is rather heart-warming, though the story is given to one-too-many cliché. ★★½ DVD: $19.99, VHS: $9.99

A Big Hand for the Little Lady
(1966, 95 min, US, Fielder Cook) *Henry Fonda, Joanne Woodward, Jason Robards, Burgess Meredith, Kevin McCarthy, Paul Ford.* Fonda and Woodward are in fine form in this sly western comedy. Fonda plays an ex-gambler who arrives with his wife (Woodward) in the town of Laredo just as the big card tournament begins. He enters the game, and gets the hand of a lifetime. Only before he can finish the hand, he suffers a heart attack. When his wife takes his place, the now-penniless woman has some fancy talking to do to stay in the game. And ya gotta love that surprise ending. ★★★ VHS: $19.99

The Big Heat
(1953, 90 min, US, Fritz Lang) *Glenn Ford, Gloria Grahame, Lee Marvin, Jocelyn Brando, Jeanette Nolan.* Although the story of mob operations and political corruption is pale compared to today's headlines, Lang's direction and some potent performances lose none of their impact. Especially effective are Ford as the honest cop, Marvin as the psychotic hood and an amazing Grahame as the gangster's moll. Yes, this is the one with the coffee-throwing scene. ★★★½ DVD: $24.99

The Big Hit
(1998, 91 min, US, Che-Kirk Wong) *Mark Wahlberg, Lou Diamond Phillips, Christina Applegate, Avery Brooks, Bokeem Woodbine, Antonio Sabato, Jr., Lela Rochon, China Chow.* *The Big Hit* is a genuinely likable action-comedy offering the visceral action of director Wong's *Crime Story* and the hip dopiness of, well, someone who's infatuated with Hong Kong action epics. Wahlberg plays a hit man who kidnaps the daughter (Chow) of a Japanese businessman, only to have it turn out that she's the goddaughter of his mob boss. Soon, his well-toned assas-

Stanley Tucci (l.) and Tony Shalhoub in *Big Night*

sin partners turn turncoat and offer to bring him in. Wong is great at staging some action sequences, particularly an opening assault in a office high-rise and a furious finale in a video store. If you know that Jackie Chan's *Drunken Master II* is better than the original *Drunken Master*, you'll get a big laugh out of *The Big Hit*. ★★★ DVD Letterbox Superbit Edition: $27.99, DVD: $14.99, VHS: $9.99

The Big Kahuna
(2000, 91 min, US, John Swanbeck) *Kevin Spacey, Danny DeVito, Peter Facinelli.* Three white guys in suits, all wearing name tags, discuss the meaning of life in a garish hotel suite which stands in for a circle of hell. In a blasphemous misuse of talent, Spacey and DeVito play Larry and Phil, jaded and fading marketing foot soldiers who shill industrial lubricant and are looking for the big kahuna, the big deal which means redemption. Naïve, fresh-face, born-again Bob (Facinelli) thinks he's found redemption and is oblivious to his own pitch. The film is unfocused as it awkwardly attempts to deal with big issues without generating any real spark of connection. Perhaps this work was more compelling in its first incarnation as a stage play; something must have motivated Spacey to co-produce and star in a film version. An interesting disappointment. ★★ DVD: $14.99

The Big Lebowski
(1998, 117 min, US, Joel Coen) *Jeff Bridges, John Goodman, Steve Buscemi, John Turturro, David Huddleston, Julianne Moore, Philip Seymour Hoffman, David Thewlis, Sam Elliott.* His name is The Dude, a stoned-out aging hippie surfer. And as hilariously played by Bridges in the Coen brothers' ecstatic, loopy comedy about bowling, mistaken identity and kidnapping, The Dude can certainly lay claim to such a moniker. Sharing in common only the same birth name, The Dude (alias Jeff Lebowski) is mistaken by some small-time hoods for a millionaire businessman (Huddleston), whose young trophy wife has been kidnapped. Soon, The Dude becomes entangled in a series of comic misadventures and neo-noir intrigue throughout L.A. that would make Raymond Chandler rethink *The Big Sleep* as a Marx Brothers vehicle. A shaggy dog story brimming with broad humor, high energy and lots of laughs, the film is buoyed by the strong support of the dead-on Goodman, whose tirades and

philosophies could have been penned only by the Coens and appreciated by someone known as The Dude. ★★★½ DVD Dual: $14.99, VHS: $9.99

Big Momma's House
(2000, 98 min, US, Raja Gosnell) *Martin Lawrence, Nia Long, Paul Giamatti, Jascha Washington, Ella Mitchell.* With a nod to Eddie Murphy in *The Nutty Professor*, Lawrence goes the makeup-transformation route, but without producing the kind of laughs that (first) film generated. Lawrence plays an FBI agent who goes undercover to catch an escaped prisoner — by masquerading as an overweight, over-bearing Southern grandmother. Lawrence is a likable comedian, and he manages to create some goodwill with Big Momma, but the screenplay is lacking any substantial humor, at least the kind worthy of Lawrence's talents. ★★ DVD Pan & Scan: $14.99, DVD: $14.99, VHS Special Edition: $9.99

Big Night
(1996, 107 min, US, Campbell Scott & Stanley Tucci) *Stanley Tucci, Tony Shalhoub, Isabella Rossellini, Ian Holm, Minnie Driver, Campbell Scott, Marc Anthony.* Adding yet another chapter to the annals of grand cinematic feasts, this charming indie feature tells the tale of two Italian immigrant brothers who make a go at the American Dream. One part comedy and two parts drama, and set in the 1950s on the North Jersey shore, the story centers around Primo (Shalhoub) and Secondo's (Tucci) desperate attempt to kickstart their failing bistro. While Primo and Secondo go out of their way to present authentic and upscale Italian fare, their competitor down the street (Holm) is clobbering them with his lowbrow, "Americanized" fare. Ultimately, they gear up for one big splash as they anticipate a visit from Italo-American bandleader Louis Prima. The ensuing feast will send any viewer with so much as a twinge of epicureanism rushing to their local trattoria begging for timpano. ★★★½ DVD Letterbox: $19.99, VHS: $19.99

The Big One
(1998, 90 min, US, Michael Moore) *Michael Moore, Studs Terkel, Garrison Keillor.* Moore has crafted another refreshingly clear-eyed exploration of America's corporate culture. While on a promotional tour for his latest book, "Downsize This,"

Moore visits recently shut-down company sites, talking with the newly unemployed about their options for the future. He's at the Payday plant in Centralia when the workers find out their profit-creating performance is being rewarded by the factory's closure. Attempts to speak with corporate honchos result in amazing displays of double-talk and double-think — textbook examples of lies, damn lies and statistics. Moore handles the complex subject matter with an accessible, light touch and many humorous highlights, yet never loses focus. Remember: the word "shareholder" does not appear once in the U.S. Constitution. ★★★★

The Big Parade

(1925, 126 min, US, King Vidor) *John Gilbert, Renee Adoree.* Vidor's stunning antiwar film is one of the classics of silent cinema. Containing realistic, remarkably staged battle sequences and moments of rare powerful dramatics, *The Big Parade* follows the enlistment of an American soldier (silent screen great Gilbert) who fights in France during WWI. Though made at the infancy of American filmmaking, Vidor has a superior command of the medium, creating scenes as achingly intimate and disturbing as they are brilliantly constructed. This epic may have influenced Stanley Kubrick's *Paths of Glory*. ★★★★ VHS: $29.99

The Big Picture

(1989, 99 min, US, Christopher Guest) *Kevin Bacon, Emily Longstreth, Martin Short, Michael McKean, Jennifer Jason Leigh.* Hollywood, and the movie industry in particular, take it on the chin in this biting and funny satire. Reminiscent of *S.O.B.* and *This Is Spinal Tap*, *The Big Picture* pokes some good-natured and wacky, on-target jabs at the Hollywood establishment in its story of a student filmmaker who tries to direct his first feature film. Bacon stars as the talented newcomer who "goes Hollywood." While a couple of jokes may be too "in" for some, most of this material is accessible to all. Short is a highly outrageous agent. ★★★ DVD: $24.99

The Big Red One

(1980, 113 min, US, Samuel Fuller) *Lee Marvin, Mark Hamill, David Carradine, Bobby DiCicco.* Marvin is the sergeant, the archetypal soldier, in Fuller's *The Big Red One*, a war story from the foot soldiers' point of view. It opens at the end of WWI with the sergeant's creation of the First Infantry insignia: the big red one. The film jumps a quarter century to North Africa, and follows Marvin and his squad as they trek across a thousand miles fighting for their lives. Based on his own war experiences, the film was written and directed by Fuller, who is unequaled in revealing in intimate detail the individual's struggle against the panorama of monumental cataclysm. Deliberately paced, methodically structured and finely detailed — a quintessential war film, made with compassion but not sentiment, affection but not pathos. The film's closing sequences offer unassailable testimony that there are moments in history when the horrors of war must be borne in defiance of pure evil. And, at some time, the war is finally over. ★★★½ DVD: $14.99, VHS: $9.99

The Big Sleep

(1946, 114 min, US, Howard Hawks) *Humphrey Bogart, Lauren Bacall, John Ridgely, Dorothy Malone, Elisha Cook, Jr.* Bogart is Philip Marlowe, who's not very tall but tries to be. A classic film noir, slightly seedy and heavy on atmosphere. There's lots of tough guys and guys who are tough, lots of fast women and loose talk, cigarette

smoke you could cut with a knife, and guns, lots of guns. The plot, which has something to do with Bogey being hired to protect a young, wild heiress, is so convoluted that the guy who wrote the book (Raymond Chandler) didn't know who committed one of the murders. William Faulkner was one of the scriptwriters. Includes 20 minutes of footage not previously seen, including scenes from director Hawks' first cut. ★★★★ DVD: $19.99, VHS Theatrical Cut: $14.99, VHS Pre-release version with extra footage: $14.99

The Big Squeeze

(1996, 100 min, US, Marcus De Leon) *Lara Flynn Boyle, Peter Dobson, Danny Nucci, Luca Bercovici.* If Quentin Tarantino directed an Afterschool Special, the result might be something like *The Big Squeeze*. It's an amiable, sunny noir (a contradiction that works) about an unhappy wife and a scam artist who team to sting her born-again husband out of $130,000. *The Big Squeeze* is refreshingly upbeat, so that even its double-crossing and infidelities seem good-natured. Unfortunately, the character intros are irritatingly cutesy, and the film as a whole tends to be too sitcomish. ★★½

The Big Steal

(1949, 71 min, US, Don Siegel) *Robert Mitchum, Jane Greer.* Siegel's third feature film is his only true film noir, an exciting and well-paced thriller of a heist gone wrong. Mitchum gives a sturdy, three-dimensional performance of a man trying to capture the real culprits of the crime of which he has been accused. The film has witty dialogue, lots of action and numerous, unexpected plot twists. Watch for a great car chase scene early on that would become the prototype for action films. ★★★★

The Big Store

(1941, 80 min, US, Charles Riesner) *Groucho Marx, Harpo Marx, Chico Marx, Margaret Dumont, Tony Martin.* This Marx Brothers romp isn't really in the same caliber of *Duck Soup* or *Horsefeathers*, but it does produce a few laughs. Detective Groucho goes undercover at Dumont's department store, and finds Chico and Harpo and crooks. (DVD only available in a seven-film pack for $59.99) ★★½

The Big Tease

(2000, 86 min, US, Kevin Allen) *Craig Ferguson, Frances Fisher, Mary McCormack, David Rasche.* "Stranger in a strange land" mockumentary about a gay hairstylist (is there any other kind?) who proudly leaves "bonnie Scotland" to compete in the "Olympics of hairstyling" in L.A., only to find that he's been invited as a guest. What's a girl to do? Well, with funds running low and time running out, our hero (Ferguson) launches a plan to break into the competition by dropping the name "Sean Connery" all over Tinseltown. Never dull and often amusing, this bitchy swipe at the "beautiful people" is silly, good-hearted and totally lightweight. ★★½ DVD: $9.99, VHS: $14.99

Big Time

(1988, 87 min, US, Chris Blum) *Tom Waits.* This concert film, taken from a performance at L.A.'s Wiltern Theatre, allows us to get a taste of some of Waits' multiple personalities. The raspy-voiced singer goes from character to character while singing classic songs from "Frank's Wild Years," "Rain Dogs," and other early Waits albums. ★★★

Big Top Pee-wee

(1988, 90 min, US, Randal Kleiser) *Paul Reubens, Penelope Ann Miller, Kris Kristofferson, Valeria Golino, Susan Tyrell.* Pee-wee's heart takes flight when he meets the new trapeze artist whose circus is staying at his farm. Youngsters should like this second outing for Paul Reubens' alter ego almost as much as the first: it's got kids and animals and Danny Elfman's great score. ★★½ DVD: $14.99

Big Trouble

(1985, 93 min, US, John Cassavetes) *Peter Falk, Alan Arkin, Beverly D'Angelo.* Double Indemnity meets *Ruthless People* in this plot-twisted comedy about an underpaid insurance agent (Arkin) who falls in with a fickle femme fatale (D'Angelo) and her plot to kill her wealthy husband (Falk). Director Cassavetes shows little flair for the comedic moment, but zany situations and characterizations make this an enjoyable entry. ★★★ DVD Letterbox: $24.99

Big Trouble

(2002, 85 min, US, Barry Sonnenfeld) *Tim Allen, Rene Russo, Dennis Farina, Janeane Garofalo, Patrick Warburton, Stanley Tucci, Omar Epps.* Another instance in which a movie's title succinctly doubles as its epitaph. Allen and Russo topline an eclectic cast of misfits, idiots, hit men and hoodlums who are all embroiled in an intricate Rube Goldberg scenario involving — big laughs! — a nuclear bomb in Miami. A climax that involves the nuke slipping undetected through airport security surely won't be earning any laughs (the film was delayed after the events of 9/11 and then hastily recut for release), but even without the inevitable echoes of real-life terrorism, *Big Trouble* is just plain unfunny. ★½ DVD: $29.99, VHS: $14.99

Big Trouble in Little China

(1986, 99 min, US, John Carpenter) *Kurt Russell, Kim Cattrall, Dennis Dun, James Hong, Victor Wong.* Russell does his best John Wayne imitation in this amiable, light-hearted adventure spoof as a tough truck driver who (sort of) helps rescue his best friend's girlfriend. It seems she was kidnapped by a 2,000-year-old magician who rules a secret underground society beneath San Francisco's Chinatown. Director Carpenter crams a lot of action into the 99-minute running time, and if some of the production is overblown, there's quite a few good sequences that make it easy to like. ★★★ DVD Dual Basic Edition: $19.99, DVD 2-disc set: $26.99, VHS: $9.99

A Bigger Splash

(1974, 90 min, GB, David Hockney) *David Hockney, Peter Schlessinger.* Controversial British painter Hockney stars as himself in this penetrating, semifictitious portrait of his personal and artistic life. Centered around the actual breakup of Hockney and his lover/model, Schlessinger, this witty and revealing work meditates on the relationship of art to life. Vignettes of Hockney with friends, lovers and ex-lovers create an impressionistic study of the swirling influences in one artist's world. ★★★ VHS: $29.99

Biker Boyz

(2003, 111 min, US, Reggie Rock Bythewood) *Laurence Fishburne, Derek Luke, Orlando Jones, Djimon Hounsou, Lisa Bonet, Larenz Tate, Eriq LaSalle.* A *Fast and the Furious* rip-off, *Biker Boyz* is really nothing more than an Afterschool Special dressed in trendy clothing. "The Kid" (Luke) wants

Jamie Bell is *Billy Elliot*

to be the best street racer in California; he's got to beat his mentor, Smoke (Fishburne), the reigning king, first — and learn some trite life lessons along the way. Truly awful camerawork, ineffectual editing and a distinct lack of drama peg *Biker Boyz* as an empty knockoff early on. Pandering, street-lingo-littered dialogue and a lousy soundtrack also kill interest, but the straw that breaks this back is the fact that the races are so dull! Fishburne and Luke give more than the film deserves, but no amount of trying can save this dismissible junk. ★ DVD Letterbox Widescreen: $14.99, DVD Pan & Scan Pan & Scan: $14.99, VHS: $9.99

Bill & Ted's Bogus Journey

(1991, 98 min, US, Peter Hewitt) *Keanu Reeves, Alex Winter, William Sadler, George Carlin, Joss Ackland, Pam Grier.* That most excellent duo, Bill and Ted, are back in this bit of lunacy. With a nod to *The Terminator*, Bill and Ted are pursued by evil look-alike robots from the future who are out to kill them. The bad guys almost succeed, which causes the good guys to meet Death. In another filmic nod (this time to *The Seventh Seal*), Bill & Ted challenge Death to a game of . . . Twister! It's just as silly as the first film, and Reeves and Winter clearly are having fun, though some of the comic mileage is starting to wear thin. ★★½ DVD Letterbox: $14.99

Bill & Ted's Excellent Adventure

(1989, 90 min, US, Stephen Herek) *Keanu Reeves, Alex Winter, George Carlin, Bernie Casey.* Feeling overwhelmed by the world today? Thank goodness there's still every American's inalienable right of — stupidity. Bill and Ted are a couple of airheads who just wanna have fun. But when they're in danger of being shipped off to military school for failing history, what do they do? They resort to the best special effects Industrial Light and Magic can drum up. Carlin, playing an equally mindless muck from the future, comes to the Valley with a time machine for our homeboys to experience history firsthand. (Sequel: *Bill & Ted's Bogus Journey*) ★★½ DVD Letterbox: $14.99

A Bill of Divorcement

(1932, 69 min, US, George Cukor) *Katharine Hepburn, John Barrymore, Billie Burke.* The film that both introduced the ravishing Hepburn and started her illustrious association with director Cukor. Barrymore gives a fine performance as a veteran who returns home after a long stay at a mental hospital, trying to establish a relationship with his daughter Kate. Burke superbly plays Barrymore's wife, whose plans of remarriage significantly alter his hopes of a happy homecoming. ★★★½ VHS: $14.99

Billy Bathgate

(1991, 106 min, US, Robert Benton) *Dustin Hoffman, Nicole Kidman, Loren Dean, Bruce Willis, Steven Hill, Steve Buscemi, Stanley Tucci.* A fast-paced and tense adaptation of E.L. Doctorow's novel, recounting the fall of mobster Dutch Schultz (Hoffman) as seen through the eyes of an ambitious teenager, Billy Bathgate (Dean). Though slightly miscast, Hoffman excels as the moody gangster. Nestor Almendros' eerie cinematography imbues the film with a grim and destructive mood. ★★★ DVD: $14.99, VHS: $9.99

Billy Budd

(1962, 122 min, GB, Peter Ustinov) *Terence Stamp, Robert Ryan, Peter Ustinov, Melvyn Douglas, David McCallum.* In 1797, under the Rights of War Act, an English warship, *Avenger*, conscripts a young, good-natured innocent (Stamp) from a merchant ship at sea. *Avenger*'s master at arms (Ryan) is particularly sadistic, even by the standards of the British Navy at the time, whose officers had life and death control over their crews. Outstanding performances from the entire cast are supported by solid direction from Ustinov, who also produced and coscripted, as well as plays the ship's captain. A strong, straightforward story of morality and honor, based on the novella by Herman Melville. ★★★½ VHS: $29.99

Billy Elliot

(2000, 111 min, GB, Stephen Daldry) *Jamie Bell, Julie Walters, Gary Lewis, Jamie Draven, Jean Heywood, Stuart Wells.* It's not often a child performance comes along that makes you want to cheer, but such is the case with young Bell, who is extraordinary as an eleven-year-old coal miner's son with aspirations toward dance. Billy (Bell) lives with his coal mining family in Northern England. Instead of pursuing boxing lessons like all the other lads, Billy opts for ballet. Demonstrating a talent for the dance, Billy disregards his macho father's protestations and follows his heart, eventually vying for an opening at London's Royal Ballet School. From the producers of *The Full Monty*, the film shares in common a few elements from that hit comedy, but stands well on its own, as not only a refreshing look at adolescence but a stirring musical entertainment as well. ★★★★ DVD: $14.99, VHS Special Edition: $9.99

Billy Jack

(1971, 114 min, US, T.C. Frank [Tom Laughlin]) *Tom Laughlin, Delores Taylor.* If *Rambo: First Blood Part II* was the sociopolitical sensation of the 1980s, then this pacifist action-adventure is the 1970s equivalent. Laughlin plays the title character, a Native American karate expert who is pushed too far by the authorities. He fights back and becomes a folk hero in the process. Immensely popular, though not in its original theatrical run, but later in 1974 in a major re-release. (Sequel: *The Trial of Billy Jack*) ★★½ DVD: $14.99, VHS: $9.99

Billy Liar

(1963, 96 min, GB, John Schlesinger) *Tom Courtenay, Julie Christie, Finlay Currie, Mona Washbourne, Wilfred Pickles.* One of the benchmark films in the British "kitchen sink" school of filmmaking, Schlesinger's early effort is an outstanding examination of middle-class life. Courtenay is sparkling as a young daydreamer who is stuck in the mundanity of his boorish life. In her film debut, Christie is a wonderful young mod woman who offers Courtenay an escape into a world of fantasy. ★★★½ DVD Letterbox Criterion Collection: $39.99, VHS: $29.99

Billy Madison

(1995, 89 min, US, Tamra Davis) *Adam Sandler, Darren McGavin, Chris Farley, Steve Buscemi.* Another idiotic film from a former "SNL" regular. Sandler, who was one of the lesser gifted comics on the show, plays a moronic heir to a $600 million throne. His dad (McGavin) isn't sure whether to leave the business to his idiot son, so said idiot son goes back to school (grades 1---12) to prove he's not an idiot. What follows is a series of scatological and juvenile jokes and pranks that only Beavis and Butt-head would find funny ("Heh-heh. He said 'shit'"). It's unclear who this was intended for (preadolescents, teens, young adults), but save for one or two funny scenes, *Billy Madison* is one big loser. ★

Billy's Hollywood Screen Kiss

(1998, 89 min, US, Tommy O'Haver) *Sean Hayes, Brad Rowe, Meredith Scott Lynn, Paul Bartel, Holly Woodlawn.* Cute, gay hip, smart and funny, this romantic comedy makes for enjoyable viewing. Billy (Hayes of TV's "Will and Grace") is a handsome goateed photographer searching for Mr. Right. Frustrated by a succession of unfulfilling one-night stands, Billy thinks that he's found the man of his dreams in the person of local café waiter Gabriel (Rowe). Gaining support from his helpful best pal Georgina (Lynn), Billy tries mightily to win the heart of his dreamy object of affection. We follow Billy's often frantic attempts to figure out whether Gabriel might be interested in him romantically. A charming gay date movie. ★★★ DVD Widescreen: $14.99

Biloxi Blues

(1988, 106 min, US, Mike Nichols) *Matthew Broderick, Christopher Walken, Matt Mulhern, Corey Parker, Casey Siemaszko, Penelope Ann Miller.* The second in Neil Simon's acclaimed autobiographical trilogy (including *Brighton Beach Memoirs* and *Broadway Bound*). Broderick is the perfect reincarnation of young Simon, who here is sent to Biloxi, Mississippi, for ten weeks of boot camp. Simon's dialogue is refreshing and funny, and his work is seasoned with both poignancy and insight. Walken is at his best as the company's possibly unstable sergeant. ★★★½ DVD Letterbox: $14.99

The Bingo Long Traveling All-Stars & Motor Kings

(1976, 110 min, US, John Badham) *Billy Dee Williams, James Earl Jones, Richard Pryor, Stan Shaw, DeWayne Jessie, Ted Ross, Mabel King.* A winning screenplay, great period design, a glorious performance by Jones and terrific supporting turns by Pryor and Shaw all contribute to make this high-spirited baseball comedy one of the 1970s' most underrated and enjoyable films. Williams stars as the manager of a black barnstorming team in the late 1930s whose group of highly irregulars becomes the main attraction in the independent league circuit. ★★★½ DVD: $19.99, VHS: $9.99

Bio-Dome

(1996, 95 min, US, Jason Bloom) *Pauly Shore, Stephen Baldwin, William Atherton, Joey Adams.* Foolishness with friends Shore and Baldwin (each going to great lengths to out-dumb the other) becoming trapped in a biosphere for a year. At what point did Hollywood start to rethink Shore as a film star? This is it. Inept on every level. ★ DVD Letterbox: $14.99

Bird

(1988, 162 min, US, Clint Eastwood) *Forest Whitaker, Diane Verona, Michael Zelniker, Keith David.* Though he had many credits as director to his name before this remarkable musical biography of jazz great Charlie Parker, Eastwood for the first time demonstrated a distinctive storytelling ability. In a most challenging role, Whitaker gives a sensitive though commanding performance as the jazz man who was considered to be the greatest saxophonist of his time. In a series of flashbacks (which sometimes border on the confusing), *Bird* recalls Parker's meteoric rise in the jazz world, his troublesome home life, and the drug addiction that ultimately led to his death at the early age of 34. Verona is excellent as Parker's wife. Featuring an outstanding musical soundtrack, *Bird* is most definitely a labor of love from Eastwood. ★★★½ DVD: $19.99, VHS: $14.99

Bird on a Wire

(1990, 110 min, US, John Badham) *Mel Gibson, Goldie Hawn, David Carradine, Bill Duke, Stephen Tobolowsky, Joan Severance.* A far-fetched chase film/love story. This is commercial high-concept filmmaking at its most cynical — the whole thing is a big cut-and-paste job. Mel plays an on-the-run witness protectee who teams for some not-very-exciting misadventures with ex-girlfriend Hawn. ★½ DVD: $14.99, VHS: $9.99

The Bird with the Crystal Plumage

(1970, 98 min, Italy, Dario Argento) *Tony Musante, Suzy Kendall.* Italian maestro of the macabre Argento's directorial debut, *Bird* is a stylish murder mystery with Musante as an American author who, after witnessing an attempted homicide, becomes obsessed with solving the case himself. A string of murders are linked to this latest crime, so Musante becomes a valuable asset to a major investigation. The killer soon targets Musante and the writer comes to find himself to be both hunter and hunted. This film has all the trademarks of later Argento films: the bizarre and violent set piece murders; the red herrings; the unusual camera angles and setups; and the inquisitive outsider who holds the key to solving the mystery. An impressive beginning to a career which has gotten even better, *Bird* is a good introduction to a distinctive, European style of horror filmmaking. ★★★ DVD: $24.99

The Birdcage

(1996, 100 min, US, Mike Nichols) *Robin Williams, Nathan Lane, Gene Hackman, Dianne Wiest, Dan Futterman, Calista Flockhart, Hank Azaria, Christine Baranski.* An often hilariously funny and successfully Americanized, upliftingly pro-gay remake of the French farce *La Cage aux Folles*. The setting is Miami Beach's hip South Beach, where Armand Goldman (Williams) runs an extravagant drag revue called The Birdcage. His longtime lover Albert (Lane) is the star attraction, billed as Starina. The story remains the same: Armand's son wants to bring his fiancée and her right-wing parents over to meet the family, forcing the men to put on a "family values" show for the unsuspecting future in-laws. Hackman and Wiest wonderfully underplay their roles as an archconservative U.S. Senator and his doting wife. Williams is subtly fey and delivers the film's best lines, and Lane steals the show as the theatrically swishy diva "mom" with an ear-piercing squeal. ★★★ DVD Dual: $14.99

Birdman of Alcatraz

(1962, 143 min, US, John Frankenheimer) *Burt Lancaster, Karl Malden, Telly Savalas, Thelma Ritter.* Giving one of his most memorable performances, Lancaster assumes the real-life role of Robert "Robby" Stroud, a hard-as-nails, world-hating convict sentenced to life who becomes an authority on birds during his incarceration. Though mainly set in Stroud's prison cell, the film is devoid of claustrophobia and is compelling throughout. Deftly directed by Frankenheimer. ★★★½ DVD: $14.99

The Birds

(1963, 120 min, US, Alfred Hitchcock) *Rod Taylor, Tippi Hedren, Jessica Tandy, Veronica Cartwright, Suzanne Pleshette.* After his great success with *Psycho*, Hitchcock further pushed the boundaries of suspense and his own cinematic techniques with this harrowing nature-gone-awry tale. Hedren made her film debut as a carefree socialite whose initiation of a practical joke leads her to the small coastal town of Bodega Bay. Taylor is the stoic object of her prank. But nature soon has a joke of its own when our fine feathered friends begin attacking the townspeople with no apparent motive. Hitchcock takes his time in building the tension — which by film's end is overwhelming — with a series of spectacularly staged attacks (and all this without benefit of a musical score, which is so important in creating suspense). The birthday party, the classroom scene and the finale have all assumed legendary status in both the horror genre and the director's body of work. ★★★★ DVD Collector's Edition: $19.99, VHS: $14.99

Birdy

(1984, 120 min, US, Alan Parker) *Matthew Modine, Nicolas Cage, John Harkins, Karen Young, Bruno Kirby.* Parker's adventurous adaptation of the William Wharton best-seller poses a young man's erotic avian obsession as a logical option in a bird-brained world. Filmed largely in Philadelphia, *Birdy* features Modine as the pigeon fancier who goes to seed after a wartime trauma; Cage is his buddy, trying desperately to help his friend. ★★★½ DVD: $24.99

Birgitt Haas Must Be Killed

(1981, 105 min, France, Laurent Heynemann) *Philippe Noiret, Jean Rochefort, Lisa Kreuzer.* A former left-wing terrorist (Kreuzer) is targeted to be assassinated and it is an unscrupulous police officer (Noiret) who plots a romantic fling as bait to snare her. An engrossing and complex police thriller. ★★★

The Birth of a Nation

(1915, 190 min, US, D.W. Griffith) *Lillian Gish, Mae Marsh, Henry B. Walthall, Miriam Cooper.* Griffith was a Hollywood pioneer and his *Birth of a Nation* was Hollywood's first epic. Hailed for its groundbreaking technical advances and mounted on an unprecedented scale, this rousing saga of two families thrown into turmoil by the Civil War features an early performance by the legendary Gish. Although marred by undeniable racist sentiments (the Ku Klux Klan are depicted as the heroes!), it remains a landmark, a movie by which all others would be measured for many years. Assistant directors were Erich von Stroheim, Jack Conway and Raoul Walsh. ★★★★ DVD: $29.99, VHS: $39.99

The Bishop's Wife

(1947, 109 min, US, Henry Koster) *Cary Grant, Loretta Young, David Niven, Monty Woolley, Gladys Cooper, Elsa Lanchester.* An enchanted comedy with an unusually reserved Grant as an angel and Niven as an overwhelmed bishop in need of some heavenly assistance. When raising money for a new church becomes too taxing for the young clergyman, emissary Grant is sent to Earth to help; but instead is caught in the middle of a romantic triangle when bishop's wife Young becomes enamored with the handsome spirit. (Remade as *The Preacher's Wife*) ★★★½ DVD: $14.99

Bite the Bullet

(1975, 131 min, US, Richard Brooks) *Gene Hackman, James Coburn, Candice Bergen, Ben Johnson, Jan-Michael Vincent, Ian Bannen.* A grand, epic-sized comic western with Hackman and Coburn in good form as contestants in a 600-mile horse race, set during the turn-of-the-century. ★★★ VHS: $9.99

Bitter Moon

(1993, 135 min, France/GB, Roman Polanski) *Hugh Grant, Kristen Scott Thomas, Peter Coyote, Emmanuelle Seigner, Victor Banerjee, Stockard Channing.* This trashy but bizarrely entertaining psychosexual drama (comedy?) is about a humorously uptight British couple (Grant and Scott Thomas) who meet up with the wheelchair-bound American expatriate Oscar (Coyote) and his voluptuously sexy wife Mimi (Seigner) on a Mediterranean cruise. Much to his frustration, Grant's Nigel becomes transfixed with Oscar's near pornographic accounts of his and Mimi's tumultuous relationship — one that includes obsessive love, excessive sex, playful sado-masochism, water sports, betrayal, bitter hatred and sick revenge (it's a long cruise). The fun really begins when it's time for the obligatory sexual games and swapping. ★★ DVD: $19.99

Bitter Sugar

(1996, 104 min, Cuba, Leon Ichaso) *René Lavan, Mayte Vilán, Miguel Guitiérrez, Larry Villanueva.* *Bitter Sugar* is a provocative coming-of-age story that shows how young Communists, like Gustavo (Lavan), are wrongly placing their faith in Socialist Cuba. Though he is smart and handsome, Gustavo is naïve — he thinks that Castro will take care of him, and that "playing the game" is enough to get ahead in life. Gustavo's father (Guitiérrez) has learned this is not the case, and he is now trying to compensate for wasted years; his rebellious brother (Villanueva) has injected the AIDS virus into his bloodstream as a revolutionary act; and his girl-friend (Vilán) is developing relationships with foreigners in hope of getting to Miami. As Gustavo slowly realizes that commitment to Castro may not be the answer, he becomes politicized to an extreme degree. Director Ichaso has made a compelling film that brilliantly captures the "no future" paradox facing young Cubans today. (Spanish with English subtitles) ★★★ DVD: $19.99, VHS: $19.99

The Bitter Tears of Petra Von Kant

(1972, 124 min, Germany, Rainer Werner Fassbinder) *Hanna Schygulla, Margit Carstensen.* A lurid and stylized account of the mangled web of domination, sadomasochism and jealousy among three lesbians. One of Fassbinder's most controversial (and entertaining) works, the film takes place in a single setting — fashion designer Petra's (Carstensen) opulently appointed apartment — amid the music of Verdi and The Platters. The story focuses on the increasingly destructive power games between the mistress of the house and the object of her passion, the model Karin (Schygulla). Petra's maid also becomes involved in the mental mind games, which are played out to the hilt. (German with English subtitles) ★★★ DVD Masterworks Edition: $29.99, VHS: $19.99

Black & White

(1999, 97 min, US, Yuri Zeltser) *Gina Gershon, Rory Cochrane, Alison Eastwood, Ron Silver.* A cheap and sleazy little thriller about a cop who is a serial killer, *Black & White* benefits from Gershon's take-charge performance as Nora "Hugs" Hugosian, a sexy LAPD cop who is the prime suspect in a string of killings. When she is not breaking in her new partner, the devoted Catholic Chris O'Brien (Cochrane), on the beat and in the bedroom, Hugs may be taking justice into her own hands by shooting her perps in the eye. Although the story is far-fetched, and the number of suspects limited, there are a few red herrings to keep this otherwise routine policer interesting. Mildly diverting for B-movie fans only. ★★ DVD: $27.99

Black and White

(2000, 99 min, US, James Toback) *Oliver "Power" Grant, Robert Downey, Jr., Bijou Phillips, Ben Stiller, Brooke Shields, Allan Houston, Stacy Edwards, Scott Caan, Gaby Hoffman, Kidada Jones.* A difficult treatise on race relations in contemporary America, *Black and White* is the ambitious but unremarkable tale of disparate New Yorkers coming together — not by choice but by happenstance. Beginning with a weird, interracial three-way in Central Park, the disjointed but often compelling story follows the bumpy road of Rich Bower (Grant), a black thug who tries to go straight and make a name for himself as a hip-hop impresario. Crossing his path are a white husband-and-wife filmmaking team (Shields, Downey) who are making a documentary on white teens emulating ghetto culture, and a white cop (Stiller) determined to nab the former hood. Director Toback provides strong visuals to tell this multiracial patchwork but is let down by his own rambling screenplay. ★★½ DVD: $24.99

Black and White in Color

(1976, 90 min, Ivory Coast, Jean-Jacques Annaud) *Jean Carmet, Jacques Dufilho.* This powerful Academy Award Winner (Best Foreign Film) explores the horror and absurdity of war as French and German factions conflict in colonial West Africa before the first World War. (French with English subtitles) ★★★½ DVD Letterbox: $29.99

Black Beauty

(1994, 87 min, GB, Caroline Thompson) *Sean Bean, David Thewlis, Peter Cook, Eleanor Bron, Andrew Knott.* While the equestrian acting is outstanding, the re-creation of 19th-century England is flawless and the story line is loyal to Anna Sewell's classic book, the trials and tribulations of Black Beauty will be a bit much for most small children. The retelling of what must be one of the first animal-rights stories is moving and absorbing, and the horses are unbelievably human in their responses. Score by Danny Elfman. ★★★ DVD: $9.99, VHS: $9.99

The Black Bird

(1975, 98 min, US, David Giler) *Stéphane Audran, Elisha Cook, Jr., Lee Patrick, George Segal.* This spoof of *The Maltese Falcon* has Segal as Sam Spade, Jr. in search of the famous statue once again. Though Cook and Patrick repeat their roles from John Huston's classic, this is minimally entertaining. ★★

The Black Cat

(1934, 66 min, US, Edgar G. Ulmer) *Boris Karloff, Bela Lugosi, David Manners, Jacqueline Wells.* Karloff and Lugosi star as archenemies who use a young couple as pawns in a sinister game of chess in this atmospheric and striking suspense classic. Karloff plays a fascistic officer whose war crimes haunt Lugosi, a kindhearted doctor. One stormy night, Lugosi travels to Karloff's ultramodern home in the wilderness to have his final reckoning with the evil man. A road accident brings into the game a young engaged couple, who realize too late what is unfolding in their overnight home. Both actors are given ample opportunity to show off their talents at playing something other than monsters. With its heavily shadowed "nouveau" sets and its wonderful, emotional musical score, *The Black Cat* is one of the best Universal horror films of the 1930s. ★★★½

Black Cat White Cat

(1998, 129 min, Serbia, Emir Kusturica) *Bajram Severdzan, Srdan Todorovic, Branka Katic.* Typically whimsical and absurdist fun from celebrated director Kusturica. A pathetic con man tries to survive in former Yugoslavia amidst an array of equally bizarre characters. Episodic and very loose, *Black Cat White Cat* is a perfect example of "carnivalesque" cinema: way over-the-top performances, goofy calliope-like music, and crazy coincidences that scream an "isn't-this-the-way-life-is?" outlook. Your appreciation of the film depends completely on your taste for this sort of filmmaking. Those who love all things "Felliniesque" will find much to like here. Either way, this apolitical follow-up to what is considered Kusturica's masterpiece (*Underground*) is still quite accomplished and original. (Serbo-Croatian and Romany with English subtitles) ★★★

The Black Cauldron

(1985, 80 min, US, Richard Rich & Ted Berman) *Voices of: Grant Bardsley, Susan Sheridan, Freddie Jones, John Byner, John Hurt.* Darker and scarier than anything the Disney folks had done before or since, *The Black Cauldron* tells the tale of a young farmboy who dreams of adventure and glory through battle. He sets out to fight the evil Horned King, who's obsessed with finding the all-powerful black cauldron, which has the power to raise the army of the dead. (Yes, it sounds like *Legend*, and the similarities don't stop there.) Vocal contributions are good (especially Hurt as the Horned King), but the animation is rather clunky compared to today's fluid, computer-enhanced standards. ★★½ DVD Gold Collection: $19.99, VHS Gold Collection: $14.99

Black Christmas

(1975, 98 min, Canada, Bob Clark) *Margot Kidder, Kier Dullea, Olivia Hussey, John Saxon.* A truly mean-spirited holiday psycho/slasher flick with a sorority house setting, obscene phone calls and plastic dry cleaning bags (didn't anyone read the warning label? This is not a toy!). Director Clark would go on to direct *Porky's*. (aka: *Silent Night, Evil Night*) ★★ DVD Critical Mass Collector's Edition: $29.99

Black God & White Devil

(1964, 102 min, Brazil, Glauber Rocha) Set in arid northeast Brazil, Rocha's first major film deals with Manuel, a worker who, after killing his boss in self-defense, finds himself on the run from the law. Enlightened to the horrendous conditions of the peasants by the rich landowners, he becomes a bandit of honor, a self-styled black saint, preaching bloodshed and the return of the land to the people. A violent yet lyrical political drama that utilizes an intoxicating mixture of social realism, symbolism, myths and references to Brazilian history and culture. (Portuguese with English subtitles) ★★★½ VHS: $59.99

Black Hawk Down

(2001, 146 min, US, Ridley Scott) *Josh Hartnett, Ewan McGregor, Tom Sizemore, Eric Bana, William Fichtner, Ewen Bremner, Sam Shepard, Ron Eldard, Zeljko Ivanek, Jeremy Piven.* When a humanitarian mission by U.S. forces goes seriously awry, a 24-hour period becomes a living hell for beleaguered American soldiers caught in a firestorm of bullets, bombs and crushing defeat. Based on the best-selling novel by Mark Bowden, *Black Hawk Down* is a magnificently told film that recounts through intense imagery, realistic battle sequences and masterful storytelling what exactly happened that day when Delta Force troops and Army Rangers landed in the hostile environment of Mogadishu in October 1993. Director Scott has achieved quite an accomplishment — chaotic war scenes of astonishing power are deftly balanced with characters who resonate far beyond the usual war film. Epic in scope but without losing an intimacy that sets it apart, *Black Hawk Down* is superior, straightforward filmmaking. ★★★★ DVD Letterbox: $19.99, DVD: 3-disc Deluxe Edition: $39.99, VHS: $14.99

The Black Hole

(1979, 97 min, US, Gary Nelson) *Maximilian Schell, Anthony Perkins, Yvette Mimieux, Robert Forster, Ernest Borgnine.* Disney's nod to *Star Wars* is a cheesy sci-fi adventure about a space expedition which comes in conflict with a "mad" scientist about to explore a black hole. Nice special effects and a fine score by John Barry. ★★½ VHS Letterboxed: $14.99

Black Knight

(2001, 97 min, US, Gil Junger) *Martin Lawrence, Marsha Thomason, Tom Wilkinson, Kevin Conway.* Mark Twain's classic story "A Connecticut Yankee" now has the affable Lawrence as the unwilling time traveler who journeys to 14th-century England to find romance and adventure. A basic interpretation that has a few laughs but lacks inspiration, *Black Knight*'s updating has Lawrence as a theme-park employee who falls into a castle moat only to awaken in the past. Having a black actor play the part opens the door for a few additional jokes, but the screenplay doesn't go very far in exploiting a 21st-century attitude (Whoopi Goldberg's TV version the same year was able to do exactly that). And after all, it is the anachronistic spirit that makes or breaks Twain's comic tale. ★★ DVD: $14.99, VHS: $9.99

Black Legion

(1937, 83 min, US, Archie Mayo) *Humphrey Bogart, Erin O'Brien, Dick Foran, Ann Sheridan.* One of Warner's better 1930s social dramas, with Bogey as a factory worker whose frustration on the job leads him to join a Ku Klux Klan-like group. ★★★ VHS: $14.99

Black Like Me

(1964, 107 min, US, Carl Lerner) *James Whitmore, Roscoe Lee Browne, Will Geer.* In the late 1950s, a white journalist took drugs which darkened his skin color enough to allow him to "pass" for black. Based on his book, this is an emotional, well-produced and empathic adaptation recounting his experiences with racial prejudice. Whitmore, who stars as the reporter, used the same drugs in preparation for the role. The story is not as dated as it should be. ★★★

B

Josh Hartnett in *Black Hawk Down*

Black Lizard

(1968, 86 min, Japan, Kinji Fukasaku) *Akihiko Maruyama, Yukio Mishima.* Mix elements of *What's Up, Tiger Lily?* with *Beyond the Valley of the Dolls*, throw in lurid color schemes and weird camera angles and you'll have some idea of the make-up of this wildly campy detective yarn. Japan's most famous female impersonator, Maruyama, stars as the villainous jewel thief The Black Lizard — a fatally seductive temptress who'll stop at nothing to get her dainty hands on the fabulous Star of Egypt diamond. Yukio Mishima, who adapted the original novel for the stage, is featured in this entertaining curiosity as a naked human statue in the glamorous chanteuse's demented private museum. She's so evil! (Japanese with English subtitles) ★★★

Black Magic M-66

(1987, 60 min, Japan, Masamune Shirow) Cross *The Terminator* with *Blade Runner*, add a hint of comedy, and you have the basic plot for this superb anime from master *manga* artist Shirow. Based on a story from Shirow's comic book, this animated sci-fi thriller follows the exploits of Sybel, a video journalist investigating a failed military experiment involving android assassins. When she finds herself one step ahead of the government task force tracking down the rogue androids, Sybel goes from covering the story to becoming a player in the all-too-real drama. Shirow blends edge-of-your-seat action sequences, comedy, suspense and unforgettable characters. (Japanese with English subtitles) ★★★½ DVD: $24.99, VHS Dubbed: $14.99, VHS Subtitled: $24.99

Black Mask

(1996, 89 min, Hong Kong, Daniel Lee) *Jet Li, Ching Wan Lau, Karen Mak.* Hong Kong superstar Li plays a soldier retooled by a mad scientist to have superhuman capabilities and feel no pain. When the government decides to terminate the project and all its results, Li escapes in a bravura action scene. He attempts to live a quiet life as a librarian, but his past catches up with him, and mayhem ensues. This entertaining, inventive and gory actioner is harmed by Americanization: hokey dubbing and especially incongruous hip-hop music detract from the atmosphere and fun. Still, Li's charisma and amazing wire-work make even this watered-down version more than worthwhile. ★★½ DVD: $9.99, VHS: $9.99

Black Moon Rising

(1986, 100 min, US, Harley Cokliss) *Tommy Lee Jones, Linda Hamilton, Robert Vaughn.* A government agent hides secret information in a high-powered auto. When the car is stolen, he must battle not only the gang that stole the auto, but the hoodlums who are out to get the info back. A vigorous, better-than-average action-adventure. ★★★ DVD: $24.99, VHS: $9.99

Black Narcissus

(1946, 99 min, GB, Emeric Pressburger & Michael Powell) *Deborah Kerr, Jean Simmons, David Farrar, Sabu, Flora Robson.* This visually sumptuous tale of a group of nuns who establish a mission in a remote Himalayan outpost was once considered one of the most breathtaking color films ever made. A dramatically charged saga of physical and emotional turmoil. ★★★★ DVD Criterion Collection: $39.99

The Black Orchid

(1959, 96 min, US, Martin Ritt) *Sophia Loren, Anthony Quinn.* The ever-glamorous Loren "dresses down" in this high-strung melodrama about a lonely businessman (Quinn) whose courtship of a gangster's widow meets with resistance from his mentally unbalanced daughter. A minor league film from a major league director. ★½ VHS: $14.99

Black Orpheus

(1958, 103 min, Brazil, Marcel Camus) *Breno Mello, Marpessa Dawn.* This extravagant explosion of colorful sights and sounds is a modern reenactment of Orpheus and Eurydice's tragic tale set against the splendid backdrop of Carnival in Rio. Virtually nonstop visual and musical excitement. Winner of the Academy Award for Best Foreign Film. Scored by Antonio Carlos Jobim. (Portuguese with English subtitles) ★★★★ DVD Criterion Collection: $29.99, VHS: $29.99

Black Rain

(1989, 120 min, US, Ridley Scott) *Michael Douglas, Kate Capshaw, Andy Garcia, Ken Takakura.* Scott's overblown, relentlessly grim and humorless police thriller set in modern-day Tokyo is a routine action film under the guise of an examination of a Japanese and American culture clash in police techniques. Douglas stars as a tough, world-weary cop (is there any other kind?) who is assigned with partner Garcia to escort a New York-based hit man for the Japanese mob back to Japan. When the assassin escapes, Douglas tears apart the city of Tokyo looking for him, coming into conflict with the local police force and the mob. ★½ DVD: $19.99, VHS: $9.99

Black Rain

(1990, 124 min, Japan, Shohei Imamura) *Kazuo Kitamura, Yoshiko Matsuda.* August 6, 1945 — a date that has long been etched into the Japanese psyche, for this is when the atomic bomb was dropped on Hiroshima. Having suppressed the consequences of this national tragedy, director Imamura has, in a grimly realistic, unrelenting fashion, exposed the national wounds by dealing with both the actual bombing of the city and its terrible aftereffects. In a determinedly nonsentimental and almost documentary approach, this haunting drama follows one family who was near Hiroshima at the time of the explosion. The family attempts to rebuild their shattered lives. But within five years all grow terribly ill due to radiation. A stunningly photographed modern masterpiece. (Japanese with English subtitles) ★★★★ VHS: $19.99

Black Rainbow

(1991, 103 min, US, Dick Hodges) *Rosanna Arquette, Tom Hulce, Jason Robards.* Arquette stars as a carnival clairvoyant whose questionable abilities take a suddenly strange turn when she begins receiving psychic transmissions from people who aren't dead — yet. Robards costars as her cynical, alcoholic father, and Hulce plays a hounding reporter who's hot for her story. A well-crafted and engaging thriller. ★★★

Black Robe

(1991, 100 min, Canada, Bruce Beresford) *Aden Young, Lothaire Bluteau, Sandrine Holt, Tantoo Cardinal.* Beresford's impassioned examination of the cruelty and oppression intentionally and unintentionally imposed by the European settlers as they brought their "civilization" and Christian beliefs to the native peoples of the New World. While the story breaks little new ground, *Black Robe* is saved from familiarity by its strikingly beautiful Canadian landscapes and its absorbing and emotional drama of faith and the will to survive. Bluteau plays a 17th-century French Jesuit missionary whose religious zeal compels him to risk martyrdom in order to bring Catholicism to the Hurons of Canada. He embarks on a harrowing journey up the St. Lawrence River — a symbolic canoe ride that begins in an explosively colorful autumn and ends during a torturously inhospitable winter. ★★★½ DVD Letterbox: $19.99

The Black Room

(1935, 67 min, US, Roy William Neill) *Boris Karloff, Marian Marsh.* Karloff has a field day in this Gothic tale of twin brothers (one good, one evil, both Karloff) whose destinies are overshadowed by a family curse. ★★½

Black Sheep

(1996, 87 min, US, Penelope Spheeris) *Chris Farley, David Spade, Tim Matheson, Christine Ebersole, Gary Busey.* After the spirited hijinks of their funny *Tommy Boy*, Farley and Spade regurgitate the same plot with considerably less successful results. Once again, Farley is a screw-up who must be baby-sitted by sarcastic little twit Spade. Unfortunately, Farley is less likable, Spade is not so sarcastic, and most of their comic antics aren't that funny. The plot has to do with big brother Matheson running for governor; Farley is his younger sibling who's "Roger Clinton, Billy Carter and every Reagan family member rolled into one." If only he were that interesting. ★★ DVD Letterbox: $19.99, VHS: $9.99

The Black Stallion

(1979, 118 min, US, Carroll Ballard) *Kelly Reno, Mickey Rooney, Teri Garr, Hoyt Axton.* A heartwarming tale of a young boy and his devoted stallion as they share both adventures on an isolated island and a quest for a racing championship. The cinematography is ravishing. ★★★½ DVD: $14.99, VHS: $9.99

The Black Stallion Returns

(1983, 105 min, US, Robert Dalva) *Kelly Reno, Vincent Spano, Allen Goorwitz, Woody Strode, Ferdinand Mayne, Teri Garr.* Adequate sequel to the 1979 family favorite. Reno is back as Alec, who finds himself in the exotic Sahara in hot pursuit of his beloved horse Black, who's been kidnapped by his original owner — desert chieftain Abu Ben Ishak (Mayne). ★★½ DVD: $14.99

Black Sunday

(1960, 87 min, Italy, Mario Bava) *Barbara Steele, John Richardson, Andrea Checchi, Arturo Dominici, Ivo Garrani, Antonio Pierfederici.* This horror classic is Bava's masterpiece. Steele stars as a condemned witch who rises from the dead to seek vengeance on the descendents of those who executed her. This Gothic tale is full of atmosphere and chilling black-and-white cinematography. As with most Italian horror films, the plot is weak and sometimes silly, but the visuals are lush and creepy. A must-see for Argento fans and classic horror buffs. ★★★½ DVD: $24.99, VHS: $29.99

Black Sunday

(1977, 143 min, US, John Frankenheimer) *Bruce Dern, Robert Shaw, Marthe Keller, Fritz Weaver, William Daniels.* From the director of *The Manchurian Candidate* comes this gripping adaptation of the Thomas Harris best-seller about a terrorist plot to blow up the Super Bowl, with a little bit of help from a demented ex-POW (Dern at his maniacal best). Shaw is the government expert on the case. ★★★ DVD: $14.99, VHS: $14.99

Black Water

(1992, 105 min, US, Nicolas Gessner) *Julian Sands, Stacey Dash, Ned Beatty, Rod Steiger.* Sands is an uptight British tax attorney and Dash is the street urchin/femme fatale he plucks off the highway in this unimaginative thriller set in the Tennessee hills. After witnessing what he thinks is a murder, Sands finds he is being tailed on his way to an innocent fishing trip. Dash offers him help, but is she playing both sides of the fence? Who knows, and more importantly, who cares? ★ VHS: $79.99

Black Widow

(1987, 101 min, US, Bob Rafelson) *Debra Winger, Theresa Russell, Sami Frey, Nicol Williamson, Dennis Hopper.* Winger and Russell square off in this spine-tingling suspense story. Russell is a jet-setting sophisticate whose husbands have a habit of dying shortly after their wedding day. Winger is the FBI agent who catches on to Russell's shenanigans and sets out to uncover her deadly scheme. Instead, the two become locked in a heated tête-à-tête (or more appropriately *coeur-a-coeur*) that sizzles with underlying sexual tension. ★★★ DVD Dual: $14.99, VHS: $9.99

Blackbeard's Ghost

(1968, 107 min, US, Robert Stevenson) *Peter Ustinov, Dean Jones, Suzanne Pleshette, Elsa Lanchester.* Fluffy Disney comedy with Ustinov as the ghost of the infamous pirate Blackbeard who helps a family fight off the bad guys. ★★½ DVD: $14.99, VHS: $9.99

Blackboard Jungle

(1955, 101 min, US, Richard Brooks) *Glenn Ford, Sidney Poitier, Vic Morrow, Richard Kiley, Anne Francis, Paul Mazursky.* Ford stars in this harrowing adaptation of Evan Hunter's novel about a New York teacher who is schooled in the ways of the streets by his students. In comparison to the Uzi-toting, crack-addicted youth of today's Hollywood high schools, these mid-'50s punks seem relatively harmless. But the drama here is tense and excellent performances are registered by Poitier and Morrow. ★★★½ VHS: $19.99

Blackjack

(1998, 123 min, US, John Woo) *Dolph Lundgren, Kate Vernon, Phillip MacKenzie, Kam Heskin, Padraigin Murphy, Tony DeSantis, Fred Williamson, Saul Rubinek.* Extremely disappointing bit of nonsense from usually dynamic action maestro Woo will bore even the director's most ardent fans. Lundgren plays Jack, an ex-CIA operative who is asked by an old friend to act as a bodyguard for his vulnerable young daughter. When the girl's parents die under mysterious circumstances, she is left in the care of "Uncle" Jack. This snooze-inducing *Bodyguard* redux is punctuated by an even sillier subplot involving Dolph's fear of the color white due to a childhood trauma. Huh? Even the action scenes are tedious. ★½ DVD: $9.99, VHS: $9.99

Blackmail

(1929, 78 min, GB, Alfred Hitchcock) *Anny Ondra, John Longden, Sara Allgood, Cyril Ritchard.* In his first talkie (which initially started as a silent), Hitchcock demonstrates some of the cunning cinematic trickery that he would later define and master. Starting unusually slow for a Hitchcock film, the story picks up considerable speed once the plot is in motion. It has to do with a flirtatious shopgirl who murders her attempted rapist and is blackmailed by a sleazy eyewitness. Though awkwardly paced, the film nevertheless maintains suspense throughout, and contains several scenes that could only be described as pure Hitchcock. This includes a terrific sequence in which the girl hears only snippets of conversation: the word "knife" over and over. ★★★ DVD: $19.99, VHS: $12.99

The Blackout

(1998, 100 min, US, Abel Ferrara) *Matthew Modine, Claudia Schiffer, Beatrice Dalle, Sarah Lassez, Dennis Hopper.* A junkie movie star (Modine) alienates his girlfriend with his drunken abuse and general bad behavior. Eighteen months later, he is sober and living with a new girlfriend (Schiffer). But he's haunted by terrifying nightmares and nagging thoughts that he did something awful during his last blackout. Director Ferrara's sin-and-redemption tale is even more downbeat and hopeless than his usual fare, making the receptive audience for this film miniscule. However, despite the relentless nihilism and self-indulgence, *The Blackout* boasts effective performances and a perverse hold on one's attention. ★★ DVD Dual: $29.99, VHS: $19.99

Blade

(1998, 120 min, US, Stephen Norrington) *Wesley Snipes, Stephen Dorff, Kris Kristofferson, N'Bushe Wright, Udo Kier.* A terrific, energetic action/horror film with Snipes as a vampire hunter who, with the help of mentor Kristofferson and doctor Wright, plans to destroy upstart punk bloodsucker Dorff's mission to turn the Earth into one big vampire dinner. This extremely entertaining adaptation of the comic book captures the look and feel of a top-drawer graphic novel, thanks to a punchy script by David S. Goyer and imaginative, super-stylish direction by Norrington. *Blade* neatly avoids the jokey tone of most action/horror/sci-fi films, and while there is humor, it's never at the expense of the story or characters. Opening with a great, gory battle in a nightclub and never letting up, *Blade* comes closer than most any American film to date to duplicating the hyperkinetic pace and excitement of Hong Kong "heroic bloodshed" films. (Sequel: *Blade 2*) ★★★½ DVD: $14.99, VHS: $6.99

Blade 2

(2002, 97 min, US, Guillermo del Toro) *Wesley Snipes, Kris Kristofferson, Ron Perlman, Leonor Varela, Norman Reedus, Luke Goss.* Snipes returns as vampire hunter Blade — the half-human, half-bloodsucker known as the Daywalker — and this time he's joining forces with his former foes to wage battle against the Reapers, a race of mutant vampires who feed off the undead. While it lacks the first film's expensive spit and polish, this stylish sequel is leaner, grittier and boasts superior makeup and visual effects. The overreliance on digital vampire disintegration gags takes on a generic video game quality, which is apropos for a film stripped right out of a cult graphic novel. Mexican filmmaker del Toro proves to be an inspired choice to orchestrate the atmospheric vampiric action — and to cement the series' viability as a muscular franchise. (Sequel: *Blade: Trinity*) ★★★ DVD Letterbox Platinum Series: $26.99, DVD Letterbox: $19.99, VHS: $6.99

Blade Runner

(1982, 114 min, US, Ridley Scott) *Harrison Ford, Rutger Hauer, Sean Young, Edward James Olmos, Daryl Hannah, William Sanderson, M. Emmet Walsh, Brion James, Joanna Cassidy.* Ford stars in this jagged, futuristic thriller as an authorized exterminator of androids gone awry. Hauer and Hannah are renegade robots whose physical prowess forces Ford out of the role of hunter and into the role of hunted. Scott's space-age L.A. is a smoky, neon-drenched landscape seething with danger and decay. A stunning film adaptation of Philip K. Dick's "Do Androids Dream of Electric Sheep?" ★★★★ DVD Director's Cut: $19.99, VHS Letterboxed Director's Cut: $14.99

The Blair Witch Project

(1999, 89 min, US, Daniel Myrick & Eduardo Sánchez) *Heather Donahue, Michael C. Williams, Joshua Leonard.* Building a legend on top of a legend, *The Blair Witch Project* purports to be footage that three student filmmakers took while researching the myth in the cursed woods. Needless to say, the three were never found, and this film linearly pieces together their footage (video and 16mm) as a documentary. The trip starts bouncily enough, but as they become lost, the film becomes truly terrifying, thanks to the audience being placed in the very same situation as the "actors." Never knowing what's behind a tree, or what's in the dark, the dread relentlessly builds, especially for those with active imaginations. However, those expecting the shocks and jumps of a *Halloween* or *Scream* will be disappointed. Accept this film as it is: a "documentary" that's a totally original experiment in terror. (Sequel: *Book of Shadows: Blair Witch 2*) ★★★½ DVD: $14.99, VHS: $9.99

Blame It on Rio

(1984, 100 min, US, Stanley Donen) *Michael Caine, Joseph Bologna, Valerie Harper, Demi Moore.* This Americanized version of the French sex farce *One Wild Moment* is a surprisingly entertaining, albeit TV sitcomish, comedy about the sexual philandering between a group of friends and their ensuing bed-hopping, all under the seductive rays of Rio de Janiero. Caine is the befuddled husband who becomes the object of desire of the nymphette daughter of his best friend, Bologna. ★★½ DVD: $14.99

Blame It on the Bellboy

(1992, 78 min, GB, Mark Herman) *Dudley Moore, Bryan Brown, Bronson Pinchot, Richard Griffiths, Patsy Kensit, Alison Steadman, Lindsay Anderson.* A bumbling bellboy mixes the schedules of three travelers and serves up a comedy of errors. Moore, Brown and Griffiths are three visitors to Venice, and they are all staying at the same hotel. It is there that bellboy Pinchot sends each man on one of the other's business. This includes assassinating a crime boss, buying a villa, and escaping for a "pleasure" weekend. Though this comedy never hits the inspired heights of another 1992 farce, *Noises Off*, there are a few (if silly) laughs awaiting the patient viewer. ★★ DVD: $9.99

Blank Check

(1994, 90 min, US, Rupert Wainwright) *Brian Bonsall, Miguel Ferrer.* This *Home Alone* clone from Disney tries to do the Macaulay Culkin hit one better: What if he's home alone — but he has a million dollars at his disposal? Such is the case when misunderstood Preston (Bonsall) has his bike run over and is given a blank check by the bad guy (Ferrer) who did it. Preston buys a neat home down the street and lives every kid's ultimate fantasy life — until the bad guy and his associates come looking for him. Processed junk food. ★★ DVD: $14.99

Blankman

(1994, 96 min, US, Mike Binder) *Damon Wayans, David Alan Grier, Jason Alexander, Robin Givens.* A charming comic satire featuring "In Living Color" 's Wayans and Grier as a pair of vigilantes. With more than a few nods to the 1960s TV series "Batman," this mindlessly entertaining film follows the pair's wild adventures fighting evil while clad in bulletproof underwear and Grandma's housecoat.

Blast 'Em

(1992, 103 min, US, Joseph Blasioli) This is a highly entertaining documentary about the competition among the paparazzi that focuses on acid-tongued imp Victor Malafronte, who pursues his celebrity prey with the precision of a trained assassin. Follow Malafronte and other photographers' exploits, including the pathetic Twinkie-addicted Queerdonna, as they stalk several stars, such as Robert De Niro, Sigourney Weaver, Michael J. Fox, John F. Kennedy, Jr. and a very funny and revealing Sally Kirkland. A must-see for star gazers everywhere. ★★★

Blast from the Past

(1999, 106 min, US, Hugh Wilson) *Brendan Fraser, Alicia Silverstone, Sissy Spacek, Christopher Walken, Dave Foley, Joey Slotnik.* In this charming, funny romantic comedy, Fraser plays Adam, whose scientist father (Walken) rushes his family to the fall-out shelter in 1962 when the Cuban Missile Crisis looks to escalate. Thinking the bomb has hit, they stay underground for 35 years. It's up to Adam to surface and reconnoiter food and supplies (and avoid the mutants!). He then meets Eve (Silverstone), and it's love at first sight. It's all very sweet-natured, thanks in part to Spacek and Walken's expert playing of Adam's parents, but mostly to Fraser's wide-eyed innocent. The laughs are genuine, the social observations subtle, and there's a killer dance sequence (is there anything this guy can't do?). Silverstone is appealing, though outshined by Fraser. ★★★ DVD: $14.99, VHS: $9.99

Blaze

(1989, 108 min, US, Ron Shelton) *Paul Newman, Lolita Davidovich, Robert Wuhl.* Shelton, who authored the terrific *Bull Durham*, makes a rousing directorial debut in this sexy and funny story based on Blaze Starr's autobiographical novel about the famous stripper's "scandalous" affair with Louisiana governor Earl Long. The film tells the entertaining story of how country girl Blaze moved to the big city (New Orleans) and became mistress to the powerful "Guv'nor" Long. Shelton has a keen ear for romantic repartee, and *Blaze* is at its best in these scenes between Long and Starr. Newman gives a full-blooded, larger-than-life characterization as Long and Davidovich is well cast physically but lacks the spark to set her rising Starr apart from other film ecdysiasts. ★★★ DVD: $14.99

Blazing Saddles

(1974, 93 min, US, Mel Brooks) *Gene Wilder, Cleavon Little, Madeline Kahn, Harvey Korman, John Hillerman, Dom DeLuise, Slim Pickens, Mel Brooks.* Brooks' uproarious comedy did wonders for making racism, sexism and bodily functions laughing matters. Richard Pryor helped script this scathing spoof of the Wild West. Kahn steals the show with her on-target Marlene Dietrich impersonation. ★★★½ DVD 30th Anniversary Special Edition: $19.99, VHS: $9.99

Favorite Line: "You will be risking your lives, whilst I will be risking an almost-certain Academy Award nomination for the Best Supporting Actor."
—*Harvey Korman as Hedley Lamarr*

Bleak House

(1987, 391 min, GB, Ross Devenish) *Diana Rigg, Denholm Elliott.* Charles Dickens' scathing look at the Byzantine judicial process of 19th-century England is brought to the small screen with the usual aplomb associated with BBC television. Rigg and Elliott deliver fine performances in this classic tale that follows the plight of the Jarndyce family, whose legal problems have been dragged through the courts for generations and devastated the lives of many. ★★★★

Bleak Moments

(1971, 110 min, GB, Mike Leigh) *Anne Raitt, Eric Allen, Sarah Stephenson, Mike Bradwell.* While this early Leigh film suffers from a small budget and reduced production values, it still evidences the director's uncanny ability to sketch indelible portraits with minimal brush strokes and often with no exposition. Sylvia (Raitt) copes with caring for her mentally challenged sister (Stephenson) and a mind-numbing job as a secretary in a barren urban environment. Her relationship with a schoolteacher (Allen) is devoid of any true communication — they share stilted conversation but no connection. The appearance of a guitar-playing lodger in the garage offers a short-lived flash of spontaneity in the sisters' treadmill lives. ★★½ DVD: $29.99, VHS: $29.99

Bless the Child

(2000, 107 min, US, Chuck Russell) *Kim Basinger, Holliston Coleman, Jimmy Smits, Ian Holm, Rufus Sewell, Christina Ricci.* An inferior occult thriller that borrows a little from *Rosemary's Baby*, *The Omen* and a host of other scare 'em-ups, but fails to make a mark of its own as either original or scary. Basinger plays a nurse who raises her drug-addicted sister's daughter. Soon the aunt and child (who seems to possess heavenly powers) are the target of a satanic sect who are out to harvest the girl's power. Basinger and cast sleepwalk through this silly film, whose few good scenes are offset by slow pacing and loopy plot developments. ★½ DVD: $14.99, VHS: $9.99

Blessed Event

(1932, 78 min, US, Roy Del Ruth) *Lee Tracy, Mary Brian, Dick Powell.* Tracy stars as Alvin Roberts, a very ambitious Broadway gossip columnist who makes a name for himself through his scandalmongering. Unfortunately, he makes a lot of enemies along the way. Fast-paced dialogue highlights this Depression-era film dealing with moral and ethical dilemmas. ★★½ VHS: $19.99

Harrison Ford stalks renegade androids through the streets of a futuristic L.A. in *Blade Runner*

Blind Date

(1987, 93 min, US, Blake Edwards) *Bruce Willis, Kim Basinger, John Larroquette, William Daniels.* Though not top-notch Edwards, there are enough laughs to keep one mildly entertained. Willis is the exec who desperately needs a date for a business dinner; Basinger is the answer to his prayers — or is she? It seems once she drinks, she's uncontrollably manic, sort of like this comedy. ★★½ DVD: $9.99

Blind Faith

(1998, 121 min, US, Ernest Dickerson) *Charles S. Dutton, Courtney B. Vance, Lonette McKee, Kadeem Hardison, Garland Whitt.* Director Dickerson delivers a shockingly powerful piece of storytelling — hammering at themes of racism, social justice and homophobia — in this intense drama about a black teenager accused of murdering a white teen in 1950s Brooklyn. Charles, Jr. (Whitt) is a seemingly happy recent high school graduate and obedient son to the stern but upstanding Charles, Sr. (Dutton), a black policeman. One evening he is accused of killing a white youth in a park. The case initially looks open-and-shut, for there are witnesses to the crime and even the youth admits to the crime. But his uncle John (Vance), a determined and fiery small-time lawyer, takes on the seemingly hopeless case. The acting is first-rate, the story complex and the outcome shattering. ★★★½ VHS: $9.99

Blind Fury

(1990, 85 min, US, Phillip Noyce) *Rutger Hauer, Terry O'Quinn, Lisa Blount, Meg Foster.* Noyce has liberally culled ideas from the "Zatoichi" Japanese swordsman film series and added fine comic action-adventure footage. The incomparable Hauer stars as a Vietnam vet who, after being blinded in the jungle, is befriended by local villagers and taught the sacred art of swinging the sword. Back in the U.S., our blind, blond samurai hero battles the bad guys at every turn. With its tongue-in-cheek humor, fast-paced fight sequences and the mesmerizing screen presence of Hauer, this is a film any action fan should not miss. ★★★ DVD: $24.99, VHS: $14.99

Blind Side

(1992, 90 min, US, Geoff Murphy) *Rutger Hauer, Rebecca DeMornay, Ron Silver.* DeMornay and Silver star as a couple on a business trip to Mexico who accidentally kill a policeman and then are tormented upon their return home by a vengeful Hauer. This film may sound good on paper, but it doesn't play well on the screen. DeMornay and Silver consistently overact, though Hauer does provide comic relief. If you have a couple of friends who enjoy laughing at bad movies, this is the one to watch. ★ DVD: $14.99, VHS: $9.99

Blind Spot: Hitler's Secretary

(2003, 87 min, Germany, André Heller & Othmar Schmiderer) *Traudl Junge.* A feature-length interview with Traudl Junge, Adolf Hitler's secretary during the last years of WWII, *Blind Spot* is not an innovative film (it's basically just several talking-head shots strung together), but its subject is such a great storyteller it's of little consequence. Junge relates the events which led to her getting the job, what Hitler was like in private, and, most interestingly, she describes in detail the last days in the bunker. She was with Hitler (and Eva Braun and Goebbels) till the bitter end, and her memories of these days are utterly fascinating. She's extremely forthright in her opinion of Hitler — she found him

charming, for the most part — and her lifelong guilt after the fact. This is a powerful, important document. The candid and engaging Junge died one day after this film premiered. (German with English subtitles) ★★★½ DVD: $29.99

Blind Trust (Pouvoir Intime)

(1987, 86 min, Canada, Yves Simoneau) This riveting suspense thriller chronicles the planning, execution and bloody aftermath of a failed armed robbery attempt in Montreal. Successfully balancing its sympathy for both the criminals as well as a guard held captive in the armored truck, this taut crime caper should keep the viewer enthralled throughout. (French with English subtitles) ★★★½

Blink

(1994, 106 min, US, Michael Apted) *Madeleine Stowe, Aidan Quinn, Laurie Matcalf, James Remar.* Stowe gives a splendid performance as a gutsy but vulnerable musician, blind since childhood, who regains her vision just in time to witness a murderer fleeing the scene of the crime. Quinn is the hard-boiled detective who, not blind to her considerable charms, sets out to find the killer before he finds her. A good use of visual effects and attention to detail and character make this a cut above the usual thriller. Granted, the mystery's resolution is a little slapdash with its "watch me pull a killer out of my hat" routine, but nevertheless *Blink* is a refreshingly eye-opening chiller. ★★★ VHS: $9.99

Bliss

(1985, 112 min, Australia, Ray Lawrence) *Barry Otto, Lynette Curran.* This outrageous and daring film stars Otto as Harry Joy, a wistful Sydney advertising man whose near-fatal (or was it fatal?) heart attack launches him into a surrealistic, mind-expanding and satirical adventure. A nightmarish examination of life, death and the eternal search for happiness. ★★★½

Bliss

(1997, 103 min, US, Lance Young) *Craig Sheffer, Sheryl Lee, Terence Stamp, Casey Siemaszko, Spalding Gray.* This sexually honest tale of love and commitment stars Lee as an obsessive/compulsive housewife whose confession to husband Sheffer that she's never had an orgasm (with him) leads to much soul-searching and psychoanalysis — until he finds that she's sleeping with a sex therapist (Stamp) whose teachings skate along the edge of the law. Deciding that he'd rather be the one to help his wife come to terms with her frigidity, Sheffer enlists the therapist's aid in becoming a better lover, thus beginning a journey of sexual discovery that could heal them both. What would, in lesser hands, be yet another seamy, steamy B-video release is elevated to the level of a serious, well-mounted drama thanks to the sincerity of the cast and, above all, director Young's sensitive and intelligent script. ★★★ DVD Dual: $29.99

The Bliss of Mrs. Blossom

(1968, 93 min, GB, Joe McGrath) *Shirley MacLaine, Richard Attenborough, John Cleese, Barry Humphries.* Here's a fun-filled piece of '60s oddball British kitsch. MacLaine stars as the wife of a brassiere manufacturer (Attenborough) who keeps a man in her attic for five years! While perhaps not on the level of other British comedies of the era (*The Magic Christian, Bedazzled*), it's still an interesting period piece with a lot of funny moments. ★★★ VHS: $14.99

Blithe Spirit

(1945, 96 min, GB, David Lean) *Rex Harrison, Constance Cummings, Kay Hammond, Margaret Rutherford.* Noël Coward's enchanting classic stage production makes for an equally captivating film comedy, adapted for the screen by Coward himself. Harrison is wonderful as a cynical author whose life turns upside down when the ghost of his deceased first wife materializes after he remarries. Hammond is a delight as the returning spectre, and Cummings is splendid as the second wife. But it's the hilarious and spirited performance of Rutherford as the medium Madame Arcati that is most memorable. ★★★½ DVD: $24.99

The Blob

(1958, 80 min, US, Irvin S. Yeaworth) *Steve McQueen, Aneta Corsaut.* This '50s sci-fi minor classic is a camp favorite. A very young McQueen stars as a teenager who tries to warn everyone in his small town that an intergalactic goo is on a path of destruction. Foolish adults — they never listen! (Remade in 1988) ★★½ DVD Criterion Collection: $39.99

The Blob

(1988, 92 min, US, Chuck Russell) *Kevin Dillon, Shawnee Smith, Donovan Leitch.* Entertaining and imaginative remake of the Steve McQueen cult classic — owing more to John Carpenter's *The Thing* than to the '50s original. A gelatinous goo falls from the sky to wreak havoc on an unsuspecting small town, gobbling all in its path. Dillon and Smith are two teenagers out to stop the plasmic menace. ★★★ DVD Letterbox: $14.99, VHS: $9.99

Blonde Venus

(1932, 97 min, US, Josef von Sternberg) *Marlene Dietrich, Cary Grant, Herbert Marshall.* The ever radiant Dietrich is nothing less than stunning as a woman who leaves her husband when she becomes convinced that she is no good for him. The true highlight of the film comes when Dietrich sings "Hot Voodoo" in a gorilla suit. ★★★ VHS: $14.99

Blood & Concrete

(1990, 97 min, US, Jeffrey Reiner) *Billy Zane, Jennifer Beals, Darren McGavin, Harry Shearer.* Zane delivers a delicious performance in this contemporary film noir about a larcenously hip and dissolute Everyman. When he literally stumbles over a suicidal Beals, he finds himself drawn into a convoluted maze of conflicted loyalties amid an amazing assortment of L.A. lowlifes. Deftly directed by Reiner, who cowrote the nifty script with producer Richard LaBrie, the film pays homage to its roots with acknowledgments to Samuel Fuller, John Boorman, Richard Widmark and Lee Marvin in the closing credits. ★★★

Blood and Roses

(1961, 74 min, Italy, Roger Vadim) *Mel Ferrer, Elsa Martinelli, Annette Vadim.* Annette Vadim stars as the sexy Carmilla in this lush and provocative vampire tale. Seduced by her lesbian vampire ancestor who takes over her body, the lusty Carmilla first jumps a young maid and then her beautiful cousin. Although the cousin is engaged to be married, the women make eyes at each other throughout the film (in that Euro-soft-porn sort of way), and director Vadim plays up every lesbionic inch of it. Based on Sheridan le Fanu's "Carmilla" and later remade as *The Vampire Lovers*. ★★½ VHS: $9.99

B

Blood and Sand

(1922, 80 min, US, Fred Niblo) *Rudolph Valentino, Nita Naldi.* Matador Valentino can't decide between the good girl or the vamp, so he takes it out on the bull. While the acting style in this hyperbolic classic is humorously bug-eyed and stilted when viewed today, this proved to be one of Valentino's most popular films. ★★★ VHS: $24.99

Blood and Sand

(1941, 123 min, US, Rouben Mamoulian) *Tyrone Power, Linda Darnell, Rita Hayworth, Nazimova, Anthony Quinn.* A gorgeous-looking and exciting remake of the Rudolph Valentino 1922 silent classic. Power plays a naïve bullfighter who gets led astray by the sultry Hayworth. Darnell is the woman who loves him from afar. ★★★ VHS: $19.99

Blood & Wine

(1997, 101 min, US, Bob Rafelson) *Jack Nicholson, Michael Caine, Stephen Dorff, Judy Davis, Jennifer Lopez, Harold Perrineau, Jr.* Treacherous waters run deep in this moody thriller. Though not completely successful in its storytelling, *Blood & Wine* moves at a fast clip, and its characters are always up to something — part of its noir appeal is figuring out what. Nicholson is a Miami wine merchant whose position with the city's wealthier clientele gives him access to their property — which helps when he and slimy associate Caine decide to empty their safes. When Nicholson's wife Davis decides to leave her husband and unknowingly walks off with a stolen necklace, she and son Dorff become targets of the maniacal Caine, with Nicholson stuck in the middle. Rafelson gives the film a good look, and there's a terrific car chase scene, but there's also nothing new to the genre here, and Dorff's romantic involvement and devotion to his stepfather's mistress (Lopez) is flimsy at best. ★★½ VHS: $9.99

Blood Feast

(1963, 70 min, US, Herschell Gordon Lewis) *Tom Wood, Connie Mason.* The first of the "Sue" films from the "master of splatter" Lewis. *Blood Feast* is the gruesome tale of Fuad Ramses, Egyptian caterer and limping psychopath. With notably bad performances. Music, photography and gore-F/X (filmed in "Blood Color") by HGL. ★ DVD: $24.99, VHS: $19.99

Blood Feud

(1979, 112 min, Italy, Lina Wertmüller) *Sophia Loren, Marcello Mastroianni, Giancarlo Giannini.* A pleasant, although not exceptional, sex comedy about a Sicilian widow in the 1920s (Loren) who receives the lustful advances of both a lawyer (Mastroianni) and a shady gangster (Giannini). Not on the same artistic level as *Swept Away* or *Seven Beauties*, it is still an enjoyable little movie filled with many of the Wertmüller touches. ★★½

Blood for Dracula

See: *Andy Warhol's Dracula*

Blood Guts Bullets & Octane

(1999, 87 min, US, Joe Carnahan) *Dan Leis, Ken Rudulph, Dan Harlan, Hugh McChord.* An ultra-low-budget independent crime drama, this is fairly negligible but at least sustains a degree of interest. Two down-on-their-luck used car lot owners have a get-rich-quick scheme fall onto their laps: if they keep a vintage car (with mysterious contents in the trunk) on their lot for two days, they get $250,000. Things go predictably awry. Way too derivative of Tarantino, Stone and even Mamet, the film begins like a *Pulp Fiction*, student-film homage. Once the story is set in motion, it becomes more interesting, with enough violence, twists and occasional smart dialogue. ★★ DVD: $19.99

Blood in, Blood Out: Bound by Honor

(1993, 180 min, US, Taylor Hackford) *Damian Chapa, Jesse Borrego, Enrique Castillo, Victor Rivers, Delroy Lindo, Benjamin Bratt.* An epic (at least in the realm of time) drama about the lives of three friends born and raised on the mean *calles* of East L.A. One becomes a successful artist only to succumb to drugs; another goes from a teen thug to a respected cop; and the third, — a blond, blue-eyed Anglo-Chicano (Chapa) — becomes a macho-posturing gang member who enters into a life of crime. There's plenty of prison action, gun shooting and tired attempts at making the characters come alive. Watchable yes, absorbing, no. (aka: *Bound by Honor*) ★★ DVD: $19.99, VHS: $9.99

Blood in the Face

(1991, 78 min, US, Anne Bohlen, James Ridgeway, Kevin Rafferty) Directors Bohlen, Rafferty and Ridgeway, with Michael Moore, interview participants at a Nazi rally in Michigan. We enter a world where "Ronald Reagan works for the Jews," the Holocaust is a hoax and only whites have a conscience because they can blush (show blood in the face). Interspersed is footage of George Lincoln Rockwell likening Hitler to the second coming of Christ and (pre-plastic surgery) David Duke in Klan garb and Nazi uniform. It's tempting to chuckle as if this were a right-wing *Reefer Madness*, but pay attention to the soft-spoken housewife. When you find out who her husband is, you won't be laughing. ★★★ VHS: $19.99

Blood of a Poet

(1930, 58 min, France, Jean Cocteau) Considered one of the most influential avant-garde films of all-time, *Blood of a Poet* explores the plight of the artist and the forces of creative thought. Constructed as a collage of dreamlike situations, autobiographical revelations and enigmatic images, the film is an odyssey into the poet's imagination. Freud described the film as being "like looking through a keyhole at a man undressing." (French with English subtitles) ★★★★ DVD: $79.99, VHS: $29.99

Blood of Beasts (Le Sang des Bêtes)

(1949, 22 min, France, Georges Franju) This landmark documentary, and first film by Franju, begins by lulling the viewer with scenes of a tranquil Parisian suburb. But tranquility is far from the theme of this film, for the camera soon enters an abattoir and begins to unflinchingly chronicle a day in the life of a slaughterhouse. Disturbing in its methodical violence, we witness the actual slaughtering of cows, sheep, calves and even horses — all done by placid workers who systematically kill. Not for the faint-of-heart. Please note that the subtitles for this film are quite poor. (French with English subtitles) ★★★ VHS: $29.99

The Blood of Heroes

(1990, 97 min, US, David Peoples) *Rutger Hauer, Joan Chen, Vincent D'Onofrio.* Set in a post-apocalyptic future, this intelligent, suspenseful action film stars Hauer as the leader of sort of a minor league nomadic sports team that travels from village to village to compete against locals in a torturous, savage game called jugging, which is part football, part hockey and part bloodbath. Chen also stars as a woman so adept at the game that she joins the team in hopes of making it to "the majors" — where coveted players enjoy the good life in the confines of an underground city. ★★★ DVD: $9.99, VHS: $9.99

The Blood of Others

(1984, 130 min, Canada/France, Claude Chabrol) *Jodie Foster, Michael Ontkean, Sam Neill, Stéphane Audran, Lambert Wilson.* A great international cast cannot save this made-for-cable romance ineptly adapted from Simone de Beauvoir's 1946 novel. Set in Paris during the Second World War, the film stars Foster as a fashion designer who falls in love with an imprisoned French resistance fighter. In a successful attempt to get him released, she begins an affair with an influential German commander, only to be accused of collusion by her fellow countrymen. Cut 40 minutes from the original broadcast running time, this misfire from Chabrol is a sadly convoluted and uninvolving mess. (Filmed in English) ★

Blood on the Moon

(1948, 88 min, US, Robert Wise) *Robert Mitchum, Barbara Bel Geddes, Robert Preston.* This solid western tale boasts a good cast to tell the story of drifter Mitchum involved in shady goings-on out West. Preston is memorable as the villain. ★★★

The Blood Oranges

(1997, 105 min, GB, Philip Haas) *Charles Dance, Sheryl Lee, Colin Lane, Laila Robbins.* Comfortably expatriated Cyril and Fiona (Dance, Lee) live in unrooted self-obsession in an ancient, impoverished Italian village. It's 1970, and their marriage reflects the moral ambiguities of the time. They meet by literal accident another displaced couple. Catherine and Hugh (Robbins, Lane) have been on the road for a year, traveling with their three daughters as Hugh photographs. These two English couples, slumming in the Third World, exploiting without purpose, indulging without satisfaction, become enmeshed as Cryil and Fiona seek Catherine and Hugh's participation in their open relationship. A lushly photographed, laconically paced adaptation of the John Hawkes novel. ★★½ DVD: $24.99

Blood Relatives

(1977, 107 min, Canada/France, Claude Chabrol) *Donald Sutherland, Donald Pleasence, Stéphane Audran, David Hemmings.* Adapted from an Ed McBain novel, this pedestrian police thriller features Sutherland as a Montreal detective assigned to a particularly savage murder case. A young girl is gruesomely killed in a back alley and the only witness, her 15-year-old cousin, implicates her brother in the case. Told in a straightforward way, Sutherland investigates, attempting to piece together the puzzle of this potentially passion-driven murder. The film starts off promisingly, but it's too one-dimensional and concludes with a decidedly anticlimactic denouement. (English language) ★★ VHS: $79.99

Blood Simple

(1984, 97 min, US, Joel Coen) *John Getz, Frances McDormand, Dan Hedaya, M. Emmet Walsh.* This extremely well-crafted first feature from the Coen Brothers pays tribute to classic film noir. The story revolves around a crazy, jealous husband who hires a shady hit man to take out his wife. Although the film was done on a shoestring budget, the Coen Brothers manage to create a technically dazzling film that boasts a gleefully ghoulish sense of humor, dazzling camera acrobatics and a plot with more loops than the L.A. Freeway. Corruption and distrust ooze from every frame of this torrid tale of tangled passions in a dusty Texas town. ★★★★ DVD: $14.99

The Blood Spattered Bride
(La Novia Ensangrentada)

(1972, 101 min, Spain, Vicente Aranda) *Alexandra Bastedo, Simón Andreu, Maribel Martin, Dean Selmier.* Sexy lesbian vampires are on the prowl once again in this erotic, bloody and creepy Spanish production. A young bride is haunted by visions of knife-wielding beauties and castrated husbands. Her life is "saved" when Carmilla, a mysterious and elegant stranger, arrives. Carmilla, a centuries-old vampiress, and the innocent bride are immediately attracted to each other and plot the death of the bride's hated hubby who "Pierced my flesh to humiliate me . . . spat inside me to enslave me." A kinky horror film that brings new meaning to the problems of marital life. Take that, Mr. Man! Based on Sheridan le Fanu's "Carmilla." (Spanish with English subtitles) ★★½ DVD Widescreen: $29.99, VHS Widescreen: $14.99

Blood Wedding

(1981, 72 min, Spain, Carlos Saura) *Antonio Gades, Christina Hoyos.* The first of three collaborations between director Saura and dancer/choreographer Antonio Gades (the other two are *Carmen* and *El Amor Brujo*), this stunning flamenco adaptation of Federico Garcia Lorca's tragic play, "La Boda de Sangre," is an exquisitely realized study of the theatrical process. The camera follows Gades and his cast through the process of putting on make-up, warming up and finally a full-dress run through of Gades' interpretation of the Lorca classic. Saura's camera lovingly examines the rehearsal in precise detail, giving the viewer an intimate and exciting peek into this exquisite art form. ★★★½

Blood Work

(2002, 115 min, US, Clint Eastwood) *Clint Eastwood, Jeff Daniels, Anjelica Huston, Wanda DeJesus, Paul Rodriguez, Dylan Walsh.* Age may have added a few more wrinkles around the eyes, and his gait may be ever so slower, but turning 70 hasn't diminished Eastwood's instincts as either director or acting icon. In this taut, efficient police procedural, Clint plays Terry McCaleb, a retired FBI agent who — heart transplant and all — is called back into action to investigate the murder of a young woman. The fact that the deceased woman is the donor of his new heart makes him all the more determined to find the killer. The identity of the murderer may or may not come as a shock, as the whodunit aspect of the film isn't its only *raison d'e-tre*; director Clint and writer Brian Helgeland (who adapted Michael Connelly's novel) seem equally attentive to Terry's ability as a detective and his vulnerability. It's somehow comforting to know that after all these years Clint is still on the case, and refreshing that he doesn't just acknowledge his age but embraces it. ★★★ DVD Letterbox: $19.99, DVD Pan & Scan: $19.99, VHS: $6.99

Bloodhounds of Broadway

(1989, 101 min, US, Howard Brookner) *Matt Dillon, Jennifer Grey, Julie Hagerty, Rutger Hauer, Madonna, Esai Morales, Anita Morris, Randy Quaid.* An impressive, though rather restrained cast is the highlight of Brookner's alternately charming and forced comic mystery based on four Damon Runyon short stories. Set on New Year's Eve on Broadway in 1928, the story revolves around a group of gamblers, showgirls and aristocrats whose lives intersect after a local gangster is nearly slain. The colorful cast of characters includes Dillon as the worst gambler in New York, Grey and Madonna as

showgirls, and Quaid (who best captures the spirit of Runyon) as a dim-witted high roller in love with Madonna (that's a twosome!). ★★½ DVD: $24.99

Bloodline

(1979, 116 min, US, Terence Young) *Audrey Hepburn, Ben Gazzara, James Mason, Michelle Phillips, Omar Sharif.* Embarrassing screen version of Sidney Sheldon's best-seller with Audrey Hepburn as the heiress to a pharmaceutical company who takes over the business when her father dies under mysterious circumstances. ★ VHS: $14.99

Bloodsucking Freaks

(1978, 89 min, US, Joel M. Reed) Universally reviled blood and guts show, with the high point (or low point, depending on your tastes) being the scene in which a woman's brain is sucked out with a straw by one of the thirsty lunatics. ★ DVD: $24.99, VHS: $19.99

Bloody Mama

(1970, 90 min, US, Roger Corman) *Shelley Winters, Robert De Niro, Don Stroud, Pat Hingle, Bruce Dern.* Winters is the infamous Ma Barker, the matriarch of mayhem during the Depression. Unlike *Bonnie and Clyde*, whose characters were remotely sympathetic, this film has criminals who are totally unlikable. The film's primary assets are its players (particularly a young De Niro as one of her sons, a junkie) and its action scenes. A curiosity piece. ★★½

Bloody Sunday

(2002, 110 min, Ireland, Paul Greengrass) *James Nesbitt, Tim Pigott-Smith, Nicholas Farrell, Declan Duddy.* On January 30, 1972, a human rights rally had been planned in the city of Derry, Northern Ireland. The march had been banned by the British government, but the peaceful protest still went ahead. At the day's end, thirteen marchers were killed, and scores injured, when British troops opened fire upon an unarmed crowd. The devastating events which led up to and followed the massacre form the basis for director Greengrass's stinging drama, an overpowering story of social conscience, military irresponsibility and great human tragedy. Filmed in a semidocumentary style, which accentuates an uneasy sense of doom and underscores the chaos which followed, *Bloody Sunday* is meticulous in detailing what may have brought both sides to such a historic calamity. Greengrass's roving camera and political stance is reminiscent of Ken Loach, and the final result is a wrenching look at a day in which hatred and fear defeated the common good. ★★★½ DVD: $19.99

Blossoms in the Dust

(1941, 100 min, US, Mervyn LeRoy) *Greer Garson, Walter Pidgeon.* Garson and Pidgeon's first film together is a touching soap opera about a woman who loses her husband and child in an accident, inspiring her to found an orphanage. Features a good performance by Garson. ★★½

Blow

(2001, 120 min, US, Ted Demme) *Johnny Depp, Penélope Cruz, Franka Potente, Ray Liotta, Rachel Griffiths, Paul Reubens.* It's amazing how mundane the life of George Jung was, considering he was one of the biggest marijuana and cocaine importers in U.S. history. Worse, *Blow* doesn't seem to notice, and the lack of thrills is especially evident in the wake of *Fear and Loathing*, *Boogie Nights* and *Traffic*. As Jung, Depp immerses himself once again into character, but there's not much there to inhabit.

The story follows Jung from the early 1970s, where he starts in petty drug dealing, to his rise as a dealer working alongside Colombian drug lord Pablo Escobar. Director Demme isn't able to sustain the energy level from a good opening that nearly makes you feel for the characters. The result is a familiar jaunt down memory lane that has little else to say than "It sucks to get caught." ★★ DVD Letterbox infinifilm Special Edition: $19.99

Blow Out

(1981, 107 min, US, Brian De Palma) *John Travolta, Nancy Allen, John Lithgow, Dennis Franz.* De Palma serves up this interesting rehash of Antonioni's *Blow-Up*. Movie sound engineer Travolta inadvertently records a car accident that turns out to be no accident. Allen costars as the accident's survivor who knows more than she should. Lithgow, in a chilling performance, is the psycho on her trail. Good use of various Philadelphia locations. ★★★ DVD: $14.99

Blow-Up

(1966, 108 min, GB/Italy, Michelangelo Antonioni) *Vanessa Redgrave, David Hemmings, Sarah Miles, Jane Birkin.* Antonioni's hypnotic and provocative film stars Hemmings as a fashion photographer in swinging 1960s London who possibly sees a murder within one of his photographs. The film's lasting power lies in the way the images begin to reveal the mystery, all without the use of dialogue or sound. (Filmed in English) ★★★★ DVD Letterbox: $19.99

Blown Away

(1994, 120 min, US, Stephen Hopkins) *Jeff Bridges, Tommy Lee Jones, Suzy Amis, Lloyd Bridges, Forest Whitaker.* More concerned with plot and character, *Blown Away* mixes action with a developed narrative which is what gives it its slight edge and many weaknesses. The always reliable Bridges plays a Boston bomb squad specialist who goes one-on-one with a former IRA bomber, played by the underused Jones. As Jones targets members of Bridges' force, the race is on to locate and stop the madman from blowing up half the city. For an action film, there are surprisingly few scenes of carnage and mayhem (after all, this *is* about a psychotic bomber), although there are two sequences which are riveting. ★★½ DVD: $14.99

Blue

(1993, 76 min, GB, Derek Jarman) *Tilda Swinton, Derek Jarman, Nigel Terry.* Jarman, who died of AIDS in February 1994, had been battling the disease for six years at the time of making this film. With impaired eyesight and deteriorating health, Jarman created a startling experimental film in which he invites his audience into his sight-deprived world creating a womb-like meditative state by employing a completely blue screen throughout the film. The cast reads from Jarman's often poetic journals, recounting the director's medical complexities, thoughts on the loss of loved ones, and reflections on his own life and art. A fitting closure to an eventful career. ★★★

Blue

(1993, 98 min, France, Krzysztof Kieslowski) *Juliette Binoche, Benoit Regent.* A haunting and visually stunning film, *Blue* is the first in director Kieslowski's "color" trilogy, which would be followed by *White* and *Red*. Binoche is compelling as a grieving widow who withdraws from life after the sudden loss of her husband and daughter. Despite her efforts to remain detached from her past and present, she slowly regains her emotional balance when she uncovers her husband's secret life. The film boasts wonderful acting and beautiful cinematography but at times gets bogged down in its overladen visual symbolism. (French with English subtitles) ★★★ DVD Subtitled: $19.99, VHS: $9.99

The Blue Angel

(1930, 90 min, Germany, Josef von Sternberg) *Marlene Dietrich, Emil Jannings.* Jannings seems a paragon of order and control, a diligent and respected schoolteacher who commands attention and obedience. But behind this facade is a repressed man, a man so needy for simple human contact that he falls prey to the almost violent sensuality of Lola-Lola (Dietrich, in the role that brought her international recognition), an earthy cabaret singer. He exchanges his security for the illusion of warmth and caring, and pays for his obsession with every shred of dignity and purpose he'd ever attained. Jannings is devastating, Dietrich is mesmerizing and von Sternberg guides the performers through Expressionistic set designs with a sure hand and an unerring eye for human foibles. A film worthy of its classic status. ★★★★ DVD: $34.99, VHS: $24.99

Blue Chips

(1994, 108 min, US, William Friedkin) *Nick Nolte, Mary McDonnell, J.T. Walsh, Ed O'Neill, Shaquille O'Neal, Robert Wuhl.* Nolte is a grumpy old basketball coach in this authentic if familiar sports story. When Nolte's college team experiences a slump, he takes to the road to recruit players who expect new cars, bags of cash and even tractors in return for their premium services, all of which is, of course, illegal. With rousing basketball scenes, the film debut of NBA superstar O'Neal, a good performance by Nolte and a moving ethical dilemma, *Blue Chips* lacks a cast of interesting supporting characters to round out the story. This is surprising since it was written by Ron Shelton, who penned *Bull Durham* and *White Men Can't Jump.* ★★½ VHS: $9.99

Blue Collar

(1978, 114 min, US, Paul Schrader) *Richard Pryor, Harvey Keitel, Yaphet Kotto, Cliff De Young.* A searing drama with Pryor and Keitel as auto workers up against their corporate bosses, and their

own union, in a losing battle. Pryor and Keitel are both outstanding in what may be their best screen performances. As a fellow worker also caught up in their ill-fated fight, Kotto gives a mesmerizing performance. ★★★ DVD Widescreen: $19.99

Blue Country

(1978, 104 min, France, Jean-Charles Tacchella) *Brigitte Fossy, Jacques Sernas.* Following his success with *Cousin, Cousine,* Tacchella directed this enchanting romantic comedy about two free souls who leave the troubles of city living behind to renew their love and begin a new life amidst the idyllic French countryside. (French with English subtitles) ★★★

Blue Crush

(2002, 104 min, US, John Stockwell) *Kate Bosworth, Michelle Rodriguez, Matthew Davis, Sanoe Lake, Mika Boorem.* Based on a magazine article by Susan Orlean, *Blue Crush* follows the aquatic and romantic adventures of three young women living in Hawaii whose passion for surfing runs deep. Or at least that's what we're supposed to think, for though the characters spend most of their time in water and on their boards, none of them seem to demonstrate any real passion for the sport. That probably has much to do with John Stockwell and Lizzy Weiss' screenplay adaptation, which treads much familiar territory. There's the obligatory training, bonding, romances with hunks, and the inevitable surfing competition. The latter energizes a film somewhat marooned by its tedious pacing, though a lot of the surfing footage can be exciting. ★★ DVD Letterbox: $14.99, DVD Pan & Scan: $14.99, VHS: $9.99

The Blue Dahlia

(1946, 99 min, US, George Marshall) *Alan Ladd, Veronica Lake, William Bendix, Howard da Silva, Hugh Beaumont.* Raymond Chandler wrote the screenplay for this tense, well-produced noir thriller with Ladd suspected of murdering his wife. ★★★ VHS: $14.99

The Blue Gardenia

(1953, 90 min, US, Fritz Lang) *Anne Baxter, Richard Conte, Ann Sothern, Raymond Burr, George Reeves, Nat "King" Cole.* Hack producer Alex

Gottlieb cynically titled this standard-issue Hollywood murder mystery to exploit the public's fascination with the "Blue Dahlia" murder of 1947. What director Lang gave him was a classic noir. Baxter wakes up from a drunken night on the town with lothario Burr only to find the playboy murdered at her feet. Newspaper gossip columnist Conte and her wise-cracking roommate Sothern try to prove her innocence. Invoking a great atmosphere, Lang livens things up with his usual visual flair, penchant for long takes, and his usual brilliant mise-en-scè--ne. ★★★½ DVD: $24.99, VHS: $19.99

Blue Hawaii

(1961, 101 min, US, Norman Taurog) *Elvis Presley, Joan Blackman, Angela Lansbury.* Pleasant Presley musical with Elvis as a returning soldier who bypasses the family business to work for a local tourist agency. Blackman is the love interest, and Lansbury adds a touch of class as Presley's mom. Elvis sings "Can't Help Falling in Love" and the title tune. ★★½ DVD: $14.99, VHS: $9.99

The Blue Hour

(1992, 88 min, Germany, Marcel Gisler) *Andreas Herder, Dina Lepizig.* The vulnerability and loneliness of a pretty "rent boy" and a flighty salesgirl is the theme of this absorbing drama. Theo is a Berlin hustler, a handsome young man who, despite selling his body, retains an amazingly sweet and trusting nature. Despite living the "good life," Theo begins feeling a little old, tired and alienated. His sadness is relieved a bit when he strikes up an uneasy relationship with his next door neighbor, Marie, a punkishly outlandish French woman. Their friendship is not the stuff of high drama, but it is a simple, surprisingly touching tale of an unlikely love between two social outcasts. (German with English subtitles) ★★★ DVD: $29.99, VHS: $29.99

Blue Ice

(1993, 96 min, GB, Russell Mulcahy) *Michael Caine, Sean Young, Bob Hoskins, Ian Holm, Bobby Short.* An appealing espionage drama with the ubiquitous Caine as a spy who came in from the cold, only to find himself frostbitten when his oldest friends start turning up dead — with the only link being the beautiful femme fatale (Young) who recently entered his life. Caine's faithful performance harkens back to his old "Harry Palmer" days in *The Ipcress File* and *Funeral in Berlin.* ★★★ VHS: $9.99

Blue in the Face

(1995, 90 min, US, Paul Auster & Wayne Wang) *Harvey Keitel, Mel Gorham, Lou Reed, Roseanne, Lily Tomlin, Michael J. Fox, Giancarlo Esposito, Jim Jarmusch, Victor Argo, Madonna, Mira Sorvino, RuPaul.* Not really a sequel, the ingratiating *Blue in the Face* is a new collection of stories that concentrate on the customers of the Brooklyn smoke shop first featured in *Smoke.* Keitel returns as Auggie, the gregarious sales clerk who acts as both father-confessor and camp counselor to a fresh crop of playmates. Told in a semidocumentary and more fragmented style than the previous film, *Blue in the Face,* as with *Smoke,* revels in the diversity of its Park Slope neighborhood, here through the many talking-heads interviews, anecdotes, monologues and fictionalized stories that populate this funny film. An eclectic, engaging cast weaves its way through the skimpy narrative. Though not as totally successful or in-depth as the first film, this outing's goals are simpler but nevertheless appealingly met. ★★★½ DVD: $19.99, VHS: $9.99

Marlene Dietrich in *The Blue Angel*

Blue Jeans

(1981, 101 min, France, Hugues Burin des Roziers) This interesting curiosity follows the first loves of a 13-year-old boy who is sent to England one summer to study English. His first tentative advances with a young girl are charming. However, she is soon lured away from him by another, older boy, which leaves our hero alone. The strange twist is that he also becomes attached to the other boy and develops a crush on the unresponsive young man. A touching and sensitive look at the heartache of first love. (French with English subtitles) ★★★

The Blue Kite

(1993, 138 min, China, Tian Zhuangzhuang) Lu Liping, Pu Quanxin. This harrowing tale of a family's struggle to survive in revolutionary China is told from the perspective of a young boy, Tietou, who witnesses firsthand the cruelty of class struggle. Banned by the Chinese authorities (and ultimately resulting in the exile of filmmaker Tian), the film is strikingly similar to Zhang's To Live in that it tells the story of one family from the Great Leap Forward through the Cultural Revolution. But where To Live succeeded in drawing the viewer into the intimate lives of a small family, The Blue Kite introduces too many players and it is hard to keep them all straight. The result is a dispassionate distancing from the characters as their lives fall victim to unwarranted punishments. (Mandarin with English subtitles) ★★½ DVD: $29.99, VHS: $24.99

The Blue Max

(1966, 157 min, US, John Guillermin) George Peppard, Ursula Andress, James Mason. Peppard does an able job in this high-flying romance/adventure story portraying a German WWI pilot who has a steamy love affair with Andress. Excellent aerial photography punctuates the dogfight scenes. ★★★ DVD: $14.99, VHS: $9.99

Blue Sky

(1994, 101 min, US, Tony Richardson) Jessica Lange, Tommy Lee Jones, Powers Boothe, Carrie Snodgress, Chris O'Donnell. Shot in 1990 and on the shelf for four years, Richardson's final film is an affecting melodrama of a family in crisis which is further enhanced by two exceptional performances by Lange and Jones. Set in the early 1960s, the story concerns military nuclear engineer Jones, wife Lange and their family, who move to a new Army base where infidelity, betrayal and conspiracy await them. A flirtatious Southern belle in the Blanche DuBois/Scarlett O'Hara mold, Lange's Oscar-winning portrayal of Carly is a revelation of sexuality and naiveté, and as Carly is the heart of the story, Lange's smoldering portrait is very much the centerpiece of the film. As her understanding but perplexed idealistic husband, Jones gives a subtle portrayal of a man at odds with his conscience. ★★★ DVD: $19.99

Blue Steel

(1990, 95 min, US, Kathryn Bigelow) Jamie Lee Curtis, Ron Silver, Clancy Brown, Louise Fletcher, Tom Sizemore. Curtis delivers a cooly understated performance in this atmospheric police thriller as a rookie cop who empties her gun into an armed robber, and is promptly suspended when the dead man's gun cannot be found. Unbeknownst to her, the witness who stole the weapon is the same man she has just started dating — the man responsible for a series of killings using bullets with her name on them. Silver is effective as the serial killer.

Director Bigelow suffuses the film with the noir glow that permeated her acclaimed vampire saga, Near Dark. ★★½ DVD Dual: $14.99

Blue Streak

(1999, 94 min, US, Les Mayfield) Martin Lawrence, Luke Wilson, Peter Greene, Dave Chappelle, William Forsythe. A case of a good comedian being sabotaged by bad material, Blue Streak is an ill-paced and very frantic action-comedy that isn't half as funny as it thinks it is. Lawrence stars as a jewel thief who must impersonate a cop in order to retrieve his stolen, hidden stash. In the process, he solves a few cases and earns the admiration of his "fellow officers," all while trying desperately to grab the diamond and run. The premise isn't a bad one, but in the hands of director Mayfield and the screenwriters Lawrence is reduced to shrieking and flailing and horrible mugging — no one lets the funny set-up play out. Lawrence is too talented a comedian to be reduced to such mindless shenanigans. ★½ DVD: $14.99, VHS: $9.99

Blue Thunder

(1983, 108 min, US, John Badham) Roy Scheider, Malcolm McDowell, Daniel Stern, Candy Clark, Warren Oates. Fascism was never so much fun as in this movie with grown-up little boys playing with their war toys. Scheider is the Vietnam vet who, after a particularly bad psychotic episode, steals the government's surveillance helicopter. McDowell is the unhappy government rep out for Scheider's blood. Amazing aerial chases over Los Angeles heighten the suspense of this otherwise silly thriller. ★★ DVD: $9.99, VHS: $9.99

Blue Velvet

(1986, 120 min, US, David Lynch) Kyle MacLachlan, Laura Dern, Isabella Rossellini, Dennis Hopper, Dean Stockwell, Jack Nance, Brad Dourif, Hope Lange. Director Lynch unleashes his demented imagination with all its perversely poetic force. Both witty and luridly beautiful, the film is part mystery, part surrealist dream. Lynch uses the postcard perfect town of Lumberton to plunge into an all-embracing ritual of sinful crime, sadism and redemption. MacLachlan innocently discovers a human ear in his backyard one day and is quickly drawn into the sordid, masochistic world of a nightclub singer (Rossellini). Hopper is at his lunatic best as the all-powerful psychotic drug thug Frank Booth. Blue Velvet is a piece of primal pop art, an erotic parable with trancelike power. ★★★★ DVD Special Edition: $24.99

Bluebeard's Eighth Wife

(1938, 80 min, US, Ernst Lubitsch) Claudette Colbert, Gary Cooper, David Niven, Edward Everett Horton. Billy Wilder and Charles Brackett wrote the screenplay for this sophisticated Lubitsch sex comedy with Cooper as a playboy millionaire who meets his match in Colbert. Delightful performances. ★★★

The Blues Brothers

(1980, 133 min, US, John Landis) James Belushi, Dan Aykroyd, Carrie Fisher, Kathleen Freeman, Cab Calloway, James Brown, John Candy, Henry Gibson, Aretha Franklin, Ray Charles. From their "Saturday Night Live" sketch, Belushi and Aykroyd are Jake and Elwood Blues, good-hearted petty criminals and dedicated bluesmen. The story about a quest to find the money to save an orphanage and the possible consequences of running a red light is really just an excuse to string together as many hilarious episodes as the filmmakers can. This

movie has it all: monumental car chases (and car crashes), a mysterious killer stalking the duo, a mission from God, raucous concert scenes and cameos by almost everyone, but also full musical performances by Franklin, Charles, Brown and Calloway. The movie is briskly paced, filled equally with action and musical scenes, is tremendously funny and is a virtual tour of the city of Chicago, birthplace of the urban blues. (Sequel: Blues Brothers 2000) ★★★½

Blues Brothers 2000

(1998, 124 min, US, John Landis) Dan Aykroyd, John Goodman, Joe Morton, J. Evan Bonifant, Aretha Franklin, James Brown, B.B. King. Eighteen years after the fact, this surprisingly bad sequel to the hilarious 1980 comedy brings the Blues Brothers back to the screen — minus John Belushi, of course. Released from prison (and just learning his brother Jake has died), Elwood (Aykroyd) is "appointed" mentor to a young ne'er-do-well and decides to get the band back together. An embarrassing Morton as a policeman is in hot pursuit the whole way, until he has a change of heart in an insipid scene inspired by the gospel number in the first film. In fact, most of the film rips off its predecessor with none of the joy or humor which made that film terrific. What's more, the musical numbers are lousy. Goodman is good as a bartender along for the ride, but he's no substitute for Belushi. ★½ DVD Collector's Edition: $14.99, DVD DTS Edition: $14.99, VHS: $9.99

Blume in Love

(1973, 117 min, US, Paul Mazursky) Susan Anspach, Kris Kristofferson, Marsha Mason, George Segal, Shelley Winters. Mazursky's perceptive and engaging comedy-drama about love and rejection stars Segal as a divorce lawyer whose life is turned upside-down when his wife (Anspach) walks out on him. ★★★ VHS: $14.99

Blunt: The Fourth Man

(1992, 86 min, GB, John McGlasham) Anthony Hopkins, Ian Richardson. Hopkins is a delight as Guy Burgess, the British government official who fled England before the discovery that he and several others were spies for the Soviets. (Knowledge of this story is beneficial.) At the center of the tale is Burgess' fellow spy, Anthony Blunt (wonderfully played by Richardson), who recruited Burgess while attending Cambridge in the 1930s. Set in the early 1960s, the film shows Blunt as a well-respected art historian. When his well-ordered life is threatened, Blunt begins an elaborate cover-up and damage control campaign. His biggest challenge is protecting Burgess, his former lover and close friend. An inviting and well-produced tale whose characters can also be seen in Another Country and An Englishman Abroad. ★★★

The Boat

See: Das Boot

The Boat Is Full

(1981, 104 min, Switzerland, Markus Imhoof) Tina Engel, Curt Bois. A haunting account of a group of Jewish refugees who attempt to seek asylum in Switzerland, despite that country's strict and subtly prejudiced immigration laws. Their struggle for freedom and life provides the emotional center to this film that is both horrifying in the depiction of a peoples' racial attitudes and heartrending in another's efforts to overcome them. (German with English subtitles) ★★★½ VHS: $29.99

B

Bob & Carol & Ted & Alice

(1969, 104 min, US, Paul Mazursky) *Robert Culp, Natalie Wood, Elliott Gould, Dyan Cannon.* Mazursky's breakthrough directorial debut is a somewhat dated but nevertheless enjoyable treatise on marriage and sex (but not necessarily in that order). Culp and Wood are a married couple who try to convince friends Gould and Cannon to express themselves sexually — by wife-swapping. Both Gould and Cannon received Oscar nominations for their delightful performances. ★★★ VHS: $9.99

Bob le Flambeur

(1955, 102 min, France, Jean-Pierre Melville) *Roger Duchesne, Isabel Corey.* Melville, the Father of the French New Wave, has made a quirky, highly stylized film that revolves around Bob, an aging but elegant gangster who plans a daring robbery of the Deauville Casino. The tension builds as Bob recruits his Montmartre cohorts, plans the break-in and attempts to execute "the biggest heist of the century." An entertaining comedy of manners as well as an exciting drama. (Remade as *The Good Thief*) (French with English subtitles) ★★★½ DVD Criterion Collection: $29.99, VHS: $29.99

Bob Roberts

(1992, 103 min, US, Tim Robbins) *Tim Robbins, Giancarlo Esposito, Alan Rickman, David Strathairn, Gore Vidal, James Spader, Susan Sarandon, Lynne Thigpen, John Cusack, Bob Balaban.* Robbins wrote, directed and stars in this scathingly brilliant political satire about the senatorial campaign of a right-wing candidate. Told in a mockumentary style, reminiscent of *This Is Spinal Tap*, the film often recalls *The Player*, introducing a gallery of characters who weave in and out of the story, many of whom are portrayed by terrific celebrity cameos. But Robbins, as an actor, writer and director, has an instinctive and incisive wit which gives the film a definition all its own. As the country music-singing, neo-fascist, *laissez faire*-invoking Roberts, Robbins gives a priceless performance; there are few of his generation who can handle comedy with such finesse. ★★★★ DVD: $14.99, VHS: $9.99

Bobby Deerfield

(1977, 124 min, US, Sydney Pollack) *Al Pacino, Marthe Keller.* Pacino makes a valiant effort to breathe some life into this turgid romantic drama, but even his talents can't save this story of a race car driver who falls in love with socialite Keller, who suffers from "Ali MacGraw's Disease." (Next time, Al, leave the impressions to Rich Little.) ★ VHS: $14.99

La Boca del Lobo

(1988, 111 min, Peru, Francisco J. Lombardi) The human tragedy of the Peruvian Civil War is explored in this intense drama. Set in a poor Indian village in the Andes, the bucolic calm of the town is disturbed when a small army patrol is sent to investigate possible insurgent activity. The desperate situation explodes after a newly appointed lieutenant declares the entire village guilty of treason and leads his forces toward a horrible atrocity. A young soldier in the group must choose between blind obedience of his superior or follow the dictates of his conscience and oppose him. (Spanish with English subtitles) ★★★ VHS: $39.99

Bodies, Rest & Motion

(1993, 93 min, US, Michael Steinberg) *Bridget Fonda, Eric Stoltz, Tim Roth, Phoebe Cates, Alicia Witt, Peter Fonda.* Steinberg, who codirected *The Waterdance* with Neal Jiminez, goes solo for his second effort, a loosely structured drama about four disillusioned twentysomethings looking for themselves. Fonda plays a young woman who finds herself in a dilemma when her estranged boyfriend (Roth) just takes off one day. Stoltz (the film's coproducer) is a house painter, quite content with life in the nowhere Arizona town where the film takes place, who meets and falls in love with stressed-out Fonda. Steinberg lets things unfold simply and slowly, which is much to the film's benefit. ★★★ DVD Letterbox: $14.99, VHS: $19.99

The Body

(2001, 108 min, US/GB, Jonas McCord) *Antonio Banderas, Olivia Williams, Derek Jacobi, Jason Flemyng, John Shrapnel, John Wood.* An intriguing premise — an archaeologist (Williams) discovers what may be the bones of Christ in an ancient tomb, thus disproving His Resurrection — makes for low-keyed, occasionally involving drama. Banderas is good as the priest sent by the Vatican to disprove Williams' claim. The political and religious implications of the discovery are explored to decent dramatic effect, but the film is a bit muted and talky. A cop-out ending doesn't help, either. Still, the story will hold one's attention, and perhaps even spark some interesting debate once the film is over. ★★½ DVD Dual: $19.99, VHS: $14.99

Body and Soul

(1947, 104 min, US, Robert Rossen) *John Garfield, Lilli Palmer, Anne Revere, Canada Lee.* Garfield gives a career performance in this hard-hitting, sometimes brutal but always mesmerizing boxing drama. Garfield plays Charlie Davis, a tough, ambitious kid from the poor part of town who makes a name for himself in the boxing world. As his career takes off, he loses sight of his dreams and honor and succumbs to the easy money supplied by his gangster manager. In support, Revere and Lee, as Davis' mother and opponent-turned-trainer, respectively, are excellent. With a taut and polished screenplay by Abraham Polonsky, *Body and Soul* is an uncompromising tale of greed, corruption and redemption, brilliantly realized by director Rossen. One of the greatest of all boxing films. ★★★★ DVD: $14.99, VHS: $9.99

Body Double

(1984, 109 min, US, Brian De Palma) *Craig Wasson, Melanie Griffith, Deborah Shelton, Dennis Franz.* De Palma's acclaimed sleazy thriller about a voyeuristic actor (Wasson) whose penchant for peeping involves him in the grisly murder of a woman (Shelton) on whom he's been spying. A prestardom Griffith also stars as a porn star. De Palma borrows from Hitchcock (here *Rear Window*) once again, with successful results. ★★★ DVD: $9.99

Body Heat

(1981, 113 min, US, Lawrence Kasdan) *William Hurt, Kathleen Turner, Ted Danson, Richard Crenna, Mickey Rourke.* Simmering passions and deadly schemes are ignited under the hot Florida sun in Kasdan's remarkable, sensuous thriller which almost single-handedly brought noir back to vogue. With nods to *Double Indemnity* and *The Postman Always Rings Twice*, Kasdan's riveting tale stars Hurt as a second-rate lawyer who begins an affair with sultry and very married Turner (her memorable debut). Only her husband (Crenna) stands in the way of their happiness. Kasdan takes the traditional femme fatale tale and spices it up with sexy lovemaking scenes, crackling dialogue and twist upon twist. In their first appearance together, Hurt and Turner are simply dynamite. ★★★★ DVD: $14.99, VHS: $9.99

Body Melt

(1998, 82 min, Australia, Philip Brophy) *Gerard Kennedy, Andrew Daddo.* A scientific experiment turns an Australian community into melting zombies. The plot is weak. The acting is weaker. The special effects are truly disgusting and the film boasts a shameless group of backwoods *Deliverance*-type hicks who are more repulsive than any melting zombies. *Body Melt* tries to ride on the coattails of Peter Jackson's successful *Dead Alive*, but misses the mark by a mile. ★ DVD: $19.99, VHS: $59.99

Body of Evidence

(1992, 99 min, US, Uli Edel) *Madonna, Willem Dafoe, Anne Archer, Joe Mantegna, Julianne Moore, Frank Langella, Charles Hallahan, Jürgen Prochnow.* Basic Instinct look like the *Citizen Kane* of the whodunit-in-the-sack thrillers. The "body" in question is Madonna's over-exposed corpus, the lethal weapon in a classic case of come-and-gone lovemaking. Dafoe is a morally dubious lawyer who must prove that while S&M hellcat Madonna is a "killer" in bed (wielding handcuffs, candles and mega-developed inner thighs), she's not actually a murderer. But can he maintain professional distance and resist the pint-sized dynamo who "does it like animals do it?" Madonna's acting doesn't amount to much, but she still out-acts Dafoe, who gives the worst performance of his career. ★ DVD Letterbox: $14.99

Body Parts

(1991, 88 min, US, Eric Red) *Jeff Fahey, Kim Delaney, Brad Dourif.* Fahey loses an arm in an auto accident and his distraught wife approves emergency surgical replacement with a donated limb. The surgery is a success, but the donor — an executed murderer — wants his arm back! While the movie occasionally slips into hackneyed horror contrivance, it is often surprisingly effective in its treatment of Fahey's bizarre predicament. Where does consciousness reside? In the mind? In the soul? Or in individual body parts? ★★½ VHS: $9.99

Body Shots

(1999, 106 min, US, Michael Cristofer) *Sean Patrick Flanery, Jerry O'Connell, Amanda Peet, Tara Reid, Ron Livingston, Emily Procter, Brad Rowe.* This annoying twentysomething "exposé" deals with date rape and barhopping in the most superficial manner possible. A gaggle of attractive, shallow young adults get together for a night on the town, pausing only to turn to the camera and share their "feelings" and "insights." With the look and feel of a lower-end Fox-TV flick, phoned-in performances from its "hip" young cast, and an embarrassing reach for style and meaning by its director, *Body Shots* is a painful experience. ★ DVD: $19.99

The Body Snatcher

(1945, 77 min, US, Robert Wise) *Boris Karloff, Bela Lugosi, Henry Daniell.* Wise's second film for producer Val Lewton (the first being *Curse of the Cat People*) is an exceptionally atmospheric thriller about a 19th-century medical school professor in league with a grave robber. Based on a Robert Louis Stevenson story. ★★★

B

Body Snatchers

(1993, 96 min, US, Abel Ferrara) *Forest Whitaker, Meg Tilly, Gabrielle Anwar, Billy Wirth.* From the director of such hard-hitting hits as *Bad Lieutenant* and *King of New York* comes this eerie but redundant second remake of the 1956 sci-fi classic *Invasion of the Body Snatchers* about soul-stealing seed pods from space. Anwar toplines as a divorce-brat whose unsuspecting father accepts a job assignment relocating him to a military base now being used as an alien stronghold. ★★½ DVD: $14.99, VHS: $19.99

The Bodyguard

(1992, 129 min, US, Mick Jackson) *Kevin Costner, Whitney Houston, Gary Kemp, Ralph Waite, Robert Wuhl.* Costner plays the title character to Houston's big, big movie star in this idiotic romantic thriller. When she is plagued by death threats, Houston's manager signs on rambling man Costner, tops in his profession, but who never stays in one place too long (he's probably in constant search for a good barber). At odds from the beginning, Costner and Houston become enraptured with each other, leading to an inevitable fling. There's a good lakeside sequence, but nothing else in the film nears the level of its short-lived excitement. In her film debut, Houston is in her element vocally, but her acting is nothing out of the ordinary. ★½ DVD: $19.99, VHS Letterbox: $9.99, VHS Pan & Scan: $9.99

Boeing, Boeing

(1965, 102 min, US, John Rich) *Jerry Lewis, Tony Curtis, Thelma Ritter.* Curtis and Lewis team in this frantic sex farce which — even for the '60s — is particularly antifeminist. Curtis hams it up royally as a journalist who literally has his hands full juggling the simultaneous relationships with three live-in fiancées, all stewardesses and strangers to each other. Enter fellow reporter Lewis, who is forced to help Curtis in keeping the three women from meeting when all unexpectedly arrive at the same time. Ritter proves to be a saving grace, providing most of the laughs as Curtis' exasperated housekeeper. ★★ VHS: $14.99

Boesman & Lena

(2000, 84 min, South Africa, John Berry) *Danny Glover, Angela Bassett.* Glover and Bassett offer powerful performances in this stagey but moving adaptation of Athol Fugard's play. An allegory for the devastating effects of Apartheid on family and community, the story follows two lovers when are forced from their Cape Town home and head out on the dusty open roads of South Africa. A sad but penetrating examination of poverty, racism and society's "expendable" class. ★★★ DVD: $29.99, VHS: $19.99, VHS Letterbox: $19.99

Bogus

(1996, 111 min, US, Norman Jewison) *Whoopi Goldberg, Gérard Depardieu, Haley Joel Osment, Nancy Travis, Andrea Martin, Sheryl Lee Ralph.* Disarming despite its own shortcomings, *Bogus* is a children's fantasy which tells children the world is not always a nice place — so that's why there are such things as invisible childhood friends. Bogus is one such presence. He appears to Albert (Osment), a seven-year-old boy whose mother has been killed in a car accident. With no family, the youngster is sent to live with his mother's foster sister, Harriet (Goldberg). The story concentrates on their efforts to learn to love each other. The scenes between Bogus and Albert are the film's most appealing moments, however, Albert and Harriet's scenes are more difficult to watch and they underscore the story's sparseness. ★★½ DVD: $14.99, VHS: $9.99

Boiler Room

(2000, 120 min, US, Ben Younger) *Giovanni Ribisi, Vin Diesel, Nia Long, Ben Affleck, Nicky Katt, Scott Caan, Ron Rifkin.* Bristling with a vibrant rhythm that sets it apart from the pack, writer-director Younger's compelling *Boiler Room* has a take-no-prisoners attitude in telling its story of innocence lost, shady dealings and eventual redemption. Ribisi gives a super-charged performance as Seth, a naïve young man looking to make his mark as a stockbroker. Things spiral out of control when he joins a company involved in illegal tradings. Caught in a crisis of conscience, he is torn between easy money and doing the right thing. Ribisi is terrific as the young go-getter, a Duddy Kravitz for the millennium. As Seth briefly enjoys the sweet smell of success, the cost is high in this uncompromising, whirlwind look at ambition and corruption. Diesel is especially good in support as a rival broker. ★★★ DVD: $14.99, VHS: $9.99

Boiling Point

(1990, 98 min, Japan, Takeshi Kitano) *Takeshi Kitano, Masahiko Ono.* A stately, arty film with occasional bursts of graphic violence, *Boiling Point* is extremely brutal, deadpan, blackly comic, and Kitano's first fully realized film as director (his earlier *Violent Cop* was picked up by him in mid-production). A young baseball player/car wash attendant offends the local crimelord, and enlists the help of a seasoned, amoral criminal (Takeshi), a cold-blooded psychopath who's so bad that he's been booted from the yakuza. While it's certainly too slow for the "kill-'em-all" action crowd, *Boiling Point* may appeal to more patient crime film fans, with its elegant, at times, eerie atmosphere, fascinating characters, and unusual outlook. (Japanese with English subtitles) ★★★ DVD: $19.99, VHS: $14.99

Boiling Point

(1993, 93 min, US, James B. Harris) *Wesley Snipes, Dennis Hopper, Lolita Davidovich, Viggo Mortensen, Dan Hedaya, Seymour Cassel, Valerie Perrine.* Snipes makes an eclectic cast as a treasury agent out to avenge his partner's death (how original) at the hands of a shifty grifter (Hopper) and his trigger-happy henchman (Mortensen). While the film garnered many favorable reviews for its focus on character rather than gunplay, it is by no means the *Lethal Weapon* derivative it might have been. As a result, the movie simmers when it should have boiled. ★★½ DVD: $14.99, VHS: $9.99

Bolero

(1984, 104 min, US, John Derek) *Bo Derek, George Kennedy, Olivia d'Abo.* Derek takes her clothes off in the quest to lose her virginity. Surely there must have been one immediate taker so we wouldn't have had to suffer for 104 minutes. ★

Bombay Talkie

(1970, 108 min, India, James Ivory) *Jennifer Kendal, Shashi Kapoor.* Lucia, an American novelist, arrives in India in a desperate search for new sensations and experiences that will help her forget her approaching middle age. She soon meets and begins an affair with Vikram, a dazzling movie actor. Vikram eventually leaves his wife and family and destroys his life and career in a futile pursuit of an image that does not exist. Director Ivory and writer Ruth Prawer Jhabvala present an interesting look at culture clash, but the romantic dramatics are very much in the range of the familiar. ★★½ DVD: $29.99, VHS Letterboxed: $19.99

Bombshell

(1933, 95 min, US, Victor Fleming) *Jean Harlow, Frank Morgan, Lee Tracy.* This fast-paced, early satire on Hollywood hasn't lost a bit of its bite over the years. Harlow stars as the used and abused Hollywood starlet whose face and name are plastered across the country. And now she wants to change her image. The snappy dialogue keeps this film rolling along. Harlow, who could have been playing herself, gives one of her best performances in this hysterical film. ★★★½ VHS: $19.99

Bon Voyage & Aventure Malgache

(1944, 26/31 min, France, Alfred Hitchcock) During World War II, Alfred Hitchcock made these two shorts in an effort to boost morale, particularly that of the French Resistance. *Bon Voyage* is classic Hitchcock, a taut spy story about an RAF pilot who escapes from a POW camp that grows more and more intense with each plot twist. *Aventure Malgache* tells the story about the Resistance fighting a corrupt government in Madagascar. Though it is not as suspenseful as the first film, it is especially intriguing because it is based on a true story. Both films showcase many of the director's stylish and thematic trademarks and should not be missed by die-hard fans of the Master of Suspense. (French with English subtitles) ★★★ DVD: $24.99, VHS: $39.99

The Bone Collector

(1999, 118 min, US, Phillip Noyce) *Denzel Washington, Angelina Jolie, Queen Latifah, Michael Rooker, Ed O'Neill, Luis Guzman.* The fact that Washington is stuck in a bed for 99% of the film surprisingly takes nothing away from this intense, involving thriller. He plays a seasoned police criminologist who is paralyzed from the neck down while on a case. He is soon asked to help in an especially difficult case — a serial killer is picking up passengers in a cab and brutally skinning them. Jolie is the cop who finds the first body and is brought on to be Washington's eyes, ears and legs. A straightforward mystery that doesn't rely on convoluted twists and turns, *The Bone Collector* is a taut, efficient exercise in terror that relies on good, old-fashioned suspense to produce those goose bumps. Latifah is well cast as Washington's no-nonsense nurse. ★★★ DVD: $14.99, VHS Special Edition: $9.99

Bones

(2001, 93 min, US, Ernest Dickerson) *Snoop Dogg, Pam Grier, Khalil Kain, Michael T. Weiss.* Snoop Dogg plays Jimmy "Bones," a '70s gangsta who is betrayed, killed and buried in an abandoned hotel. Twenty years later, some kids buy the place to turn into a nightclub. Unfortunately for them, Bones wants revenge, and he wants it bloody. An oddball horror film, *Bones* is a hodgepodge of genres, grabbing elements of everything from Italian horror and blaxploitation to slapstick and urban drama. Dickerson knows his horror (with homages to *Hellraiser* and *Suspiria*, among others), and the film is stylish enough; but ultimately it's also pointless. Ultimately, these become some tired old Bones. ★★ DVD Platinum Series: $14.99, VHS: $6.99

The Bonfire of the Vanities

(1990, 125 min, US, Brian De Palma) *Tom Hanks, Kim Cattrall, Melanie Griffith, Bruce Willis, Morgan Freeman, Saul Rubinek, Andre Gregory.* Based on Tom Wolfe's runaway best-seller, this absurdly uneven film adaptation by De Palma was one of the most anticipated releases of 1990, and created one of that year's loudest thuds. This satire on greed and justice is a disappointment on numerous levels. In one of the many ill-advised changes from the book, the miscast Hanks plays a basically likable Sherman McCoy, the Wall Street wizard who is thrust into the media spotlight when he and his mistress (Griffith) are involved in the hit-and-run of a black man. Willis makes an earnest stab at the now-American author Peter Fallow, the down-on-his-heels journalist who lucks into the story of the year. ★½ DVD: $14.99, VHS: $14.99

Bongo Man

(1982, 89 min, Jamaica/West Germany, Stefan Paul) The normally peaceful island of Jamaica, rocked with dissention and bloodied by riots during the presidential elections of the early 1980s, provides the dramatic backdrop to this Reggae Sunsplash-styled concert film featuring Jimmy Cliff. The potentially explosive situation is intercut with the Rasta and reggae music of Cliff and Bob Marley and the Wailers in an effort to promote the idea that "politicians divide, musicians unite." ★★★

Bonjour Tristesse

(1958, 94 min, US, Otto Preminger) *Jean Seberg, David Niven, Deborah Kerr.* The French Riviera is the setting of this skillful adaptation of Francoise Sagan's novella about a young girl (Seberg) who drives a wedge between her rake father (Niven) and his mistress (Kerr). Exceptional performances from both Niven and Kerr. ★★★ DVD Letterbox: $29.99

La Bonne Année

(1973, 112 min, France, Claude Lelouch) *Lino Ventura, Françoise Fabian.* Veering away from his usual saccharine tendencies, Lelouch's bright romantic caper features a gangster (Ventura) who, although just paroled, plans a big robbery but instead of riches, finds his true love. (French with English subtitles) ★★★ DVD Letterbox: $24.99

Bonnie and Clyde

(1967, 111 min, US, Arthur Penn) *Faye Dunaway, Warren Beatty, Gene Hackman, Estelle Parsons, Michael J. Pollard, Denver Pyle.* Bonnie and Clyde marked the arrival of the New Hollywood in the late sixties with a burst of creative energy. An exceptional script by David Newman and Robert Benton, stylish direction by Penn, Dede Allen's brilliant editing and great performances from the entire cast (including Beatty and Dunaway as the title characters) combine to make this one of the most daring and successful of all mainstream American productions. Based on the exploits of the real-life pair who went on a crime spree through the Midwest, the movie is by turns humorous, thrilling, romantic and shocking. The climactic sequence is a tour de force of visceral filmmaking impossible to dismiss. ★★★★ DVD: $19.99

The Boogey Man

(1980, 86 min, US, Ulli Lommel) *Suzanna Love, Ron James, John Carradine.* This boring and pointless low-budget production begins as a pair of siblings murder their mother's abusive boyfriend. Shift forward twenty years (the first, but not the last horror-film cliché employed in this movie) to the brother and sister, now grown but still suffering the psychological consequences of that terrible night. In an attempt to overcome her fears, the sister returns to the scene of the crime, and the vengeful spirit is released. You can guess the rest. Amateurish and routine. ★

Boogie Boy

(1998, 104 min, US, Craig R. Hamann) *Mark Dacascos, Emily Lloyd, Jaimz Woolvett, Traci Lords, Frederic Forrest, Joan Jett.* Part Tarantino pulp drama, part drug exposé, and part bloody murder thriller, this weird flick tries for something new and settles for being a mildly intriguing find. Jessie (Dacascos) is a hunky ex-con who is reunited with his ex-cellmate (and prison lover) Larry (Woolvett) in a dark, drug-infested area of Los Angeles. Jessie has been trying to go straight: He's successful in not continuing the relationship with Larry but fails miserably when it comes to the law. A drug deal goes sour and the result is a lot of dead bodies. Jessie and Larry flee the city. They end up in an barren motel in the desert operated by a crazed codger (Forrest) and his sexpot girlfriend (Lloyd). Sure it's ridiculous, but the violence, offbeat characters and appearances by Jett and Lords may make it of interest. ★★½ DVD: $14.99

Boogie Nights

(1997, 155 min, US, Paul Thomas Anderson) *Mark Wahlberg, Julianne Moore, Burt Reynolds, Don Cheadle, William H. Macy, Heather Graham, Luis Guzman, John C. Reilly, Alfred Molina, Philip Seymour Hoffman, Philip Baker Hall.* Wahlberg sparkles in this immensely enjoyable and decidedly over-the-top trip through the '70s as seen through the filter of the adult film industry. Wahlberg is Eddie Adams, an unassuming busboy at a seedy L.A. discotheque where he is approached by XXX-film director Jack Horner (Reynolds, in a role that should have won him an Oscar). Within weeks our winsome hero is transformed from hayseed Valley Boy into the latest 100%-grade AAA beef packin' superstar of smut . . . Dirk Diggler! Director Anderson does a masterful job of piecing together this cinematic expedition from the giddy innocence of the early '70s to the paranoiac, cocaine-addled violence at the beginning of the Reagan era. Moore is stunning as Reynolds' porn-star wife, the veteran starlet who helps initiate Dirk into their tight-knit family. Includes 20 minutes of censored scenes not shown theatrically. ★★★★ DVD 2-disc Platinum Series Special Edition: $26.99

Book of Shadows: Blair Witch 2

(2000, 90 min, US, Joe Berlinger) Invention and filmic chicanery are replaced with silliness and clichés in this tired sequel to the surprise 1999 box office hit. Noted documentarian Berlinger is able to give this film an improved visual style over the original, but the screenplay he and Dick Beebe have concocted is trapped somewhere in the backwoods of mediocrity. Four fans of the first film spend a night in the Black Hills of Burkittsville, Maryland, courtesy of a local tour guide. It soon becomes apparent that there's something out there when they all descend into a nightmare of madness and murder. Too many jump-cuts add to the confusion of too many flashbacks, resulting in stock scares and little tension. A decent twist ending is lost amongst the one-dimensional characters and convoluted story. ★½ DVD: $14.99, VHS: $9.99

Boom!

(1968, 113 min, US/GB, Joseph Losey) *Elizabeth Taylor, Richard Burton, Noël Coward, Joanna Shimkus, Michael Dunn.* Adapted by Tennessee Williams from his short play, "The Milk Train Doesn't Stop Here Anymore," this is an oddly comic drama about a dying millionaress (Taylor) who becomes enamored with wondering poet and

"Angel of Death" Burton. Filmed in the sunny island of Sardina, the film is pretentious, unintentionally funny, and strangely fascinating. Coward is featured as the bitchy Witch of Capri, a role originally written for a woman and played to the hilt by Sir Noël. ★★

Boomerang

(1992, 118 min, US, Reginald Hudlin) *Eddie Murphy, Robin Givens, Eartha Kitt, Halle Berry, David Allen Grier, Geoffrey Holder, Martin Lawrence.* Murphy stars in this entertaining comedy about a way smooth, way charming advertising man in search of the ideal woman. But his cavalier use of sex to avoid communicating and his overemphasis on a woman's appearance come back at him when he meets his new boss, Givens. The film's amiable "buppy" characters and romantic sentiment put its heart in the right place, but the level of the humor rarely rises above the belt. ★★½ DVD Letterbox: $14.99

The Boost

(1988, 95 min, US, Harold Becker) *James Woods, Sean Young, Steven Hill.* A totally mishandled "say no to drugs" treatise about a hotshot salesman and his wife whose fresh new start in L.A. becomes a cocaine nightmare. Of value only as the film that sparked the real-life "fatal attraction" skirmish between stars Young and Woods. ★★ DVD Letterbox: $14.99

Das Boot (The Boat)

(1981, 209 min, West Germany, Wolfgang Petersen) *Jürgen Prochnow, Herbert Gronemeyer.* Few films convey the horror of war as powerfully as Petersen's claustrophobic account of a German U-boat's passage through hostile waters. Dispelling traditional film images of war heroism, *Das Boot* substitutes a truer vision of the waste and inhumanity inherent in battle. This is the full-length director's cut. ★★★★ DVD Letterbox: $19.99, DVD Letterbox Original Uncut 5-Hour Version: $39.99, DVD Superbit Edition: $26.99, VHS Letterbox: $19.99, VHS Pan & Scan Dubbed: $19.99

Booty Call

(1997, 77 min, US, Jeff Pollack) *Jamie Foxx, Tommy Davidson, Vivica A. Fox, Tamala Jones, Gedde Watanabe.* Infectiously silly and sporadically amusing, *Booty Call* isn't nearly as tasteless as its title would suggest. Buppie Davidson and his girlfriend of seven weeks bring along their respective best friends (who have never met) for a double date. The men make a "gentlemen's" bet to see who will bed their girl first. Not at all original but still able to produce a few laughs, *Booty Call* contains annoying gay and immigrant stereotyping, sloppy editing and moronic, sub-sitcom situations. Still, the four leads are enthusiastic and appealing, and the film is marginal, dumb fun. ★★ DVD: $14.99, DVD Bootiest Ever Special Edition: $19.99, VHS: $9.99

Bopha!

(1993, 120 min, US, Morgan Freeman) *Danny Glover, Alfre Woodard, Marius Weyers, Malcolm McDowell.* Actor Freeman makes his directorial debut with this solemn and powerful anti-Apartheid drama based on the play by Percy Mtwa. Glover stars as a black South African police sergeant whose position requires him to unwittingly enforce the country's racist laws. Labeled a traitor by his community, his world further deteriorates when he comes into conflict with his student rebel son (Weyers), who helps open his eyes to the injustices around them. As a study of racism, *Bopha!* doesn't instill anger but rather succinctly explores the ways this practice tears apart the fabric of black families. Slowly paced at times, the film helps bring to light the reality of South Africa. ★★★ VHS: $19.99

Bordello of Blood

(1996, 87 min, US, Gilbert Adler) *Dennis Miller, Angie Everhart, Erika Eleniak, Chris Sarandon, Corey Feldman, Whoopi Goldberg.* Accidentally resurrected, the Queen of the Undead (Everhart) sets up residence in a mortuary, playing madam to a group of undead ladies of the night. When a young Christian crusader (Eleniak) loses her brother to the vampiric legions, she enlists the aid of a private detective (Miller) to help find him. The gore scenes are lame and bloodless and much of the script is reminiscent of *From Dusk Till Dawn.* ★½ DVD Letterbox: $14.99

The Border

(1982, 107 min, US, Tony Richardson) *Jack Nicholson, Harvey Keitel, Valerie Perrine, Warren Oates.* Nicholson stars as a U.S. Border Guard who gets caught up in the business of transporting illegal aliens to pay for the materialistic lifestyle his wife craves. His morals come to haunt him in the form of a young Mexican mother and her child, whom he comes to care about. An engrossing film with excellent performances. ★★★ DVD: $14.99

Boris and Natasha

(1991, 88 min, US, Charles Martin Smith) *Dave Thomas, Sally Kellerman, Paxton Whitehead.* When we last left our evil villains, Boris Badenov and Natasha Fatale, they were two-dimensional characters drawn on paper — and still they had more depth than these live-action blow-ups made flesh by Thomas and Kellerman. True, Kellerman puts in a nice turn as the old-fashioned Pottsylvanian moll, and the script does retain some of the original cartoon nuttiness, but the plot . . . the animated Boris came up with better ideas. The theme song sums it up: "It's good to be bad" — but it's bad to be mediocre. ★★ VHS: $79.99

Born Free

(1966, 96 min, GB, James Hill) *Virginia McKenna, Bill Travers, Geoffrey Keen.* Heartwarming true-life story of two game wardens (played by husband and wife Travers and McKenna) who "adopt" Elsa, a lion cub, and raise her on their Kenya farm. A sweet, compelling adaptation of Joy Adamson's book, the film features a glorious score (and title tune) and inspiring scenes of nature in all its beauty. (Sequel: *Living Free*) ★★★ DVD Dual: $19.99

Born in Flames

(1983, 78 min, US, Lizzie Borden) A science fiction tale of feminist activism and "women's empowerment from the underground," *Born in Flames* is set in an imagined future, ten years after a socialist revolution that had left the patriarchal power structure intact. A band of female anarchists, led by a black lesbian and her advisor, do battle against an unresponsive government. This unusual, engaging and controversial independent feature has a cinema verité quality that lends the story the raw power of a documentary while conveying a hopeful fantasy of women of different races and sexual orientations working together against oppression. ★★★ VHS: $29.99

Born on the Fourth of July

(1989, 144 min, US, Oliver Stone) *Tom Cruise, Willem Dafoe, Raymond J. Barry, Caroline Kava, Frank Whaley, Jerry Levine, Kyra Sedgwick, Stephen Baldwin, Lili Taylor, Tom Berenger.* Stone won a much-deserved Oscar as Best Director for this gut-wrenching adaptation of Vietnam vet Ron Kovic's autobiography. Cruise gives a remarkable performance as the initially gung-ho soldier, whose life is covered in various, almost-episodic scenes, from his tour of duty and injury to the horrendous healing process to Kovic's gradual political awakening and activism. This just may be the definitive Vietnam film: for Kovic, like our country itself, began the war with undying faith, and endured a painful crippling and anguishing soul searching that ultimately suggested we hadn't done it the right thing. ★★★★

Born to Dance

(1936, 105 min, US, Roy Del Ruth) *James Stewart, Eleanor Powell.* That national treasure from the 1930s, Powell, stars with Stewart in this Cole Porter musical. The story, concerning a sailor in love, is routine; but Powell's musical numbers are sensational. Score includes "Easy to Love" and "I've Got You Under My Skin." ★★½

Born to Kill

(1947, 97 min, US, Robert Wise) *Lawrence Tierney, Claire Trevor. Born to Kill* is a tough and gritty film noir, directed by Wise early in his career when he was just beginning to explore the possibilities of the genre. This hard-boiled melodrama probes the dark side of human nature and shows the results of giving in to those urges. Tierney is harrowing as a murderer who will do anything to get what he wants — and what he wants is his wife's sister. ★★★

Born Yesterday

(1950, 103 min, US, George Cukor) *Judy Holliday, William Holden, Broderick Crawford.* Though director Cukor's staging is more stagebound than most of his stage-to-screen adaptations, *Born Yesterday* is nonetheless a thoroughly delightful comedy that earned Holliday an Oscar for her first starring role. Re-creating the part of Billie Dawn which she played on stage, Judy gives one of the classic "dumb blonde" portrayals as a gangster's moll who comes under the tutelage of "cultured" writer Holden. Crawford is her slobbish boyfriend negotiating unsavory political connections in the nation's capitol. Garson Kanin adapted his own stage hit. (Remade in 1993) ★★★½ DVD: $24.99

Born Yesterday

(1993, 101 min, US, Luis Mandoki) *Melanie Griffith, John Goodman, Don Johnson, Edward Herrmann, Max Perlich.* More appropriately titled *Born Again Yesterday,* this by-the-book remake of the 1950 Judy Holliday vehicle casts squeakbox Griffith as the airhead consort of a loutish tycoon (Goodman). When she goes along with Goodman's plans to smarten her up, she falls for the teacher: yummy Washington columnist Johnson. The updated screenplay doesn't stray too much from the original text, which accounts for the film's few laughs. But Griffith gives a superficial performance, and Johnson only goes through the motions. ★★½ DVD: $14.99

The Borrower

(1991, 97 min, US, John McNaughton) *Rae Dawn Chong, Don Gordon, Antonio Fargas.* Director McNaughton follows up his *Henry: Portrait of a Serial Killer* with this gory revamping of 1987's *The Hidden,* wherein an alien psycho-killer is sent to Earth for a lifelong prison sentence. This time, our other-worldly friend survives by tearing off and borrowing the heads of his victims, thereby acquiring personalities and memories as a side effect. ★★½ VHS: $14.99

The Borrowers

(1998, 86 min, GB, Peter Hewitt) *Jim Broadbent, John Goodman, Celia Imrie, Mark Williams, Hugh Laurie.* Based on the classic children's novels by Mary Norton, *The Borrowers* is the totally delightful story of 4-inch-tall people who live under the floorboards of a huge house and survive by "borrowing" from the humans who live upstairs. The humans, or human "beans" as they're called, are the Clock family, who have just been kicked out of their house by conniving lawyer Ocious P. Potter (Goodman). Not to worry, because the borrowers are on the case. Children will marvel at the borrowers and their adventures (the story is well-paced and imaginative), adults will appreciate the film's good wit that all ages will get. Goodman is particularly good-spirited as the mean-spirited Potter. ★★★½ DVD: $14.99

Bossa Nova

(2000, 95 min, Brazil, Bruno Barreto) *Amy Irving, Antonio Fagundes, Alexandre Borges, Debora Block, Stephen Tobolowsky.* Mary Ann (Irving) is a widowed, fortysomething English teacher living in Rio de Janeiro. She is wooed by Pedro (Fagundes), a handsome, middle-aged lawyer, and Acacio (Borges), a studly soccer star — both of whom are students of hers. Meanwhile, Pedro's brother has the hots for the new legal intern, who has the hots for Acacio, and so on and so on. The charming *Bossa Nova* is a beguiling romantic comedy that may contain a few clichés of the genre (silly fantasy sequences, last-minute chases to the airport), but its very appealing leads and the gorgeous locale erase any concerns about such familiarity. (In English and Portuguese with English subtitles) ★★★ DVD: $24.99

The Boston Strangler

(1968, 120 min, US, Richard Fleischer) *Tony Curtis, Henry Fonda, George Kennedy, Murray Hamilton.* Curtis' gripping performance as the infamous psychopath dominates this intense story — told in quasi-documentary style — of his insidious campaign of fear and subsequent capture and trial. Fonda also stars as the police detective on the case. ★★★

The Bostonians

(1984, 122 min, GB, James Ivory) *Vanessa Redgrave, Christopher Reeve, Jessica Tandy, Linda Hunt, Wallace Shawn.* An exceptionally strong performance by Redgrave and a commendable portrayal from Reeve highlight this Merchant Ivory adaptation of Henry James' novel. Set in 19th-century New England, the story concerns a love triangle in which Redgrave, an early feminist heroine, and Reeve, a reactionary Southern lawyer, battle for the love (and political soul) of a young girl. Ruth Prawer Jhabvala (who has scripted most Merchant Ivory productions) gleaned the emotional core out of James' work and her screenplay unearths the story's underlying passion. ★★★½ DVD: $29.99

Bottle Rocket

(1996, 91 min, US, Wes Anderson) *Owen Wilson, Luke Wilson, Robert Musgrave, James Caan.* In a world of diminished expectations, three disaffected misfits tackle Goal #1 of the master plan of the trio's least stable member. Too old for adolescent rebellion but with no clue of adulthood, they embark on a multi-decade program for a life of crime. This dark comedy employs engaging performances from a cast of mostly unknowns in a well-paced, quirky and surprisingly poignant tale of modern-day rites of passage. A bittersweet tale of unfocused desires and misspent energy, creating an oddly affecting and ingratiating parable about the dangers of self-delusion and misplaced trust. James Caan has an extended cameo as a consummate con artist, the ill-chosen guru of the master plan's author. ★★★ DVD: $19.99

Le Boucher

(1969, 94 min, France, Claude Chabrol) *Stéphane Audran, Jean Yanne.* The countryside in and around a small French village is the deceivingly bucolic setting for this well-paced and compelling Hitchcockian murder thriller. The stunning Audran stars as Hélène, a sophisticated schoolteacher. Emotionally scarred by a spurned love affair, she befriends a shy butcher who is tortured by his experiences in the Indochina war. Tensions mount and tragedy strikes after Hélène begins to suspect that the man is responsible for a series of sadistic killings of young women. (French with English subtitles) ★★★½ DVD: $19.99

Boudu Saved from Drowning

(1932, 87 min, France, Jean Renoir) *Michel Simon, Charles Granval.* A humane bookseller saves the life of a tramp (the wonderful Simon) who tries to commit suicide in the Seine. Disastrous results are his thanks when the uninhibited Simon moves into the man's home and proceeds to seduce his wife and maid. Unlike the 1986 remake, *Down and Out in Beverly Hills*, Renoir's tramp evades encroaching "respectability" and stays true to his anarchistic ways. (French with English subtitles) ★★★½

Boulevard

(1994, 96 min, US/Canada, Penelope Buttenhuis) *Kari Wuhrer, Rae Dawn Chong, Lou Diamond Phillips, Lance Henriksen.* A battered teen leaves her small town for the rough 'n' tumble streets of the big city. A frail, bruised but still beautiful Jennifer (Wuhrer) runs off to Toronto in an effort to escape from her abusive white-trash boyfriend. Penniless and friendless, she is clutched from the city's mean streets by Ola (Chong), a tough-talking prostitute (yes, with a heart of gold). The tired plot features an over-acting Phillips as the bad pimp, a seen-it-all cop (Henriksen) and a bevy of stereotypical whores. ★★ VHS: $79.99

Boulevard of Broken Dreams

(1993, 95 min, Australia, Pino Amenta) *John Waters, Kim Gyngell.* Experiencing a midlife crisis, Tom Garfield (Waters) returns to his native Australia after a ten-year absence. Having found great success in New York and Hollywood as a writer, he's back home to try to pick up the pieces of his scattered life — including reconciling with his estranged wife and daughter. Filmed at a snail's pace, *Boulevard of Broken Dreams* unfolds so slowly that it's rough going to get to the story's touching, second-half revelation. ★★

La Boum

(1981, 100 min, France, Claude Pinoteau) *Sophie Marceau, Claude Brasseur, Brigitte Fossey.* This charming French farce stars Marceau as a 13-year-old girl who auspiciously encounters the rites of teendom and the rituals of adulthood. An ingenious and graceful depiction of adolescent growth and familial affairs. (French with English subtitles) ★★★

Bounce

(2000, 106 min, US, Don Roos) *Ben Affleck, Gwyneth Paltrow, Joe Morton, Natasha Henstridge, Tony Goldwyn, Johnny Galecki, David Paymer, Alex D. Linz, Jennifer Grey.* Affleck plays a hotshot ad executive who gives a plane ticket to a pleasant writer (Goldwyn) who wants to see his wife (Paltrow). The plane then goes down, and while Death doesn't chase Affleck *Final Destination* style, the bottle and guilt do. A year later, he tracks down Paltrow to see how she's doing. But while not revealing himself as the guy who kinda killed her husband, he falls in love with her. An unlikely plot to be sure, but writer-director Roos takes the trappings and creates a truly winning romance between an unsavory (but with room for improvement) man and an ideal (but hurting) woman. Real-life exes Affleck and Paltrow bring whatever they learned from their relationship to the screen and the film is better for it. ★★★ DVD 2-disc set: $19.99, VHS: $9.99

Bound

(1996, 108 min, US, Andy Wachowski & Larry Wachowski) *Jennifer Tilly, Gina Gershon, Joe Pantoliano.* In this stunning debut feature, the brothers Wachowski have accomplished a remarkable feat: They've taken a tried-and-true cinematic formula (film-noirish plans, scams and betrayal) and added a very '90s sensibility to it, not to mention a major lesbian plot angle, without losing any of the thrill, intrigue, or snappy dialogue that characterized its '40s counterparts. Gershon and Tilly star as neighbors who become lovers first, then partners in crime. Or as Gershon says, "I can fuck somebody when I've just met them; but to steal with them, I have to know them better than myself." The question for the rest of the film then becomes who will betray whom. The intelligent script avoids every cliché it approaches and is constantly taking the viewer into new angles of the familiar story line. ★★★★ DVD Letterbox Unrated: $14.99

Bound and Gagged: A Love Story

(1993, 96 min, US, Daniel Appleby) *Elizabeth Saltarrelli, Ginger Lynn Allen, Chris Denton, Karen Allen, Chris Mulkey.* This frantic "My girlfriend's left me, but I'm gonna get her back" lesbian comedy is a self-assured independent film by Appleby. Cliff (Denton) is a hetero slacker who is thrown into a suicidal funk by his wife's gleeful, vindictive departure. His best friend is Elizabeth (Saltarrelli), a fun-loving but irrational bisexual who sleeps with men but is

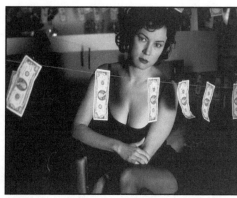

Jennifer Tilly in *Bound*

hopelessly in love with Leslie (Allen), a young woman stuck in a marriage with an abusive husband (Mulkey). When Leslie's hubby demands that the two stop seeing each other, Elizabeth, with a befuddled Cliff in tow, abducts Leslie and goes on the road, roaming the Midwest in a queer *Thelma and Louise* fashion. A snappily bizarre romp filled with weird, zany, and not always likable characters that mischievously explores the mysteries of obsessive but elusive love. ★★★

Bound for Glory

(1976, 149 min, US, Hal Ashby) *David Carradine, Melinda Dillon, Ronny Cox, Randy Quaid, Gail Strickland.* A Best Picture nomination went to this acclaimed biography of the great singer-composer Woody Guthrie. Carradine gives an exceptional performance as Guthrie, whose travels across the country during the Depression would inspire his legendary folk songs. Superb cinematography by Haskell Wexler. ★★★½ DVD: $19.99

The Bounty

(1984, 130 min, Australia, Roger Donaldson) *Anthony Hopkins, Mel Gibson, Laurence Olivier, Edward Fox, Daniel Day-Lewis, Bernard Hill.* Donaldson's lavish and sensual production presents a decidedly different and allegedly more authentic version of the infamous nautical mutiny. Hopkins as Captain Bligh is not a tyrannical madman, but rather a puritanically moral and unflinchingly formal seaman. Gibson is Fletcher Christian, former friend of the captain, who becomes a reluctant figurehead in the takeover. ★★★ DVD: $14.99

The Bourne Identity

(2002, 118 min, US, Doug Liman) *Matt Damon, Franka Potente, Chris Cooper, Clive Owen, Brian Cox, Julia Stiles.* Echoing such gritty thrillers as *Bullitt* and *The Taking of Pelham One, Two, Three*, even while wrapped up in a typically ludicrous Robert Ludlum plotline, *The Bourne Identity* is the type of film William Friedkin wishes he could remember how to make. Found bobbing at sea with no memory, Damon's Jason Bourne gradually finds clues to his identity; his gains in knowledge are met with increasing hostility from rogue CIA agents (including a sinister Cooper) and hired assassins. Massive car chases, a steamy romance (between Damon and the fetching Potente) and brutal fisticuffs

Matt Damon (l.) and Franka Potente find intrigue and adventure in *The Bourne Identity*

are kept rooted by Liman's matter-of-fact direction and keen attention to the intimate, interpersonal relationships that arise from any conflict, no matter how outrageous. The hoary device of a hero with amnesia is still a damn good one, and helps make Damon's transformation from Talented Mr. Character Actor into Kickass Superspy a little more believable than the earlier attempts by his bosom buddy Ben Affleck. (Sequel: *The Bourne Supremacy*) ★★★½ DVD Letterbox Explosive Extended Edition - Widescreen: $29.99, DVD Explosive Extended Edition - Fullscreen: $29.99, VHS: $14.99

Bowfinger

(1999, 94 min, US, Frank Oz) *Steve Martin, Eddie Murphy, Heather Graham, Christine Baranski, Terence Stamp.* Martin wrote and stars in this good-spirited, funny look at a hack Hollywood producer who will go to any lengths to get his film made. Martin is Bobby Bowfinger, a movie producer who has some pathetic titles under his belt. He is convinced that he can sell his newest picture with superstar Kit Ramsey's (Murphy) participation. Ramsey won't do it, so Bowfinger hires a lookalike (Murphy again) and edits him with surreptitious footage of the real star. Some good-hearted laughs occur as Bowfinger resorts to every trick in the book, and Ramsey sees conspiracy all around him. Martin resorts to his manic personality with good results, and Murphy — certainly in on the joke — has a great time as the pampered movie star and his slow-witted double. ★★★ DVD: $14.99

Bowling for Columbine

(2002, 120 min, US, Michael Moore) *Michael Moore, Charlton Heston, Marilyn Manson, Matt Stone, Dick Clark.* Who better than Michael Moore to handle the most serious of issues with humor and humanity, and communicate complexities with clear, concise vision? The Capraesque documentarian examines the American culture of violence through a pastiche of interviews, conversations, news footage and 911 calls; and presents a collection of statistics that everyone is familiar with, but when presented en masse is profoundly overwhelming. As Moore gets a free gun on opening a checking account and buys ammo in a barber shop, he discusses the atmosphere of violence which has permeated U.S. consciousness from the inception of the country. *Bowling* (reportedly, the shooters went bowling the morning of the

massacre) shows Littleton, Colorado, as on the surface the embodiment of the American Dream, where "two young men made very bad, very wrong decisions"; yet, under the docile morning-in-America façade, is subject to the same pervasive undercurrents affecting the country as a whole. The film is brilliant and incendiary, sure to outrage and to incite as much considered discussion as hostile reaction. Academy Award winner for Best Documentary. ★★★★ DVD Letterbox Special Edition: $19.99, VHS: $49.99

Box of Moonlight

(1997, 111 min, US, Tom DiCillo) *John Turturro, Sam Rockwell, Catherine Keener, Dermot Mulroney.* On the heels of DiCillo's uproarious *Living in Oblivion*, this bizarre existential amusement is a disappointment. Turturro stars as Al Fountain, an anal-retentive electrical engineer overseeing the installation of a generating turbine in a small Appalachian hamlet. Al begins to see odd hallucinations (coffee pouring out of a cup backward, etc.), and when the plug gets pulled on his project, he decides to go on a capricious search for a lake resort of childhood memory. His quest ultimately lands him in the lap of a twisted Peter Pan-like oddball (Rockwell) who refers to himself only as Kid. It's all too obvious that this imp is going to be Al's spiritual mentor and that's precisely what makes *Box of Moonlight* dissatisfying: it's all too obvious. Turturro gives an uncharacteristically wooden performance, thankfully offset by Rockwell's spirited turn. ★★ DVD: $19.99

Boxcar Bertha

(1972, 97 min, US, Martin Scorsese) *Keith Carradine, Barbara Hershey, John Carradine.* Scorsese's first feature-length film is not what you'd expect from a Roger Corman production with a title like this. Hershey gives a fine performance as a Depression-era orphan whose life is radicalized through association with renegade Carradine. ★★★ DVD Letterbox: $19.99

The Boxer

(1997, 109 min, Ireland, Jim Sheridan) *Daniel Day-Lewis, Emily Watson, Ciaran Fitzgerald, Brian Cox.* This third collaboration between director Sheridan and actor Day-Lewis (*My Left Foot, In the Name of the Father*) is an engaging drama but is by far the least accomplished of their three films

together. Day-Lewis plays Danny Flynn, a thirty-ish Irish boxer and former IRA member recently released from prison after 14 years who tries to make a new start by reopening his old gym and allowing both Catholics and Protestants to join. Predictably, things don't go as smoothly as hoped. Sheridan's well-meaning film has strong moments, but it can't fully create the righteous anger of *Father* or the rich characterization of *Foot*. But the acting is uniformly excellent; Lewis, Watson and Cox give strong portrayals. The film also has the pleasantly nostalgic feel of an early '80s British crime thriller, but like many of those films, the end result is involving, unremarkable entertainment. ★★★ DVD: $34.99, VHS: $14.99

The Boxer and Death

(1962, 107 min, Czechoslovakia, Peter Solan) *Stefan Kvietik.* A Polish amateur boxer, imprisoned in a German concentration camp, is forced to literally fight for his life after the camp's burly commandant, a boxer himself, spares him from death, but forces him into pummeling fighting matches. Initially stunned when he begins to receive special treatment while the commandant "fattens" him up for the kill, the prisoner faces not only the resentment of his fellow prisoners, but must decide whether to resolve to continue playing the patsy or risk his life by beating the egocentric commandant. Holding little back in depicting the wretched conditions of the death camps, the film is an unforgettably harrowing tale of bitter survival. (Czech and German with English subtitles) ★★★ VHS: $29.99

Boxing Helena

(1993, 95 min, US, Jennifer Lynch) *Julian Sands, Sherilyn Fenn, Bill Paxton, Art Garfunkel, Kurtwood Smith.* Only a child of the '80s, who was raised on "Dallas" and MTV, could think it acceptable to resolve a dramatic conflict with an "it was all a dream" sequence disguised as a music video. And twentysomething director Lynch shows her age in this immature study of love and image. Though the leads (Sands and Fenn) are undoubtedly physically attractive, Sands' twitchy, insecure performance makes the film extremely difficult to watch, even before the "dismember the one you love" theme comes to bear. ★½ DVD: $14.99

A Boy and His Dog

(1975, 87 min, US, L.Q. Jones) *Don Johnson, Jason Robards Jr..* A quirky, sci-fi comedy that envisions a future of roving scavengers and secluded townspeople. A young Johnson, accompanied by his highly intelligent talking dog, enters a surreal world of Americana only to be faced with imprisonment and the spectre of becoming a semen-producing machine for the women of the town. A cult favorite based on Harlan Ellison's WWIII sci-fi novella. ★★★ DVD Letterbox: $24.99, VHS: $29.99

The Boy with Green Hair

(1948, 82 min, US, Joseph Losey) *Dean Stockwell, Pat O'Brien, Robert Ryan.* An involving WWII drama about a young war orphan who becomes a social outcast when overnight his hair turns green. A very young Stockwell stars as the youth who is passed around from relative to relative, and ultimately becomes a symbol of the futility of war. ★★★

The Boyfriend

(1971, 141 min, GB, Ken Russell) *Twiggy, Christopher Gable, Tommy Tune, Glenda Jackson.* All-out musical numbers and spectacle abound in this lavishly entertaining musical — a glamorous tribute to Busby Berkeley. In a cameo appearance, Jackson is the star who, before opening night of the "big show," breaks her leg, forcing her mousy understudy (Twiggy) into the spotlight and onto the road to superstardom. The film was recently restored with additional footage. ★★★

Boyfriends

(1997, 82 min, GB, Neil Hunter & Tom Hunsinger) *James Dreyfus, Mark Sands, Michael Urwin, Andrew Abelson.* This insightful and vastly entertaining comedy-drama, depicting three troubled gay male couples, is both knowingly funny and unflinchingly on target. The story revolves around an Easter weekend country retreat arranged for six young gay friends and bedmates. But what begins as a relaxing time soon unravels into a series of bed-hopping, ego-bruising emotional turmoil to rival the granddaddy of gay male angst films, *The Boys in the Band.* A hilariously painful dissection of gay men's relationships — almost required viewing before calling U-Haul. ★★★ DVD: $29.99, VHS: $29.99

Boyfriends and Girlfriends (L'Ami de Mon Amie)

(1987, 103 min, France, Eric Rohmer) *Emmanuelle Chaulet, Sophie Renoir.* This, Rohmer's sixth in his series of "Comedies & Proverbs," comes dangerously close to being a parody of his best work. Intellectually lightweight with only a wisp of a plot, the film revolves around a group of young, attractive and rich friends who, when not being shallow and self-centered, are on the prowl for sex. Set in the beautifully designed but emotionally cold new city of Cergy outside of Paris, Rohmer observes these people's love follies with his usual detached amusement. (French with English subtitles) ★★ DVD: $29.99, VHS: $19.99

Boys

(1996, 87 min, US, Stacy Cochran) *Winona Ryder, Lukas Haas, James LeGros, Skeet Ulrich, John C. Reilly, Chris Cooper, Jessica Harper.* As *Boys* illustrates through rather clichéd dramatics: Left to their own devices, boys will be boys. This film also illustrates: A contrived script left underdeveloped will soon be forgotten. *Boys* is based on a short story by James Salter, and the premise would stretch the limits of a 20-minute short. Haas plays a high school senior at a boys' academy who shelters injured Ryder, who's avoiding the authorities; though why is a mystery. As the school becomes abuzz about a girl on campus, the young teen falls for the hard-partying "older" woman. Scenes are dragged on too long, and it takes forever to get to the puzzle of what happened — and by then you just won't care. ★½ DVD: $9.99, VHS: $14.99

The Boys

(1997, 85 min, Australia, Rowan Woods) *David Wenham, Toni Collette, Lynette Curran, John Polson.* Reminiscent of the smashing *Once Were Warriors, The Boys* is a well-wrought study of a brutal family dynamic. Brett (Wenham) returns from a stint in jail to the bleak poverty of home. He sees himself as the head of the household, but is actually the catalyst for its dissolution, imposing the illusion of order and normalcy through fear and intimidation. The family feeds on shared distrust and a casual, base violence that erupts with regularity and explosive force. The film's power lies in its ability to strip away all pretense from raw emotion and resonate with the primordial, blind fury of its protagonists. ★★★

Boys and Girls

(2000, 95 min, US, Robert Iscove) *Freddie Prinze, Jr., Claire Forlani, Jason Biggs, Amanda Detmer, Heather Donahoe, Alyson Hannigan.* An awful teen comedy, the generically titled *Boys and Girls* reteams the star and director of *She's All That,* but cannot duplicate that film's meager charms. The "plot" finds Prinze dumped by his girlfriend — or rather, she asked her roommate (Forlani) to tell him he's dumped. Shockingly, Prinze and Forlani start to fall in love, and that's when boredom sets in. Annoying, moldy one-liners alternate with crappy bubblegum music to grate on your last nerve. Forlani is terribly miscast and Prinze is merely terrible. ★ DVD: $19.99, VHS: $9.99

Boys Don't Cry

(1999, 116 min, US, Kimberly Peirce) *Hilary Swank, Chloë Sevigny, Peter Sarsgaard, Brendan Sexton III, Alison Folland, Alicia Goranson, Matt McGrath.* A brutal, enthralling examination of sexual identity, this fictionalized drama focuses on the tragic real-life story of Brandon Teena, a woman (Teena Brandon) who decided quite early to live her life as a man. Oscar winner Swank is riveting as Brandon, a sweet but far-from-perfect 21-year-old drifter. The harrowing tale, set in a trailer-trash Nebraska town, follows Brandon as he befriends and moves in with a group of poor but fun-loving people. He also falls in love with Lana (Sevigny in an equally impressive performance), a tough-talking gal who finally meets a man who respects her and treats her right. But when Brandon is exposed as a woman, ignorance, fear and homophobia drives two of her male friends to violently confront him. Unflinching in its depiction of the working-class environment and complex in its handling of all of the characters, the film humanizes a person whose only crime was to express his true sexual identity. ★★★★ DVD: $14.99, VHS: $9.99

The Boys from Brazil

(1978, 123 min, US, Franklin J. Schaffner) *Laurence Olivier, Gregory Peck, James Mason, Uta Hagen, Lilli Palmer, Steve Guttenberg, Denholm Elliott.* Olivier stars in this high-tension political thriller as a Nazi-hunter who uncovers the existence of a war criminal (Peck) and his plans to resurrect the Third Reich by cloning Adolph Hitler. Based on the novel by Ira Levin. ★★★ DVD: $14.99, VHS: $9.99

The Boys in the Band

(1970, 118 min, US, William Friedkin) *Kenneth Nelson, Leonard Frey, Cliff Gorman, Laurence Luckinbill, Frederick Combs, Robert La Tourneaux.* Historically and politically significant despite (or because of) the pervading self-loathing and wallowing self-pity of its gay characters, *The Boys in the Band* — based on Matt Crawley's off-Broadway hit — is a stage-bound, hyperventilating comedy-drama about eight friends who get together for a simple birthday party. What ensues during the course of the evening is enough emotion, acid-laced barbs and self-analysis to last a lifetime. With a screenplay peppered with many memorable lines, *The Boys in the Band* is a pre-liberation classic that is dated but hilarious and at times surprisingly offensive to '90s gay sensibility. It's also an important step in the depiction of gays in film. ★★★

The Boys Next Door

(1985, 91 min, US, Penelope Spheeris) *Charlie Sheen, Maxwell Caulfield, Christopher McDonald, Patti D'Arbanville, Moon Zappa.* Sheen and Caulfield are Bo and Roy, respectively, two California high school grads who vent their frustrations by going on a killing spree. In a hard-hitting, semidocumentary style, the film examines the damaged psyches of these two killers as they wend their way throughout Los Angeles randomly choosing and then murdering their victims. The murder scenes are especially brutal, but don't border on the gratuitous as they serve to illustrate the duo's twisted minds. There's a subplot of gay bashing (one of the film's most disturbing sequences) which brings to light Roy's closeted homosexual feelings. ★★★ DVD Letterbox: $9.99

The Boys of St. Vincent

(1992, 184 min, Canada, John N. Smith) *Henry Czerny, Johnny Morina, Sebastian Spence.* This compelling two-part drama of physical and sexual abuse at a Canadian boys' orphanage unravels like a wrenching sexual horror film and makes for a riveting, if uncomfortable, viewing. Part One, set in a Newfoundland school in 1975, centers on a withdrawn ten-year-old boy who is the sexual pet of Brother Lavin (Czerny), the dictatorial and devil-like principal. It takes a sympathetic janitor to call the police, but Church complicity and police reluctance to interfere conspire to cover up the problem in a veil of secrecy. Part Two, set 15 years later, finds the boys, now emotionally scarred men, successfully initiating charges against the brothers involved. The story, based on true events, is quite disturbing, and the scenes of physical and sexual abuse are almost too painful to watch. ★★★ VHS: $14.99

Boys on the Side

(1995, 117 min, US, Herbert Ross) *Whoopi Goldberg, Mary-Louise Parker, Drew Barrymore, James Remar, Matthew McConaughey, Estelle Parsons, Billy Wirth.* Singer-musician Joan (Goldberg), reeling from the break-up of her latest band, takes a ride-share to L.A. with Robin (Parker), a seemingly pristine yuppie who bemoans the crash of the real estate market. En route, they stop to visit Joan's friend Holly (Barrymore), interrupting her savage beating at the hands of her scummy boyfriend. The swiftly moving odyssey that follows is punctuated by strong characterizations. Fine cinematography indulges the glowing desert vistas of Tucson, a pit stop that extends to include birth and death. The film

Boys Don't Cry

flirts with mawkishness during the last half hour, only momentarily crossing the line. While comparisons to *Thelma and Louise* are to be made, the film's more about survival than allegory. And that's its gritty strength. ★★★ DVD: $14.99, VHS: $9.99

Boys Town

(1938, 96 min, US, Norman Taurog) *Spencer Tracy, Mickey Rooney.* Fine sentimental drama with Tracy winning an Oscar for his poignant portrayal of Father Flanagan, the founder of a school and community for troubled youths. Rooney is a streetwise delinquent. ★★★ VHS: $14.99

Boyz N the Hood

(1991, 107 min, US, John Singleton) *Cuba Gooding, Jr., Ice Cube, Laurence Fishburne, Morris Chestnut, Nia Long, Tyra Ferrell, Angela Bassett.* Singleton's powerful directorial debut is a brilliant examination of the crises facing young black men in the '90s, as well as a searing indictment of the culture of violence that holds sway in American ghettoes today. Set in the rough-and-tumble of South Central Los Angeles, the film tells the story of three black teens who face the unrelenting, and often deadly, realities of urban life. Singleton successfully avoids stereotyping his three heroes as inner-city misfits and instead portrays them as average American youth caught in an untenable situation. ★★★★ DVD: $19.99, DVD Anniversary Edition: $27.99, VHS: $12.99

The Brady Bunch Movie

(1995, 89 min, US, Betty Thomas) *Shelley Long, Gary Cole, Christine Taylor, Jennifer Elise Cox, RuPaul, Jean Smart.* The millions who loved — or hated — "The Brady Bunch," have reason to rejoice in this hilarious polyester and plaid restoration that asks the question, "What would happen if America's favorite family of the '70s ever collided with the naughty '90s?" In true sitcom fashion, this week's episode finds the Bradys on the verge of losing their groovy pad unless they can raise the $20,000 they owe in back taxes. And to add to the stew, Jan's sibling rivalry with "Marcia! Marcia! Marcia!" reaches fever pitch; and Marcia's best friend at school has a lesbian crush on her. Chock full of in-jokes and cameos, this double-knitted comedy strikes a nostalgic chord even as it hits the funny bone. (Sequel: *A Very Brady Sequel*) ★★★ DVD: $14.99, VHS: $9.99

Brain Damage

(1988, 94 min, US, Frank Henenlotter) *Rick Herbst, Gordon MacDonald.* If you loved *Frankenhooker* or *Basket Case*, then this offbeat gem is for you. In a sharp parable about drug addiction, Herbst must cater to his talking parasite's every whim or be deprived of its euphoria-inducing excreta. Horror show host Zacherley supplies the voice for the wise-cracking slug. ★★★ DVD Letterbox: $24.99, VHS: $59.99

Brain Dead

(1989, 85 min, US, Adam Simon) *Bill Pullman, Bill Paxton, Bud Cort.* Well-intentioned psychological thriller that asks the question, "Are we the dreamer or the dream?" Pullman stars as a scientist whose brain research leads to the recesses of his own mind. To say more would be to give the show away, but suffice it to say that the film is highly original and well-staged. ★★★ DVD: $19.99, VHS: $14.99

Brain Donors

(1992, 79 min, US, Dennis Dugan) *John Turturro, Bob Nelson, Mel Smith, Nancy Marchand.* The always impressive Turturro gets a chance to tickle his (and our) funny bone as he takes on the ambitious role of Groucho Marx. Updated and restaged to the world of ballet, this well-meaning remake of the Marx Brothers' classic *A Night at the Opera* benefits from Turturro's frenetic turn as an ambulance-chasing shyster masquerading as an impresario of the dance. Marchand pays ample tribute to Margaret Dumont. ★★½ VHS: $14.99

The Brain from Planet Arous

(1958, 70 min, US, Nathan Juran) *John Agar, Joyce Meadows.* In this precursor to *The Hidden*, a lascivious criminal brain from another galaxy commandeers the body of nuclear scientist Agar. Another brain from Arous, this one benevolent, comes to Earth and enlists the help of Agar's girlfriend, her father and her dog (which it inhabits) in an attempt to foil the plans of the evil brain, named Gor. Engaging in a campy way, this is 1950s sci-fi schlock, complete with cheesy special effects and one-dimensional plot and characters. ★★ VHS: $19.99

The Brain That Wouldn't Die

(1963, 81 min, US, Joseph Green) *Herb (Jason) Evers, Virginia Leith.* A scientist wants to graft the body of a hooker onto the decapitated head of his girlfriend. The seven-foot tall mutant in the closet doesn't think that's such a good idea. With occasional moments of gore, this is so bad, it's . . . well, bad. It's also cheesy, late-nite fun. ★½ DVD: $24.99

Brainscan

(1994, 96 min, US, John Flynn) *Edward Furlong, Frank Langella, T. Ryder Smith, Amy Hargreaves.* This high-tech horror yawn fest shamelessly borrows from the *Nightmare on Elm Street* films. A teenage video game addict (Furlong) orders a new interactive game which penetrates his subconscious. When friends and neighbors start turning up dead, he becomes the center of an investigation, while at the same time he's coaxed by a CD-ROM-spawned villain named The Trickster (Smith). Long on dazzling special effects but lacking in plot. ★★ DVD Letterbox: $24.99, VHS: $9.99

Brainstorm

(1983, 106 min, US, Douglas Trumbull) *Natalie Wood, Christopher Walken, Louise Fletcher, Cliff Robertson.* Forever to be remembered chiefly as Wood's last film (a double was used to finish some scenes), this energetic, highly original sci-fi yarn covers a lot of the same ground as *Flatliners*, but with better special effects (director Trumbull did the magic for *2001: A Space Odyssey*, after all). Fletcher is a knockout as a scientist grappling with the moral repercussions of a euphoria-making sensory device. ★★★ DVD: $19.99, VHS: $14.99

Bram Stoker's Dracula

(1992, 127 min, US, Francis Ford Coppola) *Gary Oldman, Keanu Reeves, Winona Ryder, Anthony Hopkins, Cary Elwes, Richard E. Grant, Bill Campbell, Tom Waits, Sadie Frost.* Coppola's extravagant adaptation of the literary classic delivers the goods with visceral, almost apocalyptic images of carnage juxtaposed with lush, Gothic visuals befitting an Anne Rice novel. These elements coupled with a truly seductive performance by Oldman as the bloodsucking antihero makes for a riveting journey through time. The film opens in the 14th century, when Vlad the Impaler (sometimes

thought to be Stoker's inspiration for his novel) renounces God in favor of evil following his beloved's premature death. The film then jumps to 19th-century England where Vlad, now known as Count Dracul, finds his eternal love reincarnated as a young beauty, portrayed by Ryder. A boldly original and satisfying interpretation of vampire lore. ★★★½ DVD Letterbox Superbit Edition: $27.99, DVD: $19.99, VHS: $9.99

Branded to Kill

(1967, 91 min, Japan, Seijun Suzuki) *Jo Shishido, Mariko Ogawa, Annu Mari.* This bizarre gangster thriller is a remarkable, audacious piece of filmmaking. It tells the story of Hanada (Shishido), the underworld's "Number Three Killer," a dead shot with either pistol or rifle who also becomes sexually aroused when he sniffs boiled rice. After he shoots Number Two Killer, he is given four extremely difficult assassinations to save face. He carries out three of them (all imaginatively staged), but the fourth is bungled, so he is marked for death. Eventually, Number One Killer comes out of the shadows and begins a long, tense showdown with Hanada. Highly original, the film thumbs its nose at both linear story telling and Japanese filmmaking. However, Suzuki's compositions are brilliant, using the black-and-white widescreen frame in new, inventive ways. While not for everyone — its story is very confusing and impressionistic — this is a wild piece of entertainment. (Japanese with English subtitles) ★★★½ DVD Criterion Collection: $29.99, VHS: $29.99

The Brandon Teena Story

(1997, 88 min, US, Greta Olafsdottir & Susan Muska) A powerful and emotionally moving documentary that delves into the nature of sexual identity as it relates to the senseless injustice of the brutal murder of a young female-to-male transsexual. In 1993, Brandon Teena was a fresh-scrubbed young man of twenty who moved to the small town of Falls City, Nebraska. He soon began dating girls. But the truth came out that he was biologically a woman, a discovery that prompted his murder. A bleak tale, but one that is given exhaustive and heart-felt handling by the filmmakers who had extraordinary access to all of the involved. Much of the information in the film formed the basis of the 1999 fiction film *Boys Don't Cry*. ★★★½ DVD: $29.99, VHS: $24.99

Brassed Off

(1997, 107 min, GB, Mark Herman) *Pete Postlethwaite, Ewan McGregor, Tara Fitzgerald, Stephen Tompkinson.* In the wonderful tradition of "small" British social comedies comes this unexpected pleasure with one of the most unlikely topics for a delectable comedy: a brass band competition. In the small Northern England mining town of Grimley, miners have proudly played in the town's brass band for over a century. But the imminent closing of the mines threatens not only the livelihood of an entire town, but the band as well. Under the direction of Postlethwaite (whose solid performance anchors the film), the band tries to persevere as the championship and an uncertain future lie ahead. Writer-director Herman has created an absolute joy — its humor is sharp, its political observations sharper, and the film is peopled with most appealing and nicely defined characters. Tompkinson gives a brilliant portrayal of comic verve and touching desperation as Postlethwaite's devoted son. ★★★½ DVD: $19.99, VHS: $9.99

The Brave Little Toaster

(1987, 90 min, US, Jerry Rees) *Jon Lovitz, Phil Hartman.* Cute animated musical adventure of a dejected toaster who rounds up the other household appliances — the vacuum cleaner, electric blanket, bedside lamp and radio — and leaves their country cottage for the big city in search of their beloved owner. ★★★ DVD: $24.99, VHS: $14.99

Braveheart

(1995, 180 min, US, Mel Gibson) *Mel Gibson, Sophie Marceau, Patrick McGoohan, Catherine McCormack, Ian Bannen, Brendan Gleeson.* Gibson's second feature film as director is an accomplished, realistically staged historical epic about 13th-century Scottish patriot and freedom fighter William Wallace. Written by Randall Wallace, reportedly a descendant of the hero himself, it shows us William's youth, courtship of his wife, his reluctant entry into "the Troubles" with the English King Edward the Longshanks (McGoohan), and his eventual embrace of the military leadership of his country. Three hours in length, *Braveheart* is remarkably never dull — a credit to Gibson's direction since the script must juggle several story lines. The most amazing thing about the film, however, is its savagely authentic battle scenes, two of which are of an epic scale not seen in film since *Spartacus.* Winner of 5 Academy Awards, including Picture and Director. ★★★½ DVD Letterbox: $19.99, VHS Letterbox: $14.99, VHS Pan & Scan: $14.99

Brazil

(1985, 131 min, US, Terry Gilliam) *Jonathan Pryce, Robert De Niro, Kim Greist, Ian Holm, Katherine Helmond, Bob Hoskins.* The second in Gilliam's "trilogy" about the realm of fantasy intruding into everyday life (the first being *Time Bandits,* the last *The Adventures of Baron Munchausen*), this darkly comic film is the best of the three. Pryce is a bureaucrat stuck in a chaotic government styled in equal parts after *1984* and *Modern Times.* He accidentally discovers a mistake made by an authoritarian wing of the government where a man was tortured to death because of a clerical error. His struggle with both his conscience and with the authorities who are now after him is interwoven with his increasingly frequent flights of fancy involving a mysterious stranger he loves and a huge samurai-like demon he must defeat to save her. Gilliam's vision is perfectly realized here; his futuristic society is a black, towering megalith of ductwork, fascist architecture and machinery crammed into every possible space. A towering achievement for Gilliam, especially considering the struggle he reportedly had to have the film released in its original form — a struggle with a mindless bureaucracy not unlike the one experienced by Pryce in this work of "fiction." ★★★★ DVD Criterion Collection: $59.99

Bread and Chocolate

(1974, 109 min, Italy, Franco Brusati) *Nino Manfredi, Anna Karina.* An uproarious comedy about an Italian immigrant working odd jobs in Switzerland and trying desperately, without success, to fit in. (Italian with English subtitles) ★★★½ VHS: $24.99

Bread & Roses

(2000, 112 min, GB, Ken Loach) *Adrien Brody, Pilar Padilla, George Lopez, Elpidia Carrillo.* British director Loach, whose body of work has often focused on working people and issues of polit-

Bread & Roses

ical and social struggles, ventures to Southern California to create an affecting humanistic drama whose politics could be accused of being somewhat simplistic but whose heart and candor could not. Maya (a striking Padilla) is a recent illegal Mexican immigrant who has moved in with her sister Rosa in Los Angeles. Maya gets a job as a janitor in the high-rise office building where Rosa works. However, Maya soon becomes involved in an attempt to unionize the workers there, and is torn between Max (Brody), the American union organizer, and a Mexican coworker striving for a law degree. Loach captures the strong family life of Mexican-Americans while revealing an economic exploitation most Americans would rather ignore. Poignantly unmasking a face to a mostly faceless work force, Loach delivers a tense, involving story of people searching for a piece of the elusive American Dream. (English and Spanish with English subtitles) ★★★½ DVD: $24.99

Bread & Tulips

(2001, 116 min, Italy, Silvio Soldini) *Licia Maglietta, Bruno Ganz, Giuseppe Battiston, Antonio Catania.* Director Soldini's charming character study is a light-hearted story about an unappreciated, middle-aged housewife struggling between her familial duties and a newfound sense of freedom and happiness. The ordinary Rosalba (the very appealing Maglietta) is left behind at a rest stop while vacationing with her boarish husband and two teenage sons. Instead of waiting for her more-angry-than-concerned husband, she hitchhikes a ride with the intention of going home but ultimately ends up in Venice — where she has never been before. Rosalba becomes enamored with the new friends and freedom she finds in Venice and the longer she remains there the more obvious it becomes that she won't be leaving her new home. The story may border on the predictable, but the film is buoyed by a delightful ensemble and the beauty of Venice itself. It is also highly commendable to see a film about an "ordinary" middle-aged woman finding herself. Hollywood should take notes. (Italian with English subtitles) ★★★ DVD Letterbox: $29.99

Break of Hearts

(1935, 80 min, US, Philip Moeller) *Katharine Hepburn, Charles Boyer.* Hepburn and Boyer offer good performances in this gentle romantic drama about a young composer (Kate) and her love affair with a famous conductor (Boyer). ★★½ VHS: $19.99

Breakdown

(1997, 93 min, US, Jonathan Mostow) *Kurt Russell, Kathleen Quinlan, J.T. Walsh.* Somewhere in the Texas desert, a husband and wife (Russell and Quinlan) are "taking the scenic route" on their way to San Diego and a new life. The financial worry they share is nothing compared to the trouble which lay ahead when she disappears in this tension-filled thriller. Stranded in the middle of nowhere, Quinlan accepts a ride from a friendly trucker (Walsh) while Russell stays with the car. But when Russell meets up with Walsh, he insists they've never met and knows nothing about his wife. The story follows Russell as he desperately tries to piece the puzzle together and locate his wife. Director Mostow creates quite a lot of suspense from the simple premise, and manages to do so with only barren landscape and narrative thrift. ★★★ DVD Letterbox: $24.99, VHS Pan & Scan: $9.99

Breaker Morant

(1979, 107 min, Australia, Bruce Beresford) *Edward Woodward, Bryan Brown, Jack Thompson, John Waters.* "Breaker" Morant, a cavalry officer serving in South Africa's Boer War, was tried for war crimes and murder along with two other Australian soldiers. They were defended by an inexperienced but spirited military defense attorney who valiantly tried to expose the political nature of the trial. This fact-based drama stars Woodward, in a sterling performance, as Morant, a heroic soldier who also happened to be a sensitive poet and sometime philosopher. Contrasted with him are the other two soldiers on trial: one a rowdy ne'er-do-well (Brown) and the other an inexperienced introvert. Beautifully filmed, *Breaker Morant* incorporates exciting flashbacks as the facts are presented in the courtroom. It's also profoundly moving, a riveting exposition of a series of events open to many interpretations which lead to a definite conception of what truth is. ★★★★ DVD: $19.99, VHS: $14.99

Breakfast at Tiffany's

(1961, 114 min, US, Blake Edwards) *Audrey Hepburn, George Peppard, Patricia Neal, Mickey Rooney.* Based on a Truman Capote story, this winning romantic comedy stars Hepburn as small-town Texas girl Holly Golightly, who leaves home to conquer the Manhattan party scene. There's zesty direction by Edwards and a fanciful Henry Mancini score including the Oscar-winning "Moon River." ★★★½ DVD Letterbox: $14.99, VHS: $9.99

The Breakfast Club

(1985, 92 min, US, John Hughes) *Emilio Estevez, Anthony Michael Hall, Judd Nelson, Molly Ringwald, Ally Sheedy, Paul Gleason.* Perceptive and entertaining teen drama written and directed by Hughes. Five high school students spend a Saturday detention at the school library. Each of the students comes to learn a little about themselves, as well as their newly acquainted classmates. Its young cast has rarely been better. ★★★ DVD: $19.99, VHS: $9.99

Breaking Away

(1979, 100 min, US, Peter Yates) *Dennis Christopher, Daniel Stern, Paul Dooley, Barbara Barrie, Dennis Quaid.* A funny, exhilarating ode to growing up. Four recent high school graduates compete against insecurity, frustration and an Italian bicycle racing team. Sensitively directed by Yates. ★★★★ DVD Dual: $14.99, VHS: $6.99

Breaking Glass

(1980, 104 min, GB, Brian Gibson) *Hazel O'Connor, Phil Daniels, Jonathan Pryce.* The rise to stardom is old fodder for the story mill and this unexceptional punk/new wave success story does nothing to give it new life. This is a fairly predictable tale of the exploits of Hazel O'Connor as she works her way out of the dingy clubs of London to become a punk superstar. Only exceptional performances save this film from complete mediocrity. ★★

Breaking In

(1989, 91 min, US, Bill Forsyth) *Burt Reynolds, Casey Siemaszko, Sheila Kelley, Maury Chaykin.* This heist comedy by Forsyth was anticipated by many in the film community with great relish. Couple Forsyth's knack for putting together charming, off-kilter comedies and the screenwriting genius of John Sayles; add to the mix the inimitable talents of Reynolds and the youthful energy of newcomer Siemaszko and it's easy to see why so many people were expecting so much from this story about an aging safecracker (Reynolds) and his overly enthusiastic apprentice (Siemaszko). The result, however, is a somewhat mild, not overly ambitious comedy of errors. ★★½ DVD Dual: $14.99, VHS: $14.99

Breaking the Code

(1986, 90 min, GB, Herbert Wise) *Derek Jacobi, Harold Pinter, Prunella Scales, Amanda Root, Alun Armstrong, Richard Johnson.* Re-creating his Tony Award-winning performance for this exceptional play-on-film, Jacobi is outstanding as mathematician and WWII hero Alan Turing, who was naïvely open about his homosexuality in an intolerant society. A mathematical genius, Turing was responsible for single-handedly breaking the impenetrable Nazi Enigma code, a breakthrough which virtually guaranteed an Allied victory against the German navy. Hugh Whitemore's intelligent screenplay, (which was based on Andrew Hodges' novel "Alan Turing: The Enigma"), traces Turing's life as a university student, his time working for British intelligence, and his postwar years as a government researcher in crystal-clear flashbacks. Complex, often humorous and intellectually satisfying, Whitemore's story, while paying tribute to Turing, is a stinging indictment of homophobia. As the stuttering, nail-biting Turing, Jacobi mesmerizes with a stunning portrayal rich in subtle shadings and honest emotions. ★★★★ VHS: $19.99

Breaking the Rules

(1992, 100 min, US, Neal Israel) *Jason Bateman, Jonathan Silverman, C. Thomas Howell, Annie Potts.* A tedious tale of three young men who reunite a few years after college to confront their past and their futures which sadly breaks no rules and blazes no new trails. In all fairness, the three young leads do their best with a lethal script which follows the trio as they set off on a cross-country road trip after Bateman reveals to them that he is dying of cancer. Potts enlivens things as a small-town waitress who joins them on their trail of tears. (Filmed in 1989 but released three years later.) ★½ VHS: $14.99

Breaking the Waves

(1996, 156 min, GB/Scotland, Lars von Trier) *Emily Watson, Stellan Skarsgård, Katrin Cartlidge, Jean-Marc Barr, Udo Kier.* Danish director von Trier has managed to tightrope his way toward straight narrative while at the same time making a thoroughly unconventional movie. And it must be said at the outset that this 156-minute marathon is definitely not for all tastes. But for those who are not put off by a claustrophobic, handheld, ultra-intimate character study of the pitiful lives of a few hardy souls in an inhospitable Scottish hamlet on the North Sea coast, the result is a riveting and thought-provoking examination of obsessive love and one's relationship to God. Bess (Watson) is an emotionally unstable young woman who breaks the village taboo by marrying an outsider, Jan (Skarsgård), an oil rigger. When he returns to his rig, she breaks apart mentally and thus begins her slide into all-out obsession. Bess regularly throughout the film holds intimate two-way conversations with God — as hokey as they could have been, Watson miraculously pulls them off. Ultimately the film seems as confused about faith as its characters are, but that by no means diminishes its effectiveness as a philosophical puzzler. ★★★★

Breaking Up

(1997, 89 min, US, Robert Greenwald) *Russell Crowe, Salma Hayek.* Though played engagingly by both Crowe and Hayek, this minor romantic comedy has some good ideas and inventive visuals, but is sabotaged by a rambling screenplay and sometime static direction. The story follows the ups and downs of a relationship — they love, they split, they argue, they reconcile, they make love, they split. Much more suited to the stage than the screen, *Breaking Up* has an energy level that is almost exhausting — detailing a break-up and reconciliation doesn't necessarily need to make the viewer feel they, too, have sweated the anxiety of this volatile affair. ★★ DVD Letterbox: $19.99, VHS: $14.99

A Breath of Scandal

(1960, 98 min, US, Michael Curtiz) *Sophia Loren, John Gavin, Maurice Chevalier.* The ghost of Ernst Lubitsch was vainly resurrected for this uneven adaptation of the Ferenc Molnar play. Loren gives a gallant attempt to be sexy and funny, playing an Austrian princess. Unfortunately, she's cast opposite the monotonous Gavin as an American businessman who enters her life and with whom she falls in love. Director Curtiz evokes a small degree of playfulness, but misses many comic opportunities. Lubitsch leading man Chevalier appears as Loren's father, and he elevates every scene in which he appears. ★★ VHS: $9.99

Breathless

(1959, 89 min, France, Jean-Luc Godard) *Jean-Paul Belmondo, Jean Seberg.* Godard shook the film world with his dynamic style of editing, sound usage, character development and plot progression in this, his first feature film. Belmondo is the two-bit, existential hood engaged in a fateful affair with Seberg. (Remade in 1983) (French with English subtitles) ★★★★ DVD: $24.99, VHS: $19.99

A Breed Apart

(1984, 101 min, US, Philippe Mora) *Donald Pleasence, Powers Booth, Rutger Hauer, Kathleen Turner.* Millionaire egg collector Pleasence wants two rare Bald Eagle eggs, even if it means extinguishing the species. He offers $150,000 to world-famous mountain climber Boothe to scale the rock face on which the nest sits, on an island owned by Vietnam vet turned back-to-nature survivalist Hauer. An idiosyncratic little film saved from its shortcomings by the performances of its cast. ★★½

Brenda Starr

(1992, 94 min, US, Robert Ellis Miller) *Brooke Shields, Timothy Dalton, Tony Peck, Diana Scarwid, Charles Durning, Eddie Albert, Henry Gibson.* It took four painstaking years to bring Dale Messick's popular comic strip character straight to home video, and this is so bad it's easy to see why it was never released theatrically. Shields stars as the star reporter for *The Flash* who, along with her dashing mystery man Basil St. John (Dalton), is hot on the trail of the scoop of the century: a new, secret formula created by an ex-Nazi scientist that could open the door to star travel. It has to be seen to be disbelieved. ★ DVD: $14.99, VHS: $14.99

Brewster McCloud

(1970, 101 min, US, Robert Altman) *Bud Cort, Sally Kellerman, Shelley Duvall, Michael Murphy, Margaret Hamilton.* A quirky oddity that, although seemingly dated today, still should please fans of fantasy as well as devotees of director Altman. Cort stars as the misunderstood young man who lives within the catacombs of Houston's Astrodome and dreams of flying on his own. Kellerman is his fairy godmother who helps make it happen, and the delightful Duvall plays a Dome tour guide who befriends him. A funny fable about man's lofty ambitions as well as the forces of self-destruction. ★★★ VHS: $19.99

Brewster's Millions

(1985, 101 min, US, Walter Hill) *Richard Pryor, John Candy, Lonette McKee, Hume Cronyn.* Though Pryor and Candy are appealing performers and work rather well together, there's not much to recommend in this oft-told tale. Pryor plays a baseball player who stands to collect $300 million — but only if he can spend $30 million in exactly one month. ★★ DVD: $14.99

Brian's Song

(1970, 73 min, US, Buzz Kulik) *James Caan, Billy Dee Williams, Jack Warden.* Well-made and moving TV drama about Chicago Bears player Brian Piccolo, and his special friendship with teammate Gale Sayers when the former is diagnosed with cancer. Caan as Piccolo and Williams as Sayers bring remarkable heartfelt conviction to their roles. (Remade in 2001) ★★★ DVD: $19.99, VHS: $9.99

The Bride

(1985, 118 min, US, Franc Roddam) *Sting, Jennifer Beals, Clancy Brown, David Rappaport, Quentin Crisp, Geraldine Page, Cary Elwes.* Sting plays Dr.

Frankenstein whose monster (Brown) runs away from the lab after being rejected by his newly created bride-to-be (Beals). On the road, the goodhearted but muddled monster is befriended by a conniving midget (Rappaport). The friendship that develops is both funny and touching and makes the film worth watching despite the inane activities going on back at Frankenstein's castle. ★★½ DVD Letterbox: $9.99

The Bride Came COD

(1941, 92 min, US, William Keighley) *Bette Davis, James Cagney, Jack Carson, George Tobias.* Though neither was known specifically for comedy, Davis and Cagney bring a lot of life to this zesty 1940s romp about flier Cagney kidnapping bride-to-be Davis at her millionaire father's request. The fireworks start when they crash-land in the desert. ★★★ VHS: $19.99

Bride of Chucky

(1998, 89 min, US, Ronny Yu) *Jennifer Tilly, Brad Dourif, John Ritter, Katherine Heigl, Nick Stabile, Alexis Arquette.* Chucky gets lucky in this third installment of the popular horror franchise, but so, too, does the viewer as director Yu and writer Don Mancini have created a campy, over-the-top horror comedy that piles on the laughs as much as the scares. Tilly is priceless as Tiffany, a black magic woman who brings Chucky back to life (after his demise in *Child's Play 2*). But Chucky has other plans, and soon, Tiffany is now a pint-sized dolly herself, and the deadly duo are on the road on a fun-packed killing spree. Put the logic on hold, and enjoy this for what it is — a crazy, funny, irreverent gross-out fest. Better than either of its predecessors. ★★★ DVD: $14.99

The Bride of Frankenstein

(1935, 75 min, US, James Whale) *Boris Karloff, Colin Clive, Elsa Lanchester.* Dr. Frankenstein (Clive) makes a bride for his creature (Karloff), and all hell breaks loose. Arguably better than the original — both emotionally and stylistically — Whale's moody sequel to his 1931 classic *Frankenstein* best illustrates the director's macabre sense of humor and filmmaking talent. Lanchester plays a dual role as "the bride" and as author Mary Shelley. Whale personally designed Lanchester's spiffy hairdo. (Sequel: *Son of Frankenstein*) ★★★★

Bride of Re-Animator

(1990, 99 min, US, Brian Yuzna) *Jeffrey Combs, Bruce Abbott.* This sequel to the horror cult classic *Re-Animator* carries on the tradition of presenting graphic bloodshed so outrageous it's goofy. Combs reprises his role as Herbert West, the thoroughly demented medical student who is obsessed with reanimating dead tissue. Here, Herbert launches a new project at med school. Filled with hilarious one-liners and ludicrous scenarios only possible in films like this, *Bride of Re-Animator* is silly and entertaining, equal parts comedy and horror. ★★½ DVD: $14.99, VHS: $9.99

Bride of the Monster

(1956, 69 min, US, Edward D. Wood, Jr.) *Bela Lugosi, Tor Johnson, Loretta King, Tony McCoy, Harvey Dunn, Dolores Fuller, Paul Marco.* Bela's last screen appearance, where he conducts radiation experiments on men (and creates a giant killer rubber octopus). Tor plays his monstrous servant. Low-grade, low-budget craziness from Wood. ★ DVD: $24.99, VHS: $19.99

The Bride with White Hair

(1993, 111 min, Hong Kong, Ronny Yu) *Leslie Cheung, Brigitte Lin.* Set in a fantasy world that sometimes resembles feudal China and sometimes looks like Rudyard Kipling on acid, this expensive Hong Kong film is about a young warrior (Cheung), the successor to the leadership of the clan Wu Tang, who falls in love with a powerful warrior/witch (Lin) who is the bound slave of a pair of evil siblings whose intent is to destroy Wu Tang and rule the world. These star-crossed lovers make a pact to run away together, but things naturally go awry and betrayal rears its ugly head, leaving bloodshed in its wake. Filled with the usual Hong Kong action setpieces, *Bride* is distinguished by its adult tone and heartfelt love story. (Cantonese with English subtitles) ★★★★ DVD: $19.99, VHS: $19.99

The Bride with White Hair 2

(1993, 80 min, Hong Kong, David Wu) *Brigitte Lin, Sunny Chan, Christy Chung, Leslie Cheung.* Made right on the heels of *Bride* part one, this dull and pointless sequel picks up ten years after the events of the original. Ni-chang (Lin), the white-haired witch, is now inexplicably the leader of a man-hating cult. Seeking to destroy the remnants of the Wu Tang clan, Lin kidnaps the bride of the nephew of Cho Yi-hang (Cheung), the man who originally betrayed her. The nephew, of course, must rally his forces and storm the fortress of the evil cult to rescue his beloved. Tepid, lackluster and sorely missing the style of the first production, *Bride 2* only becomes worthwhile during its last ten minutes, when Lin and Cheung are finally (and inevitably) reunited. Unfortunately, it's too long to wait. (Cantonese with English subtitles) ★½ DVD: $19.99, VHS: $19.99

The Bride Wore Black

(1967, 107 min, France, François Truffaut) *Jeanne Moreau, Claude Rich, Jean-Claude Brialy.* Moreau stars as the inscrutable femme fatale with a murderous mission in Truffaut's haunting, suspense-filled homage to Hitchcock. Widowed on her wedding day, Moreau vows vengeance on her husband's killers. Stylish and extremely satisfying with a score by Bernard Herrmann. (French with English subtitles) ★★★½

The Bride Wore Red

(1937, 103 min, US, Dorothy Arzner) *Joan Crawford, Franchot Tone, Robert Young.* In a nod to "Pygmalion" and with a touch of "Cinderella," an eccentric count, trying to prove his theory about class difference, sends nightclub singer Crawford off to a posh Austrian resort. There she poses as royalty, meets postman Tone and rich playboy Young. Director Arzner isn't afforded the luxury of a classic screenplay, but manages to infuse a degree of high spirits into her social comedy. Crawford is well cast and looks great. ★★★ VHS: $19.99

Brides of Dracula

(1960, 85 min, GB, Terence Fisher) *Peter Cushing, David Peel.* Dracula's back and this time he's a blond! Peel stars in this quasi-Freudian take on the vampire legend as a bloodthirsty count whose dining-out privileges are revoked by his mother, who keeps him locked in the castle tower. Who says blonds have more fun? Cushing reprises his role as Professor Van Helsing. ★★★

Brideshead Revisited

(1980, 660 min, GB, Charles Sturridge & Michael Lindsay-Hogg) *Jeremy Irons, Phoebe Nicholls, Anthony Andrews, Simon Jones, Claire Bloom, Laurence Olivier, John Gielgud, Diana Quick.* A brilliant and haunting adaptation of Evelyn Waugh's best-loved novel. Don't be put off by the length of this miniseries as it is divided into six easily viewed and totally captivating episodes which chronicle a young man's enigmatic and obsessive relationship with a rich, aristocratic British family. Spanning three decades, from the early 1920s to the end of WWII, the story begins as a disenchanted British army captain, Charles Ryder (Irons), looks back on his earlier life, in happier days. It was then he first encountered Sebastian Flyte — the dazzling ill-starred son of Lord and Lady Marchmain. Sebastian brings Charles to the family home of Brideshead, beginning Charles' compulsive love affair with this strange, doomed family. Irons is outstanding in what may be the finest miniseries on video. ★★★★ DVD 3-disc set: $79.99, VHS 5-tape box set: $99.99

The Bridge

(1959, 102 min, West Germany, Bernhard Wicki) *Volker Bohnet, Fritz Wepper.* Based on the autobiography of one of the participants, *The Bridge* is set during the final days of WWII, when Allied armies were triumphantly advancing across the German countryside and the Nazi war machine was grinding to a halt. In desperation, Hitler and his generals tapped the last resource available to defend their homeland: children. The film tells the story of a group of boys who enthusiastically take up rifles and don uniforms to defend their hometown. After the rest of the nearby German army retreats past them, they remain at their posts to face the approaching Americans, without a wiser, guiding force to tell them when to retreat or surrender. A strong antiwar film which paradoxically contains some remarkable battle sequences. You won't soon forget its harsh picture of children forced to die like men. (German with English subtitles) ★★★½

The Bridge on the River Kwai

(1957, 161 min, GB, David Lean) *Alec Guinness, William Holden, Jack Hawkins, Sussue Hayakawa.* This magnificent wartime drama won seven Academy Awards and stands out as one of the greatest and most powerful films ever made about war and its degenerative effect on the minds of men. Filled with high-powered action sequences and intense psychological torture. ★★★★ DVD Letterbox: $24.99, DVD Limited Edition: $27.99, VHS: $14.99

Bridge to Nowhere

(1986, 82 min, Australia, Ian Mune) *Bruno Lawrence, Alison Rutledge.* A tense action-adventure film about five teenagers who, on an outdoor camping trip, cross paths with a psychotic hermit. Their struggle for survival reminds one of an Aussie *Deliverance.* ★★★

A Bridge Too Far

(1977, 175 min, GB, Richard Attenborough) *Dirk Bogarde, James Caan, Sean Connery, Robert Redford, Gene Hackman, Laurence Olivier, Liv Ullmann.* Though most will regard this as "a film too long," Attenborough's adaptation of Cornelius Ryan's book about a disastrous raid behind German lines in WWII Holland does offer a meticulous examination of the ill-fated mission. ★★★ DVD: $14.99

The Bridges at Toko-Ri

(1954, 103 min, US, Mark Robson) *William Holden, Grace Kelly, Fredric March, Mickey Rooney.* Holden stars in this powerful Korean War drama based on James Michener's novel about a civilian lawyer recalled to military duty overseas. Kelly also stars as his wife who patiently waits at home. Holden and Kelly give fine performances, as do March as a world-weary admiral and Rooney as a fellow pilot. ★★★½ DVD: $14.99, VHS: $9.99

The Bridges of Madison County

(1995, 135 min, US, Clint Eastwood) *Clint Eastwood, Meryl Streep, Annie Corley, Victor Slezak, Jim Haynie.* Robert James Walker's best-selling novel makes for a grand love story, beautifully evoking the romanticism of the novel and further illustrating the lyricism and range of director Eastwood. Streep plays Francesca Johnson, an Iowa housewife and Italian émigré whose children, upon her death, discover their seemingly staid mother was involved in an extramarital affair. As the film flashes back to the mid-1960s, the story focuses on the four-day romance between Francesca and a photojournalist, Robert Kincaid (Eastwood). A truly romantic, knowing drama marred only by one or two slowly paced scenes. The remarkable Streep has a rapport with Eastwood like no other actress with whom he's appeared. And he is commendable in a role which seems to have the Robert Redford stamp all over it. ★★★½ DVD: $14.99, VHS: $14.99

Bridget Jones's Diary

(2001, 95 min, GB, Sharon Maguire) *Renée Zellweger, Colin Firth, Hugh Grant, Jim Broadbent, Gemma Jones.* It doesn't take long for the clichés to start. Not even minutes into the film, the main character, Bridget (Zellweger), an ever-so-slightly overweight single woman approaching her 30s, lip-synchs a song (in this case, "All By Myself"). It's been done to death for decades, now. But damn if Zellweger doesn't make it seem fresh and new; bestowing that scene and others to follow with such charm as to make anyone forget that we've seen all

Renée Zellweger in Bridget Jones's Diary

this before. Based on the best-seller by Helen Fielding, the story follows Bridget and her search for Prince Charming. Firth is the stuffy lawyer with whom it's hate-at-first-sight, and the debonair Grant is Bridget's womanizing boss with whom she thinks she's found true love. Though not able to fully establish Bridget's multifaceted personality so clearly delineated in the book, this whimsical adaptation is nevertheless abundant with good humor, quality laughs, and features a first-rate performance by the adorable Ms. Zellweger. ★★★ DVD: $19.99, VHS: $9.99

Brief Encounter

(1946, 86 min, GB, David Lean) *Trevor Howard, Celia Johnson.* A masterpiece from Britain's postwar cinema, this extraordinary romantic drama stars Howard and Johnson, both giving impeccable performances, as two ordinary, middle-aged people involved in a short but compassionate extramarital affair. Subtle, masterful direction from Lean. Based on Noël Coward's one-act play, "Still Life." ★★★★ DVD Criterion Collection: $39.99

A Brief History of Time

(1992, 80 min, US, Errol Morris) *Stephen Hawking.* This fascinating, intellectually demanding documentary examines the life of British theoretical physicist Hawking, based on his own best-selling book. Interweaving biographical and academic information, the film balances its time between insightful glimpses into Hawking's past and colleagues expounding on his scientific theories. A victim of ALS (Lou Gehrig's disease), Hawking is completely paralyzed and confined to a wheelchair, but his amazing inner strength and incredible intellect shine through, making his ideas and the film itself all the more mesmerizing. It's the most stimulating Advanced Physics class you'll never attend. ★★★½

Brigadoon

(1954, 109 min, US, Vincente Minnelli) *Gene Kelly, Van Johnson, Cyd Charisse.* Kelly and Johnson play two American hunters who stumble upon a magical 18th-century village in the Scottish Highlands — a village that comes alive only once every 100 years. Charisse also stars in this enchanting adaptation of the Broadway musical. ★★★ DVD: $19.99, VHS: $14.99

Bright Eyes

(1934, 83 min, US, David Butler) *Shirley Temple, James Dunn, Jane Withers.* Temple sings "On the Good Ship Lollipop." Who could ask for anything more? The story has to do with a custody battle over little Shirley. ★★★ DVD: $19.99, VHS: $9.99

Bright Lights, Big City

(1988, 110 min, US, James Bridges) *Michael J. Fox, Kiefer Sutherland, Phoebe Cates, Frances Sternhagen, Swoosie Kurtz, Dianne Wiest.* Uptown boy Fox doesn't realize that he should just say "No" in this fair adaptation of Jay McInerney's best-seller. Fox gives an earnest performance as the young magazine editor whose life becomes entrapped by an endless cycle of work, drugs and decadent nightlife. Sutherland is well cast as Fox's sleazy bar pal, Tad. ★★½ DVD: $14.99

A Bright Shining Lie

(1998, 120 min, US, Terry George) *Bill Paxton, Amy Madigan, Eric Bogosian, Donal Logue.* Episodic docudrama based on Neil Sheehan's acclaimed account of the slipshod machinations — both the U.S. and South Vietnamese governments

— behind the Vietnam War. Paxton stars as a lieutenant colonel who resigns in disgust with the U.S. military's botched handling of the war. His passion to do the right thing and win the war drives him to secure a position as a civilian advisor to the military, where, after a short while, he loses his way once again. What could have been a searing, fascinating exposé or a compelling tragedy of one man's misguided passion (or, in the right hands, both), is instead a middle-of-the-road, faintly interesting copout. *A Bright Shining Lie* is dramatically hollow, and aside from several fly-on-the-wall sequences depicting the decision makers at work, there's precious little you haven't seen before. ★★½ DVD: $9.99, VHS: $9.99

Brighton Beach Memoirs

(1986, 108 min, US, Gene Saks) *Jonathan Silverman, Bob Dishy, Blythe Danner, Judith Ivey, Jason Alexander.* The first of playwright Neil Simon's autobiographical trilogy on his coming-of-age. The story focuses on the Jeromes, a tight-knit Jewish family living in a poor Brooklyn neighborhood in the late 1930s. Silverman makes a personable young Simon, and Danner has some good moments as his mother. Not as successful as the second film, *Biloxi Blues*, but entertaining all the same. ★★★ DVD Letterbox: $14.99

Brighton Rock

(1947, 87 min, GB, John Boulting) *Richard Attenborough, Carol Marsh, Hermione Baddeley.* A tense drama, based on the novel by Graham Greene, examining the criminal underworld in Brighton. A young and menacing Attenborough is Pinky, an inexperienced but ambitious thug who, with his ragtag gang of hooligans, begins to stake out his turf on the bustling streets of Brighton. Marsh is the innocent waitress who tragically falls in love with the soulless, immoral killer. ★★★½ VHS: $39.99

Brimstone and Treacle

(1982, 85 min, GB, Richard Loncraine) *Sting, Denholm Elliott.* A satanic young man (Sting) methodically forces his way into the lives of a middle-class suburban family by claiming to be the suitor of their mute and immobilized daughter. This unusual and malevolent thriller is not for the faint of heart, but will pay off for those with a need for something out-of-the-ordinary. ★★★ DVD Letterbox: $19.99

Bring It On

(2000, 99 min, US, Peyton Reed) *Kirsten Dunst, Gabrielle Union, Eliza Dushku, Jesse Bradford, Ian Roberts.* Dunst is voted captain of her cheerleading squad, and must defend their first-place status in the all-important squad competition. This year, however, they may have to face off against the superb Compton squad, whose routines Dunst's group have been "borrowing." A lightly amusing teen film, *Bring It On* is bolstered by assured direction, some surprisingly sharp satire and Dunst's solid performance. With fun support from Dushku as the tough-ass new chick on the squad, this is a touch more sophisticated than one might expect. ★★★ DVD: $19.99, VHS Special Edition: $9.99

Bring Me the Head of Alfredo Garcia

(1974, 112 min, US, Sam Peckinpah) *Warren Oates, Isela Vega, Gig Young, Robert Webber.* Oates is a piano player who becomes a bounty hunter when the title command is proclaimed by a rich Mexican landowner. Oates sets off across the dirty, dusty modern landscape to find and deliver that head, which belongs to the father of the landowner's daughter's child. Oates is helped by Vega, his sometimes lover who knows Garcia's last whereabouts. Every character is sweaty, miserable and unattractive, double-crossing and betraying each other constantly. An uncharacteristic film for Peckinpah, *Alfredo Garcia* is somber and rather downbeat, but it will please those who are willing to take a brief interest in the struggling lives of its unhappy characters. ★★★

Bringing Down the House

(2003, 105 min, US, Adam Shankman) *Steve Martin, Queen Latifah, Eugene Levy, Joan Plowright, Jean Smart, Betty White.* Tax attorney Martin's life is turned upside down by unjustly jailed Latifah, who won't let him rest until he's helped her clear her name. In the process, typical race-comedy hijinks ensue, and Martin learns to get in touch with his inner black man. Not quite the return to form Martin fans may have been hoping for, this is Latifah's *House* all the way and she's great, even helping make palatable the potentially offensive material. While nothing here even approaches the edginess or laughs of *Bulworth*, there are giggles and smiles to go along with the groans, and the hugely appealing wave of energy that is Queen Latifah makes up for the sitcom-pat resolutions and an appalling, cloying score. An underachieving, too-conventional comedy that at least had the smarts to cast the always-welcome Levy in a key supporting role. ★★ DVD Pan & Scan: $29.99, DVD: $29.99, VHS: $24.99

Bringing Out the Dead

(1999, 121 min, US, Martin Scorsese) *Nicolas Cage, John Goodman, Patricia Arquette, Ving Rhames, Tom Sizemore.* Director Scorsese brings his usual gritty eye to this story of an EMT worker (Cage) who becomes haunted by the spirit of a woman he could not save. As the hallucinations (or are they?) continue, he spirals out of control in a binge of alcohol, drugs and recklessness. Scorsese's visuals compensate for the sporadic dramatic lapses, and a great supporting cast is in good form. ★★★ DVD: $19.99, VHS: $14.99, VHS Letterbox: $14.99

Bringing Up Baby

(1938, 102 min, US, Howard Hawks) *Katharine Hepburn, Cary Grant, Charlie Ruggles, May Robson, Barry Fitzgerald, Fritz Feld.* The definitive screwball comedy, and one of the funniest films ever made. Grant gives his best comic performance as a hilariously befuddled, bespectacled anthropologist who becomes mixed up with daffy but determined heiress Hepburn (also in one of her funniest performances). Together, they tear apart the Connecticut countryside searching for leopards, pet terriers and an intercostal clavicle; all the while being mistaken for the notorious "Leopard Gang," big game hunters and nuts from Brazil. Grant and Hepburn's flawless comic timing and Hawks' inspired direction combine to make this a timeless and much-adored classic. ★★★★ VHS: $19.99

Brink of Life

(1958, 82 min, Sweden, Ingmar Bergman) *Eva Dahlbeck, Ingrid Thulin, Bibi Andersson, Max von Sydow.* A simple direct drama by Bergman with a great "Bergman cast." The film focuses on three women facing childbirth during a 24-hour period in a maternity ward. Bergman won the Best Director prize at Cannes for this effort. (Swedish with English subtitles) ★★½ VHS: $29.99

Katharine Hepburn and Cary Grant in the quintessential screwball comedy *Bringing Up Baby*

The Brinks Job

(1978, 103 min, US, William Friedkin) *Peter Falk, Peter Boyle, Gena Rowlands, Warren Oates, Allen Garfield, Paul Sorvino.* One of director Friedkin's most entertaining films, this splendid caper comedy re-creates the famous heist that rocked Boston in 1950. ★★★

Britannia Hospital

(1982, 115 min, GB, Lindsay Anderson) *Leonard Rossiter, Graham Crowden, Malcolm McDowell, Joan Plowright.* This scathingly funny and winningly absurd black comedy sums up the ailing state of the once mighty British Empire. Preparations for a visit by the Queen Mother to a floundering medical institution are set against the backdrop of violent protests against the specialized care given to a ruthless African dictator. In the midst of the melee, every possible (and impossible) catastrophe arises until Crowden (as the inimitably insane Dr. Millar) eloquently sums up the meaning of human existence. ★★★½ DVD: $19.99

Broadcast News

(1987, 131 min, US, James L. Brooks) *Holly Hunter, Albert Brooks, William Hurt, Jack Nicholson, Joan Cusack.* An extraordinary study of the ethical proprieties of television journalism, this is a surgically fine and remarkably funny dissection of the daily goings-on of a TV newsroom. Hunter is nothing short of brilliant as the slightly neurotic but talented producer who is saddled with undisciplined newcomer Hurt, a superficial neophyte with whom she begins an affair. As Hunter's coworker and pal, Brooks gives one of the great comic performances of recent years. J.L. Brooks has written a superbly detailed and intelligent screenplay, and his direction is equally as commanding. ★★★★ DVD: $29.99, VHS: $14.99

Broadway Damage

(1997, 110 min, US, Victor Mignatti) *Michael Shawn Lucas, Aaron Williams, Mara Hobel, Hugh Panaro.* A sunny, boys-in-love romanticism permeates this sugary gay romantic comedy. The story revolves around the ambitions and loves of three wide-eyed dreamers trying to become a success in Manhattan. They include aspiring actor Marc (Lucas); his mop-headed best friend and would-be musical composer Robert (Williams), who's secretly in love with Marc; and Marc's ditsy Greenwich Village roommate Christina. Lacking any real insight, the film is at times funny and occasionally charming in its innocence. ★★½ DVD: $24.99, VHS: $24.99

Broadway Danny Rose

(1984, 83 min, US, Woody Allen) *Woody Allen, Mia Farrow, Nick Apollo Forte, Milton Berle.* Allen stars as a hopelessly inept talent agent in this charming comedy, doggedly plugging his fourth-rate clients on the borscht circuit. Forte, as a beefy lounge crooner, is his prize attraction, and Farrow is a gum-chewing moll in distress. ★★★½ DVD: $19.99

The Broadway Melody

(1929, 104 min, US, Harry Beaumont) *Bessie Love, Anita Page.* The first musical to win a Best Picture Oscar, this backstage tuner shows its age. The story is about two sisters trying to make it on Broadway. Love and Page play the starstruck siblings, and there's a pleasant score. Billed as "The First All-Talking, All-Singing, All-Dancing Musical" — and it was. ★★½ VHS: $14.99

Broadway Melody of 1940

(1940, 102 min, US, Norman Taurog) *Fred Astaire, George Murphy, Eleanor Powell.* A sparkling backstage musical. Excellent dance numbers, and a lovely Cole Porter score including "Begin the Beguine" and "I've Got My Eyes on You" set the tone. ★★★ DVD: $19.99

Brokedown Palace

(1999, 100 min, US, Jonathan Kaplan) *Claire Danes, Kate Beckinsale, Bill Pullman, Lou Diamond Phillips, Jacqueline Kim.* It's *Clueless* meets *Midnight Express* as Danes and Beckinsale play a couple of young naïve travellers and recent high school grads who soon find themselves trapped in a Thai prison, trying desperately to get a hearing before the nation's kangaroo-court justice system. The territory feels too well trodden here, but the performances are convincing and there are undeniable moments of tension throughout. Pullman is the American lawyer who defends the two girls. ★★ DVD: $9.99, VHS: $9.99

Broken Arrow

(1950, 93 min, US, Delmer Daves) *James Stewart, Jeff Chandler, Will Geer, Jay Silverheels.* After his great success in *Winchester 73*, Stewart jumped back in the saddle for this acclaimed "pro-Indian" saga with Stewart as an ex-military officer acting as mediator between the Army and Apache chief Cochise (well played by Chandler). One of the first of those great '50s westerns to sympathetically portray Native Americans. ★★★ VHS: $14.99

Broken Arrow

(1996, 110 min, US, John Woo) *John Travolta, Christian Slater, Samantha Mathis, Delroy Lindo, Bob Gunton, Frank Whaley, Howie Long.* Travolta and Slater star as Air Force pilots and steadfast buddies who fly a test run of a new B3 bomber. With nuclear weapons aboard the plane, Travolta ejects them and then himself, leaving his friend aboard the plummeting aircraft. Slater survives and teams up with a park ranger (Mathis), together going after Travolta who is in league with terrorists who plan to sell the weapons back to the government. Much of *Broken Arrow* is undermined by an inane script which eventually throws logic out the window to facilitate its major action sequences. Though somewhat (if brainlessly) entertaining, the film is indistinguishable from any other garden-variety action flick. ★★½ DVD Letterbox: $14.99, VHS: $9.99, VHS Letterbox: $19.99

Broken Blossoms

(1919, 95 min, US, D.W. Griffith) *Lillian Gish, Richard Barthelmess, Donald Crisp.* Griffith directed this silent classic of a self-appointed Asian emissary of peace (Barthelmess) and his efforts to protect a young girl (Gish) from exploitation and abuse by her London thug father (Crisp). This sepia and blue-tinted video contains a short introduction by Ms. Gish. The original musical score strongly supports the film's dramatic undercurrents. ★★★½ DVD: $29.99, VHS: $24.99

Broken English

(1997, 92 min, New Zealand, Gregor Nicholas) *Aleksandra Vujcic, Rade Serbedzija, Julian Arahanga, Temuera Morrison.* A somber drama about having to choose between love and family, *Broken English* depicts the sensitive relationship between Nina (Vujcic), a former Yugoslavian living in New Zealand, and Eddie (Arahanga), a Maori. This gritty film wants to make a powerful statement about the way cultures are assimilated and/or vanished, only it lacks the impact of the producer's previous film, *Once Were Warriors*. Although *Broken English* earned a NC-17 rating for one graphic sexual encounter, viewers not looking for a worthwhile but heated sociopolitical film will be disappointed. ★★★

The Broken Hearts Club: A Romantic Comedy

(2000, 91 min, US, Greg Berlanti) *Timothy Olyphant, Dean Cain, Matt McGrath, Ben Weber, Zach Braff, Billy Porter, Nia Long, John Mahoney, Andrew Keegan, Jennifer Coolidge.* In his feature film debut, writer-director Berlanti has crafted an often funny, touching slice-of-life portrait on the lives, loves and dramas of a group of gay West Hollywood friends. The characters include Dennis (Olyphant), a promising photographer and his often dysfunctional friends: his housemate Cole (Cain), a charming man-stealing actor; and Benji (Braff), a punkish gym bunny fancier. They all hang out together at a restaurant run by the group's unofficial patriarch, Jack (Mahoney) and play together on a softball team coached by Jack. Dramas abound especially when Cole seduces and abandons the fragile, just-out-of-the-closet Kevin (Keegan) leaving Dennis to help pick up Kevin's emotional pieces. The film loses steam towards the end as Berlanti isn't quite sure how to wrap things up, but his film is witty and always entertaining. ★★★ DVD: $29.99, VHS: $9.99

Broken Lance

(1954, 96 min, US, Edward Dmytryk) *Spencer Tracy, Richard Widmark, Robert Wagner.* This remake of *House of Strangers* has been transferred out West, and bears more than a little resemblance to "King Lear." Tracy is dynamic as the patriarch of a cattle dynasty whose three sons become at odds with their father and each other. ★★★

Broken Noses

(1987, 75 min, US, Bruce Weber) *Andy Minsker.* The provocative photographer famed for his salacious Calvin Klein underwear ads, Weber has produced, in this low-budget short feature, a surprisingly touching and strikingly provocative documentary on Golden Gloves champion Andy Minsker and the boys of the Mount Scott Boxing Club. Weber takes his camera into Andy's home, where he, his family and friends talk about the rigors of professional boxing and his obvious role as another "Great White Hope." The camera captures the romantic and sensual machismo of the young boxers and the film features the music of Julie London, Chet Baker and Gerry Mulligan. ★★★ VHS: $29.99

Broken Vessels

(1999, 91 min, US, Scott Ziehl) *Jason London, Todd Field, Roxanna Zal, Susan Traylor.* While it will invariably be compared to Martin Scorsese's *Bringing Out the Dead* for traversing the same territory — the nerve-wracking lives of EMT workers — *Broken Vessels* is, nevertheless, a good film in its own right. London plays Tom, a guy from Altoona who relocates to Los Angeles to escape a tragedy in his past. Working as a lifesaver, Tom is soon fighting another personal battle when his partner Jimmy (the excellent Field) hooks him on copious amounts of drugs as an antidote to their thankless profession. As Tom and Jimmy descend further into addiction, it is only a matter of time before they crash and burn. Director Ziehl starts the film out episodically before it culminates in its harrowing finale. ★★★ DVD: $9.99, VHS: $14.99

Broken Vows

(1986, 95 min, Canada, Jud Taylor) *Tommy Lee Jones, Annette O'Toole, David Strathairn, M. Emmet Walsh, Frances Fisher, Milo O'Shea.* This atrocious religious drama stars Jones as a priest who undergoes a spiritual conflict when he falls in love. His troubles begin when he becomes obsessed with finding a killer. He befriends the deceased man's girlfriend (O'Toole), and while trying to piece together the puzzle, they fall in love. Jones must have needed rent money, for he walks through his role with little conviction. The direction is sluggish and the script astonishingly bad. ★ VHS: $19.99

Bronco Billy

(1980, 119 min, US, Clint Eastwood) *Clint Eastwood, Sondra Locke, Geoffrey Lewis, Scatman Crothers.* One of Eastwood's most underrated films, this endearing western fable follows the adventures of a traveling Old West show run by cowboy Clint. ★★★ DVD: $14.99, VHS: $14.99

A Bronx Tale

(1993, 122 min, US, Robert De Niro) *Robert De Niro, Chazz Palminteri, Lillo Brancato, Francis Capra, Taral Hicks, Katherine Narducci, Joe Pesci.* In his directorial debut, De Niro recalls the films of his longtime director Martin Scorsese with this beautifully shot and eloquent crime drama based on the play by Chazz Palminteri. Set in the early 1960s, the story traces the relationship between a Bronx

youth, Calogero, and a local gangster, Sonny (effectively played by Palminteri), whom the boy refused to identify in a gangland slaying. As "Cee" grows up, he forms a bond with Sonny much to the dismay of his ethical father (De Niro in a subtle performance). Capra and Brancato as the child and teenaged Cee, respectively, both create memorable characterizations. ★★★½ DVD Letterbox: $14.99

The Brood

(1979, 90 min, Canada, David Cronenberg) *Samantha Eggar, Oliver Reed, Art Hindle.* The shape of rage is the subject of Cronenberg's fourth visceral medical horror feature — and also the title of the book written by Reed's character, a renowned but controversial psychiatrist whose "psychoplasmics" method of therapy encourages patients to give physical form to their emotions and fears. Eggar, Reed's star patient, is undergoing intensive treatment at his New Age-type colony in the woods. It is there she gives life to a bizarre group of mutant children who murder her enemies. *The Brood* has the framework of an ordinary horror film, but it is distinguished by an intelligent exploration of the darkest pathologies of the human psyche. ★★★ DVD Letterbox: $14.99

Brother

(2001, 113 min, US/Japan, Takeshi Kitano) *Takeshi Kitano, Omar Epps, Claude Maki.* In playing the brooding Aniki, Kitano again dons his acting moniker "Beat Takeshi," signifying another adventure of a brutal, loyal and unsatisfied Yakuza member. A higher-up in Japan who becomes untrusted, Aniki flees to Los Angeles, where he has a half-brother (Maki), a budding gangster with a few underlings. After rescuing them from a bad drug deal, Aniki finds that the local territory is easy to take and eventually starts his own Yakuza group, ready to take on the Italians. Obviously not an English speaker, Kitano provides little direction to the American cast and demonstrates a weakness for sentiment and pretension. But he's also a master of sudden violence, and shows his comedy roots in, of all things, a hilarious basketball scene. Epps shows incredible range as Aniki's protégé (even if it resembles an actor's exercise) while the others flail in the absence of direction. (English and Japanese with English subtitles) ★★½ DVD: $24.99, VHS: $9.99

The Brother from Another Planet

(1984, 110 min, US, John Sayles) *Joe Morton, Darryl Edwards, David Strathairn, Maggie Renzi, John Sayles.* After his spaceship plummets into New York harbor, a mute black alien (Morton) stumbles into Harlem and learns the earthly ropes. Sayles' comic version of a stranger in a strange land is slyer than *Starman*, earthier than *E.T.* and a potent commentary on the everyday alienation of urban inhabitants. ★★★½ DVD Letterbox: $19.99

Brother of Sleep

(1996, 127 min, Austria, Joseph Vilsmaier) *Andre Eisermann, Dana Vavrova, Ben Becker.* A hypnotic tale set in a remote Alpine village, *Brother of Sleep* is a strange combination of religious parable and tragic love story. Writer-director-cinematographer Vilsmaier has succeeded admirably in capturing the film's palpable atmosphere, but the magnificent visuals are sadly diminished on video. Screenwriter Robert Schneider adapted his own novel depicting the jealousies and prejudices of the residents of Eschberg, a hateful little hamlet that is blessed — or cursed — with the bastard birth of Elias Alder (Eisermann). Elias possesses exceptional hearing

B

and he soon becomes the town's celebrated church organist. Complicating Elias' natural gift is his love for his half-sister, Elsbeth (Vavrova), and the bitter rivalry of his friend Peter (Becker) for her affection. Although the film is slow going at times, the unerring performances keep the film focused when the action sags. (German with English subtitles) ★★★

Brother Sun, Sister Moon

(1973, 121 min, GB/Italy, Franco Zeffirelli) *Graham Faulkner, Alec Guinness, Valentina Cortese.* Sappy, meandering, hippie-esque (in the bad sense of the word) and plagued by a soundtrack by Donovan, Zeffirelli's romantic story of 13th-century St. Francis of Assisi is quite enjoyable nonetheless. A young man from a wealthy family has a burning quest for spiritual fulfillment that causes him to abandon all worldly possessions and pleasures and live a simple life among nature and the poor. Spectacularly beautiful scenery and sumptuous costumes highlight the tale. ★★½ DVD Letterbox: $14.99, VHS: $14.99

Brother's Keeper

(1992, 105 min, US, Bruce Sinofsky & Joe Berlinger) The quiet, nearly impoverished farming community of Munnville, New York, became the center of a media barrage in 1990 when semi-literate farmer Delbert Ward was arrested for killing his 60-year-old brother while their two brothers slept nearby. Having been arrested and signed a confession under duress, Delbert was subsequently released on bail with the support of the local townspeople who believed in his innocence. This award-winning documentary, while scrutinizing the particulars of the case, becomes a fascinating probe into the mindset of rural America. It's a mesmerizing sociological and legal look at an almost forgotten piece of the American pie. ★★★★ DVD: $24.99, VHS: $24.99

A Brother's Kiss

(1996, 93 min, US, Seth Zvi Rosenfeld) *Nick Chinlund, Michael Raynor, Talent Harris, John Leguizamo, Cathy Moriarty, Rosie Perez, Michael Rapaport.* A hard-hitting and absorbing debut from writer-director Rosenfeld, *A Brother's Kiss* astutely develops the bond between two siblings on opposite sides of the law. Lex (Chinlund) is the older brother, whose failures in hoops and marriage lead him to a life of crime. Mick (Raynor) is the baby, a sensitive cop devoted to keeping their broken family together. The story, told in a lengthy flashback, shows the terrible event that forces Lex to protect Mick as a kid, and the efforts the adult Mick takes to save Lex when the world starts closing in on him. Although some of the plotting is a bit contrived, both leads are given an opportunity to show their tremendous range as actors. Tough, but tender, *A Brother's Kiss* is an affecting urban drama. ★★★ DVD: $9.99, VHS: $9.99

Brotherhood of the Wolf

(2002, 144 min, France, Christophe Gans) *Samuel Le Bihan, Vincent Cassel, Émilie Dequenne, Monica Bellucci, Jeremie Renier, Mark Dacascos.* Who says the French can't make a good action film? Combining European stateliness, Hong Kong-style action and Hollywood technique, *Brotherhood of the Wolf* is a highly entertaining adventure tale that marries such unlikely genres as martial arts, romance, werewolfs and the costume epic. That the film works at all is due in large part to director Gans' snappy direction, and that no cast member is taking any of this all too seriously. The handsome

Morgan Freeman and Jim Carrey in *Bruce Almighty*

Le Bihan is Gregoire, who with his Iroquois, kung-fu fightin' blood brother Mani (Dacascos) travels to a mid-18th-century country village being terrorized by a mythical beast. He soon learns there may be Church involvement, and becomes a target of local government. Thanks to swift pacing, the film belies its two-hour-plus running time, and Gans captures the atmosphere of a chiller while simultaneously giving the film an art-house pedigree. Improbable but true, the film is based on a series of actual events when the "Beast of Gevaudan" gave 1765 France something else to talk about besides Louis XV's ineffectual reign. (French with English subtitles) ★★★ DVD Letterbox: $19.99, VHS Subtitled: $9.99, VHS Dubbed: $9.99

The Brothers Karamazov

(1958, 146 min, US, Richard Brooks) *Yul Brynner, Lee J. Cobb, William Shatner, Maria Schell.* Epic adaptation of Fyodor Dostoyevsky's novel set in 19th-century Russia. Four brothers of disparate temperament react to the death of their tyrannical father. A psychological study well scripted by director Brooks and competently acted by its cast. ★★★

The Brothers McMullen

(1995, 97 min, US, Edward Burns) *Jack Mulcahy, Edward Burns, Mike McGlone, Maxine Bahns, Elizabeth P. McKay.* Burns' directorial debut is an unaffected, refreshing and surprisingly involving look at three Irish-American brothers. As they bury their abusive, alcoholic father, they are advised by their mom not to make the same mistakes she did. She leaves from the cemetary to catch a plane to Ireland to be with the man she's always loved. Committment is a struggle for the three siblings — one married, one engaged, one adamantly unattached — a struggle made no easier by their mother's revelation after their lifelong witness to the pain of an unhappy union. Mulcahy, McGlone and Burns convey the relaxed familiarity of brothers, giving subtle and natural performances. The women in their lives don't get as much screen time, but their presence rings as affably true as the men's. ★★★ DVD: $9.99, VHS: $9.99

The Browning Version

(1951, 93 min, GB, Anthony Asquith) *Michael Redgrave, Jean Kent, Nigel Patrick.* Redgrave gives a stirring performance in this outstanding drama about a stodgy English boarding school-teacher who finds himself being forced out of his teaching position and discovers his wife's infidelity. He finds redemption in an unexpected act of kindness when one of his young students gives him a copy of "The Browning Version" of Aeschylus' "Agamemnon," a play which he has translated. Terence Rattigan scripted this adaptation of his own play, and his poignant screenplay, Redgrave's classic portrayal and a splendid supporting cast make this must-viewing. (Remade in 1994) ★★★★ VHS: $19.99

The Browning Version

(1994, 97 min, US, Mike Figgis) *Albert Finney, Greta Scacchi, Matthew Modine, Michael Gambon, Julian Sands, Ben Silverstone.* This elegantly produced and deliberately paced film explores the sterile isolation of a profoundly unhappy professor at what appears to be the anticlimactic end of his career. Finney is a marvel of nuance and understatement as the tightly controlled and rigidly repressed teacher. Transferred to another school, his departure marks a loss of prestige and place, mirrored with intense disdain in the eyes of his embittered, spiteful wife (Scacchi). A chance gift from an appreciative student serves as catharsis for the beleaguered scholar, precipitating a reevaluation of a life hitherto defined by unspoken recriminations and calcified regrets. Finney's performance is matched by his supporting cast, especially Silverstone as the young student whose compassion and understanding greatly exceeds his years. ★★★ DVD: $14.99, VHS: $19.99

Brubaker

(1980, 132 min, US, Stuart Rosenberg) *Robert Redford, Jane Alexander, Yaphet Kotto, Morgan Freeman.* Based on a true story, Redford stars as a newly appointed warden of an Arkansas prison whose humane reforms uncover a web of corruption and murder. Slightly overlong, this is nevertheless a compelling drama with earnest performances. ★★★ DVD: $14.99, VHS: $9.99

Bruce Almighty

(2003, 100 min, US, Tom Shadyac) *Jim Carrey, Morgan Freeman, Jennifer Aniston, Philip Baker Hall, Catherine Bell, Nora Dunn, Sally Kirkland.* After trying a different career path with *The Truman Show* and *The Majestic*, Carrey is back in the kind of high-concept comedy that has made him a top box-office attraction. Unfortunately, in addition to the return of wacky Jim and numerous big laughs are also the pitfalls that have defined most of his comedies. The concept here is a doozy: TV news reporter Bruce Nolan (Carrey) curses God after a series of setbacks only to have the Creator bestow on Bruce His almighty powers. As portrayed by Freeman, God (a Yankees fan, by the way, which explains a lot) is a benign deity who happily hands over His job to Bruce, allowing Him a first vacation since the Dark Ages. Bruce then sets forth to put right his life. And that's when the film begins to fall apart. Beyond a few good sight gags and a hilarious newscast, Bruce uses his powers for the mundane, mostly trying to get back with his girlfriend (Aniston), which almost brings the film to a halt. Sappy and sentimental when it should zing, the story never allows Carrey to get totally wild and

B

crazy, failing to fully exploit what Jim Carrey could really do with such power. The filmmakers seem content in producing only a few amusing jokes when the sky, the world, the universe was the limit. ★★ DVD Letterbox: $26.99, DVD Pan & Scan: $26.99, VHS: $14.99

Bruiser

(2001, 99 min, US/Canada, George A. Romero) *Jason Flemyng, Peter Stormare, Leslie Hope, Nina Garbiras.* A picked-upon schlub (boss consistently humiliates him, friends cheat him, wife is sleeping around) wakes up one morning without a face. He turns this to his advantage by "anonymously" offing those who have wronged him. A clever revenge fantasy, *Bruiser* is extremely well directed by Romero, proving he's still got his chops. His script, however, is problematic, especially in its final third. Since the lead wears a mask the entire time, there's always a question of whether his lack of facial features is all in his mind. This ambiguity isn't played on enough by the end, and the killings get silly during the climax. The ending may fizzle, but the buildup is intriguing. Worth a look. ★★½ DVD: $19.99

Brussels-Transit

(1980, 90 min, Belgium, Samy Szlingerbaum) With blurry images of a cold, impersonal subway station and tram cars slowly moving through the fog of a northern European city, a woman's voice begins to sing a heartfelt poem in Yiddish. So begins this fascinating "art" film that delves into one Jewish family's life when they leave Lodz, Poland, after WWII. Narrated by the director's mother, the film uses her reminiscences of her family's life as she, her tailor husband and their two small children eventually settle in Brussels and attempt to eke out an existence despite a devastated Europe and ignorance of the language and customs. Spanning the years 1947 through the early 1950s, this is an unusual, somber yet touching document of one family's determination to survive. (Yiddish with English subtitles) ★★★

El Bruto (The Brute)

(1952, 83 min, Mexico, Luis Buñuel) *Pedro Armendariz, Katy Jurado, Andres Soler, Rosita Arenas.* This is the ironic tale of a not-too-bright but tender-hearted brute who is hired by a rich landlord to evict a group of striking tenants. He does his job only too well, resulting in the death of an elderly man. The young wife of the landlord, like a moth to flame, is fatally attracted to this "primeval man" and in quick succession seduces the hulking worker, abandons her husband and runs off with her lover. The price for her infidelity is increasing sexual torment and a descent into madness. A passionate exploration of the mechanisms of desire and the potential consequences of its fulfillment. (Spanish with English subtitles) ★★★ VHS: $24.99

The Brylcreem Boys

(1996, 106 min, Ireland, Terence Ryan) *Bill Campbell, Angus MacFadyen, Gabriel Byrne, Jean Butler, William McNamara.* Dramatizing a little-known historical fact, *The Brylcreem Boys* is set in an Irish P.O.W. camp during WWII. In an effort to keep its neutrality during the war, Ireland interned both Allied and German soldiers captured on Irish soil. The two enemies were kept in separate camps, very visible to each other. Escape was discouraged on both sides because both the English and German governments considered Irish waterways vital. An often interesting war drama that is sometimes hindered by subpar production values and a frivolous romantic subplot, *The Brylcreem Boys* follows two pilots, one Canadian (Campbell) and the other

German (MacFadyen), as they adapt to captivity and eventually to each other. ★★½ VHS: $9.99

Bubba Ho-Tep

(2003, 92 min, US, Don Coscarelli) *Bruce Campbell, Ossie Davis, Ella Joyce, Heidi Marnhout.* Elvis hasn't left the building . . . yet. He's been holed up at a Texas retirement home recouperating from a coma after switching places with an especially talented Elvis impersonator. Frail and full of regrets, Elvis (the incomparable Campbell) soon learns what's behind a rash of deaths at the old folks home: a 3,000-year-old Egyptian mummy who's sucking the souls of the living to stay alive. He's stumbled upon this with the help of John F. Kennedy — yes, the former president — who is also alive and now black (played by a good-spirited Davis). An outrageous premise that mixes humor and scares is, for the most part, cleverly handled, though the film does run out of a little steam by the end. No matter, though, for Campbell and Davis are game for quirky hijinks, and the chill/laugh ratio is enough to keep one amused and entertained. ★★★ DVD Letterbox Special Edition: $27.99

Favorite Line: "Never, never fuck with the king!" —*Bruce Campbell as Elvis Presley*

Bubble Boy

(2001, 84 min, US, Blair Hayes) *Jake Gyllenhaal, Swoosie Kurtz, Marley Shelton, Danny Trejo, John Carroll Lynch, Verne Troyer.* Well, this is certainly a weird one. Gyllenhaal plays a boy who, thanks to his ultraconservative and protective mom (Kurtz), has never left the house or the protection of his plastic bubble. With his knowledge of the world outside limited to reruns of "Land of the Lost" and the view from his window, he's obviously primed for a fish-out-of-fishbowl road comedy. So when his beautiful friend (Shelton) leaves from California to Niagara Falls to get married, our intrepid bubble boy heads east to proclaim his unrequited love for her. A slapdash, sometimes sentimental gross-out comedy, *Bubble Boy's* humor is too often victimized by bad pacing, sanitized dialogue and the episodic road trip conventions. ★★ DVD Letterbox: $14.99, VHS: $9.99

Buck Privates

(1941, 84 min, US, Arthur Lubin) *Bud Abbott, Lou Costello, The Andrews Sisters.* One of Abbott and Costello's funniest comedies. The Andrews Sisters also star. Bud and Lou join the Army, with predictable comedic results; Patty, Maxine and Laverne sing. DVD: $24.99 (DVD includes 7 other Abbott and Costello films) ★★★½

A Bucket of Blood

(1959, 66 min, US, Roger Corman) *Dick Miller, Barboura Morris.* With exception to *Little Shop of Horrors*, this sly horror parody is director Corman's best work from his early and extremely low-budget days. That great character actor Miller is center stage as a beatnik coffeehouse waiter whose newly found prominence as a sculptor is helped greatly by the dead bodies underneath his clay. ★★★ DVD: $14.99

The Buddha of Suburbia

(1993, 222 min, GB, Roger Michell) *Naveen Andrews, Roshen Seth, Brenda Blethyn, Steven Mackintosh.* Hanif Kureishi's serio-comic novel of life among the bohemians and bohemian-wannabes

Bruce Campbell (l.) and Ossie Davis in *Bubba Ho-Tep*

in 1970s London is the basis for this accomplished BBC miniseries. The story focuses on handsome Karim (Andrews), a bisexual teenager of an unconventional English mother (Blethyn) and a surprisingly eccentric Indian father (Seth). The film — and Karim — comes into its own when the family moves to a frenetic, punk-filled London when Dad becomes a guru in the '70s Buddhist scene. Sort of an English *Tales from the City*, this sprawling slice-of-life story features music by David Bowie. ★★★ VHS: $29.99

Buddy

(1997, 84 min, US, Caroline Thompson) *Rene Russo, Alan Cumming, Robbie Coltrane, Paul Reubens, Irma P. Hall.* Based on the book by Gertrude Lintz ("Animals Are My Hobby"), this appealing, true story chronicles the exploits of Buddy, a gorilla who spent most of his 54 years in the Philadelphia Zoo, living longer than any other gorilla. Trudy (warmly portrayed by Russo) is a true animal lover lucky enough to live in a large mansion where, with the support of her loving husband (Coltrane), she keeps hundreds of animals. Buddy is an infant and near death when she rescues him from the Zoo. She nurses him back to health and he matures on their estate. Trudy eventually creates an open-air environment at the zoo for Buddy and its fellow gorillas. The gorilla effects by Jim Henson Productions and the live chimpanzees are especially good. ★★½ DVD: $19.99, VHS: $14.99

Buddy, Buddy

(1981, 96 min, US, Billy Wilder) *Jack Lemmon, Walter Matthau, Paula Prentiss, Klaus Kinski.* This American version of the French film *A Pain in the A—* is a low-key black comedy highlighted by the pairing of Lemmon and Matthau. Lemmon plays a hit man whose job is interrupted by an obnoxious hotel neighbor played by Matthau. The magic between them makes up for the fair script. ★★★

The Buddy Holly Story

(1978, 113 min, US, Steve Rash) *Gary Busey, Charles Martin Smith, Don Stroud.* The life of Buddy Holly, the legendary rockabilly king, is brought to the screen with Busey in the title role. In an amazing metamorphosis, Busey transforms himself into the rock 'n' roll pioneer; not only in looks, but also with his singing. Songs include "That'll Be the Day," "Peggy Sue," "Rave On," "Maybe Baby" and more. ★★★½ DVD: $24.99

B

The Buddy System

(1984, 110 min, US, Glenn Jordan) *Susan Sarandon, Richard Dreyfuss, Wil Wheaton, Nancy Allen.* Wheaton plays matchmaker for his mom (Sarandon) and his school security guard (Dreyfuss). The couple experience hate at first sight but, of course, they eventually fall in love. The story here is obviously nothing new, but the performances are the main attraction. ★★½ VHS: $59.99

Buena Vista Social Club

(1999, 105 min, US/Cuba, Wim Wenders) *Ry Cooder, Ibrihim Ferrer, Rubén González.* One would assume that a Wim Wenders documentary about some old-time Cuban musicians would be an all-out celebration of the joy and swagger of the Afro-Caribbean beat — and *Buena Vista Social Club* is that. But more to the core of this riveting peek into the world of old and new Havana is a fascination with the human spirit. What Wenders and guitarist Cooder uncover is a group of men (and one woman), mostly in their late-70s and early-80s (they were all world-class musicians of the '30s and '40s), whose inextinguishable passion for their music is as palpable today as it was over 40 years ago. Several of the musicians in the Buena Vista Social Club had not made music in over a decade and amazingly, it doesn't show a bit! Wenders weaves back and forth from interviews with his principals, a recording session in Havana and a triumphant Carnegie Hall performance creating a tapestry that owes as much to the fortitude and joie de vivre of these remarkable troubadours as it does to the music. ★★★★ DVD: $14.99, VHS: $9.99

Buffalo Bill and the Indians, or Sitting Bull's History Lesson

(1976, 135 min, US, Robert Altman) *Paul Newman, Burt Lancaster, Geraldine Chaplin, Joel Grey, Harvey Keitel, Shelley Duvall.* The wild, wild West — Robert Altman style. Based on the off-Broadway hit "Indians" by Arthur Kopit, Newman stars as the legendary Buffalo Bill, who is now a carnival attraction reliving the mythic adventures of his youthful Indian-fighting days and believing it's all true. A cynical examination of heroes, legends and show business. ★★★ DVD: $19.99

Buena Vista Social Club

Buffalo '66

(1998, 110 min, US, Vincent Gallo) *Vincent Gallo, Christina Ricci, Ben Gazzara, Rosanna Arquette, Anjelica Huston, Kevin Corrigan, Mickey Rourke, Jan-Michael Vincent.* An impressive directorial debut for actor Gallo, this is the kind of personal filmmaking that hasn't been seen since the '70s. Rampantly experimental, with multiple screens, bizarre freeze-frames and ersatz, Dennis Potteresque musical interludes, *Buffalo '66* was shot on color reversal film stock, giving the film a grainy, contrasty look. A bit off-putting initially, the film begins as a just-released ex-con (Gallo), a seemingly repellent character, kidnaps trailer park nubile Ricci from her tap-dancing class and forces her to pretend to be his wife (he's visiting his estranged parents, and wants to make a good impression). After meeting his horrifying parents (Gazzara and Huston) and getting to know Gallo more fully, both the viewer and Ricci (terrific, as always) gain a bit more sympathy for this loser. Unpredictable, with a smashing set-piece finale. ★★★½ DVD: $14.99

Buffalo Soldiers

(2003, 99 min, US, Gregor Jordan) *Joaquin Phoenix, Ed Harris, Scott Glenn, Anna Paquin, Elizabeth McGovern, Leon, Gabriel Mann, Dean Stockwell.* This cynical and decidedly anti-military black comedy sat on the shelf for two years awaiting release, its distributor weary of the film's perceived unpatriotism in a post-9/11 support-our-troops climate. Set in 1989 on a West German U.S. Army base, the story centers on the shifty Ray Elwood (Phoenix), a battalion clerk turned black market profiteer and heroin dealer who runs afoul of the snarly new Top Sergeant (Glenn), a tense situation that escalates to a fever pitch when Elwood puts the moves on Top's rebellious daughter (Paquin). Harris portrays the disillusioned and perpetually oblivious base commander. The film doesn't quite rise to the anarchistic heights of brass-knocking satires like *M*A*S*H* and *The Last Detail*, but Phoenix's badboy charm makes for a likeable anti-hero worth rooting for. ★★★ DVD: $29.99

Buffet Froid (Cold Cuts)

(1979, 102 min, France, Bertrand Blier) *Gérard Depardieu, Geneviéve Page, Bernard Blier, Michel Serrault.* A surrealist urban landscape is the setting for this absurdist comedy of despair in which violence is a way of life and everyone is either a murderer or his victim. Depardieu stars as a drifter who is obsessed with death. After stabbing a man, he runs home to his wife and confesses the crime. Unperturbed, she simply throws the knife into the dishwasher. But before the machine completes its last cycle, she, in turn, is killed by an intruder. In the bewildering course of events that follow, Depardieu meets and befriends both an amoral police chief as well as his wife's killer. Director Blier maliciously blends elements of urban terror gone berserk with a Kafkaesque sense of an individual trapped in a world of desensitized and twisted logic. (French with English subtitles) ★★★

Buffy the Vampire Slayer

(1992, 86 min, US, Fran Rubel Kuzui) *Kristy Swanson, Luke Perry, Donald Sutherland, Paul Reubens.* A potentially amusing horror spoof that unfortunately gets mired in an internal confusion over whether to be *Bill & Ted* meets *The Lost Boys* or *Heathers* meets *Dracula*, *Buffy* is a vampire saga in search of some bite. Buffy (Swanson) is an average airhead California cheerleader before Sutherland shows up to inform her that it is her destiny to rid the earth of the evil bloodsucking undead. Joining Buffy in her quest is Hunk-of-the-Month Perry. *Buffy* is about as stimulating as a weekend at the mall, though at least it has the good sense to visit the nicer clothing stores. ★★ DVD: $14.99, VHS: $9.99

A Bug's Life

(1998, 95 min, US, John Lasseter) *Voices of: Dave Foley, Kevin Spacey, Julia Louis-Dreyfus, Denis Leary, Phyllis Diller.* Disney and Pixar, who gave us the (first) all-computer-animated film *Toy Story*, have struck paydirt again with this jubilant, bedazzling family feature. The story begins when a loner ant Flik (Foley) accidentally ruins the colony's sacrificial food tribute to the local grasshopper gang, led by the nasty Hopper (voiced with gleeful menace by Spacey). Flik is sent on a scouting mission and finds a gaggle of "tough bugs" to help — only he doesn't know they're actually circus performers. While livelier and funnier than the similarly themed *Antz*, most of the humor here is aimed at the kids. There's plenty of clever visual and verbal gags flying around, the bright, shimmering animation is stunning, and the voices are well cast — it's all so much fun. ★★★½ DVD 2-disc Collector's Edition: $29.99, VHS: $22.99

Bugis Street (Yao jie huang hou)

(1994, 101 min, Singapore, Yonfan) *Hiep Thi Le, Michael Lam, Grego, David Knight.* The teeming (and often steamy) world of transvestite and transsexual prostitution in 1970s Singapore is vividly brought to the screen in this deliciously tawdry and campily funny melodrama. A wide-eyed and naïve country girl (Le) comes to the big city and begins work as a maid in what she thinks is a classy hotel — but the Sin Sin Hotel is actually the sleazy home and work site for a bevy of gorgeously attired, lovelorn transvestite prostitutes. In this wonderfully hyperventilating film, the director obviously has a soft spot for these tough but tender gals whose romanticism remains undimmed on this street of cheap sex and unrealized dreams. (Cantonese with English subtitles) ★★★

B

Bugsy

(1991, 135 min, US, Barry Levinson) *Warren Beatty, Annette Bening, Ben Kingsley, Harvey Keitel, Elliott Gould, Joe Mantegna, Bebe Neuwirth, Robert Beltran.* Though *Bugsy* boasts an intelligent screenplay, outstanding production values and strong direction, it's Beatty's fascinating and remarkably complex performance which dominates Levinson's colorful gangster saga. Beatty is "Bugsy" Siegel, a New York crime lord who was sent by the mob to Hollywood in the 1940s, eventually helping to found Las Vegas and its first casino, the Flamingo. Bening is terrific as Virginia Hill, an aspiring actress who becomes involved with Bugsy. The film evenly — and quite successfully — divides its time between the volatile relationship between Bugsy and Virginia, and Bugsy's near-obsessive quest to build his desert resort. ★★★½ DVD: $9.99

Bugsy Malone

(1976, 93 min, GB, Alan Parker) *Scott Baio, Jodie Foster, Florrie Augger.* Doing a mean Joan Blondell imitation, Foster steals the show in this charming children's musical which features an all-child cast. This parody of 1930s gangster flicks pits two crime bosses against each other for control of the town. Baio is the likable hero who falls in with the wrong crowd. Foster plays a nightclub headliner who can zing a one-liner with the best of them. Paul Williams wrote the unmemorable score. And parents, don't worry — there are no bullets, only whipped cream. ★★★ VHS: $14.99

Bull Durham

(1988, 108 min, US, Ron Shelton) *Kevin Costner, Susan Sarandon, Tim Robbins, Robert Wuhl.* Costner stars in this entertaining, literate and very sexy comedy as a veteran catcher who joins the minor league Durham Bulls and is relegated to playing babysitter to a hotshot pitcher (Robbins). Both become involved with the town's leading baseball authority/groupie, the ever-incredible Sarandon. A major achievement from first-time director Shelton. ★★★½ DVD Dual: $14.99

Bulldog Drummond

(1929, 85 min, US, F. Richard Jones) *Ronald Colman, Joan Bennett, Montagu Love.* In his first sound film, Colman's splendid performance illustrates why he was one of the most popular actors of his time. Colman is the ever-glib and suave Capt. "Bulldog" Drummond, the ex-British Army officer looking for excitement. He finds it when he places an ad offering his services to anyone for anything. It's Bennett who answers, involving Drummond in a kidnapping, blackmail and murder scheme, as her uncle is being held against his will. The film holds up surprisingly well, and features a nifty plot, good humor and fun characters. ★★★½ VHS: $14.99, VHS Box Set: $79.99

Bullet in the Head

(1990, 118 min, Hong Kong, John Woo) *Tony C W Leung, Jacky Cheung, Waise Lee.* Woo's dark, grim, brutally violent tale of three friends in 1967 Hong Kong, whose exploits include smuggling, gun-turf wars, gold theft, greed-induced betrayal and more. With the Vietnam War, political unrest, cold-blooded assassinations and merciless executions serving as a backdrop, this must-see departure from Woo's "spaghetti Eastern" style of filmmaking leaves one drained, emotionally and physically. (Chinese with English subtitles) ★★★½ DVD: $49.99, VHS: $19.99

Bullet to Beijing

(1997, 105 min, GB, George Mihalka) *Michael Caine, Jason Connery.* This latter-day installment in the Henry Palmer series is a truly disappointing and flat entertainment. Caine sleepwalks through his role as the bespectacled thief-turned-agent, who, in '60s espionage thrillers such as *The Ipcress File* and *Billion Dollar Brain*, provided a fun, slightly intellectual alternative to the James Bond films. Here, we're treated to an uninvolving story about laid-off superagents-for-hire searching for a deadly gas. Or something like that. The slack pacing, metronome editing, listless action scenes and endless parade of talking heads make for gruelling viewing. ★ VHS: $7.99

Bulletproof

(1996, 85 min, US, Ernest Dickerson) *Adam Sandler, Damon Wayans, James Caan.* An annoying, screechy comedy, *Bulletproof* is barely watchable even for hard-core fans of the two leads. Sandler and Wayans are good friends who steal expensive cars for a living, and wish to move up the ladder by working for TV car huckster Caan (in another phoned-in, sleazy villain role). It's soon revealed, however, that Wayans is an undercover cop, earning Sandler's trust so he can nail Caan. During a bust gone bad, Sandler shoots Wayans in the head (don't ask); Wayans rehabilitates himself and is forced to join Sandler again as the two are chased by the bad guys, bickering the whole time. Badly plotted, this infantile movie is unexciting, uninvolving and virtually laughless. ★ DVD: $14.99, VHS: $9.99

Bulletproof Heart

(1995, 96 min, US, Mark Malone) *Anthony LaPaglia, Mimi Rogers, Matt Craven, Peter Boyle.* LaPaglia and Rogers dance a lethal pas de deux in this sly if formulaic thriller about a coldhearted hit man hired to kill a gorgeous socialite/dominatrix who, for mysterious reasons, is quite ready and willing to die. Intrigued by his latest "client," he sets out to unlock the secret of her past and ends up in a torrid affair that leads to a twist ending. Malone's film is an interesting addition to the so-called "cinema of amorality" heralded by such films as *The Last Seduction* and *Red Rock West.* ★★½

Bulletproof Monk

(2003, 101 min, US, Paul Hunter) *Chow Yun-Fat, Seann William Scott, Jaime King, Karel Roden, Victoria Smurfit.* Seconds after being named the successor to his mentor as guardian of a sacred scroll, Chow Yun-Fat must battle evil Nazis intent on using it for nefarious deeds. Sixty years later (magically kept young by the scroll), the monk must discipline a young ne'er-do-well to become his successor, and continue protecting the scroll from evil forces. He finds his man in the person of . . . Stifler? Yes, the perpetually smirky Scott (of the *American Pie* films), who has a high old time, well, smirking his way through the film. *Monk* is such a poorly directed, unimaginatively written and tedious piece of derivative junk, even Chow looks bored. It's just a series of rote chase scenes and false emoting, leading to a desperate, kiddie-show-esque climax. ★ DVD Letterbox: $14.99, VHS: $9.99

Bullets over Broadway

(1994, 99 min, US, Woody Allen) *John Cusack, Dianne Wiest, Chazz Palminteri, Jennifer Tilly, Jim Broadbent, Tracey Ullman, Rob Reiner, Mary-Louise Parker.* Set in 1920s New York City, one of Allen's brightest and funniest films blends his own comic sensibilities with a touch of Damon Runyon to tell the tale of a political idealist and playwright (Cusack) desperate to get his play on Broadway. His only source of funding is a mobster who insists that his moll (a perfectly cast Tilly) star in the show. Pride tossed aside, he begins rehearsals only to find his leading lady accompanied by a nettlesome and opinionated bodyguard (Palminteri). His oddball cast is rounded out by a wifty stage legend (Wiest, who won a much-deserved Oscar) and an overeating leading man (Broadbent). While Wiest received the Academy's recognition, kudos must also go to Palminteri who dominates his interactions with Cusack and gives the film a solid narrative anchor. ★★★★ DVD: $14.99, VHS: $9.99

Bullitt

(1968, 113 min, US, Peter Yates) *Steve McQueen, Jacqueline Bisset, Robert Duvall.* Yates' exceptionally exciting police thriller redefined the chase sequence for years to come. McQueen is a tough San Francisco detective on the trail of a witness's killers. Though the film is noted for the classic car chase scene, there's much more to recommend here. ★★★ DVD: $19.99, VHS: $14.99

Bully

(2001, 115 min, US, Larry Clark) *Brad Renfro, Bijou Phillips, Rachel Miner, Michael Pitt, Kelli Garner, Nick Stahl.* Another vicious kick-in-the-gut tragedy of disaffected youth from Clark. Bobby (Stahl) is a college-bound self-loathing homophobe (and possible closet case) who vents his frustrations by beating up and tormenting his slowwitted surfer buddy Marty (Renfro). When Marty's new girl (Miner) and her best friend (Phillips) are subjected to Bobby's relentless abuse, they devise a plan to get rid of the bully once and for all. Were it not based on actual people and events, you'd never believe the teens in *Bully* could be so sickeningly heartless. While there's no denying the sumptuous polish of Clark's sun-splashed imagery (and, as in *Kids*, his ogling camera lingers over tight young tan flesh), the gruesome subject matter combined with Clark's icy, indifferent point of view makes for an unshakably queasy cinematic experience. ★★★ DVD: $24.99

Bulworth

(1998, 109 min, US, Warren Beatty) *Warren Beatty, Halle Berry, Oliver Platt, Don Cheadle, Paul Sorvino, Jack Warden, Joshua Malina, Isaiah Washington, Laurie Metcalf, Sean Astin, Christine Baranski, Ariyan Johnson, Michèle Morgan.* A blistering, hilarious, razor-sharp social comedy that takes aim at American politics and political correctness and skewers them both with equal contempt and veracity, *Bulworth* hits new heights in American political comedies. Beatty has taken his well-known penchant for politics and (even at the risk of biting the hands that feed him) has fashioned a frontal assault on the contemporary political scene. He stars as Senator Jay Bulworth: Democrat, near financial ruin, and in the midst of a nervous breakdown. It's just days before the 1996 California primaries, and the suicidal Bulworth has hired an assassin to kill him. But before the inevitable hit happens, Bulworth's sleepless, alcohol-driven delirium has him shooting from the hip, spouting un-PC remarks to and about one and all. In remarkable, non-gimmicky set pieces of rap and rhyme that escalate in brilliantly written and performed barrages, Bulworth discovers a voice inside him which gives him the will to live — but is it too late? Not merely content to just poke fun with an insider's wink of an eye, Beatty tackles themes and says truths that will undoubtedly ruffle some, but underneath it all there's no denying that his is a voice that is clear and assured. No tail wagging this dog, *Bulworth* is an original. ★★★★ DVD Letterbox: $14.99, VHS: $6.99

Buona Sera, Mrs. Campbell

(1968, 113 min, US, Melvin Frank) *Gina Lollabrigida, Peter Lawford, Phil Silvers, Telly Savalas, Shelley Winters, Lee Grant.* The premise reeks of '60s dreck: Lollabrigida plays an Italian mother who has been accepting child support for 20 years from three American WWII vets — who each thinks her daughter is his — and now they are all returning for a reunion to her small village. But this one-joke comedy is a lot funnier than it has a right to be, for it is a constant source of well-earned laughs. Lollabrigida has probably never been funnier on screen, and she has the good fortune to play off the considerable comedic skills of a skilled supporting cast. ★★★

The 'burbs

(1989, 103 min, US, Joe Dante) *Tom Hanks, Carrie Fisher, Bruce Dern, Henry Gibson.* This sometimes humorous, shallow comedy plays like "Leave It to Beaver" meets "The Munsters" rather than the dark, crazy romp it could have been. Hanks plays the suburban Everyman whose voice of sanity amongst the insanity around him is soon stifled when he and his neighbors begin to suspect that the new and very strange family which just moved in are cannibalistic murderers. ★★ DVD: $14.99, VHS: $9.99

Burden of Dreams

(1982, 94 min, US, Les Blank) Blank's revealing documentary of Werner Herzog's inexorable pursuit in filming *Fitzcarraldo* is a gripping portrait of artistic obsession and the creative process. Captured in this absorbing film are the moments of frustration and boredom, elation and prophecy which seized Herzog's crew (and himself) during their stay in the South American wilderness. ★★★ VHS: $59.99

Burglar

(1987, 102 min, US, Hugh Wilson) *Whoopi Goldberg, Bobcat Goldthwait, John Goodman, Lesley Ann Warren.* Though Goldberg tries her best with this mediocre material, and Goldthwait is a very appealing supporting character, there's not much to recommend in this comic mystery with Whoopi as a second-rate burglar who witnesses a murder and, being the number one suspect, tries to solve it herself. ★★ DVD: $9.99

The Burglar

(1987, 83 min, USSR, Valery Ogorodnikov) *Konstantin Kinchev.* Soviet rock star Kinchev stars as a Western-influenced rocker determined to make it big at any cost. His ambition gets him in trouble after he steals a synthesizer for his group. The situation gets even more complicated after Senka, his "good brother," tries to take the heat by claiming that he stole the instrument. An unusual post-*glasnost* slice-of-life drama. (Russian with English subtitles) ★★★ VHS: $59.99

Burke and Wills

(1987, 140 min, Australia, Graeme Clifford) *Jack Thompson, Nigel Havers, Greta Scacchi.* This may not be the film that you'll want to watch on a hot summer's day — an epic retelling of an expedition into the searing heat of the Australian Outback. Thompson and Havers star as the 19th-century explorers whose ambition it is to cut a path through uncharted South Australian territory — distancing over 1,000 miles. Both actors give bravura performances as a pair of men determined to chart the uncharted no matter what the cost. The film's dazzling Cinemascope images may be lost on video, but the taut drama and heroic vision will not. ★★★½

The Burmese Harp

(1956, 116 min, Japan, Kon Ichikawa) *Shoji Yasui, Rentaro Mikuni.* A magnificent, poetic piece of filmmaking. The action takes place during the closing stages of the war in Burma. A young Japanese soldier, a musician and mystic, hears a call to remain behind with his harp to minister to the dead, both friend and foe alike. (aka: *Harp of Burma*) (Japanese with English subtitles) ★★★½ VHS: $29.99

Burn! (Queimada)

(1969, 112 min, France/Italy, Gillo Pontecorvo) *Marlon Brando, Evarist Marquez.* Brando is brilliant as the Machiavellian Sir William Walker, a soldier-of-fortune sent by a British company to investigate a slave uprising on a sugar-producing Caribbean Island governed by repressive Portuguese colonials during the mid-1800s. After witnessing the brutal exploitation of the peasants and feeling that he can offer a better deal, Walker helps instigate a successful native rebellion. But when the revolt turns financially sour for the British, he switches sides and battles the leaders of the fledgling nation. A complex, anticolonial political drama. ★★★

Burn Hollywood Burn

(1998, 86 min, US, Alan Smithee) *Ryan O'Neal, Coolio, Chuck D, Eric Idle, Sylvester Stallone, Whoopi Goldberg, Jackie Chan, Richard Jeni, Harvey Weinstein, Sandra Bernhard, Stephen Tobolowsky.* After raking in millions for scripts like *Showgirls* and *Basic Instinct*, writer Joe Eszterhas bites the hand that feeds him with this satire of the way Tinseltown works. This is meant to be a hip, guerrilla, black comedy that pulverizes the wheelings and dealings of the movie business. But Eszterhas' hipness quotient appears to be up there with Newt Gingrich's, thanks to the weary salvos hurled at Hollywood here. The story posits Idle as Alan Smithee, a former film editor whose first directorial effort is *Trio*, a $212 million actioner. When evil producer O'Neal threatens to re-edit it, Idle responds by threatening to torch the film's only existing print. A similar premise worked in *S.O.B.*, but Eszterhas, who actually wrested control of this film from original helmer Arthur Hiller (who, in turn, replaced his name with "Alan Smithee" on the final credits!), has a penchant for chaos in his comedy, and this has the comic subtlety of a Godzilla rampage. ★½ DVD: $19.99

The Burning Season

(1994, 100 min, US, John Frankenheimer) *Raul Julia, Edward James Olmos, Sonia Braga, Kamala Dawson, Esai Morales, Luis Guzman.* Julia delivers his final performance, giving a pristine portrayal of Chico Mendes, the Brazilian union leader murdered while trying to preserve the rain forest and, with it, his way of life. The HBO docudrama opens with Mendes as a young boy getting his first lesson in exploitation by watching his father be grossly underpaid for a rubber delivery. In later years, the conflict between the rubber harvesters and the land barons is delineated in the larger stories of international investments and ecological issues; but the focus never strays too far from one man's passion to protect and serve his community. An impassioned, successful piece of filmmaking. Julia won a posthumous Best Actor Emmy for his work here. ★★★½ VHS: $19.99

Burning Secret

(1988, 110 min, GB, Andrew Birkin) *Faye Dunaway, Klaus Maria Brandauer, David Eberts.* Dunaway and Brandauer give affecting performances in this beautifully filmed period piece set in 1919 Vienna about the love affair between the repressed wife of an American diplomat (Dunaway) and a war-battered Austrian nobleman (Brandauer). Most remarkable is Eberts as Dunaway's young, asthmatic son, who introduces the two lovers and becomes an unlikely protagonist in a most unusual triangle. ★★★

Burnt by the Sun

(1994, 134 min, Russia, Nikita Mikhalkov) *Nikita Mikhalkov, Oleg Menchikov, Nadia Mikhalkov.* The simplicity of a family outing on a tranquil Sunday afternoon is a potent and deceiving backdrop for betrayal and corruption in Mikhalkov's powerful yet lyrical Oscar-winning drama. An allegory for Stalin's clandestine reign of terror which engulfed the Russian landscape in the mid-1930s, the Chekhovian *Burnt by the Sun* tells the story of a Russian civil war hero (played with gusto by the director), his wife and child (Mikhalkov's real-life daughter and she's a real charmer). Set during one summer's day, the action takes place at the family's dacha where the wife's former lover has returned. And it soon becomes clear this clownish, charming man has a sinister, ulterior motive. Director Mikhalkov's success lies in both his leisurely pacing, which is cunning, and his sharp, subtle portrait of malevolence, which is unexpected. (Russian with English subtitles) ★★★½ DVD Letterbox: $29.99, VHS: $19.99

Burnt Offerings

(1976, 115 min, US, Dan Curtis) *Bette Davis, Karen Black, Oliver Reed, Lee Montgomery.* A chilling haunted house film from the cocreator of "Dark Shadows." A family moves into a luxurious country estate, where one by one they succumb to the unknown force surrounding the house. ★★★ DVD Letterbox: $14.99

Burroughs

(1983, 87 min, US, Howard Brookner) *William Burroughs.* Celebrated novelist William S. Burroughs is vividly profiled in this informative and fascinating study of his life and work. The author of "Junkie," "Naked Lunch" and "Nova Express" recounts with several of his friends the momentous episodes of a wildly eventful existence. A splendid glimpse into the mind of a true literary maverick. ★★★½ VHS: $41.99

Bus Stop

(1956, 96 min, US, Joshua Logan) *Marilyn Monroe, Don Murray, Arthur O'Connell, Eileen Heckart.* Monroe displays her usual sex appeal as well as surprising pathos in this delightful adaptation of the William Inge comedy. MM stars as a torchy cafe singer who becomes the object of affection — and obsession — of young naïve cowpoke Murray (who received an Oscar nomination for his sensationally wild performance). ★★★½ DVD: $14.99, VHS: $6.99

The Bushido Blade

(1979, 104 min, Japan, Tom Kotani) *Richard Boone, Toshiro Mifune, James Earl Jones, Mako, Sonny Chiba.* In his final performance, Boone is exceptionally hammy as the leader of a group of Shogun warriors. Their mission is to search for a coveted sword through 19th-century Japan. A pretty but not very satisfying kung-fu action tale. Lots of beheadings keep you from falling asleep. Filmed in English. ★½ VHS: $69.99

Bushwhacked

(1995, 90 min, US, Greg Beeman) *Daniel Stern, Jon Polito, Brad Sullivan.* An inferior, terribly conceived family comedy in which Stern's wild-eyed antics and bumbling, slapstick acting style wear thin quickly. He plays Max Grebelski, a package delivery man who is framed for murder and chased by the FBI. He sets off for Devil's Peak, a remote mountaintop, upon learning that proof of his innocence may be there. Along the way, he is mistaken for a top-notch scout leader and forced to lead four boys and a girl on an overnight hike. ★½ VHS: $9.99

Business as Usual

(1987, 89 min, GB, Lezli-An Barrett) *Glenda Jackson, Cathy Tyson.* Jackson delivers a typically strong performance in this interesting but somewhat preachy discourse on sexual harassment in the workplace. Jackson plays a Liverpool boutique manager who is fired after she files a complaint against her boss on behalf of a coworker (Tyson). Based on a true story that became a *cause célèbre* in England. ★★ VHS: $19.99

Buster

(1988, 102 min, GB, David Green) *Phil Collins, Julie Walters.* Collins makes his film debut as Buster Edwards, the only conspirator in the Great Train Robbery (the biggest heist in British history) who managed to elude police. Both Collins and Walters (as his neglected wife) are good in this otherwise ordinary caper film. ★★½ DVD Letterbox: $14.99

Bustin' Loose

(1981, 94 min, US, Oz Scott) *Richard Pryor, Cicely Tyson.* Pryor is in splendid comic form as an ex-con who drives teacher Tyson and a busload of orphaned and problem children cross-country. Pryor and Tyson make an appealing team. ★★★ DVD: $19.99

Busting

(1973, 89 min, US, Peter Hyams) *Elliott Gould, Robert Blake, Antonio Fargas, Allen Garfield, Michael Lerner.* Patently offensive to gays, lesbians, blacks and other members of the disenfranchised, this standard police comedy-drama doesn't pit cops against robbers, but rather cops against the "socially and sexually deviant." Quite despicable and at times painful in its violent racism and homophobia. Gould and Blake as two out-of-control vice cops, rampaging through the underworld of prostitution and gay bars undeterred by the Bill of Rights and basic justice. Though this was probably intended to be more of a social comedy "exposing" the misdirection of a corrupt police force, antigay slurs abound, and over time its noxious depiction of gays is what one remembers. ★

But I'm a Cheerleader

(2000, 90 min, US, Jamie Babbit) *Natasha Lyonne, Mink Stole, Bud Cort, RuPaul Charles, Cathy Moriarty, Clea DuVall.* A high-spirited if sometimes forced comedy that pokes fun at homophobia as well as lesbian and gay stereotypes — but all in good fun. Poor Megan (Lyonne); she may be a pretty high schooler, model student and cheerleader, but her loving parents can't ignore those Melissa Etheridge records. She is quickly carted off to True Directions, a scarily cheerful five-step de-homofication rehab camp. Sapphic sparks fly when Megan locks eyes with Graham (DuVall), a tomboy beauty with no intention of going straight. Director

Babbit aims for anarchic, John Waters-like hijinks, which doesn't always hit the bull's-eye, but nevertheless the film is marked by good humor and just a touch of subversion. ★★½ DVD: $14.99

Butch Cassidy and the Sundance Kid

(1969, 110 min, US, George Roy Hill) *Paul Newman, Robert Redford, Katharine Ross.* Classic western (and box-office smash) with Newman and Redford as outlaws on the run from a relentless posse. Told with great humor and infinite style. Winner of four Academy Awards, including William Goldman's screenplay, Score and Song ("Raindrops Keep Falling on My Head"). ★★★★ DVD Special Edition: $14.99, VHS: $6.99

The Butcher Boy

(1998, 106 min, Ireland, Neil Jordan) *Eammon Owens, Stephen Rea, Alan Boyle, Fiona Shaw, Sinéad O'Connor, Ian Hart, Milo O'Shea.* A remarkable tale of troubled youth told with the utmost authority, intelligence and imagination, *The Butcher Boy*, ripe with dark humor and darker insights, tells the story of a misfit 12-year-old, Francie (Owens). It's the height of the Cold War, and even in his rural Irish village, the events of the Cuban Missile Crisis have their toll on Francie's fellow townspeople. But Francie is more concerned with having good times with his best friend Joe, the only distraction from his mentally unstable mum and his abusive dad (Rea). Francie begins seeing neighbors as villains and visions of the Virgin Mary (O'Connor), and soon withdrawals into his own private world, part reality/part fantasy, until his fill of loneliness and confusion lead to their inevitable climax. Though essentially a story of mental breakdown, *The Butcher Boy* is surprisingly effervescent, sweetened by a startlingly astute screenplay by Jordan and Patrick McCabe (based on McCabe's novel), and fine, literate direction. ★★★★ VHS: $14.99

The Butcher's Wife

(1991, 107 min, US, Terry Hughes) *Demi Moore, George Dzundza, Jeff Daniels, Frances McDormand, Mary Steenburgen, Max Perlich, Miriam Margolyes.* Moore has the title role in this whimsical romantic comedy as a Southern clairvoyant who impulsively marries a doughy butcher (Dzundza) from Greenwich Village. In her new surroundings, she sets off a farcical chain reaction of sexual trysts through her predictions of love to a neighborhood starving for it. She also finds romance with neighbor/psychiatrist Daniels. Moore is actually quite appealing here and makes the most of the material. ★★★ DVD Letterbox: $14.99, VHS: $14.99

Butley

(1974, 104 min, US/GB, Harold Pinter) *Alan Bates, Jessica Tandy, Richard O'Callaghan.* Pinter made his directorial debut with this American Film Theatre production of the play by Simon Gray. Bates is splendid as an acerbic, self-destructive professor who drives away both his long-suffering wife and his younger male lover with his bitter verbal assaults. Brimming with caustic wit, the play provides a perfect vehicle for the energetic Bates. ★★★½ DVD: $29.99, VHS: $24.99

Butterfield 8

(1960, 109 min, US, Daniel Mann) *Elizabeth Taylor, Laurence Harvey, Eddie Fisher.* Taylor won an Oscar (though many say it was because of her nearly dying of pneumonia) for her sultry portrayal of an expensive call girl who lives with her mom and doesn't think she's a prostitute. The film fea-

The Butcher Boy

tures great histrionics and a swell supporting cast. A good, old-fashioned soaper with some fine, campy dialogue. ★★½ DVD: $19.99, VHS: $14.99

Butterflies Are Free

(1972, 109 min, US, Milton Katselas) *Goldie Hawn, Eileen Heckart, Edward Albert.* Based on the Broadway play, *Butterflies are Free* is a sensitive and touching comedy-drama about a blind young man (Albert) who is determined to be independent. Leaving his family home he ventures to San Francisco where he befriends his eccentric next door neighbor, played by Hawn. They become friends and lovers, only to have their burgeoning relationship hampered by the over-protective mom, played by Heckart, who won an Academy Award. ★★★ DVD: $19.99

Butterflies on the Scaffold (Mariposas en el Andamio)

(1996, 75 min, Cuba, Luis Bernaza & Margaret Gilpin) *Butterflies on the Scaffold* is a rare view of what day-to-day life is like for the gay and drag community in modern Cuba. This award-winning documentary is the first since the 1959 revolution to examine the issues gays and transvestites face in the context of evolving attitudes towards homosexuality in Cuba, where people are judged first on what they achieve for their country. It is a highly unusual look at how a group of working-class drag queens in a small town have become an integral part of their neighborhood. With their stunningly emotive performances to the passionate music of Latin America, these queens really are like Butterflies on the Scaffold — vibrant, proud, and unexpected. (Spanish with English subtitles) ★★★ VHS: $39.99

Butterfly Kiss

(1995, 90 min, GB, Michael Winterbottom) *Amanda Plummer, Saskia Reeves.* Plummer joins the ranks of film's most notorious lesbian killers in this disturbing and hypnotically black psycho/comedy. Obsessed with Judith, the only woman to have really loved her, Eunice (Plummer), a tough North of England lass, goes on a bloody search for her. On the way she meets, captivates and seduces a female gas station attendant (Reeves) who quickly becomes her accomplice. An intelligent, quirky tale that will be sure to upset some and entrance others. ★★★ DVD: $29.99, VHS: $19.99

By Dawn's Early Light

(1990, 100 min, US, Jack Sholder) *Powers Boothe, Rebecca De Mornay, Martin Landau, James Earl Jones.* This made-for-cable nuclear drama is a classy, edge-of-your-seat thriller combining elements of *Fail Safe* and *The Hunt for Red October*. Boothe and De Mornay star as romantically involved pilots who face a moral and personal dilemma when they are assigned to drop the bomb against the "enemy" when Washington D.C. is devastated in an accidental attack. Landau is the cautious and concerned President whose presumed death brings the country to the brink of nuclear catastrophe. ★★★½ VHS: $9.99

By Design

(1981, 88 min, Canada, Claude Jutra) *Patty Duke Astin, Sara Botsford.* The sexual revolution travels north in this quirky comedy directed by Quebecer Jutra. Duke Astin (Helen) and Botsford (Angel) star as two fashion designers, business partners and lovers who decide they want to have a baby. Rejected by the adoption agency and finding artificial insemination "gross," the frustrated pair decide that a stud is needed. After slapstick encounters cruising the straight discos, bars and construction sites of Vancouver, Helen and Angel choose Terry, an oafish photographer who eagerly accepts the mission. The deft handling of the relationship between the trio makes this an offbeat and touching comedy. ★★½

Bye Bye Birdie

(1963, 112 min, US, George Sidney) *Dick Van Dyke, Ann-Margret, Paul Lynde, Janet Leigh.* It's like an episode of "Dobie Gillis" with songs in this rather benign satire on the foibles of rock 'n' roll. Before reporting for his military service, an Elvis-like character makes a visit to a small Midwestern town. And wouldn't you know it, those darn teenagers just get all silly. Van Dyke repeats his star-making Broadway role and is helped by pleasant performances from Ann-Margret and Lynde. Enjoyable tunes like "Put on a Happy Face" and "Kids" enliven this ever-so-amusing confection. (Remade in 1999) ★★★ DVD: $29.99, VHS: $14.99

Bye Bye Blues

(1990, 110 min, US, Anne Wheeler) *Rebecca Jenkins, Luke Reilly, Stuart Margolin, Michael Ontkean, Kate Reid.* A provocative romantic drama set during WWII. The wife of a military doctor captured by the Japanese, in an effort to make ends meet, takes a job with a local swing band and falls in love with the lead singer. A stylish and tuneful exploration of one woman's liberation. ★★★ VHS: $29.99

Bye Bye Brazil

(1979, 110 min, Brazil, Carlos Diegues) *Jose Wilker, Betty Fario, Fabio Junior.* Diegues' lyrical journey across Brazil is part road movie, part travelogue sprinkled with hints of political message and a touch of magical realism. Wilker stars as Lord Gypsy, the leader of a troupe of traveling performers known as Caravana Rolidei. The film follows this group in a quasi-documentary style on a revelatory trip across the Trans-Amazon highway and beyond. Faria costars as Salome, Queen of the Rumba. Diegues and his cast and crew actually embarked on a 9,000-mile journey to make the film letting much of the material come to them along the way. The resulting "journal" is not always successful, but is at times mesmerizing and offers a unique look at the rapidly changing face of Brazil. (Portuguese with English subtitles) ★★★

Bye Bye, Love

(1995, 107 min, US, Sam Weisman) *Janeane Garofalo, Matthew Modine, Paul Reiser, Randy Quaid, Rob Reiner.* Thanks to three appealing performances by Modine, Reiser and Quaid and an involving screenplay, *Bye Bye, Love* is a most pleasant surprise. Three divorced fathers meet regularly at McDonald's for the exchange of children with the ex-wives. In the course of a weekend, the story follows them as they toss one-liners, date, commiserate and fulfill their parental duties. To its credit, the film never trivializes divorce, only finding comic and sometimes touching fallout from it; though to its discredit, the wives' parts are sketchily written. Quaid is extremely funny, and his scenes with blind date Garofalo, herself hilarious, are among the film's best. ★★★

Cabaret

(1972, 124 min, US, Bob Fosse) *Liza Minnelli, Michael York, Joel Grey, Helmut Griem, Marisa Berenson.* Fosse's savory depiction of Christopher Isherwood's '30s Berlin stars an effervescent Minnelli as nightclub singer and carefree bohemian Sally Bowles and York as Isherwood's alter ego Brian Roberts. The short-lived decadent world of pre-Hitler Berlin as well as the rising nationalistic tide of Fascism are effectively captured in this trendsetting musical. Griem is a wealthy and debonair baron who sweeps both Sally and Brian off their feet. The musical numbers performed at the Kit Kat Klub are just some of the film's rousing highlights, a collection of great songs belted by both Minnelli and Academy Award winner Grey as the devilishly cynical Master of Ceremonies. ★★★★ DVD: $19.99

Cabaret Balkan

(1999, 102 min, Serbia, Goran Paskaljevic) *Nikola Ristanovski, Lazar Ristovski, Mirjana Jokovic.* Belgrade is a rough town, almost like the Wild West, and this is a rough wild West movie. With five parallel stories of postwar Balkan life, this biting comedy doesn't have a clear plot line, but as a pastiche it works beautifully. A bus is about to be hijacked by a slightly deranged anarchist. The Cabaret Balkan of the title features another slightly deranged man, but this one is performing an anarchist politcal cabaret act. Cascading from tale to tale without warning, there's one constant: a dark aura, almost surreal. The story reeks of a corrupt society where people are questioning the moral thread that has held them together for centuries. It's amazing that such a significant message is delivered in a film that manages to amuse as well as enlighten. (Serbo-Croatian with English subtitles) ★★★½ VHS: $102.99

Cabeza de Vaca

(1992, 108 min, Mexico, Nicholas Echevarria) *Juan Diego, Daniel Gimenez Cacho.* In 1528, a Spanish expedition shipwrecks off the coast of Florida — 600 of the men aboard die. One survivor roams the countryside searching for his comrades, but instead finds the Iguase, an ancient Indian tribe. Over the next eight years, the survivor, Cabeza de Vaca, learns their culture, becoming a healer and a leader. But he soon has to confront his past when newly arriving conquistadors seek to enslave the Indians. A vividly entertaining, large-scale film with stunning visuals and a sometimes surrealistic story that at times drifts into territory blazed by films such as *El Topo* and *A Man Called Horse*. (Spanish with English subtitles) ★★★½ VHS: $9.99

Cabin Boy

(1994, 81 min, US, Adam Resnick) *Chris Elliott, Ann Magnuson, David Letterman.* A television skit stretched to a barely feature-length 81 minutes, this initially funny but ultimately tedious comedy stars Elliott as an obnoxious rich boy (forget the fact that he's balding and in his thirties) who mistakenly embarks on an "it's gonna make you a man" high-seas adventure. Playing the self-centered, moronic innocent character to the hilt, Elliott brings some antic humor to the otherwise disappointing tale. Letterman has some fun in an early cameo (you get to see him before slumber sets in) and Magnuson is featured as a vampish, six-armed creature from the sea. ★½ DVD: $9.99, VHS: $19.99

Cabin Fever

(2003, 94 min, US, Eli Roth) *Rider Strong, Jordan Ladd, Joey Kern, Cerina Vincent.* Herein lay the hor-

Cabaret: Liza Minnelli and Joel Grey know that "money makes the world go 'round"

ror movie equivalent of one of those K-Tel greatest hits albums — a gruesome, carcass-strewn compilation of signature moments from at least a dozen better pioneering cult flicks. A generic gaggle of sex-starved dweebs and debs camps out in a creepy cabin, one by one succumbing to a nasty flesh-eating virus spreading throughout the woods. The local country yokels, filmic descendents of the hillbillies from *Deliverance*, are convinced the libidinous campers are the source of the virus and thusly take appropriate, grisly action. Some racy sexual hijinx and an unexpected dash of zesty culture-baiting humor add some flavor to this otherwise bland, undercooked stew, though splatter-geeks will thrill to the conventional-vs.-CGI approach to rendering the abundant gore. ★★ DVD: $26.99, VHS: $49.99

The Cabin in the Cotton

(1932, 77 min, US, Michael Curtiz) *Bette Davis, Richard Barthelmess, Dorothy Jordan.* Okay, trivia buffs, one of Davis' most repeated lines is: "Ah'd love to kiss ya but I just washed my hay-uh." And it's said in this period melodrama, an important step in Davis' rise to stardom. In a supporting part, Davis had her first "bad girl" role as a Southern vixen out to set honest sharecropper's son Barthelmess (a silent screen actor whose star was fading) on the road to ruin. Bette is terrific in this otherwise routine drama. ★★

Cabin in the Sky

(1943, 99 min, US, Vincente Minnelli) *Eddie Anderson, Lena Horne, Louis Armstrong, Ethel Waters, Duke Ellington.* A stellar black cast is featured in Minnelli's musical fable about the forces of good and evil vying for the soul of Little Joe (Anderson). ★★★

The Cabinet of Dr. Caligari

(1919, 69 min, Germany, Robert Wiene) *Conrad Veidt, Werner Krauss.* Setting in motion the wave of German Expressionism, director Wiene created this nightmarish universe which lies beneath the facade of order and reason. This horror classic employs dazzling use of art direction, lighting and cubist set design to tell its chilling tale of a carnival hypnotist using a somnambulist for the former's evil purposes. (Silent with musical accompaniment) ★★★★ DVD: $24.99, VHS: $24.99

Cabiria

(1914, 123 min, Italy, Giovanni Pastrone) The most ambitious and spectacular of the historical epics for which Italy was famous before WWI, *Cabiria* set the standard for big-budget feature-length movies and opened the way for D.W. Griffith and Cecil B. DeMille. During the war between Carthage and Rome, a girl — Cabiria — is separated from her parents. In her odyssey through the world of ancient Rome, she encounters an erupting volcano, the barbaric splendor of Carthage, human sacrifice and Hannibal crossing the Alps. Mastered from a 35mm archive, *Cabiria* features a newly recorded soundtrack from the original 1914 score. ★★★ DVD: $29.99, VHS: $24.99

The Cable Guy

(1996, 91 min, US, Ben Stiller) *Jim Carrey, Matthew Broderick, Leslie Mann, George Segal, Diane Baker, Jack Black, Janeane Garofalo, Andy Dick, Eric Roberts.* Carrey attempts the difficult genre of black comedy stamped with his own unique brand of humor. However, humor is not what you get with this unfunny, undisciplined comedy.

Cabin in the Sky

Carrey plays an obnoxious cable man whose present of free cable to customer Broderick turns the latter's life upside down. As Carrey latches on to — even stalks — the protesting Broderick, his family and friends see only one swell guy. The scenario can lend itself to many humorous situations, as *What about Bob* proved; however, the result here is mean-spirited — its malice underscored by a deficiency of laughs — and lacking in ironic counterpoint (*The War of the Roses* is a successful example of that). ★½ DVD Letterbox: $14.99, VHS: $9.99, VHS Letterbox: $19.99

Cactus

(1986, 96 min, Australia, Paul Cox) *Isabelle Huppert, Norman Kaye, Robert Menzies.* Huppert stars as a young French woman visiting Australia who begins to lose her sight after a car accident. Her acceptance of the possibility of total blindness is difficult until she meets Robert, a wise and witty young man who was born blind. They fall in love and they both help each other accept their limitations and handicaps. While not totally successful, this film does feature a hypnotic score and many affecting scenes between the lovers. ★★½ DVD: $24.99

Cactus Flower

(1969, 103 min, US, Gene Saks) *Walter Matthau, Ingrid Bergman, Goldie Hawn, Jack Weston.* The enchanting performances of the three leads make this lackluster screen version of Abe Burrows' Broadway hit tolerable. Walter plays a dentist secretly in love with his nurse Ingrid, though he's having an affair with Goldie. Hawn won the Oscar for her delightful screen debut. ★★½ DVD: $19.99

Caddie

(1976, 107 min, Australia, Donald Crombie) *Helen Morse, Jack Thompson.* An affectionate account of a determined woman struggling for independence in Sydney during the 1920s and '30s. Morse excels as the strong-willed heroine. ★★★ VHS: $59.99

The Caddy

(1953, 95 min, US, Norman Taurog) *Jerry Lewis, Dean Martin, Donna Reed.* Lewis supplies most of the laughs in this minor Lewis and Martin comedy. Jerry is the son of a golf pro who's afraid of crowds. Dino sings "That's Amore." ★★½ VHS: $14.99

Caddyshack

(1980, 98 min, US, Harold Ramis) *Michael O'Keefe, Chevy Chase, Rodney Dangerfield, Bill Murray, Ted Knight.* Depending on your comedic tastes, this wacky comedy will either cause moments of silly hysteria or pains of anguish. Either way, good taste is thrown by the wayside. Chase and Dangerfield (in a terrifically funny performance) are just two of the crazy members of an exclusive country club. Murray chases gophers a lot. (Sequel: *Caddyshack II*) ★★½ DVD: $19.99, VHS: $14.99

Caddyshack II

(1988, 93 min, US, Allan Arkush) *Chevy Chase, Dan Aykroyd, Dyan Cannon, Jackie Mason, Robert Stack.* As in the original *Caddyshack*, a seasoned comedian (Rodney Dangerfield in the first, Mason in the sequel) is the only reason to even consider this otherwise sophomoric comedy. For the rest of the cast, it's merely career low points. ★½ DVD: $9.99, VHS: $9.99

Cadillac Man

(1990, 97 min, US, Roger Donaldson) *Robin Williams, Tim Robbins, Pamela Reed, Annabella Sciorri, Lori Petty.* Williams is a fast-talking, womanizing car salesman and Robbins is the gun-toting jealous husband who decides to take Williams and his dealership hostage. Williams does his usual schtick, but this one should have been better. ★★½ DVD Dual: $14.99

Caesar and Cleopatra

(1946, 127 min, GB, Gabriel Pascal) *Vivien Leigh, Claude Rains, Flora Robson.* No this isn't Shakespeare, this is Shaw. Rains and Leigh star in this sluggish rendition of George Bernard Shaw's play about the aging Roman conqueror and the beautiful, soft-headed Queen of the Nile. Great performances capture some of Shaw's unique wit, but the plot has a tendency to drag. ★★½

Café au Lait

(1993, 94 min, France, Mathieu Kassovitz) *Julie Mauduech, Hubert Kounde, Mathieu Kassovitz.* A racially charged, but ultimately tame tale about an interracial ménage-à-trois. The film's impressive opening credits take place over a lightning-paced bicycle-wheel's-eye ride through Paris that leads to the collision of Felix (Kassovitz), a gawky Jewish bicycle messenger, and Jamal (Kounde), the handsome son of an African ambassador. Unbeknownst to either, they have shared the affections of Lola (Mauduech), a light-skinned beauty of Carribean descent. When she informs them that she is pregnant and doesn't know who the father is the two men joust over race and ego, tossing epithets at each other with little reserve. *Café au Lait*'s problem is that while it tries to be lighthearted comedy, the slurs are laid on a little too thick. Kassovitz fails to take a serious subject and inject humor into it; he simply turns comedy serious. It doesn't work. (French with English subtitles ★★ VHS: $29.99

Café Express
(1981, 89 min, Italy, Nanni Loy) *Nino Manfredi, Gigi Reder, Adolfo Celi.* Manfredi stars in this top-notch Italian comedy about a charming flim-flam man's attempts to aid his ailing son, outwitting the dim-witted police in the process. A lovable, compassionate portrait by Italy's most inventive comedy director, Loy. (Italian with English subtitles) ★★★

Café Flesh
(1982, 75 min, US, Rinse Dream) *Pia Snow, Marie Sharp, Andrew Nichols, Kevin James.* "Post-nuke thrill freaks looking for a kick!" Decadent hardly suffices in describing this concoction of tongue-in-cheek punk pornography. In the post-apocalyptic future, those capable of engaging in sex (positives) are employed to perform for the vast majority of impotent onlookers (negatives), who succumb to nausea at the very outbreak of foreplay. Demented, you say? You'll never take sex for granted again. ★★ DVD: $39.99, VHS: $39.99

Café Society
(1995, 104 min, US, Raymond DeFelitta) *Frank Whaley, Peter Gallagher, Lara Flynn Boyle, Anna Thomson, David Patrick Kelly.* Fact-based drama about Mickey Jelke (Whaley), a sophisticated New York playboy whose cushy lifestyle of booze and broads is brought to a screeching halt by a headline-grabbing scandal. When Jelke declares his love for the sultry but subpar Patricia Ward (Boyle), his mother cuts him off without a cent. To maintain his extravagant standard of living, Jelke begins to prostitute Pat, and his downfall really begins. This stylish film captures the essence of how the 1950s could not tolerate the socially irresponsible, especially if they were monied. Whaley is terrific in the lead role, and Boyle is equally impressive as the tough-minded girlfriend. ★★★

La Cage aux Folles
(1978, 91 min, France/Italy, Edouard Molinaro) *Ugo Tognazzi, Michel Serrault, Michel Galabru, Benny Luke.* This frolicsome farce that finally made drag respectable stars Tognazzi and Serrault as gay lovers who must, amid mounting complications, pose as mom and dad for the sake of a prospective daughter-in-law and her straight-laced parents. The laughs are plentiful, and Serrault creates an endearing, even resilient characterization of the drag queen Alban. Followed by two sequels, an American remake (*The Birdcage*), and adapted into an award-winning Broadway musical. (French with English subtitles) ★★★½ DVD Letterbox: $19.99

La Cage aux Folles II
(1980, 101 min, France, Edouard Molinaro) *Ugo Tognazzi, Michel Serrault, Marcel Bozzuffi, Benny Luke.* This sequel to the popular comedy reunited the original stars (Tognazzi & Serrault) who, as gay lovers Alban and Renato, become involved with spies and are forced to flee the country. Alban's valiant attempts to masquerade as a Sicilian peasant

woman is one of the hilarious highlights to this otherwise uneven sequel. (French with English subtitles) ★★½ DVD Letterbox: $19.99, VHS: $19.99

La Cage aux Folles III: The Wedding
(1985, 88 min, France, Georges Lautner) *Michel Serrault, Ugo Tognazzi, Michel Galabru, Benny Luke, Stéphane Audran.* Who saw this film when it came out theatrically? Judging from the box office receipts, not many. Gay cabaret star Alban learns he is to inherit a fortune — but only on the condition that he marry and provide an heir in 18 months. The magic is gone, though Tognazzi and Serrault are still a joy to watch. ★½

Caged Heat
(1974, 84 min, US, Jonathan Demme) *Juanita Brown, Erica Gavin, Barbara Steele.* This ain't no party, this ain't no disco, this ain't no *Stop Making Sense.* Demme's first-time directorial touch raises this women-behind-bars low-budget potboiler above the norm. Surprisingly competent performances in this semi-skin-flick morality tale. Remember: It is unlawful to transport weapons or narcotics into a federal penal institute. ★★½ DVD: $14.99, VHS: $9.99

The Caine Mutiny
(1954, 125 min, US, Edward Dmytryk) *Humphrey Bogart, Fred MacMurray, Van Johnson, Jose Ferrer, Lee Marvin.* In his last great role, Bogart stars as the neurotic Captain Queeg in this sensational screen version of Herman Wouk's Pulitzer Prize-winning novel. During a fierce typhoon, the men of the USS Caine relieve their captain of command when he suffers a breakdown, leading to a court-martial of the executive officers behind the "mutiny." (Remade in 1988) ★★★★ DVD: $19.99

The Caine Mutiny Court-Martial
(1988, 100 min, US, Robert Altman) *Brad Davis, Jeff Daniels, Peter Gallagher, Eric Bogosian.* Altman's made-for-TV movie is a solid translation of the Herman Wouk play. Altman briskly takes us through 100 minutes' worth of interrogation, all the while building and never losing the dramatic tension. Featuring some trademark Altman touches including, of course, multilayered dialogue, the film includes a number of powerful performances. Davis plays the infamous Lt. Commander Queeg, Daniels is the lieutenant on trial for mutiny, and Bogosian puts in a brilliant performance as the complex, first-time defense lawyer. ★★★½

Cal
(1984, 94 min, Ireland, Pat O'Connor) *Helen Mirren, John Lynch, Donal McCann.* A Catholic youth (Lynch) who lives in a predominantly Protestant section of Ulster becomes romantically involved with the widow of a Protestant policeman. His political belief structure is severely tried when he realizes that he was a participant in her husband's death. This powerful, gut-wrenching drama features Mirren in a superlative performance. ★★★½ VHS: $19.99

Calamity Jane
(1953, 101 min, US, David Butler) *Doris Day, Howard Keel.* Day gives one of her most appealing performances in this entertaining western musical as the legendary Calamity Jane, the tomboyish sharpshooter who changes her ways when she falls for Wild Bill Hickok (Keel). Musical score includes the Oscar-winning "Secret Love." ★★★ DVD: $19.99, VHS: $14.99

Calendar
(1993, 74 min, Canada/Germany/Armenia, Atom Egoyan) *Arsinée Khanjian, Ashot Adamian, Atom Egoyan.* Egoyan directed and stars in this hypnotic tale as a photographer whose wife leaves him for another while they are on assignment in Armenia. *Calendar* explores the nature of voyeurism and sexual obsession with an inventive, compelling structure. (English and Armenian with English subtitles) ★★★ DVD: $29.99

Calendar Girl
(1993, 90 min, US, John Whitesell) *Jason Priestley, Jerry O'Connell, Emily Warfield, Maxwell Caulfield.* Priestley tries to shed his "90210" image with a fast-talking, tough-guy numbers-runner characterization in this tiresome comedy. Set in 1962, the film follows the misadventures of a group of boyhood friends who decide to take a road trip to Hollywood to try and get Marilyn Monroe in the sack. ★½ VHS: $9.99

Calendar Girls
(2003, 108 min, GB, Nigel Cole) *Helen Mirren, Julie Walters, Penelope Wilton, Celia Imrie, Annette Crosbie, Linda Bassett, Geraldine James.* This very enjoyable if lightweight comedy has already been dubbed "a female *Full Monty*," and for good reason — that's exactly what you get as a group of middle-aged women bare it all to raise a little cash. Mirren

Calendar Girls

plays a slightly bored housewife/mother who shakes up her fuddy-duddy women's group by suggesting that they pose nude for a calendar — the proceeds of which would go toward a more comfortable waiting-room couch at the local hospital, in honor of her best friend's late husband. The predictable shocked reactions, squabbles and smiles ensue. This is all better than it ought to be, thanks mainly to Mirren and Walters (both of whom still look great), and firm direction, writing and a game supporting cast. The last third or so, when the now-infamous women head to Hollywood, turns a bit too serious and strained, but this remains an engaging comedy-drama. ★★★ DVD: $29.99, VHS: $24.99

California Suite

(1978, 102 min, US, Herbert Ross) *Jane Fonda, Alan Alda, Maggie Smith, Michael Caine, Walter Matthau, Elaine May, Richard Pryor, Bill Cosby.* An often very funny film version of Neil Simon's stage hit, which focuses on four disparate groups of families and friends who stay at the Beverly Hills Hotel. Here the stories are interwoven, so the weaker of the four never really drags the film down. The best of the chapters is the touching and extremely well-acted tale of Britishers Smith and Caine coming to town for the Oscars. Ironically, Smith won an Academy Award for her wonderful portrayal of a nominated actress; Caine plays her bisexual husband with great depth and conviction. ★★★ DVD Dual: $14.99

Caligula

(1979, 156 min, US, Bob Guccione & Tinto Brass) *Malcolm McDowell, John Gielgud, Peter O'Toole, Helen Mirren, Teresa Ann Savoy.* No, this isn't an ersatz PBS documentary. Despite its prestigious cast, this controversial production manages to steer clear of most socially accepted standards of decency. But for those chagrined at having missed the decadence and excess of the Roman Empire, this X-rated epic is as satisfying as a day of debauchery. ★ DVD 20th Anniversary: $29.99

Call Northside 777

(1948, 111 min, US, Henry Hathaway) *James Stewart, Lee J. Cobb, Richard Conte, Helen Walker.* This true story stars Stewart as a 1940s Chicago newspaperman whose investigation into an 11-year-old crime helps set free an innocent man. Directed in fascinating semidocumentary style by Hathaway, the film traces the route taken by Stewart as he slowly uncovers evidence of police corruption and conspiracy. Cobb is very good as Stewart's editor, and Conte is the unjustly convicted prisoner. Hathaway creates a tension throughout even though the outcome is obvious. ★★★½ VHS: $19.99

Calle 54

(2001, 105 min, France/Italy/Spain, Fernando Trueba) *Tito Puente, Gato Barbieri, Michel Camilo, Paquito D'Rivera.* Like Wim Wenders' *Buena Vista Social Club* before it, *Calle 54* endeavors to demonstrate the vibrancy of Latin jazz through a series of performances. Unlike Wenders' acclaimed documentary, Trueba's paean to musical legends like Bebo Valdes, Chano Dominguez and Tito Puente foregrounds the performances themselves, eschewing personal, social and national histories that necessarily inform the music. Not a bad thing, per se, because these musicians captured by the film are indeed geniuses at the top of their collective game. But *Calle 54* is, as a result, not a documentary that narrates and instructs; it is instead one that illustrates — with enthusiasm, sincerity and mucho gusto — the vivid splendor of salsa. ★★★ DVD: $14.99, VHS: $9.99

Came a Hot Friday

(1985, 101 min, New Zealand, Ian Muneli) *Philip Gordon, Peter Bland.* A rollicking comic adventure about two con men who roam through the New Zealand countryside cheating bookmakers and hustling the locals. As their fortunes turn bad, they form an alliance with an insane eccentric with a pronounced Zorro fetish. A silly and mirth-filled examination of the underbelly of the capitalistic urge. ★★★ VHS: $19.99

Camelot

(1967, 175 min, GB, Joshua Logan) *Richard Harris, Vanessa Redgrave, Franco Nero, David Hemmings, Lionel Jeffries.* This big-budget film version of the Lerner and Loewe Broadway hit is tragically short on excitement and none of those in the cast can really sing. Harris (who would go on to perform the role in a successful revival in the '80s) is a capable King Arthur, who recounts his story of chivalry, romance and betrayal. Redgrave, though miscast, is a lovely Guinevere, Arthur's betrothed and future queen. Jeffries is an almost amusing Merlin. ★★ DVD Letterbox: $19.99, VHS: $19.99, VHS Letterbox: $19.99

The Cameraman

(1927, 70 min, US, Edward Sedgwick) *Buster Keaton, Marceline Day.* In his first film under the constricting dictates of the M-G-M front office (read: Mayer, Thalberg), Keaton still manages many fine moments of comedic poetry as an inept newsreel photographer who gets mixed up with gangsters. ★★★ VHS: $29.99

The Cameraman's Revenge & Other Fantastic Tales

(1912, 80 min, France/Russia, Ladislaw Starewicz) A treat for everyone in the family, this is truly a treasure-trove of animation. There is much to be said for Starewicz's art, the influence of which is evident in the work of Tim Burton, the Brothers Quay and other surrealist animators. Each piece in this collection shows a growing understanding of manipulating the media, culminating in true mastery of the craft in works like *Mascot* and *Voice of the Nightingale*. The musical accompaniment of the earlier works is sloppy and undistinguished, but with the advent of sound in the later works, the true richness of music fully compliments his work. It is interesting to note that in Starewicz's "relocation" to Paris in the early '20s, he changed his name and became much more commercial and made his allegories less striking. (Russian with English subtitles) ★★★★ DVD: $29.99, VHS: $29.99

Camila

(1984, 105 min, Argentina, Maria Luisa Bemberg) *Susu Pecararo, Imanol Arias.* Taken from a true story that was one of Argentina's most notorious scandals, *Camila* tells the haunting tale of a doomed and forbidden love. In 1847, Camila, daughter of a wealthy politican, falls in love with a Jesuit priest. Unable to suppress their desire, the couple are forced to flee. However, the government, her family and the Church, outraged by their "sacrilege," unite in an effort to hunt them down. A gripping, elegant and erotic love story. (Spanish with English subtitles) ★★★ DVD Subtitled: $29.99, VHS Subtitled: $29.99

Camilla

(1994, 90 min, Canada, Deepa Mehta) *Jessica Tandy, Bridget Fonda, Elias Koteas, Maury Chaykin, Hume Cronyn, Graham Greene.* The last theatrical film of the great Tandy is an appealing road movie with the actress in wonderful form. She plays the title character, a retired concert violinist who lives in a past of accolade and romance. She begins a cross-country trip from her Georgia home to Toronto with Fonda, a fellow if untalented musician with an uncertain future. On the way, they meet a select group of eccentrics and try to come to terms with their individual concerns. Both actresses are delightful, and it's to their credit that each is able to overcome the generic dialogue and predictable dramatics. Cronyn also appears as Tandy's old flame, and their scenes together are poignant beyond words. ★★½ DVD: $14.99, VHS: $9.99

Camille

(1936, 110 min, US, George Cukor) *Greta Garbo, Robert Taylor, Henry Daniell.* Classic 1930s tearjerker with Garbo in one of her best roles (most Garbo-ites feel this is her definitive portrayal) as Alexander Dumas' doomed courtesan. One of the better examples of those opulent M-G-M productions which the studio either excelled at (as in this instance) or overproduced and ultimately butchered. They could have found a better Armand than Taylor, but Daniell is sensational as the villainous Baron de Varville. ★★★½ VHS: $19.99

Camille Claudel

(1988, 149 min, France, Bruno Nuytten) *Isabelle Adjani, Gérard Depardieu, Laurent Grevill.* The twin titans of French cinema, Adjani and Depardieu, star in this stirring look at the troubled life of the young sculptress Camille Claudel and her fateful relationship with Auguste Rodin. The movie examines the young artist and the creative fire which burned in her soul and eventually thrust her to the perilous heights of the male-dominated and very misogynist Parisian art world. Her romantic obsession with her mentor and lover, Rodin, eventually plunged her into a world of loneliness and madness. A haunting love story featuring a mesmerizing performance by Adjani. (French with English subtitles) ★★★ DVD: $19.99

Camille 2000

(1969, 115 min, Italy, Radley Metzger) File this cheesy Italian soap opera under campy sexploitation! Poor Dumas' classic tale gets trashed in this "naughty" exposé of heated passions, duplicitous lovers, cheating wives, horny but handsome men and sexually overcharged women and, last but not least, true love. The poor acting actually helps in giving this trash some camp value, but fans of Italian erotica and art had better steer clear. ★ DVD: $24.99, VHS: $19.99

Camp Nowhere

(1994, 96 min, US, Jonathan Prince) *Christopher Lloyd, Jonathan Jackson, M. Emmet Walsh, Tom Wilson, Wendy Makkena.* A zany and surprisingly funny romp which borrows just a little from the semi-classic British comedy *The Happiest Days of Your Life*. A group of adolescents who are all being shipped off to various theme camps for the summer (military, diet, computer, etc.), unite their resources and rent a rundown location all their own. This is done with the help of flaky drama teacher Lloyd. The kids enjoy their adult-free vacation until the moms and dads decide to visit, prompting a wacky, complicated ruse. Lloyd is quite good, combining his unique brand of kookiness with some amusing impersonations. Silly shenanigans and a deft directorial touch make this as fun as a child's summer day. ★★★ DVD: $9.99

Can-Can

(1960, 131 min, US, Walter Lang) *Shirley MacLaine, Frank Sinatra, Louis Jordan, Maurice Chevalier.* A powerhouse cast isn't enough to offset the many lethargic moments in this only occasionally entertaining Cole Porter musical. Shirley wants to dance the "shameful" title dance; the police say no, lawyer Frank says she can-can. Songs include "I Love Paris" and a few not in the original stage production. ★★½

Can She Bake a Cherry Pie?

(1983, 90 min, US, Henry Jaglom) *Karen Black, Michael Emil, Frances Fisher.* As quirky comedies go, this one takes the cake, so to speak. Jaglom delivers an eccentric love story among a group of decidedly peculiar New York neurotics. Black is Zee, an emotional wreck, frazzled by her recent break-up with her husband and starved for affection. She meets Eli (Emil), a balding, opinionated, health-obsessed rationalist, who goes so far as to measure his pulse during sex to gauge the strength of his orgasms. Pure emotion meets pure logic and the result is an oddly charming couple. ★★★ DVD: $24.99, VHS: $19.99

Can't Buy Me Love

(1987, 94 min, US, Steve Rash) *Patrick Dempsey, Amanda Peterson, Dennis Dugan.* Dempsey and Peterson make for an attractive twosome in this well-played though slight teen comedy with Dempsey as a high school nerd paying school beauty Peterson to pretend to be his girlfriend. ★★½ DVD: $19.99, VHS: $9.99

Can't Hardly Wait

(1998, 101 min, US, Deborah Kaplan & Harry Elfont) *Ethan Embray, Jennifer Love Hewitt, Lauren Ambrose, Charlie Korsmo, Seth Green, Peter Facinelli.* Can't Hardly Wait takes its cue from those John Hughes films of the '80s and puts a '90s spin on it. The majority of the action takes place on graduation night at what will be the biggest party of the year. Preston (Embray), an aspiring writer, attends in a last ditch effort to let Amanda (Love Hewitt) know how he feels about her. That's about it for story. The film is more a series of situations, some funnier than others, some not very funny at all. What the directors have captured is, in some cases, a dead-on parody of the many social cliques (Trekkie/X-File loving geeks, jocks, goth kids, homeboy wannabes, etc). It's hard to imagine any of these people attending the same social gathering, but the writers seem to know this and have a lot of fun with the improbability of the situation. ★★½ DVD: $14.99, VHS: $9.99

Can't Stop the Music

(1980, 123 min, US, Nancy Walker) *Steve Guttenberg, Bruce Jenner, Valerie Perrine, The Village People, Paul Sand, Tammy Grimes.* An all-male water ballet, a hunk-filled locker room, Bruce Jenner in lycra, and The Village People to boot! Director Walker throws in everything but the kitchen sink . . . wait, that's there, too! A campy (duh!) look at the music industry with a couple of nifty musical numbers. ★★½ DVD Letterbox: $14.99

Canadian Bacon

(1994, 91 min, US, Michael Moore) *John Candy, Alan Alda, Rhea Perlman, Kevin Pollak, Rip Torn, Steven Wright, James Belushi.* After a terrific debut with *Roger & Me*, Moore misfires with this silly farce about the President of the United States declaring war on Canada in order to win support for his reelection campaign. ★½ DVD: $14.99

The Candidate

(1972, 109 min, US, Michael Ritchie) *Robert Redford, Peter Boyle, Melvyn Douglas, Allen Garfield, Don Porter.* Potent and vastly entertaining political satire and exposé. Redford stars as an idealistic, dark-horse senatorial candidate running against a powerful, conservative incumbent. The extremely authentic flavor to the behind-the-scenes meetings and powwows, and an incisive screenplay by Oscar-winner Jeremy Larner add greatly to the success of the film. Great supporting cast. ★★★½ DVD: $19.99, VHS: $14.99

Candide

(1991, 147 min, US/GB, Humphrey Burton) *Jerry Hadley-Land, June Anderson.* Performed in 1989 at London's Barbican Centre, Leonard Bernstein's rousing musical — first performed on Broadway in 1956 — is based on Voltaire's satiric book. With a youthfully animated Bernstein conducting, this production stars Hadley-Land as Candide and Anderson as Cunegonde. With lyrics by Lillian Hellman, Dorothy Parker and Stephen Sondheim, the show follows the adventures that befall Candide in his search for "The Best of All Possible Worlds." ★★★

Candy

(1968, 124 min, US/France/Italy, Christian Marquand) *Ewa Aulin, Richard Burton, Marlon Brando, Charles Aznavour, James Coburn, Ringo Starr, John Astin, Walter Matthau, John Huston.* A cause celebre in the 1960s, this often funny but quite silly sex comedy follows naïve high school student Candy and her many sexual adventures with the opposite sex. Some good cameos (especially Burton as a drunken poet and Starr as the Mexican gardener) propel a far-out blend of '60s sexual liberation and hippie hijinks. Astin gets the best marks in the dual roles of Candy's staid father and lecherous uncle. Buck Henry adapted the novel by Terry Southern. ★★½ DVD Collector's Edition: $19.99, DVD: $19.99, VHS: $14.99

Candy Mountain

(1988, 91 min, US, Robert Frank & Ruth Wurlitzer) *Kevin J. O'Connor, Tom Waits, David Johansen, Leon Redbone.* Infused with a '50s Beat mentality, *Candy Mountain* is an engagingly charming and funny road movie. O'Connor plays an impassive, down-on-his-heels rocker who hits the road in search of the mythical master guitar maker Elmore Silk. His travels are punctuated with a bevy of oddball, on-the-fringe characters. A quirky, decidedly American low budgeter reminiscent of such road sagas as *Easy Rider* and *Stranger Than Paradise*. ★★★ VHS: $14.99

Candyman

(1992, 101 min, US, Bernard Rose) *Virginia Madsen, Tony Todd, Xander Berkeley, Vanessa Williams.* Rose follows up his 1988 film *Paperhouse* with this solid adaptation of goremeister Clive Barker's short story, "The Forbidden." Madsen gives a gutsy performance as a graduate student whose research into contemporary myths and legends summons the vengeful hook-handed spirit of a slave (Todd) who was murdered for daring to love a white woman. In possibly the first horror movie with an interracial love theme, Rose sacrifices cheesy special effects in favor of interesting characterizations and bizarre set designs, making this an enduring horror movie for the art-house set. (Followed by 2 sequels) ★★★ DVD: $14.99, VHS: $9.99

Candyman 2: Farewell to the Flesh

(1995, 95 min, US, Bill Condon) *Tony Todd, Kelly Rowan, Veronica Cartwright.* When a young woman (Rowan) loses both her father and husband to the Candyman (Todd), she comes to realize that maybe the two are bound by more than just coincidence. Clive Barker's hook-handed menace returns in this savage sequel that explains how the urban legend came to be. Taking place as though the original never happened, Condon's film more directly tackles the topic of racial harmony and intolerance, though it relies less on mysticism than on sheer blood-and-guts horror. Philip Glass' mesmerizing and passionate score adds just the right note of poetic justice to this tragic tale. ★★½ DVD Letterbox: $14.99

Cane Toads

(1987, 47 min, US, Mark Lewis) Sardonic wit and imaginative direction elevate this unusual documentary above the level of mere agricultural travelogue. The film details the introduction of cane toads from Hawaii to North Queensland, Australia, in 1935 to combat a cane grub infestation that was ravaging the sugar industry. Prolific breeders who lacked natural enemies in their new home, the toads quickly overwhelmed over 40% of Queensland and, at the time of filming, were expanding down the coast, rapidly adapting to new environments and killing off natural wildlife. This film is a fascinating look at a man-made catastrophe, a magnificently bungled attempt to alter the natural order. ★★★ DVD: $24.99, VHS: $19.99

Cannery Row

(1982, 120 min, US, David S. Ward) *Nick Nolte, Debra Winger, M. Emmet Walsh, Audra Lindley.* Nolte and Winger are well-matched in this appealing, if unusual romantic comedy-drama based on the John Steinbeck stories, "Cannery Row" and "Sweet Tuesday." Nolte is a former baseball player-turned-biologist who is thrown together with feisty good-time girl Winger, thanks to the denizens of Cannery Row. Directorial debut for writer Ward (*The Sting*). ★★★ VHS: $19.99

Cannibal Man
(La Semana del Asesino)

(1971, 98 min, Spain, Eloy de la Iglesia) *Emma Cohen, Eusebio Poncela, Vicky Lagos, Ismael Merlo, Fernando Sanchez Polack, Charlie Bravo, Vincent Parra.* A creepy, grisly and disturbing horror film and quite an unusual departure for director de la Iglesia. Parra is Marcos, a slaughterhouse worker who, after killing a cab driver in self-defense, loses his grip on sanity and begins a murderous rampage throughout the city. But what to do with the bodies? Banned in many countries for its graphic violence, this intense study of a decent man driven to obscene murder is being released in its original uncut and uncensored version. (aka: *The Apartment on the 13th Floor*) ★★★ DVD: $29.99

Cannibal! The Musical

(1996, 90 min, US, Trey Parker) *Trey Parker, Dian Bachar, Ian Hardin, Jason McHugh, Toddy Walters.* The sole survivor of an ill-fated mining expedition tells how his taste for gold was replaced by that of human flesh. And, yes, Virginia, it is a musical. You'll have a perfectly schpedoikle time with this bizarre, intentionally campy blend of show tunes and fresh, raw meat. Made way before Parker (billed here as "Juan Schwartz") hit it big with "South Park." ★★★ DVD: $24.99, VHS: $14.99

The Cannonball Run

(1981, 95 min, US, Hal Needham) *Burt Reynolds, Roger Moore, Farrah Fawcett, Dom DeLuise, Dean Martin, Sammy Davis, Jr., Jamie Farr.* It's *Gumball Rally* gone smug, as Reynolds and his former in-crowd stage a cross-country race. Much ad-libbing, mugging, and car crashes. After watching Reynolds almost break up laughing at his own lines for the tenth time, you'll put up the red flag. (Sequel: *Cannonball Run II*) ★½ DVD: $9.99, VHS: $9.99

A Canterbury Tale

(1944, 123 min, GB, Emeric Pressburger & Michael Powell) *Eric Portman, Sheila Sim, Sergeant John Sweet, Dennis Price.* One of the most original films to come out of wartime Britain, this Powell/Pressburger tale bears no relation to the Chaucer story. It is, instead, an offbeat tale about a young woman, a British officer and an American sergeant who arrive in the small village of Kent, befriend each other and become involved in an effort to apprehend the "glue man" — a mysterious individual who has been pouring glue on the heads of young ladies escorting soldiers. Filled with interesting commentary on the effects of war on a small community, this film is a very entertaining and thought-provoking WWII classic. ★★★½ VHS: $29.99

The Canterbury Tales

(1971, 109 min, Italy, Pier Paolo Pasolini) *Laura Betti, Ninetto Davoli, Hugh Griffith.* Pasolini's second film in his "Trilogy of Pleasure" adopts six of the ribald stories contained in Chaucer's classic. Set in England and featuring the director as Chaucer himself, the film seeks out the raciest, most exotic and controversial aspects of life in the Middle Ages. Rumor has it that Pasolini, long known for working with nonprofessionals in his films, even used hitchhikers he picked up during his travels in England for major roles in the film. (Italian with English subtitles) ★★★

The Canterville Ghost

(1944, 96 min, US, Jules Dassin) *Charles Laughton, Robert Young, Margaret O'Brien, Una O'Connor.* He may be a hambone, but what great fun when Laughton is on the screen as the haunter of a 17th-century castle. It can't leave until descendant Young does one heroic act — besides not murdering O'Connor to stop her incessant screeching. Adapted from an Oscar Wilde tale. ★★★ VHS: $19.99

Cape Fear

(1962, 105 min, US, J. Lee Thompson) *Gregory Peck, Robert Mitchum, Polly Bergen, Martin Balsam, Telly Savalas.* One of the most nerve-wracking and suspenseful films of all time, this thriller is set in the seemingly tranquil Louisiana bayous. The story centers around Peck, an upstanding criminal prosecutor whose family falls under the terror of a man whom Peck sent to jail years earlier — the menacing Mitchum. Through a series of chilling yet all-too-believable scare tactics, Mitchum enacts his revenge on Peck's family with such cool-headedness that the film at times becomes almost too intense to watch. Brilliant cinematography, a terrific score and outstanding performances elevate this often-imitated thriller to an almost unbearable level of tension. (Remade in 1991) ★★★½ DVD Collector's Edition: $24.99

Cape Fear

(1991, 130 min, US, Martin Scorsese) *Robert De Niro, Nick Nolte, Jessica Lange, Juliette Lewis, Robert Mitchum, Gregory Peck, Martin Balsam.* Scorsese's masterful updating of the 1962 thriller. Upon his release from a 14-year prison term, Max

Cady (De Niro) travels to the hometown of his former defense attorney, Sam Bowden (Nolte). Because of the atrocious nature of the crime, Bowden suppressed information and lost the case. And now Cady has come to instruct his counselor on the meaning of loss. As the sociopath Cady, De Niro delivers an intense, breathtaking portrait of evil. As the family he terrorizes with half-truths and innuendo, Nolte, Lange (as his wife) and Lewis (as their daughter) are uniformly fine. Lewis and De Niro's scene set in a school auditorium is a mesmerizing exercise in corruption. ★★★½ DVD 10th Anniversary: $19.99, VHS: $9.99, VHS Letterbox: $9.99

Capitaine Conan

(1996, 130 min, France, Bertrand Tavernier) *Philippe Torreton, Samuel Le Bihan, Bernard Le Coq, Catherine Rich.* In the hell of WWI trench warfare, Capitaine Conan (Torreton) leads an elite squad expert in hand-to-hand, guerrilla combat. He's a man with no illusions, infinitely adaptable, his own code of ethics carved in stone. The film opens on the eve of the big push into no-man's-land — battlefields of orchestrated slaughter and mass insanity. As the dead are carried off, military bureaucracy gets bogged down in the war after the war. Soldiers who've fought without respite for years are kept on duty for months after Armistice. The system turns against its own, and those who've risked their lives in battle face the firing squad for the "theft" of a few blankets. Director Tavernier crafts a sweeping indictment of man's capacity for savagery with finely etched, sharply honed portrayals. The haunted visage of an aging, diminished Conan is testament to the price of war. (French with English subtitles) ★★★½ DVD: $29.99, VHS: $24.99

Captain Blood

(1935, 99 min, US, Michael Curtiz) *Errol Flynn, Olivia de Havilland, Basil Rathbone.* The first of the many Curtiz-Flynn-de Havilland swashbucklers and an immensely entertaining film. Flynn stars as an Irish doctor who is sentenced to lifelong servitude in the Americas after treating a wounded rebel. He later escapes to captain a pirate ship. Contains one of the best sword fight scenes in the movies: Flynn and Rathbone dueling it out on a rocky beach. ★★★½ VHS: $14.99

Captain Corelli's Mandolin

(2001, 127 min, US, John Madden) *Nicolas Cage, Penélope Cruz, John Hurt, Christian Bale, Irene Papas, David Morrissey.* Attempting to evoke the romanticism of those glorious morale boosters made during WWII, *Captain Corelli's Mandolin* is a glossy hybrid of war and romance that fails to ignite even the smallest of sparks. Long, lifeless and devoid of any romantic chemistry between its two stars, director Madden's follow-up to *Shakespeare in Love* features Cage (sporting Italian accent and trying his best) as a captain whose company has taken over a small Greek seaside village. There he falls for the beautiful Pelagia (Cruz), a wife whose husband is away fighting. Of course, romance blossoms, thanks in part to Pelagia's father (Hurt), who doesn't seem to mind her daughter fraternizing with the enemy. The idea of Italians and Greeks getting along side by side during wartime worked quite well in *Mediterreaneo*, but here it just seems contrived. ★½ DVD Letterbox: $14.99

Captain Horatio Hornblower

(1951, 117 min, GB, Raoul Walsh) *Gregory Peck, Virginia Mayo, Christopher Lee.* Peck is appropriately gallant in the title role as Britain's dashing naval hero in this lively adaptation of the C.S.

Forester novels. It's the Napoleonic Wars, and England is at a crisis. Not to worry, though, for Capt. Hornblower is at the helm. The good captain takes on the French, a Spanish rebel, and saves the day. Things really get explosive when he rescues her ladyship Mayo who's adrift at sea. There's a couple of nifty battle scenes and even a romantic subplot doesn't drag the action. Hornblower looks good in his early 19th-century costumes; he's got a funny name, though. ★★★ VHS: $19.99

Captain January

(1936, 75 min, US, David Butler) *Shirley Temple, Guy Kibbee, Buddy Ebsen.* Little Shirley lets the tears flow in this sentimental tale of a young orphan being taken away from her adoptive father (Kibbee). She sings "The Codfish Ball." ★★½ VHS: $14.99

Captain Newman M.D.

(1963, 126 min, US, David Miller) *Gregory Peck, Tony Curtis, Angie Dickinson, Bobby Darin.* Compelling comedy-drama starring Peck as a dedicated military doctor treating mentally disturbed soldiers stateside during WWII. ★★★ VHS: $14.99

Captain Ron

(1992, 99 min, US, Thom Eberhardt) *Kurt Russell, Martin Short, Mary Kay Place.* In this amiable variation of *What about Bob?*, Short is a mild-mannered family man who inherits a boatload of trouble when he takes his family sailing with the help of lovable, ne'er-do-well Captain Ron (Russell). Like Richard Dreyfuss' psychiatrist, Short's exasperated father is the only one to notice a bumbler's shortcomings that the rest of the family is blind to. Short's comic instincts are still on the mark, but it is Russell's surprising flair for comedy that makes these hijinks seaworthy. ★★½ DVD: $9.99

The Captain's Paradise

(1953, 80 min, GB, Anthony Kimmins) *Alec Guinness, Yvonne De Carlo, Celia Johnson.* Guinness is true to form in this romping farce about a ferry boat captain who gives life to the saying "a woman in every port." Thinking he has conquered life's ills, he shuttles merrily back and forth between his betrothed, one in Tangier and one in Gibraltar. But the comedy heats up when his scheme begins to unravel. ★★★½

The Captain's Table

(1958, 90 min, GB, Jack Lee) *John Gregson, Peggy Cummins, Donald Sinden.* This fluffy British comedy follows the exploits of Captain Epps who, after serving 30 years as skipper of a run-down cargo vessel, is suddenly transferred to the luxurious *SS Queen Adelane*. More adept at hauling cargo than people, the captain becomes a fish out of water with occasional hilarious results. ★★★ VHS: $19.99

Captains Courageous

(1937, 116 min, US, Victor Fleming) *Spencer Tracy, Freddie Bartholomew, Melvyn Douglas, Lionel Barrymore, Mickey Rooney.* Well-produced, exciting adaptation of Rudyard Kipling's adventure story. A rich, pampered youth falls off a ship and is rescued by a Portuguese fisherman, teaching the boy his love for the sea. Spencer Tracy won the first of his two Oscars as the fisherman. ★★★½ VHS: $14.99

Captives

(1996, 99 min, GB, Angela Pope) *Tim Roth, Julia Ormond, Keith Allen, Siobhan Redmond, Peter Capaldi.* When she accepts a part-time position as dentist at a maximum security prison in London, a newly divorced woman begins a hesitant affair with a prisoner and is thrust into perilous circumstances. *Captives* may not feature the most original plotline, but thanks to extremely appealing performances from its two leads and a well-versed screenplay, this romantic drama/thriller is consistently engaging. Ormand is captivating as a woman caught off guard, and Roth plays her lover with smoldering intensity. *Captives* never relies on the obvious, instead creating a believable and sensual relationship between the two characters while pitting them against outside forces. ★★★ DVD: $19.99, VHS: $9.99

Capturing the Friedmans

(2003, 107 min, US, Andrew Jarecki) *Capturing the Friedmans* began life as a documentary about children's entertainers. When director Jarecki interviewed NYC party clown David Friedman, he uncovered a story far more intriguing. That story was of a middle-class suburban Jewish family torn apart by charges that both David's father Arnold and his younger brother Jesse were child molesters. Using highly skilled editing techniques, obsessive videos and films from the family, news reports and interviews, the director creates a story that is nothing less than riveting. Arnold was a pedophile — this much is a fact. He was set up by the authorities to buy some child porn from Denmark. As police began to dig deeper, they started questioning the students in Arnold's computer classes, who began to make statements that Arnold and Jesse staged orgies in their basement classroom. After plea bargains, both Friemans went to prison. These are the facts, but the filmmaker shows us more: weaving interviews with a psychologist who specializes in these cases, a police officer prone to exaggerating, a young "victim" with a faulty memory and the Friedman's themselves. One sees many sides to this complex issue. The filmmaker makes no judgments on the Friedmans' guilt — he lets us see the whole picture. And it is that subjectivity and the accompanying doubt that makes this such an enthralling, unusual film experience. ★★★★ DVD 2-disc set: $29.99

The Car

(1977, 96 min, US, Eliot Silverstein) *James Brolin, Kathleen Lloyd, John Marley, Ronny Cox, R.G. Armstrong.* A rather dour car, seemingly out of a Bergman movie, has some existential problems — no driver, no purpose in life, no license plates. So can you blame it when it decides to become a killing machine?

Career Girls

One of the more preposterous villians in cinema is treated as a dead-serious menace, especially by our hero Brolin. Bizarre stuff indeed. ★★ DVD: $24.99

Car 54, Where Are You?

(1994, 89 min, US, Bill Fishman) *David Johansen, John C. McGinley, Al Lewis, Fran Drescher, Nipsey Russell, Rosie O'Donnell, Daniel Baldwin, Jeremy Piven.* Big-screen version of the 1960s TV comedy series about a group of bungling New York City police officers. Lewis re-creates his TV role of Officer Schnauzer. The original series was no "Gilligan's Island" (you can take that as either a compliment or a razz), but this would hardly entertain a six year old just discovering Nick at Nite. ★½ DVD Pan & Scan: $14.99

Car Trouble

(1985, 93 min, GB, David Green) *Ian Charleson, Julie Walters.* Vicious *War of the Roses*-style comedy about a harried air-traffic controller and his long-suffering wife of nine years whose lives become a nightmare when he takes on a mistress — a jazzy red sports car! A caustic comedy of the blackest sort, marred only by its implausible ending. ★★½

Car Wash

(1976, 97 min, US, Michael Schultz) *Richard Pryor, Antonio Fargas, Ivan Dixon, Franklin Ajaye, Sully Boyar, George Carlin.* Appealing and often funny, this episodic, hit-or-miss comedy follows the comic exploits of a group of Los Angeles car wash employees in the disco-swinging '70s. A good musical score and some hearty laughs await. Includes the immortal line (you heard it hear first, folks) by Fargas: "I'm more man that you'll ever be and more woman than you'll ever get." Written by Joel Schumacher. ★★½ DVD Letterbox: $14.99

Caravaggio

(1986, 93 min, GB, Derek Jarman) *Nigel Terry, Sean Bean, Tilda Swinton.* Michelangelo Merisi Caravaggio (1573–1610) was the last, perhaps the greatest, and certainly the most controversial painter of the Italian Renaissance. This stylish, adventurous tribute to the outlandish artist is directed by Jarman and is further proof of his ability to stretch artistic invention. The temperaments of Jarman and Caravaggio are well suited; the result is a bold and quirky film with contemporary touches, spectacular camera work and an impressionistic feel. ★★★ VHS: $39.99

Career Girls

(1997, 87 min, GB, Mike Leigh) *Katrin Cartlidge, Lynda Steadman, Mark Benton, Kate Byers.* In this wry, nicely crafted character study, Cartlidge and Steadman costar as Hannah and Annie, respectively, a pair of college roommates who meet up in London years later for a personal reunion. Through a series of flashbacks, Leigh depicts the wild days of their raucous, punked-out youth living in a seedy London flat, pursuing their studies and loves, and consulting Emily Brontë's "Wuthering Heights" as an oracle. The young Hannah is frenetic and high-strung, while Annie is a study in timidity — a strange pair, but they form a deep bond nonetheless. A decade later, both have matured, yet they awkwardly circle around each other searching for that nexus that brought them together in the first place. Leigh is a master of portraying the complex subtleties of the human condition as he delves into his protagonists' fragile psyches. ★★★½ VHS: $14.99

Career Opportunities

(1991, 85 min, US, Bryan Gordon) *Frank Whaley, Jennifer Connelly, Dermot Mulroney, John Candy.* John Hughes wrote the screenplay for this farfetched, underdeveloped comedy, sort of an adult *Home Alone*. Whaley plays a night janitor at a discount store who comes across rich kid Connelly, who got locked in. Together they defend the store against two burglars who are about to clean the place out. ★½ DVD: $14.99

Carefree

(1938, 80 min, US, Mark Sandrich) *Fred Astaire, Ginger Rogers, Ralph Bellamy, Luella Gear, Jack Carson, Franklin Pangborn.* Though this Astaire-Rogers musical's dance sequences can't compare to some of their 1930s contemporaries, *Carefree* boasts one of the duo's strongest screenplays. A lively screwball outing, the story deals with radio star Ginger falling for psychiatrist Fred, even though she's engaged to his best friend (perennial best friend Bellamy). Ginger, probably because she's the romantic aggressor for once, is at her most spirited as she lets her subconscious roam wild to remain a patient. Irving Berlin's score is pleasant but not among his best, though "Dancing in the Dark" and an elaborately choreographed tour through a country club are sublime. ★★★ VHS: $14.99

Careful

(1992, 100 min, Canada, Guy Maddin) *Kyle McCulloch, Gosia Dobrowolska, Sarah Neville, Brent Neale.* A culture of repression and paranoid caution inhabits a small mountain valley community living in stringently enforced guilt, guarding against the threat of avalanche. This alternate world is described by director Maddin (*Tales of Gimli Hospital*) in saturated colors and stark imagery coupled with kitschy detail, creating a hyperreality of repressed passions; a rigidly organized hotbed of Freudian conflicts where dead fathers try to caution Oedipal sons, and daughters vie for fathers' affections. Visually sumptuous, witty and truly unique, *Careful* can be described as "David Lynch meets German Expressionism" via dream therapy. It's both stimulating and adventurous. ★★★ DVD: $29.99, VHS: $24.99

Careful, He Might Hear You

(1983, 116 min, Australia, Carl Schultz) *Wendy Hughes, Robyn Nevin, Nicholas Gledhill, John Hargreaves.* This poignant and emotionally charged drama digs deep to expose the underlying spitefulness of a quietly waged battle between two sisters vying for the custody of their displaced nephew. Directed by Schultz with epicurean zeal, the film benefits from brilliant performances by the ensemble. ★★★ DVD Letterbox: $24.99

Caresses

(1997, 96 min, Spain, Ventura Pons) *David Selvas, Laura Conejero, Julieta Serrano, Montserrat Salvador, Agustín González, Naim Thomas, Mercè Pons, Roger Coma, Rosa María Sard.* Fasten your seat belts for this visually torrid tour through the streets of Barcelona and into the violently emotional world of its love-starved inhabitants. Director Pons proves to be a daring and original filmmaker as he weaves several seemingly unconnected stories into a complex tapestry of people trapped by their sexual desires and who find their passions ignited and muted — all in an effort for some kind of human tenderness. The cutting is rapid, the images glossy, and the issues lurid and controversial. A drama of human detachment that will excite and mesmerize the viewer. (Catalan with English subtitles) ★★★½ DVD: $29.99, VHS: $29.99

Carla's Song

(1996, 127 min, Nicaragua/Scotland, Ken Loach) *Robert Carlyle, Oyanka Cabezas, Scott Glenn, Salvador Espinoza.* Carlyle evidences the same earthy naturalism he brought to *The Full Monty* as George, a Glasgow bus driver whose simple act of kindness precipitates an unexpected journey. George is enthralled by Carla (Cabezas, in a mesmerizing performance), a beautiful, impoverished woman with a troubled history. The petty bureaucracy faced by George fades to insignificance compared to the stark horror of Carla's past in her native Nicaragua. They return there together to confront the memories that haunt her sleep. Director Loach again offers many crystalline moments of human interaction; from a debate on movie dialogue to the full disclosure of Carla's traumatic experiences. A surprising film of power and kind regard for its two main protagonists, each of whom experiences self-discovery and some degree of closure. ★★★ DVD: $14.99, VHS: $14.99

Carlito's Way

(1993, 141 min, US, Brian De Palma) *Al Pacino, Penelope Ann Miller, Sean Penn, John Leguizamo, Adrian Pasdar, Luis Guzman.* Scarface star Pacino and director De Palma reunite to create another Hispanic gangster drama. But unlike that film's Tony Montana, Carlito Brigante (Pacino) is a man defined by romanticism and simplicity. After serving five years in prison, Carlito simply wants to go to the Bahamas to start a car-rental agency. However, loyalties to his friend David Kleinfeld (stunningly portrayed by Penn), a corrupt and double-dealing lawyer, threaten to drag him down. Pacino delivers a solid performance, and there's amazing camerawork; though one can only feel that this territory has already been heavily traveled. ★★½ VHS: $9.99, VHS Letterbox: $14.99

Carlton-Browne of the F.O.

(1959, 88 min, GB, Jeffrey Dell & Roy Boulting) *Peter Sellers, Terry-Thomas.* A hilarious screwball farce about the Island of Gallardia — a British protectorate that has somehow been forgotten for 50 years. When this circumstance is uncovered, the blundering Terry-Thomas is sent to lead the Foreign Office. A scathing satire on diplomacy. ★★★

Carmen

(1984, 130 min, France/Italy, Francesco Rosi) *Placido Domingo, Julia Migenes-Johnson.* In a season of several Carmens, Rosi's stirring version is certainly truest to the Bizet opera. As the gypsy heroine, Johnson is a lusty fireball of unkempt virtue. Domingo brings his robust tenor to the role of the soldier broken by her powerful allure. (French with English subtitles) ★★★ DVD: $27.99, VHS: $19.99

Carmen Jones

(1954, 105 min, US, Otto Preminger) *Dorothy Dandridge, Harry Belafonte, Pearl Bailey, Diahann Carroll, Brock Peters.* Directed by Preminger and scored by Oscar Hammerstein, Bizet's famous opera is transformed into an all-black musical starring Dandridge as a flirtatious party girl who causes soldier Belafonte to go off the deep end because of his passion for her. Laced with many fine performances, this highly entertaining

songfest also made Dandridge the first black performer nominated for an Oscar in a leading role. ★★★ DVD Letterbox: $14.99, VHS: $6.99

Carnal Knowledge

(1971, 97 min, US, Mike Nichols) *Jack Nicholson, Art Garfunkel, Candice Bergen, Ann-Margret, Rita Moreno.* Director Nichols collaborated with Jules Feiffer to create this brutally honest and surprisingly perceptive examination of American sexual politics, seen over the course of two decades through the eyes of two college buddies and their relationships with various women. The camera is unflinching and revelatory, capturing the most ephemeral of moments: the awkward tentativeness of youthful encounters, the exploitative cynicism of middle-aged desperation, the self-deceptive smug assuredness that accompanies the acquisition of a new partner. Nicholson is brutally honest in his depiction of a man for whom women are at best a pleasure and at worst an alimony payment. Garfunkel is the best friend who likes to think of himself as more highly evolved. Bergen and Ann-Margret are two of the women who pass through their lives. All give superior performances in a remarkable piece of work. ★★★★ DVD: $19.99, VHS: $14.99

Carnival of Souls

(1962, 83 min, US, Herk Harvey) *Candace Hilligoss, Sidney Berger.* This eerily chilling and angst-ridden cult classic follows Mary Henry (icily portrayed by Hilligoss), a taciturn organist who miraculously survives a near-fatal car accident. Shaken, she decides to start life anew, and sets out for new pastures. No sooner has she hit the road than she is haunted by a ghoul who is invisible to all but her. Filmed in shadowy black and white, the film's visual power — which set precedent for such chillers as *Night of the Living Dead*, etc. — evokes an undeniably menacing and twisted tone. *Carnival of Souls* takes us back to an era when the horror genre probed the supernatural with an eye to the psyche and spirit rather than gut-bucket gore. (Remade in 1998) ★★★ DVD Criterion Collection: $39.99, VHS: $6.99

Carnival Rock

(1958, 80 min, US, Roger Corman) *Susan Cabit, Dick Miller, The Platters.* Thrill-seeking kids, grimy gangsters and psychopathic teens clash in a rockabilly, rhythm 'n' blues, rock 'n' roll nightclub. ★★ VHS: $7.99

Carmen Jones

Carnosaur

(1993, 83 min, US, Adam Simon) *Diane Ladd, Rapheal Sbarge, Jennifer Runyan.* Roger Corman produced this shocker with Ladd as a genetic engineer who develops a virus that can turn a mild-mannered chicken embryo into a bloodthirsty Tyrannosaurus Rex. Fueled by the amphetamine-overdrive performance of Ladd, well-paced snatches of humor, cheesy special effects that can only be rivaled by the children's show "Land of the Lost," and jabs at *Jurassic Park*, this entertaining schlockfest is sure to appeal to those who like heavy doses of vitamin "B" in their viewing diet. (Followed by 2 sequels) ★★½ VHS: $14.99

Carny

(1980, 107 min, US, Robert Kaylor) *Jodie Foster, Gary Busey, Robbie Robertson, Kenneth McMillan, Meg Foster, Craig Wasson.* A quirky, moody drama about life on the road with a carnival. Busey and Robertson are carnival hustlers, or "carnys," whose lives are interrupted when they take in teenage runaway Jodie. Unusual and offbeat, though very satisfying. ★★★ VHS: $19.99

Caro Diario (Dear Diary)

(1994, 100 min, Italy, Nanni Moretti) *Nanni Moretti, Jennifer Beals, Alexandre Rockwell.* An endearing and delightful odyssey in three parts based on director Moretti's personal diaries, *Caro Diario* ("Dear Diary") is an amusing, insightful and illuminating journey. In the first segment, "On My Vespa," Moretti zooms around Rome and its adjoining neighborhoods making wry commentary on the architectual styles, inhabitants and social trends. "Islands" finds Moretti and a friend traveling to Italy's Lipari Islands in search of a relaxing place to work, only to be put off by the increasing eccentricities of each successive archipelago. In the final tale, "Doctors," Moretti comes face to face with the medical profession in an attempt to root out the cause of a mysterious skin ailment — any who have suffered at the hands of "specialists" will find this particularly humorous. (Italian with English subtitles) ★★★½

Carousel

(1956, 128 min, US, Henry King) *Gordon MacRae, Shirley Jones, Cameron Mitchell.* Invigorating screen version of the Rodgers and Hammerstein musical (based on Molnar's "Liliom") about a roguish carnival barker (MacRae) who tries to change his ways when he falls for Jones. Songs include "Soliloquy (My Boy Bill)," "June Is Busting Out All Over" and "You'll Never Walk Alone." ★★★ DVD Letterbox: $19.99, VHS: $14.99, VHS Letterbox: $19.99

Carpool

(1996, 90 min, US, Arthur Hiller) *Tom Arnold, David Paymer, Rhea Perlman, Rod Steiger.* This icky "family comedy" equates reckless driving and the mass destruction it causes with getting in touch with your inner child. Or that may be, at least, one subtext to think about to keep yourself awake while watching this almost laughless, frequently annoying mess. Arnold plays a would-be thief who takes ad exec Paymer and the five kids in his carpool hostage after a botched robbery. Everybody ends up smiling in one of those warm and fuzzy, artificial endings that's actually quite depressing. ★½ DVD: $14.99

Carrie

(1952, 118 min, US, William Wyler) *Jennifer Jones, Laurence Olivier, Miriam Hopkins, Eddie Albert, Basil Rathbone.* A turn-of-the-century country girl (Jones) comes to Chicago to pursue a life on the stage. There she becomes involved with wealthy, married man (Olivier), whose relationship with the actress leads to his downfall. Based on Theodore Dreiser's satirical novel "Sister Carrie." Olivier is simply brilliant, and Jones gives one of her most accomplished performances. ★★★

Carrie

(1976, 97 min, US, Brian De Palma) *Sissy Spacek, Piper Laurie, John Travolta, William Katt, Nancy Allen, Betty Buckley, Amy Irving.* De Palma's chilling adaptation of the Stephen King novel tells the story of a mousy high school girl taunted by classmates. What her tormentors don't know is that Carrie posseses frightening telekinetic powers, eliciting film's most famous temper tantrum. Perhaps the worst mother-daughter relationship since Joan and Christina, Spacek and Laurie, as Carrie and her bible-thumping mother, respectively, were both nominated for Oscars and deservedly so. (Remade in 2003) ★★★½ DVD Letterbox Special Edition: $19.99, VHS 25th Anniversary: $9.99

Carried Away

(1996, 105 min, US, Bruno Barreto) *Dennis Hopper, Amy Locane, Julie Harris, Hal Holbrook, Gary Busey, Amy Irving.* A low-key but quite involving romance based on the novel "Farmer" by Jim Harrison. Hopper plays a small-town farmer and schoolteacher who can't quite commit to marrying longtime girlfriend Rosealee (Irving). When a young, sexy student (Locane) enters his classroom, his life changes irrevocably. What sounds like a *Fatal Attraction* ripoff is actually an understated, quietly powerful sleeper about a man's midlife crisis, handled with sensitivity and a minimum of clichés. *Carried Away* unfolds with the tempo of a rich novella — it's not epic in scope but nevertheless creates moments of unexpected joy. ★★★

Carrington

(1995, 123 min, GB, Christopher Hampton) *Jonathan Pryce, Emma Thompson, Steven Waddington, Rufus Sewell, Samuel West, Penelope Wilton, Janet McTeer, Jeremy Northam.* Based on the book "Lytton Strachey" by Michael Holyroyd, *Carrington* is the story of the relationship and attraction between artist Dora Carrington (Thompson) and gay Bloomsbury Group writer Lytton Strachey (Pryce). Their unconventional but enduring friendship and love story begins when Strachey becomes attracted to what he thinks is a boy. He is embarrassed to find out the "boy" is actually Dora Carrington. A tentative kiss by Strachey does not lead to sexual relations, but Carrington does fall in love with him. They eventually move in together and sleep together and even find themselves attracted to the same men, including Carrington's future husband. Bearded, painfully thin and always ready with the satiric quip, Pryce's Strachey is a revelation. Director Hampton has fashioned a fine, sometimes dark period piece, complete with lush surroundings and it is well-served by an intelligent screenplay. ★★★½ DVD Letterbox: $14.99

Carry Me Back

(1982, 93 min, Australia, John Reid) *Grant Tilly, Kelly Johnson.* Two brothers and their cantankerous father venture from their family farm to watch a rugby match hundreds of miles from home. During the match the old codger dies in the hotel room. Problems arise when the brothers discover that in order to inherit the family estate, the father must die on the family's property. What ensues is a series of

sometimes funny complications as the two attempt to smuggle old dad home without anyone knowing he's a stiff. ★★½

Carry on Cleo

(1968, 92 min, GB, Gerald Thomas) *Sidney James, Amanda Barrie, Kenneth Williams, Jim Dale.* One of the best of the *Carry On* series. This is admittedly a qualified endorsement which can only be taken with so much seriousness, but this witty reworking of ancient history features lots of silly hijinks, along with Cleopatra, Caesar, Marc Antony and lots of vestal virgins. ★★½

Carry on Cruising

(1962, 89 min, GB, Gerald Thomas) *Sidney James, Kenneth Williams, Liz Fraser.* The zany, pre-Python *Carry On* gang unleash themselves on a Mediterranean cruise ship. Though not a serious thesis on the state of human existence, the film has lots of slapstick gags and lowbrow humor, which in most cases will suffice. ★★½

Carry on Doctor

(1968, 95 min, GB, Gerald Thomas) *Frankie Howard, Kenneth Williams, Jim Dale.* More hijinks from the *Carry On* crew with their sights set this time on the medical profession. This romping farce is set at an English hospital filled with crazy doctors, crazier patients and a bevy of sex-starved nurses. ★★

The Cars That Ate Paris

(1974, 92 min, Australia, Peter Weir) *Terry Camillieri, Kevin Miles.* A bizarre horror tale of a mutated town struggling to survive by cannibalizing the vehicles of unsuspecting travelers and leaving the inhabitants either dead or "veggies" for medical experimentation. A tongue-in-cheek shot at automotive madness. Original full-length version. (aka: *The Cars That Eat People*) (DVD double feature with *The Plumber*) ★★★ DVD: $29.99, VHS: $19.99

Cartouche

(1961, 115 min, France, Philippe de Broca) *Jean-Paul Belmondo, Claudia Cardinale.* He robs from the rich and gives to the poor. Sound familiar? Director de Broca presents his variation of the Robin Hood legend in the always suave Belmondo as Cartouche, the once-petty thief turned avenger of the poor. This slapstick adventure has Belmondo fighting the foes with a quick sword and a witty tongue and romancing the women with pretty much the same. Slow and dated, it's fairly enjoyable nevertheless. (French with English subtitles) ★★ DVD Letterbox: $19.99, VHS: $29.99

Casa de los Babys

(2003, 96 min, US, John Sayles) *Maggie Gyllenhaal, Daryl Hannah, Marcia Gay Harden, Susan Lynch, Mary Steenburgen, Lili Taylor, Rita Moreno.* A rather off-putting title will most likely prevent casual viewers from giving this film a chance, but fans of writer-director Sayles, as well as fans of absorbing low-key ensemble pieces, should definitely make time for this involving drama. A disparate group of women bide their time in a Mexican hotel (run by Moreno), waiting out a convoluted, frustrating infant adoption process. In good form here, Sayles relies on his keen ear for dialogue, and brings his customary political eye to focus as the events from both the foreigners' and locals' perspectives are seen. All the performances are excellent (particularly Gyllenhaal and Hannah), and the local flavor and atmosphere are spot-on. There's almost no story, and little dramatic thrust (thus *Babys* is not nearly in the same league as

Sayles' *Lone Star*), but the compelling characters and unusual setting and premise hold one's interest throughout. ★★★ DVD Letterbox: $29.99

Casablanca

(1942, 102 min, US, Michael Curtiz) *Humphrey Bogart, Ingrid Bergman, Claude Rains, Paul Henreid, Petér Lorre, Sydney Greenstreet.* As time goes by, no film equals the popularity of this indisputable classic. In quintessential roles, Bogart and Bergman are former lovers reunited in wartorn Casablanca. Bogey is the cynical cafe owner who lives by his own moral code and sticks his neck out for "no one." Bergman, as the beautiful wife of Resistance leader Paul Henreid, finds herself torn between two lovers when she reenters Bogey's life. The film's great success lies in the inimitable pairing of its two stars, a thoroughly romantic story line, terrific humor and numerous moments of suspense. Of course, that great ending helps, too. Studio filmmaking from the 1940s doesn't come better than this, and director Curtiz masterfully handles the action, comedy and romance. Nearly stealing the film is Rains as a "poor, corrupt official" who as a Nazi puppet soon discovers the beginning of a beautiful friendship. Academy Award winner for Best Picture. ★★★★ DVD: $19.99, DVD 2-disc Special Edition: $26.99, VHS: $9.99

Casanova's Big Night

(1954, 86 min, US, Norman Z. McLeod) *Bob Hope, Joan Fontaine, Basil Rathbone, Raymond Burr, Vincent Price.* The laughs are plentiful in this engaging Hope spoof with Bob mistaken as the legendary ladies' man and doing nothing to correct the error. No one plays ham like Hope. ★★★ VHS: $14.99

Casino

(1995, 177 min, US, Martin Scorsese) *Robert De Niro, Sharon Stone, Joe Pesci, James Woods, Don Rickles, Alan King, Kevin Pollak, Dick Smothers.* A gangster who lives by his own moral code; a hot-headed hit man with a hair-trigger temper; a fascinating peek into the inner workings of underworld crime; these are all familiar trappings of director Scorsese's best-known works. And in *Casino*, his ambitious examination of a mob-controlled Las Vegas, these familiarities both enhance and hinder the director's epic story of love among the slots. De Niro plays a crafty casino manager whose life is intruded upon by two opposing forces — a volatile mob associate (Pesci) who invades his business and a gorgeous ex-prostitute (Stone) who captures his heart. *Casino* is at its best during the first half, introducing its gallery of players and detailing the daily operation of the casino; but eventually it somewhat loses its balance and momentum. Stone is terrific in a breakthrough role. ★★★

Casino Royale

(1967, 130 min, GB, John Huston, Joseph Mc, Ken Hughes, Robert Parrish) *Peter Sellers, David Niven, Ursula Andress, Woody Allen, Orson Welles, Jacqueline Bisset, Deborah Kerr, Peter O'Toole, Jean-Paul Belmondo, William Holden, Charles Boyer.* A grand spoof of the James Bond genre. Often muddled, perhaps by the multitude of talents more than anything else, the film is nonetheless filled with hilarious moments and is guaranteed to please comedy buffs. ★★½ DVD Letterbox: $14.99

Casper

(1995, 95 min, US, Brad Silberling) *Bill Pullman, Christina Ricci, Cathy Moriarty, Eric Idle, Malachi Pearson, Dan Aykroyd, Clint Eastwood, Mel Gibson.* Children of all ages should delight in this special effects charmer filled with spiffy cameos, amazing ghostly creatures and a dash of mischief. Pullman and Ricci are a ghostbusting father and his unconventional daughter who move into a haunted house to rid it of prankish poltergeists. Though the screenplay is very much on a sitcomish level, the film exhibits great effects as Casper and his three devilish uncles haunt, eat, fight, drink and fly about. Casper is a "fleshed"-out kid with humor and spunk, and Ricci is adorable (though she's not given the wondrous zingers like in the *Addams Family* films). ★★★ DVD Letterbox: $19.99, DVD Pan & Scan: $19.99

Cass

(1981, 90 min, Australia, Chris Noonan) *Michelle Fawden, John Waters, Judy Morris.* This wrenching drama deals with a young female filmmaker whose life is thrown into crisis after making a film about a primitive, tribal society. She returns to "civilized society" and her husband, but becomes isolated from him. She soon falls in love with another woman. The film focuses on her attempts to resolve her newly discovered inner conflicts. ★

Cass Timberlane

(1947, 119 min, US, George Sidney) *Spencer Tracy, Lana Turner, Zachary Scott.* A very standard 1940s romantic drama based on Sinclair Lewis' novel of class distinction and self-discovery. In a small

Midwestern town, a middle-aged, widowed judge (Tracy) is charmed by a young artist (Turner) who's from the wrong side of the tracks. The story focuses on their May-December romance. Tracy and Turner are a compatible couple, but neither is helped by clichéd situations and characters. ★★ VHS: $19.99

The Cassandra Crossing

(1977, 127 min, GB, George Pan Cosmatos) *Richard Harris, Sophia Loren, Burt Lancaster, Ava Gardner, Martin Sheen, Lee Strasberg, O.J. Simpson.* A '70s all-star cast and one helluva train wreck are the highlights of this melodramatic, occasionally entertaining disaster film. The individual stories range from compelling to inane but, hey, we don't watch these kinds of epics for the stories. Mangled steel, frayed nerves and careers-on-the-verge-of-ruin are the attraction. What story there is has to do with passengers on a train becoming exposed to plague, and no one will let them stop — sending them to a bridge ready to collapse. ★★½ DVD: $14.99, VHS: $9.99

Cast a Deadly Spell

(1991, 92 min, US, Martin Campbell) *Fred Ward, David Warner, Julianne Moore, Clancy Brown.* Ward is a delight as H. Philip Lovecraft, the only private eye in 1948 Los Angeles who *not* use magic in his daily life. Lovecraft is hired by Warner to retrieve a book containing the secrets of ultimate power and world domination. Warner's daughter, when not hunting unicorns on the estate grounds, complicates Lovecraft's quest for the tempting tome and alters the fate of mankind. There's also a femme fatale chantuese, really spiffy clothes, great noirish dialogue and enticing special effects. Made for cable with tongue in cheek, *Cast a Deadly Spell* pays loving homage to the horror and supernatural genre. ★★★½ VHS: $9.99

Cast Away

(2000, 143 min, US, Robert Zemeckis) *Tom Hanks, Helen Hunt, Nick Searcy, Jenifer Lewis, Chris Noth.* In *Cast Away*, an ultimately satisfying adventure, Hanks as an actor's dream of a lifetime — to be solo for most of a film — and single-handedly transforms it into a compelling, often spellbinding tale of survival. Chuck Norland (Hanks) is a workaholic Federal Express systems engineer whose plane crashes (one helluva scene) and strands him on a deserted island. Alone and ill-prepared, Chuck must summon all his courage and shrewdness to survive this new ordeal. How he manages to discover both makes for often rousing entertainment. Blessed with gorgeous cinematography, *Cast Away* is able to fully maintain interest even as Chuck goes about the most mundane tasks. Hanks is so good he can make an emotional attachment to a volleyball seem the norm. ★★★ DVD Letterbox 2-disc set: $26.99, DVD Letterbox Basic Edition: $14.99, DVD Basic Edition: $14.99, VHS Special Edition: $9.99

The Castle

(1968, 89 min, West Germany, Rudolf Noelte) *Maximilian Schell, Cordula Trantow.* A stylized, if somewhat indistinct version of Franz Kafka's novel. Schell stars as a stranger known as "K" who arrives at a small village claiming he is the new land surveyor for a nearby castle. However, in true Kafkaesque fashion, K, confronted with a sinisterly bureaucratic and regimented populace, cannot gain admittance to the fortress. (Filmed in English) ★★½

Casual Sex?

(1988, 97 min, US, Genevieve Robert) *Lea Thompson, Victoria Jackson, Andrew Dice Clay.* Harmless, diverting sex comedy with Thompson and Jackson as single women in search of more than a one-night stand in the age of AIDS. Clay plays a sexist creep who turns out to be Mr. Nice Guy. ★★½ DVD Letterbox: $14.99, VHS: $9.99

Casualties of War

(1989, 113 min, US, Brian De Palma) *Michael J. Fox, Sean Penn, John C. Reilly, John Leguizamo, Thuy Thu Le.* Set in 1966 Vietnam, this harrowing, fact-based story is about a Vietnamese woman who is kidnapped, raped and murdered by four soldiers. Fox stars as a newly arrived private who is forced to participate; Penn is the near-maniacal platoon sergeant who heads the assault. Superbly directed by De Palma, the film divides its running time between the horrific act and its aftereffect; on Fox in particular, who, though passively resistant during the ordeal, ultimately brings the men to trial. Le is heartbreaking as the murdered woman. ★★★½ DVD Letterbox: $9.99, VHS: $9.99

Cat and Mouse

(1975, 107 min, France, Claude Lelouch) *Jean-Pierre Aumont, Michèle Morgan.* This mesmerizing and ingenious Parisian murder mystery is full of unexpected twists and humorous turns as an unorthodox detective delves into the death of a millionaire. The murder, thinly disguised as suicide, leads the detective to a variety of suspects and many baffling questions. (French with English subtitles) ★★★½

The Cat and the Canary

(1927, 81 min, US, Paul Leni) *Laura La Plante, Creighton Hale, Tully Marshall.* This delightfully eerie thriller — to which director Leni brings the Gothic sensibilities of his native Germany — is a classic of the horror genre and set the style for the famous Universal horror films of the 1930s. A group of relatives gather at midnight in an abandoned mansion to read the will of an old man. The dead man's niece is the heiress, but only if she spends the night in the house. During the course of the spooky night, she encounters clutching hands, sliding panels, revolving bookcases and a catlike apparition. Also includes a good Harold Lloyd short, 1920's *Haunted Spooks*. (Silent with musical accompaniment) ★★★½ VHS: $29.99

Cat Ballou

(1965, 96 min, US, Elliot Silverstein) *Jane Fonda, Lee Marvin, Michael Callen, Dwayne Hickman, Stubby Kaye, Nat King Cole.* Fonda sparkles in the lead role in this wonderful western spoof as a schoolteacher who turns outlaw to avenge her father's murder. But it was Marvin who walked away with an Oscar for his performance in dual roles — he plays both the film's villain and the washed-up, alcoholic gunman who is forced out of retirement to hunt him down. Cole and Kaye spice up the film with intermittent musical numbers as a pair of wandering minstrels. A breezy, comedic homage to the classic western take on the conflict between good and evil. ★★★½ DVD Special Edition: $19.99, VHS: $14.99

The Cat O'Nine Tails

(1971, 89 min, Italy, Dario Argento) *Karl Malden, James Franciscus, Catherine Spaak.* Argento's neo-Hitchcockian thriller is a confusing murder mystery involving industrial espionage in the world of experimental genetics. Malden is a blind ex-newspaper reporter who may hold some important information

Leonardo DiCaprio and friends in *Catch Me If You Can*

about the mysterious accidental death of a scientist. He contacts Franciscus, himself a reporter, and the two of them begin an investigation that leads them closer to the truth and into a deadly race with the killer. The story is needlessly confusing and not very engaging even when it is clarified at the end. (Filmed in English) ★★ VHS: $12.99

Cat on a Hot Tin Roof

(1958, 108 min, US, Richard Brooks) *Elizabeth Taylor, Paul Newman, Burl Ives, Judith Anderson, Madeleine Sherwood, Jack Carson.* Everyone has a skeleton in their closet in Tennessee Williams' Pulitzer Prize-winning drama. Taylor sinks her claws into the role of Maggie the Cat, the tormented, sexually frustrated wife of guilt-ridden ex-jock Brick (Newman). The prototypic tale of family conflict and confrontation. ★★★ DVD: $19.99

Cat on a Hot Tin Roof

(1984, 122 min, US, Jack Hofsiss) *Jessica Lange, Tommy Lee Jones, Rip Torn, Kim Stanley, David Dukes, Penny Fuller.* An excellent made-for-TV adaptation of the Tennessee Williams play, with particularly strong performances from Lange as Maggie the Cat; Torn as Big Daddy; and Jones as Brick, Big Daddy's favorite son, an alcoholic ex-jock with a burden from his past that he cannot resolve. ★★★½ DVD: $29.99, VHS: $19.99

Cat People

(1942, 70 min, US, Jacques Tourneur) *Simone Simon, Kent Smith, Jane Randolph.* Of the eight horror films Val Lewton produced for RKO Pictures in the 1940s, this moody and suspenseful thriller — awash in stark shades of black and white — is his classic. Simon stars as a mysterious woman who refuses to consummate her marriage to architect Smith on the belief that she is descended from a race of cat people and if sexually aroused, she will transform into a panther. (Remade in 1982) ★★★½

Cat People

(1982, 118 min, US, Paul Schrader) *Nastassja Kinski, Malcolm McDowell, John Heard, Annette O'Toole, Ruby Dee.* Schrader's gory remake of the 1942 classic chiller is shameless fun, even more so with the director's psychological baggage to laugh at. McDowell and Kinski play kissin' cousins who can't get down from their family tree. The whole

production exudes an all-pervasive air of fetid evil, perversity and eroticism — much like the city in which it is set: New Orleans. ★★½ DVD: $24.99

Cat's Eye

(1985, 94 min, US, Lewis Teague) *Drew Barrymore, James Woods, Alan King, Robert Hays, James Naughton.* Stephen King's uneven horror trilogy about a clinic which helps smokers quit; a mobster who gets even with his wife's lover; and (the best sequence) a cat who protects a young girl from a deadly troll. ★★½ DVD Letterbox: $19.99, VHS: $9.99

Cat's Play

(1974, 115 min, Hungary, Karoly Makk) *Margit Dayka, Margit Makay.* A contemplative drama about rekindled passion, love, friendship and growing old. Two sisters, living in different regions of the country, continue to communicate through letters and phone calls. The correspondence, usually centering on earlier, happier times, turns darker when one of them falls desperately in love with her old flame. Despite her sister's imploring, the normally sedate woman becomes girlish in her efforts to restart the affair, and becomes despondent and self-destructive when it fails. Told in the form of an epistolary novel and utilizing vivid images to convey the character's innermost thoughts, the film is a serious, stylistically daring and deeply involving drama. (Hungarian with English subtitles) ★★★½ VHS: $29.99

Catamount Killing

(1974, 93 min, US/West Germany, Krzystof Zannusi) *Horst Bucholz, Ann Wedgeworth.* Polish director Zanussi (*A Year of the Quiet Sun*) tries his hand at film noir in this English-speaking thriller set in a bucolic Vermont town. Bucholz stars as a newly arrived bank manager who seduces an older woman and then involves her in the faking of a robbery at his bank. Their plans go awry, however, resulting in murderous cover-ups. It has its moments, but there's nothing new here. ★★½ VHS: $79.99

Catch-22

(1970, 121 min, US, Mike Nichols) *Alan Arkin, Jon Voight, Martin Sheen, Orson Welles, Art Garfunkel, Richard Benjamin, Paula Prentiss, Bob Newhart, Anthony Perkins, Jack Gilford, Buck Henry.* Brilliant screen adaptation of Joseph Heller's bestselling antiwar novel. Arkin heads a first-rate all-

star cast as a WWII Army pilot caught up in the absurdities of military life. What a cast. A powerful and subversively funny black comedy. ★★★★ DVD: $14.99, VHS: $9.99

Catch Me If You Can

(2002, 140 min, US, Steven Spielberg) *Leonardo DiCaprio, Tom Hanks, Christopher Walken, Martin Sheen, Nathalie Baye, Amy Adams.* Frank Abagnale, Jr. was a charismatic, handsome teenager who in the mid-to-late 1960s scammed millions from banks and successfully impersonated a pilot, doctor and lawyer even though he had no college education. His story would have been an outrageous invention had it all not been true. Capturing the breeziness of those fanciful comedies of the time period, Spielberg has fashioned a delightful, buoyant comedy of, among other things, crime, money, sex, family and salvation. DiCaprio is Abagnale, who begins a career in forgery after running away from home at age sixteen. It's not long before the skilled teen has the FBI on his trail, headed by special agent Frank Hanratty (Hanks), who is determined to catch his man. The ensemble is uniformly terrific, with DiCaprio giving one of his best performances as a youth coerced into adulthood. Hanks is first-rate as the relentless agent, and Walken is superb as Abagnale, Sr., a father beset by financial and familial woes. Always a master in storytelling, Spielberg is in an unusually good mood, making sure that everyone involved in this airy, entertaining romp is having fun. Everyone is — but no one more than those watching it. ★★★½ DVD Letterbox 2-disc set: $19.99, VHS: $9.99

The Catered Affair

(1956, 93 min, US, Richard Brooks) *Bette Davis, Ernest Borgnine, Debbie Reynolds.* Good performances distinguish this absorbing family drama. Davis is in fine form as the wife of Bronx cabbie Borgnine whose determination to give daughter Reynolds an elegant wedding far exceeds the family's income. ★★★ VHS: $19.99

Cats and Dogs

(2001, 87 min, US, Lawrence Guterman) *Jeff Goldblum, Elizabeth Perkins, Alexander Pollock, Voices of: Tobey Maguire, Alec Baldwin, Sean Hayes, Susan Sarandon, Michael Clarke Duncan, Joe Pantoliano.* The Jeff Goldblum hot streak continues; simply by appearing forgettably in a special effects film, it becomes a blockbuster. Here, he's upstaged by talking cats and dogs, in an impressive blend of real critters and computer animation. Seems the two species have been at global war since ancient times, with the jealous cats trying to rid the world of intrepid dogs, aka man's best friend. A beagle puppy (voiced by Maguire) finds himself at the center of the latest high-tech battle, and rises to the historic occasion. *Cats & Dogs* is almost wall-to-wall mayhem, but the slapstick truly is funny and surprisingly good natured. ★★★ DVD Letterbox: $19.99, DVD Pan & Scan: $19.99, VHS: $6.99

Cats Don't Dance

(1997, 75 min, US, Mark Dindal) *Voices of: Scott Bakula, Jasmine Guy, Natalie Cole, Kathy Najimy, Don Knotts, John Rhys-Davies, George Kennedy, Hal Holbrook.* A good vocal cast adds depth and character to this wonderful animated musical. Danny is a small-town cat seeking fame and fortune in Hollywood. There he meets Sawyer, the charming secretary of the animal talent agent. Danny's big dreams are soon crushed when he finds out that animals are limited to bit parts and are not allowed to speak or sing. Danny and Sawyer eventually overcome the odds and triumphantly sing and dance their way to the top, taking lots of other underappreciated animals with them. The blind loyalty paid to Disney productions often causes gems like this to be overlooked. ★★★½ DVD: $12.99, VHS: $14.99

Caught

(1949, 88 min, US, Max Ophüls) *Barbara Bel Geddes, Robert Ryan, James Mason.* Intriguing film noir psychodrama with Bel Geddes as a mistreated wife caught between her villainous millionaire husband (Ryan) and a caring doctor (Mason). ★★★ VHS: $19.99

Caught

(1996, 109 min, US, Robert M. Young) *Edward James Olmos, Maria Conchita Alonso, Arie Verveen, Steven Schub, Bitty Schram.* Nick (Verveen), a "mysterious drifter," is taken in by Joe (Olmos), a fish shop owner, and his wife, Betty (Alonso). He's given a job and the bedroom of their son, who's in Hollywood trying to break into movies. Things are rosy until Betty and Nick start having an affair, and things get really tense when son Danny pays a surprise visit. While the scenario and conclusion fit neatly into the glib "adultery-never-pays" agenda of most erotic thrillers, *Caught* is far more believable and involving than one would expect, with good performances and a deliberate pace that allows scenes to unfold naturally. ★★★

Caught in the Draft

(1941, 82 min, US, David Butler) *Bob Hope, Eddie Bracken, Dorothy Lamour, Lynne Overman.* Hope gets *Caught in the Draft* and the service will never be the same. Congress has just legalized the draft, and movie star Hope schemes to avoid both induction into the Army and marriage to colonel's daughter Lamour. Of course, it all backfires, and Hope, who faints at the sound of a gun shot, is thrust on an unsuspecting military. This winning comedy is an arsenal of one-liners and sight gags, and its screenplay adheres to a much tighter structure than the standard Hope comedy. Bracken and Overman are tops in support as Hope's henchmen. ★★★ DVD Double Feature: $14.99, VHS: $9.99

Caught Up

(1998, 98 min, US, Darin Scott) *Bokeem Woodbine, Cynda Williams, Clifton Powell, Tony Todd, Basil Wallace, Jeffrey Combs, Snoop Doggy Dogg, LL Cool J.* A poorly written urban crime drama that would work better as a sketch in *Hollywood Shuffle*, *Caught Up* stars Woodbine as an ex-con trying to go straight. He meets Trish (a mediocre Williams), a psychic being chased by an evil Rastafarian (don't ask). Trouble starts when he agrees to help her. Every stereotype and cliché is here, not to mention howlingly bad dialogue ("Nobody was waiting for me but a dude named destiny") and cameos from yesterday's heroes (Dogg, Cool J). ★ DVD: $9.99, VHS: $9.99

Cavalcade

(1933, 110 min, US, Frank Lloyd) *Clive Brook, Diana Wynyard, Una O'Connor.* Noël Coward's 1930s stage hit is given superior treatment in this Oscar-winning adaptation. Brook and Wynyard head an upper-class British family at the turn-of-the-century. The film follows their lives through the first World War and into the 1930s. Wynyard's performance seems exaggerated and dated, but the film does not. First-rate production values and an engrossing story make this one of the classics from its era. ★★★½ VHS: $19.99

The Caveman's Valentine

(2001, 100 min, US, Kasi Lemmons) *Samuel L. Jackson, Colm Feore, Ann Magnuson, Aunjanue Ellis, Anthony Michael Hall, Rodney Eastman, Tamara Tunie.* Director Lemmons treads a fine line between bravura and excess but is able to find middle ground thanks to a fascinating, concrete performance by Jackson. With a screenplay by George Dawes Green, who adapted his own novel, *The Caveman's Valentine* features Jackson as Romulus Ledbetter, a once-promising pianist and now schizophrenic who investigates the death of a fellow homeless person. A quite unusual detective story, the film is a hallucinatory odyssey in which our Columbo is quite mad and we're not sure as to the validity of his findings or when his next outburst will surface. It's hard to imagine this absorbing, novel film working without the presence of Jackson. His is a bold, passionate performance that anchors this tricky, even illuminating puzzle. ★★★ DVD: $14.99

CB4

(1993, 83 min, US, Tamra Davis) *Chris Rock, Allen Payne, Chris Elliott, Phil Hartman, La Wanda Page.* Rock cowrote with former music critic and author Nelson George this hip-hop, gangsta rap parody. The film, which starts out as a hysterically funny pseudo-documentary, strays from its course by turning into a narrative tale and morality play. The film is filled with hilarious moments that are sharp-witted comments on African-American, B-Boy stereotypes, but all of that is lost in a weak story. ★★½ DVD Letterbox: $19.99, VHS: $9.99

Cecil B. Demented

(2000, 87 min, US, John Waters) *Stephen Dorff, Melanie Griffith, Patricia Hearst, Mink Stole, Ricki Lake, Alicia Witt, Kevin Nealon, Adrian Grenier, Harriet Dodge, Maggie Gyllenhaal.* Waters returns to the guerrilla moviemaking style of his earlier, unconventional days, but the result is far from revolutionary. Ostensibly a broad farce on Hollywood filmmaking, the lifeless *Cecil B. DeMented* is so scattershot and devoid of direction that it's difficult to tell exactly what it wants to be. Dorff is the titular underground filmmaker who kidnaps superstar Honey Whitlock (Griffith) and forces her to appear in his independent film *Raving Lunatic*. Waters uses this setup as a frontal assault on mainstream cinema, as characters go about attacking the system and anyone in their way. Anarchy and mayhem prevail. You'd think Waters would be inspired by this premise, but he's unable to deliver on hardly any of his punch lines, making this unfunny mess the director's least satisfying work. ★½ DVD: $14.99, VHS: $9.99

The Celebration

(1998, 106 min, Denmark, Thomas Vinterberg) *Ulrich Thomsen, Henning Moritzen, Thomas Bo Larsen, Paprika Steen.* A hugely dysfunctional family arrives at a secluded hotel for a 60th birthday party for the family patriarch. Suffice it to say, things don't go as cheerily as hoped. A searing, uncompromising drama, *The Celebration* is also incredibly involving and highly entertaining, and despite the subject matter (alcoholism, incest, rape, racism, to name a few), it sidesteps heavy artiness and Jerry Springer-like wallowing. Amazing performances, incisive writing and spot-on direction combine to make this quite memorable. Under the tenets of the "Dogma '95" idea, which sets strict rules about realism in cinema and is espoused by a number of European directors, *The Celebration* achieves an almost unbearable, in-your-face tension — it cuts right to the bone. (German with English subtitles) ★★★½ DVD: $19.99

Celebrity

(1998, 113 min, US, Woody Allen) *Kenneth Branagh, Judy Davis, Winona Ryder, Leonardo DiCaprio, Joe Mantegna, Melanie Griffith, Bebe Neuwirth, Charlize Theron, Famke Janssen, Hank Azaria, Dylan Baker.* Woody asks "What price fame?" and then comes up with a few desirable and not-so-desirable answers in this often amusing, scattershot comedy shot in black and white. Taking over the "Woody" role (neurotic, stammering author) is Branagh, who plays Lee Simon, a self-absorbed writer about to fall down the celebrity rabbit hole. The assorted people he meets on his crazy journey include Griffith as a pampered actress; DiCaprio, effective as a spoiled DiCaprio-like superstar; and Ryder, as a down-to-earth actress. Woody's dialogue is zesty, and though the story isn't quite as developed as one would like, the humor and a good cast certainly compensate. Davis sparkles as Simon's ex-wife who achieves her own unexpected fame. ★★★ DVD: $14.99, VHS: $9.99

Celeste

(1981, 107 min, Germany, Percy Adlon) *Eva Mattes, Jurgen Arndt.* With no plot to speak of, this subtle yet involving and ultimately inspiring love story chronicles the daily routine of an uneducated peasant girl (the wonderful Mattes) who is hired as the housekeeper for the ailing author, Marcel Proust. The film's power lies in the evolving relationship between the intellectual Proust and the simple, caring woman who in the course of nine years not only tends to his house but becomes his companion, secretary, friend and surrogate mother. Based on the memoirs of the real Céleste Albaret. (German with English subtitles) ★★★ VHS: $29.99

Celestial Clockwork

(1994, 86 min, France/Venezuela, Fina Torres) *Ariadna Gil, Arielle Dombasle, Evelyne Didi.* Exuberant, fanciful and infused with magical realism, this "Alice in Wonderland/Cinderella"-like comedy is a delightful celebration of the pursuit of individual happiness and sexual open-mindedness. In dusty Caracas, the lovely Ana leaves her husband-to-be at the altar. She jumps aboard the next Paris-bound plane and takes up residence in a funky crash pad with her old friend Alma. The apartment is right out of Almódovar, populated by a bevy of Latina exiles aggressively exercising their free will and indulging in outrageous Parisianne chic. Brimming with oddball characters and loopy plot twists, the film is a highly entertaining ride with Ana on her picaresque journey to self-fulfillment. (Spanish and French with English subtitles) ★★★½ VHS: $98.99

Celine and Julie Go Boating

(1974, 193 min, France, Jacques Rivette) *Dominique Labourier, Juliet Berto.* A truly magical cinematic journey, this 1970s art-house classic is "Alice in Wonderland" meets Cocteau. Celine (Berto) is a magician who becomes fast friends with librarian Julie (Labourier) after they meet at the steps of Montmarte. Forming an uncanny, symbiotic bond, they move into the same flat and begin sharing completely of each others' lives: bed, clothes, boyfriend, etc. Ultimately, they begin sharing the same alternate reality when they partake of a magic candy that transports them into an imaginary (or is it) haunted house, where they become involved in the drama of its inhabitants. Just as this reaches a climax, the hallucination ends and Celine and Julie must begin again. Rivette commits a huge cinematic risk by presenting this scene again and again as each time it inches closer to its conclusion (hence the 193-minute run time) and voila! It pays off. As delightful and engaging as its two main characters. (French with English subtitles) ★★★★ VHS: $19.99

The Cell

(2000, 107 min, US, Tarsem Singh) *Jennifer Lopez, Vincent D'Onofrio, Vince Vaughn, Dylan Baker, Marianne Jean-Baptiste.* The plot, and any attempt at describing *The Cell*, sounds quite tired. A psychologist (Lopez) must enter the mind of a serial killer (D'Onofrio) to find a dying victim; she does this by infiltrating his dream state, and must learn to control this false reality. Knowing all that, it's all the more incredible to find out how original this thriller is. Breathtaking stream-of-conciousness sequences through a tense carnival-of-horrors fantasy world are the highlight of this trippy film destined for cult status. With bizarre violence and an experimental technique, director Singh is superficially reminiscent of David Fincher, but this big-screen debut is full of hope and lacks Fincher's nihilistic tendencies. ★★★ DVD: $14.99, VHS: $14.99

The Celluloid Closet

(1995, 102 min, US, Jeffrey Friedman & Rob Epstein) *Narrated by: Lily Tomlin, Susan Sarandon, Whoopi Goldberg, Shirley MacLaine, Tony Curtis, Tom Hanks, Gore Vidal, Quentin Crisp.* Inspired by Vito Russo's seminal book on the depiction of homosexuality in Hollywood cinema, this funny, informative and occasionally moving documentary offers — through interviews and a vast assortment of film clips — a candid minihistory of gays and lesbians on-screen. *The Celluloid Closet* takes a chronological approach to the subject, offering clips from film ranging from the turn of the century thru the mid-1990s. While encompassing in scope, the film is too simplistic and suffers from the lack of critical analysis and a central point of view. And, too many actors have nothing really to say — only Tony Curtis and Susan Sarandon offer insight into the queer roles they have played. With that said, however, *The Celluloid Closet* is more than recommended, but for something deeper, it is best to read Russo's book. ★★★ DVD Special Edition: $29.99

The Cement Garden

(1996, 108 min, GB, Andrew Birkin) *Andrew Robertson, Charlotte Gainsbourg, Alice Coultard, Ned Birkin.* Based on a novel by Ian McEwan ("The Comfort of Strangers"), this bizarre and twisted tale of adolescence run amok is at once fascinating and seductively repulsive. On the edge of some barren,

unidentified British city stands a lone remaining house. Its four young occupants suddenly find themselves orphaned. They decide to dispose of mum's body and avoid the orphanages and thus begins a summer of complete descent into childish fantasy that's a pointed allegory — à la "Lord of the Flies" — about the decay of social behavior in a crumbling industrial society. The film teases the viewer with snippets of coherency only to settle back into an infuriatingly alluring moral ambiguity. ★★★ DVD: $19.99, VHS: $14.99

The Cemetery Club

(1992, 106 min, US, Bill Duke) *Ellen Burstyn, Olympia Dukakis, Diane Ladd, Danny Aiello, Lainie Kazan, Christina Ricci, Wallace Shawn.* A talented cast attempts to breathe life into this sappy adaptation of the failed Broadway comedy. Sadly, this meandering saga of three middle-aged widows who gather at the cemetery to toss one-liners at their husbands' graves falls well wide of its mark — straddling the line between comedy and drama, but failing to be either funny or dramatic. Burstyn gives the most charming performance of the film as a widow who finds romance. ★★ DVD: $9.99, VHS: $9.99

Cemetery Man

(1994, 100 min, US/Italy, Michele Soavi) *Rupert Everett, Anna Falchi, Francois Hadji-Lazaro.* Dario Argento's protégé Soavi comes wholly into his own with this highly original adaptation of a novel by Italian pop writer Titiano Sclavi. Everett stars as Francesco Dellamorte, caretaker of the Buffalore Cemetery. What would seem a quiet job has recently become quite a problem, however, as the dead have been returning to life soon after burial, and it is up to Dellamorte to put them permanently back into their graves. Soon Dellamorte is killing the living in order to keep them from rising from the dead and he can no longer distinguish between fantasy and reality. Somewhat convoluted, though entertaining and enticing, the film is not for the casual viewer, but those who visit the graveyard several times a week will find rewards in store. (Filmed in English) ★★★ VHS: $29.99

Center Stage

(2000, 116 min, US, Nicholas Hytner) *Amanda Schull, Peter Gallagher, Susan May Pratt, Ethan Stiefel, Donna Murphy.* Best of the best of ballet students vie for positions in the American Ballet Academy while dealing with the usual mélange of personal troubles. Slow-paced, overlong but mildly involving, *Center Stage* benefits greatly from decent performances and an appealing lead (the beautiful-in-a-perky-way Schull), but the film is terminally shallow and derivative. There's nothing here you haven't seen in countless "gotta-be-the-best" films (whether about singers, athletes, chess players or dancers), but like its antecedents, *Center Stage* shines in its performance scenes. ★★½ DVD: $14.99, VHS: $9.99

Central Station

(1998, 115 min, Brazil, Walter Salles) *Fernanda Montenegro, Marilia Pera, Vinicius de Oliveira.* Heartrending without being maudlin, *Central Station* is a poignant, accomplished drama featuring an outstanding performance from Brazil's grand dame of cinema, Montenegro. At the Rio De Janeiro central train station, Dora (Montenegro), a retired schoolteacher, writes and posts letters for the illiterate to "make ends meet." When a woman is killed

in a bus accident, Dora begins an odyssey of self-awakening when she reluctantly escorts the deceased woman's nine-year-old son Josué (de Oliveira) to his long-lost father hundreds of miles cross-country. Montenegro has made Dora a fascinating character: complex, contradictory, and ultimately sympathetic; Montenegro can say more with her eyes than a page of dialogue. Young de Oliveira is a heartbreaker as Josué; he's adorable without the precociousness. A beguiling and touching journey, the Oscar-nominated (Best Foreign Film, Best Actress) *Central Station* is rich in emotion and honesty, and marvelously done. (Portuguese with English subtitles) ★★★★ DVD: $29.99

La Cérémonie

(1996, 111 min, France, Claude Chabrol) *Isabelle Huppert, Sandrine Bonnaire, Jacqueline Bisset, Jean-Pierre Cassel.* Director Chabrol casts a sideways glance at class warfare in this somewhat off-center thriller that examines the tentative relationship between the modern aristocracy and their domestics. Bonnaire stars as the newly appointed maid for Bisset and her industrialist husband Cassel. Into the picture walks Huppert (radiant as ever), as a smart-ass postal worker with a rocky past of her own. The atmosphere is tense throughout as Bonnaire's perfect veneer begins to crack and the family becomes increasingly intolerant of her rebelliousness and her budding friendship with Huppert. Chabrol explores this territory with characteristic understatement and a "classical" panache that makes the film feel more "arty" than it really is, but his intricate study of character makes this captivating viewing nonetheless. (French with English subtitles) ★★★½ VHS: $19.99

César

(1936, 117 min, France, Marcel Pagnol) *Raimu, Pierre Fresnay.* Emboldened by the success of *Marius* and *Fanny*, Pagnol directed the final installment of his stage trilogy himself. Once again Raimu steals the film as Marius' father, but this time the film bares his name so it's all right. Short on plot but long on everything else (especially running time), *César*, like all of the films to come out of Pagnol's studio, is full of people whose company one enjoys, all of whom inhabit a little village in which one would have loved to have lived. The plot concerns Fanny's young son who discovers that Marius is her real father. Through his efforts, they are reunited after 20 years. (French with English subtitles) ★★★ DVD Trilogy 3-pack: $79.99

César and Rosalie

(1972, 110 min, France, Claude Sautet) *Yves Montand, Romy Schneider, Sami Frey.* Montand and Schneider give compelling performances in this charming comedy, a bittersweet tale of friendship and love. Schneider plays a divorcée living with tycoon Montand who becomes involved with young artist Frey. Quite unexpectedly, however, the two men, who at first see each other as nothing more than rivals, become friends; laying the framework for an unusual and caring relationship between the three lovers. (French with English subtitles) ★★★½ DVD: $24.99, VHS: $19.99

Chain Lightning

(1950, 95 min, US, Stuart Heisler) *Humphrey Bogart, Eleanor Parker, Raymond Massey.* Actual war and aerial footage highlight this routine aviation adventure, with Bogart hitting the skies as a former WWII bomber pilot who tests the new jets. Massey is the multibillionaire with a fascination for airplanes who funds the tests. ★★½ VHS: $19.99

Celine and Julie Go Boating

Chain of Desire

(1992, 105 min, US, Temistocles Lopez) *Linda Fiorentino, Malcolm McDowell, Seymour Cassel, Kevin Conroy, Elias Koteas, Patrick Bauchau, Grace Zabriskie.* From the director of the intriguing *Exquisite Corpses* comes this stylistically inventive and wittily droll observation and AIDS allegory on sexual yearning and unrequited love. Fiorentino is Alma, a singer in a slick New York nightclub who sleeps with Jesus, a married Hispanic worker. This successful coupling begins a humorous but sexually frustrating daisy chain of purely sexual encounters with a succession of New York characters. A titillating highlight is a three-way, voyeuristically charged masturbation scene (both gay and straight) between three people in three different curtainless high-rise apartments. An erotic updating of *La Ronde* exploring sexual desire. ★★★ VHS: $99.99

Chain Reaction

(1996, 100 min, US, Andrew Davis) *Keanu Reeves, Morgan Freeman, Rachel Weisz, Fred Ward.* Reeves takes his turn as the unjustly accused in Davis' attempted reworking of *The Fugitive*. Reeves stars as a young machinist working on a university physics project attempting to find a new, cheap source of energy. Once the team makes its discovery, dark forces take over and the lab is blown to smithereens. Only Reeves and a young associate hold the secret to the discovery. Framed for murder, they must run for their lives, both from the police and from the nefarious forces behind the setup. Tedious, overlong and full of gaping plot holes. ★ DVD: $14.99, VHS: $9.99

Chained

(1934, 76 min, US, Clarence Brown) *Clark Gable, Joan Crawford, Otto Kruger.* Gable and Crawford enjoy a brief encounter aboard a cruise ship in this familiar romantic drama. Gable pursues Crawford until she gives in, but when she returns to New York and lover Kruger, she becomes torn between the two men. ★★

Chained Heat

(1983, 97 min, US, Paul Nicholas) *Linda Blair, Sybil Danning, John Vernon, Tamara Dobson, Stella Stevens.* Sex, violence, showers, sex, drugs, prostitution, white slavery, sex, corruption (did we mention sex?) from the producer of *The Concrete Jungle*. One of the great treats (meaning sleaziest) in the women-in-prison genre, this violent and sexually explicit exploitation film stars the genre's reigning queens: Blair and Danning. Blair plays the innocent who's in for a quick and brutal education, as the prison is run by a drug-dealing wretch of a warden, and populated with hard-as-nails, knife-wielding peroxide babes. If Blair thought being possessed by the Devil was tough, she's never spent time in a women's prison. ★★½

Chained Heat 2

(1993, 98 min, US, Lloyd Simani) *Brigitte Nielsen, Paul Koslo.* All hope seems lost for pretty strawberry blonde Alex when she is falsely imprisoned in a hellish all-female Czechoslovakian prison for drug smuggling. The hellhole is run by a suit-and-tie attired warden (played by Nielsen) who, aided by her knife-wielding, cigar-chomping, Lotte Lenya-wannabe henchwoman, rules her roost. Filmed in an actual Prague prison, the film is laughably bad, featuring the requisite bevy of beauties, plenty of gratu-

itous flesh and several lesbian lovemaking scenes. How would you like your exploitation? With cheese, please. ★½ VHS: $14.99

Chairman of the Board

(1998, 95 min, US, Alex Zamm) *Carrot Top, Courtney Thorne-Smith, Larry Miller, Raquel Welch, Jack Warden, Bill Erwin, M. Emmet Walsh.* It's tempting to simply call this: "Pee-wee Herman *is* the Hudsucker Proxy." But that'd be an insult to both of them. Carrot Top is a surfer dude (ugh!) who strikes up a brief friendship with tycoon Warden. When the latter dies, Mr. Top is left the (cue: film title) of his huge invention business. Despite some cool doodads, and maybe a few amusing scenes, *Chairman of the Board* does star Carrot Top and his screechy voice. And the jokes, well, they seem to have been written during the Bush (Sr.) administration. ★½ DVD: $19.99

The Chalk Garden

(1964, 106 min, GB, Ronald Neame) *Deborah Kerr, Hayley Mills, John Mills, Edith Evans.* Kerr gives a beautiful performance as a governess who helps a troubled youngster coming of age. Hayley is affecting as the young girl; her father John and Evans offer solid support. ★★★

The Chamber

(1996, 110 min, US, James Foley) *Chris O'Donnell, Gene Hackman, Faye Dunaway, Lela Rochon, Robert Prosky.* In *A Time to Kill*, race relations is the focal point to a complex and involving tale. In this Grisham adaptation, race relations once again plays a major role in the story, but it's watered down and merely a plot device to a uneventful drama. O'Donnell sleepwalks through his role as a young lawyer who attempts to get a stay of execution for his grandfather (Hackman), a racist KKK member and convicted murderer sentenced to death. As he races against the clock, he tries to get to know a man he never knew who is unwilling to either defend himself or reconcile. Hackman's good performance is offset by the film's flat character development and a plodding pace. ★★ DVD: $14.99, VHS: $7.49

The Chambermaid on the Titanic

(1998, 96 min, France, Bigas Luna) *Olivier Martinez, Romane Bohringer, Aitana Sánchez-Gijón, Didier Bezace.* This tragicomic love story about the fictionalized, nonsexual relationship

between the handsome foundry worker Horty (Martinez) and Marie (Sanchez-Gijon), the beautiful chambermaid of the title, is all promise and no payoff. Director Lunas tries to create a charming period piece about love, trust, and truth, but this joyless film lacks depth and passion. As Horty recounts his adventures to his friends about how he helped Marie when she was stranded the night before the ocean liner sailed, the excitement his coworkers feel hearing his tale is not shared by the viewer. The two leads ooze sex appeal, and a scene in which they share kisses under a dining room table generates some heat, yet there is little else of interest in their chaste relationship. Horty's wife Zoe (Bohringer) complicates matters in the final third, but by that time, *The Chambermaid on the Titanic* has capsized almost completely. (French with English subtitles) ★★ VHS: $29.99

Chameleon Street

(1988, 98 min, US, Wendell B. Harris Jr.) *Wendell B. Harris Jr, Angela Leslie, Richard Kiley.* One of the merits of video is that it allows such overlooked gems as this to finally have their day in the sun. Fledgling filmmaker Harris wrote, directed and stars in this hip comedy (based on a true story) about a man who impersonates various upstanding members of society — and getting away with it! Harris's witty, world-weary narration adds just the right touch, imbuing the film with a '90s attitude offset by '70s sensibilities. ★★★ VHS: $19.99

The Champ

(1931, 87 min, US, King Vidor) *Wallace Beery, Jackie Cooper, Irene Rich.* Beery won an Academy Award for his knockout performance as a washed-up boxer attempting a comeback. A wonderful mixture of sentiment and involving dramatics, the film is smartly written and sensitively directed. As Beery's idolizing young son, Cooper gives an astonishing portrayal — child performers for decades would be measured against it. (Remade in 1953 as *The Clown* and in 1979) ★★★½ VHS: $14.99

Champion

(1949, 90 min, US, Mark Robson) *Kirk Douglas, Arthur Kennedy, Marilyn Maxwell, Ruth Roman.* Hard-nosed boxing tale without *Rocky* schmaltz

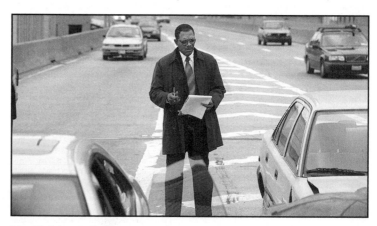

Samuel L. Jackson in *Changing Lanes*

about a nasty fighter (Douglas) who sacrifices everything as he punches his way to the top. Douglas gives an exceptional performance as the would-be champ. ★★★½ DVD: $14.99, VHS: $14.99

Chan Is Missing

(1982, 80 min, US, Wayne Wang) *Wood Moy, Marc Hayashi.* Wang's first feature film was shot in the director's hometown of San Francisco for a mere $20,000. The film follows the wanderings of a middle-aged cab driver and his wise-cracking nephew as they search all over Chinatown for Chan — who has mysteriously disappeared with the $2,000 meant to buy their taxi permit. A sophisticated statement about the trials and tribulations of ethnic assimilation. ★★★½ VHS: $79.99

Chances Are

(1989, 108 min, US, Emile Ardolino) *Robert Downey, Jr., Cybill Shepherd, Mary Stuart Masterson, Ryan O'Neal.* A routine "switch" comedy saved by Downey's charming performance. The spirit of Shepherd's deceased husband turns up in her daughter's boyfriend (Downey). With Masterson and O'Neal as the confused partners of Downey and Shepherd. ★★ DVD: $29.99

Chanel Solitaire

(1981, 120 min, France, George Kaczender) *Karen Black, Rutger Hauer, Marie-France Pisier, Timothy Dalton.* This melodramatic biopic stars Pisier as Coco Chanel, the famous couturiere who overcame a poor childhood to conquer Paris and the world with her fabulous designs. (Filmed in English) ★★ VHS: $19.99

Chang

(1927, 67 min, US, Ernest B. Schoedsack & Merian C. Cooper) Remastered from an original negative, this entertaining and exciting documentary/fiction film was shot entirely in the jungles of Siam. The story follows a native family who lives in a treehouse on the edge of the dark, potentially dangerous jungle. The film depicts their everyday routine of farming, hunting and family life, until disaster strikes when a spectacularly filmed elephant stampede overruns their village. A tender tale of survival that features a new musical score by composer Bruce Gaston. ★★★ VHS: $39.99

The Changeling

(1979, 109 min, Canada, Peter Medak) *George C. Scott, Melvyn Douglas, Trish Van Devere.* Creepy and very effective ghost story/murder mystery about a composer (Scott) whose recent loss of wife and daughter make him receptive to the hauntings of a murdered child. You would never think a wheelchair could be so frightening. ★★★ DVD: $14.99, VHS: $9.99

Changing Lanes

(2002, 98 min, US, Roger Michell) *Ben Affleck, Samuel L. Jackson, Toni Collette, Sydney Pollack, William Hurt, Amanda Peet.* A searing melodrama set on and off the busy lanes of Manhattan's FDR Drive isn't exactly the kind of film one would expect from the director of such stately British films as *Persuasion* and *Notting Hill.* But that is exactly what you get with director Michell's taut, smart *Changing Lanes,* that's part thriller and part morality tale. Jackson plays a father fighting for custody of his sons. Affleck is a hotshot lawyer whose latest case is nearing an important deadline. When these men collide on the FDR, a torturous game of one-upmanship begins a dangerous spiral as each tries to outdo the other in acts of revenge. That there is no hero or villain in the piece

— only well-shaded characters caught in an out-of-control maelstrom of rage — speaks volumes of director Michell's attention to character, rather than resorting to elements of Hollywood cliché. His pacing is swift, but it is the protagonists' thoughts as well as actions that make *Changing Lanes* move. Jackson and Affleck (who thankfully abandons his frat-boy persona) are both first-rate, carefully creating dimensional beings trapped by their own emotions. ★★★ DVD Letterbox: $14.99, VHS: $9.99

Chaos

(1999, 90 min, Japan, Hideo Nakata) *Masato Hagiwara, Ken Mitsuishi.* Invoking the spirit of Hitchcock with more of a haunting restraint, Nakata helms this stunning addition to the crime thriller genre. *Chaos's* narrative of time jumps and mind-bending plot twists tells the story of an amateur kidnapper whose sadistic aggressiveness with his captive leads to dire consequences. Yet this cryptic, labyrinthine puzzler carefully reveals how all is not what it seems in the world of these characters. Nakata is crafty with the way he plays with audience expectations, defying genre conventions while borrowing from their best elements. A film of eerie unpredictability and intelligence, *Chaos* drives a knife into the chest of the typical mystery movie. (Japanese with English subtitles) ★★★½ DVD Subtitled: $29.99, VHS Subtitled: $24.99

Chaplin

(1992, 140 min, US/GB, Richard Attenborough) *Robert Downey, Jr., Dan Aykroyd, Kevin Kline, Geraldine Chaplin, Anthony Hopkins, Diane Lane, Penelope Ann Miller, Marisa Tomei, James Woods.* Director Attenborough's biopic of Charlie Chaplin aspires towards the sweep of his many epics and, while it's fine for the bigger scenes, it leaves the smaller, more personal moments lacking emotion. As Chaplin, Downey dons astonishingly accurate movements, gestures and expressions (and received an Oscar nomination for it), but never really gets into Chaplin's mind or soul. The story covers Chaplin's poor childhood in England to his arrival in America and eventual stardom and the many ups and downs throughout his career. Geraldine Chaplin plays her own grandmother, Charlie's mentally unstable mom. ★★½ DVD Letterbox: $14.99, VHS: $9.99, VHS Letterbox: $14.99

Character

(1997, 114 min, Netherlands, Mike van Diem) *Jan Decleir, Fedja van Huet, Betty Schuurman, Tamar Van Den Dop, Victor Low, Hans Kesting.* This outstanding, Oscar-winning period drama about a son in 1920s Rotterdam trying to reconcile his relationship with his abusive father is eerily compelling. The film opens with the murder of Dreverhaven (Decleir), but the story is more of a whydunnit than a whodunnit. Flashbacks reveal the hateful Dreverhaven as a powerful, controlling man who is feared by all and loved by none. His illegitimate son Katadreuffe (van Huet) is the most likely suspect, as he has spent his entire life trying to get out from under his father's oppressive thumb. Van Diem has crafted a highly stylized, emotional film, with a mesmerizing look: the chiaroscuro lighting, the roving camera and the period detail all contribute to the film's beautiful but stark atmosphere. Likewise the full-bodied performance by Decleir is well balanced by van Huet's reluctant hero. (Dutch with English subtitles) ★★★★ DVD Letterbox: $29.99

Charade

(1963, 114 min, US, Stanley Donen) *Cary Grant, Audrey Hepburn, Walter Matthau, James Coburn,*

George Kennedy. The ever radiant Hepburn and the dapper Grant star in this delightfully comic ode to Hitchcock. The recently widowed Hepburn finds herself terrorized by the gang of her late husband's ex-associates all bent on finding his missing fortune. Not knowing where to turn, she seeks safety with Grant, but is he all he's cracked up to be? A twisting tale of intrigue. (Remade in 2002 as *The Truth about Charlie*) ★★★½ DVD Letterbox Criterion Collection (Single-Disc Edition): $39.99

The Charge of the Light Brigade

(1936, 116 min, US, Michael Curtiz) *Errol Flynn, Olivia de Havilland, David Niven, Nigel Bruce.* Rousing Flynn adventure inspired by Tennyson's poem about the famous British infantrymen fighting to the death in 19th-century India. De Havilland (who else?) plays Flynn's love interest. ★★★ VHS: $14.99

Chariots of Fire

(1981, 123 min, GB, Hugh Hudson) *Ben Cross, Ian Charleson, Ian Holm, Nigel Havers, Dennis Christopher, John Gielgud, Alice Krige, Brad Davis.* This occasionally heavy-handed portrait of the passionate careers of British track stars Eric Liddell and Harold Abrahams is nonetheless an elegant and poignant drama about religious and social differences in the England of 1924. The stories of Lidell, a deeply religious Scotsman, and Abrahams, one of the first Jews to attend Cambridge, unfold with a depth and grace that made this film a rousing international success. Academy Award winner for Best Picture. ★★★½

Charleen/Backyard

(1978/1976, 59/40 min, US, Ross McElwee) Die-hard fans of director McElwee (*Sherman's March*) should appreciate these two early documentaries focusing on his friends and family in North Carolina. *Charleen* (1978) is a personal portrait of a chatty, and, at times, remarkable woman who teaches poetry to poor children and who had befriended Ezra Pound and e.e. cummings. *Backyard* (1976) chronicles the minidramas of McElwee's friends, family and their (indentured?) household staff back in Charlotte, North Carolina. Mildly interesting stuff. ★★ VHS: $29.99

The Charles Bukowski Tapes

(1987, 240 min, US, Barbet Schroeder) *Charles Bukowski.* Bukowski, the grizzled, drunken Beat poet whose writings ("Barfly," "Tales of Ordinary Madness") as well as his own life reflect the tragic beauty and painful loneliness of the "defeated, demented and damned," is profiled in this stimulating documentary/interview. Broken up in numerous segments, the film lets Bukowski ramble on, usually tanked up on beer or wine, about everything: his travels throughout the seedy terrain of American cities, the forces behind creativity, sleazy sex, even the pleasures of pollution. Whether in his rundown L.A. home or in his old childhood home, Bukowski proves to be both a pontificating drunk and a chronicler of the losers as well as a fascinating if self-indulgent philosopher — an American original. ★★★★

Charles et Lucie

(1979, 96 min, France, Nelly Kaplan) *Daniel Ceccaldi, Ginette Garcin.* This Gallic comedy is the rags-to-riches-to-rags story of a poor Parisian couple who find that they have inherited a beautiful mansion on the Riviera. The only catch is that they must sell all their furniture in order to pay the lawyer fees. But sell they do, as they go driving off to the Riviera with their dreams of riches. The couple confront a

Cate Blanchett in *Charlotte Gray*

series of adventures that rekindle their love and taste for living. A delightfully refreshing love story. (French with English subtitles) ★★★½

Charlie's Angels

(2000, 95 min, US, McG) *Cameron Diaz, Drew Barrymore, Lucy Liu, Bill Murray, Sam Rockwell, Tim Curry, Kelly Lynch, Crispin Glover, Matt LeBlanc, LL Cool J, Tom Green, Luke Wilson, John Forsythe.* Or, *The Powerpuff Girls: 20 Years Later.* Except for that omnipresent speakerphone, you'd never know this was based on the TV show, and unlike the many TV adaptation bombs, *Charlie's Angels* is remarkably unforced and damn fun. Hey, you've got Cameron Diaz dancing in her Underoos, why not let the scene linger a little? The sweet ditzy blonde (Diaz), the bad red-headed grrl (Barrymore) and the brainy brunette (Liu) all know how to use their hair and their kung-fu to fight crime on behalf of benevolent Charlie. They get Hong Kong-style showdowns with plenty of wirework in a serviceable and self-aware plot that doesn't get in the way of the girl power and T&A. McG knows it's cheesy, but the Angels don't, and that makes them even more charming. An infectious if lightweight delight. (Sequel: *Charlie's Angels: Full Throttle*) ★★★ DVD 2-disc Superbit Deluxe: $19.99, VHS: $14.99

Charlie's Angels: Full Throttle

(2003, 105 min, US, McG) *Cameron Diaz, Drew Barrymore, Lucy Liu, Demi Moore, Bernie Mac, Crispin Glover, Justin Theroux, Robert Patrick.* The girls are back in a sequel that can only be termed lackluster, despite a pace that makes the first film look like Tarkovsky at his most contemplative. Moore is the villainess this time, portraying a rogue ex-Angel who wants to sell a list of Witness Protection Program names to a gallery of baddies. While there's tons of action and teasing shots of the three leads, *Full Throttle* is mostly bland and lifeless. It begins amusingly enough — but when everything is absurd, there's no resemblance to real-life motivations or even rudimentary physics, the film just becomes a flurry of images taking up space on the screen.

Glover shows up for a fun but all-too-brief supporting role, and there are one or two funny cameos. Bill Murray, however, is sorely missed, especially when he's been replaced by the unfunny (at least in this film) Mac. The Angels themselves are oddly unappealing this time around. ★½ DVD Letterbox Unrated: $19.99, DVD Pan & Scan PG-13 Rated: $19.99, VHS Unrated: $14.99

Charlotte Gray

(2001, 121 min, Australia/GB, Gillian Armstrong) *Cate Blanchett, Billy Crudup, Michael Gambon, Rupert Penry-Jones, James Fleet.* The extraordinary bravery of Resistance fighters during World War II would be a great subject for almost any movie. The daily heroism and near-death adventures of the survivors, the sacrifice of those killed, would be testament to all who served. Charlotte Gray, heroine of this adaptation of Sebastian Faulks' novel, displays such courage. But unfortunately, the film that honors her — and in essence all the women who risked their lives — is slow moving, clichéd, and lacking in lyricism or intrigue. Not that this should be needlessly romanticized, but it should be at least interesting. Blanchett tries her best as Charlotte, a Scotswoman who joins Britain's Special Operations corps as a spy after her RAF boyfriend is shot down over France. She parachutes into occupied territory, participating in raids and acts of sabotage against Vichy and the Nazis. She also falls for the group's leader (Crudup). Charlotte is a heroic figure, but the film doesn't allow her much heroics; instead she is trapped in a predictable romance, and her guerrilla fighting becomes an afterthought. Not a good place to go for a story of a Resistance fighter. ★★ DVD: $14.99, VHS: $14.99

Charlotte Sometimes

(2003, 85 min, US, Eric Byler) *Jacqueline Kim, Eugenia Yuan, Matt Westmore, Michael Idemoto, Shizuko Hoshi, Kimberly-Rose Wolter.* A handsome, intelligent, but withdrawn young man secretly yearns for his sexy tenant, who lives next door. On an almost nightly basis, he listens to her and her boyfriend have raucous sex, then dutifully lets her in to hang out platonically with him when her boyfriend goes to sleep. This frustrating routine is broken when he begins a relationship with a beautiful and alluring stranger, but his friendship with his tenant may be destroyed because of it. Good, realistic, satisfying drama is filled with a lot of truth, many telling details, and excellent performances by everyone. A bit pat at times, a little too vague at others, *Charlotte* is mostly an affecting, warm but levelheaded and believable slice of life. ★★★ DVD Letterbox: $24.99, VHS: $59.99

Charlotte's Web

(1973, 94 min, US, Charles A. Nichols) *Voices of: Debbie Reynolds, Henry Gibson, Paul Lynde, Charles Nelson Reilly.* Captivating animated feature based on the writings of E.B. White, centering on the friendship of a spider and a pig. ★★★ DVD Letterbox: $19.99, DVD Pan & Scan: $19.99, VHS: $9.99

Charming Billy

(1998, 80 min, US, William R. Pace) *Michael Hayden, Sally Murphy, Chelcie Ross.* Director Pace has fashioned an understated yet profoundly disturbing psychological portrait of a quiet, nondescript Everyman who sinks under the weight of life's daily banalities with most tragic results. There's a palpable undercurrent of terror as beleaguered Billy disconnects. He's less and less able to handle the unceasing commonplace, petty harassments that beset us all. As the pressure builds, Billy finally frees himself — gun

in hand — atop a water tower in an endless stretch of Midwestern farmland. *Charming Billy* is an unnerving and intriguing exploration of numbing alienation. ★★★ DVD: $9.99, VHS: $9.99

The Chase

(1966, 135 min, US, Arthur Penn) *Marlon Brando, Jane Fonda, Robert Redford, Angie Dickinson, James Fox, Janice Rule, Robert Duvall.* Redford is an escaped prisoner who returns to his small Texas town, stirring up both trouble and passions. Brando is the sheriff, and Fonda the old girlfriend. Screenplay by Lillian Hellman, based on Horton Foote's novel. Though there's a lot of talent involved here, this notoriously troubled production suffers from too many chiefs (producer Sam Spiegel's constant interference); however, there are some interesting moments. ★★½ DVD: $24.99

The Chase

(1994, 87 min, US, Adam Rifkin) *Charlie Sheen, Christy Swanson, Ray Wise, Cary Elwes, Henry Rollins.* When not dwelling on the sappy romance at its core, *The Chase* is almost remarkable in its skewering of the feeding frenzy network news has become. Sheen stars as a wrongly accused fugitive who accidentally takes a millionaire's daughter (Swanson) hostage, thereby setting off a high-speed run for the border — with full media circus in tow. Rifkin's satire mixes hip, self-assured MTV-style photography with dead-on lampoons of media-ocrity to create an alternately appealing comedy. ★★½ VHS: $9.99

Chasers

(1994, 102 min, US, Dennis Hopper) *Tom Berenger, William McNamara, Dennis Hopper, Dean Stockwell, Gary Busey, Crispin Glover.* McNamara plays a wise-cracking naval officer who gets paired up with a tough sergeant (Berenger) in order to escort a "sexy and sassy" prisoner (Eleniak) in this *Last Detail* rip-off. If you used your imagination to predict wild and wacky misadventures for the three to encounter, you'd be doing more than the screenwriters. With this cast you'd think there would be something of interest here. This film does prove one positive thing: Hopper must have a lot of devoted friends. ★ DVD: $9.99, VHS: $9.99

Chasing Amy

(1997, 105 min, US, Kevin Smith) *Ben Affleck, Joey Lauren Adams, Jason Lee, Dwight Ewell, Jason Mewes, Kevin Smith, Matt Damon.* Making a hyperspace jump from his previous two efforts, writer-director Smith has fashioned a very funny, insightful and painfully honest romantic comedy for the '90s. Affleck plays a popular comic book artist who befriends Amy (Adams), a lesbian, at a comic book convention. Their friendship develops, but he finally breaks down and confesses his love for her. At first angry, she soon declares similar feelings and they begin a relationship. That is, until he discovers her sordid, straight past, which he can't stop obsessing over. An accomplished, enjoyable movie which accurately pokes fun at a variety of modern relationships (straight, gay and bi) and even manages a few honest tear-jerking sequences. Lee has also come a long way from *Mallrats*, bringing humor and texture to the role of the "other man." ★★★½ DVD Criterion Collection: $19.99, VHS: $9.99

Chasing Sleep

(2000, 104 min, US, Michael Walker) *Jeff Daniels, Emily Bergl, Gil Bellows.* Daniels gives one of his best performances in this creepy psychological thriller/mood piece. He plays an extremely unhappily married professor who wakes up one morning to find his wife hasn't come home from her job. The tension slowly builds as the police and his wife's lover begin to suspect that Daniels did her in, and Daniels himself begins to hallucinate. Unsettling and a bit depressing, *Chasing Sleep* never quite achieves the horrific paranoia and insanity that Poe and Polanski brought to very similar material, but it is nonetheless effectively claustrophobic and compelling. ★★★ DVD: $19.99

Le Chat (The Cat)

(1970, 88 min, France, Pierre Granier Deferre) *Simone Signoret, Jean Gabin.* Signoret and Gabin are an elderly married couple of 25 years whose early love has turned into a silent hate. Set in a decaying and soon-to-be-demolished apartment house, the film explores the relationship of the two, who have no one else and who refuse to talk to each other. The probing of the reasons for the embittered separation are acted out in this sad yet unforgettable drama. Brilliantly acted. (French with English subtitles) ★★★

The Château

(2002, 92 min, France, Jesse Peretz) *Paul Rudd, Romany Malco, Didier Flamand, Sylvie Testud.* Two American brothers — Graham, goofy, inept and white, and Allen, hip, suave and black — come to France to check out their newly inherited château. They soon learn that they have also inherited crumbling masonry, massive debt and a quartet of servants who have no intention of going anywhere. As Graham, Rudd is a marvel of misdirected good intention. Malco as Allen, who wants to be called Rex, is at first all business, wanting only a quick sale of the property and a hasty exit with the resulting profits. But the servants have other plans and unlimited resourcefulness in sabotaging all attempts to sell their longtime home. *The Château* moves from broad, absurdist comedy to moments of touching vulnerability and revelation, serving up delectable offerings of deception, cover-up, and double-and triple-crosses. (In English and French with English subtitles) ★★★½ DVD Dual: $14.99, VHS: $49.99

Chattahoochee

(1990, 98 min, US, Mick Jackson) *Gary Oldman, Dennis Hopper, Frances McDormand, Pamela Reed.* When a Korean War veteran (Oldman) disrupts life in his sleepy, small Florida town by firing off a barrage of ammunition in a clumsy attempt to get himself killed, he's promptly shipped off to an asylum that makes *The Snake Pit* look like a politician's prison. Oldman is remarkable as the incarcerated vet who rediscovers himself as he opposes the insanity of the institution that confines him. ★★★ DVD Dual: $14.99

The Cheap Detective

(1978, 92 min, US, Robert Moore) *Peter Falk, Eileen Brennan, Ann-Margret, Madeline Kahn, Dom DeLuise, Stockard Channing, James Coco, Sid Caesar, Phil Silvers.* There are lots of laughs in Neil Simon's follow-up to *Murder by Death.* Falk stars in this private-eye parody, *The Maltese Falcon* in particular, ably assisted by a great comic cast. Who cares if some of the jokes are forced; the film is in good humor and what a cast! ★★★ DVD: $19.99

Cheaper by the Dozen

(1950, 85 min, US, Walter Lang) *Clifton Webb, Myrna Loy, Jeanne Crain.* Webb is well cast in this charmingly sweet comedy as an efficiency expert and father of twelve. The ever-classy Loy is his wife, who really keeps the household going. (Remade in 2003) (Sequel: *Belles on Their Toes*) ★★★ DVD: $14.99

The Cheat

(1915, 59 min, US, Cecil B. DeMille) *Sessue Hayakawa, Fannie Ward.* Racist — racy — deMille at his best, before his bombast interfered with his pandering to his middle-class clientele. A vivacious socialite becomes the Occidental tourist when she loses the community chest fund in a bad stock deal. Salvation comes in the form of a wily, Asian gentleman who prefers to take his interest out in trade, branding her — literally — a scarlet woman. Hayakawa gives a wonderfully modulated performance, his Zenlike calm evoking still waters against the raging torrents of stock company histrionics. Also: *A Girl's Folly* (1917, 30 min, US, Maurice Tourneur), a behind-the-scenes look at the day-by-day workings of a film studio. A gentle satire of a nascent industry, the film is alive with warmth and it is that which survives the intervening decades. ★★★½ DVD: $29.99, VHS: $29.99

Checking Out

(1989, 90 min, US, David Leland) *Jeff Daniels, Melanie Mayron, Michael Tucker.* Hypochondriac Daniels thinks he's going to die — after 15 minutes, you wish he would. Disappointing comedy wastes its intriguing premise. You know you're in trouble when the film's best joke is "Why don't Italians barbeque?" (Because the spaghetti falls through the grill.) ★ DVD: $14.99

Cheech & Chong's Next Movie

(1980, 99 min, US, Tommy Chong) *Cheech Marin, Tommy Chong, Evelyn Guerrero, Edie McClurg, Paul Reubens, Phil Hartman.* Cheech and Chong appear in the follow-up to their hit *Up in Smoke*, with lots more dope jokes. The duo hit the road for a series of rather crude adventures, which are only intermittently amusing. Not nearly as funny as *Smoke*. ★★ DVD Letterbox: $19.99, VHS: $9.99

A Chef in Love

(1996, 98 min, France/Georgia, Nana Dzhordzadze) *Pierre Richard, Nino Kirtadze.* This amusing but ultimately meandering yarn makes a trek through the Caucuses circa the 1920s on the heels of a happy-go-lucky French chef known as Pascal Ichak (Richard). The film begins in a 1990s Paris art gallery, where a young Franco-Georgian is preparing an exhibit of the Georgian painter Niko Pirosmani. He is introduced to a mysterious woman who claims he has papers written by his mother that she would like him to translate. This precipitates a series of flashbacks describing his mother's pre-Communist jaunt through the Georgian countryside as Ichak's lover and confidant. Richard is a pleasure to watch, and his sexual chemistry with Kirtadze is surprisingly easygoing and believable. But none of this can overcome the film's rambling lack of focus as it tries to be both uplifting tale of culinary and lustful delight and cautionary tome on the evils of armed revolution. (French and Georgian with English subtitles) ★★

Chelsea Walls

(2002, 109 min, US, Ethan Hawke) *Uma Thurman, Rosario Dawson, Vincent D'Onofrio, Kris Kristofferson, Tuesday Weld, Natasha Richardson, Steve Zahn, Robert Sean Leonard, Frank Whaley, Isaac Hayes, Christopher Walken.* A good cast cannot save this self-indulgent, uninvolving and frequently annoying directorial debut by Hawke. *Chelsea Walls*, adapted by Nicole Burdette and based on her stage play, looks at a collection of aspiring artists, musicians, junkies and oddballs who make up the guests staying at the once-great Chelsea Hotel, which was the homestead for many '60s and '70s icons. Unfortunately, the mighty building is now a shadow of its former self, and the current crop of wannabes struggle to find inspiration there while going through rather dull personal problems. This could've made a decent short, but at nearly two hours, and with nary a character to really care about, this becomes deadening rather quickly. ★½ DVD Letterbox: $14.99

Cherry Falls

(2000, 92 min, US, Geoffrey Wright) *Brittany Murphy, Michael Biehn, Jay Mohr.* A neat, witty inversion of the usual slasher film cliché: In the small town of Cherry Falls, a serial killer appears to be targeting a very specific demographic — virgins. The town's sexually inexperienced teens then schedule a sex party, all in the name of self-preservation. *Cherry Falls* is an accomplished mix of black humor, satire and horror, making it a better-than-average slasher, with muscular direction from Wright, good performances by Biehn and Murphy, and a terrifically funny/brutal wrap-up at the aforementioned party. Don't be put off by the fact that this went straight to video; *Cherry Falls* is the real deal. ★★★

Cherry, Harry & Raquel

(1969, 71 min, US, Russ Meyer) *Uschi Digard, Astrid Lillimor, Linda Ashton, Charles Napier.* Set in a dusty Arizona border town, *Cherry, Harry and Raquel* depicts double-crossing drug smugglers involved in power struggles, interspersed with various sexual encounters both lesbian and heterosexual. ★★ DVD: $39.99

Cherry 2000

(1988, 93 min, US, Steve DeJarnatt) *Melanie Griffith, Ben Johnson, Harry Carey, Jr., Tim Thomerson.* Futuristic, post-apocalyptic adventure with Griffith as a mercenary who helps a husband looking for the prototype of his robot-wife — stored in a factory located in a forbidden zone. An enjoyable sci-fi outing that wants to please, and for the most part succeeds. ★★½ DVD: $14.99

La Chèvre

(1981, 91 min, France, Francis Veber) *Gérard Depardieu, Pierre Richard.* Richard and Depardieu, the hilarious sleuthing duo of *Les Compares*, are reunited in this "prequel." Private-eye Depardieu reluctantly teams up with the bungling Richard as they travel to Mexico to find a missing woman. What follows is a series of misadventures of epic proportions. The stone-faced Depardieu is surprisingly delightful as the straight man to Richard's never-ending encounters with slamming doors, crashing planes and even lethal drinking straws in this comedy for all ages. (American remake: *Pure Luck*) (French with English subtitles) ★★★ DVD: $29.99, VHS: $24.99

Cheyenne Autumn

(1964, 158 min, US, John Ford) *Richard Widmark, Carol Baker, Karl Malden, Edward G. Robinson, James Stewart, Sal Mineo.* Ford's last western is a sprawling account of the Cheyenne Nation's 1,500-mile journey from the arid Southwest to their northern homeland. Ford depicts multiple aspects of the story: the influence of land speculators in Washington, sensationalization by the press, the varying attitudes of Army personnel, and the overwhelming hardships of the Cheyenne. Fine performances throughout. Shot in 70mm, the visual impact of the landscapes is retained on the small screen. Note: The Dodge City sequence, with a very funny James Stewart, was cut after first release; it's restored on video. ★★★ VHS: $19.99

The Cheyenne Social Club

(1970, 103 min, US, Gene Kelly) *Henry Fonda, James Stewart, Shirley Jones.* Fonda and Stewart dusted off their spurs to team together in this appealing though formula western comedy with the two Hollywood legends playing aging cowpokes who hang their hats at a new home — Stewart's newly acquired bordello. Jones runs the place. ★★½ VHS: $9.99

Chicago

(2002, 113 min, US, Rob Marshall) *Renée Zellweger, Catherine Zeta-Jones, Richard Gere, Queen Latifah, John C. Reilly, Christine Baranski, Taye Diggs.* "Give 'em the old razzle-dazzle" sings lawyer Billy Flynn (Gere) in one of the many splashy production numbers in this rollicking screen version of the Broadway musical. That advice is taken to heart by director Marshall in adapting the Kander & Ebb tuner (which was originally staged by Bob Fosse in 1975), for *Chicago* is a dazzling display of music, editing, dance and technique. A cynical contemplation of celebrity and crime, the story follows Roxie Hart (marvelously played by Zellweger), who murders her lover and finds in prison the fame that had eluded her in life. With this notoriety comes high-profile attorney Flynn to defend her, and an almost-friendly rivalry with fellow murderess/prisoner Velma Kelly (Oscar winner Zeta-Jones), herself looking for legal, though not necessarily moral, salvation. In adapting the screenplay, writer Bill Condon has reduced Velma to a supporting character, cut songs, and the revuelike musical numbers are now part of Roxie's fantasy life.

Chicago

112

But, damn if it all doesn't work. Director Marshall, whose staging and editing recall Fosse's own *Cabaret* at times, has created a razzle-dazzle tour de force — a pulsating, foot-tapping, scintillating masterwork of song, dance and all that jazz. Winner of 6 Academy Awards, including Best Picture. ★★★★ DVD: $29.99, VHS: $24.99

Chicken Run

(2000, 84 min, US, Nick Park & Peter Lord) *Voices of: Mel Gibson, Miranda Richardson, Julia Sawalha.* Masters of the claymation short Park and Lord (from Aardman studios, home of "Wallace & Gromit") find none of their whimsy diluted in their first full-length entry. The plot is an homage/take-off of prisoncamp movies, from *The Great Escape* to *Stalag 13*, that will literally fly over the heads of rapt youngsters who are just in it for the chickens. Ginger (voiced by Sawalha) is a headstrong hen on evil Mrs. Tweedy's farm, whose plots to escape become more urgent upon the arrival of an on-site chicken pie factory. Enter American flyboy rooster Rocky (Gibson), who can teach them to fly the coop (he hopes). Richly detailed, *Chicken Run* is grand entertainment that invites repeat viewing for all ages. ★★★★ DVD: $19.99, VHS: $9.99

Un Chien Andalou / Land without Bread

(1928, 17/45 min, France/Spain, Luis Buñuel & Salvador Dalí) Beginning with a pristine copy of *Un Chien Andalou*, this video of two of Buñuel's earliest works also includes his documentary on the unbelievably impoverished Spanish region of Hurdanos. Told with English narration, this moving and sad account of these stoic people is an unusual departure for Buñuel, for he forsakes his trademark humor and surrealism and instead takes the job of a social realist as he photographs the parched, mountainous area and films the people in their medieval-like towns, virtually untouched by the wealth and conveniences offered in the 20th century. An unrelenting and somber portrait of a people and one that was immediately banned by the Franco government. ★★★★ VHS: $24.99

La Chienne

(1931, 100 min, France, Jean Renoir) *Michel Simon, Janie Mareze.* This somber, naturalistic melodrama, whose surprisingly modern theme of sexual obsession and violence created tremendous controversy when first released in France, did not receive its American premiere until 1976. Realistically filmed on the noisy streets of Montmartre, this story of uncontrolled passion is about an unhappily married clerk (Simon) who falls in love with a prostitute, steals for her, then, in a fit of rage, murders her and keeps quiet while her pimp goes to the guillotine. Reportedly, the film's producer vainly attempted to reedit the film; Renoir regained control. (American remake: *Scarlet Street*) (French with English subtitles) ★★★½ VHS: $24.99

A Child Is Waiting

(1962, 102 min, US, John Cassavetes) *Judy Garland, Burt Lancaster, Gena Rowlands.* Garland is splendid in this poignant tale of a sympathetic woman's relationship with a mentally retarded boy. *A Child Is Waiting* pulls no punches in portraying the inadequacy and frustration teachers feel in trying to reach the youngsters, and the guilt parents bear in surrendering their children to mental hospitals. Most touching of all, though, are the performances of the children; they are joyous and innocent, and truly in the heart of everyone they touch. ★★★

Child's Play

(1988, 87 min, US, Tom Holland) *Catherine Hicks, Chris Sarandon, Alex Vincent, Brad Dourif.* Chucky is a popular talking doll, sweet as peaches and cream (and a complexion to match). That is until one of the dolls is possessed by the spirit of a murderer; then little Chucky is spewing forth naughty words and hacking people to death. Unchallenging, silly and slickly made, it does manage to produce a few chills. (Followed by 4 sequels) ★★½ DVD: $14.99, VHS: $9.99

Child's Play 2

(1990, 85 min, US, John Lafia) *Alex Vincent, Jenny Agutter, Gerrit Graham, Grace Zabriskie.* Chucky's back, and this time he's powered by an even more insidious force: capitalism! Chucky tries to take possession of young Andy's body once again, lest he remain in the valley of the dolls forever. Enter Zabriskie as a child welfare worker who won't believe Andy's "boy who cried doll" stories. A bad *Fatal Attraction* for the preschool set. ★ DVD: $14.99, VHS: $19.99

The Children Are Watching Us (I Bambini Ci Guardano)

(1942, 89 min, Italy, Vittorio De Sica) *Luciano de Ambrosis, Isa Pola.* One of De Sica's most heartrending films as well as an unusually critical look at Mussolini's Italy. The story focuses on the effects that a marital breakup and a suicide have on a lonely and unwanted four-year-old boy. A sad and touching story from the master of Italian neorealism. (Italian with English subtitles) ★★★½ VHS: $29.99

Children of a Lesser God

(1986, 119 min, US, Randa Haines) *Marlee Matlin, William Hurt, Piper Laurie, Philip Bosco.* Matlin won an Oscar for her immensely moving portrait of an embittered deaf woman reluctant to commit herself to a relationship. Hurt is equally as compelling as the idealist special education teacher who falls in love with her. ★★★ DVD: $14.99, VHS: $14.99

Children of Heaven

(1998, 88 min, Iran, Majid Majidi) *Mohammad Amir Naji, Mir Farrakh Hashemian, Bahareh Seddiqi.* A simple but outstanding film, *Children of Heaven* — like *The White Balloon* before it — shows life in a very foreign country through the eyes of a child. Ali (Hashemian) is a nine-year-old boy who loses his sister Zara's sneakers on the way home from the repair shop. Rather than incur their poor father's wrath, they agree to share Ali's shoes to get to and from school. This arrangement soon causes both children grief. The solution to their problem comes in the form of a race, which Ali enters, hoping to win the third place prize — a new pair of sneakers. A deserved Academy Award nominee for Best Foreign-Language Film, *Children of Heaven* features heartbreaking performances by the two children. (Farsi with English subtitles) ★★★★ DVD: $14.99, VHS: $9.99

Children of Nature

(1991, 85 min, Iceland, Fridrik Thor Fridriksson) *Gisli Halldorsson, Sigridur Hagalin, Bruno Ganz.*

Un Chien Andalou

Nominated for a Best Foreign Film Oscar, this lushly photographed and deliberately paced film follows the odyssey of a man nearing the end of his life. After an uncomfortable attempt at living with his daughter and her family, he enters a nursing home, where he meets a woman he knew in his youth. Her fiesty exuberance compliments his stoic strength; their shared desire for independence unites them in a journey of adventure and discovery. These two protagonists are portrayed with warmth and gentle vigor in a film peppered with telling moments of quiet revelation. A lyrical meditation on humankind's relationship with nature and society. (Icelandic with English subtitles) ★★★ VHS: $19.99

Children of Paradise
(Les Enfants du Paradis)

(1945, 189 min, France, Marcel Carné) *Jean-Louis Barrault, Arletty, Pierre Brasseur.* Considered by many to be one of the greatest films ever made, this intensely romantic melodrama wonderfully re-creates the teeming excitement of the early 1800s — both for the French theatre as well as Paris' *Boulevard du Crime.* In a complicated series of events, the film follows the interlocking fates of four central characters: Frederick (Brasseau), a haughty actor who communicates through words; Baptiste (Barrault), a sensitive pantomimist; Garance (Arletty), an elusive, glamorous woman of easy virtue who stands between them and the fourth character, a murderous thief. Using the theatre as a metaphor for life, the Jacques Prévert-scripted story is a richly entertaining, immense masterpiece of postwar cinema. (French with English subtitles) ★★★★ DVD Criterion Collection: $39.99, VHS: $29.99

Children of the Corn

(1984, 93 min, US, Fritz Kiersch) *Peter Horton, Linda Hamilton, R.G. Armstrong.* Silly Stephen King horror story about a young couple who arrive in a small Iowa town controlled by demonic children. (Followed by six atrocious sequels) ★ DVD: $14.99, VHS: $9.99

Children of the Revolution

(1997, 102 min, Australia, Peter Duncan) *Judy Davis, Geoffrey Rush, Sam Neill, F. Murray Abraham, Richard Roxburgh, Rachel Griffiths.* A boisterous political farce/satire that supposes what might become of Joseph Stalin's illegitimate son if he were raised by an ardent Communist mom in middle-class Australia. Davis is in top form as Joan Fraser, a vociferous 1950s era radical who writes love letters to "Uncle Joe." The aging and lonely Stalin (Abraham) catches wind of her ardor and invites her to the Kremlin for a bit of a dialectical frolic. The rest, as they say, is history. Davis returns to Oz pregnant, but is the child Stalin's or that of

Australian double agent spy Neill? Writer-director Duncan takes his narrative over the top with conviction and gusto, making *Children of the Revolution* a capricious and thoroughly agreeable romp through a mock history as seen through a fun house mirror. ★★★½ DVD: $19.99, VHS: $9.99

Children Shouldn't
Play with Dead Things

(1972, 85 min, US, Benjamin [Bob] Clark) *Alan Ormsby, Anya Ormsby, Jane Daly.* Cheapie horror film (from the director of *Porky's*, no less) about young film students making a movie in a graveyard and resurrecting the dead. Eeek. ★½

The Children's Hour

(1961, 108 min, US, William Wyler) *Shirley MacLaine, Audrey Hepburn, James Garner, Miriam Hopkins, Veronica Cartwright.* Wyler's compelling though stagey second treatment of Lillian Hellman's play (1936's *These Three* was the first) tells of the devastating effects of gossip and scandalous rumors about two women. Hepburn and MacLaine are teachers at an all-girls' boarding school. When a vindictive little girl accuses the two of having an affair, their lives (and their careers) are ruined after a self-righteous community believes the unsubstantial allegations (shades of McCarthyism!). However, the rumor also forces MacLaine to come to terms with her closeted lesbian feelings. Attempting to right the wrong of his original film, which was not allowed to discuss the theme of lesbianism, Wyler rather flimsily addresses it here. ★★½ DVD: $19.99

Chill Factor

(1999, 102 min, US, Hugh Johnson) *Cuba Gooding, Jr., Skeet Ulrich, Peter Firth, David Paymer, Kevin J. O'Connor.* Military scientist Paymer is developing a new chemical weapon that becomes colossally deadly when its temperature drops below 50 degrees. A major accident occurs (of course) and many soldiers are killed, but since Paymer is valuable to the military, the conscientious colonel of the mission is the fall guy. Ten years later, he is released from prison with revenge in mind. It's up to ice-cream truck driver Gooding and night clerk Ulrich to put a stop to him. This *Speed* rip-off is sorta fun in a *completely* mindless, cliffhanger serial way. Gooding and Ulrich's banter becomes annoying after a while. But it's never dull, though easily forgotten ten minutes after the credits roll. ★★ DVD: $14.99, VHS: $14.99

Chilly Scenes of Winter

(1982, 99 min, US, Joan Micklin Silver) *John Heard, Mary Beth Hurt, Peter Riegert, Kenneth McMillan, Griffin Dunne.* Silver's bittersweet comedy on the trials and triumphs of love. Heard portrays the quirky but amiable civil servant whose desperate passion confuses the reluctant object of his adoration, Hurt. A warm, beguiling film on the fragile bliss of romance. ★★★½

China Girl

(1987, 88 min, US, Abel Ferrara) *James Russo, Sari Chang.* Absorbing, gritty update of "Romeo and Juliet" set in New York's Little Italy and Chinatown, with Italian Russo and Chinese Chang falling in love against a gangland backdrop. ★★★

China Moon

(1994, 99 min, US, John Bailey) *Ed Harris, Benicio del Toro, Madeleine Stowe, Charles Dance.* Q): What do you get when you mix a rich husband, a beautiful wife and a tough guy who should know better? A): This umpteenth steamy, hard-boiled film

noir *Body Heat* rip-off. Harris stars as a savvy police detective who becomes involved with rich banker's wife Stowe. When her husband (Dance) turns up dead, Harris must help her erase any clues to the crime. But is he being set up as patsy? *China Moon* has its moments, but this is mostly run of the mill material. ★★ DVD Dual: $14.99

China, My Sorrow

(1989, 86 min, China, Dai Sijie) *Guo Yiang Yi, Tieu Quan Nghieu.* A wonderful story of imprisoned men in a mountain camp for noncompliant citizens under Chairman Mao. The story follows young "Foureyes" as he is sent to the reeducation center for playing music unsuitable to a young comrade (oddly enough, the song sounds much like the patriotic tune from *Yellow Earth*). "Four-eyes" and the other undesirables are put through grueling days of hard labor and dehumanizing treatment in hopes of turning them into "good workers." The story line is deeply spiritual and the photography rivals Zhang Yimou's works. (Mandarin and Shanghaiese with English subtitles) ★★★ VHS: $29.99

China Seas

(1935, 88 min, US, Tay Garnett) *Clark Gable, Jean Harlow, Rosalind Russell, Wallace Beery, Hattie McDaniel.* A good cast highlights this box-office hit with Gable as a steamship captain — transporting a secret cargo to China — who becomes romantically involved with passengers Harlow and Russell. ★★★

The China Syndrome

(1979, 123 min, US, James Bridges) *Jane Fonda, Michael Douglas, Jack Lemmon, Wilford Brimley, Scott Brady, James Karen.* Though this nuclear thriller greatly benefitted from the timely publicity from the Three Mile Island accident, this outstanding drama would have succeeded without it. Fonda is excellent as a television reporter who inadvertently films an accident at a nuclear power plant, involving her in political intrigue. Lemmon gives a superlative portrayal of a loyal plant supervisor whose search for the truth leads to tragedy. Douglas is well cast as Fonda's radical cameraman who helps in the investigation. A tension-filled examination of corporate cover-up that is both cautionary and unrelentingly suspenseful. ★★★★ DVD: $14.99

Chinatown

(1974, 131 min, US, Roman Polanski) *Jack Nicholson, Faye Dunaway, John Huston, Perry Lopez.* A superb, Oscar-winning script and consistently outstanding peformances are supported by meticulous production values to deliver a classic tale of intrigue, conflicted loyalties, overwhelming greed and the futility of honor in a corrupt world. Nicholson plays Jake Gittes, a Los Angeles private eye called into what at first appears to be a simple case of marital infidelity. Dunaway arrives at his offices to declare that she is the real wife of the man Gittes has been paid to follow, and she has no desire to see her husband tailed. Gittes, with more curiosity than forethought, delves even deeper into the mystery; the governmental malfeasance he uncovers is child's play compared to the murky family secrets lying even deeper below. A contemporary American film classic featuring one of Nicholson's best performances. (Sequel: *The Two Jakes*) ★★★★ DVD: $14.99, VHS: $14.99, VHS Letterbox: $14.99

Chinese Boxes

(1984, 87 min, GB, Chris Petit) *Robbie Coltrane, Will Patton.* An unusual though compelling thriller about an American tourist (Patton) caught up in international intrigue in West Berlin after the death of a drug pusher. ★★½ VHS: $69.99

A Chinese Ghost Story

(1987, 95 min, Hong Kong, Siu-Tung Ching) *Leslie Cheung, Joey Wong, Ma Wu, Dawei Hu, Jin Liang.* Moving from his commercially successful martial arts flicks, director Ching has gone the way of *Ghost* with this entertaining and atmospheric supernatural love story with surprisingly impressive special effects. Set during the Ming Dynasty, the story features a wandering scholar who, while visiting a haunted temple, meets and falls in love with a glamorous female ghost. But their love is never tranquil as he soon finds that he must do battle with a hoard of hellish creatures out to end their relationship. (Cantonese with English subtitles) ★★★ DVD: $49.99, VHS: $19.99

Chinese Roulette

(1976, 86 min, West Germany, Rainer Werner Fassbinder) *Margit Carstensen, Ulli Lommel, Anna Karina, Brigitte Mira, Andrea Schober, Volker Spengler.* Set during a weekend retreat in a castle, this elegant Gothic thriller follows the consequences when a crippled girl (Schober) organizes a bizarre and fiendish truth game in order to psychologically attack her philandering parents and their respective lovers. With sweeping camera movement, lush scenery and music, this cruelly humorous melodrama is pure Fassbinder. (German with English subtitles) ★★★ DVD Subtitled: $24.99, VHS: $19.99

Chitty Chitty Bang Bang

(1968, 143 min, US, Ken Hughes) *Dick Van Dyke, Sally Ann Howes, Lionel Jeffries.* Van Dyke stars as a slightly crackpot scientist who turns an old racing car into a magical flying machine. Unmemorable songs dampen the amiable spirits of this otherwise genial children's musical, which should entertain those in the preteen years. ★★½ DVD: $14.99, DVD 2-disc Special Edition: $29.99, VHS: $9.99

Chloë in the Afternoon

(1972, 97 min, France, Eric Rohmer) *Bernard Verley, Zou Zou, Françoise Verley, Marie-Christine Barrault.* Rohmer's final entry in his series of "Moral Tales" continues with the theme of temptation met and mastered in this fascinating story of a happily married suburban man who struggles to stay faithful after he meets an unstable woman out of his past. Although constantly harboring lecherous tendencies, our chaste Don Juan must decide between fidelity and the rueful charms of Chloë, a young, attractive free spirit intent on seducing him. An elegant comedy of sexual mores. (French with English subtitles) ★★★★ DVD: $19.99, VHS: $14.99

Chocolat

(1988, 105 min, France, Claire Denis) *Mireille Perrier, Emmet Judson.* This surprisingly assured and quietly emotional film is a most impressive debut for director Denis. The story centers around a young white woman who returns to Cameroon, recalling her life there as a child of the French colonial governor. Her reminiscences — that of a young girl isolated in an exotic but foreign land — evoke the repression of the people, but focus primarily on the special relationship she had with the family's black houseboy. (French with English subtitles) ★★★ DVD Letterbox: $19.99

Chocolat

(2000, 121 min, GB, Lasse Hallström) *Juliette Binoche, Johnny Depp, Judi Dench, Alfred Molina, Lena Olin, Carrie-Anne Moss, Peter Stormare, Leslie Caron, Victoire Thivisol, John Wood.* A sweet confection whose ingredients of romantic lyricism

Juliette Binoche radiates in Lasse Hallström's *Chocolat*

and magical culinary delights provide a tasty complement to a trifling story of social oppression, *Chocolat* is a lightweight fable that charms through sheer determination. The alluring Binoche is Vianne, who arrives at a small French village and opens a chocolate shop. Vianne soon becomes embroiled in the town's political bureaucracy when she stands up to the petty-minded mayor (Molina) who wants the free-spirited entrepreneur run out of town. Binoche is captivating as the winsome Vianne, who slowly wins over many of the townspeople. Like the delicious concoctions that Vianne prepares, *Chocolat* is sure to please — just don't expect anything too filling. ★★★ DVD Collector's Edition: $19.99, VHS With Making-of Featurette: $9.99

The Chocolate War

(1988, 106 min, US, Keith Gordon) *Ilan Mitchell-Smith, John Glover, Bud Cort, Adam Baldwin.* First-time director Gordon has fashioned a somber but thoughtful version of the "high school hell" film. Set in an oppressive Catholic school, young Jerry (Mitchell-Smith) refuses to conform with his classmates by declining to participate in the school's annual fund-raising effort — the chocolate bar sale. In response, the entire student body bombards him with both physical and emotional retribution. At first glance, *The Chocolate War* appears to be a simple us-against-them film, but on a deeper level, it is a scathing comment on fascism and authoritarian rule. ★★★

Choice of Arms

(1983, 117 min, France, Alain Corneau) *Gérard Depardieu, Yves Montand, Catherine Deneuve.* Reminiscent of the best works of Claude Chabrol and Jean-Pierre Melville, this classy gangster film adroitly explores the complex and often-times violent relationship between a reformed underworld chieftain (Montand) and his recently paroled crony: a wonderfully bestial and explosive Depardieu. A taut, psychologically charged thriller. (French with English subtitles) ★★★½

The Choirboys

(1977, 120 min, US, Robert Aldrich) *James Woods, Jack DeLeon, Vince Tayback, Burt Young.* An awful screen adaptation of Joseph Wambaugh's novel, this lowbrow, homophobic, rambling piece of

trash follows the supposedly comic exploits of a group of L.A. cops who violate civil rights and generally act like a bunch of morons to help alleviate the pressures of the job. Arguably the worst mainstream film of the 1970s. ★

Choose Me

(1984, 114 min, US, Alan Rudolph) *Keith Carradine, Geneviève Bujold, Lesley Ann Warren, Rae Dawn Chong.* Rudolph looks at the mate-swapping, bed-hopping antics of L.A. singles looking for love under all the wrong sheets. Carradine is the sinuous Lothario pursuing various women with amorous abandon. ★★★½ DVD Letterbox: $19.99

Chopper

(2000, 93 min, Australia, Andrew Dominik) *Eric Bana, Simon Lyndon, David Field, Kate Beahan.* A character study like few others, *Chopper* mixes humor and extreme violence in telling its tale of Mark "Chopper" Read, a larger-than-life career criminal and tinderbox of violent contradictions. Based on Read's best-selling memoirs, the film begins in an Australian maximum security penitentiary where Chopper is serving time for murder. He is an emotionally complex bruiser of a man, alternately liked, respected and hated by his fellow inmates. As played by Bana, the bombastic, pathological Chopper is fascinating to watch in all of his contradictions. It's only a matter of time before this environment of caged men explodes — but the violence and acts of revenge are all unexpected. The final part of the film, set eight years later outside the prison walls, shows a freed Chopper forced to deal with life on the outside. Far from a simple look at a criminal, *Chopper* uses wicked humor in a relentless portrait of a mesmerizing young man; watching his life unfold is like staring at an impending train wreck. ★★★½ DVD: $24.99, VHS: $9.99

A Chorus Line

(1985, 113 min, US, Richard Attenborough) *Michael Douglas, Terrence Mann, Alyson Reed, Audrey Landers, Janet Jones, Cameron English.*

Those who did not see the Broadway production of this Pulitzer Prize- and Tony Award-winning musical may appreciate Attenborough's lifeless adaptation. All others will long for the class of the original. The story, of course, is about a group of dancers auditioning for the chorus of a Broadway musical. The show's famous song, "What I Did for Love" (the song, a dancer's anthem, has been changed from "What if I couldn't dance anymore" to a whiny lovers' lament), is thrown away by Attenborough's over-the-shoulder, offhanded nonchalance; and the classic finale "One" is considerably less than showstopping. ★★ DVD: $14.99

A Chorus of Disapproval

(1989, 92 min, GB, Michael Winner) *Jeremy Irons, Anthony Hopkins, Prunella Scales, Jenny Seagrove.* Alan Ayckbourn's award-winning play about the comic transformation of a timid widower into a heart-breaking Lothario is brought to the screen in this humorous, engaging and finely acted farce. Irons plays Guy Jones, a reserved and recently widowed young man who moves into a new town in northern England and, in an effort to "have fun and meet friends," joins the local amateur acting company's production of "The Beggar's Opera." The heads (and pelvises) of the ladies in the troupe are all turned on young Guy as he sheds his shyness and becomes entangled in a few love affairs. Hopkins is wonderful as the play's blustering and tempestuous director. ★★★ VHS: $19.99

The Chosen

(1981, 108 min, US, Jeremy Paul Kagan) *Robby Benson, Barry Miller, Rod Steiger, Maximilian Schell.* An extraordinarily tender and moving screen version of Chaim Potok's novel about the friendship and conflicting loyalties of two Jewish teenagers: Hasidic Benson and liberalized Miller. The film is a loving re-creation of 1940s Brooklyn, and features a stellar cast. ★★★½ DVD: $14.99

Les Choses de la Vie
(The Things of Life)

(1969, 90 min, France, Claude Sautet) *Michel Picoli, Romy Schneider, Lea Massari.* This appealing romantic comedy centers on an architect who, after suffering a near fatal auto accident, takes the time to reflect on his life and loves. The always capable, ubiquitous Picoli stars as a sensitive man torn between his love for his estranged wife (Massari) and his mistress (Schneider). A nicely observed tragicomedy that builds to a moving examination of the fragility of life and relationships. (American remake: *Intersection*) (French with English subtitles) ★★★ VHS: $29.99

Christ Stopped at Eboli

(1979, 145 min, Italy, Francesco Rosi) *Irene Papas, Gian Maria Volonte.* Rosi's award-winning adaptation of Carlo Levi's classic is a rich, resonant film about a writer/artist and political exile, who is banned to a village in southern Italy by Mussolini in 1935. The exile's experiences in this world of poverty and quiet despair open his eyes to the unshakable values of the resolute villagers. A film full of faith in human values, stunningly directed. (Italian with English subtitles) ★★★½ DVD: $29.99, VHS: $29.99

Christabel

(1989, 149 min, GB, Adrian Shergold) *Elizabeth Hurley, Stephen Dillon.* This outstanding BBC production tells the true-life story of Christabel Bielenberg, an aristocratic English woman who marries a German lawyer and finds herself plunged into

the nightmare of Nazi Germany. Having joined the Resistance, her husband is arrested and sent to the notorious Ravensbruck concentration camp. Based on her autobiography, the film follows Bielenberg as she travels across war-ravaged Germany and takes on the Nazi beauracracy and the Gestapo in an effort to free her husband. Written by Dennis Potter. ★★★½

Christiane F.

(1981, 124 min, Germany, Uli Edel) *Natja Brunhurst, Thomas Haustein, David Bowie.* The spine-tingling account of a young German girl lost in the dark abyss of drug dependency and prostitution. Based on a true story, the film has a striking authenticity acquired through the use of actual locales (Berlin's seamiest junkie havens) and a pallid complexioned cast. Bowie provides the soundtrack music. ★★★ DVD: $24.99

Christina's House

(2000, 97 min, US, Gavin Wilding) *Brendan Fehr, Allison Lange, Brad Lowe, John Savage.* Christina's House is idiotic, unscary drivel that offers only the prurient pleasure of a scantily clad young woman to keep one barely awake. Christina lives with her jackass younger brother and overprotective dad (Savage — whatever happened to this guy?) in a creepy house. She starts to hear strange noises, then some of her friends start disappearing. Poorly written and directed, with no suspense or mystery, Christina's House will enchant only the most forgiving (or lascivious) viewer. ★ DVD: $9.99

Christine

(1983, 111 min, US, John Carpenter) *Keith Gordon, Robert Prosky, Harry Dean Stanton, John Stockwell.* Horror mavens Carpenter and Stephen King joined forces for this stylish though basic adaptation of King's novel with Gordon making the most of a shy teenager who is under the spell of a demonic '58 Plymouth. ★★ DVD: $14.99, VHS: $9.99

A Christmas Carol

(1951, 86 min, GB, Brian Desmond Hurst) *Alastair Sim, Kathleen Harrison, Michael Hordern, Patrick MacNee.* A wonderful, heartwarming rendition of Charles Dickens' classic tale, featuring a terrific performance by the delightful Sim as Scrooge. A hardy perennial that has become a well-loved part of the Christmas experience. ★★★★ DVD: $14.99, DVD Black & White and Color Versions: $19.99, VHS: $9.99

Christmas in Connecticut

(1945, 101 min, US, Peter Godfrey) *Barbara Stanwyck, Dennis Morgan, Sydney Greenstreet, S.Z. Sakall, Reginald Gardiner, Una O'Connor.* A breezy if lightweight comedy of mistaken iden-

tity. Stanwyck plays a successful writer for a women's magazine who's been faking her housekeeping abilities. When a war hero (Morgan) is to stay on "her" farm for the weekend, Stanwyck is forced to impersonate the woman her readers think she is. Of course, love blossoms between Stanwyck and Morgan, even though he thinks she is really married (an unusual comedic swipe at adultery for the '40s). Stanwyck's funny and effortlessly charming, Morgan doesn't make much of a presence, though Greenstreet and the delightful Sakall supply good support. The laughs aren't consistent but it's fun nonetheless. ★★½ VHS: $14.99

Christmas in July

(1940, 67 min, US, Preston Sturges) *Dick Powell, Ellen Drew, William Demarest.* A practical joke escalates into a frenzy of consumerism and wish-fulfillment in this whimsical Sturges look at the American Dream. Powell thinks he's won $25,000 in a slogan contest; but does money really buy happiness? Or, as the boss said to Jimmy, "Now that you're a capitalist, I don't know how you feel about working for a living. . ." ★★★½ VHS: $9.99

A Christmas Story

(1983, 98 min, US, Bob Clark) *Darren McGavin, Melinda Dillon, Peter Billingsley.* An absolutely charming adaptation of Jean Shepherd's short story. A delight for both children and adults, this endearing reminiscence of the holiday season circa 1940 captures the everyday life of the era, as young Billingsley hopes (anguishes is more accurate) for a Red Ryder BB gun. McGavin and Dillon are simply wonderful as his somewhat unconventional parents. A perennial. (Sequel: *My Summer Story*) ★★★½ DVD 2-disc Special Edition: $26.99, VHS: $14.99

Favorite Line: "You'll shoot your eye out, kid!" —*Santa to Ralphie Parker (Peter Billingsley)*

Christopher Columbus: The Discovery

(1992, 121 min, US, John Glen) *Marlon Brando, Tom Selleck, Rachel Ward, George Corraface, Nigel Terry.* From the production team that brought us *Superman* (Alexander and Ilya Salkind) comes this equally mythological depiction of the seafaring Genoan of American folklore, Cristóbal Colón. Brimming with lots of overblown production values, the film sets sail into the murky waters of historical narrative with its compass askew and its rigging tangled. Despite these failings, however, the film will still be satisfying viewing to lovers of melodramatic adventure on the high seas. Corraface performs ably in the title role, making the best of a bad script. ★★

Christopher Strong

(1933, 77 min, US, Dorothy Arzner) *Katharine Hepburn, Colin Clive, Billie Burke.* One of the few female directors of her time, Arzner brings an enchanting perspective to this capable romantic drama with Hepburn in her element as an aviatrix in romantic and professional conflict. Clive is one of the reasons for both. ★★★

Chronically Unfeasible

(2000, 101 min, Brazil, Sérgio Bianchi) *Patrick Alencar, Leonardo Vieira, Daniel Dantas, Betty Gofman, Umberto Magnani, Dira Paes, Dan Stulbach, Cecil Thiré.* Set in exotic Brazil, director Bianchi's bitterly sarcastic political comedy skewers race and class relations with witty precision as it presents a society in chaos. Filmed in an original style

A Christmas Story

using both dramatic and quasi-documentary elements, the story revolves around six characters in and around a restaurant in São Paulo. This disparate group serves as a microcosm of modern Brazil, a people besieged by corruption, exploitation and social discord. How these characters interact and struggle for identity is at the core of a controversial, original and unsettling look at the long-simmering class struggles, racial and regional differences in that polyglot country. The film nicely balances biting social criticism, memorable characters and humor tinged with the realities and hypocrisies of everyday life. (Portuguese with English subtitles) ★★★ DVD: $24.99, VHS: $24.99

Chuck & Buck

(2000, 97 min, US, Miguel Arteta) *Mike White, Chris Weitz, Lupe Ontiveros, Beth Colt, Paul Weitz, Maya Rudolph.* At times weird, at times disturbing, but ultimately and unexpectedly poignant, the highly original and sometimes creepy *Chuck & Buck* plays like a gay *Fatal Attraction* as interpreted by Forrest Gump. Screenwriter White has given himself quite a part. Buck is an emotionally stunted 27-year-old man who is fixated on his childhood friend (and possible lover) Chuck. When Buck's mother dies, he travels to Los Angeles in an attempt to reestablish a relationship with Chuck. In-between finding work with a downtown theatre group, Buck begins stalking his former friend who no longer wants anything to do with him. Told with a delightfully twisted sense of humor and an even stranger perspective, *Chuck & Buck* will never win awards from gay activist groups. However, for a sardonic look at obsessive love and emotional instability, director Arteta's no-he-didn't-say-that comedy is hard to beat. ★★★½ DVD: $14.99, VHS: $9.99

Chuck Jones Extremes & Inbetweens: A Life in Animation

(2000, 85 min, US, Margaret Selby) *Chuck Jones, Celebrity appearances by: Whoopi Goldberg, Matt Groening, Ron Howard, John Lasseter, Leonard Maltin, Steven Spielberg, Robin Williams.* A joyous celebration into the life of animator Chuck Jones, the creative genius behind Bugs Bunny, Porky Pig, Daffy Duck and all their friends from the Warner Brothers lot. Includes interviews with celebrity fans (Spielberg accurately calls Jones' 1955 *One Froggy Evening*, "the *Citizen Kane* of animated shorts"), as well as insight from Jones himself. And, of course, numerous clips from his great cartoons. ★★★½ VHS: $9.99

C.H.U.D.

(1984, 88 min, US, Douglas Cheek) *John Heard, Daniel Stern, John Goodman, Kim Greist, Jay Thomas, Patricia Richardson.* If you're a fan of spoofy-played-for-straight horror films, then this *C.H.U.D.*'s for you. All others, however, may not enjoy this tale of street people becoming Cannibalistic Humanoid Underground Dwellers when they become exposed to radioactive gunk and begin a murderous rampage. (Sequel: *C.H.U.D. II: Bud the Chud*) ★★ DVD: $9.99, VHS: $9.99

Chungking Express

(1994, 103 min, Hong Kong, Wong Kar-Wai) *Brigitte Lin, Takeshi Kaneshiro, Tony Leung, Faye Wong.* The stories of two Hong Kong police officers who are dumped by their girlfriends are interwoven in this brilliant, engrossing, yet low-budget pastiche. Made while working in postproduction on his angst-ridden swordsman movie *Ashes of Time, Chungking*'s swift genesis and execution shows. It is vibrant, immediate and exudes a truthfulness and poignancy

which can be attributed to its lack of rewrites and production tinkering. Slow motion, jump cuts, pixellated movement and the recurrent use of a handful of pop tunes all combine to make the film very different from its Hong Kong brethren yet set firmly within that diverse genre. There is also at least a kernel of truth for most people in this film about romantic relationships and how we adapt to our beginnings as well as their ends. (Cantonese with English subtitles) ★★★★ DVD Letterbox: $14.99, VHS: $9.99

Chunhyang

(2000, 120 min, Korea, Im Kwon Taek) *Lee Hyo Jung, Cho Seung Woo, Kim Sung Nyu, Lee Jung Hun.* Pansori is an ancient operatic Korean art form, performed by few in contemporary Korea. One of that country's most popular folk stories is that of Chunhyang, the daughter of an 18th-century courtesan whose love for her husband would inspire a nation. Director Im has combined pansori and the rapturous story of Chunhyang to make a luscious costume drama of true love, fidelity and class struggle. Framed in a pansori performed by Korean master Cho Sang Hyun, the film chronicles the love affair between Mongryong, the handsome son of a provincial governor, and the beautiful Chunhyang. Though of different classes, they secretly marry, only to be separated when Mongryong moves to Seoul to attend university. Director Im, a Korean legend with over 90 films to his credit but with this film receives his first American release, embues *Chunhyang* with the sweetness of a fable and the sweep of epic storytelling. Though American audiences may initially find the pansori narration a bit distracting, the art form soon grows on you, adding another dimension of time and place to this glorious tale. (Korean with English subtitles) ★★★★ DVD Letterbox: $29.99, VHS Letterbox: $19.99

The Church

(1990, 110 min, US/Italy, Michele Soavi) *Tomas Arana, Hugh Quarshine.* Dario Argento produced this so-so chiller about a group of people trapped in a church built on top of a satanic burial ground. Director Soavi delivers all the style of the master, but few of the shocks. This is the unrated version. ★★ VHS: $79.99

Ciao! Federico!

(1970, 62 min, US, Gideon Bachmann) This absorbing look at the great Italian filmmaker Federico Fellini is recorded during the making of *Fellini's Satyricon*. Includes interviews with the director and scenes from the classic film. (Italian with English subtitles) ★★★ VHS: $19.99

Ciao! Manhattan

(1965-1971, 91 min, US, David Weisman & John Palmer) *Edie Sedgwick.* This kaleidoscopic journey through the life of Warhol superstar Edie Sedgwick is both a searing psychodrama of burnout syndrome and a dynamic potpourri of Sixties cultural paraphernalia. From Edie's rise to the throne of the pop underground to her tragic plummet into drug abuse and mental illness, *Ciao!* manages to be comical, perplexing and poignant. Filming began in 1965, capturing the orgiastic frenzy of the Warhol Factory's heyday. Work resumed years later with a crumbling Edie living at the bottom of a swimming pool on the West Coast. Only months after the completion of filming, Edie died of a barbiturate overdose. She was 28 years old. ★★★½ DVD Clearance Price: $24.99

Ciao, Professore!

(1994, 99 min, Italy, Lina Wertmüller) *Paolo Villaggio, Isa Dabieli.* A flip soundbite for this breezy comedy-drama would be to call it a pubescent spaghetti *To Sir with Love*. A portly middle-aged teacher (Villaggio) from northern Italy is accidentally sent to a poverty stricken seaside town near Naples. What he finds when he arrives is a beleaguered school and a class full of truant third graders. His formidable task is to round up the group of streetwise kids, gain their trust and begin to teach them. Wertmüller overcomes the hackneyed and predictable plot through the inspired casting of the children — all of them tough but cute mini-adults, each with a personality that would soften the most curmudgeonly heart. (Italian with English subtitles) ★★★ DVD: $19.99

The Cider House Rules

(1999, 131 min, US, Lasse Hallström) *Tobey Maguire, Charlize Theron, Michael Caine, Delroy Lindo, Paul Rudd, Jane Alexander, Kathy Baker, Erykah Badu, Kieran Culkin, Heavy D.* Heartwarming and inspiring aren't exactly the first two sentiments you'd expect from a filmization of a John Irving novel, but that's precisely what you do get with this moving, beautifully acted adaptation of the author's best-seller. A marvelously understated Maguire is Homer, a serious young man who has spent his entire life in an orphanage in rural Maine. The orphanage is run by the kindly Dr. Larch (Caine in his poetic Oscar-winning performance). Dr. Larch has prepared Homer to take over as caregiver for the orphans, even though Homer isn't schooled in medicine. However, when Homer meets a stranded couple, it prompts him to leave his lifelong home and head out into an unchartered country awash in turmoil from poverty, racism and the second world war. Irving has adapted his own novel, which may explain why the characters resonate with such emotional clarity. Director Hallström supplies exquisite pacing and superior evocation of wartime America. ★★★½ DVD: $19.99, VHS: $9.99

The Cigarette Girl of Mosselprom

(1924, 78 min, USSR, Yuri Zhelyabuzhsky) A delightful and boisterous comedy satirizing Soviet life and filmmaking in the 1920s. The story follows the exploits of a young woman who is tossed from street vending into the movies when she is cast in a romantic melodrama. (Silent with orchestral accompaniment) ★★★ VHS: $29.99

Cimarron

(1931, 124 min, US, Wesley Ruggles) *Irene Dunne, Richard Dix.* The first western to win an Oscar for Best Picture is a severely dated and rather lumbering period piece based on an Edna Ferber story about American pioneers in the Old West. Dix gives the kind of performance that is subject to parody, though Dunne's solid portrait certainly elevates the production. (Remade in 1960) ★★ VHS: $14.99

Cinderella

(1950, 74 min, US, Wildred Jackson) Walt Disney's classic animated feature is a remarkable achievement, and one of his best loved. The story, of course, follows "poor Cinderella" from abused stepsister to belle of the ball. It is the combination of the superb animation, the enchanting songs and a wonderful gallery of characters that makes *Cinderella* a timeless masterpiece. ★★★★

Cinderella

(1964, 77 min, US, Charles S. Dubin) *Lesley Ann Warren, Ginger Rogers, Walter Pidgeon, Stuart Damon, Celeste Holm.* Rodgers and Hammerstein wrote the score for this enchanting musical based on the fairy tale classic, and it's ideal for younger viewers. Warren sweetly plays the title character. ★★★

Cinderella Liberty

(1973, 117 min, US, Mark Rydell) *James Caan, Marsha Mason, Eli Wallach, Kirk Calloway.* Two strong performances from Caan and Oscar-nominee Mason highlight this touching drama about a sailor who becomes involved with a prostitute and her illegitimate black son. Caan has never been better, here playing the good-natured seaman who falls for the hard-bitten Mason. The film effectively combines the gritty realism of the surroundings and the classic elements of the star-crossed romantic melodrama. ★★★ VHS: $59.99

Cinema Paradiso

(1990, 123 min, Italy, Giuseppe Tornatore) *Philippe Noiret, Salvatore Cascio.* A wonderfully endearing and emotionally satisfying story of remembrance and love. The story is about the developing relationship and love between a precocious fatherless boy of eight, Toto (engagingly played by Cascio), and a crusty old projectionist, Alfredo (a perfectly cast Noiret). Set mostly in a movie theater in a dusty Sicilian town after WWII, these two characters, seemingly so different, are drawn together and soon develop an unusual attachment. The movie is told in a series of flashbacks when Toto, now a successful film director in Rome, prepares to return to his boyhood village for the funeral of Alfredo. His loving memories of early childhood and adolescence provide the emotional core. For all but the most jaded, *Cinema Paradiso* will prove to be a rare, tender and unforgettable film. Includes the original 173-minute European cut. (Italian with English subtitles) ★★★★ DVD Letterbox: $29.99, VHS The New Version: $9.99

Circle of Friends

(1995, 114 min, Ireland, Pat O'Connor) *Chris O'Donnell, Minnie Driver, Colin Firth, Geraldine O'Rawe.* Director O'Connor is in a sweetly romantic mood and creates a picturesque atmosphere for an improbable love story with this beguiling adaptation of Maeve Binchy's novel. Benny (Driver) could probably be called the "ugly duckling" among her group of childhood friends, and growing up in a

small Irish town in the late 1950s hasn't exactly given her the opportunity for romantic or social encounters. But that's all about to change when Benny enters university and falls under the spell of the soccer team's handsome star player (O'Donnell). While "plain Jane" Cinderellas have found their Prince Charmings before, it's done so with a refreshing voice and a very grounded view of the world. ★★★½ DVD: $9.99

Circle of Iron

(1979, 102 min, US, Richard Moore) *David Carradine, Jeff Cooper, Roddy McDowall, Eli Wallach, Bruce Lee.* Offbeat martial arts adventure (filmed in Israel and started by Bruce Lee before his death) about a young karate master in search of spiritual perfection and a sacred book of knowledge. ★★½

Circle of Passion

(1996, 94 min, France/GB, Charles Finch) *Sandrine Bonnaire, Jane March, Charles Finch, Jean Rochefort, James Fox.* This sappy love story overcomes a wretched opening titles montage to become a palatable if slightly cheesy romance. A British banker, working in his father-in-law's Paris branch, puts his job, reputation and loveless marriage on the line when he has a torrid affair with a French beauty (the luminous Bonnaire). Will he do the responsible thing or follow his bliss? Swank Parisian locations and decent performances go a long way toward making this near-vanity production watchable (star, writer and director Finch does sort of grow on you — if you can get past the slow-motion, shirtless shadow-boxing sequences). This is classy trash, though — beautiful faces and scenery can't completely disguise the cliché-ridden story and overbaked dialogue. (aka: *Never Ever*) ★★½

Circuit

(2001, 130 min, US, Dirk Shafer) *Jonathan Wade Drahos, Andre Khabazzi, Paul Lekakis, William Katt, Kiersten Warren, Randall Kleiser, China Cat, Bruce Vilanch, Nancy Allen, Jim J. Bullock, Daniel Kukan.* Director Shafer's hyperkinetic film is set in the world of the circuit party, a fabulously bumpy scene where the boys have perfect pecs, designer drugs flow freely and weaker lives tend to crumble. After being outed in his small conservative town, gay cop John (Drahos) moves to West Hollywood. Befriending Hector, a high-end prostitute, John becomes wrapped up in the all-night-into-morning

dance parties. He also falls in love with Gill, who has already been through this scene and survived. As John falls deeper and deeper into drugs and partying, most of his friends lose patience, but Gill holds on. Events culminate at the annual White Party in Palm Springs where lives are changed. The circuit scene has both wondrous and scary sides, and these parallel elements are explored in this insightful film. ★★★ DVD Unrated: $19.99, VHS Unrated: $9.99

Circuitry Man

(1989, 85 min, US, Steven Loy) *Vernon Wells, Dana Wheeler-Nicholson.* Cheap sci-fi actioner about a post-apocalyptic age where the Earth's oxygen has been depleted, everybody lives underground, and the last remaining frontier is the human mind. ★½ DVD Double Feature: $24.99

The Circus

(1928, 71 min, US, Charles Chaplin) *Charlie Chaplin, Merna Kennedy.* The Circus has the Little Tramp as a member of the greatest show on Earth. This rarely seen gem features fantastic sight gags and lots of Chaplin's trademark physical humor. ★★★★

The Cisco Kid

(1993, 95 min, US, Luis Valdez) *Jimmy Smits, Cheech Marin.* Mildly entertaining action-comedy which tells the story of the famous south-of-the-border bandit with about as much accuracy as a counterfeit Rolex. The suave Smits stars as the Cisco Kid, who teams up with Pancho (Marin) as he tries to save Mexico from corrupt politicians and nefarious Frenchmen. Spiced with many stunts and ill-placed jokes for lack of a real story. ★★

The Citadel

(1938, 112 min, US/GB, King Vidor) *Robert Donat, Rosalind Russell, Ralph Richardson, Rex Harrison.* An extraordinary retelling of A.J. Cronin's novel featuring superior performances by Donat and Russell. Donat is an idealistic and hard-working London doctor whose flirtation with the rich (and an easier caseload) leads him to ignore his principles and his wife (Russell). Richardson is terrific in support as an old family friend. ★★★★ VHS: $24.99

Citizen Cohn

(1992, 112 min, US, Frank Pierson) *James Woods, Joe Don Baker, Ed Flanders, Frederic Forrest, Joe Bologna, Lee Grant.* Based on the novel by Nicholas von Hoffman, this engrossing biographical and political drama on the life of Roy Cohn — Communist headhunter, ruthless lawyer and closeted homosexual who died of AIDS in 1986 — is great explosive fun. Using his trademark hyper-energy coupled with his on-edge, often grating on-screen personality to unforgettable use, Woods stars as the charismatic but at times demonic Cohn. Made for HBO, the film is structured in a series of flashbacks, as the now disbarred Cohn lies semiconscious in a hospital bed, dying of AIDS and hallucinating on many of the contentious incidents from his life. ★★★½ DVD: $14.99

Citizen Kane

(1941, 119 min, US, Orson Welles) *Orson Welles, Joseph Cotten, Everett Sloane, Agnes Moorehead.* This masterful union of form and content stretched the boundaries of cinema with its ingeniously crafted narrative and stunning shot construction. The tale of Charles Foster Kane contains all the vital elements of epic tragedy: greed, jealousy, scandal and failure. A devastating critique of the American

Cinema Paradiso

Dream and an unmatched singular tour de force by producer, director, star and coauthor Welles. ★★★★ DVD 2-disc set: $26.99

Citizen Ruth

(1996, 104 min, US, Alexander Payne) *Laura Dern, Swoosie Kurtz, Kurtwood Smith, Mary Kay Place, Kelly Preston, Burt Reynolds, Tippi Hedren, Diane Ladd.* A scathingly funny satire that dares to take on the super-charged issue of abortion. Dern is Ruth Stoops, a hard-core skid-row regular. Pregnant and hauled before a local magistrate, she's ordered by the court to have an abortion. Just like that she finds herself at the center of a mushrooming controversy. The first to "adopt" her are local pro-lifers Place and Smith, who attempt to make a good Christian of her. Eventually, the other side catches wind and she's stolen away by a couple of radical lesbians (Kurtz and Preston). Though writer-director Payne seems to express a mildly pro-choice point of view, he leaves no one unscathed as he lampoons both sides for their unyielding zealotry with hilarious results. ★★★½ VHS: $14.99

Citizen X

(1995, 103 min, US, Chris Gerolmo) *Stephen Rea, Donald Sutherland, Max von Sydow, Joss Ackland.* Made for HBO, *Citizen X* is a tense, carefully detailed thriller about Russia's most horrific serial killer and the years-long search for him. Rea is a forensics expert and amateur detective who, upon the discovery of several bodies in a secluded wooded area, is assigned to head the investigation to track the killer. His task is made all the more difficult by an uncooperative Russian bureaucracy and antiquated investigatory procedures. Sutherland is well cast as Rea's superior, who may or may not be on his side. Adult in nature, the story doesn't flinch from the realities of its subject, and writer-director Gerolmo casts an eerie, ominous spell. ★★★½ DVD: $14.99

Citizen's Band

(1977, 98 min, US, Jonathan Demme) *Paul Le Mat, Candy Clark, Ann Wedgeworth, Marcia Rodd.* A delightful slice of Americana, this satire on the CB craze interweaves several stories revolving around an odd and lovable assortment of characters, all obsessed with their short wave radios. A quirky original from director Demme. (aka: *Handle with Care.*) ★★★½ VHS: $7.99

The City (La Ciudad)

(1999, 88 min, US, Davd Riker) Filming in gritty black and white over a five-year period (1992-1997), director Riker used immigrant workers in New York City to shoot a series of vignettes, creating a timeless metaphor on survival and the quest for opportunity and a better life. With images as earthy as Eisenstein in Mexico, several short stories link together to reveal the reality of the underclass; day laborers scrambling for work or crammed into sweltering factories for hours of tedious, low-paying piece work. Riker tells his stories of the displaced trying to find roots in an alien environment with a documentary directness and a neorealist compassion. (In English and Spanish with English subtitles) ★★★½ VHS: $89.99

City by the Sea

(2002, 108 min, US, Michael Caton-Jones) *Robert De Niro, Frances McDormand, James Franco, Eliza Dushku, William Forsythe, George Dzundza, Patti LuPone.* De Niro is in top form as NYPD officer Vince LaMarca, a man whose family is marked by violence. His father was executed for kidnapping and killing a small child when Vince was only a kid; and it seems his estranged,

Citizen Kane

junkie son (Franco) has murdered someone himself in Vince's old precinct in the rundown shore town, Long Beach. Caton-Jones (who directed De Niro in *This Boy's Life*) handles the father-son scenes rather well and makes excellent use of the terrific and haunting Long Beach locations. Structurally, however, *City* is uneven; the early junkie scenes are (despite the convincing locale) dramatically awkward, and exposition is nearly always spoken rather than shown. The film is also a hair overlong, and can't really mesh its dramatic and thriller story threads satisfactorily. Nevertheless, De Niro, McDormand and Franco all give quietly powerful performances, making *City by the Sea* seem more moving and possibly more satisfying than it really is. ★★½ DVD Letterbox: $14.99, DVD Pan & Scan: $27.99, VHS: $22.99

City Hall

(1996, 110 min, US, Harold Becker) *Al Pacino, John Cusack, Bridget Fonda, Danny Aiello, David Paymer, Martin Landau, Anthony Franciosa.* The story of a small-town boy's adventures in the big city gets another telling in this occasionally gritty political drama. Cusack plays the deputy mayor of New York City, an idealistic, loyal foot soldier to Pacino's gregarious and often charming mayor. When a young child is killed during a gangland/police shootout, the administration gets into high gear investigating the murder and playing damage control. As Cusack digs deeper, he discovers a trail of cover-ups and widespread corruption. Cusack ably conveys the turmoil of a naive politico suddenly learning how to play hardball, while Pacino is able to carve emotion from a rather one-dimensional character. *City Hall* presents an intriguing view of a machine at work, it's just so indifferent about it all it's hard to get really excited. ★★½ DVD: $9.99, VHS: $9.99

City Heat

(1984, 98 min, US, Richard Benjamin) *Clint Eastwood, Burt Reynolds, Jane Alexander, Madeline Kahn, Irene Cara, Richard Roundtree, Rip Torn.* A good cast is, sadly, not enough to elevate the enjoyment level of this disappointing '30s-style gangster take-off. ★★ DVD: $19.99, VHS: $14.99

City Lights

(1931, 90 min, US, Charles Chaplin) *Charlie Chaplin, Virginia Cherrill, Harry Myers, Hank Mann.* Chaplin's final silent film is one of the screen's true masterworks. Charlie plays the Little Tramp, who falls in love with a blind flower girl and vows to obtain the money needed for an operation to restore her sight. Filled with great humor and overwhelming emotional poignancy. ★★★★ DVD 2-disc set: $29.99, VHS: $14.99

City Limits

(1985, 85 min, US, Aaron Lipstadt) *Rae Dawn Chong, Kim Cattrell, Robby Benson, James Earl Jones.* It's another postapocalyptic thriller with gangs of youths roving barren cities on motorcycles. This second feature from the team that produced *Android*, while not as successful as their earlier effort, still manages to rise slightly above its overworked premise. ★★ VHS: $79.99

City Lovers/Country Lovers

(1982, 105 min, South Africa, Barney Simon & Mamie van Rensberg) Two works by South African dramatist Nadine Gordimer. In *City Lovers*, a middle-aged white geologist begins an affair with a black cashier; in the latter story, the son of a wealthy white farmer and the daughter of a black farmhand, who have grown up together, are secret lovers. The unifying theme in both of Gordimer's works is that the lovers must suffer the consequences of their relationships from the strict, oppressive South African government. ★★★ VHS: $69.99

City of Angels

(1998, 114 min, US, Brad Silberling) *Nicolas Cage, Meg Ryan, Dennis Franz, Andre Braugher, Colm Feore.* In remaking Wim Wenders' *Wings of Desire*, director Silberling had a difficult choice to make: keep the flavor of the original or totally Americanize it for the romantic crowd. The end result of his *City of Angels* is a little of both, which is why the film is successful and unsatisfying at the same time. A morose Cage plays Seth, an angel who is one of many in Los Angeles who look after and hear the thoughts of the mortals around them. When Seth crosses paths with Dr. Maggie Rice (Ryan), he begins to fall in love and soon questions his role as an angel. The film's first half manages to capture the pacing, style, and even the meloncholy of *Wings*. The second, and more conventional, half is strictly a by-the-books Hollywood romance haunted by the predictability and essence of other melodramas. ★★½ DVD Letterbox Special Edition: $14.99, VHS: $9.99, VHS Letterbox: $9.99

City of God

(2003, 130 min, US/Brazil/France, Fernando Meirelles & Kátia Lund) *Matheus Nachtergaele, Seu Jorge, Alexandre Rodrigues.* Sustaining a creative intensity and energy from beginning to end that sets it apart, *City of God* — a film of rare emotional power and rule-breaking cinematic invention — never trades humanity for style, allowing both to coexist in a narrative that cuts to the core. Based on firsthand accounts from a book by Paolo Lins, the film tells the complex story of a group of boys in a Rio de Janeiro housing project where crime is rampant and guns are plentiful. It chronicles the boys' rises to power, falls from grace and all of the tragedy in-between through three decades. The filmmakers mix the stark imagery of gun-wielding nine year olds with a bevy of aggressive film techniques to keep our eyes wide open and our hearts heavy as we watch how the cycle of violence revolves through generations. A chaotic journey into a world that isn't far from resembling life in America's poorest projects, *City of God* works as a brilliant cautionary tale of neglected lives and misdirected dreams. (Portuguese with English subtitles) ★★★★ DVD: $29.99, VHS Subtitled: $102.99

City of Hope

(1991, 129 min, US, John Sayles) *Vincent Spano, Tony Lo Bianco, David Strathairn, Joe Morton, John Sayles, Angela Bassett.* Sayles' take on the decline of the American city during the Reagan-Bush years is a masterfully layered exposé of corruption, greed, political favoritism, street crime and neighborhood vigilantism. Spano stars as the disillusioned son of a corrupt city contractor who, fed up with graft, quits his "ghost job" on a high-rise construction project only to find himself at the center of a swirling web of local political intrigue. Sayles manages to tinge his story with just about every major news item of the early '90s and then some. Among a good cast, Strathairn is terrific as a street person witness to it all. ★★★½

City of Industry

(1997, 97 min, US, John Irvin) *Harvey Keitel, Timothy Hutton, Stephen Dorff, Famke Janssen.* Keitel is Roy Egan, a retired criminal brought into one last jewel heist by his brother Lee (Hutton). To realize the American Dream of the last big score, Lee calls in Skip Kovich (Dorff), whose edgy near-psychosis and lack of allegiance sharply contrast with both Roy and Lee. Planned with precision and executed with exactly orchestrated violence, the job goes as planned. But Skip is greedy. Roy literally crawls away from death to scour the infested maze of L.A. in a personal quest for vengeance and honor. Director Irvin seeds the violence with small personal moments which reveal intimate aspects of the protagonists' personalities, humanizing a world in which grand theft auto, gun sales in parking lots are a way of life. Immersed in a desperate milieu, the film is an intriguing character study adeptly handled by the cast. ★★★ DVD: $14.99

City of Joy

(1992, 134 min, GB, Roland Joffé) *Patrick Swayze, Pauline Collins, Om Puri.* An aimless and disillusioned American surgeon (Swayze) attempts to lose himself in the back streets of Calcutta. Against his will, he's drawn into the operations of a health clinic run by a nurse (Collins), who's committed to the clinic's survival with pragmatic optimism and iron will. Together, they battle against the overwhelming need and abject poverty of their patients, and confront a brutal and exploitive local boss. Some engaging performances and arresting location shooting elevate the film above its predictable story line. ★★½ DVD: $19.99, VHS: $9.99

The City of Lost Children

(1995, 112 min, France, Jean-Pierre Jeunet & Marc Caro) *Ron Perlman, Daniel Emilfork, Judith Vittet, Dominique Pinon.* A fascinating, engrossing and disturbing fractured fairy tale. Set in and around an eerie, oddly futuristic yet late-19th-century waterfront (it's a setting seemingly inspired by Samuel Beckett and Fritz Lang), the film follows a hulking but pea-brained circus strongman (Perlman) known only as "One," who is on a desperate search to find his abducted ward, Little Brother. The search ultimately leads to a sea platform/laboratory where Krank, the genetically created orphan of a mad scientist, lords over his siblings (including a talking brain in a box) and conducts diabolical dream experiments. Though not as seamless as their previous *Delicatessen*, the directors have crafted a truly unique tale that is complemented by good performances, mind-blowing imagery and superb special effects. ★★★½ DVD: $27.99

City of Women

(1981, 139 min, Italy, Federico Fellini) *Marcello Mastroianni, Ettore Manni, Anna Prucnall.* Mastroianni stars as the bruised, baffled and bedazzled man who stumbles into a feminist convention, which sets off a series of wild, surrealistic fantasies. Fellini continues his eternal search into his psyche with an eloquent flourish. (Italian with English subtitles) ★★★ DVD: $29.99, VHS: $19.99

City Slickers

(1991, 108 min, US, Ron Underwood) *Billy Crystal, Daniel Stern, Jack Palance, Bruno Kirby, Patricia Wettig, Helen Slater, David Paymer, Josh Mostel.* An often hilarious and heartwarming farce about three adventure-seeking Manhattanite buddies who sign up for an "authentic" Western cattle drive. Along the way, they confront their fears, unfulfilled childhood fantasies, and their respective midlife crises. This may sound like a recipe for cheap sentimentality, but thanks to solid performances and razor-sharp, quick-witted dialogue, the film is a fun-filled and poignant examination of the disillusionment of middle age. Palance (who won an Oscar) steals the show as the real-life cowboy who leads the round-up. (Sequel: *City Slickers II*) ★★★½ DVD: $14.99

City Slickers II: The Legend of Curly's Gold

(1994, 105 min, US, Paul Weiland) *Billy Crystal, Daniel Stern, Jack Palance, Jon Lovitz, Patricia Wettig.* A genial sequel which is less a continuation and more a carbon copy of the original. Crystal learns that Curly (the Palance character who died in the first film) may have left behind a fortune in gold. He, Stern and brother Lovitz head west to search for it. On the way, Curly's twin brother shows up (Palance) and all face the same series of western misadventures as in the first film. Though there's no lack of funny lines, and Crystal is a delight to watch, the sorry subplot of Lovitz and Crystal's strained relationship and an overwhelming feeling of *deja-vu* make this only intermittently entertaining. ★★½ DVD: $19.99, VHS: $9.99

La Ciudad y los Perros (The City and the Dogs)

(1987, 135 min, Peru, Francisco J. Lombardi) Although very few of its films reach the United States, this powerful drama of personal terror amidst rampant terror proves that Peruvian cinema is quite vibrant. The story is set in a boy's military academy outside Lima. Within the confines of the repressive structure, four angry cadets form a private circle that begins to victimize and dominate the other cadets. It is only after a theft escalates into possible murder that a brave young man confronts the group. A hard-hitting and absorbing drama from Mario Vargas Llosa's classic novel. (Spanish with English subtitles) ★★★

A Civil Action

(1998, 113 min, US, Steve Zaillian) *John Travolta, Robert Duvall, Kathleen Quinlan, William H. Macy, Tony Shalhoub, John Lithgow, James Gandolfini, Dan Hedaya.* What's this: An intriguing, complex courtroom drama *not* penned by John Grisham? Based on the best-seller by Jonathan Harr, this classy production, which is based on a true-life incident, shares with Grisham a judicial setting, but *A Civil Action* has its own, distinctive flavoring in which justice may not always be served. Travolta is commendable as Jan Schlichtmann, a hotshot, cynical personal injury lawyer who agrees to represent eight families from a small Massachusetts town against two large corporations whose dumping of toxic materials may have caused a breakout of leukemia. The outcome is unexpected, and director Zaillian's screenplay adaptation contains many sharp observations of the legal profession, and on ethics vs. the law. ★★★ DVD: $14.99, VHS: $9.99

Civilization

(1916, 86 min, US, Raymond B. West) *Howard Hickman, Enid Markey.* Contemporary with Griffith's *Intolerance*, producer Thomas Ince proved himself every bit the director's equal with this impressive silent exhibiting strong plot construction and narrative economy. Set in the mythical kingdom of Teutonic, the story depicts that country's plunge into the surreal madness of war. Only when Christ himself returns to take the sover-

City of God

eign on an amazing journey to see the resulting carnage is the country saved. *Civilization* was both a commercial and critical success upon its release in 1916, and was not only used to help reelect President Wilson but also was a rallying cry against America's entry into WWI. The film became frightfully out of fashion when America entered the war. ★★★ VHS: $29.99

The Claim

(2000, 121 min, Canada, Michael Winterbottom) *Wes Bentley, Milla Jovovich, Nastassja Kinski, Sarah Polley, Peter Mullan.* Director Winterbottom's second adaptation of Thomas Hardy (the first being *Jude*) is equally glum, but *The Claim* does have some rewards. Based on "The Mayor of Casterbridge," the film stars Mullan as the "king" of a small but flourishing mining town in the Old West, who runs the town with a strict but fair hand. Railroad company man Bentley arrives to survey the town on the same day as Kinski — a figure from Mullan's shady past — and her lovely daughter (Polley). Soon all these lives intersect. *The Claim* is as grimy and gritty as most Hollywood westerns are sweeping and artificial, but the film suffers in comparison to the similarly atmospheric *McCabe and Mrs. Miller*, which had a great deal more to say about its time and place. ★★½ DVD Letterbox: $14.99, VHS: $9.99

Claire Dolan

(1998, 95 min, US, Lodge Kerrigan) *Katrin Cartlidge, Vincent D'Onofrio, Colm Meaney.* Employing the same disciplined, spare style as his debut film *Clean, Shaven*, Kerrigan's follow-up is another cold film with a warm center. Featuring characters and a narrative a little less compelling than his debut work, the challenging *Claire Dolan* follows the story of an Irish immigrant (Cartlidge), a high-class prostitute who owes her sleazy pimp (Meaney) money and is working only until her debt is paid. She attempts to escape her existence by moving to Long Island, where she begins dating a kindly cabbie (an excellent D'Onofrio). Her past, of course, catches up with her. Some terrific individual moments, sturdy performances and an effective score give relief from the film's depressing tone; ultimately, this unusual character study moves in unexpected ways. ★★★ VHS: $29.99

Claire of the Moon

(1992, 106 min, US, Nicole Conn) *Trisha Todd, Karen Trumbo, Faith McDevitt.* While not the breakthrough lesbian film, *Claire of the Moon* is an earnest, if amateurish drama of simmering female sexual desire and equally strong denial. At an oceanside women writers' retreat in Oregon, Dr. Noel Benedict (Trumbo), an author of "serious" books, finds herself rooming with her opposite — Claire (Todd), a willowy yet cynical straight blonde woman who is determinedly messy and fun-loving. Their budding relationship becomes a tense and inadvertently amusing cat-and-mouse game of "I want you . . . I don't want you" as they alternately try to overcome their insecurities and accept their true feelings. A refreshingly intimate lesbian romance that works as a love story despite being a talky and didactic soap. ★★ DVD 2-disc Collector's Edition: $24.99, VHS: $19.99

Claire's Knee

(1970, 106 min, France, Eric Rohmer) *Jean-Claude Brialy, Aurora Cornu, Beatrice Romand, Laurence de Monaghan.* The fifth in director Rohmer's series of "Moral Tales," *Claire's Knee* is a

sophisticated comedy of lust, unfulfilled desire and fidelity. The film tells the story of a young diplomat, recently engaged, who harbors a peculiar obsession for the teenage sister of his fiancée. A literate satire on sexual temptations with fine cinematography by Nestor Alemendros. (French with English subtitles) ★★★ DVD: $19.99, VHS: $14.99

Clara's Heart

(1988, 108 min, US, Robert Mulligan) *Whoopi Goldberg, Neil Patrick Harris, Michael Ontkean, Kathleen Quinlan, Spalding Gray.* A heartwarming performance by Goldberg dominates this uneven drama about a Jamaican maid whose loving influence on a young boy (Harris) helps him through family difficulties. Ontkean and Quinlan are the youth's parents — grief-stricken over the death of their infant — who inadvertently ignore their other child. ★★ VHS: $14.99

Clash by Night

(1952, 105 min, US, Fritz Lang) *Barbara Stanwyck, Robert Ryan, Paul Douglas, Marilyn Monroe, Keith Andes.* Stanwyck gives a dynamic performance in this steamy psychodrama as the penned-up wife of a boring fishing boat captain (Douglas) whose yearning for excitement leads her to her husband's best friend (Ryan). ★★★

Clash of the Titans

(1981, 118 min, GB, Desmond Davis) *Harry Hamlin, Judi Bowker, Laurence Olivier, Maggie Smith.* Special effects by Ray Harryhausen (his final film before retirement) highlight this appealing if listless Greek mythology adventure set during ancient times. ★★ DVD Letterbox: $14.99

Class

(1983, 98 min, US, Lewis John Carlino) *Jacqueline Bisset, Rob Lowe, Andrew McCarthy, Cliff Robertson, John Cusack, Alan Ruck, Casey Siemaszko, Joan Cusack.* Bisset finds herself unknowingly involved with her son's college roommate. Lowe is her offspring, McCarthy is her youthful lover. Bisset brings more class to this uninspired teen comedy than it deserves. ★½ DVD: $14.99

Class Act

(1992, 98 min, US, Randall Miller) *Christopher Reid, Christopher Martin, Meshach Taylor, Doug E. Doug.* Blend the hip-hop hijinks of Kid 'n Play's previous hit, *House Party*, throw in a little of the antic, slap-and-ouch comedy of the Three Stooges and a 1990s black version of Hope and Crosby, and you get some idea of what is in store in this agreeably inane teen comedy. Teen genius Kid (Reid) finds himself in a foul-up that has him changing places with one of his school's fun-loving bums, Play (Martin). Although all of the goings-on are predictable, the film's infectious desire to entertain and amuse pays off, creating a harmless, antidrug comedy that is pure fun. ★★★ VHS: $19.99

Class Action

(1991, 110 min, US, Michael Apted) *Gene Hackman, Mary Elizabeth Mastrantonio.* Hackman's dominant performance highlights this routine though intriguing courtroom drama — though he's not on screen nearly enough. He plays a dedicated attorney who on behalf of an injured motorist takes a powerful corporation to court — with his daughter Mastrantonio as the opposing council. Part mystery and part courtroom intrigue, the film has moments of interest, but some of the twists are rather contrived. ★★

The Class of Miss MacMichael

(1978, 93 min, GB, Silvio Narizzano) *Glenda Jackson, Oliver Reed, Michael Murphy, Rosalind Cash.* Jackson stars as a fiesty trade schoolteacher who struggles to gain the respect of her unruly students. Reed plays the school's menacing principal. The combination of comedy and melodrama is illserved here. ★½

Class of 1984

(1982, 93 min, US, Mark L. Lester) *Perry King, Timothy Van Patten, Roddy McDowell, Michael J. Fox.* The new teacher (King) gets tormented by his students — and by Van Patten in particular — at an inner-city high school. Without the pretensions of a serious-minded examination of teacher-student relations, this half-baked, violent actioner is strictly for thrills — though it produces only a few. ★★

Class of 1999

(1989, 99 min, US, Mark L. Lester) *Malcolm McDowell, Stacy Keach, Pam Grier.* In the wake of *The Terminator* comes this not-too-shabby rip-off (but rip-off nonetheless) about a high school from hell where gangbangers meet their match in a group of malfunctioning renegade robot teachers. ★★½

Clay Pigeons

(1998, 104 min, US, David Dobkin) *Janeane Garofalo, Vince Vaughn, Joaquin Phoenix, Georgina Cates, Scott Wilson.* A playful noir thriller that ambles at its own speed but has a few, nice surprises along the way. Both comic and dark, the story follows down-on-his luck Clay (an engaging Phoenix), a small-town cowboy who's having an affair with his best friend Earl's wife. But Earl has a plan and he's gone through with it — commit suicide and frame Clay for murder. It's up to Clay to straighten things out. Enter Lester Long (Vaughn), an enigmatic stranger who befriends Clay. In no time, more dead bodies, the F.B.I. and a serial killer who may or may not be Lester cross Clay's path. Dobkin makes good use of the dusty locale, nicely capturing the pace and environment for their satiric and atmospheric qualities. Vaughn mixes menace with charm to make a most believable scoundrel. ★★★ DVD: $9.99

Clean and Sober

(1988, 122 min, US, Glenn Gordon Caron) *Michael Keaton, Morgan Freeman, Kathy Baker, M. Emmet Walsh.* Keaton, in a departure from his comic portrayals, gives a first-rate performance as a drug-addicted businessman who hides out in a drug rehab; this forces him to come to terms with his addiction. While lacking the strong narrative of *The Lost Weekend* or *The Days of Wine and Roses*, the film nevertheless is a forceful drama told in a truthful, no-holds-barred manner. Excellent support from Freeman as a dedicated counselor and Baker as a weary addict. ★★★ DVD: $14.99

Clean, Shaven

(1995, 109 min, US, Lodge Kerrigan) *Peter Greene, Robert Albert, Jennifer MacDonald.* Kerrigan's first film is a vivid, gut-wrenching study of paranoid schizophrenia, told from the point of view of the disturbed individual. Greene stars as a recently released mental patient who begins an obsessive quest to find his young daughter. When his tortured journey takes a murderous turn, a manhunt begins and he is pursued by an equally obsessive detective. The film's soundtrack is particularly innovative, layering various elements such as radio broadcasts, overheard conversations and random noises within and around the dialogue itself. Very experimental in nature, and definitely not for the squeamish, *Clean, Shaven* is a highly original vision which succeeds as both social commentary and as a radically new method of exposition. ★★★ DVD: $19.99

Clean Slate

(1994, 107 min, US, Mick Jackson) *Dana Carvey, Valeria Golino, James Earl Jones, Kevin Pollak, Michael Murphy, Michael Gambon.* This amusing, gimmick-ridden piffle stars Carvey as a mild-mannered private eye whose plans to testify against a crime boss are thwarted when a rare form of amnesia makes him forget everything that happened the day before. Not very memorable, and that's the point. ★★ DVD Dual: $14.99

Clear and Present Danger

(1994, 142 min, US, Phillip Noyce) *Harrison Ford, Willem Dafoe, Anne Archer, James Earl Jones, Donald Moffat, Joaquim de Almeida, Ann Magnuson, Benjamin Bratt, Thora Birch.* Ford reprises his role from *Patriot Games* in this third Jack Ryan tale. An efficient and exciting thriller, *Danger* begins as Ryan takes over as acting deputy director of the CIA. He soon finds himself in political hot water and immediate danger when he uncovers evidence of White House duplicity with a drug cartel. Though the film is slightly overlong, it never fails to entertain, and there's a slam-bang ambush scene which is breathtaking. As usual, Ford is a commanding presence and his heroic Everyman character is well served here. More thrilling than *Games* and on par with *Hunt for Red October*, *Danger* is a helluva ride. ★★★½ DVD Letterbox Special Collector's Edition: $19.99, VHS: $9.99, VHS Letterbox: $9.99

Clearcut

(1992, 98 min, Canada, Richard Bucaski) *Graham Greene, Ron Lea, Floyd "Red Crow" Westerman.* This Native American *Deliverance* serves as an impassioned cry against environmental atrocities committed in the Canadian wilderness by big timber and paper companies. Greene plays Arthur, an irate Native who, upon learning of yet another court decision against his tribe, takes matters into his own hands and abducts the foreman of the local paper mill and the lawyer representing his tribe and takes them to the forest for a harrowing lesson in humility. Greene gives a sturdy performance in this sometimes compelling drama. ★★½ VHS: $79.99

Cleo from 5 to 7
(Cleo de cinq à sept)

(1961, 90 min, France, Agnès Varda) *Corinne Marchand, Antoine Bourseiller, Dorothee Blanck, Michel Legrand, Anna Karina, Jean-Luc Godard, Eddie Constantine.* An intelligent and absorbing film which examines a woman at the crossroads of life. A successful Parisian songstress, fearing the worst, is forced to reevaluate her life while waiting two hours for a medical report on her health. (French with English subtitles) ★★★½ DVD Criterion Collection: $29.99, VHS: $29.99

Cleopatra

(1963, 248 min, US, Joseph L. Mankiewicz) *Elizabeth Taylor, Richard Burton, Rex Harrison, Roddy McDowall, Hume Cronyn, Martin Landau.* Notorious epic about the queen of the Nile. Whether it's more noted for the Taylor-Burton angle (they met and fell in love) or the colossal sum spent on it, the film, though spectacular looking, is a tough four-hour viewing. However, it does feature two award-calibre performances by Harrison (who was Oscar

Cleo from 5 to 7

nominated) and McDowall (who wasn't because of a clerical error). ★★ DVD Five Star Collection: $26.99, VHS: $12.99

Cleopatra Jones

(1973, 89 min, US, Jack Starrett) *Tamara Dobson, Shelley Winters, Antonio Fargas.* There's lots of action in this violent adventure with Dobson as a lovely but lethal martial arts-trained government agent out to bust drug kingpins — including the hilariously preposterous Winters. (Sequel: *Cleopatra Jones and the Casino of Gold*) ★★½ DVD: $9.99, VHS: $9.99

Cleopatra Jones
and the Casino of Gold

(1975, 94 min, US, Chuck Bail) *Tamara Dobson, Stella Stevens, Norman Fell.* Don't let an incoherent plot and ludicrous acting keep you away from this fun if less-than-stellar follow-up to *Cleopatra Jones*. The leggy Dobson returns as the brave and sexy drug agent out to wipe out a notorious Hong Kong drug ring. Stevens camps it up as the villainous "Dragon Lady." ★★ VHS: $9.99

Clerks

(1994, 89 min, US, Kevin Smith) *Brian O'Halloran, Jeff Anderson, Marilyn Ghigliotti, Kevin Smith, Jason Mewes.* The two-store location in *Clerks*, a ferociously entertaining gem, doesn't even count as a mall — it's just a parking lot anchored by third-rate video and convenience stores. To work in either establishment is more serving time than being employed. The convenience store clerk tries to maintain a sense of direction in the face of futility; the video store guy has abandoned hope long ago. Waiting in limbo, without even the comforting illusion of Godot, these Generation Xers structure their pointless day with corpse abuse, analyses of working-class exploitation, unrequited love and sponging friends. This original, highly inventive low-budget surprise stirs its disparate elements into a '90s examination of meaning and purpose. It all culminates with the delivery of spontaneous satori in the face of existential despair. And it's damn funny, too. ★★★½ DVD: $19.99, VHS: $9.99

The Client

(1994, 124 min, US, Joel Schumacher) *Brad Renfro, Susan Sarandon, Tommy Lee Jones, Will Patton, Anthony LaPaglia, Mary-Louise Parker, Anthony Edwards.* This adaptation of John

Grisham's novel falls short of its expectations. Sarandon stars as a struggling Memphis attorney who sees a golden opportunity walk in her door in the person of a young boy — a witness to the suicide of a mob lawyer — who hires her to help keep the Feds off his back. Of course, the bad guys show up, and the little guy finds himself on the run from both relentless G-man Jones and villainous underworld kingpin LaPaglia. While at times entertaining, the film suffers from too many incredulities and a slack plot full of deadly breaks in the action. ★★½ DVD: $14.99, VHS: $9.99

Cliffhanger

(1993, 118 min, US, Renny Harlin) *Sylvester Stallone, John Lithgow, Michael Rooker, Janine Turner, Paul Winfield, Caroline Goodall, Leon, Max Perlich.* An unbelievably hair-raising, excessively violent actioner which, when flexing its special effects and cinematographic muscles, is nothing short of remarkable. However, these first-rate action scenes are offset by one-dimensional characters, clichéd plot developments and flat dialogue. Stallone plays an expert mountain climber haunted by the edge-of-your-seat opening tragedy. Reluctantly, he returns to the same locale when skyjackers crash land in the mountains. Thrills, lots of blood, gruesome deaths, amazing climbing footage and a caveload of bats await them. ★★½ DVD Letterbox Collector's Edition: $14.99, VHS: $9.99

The Clinic

(1984, 93 min, Australia, David Stevens) *Chris Haywood, Simon Burke.* A comedy about social disease? It may sound strange, possibly in bad taste and potentially off-putting, but *The Clinic* is a surprisingly fresh and funny frolic about one day in the life of a Sydney V.D. clinic. Chock full of bawdy doctor/patient vignettes, the film is never derisive and maintains a gentle understanding for the afflicted denizens of this madcap milieu. ★★★

Cloak and Dagger

(1946, 106 min, US, Fritz Lang) *Gary Cooper, Lili Palmer, Robert Alda.* A routine spy thriller that is more cloak than dagger. Cooper stars as an American scientist who is sent to Germany during WWII to uncover military secrets. Palmer is the femme fatale with whom he becomes involved. ★★½ VHS: $19.99

Cloak and Dagger

(1984, 101 min, US, Richard Franklin) *Henry Thomas, Dabney Coleman, Michael Murphy.* Enjoyable and even suspenseful children's thriller with Thomas as a young boy who becomes involved with spies when he obtains secret microfilm. Coleman plays dual roles as his father and his imaginary James Bond-ish playmate. ★★½ VHS: $19.99

The Clock

(1945, 90 min, US, Vincente Minnelli) *Judy Garland, Robert Walker, James Gleason.* A lovely romantic drama featuring one of Garland's best dramatic performances. Judy plays an office worker who meets soldier Walker while he's on a two-day pass; the two fall in love while spending the day together. ★★★½ VHS: $19.99

Clockers

(1995, 129 min, US, Spike Lee) *Harvey Keitel, Delroy Lindo, John Turturro, Keith David, Mekhi Phifer.* Lee collaborated with Martin Scorsese (he produced) on this adaptation of Richard Price's best-selling novel. In a very good debut performance, Phifer plays Strike, a smart youth who has gotten involved with a local crime lord, Rodney (Lindo). Strike is a "clocker," a dealer who can be found working around the clock from his perch on a park bench. When a murder occurs, a sympathetic homicide detective (Keitel) on the case refuses to believe the self-defense story given by Strike's brother, who has confessed to the crime. The officer probes deeper into Strike's world, pressuring the young man to come clean and give up Rodney. A complex tale of loyalty, betrayal and honor, and powerful without being maudlin. *Clockers* may not be particularly distinguished, but it is entertaining, engrossing and enlightening. ★★★ DVD: $14.99, VHS: $9.99

The Clockmaker

(1973, 105 min, France, Bertrand Tavernier) *Philippe Noiret, Jean Rochefort, Jacques Denis.* Based on a novel by Georges Simenon, this fascinating and thought-provoking drama stars Noiret as a clockmaker in Lyon whose life is drastically changed after he learns that his son was involved in leftist terrorist acts. With the arrest of his son, the man's placid and ordered life must be reviewed as he tries to understand his role in the world. One of the finest French films of the 1970s. French with English subtitles) ★★★★ DVD: $29.99, VHS: $24.99

Clockwatchers

(1997, 96 min, US, Jill Sprecher) *Toni Collette, Parker Posey, Lisa Kudrow, Alanna Ubach, Paul Dooley.* Collette stars as an ambitious temp worker who gets a job at a credit agency. She immediately befriends three other temps there, and the surprisingly close quartet soon have their friendships and loyalties tested when they are suspected in a rash of thefts. Anyone who's ever worked as a temp will instantly recognize many dead-on details and situations, and the atmosphere captured by director Spencer is totally accurate. The first half of *Clockwatchers* is an extremely funny, lightly satiric view of office politics (Posey has all the best moments here). But when the plot mechanics start to grind, the picture becomes too self-serious, its light touch lost for good. ★★★ DVD: $24.99, VHS: $14.99

Clockwise

(1986, 98 min, GB, Christopher Morahan) *John Cleese, Penelope Wilton, Alison Steadman.* Monty Python's Cleese is in rare comic form in this delightful and uproarious comedy as a fastidious headmaster whose perfunctory life is turned upside-down when he boards the wrong train for an important conference. ★★★½ DVD: $19.99

A Clockwork Orange

(1971, 135 min, GB, Stanley Kubrick) *Malcolm McDowell, Patrick Magee, Adrienne Corri.* Little Alex and his grahzny droogs prowl the streets in search of sladky devotchkas. Kubrick's brilliant adaptation of the Anthony Burgess novel assaults the screen with snakes, Ludwig von, the old in-out and oodles more. Don't be oddy-knocky, take this tape home and viddy the meaning of it, all my brothers. ★★★★ DVD: $19.99, VHS: $19.99

A Clockwork Orange

Close Encounters of the Third Kind

(1977, 152 min, US, Steven Spielberg) *Richard Dreyfuss, Melinda Dillon, Teri Garr, François Truffaut, Bob Balaban.* Spielberg's classic sci-fi film. Dreyfuss and Dillon are just two of the many Earthlings to see an alien craft — and are compelled to travel to Devil's Tower in Wyoming. The special effects, including the mother ship and the aliens, are second to none, and John Williams' lush, magical score is extraordinary. (This is the "special edition," which includes scenes not in the original 1977 release) ★★★★ DVD Letterbox 2-disc set: $27.99, DVD Letterbox Basic Edition: $19.99, VHS: $12.99

Close to Eden

(1992, 106 min, Russia, Nikita Mikhalkov) *Badema, Byaertu, Vladimir Gostukhin.* This exquisitely rendered fable examines the effects of modernization on a family living on the Mongolian steppes just inside the Chinese border. After giving shelter to a stranded Russian truck driver, the family begins to question their own traditional lifestyles, leading the father to make a hilarious yet sobering journey to the nearest big city in search of such modern amenities as a television and condoms. Mikhalkov masterfully depicts their simple yet noble lives as contrasted with the polluted degradation of the industrialized city and keeps the pace lively despite the film's essentially static nature. (Russian with English subtitles) ★★★★ VHS: $7.99

Closely Watched Trains

(1966, 89 min, Czechoslovakia, Jiri Menzel) *Vaclav Neckar, Jitka Bendova, Josef Somr.* This Oscar-winning Best Foreign Film is a charming, bittersweet tragicomedy about a young, naive train dispatcher and his attempts to find love during the Nazi occupation. (Czechoslovakian with English subtitles) ★★★½ DVD Criterion Collection: $29.99, VHS: $29.99

The Closet

(2000, 85 min, France, Francis Veber) *Daniel Auteuil, Gérard Depardieu, Thierry Lhermitte, Michèle Laroque, Michel Aumont.* François Pignon (Auteuil) is a mild-mannered accountant who lost his wife to boredom, his son thinks him ordinary, and he's about to be fired from his job at the condom factory. When his new neighbor suggests that he create a fake "coming out" to stave off his job problems, he reluctantly agrees. Not only does François keep his job, but he thrives as a new "out gay man." He is offered a promotion at work, a former homophobe (Depardieu) appears to have fallen in love with him, and he's fallen for a woman who thinks him gay! *The Closet* uses the new cinematic tolerance for gays as fodder for laughs, and it does produce a few. It's more sensi-

tive and funnier than the similarly themed *Three to Tango*, but ultimately it's just another gay joke without a fully realized punch line. (French with English subtitles) ★★½ DVD Letterbox: $14.99, VHS Subtitled: $9.99

Closet Land

(1991, 95 min, US, Radha Bharadwaj) *Alan Rickman, Madeleine Stowe.* In a nameless country, a woman, the writer of children's books, is taken to a secluded room with no apparent exit or entrance. There she is interrogated by a seemingly benign officer. But when his requests for a confession to political subversion are denied, he becomes increasingly violent, inflicting mental and physical torture to achieve his goal. Stowe and Rickman give tremendous performances in this political allegory, a powerful and fascinating study of the individual struggle to control one's own thoughts, and an acknowledgement of the resiliency of the human spirit. ★★★

The Clouded Yellow

(1951, 85 min, GB, Ralph Thomas) *Trevor Howard, Jean Simmons, Kenneth More.* An exciting psychological thriller and whodunit. Howard plays a British secret agent who is forced into retirement. He accepts a job in the country looking forward to peace and relaxation. There he meets emotionally scarred Simmons, who becomes the prime suspect in the murder of a hired hand. Together, Howard and Simmons flee the countryside in a determined effort to prove her innocence. The film takes its time setting up characterization, but once the chase begins, *The Clouded Yellow* (named after an elusive butterfly) shifts gears and becomes an unpredictable Hitchcock-like chase story that stays suspenseful until the final credits. ★★★½ VHS: $39.99

Clouds over Europe

(1939, 78 min, GB, Tim Whelan) *Laurence Olivier, Ralph Richardson, Valerie Hobson.* Olivier and especially Richardson are in terrific form in this taut espionage thriller which — à la *The Thin Man* — combines unusually witty comedy with a darn good mystery. Set in England at the start of WWII, the film stars Richardson as a government agent who is investigating the disappearance of top secret British aircraft. Olivier is one of the pilots who helps crack both the case and the skulls of the Nazis behind the scurrilous plot. (aka: *Q Planes*) ★★★½

The Clowns

(1970, 90 min, Italy, Federico Fellini) This "documentary" within a film is a three-ring circus of spectacle, slapstick and sensation. Fellini (acting in the film as head of the camera crew) lovingly pays homage to the circus clowns of his childhood. (Italian with English subtitles) ★★★ VHS: $19.99

The Club

(1980, 93 min, Australia, Bruce Beresford) *Jack Thompson, Graham Kennedy, John Wood.* An entertaining if pedestrian sports drama. Thompson is terrific as the inspirational coach of a soccer club who must change his team's losing ways and rally them to a championship. The film's not brain surgery but at least it's better than *The Fish That Saved Pittsburgh*. ★★½

Club des Femmes

(1936, 90 min, Jacques Deval) *Danielle Darrieux.* Darrieux stars as a nightclub entertainer who lives with several other women in a hotel in Paris where men are banned. The women's lives and fates unravel in this entertaining, playfully energetic farce. (French with English subtitles) ★★★

Club Extinction

(1990, 112 min, France/Italy/West Germany, Claude Chabrol) *Jennifer Beals, Alan Bates, Andrew McCarthy.* A stunning futuristic tale about a German society plagued by a series of violent, unexplained suicides. Originally titled *Dr. M.* (perhaps in homage to Fritz Lang's entropic character), the film stars Bates as the megalomaniacal Dr. Marsfeldt, head of an all-powerful media organization and self-professed "travel agent" for whom death is the ultimate vacation. Beals is oddly (but effectively) cast as Marsfeldt's unwitting ally. Fans of the cerebral science fiction of the '70s will find this a welcome treat. (Filmed in English) ★★★

Club Paradise

(1986, 96 min, US, Harold Ramis) *Robin Williams, Peter O'Toole, Rick Moranis, Jimmy Cliff, Joanna Cassidy, Twiggy, Adolph Caesar.* A waterlogged comedy about a disabled firefighter (Williams) who becomes partners with a reggae nightclub owner (Cliff) in a broken-down Caribbean resort. ★★

Clue: The Movie

(1985, 96 min, US, Jonathan Lynn) *Eileen Brennan, Christopher Lloyd, Madeline Kahn, Tim Curry, Lesley Ann Warren, Michael McKean.* A good cast is wasted in this limp, gimmicky mystery-comedy based on the popular board game. Was it Mrs. Peacock in the library with the candlestick? Or was it Col. Mustard in the hall with the rope? Who cares? ★ DVD: $14.99, VHS: $14.99

Clueless

(1995, 97 min, US, Amy Heckerling) *Alicia Silverstone, Stacey Dash, Brittany Murphy, Paul Rudd, Julie Brown, Jeremy Sisto, Dan Hedaya, Wallace Shawn.* What writer-director Heckerling did for the 1980s with *Fast Times at Ridgemont High* she does for the '90s in this hilariously witty send-up of high school life and adolescence (specifically California upper-middle class). The superficial but naively intelligent Cher (Silverstone) comes to a life decision to use her good looks and popularity for good causes. She sets out on a glorious quest to play matchmaker and good samaritan to anyone within arm's reach — but will she herself find true love? Heckerling's delicious updating of Jane Austen's "Emma" is one mirthful exposition after another, playfully lampooning the teenage milieu — there's a gallery of funny one-liners and comic vignettes. ★★★½ DVD: $14.99, VHS: $9.99

Coal Miner's Daughter

(1980, 125 min, US, Michael Apted) *Sissy Spacek, Tommy Lee Jones, Beverly D'Angelo, Levon Helm.* Spacek won an Oscar for her stirring portrait of country singer Loretta Lynn in this accomplished musical biography. The film follows Lynn's rise from a poor Kentucky mining town to country music superstar. Jones gives a fine performance as Lynn's husband, and D'Angelo is sensational as Patsy Cline. ★★★½ DVD Letterbox Collector's Edition: $14.99, VHS: $9.99

Cobb

(1994, 128 min, US, Ron Shelton) *Tommy Lee Jones, Robert Wuhl, Lolita Davidovich.* Ty Cobb was one of the greats on the field, but off it he was despised by the players and public alike. *Cobb,*

Shelton's demanding adaptation of Al Stump's myth-shaking novel, makes it easy to see why. Jones gives a big, brash performance as the baseball great, now in his 70s. He's just hired second-string reporter Stump (Wuhl) to write his biography. As Stump gathers biographical information, he soon comes to realize that the legend of the player is greatly contradicted by the actions of the man. Shelton takes the chance of alienating most viewers. But it only underscores his story about the demystification of our heroes and the price it extracts. ★★½ DVD: $19.99, VHS: $14.99

Cobra

(1925, 75 min, US, Joseph Henabery) *Rudolph Valentino, Nita Naldi.* One year before his death, Valentino went independent with this enjoyable melodrama about a modern-day Don Juan — a promiscuous Italian count who abandons his homeland for anonymity in New York — who becomes mesmerized by his boss' wife. Only Valentino could hold his own against the lavish sets of William Cameron Menzies and the costuming of ledgendary fashion maven Adrian. But he does so with aplomb. ★★★ DVD: $24.99, VHS: $24.99

Cobra

(1986, 87 min, US, George P. Cosmatos) *Sylvester Stallone, Reni Santoni, Brigitte Nielsen.* Stallone does his *Dirty Harry* bit with far less successful results as a Los Angeles detective hunting a serial killer. Dramatically sloppy and very grisly. ★ DVD: $14.99, VHS: $14.99

The Coca-Cola Kid

(1985, 94 min, Australia, Dusan Makavejev) *Greta Scacchi, Eric Roberts.* Makavejev directed this strangely enjoyable, captialist/sexual comedy that stars Roberts as an overly motivated American corporate whiz kid in search of new markets. Landing in Australia, he encounters difficulty with several stubbornly eccentric Aussies. Makavejev weaves his plot with characteristic absurdity and sensuality. ★★★ DVD: $14.99, VHS: $14.99

Cocaine Cowboys

(1979, 87 min, US, Ulli Lommel) *Jack Palance, Tom Sullivan, Andy Warhol, Suzanna Love.* A strange story of a rock 'n' roll band who smuggle cocaine to help pay their expenses. They fall into trouble with their underworld financiers when a shipment of coke is lost in the ocean. Produced by Warhol. ★ DVD: $16.99

El Cochecito

(1960, 90 min, Spain, Marco Ferreri) This tragi-comedy is something of a perverse one-joke film — old dad, perfectly fit, nonetheless demands from his son a motorized wheelchair in order to socialize properly with his crippled friends. This film wears thin after a while, but it does contain moments of truly bizarre black comedy while making points about the elderly and their loneliness. (Spanish with English subtitles) ★★

Cock & Bull Story

(1992, 80 min, US, Billy Hayes) *Trevor Goddard, Mark Sheppard.* "Midnight Express" author Hayes directed this potent two-man drama videotaped before a live audience. The story is set in a small English town in a gym locker room where Jacko (Sheppard) trains for an upcoming boxing event. His best mate, the fast-talking Travis (Goddard), hangs around and they engage in a series of tension-filled, sexually charged admissions and revelations about their personal feelings. Amidst the taunts and macho posturing by the working-class youths comes

the reality that the two can only express themselves through violence, despite their deep feelings to the contrary. Flat sound quality due to the live recording mars this otherwise gripping story. ★★★

Cockfighter

(1974, 83 min, US, Monte Hellman) *Warren Oates, Patricia Pearcy.* Oates stars as a trainer of fighting cocks whose illegal profession threatens his relationship with girlfriend Pearcy. A fascinating, offbeat drama from Hellman (*Two-Lane Blacktop*). ★★★ DVD: $29.99, VHS: $14.99

Cocktail

(1988, 100 min, US, Roger Donaldson) *Tom Cruise, Bryan Brown, Elisabeth Shue, Kelly Lynch, Gina Gershon.* A completely witless, slick and formulaic piece of celluloid junk food. Cruise stars as a young go-getter who arrives in the Big Apple, ready to cut himself a slice of the Wall Street action. To his dismay, he ends up working in a trendy Uptown bar where — under the tutelage of master bartender and part-time philosopher Brown — he's seduced by the life of quick money and easy women. ★½ DVD: $14.99, VHS: $9.99

Cocktail Molotov

(1980, 100 min, France, Diane Kurys) *Elise Caron, Philippe Lebas, François Cluzet.* Sequel to Kurys' *Peppermint Soda* has Caron encountering political students in Venice, but they all long to be back in Paris, in the midst of the student rebellions. Light and sweet, a wonderful look at 18 year olds discovering themselves while traveling through Europe. (French with English subtitles) ★★★ VHS: $29.99

The Cocoanuts

(1929, 96 min, US, Joseph Santley) *Groucho Marx, Harpo Marx, Chico Marx, Zeppo Marx, Margaret Dumont.* The Marx Brothers' first cinematic exercise in mayhem has the feel of the Vaudeville stage where they cut their teeth. The setting is a Florida hotel rapidly losing money under Groucho's management. All the elements of inspired madness are here, not the least of which is rapid-fire double-talk. ★★★

Cocoon

(1985, 117 min, US, Ron Howard) *Don Ameche, Jessica Tandy, Hume Cronyn, Wilford Brimley, Steve Guttenberg, Maureen Stapleton, Jack Gilford, Gwen Verdon, Brian Dennehy, Barret Oliver.* Pleasant, sentimental sci-fi fantasy about a group of Florida senior citizens who discover a fountain of youth — courtesy of the planet-hopping aliens next door. An exceptional cast of veterans keep it endearing. Ameche won an Oscar. (Sequel: *Cocoon: The Return*) ★★★ DVD: $14.99, VHS: $9.99

Cocoon: The Return

(1988, 116 min, US, Daniel Petrie) *Don Ameche, Jessica Tandy, Hume Cronyn, Wilford Brimley, Maureen Stapleton, Gwen Verdon, Steve Guttenberg.* All the stars of the highly successful *Cocoon* return in this frequently charming though ordinary sequel which brings the aging space travellers back to Earth for a four-day visit. The plot borrows greatly from the original and the story is too syrupy and heavy-handed, but the cast helps to capture a little of the magic of the first film. ★★ DVD: $14.99

Un Coeur en Hiver

(1992, 100 min, France, Claude Sautet) *Emmanuelle Béart, Daniel Auteuil, Andre Dussollier.* Sautet's emotionally cool and complex film is a startling look at love, passion and miscommunication. Dussollier plays a man who leaves his wife for a young, beautiful concert violinist (Beart). After meeting her lover's business partner (Auteuil), she soon falls in love with him. Auteuil's performance as the cold and emotionally void object of affection is an underrated gem. (French with English subtitles) ★★★½

Coffy

(1973, 91 min, US, Jack Hill) *Pam Grier, Booker Bradshaw.* Duck for cover! Hipswinging Grier, the queen of blaxploitation, is packing and out for violent revenge! Spurred by her little sister's drug overdose, nurse Coffy becomes a one-woman execution squad as she seeks out the people responsible. Sexy, smart and always willing to bare her considerable assets in the line of duty, our sweet heroine poses as a prostitute as she battles crooked politicians, L.A. cops on the take, Italian drug pushers and Super Fly-attired pimps. She blows them all away in this violent, action-packed thriller. ★★½ DVD: $14.99

Cold around the Heart

(1997, 96 min, US, John Ridley) *David Caruso, Kelly Lynch, Stacey Dash, Chris Noth, John Spencer.* Though ultimately just another nail in the coffin of career suicide Caruso, this Jim Thompson-esque journey into amorality (written by director Ridley) can be summed up as *Bonnie and Clyde* meets *The Last Seduction.* Caruso is strangely endearing as a pony-tailed, Mamet-spouting "ewok" who goes hunting for his double-crossing, ice-goddess girlfriend (Lynch) when she takes off with the loot and sticks him with the cops. Dash, on the run from an abusive father, tags along for some light sexual tension, but her character is basically an afterthought to Lynch's bleached-blonde lethal weapon in jeans. ★★½ VHS: $79.99

Cold Blood

(1978, 90 min, West Germany, Gunter Vaesse & Ralf Gregan) *Rutger Hauer, Vera Tschechowa.* This "dishonor among thieves" drama features a hot-blooded, miniskirt-clad young woman who falls for the charming but coldly opportunistic Hauer and ends up in a nightmarish adventure. The film keeps one's attention, but the ending is ridiculous. ★★

Cold Comfort Farm

(1995, 99 min, GB, John Schlesinger) *Kate Beckinsale, Eileen Atkins, Ian McKellen, Rufus Sewell, Sheila Burrell, Stephen Fry, Freddie Jones, Joanna Lumley, Miriam Margolyes.* What begins as a seemingly familiar "Masterpiece Theatre" and Merchant Ivory-style upper-class English drama soon turns into a raucously funny satire that's a true delight. In the 1930s, pretty but naive Flora Poste (Beckinsale) finds herself an orphan (and penniless), so she decides to claim her "rights" by moving to the estate of her rural relatives, the Starkadders of Sussex. And that is where the drawing room familiarity ends; for the doom-laden Starkadders, saddled by an ancient curse, are one sorry lot. They live in medieval squalor, talk in olde English and are far from accomodating to their high-falootin cousin. But Flora rolls up her sleeves and, with a smile on her pretty face, pulls the family into the 20th century. Adapted from Stella Gibbons' 1932 parody. ★★★★

Cold Creek Manor

(2003, 118 min, US, Mike Figgis) *Dennis Quaid, Sharon Stone, Stephen Dorff, Juliette Lewis, Christopher Plummer, Kristen Stewart.* Ne'er-do-well hick Dorff gets behind on his payments on the family estate, so well-off couple Quaid and Stone, tired of dangerous big-city living, buy the country mansion at auction for a steal. Thus begins an antagonistic relationship between city and country, haves and have-nots, clichés and. . . well, more clichés. Figgis and his actors bring some immediacy and tension to some scenes, but many moments feel rote and uninspired. The film is watchable enough for a while, but the promise (at least from the trailer) that the horror has supernatural roots is false, and the "big surprise" turns out to be a big yawn; the climax is as artificial and unsatisfying as these things get, making one wish they'd spent their two hours elsewhere. ★½ DVD: $29.99, VHS: $102.99

Cold Feet

(1984, 96 min, US, Bruce van Dusen) *Griffin Dunne, Marissa Chibas, Blanche Baker.* Dunne and Chibas, both involved in nongratifying relationships, take a chance on each other in a final stab at romance. Baker has some good scenes as Dunne's ex-wife in this otherwise static comedy. ★★ VHS: $59.99

Cold Feet

(1989, 94 min, US, Robert Dornhelm) *Keith Carradine, Sally Kirkland, Tom Waits, Rip Torn, Bill Pullman.* Screenwriter and novelist Tom McGuane's engrossing comedy, set in Montana, stars Carradine as the sanest in a trio of modern-day desperados whose partners include his oversexed wife-to-be Kirkland and Waits as a charming but dangerous killer bent on revenge after being jilted out of the money from their last heist. The couple's attempts to settle down in anonymity with their loot prove to be as elusive as the law, and their own lust and greed finally undermine their demented idea of the American Dream. This outrageous comedy is engaging and fun, although the writing seems forced at times with zany characters trying a bit too hard to be "weird." ★★★ DVD: $14.99

Cold Fever

(1995, 85 min, Iceland, Fridrik Thor Fridriksson) *Masatoshi Nagase, Lili Taylor, Fisher Stevens, Gisli Halldorsson.* A young Japanese executive, Atsuhi Hirata (Nagase), forgoes a sunny golfing holiday in Hawaii in order to conduct a traditional memorial ceremony in honor of his dead parents. To complete this ritual, he must travel to the harsh, wintry wilderness of Iceland, where he meets an oddball assortment of eccentric characters. As Hirata travels through the frozen wasteland, his journey of making peace with the dead becomes a personal quest for inner solace, made all the more powerful and mesmerizing by the film's spellbinding cinematography. *Cold Fever* shifts from quirky comedy to contemplative, existential drama and coalesces into a meditative comment on spirituality and an individual's place in the world. (In English and Japanese and Icelandic with English subtitles) ★★★½ VHS: $19.99

Cold Heaven

(1992, 105 min, US, Nicolas Roeg) *Theresa Russell, Mark Harmon, Will Patton, Talia Shire.* Anyone who thinks the age of chivalry is dead should take a look at the career of director Roeg who seems content to simply make movies to keep his wife (actress Russell) employed. Case in point: this unabashedly moralistic drama that veers wildly between being a supernatural thriller and a Hallmark greeting card. Russell essays the role of an unfaithful wife who experiences extreme Catholic guilt when her husband (Harmon) is killed before she can make amends. ★ VHS: $14.99

Cold Mountain

(2003, 155 min, US, Anthony Minghella) *Jude Law, Nicole Kidman, Renée Zellweger, Kathy Baker, Brendan Gleeson, Philip Seymour Hoffman, Donald Sutherland, Natalie Portman, Ray Winstone, Charlie Hunnam, Eileen Atkins, Giovanni Ribisi.* A terrific ensemble brings to life Charles Frazier's award-winning novel of love and sacrifice in the Old South during the final days of the Civil War. Featuring strong direction from Minghella (*The English Patient*), superior production design and a touching story of thwarted love, *Cold Mountain* melds the romantic and horrific onto a handsome package whose episodic stories can't help but engage. A miscast Kidman is Ada, the daughter of a minister who tries to keep the family estate intact after her father's death. Law is excellent as Inman, a Confederate soldier who leaves behind the bloody battlefields to return to her. The story interweaves these two plots as Inman must elude detection as a deserter and Ada struggles against the elements and greedy land developers. Zellweger, who won an Oscar for her gritty portrait of a tenacious drifter, is a breath of fresh air as Ruby, who helps Ada farm the land and maintain her sanity. Minghella's battle sequences are superb, leaving little doubt as to why Inman would risk capture and death to return home. On the road, Inman meets a marvelous gallery of characters, the best being the wonderful Hoffman as a defrocked priest, Atkins as a mountain woman and Portman as a young mother. Interestingly, the film avoids tackling issues of slav-

Renée Zellweger (l.) and Nicole Kidman in *Cold Mountain*

ery, unusual for a Civil War-themed, Southern-based story. A minor flaw (though what about Nicole never getting dirty being a farmer!) for an otherwise enthralling tale of war, romance and what it takes to stay alive. ★★★½ DVD 2-disc Special Collector's Edition: $29.99, VHS: $24.99

Cold Sassy Tree

(1989, 100 min, US, Joan Tewkesbury) *Faye Dunaway, Richard Widmark, Neil Patrick Harris, Frances Fisher.* Dunaway and Widmark give affecting performances in this wonderful May-December romance about Northerner Dunaway and widower Widmark's affair shocking his turn-of-the-century Southern town. ★★★ VHS: $14.99

Cold Turkey

(1971, 99 min, US, Norman Lear) *Dick Van Dyke, Bob Newhart, Tom Poston, Vincent Gardenia, Jean Stapleton, Edward Everett Horton.* A '60s-ish comedy about a small town and their efforts to stop smoking for a month to win $25 million in prize money. A pleasant romp, with Van Dyke as the priest spearheading the campaign, and a good supporting cast. ★★★

Colegas

(1980, 117 min, Spain, Eloy de la Iglesia) A fine drama about the friendship between three teenagers in present-day Madrid. Jose and Antonio have been friends for most of their lives, but their relationship is severely tested after it is discovered that Antonio's sister, Rosario, is pregnant by Jose. Their efforts to get an abortion in Catholic Spain lead them to Morocco and the dangerous drug trade. (Spanish with English subtitles) ★★★ VHS: $59.99

The Collection

(1978, 64 min, GB, Michael Apted) *Laurence Olivier, Alan Bates, Malcolm McDowell, Helen Mirren.* A great cast deliver outstanding performances in this gripping adaptation of Harold Pinter's critically acclaimed 1960 play. Harry (Olivier) and Bill (McDowell) are an embittered gay couple who come under attack from the menacing Bates when he accuses the younger Bill of sleeping with his wife (Mirren). Veiled threats and jealousy give way to deception, disappointment and betrayal as all four characters become trapped in a series of recriminations. ★★★½

La Collectionneuse

(1966, 88 min, France, Eric Rohmer) *Patrick Bachau, Daniel Pommereulle, Haydeé Politoff.* An interesting investigation of gender politics as well as modern notions of art, beauty and truth, Rohmer's "fable," the fourth in a series of six, offers an unusual parable for those unschooled in the complex games of sexual pairing. The story revolves around Adrian, a self-important would-be gallery owner, his painter friend Daniel and a Lolita-esque nymphette (Politoff). Adrian attempts to protect his solitude after he finds himself sharing a villa with the others on the Riviera. Though he first resists her, Adrian later becomes obsessed with the young girl's charms. Though Adrian's voice-overs are at times overbearing and didactic, the film maintains an even pace, thorough characterization and a solid story. (French with English subtitles) ★★★ DVD: $29.99, VHS: $19.99

The Collector

(1965, 119 min, GB, William Wyler) *Terence Stamp, Samantha Eggar, Mona Washbourne.* Searing psycho-

logical thriller with Stamp kidnapping Eggar and keeping her prisoner in his basement. Superior performances from the two leads. ★★★½ DVD: $24.99

College

(1927, 66 min, US, James W. Horne) *Buster Keaton, Ann Cornwall.* Keaton stars as a scholar who looks down on athletics but is forced to participate in order to win the attention of his girl. Compared to other Keaton comedies, this is minor, but it is elevated by some memorable gags. ★★★ DVD: $29.99, VHS: $29.99

College Swing

(1938, 86 min, US, Raoul Walsh) *Bob Hope, George Burns, Gracie Allen, Martha Raye, Edward Everett Horton.* Hope's second film is an intermittently amusing hodgepodge of music, laughs, swing, academia and romance. The film's palatable when the five leads are on screen. But some of the musical numbers, an icky romance subplot, and a few comic sequences are rough going. However, it's one of the few films from the 1930s to actually show living and breathing teenagers. They're the real *Swing Kids.* ★★ DVD Double Feature: $14.99

Colonel Redl

(1984, 144 min, Germany/Hungary, István Szabó) *Klaus Maria Brandauer, Armin Mueller-Stahl, Gudrun Landgrebe.* Brandauer gives a bravura performance as a man driven by a lust for power to rise from the son of a poor railway worker to become head of military intelligence and commander of the 8th Army in Prague. A sweeping historical epic of intrigue, love and treason set in Austria during the turbulent years leading up to WWI. (German with English subtitles) ★★★ DVD Letterbox: $29.99, VHS: $14.99

Color Me Blood Red

(1965, 79 min, US, Hershell Gordon Lewis) *Don Joseph, Candi Conder, Elyn Warner, Patricia Lee, Jerome Eden.* A struggling artist (Joseph) finds that blood supplies the perfect color for his newest painting. He begins getting his art suuply from the dripping fingers of his girlfriend, which in turn leads to headsmashing against the canvas — instant art! With the usual bad acting and homemade, disturbing gore, this is the final in Lewis' blood trilogy which includes *Blood Feast* and *Two Thousand Maniacs.* ★ DVD: $24.99

The Color of Money

(1986, 119 min, US, Martin Scorsese) *Paul Newman, Tom Cruise, Mary Elizabeth Mastrantonio, Helen Shaver, John Turturro, Forest Whitaker.* Newman won an Oscar for re-creating his acclaimed role as Fast "Eddie" Felson, ex-pool hustler turned liquor retailer, who vicariously relives the glory days of his youth through a hotshot pool player (Cruise). With Scorsese's inventive direction and Robbie Robertson's smoky score, this is a rare film experience. ★★★★ DVD: $14.99, VHS: $9.99

Color of Night

(1994, 140 min, US, Richard Rush) *Bruce Willis, Jane March, Ruben Blades, Lesley Ann Warren, Scott Bakula, Lance Henriksen, Kevin J. O'Connor.* Sigmund Freud meets a limp *Die Hard* in this mildly diverting but far from mysterious murder mystery starring Willis as a troubled psychologist who gets caught up in a series of murders. After one of his patients throws herself from his New York penthouse, he moves to L.A., where he becomes involved in murder, car chases, a group therapy session from hell, and a mystery woman. Includes the controversial frontal nude scenes of Willis. Prepare to be disappointed. ★★ DVD: $14.99, VHS: $9.99

The Color of Paradise

(1999, 90 min, Iran, Majid Majidi) *Hosein Mahjoob, Salameh Feyzi.* Director Majidi, who helmed the exquisite *Children of Heaven*, weaves another moving, lyrical story that is certain to touch the heart. Mohammad is a young blind boy who returns home from the Institute of the Blind for the summer. Happy to be reunited with his father and grandmother, the child maintains a wondrous perspective on life even though it becomes clear that his father plans on disowning him. A haunting look at childhood innocence and the beauty that surrounds us. (Farsi with English subtitles) ★★★½ DVD: $29.99, VHS: $21.99

The Color of Pomegranates

(1969, 80 min, Armenia/USSR, Sergei Paradjanov) *Sofiko Chiaureli, M. Aleksanian.* Shelved after being termed "hermetic and obscure" by Soviet authorities, this poetic masterpiece was the last film director Paradjanov made before his five-year imprisonment in 1974. *The Color of Pomegranates* focuses on the powerful works and spiritual odyssey of 17th-century Armenian poet Sayat Nova. Filled with oblique, symbolic imagery, this exotic mosaic of a film is divided into eight sections, each depicting — from childhood to death — a period of the poet's life. A tribute not only to Nova but to the spirituality of the Armenian people. (Armenian with English subtitles) ★★★½ DVD: $34.99, VHS: $29.99

The Color Purple

(1985, 153 min, US, Steven Spielberg) *Whoopi Goldberg, Danny Glover, Oprah Winfrey, Margaret Avery, Rae Dawn Chong, Adolph Caesar.* Spielberg's acclaimed though controversial screen version of Alice Walker's Pulitzer Prize-winning novel. Goldberg made a triumphant film debut as a black woman who tries to overcome the hardships of her arranged marriage to ill-tempered Glover to find her own identity. Winfrey and Avery are both terrific in support as, respectively, the live-in maid to an oppressive white family and Glover's mistress, a cabaret singer who contributes greatly to Goldberg's flourishing. ★★★½ DVD 2-disc set: $26.99, VHS: $19.99

Colors

(1988, 120 min, US, Dennis Hopper) *Robert Duvall, Sean Penn, Maria Conchita Alonso, Damon Wayans.* A clamorous vision of gang warfare in Los Angeles directed by Hopper, with his patented flair for the unusual and bizarre. Duvall and Penn are fine in their roles as L.A. cops, but what really gives the film its edge is the presence of actual gang members whom Hopper cast to play the Bloods and the Crips — the city's largest rival gangs. Without totally departing from action movie conventions, *Colors* brims with flavor and detail and features a tremendous soundtrack. ★★★ DVD Letterbox: $14.99

Coma

(1978, 113 min, US, Michael Crichton) *Geneviève Bujold, Michael Douglas, Richard Widmark, Elizabeth Ashley, Tom Selleck, Rip Torn.* Solid medical thriller adapted and directed by former med student Crichton. Bujold is a Boston doctor whose investigations into a series of inexplicable hospital deaths leads her to a horrifying conspiracy. Douglas is her disbelieving boyfriend, and Widmark is well-cast as a hospital administrator. ★★★ DVD: $9.99, VHS: $14.99, VHS Letterbox: $19.99

Combination Platter

(1993, 85 min, US/China, Tony Chan) *Jeff Lau, Colleen O'Brien.* Director Chan elicits finely drawn characterizations with minimal exposition in this low-budget independent feature. Centering around the efforts of a young, newly arrived Hong Kong emigré to get his green card, the deceptively simple story line allows a good ensemble cast to reveal the distinct personalities of a group of restaurant employees dealing with interpersonal conflicts, annoying customers, Department of Immigration agents and familial expectations. A small film, but knowing and direct in its execution. (In English and Chinese with English subtitles) ★★★ VHS: $79.99

Come and Get It

(1936, 99 min, US, Howard Hawks & William Wyler) *Edward Arnold, Joel McCrea, Frances Farmer, Walter Brennan.* An aggressive entrepreneur in the Northwest timber country abandons true love for the boss' daughter. Many years later, he's deluded into believing that he can revoke that decision of youth. Robust performances throughout. Brennan won his first of three Oscars. ★★★ VHS: $14.99

Come and See

(1985, 142 min, USSR, Elem Klimov) *Alexei Kravchenko, Olga Mironova.* The theatrical availability in 1987 of this remarkably powerful Russian film by the long-ostracized director Elem Klimov was one of the first tangible results of *glasnost* in the Soviet Union. Told with a barrage of electrifying imagery, *Come and See* is an account of the brutal invasion suffered by the Russians at the hands of Hitler. Episodes shift back and forth between the ultra-realistic and a dreamlike surrealism that borders on hallucinogenic. As seen through the eyes of a young boy, the Nazi atrocities against his village burn the screen with fierce images that will linger for a long time to come. A powerful cinematic achievement. (Russian with English subtitles) ★★★★ DVD Restored: $29.99, VHS Restored: $24.99

Come Back, Little Sheba

(1952, 99 min, US, Daniel Mann) *Burt Lancaster, Shirley Booth, Terry Moore.* Though she'll probably always be remembered as TV's "Hazel," Booth's finest hour came when she set the stage and screen afire with her unforgettable Oscar-winning performance as the downtrodden wife of an alcoholic (Lancaster). In this brilliant screen version of William Inge's play, Booth and Lancaster rent their home to young Moore, setting the stage for jealousy and recriminations. ★★★★ VHS: $14.99

Come Back to the 5 & Dime, Jimmy Dean, Jimmy Dean

(1982, 110 min, US, Robert Altman) *Cher, Sandy Dennis, Karen Black, Kathy Bates, Sudie Bond.* The stage is set for emotional warfare of a James Dean Fan Club reunion in a dust-bowl Texas town. Sandy's psyche, Cher's chest, Karen's contours and Kathy's sobriety are all in question as every skeleton tumbles from the closet in Altman's bitchy, Southern cat fight. ★★★

Come Blow Your Horn

(1963, 112 min, US, Bud Yorkin) *Frank Sinatra, Lee J. Cobb, Molly Picon, Barbara Rush, Jill St. John, Tony Bill.* Based on Neil Simon's stage play, this free-wheeling comedy charts swinging Sinatra's bachelorhood as he tries to guide his younger brother (Bill in

his screen debut) on the same road. Cobb is excellent as Sinatra's traditional father not happy with the course his sons are taking. ★★★ VHS: $14.99

Come Dance with Me

(1959, 91 min, France, Michel Boisrond) *Brigitte Bardot, Henry Vidal.* In this fluffy comedy-thriller, Bardot does some Nancy Drew-like sleuthing into the murder of a female dance studio owner, a murder that the police believe was committed by her dentist husband. Shot in bright colors and in a breezy style, the film follows Virginia (BB) as she gets a job as a dance instructor at the studio and tries to figure out whodunit. (French with English subtitles) (aka: *Do You Want to Dance with Me?*) ★★½ DVD: $29.99

Come See the Paradise

(1990, 138 min, US, Alan Parker) *Tamlyn Tomita, Sab Shimono, Dennis Quaid.* In this story of the internment of Japanese-Americans in camps during WWII, Parker gets credit for tackling a subject heretofore untouched by any American film, though one wishes the story had more dramatic structure. The first half of the film follows the love affair between a projectionist (Quaid) and his Asian boss' daughter (Tomita). Married for only a short time, they are separated after the bombing of Pearl Harbor. Quaid is drafted, and Tomita and her entire family are uprooted and sent to the camps. The remainder of the film centers on the heartbreaking conditions they face. ★★★ VHS: $19.99

The Comedy of Terrors

(1963, 84 min, US, Jacques Tourneur) *Boris Karloff, Vincent Price, Peter Lorre, Basil Rathbone.* A real treat from Val Lewton's disciple Tourneur. Two bumbling undertakers (Price, Lorre) supplement their business by murdering elderly potential clientele. Karloff is Price's father-in-law, and Rathbone plays a vengeful landlord who accidentally becomes an on-again, off-again customer. With a hilarious and extremely literate script by Richard Matheson, superb art direction, beautiful cinematography and an impressive score, *The Comedy of Terrors* succeeds as both black comedy and tongue-in-cheek horror camp. ★★★½ DVD Letterbox: $14.99

Comes a Horseman

(1978, 118 min, US, Alan J. Pakula) *Jane Fonda, Jason Robards, James Caan, Richard Farnsworth, George Grizzard.* In Montana after the second world war, ranch owner Robards wants Fonda's spread because he knows something she doesn't — there's oil under her land. The only thing stopping him: tough cowboy Caan. Farnsworth is terrific as Fonda's dedicated ranch hand. ★★★ DVD Letterbox: $14.99

Comfort and Joy

(1984, 90 min, Scotland, Bill Forsyth) *Bill Paterson, Eleanor David.* Forsyth's whimsical mixture of "Alice in Wonderland" and *Sullivan's Travels.* When his kleptomaniacal, live-in lover abandons him, Alan (a cheerfully bland Glasgow radio personality) falls into a frightful funk and, aimlessly searching for salvation, stumbles into the midst of a gangland battle between rival factions of an ice cream cartel. ★★★ VHS: $9.99

The Comfort of Strangers

(1991, 102 min, GB, Paul Schrader) *Rupert Everett, Natasha Richardson, Christopher Walken, Helen Mirren.* Director Schrader delves into the dark side of human nature with this visually exquisite production of Harold Pinter's screenplay about a young English couple (Everett, Richardson) who retreat to Venice to reevaluate their relationship and find themselves pawns in the twisted games of an Italian nobleman

and his invalid wife (Walken, Mirren). Marred only slightly by a seemingly unmotivated shock ending, this is quirky entertainment. ★★★

Comic Book Confidential

(1990, 85 min, US, Ron Mann) For devotees of animation, comic books and the creative forces behind them, this fascinating and delightful documentary is required viewing. The film combines historical footage, montages of comic art and a series of amusing interviews with many of the leading independent artists of the last 20 years, including William M. Gaines (of *Mad Magazine* fame), Stan Lee, Robert Crumb, Linda Barry, Art Spiegelman and many others. From the very first comic, "Funnies on Parade," to the avant-garde "Raw," the film provides an entertaining and informational peek behind the animated doors of comics and their creators. ★★★

Coming Home

(1978, 127 min, US, Hal Ashby) *Jane Fonda, Jon Voight, Bruce Dern, Penelope Milford, Robert Carradine.* The stunning, Oscar-winning performances of Voight and Fonda dominate this moving Vietnam war drama about disabled Voight beginning an affair with married Fonda, whose husband Dern is overseas. A poignant love story and gripping anti-war film which unfortunately over-dramatizes some of its key scenes. ★★★ DVD Letterbox: $19.99

Coming Out

(1989, 109 min, Germany, Heiner Carow) *Matthias Freihof, Dirk Kummer, Michael Gwisdek, Dagmar Manzel.* This was East Germany's first and only gay-themed film, which reportedly received its premiere on the same night the Berlin Wall came down. It is a gripping study of a man searching for his true sexual identity. Philip is a "straight" schoolteacher whose repressed homosexuality is ignited after meeting an old school chum with whom he had a gay affair. Reminiscent of quasi-autobiographical films like *Taxi Zum Klo* and *Nighthawks*, this is a sentimental but frank tale. (German with English subtitles) ★★★ DVD: $29.99, VHS: $24.99

Coming to America

(1988, 116 min, US, John Landis) *Eddie Murphy, Arsenio Hall, James Earl Jones, Samuel L. Jackson, Cuba Gooding, Jr..* Only sporadically funny, this Murphy comedy is surprisingly good-natured, a change of pace for the comic. An African prince (Murphy) engaged to a native woman decides to leave his home and head to New York in search of true love. Hall is his "man Friday" who accompanies the prince on his quest. What ensues is a rather formulaic fish-out-of-water tale with most of its jokes telegraphed hours before they arrive. ★★½ DVD: $14.99, VHS: $14.99

Coming Up Roses

(1986, 93 min, Wales, Stephen Bayly) *Dafydd Hywel, Iola Gregory.* A mildly amusing updating of *The Smallest Show on Earth.* Against the grim landscape of Thatcher's England, three employees of a dilapidated movie theatre struggle to save the old house. (Welsh with English subtitles) ★★½

Command Decision

(1949, 113 min, US, Sam Wood) *Clark Gable, Walter Pidgeon, Van Johnson, Brian Donlevy.* Gable stars as an Air Force general wrestling with his conscience about sending young men off to a certain death in order to achieve a strategic victory. Pidgeon plays Gable's superior officer; Johnson is a raw recruit. A gripping and thoughtful war adventure based on the '40s stage hit. ★★★ VHS: $19.99

Commandments

(1997, 87 min, US, Daniel Taplitz) *Aidan Quinn, Courteney Cox, Anthony LaPaglia, Pamela Gray.* An ambitious but misguided quasi-religious comedy-drama, *Commandments* features the underrated Quinn as an emotionally troubled physician who attempts to come to terms with his life after facing a series of traumatic experiences. Losing his wife, job, house and even his dog, Quinn tries to commit suicide, but even that doesn't work out. He lands in a hospital where he recounts his mess-of-a-life and decides the only retribution for his problems is breaking all ten commandments. First-time director Taplitz (who also scripted) never finds a proper tone, and the film veers from brooding to cynical to mystical to light-hearted. Intriguing premise, game cast, but it just doesn't come together. ★★ VHS: $9.99

Commando

(1985, 90 min, US, Mark L. Lester) *Arnold Schwarzenegger, Rae Dawn Chong, Dan Hedeya.* This fast-paced, often amusing adventure thriller (though violent and cluttered) is one of Schwarzenegger's best action films from the early part of his career. Arnold plays a retired Army colonel who sets out to rescue his young daughter, kidnapped by an exiled Latin American dictator. ★★½ DVD: $14.99, VHS: $9.99

Commissar

(1967, 105 min, USSR, Alexander Askoldov) *Nonna Mordyukova, Rolan Bykov.* Banned for 21 years by Soviet authorities, this remarkable human drama shocked the censors with its bold themes of anti-Semitism and women's rights. Set in 1920 during the Russian Civil War, the story follows the austere Claudia, whose military career as a Red Army Commander is jeopardized when she becomes pregnant by a comrade. She moves in with a poor Jewish family in the countryside until the child is born. Initially hostile to the family's religion and peasant ways, she soon finds herself softening and appreciating the cultural differences they have as well as the common bonds they all share. After the child is born, she faces the difficult choice of staying or rejoining the army. (Russian with English subtitles) ★★★½ VHS: $59.99

Commissioner of the Sewers

(1986, 60 min, US, Klaus Maeck) *William Burroughs.* From the publication of his novel "Junkie" in 1963 through the present with the Hollywood-backed film version of his "Naked Lunch," William S. Burroughs has remained a controversial and fascinating figure. This documentary doesn't uncover anything new for seasoned Burroughs-philes, but for the uninitiated, it will prove to be enlightening as Burroughs — with his deadpan wit and outlandish theories — pontificates on everything from his beliefs on death after life, art and artists, to the meaning of his cut-up style of writing. He concludes with a reading of his now famous, and bitterly sarcastic, "Thanksgiving Prayer." ★★½

The Commitments

(1991, 118 min, Ireland, Alan Parker) *Robert Arkins, Michael Aherne, Colm Meaney, Angeline Ball.* Parker's exuberant homage to the Dublin music scene has at its heart a highly talented cast of non-actors recruited for their musical skills. The story follows Jimmy, a determined young hustler who can't rest until he realizes his dream of putting together a soul group. What the film lacks in plot is more than amply made up for in raw energy and outstanding musical numbers, all of which were actually performed by the cast. Some of the versions of soul standards ("Try a Little Tenderness," "Mustang Sally") compare very favorably with the originals. ★★★½ DVD Letterbox 2-disc Collector's Edition: $26.99

Committed

(1984, 77 min, US, Lynne Tillman & Sheila McLaughlin) *Committed* tells the striking story of film star/leftist iconoclast Frances Farmer. While dealing with the same subject as *Frances*, with Jessica Lange, this independent production avoids some of the theatrics in this feminist interpretation of her life. In 1935, Farmer was an overnight Hollywood sensation; within ten years she was in a state mental hospital. From stardom to a locked ward to a lobotomy, the film reconstructs a compelling and many-layered look at the life and repression of this culturally defiant woman. ★★★ VHS: $29.99

Common Threads: Stories from the Quilt

(1989, 79 min, US, Jeffrey Friedman & Robert Epstein) *Narrated by: Dustin Hoffman, Cleve Jones.* In this Academy Award-winning documentary, Epstein and Friedman talk with surviving relatives and friends of five people who died of AIDS and were memorialized by the AIDS Quilt. The film presents an emotionally charged look into their lives, as told by those left behind through recollection, photographs and film. Of course, there is great poignancy to these stories. But the storytellers also infuse a spirit of being to the departed which obviously helps keep the memory of those loved ones alive. Not a eulogistic memorial, but rather personal and heartfelt reminiscences. ★★★½ DVD: $29.99

Communion

(1989, 109 min, US, Philippe Mora) *Christopher Walken, Lindsay Crouse, Frances Sternhagen.* Based on Whitley Strieber's best-seller, which detailed his experiences with alien beings, this serious-minded sci-fi thriller is far more interesting for the allegations presented by the author than for the outcome of the film. Walken, usually adept at playing eccentric characters, gives a truly strange performance as Strieber. The only cast member to really come out of this muddle totally unscathed is Sternhagen, who plays a psychiatrist all too familiar with close encounters of the third kind. ★★ VHS: $14.99

The Company

(2003, 112 min, US, Robert Altman) *Neve Campbell, Malcolm McDowell, James Franco.* A fictional, documentary-style film set in the world of ballet (and featuring members of Chicago's Joffrey company), *The Company* has much in common with Altman's *Ready to Wear* except for the fact that this one is actually good. The plot, cooked up by producer/star Campbell and tuned by longtime Altman collaborator Barbara Turner, is (perhaps neccessarily) quite familiar. Campbell plays a protégée who gets a big break, becomes a star, and finds romance, all leading up to the big production number at the end. Yet despite these machinations (and a stringently heterosexual storyline), the casual dialogue, cattiness and extreme pressure behind the scenes make for convincing and compelling passages. Best of all, roughly half of the running time focuses on the electrifying ballet performances, both in rehearsal and live on stage. Always an expert at using weather for effect, Altman stages a masterful pas de deux during a thunderstorm that features Campbell; she was trained as a ballerina, and though not quite able to perform on pointe, puts a lot of emotion into her dancing. These dance sequences are jazzed up with plenty of cuts and camera movement, but also take care to concentrate on the feet and the inherent artistry; anyone who doesn't "get" ballet will leave with a damn good (and most entertaining) education. ★★★ DVD: $26.99

The Company of Wolves

(1985, 95 min, GB, Neil Jordan) *David Warner, Angela Lansbury, Stephen Rea.* An offbeat Freudian adaptation of "Little Red Riding Hood" that intriguingly explores some of the adult subtexts of the classic story. An atmospheric mixture of dreams and fantasy, the film teeters on the edge of the downright bizarre, but it remains a frighteningly mysterious and slightly sexy thriller. ★★★ DVD Letterbox: $24.99

Company: Original Cast Album

(1970, 58 min, US, D.A. Pennebaker) *Elaine Stritch, Dean Jones, Barbara Barrie, Charles Kimbrough, Harold Prince.* Behind-the-scenes look at the recording sessions of Stephen Sondheim's award-winning Broadway musical "Company." The original Broadway cast, including Elaine Stritch, Barbara Barrie and Charles Kimbrough, and Dean Jones, who replaced lead Larry Kert after three weeks, shine and grind it out in this truly revealing documentary of the creative process at work. To anyone who cherishes the cast recording, and especially Stritch's classic rendering of "The Ladies Who Lunch," this is a must. ★★★½ DVD: $29.99

Les Compéres

(1983, 92 min, France, Francis Veber) *Gérard Depardieu, Pierre Richard, Anny Duperey.* This very funny farce features the odd-couple Depardieu and Richard as the two former lovers of a woman who is desperately looking for her runaway son and who enlists each of them to help find him by telling them both that he is the child's father. Depardieu, as an ox-like journalist, and Richard, as a bumbling depressive, prove to be a winning combo. (American remake: *Father's Day*) (French with English subtitles) ★★★½ DVD: $29.99, VHS: $24.99

The Competition

(1984, 129 min, US, Joel Olianski) *Richard Dreyfuss, Lee Remick, Sam Wanamaker, Amy Irving.* Concert pianists Irving and Dreyfuss compete against one another for the same prize — only to find romance blossoming between them. It's predictable melodramatics, but the two stars are sincere and the concert footage nicely balances the film. ★★½

The Complete Monterey Pop Festival

(1967, 238 min, US, D.A. Pennebaker) *The Mamas and the Papas, Canned Heat, The Byrds, Laura Nyro, Al Kooper, Simon & Garfunkel, Jefferson Airplane, Janis Joplin, The Who, Otis Redding, The Jimi Hendrix Experience, Ravi Shankar.* The first and the best of the great rock festivals features the dynamic performances of Jimi Hendrix, The Who, Jefferson Airplane, Janis Joplin, Otis Redding and The Animals. Great footage of a time and place worth remembering. ★★★ DVD Criterion Collection: $79.99, VHS 2-tape set: $29.99

Le Complot

(1973, 120 min, France, René Granville) *Jean Rochefort, Michel Bouquet.* This taut espionage thriller is not in the same class as *Z* or *Day of the Jackal* (based on the same historical episode), but is still gripping entertainment. In 1960, Charles DeGaulle, frustrated by its bloody insurrection, granted Algeria independence, much to the shock of millions of Frenchmen who viewed Algeria as an integral part of French domain. The political unrest spawned by DeGualle's actions resulted in an underground terrorist movement, organized by French-Algerians, fanatical right-wing patriots and disillusioned officers formerly stationed in the North African colony. The labyrinthine webs of alliances, surveillance, deceit and betrayal are revealed as the film follows police and government agencies seeking to destroy the terrorist organization before the Republican order is threatened. (French with English subtitles) ★★★

Compromising Positions

(1985, 98 min, US, Frank Perry) *Susan Sarandon, Judith Ivey, Raul Julia, Joe Mantegna, Edward Herrmann, Mary Beth Hurt.* This offbeat comic mystery is, for the most part, an entertaining sleeper with the terrific Sarandon as a Long Island housewife who sets out to find just who killed dentist Mantegna. As her investigation ensues, she discovers the womanizing doctor could have been done in by any one of his female patients. Though the film's resolution is not up to par, it's certainly fun getting there. Among the supporting cast, Ivey is terrific as Sarandon's acerbic friend. ★★★ VHS: $14.99

Compulsion

(1959, 105 min, US, Richard Fleischer) *Dean Stockwell, Bradford Dillman, Orson Welles, E.G. Marshall.* An outstanding, thought-provoking and ultimately suspenseful account of the Leopold-Loeb murder case, *Compulsion* is an enthralling, fictionalized telling of the notorious murder trial. Stockwell and Dillman as Judd and Artie, two rich geniuses who, seemingly friendless, are involved in a "dangerously close" relationship ('50s code for gay). The first third of the film examines their friendship, in which they kidnap a local boy and murder him. The murder investigation fills the middle third of the film, and the inevitable murder trial follows. Welles appears as their agnostic defense attorney, who is based on Clarence Darrow. In a magnificent portrayal, Welles delivers some of the most moving courtroom speeches outside of *Inherit the Wind.* ★★★★ VHS: $19.99

Con Air

(1997, 115 min, US, Simon West) *Nicolas Cage, John Malkovich, John Cusack, Steve Buscemi, Ving Rhames, Colm Meaney, Mykelti Williamson.* Producer Jerry Bruckheimer calls on Cage to deliver more of the same high-octane excitement of their previous smash, *The Rock.* More of the same is what you get with Con Air, a high-voltage, hyperventilating ride that copies much of *The Rock's* action framework without necessarily improving upon it. Cage plays a former Army ranger unjustly sentenced to prison. Upon his parole and flight home, his plane is commandeered by a group of ruthless criminals en route to maximum security. Though offering many slam-bang action sequences, the film suffers from the lack of truly inventive action set pieces, though the humor is hip and it maintains a degree of tension throughout. ★★½ DVD Letterbox: $19.99, VHS: $9.99, VHS Letterbox: $9.99

Conan the Barbarian

(1981, 130 min, US, John Milius) *Arnold Schwarzenegger, Sandahl Bergman, James Earl Jones, Max von Sydow, Mako, Franco Columbu.* Robert E. Howard's pulp fantasy hero is given full fleshy form by Schwarzenegger. The story, very faithful to the tone of the original novels, takes us from Conan's barbarian boyhood and his enslavement and training as a pit fighter through sundry

Drew Barrymore and Sam Rockwell in George Clooney's *Confessions of a Dangerous Mind*

minor adventures and escapades, bringing it full circle as he confronts the murderer of his parents and destroyer of his village, the evil sorcerer Thulsa Doom (Jones). A rousing adventure with plenty of chest-thumping, sword-hacking, male-bonding fun. The testosterone-laden script, by cowriters Milius and Oliver Stone, wisely gives most of the lines to everyone *but* Arnold, and moves briskly along. (Sequel: *Conan the Destroyer*) ★★★ VHS: $9.99

Conan the Destroyer

(1984, 103 min, US, Richard Fleischer) *Arnold Schwarzenegger, Grace Jones, Mako, Wilt Chamberlain, Tracey Walter, Sarah Douglas, Olivia d'Abo.* The emphasis is on comedy, rather than revenge, in this disappointing sequel. This time around, Conan and cohorts (including a laughable Chamberlain) must rescue a princess from the clutches of an evil wizard. This story, however, is needlessly complicated, lacking the simplicity of the original film's script, which was its saving grace. Arnold is given too many lines to say this time around, but manages an admirable performance when he sticks to swinging a sword and flexing his pecs. ★½ VHS: $9.99

The Conductor

(1979, 110 min, Poland, Andrzej Wajda) *John Gielgud, Krystyna Janda.* Dubbed with a jarringly inappropriate Polish voice, Gielgud nevertheless is quite commanding as an elderly Polish émigré and internationally renowned maestro who returns to his homeland after a 50-year absence. There, he rouses the provincial Gdansk Orchestra with a stirring version of Beethoven's "Fifth Symphony." Gielgud is believable as the baton-twirling conductor although the film never comes together. (Polish with English subtitles) ★★ VHS: $79.99

Coneheads

(1993, 87 min, US, Steve Barron) *Dan Aykroyd, David Spade, Jane Curtin, Jason Alexander, Phil Hartman, Michelle Burke, Michael McKean, Jon Lovitz, Sinbad, Chris Farley, Ellen Degeneres.* Surprisingly sophisticated humor, winning performances and neat special effects redeem what might have been just another bastard child sprung from

the loins of *Saturday Night Live.* Aykroyd and Curtin reprise their roles as Beldar and Primaat Conehead, who become trapped in suburbia USA. What initially reads as a one-joke premise (and one of the more tedious of the *SNL* sketches) is adroitly expanded into ideal entertainment for those who like their comedy off the wall. ★★★ DVD: $14.99, VHS: $14.99

Confessions of a Dangerous Mind

(2002, 113 min, US, George Clooney) *Sam Rockwell, Drew Barrymore, George Clooney, Julia Roberts, Rutger Hauer, Maggie Gyllenhaal.* When he wasn't corrupting American minds with his lowbrow, pre-reality fare like "The Dating Game" and "The Gong Show," Chuck Barris (Rockwell) was a CIA-trained assassin. Or so he'd have you believe, in this biographical-in-spirit adaptation of Barris' own 1982 "unauthorized autobiography." Opening on a despondent Barris in his trashed hotel room, this unusually absorbing comedy flashes back to follow his rise to game show fame in the '70s, his trips abroad to take down Communists, and subsequent fall at the hands of cancellation. Barris' self-loathing, professional doubt and aimless philandering are played to poignantly comic effect, aided by Rockwell's completely immersive performance. In addition to his role as a CIA recruiter, director Clooney — seemingly inspired by the Coen brothers — throws in everything but the kitchen sink while emphasizing the comedy. Leave it to screenwriter Charlie Kaufman to expertly adapt this mixture of life and fiction, and to make the product actually more linear, coherent and ultimately compelling than the original. ★★★½ DVD: $29.99, VHS: $14.99

Confessions of a Serial Killer

(1992, 80 min, US, Mark Blair) This disturbing fact-based account of self-confessed real-life mass murderer Henry Lee Lucas is vividly and graphically told in flashback after his capture by Texas Rangers. This is a film so lurid and perverse that even avid fans of the genre may want to take a shower after watching. ★ VHS: $79.99

Confidence

(2003, 98 min, US, James Foley) *Edward Burns, Rachel Weisz, Andy Garcia, Dustin Hoffman, Paul Giamatti, Donal Logue, Luis Guzmán, Morris Chestnut, Robert Forster.* A group of grifters, led by Burns, has unwittingly pulled a scam that drained the bank account of feared and flaky crime boss The King (Hoffman). So they cut a deal to make a new con that will repay The King, until some twists that are hidden from the audience make it impossible to tell who's playing who. Even in the nascent days of Tarantinoism, this concept would have seemed tired, but the stellar cast seems not to notice, giving some extremely engaging performances. Hoffman in particular is let loose, combining his Ratso Rizzo and Tootsie in creating a violently fey menace. The plot breezes along, aided by Foley's slick direction, but those looking for a reprise of Foley's *Glengarry Glen Ross* should note that first-time screenwriter Doug Jung is no Mamet. ★★½ DVD: $14.99

Confidential Report

(1955, 99 min, GB, Orson Welles) *Orson Welles, Michael Redgrave, Akim Tamiroff.* Welles takes a factual mysterious occurrence and weaves a mesmerizing, convoluted tale of intrigue, deception and false identity. Welles plays Gregory Arkadin, a man of immense wealth and power, who commissions a petty gangster to compile a dossier on the origins of . . . Gregory Arkadin. Pay attention: the action moves very swiftly. Remastered print. (aka: *Mr. Arkadin*) ★★★ VHS: $29.99

Confidentially Yours

(1984, 111 min, France, François Truffaut) *Fanny Ardant, Jean-Louis Tringtignant.* Truffaut's final film is a joyously spirited blend of screwball antics and film noir intrigue. The zesty Ardant is an intrepid Girl Friday determined to clear her boss of a murder charge. This supremely stylish romantic comedy sparkles with the director's joie de vivre. (French with English subtitles) ★★★½ DVD: $19.99, VHS: $14.99

Conflict

(1945, 86 min, US, Curtis Bernhardt) *Humphrey Bogart, Sydney Greenstreet, Alexis Smith.* An interesting misfire for Bogart. He plays a wife killer who becomes involved in a psychological cat-and-mouse game with psychiatrist Greenstreet, who devises a scheme to get the murderer to admit his guilt. Smith is especially good as the younger sister of Bogart's deceased wife. ★★ VHS: $19.99

The Conformist

(1969, 115 min, Italy, Bernardo Bertolucci) *Jean-Louis Trintignant, Dominique Sanda, Stefania Sandrelli.* This fascinating exploration of the emotional roots of Fascism in prewar Italy ranks as one of the best Italian films of the 1970s. Trintignant stars as Marcello, a repressed homosexual traumatized by a childhood incident in which he shot the family chauffeur after a seduction attempt. Now as an adult, Marcello longs for conformity and appears to find it when he joins the Italian Fascist Secret Service. Sent to assassinate his former professor who is now a leading dissident, he meets and is "attracted" to a lesbian and antifascist (the alluring Sanda), who eventually develops into the moral adversary to Marcello's perverted beliefs. Sanda, who performs an exhilarating tango with Sandrelli, is a strong counterweight to Trintignant's Marcello. (Italian with English subtitles) ★★★★

Congo

(1995, 109 min, US, Frank Marshall) *Dylan Walsh, Ernie Hudson, Tim Curry, Laura Linney, Joe Don Baker, Bruce Campbell, Adewale Akinnuoye-Agbaje, Stuart Pankin, James Karen.* An expedition into the Congo to return a talking ape (don't ask!) to her native habitat turns deadly when the troop stumbles across a legendary diamond mine guarded by a race of killer gorillas. One might expect that such a premise by the author of *Jurassic Park* would have some degree of style and suspense. Look elsewhere. Marshall's uninspired direction and a hodgepodge screenplay strips away all but the barest of sci-fi nuance. Only Hudson's tongue-in-cheek portrayal of a "great white hunter" provides enjoyment. ★★ DVD Letterbox: $14.99, VHS: $9.99

A Connecticut Yankee

(1931, 95 min, US, David Butler) *Will Rogers, Maureen O'Sullivan, Myrna Loy.* Mark Twain's novel gets the Hollywood treatment once-over. Rogers was a force to be reckoned with back in the 1930s, with his "I only know what I read in the papers" attitude softening the sting of his satire that would have gotten him branded a "fellow traveler" in the dark ages of the '50s. This version starts in a haunted house with radio repairman Rogers getting blasted back to the 6th century and ends with Model Ts riding to the rescue of King and country. Unlike the Bing Crosby version, Rogers never sings. ★★★ VHS: $19.99

A Connecticut Yankee in King Arthur's Court

(1949, 107 min, US, Tay Garnett) *Bing Crosby, Rhonda Fleming, William Bendix, Cecil Hardwicke.* Musicalized, pleasant third screen version of the Mark Twain tale, with Crosby as a 20th-century blacksmith who is transported back in time to the court of King Arthur. Bing croons a couple of tunes. ★★½ DVD Double Feature: $14.99

The Conqueror Worm

(1968, 88 min, GB, Michael Reeves) *Vincent Price, Ian Ogilvy.* In 17th-century England during the struggle between Cromwell and the Crown, Matthew Hopkins (Price) and his associates seek out and persecute "witches," as well as anyone else who incurs their wrath. When Hopkins executes the priest of a small town for being a warlock, he and his partner find themselves the target of a young soldier. The movie is immensely engrossing and captures the English period detail remarkably well for a low-budget production. Price is at his menacing, sadistic best. For some reason, the film's original orchestral score has been replaced by a totally inappropriate and repetitive synthesizer track. (aka: *Witchfinder General*) ★★★½

Conquest

(1937, 112 min, US, Clarence Brown) *Greta Garbo, Charles Boyer.* Good romantic costumer with Garbo as Napoleon's Polish mistress, Marie Walewska. Boyer effectively plays the French conqueror. ★★★ VHS: $19.99

Conquest of the Planet of the Apes

(1972, 87 min, US, J. Lee Thompson) *Roddy McDowall, Ricardo Montalban, Natalie Trundy, Don Murray.* Fourth in the *Apes* series. Back on present-day Earth, domesticated apes, who have been made slave-like servants, begin to rebel against the humans. The appeal of the series had begun to run its course, but this still manages to entertain in spite of itself. (Sequel: *Battle for the Planet of the Apes*) ★★½

Consenting Adult

(1985, 100 min, US, Gilbert Cates) *Martin Sheen, Marlo Thomas, Barry Tubbs.* A compelling, well-made if ever-so-sincere TV movie based on the Laura Hobson ("Gentleman's Agreement") best-seller and updated by a decade to include such topics as AIDS and antigay crime. Thomas has one of her best roles as the mother of a college athlete who must come to terms with her son's homosexuality when she discovers he is gay. ★★★

Consenting Adults

(1993, 99 min, US, Alan J. Pakula) *Kevin Kline, Mary Elizabeth Mastrantonio, Kevin Spacey, Forest Whitaker.* Yet another in the glut of "steamy erotic thrillers," this one from the director of *Presumed Innocent.* A night of passion erupts into murder and betrayal when a married man (Kline) finds his neighbor's wife too tempting to resist. Mastrantonio is the betrayed wife, and Spacey is the cuckold husband — or is he? What could have been an A-1 thriller is defeated by ridiculous plot contrivances and oh-so-predictable twists and turns. ★½ DVD: $14.99

Consolation Marriage

(1931, 82 min, US, Paul Sloane) *Irene Dunne, Pat O'Brien.* Dunne and O'Brien offer appealing performances in this standard romantic drama about jilted lovers who meet and marry, only to question their love when their former partners return. ★★½ VHS: $19.99

Conspiracy Theory

(1997, 135 min, US, Richard Donner) *Mel Gibson, Julia Roberts, Patrick Stewart, Alex McArthur, Sean Patrick Thomas, Dean Winters.* Jerry Fletcher (Gibson) is a slightly paranoid New York cab driver who has an opinion on everything. You can read all about them in his newspaper, which has a circulation of five. However, when he's kidnapped by mysterious government agents, he may not be as paranoid as either he, we, or Alice (Roberts), a Justice Department lawyer with whom he continually con-

A Connecticut Yankee

fides, may think. Crisply directed by Donner, *Conspiracy Theory* is an exciting, well-paced thriller that doesn't always follow logic but is fun nevertheless as it wends its way through intricate plot developments, unexpected twists and a dose of some old-fashioned suspense. Gibson neatly overplays his part, though Roberts isn't given all that much to do but to react. ★★★ DVD: $14.99, VHS: $9.99, VHS Letterbox: $9.99

Consuming Passions

(1988, 98 min, GB, Giles Foster) *Vanessa Redgrave, Jonathan Pryce, Sammi Davis.* A floundering family-owned chocolate factory finds the recipe for success when three employees take an accidental dip in the mixing vats. If this sounds like an absurd premise, it is, but still there are occasional flashes of hilarity. Based on a short play by Terry Jones and Michael Palin. ★★½

Contact

(1997, 150 min, US, Robert Zemeckis) *Jodie Foster, Matthew McConaughey, Tom Skerritt, Angela Bassett, John Hurt, David Morse, James Woods, William Fichtner, Rob Lowe.* Director Zemeckis' take on Carl Sagan's novel is remarkably thoughtful and profound. About to begin a mythic journey that would make even Joseph Campbell proud, Dr. Eleanor Arroway (Foster) is an astrophysicist whose life's work involves searching infinitesimal radio bandwidths for signs of extraterrestrial intelligence. Sagan's screenplay (he worked arduously on the filming until his death from cancer just prior to its completion) brilliantly intertwines Arroway's endeavor with her need for resolution of her father's death as she struggles with a sense of existential alienation and spiritual ambiguity. As directed by Zemeckis, the film is briskly paced (even at 150 minutes running time) and delivers its share of high-tech sci-fi wizardry which, combined with its lofty contemplations on life, the universe and everything, makes *Contact* a rare cinematic treat that tickles multiple pleasure zones. ★★★★ DVD Letterbox: $14.99, VHS: $9.99, VHS Letterbox: $9.99

Contempt

(1963, 103 min, France/Italy, Jean-Luc Godard) *Brigitte Bardot, Jack Palance, Fritz Lang, Michel Piccoli.* A piercing, alienating film about film. Godard tackles communication problems and the difficulties of creating a motion picture — the compromises, frustration, idiocy and sacrifice. Bardot is the contemptuous wife of a writer (Piccoli) who sells out. (French with English subtitles) ★★★½ DVD Letterbox Criterion Collection: $39.99

Jodie Foster in *Contact*

The Contender

(2000, 125 min, US, Rod Lurie) *Joan Allen, Gary Oldman, Jeff Bridges, Christian Slater, Sam Elliott, William Petersen, Philip Baker Hall, Saul Rubinek, Mariel Hemingway.* With his sophomore production, writer-director Lurie continues exploring the political themes found in his first film *Deterrence*, but here they resonate much further as to coalesce into a stately, moving study of honor and backroom political maneuverings. In an exemplary performance, Allen is Laine Hanson, a U.S. Senator who is chosen by the President (an exceptional Bridges) to fill the vacancy of the late Vice President. What should be a smooth appointment becomes political wheeling and dealing when the head of the confirmation committee (Oldman) uncovers a sex scandal which Hanson may have been involved in years earlier. On the heels of the Clinton-Lewinsky affair, this discourse on the blurring of public service and private lives takes aim at a contemporary phenomena, squarely finding fault with ambitious politicians, a hungry press and a nation eager to learn the next dirty little secret. Oldman (who also executive produced) is outstanding as the vengeful Congressman. A gripping, smart (and in the end even Capra-esque) morality play. ★★★★ DVD: $9.99

Continental Divide

(1981, 103 min, US, Michael Apted) *John Belushi, Blair Brown, Allen Garfield.* Belushi shows his acting range in this likable little romantic comedy about a hard-nosed, cynical urbanite who travels to the Rockies to interview a reclusive, self-reliant ornithologist (Brown). Written by Lawrence Kasdan. ★★½ DVD: $9.99

Contraband

(1940, 88 min, GB, Michael Powell) *Conrad Veidt, Valerie Hobson, Esmond Knight, Leo Glenn.* A briskly paced thriller in the edge-of-his-seat tradition of early Alfred Hitchcock. Set in 1939, the story begins on a commercial boat captained by Veidt. The chase is on when two of his passengers jump ship while docked for an inspection. Veidt follows the two into a blackout shrouded London where intrigue and murky dangerous characters seem to be at every corner. Set in flashy Soho nightclubs and dank warehouses, he unwittingly becomes ensnared in a Nazi espionage ring. *Contraband* offers a light, even humorous approach while still keeping the viewer wide-eyed in the labyrinthine spy world. (aka: *Blackout*) ★★★★ DVD: $29.99, VHS: $24.99

Contract Killer

(1998, 103 min, Hong Kong, Wei Tung) *Jet Li, Eric Tsang, Simon Yam.* Yet another retitled Hong Kong release starring Li (originally called *Hitman*), this one is a standard modern-day thriller enlivened by some great action. Li plays a down-on-his-luck hit man who's really a good guy at heart. When he's given the chance to earn $100 million dollars to get revenge for a yakuza boss' murder, he finds the job a bit more difficult than expected. A not-bad Li vehicle is rendered almost unwatchable by this retooling: terrible dubbing (not in a fun way, either) and some appalling hip-hop, which is blasted during most of the action scenes, all but ruin the mild fun. Try to seek out the original Hong Kong release. ★★ DVD: $24.99, VHS Dubbed: $102.99, VHS Subtitled: $102.99

The Convent

(2001, 84 min, US, Mike Mendez) *Joanna Canton, Coolio, Adrienne Barbeau.* Though bordering on the silly, *The Convent* is an endearing horror/comedy that is best viewed with a rowdy crowd. The typical

horror movie setup — a group of teens are chased by demonic zombies in a haunted church — is enlivened by enthusiastic performances, goofy but fun monsters, and especially Barbeau as a shotgun-wielding, motorcycle-riding zombie killer. Not quite in the same league as gore slapstick classics like *Dead/Alive* and *Evil Dead 2*, and weakened by a lame ending, *The Convent* is still a good time for genre fans. ★★½ DVD: $19.99

The Conversation

(1974, 113 min, US, Francis Ford Coppola) *Gene Hackman, Robert Duvall, Frederic Forrest, Harrison Ford, Allen Garfield.* This harrowing and brilliant film on the ethical and moral dilemmas of wiretapping and its consequences on personal liberties is Coppola's best film outside of the *Godfather* series. Hackman gives a bravura performance as a surveillance specialist who comes to question the propriety of his profession, only to become a victim himself. Hackman tearing his apartment to shreds is one of the most devastating sequences ever put to film. ★★★★ DVD: $19.99, VHS: $14.99

Conversation Piece

(1974, 122 min, Italy, Luchino Visconti) *Burt Lancaster, Silvana Mangano, Helmut Berger, Claudia Marsani.* Lancaster is memorable as a retired intellectual whose life of solitude amid his books, paintings and art is abruptly invaded by the arrival of a garish "modern" family who move in upstairs. His old-world comforts are shattered as he is both drawn to and forced to participate in their tawdry and hedonistic lifestyle. The invading family (which brings a breath of fresh air, life and love into the professor's life) includes the enchanting countess (Mangano), her daughter (Marsani) and the Countess' student revolutionary boy-toy (Berger). (Filmed in English) ★★★

The Conviction

(1993, 92 min, Italy, Marco Bellocchio) *Vittorio Mezzogiorno, Claire Nebout, Andrzej Seweryn.* Attempting to capture some of the money-generating controversy of his sexually explicit *Devil in the Flesh*, Bellocchio's *The Conviction* tackles the murky but volatile subject of sexual harassment. A man and a woman get locked in a castle/museum after closing. The man, Lorenzo, and the woman, Sandra, play out a cat-and-mouse dance of domination and submission that eventually leads to a furious sexual conclusion. When the passions are spent, Lorenzo produces a key, prompting Sandra to feel used and abused. She initiates legal action claiming she was raped. What follows is a debate on sexuality and the problems between the sexes. (Italian with English subtitles) ★★½ VHS: $19.99

Coogan's Bluff

(1968, 100 min, US, Don Siegel) *Clint Eastwood, Lee J. Cobb, Susan Clark, Tisha Sterling.* Siegel directs with his usual manic pace as Arizona sheriff Clint becomes a fish out of water when he comes to the Big Apple to capture an escaped hood convicted of murder. ★★★ DVD Letterbox: $14.99

The Cook, the Thief, His Wife and Her Lover

(1990, 126 min, GB, Peter Greenaway) *Helen Mirren, Michael Gambon, Richard Bohringer, Alan Howard, Tim Roth.* One of the most controversial films in years, the title of this Jacobean revenge-tragedy, set in an upscale French restaurant, says it all. The restaurant is visited nightly by the sadistic Thief (played ferociously by Gambon). His battered Wife (Mirren in a heartbreaking performance) seeks

Bardot abed in *Contempt*

solace in her secret Lover whom she meets one evening while dining. The sympathetic Cook rounds out the cast. A surreal theatre piece combining moments of tender tragedy and stomach-turning physical and mental cruelty, the film suggests that revenge is not always sweet: it sometimes has a few bones. ★★★½ DVD Letterboxed: $14.99, VHS Letterboxed: $9.99

Cookie

(1989, 93 min, US, Susan Seidelman) *Peter Falk, Emily Lloyd, Dianne Wiest, Brenda Vaccaro, Jerry Lewis, Rikki Lake, Adrian Pasdar.* Seidelman gets a couple of spirited performances in this cute tale by Nora Ephron. Smart-ass teenager Lloyd finally hooks up with the father (Falk) she never knew when she becomes his chauffeur after he is released from jail. ★★½ VHS: $14.99

Cookie's Fortune

(1999, 118 min, US, Robert Altman) *Glenn Close, Charles S. Dutton, Julianne Moore, Liv Tyler, Chris O'Donnell, Patricia Neal, Ned Beatty, Courtney B. Vance, Donald Moffat, Lyle Lovett.* Lyrical, endearing and as satisfying as a cool lemonade, Altman's playful comedy set in a most-inviting small Mississippi town finds the director in a most unusually good mood. Altman utilizes a sublime cast for this Gothic parable about deception, loyalty and great catfish enchilada. In a brief but stunning turn, the elegant Neal is Cookie, a widow whose closest friend is her caretaker, Willis (Dutton). Estranged from family and missing her husband, Cookie commits suicide. The body is found by her conniving niece Camille (Close), who, rather than have a public scandal, makes it look like a murder/robbery. In doing so, Willis becomes the prime suspect. Altman takes his sweet time with this deceptive tale, allowing the characters to grow on you as the story unfolds. The cast is exemplary, though Dutton steals the show as the Wild Turkey-swilling, down-home Willis. ★★★½

A Cool, Dry Place

(1999, 120 min, US, John N. Smith) *Vince Vaughn, Joey Lauren Adams, Monica Potter, Bobby Moat.* Russ, a Midwestern lawyer, basketball coach and single father, is an atypical role for the magnetic Vaughn, but he still turns in another charming performance. In fact, he is the best reason to watch this thinly plotted domestic drama that has Russ vacillating between Beth (Adams), his potential new girlfriend, and Kate (Potter), the

wife who left him. Smith has made a largely unremarkable slice of life, but *A Cool, Dry Place* is absorbing, and its heart is in the right place. Moat is a real find, though the film strains when Potter is on-screen — her character is the weakest element in the film. ★★½ DVD: $9.99

Cool Hand Luke

(1967, 126 min, US, Stuart Rosenberg) *Paul Newman, George Kennedy, Strother Martin, Anthony Zerbe, Harry Dean Stanton, Dennis Hopper.* Newman is splendid as the chain gang convict who's always in trouble with the boss and subsequently becomes hero to all of his fellow prisoners. The film is highlighted by the now famous egg eating scene. An excellent supporting cast is headed up by Martin ("What we got here is a failure to communicate"). ★★★★ DVD Letterbox: $19.99, VHS: $14.99, VHS Letterbox: $14.99

Cool Runnings

(1993, 98 min, US, Jon Turtletaub) *Leon, Doug E. Doug, John Candy, Rawle D. Lewis, Malik Yoba.* Disney's interpretation of the true-life story of the Jamaican bobsled team is a slightly trivial but amusing and uplifting saga. Relying on the tried-and-true formula of the underdog competing against all odds, the story follows Derice, a determined young Jamaican sprinter whose bid for the Olympics is tragically dashed. Intent on becoming an Olympian at any cost, he turns to the unlikely sport of bobsledding, assembling a ragtag crew to man his chariot and turning to ex-Olympian Candy for coaching. Briskly paced and well stocked with both funny and touching moments. ★★★ DVD: $14.99, VHS: $9.99

Cool World

(1992, 101 min, US, Ralph Bakshi) *Gabriel Bryne, Brad Pitt, Kim Basinger.* Byrne stars as an ex-con and cartoonist who discovers that his cartoon creations have a life of their own in a parallel universe known as Cool World. Director Bakshi follows the Roger Rabbit lead and combines live-action actors with his visually wild animation. On a technical level, the film is fascinating; Bakshi's trademark dark and leering imagery is as hip as ever. But the film is curiously unsatisfying — the story is muddled and the action unfocused. ★ DVD: $14.99, VHS: $14.99

The Cooler

(2003, 101 min, US, Wayne Kramer) *William H. Macy, Maria Bello, Alec Baldwin, Ron Livingston, Shawn Hatosy, Paul Sorvino.* Bernie Lootz (Macy) is one of life's endearing losers — it's all written there in his eyes, his face, in his walk, but especially his job: Bernie is a cooler. His bad luck is such that if Bernie comes near you, your good luck changes instantly. But lady luck may be about to change for Bernie, and how this comes about forms the core of writer-director Kramer's engaging character study that's an unlikely charmer. The new Las Vegas is a town for baby carriages and minivans, at least that's the way Shangri-La Casino operator Shelly Kaplow (Baldwin) sees it, and why he wants his casino, the last of a dying breed, to remain as it is. Here the ghosts of Frank Sinatra and Bugsy Siegel are palpable, and to Shelly, Bernie has his place, too. That's why he's concerned Bernie is planning to leave, a plan that may be put on hold when Bernie finds romance with a beautiful cocktail waitress (Bello), and his estranged son enters the picture. What makes Kramer's often comic, even cynical tale so refreshing is the resiliency of his characters, who while certain of their lot in life never abandon the faintest hopes of something better when a chance comes along. Macy is terrific as Bernie, and his scenes with the equally good Bello have honesty, hopefulness and, most of all, chemistry. But it is Baldwin who steals the film with a blistering portrait of a casino boss who still lives by his own, misguided code of honor, and whose humanity has long ago been relinquished. ★★★ DVD: $26.99

Cooley High

(1975, 107 min, US, Michael Schultz) *Glynn Turman, Lawrence Hilton-Jacobs.* Affectionate reminiscence about a group of black high school students in mid-1960s Chicago. The basis for the TV series "What's Happening." ★★★ DVD: $14.99, VHS: $9.99

Cop

(1987, 110 min, US, James B. Harris) *James Woods, Leslie Ann Warren, Charles Durning.* Routine suspense thriller is given a boost by Woods' over-the-top portrayal of a cop whose domestic strife interferes with his pursuit of a serial killer. Based on the novel "Blood on the Moon" by James Ellroy. ★★

Cop and a Half

(1993, 93 min, US, Henry Winkler) *Burt Reynolds, Norman D. Golden III, Ruby Dee, Ray Sharkey.* This unbearably wooden action comedy has more troubles than its star Reynolds had in divorce court. Devon (Golden) is a precocious eight-year-old who, upon witnessing a mob hit, strikes a deal with the local police: If they make him a cop, he'll tell them everything he knows. Reynolds plays the hard-nosed, rule-busting detective who is given the task of taking young Devon on patrol — and wouldn't you know it, Burt hates kids. ★ DVD: $14.99, VHS: $7.49

Cop Land

(1997, 105 min, US, James Mangold) *Sylvester Stallone, Robert De Niro, Harvey Keitel, Ray Liotta, Janeane Garofalo, Peter Berg, Michael Rapaport, Robert Patrick, Cathy Moriarty, Annabella Sciorra.* An enthralling police drama about corruption and redemption, *Cop Land* also marks the best performance of Stallone's career. Splendidly written and directed by Mangold, the film is set in fictional

Garrison, New Jersey, a small town mostly populated by New York City police officers. Stallone plays Freddie Heflin, Garrison's half-deaf sheriff who is merely tolerated by those he most desires to emulate. When a young officer (Rapaport) is involved in an off-duty shooting, cover-up, betrayal and murder force Freddie to re-evaluate loyalties and stand up against these men. Stallone's characterization of Freddie is a subtle combination of frustration, longing, self-doubt and decency, and the actor manages to make Freddie sympathetic, pathetic and believable. Liotta steals the film with his gritty, dynamic portrait of a cop on the edge. ★★★½ DVD Letterbox Director's Cut: $19.99, VHS: $14.99, VHS Letterbox: $9.99

Copacabana

(1947, 92 min, US, Alfred E. Green) *Groucho Marx, Carmen Miranda.* Miranda can't get a gig, until manager and erstwhile boyfriend Marx lands two jobs for her. At the same club. As two different people. It becomes a bit of a strain, what with one being Brazilian and the other French. There's lots of flashy musical production numbers, and the usual wise-cracking encounters with officious officials. ★★½ DVD: $14.99, VHS: $19.99

Cops and Robbers

(1973, 93 min, US, Aram Avakian) *Joseph Bologna, Cliff Gorman.* Two fine performances from Bologna and Gorman as two cops who decide to pull off one perfect heist and then retire highlight this caper film that manages to be both funny and suspenseful. From the novel by Donald Westlake. ★★★ DVD Pan & Scan: $14.99

Cops and Robbersons

(1994, 95 min, US, Michael Ritchie) *Chevy Chase, Jack Palance, Dianne Wiest, Robert Davi.* Chase is a suburban dad (and would-be detective) who sees his big break in the form of a crotchety ol' police captain (Palance) who moves in with the family to stakeout the murderous counterfeiter next door. There are a few amusing gags, and Palance's patented sneering and growling makes this tolerable, but it's predictable and routine. ★★ DVD: $19.99, VHS: $9.99

Copycat

(1995, 123 min, US, Jon Amiel) *Holly Hunter, Sigourney Weaver, Will Patton, Dermot Mulroney, Harry Connick, Jr., William McNamara.* Despite its derivative shocks and improbabilities, *Copycat* manages to serve a few chills that should give less-than-demanding thriller fans a cheap scare or two. Weaver is a renowned author and criminologist who is nearly killed by a psycho (Connick). When a copycat serial killer begins terrorizing the city, cops Hunter and Mulroney convince the agoraphobic and homebound expert to help track him. The film is full of twists (some predictable, some not), but a few of the sequences needed to set up the next scare lack either credibility or depth. Weaver and Hunter play well off each other. ★★½ DVD: $14.99, VHS: $9.99

Coquette

(1929, 75 min, US, Sam Taylor) *Mary Pickford, Johnny Mack Brown.* Pickford was the second recipient of a Best Actress Oscar, and with her win came the Academy's first controversy. Complaints were made that it was merely a popularity contest, and Pickford's histrionic portrayal of a flirtatious Southern belle only confirms those critics' charges. Pickford does get to break down on the stand, and

grieve over her lover's dead body, but this tale of the Old South creaks at the seams. Beware of poor sound quality in certain scenes. ★★ VHS: $19.99

The Core

(2003, 133 min, US, Jon Amiel) *Aaron Eckhart, Hilary Swank, Delroy Lindo, Stanley Tucci, Alfre Woodard, DJ Qualls.* Freakish worldwide occurrences (scores of people with pacemakers suddenly drop dead, pigeons seemingly go mad and cause havoc in London) lead the military and top science professor Eckhart to discover that the Earth's core has stopped spinning. This will eventually cause the death of everyone on the planet. Luckily, brilliant Lindo has developed a Jules Verne-esque ship capable of transporting a crew to the core to get it back in rotation. *The Core* begins well, building suspense and featuring solid acting, but becomes more commonplace (and tedious) as it goes along. Still mildly entertaining in a retro way (it feels less akin to *Armageddon* than, say, 1979's *Meteor*), but more energy and fewer stock characters and situations would have made this a great deal more satisfying. ★★½ DVD Letterbox: $29.99, DVD Pan & Scan: $29.99, VHS: $102.99

Corky Romano

(2001, 90 min, US, Rob Pritts) *Chris Kattan, Vinessa Shaw, Peter Falk, Peter Berg, Chris Penn, Fred Ward, Richard Roundtree.* "SNL" regular Kattan plays a character *not* based on that show, the bungling son of a mafia don who infiltrates the FBI to retrieve his father's file. Was this idea any good when it was called *Blue Streak*? What a waste of a good supporting cast. ★ DVD Letterbox: $14.99, VHS: $9.99

The Corn Is Green

(1945, 114 min, US, Irving Rapper) *Bette Davis, John Dall.* Davis shines in one of her most heartfelt performances as Miss Moffat, a lonely schoolteacher in a small Welsh mining town who dedicates herself to a gifted student (Dall), with the hope that the youth will leave his oppressive environment and one day enter Oxford. A superior, sentimental adaptation of Emlyn Williams' play. Davis would reprise the role in the ill-fated musical "Miss Moffat." (Remade in 1979) ★★★ VHS: $19.99

Cornered

(1945, 102 min, US, Edward Dmytryk) *Dick Powell, Walter Slezak.* Powell reaffirmed his tough-guy persona (after *Murder My Sweet*) with this taut thriller set post-WWII. Powell plays a war veteran whose wife died at the hands of Nazi collaborators. He winds up in Buenos Aires after circling the globe in search of a group of escaped fascists — his wife's killer among them. ★★★ VHS: $19.99

Corrina, Corrina

(1994, 115 min, US, Jessie Nelson) *Whoopi Goldberg, Ray Liotta, Tina Majorino, Joan Cusack, Don Ameche, Larry Miller, Patrika Darbo.* In an impressive debut as both writer and director, Nelson has fashioned a charming, sweet romantic comedy-drama and semiautobiography set in the 1950s. Liotta is a recent widower coping with raising his traumatized seven-year-old daughter (marvelously played by Majorino). Goldberg costars as their new housekeeper Corrina, who takes the young girl under her wing and who eventually becomes involved in an interracial romance with Liotta. Both Liotta and Goldberg offer sensitive, understated performances; and the film is thankfully devoid of any hokiness and sentimentality. ★★★ DVD: $9.99, VHS: $6.99

Corrupt

(1983, 99 min, Italy, Roberto Faenza) *Harvey Keitel, Nicole Garcia, Johnny Lydon, Leonard Mann, Sylvia Sidney.* An auspicious film debut by the notorious Lydon (aka Rotten). A sleazy heir to wealth, Lydon insinuates himself into a sado-masochistic relationship with a N.Y.C. police inspector (Keitel), stripping his personality to the bone. Relentlessly demented and frequently bristling with hostile humor, this is a kinky, punkist policer. (aka: *Cop-Killer* and *Order of Death*) ★★★

The Corruptor

(1999, 110 min, US, James Foley) *Chow Yun-Fat, Mark Wahlberg, Ric Young.* Stylish and ultra-violent, *The Corruptor* comes close to being a Hong Kong action film, right down to the central themes of male friendship and betrayal. Unfortunately, it also tries to be a cop-buddy movie, a car chase fest, and a murder mystery. The smashing opening, reminiscent of *A Better Tomorrow*, is Yun-Fat at his best, gunning down Fuk gang members in an antique shop. Against charisma like his, Wahlberg looks a bit lost. There's a great car chase in the middle, with pedestrians at the mercy of blazing guns, but like the other elements, the parts never gel into a solid film. ★★½ DVD: $9.99, VHS: $9.99

Cosi

(1997, 100 min, Australia, Mark Joffe) *Toni Collette, Ben Mendelsohn, Barry Otto, Colin Friels, Rachel Griffiths.* This whimsical little fairy tale follows Lewis (Mendelsohn), a young man who, having lost his sense of purpose in life, takes the first job he can get — directing a theatre troupe in a mental institution. His first assignment: Mozart's comic opera "Cosi Fan Tutte." The film refreshingly does not try to portray its mental patients as spiritually transcendent or morally superior to their "sane" counterparts, they are just what they appear to be. Instead the focus is on Lewis' slow awakening to a sense of self-confidence. At times scattered and unfocused, *Cosi* nonetheless is an enjoyable and even uplifting oddity. ★★★ DVD: $19.99, VHS: $14.99

The Cosmic Eye

(1985, 76 min, US, Faith Hubley) *Maureen Stapleton, Dizzy Gillespie, Linda Atkinson.* A charming feature from one of our great animators. Expanding on the work she did with her late husband John, Hubley creates a free-form visual poem about the rights and responsibilities of human-kind. Its positive message never gets old, and it seems so simple, too. ★★★ VHS: $19.99

Cosmic Slop

(1994, 90 min, US, Kevin Rodney, Reginald Hudlin, Warrington Hudlin) The creators of the *House Party* series and *Boomerang* succeed on all levels with this hip, Afro-centric "Twilight Zone"-inspired trilogy hosted by master funkateer George Clinton. Provocative, funny and always socially aware, this trio of tales tackles many of today's important issues such as domestic violence, gun control, religion and racism in a light-handed and sometimes humorous fashion. Despite its casual attitude, this clever and offbeat film manages to provide enough entertainment to satisfy those in search of something a little different. ★★★ VHS: $14.99

Costa Brava

(1995, 92 min, Spain, Marta Balletbo-Coll) *Marta Balletbo-Coll, Desi Del Valle.* Director Balletbo-Coll stars in this breezy English-language romantic comedy as a ditsy-esque tour guide and aspiring stand-up comedienne/playwright who falls in love with a beautiful not-ready-yet-ready-for-full-time-lesbianism university instructor from Israel (del Valle). Quirky, funny, endearing and fresh with realistic sounding dialogue — it feels a lot like a lesbian *Annie Hall*. ★★★

The Cotton Club

(1984, 127 min, US, Francis Coppola) *Richard Gere, Diane Lane, Laurence Fishburne, Bob Hoskins, Lonette McKee, Gregory Hines, James Remar, Nicolas Cage, Allen Garfield, Gwen Verdon, Joe Dallesandro.* Coppola's musical gangster film is a visual tour de force betrayed by a lack of dramatic substance. A good supporting cast totally overshadows leads Gere and Lane. ★★½ DVD Letterbox: $19.99

Cotton Comes to Harlem

(1970, 97 min, US, Ossie Davis) *Godrey Cambridge, Raymond St. Jacques, Redd Foxx, Cleavon Little.* Made just prior to the explosion of blaxploitation films in the '70s, this fine adaptation of the Chester Himes novel stars Cambridge and St. Jacques as policemen Coffin Ed Johnson and Gravedigger Jones. Actor-turned-director Davis does a fine job in telling their story as they try to expose a radical back-to-Africa preacher who they believe "ain't nothing but a cheat." A splendid blend of action and comedy, the film is also a spirited re-creation of 1950s Harlem. ★★★ DVD: $14.99

Cotton Mary

(2000, 124 min, GB, Ismail Merchant) *Greta Scacchi, Madhur Jaffrey, James Wilby, Prayag Raaj.* In this Merchant/Ivory production, the proficient technical qualities usually associated with this great filmmaking team are ill-served by a rambling story and static direction. Set in 1947 in post-colonial India, the story traces the disabling effect that an unstable Indian nurse, Cotton Mary (Jaffrey), has on a British household after she insinuates herself into their home. Scacchi has little to do other than gardening and serving tea as the wife who slowly loses control of her household to an increasingly mad Mary. Less a poignant statement on British imperialism, *Cotton Mary* can't escape its melodramatic conventions even though the story seems on the verge of having something interesting to say. ★★ DVD: $14.99

A Couch in New York

(1997, 104 min, US, Chantal Akerman) *William Hurt, Juliette Binoche.* New York psychoanalyst Hurt, needing a change of pace, swaps apartments with Parisian Binoche. She's barely unpacked in his apartment when she's mistaken as Hurt's analyst fill-in by one of his more neurotic patients, an error she doesn't clear up. Things get even wackier when Hurt comes home earlier than expected. Abandoning her experimental filmic techniques but maintaining the same light touch evident in her earlier films, Akerman has made an uneven yet disarming romantic comedy. Though it's fluff, there's an unexpected frothiness, and at the odd moment it beguiles. ★★½ DVD: $24.99, VHS: $14.99

The Couch Trip

(1988, 97 min, US, Michael Ritchie) *Dan Aykroyd, Walter Matthau, Charles Grodin, Donna Dixon.* Aykroyd brings a charm to this standard comedy about a mental patient who escapes by impersonating a radio talk show psychologist in Beverly Hills. ★★½ DVD: $14.99

Count Dracula

(1970, 98 min, Italy/Spain/West Germany, Jesse Franco) *Christopher Lee, Herbert Lom, Klaus Kinski.* Lee dons tooth and cape in this slowly paced but faithful updating of Bram Stoker's "Dracula." A lawyer and his fiancée encounter the prince of darkness in Transylvania. ★★½ VHS: $9.99

The Count of Old Town

(1935, 75 min, Sweden, Edvin Aldolphson & Sigurd Wallen) *Ingrid Bergman, Edvin Adolphson.* Bergman made her film debut in this buoyant comedy as a maid in a cheap hotel who falls in love with a roguish thief. (Swedish with English subtitles) ★★★ VHS: $19.99

Country

(1984, 109 min, US, Richard Pearce) *Jessica Lange, Sam Shepard, Wilford Brimley, Matt Clark.* Lange and Shepard star as farmers who fight to save their land when the government threatens foreclosure and who struggle to save their family from the ravages of crisis. A well-made and topical film. Lange's performance is remarkable. ★★★ DVD: $9.99

The Country Girl

(1954, 104 min, US, George Seaton) *Grace Kelly, William Holden, Bing Crosby, Gene Reynolds.* Three stand-out lead performances distinguish this absorbing Clifford Odets adaptation with Kelly in her Oscar-winning role as the wife of alcoholic actor Crosby. Holden is the dedicated director trying to help him in his comeback, becoming romantically involved with Grace in the process. ★★★½ VHS: $14.99

Country Life

(1995, 115 min, Australia, Michael Blakemore) *Sam Neill, Greta Scacchi, John Hargreaves, Kerry Fox, Michael Blakemore.* Concentrating more on the comedy of culture clash and romantic escapades than the drama of emotional chasms, this sometimes giddy interpretation of Chekhov's "Uncle Vanya" is set on a sheep ranch in post-WWII Australia. A sweetly romantic Neill stars as Dr. Askey, an idealistic boozer who falls in love with Deborah (Scacchi), the young wife of the estate's owner who has returned after a long absence. Unrequited love, social upheaval and regret are themes still present, though this comedy of manners treads softly. Not every scene of this liberal translation reaches its potential, but as an immensely appealing ensemble proves, *Country Life* has its merits. ★★★½ DVD Letterbox: $14.99, VHS: $9.99

Countryman

(1982, 100 min, GB/Jamaica, Dickie Jobson) *Hiram Keller, Kristine Sinclair.* Although ladened with a poor script, unprofessional acting and muddled politics, this lively story of the power of the Rastafarian is still good viewing. A peaceful Rastafarian fisherman (Keller) rescues two Americans from a plane crash. But instead of simple thanks, he is thrown into a cauldron of political intrigue that forces him to flee into the lush Jamaican jungle. It is there that he attains supernatural powers and is able to battle the elements and foe alike. The film is highlighted with a sampler-style reggae soundtrack featuring the music of Bob Marley, Toots and the Maytals, Scratch Perry, Aswad and Steel Pulse. ★★½ DVD: $14.99

Coup de Grâce

(1976, 98 min, West Germany, Volker Schlöndorff) *Margarethe von Trotta, Matthias Habich, Matthieu Carriere.* Understated, yet subtly disquieting, this drama explores destructive human behavior — both in personal relationships as well as politics. Set in 1919 in a forlorn country Baltic

estate, the story traces the lives of a middle-aged woman (von Trotta), her brother and a German lodger who find themselves slowly impoverished by the civil war and anxious over the advancement of Red troops on their land. The woman, desperate for affection, falls obsessively in love with a Soviet soldier, a man who does not return the love and is soon driven away by her erratic and at times virulent behavior. A serious portrait of bitterly restrained people caught in the whirlwind of change. (German with English subtitles) ★★★ DVD Letterbox Criterion Collection: $29.99, VHS: $29.99

Coup de Tête (Hothead)

(1978, 100 min, France, Jean-Jacques Annaud) *Patrick Dewaere, Jean Bouise, Michel Aumont.* This engaging comedy follows the exploits of a crazed soccer player whose antics and off the field cause him to lose his position, get fired and end up in jail. He gets out, however, and soon extracts his "revenge." A bristling comedy with Dewaere in one of his best roles. ★★★

Coup de Torchon (Clean Slate)

(1981, 128 min, France, Bertrand Tavernier) *Philippe Noiret, Isabelle Huppert, Stéphane Audran, Guy Marchant.* A diabolical black comedy that spits in the face of morality. Noiret is the ineffectual law enforcer in an African village who one day abandons his policy of nonconfrontation and embarks on a systematic shooting spree. Based on the novel "Pop. 1280" by Jim Thompson. (French with English subtitles) ★★★½ DVD Criterion Collection: $29.99, VHS: $29.99

Coupe de Ville

(1990, 99 min, US, Joe Roth) *Alan Arkin, Daniel Stern, Patrick Dempsey, Ayre Gross, Joseph Bologna, Annabeth Gish.* A sentimental though engaging road movie — and a heart-on-the-sleeve tribute to Dad. Three estranged brothers are reunited on a cross-country trip to deliver a birthday present, a 1954 Coupe de Ville, to their mom. Of course, en route, the boys not only discover a little something about each other, but about themselves as well. Though the film tries to be insightful, it borders on manipulative and, at times, heavy-handed sentimentality. However, there are some funny lines and attractive performances. ★★½ VHS: $9.99

Courage Mountain

(1990, 96 min, US, Christopher Leitch) *Charlie Sheen, Leslie Caron, Juliette Caton.* A beautifully photographed family film, this new version of the famed "Heidi" story won't make anyone forget the beloved 1937 Shirley Temple classic, but it is nevertheless an earnest, well-paced and sincerely acted adventure which should more than entertain pre-adolescent viewers. Young Caton ably plays the little heroine who, on the eve of WWI, moves from her Swiss Alps home to a fancy boarding school across the border in Italy. Once there, however, Heidi and a group of friends are separated from their headmistress and are taken to a local orphanage and used for slave labor. ★★★

Courage under Fire

(1996, 115 min, US, Edward Zwick) *Denzel Washington, Meg Ryan, Lou Diamond Phillips, Michael Moriarty, Matt Damon, Bronson Pinchot, Scott Glenn, Zeljko Ivanek, Sean Astin.* Washington plays an Army commander who is investigating the case of a posthumous Medal of Honor going to a female pilot (a very effective Ryan) killed in action. What should be a simple process soon becomes

Marie-France Pisier in *Cousin, Cousine*

complicated when witnesses begin to contradict each other's stories — and it's uncertain if she died a hero or a coward. As Washington digs deeper to uncover the truth (which places him in conflict with military brass), Ryan's story is told in riveting, *Rashomon*-like flashbacks. Highlighting a marvelous ensemble, Phillips is exceptional as a soldier who knows more than he's saying. An intelligent look at both the Gulf War and women in the military. ★★★½ DVD: $19.99, VHS: $9.99, VHS Letterbox: $19.99

The Court Jester

(1956, 101 min, US, Melvin Frank & Norman Panama) *Danny Kaye, Basil Rathbone, Angela Lansbury, Glynis Johns.* Kaye has one of his best roles in this beloved comedy classic which rates as one of the funniest comedies of all time. To help restore the throne to its rightful heir, Kaye goes undercover, posing as a court jester; and in the process, of course, turns the palace upside down. Basil Rathbone and young Johns and Lansbury also star. And don't forget: "The pellet with the poison's in the vessel with the pestle." Or is that "the flagon with the dragon?" ★★★★ DVD: $14.99, VHS: $9.99

The Courtesans of Bombay

(1974, 74 min, India, Ismail Merchant) *Kareem Samar, Zohra Segal, Saeed Jaffrey.* An intriguing and entertaining story that follows the inhabitants of Pavanpul, the courtesan quarters, who by day carry on their daily domestic lives and by night, thrill and delight with exuberant singing, dancing and sex. Filmed in a pseudo-documentary style, the film is more of interest for its sociological stance rather than entertainment value. Merchant's directorial debut. ★★½

The Courtship of Eddie's Father

(1963, 117 min, US, Vincente Minnelli) *Glenn Ford, Shirley Jones, Ron Howard, Stella Stevens, Jerry Van Dyke.* Heartwarming comedy (and inspiration for the popular 1970s TV sitcom) about young Howard looking for an eligible wife for his widower dad (Ford). ★★★ DVD: $19.99, VHS: $14.99

Cousin Bette

(1998, 108 min, GB, Des McAnuff) *Jessica Lange, Elisabeth Shue, Bob Hoskins, Geraldine Chaplin, Hugh Laurie.* Skating dangerously close to *Dangerous Liaisons* territory, director McAnuff tackles Balzac's story of class rivalry, sexual treachery and revenge, and though his production lacks the sizzle of Stephen Frears' classic, this poor cousin manages to stand on its own. Lange stars as the uncomely title character, poor relations to the wealthy Hulot family in 19th-century France. Rebuffed by Hector Hulot (Laurie), Bette lets loose her wrath on the family one by one, with a little help from the Hulots' individual vices. Lange settles into the role nicely, though she's rarely given the opportunity to strut her stuff. The same can be said for McAnuff's direction — it's extremely competent but at times lacks a true passion. ★★★ DVD: $9.99

Cousin Bobby

(1992, 69 min, US, Jonathan Demme) A provocative and sincere documentary about director Demme's long-lost cousin, Bobby Castle, a politically radical Episcopal priest who militantly crusades for the poor parishoners of his Harlem church. Demme goes about filming his story as if it were a home movie, documenting his own rediscovery of a distant relation with handheld camera work and microphone booms exposed. Demme splits the film between this familial reunion and Castle's history as a civil rights leader, concentrating especially on his close friendship in the '60s with Black Panther Party member Isaiah Rowley. Eloquent and outspoken, Castle, along with cousin Jonathan, makes a powerful and compelling case for economic equality and social justice. ★★★½ VHS: $19.99

Cousin, Cousine

(1975, 95 min, France, Jean-Charles Tacchella) *Marie-Christine Barrault, Marie-France Pisier, Victor Lanoux, Guy Merchant.* An engaging look at love among the members of a large French family. Trouble brews when two cousins by marriage discov-

er they have more in common than their in-laws. A sexy, romantic comedy. (American remake: *Cousins*) (French with English subtitles) ★★★½ VHS: $29.99

Cousins

(1989, 110 min, US, Joel Schumacher) *Ted Danson, Isabella Rossellini, William S. Petersen, Sean Young, Norma Aleandro, Lloyd Bridges.* An amiable if unremarkable rehash of *Cousin, Cousine* highlighted by a handful of sincere and appealing performances, including Danson and Rossellini, as two cousins who fall in love. Bridges and Aleandro both give the film a dash of vitality as a pair of high-spirited sexagenarian lovers. ★★½ DVD Letterbox: $14.99, VHS: $19.99

Cover Girl

(1944, 107 min, US, Charles Vidor) *Gene Kelly, Rita Hayworth, Eve Arden, Phil Silvers.* This delightful Kern-Gershwin musical has Kelly's brilliant dancing, Silvers' burlesque routines, Arden's wisecracks and Hayworth's beauty, all packaged in lush Technicolor by the sure hand of director Vidor. ★★★½ DVD: $24.99, VHS: $19.99

Cover Me

(1995, 94 min, US, Michael Schroeder) *Stephen Nichols, Courtney Taylor.* Playboy Films' first video release is this tepid, seen-it-before murder mystery set amidst the sex industry of L.A. in which a serial killer stalks models who have appeared on the cover

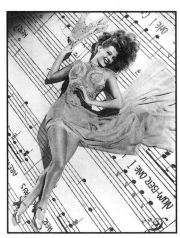

Rita Hayworth in a pose from *Cover Girl*

of a local skin magazine. Demi/Dimitri's (Nichols) MO is to don women's clothing, go to a strip club, pick up a prostitute/dancer and take her home presumably for a night of paid lesbian sex. But girl-girl lovemaking soon turns to boy-girl killing and it takes a sultry policewoman (Taylor) to go undercover to capture the sicko. ★ VHS: $79.99

Cover-Up

(1988, 76 min, US, Barbara Trent) After releasing the right-wing documentary *Oliver North*, distributor MPI Video then produced this left-leaning probe into the shady dealings of the Iran-Contra Affair. The story alleges that the 1980 Reagan-Bush campaign bargained with the Iranians to delay the hostages' release to insure a victory over President Carter. ★★★ VHS: $14.99

The Covered Wagon

(1923, 60 min, US, James Cruze) *J. Warren Kerrigan, Lois Wilson, Alan Hale.* Beautifully photographed epic of the Old West, introducing some of the elements of the genre that others would later exploit more fully. One of the biggest box-office smashes of the 1920s. ★★★ VHS: $9.99

Coyote Ugly

(2000, 101 min, US, David McNally) *Piper Perabo, John Goodman, Adam Garcia, Maria Bello, Melanie Lynskey.* A young waitress (Perabo) leaves her small Jersey town behind to pursue her dreams of a songwriting career in the Big Apple. She's forced to take a job at the title bar, however, where she must wear skimpy clothes and serve horny men drinks. Surprisingly retro (in the worst sense), this artificial film plays its Horatio Alger story line straight — this is a squeaky-clean movie, with not a whiff of sexuality. It plays like *Showgirls* remade as an "Afterschool Special" — only it's not even as fun as that might sound. ★ DVD: $19.99, VHS: $9.99

CQ

(2002, 91 min, US, Roman Coppola) *Jeremy Davies, Angela Lindvall, Élodie Bouchez, Gérard Depardieu, Giancarlo Giannini, Jason Schwartzman, Billy Zane.* Graduating from music video direction, Francis' son Roman (and Sofia's bro) continues the family tradition with this admirable feature debut. Invoking the style of the French New Wave, *CQ* is a film-within-a-film, an entertaining, loopy spoof of '60s sci-fi/secret agent flicks. Davies plays Paul, a self-obsessed American filmmaker living in Paris who is directing a filmic diary. He's financing it by toiling as editor on the cheap French sci-fi opus *Dragonfly*, that is until its director careens his sports car into a wall and Paul is thrust onto the director's chair. Now, how to juggle directing two films and keeping his high-maintenance girlfriend from walking out. Coppola clearly enjoys his friendly jabs at the filmmaking trade, and his re-creation of *Dragonfly* shows a true appreciation of the genre. With some spot-on cameos, this is part camp, part homage and all fun. ★★★ DVD Special Edition: $14.99

Le Crabe Tambour

(1977, 120 min, France, Pierre Schoendoerffer) *Jacques Perrin, Jean Rochefort, Claude Rich.* Haunting and provocative, Schoendoerffer's unconventional war drama lays bare the primitive sentiments of men in battle. Based on the actual exploits of a legendary French officer, nicknamed Le Crabe Tambour (The Drummer Crab), the film furrows through the complexities of honor and military chivalry. Perrin portrays the title character with a fascinating elusiveness — projecting the oblique demeanor of a perennial soldier. Accentuating the rich performances is Raoul Coutard's boldy adventurous cinematography, with its many spellbinding evocations of the elements. (French with English subtitles) ★★★½

Crackers

(1983, 91 min, US, Louis Malle) *Donald Sutherland, Jack Warden, Sean Penn, Wallace Shawn.* Malle's remake of the Italian classic *Big Deal on Madonna Street* is long on charm, but falls short when it comes to delivering either story or laughs. The film centers around a group of losers who keep off the mean streets of San Francisco by hanging out at a local pawn shop. When they concoct a scheme to crack the safe in the shop, the comedy is supposed to gear up, but somehow, the film never really gets on track. ★★ VHS: $59.99

Cradle 2 the Grave

(2003, 110 min, US, Andrzej Bartkowiak) *Jet Li, DMX, Anthony Anderson, Kelly Hu, Tom Arnold, Gabrielle Union, Mark Dacascos.* A wretched action film, *Cradle 2 the Grave* has DMX and Li searching for some pricey gems (which are actually deadly weapons) before baddie Dacascos can sell them to the highest, most evil bidder. The always annoying Anderson is on hand to enhance the pain, and Union winds up with an extremely tacky, chauvinistic role. Even the action (barring a watchable four-wheeler chase scene) is dull; a can't-miss, climactic, duel-to-the-death between Li and Dacascos is botched by excessive cross-cutting to other characters' fights, and some truly corny special effects. With *Romeo Must Die, Exit Wounds* and now *Cradle*, Bartkowiak is shaping up to be one of the worst action directors of all time. Even diehard Li fans can skip this clunker. ★ DVD Letterbox: $27.99, DVD Pan & Scan: $27.99, VHS: $6.99

Cradle Will Rock

(1999, 133 min, US, Tim Robbins) *Hank Azaria, Ruben Blades, Joan Cusack, John Cusack, Cary Elwes, Philip Baker Hall, Cherry Jones, John Angus MacFayden, Bill Murray, Vanessa Redgrave, Susan Sarandon, Jamey Sheridan, John Turturro, Emily Watson.* It's 1937 in America. The poor form bread lines, the rich rail against Communism, and 22-year-old upstart Orson Welles joins John Houseman to put on a show — a Federal Theatre production of Marc Blitzstein's musical "Cradle Will Rock." What Welles and Houseman see as a play, others see as an arm of the Red Menace. The Federal Theatre Project itself is under attack as un-American, foreshadowing NEA struggles today. Director Robbins weaves multiple story lines in this complex exploration of an era of social upheaval and ideological confrontation, and his evocation of 1930s New York City is complete and convincing. The film's structure, while at times somewhat cumbersome, allows the protagonists to reflect each other, like facets of a prism. They give voice to the myriad opinions of the day, capturing a sense of excitement and urgency. The film's final shot is wry and cautionary and pretty damn sobering. An entertaining and thought-provoking film. ★★★½ DVD: $14.99, VHS: $9.99

The Craft

(1996, 100 min, US, Andrew Fleming) *Robin Tunney, Fairuza Balk, Neve Campbell, Rachel True, Cliff De Young, Helen Shaver. Heathers* meets *Carrie* in this psychologically mature tale of teen angst and retribution about a circle of student misfits whose prankish use of witchcraft against their tormentors gets out of hand when one of them (Balk) loses control of her own personal demons and becomes a bitch of a witch. Director Fleming takes what might have been more "Gen-X" drivel and invests it with surprisingly keen insight and malicious wit. ★★★ DVD Letterbox Special Edition: $14.99, VHS: $14.99

Craig's Wife

(1936, 75 min, US, Dorothy Arzner) *Rosalind Russell, John Boles, Jane Darwell, Billie Burke.* Russell is outstanding as the selfish, materialistic wife whose obsessive social climbing ruins her marriage. (Remade in 1950 as *Harriet Craig*) ★★★

The Cranes Are Flying

(1957, 94 min, USSR, Mikhail K. Kalatozov) *Tatyana Samoilova, Alexei Batalov.* Made during the "thaw" of the Cold War that resulted in greater liberty for filmmakers, this lyrical and poignant love story is set during WWII and follows the sad tale of two young lovers who are separated by the war. Tragedies soon befall the girl after her sweetheart volunteers to fight, leaving her in the hands of his brutish cousin. With sweeping and lush camera work, moving performances and an unusual absence of political propaganda, this is a tender, realistic portrayal of a love that triumphs in the face of adversity. (Russian with English subtitles) ★★★½ DVD Criterion Collection: $29.99

Crash

(1997, 100 min, Canada, David Cronenberg) *James Spader, Holly Hunter, Elias Koteas, Debra Unger, Rosanna Arquette.* Banned in London and cheered and hissed at the Cannes Film Festival, Cronenberg's controversial adaptation of J.G. Ballard's novel rumbles on the fumes of its outlaw reputation. Like *Naked Lunch* and *Videodrome*, this eerie effort finds a netherworld where technology, obsession and sex meet; then it sets them against each other in the horrific battlefield of the mind. Spader plays a Toronto film producer whose unquenchable sexual desires take a new turn after he's involved in a car accident that kills the husband of passenger Hunter. Despite the tragedy and subsequent injuries, Hunter and Spader begin a carnal relationship that

Angela Lindvall stars as secret agent Dragonfly in *CQ*

eventually leads to an unusual medical researcher (Koteas), who gets his kicks staging the car accidents of the deceased and famous (James Dean, Jayne Mansfield). Spader eventually brings wife Unger into the fray. Story line and character development take a backseat to mood and the psychological surveying going on here. Heated yet chilly at the same time, the fairly heated sex scenes turn unsettling when played against the frenzy of the adrenaline-charged car crash sequences. ★★★ DVD: $24.99

Crash Dive

(1943, 105 min, US, Archie Mayo) *Tyrone Power, Dana Andrews, Anne Baxter.* Power stars as a naval officer who is assigned to commander Andrews' sub. In between daring attacks on the Germans, he falls in love with Andrews' fiancée Baxter. The story nicely mixes romance, comedy and wartime heroics, the special effects are commendable, and the film's rich color is an asset. ★★★ DVD: $14.99

The Crazies

(1973, 103 min, US, George Romero) *Lane Carroll, W.G. McMillan, Harold Wayne Jones.* An early thriller from director Romero about a bungled Army experiment contaminating a small town's water supply, turning its citizens into crazed killers. ★★ VHS: $14.99

crazy/beautiful

(2001, 95 min, US, John Stockwell) *Kirsten Dunst, Jay Hernandez, Bruce Davison, Lucinda Jenney, Taryn Manning.* A wealthy but mixed-up girl (an effective-as-usual Dunst) and a Latino boy (an equally good Hernandez) from the wrong side of the tracks meet cute and fall in love. Unfortunately, her erratic behavior and psychological problems threaten to crush his dream of becoming a Navy pilot. An engaging teen film, *crazy/beautiful* is a breath of fresh air after the countless moronic comedies of the past few years aimed at high schoolers. While one wishes writer-director Stockwell had gone dramatically further with these characters (and apparently his studio-nixed director's cut did so), this is still stronger than the vast majority of teen films. Davison is quite good as Dunst's congressman father, who is surprisingly as concerned with Hernandez's future (and Dunst's negative impact on it) as he is his own daughter's. ★★★ DVD Letterbox: $14.99, VHS: $9.99

Crazy from the Heart

(1991, 94 min, US, Thomas Schlamme) *Christine Lahti, Ruben Blades, William Russ.* A compelling drama about a high-school teacher who falls for a Hispanic janitor, causing an uproar in their small town. Both Lahti and Blades give convincing performances in this examination of self-confidence and individuality. ★★★ VHS: $79.99

Crazy in Alabama

(1999, 113 min, US, Antonio Banderas) *Melanie Griffith, Lucas Black, Meat Loaf, Rod Steiger, David Morse, Cathy Moriarty, Elizabeth Perkins, Robert Wagner, Richard Schiff.* Evidencing influences from his early work with Pedro Almodóvar, Banderas balances with agility broad farce and considered gravity. It's summer in Alabama, 1965, and Lucille (Griffith) has just poisoned her brutish husband and deposited her 7 children on her mother's doorstep to leave to pursue her dream of appearing on an episode of "Bewitched." The story is seen through the eyes of her nephew Peejoe (a rock-solid Black), who, through the simple expedient of truth, becomes a participant in the burgeoning Civil Rights move-

ment. The film is snappily paced as it contrasts Lucille's road trip insanity with the societal insanity of segregation. Credit goes to Banderas for maintaining two such dissimilar tones with the same film; which, with the exception of a bogged-down courtroom finale, he does with surprising success. ★★★ DVD: $9.99, VHS: $9.99

Crazy in Love

(1992, 93 min, US, Martha Coolidge) *Holly Hunter, Gena Rowlands, Bill Pullman, Julian Sands, Frances McDormand.* Director Coolidge has crafted a lyrical and mature examination of the bonds of family and the complications that arise out of compulsive passions. Hunter fears her husband (Pullman) is losing interest in their marriage when she meets an enchanting photographer, Sands. Filmed to good effect in and around Seattle, the film sports earnest dialogue and characterizations along with moments of touching intimacy. ★★½ VHS: $79.99

Crazy Mama

(1975, 82 min, US, Jonathan Demme) *Ann Sothern, Cloris Leachman, Linda Purl, Stuart Whitman, Jim Backus, Donny Most, Tisha Sterling, Sally Kirkland.* Director Demme's talents are very much in evidence in this early exploitation film made for Roger Corman. Three generations of women go on a riotous crime spree from California to Arkansas. An action/comedy/drama similar to Demme's later *Married to the Mob.* ★★½ DVD The Director's Series: $14.99, VHS: $9.99

Crazy Moon

(1987, 98 min, Canada, Allan Eastman) *Kiefer Sutherland, Vanessa Vaughn.* An innocuous variation on the *Harold and Maude* theme (society misfits in love). Sutherland stars as an '80s teenager caught up in '40s nostalgia who falls in love with a deaf girl. Cinema from the Great White North does not send Hollywood packing, but it's entertaining nonetheless. ★★½

Crazy People

(1990, 90 min, US, Tony Bill) *Dudley Moore, Daryl Hannah, Paul Reiser, Mercedes Ruehl, J.T. Walsh.* Moore stars as an advertising executive whose policy of "truth in advertising" lands him in the loony bin. There he becomes mixed up with a group of fellow patients. This is simply *The Dream Team* on Madison Avenue. When it is lampooning TV and print advertising, it is funny. But unfortunately, the rest of it is awkward and maudlin. ★★ DVD: $14.99

The Crazy Ray/Entr'acte

(1923/1924, 36 min, France, René Clair) *The Crazy Ray,* Dadaist Clair's first film, is a fanciful and amusing story of a mad scientist who invents a ray gun and puts the entire city of Paris in suspended animation. *Entr'acte,* conceived as a filmic intermission to be shown during the Dada ballet "Relache," has endured well beyond the original intention to become one of the important surrealist films of the period. Plotless, the film, in frantic movements designed to offend its original audience, includes a chase through Paris with a runaway hearse. (Silent with musical accompaniment) ★★★ VHS: $39.99

Creation of Adam

(1993, 93 min, Russia, Yuri Pavlov) *Alexander Strizhenov, Anzhelika Nevolina.* The first gaythemed film from Russia, this mystical drama will disappoint many by its oblique handling of the gay angle. Set in the industrialized port of St. Petersburg,

the story follows handsome designer Andrei (Strizhenov) who is stuck in an unfulfilling relationship with his equally unhappy wife. After saving an effeminate teen from a group of queer-bashers, he is quickly accused — by both the thugs and his wife — of being homosexual. His life is transformed when he meets Philip, a mysterious, self-assured young man. Their ensuing relationship, handled in a weird, dreamlike manner, is one of both seduction and brotherlike guidance. (Russian with English subtitles) ★★½ VHS: $39.99

Creation of the Humanoids

(1962, 75 min, US, Wesley E. Barry) Andy Warhol's favorite film features Forrest J. Ackerman (creator of "Famous Monsters of Filmland") and makeup by Jack Pierce, who created all the great monsters like Frankenstein and The Wolfman. After the next big one, humanoids are created to replace all the dead Third World people who used to do our menial work. ★

Creator

(1985, 108 min, US, Ivan Passer) *Peter O'Toole, Mariel Hemingway, Vincent Spano, Virginia Madsen.* Middling sci-fi comedy with O'Toole as a Nobel Prize-winning biologist who attempts to clone his long-deceased wife, with the help of a young med student (Spano). ★★

Creature Comforts

(1990, 30 min, GB, Boris Kossmehl, Nick Park, Peter Lord) Park, and the Aardman studios, burst onto the animation scene with "Creature Comforts," a hilariously dry five-minute claymated short that is so bursting with detail and humor that it must be watched more than once. Taking the form of a BBC news item, clay-animated animals are interviewed in their zoo cages, but they're voiced by real-life British citizens complaining about their dwellings! In addition to this Oscar-winner for Best Animated Short is: Kossmehl's hilarious, expressionistic "Not Without My Handbag," showing materialstic folk in the afterlife, and Lord's "Wat's Pig" and "Adam," the first a fable about twins separated into different class structures. ★★★★ DVD: $9.99, VHS: $9.99

Creature from the Black Lagoon

(1954, 79 min, US, Jack Arnold) *Richard Carlson, Richard Denning, Whit Bissell, Julie Adams.* What '50s monster movie could be any good without Carlson, Denning or Bissell? Well, this film's got all three! Plus the neatest monster this side of the sushi bar. The film exhibits a surprising lyricism in its underwater sequences, especially the aquatic pas de deux with the heroine. Features the classic line, "David, you still don't look like an ekistiologist." Originally shown in 3-D. (Sequel: *Revenge of the Creature*) ★★★ VHS: $9.99

The Creeper

(1948, 64 min, US, Jean Yarbrough) *Onslow Stevens, Eduardo Ciannelli.* A surprisingly stylish low-budget horror film about a mad doctor whose nostrum turns men into killer cats. ★★½

The Creeping Flesh

(1970, 89 min, GB, Freddie Francis) *Peter Cushing, Christopher Lee.* A lesser Hammer Studios production perhaps, but any horror film with Cushing and Lee is bound to provoke a few chills. The plot features (you guessed it) a mad scientist who is obsessed with harnessing the "essence of evil." It's an old-fashioned affair, filled with monsters, evil spirits and numerous subplots. ★★★

Creepshow
(1982, 120 min, US, George Romero) *E.G. Marshall, Hal Holbrook, Adrienne Barbeau, Ted Danson, Leslie Nielsen, Ed Harris.* Five horror stories written by Stephen King offer a few chills, especially the final one about paranoid high-rise dweller Marshall and his newly arrived guests — hundreds of cockroaches. ★★★ DVD: $9.99, VHS: $9.99

Creepshow 2
(1987, 89 min, US, Michael Gornick) *Lois Chiles, George Kennedy, Tom Savini, Dorothy Lamour.* Three more Stephen King stories, here adapted by George Romero. Doesn't deliver the same number of chills as the original, but undemanding horror fans shouldn't mind. ★★ DVD: $24.99, VHS: $9.99

The Crew
(1994, 99 min, US, Carl-Jan Colpaert) *Viggo Mortensen, Jeremy Sisto, Pamela Gidley, Donal Logue.* Funny, nasty and suspenseful, this psychological thriller revolves around a group of five people whose Caribbean cruise turns into a nightmare after their boat is hijacked by two men, including a preop transsexual out to raise enough money for his sex change. A richly detailed action/drama which touches upon homophobia, and offers one of the least likely heroes one will ever encounter. ★★★

The Crew
(2000, 88 min, US, Michael Dinner) *Burt Reynolds, Richard Dreyfuss, Carrie-Anne Moss, Seymour Cassel, Dan Hedaya, Jennifer Tilly, Lainie Kazan, Miguel Sandoval, Jeremy Piven.* A seasoned cast makes the most of this amiable comedy about four aged small-time hoods and their last hurrah. Sort of a *Grumpy Old Wiseguys*, the story follows the comic exploits of Reynolds, Dreyfuss, Cassel and Hedaya, former Jersey boys now retired and living in South Beach. When it appears they will lose their retirement home, they band together for a little con. While a lot of this is familiar territory, the pairing of these four pros and some genuinely amusing moments make *The Crew* a likable, entertaining bit of nonsense. ★★½ DVD: $19.99, VHS: $9.99

Cria!
(1975, 107 min, Spain, Carlos Saura) *Geraldine Chaplin, Ana Torrent.* This beautifully acted, haunting film stars Torrent as a nine-year-old heroine with an uncanny talent for observing scenes not meant for her eyes, specifically the death of her father. An evocative film about the darker side of childhood, superstition, knowledge and the inevitable loss of innocence. (Spanish with English subtitles) ★★★½ VHS: $29.99

Cries and Whispers
(1972, 106 min, Sweden, Ingmar Bergman) *Liv Ullman, Ingrid Thulin, Harriet Andersson, Kary Sylway, Erland Josephson.* Bergman delves into the tumultuous world of familial hates, longings and frustrations in this beautifully rendered, multilayered classic. Ullmann is superlative as a repressed woman unable to cope with her sister's slow death to tuberculosis. An unforgettable, shattering portrait of the conscious and subconscious. (Swedish with English subtitles) ★★★★ DVD Letterbox Criterion Collection: $29.99, VHS: $29.99

Crime and Punishment
(1935, 110 min, France, Pierre Chenal) *Harry Baur, Pierre Blanchar.* Dostoyevsky's complex, brooding novel is brilliantly brought to the screen in this haunting and menacing adaptation. Baur stars as Raskolnikov, a tormented student who murders a moneylender and her daughter and soon finds himself stalked by the cunning magistrate Porfiry. Light years ahead of Josef von Sternberg's Hollywood version released that same year, director Chenal stages most of the action in a claustrophobic and atmospheric studio set — the result being an almost airless and unrelentingly intense drama. (French with English subtitles) ★★★★

Crime and Punishment
(1935, 88 min, US, Josef von Sternberg) *Peter Lorre, Edward Arnold, Marian Marsh.* Not as intense as the French adaptation of Dostoyevsky's existential novel, von Sternberg's version is at least more palatable entertainment. Lorre gives a stellar performance as the brooding intellectual, Raskolnikov, who murders a greedy pawnbroker, deeming her "unfit to live." The omission of the accidental killing of the pawnbroker's retarded daughter lessens the guilt Raskolnikov battles in the novel. The story is lightened just a bit by this and Lorre's character appears a little more amiable because of it. ★★½

Crime and Punishment
(1970, 200 min, USSR, Lev Kulidzhanov) *Georgi Taratorkin, Victoria Fyodorova.* This Russian version of Dostoyevsky's literary classic about a student who murders a pawnbroker and her daughter is an authentic and brilliant translation of the much-filmed novel. The impoverished Raskolnikov, racked by guilt for his crimes, is eventually hunted by Police Inspector Porfiry and confesses. Much longer than the U.S., English and French versions, the film probes the intense mental anguish of Raskolnikov and provides a haunting image of the man's tortured soul. (Russian with English subtitles) ★★★½

The Crime of Monsieur Lange
(1935, 85 min, France, Jean Renoir) A delightfully droll black comedy, scripted by Jacques Prévert and Renoir, that mixes fantasy and politics in its story of a worker uprising. When the crooked and lecherous boss of a publishing house suddenly disappears, the exploited workers of the company unite to form a cooperative and succeed in making the company a huge success. When the boss returns to take over, he finds the workers, led by M. Lange, a timid writer of pulp westerns, united in opposition. (French with English subtitles) ★★★★ VHS: $24.99

The Crime of Padre Amaro
(2002, 120 min, Mexico, Carlos Carrera) *Gael García Bernal, Sancho Gracia, Ana Claudia Talancón, Damián Alcázar.* As if the Roman Catholic Church doesn't already have a bad rep, this adept Mexican drama drives one more stake into the heart of Catholic ideals. When young new priest Father Amaro (Bernal) joins the parish of a small Mexican town, he arouses spiritual interests from many and *other* interests from local teenager Amelia (Talancón). One thing leads to another and soon the new priest is taking Amelia to private locations to "prepare her to be a nun" as described to one inquisitor. Father Amaro climbs aboard the same corruption train that carries his mentor Father Benito (Gracia), another fornicating priest who also has been accepting drug money to build a new hospital. With such controversial themes, the film is still handled with class and without the feeling of a dime store pulp novel. Bernal sensitively approaches this material and generates humanity out of a priest whose unwise and disturbing choices are borne from a fractured religious consciousness. (Spanish with English subtitles) ★★★ DVD Letterbox $19.99, VHS Subtitled: $14.99

Crime of the Century
(1996, 110 min, US, Mark Rydell) *Stephen Rea, Isabella Rossellini.* In the 1930s, the Lindbergh baby kidnapping/murder case and its subsequent trial was an unprecedented media event. When the trial was over, a German emigrant named Hauptmann was found guilty and executed. But through the years, many historians have speculated that Hauptmann may have been innocent, a victim of an inferior defense, a zealous police investigation and a prejudiced court system. The methodically paced but riveting *Crime of the Century*, a made-for-HBO drama, takes this view and succinctly presents the facts as they *could* have been. It not only makes for great viewing, but a damn good argument for a miscarriage of justice, as well. ★★★½ VHS: $79.99

Crime Story
(1993, 90 min, Hong Kong, Kirk Wong) *Jackie Chan, Kent Cheng.* A real-life incident serves as the inspiration for a rare dramatic turn by Chan. Jackie is an ace Hong Kong cop called in to work on a tough kidnapping case. Little does he know that his own partner (Cheng) is involved in the scam. Very few Hong Kong action films reach the emotional intensity of this film. Highly recommended for traditional action fans and those looking for another side of Jackie's star persona. Unfortunately, the film has been released in an atrociously dubbed version that severely detracts from its serious tone. ★★★½

Crime Zone
(1988, 93 min, US, Louis Llosa) *Sherilyn Fenn, David Carradine, Peter Nelson.* A low-budget, futuristic *Bonnie and Clyde*, *Crime Zone* tells the tale of two young "sub-grades," Bone (Nelson) and Helen (Fenn). They are hired by a mysterious man (Carradine) to steal an important government computer disk and soon find themselves the targets of an all-out police dragnet. Roger Corman produced this imaginative, entertaining if somewhat cheesy sci-fi thriller. ★★½ VHS: $79.99

Crimes and Misdemeanors
(1989, 97 min, US, Woody Allen) *Woody Allen, Mia Farrow, Martin Landau, Anjelica Huston, Alan Alda, Jerry Orbach.* Allen's fascinating blend of humor and gripping melodrama follows the intersecting stories of two men: a successful opthalmologist (Landau), who arranges the murder of his mistress; and an out-of-work filmmaker (Allen) who falls in love with his producer (Farrow). It is Allen's remarkable irony that one man's deep-rooted religious principles are betrayed at an insignificant cost, and integrity is ill-rewarded. ★★★★ DVD: $19.99

Crimes of Passion
(1984, 107 min, US, Ken Russell) *Anthony Perkins, Kathleen Turner, John Laughlin.* This sizzling tale of a sexually repressed street preacher and a mysterious prostitute carries as resounding a wallop as could only come from the inim-

itable talents of Russell. Perkins stars as the deranged reverend who's hell-bent on saving the soul of China Blue (Turner) — a well-respected fashion designer by day who becomes a slinky streetwalker at night. Overflowing with camp humor and bizarre twists, the film is a visual treat in which seductive waves of saturated neon splash across the screen. (Unrated version) ★★★ DVD Letterbox Unrated: $19.99

Crimes of the Heart

(1986, 105 min, US, Bruce Beresford) *Sissy Spacek, Diane Keaton, Jessica Lange, Tess Harper.* In the 1940s, this offbeat comedy would have been classified as a "woman's picture"; today, it is called a "star vehicle." Spacek, Keaton and Lange breathe life into Beth Henley's Pulitzer Prize-winning play about three Southern sisters reunited in time of crisis, and of their estrangement and reconciliation. A sweet-natured film that garnered Oscar nominations for Spacek, costar Harper and its screenplay adaptation. ★★★ DVD Letterbox: $14.99

Crimetime

(1996, 95 min, GB, George Sluizer) *Stephen Baldwin, Pete Postlethwaite, Sadie Frost, Geraldine Chaplin, Karen Black.* Tabloid TV gets the *Network* treatment with this stylish-looking thriller that very nearly sinks into its own smartness. Postlethwaite plays a serial killer who picks up his first victim. A rather gruesome murder, it catches the attention of a TV magazine show (run by Black doing her worst Faye Dunaway imitation) that restages sensationalistic crimes. Baldwin is the actor who gets his 15 minutes playing the murderer. Alternating between black comedy and suspense, *Crimetime* becomes more bizarre as the murders continue and Baldwin and Postlethwaite form a bond. Postlethwaite appears to be having fun hamming it up. ★★ DVD: $14.99

Crimewave

(1986, 83 min, US, Sam Raimi) *Louise Lasser, Paul L. Smith, Bruce Campbell.* Long before *Darkman* or *Miller's Crossing*, Raimi and the Coen Brothers — Joel and Ethan — joined forces to make this alternately amusing black farce about a couple of bungling rat exterminators who set their sights on two-legged mammals instead. ★★½

Criminal Law

(1989, 117 min, US, Martin Campbell) *Gary Oldman, Kevin Bacon, Joe Don Baker, Karen Young, Tess Harper.* Oldman and Bacon dance a psychotic pas de deux in this muddled thriller about a rich-kid serial killer (Bacon) who, having been caught, tried, and found not guilty, taunts his defense attorney (Oldman) with the knowledge that he's really guilty and plans to kill again. Britisher Oldman does a knock-out American accent, but it's not enough to overcome the shaky story line and plotting. ★★½

The Criminal Life of Archibaldo de la Cruz

(1955, 91 min, Mexico, Luis Buñuel) *Ernesto Alonso, Ariadne Welter.* Director Buñuel ended his self-exile in Mexico with this slyly humorous black comedy of one man's dark, sexual and murderous obsessions. After a traumatic experience in which a boy enjoys a secret sexual thrill on the accidental death of the family maid, he grows up one sick little pup. Years later he is now an aristocratic gentleman,

and Archibaldo's secret thoughts harbor a guilt-fueled fantasy of sexual kinkiness, crime and murder against women; but, in true Buñuelian fashion, his criminal desires are thwarted at every turn. With surrealistic touches and macabre fetishism, Buñuel pokes wicked fun at the bourgeoisie, Catholicism and the Latino male. (Spanish with English subtitles) ★★★★ VHS: $29.99

The Crimson Pirate

(1952, 104 min, US, Robert Siodmak) *Burt Lancaster, Nick Cravet, Eve Bartok, Christopher Lee.* Lancaster is in top form, both as actor and athlete, in this supremely entertaining swashbuckler with Lancaster and fellow acrobat Cravat fighting the bad guys in the Mediterranean. ★★★ DVD: $19.99

The Crimson Rivers

(2001, 105 min, France, Mathieu Kassovitz) *Jean Reno, Vincent Cassel.* An adequate serial killer movie, *The Crimson Rivers*, based on a French best-seller, is ultimately too "American" and uneven to be totally successful. Reno and Cassel are two detectives whose cases converge. They team up to stop some gruesome killings near a very exclusive university nestled in the French Alps. The two leads are quite appealing, but the story . . . well, we've seen it a million times, and the denouement is rather silly and underwhelming. There's also a defiantly gratuitous martial arts fight halfway. Still, *The Crimson Rivers*, from the director of the riveting *Hate*, is certainly watchable, especially if expectations aren't too high. ★★½ DVD Special Edition: $24.99, VHS Dubbed: $14.99

Crimson Tide

(1995, 113 min, US, Tony Scott) *Denzel Washington, Gene Hackman, Matt Craven, George Dzundza, Viggo Mortensen, Lillo Brancato Jr., Jason Robards.* If *The Hunt for Red October* brought an end to the Cold War at a theatre near you, then another submarine thriller, *Crimson Tide*, certainly tries to rekindle the sleepy politics of paranoia. And it does so in an exceedingly efficient manner. Washington stars as the newly appointed second-in-command of the nuclear submarine *USS Alabama* who comes in conflict with hard-nosed captain Hackman over what action to take when a renegade Russian general takes control of a Soviet sub and threatens nuclear war. Fairly authentic and exciting throughout, *Crimson Tide* is more credible than Scott's other military saga *Top Gun*. ★★★ DVD: $19.99, VHS: $9.99

Criss Cross

(1949, 87 min, US, Robert Siodmack) *Burt Lancaster, Yvonne DeCarlo, Dan Duryea, Stephen McNally, Tony Curtis.* Lancaster returns from prison looking to go straight. Plans go awry when he runs into ex-wife DeCarlo and her double-crossing plan for an armored car stick-up. A terrific sense of atmosphere and shadowy suspense make this "B" noir one not to miss. ★★★

Critical Care

(1997, 109 min, US, Sidney Lumet) *James Spader, Kyra Sedgwick, Albert Brooks, Helen Mirren, Anne Bancroft, Jeffrey Wright, Wallace Shawn.* In this entertaining satire, Spader plays a callous, burned-out doctor at a major hospital who gets caught between two sisters fighting over their comatose father. One a spacey holy roller, wants him kept alive; the other, a manipulative fashion model, wants to pull the plug. Several subplots wind their way through the central story, making some caustic obser-

vations on the business of saving lives. Though *Critical Care* doesn't pull its punches, it could have been tougher and gone more for the jugular as, say, *Wag the Dog*. The film has an otherworldly story line involving the afterlife which completely misfires, and the ending may be too pat, but there are a great many delicious moments to savor. ★★★ DVD: $9.99, VHS: $9.99

Critical Condition

(1987, 100 min, US, Peter Faiman) *Richard Pryor, Rachel Ticotin, Ruben Blades, Joe Mantegna, Joe Dallesandro.* Harmless though silly Pryor comedy with Pryor as a developer who feigns insanity to stay out of jail. But when he escapes from the mental ward, he is mistaken for a doctor and proceeds to turn the hospital topsy-turvy. ★★ DVD: $14.99

Critters

(1986, 86 min, US, Stephen Herek) *Dee Wallace Stone, M. Emmet Walsh, Billy Zane, Don Opper, Terrance Mann.* Offbeat comic horror film about some hairy tumbleweed-like monsters who arrive from another planet and terrorize a small Kansas town. An enjoyable, silly romp with both laughs and chills going for it. (Followed by 3 sequels) ★★½ DVD: $19.99, VHS: $14.99

"Crocodile" Dundee

(1986, 95 min, Australia, Peter Faiman) *Paul Hogan, Linda Kozlowski.* A surprise and huge box-office hit, *"Crocodile" Dundee* is a tepid comedy about an Australian Everyman (played by Hogan, which would be like saying that Sylvester Stallone is an American Everyman) who finds adventure in the wilds of New York City. Admittedly, Hogan has a genial charm to him (if you can ignore his homophobia), but the film casts him in too many clichéd antics, and most of the comedy just isn't funny. (Followed by 2 sequels) ★★ DVD Letterbox: $14.99, VHS: $9.99

"Crocodile" Dundee 2

(1988, 111 min, US, John Cornell) *Paul Hogan, Linda Kozlowski.* For the record, Mick "Crocodile" Dundee (Hogan) must save his girlfriend (Kozlowski) from ruthless drug dealers. For the record, this is a witless, though very profitable sequel. For those who liked the original, there's probably nothing we can say to dissuade you from watching this (and there are a lot of you). For those who didn't, avoid this at all costs. ★ DVD Letterbox: $19.99, VHS: $9.99

"Crocodile" Dundee in Los Angeles

(2001, 95 min, US, Simon Wincer) *Paul Hogan, Linda Kozlowski, Jere Burns.* A belated and bland retread, *"Crocodile" Dundee in L.A.* provides barely enough juvenile chuckles to qualify as a time killer. Mick Dundee goes to L.A. to take part in more fish-out-of-water jokes, and gets involved in a smuggling ring, which provides all the high-test thrills of a kids' TV show. Craggy and corny, Hogan tries to exude some charm, even when recycling the same old gags, but this is very much a minor Dundee. ★½ DVD Letterbox: $19.99, VHS: $9.99

Cronica del Alba

(1982, 82 min, Spain, Antonio J. Betancor) Like Truffaut's Antoine Donel series, *Cronica del Alba* is the second film in the life story of a young boy growing into manhood. Jose Garces, or "Pepe," last seen in *Valentina*, is now 15 years old and in his first year at the university. The setting is Zaragoza in 1919, on the eve of the anarchist rebellion, and our hero is caught between his continued love for the now ravishing Valentina, his bourgeois origins and his developing revolutionary ideals. Adapted from the novel by Ramon J. Sender. (Spanish with English subtitles) ★★★

Cronos

(1993, 92 min, Mexico, Guillermo del Toro) *Federico Luppi, Ron Perlman, Claudio Brook, Margarita Isabel.* This delicious and chilling little oddity from Mexico tells the tale of an aging antiques dealer who happens upon an ancient device, built by an alchemist bent on achieving immortality, which transforms its user into a vampire. Upon accidentally discovering the scarab-shaped machine's purpose, the old man becomes addicted to its power and is soon on the road to ruin. Into the picture comes a wealthy American industrialist who is dying of cancer and will stop at nothing to get his hands on the box. Though at times gruesome and grisly, the film has a fair share of good humor and at its core is a touching tale about the relationship between the old man and his grandchild. (Spanish with English subtitles) ★★★ DVD Letterbox: $19.99

Crooklyn

(1994, 114 min, US, Spike Lee) *Alfre Woodard, Spike Lee, Zelda Harris, Delroy Lindo.* Occasionally funny and at times abrasive, this semiautobiographical film directed by Spike and cowritten by Lee and his siblings focuses on the Carmichael family as they experience a summer in their crowded but comfortable Brooklyn neighborhood. Centering on the relationship between the Carmichaels' matriarch (Woodard) and her young daughter (skillfully played by Harris), this patchwork quilt pieced together with vintage "Soul Train" footage and Afro Sheen commercials has wonderful moments but may be a little on the long side for those with short attention spans. Note: One painfully long sequence is shot in Cinemascope, so do not attempt to adjust your sets. ★★★ DVD: $14.99, VHS: $9.99

Cross Creek

(1983, 122 min, US, Martin Ritt) *Mary Steenburgen, Rip Torn, Alfre Woodard, Peter Coyote, Dana Hill.* Based on the memoirs of Marjorie Rawlings ("The Yearling"), this compelling drama stars Steenburgen as the authoress, who ventures into Florida's backwoods and composes the novel that life there inspired. Sterling support from Torn and Woodard. ★★★ DVD Letterbox: $19.99, VHS: $9.99

Cross My Heart

(1987, 100 min, US, Armyan Bernstein) *Martin Short, Annette O'Toole, Paul Reiser.* Short and O'Toole are well cast as two romantics on a first date — where everything goes wrong. An insightful though slow-moving comedy not without considerable charm. ★★½ VHS: $9.99

Cross My Heart

(1990, 105 min, France, Jacques Fansten) French films will rarely come sweeter than this charming, offbeat story about a group of classmates united in protecting a fellow student after his mother suddenly dies. Twelve-year-old Martin, fearful that he will be sent to an orphanage, tries to cover up her death. His resourceful classmates soon discover the situation, swear secrecy and begin an elaborate plan to keep Martin away from the authorities by supplying food and money, forging letters to an increasingly suspicious principal and even burying mom in an old grandfather's clock! A heartwarming and winsome tale of growing up. (French with English subtitles) ★★★ VHS: $19.99

Cross My Heart and Hope to Die

(1994, 96 min, Norway, Marius Holst) *Martin Dahl Garfalk, Jan Kornstad.* A haunting Norwegian film about a young boy's coming of age. When Otto (Garfalk) is the only child left in town during summer vacation, he befriends Frank (Kornstad), a mysterious stranger who shows up one day out of nowhere. Almost immediately, weird things start happening: they find a body in the lake; Otto's mother may be having an affair with Frank; and the boy's father is crippled in an accident. The tension builds inexorably as Otto suspects his new friend of foul play — but do his eyes deceive him? Director Holst films everything impeccably, slowly revealing the truth. *Cross My Heart* is at times unsettling — there is an awful incident with a rat — but it is hypnotic nonetheless. (Norwegian with English subtitles) ★★★½ DVD: $29.99, VHS: $79.99

Cross of Iron

(1977, 120 min, GB/West Germany, Sam Peckinpah) *James Coburn, Maximilian Schell, James Mason, David Warner, Senta Berger.* Notable for being the great action director Peckinpah's first war film, this nonetheless represents the director's decline and is only intermittently interesting. It tells the story of a group of German soldiers on the Russian front in 1943 — a compelling idea that isn't given its full due. There is, however, a brilliantly staged battle scene near the end of the film that may, or may not, make it worth sitting through. ★★ DVD: $29.99

Crossfire

(1947, 85 min, US, Edward Dmytryk) *Robert Mitchum, Robert Ryan, Robert Young, Gloria Graham.* One of the first Hollywood films to deal with racial bigotry, this low-budget but engrossing thriller was shot entirely at night. In a New York City hotel, a Jewish man is murdered and three G.I.s just back from the war are suspected. Interestingly, the original victim in the Richard Brooks novel, "The Brick Foxhole," on which the film is based, was a homosexual. Ryan (in an Oscar-nominated role) is especially good as a bigoted soldier. ★★★★ VHS: $19.99

Crossing Delancey

(1988, 97 min, US, Joan Micklin Silver) *Peter Riegert, Reizl Bozyk, Jeroen Krabbé, Sylvia Miles, Amy Irving.* A charming tale of a "modern" woman searching for love and identity in an all-too-often inhumane "modern" world. Irving is radiant as a young urbanite who has fled her ethnic roots to become a member of the "in" Greenwich Village literary scene. When her aging Lower East Side Jewish grandmother, Bubbie, hires a matchmaker to find her a hubbie — a local pickle maker (wonderfully portrayed by Riegert) — her flight becomes all the more urgent. But despite all of her efforts to deny him, he possesses an undeniably sincere charm which plunges her into a true crisis of identity. Bozyk is a delight as the overbearing but lovable Bubbie. ★★★ VHS: $14.99

The Crossing Guard

(1995, 114 min, US, Sean Penn) *Jack Nicholson, David Morse, Anjelica Huston, Robin Wright, Piper Laurie, Richard Bradford, Robbie Robertson, John Savage.* Writer-director Penn has crafted an actors' vehicle in this somber treatment of guilt and redemption. The story opens on the day John Booth (Morse) is released from prison after serving his sentence for the drunk driving death of a young girl, whose father

Freddy Gale (Nicholson) has vowed revenge. Both Morse and Nicholson deliver powerful yet nuanced performances as each struggles with his own personal hell. As the characters confront and rebuff each other, a more complete version of their lives emerges. A solid supporting cast and exquisite cinematography propel a sometimes lumbering story line to its resolution, unexpected in its emotional release. ★★★ DVD: $9.99, VHS: $9.99

Crossing the Bridge

(1992, 103 min, US, Mike Binder) *Josh Charles, Jason Gedrick, Stephen Baldwin, Cheryl Pollak, Richard Edson.* Detroit, 1975, is the setting for this rambling, finally-coming-of-age drama about three high school buddies drifting nowhere three years after graduation. Told through the eyes of Mort (an aspiring Jewish writer), the story concerns the growing up that occurs when the gang considers smuggling drugs from Canada. Writer-director Binder's film comes off as a dramatically enhanced autobiography depicting what might have been his "good old days," but the screenplay at its worst gives way to clichés about tough, young adulthood. ★★ DVD: $9.99

Crossover Dreams

(1985, 85 min, US, Leon Ichaso) *Ruben Blades, Shawn Elliott, Elizabeth Peña.* Although American made, the Latin setting in New York's Spanish Harlem gives a feel of America as a foreign land. Blades delivers a mesmerizing acting and singing performance in this gritty, bittersweet comedy about a musician who vainly strives to "cross over" to the pop music mainstream. This is a compelling tale about betraying one's roots and friends for the sake of success, and marks an impressive screen introduction for Blades. ★★★

Crossroads

(1986, 100 min, US, Walter Hill) *Ralph Macchio, Joe Seneca, Jami Gertz, Joe Morton.* Macchio is a musical prodigy who, with the help of a legendary bluesman, hits the road for fame and fortune. He also battles the Devil for his immortal soul. Ry Cooder wrote the score; good as it may be, it doesn't help. ★½

Crossroads

(2002, 97 min, US, Tamra Davis) *Britney Spears, Anson Mount, Zoe Saldana, Taryn Manning, Kim Cattrall, Dan Aykroyd.* The transition from pop star to big-screen icon is often perilous at best, and while *Crossroads* isn't exactly *Shanghai Surprise*, Britney ain't doing herself no favors. Virginal Brit packs her bags and sets off on a road trip with her girlfriends, heading to L.A. for a music audition (natch). They bring along a typical rebel with a heart of gold — Brit eventually gives "it" up for him, so those looking for a role model beware. The road trip formula is basically an excuse to spotlight Ms. Spears without requiring her to carry a real narrative, the most shameless showcase being a Karaoke competition. The Karaoke craze is over, and so, too, may be her acting career. ★½ DVD Letterbox Special Collector's Edition: $14.99, VHS: $9.99

Crouching Tiger, Hidden Dragon

(2000, 119 min, Taiwan, Ang Lee) *Chow Yun-Fat, Michelle Yeoh, Zhang Ziyi, Chang Chen, Cheng Pei Pei.* With one master stroke, director Lee has simultaneously made the art film accessible, the martial arts film artful, and combined several genres to create a poetic, exciting and awe-inspiring story of master warriors, gravity-defying fights and the ultimate battle for the legendary Green Destiny sword. Yun-Fat is

The extraordinary Zhang Ziyi in *Crouching Tiger, Hidden Dragon*

Li Mu Bai, the land's most celebrated soldier, who returns to his village to leave behind the ways of the samurai. Fate, however, has other plans as Li comes face to face with his fiercest of enemies, the Jade Fox (Pei). Caught in the middle is Jen (an extraordinary Ziyi), the daughter of the local governor who is promised in an arranged marriage. Destinies and passions soon collide in a beautiful, swirling mixture of acrobatics and romantic sweep. The fight scenes are simply astonishing; bordering on the fantastic but possessing such grace as to never appear absurd. The story, based on the novel by Wang Du Lu, stands on its own as a study of tradition and defiance; with the Hong Kong-style fight scenes, it's a perfect blending of action and grand drama. Winner of 4 Academy Awards, including Best Foreign-Language Film. (Mandarin with English subtitles) ★★★★ DVD Letterbox: $14.99, DVD Letterbox Superbit Edition: $27.99, VHS Subtitled: $9.99, VHS Dubbed: $9.99

Croupier

(1998, 91 min, GB, Mike Hodges) *Clive Owen, Kate Hardie, Alex Kingston, Gina McKee, Nicholas Ball.* Jack Manfred (Owen) suffers writer's block by day and deals cards by night, the croupier job suggested by his small-time-hood dad. Jack dyes his bleached hair black and recedes behind his tuxedo, unreadable, while unerringly reading the gamblers. He uses a keen perception of human nature while dealing that he cannot harness for writing. Breaking a cardinal rule, Jack gets involved with a beautiful player (Kingston), who leads him down a crooked path. Addiction lives on both sides of the betting table, inducing lapses of judgment and enabling convoluted patterns of betrayal. *Croupier* is an intriguing, devastatingly cynical meditation on loyalty, allegiance and the mathematics of risk, delivered with a delicious noir sentiment and an appropriate lack of sentimentality. ★★★½ DVD Letterbox: $19.99

The Crow

(1994, 105 min, US, Alex Proyas) *Brandon Lee, Ernie Hudson, Michael Wincott, David Patrick Kelly, Rochelle Davis, William H. Macy.* The Crow was expected to be Lee's breakout film. Instead, at age 28 he was killed on the set, just as his father, Bruce Lee, also died at an early age when his film career was expected to explode. The film itself is almost overshadowed by these events, but stands on its own as an entertaining actioner with a driving love story. In a darkly luminous, decaying inner city, Lee and his fiancée are brutally murdererd for standing up to a slimy urban developer. Lee emerges from his grave after a year's regeneration, seeking vengeance to gain his final peace. Lee exhibits an engaging screen presence in this well-paced, starkly shot neo-noir. His future work would have been eagerly anticipated. ★★★½ DVD Letterbox Collector's Edition: $19.99, VHS: $9.99, VHS Letterbox: $9.99

The Crow: City of Angels

(1996, 86 min, US, Tim Pope) *Vincent Perez, Mia Kirshner, Iggy Pop, Richard Brooks.* Using the same mythology created in the original but building a completely separate story from it, a new team of filmmakers has made a darker vision of the undead avenger. Ash (Perez), a single father, is killed for accidentally witnessing a murder one night — the vengeance of the Crow rises. Ash is informed of his dark purpose by Sarah (Kirshner), the only character to appear in both films, and soon sets his sights on a drug lord and his crew. Looking like a music video spawned in Clive Barker's nightmares, this sequel is filled with ritualistic tattoos, piercings, and enough religious imagery and symbolism to elevate it above its pulp-action roots. ★★★ DVD Letterbox Collector's Edition: $14.99, VHS: $9.99, VHS Letterbox: $19.99

The Crowd

(1928, 104 min, US, King Vidor) *Eleanor Boardman, James Murray.* This classic silent drama tells the tale of a newlywed couple's hard times in New York City. Boardman and Murray give refreshingly subtle performances as the young lovers who learn that it is their love for each other that prevents them from being swallowed up by the big city's faceless crowd. ★★★★ VHS: $29.99

The Crucible

(1996, 123 min, US, Nicholas Hytner) *Daniel Day-Lewis, Winona Ryder, Paul Scofield, Joan Allen, Bruce Davison, Jeffrey Jones.* Arthur Miller's 1953 play about the Salem witch-hunts was a thinly veiled allegory on McCarthyism, and the critical reception to it was lukewarm at best. In time, McCarthyism died along with him, and the play was recognized as a masterwork of the American theatre. Adapted for the screen by Miller himself, this ominous, viscerally powerful film version is faithful to the text and maintains a larger-than-life feel. The story centers on the hysteria that results when lovestruck teen Abigail Williams (Ryder) falsely accuses neighbors of witchcraft — which ultimately leads to John Proctor (Day-Lewis) and his wife Elizabeth (the terrific Allen). There needn't be a topical political or social relevance to appreciate this remarkable film; *The Crucible* provides an acidly ironic contrast to contemporary trials in which, rather than the innocent being persecuted, the guilty are set free. ★★★★ DVD: $14.99, VHS: $9.99, VHS Letterbox: $9.99

Cruel Intentions

(1999, 97 min, US, Roger Kumble) *Sarah Michelle Gellar, Ryan Phillippe, Reese Witherspoon, Selma Blair, Sean Patrick Thomas, Joshua Jackson.* Choderlos de Laclos's novel "Les Liaisons Dangereuses" has been made into three great movies already; this fourth leads one to believe that it can do no wrong. The exploits of Valmont (Phillippe) and Merteuil (Gellar) are updated to the politically incorrect '90s in Manhattan, and given a terrifically trashy twist by writer-director Kumble. The step-siblings set up a wager for Phillippe to seduce Witherspoon; Merteuil's prize? "I'll fuck your brains out." No pretentiousness here, just catty talk and vile acts. A good-looking flick with a great-looking cast and a slick soundtrack, *Cruel Intentions* is a fun hoot from start (the ruin of a psychiatrist) to inevitable finish (the slow-motion comeuppance of Merteuil). ★★★ DVD: $14.99, VHS: $9.99

Cruel Intentions 2

(2000, 87 min, US, Roger Kumble) *Robin Dunne, Sarah Thompson, Mimi Rogers, Amy Adams.* This oddball, straight-to-video trash is an almost scene-for-scene remake of the original, made by the same writer-director (couldn't he have found any other projects to keep him busy?). The characters are all the same in this sequel (even though not all of them survived last time), and the situations are almost identical, with some tiny variations here and there. A half-hearted, junior high drama class run-through of the first film. ★½ DVD: $19.99, VHS: $9.99

The Cruel Sea

(1953, 121 min, GB, Charles Frend) *Jack Hawkins, Donald Sinden, Denholm Elliott, Stanley Baker, Virginia McKenna, Alec McCowen.* Recalling the 1940s classic British war films in both its pacing and structure, the often riveting *The Cruel Sea* follows the wartime experiences of the crew of a British warship patrolling the Atlantic during WWII. Hawkins stars as the ship's captain who witnesses the sacrifice and dehumanizing effect of combat as he and his men battle a literally unseen enemy underneath the ocean, the German U-boats. From the young faces of the dead to a mesmerizing sequence of a ship sinking, the film delves into the often harsh daily lives of men at war. Stunning cinematography, location shooting and actual war footage only accentuate the realism the film successfully conveys. ★★★½

Cruel Story of Youth

(1960, 97 min, Japan, Nagisa Oshima) *Yusuke Kawazu, Miyuki Kuwano.* Dazzling, audacious and strangely contemporary, Oshima's searing depiction of youthful alienation centers around the doomed affair of two teenaged lovers. The film shows a perversely Americanized post-WWII Japan and a disillusioned generation of reckless thrill-seekers. Behind his Ray-Bans and his cat-that-ate-the-bird grin, the lead character charts a course toward a tragic end and drags his sexually exploited girlfriend down with him. (Japanese with English subtitles) ★★★★ VHS: $19.99

The Cruise

(1998, 76 min, US, Bennett Miller) Plato had it wrong: Some lives *should* be unexamined. Case in point: one Timothy "Speed" Levitch, a tour bus guide with a penchant for free-associating like a mental patient. Now share the insanity with family and friends with this engaging documentary. Enjoy the musings of a typical "colorful character" as he waylays the unsuspecting onto a double-decker bus for a ride 'round the nine circles of Hell — with his own ego at the center. Be amazed as this autodidact preens and poses, whines and rails, offering insights of the myopic. Few street philosophers have ever been more pedestrian — or in his own odd way, entertaining. ★★★ VHS: $102.99

Cruising

(1980, 106 min, US, William Friedkin) *Al Pacino, Paul Sorvino, Karen Allen, Don Scardino, Joe Spinell, James Remar, Powers Boothe, Leo Burmester.* Pacino goes undercover in the Village's gay community and director Friedkin lets loose a homophobic assault. Pacino plays a police officer assigned to investigate a series of murders committed against gay men. So he dons leather cap and jacket and hits the clubs. This thriller has been aptly described as a "gay horror story," for Friedkin's vision of the gay world is both horrific and inaccurate. ★

Crumb

(1995, 119 min, US, Terry Zwigoff) R. Crumb certainly never wore any flowers in his hair that Summer of Love when he invented Underground Comics. Indeed, in each succeeding issue of *Zap* he spewed forth page after foolscap page of Hogarthian bile documenting the delusional nature of our Aquarian innocence. Director Zwigoff has captured the complexity of this man in his straightforward, riveting documentary, allowing the helplessly voluble Crumb to tell us more than he ever meant to — just like he does in his comics. ★★★½ DVD: $27.99

Crush

(1992, 97 min, New Zealand, Alison MacLean) *Marcia Gay Harden, Donough Rees, Caitlin Bossley.* This unnerving psychological thriller is infused with a brooding sense of doom. Set against the bubbling geysers of rural New Zealand, the story examines themes of passion, betrayal, desire, jealousy, seduction and revenge. Two women, Lane (Harden) and Christina (Rees), are involved in a car accident, leaving Christina severely injured and Lane (whose carelessness was the cause of the accident) unscathed. Lane inexplicably abandons her comatose friend, eventually befriending a novelist, Colin, and his 15-year-old boyish daughter, Angela. Angela, in turn, befriends the slowly recovering Christina, thereby precipitating an emotional showdown between the characters. A twisted, stylish, tension-filled feature which works best when delving into the three women's constantly shifting relationships and subtle sexual games. ★★★ VHS: $14.99

The Crush

(1993, 89 min, US, Alan Shapiro) *Cary Elwes, Alicia Silverstone, Jennifer Rubin, Kurtwood Smith.* When a handsome young journalist (Elwes) rents the guest house of an affluent couple, he becomes the object of their precocious teenage daughter's (Silverstone) dangerously obsessive affections. With a sexy 14-year-old seductress as the protagonist, a

victim who is so clueless that one is tempted to yell "just get out of the house already stupid," and a wonderfully inane plot twist involving a used condom, *The Crush* has a sort of shamelessness about its own cheesiness. ★★½ DVD: $9.99, VHS: $14.99

Crush

(2001, 112 min, GB, John McKay) *Andie MacDowell, Imelda Staunton, Anna Chancellor, Kenny Doughty, Bill Paterson.* Undoubtedly an attempt to ride the coattails of the wildly successful "Sex and the City," this study in female angst at age 40 is as unconvincing as it is tedious. The story revolves around three professional women — Kate (MacDowell), Molly (Chancellor) and Janine (Staunton) — who seem to look for love in all the wrong places and who seem to revel in their misery within a haze of cigarette smoke and idle chatter. These women all seem unabashedly sad and perhaps if writer-director McKay's script were content to acknowledge this and engage in a simple character study limited by the very real concerns of middle-aged single women, *Crush* might have been a worthwhile entertainment. ★★ DVD Letterbox: $19.99, VHS: $14.99

Crusoe

(1989, 95 min, US, Caleb Deschanel) *Aidan Quinn, Ade Sapara, Timothy Spall.* "Just sit right back and you'll hear a tale, the tale of a fateful trip." This is indeed a fateful trip into the darkened heart of the colonial imperialist. A trip on which director Deschanel perilously sets out to explore the moral ineptitude of a 19th-century slave trader. Not that this isn't a noble purpose, but what results here is an overburdened and laboring rendition of the Robinson Crusoe story. The film is not entirely without merit, however: the cinematography offers a splendid view of the Seychelles and Quinn is compelling as a Crusoe who is forced to reevaluate his assumptions about life, power and greed. ★★

Cry-Baby

(1990, 85 min, US, John Waters) *Johnny Depp, Amy Locane, Willem Dafoe, David Nelson, Patricia Hearst, Traci Lords, Ricki Lake, Susan Tyrrell, Joe Dallesandro, Troy Donohue, Iggy Pop, Polly Bergen.* Waters' musical spoof of 1950s teen flicks is set (where else?) in Baltimore and stars Depp as "Cry-Baby" Walker, a tough-as-nails, pretty-boy

Crumb

delinquent and leader of the ultra-cool Drapes who falls in love with Allison, a squeaky clean rich girl who has that itch to go "bad." But for those of us who were teased by the uproarious *Hairspray* and have been waiting for his definitive "suburban mall period" classic, sadly, this is not the one. Although it falls a little flat, it is still enjoyable, especially for its many Waters touches. ★★★ VHS: $6.99

Cry Freedom

(1987, 157 min, GB, Richard Attenborough) *Denzel Washington, Kevin Kline, Penelope Wilton, Kevin McNally, John Thaw, Timothy West, Zakes Mokae, Alec McCowen.* Attenborough's superbly rendered film about the life and death of South African activist Stephen Biko is a compelling vision of the violence and strife which tears at the heart of the black townships. The story is told through the eyes of Biko's white journalist friend, Donald Woods (excellently portrayed by Kline). As Biko, Washington delivers a moving performances. The film was criticized for concentrating more on the plight of Woods and his family than on black South Africa, but in fact, the film stands as a stirring portrait of how injustice for some leads to injustice for all. ★★★½ DVD: $14.99

A Cry in the Dark

(1988, 121 min, Australia, Fred Schepisi) *Meryl Streep, Sam Neill, Bruce Myles.* With an astonishing characterization, here portraying a mother on trial for the murder of her child, Streep once again gives proof that she is the finest actress of her generation. Lindy Chamberlain (Streep), a housewife and mother, is wrongfully arrested when her baby is killed by a dingo. The film recounts the tragedy and its aftermath, and not only explores the unbelievable strain on the Chamberlain household during the trial, but also the power of public opinion and a cynical press. A serious and intelligent film directed with a subtle hand. ★★★½ DVD: $9.99, VHS: $14.99

Cry of the Banshee

(1970, 92 min, GB, Gordon Hessler) *Vincent Price, Elisabeth Bergner, Hugh Griffith.* This bad period horror film has virtually no redeeming value save the performance of Price, who is clearly working well below his talent here. He plays a village magistrate who exterminates a group of Satan worshippers. He has a curse placed upon his household by the leader of the group. The film then turns into a sort of slasher/monster movie, with various members of his household being dispatched in various gory ways. Good production design is offset by a ludicrous and offensive script. ★

Cry, the Beloved Country

(1951, 111 min, GB, Zoltan Korda) *Canade Lee, Sidney Poitier, Charles Carson.* One of the first films to confront the injustices of Apartheid in South Africa, this Korda classic, based on the Alan Paton novel, tells the tale of a black rural priest (Lee) who travels to Johannesburg to find his son. Once there, he is confronted by the brutal realities of urban crime and the dehumanizing conditions of the segregationist townships. Poitier costars as an urban cleric who helps Lee in his search. (Remade in 1996) ★★★½ VHS: $69.99

Cry, the Beloved Country

(1996, 109 min, US/South Africa, Darrell James Roodt) *James Earl Jones, Richard Harris, Vusi Kunene, Charles S. Dutton.* A second screen version of Alan Paton's novel of racial inequality in 1940s South Africa, *Cry, the Beloved Country* is compassionate storytelling which is lacking a thoroughly fluid narrative but is enriched by two terrific actors.

Jones plays Rev. Stephen Kumalo, a rural priest who travels to Johannesburg in search of his lost son, who is on trial for killing a white man in a robbery attempt. Harris plays James Jarvis, the victim's father, a supremacist and neighbor of Rev. Kumalo. The story constructs each grieving father's journey, eventually leading to their paths crossing. A reverent, almost solemn adaptation, the film's strengths lie in Jones and Harris' remarkable performances, and from a dramatically involving story that examines the plight of both fathers and their eventual reconciliation with their sons. ★★★ DVD: $19.99, VHS: $19.99

The Crying Game

(1992, 112 min, GB, Neil Jordan) *Stephen Rea, Jaye Davidson, Forest Whitaker, Miranda Richardson, Jim Broadbent, Adrian Dunbar.* In a brilliant marketing coup, the folks at Miramax Films released this film strongly advising people not to give away its "secret." Word of this "secret" quickly swept the nation and everybody was dying to see what would have otherwise been another *Defence of the Realm* or *Hidden Agenda*. Thankfully, director Jordan's tautly realized political thriller is worthy of all the praise and press it generated. Rea plays an IRA terrorist with a troubled conscience who promises a captured British soldier (Whitaker) that he'll look after his girlfriend. Sometime later, Rea has opted out of the terror game and is trying to lead a quiet life of obscurity in London, where he decides to look her up. Newcomer Davidson's portrayal of the slender and exotic hairdresser is a knockout. Trouble comes in spades when one of Rea's old Republican comrades (the exhilirating Richardson), shows up to test his loyalties. An exciting and highly entertaining story sprinkled with drama, comedy and plenty of intrigue. ★★★★ DVD: $14.99

Cuba

(1979, 126 min, US, Richard Lester) *Sean Connery, Brooke Adams, Hector Elizondo, Denholm Elliott, Jack Weston, Chris Sarandon, Lonette McKee.* Director Lester imbues a high style to this political thriller about a doomed love affair between Connery and Adams as the Batista government collapses around them. ★★★ DVD Letterbox: $19.99

Cube

(1998, 90 min, Canada, Vincenzo Natali) *Nicole DeBoer, Nicky Guadagni, David Hewlett, Maurice Dean Wint.* A taut little paranoid suspense thriller, the low-budget *Cube* follows a handful of diverse people who wake up inside a uniquely designed prison — a gigantic cube with individual chambers that are constantly changing configuration, much like a rotating Rubik's Cube. It's a simple Darwinian tale of survival of the fittest as the prisoners ponder the nature and identity of their jailors and struggle to find a way out. Despite a rather predictable screenplay full of randomly stilted dialogue and some shakily amateurish performances, *Cube* is salvaged by a terrific production design, some inventive and very convincing visual effects and a rich soundtrack. (Sequel: *Cube²: Hypercube*) ★★½ DVD Signature Series: $19.99

Cube²: Hypercube

(2002, 94 min, US, Andrzej Sekula) *Geraint Wyn Davies, Kari Matchett, Neil Crone, Matthew Ferguson.* Take all of the weaker elements of *Cube*: the stilted acting, the cheap sets and the constant blather of stressed-out participants, and subtract the scares, the gore, the utter mathematical logic of it all, and you get *Cube²*. Like the first, eight people who

are semi-related each wake up in a white room, with doors on all six sides leading to other seemingly identical rooms. Yet there's little rhyme to the layout, with space, time and alternate realities shifting seemingly at random. With so much unexplained for the first hour, it's an admittedly intriguing ride, until the realization sets in that none of it really matters and nothing too exciting is going to happen. ★½ DVD Letterbox: $24.99

La Cucaracha

(1999, 95 min, US/Mexico, Jack Perez) *Joaquim De Alemeida, Tara Crespo, Victor Rivers, James McManus, Eric Roberts.* Roberts is a desperate drifter stranded south of the border who's offered a second chance when a Mexican monarch offers him $100,000 to kill the man who raped and murdered his 16-year-old son. As he debates whether or not to do it, his life is put in danger by the very men offering him the contract. Costar McManus wrote this strangely moving tale of revenge and redemption that's a notch above the usual B-movie actioner. ★★½ DVD: $9.99, VHS: $102.99

Cujo

(1983, 91 min, US, Lewis Teague) *Dee Wallace, Danny Pintauro, Ed Lauter.* Only Stephen King could write a book about a mother and son trapped in a broken-down car and being terrorized by a rabid St. Bernard and get away with it. If you think this premise sounds silly, think again because this ably made film adaptation is at times terrifying and filled with tension that builds to an excellent climax. ★★★ DVD: $14.99, VHS: $9.99

The Cup

(2000, 94 min, Bhutan, Khyentse Norbu) *Jamyang Lodro, Orgyen Tobgyal, Neten Chokling.* In a Tibetan monastery in exile in the mountain regions of India, two young cousins safely arrive after a perilous journey from Tibet. Their adaptation to austere monastic life includes an unexpected wrinkle — their introduction to World Cup Soccer! Even in this isolated, ethereal locale, soccermania is rampant. When, just before the 1998 World Championship match, it becomes necessary to obtain a TV and satellite dish, the entire monastery gets involved with the project. *The Cup* maintains a wacky, caper ambience while never losing sight of the circumstances that brought these Tibetan Buddhists to their present location. Delightful character portrayals and sure-handed direction combine to deliver an engrossing entertainment in which exotic ritual coexists with a contemporary sports milieu. Based on actual events. (Bhutanese with English subtitles) ★★★½

Cup Final

(1991, 107 min, Israel, Brian Riklis) *Moshe Ivgi, Muhamad Bacri.* A quiet, slightly comic and refreshing examination of the futile hatred between Israelis and Palestinians. The story follows Cohen, a young nebbishy Jewish soldier whose planned trip to Spain for the World Cup soccer finals is dashed when he is captured by a PLO band. Forced to join them on their trek to Beirut, where they hope to find safe haven, he slowly overcomes his resentment towards his captors and even finds room to bond with them when he discovers that he and their charismatic commander, Ziad, are both rooting for the Italian team in the Cup Final. Filled with irony and gentle humor, the film exploits the situation to expose the prejudices of both sides while offering a glimmer of hope that their conflict is not intractable. (Hebrew and Arabic with English subtitles) ★★★ DVD: $29.99, VHS: $24.99

Curdled

(1996, 94 min, US, Reb Braddock) *William Baldwin, Angela Jones, Lois Chiles, Daisy Fuentes, Mel Gorham, Barry Corbin.* In an enticing but bizarre performance, Jones stars as Gabriela, a young woman fascinated by the sight and smell of human blood. In order to satisfy this craving for gore, she takes a job with a cleaning service specializing in post-forensic jobs. Their latest moneymaker is cleaning up after the "Blueblood Killer," a serial killer preying on wealthy socialites. After she finds a clue to his identity lurking beneath a pool of coagulated blood, she becomes the target of the murderer. *Curdled* is often satisfying for those who can stomach its subject matter. One could complain, however, that the filmmakers did not take the premise far enough; instead they make Gabriela a garden-variety Nancy Drew. ★★½ DVD: $19.99

The Cure

(1995, 95 min, US, Peter Horton) *Brad Renfro, Joseph Mazzello, Annabella Sciorra, Diana Scarwid, Bruce Davison.* A moving, sometimes stilted story of a boy with AIDS and his friendship with a precocious neighbor. Renfro and Mazzello are the kids of single mothers (Scarwid and Sciorra in flatly drawn roles). New to town, Renfro befriends HIV-positive Mazzello. On a quest to find a cure, the story ends up as almost a preteen version of *Midnight Cowboy* complete with bus rides and sickness, stealing and shivering. ★★½

Curly Sue

(1991, 102 min, US, John Hughes) *James Belushi, Alisan Porter, Kelly Lynch.* Hughes butchers the memory of *Paper Moon* with this maudlin rehash about a father and daughter con artist team on the grift. Drifter Belushi and young Porter hit Chicago and immediately put the sting on yuppie lawyer Lynch. After hitting Belushi twice with her car, she invites them to stay at her swank penthouse. Once together, of course, she falls victim to their charm, and vice versa. Hughes' screenplay is ludicrous and manipulative (even for him), and his attempts to mix the bittersweet with slapstick are ill-served. ★ DVD: $9.99

The Curse

(1987, 92 min, US, David Keith) *Wil Wheaton, Claude Akins, Cooper Huckabee, David Keith.* An alien meteorite lands on a Tennessee farm, setting off a battle between the young boy who lives there and the surrounding neighbors, who have now been driven crazy from the meteor's effects. An interesting if flat sci-fi tale based on H.P. Lovecraft's "The Color Out of Space," which was previously filmed as *Die, Monster, Die.* ★★

The Curse of Frankenstein

(1957, 93 min, GB, Terence Fisher) *Peter Cushing, Christopher Lee, Hazel Court.* When their programmer *The Quatermass Experiment* became a "monster" hit, Hammer Studios wanted to know why. Was it the sci-fi? Or the monster? Marketing research came back with facts to prove that it was the latter, so Fisher was assigned to direct a new version of Mary Shelley's classic — this time with all the blood and guts that Eastman color and an X certificate would allow. The results made Cushing and Lee stars and Hammer Studios the Universal of the Thames. This doctor is no madman, just intellect

No, Mia's not pressing charges, but Woody is facing the law in *The Curse of the Jade Scorpion*

personified; and in this series of films it is he, not the monster, that is the unifying thread. ★★★½ DVD Letterbox: $19.99, VHS: $14.99

The Curse of Her Flesh

(1968, 75 min, US, Michael Findlay & Roberta Findlay) Take a little New York avant-garde theatre, blend in some psychedelic '60s sexual revolutionism and some purely gratuitous "T&A" action and the result is this entertainingly weird low budgeter. For those who appreciate lines like, "I was once told by a girlfriend that my big toe was better than any man's," this video was made for you. Oh, and the plot? Something about a nightclub owner on a killing spree. ★★

The Curse of the Cat People

(1944, 73 min, US, Gunther von Fritsche & Robert Wise) *Simone Simon, Kent Smith, Jane Randolph.* This moody sequel to the classic *Cat People* is an effective psychological thriller about a young girl who is befriended by the spirit of her father's deceased first wife. Simon returns from the original as the ghostly visitor. ★★★ VHS: $19.99

Curse of the Demon

(1957, 82 min, GB, Jacques Tourneur) *Dana Andrews, Peggy Cummins.* From the director of the original *Cat People* comes this low-budget, terrifying tale about a psychologist who investigates the death of a colleague, who may have been the victim of an ancient curse. Andrews is the sleuthing shrink. A wonderfully atmospheric film that is marred only by its wooden-looking monster, included at the insistence of its American distributors. ★★★½ DVD Double Feature: $24.99

The Curse of the Jade Scorpion

(2001, 102 min, US, Woody Allen) *Woody Allen, Helen Hunt, Dan Aykroyd, Charlize Theron, David Ogden Stiers, Wallace Shawn, Elizabeth Berkley, John Schuck.* You'd think that Woody Allen and an homage to screwball comedies would go together like Katharine Hepburn and Cary Grant. Alas, with *The Curse of the Jade Scorpion*, an occasionally

amusing though muddled comedy set in the 1940s, writer-director Allen isn't fully up to homage, screwball or comedy. Allen plays C.W. Briggs, an insurance investigator who is hypnotized by a nightclub magician (Stiers) into using his expertise to rob rich clients. Then, he is given the task of investigating the crimes that he himself committed but of course cannot remember. It's a premise that's ripe for laughs, but Woody is only able to partially deliver the goods, often delivering silly jokes and forced punch lines. Sure Allen's been silly before, but he's been able to counter with big laughs, and there aren't enough here. Woody gives the film slap-happy pacing, and the cast is eager to please, but lacking a few big comic set pieces, *The Curse of the Jade Scorpion* comes off merely jokey without the substance. ★★½ DVD: $14.99, VHS: $9.99

Curse of the Queerwolf

(1987, 90 min, US, Mark Pirro) *Michael Palazzolo, Cynthia Brownell, Kent Butler, Darwyn Carson, Jim Bruce, Taylor Whitney.* One of the funnier (if lamebrained) low-budget horror/sexploitation flicks to come around in some time, this wacky variation on the werewolf legend is marred only by an insidious streak of homophobia. The story follows Larry, a typical straight-as-an-arrow guy who, much to his horror, is bitten on the ass by a pretty "girl," turning him into a queerwolf — male by day and tarty, heavily rouged "lady" by full moon. The target of the film's antic humor is primarily gay men and innocent little dogs. But while offensive to some, it is more harmless camp than incendiary hatred. ★★ DVD Special Edition: $9.99

The Curse of the Starving Class

(1994, 102 min, US, J. Michael McClay) *James Woods, Kathy Bates, Henry Thomas, Randy Quaid, Louis Gossett, Jr., Kristin Fiorella.* Ostensibly a quirky, comedy-tinged family melodrama about a clan of failing Nevada farmers, this adaptation of Sam Shepard's stage play feels mushy, contrived and disjointed in its examination of a po' white trash family. Woods is the alcoholic, good-for-nothing dad, who has been exiled from home by his more sober, but no-less-dysfunctional wife (Bates). Both seem to derive sick pleasure from not only tormenting each other, but their uneasy son (Thomas) and precocious daughter (Fiorella), as well. At issue is the family farm, which both parents are plotting to sell behind each other's backs. ★★ VHS: $14.99

The Custodian

(1993, 110 min, Australia, John Dingwall) *Anthony LaPaglia, Barry Otto, Hugo Weaving.* This stinging indictment of police corruption stars LaPaglia as an honest cop who implicates himself in an internal affairs investigation as part of a scheme to bring down his crooked partner (Weaving). Top-notch performances and nail-biting suspense make this a most pleasant surprise. ★★★ VHS: $79.99

Cutter's Way

(1981, 105 min, US, Ivan Passer) *Jeff Bridges, John Heard, Lisa Eichhorn.* Passer's taut and complex thriller has a trio of social misfits stalking a possible murderer for their own muddled purposes. Heard lends poignancy to the role of a crippled Vietnam War vet and Bridges is his drifting Ivy League buddy. ★★★ DVD Letterbox: $19.99

Cutthroat Island

(1995, 118 min, US, Renny Harlin) *Geena Davis, Matthew Modine, Frank Langella, Maury Chaykin, Stan Shaw, Rex Linn.* Director Harlin's attempt to make his wife Davis into a blockbuster action heroine is fun for awhile, but this pirate adventure is without a brain in its well-costumed head. A return to the swashbuckling sagas and serials of the 1930s, *Cutthroat Island* is the familiar story of buried treasure, coded maps, uneasy alliances, treacherous kin, barroom brawls and narrow escapes and capped by a big sea battle at the end. Davis and Modine do most of their own stunts, which the director — in Jackie Chan-style — makes obvious with a zooming camera. ★★ DVD: $9.99, VHS: $9.99, VHS Letterbox: $14.99

Cyber Ninja

(1991, 80 min, Japan, Keita Amemiya) Nonstop cartoonlike action and outrageous special effects are sure to keep you on your toes in this highly original and bizarre *Star Wars* inspired sci-fi/martial arts epic. With the story taking place amid the chaos of a destructive war, a warrior princess is kidnapped by the underlings of a dark overlord. Intended to be the main course in a blood sacrifice that will unleash evil upon the land, the princess' only hope is a rebel band of soldiers and the mysterious Cyber Ninja to rescue her before it's too late. The film manages to save itself by spicing things up with the use of some truly hallucinatory visuals and unexpected twists. ★★★

Cyborg

(1989, 86 min, US, Albert Pyun) *Jean-Claude Van Damme, Deborah Richter.* Silly and violent sci-fi actioner with Van Damme fighting vicious gangs in the post-apocalyptic future. (Followed by 3 sequels) ★ DVD: $14.99

Cyclo

(1995, 124 min, Vietnam, Tran Anh Hung) *Le Van Loc, Tony Leung-Chiu Wai, Tran Nu Yen Khe.* As he did in his previous film *The Scent of Green Papaya*, writer-director Hung unfolds a tale of corruption and redemption in a world that is both beautiful and dangerous. The result is a mesmerizing glimpse into the lives of a handful of characters on the brink of despair. The bustle of Ho Chi Minh City proves almost too difficult for a cyclo (pedicab) driver to earn his living, and he soon gets mixed up with a tough crime lord. To complicate matters, his sister, working as a prostitute, falls in love with the gangster, and a power struggle ensues. The story may sound familiar, but it looks unique; Benoît Delhomme's dazzling cinematography is unparalleled. Often lush and disturbing at the same time, Hung evokes a very distinctive, albeit depressing environment for his unusual character study. (Vietnamese with English subtitles) ★★★½ DVD Letterbox: $29.99, VHS: $19.99

Cyrano de Bergerac

(1950, 113 min, US, Michael Gordon) *Jose Ferrer, Mala Powers, William Prince.* Ferrer won an Oscar for his stirring portrayal of one of literature's favorite heroes: the swashbuckling poet with the protruding proboscis — Cyrano de Bergerac. Though the film is technically uneven, it is more than made up for by Ferrer's classically flamboyant performance. Steve Martin (*Roxanne*), Gérard Depardieu and Derek Jacobi all appear in other versions of the Edmond Rostand classic and each actor is singularly brilliant. ★★★ DVD: $19.99

Cyrano de Bergerac

(1984, 176 min, GB, Terry Hands) *Derek Jacobi, Sinéad Cusack, Pete Postlethwaite.* The Royal Shakespeare Company's elaborate and stunning 1984 Broadway production of Edmond Rostand's classic. Jacobi is mesmerizingly brilliant in the title role (he won a Tony Award), and there's an exceptional supporting cast. ★★★★

Cyrano de Bergerac

(1990, 135 min, France, Jean-Paul Rappeneau) *Gérard Depardieu, Jacques Weber, Anne Brochet, Vincent Perez.* Rappeneau's outstanding realization of Edmond Rostand's classic play is an overwhelming cinematic achievement, made only more so by the monolithic screen presence of Depardieu in the title role. For his part, Depardieu delivers the performance of a lifetime as he sinks his teeth into the romantic heart of Cyrano with panache and punctuates every action with a flourish. Everything else in the film falls into place around him: the lavish set pieces, the swashbuckling action, the beautiful rhyming verse and the brilliant cinematography. A most exciting and emotionally rewarding film experience. (French with English subtitles) ★★★★ DVD: $19.99

Da

(1988, 102 min, US, Matt Clark) *Martin Sheen, Barnard Hughes, William Hickey.* Hughes reprises his award-winning stage role in this endearing adaptation about a man (Sheen) who returns to his native Ireland for his estranged father's funeral; coming to terms with his deceased parent when the man materializes after the funeral. A rewarding, funny examination of familial responsibilities and misgivings. ★★★

Dad

(1989, 117 min, US, Gary David Goldberg) *Jack Lemmon, Ted Danson, Olympia Dukakis, Ethan Hawke, Kevin Spacey, Zakes Mokae.* As with the similarly themed *Da*, a son attempts to reconcile himself with his father, though in this instance his dad is not deceased but dying. Though not as successful as Matt Clark's comedy, Lemmon's terrific performance compensates for the film's occasional dramatic lapses. ★★½

Daddy Long Legs

(1955, 126 min, US, Jean Negulesco) *Fred Astaire, Leslie Caron, Terry Moore, Thelma Ritter.* An enchanting musical romance with playboy Astaire anonymously sponsoring orphan Caron's education, the two eventually falling in love. Score includes "Something's Got to Give." ★★★ VHS: $19.99

Daddy Nostalgia

(1990, 105 min, France/GB, Bertrand Tavernier) *Dirk Bogarde, Jane Birkin, Odette Laurie.* In this tender and wise story of the complex relationship between an aging, sick father, his wife and their daughter, Bogarde — in what may be his valedictorian performance — is simply brilliant as the fastidious and at times insufferable father. Birkin plays his gangly screenwriter daughter who travels to her parents' sun-splashed Côte d'Azur villa when her father

takes ill. Completing the trio is Bogarde's wife (Laurie), a French woman who has become distant after enduring years with her grouchy, emotionally diffident husband. Director Tavernier insightfully delves into the characters' lives, thoughts and feelings as they attempt to understand each other and express their love. ★★★★

Daddy's Dyin' . . . Who's Got the Will?

(1990, 97 min, US, Jack Fisk) *Beau Bridges, Beverly D'Angelo, Tess Harper, Judge Reinhold, Amy Wright, Keith Carradine.* A wacky Texas family reunites at Daddy's deathbed, where secrets, accusations and grudges spew forth as its members wait to see exactly what they're gonna git. Amiable shenanigans. ★★½

Dagon

(2001, 98 min, US/Spain, Stuart Gordon) *Ezra Godden, Francisco Rabal, Raquel Merono.* Director Gordon's dream project for years has been an adaptation of H.P. Lovecraft's terrific short story, "The Shadow over Innsmouth." He and screenwriter Dennis Paoli hit pay dirt twice before with Lovecraft — *From Beyond* and especially *Re-Animator* — and they've basically done it again with this sometimes uneven but often chilling film. A rather dorky (but gradually appealing) computer nerd and his girlfriend are shipwrecked off the coast of a mysterious Spanish village. They seek help from the oddball locals, but soon discover these folks are even creepier than they appear. After a bumpy start, the low-budget *Dagon* gains its footing, capturing the terrifying nightmare flavor of the short story. ★★★ DVD: $14.99

Daisy Miller

(1974, 93 min, US, Peter Bogdanovich) *Cybill Shepherd, Cloris Leachman, Eileen Brennan, Mildred Natwick.* Visually striking adaptation of Henry James's novel with Shepherd as the 19th-century heroine Daisy, a young American woman who shocks European high society with her liberated sexual attitudes. Though Shepherd's flirtatious performance fails to fully capture the spirit and complexity of James' character, she is surrounded by a first-rate supporting cast, including

Leachman as Daisy's mother, and especially Brennan as a snobbish socialite. ★★★ DVD Letterbox: $9.99, VHS: $14.99

Damage

(1993, 112 min, GB, Louis Malle) *Jeremy Irons, Juliette Binoche, Miranda Richardson, Rupert Everett, Ian Bannen, Leslie Caron. Damage* is an arousing film, not just for the voyeuristic thrill of the much ballyhooed sex scenes between Irons and Binoche, but for the peek into the sumptuous London flats, elegant country estates and luxurious antiqued European hotels that serve as the film's backdrop. Irons plays an English cabinet minister who finds himself drawn to his son's exquisite and emotionally bruised new lover (Binoche). Richardson is Iron's restrained but ultimately tortured wife, and Graves is the betrayed son and lover. Not much in terms of plot, but high on atmosphere and tension (both carnal and familial), *Damage* is at times an almost savage look into the sexual psyche. (Unrated version) ★★★ DVD: $24.99

Dames

(1934, 90 min, US, Ray Enright) *Dick Powell, Ruby Keeler, Joan Blondell, ZaSu Pitts.* One of the best of the 1930s musicals, this backstage tuner features some great standards ("I Only Have Eyes for You," and the title tune among them) and those terrific Busby Berkeley dance routines. Forget the plot — it's another "let's put on a show" — it's the singing and dancing and comedy that's the main attraction here, and it's a hoot. Blondell is a standout as a wisecracking chorine. ★★★

Damn the Defiant!

(1962, 101 min, GB, Lewis Gilbert) *Alec Guinness, Dirk Bogarde, Anthony Quayle.* Guinness is stellar as a British naval captain who must fend off a challenge for power by his first mate (Bogarde), a fierce and merciless officer who is reviled by the crew. Set during the Napoleonic wars, the movie was filmed with an acute sense of historical detail. ★★★ DVD: $24.99, VHS: $14.99

Damn Yankees

(1958, 110 min, US, George Abbott) *Gwen Verdon, Ray Walston, Tab Hunter, Jean Stapleton.* "Whatever

George Burns and Gracie Allen join Fred Astaire in *A Damsel in Distress*

Lola wants, Lola gets," and what Lola gets is this sparkling screen adaptation of the Tony Award-winning Broadway musical. Hunter is Joe Hardy, the youthful reincarnate of a middle-aged die-hard Washington Senators fan who makes a pact with the Devil so he can help beat those damn New York Yankees. Re-creating their award-winning stage roles are the miraculous Verdon as Lola, who helps tame Joe, and Walston, who gives an irrepressible comic performance as the Devil. With splashy choreography by Bob Fosse (who also appears in one dance sequence), a good-natured and memorable score and appealing characters, *Damn Yankees* is a definite winner. ★★★½ VHS: $14.99

The Damned

(1969, 157 min, Germany/Italy, Luchino Visconti) *Dirk Bogarde, Ingrid Thulin, Helmut Berger, Charlotte Rampling.* A frantic international cast depicts Visconti's panorama of prewar German decadence and Nazi narcissism. Visconti captures all the horrors of the era, culminating with the infamous slaughter of the "Night of the Long Knives." Berger is exceptional with his elaborate impersonation of Marlene Dietrich. (Filmed in English) ★★★½ DVD Letterbox: $19.99

A Damsel in Distress

(1937, 101 min, US, George Stevens) *Fred Astaire, Joan Fontaine, George Burns, Gracie Allen.* Astaire's best musical of the 1930s made without Ginger Rogers. Though Fontaine lacks Ginger's musical skill and screen charm, costars Burns and especially Allen make one forget about the leading lady with their delightful supporting turns. Fred plays a famous dancer performing in London who falls for Lady Joan. The film contains one of the most remarkable musical production numbers ever conceived, "The Funhouse" sequence, and other Gershwin numbers include "A Foggy Day" and "Nice Work If You Can Get It." ★★★½ VHS: $14.99

Dance, Girl, Dance

(1940, 90 min, US, Dorothy Arzner) *Maureen O'Hara, Lucille Ball, Louis Hayward.* In possibly her most explicitly feminist film, director Arzner pairs O'Hara, as an idealistic young woman who dreams of becoming a ballerina, with Ball, the tough-as-leather show girl who doesn't take any shit from her leering, drunken audience. Ball convinces O'Hara to become partners in a burlesque troupe in this entertaining "the vamp and the virgin" comedy-drama. As "Bubbles," Ball is in great form. ★★★

Dance Me Outside

(1994, 91 min, Canada, Bruce McDonald) *Ryan Black, Adam Beach, Lisa LaCroix, Michael Greyeyes, Kevin Hicks, Sandrine Holt.* Energized and completely unaffected performances from a talented young cast imbue a finely crafted coming-of-age story with gritty realism. Set in the present day on a Canadian Indian reservation, a young woman's murder is the focal point of many intertwining stories of relationship, family, friendship, racial prejudice and the search for identity and purpose. Black and Beach play two young men trying to get into an auto mechanics school in Toronto. They need to write an essay as part of the entrance exam, but have nothing to say until the brutal murder of one of their friends provides the material — not only for the essay, but for their own personal quests for definition and adulthood. This independent winner details the course of many lives with humor, insight and compassion, without maudlin sentimentality or gilded heroics. ★★★ VHS: $79.99

Dance of Hope

(1990, 75 min, US, Deborah Shaffer) The brutal excesses of power of the Argentine military government and the heart-rending plight of *los desaparacidos* have been well documented. But the equally repressive actions of the Pinochet regime in neighboring Chile is only now being uncovered. This film by Academy Award-winning director Shaffer probes the sad story of the relatives of the thousands of people who "disappeared" and their efforts to get the government to provide answers. The title of the film refers to the *cueca*, Chile's national dance of passion and courtship: the mothers, wives and relatives of the missing citizens perform this dance alone to emphasize the loss of their partner. (Spanish with English subtitles) ★★★ VHS: $59.99

Dance with a Stranger

(1985, 101 min, GB, Mike Newell) *Miranda Richardson, Rupert Everett, Ian Holm, Joanne Whalley.* This critically acclaimed tale of passion and mystery follows the path of the romantic self-destruction of Ruth Ellis, the last woman to be executed in Great Britain. This gripping examination of a murderous romance stars Richardson (in a sensational film debut) as a dance hall girl who murders her abusive lover. As the selfish murdered boyfriend, Everett gives a convincing and sensual performance of an emotionally shallow upper-class beauty whose slumming leads to his demise. Holm is outstanding in support as another of Ellis' men. ★★★½ DVD: $19.99

Dance with Me

(1998, 126 min, US, Randa Haines) *Vanessa L. Williams, Chayanne, Kris Kristofferson, Joan Plowright.* An insipid attempt at a fluffy date movie as both romance and dance film. Chayanne plays a Cuban dancer who comes to Texas to work in a dance studio owned by Kristofferson, an old flame of his mother's. Although he's hired as a handyman, our slick hero quickly displays his rug-cutting prowess and is invited to take part in a national dance contest in Vegas. Hokey dialogue, lame humor, stilted acting and unexciting dancing sink this snoozer quick. ★½ DVD: $19.99, VHS: $9.99

Dance with the Devil

(1998, 121 min, US, Álex de la Iglesia) *Rosie Perez, Javier Bardem, James Gandolfini, Harley Cross, Aimee Graham, Don Stroud, Alex Cox.* Violent and weird for weird's sake, this noir thriller follows the road adventures of a deranged couple: a fiery Mexican-American (Perez) and her cult-leader boyfriend (Bardem). They kidnap a young couple and plan to use them in a bizarre religious sacrifice. But not before intercepting a truckload of fetuses for a mob boss. (aka: *Purdita Durango*) ★★ DVD: $9.99, VHS: $14.99

Dancer in the Dark

(2000, 139 min, US/Denmark, Lars von Trier) *Björk, Catherine Deneuve, David Morse, Peter Storemare, Vladan Kostic, Jean-Marc Barr, Joel Grey, Udo Kier, Zeljko Ivanek.* Björk imparts a strong, naturalistic presence as Selma, a displaced Czech in small-town, 1960s America. Going blind from a hereditary disease, Selma is fighting an unrelenting deadline, working tedious jobs, and scrounging for money for her son's eye operation. She can transmute the noises of her factory job into music, imagining elaborate dance numbers like those she barely sees on the silver screen. She's an innocent in a world of opportunistic betrayal, a grounded element in a broad allegory of sacrifice.

The film presents a premise with strong potential but suffers somewhat from a rambling self-indulgence. Yet, there are moments of charming whimsy, moments of gut-wrenching anguish, delivered with a sure hand by a remarkable cast who prevent the pathos from devolving into bathos. ★★★½ DVD: $24.99

Dancer, Texas Pop. 81

(1998, 97 min, US, Tim McCanlies) *Breckin Meyer, Peter Facinelli, Ethan Embry, Eddie Mills, Patricia Wettig.* Good-natured slice-of-life tale about four young men, graduating from high school in their small Texas town, attempting to keep their promise to each other to move to L.A. together, despite pressures from family and friends. This surprisingly lightweight though compelling drama unfolds at just the right pace, nicely juggling the four men's stories, leading to a satisfying, though not too schmaltzy or pat, conclusion. Writer-director McCanlies captures the feel and attitude of a small town, highlighting both the positive and negative aspects of growing up in such a place. *Dancer* has its hokey moments, but they are minor and don't detract from a good entertainment. ★★★ DVD: $19.99

Dancers

(1987, 98 min, US, Herbert Ross) *Mikhail Baryshnikov, Leslie Browne, Mariangela Melato, Tommy Rall.* From the director and star of *The Turning Point* comes this inferior tale of an egocentric ballet star (Baryshnikov) who tends to seduce every young woman with whom he dances. When he turns his eye towards a young ballerina, he gets an unexpected lesson in love. ★ VHS: $14.99

Dances with Wolves

(1990, 183 min, US, Kevin Costner) *Kevin Costner, Mary McDonnell, Graham Greene, Rodney A. Grant.* Costner's directorial debut is this emotionally charged Academy Award-winning tribute to the Sioux Indians of the Dakota plains. Costner himself stars as Lt. John Dunbar of the Union Army, a man whose life is changed forever when he befriends the Lakota. Beautifully photographed and filled with amazing stunts, *Dances with Wolves* presents a majestically sweeping vision of the grandeur of the great American West. The acting throughout is wonderful with Greene particularly memorable as Kicking Bird. A wonderful cinematic achievement in which Costner brings back the epic western. (English and Lokata with English subtitles) ★★★★ DVD Special Edition: $29.99, DVD Basic Edition: $14.99, VHS: $9.99

Dancing at Lughnasa

(1998, 94 min, Ireland, Pat O'Connor) *Meryl Streep, Catherine McCormack, Michael Gambon, Kathy Burke, Sophie Thompson, Brid Brennan, Rhys Ifans.* As captivating as the Irish hills in which it's set, *Dancing at Lughnasa* is a poetic memory piece based on the award-winning play by Brian Friel. Set in the 1930s, it's about the last summer one family will spend together. Heading a remarkably fine cast is Streep, who absolutely shines as Kate, the eldest of five sisters who are reuniting with their beloved brother Jack, a missionary who has been abroad for 25 years. The reunion, however, is tinged with melancholy when it becomes apparent he has suffered a mental breakdown. The pulse of Friel's story is the poignant relationship of the sisters, who are ruled over by Kate. Eventually, each sister — including Kate herself — breaks free of some form of repression. This culminates in a thrilling dance performed by the sisters that ultimately bonds and then separates them. ★★★ DVD: $29.99

Dancing in the Dark

(1986, 98 min, Canada, Leon Marr) *Martha Henry, Neil Munro.* Henry gives a mesmerizing performance as a woman whose life is defined by the minutiae of her 20-year marriage. When her protective shell of illusion cracks, she forfeits her tenuous grasp on reality for a moment of catharsis. Well-crafted and somber, with thoughtful direction by Marr. ★★★ VHS: $14.99

Dancing Lady

(1933, 94 min, US, Robert Z. Leonard) *Joan Crawford, Clark Gable, Franchot Tone, Nelson Eddy, The Three Stooges.* An appealing if ordinary M-G-M musical about chorus girl Crawford making it to the top while involved with stage director Gable and playboy Tone. Astaire made his film debut. ★★½ VHS: $19.99

Dandelions

(1974, 92 min, Netherlands, Adrian Hoven) *Rutger Hauer, Dagmar Lassander.* A young Hauer stars in this cartoonish sex drama that is dubbed in a style reminiscent of *What's Up, Tiger Lily?* Rutger appears as a boozing, womanizing, self-hating low-life — or as one of the women he torments in the film calls him, "a cesspool of depravity." The characters, when they are not naked or gyrating in sexual contortions, are clothed in outlandish '70s mod outfits. Did people really dress like that? ★★

Dangaio

(1988, 45 min, Japan, Toshihiro Hirano) With names like Ramba and Pi Thunder, this cross-cultural animated space story involves four Esper-Warriors (three teenage girls and a boy), who are brainwashed and then altered into "augmented humans" or androids by a cunning scientist. This samurai-influenced story follows their adventures through space as they fight a powerfully evil blond cyborg as well as other galactic despots, all the while seeking the truth of their actual identities. The battles are mostly in space, but in one funny sequence, poor Tokyo again finds itself an impotent victim to a Godzilla-like thrashing. ★★★ VHS: $34.99

Danger Diabolik

(1968, 99 min, Italy, Mario Bava) *John Phillip Law, Marisa Mell, Michel Piccoli, Terry-Thomas.* In this campy, colorful, wild adaptation of a popular Italian comic book, director Bava has created a fun romp that echoes and spoofs everything from James Bond to those "big heist" films of the early 1960s. Law plays Diabolik, a master criminal who surrounds himself with electronic gadgets, beautiful women and wealth. Too much fun to seriously criticize and too ludicrous to take too seriously, the movie succeeds at just the level it was meant to: as a live-action comic book that has the viewer constantly rooting for its ultimate super (anti)hero. (Filmed in English) ★★★

Dangerous

(1935, 72 min, US, Alfred E. Green) *Bette Davis, Franchot Tone.* Davis won an Oscar for her performance in this glossy soaper, but it was more for the snub the year earlier when she was overlooked for *Of Human Bondage.* However, Davis is quite good as an actress on the skids who captivates architect Tone. ★★½ VHS: $14.99

Dangerous Beauty

(1998, 112 min, US/GB, Marshall Herskovitz) *Catherine McCormack, Rufus Sewell, Oliver Platt, Moira Kelly, Fred Ward, Jacqueline Bisset.* McCormack stars as a strong-willed woman of lower station in 16th-century Venice who, when spurned by her true love (who refuses to marry below his station), becomes a very popular courtesan. *Dangerous Beauty* is artless art-house lite, a repeatedly dull and pandering film with a potentially intriguing premise: how does an intelligent, independent woman get by in a society where women are treated as little more than objects? The clichéd answer that a whore is master of the man is given a spirited reading by McCormack, but the film as a whole can't transcend the mundane. ★★ DVD: $14.99, VHS: $14.99

Dangerous Game

(1993, 107 min, US, Abel Ferrara) *Harvey Keitel, Madonna, James Russo.* Ferrara continues his examination of moral ambiguity (*Bad Lieutenant*) with this verité pas de trois between a film director (Keitel) and his two leads (Madonna and Russo). They're working on a nauseating little film in which Russo plays a husband who continually abuses his wife (Madonna) and subsequently both attempt to escape their life of drug abuse and debauchery. Using the device of a film within a film, Ferrara warps the distinction between illusion and reality as the three principals become ever more enmeshed in their on- and off-the-set shenanigans. Ferrara shows a deft directorial hand, but that won't help most viewers overcome the film's repugnant core and unrelentingly nihilistic viewpoint. (Unrated version) ★½ VHS: $79.99

Dangerous Ground

(1997, 96 min, US/South Africa, Darrell James Roodt) *Ice Cube, Elizabeth Hurley, Ving Rhames, Eric Miyeni.* Cube plays a native of South Africa who returns to the U.S. after his father dies. Now a San Francisco social worker, Cube finds the old neighborhood ain't like it used to be: instead of white pro-Apartheid thugs, he now has to face black mobsters dealing in drugs. He also discovers that his brother is indebted to a Nigerian druglord (Rhames), and tries to locate and help his sibling. Despite the potentially interesting background and political milieu, *Dangerous Ground* isn't much better than most direct-to-video thrillers. Roodt just can't get the mix of action and intrigue right. This ground is not only dangerous, but shaky as well. ★½ DVD: $9.99, VHS: $9.99

Dangerous Liaisons

(1988, 120 min, US, Stephen Frears) *Glenn Close, John Malkovich, Michelle Pfeiffer, Swoosie Kurtz, Keanu Reeves, Uma Thurman, Mildred Natwick, Peter Capaldi.* Sexual corruption, insidious power games, deceitful duplicity and seductively witty dialogue are some of the unusual ingredients in this sumptuously enticing film. Close stars as the Marquise de Merteuil, an elegantly detached woman who along with her former lover, the similarly cunning Valmont (Malkovich), enters into a wager on whether he can seduce the innocent Pfeiffer. Their amoral sexual sport entangles them and all who enter their lives as it follows its inevitably destructive course. Close revels in the role of the acrimonious aristocrat, and Malkovich, although cast against type, still captures the dangerously seductive charms of a snake dressed in gentleman's clothing. A special

cinematic treat that should entertain the entire spectrum of tastes — from the romantic to the Machiavellian. ★★★★ DVD: $14.99

A Dangerous Man: Lawrence after Arabia

(1990, 104 min, GB, Christopher Menaul) *Ralph Fiennes, Denis Quilley, Paul Freeman, Nicholas Jones, Siddig el Fadil.* This BBC production features Fiennes in one of his earliest efforts, and his subdued performance is a little too minimalist and understated. It shows how far he has come as an actor. Rarely blinking or moving his lips, Fiennes does little to liven up this filmed history lesson. *A Dangerous Man*, picking up after the events of David Lean's *Lawrence of Arabia*, chronicles Lawrence's attempts to convince the British and French governments to bestow the countries of Syria and Damascus unto his close friend, the Emir Faisel (who gave Lawrence *that* robe). Chock full of historical facts and figures, this would be a suitable film to show in history class, but nowhere else. ★½ DVD: $19.99

Dangerous Minds

(1995, 94 min, US, John N. Smith) *Michelle Pfeiffer, George Dzundza, Courtney B. Vance, Robin Bartlett.* As gritty as a high school prom, *Dangerous Minds*, based on LouAnne Johnson's autobiography "My Posse Don't Do Homework," treads the well-worn hallways and classrooms of nearly every self-sacrificing teacher film from *Blackboard Jungle* to *Stand and Deliver*. And while *Minds* is clichéd, predictable and sentimental, it offers Pfeiffer as Johnson a chance to deliver an affecting performance — it helps gloss over the film's otherwise formulaic structure. Johnson turns around the lives of her apathetic, "socially troubled" students (mostly black and Hispanic) while battling school administration and other outside forces. The unruly students are mostly Screenplay 101 concoctions — their tongues may be sharp but what makes them tick is noticeably absent. ★★½ DVD: $14.99, VHS: $9.99

Dangerous Moonlight

(1941, 83 min, GB, Brian Desmond Hurst) *Anton Walbrook, Sally Gray, Cecil Parker.* This wartime classic tells the story of a Polish concert pianist (Walbrook) who, against the strenuous objections of his wife, puts aside his music and flies for the RAF. Wonderfully directed and superbly acted, the film makes excellent use of its classical music score. ★★★½

Dangerous Moves

(1983, 110 min, Switzerland, Richard Dembo) *Michel Piccoli, Leslie Caron, Liv Ullmann.* Set amid the tranquil lakeside of Geneva at the site of an international chess match, this Academy Award-winning film is imbued with a power, literacy and complexity that belies its sedate environment. The physical movements may be minimal but the tension between the two grand masters is visceral and exciting. ★★★ DVD Letterbox: $19.99

A Dangerous Woman

(1993, 99 min, US, Stephen Gyllenhaal) *Debra Winger, Gabriel Byrne, Barbara Hershey, David Strathairn, Chloe Webb, Laurie Metcalf, Jan Hooks.* Winger is riveting as an innocent, childlike woman living in a small Southern town. Though somewhat shielded by her aunt's (Hershey) position of power and influence, her naïve inability to tell socially expected lies throws her into conflict with others in her community. She is also ill-equipped to deal with the emotional upheaval she experiences at the hands of an itinerant laborer (Byrne). Ironically, her turmoil mirrors that of her sister's conflicted relationship with a married man, offering acerbic commentary on our lack of control in affairs of the heart. Though the narrative gets somewhat muddled, the film is ably carried by a fine ensemble cast. ★★½ VHS: $14.99

Daniel

(1983, 129 min, US, Sidney Lumet) *Timothy Hutton, Mandy Patinkin, Lindsay Crouse, Ed Asner, Amanda Plummer.* This gripping political drama based on the Julius and Ethel Rosenberg case divides its story between two eras: the 1950s, when the Rosenbergs were (unjustly?) sentenced to death; and the late 1960s, where their surviving children grapple with the memory of their parents (Patinkin, Crouse). Hutton plays the title character, whose search for the truth about his mom and dad (here called the Isaacsons) ushers a wave of recollections about them. Expertly acted, this rewarding film moves slowly, but never fails to move the viewer. ★★★ VHS: $7.99

Danny Boy

(1984, 92 min, Ireland, Neil Jordan) *Stephen Rea, Veronica Quilligan, Donal McCann, Ray McAnally.* This bleak Irish drama is a taut portrait of a young saxophone player who witnesses the murder of his manager. Haunted by violent images of one of the assailants, he sets out to hunt him down and avenge the atrocity. A dark and moody character study whose style is too self-serving and which is only occasionally intriguing. Rea appears in his film debut as the young musician. ★★ VHS: $59.99

Dante's Inferno

(1969, 90 min, GB, Ken Russell) *Oliver Reed.* Russell's filmic fascination with artists tortured by personal weaknesses (*The Music Lovers, Mahler, Valentino*) is amply evident in this early, rarely seen film. Reed plays Dante Gabriel Rossetti — a morose, brilliant and drunken painter-poet who, as Russell sees it, was more interested in his flamboyant and excessive lifestyle than his artistic output. Russell re-creates the period wonderfully in this engrossing tale of art, poetry, booze and sex. ★★★

Dante's Peak

(1997, 100 min, US, Roger Donaldson) *Pierce Brosnan, Linda Hamilton. Dante's Peak* should have been an F/X blast. But with only adequate effects and a transparent and cluttered story, this disaster adventure — the first and least of 1997's volcano movies — disappoints on all levels. Clearly needing lunch money, Brosnan plays a scientist who predicts a major volcanic eruption in the Pacific Northwest. No one believes him, except the spunky mayor (Hamilton) of the town located next to the mountain he thinks is ready to blow. The film teases throughout until the eventual explosion, but only after a stockpile of clichéd characters and plot lines limp across the screen. ★ DVD Letterbox Collector's Edition: $14.99, DVD DTS sound: $14.99

Danton

(1982, 136 min, France/Poland, Andrzej Wajda) *Gérard Depardieu, Wojciech Pszoniak.* Wajda directs his camera toward the social upheaval and political treachery of the French Revolution, and by doing so, draws an obvious allegory to the political situation in his native Poland in the 1980s. Depardieu is the boisterous people's champion, Danton, who is betrayed by the coldly civilized

Ben Affleck as *Daredevil*: Blind/bland crime-fighter or fledgling leather queen? You be the judge.

Robespierre as they maneuver for leadership of the New Republic. (French with English subtitles) ★★★★ VHS: $29.99

Danzón

(1991, 103 min, Mexico, Maria Novaro) *Maria Rojo, Carmen Salinas.* The sudden disappearance of her longtime dancing partner compels Julia (the endearing Rojo), a demure Mexico City telephone operator, to begin a search that escalates into a personal odyssey. She begins her road trip guarded and aloof, but before long is getting invaluable fashion advice from a cabaret-performer transvestite and warm emotional support from her hotel's craggy conciérge as well as the resident ladies of the evening. She greets this cavalcade of intriguing characters and exotic circumstances with a newly informed independence and a revitalized sense of self. Dance music pulsates throughout the film. A grown-up fairy tale awash with light and vibrant color. (Spanish with English subtitles) ★★★

Darby O'Gill and the Little People

(1959, 93 min, US, Robert Stevenson) *Albert Sharpe, Sean Connery, Janet Munro, Estelle Winwood.* Sharpe is the Irish caretaker whose tendency to spin the blarney causes no one to believe him when he becomes the guest of the Leprechauns in their underground home. Great special effects create a timeless atmosphere of charm and fantasy. ★★★

Daredevil

(2003, 103 min, US, Mark Steven Johnson) *Ben Affleck, Jennifer Garner, Michael Clarke Duncan, Colin Farrell, Joe Pantoliano, Jon Favreau, David Keith.* Pure trash, this lifeless, sloppily directed adaptation of the Marvel comic about a crime-fighting blind lawyer is lacking in excitement, humor and story — the trademarks of comic books regaling the adventures of superheroes. Affleck, who is quickly wearing out his welcome as a film star, is bland beyond belief as Daredevil, a dour attorney/vigilante who was blinded as a child. Now an adult, he uses his superpowers to fight evil — here in the form of Duncan's cardboard villain known as the Kingpin. Director Johnson brings no sense of fun or fantasy to this fantastic story, only a brooding hero, dark action scenes and a deadened pace. At least Garner and Farrell look good while they go through the gestures

of pretending to care. ★ DVD Letterbox Special Edition: $19.99, DVD Pan & Scan Special Edition: $19.99, VHS Special Edition: $12.99

Dario Argento's Phantom of the Opera

(1998, 100 min, Italy, Dario Argento) *Julian Sands, Asia Argento, Andrea Di Stefano, Nadia Rinaldi.* Dario's beautiful daughter Asia plays opera singer ingenue Christina and Sands is the Phantom in this disappointing period adaptation of the oft-filmed classic. The pace is leaden, Argento's trademark visual flair is largely absent, and the film has no spark. There are some bizarre changes to the original story — the surprisingly handsome, unscarred Phantom has been raised by rats(!), and a pair of comic-relief rat catchers make their jobs easier by building a rat-catching mobile. Asia and Sands are unremarkable, the music is good, the period atmosphere is convincing, though there isn't any of the bravura set pieces fans have come to expect from Dario. ★★ DVD Unrated Director's Cut: $9.99

The Dark Angel

(1935, 110 min, US, Sidney Franklin) *Fredric March, Merle Oberon, Herbert Marshall, Janet Beecher, John Halliday.* Lillian Hellman cowrote the screenplay for this affecting melodrama of three childhood friends, and their experiences after one is injured in World War I. Based on the 1925 silent starring Ronald Colman and Vilma Banky. ★★★

The Dark Angel

(1987, 148 min, GB, Peter Hammond) *Peter O'Toole, Jane Lapotaire, Beatie Edney.* O'Toole is an indulgent study of heavy-lidded menace in this wonderfully Gothic tale of a trusting maiden, a tragic death, a large inheritance, a mysterious and nasty Frenchwoman and a deceptively helpful uncle. This is all based on J.S. LeFanu's "Uncle Silas," written in 1864, which is generally regarded as the first psychological thriller. Encroaching danger is presaged by the strange French governess' incessant probing of her innocent charge, Maude (Lapotaire), regarding the existence of her father's will. Maude's father reveals to her the key to the chest in the library, but not enough family secrets to save her from horrific malice from those she's been told to trust. The cast revels in their deliciously exaggerated characterizations, and the production is a feast of fine detail. ★★★ VHS: $19.99

The Dark at the Top of the Stairs

(1960, 123 min, US, Delbert Mann) *Robert Preston, Dorothy McGuire, Angela Lansbury, Eve Arden, Shirley Knight.* An expertly acted, deeply affecting film version of William Inge's Pulitzer Prize-winning play. Preston heads an exceptional cast as the patriarch of an Oklahoma family in the 1920s. As seen through the eyes of a young boy coming of age, the story focuses on a family's fortunes and misfortune, misunderstandings and prejudice. ★★★

Dark Blue

(2003, 116 min, US, Ron Shelton) *Kurt Russell, Scott Speedman, Brendan Gleeson, Ving Rhames, Lolita Davidovich, Michael Michele.* There's an air of familiarity that hovers over *Dark Blue*, a story of police corruption in Los Angeles. As written by David Ayer (based on a James Ellroy story), who also wrote *Training Day*, there is a battle of wills between a crooked veteran officer and his young partner that leads to a crisis of conscience. And, as with *Training Day*, there's a terrific portrayal at the heart of the film. Russell is excellent as Eldon Perry, an L.A.P.D. detective whose investigation into a liquor store homicide is deliberately mishandled. Director Shelton gives the film a tough, gritty look, and having the action set against the 1992 Rodney King trial should give it purpose. But too often the racially charged backdrop is merely set decoration, providing little insight into social or racial conflict or even how any of the characters are affected by such an incendiary event. Ayer's screenplay is ambitious, though, and the action is often taut and menacing; it's just there's little to suggest other than we've seen it all before. ★★½ DVD Dual: $14.99, VHS: $9.99

Dark Blue World

(2001, 115 min, Czech Republic, Jan Sverak) *Ondrej Vetchy, Krystof Hadek, Tara Fitzgerald, Oldrich Kaiser, Charles Dance.* Pearl Harbor without that film's big budget and poor script, *Dark Blue World* is an often moving war drama that follows a group of Czech pilots who join the British RAF to fight the Nazis, who have occupied their homeland. The tired cliché of two friends falling for the same woman (one of the many drawbacks of that Hollywood blockbuster) nearly sinks this passionate film, but *Dark Blue World*'s quiet power and steely intensity remains untarnished. (In English and Czech with English subtitles) ★★½ DVD Letterbox Special Edition: $29.99, VHS: $14.99

Dark City

(1990, 98 min, GB/Zimbabwe, Chris Curling) The struggle of black South Africans for justice and equality in their own land is the theme of this impassioned political thriller filmed entirely in Zimbabwe with a cast made up primarily of the members of Johannesburg's Market Theatre. When a peaceful march to the mayor's house of a black township turns violent, the police begin a crackdown, arresting seven innocent people. As they are put on trial in a kangaroo court, the black leaders are faced with accepting the injustice or fighting back. The film examines the rifts within the black independence movement which often ferment violence within the community, pitting black against black and rarely involving the true antagonists: the white authorities. ★★★ VHS: $29.99

Dark City

(1998, 100 min, US, Alex Proyas) *Rufus Sewell, Kiefer Sutherland, Jennifer Connelly, William Hurt.* In an unnamed city with striking architectural design (think *Metropolis* and Tim Burton's *Batman*), a young man (Sewell) wakes up in a bathtub, a corpse in the next room. All evidence points to his being a serial killer, but he has no memory whatsoever. Did he really do it? Aided in his investigation by an initially antagonistic police detective (an excellent Hurt) and a wife he can't remember (Connelly), Sewell begins to unravel the truth behind the mysteries. Director-cowriter Proyas' superior follow-up to *The Crow* is a riveting, gorgeous sci-fi thriller, as well as a fascinating examination of memory, identity and free will. Some may feel the eye-popping effects overwhelm a thin story, but the visuals are truly in the service of an exciting, well-crafted tale. ★★★½ DVD Letterbox: $9.99

The Dark Corner

(1946, 99 min, US, Henry Hathaway) *Lucille Ball, Clifton Webb, Mark Stevens.* An unfairly neglected film noir mystery that is both exciting and well acted. Lucy plays a secretary who sets out to prove the innocence of her private detective boss (Stevens), who's been framed for murder. Webb costars as the caustic, wealthy art dealer who's behind the frame-up. ★★★ VHS: $59.99

The Dark Crystal

(1983, 94 min, GB, Frank Oz & Jim Henson) *The Muppets.* Muppet masters Henson and Oz deliver their take on a Tolkienesque world peopled with furry dwarf creatures and evil sorcerers with their unmistakable zaniness and a healthy dose of plain-old good storytelling. The story concerns Jen, a young male "Gelfling," who sets out on a harrowing and heroic journey to rid his magical realm of the evil rule of the "Skeksis," a bilious and physically repugnant race that resemble decaying vultures. While a little short on plot, the film's characterizations are top-notch and should delight adults as well as kids. ★★★ DVD Letterbox Superbit Edition: $26.99, DVD Letterbox: $49.99, DVD: $19.99, VHS: $14.99

Dark Eyes

(1987, 115 min, Italy, Nikita Mikhalkov) *Marcello Mastroianni, Silvana Mangano, Marthe Keller.* Mastroianni is nothing short of brilliant as Romano, an irresolute dreamer seduced by both love and money in this charming romantic fable by Russian émigré Mikhalkov. The story begins on an ocean liner where the garrulous Romano recounts his tumultuous and tragic life story to a rapt elderly newlywed. His tale is one of lost ambitions, luxury and boredom changed forever after he meets and falls deliriously in love with a mysterious Russian beauty. A funny, enchanting and, most of all, entertaining film. (Italian with English subtitles) ★★★½

Dark Habits

(1983, 96 min, Spain, Pedro Almodóvar) *Carmen Maura, Julieta Serrano, Christina Pascual.* While not Almodóvar's best work, *Dark Habits* nonetheless manages to carry the director's unparalleled sense of twisted, subversive and blacker-than-black humor. When Yolanda's boyfriend dies of an overdose of heroin, she decides it's better to run and hide than face the law. She winds up at the doorstep of the "Humble Redeemers," an order of heroin-addicted nuns who specialize in cases like hers — indeed they were all once cases like her! The cast includes some of the familiar Almodóvites: Serrano stars as the Mother Superior and Maura appears as the cloister's resident tiger keeper, Sister Sin. (Spanish with English subtitles) ★★½ DVD: $24.99, VHS: $19.99

The Dark Half

(1993, 121 min, US, George Romero) *Timothy Hutton, Amy Madigan, Michael Rooker, Julie Harris, Robert Joy.* Hutton stars in this well-

Darling

mounted but uninvolving story from the undisputed master of recycled horror, Stephen King. Hutton is adequate in the role of a "serious" author who is forced by a blackmailer to publicly bury his cheesy pulp fiction-writing pseudonym, "George Stark." But, like most dead things in horror movies, Stark doesn't take extinction lying down; he springs to life and goes on a killing spree. Romero's sure-footed direction is light-years away from the low-budget material that he has come to be associated with; it just isn't very scary. ★★½ DVD: $14.99

Dark Journey

(1937, 79 min, GB, Victor Saville) *Vivien Leigh, Conrad Veidt, Joan Gardner.* An efficient espionage yarn, *Dark Journey* features the luminous Leigh as a Stockholm dress shop owner whose successful business is really a front for her spying for the German government. Veidt is a German playboy who courts her. Of course, there's more than that going on here. Through the years we've seen so many films of this sort that the answers may not be all too difficult to come up with, but *Dark Journey* keeps your interest throughout, is well played by the entire cast, and a couple nightclub scenes offer a keen look at trendy high society in the late teens. ★★★ VHS: $19.99

The Dark Mirror

(1946, 85 min, US, Robert Siodmak) *Olivia de Havilland, Lew Ayres, Thomas Mitchell.* De Havilland, in a dual role, gives an entertainingly over-the-top performance as identical twins: one a virtuous young lady, the other a psychotic, deranged murderer. This Freudian thriller, both tense and fast-paced, revolves around the police and a psychiatrist's baffled efforts to determine which of the two women is innocent and which is the killer. ★★★ VHS: $14.99

Dark Passage

(1947, 106 min, US, Delmer Daves) *Humphrey Bogart, Lauren Bacall, Agnes Moorehead.* Bogart stars in this stylish film noir as a falsely accused convict who escapes prison and changes his appearance (via plastic surgery) in order to smoke out the real culprit. Bacall is on hand as the socialite who believes in him. Good use of subjective camerawork, in which the first half hour of the film is shown from the point of view of the escaped con — whose face we don't see until he becomes Bogart. Moorehead is especially good in support. ★★★ DVD: $19.99, VHS: $19.99

Dark Victory

(1939, 106 min, US, Edmund Goulding) *Bette Davis, George Brent, Geraldine Fitzgerald, Humphrey Bogart, Ronald Reagan.* In one of her greatest triumphs, Davis stars in this classic soaper as a jet-setting socialite who discovers she has only a few months to live. As she slowly accepts her fate, she becomes more responsible, living her remaining months "beautifully and finely," as her doctor/lover (Brent) suggests. ★★★½ DVD: $19.99, VHS: $14.99

The Dark Wind

(1993, 111 min, US, Errol Morris) *Lou Diamond Phillips, Gary Farmer, Fred Ward, Guy Boyd.* Director Morris imbues *Dark Wind* with the same hypnotic realism which permeated his *The Thin Blue Line.* Phillips is at his best as Jim Chee, the Navajo cop who studies to be a medicine man. A corpse mutilated by a Navajo skinwalker is found on Hopi ground, involving the police in intertribal politics and the spectre of witchcraft. The FBI and major drug transactions rapidly surface in this tale of a long-festering lust for revenge and rampant greed. Neil Jiminez (*The Waterdance*) cowrote the story, based on one of Tony Hillerman's many books set in the Arizona territories. ★★★ DVD: $14.99

Darkman

(1990, 120 min, US, Sam Raimi) *Liam Neeson, Colin Friels, Frances McDormand, Larry Drake.* Spectacular stunts and excellent special effects highlight this superhero adventure story. Neeson stars as a scientist whose unfortunate run-in with the mob leaves him horribly disfigured and transforms him into a shadowy crime fighter. Director Raimi continues to impress with his inventiveness as he and his scriptwriters unleash a slew of clever plot twists and come up with at least a half-dozen new ways to dispose of the bad guys. Friels and McDormand offer fine support as, respectively, an evil real estate tycoon and Neeson's lawyer girlfriend. (Followed by 2 sequels) ★★★ DVD: $14.99, VHS: $9.99

Darkness Falls

(2003, 85 min, US, Jonathan Liebesman) *Chaney Kley, Emma Caulfield, Lee Cormie.* It was only a matter of time till they got around to a horror film about the Tooth Fairy. Unfortunately, it's *Darkness Falls.* After an effective opening, wherein a boy places a tooth under his pillow and is terrorized by said creature, the derivative and silly plot takes hold. Years later, the now grown man returns home to help out a childhood friend's young brother, who's suffering the same sleepless nights, and the Tooth Fairy is back on the rampage. Despite a few good scares, the film never catches on, due in large part to a screenplay that doesn't always make sense. But the direction is often stylish, and at least the snappy pacing keeps the incomprehensible moving along. ★½ DVD Special Edition: $19.99

Darling

(1965, 122 min, GB, John Schlesinger) *Julie Christie, Dirk Bogarde, Laurence Harvey.* This highly influential classic brilliantly captures many of the manners, morals, and mores of mod mid-'60s London. Christie, who is nothing less than radiant, deservedly won an Oscar for her portrayal of a young London model who quickly climbs the social ladder by strategically jumping in and out of assorted beds. Bogarde also stars as one of her conquests, and Harvey is featured as one who escapes her enticing trap. Schlesinger received an Oscar nomination for his perceptive direction, and the film itself was a Best Picture nominee. ★★★★ DVD Letterbox: $19.99

D.A.R.Y.L.

(1985, 99 min, US, Simon Wincer) *Mary Beth Hurt, Michael McKean, Barret Oliver, Colleen Camp.* An engaging if low-keyed children's fantasy about a young boy, half-android, who runs away from his government lab and is befriended by a childless couple. Oliver nicely plays the youth. ★★½ VHS: $14.99

Daughters of Darkness

(1971, 100 min, Belgium, Harry Kumel) *Delphine Seyrig, Daniele Ouimet, John Karlen.* One from the vaults! Seyrig stars as a Hungarian countess and present-day vampiress who, in order to continue her daily blood baths (a youth and beauty preservative), must continually prowl for nubile virgins. Her blood-gathering soirees take her to Belgium where she, along with her lesbian secretary, seductively stalks the hotel for a quick fix. Bela Lugosi she's not. Campy, funny and erotic, this Gothic tale explores the darker side of sexuality with shocking frankness. (Filmed in English) ★★★ DVD: $19.99

Daughters of the Dust

(1991, 114 min, US, Julie Dash) *Cora Lee Day, Alva Rodgers, Barbara O.* Independent filmmaker Dash has fashioned a lyrical, visually stunning drama about an African Gullah family off the coast of Georgia, circa 1902. Centering on the family's struggles, the film shows how half the family wants to move to the mainland, while the other half worry that their traditional African culture will be forever lost. Gorgeous and exquisite. ★★★½ DVD: $34.99, VHS: $24.99

Dave

(1993, 110 min, US, Ivan Reitman) *Kevin Kline, Sigourney Weaver, Frank Langella, Kevin Dunn, Ving Rhames, Charles Grodin, Ben Kingsley, Arnold Schwarzenegger.* A crowd-pleaser in every sense of the word, *Dave* is a wonderfully funny comedy worthy of bipartisan support. The appealing Kline plays Dave, a likable, good-hearted schmoe who's a dead ringer for the President of the United States. Which is why, when the Commander in Chief suffers a stroke, he's chosen to impersonate him. Under the tutelage of the scheming Chief of Staff (Langella), Dave charms all, including his First Lady (Weaver), as he sets forth his own political agenda. Writer Gary Ross revels in the fish-out-of-water scenario, and taps into a Capra-esque tone in celebration of the Average Joe. There's also four score and seven cameo appearances — and to give one of them away is grounds for impeachment. ★★★½ DVD: $19.99, VHS: $9.99

David

(1979, 106 min, West Germany, Peter Lilienthal) *Mario Fischel, Walter Taub, Eva Mattes.* A suspenseful, understated account of the devastating rise of fascism and its effect on one particular family. David, a Jewish teenager growing up in Berlin in the 1930s, is temporarily insulated from the Nazis' horrific policies by his naively optimistic middle-class family. Told on a human scale, the film follows David as he witnesses the destruction of his community and home; is separated from his parents; and experiences personal persecution by brutal authorities and neighbors. His will to survive is well-portrayed in this moving drama. (German with English subtitles) ★★★ VHS: $29.99

David and Lisa

(1962, 94 min, US, Frank Perry) *Keir Dullea, Janet Margolin, Howard da Silva.* Perry's acclaimed drama about the relationship between two mentally ill teenagers, played with great sensitivity by Dullea and Margolin, is a sympathetic, rewarding look at young love and institutionalization. Da Silva gives a wonderful performance as their sympathetic doctor. ★★★½ DVD: $14.99, VHS: $9.99

David Copperfield

(1935, 130 min, US, George Cukor) *Freddie Bartholomew, W.C. Fields, Edna May Oliver, Lionel Barrymore, Maureen O'Sullivan, Roland Young, Basil Rathbone.* Cukor's superbly crafted adaptation of Charles Dickens' classic novel (the author's favorite among his own work) was one of the box-office giants of the 1930s, and with good reason. Bartholemew, in perhaps his finest role, heads a stellar all-star cast as Dickens' young hero, experiencing the hardships and sorrows of orphaned life in 19th-century England. Fields is the perfect incarnation of Micawber, David's ne'er-do-well mentor, and Oliver is splendid as David's eccentric Aunt Betsy. One of the finest filmic interpretations of classic literature. ★★★★

David Holzman's Diary

(1967, 74 min, US, Jim McBride) *L.M. Kit Carson, Louise Levine.* Selected as one of the American cultural treasures in the Library of Congress' National Film Registry, this amazingly self-assured and uncomfortably perceptive first film by McBride (*The Big Easy*) is an audacious, groundbreaking independent film. David, an obsessively neurotic aspiring filmmaker attempting to unravel the mysteries of life, decides to make a movie on his life. But instead of learning from the study, the young man's film diary becomes his undoing, alienating his friends and girlfriend, distorting any real meaning and finally turning him into an alienated, frustrated and voyeuristic basketcase. Filmed in a wickedly *faux*

Daughters of Darkness

cinema verité style, this clever satire captures both the feeling of the tumultuous '60s era and the folly of its self-seeking "artists." ★★★★ VHS: $19.99

David Lynch's Hotel Room

(1992, 100 min, US, David Lynch & James Signorelli) *Harry Dean Stanton, Glenne Headly, Griffin Dunne, Chelsea Field, Crispin Glover, Alicia Witt, Deborah Unger.* A documentary about the places director Lynch stays when he travels — now *that* would be interesting! Here, rather, is a collection of three odd tales set in the same hotel room in various eras. *Tricks* is a basic weird-for-the-sake-of-weird story involving a hooker and an unexpected guest checking into room 603 in 1969. An ominous tone, but nothing really adds up. *Blackout*, the third segment and set in 1936, finds Lynch mining the spirit, but not the style, of *Eraserhead* to produce an awkward conversation between a young Oklahoma couple (Witt, Glover). The second segment provides the only real spark in the program. Directed by Signorelli, *Getting Rid of Robert* is a campy black comedy concerning three young socialites as they anticipate the arrival of a soon-to-be ex-boyfriend. ★★

Dawn of the Dead

(1979, 125 min, US, George Romero) *David Emge, Ken Foree, Scott Reiniger.* In this second installment of the *Night of the Living Dead* trilogy, the zombies get their just deserts when a Philadelphia SWAT team gets trapped in their hang-out — a large suburban shopping mall. There's lots of sly humor, blood and guts, making this bizarrely entertaining horror film a classic of the genre. (Sequel: *Day of the Dead*) (Remade in 2004) ★★★½ DVD: $19.99

Dawn of the Dead

(2004, 100 min, US, Zack Snyder) *Sarah Polley, Ving Rhames, Jake Weber, Mekhi Phifer, Ty Burrell.* George Romero's classic 1979 horror tale gets updated for the 21st century with this good reinterpretation that takes the old story of rampaging zombies and freshens it with a little technical wizardry. Not as gory as the original but certainly with enough blood and guts to satisfy any zombie-phile, this new *Dawn* begins at breakneck speed. Polley is a nurse who returns home and is promptly fighting off the neighbor's kid and her husband, who both have a taste for blood. In this version, however, getting away isn't as easy, since these zombies can run. When she and a group of other stranded mortals meet up at the mall, they all have their hands full from the hungry mob milling outside, militaristic mall security guards and dying cohorts about to become the living dead. As in the original, director Snyder milks many a scene for laughs, and the mix of scares and laughs works well. Rhames makes for a great zombie fighter; he, Polley, Weber and Phifer bring top-level talent to an already prime horror story, making this fun for all. ★★★ DVD Letterboxed: $29.99

The Dawn Patrol

(1938, 103 min, US, Edmund Goulding) *Errol Flynn, Basil Rathbone, David Niven, Donald Crisp.* Flynn had one of his best roles as a WWI flying ace assigned to keep the Germans behind enemy lines. Rathbone is in good form as a tough officer who must send new recruits to almost certain death. ★★★

The Dawning

(1991, 96 min, Ireland, Robert Knights) *Anthony Hopkins, Rebecca Pidgeon, Jean Simmons, Hugh Grant, Trevor Howard.* An affecting tale about a young woman's coming-of-age in 1920s Ireland and a mysterious man who she thinks may be her long-lost

father. Set just outside Dublin at the height of the Republican campaign for independence, the story centers around Nancy, who, surrounded by wealth, has little knowledge of the political violence and turmoil engulfing her country. On her 18th birthday, she encounters a rough-hewn rogue (Hopkins) in her secret hideaway by the beach. Reminiscent of many a Masterpiece Theatre production, the film sports some able performances and is enjoyable viewing, although ultimately it glosses over the political and emotional issues it purports to address. ★★ VHS: $79.99

The Day After

(1983, 126 min, US, Nicholas Meyer) *Jason Robards, JoBeth Williams, John Lithgow, Steve Guttenberg, Amy Madigan, John Cullum.* Powerful made-for-TV movie detailing life in a small Kansas town before and after a nuclear strike. Powerful images fill the screen with what Americans would have to look forward to in the case of the unthinkable. Though not as subtle as the similarly themed *Testament*, it is, however, not as devastatingly graphic as the haunting British counterpart, *Threads*. ★★★ DVD: $14.99

The Day After Trinity

(1980, 89 min, US, Joe Else) The scientific research that ushered in the dawn of the nuclear era is examined in this penetrating documentary. The site is Los Alamos, New Mexico, where, in 1941, J. Robert Oppenheimer and a group of brilliant scientists worked on a government project to end the war — with the result being a weapon of such power and destructive capability that its use in 1945 irrevocably changed the world. With footage of actual explosions and interviews with the people involved in the research, the film explores the moral anguish experienced by the naive scientists whose peace-inspired work resulted in the creation of a new generation of terrifying weapons. ★★★ DVD: $24.99, VHS: $39.99

A Day at the Races

(1937, 111 min, US, Sam Wood) *Groucho Marx, Harpo Marx, Chico Marx, Margaret Dumont, Maureen O'Sullivan, Allan Jones.* Fair maiden O'Sullivan is about to lose her health spa unless she receives financial assistance from hypochondriac millionairess Dumont. And who best to woo the symptom-laden lady than the ever-amorous Dr.

Hugo C. Hackenbush, played by — guess who? — Groucho Marx. Chico and Harpo masquerade as his medical assistants, and the day is saved by a horse. ★★★½ DVD: $19.99

Day for Night

(1973, 120 min, France, François Truffaut) *François Truffaut, Jean-Pierre Léaud, Jacqueline Bisset, Jean-Pierre Aumont, Valentina Cortese.* A loving ode to the intricacies of filmmaking. Truffaut portrays the compassionate director of a beleaguered production. Léaud is a spoiled young actor and Bisset is the beautiful heroine of the film within a film. Cortese is splendid as an actress who just can't get that one take right. An exhilarating and affectionate satire that captured the Best Foreign Film Oscar. (French with English subtitles) ★★★★ DVD Letterbox includes both subtitled and dubbed versions: $19.99

A Day in the Country

(1936, 40 min, France, Jean Renoir) *Sylvia Bataille, Georges Darnoux, Jane Marken, Andé Gabriello, Paul Temps.* A Parisian mother and daughter are seduced during an afternoon outing, but what exhilarates one proves to be a rude awakening for the other. Renoir's lyrical, impressionistic work is taken from a de Maupassant short story. (French with English subtitles) ★★★★ VHS: $24.99

A Day in the Death of Joe Egg

(1972, 106 min, GB, Peter Medak) *Alan Bates, Janet Suzman, Elizabeth Robillard.* Bates and Suzman give intense performances as a couple whose marriage is coming undone by the stress of caring for their spasmodic daughter. A black comedy of the darkest imaginable shade. ★★★

Day of the Beast

(1996, 99 min, Spain, Álex de la Iglesia) *Álex Angulo, Armando de Razza, Santiago Segura, Terele Pavez.* Father Angel, a laconic, devout priest, is convinced that Satan has come to Earth to claim its as his own, and, with the help of a beefy music store clerk, decides to stop him. Very Catholic and very Spanish, *Day of the Beast* is an effectively offbeat film that will strongly appeal to fans of outrageous humor. Not for all tastes, certainly (hardcore horror fans may find it too jokey, mainstream audiences will find it too over the top and bizarre), this is a flawed

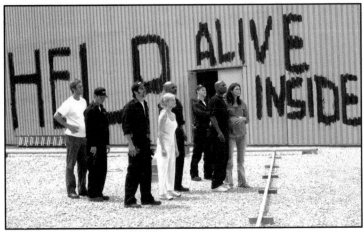

Zombies walk the earth in the remake of *Dawn of the Dead*

but original and entertaining work. It's a certain contender for cult favorite status. Winner of 6 Spanish Goya awards. (Spanish with English subtitles) ★★★

Day of the Dead

(1985, 102 min, US, George Romero) *Lori Cardille, Terry Alexander, Joseph Pilato.* Romero's final entry in his "zombie" series, following *Night of the Living Dead* and *Dawn of the Dead*. A group of scientists and military personnel become trapped in an underground missile silo, and hordes of the living dead lie between them and freedom. This claustrophobic horror film lacks the suspense of the first film and the special effects wizardry of the second. ★½ DVD Letterbox 2-disc Special Edition: $29.99

The Day of the Jackal

(1973, 141 min, GB, Fred Zinnemann) *Edward Fox, Alan Badel, Cyril Cusack, Delphine Seyrig, Derek Jacobi.* Zinnemann's taut political thriller chronicles the international manhunt for a professional assassin (Fox) on assignment to kill Charles de Gaulle. Though history tells us of the assassin's failure, the film maintains a remarkable tension throughout, and builds to an incredibly suspenseful ending. (American remake: *The Jackal*) ★★★½ DVD: $9.99

The Day of the Locust

(1975, 144 min, US, John Schlesinger) *Donald Sutherland, Karen Black, William Atherton, Burgess Meredith, Geraldine Page.* A powerful, beautifully filmed screen version of Nathaniel West's novel of aspirations and forgotten dreams in 1930s Hollywood. Black gives one of her best performances as an opportunistic, aspiring actress involved with both young studio set director Atherton and lonely, slightly slow-witted Sutherland (in a mesmerizing portrayal). Meredith received a well-deserved Oscar nomination as Black's boozing, sickly ex-vaudevillian father. An unforgettable though demanding film experience; the Hollywood premiere at the finale remains one of the most chilling sequences ever put to film. ★★★½ DVD Letterbox: $14.99

The Day of the Triffids

(1963, 95 min, GB, Steve Sekely) *Howard Keel, Nicole Maurey, Janet Scott.* Lying in a London hospital bed with bandages around his eyes, Keel is one of the few people on Earth to miss a spectacular meteor display in the skies. He wakes up the next morning to discover that most of the population has disappeared and the few remaining people have lost their sight. And to make matters worse, man-eating plants are slowly taking over the city. This is the fascinating premise of this low-budget but smart sci-fi thriller that puts as much accent on characterization and plot as it does on chills. The killer plants are kind of cheesy, but that only adds to the fun. ★★★ DVD: $24.99, VHS: $19.99

The Day the Earth Stood Still

(1951, 92 min, US, Robert Wise) *Michael Rennie, Patricia Neal, Hugh Marlowe, Sam Jaffe, Billy Gray.* 1950s science fiction doesn't come any better than this classic tale of alien beings and Earth's redemption. Rennie plays Klaatu, an emissary from outer space who arrives in the nation's capital to deliver a message of doom. Shot on sight and tiring of lip service from the political hacks (it *is* Washington, D.C.), he decides to mingle with the general population, and befriends widow Neal and her precocious son Gray. Meanwhile, there's the matter of the eight-foot robot, Gort, standing guard of Klaatu's spaceship, and his mission of peace.

Edward Fox in *The Day of the Jackal*

Made at a time when most sci-fi stories featured killer aliens, Wise's poetic, cautionary film presented a benevolent spaceman, and it did so in a suspenseful manner with touches of wit and political awareness. Jaffe's enlightened scientist is particularly appealing. *Klaatu Barada Nikto*. ★★★★ DVD: $14.99, VHS: $9.99

The Day the Sun Turned Cold

(1994, 99 min, China/Hong Kong, Yim Ho) *Siqin Gowa, Tuo Zhong Hua.* This coproduction between mainland China and Hong Kong filmmakers is a powerful and sad exploration of grief, regret and responsibility that is haunting in its stark emotions. Set in a tiny rural area in northern China, the story centers on a patriotic young factory worker who goes back to his childhood village to accuse his mother of secretly poisoning his father many years before. Through flashback, we learn of the stern habits of the father, a possible extramarital affair by the mother, and a kindly stranger who may have been a catalyst for the supposed murder. While uninvolving on a visual level, the film is thoroughly engrossing through its well-developed characters and thought-provoking story. (Mandarin with English subtitles) ★★★½ VHS: $24.99

Daybreak

(1993, 91 min, US, Stephen Tolkin) *Moira Kelly, Cuba Gooding, Jr., Martha Plimpton, Omar Epps, Alice Drummond.* Tolkin's adaptation of the off-Broadway play "Beirut" is set in the near future of New York City as an epidemic sweeps across the nation infecting hundreds of thousands of people. The government places the "positive" individuals into isolation camps. Kelly plays a young woman whose eyes are opened to what really is happening when she meets a group of resistance fighters led by Gooding, who tend and care for the infected. While this made-for-cable film is an obvious AIDS metaphor, it never really etches itself into believability despite competent performances by the leads. ★★ VHS: $9.99

Daylight

(1996, 115 min, US, Rob Cohen) *Sylvester Stallone, Amy Brenneman, Viggo Mortensen, Dan Hedaya, Claire Bloom, Stan Shaw.* Dull and dreary from start to finish, this is less "*Die Hard* in a tunnel" and more "*The Poseidon Adventure* underground." Stallone is a former New York emergency services specialist who's on the scene when the Lincoln Tunnel collapses trapping a handful of survivors. Sly must enter the tunnel (the best sequence in the film, unfortu-

nately at the very beginning) and lead the dazed survivors out. But after the spectacular tunnel collapse and Stallone's entry, the film goes steadily downhill. The victims are a mixed bag of stereotypical disaster movie characters. ★★½ DVD Letterbox Collector's Edition: $14.99, DVD DTS sound: $14.99

The Days of Being Dumb

(1992, 98 min, Hong Kong, Sau Leung Ko) *Jacky Cheung, Tony Leung.* This charmingly slap-dash comedy is a fun example of Hong Kong action/comedy features. Fred (Cheung) and Keith (Leung) are inseparable boyhood friends and inept gangster wannabes. Their attempts to join the Hong Kong underworld are hampered because every time they join, they accidentally cause the quick death of their crime boss. Try as they might, the two just can't stay in a gang and soon earn the reputation as jinxes. They decide to go independent, but their first scheme — pimping — turns into a disaster when their first prostitute from Singapore turns out to be a lovelorn lesbian. Not of "international" standards, the film is nonetheless great, mindless fun. (Cantonese with English subtitles) ★★½ VHS: $59.99

Days of Heaven

(1978, 95 min, US, Terrence Malick) *Richard Gere, Brooke Adams, Sam Shepard, Linda Manz.* Malick's lyrical film of a triangular love affair is set in the Eden-like vistas of the golden wheat fields of Texas. Gere stars as a Depression-era drifter who, with his sister Manz and girlfriend Adams, finds employment on the farm of lonely landowner Shepard. A beautiful, haunting version of the pastoral dream. ★★★★ DVD Letterbox: $14.99, VHS: $9.99, VHS Letterbox: $14.99

Days of Thunder

(1990, 107 min, US, Tony Scott) *Tom Cruise, Robert Duvall, Nicole Kidman, Cary Elwes, Michael Rooker.* Cruise, who acquired Paul Newman's fascination for race driving when they appeared together in *The Color of Money*, takes to the track in this heavily clichéd racing drama. Cruise plays a boy wonder behind the wheel and under the sheets. Duvall and Kidman benefit from his areas of expertise. ★★ DVD: $14.99, VHS: $9.99

Days of Wine and Roses

(1962, 117 min, US, Blake Edwards) *Jack Lemmon, Lee Remick, Charles Bickford, Jack Klugman.* Though he is mainly considered a comedic filmmaker, Edwards directed two impressive dramas in the early 1960s: *Experiment in Terror*, and this harrowing story about alcohol abuse. Lemmon and Remick give outstanding performances as a newly married couple whose lives are devastated by the rigors of their incessant drinking bouts. On par with Billy Wilder's *The Lost Weekend*. ★★★½ DVD: $19.99, VHS: $14.99

The Daytrippers

(1997, 87 min, US, Greg Mottola) *Hope Davis, Stanley Tucci, Parker Posey, Liev Schreiber, Anne Meara, Pat McNamara, Campbell Scott.* Writer-director Mottola's first film is a prime example of what independent filmmaking should be. Take a simple story about a highly dysfunctional family and shoot it on location for next to no money, and put together a compelling little comedy-drama. The action begins when Davis discovers a cryptic post card — which suggests an extramarital affair — that's fallen from husband Tucci's night stand. This prompts a familiy trip into the city to confront hubby. Thus begins a smartly concocted and at times

Independent film just wouldn't be the same without the triumvirate of Hope Davis, Liev Schreiber and Parker Posey, pictured here in *The Daytrippers*

hilarious, picaresque ride from Long Island to Manhattan and environs. Whenever things seem about to fizzle, Mattola's ingeniously written script unveils another intricate exploration of family dynamics as it heads toward a couple of dramatic denouements. ★★★½

Dazed and Confused

(1993, 113 min, US, Richard Linklater) *Wiley Wiggins, Jason London, Sasha Jenson, Rory Cochrane, Milla Jovovich, Anthony Rapp, Matthew McConaughey.* The second film by director Linklater moves at a slacker's pace, ambling here, ambling there, all the while telling the eclectic and engaging tale of a group of teenagers celebrating the last day of school in 1976. The pacing befits the film's message, which basically says that "the '70s suck and nothing happens." With a virtually nonexistent plot, the story follows a core cast of eight teenagers through their haze of alcohol, music and drugs (lots-o-pot). The young actors have understated styles that make their boredom seem genuine and their anticipation of the "coolness of the Eighties" seem slightly pathetic. If none of the characters in this film seem familiar to you, your teenage years were definitely spent pre-Woodstock. ★★★

The Dead

(1987, 88 min, Ireland, John Huston) *Anjelica Huston, Donal McCann, Donal Donnelly.* Director Huston's last film is a remarkable tribute to the poetic mastery of James Joyce. Deftly capturing the essence of Joyce's prose, Huston has fashioned a film brimming with incredible detail and richly imbued with the Irish spirit. The story may be a disappointment to some, however; for no matter how one approaches it, the viewer is simply an uninvited guest at a Christmas dinner party at which nothing really happens. Huston saves any emotional wallop for the film's ending passage in which the narrative poetry finally draws the audience into a long-awaited catharsis; considering the film's rich atmosphere, it's a worthwhile wait. ★★★½

Dead Again

(1991, 107 min, US, Kenneth Branagh) *Kenneth Branagh, Emma Thompson, Derek Jacobi, Robin Williams, Hanna Schygulla.* Actor-director Branagh goes giddy with this wildly imaginative comedy-thriller. He stars as Mike Church, a Los Angeles detective who comes to the aid of a mysterious amnesiac woman (Thompson). She is haunted by memories from 40 years earlier in which a renowned composer (Branagh again) may have murdered his wife (Thompson again). Jacobi costars as a psychic who tries to help them sort things out. Branagh uses this preternatural premise and runs it over the top, taking the audience on a wonderfully tongue-in-cheek roller-coaster ride replete with surprise twists and a Hitchcockian ending. ★★★½ VHS: $9.99

Dead Ahead:
The Exxon Valdez Disaster

(1992, 90 min, US/GB, Paul Seed) *John Heard, Christopher Lloyd, Rip Torn, Michael Murphy, Bob Gunton.* Meticulously researched, superbly acted and thoroughly engrossing, this HBO/BBC production is a fast-paced exposé on the chain of events set in motion when the Exxon tanker Valdez dumped millions of gallons of crude oil into the pristine Alaskan waters of Prince Williams Sound. The accident itself, caused by drunken carelessness, was horrible enough; even more terrifying was the response to it. The film presents a parade of company executives and government and military officials more interested in spin doctoring than solving the problem at hand. ★★★½

Dead Alive

(1991, 97 min, New Zealand, Peter Jackson) *Timothy Balme, Elizabeth Moody.* Before *Heavenly Creatures*, Jackson made this wild zombie splatterthon that ranks without a doubt as the goriest film ever made, bar none! Originally filmed as *Brain Dead*, this coal-black comedy barrage of pus-spewing, entrail-eating wackiness follows the story of an overbearing mother, her charming but somewhat wimpy son, his spicy Latina lover, a kung fu-fighting priest and a very rabid Sumatran rat-monkey. This highly entertaining, limb-shredding homage to such directors as George Romero and Sam Raimi is a must-see for those who like heavy doses of slapstick mixed with their horror. ★★★½ DVD: $19.99

Dead Calm

(1989, 96 min, Australia, Phillip Noyce) *Sam Neill, Nicole Kidman, Billy Zane.* Nail-biting suspense abounds in this high-seas thriller about a married couple who take to the Pacific in their yacht to find peace of mind after the death of their infant son. Their tranquility is shattered, however, when they take aboard the lone passenger of a sinking yacht, unaware that the man is a psychopath. Director Noyce effectively uses the tiny confines of the boat to develop a frenzied atmosphere of claustrophobia and terror. Neill and Kidman give grounded performances as the victimized couple, and Zane is a perfect embodiment of evil as the maniacal visitor. ★★★ DVD Letterboxed: $19.99, VHS: $14.99

Dead Connection

(1993, 93 min, US, Nigel Dick) *Michael Madsen, Lisa Bonet, Gary Stretch.* Madsen is a cop on a mission in this mean-spirited suspenser about a vicious psychopath (Stretch) who uses his exceptional good looks to attract women; then, he beats them to death and rapes them (in that order). Interesting characterizations and a few twists can't distract from the formulaic story and its execution. ★★

Dead End

(1937, 93 min, US, William Wyler) *Humphrey Bogart, Sylvia Sidney, Joel McCrea, Claire Trevor, The Dead End Kids.* Director Wyler elicits remarkable performances from his entire cast in this classic drama, based on Sidney Kingsley's Broadway hit, about life in a New York City tenement. Lillian Hellman wrote the screenplay adaptation. ★★★½

Dead Heat

(1988, 86 min, US, Mark Goldblatt) *Treat Williams, Joe Piscopo.* Two L.A. cops investigate a series of robberies only to discover the culprits are the living dead. The criminals may have been brought back to life, but this film is dead and buried. An embarrassment for the otherwise respectable Williams. ★ VHS: $14.99

Dead Man

(1996, 120 min, US, Jim Jarmusch) *Johnny Depp, Gary Farmer, Lance Henriksen, Gabriel Bryne, Robert Mitchum, John Hurt, Iggy Pop, Billy Bob Thornton, Crispin Glover.* Director Jarmusch uses the elements of the traditional western to craft a grim and gritty tale of one man's odyssey through a harrowing, alien environment. Depp is the perfect embodiment of a wanderer adrift in a world he never made, searching for meaning and direction in a hostile landscape fraught with danger, studded with pitfalls, and muddled by one miscommunication after another. *Dead Man* is part existential allegory, part fairy tale; and in it Depp is basically the knight errant who must overcome a series of trials on his path. In its starkness and simplicity, *Dead Man* returns to the crystalline laconicism of Jarmusch's *Stranger Than Paradise*; and though we may sense that this saga is essentially without hope, we are still wryly bemused and frequently amused. ★★★ DVD: $19.99, VHS: $9.99, VHS Letterbox: $14.99

Dead Man on Campus

(1998, 94 min, US, Alan Cohn) *Tom Everett Scott, Mark-Paul Gosselaar, Alyson Hannigan.* Two college roommates, failing their classes, decide to save their skins by taking advantage of a university rule that allots a 4.0 average to anyone whose roommate commits suicide. They search for the perfect candidate. Gosselaar and Scott give engaging performances under trying circumstances, and there's a few more laughs than would be expected. Still, this is an unpleasant, tasteless premise, and irresponsible partyers are amusing for only so long. John Waters may

D

have been able to mine this dangerous comic field, but Cohn doesn't have a first clue. ★★ DVD: $19.99, VHS: $14.99

Dead Man Walking

(1995, 125 min, US, Tim Robbins) *Susan Sarandon, Sean Penn, Robert Prosky, Raymond J. Barry, R. Lee Ermey, Lois Smith.* Powerful performances from Penn and Sarandon and the deft directorial touch of Robbins distinguish this gripping examination of capital punishment. Sarandon stars as Sister Helen Prejean (upon whose book the film is based), a Louisiana nun who attempts to aid a death row inmate, Matthew Poncelet (Penn). Most of the film revolves around these two characters as Sister Helen tries to draw out some shred of humanity from the remorseless Poncelet. As an analysis of a hot political issue, *Dead Man Walking* manages, remarkably, to find the center by concentrating on the totality of the human tragedy in both the initial crime and the concept of execution. Sarandon and Penn play off each other brilliantly (Sarandon won an Academy Award; Penn was nominated) in a film that depends heavily on the intimate and emotionally gut-wrenching scenes between the two of them. ★★★★ DVD Letterbox: $19.99

Dead Men Don't Wear Plaid

(1982, 90 min, US, Carl Reiner) *Steve Martin, Rachel Ward, Reni Santoni, George Gaynes.* A vastly entertaining and clever mystery spoof with Martin as a private eye who mixes it up on screen with Humphrey Bogart, Bette Davis, Barbara Stanwyck, Burt Lancaster and Alan Ladd — thanks to old movie clips and ingenious editing. ★★★ DVD: $24.99, VHS: $9.99

Dead of Night

(1945, 102 min, GB, Alberto Cavalcanti, Basil Dearden, Charles Crichton, Robert Hamer) *Michael Redgrave, Basil Radford, Sally Ann Howes.* An eerie and chilling horror masterpiece about five people gathered together to tell strange tales. Made in 1945, the film was the standard for all subsequent horror anthologies to follow. The highlight is the final tale with Redgrave as a ventriloquist — it'll definitely leave you hearing all of those things that go bump in the night. ★★★★ DVD Double Feature: $29.99

Dead of Winter

(1987, 100 min, US, Arthur Penn) *Mary Steenburgen, Roddy McDowell, Jan Rubes.* Steenburgen is in good form playing three roles in this tense chiller. An out-of-work actress must fight for her life when she accepts a part in a movie being produced by an eccentric recluse (Rubes) at his remote country mansion. McDowall is splendid as a mild-mannered though psychotic henchman. ★★★ DVD: $14.99

Dead Poets Society

(1989, 128 min, US, Peter Weir) *Robin Williams, Robert Sean Leonard, Ethan Hawke, Josh Charles, Kurtwood Smith, Lara Flynn Boyle, Al Ruggiero.* Director Weir's surprise hit is an often hilarious, sometimes deeply moving and somber treatise on the fires of youth and the creative spirit which they enkindle. Williams gives a spirited performance as Jack Keating — an unconventional English teacher at a New England boarding school for boys who finds himself at odds with the school's administration. And while no one here will deny the brilliance of Williams' work, the movie really doesn't belong to him: it belongs to the young actors who play his students. Leonard and Hawke head the ensemble of talented teenagers who make this movie a true success; their performances, as a group, are nothing less than marvelous. ★★★ DVD: $19.99, VHS: $9.99

The Dead Pool

(1988, 91 min, US, Buddy Van Horn) *Clint Eastwood, Jim Carrey, Liam Neeson, Patricia Clarkson.* In his fifth appearance as detective Harry Callahan, Eastwood finds himself hunting down the perpetrator(s) of a hit list known as the "dead pool." Not as exciting as its predecessors, still the film has all of the action and gunplay one comes to expect from *Dirty Harry* movies. ★★½ DVD Letterbox: $14.99, VHS: $9.99

Dead Presidents

(1995, 119 min, US, The Hughes Brothers) *Larenz Tate, Keith David, Chris Tucker, Rose Jackson, Bokine Woodbine, N'Bushe Wright, Seymour Cassel.* The Hughes Brothers follow their scintillating debut *Menace II Society* with this less impressive though not uninteresting morality tale about a young black Vietnam vet trying to build a life after the war. The film has all the elements required to be a fascinating study of this young man's struggle to reintegrate, and his fall from virtue to disgrace. But it can't seem to decide what to be: Is it a touching ghetto melodrama; harrowing Vietnam War exposé; or shoot-'em-up heist flick? Tate imbues his role with more complexity than seems to have been in the script. The Hughes' once again employ a hands-off approach to their characters' moral integrity, a stance that paid off in *Menace* but here backfires in the face of the lead's questionable final choices. ★★½ DVD Letterbox: $14.99, VHS: $9.99

Dead Reckoning

(1947, 100 min, US, John Cromwell) *Humphrey Bogart, Lizabeth Scott.* Departing slightly from his tough guy roles, Bogart plays a noir hero who, when he investigates the disappearance of an Army buddy, becomes entangled in a web of intrigue well beyond his control. A cynical tale where the hunter becomes the hunted. Scott is luminously attractive as the duplicitous young lady who entraps Bogie. A taut mystery that will keep you guessing right up to the end. ★★★ DVD: $24.99, VHS: $19.99

Dead Ringer

(1964, 115 min, US, Paul Henreid) *Bette Davis, Peter Lawford, Karl Malden.* Davis' follow-up to her smash hit *Whatever Happened to Baby Jane?* may be a silly psychological thriller, but thanks to Davis' histrionics, it's certainly a lot of fun. Bette chews the scenery as estranged twins: one good and one evil. When the latter kills the former, she changes places with her wealthy sister to live the good life. Will anyone suspect the imposter? Police inspector Malden has his doubts. ★★★ DVD: $19.99

Dead Ringers

(1988, 115 min, Canada, David Cronenberg) *Jeremy Irons, Geneviève Bujold, Heidi von Palleske.* The good twin-bad twin genre gets an unusual and fascinating once-over in this intense, often gruesome and quite disturbing psychological horror film based on an actual incident. Irons stars as identical twin brothers whose drug dependency and romantic involvement with the same woman (Bujold) triggers their emotional and professional decline. Irons gives a truly magnificent performance as the two doctors, giving each brother a distinctive and subtle shading. Bujold is excellent as the actress caught between them. The faint of heart beware. ★★★½

Dead Tired (Grosse Fatigue)

(1994, 85 min, France, Michel Blanc) *Michel Blanc, Carole Bouquet, Philippe Noiret, Charlotte Gainsbourg, Thierry L'Hermitte, Roman Polanski.* Director and writer Blanc plays dual roles as himself and a mischievous double in this wicked little farce dotted with actors, directors and the occasional agent, all playing themselves. Blanc finds himself in a waking nightmare, accused of nefarious deeds by friends and acquaintances of long standing. He retreats to the countryside to regain his composure, but that only leads him deeper into the abyss. Spurred into action by his friend Bouquet, they embark on an odyssey to discover the source of his inexplicable predicament. A delightful romp with many sly observances on fame and the cult of celebrity. (French with English subtitles) ★★★ DVD: $19.99, VHS: $19.99

The Dead Zone

(1983, 103 min, US, David Cronenberg) *Christopher Walken, Martin Sheen, Brooke Adams, Herbert Lom, Colleen Dewhurst, Anthony Zerbe.* From "goremeister" Cronenberg comes this unusually tame yet excellent adaptation of the Stephen King

Sean Penn and Susan Sarandon in *Dead Man Walking*

novel about an average Joe (Walken) who wakes from a five-year coma with the ability to see the future of anyone he touches. ★★★ DVD: $14.99, VHS: $9.99

Deadline at Dawn
(1946, 83 min, US, Harold Clurman) *Susan Hayward, Bill Williams, Paul Lukas.* With a crackling screenplay by Clifford Odets and an ominous and steamy New York-at-night backdrop, this fast-paced murder mystery stars Hayward as a streetwise but softhearted dance hall girl who gets involved with a naïve sailor in their frantic search for the killer of a female blackmailer. She soon becomes enmeshed in a maze of suspects and seedy characters all offering good reasons for having knocked off the broad. ★★★

Deadlock
(1991, 103 min, US, Lewis Teague) *Rutger Hauer, Mimi Rogers, Joan Chen, James Remar. The Defiant Ones* with a twist: Hauer and Rogers costar in this slick, entertaining made-for-cable thriller as a pair of criminals, shackled together at their necks by an explosive collar. They escape from an experimental maximum security prison to recover $25 million in stolen diamonds from Hauer's double-crossing partners in crime. ★★★ VHS: $19.99

The Deadly Companions
(1961, 90 min, US, Sam Peckinpah) *Maureen O'Hara, Brian Keith, Chill Wills.* Peckinpah's first film lacks the director's later accomplished visual style, but this is nevertheless an interesting western drama. O'Hara is a pioneer woman whose young son is accidentally killed; Keith is the ex-Army officer responsible for the boy's death — who escorts the woman cross-country for the boy's burial. ★★★ VHS: $14.99

Deadly Currents
(1991, 114 min, Canada, Simcha Jacobovici) An involving documentary concerning the Israeli-Palestinian conflict, this surprisingly evenhanded examination gives equal time to both sides, as well as three people caught in the middle. Soldiers, policemen, children, political leaders and terrorists all have their say — and the film avoids both sentimentality and a politically correct viewpoint. The conflict is seen through the eyes of its protagonists, not the eyes of (Western) onlookers. *Deadly Currents* offers an intimate look at everyday life in the West Bank, an existence marked by the commonality of violence and hatred. No pat resolutions, here; no one offers a viable solution to the conflict, and few offer any hope. (Hebrew and Arabic with English subtitles) ★★★½ VHS: $29.99

Deadly Friend
(1986, 99 min, US, Wes Craven) *Matthew Laborteaux, Kristy Swanson.* Teenage genius implants a chip into the brain of a dead friend, bringing her back to life — as a rampaging killer. Craven has certainly done better. ★

The Deadly Mantis
(1957, 78 min, US, Nathan Juran) *Craig Stevens, William Hopper.* Released by an earthquake in the Arctic, a giant praying mantis hops to the East Coast, causing destruction in Washington, D.C., and New York City before being gassed to death in the Holland Tunnel. Fun 1950s schlock with good F/X and lots of stock footage. ★★½

Deadtime Stories
(1986, 83 min, US, Jeffrey S. Delman) *Scott Valentine, Michael Mesmer.* An average horror trilo-

gy, whose stories of witches, werewolves and murderesses is highlighted by the final and funny "Goldilocks" story. ★★

Deal of the Century
(1983, 99 min, US, William Friedkin) *Chevy Chase, Sigourney Weaver, Gregory Hines, Wallace Shawn.* An embarrassing political comedy about weapons dealers involved with the Third World. ★

Dear God
(1996, 112 min, US, Garry Marshall) *Greg Kinnear, Laurie Metcalfe, Hector Elizondo, Maria Pitillo, Tim Conway, Roscoe Lee Browne, Nancy Marchand, Jack Klugman.* Very nearly smirking his way to cynically cool, Kinnear is nevertheless submerged in the same sap and nonsense he so adroitly lampooned on "Talk Soup." He plays a scam artist who is forced to take a job at the post office's dead letter department. There, he begins reading letters written to God — and inadvertently helps the beleaguered authors (the letter writers, not the scriptwriters) in an escalating "do-good" campaign. Marshall's wooden direction only underscores the screenplay's lack of laughs. ★★ DVD: $14.99, VHS: $14.99

Death and the Maiden
(1994, 103 min, GB, Roman Polanski) *Sigourney Weaver, Ben Kingsley, Stuart Wilson.* A grim, involving chamber piece based on Ariel Dorfman's stage play, *Death and the Maiden* stars Weaver as a former brutalized political prisoner. Now living peacefully with her husband (Wilson), whom she had protected, Weaver's seemingly calm exterior is shattered one night when she hears the voice of an acquaintance of her husband — the man who had tortured her. Thus sets in motion a game of revenge as the man (a marvelously controlled Kingsley), now being held hostage, firmly denies being him and Weaver will do anything to prove that he is. But who is right? Weaver's forceful but one-note portrayal and Polanski's stage-bound direction don't completely undermine an otherwise compelling scenario. ★★½ DVD: $19.99

Death Becomes Her
(1992, 115 min, US, Robert Zemeckis) *Meryl Streep, Goldie Hawn, Bruce Willis, Isabella Rossellini, Sydney Pollack.* Vanity, thy name is woman — or, more specifically, Streep and Hawn in this hilariously vicious black comedy. Youthful lovers Hawn and Willis are engaged; that's until Broadway star Streep gets in the way. Years later, Hawn plots her revenge: Streep's death. But there's a catch — Streep has found the secret to immortality. Black comedy doesn't often get sharper than this, and there are some staggering special effects to help underscore the film's delightful nastiness. Streep once again amazes as she revels in the role of a vain, aging actress; her satiric performance is at once subtle, cunning and totally brilliant. And wait until you see Goldie as a 400-pound eating machine — it alone is worth the rental fee. ★★★½ DVD: $14.99

Death in Brunswick
(1990, 106 min, Australia, John Ruane) *Sam Neill, Zoe Carides, John Clarke.* Neill is Cal, a 34-year-old unemployed cook under the thumb of his meddling mom and living in squalor with no clear ambitions. A job in a sleazy nightclub introduces him to a vibrant young woman and an odyssey involving inadvertent murder, a crazed bouncer, illicit drugs, corpse defilement, firebombing and signs from God. A darkly funny, low-budget surprise, with the gritty sense of realism often present in Australian films. Neill is

matched by the supporting cast in whimsical portrayals of marginal small-town characters who handle life's eccentricities with more heart than reason. ★★★

Death in the Garden (La Mort en ce Jardin)
(1956, 90 min, Mexico, Luis Buñuel) *Georges Marchal, Simone Signoret, Charles Vanel.* Using a more conventional narrative, Buñuel's *Death in the Garden* may prove a disappointment to fans of the great surrealist director. Based on a novel by Jose Andre Lacour, the film tells the story of diamond miners in post-WWII South America. When military officials announce that all mining will be controlled by the government, the town erupts into riotous chaos. A motley group of refugees eventually flees the militia on a riverboat for Brazil, their notions of identity and power stripped by the brutal conditions of travel. Ultimately the film's structure breaks down to reveal what is an existential polemic, rather than a social critique — and at best, an interesting historical document that testifies to the dangers of colonialism. (French and Spanish with English subtitles) ★★½

Death in Venice
(1971, 130 min, Italy, Luchino Visconti) *Dirk Bogarde, Mark Burns, Björn Andresen, Nora Ricci, Marisa Berenson, Silvana Mangano, Carole André.* Visconti's adaptation of the Thomas Mann novella of an artist in search of purity and beauty but who ultimately becomes fatally obsessed with an exquisite teenaged boy is a melancholy experience. Set in turn-of-the-century Venice, this languidly paced, darkly atmospheric film stars Bogarde as Aschenbach, an older man enamored with a flirtatious but unattainable blind youth (Andresen), and who is gradually weakened by the cholera epidemic sweeping the city. Visconti changed Aschenbach's profession from writer to composer, enabling him to fill a largely wordless film with the wondrous music of Gustav Mahler. (Filmed in English) ★★★ DVD Dual: $19.99

Death of a Bureaucrat
(1966, 87 min, Cuba, Tomás Gutiérrez Alea) *Salvador Wood, Silvia Planas.* When it comes to uproarious comedies, one rarely identifies the films of the Communist bloc, in general, and Castro's Cuba, in particular, as a source. But this madcap comedy is nothing if not a joy from beginning to end. Combining surrealist humor and pratfall antics, Alea's story concerns a young man whose recently widowed mother finds that she cannot receive her pension without his union card — which was buried with him! He finds himself in a classic Catch-22 as he tackles an endless array of red tape in his bewildering efforts to first get his father exhumed and then to get him reburied. A very funny black comedy that pokes wildly subversive fun at the powers-that-be. (Spanish with English subtitles) ★★★½ VHS: $19.99

Death of a Salesman
(1985, 150 min, US, Volker Schlöndorff) *Dustin Hoffman, John Malkovich, Kate Reid, Stephen Lang, Charles Durning.* Remarkably successful play-on-film version of Arthur Miller's classic drama, with Hoffman giving a stunning performance as Willy Loman, the aging Brooklyn salesman whose career and home life slowly unravel about him. A superior supporting cast includes Malkovich and Lang as his sons, and Reid as his loyal wife. ★★★★ DVD: $24.99, VHS: $19.99

The Decalogue

Death of a Soldier

(1985, 93 min, Australia, Philippe Mora) *James Coburn, Reb Brown, Bill Hunter.* A well-mounted recounting of the true story of a U.S. Army private stationed in Australia during WWII who murders three local women, and of his subsequent trial and execution. ★★½ VHS: $79.99

Death on the Nile

(1978, 135 min, GB, John Guillermin) *Peter Ustinov, Bette Davis, David Niven, Angela Lansbury, Maggie Smith, Mia Farrow, Simon MacCorkindale, Jack Warden.* Lavish Agatha Christie mystery highlighted by sumptuous locales and a solid cast. Ustinov is a delightful Hercule Poirot, who investigates the shipboard murder of a spoiled heiress. Who done it? We'll never tell. Lansbury is a stand-out among these accomplished performers. ★★★ DVD: $14.99, VHS: $9.99

Death Race 2000

(1975, 80 min, US, Paul Bartel) *David Carradine, Sylvester Stallone, Mary Woronov.* Frankenstein (Carradine) is the survivor of a number of deadly crashes, outfitted with a number of artificial limbs and devices taking on his challenger Machine Gun Viterbo (Stallone) in this funny, somewhat campy but exciting action-satire. ★★★ DVD: $14.99, VHS: $14.99

Death Takes a Holiday

(1934, 78 min, US, Mitchell Leisen) *Fredric March, Evelyn Venable, Guy Standing, Gail Patrick.* Maxwell Anderson's acclaimed Broadway drama makes for a fascinating and surreal film adaptation. March plays Death, who decides to take a three-day holiday. Disguising himself as royalty, he stays at a Spanish villa where he observes humans up close for the first time and, to his surprise, falls in love. (Remade as *Meet Joe Black*) ★★★½

Death to Smoochy

(2002, 109 min, US, Danny DeVito) *Robin Williams, Edward Norton, Catherine Keener, Danny DeVito, Jon Stewart, Harvey Fierstein.* Our sentiments exactly. Williams desperately tries to wriggle his way out of the pigeonhole of having portrayed a string of syrupy saps in smug, feel-good dramas. Here, he does an about-face as Rainbow Randolph, the much-adored host of a popular kids' variety show who's disgraced after the FBI busts him during a pay-

ola sting. Rainbow's embarrassed network seeks out a new, morally upright host for their show. Enter Norton as the titular Smoochy, a fuchsia rhino so squeaky-clean and boring even Barney the Dinosaur would consider him a wuss. As Smoochy helps the network rebound, dejected Rainbow becomes a vicious stalker, scheming to rid the world of this one-horned menace. It's indeed a nice change of pace to see Williams foam at the mouth and hurl colorful vulgarities, but his venomous, one-note schtick quickly gets tedious. Worse, the movie thinks it's skewering the mass marketing mentality of puritanical children's icons, but instead of poking Barney a new orifice, the film stabs itself squarely in the foot. A chaotic, insufferably unfunny mess. ★ DVD Letterbox: $19.99, DVD Pan & Scan: $19.99, VHS: $14.99

Death Warrant

(1990, 90 min, Canada, Deran Sarafian) *Jean-Claude Van Damme, Cynthia Gibb, Robert Guillaume.* A cop (Van Damme) goes undercover in a violent penitentiary, seeking out those responsible for a series of brutal prison murders. Violent and only sporadically interesting. ★★ DVD: $14.99

Death Wish

(1974, 93 min, US, Michael Winner) *Charles Bronson, Vincent Gardenia, Hope Lange, Steven Keats, Olympia Dukakis, Jeff Goldblum, Christopher Guest.* In the film that started the "vigilante" action genre, Bronson stars as a New York businessman who seeks vengeance against society's criminal underworld for the murder of his wife. The film tries to balance gritty, violent action sequences with a thoughtful treatise on crime and punishment, but it's nothing more than an excuse for Bronson to blow away punks and street scum and having the audience cheer him while he's doing it. As a detective on Bronson's trail, Gardenia is actually quite good, giving more conviction to his part than it deserves. (Followed by 4 sequels) ★★½ DVD: $19.99, VHS: $14.99

Deathtrap

(1982, 116 min, US, Sidney Lumet) *Michael Caine, Christopher Reeve, Dyan Cannon, Irene Worth.* Ira Levin's hit Broadway murder mystery is brought to the screen in only a satisfactory adaptation. Caine plays a down-on-his-luck playwright who sees a chance at reclaiming success when a former student (Reeve)

shows up with a sure hit script. Caine plots to murder him and take the play as his own. But plot twists and red herrings await them. The two twist endings are neatly written, but the entire production suffers from a dreariness due, in most part, to Lumet's stage-bound direction. ★★½ DVD: $9.99, VHS: $19.99

Deathwatch

(1980, 128 min, France/West Germany, Bertrand Tavernier) *Romy Schneider, Harvey Keitel, Max von Sydow, Harry Dean Stanton.* This unusual, present-day science-fiction film features Schneider as a terminally ill woman whose slow death is being witnessed by a mass audience through a tiny video camera implanted in the eyes of an undercover TV reporter (Keitel). A fascinating film which speculates on the abuses of the media as well as the rise of Big Brother. (Filmed in English) ★★★

A Decade under the Influence

(2003, 180 min, US, Richard LaGravenese & Ted Demme) *Robert Altman, Martin Scorsese, Peter Bogdanovich, Dennis Hopper, Ellen Burstyn, William Friedkin, Jon Voight, Julie Christie.* Highly entertaining documentary (codirected by Oscar-nominated screenwriter LaGravenese and Demme, who died during production) about the movies, directors and stars of the 1970s, when more personal filmmaking was at its height. Tracing the rise of the young turk directors who gained power when out-of-touch studios desperately craved the lucrative teen market, to their decline with the reemergence of the escapist blockbuster via *Jaws* and *Star Wars*, *Decade* is a terrific primer for those unfamiliar with the era. For film nuts, most of the information will be old hat, but the interviews (with Coppola, Friedkin, Scorsese, et al) are always interesting, at times moving and will surely rekindle a desire to catch up with some films you may have missed (or revisit some classics). ★★★½ DVD: $24.99

The Decalogue

(1988, 571 min, Poland, Krzysztof Kieslowski) The director of the "Three Colors" trilogy (*Blue*, *White* and *Red*) had already created his masterpiece by the time those films hit these shores. In fashioning ten short films for Polish television, each inspired by one of the Ten Commandments, Kieslowski explores dark, difficult moral and ethical dilemmas in his trademark brooding, moody style. Each episode is deeper than it appears; the fifth film, "Thou Shalt not Kill," is not merely a murder story, but a treatise on capital punishment. And the ten films, while working individually, are most powerful as a whole; all taking place in the same area, characters from some episodes make cameo appearances in others. This is a fully realized masterwork, worthy of its legendary status. ★★★★ DVD 3-disc Box Set: $79.99, VHS: $99.99

The Decameron

(1970, 111 min, Italy, Pier Paolo Pasolini) *Franco Citti, Ninetto Davoli.* Boccaccio's bawdy and earthy stories of sexual adventures during the 14th century receive the Pasolini treatment. Told in several episodes, the stories illustrate the different facets of uninhibited human sexuality. The film takes special pleasure in depicting the Church's sexually repressed clerics frolicking lecherously amongst their flocks. *The Decameron*, Pasolini's first film in his trilogy of medieval tales, is perhaps his funniest and is certainly one of the director's best films. (Italian with English subtitles) ★★★½ DVD: $19.99

Deceived

(1991, 103 min, US, Damian Harris) *Goldie Hawn, John Heard, Jan Rubes, Beatrice Straight, Kate Reid.* Hawn delivers an understated performance as a woman who slowly comes to discover that her recently deceased husband (perennial yuppie bad-guy Heard) may not have been all the good things that she thought he was. In fact, he may not even be dead. Crisp direction and stylish settings keep a predictable plot moving briskly. ★★½ DVD: $14.99

Deceiver

(1998, 102 min, US, Jonas & Joshua Pate) *Tim Roth, Renée Zellweger, Chris Penn, Michael Rooker, Rosanna Arquette, Ellen Burstyn.* A twisty bit of trickery, *Deceiver* is gripping without ever being really good. Slickly written and directed, this psychological mystery concerns two cops, Braxton (Penn) and Kennesaw (Rooker), who are administering a polygraph test to murder suspect James Walter Wayland (Roth). James suffers from temporal lobe epilepsy, and he may have killed a prostitute (Zellweger, seen only in flashback) during one of his seizures. However, while the cops do not have any hard evidence, James has some dirt on them. As the tables turn on all of the characters, and nasty secrets are revealed, it almost never becomes clear just who is deceiving whom. ★★½ DVD Dual: $14.99

The Deceivers

(1988, 112 min, GB, Nicholas Meyer) *Pierce Brosnan, Saeed Jaffrey, Shashi Kapoor, Keith Michell.* Brosnan stars as a 19th-century British officer who goes undercover to investigate a series of ritual killings by the secret brotherhood of the Thuggees. Posing as an Indian, the officer infiltrates the fiendish sect and finds himself mysteriously drawn into its power, endangering not only his mission, but his life as well. At times a bit muddled, the film nonetheless is an often exciting and interesting sojourn to a little-traveled time in history. ★★½

December Flower

(1984, 650 min, GB, Judy Allen) *Jean Simmons, Mona Washbourne.* This tender story about the flowering relationship between a middle-aged widow and her aging aunt is a beautiful tribute to the resilience of the elderly. ★★★

Deception

(1946, 112 min, US, Irving Rapper) *Bette Davis, Paul Henreid, Claude Rains.* Davis is in great form as a suffering pianist torn between Rains and Henreid. Rains matches La Davis every step of the way with a grand portrayal of her mentor. One of Davis' most entertaining soaps. ★★★

Deception

(1992, 90 min, US, Graeme Clifford) *Andie MacDowell, Liam Neeson, Viggo Mortensen, Jack Thompson.* What could elevate this by-the-book mystery about a harried housewife (MacDowell) who crisscrosses the globe in search of answers after her flyboy husband dies surrounded by shady dealings? Why Neeson, as a shyly charismatic "Feed the World" worker, of course. MacDowell gives, as usual, a one-note performance. ★★ DVD: $14.99, VHS: $9.99

The Decline of the American Empire

(1986, 101 min, Canada, Denys Arcand) *Dominique Michel, Dorothee Berryman, Louise Portal, Genevieve Rioux, Pierre Curzi.* Arcand's comically incisive film examines a group of male and female French Canadian academicians as they analyse the worlds of sex and human mortality. As their discussion unfolds, many in the group arrive at varying degrees of self-discovery. Arcand skillfully weaves his way through the many viewpoints and compassionately presents his characters as they turn to sexuality as a hedge against death. (French with English subtitles) ★★★ DVD: $39.99, VHS: $39.99

The Decline of Western Civilization

(1980, 100 min, US, Penelope Spheeris) Spheeris' absorbing, close-up look at the hardcore lifestyle on the wild and wooly West Coast features the serene sounds of X, Black Flag, Fear, Germs and Catholic Discipline. ★★★

The Decline of Western Civilization, Pt 2: The Metal Years

(1988, 90 min, US, Penelope Spheeris) Director Spheeris' raucous follow-up to her acclaimed docu-musical probes the headbanging fans and fast-living stars of the heavy metal world. Plenty of music and amusing interviews with demigods Ozzy Ozbourne, Aerosmith, Gene Simmons and Alice Cooper. ★★½

Deconstructing Harry

(1997, 96 min, US, Woody Allen) *Woody Allen, Kirstie Alley, Elisabeth Shue, Judy Davis, Demi Moore, Billy Crystal, Robin Williams, Julia Louis-Dreyfus, Mariel Hemingway, Amy Irving, Eric Bogosian, Julie Kavner, Bob Balaban, Hazelle Goodman.* With the most infuriatingly honest, darkest and derisive film of his career, Allen's funny comedy finds the writer-director in new territory as he opens the wounds of his private life in language, situation and character. Woody plays Harry Block, a writer in the throes of crisis with ex-wives, ex-girlfriends, career and conscience. These are themes are presented in such an in-your-face cinematic style and bantered about with uncharacteristic off-color dialogue, that Woody's self-revelatory exploration of an unapologetically immature husband, father and artist will certainly divide even his most loyal fans. The story, which inventively and successfully mixes past and present, and reality and fiction, follows Block as he prepares to accept an award from his alma mater. In brief appearances, Alley as an ex-wife, Davis as a former in-law, Crystal as the Devil, and Williams as a fictional character stand out among the large, cameo-driven all-star cast. ★★★½ DVD: $24.99, VHS: $14.99, VHS Letterbox: $14.99

Decoration Day

(1990, 99 min, US, Robert Markowitz) *James Garner, Bill Cobbs, Laurence Fishburne, Judith Ivey, Ruby Dee.* Garner stars in this made-for-TV drama about a retired Georgia judge who reluctantly searches for his estranged boyhood friend, a black WWII vet who refuses to accept a long overdue Congressional Medal of Honor. An intelligent screenplay, incisive direction and exceptional performances contribute to elevate this well above standard TV-movie fare. ★★★½ DVD: $19.99, VHS: $14.99

The Deep

(1977, 123 min, US, Peter Yates) *Nick Nolte, Jacqueline Bisset, Louis Gossett, Jr., Robert Shaw.* Nolte and Bisset play lovers on a romantic vacation in Bermuda who stumble upon a sunken wreck from WWII and get entangled with a Haitian drug dealer (Gossett) and an old treasure hunter (Shaw). The cinematography captures the lushness of the surroundings, but a flat screenplay sinks to the bottom. ★★ DVD: $9.99

Deep Blue Sea

(1999, 105 min, US, Renny Harlin) *Saffron Burrows, Thomas Jane, Samuel L. Jackson, LL Cool J, Michael Rapaport, Stellan Skarsgård.* Borrowing quite liberally from just about every popular horror/thriller of the last couple decades, this underwater thriller still manages to entertain in spite of its creaky story and cartoonish effects. Scientist Burrows is searching for an Alzheimer's cure by toying with shark DNA. Only thing is, her tests have elevated the sharks up the evolutionary scale a notch or two. And now the great whites have flooded the underwater lab the small crew inhabits — and they're pissed. The production design is actually quite good, but is offset by the less-than-menacing sharks. At least it's fun to watch each member become dinner in a wide variety of attacks. The cast is mostly competent, however, Burrows must have taken acting lessons from Steven Seagal. ★★½ DVD: $19.99, VHS Collector's Edition: $9.99, VHS Letterbox Collector's Edition: $9.99

Deep Cover

(1980, 81 min, GB, Richard Loncraine) *Donald Pleasence, Denholm Elliott, Tom Conti.* Dennis Potter wrote the screenplay for this brooding made-for-TV drama which mixes cryptic dialogue, paranoia, sexual duplicity and a notorious 1930s British scandal. Pleasence stars as a reclusive author whose home is visited by an enigmatic stranger (Conti), claiming to be writing his thesis on one of his books. As he ingratiates himself into the household, it becomes apparent that he has ulterior motives. Potter sets the pace of his scenario slowly as characters playfully banter back and forth, with the author playfully giving bits of information only when needed. The cinematography gives the film a storybook glow that belies the characters' malevolent intents. (aka: *Blade on the Feather*) ★★½

Deep Cover

(1992, 107 min, US, Bill Duke) *Jeff Goldblum, Laurence Fishburne, Victoria Dillard, Charles Martin Smith, Clarence Willliams III, Glynn Turman.* In this gritty urban thriller, Fishburne is magnetic as a cop who finds himself being seduced by a life of crime when he is sent into "deep cover" as a drug dealer. With a story as streetwise as anything this side of Scorsese, the screenplay by maverick writer Michael Tolkin (*The Player*) adds an extra level of depth and decadence to the characterizations — particularly Goldblum's turn as an ultra-smarmy attorney who wants to market his own designer drug. ★★★½ DVD: $14.99, VHS: $9.99

Deep Crimson

(1996, 110 min, Mexico, Arturo Ripstein) *Daniel Giménez Cacho, Regina Orozco, Marisa Paredes, Verónica Merchant.* This is a truly odd film, based on the same ultrastrange true case that inspired the cult movie *The Honeymoon Killers*. There's no camp in this one, just a straightforward retelling of the tale of the doomed lovers and their nasty scheme to rip various spinsters and widows out of their fortunes after marrying and murdering them. Fans of *Honeymoon Killers* will either enjoy this for its different take on the case or be put off by the film's rather sluggish pacing. (Spanish with English subtitles) ★★ VHS: $29.99

The Deep End

(2001, 99 min, US, David Siegel & Scott McGehee) *Tilda Swinton, Goran Visnjic, Jonathan Tucker, Peter Donat, Josh Lucas, Raymond Barry.*

Lake Tahoe, California. Margaret Hall (Swinton) wakes early one morning to find the body of her gay 17-year-old son's lover impaled on an anchor on the beach of their lakefront home. With her husband away and nowhere to turn, she makes a reckless decision to move the body and hide it in the lake, only to find herself and her family in even greater danger when the body is found, and she is confronted by blackmailers. A taut, compact thriller, *The Deep End* takes an ordinary mom and places her in extraordinary circumstances. Deals are made and broken, sleazy businessmen blackmail, and there's more going on under the surface than either we or she can see. Swinton gives a nuanced, sympathetic performance, which goes a long way in making one care about her and her family's plight. "E.R."'s Visnjic makes a good impression as a hood who may or may not be on the Halls' side. ★★★½ DVD: $14.99, VHS: $9.99

Tilda Swinton in *The Deep End*

The Deep End of the Ocean

(1999, 106 min, US, Ulu Grosbard) *Michelle Pfeiffer, Treat Williams, Whoopi Goldberg, Jonathan Jackson, Ryan Merryman.* A minor, TV movie-of-the-week story brought to life by an A-list cast, this earnest drama follows the hardships endured by a family after their youngest child disappears. In an engaging portrayal that manages to overcome the clichés of the story, Pfeiffer is Beth, who loses her son Ben in a crowded lobby. Ben is never found, leading to a series of accusations by both parents. A few years later, however, Beth sees a neighborhood boy who she thinks may be Ben. Is he? And if he is, will he choose to live with his new family? By then it won't matter much, for the story becomes strained as it pretends to examine the moral dilemma — but it's all so superficial. ★★ DVD: $14.99, VHS: $9.99

Deep Impact

(1998, 121 min, US, Mimi Leder) *Robert Duvall, Téa Leoni, Morgan Freeman, Maximilian Schell, Elijah Wood, Vanessa Redgrave.* A visually striking end-of-the-world flick, *Deep Impact* focuses more on human emotion rather than special effects, which immediately separates it from 1998's other disaster film, *Armageddon*. Young astronomer Wood discovers a huge comet hurdling towards Earth. This sets in motion the inevitable panic as the President (a stately Freeman) responds accordingly. Leoni is a TV reporter who breaks the news, and the story shuttles between the emotional toll being taken on the doomed characters, and the space mission that attempts to destroy the comet. The effects at the end are good, but there's little of them, which could make one feel cheated. ★★½ DVD Letterbox: $14.99, VHS: $9.99

Deep in My Heart

(1954, 132 min, US, Stanley Donen) *Jose Ferrer, Merle Oberon, Paul Henreid, Gene Kelly, Cyd Charisse.* Entertaining production numbers highlight this otherwise by-the-books musical biography of Hungarian composer Sigmund Romberg ("The Student Prince," "The Desert Song"), with Ferrer as the songwriter. ★★½

Deep in the Woods

(2000, 90 min, France, Lionel Delplanque) *Clotilde Courau, Clément Sibony, Vincent Lecoeur, Alexia Stresi.* This Gallic slasher is basically the same old stuff, but it has the whiff of something classier and contains enough stylish moments to almost recommend it to stalwart horror fans. A troupe of shallow young actors are summoned to a wealthy estate in the woods to put on a show for an invalid child. The play is a success, but then the kids

start getting picked off one by one (mostly after having sex, of course). As usual with lesser gore films, you don't care one whit for the victims, so there's little in the way of suspense, despite the efforts of the talented director. Some nice atmosphere and camera work help, but this premise was handled far more effectively in Michele Soavi's *Stagefright*. (aka: *Aquarius*) (French with English subtitles) ★★ DVD Dual Dubbed: $14.99, VHS Dubbed: $9.99

Deep Red

(1975, 98 min, Italy, Dario Argento) *David Hemmings, Daria Nicoldi, Gabriele Lavia.* Hemmings stars in this chilling horror-mystery as a British musician in Rome who witnesses the "Hatchet Murder" of a psycho. He then becomes obsessed with solving the case, finding clues, corpses and some bizarre drawings along the way. Filled with tension and atmosphere. ★★★ DVD: $19.99

Deep Rising

(1998, 106 min, US, Stephen Sommers) *Treat Williams, Famke Janssen, Anthony Heald, Kevin J. O'Connor, Wes Studi, Djimon Hounsou.* Cookie-cutter moviemaking, *Deep Rising* is an odd, uneven hybrid of *The Poseidon Adventure*, *Speed 2*, *Die Hard*, *Predator* and all four *Alien* films. Defying logic and coherence, the film puts a colorful assortment of gleefully underwritten characters in jeopardy when a luxurious cruise ship is undertaken by bad guys with guns. The twist is that a gigantic underwater creature has come up from the depths for supper. Lots of prefab suspense and bloody mayhem ensues, though the effects are distractingly cheesy. Still, there's campy, B-movie fun to be had. ★★ DVD: $14.99, VHS: $9.99

DeepStar Six

(1988, 103 min, US, Sean S. Cunningham) *Greg Evigan, Nancy Everhard, Taurean Blacque, Miguel Ferrer.* A group of deep-sea explorers attempt to establish a second naval base on the ocean floor, but they discover there's a terror in the ocean depths. Nothing could be as scary, though, as this film's screenplay, acting and directing. ★ DVD: $14.99, VHS: $9.99

The Deer Hunter

(1978, 183 min, US, Michael Cimino) *Robert De Niro, Christopher Walken, Meryl Streep, John Cazale, John Savage, George Dzundza, Shirley Stoler.* This Oscar-winning Best Picture is an unusual Vietnam War film in that it shows its characters before, during and after their war experience. The Vietnam episode is only a third of the film, but it is so devastating that it stays with you until the film's end. Among the extraordinary ensemble, Walken won an Oscar for his emotionally scarred soldier. ★★★★ DVD Letterbox: $19.99, VHS: $9.99, VHS Letterbox: $9.99

Def by Temptation

(1990, 95 min, US, James Bond III) *Cynthia Bond, Kadeem Hardison, James Bond III, Bill Nunn, Melba Moore, Samuel L. Jackson.* An all-black cast invigorates this original treatment about a virginal "man of God" (Bond) who must avenge his father's downfall by doing battle with a demon (Cynthia Bond, the director's sister) who preys on sexually dishonest souls. Director Bond makes the most of his low, low budget while serving up a horror treat that harks back to the "blaxploitation" era of *Blacula*, but without the gratuitous exploitation of that genre. ★★★ DVD: $14.99, VHS: $14.99

Defence of the Realm

(1987, 96 min, GB, David Drury) *Gabriel Byrne, Greta Scacchi, Denholm Elliott, Ian Bannen.* Engrossing political thriller about a journalist who uncovers an explosive sex scandal involving a Member of Parliament and a KGB agent, which leads the reporter on the trail of a governmental cover-up of a nuclear mishap on an American military base. Elliott gives a smashing performance as Byrne's seasoned editor. ★★★ DVD: $14.99

The Defender

(1994, 100 min, Hong Kong, Corey Yuen) *Jet Li, Christy Chung.* The inimitable Li is saddled with third-rate material here. Basically a Hong Kong remake of *The Bodyguard*, *The Defender* has Beijing bodyguard Li assigned to protect lovely young Chung from a bunch of baddies. The usual dull antagonism between the two is protracted, and it's nearly an hour before the first real action scene. Li's charisma is the only thing holding one's attention until the terrific climax, with Li going mano-a-mano with the baddest of the bad guys. (aka: *The Bodyguard from Beijing*) ★★ DVD: $14.99, VHS: $9.99

Defending Your Life

(1991, 112 min, US, Albert Brooks) *Albert Brooks, Meryl Streep, Rip Torn, Lee Grant, Buck Henry.* One of the most innovative and freshest comedies of the '90s, this low-key, quirky and very funny fantasy follows businessman Brooks' adventures in the hereafter. Killed in a car accident, he goes on trial to determine his next plane of existence. During his stay at Judgment City — where you can eat as much as you like and never gain weight — he falls in love with Streep, who is certainly on a higher spiritual plateau. The film, written and directed by Brooks, finds most of its humor with our conceptions concerning death, love and commitment. ★★★½ DVD: $19.99

The Defiant Ones

(1958, 97 min, US, Stanley Kramer) *Tony Curtis, Sidney Poitier, Theodore Bikel, Lon Chaney, Jr.* Kramer had a thing for films about prejudice (*Guess Who's Coming to Dinner*, *Judgment at Nuremberg*), but this taut drama is probably the best of them all. Curtis and Poitier play two escaped convicts cuffed to each other, fleeing the police in the South. Their performances are remarkably well-defined. ★★★★ DVD Letterbox: $14.99

Déjà Vu

(1998, 115 min, US/GB, Henry Jaglom) *Stephen Dillane, Victoria Foyt, Vanessa Regrave, Rachel Kempson, Noel Harrison, Anna Massey.* Another anxious romance from writer-director Jaglom, *Deja Vu* will please his dedicated fans, and it may actually earn him some new ones. Foyt (Jaglom's wife, and the film's cowriter) stars as Dana, a woman who believes — based on a set of coincidences — that her soulmate is Sean (Dillane), a painter. As the couple hopscotch around the globe, and each other's hearts,

D

they allow fate and destiny to take control of their lives. *Deja Vu* has some lovely, romantic moments when its characters' neuroses are not too overbearing, and happily, Jaglom's direction is a bit less intrusive than usual. Dillane is an engaging romantic hero, and the film is graced with the elegant presence of Redgrave. ★★★ DVD: $19.99, VHS: $14.99

The Delicate Delinquent

(1957, 90 min, US, Don McGuire) *Jerry Lewis, Darren McGavin, Martha Hyer.* Lewis plays a bumbling (what else?) janitor who hangs out with the crowd from the wrong side of the tracks but ends up becoming a police officer. His first movie without Dean. ★★★ VHS: $14.99

Delicatessen

(1991, 97 min, France, Jean-Pierre Jeunet & Marc Caro) *Dominique Pinon, Marie-Laure Dougnac, Jean Claude Dreyfus.* Displaying a playfully inventive virtuosity with the camera, and offering as its theme the socially indigestible subject of cannibalism, *Delicatessen* is a hilariously witty and sweetly outrageous story of a fairy-tale romance set amidst the ruins of a post-apocalyptic world. The story revolves around an enterprising butcher who stays in business by adding some human flesh to his meats and sausages. Life changes for the butcher and his odd-ball tenants when Louison (Pinon), a sweet-natured, clown-on-the-lam comes looking for a job and a place to live. Before you can say, *"filet mignon au poivre,"* Louison falls in love with the butcher's willowy, near-sighted daughter. As poor Louison has to stay one step ahead of the butcher's cleaver, the directors gleefully notch up the speed and unleash a flurry of chaos as the film races to an inspired comicbook conclusion. (French with English subtitles) ★★★★ VHS: $7.99

Delirious

(1983, 70 min, US, Bruce Gowers) *Eddie Murphy.* Murphy live in concert, recorded in Washington D.C. in 1983, at the beginning of his phenomenal film career. Brimming with the humor — adult-oriented, often side-splitting and usually offensive — which has become the comic's trademark. ★★★

Deliver Us from Eva

(2003, 105 min, US, Gary Hardwick) *LL Cool J, Gabrielle Union, Duane Martin, Essence Atkins.* An updated reworking of Shakespeare's "Taming of the Shrew," the amiable and marvelously titled *Deliver Us from Eva* provides a few laughs, but is unable to compensate for a story mired in predictability and cliché. Union is Eva, the eldest of the four beautiful Dandridge sisters. Abrasive, sharp-tongued and single, Eva's constant interference in her sisters' relationships is the cause of much dismay for the men in their lives. This sets in motion a ruse in which handsome Lothario Ray (LL Cool J) is hired to romance Eva in the hopes she'll have little time for meddling. Of course, self-acknowledged player Ray starts to fall for Eva, and she for him. The premise has long been a good one, but the filmmakers are unable to freshen it, relying instead on a few funny lines, caricatures and nice chemistry between Union and LL Cool J. ★★ DVD Letterbox: $19.99, DVD Pan & Scan: $19.99, VHS: $9.99

Deliverance

(1972, 109 min, US, John Boorman) *Jon Voight, Burt Reynolds, Ned Beatty, Ronny Cox.* James Dickey's best-seller makes for a stirring adventure-drama about four business associates whose weekend in the wilds turns tragic. Voight and Reynolds

Delicatessen

are fine as two of the execs, and completing the quartet, Beatty and Cox both make impressive film debuts. ★★★½ DVD Letterbox: $14.99, DVD Fullscreen: $14.99, VHS: $14.99, VHS Letterbox: $14.99

The Deluge (Potop)

(1974, 290 min, Poland, Jerzy Hoffman) Set in the mountainous ravines of the Carpathians and filled with burning villages, opulent castles and spurting blood, this impressive 17th-century war epic chronicles the patriotic glory and bloody violence during the Polish-Swedish War. The story is told through the romantic eyes of Andrzej, a courageous adventurer who finds more than a little time for amorous interludes. Based on the novel by Henryk Sienkiewicz, this Polish *Tom Jones* was nominated for the Academy Award for Best Foreign Language Film. (Polish with English subtitles) ★★★ DVD: $49.99

Delusion

(1990, 95 min, US, Carl Colpaert) *Jim Metzler, Jennifer Rubin, Kyle Secor.* On a trip to Reno through a preternaturally desolate expanse, an altruistically motivated embezzler gives a lift to the wrong young couple. The eerily depopulated, incandescent desert becomes a mute observer as the mob lackey with a bad stomach and his would-be chanteuse kidnap the executive and introduce a slight detour into his travel plans. An engaging cast, a clever script and attentive direction combine to create a nifty noir-ish mystery with an existential slant. ★★★

Delusions of Grandeur

(1976, 85 min, France, Gerard Oury) *Yves Montand, Louis De Funes.* A delightful, fast-paced comedy of royal intrigue in 17th-century Spain. Louis De Funes is an evil, all-powerful minister of the king who, when exiled by the queen, plots to get even. He is aided by his clever, good-natured servant, Blaze (Montand). (French with English subtitles) ★★★

Dementia 13

(1963, 81 min, US, Francis Ford Coppola) *William Campbell, Luana Anders.* Coppola made his feature film debut with this Roger Corman cheapie about an ax-murderer on the loose on an Irish castle. Often

very gory, Coppola effectively uses black and white to enhance the horror of this Gothic thriller. Worth a look as both low-budget horror film and as first film for a major American director. ★★★ DVD: $9.99

Demetrius and the Gladiators

(1954, 101 min, US, Delmer Daves) *Victor Mature, Susan Hayward, Anne Bancroft, Ernest Borgnine, Michael Rennie, Debra Pagent.* A good cast is featured in this inferior sequel to 1953's *The Robe,* which centers on the search for the robe that Christ wore before He was crucified. ★★ DVD: $14.99, VHS: $6.99

Demolition Man

(1993, 114 min, US, Marco Brambilla) *Sylvester Stallone, Wesley Snipes, Sandra Bullock, Nigel Hawthorne, Rob Schneider, Benjamin Bratt, Bob Gunton, Denis Leary, Glenn Shadix.* In this surprisingly effective and comical action film, Stallone plays a renegade cop whose battle with bad-guy Snipes leads to the deaths of innocent civilians. Both are frozen as punishment. Thirty-five years later, in a grotesquely funny fascist Utopian society, Snipes escapes, and an ill-equipped police department defrosts Sly to help them catch him. First-time director Brambilla has a good eye in creating an off-center future, and his action sequences are well-staged. As the over-the-top villain, Snipes clearly seems to be enjoying himself. ★★★ DVD: $14.99, VHS: $9.99

Demon Barber of Fleet Street

(1936, 68 min, GB, George King) *Tod Slaughter, Bruce Seton, Stella Rho, Eve Lister.* The cruelties of man are more wondrous than Peru in this true story of barber Sweeney Todd, who would kill bad-tipping customers and turn them into meat pies. (No singing in this film.) Slaughter's most famous exercise in the Grand Guignol, rumored to feature asylum inmates in minor roles (mostly in front of the camera). ★★½ VHS: $9.99

Demon Knight

(1995, 93 min, US, Ernest Dickerson) *Billy Zane, William Sadler, Jada Pinkett, Brenda Bakke, Thomas Haden Church, CCH Pounder, Dick Miller.* The Crypt Keeper from TV's "Tales from the Crypt" makes his way to the big screen in this tongue-in-cheek tale. The film, like the series, is alternately ghoulish, coolish and humorous, but it doesn't quite succeed in becoming the triple threat it so wants to be. Director Dickerson creates a chilling atmosphere, but he's working from an undeveloped script. It has to do with the Devil (Zane) battling the mortal guardian (Sadler) of a key containing the blood of Christ. Gory effects and macabre humor follow as he plays a demonic game of Ten Little Indians. ★★ DVD Letterbox: $14.99, VHS: $14.99

Demon Seed

(1977, 97 min, US, Donald Cammell) *Julie Christie, Fritz Weaver, Robert Vaughn*. Christie plays a housewife who's caught in the deadly plot of a powerful computer system as it attempts to secure immortality and take over the world. ★★½

demonlover

(2002, 117 min, US, Olivier Assayas) *Charles Berling, Gina Gershon, Connie Nielsen, Chloë Sevigny*. A strange, at-times beguiling film, the ambitious *demonlover* unfortunately loses its way and reveals itself to be much less than the sum of its parts. Slow-paced but intriguing, this corporate espionage tale for most of its running time has dreamy, captivating cinematography and excellent performances (not to mention a guilty-pleasure cat fight between Nielsen and Gershon) to glide over the bumpy parts; but director Assayas lets his grip on the material slip in the second half, which, while faster paced, becomes sillier and sillier as it goes. Vague, frustrating, at times annoying, but also oddly compelling if you're in the mood for something unusual. ★★★★ DVD: $24.99

Demons

(1986, 89 min, Italy, Lamberto Bava) *Urbano Barberini, Natasha Hovey*. Stylish, eerie (if somewhat implausible) horror film cowritten and produced by Italian horror master Dario Argento about a movie preview audience watching a slasher film, while the horror on screen extends itself into the real world. (Sequel: *Demons 2*) ★★★ DVD: $29.99, VHS: $14.99

Demons in the Garden

(1982, 100 min, Spain, Manuel Gutiérrez Aragón) *Angela Molina, Ana Belen, Eusabio Lazáro*. A child's magical memory of his father's hypocrisy and deceit is the subject of this engrossing tale about life after the end of the Spanish Civil War. A young boy grows up spoiled and manipulative as his mother, aunt and grandmother vie for influence over him. A trio of Spain's finest actresses etch memorable portraits that embody the divided nature of the Spanish character. (Spanish with English subtitles) ★★★

Dennis Potter: The Last Interview

(1994, 70 min, GB, Tom Poole) Betrayed by his body, sipping morphine from a flask, Dennis Potter, writer of such masterworks as "The Singing Detective," "Pennies from Heaven" and "Brimstone and Treacle," talks about his life, his art and his impending death in this often fascinating interview. The location for this gentle interrogation is appropriate: a TV studio empty save for two chairs, a small table, the interviewer and his clipboard, and Potter himself. Only minutes into the program, the playwright can no longer maintain his adopted role as Britian's bitterish curmudgeon — or perhaps, like so many of the characters who populate his plays, he just gives it more complexity and greater depth. ★★★ VHS: $29.99

Dennis the Menace

(1993, 94 min, US, Nick Castle) *Walter Matthau, Joan Plowright, Mason Gamble, Christopher Lloyd, Lea Thompson, Paul Winfield*. This updating of the "Dennis the Menace" saga has its moments, like the one where Dennis (Gamble) explains to Mrs. Wilson why his parents want to be left alone for their weekly Sunday morning "wrestling" sessions. Unfortunately, moments like these are few and far between and the story consequently sags around John Hughes' by now worn-out plot involving a burglar (Lloyd) who gets nailed by a precocious eight-year-old. Most of the performances are bland, with the exception of Matthau as the curmudgeonly Mr. Wilson and Plowright as his understanding wife. ★★ DVD Letterbox 10th Anniversary: $14.99, VHS: $9.99

The Dentist

(1996, 93 min, US, Brian Yuzna) *Corbin Bernsen, Linda Hoffman*. Rather than being a *Dr. Giggles*-like slasher movie, this ambitious but failed project is more along the lines of a psychological thriller with teeth. Bernsen stars as a successful dentist with a beautiful wife, luxurious home and lucrative practice. This, however, is all an illusion, as he's slowly losing it all. While there is some effective satire, the film unfortunately concentrates too much on the collapse of the doctor's mind. Fans expecting a slasher pic will be sorely disappointed. Dentistry was more chilling in *Marathon Man*. (Sequel: *The Dentist 2*) ★★ DVD: $14.99

Le Départ

(1966, 90 min, Belgium, Jerzy Skolimowski) *Jean-Pierre Léaud, Catherine Duport*. Mark (Léaud) is a 19-year-old with a mania for Porsches and car racing. His determination to enter a race (and find a Porsche in the process) is undermined when he meets and falls in love with Michele. A funny, visually eclectic story of one's dreams confronting reality. (French with English subtitles) ★★★

Deranged

(1974, 88 min, US, Alan Ormsby & Bob Clark) *Roberts Blossom, Cosette Lee*. Based on the real-life activities of Wisconsin necrophile/murderer Ed Gein, *Deranged* stars Blossom as "the butcher of Woodside," a mother-obsessed weirdo who digs up his mom, stuffs her and soon begins to kill other women to keep her company. Shocking, graphic, and at times semihumorous, this unusual release is truly a "you've got to see it to believe it," but is recommended only for horror fans with a strong stomach. ★★

Le Dernier Combat (The Last Battle)

(1983, 93 min, France, Luc Besson) *Pierre Jolivet, Jean Bouise, Jean Reno, Fritz Wepper*. Besson makes an impressive directorial debut with this offbeat, black-and-white sci-fi adventure set in a postnuclear world where the few surviving men battle each other over territory and the last remaining women on Earth. Though Besson's film, which has no dialogue, follows the conventions of the postapocalyptic genre, his visuals are striking and he creates a disturbing sense of atmosphere. ★★★ DVD Letterbox: $29.99

Dersu Uzala

(1975, 160 min, Japan/USSR, Akira Kurosawa) *Yuri Solomin, Maxim Munzuk*. Kurosawa's Oscar-winning epic, a magnificent and sweeping production, explores the tremendous bond between an early 20th-century Russian explorer and his faithful guide Dersu.

Kurosawa's immense visual artistry vividly captures nature's beauty and wrath. (Japanese with English subtitles) ★★★★ DVD: $29.99, VHS: $24.99

Desecration

(1999, 88 min, US, Dante Tomaselli) *Irma St. Paule, Christie Sanford, Danny Lopes*. Weird and dreamlike, the intriguing *Desecration* from first-time director Tomaselli is loaded with atmosphere and bizarre Catholic/mother imagery once the silly plot kicks in. A young ne'er-do-well at a Catholic school accidentally kills a nun — with his remote control airplane! That unintentionally funny scene out of the way, *Desecration* becomes a rather likable, guilt-trip nightmare that, at its best, recalls classic dream/horror films like *Phantasm*. Very uneven, very low-budget, and very goofy, one wishes *Desecration* were a little scarier, a bit more outrageous; but, all things considered, it's a nice surprise. ★★½ DVD: $9.99, VHS: $9.99

Desert Bloom

(1986, 103 min, US, Eugene Corr) *Jon Voight, Annabelle Gish, JoBeth Williams, Ellen Barkin*. This underrated, extremely well-acted drama is set in 1950s Nevada at the dawn of the A-Bomb testing. Gish offers a sincere performance as a young girl coming-of-age living with her mom (Wiliams) and troubled stepdad (Voight). Barkin is terrific as Gish's sympathetic, flamboyant aunt. ★★★½ DVD: $24.99

Desert Blue

(1999, 90 min, US, Morgan J. Freeman) *Christina Ricci, Brendan Sexton III, Casey Affleck, Kate Hudson, Sara Gilbert*. When a trucker spills a feared contaminant and dies, a small California town is quarantined. Blue (Sexton) is the son of the town's founder, and he falls in love with Skye (Hudson), a TV actress stranded in the town during an ill-timed visit. Meanwhile, Ely (Ricci), who likes to blow things up, and her boyfriend Peter (Affleck), have run-ins with the FBI. As tempers flare, secrets are revealed, and love blossoms in the desert, writer-director Freeman (*Hurricane Streets*) makes things compelling even when they get contrived. ★★½ DVD: $14.99

The Desert Fox

(1951, 88 min, US, Henry Hathaway) *James Mason, Cedric Hardwicke, Jessica Tandy*. A tour-de-force performance by Mason highlights this standout WWII war drama about Field Marshall Rommel and the Nazi general's defeat in the African campaign. ★★★½ DVD: $14.99, VHS: $9.99

Desert Hearts

(1985, 93 min, US, Donna Deitch) *Helen Shaver, Patrice Charbonneau, Audra Lindley, Gwen Welles, Alex McArthur*. Truly a landmark film in its positive and very realistic depiction of a love affair between two attractive and intelligent women, offering the viewer a human-scale, tender treatment of two women in love. A dude ranch in Reno, Nevada, in 1959 is the setting for the meeting of an uptight Columbia University professor awaiting her divorce and a free-spirited and openly gay sculptress who lives on the ranch. Shaver and Charbonneau both give warm, expansive performances. ★★★½ DVD: $19.99, VHS: $19.99

The Desert Rats

(1953, 88 min, US, Robert Wise) *Richard Burton, Robert Newton, James Mason*. Mason repeats his role from *The Desert Fox* as Field Marshal Rommel in this exciting WWII actioner. Set in North Africa,

D

Rommel wages a battle of wits with a British commander (Burton) in the Allied offensive at Tobruk. ★★★ DVD: $19.99, VHS: $9.99

Design for Living

(1933, 90 min, US, Ernst Lubitsch) *Miriam Hopkins, Fredric March, Gary Cooper, Edward Everett Horton.* A smart and very funny adaptation of Noël Coward's stage play, substantially rewritten for the screen by Ben Hecht. The story involves three struggling bohemian artists in 1930s Paris. Cooper is an artist, March is a writer, and the enchanting Hopkins is in love with both of them. Even though much of Coward's sexual innuendo has been removed, this is still enjoyable in part to the great lead performances and the director's deft "touch." Horton stands out as Hopkins' fussy cliché-spouting husband. ★★★½

Designing Woman

(1957, 118 min, US, Vincente Minnelli) *Gregory Peck, Lauren Bacall, Mickey Shaughnessy.* This pleasant romantic comedy is reminiscent of *Woman of the Year*. Sportswriter Peck and fashion designer Bacall fall in love and marry while visiting California. Once back in their native New York, however, the honeymoon is over as the mismatched couple must contend with each other's crazy friends, jealous former partners and big city thugs. It's an engaging romp brightened by two star performances, but lacks the depth of the Spencer Tracy-Katharine Hepburn comedies it imitates. The film features (probably) the first choreographed kickboxing scene — by a fey dancer, no less. ★★★ DVD Letterbox: $19.99, VHS: $14.99

Desire

(1993, 108 min, Canada/France/West Germany, Andrew Birkin) *Greta Scacchi, Vincent D'Onofrio, Claudine Auger.* With its gorgeous multicontinental locales, attractive cast, and the beginnings of a passionate "lost love"-type story, *Desire* starts off with a romantic bang, but slowly peters out into just another repetitive romp in the proverbial sand. Scacchi plays the daughter of European intellectuals who spend their holidays in the Scottish countryside. One summer Scacchi experiences a sexual awakening with farmer/fisherman D'Onofrio. Their subsequent brief encounters haunt Scacchi through her marriage, divorce and move to America. ★★ VHS: $89.99

Desire and Hell at Sunset Motel

(1992, 87 min, US, Alien Castle) *Sherilyn Fenn, Whip Hubley, Paul Bartel, David Johansen, David Hewlett.* A bickering young couple (Fenn, Hubley) takes a room in a moderately sleazy motel in sunbaked Southern California in 1958. Their contemptuous combat is punctuated with periods of blackout, flashbacks (flashforwards?), illicit and would-be lovers, a peeping-tom motel manager and a disappearing body in the pool. You won't know who's loyal to whom until the very end. An intriguing look at the dark side of Ozzie and Harriet America. Director Castle also wrote the satisfyingly convoluted script. ★★½ VHS: $19.99

Desire under the Elms

(1958, 111 min, US, Delbert Mann) *Anthony Perkins, Sophia Loren, Burl Ives.* A curiously uneven but seductive adaptation of Eugene O'Neill's drama. Set in mid-19th-century New England, the film stars Perkins as the son of farmer Ives. He begins an affair with his stepmother (the miscast but alluring Loren). ★★½ VHS: $19.99

Desiree

(1954, 110 min, US, Henry Koster) *Marlon Brando, Jean Simmons, Merle Oberon, Michael Rennie.* A rather muddled costume drama chronicling the love affair between young officer Napoleon and his mistress Desiree. More attention was paid to sets and costumes than historical accuracy, and the film suffers for it. Brando is an animated Napoleon, Simmons is a lovely Desiree, and Oberon is quite stunning as Josephine, but even these talents can't help salvage this production from mediocrity. ★★ VHS: $19.99

Desk Set

(1957, 103 min, US, Walter Lang) *Katharine Hepburn, Spencer Tracy, Joan Blondell, Gig Young.* Tracy and Hepburn, in their eighth film together, are both splendid in this spirited version of the Broadway hit. Kate runs the research department of a TV network; Spence is the efficiency expert whose computer is about to replace her and her staff. And though they're initially at odds, romance ensues. Blondell is particularly snappy in support. ★★★½ DVD Letterbox: $14.99, VHS: $14.99

Desolation Angels

(1995, 90 min, US, Tim McCann) *Michael Rodrick, Peter Bassett, Jennifer Thomas, Quentin Crisp.* It seems nearly every independent film released these days falls into one of two camps — the touchy-feely twentysomething relationship movie, or the gritty, cynical "this-is-reality" cinema verité. *Desolation Angels*, detailing a working-class man's pursuit of vengeance for the alleged rape of his girlfriend, falls into the latter category. With its constant handheld camerawork, real locations and unpleasant situations, the film aims for harsh realism, and succeeds much of the time. But the two male leads are thinly drawn and uninteresting, and the supporting characters are stock; only Thomas gives a performance of merit. ★★½ DVD: $9.99, VHS: $9.99

Despair

(1978, 119 min, Germany, Rainer Werner Fassbinder) *Dirk Bogarde, Andrea Ferreol, Volker Spengler.* This critically maligned psychological drama, based on Tom Stoppard's adaptation of a Vladimir Nabokov novel, is an interesting, even riveting but ultimately muddled puzzle. Bogarde stars as Russian émigré Hermann Hermann, a 1930s chocolate manufacturer who attempts to elude the Nazis by exchanging identities with a working-class double. The French title, *The Mistake*, might better describe Hermann's unbalanced schizoid state of mind when he concocts a plan of murdering his "double," collecting the insurance and then fleeing to Switzerland using the dead man's identity papers. (Filmed in English) ★★½

Desperado

(1995, 106 min, US, Robert Rodriguez) *Antonio Banderas, Salma Hayek, Joaquim de Almeida, Cheech Marin, Steve Buscemi, Quentin Tarantino.* Sophmore director Rodriguez returns to the scene of the crime with this occasionally dazzling sequel to his *El Mariachi*. Rodriguez has all the right elements in place: sexy Banderas; a strikingly beautiful, strong female lead in Hayek; and a budget for enough pyrotechnics to blow up an entire city block. Sadly, however, *Desperado*, though flawlessly filmed and edited, fails to capture the good-humored slapstick zaniness of its predecessor and commits the sin of taking itself too seriously. Following a wonderfully moody setup in which Buscemi tells some tall tales in a sleazy Mexican bar, Banderas breezes into town seeking vengeance. The ensuing gun battles will stand up proudly against the best of John Woo for their outstanding choreography and bubblegum hilarity. But Rodriguez blows all his ammunition in the first 40 minutes and the remaining hour sees the action become increasingly sporadic and inane. ★★½ DVD Letterbox Superbit Edition: $27.99, DVD: $19.99, VHS: $9.99

Desperate

(1947, 74 min, US, Anthony Mann) *Steve Brodie, Audrey Long, Raymond Burr.* Refusing to take the rap for a fur heist he was conned into, honest ex-vet Brodie is forced to flee from both the police as well as the thug ringleader (the unsettlingly villainous Burr). His life on the lam is fraught with danger for him and his pregnant wife until he decides to fight back. A taut and engrossing low-budget film noir. ★★★

Desperate Characters

(1971, 88 min, US, Frank D. Gilroy) *Shirley MacLaine, Kenneth Mars, Gerald S. O'Loughlin, Sada Thompson.* As seen through the eyes of the characters of this edgy drama, New York City seems to be a breeding ground of lives of quiet desperation. Addressing burgeoning themes whose topicality has not faded, Gilroy's adaptation of Paula Fox's novel is a moody character study that taps into the white fears of urban living in the early 1970s. The story follows the tedium that is the life of married couple MacLaine and Mars as they eke out a daily existence. That the film is never tedious is as much a credit to director Gilroy's deft touch as it is to the two excellent performances by MacLaine and Mars. ★★★

The Desperate Hours

(1955, 112 min, US, William Wyler) *Humphrey Bogart, Fredric March, Martha Scott, Arthur Kennedy, Gig Young.* A suburban nightmare movie that predates *Blue Velvet*. Bogart is an ex-con who holds a perfect Eisenhower-era family (suit-and-tie dad, doting mom, attractive daughter and precocious young son) hostage in their own home. March is the strong-willed father, afraid for his family's safety, who wages a battle of wits and guts with Bogey. (Remade in 1990) ★★★½ DVD: $14.99, VHS: $14.99

The Desperate Hours

(1990, 105 min, US, Michael Cimino) *Mickey Rourke, Anthony Hopkins, Lindsay Crouse, Mimi Rogers, Kelly Lynch.* A disappointing remake of the 1955 Humphrey Bogart thriller. Rourke stars as a psychotic who, with the help of his laywer, busts out of jail. They hide out in the house of a recently separated couple (Hopkins, Rogers). Crouse is a tough-talking FBI agent hot on Rourke's tail. Cimino fails to deliver on what could have been a taut little thriller, choosing unwisely to "open" the film up; but he does manage to keep the suspense high and deliver some jarring moments. ★★ DVD Letterbox: $14.99

Desperate Journey

(1942, 107 min, US, Raoul Walsh) *Errol Flynn, Raymond Massey, Ronald Reagan, Alan Hale.* A rather exciting war adventure that mixes suspense, comedy and patriotism. Flynn plays an Australian commander who leads a group of Allied airmen (including wise-cracking Reagan) on a bombing mission in Germany. When they're shot down over enemy territory, he leads them on a perilous journey across Germany — in-between acts of sabotage and imprisonment — to England and freedom. Hale provides the comic relief, and Massey is a relentless Nazi officer on their trail. ★★★ VHS: $19.99

Desperate Living

(1977, 90 min, US, John Waters) *Mink Stole, Edith Massey.* A motion picture malignancy which "spread like cancer in Waters' brain." Stole stars as a society dame who kills her hubby and goes on the lam with her 400-pound black maid Grizelda. They find refuge in Mortville, a haven for perverts, murderers and worse, ruled over by porcine despot Queen Carlotta (Massey). A high-volume, determinedly offensive camp comedy. ★★★ VHS: $19.99

Desperate Measures

(1997, 100 min, US, Barbet Schroeder) *Michael Keaton, Andy Garcia, Brian Cox, Marcia Gay Harden.* Utterly preposterous suspense yarn with Keaton as an imprisoned psycho-killer who just happens to be the sole match for a bone marrow transplant that will save the life of a cop's (Garcia) 10-year-old son. During the operation, Keaton stages a daring breakout, and the rest of the film is basically a cat-and-mouse chase throughout a hospital. In spite of a couple well-staged scenes, the thrills are canned and the one-liners flat. Keaton's taunting genius is so obviously a reflection of Hannibal Lecter that the film strains credibility from the outset. ★½ DVD: $9.99, VHS: $9.99

Desperate Remedies

(1993, 92 min, New Zealand, Peter Wells & Stewart Main) *Jennifer Ward-Lealand, Cliff Curtis, Kevin Smith.* Campy to an outrageously shameless fault, this enjoyable and visually explosive costume romp is infused with more than its fair share of hyperventilating passions, luscious bosom-popping women and seductively thick-lipped men yearning for fulfillment. All this presented in blinding colors and with a convoluted plot that seems to have combined a dozen Harlequin romance novels. Set in Hope, a rugged 19th-century New Zealand pioneer seaport, the story revolves around the efforts of Doretha (Ward-Lealand), a strong-willed rich girl, and a sneering fop, Fraser (Curtis), to set up her pregnant opium-and-love-addicted sister Anna with the newly arrived but befuddled hunk Lawrence (Smith). A delightful romp that should have all howling with laughter. ★★★ VHS: $7.99

Desperately Seeking Susan

(1985, 104 min, US, Susan Seidelman) *Rosanna Arquette, Madonna, Aidan Quinn, Laurie Metcalf, Steven Wright, Ann Magnuson, John Turturro.* This hip comic adventure stars Arquette as a bored New Jersey housewife thrust into the heart of Greenwich Village bohemianism by a konk on the head. Madonna made her feature film debut as Susan, the free spirit whose life Arquette follows through the personals in *The Village Voice*. ★★★ DVD: $19.99

Destination Tokyo

(1943, 135 min, US, Delmer Daves) *Cary Grant, John Garfield, Alan Hale, Dane Clark.* Grant heads a good cast in this taut WWII submarine tale about the crew whose invasion of mainland Japan laid the groundwork for the aerial strike of Tokyo (for that story, see *Thirty Seconds over Tokyo*). Though the characters are pure 1940s caricatures of fighting men, the sincerity of the actors portraying them and the solid action and suspense more than compensate. ★★★½ DVD: $19.99

Destiny (al Massir)

(1997, 135 min, Egypt, Youssef Chahine) *Nour el-Cherif, Laila Eloui, Mahmoud Hemeida.* When a disciple of Averroes (a 12th-century philosopher) is burned at the stake for heresy, his young son journeys to Andalusia to study with his father's mentor. There, the teenager becomes involved in romance, adventure, musical dance numbers, and a rip-roaring fight against an evil shiek. The exotic locales, frenzied plot and vibrant storytelling help make this a real discovery and treat. (Arabic with English subtitles) ★★★ VHS: $29.99

Destiny Turns on the Radio

(1995, 101 min, US, Jack Baran) *Dylan McDermott, Nancy Travis, James LeGros, James Belushi, Quentin Tarantino, Allen Garfield, Bobcat Goldthwaite, Richard Edson.* Julian (McDermott) breaks out of jail after three years to find out from his partner in crime Thoreau (LeGros) that the money from their bank job is gone and his girl (Travis) has taken up with another (Belushi). Reality is heightened by confluences of chance and predestination; forays into the supernatural can be initiated by filling up the pool, and maintaining a healthy respect for animistic spirits and 20th-century rituals. The cast is uniformly engaging, and Baran provides some witty directorial touches to the tragically hip script. ★★½ VHS: $9.99

Destry Rides Again

(1939, 94 min, US, George Marshall) *James Stewart, Marlene Dietrich, Brian Donlevy, Mischa Auer.* A gunslinger spoof — with a serious side — starring Stewart as a nonviolent sheriff who tames a Wild West town. There's plenty of action, lots of laughs and Dietrich, as a sexy saloon singer, even gets to sing a song or two. ★★★★ DVD: $14.99

Details of a Duel

(1989, 97 min, Argentina, Sergio Cabera) A teacher and a butcher leave home to go about their business of the day, including preparing for death. Contrary to their true nature, one must kill the other by midafternoon. Egged on by the clergy, the militia and the town's bureaucrats, the private conflict between the two men is soon escalated into a gladiatorial spectacle. Set in the Argentine Andes in the 1950s, this wry and subtle comedy mischievously exposes the machismo code of honor, a tradition that dictates a duel and possible death — all in the name of manly protocol. (Spanish with English subtitles) ★★★ VHS: $24.99

Detective

(1985, 95 min, France, Jean-Luc Godard) *Claude Brasseur, Nathalie Baye, Johnny Hallyday, Laurent Terzieff, Jean-Pierre Léaud, Julie Delpy.* Another one of Godard's difficult films, *Detective* has all of the hallmarks of the famed French New Wave director's later works: repetitive images, intermittent music and sound, and inscrutable scenes depicting the relationships between art, sex, death and culture. While the twin plotlines have something to do with an unsolved murder, and a couple's attempt to recover money owed to them by a boxing manager, the film is really about stylistic excess and the creation of desire. Godard constantly toys with the audience, occasionally filling the frame with static shots that are nice to look at, but ultimately meaningless. It's a relief when the final shootout finally takes place, because it provides the only real action in this otherwise inert film. (French with English subtitles) ★★½

The Detective

(1954, 91 min, GB, Robert Hamer) *Alec Guinness, Peter Finch, Joan Greenwood, Cecil Parker.* A sterling adaptation of the G.K. Chesterton novel. Guinness is in masterful form in this lively comedy-thriller as the priest-turned-sleuth on the trail of stolen religious artifacts. (aka: *Father Brown*) ★★★ VHS: $19.99

The Detective

(1968, 114 min, US, Gordon Douglas) *Frank Sinatra, James Inman, Robert Duvall.* Frank plays a jaded New York City cop searching for a killer in this gritty actioner set for the most part in the city's nefarious homosexual haunts. A wealthy gay man has been found brutally murdered, and Frank and his homophobic partner comb the gay bars and cruising areas looking for the killer. Wrongly accused suspects, police cover-up, influential closet cases exposed and lots of foot work follow. ★★★

Deterrence

(2000, 104 min, US, Rod Lurie) *Kevin Pollak, Timothy Hutton, Sheryl Lee Ralph, Sean Astin.* Former *L.A. Magazine* film critic Lurie makes a promising directorial debut with this thinking person's thriller that's sort of a cross between *Miracle Mile* and *Fail-Safe*. During a severe snowstorm, the U.S. President (Pollak), a couple of his advisors and some locals are stranded at a roadside diner in a small

Marlene Dietrich (c.) in *Destry Rides Again*

Colorado mountain town. While there, the president becomes involved in a showdown with the Iraqi government, a confrontation that could lead to global nuclear war. A one-setting piece, the film is rarely claustrophobic, and the ensemble is effective in giving a for-the-most-part actionless story the impression of action. ★★½ DVD: $29.99, VHS: $14.99

Detour

(1945, 68 min, US, Edgar C. Ulmer) *Tom Neal, Ann Savage.* Made for almost nothing in only five days by a small-time studio, this film noir classic probes the plight of an "innocent" man trapped in circumstances beyond his control. While hitchhiking across the U.S. to meet his girlfriend in Los Angeles, a man is accused of murder by a tough-talking tomato, who threatens to tell the police if he does not follow her every demand. Entrapped by this increasingly dangerous psychopath, the man must plot his escape. Infused with snappy dialogue, fog-shrouded city streets and a wonderfully evil femme fatale, this dark drama will prove to be a delight for all noir fans. ★★★½ DVD: $24.99, VHS: $24.99

Detroit 9000

(1973, 106 min, US, Arthur Marks) *Alex Rocco, Hari Rhodes, Vonette McGee, Scatman Crothers.* This blaxploitation crime thriller is a moderately entertaining (if overlong) entry in the '70s nostalgic sweepstakes. Rocco plays the "white cop" on a major, racially charged case — masked men rob the wealthy (mostly African-American) crowd at a fundraiser for a Detroit politician. He's paired with a black cop (Rhodes) to help smooth things over, and the duo chase suspects, have some shootouts, and wear stylin' clothes. Though the story is uneven, there's some funky music, Rocco's solid turn, and a few decent action scenes. It can be pretty nifty. ★★½ DVD: $9.99, VHS: $9.99

Detroit Rock City

(1999, 95 min, US, Adam Rifkin) *Edward Furlong, Natasha Lyonne, Sam Huntington, James DeBello.* From the director of *The Chase* comes another rambunctious party suited for late-night basic cable broadcast. Four high school friends head to the Motor City for a Kiss concert in 1978. When they lose their tickets, they go about scoring new ones. *Detroit Rock City* is more about the fans than the band (these over-the-hill musicians appearing as themselves are no more than a cameo), and the humor is gross and silly. The film does have a nice '70s vibe to it, and the credit sequence is kinda cool. ★★ DVD Platinum Series: $14.99

Deuce Bigalow: Male Gigolo

(1999, 88 min, US, Mike Mitchell) *Rob Schneider, William Forsythe, Eddie Griffin, Arija Bareikis, Oded Fehr, Jackie Titone.* There are some comics for whom it should be unlawful to star in their own films. Tom Arnold is one. Rob Schneider is another. The former "SNL" comedian actually has made a reputation for himself as a comic foil in supporting roles; but carrying an entire film is a whole other matter. Case in point is this horrid little comedy with Schneider as a fish-out-of-water fish-tank cleaner who stumbles into male prostitution — and succeeds! The jokes are tired, the story ridiculous, and the dumb-dumber schtick fails to produce even the mildest of groans. ★ DVD: $14.99, VHS: $9.99

Devi

(1960, 96 min, India, Satyajit Ray) *Chhabi Biswas, Sharmilla Tagore, Soumitra Chatterjee.* Ray's dreamily sensual film is about a Bengalese girl of astounding beauty who is declared to be a reincarna-tion of a goddess by her wealthy father-in-law. When he starts a cult of worship in her honor, she gradually becomes convinced of her own divinity. This ironic examination of India's decadent upper classes was banned from export until the intercession of Nehru. (Bengali with English subtitles) ★★★ VHS: $24.99

The Devil and Daniel Webster

(1941, 109 min, US, William Dieterle) *Edward Arnold, Walter Huston, James Craig, Simone Simon.* Terrific screen version of Stephen Vincent Benet's novel with Arnold and Huston giving terrific performances as Daniel Webster and Mr. Scratch (aka the Devil), respectively. The famous statesman defends a farmer who has sold his soul. The case is prosecuted by Scratch and the jurors are the cursed from Hell. (aka: *All That Money Can Buy*) ★★★½ DVD Criterion Collection: $39.99, VHS: $24.99

The Devil and Max Devlin

(1981, 95 min, US, Steven Hillard Stern) *Elliott Gould, Bill Cosby.* After getting pummeled by a bus, the deceased Max Devlin (Gould) strikes a deal with the Devil (Cosby) to have his life restored if he can convince three people to sell their souls. An unexciting execution of a timeworn premise. ★★ DVD: $24.99

The Devil and Miss Jones

(1941, 92 min, US, Sam Wood) *Charles Coburn, Jean Arthur, Robert Cummings, Edmund Gwenn.* Captivating Capra-esque comedy about a millionaire (Coburn) who goes undercover at his own department store to find out what his disgruntled employees are complaining about. The strength of Norman Krasna's script and the charm of stars Arthur, Cummings and Coburn transcend the clichés and make for a most enjoyable romp. ★★★

The Devil Bat

(1941, 69 min, US, Jean Yarbrough) *Bela Lugosi, Dave O'Brien.* Lugosi charges up his giant bats with electricity and then sics them on people wearing his specially formulated cologne, only to be done in by a father of three wearing too much Old Spice. (Sequel: *The Devil Bat's Daughter*) ★★½ VHS: $12.99

The Devil-Doll

(1936, 79 min, US, Tod Browning) *Lionel Barrymore, Maureen O'Sullivan.* Barrymore has a field day in this fun horror film as a scientist who shrinks humans to the size of dolls to get even with his enemies. ★★★ VHS: $19.99

Devil Girl from Mars

(1954, 77 min, GB, David MacDonald) *Patricia Laffan, Hugh McDermott.* A Scottish inn and its inhabitants are terrorized by a beautiful but ruthless Martian (Laffan) in black leather. One of the first films with aliens seeking Earthlings for breeding stock. ★★ DVD: $14.99, VHS: $14.99

Devil in a Blue Dress

(1995, 102 min, US, Carl Franklin) *Denzel Washington, Tom Sizemore, Jennifer Beals, Don Cheadle.* Washington, that master of subtle characterization, has created another persona rooted in a specific time and place with striking authenticity. Washington is Easy Rawlins (the character in Walter Mosley's books), a WWII vet whose recent unemployment coupled with mortgage payments induces him to agree to DeWitt Albright's (Sizemore) request to locate Daphne Money (Beals). She's an enigmatic beauty publicly tied to a local politico, and she's recently dropped out of sight. Soon Rawlins finds that he's fallen down the rabbit hole. He calls on an old acquaintance for support, Cheadle in a hyperkinetic turn as Mouse, who shoots first and rarely asks questions. Director Franklin has delivered a fitting follow-up to *One False Move*, meticulously re-creating late 1940s Los Angeles and bathing it in the golden glow of reminiscence. ★★★½ DVD: $14.99

Devil in the Flesh
(Le Diable au Corps)

(1947, 110 min, France, Claude Autant-Lara) *Gerard Philipe, Micheline Presle.* A beautifully acted and exquisitely filmed tale of the passionate and tragic involvement between a young student and a mature married woman set during World War I. While relatively calm by today's jaded standards, this shocking love story caused quite a controversy when it was first released. (Remade in 1987) ★★★½ VHS: $34.99

Devil in the Flesh

(1987, 110 min, France/Italy, Marco Bellocchio) *Maruschke Detmers, Federio Pitzalis.* Bellocchio's notorious updating of the classic Maurice Radiquet novel tells the story of a sizzling love triangle between an imprisoned terrorist, his sultry girlfriend, and a teenage boy she lures right from the schoolyard. The themes of political intrigue, betrayal and madness take a back seat to the erotic couplings and explicit oral sex scenes between the sensuous young woman (Detmers), and her handsome enamored young victim (Pitzalis). (Italian with English subtitles) ★★★

The Devil Is a Woman

(1935, 83 min, US, Josef von Sternberg) *Marlene Dietrich, Cesar Romero, Lionel Atwill, Edward Everett Horton.* This breathtaker's history is marked by legend: The Franco government demanded that every copy be destroyed lest diplomatic ties be strained. Long thought lost, Dietrich herself supplied a copy for a 1960s retrospective. Outdoing himself with costumes and sets, von Sternberg's rich tale, set during Carnival in Seville, Spain, is a story of love's dark side. An older man (Atwill) recounts his humiliation at the hands of a siren (Dietrich), and warns his young friend (Romero) vainly to save himself from wreckage. Dietrich's beauty and humor and the director's eye for contrast inspire a reverence akin to that which one feels in a great cathedral. All of the Dietrich/von Sternberg collaborations were high art; this is one of the highest. ★★★½ VHS: $14.99

The Devil, Probably

(1977, 95 min, France, Robert Bresson) *Antoine Monnier, Tina Irissari, Henri de Maublanc, Laetitia Carcano.* In a world dying from human pollution, young, angelic Charles (Monnier) finds no solace in radical politics, religion, sex, psychology or the arts. Unanchored, he vacilates between two women who love him: Edwige (Carcano), who waits for him stoically, and Alberte (Irissari), who leaves her lover Michel (de Maublanc) to care for the increasingly alienated Charles. His death wish is a microcosm of the planet's unraveling, and the combined support and caring of his friends and lovers have no impact on his downward spiral. Young, attractive, intelligent and loved, why is Charles suicidal? But then, why are we killing ourselves as a species? Bresson's polemic on the human penchant for self-destruction and inability to commit is kaleidoscopic, visionary; at once frenetic and stilted, energized and stolid, blistering and melancholy. (French with English subtitles) ★★★½ VHS: $19.99

Devil's Advocate

(1997, 140 min, US, Taylor Hackford) *Al Pacino, Keanu Reeves, Charlize Theron, Judith Ivey, Craig T. Nelson, Jeffrey Jones, Connie Nielsen, Tamara Tunie, Heather Matarazzo, Leo Burmester, Delroy Lindo.* Pure pulp fiction here, with Pacino in rabid, scene-chewing mode as Lucifer himself. In what amounts to Grisham's *The Firm* on a theological scale, a young hotshot lawyer (Reeves) is seduced by the allure of a high-powered New York law firm and discovers that the price for selling out is his soul. This crackerjack thriller is given a boost not only from Pacino's deliciously over-the-top histrionics, but from Hackford's clever direction, a slick production design, some eye-popping special effects, and an effectively creepy musical score. It also helps that just beneath the high-gloss surface, nobody is taking this preposterous fluff too seriously. ★★★ DVD Letterbox: $19.99, VHS: $9.99, VHS Letterbox: $14.99

The Devil's Backbone

(2001, 106 min, Spain, Guillermo del Toro) *Fernando Tielve, Marisa Paredes, Federico Luppi, Eduardo Noriega.* It could be the surface of the moon, except for the rusted, dilapidated vehicle heading toward the decrepit, ramshackle building looming in the middle of nowhere. Ten-year-old Carlos doesn't know that his stay at this forlorn orphanage is indefinite. The inhabitants of this questionable refuge are all collateral damage of the Spanish Civil War outside, whose presence is manifested by the unexploded aerial bomb imbedded in the middle of the courtyard. Carlos becomes aware of the conflicted interrelations of the adults (as children always do) as he becomes aware of a restless spirit, "the one who sighs," permeating the environs. Director Del Toro creates an effectively eerie atmosphere, drawing the audience into this isolated community of souls who seem to teeter on the brink of the spirit world. A secret is revealed and a death avenged, and poverty and disease are discovered to be without doubt the devil's backbone. (Spanish with English subtitles) ★★★½ DVD Letterbox: $29.99, VHS Subtitled: $14.99

The Devil's Disciple

(1959, 83 min, US, Guy Hamilton) *Burt Lancaster, Kirk Douglas, Laurence Olivier, Harry Andrews, Janette Scott, George Rose.* Lancaster, Douglas and Olivier bring splendor to the words of George Bernard Shaw in this glorious Revolutionary tale based on Shaw's play. Lancaster plays a small-town pastor, indifferent to the war around him, who gets a loud wake-up call to arms when he crosses paths with an American rebel (Douglas) and British General Burgoyne (Olivier). There's wit and vitality to Shaw's clever dialogue: no boring discourse here. The performances of the three actors befit their legendary stature. ★★★½

The Devil's Eye

(1960, 90 min, Sweden, Ingmar Bergman) *Bibi Andersson, Gunnar Björnstrand.* One of Bergman's few comedies, this captivating adaptation of G. B. Shaw's "Don Juan in Hell" begins with the old Irish proverb, which says, "A maid's chastity is a sty in the eye of the Devil." We follow the determined efforts of Satan who, on a promise of reduced time in Hell, sends Don Juan to earth in order to rob the virginity of bride-to-be Andersson. Will the Devil's eye problem clear up, or will human goodness triumph? (Swedish with English subtitles) ★★★ VHS: $29.99

Al Pacino raises hell in *Devil's Advocate*

The Devil's Own

(1997, 110 min, US, Alan J. Pakula) *Harrison Ford, Brad Pitt, Margaret Colin, Ruben Blades, Treat Williams, George Hearn.* The teaming of Ford and Pitt works surprisingly well to create an absorbing if somber drama that balances social and moral issues, good action sequences, and an affecting tale of a surrogate father and son. Showing few signs of its high-profile on-set difficulties, *The Devil's Own* casts Pitt as an IRA commander whose latest battle with the British forces him into hiding in America. He is placed with unsuspecting New York cop Ford, and while playing the part of the gracious visitor he is actually preparing a return to Ireland with a boatload of missiles. The strong performances by Ford and Pitt firmly establish their bond of friendship and the sting of its eventual betrayal. Its screenplay sometimes looks patchy (it was often written daily), but the overall finished product is sleek and engrossing. ★★★ DVD: $14.99, VHS: $9.99

Devil's Playground

(2002, 72 min, US, Lucy Walker) This absorbing documentary traces the paths of four Amish teenagers during their period of "rumspringa" — translated literally as "running around," it's the time following an Amish teen's 16th birthday when s/he is set loose into English society to explore all the material trappings and personal freedoms inherently forbidden within the constrictions of the Mennonite lifestyle. "Rumspringa" concludes when that young adult vows a lifetime commitment to the Amish church and is thenceforth baptized. These culture-shocked kids are flung into a strange new world in which their sturdy religious upbringings are tested against the intoxicating — and unchecked — lures of designer clothing, fast cars, video games, loud music, booze, cigarettes and drugs. The choices these unprepared teens make may surprise, and the mistakes that trip them up along the way provide for a compelling peek inside a little-seen culture. ★★★ DVD: $24.99, VHS: $59.99

The Devil's Wanton

(1949, 78 min, Sweden, Ingmar Bergman) *Doris Svedlund, Eva Henning.* Bergman's sober interpretation of hell on earth, told from the point of view of a girl trying to find happiness with a man who was deserted by his wife after her lover had their baby killed. This arty drama is filled with many of the master's signatures and cinematic techniques. (Swedish with English subtitles) ★★½

The Devils

(1971, 109 min, GB, Ken Russell) *Oliver Reed, Vanessa Redgrave, Dudley Sutton, Gemma Jones, Max Adrian.* Reed is the martyred cleric and Redgrave is the sexually repressed nun in Russell's gruesome and graphic account of witchcraft hysteria in the 17th century. Both Reed and Redgrave are superb in this frenzied adaptation of Aldous Huxley's book "The Devils of Loudon." Filmed with Russell's usual sobriety and reserve. ★★★½ VHS: $19.99

The Devils Playground

(1976, 105 min, Australia, Fred Schepisi) *Arthur Dignam, Nick Tate, Simon Burke.* This compelling drama, set in a boys' seminary, probes the torment of young students and their instructors as they grapple with sexual yearning and the harsh codes of religious discipline. The story concerns one particular boy's struggle to deal with both his divine calling and his pent-up sexual needs. A sometimes funny, always hard-hitting indictment of repression. ★★★ DVD: $29.99, VHS: $29.99

Diabolically Yours

(1967, 94 min, France, Julien Duvivier) *Alain Delon, Senta Berger.* Rivaling Brigitte Bardot for the title for the greatest number of forgettable, grade-B French films, dashing Delon gives his all in this psycho thriller about a man's desperate search for his sanity. After a near-fatal car accident that left him in a coma for three weeks, Delon awakens to find that his memory is completely lost. Paranoia overwhelms him when he begins to suspect that the woman who claims to be his loving wife, the doctor who is supposed to be his best friend and the relatives who visit are merely staging an elaborate charade in some kind of secret conspiracy to drive him crazy. ★★½ VHS: $59.99

Diabolique

(1954, 107 min, France, Henri-Georges Clouzot) *Simone Signoret, Vera Clouzot, Paul Meurisse, Michel Serrault.* This white-knuckled thriller is set in a shabby boys' school and stars Signoret as a battered mistress who plots a murder with her lover's wife (Clouzot). In grisly fashion, they drug the husband, drown him in the tub and dump the corpse in a pool. But mysteriously, the body disappears and evidence of their crime begins to haunt them. The heart-stopping climax and twist ending will have you on the edge of your seat. (American remake made in 1996) (French with English subtitles) ★★★★ DVD Criterion Collection: $29.99, VHS: $29.99

Diabolique

(1996, 105 min, US, Jeremiah C. Chechik) *Sharon Stone, Isabelle Adjani, Chazz Palminteri, Kathy Bates, Spalding Gray, Shirley Knight.* An inferior,

Grace Kelly caught unaware in
Dial M for Murder

lifeless remake of the 1954 classic French thriller. Stone and Adjani are teachers at a boarding school who plot and kill Adjani's tyrannical husband (Palminteri), the school's headmaster. They get away with it, but when the body turns up missing, it appears he may not be dead. Bates adds a little life as a detective investigating the disappearance. Not even a '90s bent on the two women's sexual relationship makes this of interest. ★½ DVD: $19.99, VHS: $19.99

Dial M for Murder
(1954, 105 min, US, Alfred Hitchcock) *Grace Kelly, Ray Milland, Robert Cummings, John Williams.* Kelly is the rich and beautiful wife of the diabolical Milland. He hires a hit man to bump her off, but she kills the would-be assassin and faces the electric chair. In his inimitable fashion, Hitchcock forces the culprit husband to reveal his guilt. (Originally filmed in 3-D) (Remade as: *A Perfect Murder*) ★★★

Diamonds Are Forever
(1971, 119 min, GB, Guy Hamilton) *Sean Connery, Jill St. John, Charles Gray, Jimmy Dean.* Connery returns for his next-to-last appearance as 007. His mission: to track down a diamond smuggler; which, of course, requires a whirlwind, worldwide adventure through Amsterdam, Los Angeles and Las Vegas. Lots of fun. (Sequel: *Live and Let Die*) ★★★

Diary of a Chambermaid
(1946, 86 min, US, Jean Renoir) *Paulette Goddard, Burgess Meredith, Judith Anderson, Hurd Hatfield.* This bewitching but distinctively odd adaptation of the Octave Mirbeau novel was one of Renoir's last films made during his sojourn in Hollywood during the war. Coproduced and scripted by Meredith, this romantic comedy stars Goddard as the keyhole-peeping, gold-digging chambermaid whose arrival at a provincial mansion brings havoc to its decadent inhabitants. The film features Meredith as an eccentric, flower-eating neighbor, and Anderson as the matriarch of the household who rules with an iron fist. Though not as bitterly savage as the Luis Buñel version, Renoir's film is still sharp in its satire of the upper classes. ★★½

Diary of a Chambermaid
(1964, 79 min, France, Luis Buñuel) *Jeanne Moreau, Michel Piccoli, Georges Geret.* Moreau stars as a reserved and well-cultured woman from Paris who begins to work for an upper-class family

in the Provinces in 1939. The new maid soon discovers that the family is a thoroughly decadent group of characters as she finds herself enmeshed in the midst of a hotbed of hypocrisy and perversion. Their seemingly innocuous habits, like the grandfather's foot fetish, prove to be not-so-harmless when a young girl is found murdered and Moreau becomes obsessed with exposing the killer. Buñuel's sly comic touches are in evidence, but the film retains a biting edge as he equates the gentry's oppression with the rise of fascism. (French with English subtitles) ★★★½ DVD Letterbox Criterion Collection: $29.99, VHS Letterbox: $29.99

Diary of a Country Priest
(1950, 120 min, France, Robert Bresson) *Claude Layou, Jean Riveyre.* Bresson's uniquely austere style of filmmaking is beautifully rendered in this somber work on the life and death of a young priest and his unsuccessful attempts to minister his first parish. (French with English subtitles) ★★★½ DVD: $39.99, VHS: $24.99

Diary of a Hitman
(1991, 90 min, US, Roy London) *Forest Whitaker, Sherilyn Fenn, James Belushi, Seymour Cassel.* Though miscast, Whitaker makes a good showing as a hit man who studiously saves the earnings from his murderous profession for a down payment on his co-op apartment. Fenn is a drug-addicted wannabe cheerleader who stands in Whitaker's way for one last completed assignment. An intriguing premise executed with style, and it's fairly suspenseful. ★★★ VHS: $14.99

Diary of a Lost Girl
(1929, 100 min, Germany, G.W. Pabst) *Louise Brooks, Fritz Rasp.* The alluring and enigmatic Brooks stars in this parable of a woman's road to ruin. Brooks is a wronged innocent who is banished from respectability for having a baby out of wedlock. Forced to stay in a hellish house of correction, she escapes only to land in a brothel where she finds her ultimate redemption. (Silent with musical soundtrack) ★★★½ DVD: $29.99, VHS: $24.99

Diary of a Mad Housewife
(1970, 94 min, US, Frank Perry) *Carrie Snodgress, Richard Benjamin, Frank Langella.* A perceptive study of housewife Snodgress' psychological deterioration at the hands of social climbing, philandering husband Benjamin and charmingly egocentric writer Langella, with whom she has a brief, tempestuous affair. Superb performance by Snodgress and good support from Langella. ★★★

Diary of a Mad Old Man
(1987, 90 min, Belgium/France, Ralph Michael) *Derek De Lint, Ralph Michael, Beatie Edney.* This Ingmar Bergman-influenced drama is a tepid examination of an old man as he nears the end of his life. Marcel is a rich and self-absorbed businessman who forsakes the love of his devoted wife for a never-consummated sexual obsession with his son's attractive wife. The indignities of the aging process do not stop him from pursuing the young woman, even at the expense of his family and health. For a better look at an old man's reflection on his nearly completed life, watch *Wild Strawberries*. (Filmed in English) ★½

Diary of a Seducer
(1995, 95 min, France, Daniele Dubroux) *Chiara Mastroianni, Jean-Pierre Léaud, Melvil Poupaud.* *Diary of a Seducer* derives its plot from a magic book that forces its readers to fall in love with the

giver. While this story line has the potential for a *La Ronde*-type of farce, writer-director Dubroux shuns this approach and instead labors to feature bizarre characters and a dead body. These elements would have benefitted from a subversive touch á la Buñuel, but Dubroux opts for a too cool tone. When Claire (Marcello's daughter Chiara) is given the Kierkegaard book of the title by Gregoire (Poupaud), she becomes entranced by him. Meanwhile, various acquaintances, including her therapist, develop an interest in Claire. There are the inevitable misunderstandings, but there is no real tension between the characters or their predicaments. *Diary of a Seducer* is billed as a comic thriller, but it is neither funny nor thrilling. And what's more, it's not even seductive. (French with English subtitles) ★★ VHS: $79.99

The Diary of Anne Frank
(1959, 156 min, US, George Stevens) *Millie Perkins, Joseph Schildkraut, Shelley Winters, Ed Wynn, Richard Beymer, Lou Jacobi.* One of the most gripping and heartfelt stories to emerge from the Holocaust, this magnificent adaptation of the acclaimed play is based on the writings of Dutch teenager Anne Frank, whose diaries documenting years of hiding during WWII captured the hearts of millions around the world. Perkins deftly plays Anne, who hid with her family in the attic of an Amsterdam warehouse to elude the Nazis. A superior supporting cast includes Oscar winner Winters. ★★★★ DVD: $19.99, VHS: $14.99

Diary of Forbidden Dreams
(1972, 94 min, Italy, Roman Polanski) *Marcello Mastroianni, Sydne Rome.* Originally titled *What?*, this Polanski oddity is a ribald comedy about the sexual misadventures of an innocent but irresistible young woman. Her bizarre ordeal begins when she seeks shelter in an eccentric's mansion on the Italian Riviera. Her docile host turns lecherous tiger — but that only opens up a can of sexual worms as several other weird men descend for a bite. Funny and just a bit strange. ★★½

Dick
(1999, 92 min, US, Andrew Fleming) *Kirsten Dunst, Michelle Williams, Dan Hedaya, Will Ferrell, Bruce McCulloch, Teri Garr, Dave Foley, Jim Breuer, Harry Shearer, Saul Rubinek.* "Muckracking bastard journalists" Bob Woodward and Carl Bernstein won a Pulitzer Prize for breaking the Watergate scandal, relying heavily on a source named "Deep Throat." But who was this source? According to *Dick*, it was two 15-year-old girls who were in the wrong place at the right time. As directed by Fleming, *Dick* is given a light, even cute satirical touch that hits lots of easy targets without saying anything deep. Dunst and Williams, making a winning couple, witness the burglary at the hotel and later see paper shredding and even Dick's recording system (on which Williams leaves an 18½-minute love paean to him). Anyone familiar with the scandal will enjoy the references, but the jokes are predictable, until the film thuds to an ending with a labored *Dick* joke. ★★½ DVD: $19.99, VHS: $9.99

Dick Tracy
(1990, 104 min, US, Warren Beatty) *Warren Beatty, Al Pacino, Dustin Hoffman, Glenne Headly, Madonna, Charlie Korsmo, William Forsythe, Seymour Cassel, Charles Durning, Mandy Patinkin, Dick Van Dyke, Paul Sorvino, James Caan, Estelle Parsons.* Beatty's colorful adaptation of the Chester Gould comic strip is a dazzling display of costumery

and scenery. The performances in the film are, for the most part, splendid. Pacino's rendition of Tracy's arch-rival Big Boy Caprice is sensational. In the title role, Beatty delivers an appropriately heroic performance; Headly is charming as his girlfriend Tess Trueheart; and Madonna gets to sing a couple of breathy show tunes penned by the inimitable Stephen Sondheim, and all of her other attributes are used to perfection. ★★★ DVD: $14.99, VHS: $9.99

Die Another Day

(2002, 132 min, GB, Lee Tamahori) *Pierce Brosnan, Halle Berry, Toby Stephens, Judi Dench, Rosamund Pike, Rick Yune, John Cleese, Madonna, Will Yun Lee, Samantha Bond.* Let's see . . . extreme surfing, diamond smuggling, an invisible Aston Martin, a headquarters made of ice, a gigantic satellite weapon, an insomniac villain, a few sexy temptresses, and one martini — shaken, not stirred. Yes, James Bond is back for his 20th official film, in a coherently action-packed entry that recalls the grittiness of the Timothy Dalton films while sporting a better cast, including the born-to-be-Bond Brosnan. Berry is a welcome addition to the Bond Girl canon as Jinx, an independent American agent who attracts James even as she gets in his way. Yune is a memorable heavy, with good kung-fu moves and diamonds for acne. If there's a weakness here it's Madonna, who continues her remarkable losing streak with a rare trifecta: a terrible title song, irritating closing remix and stiff cameo performance. ★★★ DVD Letterbox 2-disc Special Edition: $14.99, DVD Pan & Scan Special Edition: $14.99, VHS Special Edition: $9.99

Die! Die! My Darling!

(1965, 97 min, GB, Silvio Narizzano) *Tallulah Bankhead, Stefanie Powers, Peter Vaughan, Donald Sutherland.* The legendary Bankhead stars in this campy *Baby Jane*-style thriller about a psychotic old woman who keeps her son's fiancée (Powers) hostage in her attic. Screenplay by Richard Matheson. (aka: *Fanatic*) ★★½

Die Hard

(1988, 132 min, US, John McTiernan) *Bruce Willis, Bonnie Bedelia, Alan Rickman, Alexander Godunov, Reginald Vel Johnson, Hart Bochner, William Atherton.* First-rate action thriller starring Willis as a tough New York City policeman whose L.A. vacation is cut short when he finds himself up against a group of terrorists — armed only with his wits — who have taken control of a 40-story office building, among whose hostages include his wife. The action scenes are extremely well directed and maximize suspense, and Willis' cynical cop is afforded some great one-liners as he battles the bad guys. (Followed by two sequels) ★★★½ DVD Letterbox 2-disc Special Edition: $26.99, VHS Special Edition: $9.99, VHS Letterbox: $12.99

Die Hard 2

(1990, 122 min, US, Renny Harlin) *Bruce Willis, Bonnie Bedelia, William Atherton, Franco Nero, John Amos, Reginald Vel Johnson, John Leguizamo, Robert Patrick.* Willis is back in this fast-paced pyrotechnic sequel. This time, he's at Dulles Airport in Washington, D.C., waiting for his wife (Bedelia) to land, when the place is taken over by a mercenary commando squad trying to hijack a Noriega-like dictator to safety. Not as tense, or as comprehensible, as the first film, but the large scale special effects and stunt work are amazing and the film packs a visceral jolt. ★★★ DVD Letterbox Five Star Collection: $29.99

Die Hard with a Vengeance

(1995, 112 min, US, John McTiernan) *Bruce Willis, Samuel L. Jackson, Jeremy Irons, Graham Greene, Colleen Camp.* Willis' N.Y.C. cop John McClane gets to play on his home turf in this action-packed if derivative third entry. McClane is called into a terrorist bombing case when the perp (Irons), called Simon, asks for him by name. The brother of one of McClane's victims, Simon's out for revenge by playing cat-and-mouse all over the city with our hapless hero, who is now partnered with a Harlem store owner (Jackson) to help track down the bomber. *With a Vengeance* features some great action sequences; but even in light of the likable pairing of Willis and Jackson, the film has less to offer than the first two. ★★½ DVD Letterbox Five Star Collection: $29.99

Different for Girls

(1996, 97 min, GB, Richard Spence) *Rupert Graves, Steven Mackintosh, Miriam Margolyes, Saskia Reeves, Charlotte Coleman.* An endearing, highly enjoyable and offbeat romantic transgender comedy. Paul (Graves) and Karl (Mackintosh) were childhood best friends. Separated after nearly 20 years, they meet up again in London. But things have changed a bit: Karl has undergone a sex change operation and is now called Kim. She is organized and genteel, with a career as a writer in a greeting card company. Paul has become a rebellious character, working as a motorcycle courier by day and a pub crawler at night. How they overcome society's prejudices and, more importantly, their own differences, is executed in a breezy, refreshingly warm fashion. ★★★ DVD: $14.99, VHS: $9.99

A Different Story

(1978, 108 min, US, Paul Aaron) *Perry King, Meg Foster, Valerie Curtin.* A gay man (King) and a lesbian (Foster) marry to prevent his deportation, and then fall in love, have kids and go straight — each surrendering his/her sexual identity. The film uses the gay subtext simply as a gimmick, dwelling little on their original sexual orientation and more on their affair. Curtin is shrill and offensive as Foster's former lover; some of the other characters are merely stereotypes, as well. Addressing the sexual politics, the film is questionable in the notion that queers can be cured with a good heterosexual fuck. Politics, aside, it's just not funny, ★½

Digging to China

(1998, 103 min, US, Timothy Hutton) *Kevin Bacon, Mary Stuart Masterson, Cathy Moriarty, Evan Rachel Wood.* Sentimental, without being cloying, *Digging to China* is the directorial debut by actor Hutton, who coaxes a wonderful lead performance from young Wood. Harriet, a loquacious 10-year-old who marches to the beat of a different drummer, lives in a North Carolina cabin lodge operated by her mother (Moriarty) and her older sister Gwen (Masterson). Constantly dreaming of escape, Harriet is given over to flights of fancy, and when she meets Ricky (Bacon), a mentally retarded man, she finds a coconspirator for her projects. However, fearing more than just a friendship, Gwen tries to keep them apart. The screenplay addresses the way love can overcome grief, though some of the drama feels forced. ★★½

Diggstown

(1992, 98 min, US, Michael Ritchie) *James Woods, Louis Gossett, Jr., Oliver Platt, Bruce Dern, Heather Graham.* Woods offers a sturdy performance in this familiar but likable Runyonesque comedy about a grifter par excellence, his semiretired partner (Gossett), and their screwball scheme to swindle an entire town. Though not as intricately plotted as *The Sting*, nor as stylish, the film offers good performances and some nice action sequences. ★★½ DVD Letterboxed: $14.99

Dim Sum: A Little Bit of Heart

(1984, 89 min, US, Wayne Wang) *Laureen Chew, Kim Chew, Victor Wong, Joan Chen.* Once again, director Wang reveals the communality of human experience through a sharply focused examination of a distinctive culture. The relationship between a Chinese-American mother and daughter is central to this warm observation of the familial bonds and cultural strengths of an Asian family in San Francisco. ★★★

Brosnan . . . Pierce Brosnan and Berry . . . Halle Berry in *Die Another Day*

Diner

(1982, 110 min, US, Barry Levinson) *Kevin Bacon, Steve Guttenberg, Daniel Stern, Mickey Rourke, Ellen Barkin, Timothy Daly, Paul Reiser, Michael Tucker.* A scintillating slice-of-life served with a sprinkling of '50s nostalgia and a robust helping of male camaraderie. Levinson has created one of the most charming and humorous documentations of the often awkward transition from youth to adulthood. Impeccable ensemble acting. ★★★★ DVD: $9.99, VHS: $14.99

Dinner at Eight

(1933, 111 min, US, George Cukor) *Lionel Barrymore, Billie Burke, John Barrymore, Marie Dressler, Wallace Beery, Jean Harlow, Edmund Lowe.* An all-star cast highlights this elegant Cukor classic based on George S. Kaufman and Edna Ferber's stage hit. Park Avenue shipping magnate Barrymore and his social-climbing wife Burke throw a dinner party for a visiting British lord. On the guest list are fading screen idol Barrymore (before his own decline); aging stage legend Dressler; and obnoxious financier Beery and his blowsy wife Harlow. How their lives and problems intertwine is the stuff that great moviemaking is made of. Dressler and Harlow steal the show. (Remade in 1996) ★★★★

The Dinner Game

(1999, 81 min, France, Francis Veber) *Thierry Lhermitte, Jacques Villeret, Francis Huster, Catherine Frot.* In this biting French comedy, a group of friends meet each week for a dinner party in which each tries to bring the most boring dinner guest. When Pierre thinks he has a winner in unsuspecting accountant François, the tables are soon turned on the unsuspecting Pierre as he can't get rid of François no matter how hard he tries. Hilarious jokes and sight gags punctuate this subversive gem. (French with English subtitles) ★★★½ DVD: $14.99, VHS: $9.99

Dinner Rush

(2002, 99 min, US, Bob Giraldi) *Danny Aiello, Edoardo Ballerini, Vivian Wu, Mike McGlone, Kirk Acevedo, Sandra Bernhard, John Corbett, Summer Phoenix, Polly Draper.* The chaotic, behind-the-scenes dramas of a TriBeCa Italian restaurant forms the core of this frantic, funny romp by Giraldi — a music video director ("Beat It") and restaurateur — making his feature film debut. Using as inspiration his own eatery Gigino's Trattoria, Giraldi creates a rapid-fire tale of gangsters, gourmet food, high-flying chefs, bookies and obnoxious patrons all made real with snappy dialogue and an experienced ensemble cast. Aiello is at his best as a longtime Italian restaurant owner who's at odds with his gourmet chef son over the new menu, even though the place is now a hit with the critics and public alike. A delicious blend of humor, endearing characters, culinary delights and unexpected poignancy. ★★★ DVD Dual: $19.99, VHS: $9.99

Dinosaur

(2000, 82 min, US, Eric Leighton & Ralph Zondag) *Voices of: D.B. Sweeney, Julianna Margulies, Joan Plowright, Ossie Davis, Alfre Woodard, Della Reese.* Cool computer animation of dinosaurs trying to avoid the effects of a meteor crashing into the Earth highlight this uneven animated rip-off of *Land Before Time.* Since it's a Disney film, the dinos talk (though don't sing), and band with lemurs to save themselves from extinction while on a march to their breeding

Audrey Tautou in Stephen Frears' *Dirty Pretty Things*

ground. Unfortunately, the $125 million movie is at the service of a 98¢ script, a clichéd road movie that goes nowhere new. ★★ DVD: $39.99, VHS: $26.99

Diplomaniacs

(1933, 63 min, US, William A. Seiter) *Bert Wheeler, Robert Woolsey, Marjorie White.* The comedy team of Wheeler and Woolsey star in one of their best comic outings, a totally crazy and hilarious romp (in every sense of the word) as barbers on an Indian reservation, being mistaken for diplomats and sent to Geneva to attend a peace conference. Silly and quite enjoyable fun. ★★★ VHS: $19.99

El Diputado

(1979, 110 min, Spain, Eloy de la Iglesia) *Jose Sacristan, Maria Luisa San Jose, Jose Alonso.* This highly praised and powerful thriller follows the political and sexual coming-out of a young married politician in post-Franco Spain. A congressman's repressed homosexual desires are awakened while serving a brief prison term for a political matter. After a first encounter, he furtively seeks out sexual partners until he falls in love with a 16-year-old street hustler. The film deals with the delicate balance between his life, his loving wife and his political goals. (Spanish with English subtitles) ★★★ VHS: $59.99

Directed by Andrei Tarkovsky

(1988, 105 min, USSR, Michel Leszczylowski) This "investigative" documentary into the life and works of the Soviet Union's greatest modern director was produced by the Swedish Film Institute and directed by Tarkovsky's longtime friend and editor Leszczylowski. Filmed in Sweden during the making of his final feature, *The Sacrifice,* and while he was gravely ill with cancer, the film attempts to capture, through interviews and footage from his films, the essence behind this brooding intellectual genius. ★★★ DVD: $39.99, VHS: $29.99

Dirty Dancing

(1987, 105 min, US, Emile Ardolino) *Patrick Swayze, Jennifer Grey, Jerry Orbach, Cynthia Rhodes, Jack Weston.* This sleeper hit of 1987 is a wonderfully nostalgic coming-of-age tale set in

a Catskill Mountains resort in 1963. Swayze became a star thanks to his role as the handsome dance instructor who becomes involved with innocent teenager Grey. Some good dancing and golden oldies highlight the film. ★★★ DVD Letterbox 2-Disc Ultimate Edition: $19.99, VHS: $9.99

Dirty Dishes

(1982, 99 min, France, Joyce Buñuel) *Carol Laurie, Pierre Santini.* After ten years of cooking, cleaning and taking care of her husband, a housewife's life has become so dulled by these domestic chores that even an affair with a younger man and other incidents cannot seem to break her out of her crazed boredom. A deceptively comic *Diary of a Mad Housewife.* The director is Luis Buñuel's daughter-in-law. (French with English subtitles) ★★★

The Dirty Dozen

(1967, 150 min, US, Robert Aldrich) *Lee Marvin, Charles Bronson, John Cassavetes, Donald Sutherland, Robert Ryan, Ernest Borgnine, George Kennedy, Telly Savalas, Jim Brown.* Classic WWII adventure with Marvin leading 12 condemned prisoners on a daring raid of a Nazi stronghold. Not a dull moment in its two and a half hours, the first half of the film follows the rigorous training the men go through, and the second covers the crackerjack assault. ★★★½ DVD: $14.99, VHS Special Edition: $9.99, VHS Letterbox Special Edition: $9.99

Dirty Hands

(1976, 102 min, France/Germany/Italy, Claude Chabrol) *Romy Schneider, Rod Steiger, Paoli Giusti, Jean Rochefort.* Chabrol, France's master of the suppressed but always torrid urges and desires of the bourgeoisie, directed this familiar though atmospheric tale of treachery, murder and mystery. A woman and her lover plot to murder her husband — but with unexpected results. ★★

Dirty Harry

(1971, 103 min, US, Don Siegel) *Clint Eastwood, Harry Guardino, Andy Robinson, John Vernon.* The first of Eastwood's *Dirty Harry* series is a classic action-thriller. In this flavorful and exciting police story, Harry Callahan chases after a psychopathic rooftop sniper. (Sequel: *Magnum Force*) ★★★ DVD: $19.99, VHS: $9.99, VHS Letterbox: $9.99

Dirty Pretty Things

(2003, 94 min, GB, Stephen Frears) *Chiwetel Ejiofor, Audrey Tautou, Sergi Lopéz, Sophie Okonedo.* London's nighttime takes on a menacing afterglow in this atmospheric, tough-minded thriller that's as suspenseful as it is disturbing and hypnotic. Combining elements of political thriller, dark comedy and poignant romance, director Frears aims for the jugular and isn't afraid to draw blood. Okwe (Ejofor) is a Nigerian immigrant (and former doctor) living in London who has traded his stethoscope for the wheel of a cab by day and a hotel counter by night. His and the life of a friend, Senay (Tautou), a Turkish immigrant working as a maid, soon become endangered when Okwe learns of a ruthless organized crime syndicate working at the hotel trading kidneys for visas. Frears shows us a dirty London not in the tour books, where immigrants are routinely exploited without voice or recourse, and principle is an extravagance one can ill afford. *Dirty Pretty Things* is a chilling but rewarding film, remarkably told and acted to perfection by an outstanding ensemble. ★★★½ DVD Letterbox: $29.99, VHS: $102.99

Dirty Rotten Scoundrels

(1988, 110 min, US, Frank Oz) *Michael Caine, Steve Martin, Glenne Headly, Barbara Harris.* Caine and Martin make an unlikely but very funny and effective comic duo in this hilarious yarn about a couple of con men competing for control of a town on the French Riviera. Caine is superb as the established swindler who masquerades as a deposed prince. When rival Martin (who is in his element as the rude and crude American) lands on the scene, Caine is faced with a serious challenge to the control of his turf; where the two become enmeshed in a wacky series of attempts to outscheme each other. Headly more than holds her own as their mutual target. (Remake of 1964's *Bedtime Story*) ★★★½ DVD: $14.99

Dirty Work

(1998, 82 min, US, Bob Saget) *Norm MacDonald, Jack Warden, Artie Lange, Christopher McDonald, Chevy Chase, Don Rickles, Adam Sandler, Chris Farley.* Dirty work, indeed. Norm Macdonald is onscreen for about 82 minutes. As a TV comic-type, Macdonald gets his smart-ass stream-of-consciousness shtick to work in little five-minute bits — but in his own movie? Yikes. Basically, wacky stuff happens to Norm and fat-guy sidekick Lange when they open a Revenge-for-Hire business. The stupid jokes are all Norm's and they all seem to be related to his "Note to self" mini tape-recorder bit from *SNL*. Unless you're really into this sort of thing, let someone else watch it for you. ★½ DVD: $14.99, VHS: $14.99

The Disappearance of Garcia Lorca

(1997, 113 min, US/Spain, Marcos Zurinaga) *Andy Garcia, Esai Morales, Edward James Olmos, Jeroen Krabbé, Giancarlo Giannini, Miguel Ferrer.* Poet Federico Garcia Lorca was one of the first victims of Franco's fascist regime, which took power after winning the Spanish Civil War in 1936. *The Disappearance of Garcia Lorca* follows a journalist who returns to his boyhood home in Spain to uncover the mystery surrounding the death of Lorca, whose writings and homosexuality branded him as a subversive by the government. The cast, including Olmos and Ferrer, is uniformly good, but it is Garcia's standout performance as Lorca that elevates the film. Flashbacks — told *Rashomon*-like from several conflicting sources — are confusing at times. Overall, though, the film is compelling and the cinematography is gorgeous. (Filmed in English) ★★★

The Disappearance of Kevin Johnson

(1995, 105 min, US, Francis Megahy) *Michael Brandon, Pierce Brosnan, James Coburn, Dudley Moore, Kari Wuhrer.* If you thought *The Player* was a hoot, this mockumentary is just what the doctor ordered: a dark, witty Hollywood biz satire with some interesting curves to boot. A TV crew from England working on a documentary on Brits living in L.A. discovers that Kevin Johnson, a millionaire British film producer, has mysteriously disappeared. Led by an anonymous, offscreen filmmaker-narrator, the TV crew decides to find out what happened to Johnson. Writer-director Megahy has lots of fun with this premise, even aping real-life documentarian Nick Broomfield's *Heidi Fleiss: Hollywood Madam* with his accent and persistent, probing questions. Anyone who reads *Variety* on a regular basis, or has surfed the Ain't It Cool News website, should enjoy watching Tinseltown jerks get theirs one more time. ★★★

Disclosure

(1994, 128 min, US, Barry Levinson) *Michael Douglas, Demi Moore, Donald Sutherland, Dennis Miller, Caroline Goodall, Roma Maffia.* Douglas, the self-appointed spokesman for the victimized white heterosexual male, is cast as such once again as a successful computer engineer and all-around good guy who is sexually harassed by his new boss and ex-flame Moore. She in turn brings charges against him. This sets in motion a battle to prove his innocence. Forgetting the obvious complaint of a female aggressor in Hollywood's first film about sexual harassment, there are other points which make *Disclosure* an irritating piece of trash. Though slickly made by Levinson, the film is a cheap sleight of hand which is no more about harassment than *Philadelphia* is about AIDS. It's a misogynist, calculated foray into sexual politics whose only point is that women as much as men can abuse power. ★★ DVD: $19.99, VHS: $9.99

The Discreet Charm of the Bourgeoisie

(1972, 100 min, France, Luis Buñuel) *Fernando Rey, Delphine Seyrig, Jean-Pierre Cassel, Bulle Ogier, Michel Piccoli, Stéphane Audran.* A witty, anarchistic social comedy about six upper-crust Parisians and their unsuccessful attempts to dine in a civilized manner. Buñuel's sardonic statement on the amoral world of the ruling class. (French with English subtitles) ★★★★ DVD Criterion Collection: $39.99, VHS: $29.99

The Disenchanted (La Désenchantée)

(1990, 78 min, France, Benoît Jacquot) *Judith Godrèche, Marcel Bozonnet.* Slight but not uninteresting, *The Disenchanted* concerns the 17-year-old Beth (Godreche) as she grapples with her sexuality. This sparse but not entirely revealing character study opens with Beth's boyfriend challenging her to sleep with ugly men, and ends with Beth being the unwilling object of a sugar daddy's attention. In between, she meets A.D. (Bozonnet), a potential suitor who forces her to reevaluate her feelings and goals in life. Writer-director Jacquot deliberately keeps the drama subtle, but the tension is often quite palpable. The lovely Godreche gives a finely nuanced performance, but the film is detached and uninvolving, and this moodiness casts a pall over the entire film. (French with English subtitles) ★★½ DVD: $29.99, VHS: $14.99

The Dish

(2001, 101 min, Australia, Rob Sitch) *Sam Neill, Kevin Harrington, Tom Long, Patrick Warburton, Genevieve Mooy.* It's July 1969. The largest radio telescope in the Southern hemisphere, located in the middle of a sheep paddock in Parkes, Australia, is preparing to carry the TV signals of man's first steps on the surface of the moon. Days before the event, a power surge causes a momentary blackout of the region — long enough to wipe out the computer's data and lose *Apollo 11*'s signal. As the technical crew scrambles to get back on line, the rustic town of Parkes plays host to the U.S. Ambassador and its own Prime Minister, joining the other 600 million on Planet Earth waiting to witness the historic event. *The Dish* is quirky, witty, warm and affectionate as it recounts the political maneuvering, human idiosyncrasy, budding romance and personal loss of the ensemble characters, deftly portrayed by an exceptional cast headed by Neill as the dish's contemplative chief of operations. ★★★ DVD Letterbox: $19.99, VHS: $14.99

Dish Dogs

(1998, 96 min, US, Robert Kubilos) *Sean Astin, Brian Dennehy, Matthew Lillard, Shannon Elizabeth.* Astin's winning performance is the sole saving grace of this mostly uninvolving comedy about a philosophy-spouting "career dishwasher" who is unwilling to let anything — even a beautiful stripper (Elizabeth) — interfere with his quest for spiritual "epiphany." Lillard puts in his usual overbearing act as the best friend who gives it all up for love, and Dennehy has a limited role as the boys' mentor. Released in time to cash in on the *American Pie* craze. ★★ DVD: $24.99

The Disorderly Orderly

(1964, 90 min, US, Frank Tashlin) *Jerry Lewis, Glenda Farrell, Kathleen Freeman.* Lewis is a young practicing med student who seems to have more of a flair for comedy than healing (unless you believe in the healing power of laughter). ★★★ VHS: $9.99

Disorganized Crime

(1989, 101 min, US, Jim Kouf) *Lou Diamond Phillips, Fred Gwynne, Corbin Bernsen, Ruben Blades, William Russ.* Disorganized comedy about a group of small-time criminals who attempt the ultimate heist, but who are faced with a few problems, such as the loss of their leader and no plan whatsoever. ★★ DVD: $9.99

Disraeli

(1929, 87 min, US, Alfred E. Green) *George Arliss, Florence Arliss, Joan Bennett.* Arliss, such a distinguished actor of his day that in this film he is billed "Mr. George Arliss," won a much-deserved Best Actor Oscar for re-creating his legendary Broadway performance. This intelligent, if stagey, adaptation centers on England's Jewish Prime Minister of the late 19th century and his efforts to secure the Suez Canal for Britain — which includes going head-to-head with Russian spies and anti-Semitism. Arliss' wife Florence is ideally cast as Disraeli's spouse. Arliss had played the role once before in a 1921 silent. ★★★½ VHS: $14.99

Distant Thunder

(1973, 92 min, India, Satyajit Ray) *Soumitra Chatterjee, Sandhya Roy.* Set in a remote village in Bengal during the outbreak of WWII, this harsh and vividly filmed story chronicles the lives of several families when the area is shaken by a famine and their world is disastrously uprooted. A riveting drama of great scope and power. (Hindi with English subtitles) ★★★½ VHS: $49.99

Distant Thunder

(1988, 114 min, US, Rick Rosenthal) *John Lithgow, Ralph Macchio, Janet Margolin.* An emotionally scarred Vietnam vet (Lithgow) leaves his secluded life in Washington's rain forest to see the son (Macchio) he hasn't seen in fifteen years. Lithgow's sensitive performance can't offset the sentimental melodramatics and clichéd characterizations. ★★ VHS: $14.99

Distant Voices, Still Lives

(1988, 85 min, GB, Terence Davies) *Freda Dowie, Pete Postlethwaite, Angela Walsh.* Davies' autobiographical and unblinking account of a family's oppressive lifestyle in pre- and postwar England. A timeworn photo album on film, the story traces the adolescence of Davies and his older sisters struggling to mature despite their abusive father's tyranny; and also the grown children's disenchantment, told through song at the local pub. *Distant Voices, Still Lives* is a passionate and rich film. ★★★½ VHS: $89.99

The Distinguished Gentleman

(1993, 112 min, US, Jonathan Lynn) *Eddie Murphy, Sheryl Lee Ralph, Joe Don Baker, Lane Smith, Grant Shaud.* More homogenized humor from former four-letter-wordsmith Murphy. This time out he tackles the role of a grifter who scams his way into Congress in search of streets paved with gold, only to discover that he has a heart of gold himself. Awww, shucks. It's pretty funny, though, even without the profanity. ★★½ DVD: $9.99, VHS: $9.99

Le Distrait (The Daydreamer)

(1978, 101 min, France, Pierre Richard) *Pierre Richard, Bernard Blier, Maris-Christine Barrault.* Richard continues his bungling and frantically funny misadventures in this Gallic farce about an ad executive who just can't keep fantasy away from reality. Richard himself directed this funny escapade. (French with English subtitles) ★★★

Disturbing Behavior

(1998, 84 min, US, David Nutter) *James Marsden, Katie Holmes, Nick Stahl, Bruce Greenwood, William Sadler, Ethan Embry.* Disturbing Behavior is an underachieving thriller that is, at best, a passable adolescent tragic melodrama. A mildly dysfunctional family, recovering from the suicide of their 11-year-old son and brother, moves to the all-American town of Cradle Bay. Before you can say *The Stepford Wives*, our teen heroes discover a bizarre conspiracy by the adults to turn their rebellious kids into obedient, scholarly model citizens. While hardly original, the premise is at least intriguing. The film looks crisp, however, last-minute studio cuts may be to blame for the lack of coherence and character motivation. ★★ DVD: $14.99, VHS: $9.99

Diva

(1981, 123 min, France, Jean-Jacques Beineix) *Wilhemina Fernandez, Frederic Andrei, Richard Bohringer, Dominique Pinon, Thuy An Luu.* Beineix's stunning film debut is a dashing, eclectic adventure that shimmers with style and humor. The unpredictable escapades begin when a young postal messenger secretly tapes the performance of a determinedly unrecorded operatic star. The chase begins when he flees from a skinhead punk, a pair of inescapable Taiwanese record pirates, and the police. A rapturous thriller that is an amalgam of pop-cul-

ture paraphernalia, B-movie clichés and prodigious flair. (French with English subtitles) ★★★½ DVD: $24.99, VHS: $14.99

Dive Bomber

(1941, 130 min, US, Michael Curtiz) *Errol Flynn, Fred MacMurray, Ralph Bellamy.* A dashing young Navy flight doctor (Flynn) attempts to discover a way to prevent "pilot blackout" at the end of a power dive. MacMurray and Bellamy are a veteran pilot and chief flight doctor, respectively. Their interaction with Flynn is good, but this film follows conventions like there's no tomorrow. Spectacular aerial photography highlights an otherwise solid by-the-numbers film. ★★★

Divided We Fall

(2000, 117 min, Czech Republic, Jan Hrebejk) *Boleslav Polivka, Anna Siskova, Jaroslav Dusek, Csongor Kassai.* Sacrifice and the boundless limits of friendship are at the core of the emotionally stirring *Divided We Fall*, a thoughtful, sometimes witty examination of a Czech village and a married couple under attack from the ravages of Nazism. It's World War II, and the Germans have taken control of Josef and Marie's town. The Jewish son of Josef's employer, David, has been carted off to the concentration camps, and Josef is now out of work. He balances his time trying to stay on the good side of a Nazi-sympathizer "friend," and avoiding the stares of his neighbors. An unusual series of events unfolds when David escapes, and Josef and Marie hide him in their closet, setting in motion heroic actions neither Josef nor Marie would have thought possible. An Oscar nominee for Best Foreign-Language Film. (Czech with English subtitles) ★★★½ DVD: $29.99

Divine Madness

(1980, 95 min, US, Michael Ritchie) *Bette Midler.* La Belle Bette, the Divine Miss Midler, in concert. No joke is too cheap, no gag too crass as evidenced by the raunchy stage performance of Bette and her Harlettes. And she sings, too. ★★★ DVD: $9.99

The Divine Nymph

(1979, 90 min, Italy, G.P. Griffi) *Laura Antonelli, Marcello Mastroianni, Terence Stamp.* This sexy romp features Laura Antonelli as a young and sensu-

ous woman who becomes involved in a tragic love triangle with Mastroianni and Stamp. A predictable story of decadence, obsession and deception. ★★

Divine Secrets of the Ya-Ya Sisterhood

(2002, 110 min, US, Callie Khouri) *Ellen Burstyn, Sandra Bullock, Ashley Judd, James Garner, Maggie Smith, Fionnula Flanagan, Shirley Knight, Angus MacFadyen, Cherry Jones.* The Southern female ensemble film, fast becoming a genre all its own, won't have its current reigning champ *Fried Green Tomatoes* dethroned quite yet, as this film adaptation of two popular Rebecca Wells novels comes up a bit short in the "make-'em-laugh-make-'em-cry" department. Buoyed by a strong all-star cast, *Ya-Ya* traces the rocky relationship of a mother and daughter (Burstyn, Bullock), two equally headstrong women, and the attempt of the mother's childhood friends (known as the Ya-Yas) to bring them together. The story also recalls the troubled road Mom had taken when she was younger, complete with flashbacks and forwards. Unlike a *Steel Magnolias*, the dialogue isn't quite funny enough to overcome uneven pacing, middling characters and patchy editing. But it does have that good ensemble, who seem very eager to please despite having to portray characters that are one-dimensional and — more often than not — not all that interesting. ★★ DVD Letterbox: $14.99, DVD Pan & Scan: $14.99, VHS: $6.99

Divorce — Italian Style

(1961, 104 min, Italy, Pietro Germi) *Marcello Mastroianni, Daniela Rocco.* Mastroianni is pure magic in this frantic satire on love and marriage — the first, and best, of the Italian sex comedies of the 1960s. Mastroianni plays an aging nobleman who, in order to marry his vivacious teenage cousin, must first get rid of his wife — a difficult task in a no-divorce country. His convoluted plan soon involves him acting as a jealous husband who, on finding his wife in bed with another man, kills her off in a fit of passion — the only problem is finding the "other man." A delightful comedy that won the Academy Award for Best Original Screenplay. (Italian with English subtitles) ★★★★ DVD: $29.99, VHS: $24.99

The Divorce of Lady X

(1938, 92 min, GB, Tim Whelan) *Laurence Olivier, Merle Oberon, Ralph Richardson.* This witty,

Diva

sophisticated comedy examines the problems of a London barrister who allows a pretty young lady to spend an "innocent" night in his flat, only to later be named as a correspondent in a subsequent divorce action. A frothy comedy. ★★★

The Divorcee

(1930, 83 min, US, Robert Z. Leonard) *Norma Shearer, Chester Morris, Conrad Nagel, Robert Montgomery.* Shearer won an Oscar for her portrayal of a married woman who suffers through her husband's infidelity before deciding to give him a taste of his own medicine. Shearer's performance makes this hoary melodrama of interest. ★★½ VHS: $14.99

Do the Right Thing

(1989, 120 min, US, Spike Lee) *Danny Aiello, Ossie Davis, Ruby Dee, Spike Lee, John Turturro, Giancarlo Esposito, Bill Nunn, Richard Edson, Paul Benjamin, Samuel L. Jackson, John Savage, Rosie Perez, Martin Lawrence.* Lee's brilliant, controversial and thought-provoking *Do the Right Thing* bulldozed its way into the American consciousness — forcing people to take sides on many of Lee's radical assertions and making race relations the hot topic of the summer of '89. The story revolves around a single street in the Bed-Stuy section of Brooklyn during one of the hottest days of summer. Spike's attention is given to the citizens of the street from 'da Mayor (Davis is terrific as the suds-soaked elder who offers snatches of street wisdom) to Mother Sister (wonderfully rendered by Dee) to Mookie (Lee is his rambunctious self as the unenlightened delivery boy for Sal's Pizzeria). Aiello also shines as Sal. Superbly acted and filmed, *Do the Right Thing* is not simply incendiary — it is downright great filmmaking. ★★★★ DVD Criterion Collection: $39.99, VHS: $9.99

Do You Remember Dolly Bell

(1981, 105 min, Yugoslavia, Emir Kusturica) Made a few years before his highly successful *When Father Was Away on Business,* director Kusturica's perceptive and amusing coming-of-age drama is set in 1960s Sarajevo. The story centers around the family life of Dino, an amiable 16-year-old who befriends a caustic but engaging young prostitute, nicknamed Dolly Bell. An engrossing film that delves into Yugoslavia's ever-shifting nature of nonaligned Communism and its effect on the family, especially the young. (Serbian with English subtitles) ★★★

D.O.A.

(1950, 83 min, US, Rudolph Mate) *Edmond O'Brien, Pamela Britton, Luther Adler, Beverly Garland.* O'Brien walks into a police station and reports a murder: his own. Thus begins Mate's tense, enthralling mystery about a man who only has three days to find out who gave him a slow-acting lethal poison. Filmed on location in Los Angeles and San Francisco, this classic film noir will have you on the edge of your seat right up to the end. (Remade in 1988) ★★★½ DVD: $19.99, VHS: $19.99

D.O.A.

(1988, 96 min, US, Annabel Jankel & Rocky Morton) *Meg Ryan, Charlotte Rampling, Daniel Stern, Dennis Quaid.* Codirectors Morton and Jankel's music video background is much in evidence in this slick style-over-substance remake of the 1950 film noir classic about a man (Quaid) who spends his final hours of life looking for the person who slipped him a slow-acting poison. Though much maligned as a remake, the film is a fairly enjoyable thriller in its own right. ★★½ DVD: $14.99

Doc Hollywood

(1991, 105 min, US, Michael Caton-Jones) *Michael J. Fox, Bridget Fonda, Woody Harrelson, Julie Warner, Barnard Hughes, David Ogden Stiers, Frances Sternhagen.* A hotshot big-city doctor is forced to offer his services to a small, backwoods town populated with a collection of offbeat and endearing characters. No, it's not "Northern Exposure." It's *Doc Hollywood,* a surprisingly charming comedy with Fox as the doctor in question, a Washington D.C. surgeon waylaid in a Southern community on his trek west. Fox gives an attractive performance as the Doc, discovering a maturity heretofore unseen on-screen. ★★★ DVD: $9.99

Docks of New York

(1928, 76 min, US, Josef von Sternberg) *George Bancroft, Betty Compson.* Lacking the mannered bombast of his later melodramas, von Sternberg's efficient, superb drama chronicles a stevedore's developing love for a woman he saved from suicide. The director's mastery of the language of silent film is most evident in his slow dissolves — either to compress time, or to accentuate the internal turmoil of a character. ★★★★ VHS: $7.99

The Doctor

(1991, 125 min, US, Randa Haines) *William Hurt, Christine Lahti, Elizabeth Perkins, Mandy Patinkin, Adam Arkin, Charlie Korsmo.* Yet another in 1991's spate of moral redemption films (*Regarding Henry, The Fisher King, Doc Hollywood*), this one gets by thanks to its big heart. Hurt gives a solid performance as Jack McKee, a successful and respected surgeon who finds himself on the other side of the emergency room door when he is diagnosed with throat cancer. In coming to grips with both his illness and the indifference of his colleagues, he soon realizes his own shortcomings as a doctor and husband. Perkins excels as a terminally ill woman. ★★★ DVD: $19.99

The Doctor and the Devils

(1985, 93 min, GB, Freddie Francis) *Timothy Dalton, Jonathan Pryce, Twiggy, Julian Sands, Stephen Rea, Patrick Stewart, Phyllis Logan.* Another unusual production from Brooksfilms (Mel Brooks' production company), this Gothic tale is based on a 1940s screenplay by Dylan Thomas. It concerns two of the most famous villains in British history, Broom and Fallen, who provided corpses for the anatomical research of Dr. Thomas Rock. A grisly tale that evokes images of the old Hammer classics. ★★★ VHS: $79.99

Dr. Bethune

(1990, 115 min, Canada/China/France, Phillip Borsos) *Donald Sutherland, Helen Mirren, Helen Shaver, Anouk Aimée.* In a mesmerizing performance, Sutherland brings subtle shading to the many facets of Dr. Norman Bethune, a complex man whose rude arrogance is tempered by his compassionate devotion to the cause of universal medical treatment. With a history as social and medical crusader, Bethune is summoned in 1938 to Yunan by Chairman Mao to be chief medical advisor to 100,000 troops. In flashbacks, the film concentrates on his efforts there; and his prior achievements, as well. Beautifully photographed and finely crafted. ★★★½ VHS: $19.99

Dr. Caligari

(1991, 80 min, US, Stephen Sayadian) *Madeleine Reynal, Fox Harris.* The director of the stylish porno-punk *Cafe Flesh* goes "legit" with this colorful takeoff on the classic German silent *The Cabinet*

of *Dr. Caligari.* Now it is his granddaughter who is in charge of the asylum and her radical new form of therapy consists of gender bending until the patient snaps from severe mental fatigue. ★★

Dr. Cyclops

(1945, 75 min, US, Ernest Schoedsack) *Albert Dekker, Janice Logan.* Until the late 1950s, it was rare for color films to have many special effects. It was even rarer for a horror film to be made in color. Dekker plays a mad doctor living in the jungle who shrinks anyone who visits him for no other reason than because he can. Good premise and nicely done. ★★★

Doctor Detroit

(1983, 91 min, US, Michael Pressman) *Dan Aykroyd, Donna Dixon, Fran Drescher, Howard Hesseman, Lynn Whitfield, Glenne Headly.* Aykroyd plays a mild-mannered college professor who finds himself caught up in a power struggle with the Chicago mob when he takes care of five beautiful prostitutes. Some good laughs in this playful comedy. ★★½

Doctor Dolittle

(1967, 151 min, US, Richard Fleischer) *Rex Harrison, Samantha Eggar, Anthony Newley, Richard Attenborough, Geoffrey Holder.* Harrison talks to the animals and sails around the world in a giant snail. Children may enjoy this musical fable, though adults will find some of it difficult to take. A beguiling score includes "Talk to the Animals" (Oscar winner). (Remade in 1998) ★★½ DVD: $14.99, VHS: $9.99

Dr. Dolittle

(1998, 85 min, US, Betty Thomas) *Eddie Murphy, Ossie Davis, Oliver Platt, Peter Boyle, Jeffrey Tambor, Chris Rock, Norm MacDonald, Ellen Degeneres, Albert Brooks, John Leguizamo, Paul Reubens.* Murphy proves he *can* talk to the animals in this funny and entertaining family comedy based on the 1967 musical. As with his *Nutty Professor,* Murphy has updated a '60s semiclassic to produce a laugh-laden hit that stands on its own. Much to his regret, Dolittle learns he has the ability to understand animals — all animals. Unlike Harrison's doc, Murphy is not happy about his gift, and it wreaks havoc with family and business associates. Though some of the family segments border on the sentimental, the humor is much more broad. Director Thomas (*The Brady Bunch Movie*) has once again created a winning comedy for the whole family. (Sequel: *Dr. Dolittle 2*) ★★★ DVD Pan & Scan: $14.99, DVD: $14.99, VHS: $9.99

Dr. Dolittle 2

(2001, 81 min, US, Steve Carr) *Eddie Murphy, Kristen Wilson, Jeffrey Jones, Kevin Pollak, Voices of: Steve Zahn, Norm MacDonald, Isaac Hayes.* The animals are back, and so is Edddie, in this inferior sequel that's harmless but only occasionally manages to produce a laugh or two. This time out, Doc Dolittle teams with a circus bear (voiced by Zahn) to save the forest from greedy developers. The talking animals are still cute, though some of the jokes are a little cruder than before. ★★ DVD Pan & Scan: $14.99, DVD Special Edition: $14.99, VHS: $9.99

Doctor Faustus

(1968, 93 min, GB, Richard Burton) *Richard Burton, Andreas Teuber, Elizabeth Taylor.* Colorful rendering of the Faustus legend with first-time director Burton in the title role as a man who sells his soul to the Devil for personal gain. While not the best telling of the tale, the film is notable for a cameo appearance by the director's wife in the role of "Helen of Troy." ★★ DVD: $24.99

Dr. Giggles

(1992, 96 min, US, Manny Coto) *Larry Drake, Holly Marie Combs, Glenn Quinn.* With a razor-thin scalpel in hand, a menacingly diabolical giggle and a penchant for involuntary organ transplants, Dr. Giggles is no ordinary Marcus Welby. Drake draws more than just a few chuckles as the deranged son of a mad doctor who escapes from an asylum and sets out to exact vengeance on the town that killed his father. The film fails to deliver the goods as a hardcore splatter film, but it has spoofy moments that will have some viewers placing their hands over their eyes. ★★

Doctor in the House

(1954, 92 min, GB, Ralph Thomas) *Dirk Bogarde, Muriel Pavlow, Kenneth More, Donald Sinden, Kay Kendall.* Bogarde stars in this hilarious farce about medical school students based on the story of Richard Gordon. This was the first of a series of sophisticated takeoffs on the *Carry On* films. ★★★

Dr. Jekyll And Mr. Hyde

(1920, 96 min, US, John S. Robertson) *John Barrymore, Martha Mansfield.* Barrymore gives a virtuoso performance as Robert Louis Stevenson's tormented doctor in this silent classic. Filmed many times since, including the 1932 Fredric March version, which has yet to be surpassed. ★★★ DVD: $24.99, VHS: $24.99

Dr. Jekyll and Mr. Hyde

(1932, 82 min, US, Rouben Mamoulian) *Fredric March, Miriam Hopkins, Halliwell Hobbes.* Robert Louis Stevenson's classic thriller of split personality and dementia has been done so many times and on so many different levels, that it, like "Frankenstein," has somehow lost not only its freshness, but also its ability to cause fear or to shock. This 1932 version is an exception. March, who won the Oscar for Best Actor, brings both tenderness and ferocity to the character that, despite the film's age, makes it hard to imagine anyone else in the role. Hopkins is unforgettable as the doomed prostitute who takes up with Mr. Hyde, and had there been a Supporting Actress category in 1932, she probably would have been an Oscar winner as well. Armenian-born director Mamoulian used his innovative camerawork and direction to create a truly tragic figure. (DVD double feature with 1941 version) ★★★★ DVD: $19.99, VHS: $14.99

Dr. Jekyll and Mr. Hyde

(1941, 114 min, US, Victor Fleming) *Spencer Tracy, Ingrid Bergman, Lana Turner.* Slick remake of the Robert Louis Stevenson story with Tracy as the mad doc, Bergman as Hyde's ill-fated Cockney mistress and Turner as Jekyll's bride-to-be. (DVD double feature with 1932 version) ★★★ DVD Double Feature: $19.99

Dr. Jekyll & Ms. Hyde

(1995, 95 min, US, David Price) *Tim Daly, Sean Young, Lysette Anthony, Harvey Fierstein.* When network TV shows nothing but "Hee-Haw," when an ushers' strike closes down the cinema, and when video stores are stocked with only Sylvester Stallone flicks, only then should this ludicrous film be watched. A tired variation of the Jekyll and Hyde tale, this insipid comedy features Daly as a eccentric scientist who accidentally turns into a power-hungry woman (Young). Yes, sexual hijinks ensue as men

fall under his/her murderous attractiveness. The best thing that can be said about this film is that it does not cause cancer (although not all of the studies are in). ★ VHS: $14.99

Dr. Jekyll and Sister Hyde

(1972, 94 min, GB, Roy Ward Baker) *Ralph Bates, Martine Beswick.* Friends of Freud should have a field day with this intriguing, but at times lifeless, variation of the Robert Louis Stevenson chiller with Bates as the insanely curious doctor who manages to isolate his dark side only to find that it is actually feminine! As with most treatises on the nature of good and evil, evil is more fun as evidenced by Beswick's villainous performance as Sister Hyde. ★★★ VHS: $9.99

Dr. No

(1963, 111 min, GB, Terence Young) *Sean Connery, Ursula Andress, Joseph Wiseman.* Connery stars in the first and foremost James Bond adventure. There's sex, violence, exotic locales and the master fiend Dr. No. This is agent 007 at his finest. (Sequel: *From Russia with Love*) ★★★½

Dr. Phibes Rises Again

(1972, 89 min, GB, Robert Fuest) *Vincent Price, Peter Cushing, Terry-Thomas, Beryl Reed.* A disfigured madman (Price) and his deceased wife go boating down the Underground River of the Dead in this sequel to *The Abominable Dr. Phibes.* Everybody's in it for the laughs — even the set designer. ★★½ DVD: $14.99, VHS: $9.99

Dr. Seuss' How the Grinch Stole Christmas

(2000, 105 min, US, Ron Howard) *Jim Carrey, Taylor Momsen, Jeffrey Tambor, Molly Shannon, Christine Baranski, Bill Irwin; Narrated by Anthony Hopkins.* As prepackaged as a seasonal fruitcake, and about as appealing, this live-action version of the 1960s cartoon favorite has great costumes, astonishing makeup and marvelous sets — everything, it seems, except story, humor and heart. Under Oscar-winning green makeup for days, Carrey is the one and only Grinch who lives on the outskirts of pleasant Whoville where all the Whovillians live and prosper. Of course, as the story goes, he sets out to stop Christmas, only to be thwarted by young Cindy Lou Who (Momsen). Dr. Seuss' immortal story has lived on through Chuck Jones' 1966 animated short, a perfect rendering of the tale. But director Howard's overblown take is sappy, loud and —when Carrey isn't on-screen — boring. Even when Carrey is on-screen, the jokes aren't fully realized. You don't have to be a "mean one" to not particularly enjoy this holiday present that has about as much thought behind it as giving a tie for Christmas. ★★ DVD Letterbox: $19.99, DVD Pan & Scan: $19.99, DVD Limited Edition: $39.99, DVD 2-disc set: $29.99, VHS: $14.99, VHS Gift Set with Grinch Plush: $29.99

Dr. Strangelove

(1964, 93 min, GB, Stanley Kubrick) *Peter Sellers, George C. Scott, Sterling Hayden, Slim Pickens, Keenan Wynn.* Kubrick's unforgettable and hilarious black comedy is undeniably one of the greatest indictments of the Cold War ever to be seen in the cinema. From the legendary performances by the cast to Kubrick's brilliant use of the cinematic form, the film is an undaunted piece of mastery. The film's profound message about the dangers of aggression in

Peter Sellers as *Dr. Strangelove*

the nuclear age is as timely now as it was when it was released — a superior cinematic achievement. ★★★★ DVD Special Edition: $19.99

Dr. T & the Women

(2000, 121 min, US, Robert Altman) *Richard Gere, Helen Hunt, Laura Dern, Farrah Fawcett, Shelley Long, Tara Reid, Kate Hudson, Liv Tyler, Lee Grant, Janine Turner, Robert Hays, Andy Richter, Matt Malloy.* Director Altman has always brought out the best in his actors, and here he has done the impossible: coaxed a smart, rich and winning performance out of old stoneface, Richard Gere. He plays an obstetrician/gynecologist around whom many Dallas women's lives seem to revolve, in typical multicharactered Altman style. While he's the object of some misplaced affection, he is wholly devoted to his wife; when she has a mental breakdown and reverts to childish ways, his formerly perfect life is thrown into turmoil. The emphasis is on humor, as Altman's positive outlook sees no difference between quirky little problems (Dern's tipsy sister-in-law) and the ones that initially seem huge (engaged daughter Hudson's lesbian affair) — in the end, life goes on. Long is a particular comic standout as Dr. T's harried and too-devoted head nurse. ★★★ DVD: $9.99, VHS: $9.99

Dr. Terror's House of Horrors

(1965, 98 min, GB, Freddie Francis) *Peter Cushing, Christopher Lee, Donald Sutherland.* Intriguing, episodic horror film from the director of *The Doctor and the Devils.* Five fellow travelers have their tarots read by a mysterious doctor as they ride on a train headed — where? ★★★

Doctor Zhivago

(1965, 197 min, US, David Lean) *Julie Christie, Omar Sharif, Geraldine Chaplin, Rod Steiger, Alec Guinness, Tom Courtenay, Rita Tushingham, Ralph Richardson.* Through his retelling of Boris Pasternak's novel of the Russian Revolution, Lean succeeds in creating both a mammoth spectacle and an impressive and absorbing account of one of the most fascinating and important periods in human history. An incredible ensemble is headed by the exceptional Christie and handsome Omar, with Steiger and Courtenay excelling among the fine ensemble cast. ★★★½ DVD Letterbox 2-disc Special Edition: $26.99, VHS Pan & Scan: $14.99, VHS Letterbox: $19.99

Dodes'ka-den

(1970, 140 min, Japan, Akira Kurosawa) *Yoshitaka Zushi, Junzaburo Ban.* A stunning and masterful examination of the downtrodden lives and glorious dreams of a number of Tokyo slum dwellers. Kurosawa's first film in color is an eloquent and impassioned affirmation of life and the awesome power of hope. Oddly, the film was not very well received by the critics and was a big disappointment at the box office, causing Kurosawa to abandon filmmaking for several years. (Japanese with English subtitles) ★★★ VHS: $29.99

Dodge City

(1939, 101 min, US, Michael Curtiz) *Errol Flynn, Olivia de Havilland, Ann Sheridan, Bruce Cabot, Alan Hale.* Flynn trades in his sword and tights for a pistol and cowboy boots as the new sheriff in a trigger-happy town. Flavorful western fun. ★★★ VHS: $14.99

Dodsworth

(1936, 101 min, US, William Wyler) *Walter Huston, Mary Astor, Ruth Chatterton, David Niven, Paul Lukas, Maria Ouspenskaya.* Superb film version of Sinclair Lewis' novel about a retired industrialist and his wife who travel abroad; each coming to re-examine the purpose and value of their lives. Huston, Chatterton and Astor all give outstanding performances. ★★★★ DVD: $19.99

Dog Day (Canicule)

(1983, 101 min, France, Yves Boisset) *Lee Marvin, Miou-Miou, Jean Carmet.* This gritty, macabre little gem is a pristine manifestation of the Gallic infatuation with American gangsters. Marvin stars as Jimmy Cobb, a chiseled-faced personification of the amoral yet honorable hood, who is on the run after a botched stick-up job. He finds himself at the dubious mercy of a farming family, whose interrelationships and sense of loyalties make the word "criminal" inoperative. Like Godard's *Alphaville* and Melville's *Bob le Flambeur*, this is a parable of existential man told against the backdrop of the chimerical safety of small-caliber weapons and the illusive salvation of the big score. ★★★½

Dog Day Afternoon

(1975, 130 min, US, Sidney Lumet) *Al Pacino, Charles Durning, Chris Sarandon, John Cazale, Carol Kane, Sully Boyar, James Broderick, Lance Henriksen.* Before Pacino embarrassed himself *Cruising* the leather bars, he gave a first-rate performance as a gay thief whose attempt to rob a bank (to pay for his lover's sex change) brings the city of New York to a standstill. An often delightful comedy, director Lumet flavors his film with warm characters and deft humor. In supporting roles, Durning as a police liaison and Oscar-nominee Sarandon as Pacino's lover are standouts. Based on a true incident. ★★★½ DVD: $14.99, VHS: $14.99

Dog Days

(2001, 120 min, Austria, Ulrich Seidl) *Maria Hofstätter, Alfred Mrva, Erich Finsches, Gerti Lehner, Franziska Weiss, Rene Wanko.* If Norman Rockwell grew up watching Tarantino and John Waters, he might have ended up with suburban portraits like those in the improvised yet intricately mannered *Dog Days.* In delving into the sordid lives of six marginally connected groups of down-and-out Austrians, director Seidl paints indelible portraits with the darkest tinge of black comedy. Most memorable are a chatterbox hitchhiker who possesses little social decorum (eventually meeting a horrifying fate), and an aged widower who dresses his frumpy housemaid in his late wife's dresses in an attempt to fill the void in his life. Like *21 Grams* (which came later), the stories jump back and forth seemingly at

random, eventually making sense at the end. It can be an exhausting process, but with characters this fascinating, it's one that's most rewarding. The rich color cinematography by Wolfgang Thaler is mesmerizing. (German with English subtitles) ★★★ DVD Unrated Director's Cut: $29.99

Dog Soldiers

(2002, 105 min, GB, Neil Marshall) *Sean Pertwee, Kevin McKidd, Liam Cunningham, Emma Cleasby.* A group of British soldiers, on a training mission in a desolate forest, find themselves fighting to survive an attack by a pack of vicious werewolves. Another example of a bloody good video find, this is a tense, exciting horror tale that provides the thrills much like *Brotherhood of the Wolf*, though on a smaller sale (and without the accents). ★★★ DVD: $9.99, VHS: $102.99

Dogfight

(1991, 92 min, US, Nancy Savoca) *River Phoenix, Lili Taylor, Brendan Fraser, Holly Near, Anthony Clark, Richard Panebianco, Mitchell Whitfield.* The heavily anticipated second effort from director Savoca is every bit as marvelous as her debut, *True Love.* Phoenix stars as a young Marine who sets out with his buddies on a dogfight — a search for the ugliest girl in town to escort to a dance. He charms Taylor, a plump and awkward aspiring folk singer who soon discovers his cruel deception. To make amends, he convinces her to go on a "real" date and they wind up spending the night together — a night of revelation and intimacy that neither would soon forget. Phoenix, as always, is first-rate, but it is Taylor's superb portrayal which elevates the film. An honest slice-of-'60s life captured with sensitivity and awareness. ★★★½ DVD Letterbox: $19.99, VHS: $19.99

Dogma

(1999, 125 min, US, Kevin Smith) *Linda Fiorentino, Chris Rock, Salma Hayek, Jason Lee, Alan Rickman, Matt Damon, Ben Affleck, Jason Mewes, Kevin Smith, Alanis Morissette.* Protests surrounding irreverent Catholic movies are generally a good sign (i.e. *Last Temptation of Christ*, *Priest*); Smith's *Dogma* lives up to the oblivious protests. Smith's story concerns Bethany (Fiorentino), an abortion clinic worker, who must go on a pilgrimage to New Jersey to save the world from two fallen angels (Damon and Affleck, natch). It seems God has gone missing after a skee-ball expedition, so

Bethany will need the help of stoner prophets Jay and Silent Bob, and Rufus (Rock), the black 13th apostle. Wait, wait, put your pickets down . . . Smith has done his homework. Within these outrageous trappings are reverent ideas that preach a personal relationship with God, rather than simple servitude before an organized religion. These mature themes are presented in an often hilarious package, with Rock delivering fall-down-funny dialogue guaranteed to spark conversation. The plot becomes a bit ponderous; but after seeing God do a handstand and explain the meaning of life, all is forgiven in this ambitious, fantastic parable. ★★★½ DVD: $19.99, DVD Special Edition: $29.99, VHS: $9.99

Dogs in Space

(1987, 109 min, Australia, Richard Lowenstein) *Michael Hutchence, Saskia Post.* This "drugged-up punks in love" picture explores the underground subculture of Australia's alienated youth, circa 1978. Hutchence, lead singer of INXS, stars as the immovably passive leader of a commune of punks who hangers-on living in comfortable squalor in a ramshackle house in Melbourne. Infused with loud music, countless subplots and characters, the film, like its denizens, is incoherent and rambling. Yet, despite the problems, it is entertaining and amusing. ★★½ VHS: $79.99

The Dogs of War

(1980, 101 min, GB, John Irvin) *Christopher Walken, Colin Blakely, Tom Berenger, JoBeth Williams.* This film stretches the boundaries of political reason by idolizing a group of mercenaries who are hired to overthrow the dictator of a newly formed West African nation. A somber but solid adaptation of Frederick Forsythe's novel. ★★★ DVD Letterbox: $14.99

Dogtown and Z-Boys

(2002, 91 min, US, Stacy Peralta) *Narrated by: Sean Penn.* Tight and informative, *Dogtown and Z-Boys* is a highly entertaining documentary about the Zephyr Team, a group of California skateboarders who revolutionized the sport. The film traces the team from its start as an outcast band of surfers, to their creative use of empty swimming pools during a drought in the early '70s, to their international stardom in the latter part of the decade. While one might think that the film being directed and cowritten by Peralta — who was one of the most successful of the

Chris Rock, Kevin Smith, Jason Mewes and Linda Fiorentino in *Dogma*

Z-Boys — would result in extreme bias, the film is actually enhanced greatly by his expertise on the sport and inside knowledge of what really went on. Fast-paced and fascinating, *Dogtown and Z-Boys* will suck you in even if you think you have no interest in the subject. For fans, of course, the film is an absolute must. ★★★½ DVD Special Edition: $19.99, VHS: $9.99

Doin' Time on Planet Earth
(1988, 83 min, US, Charles Matthau) *Matt Adler, Adam West, Candy Azzara.* A harmless, dopey comedy about teenage alienation — as in alien from outer space. Adler is trapped in a dull, small Arizona town. Life seems aimless. Until he comes to the conclusion he's really from another planet. He meets up with West and Azzara, who convince him not only that he is right, but he's their leader who's destined to take them home. The film pokes fun at the extraterrestrial craze, and produces a few smiles. ★★ VHS: $19.99

La Dolce Vita
(1961, 176 min, Italy, Federico Fellini) *Marcello Mastroianni, Anita Ekberg, Anouk Aimée, Lex Barker.* A staggering, trendsetting film that examines the hollow lives of Rome's decadent upper crust through the eyes of a cynical columnist. Mastroianni became an international star thanks to his swaggering portrayal of the lustful gossip columnist, and Fellini sharply observes the mores and morals of a generation. (Italian with English subtitles) ★★★★

Dolemite
(1974, 88 min, US, D'Urville Martin) *Rudy Ray Moore.* He's bad, the man is out-a-sight . . . he's Dolemite! Spewing hilarious invective-filled poetry that would make Eddie Murphy blush, Moore single-handedly brings back those halcyon days at Philadelphia's Goldman Theatre when pimps in fluorescent polyester jumpsuits, fur hats and gravity-defying Afros ruled the cinematic land. Ignore the ludicrous acting and production values and just sit back and enjoy Dolemite as he faces crooked white cops, double-dealing thugs and scantily clad "hos" in this blaxploitation classic. ★★★ DVD: $19.99, VHS: $19.99

A Doll's House
(1973, 83 min, GB, Joseph Losey) *Jane Fonda, Edward Fox, Trevor Howard, David Warner,*

Delphine Seyrig. Fonda's controversial interpretation of Henrik Ibsen's 19th-century liberated woman is the centerpiece of Losey's cinematic adaptation of the classic play. Fonda plays Nora, who risks destruction in order to save her husband only to suddenly and dramatically have to assert her independence when he confronts her with unabashed male arrogance. ★★★

Dollar
(1938, 78 min, Sweden, Gustaf Molander) *Ingrid Bergman.* An uncharacteristically light *Rules of the Game*-like comedy about three society couples who set out on a group skiing vacation. (Swedish with English subtitles) ★★½ VHS: $19.99

The Dollmaker
(1984, 140 min, US, Daniel Petrie) *Jane Fonda, Geraldine Page, Amanda Plummer, Levon Helm.* Fonda won an Emmy Award for her stirring performance in this first-rate TV drama as an impoverished farm woman who moves her family to Detroit when her husband lands a factory job. The film evokes a fine feel for 1940s America, and there's a stellar supporting cast. ★★★½

Dolores Claiborne
(1995, 125 min, US, Taylor Hackford) *Kathy Bates, Jennifer Jason Leigh, Christopher Plummer, David Strathairn, Eric Bogosian.* This heartfelt adaptation of Stephen King's best-seller is distinguished by yet another Oscar-caliber performance by Bates as a downtrodden New England housewife who must vindicate herself in the murder of her employer even as she unlocks the secrets that separate her from her neurotic, chain-smoking daughter (Leigh). Hackford deftly and seamlessly switches from present day to flashback, creating a richly woven tapestry of mystery and suspense. ★★★½ DVD Letterbox: $9.99, VHS: $9.99, VHS Letterbox: $9.99

The Dolphin (O Boto)
(1987, 95 min, Brazil, Walter Lima Jr.) *Carlos Alberto Riccelli, Cassia Kiss.* This steamy fantasy is derived from a Brazilian myth about "O Boto," a lustful "were-dolphin" who, on the night of the full moon, becomes a handsome young man and lures unsuspecting women to the water where he bewitches and seduces them. Set in a small village on the northern coast of Brazil, the film tells the tale of

Tereza, the daughter of a fisherman who falls under "O Boto"'s spell. When she gives birth to his son, the town becomes victim to a terrible curse in which the local waters become devoid of fish. This erotic drama is tinged with a smattering of black humor and filmed in sensuous shades of midnight blue. (Portuguese with English subtitles) ★★★

Domestic Disturbance
(2001, 100 min, US, Harold Becker) *John Travolta, Vince Vaughn, Teri Polo, Matt O'Leary, Steve Buscemi.* A ludicrous thriller that could give "trashy" a bad name, *Domestic Disturbance* pits father against stepfather in an ultimate fight for survival. Usually with this kind of dreck, it's the wife who is caught in the middle and suffers accordingly. Here, it's a young boy, and it only makes this more infuriating. Travolta plays a nice-guy divorced dad who is the only one to believe his son when the youth says he witnessed his new stepdad commit murder. This puts both parent and child in danger. Shallow characters, an inept screenplay and slack direction make it impossible to care about anything that's going on. ★ DVD Letterbox: $14.99, VHS: $9.99

Dominick & Eugene
(1988, 111 min, US, Robert M. Young) *Tom Hulce, Jamie Lee Curtis, Ray Liotta, Todd Graf. Rain Man* has nothing on this similarly themed, criminally neglected drama. Set in Pittsburgh, the film details the complex relationship between twin brothers who have a dark secret buried in their past. Dominick (Hulce) is a slow-witted man-child whose job as a trash collector subsidizes his brother's medical school tuition. Eugene (Liotta) realizes his financial dependence on his brother — and Dominick's emotional dependence on him — is becoming burdensome, forcing him to consider some tough decisions about their future. Hulce gives a brilliantly textured performance and it probably should have been him, not Dustin Hoffman, to win that year's Oscar for a portrayal of a mentally disabled sibling. ★★★★ DVD Letterbox: $19.99

Don Giovanni
(1979, 186 min, France/Italy, Joseph Losey) *Ruggero Raimondi, Jose van Dam, Kiri Te Kanawa, Teresa Berganza.* Losey's brilliant screen adaptation of Mozart's operatic masterpiece features what amounts to an all-star cast of singers including van Dam, Te Kanawa, Raimondi and Berganza. Using a subtle blend of commedia dell'arte and morality play, Losey's interpretation of this Don Juan-based legend is a beautiful and bold marriage of opera and cinema. (Italian with English subtitles) ★★★★ DVD Letterbox: $29.99, VHS: $24.99

Don Juan
(1926, 111 min, US, Alan Crosland) *John Barrymore, Mary Astor, Myrna Loy.* The first sound feature (only music and sound effects, no dialogue; thus no mention in the history books). Barrymore is at his swashbuckling best, running when others would walk, jumping when others would sit down. If he weren't such a kinetic ball of energy, he would get lost in the sumptuous sets. ★★★½ VHS: $29.99

Don Juan DeMarco
(1995, 90 min, US, Jeremy Leven) *Johnny Depp, Marlon Brando, Faye Dunaway, Rachel Ticotin.* In this deliriously romantic fable about the power and magic of love, Depp stars as a possibly delusional young man who, insisting that he is the legendary lover Don Juan, decides to end his life because he cannot have the one woman he truly loves. Enter

La Dolce Vita

Brando as the retiring psychiatrist who tries to unlock the mystery of "the greatest lover that ever lived," all the while being seduced by the rhapsodic tales Depp spins during his therapy. First-time director Leven (a clinical psychologist and author) serves a delicious mixture of erotic love and comedy. *Don Juan* is a natural charmer — as only Depp could play him. ★★★ DVD: $9.99, VHS: $9.99

Don Juan My Love

(1990, 96 min, Spain, Antonio Mercero) *Juan Luis Galiardo, Rossy De Palma.* This delightful fable is a thoroughly enjoyable and, at times, hilariously wicked comedy. The date is October 31, All Souls' Day eve, when the tormented ghost of the womanizing Don Juan rises from his grave and, as he has been doing for hundreds of years, begins a 24-hour attempt to end his term in purgatory by doing a good deed. The comedy of errors begins when he is mistaken for an obnoxious actor who is playing Don Juan in a theatrical production. Drug-smuggling actors, corpulent knife-wielding grandmothers, castanet-speaking production assistants and coke-filled angels all pop up in this wild romp that juxtaposes the romantic memory of old Spain with the harsh reality of a modern one. (Spanish with English subtitles) ★★★ VHS: $19.99

Don King: Only in America

(1997, 112 min, US, John Herzfeld) *Ving Rhames, Vondie Curtis-Hall, Jeremy Piven, Loretta Devine, Keith David.* HBO's freewheeling, wholly enjoyable account of the life and times of the badass promoter, Don King. Based on Jack Newfield's controversial book, this production is a showcase for Rhames, boldly bald in past roles, now electri-follicled as the motor-mouthed huckster. Director Herzfeld and screenwriter Kario Salem chronicle the events that put King on boxing's throne, beginning with his numbers runnings days in 1950s Cleveland and two jail stints before emphasizing his relations with boxing's greats, his role in such major matches as "Rumble in the Jungle," and his wheelings and dealings behind the scenes, arranging TV deals, and duping business rivals and fighters alike. At one point toward the film's end, Rhames, in all of his galvanizing glory, addresses the camera from inside the boxing ring. He says, "I made you HBO motherfuckers a lot of money." Talk about guts and glory. ★★★½ DVD: $19.99, VHS: $9.99

Don Segundo Sombra

(1969, 110 min, Spain, Manuel Antin) *Juan Carballido, Juan Carlos Gene.* Based on Ricardo Guiraldes' novel, the title character narrates the story of Fabio Caceres as he grows into adulthood. Don Segundo Sombra, an old "gaucho," is his mentor and model: he teaches the youth moral and human values through his behavior, his stories and his example. (Spanish with English subtitles) ★★½ VHS: $29.99

Don's Party

(1976, 91 min, Australia, Bruce Beresford) *John Hargraves, Pat Bishop, Graham Kennedy.* A hilariously vulgar, 100-proof comedy that directs an unrelenting attack on Australian politics and suburbia. Don invites his friends over for an election night party, but what begins as a quiet victory celebration soon succumbs to riotous boozing, arguments, partner swapping, fights and crumbling marriages. Great fun! ★★★ DVD: $29.99, VHS: $19.99

Don't Bother to Knock

(1952, 76 min, US, Roy Baker) *Marilyn Monroe, Richard Wodmark, Anne Bancroft, Jim Backus.*

Billed for the first time above the title, Marilyn plays an emotionally disturbed baby-sitter who's a danger to herself and the young girl she's watching. Widmark lives across the courtyard and comes to the rescue. As a lounge singer involved with Widmark, Bancroft makes her film debut. A contrived melodramatic suspenser that's made bearable thanks to a few exciting scenes, and MM and her durable costar. ★★½ DVD: $14.99, VHS: $6.99

Don't Do It

(1994, 95 min, US, Eugene Hess) *Alexis Arquette, Heather Graham, James LeGros, Sheryl Lee, James Marshall, Esai Morales, Balthazar Getty.* Essentially a series of vignettes, this uninspired look at twentysomething relationships advertises itself as "The Generation X Comedy," with a display box that says more about the musical score than the story line. For good reason. Ill-using its large group of up-and-coming actors, many of whom have previously given competent performances, the film tries to be a contemporary comedy of manners, complete with requisite AIDS reference, but it collapses in on itself with derivative tedium. Don't Watch It! ★

Don't Drink the Water

(1969, 100 min, US, Howard Morris) *Jackie Gleason, Estelle Parsons, Ted Bessell.* Mildly entertaining version of Woody Allen's hit play with Gleason and Parsons as American tourists on a European vacation who are accused of spying and held captive in the Iron Curtain country of Vulgaria. (Remade in 1999) ★★½

Don't Let Me Die on a Sunday

(1999, 86 min, France, Didier Le Pecheur) *Élodie Bouchez, Jean-Marc Barr, Martin Petitguyot, Patrick Catalifo.* A handsome morgue worker eyes a hot young woman on the slab; he locks the door and does the unmentionable. Teresa, the young woman, had a drug overdose at a rave, and she comes back to life after the experience. She befriends Ben, the morgue worker, and they go on a journey of bisexual S&M orgies where anything goes. The uneven film is difficult to follow, with little reward at the end. (French with English subtitles) ★★ DVD: $29.99, VHS: $79.99

Don't Look Back

(1967, 96 min, US, D.A. Pennebaker) *Bob Dylan.* D.A. Pennebaker's intimate portrait of a young Bob Dylan follows the iconoclastic troubadour on his 1965 British tour as he encounters adoring fans, skeptical critics and bothersome comparisons to Donovan. ★★★½ DVD: $24.99, VHS: $19.99

Don't Look Now

(1973, 110 min, GB, Nicolas Roeg) *Donald Sutherland, Julie Christie, Hilary Mason.* This stylish, visually beautiful mystery based on a novel by Daphne du Maurier established Roeg as a leading auteur. In addition to creating one of the most famous sex scenes in the history of the cinema, Roeg brilliantly taps into one of the most primal fears of many adults — the death of a child. Christie and Sutherland are the bereaved parents who attempt to contact their child through a medium. Roeg's haunting imagery of winter in Venice is breathtaking. ★★★½ DVD Letterbox: $14.99, VHS: $19.99

Don't Play Us Cheap

(1972, 95 min, US, Melvin Van Peebles) *Esther Rolle, Avon Long, Mabel King, Rhetta Hughes, Joe Keyes Jr..* Based on Van Peebles' endearing stage musical celebrating through song and dance the

resilience of the African-American culture, this slightly dated and stagey filmic adaptation nicely captures the essence of the original piece. Featuring the original cast, the film is the playful and comic tale of two minions of the Devil whose perpetual assignment of breaking up parties leads them to crash a festive Saturday night get-together in Harlem. Rolle is the hostess, and she and her guests unknowingly and successfully counter each and every serve thrown at them. Van Peebles experiments with editing and overlapping, which he sometimes allows to go on too long. Tony Award nominee Long is particularly memorable as a devil's disciple. ★★★ VHS: $79.99

Don't Say a Word

(2001, 95 min, US, Gary Fleder) *Michael Douglas, Sean Bean, Brittany Murphy, Oliver Platt, Famke Janssen.* Slick, preposterous and not without a few effective scenes, *Don't Say a Word* is another in a long line of generic thrillers that paints both its characters and plot strictly by the numbers, but manages to push a thrill button or two in spite of itself. In a role he can do in his sleep, Douglas plays a noted psychiatrist whose daughter is kidnapped by a group of jewel thieves. They want him to retrieve information from a comatose girl (Murphy, whose "I'll never tell" was the movie catchphrase of 2001), and he has only 24 hours. The film is full of coincidences, most of which are tough to overlook, though director Fleder does try to compensate by maintaining some degree of suspense — he's only marginally successful. ★★ DVD Letterbox: $14.99, VHS: $9.99

Don't Tell Mom the Babysitter's Dead

(1991, 105 min, US, Stephen Herek) *Christina Applegate, Joanna Cassidy, Keith Coogan.* Left in the care of a tyrannical baby-sitter for the summer while their mother is away, Applegate and siblings get a reprieve when nanny unexpectedly dies. With no money to live on, sis is sent into the working world. There are a few laughs, but this amiable comedy is very one-note. ★★ DVD: $14.99

Doña Flor and Her Two Husbands

(1976, 106 min, Brazil, Bruno Barreto) *Sonia Braga, Jose Wilker.* The humorous account of a young woman (Braga) whose first husband is beckoned from the grave when her second fails to satisfy her sexual needs. Barreto's hedonistic excursion simmers with the sights and sensuality of Brazil. (American remake: *Kiss Me Goodbye*) (Portuguese with English subtitles) ★★★

Doña Herlinda and Her Son

(1986, 90 min, Mexico, Jaime Humberto Hermosillo) *Guadalupe del Toro, Marco Antonio Trevino, Arturo Meza.* A funny and subversively heartwarming love story about Doña Herlinda, a shrewd yet always placid mother who wishes for her son only that he live happily with Mom, his wife . . . and another man if need be. Her son, a sexually confused surgeon, is having a relationship with Ramon, a handsome music student. When Mom realizes that their relationship is romantic and deep, she helps things out by inviting her son's lover to stay with them, reasoning, "Rodolfo has such a large bed!" A wickedly funny and uplifting Mexican comedy of manners that sympathetically portrays gay love. (Spanish with English subtitles) ★★★½ DVD: $19.99

Donkey Skin

(1970, 90 min, France, Jacques Demy) *Catherine Deneuve, Jean Marais, Delphine Seyrig.* This enchanting and lyrical fairy tale is set in a small kingdom where the beloved queen is dying. Her final wish is that her husband, the king, only marry someone who is as beautiful as she. To the king's consternation, the only woman is his daughter! Filmed in sumptuous color, this adaptation of Charles Perrault's story is consistently entertaining. (French with English subtitles) ★★★

Donnie Brasco

(1997, 115 min, US, Mike Newell) Al Pacino, Johnny Depp, Anne Heche, Michael Madsen, Bruno Kirby, James Russo, Zeljko Ivanek. Director Newell concisely captures the nuance and flavor of 1970s gangland New York in this crisp, extremely well-acted gangster drama based on the real-life experiences of undercover FBI agent Joe Pistone. Depp is Donnie Brasco (alias Pistone), who infiltrates the mob. Befriending midlevel wiseguy Lefty Ruggiero (Pacino), Donnie secures a place for himself with Lefty as his mentor, all the while dispatching vital information. The strength of the film is the human face placed on all its characters. The best of these is Pacino's Lefty, an anonymous foot soldier who sees in Donnie a chance to pass along his limited worldly wisdom. Pacino is superb in etching the fragile shadings of unfulfilled ambition, and Depp is equally adept in relaying the inner conflict of a man slowly losing his emotional grip. Donnie Brasco brings a fresh attitude to an often overplayed genre. ★★★½ DVD Letterbox: $14.99, VHS: $9.99

Donnie Darko

(2001, 112 min, US, Richard Kelly) Jake Gyllenhaal, Jena Malone, Drew Barrymore, Mary McDonnell, Katharine Ross, Patrick Swayze, Noah Wyle, Maggie Gyllenhaal. Owing a passing debt to David Lynch and P. T. Anderson, director Kelly makes an impressively hypnotic debut with this (perhaps too) ambitious indie sci-fi thriller. J. Gyllenhaal plays the title character, a doubly troubled teen circa 1988 who's disaffected and schizophrenic. His dreams are haunted by a demonic rabbit named Frank, who gives Donnie apocalyptic prophecies and spurs him to do delinquent deeds. Still, he manages to find a kindred spirit in Gretchen (Malone), a girl new to the community and just as alienated as Donnie. But what does Frank have in store for him? Kelly ratches the suspense by slowing things down, using long fluid takes (that utilize the full widescreen frame) and changing film speeds; the effect is mesmerizing. This otherwise remarkable

effort is marred only by a protracted ending that not only makes little sense but also contradicts much of the science that came before it. ★★★½ DVD: $14.99, VHS: $9.99

Donovan's Brain

(1953, 83 min, US, Felix Feist) Lew Ayres, Gene Evans, Nancy Davis. Another scientist with a social problem. This one is Ayres, and he's being controlled by the disembodied and quite living brain of an evil industrialist. ★★★ DVD: $14.99

The Doom Generation

(1995, 85 min, US, Gregg Araki) Rose McGowan, James Duval, Johnathon Schaech, Parker Posey, Heidi Floss, Margaret Cho, Amanda Bearse. Araki's "teens-on-the-run" epic is dripping with homoerotic undertones, foul language, and violence that borders on the sadistic. On what was supposed to be a simple date, the tough-as-nails Amy (McGowan), an angry Valley Girl with a checkered past, and Jordan (Duval), a sweetly naïve cutie, meet up with the dangerously sexy X (Schaech). He soon gets them involved in a Quickie Mart robbery that turns deadly. And with bloody Twinkies in hand, the three escape into the neon night. Of course, just like those horny mall rats of suburbia, sex is always on their minds, resulting in various couplings. Mocking mid-American values, The Doom Generation is a viciously funny, tumultously nihilistic ride through a hellish California. Buckle up. ★★★½ DVD Unrated: $24.99

The Doors

(1991, 141 min, US, Oliver Stone) Val Kilmer, Meg Ryan, Kevin Dillon, Frank Whaley, Kyle MacLachlan. A daring, provocative and hallucinogenic tribute, ostensibly a biography but much more, of the founding member of the 1960s rock group The Doors — Jim Morrison. Director Stone sees Morrison as a lost poet of his generation, which he probably was, and the film never condescends to either the era (which is difficult to recapture on film, but Stone has done so amazingly) or Morrison himself. Kilmer is an uncanny look-alike of the singer, but his portrayal goes far beyond simple impersonation; Kilmer embodies the passion and the firebrand of the pop star who was Jim Morrison. The live performances are particularly impressive, featuring most of the group's classic material. ★★★½ DVD Special Edition: $14.99, VHS: $9.99

Double Dragon

(1994, 96 min, US, James Yukich) Robert Patrick, Mark Dacascos, Scott Wolf, Alyssa Milano. Another witless, empty attempt to cash in on the success of a video game. The results are just a cut above a Saturday morning cartoon. In postapocalyptic Los Angeles where street gangs rule and even the cops are afraid to go out after dark, the nefarious Koga Shuko (Patrick looking like a refugee from a Prince video) attempts to wrest the second half of a mystical medallion from the two perky kickboxing orphans (Dacascos and Wolf) charged with protecting it. Anemic fighting sequences and only one decent special effect make this strictly for the pre-teen set. ★½ DVD: $19.99

Double Face

(1977, 84 min, GB/Italy/West Germany, Robert Hampton) Klaus Kinski. Atrocious in so many ways — cheesy special effects, cartoonish acting, overly serious plot and the just-not-quite-right dubbing — this baf-

fling and hyperventilating murder mystery is nevertheless strangely enjoyable. Kinski gives a wonderfully constipated, clenched-jaw performance as the cuckold husband of a wealthy industrialist who dies in a suspicious car accident. Did she die innocently or was she killed — or better yet, was her death faked with her lesbian lover? Not content to simply run the company and enjoy the money, our hero begins his own investigation into the byzantine circumstances and finds out more than he ever wanted to know. Great trash. ★★ VHS: $49.99

Double Happiness

(1995, 87 min, Canada/China, Mina Shum) Sandra Oh, Alannah Ong, Stephen Chang, Frances You, Johnny Mah, Callum Rennie. This delightfully offbeat drama-comedy is a promising feature film debut from writer-director Shum. Set in Vancouver, the story follows Jade Li (Oh), a spunky 22-year-old Chinese-Canadian woman who, when not working for her big break in acting, tries to find romance — two goals that upset her traditional-minded parents who just want her to find a "nice Chinese man and settle down." Interracial romance blooms when Jade falls for a cutely dorky white guy (Rennie) while her parents (Chang, Ong) desperately try to set her up with a handsome, debonair and Chinese (but gay) lawyer (Mah). The complex family dynamics of an immigrant family clinging to the ways of the old world are wonderfully exposed in this spirited, thoughtful film. ★★★ VHS: $19.99

Double Impact

(1992, 107 min, US, Sheldon Lettich) Jean-Claude Van Damme. Van Damme really cuts his acting teeth (okay, maybe not) in this effective kickfest as twin brothers separated at birth who reunite years later to avenge the brutal murder of their parents. Though not a horror movie, it's scary to think Jean-Claude actually does seem to be two different people. ★★ DVD: $14.99

Double Indemnity

(1944, 106 min, US, Billy Wilder) Barbara Stanwyck, Fred MacMurray, Edward G. Robinson. Considered to be the definitive film noir. The stunning Stanwyck plays an alluring vixen who cons unsuspecting insurance investigator MacMurray into a murderous web of intrigue. A very sexy film, rich in subtlety. Robinson is especially good as a wily investigator. Director Wilder at his best. ★★★★

Double Jeopardy

(1999, 105 min, US, Bruce Beresford) Ashley Judd, Tommy Lee Jones, Bruce Greenwood, Annabeth Gish. If you've seen the trailers, you've seen the movie. Framed for murdering her husband, a woman (Judd) serves seven years for the crime. When she discovers that he isn't dead, she breaks parole and goes hunting for him. Jones, who doesn't appear until a half-hour into the film, plays her embittered parole officer who chases her across the country. There's one especially good scene involving handcuffs, a car, a ferry and both Judd and Jones going overboard. But other than that, this thriller is standard issue, by-the-books and often implausible. ★½ DVD: $14.99, VHS: $9.99

A Double Life

(1947, 104 min, US, George Cukor) Ronald Colman, Shelley Winters, Edmond O'Brien. Colman won an Oscar for his triumphant performance as an acclaimed stage actor who can no longer separate his on- and off-stage lives — and now he's playing "Othello." Winters

Fred MacMurray and Barbara Stanwyck in *Double Indemnity*

is terrific in support as his fateful girlfriend. A superior suspense drama directed with great relish by Cukor. ★★★½ DVD: $14.99, VHS: $14.99

The Double Life of Veronique

(1991, 97 min, France/Poland, Krzysztof Kieslowski) *Iréne Jacob, Philipe Volter.* Jacob is mesmerizing in dual roles in this beautifully photographed, dreamlike exploration of psychic bonds and parallel lives. Jacob plays two women, born at the same time but a thousand miles apart, who are as inextricably bound as Siamese twins. Lush, golden lighting imparts an ethereal sense of myth and fairy tale as Veronique/Veronika searches for an understanding of her pervasive emotional reality. A revelatory inquiry into the transience of human existence and the devastation of loss. (French and Polish with English subtitles) ★★★½

Double Suicide

(1969, 105 min, Japan, Masahiro Shinoda) *Kichieman Nakamura, Shima Iwashita, Hosei Komatsu.* Set in 18th-century Japan and faithful to the Bunraku puppet theatre tradition for which it was originally written, this delicate, stylistic and erotic film tells the tragic tale of a middle-class merchant who, blinded by passion, loses his family and business in his relentless pursuit of an alluring prostitute. Based upon a work by Japan's greatest playwright, Monzaemon Chikamatsu (1653–1724), *Double Suicide* moves continually between the realistic and the formality of the Bunraku Puppet Theatre, which links it to the original play. Remastered print. (Japanese with English subtitles) ★★★ DVD Criterion Collection: $29.99, VHS: $29.99

Double Take

(1997, 86 min, US, Mark L. Lester) *Craig Sheffer, Costas Mandylor, Brigitte Bako.* Sheffer (sporting a truly distracting haircut) plays a respected novelist with a serious case of writer's block who witnesses the shooting death of a jeweler friend. He testifies against the suspect, certain of the man's guilt. But, several days after the conviction, Sheffer sees the guy's double on the street — could he have nabbed the wrong guy? Halfway intriguing premise holds one's attention for about half the running time, but the film has no surprises or twists. ★★ VHS: $79.99

Double Team

(1997, 91 min, US, Tsui Hark) *Jean-Claude Van Damme, Dennis Rodman, Mickey Rourke, Paul Freeman.* Lightning strikes a fourth time, as a talented Hong Kong action director (Hark) succumbs to the dubious talents of star Van Damme (Yuen Kwai, John Woo and Ringo Lam were before him). Van Damme is a covert agent whose identity is erased and then sent to a top-secret island facility called the Colony. In the movie's only moderately well-written action set piece, he escapes; thus begins the hunt for his nemesis, this time with the aid of a tattooed weapons expert (the similarly attired Rodman). Only a furious kung fu fight between Van Damme and Chinese stuntman and movie villain Xiong Xin-Xin will quicken the pulse. ★½ DVD: $14.99, VHS: $9.99

Double Vision

(2003, 110 min, Hong Kong, Kuo-fu Chen) *Tony Leung, David Morse, Rene Liu.* A diverting buddy cop film/supernatural thriller, Double Vision has "Ugly American" Morse assisting burned-out Leung in investigating a series of bizarre deaths, each involving an odd black fungus found on the victims — a man freezes to death in his office on a swelter-

ing summer day, a woman burns to death in her apartment with no other signs of a fire. This intriguing "X-Files"-esque premise is complemented by nice chemistry between the two leads and some effective scenes. However, there's little action to the film, and it never quite grabs you the way it should to totally compel. ★★½ DVD: $24.99, VHS: $102.99

Double Wedding

(1937, 87 min, US, Richard Thorpe) *William Powell, Myrna Loy, Florence Rice, John Beal, Jesse Ralph.* Asking the probing question, "Why do Bohemians have to stay up all night?," this breezy screwball comedy stars Powell as an eccentric artist who crosses paths with rigid businesswoman Loy when she thinks he's in love with her younger sister (Rice). A slew of zany characters are thrown into the stew as the two slowly fall in love. These include Beal, a catatonic wonder, as Rice's real fiancé, and Ralph as a fiery old broad and friend to Powell. The ending is right out of a Marx Brothers film. Based on the play "Great Love" by Ferenc Molnar ("The Guardsman"). ★★★ VHS: $19.99

Doubting Thomas

(1935, 78 min, US, David Butler) *Will Rogers, Billie Burke.* It's comedy of a high order when Rogers' wife Burke gets the lead in a small-town amateur theatrical production. One of Rogers' best films is a truly funny adaptation of George Kelly's play, "The Torch Bearers." A good starter for those unfamiliar with the wonderful, homespun Rogers. ★★★ VHS: $19.99

Le Doulos

(1962, 108 min, France, Jean-Pierre Melville) *Jean-Paul Belmondo, Michel Piccoli, Serge Reggiane, Jean Dessaily.* Melville's remarkable 1962 "nocturnal western" is adapted from a French detective novel and set in the French underworld. Belmondo stars as a mysterious, cryptic informer caught up in the complex relationship between criminal and policeman. In this tightly written and subtly acted film, Melville has created a man's world rich with male rituals and solidly sensuous women, all involved in a Pirandellian plot that none of the characters fully understands. Stylishly and brilliantly photographed in black and white, and filled with Melville's passionate love of film noir and the language of film. (French with English subtitles) ★★★

Down and Dirty

(1976, 115 min, Italy, Ettore Scola) *Nino Manfredi, Francesca Annibaldi.* Can you believe that Scola, the esteemed director of such high-brow hits as *Passion D'Amore* and *La Nuit de Varennes*, would also be responsible for this hilarious Italian "version" of *Pink Flamingos*!? Italy's urban poor, long ennobilized in neorealist films, are seen in an entirely different light in this demented and scathing black comedy. Manfredi stars as the brutish patriarch of a morally depraved family whose interests include adultery, murder, revenge and incest. This thoroughly sick, no-holds-barred romp about Rome's lowlife will have you crossing the street screaming the next time you are approached by a vagrant. (Italian with English subtitles) ★★★

Down and Out in Beverly Hills

(1986, 97 min, US, Paul Mazursky) *Nick Nolte, Richard Dreyfuss, Bette Midler, Little Richard, Elizabeth Peña, Alexis Arquette.* Mazursky's boisterously funny social comedy stars Nolte as a street person who is taken in by a nouveau riche Beverly Hills family when he tries to drown himself in their swimming pool. Dreyfuss and Midler are in top form

as the husband and wife whose lives are turned upside down by their new boarder. Modern remake of the Jean Renoir 1932 classic *Boudu Saved from Drowning.* ★★★ DVD: $14.99, VHS: $9.99

Down by Law

(1986, 107 min, US, Jim Jarmusch) *John Lurie, Tom Waits, Roberto Benigni, Ellen Barkin.* Jarmusch continues on the theme of alienated outsiders in this razor-sharp and decidedly different "road picture." Lurie and Waits (wonderfully cast as a gravel-voice D.J./hipster) meet up in a Louisiana prison where they team with an irrepressible Italian tourist who leads them on a jailbreak through a stark eerie swamp and beyond. An offbeat comedy from one of the most original American filmmakers of today. ★★★ DVD Letterbox Criterion Collection: $39.99

Down in the Delta

(1998, 115 min, US, Maya Angelou) *Alfre Woodard, Al Freeman, Jr., Wesley Snipes, Esther Rolle, Mary Alice.* Poet Maya Angelou's stellar directorial debut is a beautifully realized portrait of the highs and the lows of African-American life. Woodard stars as Loretta, a screwed-up, boozing mom living in the projects of Chicago. Her son and daughter are under the kindly supervision of Grandma (Alice, graceful as always) who finally have enough of Loretta's addictive ways — she sends Loretta and her kids on a bus for the Mississippi Delta to spend a summer with Uncle Earl (Freeman). Once there, of course, Loretta undergoes a slow transformational healing. Though just a little conventional, it doesn't deter a splendid cast from elevating this into a serious and sensible family drama that is filled with a sense of triumph and a profound connection to history. ★★★ DVD: $14.99, VHS: $9.99

Down Periscope

(1996, 92 min, US, David S. Ward) *Kelsey Grammer, Lauren Holly, Bruce Dern, Rob Schneider, Rip Torn, Harry Dean Stanton.* Another small-to-big-screen casualty, *Frasier's* Grammer forgoes his very funny TV persona for a smug submarine commander in his first, disaster-prone mission. The usual assortment of misfits and slackers are on hand, with a slightly bemused Grammer enduring his crew's shenanigans; after all, damn it, they're a great bunch of guys. Director Ward does manage to inject some humor, but it's of the knucklehead variety. ★★ DVD Dual: $14.99

Down to Earth

(2001, 87 min, US, Paul Weitz & Chris Weitz) *Chris Rock, Regina King, Mark Addy, Chazz Palminteri, Eugene Levy, Frankie Faison, Jennifer Coolidge.* In remaking both *Here Comes Mr. Jordan* and *Heaven Can Wait*, it would seem that writer and actor Rock would have found the perfect backdrop — that of stand-up comedy — to replace the sports themes of the previous two films. Unfortunately, unmemorable one-liners, mostly about race and sex, and static pacing are what make up *Down to Earth*, an uninspired concoction with too few laughs. Rock plays a struggling comedian who is spirited away to Heaven before his time. The man in charge, Mr. King (Palminteri, who plays this angel as a Sinatra-loving goodfella), finds him another body — that of a rich, white businessman. He falls for a neighborhood activist while trying for a comedy spot at the Apollo. The plotting is fairly identical to the first two films, but the laughs are noticeably missing. With this premise and cast, you expect Richard Pryor but get amateur night on the WB. ★★ DVD: $14.99, VHS Special Edition: $9.99

Down to You

(2000, 89 min, US, Kris Isacsson) *Freddie Prinze, Jr., Julia Stiles, Selma Blair, Shawn Hatosy, Henry Winkler, Zak Orth.* A romantic comedy that lives up — or is it down? — to its title, *Down to You* benefits from having two cute stars, but it gives them little to do. Al (Prinze) is a chef in college who meets and falls in love with Imogen (Stiles), a designer. They have friends who direct porn films (Orth) or star in them (Blair), and they stay generally smitten except when Al suspects Imogen of having an affair, and then he actually has one himself. Prinze and Stiles try their best, but are stuck in a futile film that fails to fully take advantage of anyone's talents. ★½ DVD: $19.99, VHS: $9.99

Down with Love

(2003, 102 min, US, Peyton Reed) *Renée Zellweger, Ewan McGregor, David Hyde Pierce, Sarah Paulson, Tony Randall.* It plays like *Pillow Talk*, it sounds like *Sex and the Single Girl* and, geez, it looks just like it was shot in 1962, from the elaborately artificial sets to the glorious Cinemascope logo that opens the film. But *Down with Love* is more than a carbon copy of the delightfully innocuous sex comedies of the '60s. Like *Far from Heaven*, it updates the characters a bit, bringing issues like homosexuality bubbling to the surface, while detailing the corners of the frame with a loving touch that was absent from the simply manufactured originals. Zellweger plays a modern woman who writes a hit self-help book, advocating sex without love for the repressed female masses. Enter the dashing McGregor as Catcher Block, the Lothario who wants to write an exposé on her and prove that all she wants is love. The plot machinations lead to a winning mating dance peppered with more double entendres than an episode of "The Match Game." Pierce is brilliantly cast as the Tony Randall type: a fey would-be ladies' man who's plagued by the image that he's really bedding his best friend Catcher. That Randall himself appears as Zellweger's two-initialed publisher is just icing on this delectable cake. ★★★ DVD Pan & Scan: $19.99, DVD Letterboxed: $19.99, VHS: $12.99

Favorite Line: "Who are you calling Nancy?" — *David Hyde Pierce as Peter MacMannus*

Downhill Racer

(1969, 102 min, US, Michael Ritchie) *Robert Redford, Gene Hackman, Dabney Coleman.* Redford is the ski bum who gets a chance for an Olympic try-

Down with Love

out. Hackman is the compassionate coach. An involving drama heightened by superior ski sequences. ★★★ VHS: $14.99

Downtown

(1990, 96 min, US, Richard Benjamin) *Anthony Edwards, Forest Whitaker, Penelope Ann Miller, Joe Pantoliano.* Though Edwards and Whitaker are extremely likable actors, there's little to recommend in this buddy-cop comedy set in urban Philadelphia (though locals may not recognize all the scenery). Edwards is the naïve white cop partnered with street-wise black cop Whitaker, together tracking down a stolen-car ring. ★★ VHS: $19.99

Dr. Seuss' The Cat in the Hat

(2003, 82 min, US, Bo Welch) *Mike Myers, Alec Baldwin, Kelly Preston, Dakota Fanning, Spencer Breslin, Sean Hayes.* Poor Dr. Seuss . . . he must be rolling over in his grave. After the botched film adaptation of his wonderful story "The Grinch Who Stole Christmas," now they've gone and done it again with his classic "The Cat in the Hat." Myers is the "witty, cultured" cat in the hat, a mischievous prankster whose shenanigans spell comic doom for two small children. That's all well and good, but the way Myers plays the part, "witty" and "cultured" are missing in action. There are bits of Austin Powers, Linda Richman and Wayne hidden under all that makeup, and the actor never creates a singular character, unlike Carrey's resourceful Grinch. But blame for this train wreck of a movie isn't Myers' entirely, as he's been given little help in the writing or directing departments. Too bad the art directors didn't helm the film — they at least give the impression they knew what they were doing. He's the cat in the hat/And he's come here today/To show you some fun/But forgotten the way. ★ DVD Letterbox: $26.99, DVD Pan & Scan: $26.99, VHS: $24.99

Dracula

(1931, 75 min, US, Tod Browning) *Bela Legosi, Dwight Frye, David Manners, Helen Chandler.* Classic Hollywood horror film with Legosi as the quintessential Count Dracula, that pain-in-the-neck vampire who here is on the loose in foggy old London. Director Browning creates an effectively eerie atmosphere to play out his tale, played to the hilt by Legosi. Frye makes a memorable Renfield. (Sequel: *Dracula's Daughter*) ★★★½

Dracula: The Spanish Version

(1931, 104 min, US, George Melford) *Carlos Villarias, Lupita Tovar.* One from the vaults! Filmed simultaneously with the original 1931 Bela Lugosi classic, this long-lost gem features the same sets and script translated into Spanish. Ripe with sensuality and atmosphere, many feel this version is more chilling than its English-language counterpart. With Villarias as the infamous Count. (Spanish with English subtitles) ★★★½

Dracula

(1973, 100 min, US, Dan Curtis) *Jack Palance, Simon Ward, Nigel Davenport.* Having made a fortune serializing the vampire legend with "Dark Shadows," producer-director Curtis returns to the original source with this made-for-TV adaptation of the Bram Stoker novel. Hollywood ham Palance dusts off his formal attire for the title role of the Count who, well, you know the story. Teleplay by Richard Matheson. ★★½ DVD: $14.99, VHS: $59.99

Dracula

(1979, 109 min, US, John Badham) *Frank Langella, Kate Nelligan, Laurence Olivier, Donald Pleasance, Trevor Eve.* This cinematic interpretation of the Broadway hit highlights the sexual subtext that is really at the heart of the vampire legends. Still, director Badham doesn't ignore the frights in this dark romance featuring Langella as the sensual count locked in immortal conbat with Dr. Van Helsing (Olivier). Features an excellent score by John Williams. ★★★

Dracula 2000

(2000, 90 min, US, Patrick Lussier) *Jonny Lee Miller, Justine Waddell, Gerard Butler, Jennifer Esposito, Sean Patrick Thomas, Omar Epps, Christopher Plummer.* A group of hi-tech (but really stupid) thieves decide to rob the Van Helsing vault — and discover a sealed coffin. Hmmm . . . better open it right then and there! Silly but surprisingly enjoyable film has some choice lines ("I don't drink . . . coffee") a lush look (courtesy of *Crouching Tiger* cinematographer Peter Pau) and a classy Van Helsing in Plummer. However, there is an abundance of product placement, and a colossal mistake by the filmmakers that occurs more than halfway through, from which the film never recovers. ★★½ DVD: $22.99

Dracula: Dead and Loving It

(1995, 90 min, US, Mel Brooks) *Leslie Nielsen, Peter MacNicol, Steven Weber, Harvey Korman, Amy Yasbeck, Mel Brooks, Lysette Anthony, Anne Bancroft.* Brooks is close to speed with this funny if sometimes obvious spoof on vampire films. Nielsen clearly is enjoying himself as the Count, neatly satirizing every vamp from Lugosi to Oldman. The story is basically the same: Dracula comes to England, and becomes a real pain in the neck until Professor Van Helsing (Brooks) gets on his trail. Brooks and his cowriters aren't on target with every joke, but many of the ones which do work are surprisingly fresh (such as Dracula dancing in front of a mirror or a hysterical scene of a staking). ★★½ DVD: $19.99

Dracula Has Risen from the Grave

(1968, 92 min, GB, Freddie Francis) *Christopher Lee, Rupert Davies, Veronica Carlson.* In this Hammer vampire horror tale, Lee emerges from a watery hibernation — looking more constipated than usual — to take sweet vengeance on a haughty monsignor (Davies) by claiming his beautiful niece. Hokey, campy fun. ★★½ DVD: $19.99

Dracula: Prince of Darkness

(1965, 90 min, GB, Terence Fisher) *Christopher Lee, Andrew Keir, Barbara Shelley.* Lee is back as the epitome of evil. Only this time around, he doesn't say one word! Not to worry, however: his physical presence speaks volumes. A group of four English travelers stumble upon Castle Dracula in the mountains of Transylvania and unwittingly participate in his resurrection by a faithful human servant. More atmospheric than previous entries in the cycle, *Prince of Darkness* is another subtle masterwork by director Fisher. ★★★ VHS: $14.99

Dracula's Daughter

(1936, 70 min, US, Lambert Hillyer) *Gloria Holden, Otto Kruger.* With a decided taste for female blood, the screen's first vampire of the fairer sex, Holden, stars in this moody sequel to the Bela Lugosi classic. Holden stars as the titular vampire, whose attempts to escape her bloodthirsty inclinations (through the help of a sympathetic doctor) are dashed when she develops an affinity for a young woman whom she seduces and vampirizes. The first of what would be a long line of lesbian-themed vampire films. ★★★ VHS: $14.99

Dragnet
(1954, 89 min, US, Jack Webb) *Jack Webb, Ben Alexander.* Webb is Sergeant Joe Friday and Alexander is Officer Frank Smith in this first film version of two Los Angeles detectives, here investigating a mob slaying. Webb also teamed up with Harry Morgan in the 1960s TV series. (Remade in 1987 as a comedy) ★★½

Dragnet
(1987, 106 min, US, Tom Mankiewicz) *Tom Hanks, Dan Aykroyd, Harry Morgan, Christopher Plummer, Dabney Coleman.* "Just the facts . . ." Okay, this mediocre comic remake of the movie and famed TV series is a bust. Hanks and Aykroyd try their best to bring some lightheartedness into their roles, but they just aren't given any good material. ★½ DVD: $24.99, VHS: $14.99

Dragon Chow
(1987, 75 min, Germany, Jan Schütte) *Ric Young, Bhasker, Buddy Uzzaman.* Schütte's evocative and moving study of the hopes and ambitions of a pair of immigrant Pakistanis in Hamburg, West Germany, is as unpretentious and pristine as its simple black-and-white photography. The story follows Shezad and Rashid, who live in a barren welfare hotel filled with Hamburg's *gastarbeiter* (guest workers). Shezad's dream is to break into the restaurant business. He gets his start when he lands a job at a local Chinese restaurant and joins forces with one of the waiters. Together, they set out to open their own business, but find the West German environment less than hospitable. Schütte's story is simple and understated, but his treatment of this stranger-in-a-strange-land theme is flavorful and at times captivating. (German with English subtitles) ★★★½ VHS: $19.99

Dragon Fist
(1984, 95 min, Hong Kong, Lo Wei) *Jackie Chan.* Chan stars as kung fu artist Yuan, who seeks vengeance for the death of his master. Traveling with the master's widow and her daughter, they journey to a distant village where they uncover the killer. To their surprise, however, he has mutilated himself out of guilt for his deed. Revenge, honor, soap-opera melodrama and great fight scenes galore make this an above-average martial arts film. ★★★ DVD Letterbox: $14.99, VHS: $19.99

Dragon Inn
(1992, 105 min, Hong Kong, Raymond Lee) *Maggie Cheung, Brigitte Lin, Tony Leung, Donnie Yen.* A needlessly dense and lengthy prologue sets up the premise for this Hong Kong actioner: bad guys want to kill the good guys. Most of the film takes place in the titular locale: the only shelter for many miles in a vast desert. After a sluggish first half, the film kicks into high gear with the type of kinetic and imaginative fight scenes fans have come to expect from producer Tsui Hark. With a lot of trimming (this cut is actually longer than the original), this could have been first-rate. As is, it's uneven and mildly enjoyable. (Cantonese with English subtitles) ★★½ DVD Special Edition: $19.99, VHS Dubbed: $19.99, VHS Subtitled: $19.99

Dragon Seed
(1944, 149 min, US, Harold S. Bucquet & Jack Conway) *Katharine Hepburn, Walter Huston, Agnes Moorehead.* Pearl S. Buck's novel of patriotism and heroism in war-torn China is the basis for this Hepburn vehicle. Kate plays a young Chinese peasant who becomes a guerrilla fighter when the Japanese army invades her small village. Anglo-Americans portraying Asians may disarm some viewers, but this well-intentioned war drama did serve as allegory and morale booster for the American fight against Nazism at the time. ★★½ VHS: $14.99

Dragon: The Bruce Lee Story
(1993, 119 min, US, Rob Cohen) *Jason Scott Lee, Lauren Holly, Robert Wagner, Michael Learned, Nancy Kwan.* This rousing chop-socky story of Bruce Lee rises above its mediocre biopic roots thanks to the winning combination of its undeniably exciting subject, a breezy and witty screenplay, elaborately staged fight sequences, and the riveting presence of Jason Scott Lee in the lead role. The film follows B. Lee from his early days in Hong Kong to his life as an ambitious American immigrant, his short-lived American TV stint in "The Green Hornet," to his career as a martial arts star, suddenly dying at age 32. J.S. Lee's smile, body and personality carry the adulatory movie, adapted from the book by Lee's widow, Linda Lee Cadwell. While the film's love story is "nice," it is the fight sequences that are mesmeric — capturing the exaggerated look of kung fu fights, with their gravity-defying leaps, flailing legs and fists that would pulverize any mere mortal. ★★★½ DVD Collector's Edition: $14.99, VHS: $9.99

Dragonheart
(1996, 108 min, US, Rob Cohen) *Dennis Quaid, David Thewlis, Julie Christie, Pete Postlethwaite, Voice of: Sean Connery.* This film will be remembered, at the very least, for featuring the first completely computer-generated main character, Draco the Dragon (voiced by Connery). Quaid stars as an errant knight who lives to slay dragons. He meets his match in Draco, whom he discovers is the last of his kind. They soon learn they were each partially responsible for the evil deeds and villainy of the country's tyrannical ruler (Thewlis). Naturally, they join forces to destroy the evil king and restore goodness to the land. While the computer effects are stupendous and the scenes between Draco and Quaid are the best of the film, the overall tone of the movie is far too juvenile for adults and too heavy, even dull at times, for kids. ★★½ VHS: $14.99

Dragonslayer
(1981, 109 min, US, Matthew Robbins) *Ralph Richardson, Peter MacNicol, Caitlin Clarke.* When his mentor (Richardson) suddenly shuffles off his mortal coil, a young sorcerer's apprentice (MacNicol) finds himself thrust into battle with a massive serpent. This exciting tale will be sure to please fans of medieval myth and fantasy as well as lovers of good action-adventure. The dragon sequences are terrific. ★★★ DVD: $14.99, VHS: $14.99

The Draughtsman's Contract
(1982, 103 min, GB, Peter Greenaway) *Anthony Higgins, Janet Suzman, Joss Buckley, Steve Ubels, Anne Louis Lambert, Hugh Fraser.* This bizarre tale of adultery, blackmail and murder is set amidst the genteel countryside of late 17th-century England. An early effort from director Greenaway (*The Cook, The Thief*), this provocative and ribald puzzle of a film concerns an artist's rather unusual bargain to sketch the estate of a wealthy landowner: £8 per drawing and the use of the man's wife for sexual favors. ★★★ DVD: $19.99, VHS: $14.99

Dream for an Insomniac
(1997, 87 min, US, Tiffanie Debartolo) *Ione Skye, Jennifer Aniston, Mackenzie Astin, Michael Landes, Seymour Cassel.* This dopey little story could be called *Cure for Insomnia.* With a sanitized San Francisco as backdrop, the movie borrows its unnaturally tidy coffee-shop setting from "Friends," the TV home of Aniston and contains a lot of inane banner about caffeine. And don't adjust your sets: the first quarter is in black and white, building to one of the worst abuses of the "Oz effect." This cream puff is overstuffed with an almost uninterrupted soundtrack of goofy swing instrumentals or tunes by alterna-bands of the moment, so that in some scenes the wannabe-witty dialogue is all but drowned out. ★★ DVD Letterbox: $24.99, VHS: $14.99

Dream Lover
(1994, 103 min, US, Nicholas Kazan) *James Spader, Madchen Amick, Bess Armstrong, Larry Miller.* Spader plays a successful architect who meets in the person of Amick his dream woman. Low-keyed and set at a lethargic pace, the film (ever so) slowly has Spader soon wondering if his new wife and the mother of his child is not only having an affair but if she is really who she says she is. *Dream Lover* does become mildly interesting when the con becomes evident, and builds to a rather neat twist ending. ★★ DVD: $14.99

A Dream of Passion
(1978, 106 min, Germany, Jules Dassin) *Ellen Burstyn, Melina Mercouri, Irene Emirza, Andreas Filippides.* This interesting film focuses on the parallel Medea-like lives of two women in modern day Athens. Burstyn delivers a powerful performance as an American woman jailed in Greece for murdering her three children in a fit of rage over her unfaithful husband. Mercouri is an international actress who returns to Greece to play the role of Medea in a play. She soon becomes obsessed with Burstyn's plight and the two women's lives become inextricably connected through tragedy. (Filmed in English) ★★

The Dream Team
(1989, 113 min, US, Howard Zieff) *Michael Keaton, Christopher Lloyd, Peter Boyle, Stephen Furst, Lorraine Bracco.* Keaton heads a solid cast in this literally crazy comedy about the misadventures of four mental patients on the loose in New York City. They're left to fend for themselves on the mean streets when their doctor witnesses a murder and is left for dead. ★★★ DVD Letterbox: $9.99

Dream with the Fishes
(1997, 96 min, US, Finn Taylor) *David Arquette, Brad Hunt, Cathy Moriarty, Kathryn Erbe, Patrick McGaw.* Arquette stars as a voyeuristic, suicidal schlub who becomes involved with his low-life, terminally ill neighbor. Not at all the "Afterschool Special" it may sound like, *Dream with the Fishes* allows the cast to flesh out the characters, warts and all. The basic story, of an introvert who is brought out of his shell by his opposite, is a well-worn tale; but writer-director Taylor brings an individuality to the film that makes it seem *almost* fresh. While *Dream* is marred by a sometimes trendy soundtrack and attitude, and a near-absence of narrative drive, there are a few shining moments. Unfortunately, Taylor's screenplay doesn't cut deep enough. ★★½

D

Dreamcatcher

(2003, 135 min, US, Lawrence Kasdan) *Morgan Freeman, Thomas Jane, Jason Lee, Damian Lewis, Timothy Olyphant, Tom Sizemore, Donnie Wahlberg.* If the screenplay to this film hadn't had the words "Based on the novel by Stephen King" typed on it, it's highly improbable it would've been made. For *Dreamcatcher* is the loopiest, oddest major studio release in years — but in a good way. The film contains slimy aliens that are "born" by way of human rectums, an Army general gone mad, four lifelong pals who are psychically linked, an evil alien who speaks with a foppish British accent, an *Independence Day*-style battle between U.S. military choppers and an alien spacecraft — and much, much more. There's no way all this could have held together, so it's to Kasdan's, coscreenwriter Goldman's and their excellent cast's credit that it almost does. A ridiculous, absurd mess, to be sure; it's also highly entertaining, if you go with it. ★★½ DVD Letterbox: $19.99, DVD Pan & Scan: $19.99, VHS: $8.99

Dreamchild

(1985, 94 min, GB, Gavin Millar) *Coral Brown, Peter Gallagher, Ian Holm, James Wilby.* This lavish fantasy/drama tells the story of the 80-year-old Alice Hargreaves who, as a child, inspired Lewis Carroll to write his immortal "Alice in Wonderland." As Mrs. Hargreaves prepares to attend a symposium at Columbia University celebrating the 100th anniversary of Carroll's birth, she becomes haunted by fantastic images of the classic story, her youth, and her relationship with Mr. Carroll. Holm is superb as the stuttering Carroll, and Brown is unforgettable as the elder Alice. ★★★½

Dreamers of the Day

(1990, 94 min, Canada, Patricia Spencer & Philip Wood) *Lorna Harding, Julie Lemieux.* From the *Claire of the Moon* school of lesbian love and sexual coming out is this enjoyable if a bit amateurish drama. Set in Toronto, the story revolves around the friendship between openly lesbian Andra (Harding), an aspiring filmmaker, and Claire (Lemieux), a married, professionally successful film producer. The film follows their budding friendship, which is undermined by Andra's attraction to the "straight" Claire, and their eventual romantic relationship. A tender and believable love story, the film suffers a bit from a standard story line, often stilted acting, and a static camera. ★★

Dreaming of Joseph Lees

(1999, 114 min, GB, Eric Styles) *Samantha Morton, Lee Ross, Rupert Graves.* A somber drama about an unhappy love triangle, *Dreaming of Joseph Lees* is set in dreary Somerset, England, circa 1958. Eva (Morton) is a young girl who loves her cousin Joseph (Graves), but sees little of him. She is courted by Harry (Ross), a young man who offers her temporary happiness, and she eventually moves in with him. Yet, when Eva reunites with Joseph, she finds her feelings for him cannot be denied. *Dreaming of Joseph Lees* deliberately paces its first hour where very little happens, only to gum up the works by rushing things in the last thirty minutes. The film captures the stifling atmosphere well, but like the characters, the audience suffers. ★★ VHS: $102.99

Dreaming of Rita

(1994, 108 min, Sweden, Jon Lindstrom) *Per Oscarsson, Marika Lagercrantz.* From the less serious side of Swedish filmmaking comes this wacky, but sadly not entirely successful, road comedy. The action kicks off when the recently widowed Bob

(Oscarson) flips his lid, and runs off in search of a Danish sweetheart of some thirty years earlier. This precipitates a chase in which his daughter, Rita (named after Miss Hayworth), tracks him down and together they journey on to Copenhagen all the while exploring their past à la *Wild Strawberries*. The film ultimately lands nowhere and its pat ending leads to no revelations; still, *Dreaming of Rita*'s amiable atmosphere and curious characters make it amusing, if not wholly worthwhile, viewing. (Swedish with English subtitles) ★★½ VHS: $14.99

The Dreamlife of Angels

(1999, 113 min, France, Erick Zonca) *Élodie Bouchez, Natacha Regnier, Gregoire Colin.* An intimate and deceptively simple film, *The Dreamlife of Angels* nevertheless packs an indelible emotional wallop. Isa (Bouchez) is a wanderer who meets factory-worker Marie (Regnier) when she stops in the northern French town of Lille. These two very different women soon forge a complex and unlikely friendship. Director Zonca chronicles the survival instincts and self-destructive tendencies of both Isa and Marie as they conduct their affairs, filming much of the action in real time. The naturalistic performances by the three leads are uniformly outstanding, and the film's stark directorial style only reinforces the despair of the lives on display. Emotionally complex and ultimately devastating. (French with English subtitles) ★★★½ DVD: $29.99, VHS: $14.99

Dreams

(1955, 87 min, Sweden, Ingmar Bergman) *Harriet Andersson, Gunnar Björnstrand, Eva Dahlbeck.* This probing study into the psychology of desire follows the activities of a photography agency head and her top model who, while visiting another city for work, each have an affair. The setting is but a pretense for Bergman to explore women's dreams, torments and sexual obsessions; and how all of this affects their relationships with men. (Swedish with English subtitles) ★★★ VHS: $29.99

Dreamscape

(1984, 99 min, US, Joseph Ruben) *Kate Capshaw, Max von Sydow, Christopher Plummer, Dennis Quaid.* Telepathic spies romp through the president's nightmares in this imaginative sci-fi thriller. Good dream sequences. ★★★ DVD: $14.99, VHS: $19.99

The Dress Code

(1999, 108 min, US, Shirley MacLaine) *Alex D. Linz, Shirley MacLaine, Gary Sinise, Stacey Halprin, Kathy Bates, Jennifer Tilly, Joey Lauren Adams, Gwen Verdon.* Full of sweetness and charm, *The Dress Code* is the story of the cross-dressing eight-year-old and his 450-pound mother. Bruno has two unusual characteristics: he loves to wear dresses and he's a champion speller. Grandmom (MacLaine), Dad (Sinise) and Mother Superior (Bates) are uncomfortable with the whole situation, that is until each is convinced in their own unique way. Comparisons to *Ma Vie en Rose* are obvious, but *The Dress Code* is a bit wackier and grounded less in fantasy. The acting is first-rate, especially Linz as Bruno, who brings such nuance and humor to Bruno you'd swear he was a pint-sized Tom Hanks. Although MacLaine directs this winning comedy-drama about acceptance and cross-dressing with the occasional heavy hand, David Ciminello's smart, involving screenplay makes sure its message of individuality is not lost in a story both funny and touching. (aka: *Bruno*) ★★★ DVD: $9.99

Dress Gray

(1986, 208 min, US, Glenn Jordan) *Alec Baldwin, Eddie Albert, Hal Holbrook, Lane Smith, Lloyd Bridges, Patrick Cassidy, Timothy Van Patten.* This riveting murder mystery set in a military academy during the Vietnam War is based on the novel by Lucian K. Truscott IV and adapted by Gore Vidal. Baldwin stars as a cadet who becomes embroiled in the murder case of another cadet who had been raped before his murder. Fearing a scandal, the embarrassed commandant (Holbrook) covers up the death. Soon Baldwin is a suspect and handcuffed by the military's code of honor. Like a high stakes Hardy Boys mystery, he attempts to clear his name and uncover the real killer with the mystery unraveling in a genuinely tense and exciting fashion. *Dress Gray* is both a well-told story and a well-developed allegory for America's involvement in Vietnam. ★★★½

Dressed to Kill

(1979, 105 min, US, Brian De Palma) *Michael Caine, Angie Dickinson, Nancy Allen, Keith Gordon, Dennis Franz.* De Palma's homage to Hitchcock stars Caine as an inquisitive psychiatrist and Dickinson as a woman whose promiscuity leads her to become the first victim of a schizophrenic transvestite murderer. De Palma succeeds in creating both atmosphere and suspense. ★★★ DVD Special Edition: $14.99

The Dresser

(1983, 118 min, GB, Peter Yates) *Tom Courtenay, Edward Fox, Michael Gough, Albert Finney.* Finney and Courtenay are both outstanding as, espectively, a grandiloquent, aging actor and his devoted dresser. Finney is the head of a second-rate touring company besieged by financial and wartime woes; Courtenay is his gay confidant/secretary/valet who watches over him with the eye of a hawk and the perseverance of a den mother. A brilliant, moving and often funny peek behind the curtain of theatre life. ★★★½ DVD: $19.99

The Dressmaker

(1989, 92 min, GB, Jim O'Brien) *Joan Plowright, Billie Whitelaw, Pete Postlethwaite, Jane Horrocks.* Set in Liverpool in 1944, this intricate character study subtly probes the complexities of three women. When Rita, a timid, young waif, befriends a randy American soldier who is stationed in town, a bitter struggle for her soul ensues between her two aunts: the fun-loving Margo (beautifully played by Whitelaw) and the disapproving, repressed spinster Nellie (icily portrayed by Plowright). Based on the novel by Beryl Bainbridge, this extremely well-acted and absorbing family drama is taunt with sexual tensions and impending disaster. ★★★ VHS: $79.99

Drifting

(1983, 80 min, Israel, Amos Gutman) *Jonathan Sagalle, Ami Traub.* Gutman's acclaimed first feature is also the first gay film made in Israel. The story follows Robi, a 24-year-old would-be filmmaker who isolates himself completely in the gay world and grows increasingly troubled; not by the political turmoil in his country, but by his increasingly aimless and frustrated life. His ennui causes him to reject his friends and lover and withdraw into self-destruction. A sensitive and moving drama. (Hebrew with English subtitles) ★★★

Drifting Weeds

(1959, 119 min, Japan, Yasujiro Ozu) *Ganjiro Nakamura, Machiko Kyo.* A remake of his own silent film *A Story of Silent Weeds*, Ozu's lyrical drama is about rivalries among a traveling acting troupe. The film is marked by Ozu's spare directorial style and the beautiful photography by Daiei cameraman Miyagawa. (Japanese with English subtitles) (aka: *Floating Weeds*) ★★★½

Drive Me Crazy

(1999, 91 min, US, John Schultz) *Melissa Joan Hart, Adrian Grenier, Stephen Collins, Susan May Pratt.* Attractive opposites Nicole (Hart) and Chase (Grenier) are next-door neighbors and seniors in high school. When their respective partners dump them before the big centennial dance, Nicole and Chase pose as a couple to win back their true loves. Of course, while they "scam" everyone with their act, the pair end up falling for each other. Though the plot is clichéd and contrived, it's given some degree of freshness thanks to the two leads. Hart is kinda adorable as the perky go-getter, while Grenier is endearing as the social outcast who bonds with the in-crowd. ★★½ DVD: $9.99, VHS: $9.99

Driven

(2001, 108 min, US, Renny Harlin) *Sylvester Stallone, Burt Reynolds, Kip Pardue, Til Schweiger, Gina Gershon, Estella Warren, Robert Sean Leonard.* The reteaming of *Cliffhanger* collaborators Stallone and director Harlin results in a clichéd racing drama punctuated by often exciting race sequences. Sly is an ex-racing champ who takes up-and-comer Pardue under his wing. Of course, as scripted by Stallone, *Driven* allows the young'un to be taught some life lessons as well. Uneven, at times painfully corny, *Driven* gets pulpier in its second half, featuring a tolerable performance by Stallone and scenery-chewing ones by Leonard and Gershon. Though with Harlin at the wheel, the many CGI effects are obvious and phony. ★★ DVD Letterbox: $24.99, VHS: $14.99

The Driver

(1978, 131 min, US, Walter Hill) *Bruce Dern, Ryan O'Neal, Isabelle Adjani.* Some spectacular car chase sequences highlight this unusual action-adventure with Dern as a cop obsessed with catching jewel thief O'Neal. ★★★ VHS: $59.99

Driving Miss Daisy

(1989, 99 min, US, Bruce Beresford) *Morgan Freeman, Jessica Tandy, Dan Aykroyd, Esther Rolle, Patti LuPone.* Based on Alfred Uhry's play, this is an extremely well acted and literate examination of the four-decade relationship between an elderly, Southern Jewish widow and her ever-patient black chauffeur. Oscar-winner Tandy and Freeman give magnificent performances as Daisy and Hoke, whose working relationship, beginning in 1948, slowly develops into one of friendship; reflecting the changing social mores around them. Oscar winner for Best Picture, though there were far more worthy films nominated that year. ★★★½ DVD: $19.99, VHS: $9.99

Drôle de Drame

(1937, 109 min, France, Marcel Carné) *Michel Simon, Louis Jouvet, Francoise Rosay.* Carné and Prévert fashioned this exuberant farce/burlesque-mystery with an all-French staff playing a group of Victorian Englishmen, enmeshed in a web of disguises, lies, murder and romance. An acute, humorous examination of how the French thought of their channel-mates, the British. (French with English subtitles) ★★★ DVD: $19.99

Drop Dead Fred

(1991, 98 min, US, Ate de Jong) *Phoebe Cates, Rik Mayall, Marsha Mason.* A poor man's *Beetlejuice,*

this sporadically funny though annoying comedy manages to entertain in spite of itself. Cates returns home to her shrewish mother (Mason) after her husband dumps her. There she is revisited by her "imaginary" childhood friend, Drop Dead Fred. As played by Mayall (of "The Young Ones"), Fred is a nose-picking, mischievous tornado of activity, eager to help straighten out the life of his former friend. Mayall's over-the-top mugging will either cause chuckles or spasms. ★★ DVD: $14.99, VHS: $9.99

Drop Dead Gorgeous

(1999, 99 min, US, Michael Patrick Jann) *Kirstie Alley, Kirsten Dunst, Denise Richards, Ellen Barkin, Allison Janney.* A scintillating premise is allowed to be flushed down the drain thanks to static direction and a script that doesn't live up to its potential. Told as a faux documentary, the story sends-up beauty pageants and the mothers and daughters who live for them — and would kill for them. That the film hits a few of its targets in parodying the contestants and their families makes it only more disappointing. Alley and Richards are in good form as the haughty mother and daughter determined to win at any cost, and Barkin is just right as Dunst's trailer-trash mom. Too bad the satire they've all been given to do is so obvious. ★★ DVD: $9.99, VHS: $9.99

Drop Zone

(1994, 101 min, US, John Badham) *Wesley Snipes, Gary Busey, Michael Jeter, Yancy Butler, Grace Zabriskie.* Exhilarating aerial photography punctuates this otherwise by-the-numbers rehash of *Die Hard* and *Point Break.* Snipes stars as a U.S. Marshall who goes undercover in the world of skydiving to locate a gang of gonzo parachutists planning to "drop in" on the DEA, steal the names of every undercover agent working in the field, and sell them to the highest bidder. Obviously this is the kind of film where macho posturing replaces acting, and stuntwork supplants action, but Snipes and Busey make the best of it. ★★½ DVD: $14.99, VHS: $9.99

Drowning by Numbers

(1987, 121 min, GB, Peter Greenaway) *Joan Plowright, Juliet Stevenson, Joely Richardson, Bernard Hill.* Wildly imaginative and entertaining, this offbeat comedy is a decidedly different twist on the battle between the sexes. The film follows the saga of three women (all named Cissie) who drown their husbands and then, attempting to cover up their crimes, engage in a bizarre game of sexual innuendo with the local coroner, Madgett. This outrageous tryst becomes the centerpiece of Greenaway's operative metaphor; namely, the games people play. The film is literally filled with games, mostly played by Madgett and his prepubescent son. Additionally, the film itself is one long game of numerical hide-and-seek — video viewers beware, the small screen may make it difficult to participate. A terrific ensemble is featured. ★★★½

Drowning Mona

(2000, 107 min, US, Nick Gomez) *Danny DeVito, Bette Midler, Neve Campbell, Jamie Lee Curtis, Casey Affleck, Will Ferrell, William Fichtner, Marcus Thomas.* A good premise that is rarely fulfilled, *Drowning Mona* tries desperately to recapture the dark humor of *Ruthless People,* DeVito and Midler's hilarious first film together, but their reunion unfortunately lacks that film's wit. Midler is Mona Dearly, who at the film's beginning sails off a cliff in her new Yugo into the depths of a local lake. It soon becomes apparent that it was murder. But who did

it? Through a series of flashbacks, it looks as if the whole town had reason to bump off the mean-spirited Mona. The scenario is ripe for black comedy, but director Gomez has little command for either frantic farce or subtle comedic escapades, and as such most of the comedy just sits there — despite an eager cast. ★★ DVD: $9.99, VHS: $9.99

The Drowning Pool

(1976, 108 min, US, Stuart Rosenberg) *Paul Newman, Joanne Woodward, Anthony Franciosa, Melanie Griffith.* This sequel to *Harper* finds Newman deep in the heart of Dixie trying to help old lover Woodward out of a jam and only making matters worse. Griffith makes a delightful film debut as Woodward's precocious daughter. ★★½ VHS: $14.99

Drugstore Cowboy

(1989, 100 min, US, Gus Van Sant) *Matt Dillon, Kelly Lynch, James LeGros, Heather Graham, William S. Burroughs, James Remar, Max Perlich, Grace Zabriskie.* Van Sant's gritty and provocative exposé of the down-and-out lives of four drug addicts living in the Pacific Northwest in the 1970s is highly original and profoundly honest. Dillon is perfectly cast as an icy-cool and unrepenting "drug fiend" who plays daddy to a rogue family of three fellow junkies — Lynch as his statuesque wife and LeGros and Graham as his mindless junkie pals. Drawing its power from a surprisingly wry sense of humor and its wholly unapologetic tone, the film follows Dillon and crew as they wantonly romp from town to town and burgle the drugs they need from local apothecaries. It seems inconceivable that in the Reagan-Bush era of rampant antidrug hysteria a film as brazenly nonjudgmental on this issue could have been made, much less enjoy the tremendous acclaim which this film deservedly received. Burroughs has a terrific cameo as a weathered drug addict. ★★★★ DVD Special Edition: $14.99, VHS: $9.99

Kirsten Dunst and Denise Richards in *Drop Dead Gorgeous*

Drumline

(2002, 118 min, US, Charles Stone III) *Nick Cannon, Zoe Saldana, Orlando Jones, Leonard Roberts. Drumline* uses the old Hollywood formula of the arrogant talent who has to lose before he can truly win. But who said formula is a bad thing if the end result is entertaining and fresh? Exploring the subject of band competitions between predominately black universities, the film traverses some unchartered musical territory. Its love stories and power struggles are effectively handled, thanks to competent performances from Cannon and an understated Jones. Nonetheless, these issues take a bit of a backseat to the infectious rat-tat-tat of some wildly entertaining drummers. Even though *Drumline* is a love letter to those who opted for band in school, it'd be difficult for even the biggest jock not to groove to these rhythms. This is both a feel-good *and* sound-good movie — just try to keep your foot from tapping. ★★★ DVD Letterbox: $19.99, DVD: $19.99, VHS: $12.99

Drums

(1938, 104 min, GB, Zoltan Korda) *Roger Livesey, Raymond Massey, Sabu, Valerie Hobson.* Korda's beautifully filmed colonial adventure features Livesey as a patriotic British officer who forms an alliance with a young Indian prince (Sabu) to help him battle his scheming uncle (Massey). ★★★

Drums along the Mohawk

(1939, 103 min, US, John Ford) *Henry Fonda, Claudette Colbert, Edna May Oliver, John Carradine.* Released the same year as his classic western *Stagecoach*, Ford heads East with this sumptuous historical drama mixed with humor and rousing adventure sequences. Fonda and Colbert star as colonists during the Revolutionary War who must protect themselves from Indian uprisings in the backwoods of upstate New York. Gorgeous cinematography in glorious Technicolor. ★★★ VHS: $19.99

Drunken Angel

(1948, 102 min, Japan, Akira Kurosawa) *Toshiro Mifune, Takashi Shimura.* An older doctor attempts to cure and rehabilitate a tubercular young gangster (Mifune) in this sinister and disturbing allegory on the human condition. This early Kurosawa work pays tribute to American film noir. (Japanese with English subtitles) ★★★ VHS: $19.99

Drunken Master

(1978, 107 min, Hong Kong, Yuen Woo-Ping) *Jackie Chan, Cassanova Wong, Simon Yuen, Pan Pan Yeung.* This piece of early Jackie fun, Chan plays an unruly teen with an authority problem who comes into his own as a man and a martial artist when he is taught the art of drunken fighting. Not much plot to speak of, but plenty of action, and the pace is brisk. The dubbing on this current domestic release is atrocious, only adding to the late-'70s, Saturday afternoon, "chopsocky" feel of the film. Chan fans shouldn't miss it, but casual viewers might find a lot to enjoy here as well, as the film's downtime is marked by plenty of Chan-style humor. (Sequel: *Drunken Master II*) ★★★ DVD: $19.99, VHS Dubbed: $9.99

Drunken Master II

(1994, 102 min, Hong Kong, Liu Chia Liang) *Jackie Chan, Anita Mui, Andy Lau.* In this terrific action comedy (many fans think this may be Jackie's best), the martial arts superstar plays Wong Fei Hun, a ne'er-do-well who battles the bad guys with a bizarre secret weapon: the more he drinks, the more

amazing a fighter he becomes. This film contains two of the greatest fight scenes ever filmed: an extremely energetic bamboo-stick fight, and the lengthy, climactic, mano-a-mano. This is a must-see for action nuts, and a must-own for Jackie fans. (Cantonese with English subtitles) (aka: *The Legend of Drunken Master*) ★★★★ VHS: $19.99

Drunks

(1997, 88 min, US, Peter Cohn) *Richard Lewis, Faye Dunaway, Dianne Wiest, Amanda Plummer, Howard E. Rollins, Jr., Parker Posey, Spalding Gray.* A small group of recovering alcoholics gather in the basement of a Times Square church for an intense AA meeting. One member (Lewis) ducks out early to walk the streets of New York City — will he revert to his old ways? Well-intentioned but rather flat, *Drunks* is basically a succession of talking heads, each giving his or her story of addiction and misery. This is an adaptation of the play "Blackout," and its theatrical origins show. The acting is uniformly good, but the overall effect is artificial and unconvincing. It has the feel of an actor's workshop and screams to be left on the stage. ★★ DVD: $24.99, VHS: $14.99

Dry Cleaning

(1999, 97 min, France, Anne Fontaine) *Miou-Miou, Charles Berling, Stanislas Merhar.* This compelling French psychosexual drama revolves around a staunchly "normal" married couple and how their dormant sexuality is ignited when a young man — a bisexual drag queen performer — enters their lives. Nicole (Miou-Miou) and Jean-Marie (Berling) are a strait-laced married couple who operate a small-town dry cleaning shop. One night, they visit a club where they become entralled by a brother-sister drag act. Through circumstances, the brother, Loic, begins to work at the couple's shop. The story focuses on how both Marie and Jean-Marie are attracted to him. The drama provocatively probes the shifting emotions, pent-up sexual longings and fears of the three. (French with English subtitles) ★★★ DVD: $29.99

A Dry White Season

(1989, 97 min, US, Euzhan Palcy) *Donald Sutherland, Zakes Mokae, Jürgen Prochnow, Susan Sarandon, Marlon Brando.* South African director Palcy powerfully confronts the violence and inhuman brutality of Apartheid. Sutherland is excellent as Ben du Toit, a well-respected Afrikaner schoolteacher asked to use his influence to help find his gardener's missing son. Du Toit quickly finds himself entangled with the dreaded Special Branch — a rather noxious element of the South African security system. The movie draws its power as we witness du Toit, ostracized, humiliated and beaten, in his transformation from ignorant patriot to outraged citizen. Excellent supporting cast. ★★★½

DuBarry Was a Lady

(1943, 100 min, US, Roy Del Ruth) *Red Skelton, Lucille Ball, Gene Kelly, Zero Mostel.* Those two crowned heads of comic tomfoolery, Skelton and Ball, take over the Bert Lahr and Ethel Merman roles of this entertaining adaptation of the Cole Porter musical. And though Red and Lucy are just fine, Hollywood once again outsmarted itself in the translation of a stage musical, here keeping only three of Porter's songs ("Friendship," "Do I Love You" and "Katie Went to Haiti"). Red's in love with nightclub entertainer Lucy. He sips a mickey and dreams he's Louis XV of France to Lucy's Madame DuBarry. ★★★ VHS: $19.99

duBEAT-E-O

(1984, 84 min, US, Alan Sacks) *Ray Sharkey.* Punky, irreverent and cocky, but marred by a nasty misogynist, violent and antigay streak, this low-budget musical-comedy is a wonderful illustration of the vastly different independent filmmaking worlds of L.A. and New York. Sharkey plays a sleaze-ball filmmaker who, on the "forceful" insistence of his producer, must finish his rock opus on Joan Jett within 31 hours. With offscreen narration and commentary by the actual filmmaker and his friends, the film's hipper-than-thou approach will remind many of the much funnier and similarly themed *Tapeheads.* ★★½ VHS: $59.99

Duck Soup

(1933, 70 min, US, Leo McCarey) *Groucho Marx, Harpo Marx, Chico Marx, Zeppo Marx, Margaret Dumont, Edgar Kennedy.* The best Marx Brothers by most standards, this wacky tale follows the boys' exploits in the tiny country of Freedonia (Land of the Spree and Home of the Knave). Groucho is memorable as the celebrated Rufus T. Firefly, newly

Drumline

appointed president; Harpo and Chico are enemy spies, and Zeppo is a tenor. Dumont is her usual resilient self. ★★★★

Favorite Line: "We're fighting for this woman's honor, which is more than she ever did." — *Groucho Marx as Rufus T. Firefly*

Dude, Where's My Car?

(2000, 83 min, US, Danny Leiner) *Ashton Kutcher, Seann William Scott, Jennifer Garner, Marla Sokoloff, Kristy Swanson.* Two stoners, Chester and Jesse (Kutcher, Scott), have such a wild night partying they wake up not remembering a thing. They spend the entire film trying to piece together what happened. Not exactly a premise that would have had Billy Widler jumping up and down, but one that has a certain amount of promise in the dumb slacker comedy genre. What transpires is a curiously sweet but laughless exercise in pot jokes, sex jokes and alien encounters. A lesser Bill and Ted, Kutcher and Scott are agreeable enough, but the tame screenplay reduces them to jokes borrowed from Abbott and Costello, Cheech and Chong, Parker and Stone, without any identity of their own. ★½ DVD: $14.99, VHS: $9.99

Dudley Do-Right

(1999, 83 min, US, Hugh Wilson) *Brendan Fraser, Sarah Jessica Parker, Alfred Molina, Eric Idle, Robert Prosky, Alex Rocco.* Trying to capture the same sense of silly fun that made *George of the Jungle* such a hit, this amiable comedy — based on another Jay Ward cartoon — certainly gets the silly part down. With the same toothy enthusiasm he brought to *George*, Fraser is Dudley Do-Right, that luckless Canadian Mountie who forever is being outsmarted by that dastardly villain Snidely Whiplash. The story, which is backseat to pratfalls and goofy shenanigans, has to do with Snidely faking a gold rush so that his town can reap the rewards. There are quite a few laughs, most at the expense of Dudley, but the silliness ratio becomes a little too high after a while. ★★½ DVD: $9.99

Duel

(1971, 90 min, US, Steven Spielberg) *Dennis Weaver, Lucille Benson.* Spielberg's career-launching film is a first-rate made-for-TV thriller starring Weaver as a businessman being terrorized by an unseen truck driver who is apparently, and for no known reason, out to kill him. Inventive and highly suspenseful. ★★★ VHS: $9.99

Duel at Diablo

(1966, 103 min, US, Ralph Nelson) *Sidney Poitier, James Garner, Bibi Andersson, Dennis Weaver.* An exciting western with Garner as an Indian scout, seeking revenge for the murder of his wife, who helps transport guns across Indian territory. Poitier is an ex-Army officer. Together, they hold off an Indian attack. ★★★

Duel in the Sun

(1946, 130 min, US, King Vidor) *Gregory Peck, Jennifer Jones, Joseph Cotten, Lillian Gish, Lionel Barrymore, Butterfly McQueen.* Producer David O. Selznick's sexy epic western about the rivalry between two brothers (Peck, Cotten) for the love of a beautiful half-breed Indian girl, played with sultry authority by Jones. One of the most popular films of the 1940s, the film, though very entertaining, sometimes seems to border on high camp. ★★★ DVD: $14.99, VHS: $9.99

Duel to the Death

(1982, 100 min, Hong Kong, Ching Siu-Tung) *Damian Lau, Flora Cheung, Norman Tsui.* Two outstanding swordsmen from rival schools, one Japanese and one Chinese, are forced to do battle in a traditional tournament that is held once every 100 years. But these are not ordinary swordsmen; they can fly through the air and summon supernatural powers to aid them in combat. Unexpectedly, the two become friends, combining their awesome abilities to defeat their enemy. In his debut film, Ching features all the trademark attractions of his later works: gravity-defying swordsmen, chaotic camerawork, themes of loyalty and duty, a bit of humor to lighten the drama and sumptuous visuals. A great introduction to Hong Kong action cinema, but also a forgotten gem sure to please even veteran fans. (Cantonese with English subtitles) ★★★½ DVD: $9.99

The Duellists

(1977, 100 min, GB, Ridley Scott) *Keith Carradine, Harvey Keitel, Edward Fox, Tom Conti, Albert Finney.* Scott's first feature film is an eccentric rendering of the Joseph Conrad story about an inexplicable feud between two officers of the Napoleonic army. Carradine and Keitel personify the passion, honor and violence that are the heart of Conrad's story. A visually stunning film. ★★★½ DVD Special Collector's Edition: $14.99, VHS: $14.99

Duet for One

(1986, 107 min, GB, Andrei Konchalovsky) *Julie Andrews, Alan Bates, Max von Sydow, Rupert Everett.* Andrews, taking a break from musical comedy, gives a sensitive performance in this routine tragic tale of a world-renowned concert violinist whose career is brought to an abrupt end with the onset of multiple sclerosis. Adapted from the play by Tom Kempinski, who based his story on Jackie du Pre (whose own story would be told in *Hilary & Jackie*). ★★½

Duke of the Derby
(Le Gentleman D'Epsom)

(1962, 83 min, France, Jacques Juranville) *Jean Gabin.* Veteran French actor Gabin breezes his way through this lightweight but entertaining comedy-drama as a charming old snob who lives in the sordid world of horse racing and gambling. Similar to the trend-setting *Bob le Flambeur*, the film follows him through the betting circles and races as he charismatically scams his way through every crisis that confronts him. (French with English subtitles) ★★½

Dulces Navajas (Navajeros)

(1981, 100 min, Spain, Eloy de la Iglesia) *Isela Vega.* Within the slums and bordellos of Madrid, an illiterate 16-year-old gang leader battles police, prison authorities and rival youth gangs for love and acceptance. A hard-hitting, sexually charged film based on a true story. (Spanish with English subtitles) ★★★

Dumb and Dumber

(1994, 106 min, US, Peter Farrelly) *Jim Carrey, Jeff Daniels, Teri Garr, Lauren Holly, Charles Rocket.* This sophomoric, scatological road comedy follows Lloyd and Harry, two bumbling, dim-witted roommates who travel cross-country to locate Lloyd's dream woman (Holly). On the way, their stupid shenanigans involve them with blackmailers, murderers and high society. Anyone who has seen a Jerry Lewis or Bob Hope comedy has seen this all before. Ironically, it's Daniels as Harry who supplies most of the laughs, including a hilarious sequence

set on the slopes of Aspen with Holly as a Margaret Dumont-like foil. Carrey, in turn, gives a hammy performance. (Prequel: *Dumb and Dumberer: When Harry Met Lloyd*) ★½ DVD: $19.99

Dumb and Dumberer:
When Harry Met Lloyd

(2003, 83 min, US, Troy Miller) *Eric Christian Olsen, Derek Richardson, Eugene Levy, Rachel Nichols, Mimi Rogers, Luis Guzman.* A calculated, stillborn, cash-in prequel, *Dumberer* tells the story of how Lloyd and Harry (Jim Carrey and Jeff Daniels from the first film) met and became pals in high school, and how they unwittingly take on their evil principal (Levy). Even with a good supporting cast (Levy, Oteri and "Mr. Show" 's Posehn), there's little to laugh at thanks to sluggish direction and sloppy writing. To his credit, though, Olsen embodies Carrey completely as Lloyd — it's almost eerie at times. Finally, however, *Dumberer* is too obviously a money-grubbing product — and just not funny. ★ DVD: $19.99, VHS Pan & Scan: $6.99

Dumbo

(1941, 64 min, US, Ben Sharpsteen) After the (initial) financial disappointment of *Fantasia*, Disney needed some cash, and fast, or his studio was going to be converted into a hospital. This film was made quick and cheap, and that's what gives it its energy and charm. Clean and simple design, charming songs, and all the vitality of the classic shorts, *Dumbo* found Disney returning to form. ★★★★ DVD 60th Anniversary: $29.99, VHS 60th Anniversary: $22.99

Dune

(1984, 137 min, US, David Lynch) *Jose Ferrer, Francesca Annis, Sting, Max von Sydow, Brad Dourif, Kyle MacLachlan, Patrick Stewart.* Lynch brings Frank Herbert's sci-fi classic to the screen in this wildly uneven but thought-provoking adaptation. In the distant future, the most coveted substance is the druglike spice known as Melange. Valued for its mind-expanding properties, the sole source of the spice is the desert planet Arrakis, or Dune. Thus, the superpowers clash over the control of Arrakis; for whoever owns the spice owns the universe. Although inconsistent, the set and costume design, as well as Lynch's directorial touches, make *Dune* a film that challenges the imagination. (Remade in 2000) ★★½

Dune

(2000, 270 min, US, John Harrison) *William Hurt, Alec Newman, Giancarlo Giannini, Uwe Ochsenknecht, Matt Keeslar, Ian McNiece, Saskia Reeves.* One of the most damning criticisms of David Lynch's trippy 1984 adaptation of Frank Herbert's classic sci-fi saga is that Lynch's film compressed a dense, labyrinthine plot into 140 minutes of movie. Produced for the Sci-Fi Channel, this new miniseries runs a marathon four-and-a-half hours yet, despite the opportunity to flesh out characters and expound on shady alliances and secret betrayals, this longer *Dune* is just as confounding. Some truly cool special effects are offset by shoddy visuals, and the semi-impressive production design is wrecked by the overuse of colored lighting effects to establish locale and mood. ★★ DVD Letterbox Special Edition Director's Cut (3-Disc Set): $19.99, VHS: $14.99

D

The Dunera Boys

(1985, 150 min, Australia, Sam Lewin) *Bob Hoskins, Joe Spano.* Hoskins stars in this film about a group of Jewish refugees during WWII who are suspected of being Nazi informants by the British army. They are deported to a prison camp in Australia. Hoskins is absolutely brilliant as one of the refugees who is forced to prove his loyalty to England. Marred only by its length, this is an intelligently written and powerfully acted film. ★★★ VHS: $79.99

Dunston Checks In

(1995, 85 min, US, Ken Kwapis) *Jason Alexander, Faye Dunaway, Eric Lloyd, Rupert Everett, Paul Reubens, Glenn Shadix.* Parents, beware: When Dunston checks in, your brain checks out. Dunston is an orangutan whose owner (Everett) passes for a British lord but who is in fact a thief with a primate assistant. The two of them check into a five-star hotel run by Alexander. And then the shenanigans begin. Neither the strong cast nor the excellent production values can overcome the convoluted and drawn-out story line. ★★ DVD: $14.99, VHS: $6.99

The Dunwich Horror

(1969, 90 min, US, Daniel Haller) *Dean Stockwell, Sandra Dee, Ed Begley.* Roger Corman produced this effective adaptation of the classic H.P. Lovecraft story. Stockwell's interest in a rare book called "The Necronomicon" soon requires more than an attentive reading and begins to impinge on his relationship with girlfriend Dee. Begley, in his last role, is the professor who puts a stop to all this evil. ★★½ DVD Letterbox: $14.99, VHS: $9.99

Dust

(1985, 88 min, Belgium/France, Marion Hansel) *Jane Birkin, Trevor Howard.* Set on an isolated South African farm, this Venice Film Festival winner charts, with fearful precision, the mental disintegration of a lonely and sexually desperate young woman (Birkin) who murders her tyrannical father (Howard). Based on J.M. Cotzee's novel, "In the Heart of the Country." ★★★

Dust Devil

(1992, 87 min, GB, Richard Stanley) *Robert Burke, Chelsea Field, Zakes Mokae.* From the writer-director of the visually interesting (but ultimately disappointing) *Hardware* comes this mystical tale of a demon (Burke) who walks the South African veld looking for doomed souls to revitalize his life force. Once again, style tends to overpower director Stanley's story line, thereby lessening the chill factor. ★★ VHS: $7.99

Dusty

(1985, 89 min, Australia, John Richardson) *Bill Kerr, Noel Trevarthen.* A heartwarming tale of an aging Outback prospector, played by Kerr, who befriends a half-wild sheepdog named Dusty. A moving family adventure in the tradition of *Old Yeller.* ★★★ VHS: $39.99

Dutch

(1991, 105 min, US, Peter Faiman) *Ed O'Neill, JoBeth Williams, Ethan Randall.* John Hughes returns to one of his successful formulas (*Planes, Trains and Automobiles*) with considerably less successful results. Working-class stiff O'Neill is engaged to upper-crust Williams. It's Thanksgiving vacation, and Williams' preppy teenage son (Randall) is stuck at school. So O'Neill is sent to escort the lad home. You won't need a crystal ball to predict plot developments, such as the two of them

won't hit it off, or the cross-country trip becomes a comedy of errors, or they become best buddies. Randall is appropriately obnoxious — to the point of wanting to hit him with a snow shovel. ★½

Dying Young

(1991, 105 min, US, Joel Schumacher) *Julia Roberts, Campbell Scott, Colleen Dewhurst, Vincent D'Onofrio, Ellen Burstyn.* In a terribly written role (which shamelessly copies her *Pretty Woman*), Roberts is a working-class woman who takes a job as nurse to a terminally ill man (Scott). As the rich man intellectually enlightens her, she brings a much-needed spark of energy to an otherwise privileged, lonely person. Set in San Francisco and full of AIDS awareness messages in the background, the film is a tedious allegory for that disease and its wasting of young lives — if only the filmmakers had the guts to make the movie that this self-consciously tries to be. ★ DVD: $14.99

E.T. The Extra-Terrestrial

(1982, 115 min, US, Steven Spielberg) *Henry Thomas, Dee Wallace, Drew Barrymore, Robert MacNaughton, Peter Coyote.* A classic sci-fi adventure, and one of the most popular pictures of all time. An alien lands in suburban California and is befriended by a ten-year-old boy (Thomas), who helps the space traveler return home. It's magical, mystical, funny and extremely touching; and E.T. itself is a marvel of makeup and effects. Barrymore is a delight as Thomas' younger sister. This is our generation's *The Wizard of Oz.* ★★★★ DVD Pan & Scan Limited Edition 2-disc set: $29.99

Each Dawn I Die

(1939, 92 min, US, William Keighley) *James Cagney, George Raft, George Bancroft.* Cagney plays

a reporter who is framed and sent to prison. Raft is the tough con he tangles with. This routine Warner programmer features its stars in good form but is mired by a convoluted second half. ★★½ VHS: $19.99

The Eagle

(1925, 77 min, US, Clarence Brown) *Rudolph Valentino, Louise Dresser, Vilma Banky.* Full of romance, action and adventure, this silent costume adventure yarn was adapted from an Alexander Pushkin story. Valentino plays a young Russian officer who rejects the advances of the evil Czarina (Dresser). As a result, he is banished. But he returns as The Eagle, a Tartar Robin Hood out to take vengeance against the Czarina as well as win the hand of the woman (Banky) he loves. Great fun and Valentino cuts a fine swash. ★★★½ DVD: $24.99

The Eagle and the Hawk

(1933, 68 min, US, Stuart Walker) *Fredric March, Cary Grant, Carole Lombard, Jack Oakie.* March and Grant make a formidable team in this first-rate antiwar film set during WWI. They play American pilots stationed in France, each learning a lesson about heroism and friendship. Lombard is the society girl torn between them. ★★★½

The Eagle Has Landed

(1977, 123 min, GB, John Sturges) *Michael Caine, Donald Sutherland, Robert Duvall, Donald Pleasence, Treat Williams, Larry Hagman.* Fast-moving, intricately plotted and solidly entertaining, this WWII action-adventure makes full use of an excellent cast. Based on the novel by Jack Higgins about an attempt by the Germans to kidnap Winston Churchill. ★★★ DVD: $9.99, VHS: $9.99

The Eagle Has Two Heads
(L'Aigle à Deux Têtes)

(1947, 99 min, France, Jean Cocteau) *Jean Marais, Edwige Feuillere.* This extravagant and romantic melodrama was adapted from Cocteau's hugely successful play. Set in the 19th century, the film stars Marais as a lederhosen-clad poet/anarchist (and double for the dead king) who sets out to assassinate the beautiful queen (Feuillére), but when the two lock eyes, it is love at first sight. In keeping

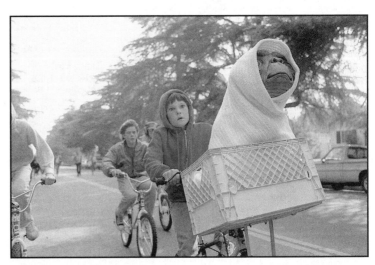

E.T. The Extra-Terrestrial

with Cocteau's passion for linking love with death, the couple meets a tragic end. Probably the least successful of Cocteau's films. (French with English subtitles) ★★½ VHS: $29.99

An Early Frost

(1985, 100 min, US, John Erman) *Aidan Quinn, Gena Rowlands, Ben Gazzara, Sylvia Sidney, D.W. Moffett, John Glover.* The first TV movie to deal with the subject of AIDS, *An Early Frost* is a thoughtful and undeniably powerful drama. Quinn stars as Michael, a successful gay lawyer who decides to tell his family that he is gay and HIV-positive. The effect of his announcement on him and his family is at the core of the heartfelt story. Quinn gives a sensitive though commanding performance, and Rowlands, Gazzara and especially Sydney offer strong support as his parents and grandmother. An Emmy Award winner for Best Screenplay. ★★★½

Early Summer (Bakushu)

(1951, 135 min, Japan, Yasujiro Ozu) *Ichiro Sugai, Chishu Ryu.* The essence of Japanese family life is masterfully captured in this illuminating, passionate and, at times, humorous work that must be considered one of director Ozu's best postwar films. Noriko, an intelligent and independent woman of 28, is faced with an arranged marriage to an unloved and unloving man, but her sense of individualism conflicts with her feelings of obligation towards her family. A restrained, succinct observation on the inevitable tides of change on family traditions and bonds, and their effect on Japanese culture. (Japanese with English subtitles) ★★★★ VHS: $29.99

The Earrings of Madame de . . .

(1945, 105 min, France, Max Ophüls) *Charles Boyer, Danielle Darrieux, Vittorio De Sica.* This wonderfully captivating film tells the ironic and ultimately tragic tale of a woman and a set of diamond earrings which are given to her by her husband, pawned by him when in debt, and then given again to her, but this time by her lover. A remarkable portrait of the vanity and frivolous nature of the upper classes in 19th-century Paris. (French with English subtitles) ★★★ VHS: $14.99

Earth

(1930, 90 min, USSR, Alexander Dovzhenko) *Semyon Svashenko, Mikola Nademsy.* One of the last silent movies and a masterpiece in Soviet cinema, *Earth* is a lyrically told poem to man's love of nature, his endeavors to adapt it to his needs, and of man's death as part of the cycle of life. In Ukraine, a collective of poor peasants attempt to farm the vast lands of the Kulaks, the landed gentry, who in turn oppose them. Dovzhenko paints an indelible portrait of a people's struggle against superstition, rich landowners and nature itself in their fight to make their dreams reality. (Silent with orchestral accompaniment) ★★★★ DVD: $24.99, DVD Triple Feature: $29.99, VHS: $24.99

Earth Girls Are Easy

(1989, 102 min, US, Julien Temple) *Jeff Goldblum, Jim Carrey, Geena Davis, Damon Wayans, Julie Brown.* Davis awakens to find a spaceship in her swimming pool; a ship with shaggy Goldblum, Carrey and Wayans aboard. Doing her best for interplanetary relations, she takes the visitors under her wing, and in the process falls in love with Captain Jeff. The film never reaches the comic fever pitch it sets out to capture, though the cast manages to make the most of the uneven screenplay. ★★½ DVD: $14.99, VHS: $9.99

East Is East

Earth vs. the Spider

(2001, 90 min, US, Scott Ziehl) *Dan Aykroyd, Devon Gummersall, Amelia Heinle, Theresa Russell.* A lily-livered, comic book-devouring security guard is injected with a super spider serum during a robbery at the pharmaceutics company where he works. He slowly begins mutating into a superhero . . . or is he becoming a monster? A neat cross-pollination of *Spider-Man* and Cronenberg's *The Fly*, this made-for-Showtime remake of the 1958 low-budget AIP chiller is entertaining throughout, despite tonal problems (its jazzy, satiric score suggests goofy fun while tragedy unfolds onscreen) and inevitable comparisons to Cronenberg's superior outing. The effects (by Stan Winston) are extremely well done, helping to compensate for some slow pacing and questionable plot developments. ★★½ DVD: $24.99, VHS: $14.99

Earth vs. the Flying Saucers

(1956, 83 min, US, Fred F. Sears) *Hugh Marlowe, Joan Taylor.* Splendid special effects by wizard Ray Harryhausen highlight this sci-fi favorite about aliens demanding Earth's surrender. ★★★

Earthquake

(1974, 129 min, US, Mark Robson) *Charlton Heston, Geneviève Bujold, George Kennedy, Ava Gardner, Richard Roundtree, Lorne Greene, Marjoe Gortner, Victoria Principal.* Well, it *did* win an Oscar for some outstanding special effects, but aside from a dexterity at leveling miniature models of L.A., the film offers little else. Greene plays Gardner's father! ★★

East Is East

(2000, 96 min, GB, Damien O'Donnell) *Om Puri, Linda Bassett, Jimi Mistry, Jordan Routledge.* A highbrow cultural comedy with a penchant for gross-outs, this curiously entertaining import beat out *Notting Hill* for the British Academy Award for Best British Picture. Puri plays George, a Pakistani immigrant in Manchester. His family, including Anglo wife Ella (Bassett) and their seven kids, is growing up in the early '70s; circumcision, arranged marriage and George's other Muslim family values don't rub well in this time of cultural upheaval.

Likewise, neither does their mixed family fit in with the xenophobic locals. The comedy is excellent; from subtle commentary to broad strokes, it's all winningly acted by the young ensemble, especially Puri. However, when the script takes occasional sharp turns to the serious, the tone shift is so jarring as to take you out of the movie. There's a good little comedy in here; the attempt at something more relevant taints the film as much as it tarnishes Puri's character. ★★★ DVD: $14.99, VHS: $9.99

The East Is Red

(1992, 95 min, Hong Kong, Ching Siu-Tung) *Brigitte Lin-Ching Hsia.* Move over, Supergirl. Your days are numbered, Wonder Woman. Asia the Invincible, the first transsexual lesbian superhero, is now the reigning queen. This spectacular kung fu fantasy is 95 minutes of nonstop action featuring awesome special effects and enough flailing bodies and exhilarating fight sequences to keep any fan of the genre enthralled. With magical powers (including flying across the screen and flinging killer needles at her foes), Asia (Ching-Hsia) is a fiery villain/hero who goes on a rampage, fighting neighboring armies, Spanish conquistadors and even a bevy of fake Asias, to regain the hand of Snow, the woman she loves. ★★★ DVD: $29.99, VHS: $39.99

East of Eden

(1955, 115 min, US, Elia Kazan) *James Dean, Julie Harris, Raymond Massey, Jo Van Fleet.* Dean gives an affecting and sincere performance as a rebel with a cause in this Kazan classic. Based on John Steinbeck's novel, this was Dean's starring debut as a misunderstood youth, yearning for his father's approval while searching for the truth about his mysteriously absent mother. Harris and Massey give fine performances in support, and Van Fleet was an Oscar winner for her portrayal of Dean's bitter mom. ★★★★

East Side Story

(1997, 78 min, Germany, Dana Ranga) *East Side Story* is a terrific documentary that offers a history of the Communist musical. Told through narration, interviews and wonderful film clips, it's a fascinating history indeed. We see scenes from

Stalin's favorite film — a cheesy "song for the common man"; clips from films considered subversive by censorious governments, and hilariously campy '60s teen musicals influenced by U.S. and British films. While the clips themselves are the real draw here, the interviews provide an enticing inside look at how artists work within the heavy constraints of a Communist regime. The only real drawback is that it is an inadvertent tease: these tantalizing clips are likely the only glimpses we'll get of these films. (German and various other languages with English subtitles) ★★★★ DVD: $29.99, VHS: $24.99

East Side, West Side

(1949, 108 min, US, Mervyn LeRoy) *Barbara Stanwyck, James Mason, Ava Gardner, Van Heflin.* The foibles of New York's society darlings are under scrutiny in this capable though shallow melodrama based on the Marcia Davenport novel. Stanwyck and Mason are a wealthy couple whose marriage is coming apart, especially with Gardner and Heflin waiting for them in the wings. Good performances by all help gloss over the occasional dramatic potholes. ★★½ VHS: $19.99

East/West (Est/Ouest)

(1999, 125 min, France/Russia, Régis Wargnier) *Sandrine Bonnaire, Oleg Menchikov, Catherine Deneuve, Sergi Bodrov, Jr., Ruben Tupiero.* Alexei Golovine (Menchikov) is a young Russian doctor living in France in 1946, when Stalin issues an open invitation to all expatriates to return to Mother Russia. With his French wife Marie (Bonnaire) and their young son, he joins the last wave of the WWII diaspora, only to receive their first lesson in the institutional insanity that is Stalinist Russia. Essentially hijacked and shipped to Kiev, they are little more than prisoners. Alexei is more fully aware of his family's peril; as he struggles with the guilt of placing them in this situation, he plays to the country's need for medical practitioners. As he did in *Indochine*, director Wargnier explores epic, historical events through personal, intimate human moments. The performances are excellent, especially Menchikov's turn as the father who never lost sight of the long view regarding his family's safety. (French and Russian with English subtitles) ★★★½ DVD: $29.99, VHS: $21.99

Easter Parade

(1948, 104 min, US, Charles Walters) *Judy Garland, Fred Astaire, Ann Miller, Peter Lawford.* Tuneful Irving Berlin musical with Astaire and Garland as a song-and-dance team during the early 1900s. Songs include "Steppin' Out with My Baby," "A Couple of Swells" and the title tune. ★★★½ VHS: $14.99

The Easy Life (Il Sorpasso)

(1963, 105 min, Italy, Dino Risi) *Vittorio Gassman, Jean-Louis Trintignant.* Capturing the optimistic and carefree outlook in a rapidly modernizing Italy, this comedy-drama stars Gassman as a pleasure-seeking middle-aged playboy who meets his opposite in a young Trintignant, a meek, serious law student whom he takes under his wing. The fast-talking and equally fast-driving Gassman convinces the young man to accompany him on a trip to northern Italy and taste life's sweet offerings. A likable, off-beat film, well-played by the two charming leads. (Italian with English subtitles) ★★★

Easy Living

(1937, 88 min, US, Mitchell Leisen) *Jean Arthur, Ray Milland, Edward Arnold, Franklin Pangborn, William Demarest.* Preston Sturges wrote the screenplay for this consistently funny screwball comedy. In a wonderfully wacky performance, Arthur sparkles as a working girl whose life turns upside down when tycoon Arnold throws his wife's mink out the window, landing on Arthur. Milland costars as Arnold's son who romances her. There's a great slapstick scene at an automat, and Pangborn, as a catty salesclerk, proves when it comes to dishing the dirt, he's second to none ("Where there's smoke, there must be . . . somebody smoking"). ★★★½ VHS: $14.99

Easy Living

(1949, 77 min, US, Jacques Tourneur) *Victor Mature, Lucille Ball, Lizabeth Scott.* Mature plays an aging football star facing retirement. Ball plays the team secretary in love with him. Scott plays Mature's possessive wife. A compelling and thoughtful drama accented by three smart performances. ★★★ VHS: $99.99

Easy Money

(1983, 95 min, US, James Signorelli) *Rodney Dangerfield, Joe Pesci, Candy Azzara, Geraldine Fitzgerald.* Dangerfield delivers some good laughs in this easygoing comedy about a slobbish baby photographer who stands to inherit millions — if he can give up drinking, smoking, gambling and over-eating. ★★★ DVD: $19.99

Easy Rider

(1969, 94 min, US, Dennis Hopper) *Peter Fonda, Dennis Hopper, Jack Nicholson.* This low-budget phenom sent shock waves through Hollywood and the nation. Fonda and Hopper are the hippie bikers whose trek across America blithely caught the mood of the times. Nicholson is unforgettable as the alcoholic lawyer with an itch to drop out. ★★★½ DVD Letterbox Special Edition: $14.99, VHS: $14.99

Easy Virtue

(1927, 79 min, GB, Alfred Hitchcock) *Isabel Jeans, Ian Hunter.* Hitchcock meets Noël Coward. It's tempting to simply leave it at that. Based on a story by Coward, this early silent Hitchcock feature comes up a little short dramatically, but it does have flashes of the director's later style. The story has to do with the melodramatic sufferings an alcoholic's wife (Jeans) endures. ★★½ VHS: $12.99

Eat a Bowl of Tea

(1989, 102 min, US, Wayne Wang) *Cora Miao, Russell Wong, Victor Wong, Jessica Harper.* Shortly after WWII, young Ben Loy is sent to Hong Kong by his father, Wah Gay, to find a bride. He returns with Mei Oi — a very modern and independent young woman with whom he has fallen deeply in love. Unfortunately, the choice is not one which sits so well with Wah Gay. What follows is a wry and irreverent, often offbeat and always endearing treatise on the struggle between old and new in the Chinese community. It is pulled together with the dizzyingly frantic pace of a 1930s screwball comedy. Once again, Wang has succeeded in making a purely Chinese-American movie that will appeal to all. (English and Chinese with English subtitles) ★★★

Eat Drink Man Woman

(1994, 120 min, Taiwan, Ang Lee) *Sihung Lung, Ah-Leh Gua, Winston Chao, Yu-Wen Wang, Chien-Lien Wu, Kuei-Mei-Yang, Lester Chen.* A heartfelt, humorous examination of the romantic aspirations of an aging widower and his daughters. Featuring the most visually sumptuous cinematic food since *Like Water for Chocolate* and *Babette's Feast*, the film opens with a bang — the viewer being drawn into an ornate ritual of food prep as old Tao Chu readies an "average" Sunday family dinner. His three daughters are a study in diversity: Jia-Jen, the eldest, is a devoutly Christian schoolteacher; Jia-Chien, the middle, is a rebellious spitfire and successful businesswoman; Jia-Ning, the youngest, seemingly infatuated with American "mall culture." Lee's acute eye for character uses this quartet to paint a stirring and highly humorous picture of emotional isolation against a backdrop of Taiwan's rapidly modernizing culture. (Mandarin with English subtitles) ★★★★ DVD Letterbox: $19.99, VHS: $14.99

Eat the Peach

(1986, 95 min, Ireland, Peter Ormrod) *Stephen Brennan, Eamon Morrissey.* Two unemployed Irish fellows, inspired by a scene in Elvis Presley's bike movie, *Roustabout*, conspire to construct a "Wall of Death" upon which they will ride their cycles and defy gravity. Of course, their families and friends think they've gone mad, but Vinnie and Arthur persevere, resorting to smuggling and petty theft to realize their dream. An amiable comedy, filled with down-home Irish charm. ★★½ VHS: $79.99

Eat the Rich

(1988, 92 min, GB, Peter Richardson) *Nosher Powell, Lanah Pellay, Miranda Richardson.* The outrageous British comedy troupe The Comic Strip (*The Supergrass*) serves some heaping portions of over-the-top comedy in this biting attack on England's class system. Having been fired from a very posh and unbearably snobby London restaurant, a transsexual waiter gangs up with a couple of fellow disenfranchised citizens and vows to start the revolution. They begin by taking over the restaurant and renaming it "Eat the Rich" — which, as it turns out, is exactly what the patrons unwittingly do. A marvelous example of Thatcher-era humor. ★★★ VHS: $19.99

Eaten Alive

(1976, 96 min, US, Tobe Hooper) *Neville Brand, Mel Ferrer, Carolyn Jones, Robert Englund.* From the director of *The Texas Chainsaw Massacre* comes this horror outing about a psychopathic hotel owner who has a bad habit of feeding his guests to his pet crocodile. Hooper's debut feature is bizarre though occasionally scary. ★★ DVD: $14.99

Eating

(1990, 110 min, US, Henry Jaglom) *Frances Bergen, Lisa Richards, Gwen Welles.* Jaglom takes us on a wonderfully entertaining afternoon outing to a fine suburban L.A. home where a group of women come together for a birthday party and where everyone's favorite topic of discussion is food, food, food. Filmed with an all-female cast, the comedy is much more consistent and funnier than Jaglom's previous outings as the wacky cast of Left Coast caricatures chatter, bemoan and marvel in their collective guilt for and obsession of food and eating. The film is loosely structured, allowing the actresses to improvise, with the results being many hilariously memorable and perceptive lines. ★★★½ VHS: $7.99

Eating Raoul

(1982, 83 min, US, Paul Bartel) *Paul Bartel, Mary Woronov, Robert Beltran, Ed Begley, Jr., Edie McClurg.* Paul and Mary Bland, a mild-mannered couple, devise a diabolical scheme to raise funds for their entrepreneurial dreams. Placing an ad in the local sex publication, they lure unsuspecting degenerates to their abode, club them with a frying pan and empty their wallets. Hunky Beltran also stars as the not-as-clever-as-he-thinks-he-is hustler Raoul who may become their next victim. Bartel's cannibalistic comedy serves up a healthy portion of laughs in his most consistently outrageous comedy. ★★★½ DVD Letterbox: $19.99

The Ebony Tower

(1987, 80 min, GB, Robert Knights) *Laurence Olivier, Greta Scacchi, Roger Rees, Toyah Wilcox.* Olivier stars as an aging painter who, out of disdain for the art world, cloisters himself with two beautiful female art students in a remote French chateau. Their peaceful retreat is sent into chaos, however, by the arrival of a young artist (Rees). John Mortimer adapted the John Fowles novel. ★★★

Echo Park

(1986, 92 min, US, Robert Dornhelm) *Tom Hulce, Susan Dey, Michael Bowen, Christopher Walken, Cheech Marin.* An offbeat charmer about a would-be actress (Dey) and her relationship with two boarders, a songwriting pizza delivery man (the very likable Hulce) and a budding bodybuilder (Bowen), both of whom share her rundown duplex in East Los Angeles. ★★★ DVD Dual: $19.99

Echoes of Paradise

(1987, 92 min, Australia, Phillip Noyce) *Wendy Hughes, John Lone.* Hughes stars as a happily married mother of three whose idyllic suburban life is shattered after she discovers that her husband has been in a series of affairs for years. In an effort to escape the emotional turmoil at home, she travels with a friend to exotic Thailand where she meets a handsome Balinese dancer (Lone). The film treads no new territory; and with seductive lines like, "You look tense. Let me give you a massage," the viewer should take the film more as a beautiful travelogue and less as anything insightful. ★★

The Eclipse (L'Eclisse)

(1962, 123 min, Italy, Michelangelo Antonioni) *Monica Vitti, Alain Delon.* The concluding film in Antonioni's existential trilogy, which includes *L'Avventura* and *La Notte*, continues with the theme of the barriers to human communication as part of an increasingly stark contemporary world. Vitti stars as a young woman who, hours after leaving her old lover, meets a passionate young man (Delon). Whether she'll really end her old affair or if the fledgling new one will even begin is at the heart of the conflict in this existential "art" film. The plot, however, takes a back seat to Antonioni's experimental film techniques and abstract style. (Italian with English subtitles) ★★★

Ecstasy

(1933, 82 min, Czechoslovakia, Gutsav Machaty) *Hedy Lamaar, Jaromir Rogoz.* A true curiosity! This slow-moving, predictable Czech film would have long been used for landfill had it not been for its scandalizing nude scenes of a pre-Hollywood Lamarr. This uncut version has Lamarr in all her natural beauty as a young woman whose marriage to a fastidious older man sours on their wedding night. She soon leaves him and finds solace in the arms of a handsome young engineer. Filmed mostly as a silent film, the acting is overly expressive by today's standards. (German with English subtitles) ★ DVD: $24.99, VHS: $19.99

Ed Gein

(2000, 90 min, US, Chuck Parello) *Steve Railsback, Carrie Snodgress, Brian Evers.* Gein was the real-life serial killer/all-around weirdo from Wisconsin who was the inspiration for both *Psycho* and *The Texas Chainsaw Massacre.* This rather belated biopic, sadly, can't hold a candle to either of those classics, or to the only other (largely fictionalized) Gein film, the effective *Disturbed*, which features an inspired performance by Roberts Blossom. Here Gein is well played by Railsback, but the film itself is tired and without inspiration. *Ed Gein* isn't a terribly bad movie, just a redundant and pointless one. (aka: *In the Light of the Moon*) ★★ VHS: $7.99

Ed Wood

(1994, 128 min, US, Tim Burton) *Johnny Depp, Sarah Jessica Parker, Martin Landau, Bill Murray, Patricia Arquette, Vincent D'Onofrio, Jeffrey Jones, G.D. Spradlin, Lisa Marie.* Depp stars as the titular character in this ideally crafted biopic of the 1950s film director who single-handedly molded the grade-B aesthetic. Shot in black and white and imitating the cheesy production values of Wood's immortal cult classics, the film is a perfect tribute to the man whose charming incompetence as a filmmaker was equally matched by an unrelenting enthusiasm for the medium. Depp's portrayal of Wood, a WWII vet with an insatiable appetite for angora and women's clothing, is right on the money, but it is Landau's astonishing portrait of Bela Lugosi that steals the show. Landau's Oscar-winning performance transforms the film from simple biography to an inspirational tale of friendship and redemption. Fortunately, director Burton tempers the film's serious underbelly with generous doses of hilarity and wit, or to quote Depp as Wood, "Transvestites! Get me transvestites!" ★★★★

Ed Wood, Look Back in Angora

(1994, 51 min, US, Ted Newsom) A fitting companion piece to Tim Burton's *Ed Wood*, this engagingly frenetic examination of the blazingly eccentric director-writer-actor crosscuts clips from his one-of-a-kind movies with interviews from those who knew him. Interviewees include an ex-Marine who fought with him in the Pacific during WWII; movie industry types of the most marginal sort; and his long-suffering, ever-devoted wife. Director Newsom lets Wood's films speak for the tormented, would-be auteur, creating an affectionate and intimate biography of an obsessive whose ambitions greatly exceeded his talents. A stirring tribute to the man who created some of the worst movies ever made. ★★★½ VHS: $9.99

Eddie

(1996, 100 min, US, Steve Rash) *Whoopi Goldberg, Frank Langella, Dennis Farina, Richard Jenkins.* In this predictable though amiable sports comedy, Whoopi plays a die-hard New York Knicks fan who becomes the slumping team's head coach. *Eddie* bears no more originality than similarly themed kids' films like *Rookie of the Year* and *Little Big League*, and it unfortunately promises more than it can deliver. Whoopi is agreeable and often amusing, but her comic prowess alone cannot keep this comedy courtside. ★★½ DVD: $9.99, VHS: $9.99

Eddie and the Cruisers

(1983, 92 min, US, Martin Davidson) *Tom Berenger, Michael Paré, Ellen Barkin.* A popular 1960s rock band leader presumably died in an accident — but he may have faked his death and returned to his old neighborhood. Barkin is the TV reporter investigating the story; Paré is the legendary Eddie. (Sequel: *Eddie and the Cruisers II*) ★★½ DVD Letterbox: $14.99, VHS: $4.99

Eddie Murphy: Raw

(1987, 90 min, US, Robert Townsend) *Eddie Murphy.* This aptly titled movie is Murphy's second concert film. He's often very funny and has a great deal of energy, but he's as enamored with his anatomy as ever. If you like Murphy and enjoy his style of humor, this R-rated (well justified) romp is the one for you. ★★ VHS: $9.99

Eden

(1998, 106 min, US, Howard Goldberg) *Joanna Going, Dylan Walsh, Sean Patrick Flanery.* No more than a TV movie of the week with a handful of four-letter words, *Eden* concerns a housewife, Helen Kunen (Going), who is having out-of-body experiences. This film tries to address the mind/body/spirit problem, but, like its heroine, it has no real energy. Helen, who suffers from multiple sclerosis, has a series of dream-flights where she can see and feel the lives of others. Her stick-in-the-mud husband does not appreciate the changes in his wife, but she forms a bond with one of her failing students. Frankly, none of this is very moving, since the film touches on the issues, rather than tackles them. At least *Eden* is never offensive or insulting. ★½ DVD: $14.99, VHS: $14.99

The Edge

(1997, 117 min, US, Lee Tamahori) *Anthony Hopkins, Alec Baldwin, Elle Macpherson, Harold Perrineau.* Set against the beautiful mountaintops and lakes of remote Alaska, *The Edge* is a taut action adventure that pits man against beast as well as man against man. Hopkins plays a multimillionaire who travels along with his supermodel wife on a fashion shoot. When he and photographer Baldwin become trapped in the wilderness after a plane crash, they must use their wits to fight the elements — including a killer Kodiak bear — and eventually themselves. David Mamet's screenplay is terse and economical, and there are some dazzling scenes involving the bear. If the pacing falls apart somewhat by story's end, *The Edge* has still provided some chilling moments. ★★★ DVD: $14.99, VHS: $9.99, VHS Letterbox: $19.99

Johnny Depp and Martin Landau in *Ed Wood*

Johnny Depp as *Edward Scissorhands*

Edge of Darkness

(1943, 120 min, US, Lewis Milestone) *Errol Flynn, Ann Sheridan, Walter Huston, Ruth Gordon, Judith Anderson.* From the director of the classic antiwar film *All Quiet on the Western Front* comes that film's antithesis, a gripping WWII drama and passionate call to arms. Flynn and Sheridan head a splendid ensemble cast as leaders of the underground movement of their small Norwegian village, which the Nazis occupy. Featuring exceptional cinematography, this well-detailed film examines daily life under oppressive German rule and the birth of the town's Resistance movement. A dashing Flynn, a no-nonsense Sheridan and a heart-tugging performance by Gordon all contribute to make *Edge of Darkness* stand out among other war-era films. ★★★½ VHS: $19.99

Edge of Darkness

(1986, 307 min, GB, Martin Campbell) *Bob Peck, Joanne Whalley, Joe Dan Baker.* This stylishly produced BBC thriller is filled with espionage and intrigue and won six British "Emmy" awards. Peck stars as a London police detective whose life is brutally torn apart when his young daughter is found murdered. As he follows the trail of her killer(s), he uncovers a tangled web of conspiracy involving government agents, a maverick CIA operative, multinational corporations and a radical environmental group. Good, solid action entertainment. ★★★ VHS: $29.99

Edge of Sanity

(1988, 90 min, GB, Gerald Kikoine) *Anthony Perkins, Glynis Barber.* Turgid, uninvolving and ineptly directed, this Dr. Jekyll and Mr. Hyde horror spin-off features a bug-eyed Perkins as a doctor who accidentally concocts a mixture that turns him into a pasty-faced killer with a predilection for sleazy prostitutes. Set in Victorian London, this updated version of the Stevenson classic is a disappointment that is not enjoyable even on a camp level. ★ DVD Dual: $14.99

Edison the Man

(1940, 107 min, US, Clarence Brown) *Spencer Tracy, Rita Johnson, Charles Coburn.* Fine sequel to *Young Tom Edison* (which starred a youthful Mickey Rooney) with Tracy as the adult inventor. The film follows Edison's fascination with devices, and though some of the story is Hollywood-ized, it's a rewarding homage to the American genius. ★★★ VHS: $19.99

Edith and Marcel

(1983, 140 min, France, Claude Lelouch) *Marcel Cerdan Jr., Evelyne Bouix, Charles Aznavour.* The love affair between singer Edith Piaf and boxing champion Marcel Cerdan, who died in a plane crash in 1944, is romantically brought to the screen by Lelouch. The entrancing music of actual Piaf recordings and the casting of real-life son Cerdan, Jr. in the lead role adds pathos to this tragic love story. (French with English subtitles) ★★½

EDtv

(1999, 122 min, US, Ron Howard) *Matthew McConaughey, Jenna Elfman, Woody Harrelson, Ellen Degeneres, Martin Landau, Sally Kirkland, Rob Reiner, Dennis Hopper, Elizabeth Hurley, Clint Howard.* EDtv is no *Truman Show* — oh, wait, yes it is. Similar in premise though not in accomplishment, Howard's lively though unremarkable comedy has video store clerk McConaughey having his every move televised for the amusement of his home viewing audience — 24 hours a day. *EDtv* sometimes drags between the often funny scenes of Ed's latest TV melodramas, which are lapped up by fans across the nation. The ensemble is very effective; McConaughey is quite appealing with his aw-shucks, average-guy bit, and Harrelson has a few good scenes as his brother. However, it's DeGeneres who gives the film's best performance as the series' producer. You often find yourself rooting more for her than for Ed. That's show biz. ★★½ DVD Letterbox Collector's Edition: $9.99, DVD DTS sound: $9.99

Educating Rita

(1983, 110 min, GB, Lewis Gilbert) *Michael Caine, Julie Walters.* Walters is delightful as the Cockney dynamo who enrolls in a course at the Open University and comes under the tutelage of the cynical and boozy Caine. Driven by her thirst for knowledge, Rita exchanges the chatter of the ladies' hair salon for discussions on Chekov and Blake, while at the same time breathing new life into a moribund teacher. A warm and witty comedy from Willy Russell's hit West End play. ★★★½

The Education of Little Tree

(1998, 117 min, US, Richard Friedenberg) *James Cromwell, Tantoo Cardinal, Joseph Ashton, Graham Greene.* An adaptation of Forrest Carter's novel, the beautifully made *The Education of Little Tree* tells the story of Little Tree, a Cherokee boy (Ashton) who leaves the confines of his rural town to live with his grandparents (Cromwell and Cardinal) in the hills of Tennessee's Smoky Mountains during the Depression. There, the grandfather teaches Little Tree the ways of "mountain folk" and instills in him a cultural pride with the help of a spiritual Indian friend, Willow John (Greene). More than just a quaint slice of Americana, *The Education of Little Tree* brings the attitudes of the era and its people into sharp perspective — a reality that never would be found on an episode of "The Waltons." Brought to marvelous life by the cast and exquisite cinematography, *The Education of Little Tree* is an affecting vision of a time when people's bitter life lessons are often peppered with steps toward belief in oneself. ★★★½ DVD Letterbox: $14.99, VHS: $9.99

Edvard Munch

(1974, 168 min, Norway, Peter Watkins) *Geir Westby, Gro Fraas.* Though labeled by his contemporaries as a sick madman, Edvard Munch (1863–1944) is considered one of the most impor-tant and influential painters in the Expressionistic Movement. This abstract examination into the psyche of the artist traces Munch's professional and private lives through the combination of narrative and dialogue (some taken directly from his diary), reenactments, and documentary-like interviews. The collage design of the film produces an overlaying of image and sound, a hodge-podge of short scenes and repetition of events, and its running time of 167 minutes may push some viewers to wonder if they could be the model for Munch's most famous work: The Scream. (Norwegian and German with English subtitles) ★★½

Edward II

(1991, 91 min, GB, Derek Jarman) *Steven Waddington, Andrew Tiernan, Tilda Swinton, Nigel Terry.* Director Jarman has reworked Christopher Marlowe's play into a homoerotic, sexually charged, radically relevant work for our times. Graphically brutal, moving, surprisingly funny and always erotic, Jarman blends Marlowe's prose with contemporary jargon and costumes, replete with positive portrayals of queer sex, profanity and ACT-UP activists for a truly mesmerizing experience. Brilliant, daring and innovative, *Edward II* is contemporary filmmaking at its finest, and one of the best examples of modern queer cinema. ★★★★

Edward Scissorhands

(1990, 98 min, US, Tim Burton) *Johnny Depp, Winona Ryder, Dianne Wiest, Alan Arkin, Vincent Price, Kathy Baker, Anthony Michael Hall, Conchata Ferrell.* Having paid his dues to Hollywood several times over with *Batman*, director Burton presents this small-scale gem about a boy with scissors for hands. This heartbreaking and highly original parable on conformity casts Depp as a social misfit who's taken by Wiest to live in her "average suburban household" where he falls in love for the first time, becomes all the rage as a hairdresser to the neighborhood's wives, and learns the high cost for societal conventions. Burton has fashioned in this beautifully filmed and comic fantasy the ultimate tale of the outsider as misunderstood and victimized innocent. ★★★½ DVD Pan & Scan: $14.99, DVD: $14.99, VHS: $9.99

The Eel

(1997, 117 min, Japan, Shohei Imamura) *Koji Yakusho, Misa Shimizu.* A workaday Everyman

Marcello Mastroianni in *8½*

(Yakusho) learns of his wife's infidelity. He seems quietly surprised when he brutally stabs his wife to death, and hums a gentle tune as he bicycles to the police station to turn himself in. Eight years later, he is released to the care of his parole officer, with the pet eel that had been his best companion during his incarceration. He has a hard time unlearning the habits of his confinement, but his intervention in a young woman's suicide attempt proves the catalyst that enables him to reconnect with life. In this compassionate yet unsentimental look at base cruelty and exalted empathy, director Imamura has constructed a sagacious consideration of the societies we construct and the raw emotion always lying just beneath the surface. (Japanese with English subtitles) ★★★ DVD Letterbox: $29.99, VHS: $19.99

Effi Briest

(1974, 140 min, Germany, Rainer Werner Fassbinder) *Hanna Schygulla, Wolfgang Schneck, Ulli Lommel.* Schygulla is luminous as the title character in Fassbinder's accomplished adaptation of the 1895 novel by Theodore Fontane. Fassbinder once again explores the subject of societal restraints in this beautifully photographed and elegantly mounted production. When Effi's much-older husband finds evidence of a long-dead affair, a chain of events is inexorably initiated, and Effi is its primary victim. Schygulla's performance is subtle, delicately layered and compelling. One of the director's best works. (German with English subtitles) ★★★★ DVD: $24.99, VHS: $19.99

The Efficiency Expert

(1992, 85 min, Australia, Mark Joffe) *Anthony Hopkins, Alwyn Kurts, Angela Punch McGregor, Bruno Lawrence.* In the tradition of *Local Hero* comes this warm, low-key comedy from Australia. Set in 1960s Melbourne, the film is about a management specialist's (Hopkins) efforts to "update and modernize" a small, family-run moccasin company. Instead of focusing on the ins and outs of the efficiency business, director Joffe's film is about decent working people trying to treat each other decently. In a richly textured but subtly moving performance, Hopkins plays a man in the midst of both a personal and a professional crisis of ethics. While the film may not break any new ground, it treads familiar territory gently and pleasantly. ★★★ VHS: $14.99

Egg

(1988, 58 min, Netherlands, Danniel Danniel) *Johan Leysen, Marijke Vengelers.* This engaging and delightful film centers around a sweet but lonely 35-year-old baker whose quietly efficient life is put in turmoil after a personal ad he placed in an out-of-town newspaper produces a determined woman at his doorstep. His tenuous attempts at a relationship soon involve the entire town's population. A humorous fable that takes a subdued approach and relies more on the actions of the characters rather than dialogue to tell its tale. (Dutch with English subtitles). ★★★ VHS: $59.99

The Egg and I

(1947, 108 min, US, Chester Erskine) *Claudette Colbert, Fred MacMurray, Marjorie Main, Percy Kilbride.* Big city socialite Colbert experiences culture shock at new hubby MacMurray's chicken farm. Colbert sparkles; she and MacMurray highlight a strong supporting cast of seasoned character actors in this delightful, witty and fun excursion into the green acres of the American heartland. One of the smash hits of the 1940s, the film introduced Main and Kilbride as "Ma and Pa Kettle." ★★★

Marshall Mathers, er, Eminem in Curtis Hanson's *8 Mile*

The Egyptian

(1954, 140 min, US, Michael Curtiz) *Victor Mature, Edmund Purdon, Jean Simmons, Peter Ustinov.* Hollywood doesn't make 'em like this anymore — and for most of us that's probably good news. An abandoned baby grows up to be the Pharaoh's physician. Based on a true story. A lifeless biblical epic. ★ VHS: $19.99

8½

(1963, 135 min, Italy, Federico Fellini) *Marcello Mastroianni, Claudia Cardinale, Anouk Aimée.* Fellini's masterful statement on his life and art stars Mastroianni as a filmmaker paralyzed by creative block and slipping deeper into a world of dream and fantasy. Cardinale portrays his sensuous apparition. (The inspiration for the Broadway musical "Nine.") (Italian with English subtitles) ★★★★ DVD Letterbox Basic Edition: $19.99, DVD Criterion Collection: $39.99, VHS: $19.99

8 Heads in a Duffel Bag

(1997, 95 min, US, Tom Schulman) *David Spade, Joe Pesci, Andy Comeau, Kristy Swanson, Todd Louiso, George Hamilton, Dyan Cannon.* Anyone expecting a dark comedy hybrid of *Weekend at Bernie's* and *Goodfellas* will be horribly disappointed by this strained and unfunny comedy about a mobster (Pesci) whose bag containing the heads of his boss' rivals is accidentally switched with that of a college schmoe (Comeau) trying to make a good impression on his fiancée's parents. Pesci has the thankless task of having to rehash his mobster schtick without the edge or the profanity ("friggin" is the word of choice, here), and spends the entire movie bullying and torturing Comeau's roommates (Spade and Louiso) into revealing his whereabouts. ★½ DVD Dual: $9.99

Eight Legged Freaks

(2002, 99 min, US, Ellory Elkayem) *David Arquette, Kari Wuhrer, Scott Terra, Scarlett Johansson, Doug E. Doug, Rick Overton.* A tongue-in-cheek comedy/horror homage to those giant insect films of the 1950s (*Them, Tarantula,* etc.), *Eight Legged Freaks* can't quite juggle the laughs and frights effectively, but there are moments of fun to be had in spite of it all. Arquette, looking bothered and bewildered, plays a slacker who returns to his small hometown just in time to help lead the fight against mutant spiders, which are now on the attack. The digital effects of rampaging spiders don't always create a sense of terror, but at least they look cool as they devour everyone in their path. The ensemble appears to be having fun, even though they are called upon to say and do some silly things. ★★½ DVD Letterbox: $14.99, DVD Pan & Scan: $14.99, VHS: $14.99

Eight Men Out

(1988, 119 min, US, John Sayles) *John Cusack, D.B. Sweeney, Christopher Lloyd, David Strathairn, John Mahoney, Charlie Sheen, Michael Lerner, Michael Rooker.* A beautiful period piece rich in emotion about the infamous "Black Sox Scandal" of 1919. It was a time when baseball players were the heroes of the day, until the underpaid and underappreciated players of the Chicago White Sox threw the World Series and brought shame to our national pastime. Examining the events that led up to the darkest days in the history of American sports, Sayles has assembled a fine team of young, talented actors. Sayles should be commended as both writer and director for the depth and clarity he brings to the almost 20 characters whose individual stories seem to effortlessly intertwine to tell this fascinating and sorrowful tale. ★★★★ DVD: $14.99

8 Mile

(2002, 111 min, US, Curtis Hanson) *Eminem, Kim Basinger, Brittany Murphy, Mekhi Phifer, Evan Jones.* One of the few white boys raised in Detroit's tough 313 area code, a brooding hip-hop poet unafraid to pick a fight and stand up for himself, Jimmy "Bunny Rabbit" Smith (Eminem) mirrors the accepted, possibly mythical history of the man who portrays him. Still living (like most of his friends) with his mom and working a steady industrial job, bouncing from girlfriend to new girlfriend (Murphy in an energetic if token performance), Rabbit comes alive onstage at the regular rap slams where his artistic skills and ego come together in brilliant fashion. At least when he's not dying of stage fright. His character arc is predictable enough that it might as well be written on the popcorn tub, and the one-note friends border on spoofs ("Conspiracy Brother" in particular outstays his welcome). But Hanson's surprisingly gritty direction keeps the events vibrant, and the climactic one-on-one slam is as electrifying as the best western showdowns. The film's ultimate success, however, is due to a terrific, sensitive performance by first-time actor Eminem, who also contributes songs so controversial, creative and smart that Oscar never saw them coming. ★★★½ DVD Letterbox Uncensored Bonus Features: $19.99, DVD Pan & Scan Uncensored Bonus Features: $19.99, VHS: $9.99

8MM

(1999, 119 min, US, Joel Schumacher) *Nicolas Cage, Joaquin Phoenix, Peter Stormare, James Gandolfini, Catherine Keener, Anthony Heald, Chris Bauer.* An instance in which *8* isn't greater than *Seven*, this slick but lurid thriller attempts to be sexually provocative with its adult movies backdrop, but ultimately disintegrates into a formulaic, tired revenge flick. Written by Andrew Kevin Walker, the author of the terrific *Seven*, the dark-hued, somber *8MM* follows private investigator Tom Welles (a sullen Cage) and his dark journey into the darker side of the pornography industry when he is hired to determine if a "snuff movie" is real or not. Soon it gets ugly as Welles finds what he's looking for. The story is lacking in the human element it pretends to care about, though the film does offer some bloody thrills — but they're neither edgy nor satisfying. ★★ DVD: $19.99, VHS: $9.99

8 Million Ways to Die

(1986, 115 min, US, Hal Ashby) *Jeff Bridges, Rosanna Arquette, Andy Garcia.* Slick though unremarkable crime thriller with Bridges as an ex-Los Angeles sheriff who tries to crack a cocaine ring and help a prostitute (Arquette) break free of her obsessive pimp. Garcia is terrific as Arquette's menacing pimp. ★★★ VHS: $19.99

8 Women

(2002, 103 min, France, François Ozon) *Danielle Darrieux, Catherine Deneuve, Isabelle Huppert, Emmanuelle Béart, Fanny Ardant, Virginie Ledoyen.* Ozon has done his homework on female-driven Hollywood classics. With *8 Women*, the director is all about *All about Eve* references and women who rule with this homage to the glory years of female power and edginess on-screen. When a murder (of the only male in the film) occurs at a country estate, the eight women of the title all become suspect. Trying to figure out whodunnit leads to many skeletons being released from many closets. Both soap-operatic deception and a few carefully placed musical numbers create a playful atmosphere in the midst of some dark themes. Using his ever-increasing clout, Ozon assembles an A-list of French actresses and has them delightfully chew up the scenery. Deneuve and Huppert in these showy, uncharacteristic roles are a joy, and *8 Women* glimmers with a sassiness that Bette Davis would have appreciated. (French with English subtitles) ★★★½ DVD Subtitled: $29.99, VHS Subtitled: $9.99

1860

(1933, 80 min, Italy, Alessandro Blasetti) *Aida Bellia, Andrea Checchi, Vasco Crepi.* The struggle for the unification of Italy, and especially the Sicilian peasant revolt against the Prince of Naples, provide the historical backdrop to this elegant war drama. Using nonprofessional actors, location shooting and natural lighting, the film brings an almost documentary feel to the story of one peasant's role during the battles and is considered a stylistic precursor to the Italian neorealist movement of the 1940s. (Italian with English subtitles) ★★★ VHS: $29.99

The 18th Angel

(1998, 100 min, US, William Bindley) *Christopher McDonald, Rachael Leigh Cook, Stanley Tucci, Maximilian Schell, Wendy Crewson.* A group of kooky Etruscan monks, led by Schell, are looking for eighteen "angels" — children and young teens whose innocence and beauty, along with the aid of an evil ancient clock, will bring about the ascendance of

Satan. How? Who knows? Who cares? Certainly not *Omen* scribe David Seltzer, who wrote this dreck. The main story centers around a young beauty and her widower father, who are invited to Rome under odd circumstances; of course, those nasty Etruscans want the beautiful girl as the 18th angel. Clichéd, moronic and unsuspenseful. ★ VHS: $9.99

The Eighth Day

(1996, 114 min, France, Jaco van Dormeal) *Daniel Auteuil, Pascal Duquenne, Miou-Miou.* Optimistic Belgian director van Dormeal is given over to some wonderful flights of fancy, but his message about living life to the fullest is still cliché no matter how he dresses it up. George (Duquenne), a young man with Down's Syndrome, has a child-like sense of wonder. Harry (Auteuil), an uptight salesman, fails to appreciate what he has. When these two characters meet in an accident one stormy night, they, of course, have a transforming effect on one another. Van Dormeal can achieve great moments of sadness and magic in the film, but there is too much filler between the scenes that truly captivate. However, Duquenne is truly inspired as George, and Auteuil deftly shows how Harry melts from his cold, unfeeling personality into a caring human being. (French with English subtitles) ★★½

The Eighties

(1983, 82 min, Belgium/France, Chantal Akerman) *Aurore Clement, Lio, Magali Noel.* The creative genesis of art and the filmmaking process is examined and deconstructed in this unusually fascinating and pleasurable film. Unlike director Akerman's previous somber films, this is a giddy work: a musical set in a suburban shopping mall. The first part of the film features a series of confusingly repetitive and jumbled scenes of a group of women singing, talking, discussing and arguing. The film changes direction completely in the second half to reveal the end result of all this confusion — a deliriously fun musical extravaganza. A witty, tongue-in-cheek film that can be frustrating but proves to be well worth the wait. (French with English subtitles) ★★★ VHS: $79.99

84 Charing Cross Road

(1987, 97 min, US/GB, David Jones) *Anne Bancroft, Anthony Hopkins, Judi Dench, Mercedes Ruehl.* Bancroft and Hopkins give splendid performances in this lovely film version of Hugh Whitemore's play (based on the memoirs of Helen Hanff) about the 20-year, transatlantic correspondence between a London bookseller (Hopkins) and one of his customers, a New York City woman (Bancroft). ★★★½ DVD: $19.99, VHS: $19.99

Eijanaika

(1981, 151 min, Japan, Shohei Imamura) *Ken Ogata, Shigeru Izumiya.* This chaotic portrait of Japanese society in the throes of a violent transition is masterfully directed by Imamura. Set in a bustling 19th-century Tokyo, the film depicts the loss of power by the Samurai Class at the hands of the new Imperial forces as well as outside business interests. Filmed against a backdrop of corruption, anarchy, bloodshed and eroticism, the story follows Genji, who returns to Tokyo after a five-year absence and finds that his wife has run off with a gangster. This mosaic portrait of Japanese culture run amok climaxes in a revolutionary frenzy and one of the most highly charged and dramatic spectacles in modern Japanese cinema. (Japanese with English subtitles) ★★★½

The Einstein of Sex

(1999, 98 min, Germany, Rosa von Praunheim) *Friedel Von Wangenheim, Ben Becker, Wolfgang Völz, Otto Sander, Meret Becker, Monika Hansen.* Director von Praunheim explores the extraordinary life and work of pioneering gay sexologist Magnus Hirschfeld in this lush if clinical historical drama. The story takes a chronological approach to tell the story of the German doctor who dedicated his life to the study of homosexuality. A gay Jew living in Berlin at the turn of the century, the young Hirschfeld formed a gay political group in 1897, and set up a medical practice catering to homosexuals. This practice eventually become "The Institute of Sexual Science." The rising power of Fascism in the early 1930s, however, threatened his life and work. By nature of its subject matter alone, this is an interesting look at queer history. (German with English subtitles) ★★½ DVD Letterbox: $19.99, VHS: $9.99

El (This Strange Passion)

(1952, 82 min, Mexico, Luis Buñuel) *Arturo de Cordova, Delia Garces.* This overheated story of passion, jealousy and violence is one of Buñuel's most entertaining films from his Mexican period. A biting anticlerical satire full of bizarre touches and one that continues his theme of *amour fou*, which he first dealt with in *L'Age D'Or*. Francisco, a seemingly normal and devout aristocrat (but secret foot fetishist), becomes obsessed with a woman he sees in church. He pursues her and eventually marries the woman, but soon changes from a loving husband to a man crazed with murderous and unjustifiable jealousy. Buñuel's wry sense of humor is clearly intact in this memorable black comedy. Please note that there is a slight problem with reading the white subtitles when there is a white background. (Spanish with English subtitles) ★★★ VHS: $59.99

El Cid

(1961, 185 min, US, Anthony Mann) *Charlton Heston, Sophia Loren, Raf Vallone, Geneviéve Page.* Sprawling historical epic with Heston as the legendary Spanish hero who drove the Moors from his homeland. A smart costume epic complete with impressive battle sequences, a better-than-average romance, and a story line none-too-difficult to follow. ★★★

El Dorado

(1967, 126 min, US, Howard Hawks) *John Wayne, Robert Mitchum, James Caan, Edward Asner, Christopher George.* Hawks' follow-up to his classic western *Rio Bravo*, *El Dorado* is an exciting western adventure with fine touches of comedy. Aging gunfighter Wayne and sheriff Mitchum team up against a ruthless cattle baron. ★★★ DVD: $14.99, VHS: $9.99

El Norte

(1983, 139 min, US, Anna Thompson & Gregory Nava) *David Villalpando, Zaide Silvia Gutierrez, Ernesto Cruz.* After their parents are murdered by a government death squad, a brother and sister flee their remote Guatemalan village and begin a hazardous trek to the "promised land" of America. A stunning, poetic tale of survival. ★★★½

El Super

(1979, 80 min, US, Leon Ichaso & Orlando Jiminez-Leal) *Raymundo Hidalgo-Gato, Orlando Jiminez-Leal, Elizabeth Peña.* Made in New York, this humorous, nonsentimental story of the trials of a homesick Cuban immigrant is both accomplished and heartwarming. Roberto, a Cuban exile for 10 years,

Reese Witherspoon in *Election*

works as a super in a New York apartment house and lives in its basement. Still not assimilated into this strange new land of snow, garbage and crime, he dreams of the palm trees, warmth and friendliness of his former land. This comical sad tale of a reluctant émigré is reminiscent of *Bread and Chocolate*. (Spanish with English subtitles) ★★★ VHS: $19.99

Elaine Stritch: At Liberty

(2002, 140 min, US, Rick McKay) *Elaine Stritch.* Diminutive in size but possessing a larger-than-life stage presence suggesting she's ten-feet tall, Broadway star and certified grand dame of the theatre Stritch stands alone center stage with nothing more than her memories of a career spanning over 50 years and black leotards shaping a pair of legs that blatantly defy that longevity. In her Tony Award-winning one-woman show, Stritch bares her soul of a career and all its ups and downs and makes theatrical history in the process. Funny, moving, bittersweet and completely spellbinding, this literal performance of a lifetime includes musical sequences and reminiscencs of fellow performers (from Ethel Merman to Judy Garland), her love affairs and her professional life. It's a story told in wry, entertaining bits of history and gossip, reverence and mockery, without ego or flattery. A one-of-a-kind theatrical experience performed by a one-of-a-kind stage legend. ★★★★ DVD: $24.99

The Eleanor Roosevelt Story

(1965, 90 min, US, Richard Kaplan) When a Boswell, due to propriety, chooses to ignore the defining crisis in its subject's life, then any possibility of framing a coherent profile is relinquished. This by-the-numbers collage of newsreel footage and snapshots narrated with an almost comically stentorian voice-over by Eric Severeid won an Academy Award as Best Documentary in 1965. Now "freshened up" for home video with a few pointless words from Hillary Rodham Clinton, *The Eleanor Roosevelt Story* is hindered by an incessant tone of veneration, endemic of its era before Watergate. We only learn what she did; never really *why*. What was it that caused this sheltered woman of privilege to suddenly betray her class and become a rare advocate for the poor and disenfranchised? Maybe such things weren't discussed during the mid-'60s, but in ignoring the more controversial issues, their absence is only magnified. ★★ DVD: $29.99

Election

(1999, 105 min, US, Alexander Payne) *Matthew Broderick, Reese Witherspoon, Chris Klein, Jessica Campbell, Colleen Camp.* Citizen Ruth director Payne once again tackles political processes, this time within a public high school. Running for school president is perky overachiever Witherspoon; her nemesis here is Broderick, as a teacher (not a Bueller) who looks for ways to defeat her. No one in this scattershot satire is safe, with teacher-student sex, budding lesbianism, campaign politics and perfectionist parents among the dozens of targets. It's completely hilarious, and even when the viciousness is shocking, it rings very true. Witherspoon shines, and Broderick is a revelation, playing the most complex and adult (if not exactly grown-up) part of his career. *Election* is a scintillating slap at the forces of comformity, cheer and good fortune. ★★★½ DVD: $14.99, VHS: $14.99

The Electric Horseman

(1979, 120 min, US, Sydney Pollack) *Robert Redford, Jane Fonda, Valerie Perrine, John Saxon, Willie Nelson, Wilford Brimley.* An unusual though entertaining drama about a cowboy (Redford) who steals a $12 million horse and escapes into the Nevada desert. There he is followed by TV reporter (Fonda) and romance ensues. ★★★ DVD: $14.99

The Elegant Criminal

(1991, 120 min, France, Francis Girod) *Daniel Auteil, Jean Poiret.* Long dependent on Hollywood for its cinematic diet of lurid depictions of evil, the French now have an evil genius to call their own. In this fascinating portrait, based on the true story of the notorious 19th-century murderer Pierre-Francois Lacenaire, director Girod has avoided the cheap, gory route and instead has fashioned an intimate, witty look into the dark abyss of unrepentant evil. Auteil is riveting as Lacenaire — a failed playwright, refined gentleman, homosexual, as well as thief, con man and knife-wielding mass murderer — who despite (or because of) it all, received the respect of his jailers and became a national celebrity. (French with English subtitles) ★★★

The Element of Crime

(1989, 104 min, Denmark, Lars von Trier) *Michael Elphick, Esmond Knight, Jerold Wells.* This dark and brooding police thriller follows the story of an emotionally fragile cop who, after spending years in self-exile in Egypt, returns to a postnuclear Europe — a continent plunged into inexplicable darkness, constant rain, and which is crumbling into chaos and senseless crime. Hired to track down the elusive killer responsible for a series of horrifying mutilations of young girls, the detective attempts to solve the killings by using the revolutionary theory of his former mentor: re-creating the exact events leading up to each murder. Filmed in mute black and white, the film's labyrinthine plot and bizarre imagery combine to make this a beguiling yet satisfying murder-mystery. (Filmed in English) ★★★ DVD Criterion Collection: $39.99, VHS: $19.99

The Elementary School

(1991, 100 min, Czechoslovakia, Jan Svêrák) *Jan Triska, Libuse Safrankova.* In a small Czech village at the end of WWII, young boys use abandoned tanks as jungle gyms and drive their teacher to distraction. Their overwrought instructor is replaced by a man of military bearing with many stories of brave exploits to tell. The students' childhood confidences and explorations are juxtaposed against the ambiguous

realities of the adult world, where no truth is pristine and the behavior of a perceived hero is often questionable. What the film may lack in cohesion is more than compensated for in its warmth and compassion. In the manner of *Hope and Glory*, the film is a series of youthful reminiscences told in the golden glow of adult reflection on that time when Czechoslovakia basked in the expectation of socialism with a human face. (Czech with English subtitles) ★★★

Eléna and Her Men

(1956, 98 min, France, Jean Renoir) *Ingrid Bergman, Jean Marais, Mel Ferrer.* A blithely old-fashioned, highly stylized creation from director Renoir starring Bergman as an impoverished 1880s Polish countess. On Bastille Day in Paris, Bergman becomes romantically involved with a debonaire count and a high-ranking soldier. This lush *fantaisie musicale* follows the countess' days as she must choose between the men and, of course, live happily ever after. This film, which Bergman specifically asked the director to make for her, was long thought lost. This is the full-length, restored version. (French with English subtitles) (aka: *Paris Does Strange Things*) ★★★ VHS: $24.99

Eleni

(1985, 117 min, US, Peter Yates) *John Malkovich, Kate Nelligan, Linda Hunt, Dimitra Arliss.* Based on Nicholas Gage's autobiographical best-seller, this uninvolving adaptation stars Malkovich as a *New York Times* reporter who returns to his native Greece to investigate the death of his mother at the hands of Communist guerrillas 30 years earlier. Nelligan is excellent as Gage's mother, whose story is told in flashback. ★★

Elephant

(2003, 80 min, US, Gus Van Sant) *Alex Frost, Eric Deulen, John Robinson, Elias McConnell, Jordan Taylor, Carrie Finklea.* Continuing to film with the minimalistic style of *Gerry*, writer-director Van Sant hauntingly distills the events surrounding a Columbine-like high school shooting to its most basic elements. In taking the time to get to know several sets of interlinked students, the tragedy becomes more profound yet even more senseless. Perhaps echoing the frustration of endless news coverage that demands explanations, however superficial, Van Sant introduces many possible causes and debunks them: deficient parents, peer pressure, drug use, insecurity, sexual issues (gay and straight) — in short, life in a typical high school. The easy availability of guns and violent entertainment may be contributors, but are they triggers, facilitators, or mere conveniences? Much of *Elephant* is shot from a first-person-shooter video game perspective, but it's hard to imagine a movie so grueling being an inspiration to violence. The identity of the shooters isn't even revealed until halfway through, forcing the audience into a fruitless guessing game, a search for nonexistent answers. These are misunderstood kids, and there's no way an 80-minute movie is going to understand them either. Instead, Van Sant lets us watch, intimately, and maybe experience just a little bit of what it was like for an entire generation to lose its innocence. And that's more than enough. ★★★½ DVD: $27.99, VHS: $26.99

The Elephant Man

(1980, 125 min, US, David Lynch) *John Hurt, Anthony Hopkins, Anne Bancroft, John Gielgud, Wendy Hiller.* An eerie and hypnotic account on the life of John Merrick — a man so hideously deformed by disease that he was forced to make a

Joseph Fiennes and Cate Blanchett in *Elizabeth*

living as a sideshow freak. Filmed in stark black and white, Lynch's camera acutely captures the darker corners of Victorian London and draws us into a world of shadows and despair. (Not associated with the Tony Award-winning play.) ★★★★ DVD Letterbox: $19.99, VHS: $14.99

Elephant Walk

(1954, 103 min, US, William Dieterle) *Elizabeth Taylor, Peter Finch, Dana Andrews.* A new wife travels to her husband's exotic plantation, where a battle ensues with nature. No, it's not *The Naked Jungle*, which had those neat killer ants, but the inferior *Elephant Walk*, which can only boast rampaging elephants. (Taylor replaced Vivien Leigh, who can be seen in certain shots.) ★★ VHS: $14.99

11 Harrowhouse

(1974, 95 min, GB, Aram Avakiam) *Charles Grodin, Trevor Howard, Candice Bergen, James Mason, John Gielgud.* Grodin stars as a diamond salesman enlisted by a crazy millionaire (Howard) to steal one million dollars' worth of diamonds. An unusual action spoof. ★★½ VHS: $29.99

Elizabeth

(1998, 124 min, GB, Shekhar Kapur) *Cate Blanchett, Geoffrey Rush, Joseph Fiennes, Richard Attenborough, Christopher Eccleston, Fanny Ardant.* With its graphic opening sequence of a trio of Protestant heretics being burned at the stake, one knows right away that this look at the tumultuous rise to power of Elizabeth I will not be the fluff of light costume drama. The year is 1554 and Elizabeth's Catholic half-sister Mary is on the throne. She's dying of cancer and amidst the religious strife that's tearing England apart, Elizabeth becomes the last hope for the country's Protestants. Naturally, the palace is awash in intrigue, and everyone's being carted off to the Tower — including Elizabeth. Kapur paints a London reluctantly climbing out of the grit of the Middle Ages and into the opulence of the Renaissance. Blanchett is dazzling as Elizabeth, offering a radiant portrayal of a young woman who though cunning and guilelessness is struggling to hang on to every shred of her inno-

cence. Moody, gloomy and ultimately triumphant, with a flawless evocation of 16th-century England. ★★★★ DVD: $14.99, VHS: $9.99

Elmer Gantry

(1960, 147 min, US, Richard Brooks) *Burt Lancaster, Jean Simmons, Shirley Jones, Dean Jagger.* Lancaster won a Best Actor Oscar for his dynamic portrayal of a shady evangelist who charms himself into a religious troupe and the heart of Simmons. Jones also won an Oscar for her sensational performance as Lancaster's former girlfriend-turned-prostitute. Based on Sinclair Lewis' best-seller. ★★★½ DVD: $14.99

The Elusive Corporal

(1962, 106 min, France, Jean Renoir) *Jean-Pierre Cassel, Claude Brasseur.* This intentionally lighthearted comedy about various attempts of three French soldiers to escape from a POW camp during World War II may bring to mind Renoir's antiwar classic *La Grande Illusion*. But the intent of the director was less on the examination of class and regional differences and more on the solidarity and friendship of his characters. Cassel is the charming and educated corporal who dedicates himself to breaking out of prison by any means possible. A wry, gentle comedy, featuring lively performances, and one of Renoir's most entertaining films. (French with English subtitles) ★★★½ VHS: $59.99

The Elusive Pimpernel

(1950, 107 min, GB, Emeric Pressburger & Michael Powell) *David Niven, Margaret Leighton, Cyril Cusack.* Longtime collaborators Powell and Pressburger's excellent version of the daring exploits of Baroness Orczy's famous character is every bit as entertaining as the 1935 original, *The Scarlet Pimpernel*. Niven is excellent as the heroic adventurer who rescues French aristocrats from the guillotine while doubling as an "indolent dandy of London." Originally filmed as a musical, all of the numbers were edited out, which is probably all the better. ★★★ VHS: $29.99

Elvira Madigan

(1967, 89 min, Sweden, Bo Widenberg) *Pia Degermark, Thommy Berggren.* Considered one of the cinema's most beautiful films, this tale of star-crossed love follows a young officer who meets a beautiful circus dancer and takes off to create a fragile life in isolation that must surely destroy them both. This exquisitely photographed, superbly performed film explores the consequences of love in a lyrical, poignant manner. (Swedish with English subtitles) ★★★★

Elvira, Mistress of the Dark

(1988, 96 min, US, James Signorelli) *Cassandra Peterson, Jeff Conaway, Edie McClurg.* A feature film may seem like an unlikely vehicle for Elvira, the late night horror show hostess. It does not take long, however, for this disarming comedy to win you over. In the same vein as Pee-wee Herman, Cassandra Peterson's outrageous alter ego travels to Salem, Massachusetts, to collect an inheritance. Her confrontations with the straight-laced residents are funny and surreal. ★★½ DVD Letterbox: $9.99

The Emerald Forest

(1985, 113 min, US, John Boorman) *Powers Boothe, Charley Boorman, Meg Foster.* Director Boorman's son Charley plays the kidnapped child of an American engineer stationed deep within the Amazon. Boorman captures the beauty and mystery

of these precious rain forests, while weaving subtle messages of the importance of cultural diversity and environmental respect into this taut action-packed adventure. Boothe plays the father who spends ten years searching for his son. ★★★½ DVD: $19.99

Emily Brontë's Wuthering Heights

(1992, 106 min, GB, Peter Kosminsky) *Ralph Fiennes, Juliette Binoche.* Fiennes and Binoche appearing as star-crossed lovers Heathcliff and Cathy certainly demands a certain amount of expectations. But unfortunately, neither performer is allowed to really shine under the misguided direction of Kosminsky, and only occasionally is this newest version of Brontë's classic worthy of either author or star. Fiennes plays Heathcliff with passionate despair and anger, but forgets that ultimately this is a man driven by loss of love, not hate. Binoche would be more at home as Scarlett O'Hara, playing Cathy more as a flirt while not fully exploring her divided romantic loyalty. Kosminsky's pacing is most at fault, however, as the film never establishes its own tempo and finally is nothing more than a collection of beautiful set pieces unable to fully capture the story's splendor and romanticism. ★★ DVD: $19.99, VHS: $14.99

Emma

(1996, 107 min, GB, Diarmuid Lawrence) *Kate Beckinsale, Mark Strong, Prunella Scales, Samantha Morton.* In this sterling television adaptation, Beckinsale upstages Gwyneth Paltrow's recent take on the title character (though Paltrow brings her own sparkle) with a very mannered but nonetheless mischievous look at Austen's would-be Cupid. Having found true love for her one-time nanny, Emma Woodhouse declares herself a bonafide matchmaker and sets out to sow the seeds of amorous bliss for her best friend. Her plan goes terribly awry, however, and in the end, she's squarely confronted with her own shortcomings. It's a marvelously moral tale that is presented here with all the manners and propriety that Austen herself could have hoped for. ★★★★ DVD: $19.99, VHS: $14.99

Emma

(1996, 111 min, GB, Douglas McGrath) *Gwyneth Paltrow, Alan Cumming, Jeremy Northam, Greta Scacchi, Toni Collette, Juliet Stevenson, Ewan McGregor, Polly Walker.* An absolutely charming, albeit commercial, rendition of Jane Austen's novel about a meddlesome young woman whose attempts to sow the seeds of romance go hopelessly awry. A radiant Paltrow brings an abundance of youthful exu-

Gwyneth Paltrow as *Emma*

berance to the title role while exceeding all expectations of her American pop film pedigree. And while her Emma is a peppy, somewhat modernized interpretation, in the context of director McGrath's fanciful take on the tale, it's right on the money. An array of British talent surrounds Paltrow, and all excel in supporting roles while lending that air of authenticity that only British actors can. There's no reason for anyone not to be swept up in the sheer fun of it all. ★★★½ DVD: $14.99, VHS: $9.99

Emma's Shadow

(1988, 93 min, Denmark, Soeren Kragh-Jacobsen) *Bjorje Ahistedt, Line Kruse.* The unlikely friendship between a willful, lonely 11-year-old girl with a slow-thinking, middle-aged sewer worker is the center of this small but affecting drama set in 1930s Copenhagen. Little rich girl Emma, frustrated by her parents' inattention, stages her own kidnapping and runs away from home, eventually hiding out at Malthe's ramshackle flat in the poor section of town. They form an unlikely alliance — with the clumsy but affectionate man passing the little girl off to his friends and neighbors as his niece. This Cannes Film Festival winner is a touching, gentle, lyrical movie about two lonely outcasts who find love and understanding. (Danish with English subtitles) ★★★

Billy Dee Williams and Harrison Ford in *The Empire Strikes Back*

Emmanuelle

(1974, 94 min, France, Just Jaeckin) *Sylvia Kristel, Alain Cuny.* Until Perrier hit these shores, director Jaeckin's classy come-on reigned as France's most popular export. Kristel plays the inquisitive neophyte who sets out to satiate her carnal desires. A film classic which depicts virtually every variation on sexual activity as the heroine pursures the peaks of pleasure and desire. (French with English subtitles) ★★½ DVD Dubbed: $29.99, VHS Dubbed: $19.99

Emperor Jones

(1933, 72 min, US, Dudley Murphy) *Paul Robeson, Dudley Digges.* Robeson plays Brutus Jones, a strong-willed, egotistical railroad pullman who becomes king on a small island in the South Seas. Though this screen adaptation of Eugene O'Neill's acclaimed stage play is rather stagey, it is well worth a look for Robeson's incredibly commanding performance. ★★★ DVD: $19.99

The Emperor's Club

(2002, 109 min, US, Michael Hoffman) *Kevin Kline, Emile Hirsch, Embeth Davidtz, Rob Morrow, Edward Herrmann, Harris Yulin, Joel Gretsch, Steven Culp, Patrick Dempsey, Jesse Eisenberg, Rishi Mehta, Paul Dano, Roger Rees.* Professor William Hundert may well be the most popular teacher at the exclusive St. Benedict's Academy for Boys. Serious, slightly arrogant, but not without a sense of humor, Hundert is the kind of academic movies love to exalt. Unfortunately, *The Emperor's Club* doesn't allow Hundert — played with authority by Kline — to fully distinguish himself from Mr. Holland, Miss Dove or their countless contemporaries. The story recalls one particular school year when Hundert attempted to connect with a troubled student and self-appointed school rebel. *The Emperor's Club* does try to set itself apart by underscoring philosopher Heraclitus' maxim "A man's character is his fate," so fondly recalled by Hundert, but the screenplay only occasionally rises above the familiar teacher-student formula. ★★½ DVD Letterbox: $14.99, DVD Pan & Scan: $14.99, VHS: $9.99

The Emperor's New Groove

(2000, 77 min, US, Mark Dindal) *Voices of: David Spade, John Goodman, Eartha Kitt.* Though its animation isn't up to Disney's usual standards, this madcap romp is elevated by a bouncy screenplay whose accent is most definitely on jokey one-liners and spirited hijinks. Spade provides good vocals for Kuzco, a self-centered king nearing his 18th birthday. When he fires his advisor Yzma (Kitt), she retaliates by turning him into a llama. He teams with peasant Pacha (Goodman) to return to the castle and his former self. The jokes are lively and keep coming, thanks to Spade's vainglorious reading. Though it could have used better songs, *The Emperor's New Groove* is fun all around. ★★★ DVD Letterbox: $29.99, DVD The Ultimate Groove: $39.99, VHS: $26.99

Empire of the Sun

(1987, 152 min, US, Steven Spielberg) *Christian Bale, Ben Stiller, John Malkovich, Miranda Richardson, Nigel Havers, Joe Pantoliano.* Spielberg's ambitious project is an enthralling, spectacularly filmed if not totally successful tale of a young, privileged British boy (Bale) living in 1940s China who is separated from his parents when the Japanese invade. Sent to an internment camp, the youth quickly adapts to his environment; aided, in part, by sleazy American Malkovich and frustrated Richardson. ★★★½ DVD: $19.99, VHS: $14.99

Empire State

(1987, 104 min, GB, Ron Peck) *Cathryn Harrison, Martin Landau, Ray McAnally.* Independent filmmaker Peck goes "mainstream" with this underworld crime thriller set amidst the 1980s boom of the rapidly gentrifying docklands of London's East End. Seemingly countless characters and subplots are weaved through this violent tale of drugs, scheming real estate speculation, greedy yuppies, bruising boxers, male prostitutes and elegant moles. The central story follows the attempt of a former male prostitute to try to take over a glitzy gay/straight nightclub. The provocative though uneven film opens promisingly, but concludes in a mess of unanswered questions. ★★½ VHS: $79.99

The Empire Strikes Back

(1980, 124 min, US, Irvin Kershner) *Mark Hamill, Harrison Ford, Carrie Fisher, Billy Dee Williams, Anthony Daniels, David Prowse, Alec Guinness, Clive Revill, James Earl Jones.* This second and arguably best installment of the *Star Wars* trilogy picks up the story as the Rebellion is consolidating its power and internal structure. An Imperial probe droid soon interrupts their work and puts them on the defensive against a newly reorganized and newly vengeful Empire, led by the evil Darth Vader. The Rebel leaders disperse: Luke heading off to a swamp planet to complete his Jedi training, and Han and Leia taking an extended detour through an asteroid belt and a city in the clouds. By far the darkest of the trilogy, *Empire* sustains a high level of tension throughout the film, especially since there exists the real possibility of evil triumphant. *Empire* improves upon the original and leaves the viewer wanting more, more, more. ★★★★ Available in a DVD Letterboxed Trilogy-pack for $69.99

Employees' Entrance

(1933, 75 min, US, Roy Del Ruth) *Warren William, Loretta Young, Wallace Ford.* This Depression-era melodrama puts *Wall Street* to shame. William stars as a department store manager who fires employees at the drop of a hat and is constantly fighting the managing directors, but he also keeps profits up. Young is a new employee who finds herself at odds with him when her fiancé becomes his assistant. Can she keep him from becoming as unscrupulous as the boss? With some racy dialogue and humorous moments, this is a thinly veiled debate about management's treatment of labor and its lack of morality. ★★★ VHS: $19.99

Empty Canvas

(1964, 118 min, Italy, Damiano Damiani) *Bette Davis, Horst Bucholtz, Catherine Spaak.* International casting of stars for film productions was quite the rage in Europe in the mid-Sixties. Which explains how Davis, with a Southern accent and blond Dutchboy wig, ended up in this interesting but convoluted Italian production. Art student Bucholz's love for a seductive model is frustrated by his domineering and blustery and immensely wealthy mother (Davis). A treat for Davis fans, but overall the story fails to excite. (Filmed in English) ★★

The Empty Mirror

(1996, 118 min, US, Barry J. Hershey) *Norman Rodway, Camilla Soeberg, Joel Grey, Peter Michael Goetz, Doug McKeon.* Through archival footage, hallucinatory flashbacks, and subjective self-analysis, history's most notorious mass murderer, Adolf Hitler, lays bare his own psyche while reveling in his own genius. Rodway's powerful performance (shot basically in the form of a one-man show) and Hershey's mesmerizing camera cannot overcome the unpleasantness of having to spend two hours inside the mind of an unrepentant monster. As the title suggests, the mirror — and indeed the experience — is truly quite empty. ★½ DVD: $14.99, VHS: $9.99

Enamorada (In Love)

(1965, 81 min, Mexico, Emilio Fernandez) A classic of the Mexican cinema. Beatriz is the beautiful daughter of a very wealthy man. Jose, a general committed to social and political change, is deeply in love with her. But the woman, blinded by a life's teaching that class is more important than love, has only contempt for this peasant-born young man. A fiery and passionate tale of love overcoming social pressures. (Spanish with English subtitles) ★★★½

Enchanted April

(1991, 104 min, US, Mike Newell) *Miranda Richardson, Josie Lawrence, Joan Plowright, Polly Walker, Alfred Molina, Jim Broadbent, Michael Kitchen.* A heartwarming adaptation of Elizabeth von Arnim's 1922 romantic comedy about four English women who run off to an Italian seaside castle for emotional revitalization. The theme is a familiar one to English literature (uptight Brits flee their rainy island to the Italian sun where they finally let loose, a little) and it's done full justice here. Filmed in the actual villa in Portofino, Italy, where von Armin penned her book, the film lovingly re-creates the ambience of the era while telling its charming tale of four women who start off as unlikely traveling companions and wind up best of friends. The acting is uniformly excellent. ★★★★ VHS: $19.99

The Enchanted Cottage

(1945, 92 min, US, John Cromwell) *Dorothy McGuire, Robert Young, Herbert Marshall, Mildred Natwick.* Isolated from society by physical deformities resulting from different sets of circumstances, a young man and woman learn to see themselves through each other's eyes. Touching performances from McGuire and Young elevate what could have been mawkish melodrama. Instead, this is a fantasy parable about the healing power of unconditional love. This film was used as an allegorical reference in Joseph Wambaugh's "The Secrets of Harry Bright." ★★★

Encino Man

(1992, 88 min, US, Les Mayfield) *Pauly Shore, Brendan Fraser, Sean Astin, Megan Ward.* In a move that might seem tantamount to box-office suicide, Hollywood has given us a movie starring quite possibly the most irritating creature ever put before the camera. The punchline is . . . for the most part, it works. Shore plays the world's oldest-looking high school student who becomes part of the in-crowd when his best friend (Astin) unearths a prehistoric man in his backyard. Though a wee bit lethargic in the laughs department, a debuting Fraser steals the pic hands down with his money's-worth performance as the title character. ★★½ DVD: $9.99

Encore

(1952, 87 min, GB, Anthony Pelissier, Harold French, Pat Jackson) *Glynis Johns, Kay Walsh, Nigel Patrick.* An intriguing trilogy based on three short stories by W. Somerset Maugham. In the first, a playboy battles with his brother over money; in the second, an irascible spinster makes life miserable for the unfortunate passengers on an ocean crossing; in the third, a circus high-diver gets the jitters. ★★★½

The End

(1978, 100 min, US, Burt Reynolds) *Burt Reynolds, Dom DeLuise, Sally Field, Joanne Woodward, Carl Reiner, David Steinberg, Kristy McNichol, Robby Benson, Myrna Loy.* Scandalously funny, this wicked black comedy features Reynolds as a man who is told that he has only a few months to live and decides to commit suicide. Featuring hilarious appearances by the entire cast, especially DeLuise who is wonderfully deranged as Reynolds' schizophrenic best friend. The film takes a sharp satiric swipe at the hypocrisy of compassion as well as the sanctity of life. ★★★ DVD: $14.99

End of Days

(1999, 118 min, US, Peter Hyams) *Arnold Schwarzenegger, Gabriel Byrne, Robin Tunney, Kevin Pollak, Rod Steiger.* "Ah-nuld" produces a medium bang in this bizarre mix of generic action flick and fire-and-brimstone apocalyptic thriller. Arnold plays a scruffy New York cop who must protect a cynical woman from the vile clutches of Satan himself (Byrne, whose sinister bent and malevolent pranks provide the only source of much-needed humor in this otherwise grim and heartless movie). Tired cop-movie clichés and digital special effects dominate as the forces of evil threaten the forces of light. Knowing what he's up against, the film flirts with ludicrosity far too often by making him blast away at Beelzebub with a Rambo-sized arsenal. Steiger has some fun chewing his ham and everyone else's scenery. ★★ DVD: $14.99, VHS Special Edition: $9.99

The End of Innocence

(1990, 102 min, US, Dyan Cannon) *Dyan Cannon, John Heard, George Coe, Michael Madsen, Renee Taylor.* Cannon wrote, directed and stars in this personal story of an overachiever who's determined to be everything to everybody: the perfect daughter, the perfect employee, the perfect lover, the perfect woman. Slowly, she comes to terms with the responsibility of making her own happiness. ★★★ VHS: $79.99

The End of St. Petersburg

(1927, 69 min, USSR, Vsevolod Pudovkin) *Ivan Chuvelov.* Made on the commemoration of the Tenth Anniversary of the 1917 Revolution, this ambitious drama follows the plight of a common laborer who is forced to leave his failing farm only to then suffer at the hands of capitalist factory owners and eventually witness the horrors of war. The film, in not a subtle fashion, details the pains and humiliation the people had to endure before experiencing the social upheavals and resulting freedoms of the Revolution. (Silent with orchestral accompaniment) ★★★ DVD Double Feature: $24.99, VHS: $24.99

The End of the Affair

(1999, 101 min, GB, Neil Jordan) *Ralph Fiennes, Julianne Moore, Stephen Rea, Ian Hart.* Jordan's exquisite and mostly faithful adaptation of Graham Greene's semiautobiographical novel, *The End of the Affair* features remarkable performances and

gorgeous cinematography. Maurice Bendrix (Fiennes) begins an erotic affair with Sarah Miles (Moore), who ends things for no apparent reason. Two years later, Maurice and Sarah reunite through her cuckolded husband, Henry (Rea), and emotions begin to simmer again. Jordan keeps the tension mounting, yet what makes the film so passionate is that in the present or in the past, every touch between the lovers is palpable and heartfelt. The second screen version of Greene's novel, this *End of the Affair* is heartbreaking and very moving. ★★★½ DVD: $27.99

The End of Violence

(1997, 122 min, US, Wim Wenders) *Bill Pullman, Andie MacDowell, Gabriel Byrne, Loren Dean, Traci Lind, Udo Kier, Sam Fuller.* Director Wenders' disdain for contemporary Hollywood and fear of Los Angeles is evident in almost every scene of *The End of Violence.* Pullman plays a producer specializing in blood-and-bullets epics who is so absorbed in financing his latest movie that when wife MacDowell announces she's leaving him, he barely reacts. Then, he is carjacked by two thugs, who are murdered, giving Pullman a chance to start a new life for himself — working anonymously with a group of Latino gardeners. At the same time, scientist Byrne is busy developing a surveillance system for the L.A. area. When one of Byrne's cameras catches the killing of Pullman's assailants, strange things start to occur and skeletons are pulled out of both men's closets. Part thriller, part Hollywood business satire and part marital drama, *The End of Violence* is a haunting meditation on living and dying in L.A., a place where a wife uses a cell phone to tell her husband she wants a divorce while sitting a few feet away. ★★★ DVD: $19.99

Endangered Species

(1982, 92 min, US, Alan Rudolph) *Robert Urich, JoBeth Williams, Hoyt Axton, Paul Dooley, Peter Coyote, Dan Hedaya.* Low-keyed performances enhance this fact-based suspense thriller about a New York detective (Urich) assigned to investigate a string of bizarre cattle mutilations out West. Williams costars as the country sheriff also on the case. Slow-moving at times, but the patient viewer will be rewarded. ★★★

Endgame

(2001, 113 min, GB, Gary Wicks) *Mark McGann, John Benfield, Daniel Newman, Corey Johnson, Toni Barry.* This moody English thriller stars Newman as Tom, a rent boy who is kept by George (McGann), a sadomasochistic gangster. Tom is kept in high style in a London flat filled with pop art and a bedroom set up not only for sex but also for blackmail, with a hidden camera focused on the red silk sheets. Tom is drawn into a nasty scheme involving drugs, dirty money and protection by George's connection with a crooked gay cop. Things turn nasty rather quickly in this violent film, with beatings, extortion and corruption. The sumptuous apartments are as stunning as the Welsh countryside, where Tom makes his getaway after an accidental death. A good script and some fancy editing make sure that this familiar crime saga remains entertaining and suspenseful. ★★★ DVD: $19.99, VHS: $9.99

Endless Love

(1981, 115 min, US, Franco Zeffirelli) *Brooke Shields, Martin Hewitt, Don Murray, Shirley Knight, Richard Kiley, Beatrice Straight, Tom Cruise, James Spader.* The film which will always be remembered as the butt of Bette Midler's classic

Oscar-night joke: "That endless bore — *Endless Love*." It's about two teenagers (Shields, Hewitt) with the hots for each other. Despite being one of the worst films of its decade, debuting actors Cruise and Spader were able to get work after this. ★

Endless Night

(1971, 95 min, GB, Sidney Gilliat) *Hayley Mills, Hywel Bennett, Britt Ekland, George Sanders, Per Oscarsson*. Suspenseful Agatha Christie thriller about a rich American girl (Mills) who marries her chauffeur (Bennett). When they move into her mansion, their new life is anything but blissful when blackmail and murder enter the scene. ★★★ DVD: $14.99, VHS: $9.99

Enemies: A Love Story

(1989, 119 min, US, Paul Mazursky) *Ron Silver, Anjelica Huston, Lena Olin, Margaret Sophie Stein, Paul Mazursky, Alan King*. Featuring a superb evocation of post-WWII New York, director Mazursky has created a career milestone with this darkly comic tale about a Jewish immigrant (Silver), scarred from his wartime experiences, who suddenly finds himself with three wives. An extraordinary cast includes Huston as his strong-willed first wife thought killed in the camps; Stein as his gentile, slave-like second; and the remarkable Olin as a lusty socialist whose passion most ignites the stolid Silver. ★★★★ DVD Letterbox: $19.99

Enemy at the Gates

(2001, 131 min, GB, Jean-Jacques Annaud) *Jude Law, Joseph Fiennes, Rachel Weisz, Ed Harris, Bob Hoskins, Ron Perlman, Eva Mattes, Gabriel Marshall-Thomas*. Stunning battle sequences collide with the familiar subplot of two soldiers in love with the same woman, making the visually exciting *Enemy at the Gates* a rousing if routine war film. Based on the experiences of real-life Russian hero Vassili Zaitsev (Law), the story introduces Vassili at the battle of Stalingrad, where he has distinguished himself as a marksman. In an effort to bolster morale, a writer follows Vassili's successful sniper attacks on German officers, turning him into a national hero. This also attracts the attention of the Nazis, who send a cold-blooded assassin (a sensational Harris) to hunt him down. *Enemy at the Gates* is at its best detailing the components of war, from bloody battle to the final hunt. It loses much of its dramatic momentum by giving equal time to an uninvolving love triangle. ★★½ DVD Letterbox: $19.99, VHS: $9.99

The Enemy Below

(1957, 98 min, US, Dick Powell) *Robert Mitchum, Curt Jurgens, David Hedison, Theodore Bikel*. Solid WWII yarn with Mitchum as an American warship commander and Jurgens as a Nazi U-boat captain engaged in a battle of wits as the Yanks hunt down a German sub. The film explores the interpersonal relationships between the men of both crews, and also features Oscar-winning special effects. ★★★ DVD: $14.99

Enemy Mine

(1985, 108 min, US, Wolfgang Petersen) *Louis Gossett, Jr., Dennis Quaid*. From the director of *Das Boot* comes this visually striking sci-fi adventure about two interplanetary enemies, a pilot from Earth and a warrior from the planet Drac, who become stranded together on a distant, deserted planet. A space-age *Hell in the Pacific*. ★★★ DVD: $24.99

Enemy of the State

(1998, 127 min, US, Tony Scott) *Will Smith, Gene Hackman, Jon Voight, Regina King, Loren Dean, Jason Lee, Gabriel Byrne, James LeGros, Ian Hart*. In this exciting political thriller, Smith is Robert Dean, a wily lawyer who is forced to use all his wiles when government goons mistake him for an agent with damaging evidence against their covert syndicate. Dean then spends the rest of the film dashing in and out of trouble in tense, even plausible cat-and-mouse games. He gets a little help from a reclusive surveillance expert (Hackman in another saving-grace supporting turn) who teaches him a few tricks in the book. The film starts a little slow in setting up the game, but once the game's afoot, *Enemy of the State* is an often crackerjack espionage tale. ★★★ DVD: $19.99, VHS: $9.99

Enemy Territory

(1987, 90 min, US, Peter Manoogian) *Gary Frank, Ray Parker Jr., Jan-Michael Vincent*. Effective urban thriller about a naïve insurance salesman and a street-smart phone workman who join forces when they become trapped in a ghetto apartment building under siege by a neighborhood gang. ★★½ VHS: $79.99

The Enemy Within

(1994, 86 min, US, Jonathan Darby) *Forest Whitaker, Sam Waterston, Dana Delany, Jason Robards, George Dzundza, Josef Sommers*. In this updated remake of *Seven Days in May*, the president (Waterston) has seven days to sign a bill which increases the military budget by 30%. He does not intend to sign it. Whitaker turns in a solid performance as the colonel who inadvertently uncovers a plot to overthrow the presidency — perpetrated by the U.S. military. Robards exudes controlled mania as the general who orchestrates the military maneuvers. A tautly paced and finely detailed HBO production. ★★★ VHS: $9.99

Les Enfants Terribles

(1950, 107 min, France, Jean-Pierre Melville) *Edouard Dermithe, Nicole Stephane*. A landmark of French cinema and a strong influence on the New Wave filmmakers, this collaboration with Jean Cocteau (who scripted the film and oversaw its production) is a haunting cinematic poem about the love and confused narcissism of a brother and sister, whose passion for each other is so intense that it flowers into perversity and eventual death. Please note that the only available videos of this classic, taken from a 16mm film, are in only fair condition. (French with English subtitles) ★★★ VHS: $29.99

L'Enfer

(1993, 100 min, France, Claude Chabrol) *Emmanuelle Béart, François Cluzet*. There's an unsettling discord between the open, sun-drenched country inn where *L'Enfer* is set, and the spiraling descent into madness that the film depicts. A husband (Cluzet) becomes increasingly obsessional regarding his wife's (Béart) supposed infidelities. While the film is sometimes ambivalent about her actual culpability, there is no doubt that Cluzet has crossed into a reality of his own making. Chabrol's masterly command of the medium allows the viewer to enter the mind of a man driven to hallucinatory extremes fueled by his paranoid distrust. The great director Henri-Georges Clouzot wrote the screenplay in 1963 with the intent of directing it. (French with English subtitles) ★★★★ DVD: $29.99, VHS: $19.99

The Enforcer

(1951, 87 min, US, Bretaigne Windust) *Humphrey Bogart, Zero Mostel, Everett Sloane*. Tough Bogart drama with Bogey as a hard-boiled district attorney out to break a crime ring. ★★★ DVD: $14.99, VHS: $9.99

The Enforcer

(1976, 96 min, US, James Fargo) *Clint Eastwood, Tyne Daly, Harry Guardino*. Eastwood encores as Dirty Harry in this third installment of the series. Daly costars as his partner as they comb San Francisco in search of a terrorist group. (Sequel: *Sudden Impact*) ★★★ DVD Letterbox: $14.99, VHS: $9.99

The English Patient

(1996, 162 min, US, Anthony Minghella) *Ralph Fiennes, Kristin Scott Thomas, Juliette Binoche, Willem Dafoe, Colin Firth, Naveen Andrews, Jürgen Prochnow*. From its opening frames, *The English Patient* evokes an exhilarating sense of time and place. Told with sweeping economy and the lyricism that only great art can author, this breathlessly romantic epic is a rare reminder of the pleasures made available from consummate filmmaking. The story effortlessly narrates two time periods: prewar Northern Africa and war-torn WWII Italy. Fiennes plays a severely burned amnesiac tended by a caring nurse (the Oscar-winning Binoche), dealing with her own scars. His love affair with a married woman is told through flashback. Scott Thomas revels in the role of the beautiful sophisticate, giving a smart, alluring performance. Adapted from Michael Ondaatje's novel by director Minghella, *The English Patient* is keenly observed and replete with the kind of romanticism and intelligent dialogue audiences ache for. Winner of 9 Academy Awards, including Best Picture. ★★★★ DVD Collector's Edition: $29.99, VHS: $9.99

An Englishman Abroad

(1985, 63 min, GB, John Schlesinger) *Alan Bates, Coral Browne*. Bates gives a riveting performance in this brilliantly staged drama made for British TV (and based on a true incident). Guy Burgess (Bates), the infamous British spy, traitor and gay outcast, defected to Russia in the 1940s. During a 1958 theatrical performance in Moscow featuring visiting actress Browne (appearing as herself), a drunken Burgess promptly crashes backstage and sets up a friendship with the actress. Browne, who is intrigued by this disheveled and eccentric outsider, comes to pity, despise and assist him after he invites her to his shabby flat — and comes to understand this almost broken man. A touching and humorous film with a witty, concise screenplay. ★★★★

The Englishman Who Went up a Hill, But Came down a Mountain

(1995, 99 min, GB, Christopher Monger) *Hugh Grant, Tara Fitzgerald, Colm Meaney, Ian Hart, Kenneth Griffiths*. Recalling the effervescence and whimsy of those wonderful Ealing comedies of the '50s and '60s, this is a thoroughly engaging if understated romp that charms at the most unexpected moments. Set in 1917, the film stars Grant as an English mapmaker who travels to a small Welsh village to measure the town's mountain, which appears to be the only source of pride for the villagers. When they discover their mountain's height only qualifies as a hill, and will therefore be ineligible to be included on the map, the entire populace engages in a crazy scheme to make up the difference and to keep Grant in town to remeasure it. Director Monger sets an easygoing pace that befits the story's unconventional comedy and budding romance. ★★★ DVD: $9.99, VHS: $9.99

Enjo

(1958, 98 min, Japan, Kon Ichikawa) *Raizo Ichikawa, Ganjiro Nakamura.* Although *Enjo* takes place in a world that is alien to most of us, there are emotions explored that transcend all bounderies. Goichi Mizoguchi (Ichikawa) is a young monk who is lonely and misunderstood. After his father's death, Mizoguchi leaves his poor temple and arrives at the famous Shukaku temple. He is accepted at first by the head priest who is an old friend of his father's. But Mizoguchi soon proves to be inept at most everything he tries, with exception to his love for the temple. While political infighting and scandal dominate the rest of the monks' time, the ostracized Mizoguchi only wants to care for Shukaku. Beautifully shot, *Enjo* is another masterpiece from Ichikawa. Based on Yukio Mishima's novel. (Japanese with English subtitles) ★★★½ VHS: $19.99

Enormous Changes at the Last Minute

(1983, 115 min, US, Ellen Hovde & Mirra Bank) *Ellen Barkin, Kevin Bacon, Maria Tucci, Lynn Milgran.* Based on the charming, humanistic tales of novelist Grace Paley, *Enormous Changes . . .* unites a crisp John Sayles-Susan Rice script and glorious performances. This trilogy from Paley's second collection glistens with the dignity of contemporary urban women struggling against setbacks but determined to get their fair share from life. A funny, gracefully optimistic work. ★★★ VHS: $79.99

Enough

(2002, 115 min, US, Michael Apted) *Jennifer Lopez, Billy Campbell, Juliette Lewis, Dan Futterman, Noah Wyle, Fred Ward, Bill Cobbs.* Lopez stars as a waitress who's swept off her feet by wealthy hunk Campbell, and within minutes, it seems, they're married with dream house and cute daughter. But when she finds he's been cheating on her, he suddenly becomes the husband from hell, until she decides she's had . . . enough! The title of this film should really have been "You Go Girl!," as that's seemingly the only desired reaction hoped for from its intended audience. Characters aren't very believable or interesting, and the situations aren't exactly two-sided, either. It boils down to: J-Lo good, Billy C. bad. And we wait (and wait) for her to kick his ass. An ordinary and derivative film, *Enough*'s ending works on a pandering, black-and-white level. Good luck making it that far. ★★ DVD Dual: $14.99, VHS: $14.99

Ensign Pulver

(1964, 104 min, US, Joshua Logan) *Robert Walker, Walter Matthau, Tommy Sands, Larry Hagman, James Coco, Jack Nicholson.* Inferior sequel to *Mister Roberts* with Walker taking over the Jack Lemmon role. Ensign Pulver continues his wartime shenanigans aboard a naval ship. ★★ VHS: $14.99

Enter the Dragon

(1973, 103 min, US, Robert Clouse) *Bruce Lee, John Saxon, Jim Kelly.* The first American/Hong Kong coproduction is arguably the best martial arts film ever made. Lee (appearing in his final film) goes underground to track down an opium ring. ★★★½ DVD Letterbox: $26.99, DVD: $19.99, VHS: $12.99, VHS Letterbox: $12.99

The Entertainer

(1960, 100 min, GB, Tony Richardson) *Laurence Olivier, Joan Plowright, Daniel Massey, Alan Bates, Albert Finney.* Olivier gives an extraordinary performance in Richardson's depiction of a seedy vaudevillian on the skids who unwittingly destroys those around him. As the egotistical Archie Rice, Olivier captures the grotesque demeanor and futile yearnings of a defeated man. Based on John Osborne's play. ★★★½ DVD: $19.99, VHS: $24.99

Entertaining Mr. Sloane

(1970, 94 min, GB, Douglas Hickox) *Beryl Reid, Harry Andrews, Peter McEnery.* Playwright Joe Orton's scathing black comedy about a young stud's entry into the lives of a middle-aged brother and sister. Reid is the sex-starved, man-hungry sister, Andrews is her latently homosexual brother and McEnery is the menacing hustler. This is a superbly acted and boldly presented rendition of one of Britain's most daring late-great playwrights. ★★★

Entrapment

(1999, 120 min, US, Jon Amiel) *Sean Connery, Will Patton, Catherine Zeta-Jones, Ving Rhames.* A tame thriller given much more class by its two stars than it really deserves, *Entrapment* stars Zeta-Jones as an insurance investigator who tracks down world-class thief Connery when a priceless painting is stolen. She cons her way into a scheme with him, but is she really there to trap him? The story has a twist every half hour or so, but none will produce more than a mild "oh" as director Amiel approaches the material with a nonchalant ambivalence. The two elaborate thefts that bookend the film sustain interest and even generate a moment or two of suspense, but the numerous cat-and-mouse games go nowhere. ★★ DVD Pan & Scan: $14.99, DVD: $14.99, VHS: $9.99

Entre Nous

(1983, 110 min, France, Diane Kurys) *Miou-Miou, Isabelle Huppert, Guy Marchand.* Kurys' largely autobiographical work is a beautiful rendering of the strength and complexity of friendship. Huppert portrays Lena, a reticent housewife resigned to the numbing security of her husband and family. Through a chance encounter, she meets Madeleine (Miou-Miou), a vibrantly bohemian sculptress whose love and companionship open the door to Lena's self-discovery. The film radiates with the delicate nuances of a woman's sensibility and sensuality. (French with English subtitles) ★★★★

Equilibrium

(2002, 107 min, US, Kurt Wimmer) *Christian Bale, Emily Watson, Taye Diggs, Angus MacFadyen, Sean Bean, William Fichtner.* In his 1982 film, *One Down, Two to Go,* blaxploitation icon Fred Williamson pulls a pistol on a martial artist, uttering the immortal line, "You may be an expert in kung fu, but I'm an expert in *gun* fu!" Twenty years later, it seems writer-director Wimmer has taken this sentiment to heart by making what may be the first "gun fu" film. In an oppressive future, a "cleric" (Bale), trained in a firearms-based martial art, hunts "sense offenders" — citizens who've stopped taking their emotion-deadening drugs. That is until he forgets to take his own meds. This derivative, silly premise is the springboard for some terrific gunfight set pieces that elevate the moderately involving if nonsensical story to the realms of irresistible guilty pleasure. ★★½ DVD: $19.99, VHS: $9.99

Equinox

(1993, 107 min, US, Alan Rudolph) *Matthew Modine, Lara Flynn Boyle, Fred Ward, Tyra Ferrell, Marisa Tomei, Kevin J. O'Connor, Tate Donovan, M. Emmet Walsh.* An elderly, indigent woman lies dying in a New York City street. She clutches a scrap of paper, closed with sealing wax, that catches the eye of a curious, would-be-writer morgue attendant, initiating a quest to uncover the truth behind a 30-year-old blind trust. Director Rudolph's relentless pacing is magnified by the constant, pounding ambient noise which underscores the desperation of characters tightly interwoven by proximity but with no emotional contact. As is usual with Rudolph films, there's an eclectic mix of talented players. Every element of the production is on target and highlighted by a mesmerizing soundtrack. ★★★½

Equinox Flower

(1958, 118 min, Japan, Yasujiro Ozu) *Shin Saburi, Kinuyo Tanaka.* Ozu's deceptively serene style of filmmaking is showcased in this family drama about the postwar generation gap between a tradition-bound businessman and his more modern-minded daughter. Although sympathetic to the independence of his friends' children, Hirayama confronts rebellion in his own family after his daughter announces her engagement to a young man without seeking his approval. Shooting from about three feet from the ground with a rock-steady camera and featuring a bold use of color (his first film in color), Ozu provides a gentle drama of familial misunderstanding and reconciliation, a beautifully designed and moving work. (Japanese with English subtitles) ★★★

Equus

(1977, 138 min, US, Sidney Lumet) *Richard Burton, Peter Firth, Jenny Agutter, Joan Plowright.* Peter Shaffer's shattering play is faithfully brought to the screen with Burton as the troubled psychiatrist who attempts to unlock the secret that triggered a disturbed stable boy (Firth) to blind six horses. Both Burton and Firth are especially good. ★★★ DVD: $19.99

Eraser

(1996, 115 min, US, Charles Russell) *Arnold Schwarzenegger, James Caan, Vanessa L. Williams, James Coburn, James Cromwell.* Arnold's megabudget action movies have nearly attained a status not unlike Greek mythology: Everybody knows the stories and how they'll end, so just add explosions. This story-lite, gun-heavy vehicle is one of the worst offenders. Combining plot elements from a half-dozen earlier (and better) Schwarzenegger efforts, *Eraser* gives us Arnold as a U.S. Marshal charged with protecting star witness Williams. And this time he's up against one of his own guys. Full of by-the-numbers stunts and explosions, this will only entertain diehard fans. ★★ DVD: $19.99, VHS: $9.99, VHS Letterbox: $9.99

Eraserhead

(1977, 90 min, US, David Lynch) *Jack Nance, Charlotte Stewart, Jeanne Bates.* Lynch's fiendish cult classic adopts the logic of dreams and nightmares as layers of reality dissolve, sucking you into the eerie world of a warped mind. The befuddled protagonist Henry struggles against the powers of his child, a shrieking mutant blob, in this demented gem. In heaven, everything is fine. Based, in part, on the director's brief stay in Philadelphia. ★★★½

Erendira

(1982, 103 min, France/Mexico/West Germany, Ruy Guerra) *Irene Papas, Claudia Ohana, Michael Lonsdale.* Director Guerra paints a surreal fresco of passion and revenge in this darkly humorous tale of a young girl forced into prostitution by her demented grandmother (Papas). Based on a short story by Gabriel Garcia Márquez. (Spanish with English subtitles) ★★★ VHS: $24.99

Erik the Viking

(1989, 100 min, GB, Terry Jones) *Tim Robbins, Mickey Rooney, Eartha Kitt, John Cleese, Terry Jones, Antony Sher.* Monty Pythonite Jones directed this funny, offbeat comic adventure that dares to ask the pertinent question, "Why rape, pillage and kill if you don't really feel like it?" Robbins stars as the sensitive Norseman, Erik, who questions the rather violent way of life of a 12th-century Viking after he is affected by a woman he has accidentally killed. The director appears as the king of an island teeming with Julie Andrews wannabes. ★★½

Erin Brockovich

(2000, 126 min, US, Steven Soderbergh) *Julia Roberts, Aaron Eckhart, Peter Coyote, Marg Helgenberger, Cherry Jones, Albert Finney.* Roberts (who won a Best Actress Oscar) shines as the title character, a single mother of three with no formal training who was instrumental in a class-action lawsuit against California's powerful PG&E. Based on a true story, this always compelling, often funny and unexpectedly touching film traces Erin's road in helping score the largest settlement in U.S. history. Director Soderbergh's first commercial film is a winner — the king of the independents is right at home with the rhythm of an underdog story, the demands of a big-budget film, and showcasing to great effect Hollywood's biggest female star of the '90s. This is a Julia Roberts movie for those who don't like Julia Roberts movies. ★★★½ DVD: $14.99, VHS: $9.99

Ermo

(1995, 93 min, China, Zhou Xiaowen) *Alia, Liu Peiqi, Ge Zhijun.* Not the uproarious comedy the video box would imply, *Ermo* is actually a scathing social satire on the rapidly changing economic and political changes currently underway in Communist China. Set in that country's impoverished rural interior, the story focuses on Ermo, a wife and mother who becomes determined to "keep up with the Joneses" in her effort to own the biggest television in the village. In order to get the money for her dream appliance, Ermo becomes the epitome of a capitalist-crazed entrepreneur when she turns her simple homemade noodles into an ever-expanding enterprise. For the politicos, it can be seen as an indictment on the encroaching consumerism and for others less didactically inclined, simply a wry comedy-drama about ambition, family and the hidden joys of the simple ways of life. (Mandarin with English subtitles) ★★★

The Ernest Green Story

(1991, 101 min, US, Eric Laneuville) *Morris Chestnut, CCH Pounder, Ossie Davis, Ruby Dee.* This stirring, superb production from the Disney family entertainment line tells the true story of the first black student to graduate from a white high school in the South. Battling intense hatred, the Arkansas government and even the Arkansas National Guard, nine brave teenagers chose to take a stand for equal education by leaving the safety of their black high school to enroll in a prestigious white Little Rock school. ★★★★

Ernesto

(1979, 95 min, Italy, Salvatore Samperi) *Michele Placido, Martin Halm.* This lush period drama revolves around the emotional and sexual coming-of-age of an impetuous Italian teenager who quickly discovers the power of youth, beauty and money. Set in the town of Trieste in 1911, the story follows

Julia Roberts as *Erin Brockovich*

Ernesto, the son of a wealthy merchant who, wielding his emerging sexuality with wanton abandon, becomes involved with a hunky stevedore, only to cruelly discard him. The lad immediately enters into an unlikely love triangle with a younger boy and his twin sister. Throughout his amorous romps, Ernesto — not a particularly likable youth — remains a figure of vacillating loyalties and reckless sexuality. The handsome Placido is perfectly cast as the helplessly infatuated workman. (Italian with English subtitles) ★★★ VHS: $49.99

Ernesto Che Guevara: The Bolivian Diary

(1997, 94 min, France/Switzerland, Richard Lindo) In a quietly moving documentary portrait, director Lindo has succeeded in delicately mythologizing one of the century's great idealists. *The Bolivian Diary* begins with Ernesto "Che" Guevara's exile from the state he helped revolutionize, due to his adversity toward Cuba's friendly relations with the Soviets. Building a narrative from Che's own handsomely scripted journal entries, the viewer travels within Bolivian underbrush, down narrow river canyons and through one-street villages in the footsteps of the guerillas. Archival films and stills of Fidel and party officials are complemented by grainy, sun-washed and lyrical video footage of testimony from surviving guerillas and Bolivian soldiers, as well as the peasants with whom Che interacted during his 11 months as leader of the revolution run aground. ★★★ VHS: $29.99

The Escape

(1995, 91 min, US/Canada, Stuart Gillard) *Patrick Dempsey, Brigitte Bako, Colm Feore.* A routine escaped convict tale with artsy pretenses. *The Escape* is a stylishly made thriller that can't escape the formula of the genre. Dempsey is a convicted murderer who becomes a fugitive when he runs away from his brutal guards while working in a remote wooded area. During a thunderstorm, he hides out in an abandoned house, only to save the life of a young, beautiful cellist (Bako) whose car has careened in a nearby lake. Together they wait

out the storm, and Dempsey finds romance and possible redemption with the young woman. The film starts briskly, but the romantic angle slows things considerably. ★★½

Escape from Afghanistan

(1994, 88 min, Russia, Timur Bekmambetov & Gennadi Kayumov) *Barry Kushner, Viktor Verzbitsky.* Filmed in 1994 under the title *Peshavar Waltz*, this Russian film may have originally been a somewhat intelligent war film (winning Best Director honors at the Karlovy Vary International Film Festival), but is undermined by a horrendous English dubbing. Because this home release version is so bad it is difficult to know if the faults rest on the shoulders of the original film. It's a shame because the film admirably tackles the rarely explored terrain of the Soviet-Afghanistan war. The story is narrated and told from the point-of-view of an American journalist, who is taken hostage by mistreated Russian soldiers in a Pakistani POW camp. When the Russians barricade themselves in an underground "bunker," it becomes apparent that all parties would just as soon prefer them dead. Though the film's low budget lends a gritty documentary feel, the editing is at times confusing and the ending is predictable and of the oft-used "horrors-of-war" cliché variety. ★ DVD: $19.99, VHS: $49.99

Escape from Alcatraz

(1980, 112 min, US, Don Siegel) *Clint Eastwood, Patrick McGoohan, Fred Ward, Danny Glover, Roberts Blossom.* A true story of the only three men ever to escape from Alcatraz. Eastwood stars as Frank Morris, the bank robber who masterminds the escape. An exciting and accomplished thriller. ★★★½ DVD: $24.99, VHS: $14.99

Escape from L.A.

(1996, 100 min, US, John Carpenter) *Kurt Russell, Steve Buscemi, Stacy Keach, Peter Fonda, Cliff Robertson, Pam Grier, Bruce Campbell, Paul Bartel.* Both a remake and a sequel to his 1981 cult classic *Escape from New York*, Carpenter's *Escape from L.A.* marks the return of the world's most unlikely one-eyed hero, Snake Plissken (Russell). This time, he must enter the island of Los Angeles, now serving as a spot of exile for those deemed undesirable to the fascist regime ruling what remains of the United States. There he has to retrieve both a lethal satellite control mechanism and the president's loony daughter, in that order. Overall the lackluster computer effects, forced humor and sense of "we've seen all this before" work too much against it. ★★½ DVD: $24.99, VHS: $9.99

Escape from New York

(1981, 106 min, US, John Carpenter) *Kurt Russell, Lee Van Cleef, Ernest Borgnine, Donald Pleasence, Isaac Hayes, Adrienne Barbeau.* In 1997, New York City is a walled, barricaded maximum security prison. Air Force One, with the president aboard, is hijacked and crash-lands inside the prison. Snake Plissken (Russell), one-time war hero and just sentenced to life, is volunteered as a one-man rescue team. *Escape from New York* effectively blends action-adventure and tongue-in-cheek comedy with consistently engaging performances from its cast. Imbued with trademark Carpenter directorial touches, not the least of which is the musical score, this director's cut includes the original trailer and a revealing interview with Carpenter. ★★★½ DVD Letterbox Special Collector's Edition: 2-Disc Set: $29.99, DVD: $14.99

Escape from the Planet of the Apes

(1971, 97 min, US, J. Lee Thompson) *Roddy McDowell, Kim Hunter, Ricardo Montalban, Sal Mineo.* In the third entry of the *Apes* series, futuristic apes McDowall and Hunter travel back in time to present-day Los Angeles. Though all the *Ape* sequels lack the energy and creative spark of the first film, this is nevertheless a lot of fun and the simian cast is clearly enjoying itself. (Sequel: *Conquest of the Planet of the Apes*) ★★★

Escape Me Never

(1947, 103 min, US, Peter Godfrey) *Errol Flynn, Ida Lupino, Alexis Smith.* Lupino sparkles as the waif with a heart o' gold in this musical melodrama set in northern Italy. She's a single mother crooning for her cappucino while her beau, charming composer Flynn, smooth-operates on aristocrat Parker. Even after making an honest woman out of Lupino, Flynn can't curb his lust. Predictable yes, but Lupino is a delight. ★★½ VHS: $19.99

Escape to Witch Mountain

(1975, 97 min, US, John Hough) *Eddie Albert, Donald Pleasence, Ray Milland.* Two orphans with psychic powers search for their origins with the help of Albert in one of Disney's better mystery/fantasies. Pleasence is a psychic investigator and Milland plays an evil tycoon. ★★★ DVD: $24.99, VHS: $19.99

Essex Boys

(2000, 102 min, GB, Terry Winsor) *Sean Bean, Alex Kingston, Charlie Creed-Miles, Tom Wilkinson, Larry Lamb.* Edgy Jason is just out after a five-year stint in prison. After corralling Billy to be his driver, he immediately performs various acts of extreme brutality, seeking vengeance on those who've betrayed him, seeing betrayal where none exists. Billy is the relative innocent, an amateur who is both intrigued and unsettled at finding himself caught up in the escalating mayhem. The film has just enough visual flair to entertain the die-hard action-thriller aficionado, but it's also predictable, serving up the expected smorgasbord of plot elements: complications, double-crosses, big scores gone bad. Although it looks slick enough to justify its self-references to such films as *Pulp Fiction* and *Reservoir Dogs*, it has no innovation and little wit. ★★ DVD: $19.99, VHS: $9.99

L'Etat Sauvage

(1978, 111 min, France, Francis Girod) *Jacques Dutronc, Marie-Christine Barrault, Michel Piccoli.* An unusually hard-hitting French political thriller that deals with the ambiguous relationship and underlying racism between France and one of her former colonies — a developing central African country. Set in the early 1960s, the story revolves around a young French couple who find themselves adrift in the politically charged atmosphere of a recently established black state. The man (Dutronc) is a UNESCO official who finds that his wife (Barrault) is having an illicit affair with the powerful Minister of Health. Filmed under the punishing sun of French Guinea, the film is an accomplished and taut drama of corruption, hatred and deceit. (French with English subtitles) ★★★

L'Été Meurtrier
(One Deadly Summer)

(1983, 134 min, France, Jean Becker) *Isabelle Adjani, Alain Souchon.* This sizzling psychological drama captured four Césars in 1983, including the Best Actress Award for Adjani. The story is set in a provincial village where a cartoonish tramp, played

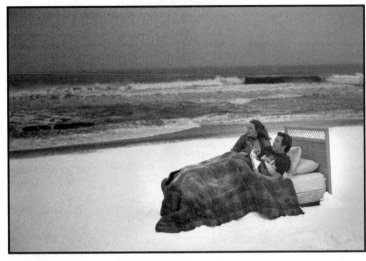

Jim Carrey and Kate Winslet in *Eternal Sunshine of the Spotless Mind*

to the hilt by Adjani, struts into town throwing male libidos into a frenzy. Though dismissed as a whore by the townsfolk, little do they know that beneath the unpredictable exterior lurks a cunningly vengeful woman, determined to wipe away the remembrances of a haunting personal tragedy. (French with English subtitles) ★★★

The Eternal

(1999, 95 min, US/Ireland, Michael Almereyda) *Alison Elliot, Jared Harris, Christopher Walken, Lois Smith.* An alcoholic couple (Elliot and Harris, who are both good) with a young son decide to kick the bottle by visiting Elliot's family in Ireland. They arrive to meet crazy Uncle Bill (Walken), who's keeping a mummified witch in the basement. The setup promises to be a funny/creepy variation of the classic *The Old Dark House*. Unfortunately, it's just a moderately interesting mishmash. While there's a little humor (thanks to Walken), the film mostly opts for murky pretension and vague "scares," neither of which work. (aka: *Trance*) ★★ DVD: $24.99

The Eternal Return (L'Eternal Retour)

(1943, 100 min, France, Jean Delannoy) *Jean Marais, Madeleine Sologne.* Written by Jean Cocteau, this modern retelling of the Tristan and Isolde legend is a lavishly romantic and tender love story. Marais is Patrice, the nephew of a wealthy widower, who arranges a marriage (albeit loveless) between Nathalie, a beautiful young woman he meets, and his uncle. With the help of a love potion, Patrice and Nathalie are irrevocably attracted to each other, threatening the family with their forbidden love. A poetic fable of tragic love. (French with English subtitles) (aka: *Love Eternal*) ★★★ VHS: $24.99

Eternal Sunshine of the Spotless Mind

(2004, 108 min, US, Michel Gondry) *Jim Carrey, Kate Winslet, Kirsten Dunst, Mark Ruffalo, Elijah Wood, Tom Wilkinson, Jane Adams.* When every other TV ad offers a pill for the eradication of any conceivable physical and mental ailment, wouldn't the next logical step be to zap the memory of sad thoughts? (Bad brain!) But just as with all those tablets of instant gratification (Side effects may

include . . .), there's a price to pay for immediate relief. *Eternal Sunshine* takes place next week or next year, in a very familiar-looking future. A new medical procedure erases specific memories and their attached heartache and grief. It also cuts off emotional experiences and eradicates the life lessons to be learned from them. Carrey and Winslet are two of several characters to have the procedure, only to once again engage in the activity they wanted so desperately to forget. Heading a very engaging cast, the two leads are cast most successfully against type as one pairing of protagonists. Carrey imbues his portrayal of Joel Barish with a sweet, vulnerable wistfulness diametrically opposed to his usual manic screen persona. You could make the case that this subtle characterization is his most accomplished performance to date. Winslet as Clementine Kruczynski, the apple of Barish's eye, is modern, brittle, wounded, caustic and uncomfortably recognizable. Director Gondry takes masterful command of another sterling Charlie Kaufman screenplay (cowritten with the director), successfully creating the fluid reality of dreams and the often ethereal nature of waking life. *Eternal Sunshine* is a meditation on identity, bonding, love and pain; at its heart, the film is a most unexpected, most deeply moving love story. ★★★★ DVD Letterbox: $29.99

Ethan Frome

(1993, 107 min, US, John Madden) *Liam Neeson, Patricia Arquette, Joan Allen, Tate Donovan.* Anyone who has read Edith Wharton's bleak tale of one man's catastrophic grasp at passion knows its movie adaptation is not destined to be "the feel good hit of the season." Neeson is perfectly cast as the poor farmer whose desire for his wife's cousin (Arquette) ends in a tragic accident. Neeson's face transforms from twisted and bitter to smooth and handsome as this classic tale flashes between post- and pre-accident. Arquette is similarly well-suited, eschewing coquettishness for a more heart-pounding, lump-in-your-throat, clumsy sense of desire. The pace is slow and there is rarely any relief from the oppressiveness of the story, but the superb acting and intensity of its emotions more than compensate. ★★★ DVD: $19.99, VHS: $9.99

Eureka

(1983, 130 min, GB, Nicolas Roeg) *Gene Hackman, Rutger Hauer, Theresa Russell, Mickey Rourke.* Roeg's tale of a gold prospector (Hackman) who strikes it rich in the Yukon and, years later, must fight gangsters and a son-in-law who might be a sorcerer is told in the director's familiar mythic style. His trademarks — breathtaking cinematography, jagged editing, and temporal jumps — are all present in this mystical story of greed and lust. ★★½ DVD Letterbox: $19.99

Europa, Europa

(1991, 110 min, France/Germany, Agnieszka Holland) *Marco Hofschneider, Klaus Abramowsky, Julie Delpy.* This sweeping statement on the resilience of the human spirit is one of the most powerful films to address the Holocaust. A brilliant mix of gut-wrenching drama and dark humor, *Europa, Europa* is based on the harrowing true story of Solomon Perel, a Jewish teenager who miraculously survived the war by passing himself off as Aryan; so well, in fact, that he unwittingly wound up in the Nazi Youth. Set adrift in a historical tide of events beyond his control, young Solomon desperately clings to his identity while at the same time having to forsake it. Holland adeptly seizes Perel's story and punctuates the horror of his situation without overemphasizing the psychological strain such an ordeal might have had on its young hero. (German and Russian with English subtitles) ★★★★ DVD Subtitled: $19.99

The Europeans

(1979, 92 min, US, James Ivory) *Lee Remick, Lisa Eichhorn, Robin Ellis.* A lush adaptation of Henry James' novel about a 19th-century New England family whose lives are disrupted by the arrival of two European cousins — one a meddlesome, fortune-hunting countess. ★★★ VHS: $19.99

Eurotrip

(2004, 90 min, US, Jeff Schaffer) *Scott Mechlowicz, Jacob Pitts, Michelle Trachtenberg, Travis Webster, Jessica Boehrs, Lucy Lawless, Vinnie Jones.* The producers of *Road Trip* have struck again in this insipid cobbling of grotesquely unfunny culture-clash moments between a bland bunch of cutesy American horn-dogs and a continent's worth of freaky-deaky Europeans. If half-baked gags concerning homophobia, incest, battery and anal rape are your idea of *haute humour*, if your enjoyment of a sloppy travelogue romp is commensurate with the amount of T+A flashed onscreen, if the spirit of rampant American xenophobia run amok strikes a jolly chord, then this bad *Trip* is for you. Matt Damon and Jeffrey Tambor appear unbilled — wise moves. ★ DVD Unrated: $26.99

Eve and the Handyman

(1960, 65 min, US, Russ Meyer) At times reminiscent of a Buster Keaton silent comedy, this early work by Meyer emphasizes sight gags and features a detective novel-style narrative by Eve Meyer as she tracks her man through his daily routine, noting his attempts to ignore a series of trademark Meyer women. Filmed on location in San Francisco, and featuring a thumping strip-tease soundtrack, *Eve and the Handyman* comments on sex and society in a lighter fashion than Meyer's later works. ★★½

Eve of Destruction

(1991, 95 min, US, Duncan Gibbons) *Renée Soutendijk, Gregory Hines, Kevin McCarthy.* The sexy Soutendijk is superbly preposterous as a spike-heeled, nuclear warhead-equipped humanoid in this otherwise disappointing sci-fi thriller. Eve VIII, an experimental cyborg invented by a sexually repressed doctor (also played by Soutendijk), is accidentally activated and becomes stuck in her "Battlefield mode" of programming. Hines, acting as though this were Shakespearean drama, is ridiculous as the determined cop on her bloody trail. A great idea never realized. ★½ DVD: $14.99, VHS: $6.99

Eve's Bayou

(1997, 109 min, US, Kasi Lemmons) *Samuel L. Jackson, Lynn Whitfield, Debbi Morgan, Jurnee Smollett, Meagan Good, Diahann Carroll.* Lemmons has created a stunning, bittersweet and good-humored memory piece that evokes the wistful recollections of youth as wisely as *To Kill a Mockingbird.* An adult narrator looks back at her youth in the South and on her relationship with her father. As ten-year-old Eve (Smollett) recalls in the film's opening, it is 1962 and the year "I killed my father." In the small Louisiana town of Eve's Bayou, young Eve's father, Dr. Batiste (Jackson), appears to be the idol of all the women in the area. When she spies him having sex with a neighbor, the entire family is thrown into emotional turmoil that eventually brings to light sibling rivalry, patricide, voodooism, parapsychology and incest. Jurnee is an absolute wonder as Eve. As Eve's emotionally scarred aunt, Morgan gives a knockout performance that is all at once touching, majestic, persuasive and, most of all, full of grace. ★★★★ DVD Lions Gate Signature Series: $19.99

Evelyn

(2002, 94 min, Ireland, Bruce Beresford) *Pierce Brosnan, Aidan Quinn, Julianna Marguiles, Sophie Vavasseur, Stephen Rea, Alan Bates.* Playing on the heartstrings quite unapologetically, *Evelyn* is the touching true story of what lengths one father would go to regain custody of his children. In 1953 Dublin, Desmond Doyle (Brosnan) has his daughter and two sons taken away from him. With the help of an American lawyer (Quinn) and a retired barrister (Bates), Desmond challenges the very law that allowed his children to be removed — in the Irish Supreme Court. *Evelyn* absolutely drips with sentiment, especially when daughter Evelyn (a spunky mix of Hayley Mills and Margaret O'Brien)

is on-screen. The drama, though, becomes more focused when it concentrates on the legal maneuvers of this motley group, whose actions would be scrutinized by a nation. In the end, it unexpectedly beguiles — sugar coating and all. ★★★ DVD Letterbox: $14.99, VHS: $9.99

Even Cowgirls Get the Blues

(1994, 100 min, US, Gus Van Sant) *Keanu Reeves, Uma Thurman, John Hurt, Rain Phoenix, Lorraine Brocco, Crispin Glover, Roseanne, Udo Kier, Faye Dunaway, Steve Buscemi.* A disappointingly vapid and lifeless misfire, this attempt to capture the hippie-dippy effervescence of Tom Robbins' 1976 novel completely fails to come to cinematic life. Thurman plays the pleasant if vacuous Sissy Hankshaw, a young beauty who is blessed/cursed with abnormally large thumbs and who lives the free life of the road. Sissy soon becomes embroiled in a cowgirl uprising headed by the "charismatic" Bonanza Jellybean (the catatonic Phoenix). Though a failure on every level, and saddled by its attempts to be both post-modern camp and politically and sexually relevant, *Cowgirls* is nonetheless easy to watch and does sport moments of fun. ★★

The Evening Star

(1996, 129 min, US, Robert Harling) *Shirley MacLaine, Juliette Lewis, Bill Paxton, Miranda Richardson, Marion Ross, Ben Johnson, Jack Nicholson, Scott Wolf.* MacLaine repeats her *Terms of Endearment* role as Aurora Greenway in this strained if occasionally compelling sequel. *The Evening Star* takes place 13 years after the death of Aurora's daughter Emma. Aurora has raised her three grandchildren, but they are mostly problem kids. As the jagged, episodic story introduces its characters, Aurora tentatively initiates an affair with a younger man (Paxton) while her teenaged granddaughter (Lewis) is ready to run away to Los Angeles. *The Evening Star* doesn't have the original's rich material exploring the complex relationship between mother and daughter. And it's manipulative and sentimental. But it has a surprising emotional impact, probably due to the very able cast. Oh, Jack's back, too. ★★½ DVD: $14.99, VHS: $9.99

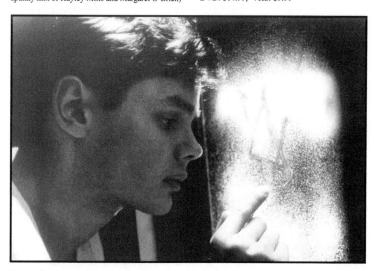

Europa, Europa

Event Horizon

(1997, 97 min, US, Paul Anderson) *Laurence Fishburne, Sam Neill, Kathleen Quinlan, Joely Richardson.* Innovative visuals and an inspired production design can save an otherwise mediocre film. This is almost true in the case of *Event Horizon*, but not quite. Its lame-brained script, underdeveloped characters and seen-it-all-before feel work too strongly against it. Fishburne stars as the commander of an interstellar rescue team that is sent to investigate a previously "lost" ship, the *Event Horizon*. Once on-site, they find out that the *Event Horizon* is a sort of ghost ship that begins to exert harmful psychological influences over the rescue team. ★★ DVD: $14.99, VHS: $9.99

Ever After

(1998, 121 min, GB, Andy Tennant) *Drew Barrymore, Anjelica Huston, Dougray Scott, Jeroen Krabbé, Jeanne Moreau.* An absolutely delightful film. Barrymore drops the Gen-X bad-girl image for a change and delivers a bravura performance (faltering fake accent notwithstanding) as the Cinderella-inspired heroine. Barrymore is Danielle, a servant girl whose loving father (Krabbe) kicks the bucket only days after bringing home his new wife (Huston), who's tailor-made to play the evil step mom) and her two daughters. It's all done with a healthy sense of good-natured fun and the result is alternately touching, hilarious, romantic and thought-provoking. ★★★½ DVD PG-13 Rated: $14.99, VHS PG-Rated: $6.99

Everest

(1998, 48 min, US, MacGillivray Freeman) *Narrated by Liam Neeson.* Meant for a huge IMAX screen, this will certainly lose its impact on a home TV. Though flawed, it's a worthwhile experience, filmed during the 1996 climbing disaster that cost several lives (and was the inspiration for the film *Into Thin Air*). The footage of Mt. Everest is impressive, and the minutiae of the climbers' preparation and actual climb are fascinating. Still, like most IMAX films, *Everest* is far from accomplished filmmaking, and as a documentary it owes more to "Hard Copy" and less to the Maysles Brothers. ★★½ DVD: $19.99, VHS: $9.99

Evergreen

(1934, 91 min, GB, Victor Saville) *Jessie Matthews, Sonnie Hale.* Saville's musical comedy features a dazzling performance from Matthews as a young unemployed chorus girl who rises to fame by imitating her long-retired but once-famous mother. Fabulous set pieces make a wonderful backdrop for Matthews' splendid dancing. Punctuated by a lively Rodgers and Hart score. ★★★½

An Everlasting Piece

(2000, 103 min, Ireland, Barry Levinson) *Barry McEvoy, Brian F. O'Byrne, Anna Friel, Billy Connolly.* Director Levinson has crafted an absurdist gem in *An Everlasting Piece*, in which Colm (McEvoy) and George (O'Bryne), barbers at the local insane asylum (which, in Belfast in the 1980s, is actually a bit more sane than the outside environs), take over the client list of the new inmate, the Scalper (Connolly). The Scalper, who was the sole purveyor of quality hairpieces in all of Northern Ireland, cracks one day and literally scalps four of his erstwhile clients. The two young men soon discover that sales is no walk in the park, what with unexpected competitors to their exclusive control of the territory, random searches at military check-

points, and unscheduled meetings with roving bands of IRA militia. Engaging portrayals, a serendipitous sensibility and lots of really fine music combine in this most pleasant surprise. ★★★½ DVD Letterbox: $26.99, VHS: $14.99

The Everlasting Secret Family

(1987, 93 min, Australia, Michael Thornhill) *Mark Lee, Arthur Dignam.* With an outrageous premise — a highly organized secret society of pederasts stalk schools for young male victims — this as an enjoyably ludicrous drama that despite its sinister idea still makes for strangely riveting entertainment. Lee plays a gorgeous young boy who is spirited away by a wealthy middle-aged senator. He soon tolerates the sex and begins to enjoy the power and prestige he attains as the boy-toy of the politician. But as is wont for a finicky pederast, the senator soon drops him for younger flesh. Now fully indoctrinated into the society, and aging rapidly, Mark must go off himself in search of an innocent victim; and the boy he chooses is the senator's young son. Enjoyable camp once you ignore its incendiary harangues. ★★

Every Day's a Holiday

(1937, 79 min, US, A. Edward Sutherland) *Mae West, Edmund Lowe, Charles Winninger, Louis Armstrong.* The imitable West tips her hat to the screwball genre with this amusing romp set at the turn of the century. Written by West, the story follows Mae as con artist/performer Peaches O'Day and her series of misadventures trying to elude the police, masquerade as a dark-haired French chanteuse, and organize a mayoral race. Mae manages to turn a catchphrase or two ("Keep a diary, and someday it'll keep you"), but most of the film's comedy is courtesy of lots of hare-brained hijinks. Mae proves herself quite handy with a pair of drumsticks. ★★★

Every Girl Should Be Married

(1948, 84 min, US, Don Hartman) *Cary Grant, Betsy Drake, Diana Lynn, Franchot Tone.* In a role reversal from most '30s and '40s comedies, shopgirl Drake sets her eyes on eligible bachelor Grant, and *she* pursues *him*. Of course, Grant is happily unmarried with a preference to stay that way. Grant's charm makes this ordinary comedy more frothy than it really is. ★★½ VHS: $19.99

Every Man for Himself and God Against All

(1974, 110 min, West Germany, Werner Herzog) *Bruno S., Brigitte Mira, Walter Ladengast.* A young man, imprisoned in a cellar and locked away from society for most of his life, reemerges and must begin the arduous task of readjusting to an illogical and iniquitous world. Bruno S. gives an astounding performance as Kasper Hauser. (German with English subtitles) (aka: *The Mystery of Kasper Hauser*) ★★★½

Every Which Way But Loose

(1978, 115 min, US, James Fargo) *Clint Eastwood, Sondra Locke, Ruth Gordon, Geoffrey Lewis.* Amazingly, this boisterous, feeble backwoods comic adventure of a barroom brawler and his pet orangutan is Eastwood's most successful film to date. Go figure. Clint has certainly done better (and so has Clyde). (Sequel: *Any Which Way You Can*) ★½ DVD Letterbox: $19.99

Everybody Wins

(1990, 98 min, US, Karel Reisz) *Nick Nolte, Debra Winger, Will Patton, Jack Warden.* Nolte is a small-town private investigator hired by local free-spirit Winger to prove a friend innocent of murder. Ill-conceived from the start, the ludicrous screenplay is by Arthur Miller. ★

Everybody's All-American

(1988, 127 min, US, Taylor Hackford) *Jessica Lange, John Goodman, Timothy Hutton, Carl Lumbly, Dennis Quaid.* An involving drama about love and broken dreams with Quaid as a college football star and Lange as his beauty queen girlfriend who marry and search for the American Dream. ★★★ DVD Letterbox: $14.99, VHS: $14.99

Everybody's Famous!

(2000, 99 min, Belgium, Dominique Deruddere) *Josse De Pauw, Eva Van Der.* Forget stage mothers, it's stage fathers you have to worry about. Middle-aged, blue-collar Jean is obsessively dedicated to his teenaged daughter Marva's nonexistent career. Refusing to be deterred by reason or sanity, Jean pushes Marva to unceasingly disastrous performances at every talent show he can find. When he loses the security of his job, he breaks his tenuous hold on any recognizable reality and kidnaps his small country's biggest pop star. While *Everybody's Famous* doesn't quite measure up to any expectation generated by its Oscar nomination for Best Foreign-Language Film, it does exhibit a perverse humor and frenetic energy that holds your attention, sometimes against your will. It's also consistently amazing to see evidence of the universal culture of media saturation, in which one's life is meaningless unless it gets airtime. Director Deruddere has fashioned a contemplation of contemporary culture at once bemused and frenzied. (French, Danish and Flemish with English subtitles) ★★★ DVD: $14.99, VHS: $14.99

Everybody's Fine

(1991, 115 min, Italy, Giuseppe Tornatore) *Marcello Mastroianni, Salvatore Cascio.* Much less saccharine than his delightful art-house hit *Cinema Paradiso*, director Tornatore's family drama is a bittersweet tale of illusion and disenchantment. Mastroianni stars as a simple old man who decides to visit his five "successful and happy" grown children who are dispersed throughout Italy. Unprepared for his surprise visits, his children try to bolster his mistaken belief that they lead problem-free lives, but their charades quickly fall apart, forcing him to come to grips with reality and let go of his cherished and idealized images of their childhoods. (Italian with English subtitles) ★★★

Everyone Says I Love You

(1996, 100 min, US, Woody Allen) *Woody Allen, Goldie Hawn, Alan Alda, Julia Roberts, Edward Norton, Drew Barrymore, Tim Roth, Lukas Haas, Gaby Hoffmann, Natalie Portman.* Not everyone will be echoing the sentiments of the title of Allen's musical comedy valentine to New York, Paris and big city neurotics. Often entertaining and funny though insubstantial with lightweight character development, the film is a pastiche of bygone Hollywood musicals where characters just break into song. But whereas those musicals featured performers with good voices, here actors not known for their singing talents (and for good reason) use their own voices. A few are used to good effect (Hawn, Norton), but most are not. It's a distracting gimmick. Hawn is radiant as Allen's ex-wife, and the two engage in a wonderful dance sequence on the banks of the Seine. ★★½ DVD: $14.99, VHS: $9.99

Everything Put Together

(2001, 87 min, US, Marc Forster) *Radha Mitchell, Megan Mullally, Catherine Lloyd Burns, Alan Ruck, Michele Hicks, Judy Geeson.* In a first-rate performance that could take her off the B-list, Mitchell stars as a suburban mother-to-be whose friends all happen to be new or expecting mothers. Everything is rosy until her beautiful baby boy dies from SIDS just hours after his birth. She is understandably devastated — even more so when her friends, in cowardice and cruelty, ostracize her because the situation is too "awkward" for them to bear. As a result, her grip on reality slides. With the look and atmosphere of a low-budget horror film, the shot-on-digital video *Everything Put Together* can be depressing but is also chilling and unsettling. Director Forster (who made this film a year before his *Monster's Ball*) unfortunately lets the dark suburban satire slip into grotesquerie now and again, but does an admirable job maintaining a feeling of dread and grief throughout, with a perfectly ambiguous ending. ★★★ DVD: $24.99, VHS: $39.99

Everything You Always Wanted to Know about Sex . . . But Were Afraid to Ask

(1972, 87 min, US, Woody Allen) *Woody Allen, Burt Reynolds, Gene Wilder, Tony Randall, Lynn Redgrave, Lou Jacobi.* Allen's hilarious assault on Dr. David Reuben's ridiculous best-seller is full of crude jokes, potentially obscene skits and Woody's unforgettable portrayal of the reluctant, existential sperm. ★★★ DVD: $19.99, VHS: $14.99

Evil Cat

(1987, 90 min, Hong Kong, Dennis Yu) *Chow Yun-Fat.* Incredible fantasy-based martial arts/horror flick where an ancient catlike being enters our world from a subterranean home to unleash its destruction of our society. ★★★½ VHS: $59.99

The Evil Dead

(1983, 85 min, US, Sam Raimi) *Bruce Campbell, Helen Sandweiss, Betsy Baker.* This low-budget horror film has more scares in it than all the *Friday the 13th*s put together. Five friends head to the woods for a secluded, quiet weekend. However, things are anything but quiet when they awaken a demonic spirit. Director Raimi concentrates more on the suspense than the gore (though there's plenty of that, too), which immediately separates it from the usual, mindless horror film. (Sequel: *Evil Dead 2*) ★★★ DVD Elite Entertainment Special Edition: $14.99, DVD Book of the Dead: $49.99, VHS: $9.99

Evil Dead 2: Dead by Dawn

(1987, 85 min, US, Sam Raimi) *Bruce Campbell, Sarah Berry, Dan Hicks.* In this spectacularly entertaining and frightening horror sequel, director Raimi accomplishes the near-impossible: he tops his terrific original. Campbell returns once again to battle the demonic spirits at secluded cabin in the woods. There's a lot more humor here, and the special effects are sensational. Campbell gives an over-the-top performance, which helps immensely in the enjoyment of this outrageously original chiller. (Sequel: *Army of Darkness*) ★★★½ DVD: $19.99, VHS: $14.99

The Evil of Frankenstein

(1964, 98 min, GB, Freddie Francis) *Peter Cushing, Duncan Lamont.* Dr. Frankenstein discovers that his monster has been preserved in ice, but has fallen under the spell of a hypnotist and is rampaging once again. Cushing plays Doctor Frank in this entertaining though familiar Hammer Films production. ★★ VHS: $14.99

Evil under the Sun

(1982, 112 min, GB, Guy Hamilton) *Peter Ustinov, James Mason, Maggie Smith, Roddy McDowall, Diana Rigg, Sylvia Miles.* Ustinov returns as Hercule Poirot in this Agatha Christie mystery. Though not up to par with *Murder on the Orient Express* or *Death on the Nile*, this effective whodunit will nevertheless keep you guessing right up to the end. Poirot investigates the murder of a bitchy actress. ★★½ DVD: $14.99, VHS: $9.99

Evita

(1996, 135 min, US, Alan Parker) *Madonna, Antonio Banderas, Jonathan Pryce, Jimmy Nail.* Never having given a truly tantalizing performance on-screen despite having a superstar profile, Madonna finally hits the big time in the movies. She gives an extremely capable performance as Argentina's first lady Eva Peron in this well-crafted adaptation of Andrew Lloyd Webber's musical. Though Parker's direction sometimes teeters on overkill, he has staged some knockout musical sequences. Closely following the stage show, the story follows the rise of Eva Duarte from poor beginnings to stardom as a (second-rate) actress to becoming her country's first lady and sometime spiritual voice. Webber acknowledges Eva's status as a controversial figure, but straddles the fence in political terms. Still, the music is his best. The real surprise is Banderas, who is splendid in both voice and performance as the story's narrator and social conscience. ★★★½ DVD Letterbox: $14.99, VHS: $9.99

Evolution

(2001, 103 min, US, Ivan Reitman) *David Duchovny, Julianne Moore, Orlando Jones, Seann William Scott, Ted Levine.* The next stage of evolution for the *Ghostbusters* series has a heap of trouble adapting to the environment. The obsession with bodily functions already seems out of date, while the story structure is still rooted in the '80s. Reitman's formula brings together two laid-back professors (Duchovny and Jones) to investigate a meteorite, discovered by a bumbling fireman-in-training (Scott). The meteorite brought something with it: an alien ecosystem that rapidly adapts to the surrounding environment, threatening to gross out the affluent community and spread across the earth. Who you gonna call? The effects are nothing great, and the scripted jokes are pretty flat. Still, Reitman keeps the tone light and the cast loose (though Moore is in danger of revoking her Meryl Streep Club membership). ★★ DVD: $14.99, VHS: $9.99

The Ex-Mrs. Bradford

(1936, 80 min, US, Stephen Roberts) *William Powell, Jean Arthur, James Gleason.* Powell goes sleuthing with ex-wife Arthur. Is Powell ever not suave and debonair? Is Arthur ever not sparkling and charming? Apparently not. Stylish, witty fun, with a darned clever resolution to the murders at hand. Powell is in familiar Nick Charles territory here. ★★★

Excalibur

(1981, 140 min, GB, John Boorman) *Nigel Terry, Nicol Williamson, Helen Mirren, Gabriel Byrne, Liam Neeson, Patrick Stewart.* This spellbinding saga is steeped in the rich lore of gallant knights and sinister sorcery. A lavish production, aswirl with sensuous colors and breathtaking imagery, *Excalibur* is a superlative rendition of the Arthurian legend with added mystical and sexual overtones. It is a brilliant illumination of why these tales have survived so vividly in our imaginations. Williamson steals the show as Merlin. ★★★★ DVD: $14.99, VHS: $9.99

Excess Baggage

(1997, 101 min, US, Marco Brambilla) *Alicia Silverstone, Benicio del Toro, Christopher Walken, Harry Connick, Jr., Jack Thompson.* In the unappealing *Excess Baggage*, an equally unappealing Silverstone plays Emily Hope, an heiress who fakes her own kidnapping. More interested in his business deals, her father sends old friend Uncle Ray (Walken) to deal with the mess. Meanwhile, Emily's "captor" is Vincent (the deliciously bizarre Del Toro), who comes off more as sociopath than thief-with-a-heart-of-gold. There's zero chemistry between the two leads. The only chemistry on-screen is between Vincent and Ray, and these scenes are all too brief. If the writers had them ditch Emily at a truck stop and head off as a duo, there could've been a decent road movie in the making. ★★ DVD: $9.99, VHS: $9.99

Executioners (The Heroic Trio 2)

(1993, 90 min, Hong Kong, Ching Siu-Tung & Johnny To) *Anita Mui, Michelle Yeoh, Maggie Cheung, Anthony Wong.* The female superhero trio is back, but this time in a sober, nihilistic postapocalyptic world of the future where water is a precious commodity and power-mad politicians vie for the support of the beleaguered population. Deemphasizing the comedy almost to an extreme, this sequel is satisfying in its own way, but lacks the campy fun and vivaciousness of the first film. Our three original heroines return, but do not team up as the Trio proper until nearly the end. Without as much action or comedy as its predecessor, *Executioners* relies instead on its bleak tone and future-noir art direction to retain interest; it is, however, more stylishly shot and edited than the first *Trio* film. (Cantonese with English subtitles) ★★½

Executive Decision

(1996, 133 min, US, Stuart Baird) *Kurt Russell, Halle Berry, John Leguizamo, Oliver Platt, Steven Seagal, Joe Morton, Len Cariou, B.D. Wong, J.T. Walsh.* It would be easy to call *Executive Decision* another *Under Siege* clone, for it does bear many similarities: terrorists have taken control of a mode of transportation and it's up to our hero to set things right. But this exciting actioner relies less on explosions, and more on suspense, paying greater attention to how they do it. Mideast terrorists have taken control of an American airliner, and in a daring midflight linkup, the good guys board the plane in their effort to thwart the bad guys' plans to bomb the Eastern seaboard. ★★★ DVD: $19.99, VHS: $9.99, VHS Letterbox: $19.99

Executive Suite

(1954, 104 min, US, Robert Wise) *Barbara Stanwyck, William Holden, Fredric March, June Allyson, Walter Pidgeon, Shelley Winters, Paul Douglas.* When the president of a major furniture-manufacturing company suddenly dies, the members of the board scramble to replace him quickly and quietly. Each man is driven by his own motives, be it avarice or altruism. An all-star cast is entangled in many subplots that complement the big business focus. A very involving drama adapted from Cameron Hawley's best-selling novel. ★★★

eXistenZ

(1999, 97 min, Canada, David Cronenberg) *Jennifer Jason Leigh, Jude Law, Willem Dafoe, Ian Holm, Sarah Polley, Christopher Eccleston.* Allegra Geller (Leigh) has created her newest game, eXistenZ, whose virtualism is so real that players need to attach the game directly to their spines. Once hooked up, players can touch, taste, feel the environment; but what effect does this have on their reality? Complicating matters is the self-reflexivity of eXistenZ, where players hook up to new games within the game. Ostensibly a meditation on our decreasing grip on reality, it seems more an excuse for Cronenberg to explore orifices (the anus-like "bio-ports" that the game hooks up to), gore, and other favorite themes. It's a fun ride, and certainly very creepy, especially the game unit and umbilical cord that are made from flesh and blood. ★★★ DVD: $9.99, VHS: $9.99

Exit to Eden

(1994, 113 min, US, Garry Marshall) *Dan Aykroyd, Rosie O'Donnell, Dana Delany, Paul Mercurio, Iman, Stuart Wilson, Hector Elizondo.* Based on the Anne Rice novel, *Exit to Eden* is a tedious comedy that mixes mild S&M fantasy with a ridiculous story of jewel thieves. Mercurio stars as a hunky photographer with specialized sexual tastes (read: S&M) who unknowingly takes photos of two thieves in the middle of a heist. Pursued by cops Aykroyd and O'Donnell, the bad guys follow Mercurio to a tropical island resort named Eden, a kinky sexual Disneyland run by dominatrix Delany. Director Marshall tries to create a sophisticated, wacky romp when all the characters come together, but this contrived flop is enough to give sex a bad name. ★ DVD: $14.99, VHS: $9.99

Exit Wounds

(2001, 103 min, US, Andrzej Bartkowiak) *Steven Seagal, DMX, Isaiah Washington, Anthony Anderson, Bill Duke, Tom Arnold, Jill Hennessy.* A cop with unorthodox methods ticks off too many superiors, and is sent to the worst precinct in town. There, he brings his own brand of justice (yawn) to bring down a cadre of corrupt cops (yawn again). Seagal's "comeback" film is rather fitting: it's as ridiculous and dull as the majority of his late '80s/early '90s output (with exception of *Under Siege*). This isn't even amusing on a trash level: do not operate heavy machinery while watching this snoozer. ★ DVD Letterbox: $14.99, VHS: $6.99

Exodus

(1960, 213 min, US, Otto Preminger) *Paul Newman, Eva Marie Saint, Ralph Richardson, Sal Mineo, Lee J. Cobb, Peter Lawford.* An epic version of Leon Uris' mammoth novel detailing the struggles of the new Israeli state. Newman plays an Israeli resistance leader, involved with Army nurse Saint. ★★★ DVD Letterbox: $19.99

The Exorcist

(1973, 121 min, US, William Friedkin) *Ellen Burstyn, Max von Sydow, Lee J. Cobb, Linda Blair, Jason Miller.* The film that brought the devil back into vogue and spurred a host of imitations. Blair gives her all in a role that requires her to turn green and rotate her head 360 degrees. Don't say we didn't warn you. (Followed by 3 sequels) ★★★½

Exorcist II: The Heretic

(1977, 110 min, US, John Boorman) *Richard Burton, Linda Blair, Ellen Burstyn, Max von Sydow,*
Lee J. Cobb. It's a few years after the infamous possession, and Blair's being visited by unwanted guests again. Burton is the priest who tries to evict 'em in Boorman's over-the-top sequel featuring some really wild special effects, campy performances and lots of silly religious mumbo-jumbo. ★½ DVD Letterbox: $19.99

The Exorcist III

(1990, 110 min, US, William Peter Blatty) *George C. Scott, Ed Flanders, Jason Miller, Nicol Williamson, Scott Wilson, Brad Dourif.* Author William Peter Blatty takes matters into his own (directorial) hands with this adaptation of his "Exorcist" sequel, "Legion." Police detective Lt. Kinderman returns (now in the persona of Scott), and is on the trail of a serial killer. When evidence suggests that the killings are the handiwork of more than one person, he begins to suspect the presence of greater evil. The plot, undone by its own complexity, does manage to work up a good chill. ★★½ DVD: $9.99, VHS: $9.99

The Exorcist: The Version You've Never Seen

(2000, 132 min, US, William Friedkin) *Ellen Burstyn, Max von Sydow, Lee J. Cobb, Linda Blair, Jason Miller.* Friedkin and writer William Peter Blatty have restored some cut scenes, pumped up the sound and added some visual effects in what may best be described as a "writer's cut" of the film. Some of the cut scenes were previously available on video, but here they're integrated into the film, adding to the story but crippling the pace in parts. The new effects are pretty spiffy. A nice companion to the original, as neither version is definitive. ★★★ DVD: $19.99, VHS: $9.99

Exotica

(1995, 104 min, Canada, Atom Egoyan) *Bruce Greenwood, Mia Kirshner, Elias Koteas, Victor Garber.* A beguilingly cryptic, haunting psychological thriller. In Robert Altman-style, Egoyan weaves several characters and their stories together as he explores such ominous themes as voyeurism, grief, betrayal and the search for healing, forgiveness and salvation. There is Thomas, a gay pet shop owner involved in illegal importation of exotic bird eggs; and Francis (Greenwood), a tax advisor who spends his sullen nights at a strip club called Exotica where he quietly obsesses over one particular dancer, Christina (Kirshner). She, in turn, is involved in a relationship with Zoe, the club owner and object of jealous affection by the violent D.J., Eric (Koteas). Nothing is as it seems as Egoyan stingily offers bits of information to the byzantine connections that thread the characters together. An intelligent, even mesmerizing black comedy, *Exotica* will entrance those with the patience to consider the complexities of this demanding film. ★★★½ DVD: $9.99, VHS: $9.99

Experience Preferred ... but Not Essential

(1983, 80 min, Wales, Peter Duffell) *Elizabeth Edmonds, Sue Wallace.* A delightful little comedy about a schoolgirl's summer experiences at a resort hotel on the Welsh coast. Annie (Edmonds) begins her life's education when she encounters the eccentric and slightly daft employees of the Hotel Grand. Included in the colorful crew are the Scottish cook who romances her out of her "wellies" and a burly somnambulist prone to nocturnal wanderings in the nude. A warm, charming film with unexpectedly good performances. ★★★

Das Experiment

(2002, 114 min, Germany, Oliver Hirschbiegel) *Moritz Bleibtreu, Maren Eggert, Christian Berkel, Justus Von Dohnanyi.* A disparate group of men volunteer (with pay) to take part in a study, wherein some of them will be prisoners, some will be guards. Of course, human nature being what it is, things go horribly awry. Obvious parallels to Nazi-era Germany and extremely contrived, artificial character motivations really sink this would-be thriller, based on Mario Giordano's novel "Black Box," itself probably inspired by the 1971 Stanford University experiment. The film starts off well, with a palpable sense of "calm before the storm"; unfortunately, the storm itself is predictable and overwrought. None of this is Bleibtreu's fault; he's quite good and appealing as the lead. The absolutely gorgeous Eggert, in a thankless role as the woman waiting for him in the real world, also makes a decent impression in this otherwise disappointment. (German with English subtitles) ★★ DVD: $29.99, VHS: $102.99

Experiment in Terror

(1962, 123 min, US, Blake Edwards) *Glenn Ford, Lee Remick, Stefanie Powers, Ross Martin.* Good performances highlight this exciting thriller about a psychopath who kidnaps a bank teller's sister, thus blackmailing the woman into stealing from her employer. Ford is the agent assigned to the case, and Powers is the abducted sister. As the cashier, Remick is first-rate, and Martin — before his celebrated "Wild Wild West" good-guy role on TV — is chilling as the killer. ★★★ DVD: $19.99

Explorers

(1985, 100 min, US, Joe Dante) *River Phoenix, Ethan Hawke, Jason Presson, Amanda Peterson, Dana Ivey, James Cromwell.* This lighthearted and wacky sci-fi comedy follows the adventures of three young boys who build a makeshift spacecraft and head for the stars. Phoenix (as the brainy nerd!), Hawke and Presson are the kids, and their confrontation with alien creatures is delightful. ★★★ VHS: $14.99

Expresso Bongo

(1959, 101 min, GB, Val Guest) *Laurence Harvey, Cliff Richard, Sylvia Syms.* Director Guest brings lots of energy and panache to this fast-moving teen pic. *Expresso Bongo* follows the exploits of an opportunistic music agent (played with speed freak freneticism by Harvey), who "discovers" singer/bongo player Richard and proceeds to make him a star, at the expense of his girlfriend/client, a stripper who spies greener pastures. Like most studio-financed, trendy teen flicks, this is more square than it thinks it is, with all the "teens" played by actors in their late 20s and early 30s, and featuring kitschy (but catchy) musical numbers. For a happy-go-lucky piece of fluff, though, there are some witty barbs, snappy dialogue and snazzy visuals to spare. Not up to the director's great sci-fi tales, or as audaciously campy as *Beat Girl* or *Winter-a-Go-Go*, *Expresso Bongo* is a good time on its own terms. ★★★ DVD: $24.99, VHS: $19.99

Exquisite Corpses

(1989, 95 min, US, Temistocles Lopez) *Zoe Tamerlaine Lund, Gary Knox, Daniel Chapman.* A young man with a trombone and a stetson, fresh from the American heartland, gets off the bus in New York City. In no time at all, he's had his luggage stolen and found out that his fiancée is shacked up with another guy. In not very much more time, he's subjected to every con and con artist in the book (all those guys in ponytails); but he also gets a dose of urban myth and magic. Before long, our newly issued midnight cowboy is *the* hot new cabaret star. But the path of our hero's quest to become the new idol for the jaded masses is littered with dead bodies. Writer-producer-director Lopez has fashioned a witty, sly, sardonic little gem, peopled with characters only slightly exaggerated. ★★★

The Exterminating Angel

(1962, 95 min, Mexico, Luis Buñuel) *Silvia Pinal, Enrique Rambal.* Buñuel's scathing wit is amply displayed in one of his most complex works. The guests of a dinner party are simply unable to leave their host's home when they are ready to depart. Within this claustrophobic microcosm, Buñuel lampoons society's decadence and corruption. (Spanish with English subtitles) ★★★★ VHS: $24.99

Extramuros (Beyond the Walls)

(1985, 120 min, Spain, Miguel Picazo) *Carmen Maura.* A fascinating and often strange story of lesbian love and lusty ambition behind a convent's walls. While the Plague ravages all around, a poverty-stricken convent becomes the center of attention after Sister Angela injures her hands and fakes the miracle of Stigmata. The nun, with her lover Sister Ana (Maura), staves off the despotic Mother Superior to eventually become prioress herself, until the members of the Inquisition pay a not-so-friendly visit to the "saint." An unusual melodrama that borders on the deliriously unreal — a curious mix of the combined excesses of Ken Russell's *The Devils* and the Watergate conspiracy. (Spanish with English subtitles) ★★★ VHS: $19.99

The Extraordinary Adventures of Mr. West in the Land of the Bolsheviks

(1924, 78 min, USSR, Lev Kuleshov) *Vsevolod Pudovkin, Boris Barnet.* This sharply satiric comedy has all of the action and pratfalls of a Chaplin film in telling its story about the wildly misconceived notions Americans had (and still possess) of Soviet Russia. Mr. West, a naive and nervous American, travels to Russia to see firsthand this nation of raging Bolsheviks and deranged radicals. But with the "help" of some mischievous pranksters, his travels turn into a wild adventure peopled by an increasingly strange procession of weirdos. An inspired and still timely farce. (Silent with orchestral accompaniment) ★★★ VHS: $29.99

Extreme Justice

(1993, 105 min, US, Mark L. Lester) *Lou Diamond Phillips, Scott Glenn, Chelsea Field, Yaphet Kotto.* Interesting but highly uneven — and at times wooden — drama about the L.A.P.D.'s unique crimefighting task force, the S.I.S. (Special Investigation Squad) and their highly unorthodox methods of taking hard-core criminals off the streets. ★★ DVD Pan & Scan: $14.99, VHS: $14.99

Extreme Measures

(1996, 117 min, US, Michael Apted) *Gene Hackman, Sarah Jessica Parker, Hugh Grant, David Morse, Debra Monk, Bill Nunn.* A blurry look at the halls of medicine, *Extreme Measures* asks if the ends can justify the means when one prominent doctor (Hackman in another skilled portrayal) takes both lives and shortcuts to find a cure for the incurable. Grant, with his charm and perfectly just-out-of-place hair, is the unknowing physician caught in the conspiracy. This stunted wandering never reaches a vasteness of any thrill, with its fre-

quent plot turns leaving viewers knowing where it will lead without a proper explanation of how it arrived there. ★★ DVD: $19.99, VHS: $19.99

Extreme Prejudice

(1987, 104 min, US, Walter Hill) *Nick Nolte, Powers Booth, Maria Conchita Alonzo, Rip Torn.* Appealing actioner with boyhood friends Nolte and Booth finding themselves at odds when one grows up to be a drug king and the other a Texas Ranger. ★★½ DVD: $9.99, VHS: $9.99

Extremities

(1986, 90 min, US, Robert M. Young) *Farrah Fawcett, Alfre Woodard, Diane Scarwid, James Russo.* Fawcett, who appeared in William Mastrosimone's hit off-Broadway play, repeats her stage role as an attempted rape victim who overcomes her attacker and holds him hostage. Farrah's attempt to prove herself a serious actress, for the most part, is a success: she gives a compelling performance. Woodard and Scarwid ably play Farrah's roommates caught in the moral dilemma, and Russo makes an intense psycho. ★★½ DVD Dual: $14.99

The Eye

(2003, 98 min, Thailand, Danny Pang & Oxide Pang) *Angelica Lee.* A blind woman receives an eye transplant, and is given the gift of sight. Unfortunately, she's also given the dubious gift of second sight — she's able to see the dead. What follows are a handful of creepy setpieces involving *Sixth Sense*-like visions of dead people. This includes a particularly frightening elevator sequence that'll send you to the stairs, and an apocalyptic, show-stopping climax. However, the film isn't consistently on the artistry level of *Ringu*, to which it is similar in many ways. *The Eye* does provide old-school horror movie jolts and jumps alongside the more ethereal creep-outs, making it surefire, edge-of-your-seat fun. (Cantonese with English subtitles) ★★★ DVD: $24.99, VHS: $59.99

Eye for an Eye

(1996, 105 min, US, John Schlesinger) *Sally Field, Ed Harris, Kiefer Sutherland, Joe Mantegna, Beverly D'Angelo, Charlayne Woodard.* Field takes a cue from the *Death Wish* series as a mother who seeks vengeance against the man who raped and murdered her daughter, and then walked free. About as dramatically defined as any of the Bronson sequels, *Eye for an Eye* features incredibly overdrawn characters who all wear their caricatures on their sleeves. The film could have veered into an interesting examination of the mother's dilemma, but opts for the ridiculous scenario of a gun-toting Field stalking the low-rent district of L.A.'s downtown (rich people = good; poor people = bad). ★½

Eye of God

(1997, 88 min, US, Tim Blake Nelson) *Martha Plimpton, Kevin Anderson, Hal Holbrook, Nick Stahl, Margo Martindale, Richard Jenkins.* One of the most chilling films in recent memory, *Eye of God* uses the biblical tale of Abraham and Isaac to dovetail two riveting stories — Ainsley Dupree's (Plimpton) increasingly repressive marriage to an ex-con (Anderson), and a devastated young boy's (Stahl) response to witnessing a gruesome murder. Writer-director Nelson has a remarkable grasp of the dead-end lives of his characters, and the performances are uniformly excellent. Using an ominous flash-forward/flashback time sequence to create a brilliant mosaic that show these very different characters' lives intersect, Nelson depicts the hope and

suffocation each individual feels as they faithfully try to start families, and find work. The only drawback to this simple, yet extraordinarily powerful film is the graphic, disturbing ending that reinforces the evil that prompts the grisly murder. A haunting, unforgettable experience. ★★★½ DVD: $14.99

Eye of the Beholder

(2000, 101 min, US, Stephan Elliott) *Ashley Judd, Ewan McGregor, Jason Priestley, Geneviève Bujold, Patrick Bergen, k.d. lang.* A film so bad it will bring a greater appreciation of grade-B, direct-to-video thrillers, *Eye of the Beholder* takes a ludicrous story and then makes it totally incomprehensible with flashy camerawork, weird editing and weirder plot developments. A comatose McGregor plays a British intelligence officer haunted by his wife and daughter leaving him. While on assignment, he witnesses a woman (Judd) kill a man. Instead of turning the sexy suspect in, he tracks her across the country as she goes on a killing spree. Then things get even sillier. ★ DVD: $9.99, VHS: $9.99

Eye of the Needle

(1981, 112 min, US, Richard Marquand) *Donald Sutherland, Kate Nelligan, Ian Bannen.* Excellent WWII spy thriller starring Sutherland (in one of his best roles) as the notorious Nazi assassin, "The Needle," who must keep his identity secret when he becomes stranded on an island inhabited by a war-wounded Brit and his lonely and frustrated wife (Nelligan). Based on the best-selling novel by Ken Follett. Riveting from start to its pulse-pounding finish. ★★★½ DVD Letterbox: $14.99

Eye of the Storm

(1991, 98 min, US, Yuri Zeltser) *Lara Flynn Boyle, Dennis Hopper, Craig Sheffer, Bradley Gregg.* Adequate performances and a flashy build-up somehow can't quite sustain this stylish exercise in suspense. A downtrodden wife (Boyle) takes a wrong turn when she and her abusive husband (Hopper, renewing his "psycho" patent), pull into a lonely desert hotel run by a strange young man (Sheffer) and his blind brother (Gregg). ★★ VHS: $14.99

Eyes of Laura Mars

(1978, 104 min, US, Irvin Kershner) *Faye Dunaway, Tommy Lee Jones, Brad Dourif, Rene Auberjonois, Raul Julia.* Bondage chic ever so commercial in Kershner's tale of a psychic fashion photographer (Dunaway) and a troubled policeman (Jones) searching for the identity of an ice pick murderer. A few good scares are interspersed with a muddled story. ★★½ DVD: $14.99

The Eyes of Tammy Faye

(2000, 79 min, US, Fenton Bailey & Randy Barbato) *Tammy Faye Bakker, Jim Bullock, Jerry Falwell, Pat Robertson, Narrated by: RuPaul.* A wonderfully original, surprisingly sympathetic and oftentimes hilarious documentary. Young Tammy had it all: she was a Southern beauty, she had a handsome, adoring husband, and they together produced a theme park and a highly rated television show that generated enough money to keep her in blush and eyelashes well into the next millennium. Yet it all fell apart. Husband number one (Jim) is in jail, number two is in jail, daughter's a runaway, son is wallowing in booze and drugs and the religious cash cow empire is destroyed. It's a *Citizen Kane* for the Right Wing religious sect, one hell of a documentary as Bailey and Barbato capture the many facets of a surprisingly complex, misunderstood personality. ★★★½ DVD: $14.99, VHS: $9.99

Eyes Wide Shut: Kubrick's final film; Tom and Nicole's last dance

The Eyes, the Mouth

(1982, 100 min, France/Italy, Marco Bellocchio) *Lou Castel, Angela Molina, Emmanuelle Riva.* A compelling examination of a family ravaged by the suicide of a brother, and of the lengths that the brother's twin must go to to separate himself from the crippling ties of the past. (Italian with English subtitles) ★★★ VHS: $19.99

Eyes Wide Shut

(1999, 159 min, GB, Stanley Kubrick) *Tom Cruise, Nicole Kidman, Sydney Pollack, Marie Richardson, Rade Sherbedgia, Todd Field.* Cruise and Kidman are William and Alice Harford, a physically beautiful, emotionally stunted, psychologically impaired couple living in opulence in New York City. He is a top-dollar doctor, she once ran an art gallery. William finds himself drawn into an underground world of sexual excess while obsessed by his wife's disclosure of an unfulfilled fantasy — a fantasy that becomes as real to him as his waking life. He crashes a party to find a ritual mass of depravity, precipitating a series of events that seem to threaten his very life. Kubrick has crafted an exploration of how our internal lives conform our perception of reality, warping our view of the world to mirror our lust and shame and fear. In his final opus, the director utilizes to great effect his signature, striking visual imagery in constructing a mystery both visceral and abstract. ★★★½ DVD: $19.99, VHS: $19.99

Eyes without a Face

(1959, 90 min, France, Georges Franju) *Alida Valli, Pierre Brasseur.* This elegantly moody horror film concerns a deranged plastic surgeon who, after being responsible for a car accident that leaves his young daughter hideously disfigured, becomes determined to give her a new face — a face whose skin is grafted from the bodies of beautiful women his assistant kidnaps off the streets of Paris. A macabre and frightening story that creates its horror not through histrionics or blood but through an elegantly dark style, similar to the works of Jean Cocteau and the early German expressionists. (French with English subtitles) (aka: *The Horror Chamber of Dr. Faustus*) ★★★½

Eyewitness

(1981, 102 min, US, Peter Yates) *William Hurt, Sigourney Weaver, James Woods, Christopher Plummer, Irene Worth.* A slickly produced murder mystery about a janitor (Hurt) who pretends to have knowledge of a murder being investigated by a hot-shot reporter (Weaver), in order to become involved with the beautiful journalist. ★★★ VHS: $14.99

F/X

(1986, 106 min, US, Robert Mandel) *Bryan Brown, Brian Dennehy, Cliff DeYoung, Diane Venora, Jerry Orbach.* Imaginative and taut thriller with Brown as a movie special effects expert who is hired by the Justice Department to fake the assassination of a mobster, only to be framed for the murder. The film features fine F/X and makes good use of New York City locales. Dennehy is particularly good as a cop on Brown's trail. (Sequel: *F/X 2*) ★★★ DVD: $14.99

F/X 2

(1991, 109 min, US, Richard Franklin) *Bryan Brown, Brian Dennehy, Rachel Ticotin, Joanna Gleason, Philip Bosco, Kevin J. O'Connor, Jose DeGuzman.* This more-than-capable sequel to the 1986 hit picks up five years later. F/X expert, and now toy manufacturer, Brown is convinced to help his girlfriend's ex-husband in a police sting. But when the latter is killed, Brown discovers a cover-up and enlists the help of pal Dennehy to find out what happened. Though not entirely as successful as the original, the film nevertheless is an exciting mystery story peppered with some good special effects. ★★½ DVD: $14.99, VHS: $9.99

The Fable of the Beautiful Pigeon Fancier

(1988, 73 min, Brazil/Spain, Roy Guerra) *Claudia Ohana, Tonia Carrero.* From Gabriel Garcia Marquez comes this lyrical, dreamlike fable, filled with mystical forboding, dealing with the love of an older man for an alluringly mysterious woman. Don Orestes, a Dali-esque dandy of a man, lives off the wealth of his family in a poverty-stricken town in 19th-century Brazil. His highly structured life, dominated by his mother, is thrown into a whirlwind after he meets and falls in love with Fulvia (Ohana), a beautiful dark-haired woman who tends pigeons and lives in seclusion on the edge of town with her husband and baby. The two are inexplicably drawn together, culminating in a fateful conclusion. Note: This film, made for Spanish television, was filmed in Brazil. The actors spoke Portuguese which was then dubbed into Spanish. (Spanish with English subtitles) ★★★

The Fabulous Baker Boys

(1989, 113 min, US, Steve Kloves) *Jeff Bridges, Michelle Pfeiffer, Beau Bridges, Jennifer Tilly.* This vibrant, sexy romantic comedy-drama is an extremely well-written, acted and executed adult entertainment set against the sometimes tacky world of the lounge act. Pfeiffer gives a smoldering performance as Susie Diamond, the singer who enters the lives of two brothers (the fabulous Bridges boys) whose piano act is dying a slow death. The film follows the love affair between cynical Jeff and sultry Michelle, almost effortlessly evoking the mood of those great 1940s screen romances. The smokey atmosphere is further enhanced by Dave Grusin's outstanding jazz score. ★★★½ DVD: $24.99, VHS: $14.99, VHS Letterbox: $14.99

Face

(1997, 107 min, GB, Antonia Bird) *Robert Carlyle, Ray Winstone, Steven Waddington, Philip Davis, Lena Headey.* A moderately intriguing British crime drama, *Face* proves that old adage: There is no honor among thieves. When a gang of five men, lead by Ray (Carlyle), commit armed robbery, the take is less than expected. Then, when the money that has been divided up equally starts to disappear, Ray and his pals have to figure out who is taking the cash and leaving bodies behind. *Face* has a few tense action sequences to recommend it, but the pacing is sometimes slow and the thick accents occasionally troublesome. Director Bird has made a gritty little picture, and Carlyle is quite effective in the lead role, but anyone looking for another *Lock, Stock and Two Smoking Barrels* will be mildly disappointed. ★★½ VHS: $19.99

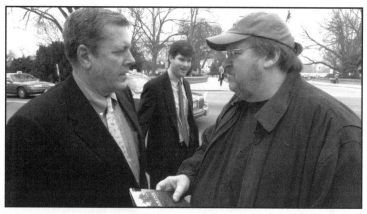

Michael Moore (right) attempts to convince congressmen to send their sons to Iraq in a scene from his blistering anti-Bush film *Fahrenheit 9/11*

A Face in the Crowd

(1957, 126 min, US, Elia Kazan) *Andy Griffith, Patricia Neal, Walter Matthau, Lee Remick, Anthony Franciosa.* The writer (Budd Schulberg) and director of *On the Waterfront* were reunited for this compelling drama about a homespun hillbilly entertainer whose TV success transforms him into a power-hungry demagogue. Griffith is quite good in his film debut. ★★★½ VHS: $19.99

Face of Another

(1966, 124 min, Japan, Hiroshi Teshigahara) *Tatsuya Nakadai, Machiko Kyo.* A scientist, his face horribly disfigured in an industrial accident, is fitted with a handsome mask; but instead of gaining renewed confidence and self-esteem, he retreats into self-pity and mistrust, eventually seducing his wife and then accusing her of adultery. Using surreal techniques, this psychological drama examines the dehumanization and isolation of man in present-day Japan. A chilling and fatalistic tale of alienation that was coscripted by Teshigahara and Kobo Abe, whose previous collaboration was *Woman in the Dunes.* (Japanese with English subtitles) ★★★ VHS: $59.99

Face/Off

(1997, 138 min, US, John Woo) *John Travolta, Nicolas Cage, Joan Allen, Gina Gershon, Nick Cassavetes, Harve Presnell, Margaret Cho, CCH Pounder, Colm Feore.* Woo hits his stride in American cinema with this highly textured, complicated film which nearly equals the excellent work he did in Hong Kong. The inventive script sets up a situation that, although it is completely implausible, plays right into Woo's strength: an intimate conflict between two inextricably connected men of action. Travolta is Sean Archer, an FBI agent committed to the capture of terrorist Castor Troy (Cage), who murdered Archer's son in a botched assassination attempt. Troy is captured, but put into a coma, and Archer assumes his identity. But Troy soon wakes up, assumes Archer's identity and takes over his old life. They soon share a bond that is more complex than that of traditional hero and villain. The action sequences are brilliantly staged and the dramatic content of the film finally lives up to Woo's famous pyrotechnic sequences. ★★★½ DVD Letterbox: $19.99, VHS: $9.99, VHS Letterbox: $9.99

Faces

(1968, 129 min, US, John Cassavetes) *Gena Rowlands, John Marley, Lynn Carlin, Seymour Cassel, Fred Draper.* Cassavetes was a master of truth-telling without compromise, whose unrepentant exposure of human hypocrisy was tempered by his astounding empathy for human suffering — even when self-inflicted. This is an unflinching examination of a middle-aged, middle-class couple in the throes of marital breakup, and the emotionally ravaging effects of their midlife attempts to establish new relationships. The couple (Carlin, Marley), their friends and acquaintances (Rowlands is devastating as the other woman) are fully revealed as they confront the artificial confines of their societal roles. The film is brutal in its depiction of the underlying assumptions of the sexual mores of the time, which now seem almost Victorian yet uncomfortably familiar. ★★★½ DVD: $24.99

Faces of Women

(1987, 103 min, Ivory Coast, Désiré Ecaré) *Eugénie Cissé Roland, Sidiki Bakaba.* Ecaré's debut is an exuberant blend of raucous comedy, pulsating African music and dance, and steamy eroticism.

Two stories, filmed ten years apart with two separate casts, are woven together with the chants and dances of an energetic female chorus. Both segments concern the place of African women in marriage, sex and society. The first and pivotal story offers an erotic, feminist slant on lust and cuckolding, with lovemaking so candid that the film was barred for many years from its native country. The second tale focuses on a middle-aged, successful businesswoman confronting resistance from a stern patriarchal society. Having created a bold, vibrant film, Ecaré uses a new-wave-influenced directorial style to examine the eternal battle of the sexes. (French with English subtitles) ★★★ VHS: $29.99

The Faculty

(1998, 105 min, US, Robert Rodriguez) *Elijah Wood, Clea DuVall, Jordana Brewster, Josh Hartnett, Laura Harris, Robert Patrick, Piper Laurie, Bebe Neuwirth, Salma Hayek, Jon Stewart.* If Shakespeare, Jane Austen and Laclos can return to high school, why not those damn pod people? In another teenage updating, this time of *Invasion of the Body Snatchers*, teens take on a group of aliens who are taking control of their small town. There's nothing new here, but director Rodriguez at least has a degree of fun with the tale. The few effects are good, and there are a couple of swiftly paced scenes. A cast obviously enjoying themselves helps gloss over the slow patches and obligatory pop culture references that become annoying after awhile. ★★½ DVD: $19.99, VHS: $9.99

Fade to Black

(1980, 102 min, US, Vernon Zimmerman) *Dennis Christopher, Tim Thomerson, Normann Burton, Mickey Rourke.* It seems that whenever a high-profile murder makes the national news, someone is quick to blame it on Hollywood. *Fade to Black* put a literal face on this two decades ago, with Christopher playing a movie freak who loses his grip on reality and starts copying the killers in his favorite films. Ultra-violent and not entirely successful horror flick, but with its right-wing reactionary subtext, still very timely. (DVD double feature: *Hell Night*) ★★½ DVD: $14.99, VHS: $14.99

Fahrenheit 451

(1967, 111 min, France, François Truffaut) *Julie Christie, Oskar Werner, Cyril Cusack.* This intriguing adaptation of the famed Ray Bradbury novel is a frightening vision of a not-too-distant future where books are outlawed and firemen incinerate "antisocial rubbish." Truffaut creates an eerie atmosphere of repression in this intelligent sci-fi tale. (Filmed in English) ★★★ DVD: $14.99

Fahrenheit 9/11

(2004, 121 min, US, Michael Moore) *Michael Moore, Lila Lipscomb.* Moore's documentarian skills reach a new level of maturity in *Fahrenheit 9/11*, his scathing indictment of President George W. Bush's occupation of the Oval Office. Moore communicates massive quantities of complex information with clarity, humor and a decidedly anti-administration, leftist bent. He brilliantly uses news footage and taped interviews to let the protagonists speak for themselves, intercutting recent assertions with past statements to the contrary, documenting business ties over the past thirty years between the Bush family and the bin Laden family, and in general asserting that the emperor is buck naked. The film starts in Florida during the 2000 presidential election, as a grinning Dubya assures a reporter that, don't worry, he's gonna win this state. The next few

years are related with minimum exposition: a dark screen reveals the terrified faces of people staring up unbelievingly at inconceivable horror, looking at images now etched into our national psyche; months earlier, intelligence reports to the White House warned against bin Laden's plans to execute terror attacks. But Dubya had other things on his mind, like finding a reason to attack Saddam Hussein. Even when relating the most abstract and convoluted data, Moore never loses sight of the people most immediately affected. We meet a woman who was proud when her son joined the military, but has come to wonder if he died for a just cause. We meet young men for whom the military is their best economic option. The film grabs you for its full 121 minutes, and stays with you for hours, days, afterwards. *Fahrenheit 9/11* is a monumental achievement that will elicit with equal power anger and grief. ★★★★

Fail-Safe

(1964, 111 min, US, Sidney Lumet) *Henry Fonda, Larry Hagman, Walter Matthau, Dan O'Herlihy, Dom DeLuise, Fritz Weaver.* One of the most effective films about the futility and horror of nuclear war, this taut and suspenseful adaptation of Burdick-Wheeler's best-seller is a nightmare "what-if" scenario: Through computer error, we've sent a plane to bomb Moscow — and the President must convince the Russians it was an accident and also decide how to rectify the situation. Fonda is appropriately low-keyed as the Commander-in-Chief, and a young Hagman ably plays the interpreter. ★★★½ DVD: $24.99

Fair Game

(1985, 88 min, Australia, Mario Andreacchio) *Cassandra Delaney, Peter Ford, David Sandford.* Mindless revenge flick about an outback animal preservationist who finds herself in a sadistic game of one-upmanship with a psychotic poacher and his brain-dead cohorts. *Fair Game* isn't as exploitative as it sounds; however, one cannot help wondering if this is not yet another heroine trying to follow in the lucrative footsteps of *Alien's* Sigourney Weaver. ★ DVD: $19.99, VHS: $29.99

Fair Game

(1995, 90 min, US, Andrew Sipes) *William Baldwin, Cindy Crawford, Steven Berkoff, Jenette Goldstein.* Acting more with the variety of T-shirts she wears than with her emotions, Crawford makes her acting debut as a divorce lawyer who is hunted by an ex-KGB agent. This latest Eurotrash villain (Berkoff) and his gang of thugs try to blow up Cindy because she is inadvertently delving too deep in their business. Baldwin is the chummy cop-on-the-edge who rescues her, and the two run for their lives, pursued by the bad guys. The action sequences are boring, the acting is bad, and even the sight of a villain targeting Baldwin's ass-crack with a laser while in flagrante delicto with Crawford in a moving boxcar cannot enliven this bloated mess. ★ DVD: $14.99, VHS: $9.99

Fairy Tale: A True Story

(1997, 97 min, GB, Charles Sturridge) *Florence Heath, Elizabeth Earl, Phoebe Nicholls, Peter O'Toole, Harvey Keitel, Mel Gibson.* At the turn of the century, well before New Age lifting from shoppes in every city's version of Greenwich Village, spiritualism was all the rage. In post-WWI England, theosophy stepped out of dark parlour trickery and into the light of the headlines via a series of photographs — of fairies. *Fairy Tale* is the true story of two young girls who supposedly took these photographs. Keitel is Houdini, the no-bullshit ghostbusting illusionist with a wise, never-give-an-inch sense of sympathy toward the possibilities and truth behind the girls' story. This wonderful family film, awash in playful special effects, will surely entertain both child and adult, alike; but there may be some answering of some "big questions" to the wee-ones. ★★★½ DVD: $14.99, VHS: $14.99

Faithless

(2000, 142 min, Sweden, Liv Ullmann) *Lena Endre, Erland Josephson, Krister Henriksson, Thomas Hanzon.* An older gentleman, well-groomed and articulate, sits at his desk in his stately coastal home talking to a beautiful woman, who may or may not really exist. That's at least what he tells himself as she recounts the story of her adulterous affair that tore her family apart many years before. In bringing film legend Ingmar Bergman's thoughtful, absorbing semiautobiographical screenplay to the screen, director Ullmann — Bergman's greatest leading lady — demonstrates a gift nearly worthy of her mentor for dissecting the conflicting emotions and inner turmoil of her characters. Ullmann elicits wonderful performances from her cast, allowing each performer to fully explore the shadings of their characters, all of whom experience the pain, passion and regret of a single act that leads to an inevitably harrowing conclusion. (Swedish with English subtitles) ★★★½ DVD: $14.99, VHS: $9.99

The Falcon and the Snowman

(1985, 131 min, US, John Schlesinger) *Sean Penn, Timothy Hutton, Lori Singer, Pat Hingle.* Acclaimed espionage thriller based on the true-life story of Christopher Boyce and Dalton Lee, who sold national secrets to the Soviets. Hutton and Penn are both outstanding as the accused, conflicted teens. ★★★ DVD Letterbox: $14.99, VHS Pan & Scan: $14.99, VHS Letterbox: $19.99

Fall

(1997, 90 min, US, Eric Schaeffer) *Eric Schaeffer, Amanda De Cadenet, Francie Swift, Lisa Vidal, Rudolf Martin, Roberta Farnham Maxwell.* It is perhaps damning with faint praise to say that Schaeffer's vanity production *Fall,* which he wrote, produced, directed and stars in, is better than his last film, *If Lucy Fell.* As Michael Shiver, a cab driver who begins a heated affair with married supermodel Sarah Easton (De Cadenet), Schaeffer will either charm or annoy viewers with his cutesy-poo petulance. Chronicling this unlikely relationship, Schaeffer seems to be bringing his sexual fantasies to the screen, allowing Michael to sex-talk Sarah to orgasm in one scene followed by Sarah tying up and screwing Michael in another. At least this boy-meets-supermodel romance has a terrific soundtrack to keep it moving, since there is too much dialogue and too little plot. ★★½

The Fall of the House of Usher

(1960, 85 min, US, Roger Corman) *Vincent Price, Myrna Fahey, Mark Damon.* Corman graduated (for a time, anyway) from quickly produced exploitation pictures to heavily atmospheric, adult-themed horror films with this, his first of eight film adaptations of the works of Edgar Allan Poe. Price stars as the tragic Roderick, last in the doomed line of Ushers. Philip Winthrop (Damon) arrives at the House of Usher to sweep away his fiancée Madeline, Roderick's sister. Roderick, however, will not allow her to leave, and Damon becomes a hopeless bystander. *House of Usher* is an unusually realized Gothic horror story, and Richard Matheson's chilling screenplay was also a remarkable beginning in a line of Poe adaptations. ★★★ DVD: $14.99, VHS: $14.99

Fall of the Romanov Dynasty

(1927, 90 min, USSR, Ether Shub) With innovative editing of remarkable archival footage, this is the first historical documentary produced in the Soviet Union. It's a stirring account of the events that led up to the overthrow of the Czarist regime and the subsequent rise of the people's republic. Director Shub skillfully utilizes newsreel footage as well as Czar Nicholas' home movies in bringing to life those fateful years between 1912 and 1917. (Silent with piano accompaniment) ★★★ VHS: $29.99

Fall Time

(1994, 88 min, US, Paul Warner) *Mickey Rourke, Stephen Baldwin, David Arquette, Jonah Blechman, Jason London.* This kinky crime thriller uses Tarantino-style violence and a bevy of pretty boys to create an improbable tale dripping with homoerotic undertones. Leon (Baldwin) and Florence (Rourke) are two gun-toting crooks (and possible lovers) looking to hit a bank in a Southern town. Their scheme is foiled when three freshly scrubbed teens get in the way. The boys — ringleader David (Arquette), cute Joe (Blechman) and chiseled beauty Tim (London) — are soon held hostage by the hoods. The film then takes a decidedly S&M bent as knives and guns are brandished (often times towards their captives' mouths — duh, symbolism?), pants are dropped and a bondage fantasy right out of a violent porn novel is acted out as Leon and Florence torment the youths while figuring out their next move. ★★★ DVD: $9.99

Fallen

(1998, 115 min, US, Gregory Hoblit) *Denzel Washington, John Goodman, Donald Sutherland, Embeth Davidtz, James Gandolfini, Elias Koteas, Robert Joy, Al Ruggiero.* In this not altogether unsuccessful merging of supernatural thriller and police procedural, Washington plays a Philadelphia detective who, in the film's opening, watches the vicious serial killer (Koteas) he captured sizzle in the electric chair. Shortly thereafter, several murders take place with the very same M.O. as before — are they copycat killings, or is the explanation supernatural? Director Hoblit and screenwriter Nicholas Kazan approach their well-worn premise with a realistic, earthbound feel, but with mixed results. Ironically, the gritty atmosphere Hoblit brings to the picture allows the already silly scare scenes to appear even sillier. However, *Fallen* is reasonably compelling, admirably dark and creepy, and has a nice twist ending — and a good use of Philly exteriors. ★★½ DVD: $14.99, VHS: $9.99, VHS Letterbox: $14.99

Fallen Angels

(1995, 96 min, Hong Kong, Wong Kar-Wai) *Leon Lai Ming, Michele Reis, Takeshi Kaneshiro.* A companion piece to his terrific *Chungking Express,* director Kar-Wai's *Fallen Angels* is a similarly atmospheric, stunningly visual treat. Two tenuously related story lines are interwoven here: a young hit man considers a career change, and a slacker who lives with his pop earns a living by breaking into shops after hours and selling the goods. As with *Chungking,* the stories in *Angels* aren't as important as the characters and the details of their day-to-day lives, their feelings, outlooks and relationships. Kar-Wai's restless camerawork and editing, multiple film stocks, ultracool soundtrack and stylized — though brief — gunfights signal the emergence of a hip, very talented craftsman and artist; it's his humanism and warmth that really stands out and sets him apart. Languid, moody and moving, *Fallen Angels* is truly memorable. (Cantonese with English subtitles) ★★★½ DVD: $29.99, VHS: $19.99

Fallen Champ: The Mike Tyson Story

(1993, 93 min, US, Barbara Kopple) Mike Tyson went from Brownsville, Brooklyn, welfare kid to Heavyweight Champion of the World to convicted rapist, all before his 25th birthday. Kopple traces the many influences in his life which led him from obscurity to adulation, and ultimately, to his incarceration. Powerful, lucid and unflinching, this documentary offers compelling commentary on Tyson as an individual as well as on being black in America. ★★★ VHS: $14.99

The Fallen Idol

(1948, 95 min, GB, Carol Reed) *Ralph Richardson, Bobby Henrey, Michèle Morgan, Jack Hawkins.* Richardson stars in this outstanding realization of Graham Greene's story about the friendship between an upper-class boy and a house servant who is suspected of murder. Reed skillfully probes the psychological depths of his characters while creating a fascinating examination of the schism between adults and children in their views of reality. ★★★★ VHS: $29.99

Falling Down

(1993, 112 min, US, Joel Schumacher) *Michael Douglas, Robert Duvall, Barbara Hershey, Frederic Forrest, Tuesday Weld, Rachel Ticotin, Lois Smith.* In this over-the-edge, misanthropic black comedy, Douglas plays a slightly psychotic, unemployed defense worker whose pent-up hostilities against what he perceives as an increasingly foreign society explode in the sweltering heat and insufferable traffic jams of Los Angeles. At times wildly entertaining, at others shockingly violent and disturbing, the film follows Douglas as he treks across L.A., unleashing his fury on Latinos, Asians, neo-Nazis and other "bogeymen" standing between him and the American dream. Duvall injects a voice of reason in the film as a henpecked cop who must come to grips with his own sense of inadequacy before confronting Douglas. A reactionary though simple message of white fear in an increasingly non-white society. ★★★ DVD: $14.99, VHS: $9.99

Falling in Love

(1984, 107 min, US, Ulu Grosbard) *Meryl Streep, Robert De Niro, Harvey Keitel, Dianne Wiest.* A curiously unaffecting film, given the high-power cast. De Niro and Streep allow a chance encounter on a commuter train to blossom into an affair. They provide their usual professional performances, as do supporting players Keitel and Wiest, among others. There just isn't very much to work with. Interesting as evidence of a seldom-exposed aspect of the De Niro persona and a chance to see Streep do a toned-down, suburban Annie Hall. ★★½ DVD Letterbox: $14.99, VHS: $14.99

Fame

(1980, 134 min, US, Alan Parker) *Irene Cara, Barry Miller, Paul McCrane, Lee Curreri, Anne Meara, Richard Belzer, Albert Hague, Gene Anthony Ray, Debbie Allen.* Parker follows a group of students at the New York High School of the Performing Arts from their auditions in dance, voice, drama and music through their graduation ceremony. Hot lunches, hard lessons and dancing in the street. Cara sings the Oscar-winning title song. ★★★ DVD: $14.99

The Family

(1987, 130 min, Italy, Ettore Scola) *Vittorio Gassman, Fanny Ardant, Philippe Noiret.* Utilizing a relaxed and intimate filmmaking style, Scola chronicles the 80 years of one typical family's life, loves and losses. By confining the entire story within the walls of a grand Roman apartment, Scola's attention is not on the tumultuous events of the 20th century but rather on the more mundane but equally compelling story of a middle-class family headed by Gassman. A touching and finely detailed soap opera. (Italian with English subtitles) ★★★

Family Business

(1989, 115 min, US, Sidney Lumet) *Sean Connery, Dustin Hoffman, Matthew Broderick, Rosana De Soto.* Endearing misfire written by Vincent Patrick (*The Pope of Greenwich Village*) about three generations of small-time crooks (Connery, Hoffman, Broderick) who decide to pull one last heist together. Though Patrick's screenplay has the same "homespun" feel that made *Pope* such a joy, the three strong leads tend to overpower the material. Efficiently directed by Lumet. ★★ DVD Letterbox: $19.99, VHS: $9.99

The Family Game

(1983, 107 min, Japan, Yoshimitsu Morita) *Junichi Tsujita, Yusaku Matsuda.* The contemporary Japanese middle class are mercilessly lampooned in this hilarious farce. The story, brimming with style and invention — from its extraordinary visual design to its incredulously quirky soundtrack — revolves around a family's decision to hire a tutor for their academically troubled son. The unorthodox and anarchistic instructor proceeds to wreak havoc in their previously tranquil lives. A wickedly satiric and endlessly surprising film. (Japanese with English subtitles) ★★★

Family Life

(1971, 108 min, GB, Ken Loach) *Sandy Ratcliff, Grace Cave, Bill Dan, Hilary Martyn.* An indictment of the generation gap, the mental health care system and society at large. This fictional documentary by Loach details the deteriorating mental state of a severely disturbed 19-year-old girl with an identity crisis, who becomes pregnant and is forced by her parents into an abortion. A harrowing portrait of mental illness and one that comes down hard against drug treatments and electroshock therapy. (aka: *Wednesday's Child*) ★★★ VHS: $9.99

The Family Man

(2000, 126 min, US, Brett Ratner) *Nicolas Cage, Téa Leoni, Don Cheadle, Jeremy Piven, Saul Rubinek.* Sharing more in common with *Mr. Destiny* than with *It's a Wonderful Life* for which it so desperately strives, this moderately enjoyable fantasy benefits from a nice turn by Leoni. Cage plays Jack, a successful Wall Street businessman who awakens on Christmas day to find himself in a parallel life: husband to Kate (Leoni), the woman he left behind 13 years earlier. Trapped in this new existence, Jack lives out this new life all the while trying to return to his reality. Balancing family comedy, sentimental dramatics and flights of fancy is a tall order, and director Ratner has difficulty in fully realizing and juggling these various tones. What success the film does achieve comes from the genial performances and a cute premise that delivers half of the time. ★★½ DVD Letterbox Collector's Edition: $19.99, VHS Special Edition: $9.99

Family Plot

(1976, 120 min, US, Alfred Hitchcock) *Bruce Dern, Barbara Harris, William Devane, Karen Black, Ed Lauter, Katherine Helmond.* The 53rd and final film in Hitchcock's illustrious career is a quirky blend of sinister humor and mystery. Harris, in a wonderfully kooky performance, is a phony (?) medium who, along with boyfriend Dern, stumbles onto the kidnapping pastime of diabolical Devane and Black. A supremely droll study of coincidence and the criminal urge. ★★★½ DVD: $19.99

A Family Thing

(1996, 110 min, US, Richard Pearce) *James Earl Jones, Robert Duvall, Michael Beach, Irma P. Hall, David Keith, Grace Zabriskie, Regina Taylor.* Jones and Duvall deliver subtle, finely drawn characterizations as half-brothers who are reunited after a separation of many decades, hundreds of miles, and the chasm of American racial relationships. Raised as white, Duvall receives a posthumous letter from his mother informing him that in fact his birth mother was a black woman who worked for the family and who died at his birth. He embarks on an odyssey of self-discovery, traveling to Chicago to find his brother and his history. The script, wonderfully understated and studded with wry, poignant glimpses at human foibles, was cowritten by Billy Bob Thornton. The supporting cast is uniformly competent, with Hall in a standout performance as Aunt T., the family's backbone and historian. *A Family Thing* is a small gem of surprising emotional impact, a story of ordinary people that encapsulates larger issues in a personal framework. ★★★½ DVD Letterbox: $14.99

Family Viewing

(1987, 86 min, Canada, Atom Egoyan) *David Hemblen, Aidan Tierney, Arsinée Khanjian.* Told with salacious humor and effective drama, this unusual black comedy is a droll observation of the goings-on of a denuclearized family. Dad is a middle-class, sadomasochistic VCR repairman who, after driving his wife away with his obsession for kinky phone sex, lives in domestic bliss with his sexy bimbo. His son, Stan, is a pasty-faced teenage couch potato. The son finally escapes from his father and moves in with his girlfriend who, unbeknowst to him, works at the phone sex company and has a peculiar sexual relationship with his father. This story of contemporary familial corruption is an intelligent and promising start for a talented filmmaker. ★★★ DVD 2-disc set: $34.99

The Fan

(1981, 95 min, US, Edward Bianchi) *Lauren Bacall, James Garner, Maureen Stapleton, Michael Biehn, Hector Elizondo, Griffin Dunne.* Bacall plays a legendary stage and screen star who is stalked by a psychotic fan. A creepy and rather unlikable thriller based on Bob Randell's novel. ★½ DVD Letterbox: $24.99, VHS: $14.99

The Fan

(1996, 116 min, US, Tony Scott) *Robert De Niro, Wesley Snipes, Ellen Barkin, John Leguizamo, Benicio del Toro, John Kruk.* As slick, cold and transparent as ice, *The Fan* is a twisted, by-the-books thriller that offers few thrills or any redeeming qualities. De Niro is a Willy Loman-like salesman and obsessed San Francisco Giants fan about to lose his grip. Snipes is the Ken Griffey-like superstar who becomes De Niro's object of obsession. The suspense supposedly starts when they cross paths, but it's more like a lesson in Screenplay Coincidence 101. Barkin has little to do as a sports announcer. The background baseball sequences add little excitement. ★½ DVD: $9.99

Fancy Pants

(1950, 92 min, US, George Marshall) *Bob Hope, Lucille Ball, Bruce Cabot.* Hope and Ball are in good form in this spirited remake of *Ruggles of Red Gap.* Bob is the cowardly valet who heads West with wild-and-woolly Lucy. She also sings the title song. ★★★ DVD: $14.99, VHS: $14.99

Fandango

(1985, 91 min, US, Kevin Reynolds) *Kevin Costner, Judd Nelson, Sam Robards, Chuck Bush, Suzy Amis, Glenne Headly.* Five college roommates, having just graduated, go on a last fling together across the Texas Badlands. An interesting youth drama with good performances from its cast. ★★½ VHS: $9.99

Fanny

(1932, 120 min, France, Marc Allégret) *Raimu, Charpin, Orane Demazis, Pierre Fresnay.* In this second segment of the remarkable Pagnol Trilogy, Marius' father César (played by the unforgettable character actor Raimu) comforts Fanny after being deserted by his son. Pregnant, she accepts the hand of Panisse, a kindly but older friend of César's. The film provides a rich portrait of complex familial relationships. (French with English subtitles) ★★★½ DVD Trilogy 3-pack: $79.99

Fanny

(1961, 133 min, US, Joshua Logan) *Leslie Caron, Maurice Chevalier, Charles Boyer, Horst Buchholz.* Acclaimed reworking of Marcel Pagnol's timeless story, based on the Broadway musical but *without* the songs (similar to 1963's *Irma La Douce*), with Caron as the young waif abandoned by a sailor. Enchanting performances. ★★★ VHS: $14.99

Fanny and Alexander

(1982, 197 min, Sweden, Ingmar Bergman) *Pernilla Allwin, Bertil Guve, Gunn Wallgren, Erland Josephson, Harriet Andersson.* Bergman's joyous and engrossing portrait of a civilized Swedish family gracefully details the trauma and triumphs they encounter over the course of a year. Abandoning the dour tone of his earlier works, Bergman creates an enchanting tapestry of life's amplitude in this wise and witty Academy Award winner. (Swedish with English subtitles) ★★★★

Fanny and Alexander

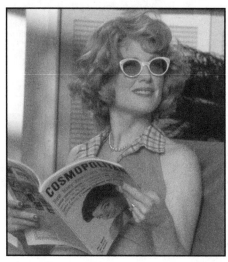

Julianne Moore in *Far from Heaven*

Fanny Hill

(1983, 80 min, GB, Gerry O'Hara) *Lisa Raines, Shelley Winters, Oliver Reed.* The extremely curvaceous Raines stars in this bawdy Playboy production rendition of the famous English folktale. The story follows the adventures of Fanny, a young country girl, orphaned in her adolescence, who moves to London where she falls into the good graces of Mrs. Cole (Winters), the cheerful proprietress of a house of pleasure. ★★

Fantasia

(1940, 120 min, US, Dick Huemer & Joe Grant) This Walt Disney masterpeice is a consummate collection of seven animated shorts, each utilizing a classical score for their background, and all under the direction of Leopold Stokowski. The selections include "The Sorcerer's Apprentice," starring Mickey Mouse; the brilliantly animated "The Rites of Spring"; and the stirring finale, "A Night on Bald Mountain." ★★★★ DVD: $29.99

Fantasia 2000

(2000, 75 min, US, Various Directors) *Hosts: Steve Martin, Itzhak Perlman, Quincy Jones, Bette Midler, James Earl Jones, Penn, Teller, James Levine, Angela Lansbury.* Despite the inclusion of "The Sorcerer's Apprentice," this is not a reworking of the original *Fantasia* (as Walt Disney originally intended) so much as a brand-new film in the same spirit, using computer technology and IMAX to make it technically up-to-date. Astonishingly rich in detail, with a surround-sound score by the Chicago Symphony, *Fantasia 2000* is a worthy successor, and at a too-brief 75 minutes, leaves one begging for a third installment. Like the original, it's a little heavy on dancing animals. Refreshingly, there's some new style here too: an urban, Abe Hirschfeld-inspired "Rhapsody in Blue" is closer to Warner than Disney and is most welcome. ★★★½ DVD: $29.99, VHS: $26.99

Fantastic Planet

(1973, 74 min, France, René Laloux) An unusual and provocative combination of science fiction and animation. Jammed with original ideas and visualizations, this French production is an imaginative allegorical tale about a futuristic planet where men are tolerated as tame, tiny pets. Also included are three shorts from Laloux: *Les Dents du Singe (Monkey's Teeth), Les Temps Morts (Idle Time)* and *Les Escargots (The Snails)*. (In English) ★★★ DVD: $19.99, VHS: $14.99

Fantastic Voyage

(1966, 100 min, US, Richard Fleischer) *Stephen Boyd, Raquel Welch, Donald Pleasence, Edmond O'Brien.* The special effects in this highly entertaining mid-'60s sci-fi classic may seem simple by today's standards, but at the time, they were nothing less than breathtaking. Members of a medical team are miniaturized and then injected into the body of the president in order to perform some truly up-close surgery. ★★★ DVD Double Feature: $14.99, VHS: $14.99

Far and Away

(1992, 140 min, US, Ron Howard) *Tom Cruise, Nicole Kidman, Robert Prosky, Thomas Gibson, Barbara Babcock, Colm Meaney.* Cruise and Kidman manage to ignite a few sparks in this handsomely produced romantic epic set in late 19th-century Ireland and America. Essentially a three-act story, the first part, set in Ireland, finds poor farmer Cruise and rich landowner's daughter Kidman meeting after he attempts to murder her father. The second act takes place in Boston, where the two have emigrated, finding only poverty and corruption. The final is set in the Old West, where all have surfaced to strike a claim. Though the film's Boston scenes are overly melodramatic, it is the first and last acts in which director Howard distinguishes himself. The lush Irish landscapes and the vast Western skies provide a thrilling backdrop for what becomes, ultimately, a surprisingly rousing entertainment. ★★★ DVD Letterbox: $14.99

Far Away, So Close

(1993, 140 min, Germany, Wim Wenders) *Otto Sander, Peter Falk, Willem Dafoe, Lou Reed.* Wenders continues his "Angels over Berlin" saga with this less-than-successful follow-up to the brilliant *Wings of Desire*. Angel Cassiel (Sander) comes down to earth because he wants to make things better. Instead, he falls victim to all of the human ailments he had hoped to remedy. Wenders takes a very grim view of the post-Cold War world, using Berlin as the perfect setting for a tale of impending social anarchy brought about by the collapse of old systems. Too often, however, Wenders allows his narrative to run wild and his flights of fancy can't keep things interesting. (German with English subtitles) ★★ VHS: $14.99

The Far Country

(1955, 97 min, US, Anthony Mann) *James Stewart, Ruth Roman, Walter Brennan.* A sturdy western adventure with Stewart in typically good form as a cowboy whose cattle drive to Alaska turns disastrous when he is swindled by outlaws. Good scenery and character interplay highlight this exciting tale. ★★★ DVD: $14.99, VHS: $9.99

Far East

(1982, 90 min, Australia, John Duigan) *Bryan Brown, Helen Morse.* Tepid drama about the owner of a sleazy tourist bar in Southeast Asia and his relationship with the wife of a crusading journalist. This mixture of political intrigue and romance has been done time and time again — with better results. ★

Far from Heaven

(2002, 107 min, US, Todd Haynes) *Julianne Moore, Dennis Quaid, Dennis Haysbert, Patricia Clarkson, Viola Davis, James Rebhorn.* From the gorgeous cinematography by Edward Lachman to Elmer Bernstein's luscious score to spectacular sets and costumes that evoke such a specific period in time — that of 1950s America — writer-director Haynes' reworking of Douglas Sirk's *All That Heaven Allows* is a remarkable achievement. The Whitakers appear to be the perfect Eisenhower couple. Frank (Quaid) is a successful salesman and Kathy (Moore) is the perfect suburban housewife. The façade is shattered, however, when Frank begins to act upon his dormant homosexual feelings, sending Kathy into the arms of their kindly black gardener Raymond (Haysbert). Conventions have been broken, and tongues soon begin to wag. The three lead actors are superb in difficult roles that require a subtleness in what is not said as much as what is. Moore especially shines as a confused wife who finds comfort and — for the first time? — compassion in a man that society will not allow her to befriend. Though it may find its inspiration in another film, *Far from Heaven* is a truly original work born of intelligence, passion and craftsmanship. ★★★★ DVD Letterbox: $19.99, VHS: $9.99

Far from Home

(1989, 86 min, US, Meiert Avis) *Drew Barrymore, Matt Frewer, Richard Masur, Susan Tyrrell, Jennifer Tilly.* Barrymore headlines this standard B-thriller about a budding teenaged nymphet who is stalked by an unknown killer while vacationing with her estranged father (Frewer). Nothing special, but a few unexpected touches (including a well-handled lesbian couple) spice things up. ★★ DVD: $14.99, VHS: $9.99

Far from Home: The Adventures of Yellow Dog

(1995, 81 min, US, Phillip Borso) *Mimi Rogers, Bruce Davison, Jesse Bradford.* An adolescent boy is lost in the wilds and faces certain horrors as he attempts to find his way back home. Set at a lethargic pace and given to clichés of the genre, *Far from Home*'s main appeal is the "boy and his dog" story that punctuates the survival dramatics. The film offers beautiful scenery (shot on location in British Columbia), but fails to maintain any excitement in the boy's rescue attempts. ★★ VHS: $9.99

Far from Poland

(1984, 106 min, US, Jill Godmilow) Denied a visa to shoot a film in Poland, left-leaning independent filmmaker Godmilow is forced to construct her documentary on the Solidarity movement from her studio in New York. This serious, nonfiction film delves into the perception and representation of "truth" as it charts the rise of the Solidarity movement in the shipyards of Damansk in early 1980 to its suppression by martial law in December 1981. From a number of various angles, Godmilow aims to present the reality of the situation without succumbing to easy, prejudicial conclusions. ★★★ VHS: $69.99

Far from the Madding Crowd

(1967, 169 min, GB, John Schlesinger) *Julie Christie, Alan Bates, Peter Finch, Terence Stamp.* Christie stars as a ravishing femme fatale who manages to make emotional mince meat out of three men's lives (Bates, Finch, Stamp). Director Schlesinger's masterful touch combined with the brilliant cinematography of Nicolas Roeg make this an extraordinary viewing experience. ★★★½ VHS: $14.99

Far North

(1988, 92 min, US, Sam Shepard) *Jessica Lange, Charles Durning, Tess Harper, Patricia Arquette, Donald Moffat, Ann Wedgeworth.* Lange and Durning head a strong cast in this allegorical tale written by Shepard, here making his directorial debut. When the head of a Minnesota farming family is almost killed by one of his most obstinate horses, he wants his strong-willed daughter to destroy the dangerous animal, with unexpected consequences. ★★★

A Far Off Place

(1993, 105 min, US, Mikael Salomon) *Reese Witherspoon, Ethan Randall, Sarel Bok, Maximilian Schell, Jack Thompson.* Based on a pair of novels by Laurens van der Post, this passable Disney adaptation recounts the adventures of a pair of white teenagers and their Bushman friend who, in order to evade a gang of murderous poachers, flee into southern Africa's Kalihari Desert. The story of orphaned children fleeing evil adults appears to be the perfect Disney fit; but despite this, or perhaps because of it, the film occasionally gets bogged down in formulaic predictability. ★★½

Farewell My Concubine

(1993, 155 min, China, Chen Kaige) *Leslie Cheung, Zhang Fengyi, Gong Li.* Told on an epic scale, this big-budget spectacle recounts the tempestuous relationship between two Peking Opera stars as they live through five decades of turbulent Chinese history. In a repressive 1920s opera school, an androgynous young boy, Dieyi, begins a lifelong involvement with another student, Xiaolou. Years later, the two achieve national stardom. As their professional lives soar, their relationship becomes strained as the gay Dieyi falls in love with his affectionate but heterosexual costar. Even after Xiaolou (Zhang) marries a fiery former prostitute (superbly played by Gong), the two men's lives remain intractably intertwined. Exotic locations, sweeping photography, colorful costumes and an emotional story line make this a riveting experience. (Chinese with English subtitles) ★★★★ DVD Director's Cut: $14.99, VHS: $9.99

Farewell, My Lovely

(1975, 98 min, GB, Dick Richards) *Robert Mitchum, Charlotte Rampling, Sylvia Miles, Anthony Zerbe, Sylvester Stallone.* Wonderfully evoking the time and mood of Raymond Chandler's 1940s Los Angeles, this film noir detective drama stars Mitchum as an aging, down-on-his-heels Philip Marlowe who is pursuaded to take on a case involving a nightclub singer missing for six years. Rampling is confusingly and destructively alluring as the femme fatale and Miles is unforgettable as an alcoholic floozy who "sings" for a bottle. A complex, dark and entertaining film that more than holds its own with the original, *Murder My Sweet.* ★★★½ VHS: $14.99

A Farewell to Arms

(1932, 78 min, US, Frank Borzage) *Gary Cooper, Helen Hayes, Adolph Menjou.* Hemingway's nihilistic novel of profane love and war deflated the 1920s' romantic ideals, but Depression-era Hollywood wanted something to believe in after the death of God and Country. Enter director Borzage, whose faith in the transcendence of physical love elevates Hemingway's bumbling paramours, finding something sacred in their union. Everything is painted in extremes: candid, naturalistic dialogue bumps into silent-era expressionism; tiny thespian Hayes and huge hunk Cooper cut iconic figures. A remarkable achievement, for those with a stomach for it, less a literal translation than a metamorphosis of the medium, perhaps to be paired with Lewis Milestone's underrated *Rain* for a taste of what hot, steamy places were American cinemas in that desperate year of 1932. (Remade in 1957) ★★★½ DVD: $24.99

Farewell to the King

(1989, 117 min, US, John Milius) *Nick Nolte, James Fox, Nigel Havers.* From the macho writer-director Milius comes this visually stunning, thematically stunted adventure epic of a WWII Army deserter (Nolte) who faces a crisis of conscience when the island paradise he has ruled in peace is invaded by the British-Japanese conflict. Based on a novel by Pierre Schoendoerffer. ★★

Fargo

(1996, 90 min, US, Joel Coen) *Frances McDormand, William H. Macy, Steve Buscemi, Peter Stormare, Harve Presnell.* The peculiarly heightened reality that is a trademark of Coen Brothers' films is well-suited to this bizarre tale of a seemingly solid, middle-class man (Macy) whose proximity to financial ruin precipitates a hare-brained scheme for quick monetary reward. His plan — to arrange his wife's kidnapping and split with the hired kidnappers the ransom to be paid by his wealthy father-in-law — is conceived in gnawing greed and blind stupidity, and culminates in horrific tragedy imbued with macabre humor. All of the performances are remarkable, overtly broad yet cunningly subtle. But the absolute delight is Oscar-winning McDormand as Margie the pregnant police chief, offhandedly battling morning sickness as she examines a triple-homicide crime scene. Minnesota's vast frozen expanses endow physicality to the desperate isolation that underlies this winter's tale. ★★★★ DVD Dual Special Edition: $19.99

Farinelli

(1994, 110 min, Belgium, Gerard Corbiau) *Stefano Dionisi, Enrico Lo Verso, Jeroen Krabbé.* The tumultuous life of castrato singer Farinelli (nee Carlo Broschi), along with his codependent relationship with his brother, is bombastically explored in this absorbing if predictable period drama. Set in 18th-century France, the story revolves around the ambitious singer (Dionisi), whose beautiful voice — preserved through a traumatic castration as a boy — becomes his instrument for success. Riding the coattails of that success is his brother Ricardo (Lo Verso), a much less talented composer, and their intense love/hate relationship extends to their careers and romantic affairs. Krabbé is very good as composer Handel who both admires, envies and admonishes the young singer. An elegant drama of unchecked ambition that sadly suffers from operatic excess. (French and Italian with English subtitles) ★★½ DVD: $29.99, VHS: $19.99

The Farmer's Daughter

(1947, 97 min, US, H.C. Potter) *Loretta Young, Joseph Cotten, Ethel Barrymore, Charles Bickford.* Young won an Academy Award for her enchanting performance as a Swedish farm girl who takes a job as a maid for a Congressman's family and finds love and political career opportunities. A charming comedy with sublime performances from the cast. (Basis for a 1960s TV series.) ★★★

The Fast and the Furious

(2001, 101 min, US, Rob Cohen) *Vin Diesel, Paul Walker, Michelle Rodriguez, Joseph Cotten, Rick Yune, Ted Levine.* Hot cars, hotter racing action and gorgeous babes and hunks are the main attraction in this throwback to the low-budget B racing car dramas of the 1950s and '60s, only souped up for 21st-century sensibilities. The characters still conform to cheesy dialogue and are one-dimensional cutouts, but the car racing scenes, flashy editing and high-octane camera work more than make up for the film staying true to the roots of the genre. Diesel plays Dominic, the leader of a street racing gang (though he prefers "team") who are possible suspects in a string of truck hijackings. Walker is Brain, an undercover cop who infiltrates the gang, er, team, falling for Dominic's sister Mia (Brewster) in the process. That's the excuse for a succession of motorcycle and car races, chases and explosions, and some of them are a doozy. *The Fast and the Furious* is great junk food thanks to its fast pace, knockout driving sequences, and a general desire to entertain in spite of all its limitations. (Sequel: *2 Fast 2 Furious*) ★★★ DVD Letterbox Tricked Out Edition: $26.99, VHS Special Edition: $9.99

Fast, Cheap, and Out of Control

(1997, 82 min, US, Errol Morris) Another quirky factual film from maverick documentarian Morris, this look at four men who have found infatuation and fascination with their eccentric lines of work is the story of obsession by an obsessive. They include: Hoover, an animal trainer; Mendez, a naked mole rat researcher; inventor Brooks, who developed an insect-like robot; and Mendonca, a topiary gardener with the ability to shape bushes into spitting images of animals. On the surface, they seem like regular guys. Delve a little deeper, however, and their obsessive streak becomes more apparent, as they espouse on their particular field of expertise while tinkering with science and nature. As is his nature, Morris loves tinkering himself, using old movie clips, staged sequences, hypnotic music and a mix of film and video textures to supplement his interview footage. Morris' inventive flourishes help show us that even the most ordinary people can be extraordinary at times. ★★★ VHS: $24.99

Fast Food Fast Women

(2001, 96 min, US, Amos Kollek) *Anna Thomson, Jamie Harris, Louise Lasser, Robert X. Modica, Victor Argo, Angelica Torn, Lonette McKee.* A look at a handful of oh-so-quirky New Yorkers, *Fast Food Fast Women* follows the romantic ups and downs of patrons of a coffee shop and their desire to find fulfilling sex and love lives. What you get, however, is one annoyingly cutesy scene after another in an uninvolving comedy underscored by dreadful, "aren't-we-having-fun?" tango music. It's rare to see a movie deal with the subject of older people seeking companionship and sex, so Kollek's cowardly retreat to sitcom-level dialogue and resolutions is particularly upsetting. Saddled with a ridiculous ending, *Fast Food Fast Women* achieves little more than placing irritating characters in irritating situations. ★½ DVD: $19.99, VHS: $14.99

The Fast Runner

(2002, 161 min, Canada, Zacharias Kunuk) *Natar Ungalaaq, Sylvia Ivalu, Peter-Henry Arnatsiaq.* In this retelling of an Inuit legend, a curse upon a clan continues to the next generation as Atanarjuat, the son of a deposed tribal leader, holds the heart of the woman betrothed to the son of his father's usurper. Though he wins his claim with honor and legitimacy, long-festering animosities and jealousies explode in murder and precipitate a frenzied flight across an endless expanse of ice. The windswept, unforgiving wasteland provides the physical challenges that Atanarjuat faces, as well as manifesting the chilled, exiled isolation he suffers in his heart. Yet the alien environment seems only to reinforce the universality of the human emotions that push these protagonists to their fate. The lack of self-consciousness and the primal spontaneity of the actors lend an almost documentary feel to the film, creating for the viewer the sense of being present, of observing the proceedings firsthand. The film at times requires patience, but offers more than adequate reward. (Inuktitut with English subtitles) ★★★½ DVD Letterbox: $27.99, VHS Subtitled: $102.99

Fast Talking

(1986, 93 min, Australia, Ken Cameron) *Steve Bisley, Tracey Mann.* A sensitive comedy about the coming-of-age of a streetwise Australian youth who yearns to break out of the restricting confines of school and family life. A movie about hope, defiance and emotional honesty. ★★½

Fast Times at Ridgemont High

(1982, 92 min, US, Amy Heckerling) *Jennifer Jason Leigh, Judge Reinhold, Sean Penn, Phoebe Cates, Forest Whitaker, Eric Stoltz, Anthony Edwards, Robert Romanus, Brian Backer, Ray Walston, Vincent Schiavelli.* "Hey dude, let's party." With these infamous four words, Penn introduced the California Valley boy in this entertaining, wacky comedy whose moments of insight into the rigors of growing up elevate it far above the usual teenager-obsessed-with-sex flick. A few of these students would go on to make a name for themselves. Heckerling's directorial debut. ★★★ VHS: $9.99

Favorite Line: "People on 'ludes should not drive." —*Sean Penn as Jeff Spicoli*

Faster, Pussycat, Kill! Kill!

(1966, 83 min, US, Russ Meyer) *Tura Satana, Lori Williams, Haji.* Tura Satana stars as Varla, the tough-talking ringleader of a wild gang of out-of-control go-go girls(!) in this thoroughly outrageous cult classic. Varla, the protolesbian killer with a taste for fast cars and helpless girls, rules with a leather-gloved fist over blonde beauty Billie (aka Boom Boom) (Lori Williams) and dark toughie Josie (Haji), two hot-rodding chicks in skin-tight clothes (calling them buxom would be redundant when talking about a Russ Meyer babe). Set in the California desert, these violent femmes kill a man and kidnap his bikini-wearing cutie pie girlfriend and go on a reckless road to inevitable ruin. Filled with hilarious dialogue and hellacious catfights, this potboiler is one of Meyer's best. ★★★

Fat City

(1973, 96 min, US, John Huston) *Stacy Keach, Jeff Bridges, Susan Tyrrell, Candy Clark.* After a period of intermittent critical and commercial success, Huston delivered this powerful portrayal of lonely outcasts on the fringes of the boxing world in California. Keach

The Fast Runner

plays a down-and-out veteran of the ring and Bridges is a hungry newcomer. Tyrrell is outstanding in support, giving a heartbreaking performance as a boisterous barfly. ★★★½ VHS: $19.99

Fat Man and Little Boy

(1989, 126 min, US, Roland Joffé) *Paul Newman, Dwight Schultz, Bonnie Bedelia, John Cusack, Natasha Richardson, Laura Dern.* An absorbing drama about the birth of the atom bomb. Newman, in an uncharacteristically unsympathetic and cold portrayal, stars as General Leslie Groves, the military leader who oversaw the project headed by the scientist J. Robert Oppenheimer. From this project would come the bombs that would be dropped on Hiroshima and Nagasaki. The film tries to create a mood of suspense in whether the scientists will succeed, but is far more interesting for the cat-and-mouse psychological games played between Groves and Oppenheimer in their race to develop and ultimately use the bombs. ★★½ DVD: $14.99, VHS: $14.99

Fatal Attraction

(1987, 119 min, US, Adrian Lyne) *Michael Douglas, Glenn Close, Anne Archer, Fred Gwynne, Stuart Pankin, Ellen Foley, Mike Nussbaum.* A box-office sensation, this psychological thriller is a not-too-subtle cautionary tale about adultery in the age of AIDS. Married exec Douglas has a one-night stand with Close and lives to regret it. Archer is the wife who is most hurt (literally) by the indiscretion. The film received a Best Picture nomination — a nod more to the sociopolitical impact of the story than a recognition of great filmmaking. ★★★ DVD Letterbox Special Collector's Edition: $14.99, VHS: $9.99, VHS Letterbox Director's Cut: $19.99

Fatal Beauty

(1987, 104 min, US, Tom Holland) *Whoopi Goldberg, Sam Elliott, Ruben Blades, Jennifer Warren, Brad Dourif, Cheech Marin.* This attempt to cash in on the success of *Beverly Hills Cop* stars Goldberg as an L.A. cop who's tracking down the source of a lethal batch of cocaine known as "Fatal Beauty." Very few thrills and an inferior story line is only partially offset by Goldberg's mugging. ★½ DVD: $14.99

Fatal Error

(1980, 90 min, Netherlands, Wim Verstappen) *Rutger Hauer, Rijk de Gooyer.* As imaginative as its title, this limp cop caper is another of the seemingly

endless stream of grade-B European action flicks Hauer made before he found fame (and better scripts) Stateside. This Dutch *Lethal Weapon* has a boyish Rutger as a bungling but charming detective who becomes embroiled in the mysterious suicide of a heroin dealer. They go undercover in the violent underbelly of Amsterdam's drug subculture. (aka: *The Outsider*) ★★

Fatal Instinct

(1993, 85 min, US, Carl Reiner) *Armand Assante, Sean Young, Kate Nelligan, Sherilyn Fenn, Christopher McDonald, James Remar, Tony Randall.* Unjustly maligned upon its release, *Fatal Instinct* is a sometimes very funny takeoff on film noir — and some of the targets include *Body Heat, Basic Instinct* and *Double Indemnity.* Though no Leslie Nieslen, Assante proves himself quite adept at parody, playing a cop/lawyer whose work for client Young puts him on the road to danger. As with most comedies of this sort, not all the gags work, but there's an abundance of laughs that do, thanks to a cast which clearly is having a lot of fun. Our favorite gag: Young's *Fatal Attraction* roller coaster ride. ★★★ DVD: $14.99

Fatal Vision

(1984, 192 min, US, David Greene) *Karl Malden, Eva Marie Saint, Gary Cole, Barry Newman, Andy Griffith.* Critically acclaimed adaptation of the Joe McGinness best-seller in which an ex-Green Beret is accused of murdering his pregnant wife and two young daughters, and his in-laws' relentless search for justice. Based on a true story. ★★★

Father

(1966, 89 min, Hungary, István Szabó) *Andras Balint, Miklos Gabor.* A sensitive and involving look at a young man's maturation as he searches for the real conditions that caused his father's death in World War II. (Hungarian with English subtitles) ★★★ VHS: $24.99

Father

(1991, 106 min, Australia, John Power) *Max von Sydow, Carol Drinkwater.* Set in modern-day Melbourne, this touching, emotional story concentrates on a middle-class family who runs a small hotel and restaurant. An anonymous phone call urges the young mother to watch a TV documentary one night, so as to learn the "real past" of her father. In a riveting moment, the woman is forced to delve into her father's questionable past: Was her father involved in a hideous and brutal war crime, and if so, then what has he been pretending to be all these years? Reminiscent of Costa-Gavras' much slicker *Music Box*, *Father* is smaller in scale, but packs more power, due in large part to von Sydow's tortured and pained portrayal. ★★★ VHS: $19.99

Father Goose

(1964, 116 min, US, Ralph Nelson) *Cary Grant, Leslie Caron, Trevor Howard.* Grant gives beach bum in this entertaining, sporadically funny comic adventure, the next-to-the-last film the actor would make. Set during WWII, the film casts Grant as a beachcomber living alone on a small South Seas island who is "drafted" by the Australian navy as a lookout. Complications, romance and some laughs arise when he rescues a French schoolmistress and six refugee children adrift at sea. ★★★ DVD: $14.99, VHS: $9.99

Father of the Bride

(1950, 93 min, US, Vincente Minnelli) *Spencer Tracy, Joan Bennett, Elizabeth Taylor, Billie Burke, Leo G. Carroll, Russ Tamblyn.* In this delightful family comedy, Tracy may have proved the inspiration for every sitcom father who has ever had to deal with a teenager. But few have done it better; it's hard to believe someone could be so funny just lifting an eyebrow. The story follows father Tracy and mother Bennett readying for daughter Taylor's wedding. (Sequel: *Father's Little Dividend*) (Remade in 1991) ★★★½ DVD: $19.99, VHS: $14.99

Father of the Bride

(1991, 105 min, US, Charles Shyer) *Steve Martin, Diane Keaton, Martin Short, B.D. Wong, Kimberly Williams.* Martin takes over the Spencer Tracy role from the 1950 classic comedy about a family preparing for their eldest daughter's wedding. Martin, who doesn't attempt to compete with Tracy, gives a funny performance as the exasperated dad, but the film manages to be only mildly amusing. As with the original, Mom (played endearingly by Keaton) and Dad become overwhelmed by all the arrangements. From the in-laws to the caterers (Short and Wong in offensively gay stereotypes), it's a never-ending calamity which the father of the bride handles with one-liners, pratfalls and humiliation. Ultimately, this *Father* is only a stand-in for the original. (Sequel: *Father of the Bride, Part II*) ★★½ DVD: $19.99, VHS: $9.99

Father of the Bride, Part II

(1995, 106 min, US, Charles Shyer) *Steve Martin, Diane Keaton, Martin Short, Kimberly Williams, Kieran Culkin, B.D. Wong.* This painfully unfunny, sugar-coated follow-up to the 1991 film (and based on the screenplay of the 1951 film *Father's Little Dividend*), is a flimsy excuse for a movie. Martin is back as George Banks, the grumpy and whiny husband of Nina (an often-out-of-focus Keaton), the 1950s idea of the perfect wife. The premise is that both his wife and daughter become pregnant (and that's it folks — that's the plot) — they each deliver a baby and then the movie ends!). Short and Wong return from the '91 original reprising their offensive roles as swishy and shrill decorators. ★ DVD: $19.99, VHS: $9.99

Father's Day

(1997, 98 min, US, Ivan Reitman) *Robin Williams, Billy Crystal, Nastassja Kinski, Charlie Hofheimer, Julia Louis-Dreyfus, Bruce Greenwood.* Admittedly, the thought of Williams and Crystal costarring in their first film together would seem almost heaven-sent. Expectations aside, however,

their first joint venture is only occasionally funny, and director Reitman doesn't give his stars ample room in which to explore the comic possibilities of the scenario. Based on the French comedy *Les Comperes*, the story begins when former lover Kinski tells both Williams and Crystal that her missing son is his. They eventually unite to locate the teenager, and their incompatability sets the stage for a few laughs. The two stars have a great rapport, but the screenplay just isn't consistently funny. Instead of nonstop hilarity, we get two incredibly gifted but underused leads. ★★½ DVD: $9.99, VHS: $9.99

Father's Little Dividend

(1951, 82 min, US, Vincente Minnelli) *Spencer Tracy, Elizabeth Taylor, Joan Bennett, Billie Burke.* Cheerful sequel to the hit comedy *Father of the Bride*. All the main leads all repeat their roles as newlywed Taylor returns home — expecting. (Remade in 1995 as *Father of the Bride II*) ★★★ VHS: $19.99

Fatherland

(1994, 100 min, US, Christopher Menaue) *Rutger Hauer, Miranda Richardson, Peter Vaughan, Jean Marsh, Michael Kitchen.* It's 1964. Hitler, having won WWII, dominates Europe (now known as Germania), but is still battling guerrillas in Russia. Needing an alliance with the United States, Germany opens its borders to American journalists for the first time since the war. The Reich readies for a celebration of the Fuhrer's 75th birthday, and there are rumors of a summit with U.S. President Joseph Kennedy, Sr. Through unusual elements in a murder investigation, SS Major Hauer (the SS is now the peacetime police) and U.S. journalist Richardson cross paths while tracking down a decades-old mystery. This HBO production is a well-executed thriller that makes good use of an intriguing premise and is uncomfortably effective in imagining life in a prosperous authoritarian state. ★★★½

Fatso

(1980, 94 min, US, Anne Bancroft) *Dom DeLuise, Anne Bancroft, Ron Carey, Candice Azzara.* First-time director Bancroft treads into husband Mel Brooks' territory with this occasionally amusing though disappointing comedy about an obese man's attempts to diet. DeLuise makes the most of the material ("Get the honey!"), but even his larger-than-life comedic talents aren't enough to warrant a recommendation. ★★ VHS: $12.99

Faust

(1926, 116 min, Germany, F.W. Murnau) *Emil Jannings, Gosta Ekman, Camilla Horn, Wilhelm Dieterle.* This lavishly produced expressionistic fable is one of the classics of silent film. The story begins with a wager between God and the Devil over the soul of an elderly scientist named Faust. Jannings stars as Mephistopheles, a conniving evildoer sent to a plague-stricken Europe to convince Faust to sell his soul in exchange for youth, pleasure and power. Jannings is superb as the wide-eyed, satin-caped Mephisto — an impish figure who takes malicious delight in destroying people's lives. With elaborate, medieval *Caligari*-like sets, experimental special effects, vivid imagery and a timeless tale, the film is Murnau's masterpiece and one that is just as striking when viewed today. ★★★½ DVD: $29.99, VHS: $24.99

Faust

(1994, 97 min, Czech Republic, Jan Svankmajer) A warped, hypnotic retelling of the Faust legend. Anyone familiar with Czech animator Svankmajer knows he's not going to helm the next *Winnie the Pooh* episode. His films are adult, dark, obsessive and truly surreal. *Faust* is definitely no exception. Making use of marionettes, live action and stop-motion animation, Svankmajer arguably has made his most mature, haunting and affecting film to date — after a slow start, this becomes fascinating and enthralling. Svankmajer is able to take clay figures and clunky puppets and creak memorable images that are disturbing and hilarious, revolting and gorgeous. A real pleasure for fans of the bizarre. ★★★½ DVD: $29.99, VHS: $19.99

Faust: Love of the Damned

(2000, 92 min, US, Brian Yuzna) *Mark Frost, Isabel Brook, Jeffrey Combs, Andrew Divoff.* A horrible adaptation of the pretty cool graphic novel. When the protagonist's girlfriend is murdered, he sells his soul to the Devil to get revenge. But, bummer for him, the Devil wants him to keep killing enemies of evil so he may accomplish some muddy goal of his. The two leads give turgid performances, and even cult fave Combs is subpar here, despite sporting some nifty rockabilly sideburns. The story and dialogue are guffaw-inducing, and the effects wouldn't pass muster on a website for a local diner. A crappy *Crow/Spawn* rip-off. ★ DVD Letterbox: $14.99

The Favor

(1994, 97 min, US, Donald Petrie) *Harley Jane Kozak, Elizabeth McGovern, Bill Pullman, Brad Pitt, Larry Miller, Ken Wahl.* When married Kathy (Kozak) can't get her old flame (Wahl) out of her amorous fantasies, she convinces her semisingle friend Emily (McGovern) to act as her . . . well, as her proxy in love, thereby being able to enjoy an extramarital affair vicariously. Of course, a few problems arise, like the protests of Emily's young beau (Pitt). A tepid comedy buoyed by McGovern's quirky charms. ★★ DVD Dual: $14.99, VHS: $6.99

The Favor, the Watch and the Very Big Fish

(1991, 89 min, GB, Ben Lewin) *Bob Hoskins, Jeff Goldblum, Natasha Richardson, Michel Blanc, Jean-Pierre Cassel.* Hoskins photographs religious tableaus for the greater glory of the Mother Church. He's given the assignment to find a new Christ on the same day a friend asks a favor, in the execution of which he meets Richardson, an enchanting young woman with an incredible story about a watch. Blanc and Goldblum join them in this fanciful and irreverent tale of the foibles of belief and the dangers of misplaced faith. Lewin directs his delightful script with wit and vigor, and the cast is engaging. As the two guys at the river bank note, "I just saw someone trying to walk on the water." "It happens. Go to sleep." ★★★ VHS: $9.99

Fear (La Paura)

(1954, 84 min, Italy, Roberto Rossellini) *Ingrid Bergman, Mathias Wiedman.* Rossellini's last and darkest film shows a marriage stumbling across lines of suspicion, mistrust and fear. An unfaithful wife (Bergman) is blackmailed by her lover's ex-girlfriend (and husband?). Her guilt drives her further into a series of lies leading to tragedy. (Filmed in English) ★★½

Fear

(1996, 95 min, US, James Foley) *Mark Wahlberg, Reese Witherspoon, William L. Petersen, Amy Brenneman, Alyssa Milano.* When adorable adolescent Witherspoon finds herself the object of obsession of bad-boy Wahlberg, bad things ensue, especially bad things for — surprise — the family pet and the sensitive best friend. The screenplay appears to have been written with much help from a psychology textbook as there is no shortage of *quien es mas macho* posturing between boyfriend and Mr. Father Knows Best (Petersen) and a "You're not my mother" conflict between daughter and stepmom. A standard, predictable genre thriller. ★½ DVD: $14.99, VHS: $9.99

Fear and Loathing in Las Vegas

(1998, 119 min, US, Terry Gilliam) *Johnny Depp, Benicio del Toro, Ellen Barkin, Cameron Diaz, Gary Busey, Christina Ricci, Lyle Lovett.* Occasionally video offers a new lease on life for films neglected in the theatres: this hopefully will be the case for *Fear and Loathing in Las Vegas*, a hallucinatory, extravagantly funny and unapologetic look at writer Hunter S. Thompson's drug-induced haze in late-1960s Las Vegas. The film was ripped apart by most critics, which could lead one to speculate that maybe its non-antidrug posture was too much in these "just say no" times. Depp is remarkable as Thompson, who is assigned to cover a sporting event for an unnamed magazine. Accompanied by his overweight Samoan lawyer (an almost unrecognizable Del Toro), Thompson begins a descent into cultural hell as the backyard of America's playground lays waste to unceasing drug and alcohol binges. Based on Thompson's cult novel, *Fear and Loathing* is a visual tour de force of acid trips, tacky art direction and oblivious destruction, and Gilliam and his cowriters have taken no prisoners in translating the essence of a counterculture classic. This wild, dizzying ride sputters now and then, but like any good amusement, it takes us by the throat and rattles us around till we're not sure which way is up. And if Thompson and friends didn't, why should we have such an advantage? ★★★½ DVD Criterion Collection: $39.99, VHS: $9.99, VHS Letterbox: $14.99

Fear City

(1984, 93 min, US, Abel Ferrara) *Tom Berenger, Melanie Griffith, Billy Dee Williams, Rae Dawn Chong.* From the director of *King of New York* comes this grade-B thriller about New York City strippers getting sliced and diced by a self-righteous martial arts expert hellbent on cleansing the city. ★★½ DVD: $24.99, VHS: $9.99

The Fear Inside

(1992, 100 min, US, Leon Ichaso) *Christine Lahti, Dylan McDermott, Jennifer Rubin, Thomas Ian Nicholas.* The ever-underrated Lahti headlines this sterling nail-biter about a woman suffering from acute agoraphobia, making it impossible for her to leave the house — even when it is taken over by a psychotic couple on the run. Nostalgia fans will undoubtedly recognize this as an updating of the 1964 cult classic *Lady in a Cage*. By changing the prison from a physical one to one of the mind, the terror and helplessness are made all the more real. ★★★

Fear of a Black Hat

(1994, 86 min, US, Rusty Cundieff) *Mark Christopher Lawrence, Larry B. Scott, Rusty Cundieff, Kasi Lemmons.* First-time director Cundieff wears many hats, including writer and star, in this often hilarious, sophisticated *This Is Spinal Tap*-like parody about the making of a documentary of a "rags to riches" Public Enemy-like rap group called N.W.H. ("Niggaz with Hats"), whose members display an obscene fascination for "booty," guns and hats. The insipid head of the group, Ice Cold (Cundieff), and his daffy cohorts are seen in interviews and personal moments, all of them blistering funny. But the film's true genius lies in its scathing skewering of rap industry infighting, as well as the group's off-the-cuff, outlandish "PC" justifications for the sexism, misogyny, racism amd violence strewn throughout their music. ★★★½ DVD: $19.99

Fear Strikes Out

(1957, 100 min, US, Robert Mulligan) *Anthony Perkins, Karl Malden.* Unflinching examination of baseball player Jimmy Piersall, whose battle with mental illness is tensely brought to the screen by a stand-out portrayal from Perkins (who truth be told doesn't make the most convincing ballplayer). Another strong performance from veteran Malden as Piersall's father. ★★★ DVD: $14.99, VHS: $14.99

Feardotcom

(2002, 98 min, US, William Malone) *Stephen Dorff, Natascha McElhone, Stephen Rea, Jeffrey Combs.* A series of resplendent visuals aren't quite enough to compensate for a nonsensical story line in this mixed bag of a horror tale. Dorff is a detective investigating the seemingly unconnected deaths of people with the same symptoms: bleeding from the nose and eyes, and a look of abject terror frozen on their faces. He and health inspector McElhone soon discover these folks had all logged onto a snuff website before they died. The story (such as it is) is derivative of several Japanese horror films, and specific visual ideas are borrowed from a variety of U.S. and European horrors. Though the film's a mess, it's oddly compelling; individual scenes, even certain shots, can be at once disturbing, moronic, gorgeous and incongruous. ★★ DVD Letterbox: $26.99, VHS: $6.99

Fearless

(1993, 122 min, US, Peter Weir) *Jeff Bridges, Rosie Perez, Isabella Rossellini, Tom Hulce, John Turturro, Benicio Del Torro.* Weir returns to form with this unnerving character study, reminiscent of the director's more complex Australian works. Bridges is remarkable as an airplane crash survivor who undergoes a dramatic change of personality. Having saved several lives on the plane, Bridges begins to assume a Christ-like persona as he moves further away from his loved ones and forms a bond with another survivor (Perez in a riveting performance), a mother whose two-year-old died in the crash. Perez and Bridges' scenes together possess a rare intensity, and both actors are the driving force of the film. Weir is successful in both examining the damaged psyches of his characters, and keeping a firm hand on an extremely well-directed crash sequence, told mostly through flashback. ★★★½ DVD: $14.99, VHS: $14.99

The Fearless Vampire Killers

(1967, 107 min, GB, Roman Polanski) *Roman Polanski, Jack MacGowran, Sharon Tate, Alfie Bass.* The restored version of this horror comedy adds over fifteen minutes of material to Polanski's loving tribute to the vampire films of Hammer Studios. Polanski himself plays one of the hunters out to rid the world of vampirism. The full title is *The Fearless Vampire Killers or Pardon Me, But Your Teeth Are in My Neck.* (The basis for the Broadway musical "Dance of the Vampires") ★★★

Feast of July

(1995, 118 min, GB, Christopher Menaul) *Embeth Davidtz, Tom Bell, Gemma Jones, Greg Wise, James Purefoy.* While this Ismail Merchant production would be but a minor addition to the oeuvre of his directing partner James Ivory, it is a decent first outing for British TV helmer Menaul. True to decorative detail and languid rhythms we associate with that era, *Feast of July* is a wistful pleasantry, needing only Alastair Cooke's gently guiding introduction to make one feel certain it is a quiet Sunday evening and "Masterpiece Theatre" is on the telly. Davidtz embodies the broken and battered Bella Ford, a woman led astray in a town and a time not known to be forgiving. She is forced to bury her stillborn baby in the rough earth and seek sanctuary in the house of a lamplighter and his marriageable sons. Whether tragedy or happiness is to be found there is wherein hangs the tale, one that is engrossing during its telling but forgotten at its end. ★★½ DVD: $14.99, VHS: $19.99

Fedora

(1978, 114 min, US/West Germany, Billy Wilder) *William Holden, Marthe Keller, Jose Ferrer, Frances Sternhagen, Henry Fonda, Michael York.* This fascinating curiosity from Wilder, toward the end of his career, stars Holden as an independent film producer who goes to Greece in search of Fedora, an actress from Hollywood's glamour years who now lives in a secluded villa. The film demonstrates a more romantic side of Wilder, but his potshots at contemporary Hollywood lack the bite of his more classic turns in the director's chair, most notably *Sunset Boulevard*. ★★★

Feeling Minnesota

(1996, 95 min, US, Steven Baigelman) *Keanu Reeves, Vincent D'Onofrio, Cameron Diaz, Delroy Lindo, Courtney Love, Tuesday Weld, Dan Aykroyd.* As pseduo-hip and annoying as the worst Tarantino rip-off, *Feeling Minnesota* fails as thriller, Generation X road movie, and Tarantino-wannabe. The dull plot concerns a prodigal son named Jjaks (gosh, how cool!) who returns home for his loathsome brother's wedding to a bombshell (Diaz), only to run off with sister-in-law. A corrupt cop (Aykroyd) and a friendly waitress (well played by Love) also pop in and out of the film, which is basically a series of fistfights and shouting matches set to an alternative beat. With the exception of Love's waitress, all the characters are scum, and the "big twist" is as illogical and obvious as the surprise ending of a minor "Hart to Hart" episode. ★½ DVD: $9.99, VHS: $4.99

Felicia's Journey

(1999, 111 min, GB, Atom Egoyan) *Bob Hoskins, Elaine Cassidy.* A young runaway is befriended by a gentlemanly chef, a serial killer who has been murdering young women who find themselves in desperate situations. Director Egoyan explores the psyche of a mass murderer with restraint, concentrating on emotional conflict rather than violence. Hoskins' serene, textured performance belies his character's malevolent intent, which only adds to the intensity of this subtle, brooding tale. ★★★ DVD: $19.99

Fellini Satyricon

(1969, 129 min, Italy, Federico Fellini) *Martin Potter, Capucine, Hiram Keller, Salvo Randone.* A wild and shocking phantamagoria set in a world of hermaphrodites, dwarves, prostitutes, nymphomaniacs and homosexual youths. Boldly bizarre in the unmistakable Fellini manner. (Italian with English subtitles) ★★★½ DVD: $19.99, VHS: $19.99

Fellini's Roma

(1972, 128 min, Italy, Federico Fellini) *Peter Gonzales, Fiona Florence, Anna Magnani, Gore Vidal.* Nostalgic and lavishly impressionistic, this "story of a city" is an engrossing tour of the Eternal City. Spanning from the '30s to the turbulent Rome of the '70s, Fellini offers a diverse view of his home through a mélange of deeply personal images of this vital, passionate land. (Italian with English subtitles) ★★★ DVD: $19.99, VHS: $19.99

Fellow Traveler

(1989, 97 min, GB, Philip Saville) *Ron Silver, Hart Bochner, Daniel J. Travanti, Imogen Stubbs.* *Fellow Traveler* is a totally engrossing psychological mystery about a blacklisted Hollywood writer living in England who learns of the suicide of his best friend. Silver is splendid as the writer who, haunted by the memory of his friend (Bochner), tries to piece together the reason and circumstance of his death — even at the risk of his own safety. An intriguing glimpse into the days of blacklisting and anti-Communist hysteria, and of the pain endured by those blacklisted. ★★★

Female

(1933, 60 min, US, Michael Curtiz) *Ruth Chatterton, George Brent.* This early directorial effort by Curtiz is a foreshadowing of his greatness to come. Chatterton is the head of an automobile factory. She's never found a man who's an equal match, although she's had some fun along the way. Brent plays a new employee who's not afraid to say no to her. Looking for a man who wants her for herself and not her money, she struggles with her identity: can she be a hard-working woman and still be "feminine"? Never too melodramatic and surprisingly explicit, the film's subject matter is still relevant today. ★★★½ VHS: $19.99

Female Perversions

(1996, 113 min, US/Germany, Susan Streitfeld) *Tilda Swinton, Amy Madigan, Karen Sillas, Clancy Brown, Frances Fisher, Paulina Porizkova.* *Female Perversions* is pretentious, arty and angry — three qualities which make it both intriguing and tough going. Swinton stars as Eve, a high-profile lawyer preparing for an interview with the governor in the hopes of being appointed a judge. In the meanwhile, she must contend with her estranged, kleptomaniac sister (Madigan), a workaholic boyfriend (Brown), a somewhat hesitant female lover (Sillas), and her own inner demons and film-school nightmare visions. *Female Perversions* does indeed resemble a grad film student's thesis — heavy-handed, issue-laden, mouthpieces serving as supporting characters and a handful of technical mistakes (boom mikes and production personnel refelcted on car hoods). But the material offers strong compensations — solid acting (Swinton in particular, playing the definitive neurotic), some insightful dialogue and a thoughtful ending. ★★½ DVD: $9.99

Female Trouble

(1974, 95 min, US, John Waters) *Divine, Edith Massey, Mink Stole.* Follow the trials and tribulations of Dawn Davenport (Divine): from cha-cha heel obsessed teen to rape victim to murderess to electric chair victim. Waters' ode to misguided teen traumas and prison melodrama includes satirical blasts at middle-class values, performance art, and really bad makeup. ★★★ VHS Uncut: $19.99

Femme Fatale

(2002, 110 min, US, Brian De Palma) *Antonio Banderas, Rebecca Romijn-Stamos, Peter Coyote, Gregg Henry.* This silly but fascinating noir riff is pure, undiluted De Palma. Romijn-Stamos (who acquits herself well, despite some goofball dialogue) is a thief who screws over her crew after a heist at the Cannes Film Festival goes wrong. She escapes Paris, and begins life anew in the States. When she is forced to come back to France, she is again pursued by her former cronies, thanks to Banderas' paparazzo snapping a picture of her that is made public. Often ridiculous, with ludicrous plot twists, *Femme Fatale* is also a ragingly cinematic, gorgeously stylish film, with its mesmerizing split screen, witty film tricks, terrific slow-motion set-pieces and a great opening heist. There's an extremely hot striptease, to boot, and the whole thing seems to be De Palma's comment on the myth of femmes fatales in movies. Forget the slightly draggy midsection and the film's goofy story and revel in the dazzling visuals and delightful conceits. ★★★ DVD Letterbox: $19.99, VHS: $22.99

La Femme Nikita

(1990, 117 min, France, Luc Besson) *Anne Parillaud, Jean-Hugues Anglade, Tcheky Karyo, Jean Reno, Jeanne Moreau.* Action-packed and filled with mega-violence, Besson's wonderfully entertaining romantic thriller is one part *Clockwork Orange*, and two parts "Pygmalion." The seductively pouty and dazzlingly leggy Parillaud debuts as Nikita, a modern-day Liza Doolittle with a vicious mean streak. Besson's story follows her somewhat Orwellian transformation from savagely criminal, punked-out heroin addict to well-groomed, cold-blooded assassin for the French government. Soon, however, she begins to experience stirrings of humanity, which elevates *La Femme Nikita* above its action-adventure status. Besson bathes his visuals in neon-drenched colors and captures the action with a high-fashion, nouveau-chic panache. (American remake: *Point of No Return*) (French with English subtitles) ★★★½ DVD Special Edition: $24.99

Femmes de Paris (Peek-a-Boo)

(1953, 83 min, France, Jean Loubignac) *Robert Dhery, Collette Brosset.* A delightful backstage comedy set in a burlesque hall and featuring the "Bluebell Girls" who provide the beauty (and some daring nudity!) and Louis de Funes who delivers the comedy. Adapted from the play "Ah, Les Belles Bacchantes." (French with English subtitles) ★★★

Ferngully: The Last Rainforest

(1992, 72 min, US, Bill Kroyer) *Voices of: Robin Williams, Tim Curry, Samantha Mathis, Christian Slater.* Excellent animation and a very timely message more than compensate for the relatively weak tale of fairies and humans engaged in a power struggle over the valuable rainforest. The fairies and their friends are happily living in a magical rainforest until the humans, while thoughtlessly cutting down trees, unleash the mysterious, evil monster Hexxus. While over-simplistic, the themes serve to promote ecological awareness at an early age. (Sequel: *Ferngully 2: The Magical Rescue*) ★★★ DVD: $14.99

Ferris Bueller's Day Off

(1986, 103 min, US, John Hughes) *Alan Ruck, Matthew Broderick, Mia Sara, Jeffrey Jones, Jennifer Grey.* Often hilarious Hughes teen comedy with Broderick in great form as a high school student whose charm and ingenuity are able to get him into — and out of — any situation of his choosing. The story follows Bueller and his friends playing hooky and visiting downtown Chicago. ★★★½ DVD: $14.99, VHS: $9.99

A Few Good Men

(1992, 138 min, US, Rob Reiner) *Tom Cruise, Demi Moore, Jack Nicholson, Kiefer Sutherland, Kevin Bacon, Kevin Pollak, Cuba Gooding, Jr., J.T. Walsh, Noah Wyle.* Cruise's high-octane performance as a cocky underdog helps energize an already compelling courtroom drama and murder mystery. He plays a Navy lawyer who is chosen to defend two Marines accused of killing a fellow soldier. The question is: Were the two young cadets acting on their own, or were they under orders from a superior officer? As Cruise and fellow lawyers Moore (who is actually fully clothed here) and Pollak feverishly investigate the killing, they are thwarted by military red tape at every turn. In a small but pivotal role, Nicholson gives a spellbinding performance as an over-zealous commander. ★★★½ DVD Special Edition: $14.99

Anne Parillaud in *La Femme Nikita*

The Fifth Element

ffolkes

(1980, 99 min, GB, Andrew V. McLaglen) *Roger Moore, Anthony Perkins, James Mason.* A surprisingly entertaining high-seas actioner with Perkins chewing the scenery as the leader of a group of terrorists who have taken over a supply ship. Moore, in a playful mood, is the disheveled hero out to stop them. ★★★ DVD Letterbox: $14.99, VHS: $59.99

Fiddler on the Roof

(1971, 181 min, US, Norman Jewison) *Chaim Topol, Norma Crane, Leonard Frey, Molly Picon.* Magnificent screen version of the smash Broadway musical based on the stories of Sholem Aleichem. Topol plays Tevye the milkman (and he almost makes one forget about Zero Mostel), a poor Jewish husband and father of five who grapples with changing religious and social mores in Czarist Russia. The musical sequences are outstanding, and the classic score includes "If I Were a Rich Man" and "Sunrise, Sunset." ★★★★ DVD Letterbox Special Edition: $19.99

The Field

(1990, 110 min, Ireland, Jim Sheridan) *Richard Harris, Brenda Fricker, Tom Berenger, John Hurt, Sean Bean.* Harris' excellent performance dominates this emotionally satisfying, leisurely paced and beautifully filmed story of obsession and murder. Harris plays (appropriately named) Bull McCabe, a poor farmer working the fields of the gorgeous Irish countryside whose determination and inflexibility toward acquiring a piece of land — one he had been cultivating for decades — leads to tragedy. ★★★½ DVD: $14.99, VHS: $9.99

Field of Dreams

(1989, 106 min, US, Phil Alden Robinson) *Kevin Costner, James Earl Jones, Amy Madigan, Ray Liotta, Burt Lancaster, Frank Whaley, Gaby Hoffman.* "If you build it, he will come." This is what novice farmer Costner hears in his cornfield one day, accompanied by a vision for him to build a baseball field. Acting on faith alone, he builds it, and "he" does come; he being the ghost of the great "Shoeless" Joe Jackson. This warm and humorous fantasy is a profoundly moving and magical fable about faith, redemption and our national pastime. An idealistic Costner excels as the farmer; as does Jones as a reclusive, iconoclastic 1960s author who journeys with Costner. ★★★★ DVD Letterbox 2-disc Anniversary Edition: $26.99, DVD Pan & Scan 2-disc Anniversary Edition: $26.99

Field of Honor

(1988, 87 min, France, Jean-Pierre Denis) *Cris Campion, Eric Wapler.* Set in 1870 France, this subtle but moving drama concerns a naïve farm boy who, as was common at the time, is paid by a rich merchant to take the place of his son in the army. But he is soon disillusioned once he witnesses the horrors of war. (French with English subtitles) ★★★ VHS: $19.99

Fiend without a Face

(1958, 74 min, GB, Arthur Crabtree) *Marshall Thompson, Kim Parker.* Lifting a lesson from the Krell, a scientist using simple everyday objects manages to materialize his thoughts. Unfortunately, he's thinking about brains that crawl around on their spinal cords and suck the mental matter out of the heads of the local villagers who are revolted and revolt. The special effects are surprisingly good, and the film is both very effective and frightening. ★★★ DVD: $39.99, VHS: $19.99

Fierce Creatures

(1997, 98 min, US/GB, Fred Schepisi & Robert Young) *John Cleese, Jamie Lee Curtis, Kevin Kline, Michael Palin.* The cast of 1988's classic *A Fish Called Wanda* reunites for this not-really-a-sequel. The plot concerns a rich Australian tycoon (Kline) who overtakes a British company that controls, among other things, a zoo. Kline also plays the tycoon's oversexed, ne'er-do-well son, and he and the sexy Curtis supervise the promotional overhaul of the zoo. In an effort to boost profits and give patrons the carnage they *really* want, only fierce animals are to be kept on hand. This sets up all sorts of comic situations in which the animal caretakers try to B.S. new director Cleese into thinking that various cute little critters are actually rabid, carnivorous vermin. The film has a few clever bits, but the pitch-black humor and cheerful malevolence of the first film are substituted for cute, family-friendly hijinks. ★★½ DVD: $24.99

15 Minutes

(2001, 121 min, US, John Herzfeld) *Robert De Niro, Edward Burns, Kelsey Grammer, Karel Roden, Oleg Taktarov, Kim Cattrall.* De Niro and Burns make a decent team in this otherwise unsatisfying thriller/satire. De Niro is an alcoholic celebrity cop on the trail of two thrill-killing, East European immigrants (Roden, Taktarov); Burns is an arson investigator who gets caught up in the case. The weak satire comes into play when the villains decide to videotape their killings, plead insanity when caught, then make millions selling their story.

15 Minutes is a bit of a mess: as a thriller, it's far too unpleasant and lethargic, and as satire, it's at once obvious and confused. The reactionary ending would've been far more effective in an adolescent, Chuck Norris-type film; here, it just feels cheap and ugly, and erases any potency the subject matter might've had. ★★ DVD Letterbox infinifilm Special Edition: $14.99, VHS: $9.99

The Fifth Element

(1997, 127 min, US, Luc Besson) *Bruce Willis, Gary Oldman, Ian Holm, Milla Jovovich, Chris Tucker, Luke Perry.* Besson's Gallic sensibilities serve him well in this sci-fi near-epic starring Willis as a cab driver who saves the world. Corbin Dallas, a decorated ex-soldier, is called upon to do his duty again when a gigantic, indestructible black flame is discovered to be advancing toward the Earth. Luckily, Corbin has the assistance of the Fifth Element, the Supreme Being of the Universe, a very cute and very deadly orange-haired alien (Jovovich). Standing in their way is a weapons magnate (Oldman) with big buck teeth and an accent to rival Foghorn Leghorn's. The effects and overall visual design of the film are stunning. Unfortunately, the story itself does not live up to its look and feel. Alternately goofy and flashy, and sometimes too serious for its own good, it succeeds as fantastic popcorn entertainment, but falls short of being a speculative science fiction classic. ★★★ DVD Letterbox Superbit Edition: $27.99, DVD: $19.99, VHS: $9.99

The Fifth Monkey

(1990, 93 min, Brazil/GB, Eric Rochat) *Ben Kingsley.* A lushly photographed though slow-moving version of Jacques Zibi's novel, "Le Cinquieme Singe." Kingsley plays a peasant animal trader whose discovery of four chimpanzees in the Brazilian wilderness seems to be the answer to his matrimonial money problems. En route through the jungles to sell the animals, however, Kingsley comes up against mercenaries and corrupt officials. ★★

Fifth of July

(1983, 116 min, US, Kirk Browning & Marshall W. Mason) *Richard Thomas, Jeff Daniels, Swoosie Kurtz, Jonathan Hadary.* An extremely well-acted, first-rate adaptation of Lanford Wilson's acclaimed Broadway comedy-drama, with most of the original cast reprising their roles. The show is slightly opened up yet still retains its intimate theatricality. In a splendid performance, Thomas plays a gay schoolteacher and disabled Vietnam vet who faces an emotional crisis upon returning to the classroom. Daniels is his supportive lover whose even temper and goodwill are put to the test when Thomas' college friend Kurtz (who won a Tony Award), a free-spirited and now successful singer, arrives with her entourage for a short stay. As the characters recall the past and face the future, secret passions, betrayals and insecurities are brought to the surface. Wilson's poetic dialogue is funny, tender, intelligent and remarkably assured. ★★★★ DVD: $24.99

50 First Dates

(2004, 96 min, US, Peter Segal) *Adam Sandler, Drew Barrymore, Rob Schneider, Sean Astin, Dan Aykroyd, Blake Clark.* After the sundry charms of *The Wedding Singer*, maybe it was too much to expect that a Sandler-Barrymore reunion would capture a similar magic. While the chemistry is still there in this equally sentimental romantic comedy, Sandler's preferred lowbrow gags are out in such force as to quash any remaining goodwill.

Barrymore plays a young Hawaiian who, thanks to a car accident, wakes up each morning thinking it's her dad's birthday (no, not Groundhog Day). Sandler is a ladies' man who finally thinks of settling down when he meets this difficult catch. Of course, each morning he must struggle with how to re-meet her and inform her of their budding relationship. If the film was nothing more than *50 Meet Cutes* it might have worked. But then comes the poorly timed sophomoric humor, like clockwork, to ruin it. Walrus vomit? Check. Rob Schneider bleeding from a shark bite? Check. Adam Sandler hurting his balls? Double check. Even the modest success of *The Wedding Singer* now seems a total fluke, as Sandler is apparently content unambitiously catering to the 15-and-under crowd. ★★ DVD Letterbox: $28.99, DVD Pan & Scan: $28.99

55 Days at Peking

(1963, 154 min, US, Nicholas Ray) *Charlton Heston, Ava Gardner, David Niven, Flora Robson, Paul Lukas.* Sprawling, exciting epic about a group of Europeans involved in the Chinese Boxer Rebellion of 1900. ★★★

54

(1998, 93 min, US, Mark Christopher) *Ryan Phillippe, Salma Hayek, Mike Myers, Sela Ward, Breckin Meyer, Neve Campbell, Heather Matarazzo, Michael York, Lauren Hutton.* There's another reason to hate the disco era: writer-director Christopher's *54*, a clichéd morality tale of dance, drugs and redemption. In yet another boy-comes-to-the-big-city plot line, Phillippe stars as Shane, a naïve, good-looking 19-year-old from Jersey City whose dream of getting into Studio 54, the shining star of New York dance clubs, becomes a reality when he becomes employed there. Quicker than you can snort a hit of coke, he's doing drugs and having anonymous sex. As a story of corrupted youth, *54* has little to offer; its limited appeal lies in the peripheral characters who populate the club. Best of these is Myers, who gives an engaging performance as Steve Rubell, 54's owner. The music is good, the drug angle moralizing, the feel authentic, and too many spot-the-star cameos. ★★ DVD: $14.99, VHS: $9.99

52 Pick-Up

(1986, 114 min, US, John Frankenheimer) *Roy Scheider, Ann-Margret, Vanity, John Glover, Clarence Williams III.* Elmore Leonard's best-selling novel makes for an exciting screen thriller. Scheider plays a successful businessman who takes on a group of blackmailing pornographers. Solid support from Glover as the villainous ringleader. ★★★

Fight Club

(1999, 139 min, US, David Fincher) *Brad Pitt, Edward Norton, Helena Bonham Carter, Meat Loaf, Jared Leto.* A smart and sexy adrenaline rush, the subversive *Fight Club* bids farewell to the old millennium and greets the new as it tears apart the mores and morals of the late, great 20th century. Fincher brings gut-level tension to this nihilistic tale of white, disenfranchised blue-collar men who find emotional release in nightly bareknuckle fighting — but in the form of a vibrant, hyperventilating black comedy. Norton is the Narrator, an angst-ridden businessman whose life dramatically changes when he meets the mysterious Tyler Durden (Pitt). Together they start Fight Club, a movement that catches on like wildfire. Violent and vibrant, the film is a ravaging attack on consumerism and a bloody exercise in machismo, as members beat each other senseless in superbly choreographed fight scenes. But this is a film where not

everything is as it appears, and Fincher takes delight in confounding and provoking. ★★★½ DVD Basic Edition: $19.99, VHS: $9.99

Fight for Us

(1989, 92 min, Philippines, Lino Brocka) *Phillip Salvador, Dina Bonnevie.* Filmed clandestinely, director Brocka's stirring drama explores the political chaos and repression in The Philippines after a bloody revolution brings down a dictator only to install an equally corrupt "democracy." Jimmy Cordero is a former priest and dissident freed from jail after Marcos' downfall. He finds his efforts to resume a normal life interrupted when he is forced to confront a group of vigilantes. His efforts to bring these men to justice and to expose their connection to the government embroils him in a bloody fight that threatens an entire village as well as his wife, friends and children. ★★★

The Filth and the Fury

(2000, 103 min, GB, Julien Temple) *John Lydon, Paul Cook, Sid Vicious, Glen Matlock, Steve Jones, Malcolm McLaren.* The Filth and the Fury opens with newsreel footage of the violent street protests that permeated Great Britain in the late 1970s. It now seems inevitable that the band The Sex Pistols would skyrocket to infamy during this period of profound social unrest. Director Temple has brilliantly documented the period's social chaos with an intimate portrait of the band — delivered with affection and without blinders on. In only 26 months, The Sex Pistols were hired and fired by three major record companies, banned and condemned throughout England. As punk is absorbed into the mainstream, the Sex Pistols descend into their final dissolution. A very entertaining documentary for both lovers and haters of punk. ★★★½ DVD: $24.99, VHS: $14.99

Final Analysis

(1992, 124 min, US, Phil Joanou) *Richard Gere, Kim Basinger, Uma Thurman, Keith David, Eric Roberts.* First teamed in *No Mercy*, where they caused very few sparks, Gere and Basinger are together again in this routine but flashy thriller. A low-key Gere plays a successful San Francisco psychiatrist who becomes involved with a relative of one of his patients. The patient: Thurman, who shows up

with new and interesting stories. The relative: Basinger, a beauty who could use a few hours on the couch herself. As Gere becomes spellbound by Basinger, he finds himself caught in a deadly game of cat and mouse between Basinger and her gangster husband Roberts. ★★½ DVD: $14.99, VHS: $9.99

The Final Countdown

(1980, 104 min, US, Don Taylor) *Kirk Douglas, Martin Sheen, Katharine Ross, James Farentino.* Intriguing and imaginative sci-fi outing with Douglas as the commander of an aircraft carrier who is suddenly transported — with his ship and crew — back to the Pacific just days before the Pearl Harbor attack. ★★★ DVD: $29.99

Final Destination

(2000, 93 min, US, James Wong) *Devon Sawa, Ali Larter, Kerr Smith, Kristen Cloke, Daniel Roebuck.* An overacting high schooler (Sawa) has a premonition that the plane he and his classmates are on will explode. He makes a scene, and he and several of his friends are thrown off the plane . . . which does explode. But Death is unhappy that Sawa has ruined his Design, and proceeds to pick off the survivors one by one. Despite the silly but interesting premise, the filmmakers can only come up with one or two creepy/funny touches. (Sequel: *Final Destination 2*) ★½ DVD Platinum Series: $14.99, VHS: $9.99

Final Destination 2

(2003, 88 min, US, David R. Ellis) *Ali Larter, A.J. Cook, Michael Landes.* From its oxymoronic title to its silly metaphysical musings to its slapstick gore scenes, *Final Destination 2* is a guilty pleasure, through and through. After a young woman has a premonition of a particularly grisly highway pileup, she convinces some of the drivers involved to stay off the road. Of course, these "survivors" have cheated Death and are now being picked off one by one in a succession of freak accidents. To watch this, you've got to be in the mood to cackle while human beings are sliced, diced, gutted and crushed in the most grisly manner possible. Don't expect anything resembling a screenplay; still, the direction is crisp, the actors are game, and it flies along like a bat outta hell. ★★ DVD infinifilm Special Edition: $27.99, VHS: $8.99

Brad Pitt (l.) and Ed Norton in *Fight Club*

Finders Keepers, Lovers Weepers

(1968, 72 min, US, Russ Meyer) *Ann Chapman, Lavelle Roby, Jan Sinclair.* Inspired by Don Siegel's gangster movies, *Finders Keepers, Lovers Weepers* is about a robbery attempt in a go-go dance bar that gets out of hand. There's a memorable sequence of a couple making love out with a demolition derby. ★★

Finding Forrester

(2000, 136 min, US, Gus Van Sant) *Sean Connery, Rob Brown, F. Murray Abraham, Anna Paquin, Busta Rhymes.* Connery gives a career-topping performance as a brilliant, reclusive writer in this compelling drama from the director of *Good Will Hunting.* Sharing in common with that film the themes of mentorship and academia, *Finding Forrester* follows the friendship of 16-year-old Jamal (Brown), a high-school basketball star with a secret passion for writing, and William Forrester (Connery), a celebrated author who's as famous for his privacy as he is for his artistic output of one (Pulitzer Prize-winning) novel. The touching, often humorous story explores the bond that grows between them and how each has something to teach the other. Young Brown — in his film debut — keeps pace nicely with the seasoned cast around him. ★★★ DVD: $14.99, VHS: $14.99

Finding Nemo

(2003, 101 min, US, Andrew Stanton) *Voices of: Albert Brooks, Ellen Degeneres, Eric Bana, Willem Dafoe, Geoffrey Rush, John Ratzenberger.* Pure aquatic bliss from start to finish, this delightful under-the-sea adventure from Pixar boasts the most astonishing computer-generated animation concocted yet, and its highly neurotic characters are infectiously endearing. Brooks lends voice to Marlin, a nebbish clownfish whose overprotectiveness prompts only-spawn Nemo to perform an insolent stunt that results in the little guy's capture by a sadistic dentist. The chase is on as Marlin swims across the Great Barrier Reef to rescue his son. Along the way he pairs up with Dory (DeGeneres), a wired blue tang prone to lapses in short-term memory; both nearly become lunch for a Sharks Anonymous support group. Meanwhile, Nemo and his fellow aquarium captives hatch a daring plan for a great escape. The combination of Disneyfied pathos and boisterous humor has never felt so casually sublime, and the requisite emotional tides are, miraculously, schmaltz-free. ★★★★ DVD 2-disc Collector's Edition: $29.99, VHS: $24.99

There's plenty of neuroses under the sea in Pixar's *Finding Nemo*

A Fine Madness

(1966, 104 min, US, Irvin Kershner) *Sean Connery, Joanne Woodward, Jean Seberg, Colleen Dewhurst.* Elliot Baker did a fine adaptation of his own satiric novel, retaining much of its bite and a lot of its slapstick. Taking a break from his role as 007, Connery plays an egocentric poet at odds with the world, including wife Woodward. ★★★ VHS: $14.99

A Fine Mess

(1986, 100 min, US, Blake Edwards) *Ted Danson, Howie Mandel, Richard Mulligan.* Danson and Mandel are two get-rich-quick schemers chased throughout Los Angeles by two petty, inept thieves. Unfortunately, there is nothing worth recommending in this stupid and unfunny comedy. ★

Fingers

(1978, 91 min, US, James Toback) *Harvey Keitel, Jim Brown, Tisa Farrow, Danny Aiello, Michael V. Gazzo.* Gritty Scorsese-esque character study of an aspiring concert pianist (Keitel) who moonlights as a debt collector for his aging mafioso father. Though favorably reviewed upon its initial release, the film failed to receive audience support, and over the years has attained a certain cult status. ★★★ DVD Letterbox: $19.99, VHS: $14.99

Finian's Rainbow

(1968, 145 min, US, Francis Ford Coppola) *Fred Astaire, Tommy Steele, Petula Clark, Keenan Wynn, Al Freeman, Jr..* Coppola's glossy but rather stilted song-and-dance is based on the Burton Lane-E.Y. Harburg Broadway musical. Astaire, bringing a touch of dignity and immeasurable charm, has scene-stealing Steele and Clark, as Astaire's spirited daughter, star in this story of racism, leprechauns and a stolen crock of gold. ★★½ VHS: $19.99

Finnegan Begin Again

(1984, 112 min, US, Joan Micklin Silver) *Mary Tyler Moore, Robert Preston, Sam Waterston, Sylvia Sydney.* Moore and especially Preston offer strong performances in this delightful made-for-cable movie about the relationship between a sixtysomething newspaper man and a 40-ish schoolteacher. ★★★

Fiorile

(1992, 118 min, Italy, Paolo & Vittorio Taviani) *Michael Vartan, Galatea Ranzi.* A wonderful tale spanning three hundred years in a family's history of unrequited love. A poor farmer's daughter, Fiorile Benedetti, falls in love with a soldier of Napoleon's troops sent to insure safe passage of a chest of gold. While they tryst, her brother finds the gold on the back of a stray mule. Rather than return the gold, the brother keeps it, prompting the French to kill the soldier; which, in turn, leaves Fiorile listless and pregnant. She places a curse on the person who caused her lover to be killed. This sets off the continuation of the theme through every other generation of Benedettis. Sibling rivalry, greed, power and the rest of the expected fare are featured in this beautifully photographed, sweeping costume drama. (Italian with English subtitles) (aka: *Wildflower*) ★★★

Fire

(1997, 104 min, Canada/India, Deepa Mehta) *Shabana Azmi, Nandita Das.* An original and emotionally charged drama about the forbidden love between two women. The newly wed Sita (Das) is a young and beautiful woman who comes to live with her husband's brother and his wife Rahda (Azmi) in New Dehli. Restless and independent and realizing that her arranged-marriage husband is far from

faithful, Sita quickly finds her new world stifling. The older Rahda, on the other hand, offers the face of complacency, all the while holding within her rage and loneliness. Within this volatile atmosphere the two women strike up a natural friendship which leads to smoldering passions and a sensual but secretive romance. Mehta has created a taut, brave and invigorating love story that challenges the place of women in Indian society. (Filmed in English) ★★★½ DVD: $29.99, VHS: $29.99

Fire and Ice

(1983, 83 min, US, Ralph Bakshi) This animated sword and sorcery film is many cuts above its live-action brethren thanks to a fine script from ace comic writers Roy Thomas and Gerry Conway, striking graphic designs by Frank Frazetta, and powerful animation by Bakshi. ★★★

Fire Down Below

(1957, 116 min, US, Robert Parrish) *Jack Lemmon, Robert Mitchum, Rita Hayworth, Herbert Lom, Anthony Newley.* Solid performances from Lemmon and Mitchum and the particularly hypnotic presence of Hayworth barely compensate for the wooden direction from Parrish in what should have been a rollicking scorcher of a movie. Refugee Hayworth has no papers. Sea-faring buddies Lemmon and Mitchum are paid to smuggle her from one Carribean island to another. During the voyage, both fall for her. Hard. ★★½ DVD: $24.99

Fire Down Below

(1997, 103 min, US, Felix Enriquez Alcala) *Steven Seagal, Marg Helgenberger, Kris Kristofferson, Harry Dean Stanton, Randy Travis.* If Dylan could go electric, why can't Seagal go country? Well, Seagal does go country in this, the monosyllabic martial arts maven's second ecological actioner. He's an EPA agent sent to Kentucky to find out who killed a former compadre who discovers that the environment is being polluted by Kristofferson, a good ol' boy tycoon. This is passable genre fodder, until the end when pony-tailed palooka makes like Superman and Al Gore at the same time, and getting all political about the hazards of pollution. Didn't he get all that out of his system in his laughable *On Deadly Ground*? ★★ DVD: $9.99

Fire in the Sky

(1993, 111 min, US, Robert Lieberman) *Robert Patrick, D.B. Sweeney, James Garner, Peter Berg, Craig Sheffer, Henry Thomas.* In a small Southwestern town, five loggers report the disappearance of their coworker. But what has the police and community up in arms is their story — that he was abducted by a UFO. Based on an actual sighting, *Fire in the Sky* is a surprisingly engrossing and credible recounting of the young man's story and the dilemma faced by his friends. The film's success is due in large part to its focus on the community and its reactions to the alleged event. Well crafted and nicely acted by a strong cast, this underrated and unexpectedly engaging film is worth checking out by skeptics and believers alike. The scenes aboard the spacecraft are particularly effective. ★★★ VHS: $19.99

Fire over England

(1937, 89 min, GB, William K. Howard) *Laurence Olivier, Flora Robson, Vivien Leigh, Leslie Banks, Raymond Massey, James Mason.* A handsomely produced costume epic set during the 1500s British-Spanish naval conflict, *Fire over England* is a forcefully acted, well-written historical drama highlighted by the outstanding performance by Robson as

Vivien Leigh in *Fire over England*

Queen Elizabeth. Though stagey in parts, the action moves swiftly as the story follows British loyalist Olivier trying to uncover an assassination plot on the queen, eventually being sent to Spain to impersonate a traitor. A young and vibrant Leigh plays one of the queen's ladies who is in love with Olivier. Both give sincere portrayals that hint at the greatness to come; though it is Robson as the willful, self-pitying but ever-commanding monarch who anchors the film. ★★★ VHS: $19.99

The Fire Within (Le Feu Follet)

(1963, 104 min, France, Louis Malle) *Maurice Ronet, Lena Skerla.* Stylish photography — perfectly capturing the "Swinging Paris" so familiar in the New Wave films of Godard, Truffaut and Rivette — is contrasted with an austere, melancholy account of a young man's final 48 hours in this, one of Malle's best works. Alain (Ronet), a handsome man of about thirty, is a recovering alcoholic about to release himself from a clinic. Disinterested in his former lifestyle as a bon vivant, and infused with an existential angst, he seeks out his friends in a dispirited attempt in finding some reason to live. A serious, somber drama of emptiness, regret and lost love. (French with English subtitles) ★★★½ VHS: $29.99

Firefox

(1982, 124 min, US, Clint Eastwood) *Clint Eastwood, Freddie Jones, Nigel Hawthorne.* Eastwood's lukewarm espionage thriller concerns a retired U.S. pilot who sneaks behind Russian lines to steal their latest MiG. The film is peppered with occasional sparks of high-flying action and, despite its plodding pace, provides some entertaining moments. ★★ DVD Letterbox: $14.99, VHS: $14.99

Firelight

(1998, 104 min, France/GB, William Nicholson) *Sophie Marceau, Stephen Dillane, Kevin Anderson, Joss Ackland, Lia Williams.* A predictable, barely fresh story of passion's power that manages to involve nonetheless. A Swiss woman, Elizabeth, is paid to bear a child for a secretive wealthy Englishman, Charles. Of course, during the fun part of their "transaction," sparks begin flying and they fall in love. However, circumstances dictate they must part, and the baby is shipped off. Seven years later, Elizabeth tracks her child — Louisa, a spoiled brat from hell whom Daddy merrily enables.

Elizabeth then becomes the child's governess, and soon old feelings are reignited. Though the script and direction are uncluttered, there's little grit or grime in the storytelling, which could have been used to avoid the Hallmarkesque atmosphere. An ultimately average period piece. ★★ VHS: $19.99

The Firemen's Ball

(1967, 73 min, Czechoslovakia, Milos Forman) *Vaclav Stockel, Josef Svet.* Forman aims his satiric wit at Slavic bureaucracy in this, one of his earliest films. The setting is a ball honoring an aged fire chief, but he is quickly forgotten and it gives way to a torrent of disasters, including one of the funniest and most wonderfully demoralizing beauty contests ever conceived. (Czech with English subtitles) ★★★ DVD Letterbox Criterion Collection: $29.99, VHS: $29.99

Fires on the Plain (Nobi)

(1959, 105 min, Japan, Kon Ichikawa) *Eiji Funakoshi, Osamu Takizawa.* This hard-hitting antiwar outcry revolves around the retreat of a group of Japanese soldiers in the Philippines during WWII. Hiding in the hills, the soldiers must resort to cannibalism in order to survive. A harrowing, depressing and graphic account of the horrors of war. (Japanese with English subtitles) ★★★ VHS: $29.99

Fires Within

(1991, 90 min, US, Gillian Armstrong) *Jimmy Smits, Greta Scacchi, Vincent D'Onofrio.* Smits and Scacchi score high marks based on sex-appeal quotient with this slow-moving though compelling romantic love triangle set against the backdrop of political imprisonment and social injustice. Having just been released from eight years of prison in Castro's Cuba, Smits joins his family in Miami only to find that his wife (Scacchi) has become involved with a local (D'Onofrio) and his young daughter cannot remember him. In his struggle to assimilate and win back his family's love, Smits finds he must choose between his new life and the old comrades of his homeland. ★★½ DVD Dual: $19.99, VHS: $14.99

Firestarter

(1984, 115 min, US, Mark Lester) *George C. Scott, Drew Barrymore, Martin Sheen, Louise Fletcher, Art Carney.* Scott and Barrymore strike sparks in this Stephen King horror story about a little girl who can induce a conflagration through mere thought. ★★½ VHS: $9.99

Firestorm

(1998, 89 min, US, Dean Semler) *Howie Long, Scott Glenn, Suzy Amis, William Forsythe.* Ex-NFL star Long plays a gung-ho firefighter who must battle a raging forest fire and the prison-breaking convicts who started it as a cover for their escape. After a hilariously idiotic opening rescue scene, *Firestorm* becomes *so* ludicrous that it ceases to be even unintentionally amusing. The action scenes are listless, the dialogue despicable, and the comic relief just plain sad. Long is akin to a live-action Dudley DoRight. ★ DVD: $9.99, VHS: $9.99

Fireworks (Hana-Bi)

(1998, 103 min, Japan, Takeshi Kitano) *Takeshi Kitano, Ren Osugi, Kayoko Kishimoto.* The Japanese cryptogram for "fireworks" contains the symbol for "flower" and the symbol for "fire"; creation and destruction, an apt metaphor for this action-packed chamber piece of three people searching for a "furious peace." While visiting his dying wife in the hospital, a tough detective (played with Rayband stoicism by writer-director Kitano) escapes an ambush of his partners by a gang of ruth-

less criminals. Now he must find justice and redemption for sins he did not commit yet haunt him still. By choosing to tell a tale as familiar as a Noh play, Kitano is free to concentrate on the characters, slowly revealing their scarred souls in an exhilarating, nonlinear fashion, letting images play off one another in a uniquely cinematic, pyrotechnic display. A bad-boy filmmaker/actor/comic/pop icon known as "Beat" in his native Japan, Kitano (who also helmed *Sonatine*) displays an uncanny ability to mix action, comedy and attitude; his film has style to spare. (Japanese with English subtitles) ★★★½ DVD: $29.99, VHS: $19.99

The Firm

(1993, 153 min, US, Sydney Pollack) *Tom Cruise, Gene Hackman, David Strathairn, Jeanne Tripplehorn, Holly Hunter, Ed Harris, Wilford Brimley, Hal Holbrook, Gary Busey.* In this exciting adaptation of John Grisham's best-selling novel of corporate intrigue, Cruise plays a Harvard law graduate who accepts a golden opportunity job with an upscale Memphis firm. However, Cruise soon learns all is not as it appears when the Orwellian company not only has a firm grasp on his life, but they may have even murdered employees. As this relentless thriller unfolds, Cruise finds himself caught between government agents and hired killers who are on his trail. *The Firm* is a constant source of pulse-pounding suspense, and benefits greatly from an outstanding ensemble cast. Hackman heads this group as a seasoned lawyer who takes Cruise under his wing, and the shimmering Hunter is a helpful and wily secretary. Director Pollack keeps the action at a brisk pace which belies the two-and-a-half-hour running time. ★★★½ DVD: $14.99

First Blood

(1982, 97 min, US, Ted Kotcheff) *Sylvester Stallone, Brian Dennehy, David Caruso, Richard Crenna.* The film that introduced Rambo. Stallone plays an ex-Green Beret who is falsely arrested by small town authorities (led by Dennehy); he exacts his revenge in particularly violent ways. Though it's not saying much, this mindless, violent actioner is the "best" of the trilogy. (Sequel: *Rambo: First Blood Pt. 2*) ★★ DVD Letterbox Special Edition: $14.99, VHS: $9.99, VHS Letterbox: $14.99

The First Deadly Sin

(1980, 112 min, US, Brian G. Hutton) *Frank Sinatra, Faye Dunaway, Brenda Vaccaro, David Dukes, James Whitmore.* Sinatra stars as a New York City police detective trying to uncover a serial killer while at the same time trying to cope with his wife's impending death. Dunaway plays his bed-ridden spouse. Too sluggish to be an interesting action film and too convoluted to be of interest as a thriller. ★★ DVD: $9.99, VHS: $9.99

. . . First Do No Harm

(1996, 94 min, US, Jim Abrahams) *Meryl Streep, Fred Ward, Seth Adkins.* A middle-class couple's (Streep, Ward) emotional and economic hardships when faced with the news that their youngest son has epilepsy is at the center of this earnest, moving made-for-TV drama. At first, the family is able to offer one another support and everything seems fine on the surface, but when Ward's health insurance is discontinued, tensions rise. While it occasionally conforms to its TV "disease of the week" roots, this is believable and well made, helped immeasurably by Ward, Streep and young Adkins as the young boy, whose realistic performance makes the seizures especially wrenching. An effectively somber yet hopeful drama. ★★★ DVD: $9.99, VHS: $19.99

First Family

(1980, 104 min, US, Buck Henry) *Bob Newhart, Madeline Kahn, Gilda Radner, Rip Torn, Julie Harris, Harvey Korman.* Henry wrote and directed this aimless political satire about a time in our not-too-distant future (perhaps even in your lifetime) when we have an ineffectual president (Newhart), with a dipsomaniac first lady (Kahn) and a promiscuous daughter (Radner), and his funny adventures with that ever-wacky Third World. ★★ VHS: $14.99

First Kid

(1996, 101 min, US, David Mickey) *Sinbad, Brock Pierce, Robert Guillaume, Timothy Busfield, James Naughton, Zachary Ty Bryan.* A mildly amusing family comedy, *First Kid* is sort of a *Guarding Tess* for the prepubescent set. Sinbad plays a Secret Service agent who wants to guard the president. But he's assigned to the Commander-in-Chief's bratty, trouble-making adolescent son instead. The film manages to produce a few laughs at the expense of Sinbad and his efforts to hide his charge's mischievous nature. But a lot of time is also spent on the youth's self-pitying, which would bore even its target audience. Sinbad and young Pierce have a pleasant rapport. ★★ DVD: $19.99, VHS: $9.99

First Knight

(1995, 132 min, US, Jerry Zucker) *Sean Connery, Richard Gere, Julia Ormond, Ben Cross, John Gielgud.* With *First Knight*, one actually gets two movies in one sitting. The first is the familiar though nicely played story of King Arthur (played with gusto by Connery) and his reign at Camelot. The second concentrates on the love story between Lancelot and Guinevere — and it's a preposterous one at that. Gere's Lancelot is a swaggering *Yankee in King Arthur's Court* who acts more like Fred Astaire pursuing Ginger Rogers than a man burnt by the embers of love. Set against an impressive evocative backdrop, it's still not quite enough to offset Gere's miscasting and a ludicrous screenplay. ★★½ DVD, VHS: $9.99

First Love

(1970, 90 min, GB, Maximilian Schell) *Maximilian Schell, Dominique Sanda, John Moulder-Brown.* Based on a story by Russian novelist Ivan Turgenev, this lyrical drama — photographed by Sven Nykvist — features a very attractive love interest in Sanda and Moulder-Brown. Set in a Russian dacha during the calm before World War I, the story involves a teenager's (Moulder-Brown) first love with the lovely yet bedeviling daughter of an impoverished and eccentric old woman who moves in next door. Our lovesick young man's attempts to capture her interest are thrown into confusion when he discovers that she is his father's mistress! The excitement, pain and mystery of young love are captured in this Barry Levinson-produced film. ★★★

First Love Last Rites

(1998, 94 min, US, Jesse Peretz) *Natasha Gregson Wagner, Giovanni Ribisi, Donal Logue, Robert John Burke.* Ribisi and Wagner are young lovers who, after some arousing sex scenes, start to finally learn about each other. And what could be more terrifying than learning that her dad is Robocop 3? *First Love Last Rites* attempts to build drama out of eel fishing, a mysterious rat, and a woman who has such winning lines as "You've got such long eyelashes; they remind me of my dog." At least she has good taste in music; a toy record player in her pad is always

spinning Shudder To Think 45s (until she boils them; don't ask). Wagner continues to prove that while beauty is inherited, talent is not. She gives blank readings to empty dialogue. Ribisi has something going on, however, from his nervous little laugh to his fleeting full frontal. Still, even when the chemistry is there, the distinct lack of significant events makes this a snoozer. ★★

First Men in the Moon

(1964, 103 min, GB, Nathan Juran) *Lionel Jeffries, Edward Judd, Martha Hyer.* Master stop-motion animator Ray Harryhausen adapts H.G. Wells' speculative novel to his own needs, adding lots of grasshopper-like moonmen, giant slug-cows and huge underground factories. Jeffries gives an amusing performance as the bumbling scientist, as does Judd as his unwilling compatriot. ★★★ DVD Letterbox: $24.99

First Name: Carmen

(1983, 87 min, France/Switzerland, Jean-Luc Godard) *Maruschka Detmers, Jacques Bonnaffe, Jean-Luc Godard.* This deconstructionist version of Merimee's classic tale finds Godard, loopy and pithy as ever, transforming the gypsy femme fatale into a filmmaker-cum-bank-robbing revolutionary whose politics aren't nearly as well developed as are her libidinal urges. Joseph is the befuddled bank guard who is captivated by her sexual charms in the midst of a botched heist. Offering his asides and snide observations is her uncle, a washed-up fraud of a film director named Jean-Luc Godard, played with understated conviction by Godard himself! (French with English subtitles) ★★★

The First Power

(1990, 99 min, US, Robert Resnikoff) *Lou Diamond Phillips, Tracy Griffith, Mykelti Williamson.* Lackluster horror film offers little in chills or originality as L.A. cop Phillips is up against the spirit of a recently executed murderer. ★ DVD Letterbox: $14.99

The First Wives Club

(1996, 102 min, US, Hugh Wilson) *Bette Midler, Goldie Hawn, Diane Keaton, Maggie Smith, Sarah Jessica Parker, Dan Hedaya, Stephen Collins, Victor Garber.* If Hell hath no fury like a woman scorned, then the three divas of comedy doth more than their fair share of fun in *The First Wives Club*, a funny, spirited romp that postulates that revenge is not only sweet but profitable. With not an ego in sight, Midler, Hawn and Keaton play former college roommates who are reunited after 25 years and form a bond (and later a company) to get even with their not-so-better halves. Based on Olivia Goldsmith's best-seller, the buoyant screenplay mixes physical comedy with sharp one-liners. But the real story here is the impeccable timing and teaming of Midler, Hawn and Keaton; singularly and together they ignite the film with sparkling energy and wit. ★★★ DVD: $14.99, VHS: $9.99

A Fish Called Wanda

(1988, 108 min, GB, Charles Crichton) *Kevin Kline, Jamie Lee Curtis, John Cleese, Michael Palin.* What happens when two scheming American jewel thieves join forces with a pair of double-crossing British thugs? All hell breaks loose, that's what. This slapdash, high-speed comedy is certainly one of the funniest films of the 1980s. Cleese is wonderful as an uptight barrister who inadvertently gets tangled in the mess. Palin has some very funny scenes as the bumbling, stuttering sidekick, and Curtis simply enchants as the manipulative American bombshell.

But the laurels go to Oscar winner Kline, who as Curtis' psychotic boyfriend ("Don't call me stupid") climbs all over the screen in one of the finest comic performances in years. A fabulously entertaining caper comedy featuring a wickedly funny running gag about some very unlucky dogs. (Sequel: *Fierce Creatures*) ★★★½ DVD: $14.99

The Fisher King

(1991, 138 min, US, Terry Gilliam) *Jeff Bridges, Robin Williams, Mercedes Ruehl, Amanda Plummer, Michael Jeter, David Hyde Pierce, Kathy Najimy, Harry Shearer, Tom Waits.* Gilliam's magical fable for modern times is an original and delightful masterwork complete with love, desperation and redemption. A hypnotic and exceptionally funny parable, the film stars Bridges as a hotshot D.J. whose world collapses when he feels responsible for a restaurant shooting. A few years later, he finds possible salvation in the form of street person Williams, a former professor whose wife was killed in the slayings. In a quest worthy of the Holy Grail, Bridges sets out to make amends for two of the lives touched by the tragedy. Williams gives one of his best performances: his manic, machine-gun comic delivery is much in evidence, of course, but never has the actor demonstrated such vulnerability and tenderness. Bridges, in a very subdued role, is equally impressive and Oscar-winner Ruehl is smashing as his lusty girlfriend. ★★★★ DVD: $14.99

A Fistful of Dollars

(1964, 96 min, Italy, Sergio Leone) *Clint Eastwood, Gian Marie Volante.* The first of Leone's "spaghetti westerns" is an exciting and entertaining working of Kurosawa's *Yojimbo*. Eastwood became a star thanks to his role as the "Man with No Name," a mysterious stranger who gets involved in a feud between two rival families. ★★★ DVD: $14.99

A Fistful of Dynamite

(1971, 138 min, Italy, Sergio Leone) *James Coburn, Rod Steiger, Romolo Valli.* Coburn stars in this high-voltage war adventure as an Irish terrorist who hooks up with peasant Steiger during the Mexican Revolution. (aka: *Duck You Sucker*) ★★★

Fitzcarraldo

(1982, 157 min, West Germany, Werner Herzog) *Klaus Kinski, Claudia Cardinale.* Herzog chronicles the bizarre history of a strong-willed visionary whose dream is to construct an opera house in the heart of the Peruvian jungle. A beguiling tale laced with the director's usual dose of mysticism and madness and featuring yet another appropriately lunatic performance by Herzog favorite Kinski in the title role. ★★★★ DVD: $34.99

Five Card Stud

(1968, 103 min, US, Henry Hathaway) *Robert Mitchum, Dean Martin, Inger Stevens, Roddy McDowall.* A tame western adventure with Martin as a gunslinger (and part-time gambler) investigating the murders of the members of a lynch gang. ★★ DVD Letterbox: $14.99, VHS: $9.99

Five Corners

(1988, 98 min, US, Tony Bill) *Tim Robbins, Jodie Foster, John Turturro, Elizabeth Berridge, Todd Graff.* With plot developments as capricious as life itself, this story of five teenagers living in the Bronx in 1964 is writer John Patrick Shanley's follow-up to *Moonstruck*. Turturro gives a stand-out performance as a psychotic ex-con whose infatuation with Foster leads to an evening of tragedy. ★★★ VHS: $14.99

Five Days One Summer

(1983, 108 min, US, Fred Zinnemann) *Sean Connery, Betsy Brantley.* Connery plays a middle-aged doctor vacationing in a remote Swiss village in the early 1930s. There, he is accompanied by a young woman (Brantley) who is posing as his wife. However, as their relationship is explored, their dark secrets soon surface. This soap opera is set at a lethargic pace, and even Connery can't make you feel for the characters' plight. ★★ VHS: $14.99

Five Easy Pieces

(1970, 98 min, US, Bob Rafelson) *Jack Nicholson, Karen Black, Lois Smith, Susan Anspach.* This fascinating character study follows an aimless drifter who abandons the accoutrements of middle-class existence (and a promising musical career) for a life on the road spent amongst the squalor of cheap bars and shabby motels. Nicholson gives a virtuoso, career-making performance, and Black and especially Smith as Nicholson's sister are outstanding in support. ★★★★ DVD: $14.99

Five Fingers

(1952, 108 min, US, Joseph L. Mankiewicz) *James Mason, Michael Rennie, Danielle Darrieux.* The allegedly true story of how the Nazis came upon the plans for the Allied's Normandy invasion makes for a riveting and witty spy story that forgoes cloak and dagger in favor of an intelligent character study. Mason is excellent as the suave valet to a high-ranking British diplomat who finances his planned retirement by selling secrets to the Germans. Rennie is the agent on his trail. A complex tale of espionage that explores class differences as well, *Five Fingers* has not one but two great twists at its exciting finale. ★★★★ VHS: $19.99

Five Fingers of Death

(1973, 105 min, Hong Kong, Cheng Chang Ho) *Lo Lieh.* The film that opened the floodgates of the martial arts/kung fu flicks that became popular in the 1970s comes complete with gravity-defying fight scenes, the usual vengeance plot and the inept dubbing that will make you wonder if the voices were borrowed from a 1960s Hercules film. Great fun, and one of the best of the genre. ★★★ VHS Letterbox: $19.99

Five Graves to Cairo

(1943, 96 min, US, Billy Wilder) *Franchot Tone, Anne Baxter, Akim Tamiroff, Erich Von Stroheim.* With a wit and style usually not associated with WWII dramas, director Wilder has crafted a suspenseful espionage tale that is at once taut and relaxed. Tone stars as a British corporal who is stranded in the North African desert. Stumbling upon a hotel run by Tamiroff and Baxter, he is forced to impersonate a German agent when Field Marshal Rommel arrives in his push towards Cairo. Von Stroheim ably plays Rommel as a blustery, egocentric militarist. Tone is quite affable as an ordinary man thrust into danger — he would have been quite at home in *The 39 Steps* or *The Lady Vanishes*. ★★★½

The Five Heartbeats

(1991, 122 min, US, Robert Townsend) *Robert Townsend, Michael Wright, Tico Wells, Diahann Carroll.* Townsend's flavorful but uneven musical drama is about the rise and fall of a black singing group in the 1960s. Townsend, who wrote the screenplay with Keenan Ivory Wayans, plays the group's leader and songwriter, who takes The Five Heartbeats from obscurity to stardom. There are many fine moments, especially the musical sequences, which have an indestructible energy; but some of the film's dramatic scenes are heavy-handed and border on music industry cliché. ★★½ DVD Letterbox: $14.99, VHS: $6.99

The 5,000 Fingers of Dr. T

(1953, 88 min, US, Roy Rowland) *Peter Lind Hayes, Hans Conreid.* Dr. Seuss wrote this imaginative and unusual children's entertainment about a young boy (Hayes) who fantasizes that his piano teacher (Conreid) is really the diabolical Dr. T., who kidnaps and imprisons youths, forcing them to participate in daily piano rehearsals. Clever set designs, wild choreography and an abundance of youthful escapades make this curiosity all the more intriguing. ★★★ DVD: $24.99, VHS: $14.99

The Fixer

(1968, 132 min, GB, John Frankenheimer) *Alan Bates, Dirk Bogarde, David Warner, Georgia Brown, Ian Holm, Hugh Griffith.* In an Oscar nominated role, Bates is extraordinary as Yakov Bok, a Jewish handyman living in early 20th-century Russia. Based on the Pulitzer Prize-winning novel by Bernard Malamund, the film explores anti-Semitism in Czarist Russia as Bok is wrongly accused and imprisoned for brutally killing a child. An intense story of the endurance and triumpg of the human spirit. ★★★½

The Flamingo Kid

(1984, 98 min, US, Garry Marshall) *Matt Dillon, Hector Elizondo, Richard Crenna, Jessica Walter.* Dillon is well cast in this endearing teen comedy about a Brooklyn high school grad who takes a summer job at an exclusive Long Island club. The film abandons the usual sex-obsessed hijinks of most teen comedies, opting instead for a surprisingly sweet reminiscence of the times. An excellent supporting cast includes Elizondo as Dillon's dad, Walter as a snobbish patron, and, in a dynamic performance, Crenna as an unscrupulous car salesman whose influence on the naive Dillon proves to be an eye-opener. ★★★ DVD: $14.99, VHS: $14.99

Flamingo Road

(1949, 94 min, US, Michael Curtiz) *Joan Crawford, Zachary Scott, Sydney Greenstreet.* Crawford gives one of her better performances in this highly entertaining melodrama that skewers small-town Americana and the political process. Crawford plays a carnival dancer who becomes stranded in Smalltown, USA. There, she falls in love with the town deputy (Scott), but the sheriff and town boss (the ever-evil Greenstreet) have other ideas. When the latter frames Joan and sends her to prison, it's get-even time when Joan is released. Crawford suffers gallantly, and is ever-ready with the next witty barb. ★★★ VHS: $19.99

Flash Gordon

(1980, 110 min, US, Mike Hodges) *Sam J. Jones, Max von Sydow, Topol, Timothy Dalton, Mariangelo Melato, Ornella Muti, Brian Blessed.* Though this updated sci-fi adventure failed to set a spark at the box office, it's a guaranteed fun ride as football hero Flash Gordon (Jones) and reporter Dale Arden (Anderson) travel to the planet Mongo with Dr. Zarkov (Topol) to stop the destruction of Earth at the hands of evil emperor Ming (the Merciless, that is), played with great relish by von Sydow. Features splendid sets and costumes, good special effects and a wonderful comic touch to the action. Score by Queen. ★★★ VHS: $9.99

A Flash of Green

(1985, 122 min, US, Victor Nunez) *Ed Harris, Blair Brown, Richard Jordan, John Glover.* In this compassionate tale of corruption and greed, an investigative journalist (Harris) becomes involved in a local real estate dispute between a corrupt politician and a homeowner. ★★★

Flashback

(1990, 108 min, US, Franco Amurri) *Dennis Hopper, Kiefer Sutherland, Carol Kane, Richard Masur.* Hopper makes the most of his role as a '60s fugitive captured by the FBI in this slight comedy. It's Hopper's show all the way, actually, playing an Abbie Hoffman-like radical who is being transported by uptight agent Sutherland. It's sort of a poor man's *Midnight Run* with a political flavor as Hopper continually outwits his guardian till each discovers a respect for the other. ★★½ DVD Letterbox: $14.99, VHS: $14.99

Flashdance

(1983, 96 min, US, Adrian Lyne) *Jennifer Beals, Michael Nouri, Belinda Bauer, Lilia Skala.* Gnash your teeth if you will, but there's no denying this film's impact on Hollywood and pop culture (not to mention the welding industry). You certainly didn't find torn sweatshirts at Bloomie's before. In spite of its stilted plot, *Flashdance* is a viscerally entertaining musical with imaginative dance routines and a pulsating score. C'mon now, "What a feeling . . ." ★★ DVD Letterbox: $14.99, VHS: $9.99

Flatliners

(1990, 105 min, US, Joel Schumacher) *Julia Roberts, Kiefer Sutherland, Kevin Bacon, William Baldwin, Oliver Platt, Kimberly Scott.* This psychological thriller, about a group of medical students who embark on a series of other-worldly experiments, brims with a dark sense of dread and classic horror. Sutherland is ideally cast as an intern who dreams up the idea of killing himself so that his fellow classmates can bring him back to life — thereby experiencing death. One by one, they go under, for longer and longer periods, but as they return from death, these modern-day Frankensteins find that they don't always return alone. Filled with psychological underpinnings, *Flatliners* is as much about healing childhood wounds as it is a horror film. ★★★ DVD: $14.99, VHS: $12.99

Max von Sydow (l.) is Ming the Merciless in 1980's *Flash Gordon*

The Flavor of Corn

(1991, 93 min, Italy, Gianni da Campo) *Marco Mestriner, Lorenzo Lena.* Similar in theme to the more explicit Dutch film *For a Lost Soldier*, this tender drama of friendship and enveloping love between a teacher and a 12-year-old boy is hampered by amateurish acting and an overly serious tone. University student Lorenzo (Lena) travels to a rural region of northern Italy for his first teaching assignment. He discovers that one of his pupils, Duilio (Mestriner), is in "puppy love" with him. They become friends, and after Lorenzo breaks up with his girlfriend, he considers a sexual attraction to the youth. A surprisingly tasteful, restrained and bittersweet tale of first love and the internal conflict of accepting one's sexual feelings. (Italian with English subtitles) ★★½ VHS: $59.99

Flawless

(1999, 110 min, US, Joel Schumacher) *Robert De Niro, Philip Seymour Hoffman, Barry Miller, Joey Arias, Jackie Beat.* *Flawless* might be better titled *Shameless*, for its story rips off *Outrageous!* and *The Queen*. Director Schumacher takes a true incident that happened to a friend of his and turns it into a second-rate melodrama, complete with stereotypes and ridiculous subplot. De Niro is Walt, a retired security guard living in the same rundown East Village building as Rusty, a flamboyant drag queen. When Walt suffers a stroke that partially paralyzes his speech, he takes singing lessons from Rusty to strengthen his vocal cords. As expertly played by Hoffman, Rusty is a larger-than-life, line-quoting, all-out drag queen who doesn't seem to stop "being on" for a minute. But his performance isn't quite enough to compensate for all the clichés, misguided sincerity and the eventual tacky run-in with small-time crooks. ★★ DVD: $14.99

Fled

(1996, 98 min, US, Kevin Hooks) *Laurence Fishburne, Stephen Baldwin, Will Patton, Salma Hayek, Robert Hooks.* A low-rent knock-off of *The Defiant Ones*, *Fled* pits a black man and a white man against each other, both of whom are escaped convicts and handcuffed together. But wait — this isn't an old boring examination of moral conflict or a complex story of two men grappling with prejudice and inner pain. This is an action movie. Set in the high-tech '90s. Where computer software replaces human interest. Fishburne is saddled with dopey Baldwin, together fleeing police and mysterious underworld figures on their trail. They bicker, they argue, they fight, they fall down a lot — they do everything but walk into the sunset together. ★★ DVD: $14.99

Flesh

(1968, 89 min, US, Paul Morrissey) *Joe Dallesandro, Candy Darling, Jackie Curtis, Patti D'Arbanville, Maurice Braddell.* A true artifact of the '60s sexual revolution as well as a great example of the quirky New York independent filmmaking that came out of the Warhol film factory. The film is an homage to the personality and body (with the emphasis on body) of Dallesandro. The plot is simply a day-in-the-life of gay hustler Joe who utters immortal lines such as, "How am I going to make any money without clean underwear!" The story is told in vignettes and features old Warholian favorites Darling and Curtis. There are priceless drug-induced dialogues throughout including the great philosophical thought, "The more you learn the more depressed you get." ★★★

Flesh & Blood

(1985, 126 min, Netherlands, Paul Verhoeven) *Rutger Hauer, Jennifer Jason Leigh, Tom Burlinson, Susan Tyrrell, Jack Thompson, Bruno Kirby.* Given a big budget for the first time, Verhoeven weaves a colorful, erotic and gritty story of a ragtag group of mercenary soldiers during Europe's feudal wars. This rowdy adventure tale lives up to its title and fascinates us with battles at castle gates, treacherous kings and princesses in distress. Don't miss this one. (Filmed in English) ★★★½ DVD: $14.99

Flesh and Bone

(1993, 124 min, US, Steve Kloves) *Gwyneth Paltrow, Meg Ryan, James Caan, Dennis Quaid, Scott Wilson.* From its intense opening sequence to its haunting end, *Flesh and Bone* manages to be stylish and suspenseful without being flashy or shocking. Quaid is mesmerizing as a lonely Texas vending-machine supplier whose dark past suddenly sneaks up on him. As in his first film, *The Fabulous Baker Boys*, writer-director Kloves frames his eye just below the surface of the ordinary to reveal secret things we wish we hadn't seen. Paltrow gives a delightfully droll and dangerous performance. ★★★ DVD: $14.99

Flesh and the Devil

(1926, 95 min, US, Clarence Brown) *Greta Garbo, John Gilbert, Lars Hanson.* Garbo gives a seductive performance in her first American film as a beautiful schemer who comes between lifelong friends Gilbert and Hanson. Garbo and Gilbert are an inspired romantic duo. ★★½

Flesh for Frankenstein

See: *Andy Warhol's Frankenstein*

Flesh Gordon

(1974, 90 min, US, Howard Ziehm & Michael Benveniste) *Jason Williams, Suzanne Fields, Joseph Hudgins, William Hunt, John Hoyt.* Flesh and his companions Prince Precious and Dr. Jerkoff explore the inner and outer regions of space. Late-nite cult fun that parodies the story's sci-fi origins, and includes lots of sex and cheesy sets and F/X. ★★ DVD: $29.99, VHS: $29.99

Fletch

(1985, 98 min, US, Michael Ritchie) *Chevy Chase, Tim Matheson, Geena Davis, M. Emmet Walsh, George Wendt.* This may be Chase's funniest screen comedy. Chevy plays an investigative reporter who, while undercover, is offered $50,000 by a millionaire (Matheson) to murder him. Plenty of sharp dialogue and Chase is very funny. (Sequel: *Fletch Lives*) ★★★

Fletch Lives

(1989, 95 min, US, Michael Ritchie) *Chevy Chase, Hal Holbrook, Cleavon Little, R. Lee Ermey.* In this surprisingly funny sequel, Chase returns as the glib, wisecracking reporter Fletch who here travels to the heart of Dixie when he inherits an old Southern mansion. There, he quickly becomes involved with the Klan, toxic waste, a TV evangelist, and murder. Chase can deliver a put-down with the best of them, and his impersonations of an array of characters are quite amusing. ★★★ DVD Letterbox: $19.99

A Flight of Rainbirds

(1981, 94 min, Netherlands, Ate de Jong) *Jeroen Krabbé.* From the director of *Drop Dead Fred* and *Highway to Hell* comes this seriocomedy about love, sex and religion. Reportedly one of the highest grossing films in Dutch history, *A Flight of Rainbirds* stars Krabbé in dual roles. In one, he is a timid and repressed scientist who one night dreams that he must lose his virginity in seven days or die. His more debonair alter ego is hence forced to come to the rescue. (Dutch with English subtitles) ★★½ VHS: $29.99

Flight of the Dragons

(1992, 98 min, US, Arthur Rankin Jr. & Jules Bass) *James Earl Jones, John Ritter, Harry Morgan.* Four wizard brothers in the time of King Arthur band together to preserve the disappearing world of magic. Although they are aided by dragons, knights, and even a man from the 20th century, they are thwarted by one of the evil brothers who sees this as an opportunity to take all of the magic for his own malevolent purposes. While the voices add solidity, the animation's poor quality pulls the production down. ★★½

The Flight of the Eagle

(1982, 139 min, Sweden, Jan Troell) *Max von Sydow, Goran Stangertz.* This Swedish epic by Troell chronicles the brave but foolhardy trek of several men who attempt a balloon mission to the North Pole in 1897. Von Sydow heads the group who are stranded in the frozen North and are confronted with eerie silence and the very real possibility that they will not survive. A gripping existential drama. (Swedish with English subtitles) ★★★

Flight of the Innocent

(1993, 105 min, Italy, Carlo Carlei) *Manuci Colao, Francesca Neri.* When a loving 10-year-old boy witnesses the murder of his entire gangster family by a rival crime syndicate, the stage is set for this edge-of-your-seat, run-for-your-life thriller that marks the auspicious debut of director Carlei. While inarguably the best foreign actioner to come out of Europe since *La Femme Nikita*, the film also merits strong praise as an art film for its masterful juxtaposition of gorgeous dreamlike imagery with scenes of horrendous violence reminiscent of Peckinpah at his peak. Young Colao gives a striking performance as the boy evading both the mob and the police. (Italian with English subtitles) ★★★★ DVD: $19.99

Flight of the Intruder

(1991, 114 min, US, John Milius) *Danny Glover, Willem Dafoe, Brad Johnson, Rosanna Arquette, Tom Sizemore.* Vietnam War adventure film with Glover as a Navy commander saddled with hot-shot pilots Johnson and Dafoe, who disobey orders and fight the enemy in the way they think they should be fought. Plays like a right-wing fantasy, and a boring one, at that. ★ DVD: $14.99, VHS: $14.99

Flight of the Navigator

(1986, 90 min, US, Randal Kleiser) *Veronica Cartwright, Joey Cramer, Cliff De Young, Voice of: Paul Reubens.* Enjoyable if lightweight science-fiction tale about a 12-year-old boy (Cramer) who is kidnapped by an alien spacecraft and accidentally returned — unchanged — eight years later. ★★½ DVD: $19.99

The Flight of the Phoenix

(1965, 147 min, US, Robert Aldrich) *James Stewart, Richard Attenborough, Peter Finch, Ian Bannen, Hardy Kruger, Ernest Borgnine.* First-rate adventure film about a group of plane crash survivors stranded in the Sahara Desert. Stewart heads a good cast. ★★★½ DVD: $14.99

The Flintstones

(1994, 92 min, US, Brian Levant) *John Goodman, Rick Moranis, Rosie O'Donnell, Elizabeth Perkins, Kyle MacLachlan, Elizabeth Taylor.* With as much about it to like as to dislike, *The Flintstones* is an appropriately cartoonish live-action version of the adored 1960s animated TV series. Featuring some neat special effects, playful performances and a less-than-beguiling script, the film is aided nicely by the near-perfect casting of Goodman and Perkins as Fred and Wilma, and Moranis and O'Donnell as Barney and Betty. The sluggish story has to do with Fred being promoted and used as a patsy by his devious supervisor. Sad to say, some of the TV episodes had more humor. ★★½ DVD DTS sound: $19.99, VHS: $9.99

The Flintstones in Viva Rock Vegas

(2000, 91 min, US, Brian Levant) *Mark Addy, Alan Cumming, Stephen Baldwin, Kristen Johnston, Thomas Gibson, Jane Krakowski, Harvey Korman, Joan Collins.* They may be a modern stone-age family, but the dialogue Fred and Wilma, Barney and Betty are forced to recite is old hat indeed. In this prequel, the story follows the adventures of a younger, unmarried Fred and company as they meet and fall in love with their soon-to-be spouses. Addy is an able Fred, playing him more like Ralph Kramden, which is okay because he was the inspiration for Fred, anyway. Barney is played by a limber Baldwin, who actually moves like a cartoon character. But the screenplay works against the fun the entire cast tries to have. ★★ DVD: $24.99, VHS: $14.99

Flipper

(1963, 90 min, US, James Clark) *Chuck Connors, Luke Halpin.* Irresistible to children, this charming family film became the basis of the popular TV series. A fast bond develops between young Luke and Flipper after the boy saves the dolphin's life. ★★½ VHS: $14.99

Flipper

(1996, 96 min, US, Alan Shapiro) *Paul Hogan, Elijah Wood, Chelsea Field, Jonathan Banks, Isaac Hayes.* Originally a feature film in 1963, then a popular TV series, the story of a boy and his dolphin is back in this updated, benign family adventure. No longer a tale of a father and his sons, this time a young divorce orphan spends a summer with his bohemian uncle on a remote Caribbean island. It is here he befriends Flipper, who has lost his mate due to an evil fisherman. Of course, Flipper helps in exposing him, and makes new friends in the process. The underwater sequences of *Flipper* are rather impressive, and the locales are beautiful. ★★½ DVD Letterbox: $14.99, VHS: $9.99

Flipping

(1997, 102 min, US, Gene Mitchell) *Keith David, David Proval, David Amos, Gene Mitchell.* This Tarantino-inspired crime drama treads some very familiar (and some surprisingly original) ground in its telling of a gang of criminals who go on a bloody rampage. Square-jawed Mike (Amos) is a deceptively quiet thug who decides to take over control of

a small-time syndicate lorded over by an alternately sadistic and fatherly Leo (David). There's loads of killings, some good dialogue and even occasional humor, but what makes this tale especially unusual is the gay subplot between the good-looking Mike and an undercover cop (Proval). ★★★ VHS: $7.99

Flirt

(1995, 85 min, US, Hal Hartley) *Bill Sage, Michael Imperioli, William Sage, Parker Posey, Martin Donovan, Dwight Ewell, Miho Nikaidoh.* Hartley tells a short story of a love affair at the brink of commitment. He tells it three times, in three cities with three casts, using much of the same dialogue each time. In each retelling, there's a gun and a defining moment, changing one protagonist's life unalterably. And yet, it's a commonplace occurrence, whether in New York or Berlin or Tokyo. The repetition, across cultural boundaries, across issues of sexual orientation and class identity, serves to emphasize the story's universality. Daffy and romantic, *Flirt* is about love's pain and exaltation, its nature as solid as a rock and as ephemeral as happiness; it's also about flirting and flirting's role in human relations. Godardian in nature, *Flirt* is an energetic delight, filled with wry observance and urbane compassion. ★★★

Flirtation Walk

(1934, 98 min, US, Frank Borzage) *Dick Powell, Ruby Keeler, Pat O'Brien.* With more in common with *This Is the Army* than *42nd Street*, this cornball musical is a singing Armed Forces advertisement for a peacetime America. Powell plays a flip Army private who falls for the general's daughter, the non-dancing Keeler. Powell's repartee and most of the comedy are passable, but when buddy O'Brien starts crying amid an extended military parade, it's all too much. ★★½ VHS: $19.99

Flirting

(1990, 100 min, Australia, John Duigan) *Noah Taylor, Thandie Newton, Nicole Kidman.* Director Duigan's follow-up to *The Year My Voice Broke* is one of those purely delightful cinematic surprises — an insightful, intelligent and superbly crafted tale of coming-of-age. Set in early 1960s Australia, the story follows Danny Embling, a pimply-faced youth with leftist leanings and a commanding intellect who is suffering through his time at a posh, all-boys boarding school. Scandal ensues when he becomes involved with Thandiwe Adjewa, a Ugandan student (whose father is fleeing the regime of Idi Amin) from the sister school across the lake. Kidman is solid in support as a bitchy student who tries, at first, to sabotage their relationship. Filled with humor, mirth and unwavering humanism, *Flirting* is a small gem of a movie. ★★★★ DVD Letterbox: $19.99

Flirting with Disaster

(1996, 92 min, US, David O. Russell) *Ben Stiller, Patricia Arquette, Téa Leoni, Mary Tyler Moore, George Segal, Lily Tomlin, Alan Alda, Josh Brolin, Richard Jenkins.* A relentlessly funny film about a young couple who set out on a cross-country drive in search of a name for their new baby. The trouble begins when Stiller (an adoptee) becomes obsessed with finding his birth parents before bestowing his newborn son with an appelation. In steps Leoni, a long-legged, ravishing and slightly batty psychology student who's sent by the adoption agency to help him in his search. Along the way several uproarious blunders and mistaken identities are made and Stiller and Leoni do a little of their own "flirting with disaster." Into the mix are thrown a pair of federal

agents, one of whom happens to be Arquette's former boyfriend, and the sexual hijinks really begin to heat up. Hilarious supporting work comes from Moore and Segal as Stiller's adoptive parents and Alda and Tomlin as his real ones. As written and directed by Russell, the film is a rollicking, quixotic journey that unleashes a barrage of side-splitting gags and awkward situations, culminating in a mind-bending denouement that will warm the cockles of any ex-hippie's heart. ★★★★ DVD: $19.99

The Florentine

(1999, 104 min, US, Nick Stagliano) *Michael Madsen, Hal Holbrook, Virginia Madsen, Tom Sizemore, Mary Stuart Masterson, Luke Perry, James Belushi.* The day-to-day dramas of a handful of friends in a dying steel town are trotted out in this cliché-ridden film, executive produced by Francis Ford Coppola. M. Madsen is Whitey, owner of the local hangout bar, the Florentine, whose sister (real-life sister Virginia) is to be married in a few days. Things get "complicated" when Virginia's old flame returns to town. A game cast and nice location work (in and around the Lehigh Valley in Pennsylvania) almost compensate for a deadeningly familiar, artificial script. ★★ VHS: $94.99

A Florida Enchantment

(1914, 64 min, US, Sidney Drew) *Edith Storey.* Considered one of the earliest films to feature ambiguous sexual attraction, this cross-dressing comedy, based on an 1896 Broadway play, is set at an elegant Florida resort. A young woman (Storey), frustrated at her fiancé's philandering, ingests magic seeds from the African Tree of Sexual Change which quickly transforms women into men and vice versa. While she remains feminine looking, she immediately assumes the behavior of a man. The seeds ultimately fall into the hands of her former fiancé, who becomes an effeminate female in a male body. An ahead-of-its-time comedy that humorously explores men and women's sexual roles. ★★★ VHS: $39.99

Floundering

(1994, 97 min, US, Peter McCarthy) *James LeGros, John Cusack, Ethan Hawke, Lisa Zane, Steve Buscemi, Jeremy Piven, Viggo Mortensen, Alex Cox.* McCarthy, who produced *Repo Man* and *Sid & Nancy*, makes his directorial debut with this umpteenth "Generation X" comedy which plays like "This Is Your Life." Set in the seedy surroundings of Venice Beach, California, the film stars LeGros as John Boyz, a twentysomething slacker who aimlessly wanders the streets of Venice. As friends pretentiously philosophize the meaning of their existence, the possibility of a plot rears its ugly head — John's failing attempts to find work. The film has some very funny moments, especially the cameos by Cusack and Buscemi. But the generic screenplay is hit-or-miss, turning the film into a series of vignettes rather than a full-length feature. ★★

Flower Drum Song

(1961, 133 min, US, Henry Koster) *Nancy Kwan, James Shigeta, Jack Soo, Miyoshi Umeki, Juanita Hall.* Though not one of Rodgers and Hammerstein's best musicals, this pleasant adaptation of their Broadway show manages to capture some lightheartedness and whimsical spirits. It's a tale about the conflict of old and new traditions in San Francisco's Chinatown district. The score's best songs include "I Enjoy Being a Girl" and "A Hundred Million Miracles." ★★½

The Flower of My Secret

The Flower of My Secret

(1995, 105 min, Spain, Pedro Almodóvar) *Marisa Paredes, Juan Echanove, Chus Lampreave, Rossy De Palma, Joaquin Cortes.* Almodóvar continues his fascination with women on the verge in this uncharacteristically serious, even somber tale of lost love. The gorgeous and wealthy Leo (Paredes), a disenchanted writer of trash romance novels, is in the midst of the painful dissolution of her marriage. To make matters worse, her best friend is having an affair with Leo's husband; and her mother and sister — played with true familial tragicomedy by Lampreave and De Palma — are perennially at each other's throats. Needing a change in her life, Leo becomes a literary critic, but under a pseudonym. Her first assignment: do a negative review of her most recent novel. While short on a coherent plot, the characters are engaging, as Almodóvar takes a more mature approach to love and the lack of it. (Spanish with English subtitles) ★★½

Flowers in the Attic

(1987, 95 min, US, Jeffrey Bloom) *Louise Fletcher, Victoria Tennant, Kristy Swanson.* Four children are brought by their mother to stay at their grandmother's and are locked in the attic, presumably not to be let out again. The best-selling novel is given a flat screen translation, and the drab performances of Tennant and Fletcher (who can be tremendous in these types of roles) dampen an already preposterous film. ★ DVD: $24.99, VHS: $14.99

Flubber

(1997, 93 min, US, Les Mayfield) *Robin Williams, Marcia Gay Harden, Christopher McDonald, Clancy Brown, Ted Levine, Wil Wheaton.* Disney updates another one of its comedies, this time the popular 1961 film *The Absent-Minded Professor.* Like the original, it's about a scientist who invents flubber — flying rubber. Taking over the Fred MacMurray role with considerable comedic splash is Williams, who is able to somewhat control his manic personality. Unfortunately, the writers haven't given him too much to do, and ultimately *Flubber* is no more than an occasionally amusing family comedy which lets down throughout. ★★½ DVD: $19.99, VHS: $9.99

The Fluffer

(2001, 95 min, US, Richard Glatzer & Wash West) *Scott Gurney, Michael Cunio, Roxanne Day, Debbie Harry, Guinevere Turner, Robert Walden, Chi Chi LaRue.* Sexy without being nasty, provocative but not shocking and topped off with a healthy dose of cynicism, *The Fluffer* is a low-budget surprise set amid the underbelly of the gay porn industry. Sean (Cunio) has been renting the classics and by error gets *Citizen Cum* instead of *Citizen Kane.* The film's star is Johnny Rebel (Gurney), a hot "gay for pay" porn star with drug, relationship and stability problems. Sean becomes so smitten with Johnny that he applies for work at the film's studio, Men of Janus. He's hired as Johnny's fluffer (one who performs oral sex so that the porn performer is hard on camera), becoming more enamored with Johnny, whose life is spiraling out of control. Non-sexually explicit, this is director West's first non-adult film, a loopy tale of obsession that manages to illustrate the allure of the porn business while telling a fairly difficult tale of obsession. ★★★ DVD Letterbox Unrated: $24.99, VHS Unrated: $19.99

Fluke

(1995, 96 min, US, Carlo Carlei) *Matthew Modine, Nancy Travis, Eric Stoltz, Max Pomeranc, Samuel L. Jackson.* Modine dies in the first scene in a fiery car crash and, in a bizarre twist on *Ghost* and *The Incredible Journey,* is reincarnated — as a puppy. After befriending a bag lady (who names him Fluke), he finds a mentor in a big old mutt named Rumpo. Life goes on for Fluke, but he is continually haunted by thoughts of his former wife (Travis) and son (Pomeranc) and by some foreboding evil that seems linked to his former business partner (Stoltz). At times supremely silly, the film straddles the line, with varying degrees of success, between kid's fantasy comedy and adult melodrama. Still, it's all such feel-good fun, you can't help but like it. Jackson gives a goofy and garrulous turn as the voice of the streetwise Rumpo. ★★½ DVD: $14.99, VHS: $9.99

The Fly

(1958, 94 min, US, Kurt Neumann) *Vincent Price, Al (David) Hedison, Herbert Marshall, Patricia Owens.* Perhaps the ultimate sci-fi shocker of its day, Hedison stars as a scientist whose matter transference experiments go horribly awry when he accidentally integrates his own gene patterns with those of a common housefly. Contains the famous spider scene ("Help me, help me"). Screenplay by "Shogun" author James Clavell. (Remade in 1986) ★★★ DVD: $19.99, VHS: $9.99

The Fly

(1986, 96 min, US, David Cronenberg) *Jeff Goldblum, Geena Davis, John Getz.* Cronenberg's remake of the 1958 semiclassic is a terrifying thriller highlighted by both Goldblum's virtuoso performance as the scientist experiencing a metamorphosis and incredible makeup effects. An intense and gory horror film, and not for everyone. (Sequel: *The Fly II*) ★★★½ DVD: $14.99, VHS: $9.99

Fly Away Home

(1996, 105 min, US, Carroll Ballard) *Jeff Daniels, Anna Paquin, Dana Delany, Terry Kinney.* After her mother is killed in an auto accident, a 13-year-old Australian girl (Paquin) is sent to Canada to live with her estranged father (Daniels), an eccentric inventor. What follows is an uplifting and endearing family drama that celebrates life and its wayward souls. The story has to do with Paquin raising a family of orphaned geese who think the youngster is their mother. When they are threatened with possible captivity or worse, father and daughter devise an improbable plan to allow the domesticated geese to migrate over a thousand miles away. Probably the most skilled and enjoyable non-Disney family film since *Babe,* *Fly Away Home* is enhanced by extraordinary cinematography and a lovely score. A genuinely satisfying family film. ★★★½ DVD Special Edition: $14.99

The Flying Deuces

(1939, 67 min, US, Edward Sutherland) *Stan Laurel, Oliver Hardy.* Funny Laurel and Hardy feature with Stan and Ollie joining the French Foreign Legion to forget Ollie's ill-fated romance. ★★★ VHS: $9.99

Flying Down to Rio

(1933, 89 min, US, Thornton Freeland) *Delores Del Rio, Gene Raymond, Fred Astaire, Ginger Rogers, Eric Blore, Franklin Pangborn.* The film that first paired Astaire and Rogers. Del Rio and Raymond are the stars in this lively tuner about a dance band in Rio. Fred and Ginger's dancing is tops, and there's a knockout of a finale with chorines dancing on the wings of a moving plane. ★★★ VHS: $14.99

Focus

(2001, 106 min, US, Neal Slavin) *Laura Dern, William H. Macy, Meat Loaf Aday, David Paymer.* In his first novel, published in 1945, Arthur Miller addressed anti-Semitism in an era of rampant bigotry. Adapted for the screen in the time of 9/11, when American Muslims became the targets of indiscriminate prejudice, *Focus* would give the impression to be topical and timely. But this sincere, subtle though one-note film fails to fully ignite the passions about such an incendiary subject. Macy gives a splendid performance as Lawrence Newman, a reserved bachelor living in 1940s Brooklyn. His own experiences with prejudice begin when he is ordered not to hire Jews at the company where he is personnel director. His life takes a turn for the worse when, after getting new glasses that make him look "too Jewish," he loses his job and becomes a target by an organized neighborhood group who are terrorizing a local Jewish shopkeeper. The story's theme of prejudice clearly resonates, but director Slavin occasionally strays towards the heavy-handed and simplistic when the events and characters should speak for themselves. ★★½ DVD: $29.99, VHS: $14.99

F

The Fog

(1980, 90 min, US, John Carpenter) *Jamie Lee Curtis, Adrienne Barbeau, Hal Holbrook, Janet Leigh, John Houseman)* Carpenter's follow-up to *Halloween* reunites him with that film's star, Curtis, in this effective horror tale about a New England coastal town terrorized by a mysterious killer fog. ★★★ DVD Dual Special Edition: $14.99

The Fog of War

(2003, 105 min, US, Errol Morris) *Robert McNamara.* Warmonger to doves, peacenik to hawks, Robert S. McNamara was pulled from upper echelon corporate America by President John F. Kennedy to be Secretary of Defense. He continued to serve under Johnson and was vilified by the anti-war movement as an architect of mass murder. Director Morris, who participated in his fair share of antiwar demonstrations, paints an unexpectedly sympathetic portrait of the man. McNamara seems the soul of reason while talking down General Curtis LeMay from a full-scale military assault against Cuba. And he seems haunted when he speaks of Kennedy's plans to pull back in Vietnam, under discussion shortly before the assassination. Morris delivers a succinct history of the times using McNamara's eleven lessons, learned from his experiences (#1: Empathize with your enemy). Each lesson is delivered by McNamara with a concise focus that four decades ago seemed bloodless but now seems oddly refreshing. From the tightrope of the Bay of Pigs to his dismissal by LBJ, McNamara witnessed history in the making (and made some himself) from a unique position during that seminal period in world affairs when the phrase "brink of annihilation" entered public consciousness. He and director Morris have crafted a thoughtful examination of our volatile past which can assist in a methodic investigation of our corrupted present. ★★★½ DVD: $26.99

Follow Me Quietly

(1949, 59 min, US, Richard Fleischer) *William Lundigan, Dorothy Patrick.* The eternal confrontation between good and evil is reenacted in this well-made crime melodrama. In the dark heart of a big city, a psychopathic serial killer, called "The Judge," stalks his innocent prey, leaving only a trail of corpses in his wake. The police are stymied until one detective uses an unorthodox method of constructing a dummy of the suspect, culled from evidence and witnesses, to trap the maniacal killer. ★★★

Follow the Fleet

(1936, 110 min, US, Mark Sandrich) *Fred Astaire, Ginger Rogers, Randolph Scott, Harriet Hilliard, Lucille Ball.* Sheer musical enchantment as sailors Astaire and Scott court sisters Rogers and Hilliard (aka Harriet Nelson). Irving Berlin songs include "Let Yourself Go" and "Let's Face the Music and Dance." ★★★½ VHS: $14.99

Following

(2000, 70 min, GB, Christopher Nolan) *Jeremy Theobald, Alex Haw, Lucy Russell, John Nolan.* This skittish, edgy indie gem takes you down an obscure path with unexpected turnings. The film is artfully constructed, the story offered in glimpses, random segments that the viewer pieces together, the perceived reality changing with each additional datum. Bill (Theobald), a young man lacking purpose and identity, breaks into empty apartments after randomly stalking the occupants, whom he analyzes on the basis of their possessions. He tells himself he's conducting research for a nonexistent writing career. A seemingly chance encounter with a practicing burglar takes him to another level of invasion; as people instill their personae into physical objects, taking these things away shows them what they had, what they took for granted. This pseudo-philosophical justification for their incursions propels their activities to greater risk and daring, sending Bill down the rabbit hole to a place where nothing is as it seems. *Following* is most satisfying, an intelligent and beautifully orchestrated film; a low-budget triumph. ★★★½ DVD: $19.99

Food of Love

(2002, 112 min, US, Ventura Pons) *Kevin Bishop, Paul Rhys, Juliet Stevenson, Alan Corduner, Geraldine McEwan.* Spanish director Pons' first English-language film is this faithful, compelling adaptation of David Leavitt's "The Page Turner" about a young gay pianist, his overbearing mother and his tempestuous first love. Bishop plays Paul, a sexually repressed, aspiring pianist. When he meets his idol, the famed pianist Richard Kennington (Rhys), they embark on a passionate affair. Paul's recently divorced mother Pamela (Stevenson), oblivious to the notion that her son is gay, misinterprets Richard's amorous signals and believes he is flirting with her. Enlisting a good ensemble cast and shooting in Spain and New York, Pons crossed borders of all sorts this go-around. A moving coming-of-age tale that addresses both sexuality and the realization of one's own dreams, expectations and limitations. ★★½ DVD: $19.99, VHS: $9.99

Fool for Love

(1986, 105 min, US, Robert Altman) *Sam Shepard, Kim Basinger, Harry Dean Stanton, Randy Quaid.* Shepard's raw, elemental tragicomedy has been skillfully transferred from the stage to the screen by the ever-inventive Altman. This tale of obsessive love, set in a neon-drenched motel at the edge of the Mojave Desert, features the gorgeous and hot-tempered Basinger in a lively turn. ★★★ DVD: $14.99, VHS: $14.99

The Fool Killer

(1965, 100 min, US, Servando Gonzalles) *Anthony Perkins, Edward Albert, Dana Elcar.* Shortly after the American Civil War, an abused child (Albert) runs away from home and befriends an amnesiac war veteran (Perkins) — who may or may not be a mythical killer. A moody, provocative mystery drama. ★★★ VHS: $19.99

Foolish

(1999, 84 min, US, Dave Meyers) *Master P, Eddie Griffin, Marla Gibbs, Andrew Dice Clay, Traci Bingham.* Griffin plays Foolish Waise (if the name is too obvious for your taste, please move on to another movie), an aspiring stand-up comic who's squandering his life on booze, drugs and other clichés that affect our urban youth. His brother is played by Master P, who gives a horrible performance as a minor drug dealer, exactly the life that Foolish doesn't want for himself. That said, within this tired framework, there is the remarkable talent of Griffin, who spends roughly a third of the film (and the entire climax) doing his stand-up routines. It's Richard Pryor-style observation comedy; outrageously profane and obscenely funny. No, it's not a good movie by any means, but it can be mighty entertaining. ★★½ DVD: $14.99, VHS: $9.99

Foolish Wives

(1922, 143 min, US, Erich von Stroheim) *Erich Von Stroheim, Maud George, Mae Busch.* Set in a Monte Carlo we have never known, von Stroheim's third film is chock full of adultery, seduction, blackmail, lechery and suicide, all seasoned with a heavy hand of symbolism. Would be high camp if it weren't for the perceptive characterizations with real psychological depth. ★★★ DVD Deluxe Collector's Edition: $29.99, VHS: $24.99

Fools of Fortune

(1990, 104 min, Ireland, Pat O'Connor) *Mary Elizabeth Mastrantonio, Iain Glen, Julie Christie, Michael Kitchen.* Set against the backdrop of the bloody battle for Irish independence, this engrossing film tells the tale of a family ruined by war and reunited by courage and faith. Mastrantonio stars as a young English woman whose love for her Irish cousin (Glen) draws her into the midst of the fray. Christie costars as her aunt, a British woman fighting for the Republican cause. ★★★ VHS: $19.99

Fools Rush In

(1997, 109 min, US, Andy Tennant) *Matthew Perry, Salma Hayek, Jon Tenney, Carlos Gomez, Jill Clayburgh.* Perry plays a New Yorker working in a nightclub in Las Vegas who has a one-night stand with Hayek, an earthy, aspiring photographer. Before the bacon and eggs are made in the morning, she takes off, only to reappear a few months later, pregnant. They marry, and problems immediately kick in: culture clashes, coastal clashes, religious clashes. There's no way this relationship should work. And, until the screenwriters settle for a syrupy, storybook finale, it doesn't. There are so many differences between the characters, you wonder where the romance comes into the romantic comedy. As an old song once asked, "Why do fools fall in love?" After watching this, your answer may be: "Who cares?" ★★ DVD: $19.99

Footlight Parade

(1933, 104 min, US, Lloyd Bacon) *James Cagney, Joan Blondell, Ruby Keeler, Dick Powell, Guy Kibbee.* Cagney is in *42nd Street* territory as a stage director putting on a Broadway show. Blondell is the faithful secretary, and she's a delight. Great musical numbers (by Busby Berkeley) include "Honeymoon Hotel," "By a Waterfall" and Cagney in "Shanghai Lil." Kibbee makes a most amusing angel (that's theatrical parlance for a show's financial backer). ★★★½

Footloose

(1984, 107 min, US, Herbert Ross) *Kevin Bacon, Sarah Jessica Parker, John Lithgow, Lori Singer, Dianne Wiest, Christopher Penn.* Clichéd musical drama about a city boy (Bacon) who moves to Iowa and comes up against the town's powerful minister (Lithgow), who was instrumental in banning school dances. ★★ DVD Letterbox: $19.99, VHS: $9.99

For a Few Dollars More

(1964, 130 min, Italy, Sergio Leone) *Clint Eastwood, Lee Van Cleef, Klaus Kinski.* Eastwood stars as "The Man with No Name," who forms an uneasy alliance with Van Cleef in a search for the bandit "Indio." The good guys and bad guys, so easy to identify in the Hollywood western thanks to the wardrobe department, become as ambiguous as the landscape yet as omnipresent as Ennio Morricone's haunting score. ★★★ DVD Letterbox: $14.99

For a Lost Soldier

(1993, 92 min, Netherlands, Roeland Kerbosch) *Andrew Kelley, Maarten Smit.* The potentially explosive subject of man-boy love is delicately handled in this touchingly romantic drama of a boy's coming-of-age during WWII. Jeroen (Smit), a handsome 13-year-old, is sent by his mother to the countryside. It is there that his adolescent sexual yearnings for those of his own sex begin to take hold. Initially interested in his girl-crazy best friend, Jeroen finds true love with the older Walt (Kelley), a Canadian soldier stationed in the area. A gay version of *Summer of '42*, this wonderful love story is never sexually graphic, but the achingly romantic lovemaking scene between Jeroen and Walt is certain to shock, especially with its cavalier, naturalistic view of their tender love. (Dutch with English subtitles) ★★★½ DVD: $29.99, VHS: $79.99

For Colored Girls Who Have Considered Suicide/ When the Rainbow Is Enuf

(1982, 80 min, US, Oz Scott) *Alfre Woodard, Ntozake Shange, Lynn Whitfield, Trazana Beverly.* A filmed enactment of Ntozake Shange's stage production, originally presented by the New York Shakespeare Festival, *For Colored Girls* is a linked series of vignettes, choreographed and orchestrated blank verse poems, in which black women share stories of their lives, loves, betrayals and triumphs. Shange fashions a stylized codification of oral herstory, truths told in parable, passed down from mother to daughter, shared sister to sister, to ease hardships and trials, to celebrate moments of glory. The ensemble cast is potent and accessible, with special mention to Woodard, Whitfield and author Shange. An unusual and powerful film that retains the immediacy of its theatre origins. An American Playhouse production. ★★★½ VHS: $29.99

For Keeps

(1988, 98 min, US, John G. Avildsen) *Molly Ringwald, Randall Batkinoff, Kenneth Mars.* Straight-A student Ringwald lets her high school crush on fellow student Batkinoff lead her to the altar and the maternity ward as she learns that life can be a good deal harder than college prep algebra. ★ DVD: $24.99

For Love of Ivy

(1968, 102 min, US, Daniel Mann) *Sidney Poitier, Abbey Lincoln, Beau Bridges, Carroll O'Connor, Lauri Peters.* When their maid Ivy (Lincoln) announces she's leaving, O'Connor's children (Bridges and Peters) try to fix her up with small-time gambler Poitier in this charming comedy-drama. ★★★ VHS: $14.99

For Love of the Game

(1999, 137 min, US, Sam Raimi) *Kevin Costner, Kelly Preston, John C. Reilly, Jena Malone, Brian Cox.* Kevin Costner must have been a baseball player in his previous life. For when he's on-screen and anywhere near a baseball diamond, he comes alive. He's right at home in this romantic drama with a baseball backdrop. And the baseball scenes here are terrific. Unfortunately, they only make up about a third of the film, for the other two thirds are occupied by a run-of-the-mill, predictable romance whose story and dialogue are right out of Screenplay 101. Costner is Billy Chapel, a 40-year-old star veteran pitching what could be his last game. As he faces the Yankees and finds himself in a perfect game, Billy flashes back to the significant moments in his life — mainly his on-again, off-

again relationship with his girlfriend Jane (Preston). Raimi's camera captures the excitement of a major league game in remarkable fashion, but neither he nor Costner are able to flesh out the film's soggy romantic angle. ★★ DVD: $14.99

For Love or Money

(1993, 96 min, US, Barry Sonnenfeld) *Michael J. Fox, Gabrielle Anwar, Anthony Higgins, Michael Tucker, Udo Kier, Bob Balaban.* The sad thing about cinematographers-turned-directors is that they tend to litter their resumes with features that look great and have nothing to say, while ignoring their lower-profile works. Such is the case with Sonnenfeld, whose two *Addams Family* features turned into Gothic gold mines, while this stylish, old-fashioned romantic comedy was undeservedly vanquished to video oblivion. Fox resurfaces as a concierge extraordinaire whose dream of owning his own hotel is jeopardized when he falls for his principal investor's mistress (Anwar). Sure, it's been done before, but this fun frolic should warm many a heart. ★★★ DVD Letterbox: $14.99, VHS: $7.49

For Me and My Gal

(1942, 104 min, US, Busby Berkeley) *Judy Garland, Gene Kelly, George Murphy.* Kelly made his film debut opposite Garland in this enjoyable backstage musical. They play a vaudeville couple during WWI hoping to make it big . . . which, of course, they do. Songs include "After You've Gone" and the title tune. ★★★ DVD: $19.99, VHS: $19.99

For Richer or Poorer

(1997, 116 min, US, Bryan Spicer) *Kirstie Alley, Tim Allen, Jay O. Sanders, Michael Lerner, Wayne Knight, Larry Miller.* Alley and Allen star as a bickering and very rich Manhattan couple who are on the run from the IRS and prison after their accountant takes off with millions. They hide out in the Pennsylvania Amish country and masquerade as kinfolk to a hard-working Amish family. Featuring broad caricatures, *For Richer or Poorer* delivers a few hearty laughs at the expense of Alley and Allen's misfortunes; but most of this is silly, unfunny, and surprisingly maudlin at times. If there's really the need to see a film about hiding out in the Amish country, rent *Witness* again. ★½ DVD: $14.99, DVD DTS sound: $14.99, VHS: $14.99

For the Boys

(1991, 148 min, US, Mark Rydell) *Bette Midler, James Caan, Patrick O'Neal, Arye Gross, George Segal, Arliss Howard.* Midler is paired with the miscast Caan in this hit-or-miss tale about the turbulent partnership of a song and dance duo — from their meeting during WWII to the present. When set in the '40s, the film has vitality and purpose, but it is overly ambitious and none-too-successful in tackling the Hollywood blacklist and the Korean and Vietnam wars. As the bawdy Dixie Leonard, Midler is in excellent voice and her acting far outshines the rest of the cast, thereby propelling this otherwise mediocre film. A good soundtrack is amongst the film's few other outstanding attractions. ★★½ DVD: $14.99

For the Moment

(1993, 120 min, Canada, Aaron Kim Johnston) *Russell Crowe, Christianne Hirt.* This softly romantic film is set in Manitoba in 1942, and explores the relationship between a young woman (Hirt), whose husband of one week has been overseas for two years, and an equally young fighter pilot-in-training (Crowe). Their mutual attraction is conflicted by her loyalty to her absent husband and the tenuous nature

of their current circumstances. There's not much new ground here, but the film does possess an authentic feel for the era. Crowe and Hirt's strong performances counteract some hackneyed stereotypes and clichéd vignettes. A gentle and affectionate reminiscence of a time of great sacrifice and personal loss. ★★½ VHS: $14.99

For Whom the Bell Tolls

(1943, 188 min, US, Sam Wood) *Gary Cooper, Ingrid Bergman, Katina Paxinou, Akim Tamiroff.* A critical and commerical hit upon its initial release, *For Whom the Bell Tolls* is a beautifully photographed adaptation of Ernest Hemingway's novel that hasn't held up quite as well as other films from its era. Shot in a stylized and fragmented fashion, the film stars Cooper as an American fighting with the Spanish partisans in 1937 during their Civil War. Assigned to blow up a strategic bridge, he's teamed with peasant guerrillas led by Tamiroff and his stalwart wife Paxinou (in a dynamic Oscar-winning performance), and including refugee Bergman. As Cooper and Bergman fall in love, their future is threatened by the severity of their mission. Bergman looks impossibly beautiful, complemented more by the gorgeous Technicolor. ★★★ DVD: $26.99, VHS: $14.99

For Your Eyes Only

(1981, 128 min, GB, John Glen) *Roger Moore, Carole Bouquet, Chaim Topol.* The 12th James Bond thriller marked a deliberate return to a trimmed-down plot and a minimum of histrionic gadgetry. While subsequent productions have proven to such diversions, this effort is much closer to the stylistic intentions of the series' creator Ian Fleming. The film still features many of the Bond trademarks — spectacular chase scenes, mind-boggling stunts and a bevy of beautiful women. (Sequel: *Octopussy*) ★★★

Forbidden Choices

(1994, 109 min, US, Jennifer Warren) *Rutger Hauer, Martha Plimpton, Kelly Lynch, Patrick McGaw.* Based on Carolyn Chute's novel "The Beans of Egypt, Maine," which was the title when released in theatres, this drama of love and poverty is second-rate Dickens for 20th-century America. Plimpton stars as Earlene, an alienated, waifish young woman whose fascination with her white-trash neighbors, the Bean family, forms the core of the story. Hauer is Reuben, the unlikely Bean patriarch, and McGaw is Beal, the handsome rogue who initially inspires Earlene's romantic fantasies and who eventually becomes her husband. While the performances are uniformly fine, director Warren seems to wallow in the misfortune of the characters' lives to such an extent that you'll hear yourself saying "now what" with each passing plot development. ★★ VHS: $89.99

Forbidden Games

(1952, 87 min, France, René Clément) *Brigitte Fossey, Georges Poujouly.* Clément's poignant anti-war outcry follows two French children who become playmates during the German occupation in 1940 and soon begin to imitate the cruelty of the adult world that surrounds them. An unforgettable film experience. (French with English subtitles) ★★★★ VHS: $29.99

Forbidden Planet

(1956, 98 min, US, Fred McLeod Wilcox) *Leslie Nielsen, Walter Pidgeon, Anne Francis, Earl Holliman.* Nielsen heads a group of space travelers who land on the planet Altair Four and encounter a "mad" scientist (Pidgeon), his alluring daughter (Francis), Robbie the Robot and the power of Id. An unusually intelligent sci-fi yarn with nifty F/X, good scenic design, and a plot borrowed from Shakespeare's "The Tempest." ★★★½ DVD Letterbox: $19.99, VHS: $14.99, VHS Letterbox: $19.99

Forbidden Zone

(1980, 76 min, US, Richard Elfman) *Susan Tyrrell, Herve Villachaize, Marie-Pascale Elfman, Viva.* Horny midgets, transvestite schoolteachers, a half-chicken/half-boy, savage nymphomaniacs, obese maidens in bikinis and a dancing frog all inhabit the Forbidden Zone! Little Frenchy should never have opened that door. This ferocious farce defies description and promises to render you speechless. Original music by Danny Elfman and the Mystic Knights of the Oingo Boingo. ★★½

Force of Evil

(1948, 78 min, US, Abraham Polonsky) *John Garfield, Thomas Gomez, Marie Windsor.* Blacklisted director Polonsky's last film for over twenty years casts Garfield as a corrupt lawyer working for the mob in this powerful film noir classic. ★★★½ DVD: $14.99

Force 10 from Navarone

(1978, 118 min, GB, Guy Hamilton) *Robert Shaw, Harrison Ford, Carl Weathers, Barbara Bach, Edward Fox, Franco Nero.* Inferior sequel to *The Guns of Navarone* finds the likes of Shaw, Ford and Weathers teaming with other members of Allied forces to blow up a bridge crucial to the Nazi war effort. ★★ DVD: $14.99

Forced March

(1989, 104 min, US, Rick King) *Chris Sarandon, Renée Soutendjik, Josef Sommer.* Sarandon plays an actor who finds the walls disolving between himself and the character he is playing — Hungarian poet Mikilos Radnoli, who was killed in a Nazi concentration camp. The film evokes a certain power but the ambitious story line cannot fully explore the various subjects it presents. ★★½

Forces of Nature

(1999, 104 min, US, Bronwen Hughes) *Sandra Bullock, Ben Affleck, Maura Tierney, Blythe Danner, Steve Zahn, Ronny Cox, Richard Schiff.* An engaging romantic comedy that doesn't aim straight for the heart nor the expected, *Forces of Nature* benefits greatly from the very appealing chemistry between its two stars, Bullock and Affleck. Ben (Affleck) is a writer on his way from New York to Savannah and is due to be married the next day. When the plane nearly crashes on takeoff, he "rescues" Sarah (Bullock) who is knocked unconscious. From there, the two pair to get to Savannah, experiencing a series of setbacks and misadventures. Of course, Ben is soon uncertain of his marriage as he's "never met a woman" quite like Sarah. Director Hughes and writer Marc Lawrence bring a certain breeziness to their story while not going overboard in the how-nature-affects-the-two-lovers department. The ending isn't quite what you'd expect, but then neither are Sarah and Ben. ★★★ DVD: $9.99

A Foreign Affair

(1948, 116 min, US, Billy Wilder) *Jean Arthur, Marlene Dietrich, John Lund, Millard Mitchell.* A witty script and lively performances highlight Wilder's funny satire on the military and postwar relations. Things heat up when a straight-laced Congresswoman (Arthur) — sent to investigate the morals of G.I.s overseas — discovers that a U.S. Army captain (Lund) is more than allies with a Berlin bombshell (Dietrich). ★★★½

Foreign Body

(1986, 108 min, GB, Ronald Neame) *Victor Banerjee, Warren Mitchell, Trevor Howard, Amanda Donohoe, Denis Quilley.* Banerjee (*A Passage to India*) plays an Indian immigrant in London who, upon the prodding of a friend, finds himself posing as a chiropractor. Banerjee displays a cunning knack for comedy as he is overcome by the advances of his wealthy female patients. ★★½

Foreign Correspondent

(1940, 119 min, US, Alfred Hitchcock) *Joel McCrea, Laraine Day, George Sanders, Herbert Marshall, Robert Benchley, Albert Basserman.* McCrea is an American newspaperman stationed in London who becomes involved with a Nazi spy ring and is plunged into a series of terrifying adventures. This enthralling suspenser features a host of Hitchcock's most imaginative scenes, including the windmills that turn backward, an assassination attempt in Westminster Cathedral and a spectacular plane wreck at sea. Splendid performances. ★★★★

A Foreign Field

(1993, 90 min, GB, Charles Sturridge) *Alec Guinness, Lauren Bacall, Jeanne Moreau, Edward Herrmann, Leo McKern, Geraldine Chaplin, John Randolph.* An enchanting international cast distinguishes this impeccably produced made-for-TV BBC drama that is subdued and deliberately paced, but charming nonetheless. Infused with amiable moments of comedy, the film follows the connecting stories of several people visiting the shores of Normandy 50 years after D-Day. The ensemble includes McKern as a former British infantryman, Guinness as a mentally disabled veteran, Bacall as a different kind of war widow, and Moreau as a former flame of both McKern and ex-G.I. Randolph. ★★★

Foreign Student

(1994, 96 min, US/GB, Eva Sereny) *Marco Hofschneider, Robin Givens, Edward Herrmann, Hinton Battle, Charles S. Dutton.* Based on the novel by Philippe Labro, this low-key adaptation examines an interracial romance in the 1950s. Hofschneider plays a Parisian exchange student who spends a semester at a Southern college. There he meets a beautiful black woman (Givens), a teacher who works as a maid at the home of one of his professors. Blind to the segregation and racism of the times, he pursues her, and the two fall in love. Any interesting dramatics is countered by rather listless pacing. Hofschneider, who spoke several languages as the young hero in *Europa, Europa*, effectively handles two more here. ★★ VHS: $9.99

Forever and a Day

(1943, 105 min, US, Cedric Hardwicke, Edmund Goulding, René Clair) *Ray Milland,* *Merle Oberon, Charles Laughton, Robert Cummings, Nigel Young, Buster Keaton, Claude Rains, Victor McLaglen, Elsa Lanchester, Gladys Cooper, Roland Young.* This impressive episodic drama chronicles the lives of several generations of a family and their London home. Spanning the century-and-a-half from 1804 to the German Blitz, the film was produced as a postwar fundraiser for British reconstruction and features just about every Hollywood actor with English roots. ★★★½ DVD: $24.99, VHS: $19.99

Forever Female

(1953, 93 min, US, Irving Rapper) *Ginger Rogers, William Holden, Paul Douglas, Pat Crowley.* An engaging cast adds sparkle to this pleasant backstage comedy, written by Julius and Philip Epstein (*Casablanca*). Rogers plays a middle-aged Broadway actress still playing the ingénue. She meets writer Holden, whose new play's characters include a 19-year-old daughter and a 50-year-old mother. Guess which one Rogers wants to play? As Rogers' ex-husband, Douglas gives the film's best performance; he can sling a one-liner with the best of them. ★★★ VHS: $9.99

Forever Lulu

(1987, 85 min, US, Amos Kollek) *Hanna Schygulla, Debbie Harry, Alec Baldwin.* Baldwin made his theatrical film debut in this tale about a New York City novelist (Schygulla) who begins investigating the goings-on of a gangster's moll (Harry). A forgettable, sloppy rip-off of *Desperately Seeking Susan* with no originality of its own. ★

Forever Mary

(1990, 100 min, Italy, Marco Risi) *Michele Placido, Alesandro DiSanzo.* A tougher look into modern urban Italian life than one usually sees. This hard-hitting prison drama, set in a Palermo juvenile detention center, takes an unflinching look at the "rehabilitation" of a group of teenagers. Essentially a spaghetti *To Sir with Love*, the story follows Marco (Placido), a taciturn yet dedicated teacher who volunteers to spend some time trying to educate a clamorous group of teenagers. Their initial scorn soon turns to respect and much to the director's credit, the story avoids sentimental pitfalls and retains its hard edge. The title refers to Mario, a transvestite prostitute who falls in (puppy) love with the teacher. (Italian with English subtitles) ★★★ VHS: $39.99

Forever Mine

(1999, 117 min, US, Paul Schrader) *Joseph Fiennes, Ray Liotta, Gretchen Mol.* A towel boy (Fiennes) at a posh resort falls in love with a politician's beautiful young wife and they begin a torrid affair. When the husband finds out about it, he has the young man killed. Miraculously, the man survives the attempt on his life and . . . oh, never mind. If you stick with the film past this point, you may get a few unintentional chuckles out of it, but it's hardly worth the wait. The acting is across-the-board wretched, the story at times embarrassing, and the only evidence that Schrader's behind this is the Catholic guilt of Mol's character and the sporadic spiritual musings from Fiennes. ★ DVD Letterbox: $9.99

Forever Young

(1983, 85 min, GB, David Drury) *James Aubrey, Nicholas Gecks, Alec McCowen.* David Putnam produced this intimate and compelling story about the relationship between a 12-year-old boy and a young priest who attempts to shield him from a painful secret. ★★★

Forever Young

(1992, 115 min, US, Steve Miner) *Mel Gibson, Jamie Lee Curtis, Elijah Wood, Joe Morton, George Wendt.* Following in the footsteps of the charming independent feature *Late for Dinner* comes this likable comedy-drama of cryogenics and lost love. Gibson plays a nice guy test pilot in 1939 who, after his fiancée becomes comatose, agrees to be a human guinea pig for scientist/pal Wendt's experiment — to be frozen alive for a year. Fifty years later, Gibson is awakened by young Wood. As Gibson acclimates to life in the '90s, he tries to track down his long-lost friend. Alternately funny and shamelessly sentimental, *Forever Young* is the kind of popular mainstream entertainment that can unapologetically make one laugh and cry. ★★½ DVD: $14.99, VHS: $9.99

Forget Mozart

(1985, 93 min, Germany, Slavo Luter) *Armin Mueller-Stahl, Caterina Raacke.* Mueller-Stahl stars in this intellectual music lover's answer to *Amadeus*, which pays far more attention to historical fact than to Hollywood passions. The character of Salieri is again prominent in this story, but blame for Mozart's death is attributed to disease, a failed marriage, alcoholism and the government's inattentiveness. Mueller-Stahl is perfect as the state's investigator into Mozart's untimely demise. Focusing on the historical and political backdrop to Mozart's life, the film explores Mozart's connections with the Freemasons and their influence in this era of revolutionary change in Europe. (German with English subtitles) ★★★ VHS: $29.99

Forget Paris

(1995, 101 min, US, Billy Crystal) *Billy Crystal, Debra Winger, Joe Mantegna, Cynthia Stevenson, Richard Masur, Julie Kavner, Cathy Moriarty.* Crystal wears several hats as star/producer/director/writer of this amiable romantic comedy, which offers quite a few laughs in Crystal's inimitable comedic style but is also very familiar. The on-again, off-again love affair of Crystal and Winger is told in flashbacks as friends' dinner conversation. More serious in tone than his other romances, Crystal's film does offer many laughs, but it takes longer to get to them. Winger is a delight. ★★½ DVD: $9.99, VHS: $9.99

Forgive and Forget

(2000, 100 min, GB, Aisling Walsh) *Steve John Shepherd, John Simm, Laura Fraser, Maurice Roeves, Ger Ryan.* This edgy British drama features a solid performance by newcomer Shepherd in an absorbing character study of one man's conflict between his repressed sexuality and his love for another man. Handsome, macho David (Shepherd) is a construction worker for his father's building firm in South London. Visiting trendy Soho for casual sexual encounters, David is unable to admit to himself or anyone else that he is gay. That includes Theo (Simon), his straight best mate whom David secretly loves. Inseparable since childhood, they've always been there for each other . . . until Theo moves in with his new girlfriend, putting a strain on David's and Theo's friendship. Sexual tensions build and secrets are bared in this unapologetic drama, an uncompromising examination of sexual identity and the bonds of friendship that traces a tumultuous journey towards self-acceptance and coming out. ★★★ DVD Letterbox: $14.99, VHS: $9.99

Forgotten Silver

(1996, 55 min, New Zealand, Costa Botes & Peter Jackson) *Peter Jackson, Costa Botes, Marguerite Hurst, Leonard Maltin, Sam Neill.* New Zealand, it seems, has some issues with its self-image. After being dumped by Britain following WWII, the country was forced to develop its own societal identity. Director Jackson has used this cultural blank slate as an opportunity to manufacture his own film history. With the pretense of a newly discovered trunk of rapidly disintegrating films, Jackson and cowriter/director Botes invent a "nearly forgotten" chapter in Kiwi film history. Their discovery, director Colin McKenzie (Botes), is ostensibly the most important film innovator in New Zealand history. Suffering slightly from the *Forrest Gump*-ism of McKenzie's responsibility for every major advance in film history, the film is an ingeniously convincing, deeply humorous and richly woven fabrication. When this "mockumentary" was first presented on New Zealand television, it erroneously provided a new source of Kiwi cultural pride, prompting the network to issue an apology and explanation. ★★★½ DVD: $14.99

Forgotten Tune for a Flute

(1987, 131 min, USSR, Eldar Ryazanov) *Leonid Filatov, Tatiana Dogileva.* A breezy Soviet comedy about a bureaucrat who rediscovers a lost and suppressed part of his life. Lenny is a high-ranking government employee "happily" married to the daughter of another functionary who, after a mild heart attack, begins an affair with a sensible nurse. She, in turn, encourages him to broaden his life and take up another passion long forgotten: playing the flute. A delightful, post-*glasnost* social satire. (Russian with English subtitles) ★★★ VHS: $19.99

Formula 51

(2002, 93 min, US, Ronny Yu) *Samuel L. Jackson, Robert Carlyle, Emily Mortimer, Sean Pertwee, Ricky Tomlinson, Rhys Ifans, Meat Loaf.* Jackson plays a double-dealing drug designer who reluctantly hooks up with low-rent hood Carlyle to sell his new, ultra-powerful drug formula in England. Perhaps if this were made in the 1970s, by, say, Hal Ashby, with a bitter, satiric tone, this *Formula* could have worked. However, with stylish but hollow direction by Yu and a grating lead performance by Jackson, *Formula 51* is nothing more than a turgid experience. Aiming for a Guy Ritchie/Tarantino/Hong Kong trendiness, Yu wallows in annoying, empty amorality that will most likely appeal only to slow-witted teens, with an attitude toward the drug trade that is cartoonish at best and sickening at worst. The only saving grace here is the always reliable Carlyle, who, amazingly, milks some likability from his loser role. ★½ DVD Dual: $27.99, VHS: $9.99

Forrest Gump

(1994, 142 min, US, Robert Zemeckis) *Tom Hanks, Sally Field, Gary Sinise, Robin Wright, Mykelti Williamson.* With the nugget of folk wisdom "Life is like a box of chocolates," Hanks launches into the epic telling of the life of Forrest Gump, a small-town simpleton who finds himself at the center of just about every significant cultural event in the latter half of the 20th century. The premise leads to a host of entertaining moments. But it's all so shallow one wonders if it isn't merely the ideal contrivance to lure baby boomers to the box office — which it did in droves. Hanks' Gump is more than just an "enlightened idiot" of the Chauncy Gardner variety; he's a pure-of-heart all-American boy who never questions authority and prospers as a result. And therein lies its fundamental message, which seems to offer absolution to boomers in a sweeping apology for the bad old days of the 1960s. In support, Sinise stands out as Gump's sergeant. ★★½ DVD Letterbox 2-disc set: $19.99, VHS: $9.99, VHS Letterbox: $9.99

The Forsaken

(2001, 90 min, US, J.S. Cardone) *Kerr Smith, Brendan Fehr, Izabella Miko, Carrie Snodgress, Johnathon Schaech.* A dull, young film editor decides to deliver a swank car cross-country for some extra cash, only to be besieged by vampires along the way. This big yawn of a horror flick walks and talks like a bloodier-than-usual USA Network movie (despite a surprisingly frank opening credits image), yet this junk somehow got a major theatrical release. Boring, slow, derivative and mean without being remotely scary, *The Forsaken* also features a truly lame villain who's about as menacing as Aaron Carter. If watching a couple of twentysomething dorks drive around the desert for 90 minutes spouting annoying, trendy dialogue while looking for even more annoying, trendy vampires is your idea of a great time, look no further. ★ DVD: $19.99, VHS: $14.99

Forsaking All Others

(1934, 84 min, US, W.S. Van Dyke) *Joan Crawford, Clark Gable, Robert Montgomery.* Always an intoxicating duo, Crawford and Gable reteam for this satisfying romantic melodrama. Crawford finds her marriage to Gable on the dull side (Gable dull?), so she looks for excitement in the arms of dashing Montgomery. Will she leave her husband or realize they were meant for each other all along? The stars outperform their material. ★★½ VHS: $19.99

Fort Apache

(1948, 125 min, US, John Ford) *Henry Fonda, John Wayne, Shirley Temple, Victor McLaglen.* The first of director Ford's cavalry trilogy (followed by *She Wore a Yellow Ribbon* and *Rio Grande*) stars Fonda as a strict military commander at odds with both his men and neighboring Indians. Wayne is the more compassionate officer caught between loyalty to the soldiers in his command and duty to the martinet under whom he serves. ★★★ VHS: $9.99

Fort Apache, the Bronx

(1981, 125 min, US, Daniel Petrie) *Paul Newman, Edward Asner, Ken Wahl, Pam Grier.* Newman is the cop facing a conflict of conscience when he witnesses two policemen throw a Hispanic man off a tenement roof. Asner is the precinct captain trying to hold on to his outpost in the center of the crime-

Jack Lemmon in *The Fortune Cookie*

torn South Bronx (where the film was shot with much protest from the community, who didn't care for the portrayal of their neighborhood). Grier steals the film with her performance as a drug-crazed prostitute. ★★★ DVD: $9.99

Fortress

(1993, 92 min, US, Stuart Gordon) *Christopher Lambert, Loryn Locklin, Kurtwood Smith, Jeffrey Combs.* The director of *Re-Animator* shows us his vision of the future: an authoritarian world where, due to overpopulation, couples are limited to one child — offenders are duly sentenced to lengthy stays in corporate-managed, computer-controlled prisons. Lambert and Locklin play a husband and wife who find themselves imprisoned, with him assembling a group of prisoners to help him rescue his wife and escape the fortress. Gordon showers the set with blood, and introduces a few grisly futuristic innovations. While not for the squeamish, *Fortress* is nevertheless an enjoyable sci-fi/action hybrid. (Sequel: *Fortress 2: Re-Entry*) ★★½ DVD: $9.99, VHS: $9.99

Fortunata y Jacinta

(1969, 108 min, Italy/Spain, Angelino Fons) Based on the 1877 novel, "Historia de Dos Casadas," by Benito Perez Galdos, this elegant but shrill melodrama recounts the tragic story of two very dissimilar women who vie for the love of the same man. Juan, a young Rock Hudson look-alike, leads a privileged life, with his future assured by the planned marriage to his beautiful cousin Yacinta. Then he meets and becomes obsessed with the earthy, sexually charged peasant woman Fortunata. Their entangled loves and passions lead inevitably to heartbreak and loss. The attempt by the filmmaker to tell the entire novel in the span of two hours gives the film a frantic, Cliffnotes feel, but irregardless, this ageless story of insuppressible passion is still engaging. (Spanish with English subtitles) ★★½

The Fortune

(1975, 88 min, US, Mike Nichols) *Jack Nicholson, Warren Beatty, Stockard Channing, Scatman Crothers, Florence Stanley, Richard B. Shull.* Broad satire with Nicholson and Beatty as grifters out to murder heiress Channing for her money. Funny, fast-paced and featuring great performances (especially Channing as the hapless target). ★★★½

Fortune and Men's Eyes

(1971, 102 min, US/Canada, Harvey Hart) *Wendell Burton, Zooey Hall, Michael Greer.* John Hubert's play about homosexual brutality in prison comes to the screen in this taut, claustrophobic and sensationalistic drama. The story follows young first-timer Smitty (Burton) who finds himself the prized sexual catch to a thuggish Rocky (Hall). Sexual humiliation, domination and abuse fill the halls of the seemingly guardless prison as the inmates enact a frenzied dance for power and gratification. Greer is alternately hilarious and terrorizing as Queeny, the affectionate, limp-wristed fairy cellmate who, when threatened, turns into a dangerously violent psychopath. ★★★

The Fortune Cookie

(1966, 125 min, US, Billy Wilder) *Jack Lemmon, Walter Matthau, Ron Rich.* Matthau won an Oscar for his performance as a shyster lawyer out to parlay Lemmon's minor injury into some really big bucks. A funny, biting comedy from the pens of Wilder and partner I.A.L. Diamond. ★★★ DVD: $14.99

Fortunes of War

(1987, 180 min, GB, James Cellan Jones) *Kenneth Branagh, Emma Thompson, Rupert Graves, Robert Stephens.* This BBC production follows a British couple swept up in the struggle against Fascism in 1939 Romania. Based on the autobiographical accounts of Olivia Manning, the story follows the pair as they reluctantly and increasingly become involved with the British Secret Service. With Branagh and Thompson in the leads, the acting is, as would be expected, top-notch and this epic production whisks the viewer through such exotic locales as Bucharest, Athens and Cairo. ★★★ VHS: $29.99

Forty Carats

(1973, 110 min, US, Milton Katselas) *Liv Ullmann, Edward Albert, Gene Kelly, Binni Barnes.* Lackluster version of the Broadway hit with Ullmann as a 40-ish New Yorker who begins an affair with 20-ish Albert while on holiday in Greece. Though Ullmann is miscast, and Albert is rather emotionless, there's good support from Kelly and Barnes. ★★

48 Hrs.

(1983, 97 min, US, Walter Hill) *Eddie Murphy, Nick Nolte, James Remar, Annette O'Toole.* Murphy's dazzling big-screen debut elevates this cop-and-convict caper above the usual urban actiondrama. Murphy and the comically gruff Nolte join forces to track a pair of homicidal heavies in Hill's jagged-edged comedy-thriller. (Sequel: *Another 48 Hrs.*) ★★★½ DVD: $14.99, VHS: $9.99

The 49th Parallel

(1941, 107 min, GB, Michael Powell) *Leslie Howard, Laurence Olivier, Eric Portman, Raymond Massey, Glynis Johns.* A stirring WWII suspense drama which was one of the first of the great 1940s British films detailing both the physical and moral fight against the Nazis. When a German U-boat is sunk off the coast of Canada, its five survivors embark on a murderous, ruthless trail from one community to another in their quest to cross into the United States. This political allegory follows the stalwart fight of civilians and servicemen alike to keep the German soldiers from accomplishing their mission. (aka: *The Invaders*) ★★★★

42nd Street

(1933, 89 min, US, Lloyd Bacon) *Warner Baxter, Ruby Keeler, Bebe Daniels, George Brent, Dick Powell, Ginger Rogers.* Classic backstage musical with Baxter as the driven director and Keeler as the chorine who subs for the injured leading lady and "comes back a star." It's a little creaky by today's standards, but who cares — it's got those terrific Busby Berkeley dance numbers and a fine Warren-Dubin score. ★★★★ DVD: $19.99

The 47 Ronin: Parts 1 & 2

(1942, 112 min, Japan, Kenji Mizoguchi) Taking his inspiration from one of the most admired tales of Japanese folklore, Mizoguchi adapts for the screen the true story of the 47 masterless samurai who, in 1703, all mysteriously killed themselves by committing *seppuku*. The two-part film begins with the Lord Asano who, in

The Fountainhead

anger, draws his sword and strikes an arrogant but superior lord. With this act of insolence, he must kill himself, which leaves his loyal samurai without a leader. The ronin vow to avenge their young lord's death. And with this background our story takes off. Successfully created to inspire wartime patriotism for the war-weary public, the film reinforces traditional Japanese values as well as reminds the people of their heroism and warrior spirit. (Japanese with English subtitles) (Each VHS volume sells singularly for $29.99) ★★★ DVD: $34.99, VHS: $49.99

Foul Play

(1978, 116 min, US, Colin Higgins) *Goldie Hawn, Chevy Chase, Dudley Moore, Burgess Meredith, Rachel Roberts, Brian Dennehy.* Hawn stars in this funny mystery comedy as a San Francisco librarian who becomes involved with detective Chase and a plot to assassinate the Pope. ★★★ VHS: $14.99

The Fountainhead

(1949, 114 min, US, King Vidor) *Gary Cooper, Patricia Neal, Raymond Massey.* This highly stylized film version of the Ayn Rand novel stars Cooper as an architect, modeled after Frank Lloyd Wright, whose ideas are ahead of their time. A rugged individualist, Cooper takes on a group of federal housing bureaucrats in a struggle over the perversion of his designs. ★★★

Four Adventures of Reinette and Mirabelle

(1986, 95 min, France, Eric Rohmer) *Joelle Miquel, Jessica Forde, Beatrice Romand.* Sophisticated humor and two disarmingly charming leads highlight this low-budget account of the up-and-down relationship between two young students. Reinette, a rigorously principled, naïve country girl who is studying ethnology at the Sorbonne, meets Mirabelle, a pragmatic, worldly Parisian art student, and they decide to become flatmates. Together, they have four adventures involving several characters from the streets of Paris. As always, this Rohmer tale is a talk-fest (but entertainingly so) as the two unknown teenage actresses give beguilingly naturalistic performances. An intelligent drama filled with wisdom, idealism and beauty. (French with English subtitles) ★★★½ VHS: $29.99

Four Days in July

(1984, 99 min, Ireland, Mike Leigh) *Des McAleer, Brid Brennan, Stephen Rea.* This quirky comedy-drama is set in Northern Ireland during the middle of July, when the Protestants celebrate their national pride. Director Leigh deftly interweaves the lives of two couples, one Protestant and the other Catholic, and both expecting their first child. In his typical cinema verité manner, Leigh gently exposes the nuances of these disparate elements of Ulster society employing only simple living room conversation and other trivial daily chores — it is a quietly evocative exposé on a territory torn by strife. ★★★½ VHS: $29.99

Four Days in September

(1997, 113 min, Brazil, Bruno Barreto) *Alan Arkin, Pedro Cardoso, Fernando Torres, Fisher Stevens.* Director Barreto returned to his native Brazil for this superior thriller, a Best Foreign-Language Film nominee. In the tradition of *State of Siege* and *Missing*, this true-life tale focuses on the people caught in the middle of perilous political turmoil. The case here is Brazil in 1969, when a group of young radicals rebelling against an oppressive military government kidnap Charles Elbrick (Arkin), the U.S. Ambassador to the country. Organized by a fierce female leader (Torres), the group holds Elbrick at gunpoint while they await government powers to release 15 political prisoners from jail. Tightly wound, marvelously acted and filled with moments of bare-knuckle suspense, the film belongs on the shelf next to the best of Costa-Gavras. (In English and Portuguese with English subtitles) ★★★½ DVD: $19.99, VHS: $9.99

The Four Feathers

(1939, 115 min, GB, Zoltan Korda) *Ralph Richardson, John Clements.* A.E.W. Mason's story about a young aristocrat who resigns his military commission on the eve of an expedition to the Sudan. He is subsequently branded a coward by friends and lover alike. To prove his worthiness he joins the group and helps battle the Sudanese uprising. A great epic of British imperialism. ★★★½

The Four Feathers

(2002, 127 min, US/GB, Shekhar Kapur) *Heath Ledger, Wes Bentley, Kate Hudson, Djimon Hounsou, Michael Sheen.* This sumptuously photographed, emotionally vacuous historical adventure epic plays like a half-cocked *Lawrence, the English Patient of Arabia* for the *Tiger Beat* set. It's 1884 and the British are heading off for a desert war in the Sudan. Bright young officer Harry Feversham (Ledger) gets cold feet on the eve of combat and whiningly resigns his commission. Served four white feathers as badges of his cowardice, shunned Harry treks out across the desert on a quest to reclaim his manhood and self-respect. Crippled by disjointed editing and undermined by starchy plot melodramatics, the film benefits greatly from director Kapur's attention to exquisite period detail and his sweeping command of visual and sonic atmospherics. Alas, the potent sensory spell Kapur casts readily overpowers the flimsy human element, making for an intimate epic that's too heavy on spectacle and short on heart. ★★½ DVD Letterbox: $29.99, DVD Pan & Scan: $29.99, VHS: $9.99

Four Friends

(1981, 116 min, US, Arthur Penn) *Craig Wasson, Jodi Thelen, Michael Huddleston, Jim Metzler.* Powerful stuff from director Penn. This tale of

growing up in the sixties is a classic story of the son of a steelworker who falls in love with the girl his best friends have fallen for. It takes a decade to work out, but they figure it out. The car crashing onto the disco finale is one of the most memorable scenes in all of Penn's films. Magical score by Elizabeth Swados. ★★★½ DVD: $19.99

Four Horsemen of the Apocalypse

(1961, 153 min, US, Vincente Minnelli) *Glenn Ford, Charles Boyer, Lee J. Cobb, Ingrid Thulin, Paul Henreid.* Remake of the Rudolph Valentino silent box-office hit, with much less success, about brothers fighting on opposite sides of the war; here updated to WWII. ★★ VHS: $19.99

The 400 Blows

(1959, 99 min, France, François Truffaut) *Jean-Pierre Léaud, Claire Maurier, Jeanne Moreau.* Arguably the finest in a long line of cinematic coming-of-age efforts, *The 400 Blows* marked the emergence of a brilliant young directorial talent. Truffaut's largely autobiographical feature film debut commenced the wonderful saga of Antoine Doinel (Léaud), the director's alter ego. Oppressed by the demands of parents and teachers, the young Antoine ventures out on his own only to discover the unsettling bleakness of personal freedom. (French with English subtitles) ★★★★ DVD: $19.99, VHS: $14.99

4 Little Girls

(1997, 102 min, US, Spike Lee) Told with present-day interviews and archival footage, the riveting documentary *4 Little Girls* recounts the story of the title teens who were killed by a racist's bomb while they attended Sunday school in early 1960s Birmingham. The film also examines the attitudes of the people — both black and white — in that city at the time, and how the rest of the country reacted. Several of the interviews may move you to tears, and there's a jaw-dropping, and rather sad, talk with former Alabama Governor George Wallace. But what one comes away with most from this fascinating film is the astonishing courage and depth of spirit of the families and friends of the victims in the face of such unspeakable hatred. ★★★★ DVD: $14.99, VHS: $14.99

The Four Musketeers

(1974, 106 min, GB, Richard Lester) *Oliver Reed, Raquel Welch, Richard Chamberlain, Frank Finlay, Michael York, Christopher Lee.* Lester's impressive follow-up to *The Three Musketeers*, his romping vision of the Dumas classic, was filmed simultaneously with the original. While darker in tone than the first film, and less emphatic in its physical comedy, it is still filled with incisive period wit and lots of rollicking adventure. ★★★ VHS: $9.99

Four Rooms

(1996, 98 min, US, Alexandre Rockwell, Allison Anders, Quentin Tarantino, Robert Rodriguez) *Tim Roth, Antonio Banderas, Jennifer Beals, Marisa Tomei, Madonna, Bruce Willis, Quentin Tarantino.* While two of the four segments in this anthology film are moderately good, the other two are so bad that they very nearly make the entire project a failure. The film takes place on New Year's Eve and tells four different bizarre stories, happening in four different rooms of a hotel serviced by one very overworked bellboy (Roth in an ingratiatingly mugging performance). Anders' segment concerns a coven of witches; it's boring from start to finish. Rockwell's bit is equally bad: It stars Beals as the victim of a twisted bondage and power game and is actually painful to

The 400 Blows

watch. The film livens up substantially in Rodriguez's segment, about two children in a room by themselves, nominally supervised by Roth. And Tarantino's segment tops off the weird mix with a macabre tale of a bet made in flesh. ★½ DVD: $19.99, VHS: $9.99

The Four Seasons

(1981, 107 min, US, Alan Alda) *Alan Alda, Carol Burnett, Rita Moreno, Jack Weston, Len Cariou, Sandy Dennis.* A genuinely funny comedy on romance and relationships, director Alda has yet to equal this story about a group of friends who spend their vacations together. As the couples, Alda and Burnett, Weston and Moreno, and Cariou and Dennis and then Armstrong, all offer delightful performances. A witty, even perceptive script by Alda. ★★★

Four Weddings and a Funeral

(1994, 116 min, GB, Mike Newell) *Hugh Grant, Andie MacDowell, Kristin Scott Thomas, Simon Callow, John Hannah, Rowan Atkinson.* Grant is effortlessly charming in this enchanting romantic comedy, playing a likable Britisher whose biggest flaw seems to be his fear of commitment. Fulfilling its titular promise, the film follows Grant and a wonderful group of friends as they wind their way from one ceremony to another imparting blithe observations on love, relationships and fear of both. Featuring a marvelously written screenplay, the film only loses control at its finale with an abrupt, simplistic ending that belies the intelligence that came before it. McDowell is the film's only other flaw, giving a lifeless performance as the woman of Grant's dreams. However, Callow and Hannah, as devoted lovers, and Atkinson, immensely funny as a tongue-tied priest, are exceptional in support. ★★★½ DVD: $14.99

1492: Conquest of Paradise

(1992, 150 min, US/France/GB, Ridley Scott) *Gérard Depardieu, Sigourney Weaver, Armand Assante, Frank Langella, Loren Dean, Angela Molina.* The better of 1992's two dramatizations (the other being *Christopher Columbus: The Discovery*) about Christopher Columbus being discovered by Native Americans when he got lost trying to find a quicker trade route to Asia. Depardieu gives a fine performance as the explorer who betrays and is eventually betrayed, ultimately ending his years in obscurity and poverty. Director

Scott's eye for the striking visual serves him well in enlivening this revisionist epic which unfortunately suffers from delusions of profundity. ★★ VHS: $14.99, VHS Letterbox: $24.99

The 4th Man

(1983, 110 min, Netherlands, Paul Verhoeven) *Jeroen Krabbé, Renée Soutendijk, Thom Hoffman.* A wonderful hallucinatory thriller that bristles with dark, forboding humor and sexual paranoia. The story concerns a brooding novelist (Krabbé) entwined in the web of a mysterious beautician and her handsomely sculpted lover. Starring the hauntingly beautiful Soutendijk. (Dutch with English subtitles) ★★★½ DVD Letterbox: $29.99

The Fourth Protocol

(1987, 100 min, GB, John MacKenzie) *Michael Caine, Pierce Brosnan, Joanna Cassidy.* A superior political thriller with Caine as a government agent who stumbles upon a plot by a renegade Soviet general to destroy an American air base in England. Based on Frederick Forsyth's novel, the film, as with the author's *The Day of the Jackal*, builds an unrelenting tension until its shattering conclusion. Brosnan is the KGB agent assigned to the deadly task, and Cassidy is radiant as his contact. ★★★½

The Fourth War

(1990, 91 min, US, John Frankenheimer) *Roy Scheider, Jürgen Prochnow, Tim Reid, Harry Dean Stanton.* Scheider and Prochnow battle it out as the last of the Cold War militarists in this competent though unexciting thriller. Scheider plays an American colonel and Prochnow is a Russian commander, both willing to start WWIII for the sake of psyching out the other. ★★½ VHS: $9.99

Fox and His Friends

(1975, 123 min, Germany, Rainer Werner Fassbinder) *Rainer Werner Fassbinder, Peter Chatel, Harry Baer, Kurt Raab.* Fassbinder's first specifically male gay-themed film is a richly textured and powerful drama of the relationship between two gay men of vastly different social backgrounds. A lower-class carnival entertainer, Fox (played by Fassbinder), finds himself suddenly flush after winning 500,000DM in a lottery. He soon becomes involved in an ill-fated romance with gold-digging Eugen, a rich, manipulative young man. The eternal class struggle and the continued exploitation of the poor and working class is tragically played out as the unwitting Fox is swindled out of his money and self-respect by his bourgeois lover and his family. (German with English subtitles) ★★★★ DVD: $24.99, VHS: $19.99

The Fox and the Hound

(1981, 83 min, US, Art Stevens, Richard Rich, Ted Berman) *Voices of: Kurt Russell, Mickey Rooney, Sandy Duncan, Corey Feldman.* While the music of this potential classic is not up to Disney's current standards, this tale of friendship between the hunter and the hunted is timeless and timely. Tod is an orphaned fox cub who befriends Copper, a hound puppy who will eventually be trained to hunt foxes. Although they become best friends, their relationship is threatened by Copper's owner, who is determined to kill Tod. The thrilling climax proves that friendship is indeed more powerful than hate or revenge, and reminds kids that differences need not be dividers. The animation is first-rate. ★★★ DVD: $29.99, VHS: $22.99

Foxes

(1980, 106 min, US, Adrian Lyne) *Jodie Foster, Sally Kellerman, Randy Quaid, Cherie Currie, Scott Baio, Laura Dern, Lois Smith.* Foster stars as one of four girls who share an apartment in the Los Angeles suburbs in this sociological study that poignantly examines the restless lives of today's youth, although it presents more questions than answers. ★★½ DVD: $14.99, VHS: $9.99

Foxfire

(1996, 102 min, US, Annette Haywood-Carter) *Hedy Burress, Jenny Shimizu, Angelina Jolie, Jenny Lewis, Sarah Rosenberg, Cathy Moriarty.* A disappointing adaptation of Joyce Carol Oates' novel about a girl gang, *Foxfire* waters down important issues such as sexual harassment, drug addiction and female teenage angst as it depicts the actions of five rebellious high school girls coming to terms with their identities. Suspended from school for attacking a teacher, these disparate teens embark on a series of crimes that escalate in their severity. Like *Girls Town*, *Foxfire* takes the perspective of young women on the verge of adulthood, but much of the drama is heavy-handed and unpleasant. What could have been a fiery display of female solidarity quickly becomes a frustrating one. ★★ DVD: $24.99

Foxy Brown

(1974, 94 min, US, Jack Hill) *Pam Grier, Terry Carter, Antonio Fargas.* Mob queenpin Miss Katherine finds her harem reduced to mincemeat when Grier goes after those responsible for her brutal rape and the death of her brother. Grier is certainly a sight, but this early blaxploitation actioner is very violent and muddled. ★★ DVD: $14.99

Frailty

(2002, 99 min, US, Bill Paxton) *Bill Paxton, Matthew McConaughey, Powers Boothe, Matt O'Leary.* Fenton Mieks (McConaughey), a sullen man whose good looks are masked by resignation and pain, walks into the Dallas FBI office and informs them that his brother Adam is guilty of murders known as the "God's Hands" killings. He then proceeds to tell how his father (Paxton), twenty years before, had visions and initiated a brutal series of kidnapping/murders in the name of God. Thus begins the creepy, intense *Frailty*, a moody psychological thriller that's abundant in atmosphere and whose story maintains dread throughout until a rather unsatisfying ending. Paxton is quite good at conveying the contradictory elements of a devoted father who forces his children to a calling of murder. As young Fenton, O'Leary impresses as a son in conflict. Giving in to trend by having two twist endings, *Frailty* only falters in the last reel, having made certain, however, to give the viewer the willies way before then. ★★★ DVD: $14.99

Frameup

(1993, 91 min, US, Jon Jost) *Howard Swain, Nancy Carlin.* It's no big secret that the works of Jost are an acquired taste: his minimalistic, free-form films test the patience of most viewers and are probably of interest only to experimental filmmakers and fans thereof. *Frameup*, a monotonous, pretentiously artsy examination of a *Badlands*-like couple, holds true to the director's reputation. Husband and wife Swain and Carlin star as the ill-fated couple, who meet in Idaho and head West for relaxation, sex and murder. Comprised of a series of narrations framed by a motionless camera, the film is all talk and very little action. Carlin gives a grating

performance; Swain nearly captures the essence of a bad guy. He also has a tattoo on his penis spelling "Wow" — if there was truth in advertising it would have said "This Sucks." ★ VHS: $24.99

Frances

(1982, 140 min, US, Graeme Clifford) *Jessica Lange, Kim Stanley, Sam Shepard.* Lange gives a powerful performance as Frances Farmer, the radiant Hollywood starlet of the '30s whose nonconformity launched a tragic succession of injustices. This chilling biopic delineates the demise of Farmer's promising film career and discloses the terrifying conditions of her imposed institutionalization. ★★★ DVD: $19.99, VHS: $9.99

Francesco

(1989, 105 min, Italy, Liliana Cavani) *Mickey Rourke, Helena Bonham Carter.* A prepuffy-faced, before-his-boxing-career-skids-days Rourke is featured in this religious drama giving an emotionally raw and stirring performance as Francesco, the egotistical son of a wealthy merchant. After reading one of the first non-Latin translations of the Bible, Francesco takes the gospels literally. He gives up everything to live and suffer with the poor, gains "peace," starts the Franciscan order and becomes a saint. An elegantly told biblical epic that proves captivating even for nonbelievers. ★★★

Francis

(1950, 91 min, US, Arthur Lubin) *Donald O'Connor, Chill Wills.* The first in the popular 1950s comedy series about the comic hijinks of Francis, the talking mule. Before dazzling audiences with his fancy footwork in *Singin' in the Rain*, O'Connor had one of his first big hits as a G.I. who is befriended by the chatty and wisecracking animal. The entire series is dated but mindless fun, and this first entry is the best of them. Director Lubin went on to direct TV's "Mr. Ed." (Followed by 6 sequels) (DVD 4-pack includes *Francis Covers the Big Town*, *Francis Goes to the Races* and *Francis Goes to West Point*) ★★½ DVD: 19.99, VHS: $9.99

François Truffaut: Stolen Portraits

(1993, 93 min, France, Michel Pascal & Serge Toubiana) When director Eric Rohmer comes across his name on one of the hundreds of folders in the late Truffaut's study, he is nonplussed, irritated and a little bit frightened ("What's this?" he exclaims. "I don't keep a file on Truffaut in *my* office!"). Seemingly everyone who founding member of the French New Wave ever met was clipped, codified and arranged alphabetically in case the prolific director needed — somehow, to some degree — something of them in one of his cinematic tapestries. Well-chosen clips from the more famous of his works act as a kind of Greek chorus to the ex-wives, boyhood friends, actors and directors who tell many tales — some flattering, some not so. Obviously 90 minutes is not enough time to develop a full portrait of Truffaut, whose many contradictions — as a man and as an artist — invigorated so many of his movies. ★★★ VHS: $19.99

Frankenhooker

(1990, 85 min, US, Frank Henenlotter) *James Lorinz, Patty Mullen, Louise Lasser.* From the director of *Basket Case* and its sequels comes this tale of a girl who is dismembered by a lawn mower at her own birthday party and the efforts of her boyfriend to get her back together. While keeping her head on ice in the family freezer, he goes shopping for parts on 42nd Street to see what he can pick up. Great sick fun. ★★½

Frankenstein

(1931, 72 min, US, James Whale) *Boris Karloff, Colin Clive, Mae Clark, Dwight Frye.* The grand-daddy of all horror films. This classic stars Karloff as the man-made monster, Clive as the scientist who creates him ("It's alive!"), and Clark as the requisite damsel in distress. A masterpiece of suspense, atmosphere and design. (Sequel: *The Bride of Frankenstein*) ★★★★ VHS: $9.99

Frankenstein Meets the Wolf Man

(1942, 73 min, US, Roy William Neill) *Lon Chaney, Jr., Bela Lugosi, Patric Knowles, Maria Ouspenskaya.* It's Lugosi meets Chaney in this fifth entry in the *Frankenstein* series and sequel to *The Wolf Man.* This eerie, well-made story has Chaney searching to end his curse, only to do battle with the monster. As with the majority of the Universal horror films of the '30s and '40s, it's chilling to the bone. (Sequel: *House of Frankenstein*) ★★★ VHS: $14.99

Frankenweenie

(1984, 27 min, US, Tim Burton) *Shelley Duvall, Daniel Stern, Barrett Oliver.* Director Burton gives his special treatment to a young boy's undying devotion to his dog. Duvall and Stern are Oliver's parents in this dark, brooding examination of heartfelt loyalty in the face of rabid persecution. You'll see early glimmerings of *Edward Scissorhands* and *Batman*, evidence of Burton's already-strong signature. A very polished effort and O.K. for kids despite its somber tone. ★★★½

Frankie & Johnny

(1991, 118 min, US, Garry Marshall) *Al Pacino, Michelle Pfeiffer, Kate Nelligan, Hector Elizondo, Nathan Lane.* Pacino and Pfeiffer turn in a pair of charming performances in this pleasing romantic comedy about an ex-con (Pacino) who takes a job as a short order cook in a greasy-spoon diner and falls for the waitress (Pfeiffer). Excellent support includes Nelligan as an oversexed waitress, and Lane as Pfeiffer's gay best friend. Marshall's directing is overly sentimental and TV-ish, as with his previous outing, *Pretty Woman*, but Terrence McNally's adaptation of his own stage play, "Frankie and Johnny in the Clair De Lune," is strong enough to make this an enjoyable outing. ★★★ DVD: $14.99, VHS: $14.99

Frankie Starlight

(1995, 101 min, Ireland, Michael Lindsay-Hogg) *Anne Parillaud, Matt Dillon, Gabriel Byrne, Georgina Cates, Corban Walker, Alan Pentony.* This bittersweet Irish yarn tells the tale of a slightly psychic young French girl (Parillaud) and her Irish-born dwarf son, Frankie. Weeks before D-Day, Parillaud makes the disastrous error of predicting the invasion a day early. Stricken with grief, she stows away on an American troop ship only to be dropped off in Ireland, pregnant. She finds a benefactor in a kindly customs officer (Byrne) who helps her through hard times and becomes a surrogate father to Frankie, and plants in the young boy a love of stargazing. Later, G.I. Dillon shows up and woos them both with his Yankee charm. Not a lot transpires in *Frankie Starlight*, but its likable characters and generally mirthful outlook make it a completely enjoyable lark. ★★★ VHS: $19.99

Frantic

(1958, 94 min, France, Louis Malle) *Jeanne Moreau, Maurice Ronet.* Malle's first film is an elegant thriller about what can happen to the perfect crime. Moreau's lover is trapped in an elevator after murdering her husband. Subsequently, they become incriminated in a series of crimes they neither committed nor can deny, when their getaway car is stolen by a delinquent Parisian couple and is used for a rampage. A stylish film noir with a great Miles Davis score. (French with English subtitles) ★★★

Frantic

(1988, 120 min, US, Roman Polanski) *Harrison Ford, Emmanuelle Seigner, Betty Buckley, John Mahoney.* Ford gives a controlled but compelling performance as an American whose wife (Buckley) disappears on the first day of their French vacation. He discovers the sleazy underbelly of Paris at night as he unrelentingly searches for his missing wife. ★★★ DVD: $14.99, VHS: $9.99

Frauds

(1993, 94 min, GB, Stephan Elliott) *Phil Collins, Hugo Weaving, Josephine Byrnes.* Guilt, fate and the "Peter Pan Syndrome" collide in this dark British comedy that gives new meaning to the term "death by misadventure." Collins earns his acting wings as a game-playing insurance investigator who makes out like a bandit blackmailing a young couple (Weaver, Byrnes) who are guilty of insurance fraud — until the two find the prankster's own Achilles' heel. Good set design, winning performances and coal-black humor easily elevate this film above the level of standard "B-movie" fare. ★★★ VHS: $49.99

Freaked

(1993, 85 min, US, Alex Winter & Tom Stern) *Alex Winter, Randy Quaid, Brooke Shields, Mr. T, Bobcat Goldthwait.* Winter (the *other* guy from *Bill & Ted's Excellent Adventure*) codirected and cowrote this highly original, laugh-laden comedy. He plays a self-absorbed TV star who, upon being named spokesperson for the nefarious E.E.S. Corporation (Everything Except Shoes), is sent to the tropical paradise Santa Flan to curb rumors about the side effects of the company's toxic product. It is there he and a group of innocents are turned into sideshow freaks by a demented scientist/carnival owner (Quaid). Amazingly creative in its use of special effects. ★★★½ VHS: $89.99

Freaks

(1932, 64 min, US, Tod Browning) *Wallace Ford, Olga Baclanova.* Browning's shocking story of circus freaks who wreak vengeance against their cruel exploiters. Sometimes gruesome, yet a sympathetic look at society's outcasts driven by abuse to an act of terror. ★★★ DVD: $19.99

Freaky Friday

(1976, 95 min, US, Gary Nelson) *Barbara Harris, Jodie Foster, Patsy Kelly, John Astin, Dick Van Patten, Sorrell Booke, Ruth Buzzi, Kaye Ballard.* Long before the body-switching craze of the late 1980s, Harris and Foster played mother and daughter who switched identities for predictable comic results. This Disney comedy is charmingly done and benefits greatly from sparkling performances from the two ladies. (Remade in 2003) ★★★ DVD: $19.99

Freaky Friday

(2003, 93 min, US, Mark S. Waters) *Jamie Lee Curtis, Lindsay Lohan, Ryan Malgarini, Marc Harmon, Harold Gould.* Parents just don't understand . . . and neither do their kids. So when mildly rebellious (in a harmless Disney sort of way) daughter Annabelle and flustered mom Tess find themselves once again at each other's throat, a fortune cookie (administered by an unfortunate Chinese stereotype) has them switch places — and the real fun begins. As in the 1976 original, there are a bunch of mild life lessons to be sure, mostly involving Annabelle (Lohan, not quite Jodie Foster but likable enough) and her inability to accept that her mother has found a new beau. But feel free to ignore the preaching and concentrate on Curtis (picking up for Barbara Harris), who has the time of her life in her role as the 16-year-old in the body of a "cryptkeeper." She's the equal of Tom Hanks in *Big*, and that's saying something. Despite a plot rooted in fantasy, there are wickedly truthful insights into the minds of this family — it's all a blast of good fun that refuses to give in to sugary overkill. ★★★ DVD: $29.99, VHS: $24.99

Freddy Got Fingered

(2001, 92 min, US, Tom Green) *Tom Green, Rip Torn, Marisa Coughlin, Eddie Kaye Thomas, Julie Hagerty, Anthony Michael Hall.* Tom Green, "le roi du *gross* de 2000," starts off his debut as auteur recklessly skateboarding through a mall. This is apt, as *Freddy Got Fingered* owes its origins not to surrealism or gross-out comedy but punk skateboard videos, with their mix of loud music and outrageous antics. As such, Green is forgiven for not having much of a plot (a dolt's half-assed quest to become an animator); what's unforgivable is how shockingly unfunny and mean-spirited the episodic setups are. A master of confrontational humor, Green seems to feed off of unwilling participants on his TV show; here, the gags are left hanging lifeless on the scripted characters. In the process, he's reduced to a mere buffoon, performing for an audience of one. ★½ DVD: $9.99

Freddy vs. Jason

(2003, 97 min, US, Ronny Yu) *Robert Englund, Monica Keena, Jason Ritter, Ken Kirzinger.* The teaming of '80s horror giants Freddy and Jason arrives after many years of speculation and anticipation and the result just isn't worth the wait. *Freddy vs. Jason* begins dreadfully with Freddy telling us the premise of the film! After this stumbling block, you'd think it could only get better — just barely. The teen characters we're introduced to are as bland and annoying as any in the worst entries of the *Nightmare* or *Friday the 13th* series, and even though Mr. Krueger has kindly explained the plot to us, these dorks still have to spell it out again *ad nauseum*. Though there are one or two clever lines for longtime fans of both series, and it's certainly bloody enough, this matchup creates few sparks and ruins one helluva an idea. It's in desperate need of a bit more brains and balls. ★½ DVD Dual: $29.99, VHS: $22.99

A Free Soul

(1931, 91 min, US, Clarence Brown) *Clark Gable, Lionel Barrymore, Norma Shearer, Leslie Howard, James Gleason.* Barrymore won an Oscar for his solid portrayal of a lawyer defending mobster Gable on a murder charge. Shearer plays the attorney's daughter, who falls in love with Gable. The film is impeccably acted, and helped launch Gable on the road to stardom. ★★★ VHS: $14.99

Free Willy

(1993, 111 min, US, Simon Wincer) *Jason James Richter, Lori Petty, Michael Madsen.* Director Wincer pulls every cheap emotional trick out of his bag in this tale of a boy and his whale and, for the most part, he succeeds in his efforts. Kind of an *E.T.* of the sea, the film follows a runaway (Richter) from the foster care system who, after vandalizing a local marine park, is taken under the wing of the park's employees and befriended by their charge, an unhappy whale named Willy. But when the park's greedy owner sees profits in killing the whale and collecting the insurance, our young hero is pressed into action to save his friend. Yes, it reeks of tearjerking formulaity, but the film is nevertheless a winner amongst its target audience — kids. (Followed by 2 sequels) ★★½ DVD 10th Anniversary: $19.99, VHS: $14.99

Free Willy 2: The Adventure Home

(1995, 96 min, US, Dwight Little) *Jason James Richter, August Schellenberg, Jayne Atkinson, Michael Madsen, Elizabeth Peña, Mykelti Williamson, M. Emmet Walsh, Francis Capra.* Jesse (Richter) and his whale pal Willy are reunited for more adventure in this amiable sequel that ambitiously tackles ecological, Native American and coming-of-age themes. While on a family camping trip, Jesse makes contact with Willy, who has been reunited with his family. When an oil tanker runs aground and spills its contents, Willy and his family's lives are threatened by the spill. The first half of the film takes its time setting up the plot, and the human story of Jesse's mother's death is maudlin. However, the scenes with Jesse and Willy have an excitement to them, especially the film's finale which pits Jesse against greedy industrialists and a deadly oil fire. ★★½ DVD Letterbox: $14.99, VHS: $14.99

Free Willy 3: The Rescue

(1997, 86 min, US, Sam Pillsbury) *Jason James Richter, August Schellenberg, Annie Corley, Vincent Berry.* Young Max (Berry) finds out that he is the son of a whale poacher when he accompanies his father for the first time on a fishing trip. Jesse (Richter), back from the first two *Willy* films and now a teenager, has followed Willy to Alaska and is on a whale tracking research team. The team comes upon the whalers just as they are about to make a kill, but fail to obtain hard evidence of their crime. Max and Jesse become friends and work together to stop the poaching. Simplistic in its story and execution, there's a good ecological message for kids, but the film veers towards overkill. ★★½ DVD Letterbox: $14.99, VHS: $14.99

Freedom Is Paradise

(1989, 75 min, Russia, Sergei Bodrov) The innocent young boy in search "of freedom" or "of his father" has been a consistent theme in Russian filmmaking. Films like *Freeze, Die, Come to Life* and *Come and See* all use the boy as a symbol of a new, true Russia lost in a harsh post-Communist world. This harrowing yet lyrical drama centers on 13-year-old Sasha who, after his mother dies, begins a journey through the barren worlds of Alma Ata in middle Asia to the outskirts of Leningrad, all in a determined quest to find his long-imprisoned father. A serious and gripping tale of persistence and perseverance. (Russian with English subtitles) ★★★½ VHS: $59.99

Freefall

(1993, 96 min, US, John Irvin) *Jeff Fahey, Pamela Gidley, Eric Roberts.* B-movie bad boys Fahey and Roberts costar in this engaging espionage thriller about a photographer (Gidley) who becomes an unwitting pawn in a game of international cat and mouse when she launches into an affair with a rakish CIA operative (Roberts) who has taken a professional interest in her publishing mogul fiancé (Fahey). Despite the *Cliffhanger*esque packaging, this spy tale keeps the pulse pounding right up to the end. ★★★

Freejack

(1991, 110 min, US, Geoff Murphy) *Emilio Estevez, Mick Jagger, Anthony Hopkins.* An insipid sci-fi thriller from the producer/cowriter of *Alien* and *Total Recall*. With special effects that far outshine the acting, the film features a catatonic Estevez as a cocky race car driver who is taken from the 20th century into the future by the lunar-faced Jagger, who sports a smirk throughout the film as if to say, "And I get paid plenty for this!" Jagger is the hired hand of an evil industrialist who wants to prolong his life by transferring the life juices of our young hero into his dying body. ★½ DVD: $14.99, VHS: $14.99

Freeway

(1996, 101 min, US, Matthew Bright) *Kiefer Sutherland, Reese Witherspoon, Wolfgang Bodison, Dan Hedaya, Amanda Plummer, Brooke Shields.* Witherspoon is a revelation as Vanessa, a whitetrash gal with morals, guts and spunk who gets into a load of trouble when she decides to visit her grandmother. This darkly funny indy — written and directed by Bright — features the often miscast Sutherland as Bob, a demented psychologist who picks up the stranded Vanessa on the highway. But is he a notorious serial rapist/murderer, or just a horny guy who gets kinky with a hot teen in his car? Well, Witherspoon doesn't wait for the 6:00 News to find out and her decision leads to violence, revelations and a manhunt. Funny, vicious and quite unusual (the body count is surprisingly high). (Sequel: *Freeway 2: Confessions of a Trickbaby*) ★★★½ DVD Letterbox: $9.99, VHS: $9.99

Freeway 2: Confessions of a Trickbaby

(1999, 90 min, US, Matthew Bright) *Natasha Lyonne, Vincent Gallo, Maria Celedonio, David Alan Grier, Michael T. Weiss, John Landis, Max Perlich.* Bright's follow-up is unrelated to the original, except for its twisted tone and over-the-top grotesqueness. Yes, that's a compliment. The opening scenes show White Girl (Lyonne), a hardened criminal not even 20 years of age, being incarcerated. There she befriends psychotic Cyclona (Celedonio); they escape and set out on a road trip to find a mystic nun (Gallo). Loosely paralleling the Hansel and Gretel fairy tale (like *Freeway*'s Red Riding Hood connections), *Freeway 2* plays even more like Bright's fetish reel: girls killing, girls injecting, girls masturbating. It's all done with outrageous humor and style, and somehow Bright still pulls compelling, inhibition-free performances from his female leads. Great late-night fun. ★★★

Freeze, Die, Come to Life

(1990, 105 min, Russia, Vitaly Kanevski) *Pavel Nazarov, Dinara Drukarova.* A brutal and uncompromising look at Soviet life under the Stalin regime as seen through the eyes of a young boy. The Party faithful are rallying villagers for a May Day celebration amid the abysmal poverty and unceasingly overcast skies in a remote Siberian outpost. The young protagonist, a pint-sized rebel and unwilling scapegoat, struggles gamely against hypocrisy, toadyism and bureaucratic myopia while maintaining his high spirits and fierce sense of individuality. Filmed with a raw, documentarylike feel, the film is sometimes bitter, often funny and insightful, and has moments of touching tenderness. It's also reminiscent of the equally superlative *Come and See*. ★★★½

French Can-Can

(1955, 102 min, France, Jean Renoir) *Jean Gabin, Françoise Arnoul, Edith Piaf.* Set during La Belle Epoche in Paris' lively Montemartre, Renoir's gloriously vibrant tribute to the music hall shimmers with the brilliant colors of the director's palate. *French Can-Can* weaves a tale of jilted lovers, ambitious artists and scheming "angels." Gabin, the Gallic Bogart, portrays an amorous impresario with a dream to revive the can-can in a renovated nightclub, which will become the legendary Moulin Rouge. Surrounding him is a circus of dance, love and music, and the people swept up in the exhilarating rhythms of the theatre. (French with English subtitles) ★★★★ VHS: $24.99

The French Connection

(1971, 104 min, US, William Friedkin) *Gene Hackman, Roy Scheider, Fernando Rey.* Hackman's tour-de-force performance as real-life New York City detective Popeye Doyle dominates this slambang police adventure about Doyle hunting down an international narcotics ring. Scheider also stars as Hackman's partner. Winner of five Academy Awards, including Best Picture. (Sequel: *French Connection II*) ★★★½ DVD Five Star Collection: $26.99, VHS Special Edition: $19.99

The French Connection II

(1975, 119 min, US, John Frankenheimer) *Gene Hackman, Fernando Rey, Bernard Fresson.* Hackman returns in this exciting sequel to the original Oscar winner. Popeye Doyle continues his search for an international drug ring, headed by Rey (who also returns from the first film). ★★★

The French Detective

(1975, 100 min, France, Pierre Granier-Deferre) *Lino Ventura, Patrick Dewaere, Victor Lanoux.* An entertaining police story that pits a determined middle-aged cop (Ventura) and his cynical young partner (Dewaere) against a ruthless and elusive politician. (French with English subtitles) ★★★

French Exit

(1996, 92 min, US, Daphna Kastner) *Jonathan Silverman, Madchen Amick, Molly Hagan.* A lightweight set-in-Hollywood romantic farce, this firsttime effort from actress Kastner plays like "Four Parties and a Reconciliation." Silverman and Amick are both screenwriters who are competing for the writing assignment on a remake of *Mutiny on the Bounty* (her take: all female). Then they fall in love. Then they break up. Then they get back together again. And so on. Some of the Hollywood insider stuff is enjoyable on an elementary level, but few sparks fly between the two leads. This routine film is at its best when it tries to be daring, like having Timothy Leary (in a cameo) handing out Ecstasylaced cups of tea at one of those schmooze-fests. ★★

French Kiss

(1995, 111 min, US, Lawrence Kasdan) *Kevin Kline, Meg Ryan, Timothy Hutton, Jean Reno, François Cluzet.* Ryan plays an American émigré who's engaged to Canadian doctor Hutton. He flies to Paris for a business trip. Since she's afraid to fly, she stays home. Bad move. He meets a beautiful French woman and breaks the engagement. This sends her abroad. On the flight, she meets French jewel thief Kline, who uses her to help smuggle his latest booty. In an effort to keep track of her and the jewels, he pretends to help her win Hutton back. Of course, love blossoms. *French Kiss* is a lot more funny and endearing than the formulaic plot suggests, thanks to

Ashley Judd (l.) and Salma Hayek burn up the screen in *Frida*

the frothy pace set by director Kasdan and the pleasant performances by its two stars. Ryan and Kline wrangle fresh interpretations of parts they've played before. ★★★ DVD: $14.99, VHS: $6.99

French Lesson

(1986, 90 min, GB, Brian Gilbert) *Jane Snowden, Alexandre Sterling.* Snowden stars in this amusing little comedy of manners about a young English woman who sojourns to France where she receives a schooling in affairs of the heart. ★★½ VHS: $14.99

The French Lieutenant's Woman

(1981, 124 min, GB, Karel Reisz) *Meryl Streep, Jeremy Irons, Leo McKern.* This passionate tale of a mysterious woman's obsession shines with the excellent acting of Streep and Irons, and the intriguingly complex screenplay by Harold Pinter. ★★★ DVD Letterbox: $19.99

French Twist

(1995, 100 min, France, Josiane Balasko) *Josiane Balasko, Victoria Abril, Alain Chabat.* This whimsical French farce with a lesbian twist nicely blends all the outrageousness of its genre with some finely drawn subtleties to create a highly amusing *divertimento* that is peppered throughout with touching moments. Abril is Loli, the dutiful (and housebound) Spanish wife of a boorish French real estate broker (Chabat). Marijo (Balasko), a bohemian, cigar-smoking dyke from Paris, lands on their doorstep in the South of France with a broken-down VW minivan and, after a bit of small talk, makes a pass at Loli. Starved for the attentions of her philandering husband, Loli responds warmly to these advances, much to his outrage. Filled with the standard burlesque guffaws, *French Twist* is most impressive for its even-handed treatment of its characters. Balasko is quite fetching as a boyishly macho lesbian, Abril's range of emotion is sensational and her radiance is enough to capture the heart of any sexual persuasion. (French with English subtitles) ★★★ DVD: $19.99, VHS: $9.99

The French Way

(1952, 72 min, France, Michel Deville) *Josephine Baker, Micheline Presle.* This wartime musical comedy is generally pedestrian fare, but the presense of Baker helps make it of interest. Ms. Baker, who sings five songs in the film, plays cupid to two young lovers who cannot marry because of their feuding parents. (French with English subtitles) ★★

French Woman

(1979, 97 min, France, Just Jaeckin) *Françoise Fabian, Klaus Kinski.* A shocking sex scandal rocks the French government in this tale of blackmail and murder. Fabian stars as the real-life madam whose clientele included some of the world's most influential leaders. (aka: *Madame Claude*) ★★

Frenzy

(1972, 116 min, GB, Alfred Hitchcock) *Jon Finch, Alec McCowen, Barry Foster, Vivien Merchant, Anna Massey, Billie Whitelaw.* Brilliant latter-day Hitchcock. A suave London strangler ingeniously incriminates an innocent man in a wave of murders. A bold and crafty reassertion of Hitch's mastery of the suspense genre. ★★★★ DVD: $29.99

Frequency

(2000, 119 min, US, Gregory Hoblit) *Jim Caviezel, Andre Braugher, Elizabeth Mitchell, Dennis Quaid, Noah Emmerich.* Mixing equal parts sentiment, fantasy, thrills and the most moving father-son bond since *Field of Dreams*, *Frequency* takes a rather implausible premise and makes it work with a little bit of heart, a touch of cleverness, and plenty of "spirit and guts." Quaid plays Frank Sullivan, a heroic fireman living with his wife and young son John in 1969 Queens. Caviezel is a grown-up John, a police officer in the year 2000. When they are able to contact each other on Frank's ham radio 30 years apart, it sets in motion a remolding of fate and the hunt for a serial killer. Screenwriter Toby Emmerich plays a little fast and loose with the concepts of time and space, but he's also created a handful of characters who should win over even the most skeptical. ★★★ DVD: $19.99, VHS: $14.99

Fresh

(1994, 115 min, US, Boaz Yakin) *Sean Nelson, Giancarlo Esposito, Samuel L. Jackson, N'Bushe Wright.* Starkly realized and ingeniously crafted, this urban coming-of-age drama follows an inner-city youth as he struggles to ride out life in the mean streets of Harlem. Nelson delivers a disturbing portrayal as Fresh, a tensomething chess wizard (and a hardened drug runner) who is teetering on the edge of a life of crime. His dispassionate, calculating approach to life offers the viewer a sobering look at a vanquished generation, and his Machiavellian maneuvers and innovative survival skills make this much more than just another blighted urban/teen melodrama. Excellent support comes from Jackson as his unemployed father, a fallen chess master to whom the boy regularly turns for advice. ★★★½ DVD Letterbox Collector's Edition: $14.99, VHS: $9.99

Fresh Horses

(1988, 105 min, US, David Anspaugh) *Molly Ringwald, Andrew McCarthy, Ben Stiller, Patti D'Arbanville.* After she turned on *The Pick-Up Artist* and he scored *Less Than Zero*, it was uncertain if Ringwald and McCarthy could sink any lower in their careers. Well, they could. Essentially a wrong-side-of-the-tracks romantic drama, this totally contrived and suprisingly moribund film, about rich college student McCarthy falling for poor but sexy Ringwald, isn't even for fans of the two stars. ★ DVD: $24.99

The Freshman

(1990, 102 min, US, Andrew Bergman) *Marlon Brando, Matthew Broderick, Maximilian Schell, Bruno Kirby.* This delightfully droll comedy stars Broderick as a film student who takes a job as a messenger to a presumed Mafia don (Brando). Brando, with no apologies, patterns his role after another Mafia don he made famous in a cinema classic back in the '70s — and he's terrifically funny. Look for a show-stopping cameo by Bert Parks. ★★★½ DVD: $14.99

Frida

(1984, 108 min, Mexico, Paul Leduc) *Ofelia Medina, Juan Jose Gurrola.* The life of painter, revolutionary and woman-of-the-world Frida Kahlo is brilliantly brought to the screen in this insightful and poetic biography. Told from her deathbed in surreal flashbacks reminiscent of her own canvases, the film recalls Frida's stormy relationship with muralist Diego Rivera, her dealings with Leon Trotsky, her involvement with the cultural renaissance in Mexico in the 1930s, as well as captures the spirit and determination of one of the dominant painters of the 20th century. (Spanish with English subtitles) ★★★

Frida

(2002, 120 min, US, Julie Taymor) *Salma Hayek, Alfred Molina, Antonio Banderas, Valeria Golino, Geoffrey Rush, Ashley Judd, Edward Norton, Mia Maestro, Roger Rees.* Frida Kahlo, born to relative comfort in Mexico in 1907, was precocious, rebellious, the apple of her photographer father's eye; which helped her combat childhood polio and the excruciating lifelong aftereffects of a debilitating accident that nearly killed her. She participated in the social and political movements of her tumultuous times, and, like her mate Diego Rivera, created timeless, vibrant art. She crossed paths with Trotsky and Rockefeller, led protest marches through the streets and sat in Parisian cafes as the toast of the town. Hayek's evocation of Kahlo's spirit and vigor is a singular performance, a remarkable re-creation that does justice to Kahlo as complex persona and historical figure. The film flows effortlessly, charting her travels across continents, over decades, through her rich interior life. *Frida* moves from quasidocumentary to meditative dream with arresting images hyper-realized in saturated colors and swirling desert sand. Life transmutes into art, art reveals the inner canvas of a soul. Director Taymor delineates this remarkable life with respect, wit, humor and affection, recounting this peripatetic, multilayered herstory in a beautiful arc, with profound symmetry and completion. ★★★½ DVD 2-disc set: $19.99, VHS: $9.99

Friday

(1995, 96 min, US, F. Gary Gray) *Ice Cube, Chris Tucker, Johnny Witherspoon, Tiny Lister, La Wanda Paige.* This well-written (by Cube and DJ

Pooh) hip-hop comedy chronicles a day in the life of a pair of homeboys in South Central Los Angeles who try to raise enough money to pay a debt to a pot dealer. Spiced with acid-tongued dialogue, *Friday* is a most amusing, energetic romp. (Followed by 3 sequels) ★★★ DVD: $19.99, VHS: $14.99

Friday the 13th

(1980, 96 min, US, Sean S. Cunningham) *Betsy Palmer, Adrienne King, Kevin Bacon.* Director Cunningham started the slasher genre with this gory though unexciting thriller about an unknown killer stalking camp counselors at Camp Crystal Lake. Jason would come back for eight more helpings. ★★ DVD: $14.99, VHS: $9.99

Fried Green Tomatoes

(1991, 130 min, US, Jon Avnet) *Kathy Bates, Mary Stuart Masterson, Mary-Louise Parker, Jessica Tandy, Cicely Tyson, Chris O'Donnell, Stan Shaw, Lois Smith.* Based on Fannie Flagg's novel, this heartwarming, touching and funny film revolves around two separate stories: one present-day and one set in the 1930s. Ignored housewife Bates meets charmer Tandy at a retirement home. It is there Tandy tells her the story of Idgy and Ruth, two friends from her youth in a small, nearby Alabama town. It is the latter story that is at the core of this tender, remarkable film. And as these two women, the incredible Masterson and the wonderful Parker deliver multilayered performances worthy of their storyteller's adulation. And through these stories Bates is inspired to instill in herself newfound self-esteem. A lovely piece of pop filmmaking with indelible performances by a gifted cast. ★★★½ DVD Letterbox Collector's Edition: $19.99, VHS: $9.99, VHS Letterbox: $14.99

A Friend of the Deceased

(1998, 100 min, Ukraine, Vyacheslav Krishtofovich) *Alexandre Lazarev, Tatiana Krivitska, Eugen Pachin, Elena Korikova.* This Ukrainian twist on *It's a Wonderful Life* is poignant, funny, and, ultimately, romantic. Anatoli (Lazarev) is an unemployable translator who's wife has left him, and who has lost the will to live. Deciding to commit suicide, he hires a hit man to kill him, but a series of encounters with an old friend (Pachin), a kind-hearted prostitute (Krivitska) and a recent widow (Korikova), force Anatoli to reconsider his decision. What makes *A Friend of the Deceased* special is that Anatoli is a kind of an Everyman, dissatisfied with his place in the world, yet also unable to change it. He represents a member of post-Communist Kiev, where his opportunities are limited — unless he makes them himself. Director Krishtofovich has created a resonant drama that speaks to anyone who has ever found himself trapped in an inescapable rut. As Anatoli, the handsome Lazarev gives a great performance in this highly affecting film. (Russian with English subtitles) ★★★½

Friendly Persuasion

(1956, 138 min, US, William Wyler) *Gary Cooper, Dorothy McGuire, Anthony Perkins, Marjorie Main.* Wyler's absorbing and sensitive adaptation of Jessamyn West's novel is about a Quaker family trying to maintain their religious beliefs during the days of the Civil War. An exceptional cast. ★★★½ DVD: $19.99

Friends Forever

(1986, 95 min, Denmark, Stefan Christian Henszelman) A teenage boy's sexual and emotional development is the theme in this pleasant Danish drama. Shy Kristian is a gangly and innocent 16-year-old who becomes friends with two very different boys — Henrik, a slightly effeminate and determinedly nonconformist student, and Patrick, a blond thug. When Patrick tells him that he is gay and introduces him to his older lover, Kristian is thrown into emotional turmoil. Similar to Denmark's other adolescent gay drama *You Are Not Alone*, this simple yet unpredictable story presents a positive outlook on a young man's sexual coming out and its effect on his friends. (Danish with English subtitles) ★★★

Fright Night

(1985, 105 min, US, Tom Holland) *Chris Sarandon, William Ragsdale, Roddy McDowall, Amanda Bearse, Stephen Geoffreys.* First-time writer-director Holland takes the Gothic out of vampire lore and plops it right down in the middle of American suburbs. In this wonderfully toothsome twist on the "Boy Who Cried Wolf" story, a young teen desperately trys to convince people that his new neighbor is not the handsome lady-killer he seems to be — except the part about "lady-killer," of course. He finally enlists the reluctant help of a washed-up TV horror show host (McDowall). Sarandon is exquisite as the vampire and Ragsdale lends an over-the-top urgency to the young ghoul-chaser. Geoffreys is particularly effective as Ragsdale's hapless cohort. (Sequel: *Fright Night Pt. 2*) ★★★ DVD: $14.99, VHS: $9.99

Fright Night Pt. 2

(1988, 101 min, US, Tommy Lee Wallace) *Roddy McDowall, William Ragsdale, Traci Lind.* The sister of the vampire killed in the original is out for blood against those who killed him — including TV horror film host Peter Vincent (McDowall); until she finally sees the light about what's at stake with her degenerate lifestyle. ★★ DVD: $14.99, VHS: $9.99

The Frighteners

(1996, 110 min, US, Peter Jackson) *Michael J. Fox, Trini Alvarado, Jeffrey Combs, Dee Wallace Stone, Jake Busey, R. Lee Ermey.* Jackson proves once again that he's an original with this horror/suspense/private eye/love story/serial killer/ghost comedy. Fox is Frank Bannister, a con man ghost-hunter who has the unique power to see the dearly departed. He stumbles into the middle of a series of murders being committed by a ghastly apparition only he can see. Able to determine who will be next on this soultaker's list, he decides to use his gift to stop the malevolent spirit when a beautiful young widow (Alvarado) shows up with a number on her head. Exhilarating from start to finish, *The Frighteners* features terrific computer-generated special effects and is a brilliant fusion of comedy and horror, alternately hilarious and downright shocking. ★★★½ DVD Letterbox: $19.99, VHS: $9.99

The Fringe Dwellers

(1986, 101 min, Australia, Bruce Beresford) *Kristina Nehm, Justine Saunders.* This exotic film concerns Australia's Aborigines, whose story is similar to that of the American Indian, and the sad and frustrating fact that their tribal roots are disintegrating as they become displaced in their own land. The story follows Trilby, an Aborigine who seeks to leave her community to live out her dreams of romance and high living in the big city. ★★★ VHS: $79.99

The Frisco Kid

(1979, 122 min, US, Robert Aldrich) *Harrison Ford, Gene Wilder.* Aldrich captures the warmth and poignancy that could have so easily been lost in this tale of the Old West set in the 1850s. Bank robber Ford becomes the reluctant guide for rabbi Wilder on his way to join his congregation in California. A nice mixture of comedy and sentimental dramatics. ★★★ VHS: $14.99

Frisk

(1995, 83 min, US, Todd Verow) *Michael Gunther, Craig Chester, Jaie Laplante, Raoul O'Connell, Parker Posey, Alexis Arquette.* Verow makes a memorable if controversial feature film debut with this adaptation of Dennis Cooper's 1991 novel of homosexuality, sadism and murder. Dennis (Gunther) is a young gay man who experiences problems with his sexual persona. He meets Henry (Chester), a drugged-out masochist with no self-esteem. What begins as playfully violent sexual antics culminates in murder. Graphic in its gay sex scenes, the film escalates to an almost unwatchable intensity as the violence becomes all too real — or is it simply imagined? Technically proficient and intelligently made, *Frisk*'s ominous content prompts the question of what is being said about gay men. No easy answers here. ★★★ DVD: $29.99

Fritz the Cat

(1972, 78 min, US, Ralph Bakshi) R. Crumb's raunchy feline comes to life in this full-length X-rated cartoon crammed with good humor and bad taste. Whips up more obscenity and violence than Disney dared dream of. ★★★ DVD Letterbox: $19.99

Frogs for Snakes

(1999, 98 min, US, Amos Poe) *Barbara Hershey, Robbie Coltrane, Harry Hamlin, Ian Hart, John Leguizamo, Lisa Marie, Clarence Williams III, Debi Mazar.* Indie crime drama is an interesting failure — an attempt to meld a low-key gangster flick with an acting class. A group of New Yorkers — all acting students from the same class who moonlight as hit men and the like for off-Broadway producer and crime boss Coltrane — double-cross and murder each other, mostly in the name of securing a good stage role. While the satire is fairly original though obvious, it does get a little tiresome by the end, what with every member of the cast doing at least one monologue from a classic film or play. *Frogs for Snakes* is for crime film completists and acting students only. ★★ VHS: $14.99

From Beyond

(1986, 85 min, US, Stuart Gordon) *Jeffrey Combs, Barbara Crampton.* Gordon's effective follow-up to his acclaimed *Re-Animator*. Once again borrowing from the works of H.P. Lovecraft, Gordon fills his film with outstanding and quite eerie special effects for his story about a doctor investigating the death of a scientist, who becomes obsessed with the dead man's experiments with the "beyond." ★★★

From Beyond the Grave

(1973, 97 min, GB, Kevin Connor) *Peter Cushing, Donald Pleasence, David Warner, Ian Bannen, Margaret Leighton.* Four customers each try to rip off antique dealer Cushing in some way, and — as is always the case in these kinds of films — get their just deserts in various macabre and supernatural ways. The best story involves an old doorway that opens a portal into a sinister world which threatens to suck in and destroy a young married couple. Lots of ghoulish fun and great entertainment on a dark night. ★★½ VHS: $14.99

From Dusk Till Dawn

(1996, 107 min, US, Robert Rodriguez) *George Clooney, Quentin Tarantino, Harvey Keitel, Juliette Lewis, Cheech Marin, Fred Williamson, Salma Hayek, Tom Savini, Michael Parks.* Easily the most entertaining horror/action/comedy since *Evil Dead 2.* Two homicidal brothers (Clooney, Tarantino) take a lapsed Baptist minister (Keitel) and his family hostage on their run to the Mexican border. Once across, the only thing that stands between them and freedom is one night in a rough-and-tumble biker/trucker bar called the Titty Twister. Unbeknownst to them, the bar is home to a horde of shape-shifting vampires (including gorgeous vampiress Hayek). Screenwriter Tarantino effortlessly combines the best elements of two genres — the film begins as an escaped-convicts-road movie and turns on a dime into the realm of zombie and vampire flick. Gory and very adult themed, *From Dusk Till Dawn* will leave its audience alternately gasping, screaming and laughing. (Sequel: *From Dusk Till Dawn 2: Texas Blood Money*) ★★★½ DVD Collector's Edition: $19.99, VHS: $9.99

From Dusk Till Dawn 2: Texas Blood Money

(1998, 88 min, US, Scott Spiegel) *Robert Patrick, Bo Hopkins, Duane Whitaker, Raymond Cruz, Bruce Campbell, Tiffani-Amber Thiessen.* A straight-to-video sequel, this blood-soaked vampire tale lacks the visceral thrills and comic punch of the original. A group of good 'ol boys looks to knock off a bank, but vampires from the local Titty Twister have other ideas. The story takes forever to get started, but when the carnage commences, *Dawn 2* is quite over-the-top. It's not all that suspenseful, but it certainly has its share of vampiric activity. ★★ DVD: $14.99, VHS: $9.99

From Dusk Till Dawn 3: The Hangman's Daughter

(1999, 94 min, US/Mexico, P.J. Pesce) *Sonnia Braga, Michael Parks, Rebecca Gayheart, Marco Leonardi, Danny Trejo.* Inspired by the real-life disappearance of writer Ambrose Bierce in Mexico, *FDTD3* follows Bierce as he tangles with a variety of stereotypes before ending up at a brothel run by vampires. Unlike *FDTD2*, this film follows the exact structure as the original: it's a straight-faced (if over-the-top) western for the first hour before shifting gears and becoming a flat-out horror film. The problem is, this time we expect the horror, so surprise is nil, and while the horror scenes are OK, the buildup is not, lacking the much-needed Tarantino wit and George Clooney charisma. ★½ DVD: $14.99, VHS: $9.99

From Hell

(2001, 115 min, US, The Hughes Brothers) *Johnny Depp, Heather Graham, Ian Holm, Robbie Coltrane, Katrin Cartlidge, Jason Flemyng.* Hell is said to exist on many levels. There is hell on earth; the mythic hell of fire and brimstone; there's also one man's hell that is another's heaven. No matter what our perception of it is, it couldn't be much worse than the hell imagined by the Hughes Brothers in their merciless, gritty telling of Jack the Ripper's reign of terror in 19th-century London. Based on the graphic novel by Alan Moore and Eddie Campbell, *From Hell* captures time and place

Burt Lancaster and Deborah Kerr's quintessential embrace in *From Here to Eternity*

exceedingly well, the smallest detail not overlooked. However, this is an unsettling journey, one distinguished by an unusually good look — murder and gore have rarely looked so shockingly splendid. Depp plays an unorthodox police inspector (he's a drug addict and psychic) assigned the case of the Ripper, who is mutilating East End prostitutes. As he digs deeper — much in the same vein as the excellent *Murder by Decree* — clues begin to point to high society and the royal palace. *From Hell* is essentially a mystery story, not a horror tale, but one told with the elements of a horror film. The directors know there's no more effective monster than man at his basest, and they spare little in conveying such. For in the dark, everyone looks the same, and each approaching stranger is either salvation or doom. ★★★ DVD: $19.99, VHS: $9.99

From Here to Eternity

(1953, 118 min, US, Fred Zinnemann) *Burt Lancaster, Deborah Kerr, Montgomery Clift, Donna Reed, Frank Sinatra, Ernest Borgnine.* A brilliant cast brings to the screen James Jones' novel of pre-WWII life in an outstanding adaptation in which everything clicks — from the multilayered screenplay to director Zinnemann's focused eye to a gallery of indelible performances. Set in Pearl Harbor just before the Japanese attack, the film follows the lives of a group of soldiers stationed in Hawaii. Lancaster excels as the impassioned sergeant involved with commander's wife Kerr. In what is the performance of his career, Clift plays a trumpet-playing G.I. whose soul-searching is at odds with military sensibility. Sinatra and Reed both won Oscars in support as, respectively, a private and a dance-hall hostess. Lancaster and Kerr appear in one of the most famous lovemaking scenes of all time: sand, saltwater and seaweed never looked so good. ★★★★ DVD: $19.99, DVD Superbit Edition: $26.99, VHS: $14.99

From Mao to Mozart

(1980, 84 min, US, Murray Lerner) This Academy Award-winning documentary follows Isaac Stern on his 1979 tour of Communist China. Whether on stage performing, or encouraging budding violinists to feel their playing, Stern is always an electrifying presence. ★★★½ DVD: $24.99, VHS: $19.99

From Russia with Love

(1964, 118 min, GB, Terence Young) *Sean Connery, Lotte Lenya, Robert Shaw, Daniela Bianchi.* Super spy James Bond (Connery) must retrieve a top secret decoder machine and return it to England. The second, and many say the best, of the

Bond adventures has Lotte Lenya as a sinister spy determined to terminate Agent 007. Plenty of suspense and hair-raising encounters. (Sequel: *Goldfinger*) ★★★½

From the Earth to the Moon

(1958, 100 min, US, Byron Haskin) *Joseph Cotten, George Sanders, Debra Pagent.* Cotten and Sanders play rival munitions manufacturers teaming up to reach the moon in this unusually faithful adaptation (except for the stowaway love interest) of the Jules Verne story. Director Haskin (*War of the Worlds*) captures a good sense of place and era that imbues the film with charm, if not scientific accuracy. ★★½

From the Hip

(1987, 111 min, US, Bob Clark) *Judd Nelson, Elizabeth Perkins, John Hurt, Ray Walston.* From the director of *Porky's* comes this courtroom comedy that turns rather suspenseful at the end. Nelson is the brash upstart lawyer whose courtroom theatrics would embarrass even F. Lee Bailey, as he is faced with defending a repellent murder suspect (Hurt at his most flamboyant). ★★½ DVD Letterbox: $19.99, VHS: $9.99

From the Life of Marionettes

(1980, 104 min, West Germany, Ingmar Bergman) *Robert Atzorn, Christine Buchegger, Martin Benrath.* This harrowing and provocative film was made in West Germany during Bergman's celebrated self-exile from Sweden for tax-evasion charges. His troubled mental state could be a clue to his harrowing story of a successful but dangerously psychotic businessman who is obsessed with killing his unfaithful wife. This obsession leads him into the sleazy world of sex clubs where he brutally murders a prostitute. An unsettling film, not for everyone, but insightful for Bergmanphiles. (German with English subtitles) ★★½ VHS: $29.99

The Front

(1976, 94 min, US, Martin Ritt) *Woody Allen, Zero Mostel, Herschel Bernardi, Joshua Shelley, Lloyf Gough.* This dramatization doesn't stray from the real-life situation that too many American artists found themselves in during the Truman and Eisenhower years — a reality that seems to be re-emerging in other forms today (John Ashcroft, take a bow). In this drama with comedic overtones, director Ritt captures an era permeated with fear, necessitating Allen to front for desperate writers blacklisted for having Communist associations. The film is all the more powerful knowing that director Ritt, costars

Mostel (in a terrific supporting turn), Bernardi, Shelley, Gough and writer Walter Bernstein were all victims of the Hollywood witchhunt. ★★★½

The Front Page

(1931, 103 min, US, Lewis Milestone) *Adolphe Menjou, Pat O'Brien, Mae Clarke, Edward Everett Horton.* This early talkie starts talking and doesn't stop. Menjou plays the ruthless newspaper editor who will do anything to beat the rival papers covering the execution of a convicted murderer. O'Brien is his reporter who will abandon his fiancée and his ethics to get that interview by helping the convict escape. This first filming of the Hecht/MacArthur comedy — later gender-switched into *His Girl Friday,* then remade by Billy Wilder, and updated as *Switching Channels* — is fast and funny and as cynical as a *National Enquirer* headline. ★★★½

The Front Page

(1974, 105 min, US, Billy Wilder) *Jack Lemmon, Walter Matthau, Susan Sarandon, Carol Burnett, Vincent Gardenia, David Wayne, Allen Garfield, Austin Pendleton, Charles Durning.* In this third screen version of the Hecht-MacArthur classic, director Wilder's usual subtle comic hand is missing in action as everything is played too broadly. Lemmon and Matthau do their best as feuding newspapermen, and there are laughs inherent in the story's superior set-up, but much of the original's vitriol has been stripped of its comic essence, resulting in brittle jokes and shameless caricatures. ★★ VHS: $14.99

Frozen Assets

(1992, 96 min, US, George Miller) *Shelley Long, Corbin Bernsen, Larry Miller, Matt Clark.* This thematic mishmash manages somehow to combine plot lines about a bordello-like sperm bank, a stud-of-the-year contest and frustrated unemployed prostitutes into what appears to be a family comedy. Bernsen is a low-level executive sent to a small town to improve the finances of the community sperm bank. Long is the uptight biochemical engineer in charge of the "bank." ★ VHS: $79.99

The Fugitive

(1947, 104 min, US, John Ford) *Henry Fonda, Dolores Del Rio, Pedro Armendiaz, Sr.* Affecting political allegory set in an anticlerical, totalitarian Mexican state about a priest (Fonda) on the run from zealous government officials. Director Ford's classic tale, told with foreboding and awash with shadows, is a subdued but nevertheless arresting portrait of a corrupt state versus the indomitable faith of its people. Filmed on location in Mexico. ★★★½

The Fugitive

(1993, 127 min, US, Andrew Davis) *Harrison Ford, Tommy Lee Jones, Jeroen Krabbé, Joe Pantoliano, Julianne Moore, Sela Ward.* Though not the first, nor last, TV-to-big screen adaptation, *The Fugitive* is certainly the final word. Ford takes over the part once immortalized by David Janssen in the classic 1960s TV show: Dr. Richard Kimble, a successful surgeon falsely convicted of murdering his wife. En route to prison, Kimble escapes, setting into motion a massive manhunt led by the relentless Det. Gerard (marvelously played by Oscar winner Jones). Rather than simply rehash the original series, director Davis and his writers have updated and re-energized a quintessential TV drama with remarkable success. A breathtaking adventure and a fascinating detective story told at breakneck speed, *The Fugitive* also features some of the best chase sequences in recent memory. ★★★★ DVD Special Edition: $14.99, VHS Special Edition: $9.99, VHS Letterbox Special Edition: $9.99

The Fugitive Kind

(1959, 135 min, US, Sidney Lumet) *Marlon Brando, Anna Magnani, Joanne Woodward, Maureen Stapleton.* Disappointing though gritty version of Tennessee Williams' play, "Orpheus Descending." Brando stars as a Mississippi drifter who becomes involved with two women (Magnani and Woodward) while staying at a small Southern town. Tallulah Bankhead may have said it best: (to Williams) "Dahling, they've absolutely ruined your perfectly dreadful play." ★★

Full Contact

(1992, 99 min, Hong Kong, Ringo Lam) *Chow Yun-Fat, Simon Yam, Anthony Wong.* In this brutal Hong Kong action film, Chow plays a buzz-cut, tattooed petty thief who teams up with Judge (Yam), a creepy associate of his cousin (Wong), for a big heist. They pull off the heist, but Judge double-crosses Chow and kills his young friend and partner, leaving Chow for dead. Chow slowly recovers, building his strength and wrath for another confrontation with Judge and his traitorous cousin. A radical departure for American audiences used to John Woo's highly stylized operas, Lam's work is more Western and story-driven. His eruptions of violence are also filmed in a less balletic way, particularly in this film, where the final showdown between Chow and Judge involves point-of-view shots of the bullets speeding across the room into furniture and human skulls. (Cantonese with English subtitles) ★★★ DVD: $24.99

Full Frontal

(2002, 103 min, US, Steven Soderbergh) *Julia Roberts, Blair Underwood, Catherine Keener, David Hyde Pierce, Mary McCormack, Enrico Colantoni, Nicky Katt, David Duchovny.* Director Soderbergh returns to his independent roots for this self-indulgent long take about Hollywood and its players. Shot on video with little of the command that he demonstrated with both his Hollywood hits and indie gems, Soderbergh's tedious tale follows the intersecting lives of a group of actors working on a movie. It's told in a documentarylike narrative, and also features scenes from *Rendezvous,* the film the cast is making. Keener and Katt offer solid portrayals, but it's not enough to compensate. ★★ DVD: $19.99, VHS: $9.99

Full Metal Jacket

(1987, 120 min, US, Stanley Kubrick) *Matthew Modine, Alan Baldwin, Vincent D'Onofrio, R. Lee Ermey, Dorian Harewood, Arliss Howard.* Kubrick's brilliantly realized Vietnam War drama, told with such grace and subtlety it practically discredits all similarly themed films that precede it. Kubrick divides his film into two equally devastating parts: a brutal boot camp training sequence and a horrific war piece set amidst the rubble of the 1968 Tet Offensive. Outstanding in support are D'Onofrio (who gained 60 pounds for the part) as a dim-witted recruit, and Ermey as a merciless drill sergeant. ★★★★ DVD: $19.99, VHS: $6.99

The Full Monty

(1997, 95 min, GB, Peter Cattaneo) *Robert Carlyle, Tom Wilkinson, Mark Addy, Paul Barber, Steven Huison, Hugo Speer, Lesley Sharp.* This hard-edged but still quite funny and endearing hit follows the misadventures of a group of unemployed steelworkers who band together to take it all off. When a local performance of The Chippendales sells out, divorced dad Gaz (Carlyle) reasons anything they can do, he

can do almost as well. He rounds up a group of cohorts — all suffering under Northern England's economic crunch — to form their own strip group. The troupe features the unlikeliest candidates to draw a sell-out crowd, but their antics together most definitely are charming, often hilarious and guaranteed to keep a smile on one's face. ★★★½ DVD Letterbox: $14.99, VHS Letterbox: $9.99

Full Moon in Blue Water

(1988, 95 min, US, Peter Masterson) *Gene Hackman, Teri Garr, Burgess Meredith, Elias Koteas.* Playwright Bill Bozzone wrote this muddled screenplay about a widower (Hackman) haunted by the past and the effect it has on his relationship with his girlfriend (Garr), his father-in-law (Meredith) and his failing business on the coast of Texas. ★★ DVD Dual: $14.99

Full Moon in Paris

(1984, 102 min, France, Eric Rohmer) *Pascale Ogier, Tcheky Karyo.* Sharp dialogue and the beguiling presence of Ogier help make this Rohmer philosophical romance a gem. A headstrong self-absorbed woman, bored of her live-in lover, finds a second flat and begins another affair. (French with English subtitles) ★★★½ DVD: $29.99, VHS: $19.99

Full Speed

(1996, 85 min, France, Gael Morel) *Mezziane Bardadi.* An assured feature film debut for actor Morel (*Wild Reeds*), *Full Speed* delves into the tangled sexual lives of several young people in rural France. The moody and alienated Samir (Bardadi), a handsome teenager of Arab descent, befriends a group of young people, including Quentin, a writer, Julie, his twenty-year-old free-spirited girlfriend, and eighteen-year-old Jimmy, a gorgeous tough guy who's always in trouble. While Julie and Jimmy begin to have an affair, Samir falls violently in love with a tentatively accepting Quentin. Director Morel borrows more than he should have from his mentor André Téchiné's classic film. However, his film successfully captures the drama of young lust, bisexuality, unrequited love and racial prejudice. (French with English subtitles) ★★★

Full-Tilt Boogie

(2000, 100 min, US, Sarah Kelly) This entertaining feature-length documentary covers the making of the crime thriller/horror hybrid *From Dusk Till Dawn.* Beginning with an announcement of the project at a horror convention, and concluding with the final day of filming, *Full-Tilt Boogie* offers an intriguing look at the incredible amount of work that goes into the creation of a film. While the film is a bit ragged, and certainly isn't a fascinating portrait of a passionate artist like the terrific *Hearts of Darkness* or *The Hamster Factor,* for fans of collaborators Quentin Tarantino and Robert Rodriguez — and *From Dusk Till Dawn* in particular — *Full-Tilt Boogie* is a must. ★★★ VHS: $9.99

The Fuller Brush Girl

(1950, 85 min, US, Lloyd Bacon) *Lucille Ball, Eddie Albert.* A hilarious follow-up to *The Fuller Brush Man.* Ball and Albert play a pair of young lovers trying to scrape together enough money to buy their dream house. Desperate for money, Lucy jumps into door-to-door cosmetics sales with disastrous results. The plot is slight and some of the hijinx are a little too over-the-top, but Ball's talent for outrageous slapstick carries the day, making this an all-around good time. Red Skelton has a cameo, reprising his role as the Fuller Brush Man. ★★★ VHS: $19.99

The merry pranksters of *Funny Bones*

The Fuller Brush Man

(1948, 93 min, US, S. Sylvan Simon) *Red Skelton, Janet Blair.* Skelton gets a lot of mileage from this wacky, slapstick comedy with the gifted comedian uncovering a murder while going door-to-door. (Sequel: *The Fuller Brush Girl*) ★★★ VHS: $14.99

Fun with Dick and Jane

(1977, 95 min, US, Ted Kotcheff) *Jane Fonda, Ed McMahon, George Segal.* Fonda and Segal bring a lot of life to the 1970s social comedy as a married couple who turn to robbery to maintain their way of life after hubby Segal gets fired. ★★★ DVD Letterbox: $24.99, VHS: $9.99

The Funeral

(1984, 124 min, Japan, Juzo Itami) *Tsutomu Yamazaki, Nobuko Miyamoto.* Made before his wonderfully quirky and popular hit *Tampopo*, Itami's black comedy follows the complex, confusing and often bizarre happenings during the preparation of a traditional Buddhist funeral by an affluent bourgeois couple. At once comic, sad and moving. (Japanese with English subtitles) ★★★½ DVD: $29.99, VHS: $14.99

The Funeral

(1996, 99 min, US, Abel Ferrara) *Christopher Walken, Benicio del Toro, Chris Penn, Annabella Sciorra, Vincent Gallo, Isabella Rossellini.* Director Ferrara and screenwriter Nicholas St. John continue their exploration of morality and personal responsibility (after *The Addiction*), this time around, the gangster genre is the target, and the pair fashion a tale of organized crime in the 1930s, where the families of two surviving brothers (Walken, Penn) come together at the untimely funeral of a third. While *The Funeral* is interesting and its ensemble achieves an almost Coppola-level of success in the period gangster film genre, the film is overburdened with moralizing philosophy. And the heavy-handed ending undermines the successful drama and tragedy the fine cast worked so hard to establish. ★★½

Funeral in Berlin

(1966, 102 min, GB, Guy Hamilton) *Michael Caine, Eva Renzi, Oscar Homolka.* Caine is the British operative who must arrange the defection of a top-level Russian military officer in Berlin. The second of the "Harry Palmer" spy thrillers, filmed on location in

Berlin, has a few exciting scenes but isn't as effective as *The Ipcress File*. Based on the novel by Len Deighton. (Sequel: *Billion Dollar Brain*) ★★½

The Funhouse

(1981, 96 min, US, Tobe Hooper) *Elizabeth Berridge, Shawn Carson, Cooper Huckabee, Sylvia Miles.* A group of teenagers decide to spend a night in a carnival funhouse and are stalked by a ghoulish creature. Not very spooky, the film relies on the occasional shock for its chills. ★★ DVD: $14.99, VHS: $14.99

Funny Bones

(1995, 128 min, GB, Peter Chelsom) *Oliver Platt, Lee Evans, Jerry Lewis, Leslie Caron, Oliver Reed, Richard Griffiths.* Tommy Fawkes (Platt) is a failing comic who lives in the shadow of his near-legendary father George (Lewis). When Tommy's act bombs in Las Vegas, he immediately disappears, only to turn up in a small coastal town in England where he grew up. But what does this have to do with the opening sequence of a half-witted comedian (Evans) who's left adrift at sea? Well, to tell any more would be to give away some of the zaniest jokes, sight gags and plot developments since Mel Brooks was in his prime. An alternately hilarious and dark comedy, *Funny Bones* is a boldly original if lunatic peek into the artistic process that at the same time tries to answer that age-old question: What is funny? As the talented nutcase, Evans gives an uproarious performance combining superlative physical schtick with a sympathetic portrait of a fragile mind. ★★★★ DVD: $9.99

Funny Dirty Little War

(1983, 80 min, Argentina, Hector Olivera) *Federico Luppi, Julio de Grazia.* This anarchic and ruthless black comedy dissects the political absurdities and petty bureaucracy of a small Argentine village during the post-Peron years in the late 1950s. A full-scale civil war erupts in an otherwise peaceful, though disordered town when a local administrator becomes involved in a fanatical conflict with his governmental associates. As each political faction doggedly pursues victory, the corruption and dehumanization of war takes its toll when all involved increasingly become efficient in the practices of torture and murder. A blistering anti-war satire which is both witty and tragic. (Spanish with English subtitles) ★★★½ DVD: $29.99, VHS: $29.99

Funny Face

(1957, 104 min, US, Stanley Donen) *Fred Astaire, Audrey Hepburn, Kay Thompson.* All Paris becomes fixated when photographer Astaire pulls out all the stops to capture the heart of his new model, the radiant Hepburn. This charming musical, from the director of *Singin' in the Rain*, features a fine score by George Gershwin, including "How Long Has This Been Going On?" and "S'Wonderful." ★★★½ DVD: $14.99, VHS: $9.99

Funny Farm

(1988, 101 min, US, George Roy Hill) *Chevy Chase, Madolyn Smith.* More dumb hijinks with Chase, here as a city-bred writer whose move to the country isn't exactly what he thought it would be. Some of the jokes are very funny, but many fall flat. ★★ DVD: $14.99, VHS: $9.99

Funny Games

(1997, 108 min, Austria, Michael Haneke) *Susanne Lothar, Ulrich Mühe, Arno Frisch.* To describe this repulsive though accomplished thriller as unpleasant, horrifying or gut-wrenching would be a colossal understatement. A wealthy couple and their young son are terrorized by two preppie psychos while vacationing at a lakeside house. What might sound like a typical genre flick is anything but; while there is relatively little on-screen physical violence, the psychological brutality in *Funny Games* is intense to the nth degree. Technically polished, well directed and acted, the film is ultimately too nihilistic, cynical and depressing except for the most adventurous, daring viewer. (German with English subtitles) ★★½ DVD: $29.99, VHS: $19.99

Funny Girl

(1968, 155 min, US, William Wyler) *Barbra Streisand, Omar Sharif, Kaye Medford, Walter Pidgeon, Anne Francis.* Streisand's Oscar-winning film debut, repeating her acclaimed stage role, as the legendary performer Fanny Brice. Though the film is somewhat melodramatic for a musical biography, Streisand's singing and clowning make it all worthwhile. Good period design, and Barbra sings "My Man," "People" and "Don't Rain on My Parade." (Sequel: *Funny Lady*) ★★★ DVD: $19.99

Funny Lady

(1975, 137 min, US, Herbert Ross) *Barbra Streisand, James Caan, Omar Sharif, Ben Vereen, Roddy McDowall.* This okay sequel to *Funny Girl* finds Barbra in excellent voice reprising her role as legendary performer Fanny Brice. With Nicky in prison, Fanny takes up with Billy Rose, who would become her second husband. Caan plays Billy, Sharif has a small role encoring as Nicky, and Vereen is a standout performing "Goodtime Charley." ★★½ DVD: $24.99

A Funny Thing Happened on the Way to the Forum

(1966, 99 min, US, Richard Lester) *Zero Mostel, Jack Gilford, Michael Crawford, Phil Silvers, Buster Keaton.* A rip-roaring, bawdy and hilarious adaptation of the hit Broadway musical. Mostel (with the exception of "Fiddler on the Roof") had his best role onstage, and here on-screen, as a conniving Roman slave who sets out to obtain his freedom. Sexual innuendo, slapstick and feverish chases are the order of the day as Mostel uses every trick in the book in his glorious quest. Gilford also repeats his stage role as a fellow slave, and Crawford is their young, love-struck master. Score by Stephen Sondheim. ★★★½ DVD: $14.99, VHS: $14.99, VHS Letterbox: $14.99

Fury

(1936, 94 min, US, Fritz Lang) *Spencer Tracy, Sylvia Sidney, Walter Brennan.* Lang's masterful exposé of mob violence with Tracy in a powerful portrayal of an innocent man unjustly accused of murder. Sidney is splendid as Tracy's fiancée. ★★★½ VHS: $19.99

The Fury

(1978, 118 min, US, Brian De Palma) *Andrew Stevens, Kirk Douglas, John Cassavetes, Carrie Snodgress, Amy Irving.* Set in the paranoid post-Watergate '70s, *The Fury* tells the story of two young psychics, Stevens and Irving, who are being manipulated by a covert government agency attempting to harness their awesome powers. Stevens' father, Douglas, comes to their aid, battling the evil Cassavetes. Director De Palma's film, as with most of his work, is highly stylized and often very violent. Rick Baker's makeup wizardry is outstanding. ★★★ DVD: $19.99, VHS: $9.99

Fury Is a Woman

See: *Siberian Lady Macbeth*

Futuresport

(1998, 89 min, US, Ernest Dickerson) *Dean Cain, Vanessa L. Williams, Wesley Snipes, Rachel Shane, Adrian Hughes, Bill Smitrovich.* In 2015, professional basketball is disbanded due to scandal. It is replaced by, no, not BASEketball, but by a violent mix of rollerball, skateboarding and hockey. Ten years later, it is the country's favorite sport, and Cain is its favorite player. Meanwhile, in Hawaii, the revolutionary group Hawaiian Liberation Front is fighting guerrilla warfare. How these two factions meet makes up *Futuresport*, an entertaining, well-made futuristic actioner made for TV. The subplot about the revolutionaries is sometimes confusing, but the scenes of futuresport are exciting, and the film doesn't drag during its non-action sequences. ★★★ DVD: $14.99

G.I. Jane

(1997, 120 min, US, Ridley Scott) *Demi Moore, Viggo Mortensen, Anne Bancroft, Jason Beghe, Scott Wilson.* The initial reaction to a film starring Moore as the first female SEAL candidate was an expectant rush of cynical loathing. Instead, immersed in the pyrotechnics of director Scott's signature hyperactive style, substantive questions are raised in this extravagant Hollywood product. Moore is chosen with the influence of a U.S. Senator from Texas (portrayed with icy flint by Bancroft) with her own agenda. Moore's take on the archetypal Ripley heroine is conducted with punctuated sensory assaults by Scott, whose simulations of combat are as much a commentary on moviemaking as on the carnage of war and training for war. Moore is reminded that Israelis stopped using women in combat because male soldiers tarried when women were injured. Let's face it: The real male nightmare regarding women in the military is not women who *get* killed but women who *can* kill. *G.I. Jane* is a slickly made exploration of some button-pushing issues, presented with a budget rivaling some of your smaller wars. ★★★ DVD: $9.99, VHS: $9.99, VHS Letterbox: $9.99

Gabriel over the White House

(1933, 78 min, US, Gregory La Cava) *Walter Huston, Karen Morley, Franchot Tone.* Imagine that George Bush, shortly after being elected, was in a high-speed car accident and wound up in a deep coma. And, that when he came out of it, he began a program to wipe out poverty, erase organized crime and eliminate war. If you can picture this, you'll have some idea of what this unabashed Depression-era propaganda piece is all about. Huston stars as the president, elected by fraud and entrenched in a corrupt party system until his conversion at the hands of God. Thereafter he sets out to dissolve Congress and institute a kind of bleeding-heart liberalist dictatorship where all of the evils of the world can be eradicated. For those of us who respect the balance of power created by a trilateral government, it's a pretty frightening picture. Still, the film offers some fascinating glimpses at the social agenda in the early days of Roosevelt as well as makes some ominous predictions about the horrors of future world wars. ★★½ VHS: $19.99

Gabriela

(1983, 102 min, Brazil, Bruno Barreto) *Sonia Braga, Marcello Mastroianni.* Brazilian beauty Braga swaggers through this dreamy sex comedy as the hard-to-hold wife of a Turkish bar owner (Mastroianni) who sets an entire two-bit town on its ear. Barreto smoothly directs Jorge Amado's tale of primitive passion and derailed amour. (Portuguese with English subtitles) ★★★

Gabriela

(2001, 93 min, US, Vincent Jay Miller) *Jaime Gomez, Seidy Lopez, Zach Galligan, Lupe Ontiveros, Troy Winbush.* What happens when a nice guy falls in love with an unavailable woman? This is the question posed in *Gabriela*, Miller's directorial debut. Unfortunately, the emotional, ethical and psychological elements of such a question are never even adequately examined, much less answered. Set against the backdrop of a rather unlikely clinic where social workers spend more time socializing than anything else, Miller's tale unfolds quickly after a rather perfunctory setup of its characters: Mike (Gomez) is a good-looking stud who just can't find a beautiful woman to be in love with. Of course, handsome Mike meets the title character, a down-to-earth Mexican beauty (well played by the gorgeous Lopez) and they can only deny the chemistry for so long. Trouble is she's engaged to a hyper-Anglo attorney (Galligan) and you know the rest. Once the trio's cards are all on the table, Miller's script stalls and we are taken from one repetitive hushed conversation to the next. ★★
DVD: $14.99, VHS: $9.99

Gal Young 'Un

(1979, 105 min, US, Victor Nunez) *Dana Preu, David Peck.* Based on a story by Marjorie Kinnan Rawlings ("The Yearling," "Cross Creek"), and set in Florida during Prohibition, this passionate film follows a lonely widow (Preu) who erupts into violence when she realizes that she has been victimized by a fast-talking con man (Peck). ★★★

Galaxy Quest

(1999, 100 min, US, Dean Parisot) *Tim Allen, Sigourney Weaver, Alan Rickman, Tony Shalhoub, Sam Rockwell, Daryl Mitchell, Enrico Colantoni.* What took this so long? Spoofing the decades-old "Star Trek" TV series may not seem the most timely of subjects, but in the hands of writers Robert Gordon and David Howard, director Parisot, and a most engaging cast, it was definitely worth the wait. In this very funny sci-fi comedy, the cast members of a "Star Trek"-type TV show are thrust into intergalactic adventure when aliens think the TV stars to be real space heroes. If William Shatner hadn't made famous the role of Capt. James T. Kirk, then Allen would have been the next, clear choice. He, Weaver and Rickman (extremely funny as the "Spock" character) are surely enjoying themselves, which is why this works as well as it does. ★★★ DVD: $14.99, DVD DTS sound: $14.99

Gallipoli

(1981, 110 min, Australia, Peter Weir) *Mel Gibson, Mark Lee, Bill Kerr.* A visually striking and emotionally jarring war drama focusing on the camaraderie of two young Australians who naively enlist in the army only to meet the savage realities of World War I. Gibson and Lee star as a pair of budding athletes who encounter the butchery of trench warfare up close on a stretch of godforsaken Turkish coastline known as Gallipoli. Weir holds no punches in delivering a stinging indictment of military leadership and war in general. ★★★★ DVD Letterbox: $14.99, VHS: $14.99, VHS Letterbox: $14.99

Galaxy Quest: Not too bold about going where no man has gone before

Daniel Day-Lewis (l.) and Leonardo DiCaprio in Martin Scorsese's *Gangs of New York*

The Game

(1997, 128 min, US, David Fincher) *Michael Douglas, Sean Penn, Deborah Kara Unger, Carroll Baker, Armin Mueller-Stahl.* In this slick, tense thriller, twists, suspense and uncertainty all come together in a chilling puzzle called *The Game*. Douglas is right at home as Nicholas Van Orton, a multimillionaire investment banker whose rigid lifestyle and cold exterior have given him little time or desire to manage familial or social relationships. On his uneventful 48th birthday, Nicholas' younger brother Conrad (an underused Penn) makes a present to Nicholas of "the game," sort of a full-time fantasy camp where the subject lives out an unknown scenario. But as life-threatening and increasingly bizarre incidents occur, Van Orton learns this game, once begun, is not easily ended. Fincher is very successful in setting up his action pieces, and maintains believable, edge-of-your-seat tension throughout. ★★★ DVD: $14.99

The Game Is Over

(1966, 96 min, France, Roger Vadim) *Jane Fonda, Michel Piccoli, Peter McEnery.* Fonda's first dramatic role features her as a neglected wife who falls passionately in love with her stepson (McEnery). Her husband, Piccoli, learns of the affair and viciously plots revenge. Swinging '60s Paris comes alive in this electrifying story of decadence directed by Fonda's then-husband. (Filmed in English) ★★★ DVD: $24.99, VHS: $19.99

Game of Seduction

(1985, 95 min, France, Roger Vadim) *Sylvia Kristel, Nathalie Delon, Jon Finch.* A steamy frolic amid the boudoirs and satin bedsheets of the always decadent French bourgeoisie. Kristel stars as a sultry and beautiful woman who is happily married. Her fidelity to her husband is severely tested when a cold-blooded killer and equally cunning noblewoman place a bet that he can seduce her. (Filmed in English) ★★½

Gandhi

(1982, 200 min, GB, Richard Attenborough) *Ben Kingsley, Candice Bergen, John Gielgud, Edward Fox, John Mills, Saeed Jaffrey, Trevor Howard,* *Daniel Day-Lewis.* Kingsley brilliantly portrays Mahatma Gandhi, the spiritual and political leader of India who, driven by his dream of an independent India and guided by principles of nonviolence, struggled a lifetime to rid his country of British imperialism. A fascinating and moving portrait of a man whose commitment to nonviolence has served as a shining example to people all over the world. Winner of 8 Academy Awards including Best Picture and Actor. ★★★★ DVD: $24.99, VHS: $19.99

Gang in Blue

(1996, 99 min, US, Mario Van Peebles & Melvin van Peebles) *Mario Van Peebles, Josh Brolin, Melvin Van Peebles, Cynda Williams, J.T. Walsh, Stephen Lang.* The Van Peebles — father Melvin and son Mario — team up as codirectors and costars for this made-for-cable drama. A racist band of big-city cops has been harassing — and murdering — minorities for years. One black cop (Mario) has had enough. He tries to enlist the aid of his ex-lover (Williams), now an FBI agent, but she's disinterested. Then he's assigned a new partner — a redneck ex-Marine. This fact-based cop drama is by the numbers at times, rather heavy-handed at others, but it has some kick to it and is certainly never dull. It falls in the trap, however, of presenting racists as one-dimensional characters; a little more development would have given the film more of an edge. ★★½ VHS: $9.99

Gang of Souls

(1988, 60 min, US, Maria Beatty) *William Burroughs, Allen Ginsberg, Marianne Faithfull, Lydia Lunch.* This tribute to the Beat Generation is comprised of various interviews with members of the first generation of the '50s movement (William Burroughs, Allen Ginsberg, Gregory Corso) as well as its leading adherents a generation later (Marianne Faithfull, Lydia Lunch, Richard Hell). With quotes like "'Howl' overcame censorship trials to become one of the most widely read works of this century," the documentary is prone to hyperbole and self-boasting, but nonetheless presents a vivid hour exploring the recollections and observations of today's performers and poets who together give us a teasing glimpse into creativity in the key of Beat. ★★½ VHS: $34.99

Gang Related

(1997, 109 min, US, Jim Kouf) *James Belushi, Tupac Shakur, Lela Rochon, Gary Cole, Dennis Quaid, James Earl Jones, David Paymer.* Belushi and Shakur are cops and partners (in crime) who shake down a handful of drug dealers, murder them, and then dismiss the cases as "gang related." Their scheme hits a snag when their latest hit turns out to be an undercover DEA agent, and a full-blown investigation ensues. Their search for a suitable patsy leads to alcoholic, homeless Quaid — and their problems snowball even more. The simple premise of this modestly entertaining film is taken to its breaking point; the first two-thirds are suspenseful and involving, but it really runs out of gas towards the end. The trite, superficial ending reveals the total lack of point of view and hollowness at the film's core. ★★½ DVD Letterbox: $14.99, VHS: $9.99

The Gang's All Here

(1943, 103 min, US, Busby Berkeley) *Carmen Miranda, Alice Faye, James Ellison.* A camp classic from the Golden Age of Hollywood! Forget about the lame love story between Alice Faye and James Ellison and pay attention to the fabulously over-the-top frocks and musical dance numbers starring Carmen Miranda. "The Lady in the Tutti-Frutti Hat" is the film's showstopper. ★★★

Gangs of New York

(2002, 168 min, US, Martin Scorsese) *Leonardo DiCaprio, Daniel Day-Lewis, Cameron Diaz, Jim Broadbent, Henry Thomas, John C. Reilly, Brendan Gleeson, Liam Neeson, Alec McCowan.* The plight of immigrants, and specifically how various segments of this embattled population coexisted, is at the heart of director Scorsese's blistering epic which examines the little known turf wars of the mid-1800s that plagued lower Manhattan. While a Civil War divided a nation, civil unrest infested the Five Corners, where a brutal gang war between American-born "Nativists" and recent Irish emigrants has ordained the vile Bill "the Butcher" Cutting (Day-Lewis) as the leader of the Lower East Side's lower classes. The son of the last "worthy" opponent Cutting faced (and butchered), Amsterdam Vallon (DiCaprio), has returned after 16 years to seek his vengeance against Bill. But in a twisted irony, Bill becomes Vallon's surrogate father. Though its tale of revenge is central to *Gangs of New York*, Scorsese's extraordinary vision encompasses social and political issues of America today and yesterday: prejudice, political corruption and immigration. As a technician, Scorsese has topped himself, and as a storyteller, he's rarely been better, ably juggling many plotlines and infusing each with passion and clarity. His ensemble is first-rate, including a stunning performance from Day-Lewis, who makes the villainous Bill both human and horrible. ★★★★ DVD: $29.99, VHS: $24.99

The Gangster

(1947, 84 min, US, Gordon Wiles) *Barry Sullivan, John Ireland, Henry Morgan, Leif Erickson.* A cynical gangster (Sullivan) is confronted with a vicious out-of-towner who tries to muscle in on his territory. A tough, intriguing character study with Sullivan giving a commanding portrayal of a nefarious hood. ★★★

G

Gangster No. 1

(2000, 103 min, GB, Paul McGuigan) *Malcolm McDowell, David Thewlis, Paul Bettany, Saffron Burrows.* There's been a surge in British gangster pictures recently (*Snatch, Sexy Beast*), but the savage *Gangster No. 1* stands apart from the pack through its uncompromising willingness to strip away the irony and posturing in favor of exploring the brutality and ruthlessness of London's organized crime world. Bettany is excellent as an ambitious, psychotic hood who rises to power in swinging '60s London. The main portion of the film is a flashback, as reminisced by the gangster as an older man (played in these scenes by McDowell), upon learning the mentor (Thewlis) he set up has just been released from prison. The time period and locale are expertly captured here, and the film is both involving and superbly acted (though McDowell is perhaps a bit over the top in the penultimate scene). There are several chilling, disturbing sequences, however, so the squeamish should beware. All others will find a well-crafted crime film. ★★★½ DVD Dual: $14.99

Garbo Talks

(1984, 104 min, US, Sidney Lumet) *Anne Bancroft, Ron Silver, Harvey Fierstein, Carrie Fisher, Catherine Hicks, Steven Hill.* Bancroft's spirited performance dominates this bittersweet comedy about a son (Silver) who goes through heaven and hell to make his dying mother's last wish come true: to meet Greta Garbo. An episodic tale that features charming touches, though the film does move at a slow pace. ★★½

The Garden

(1990, 88 min, GB, Derek Jarman) *Tilda Swinton, Johnny Mills, Philip MacDonald.* As director Jarman fitfully sleeps in his garden, his cryptic dreams — culled from his subconscious and his fevered imagination — are played out in their fullest, queerest glory. The lyrical images of male love, tenderness and art are interspersed with visions of natural beauty but collide against a background of homophobia, persecution and death. An allegory for AIDS, and his friends who have died from it, the film's main narrative thrust depicts two young male lovers as they, in the manner of Jesus Christ, are taunted, arrested, tortured and then crucified for their beliefs. A stunningly filmed work of art, full of poetic images, and supported by a haunting score by Simon Fisher Turner. ★★★ VHS: $14.99

The Garden of Delights

(1970, 95 min, Spain, Carlos Saura) *Jose Luis Lopez Vincent, Lina Canelajas.* Saura drastically changes pace and theme with this bizarre black comedy on Spanish society. This cynical tale is about a rich and ruthless old man who loses his memory and suffers from paralysis after an auto accident. His monstrously greedy relatives, desperate to find out the location of his fortune, stage disturbing scenes from his boyhood in their efforts to shock him into remembering. All the while, the old man silently plots his revenge. (Spanish with English subtitles) ★★★

The Garden of the Finzi-Continis

(1970, 95 min, Italy, Vittorio De Sica) *Dominique Sanda, Helmut Berger, Lino Capolicchio, Fabio Testi, Romolo Valli.* Set in fascist Italy, De Sica's Oscar-winning Best Foreign Film depicts an aristocratic Jewish family's confrontation with sweeping anti-Semitism. Based on the semiautobiography by Giorgio Bassani, this exquisitely photographed film explores the horrors of prewar and war-torn Italy, and the complacency taken by the Finzi-Continis family, who lock themselves in the comfort of their mansion's garden far away from the realities outside their walls. (Italian with English subtitles) ★★★½ DVD Letterbox: $29.99

Gardens of Stone

(1987, 112 min, US, Francis Coppola) *James Caan, James Earl Jones, Laurence Fishburne, Anjelica Huston, D.B. Sweeney, Dean Stockwell, Mary Stuart Masterson, Lonette McKee.* Coppola's passionate though heavy-handed Vietnam War film is a showcase for some four-star acting. Caan and Jones deliver powerful performances as cynical Arlington Honor Guard officers who refer to themselves as "toy soldiers" — powerless to do anything about the onslaught of body bags except give them elegant funerals. Sweeney is the young officer itching to go to Vietnam: a gung-ho youngster who may not be ready for the experience. ★★½ DVD: $24.99, VHS: $9.99

Gas Food Lodging

(1992, 102 min, US, Allison Anders) *Fairuza Balk, Brooke Adams, Ione Skye, Donovan Leitch, James Brolin.* In her debut film, director Anders tears a page out of Wim Wenders' *Paris, Texas* with this heartfelt and emotionally penetrating tale of familial discord and redemption set against the backdrop of the American Southwest desert. Young Shade (winsomely portrayed by Balk) lives with her single mother (Adams) and her teenage sister (Skye). She spends her afternoons alternately haunting the town's deserted cinema, hanging out with her androgynous friend, Darius, and dreaming of her long-lost father. Sprinkled throughout with a wry sense of humor, the film sports some enjoyably whimsical moments, especially when Shade bridges the town's racial barrier and befriends a young Mexican boy and his deaf mother. A truly enjoyable, exquisitely rendered drama. ★★★½ DVD: $24.99

Gaslight

(1944, 114 min, US, George Cukor) *Ingrid Bergman, Charles Boyer, Joseph Cotten, Angela Lansbury.* Boyer is an effectively sinister counterpoint to Bergman's fragile, luminous innocence in Cukor's classic treatment of manipulation and betrayed love. Boyer has a hidden purpose when he woos and weds orphan Bergman; to protect his secret, he begins a systematic attempt to drive her insane. In her film debut, Lansbury is very tarty as their flirty maid. ★★★½ DVD: $19.99

The Gate

(1987, 92 min, US, Tibor Takacs) *Stephen Dorff, Christa Denton, Louis Tripp.* The Gate, which delivers a few effective frights, follows a pair of young teens who accidentally unleash a horde of demons upon their neighborhood by playing the Satanic messages of a heavy metal record. The embarrassing plot is really just an excuse to showcase the film's spectacular low-budget effects, which include a very scary walking corpse. (Sequel: *The Gate II*) ★★

Gate of Hell

(1953, 89 min, Japan, Teinosuke Kinugasa) *Kazuo Hasegawa, Machiko Kyo.* A handsomely photographed historical drama set during the 12th-century Japanese rebellion about a samurai warrior who invades a small town, falls in love with and is rejected by a married woman. Academy Award for Best Foreign Film. (Japanese with English subtitles) ★★★½ VHS: $29.99

Gates of Heaven

(1978, 82 min, US, Errol Morris) An appealingly funny documentary about pet owners and the trauma they face when their pet cemetery is sold and their animals' remains are transfered to another plot. A truly original meditation on the American soul. ★★★½

Gattaca

(1997, 112 min, US, Andrew Niccol) *Ethan Hawke, Uma Thurman, Alan Arkin, Jude Law, Tony Shalhoub, Blair Underwood, Loren Dean, Ernest Borgnine, Xander Berkeley, Elias Koteas.* The phrase "designer genes" takes on an entirely new meaning in this elegant, beautifully lensed drama that falls into the category of "thinking person's science fiction." Set in a not-too-distant future where the unborn are genetically engineered and bred to be "super yup-

G

Malcolm McDowell in *Gangster No. 1*

Uma Thurman in *Gattaca*

pies," the story centers around a physically flawed genius (Hawke) who assumes the identity of a paralyzed athlete (Law) in order to gain entrance into the elitist Gattaca Corporation space project. Director Niccol eschews the visual histrionics of, say, *The Fifth Element*, for a minimalist look and feel that is strongly reminiscent of the cerebral sci-fi classics of the '60s and '70s. ★★★ DVD Letterbox Superbit Edition: $27.99, DVD: $19.99, VHS: $9.99

The Gauntlet

(1977, 109 min, US, Clint Eastwood) *Clint Eastwood, Sondra Locke.* Eastwood is cop Ben Shockley who thinks he is escorting an ordinary witness (Locke) back to Phoenix for a trial. But he soon finds there are plenty who want to stop her from testifying against an organized crime family. A flavorful, exciting action tale nicely handled by director and star Eastwood. ★★★ DVD: $14.99, VHS: $14.99

The Gay Deceivers

(1969, 99 min, US, Bruce Kessler) *Michael Greer, Kevin Coughlin, Larry Casey, Brook Bundy, Jo Ann Harris.* What has time done to this low-budget '60s comedy about two "perfectly normal" guys who try to evade the draft by posing as homosexual lovers? Is it offensively homophobic drivel or simply a frequently hilarious, naïvely camp curiosity? Filmed in a contemporary sitcom style, the film's funniest scenes come when our hapless heroes, under investigation by a suspicious Army recruiter, must move into a gay bungalow complex, populated by the most outrageous gay stereotypes this side of Fairyland. Greer adds both a campy humor and surprising gay dignity as he steals the show as Malcolm, the boys' gay landlord. This anachronistic sex comedy should provide some laughs and an appreciation of how much things have changed in 30 years. ★★½

The Gay Divorcee

(1934, 107 min, US, Mark Sandrich) *Fred Astaire, Ginger Rogers, Edward Everett Horton, Alice Brady, Eric Blore, Erik Rhodes, Betty Grable.* In their second film together, Astaire and Rogers demonstrate such chemistry in both dancing and nonmusical scenes that it only makes sense that they'd be paired another eight times. Fred plays a noted dancer who meets and pursues Ginger all over London. But she's unhappily married and hires Fred's best friend, lawyer Horton, to set up an infidelity scam to initiate a divorce. That's all the plot that's needed to provide several exquisite dance numbers and very lively comedy. Among the routines, Fred and Ginger perform "The Continental" and "Night and Day." The hilariously effete Horton and scatterbrained Brady offer wonderful support, with Horton actually getting to perform a song ("Let's Knock Knees") and Brady given such amusing lines as "Divorces make me so sentimental." ★★★½ VHS: $14.99

Gay Purr-ee

(1962, 85 min, US, Abe Levitow) *Judy Garland, Robert Goulet, Red Buttons, Paul Frees.* Garland is in exceptionally good voice as Musette, the fairest feline in all of France. This animated tale follows her flight from country abode to the big city in search of fame and fortune. Her jilted suitor (Goulet) and small friend (Buttons) prowl after her in hot pursuit and arrive just in time to save her from the clutches of the villain Meowrice (Frees). ★★½ DVD: $19.99, VHS: $14.99

Gen-X Cops

(1999, 113 min, Hong Kong, Benny Chan) *Nicholas Tse, Stephen Fung, Sam Lee, Grace Ip.* Dorky Hong Kong action film is entertaining, clichéd cheese, but nothing more. A group of ne'er-do-well, "hip" rookie cops are recruited by a foul-up police officer to go undercover and stop a bunch of bad guys. Typical for a HK genre film, *Gen-X Cops* is wildly uneven, veering from sappy melodrama to violent action to silly slapstick, sometimes in the same sequence. Still, lotsa action and style, and an amusing, last-minute cameo from producer Jackie Chan. ★★½ DVD: $14.99, VHS: $9.99

Gen-Y Cops

(2001, 120 min, Hong Kong, Benny Chan) *Edison Chen, Stephen Fung, Sam Lee, Maggie Q, Paul Rudd.* This sequel to the mixed-bag *Gen-X Cops* is even less successful. The first half or so of the film doesn't work, repeating all the mistakes of its predecessor (trendy, annoying, slow) while trying to sell its oddball genre mishmash: sci-fi/cop drama/action film/romance/lowbrow comedy/espionage thriller. Then an incongruous entrance by American actor Rudd as a hotheaded U.S. lawman adds buddy flick to the already overstuffed list. It settles down at this point to become a mildly entertaining story of an elite task force taking on terrorists, with a couple of decent action scenes and some amusing humor to almost make it worth recommending. ★★ DVD Dubbed: $26.99, VHS Dubbed: $14.99

The Gene Krupa Story

(1959, 101 min, US, Don Weis) *Sal Mineo, Susan Kohner, James Darren, Red Nichols, Buddy Lester.* Mineo gives a good performance as the famous jazz drummer in this ordinary bio, which examines Gene Krupa's professional career and his personal life, including an almost career-ending drug addiction. ★★ DVD: $24.99

The General

(1927, 74 min, US, Buster Keaton & Clyde Bruckman) *Buster Keaton, Marion Mack, Glen Cavander, Jim Farley.* Keaton plays a Confederate engineer with two great loves: a sweet Southern belle, and his train. When both are kidnapped by Yankee spies, Buster sets out on an uproarious quest to rescue them. Keaton uses his impeccable timing and acrobatic expertise to create many of silent comedy's definitive routines. The stunts here, often involving cannons and moving trains, demonstrate what a fearless performer Keaton was. ★★★★ DVD: $24.99, VHS: $29.99

The General

(1998, 124 min, GB, John Boorman) *Brendan Gleeson, Adrian Dunbar, Sean McGinley, Jon Voight, Maria Doyle Kennedy, Angeline Ball.* Gleeson is brilliant in his portrayal of Martin Cahill, folk hero to some, violent master criminal to others. Born into abject poverty, he alternates charm with casual bru-

tality as he directs his considerable talents toward the circumvention of the law. He orchestrates a daring jewel heist deemed by the IRA as too risky to attempt, yet never misses the queue for the dole. Self-defined as the ultimate outsider, bound by no laws but his own limited but deeply held loyalties, Cahill's downfall results from rebuffing the IRA and attempting a deal with the Loyalists. Voight acquits himself well as a policeman who watches Cahill grow from truant to crime lord as he himself moves from beat cop to inspector. The film succeeds in delivering not just Cahill's story, but a feeling for the country and its people. Ranks with the director's *Hope and Glory*. ★★★½ DVD: $29.99, VHS: $21.99

General Della Rovere

(1959, 129 min, Italy, Roberto Rossellini) *Vittorio De Sica, Otto Messmer, Sandra Milo.* Brilliantly acted by De Sica, this tragic story revolves around an opportunistic con man who is persuaded by the Germans to impersonate a dead Resistance leader. Their plan backfires, however, when the man begins to assume the characteristics of the general. De Sica's transformation from scoundrel to hero and martyr is riveting. (Italian with English subtitles) ★★★★

The General Died at Dawn

(1936, 97 min, US, Lewis Milestone) *Gary Cooper, Madeleine Carroll, Akim Tamiroff.* Top-notch romantic adventure with Cooper as a mercenary in the Far East who becomes involved with spy Carroll and fights treacherous warlord Tamiroff. Script by Clifford Odets. ★★★½ VHS: $14.99

The General's Daughter

(1999, 118 min, US, Simon West) *John Travolta, Madeleine Stowe, James Cromwell, James Woods, Timothy Hutton, Clarence Williams III.* With this story of murder, betrayal and cover-up, West attempts the quintessential military murder mystery tinged with social commentary. However, the director of *Con Air* has bitten off more than he can chew. Travolta is a wily investigator for the Army's Criminal Investigation Division who is called upon to investigate the murder of a female officer. The fact that she's also a high-profile general's daughter only adds more pressure to an already tense case. The film starts promisingly, setting up the story. But the characters aren't fully developed, and West's direction is slack. He fails at creating tension during the investigation, and his red herrings can be seen a mile away. ★★ DVD: $14.99, VHS: $9.99

A Generation

(1954, 85 min, Poland, Andrzej Wajda) *Tadeusz Lominicki, Ursula Modrzynska, Zbigniew Cybulski, Roman Polanski.* The first of Wajda's "War Trilogy" (which includes *Ashes and Diamonds* and *Kanal*), this is a compelling, exceptionally told story of the underground youth movement afoot in Nazi-occupied Poland. A young man, lured by a pretty face, helps the Resistance by aiding escapees from the Warsaw Ghetto. The naiveté of the youthful freedom fighters is shown in their understanding of war as a game. Their view is soon changed with the realities of death as their innocent lives are corrupted and forever scarred. Wajda creates a mood of urgent and threatening angst. A young Polanski is featured as one of the many youthful members of the Resistance. ★★★★ VHS: $24.99

A Gentle Woman
(Une Femme Douce)

(1969, 89 min, France, Robert Bresson) *Dominique Sanda, Guy Frangin, Jane Lobre.* Bresson's first color film opens as an achingly beautiful 17-year-old Sanda leaps from her window to her death in the Paris streets below. Her husband recounts their brief courtship and marriage in a curious monotone with no emotional affect. This self-deluded, self-important man sees her (she's never given a name) only as a "sweet girl," not as an evolving personality. She is a young and impoverished orphan, leaving relatives whom she describes as sinister. He is a methodical man without spontaneity or joy. The subtle though involving film maintains a sterile atmosphere, employing no score. The viewer is witness to two lives that intersect with no real connection, and the man is left with his version of the truth. (French with English subtitles) ★★★ VHS: $29.99

Gentleman Jim

(1942, 104 min, US, Raoul Walsh) *Errol Flynn, Alexis Smith, Jack Carson, Alan Hale, William Frawley.* Flynn is in good form as turn-of-the-century boxer Jim Corbett. Interesting look at the early days of boxing. ★★★ VHS: $14.99

Gentleman's Agreement

(1947, 118 min, US, Elia Kazan) *Gregory Peck, John Garfield, Dorothy McGuire, Celeste Holm, Jane Wyatt, Dean Stockwell.* Peck stars as Skyler Green, a journalist who goes undercover as a Jew in order to collect information on anti-Semitism in this Academy Award-winning Best Picture. The premise has a tendency toward preachiness, but sadly many of the issues concerning prejudice brought up in this 1947 film are still raging through today's headlines. From the cynical vantage point of the 2000s, Skyler can appear overly earnest as he discovers anti-Semitism at almost every turn. Easing some of the heavier moments in the film, however, is Holm, who won a Supporting Actress Oscar for her delightful portrayal of Ann, a wisecracking, life-of-the-party fashion editor who befriends Skyler. A powerful, earnest treatise on prejudice. ★★★½ DVD: $14.99, VHS: $9.99

Gentlemen Prefer Blondes

(1953, 91 min, US, Howard Hawks) *Marilyn Monroe, Jane Russell, Charles Coburn, Elliott Reed, Tom Noonan.* Marilyn is the gold-digging Lorelei Lee, who's just a little girl from Little Rock. She and best pal Jane head to Paris in search of well-heeled husbands. Though Hawks' direction is sometimes static, and he may not fully understand the intricacies of the Hollywood musical, he nevertheless has created a bright and brassy musical comedy. Featuring unbeatable humor and the classic "Diamonds Are a Girl's Best Friend" production number, *Gentlemen's* wonderful story line and snappy dialogue shine through. Marilyn gives one of her most endearing performances. And Russell, who has the funniest line about a hat, is at her best. ★★★ DVD: $14.99, VHS: $6.99

Favorite Line: "You'll find I mean business."
—*Norma Varden as Lady Beekman*

"Oh, really? Then why are you wearing that hat?"
—*Jane Russell as Dorothy Shaw*

Genuine Risk

(1989, 86 min, US, Kurt Voss) *Terence Stamp, Michelle Johnson, Peter Berg.* A by-the-books erotic thriller involving a fatal love triangle. The lusty girlfriend (Johnson) of an underworld kingpin (Stamp) seduces his brooding bodyguard, igniting jealousy, rage and murder. ★★½

George of the Jungle

(1997, 91 min, US, Sam Weisman) *Brendan Fraser, Leslie Mann, Thomas Haden Church, Holland Taylor, Richard Roundtree, John Cleese.* Okay, so we didn't exactly need another movie based on an animated television series; but Disney's live-action spin on the cult Saturday morning cartoon is actually amicable, innocuous fun. Fraser stars as the accident-prone, loincloth wearing jungle boy George, and it's the sort of camp-it-up, cheerfully silly role that would humiliate an actor with either less confidence or a lesser sense of humor. He exudes charisma, and whether swinging from vine to vine through the African jungle, fighting a vicious lion, or courting a beautiful San Francisco socialite (Mann) on safari, he's a delight. Another ingredient in the film's overall enjoyment is capturing the feel of the old Jay Ward (who also did "Rocky and Bullwinkle") cartoons, down to the smart-ass narrator, bad puns, and breaking of the cinematic fourth wall. ★★★ DVD: $19.99, VHS: $9.99

George Stevens:
A Filmmaker's Journey

(1984, 100 min, US, George Stevens Jr.) A thoroughly engaging and heartfelt documentary written and directed by Stevens, Jr. about the life and career of his father, the noted film director. The program includes scenes from such Stevens classics as *Gunga Din, Woman of the Year, A Place in the Sun* and *Giant.* Stevens' approach to filmmaking is explored, and the film also includes rare color footage taken by the director during WWII. ★★★ VHS: $14.99

George Washington

(2000, 90 min, US, David Gordon Green) *Donald Holden, Candace Evanofski, Damian Jewan Lee, Curtis Cotton III.* An exquisitely shot first feature from North Carolina School of the Arts grad Green, *George Washington* signals the arrival of an original talent. A poetic, haunting drama, the film follows a small group of mostly African-American kids as they spend their summer in a backwater Southern town, whiling away their days swimming, playing and talking about their futures. While the film begins somewhat awkwardly, with (seemingly intentional) artificial dialogue and deliberate pace, it soon begins to sustain a rhythm all its own. Green's sure hand (as well as the enormous talent of cinematographer Tim Orr) allows the dramatic restraint and very adult observations by these kids (with extremely natural performances by all) to build to a moving and surprisingly optimistic movie experience. A warm, winning film. ★★★½ DVD Letterbox Criterion Collection: $39.99, VHS: $29.99

George Washington Slept Here

(1942, 93 min, US, William Keighley) *Jack Benny, Ann Sheridan, Charles Coburn, Hattie McDaniel.* Before Cary Grant as Mr. Blandings built his dream house, or Oliver and Lisa said "goodbye city life" in "Green Acres," Benny and Sheridan tore apart the countryside in this amusing comedic romp. Antique-buff Sheridan surprises city-loving husband Benny by buying a colonial home in the country. It's dilapidated, but it's okay: for George Washington once slept there. They soon find, however, that the place hasn't been touched since then as they prepare to refurbish it. Benny delivers his one-liners with zeal; and if there is a clinker among them, don't worry — there's a better one just a few lines away. Based on the Kaufman and Hart play. ★★★

Jane Russell (l.) and Marilyn Monroe in *Gentlemen Prefer Blondes*

Georgia

(1987, 90 min, Australia, Ben Lewin) *Judy Davis, Julia Blake.* Davis is an intelligent, witty, eccentric and captivating actress. And she brings all of these attributes to this slightly mystifying story of Nina Baily, an Australian tax lawyer who discovers that her biological mother was not the woman who raised her, but instead was Georgia, an erratic high society photographer who died amid tabloid rumors: "Accident or murder?" Though at times the facts are a bit hard to keep straight through the characters' thick Australian accents, the compelling story and rich characterizations make *Georgia* an extremely satisfying mystery. ★★★ VHS: $19.99

Georgia

(1995, 117 min, US, Ulu Grosbard) *Jennifer Jason Leigh, Mare Winningham, Ted Levine, Max Perlich, John Doe.* Sibling rivalry achieves new heights in this courageous but ultimately disappointing musical drama that examines the fragile relationship between two sisters. Giving a no-holds-barred performance, Leigh plays Sadie, an untalented rock singer struggling to make a name for herself in the grunge clubs of Seattle. Her sister, Georgia (Winningham), however, has made a name for herself, a success that Sadie both resents and desperately strives for. *Georgia* is at its best when exploring their unstable relationship. But the film also seems to revel in Sadie's professional and personal inadequacies, often exposing raw emotions in a dramatically involving series of events but without benefit of much subtlety. However, Sadie's final indignity is that a film about her is named after Georgia. ★★½ DVD: $19.99, VHS: $19.99

Georgy Girl

(1966, 100 min, GB, Silvio Narizzano) *Lynn Redgrave, James Mason, Charlotte Rampling, Alan Bates.* Redgrave delivers a delightful performance · in this uncommon British comedy about a frumpy young woman who's satisfied to live life vicariously through her swinging London roommate (Rampling). A delightful adult comedy-drama of modern-day morals. Mason stars as a wealthy man who desires the ugly-duckling Georgy as his mistress. ★★★½

Germany Year Zero

(1947, 75 min, Germany/Italy, Roberto Rossellini) *Edmund Moeschke.* This grim vision of destruction and chaos forms one of Rossellini's war trilogy, which includes *Open City* and *Paisan.* The setting of this neorealist classic is the ruined city of Berlin after the war, where survivors struggle to live peacefully in an environment in which their self-respect, even their humanity, is destroyed. The dispassionate camera follows 12-year-old Edmund (Moeschke), a boy whose family lives in a cramped war-damaged flat with four other families. As Edmond scavenges the city for coal, money and food, he meets Mr. Enning, a creepy middle-aged man and former Nazi schoolteacher. The old man soon involves the boy in the black market and ultimately eggs the youth to a heinous crime, an act that destroys the boy's innocence and proves the pervading power of lingering Fascism. (German with English subtitles) ★★★½ DVD: $24.99, VHS: $79.99

Germinal

(1993, 160 min, Belgium/France/Italy, Claude Berri) *Gérard Depardieu, Miou-Miou, Renaud, Judith Henry.* Based on Emile Zola's gripping novel about coal miners in the 19th century, *Germinal* provides director Berri with yet another exquisite literary adaptation. Miou-Miou and Depardieu are wonderfully typecast as the working-class hero and his wife who struggle through the tense conditions that lead to a workers' revolt. With sweeping camerawork and a pervading sense of doom, the film expertly captures the feeling of claustrophobia as to recall the power and anxiety of *Das Boot.* Berri is a true master of detail and period work, and nowhere is it more evident than in this epic saga. (French with English subtitles) ★★★½ VHS: $19.99

Geronimo: An American Legend

(1993, 115 min, US, Walter Hill) *Jason Patric, Gene Hackman, Robert Duvall, Wes Studi, Rodney A. Grant, Kevin Tighe, Matt Damon.* Patric brings intensity and intelligence to this haunting examination of Geronimo, the Apache who was the last Native American leader to elude the government's attempt to confine the Indian nations to reservations. Shot amid the dusty Utah vistas, Patric — complete with gentle Southern drawl — plays the cavalry officer who is sent to bring in Geronimo (Studi) upon his surrender. The last scenes in the film paint a vivid portrait of some of the most shameful injustices in the history of the West. ★★★ DVD: $9.99, VHS: $9.99

Gerry

(2003, 103 min, US, Gus Van Sant) *Casey Affleck, Matt Damon.* A plot synopsis is somewhat pointless when regarding the first experimental film to recieve mass distribution since Buñuel was directing, but here goes: Damon and Affleck play guys named Gerry who drive to the desert, walk a lot, become lost, walk some more, become lost a bit, and then keep walking. Summarizing "Waiting for Godot" would get you about as far since, like Beckett, Van Sant is more interested in the form and structure of his art than the text. Using a widescreen frame and gritty color film (it could never work without the sharp beauty of film, though it was originally envisioned as a digital video project), each shot is nothing less than remarkable, from a breathless close-up dolly of the two Gerrys running to perfectly framed static compositions of vistas that could make John Ford reach for his canteen. In between are a few set pieces, including a very funny bit where Gerry #1 finds himself "marooned" on a giant boulder, with no explanation as to how he got up there nor an easy way off. This is hypnotic stuff, though its impact will be inevitably lessened on the small screen, and is as likely to enrapture viewers in reverie as send them searching for the eject button. ★★★ DVD: $29.99

Gervaise

(1956, 110 min, France, René Clément) *Maria Schell, François Perier.* Based on the Emile Zola novel "L'Assommoir," this superbly acted drama of a laundrywoman's bleak life in 19th-century Paris achieves moments of brilliant realism and spellbinding dramatics but is overshadowed by the depressing lives of its characters. Nominated for Best Foreign-Language Film, *Gervaise* stars Schell in a heartbreaking performance as a crippled woman who starts life anew with her two children after her philandering husband leaves her. Happiness is short-lived, however, as her second husband turns to drink and ruins both their lives. This is a devastating tale of betrayal, revenge and star-crossed love. (Remake: *Germinal*) (French with English subtitles) ★★★ VHS: $29.99

Get Bruce!

(1999, 82 min, US, Andrew J. Kuehn) *Bruce Vilanch, Rosie O'Donnell, Robin Williams, Billy Crystal, Bette Midler, Whoopi Goldberg, Lily Tomlin, Nathan Lane, Roseanne, Carol Burnett, Shirley MacLaine.* Bruce Vilanch — with his appearances on the new "Hollywood Squares" — seems to have come out of nowhere but that is far from reality as this entertaining documentary sets out to reveal. With his wildly bushy blond hair, beard, oversized glasses and roly-poly physique, one cannot easily forget this man, but he has actually been working behind the entertainment scene for most of his 30 years as one of the industry's top comedy writers. We find out that Bruce has been making people laugh for years with his witty, often naughty lines, not as front man but as behind-the-scenes laugh doctor for leading entertainers, politicians and actors. He has also been comedy writer on almost every awards show including being head writer for the Academy Awards (and winning awards for the Billy Crystal-hosted programs). The film focuses on the former *Chicago Tribune* writer and features interviews with a litany of stars for whom he has been providing laugh lines. ★★★½ DVD: $19.99, VHS: $14.99

Get Carter

(1971, 112 min, GB, Mike Hodges) *Michael Caine, Ian Hendry, Britt Ekland.* Ushering in the neo-noir wave of the '70s, *Get Carter* saw the future and it was bleak. The devastatingly suave Caine plays Jack Carter, a magnetic gangster with a pervasive mean streak. He heads to grimy Newcastle to track down his brother's murderer. Using intimidation (for men) and seduction (for the ladies), he gets answers and issues judgment, but revenge is rarely satisfying. Hodges provides a quiet visual flair, putting the camera right where it traditionally shouldn't be, picking up other characters and some essential mood in the process. (Remade in 1971 as *Hit Man* and in 2000 as *Get Carter*) ★★★½ DVD: $19.99, VHS: $19.99

Get Carter

(2000, 102 min, US, Stephen Kay) *Sylvester Stallone, Alan Cumming, Miranda Richardson, Rachael Leigh Cook, Mickey Rourke, Michael Caine.* Sometimes, style can indeed triumph over substance. In this inconsistently dull Americanization of *Get Carter*, though, the (lack of) substance is so prevalent that the gloss is a mere distraction. This updating does more than move Carter (Stallone) to Seattle; it replaces the social cynicism of the original with the idea that revenge *can* buy happiness. And, yes, the brutal fights (especially with well-cast Rourke) and car chases are refreshing when they finally occur. But it leaves an empty feeling afterwards, one that the filmmakers don't recognize. ★★ DVD: $14.99, VHS: $9.99

Get Crazy

(1983, 98 min, US, Allan Arkush) *Malcolm McDowell, Ed Begley, Jr., Lou Reed, Daniel Stern, Fabian.* The *crazy* in the title is not misleading as a rock promoter for a Fillmore East-like theatre gets more than he bargained for when he stages a New Year's Eve concert. A few "in" cameos by famous music personalities. ★★★

G

Get on the Bus

(1996, 121 min, US, Spike Lee) *Charles S. Dutton, Ossie Davis, Roger Guenveur Smith, Andre Braugher, Isaiah Washington.* A group of 20 or so African-American men hop on a commercial bus in Los Angeles and head to the Million Man March in Washington, D.C. Along the way, friendships are forged, fights break out, and the very purpose of this cross-country trek is discussed. Director Lee gathers together a collection of "types" (ex-gang banger, wise elder, buppie, gay couple, deadbeat dad) in an enclosed space for a period of time, and like a fascinating sociological experiment, observes the results. Lee avoids heavy moralizing for the most part, concentrating instead on delicious debates on a broad range of topics concerning black males: racism, misogyny, homophobia, upward mobility, self-respect, and even the O.J. verdict. This is a well-acted, involving, fast-paced effort marred only by a dramatically unsatisfying, clunky ending. ★★★ DVD: $14.99

Get Out Your Handkerchiefs

(1978, 109 min, France, Bertrand Blier) *Gérard Depardieu, Patrick Dewaere, Carole Laurie.* A farcical comedy on unconventional love and sex. Depardieu is a husband aiming to please, Laurie is his enigmatic wife and Dewaere is a lover brought in to lift her out of her depression. An insightful look into the sexual roles of the modern relationship; both witty and perceptive. (French with English subtitles) ★★★½ DVD: $19.99

Get over It

(2001, 86 min, US, Tommy O'Haver) *Kirsten Dunst, Ben Foster, Melissa Sagemiller, Sisqo, Swoosie Kurtz, Ed Begley, Jr., Martin Short, Coolio.* The explosion of the teen comedy genre has reinforced among film executives the sinister notion that adolescent kids will flock to see anything that's raunchy and gross. That's what makes this teen flick, starring the always-endearing Dunst, a little more refreshing than the others. It's still the same old story, told against the backdrop of a high school production of "A Midsummer Night's Dream": Girl dumps Guy, Guy wants her back and can't see that Girl #2, the Girl of His Dreams, is right in front of him. But it is nicely told by director O'Haver, with some clever stunts — like kitschy production numbers and zany hallucinations — thrown in for kicks. And though it's hard to take at all seriously the notion of lovesick teenagers, Shakespeare would posit otherwise. Predictable as it may be, *Get over It* is a light-hearted if earnest entertainment. ★★½ DVD, VHS: $9.99

Get Real

(1999, 110 min, GB, Simon Shore) *Ben Silverstone, Brad Gorton, Charlotte Brittain, Stacy Hart, Kate McEnery, Patrick Nielsen, Tim Harris, Jacquetta May, David Lumsden.* A sharply observed coming-of-age story, *Get Real* is infused with charm, humor and a knowing sense of the difficulties of being a gay teen. Steven (Silverstone) is a 16-year-old living in the new British suburbia with his upper-middle-class parents. Life changes for the soft-spoken teen when he locks eyes on the school's super-jock John (Gorton). The two are attracted to each other, but John's self-hating fears threaten to tear apart their tentative relationship. Though the plot is too similar to *Beautiful Thing*, and there are some unnecessary melodramatic excesses, this tale captivates by adroitly examining what it feels like to

be an outsider. The screenplay, by Patrick Wilde, is based on his play, "What's Wrong with Angry?" ★★★ DVD: $29.99, VHS: $14.99

Get Rita

(1972, 90 min, Italy, Giorgio Capitini) *Sophia Loren, Marcello Mastroianni.* In the mood for a scoop of Italian gelato? Try the cinematic equivalent in this light, endearingly terrible comedy. Loren is Poopsie, a Milanese prostitute who finds herself "bought" by Charlie (Mastroianni), an abusive, big-time gangster. Poopsie proves to be a lot tougher than her nemesis as she seeks to undermine the low-life kingpin. Sounds serious? Don't be fooled — everyone overacts in this wacky comedy whose highlight is Loren's imitation of a dancing and singing Rita Hayworth. ★★½

Get Shorty

(1995, 105 min, US, Barry Sonnenfeld) *John Travolta, Gene Hackman, Rene Russo, Danny DeVito, Dennis Farina, Delroy Lindo, James Gandolfini, David Paymer, Bette Midler.* A thoroughly entertaining, hip and refreshing gangster comedy that takes aim at Hollywood and its players. Travolta gives a scintillating performance as Chili Palmer, a low-level but self-assured Miami mobster whose debt collection assignment takes him to Hollywood. An acknowledged film buff, Chili is soon pitching a movie deal to sleazy producer Harry Zimm (a hilarious Hackman) rather than collecting his debt. In an ever-spiraling comedic vortex of industry machinations, Chili becomes involved with Zimm's leading lady (Russo), a pretentious star (DeVito), a rival gangster (Lindo), and a Miami gangland boss (Farina in a wonderfully antic performance) out for revenge. Based on the novel by Elmore Leonard, *Get Shorty* is smart, cynical and fabulously funny; its satire goes for the jugular in the most unexpected and gratifying ways. ★★★★ DVD: $14.99

Get to Know Your Rabbit

(1972, 91 min, US, Brian De Palma) *Tom Smothers, John Astin, Orson Welles, Allen Garfield, Katharine Ross.* Quirky, smirky, mischievous and very '70s, this oddball comedy (actually filmed in 1970) was made during De Palma's inventive independent period. Smothers plays a '70s version of a yuppie who chucks the pressures of executive life and "drops out" to become a tap-dancing magician. Welles (who was an amateur magician) is his strange teacher, a bug-eyed Astin is his former boss and Garfield is a swinger with a brassiere fetish. The film is filled with wacky humor that does not always hit the mark, but overall it's a fine example of the kind of exuberant comedy popular at the time. ★★★ VHS: $19.99

The Getaway

(1972, 122 min, US, Sam Peckinpah) *Steve McQueen, Ali MacGraw, Ben Johnson, Sally Struthers, Slim Pickens, Jack Dodson.* McQueen and MacGraw capture on-screen the sparks they were striking offscreen in this violent tale of an ex-con hired by the mob to pull off a simple bank job. Even though the heist goes awry, the mob still wants their money — and they're holding his wife until they get it. This time out, director Peckinpah's penchant for balletic violence is subvervient to the story and suspenseful action sequences. (Remade in 1994) ★★★ DVD: $19.99

The Getaway

(1994, 114 min, US, Roger Donaldson) *Alec Baldwin, Kim Basinger, James Woods, Michael Madsen, David Morse, Jennifer Tilly, Philip*

Seymour Hoffman. From the director of *No Way Out* comes this glamorous, highly entertaining remake of the grungy Sam Peckinpah actioner starring real-life husband and wife Baldwin and Basinger in the roles originally played by real-life couple Steve McQueen and Ali MacGraw. Both are evenly matched as a bickering, larcenous couple on the run from a botched heist and the accomplices that set them up (including Madsen as a red-headed psycho). Special mention goes to Tilly in the comic role originally played by Sally Struthers. ★★★ DVD: $9.99

Getting Away with Murder

(1996, 92 min, US, Harvey Miller) *Dan Aykroyd, Lily Tomlin, Jack Lemmon, Bonnie Hunt, Brian Kerwin.* What was probably intended as an acerbic commentary on contemporary morals, *Getting Away with Murder* is merely plodding and muddled. Mild-mannered history professor Aykroyd suspects next-door neighbor Lemmon to be a Nazi war criminal. His interest is misread as support by Lemmon and daughter Tomlin, leading to Aykroyd's further involvement in ensuing events. However, instead of a wry, twisting morality tale, this unfocused and weak effort telegraphs its punches way too early and without a power delivery. ★ VHS: $9.99

Getting Even with Dad

(1994, 108 min, US, Howard Deutch) *Ted Danson, Macaulay Culkin, Glenne Headly, Saul Rubinek, Hector Elizondo.* A promising premise, that of a precocious 12-year-old son blackmailing his criminal dad to go straight, hasn't been exploited at all and both lifeless direction and an awful script make this a tedious bore. Danson plays an ex-con who masterminds a robbery that seems to be foolproof — only he didn't allow for a visitation from his estranged son (Culkin). The kid gets wise to Dad's plans, and forces him to spend time with him, hoping he'll forget his life of crime. Only Rubinek as Danson's partner and Headly as a cop rise above the material. ★½ DVD: $14.99, VHS: $9.99

Getting It Right

(1989, 105 min, GB, Randal Kleiser) *Jesse Birdsall, Lynn Redgrave, Peter Cook, John Gielgud.* This English comedy about a man's sexual and emotional awakening is a surprisingly touching and consistently funny coming-of-age film. Gavin Lamb (the perfectly cast Birdsall) is a slightly awkward but handsome 31-year-old London hairdresser who lives at home and dreams of one day losing his virginity. In a whirlwind two weeks his structured life is shattered when he is thrown into the arms, and beds, of three very different women. Redgrave is smashing as the "older woman" who introduces our young hero to the pleasures of the flesh. ★★★

The Getting of Wisdom

(1977, 100 min, Australia, Bruce Beresford) *Susannah Fowles, Alix Longman, Hilary Ryan, Barry Humphries.* A spirited girl encounters unhappiness at a snobbish Melbourne girls' academy in Beresford's pleasant if unimaginative coming-of-age drama. Set before the turn of the century, the story follows intelligent but impetuous Laura (Fowles), who leaves her rural home for higher education in the big city. There, she overcomes the school's petty regulations, schoolgirl rivalries and the authority's herd mentality. Humphries, the alter ego to Dame Edna Everage, appears as the school's principal in a wasted performance. ★★½

G

Gettysburg

(1993, 254 min, US, Ronald F. Maxwell) *Tom Berenger, Jeff Daniels, Martin Sheen, Sam Elliott, Maxwell Caulfield, C. Thomas Howell, Stephen Lang, Kevin Conway, Richard Jordan.* An epic re-creation of the Battle of Gettysburg, this four-hour drama may not belie its running time, but it certainly captures the flavor of its time, and brilliantly stages in painstaking detail the endless battles that marked the Civil War. Earnest performances from the ensemble distinguish the production, though Daniels and Jordan excel in their characterizations of ethical men caught in the confines of bloody combat. Though *Gettysburg's* dramatic scenes aren't on par with its battle sequences, the film features outstanding production values, and also some truly awful makeup. ★★★ DVD Letterbox: $19.99, VHS: $14.99

Ghost

(1990, 127 min, US, Jerry Zucker) *Patrick Swayze, Demi Moore, Whoopi Goldberg, Tony Goldwyn, Vincent Schiavelli.* A metaphysical romance/thriller/comedy, *Ghost* is a guaranteed crowd-pleaser filled with supernatural intrigue and lots of laughs. Swayze and Moore star as Sam and Molly, a yuppie couple whose picture-perfect romance is broken up when Sam is suddenly dispatched to the other side. As he becomes stuck between dimensions, Sam's spirit roams the streets of Manhattan in search of answers. Goldberg's Oscar-winning performance as Oda Mae Brown, a storefront spiritual advisor who becomes Swayze's reluctant link to the world of the living, is hilarious. Director Zucker moves the action along at a lively pace and makes the most of Goldberg's enormous comedic talents. ★★★ DVD Letterbox: $14.99, VHS: $9.99, VHS Letterbox: $9.99

The Ghost and Mrs. Muir

(1947, 104 min, US, Joseph L. Mankiewicz) *Gene Tierney, Rex Harrison, George Sanders, Edna Best, Natalie Wood.* A charming fantasy about a widow (Tierney) who is romanced by a crusty if ethereal sea captain (Harrison), the once and present occupant of her New England cottage. A felicitous mixture of make-believe with an acute observation of human foibles, and requiring very little suspension of disbelief. Tierney is especially engaging. Scripted by Philip Dunne, with music by Bernard Herrmann. (Remade as a TV series in the 1960s) ★★★ DVD: $14.99, VHS: $9.99

The Ghost and the Darkness

(1996, 110 min, US, Stephen Hopkins) *Michael Douglas, Val Kilmer, Bernard Hill, John Kani.* Though he doesn't appear on screen until a half-hour into the film, Douglas' big-game hunter adds just the right kick to an otherwise familiar, occasionally exciting jungle adventure. Set in late-1890s East Africa, and amazingly based on a true story, *The Ghost and the Darkness* follows the attempts to build a railroad by a British firm whose crew has come under attack by two particularly ferocious lions. Kilmer is the engineer sent to oversee construction and the elimination of the animals. Kilmer is a little too white-man-knows-it-all, but he gives an earnest interpretation; Douglas at least has some fun with a slant on the great-white-hunter adventurer. The scenery is spectacular, and the cinematography captures the beauty of the land and the terror of the beasts. Once again, nature rules. ★★½ DVD: $14.99, VHS: $9.99

The Ghost Breakers

(1940, 85 min, US, George Marshall) *Bob Hope, Paulette Goddard, Willie Best.* Though short on plot, there's plenty of laughs to this uproarious Hope ghost comedy. Radio journalist Bob helps Paulette — who's just inherited a haunted castle in Cuba — battle the bad guys and some prankish poltergeists. And Hope's got a one-liner for every occasion: Some are merely funny; others are just hilarious. Best makes the most of the role of the "scared Negro" (and he does get in a few zingers of his own), and Goddard is captivating. (Remade as *Scared Stiff*) ★★★½ DVD: $14.99

Ghost Dad

(1990, 84 min, US, Sidney Poitier) *Bill Cosby, Denise Nicholas, Ian Bannen.* Cosby plays a widowed father who dies and comes back to life, given a couple of days to straighten out his affairs for the sake of his children. Though Cosby hams it up, there's little that works in this tired ghost comedy. ★★

Ghost Dog: The Way of the Samurai

(2000, 116 min, US, Jim Jarmusch) *Forest Whitaker, John Tormey, Cliff Gorman, Henry Silva, Tricia Vessey, Victor Argo.* Ghost Dog, a typically low-key, slow-paced Jarmusch comedy-drama, is among his best. Whitaker plays a hit man for the mob who lives his life according to the code of the Japanese samurai. When a hit goes slightly wrong, he is marked for death, leading to a war of old-school philosophies. Filled with the usual Jarmusch dry-as-toast humor, *Ghost Dog* is a surprisingly effective film, juggling hilarious insights into race relations and violence with jarring shoot-outs and dramatic moments. Whitaker is superb, the cinematography is spot-on, and the old mob guys — especially Argo and Gorman — are hysterical. ★★★½ DVD: $9.99, VHS: $14.99

The Ghost Goes Gear

(1966, 79 min, GB, Hugh Gladwich) *The Spencer Davis Group, Nicholas Parson, Jack Haig, Sheila White.* The popular 1960s British pop group Spencer Davis Group follows on the heels of The Beatles' *A Hard Day's Night* and *Help!* with this lively rock comedy featuring daft blokes, mod birds, groovy tunes and ghosts gone gear. ★★★ DVD: $24.99, VHS: $14.99

The Ghost Goes West

(1936, 82 min, GB, René Clair) *Robert Donat, Jean Parker, Eugene Pallette, Elsa Lanchester.* Delightful ghost comedy about a 200-year-old spirit who, refusing to leave the Scottish castle he haunts, travels to America when it is sold and shipped abroad. Written by Robert E. Sherwood, with Donat as charming as ever in dual roles as the poltergeist and his descendant. ★★★½

Ghost in the Machine

(1994, 90 min, US, Rachel Talalay) *Karen Allen, Chris Mulkey, Jessica Walter.* The Lawnmower Man meets *Shocker* meets *The Horror Show* ad infinitum ad nauseam (emphasis on "nauseum") as a serial killer on the brink of death is uploaded into a municipal mainframe enabling him to kill anyone who's paid their electric bill. State-of-the-art effects and a couple of creatively grisly deaths can't help shock this one back to life. ★½ VHS: $9.99

Ghost in the Noonday Sun

(1973, 93 min, GB, Peter Medak) *Peter Sellers, Spike Milligan, Anthony Franciosa, Peter Boyle.* It is rumored that Sellers and director Medak had a falling-out that led to the demise of this blundering pirate comedy. Sellers stars as a rogue pirate who leads his men in search of hidden treasure, but finds that the booty is protected by a less than friendly ghost. ★

Ghost in the Shell

(1995, 80 min, Japan, Mamoru Oshii) Based on the cyberpunk manga by Masamune Shirow, *Ghost in the Shell* is a cerebral animated sci-fi tale that mixes philosophy with its high-octane action. In a future dominated by technology, a female cyborg, Major Motoko Kusanagi, is investigating a series of computer-hacking crimes with her special police unit, when it is revealed that their opponent is a new cybernetic life form. Director Oshii brings a distinct style of visual storytelling to this feature through a mix of computer and traditional cel animation. The results are breathtaking. (Japanese with English subtitles) ★★★½ DVD: $29.99, VHS Dubbed: $19.99, VHS Subtitled: $29.99

The Ghost of Frankenstein

(1942, 68 min, US, Erle C. Kenton) *Cedric Hardwicke, Lon Chaney, Jr., Lionel Atwill, Ralph Bellamy, Bela Lugosi.* In this fourth entry in Universal's popular series, Frankenstein's monster returns yet again, this time without the abnormal brain. Atmospheric though starting to show signs of wear, this occasionally fun outing is highlighted by Lugosi's turn as Ygor. Chaney fills in for Karloff as The Monster. (Sequel: *Frankenstein Meets the Wolf Man*) ★★½ VHS: $14.99

Ghost Ship

(2002, 90 min, US, Steve Beck) *Julianna Margulies, Gabriel Byrne, Ron Eldard, Desmond Harrington, Isaiah Washington.* Director Beck imbues a nice sense of atmosphere in the opening moments of *Ghost Ship*, when the passengers and crew of a Russian ocean liner all meet a gruesome fate. The clichés start to pile up, however, when a motley group of salvagers — led by Byrne — discover the long-dead floating behemoth, and one by one meet their doom in a variety of not-so-ingenious ways. The cast brings more depth to their roles than is deserving of this dead-in-the-water story, which gets sillier and sillier as the film progresses. ★½ DVD Letterbox: $19.99, DVD Pan & Scan: $19.99, VHS: $6.99

Ghost Story

(1981, 85 min, US, John Irvin) *Fred Astaire, Melvyn Douglas, Douglas Fairbanks, Jr., John Houseman, Craig Wasson, Patricia Neal.* The old guard of Hollywood showed up to make this horror film as generic as its title. Astaire (in his last film) and pals teeter through this film about a shared secret from 50 years ago that is back for revenge. ★½ DVD Letterbox: $14.99

Ghost World

(2001, 101 min, US, Terry Zwigoff) *Thora Birch, Scarlett Johansson, Steve Buscemi, Brad Renfro, Illeana Douglas, Bob Balaban, Teri Garr.* Director Zwigoff brings his ultrahip *Crumb* sensibility to his existential, angst-ridden (yet curiously refreshing) *Ghost World*, which he cowrote with Daniel Clowes, the author of the graphic novel upon which this is based. Birch is despondently perfect as Enid, who responds to the living death of her suburban hell with the sneering disdain that peaks in the senior year of high school. With best friend Rebecca (Johansson), she enters the unique limbo of that first summer after high school graduation, wandering through tract housing, strip malls and faux '50s diners in utter boredom, making plans to get an apartment but

G

Scarlett Johansson (l.) and Thora Birch in *Ghost World*

unable to hold a job. A mean-spirited prank brings her in contact with Seymour (Buscemi), Crumb redux, who becomes her alternative father figure, fellow malcontent, instructor in turn-of-the-century jazz and blues, and covert object d'amore. Enid becomes less caricature and more character as the film progresses and she finds her way through petty frustrations, the weirdness of others and her own personal foibles. A most satisfying independent offering. ★★★½ DVD Letterbox: $14.99, VHS: $9.99

Ghostbusters

(1984, 107 min, US, Ivan Reitman) *Bill Murray, Dan Aykroyd, Harold Ramis, Sigourney Weaver, Rick Moranis, Annie Potts, Ernie Hudson, William Atherton.* One of the highest-grossing comedies of all time. Murray, Aykroyd and Ramis play bumbling "paranormal investigators" who save the world, or at least New York City, from demonic apparitions. The special effects are state-of-the-art, and both highbrow and lowbrow humor abounds. Fine comic performances from Weaver and Moranis. (Sequel: *Ghostbusters II*) ★★★ DVD: $14.99, VHS: $9.99

Ghostbusters II

(1989, 102 min, US, Ivan Reitman) *Bill Murray, Dan Aykroyd, Sigourney Weaver, Harold Ramis, Rick Moranis, Annie Potts, Ernie Hudson.* This formulaic sequel has, as in the original, an evil spirit from the past haunting the present — this time in the form of a truly ugly medieval monarch who is trapped in a less-than-flattering Renaissance painting. In conjunction with his imminent release the city of New York is being inundated by the now familiar ooze called "slime." All of the characters have returned from the first film — kudos go to Weaver for being the only one in the bunch to have actually developed her character from the original. ★★½ DVD: $14.99, VHS: $12.99

Ghosts of Mars

(2001, 98 min, US, John Carpenter) *Ice Cube, Natasha Henstridge, Jason Statham, Pam Grier, Clea DuVall, Joanna Cassidy.* Henstridge plays a drug-addicted cop on a matriarchal Mars in the future, put in charge of bringing in uber-criminal Desolation Williams (Cube). Unfortunately, meddling scientist Cassidy has let Mars' former inhabi-

tants out of their tomb, and now they are possessing the colonists. Unabashedly retro and B-movie goofy, *Ghosts of Mars* can also be a bit of fun, with its hodgepodge plot culled from about 20 different movies and Cube's tuff-ass caricature. It certainly could have been scarier, but *Ghosts of Mars* defiantly supplies an abundance of old-fashioned cheese. Carpenter also delivers a good, crunchy soundtrack. ★★½ DVD Special Edition: $14.99, VHS: $14.99

Ghosts of Mississippi

(1996, 123 min, US, Rob Reiner) *Alec Baldwin, Whoopi Goldberg, James Woods, Craig T. Nelson, William H. Macy, Diane Ladd, Virginia Madsen, Michael O'Keefe, Brock Peters.* In 1963, civil rights activist Medgar Evers was assassinated in front of his Mississippi home. The murderer went free after two hung juries couldn't come to a verdict. Thirty years later, Evers' widow pushed for a new trial, eventually bringing her husband's killer to justice. This sad chapter of America's past is the focus of Reiner's commendable if unremarkable film, a detective and courtroom drama that doesn't quite have the passion of its convictions. Baldwin plays the assistant district attorney in charge of the case, and Goldberg is Myrlie Evers. Like so many Hollywood films about racial prejudice against African-Americans, the story is seen through the eyes of a white person — here Baldwin. But whereas a film like *Mississippi Burning* has energy and focus, *Ghosts of Mississippi* has professionalism but little heart. ★★½ DVD: $19.99, VHS: $14.99

Ghosts of the Abyss

(2003, 92 min, US, James Cameron) *Bill Paxton, Dr. John Broadwater, Charles Pellegrino.* Even after eleven Oscar wins for his 1997 film *Titanic*, director Cameron still can't give up the ship. This document of a real-life dive back to the sunken wreck of *Titanic* was produced as an IMAX 3-D feature, and though the awesome impact of the undersea imagery is quashed on a home video screen, the film packs so much wonderment, intrigue and drama that even the most jaded *Titanic* buff will be mystified. State-of-the-art submersibles, cameras, underwater lighting rigs and agile remote-piloted ROV's offer rare, intimate glimpses of the ghostly luxury liner, which is slow-

ly decaying on the ocean floor. The DVD edition includes an additional 30 minutes of drama not seen in IMAX presentations, concerning a real-life technical snafu that escalates into a tense search-and-rescue mission. *Titanic* costar Paxton is along for the ride, serving as the eyes and ears of the audience. ★★★½ DVD Letterbox 2-disc set: $29.99

Ghoulies

(1985, 81 min, US, Luca Bercovici) *Peter Liapis, Lisa Pelikan, Michael Des Barres, Jack Nance.* A young man inherits his father's mansion, and becomes obsessed with the demonic witchery that led to his parents' deaths. A ridiculous story line, inferior special effects and a lack of good scares don't even make this a campy pleasure. (Followed by 3 sequels) (DVD double feature with *Ghoulies II*) ★ DVD Letterbox Double Feature: $14.99

Gia

(1998, 126 min, US, Michael Cristofer) *Angelina Jolie, Elizabeth Mitchell, Kylie Travis, Mercedes Ruehl, Faye Dunaway.* A mesmerizing, fact-based drama about the tragic life of supermodel Gia Carangi, Cristofer's mercurial film boasts a sensational performance by Jolie in the title role. Gia's rise and fall from an unruly Philadelphia teenager who becomes a top model to drug addict and AIDS victim makes for spellbinding viewing. Cristofer's approach to the material is never melodramatic; however, he uses diary snippets and memories by those who knew her to depict Gia's fast life and untimely death. Although the film suffers from an overly arty style, it's mostly riveting thanks to Jolie's no-holds-barred star turn. ★★★ DVD: $9.99, VHS: $9.99

Giant

(1956, 200 min, US, George Stevens) *James Dean, Elizabeth Taylor, Rock Hudson, Sal Mineo, Mercedes McCambridge, Dennis Hopper.* Fifty years after his tragic death, Dean remains a mythic icon of youthful rebelliousness and alienation. This sprawling saga of Texas oil aristocracy provided Dean his final and most challenging role as the arrogant ranch hand, Jett Rink. A Best Director Oscar went to Stevens, while Hudson earned a nomination for his finest screen work and Taylor won acclaim as Hudson's compassionate wife. *Giant* is an epic-sized drama of greed, jealousy and loyalty, but its stars seem to outshine the penetrating screenplay and thoughtful direction. ★★★½ DVD Letterbox 2-disc Box Set: $26.99, VHS Letterboxed: $14.99

The Giant Gila Monster

(1959, 75 min, US, Ray Kellogg) *Don Sullivan, Lisa Simone.* Giant Gila monsters with funny glued-on fins attack kids in New Mexico as they listen to rock 'n' roll in their hot rods. Youth wins out. ★★ VHS: $9.99

Gidget

(1959, 95 min, US, Paul Wendkos) *Sandra Dee, James Darren, Cliff Robertson.* First of the popular series with Dee as the innocent young beach groupie in love with surfer Darren. Also with Robertson, who plays a beach bum, himself smitten by our little heroine. It's kinda sappy in a kinda cute way, but remember that it's *not* a documentary. ★★½

The Gift

(1982, 195 min, France, Michel Lang) *Clio Goldsmith, Claudia Cardinale, Pierre Mondy.* A harried bank worker meets and falls in love with a beautiful and alluring mystery woman (Goldsmith), only to discover that his coworkers "bought" her for him as a retirement gift. Though the premise is promising, this sex farce barely ignites any sparks. ★★

The Gift

(2000, 111 min, US, Sam Raimi) *Cate Blanchett, Giovanni Ribisi, Keanu Reeves, Greg Kinnear, Katie Holmes, Hilary Swank, Michael Jeter, Gary Cole.* For decades, rural folk have referred to those possessing psychic powers as having "the gift," a mixed-blessing ability to be kept from strangers and embraced only by those who believe. After what happens to Annie (Blanchett) in the atmospheric mystery thriller *The Gift*, it's little wonder as to why. In a small Georgia town, the widowed Annie barely supports herself and her three kids from government checks and psychic readings. When the daughter of the town's richest citizen goes missing, and the police have exhausted all leads, Annie is called into the investigation. Her life begins to spiral out of control when a vision leads police to the body, and puts Annie and her children at risk. This is an alternately spooky and kooky tale, one in which the apparition of a dead relative is handled with the same sincerity as that of the subplot of a wife abuser. The filmmakers try to steer clear of the clichés, and, for the most part, succeed. ★★★ DVD Letterbox: $14.99, VHS Special Edition: $9.99

The Gig

(1985, 92 min, US, Frank Gilroy) *Wayne Rogers, Cleavon Little, Warren Vache, Joe Silver, Jay Thomas.* Rogers heads a cast of wonderful actors in this engaging comedy-drama about a group of friends who get together to play jazz. All's well until they get their first professional gig. ★★★

Gigi

(1958, 116 min, US, Vincente Minnelli) *Leslie Caron, Louis Jordan, Maurice Chevalier, Hermione Gingold.* Enchanting Oscar-winning musical about a French girl (Caron), being groomed to be a courtesan, and her romance with a handsome playboy (Jordan). Chevalier is most memorable as young Gigi's guardian. Winner of 9 Academy Awards, including Best Picture. Terrific Lerner & Lowe score includes "Thank Heaven for Little Girls" and "I Remember It Well." ★★★★ DVD: $19.99

Gigli

(2003, 121 min, US, Martin Brest) *Ben Affleck, Jennifer Lopez, Justin Bartha, Lenny Venito, Al Pacino, Christopher Walken.* Affleck, tattooed and chesty, plays low-level Mafia goombah Larry Gigli (rhymes, we're told repeatedly, with *really*). He's charged by his snarly boss to kidnap the autistic brother of a prosecutor in the hopes that the feds will ease off the Big Don, but Gigli is a screw-up, so his boss assigns another "pro" to keep an eye on them — Ricki (Lopez), a curvaceous freelancer/hit woman who immediately arouses Gigli's loins. Alas, she's a lesbian, and she playfully taunts him into second-guessing his own overexaggerated masculinity. Naturally, Gigli sees himself as the one guy able to melt through Ricki's icy wall of sexual indifference, but the script's singular inventive notion concerns Ricki's reverse seduction of Gigli: The hetero-hunk doesn't "score" the lesbian so much as the lesbian responds favorably towards the closet queer's suppressed femininity. Which would make Gigli the slyest, most subversive lesbian love story ever told were it not that its leading man/dyke is too shallow/oblivious to wade into these waters . . . and were it not for the painful fact that the movie is just plain crass, tasteless and dreadfully unfunny. *Really.* ★ DVD: $19.99, VHS: $14.99

Gilda

(1946, 110 min, US, Charles Vidor) *Rita Hayworth, Glenn Ford, George Macready.* A steamy, hard-boiled classic with the ravishing Hayworth driving husband MacReady and ex-lover Ford into frenzies of lust. Boldly adventurous in its day, *Gilda* holds up as a sizzling cauldron of perverse eroticism and social aberration. Featured is Rita's grinding performance of "Put the Blame on Mame," in which she loosens libidos with the removal of a single glove. ★★★½ DVD: $19.99

Gimme Shelter

(1969, 91 min, US, Albert Maysles, Charlotte Zwerin, David Maysles) *The Rolling Stones.* Definitive film record of The Rolling Stone's 1969 U.S. Tour including footage from the infamous Altamont Speedway concert. The film starts with outstanding recordings of the Stones doing "Satisfaction," "Jumping Jack Flash" and "Honky Tonk Woman" from their Madison Square Garden performances. The sense of foreboding is recorded with the Maysles' usual spare elegance. The Altamont concert is infamous because the Hell's Angels were hired as security guards and they murdered four people at the concert. The Maysles have truly captured the clash of the Hell's Angels with 300,000 hippies that ended the summer of love. This is required viewing for lovers of rock 'n' roll films. ★★★½ DVD: $39.99, VHS: $29.99

The Gin Game

(1982, 82 min, US, Mike Nichols) *Jessica Tandy, Hume Cronyn.* Tandy and Cronyn repeat their award-winning performances in this lovely comedy-drama, a live version of their early 1980s stage hit. Written by D.L. Coburn, the play casts Tandy and Cronyn as elderly residents at a rest home whose developing relationship is put to the test during a series of lively, almost cutthroat gin games. Though the play does occasionally lapse into heavy dramatics, it is nonetheless poignant, insightful and vastly amusing. Its two legendary performers are remarkably fine. (Remade in 2003) ★★★

Ginger and Fred

(1986, 126 min, Italy, Federico Fellini) *Giuletta Masina, Marcello Mastroianni, Franco Fabrizi.* Fellini's best since *Amarcord* is a refreshingly whimsical story of two aging hoofers who are reunited after 30 years to appear on a TV variety show that is a cross between "This Is Your Life" and "The Gong Show." Both Masina and Mastroianni are entrancing as the two out-of-their-element dancers. (Italian with English subtitles) ★★★ VHS: $19.99

Ginger Snaps

(2000, 108 min, Canada, John Fawcett) *Emily Perkins, Katharine Isabelle, Kris Lemche, Mimi Rogers, Jesse Moss.* Ginger and Brigitte are sisters trapped in high school hell, a "mindless little breeders machine" that is located slightly north of the numbing suburban landscape of *American Beauty.* Both are obsessed with death, and either one makes Morticia Addams seem giddy by comparison. Quite predictably, they are the school outcasts. However, what happens to them when they taste a little too much of the macabre is anything but predictable in this scintillating comic horror/thriller that plays like *Heathers* meets *An American Werewolf in London.* Isabelle is Ginger, the eldest sister, who is attacked one night by a mysterious beast and soon gets in touch with her animal instincts. Perkins is a revelation as her younger sister, a Goth-in-training who surprises no one more than herself in taking on the dark side. Director Fawcett and writer Karen Walton creatively capture the nuance of being an outsider and the growing terror of the unknown, setting in motion a cutthroat vision of community that is underscored by some truly chilling moments of lycanthrope activity. A subversive little gem. (Sequel: *Ginger Snaps 2*) ★★★½ DVD: $9.99, VHS: $9.99

The Gingerbread Man

(1997, 114 min, US, Robert Altman) *Kenneth Branagh, Robert Duvall, Robert Downey, Jr., Daryl Hannah, Tom Berenger, Embeth Davidtz.* Grisham's first opus written directly for the screen is a surprisingly well-paced mystery about a divorced attorney (Branagh) who jumps into a relationship with a downtrodden divorcée (Davidtz) who's being stalked by her father (Duvall), the head of a backwoods cult. When Branagh uses all his legal might to get the old man committed, he places the lives of himself and his children in danger. This is not the ego-driven "clash of titans" one might expect from a cast and crew of this caliber, but rather a quiet ensemble piece with a few unexpected twists and turns (especially the ending). Altman's direction seems to add an extra dimension of thought to what might have been a more action-packed drivel. ★★★½ DVD: $9.99

Girl

(1999, 96 min, US, Jonathan Kahn) *Dominque Swain, Sean Patrick Flanery, Portia DeRossi, Summer Phoenix, Selma Blair, Tara Reid.* For those still mourning the cancellation of "My So-Called Life," rejoice: Swain does her best Clare Danes in *Girl*, which has the same look and tone of the beloved TV show as well. Swain plays a well-to-do high school virgin who has a spineless best friend (Blair), but wishes she were as strong as her other good friend, the inevitable crazy-maned, girl-with-attitude (Reid). Swain is also head over heels in lust for local rocker Flanery, and her slo-mo, luscious visions of the gorgeous guy provide the film's best kitsch moments. While obviously clichéd and derivative, *Girl* is blessed with good performances and is surprisingly engaging. ★★½ DVD: $24.99, VHS: $14.99

The Girl

(1987, 104 min, Sweden, Arne Mattsson) *Franco Nero, Bernice Stegers, Christopher Lee.* Cheesy soft-core erotic thriller with Nero as a successful, married lawyer who falls under the alluring spell of an unusually lascivious 14-year-old girl. His Lolita-esque affair soon becomes his undoing, however, when his passion leads to cross-European intrigue and murder. An unintentionally funny international mess. (Filmed in English) ★

The Girl Can't Help It

(1956, 99 min, US, Frank Tashlin) *Jayne Mansfield, Tom Ewell, Edmond O'Brien.* Mansfield stars as the quintessential "dumb blonde" in this classic cult musical. Ewell plays a talent agent hired by Mansfield's gangster boyfriend (O'Brien) to make her a famous singing star. Jayne's attributes are more visual than vocal, but included in the film are some wonderful vintage performances by Fats Domino, Gene Vincent and The Platters. ★★★ VHS: $29.99

Girl Crazy

(1943, 100 min, US, Norman Taurog) *Judy Garland, Mickey Rooney, June Allyson, Nancy Walker.* A terrific George and Ira Gershwin score highlight this enjoyable Judy-Mickey musical with Mickey as a rich kid who's sent to an all-male school to forget about girls, only to fall for Judy on arrival. Songs include "I Got Rhythm" and "But Not for Me." Choreography by Busby Berkeley. ★★★½

Girl from Hunan

(1986, 99 min, China, U Lan & Xie Fei) *Na Renhua, Deng Xiaotuang.* Spectacular landscapes of Chinese villages, mountains and rice fields provide the lush backdrop to this powerful drama of a young woman struggling to overcome sexist repression in rural China at the turn of the century. Sent to a nearby village in a prearranged marriage, 14-year-old Xiao Xiao finds herself engaged to a little boy of two. Pampered by her future father-in-law, yet independent-minded, the girl cares for her toddling husband-to-be, but as her teenage years progress, she begins to think of him more in brotherly ways and directs her budding sexual curiosities toward older men, setting up a confrontation with clan elders who strictly enforce laws against adultery. Featuring elaborately staged tribal ceremonies for marriage and death in a male-dominated society, the film's theme, much repeated in Chinese and Japanese cinema, that "women were born to suffer," is nevertheless quite powerful. (Mandarin with English subtitles) ★★★½ VHS: $29.99

The Girl in a Swing

(1989, 112 min, US/GB, Gorgon Hessler) *Meg Tilly, Rupert Frazer.* A repressed middle-aged businessman marries a mysterious German secretary (Tilly) after a whirlwind romance and gets more than he bargained for. Unfortunately, the viewer gets less than he/she hoped for in this tepid "sexy" drama, based on the 1979 novel by Richard Adams ("Watership Down"). The film is filled with many tedious tearful outbursts as well as some strange hallucinatory episodes. ★

The Girl in the Picture

(1985, 90 min, GB, Cary Parker) *John Gordon Sinclair, Irina Brook.* Sinclair, the gangly star of *Gregory's Girl*, stars in this lighthearted comedy about the frailties of modern love. Sinclair plays a young photo shop clerk who is involved in a tumultuous on-again, off-again relationship with a young college student. ★★ VHS: $79.99

Girl, Interrupted

(1999, 127 min, US, James Mangold) *Winona Ryder, Angelina Jolie, Clea DuVall, Brittany Murphy, Whoopi Goldberg, Jared Leto, Jeffrey Tambor, Vanessa Redgrave.* Susanna (Ryder) is at odds with her upper-middle-class suburban existence in 1968 America. The only student in her posh school's graduating class not going on to college, she doesn't know where she fits in, except to know it's not here. A ritualistic suicide attempt lands her in an institution, where she joins a small group of sister inmates. This includes Lisa (Jolie, in an Oscar-winning performance), a lifer, a leader, and a predator. Through her interactions with Lisa, Susanna confronts her own life choices, rediscovers her capacity for connection, and gets outside of herself long enough to feel empathy. Though it falters somewhat at the end, with ambivalence regarding Lisa's character and nature, this is a thoughtful exploration of an autobiographical book. ★★★ DVD: $14.99, VHS: $9.99

Girl on the Bridge

(2000, 92 min, France, Patrice Leconte) *Daniel Auteuil, Vanessa Paradis.* A tale of desperation, director Leconte's *Girl on the Bridge* stars Paradis as Adele, a young woman heartbreakingly unconvinced of her worth and eerily convinced of her tragic doom. Enter Gabor (Auteuil), who finds Adele — on the verge of suicide — and nimbly recruits her into his knife-throwing act. Moments of sly, paternal seduction in a world of dangerous self-destruction are far from rare in great cinema, but Adele's acquiescence is portrayed with such raw tenderness that it sets the tone for the rest of the film. Yet for all of its pathos and, at times, melodramatic self-pity, *Girl on the Bridge* remains a vivid, intelligent film. (French with English subtitles) ★★★½ VHS Letterbox: $102.99

Girl 6

(1996, 107 min, US, Spike Lee) *Theresa Randle, Isaiah Washington, Spike Lee, Debi Mazar, Jenifer Lewis, Madonna, Peter Berg, Naomi Campbell, Quentin Tarantino, John Turturro.* Myriad cameo appearances by the terminally hip (Madonna, Quentin Tarantino, etc.) and the engaging presence of Randle can't save this disjointed morality tale. Randle plays a young woman who, to pay the rent until she gets her break in show business, accepts a phone sex job. Now a number on a switchboard — Girl 6 — not a name, she sinks into the milieu, losing sight of goals as they devolve into fantasies. Clips of Dorothy Dandridge and '70s blaxploitation flicks are interspersed throughout *Girl 6*, and the closing scene is a tip of the hat to Fellini's *8½*. Is this a parable equating acting and moviemaking with prostitution? Probably. But even such touches as the visual pun of Naomi Campbell in a T-shirt bearing the legend "Models Suck" can't salvage this unfocused amalgam of vignettes punctuated by an insistent, intrusive score by Prince. ★★ VHS: $29.99

Girl Talk

(1987, 85 min, US, Kate Davis) Pinky is a spunky 13-year-old who is continually threatened with lockup for not going to school. Sometimes she chooses to sleep in the streets rather than go home. Mars has found a surrogate family among fellow employees at a strip joint. They're actually more supportive than her own family. Martha is a single 19-year-old with an infant son. Director Davis examines the lives of these three young women, the products of sexual and psychological abuse; and looks at the failure of the existing systems created to address these problems. Though the film suffers slightly from an occasional lack of focus, it is often searing in the pain it reveals. The director offers no solutions or panaceas, but simply exposes the realities of the daily lives of these women, inviting understanding and compassion. ★★★ VHS: $19.99

Girl with a Pearl Earring

(2003, 95 min, GB, Peter Webber) *Colin Firth, Scarlett Johansson, Tom Wilkinson, Judy Parfitt, Cillian Murphy, Essie Davis.* Adapted from the novel by Tracy Chevalier, *Girl with a Pearl Earring* is named for a painting by Johannes Vermeer, which poses a story behind the overtly seductive portrait atypical of the artist's style of subtle domestic interiors. In Delf, Holland, Griet (Johansson), a young Protestant girl, is sent by her destitute parents to work as a maid in the home of the Catholic painter Vermeer (Firth). Once in the house of the Flemish Master, she soon becomes an object of his fascination and a creature of suspension with regards to his neurotic wife Catharine (Davis). Though Griet is courted by the local butcher's son, she is drawn to the painter. Vermeer's patron, Van Ruijven (Wilkinson), also desires the young girl and commissions a portrait in order to get access to her. The film is visually impressive, with wide sweeping camera shots of canals and cityscapes, and a sparkling use of light — it's a highly polished, evocative period film. ★★★ DVD Letterbox: $26.99

Girl with Green Eyes

(1964, 91 min, GB/Ireland, Desmond Davis) *Rita Tushingham, Peter Finch, Lynn Redgrave, T.P. McKenna.* Classic British coming-of-age drama, with Tushingham giving an outstanding performance as a young farm girl who moves to the big city (Dublin) and falls in love with an older writer (Finch). Redgrave is terrific as Tushingham's roommate. ★★★½ DVD Letterbox: $14.99, VHS: $9.99

The Girl with the Hatbox

(1927, 67 min, USSR, Boris Barnet) *Anna Sten, Vladimir Fogel.* With heavily politicized diatribes being the norm in early Soviet filmmaking, it is an even greater pleasure to view this cheery "American-style" comedy. Sten, who later starred in films at Goldwyn, plays a poor, naïve factory girl who is given a seemingly worthless lottery ticket in lieu of pay by her unscrupulous boss, only to discover that she is a winner. The money, she soon discovers, elicits not only pleasure but the greed of those around her and devious lovers as well. (Silent with orchestral accompaniment) ★★★ VHS: $29.99

Girlfight

(2000, 110 min, US, Karyn Kusama) *Michelle Rodriguez, Jaime Tirelli, Paul Calderon.* A big winner at Sundance, this underdog story of a gutsy Brooklyn high school boxing chick has got enough raw energy and fiery talent to kick just about every other polished studio flick in the balls. Newcomer Rodriguez is a real find, her intense leer and street-smart chutzpah commanding the screen with a power and fragile confidence rarely seen by a rookie performer. She's a natural, and first-time filmmaker Kusama keeps the drama lean and unpredictable, despite — or because of — some familiar plot devices. ★★★ DVD: $14.99

Girlfriends

(1978, 86 min, US, Claudia Weill) *Melanie Mayron, Amy Wright, Anita Skinner.* A flawless performance from Mayron as a photographer who makes it "on her own" after her best friend and roommate gets married makes this independent drama well worth watching. Susan (Mayron) finds success as an artist while Ann (Skinner) struggles to balance being a wife and mother with a writing career. Weill's film touchingly and accurately explores the two women's friendship and their singular ambitions without sentimentality or heavy-handedness. ★★★ VHS: $19.99

Girl with a Pearl Earring

Gladiator: Russell Crowe (l.) and Djimon Hounsou are the headliners at the Colosseum

Girls Can't Swim

(2000, 98 min, France, Anne-Sophie Birot) *Isild Le Besco, Karen Alyx, Pascal Elso.* A sadly tepid affair, *Girls Can't Swim* is a French coming-of-age film about the troubled relationship between two teenage girls. While Le Besco makes a strong impression — and certainly has a solid career ahead of her with better films to come — the characters aren't particularly interesting or unique, and their arguments and problems become tiresome. Despite a handful of good moments, the film can be tedious and uninvolving, and a somewhat desperate attempt at a "shocking" ending doesn't so much backfire as simply not register. You've seen this film before, and you've seen it better. (French with English subtitles) ★★ DVD Letterbox: $14.99, VHS: $14.99

Girls in Prison

(1994, 82 min, US, John McNaughton) *Anne Heche, Ione Skye, Missy Crider, Bahni Turner, Jon Polito.* This spirited spoof of women-behind-bars films should delight any fan of trash cinema. Set during the "Communist Witch Hunt" of the 1950s, the film focuses on a trio of gals sent to an L.A. slammer for diverse reasons: Skye, a lesbian writer; Turner gets all medieval on a TV commentator; and Crider is an aspiring folk singer. Since the homespun Crider is the real innocent, the other women unite to get her off the hook. With the help of an outside detective, they discover that Heche, a golddigging harpy, has set up Crider in order to reap the rewards of her soon-to-be hit record. Based on an AIP film from the 1950s, *Girls in Prison* may be the final film credit of tabloid great Sam Fuller, who penned the script with Christa Lang. Director McNaughton fills the frames with garish colors, steamy shower scenes, a host of hot-to-trot cartoony characters and hard-boiled dialogue. He has a unique talent of milking sordid subjects until they're downright refreshing. ★★★½ DVD: $14.99

Girls Just Want to Have Fun

(1984, 87 min, US, Alan Metter) *Sarah Jessica Parker, Helen Hunt, Ed Lauter, Shannen Doherty.* Enjoyable, better-than-average teen comedy with Parker giving a charming performance as a teenage girl determined to enter the big video dance contest despite protestations from family and church. ★★★ DVD: $19.99, VHS: $9.99

Girls Town

(1996, 90 min, US, Jim McKay) *Lili Taylor, Anna Grace, Aunjuane Ellis, Bruklin Harris, Asia Minor.* Touching upon issues important to young women, such as date rape, spousal abuse, teen pregnancy and abortion, the story provides an intimate look at a tight-knit band of female high school seniors anxiously awaiting their last day of educational captivity. The film initially looks as if it might become painfully aimless and meandering; but when an unexpected tragedy befalls the group, *Girls Town* comes sharply into focus and the young women set out to vent their rage at the men who have screwed up their nascent lives. Set somewhere in the quasi-urban environs of Queens, the film's heroines are an unlikely mix of race and social backgrounds that have coalesced around a pride in their citified toughness and an inane rebelliousness. The performances are top-notch, and the film avoids the maudlin "Afterschool Special" mentality. ★★★½ VHS: $9.99

Gladiator

(1992, 98 min, US, Rowdy Herrington) *Cuba Gooding, Jr., James Marshall, Brian Dennehy, Robert Loggia, Ossie Davis, John Heard.* A surprisingly sensitive blood-and-gutser focusing on the friendship between two inner-city youths (Gooding, Marshall) and their entanglement with a crooked underground fight promoter (Dennehy at his most demonic). It's silly and predictable, but fans of the genre should enjoy it. ★★ DVD: $24.99

Gladiator

(2000, 155 min, US, Ridley Scott) *Russell Crowe, Joaquin Phoenix, Connie Nielsen, Oliver Reed, Richard Harris, Djimon Hounsou, Derek Jacobi.* Extraordinary spectacle and involving dramatics come together to produce the kind of epic gladiator movie that we haven't seen since the days of *Spartacus* and *Ben-Hur.* In his Oscar-winning role, Crowe is Maximus, a decorated Roman general loyal to the emperor (a splendid Harris). Knowing he is about to die, the benevolent ruler decrees Maximus his successor, which doesn't sit too well with the scheming prince Commodus (Phoenix). In retaliation, Commodus murders his father and orders Maximus and his family killed. Maximus escapes, only to be captured and enslaved, eventually proving himself in the arena to become the star attraction of the Roman Colosseum. That the film works so well falls squarely on the very broad shoulders of Crowe, who creates a sympathetic, idealistic hero who never wavers in his principles. In support, Phoenix is outstanding as the sniveling Commodus. Winner of 5 Academy Awards, including Best Picture. ★★★★ DVD Letterbox Basic Edition: $19.99, DVD: $29.99, VHS: $14.99

The Glass Bottom Boat

(1966, 100 min, US, Frank Tashlin) *Doris Day, Rod Taylor, Arthur Godfrey, Paul Lynde, Dom DeLuise, John McGiver, Edward Andrews.* Though the times they were a changin', Day, in one of her last films, steered straight ahead with this familiar and silly slapstick comedy. Doris plays a widow whose work relationship with scientist Taylor leads to romance and spies. A good supporting cast. Fun for those wishing to wax a nostalgic good time. ★★½

The Glass House

(1972, 91 min, US, Tom Gries) *Alan Alda, Dean Jagger, Vic Morrow, Billy Dee Williams, Clu Gulager, Luke Askew, Edward Bell, Scott Hylands, Roy Jenson, Tony Mancini, Kristoffer Tabori, Alan Vint.* Truman Capote cowrote the screenplay (with Wyatt Cooper) for this harrowingly realistic depiction of prison life that was a landmark made-for-TV drama. Shot in an actual Utah state prison and using real inmates as extras, the film depicts the often savage, predatory conditions in the brutal "glass house" where control lies in the thuggish hands of Hugo Slocum (Morrow) and his gang of goons. ★★★ VHS: $14.99

The Glass House

(2001, 105 min, US, Daniel Sackheim) *Leelee Sobieski, Diane Lane, Stellan Skarsgård, Bruce Dern.* Teenager Sobieski and her younger brother are taken in by kindly friends (Skarsgård and Lane) of the family after their parents are killed in a car accident. However, clue after obvious clue leads Sobieski to think maybe her surrogate folks aren't as kindly as they seem. A numbingly predictable thriller, *The Glass House* is watchable for a while, mainly due to decent performances, but the pointlessness and familiarity soon breed contempt. The kind of trash that asks us to cluck our tongues disapprovingly when Skarsgård acts even slightly lecherous towards Sobieski, while the filmmakers insist she wear tight, skimpy clothes at every opportunity — the better for us to hypocritically ogle her. ★½ DVD Dual: $14.99, VHS: $9.99

The Glass Key

(1942, 85 min, US, Stuart Heisler) *Alan Ladd, Veronica Lake, Brian Donlevy, William Bendix.* Tough-as-nails remake of the 1935 film, adapted from a Dashiell Hammett story, about a politician (Donlevy) who is implicated in a murder; Ladd is his "henchman" who tries to clear his name. ★★★½

The Glass Menagerie

(1987, 134 min, US, Paul Newman) *Joanne Woodward, John Malkovich, Karen Allen, James Naughton.* The sterling performances of the cast elevate this handsome production based on Tennessee Williams' classic play. Allen brings a heart-wrenching vulnerability to Laura, the lonely and lame daughter of faded Southern belle Woodward. Malkovich is well cast as Woodward's troubled son Tom, and Naughton rounds out the cast as the Gentleman Caller. ★★★

The Glass Shield

(1995, 101 min, US, Charles Burnett) *Michael Boatman, Lori Petty, Ice Cube, Richard Anderson, Michael Ironside, Bernie Casey, M. Emmet Walsh, Elliott Gould.* The Glass Shield begins with comic book strips of police officers on the job, but these one-dimensional figures unfortunately carry over to the live action. In this well-intentioned though heavy-handed examination of racism in police ranks, Boatman and Petty are newly placed officers who band together to expose corruption in their department. The story occasionally moves, but the rogue cops are drawn with such broad strokes they have about as much depth as a villain on a "Kojak" episode. ★★ DVD: $19.99, VHS: $9.99

Gleaming the Cube

(1989, 105 min, US, Graeme Clifford) *Christian Slater, Steven Bauer, Ed Lauter.* This skateboard thriller is of interest because of its lead performer, Slater. With a hip delivery, reminiscent of Jack Nicholson, Slater brings a coolness to his role of the eternally rebellious youth who investigates the murder of his half-brother, a Vietnamese honor student. An interesting look at sibling rivalry and cultural clashes, with impressive skateboarding scenes. ★★½

Glen and Randa

(1971, 94 min, US, Jim McBride) *Steven Curry, Shelley Plimpton.* A low-budget, postapocalyptic tale, this early feature by McBride follows the travels of a primitive "Adam and Eve" couple scrounging for survival and looking for the fabled city of Metropolis. Clearly made in the heyday of the hippie movement, this minimalist parable is slowly paced but nevertheless intriguing in director McBride's quirky visual style. (Originally rated "X" in its theatrical release — solely for a prolonged nude scene.) ★★★ VHS: $59.99

Glen or Glenda

(1953, 67 min, US, Edward D. Wood, Jr.) *Bela Lugosi, Dolores Fuller, Daniel Davis (Ed Wood, Jr.).* "Beevare the beeg green dragin!" Thus we are warned by narrator Bela Lugosi who introduces us to the hopelessly confused Glen, possessed with an uncontrollable urge to don female garb. Wood's unredeemable schlock-umentary is one of the most ill-conceived and funniest works of all time. "Vat are little boys made ov? Is it puppy dog tails? Big fat snails? Or maybe *brassieres! garters!*" (aka: *I Changed My Sex*) ★ DVD: $24.99, VHS: $14.99

Glengarry Glen Ross

(1992, 100 min, US, James Foley) *Jack Lemmon, Al Pacino, Ed Harris, Alan Arkin, Kevin Spacey, Alec Baldwin, Jonathan Pryce.* David Mamet's riveting adaptation of his own Pulitzer Prize-winning play is marvelously realized by Foley. Pacino, Lemmon, Harris, Arkin and Spacey star as a group of seedy real estate men who scratch out a living selling Florida vacation tracts to retirees, and Baldwin puts in a short but brilliant turn as a callous head honcho who gives this ragtag sales force a merciless tongue-lashing. With the proverbial "axe" hanging over their heads, they find themselves in a dog-eat-dog fight for their jobs. Mamet's screenplay, which bristles with his usual razor-sharp dialogue, tells a compelling and timely story of greed, avarice and the rich getting richer. While the entire cast is brilliant, special kudos go to both Lemmon and Pacino for their gutsy handling of Mamet's barrage of profanities. ★★★★ DVD Dual 2-disc Special Edition: $14.99, VHS: $14.99

The Glenn Miller Story

(1954, 113 min, US, Anthony Mann) *James Stewart, June Allyson, Harry (Henry) Morgan, Gene Kupra, Louis Armstrong.* Stewart had one of his more popular roles in this affectionate tribute to the great swing time bandleader Glenn Miller. The film follows Miller's rise to become one of the major influences in popular music in the 1930s and '40s. Allyson plays Mrs. Miller, and the score includes such standards as "Chattanooga Choo-Choo" and "Pennsylvania 6-5000." ★★★ DVD: $9.99

The Glimmer Man

(1996, 92 min, US, John Gray) *Steven Seagal, Keenen Ivory Wayans, Bob Gunton, Brian Cox.* This Seagal slugfest isn't his worst movie (that honor still belongs to *On Deadly Ground*), but this tired retread comes close. Instead of an interesting twist or plot, we get Seagal as a mysterious homicide detective who is skilled in martial arts and practices Chinese medicine, and Wayans as his beleaguered partner. They happen upon the trail of a mysterious cover-up involving a serial killer, the CIA and Seagal's shadowy past. The outcome, however, is boring and unimaginative and not worth the buildup. ★½ DVD: $14.99, VHS: $9.99, VHS Letterbox: $9.99

Glitter

(2001, 104 min, US, Vondie Curtis-Hall) *Mariah Carey, Max Beesley, Terrence Howard, Dorian Harewood.* Trashy diva wannabe Carey (as in "can't carry her own movie") humiliates herself completely in this clumsy, rote semiautobiographical romantic drama about a ghetto-fabulous singer's meteoric rise to superstardom, thanks to a cute but prissy DJ (Beesley) who's thunderstruck by her "angelic" voice and perpetually rosy cheeks. As Billie Frank, Mariah scores the impressive coup of remaining a nonpresence in her own starring vehicle. Gratuitously flashy Scorsese-like time-lapse transitions are sprinkled throughout for no other reason than to liven up the dullness. Stupefyingly embarrassing, mercilessly hokey, desperately humorless, *Glitter* isn't even funny *accidentally*, darn it, eliminating the possibility that this dud might ever become the cheesy cult classic we were all bracing for. ★ DVD: $9.99, VHS: $9.99

Gloria

(1980, 121 min, US, John Cassavetes) *Gena Rowlands, Buck Henry, John Adames, Julie Carmen, Lupe Guarnica.* Cassavetes' whirlwind thriller features a remarkable performance from Rowlands as an ex-gangster's moll who begrudgingly takes charge of her neighbors' child after they are brutally massacred by the mob. As she and the kid flee would-be assassins, Cassavetes' camera masterfully captures the gritty underbelly of New York City. (Remade in 1999) ★★★ DVD Letterbox: $24.99

Gloria

(1999, 108 min, US, Sidney Lumet) *Sharon Stone, Jean-Luke Figueroa, Jeremy Northam, Cathy Moriarty, George C. Scott.* Cockamamie. For those who found Gus Van Sant's *Psycho* remake unnecessary, this one rates as downright unlawful. Why Lumet would tamper with John Cassavetes' gritty thriller is incomprehensible. Stone now plays the title character originated by Gena Rowlands, a gangster's moll who looks after a young boy whose family has been rubbed out by the mob. Everything from the art design to the mix of comedy, drama and suspense fails completely. Another instance to stick to the original. ★ DVD: $9.99, VHS: $9.99

Glory

(1989, 122 min, US, Edward Zwick) *Denzel Washington, Matthew Broderick, Morgan Freeman, Andre Braugher, Cary Elwes, Jane Alexander, Donovan Leitch, John Cullum.* This powerful Civil War drama is the startlingly good, impressive and long-overdue story about a little-known chapter in American history: the first black combat unit. Broderick heads a first-rate cast as the white commander of the 54th Massachusetts Regiment, an all-black fighting unit comprised of enlisted men who were initially denied the basic rights of other soldiers; they were then forced to prove themselves in order to be treated equally. Freeman offers solid support as the company's wise sergeant and Oscar winner Washington is outstanding as a former slave. Based on the letters of Colonel Robert Gould Shaw, whom Broderick portrays. ★★★★ DVD Special Edition: $19.99, VHS: $14.99

Glory Daze

(1996, 99 min, US, Rich Wilkes) *Ben Affleck, Megan Ward, Sam Rockwell, French Stewart, Matthew McConaughey.* Amateurish to the extreme, *Glory Daze* is an infantile campus comedy about the last days of school for a group of graduating seniors. A collection of lifeless episodes and unfunny punch lines with a cast of characters either annoying or one-dimensional, this boggles the mind. The funny *PCU* proves there's always room for an imaginative updating of the *Animal House* genre, but this is just bad, lazy comedy. Affleck's a zombie, and even McConaughey's bizarre minute cameo misses the mark. ★ DVD Dual: $9.99

Glory! Glory!

(1988, 152 min, US, Lindsay Anderson) *Richard Thomas, Ellen Greene, James Whitmore.* Anderson's potent satire of televangelism stars Thomas as Bobby Joe Stuckey, an electronic preacher whose ministry is in disarray. His contributions are dwindling and cash flow is low. Things are so bad, in fact, that he hires a sexy rock 'n' roll singer (Greene) to help boost profits, and that's when the word of the Lord really starts to get turned upside down. ★★★

The Gnome-Mobile

(1967, 90 min, US, Robert Stevenson) *Walter Brennan, Matthew Garber, Karen Dotrice.* Bright Disney fluff by the director of *Mary Poppins*. Brennan, Garber and Dotrice are out to protect forest gnomes from the grasp of a greedy circus owner. ★★★ DVD: $19.99

The Glass Key

Go

(1999, 103 min, US, Doug Liman) *Desmond Askew, Taye Diggs, William Fichtner, J.E. Freeman, Katie Holmes, Jane Krakowski, Breckin Meyer, Jay Mohr, Timothy Olyphant, Sarah Polley, Scott Wolf, James Duval.* Go takes the great characterizations and kinetic energy of director Liman's *Swingers* and ups the ante with colorful widescreen cinematography and a groundbreaking narrative style. The Möbius-looping story begins as supermarket cashier Polley has a night on the town, scoring drugs and going to a rave. From there, people who works with and meets soon become the center of the film. Basically told in three acts, the nonlinear story never loses its lightning-quick pulse and always remains in focus. Thankfully, the twists are never hokey; they're done for laughs and feel natural. *Go* is an exhilarating rush. Of the great cast, Polley excels as Ronna, who comes full circle in this twisting, tantalizing puzzle of a film. ★★★★ DVD: $19.99

Go Fish

(1994, 85 min, US, Rose Troche) *Guinevere Turner, V.S. Brodie.* An unlikely candidate to join the ranks of epochal lesbian-themed films, this delightful yet knowing independent romantic comedy is more than simply the *Desert Hearts* for the '90s. Made on an extremely low budget, filmed in black and white, and featuring primarily nonprofessionals in major roles, *Go Fish*'s grittiness helps in making its characters more honest and accessible. Boyishly hip Max (Turner) is looking for love. She possibly finds it in the person of Ely (V.S. Brodie), a slightly older woman. How the two women meet, court and maybe even get together is wonderfully handled in a light, effervescent fashion that combines to paint an on-target depiction of young lesbian life. What the film lacks in professional pizzazz and slickness is more than made up for by its vividly drawn characters and witty screenplay. ★★★½ DVD: $19.99

The Go-Masters

(1982, 134 min, China, Duan Ji-Shun & Junja Sata) *Huang Zong-Ying, Du Peng.* The first Chinese-Japanese film coproduction, *The Go-Masters* is a sprawling political/historical epic spanning the turbulent years of the 1920s thru the 1950s, and a poignant exploration of love, loyalty and destiny — pitting pride against national power. The story focuses on the relationship of two families, one Japanese and the other Chinese. The son of the Chinese family is an aspiring master of Go, a chess-like strategy game, who moves to Japan under the tutelage of a Japanese Go champion. When war erupts, he is thrown into a political maelstrom, forced to choose between his allegiance to his birthplace and to his adopted land. (Chinese and Japanese with English subtitles) ★★★½ VHS: $59.99

Go Now

(1998, 86 min, GB, Michael Winterbottom) *Robert Carlyle, Juliet Aubrey, James Nesbitt.* A tough British film about a young man who develops multiple sclerosis, *Go Now* could be just another disease-of-the-week weepie. Yet in the hands of director Winterbottom, this familiar love story becomes a highly affecting drama. Carlyle stars as Nick, a footballer who falls in love with Karen (Aubrey) and learns shortly thereafter that he has M.S. Carlyle's portrayal of a man determined to understand and overcome his illness is remarkable, and his performance cements his leading man status. As his girlfriend, Aubrey is equally terrific. Her character really grapples with her feelings for Nick (and his feelings for her), and their struggle for happiness is

quite moving. *Go Now* also features a great soundtrack of soul tunes, especially the haunting title track. ★★★

Go Tell the Spartans

(1978, 114 min, US, Ted Post) *Burt Lancaster, Craig Wasson, David Clennon, Marc Singer.* Lancaster gives a well-modulated performance as an "advisory group commander" trying to keep his doubts to himself and his men alive as they traipse through the jungles of Vietnam on another pointless mission. One of the first films to look at our involvement in that war. ★★★½ VHS: $9.99

Go West

(1940, 81 min, US, Edward Buzzell) *Groucho Marx, Harpo Marx, Chico Marx, John Carroll, Diana Lewis.* Groucho, Chico and Harpo take Horace Greely's advice and head west to make their fortune and find themselves in the middle of a land swindle involving property wanted by the railroad. Even if not quite up to the standard of their earlier films, there are lots of funny bits, especially the spectacular closing train scene. (DVD only available in a seven-film pack for $59.99) ★★½ VHS: $19.99

Go West, Young Man

(1936, 80 min, US, Henry Hathaway) *Mae West, Randolph Scott, Warren William.* Though this backwoods West comedy is not on par with her best-known comedies, Mae's quips and a jab or two at Hollywood and stardom make this worthy of interest. West, who wrote the screenplay adaptation, plays a famous movie actress on tour promoting her newest film. En route to Harrisburg, she and press agent William become stranded in a small town where her arrival quickly turns everything topsy-turvy. Scott is the hunkish ('30s-style) garage mechanic who makes Mae's weekend in the country all the more enjoyable. Those expecting a western romp will be disappointed, as the punny title refers to La West and not to geographic location. ★★½

The Go-Between

(1971, 118 min, GB, Joseph Losey) *Julie Christie, Alan Bates, Margaret Leighton, Michael Redgrave, Dominic Guard.* A brilliant, richly detailed portrait of a forbidden romance and the lasting influence it has on the young boy who served as messenger for the illicit lovers. Christie is the Lady Trinigham, involved in an affair with a farmer (Bates) down the road; Guard is the twelve-year-old who acts as go-between. A visually sumptuous, fascinating study of deception and its lingering effects. Screenplay by Harold Pinter. ★★★★

The Goalie's Anxiety at the Penalty Kick

(1971, 101 min, West Germany, Wim Wenders) *Arthur Brauss, Erika Pluhar.* After being suspended for missing a penalty kick, a goalie wanders around Vienna aimlessly. He picks up a cinema cashier and, for no apparent reason, kills her. While waiting for the inevitable arrest, he searches his soul, but finds only alienation and ennui. Although slow-going, this early Wenders film is a must for his fans. The filmmaker explores the existential territory of Camus' "The Stranger" and Sartre's "Nausea." (German with English subtitles) ★★★

God Is My Witness (Khuda Gawah)

(1994, 193 min, India, Mukul S. Anand) *Amitabh Bachchan, Sridevi.* This dazzling action/adventure/romance/musical/melodrama is a heady, thrilling experience. The epic story involves Badshah Khan (Bachchan), a cocky, noble Pathan chieftan who flips for the beautiful woman warrior Benazir (Sridevi),

who won't marry him until he brings her the head of her father's murderer. Nearly all Indian films have a musical number every 20 minutes or so — no matter the genre. *God Is My Witness* is full of song-and-dance numbers, but wisely — and beautifully — uses them to further the story and flesh out characterizations. This attitude culminates in the operatic climax, a deliriously romantic, kitchen-sink crescendo rife with explosions, gunfire, reconciliations, swordplay, revenge and declarations of adulation. For those who mourn the loss of golden-age Hollywood; it didn't die, it just moved to India. (Hindi with English subtitles) ★★★★

God Told Me To

(1977, 91 min, US, Larry Cohen) *Tony LoBianco, Deborah Raffin, Sylvia Sidney, Sandy Dennis.* New York City is besieged by a series of unrelated sniper attacks, committed by seemingly ordinary citizens who said they were ordered by God to kill. LoBianco is the police detective whose investigation leads him to otherworldly powers. An imaginative if bizarre thriller that manages quite a few eerie moments. (aka: *Demon*) ★★½ DVD: $19.99, VHS: $9.99

The Godfather

(1972, 175 min, US, Francis Ford Coppola) *Marlon Brando, Al Pacino, Robert Duvall, James Caan, Sterling Hayden, John Cazale, Diane Keaton, Talia Shire.* In Coppola's brilliant crime saga, the director transformed the lowly gangster drama into an American epic capable of rivaling the western. From the wedding of Connie Corleone to the end of her brother Michael's marriage, *The Godfather* is richly imbued with the texture of life, the allure of power and the basic corruptness of capitalism. Add to this the sheer visceral pleasure of watching top actors giving superlative performances and you've got one of the masterpieces of American cinema. Brando salvaged his career as the ruthless Don Corleone, and Pacino became a star playing his son Michael. Truly an all-star cast. (Followed by 2 sequels) ★★★★ DVD: $19.99, VHS: $14.99, VHS Letterbox: $14.99

The Godfather – Part II

(1974, 200 min, US, Francis Ford Coppola) *Al Pacino, Robert De Niro, Robert Duvall, Michael Gazzo, Lee Strasberg, Talia Shire.* Following the success of the original, Coppola felt free to delve more deeply and lyrically into the inherent roots of corruption, power and greed. By cross-cutting his two major stories — the rise of Vito Corleone and the fall of Michael — Coppola creates a dialectical narrative that elevates the movie above its low genre birthright. Also, this was the first film to contradict the much abused notion that sequels must be "parts" of a larger story. De Niro is especially good as a young Vito. ★★★★ VHS: $14.99, VHS Letterbox: $14.99

The Godfather – Part III

(1990, 161 min, US, Francis Ford Coppola) *Al Pacino, Andy Garcia, Diane Keaton, Sofia Coppola, Joe Mantegna, George Hamilton, Talia Shire, Bridget Fonda.* The third and final entry in Coppola's *Godfather* trilogy is a worthy, if flawed, finale — though it certainly isn't in the same league as the two classics that came before it. Pacino, in a forceful performance, returns as the reluctant Mafia boss, Michael Corleone, who is lulled back into gangland activities after trying to go "legit." If the picture has one major flaw, it is the casting of Coppola's daughter Sofia in the pivotal role of Michael's beloved daughter, Mary. The actress doesn't have the depth required, and in some scenes other actors can be noticed "holding back." Garcia, however, is exceptional as a low-level criminal with loftier ambitions. ★★★ VHS: $14.99, VHS Letterbox: $14.99

Gods and Monsters

Gods and Monsters

(1998, 105 min, US, Bill Condon) *Ian McKellen, Brendan Fraser, Lynn Redgrave, Lolita Davidovich, Kevin J. O'Connor, David Dukes.* In a performance that is nothing short of brilliant, McKellen hypnotizes as gay film director James Whale in this moving, poetic adaptation of Christopher Bram's novel "Father of Frankenstein." The story ostensibly follows the friendship between Whale — now in his early 60s and suffering the effects of a stroke — and his handsome straight gardener (Fraser); but at the core of this lyrical tale is a study of desire and self-determination. In the 1930s, Whale made a handful of Hollywood classics (including *Frankenstein*); it's now 1957, and he is no longer able to live his life on his terms. Knowing that Whale was found dead in his swimming pool, the filmmakers have concocted a probable scenario that ends in a cynical *pièce de résistance.* Bringing compassion and elegance to Whale, McKellen's portrayal is so rich in nuance and shading that he makes you forget it's acting. Fraser is excellent as the ex-Marine who captures Whale's heart and, in turn, his respect. ★★★½ DVD: $14.99

The Gods Must Be Crazy

(1980, 109 min, South Africa, Jamie Uys) *N!xau.* All this fuss over a Coke bottle? After viewing it, one can see why this small-budget gem became such a huge international hit. On a peaceful day in Botswana's Kalahari desert, a Coca-Cola bottle falls to earth and disrupts the life of a simple tribe of Bushmen. Their efforts to return the bottle from whence it came unleashe a tide of savage satire and slapstick comedy from which virtually no one escapes. (DVD double feature with the 1990 sequel: *The Gods Must Be Crazy II*) ★★★½ DVD: $29.99

The Gods Must Be Crazy II

(1990, 97 min, South Africa, Jamie Uys) *N!xau. Crazy II* contains the same elements as the original including a propensity for surefire slapstick comedy. Bushman Xixo — played by N!xau, retaining the charm and genial sincerity which made the original such a success — returns, here having a series of misadventures searching for his two missing children. Meanwhile, a temperamental New York anthropologist is stranded in the desert with a local naturalist, and she's having a doozy of a time with the wildlife. Director Uys again displays a talent for precisely choreographed visual comedy. DVD: $29.99 (DVD double feature with 1980 original) ★★★ VHS: $19.99

Gods of the Plague

(1969, 92 min, West Germany, Rainer Werner Fassbinder) *Hanna Schygulla, Harry Baer, Margarethe von Trotta.* Deep in the backstreets of a sunless Munich, a den of sleazy gangsters and their molls stealthily plot their big heist only for it to end in betrayal and murder. Fassbinder has created a stunning and knowing tribute to film noir and the American gangster genre, combining swift camerawork with a suspenseful story line. (German with English subtitles) ★★★½ DVD Subtitled: $24.99, VHS: $19.99

The Godson

(1967, 86 min, France, Jean-Pierre Melville) *Alain Delon, Nathalie Delon.* Drained of bright colors and told in a crisp, tight style, this definitive hard-boiled gangster film features Delon as an emotionless and solitary hired killer whose airtight alibi for one of his jobs is slowly unraveled by authorities after he makes the mistake of falling in love. A classic tale of a man whose existence is as rigid, romantic and outdated as that of the Japanese samurai. ★★★

Godspell

(1973, 103 min, US, David Greene) *Victor Garber, David Haskell, Lynne Thigpen, Jerry Sroka, Katie Hanley, Robin Lamont.* Based on the hit Broadway musical, this energetic, vastly entertaining adaptation that follows the last days of Jesus Christ through song came out the same time as *Jesus Christ, Superstar.* And though *Godspell*'s score isn't as well known or as accomplished as Andrew Lloyd Weber's first hit, the film as a whole is much more satisfying. Includes "Day by Day." ★★★½ DVD: $27.99

Godzilla

(1998, 139 min, US, Roland Emmerich) *Jean Reno, Matthew Broderick, Maria Pitillo, Hank Azaria, Kevin Dunn, Michael Lerner.* With nary a hint of topicality, finesse or sense of fun, director Emmerich and writer Dean Devlin (*Independence Day*) steal, er, pay homage to everything from those grade-Z atomic monster movies of the '50s and rubber-suit *Godzilla* movies to *Jurassic Park.* The result is an emotionally empty show. Sure the effects are cool, but the movie plays like an extended computer game. And forget about seeing one panoramic shot of Godzilla trapsing against the cityscape, a cornball tradition. And the humans? They're stuck with the lamest dialogue since Ed Wood cranked out a screenplay. ★★ DVD Letterbox: $9.99, VHS: $9.99

Godzilla, King of the Monsters

(1956, 80 min, Japan, Inoshiro Honda & Terry Morse) *Takashi Shimura, Raymond Burr.* This original A-bomb allegory, and the first and best Godzilla film to date, features surprisingly effective special effects for its time, and a dark and somber tone absent from its many sequels. Godzilla, not one of the good guys in this original incarnation, rises from the sea belching radioactive breath. The inadvertent by-product of a nuclear accident, he wreaks total destruction at every turn, including the entire city of Tokyo. Edited for U.S. consumption, this version features spliced-in sequences with Burr as a reporter (named Steve Martin!) covering the events. The original Japanese release is unfortunately not yet available on video. (American remake: *Godzilla*) ★★½

Godzilla 2000

(2000, 96 min, Japan, Takao Okawara) *Takehiro Murata, Naomi Nishida, Mayu Suzuki, Hiroshi Abe, Shirô Sano.* So adherent to the Godzilla genre as to be virtually review-proof, this millennial entry is nothing if not a refreshing rebound from the bloated American behemoth. From a nifty character introduction of the big guy (still a man in a suit, though it's a new suit) to a climactic showdown with a killer space squid in mini-Tokyo, there's a lot of nostalgic ooh-ahh for grownups and cool firebreathing for kids. The interim scenes of humans talking are boring as usual (despite somewhat campy dubbing), and Godzilla disappears for a long stretch of time as the scientists deal with a zero-personality spaceship. But when the squid comes out and shoots energy bolts from his shoulder bursitis, the smiles come back, and you realize you got exactly what you expected. ★★½ DVD: $24.99, VHS: $9.99

Goin' South

(1978, 109 min, US, Jack Nicholson) *Jack Nicholson, Mary Steenburgen, Christopher Lloyd, John Belushi, Danny DeVito, Veronica Cartwright.* Nicholson is a horse thief who is saved from the noose by a little-known law, giving him the opportunity to marry a widow (Steenburgen) and take up the habits of a good prairie husband. However, he soon finds his past returning to haunt him. This is Nicholson's second directorial effort (after *Drive, He Said*). ★★★ DVD Letterbox: $14.99, VHS: $14.99

Goin' to Town

(1935, 71 min, US, Alexander Hall) *Mae West, Paul Cavanagh.* Here's a sight to behold: A sequined West dressed all in white riding a horse across the fruited plains. And darn if she doesn't look natural doing it. Mae plays a saloon singer who agrees to marry an oil tycoon/cattle rustler. When he gets killed on their wedding day, she inherits everything, and soon falls for a British earl who snubs her crude Western ways. So, the widow West heads to Buenos Aires for a crash course in society manners, horseracing and love. An enjoyable concoction with West in her element as a rustic flirt trying to make good. ★★★

Going All the Way

(1997, 103 min, US, Mark Pellington) *Ben Affleck, Jeremy Davies, Jill Clayburgh, Amy Locane, Rachel Weisz, Lesley Ann Warren, Rose McGowan.* Here's a surprise — a period coming-of-age film, shot in a very trendy, music video style (flash frames, jump cuts, etc.) with a disaffected youth as the protagonist, and it's actually good. Davies gives a mannered yet ultimately moving performance as a shy, geeky Army vet who returns home to 1950s Indianapolis to live with his painfully status quo parents. His sanity is kept intact by his friendship with a fellow vet (Affleck). Despite their differences, they become close friends, dreaming of leaving the Midwest to go to college in NYC, in the meantime getting drunk, chasing women and studying art and photography. While both its title and plot suggest otherwise, *Going All the Way* is actually an intelligent comedy-drama that touches knowingly on questions of conformity, popularity, religion, morality, and especially sexuality. ★★★

Going in Style

(1979, 96 min, US, Martin Brest) *George Burns, Art Carney, Lee Strasberg.* Burns gives a rich performance as a senior citizen who talks his buddies Carney and Strasberg into helping him rob a bank because they feel bored and forgotten. While the humorous sequences are sit-com funny, it's the tragic subtext about growing old in America which gives this small comic gem an unexpected resonance. ★★★½ DVD Letterbox: $19.99, VHS: $14.99

Going My Way

(1944, 130 min, US, Leo McCarey) *Bing Crosby, Barry Fitzgerald, Gene Lockhart, William Frawley.* Crosby gives his most winning performance (it even won him an Oscar) as Father O'Malley, whose progressive ideas don't go down well with the street punks or the old parish priest. Bing sings "Swing on a Star," and there are plenty of familiar faces, including Oscar winner Fitzgerald. Winner of 7 Academy Awards, including Best Picure. (Sequel: *The Bells of St. Mary's*) ★★★ DVD: $19.99

Going Places

(1974, 117 min, France, Bertrand Blier) *Gérard Depardieu, Patrick Dewaere, Miou-Miou, Jeanne Moreau.* Blier's energetic account of two loutish drifters who steal, molest and terrorize until they encounter a beautiful ex-convict who undermines their entire lifestyle. A weirder French film you will never see. (French with English subtitles) ★★★

Gold Diggers of 1933

(1933, 96 min, US, Mervyn LeRoy) *Dick Powell, Joan Blondell, Ruby Keeler, Ginger Rogers, Aline MacMahon, Guy Kibbee.* Classic Berkeley backstage musical. Here it's Blondell, Keeler, Powell and pals putting on a Broadway show. Songs include "We're in the Money" (in pig Latin!) and "Forgotten Man." Berkeley's production numbers are sensational. ★★★½

Gold Diggers of 1935

(1935, 95 min, US, Busby Berkeley) *Dick Powell, Adolphe Menjou, Gloria Stuart, Alice Brady, Glenda Farrell.* That "let's put on a show" gang is back, here in the forms of Powell, Menjou, Stuart and pals. Berkeley's production numbers are first-rate, and included is the remarkable "Lullabye of Broadway" (one of the great musical sequences of all time). ★★★ VHS: $14.99

The Gold of Naples

(1954, 107 min, Italy, Vittorio De Sica) *Sophia Loren, Silvana Mangano, Toto.* Departing from his neorealist tradition, De Sica constructs four vignettes ranging from the comic to the tragic in this poignant, perceptive slice of Napleanic life. A 20-year-old Loren stars as a philandering wife who loses her wedding ring during a rendezvous with a lover and convinces her baker husband that she lost it in a pizza. Toto stars in another episode as a meek husband whose house is occupied by an arrogant racketeer. De Sica himself is featured in a third story of an avid gambler who is outsmarted in cards by an eight-year-old and the final segment has Mangano as a prostitute who enters into a strange marriage with a mentally unbalanced young man. (Italian with English subtitles) ★★★ VHS: $34.99

The Gold Rush

(1925, 100 min, US, Charles Chaplin) *Charlie Chaplin, Mack Swain.* This is quintessential Chaplin. This immortal comedy features some of the Little Tramp's most memorable routines, including the dance of the dinner rolls and the shoe-eating sequence. Charlie plays a lone prospector, adrift in the frenzy of the Klondike gold rush. ★★★★ DVD Chaplin Collection - 2 disc set: $29.99

Gone with the Wind

The Golden Boat

(1993, 90 min, US/France, Râùl Ruiz) *Michael Kirby, Annie Sprinkle, Barbet Schroeder, Jim Jarmusch, Kathy Acker.* Blending surrealism with avant-garde deconstructionism and dreamlike images, Ruiz's first English-language film follows a young philosophy student and part-time rock critic for *The Village Voice*, Israel, who encounters an older homeless man, Austin, in a back alley on the Lower East Side. Before Israel can respond, Austin stabs himself and, while bleeding profusely, leads Israel on a bizarre journey through the streets of New York, all in a quest to find his true love, a Mexican soap opera star. Along the way, philosophy is discussed even while Austin compulsively kills several people — all of whom seem to come back to life in future scenes. Beguilingly obscure yet strangely wonderful. ★★★ VHS: $59.99

Golden Boy

(1939, 99 min, US, Rouben Mamoulian) *William Holden, Barbara Stanwyck, Lee J. Cobb.* Clifford Odets' searing story of a youth (Holden in his breakthrough role) torn between his love of music and his boxing career. ★★★

The Golden Child

(1986, 93 min, US, Michael Ritchie) *Eddie Murphy, Charlotte Lewis, Charles Dance.* A movie that doesn't attempt to go beyond a fingerpaint-user's idea of humor; but if you like Murphy, you may find it amusing. Jokes involve "boogers" and Pepsi cans, while Eddie looks for the "Golden Child," the kidnapped savior of the world. ★ DVD: $14.99, VHS: $14.99

The Golden Coach

(1952, 105 min, Italy, Jean Renoir) *Anna Magnani, Odoardo Spadaro.* Renoir peppered this luxuriant fable set in 19th-century South America, which follows the three transient loves of a tempestuous actress (forcefully played by Magnani) with an uncharacteristic tone of biting irony. Renoir joyfully expresses his love for the theater and theater life as he follows the commedia dell'arte through their lives and loves. (Filmed in English) ★★★½ VHS: $24.99

Golden Demon

(1953, 91 min, Japan, Koji Shina) *Jun Negami, Fujiko Yamamoto.* A spectacular look at the destructive effect of wealth in today's society. A poor young man falls in love with a middle-class woman but is rejected. Determined not to be hurt again, the man commits his life to the ruthless pursuit of wealth. After escaping a loveless marriage, the woman seeks out her old love but finds a changed person. A sensitive yet hard-hitting love story. (Japanese with English subtitles) ★★★

The Golden Voyage of Sinbad

(1974, 105 min, GB, Gordon Hessler) *John Phillip Law, Caroline Munro, Tom Baker.* A delightful rehashing of the adventures of Sinbad the sailor, which features some of Ray Harryhausen's finest "dynamation" effects including a ship's figurehead that comes to life and, even more impressive, a six-armed statue that does battle with Sinbad. A wonderfully entertaining throwback to the days of Saturday afternoon matinees. ★★★ DVD: $19.99, VHS: $14.99

Golden Years

(1991, 234 min, US, Allen Coulter) *Keith Szarbajka, Frances Sternhagen, Phillip Lenkowsky.* Stephen King tells the story of Harlan Williams, an elderly janitor who is accidentally exposed to a strange green dust in an explosion at a government defense lab. Shortly thereafter, he begins going through a series of mysterious changes which slowly turn him younger. Following this, of course, the big bad Feds show up and will stop at nothing to capture their newfound lab rat. Szarabajka plays the first aged, then youthful hall sweeper. Sternhagen is solid in support as his wife. Originally seven hours on TV, the continuity suffers somewhat in this heavily edited edition. ★★★ DVD: $14.99, VHS: $9.99

Goldeneye

(1995, 127 min, GB, Martin Campbell) *Pierce Brosnan, Sean Bean, Izabella Scorupco, Famke Janssen, Joe Don Baker, Judi Dench, Robbie Coltrane, Michael Kitchen.* Brosnan has some pretty big shoes to fill with this, the 17th film to showcase the exploits of a certain "Bond, James Bond" — and those shoes fit like a glove. This time, it's personal as Bond goes after a "00" double agent (Bean) who plans to topple the world economy using a pirated weapons satellite (codename: Goldeneye). There are, of course, the usual death-defying stunts, beautiful women and arch humor. But Brosnan makes the film his own, creating a Bond who is more mature and introspective than his predecessors. Dench is M, the new head of MI6. (Sequel: *Tomorrow Never Dies*) ★★★

Goldfinger

(1964, 111 min, GB, Guy Hamilton) *Sean Connery, Honor Blackman, Gert Frobe, Shirley Eaton, Harold Sakata.* Her majesty's finest, Agent 007, combats the wicked genius with the Midas touch and his evil Asian henchman with the deadly derby. The third in the Bond series, complete with scads of gadgetry, loads of lovelies and Connery in top form. One of the very best of the series. (Sequel: *Thunderball*) ★★★½

The Goldwyn Follies

(1938, 120 min, US, George Marshall) *Adolphe Menjou, Andrea Leeds, The Ritz Brothers.* George Gershwin's last film score highlights this okay musical about a Hollywood producer who searches for a "typical" moviegoer to judge his work. ★★ VHS: $14.99

The Golem

(1920, 75 min, Germany, Carl Boese & Paul Wegener) A classic tale of a rabbi who conjures up a cannibalistic monster of Jewish legend in order to avert an oppressive policy against Jews in Hapsburg. But once brought to life, the Golem breaks free from his master's spell and rampages through the town, causing havoc that appears to be beyond anyone's ability to stop. (Silent) ★★★½ DVD: $24.99, VHS: $39.99

Gone Fishin'

(1997, 94 min, US, Christopher Cain) *Danny Glover, Joe Pesci, Rosanna Arquette, Lynn Whitfield, Carol Kane, Willie Nelson.* In this lame-brained comedy, Glover and Pesci play two klutzy childhood chums who win a fishing vacation in the Florida Everglades. With barely a fully functioning brain between them, the duo cut a swath of accidental destruction and comic mayhem across the Sunshine State that rivals that of Hurricane Andrew. The sophomoric mentality of the film's slapstick physical humor is childish at best, and actors of such high calibre as Pesci and Glover deserve better. ★ DVD: $9.99, VHS: $9.99

Gone in 60 Seconds

(2000, 117 min, US, Dominic Sena) *Nicolas Cage, Giovanni Ribisi, Will Patton, Robert Duvall, Angelina Jolie, Delroy Lindo, Chi McBride, Scott Caan, Christopher Eccleston.* A puffed-up, way overproduced remake of the '70s H.B. Halicki drive-in classic, *Gone in 60 Seconds* has Cage stealing 50 cars in 24 hours to save his brother's hide. Typically loud, abrasive, faux-hip Bruckheimer nonsense skips his usual homophobia to allow room for some uncomfortable racism, while shoving Jolie into a surprisingly small role as "the ex." Lindo, Duvall and Patton lend a hint of class to this mess, but that's not what the film needs — it should be fast, gritty and exciting as hell; the original is hardly a triumph of content over style, but it's a lotta fun. This is shockingly dull; it's a movie about fast cars and is slow as molasses. ★ DVD: $19.99, VHS: $9.99

Gone with the Wind

(1939, 224 min, US, Victor Fleming) *Vivien Leigh, Clark Gable, Olivia de Havilland, Leslie Howard, Hattie McDaniel, Thomas Mitchell, Butterfly McQueen.* This is the big one! Based on Margaret Mitchell's epic Civil War novel, Leigh stars as Scarlett O'Hara, a beautiful, spoiled and determined Southern belle who meets her match in Rhett Butler (Gable), a dashing and rebellious charmer. Academy Awards for Best Picture, Actress (Leigh), and eight others. *GWTW* has myriad characters, wonderful production values, and is the definitive example of old, big-studio moviemaking. Little wonder this movie has been woven into the fabric of our culture. ★★★★ DVD: $19.99, VHS: $9.99

Gonza the Spearman

(1986, 126 min, Japan, Masahiro Shinoda) *Hiromi Goh, Shima Iwashita.* Filmed with stunning visuals, Shinoda's period piece is a vivid and engrossing account of what life was like during the samurai era. Gonza, a handsome but overly ambitious samurai, breaks off his engagement with a woman in order to better his position by marrying the clan leader's daughter. The brother of Gonza's former fiancée, a fellow lanceman, vows revenge for the insult to his sister and family. A classic tale of love, honor and tragedy. (Japanese with English subtitles) ★★★

Good Burger

(1997, 95 min, US, Brian Robbins) *Kenan Thompson, Kel Mitchell, Abe Vigoda, Shaquille O'Neal, Sinbad.* Silly and fun and family friendly, *Good Burger* is based on one of the more popular skits from Mitchell and Thompson's top-rated Nickelodeon TV show. When fast-food chain Mondo Burger opens up right across the street from their own emporium, the lads join forces to save it — and themselves — from certain economic ruin. Sinbad gets laughs as the once-hip high school teacher still stuck in the Black Power '70s. Holding together this airy confection is the genial comedy of Kenan and Kel, exhibiting pleasing traces of Laurel & Hardy and Martin & Lewis. And any movie sly enough to feature George Clinton as a mental patient ready to rock the ward has surely earned its street credentials. ★★★ DVD: $14.99, VHS: $14.99

The Good Earth

(1937, 138 min, US, Sidney Franklin) *Paul Muni, Luise Rainer, Walter Connolly, Charley Grapewin, Jessie Ralph, Keye Luke.* Pearl S. Buck's novel of peasant farmers in China has been brilliantly brought to the screen to create one of the 1930s greatest films. In two magnificent performances, Muni and Oscar winner Rainer portray Wang and O-Lan, a married couple who endure famine, revolution, the death of a child, betrayal, life as refugees and, in a classic sequence, a swarm of locusts. The mixing of Asian and Anglo cast members surprisingly detracts nothing from the film's power and credibility. This is due, in no small amount, to Muni and Rainer's portrayals. Franklin's direction is self-assured and his epic stagings of a mass exodus, political riot and the locust swarm are superbly juxtaposed by deeply effecting scenes of familial conflict. ★★★★

Good Evening Mr. Wallenberg

(1990, 115 min, Sweden, Kjell Grede) *Stellan Skarsgård, Erland Josephson, Katharina Thalbach.* An ambiguous, compelling drama, *Good Evening, Mr. Wallenberg* is based on the true-life experiences of Raoul Wallenberg (Skarsgord), a Swedish diplomat who attempted to save tens of thousands of Jews in Nazi-occupied Budapest near the end of WWII. Encountering Nazi bureaucrats, Hungarian collaborators and civilian hostility, Wallenberg's difficult path is detailed, and the story in unflinching honesty depicts the brutal, anti-Semitic realities of the time. Though the film may lack the epic feel and fluid narrative of the similarly themed *Schindler's List*, a wrenching power exists all the same. (Swedish, German and Hungarian with English subtitles) ★★★ VHS: $19.99

The Good Father

(1987, 90 min, GB, Mike Newell) *Anthony Hopkins, Jim Broadbent, Simon Callow.* Hopkins gives a multi-layered performance as a recently separated father exorcising his own demons through an acquaintance's custody battle. An intelligent, adult, considered exploration of male-female relationships and the dissolution of marriage. Nicely directed by Newell. ★★★

The Good Fight

(1982, 98 min, US, Mary Doe, Noel Buckner, Sam Sills) A stirring portrait of the men and women who made up the Lincoln Brigade, a group of 3,200 Americans who fought for the Spanish Republic against Franco and his fascist supporters in Spain's civil war. Told through newsreel footage, a Hollywood film and interviews with Brigade veterans, this absorbing documentary fills in the gaps of our social history and celebrates the passion and idealism of these real-life heroes. ★★★½ VHS: $29.99

The Good Girl

(2002, 93 min, US, Miguel Arteta) *Jennifer Aniston, Jake Gyllenhaal, John C. Reilly, Tim Blake Nelson, Zooey Deschanel, Mike White.* Aniston is subtle and engaging as Justine, a woman who spends her nights in her backwater Texas town lying awake next to her snoring, stoner, house painter husband Phil (Reilly). Her fellow employees at the Retail Rodeo discount store accommodate their lives each in his own way, whether born-again fervor, vegetarian-assisted cheerfulness or straight-faced verbal rebellion. Justine notices new employee Holden (Gyllenhaal), silent, brooding, just about the same age she was when she married Phil seven years ago. They form a relationship based on the shared contention that nobody gets them and they get each other. The affair precipitates events inevitable, tragic and ultimately redemptive. *The Good Girl* is an unexpected gem; small, well-faceted, with exceptional clarity and color. Director Arteta, who with writer White previously collaborated on *Chuck & Buck*, continues to impart his unique sensibility to the screen, making good use of his well-chosen cast as he and they bring these most fallible characters to life with quirky affection. ★★★½ DVD Dual: $14.99, VHS: $9.99

A Good Man in Africa

(1994, 93 min, GB, Bruce Beresford) *Colin Friels, Sean Connery, Joanne Whalley-Kilmer, John Lithgow, Louis Gossett, Jr., Diana Rigg.* The affable Friels stars as a British diplomatic attaché whose disastrous attempts to keep order backfire at every turn. A good supporting cast includes Gossett as a presidential nominee needing a rather dishonest favor from Friels; Lithgow as an uproariously pompous dignitary; and Connery as a dedicated doctor and the titular good man. *A Good Man* is low-key and often flat, but it also contains many small charms at the most unexpected moments. ★★½ VHS: $9.99

Good Morning Babylon

(1987, 115 min, Italy, Paolo & Vittorio Taviani) *Vincent Spano, Joaqui De Almeida.* The Taviani brothers' first film in English is a modern fable that chronicles the ambitions, dreams and loves of two brothers. Gifted artisans, the brothers leave their native Italy, emigrate to America and eventually work on the making of the sets for D.W. Griffith's *Intolerance*. Spano and De Almeida are the siblings (and alter egos of the directors) in this funny yet poetic homage to the magic of the cinema. (Filmed in English) ★★★

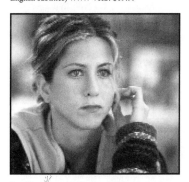

Jennifer Aniston in *The Good Girl*

Good Morning, Vietnam

(1987, 120 min, US, Barry Levinson) *Robin Williams, Forest Whitaker, Bruno Kirby, Richard Edson, Robert Wuhl, J.T. Walsh.* Williams sparkles as Adrian Cronauer, a real-life radio D.J. who found himself plunked down against his will in Saigon, 1965. What Levinson's film lacks by way of plot is more than made up for by Williams' sensational talents — his on-air scenes are pure comic genius. ★★★ DVD: $14.99, VHS: $9.99

The Good Mother

(1988, 103 min, US, Leonard Nimoy) *Diane Keaton, Liam Neeson, Jason Robards, James Naughton, Ralph Bellamy, Teresa Wright, Joe Morton, Matt Damon.* Keaton's remarkable performance elevates this involving melodrama about a divorced mother who begins an affair with a free-spirited artist; her ex-husband retaliates with child abuse charges. ★★★ DVD: $14.99

Good Neighbor Sam

(1964, 130 min, US, David Swift) *Jack Lemmon, Romy Schneider, Edward G. Robinson, Dorothy Provine.* Lemmon proves his mastery of physical comedy when he agrees to help the woman next door claim her inheritance by posing as her husband — much to his wife's annoyance. ★★½ VHS: $9.99

Good Night Michelangelo

(1989, 91 min, Canada, Carlo Liconti) *Giancarlo Giannini, Kim Cattrall, Lina Sastri.* A charming and offbeat film, this gentle comedy follows the lives of a family of immigrants in 1957 Toronto. Narrated by six-year-old Michelangelo, the film details the struggles, loves and misadventures of this boisterous family as they try to assimilate into the new English-speaking world. The family includes a grumpy grandfather, a hot-blooded widowed mother who rules with an iron fist, and an amorous Italian boarder, mischievously played by Giannini. Told with humor and a knowing nod to the family's difficulties, this Italian *Parenthood* is a pleasant portrait of a family in transition. (English language) ★★★

Good Sam

(1948, 128 min, US, Leo McCarey) *Gary Cooper, Ann Sheridan, Edmund Lowe.* A good samaritan (Cooper) has the knack for getting into trouble with each good deed he performs. A minor comedy from the otherwise sterling career of writer-director McCarey. ★★ VHS: $19.99

The Good Son

(1993, 87 min, US, Joseph Ruben) *Macaulay Culkin, Elijah Wood, Wendy Crewson, David Morse.* Director Ruben follows his muddled box-office hit *Sleeping with the Enemy* with this equally contrived thriller, which still should manage to give a few chills to those who enjoyed his previous work. Culkin reinterprets "The Bad Seed" for the '90s; he's a cherub-faced demon who delights in killing dogs, instigating a 12-car pileup and threatening the life and limb of his loved ones. Wood plays the young cousin who comes to live with Culkin and his family, and who soon discovers the truth about the little psycho. It is Wood's performance that gives the film its interest. A startling ten-minute ending sequence is evidently the film's only excuse for being made. ★★ DVD Dual: $14.99, VHS: $9.99

The Good, the Bad and the Ugly

(1967, 161 min, Italy/Spain, Sergio Leone) *Clint Eastwood, Lee Van Cleef, Eli Wallach.* The final installment of the trilogy about "The Man with No

The Good Thief

Name" finds Eastwood reluctantly teaming up with low-life Wallach in order to beat bad guy Van Cleef to a buried fortune in Confederate gold. The film rambles along like the shaggy dog tale that it is, always visually interesting, often very funny, with *the* classic film score by Ennio Morricone. ★★★½ DVD Letterbox: $14.99, DVD Letterbox Extended 3-hour version: $29.99, VHS: $9.99

The Good Thief

(2002, 109 min, GB, Neil Jordan) *Nick Nolte, Said Taghmaoui, Tcheky Karyo, Ralph Fiennes.* Reflections of moonlight shimmering in neonoir splendor, seedy underworld characters living by their own code of honor, unrelenting cat-and-mouse games between desperate thieves and world-weary cops — it's all here and then some in director Neil Jordan's thrilling remake of Jean-Pierre Melville's classic 1955 caper film *Bob le Flambeur*. Set in a French Riviera where sunlight is toxic, *The Good Thief* creates a remarkable atmosphere of conspiracy, romance and danger as its nocturnal denizens of prostitutes, thieves and con artists provide a classic crime-movie milieu. Giving his best performance in years, Nolte revels in seediness as Bob Montagret, a morose, cynical down-on-his-luck gambler whose fortune may be about to change when he's brought into a scheme to rob a Monte Carlo casino. The cool, capricious nights serve as a scintillating backdrop to the games, deceits and betrayals that lay ahead for this motley group of dreamers. ★★★½ DVD: $19.99

The Good Wife

(1987, 97 min, Australia, Ken Cameron) *Bryan Brown, Rachel Ward, Sam Neill.* Set in a pre-WWII small Australian town, the story concerns the secretive love affair between an unhappily married woman and a handsome and attentive stranger. The stars keep the ordinary story of interest. ★★½ DVD Dual: $14.99

Good Will Hunting

(1997, 122 min, US, Gus Van Sant) *Matt Damon, Robin Williams, Ben Affleck, Minnie Driver, Stellan Skarsgård, Casey Affleck.* A genuinely moving, exceptionally written and performed drama of a mathematical genius at odds with the world. Cowriter Damon (who shared a Best Screenplay Oscar with costar B. Affleck) gives a sincere performance as Will Hunting, a troubled but gifted working-class Boston youth who begins therapy to stay out of jail. These sessions with a caring psychiatrist (Oscar winner Williams) are the heart of the drama, in which both men are able to come to terms with

their demons. Director Van Sant never allows the film to wallow in sentimentality; it's low-key, but it's also as tough-minded, steadfast and unexpectedly humorous as Will himself. Driver is splendid as a Harvard student who sees in Will more than his gruff exterior and masked hurt. ★★★★ DVD Special Edition: $19.99, VHS: $9.99

Goodbye, Columbus

(1969, 105 min, US, Larry Peerce) *Richard Benjamin, Ali MacGraw, Jack Klugman, Nan Martin.* It's Benjamin (in his film debut) saying so long to university life when he falls for Jewish American Princess MacGraw in this, the best adaptation of any of Phillip Roth's books. ★★★ DVD Letterbox: $14.99

The Goodbye Girl

(1977, 110 min, US, Herbert Ross) *Marsha Mason, Richard Dreyfuss, Quinn Cummings, Marilyn Sokol.* Snappy Neil Simon comedy with Mason as a divorced mother who is forced to share her apartment with an egocentric actor (Dreyfuss in his Oscar-winning role). Cummings deftly plays Mason's sharp-tongued young daughter. ★★★ DVD: $19.99, VHS: $14.99

Goodbye Lover

(1999, 100 min, US, Roland Joffé) *Patricia Arquette, Dermot Mulroney, Ellen Degeneres, Mary-Louise Parker, Don Johnson.* A playful noir with a few good twists, *Goodbye Lover* is a consistently enjoyable comic mystery that delights in its subversive ways. Older sibling Johnson is having an affair with his brother's wife (Arquette). Younger sibling Mulroney is at his wit's end — or is he? Conspiracy's afoot when one of them ends up dead. That's when cynical cop DeGeneres enters the scene. It's a case of scam, double cross and hoodwink as allegiances are tested, morals are reinterpreted, and only the truly cunning survive. The ensemble is obviously having a good time with the lively material, with the wily DeGeneres having the most fun with her role — she's delectable. ★★★ DVD: $9.99, VHS: $14.99

Goodbye, Mr. Chips

(1939, 115 min, US, Sam Wood) *Robert Donat, Greer Garson, Paul Henreid, John Mills.* Extraordinary adaptation of James Hilton's novel about the life of a dedicated, shy schoolmaster. Donat gives a remarkable Oscar-winning performance as Chips, and Garson is exceptional in her film debut as his young wife. One of the greatest achievements of the incredible film year of 1939. (Remade in 1969 as a musical) ★★★★ DVD: $19.99, VHS: $14.99

Goodbye, Mr. Chips

(1969, 151 min, GB, Herbert Ross) *Peter O'Toole, Petula Clark, Michael Redgrave, Sian Phillips.* O'Toole's likable performance highlights this uninspired musical remake of the 1939 classic, based on the James Hilton novel. Updated to WWII, it's about a self-sacrificing teacher and his love for a dance-hall singer (Clark). Redgrave and Phillips are quite good in support. ★★ VHS: $19.99

Goodbye, New York

(1985, 90 min, Israel, Amos Kollek) *Julie Hagerty, Amos Kollek.* The comic talents of Hagerty are fully realized in this charming Israeli comedy about a ditsy New Yorker who leaves her unfaithful husband, quits her job and flees to Paris. Fate intervenes, however, as she oversleeps at the Paris stopover and ends up, without luggage or money, in the totally foreign land of Israel. She is soon befriended by a good-natured but lascivious cab driver who guides her through comic misadventures and her second education in the Holy Land. (Filmed in English) ★★★

The Goodbye People

(1986, 104 min, US, Herb Gardner) *Martin Balsam, Judd Hirsch, Pamela Reed, Ron Silver.* Bittersweet tale of a 70-year-old retiree (Balsam) who decides to reopen his Coney Island beachfront hot dog stand; aided by his estranged daughter (Reed) and an eccentric artist (Hirsch). Based on director Gardner's play. ★★ VHS: $14.99

Goodbye Pork Pie

(1981, 105 min, New Zealand, Geoff Murphy) *Tony Barry, Kelly Johnson.* A wild adventure comedy about two young men and their thousand-mile excursion in a stolen car. As the police follow in hot pursuit, the two become news-media heroes as a result of their reckless escapades. ★★★ VHS: $69.99

GoodFellas

(1990, 147 min, US, Martin Scorsese) *Robert De Niro, Lorraine Bracco, Ray Liotta, Joe Pesci, Paul Sorvino, Samuel L. Jackson.* Liotta delivers a gritty and charismatic performance as a young mob functionary in this based-on-fact, superbly crafted and high-energy look at the rise and fall of a mob insider. The film brilliantly illustrates the seduction of Liotta's early initiations, the headiness of his status as "goodfella" and the hellishness of his inevitable fall from grace. As Liotta's cold-blooded comrades, De Niro and especially Oscar-winner Pesci are mesmerizing; and Bracco sparkles as Liotta's tough-as-nails wife. Scorsese has created a modern masterpiece, as well as one of the finest gangster movies of all time. ★★★★ DVD Letterbox 2-disc Special Edition: $26.99, VHS: $9.99, VHS Letterbox: $14.99

The Goonies

(1985, 111 min, US, Richard Donner) *Sean Astin, Josh Brolin, Corey Feldman, Martha Plimpton, Anne Ramsey, Joe Pantoliano.* This fun-filled if loud children's adventure follows the comic exploits of a group of adolescents who go searching for buried treasure to save their parents' home. Strictly for kids and only for adults who have yet to lose their inner child. ★★½ DVD: $19.99, VHS: $14.99

Gore Vidal's Billy the Kid

(1989, 100 min, US, William Graham) *Val Kilmer, Wilford Brimley, Michael Parks.* Vidal's second film on the life and death of Billy the Kid, while enjoyable enough, does not come close to the complexity and nuances that were much in evidence in *The Left-Handed Gun.* Kilmer plays Billy, but a Billy who is less tormented and a bit more goofy than Paul Newman's interpretation. The story focuses primarily on the friendship between Billy and the man who finally guns him down, Pat Garrett. Kilmer is an attractive renegade, but his role is ultimately undermined by the traditional, strictly-by-the-numbers approach to the legend. ★★

Gore-Gore Girls

(1972, 70 min, US, Hershell Gordon Lewis) *Henny Youngman.* Lewis goes all out to gross out in his final and goriest film. Henny Youngman (!) is the owner of a nightclub whose dancers are butchered in various gruesome fashions. Graphic (and relatively lengthy) mutilation sequences made this one of the first films ever to receive an X rating for violence. ★

Gorgeous

(1999, 99 min, Hong Kong, Vincent Kok) *Jackie Chan, Shu Qi, Tony Leung.* A tepid romance/action film, the Hong Kong-made *Gorgeous* is a misstep in the career of Chan. The accent is all on hideously cutesy romance and a deadly dull story, with very little action or humor. ★½ DVD: $14.99, VHS: $9.99

The Gorgeous Hussy

(1936, 102 min, US, Clarence Brown) *Joan Crawford, Robert Taylor, Melvyn Douglas, James Stewart.* Other than its catchy title, the best that can be said for this opulent costumer is that it features superior production values. Crawford stars as Peggy Eaton, the infamous "Belle of Washington" during President Andrew Jackson's administration. The film traces her rise in political circles, and the scandal she caused, though it's not as interesting as it sounds. ★½ VHS: $19.99

Gorgo

(1961, 78 min, GB, Eugene Lourie) *Bill Travers, William Sylvester, Vincent Winter, Bruce Seton.* When Toho Studios made a knock-off of director Lourie's *The Beast from 20 Thousand Fathoms* called *Godzilla,* he decided to return the favor by making this man-in-a-rubber-monster-suit film, to much better results. When a traveling circus captures a giant prehistoric beast off the Scottish Sea and exhibits it in London, it becomes an instant smash — until Mom comes looking for Jr. ★★½ VHS: $14.99

The Gorgon

(1961, 83 min, GB, Terence Fisher) *Peter Cushing, Christopher Lee, Barbara Shelley.* In this Hammer film, Cushing's ward has a problem: this beauty's a Medusa, first breaking men's hearts, then turning them into stone — literally. ★★½

The Gorilla

(1939, 66 min, US, Alan Dwan) *The Ritz Brothers, Anita Louise, Patsy Kelly, Bela Lugosi.* Though the brilliance of the Ritz Brothers was never captured on film, this traditional haunted house mystery is enlivened by their silly jokes, synchronized dancing and wild slapstick. ★★½

Gorillas in the Mist

(1988, 129 min, US, Michael Apted) *Sigourney Weaver, Bryan Brown, Julie Harris.* Weaver's outstanding performance is the heart and soul of this well-produced biography on anthropologist Dian Fossey. The story covers the nearly 20 years Fossey dedicated to the mountain gorillas of central Africa, from her arrival on the continent as a census taker to her unprecedented work with the animals to her tragic murder. Brown also stars as a *National Geographic* cinematographer (and Fossey's lover) whose films on the naturalist's accomplishments helped bring about her international renown. Efficient, commanding direction from Apted. ★★★ DVD: $14.99

Gorky Park

(1983, 126 min, US, Michael Apted) *William Hurt, Lee Marvin, Brian Dennehy, Joanna Pacula.* Three corpses are found in Moscow's Gorky Park with their faces removed to make identification nearly impossible. But the key word here to Russian policeman Hurt is "nearly." And he sets out to solve the murders with Sherlockian reasoning. Marvin is chillingly effective as a shady American businessman. Dennis Potter adapted the taut and clever thriller (based on Martin Cruz Smith's novel), with gritty yet stylish direction from Apted. ★★★½ DVD: $14.99

Gosford Park

(2001, 138 min, US/GB/Italy, Robert Altman) *Michael Gambon, Derek Jacobi, Helen Mirren, Jeremy Northam, Clive Owen, Emily Watson, Kristen Scott Thomas, Maggie Smith, Ryan Phillippe, Bob Balaban, James Wilby, Alan Bates, Eileen Atkins, Richard E. Grant.* It's a wonder that Altman took so

Robert Altman's *Gosford Park*

long to direct a light murder-mystery, since it now seems so obvious that the genre is his very cup of tea. The evidence: a huge ensemble cast (with ensuing overlapping dialogue), issues of politics and social status, and plenty of room for sharp repartee; Altman even works a bit of old Hollywood into it. The occasion is a 1930s dinner and shooting party, thrown by an elite businessman (Gambon) on his vast English estate. The invitees include old money (countess Smith), new money (actor Northam), and a servant for every guest. As is his nature, Altman is a little more interested in the servants downstairs than the elite, especially since they can share the secrets that must go unsaid upstairs. After the leisurely character introductions, there is a murder of a generally disliked attendee; naturally, everyone is a suspect. Like *The Player*, Altman isn't so interested in the outcome; rather, he uses the murder as a catalyst to deeper revelations of character and class, coaxing extraordinary performances throughout. ★★★★ DVD Letterbox Collector's Edition: $14.99, VHS: $9.99

The Gospel According to Al Green

(1984, 90 min, US, Robert Mugge) Philadelphia filmmaker Mugge directed this exultant, fascinating portrait of pop superstar turned Pentacostal preacher extraordinaire Al Green. Throughout his career, Green has incorporated both a spirituality and a sensuality that moves audiences to ecstatic heights of joy and release. Mugge captures Green both in concert and on the pulpit, hypnotizing his audience with the intensity and majesty of his performance. His dedication and desire to help his audience find happiness on this planet give this spine-tingling documentary an electric, revelatory energy rarely captured on film. ★★★½ DVD: $14.99, VHS: $9.99

The Gospel According to St. Matthew

(1964, 135 min, Italy, Pier Paolo Pasolini) *Enrique Irazoqui, Margherita Caruso, Settimo Di Porto, Alfonso Gatto.* Pasolini's remarkable film is a modern interpretation of the last days of Christ. Using nonprofessionals and filmed in a realistic, pseudo-documentary fashion in the arid regions of Calabria in southern Italy, the film depicts Jesus Christ as a man of the people and a revolutionary, fighting the social injustices of the time. Yet despite his faithful use of the scriptures, the film is imbued with a Marxist ideology, a situation which produced confused acclaim from Church leaders. (Italian with English subtitles) ★★★★ DVD Letterbox: $29.99, VHS: $29.99

Gospel According to Vic

(1986, 95 min, Scotland, Charles Gormley) *Tom Conti, Helen Mirren.* In this irreverent Scottish comedy, Conti brings his prototypical comic flair to the role of Father Cobb, a chaplain who is two miracles short of successfully pleading sainthood for a certain Blessed Edith. ★★★ VHS: $79.99

Gossip

(2000, 90 min, US, Davis Guggenheim) *James Marsden, Lena Headey, Norman Reedus, Kate Hudson.* Three journalism students go too far when asked to identify the link between news and gossip. To illustrate, they create a real-life rumor about a celibate freshman and her boyfriend getting it on. When the boyfriend is wrongly arrested on date rape charges, the students realize that the rumor has gotten out of hand and has become the news. The serious issues are muddled in a pretty generic teen thriller that, like its characters, has a tenuous grip on reality. ★ DVD: $19.99, VHS: $14.99

Gotcha!

(1985, 97 min, US, Jeff Kanew) *Anthony Edwards, Linda Fiorentino, Alex Rocco.* The very likable Edwards plays a college kid on a European vacation who becomes involved in political intrigue. Fiorentino is very much a part of that intrigue. The film never really connects, but the Edwards-Farentino teaming and some amusing espionage bits compensate. ★★½ DVD Letterbox: $14.99

Gothic

(1987, 90 min, GB, Ken Russell) *Gabriel Byrne, Julian Sands, Natasha Richardson, Timothy Spall, Miriam Cyr.* Russell takes another step beyond the edge with this unusual, dreamlike psychological thriller. Set in the 1800s at Lord Byron's villa, the film depicts one hellish night spent by Byron and his guests, who included P.B. Shelley, his lover Mary, and author Dr. Polidori. The film suggests this fateful evening inspired Polidori to write "The Vampyre" and Mary (who would later marry her paramour) to pen "Frankenstein." ★★★ DVD: $14.99

Gothika

(2003, 96 min, US, Mathieu Kassovitz) *Halle Berry, Robert Downey, Jr., Penélope Cruz, Charles S. Dutton, John Carroll Lynch, Bernard Hill.* In this very mild, clichéd horror film, psychiatrist Berry wakes up one morning an inmate; apparently, she hacked up her husband with an ax, but has no memory of doing so. She also has visions of a little girl who's been dead for years. A promising if not terribly original story is given the typical Dark Castle Productions treatment: traditional "scary" ghosts, hip, nonsensical, "weird" sequences, and decent though uninspired performances from a name cast. Director Kassovitz (*La Haine, The Crimson Rivers*) does an efficient, anonymous job, and the whole thing moves at a fast clip. It's just not very involving or scary, and suffers from an odious, silly wrap-up (another Dark Castle trait) that renders the whole film unsatisfying. ★★ DVD Letterbox: $27.99, DVD Pan & Scan: $27.99, VHS: $59.99

The Governess

(1998, 105 min, GB, Sandra Goldbacher) *Minnie Driver, Tom Wilkinson, Harriet Walter, Florence Hoath, Bruce Myers, Jonathan Rhys Meyers.* A handsomely mounted, but largely uninvolving drama by writer-director Goldbacher, this story of an interloper and her affairs is more ambitious than it is good. Rosina (Driver) is a Jewess from London who passes herself as Mary Blackchurch, a governess. Employed by the Cavendish family, Rosina meets the bratty daughter, the brittle wife, and the robust patriarch (Wilkinson), an amateur photographer who takes a sexual interest in her. She also becomes the romantic obsession of Henry (Meyers), the teenage son who learns her secret. The drama is uninspired, and the passions are more tepid than torrid. It's an overheated but underwhelming romance. The cinematography, however, is beautiful. ★★ DVD: $29.99

Grace of My Heart

(1996, 115 min, US, Allison Anders) *Illeana Douglas, Matt Dillon, Eric Stoltz, John Turturro, Bruce Davison, Patsy Kensit, Bridget Fonda, Chris Isaak, Peter Fonda, David Clennon.* Douglas turns in a captivating performance as a woman searching for professional achievement and personal fulfillment in the fiercely competitive music industry. Opening in 1958 and spanning a decade and a half, the film sweeps across

the shifting tides of contemporary popular culture while exploring the life of Edna Buxton (Douglas): naïve, overprotected child of privilege with an unexpected reserve of strength. Director Anders successfully captures the look and feel of the varying eras and locales, as well as conveying the nature of the creative process as Edna's songs increasingly reflect her experiences and observations. The cast is uniformly strong in their portrayals, and the film is densely packed and leisurely paced, losing focus only briefly during the California segment. ★★★ DVD: $9.99, VHS: $9.99

Grace Quigley

(1985, 87 min, US, Anthony Harvey) *Katharine Hepburn, Nick Nolte, Elizabeth Wilson, Chip Zien.* Hepburn witnesses a murder committed by Nolte. Appreciating the professional touch, she hires him — to kill her. In the course of making the financial arrangements, a lucrative enterprise evolves; you might call it a growth industry. A quirky reflection on the perils of old age that fluctuates between farce and pathos, the film could have been better. Strong performances by Hepburn and Nolte seem ill-served by director Harvey. Another edit of the film exists, but not on video. In all this, one question is left unanswered: How can Hepburn still look that good? ★★

The Graduate

(1967, 105 min, US, Mike Nichols) *Dustin Hoffman, Anne Bancroft, Katharine Ross, William Daniels, Murray Hamilton, Marion Lorne, Alice Ghostley, Elizabeth Wilson, Buck Henry, Norman Fell, Richard Dreyfuss.* Nichols' landmark comedy made stars of Hoffman and Simon & Garfunkel, and cleared the path for the cinematic concerns of the younger generation. Effortlessly poignant and humorous, the film follows recent grad Benjamin (Hoffman) as he contemplates the future (plastics?) and becomes romantically involved with the sultry Mrs. Robinson (Bancroft in a smashing portrayal) and then her daughter (Ross). A perceptive and double-edged examination of mores and morals in 1960s America. Includes an interview with Hoffman and a documentary on the film. ★★★★ DVD Letterbox: $14.99

Favorite Line: "Mrs. Robinson, if you don't mind my saying so, this conversation is getting a little strange." —*Dustin Hoffman as Benjamin Braddock*

"Well here's to you, Mrs. Robinson": Anne Bancroft in *The Graduate*

Graffiti Bridge

(1990, 91 min, US, Prince) *Prince, Morris Day, Jerome Benton.* Prince wrote, directed and stars in this awful sequel to his 1984 hit *Purple Rain*, detailing the further musical adventures of "The Kid." Look for Mavis Staples, George Clinton and Ingrid Chavez. ★ VHS: $14.99

Grain of Sand

(1983, 90 min, France, Promme Meffre) *Delphine Seyrig, Genevieve Fontanel.* Seyrig finds herself sinking into a morass of self-doubt when she loses her job after 14 years. Her only hope: locate an old lover from her past now living on the island of Corsica. Meffre makes a striking directorial debut, deftly handling the subtle psychology of a woman unsettled just as she comes to the precipice of encroaching old age. (French with English subtitles) ★★★ VHS: $59.99

Grand Canyon

(1991, 135 min, US, Lawrence Kasdan) *Kevin Kline, Danny Glover, Mary McDonnell, Steve Martin, Alfre Woodard, Mary-Louise Parker.* Writer-director Kasdan turns his discerning eye to the fears and frustrations facing the American society in the '90s. An epic assignment, to be sure, but Kasdan and cowriter and wife Meg have fashioned an insightful and powerful examination of our times. Heading a dream cast, Kline plays a successful L.A. lawyer whose wrong turn driving home leads to an altercation with a street gang. He is rescued by truck driver Glover. The two men befriend each other, ultimately opening a wide panorama of issues and concerns facing not only them but their family and friends. The film tackles disparate themes such as racism, child abandonment, crime, violence, family mores, just to name a few, and all are handled with sensitivity and thoughtfulness. ★★★½ DVD: $9.99, VHS: $6.99

Le Grand Chemin

(1987, 104 min, France, Jean-Loup Hubert) *Anemone, Richard Bohringer, Antoine Hubert.* Poignant and tender without being maudlin, this delightful coming-of-age drama tells the story of a sensitive nine-year-old Parisian boy's experiences in the countryside after his mother leaves him with friends for the summer. The couple, a prissy but insolent woman and a rough and tumble drunkard, dote on the boy but incessantly argue as they are constantly reminded of their own child who tragically died a few years before. Rounding out the boy's education and introduction into the grown-up world is a rambunctious and wise-beyond-words tomboy. (American remake: *Paradise*) (French with English subtitles) ★★★½

Grand Hotel

(1932, 113 min, US, Edmund Goulding) *Greta Garbo, John Barrymore, Joan Crawford, Lionel Barrymore, Wallace Beery.* Garbo heads an all-star cast as the melancholic ballerina who "vants to be alone." Barrymore is the debonair jewel thief who romances her. Superior performances from the ensemble, fine direction from Goulding, and an intelligent script make this a classic from its era. Academy Award winner for Best Picture. ★★★★ DVD: $19.99

Grand Illusion

(1937, 114 min, France, Jean Renoir) *Jean Gabin, Erich Von Stroheim, Pierre Fresnay.* Renoir's humanistic masterpiece examines the chivalry and codes of honor among French POWs during WWI and their elegant German commandant (von Stroheim), divided by nationality but united by class. A monumental indictment of the savagery of war. The first foreign-language film to be nominated for a Best Picture Oscar. (French with English subtitles) ★★★★ DVD: $39.99, VHS: $29.99

Grand Prix

(1966, 171 min, US, John Frankenheimer) *James Garner, Toshiro Mifune, Eva Marie Saint, Yves Montand, Jessica Walter.* Oscar-winning Special Effects and Editing highlight this otherwise plodding racing drama about the lives and rivalries of four drivers competing for the World Championship. ★★½ VHS: $19.99, VHS Letterbox Widescreen: $19.99

Grand Tour: Disaster in Time

(1992, 99 min, US, David Twohy) *Jeff Daniels, Ariana Richards.* Science-fiction buffs have reason to cheer in this edge-of-your-seat thriller penned (and directed) by Twohy, one of the legion of screenwriters credited on *Alien³*. Daniels stars as "the boy who cried aliens" when his quaint New England town is visited by time-traveling "disaster groupies" who get their kicks playing spectator to mankind's greatest tragedies. Nail-biting suspense makes this more than just another tedious morality play in the "Star Trek" mold. ★★★ DVD Letterbox: $19.99

La Grande Bouffe

(1973, 125 min, France/Italy, Marco Ferreri) *Marcello Mastroianni, Ugo Tognazzi, Michel Piccoli, Philippe Noiret.* Director Ferreri, who can be as unrelenting and as vicious as Jonathan Swift, performs an autopsy on a dying class. Four bored businessmen are all victims of a terminal case of ennui brought on by the limitations inherent in bourgeois sensibilities. These gourmets become gourmands and decide to end it all by eating themselves to death. Ferreri vividly exposes the desperation among aging males as they attempt to retain their privileged positions — if not in the real world, than one of their own creation. Though the director evidences an attention to the scatological detail and an insistence at amplifying events to absurd proportions, these traditional elements of satire only heighten the film's comic possibilities. The big questions are asked, but only little ones are answered — unsatisfying perhaps, but then it's expected in these superficial times. (French with English subtitles) ★★★½ DVD: $24.99, VHS: $19.99

La Grande Bourgeoise

(1977, 115 min, Italy, Mauro Bolognini) *Catherine Deneuve, Giancarlo Giannini, Fernando Rey, Tina Aumont.* The repressed lust and violent emotions of the Italian upper classes in turn-of-the-century Rome make this stylish drama of love, murder and betrayal a fascinating drama. Deneuve marries older man Rey but her disturbed brother Giannini can't accept them and plots his murder. A lush, wonderfully photographed and costumed period piece. (Italian with English subtitles) (aka: *The Murri Affair*) ★★★

La Grande Guerra (The Great War)

(1959, 118 min, Italy, Mario Monicelli) *Vittorio Gassman, Alberto Sordi, Silvana Mangano.* A pardoned criminal (Gassman) becomes an unlikely soldier and together with his friend and fellow conscript, the cowardly Sordi, they find themselves becoming reluctant heroes in this diverting comedy set during World War I. (Italian with English subtitles) ★★½

Grandview, U.S.A.

(1984, 97 min, US, Randal Kleiser) *Patrick Swayze, Jamie Lee Curtis, C. Thomas Howell, Jennifer Jason Leigh, M. Emmet Walsh, John Cusack, Joan Cusack.* A good cast supplies the star power for a series of intertwining tales set in a small Midwestern town centering around the family-run auto derby. ★★ VHS: $19.99

The Grapes of Wrath

(1940, 129 min, US, John Ford) *Henry Fonda, Jane Darwell, John Carradine, Charlie Grapewin, John Qualen.* A monumental achievement in American film history, this superb adaptation of John Steinbeck's novel received compassionate and visionary guidance from director Ford, and remarkable contributions from the entire cast. Set during the Depression, the unforgettable story follows the hardships of a poor Oklahoma family, the Joads, who migrate from their dust-bowl farm to California and the promise of a better future. The outstanding cast includes Fonda, in the performance of his career, as the Joads' idealistic son, Tom; and Darwell as the stalwart matriarch. Oscars went to Ford and Darwell. ★★★★ DVD: $14.99

Grass

(2000, 79 min, US, Ron Mann) *Narrated by Woody Harrelson.* Staunch hemp lobbyist Harrelson narrates this brisk but ultimately bland documentary about our society's ever-shifting views on marijuana. Weaving together early government antidrug propaganda films with funky stock footage of the counterculture revolution, *Grass* charts the relatively short history of the drug in American culture and recounts the growing hysteria within the government apparatus that's kept dope illegal for generations. Though not as fiendishly subversive as its subject matter would suggest, this documentary nonetheless hits some irreverent, er, highs. ★★½ DVD Letterbox: $29.99, VHS: $59.99

The Grass Harp

(1996, 107 min, US, Charles Matthau) *Piper Laurie, Sissy Spacek, Walter Matthau, Jack Lemmon, Edward Furlong, Mary Steenburgen, Nell Carter, Roddy McDowall, Charles Durning.* An affecting adaptation of Truman Capote's touching novel of life in the South a couple generations ago, *The Grass Harp* is as tranquil as a calm summers' eve, which doesn't always accentuate the story's plucky characters or whimsical situations. Partly autobiographical, Capote's warm tale centers on Collin, an orphaned youth who is sent to live with his two maiden aunts. Spacek plays Verena, the younger but controlling sister, and Laurie is Dolly, a cheerful, childlike recluse. One of the strengths of *The Grass Harp* is the fine ensemble cast director Matthau has assembled, including his father Walter in a wonderful turn as Dolly's suitor. The film's gentle motion befits Capote's wistful recollections. ★★★

The Grass Is Greener

(1961, 105 min, US, Stanley Donen) *Cary Grant, Deborah Kerr, Robert Mitchum, Jean Simmons.* Stagey but mostly entertaining drawing room comedy with Grant as an English earl whose jealousy sparks a calamitous weekend affair when wife Kerr is given the royal treatment by visiting American millionaire Mitchum. Simmons is Mitchum's wife who has her own designs on Grant. Music and lyrics by Noël Coward. ★★½ DVD: $14.99

The Great Dictator: Charlie Chaplin and Jack Oakie knock Hitler and Mussolini on their Axis

Grave Indiscretion

(1995, 99 min, GB, J.P. Davidson) *Alan Bates, Sting, Theresa Russell, Lena Headey, Anna Massey.* Known as *The Grotesque* in Britain and the awfully titled *Gentlemen Don't Eat Poets* in America, this kinky but ultimately flaccid murder mystery is far from being a total waste of time. Reminiscent of *The Servant, Rebecca* and *Teorema*, the film stars Bates as Sir Hugo Cole, an eccentric paleontologist trapped in a sexless marriage with his American wife (Russell, in an amusing miscast role) who comes under the suspicious antics of his new butler Fledge (Sting). What begins as mental game playing and one-upsmanship escalates into the murder of the bisexual fiancé of the Coles' daughter. Set in an opulent home in late 1940s England, *Grave Indiscretion* should be enjoyed for its campy and sinister sexual encounters rather than for its feeble attempt at creating mystery and an air of foreboding. ★★

Gray's Anatomy

(1997, 80 min, US, Steven Soderbergh) *Spalding Gray.* America's premiere monologist Gray takes on the terror of physical trauma and myriad alternative healing beliefs in *Gray's Anatomy,* in which the author/protagonist reacts to retinal damage in his left eye by embarking on yet another journey of thousands and thousands of miles. Advised to have surgery, this child of Christian Science runs the idea by his existential realist therapist, an astral-projecting sweat lodge overseer, a nutritional optometrist, and a Filipino psychic surgeon. The staged performance piece is opened up with creative direction, and interspersed with interviews with some people who've had their own encounters with medical emergencies threatening that most-precious sense: sight. As in his past theatrical forays (*Swimming to Cambodia* most notably), Gray bares his soul and psyche with self-deprecating wit and flippant awareness of the human condition. ★★★ DVD: $14.99, VHS: $14.99

Grease

(1978, 110 min, US, Randal Kleiser) *John Travolta, Olivia Newton-John, Stockard Channing, Jeff Conaway, Eve Arden, Sid Caesar, Joan Blondell, Alice Ghostley.* Travolta and Newton-John created a small sensation in the late 1970s with this lively version of the drippy long-running Broadway musical. Set in the late 1950s, the film brought Travolta fame as a high school "greaser" who tries to hide his romance with "uncool" new girl Newton-

John. Spirited dance numbers and a pleasant score are the main attraction here. Channing steals the show as the leader of the girl greasers, and it's always nice to see the likes of Arden, Caesar, Blondell and Ghostley. (Sequel: *Grease 2*) ★★½ DVD Letterbox: $14.99, DVD Pan & Scan: $14.99, VHS: $9.99, VHS Letterbox: $9.99

Grease 2

(1982, 114 min, US, Patricia Birch) *Maxwell Caulfield, Michelle Pfeiffer, Lorna Luft, Eve Arden, Sid Caesar.* Birch, who choreographed the appealing dance sequences in the original *Grease,* directed this very unappealing sequel. Caulfield and a young Pfeiffer are the high school kids in love. ★ DVD: $19.99, VHS: $9.99

Greaser's Palace

(1972, 91 min, US, Robert Downey) *Albert Henderson, Allan Arbus.* Downey's irreverent version of the Christ Story set in the Wild West. Our Savior's descent comes in the form of Zoot Suit, a gentle song-and-dance man who arrives by parachute to work miracles and bring peace and harmony to the world. ★★½ DVD: $24.99, VHS: $19.99

Great Balls of Fire

(1989, 108 min, US, Jim McBride) *Winona Ryder, Alec Baldwin, Trey Wilson, Dennis Quaid, John Doe.* A high-energy, slick bio on rock 'n' roll legend Jerry Lee Lewis. Quaid, in a gutsy though rather one-dimensional performance, plays the rock pioneer, whose life is traced from his meteoric rise on the music scene to his controversial marriage to his teenage cousin to the infamous British tour which nearly ruined his career. Though the film is short on dramatic development, and its characters behave as music biz/Southern stereotypes, it is at its best (and agreeably entertaining) in the razzle-dazzle musical numbers featuring some of Lewis' greatest hits. Ryder deftly plays Lewis' child bride. ★★★ DVD Dual: $14.99

A Great Day in Harlem

(1994, 60 min, US, Jean Bach) *Quincy Jones, Dizzy Gillespie, Art Blakey, Art Farmer, Chubby Jackson, Paula Morris, Marian McPartland, Eddie Locke, Ernie Wilkins, Mona Hinton, Robert Benton, Sonny Rollins.* It was a beautiful day, that June morning in 1958, when fledgling photographer Art Kane and film director Robert Benton, then editor of *Esquire,* assembled some of the greatest jazz legends for a group photograph. This marked the first time that many of the greatest drummers, trumpet, piano and

sax players were at the same place at the same time where none of them were playing. Milt Hinton and his wife Mona took 8mm home movies of the event and other people took candid photos, never before seen, of the gathering. Egos can get in the way with performers, but at least the artists discuss the other performers with mutual respect and include an interesting glimpse into the after-hours "party" that took place on the front stoop of 125th St. that summer day. ★★★

The Great Dictator

(1940, 128 min, US, Charles Chaplin) *Charlie Chaplin, Paulette Goddard, Jack Oakie, Billy Gilbert.* Chaplin's first talkie stands as one of his greatest achievements. In this touching and often hilarious political spoof on the Third Reich, Chaplin plays dual roles: a poor Jew from the ghetto and Hynkel, the Hitler-inspired leader. Oakie is hilarious as Italian dictator "Napolini." ★★★★ DVD Chaplin Collection - 2 disc set: $29.99, VHS: $19.99

The Great Escape

(1963, 168 min, US, John Sturges) *Steve McQueen, James Garner, Richard Attenborough, James Coburn, Charles Bronson, Donald Pleasence, David McCallum.* Blockbuster adventure, based on a true story, about a group of Allied POWs who plan a daring escape from a German camp during WWII. A terrific all-star cast. ★★★½ DVD Letterbox: $14.99, DVD 2-disc Collector's Set: $29.99

Great Expectations

(1946, 118 min, GB, David Lean) *John Mills, Valerie Hobson, Bernard Miles, Alec Guinness, Jean Simmons, Martita Hunt.* One of the finest literary adaptations ever put to film, this stunning version of the Charles Dickens classic about a young orphan and his mysterious benefactor features masterful direction by Lean. ★★★★ DVD: $39.99

The Great Gatsby

(1974, 143 min, US, Jack Clayton) *Robert Redford, Mia Farrow, Bruce Dern, Sam Waterston, Karen Black.* Francis Ford Coppola adapted F. Scott Fitzgerald's classic for the screen with Redford as the titular character, a self-made man accepted into Long Island society back in the jazz age. The film captures neither the sensuality nor excitement of the novel, though it's a faithful adaptation. Redford and Farrow as Daisy are well matched if curiously subdued. ★★½ DVD: $19.99, VHS: $14.99

The Great Impostor

(1960, 112 min, US, Robert Mulligan) *Tony Curtis, Edmond O'Brien, Arthur O'Connell, Raymond Massey, Karl Malden.* Curtis stars in this true story as Ferdinand Waldo Demara, Jr., who in the 1950s successfully impersonated a monk, a college professor, a prison warden, a naval surgeon and a schoolteacher all before being caught and arrested. Curtis is in good form, though the episodic story only occasionally delivers. ★★½

The Great Lie

(1941, 107 min, US, Edmund Goulding) *Bette Davis, George Brent, Mary Astor, Hattie McDaniel.* Competent soaper with Davis marrying Brent, who used to be involved with Astor. He disappears in a plane crash, Mary is pregnant, and Bette then raises the child as her own. Though Bette is her usual indomitable self, the acting honors go to Academy Award winner Astor. ★★½

The Great Madcap (El Gran Calavera)

(1949, 90 min, Mexico, Luis Buñuel) *Fernando Soler, Rosario Granados.* One of the most commercial films of his career, Buñuel's engaging and gentle social comedy takes a playful look at the insensitive and irresponsible bourgeoisie, a constant theme he explores in a much more surrealist and biting fashion in *The Discreet Charm of the Bourgeoisie*. Soler plays a wealthy industrialist who, after a period of drunken carousing and free-spending ways, suffers a heart attack. On recovery, he realizes that his ingratiating and fast-living wife, son and even servants, long accustomed to milking him of money and favors, need a good lesson on the value of money and the need to work. The plot has been done before, but the story remains fresh and lively with Buñuel's satiric touch. (Spanish with English subtitles) ★★★ VHS: $79.99

The Great Man Votes

(1939, 72 min, US, Garson Kanin) *John Barrymore, Peter Holden, Virginia Weidler.* Through an ironic bit of casting, Barrymore, whose career was virtually ruined because of his drinking, had his greatest late-career role as an alcoholic given one last chance at redemption. In this wonderful mix of comedy and pathos, Barrymore plays a former professor whose wife's death leads to his drinking and decline. As he fights for custody of his two children, the now-night watchman gets a second chance: His is the deciding vote in the town's mayoral race, making him a very popular constituent. ★★★½ VHS: $19.99

The Great McGinty

(1940, 81 min, US, Preston Sturges) *Brian Donlevy, Akim Tamiroff, William Demarest, Muriel Angelus, Louis Jean Heydt.* In a flea-bitten Mexican cantina, a man who lost it all in a moment of dishonesty hears the story of a man who lost it all the first time he tried to go straight. Donlevy is terrific as McGinty, who goes from hobo to governor to bartender-on-the-lam. Sturges won an Oscar for the screenplay of this, his first directorial effort. ★★★½

The Great Moment

(1944, 83 min, US, Preston Sturges) *Joel McCrea, Betty Field, William Demarest, Franklin Pangborn.* McCrea plays Dr. W.T.G. Morton, a 19th-century dentist who discovered anaesthesia, but was not credited with such during his lifetime. Sturges' intriguing biography is an interesting failure, marred mostly by disorienting flashbacks and out-of-place slapstick. ★★ VHS: $14.99

The Great Mouse Detective

(1986, 74 min, US, John Musker) *Voices of: Vincent Price, Barrie Ingham.* Boasting impeccable animation by Disney, this delightful detective story follows the exploits of a spirited murine sleuth. Kids of all ages and adults will enjoy this gentle parody of Sherlock Holmes. It may not be one of Disney's best, but it will certainly entertain. ★★★

The Great Muppet Caper

(1981, 95 min, GB, Jim Henson) *Charles Grodin, Diana Rigg, John Cleese, Robert Morley, Peter Ustinov, Jack Warden.* The standard Muppet buffoonery makes for loads of fun as they try to solve a jewel robbery. Miss Piggy steals the show with her musical numbers (so reminiscent of

Marilyn in *Gentlemen Prefer Blondes*), but the star-studded list of cameos is still impressive. ★★★ DVD: $19.99

The Great Outdoors

(1988, 90 min, US, Howard Deutch) *John Candy, Dan Aykroyd, Annette Bening.* Very minor John Hughes-scripted comedy with Candy planning to spend a relaxing family vacation in the woods, not counting on cumbersome Aykroyd. ★½ DVD: $14.99, VHS: $9.99

The Great Race

(1965, 151 min, US, Blake Edwards) *Jack Lemmon, Peter Falk, Tony Curtis, Natalie Wood, Keenan Wynn.* Epic-sized comedy from director Edwards about an intercontinental race and its wacky participants. Though some of the jokes don't make the grade, there are plenty that do. Lemmon and Falk are the bad guys (boo, hiss) up against good guys Curtis and Wood. ★★★ DVD: $19.99

The Great Rock 'n' Roll Swindle

(1980, 103 min, GB, Julien Temple) Our only question is why the powers that be changed the title of this film from the original *Who Killed Bambi?* The original ad campaign pictured a mutilated fawn and let's face it, what better way could one summarize the insane destructiveness of the legendary Sex Pistols? This fascinating documentary features the lunacy of Johnny Rotten, Sid Vicious, Malcolm McLaren and the rest of the gang. Trash and burn was never like this before. ★★★

The Great Santini

(1979, 116 min, US, Lewis John Carlino) *Robert Duvall, Michael O'Keefe, Blythe Danner, David Keith.* An immensely absorbing family drama starring Duvall as a no-nonsense military man whose toughest battle is waged with his troubled son. Outstanding performances by Duvall, Danner and O'Keefe. ★★★½ DVD: $9.99

The Great Train Robbery

(1979, 111 min, US, Michael Crichton) *Sean Connery, Donald Sutherland, Leslie-Anne Down.* An outlandishly entertaining, knock-your-socks-off caper film from writer-director Crichton, based on an actual incident from the mid-1800s. Connery is well cast as the mastermind behind a daring train robbery who enlists the help of Sutherland and Down in the pursuit of a large gold shipment. Just try to sit still during the shaving scene! ★★★½ DVD Letterbox: $14.99

The Great Waldo Pepper

(1975, 109 min, US, George Roy Hill) *Robert Redford, Susan Sarandon, Margot Kidder, Bo Svenson, Geoffrey Lewis, Edward Herrmann.* Entertaining comic adventure starring Redford as a daredevil pilot in the Roaring '20s. He's ably assisted by Sarandon and Kidder. Good aerial photography. ★★★

A Great Wall

(1986, 100 min, US/China, Peter Wang) *Peter Wang, Sharon Iwai, Kelvin Han Yee.* The first Chinese/United States coproduction is a good natured comedy about the cultural clashes confronting a Chinese-American family when they make their first trip back to the family's hometown in mainland China. (English and Chinese with English subtitles) ★★½ DVD Letterbox: $19.99

The Great White Hope

(1970, 101 min, US, Martin Ritt) *James Earl Jones, Jane Alexander, Hal Holbrook.* Jones repeats his award-winning stage role in this commanding adaptation. Jones gives a truly magnificent performance as turn-of-the-century boxer Jack Johnson (called Jefferson here), facing as many challenges outside the ring as inside it. Alexander also repeats her stage role in a brilliant portrayal of Johnson's white mistress. ★★★

The Great White Hype

(1996, 87 min, US, Reginald Hudlin) *Samuel L. Jackson, Damon Wayans, Peter Berg, Jeff Goldblum, Jon Lovitz, Corbin Bernsen, Cheech Marin.* A playful if unruly racial and sports farce that at times goes over the edge of tastefulness and at others doesn't go far enough. Playing what could be Don King, Jackson stars as a shameless boxing promoter who engineers a championship bout to save his sagging empire — have a white opponent face his black champion (Wayans). He picks a has-been boxer turned rock singer (Berg), and proceeds to try to get the out-of-shape contender into a reasonable facsimile of a fighter. Parts of *Great White Hype* are very funny, especially when lampooning the boxing industry and skewering race relations. But often the film is undisciplined and characterizations tend to be too broad. Still, it offers many a laugh, and Jackson and his fellow cast members are highly spirited. ★★½ DVD: $9.99, VHS: $9.99

The Great Ziegfeld

(1936, 177 min, US, Robert Z. Leonard) *William Powell, Frank Morgan, Myrna Loy, Luise Rainer, Fanny Brice, Virginia Bruce, Reginald Owen, Ray Bolger.* Lavish musical biography of legendary showman Florenz Ziegfeld. Powell is a perfect incarnation of Ziegfeld, and Rainer justifiably won an Oscar as his first wife Anne Held. Loy has a good supporting role as second wife, Billie Burke (though she can't duplicate Burke's marvelous vocal quiver). It undeservedly won a Best Picture Oscar (over *Modern Times* and *Mr. Deeds Goes to Town*) but is grand entertainment nevertheless. ★★★½ DVD: $19.99, VHS Double Cassette: $19.99

The Greatest Show on Earth

(1952, 153 min, US, Cecil B. DeMille) *Charlton Heston, James Stewart, Betty Hutton, Dorothy Lamour, Cornel Wilde.* The title says it all and it's not just fairway hyperbole when Cecil gives the DeMille treatment to the circus. All thrills and spectacle, with about as much of a plot as one would find in any big-top performance. A huge cast (including Stewart as a clown) keep all three rings busy in this Oscar winner for Best Picture (though it really didn't deserve it over such classics as *High Noon* or *The Quiet Man*). ★★½ DVD: $14.99, VHS: $14.99

The Greatest Story Ever Told

(1965, 195 min, US, George Stevens) *Max von Sydow, Charlton Heston, John Wayne, Carroll Baker, Angela Lansbury, Sidney Poitier, Shelley Winters, Ed Wynn, Telly Savalas.* An all-star cast highlights this glossy though tired biblical epic about the life of Jesus. Wayne is the Roman centurian overseeing Christ's crucifixion (hope we didn't give away the ending). ★★ DVD: $19.99

Greed

(1924, 239 min, US, Erich von Stroheim) *Dale Fuller, ZaSu Pitts, Jean Hersholt.* Probably the most complete version of this psychological epic we will ever get to see. Von Stroheim's masterpiece achieves a depth of characterization through an almost obsessive use of objective correlatives. A love triangle with a gold filling, the film starts high in the mountains and ends on a burning desert. Originally over nine hours long, cut by the studio to just over two, Brownlow & Gill have restored only minutes — but important minutes — including the prologue in the mine (where much of the symbolism is set up). Features another fabulous score by Carl Davis. (Silent) ★★★★

Greedy

(1994, 109 min, US, Jonathan Lynn) *Michael J. Fox, Kirk Douglas, Phil Hartman, Nancy Travis, Bob Balaban, Olivia d'Abo, Colleen Camp.* From the writers of *Parenthood* comes more dysfunctional family humor — and though the results aren't equal to that film, this is nevertheless an appealing though predictable comedy sporting a wicked bent. Fox plays an estranged nephew who returns to the estate of his rich, dying uncle (the crotchety Douglas) at the insistence of his greedy cousins. The film is at its most entertaining when these vulturous family members (including the devilishly funny Hartman) are at each other's throats in venomous one-upsmanship. ★★½ DVD: $14.99

The Greek Tycoon

(1978, 112 min, US, J. Lee Thompson) *Jacqueline Bisset, Anthony Quinn, James Franciscus, Edward Albert.* Bisset plays the young widow of an assassinated American president who ends up marrying the richest man in the world (played by a crusty Quinn). This little-camouflaged story of the Kennedy-Onassis affair offers little of interest save some exotic locations. ★

The Green Berets

(1968, 141 min, US, John Wayne & Ray Kellogg) *John Wayne, David Janssen, Jim Hutton, Aldo Ray, Raymond St. Jacques.* Wayne appeared in a few turkeys in his long career, but none more than this Vietnam War drama. Made at the infancy of the anti-war movement, this cliché-filled story is amazing in its stupidity, and even failed as a patronage to the titular fighting force. (And yes, that *is* the sun setting in the East!) ★ DVD: $14.99, VHS: $14.99

Green Card

(1990, 108 min, US, Peter Weir) *Gérard Depardieu, Andie MacDowell, Bebe Neuwirth, Gregg Edelman, Robert Prosky, Lois Smith.* The American debut of French superstar Depardieu is this attractive tale of illegal immigration. Depardieu, while not in peak form (possibly due to language barriers), carries the film for MacDowell, who was so wonderful in *sex, lies and videotape.* Here, unfortunately, she falls flat. A definite step backward for Weir. ★★ DVD: $9.99

Green for Danger

(1946, 93 min, GB, Sidney Gilliat) *Alastair Sim, Trevor Howard, Leo Genn.* Sim camps it up as an eccentric Scotland Yard inspector investigating a series of murders in a WWII hospital unit somewhere in the English countryside. Great fun for aficionados of the classic "drawing room/country house" murder mysteries made famous by Agatha Christie. ★★★½

Green Grow the Rushes

(1951, 79 min, GB, Derek Twist) *Richard Burton, Honor Blackman, Roger Livesey.* Set in postwar rural England, this film of charming mannerisms takes its own good time setting up its peculiar story;

but once that story is in motion it's unpredictably funny. A youthfully handsome Burton plays a fisherman involved in the local smuggling of alcohol. Onto the scene stumbles roving reporter Blackman. Also on hand for this gentle send-up of bureaucracy are various local authorities and government officials — some in on the scam, others trying to uncover it. Procedure gives way to lunacy as a routine pickup literally lands itself in the middle of the town for all to see. As a crafty sea captain who handles any situation with a wry retort and deadpan diplomacy, Livesey steals the show. ★★★ VHS: $29.99

The Green Man

(1991, 150 min, GB, Elijah Moshinsky) *Sarah Berger, Michael Hordern, Albert Finney.* Adapted from a Kingsley Amis novel, this elegantly sexy thriller/ghost story stars Finney as a charming but overweight, sex-obsessed, middle-aged boozer. Along with his hard-working and all-too-understanding wife, he operates a cottage hotel outside of London that is famous for its reported ghostly visitations. Having used this ghost lore as an entertaining promotional lure, Finney, in a drunken haze, one day hallucinates that he actually sees a real ghost. After talking with the spectre, and doing some biddings for him, our inebriated hero discovers the apparition's evil intentions. A thoroughly entertaining, sophisticated and ghoulish delight. ★★★½

The Green Mile

(1999, 189 min, US, Frank Darabont) *Tom Hanks, David Morse, Michael Clarke Duncan, Bonnie Hunt, James Cromwell, Michael Jeter, Sam Rockwell, Patricia Clarkson, Harry Dean Stanton.* With his first film since his 1994 masterpiece *The Shawshank Redemption,* director Darabont returns with yet another stirring Stephen King adaptation. A little too long for its own good, *The Green Mile* is the mystical and powerful story of a physically large but mentally slow prisoner (Oscar nominee Duncan) who is transferred to the death row cellblock of a Louisiana penitentiary (known as the Green Mile) and how he comes to affect not only the guards there but his fellow prisoners as well. Hanks leads a splendid cast as the head guard who comes to realize that his prisoner may be blessed with extraordinary powers. Director Darabont creates a terrific evocation of the times and maintains such a lyrical pace it often feels poetic. ★★★½ DVD: $24.99, VHS: $14.99

The Green Pastures

(1936, 92 min, US, Marc Connelly & William Keighley) *Rex Ingram, Oscar Polk, Eddie Anderson.* First he created a Broadway hit from the writings of Roark Bradford, then Connelly took them to Hollywood in this imaginative fable on how heaven *ought* to be. Today, one less generous might see the performances as your typical "Negro" stereotype — if the film made any attempt at realism. But *Green Pastures* has the benevolence of a child dreaming in Sunday school on a warm summer's day. The play's text is actually rather subversive: The Lord God Jehovah finally gets to move from the Old Testament to the New when he learns the meaning of mercy from his most disappointing creation, Man. The film features wall-to-wall spirituals, scored by Erich Wolfgang Korngold and performed by The Hal Johnson Choir. ★★★ VHS: $14.99

The Green Room

(1978, 95 min, France, François Truffaut) *François Truffaut, Nathalie Baye.* Truffaut stars as a journalist obsessed with his mortality and the deaths of his WWI comrades. An eerie, atmospheric departure for the director. Based on the writings of Henry James. (French with English subtitles) ★★½

The Green Slime

(1968, 89 min, US/Japan, Kinji Fukasaku) *Robert Horton, Richard Jaeckel, Luciana Paluzzi.* An oozing, bubbling, slithering green slime, terrorizing an outer space station, threatens to invade Earth and wipe out civilization. Oh, the horror! ★ VHS: $19.99

The Green Wall

(1969, 110 min, Peru, Armando Robles Godoy) *Julio Aleman, Sandra Riva.* A stirring autobiographical tale of an urban family who, in a back-to-nature move, leave the pressures of Lima to hack out a new life in the challenging environment of the Peruvian jungle — the green wall. The film records their successes and obstacles, both natural and man-made, as they become determined to survive in this idyllic but cruel, rich but unyielding world. A film of spellbinding power and beauty. (Spanish with English subtitles) ★★★ VHS: $79.99

Tom Hanks (l.) and Michael Clarke Duncan in *The Green Mile*

Greetings

(1968, 88 min, US, Brian De Palma) *Robert De Niro, Gerrit Graham, Allen Garfield.* The talents of De Palma are wonderfully previewed in this early directorial effort. Clearly showing his film school background, De Palma structures this witty satire on the '60s counterculture in a series of vignettes. A very young De Niro stars as one of three friends living in New York City. The story follows their resourceful attempts to keep one of them from being drafted. Consistently funny and inventive. ★★★

Gregory's Girl

(1982, 99 min, GB, Bill Forsyth) *Gordon John Sinclair, Dee Hepburn.* Teetering on the brink of adulthood, a gangly Scottish schoolboy discovers the pleasures and perils of infatuation as he falls for a leggy lass on the soccer team. Forsyth's spirited comedy deftly conveys the invigorating effects of young love. ★★★ DVD Letterbox: $14.99

Gremlins

(1984, 106 min, US, Joe Dante) *Zach Galligan, Phoebe Cates, Hoyt Axton, Polly Holliday, Dick Miller.* Offbeat humor and garish horror successfully blend together in this box-office hit. Young Galligan gets a pet mogwai (*mog-why*) from his dad. The cute, cuddly animal (after the three rules have been ignored) spawns terrifying gremlins that proceed to destroy the town. Lots of in-jokes and neat special effects; and more importantly, the film demonstrates the many uses for a blender. (Sequel: *Gremlins 2: The New Batch*) ★★★ DVD Special Edition: $19.99, VHS: $14.99

Gremlins 2: The New Batch

(1990, 106 min, US, Joe Dante) *Zach Galligan, Phoebe Cates, Christopher Lee, John Glover, Paul Bartel.* The original *Gremlins* was a well-made thriller filled with a scathing, dark sense of humor, but much of its horror was too intense for smaller children. In *Gremlins 2*, Dante may have found what he was looking for when he made the first film. This hilarious romp is filled with hysterical self-reference and reaches such heights of absurdity that even little ones know it's all in good fun. This time around, the little nasties are set loose on a New York office tower, The Clamp Centre (aptly modeled, owner and all, after the Trump Plaza). ★★★½ DVD: $19.99, VHS: $14.99

The Grey Fox

(1982, 92 min, Canada, Philip Borsos) *Richard Farnsworth, Jackie Burroughs, Wayne Robson.* Very successful western/character study of convicted stagecoach robber Bill Miner (Farnsworth) who emerges from prison after 30 years to find that the world has left him behind. With robbery his only acknowledged trade, and horses and stagecoaches having been supplanted by steam engines and trains, what's a guy to do? Though the pacing may be a little slow for some tastes, Farnsworth's portrayal of "the gentleman bandit" is in itself worth the price of rental. Director Borsos ably mixes the inherent humor of the situation (imagine, an 80-year-old train robber) with the pathos of the character to create a film that is touching without being maudlin. ★★★½

Grey Gardens

(1976, 95 min, US, Albert Maysles, David Maysles, Ellen Hovde, Muffie Meyer) *Edith Bouvier Beale, Little Edie.* The lives of Edith Bouvier Beale and her adult daughter Edie are the subject of this moving documentary by the Maysles

brothers. Secluded in their decaying Long Island mansion, these two eccentric women allow the morbid spectacle of their private melodrama to simply play itself out in front of the camera. Some have charged the directors with exploitation, although by revealing their subjects so unsparingly they go beyond voyeurism and challenge us to feel true compassion for these lonely human beings. ★★★ DVD Criterion Collection: $39.99, VHS: $29.99

Grey Owl

(1999, 117 min, Canada/GB, Richard Attenborough) *Pierce Brosnan, Annie Galipeau, Nathaniel Arcand, Graham Greene.* A $30 million production that went straight to video, this picturesque period drama is actually better than its roots suggest. Based on a true-life incident, *Grey Owl* stars Brosnan as an Indian tracker living in the Canadian wilds whose environmental advocacy makes him a cause celebre in 1930s England. The author of magazine articles and then a best-selling book, Grey Owl goes on tour to promote the protection of the wilderness. But as his celebrity grows, his secret past soon comes to light. Attenborough directs with an epic sweep, getting the most out of the lush Canadian backdrop, but the relationship between Grey Owl and his young bride is heavy-handed where it should be tender. Fortunately, this doesn't take too much away from the story itself, which can be quite compelling. ★★½ DVD: $14.99, VHS: $9.99

The Grey Zone

(2001, 108 min, US, Tim Blake Nelson) *David Arquette, Steve Buscemi, Harvey Keitel, Mira Sorvino, Natasha Lyonne, Daniel Benzali.* Actor Nelson steps behind the camera for this affecting, harrowing Holocaust drama set in Auschwitz. A surprisingly moving Arquette heads a good ensemble to tell the story of the only uprising by Jewish prisoners at the German concentration camp. Watching Jews lead fellow unsuspecting Jews into the ovens is tough viewing, but *The Grey Zone* avoids the sensational and stirs emotions by way of its complex characters and strong dramatics. ★★★ DVD: $24.99

Greystoke: The Legend of Tarzan

(1984, 129 min, GB, Hugh Hudson) *Christopher Lambert, Ralph Richardson, Ian Holm, James Fox, Andie MacDowell.* Director Hudson followed his Academy Award-winning *Chariots of Fire* with this liberally adapted retelling of the Edgar Rice Burroughs Tarzan tale. Richardson is captivating in

Tim Roth (l.) and Tupac Shakur in *Gridlock'd*

his swan song performance and Lambert became an international sex symbol through his portrayal of the Lord of the Jungle. A visual treat and the first Tarzan film to try to bring a sophistication to the tale. ★★★ VHS: $14.99

Gridlock'd

(1997, 90 min, US, Vondie Curtis-Hall) *Tim Roth, Tupac Shakur, Thandie Newton, Vondie Curtis-Hall, Charles Fleischer, Howard Hesseman, John Sayles.* A frustration comedy about two junkies who run into bureaucratic roadblocks while trying to get clean, *Gridlock'd* is an engrossing but not quite heady trip. Solid performances by Roth and Newton prevent this potentially downbeat film from becoming a trite antidrug message movie. Yet it is the heartbreaking presence of the late rapper Shakur that really makes this gritty, dark urban tale valuable. The film's weakest element is the subplot about buddies Spoon (Shakur) and Stretch (Roth) being chased by a gangster they wronged. But at least this story line puts the rest of *Gridlock'd*'s accomplishments in bold relief. Politicized to a degree, the film makes its points within an interesting and entirely constructive framework. ★★★ DVD: $19.99, VHS: $9.99

Il Grido (The Outcry)

(1957, 115 min, Italy, Michelangelo Antonioni) *Steve Cochran, Alida Valli.* A compelling, slow moving, if not totally successful film about a man and his daughter who wander about aimlessly when their lives are placed in upheaval after the sudden departure of his fiancee. One of director Antonioni's earlier works is a moody look at psychological breakdowns and the lack of personal communication. (Italian with English subtitles) ★★½ DVD: $29.99, VHS: $24.99

Grief

(1993, 92 min, US, Richard Glatzer) *Craig Chester, Alexis Arquette, Jackie Beat, Carlton Wilborn, Paul Bartel, Mary Woronov, John Fleck.* Writer-director Glatzer has taken his personal experiences as a writer for TV's "Divorce Court" and fashioned an engaging and funny comedy-drama about friendship, love, bereavement and trash TV. Set during an eventful workweek, the film follows the misadventures of Mark (Chester), a writer for a daytime TV show, as he comes to grips with his co-workers, office politics, an office crush, homophobia and the loss of his lover. Beat plays the show's overbearing but maternal producer. Arquette also stars as a bisexual employee involved in a secret office romance. Highlighting the film are campy renditions of the TV soap opera, which includes everything from lesbian circus performers to schizophrenic divas. ★★★ DVD: $19.99

Grievous Bodily Harm

(1988, 96 min, Australia, Mark Joffe) Colin Friels, Bruno Lawrence, John Waters. Don't let the artwork on the video box fool you: this gritty, nicely acted and sexy thriller is very much *not* the grade-C exploitation film that the cover suggests. Friels plays a seedy Sydney newspaper reporter covering the murder of a porn star. Lawrence is the policeman investigating the case. And Waters (not the American director), in a first-rate performance, is the killer whose search for his presumably dead wife leads the three men on an intersecting road to danger. ★★★

The Grifters

(1990, 110 min, US, Stephen Frears) Anjelica Huston, John Cusack, Annette Bening, J.T. Walsh, Pat Hingle, Stephen Tobolowsky, Henry Jones, Charles Napier, Xander Berkeley. Director Frears' foray into the degenerate world of novelist Jim Thompson is a compelling look at life on the fringe. The story centers around a three-way power struggle between Roy, a small-time grifter, and the two women in his life: his mother and his girlfriend. Cusack sinks his teeth into the role of Roy with intense complexity. Huston dazzles as Roy's mother, Lily, a ruthless swindler who works the odds at the track for the mob. Bening is Myra, Cusack's part-time-prostitute girlfriend, who tries to lure him into the big-stakes world of the "long con." Though theirs is a world filled with mistrust and betrayal, Frears' vision of their lives is tempered with occasional moral twists and underlying humanity. Superbly acted and directed, *The Grifters* is peppered with moments of shocking brutality as it careens toward its tragic conclusion. ★★★★ DVD Collector's Edition: $14.99, VHS: $9.99

The Grim Reaper
(La Commare Secca)

(1962, 89 min, Italy, Bernardo Bertolucci) Francesco Rula, Giancarlo De Rosa, Marisa Solinas. This rarely seen work, based on a five-page outline by Pier Paolo Pasolini, was 22-year-old Bertolucci's first film as a director. Set in Rome's seedy underworld, the story involves the investigation of the police into the brutal murder of a prostitute. As they go through the list of possible suspects, the police find a beguiling maze of alibis as well as widely differing recountings of the events leading up to the woman's last day. An interesting debut and one that the director admits was made by ". . . someone who had never shot one foot of 35mm before but who had seen lots and lots of films." (Italian with English subtitles) ★★★ VHS: $29.99

Grind

(1996, 96 min, US, Chris Kentis) Billy Crudup, Adrienne Shelly, Paul Shulze, Frank Vincent. In this slight, minor diversion about "Everyday, working-class Joes," ex-con Eddie (Crudup) moves in with older brother Terry (Shulze) and his pretty wife Janey (Shelly). Eddie joins his brother and father at the factory, while getting involved in a car theft ring and pursuing his dream of drag-car racing. One of *Grind*'s better accomplishments is capturing the blue collar milieu, and there are some very effective moments. But watching the many intimate scenes between the characters gives the impression the

filmmakers wanted to make a down-to-earth, "real" alternative to Hollywood gloss and fantasy; and while an admirable idea, and much of it does work, the result doesn't necessarily guarantee exciting dramatics. ★★½ DVD: $24.99, VHS: $14.99

Groove

(2000, 86 min, US, Greg Harrison) Lola Glaudini, MacKenzie Firgens, Denny Kirkwood, Hamish Linklater. Mix together the following ingredients over a low flame: Two brothers, a great techno dance track, an easy-to-follow story line, and ecstasy for the whole cast. The final result is the engaging *Groove*. The story line loosely follows two brothers, one of whom is to announce his engagement at the rave that night, and the other is to try ecstasy for the first time. The story juggles various subplots about the partyers, nicely keeping track of an eclectic cast of characters, The soundtrack is a great assortment of techno and trance music that alone should attract lovers of the scene to this sweet movie. ★★★ DVD: $24.99, VHS: $14.99

The Groove Tube

(1974, 75 min, US, Ken Shapiro) Chevy Chase, Richard Belzer. Goofy and sometimes very funny spoof on television, with a wide variety of skits and episodes. Chase made his film debut. ★★½ VHS: $19.99

Gross Anatomy

(1989, 107 min, US, Thom Eberhardt) Matthew Modine, Daphne Zuniga, Christine Lahti, Zakes Mokae. The Paper Chase goes to medical school in this uneven but appealing comedy-drama. Modine is in fine form as the initially cocky doctor-in-training who eventually comes to learn about more than just medicine. Lahti does as well as possible in the cliché-ridden John Houseman role of tormentor/supporter. ★★½ DVD: $9.99

Grosse Pointe Blank

(1997, 109 min, US, George Armitage) John Cusack, Minnie Driver, Dan Aykroyd, Alan Arkin, Joan Cusack, Jeremy Piven, Hank Azaria, Barbara Harris. Wearing a few hats (cowriter, coproducer), Cusack plays an angst-ridden assassin in this very funny dark comedy. He plays Martin Blank, a successful hit man who returns to his high school's tenth reunion. There he is reunited with Debi (the very engaging Driver), his former sweetheart whom he stood up on prom night (never to be heard from again). Having federal agents and a rival hit man (Aykroyd) on his trail is nothing compared to the task at hand in making amends with Debi. And then there's the school dance! Like his *Miami Blues*, director Armitage brings his own wonderful, offbeat humor and rhythm to the film, and *Grosse Pointe Blank* revels in these moments of fancy. John has become the master of understatement, and he gives a ripe, humorous performance. ★★★½ DVD: $14.99, VHS: $9.99

Ground Zero

(1987, 109 min, Australia, Michael Pattison) Colin Friels, Jack Thompson, Donald Pleasance. In this suspenseful political thriller, Friels stars as a cinematographer who unwittingly becomes involved in political intrigue when he searches for the truth about the death of his father, a noted WWII cameraman killed under mysterious circumstances. In the process, he uncovers a British secret service cover-up from decades before. A thoroughly satisfying mystery with ample portions of social commentary and suspense. ★★★

Groundhog Day

(1993, 103 min, US, Harold Ramis) Bill Murray, Andie MacDowell, Chris Elliott, Stephen Tobolowsky. On the heels of his whimsical turn in What about Bob?, Murray tops himself with this extremely funny and surprisingly sweet romantic comedy, with the glib comedian giving one of his most likable and funniest performances. It's Groundhog Day, and cynical TV weatherman Murray has been sent to Punxsutawney, Pa., to cover the festivities for his Pittsburgh station. But there's one small problem: he seems to be reliving the day over and over and over again. Writer-director Ramis and cowriter Danny Rubin have milked this inventive premise for all it's worth, and they've given some hilarious and irresistible moments to Murray and his merry band of cohorts. ★★★ DVD Special Edition: $24.99, VHS: $9.99

The Group

(1966, 150 min, US, Sidney Lumet) Candice Bergen, Joan Hackett, Elizabeth Hartman, Shirley Knight, Jessica Walter, Hal Holbrook, Richard Mulligan, Larry Hagman. Bergen, Hackett and Holbrook made their film debuts in Lumet's adaptation of Mary McCarthy's novel. Following the intertwining lives of eight graduates of an exclusive women's college, the story examines each character's development as they enter adult life. In much the same way as George Cukor's The Women, the film is revelatory in exposing its underlying assumptions regarding women's nature and women's place. While it may sometimes play like a soap opera, it's an interesting document of its time. ★★★

Grown Ups

(1980, 95 min, GB, Mike Leigh) Philip Davis, Leslie Manville, Lindsay Duncan, Sam Kelly. Featuring intricate characterizations and plenty of incisive humor, Leigh's comedy-drama, though slowly paced (as are most of Leigh's earlier films), is a meticulous and startling examination of Thatcher's England. The story focuses on a young lower-middle-class couple who has just moved into their first home and are besieged by the wife's batty sister. Not helping matters is the fact that their next-door neighbor is their former high school teacher. Not a lot happens as far as plot is concerned, but Leigh's camera and sly wit make this of interest. ★★★ DVD: $29.99, VHS: $29.99

Grumpier Old Men

(1995, 100 min, US, Howard Deutch) Jack Lemmon, Walter Matthau, Ann-Margret, Sophia Loren, Burgess Meredith, Kevin Pollak, Daryl Hannah. This sophomoric sequel to *Grumpy Old Men* should tickle the funny bone of those who found enjoyment in the first film. The film introduces a new character to the small Minnesota town: the impossibly beautiful Loren. She has taken over the local bait shop and is preparing to turn it into an Italian restaurant. Thus begins a war of wills as dedicated fishermen Lemmon and Matthau turn to every dirty trick in the book to sabotage her opening; that is until Loren turns to her feminine wiles. Many of the jokes are of the sexual and flatulent variety, though in the hands of this very able cast you can't help but laugh out loud. Time may have aged the appearances of the cast, but certainly not their comic timing; and how wonderful to see romantic characters above the age of 50. ★★½ DVD: $9.99, VHS: $9.99

Grumpy Old Men

(1993, 105 min, US, Donald Petrie) *Jack Lemmon, Walter Matthau, Ann-Margret, Burgess Meredith, Ossie Davis, Daryl Hannah, Kevin Pollack.* Lemmon and Matthau reunite for the first time in 12 years and they've lost none of the chemistry that has made them one of the screen's great comedy teams. And if the script isn't exactly on par with most of their previous works, their bouyant performances make this a lively comedy. They play neighbors who have been feuding since childhood. Into their lives breezes eccentric artist Ann-Margret (looking lovely but none-too-bohemian) and the race is on to capture her affection. Though many of the film's lines are on the Bart Simpson scale ("Eat my shorts," etc.), the entire cast manages to sustain a playful cheerfulness despite what the title may suggest. (Sequel: *Grumpier Old Men*) ★★½ DVD: $14.99, VHS: $9.99

Guantanamera!

(1995, 104 min, Cuba, Juan Carlos Tabio & Tomás Gutiérrez Alea) *Carlos Cruz, Mirta Ibarra, Jorge Perugorría, Raúl Eguren.* This brilliant and hilarious skewering of the Latin passion for sex, death and bureaucracy follows a picaresque trail across Cuba and uncovers a fascinating and intimate portrait of the country along the way. Yoyita, a world-renown ex-patriot singer, returns to her home town of Guantanamo. She meets up with her old flame, Candido, and, in a moment of passionate embrace, she dies of a heart attack. Enter her niece Gina and Gina's husband Adolfo, who heads the ministry in charge of funeral arrangements. So Candido, Adolfo and Gina (along with Yoyita's corpse, of course) set off on a zany, ambling journey across the entire island that crisscrosses several times with a macho truck driver, Mariano, who was once a student of Gina's and still carries a big crush for her. Directors Alea and Tabio prove their skill at pushing the limits of acceptable critique of Castro's government and do so with considerable goodwill and humor. (Spanish with English subtitles) ★★★★ DVD: $29.99, VHS: $29.99

The Guardian

(1990, 93 min, US, William Friedkin) *Jenny Seagrove, Dwier Brown, Carey Lowell.* Seagrove is the nanny from hell, offering newborns to an evil oak in this, Friedkin's first horror tale since *The Exorcist.* The story is ridiculous, the chills are non-existent, and Friedkin's pacing is lethargic. ★ DVD: $24.99, VHS: $14.99

Guarding Tess

(1994, 98 min, US, Hugh Wilson) *Shirley MacLaine, Nicolas Cage, Austin Pendleton, Edward Albert, Richard Griffiths.* Masquerading as a gentle comedy about the tumultuous relationship between a former First Lady and one of her Secret Service agents, *Guarding Tess* quickly deteriorates into an implausible, yawn-provoking thriller without the thrills. MacLaine is right at home with her role as the widow of a former President. She gets particular joy in playfully tormenting agent Cage, a serious young man who can't wait for his time to be up. As they bicker and eventually come to understand each other, it becomes clear that someone is out to kill her. ★★ DVD: $14.99, VHS: $9.99

The Guardsman

(1931, 83 min, US, Sidney Franklin) *Alfred Lunt, Lynn Fontanne, Roland Young.* Stage legends Lunt and Fontanne make a rare screen appearance in this thoroughly entertaining version of Ferenc Molnar's

Sarah Polley in *Guinevere*

classic comedy. Reprising their acclaimed stage roles, the Lunts play a husband and wife acting team. Certain she is unfaithful to him, Lunt impersonates a dashing soldier and woos his own wife. And to his horror, she acquiesces. Though stage and screen require different acting styles, the very theatrical Lunts adapt to film with great skill. They are wonderful farceurs — what a shame they didn't return to Hollywood. Young is splendid in support as a critic who watches this comedy of errors. (Remade as *The Chocolate Soldier* and *Lily in Love*) ★★★★ VHS: $19.99

Guess Who's Coming to Dinner

(1967, 108 min, US, Stanley Kramer) *Katharine Hepburn, Spencer Tracy, Sidney Poitier, Katharine Houghton, Beah Richards, Cecil Kellaway.* Hepburn and Tracy appeared together for the last time in this acclaimed social comedy whose theme of interracial marriage may seem tame by today's standards but in 1967 created quite a stir. Poitier is wed to Tracy and Hepburn's daughter Houghton, causing varying reactions from both their families. Hepburn won an Oscar for Best Actress, and this was Tracy's final film. Houghton, incidentally, is Hepburn's real-life niece. ★★★ DVD: $14.99, VHS: $19.99

Guilty as Charged

(1991, 95 min, US, Sam Irvin) *Rod Steiger, Lyman Ward, Isaac Hayes, Lauren Hutton, Heather Graham.* In this black comedy, spoofy thriller and cult film candidate, Steiger — with a nod to Mr. Joyboy from *The Loved One* — chews the scenery as the owner of a meat packing company who moonlights as a vigilante judge and executioner. Kidnapping paroled or escaped convicted murderers, Steiger imprisons and then zaps the convicts in a homemade electric chair. ★★½

Guilty as Sin

(1993, 107 min, US, Sidney Lumet) *Rebecca DeMornay, Don Johnson, Stephen Lang, Jack Warden, Dana Ivey.* An uneven but trashily entertaining nail-biter. DeMornay is well cast as a career- and ego-driven defense attorney who bites off more than she can chew when she takes on the case of a sleek lothario (Johnson) accused of killing his wife. To say more would be to give too much away as this murder mystery snakes along with more twists than DeMornay's pistol-driven swagger. Though steamy when it wants to be, *Guilty as Sin* is a little too slick and a little too obvious. ★★ DVD: $14.99

Guilty by Suspicion

(1991, 105 min, US, Irwin Winkler) *Robert De Niro, Annette Bening, George Wendt, Martin Scorsese, Ben Piazza, Sam Wanamaker.* The Hollywood blacklist of the 1950s, though mostly ignored over the years until the 1970s — which produced *The Way We Were* and *The Front* — is the subject of this compassionate drama. De Niro is compelling as a successful film director whose personal and professional lives fall apart when he refuses to cooperate with the House Committee on Un-American Activities. Writer-director Winkler's film is full of remarkable detail, presenting its unsettling, effective story with finesse and subtlety. Bening is very good as De Niro's wife. ★★★ DVD: $14.99, VHS: $14.99

Guinevere

(1999, 105 min, US, Audrey Wells) *Stephen Rea, Sarah Polley, Jean Smart, Gina Gershon, Paul Dooley, Sandra Oh, Jasmine Guy.* There are moments of brilliance in *Guinevere*, writer-director Wells' thoughtful take on the uneasy relationship between a young girl and a much older man, but once the film makes its points, it has nowhere to go. Harper (Polley) is an insecure teen on the cusp of adulthood receiving life lessons from an aging photographer (Rea) who seduces her. While this sounds very salacious, Wells handles their relationship with extreme care and sensitivity. *Guinevere* contains a few real epiphanies, but there are an equal number of frustrating scenes, mostly involving his past lovers. The two leads are well cast, and in support, Smart is superb as Harper's disapproving mother. ★★½ DVD: $19.99, VHS: $9.99

Gulliver's Travels

(1996, 175 min, GB, Charles Sturridge) *Ted Danson, Mary Steenburgen, James Fox, Edward Fox, Omar Sharif, Alfre Woodard, Geraldine Chaplin, John Gielgud, Peter O'Toole, Kristin Scott Thomas.* Like Lewis Carroll's "Alice" books, Jonathan Swift's 1726 classic defies translation into other media. The targets for his vitriol are now lost to the ages, and this biting attack against a bulging bourgeoisie has been carved down to a harmless little fairy tale. Who, then, would have imagined a made-for-TV production would be the most faithful and entertaining adaptation yet? And whoever OK'd Danson for the role of the good ship's doctor is either a man of vision or a fool for Q ratings. But Danson does give a very good performance in a very difficult role, wisely choosing not to attempt an English accent. Of course, the *real* stars are the special effects, here supplied by Jim Henson's always reliable people. ★★★½ DVD: $14.99, VHS: $9.99

Gummo

(1997, 95 min, US, Harmony Korine) *Linda Manz, Max Perlich, Jacob Reynolds, Chloë Sevigny.* Will all those who feel a stir whenever they come across one of Calvin Klein's desolate ads for Obsession or CKOne please stand up — come on, you know who you are. You're going to love this movie! For the rest of us, this extended exercise in vapidity will prove to be sheer excruciation. Like one long, strung out (in both senses of the term) Klein ad, this directorial debut from the writer of *Kids* traipses around the central Ohio town of Xenia, which has never recovered from the tornado that hit it several years prior. As seen from the point of view of a handful of the town's unsupervised adolescents, we are given over to extended, cloying (chickenhawkish, even) shots of these young wastrels as they go about their daily activities. All this is not to say that Korine is not without talent. But none of this stuff is original. And, sure, it's rebellious, but it has no substance. ★ DVD: $24.99

Gumshoe
(1972, 88 min, GB, Stephen Frears) *Billie Whitelaw, Frank Finlay, Albert Finney.* A capricious comedy about a small-time vaudevillian who's seen too many Bogart films and decides to try some sleuthing of his own. An intriguing little crime story. ★★★

Gun Crazy
(1949, 87 min, US, Joseph H. Lewis) *John Dall, Peggy Cummins, Morris Carnovsky, Russ Tamblyn.* After a lifetime of being obsessed with guns, a young man (Dall) meets the love of his life in the form of a sexy, gun-toting carnival performer. The tough-talking dame (Cummins), a dangerous femme fatale in the most literal sense, craves the good things in life and coaxes the man into a violent series of armed robberies and eventually murder. An entertaining cult favorite, seemingly years ahead of its time, that is stylishly filmed and offers an unflinching peek, in the *Bonnie and Clyde* tradition, at ill-fated fugitives on the lam. (Remade in 1992) ★★★½ DVD: $19.99

Gun Crazy
(1992, 97 min, US, Tamra Davis) *Drew Barrymore, James LeGros, Ione Skye, Billy Drago, Michael Ironside, Joe Dallesandro.* Like a magnum in a velvet glove, Barrymore blows away this touching love-and-bullets drama that proves sometimes a cigar really is more than just a cigar, but a gun is just a gun. Barrymore slips comfortably into the role of a trailer park girl with a heart of lead who discovers the joys of gunplay when she murders her touchy-feely stepfather (Dallesandro) and falls in love with the world's only male virgin (LeGros). This made-for-cable remake owes less to the 1949 classic than it does to *Badlands* or *Bonnie and Clyde*, but it is destined to stand in its own right as an exceptional entry into the "love-on-the-run" genre. ★★★½ DVD Letterbox: $9.99, VHS: $7.99

The Gun in Betty Lou's Handbag
(1992, 89 min, US, Allan Moyle) *Penelope Ann Miller, Eric Thal, William Forsythe, Alfre Woodard, Cathy Morarity, Julianne Moore.* Disney's take on

female empowerment and self-worth won't please very many hard-core feminists, but anyone looking for a lightweight action comedy should take notice. Miller stars as the title character, a small-town underdog who makes a desperate bid for attention by confessing to a crime she didn't commit. Then things get really out of hand when crime boss Forsythe comes looking for her. ★★ DVD: $9.99

Gunfight at the O.K. Corral
(1957, 122 min, US, John Sturges) *Burt Lancaster, Kirk Douglas, Rhonda Fleming, Jo Van Fleet, Earl Holliman, Deforest Kelly.* Expert telling of the infamous gunfight between Doc Holliday-Wyatt Earp and the Clanton gang. A good companion piece covering the same story is John Ford's classic *My Darling Clementine.* ★★★½ DVD: $14.99, VHS: $9.99

The Gunfighter
(1950, 84 min, US, Henry King) *Gregory Peck, Karl Malden, Helen Westcott, Millard Mitchell, Ellen Corby.* A splendid western tale with Peck in fine form as a former gunfighter unable to rid himself of his past. The look and feel of the film is remarkably authentic, and Peck is ably supported by a good cast. ★★★½ VHS: $14.99

Gung Ho
(1986, 111 min, US, Ron Howard) *Michael Keaton, Gedde Watanabe, George Wendt, Mimi Rogers, John Turturro.* Pleasant comedy examining the cultural clash between Japanese and American workers. Keaton is certainly in his element as a Pennsylvania auto employee who convinces a Japanese interest to reopen his town's closed plant. Made a few years before the numerous headline-making Japanese takeovers. Watanabe steals the show as a harried Japanese exec. ★★½ DVD Letterbox: $14.99, VHS: $14.99

Gunga Din
(1939, 117 min, US, George Stevens) *Cary Grant, Victor McLaglen, Douglas Fairbanks, Jr., Joan Fontaine, Sam Jaffe.* Three rowdy, hard-fisted British soldiers enjoy adventures in 19th-century India battling the Thugees and dropping wisecracks all the way. Grant, McLaglen and Fairbanks are wonderful foils for each other in this rousing adventure film: the one which all others are judged by. Also with the splendid Jaffe as the most famous water carrier in literature. Based on Rudyard Kipling's poem. ★★★★

Bette Midler in *Gyspy (1993)*

Gunmen
(1993, 97 min, US, Deran Sarafian) *Christopher Lambert, Mario Van Peebles, Denis Leary, Patrick Stewart, Kadeem Hardison, Sally Kirkland.* A slightly above average adventure that excels in borrowing story lines from many other action films. A renegade DEA agent (Van Peebles) searching for $400 million belonging to a South American drug lord (Stewart) enlists the help of down-and-out Lambert, taking the pair on a wild chase with chain-smoking, wise-cracking Leary as their hunter. In spite of the fast pacing and over-the-top performances, the film is curiously aloof considering its theme and genre. ★★½ DVD: $9.99, VHS: $9.99

The Gunrunner
(1984, 92 min, Canada, Nardo Castillo) *Kevin Costner, Sara Botsford.* A then-unknown Costner stars as an idealist, circa 1926, who tries to finance guns for the Chinese Nationalist Revolution by selling bootleg liquor in Montreal. A very minor gangster saga. ★ VHS: $14.99

The Guns of Navarone
(1961, 157 min, US, J. Lee Thompson) *Gregory Peck, David Niven, Anthony Quinn, Irene Papas, Richard Harris, Anthony Quayle, James Darren.* The special effects won an Oscar, and everything else about this fast-moving, involving and action-packed WWII adventure is up to the same standard. Peck, Niven and Quinn head a strong international cast as the Allies go after a strategic Nazi placement of big guns. Based on the novel by Alistair MacLean. (Sequel: *Force Ten from Navarone*) ★★★½ DVD: $19.99, VHS: $14.99

The Guru
(2003, 95 min, US/GB, Daisy von Scherler Mayer) *Jimi Mistry, Heather Graham, Marisa Tomei, Michael McKean.* A comedy, a musical, a Bollywood homage, a calm indictment of the exclusion of Indians in Tinseltown and a satire of quick-fix spirituality in the U.S.: all in 95 minutes. *The Guru,* a fresh, fluffy comedy that's insubstantial but a lot of fun, has so many ideas, it's a small miracle that they all work together as they do. Mistry stars as Ramu Gupta, a young Indian dance teacher who leaves his home country for New York and a chance to make it big in entertainment. A series of funny circumstances takes him from performing in a porn movie to becoming a popular sex guru. The film includes a couple of high energy musical numbers and a diverse and comically gifted supporting cast. With this unconventional offering, director von Scherler Mayer makes amusing, naughty and energetic music. ★★★ DVD: $14.99, VHS: $9.99

Hollywood does Bollywood in *The Guru*

A Guy Named Joe

(1943, 120 min, US, Victor Fleming) *Spencer Tracy, Van Johnson, Irene Dunne, James Gleason, Lionel Barrymore.* Steven Spielberg liked this film so much he remade it in 1989 as *Always*. And it's hard to blame him. After being killed in action during WWII, pilot Tracy is sent back to Earth to look after young Johnson, who has become involved with Tracy's ex-girl Dunne. Okay, so the idea may sound silly, but who's to say it's not true. Pure romantic fluff, this 1940s morale booster may be sticky around the edges, but it certainly has heart. ★★½ VHS: $19.99

A Guy Thing

(2003, 101 min, US, Chris Koch) *Jason Lee, Selma Blair, Julia Stiles, James Brolin, Shawn Hatosy.* Tired, predictable and laughless, *A Guy Thing* is the kind of movie that begs the question: Why did these talented actors concede to do this movie? It's not like we've never seen a film about a groom-to-be who has second doubts after meeting "the woman of his dreams." Lee is embarrassingly awkward as the harried guy, Blair is stiff and artificial as the clueless fiancée, and Stiles seems pleased to only be on-screen for a few minutes. Too bad, for the only time the movie comes alive (a relative term) is when Lee and Stiles are on together. ★ DVD: $14.99, VHS: $9.99

Guys and Dolls

(1955, 150 min, US, Joseph L. Mankiewicz) *Marlon Brando, Frank Sinatra, Jean Simmons, Vivian Blaine, Stubby Kaye.* The Broadway musical based on Damon Runyon's colorful characters and featuring the music of Frank Loesser comes to the screen in this lavish and entertaining film. The story centers on gambler and rogue Sky Masterson's (Brando) budding affair with an innocent Salvation Army volunteer (Simmons). A razor-thin Sinatra also stars as a fellow gambler who has to find a site for their crap game. Blaine is unforgettable as Sinatra's squeaky-voiced girlfriend who stops the show with her rendition of "Adelaide's Lament." Brando in a singing role, the mesmerizing Runyon dialogue and great music combine to create an unusual, fun musical. ★★★ DVD: $14.99

Gypsy

(1962, 149 min, US, Mervyn LeRoy) *Rosalind Russell, Natalie Wood, Karl Malden, Ann Jillian.* Based on the Broadway landmark — itself based on the memoirs of stripper Gypsy Rose Lee — this stagey but entertaining musical stars Russell in the famed Ethel Merman role. Russell plays Rose, the driving force behind and mother of two child stars of the 1920s, one of whom becomes burlesque's reigning queen. Wood is the young Gypsy. Classic Stephen Sondheim-Jules Styne score includes "Everything's Coming Up Roses" and "Let Me Entertain You." (Remade in 1993) ★★★ DVD Letterbox: $19.99, VHS: $14.99, VHS Letterbox: $14.99

Gypsy

(1993, 140 min, US, Emile Ardolino) *Bette Midler, Peter Riegert, Cynthia Gibb, Ed Asner.* Taking over one of the most demanding and rewarding roles in musical theatre, that of the hard-driven stage mother Rose, Midler delivers a tour-de-force performance. It is to her credit that with the ghosts of Ethel Merman, Rosalind Russell, Angela Lansbury and Tyne Daly circling overhead (all had previously played Rose), she is able to give a fresh interpretation of a time-honored role that more than one actress had stamped her name upon. Though this small-screen version may somewhat lack the energy

and excitement of a live performance, there's little doubt that the story of Mama Rose and her daughter, actress/stripper Gypsy Rose Lee, is one of the greatest of all American musicals. ★★★½

The Gypsy

(1975, 90 min, France, Jose Giovanni) *Alain Delon, Annie Girardot.* The eternally sexy Delon plays a gypsy Robin Hood, a dashing thief who would steal anything for his beleaguered people. His criminal exploits and his valiant attempts to stay one step ahead of the police help make this an exciting and entertaining adventure film. ★★★

Habit

(1997, 112 min, US, Larry Fessenden) *Larry Fessenden, Meredith Snaider, Aaron Beall, Patricia Coleman.* Writer/director/star Fessenden portrays a New Yorker on the rebound who begins a relationship with a hot young creature he meets at a party. He's so smitten with her that even when he discovers she may be a genuine vampire, he can't bring himself to break it off. A perfectly modulated, intelligent horror film, *Habit* has a terrific NYC atmosphere, with naturalistic performances, excellent location work and a unique sense of erotic dread throughout. Snaider is an important part of the film's success as well, combining a smoldering sexuality with an alluring coldness that makes her vampire character wholly believable. ★★★½ DVD: $14.99, VHS: $14.99

Hackers

(1995, 105 min, US, Iain Softley) *Jonny Lee Miller, Angelina Jolie, Fisher Stevens, Jesse Bradford, Matthew Lillard, Lorraine Bracco.* Neither plausible nor exciting, *Hackers* stars the sullen Miller as a gifted high school hacker who moves to New York and quickly falls in with fellow trendy computer nerds. When one of their own accidentally hacks some private and incriminating files, a corporate bad guy (Stevens) and his goons set out to retrieve the disc and frame the kids. This, of course, inspires them to band together, prove their innocence and

expose the culprits. In spite of the film's sometimes impressive visuals, *Hackers* allows its clichéd teen characters' misfit hijinks to substitute for character development — and ultimately these kids are more hackneyed than hackers. ★★ DVD: $14.99

Haiku Tunnel

(2001, 86 min, US, Jacob Kornbluth & Josh Kornbluth) *Josh Kornbluth, Warren Keith, Helen Shumaker, Amy Resnick.* Josh Kornbluth stars as Josh Kornbluth in a "fictional" account of life as a temp. This is well-trod territory (somewhere between *Office Space* and *Office Killer*), but given how much time most of us spend inside offices, it's surprising there aren't more wry comedies dealing with such banalities as mailing "very important documents" and getting around the night security guards. Then again, even if these observations are original, they sure don't seem that way. *Haiku Tunnel* is at its best when the Kornbluths allow peeks into Josh's psyche, and his twisted way of avoiding responsibility while hiding behind his artistic temperament. It's not a particularly ambitious film, and shows its roots as a monologue, but Kornbluth is such an amiable kvetch that it's often hard to resist. ★★½ DVD Letterbox: $29.99, VHS: $102.99

Hail, Hero!

(1969, 97 min, US, David Miller) *Michael Douglas, Arthur Kennedy, Teresa Wright.* Douglas makes his film debut in this tense though plodding drama about an antiwar protester who enlists during the Vietnam War. ★★ VHS: $59.99

Hail Mary (Je Vous Salue Marie)

(1985, 90 min, France, Jean-Luc Godard) *Myriem Roussel, Thierry Rode.* This controversial film is truly not as blasphemous or shocking as it has been made out to be. Rather, *Hail Mary* is a reverent modern retelling of the Incarnation and Virgin Birth of Christ. The setting is 1980s France where Mary works at her father's gas station. Her selection to be the Mother of Christ, and how she deals with this, provides the central theme to this religious work. (French with English subtitles) ★★★

Hail the Conquering Hero

(1944, 101 min, US, Preston Sturges) *Eddie Bracken, William Demarest, Ella Raines, Franklin Pangborn.* Sturges' miraculous satire stars Bracken as the conquering hero of the title, a medically discharged Marine whose small hometown thinks him a war hero. Sturges lets loose a comic assault on poli-

Hail the Conquering Hero

Hamlet (Ethan Hawke)

tics, mother love and popular opinion as Bracken's Woodrow Truesmith gallantly tries to set the record straight, but is sabotaged at every turn. Bracken (as in Sturges' *Miracle of Morgan's Creek*) is priceless, and Demarest shines as a "real" war hero trying to make Bracken look the part in his mother's and sweetheart's eyes. ★★★★ VHS: $14.99

Hair

(1979, 121 min, US, Milos Forman) *Treat Williams, John Savage, Beverly D'Angelo, Annie Golden, Michael Jeter, Dorsey Wright, Cheryl Barnes, Nell Carter, Melba Moore, Don Dacus.* Forman's exuberant adaptation of the '60s landmark play shines with a wealth of cinematic finesse, heightened by Twyla Tharp's visceral choreography and the inspired performances of Williams, D'Angelo and Savage. They said it was unfilmable, and Forman proved them wrong. ★★★★ DVD: $14.99

Hairspray

(1988, 94 min, US, John Waters) *Divine, Ricki Lake, Sonny Bono, Pia Zadora, Debbie Harry, Rick Ocasek.* Waters, the Prince of Puke and sleazemaster extraordinaire, put aside his odious ways to make this glorious sendup of the "teen scene" movies of the late '50s and early '60s. Set in Baltimore (where else?), the story follows Tracy Turnblad (Lake), a heavyset teen whose main ambition in life is to be on a local TV dance program. But she is soon faced with a moral dilemma when the producers ban her black friends from attending. Waters proves up to the task of exploring the racial issue, but wisely keeps the lid on all-out polemic and heavy-handedness by sticking with his strength — namely outrageous comedy. ★★★ DVD: $19.99

Half a Loaf of Kung Fu

(1985, 96 min, Hong Kong, Chen Chi-Hwa) *Jackie Chan.* The incomparable Chan stars as a buffoonish drifter looking for work, wisdom and the ultimate kung fu master in Imperial China. From the opening credits, you'll know that this self-parodying kung fu epic approaches its subject with tongue planted firmly in cheek. ★★★ VHS: $39.99

Half-Baked

(1998, 73 min, US, Tamra Davis) *Dave Chappelle, Jim Breuer, Harland Williams, Guillermo Diaz, Rachel True, Clarence Williams III, Snoop Doggy Dogg, Cameos: Janeane Garofalo, Willie Nelson, Stephen Baldwin, Bob Saget, Jon Stewart, Tommy Chong.* Dude, this sucks. *Half-Baked* stars Chappelle as the leader of a quartet of stoners with

loser jobs. When one is jailed for the murder of a cop (he fed a diabetic police horse pounds of junk food), the rest start raising his bail by selling grade-A ganja pilfered from the hospital where Chappelle works as a custodian. But the plot doesn't really matter; the point here is to string together a few movie parodies, superfluous cameos, and, of course, lots of pothead jokes, most of which Cheech and Chong would have thought dumb. Despite the bright cast, *Half-Baked* is generally a waste; for a truly funny and completely authentic look at the stoner culture, check out *Dazed and Confused.* ★★

Half Moon Street

(1986, 90 min, GB, Bob Swaim) *Sigourney Weaver, Michael Caine, Keith Buckley.* Muddled adaptation of Paul Theroux's novel "Dr. Slaughter," with Weaver in the role of a financially depressed American Ph. D. in London who tries to make ends meet by becoming an "escort" for politically influential clientele — in this case, the ubiquitous Caine as a high-powered British diplomat. Anyone who's ever fantasized about the statuesque Ms. Weaver will find this a guilty pleasure at best, as nudity seems to have been written into her contract. ★ DVD Dual: $14.99

Half of Heaven

(1987, 127 min, Spain, Gutierrez Aragon) *Angela Molina, Margarita Lozano.* This charming story of a young woman's growth, loves and successes reads like a modern-day fairy tale with characters including two mean and ugly sisters and a grandmother imbued with special powers. Set in 1960s Franco Spain, our story follows Rosa (Molina), an ambitious and self-reliant young widow who, with her daughter, leaves her family and the peasant lifestyle to find opportunities in the city. A wonderful story of one woman determined to make it on her own. While lulling you with the film's light and entertaining style, the director throws in biting commentary on Franco Spain, imbued with a fine Buñuelian sense of humor. (Spanish with English subtitles) ★★★

Hallelujah!

(1929, 90 min, US, King Vidor) *Daniel L. Haynes, Nina Mae McKinney, William Fontaine.* Though not the first film to feature an all-black cast, this simple morality tale is probably the best of its type and time. One must look beyond the patronizing and stereotypes, for at work here is quite an accessible story of an honest man caught in the clutches of evil and his redemption. Heading a very dedicated cast, Haynes plays a trusting cotton-pickin' farmer who is led down the path of temptation by vixen McKinney. When

tragedy strikes, Haynes turns to God, only to be once again led astray. Director Vidor has crafted a gripping work, and there are spellbinding scenes that equal or surpass any film of the day, including one of a crowd being worked into a religious frenzy. There are several accomplished musical numbers as well. ★★★½

Halloween

(1978, 90 min, US, John Carpenter) *Jamie Lee Curtis, Donald Pleasence, Nancy Loomis, P.J. Soles.* Carpenter's celebrated horror film is credited with starting the "slasher" genre, which has given way to Freddy, Jason and the likes. There's more than just blood and guts here, though, in this suspenseful tale of little Michael Meyers returning to his small hometown to pick off Curtis and friends. Pleasence is the alarmed doctor trying to warn anyone who will listen. (Followed by 7 sequels) ★★★ DVD Letterbox Extended version: $19.99, DVD Letterbox 25th Anniversary: $29.99, VHS Letterboxed: $14.99, VHS Letterbox Extended version: $9.99

Halloween: H2O (Twenty Years Later)

(1998, 85 min, US, Steve Miner) *Jamie Lee Curtis, Adam Arkin, Josh Hartnett, Michelle Williams, LL Cool J, Janet Leigh, Joseph Gordon-Levitt.* Curtis returns after a 17-year absence in this enjoyable horror outing that has an overall sense of fun, lots of scares and a director who actually knows what he's doing. Curtis is Laurie Strode, who back when Carter was president seemed to be having some sibling problems with brother Michael Myers. It's now 20 years later, and Laurie is still haunted by the memories of her murderous bro. She has a teenage son, is a headmistress at a posh boarding school, and has a boyfriend on the side. Things seem good — until Michael decides to initiate a family reunion. Director Miner forgoes the splatter sensationalism and concentrates on scares and suspense, which is what distinguished the first *Halloween* film. But the best thing is Curtis, who shows she can kick ass with the best of them. Jamie's mom Janet turns up for a great cameo and in-joke. (Sequel: *Halloween: Resurrection*) ★★★ DVD: $14.99, VHS: $9.99

Halloween: Resurrection

(2002, 89 min, US, Rick Rosenthal) *Busta Rhymes, Jamie Lee Curtis, Brad Loree, Bianca Kajlich, Thomas Ian Nicholas, Sean Patrick Thomas, Tyra Banks.* Or, Number 8, for those still counting. Despite a ridiculous "explanation" for Michael Myers' still being alive, the opening of the film isn't bad, though it actually feels like the ending to a better film. The film proper is standard sequel cheese: Rhymes and Banks decide to cash in on the Myers craze by recruiting some photogenic college students to spend the night in Michael's old home in Haddonfield, while broadcasting the event live on Halloween night. The participants are equipped with personal cameras, allowing for some sub-*Blair Witch*, low-tech "scares." Poorly written, mostly unscary, and with visual references to earlier sequels, *Halloween: Resurrection* can be mildly enjoyed with a group of *Halloween*-fan friends (and a case of beer), but that's about the best that can be said for this time waster. ★½ DVD Letterbox: $19.99, VHS: $14.99

Hamlet

(1948, 153 min, GB, Laurence Olivier) *Laurence Olivier, Eileen Herlie, Basil Sydney, Jean Simmons, Stanley Holloway, Peter Cushing.* Olivier directed and stars in this superlative adaptation of Shakespeare's tragedy. Olivier embodies the melancholy Hamlet, as much a victim of his lack of decisiveness as of his circumstances. The supporting players match him in their assumptions of their roles. Oscar for Best Picture; Olivier won as Best Actor. ★★★★ DVD: $29.99

Hamlet

(1969, 114 min, GB, Tony Richardson) *Nicol Williamson, Anthony Hopkins, Marianne Faithful, Gordon Jackson, Anjelica Huston.* Richardson's little seen, imaginative interpretation was filmed at the Round House, London's equivalent of off-Broadway. Done in period dress, this *Hamlet* has a contemporary feel to it accented by dark, claustrophobic staging with little movement of the actors and a concentration on the intense faces of the leads, which include Hopkins and Faithful as Ophelia. Williamson's performance of a confused Hamlet, full of neurotic twitches and personal uncertainties, is riveting. ★★½

Hamlet

(1976, 67 min, GB, Celestino Coronado) *Quentin Crisp, Lindsay Kemp, Anthony Meyer, David Meyer, Helen Mirren.* Feverish, dreamlike and campy to a '70s fault, this outlandish interpretation of William Shakespeare's "Hamlet" is a low-budget druggy, flesh-filled drama staged by the Lindsay Kemp Company. Twin brothers play the oft-naked, much tortured lead, Mirren is both Gertrude and Ophelia, and a much made-up Crisp is Polonius. This Fellini-esque adaptation, condensed and altered a bit, takes place in front of a gauze background and is mostly suited to fans of the avant-garde. All caution is thrown to the wind as director Coronado fills the screen with erotic dances, futuristic costuming transvestites and two Hamlets running around clothed only in jockstraps. This isn't your mother's Shakespeare! ★★★ VHS: $19.99

Hamlet

(1990, 135 min, GB, Franco Zeffirelli) *Mel Gibson, Glenn Close, Alan Bates, Helena Bonham Carter, Ian Holm, Paul Scofield, Pete Postlethwaite.* In a sumptuous retelling of the classic tragedy, Gibson gives a fiery, credible and even inspired interpretation of Shakespeare's Melancholy Dane. And he is given remarkable support. Close is superlative as Hamlet's mother, Gertrude, who unknowingly marries her husband's murderer. Bates makes an arresting Claudius, Bonham Carter is a fragile Ophelia and Holm is a most amusing Polonius. Director Zeffirelli brings great energy to the work, and his stagings are carefully conceived and executed. ★★★½ DVD Letterbox: $19.99

Hamlet

(1996, 243 min, GB, Kenneth Branagh) *Kenneth Branagh, Julie Christie, Derek Jacobi, Richard Briers, Kate Winslet, Charlton Heston, Michael*

Hamlet (Kenneth Branagh)

Maloney, Jack Lemmon, Billy Crystal, Robin Williams. Attempting to film the entire four-hour verse of Shakespeare's masterpiece, the first time the entire play has been adapted for the screen, director-star Branagh has created one of the most thrilling and accessible adaptations of *Hamlet* to date. It's fairly extravagant in detail but significantly intimate in emotion. In addition to his articulate direction, Branagh as actor is revelatory as the mad Prince of Denmark. His performance never waivers in intensity or focus, and he is able to convey lighter moments heretofore unrealized. The supporting cast for the most part is examplary. Jacobi absolutely scintillates as the calculating Claudius, Christie is a regal Gertrude, and Briers' exhilaratingly new interpretation of Polonius is more politician than fool. ★★★★ VHS Letterbox: $24.99

Hamlet

(2000, 112 min, US, Michael Almereyda) *Ethan Hawke, Julia Stiles, Sam Shepard, Bill Murray, Diane Venora, Kyle MacLachlan, Liev Schreiber, Steve Zahn, Casey Affleck, Jeffrey Wright, Paul Bartel.* Director Almereyda offers an imaginative and playful interpretation as he sets Shakespeare's classic amidst the skyscrapers of 21st-century Manhattan. But while he hits the mark, several of his cast are proving iambicly challenged. In the title role, Hawke provides an interesting nihilistic hipness, but it doesn't quite play in the soliloquies. Murray trips all over himself as Polonious, but Schreiber and MacLachlan are dutiful as Laertes and Claudius respectively. Overall, it's an exciting revision of the tale, but for the definitive character interpretation, stick with Branagh's. ★★½ DVD: $19.99, VHS: $9.99

Hammers over the Anvil

(1992, 101 min, Australia, Ann Turner) *Russell Crowe, Charlotte Rampling, Alexander Outhred.* An occasionally sappy tale of a horse breaker who gets involved with an older married woman. Caught in the middle is a polio stricken boy named Alan whose dreams of riding are overshadowed by his idolizing of East Driscoll (Crowe). In addition, Alan's obvious attraction to the older Grace further complicates his quest for contentment in a life that he already finds to be quite frustrating. A rather impressive performance by Crowe in a very early role makes this film worth seeing, not to mention the opportunity to see him riding a horse naked. ★★½ DVD: $24.99, VHS: $19.99

Hammett

(1983, 97 min, US, Wim Wenders) *Frederic Forrest, Peter Boyle, Marilu Henner, Sylvia Sydney, Samuel Fuller.* After interminable delays in production, editing and distribution, Wenders' first American feature is a surprisingly intriguing, hard-boiled yarn stemming from the fictional exploits of pulp novelist extraordinaire Dashiell Hammett (Forrest). As with the best gumshoe tales, the plot is a foggy series of double crosses and blackmail schemes. The film boasts an impressive gallery of supporting players and stylish, shadowy sets. ★★★

The Hand

(1981, 104 min, US, Oliver Stone) *Michael Caine, Andrea Marcovicci, Viveca Lindfors.* When cartoonist Caine's hand is severed in a car accident, it follows him around and kills his enemies — or does it? Stone keeps his trademark stylistic flourishes well concealed in this early directorial outing. ★ VHS: $14.99

Hand Gun

(1994, 90 min, US, Whitney Ransick) *Treat Williams, Seymour Cassel, Paul Schulze.* Ransick debuts with this gritty urban slice-of-life about a career criminal whose big score proves to be his last. Cassel stars as the lone survivor of an ill-fated heist who, wounded in the ensuing gun battle, tells each of his two sons, Williams and Schulze, different clues as to the whereabouts of the stolen loot, thereby forming an uneasy and treacherous alliance between the two. Ransick mixes jarring violence with well-drawn characters to create a tale that is tense and entertaining. Williams gives a particularly charismatic performance. ★★★ VHS: $9.99

The Hand That Rocks the Cradle

(1992, 110 min, US, Curtis Hanson) *Rebecca DeMornay, Annabella Sciorra, Matt McCoy, Ernie Hudson, Julianna Moore.* A parents' nightmare makes for an enjoyably trashy if contrived thriller. Having created a sense of dread in *Bad Influence,* director Hanson resorts to all the tricks to give a potent scare or two. Sciorra and McCoy are almost the perfect new-age couple. They're madly in love, have a perfect home, perfect children . . . gee, the perfect life. Into their home comes what they think to be the perfect nanny, DeMornay. But she blames Sciorra for her husband's death and now has a score to settle. DeMornay is actually quite good as a demented Mary Poppins, and her effective performance is at the heart of *Cradle*'s modest success. ★★½ DVD: $14.99, VHS: $9.99

A Handful of Dust

(1988, 118 min, GB, Charles Sturridge) *James Wilby, Kristin Scott Thomas, Rupert Graves, Alec Guinness, Judi Dench, Anjelica Huston.* A delight for all fans of "Masterpiece Theatre," the books of Evelyn Waugh and of films which opulently depict the trials, tribulations and eventual decay of England's landed gentry in the early part of this century. Wilby stars as a naïvely contented land owner who unwittingly loses both his loves and his serenity when he allows his restless wife a "weekend" flat in London. The fun loving woman (Scott Thomas) soon falls for a penniless charmer in her frantic search for freedom and passion. Not as witty as Waugh's "Black Mischief" or "Decline and Fall," the story is nonetheless classy entertainment highlighted by a stellar cast. ★★★ VHS: $19.99

The Handmaid's Tale

(1990, 109 min, US, Volker Schlöndorff) *Natasha Richardson, Robert Duvall, Faye Dunaway, Elizabeth McGovern, Aidan Quinn.* Imagine a world so closely conformed to Phyllis Schlafly's dictates that even *she* couldn't get out of the house. In the near future, excessive environmental pollution has sterilized a majority of the population. The ruling reactionary theocracy therefore sends fertile females to the households of the ruling elite, where they are expected to copulate and procreate for the greater glory of God and state. Schlöndorff directs Harold Pinter's adaptation of Margaret Atwood's novel, fully utilizing the consumate talents of a gifted cast. ★★★ DVD: $19.99, VHS: $14.99

The Hands of Orlac

(1960, 95 min, France/GB, Edmond T. Greville) *Mel Ferrer, Christopher Lee, Donald Pleasence.* When crippled pianist Ferrer gets new hands transplanted from an executed murderer, he picks up some bad habits with them. Unimaginative and rather boring. (aka: *Hands of a Strangler*) ★ VHS: $12.99

Hands on a Hardbody

(1998, 97 min, US, S.R. Bindler) Longview, Texas, is the setting for possibly the most bizarre car promotion in history: Every year, customers compete to see who can lay their hands on a truck for the longest period of time. Last person left touching the truck wins it. Not only does this contest draw an eclectic group of characters, but it pushes them to the brink of madness as sleep deprivation and exhaustion set in (4 or 5 days usually produces a winner). As much a study in the limits of human endurance as materialism, *Hands on a Hardbody* is hilarious without being exploitative, as the participants fall into fits of delirium-induced laughter. ★★★½

Hang 'em High

(1968, 114 min, US, Ted Post) *Clint Eastwood, Dennis Hopper, Ben Johnson, Alan Hale, Jr.* When his lynching doesn't take, Eastwood wants satisfaction from the guys who did such a lousy job. This American take on Leone's spaghetti westerns lacks that director's stylish flourishes, but this still manages to entertain. ★★½ DVD: $14.99, VHS: $9.99

Hangin' with the Homeboys

(1991, 89 min, US, Joseph Vasquez) *Doug E. Doug, John Leguizamo, Mario Joyner.* Four homeboys' search for a good time on a Friday night takes them from the South Bronx to Manhattan. It's a simple premise, but Vasquez uses it to good effect in chronicling the world view of disaffected black and Hispanic youths. Produced on a shoestring budget, the film suffers slightly from an unfocused script and some inconsistent performances (with the exception of Leguizamo — who offers some of the more poignant moments), but it still manages to entertain in spite of its shortcomings. ★★★ DVD: $19.99, VHS: $14.99

The Hanging Garden

(1998, 91 min, Canada, Thom Fitzgerald) *Chris Leavins, Kerry Fox, Seanna McKenna, Peter MacNeill, Sarah Polley.* This impressively mature first feature from writer-director Fitzgerald examines the emotional tribulations of a family on the brink of destruction. The story is set in a Nova Scotia home where the extended family is reunited for a wedding. William, a young man who left the family as an obese, unhappy and closeted teenager, now returns after a 10-year absence thin, attractive and openly gay. Told with biting humor, symbolism and moments of surrealism (William's memories of his schoolboy love, who is marrying his sister, begin to stir long buried memories). Reminiscent of *Sweetie*, the film adroitly balances the ranging emotions of its characters; the result being an involving, unsettling but moving story. ★★★ DVD: $19.99

The Hanging Tree

(1959, 108 min, US, Delmer Daves) *Gary Cooper, Karl Malden, Maria Schell, George C. Scott, Ben Piazza.* Cooper brings a quiet strength to this involving western which casts the legendary star as a mysterious stranger who takes residence at an 1870s Montana gold mining town. Cooper plays a doctor with an uncertain past. Among those who cross his path are blinded immigrant Schell, seedy prospector Malden and, in their film debuts, Scott as a malicious preacher and stage actor Piazza as a potential lynch-mob victim whom Cooper saves. ★★★

Hanging Up

(2000, 95 min, US, Diane Keaton) *Meg Ryan, Diane Keaton, Lisa Kudrow, Walter Matthau.* Ryan's appeal is almost enough to make this a tolerable experience, a forced comedy-drama that awkwardly shifts between heavy-handed dramatics and sappy humor. It's the story of three sisters (Ryan, Keaton, Kudrow) who are forced to come to terms with the aging of their father (Matthau). Director Keaton has assembled a solid cast, but they're given to hysterics and only an occasion register any true emotion. ★★ DVD: $9.99, VHS: $9.99

Hanna K.

(1983, 108 min, France, Constantin Costa-Gavras) *Jill Clayburgh, Jean Yanne, Gabriel Byrne, Mohammed Bakri.* Clayburgh stars as a lawyer torn between her conflicting involvement with an Israeli lover (the District Attorney of Jerusalem) and an enigmatic Palestinian whom she defends against him in court. Caught up in the political strife, her perceptions of herself, her relationships and Israel, her adopted land, are profoundly altered. The film presents many questions which, though well-meaning, are clumsily handled. (Filmed in English) ★★

Hannah and Her Sisters

(1986, 107 min, US, Woody Allen) *Mia Farrow, Barbara Hershey, Dianne Wiest, Michael Caine, Woody Allen, Lloyd Nolan, Maureen O'Sullivan, Max von Sydow, Carrie Fisher, Sam Waterston, Daniel Stern, Julie Kavner, Joanna Gleason, Tony Roberts.* Brilliantly scripted and directed, *Hannah and Her Sisters* stands as one of Allen's greatest accomplishments. Featuring Farrow, an ascendant Hershey and the Oscar-winning Wiest as three sisters — whose lives are inextricably entwined amongst a host of friends, relatives, and lovers — *Hannah* is a skillful and subtle exploration of human interdependencies. This illuminating work features a superb supporting cast, including the wonderful, Oscar-winning Caine. ★★★★ DVD: $19.99

Hannibal

(2001, 131 min, US, Ridley Scott) *Anthony Hopkins, Julianne Moore, Ray Liotta, Gary Oldman, Giancarlo Giannini, Frankie R. Faison.* Moody, suspenseful and a little too gratuitous in its gory depiction of evil genius, *Hannibal* picks up the story of Dr. Hannibal Lecter ten years after *The Silence of the Lambs*. With a new director on board for this third chapter in the Lecter series, *Hannibal* retains the vision of director Scott much like *Silence* was a product of Jonathan Demme. Gone is the psychological cat-and-mouse games between Lecter and FBI agent Clarice Starling (Moore who replaced Jodie Foster). In its place is a visceral panorama of unbridled menace, a graphic display of malevolence captured with chilling deliberation. The story follows Starling in her attempt to track down Lecter after he is returned to the FBI's Ten Most Wanted list. Returning to the role which won him an Oscar, Hopkins delights in the sinister civility of Lecter once more, giving another precise portrait both controlled and cunning. It's the centerpiece of a devilishly entertaining, unnerving film. (Prequel: *Red Dragon*) ★★★ DVD Special Edition: $22.99, DVD Theatrical Cut: $14.99, VHS Special Edition: $9.99

Hanover Street

(1979, 109 min, US, Peter Hyams) *Harrison Ford, Leslie-Anne Down, Christopher Plummer, Alec McCowan.* American soldier Ford finds love in war-torn Britain with a married woman (Down) in this uninspired romantic drama set during WWII. ★★ DVD: $9.99, VHS: $9.99

Hans Christian Anderson

(1952, 120 min, US, Charles Vidor) *Danny Kaye, Farley Granger.* Kaye lends considerable charm to this wondrous children's tale about storyteller Hans Christian Andersen. Frank Loesser's score includes "Inch Worm" and "Ugly Duckling." ★★★ DVD: $14.99

Hanussen

(1989, 140 min, Hungary/West Germany, István Szabó) *Klaus Maria Brandauer, Erland Josephson.* Following *Mephisto* and *Colonel Redl*, this third collaboration between Szabó and actor Brandauer features Brandauer as an Austrian soldier in WWI who acquires an unsettlingly accurate ability to foretell the future. Settling in Berlin, he becomes a successful magician and clairvoyant. His comfortable life becomes entangled when he foresees fascism's rise and the persecution of the Jews, and must decide on keeping quiet or exposing them. Nominated for an Academy Award for Best Foreign Film, the film offers little dramatic punch but is beautifully photographed and has Brandauer giving a riveting performance as an ordinary man caught between powerful forces. (German with English subtitles) ★★★

Happenstance

(2001, 97 min, France, Laurent Firode) *Audrey Tautou, Faudel, Eric Savin.* While riding the metro one morning, waifish store clerk Irene (Tautou) is told by a fortune-teller that she will meet the love of her life that day. This encounter triggers a series of seemingly unrelated karmic events, prompted by a handful of disparate, lovelorn Parisians, each one unwittingly conspiring to bring Irene together with her as-yet-discovered true love. The French title "Le Battement d'Ailes du Papillon" — meaning literally "The Beating of Butterfly Wings" — concerns the chaos theory that the tiny fluttering of a butterfly can kick-start a meteorological chain reaction that results in a thunderstorm halfway around the world. As played out here, tiny moments of chance, cause and consequence send ripple effects throughout Paris and, as fate would have it, they coalesce with clock-like precision. By turns whimsical, heartbreaking and sometimes a tad too predictable for its own good, the bittersweet *Happenstance* casts a feather-weight charm — and Tautou, the doe-eyed star of *Amélie*, is sheer effervescence. (French with English subtitles) ★★★ DVD: $29.99, VHS: $19.99

The Happiest Days of Your Life

(1950, 81 min, GB, Frank Launder) *Margaret Rutherford, Alastair Sim, Joyce Grenfell.* A charming example of postwar British comedy, this small yet delightfully droll and often hilarious tale stars those two British national treasures: Sim and Rutherford. It's a new school year at the Nutbourne Academy for Boys, and when 100 girls arrive to share accomodations, it's anything but business as usual. Sim smartly plays the befuddled Nutbourne schoolmaster, and Rutherford is wonderful as his girls' school counterpart. The film's first half is full of entendres and puns (some may be lost on American audiences); the second half hits a frenzied, screwball pitch as students and faculty in both camps attempt to simultaneously conceal Nutbourne's coed status from rival school personnel and visiting parents. ★★★ VHS: $29.99

H

THE DISCERNING FILM LOVER'S GUIDE

Happily Ever After
(1986, 92 min, Brazil, Bruno Barreto) *Regina Duarte, Paul Castelli.* This electrifying drama borrows elements from such films as *After Hours* and *Montenegro* to create a slightly surreal and sexually charged atmosphere, where the unexpected can always happen and people fall prey to their own desires. Barreto fashions a humorous, suspenseful tale of a woman's unlikely experience with a man she first meets in a dream. Duarte delivers a powerfully controlled performance. Barreto's taut direction prevents the film from degenerating into just another skin flick. Menacing landscapes and Buñuelian adventures with a steady undercurrent of sexual excitement. (Portuguese with English subtitles) ★★★½ VHS: $69.99

Happiness
(1934, 69 min, USSR, Alexander Medvedkin) Subtitled "A Tale About a Hapless Mercenary Loser, His Wife, His Well-Fed Neighbor, a Priest, a Nun, and Other Old Relics," this free-wheeling slapstick farce stops at nothing in presenting its own skewed version of reality. Infused with elements of vaudeville, burlesque and even surrealism, the comedy, based on folklore, revolves around a farmer who finds a purse filled with money. Believing that he has found everlasting happiness, the farmer finds instead bizarre disaster every which way he turns. Banned in Russia for over 40 years, this satire on man's and society's greed features everything from polka-dotted horses to nuns in see-through tunics. (Silent with orchestral accompaniment) ★★★ VHS: $29.99

Happiness
(1998, 139 min, US, Todd Solondz) *Philip Seymour Hoffman, Jane Adams, Dylan Baker, Lara Flynn Boyle, Ben Gazzara, Louise Lasser, Cynthia Stevenson, Camryn Manheim, Elizabeth Ashley, Jon Lovitz.* The final word in family dysfunctionalism, *Happiness* is writer-director Solondz's harrowing follow-up to *Welcome to the Dollhouse*. As uncompromising as that film was, nothing can prepare the viewer for the gruelling, bitter, funny and insightful examination of the deterioration of a familial psyche that's on display in this brilliantly written, to-hell-and-back character piece. Effortlessly balancing the stories of its many characters, Solondz isn't wearing rose-colored glasses, for his depiction of human flaws, emotional scars and a suburban morass is brutally honest. The story follows three sisters, their family and relationships. At first we aren't even aware that most of the characters are related, but little by little Solondz gives just enough information. Each is given equal time, and none are shorted in composition. *Happiness* is often difficult to watch, but it is a riveting experience. Even in light of its integrity to character and honesty of the written word, it's not for everyone. ★★★★ DVD Signature Selection: $19.99

Happy Birthday, Gemini
(1980, 107 min, US, Richard Benner) *Alan Rosenberg, Madeline Kahn, Rita Moreno, Robert Viharo, Sarah Molcomb, David Marshall Grant.* Ridiculous stereotypes, terrible acting and a tired script make this film version of Albert Innaurato's 1970s Broadway comedy "Gemini" a messy failure. Set in the row houses of Italian South Philadelphia, the story revolves around a closet case, Francis (Rosenberg), who, while in the midst of a sexual identity crisis, must contend with his wacky neighbors, overbearing father and the unexpected arrival of two of his WASPish Harvard friends. Problems arise when schoolmate Judith (Molcomb) wants to resume their tentative college affair, but Francis is actually attracted to her blond brother Randy

(Grant). His tormented indecision finally comes to a head as he begins to accept his homosexuality. From the director of *Outrageous*. ★

Happy Gilmore
(1996, 92 min, US, Dennis Dugan) *Adam Sandler, Ben Stiller, Christopher McDonald, Julie Bowen, Frances Bay, Carl Weathers, Bob Barker.* After the abysmal *Billy Madison*, Sandler grows up ever so slightly in this equally moronic golf comedy which produces but a few (insipid) laughs. Happy Gilmore (Sandler) is a hockey nut/player with no talent for the game; in fact, he has no talent for any sport except golf, which he discovers accidentally. When his grandmother is in danger of losing her house, he sets out to win a few bucks in golf tournaments. A puerile smart aleck and perpetual loser, Happy's disregard for convention and his surprising ability make him a hero as he turns the golfing world topsy-turvy. Though *Happy Gilmore* is only marginally better than *Madison*, the jokes are still aimed at prepubescents, and in his first few film appearances Sandler has only honed the skill of being annoying. ★½

Happy, Texas
(1999, 98 min, US, Mark Illsley) *Jeremy Northam, Steve Zahn, Ally Walker, Illeana Douglas, William H. Macy.* Remember *The Gay Deceivers*, that campy little curiosity from the late '60s about two straight guys who have to pretend to be gay? It's sort of been updated for the '90s as *Happy, Texas*, a curious little comedy about two straight guys who have to pretend to be gay. There's a few laughs, and a wonderful performance by Macy as the sheriff of the small Texas town in which these two cons hide out; but ultimately it's a gay-themed comedy lacking any gay sensibility. Northam and the zany Zahn are the prison escapees who take the identity of two gay beauty pageant coordinators. Greeted with open arms by the town, they continue the charade with the intent of robbing the town's bank. It's a good premise, but the filmmakers never go far enough with it. It's innocuous fun that will make you no better or worse for having seen it. ★★½ DVD: $14.99, VHS: $9.99

Happy Together
(1997, 98 min, Hong Kong, Wong Kar-Wai) *Tony Leung, Leslie Cheung.* The title is purely ironic in Kar-Wai's melancholy dissection of a gay relationship in the throngs of dissolution. More of a mood piece rather than a traditional narrative-driven drama, the story begins with two handsome men, Ho Po-wing (Cheung) and Lai Yiu-fai (Leung), making passionate and graphic love. That physical and emotional closeness will never appear again. The two go on a tempestuous vacation to Argentina where they argue, run out of money, and drift apart in a dark, desolate, cold and wet Buenos Aries. One begins working in a nightclub to earn his money back home while the other goes for a more carefree playboy life. Their vain attempt at reconciliation is doomed — they can't reconnect yet they can't seem to leave. Filmed in an experimental style, the film is a bold look at the breakdown of love and intimacy. ★★★½ DVD: $29.99, VHS: $19.99

Harakiri
(1962, 134 min, Japan, Masaki Kobayashi) Set in 17th-century Japan after a long series of civil wars, *Harakiri* centers on the life of the samurai in peacetime. Having no lord to serve and no war to fight, the samurai can either live in poverty or commit harakiri, the suicide ritual. A young samurai appears at the door of a rich lord's castle asking permission to perform the ritual, hoping instead the lord will offer him money to get rid of him. When the lord calls the soldier's bluff, the youth's father-in-law petitions the

lord to take his son-in-law's place, but not before telling the tale of how the boy warrior came to be a samurai. Kobayashi brilliantly weaves the many stories together as he effortlessly slips back and forth through time, aided greatly by the gorgeous black-and-white cinematography of Yoshio Miyajima. *Harakiri* is a classic waiting to find its cult. (Japanese with English subtitles) ★★★★ VHS: $29.99

Hard Boiled
(1992, 127 min, Hong Kong, John Woo) *Chow Yun-Fat, Tony Leung, Philip Chan.* After an exhilarating teaming in *The Killer*, the Chinese Scorsese and De Niro, Woo and Yun-Fat, triumph again with this spectacular amphetamine-overdriven thriller. Yun-Fat plays a renegade cop named Tequila, whose mission is to halt the operation of an ultraviolent gun-smuggling ring. From the incredible opening shootout, which packs more punch than ten *Lethal Weapon*s, to the everything-but-the-kitchen-sink ending, this action epic succeeds on many levels thanks to the multilayered characterizations and story, focused and creative direction, and pulse-pounding action sequences that thrust this pulp melodrama to near-operatic grandeur. (Cantonese with English subtitles) ★★★★

Hard Choices
(1986, 90 min, US, Rick King) *Gary McCleery, Margaret Klenck, John Sayles, Spalding Grey.* A teenager (McCleery) enters the criminal justice system through an innocent involvement with a robbery, and becomes involved with the social worker (Klenck) assigned to his case. An interesting look at the process of enforcement and corrections in this country, and highlighted by an intriguing portrayal by Sayles of a jaded, flippant drug smuggler. Based on a true story. ★★½ VHS: $14.99

A Hard Day's Night
(1964, 85 min, GB, Richard Lester) *The Beatles, Wilfrid Brambell, Norman Rossington, Victor Spinetti.* Though 12 songs and filler would have made a hit, The Beatles and director Lester instead fashioned this inventive musical comedy classic filled with the frenzied emotion of early Beatlemania. Lester's early style shines through in this playful day-in-the-life look at the emerging rock stars. ★★★★ DVD 2-disc Collector's Edition: $19.99, VHS: $9.99

Hard Eight
(1997, 101 min, US, Paul Thomas Anderson) *Gwyneth Paltrow, Philip Baker Hall, John C. Reilly, Samuel L. Jackson, Philip Seymour Hoffman.* Mix the staccato, tough-talk style of David Mamet and the existential forcefulness of Melville's *Bob Le Flambeur* and you get *Hard Eight*, a scruffy independent winner that will appeal to those who, well, like scruffy independent winners. Although set in Las Vegas and Reno, the film really takes place in that neon twilight zone where glitz and seediness meet. Reilly, a naïve loser in desperate need of $6,000, gets a chance to change his luck when he meets Hall, a world-weary gambler who takes him under his wing and shows him how to turn meager earnings into thousands of dollars in freebies. After a few successful years, the mens' friendship changes when Reilly falls for Paltrow, a cocktail waitress who turns tricks on the side. Directed with icy precision by Anderson, *Hard Eight* is more concerned with atmosphere and characters than intricate plotting, though there's some surprising wrenches thrown into the story. Hall turns in a mesmerizing career performance as the obsessively controlling gambler. ★★★½ DVD: $27.99

Hard Rain

(1998, 98 min, US, Mikael Salomon) *Morgan Freeman, Christian Slater, Randy Quaid, Minnie Driver, Betty White, Richard Dysart, Ed Asner.* If you took *The Thomas Crown Affair* and breeded it with *The Poseidon Adventure*, *Hard Rain* would be their bastard son. There's lots of water, boats and assorted money-grabbing types all trying to outsmart each other, but there's no credible plotting or characterizations. Slater and Asner are security guards transferring $3 million. They get caught in flood waters, which is lucky for Freeman and pals who are after the money. After shooting Asner, the crooks chase Slater all over a flood-ravaged Midwestern small town. The technical aspects of this disaster thriller are impressive, and there are even a few good action scenes. But there's not much going on in the script department; while most fans don't watch action thrillers for their screenplay merits, you need a story now and then. ★★ DVD: $14.99, VHS: $9.99

Hard Target

(1993, 92 min, US, John Woo) *Jean-Claude Van Damme, Lance Henriksen, Arnold Vosloo, Kasi Lemmons, Wilford Brimley, Yancy Butler.* Woo, the Balanchine of Bullets, makes his first stateside effort and the result is a mostly successful, if somewhat uneven, reworking of *The Most Dangerous Game.* Van Damme is up against bad guy Henriksen, who sets up hunts for wealthy thrill seekers. The game: down-and-out combat veterans. Van Damme plays a hapless merchant marine who just wants to get out of New Orleans, but instead gets pulled into the intrigue when enlisted by a young woman whose father has disappeared. The film's first half is choppy, fraught with staccato dialogue and sporadic action. But once the chase is on, the action rises to a nonstop pitch. ★★½ DVD: $9.99

Hard Times

(1975, 97 min, US, Walter Hill) *Charles Bronson, James Coburn, Jill Ireland, Strother Martin.* Hill's directorial debut is also one of his best films. Bronson takes on all comers in bare-knuckle fights. Coburn plays his manager. Lots of action. ★★★ DVD: $14.99

The Hard Way

(1991, 115 min, US, John Badham) *Michael J. Fox, James Woods, Annabella Sciorra, Stephen Lang, LL Cool J, Christina Ricci, Luis Guzman.* Though really nothing more than a formula buddy-cop comedy, the teaming of Fox and Woods proves to be a saving grace. Fox plays a spoiled Hollywood actor who is partnered with hard-boiled New York detective Woods when the former requests training for his next film assignment. Constantly at odds, Fox and Woods milk the situation dry; eliciting laughs even when the script doesn't warrant them. An amiable, harmless romp. ★★½ DVD Letterbox: $14.99, VHS: $7.49

Hardball

(2001, 102 min, US, Brian Robbins) *Keanu Reeves, Diane Lane, John Hawkes, D.B. Sweeney, Mike McGlone.* After the disastrous results of the football comedy *The Replacements*, and the agonizingly clichéd baseball drama *Hardball*, it's time for Hollywood to pass a law: no more sports-themed films starring Keanu Reeves. This tries very hard to be *The Mighty Ducks* meets *The Bad News Bears*; ultimately, it's just bad news all around. Reeves plays a gambler who is coerced into coaching an inner-city (Chicago) baseball team. Aside from the tired premise and a dubious race perspective (do we really need another film in which a white comes to the rescue of poor blacks?), *Hardball* is just plain, bad filmmaking: thoughtless, derivative and sloppy. ★ DVD Letterbox: $14.99, VHS: $9.99

Hardcore

(1979, 108 min, US, Paul Schrader) *George C. Scott, Peter Boyle, Season Hubley, Dick Sargent.* It's every father's nightmare when Scott, playing a Calvinist from the Midwest (as is director Schrader), finds his runaway daughter making porno movies in the big city. Schrader captures the sleazy, degrading lifestyle often associated with these sorts of enterprises, but doesn't have the courage of his convictions when it comes to the ending. ★★½

Hardcore

(1984, 90 min, US, Richard Kern) *Lydia Lunch.* Performance art, New York independent filmmaking and hard-core sex and violence collide in this shocking, determinedly self-indulgent and patently offensive series of shorts. Wallowing in post-punk nihilism and featuring punk queen Lunch (as well as her poetry), the films, with background punk music by the Butthole Surfers and Sonic Youth, set out to offend all viewers with cheesy depictions of suicide, necrophilia, deviant sexual acts and really sloppy East Village apartments. ★★ VHS: $19.99

The Harder They Come

(1973, 98 min, Jamaica, Perry Penzelle) *Jimmy Cliff.* The age-old story of a country boy seeking riches in the big city, of urban corruption and coming to a bad end — reggae style! Cliff is striking as the marijuana-running punk who kills a cop in a drug bust and becomes a folk hero. Features a hypnotic reggae soundtrack. ★★★ DVD 30th Anniversary: $19.99, DVD Criterion Collection: $39.99, VHS: $14.99

Hardware

(1990, 94 min, GB, Richard Stanley) *Stacey Travis, Dylan McDermott, John Lynch, Iggy Pop.* Style-over-substance defeats this *Alien/Terminator* derivative about a postapocalyptic metalworker (Travis) whose latest sculpture turns lethal when the scrap robot head given to her by her boyfriend (McDermott) reactivates and reassembles itself. Sounds great, but never manages to overcome the director's obvious music video background. ★

Harem

(1987, 107 min, France/GB, Arthur Joffe) *Ben Kingsley, Natassja Kinski.* This curiosity has Kingsley as an OPEC oil minister who becomes enraptured by Kinski while on a business trip to America. Kingsley must have the beauty and right before he leaves, he ruthlessly kidnaps her and then places her among his 30-member harem. Passions explode when past meets present in this bizarre romantic comedy. (Filmed in English) ★ VHS: $79.99

Harlan County, USA

(1977, 103 min, US, Barbara Kopple) This Academy Award-winning documentary compellingly involves the viewer in the plight of Kentucky coal miners up against the Eastover Mining Company. The strikers are presented forthrightly, without condescension or glamorization, and with dignity. Surprisingly effective and immediate, the film retains its relevance regarding the conditions affecting American workers today. Highly recommended. ★★★★ VHS: $29.99

Harlem Nights

(1989, 115 min, US, Eddie Murphy) *Eddie Murphy, Richard Pryor, Redd Foxx, Della Reese, Arsenio Hall, Stan Shaw.* Murphy wrote, directed and stars in this gangster comedy set in late-1930s Harlem. Pryor and his "adopted" son Murphy are up against a crooked cop and a white mob kingpin who want a piece of their lucrative nightspot. Superlative sets and costumes can't mask an unfunny screenplay, in which most of the humor is one character cursing at another. Director Murphy's film lacks the energy needed to sustain the farcical romp he wants it to be; however, writer Murphy is to be applauded for giving Pryor the plum part of the film — and the veteran comic makes the most of it. Shaw is especially good in support as a punch-drunk boxer. ★★ DVD Letterbox: $14.99, VHS: $9.99

Harley Davidson and the Marlboro Man

(1991, 98 min, US, Simon Wincer) *Don Johnson, Mickey Rourke, Daniel Baldwin, Vanessa L. Williams, Giancarlo Esposito, Tom Sizemore.* Director Wincer makes a valiant effort, but this tale of two outlaw misfits who join forces to save a neighborhood bar from greedy developers is lost in a whirlwind of lackluster performances, overblown action sequences and an undernourished script. Hard-core Rourke fans might enjoy this oddity — others beware. ★½ DVD: $14.99

The Harmonists

(1999, 115 min, Germany, Joseph Vilsmaier) *Ben Becker, Heino Ferch, Ulrich Noethen, Heinrich Schafmeister.* Involving true-life story of a singing quintet — The Comedian Harmonists — who were superstars in Berlin in the '30s. Unfortunately, Hitler was coming into power, and three of the five were Jewish. This is a standard rise-and-fall-of-a-music-group drama, given dimension by the Nazism background. While there is some great music and a handful of good scenes, *The Harmonists* never really transcends its clichés or sentimentality, and a treacly ending leaves a bad taste. It holds the attention, though, and its heart is in the right place. (German with English subtitles) ★★½ DVD: $14.99, VHS: $9.99

Harold and Maude

(1971, 90 min, US, Hal Ashby) *Ruth Gordon, Bud Cort, Vivian Pickles, Cyril Cusack.* He's 20 and obsessed with death; she's 80 and full of joie de vivre. Together they combat the doldrums of life. Gordon shines as the vivacious Maude and Cort is playfully grim as the morbid young Harold. Black comedy at its darkest, this wonderful love story features the music of Cat Stevens and features a hilarious supporting role by Pickles as Harold's daffy mother. One of the most popular films ever to play TLA Cinema. ★★★★ DVD: $14.99, VHS: $9.99

Harper

(1966, 121 min, US, Jack Smight) *Paul Newman, Lauren Bacall, Robert Wagner, Janet Leigh, Julie Harris.* Newman stars as Louis Harper, a cynical Los Angeles detective hired for a missing persons case. A perfect '60s thriller, complete with scenery, California atmosphere and Newman's charisma. Bacall costars as the bedridden widow who hires Harper and she makes the most of her femme fatale charm. Sharp direction from Smith and a witty script by William Goldman make for a most entertaining thriller. (Sequel: *The Drowning Pool*) ★★★½ VHS: $14.99

H

Harry Potter and the Prisoner of Azkaban

Harriet Craig

(1950, 94 min, US, Vincent Sherman) *Joan Crawford, Wendell Corey.* In this engrossing remake of *Craig's Wife*, Crawford is in great form as she sulks and rages as the perfectionist, home-wrecking housewife who destroys her own marriage through her penchant for control. ★★★

Harriet the Spy

(1996, 101 min, US, Bronwen Hughes) *Michelle Trachtenberg, Rosie O'Donnell, Eartha Kitt.* Harriet is a precocious 11-year-old girl whose independent outlook has made her a bit of an outcast. Her beloved nanny instills in Harriet individualism and an appreciation for life. Which explains Harriet's penchant for writing in her notebook everything she sees. It's her observations and thoughts which lead to trouble in the sweet and enjoyable *Harriet the Spy*, a spirited adaptation of the Louise Fitzhugh children's book. Trachtenberg makes a very appealing Harriet; she neither down-plays Harriet's peculiarities nor does she immerse herself in them. O'Donnell is wonderful as Harriet's nanny, who imparts on the young girl sage advice while serving as loyal best friend. ★★★ DVD: $14.99, VHS: $9.99

Harry and the Hendersons

(1987, 110 min, US, William Dear) *John Lithgow, Melinda Dillon, Don Ameche, Lainie Kazan, M. Emmet Walsh.* This amusing little comedy about a suburban Seattle family who find themselves host to Bigfoot is filled with warmhearted humor. Lithgow puts in yet another solid (and yet unsung) performance as Dad. Rick Baker's makeup for the giant Harry won him an Academy Award. ★★½

Harry and Tonto

(1974, 115 min, US, Paul Mazursky) *Art Carney, Ellen Burstyn, Larry Hagman, Geraldine Fitzgerald, Melanie Mayron.* A Best Actor Academy Award went to Carney for his portrayal of an old man who, after eviction from his apartment building (about to be torn down around his ears), sets out on a cross-country odyssey with his cat. Touching, warm, humorous and sometimes very sad. In addition to *The Late Show*, perhaps the fullest use of Mr. Carney's mature talents. ★★★½

Harry Potter and the Chamber of Secrets

(2002, 161 min, US, Chris Columbus) *Daniel Radcliffe, Rupert Grint, Emma Watson, Richard Harris, Maggie Smith, Kenneth Branagh, Jason Isaacs, Robbie Coltrane, Alan Rickman, Tom Felton, Miriam Margoyles, Julie Walters.* J.K. Rowling's essential series of Potter novels is rapidly becoming a formidable film franchise, as a tremendous amount of novelistic detail is expertly condensed into this wondrous, exciting and quite breathtaking second installment. It's year two at Hogwarts School of Witchcraft and Wizardry, and after lying dormant for decades, a frightening Chamber of Secrets has been opened, the creature within out for blood. Mudblood, that is, which makes half-witch half-muggle Hermione (Watson) a prime target. So it's up to Harry (Radcliffe) to save the day . . . and is that a hint of a (yuk) budding romance between the two? Top-notch special effects and set designs bring Hogwarts to life, with such standouts as a Whomping Willow tree, a very funny lesson in harvesting mandrakes and a new, pivotal ghost by the name of Moaning Myrtle (there's one in every school). Yet the human touch is just as important: Harry, Hermione and Ron (Grint) are winning as ever, and Branagh is a delight as an egomaniacal professor who's famous for his writing ("Magical Me" is his latest) but is merely full of hot air. Harris is majestic in his final role, as the wizened wizard Dumbledore who takes Harry under his wing. (Sequel: *Harry Potter and the Prisoner of Azkaban*) ★★★½ DVD Letterbox: $19.99, VHS: $6.99

Harry Potter and the Prisoner of Azkaban

(2004, 136 min, US, Alfonso Cuarón) *Daniel Radcliffe, Rupert Grint, Emma Watson, David Thewlis, Michael Gambon, Maggie Smith, Alan Rickman, Robbie Coltrane, Gary Oldman, Emma Thompson, Julie Christie, Timothy Spall.* As the characters have grown up, so, too, has the series. That's just one of the many impressions that can be taken away from this terrific third chapter of J.K. Rowling's series, for director Cuarón (stepping in after Chris Columbus helmed the first two films) has made a more mature, darker, funnier and more menacing film in following the continuing adventures of young wizard Harry Potter. Harry, Hermione and Ron are now in their third year of schooling at Hogwarts. Nearly gone are the school rivalries and magical abstracts the school has to offer, for as this fearsome trio comes of age so do the perils and misadventures they face. And none has been greater for Harry than Sirius Black (Oldman), who betrayed Harry's parents to Voldemort, the evil wizard who murdered them. And he's just escaped Azkaban Prison, and has set out to kill Harry. Cuarón has made sure that this time out, when someone is in danger, you really doubt their safety. The film is suspenseful without being too unsettling, and these scenes are offset by some wonderful comedic moments — there may not be as many of them as compared to the last two films, but the humor is stronger. The three main characters are caught in that awkward period of adolescence and none are the worse off for it. There's even a hint at romance between Hermione and Ron, but we'll just have to wait for the fourth go-round. Meanwhile, Radcliffe as Harry has never been this assured before. Thanks to a superior supporting cast, excellent effects, and a complex but engaging story where imagination is still the limit, this just may be the best *Harry Potter* yet. ★★★★

Harry Potter and the Sorcerer's Stone

(2001, 146 min, GB, Chris Columbus) *Daniel Radcliffe, Rupert Grint, Emma Watson, John Cleese, Robbie Coltrane, Warwick Davis, Richard Griffiths, Ian Hart, John Hurt, Alan Rickman, Fiona Shaw, Maggie Smith, Julie Walters, Zöe Wanamaker.* Director Columbus, a sometimes accomplished director of kiddie films, took on the possibly thankless job of creating a faithful adaptation of the most popular book series since Dr. Seuss' heyday, and pleasing hundreds of millions of author J.K. Rowling's rabid fans. Somehow, he accomplished some wizardry of his own. There's not too much attention to conventional plot here, as young Harry learns that he has wizardry in his blood and sets off to Hogwart's School to hone his crafts. In fact, the most magical thing about *Sorcerer's Stone* is this very sense of discovery, of how fascinating it would be to find that broomsticks can fly, hats can speak, and chess pieces can do battle. The only thing one could ask for is more: More scenes in the wizards' classrooms, more about Harry's amorphous nemesis Voldemort, more time with the adorable dragon Norbert. But in a film packed to the two-and-a-half-hour point with nonstop fantastic whimsy, how would that be possible? The answer is with the upcoming sequels, a prospect that has the ten-year-old in all of us giddy with anticipation. (Sequel: *Harry Potter and the Chamber of Secrets*) ★★★½ DVD Letterbox 2-disc set: $19.99, DVD Pan & Scan 2-disc set: $19.99, VHS With deleted scenes: $6.99

Harvest

(1937, 129 min, France, Marcel Pagnol) *Fernandel, Orane Demazis.* Demazis and Fernandel, the stars of *Angele*, are reunited in this Pagnolian human drama about a peasant family and their struggle for existence. An itinerant hunter, wishing to have a family, coaxes a down-on-her-luck cabaret singer to leave her abusive companion and set up house with him in a deserted, decaying mountain village. The unlikely lovers struggle, against all odds, to till the land and keep the village alive. Innocently told by today's standards, this film was originally banned by French censors on moral grounds. (French with English subtitles) ★★★★ VHS: $59.99

The Harvest

(1992, 97 min, US, David Marconi) *Henry Silva, Harvey Fierstein, Miguel Ferrer.* Ferrer stars as a screenwriter who travels to a Mexican resort town to get away from it all and rewrite his newest screenplay. Once there, he becomes involved in a convoluted series of events which lead to illegal organ transplants, murder and cover-ups. A finely crafted neo-noir thriller, *The Harvest* is an intricate puzzle that's fun to watch unfold. ★★★

Harvey

(1950, 104 min, US, Henry Koster) *James Stewart, Josephine Hull, Victoria Horne, Cecil Kelloway, Peggy Dow, Charles Drake, Jesse White.* Stewart gives one of his most appealing performances as the tipsolated Elwood P. Dowd, whose best friend, Harvey, just happens to be a six-foot rabbit (he's actually a pooka, but why quibble). Based on Mary Chase's Pulitzer Prize-winning Broadway play, the film is a faithful and delightful adaptation, capturing all the warmth, humor and craziness that made the play one of the great sensations of the late 1940s. As Elwood's exasperated sister, Hull had the role of her career and won an Oscar for it. ★★★½ DVD: $14.99

The Harvey Girls

(1946, 101 min, US, George Sidney) *Judy Garland, Ray Bolger, Angela Lansbury, John Hodiak, Marjorie Main, Virginia O'Brien, Cyd Charisse.* Garland sings "Atchison, Topeka and the Santa Fe" as she and other well-bred young ladies head West to be waitresses at the new Fred Harvey railroad station restaurants. Though the story is pure hokum, Judy and a talented cast plus enjoyable musical numbers make this a pleasant ride. ★★★ DVD: $19.99

The Hasty Heart

(1949, 104 min, GB, Vincent Sherman) *Richard Todd, Patricia Neal, Ronald Reagan.* Based on John Patrick's sentimental stage play, this affecting tear-jerker is as sappy as it is captivating. Todd gives an immense performance as a proud Scottish soldier staying at a Burmese hospital during WWII. Arrogant and cantankerous, he makes enemies of all around him until it is learned he only has a few weeks to live. Neal is quite good as the nurse looking after him, and even the presence of Reagan as an American G.I. doesn't compromise the integrity or enjoyment level of this polished, bittersweet tale. (Remade in 1986) ★★★½ VHS: $19.99

Hatchet for a Honeymoon

(1967, 93 min, Italy/Spain, Mario Bava) *Stephen Forsythe, Dagmar Lassander, Laura Betti.* Strong on visual imagery and short on plot, Italian horror master Bava tells the tale of a cross-dressing psycho killer/fashion mogul who murders brides while haunted by the ghost of his own wife. ★★½ DVD: $24.99, VHS: $19.99

Hate (La Haine)

(1995, 94 min, France, Mathieu Kassovitz) *Vincent Cassel, Hubert Kounde, Said Taghmaoui.* Three marginalized French youths — one black, one Arab, one Jew — spend a night on the mean streets of Paris in this stunning black-and-white feature by actor-director Kassovitz. The day after a massive street riot during which a well-liked gang member was put into a coma by a police beating, the three friends set out on their normal daily activities. But there's a twist: a policeman lost his pistol during the melee and one of the three now has it, and he's vowing revenge. Violence lurks around every corner in *Hate*, and only after expectations have subsided does it show its ugly head. Low-budget though shot and edited remarkably well, the film is alternately harrowing and sad, and it paints a very bleak picture of the future of urban society via its treatment of its youth. (French with English subtitles) ★★★★

Haunted

(1995, 107 min, GB, Lewis Gilbert) *Aidan Quinn, Kate Beckinsale, John Gielgud, Anthony Andrews.* A slow-moving yet haunting ghost story about an arrogant turn-of-the-century college professor (Quinn) who, having been haunted as a child by the accidental death of his younger sister, has dedicated his life to proving there's no such thing as ghosts. But when he takes up the challenge of exorcising a country estate, he uncovers a supernatural scandal so horrifying even Casper would run screaming.

The Haunting: Julie Harris (l.) and Claire Bloom go ghost-hunting

Director Gilbert is in uncharted territory with this poltergeist patchwork, but he compensates the unlively pace and familiar scare techniques with a good screenplay (based on the novel by James Herbert), winning performances and that great shock ending. ★★½ DVD: $14.99, VHS: $9.99

Haunted Honeymoon

(1986, 84 min, US, Gene Wilder) *Gene Wilder, Gilda Radner, Dom DeLuise, Jonathan Pryce.* A sometimes amusing mystery spoof with Wilder and Radner as two 1930s radio stars who visit Wilder's aunt (DeLuise in drag) at the family estate, becoming targets for murder. Though the pairing of Wilder and Radner is irresistible, they really aren't given any good material. ★★ DVD Letterbox: $14.99

Haunted Summer

(1988, 106 min, US, Ivan Passer) *Eric Stoltz, Laura Dern, Philip Anglim, Alice Krige, Alex Winter.* Languid (read: boring), beautifully filmed (read: the countryside is more interesting than the characters), evocative period piece (read: pretentious costume drama drivel) and shocking (read: a failed attempt at titillation), this drama retreads the often-traveled grounds of the fateful summer that Percy Shelley, his lover and future wife Mary Goodwin, her half-sister Claire Claimont and the roguish poet Lord Byron spent together on the shores of Lake Geneva in 1816. For a much better film on the same subject, Ken Russell's dreamlike psychological thriller *Gothic* is a must. ★

The Haunting

(1963, 112 min, US, Robert Wise) *Julie Harris, Claire Bloom, Russ Tamblyn, Richard Johnson.* Wise's classic ghost story about a team of researchers investigating a haunted house. Harris and Bloom are both splendid as psychic investigators, and Wise can get more scares from a door than Jason or Freddy can scrape together with an assortment of knives and axes. Based on Shirley Jackson's "The Haunting of Hill House," this is a frightening, genuinely creepy and well-made chiller. (Remade in 1999) ★★★★ DVD: $19.99

The Haunting

(1999, 113 min, US, Jan De Bont) *Liam Neeson, Catherine Zeta-Jones, Lili Taylor, Bruce Dern, Owen Wilson, Marian Seldes, Todd Field.* This remake of Robert Wise's 1963 classic ghost story misses the mark in nearly every department. This second screen version of Shirley Jackson's "The Haunting of Hill House" starts promisingly. Neeson plays a psychologist who gathers three subjects (Zeta-Jones, Taylor and Wilson) for a sleep-disorder

study at the Gothic mansion Hill House. Little by little, it becomes apparent that the place may be haunted. In the original, this was accomplished through the subtle use of chills and scares; here it's done through loud noises and garish special effects. Mouths will be gaped — not by the sheer terror of it all but by the often ridiculous plot developments. ★½ DVD Letterbox: $14.99, DVD DTS sound: $14.99, VHS: $9.99

The Haunting of Julia

(1976, 96 min, Canada/GB, Richard Loncraine) *Mia Farrow, Keir Dullea, Tom Conti.* Moody and seductive supernatural thriller with Farrow as a mother haunted by the death of her young daughter, whose spirit has now returned from the dead. ★★½

The Haunting of Morella

(1991, 82 min, US, Jim Wynorski) *David McCallum, Nicole Eggert.* Roger Corman strikes again, and strikes out, in this dismal Poe adaptation that's a far cry from his 1960s efforts. McCallum is the dopey, dedicated hubby of a condemned sorceress who returns to possess their virginal daughter. A campy mix of buxom starlets and T&A in lieu of talent. ★ VHS: $79.99

Havana

(1990, 145 min, US, Sydney Pollack) *Robert Redford, Lena Olin, Raul Julia, Alan Arkin, Richard Farnsworth.* The sixth collaboration between actor Redford and director Pollack features intelligent acting and competent direction, but is plagued by an insufferably poor script. The story follows the exploits of Redford as a big-stakes American gambler who's hanging around Havana on the eve of the Communist takeover. All he's interested in is a good poker game, but when he becomes smitten by the wife of a wealthy revolutionary (Olin), he is inextricably sucked into the political fray. The film borrows heavily from films like *Casablanca*, right down to the Scandinavian-born leading lady, but falls mighty short of that film's greatness. ★★ DVD: $9.99, VHS: $9.99

Hawaii

(1966, 172 min, US, George Roy Hill) *Max von Sydow, Julie Andrews, Richard Harris, Gene Hackman, Carroll O'Connor, John Cullum.* Epic film version of James Michener's novel set in the 1800s about settlers in our 50th state and how they shaped the territory. Von Sydow is appropriately dour as a missionary, Andrews is his personable wife, and Harris is the sea captain in love with Andrews. ★★★

H

The Hawk

(1993, 84 min, GB, David Hayman) *Helen Mirren, George Castigan, Owen Teale.* When a serial killer stalks the normally peaceful English countryside, an uptight housewife (Mirren) soon begins to suspect her traveling salesman husband (Castigan), due to the many similarities between her own life and the killer's victims. The tired script, which occasionally succeeds by creating suspenseful moments, fails just as often by giving obvious clues and plot twists. Though the film rescues itself by allowing Mirren to deliver a strong performance, it's difficult to camouflage a clichéd, muddled story. ★★½ VHS: $19.99

Hawk's Vengeance

(1997, 96 min, US, Marc F. Voizard) *Gary Daniels, Vlasta Vrana, Cass Magda.* Somebody give Gary Daniels a break! The handsome action star has talent, great martial arts ability and a likable screen persona, but he is continually cast in crappy grade-Z action flicks like this one. This time, Daniels is cast as "Hawk," a British marine who comes to the U.S. to investigate the mysterious death of his half-brother, an American cop. He teams up with his ex-partner and together they take on a local ganglord. *Hawk's Vengeance* is silly from start to finish. The martial arts fights are put together so poorly and shot so slowly that no tension or excitement is left in them. ★ DVD: $19.99, VHS: $9.99

Hawks

(1988, 100 min, GB, Robert Ellis Miller) *Timothy Dalton, Anthony Edwards, Jill Bennett, Sheila Hancock, Connie Booth.* Quirky comedy-drama with Dalton and Edwards as two terminally ill cancer patients who escape from their hospital ward in search of adventure. Dalton and Edwards bring great pathos to their roles; and though the last third of the film veers on a rather strange course, this can be rewarding, if offbeat, entertainment. ★★½ VHS: $102.99

The Hawks and the Sparrows

(1965, 88 min, Italy, Pier Paolo Pasolini) *Toto, Ninetto Davoli.* This post-neorealist parable is an unconventional story featuring Italy's beloved stone-faced clown Toto as an Everyman who, with his empty-headed son, travels the road of life accompanied by a talking crow, who waxes philosophically and amusingly on the passing scene. Pasolini presents a tragic fable that shows two delightful innocents caught between the Church and Marxism. (Italian with English subtitles) ★★★ DVD Letterbox: $29.99, VHS: $29.99

He and She

(1994, 90 min, Hong Kong, Cheng Dan Shui) *Tony Leung, Cherie Chung.* Gay costume designer Tai (Leung) finds his sexuality blurred after he enters into a marriage of convenience with a pregnant friend. Happily homosexual, Tai soon begins to feel troublingly attracted to his new roommate Yee (Chung). When the married biological father challenges the validity of the marriage and fights for child custody in court, Tai is forced to acknowledge his gayness and admit the marriage was unconsummated. Despite having the marriage annulled by the court, Tai realizes that he does indeed feel heterosexual yearnings for Yee and gathers that he doesn't love women in general, just Yee. Although leaning on the soap opera-ish side, this drama is quite interesting in its realistic depiction and social acceptance of a gay man – although his eventual "conversion" will leave many unconvinced. (Cantonese with English subtitles) ★★½ VHS: $79.99

He Got Game

(1998, 130 min, US, Spike Lee) *Denzel Washington, Ray Allen, Milla Jovovich, Ned Beatty, Bill Nunn, John Turturro.* In a most accomplished portrayal, Washington plays Jake, a man serving a lengthy prison term for killing his wife. Jake is released for one week to try to convince his estranged son Jesus (Allen), a nationally known high school basketball prodigy, to accept a scholarship at the governor's alma mater, in exchange for a shortened sentence. This pulpy, almost high-concept idea is given the customary intense yet loose treatment by director Lee. A healthy cynisicm permeates the entire film, with coaches, colleges, family and friends all trying to get a piece of the young ballplayer. Beautifully edited, long but compelling and fast-paced, the only negative of the film is the less-than-defined characterizations of the women – something Lee must address in future films. The performances are uniformly good, with a surprisingly natural turn from real-life NBA star Allen. ★★★½ DVD: $14.99, VHS: $9.99

He Said, She Said

(1991, 115 min, US, Ken Kwapis & Marisa Silver) *Kevin Bacon, Sharon Stone, Elizabeth Perkins, Nathan Lane, Anthony LaPaglia.* Lightweight comedy that is actually two films in one. The story centers on the relationship of journalists Bacon and Perkins – told through the eyes of each of them. Kwapis directed the "male" point-of-view, and Silver directed the "female" counterpart. ★★ DVD Letterbox: $14.99, VHS: $14.99

He Walked by Night

(1948, 80 min, US, Alfred L. Werker) *Richard Basehart, Scott Brady, Roy Roberts, Whit Bissell, Jack Webb.* This seminal noir picture showcases the use of forensic science as the LAPD tracks a vicious and highly intelligent cop killer. Starkly shot and tautly written, the film follows the police investigation as it pieces together minute scraps of evidence, following leads with state-of-the-art technology of the time. This focus on the technical aspect of criminal investigation was unique in films by 1949, and apparently made a big impression on the actor portraying the crime lab scientist – Webb. The film's introductory voice-over opens with a description of Los Angeles, and tells us that what we are about to see is a true story – only the names have been changed . . . and taken from the files of the detective division. Sound familiar? It's the prototype for Webb's TV series, "Dragnet"; a term, incidentally, pointedly used several times in the film. ★★★ DVD: $14.99, VHS: $19.99

Head

(1968, 86 min, US, Bob Rafelson) *The Monkees, Terry (Teri) Garr, Vito Scotti, Victor Mature, Frank Zappa, Annette Funicello, Jack Nicholson.* "Hey, hey, it's the Monkees!" The pre*fab*ricated four cavort with an all-star cast including Mature (that hunk of yore) and Nicholson (who also coscripted) in this psychedelic explosion of drug-induced humor. ★★★ DVD: $19.99, VHS: $19.99

Head above Water

(1997, 92 min, US, Jim Wilson) *Harvey Keitel, Cameron Diaz, Craig Sheffer, Billy Zane.* A truly wretched comedy with a slumming Keitel as a middle-aged judge who becomes terribly jealous when he finds the dead, naked body of the old beau of his beautiful young wife in the basement. Boring misadventures follow as husband and wife team up to try to dispose of the body, while Diaz's childhood friend (Sheffer) grows suspicious. A cutesy "comic" music

score only adds to the misery as three able actors give career-low performances walking around like dull idiots. The ending is a slow death-crawl to the credits, with no buildup or climax to speak of. In fact, the ending is *so* inconsequential and casual, you may feel you have missed something. You won't want to rewind to find out what. ★ DVD: $19.99

Head Against the Wall
(La Tete Contre les Murs)

(1958, 90 min, France, Georges Franju) *Jean-Pierre Mocky, Anouk Aimée, Charles Aznavour.* Franju, along with Jean-Pierre Melville, made consistently intriguing films in the '40s and '50s that anticipated the French New Wave. Franju, cofounder of the Cinematique Francaise in 1938, was known mostly for his documentaries and shorts; this was his first feature. Taking the theme of repression and rebellion, the story – possibly influenced by James Dean's alienated youth films – follows a young man's (Mocky, who also wrote the script) escape from an insane asylum in his efforts to locate his girlfriend (Aimée) and avoid his father's desperate attempts to recommit him. (French with English subtitles) ★★★

Head of the Family

(1970, 105 min, Italy, Nanni Loy) *Leslie Caron, Nino Manfredi, Ugo Tognazzi, Claudine Auger.* Set in postwar Rome, this sensitive drama concerns a woman (Caron) whose marriage of ten years has become loveless. She must face the prospect of life alone, dealing with both its pleasures and anxieties. ★★½ VHS: $79.99

Head Office

(1986, 90 min, US, Ken Finkleman) *Judge Reinhold, Danny DeVito, Eddie Albert, Jane Seymour, Rick Moranis.* Lackluster parody of the financial world with Reinhold as a young idealist working his way up the corporate ladder. ★★ VHS: $9.99

Head On

(1998, 104 min, Australia, Ana Kokkinos) *Alex Dimitriades, Paul Capsis, Julius Garner, Tony Nikolakopoulas, Elena Mandalis, Eugenia Fragos, Paul Capsis.* In this adaptation of the book "Loaded" by Christos Tsiolkas, director Kokkinos has created a vivid portrait of a culturally and sexually confused youth in the person of Ari (brilliantly portrayed by Dimitrades), a Greek-Australian hunk. The exciting drama centers on 24 hours in Ari's life. A very closeted young man who lives with his traditionalist Greek family, the unemployed Ari spends his days with his fellow Greek friends (including a frustrated girlfriend), partying and taking drugs. And he releases his insatiable homosexual desires through quick public rest room and back alley encounters with a variety of men. The clash of his straight world and his gay yearnings come to a head one evening when he meets a handsome man. With a pulsating soundtrack and vibrant visuals, Kokkinos takes us on an intimate, narcotic ride into Ari's troubled world. ★★★½ DVD: $29.99, VHS: $29.99

Head over Heels (A Coeur Joie!)

(1967, 89 min, France, Serge Bourguignon) *Brigitte Bardot, Laurent Terzieff.* Bardot is a happily married woman who, through several years of marriage, has never cheated on her husband. Her fidelity is severely tested when, in London on a business trip, Bardot finds herself pursued by a handsome young man and must decide on staying faithful or having a "short" love affair. This drama, made for the French domestic market, is still an entertaining and knowledgeable look into the labyrinthine world of love. (French with English subtitles) ★★★

H

Head over Heels

(2001, 87 min, US, Mark S. Waters) *Monica Potter, Freddie Prinze, Jr., Shalom Harlow.* Doing her best (or is that worst?) Julia Roberts imitation, Potter joins the ranks of the seriously cute but dead-on-delivery airhead romantic leads. 'Tis a pity, for Potter demonstrates some signs of life in the film's promising beginning, playing a supposedly intelligent restorer for the Metropolitan Museum who has trouble picking the right guy. When she meets her handsome new neighbor Prinze (fast becoming the King of Bland), it's love at first sight — that is, until she thinks he's murdered someone and sets out to solve the case. What follows is a series of unfunny, sometimes tasteless and silly predicaments. A low-rent *Rear Window* populated with characters who aspire for Anita Loos but settle for John Hughes, the generically titled, generically made *Head over Heels* would give modern romantic comedies a bad name — if they didn't already have one. ★½ DVD: $14.99, VHS: $9.99

Hear My Song

(1991, 115 min, GB, Peter Chelsom) *Adrian Dunbar, Ned Beatty, Tara Fitzgerald, Shirley Ann Feld.* Made in the tradition of the Ealing Studio comedies with a splash of *Local Hero* thrown in, *Hear My Song* is a delightful frolic about a sprightly young Irishman trying to make a go of it as a nightclub operator in Liverpool. After making a series of disastrous bookings, he is forced to try and save his venue by luring the famed Irish tenor Josef Locke (Beatty) back from Ireland where he's been avoiding British tax collectors. Dunbar (who cowrote the screenplay with first-time director Chelsom) delivers a winning performance as the music promoter Mickey O'Neill. Beatty is marvelous as Locke, putting in one of his best performances. ★★★½ VHS: $19.99

Hear No Evil

(1993, 97 min, US, Robert Greenwald) *Marlee Matlin, D.B. Sweeney, Martin Sheen, John C. McGinley.* Matlin stars in this insipid thriller as a deaf aerobics instructor who inadvertently becomes involved in a murderous robbery scheme. It seems one of her clients, investigative reporter McGinley, picks up a scoop about a stolen coin worth a million dollars. And the police department of Portland, Oregon, has a rotten apple in the form of sergeant Sheen, who's involved in the heist. Sheen and his cronies then terrorize everyone in sight, and Matlin becomes the object of the bad guy's ire. Director Greenwald can't decide whether he's making a thriller or a music video as he inserts several numbers that completely break the tension. ★½ VHS: $9.99

Hearing Voices

(1990, 89 min, US, Sharon Greytak) *Erika Nagy, Stephen Gatta.* Numbed into quiet boredom by the shallow, manipulative world of fashion modeling, and physically scarred after reconstructive surgery, Erika floats aimlessly through her successful but empty life. She is saved emotionally after meeting Lee (sort of a Pauly Shore on Prozac), the gay lover of her doctor. Their relationship (sexual?) is an unusual love, which while not altogether fulfilling, and ultimately doomed, does help in their respective healing processes. This story, of a "romance" between a gay man and a straight woman, provides a great premise; but the film, hampered by languid pacing and stilted acting is reduced to an earnest but lifeless viewing experience. ★★

Heart

(1999, 81 min, GB, Charles McDougall) *Christopher Eccleston, Saskia Reeves, Kate Hardie, Rhys Ifans.* The British thriller *Heart* boasts a fine pedigree on both sides of the camera: director McDougall and writer Jimmy McGovern previously collaborated on the TV series "Cracker," McGovern wrote the excellent *Priest*, and Eccleston and Ifans have given fine performances in enjoyable films. So what the hell happened? *Heart* is a bloody mess. Eccleston plays a jealous husband with a bad ticker. He receives a heart transplant, and becomes newly invigorated. The mother of the heart donor becomes fixated on the husband and ... oh, why bother? The plot just gets more ludicrous and a predictably ghastly demise is had by all. ★ DVD: $24.99, VHS: $89.99

Heart and Souls

(1993, 103 min, US, Ron Underwood) *Robert Downey, Jr., Alfre Woodard, Charles Grodin, Tom Sizemore, Kyra Sedgwick, David Paymer, Elisabeth Shue.* While its scale may be more fitting for the small screen rather than the large one, this ghost comedy is really quite a charmer. Sedgwick, Sizemore, Woodard and Grodin are lost souls. They unexplainedly find themselves watching over a youngster, who grows up to be harried businessman Downey. As they try to put his life right, they also are given a chance to tie up the loose ends of their own lives, which each failed to do before their deaths. As he demonstrated in *Chaplin*, Downey has a real knack for physical comedy; which comes in handy since the spirits — recalling Steve Martin's *All of Me* — possess Downey's body for much of the film. ★★★ VHS: $7.49

Heart Beat

(1980, 109 min, US, John Byrum) *Nick Nolte, Sissy Spacek, John Heard, Ray Sharkey.* Fictionalized though rewarding account of the friendship of Beat poet Jack Kerouac and Carolyn & Neal Cassady. Heard is the author, and Spacek and Nolte are the Cassadys. Sharkey is a standout in support as a Ginsberg-like writer. ★★½ VHS: $19.99

Heart Condition

(1990, 98 min, US, James D. Parriott) *Bob Hoskins, Denzel Washington, Chloe Webb.* Instantly forgettable yet strangely enjoyable while it lasts, this phantasmal comedy about a racist cop who is befriended by a congenial black ghost is the perfect example of the "concept" idea of screenwriting. Hoskins, at his gruffest and most lovable, is a down-at-the-heels cop who suffers a heart attack. Washington is the recently deceased man who spectrally returns to earth after his heart is transplanted into Hoskins' body. The two form an unlikely team as they attempt to track down Washington's druglord killers. ★★½ DVD: $19.99, VHS: $9.99

The Heart Is a Lonely Hunter

(1968, 125 min, US, Robert Ellis Miller) *Alan Arkin, Sondra Locke, Stacy Keach, Laurinda Barrett, Chuck McCann, Cicely Tyson.* Based on Carson McCuller's lyrical first novel, this poignant drama stars Arkin (in an Oscar-nominated performance) as a sensitive deaf-mute who befriends, supports and, then in some quiet fashion, is betrayed by a small group of fellow social outcasts. Set in the South, this tender tale features Locke (also an Oscar nominee) and Keach in their screen debuts. ★★★

Heart Like a Wheel

(1983, 113 min, US, Jonathan Kaplan) *Bonnie Bedelia, Beau Bridges, Bill McKinney, Anthony Edwards, Hoyt Axton, Leo Rossi, Dick Miller.* This triumphant, true-life saga chronicles the uphill struggle of stock car driver Shirley Muldowney (Bedelia) to gain acceptance in the male-dominated world of motorsport racing. A thrilling tale of determination and perseverance. Bedelia gives an outstanding performance; Bridges is exceptional as racer Connie Kalitte. ★★★½

Heart of Dixie

(1989, 95 min, US, Martin Davidson) *Ally Sheedy, Virginia Madsen, Phoebe Cates, Treat Williams.* Another in the long line of well-meaning social dramas about racial discrimination in our country's past. A worthy subject to be sure, but the film lacks a perspective and a strong narrative needed to make it of interest. Sheedy gives a sincere performance as a white college student given a jolting political lesson in racial injustice. ★★½ DVD Letterbox: $9.99, VHS: $19.99

Heart of Dragon

(1985, 85 min, Hong Kong, Sammo Hung) *Jackie Chan, Sammo Hung, Emily Chu.* In one of his earliest dramatic roles, Jackie is cast as a police officer who is constantly taking care of his mentally retarded brother (director Hung), and running into myriad troubles while doing so. This HK version of *Rain Man* begins slowly, but builds to a grueling twenty-minute action climax set in a construction site which finds Jackie fighting at his fiercest to rescue his kidnapped brother. But fight scenes are not what this movie is about; it is more about Jackie's recognition of his love and responsibility for his unfortunate sibling. The two actors (who were schoolmates together) have several tender and dramatic moments together and Sammo proves that he can be sentimental without becoming maudlin. Jackie as well handles the dramatic scenes with skill and shows an uncharacteristic face of rage and frustration during the climactic fight. (Cantonese with English subtitles) ★★★ DVD Letterboxed: $9.99, VHS Subtitled: $19.99, VHS Dubbed: $19.99

Heartaches

(1981, 93 min, Canada, Donald Shebib) *Margot Kidder, Annie Potts, David Carradine.* This winsome romantic comedy and female buddy movie stars Potts as a woman who after finding herself pregnant, and not by her racing-car enthusiast boyfriend David Carradine, abandons him and goes on the road. It doesn't take her long to meet up with a zany, streetwise woman (Kidder) who takes her under her wing, and together they set up house in Toronto. Kidder gives an enjoyably manic performance in the plum role of the man-crazed peroxide blonde who takes the frumpy Potts on an unwilling series of adventures. ★★★

Heartbreak Hotel

(1988, 93 min, US, Chris Columbus) *Charlie Schlatter, David Keith, Tuesday Weld.* In this ficticious comedy, a teenager (Schlatter) kidnaps Elvis Presley (Keith) and brings "the King" home for his divorced mom (Weld). Easily forgettable. ★½ DVD: $9.99

The Heartbreak Kid

(1972, 106 min, US, Elaine May) *Charles Grodin, Cybill Shepherd, Jeannie Berlin, Eddie Albert, Audra Lindley.* One of the best American comedies to come out of the 1970s, this Neil Simon scripted film from a Bruce Jay Friedman story features

Grodin as Lenny, a nice if self-absorbed Jewish *schlemiel* who, realizing on his honeymoon that he has made a fatal mistake in marrying his sunburned, cake-guzzling wife (hilariously and pathetically played by Berlin), makes the decision to dump her for the WASPish ice-queen goddess in the body of Shepherd. His frantic efforts to bow out of his marriage and his ensuing relentless pursuit of his unattainable dream woman is mercilessly lampooned by director May. ★★★½ DVD: $14.99

Heartbreak Ridge

(1986, 130 min, US, Clint Eastwood) *Clint Eastwood, Marsha Mason, Everett McGill, Moses Gunn, Mario Van Peebles, Eileen Heckart, Bo Svenson.* Vigorous war adventure, with an accent on humor during its well-paced boot camp sequence, stars director Eastwood as a rough-talking, old-school Marine sergeant in charge of a platoon of new recruits. ★★½ DVD Letterbox: $14.99, VHS: $14.99

Heartbreakers

(2001, 123 min, US, David Mirkin) *Sigourney Weaver, Jennifer Love Hewitt, Ray Liotta, Gene Hackman, Jason Lee, Anne Bancroft, Jeffrey Jones, Nora Dunn.* Max and Page, a beautiful mother and daughter con-artist team portrayed by the beautiful Weaver and Hewitt, have just scored the latest in a long string of stings. Next, it's off to Palm Springs for these dirty rotten scoundrels, where they search for their next, rich pigeon. How they do it and what happens afterward forms the basis for this intermittently funny con comedy, which should have been a whole lot funnier but manages to flim-flam enough agreeable chuckles. Director Mirkin gives his film a polished look, but the screenplay doesn't always hit its mark, as some of the jokes are needlessly self-conscious. But Mirkin has also assembled a game cast who know how to rise above the limitations of a script, giving seasoned performers such as Weaver, Liotta and Hackman ample room to lock their sights on a joke. When they do, *Heartbreakers* can be downright pleasing. ★★½ DVD Special Edition: $14.99, VHS: $9.99

Heartburn

(1986, 108 min, US, Mike Nichols) *Jack Nicholson, Meryl Streep, Steven Hill, Richard Masur, Stockard Channing, Jeff Daniels, Maureen Stapleton, Mercedes Ruehl.* Nicholson and Streep deliver earnest performances in this faithful film version of Nora Ephron's autobiographical best-seller about a writer (Streep) who discovers that her husband (Nicholson) is having an affair both during and after her pregnancy. A grueling commentary on deception and its consequences. ★★½ DVD: $14.99

Heartland

(1979, 96 min, US, Richard Pearce) *Conchata Ferrell, Rip Torn, Lilia Skala.* Magnificent independent production set in the early 1900s about a widow (Ferrell) who heads to Wyoming to become housekeeper for a cantankerous rancher (Torn). A beautifully filmed story of pioneer life with sterling performances by Ferrell (whose film roles have been too few), Torn and Skala as a stalwart neighbor. ★★★½ DVD: $29.99, VHS: $24.99

Hearts and Minds

(1974, 110 min, US, Peter Davis) This Oscar-winning documentary examines the American psyche in the wake of the Vietnam War. A series of heartrending interviews with veterans (and others who were sucked up into the war's madness) is intercut with some of the most horrifying footage of the war to create a brutally emotional viewing experience. ★★★★ DVD Letterbox Criterion Collection: $39.99

Hearts in Atlantis

(2001, 101 min, US, Scott Hicks) *Anthony Hopkins, Anton Yelchin, Hope Davis, David Morse, Mika Boorem.* Long on reverence but a little short on dramatic substance, *Hearts in Atlantis* is director Hicks' polished, languid adaptation of Stephen King's non-horror romance. A wistful coming-of-age tale in the guise of a supernatural suspense film, the story centers on the arrival of Ted (Hopkins), an enigmatic stranger, to the boarding house run by young Bobby's mother. Bored, lonely and fascinated by his new tenant, Bobby befriends Ted, who is reluctant to get too close. But as Ted unwillingly becomes the youth's surrogate father, Bobby begins to demonstrate psychic ability, a gift already honed by Ted. Despite a sincere performance by Hopkins and a moving evocation of 1960s New England, the film never truly takes off due to the inability to establish a fluid rhythm or fully develop the main characters. ★★½ DVD Letterbox: $14.99, VHS: $9.99

Hearts of Darkness: A Filmmaker's Apocalypse

(1991, 96 min, US, Eleanor Coppola, Fax Bahr, George Hickenlooper) This mesmerizing documentary on the making of Francis Ford Coppola's Apocalypse Now was culled from over 60 hours of footage shot by Coppola's wife, Eleanor, while on location in the Philippine jungle. The film follows Coppola and crew as they wend their way up river and almost enter the eerie world of Joseph Conrad's "Heart of Darkness" themselves. Documented are all of the troubles which beset the film: Martin Sheen's near-fatal heart attack; sets being destroyed by tropical monsoons; and the delays caused when the Filipino Air Force helicopters being used as props would leave to engage in real combat with that country's Communist rebels. Coppola's quip to reporters at Cannes sums the film best, "We had access to too much money, too much equipment and we slowly went insane." ★★★½

Hearts of the West

(1975, 103 min, US, Howard Zieff) *Jeff Bridges, Andy Griffith, Alan Arkin, Blythe Danner, Donald Pleasence.* Underrated western spoof with Bridges as a farmboy who heads to Hollywood and becomes a star of Grade-B cowboy movies. Arkin is hilarious as an eccentric director. ★★★ VHS: $19.99

Heat

(1995, 173 min, US, Michael Mann) *Al Pacino, Robert De Niro, Val Kilmer, Jon Voight, Tom Sizemore, Diane Verona, Amy Brenneman, Ashley Judd, Mykelti Williamson, Wes Studi, Ted Levine.* Mann's self-described "Los Angeles crime saga" features, among other pleasures, the first on-screen meeting between thespian heavyweights De Niro and Pacino. De Niro plays a cool, icily competent thief; Pacino is the weathered, equally cool L.A. homicide detective obsessed with his capture. Most of the film is a buildup to the inevitable showdown between the two men, neither of whom is willing to back down or give up. Mann's script brings the tired cliché of "honor among thieves" to a new level as it contrasts both men. Unfortunately, the overlong film is bogged down by far too many unnecessary subplots. Also hindering the success of the film is Pacino's out-of-control performance. Despite the flaws, however, Mann's exceptional visual style shines with slickly staged chases, robberies and confrontations, making this a satisfying and moving crime drama. ★★★ DVD Letterbox: $19.99, VHS: $14.99, VHS Letterbox: $14.99

Heat and Dust

(1983, 131 min, GB, James Ivory) *Julie Christie, Greta Scacchi, Shashi Kapoor.* Ivory's lush and romantic tale of two British women's parallel absorption into the mystical and carnal realm of the Far East. Christie is the independent, contemporary woman tracing her roots and Scacchi makes a dazzling debut as her scandalous great aunt. ★★★ DVD Criterion Collection: $29.99

Heat & Sunlight

(1987, 98 min, US, Rob Nilsson) *Rob Nilsson.* The final 16 hours of a relationship between an aging, leather-clad photographer (Nilsson) and a beautiful young dancer is explored in this slow-moving, improvisational melodrama. Bringing new meaning to the phrase "vanity production," director Nilsson plays the brooding, jealous, obsessive man who is slow in realizing that his girlfriend is just not interested. ★½ VHS: $29.99

Heat of Desire (Plein Sud)

(1985, 91 min, France, Luc Beraud) *Clio Goldsmith, Patrick Dewaere, Guy Marchand, Jeanne Moreau.* This unexpectedly unpredictable tale of obsessive love follows university professor Dewaere as he meets sensuous siren Goldsmith and immediately throws off the life he had lived to that point. His involvement with her grows to include her shady family and an improbable scam that they are preparing. (French with English subtitles) ★★★

The Heat of the Day

(1991, 120 min, GB, Christopher Morahan) *Patricia Hodge, Michael Gambon, Michael York, Peggy Ashcroft.* Made for "Masterpiece Theatre," this romantic spy thriller, set against the backdrop of the London Blitz, stars Hodge as a middle-aged woman who is drawn into the espionage biz against her will. When a very mysterious and elusive Gambon shows up at her door and insinuates that her lover (York) is a Nazi spy, Hodge finds herself in a sticky ethical dilemma. Then, Gambon complicates things with his amorous advances. The three veteran actors breathe life into an otherwise moribund Harold Pinter screenplay. ★★½ VHS: $19.99

Heathers

(1989, 102 min, US, Michael Lehmann) *Winona Ryder, Christian Slater, Shannen Doherty, Kim Walker, Lisanne Falk.* Comedy comes no blacker than in this bitingly sharp satire on teenage suicide and murder. First-time director Lehmann and writer Daniel Waters have fashioned a refreshing antidote to all of those disgustingly sweet Brat Pack flicks that presume to tell Middle America what the white youth of today are thinking. The story revolves around three bitchy, self-obsessed beauties all named Heather who prance about their high school terrorizing the geeks and cock-teasing the jocks. Their newest member Veronica (Ryder) takes part in the pranks, but feels somehow empty until she meets J.D. (Slater), a decidedly different teen whose cool looks and demented sense of a good time propels her into a whirlwind week of murder, terrorism and funerals. When Veronica writes in her diary, "Suddenly my teenage angst has a body count," you know that this is no ordinary coming-of-age movie. ★★★★ DVD Letterbox: $19.99, VHS: $9.99

H

273

Heatwave

(1983, 99 min, Australia, Phillip Noyce) *Judy Davis, Chris Haywood.* Set amidst a blistering city heatwave, this complex thriller about the abuses of corporate power escalates to a stirring, nerve-shattering climax. Davis is especially good as a community organizer who opposes the uncontrolled and insensitive policies of an expansionist development company. ★★★

Heaven

(1987, 80 min, US, Diane Keaton) A lighthearted look at what lies ahead after this lifetime, from first-time director Keaton. Includes a mix of interviews and film footage addressing the subject of Heaven. ★★½ DVD: $19.99, VHS: $9.99

Heaven

(1999, 95 min, US, Scott Reynolds) *Martin Donovan, Joanna Going, Richard Schiff.* In this intriguing and wholly satisfying tale of destiny and free will, Donovan plays a gambling-addicted architect whose wife has left him and whose sole client is a scuzzy strip joint owner. After he befriends a clairvoyant transsexual stripper named Heaven, his life takes a very interesting turn. Fans of Steven Soderbergh's thrillers (*Out of Sight, The Limey*) will enjoy the constant flashbacks and forwards, which, while being visually engaging and clever, also build the story to an almost unbearably suspenseful climax. Slight and not very durable upon multiple viewings, *Heaven* is still an extremely enjoyable film, with excellent perfs from Donovan and character actor Schiff. ★★★ DVD: $19.99, VHS: $9.99

Heaven and Earth

(1993, 135 min, US, Oliver Stone) *Tommy Lee Jones, Hiep Thi Le, Joan Chen, Haing S. Ngor, Debbie Reynolds, Conchata Ferrell.* The third film in director Stone's Vietnam trilogy (*Platoon* and *Born on the Fourth of July*), based on the true-life perils of a Vietnamese peasant, Le Ly Hayslip (Le). Unique because this intensely melodramatic story looks at the war through the eyes of a woman, viewers will find themselves physically and emotionally drained as the film examines in minute detail the main character's trials, which include torture, rape, prostitution and a failed marriage to an American G.I. (Jones). Lushly photographed and laced with fine performances by Le, Jones and Chen, this fiercly impassioned film shows another side of the Vietnam conflict with insight and understanding. ★★★ DVD: $24.99, VHS: $19.99

Heaven Can Wait

(1943, 112 min, US, Ernst Lubitsch) *Don Ameche, Gene Tierney, Charles Coburn, Marjorie Main.* Superbly entertaining comic fantasy from Lubitsch with Ameche as the recently departed, retelling the story of his youthful romantic intrigues to the Devil himself. (Not associated with the similarly titled Warren Beatty comedy.) ★★★½ VHS: $19.99

Heaven Can Wait

(1978, 101 min, US, Buck Henry & Warren Beatty) *Warren Beatty, James Mason, Julie Christie, Jack Warden, Dyan Cannon, Charles Grodin.* Beatty is in fine form as both director and star in this exceptional remake of the 1941 classic *Here Comes Mr. Jordan.* He plays a pro football player who dies before his time and, with the help of angel Mason, finds a new body to inhabit. Great supporting cast, especially Cannon and Grodin as murderous and quite excitable paramours. (Remade as *Down to Earth*) ★★★½ DVD: $19.99, VHS: $14.99

Heaven Help Us

(1985, 104 min, US, Michael Dinner) *Andrew McCarthy, Mary Stuart Masterson, Donald Sutherland, John Heard, Kevin Dillon, Wallace Shawn, Patrick Dempsey, Stephen Geoffreys.* An above average and quite entertaining coming-of-age comedy set in a mid-1960s Brooklyn all-boys Catholic high school. The sometimes hilarious story follows the tight-knit group, each of whom is dealing with the inner turmoil of both being at the mercy of their ever-raging hormones and being born a Catholic. The film features an appealing cast, including Andrew McCarthy, Mary Stuart Masterson, Donald Sutherland, John Heard, Kevin Dillon, Wallace Shawn, Patrick Dempsey and, in a riotously funny turn, Stephen *Fright Night* Geoffreys as one of the boys who just can't seem to keep "it" in his pants any longer. ★★★

Heaven Knows, Mr. Allison

(1957, 107 min, US, John Huston) *Robert Mitchum, Deborah Kerr.* Two very appealing performances by Kerr (an Oscar nominee) and Mitchum highlight cowriter/director Huston's slick WWII drama that can't help but draw comparisons to his earlier, superior *The African Queen.* A Marine (Mitchum) and a nun (Kerr) become stranded on a Japanese-held island, setting aside their bickering to team against the enemy. Huston replaces sexual tension with action and humor, and though it may not all work, these two stars make you forget about how familiar it really is. ★★★ DVD: $14.99, VHS: $9.99

Heaven on Earth

(1986, 100 min, Canada, Allan Kroeker) *R.H. Thomson, Sian Leisa Davies.* This compelling and sensitive drama is based on a little known historical episode. Between the years 1867 and 1914, during the social upheaval of the Industrial Revolution, England found itself with many unwanted, abandoned and orphaned children. In an effort to alleviate the problem, these "home children," as they became known, were sent to Canada to begin new lives. This is the story of five of these children; innocents who, faced with a demanding and often times cruel existence, soon realized that their dreams of heaven on Earth were not to be realized in their new adopted land. ★★★

Heaven's Burning

(1997, 99 min, Australia, Craig Lahiff) *Russell Crowe, Youki Kudoh.* Crowe stars in this pre-*L.A. Confidential* role as the driver in a bank robbery gone wrong: to make their escape, the thieves take a hostage, a young Japanese woman (Kudoh) who has just left her husband on the last day of their honeymoon. When his cronies decide to kill the hostage, Crowe shoots one of them to save her, thus instigating an oath of vengeance from the slain lad's loony dad. With the jilted hubby and vengeful pop on their trail, Crowe and Kudoh drive through the Outback and fall in love. Their scenes are genuinely, sweetly romantic — Crowe makes a greatly appealing, chivalrous hero; and Kudoh is an incredibly cute, resilient and likable heroine. The scenes featuring the cuckolded husband, though, are atrocious, and *Heaven's Burning* tends to be too jokey and mean-spirited at times. There's an amusing cameo by Colin Hay, formerly of seminal '80s band Men at Work. ★★½ DVD: $24.99

Heaven's Gate

(1980, 220 min, US, Michael Cimino) *Kris Kristofferson, Jeff Bridges, Isabelle Huppert, Joseph Cotten, Christopher Walken.* Whadda you

Hedd Wyn

care how much this notorious $50 million bomb cost? It costs the same to rent as any of Corman's two-day wonders. Cimino lavishes his attention on the evolution of the community of Heaven's Gate — from its rough and tumble mining town origins to that of a full-blown city, as civilization begins to tame the wild frontier. ★★ DVD Letterbox: $19.99

Heaven's Prisoners

(1996, 126 min, US, Phil Joanou) *Alec Baldwin, Mary Stuart Masterson, Kelly Lynch, Teri Hatcher, Vondie Curtis Hall, Eric Roberts.* A troubled, recovering-alcoholic ex-cop (Baldwin) and his wife (Lynch) enter a hazy world of drug trafficking, cover-up and disloyalty when a small plane crashes into the Bayou not far from their boat. The only survivor is a very young Salvadorian refugee, whom the couple take into their home. The arrival of a DEA agent leads Baldwin to old childhood friend Roberts, now a drug dealer, and his perpetually intoxicated wife Hatcher. As the story progresses, layers of deceit are peeled away. Baldwin's attempts to secure the orphaned girl's safety lead him too close to the activities of a drug-smuggling ring, placing those closest to him in imminent danger. Though overly long, the film adroitly defines a mood of despondency and captures the feel of the Louisiana Bayou. ★★½

Heavenly Creatures

(1994, 99 min, New Zealand, Peter Jackson) *Melanie Lynskey, Kate Winslet, Sarah Peirse.* The provocative, imaginative true-life story of how the intense and passionate relationship of two 1950s teenagers Pauline Parker and Juliet Hulme led to the grisly murder of Pauline's mother. The film realistically and fantastically portrays the friendship of the teens, with Lynskey and Winslet giving outstanding and believable performances as Pauline and Juliet, respectively. The parents of both teens worry about their daughters' "unnatural" relationship and things go terribly wrong when they are eventually separated. Only one solution remains for the two friends. Director Jackson endows the film with such vision and substance (in addition to some amazing special effects) that the viewer is easily and quickly drawn into the lives of the lead characters. It's the most thrilling story of matricide since *Psycho*. Of interest: After serving time, Juliet became a best-selling murder mystery author, using the name Anne Perry. ★★★★ DVD Uncut: $14.99, VHS: $9.99

Heavens Above

(1963, 105 min, GB, John Boulting & Roy Boulting) *Peter Sellers, Cecil Parker, Isabel Jeans,*

H

Ian Carmichael. Sellers displays his usual comic genius as an idealistic and naive young vicar who is accidentally assigned to a small country parish. When, upon arriving, he is met with a less-than-Christian zeal by the townsfolk, he cheerfully sets out to breed a healthier atmosphere — much to the chagrin of the local power structure. This scathing satire pointedly accuses the Anglican church of acquiescing to the establishment. The film's only drawback is its somewhat heavy-handed Christian message. ★★★½ DVD Letterbox: $19.99

Heavy

(1996, 105 min, US, James Mangold) *Pruitt Taylor Vince, Liv Tyler, Shelley Winters, Deborah Harry, Evan Dando, Joe Grifasi.* Like a more modest "*Marty*" for the '90s, *Heavy* is a nicely observed, small slice-of-lifer, set mostly in an out-of-the-way greasy spoon in upstate New York, about the unrequited love between an overweight cook and a beautiful new waitress. Vince is excellent as Victor, the terribly shy but good-hearted mama's boy who dreams of both becoming a gourmet chef and having a relationship with the very appealing Callie (Tyler). Director Mangold captures many telling details that ring true — the dreary, small-town atmosphere, for example, is spot on. Though not as rich in character as one would want, Mangold makes a strong debut with this moody tale, and gets terrific performances from his cast. ★★★ DVD: $27.99

Heavy Metal

(1981, 93 min, Canada, Gerald Potterton) *Richard Romanus, John Candy, Eugene Levy, Joe Flaherty.* An animated anthology film, *Heavy Metal* is a series of fantasy and sci-fi tales which have the common theme of breasts, broadswords, badass aliens and bodacious rock 'n' roll. Source of countless adolescent erotic fantasies, the film's animation is primitive compared to contemporary works, but its nostalgic charm and historical value are hard to deny. The segments range from the terrific ("B17" and Richard Corben's "Den") and funny ("So Beautiful, So Dangerous" and Berni Wrightson's "Captain Sternn") to the overlong ("Taarna") and trite ("Harry Canyon"). The best rely on animation and music to tell the story, rather than dialogue. Boasting a soundtrack of the best of the late '70s and early '80s rock music, *Heavy Metal* is a sexy, gory, violent, fun-filled ride whose qualities will not diminish on repeated viewing. ★★★ DVD Letterbox Superbit Edition: $26.99, DVD: $27.99, VHS: $14.99

Heavy Metal 2000

(2000, 88 min, US, Michael Coldewey & Michel Lemire) *Michael Ironside, Julie Strain, Billy Idol.* A belated sequel to the 1981 cult hit, *Heavy Metal 2000* rates as a major disappointment. Periodically announced throughout the years as another anthology film, but this time mixing live action and animation, *HM2000* arrives as a fully animated, single-story film. The odd, much-sought-after glowy power thingy (the chamber of immortality) from the first film is the impetus for a snoozer story involving a bad guy (voiced by Ironside) being chased on a quest for vengeance by a hot chick. Punctuated by some fun gore and violence, the dull story meanders along with very little imagination. Animation buffs may want to watch this, but casual viewers should stay far away. ★½ DVD: $24.99, VHS: $14.99

Heavy Petting

(1989, 85 min, US, Obie Benz) *David Byrne, Sandra Bernhard, Ann Magnuson, Josh Mostel, Laurie Anderson, Spalding Grey.* Amusing and

entertaining satire on our country's repression of and obsession with sex; chronicling those "innocent" days (when "good girls didn't") with clips from '50s "B" movies and with funny, insightful and occasionally stupid anecdotes. ★★★ VHS: $19.99

Heavy Traffic

(1973, 77 min, US, Ralph Bakshi) Animator Bakshi's most ambitious project of his early career, this boldly original and revolutionary work combines live action and animation to tell the story of a New York youth who escapes the confines of his surroundings by drawing the people around him — creating a devastating portrait of the underside of city life. Rated X. ★★★ DVD: $14.99, VHS: $14.99

Hedd Wyn

(1995, 123 min, Wales, Paul Turner) *Huw Garmon, Sue Roderick, Judith Humphries, Phil Reid.* From a country where poets are revered as much as sports figures are in America comes this handsome film based on a true story. Told in a series of flashbacks remembered by a soldier wounded in battle in WWI, *Hedd Wyn* recounts the story of Ellis, a young farmer living with his large family in an impoverished Welsh village whose talent for prose has made him somewhat of a local celebrity. As he pursues the local lasses with religious fervor, Ellis tries to accomplish a poet's highest honor — winning a chair for poetry. While most of the story concentrates on Ellis' romantic and literary agendas, the film also reflects upon the Welsh tradition and speaks to the misfortunes of war (for both soldier and family left behind) in a series of carefully detailed battle scenes. Garmon, a good-looking and efficient actor, brings to Ellis a good-natured charm. (Welsh with English subtitles) ★★★ VHS: $19.99

Hedda

(1975, 100 min, GB, Trevor Nunn) *Glenda Jackson, Timothy West, Jennie Linden, Peter Eyre, Patrick Stewart.* Jackson dominates this powerful film version of Henrik Ibsen's classic play "Hedda Gabler." Taken directly from the Royal Shakespeare Company's stage rendition, Jackson's Hedda is a Nordic femme fatale — a neurotic, iron-willed controller who is nevertheless alluring to the local men. ★★★

Hedwig and the Angry Inch

(2001, 95 min, US, John Cameron Mitchell) *John Cameron Mitchell, Miriam Shor, Michael Pitt, Andrea Martin, Alberta Watson, Stephen Trask.* Based on the long-running off-Broadway show, *Hedwig* hits the screen in all its bewigged glory compliments of creators Mitchell and Trask. Mitchell directs and stars as Hansel/Hedwig, a gay aspiring rock star raised in Communist East Berlin who desperately wants to move to the West. He meets Luther, an African-American G.I. who encourages him to have a sex change, marry and escape with him to Kansas. The operation is botched and Hansel is left with a teeny weeny! Once there, in trailer park hell, Hedwig is abandoned with little more than an "angry inch." Relegated to baby-sitting gigs, she/he develops a lounge act and hits the road with her pan-Slavic band determined to right the wrongs and claim the recognition, riches and "other half" she so richly deserves. A scintillating, original, in-your-face, often hilarious experience that blurs the lines between gay performance art, exhilarating musical parody and cynical Bette Davis-like melodrama. ★★★★ DVD Platinum Series: $24.99

Heidi

(1937, 88 min, US, Allan Dwan) *Shirley Temple, Jean Hersholt, Arthur Treacher.* Little Shirley shines as the young Swiss girl taken away from her loving grandfather. ★★½ DVD: $19.99, VHS: $9.99

The Heidi Chronicles

(1995, 94 min, US, Paul Bogart) *Jamie Lee Curtis, Kim Cattrall, Tom Hulce.* Based on a play by Wendy Wasserstein (who also wrote this made-for-cable adaptation), this bittersweet drama chronicles the maturation of art historian Heidi Holland (Curtis), a tirelessly average woman naïvely caught up in the politics and fads of American life. The story begins with her high school prom in the early 1960s and then fast-forwards her through the hippie and anti-war periods, the feminist decade of the '70s, and '80s "Me Generation." Through the years, she sets forth on a voyage of self-discovery, though to her regret she doesn't always find the most satisfactory romances. Curtis gives a pleasing performance as the sometimes hapless Heidi. Hulce gives a solid performance in support as Heidi's gay friend Peter, who approaches his complex character with good humor and a level-headedness. ★★★ VHS: $14.99

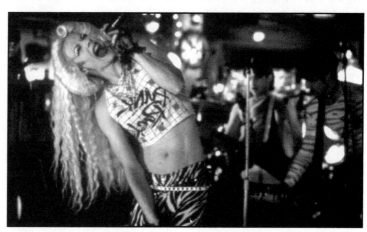

Hedwig and the Angry Inch

Heidi Fleiss: Hollywood Madam

(1995, 106 min, US, Nick Broomfield) This weirdly funny, satirical documentary — a perhaps unintentional parody of the exploitative TV newsmagazines whose clips it uses — is the perfect vehicle for this tale of Hollywood's swarmy excesses. The film concentrates on convicted panderer Heidi Fleiss' relationships with Ivan Nagy, her lover, nemesis and alleged pimp; and Madam Alex, Hollywood's grand madam for 20 years and Heidi's one-time employer and mentor. Each of the three refutes allegations from the other two, yet they all seem inextricably linked. LAPD is represented by Daryl Gates, whose brother is openly acknowledged as using such professional services. Gates details his fervor to prosecute pimps rather than johns. Yet the department has a history of protecting pimps and madams if they're good informants, a role that Fleiss apparently refused to play. Wickedly enjoyable yet ultimately unsettling, it demonstrates wretched excess permeates every aspect of this latest entry into the annals of Babylon. You'll feel the need to bathe after viewing. ★★★ VHS: $14.99

Heist

(2001, 107 min, US, David Mamet) *Gene Hackman, Danny DeVito, Delroy Lindo, Sam Rockwell, Rebecca Pidgeon, Ricky Jay, Patti LuPone.* If there is honor among thieves, some of the characters in writer-director Mamet's edgy thriller *Heist* have long forgotten such a mantra. A couple others haven't, and it's part of the fun deciphering just who is who when a veteran thief is coerced for one last big sting. As expertly played by Hackman, Joe Moore is the kind of team leader who leaves little to chance — his backup plans have backup plans. When he has no choice but to accept his fence Bergman's (DeVito) offer for a high-stakes heist, Joe and his crew embark on a dangerous mission with Bergman's wild card of a nephew in tow. Sure the setup has almost become a cliché (2001's *The Score* used the same formula to even greater effect), but whereas other heist films concentrate on the heist itself, Mamet is far more interested in his characters and how each will react to every twist. Mamet isn't as complete with the roles of Joe's wife and Bergman's nephew as other characters, and their motivations often ring false. But the strength of the piece is in Hackman's robust character and determined portrayal, elevating a story that — when it wants to be — can be quite smart. ★★★ DVD: $14.99, VHS: $9.99

Held Up

(2000, 88 min, US, Steve Rash) *Jamie Foxx, Nia Long, Barry Corbin, John Cullum, Jake Busey, Eduardo Yañez.* A moronic "action-comedy" about a loud-mouthed idiot (Foxx) whose macho-man antics cost him his new car, his girlfriend (Long, in a wasted role), and nearly his life. This feeble attempt at screwball comedy is never funny even once, and will be a major disappointment to anyone expecting the comic agility displayed by Foxx in "In Living Color." ★ DVD: $24.99

Hell Comes to Frogtown

(1988, 86 min, US, R.J. Kizer) *Roddy Piper, Sandahl Bergman, Rory Calhoun.* Enjoyable low-budget sci-fi adventure starring Piper as a post-apocalyptic mercenary (and one of the few remaining fertile men) who must rescue a group of similarly potent women. ★★½

Hell in the Pacific

(1968, 103 min, US, John Boorman) *Lee Marvin, Toshiro Mifune.* Director Boorman takes a microcosm of WWII and extrapolates a parable on the insanity of war. An American and a Japanese soldier find themselves washed up on a deserted island in the Pacific. Their mutual dependence necessitates the suppression of their hostilities. Both Marvin and Mifune are superb, managing to be both ethnic representatives and universal Everymen. Boorman directs with a sure hand. ★★★½ DVD: $14.99

Hell Is for Heroes

(1962, 90 min, US, Don Siegel) *Steve McQueen, Bobby Darin, Harry Guardino, James Coburn, Nick Adams, Bob Newhart.* A fine cast of young actors is featured in this taut WWII drama about a small American company caught behind enemy lines. ★★★ DVD: $14.99, VHS: $9.99

Hell Up in Harlem

(1973, 96 min, US, Larry Cohen) *Fred Williamson, Julius W. Harris, Margaret Avery.* Williamson sets out, in his own annihilating way, to make the ghetto safe from detestable murderers and druggies in this entertainingly violent sequel to *Black Caesar.* One of the best scenes features black maids force-feeding soul food to Mafia children. ★★ DVD Letterbox: $14.99, VHS: $4.99

Hell's Angels on Wheels

(1967, 95 min, US, Richard Rush) *Jack Nicholson, Adam Roarke.* Four bikers tangle with rival roadies and local thugs. A young Nicholson plays a brooding gas station attendant named Poet who discovers the joys of a hog. Trashy biker pic still manages to entertain in a guilty pleasure sort of way. ★★ DVD: $19.99

Hellbound: Hellraiser II

(1988, 97 min, GB, Tony Randel) *Ashley Laurence, Clare Higgins.* With this extremely gruesome sequel, British author Clive Barker continues to redefine the modern horror genre. Picking up where the original left off, Kirsty wakes up in a mental hospital. Intent on saving her father's damned soul, she enlists the help of a fellow patient, and together they descend into the bowels of Hell. Very graphic and violent — not suggested for the faint-hearted. (Sequel: *Hellraiser 3: Hell on Earth*) ★★★ DVD Unrated: $19.99, VHS Unrated: $9.99

Hellhole

(1985, 90 min, US, Pierre de Moro) *Judy Landers, Ray Sharkey, Mary Woronov.* A young woman (Landers) develops amnesia after witnessing the brutal murder of her mother, and awakens in a sanitarium. There, she is stalked by the killer (Sharkey) and a psychotic scientist (Woronov) who wants to use her as an experimental guinea pig. As bad as it sounds. ★

Hello, Dolly!

(1969, 146 min, US, Gene Kelly) *Barbra Streisand, Walter Matthau, Tommy Tune, Michael Crawford, Louis Armstrong.* Streisand shines in this elaborate and entertaining screen version of the hit Broadway musical comedy. Streisand plays turn-of-the-century matchmaker Dolly Levi, who sets her own sights on grocery store owner Horace Vandergelder (the agreeably gruff Matthau). There are wonderful dance numbers, and a whimsical score by Jerry Herman. Though some of the production is rather overblown, it detracts nothing from the film's enjoyment. Based on Thornton Wilder's comedy, "The Matchmaker." ★★★½ DVD: $14.99

Hellraiser

(1987, 93 min, GB, Clive Barker) *Andrew Robinson, Clare Higgins, Ashley Laurence.* Barker's riveting directorial debut is unquestionably one of the most serious and intelligent horror films in recent memory. Told from the perspective of Kirsty, our teenage heroine, this phantasmagorical tale of gruesome family secrets finds its beginnings with her Uncle Frank, a sinister sensualist who cracks the code of a mysterious Chinese puzzle box and thereby opens the door to another dimension. Through this threshold come the dreaded Cenobites (led by the menacing Pinhead), a punked-out crew of otherworldly sadists with a penchant for ripped flesh and steaming entrails. (Sequel: *Hellbound: Hellraiser II*) ★★★½ DVD: $19.99, VHS: $14.99

Hellraiser: Bloodline

(1996, 90 min, US, Alan Smithee) *Doug Bradley.* Makeup effects artist Kevin Yagher originally conceived and directed this fourth installment in the *Hellraiser* series as a three-part anthology film, showing the various problems that people throughout the ages have gotten into when they irresponsibly play with a Lament Configuration. Studio executives, however, decided to re-edit the film into a linear narrative with flashbacks. Primarily set in the future, the film is now about the current Lemarchand's attempt to destroy Pinhead forever. Mildly atmospheric and definitely better than the third installment of the series (*Hellraiser 3: Hell on Earth*), *Bloodline* is worth a die-hard horror fan's passing glance, but no more. ★★ DVD: $14.99, VHS: $9.99

Hellraiser: Hellseeker

(2002, 90 min, US, Rick Bota) *Dean Winters, Doug Bradley, Ashley Laurence. Hellraiser: Hellseeker,* the sixth film in the series, is just plain inexcusable. No one's expectations could have possibly been high after the dreadful fourth and fifth chapters, but this film is beyond comprehension. The talented Winters (of HBO's "Oz") is wasted as a widower having nightmarish visions after his wife apparently died in a car crash. He has these (unscary, unimaginative, pointless) visions for nearly the entire running time, until the silly surprise ending, which is a nasty slap in the face for fans of the first two films (which remain the only quality entries in the series). And what's worse: Pinhead's gotten chunky — do they have nachos in Hell? ★ DVD: $29.99, VHS: $14.99

Hellraiser: Inferno

(2000, 99 min, US, Scott Derrickson) *Craig Sheffer, Nicholas Turturro, James Remar, Doug Bradley.* The awful *Hellraiser: Inferno* is only a reminder of a better time when horror films were truly frightening and their cheap-ass knockoff sequels at least had chapter numbers in the titles. In case you're counting, "Inferno" is the fifth installment of the goth-horror series spawned by Clive Barker. Iconic boogeyman Pinhead pops up in a mere cameo in a yawningly uninspired tale of a bad cop who opens the mysterious puzzle box and takes a mind-bending plunge into Hell. Cheap production values and brittle performances wreck an already lousy script, resulting in a movie so devoid of surprise and tension it's no wonder it was condemned straight to video. Another horror series officially bites the dust. ★ DVD: $14.99, VHS: $9.99

Help!

(1965, 90 min, GB, Richard Lester) *The Beatles, Leo McKern, Eleanor Bron, Victor Spinetti, Roy Kinnear.* It's hard to top a masterpiece. Lester and

The Beatles united again in this attempt to recapture the mad-cap brilliance of *A Hard Day's Night*, and while the effort is a decidedly good one, it falls short of its predecessor. Still, any fan of The Beatles or Lester's slap-dash comic style will revel in this rockin' romp. ★★★½

Helter Skelter

(1976, 119 min, US, Tom Gries) *Steve Railsback, Nancy Wolfe, George DiCenzo.* Based on the best-selling novel by prosecuting attorney Vincent Bugliosi, this exceptional made-for-TV movie is a truly disturbing docudrama about Charles Manson and his family of disciples. Railsback's intense portrayal of Charlie is stunning. ★★★½ DVD: $19.99

Hennessey

(1975, 103 min, GB, Don Sharp) *Rod Steiger, Lee Remick, Trevor Howard.* Steiger stars in this high-paced political thriller as an Irish demolitions expert who sets out to avenge his daughter's death by bombing the Parliament on opening day — when the Royal Family attends. The action gets hot when both the IRA and the British Secret Service try to stop him. ★★★ VHS: $19.99

Henry & June

(1990, 140 min, US, Philip Kaufman) *Fred Ward, Uma Thurman, Maria de Medeiros, Richard E. Grant, Kevin Spacey.* The first film to earn the MPAA's NC-17 rating, director Kaufman's steamy adaptation of Anaïs Nin's novel about the passionate love triangle between herself, writer Henry Miller and his wife June is a glorious sexual and literary odyssey through the streets of 1930s Paris. Exquisitely photographed, *Henry & June* sumptuously evokes a frenzied carnival atmosphere and makes for an extraordinary sensual cinematic experience. Newcomer de Medeiros is dazzling as the doe-eyed Anaïs, a prolific diarist who vigorously committed herself to the pursuit of complete sexual abandon. As Miller, Ward is excellent, exuding a sleazy sexuality and the tenderness of a love-struck poet. Thurman gives a lusty portrayal of the voluptuous bombshell June. ★★★½ DVD: $9.99

Henry V

(1946, 137 min, GB, Laurence Olivier) *Laurence Olivier, Robert Newton, Leslie Banks, Renee Asherson.* A stirring version of Shakespeare's historical drama. Olivier directed as well as stars as the heroic king who fights for his kingdom in France. Filmed in Technicolor, Olivier introduces the viewer to his play on film by opening with an impressive aerial shot of a re-creation of London's 17th-century Globe Theatre. ★★★★ DVD: $39.99

Laurence Olivier's *Henry V*

Henry V

(1989, 137 min, GB, Kenneth Branagh) *Kenneth Branagh, Paul Scofield, Derek Jacobi, Ian Holm, Brian Blessed, Alec McCowan, Judi Dench, Michael Maloney, Emma Thompson.* Branagh's astonishing directorial debut remakes Shakespeare's classic, which Laurence Olivier had all but stamped his name upon. Everything about this film works. Branagh delivers a bravura performance as the young King Henry that is nothing short of inspirational. His supporting cast is as good as they come. Branagh's direction is crisp and clean, his command of the dialogue is perfect and he masterfully works Shakespeare's subtle sense of humor into the movie. ★★★★ DVD: $19.99

Henry Fool

(1998, 137 min, US, Hal Hartley) *Thomas Jay Ryan, Parker Posey, James Urbaniak, Maria Porter.* Can a lying con man be a mentor to a repressed sanitation worker? Henry Fool (Ryan) rents a room in the unhappy household of Simon Grim (Urbaniak), a young man ridiculed by clinically depressed mom Mary (Porter), slutty sister Fay (Posey) and an assortment of neighborhood toughs. Henry assumes control of these lives teetering between pointlessness and despair, mixing unabashed admiration for Simon's poetry with tales of high adventure in South American jungles. Resistance to Henry's influence is never a consideration for Simon, whose unabating sense of futility is for once pushed aside by glimmerings of self-worth. Bringing his characters to the edge of caricature, director Hartley uses their particular idiosynchracies to make broader statements about American cultural anomalities, As the protagonists blindly grope for purpose and meaning, the film's tone shifts from cerebral detachment to uncomfortable menace as Hartley crafts another sly exploration of human relation and individual salvation. ★★★ DVD: $24.99

Henry IV

(1985, 94 min, Italy, Marco Bellocchio) *Marcello Mastroianni, Claudia Cardinale.* Driven mad by unrequited love, a man (Mastroianni) spends 20 years believing himself to be a medieval emperor. A finely crafted tale of passion and illusion from Nobel Prize-winner Luigi Pirandello. (Italian with English subtitles) ★★★ DVD: $29.99

Henry: Portrait of a Serial Killer

(1986, 105 min, US, John McNaughton) *Michael Rooker, Tracy Arnold, Tom Towles.* Initially dismissed by its producers as not having enough blood and action to please the *Friday the 13th* horror crowd, this harrowing portrait of a psychotic killer was not successful until the art audience discovered it. Henry, recently released from prison for killing his mother, moves in with his old buddy Otis and his sister, Becky. Henry soon resumes his random killings, eventually initiating a more-than-willing Otis in his frenzied rampages. The real horror in the film is not the actual killings, but rather in the sympathetic and nonjudgmental approach the film takes as it follows Henry on his cooly detached and senseless pursuit of death. ★★★ DVD Director's Edition: $24.99, VHS Director's Edition: $19.99

Hera Purple: Devil Goddess

(2002, 93 min, Korea, Chung Gil-Chae) *Chung Kim, Lee Se-Chang, Lee Ho-Sung, Chung Gil-Chae.* A truly strange Korean horror/sex/detective film, *Herapurple: Devil Goddess* is fast-paced and stylish enough to overcome its incredible silliness. A happily married mother inexplicably morphs into a

vengeful sex goddess and murders unsuspecting partners in compromising positions. And they are in every position imaginable: there's sex on horseback, underwater, in the snow, on the street, straight, gay, lesbian — it's got it all. If it's sex you're after, you've come to the right place, but horror fans won't find much to get too excited about (aside from the sex, of course). The film makes little sense, and doesn't fully work as a police procedural, but it's pretty to look at (in more ways than one), zips by and makes a helluva party flick. (Korean with English subtitles) ★★½ DVD: $19.99, VHS: $19.99

Hercules

(1959, 107 min, Italy, Pietro Francisci) *Steve Reeves, Sylvia Koscina.* Muscleman Reeves stars in this sleek adventure film as the Greek hero Hercules. The film that started the "gladiator" genre which was so popular in the early '60s. ★★½

Hercules

(1997, 93 min, US, John Musker & Ron Clements) *Voices of: Tate Donovan, Danny DeVito, James Woods, Bobcat Goldthwait, Paul Shaffer, Rip Torn, Charlton Heston.* While this Disney animated feature doesn't come close to matching the magical splendor of the studio's best classics, *Hercules* is brisk, breezy fun. The animation is a bit clunky, despite the liberal use of computer-enhanced effects, and the songs are downright forgettable (something that has characterized *Pocahontas* and *Hunchback of Notre Dame*, which came before this), but the instrumental score is strong, and the vocal contributions are top-notch — including Torn as Zeus, Donovan as Herc, and, in a standout bit of cheerful malevolence, Woods as Hades, the leader of the Underworld. ★★★ DVD: $29.99, VHS: $22.99

Hercules in New York

(1970, 91 min, US, Arthur Allan Seidelman) *Arnold Schwarzenegger, Arnold Stang.* Schwarzenegger's film debut finds him pitted against Stang in a grade-Z *Clash of the Titans*-like production. The picture cuts between New York and Mt. Olympus (actually a mound of rock in Central Park) as Arnie disobeys Zeus' order not to hang out with mortals. The spectacular production values in this one might have even cost as much as $100. All of the acting is bottom-of-the-barrel and Arnie's accent was so thick at the time that all of his lines are badly dubbed. Yes, it's trash, but hey, you must admit, this is the ultimate Saturday night party tape as well as a prime candidate for "Mystery Science Theatre 3000." ★ DVD: $19.99

Herdsmen of the Sun

(1988, 52 min, France, Werner Herzog) Narrated in English by director Herzog, this fascinating, anthropologic documentary focuses on the Woodabes, a Saharan nomadic tribe. The highlight of the film is the strange mating ceremony staged by the young male members, all with exotically handsome, mesmeric features, who don fancy dress and elaborate makeup for an unusual beauty pageant that is judged by the women of the tribe. ★★★ VHS: $24.99

Here Comes Mr. Jordan

(1941, 93 min, US, Alexander Hall) *Robert Montgomery, Claude Rains, James Gleason, Evelyn Keyes, Edward Everett Horton.* Classic supernatural comedy with Montgomery in a splendid performance as a boxer who dies before his time; forced

H

to look for another body to inhabit with the help of heavenly Mr. Jordan (Rains). Special mention goes to Gleason as Montgomery's exasperated coach. (Remade in 1978 as *Heaven Can Wait* and in 2001 as *Down to Earth*) ★★★½

Here on Earth

(2000, 97 min, US, Mark Piznarski) *Chris Klein, Leelee Sobieski, Josh Hartnett, Bruce Greenwood, Annette O'Toole, Michael Rooker.* A teen *Love Story*, without much story, this near-nauseating romantic drama is enough to put anyone off romance at least into the next century. When his drag racing leads to a local diner burning to the ground, an affluent high school student (Klein) must spend the summer helping rebuild it. There he falls for the owner's daughter (Sobieski), already involved with the other drag racer (Hartnett). By-the-numbers characters populate this turgid triangle, and even though its cast has done good work elsewhere, there's zero chemistry between any of the leads. ★ DVD: $14.99, VHS: $6.99

Hero

(1992, 112 min, US, Stephen Frears) *Dustin Hoffman, Geena Davis, Andy Garcia, John Cusack, Tom Arnold, Chevy Chase, Kevin J. O'Connor.* There's a lot to like, and a lot to digest, in Frears' satire on heroism and the media. Hoffman returns to Ratso Rizzo territory with a glorious slimy performance as a petty crook who, in spite of himself, rescues a planeload of passengers after an airplane crashes right in front of him. One of those he saves is TV reporter Davis, who turns the city topsy-turvy looking for the "hero" who vanished into the night. When a substantial award is offered for him to come forward, onto the scene comes grifter and too-good-to-be-true Garcia. Not getting his due, Hoffman tries to convince anyone who will listen that he really is the hero, but no one will believe him. ★★★ DVD: $24.99, VHS: $14.99

Heroes Shed No Tears

(1985, 93 min, Hong Kong, John Woo) *Eddy Ko, Lam Ching Ying, Phillip Loffrede.* This wartime actioner doesn't quite live up to director Woo's other Hong Kong works of the late 1980s. Ko plays a mercenary sent to retrieve a wanted druglord from Thailand and bring him back to Hong Kong. He captures the general safely, but things go badly when he and his men try to escape the jungle. Not only are the general's men after him, but Ko is soon the object of vengeance of a mad colonel (Lam, in a terrific turn as the villain). Distinguished mainly by the excellent end fight scene between Ko and Lam, as well as the ongoing relationship between Ko and his son (shades of *Lone Wolf and Cub*), the remainder of the film is a by-the-books action flick. None of Woo's trademarks are evident in any abundance, but it's worth watching. (Cantonese with English subtitles) ★★½ VHS: $19.99

The Heroic Trio

(1993, 104 min, Hong Kong, Ching Siu-Tung & Johnny To) *Anita Mui, Michelle Yeoh, Maggie Cheung, Anthony Wong, Damien Lau.* Only the wild world of Hong Kong action cinema could have produced this dizzying comic book-style movie about three female superheroes and their battle against an androgynous demon. Mui is the mask-wearing Wonder Woman, who runs across electrical power lines and throws razor-sharp darts into her foes. The astonishing Yeoh is the kung fu mistress Invisible Girl, who is at first allied with the demon, but who soon learns she has a mysterious past connection

The Hidden Fortress

with Wonder Woman. Cheung plays Thief Catcher, a motorcycle-riding, shotgun-toting, leather-clad tough chick who only does good when the pay is right. An outrageous, colorful and campy romp, *Heroic Trio* is cinema for the sheer fun of it, with flying heroes/heroines and villains and gravity-defying fight scenes. (Cantonese with English subtitles) (Sequel: *Executioners*) ★★★ DVD Dubbed: $29.99, VHS Dubbed: $9.99

Hester Street

(1975, 90 min, US, Joan Micklin Silver) *Carol Kane, Steven Keats, Doris Roberts.* The first feature by Silver weaves a rich tapestry of ghetto life in New York City's Bowery at the turn of the century. Kane was given a well-deserved Academy Award nomination for her performance as Gilt, a Jewish émigré trying to assimilate as quietly as possible into her new country while still being supportive of her husband as he experiences a cultural identity crisis. ★★★ VHS: $9.99

Hexed

(1993, 91 min, US, Alan Spencer) *Arye Gross, Claudia Christian, R. Lee Ermey.* Gross stars as a nerdish hotel clerk who fancies himself a trendy big-wig. Telling fellow workers of his famous (albeit fictitious) associations with celebs, he's put to the test when one of them shows up at the hotel. She's a model with secrets of her own — one of them being that she's a murderess. Too bad she didn't take aim at the script. Director-writer Spencer tries to create a frantic farce in the mistaken identity, door-slamming tradition; what he gives life to, however, Dr. Frankenstein wouldn't lay claim to. ★ VHS: $14.99

Hey Babu Riba

(1986, 109 min, Yugoslavia, Jovan Acin) *Gala Videnovic, Nebojsa Bakocevic.* Set in 1950s Yugoslavia, this charming and funny film recounts the days of innocence of four close friends and rowing partners who all fall in love with the same girl, their beautiful blonde coxswain. The young girl, flattered by all of the attention, likes them all and wishes to remain friends but rejects their advances only to unwisely fall in love with an ambitious member of the Communist Party. A decidedly different coming-of-age film: one that explores the tender pain of first love and the bonds of loyal friendship, yet set against the political turmoil of a recently formed Communist government. (Serbo-Croatian with English subtitles) ★★★½

Hi, Mom!

(1970, 87 min, US, Brian De Palma) *Robert De Niro, Charles Durnham, Allen Garfield, Lara Parker, Jennifer Salt.* Anarchy reigns in De Palma's frenzied sequel to *Greetings*. De Niro stars as a returning Vietnam vet who takes on the roles of urban guerrilla, porno filmmaker and insurance salesman. Add to the fray a spoof of 1970s "encounter theatre" called "Be Black Baby," in which a group of black militants terrorize their white audience, and you've got a loopy and totally frantic vision of New York at the height of the counterculture generation. ★★★ VHS: $14.99

The Hidden

(1987, 98 min, US, Jack Sholder) *Michael Nouri, Clu Gulager, Kyle MacLachlan.* Alien MacLachlan gives L.A. cop Nouri a hand in capturing an incredibly violence-prone extraterrestrial hiding out in the bodies of various citizens. Stylish, clever and full of action. (Sequel: *The Hidden 2*) ★★★ DVD: $19.99, VHS: $14.99

The Hidden 2

(1994, 91 min, US, Seth Pinsker) *Raphael Sbarge, Kate Hodge, Michael Nouri.* Fans of the 1987 cult fave have little to cheer in this unworthy sequel that features none of the original cast nor none of the originality. This time around, Sbarge stars as an alien cop sent to Earth as backup to stop the original alien from reproducing and turning the world into a party planet (darn!). Though it's as bad as it sounds, it may be worth a look for fans of the horror genre. ★★ VHS: $14.99

Hidden Agenda

(1990, 106 min, GB, Ken Loach) *Brian Cox, Frances McDormand, Brad Dourif, Mai Zetterling.* Based on an amalgamation of actual scandals, this fictionalized account of official corruption in Northern Ireland is a superb addition to the already substantial library of British films which explore the machinations of the "secret" government. The tightly woven thread of intrigue begins when an American civil rights activist (Dourif) is assassinated in Belfast. McDormand and Cox are both excellent as, respectively, Dourif's girlfriend and an incorruptible Scotland Yard detective who together uncover the biggest political scandal since Watergate and Iran/Contra. ★★★½ DVD Dual: $19.99

The Hidden Fortress

(1958, 139 min, Japan, Akira Kurosawa) *Toshiro Mifune, Misa Vehara.* One of Kurosawa's most entertaining works, *The Hidden Fortress* concerns a shrewd general (Mifune) attempting to smuggle a petulant princess and her treasure trove of gold through enemy territory. Augmented by a bungling pair of peasants, the divergent group encounters enough hair-raising obstacles to sap the power of a light saber. Much in evidence is Kurosawa's sense of humor, largely embodied by Mifune's warrior who flails, cajoles and berates his ragtag crew. The inspiration for *Star Wars*. (Japanese with English subtitles) ★★★½ DVD Criterion Collection: $29.99, VHS: $29.99

Hidden Pleasures
(Los Placeres Ocultos)

(1977, 95 min, Spain, Eloy de la Iglesia) Spain's first openly gay film is an impassioned drama about a closeted bank director who prowls the street of Madrid in search of male teenage prostitutes. His life is changed after he meets and falls in love with a straight young man. The controlled, placid surface of their relationship is shattered by contradictory and sometimes violent interplay concerning differences of class, intellect and convention. (Spanish with English subtitles) ★★★ VHS: $69.99

Hide and Seek

(1980, 90 min, Israel, Dan Wolman) *Gila Almagor, Doron Tavori.* A study of adolescents in the throes of self-discovery, this film explores the sensitive issue of forbidden love. Set in the late 1940s, the crucial years before the birth of the state of Israel, the film deals with the youthful quests and adjurations of a generation which would become the backbone of the new nation. (Hebrew with English subtitles) ★★★

Hide and Seek

(1999, 100 min, US, Sidney J. Furie) *Daryl Hannah, Jennifer Tilly, Bruce Greenwood, Vincent Gallo.* An ugly, uncomfortable hostage thriller, *Hide and Seek* is a ill-fated cross between *Misery* and *The Hand That Rocks the Cradle.* Ann (Hannah) is kidnapped by Frank (Gallo) and Helen (Tilly), an unhinged couple who want the baby Ann is carrying. Chained in the basement of an isolated farmhouse, Ann tries repeatedly, and unsuccesfully, to escape at any opportunity. Meanwhile, Ann's husband, Jack (Greenwood), searches for his wife meeting frustration at every turn. Hannah suffers nobly in her role, but it is the sleazy Gallo and the extremely annoying Tilly that ham it up in this tense yet ridiculous film that ruins whatever potential this sick story had. ★★ DVD: $14.99

Hide in Plain Sight

(1980, 98 min, US, James Caan) *James Caan, Jill Eikenberry, Robert Viharo, Kenneth McMillan, Danny Aiello.* Caan makes an impressive directorial debut with this based-on-fact story about a divorced man (Caan) who loses his children when his ex-wife's husband is relocated after testifying against the mob. ★★★

Hideaway

(1995, 112 min, US, Brett Leonard) *Jeff Goldblum, Christine Lahti, Alicia Silverstone, Jeremy Sisto.* Goldblum stars in this uneventful thriller about a man who returns from the brink of death with the ability to see through the eyes of a serial killer (Sisto). Good thing, too, because the killer's next victim is: (ta-da!) Goldblum's daughter (Silverstone). Dean R. Koontz's best-selling novel is reduced to pop/psychobabble drivel centering around Goldblum's need to make amends for the accidental death of his youngest daughter by risking everything to save his eldest. Director Leonard gratuitously uses state-of-the-art F/X, but it's a clear attempt to disguise that there's nothing much going on here. Lahti is wasted as Goldblum's wife. ★½ DVD: $24.99, VHS: $14.99

Hideous Kinky

(1999, 99 min, GB, Gilles MacKinnon) *Kate Winslet, Saïd Taghmaoui, Bella Riza, Carrie Mullen.* Based on the best-selling novel by Esther Freud (a descendant of Sigmund), this sumptuously shot though emotionally distant memory piece looks at the bohemian existence and spiritual journey of a British expatriate in early-1970s Marrakech. Winslet gives a lovely performance as Julia, who — with her two young daughters in tow — has left the dreary trappings of London for the warm desert and spiritual possibilities of Morocco. Though based on the novel by the youngest child, the story is seen through Julia's eyes, which may explain why Julia is such an enigmatic character. Director MacKinnon has done an effective job in re-creating the look and feel of the era, and his brother Billy, who adapted Freud's novel, certainly understands the precious relationship between mother and daughters, but the film suffers somewhat from its lack of passion and uneven pacing. ★★½ DVD: $27.99

Hiding Out

(1987, 98 min, US, Bob Giraldi) *Jon Cryer, Keith Coogan, Annabeth Gish.* Cryer's likable performance is the sole reason to see this amiable though lifeless comedy about a stockbroker who masquerades as a high school senior to hide from the mob. ★★ DVD Letterbox: $14.99, VHS: $9.99

The Hiding Place

(1975, 145 min, US, James F. Collier) *Julie Harris, Eileen Heckert, Arthur O'Connell.* A moving true story about a Dutch family sent to a German concentration camp for hiding Jews during WWII. Produced by Billy Graham's Evangelistic Association, the film, though overtly religious, is not in any way "preachy" — and presents an unrelenting view of camp life. Good performances from the entire cast. ★★★ VHS: $19.99

High and Low

(1962, 142 min, Japan, Akira Kurosawa) *Toshiro Mifune, Kyoko Kagawa, Tatsuya Mihashi, Takashi Shimura.* This carefully paced thriller by Kurosawa stars Mifune as a business executive who is forced to pay ransom to kidnappers who mistakenly stole his chauffeur's son. Adapted from the Ed McBain novel "King's Ransom," Kurosawa vividly captures the extent to which Mifune, an innocent bystander, has to accept responsibility for the actions of the repellent kidnappers. (Japanese with English subtitles) ★★★½ DVD: $39.99, VHS: $29.99

High Anxiety

(1977, 94 min, US, Mel Brooks) *Mel Brooks, Harvey Korman, Cloris Leachman, Madeline Kahn, Ron Carey, Howard Morris.* Perceptive Hitchcock spoof from director Brooks about a psychiatrist (Brooks) who becomes the new chief of an asylum with murderously funny results. Korman and Leachman are wonderful as kinky coconspirators, and Kahn delectably brings to life the "icy blonde" persona of a 1930s namesake, Madeleine Carroll. Great fun for playing "spot the plot" with Hitchcock scholars. ★★★ VHS: $9.99

High Art

(1998, 102 min, US, Lisa Cholodenko) *Ally Sheedy, Radha Mitchell, Patricia Clarkson, Tammy Grimes, Bill Sage, Gabriel Mann, Anh Duong, David Thornton.* Faulty plumbing in a Soho walk-up leads to a chance encounter between an ambitious assistant editor at a photography magazine and a once-prominent photographer, back in New York after a decade in Berlin. As the photographer Lucy, Sheedy is a glistening, jagged edge in an almost somnambulent environment, snorting smack with her ex-Fassbinderactress lover and other denizens of her free-falling coterie. Mitchell, as the newly minted assistant editor Syd, is luminous and arresting as she tests her wings in the turbulence of the casual duplicities and reflexive back-stabbings of the artistically evolved. Syd and Lucy develop a true bond; but it is no match for the realities of the world they inhabit. Director Cholodenko stays one step back in observation, utilizing subtle, sharply etched performances; allowing the viewer to glimpse personal histories through fragments of conversation and telling glances. Syd receives first-hand experience of art and artist as disposable products for mass consumption. High art, indeed. ★★★ DVD Letterbox: $19.99

High Crimes

(2002, 118 min, US, Carl Franklin) *Ashley Judd, Morgan Freeman, Jim Caviezel, Amanda Peet, Bruce Davison, Tom Bower.* Hotshot attorney Judd is shocked when her seemingly perfect husband is accused of war crimes. She enlists the aid of alcoholic has-been Freeman to help her defend him in military court. Slick but hollow, predictable and protracted, *High Crimes* is a weak variation (read: rip-off) of both *Jagged Edge* and *Music Box.* The military's culpability in the crime (a My Lai-like village massacre) is never explored, it's just a plot device, and the guilty party is merely a lone psycho, and a boring, clichéd one at that. The revelation of the killer is especially tired, paving the way for a snoozer of a "climax." Judd and Freeman are fine in slumming mode, but the biggest crime here is the waste of director Franklin who, based on the evidence of *One False Move* and *Devil in a Blue Dress*, is capable of so much more. ★½ DVD: $14.99, VHS: $14.99

High Fidelity

(2000, 113 min, US, Stephen Frears) *John Cusack, Iben Hjejle, Catherine Zeta-Jones, Jack Black, Todd Louiso, Lisa Bonet, Joan Cusack, Tim Robbins, Sara Gilbert, Lili Taylor.* A scintillating, often hilarious look at relationships, regrets and LPs, *High Fidelity*, based on the book by Nick Hornby, maneuvers through the sometimes murky waters of modern romance with comic agility and uncommon insight. Cusack is Rob, a record shop owner in Chicago, who reexamines his life after his girlfriend leaves him. Prone to evaluating anything and everything of importance in iconoclastic top five lists, Rob sets out to discover what happened in the top five breakups of his life. Cusack is at his absolute best, giving Rob just the right balance of geeky hipster and angst-ridden romantic. There's lots of reasons to see *High Fidelity*, but the top five: 1) Cusack's great turn 2) a smart screenplay 3) what it has to say about men, women and relationships 4) perceptive direction and 5) it's just so damn funny. ★★★★ DVD: $14.99, VHS: $9.99

Gary Cooper in *High Noon*

High Heels

(1972, 100 min, France, Claude Chabrol) *Jean-Paul Belmondo, Mia Farrow, Laura Antonelli, Daniel Ivernel.* A great cast can't save this minor Chabrol comedy mystery. Playboy doctor Belmondo courts and weds Farrow, only to then meet and fall in love with her sister, Antonelli. Belmondo then goes about the task of eliminating Miss Antonelli's many suitors. (Dubbed) ★½

High Heels

(1991, 115 min, Spain, Pedro Almodóvar) *Victoria Abril, Marisa Paredes, Miguel Bose.* Almodóvar moves into new territory by looking a bit more closely at the human motives and desires he usually savages. The story revolves around a volatile estranged mother-daughter relationship; upon reuniting, they come to realize that they have been sharing the same man. Quicker than you can say *Women on the Verge*, the film fires headfirst into a series of alternately hilarious and tragic situations. The luminous Abril plays the successful but emotionally bankrupt daughter Becky. Paredes gives a virtuoso Joan Crawford-style performance as Becky's domineering, cold but ultimately caring mother. Almodóvar's trademark visuals blend with tragic and comedic melodrama to wonderful effect; he continues to be one of the most original and inventive directors working today. (Spanish with English subtitles) ★★★

High Hopes

(1989, 110 min, GB, Mike Leigh) *Philip Davis, Ruth Sheen, Edna Dore.* This bitingly sarcastic and yet poignant survival guide to Thatcher's England is often funny and always thought provoking. The story revolves around Cyril and Shirley, two lovers attempting to stay true to their leftist ideals and lifestyle despite the rising tide of heartless capitalism. The cast of memorable characters includes Cyril's embittered mother, teetering on senility; his hysterical sister, bent on obliterating her working-class roots with the plastic comforts of suburbia; and two wildly funny upper-class twits who blindly romp amidst the decay of Thatcher's New Society. ★★★½

High Noon

(1952, 84 min, US, Fred Zinnemann) *Gary Cooper, Grace Kelly, Thomas Mitchell, Lloyd Bridges, Lon Chaney, Jr., Katy Jurado.* Cooper won a second Oscar for his stirring performance in this western classic as a retiring small-town marshall who is abandoned by the townspeople when a murderer he sent away to prison returns to seek vengeance. The gunfight finale is arguably the best showdown in film. ★★★★ DVD 50th Anniversary: $19.99, VHS: $14.99

High Plains Drifter

(1973, 105 min, US, Clint Eastwood) *Clint Eastwood, Verna Bloom, Marianna Hill, Mitchell Ryan.* A solid western tale from Eastwood about the title character (Eastwood) protecting a small town from a group of prison parolees out for vengeance. ★★★ DVD Letterbox: $14.99, VHS: $7.49, VHS Letterbox: $14.99

High Road to China

(1983, 120 min, US, Brian G. Hutton) *Tom Selleck, Bess Armstrong, Jack Weston, Robert Morley, Wilford Brimley.* Having been the first choice, and unavailable, for *Raiders of the Lost Ark*, Selleck finally starred in a big-screen, tongue-in-cheek adventure — unfortunately for him, it was this pleasant but minor film. Selleck plays a daredevil flyer hired by Armstrong to find her missing father. ★★

High School Confidential

(1958, 85 min, US, Jack Arnold) *Russ Tamblyn, Mamie Van Doren, Jan Sterling, Jackie Coogan, Jerry Lee Lewis.* The legendary cult classic featuring "the smart aleck leader of the hot rod set," "the girl who has too much too soon," and "the glamorous teacher devoted to thwarting delinquency." They don't make 'em like this anymore! ★★ DVD: $14.99

High School High

(1996, 90 min, US, Hart Bochner) *Jon Lovitz, Tia Carrere, Mekhi Phifer, Louise Fletcher.* In this *Airplane*-like parody of *Dangerous Minds* and *Stand and Deliver*, Lovitz plays the idealistic son of the snobbish headmaster of a posh private school who takes a teaching job at Marion Berry High, the worst school in the city. The first third of the film is actually funny, alternating between sharp satire and so-dumb-it's-funny humor in true Z-A-Z fashion. Unfortunately, the writers run out of ideas far too quickly, and *High School High* ends up becoming a slightly comic variation of what it started out satirizing — a cheesy, feel-good, inspirational teen drama. ★★ DVD: $9.99, VHS: $9.99

High Season

(1987, 92 min, GB, Clare Peploe) *Jacqueline Bisset, James Fox, Irene Papas, Kenneth Branagh, Robert Stephens.* First-time director Peploe cowrote (along with son Mark) this tepid mishmash about the effects of tourism on a small Greek island. The beautiful Bisset competes with the scenery in her role as a photographer whose life is complicated by obnoxious tourists, inept spies and her self-important ex-husband (Fox in a suitably hedonistic role). No doubt Britain's idea of "mindless entertainment." ★★ DVD Dual: $19.99

High Sierra

(1941, 100 min, US, Raoul Walsh) *Humphrey Bogart, Ida Lupino, Joan Leslie, Arthur Kennedy, Cornel Wilde.* Bogart is at his best in this stirring tale of a tired, aging killer on the lam from the police. The theme is an old one, but it is masterfully rejuvinated by Bogart's unforgettable performance. Also contributing to the overall excellence of the film are stand-out performances by Leslie, as Bogey's goody-goody heartthrob, and the great Lupino, as the not-so-goody moll who pines for his love. ★★★½ DVD: $19.99

High Society

(1956, 107 min, US, Charles Walters) *Grace Kelly, Bing Crosby, Frank Sinatra, Celeste Holm, Louis Armstrong.* Amiable musical remake of *The Philadelphia Story* with songs by Cole Porter (including "True Love"). Kelly, Crosby and Sinatra take over the Katharine Hepburn, Cary Grant and James Stewart roles. ★★★ DVD Letterbox: $19.99, VHS: $9.99

High Spirits

(1988, 97 min, US, Neil Jordan) *Peter O'Toole, Daryl Hannah, Steve Guttenberg, Liam Neeson, Beverly D'Angelo.* O'Toole, Hannah and Guttenberg barely manage to wring a few laughs from this tepid ghost comedy with Guttenberg as an American tourist visiting an Irish castle who meets and falls in love with ghost Hannah. ★½ DVD Dual: $14.99

High Tide

(1987, 104 min, Australia, Gillian Armstrong) *Judy Davis, Claudia Karvan, Jan Adele, Colin Friels.* A well-crafted, emotionally powerful story of a woman (Davis), stranded in a small coastal town, who befriends an adolescent girl. Armstrong's fine, sensitive direction elevates this absorbing drama well above the clichéd, maudlin soap opera it very well could have been. Davis, Karvan as the young girl, and especially Adele as the girl's grandmother, all offer outstanding performances. ★★★½

Higher Learning

(1995, 127 min, US, John Singleton) *Omar Epps, Kristy Swanson, Laurence Fishburne, Michael Rapaport, Ice Cube, Jennifer Connelly, Jason Wiles.* In *Boyz n the Hood*, director Singleton shaded his story with a subtlety which belied its incendiary theme. But in an effort to punctuate his thought-provoking *Higher Learning*, about campus strife in the '90s, he has given way to stereotypes and heavy-handedness. In remarkable detail, the story shows the fractious campus life awaiting a group of college freshman. As the students come to adhere to their own agendas — racial, sexual, political — the cookie-cutter story lays the way to a tragic but inevitable climax. Among a splendid cast are Epps, very good as a black athlete on scholarship; Rapaport, who makes the most of a one-dimensional fascist; and Swanson, who is sympathetic as a white freshman "do-gooder" exploring her sexuality. Best of all, however, is Fishburne as a dedicated professor. ★★½ DVD Dual: $14.99, VHS: $9.99

Highlander

(1986, 116 min, GB, Russell Mulcahy) *Sean Connery, Christopher Lambert, Clancy Brown, Roxanne Hart.* Lambert stars as a Scottish member of a bizarre group of immortal warriors who do battle with each other down through the ages. The story skips around from 12th-century Scotland to modern-day Manhattan to 18th-century Boston (and so on) and, as a result, the film sometimes becomes narratively incoherent. But despite this shortcoming, the action is fantastic. Connery is his usual marvelous self as Lambert's mentor and Brown is his menacing adversary. (Followed by 3 sequels and a TV series) ★★½ DVD Letterbox: $14.99, DVD The Immortal Edition: $39.99, VHS: $9.99, VHS Letterbox: $9.99

Highlander 2: The Quickening

(1990, 90 min, US, Russell Mulcahy) *Christopher Lambert, Sean Connery, Virginia Madsen, John C. McGinley.* Good special effects (as well as some chintzy ones) help add to the cheesy fun of this inferior remake of the 1985 swashbuckling adventure. Connery and Lambert dust off their broadswords as they do battle with alien assassins (led by the ever-leering Ironside) out to destroy the Earth's fragile ecosystem. ★★ DVD Letterbox: $14.99, DVD Letterbox Special Edition: $19.99, VHS: $9.99, VHS Letterbox: $19.99

Highlander: The Final Dimension

(1994, 100 min, GB, Andy Morahan) *Christopher Lambert, Mario Van Peebles, Deborah Unger, Mako.* Director Morahan should have applied the Highlander credo, "There can be only one," to the making of sequels and not served up this totally inept and unsatisfying conclusion. Lambert reprises his role as the centuries-old swordsman who must now face a recently unearthed immortal (Van Peebles in an undisciplined performance). Offscreen beheadings, major plot holes and a totally gratuitous subplot about an old flame reincarnated as an antiquities expert (the fetching Unger) make this rehash about as ridiculous as it sounds. ★ DVD: $19.99, VHS: $9.99

Highlander: Endgame

(2000, 101 min, US, Douglas Aarniokoski) *Adrian Paul, Christopher Lambert.* After an abysmal third installment, the *Highlander* film series goes back to basics, reprising its popular themes of swordplay and mentorship. In this fourth chapter, Lambert teams with his TV counterpart Paul for a good-looking, sometimes exciting if by-the-books adventure tale of immortals battling each other to be "the one." Fans of the TV show and film series should enjoy this harmless actioner. (Fourteen minutes longer than the theatrical cut.) ★★½ DVD: $19.99, VHS: $19.99

The Highest Honor

(1984, 99 min, Australia, Peter Maxwell) *John Howard, Atsuo Nakamura, Scott Wilson.* Compelling WWII drama that recounts the true story of the unique friendship between two enemies: a POW and his Japanese jailer, both torn by their sense of duty and sense of humanity. This action/drama is interesting but not as riveting as the similarly themed *Merry Christmas, Mr. Lawrence.* ★★½

Highway 61

(1992, 99 min, Canada, Bruce McDonald) *Don McKellar, Valerie Buhagier, Earl Pastko.* A Canadian independent feature, this road comedy contains much of the hip and anarchic humor that distinguishes Jim Jarmusch's and Hal Hartley's works. Though not entirely successful in its send-ups and Lynch-like Americana admonishments, there's an abundance of offbeat and wildly satiric jabs at the denizens both on and off the road. McKellar, displaying a charmingly subdued persona, is a staid Canadian small-town barber taken on the ride of his life by "escapee from a heavy metal crew" roadie Buhagiar. En route to New Orleans transporting the dead body she claims to be her brother, and pursued by a man who identifies himself as Satan, the two disparate travelers wind their way down an erratic highway as loopy and disjointed as the eccentrics they meet. ★★★ VHS: $7.99

Highway to Hell

(1992, 100 min, US, Ate de Jong) *Chad Lowe, Kristy Swanson, Patrick Bergin.* Lowe and Swanson star as a young couple on their way to Las Vegas for a secret wedding. Unknowingly, the pair find a passageway to Hell, and meet the Devil himself (played by Bergin). Filled with car chases, battles with zombie bikers, cannibal freaks and someone named Hell Cop, this fast-paced horror/adventure/comedy provides mindless fun and fright for all. ★★½

Hilary and Jackie

(1998, 124 min, GB, Anand Tucker) *Emily Watson, Rachel Griffiths, David Morrissey, James Frain, Charles Dance.* A demanding but ultimately rewarding biography, *Hilary and Jackie* features two remarkable performances from Watson and Griffiths as the two British sisters, one the world-renowned cellist Jacqueline du Pré. Divided into two parts titled after each sister, the film traces their lives from childhood (where sibling rivalry was encouraged) to Jackie's success in the music field and Hilary's departure from it to Jackie's illness from multiple sclerosis. Giving bits of information in one part and then completing the story in the next adds a dimension not always associated with "disease-of-the-week" films, and the relationship between the two sisters is well rounded. Watson as Jackie and Griffiths as Hilary complement each other beautifully, each giving precise, singular portrayals. ★★★ DVD: $19.99, VHS: $9.99

Hill 24 Doesn't Answer

(1959, 106 min, Israel, Thorton Dickinson) *Edward Mulhare, Haya Harareet.* Hill 24 is one of the foothills dominating the approach to Jerusalem. Set in 1949, on the eve of the U.N. cease-fire imposed during the Israeli war of independence, this fiercely realistic drama follows the actions of four young Zionists who volunteer to defend the strategic hill in order to maintain access to the besieged city. A historically important film that successfully captures the tensions in the birth of a nation. (English dialogue) ★★★

Hillbillies in a Haunted House

(1967, 88 min, US, Jean Yarbrough) *Ferlin Husky, Joi Lansing, Lon Chaney, Jr., John Carradine, Basil Rathbone.* Two country singers and their manager spend the night in a seemingly abandoned mansion. Little do they know that a gang of foreign spies is hiding out in the basement, poised to steal a secret formula for rocket propellant. Warning: Lots of songs! ★ DVD: $19.99, VHS: $19.99

The Hills Have Eyes

(1977, 89 min, US, Wes Craven) *Susan Lanier, Robert Houston, Dee Wallace Stone.* Tense and gory horror film from director Craven. A vacationing family makes a very wrong turn in the desert — and find themselves up against a group of psychotic cannibals (are there any other kind?). (Sequel: *The Hills Have Eyes, Part 2*) ★★★ DVD Letterbox 2-disc set: $29.99

The Hills Have Eyes, Part 2

(1984, 86 min, US, Wes Craven) *Michael Berryman, Kevin Blair.* Sequel to Craven's cult horror film. This time out, it's some teenagers in trouble, as they travel through the desert. Lacks the suspense and style of the original. ★★ DVD: $24.99

Himalaya

(2000, 104 min, Nepal, Eric Valli) *Thinlen Lhondup, Karma Wangiel.* A caravan returns to its home village from a trading run across the treacherous terrain of the Himalayas. It carries with it the body of the fallen leader, whom Karma, the second in command, says attempted a dangerous route alone. The grief of the dead chief's father, Tinle, leads him on a path of suspicion and accusation that threatens to alienate him from his community. Tinle's insistence on leading the next trade expedition causes a crisis in the line of succession that splits the village along generational lines. The universal generational conflict is played out against a most harsh yet most stupendously beautiful environment; one that can change from springlike warmth to howling blizzard overnight. Against this backdrop is always at the fore a profound understanding of human nature; and a compassion that provides people sufficient loving support to allow them to comprehend their own frailties, to see the wisdom of those who oppose them, and to be capable of growth and understanding. An Academy Award nominee for Foreign-Language Film, this amazing film reveals the communality of the human experience in a most alien landscape. (aka: *Caravan*) (Tibetan with English subtitles) ★★★★ DVD Letterbox: $29.99, VHS Letterbox: $24.99

Himatsuri

(1985, 115 min, Japan, Mitsuo Yangimachi) *Kinya Kitaoji, Kwako Taichi.* One of the Japanese New Wave's best efforts so far, *Himatsuri* brilliantly explores the complex mental landscape of modern Japan, torn between advanced technology and the superstitions and mystical undercurrents that pervade the Japanese subconscious. Set in a fishing village, it follows the spiritual transformation of a rough-hewn but affable lumberjack (the superb Kitaoji) who moves from defiling the land to communication with the gods that inhabit it. (Japanese with English subtitles) ★★★½ VHS: $24.99

The Hindenburg

(1975, 125 min, US, Robert Wise) *George C. Scott, Anne Bancroft, William Atherton, Roy Thinnes, Gig Young, Burgess Meredith, Charles Durning.* A good cast is featured in this inflated disaster film, which speculates that the infamous Hindenburg crash of 1937 was actually sabotage. Outstanding special effects and actual footage interspersed heighten the tension at the end — and what a knockout ending it is. ★★ DVD: $14.99

The Hired Hand

(1971, 95 min, US, Peter Fonda) *Peter Fonda, Warren Oates, Verna Bloom.* Fonda's follow-up to *Easy Rider* is this elegiac and subversive western that bombed at the box office. Fonda stars as a mysterious wanderer who returns to his wife (the terrific Bloom) after a seven-year absence. Panned by critics, this lyrically filmed mood piece on loneliness, loyalty and the nature of love was lost in the flood of "trippy" films in the early '70s, but still, it compares favorably to other "modern westerns" championed by Peckinpah. ★★★ DVD Basic Edition: $19.99, DVD 2-disc Collector's Edition: $39.99, VHS: $19.99

Hiroshima

(1995, 165 min, Canada/Japan, Koreyoshi Kurahara & Roger Spottiswoode) *Kenneth Welsh, Tatsuo Matsumura, Richard Masur, Saul Rubinek.* Made-for-cable, this illuminating and extremely accomplished film is an even-handed depiction of the events leading to the dropping of the atomic bomb on Hiroshima and Nagasaki during WWII. Told in a quasi-documentary style, *Hiroshima* incorporates actual newsreel footage that has been masterfully tinted and juxtaposes it with an astonishingly authentic re-creation of the times and events — shot in subdued hues — to produce a jarring, fascinating narrative. The story is seen from Truman's perspective as the new commander-in-chief, and through the eyes of Japan's Prime Minister Suzuki as the Japanese high council debates their future war efforts. A large international cast excels, though Welsh as Truman and Matsumura as Suzuki ground the film with their inspired portrayals. (English and Japanese with English subtitles) ★★★½

Hiroshima Maiden

(1988, 58 min, US, Joan Darling) *Tamlyn Tomita, Susan Blakely, Richard Masur.* A young Japanese woman from Hiroshima comes to America in 1955 and stays with a family while she undergoes treatment for radiation burns. Everyone welcomes her except the oldest son, who is persuaded by his friends that she is a spy. This touching though slowly paced drama is inspired by the stories of the real-life "Hiroshima Maidens." ★★½ VHS: $29.99

Hiroshima, Mon Amour

(1959, 91 min, France, Alain Resnais) *Emmanuelle Riva, Eiji Okada.* Obsessive pasts haunt the affair of a French woman and a Japanese architect in 1950s Hiroshima. The woman's memories of her scandalous involvement with a German soldier and the piercing recollections of nuclear horror both unite and repel the two lovers. Resnais' brilliant first film was scripted by Marguerite Duras. (French with English subtitles) ★★★★ DVD Criterion Collection: $39.99, VHS: $29.99

His Girl Friday

(1940, 92 min, US, Howard Hawks) *Rosalind Russell, Cary Grant, Ralph Bellamy, Gene Lockhart, John Qualen, Roscoe Karns.* Hawks' fast-talking, wise-cracking, sex-change version of *The Front Page*. Russell is the ace reporter set to wed the less than dynamic Bellamy. Grant is her editor and ex-husband determined to thwart the match. A classic screwball comedy filmed at a machine-gun pace, the film's jokes are hilarious, the situations outlandish, and Grant and Russell are in terrific form. (Remade as *Switching Channels*) ★★★★ DVD: $24.99, VHS: $19.99

History Is Made at Night

(1937, 98 min, US, Frank Borzage) *Jean Arthur, Charles Boyer, Colin Clive.* Intriguing blend of romance, comedy and melodrama with Arthur and Boyer in fine form in the story of Arthur divorcing husband Clive and falling in love with headwaiter Boyer. ★★½ VHS: $14.99

History of the World, Part 1

(1981, 92 min, US, Mel Brooks) *Gregory Hines, Dom DeLuise, Madeline Kahn, Harvey Korman, Cloris Leachman, Sid Caesar, Bea Arthur, Narrated by: Orson Welles.* An alternately funny and fuzzy, sometimes vulgar history lesson from the not-so-professorial mind of Brooks. Vignettes tell the progress of man from primitive cave dwellers to the Roman

Empire to the French Revolution. In typical Brooks fashion, the film features outrageous comic situations, unbelievably silly jokes and an all-star cast. ★★

Hit!

(1973, 135 min, US, Sidney J. Furie) *Billy Dee Williams, Richard Pryor, Gwen Welles.* Embittered over the drug-related death of his daughter, U.S. agent Nick Allen (Williams) teams up with an underwater warfare expert (Pryor) to seek vengence against a group of drug smugglers in Marseilles. Overly detailed and lengthy at times, but more-than-exciting action and witty dialogue help to keep this one moving. ★★½ VHS: $14.99

The Hit

(1985, 98 min, GB, Stephen Frears) *Terence Stamp, John Hurt, Tim Roth, Laura del Sol.* Willie Parker (Stamp) dropped a dime on his mobster cohorts. For his confession, the British magistrate granted him clemency and a new identity in a bucolic Spanish villa. Now, ten years later, he's being hunted down by a hired killer and appears doomed to pay for his finger-pointing. However, things go peculiarly astray when this condemned man's tranquil acceptance of his death sentence throws his edgy executioner (Hurt) for a loop. In spite of its ominous subject matter and jagged action, *The Hit* harbors a sly undertow of dark humor which distinguishes it from simpler underworld thrillers. ★★★ DVD: $14.99, VHS: $14.99

The Hitch-Hiker

(1953, 71 min, US, Ida Lupino) *Edmond O'Brien, Frank Lovejoy, William Talman.* Two ordinary men are on a weekend excursion away from their wives and families when they happen to make a deadly mistake and pick up the wrong hitchhiker, an escaped fugitive and serial killer with a lazy eye and a deadly shot. What follows is an extremely suspenseful road movie as the killer makes the men drive him into Baja Mexico. O'Brien and Lovejoy are extremely good as the unwilling passengers, one stalwart in the face of death and the other slowly cracking under the strain, but it is Talman who steals the picture with his vivid portrait of a truly three-dimensional, but nevertheless horribly menacing villain. In this three-char-

acter piece, Lupino sustains the tension throughout each episode the group undertakes, whether it is quietly trying to steal gasoline in the middle of the night or make it past a police checkpoint without Talman being discovered. Highly recommended for fans of classic film noir, directed by the only woman in the field. ★★★½ DVD: $29.99, VHS: $19.99

The Hitcher

(1986, 97 min, US, Robert Harmon) *Rutger Hauer, C. Thomas Howell, Jennifer Jason Leigh.* Hauer is evil personified in this taut thriller about a young man who is terrorized by a maniacal hitchhiker. Howell, in what may easily be his best role to date, is the innocent driver whose trek across Nevada turns into a deadly game of cat and mouse. Filled with unrelenting suspense and seething with homoerotic imagery, this film, not for the faint of heart, will electrify fans of the genre. ★★★ DVD Letterbox: $14.99

Hitler's Children

(1943, 83 min, US, Edward Dmytryk) *Tim Holt, Bonita Granville, Otto Kruger, H.B. Warner.* Though the title suggests *They Saved Hitler's Brain* rather than *Watch on the Rhine*, this compelling 1940s anti-Nazi propaganda drama is very much in the latter film's league in its cautionary tale of Nazi oppression. Sort of a "Romeo and Juliet" set in the Fatherland, the story follows the friendship and romance of a Nazi youth (Holt) and an American girl (Granville) living in Germany. A big hit in its day, the title refers to the dictator's army of children undergoing fascist brainwashing. ★★★

Hobson's Choice

(1954, 107 min, GB, David Lean) *Charles Laughton, Brenda de Banzie, John Mills.* Laughton offers a priceless performance in this delicious working-class comedy about a tyrannical bootmaker who struggles to maintain his dominion over his three daughters. De Banzie plays a strong-willed daughter who defies his authority by marrying the man of her choice. ★★★½ VHS: $29.99

Hocus Pocus

(1993, 96 min, US, Kenny Ortega) *Bette Midler, Sarah Jessica Parker, Kathy Najimy, Charles Rocket, Kathleen Freeman.* This very lightweight but amiable fantasy half-heartedly recaptures the frivolity of the Fred MacMurray comedies of the 1960s. Midler, Najimy and Parker star as 17th-century witches who return to modern-day Salem and run "amok, amok, amok." With more hokum than hocus, the witches set out to steal the souls of the town's children. Their only opposition are three spunky kids. Most of the laughs are mild, and the film gives the impression of being more risque than it is — it's harmless fare. Though she's not given much to do, Midler generates some energy, and sings "I Put a Spell on You," the film's only real highlight. ★★½ DVD: $14.99, VHS: $9.99

Hoffa

(1992, 140 min, US, Danny DeVito) *Jack Nicholson, Danny DeVito, Armand Assante, J.T. Walsh, Kevin Anderson.* This sprawling biography of the tough-as-nails labor leader benefits from a gutsy performance by Nicholson in the title role, but it would have been better if it were more Hoffa and less DeVito. There are few scenes here where the costar/director's presence is not apparent, and that's the big problem: after nearly two and a half hours, we know more about DeVito's fictitious sidekick, Bobby Ciaro, than we do of James Hoffa — and that's no fault of Nicholson. The film traces Hoffa's

SHE LEARNED ABOUT MEN FROM HIM !

CARY GRANT
ROSALIND RUSSELL
HOWARD HAWKS'
"HIS GIRL FRIDAY"
RALPH BELLAMY
GENE LOCKHART

rise to power, from his determined attempts to enlist truckers to the union to his prominence as the no-nonsense Teamsters president. With no thanks to David Mamet's script, DeVito — whose visual style apes Coppola — glosses over Hoffa's personal life in favor of mano-a-mano confrontations and feverish speeches that eventually grow repetitious. ★★

The Holcroft Covenant

(1985, 112 min, GB, John Frankenheimer) *Michael Caine, Anthony Andrews, Lilli Palmer, Mario Adorf.* Master suspense director Frankenheimer is not too successful in bringing Robert Ludlum's first novel to the screen. Caine is led on a globe-trotting series of adventures as he searches for a fortune left behind by his dead father (a comrade-in-arms to Hitler). ★½ DVD: $14.99, VHS: $14.99

Hold Me, Thrill Me, Kiss Me

(1993, 110 min, US, Joel Hershman) *Adrienne Shelley, Diane Ladd, Sam Young.* If one can pay homage to Pedro Almodóvar, Russ Meyer and Woody Allen in the same film, first-time director Hershman has done it with this quirky comedy. Set in a seedy trailer park, the plot is just the old "boy meets stripper, stripper handcuffs boy to bed, boy begins to fall for stripper's animal-loving little sis" story, with a little murder and mayhem thrown in for good measure. ★★★ VHS: $79.99

Hold That Ghost

(1941, 80 min, US, Arthur Lubin) *Bud Abbott, Lou Costello, Joan Davis, Mischa Auer, The Andrews Sisters.* In one of their best films, Abbott and Costello meet their comedic equal in Davis when they spend the night in a house haunted not only by ghosts but by mobsters. A wonderful romp, and Davis is a particular delight. DVD: $24.99 (DVD includes 7 other Abbott and Costello films) ★★★

A Hole in the Head

(1959, 120 min, US, Frank Capra) *Frank Sinatra, Edward G. Robinson, Eddie Hodges, Eleanor Parker, Carolyn Jones, Thelma Ritter.* Sinatra sings "High Hopes" in this Capra sentimental favorite. Frank plays a down-on-his-heels motel owner raising a young son (Hodges) and trying to make ends meet. ★★★ DVD Letterbox: $14.99

The Holes (Les Gaspards)

(1981, 92 min, US/France, Pierre Tchernia) *Gérard Depardieu, Philippe Noiret, Michel Serrault.* A good cast and a peculiarly un-French premise makes this fantasy/comedy a real find for Francophiles. The plot is as follows: Living in the labyrinthine maze of ancient tunnels and caves deep under the streets of Paris is a society of people who want to escape the world above. Their tranquility is disturbed, however, after an ambitious Minister of Public Works begins to dig up the city for his many pet construction projects. The mole people, led by an aristocratic Noiret, take matters into their own hands by kidnapping tourists, bicyclists and even policemen in a frantic effort to keep progress at bay. Laced with many funny moments and featuring a young, mop-headed Depardieu, this strange film is imaginatively executed and wackily entertaining. ★★★ DVD: $4.99, VHS: $9.99

Holiday

(1938, 94 min, US, George Cukor) *Katharine Hepburn, Cary Grant, Doris Nolan, Edward Everett Horton, Lew Ayres.* The second and more popular version of Philip Barry's Broadway hit, this delightful comedy stars Hepburn and Grant, in their third

of four films together, as nonconformists up against an ever-restrictive world. Grant, at his most charming, plays a free spirit engaged to socialite Nolan, soon discovering he has more in common with her sister Kate. Ayres stands out as the alcoholic black sheep of the family, and Horton, repeating his role from the original 1930 film, is marvelous as Grant's mentor and friend. ★★★★

Holiday Affair

(1949, 87 min, US, Don Hartman) *Janet Leigh, Robert Mitchum, Wendell Corey.* A beautiful and young Leigh plays a war widow who must decide between Mitchum and Corey. A pleasant comedy-drama enhanced by two delightful performances by Leigh and Mitchum. ★★½ VHS: $14.99

Holiday Hotel

(1978, 109 min, France, Michel Lang) *Guy Marchand, Sophie Barjac.* The French preoccupation with both love and summer vacation is wittily explored in this sexy, cheerful comedy. Marchand is a frazzled father whose 16-year-old daughter is set loose at a small summer resort during August holiday. Lots of French skin and a giddy good time. (French with English subtitles) ★★½

Holiday Inn

(1942, 101 min, US, Mark Sandrich) *Bing Crosby, Fred Astaire, Marjorie Reynolds.* Crosby and Astaire are the top-liners (can't get any bigger than that) at Bing's holiday resort (only open during holidays, naturally). As the romantic interest, Reynolds is splendid; as is the Irving Berlin score (which includes "White Christmas"). Delightful. ★★★½

Hollow Man

(2000, 113 min, US, Paul Verhoeven) *Kevin Bacon, Elisabeth Shue, Josh Brolin, Kim Dickens, William Devane.* Verhoeven's cynical invisible man thriller is a case of a perfectly good genre flick suffocated by the constrictions of the wrong genre. In updating the classic sci-fi fantasy of invisibility, Verhoeven has chosen to spin the concept into a mean-spirited, gore-splattered stalker flick. Bacon plays the supremely arrogant super-genius in charge of a secret government research project. Zapping himself transparent was the easy part; getting back is the problem, and the longer he remains invisible, the more sinister his behavior becomes. Beyond the flimsy characters and plot, the film features flashy production design and some cool visual effects. ★★ DVD Letterbox Superbit Deluxe Edition: $29.99, DVD Special Edition: $14.99

Hollow Reed

(1997, 105 min, GB, Angela Pope) *Martin Donovan, Joely Richardson, Ian Hart, Jason Flemyng, Sam Bould.* A flawed but well-meaning drama, *Hollow Reed* takes a sensitive subject — the custody battle between a gay man and his ex-wife — and introduces an explosive plot element about child abuse. Martyn (Donovan) is living happily with his boyfriend (Hart) when he learns that his son Oliver (Bould) is being physically harmed by Tom (Flemyng), the new lover of his ex-wife Hannah (Richardson). Director Pope (*Priest*) has made an engrossing film about determining which parent is more suitable to care for Oliver, but the stress Martyn has about having his homosexuality put on trial is not properly paralleled with Hannah's feelings about loving an abuser. ★★½

Hollywood Ending

(2002, 112 min, US, Woody Allen) *Woody Allen, Téa Leoni, Treat Williams, Mark Rydell, Debra Messing, George Hamilton, Tiffani Thiessen, Barney Cheng, Lu Yu, Mark Webber.* In *Hollywood Ending*, a famed director and auteur who hasn't had an artistic success in ten years attempts a comeback with a studio production set on the streets of New York. As comically envisioned by Allen, who shares a few similarities with his fictional alter ego, *Hollywood Ending* sets out to poke fun at the moviemaking process and some of the business' players, but despite some good laughs can't quite deliver on an amusing premise. Allen plays Val Waxman, an Oscar-winning director who has been reduced to TV commercials in Canada. He gets a break when his ex-wife (Leoni), now a studio exec in L.A., gets him hired for a big-budget gangster drama. Woody is in lovable neurotic mode, so it isn't long until Val experiences a comic breakdown — in the form of going blind. *Hollywood Ending* suffers a bit from some inconsistent pacing and the comic timing seems off, but Allen has made sure there's enough good humor to go around. Leoni is quite good as Waxman's ex, but you never believe the two were once married, which detracts from the film. Great romantic comedies succeed, in part, by the audience rooting for the two leads to get together by the end of the film — here you just don't care. ★★½ DVD Letterbox: $14.99, VHS: $9.99

Hollywood Shuffle

(1987, 82 min, US, Robert Townsend) *Robert Townsend, Anne-Marie Johnson, Keenen Ivory Wayans, Damon Wayans.* A series of side-splitting vignettes tell the tale of a struggling black actor's search for a serious role in Hollywood. Stand-up comic and first-time director Townsend redefined the term "shoestring budget" when he "maxed out" his credit cards in order to pay the final production costs for this spoof. His strategy paid off and the resulting lampoon on racial inequity in tinseltown went on to reap huge and, well-deserved, rewards at the box office. ★★★ DVD Letterbox: $14.99

The Holy Innocents

(1984, 108 min, Spain, Marto Camus) *Francisco Rabal, Alfredo Lando.* In Franco's Spain, 1962, the modern world has yet to arrive at many rural communities where the feudal system of landowning gentry and peasant laborers continue. This is the setting for Camus' powerful and rousing drama of oppression and revenge. Paco and Regula, husband and wife, are gatekeepers to an aristocratic family. Their struggles — raising a family, eking out a subsistence and maintaining some self-respect — provide the soul for this touching film. (Spanish with English subtitles) ★★★

Holy Man

(1998, 114 min, US, Stephen Herek) *Eddie Murphy, Jeff Goldblum, Kelly Preston, Robert Loggia, Jon Cryer.* An insipid, empty, preachy comedy, *Holy Man* is an overlong parable almost saved by Murphy's endearing performance. Goldblum plays a desperate TV exec at a Home Shopping-like network whose ratings and sales are in the basement. After accidentally hitting an enigmatic, beatific man (Murphy) with his car, Goldblum puts this "holy man" on the air with spectacular results. Heavy-handed network satire mixed with trendy, New Age "messages" provide the non-material for Murphy to work with, yet the comic still delivers a thoughtful, change-of-pace performance. Goldblum, however, is at his most jittery — possibly to give the unfocused direction an energetic point of view. It doesn't help. ★½ DVD: $9.99, VHS: $9.99

H

Holy Smoke!

(1999, 114 min, US/Australia, Jane Campion) *Kate Winslet, Harvey Keitel, Pam Grier, Julie Hamilton.* A beautiful young Australian woman (Winslet), while vacationing in India, falls hard for a religious cult leader. Her family coerces her back home, and to spend time with a macho deprogrammer. Wildly uneven, *Holy Smoke!* boasts terrific, brave performances by Winslet and Keitel and some stylish direction, but also succumbs to cartoonish stereotyping (especially Winslet's family). The film begins and ends badly, but many of the scenes between the two leads — set in a hut in the middle of the empty, sprawling Australian Outback — are compelling, even though they never rise to the enticing war-of-wills/battle-of-the-sexes free-for-all promised early on. ★★½ DVD: $14.99, VHS: $9.99

Hombre

(1967, 111 min, US, Martin Ritt) *Paul Newman, Richard Boone, Fredric March, Diane Cilento, Martin Balsam.* Newman has a sardonic cool about him as a white man living among the Indians who journeys with a group of travelers on a stagecoach line's final voyage. Set in the last days of the Old West, director Ritt's riveting parable (based on an Elmore Leonard story) probes racial intolerance against Indians and the price of humanism as Newman and coriders March, Cilento and Balsam are up against bad guy Boone, highwaymen and the elements. A thoroughly satisfying western, featuring a terrific performance from Cilento as a gutsy widow. ★★★½ DVD: $14.99, VHS: $6.99

Home Alone

(1990, 103 min, US, Chris Columbus) *Macaulay Culkin, Joe Pesci, Daniel Stern, Catherine O'Hara, John Heard, John Candy.* John Hughes wrote the script for this box-office smash about an eight-year-old boy left behind when his family leaves for their European Christmas vacation. Little Culkin plays Kevin, whose idyllic stay home alone is interrupted by two inept burglars. Much of the film centers on Kevin's ingenious defense ploys, and the hilariously sadistic acts of sabotage he institutes against the thieves. Pesci and Stern are the unfortunate criminals. However, it's youngster Culkin who captivates with a refreshing variation on the precocious youth; and his enormous contribution to this romp should not be overlooked. (Followed by 2 sequels) ★★★ DVD: $19.99, VHS: $9.99

Home Alone 2: Lost in New York

(1992, 113 min, US, Chris Columbus) *Macaulay Culkin, Joe Pesci, Daniel Stern, Tim Curry, Rob Schneider, Dana Ivey.* The lucrative adventures of young Kevin McAllister (Culkin) continue in this by-the-numbers but amusing sequel. The action has been transplanted from the suburbs to the more exciting mean streets of Manhattan. Predictably, Kevin becomes separated from his family again, meets up with the recently escaped Wet Bandits (Pesci, Stern) and sets out to creatively foil their plot to rob a toy store. Writer-producer John Hughes sticks to his winning formula like tar to a rooftop, though this time Kevin is less an innocent child and more a preachy know-it-all. ★★½ DVD: $19.99, VHS: $9.99

Home Alone 3

(1997, 102 min, US, Raja Gosnell) *Alex D. Linz, Scarlett Johansson, Haviland Morris, Marion Seldes, Olek Krupa, Rya Kihlstedt.* While it contains no real surprises, this third installment of the popular series has a new face who's — yep — left home alone. This time, young Alex is given a remote-controlled car that is actually the hiding place for a stolen computer chip that the Army suspects has been taken by four terrorists. Once they realize that the kid has their chip, the games begin. The four spies go from cool, calm, collected secret agents to frazzled and fried victims of Alex's traps. Yawn, already. ★★ DVD: $19.99, VHS: $9.99

The Home and the World

(1984, 130 min, India, Satyajit Ray) *Victor Benerjee, Soumitra Chatterjee.* Set in 1908 British-ruled India, this is a shattering yet measured study of emancipation, commitment and love. The story concerns a liberal man's desire to free his wife of purdah and allow her to mingle with his male friends. His plan backfires, however, when she becomes fascinated by an intelligent revolutionary politician. Ray intricately explores the shifting tides of emotion between the three in this exquisite drama. (Bengali with English subtitles) ★★★

Home for the Holidays

(1995, 105 min, US, Jodie Foster) *Holly Hunter, Robert Downey, Jr., Dylan McDermott, Anne Bancroft, Charles Durning, Geraldine Chaplin, Steve Guttenberg, Cynthia Stevenson, Claire Danes.* Foster's directorial follow-up to *Little Man Tate* continues her examination of familial conflicts and off-the-fringe characters in this sometimes funny family comedy that proves "it's all relative." The slightly neurotic but sane Hunter returns home for the Thanksgiving holiday. To anyone who has suffered through family get-togethers, her anxiety is all the more empathetic as she is greeted by a varied assortment of relatives. While all the characters have their peculiarities, Foster and writer W.D. Richter ultimately exploit their endearing characteristics as well. The film is at its best up to and during the eventful dinner scene, and the closing montage nicely brings the film together. ★★½ DVD Letterbox: $14.99

Home Fries

(1998, 93 min, US, Dean Parisot.) *Drew Barrymore, Luke Wilson, Catherine O'Hara, Jake Busey, Shelley Duvall.* Barrymore is appealing in this otherwise mixed-up, where-do-we-go-next romantic/murder comedy. Flyboys and brothers Wilson and Busey buzz their dad in his helicopter, but the old guy dies of a heart attack. It seems he was fooling around and mom (a shrill O'Hara) wanted to scare him. Turns out the girl he was two-timing with is the same person who may have heard the murder on her headphones: burger drive-thru cashier Barrymore. Wilson then begins working at the place to find out what she knows. Okay, class, all who think they're gonna fall in love, raise your hands. There are a few amusing, dark scenes, but mostly this crash course in romantic cynicism runs out of gas way before the inevitable finale. ★★ DVD: $14.99, VHS: $9.99

A Home of Our Own

(1993, 104 min, US, Tony Bill) *Kathy Bates, Edward Furlong, Soon-Teck Oh, Tony Campisi, T.J. Lowther.* Bates' sturdy performance as a widowed mother of six elevates this sentimental drama, literally a poor woman's *Alice Doesn't Live Here Anymore.* Set in the early 1960s, the story follows Bates and her children as they leave their Los Angeles home and head east for greener pastures. En route, they settle in Idaho, where they scrape out a living in a small rural town and try to come together as a family all the while trying to make the titular dream come true. As Shayne, the eldest son of the "Lacey tribe," Furlong is impressive. ★★½ DVD: $14.99

Home of the Brave

(1949, 86 min, US, Mark Robson) *James Edwards, Lloyd Bridges, Frank Lovejoy, Jeff Corey.* Powerful WWII drama based on Arthur Laurents' play about a black soldier (Edwards) experiencing prejudices from fellow G.I.s while fighting in the South Pacific. Produced by Stanley Kramer. ★★★½ VHS: $19.99

Homeboy

(1988, 118 min, US, Michael Seresin) *Mickey Rourke, Christopher Walken, Debra Feuer, Ruben Blades.* After his daring performance in *Barfly*, Rourke goes even further over the edge with a highly unusual portrayal of an illiterate, monosyllabic boxer competing one last time for the title. Walken plays his unsavory manager. A downbeat but curiously appealing boxing drama which unfortunately gives in to many clichés of the genre. ★★½

Homecoming

(1948, 113 min, US, Mervyn LeRoy) *Clark Gable, Lana Turner, Anne Baxter.* In postwar roles, Gable and Turner both demonstrate a dramatic maturity together in comparison to their two earlier teamings. In this compelling if familiar wartime story, Gable stars as a society doctor who enlists and is sent overseas, where he eventually falls for headstrong nurse Turner. Baxter is Gable's wife back home: she also serving who only stands and waits. Gable's character's name is Ulysses, which suggests the film's inspiration in the story of a soldier who returns home a changed man. Baxter's scenes are perfunctory, as Gable and Turner's romance and working relationship during the war are the film's main attraction. ★★½ VHS: $19.99

The Homecoming

(1973, 111 min, GB, Peter Hall) *Cyril Cusack, Michael Jayston, Ian Holm, Vivien Merchant.* Hall's production of Harold Pinter's now-classic play is perhaps one of the finest stage-to-screen adaptations to come out of the American Film Theatre series. This riveting family saga about a young academic who returns to his parents' London home with his newlywed wife in tow is peppered with Pinter's wry humor as well as his incisive views on domestic strife. Outstanding performances abound from the cast. ★★★★ DVD: $29.99, VHS: $29.99

Homegrown

(1998, 102 min, US, Stephen Gyllenhaal) *Billy Bob Thornton, Hank Azaria, Kelly Lynch, Jon Bon Jovi, Ryan Phillippe, Judge Reinhold, Ted Danson, John Lithgow, Jamie Lee Curtis, Maggie Gyllenhaal.* Oddly marketed as a comedy, *Homegrown* is actually a trite murder mystery set against the relatively unexamined (by Hollywood standards) landscape of America's professional marijuana industry. The flimsily constructed script cashes in on both the sensationalism and the obligatory humor attached with the subject matter, and merely hedges around the larger issues connected with what is reputedly known as America's most profitable cash crop. Despite a diverse cast, the central characters are spread too thin to hide the blemishes in the predictable story line about three dopey weed farmers who become ad-hoc drug dealers after witnessing their boss' murder. Complete with three hundred pot jokes, two inferred sex scenes, one dumb plot twist, and half a high-speed car chase, *Homegrown* is still a few ounces short of a pound. ★★ DVD: $29.99

Homer and Eddie

(1989, 100 min, US, Andrei Konchalovsky) *Whoopi Goldberg, James Belushi, Karen Black, Anne Ramsey.* Belushi is Homer, a sheltered, child-like man. Goldberg is Eddie, an already-crazed woman who just found out she has a month to live. Together, this unlikely pair take to the road and learn about themselves and each other. ★★

Homeward Bound: The Incredible Journey

(1993, 90 min, US, DuWayne Dunham) *Robert Hays, Kim Greist, Jean Smart, Michael J. Fox, Sally Field, Don Ameche.* Disney's remake of their classic 1963 adventure film *The Incredible Journey* is a winsome and charming experience. Three pets are left on a neighbor's ranch while their family is temporarily away. As time passes, they become convinced that the family is in trouble and decide to make their own way back to their old house, thus beginning their "incredible journey." This is indeed one of those rare family movies that will please everyone. (Sequel: *Homeward Bound 2: Lost in San Francisco*) ★★★ DVD: $14.99, VHS: $9.99

Homeward Bound II: Lost In San Francisco

(1996, 89 min, US, David R. Ellis) *Michael J. Fox, Sally Field, Robert Hays.* With most of the original cast intact, this sequel lacks the spontaneous charm of the original. On this family vacation, the three animals escape from their cages on the airport runway, fearing that they are going to a "bad place." They must then battle their way through the animalistic streets of San Francisco, making friends and saving a child and a kitten from a raging fire along the way. Not one of the better talking animal films available. ★★ VHS: $22.99

Homicide

(1991, 100 min, US, David Mamet) *Joe Mantegna, Ving Rhames, William H. Macy.* Mamet's third outing as director is a gritty crime drama about a Jewish homicide detective struggling with his ethnic identity. Mamet regular Mantegna stars as Bobby Gold, a hard-nosed inner-city cop who is hot on the trail of a dangerous fugitive, and a probable promotion. But, when a Jewish shopkeeper is murdered, he gets lassoed into working the case by the deceased's family. Disavowing his heritage, he tries to get off the case and, at first, derides the family's hysteria over the possibly anti-Semitic nature of the crime. Mamet's characteristic terse dialogue punctuates this deftly made modern-day morality play. Mantegna's raw portrayal contributes greatly to the film's dark, moody atmosphere. ★★★★

L'homme Blessé

(1984, 100 min, France, Patrice Chereau) *Jean-Hugues Anglade.* Adrift in the French underworld of hustlers and pickups, the innocent Henri (Anglade) experiences a brutal awakening to his gay sexuality. He witnesses a trick being beaten in the train station toilet, surrenders to the culprit's fierce embrace and finds himself hopelessly lost in ardor for this mysterious thug. Suddenly drawn to rough trade, Henri undergoes a number of hardships before finding liberation in a shocking final act of conquest. A disturbing yet powerful examination of sexual obsession and one man's personal sexual odyssey. (French with English subtitles) ★★★ DVD: $29.99, VHS: $39.99

Hondo

(1953, 84 min, US, John Farrow) *John Wayne, Geraldine Page, Ward Bond.* Though not on the level of Wayne's work with director John Ford, *Hondo* is an exciting and well-made western that features a sterling film debut by Page. Wayne plays a half-Indian scout who befriends Page and her young son, who have been left alone on their ranch located dangerously close to an Apache camp. Wayne gives an overly mannered performance, but is countered by Oscar nominee Page, who gives a solid portrayal of a stalwart homesteader. ★★★ VHS: $19.99

Honey

(1978, 89 min, Italy/Spain, Gianfranco Angelucci) *Clio Goldsmith, Fernando Rey.* A sensual, erotic drama about a young woman novelist who takes her manuscript to a publisher's home and is asked to read passages from it. What unfolds is her steamy story of first sexual encounters and discovered pleasures. ★★

Honey

(2003, 94 min, US, Bille Woodruff) *Jessica Alba, Mekhi Phifer, Lil' Romeo, Joy Bryant, Lonette McKee.* Alba is unimpressive (except physically, if uber-aerobicized, cookie-cutter hotties are your thing) as the title character, a none-too-interesting club dancer with stars in her eyes. Seemingly within minutes, she's a music video dance star. . . but she (and the audience) have some lessons to learn about the big, bad world. Lightning-paced yet excruciatingly dull, *Honey* is so thin and synthetic it makes *Flashdance* look like Chekov adapted by Bergman. It's also shamelessly pandering, and even the choreography is unimaginative and tedious. ★ DVD Pan & Scan: $26.99, DVD: $26.99, VHS: $22.99

Honey, I Blew Up the Kid

(1992, 89 min, US, Randal Kleiser) *Rick Moranis, Marcia Strassman, Robert Oliveri, Lloyd Bridges.* Moranis and Strassman reprise their roles in this mildly entertaining rehash of *Honey, I Shrunk the Kids*. This time, of course, scientist Moranis blunders in the opposite direction and winds up with a 100-foot tall, two-year-old behemoth, who threatens downtown Las Vegas (temper tantrums pose a real threat now!). While the original provided entertainment for all ages, this one will be infinitely more appealing to the little ones than adults. Another disappointment is the lack of a Roger Rabbit short which preceded the original. An instance in which bigger isn't necessarily better. (Sequel: *Honey We Shrunk Ourselves*) ★★½ DVD: $14.99, VHS: $9.99

Honey, I Shrunk the Kids

(1989, 93 min, US, Joe Johnston) *Rick Moranis, Matt Frewer, Marcia Strassman.* Moranis stars as a scientist dad whose attic project goes berserk one fine afternoon and miniaturizes not only his kids, but the neighbor's as well. As bad turns to worse, the little ones find themselves stranded across the backyard, and their only hope lies in trekking across the yard — which, for them, is now the size of Kansas and bears a striking resemblence to Oz. This is a pure fluff and fun comedy-fantasy which takes its simple premise and goes a long way. (Sequel: *Honey, I Blew Up the Kid*) ★★★ DVD: $19.99, VHS: $9.99

Honey, We Shrunk Ourselves

(1997, 75 min, US, Dean Cundey) *Rick Moranis.* Moranis is the only remaining cast member in this third, and hopefully, final entry in the series. While mildly entertaining, the mediocre special effects and sappy plot dampen adult enjoyment. This episode pairs Moranis' family with his brother, sister-in-law, niece and nephew. The two wives are about to embark on a weekend getaway but discover their husbands have been accidentally shrunk — a fate they themselves suffer. Meanwhile the kids, thinking they have the house to themselves, proceed to party under the secret watch of their minute parents. ★★ DVD: $14.99, VHS: $9.99

Honeymoon in Vegas

(1992, 92 min, US, Andrew Bergman) *Nicolas Cage, Sarah Jessica Parker, James Caan, Anne Bancroft, Peter Boyle, Seymour Cassel, Tony Shalhoub.* Can a film which features 34 Flying Elvises be all bad? Writer-director Bergman is taken to task this age-old question, and in his capable hands, *Honeymoon in Vegas* is a most pleasurable comedy. Cage and Parker are madly in love, and have traveled to Las Vegas to wed. But big-time gambler Caan sees Parker, who's a dead ringer for his late wife, and promptly tricks Cage into an arrangement to spend the weekend with her. From there it's an all-out free-for-all, as Cage travels through hell and high water to get her back. Cage is at his most manic, handling each successive zany setback with frenzied comic abandon. Parker, as she was in *L.A. Story*, is a lovely comedienne. The 34 Flying Elvises, by the way, all perform admirably. ★★★ DVD: $14.99

The Honeymoon Killers

(1970, 108 min, US, Leonard Kastle) *Shirley Stoler, Tony LoBianco.* A crazed swindler and his 250-lb. lover prey on a host of lonely, gullible women for financial gain in this sinister and subversive cult classic. ★★★ DVD Criterion Collection: $29.99

The Honeymoon Machine

(1961, 87 min, US, Richard Thorpe) *Steve McQueen, Jim Hutton, Paula Prentiss, Jack Weston, Dean Jagger.* McQueen is an American sailor stationed in Venice who joins forces with scientist Hutton in an elaborate scheme to use a Navy computer to win at the roulette table. In-between fine-tuning the system and collecting their winnings, both men find time for romance. It's slightly disorienting to see McQueen in such a farcical role, but he manages to wring a few laughs; as does the scene-stealing Weston. ★★½ VHS: $19.99

Honky Tonk

(1941, 105 min, US, Jack Conway) *Clark Gable, Frank Morgan, Lana Turner, Claire Trevor.* The first of Gable and Turner's four films together is an appealing western drama. Gable is a con artist on the run who meets up with beauty Turner en route to a small Nevada town. There, Gable takes up residence, courting Turner for romance and the locals for business. Turner makes the most of her first starring role, and the dialogue is snappy and full of double-entendres. Morgan and Trevor offer good performances in support as, respectively, Turner's drunkard father and a dance-hall girl. ★★½ VHS: $19.99

Honkytonk Man

(1982, 122 min, US, Clint Eastwood) *Clint Eastwood, Kyle Eastwood, Verna Bloom, Marty Robbins.* One of Eastwood's very few misfires. Clint plays a terminally ill, Depression-era country singer who packs up and heads on the road, hoping to make it to the Grand Old Opry. Clint's son Kyle plays his nephew who accompanies him on the trip. ★★ DVD: $19.99, VHS: $14.99

The Honor of Dongfang Xu

(1988, 92 min, China, Xhang Huanxun) Kung Fu fans should enjoy the wonderfully operatic martial arts melees in this otherwise ordinary movie. Set in the early 1900s, when China was under the imperialistic domination of eight Western nations, the story revolves around Dongfang Xu, a gentle family man, whose combined martial arts agility and Zen-master's concentration lead him to be chosen to fight an "evil" Russian boxer. ★★

Hoodlum

(1997, 122 min, US, Bill Duke) *Laurence Fishburne, Tim Roth, Andy Garcia, Vanessa L. Williams, Cicely Tyson, William Atherton, Loretta Devine.* The effects of crime and the efforts of a group of black crooks to control their turf in 1930s Harlem is the subject of this minor gangster outing. Fishburne is "Bumpy" Johnson, a slick con artist just out of the slammer who wants to make his mark on New York's organized crime front. He assimilates himself into the lucrative numbers racket run by the Queen (Tyson), but soon finds the operation in trouble when veteran bad boy Dutch Schultz (Roth with a bad haircut) muscles in. Director Duke has classic aspirations, but don't have the chutzpah to put it all together. There's fine period production work and costumes, but their effort simply lacks the type of style needed to pull off an epic gangster movie. Bumpy? You bet. ★★ DVD: $14.99

Hoods

(1998, 90 min, US, Mark Malone) *Joe Mantegna, Jennifer Tilly, Kevin Pollak, Joe Pantoliano, Seymour Cassel.* Another entry in the recent mob comedy subgenre, *Hoods* is too uneven in tone to be a hit with audiences. Angelo Martinelli (Mantegna, who also produced) is having one of those days. On his birthday, his ailing father (Cassel) asks him to whack someone named Carmine Dellarosa, but no one knows who he is. While the stars are well cast, and there is one rather clever plot twist, *Hoods* is ultimately disappointing because the film unwisely shifts gears from frustration comedy into poignancy. In the process, it generates too few laughs, and even less sympathy. ★★ VHS: $9.99

Hook

(1991, 144 min, US, Steven Spielberg) *Gwyneth Paltrow, Robin Williams, Dustin Hoffman, Bob Hoskins, Maggie Smith, Caroline Goodall, Charlie Korsmo.* With this update of the Peter Pan fairy tale, Spielberg has fashioned a fun-loving romp through Never-Never-Land which will delight kids and has enough depth to captivate adults. *Hook* finds Peter Pan all grown up and in the form of a Williams, 40-year-old workaholic corporate raider-type who has no time for his kids let alone *being* one. When his old nemesis, Captain Hook (Hoffman), kidnaps Peter's tykes, he is forced to confront a past he doesn't even remember. The performances are splendid throughout: Williams revels in his boyish way; Hoffman camps it up as the decadent and snobbish Hook; Hoskins nearly steals the show as Hook's comical henchman Smee; and Smith is wonderful as the aging Wendy. ★★★ DVD: $19.99

Hoop Dreams

(1994, 171 min, US, Frederick Marx, Peter Gilbert, Steve James) This compelling look at the aspirations of two talented African-American high school basketball stars, Arthur Agee and William Gates, is both highly entertaining and deeply disturbing. The film introduces the two as they are recruited to play for an exclusive suburban Catholic Academy, St. Joseph's. Their paths eventually diverge as Arthur loses his scholarship and returns to public school while William is groomed to be the team's next star. Assembled from over 250 hours of footage shot over five years, the film impressively pinpoints each young man's basketball highlights and lowlights, creating an urgent sense of athletic drama throughout. But the film's real triumph is in its depiction of their respective families and struggles; and in acknowledging the bitter irony that so many young men place their hopes in basketball, when really it's just another level of exploitation and marketing. March Madness will never seem the same again. ★★★★ VHS: $19.99

Hoosiers

(1986, 114 min, US, David Anspaugh) *Gene Hackman, Barbara Hershey, Dennis Hopper, Sheb Wooley, Fern Parsons, Brad Boyle.* Hackman gives a dynamic performance as the new coach to an Indiana high school basketball team, determined to get them to the championships. An exciting and involving drama, with great support from Hershey and Oscar nominee Hopper as a boozy fan. Even for those who avoid sports dramas, this is a must. Excellent score by Jerry Goldsmith. ★★★½ DVD: $14.99

Hope and Glory

(1987, 113 min, GB, John Boorman) *Sara Miles, David Hayman, Derrick O'Connor, Susan Woolbridge, Sammi Davis, Ian Bannen, Sebastian Rice-Edwards.* Boorman's sweet, finely crafted and quite humorous recollection of his childhood days in England during WWII at the time of the German Blitz. Young Rice-Edwards is Billy, the director's alter ego, through whose eyes we see a unique view of war-torn Britain. Miles is splendid as Billy's mother, who struggles to keep her family together in the wake of neighborhood bombings, extramarital affairs and indifferent adolescents. Perfectly cast and boasting outstanding production values, this reminiscence, like Woody Allen's similarly themed *Radio Days*, is a brilliant evocation of early 1940s life. ★★★★ DVD: $19.99

Hope Floats

(1998, 112 min, US, Forest Whitaker) *Sandra Bullock, Harry Connick, Jr., Gena Rowlands, Mae Whitman, Michael Pare, Kathy Najimy.* This sentimental roller-coaster delivers if you're looking for a tearjerker. All others be warned that the film pulls out all the emotional stops. Birdee (Bullock) goes on a talk show and is informed, along with the national audience, that her husband has been cheating on her with the same best friend for over a year and that he is leaving her for the other woman. Devastated and shamed, Birdee and her daughter Bernice take refuge with her mother (warmly played by Rowlands) in her hometown. Enter Justin (Connick), a former high school nerd, now a sexy and sympathetic house painter. There are plenty of tragic twists and turns until the inevitable happy ending. Fine acting and some heartwarming moments help elevate the film above the maudlin plot. ★★½ DVD: $14.99, VHS: $6.99

Hopscotch

(1980, 104 min, US, Ronald Neame) *Walter Matthau, Glenda Jackson, Ned Beatty, Sam Waterston.* Matthau and Jackson are reteamed (after *House Calls*) in this entertaining spy comedy with Matthau as a weary CIA agent who decides to publish his memoirs — and tell all. Beatty is his boss who's not too keen on the idea. ★★★ DVD Letterbox Criterion Collection: $29.99

The Horn Blows at Midnight

(1945, 78 min, US, Raoul Walsh) *Jack Benny, Alexis Smith, Franklin Pangborn.* Though he often joked about this film being the turkey of the 1940s (and his career), Benny's ascent into the heavens is actually quite funny. Benny plays an angel who is dispatched to Earth to destroy it with one blow from Gabriel's horn. Though *To Be or Not To Be* is unquestionably Benny's one film classic, *Horn* is a pure lark with the comedian in wonderful form. ★★★

Horror of Dracula

(1958, 82 min, GB, Terence Fisher) *Christopher Lee, Peter Cushing, Michael Gough, Melissa Stribling.* The first of the British Hammer Films to feature Lee as Count Dracula and Cushing as the tireless Dr. Van Helsing. In this outing, the Prince of Darkness ventures from Transylvania to London in search of new blood. A well-played and atmospheric horror tale that ably compares to the 1931 Bela Lugosi classic. ★★★½ DVD Letterbox: $19.99, VHS: $14.99

The Horror Show

(1989, 95 min, US, James Isaac) *Lance Henriksen, Dedee Pfeiffer, Brion James.* A serial killer who dies in the electric chair vows to take revenge on the cop who put him away. Now, as an unstoppable force, the killer returns to terrorize the cop and his family. ★½

The Horse

(1983, 116 min, Turkey, Ali Ozgenturk) The incredible hardships endured by a father and son as they struggle against abject poverty is the plot of this compelling film. Reminiscent of *The Bicycle Thief*, the film, set in modern Turkey, details the father's attempts to earn enough money to send his son to school. A sensitive yet complex exposé of the grim realities of life, this film so upset the government that director Ozgenturk was sent to prison for several years. ★★★

Horse Feathers

(1932, 68 min, US, Norman Z. McLeod) *Groucho Marx, Harpo Marx, Chico Marx, Zeppo Marx, Thelma Todd.* The password is "swordfish" as the Marx Brothers turn academia upside-down with Groucho as the head of Huxley College, preparing the school for the big game. Harpo and Chico are part-time students as well as spies. Todd is the "big girl on campus." With the exception of *Duck Soup*, this madcap romp is the funniest of all the Marx Brothers' movies. ★★★½

Horse of Pride

(1980, 118 min, France, Claude Chabrol) *Jacques Dufilho, François Cluzet.* Chabrol, France's best-known chronicler of the foibles of the bourgeoisie turns his cinematic eye towards a drastically different type of people: the proud but poor peasants of Brittany. Set in the early 1900s and adapted from the French best-selling novel by Pierre Jakez Helias, this earthy drama follows the rituals of birth, death, marriage and harvest in a Breton village during four seasons. Chabrol captures their values and mythology in a lifestyle that has been steadily dying. (Breton with English subtitles) ★★★½

The Horse Soldiers

(1959, 119 min, US, John Ford) *John Wayne, William Holden, Hoot Gibson, Anna Lee.* Brooding Civil War drama with Wayne and Holden as ideologically opposed Union soldiers who are on a sabotage mission deep within Confederate territory. Not one of Ford's best, but nevertheless intriguing. ★★½ DVD: $14.99, VHS: $9.99

Horse Thief

(1986, 88 min, China, Tian Zhuangzhuang) Set in an isolated and impoverished village in Tibet, *Horse Thief* is a stirring yet simply told work of art. Nordo, a young and able man, is forced to steal in order to support his growing family. He is caught and, with family in tow, driven out of the village into nomadic life. In the harsh conditions of the countryside, his attempts to eke out an existence fail and he returns to repent. But he soon finds himself again attracted to theft. Full of mysterious religious rituals and haunted by images of death, this film eschews simple Communist doctrine and is more concerned with the ancient ways of dealing with the hardships and cruelties of life. (Mandarin with English subtitles) ★★★½ VHS: $24.99

The Horse Whisperer

(1998, 168 min, US, Robert Redford) *Robert Redford, Kristin Scott Thomas, Scarlett Johansson, Sam Neill, Dianne Wiest, Chris Cooper, Cherry Jones.* With the gorgeous mountains and fields of Montana as picturesque backdrop, Redford's marvelously acted, emotionally satisfying *The Horse Whisperer* is a stirring story of one young girl's coming-of-age and one woman's rediscovery of her heart. Based on the novel by Nicholas Evans, the film begins with a staggering horseback-riding accident. Thirteen-year-old Grace (Johannson) is injured in the fall, resulting in the amputation of her leg and her horse Pilgrim about to be put to sleep. Grace's emotionally reserved mother Annie (Scott Thomas), a high-powered New York magazine editor, decides to try to save the animal. She treks with Grace and Pilgrim to Montana where "horse whisperer" Tom Rooker (Redford) resides, hoping to mend both daughter and horse. It is Annie, however, who heals the most when she falls in love with Tom and regains the ability to love. Scott Thomas is extraordinary as Annie, a woman with a hard-edged exterior but whose interior is fragile. Young Johannson is also first-rate, shading Grace with vulnerability and verve — her "who will love me" scene is heartbreaking. ★★★½ DVD Letterbox: $14.99

The Horse's Mouth

(1958, 93 min, GB, Ronald Neame) *Alec Guinness, Kay Walsh, Robert Coote, Michael Gough.* Guinness' flawless portrayal of Gulley Jimson, a crotchety and eccentric old artist whose love of painting leads to incessant mischief, is unquestionably one of his finest comic performances. Walsh is also brilliant as his reluctant cohabitant in this hilarious tribute to noncomformity and art. Guinness himself wrote the screenplay from a Joyce Cary novel. ★★★½ DVD Letterbox Criterion Collection: $29.99

The Horseman on the Roof
(Le Hussard sur le Toit)

(1996, 117 min, France, Jean-Paul Rappeneau) *Juliette Binoche, Olivier Martinez, Gérard Depardieu.* France's great cholera epidemic of 1832 would hardly suggest the backdrop to a gripping story of courage, loyalty and love, but with its exquisite cinematography, compelling performances and stirringly old-fashioned story line, *The Horseman on the Roof* is exactly that. Martinez stars as Angelo, handsome Colonel of the Hussards, revolutionary and Italian expatriate, who begins a Candide-like adventure in his attempt to return home to Italy. He is accompanied on his journey by Pauline de Théris (Binoche), a beautiful countess with her own agenda for fleeing the region. As small towns in Provence become ravaged by the enveloping epidemic, the two refugees encounter fear, death, intrigue, and their own hearts. Director Rappeneau (*Cyrano de Bergerac*) has crafted an ambitious epic both ravishing and penetrating which rarely falters in its intensity, and the film is remarkably lucid in its many narrative transitions. Binoche offers a radiant performance, and Martinez is especially good as the dedicated soldier. (French with English subtitles) ★★★½ DVD: $19.99

The Hospital

(1971, 103 min, US, Arthur Hiller) *George C. Scott, Diana Rigg, Barnard Hughes, Stockard Channing, Nancy Marchand.* Biting satire by Paddy Chayefsky with Scott as a disillusioned doctor working at a New York City hospital who finds more ills in both administrative policy and his fellow physicians than he does in his patients. Chayefsky won an Oscar for his scathing screenplay. ★★★½ DVD Dual: $14.99

The Hot Chick

(2002, 100 min, US, Tom Brady) *Rob Schneider, Anna Faris, Matthew Lawrence, Michael O'Keefe, Eric Christian Olsen, Robert Davi.* Leave it to Rob Schneider to create a film that makes one wax nostalgic for such body-swapping masterpieces-by-comparison as *18 Again* and *Vice Versa*. After obtaining some magic earrings, popular girl Jessica switches places with slimy thief Clive (Schneider). In his vile body, "she" and her friends try to find out how to switch back, but not before banal adventures in urination, shaving and, most frightening, dancing. Schneider actually isn't half bad, but his modest efforts are wasted in a film with such unoriginal and lowbrow ideas. Adam Sandler appears in a cameo, playing Schneider's old "You put your *weed* in there" character from "Saturday Night Live." It smacks of desperation, but at least this in-joke is good for a laugh, unlike the rest of this sorry picture. ★½ DVD: $19.99, VHS: $9.99

Hot Shots!

(1991, 85 min, US, Jim Abrahams) *Charlie Sheen, Cary Elwes, Valeria Golino, Lloyd Bridges, Jon Cryer, Kristy Swanson.* From one of the directors of *Airplane!* comes this often hilarious parody of military and pilot films, *Top Gun* in particular. The jokes are delivered at a machine-gun pace and most of them succeed. Sheen, satirizing his *Navy SEALS* role, is the Tom Cruise-ish, hotshot pilot competing against arrogant Elwes. Bridges shows up as an admiral who is obviously related to Bridges' *Airplane!* air traffic controller. Obviously, all are in *Airplane!* territory, here. And though the film doesn't reach the comic heights of that classic, *Hot Shots* is nevertheless a high-flying romp. (Sequel: *Hot Shots! Part Deux*) ★★★ DVD Letterbox: $14.99

Hot Shots! Part Deux

(1993, 89 min, US, Jim Abrahams) *Charlie Sheen, Lloyd Bridges, Valeria Golino, Richard Crenna, Rowan Atkinson, Brenda Bakke, Miguel Ferrer.* More lowbrow hijinks courtesy of Abrahams and cowriter Pat Proft. Not as consistently funny as the first film, there are still quite a few funny bits to this spoof, which now sets its aim at *Rambo*-type films. Crenna even shows up to poke fun at his mentor role. And look for the cute cameo by Martin Sheen tipping his hat to his most famous role. ★★½ DVD Letterbox: $14.99

Hot Spell

(1958, 86 min, US, Daniel Mann) *Shirley Booth, Anthony Quinn, Shirley MacLaine, Earl Holliman, Eileen Heckart.* Exceptional performances by Booth, Quinn and MacLaine highlight this compelling drama. Booth plays a middle-aged housewife who must contend with her husband's extramarital affairs and her children's romantic problems. ★★★

The Hot Spot

(1990, 120 min, US, Dennis Hopper) *Don Johnson, Virginia Madsen, Jennifer Connelly, Charles Martin Smith, William Sadler, Barry Corbin, Jack Nance.* Based on a Charles Williams pulp novel, this atmospheric and offbeat thriller tells a tale of robbery, murder, blackmail and "good-lookin'-but-dangerous dames" set in the dusty locales of a small Texas town. In the leading roles, Johnson as a low-life drifter and Madsen as a femme fatale fail to impress. The film is elevated, however, by a host of wonderful supporting actors and a bluesy score by John Lee Hooker and Miles Davis. ★★½ DVD: $14.99

Hot to Trot

(1988, 83 min, US, Michael Dinner) *Bobcat Goldthwait, Dabney Coleman, Virginia Madsen, John Candy.* Goldthwait (who is a great stand-up comedian but who has yet to find a suitable film role) dons the Donald O'Connor role from the *Francis* movies of the 1950s in this tired talking horse comedy. ★

Hotel Colonial

(1987, 103 min, US, Dinzia T.H. Torrini) *John Savage, Robert Duvall, Rachel Ward, Massimo Troisi.* Savage is called to Bogota, Colombia, to identify the body of his brother, who has supposedly committed suicide. But after trudging through the Amazonian jungle, Savage finds that his brother is actually living in a world of drugs and depravity. A dismal drama of betrayal and corruption. ★

The Hotel New Hampshire

(1984, 110 min, US, Tony Richardson) *Rob Lowe, Jodie Foster, Beau Bridges, Nastassja Kinski, Wallace Shawn, Matthew Modine, Wilford Brimley, Amanda Plummer, Anita Morris.* A felicitous actors' exercise that follows closely the John Irving novel. The serendipitous script examines the exploits of a highly unusual American family, both at home and abroad, and ranges in mood from the almost slapstick to the nearly tragic. While the direction tends to harbor self-indulgence, each actor's portrayal is inventive and endearing. ★★★ DVD Letterbox: $9.99

Hotel Reserve

(1944, 79 min, GB, Peter Glenville) *James Mason, Lucie Mannheim, Herbert Lom.* Mason stars in this gripping drama about an Austrian refugee at a seaside resort in the south of France during WWII who helps the local police hunt down a Nazi spy. ★★★

Hotel Terminus

(1988, 27 min, US, Marcel Ophüls) Winner of both the Cannes International Critics Prize in 1988 as well as the Academy Award for Best Documentary, this groundbreaking film is a meticulous investigation into the life of Klaus Barbie, the "Butcher of Lyons," whose Nazi war crimes include the ordering of the deaths of over 4,000 people as well as 44 children of Izieu. The film spans 70 years and traces the 40-year manhunt for the ruthless war criminal. An extraordinary film that is part detective story and part a study of the complex web of international political deceit. *Hotel Terminus* can be considered the final chapter in Ophüls' trilogy on World War II which includes *The Sorrow and the Pity* and *Memory of Justice*. ★★★★

H

287

The Hound of the Baskervilles

(1939, 80 min, US, Sidney Lanfield) *Basil Rathbone, Nigel Bruce, Richard Greene, Wendy Barrie, Lionel Atwill, John Carradine.* The sun never rises on the English moor; ominous foreboding permeates even broad daylight. Stark, brooding black-and-white cinematography establishes the ambience for Mr. Sherlock Holmes' unraveling of the centuries-old curse of the Baskerville family. This first pairing of Rathbone and Bruce as Sherlock Holmes and Dr. Watson clicked so powerfully that it was followed by another 13 Sherlock Holmes films. ★★★½ DVD: $19.99, VHS: $16.99

The Hound of the Baskervilles

(1959, 88 min, GB, Terence Fisher) *Peter Cushing, Andre Morell, Christopher Lee.* The horror masters at Hammer Studios chose Arthur Conan Doyle's most macabre mystery in what they had hoped would begin a new series for them. Cushing, though a little too aged for the role of Sherlock Holmes, does a credible job, keeping the great detective cold as ice and sharp as a tack. Effective and atmospheric. ★★★ DVD Letterbox: $14.99

The Hound of the Baskervilles

(1977, 84 min, GB, Paul Morrissey) *Dudley Moore, Peter Cook, Kenneth Williams, Denholm Elliott, Spike Milligan, Terry-Thomas, Prunella Scales.* Basil Rathbone can rest easy as Morrissey's tepid spoof of Arthur Conan Doyle's classic novel falls laughlessly flat. Cowriters Moore and Cook should share the blame, as well, as their antics are deadly unfunny. Even a good supporting cast can't help. Moore slaps a happy medium, the dog runs away with the picture, and careers must be salvaged. ★

Hour of the Star

(1986, 96 min, Brazil, Suzanna Amaral) *Marcelia Cartaxo, José Dumont, Tamara Taxman, Fernanda Montenegro.* This deeply touching work harkens back to the grand neorealist style of *La Strada* and *The Bicycle Thief*, creating an unlikely heroine out of Macabea, an uneducated, obtuse girl from Brazil's northeastern provinces. Despite her impoverished surroundings, she carries herself with dignity and a surprising degree of wit. First-time director Amaral made the film when 52 years old, after raising nine children, then attending N.Y.U. (Portuguese with English subtitles) ★★★½ VHS: $79.99

Nicole Kidman in *The Hours*

Hour of the Wolf

(1967, 89 min, Sweden, Ingmar Bergman) *Max von Sydow, Liv Ullmann, Ingrid Thulin, Erland Josephson.* One of Bergman's most powerful works, *Hour of the Wolf* is a nightmarish drama of mental illness and creative intensity. A successful painter (von Sydow) and his loving wife (Ullmann) spend the summer on a barren island where, spurred by insomnia and haunted by demons both real and imagined, the man's sanity slowly unravels while his distraught wife helplessly watches. A haunting psychological horror film that mixes surrealistic touches with old-fashioned Gothic terror to create a brilliant and unforgettable vision of madness. (Swedish with English subtitles) ★★★★ DVD: $24.99

The Hours

(2002, 114 min, GB, Stephen Daldry) *Nicole Kidman, Meryl Streep, Julianne Moore, Ed Harris, Claire Danes, Allison Janney, Toni Collette, Jeff Daniels, John C. Reilly, Miranda Richardson, Stephen Dillane, Jack Rovello.* Three women, separated by time, class and geographic location, share the book "Mrs. Dalloway" by Virginia Woolf. The film opens with author Woolf in an idyllic Sussex countryside in the early 1920s. Kidman, who won a Best Actress Oscar as Woolf, offers a studied, controlled exploration of a creative spirit trapped by expectations of reason and conformity and the best intentions of those who love her. Laura Brown (Moore) enjoys the middle-class bliss of suburban Los Angeles in 1951, yet she seems curiously sad and disassociated. Her eerily prescient son Richie (a superb performance by young Rovello) observes her with understanding beyond his years. And in present-day New York City, Clarissa Vaughan (Streep) is hosting yet another party; this time for her long-time friend and confidant Richard (Harris), a poet dying from AIDS. With children or without, with men or without, these three women share a replication of activities and a communality of emotions and demands that transcend their superficial differences. The film avoids toppling under the weight of the complexity of Michael Cunningham's poetic and sprawling Pulitzer Prize-winning novel by the grace of remarkable performances from the three leads and supple, fluid direction. ★★★★ DVD Letterbox Collector's Edition: $29.99, VHS: $9.99

House

(1986, 93 min, US, Steve Miner) *William Katt, George Wendt, Richard Moll, Kay Lenz.* Tongue-in-cheek horror film about a horror novelist (Katt) who moves into the house of his deceased aunt to write about his Vietnam War experiences, and becomes terrorized by deadly, gruesome monsters. The film mixes decent horror effects with comedy, and the result is enjoyably silly. (Sequel: *House 2: The Second Story*) ★★½ DVD: $29.99, VHS: $14.99

House Arrest

(1996, 108 min, US, Harry Winer) *Jamie Lee Curtis, Kevin Pollak, Kyle Howard, Amy Sakasitz, Christopher McDonald, Wallace Shawn, Sheila McCarthy, Jennifer Tilly, Ray Walston.* On their wedding anniversary, Curtis and Pollak announce to their two children their intent to separate. Their seventh grade son Grover (Howard) decides to take radical steps and locks them in the basement in an attempt to force them to resolve their problems. Some neighborhood kids find out about the lockup and force their parents to join the prisoners, creating a house of juvenile delinquents upstairs and disgruntled adults downstairs. Though the film has a certain charm and the cast is quite engaging, *House Arrest* is too long, the ending is too pat, and there's not an abundance of funny scenes to overcome the story's banalities. ★★ DVD: $14.99, VHS: $9.99

House Calls

(1978, 98 min, US, Howard Zieff) *Walter Matthau, Glenda Jackson, Art Carney, Richard Benjamin, Candice Azzara.* Matthau and Jackson make a surprisingly effective comedic team in this funny romantic romp. Swinging divorcé Walter is a surgeon who romances no-nonsense hospital administrator Glenda. Love and laughs — though not necessarily in that order — follow. Carney is great in support as an absent-minded doc. ★★★

House of Angels

(1993, 119 min, GB/Sweden, Colin Nutley) *Helena Bergstrom, Rikard Wolff, Per Oscarsson.* Some would say the term "Swedish comedy" is an oxymoron, but thanks to British director Nutley, this delightful Nordic romp should sway all naysayers. A pixie-like Bergstrom stars as a young cabaret artist who returns to her mother's village to collect her inheritance, one of the town's prized estates. This, along with her leather-clad, motorcycle-straddling gay companion, Zac, turns the normally quiet little town into a beehive of gossip and curious disbelief. Sporting a wonderfully eccentric cast ranging from yokels to drag queens, the film is one of those marvelous contrivances which, though minor in scope, provides plenty of heartwarming good cheer. (Swedish with English subtitles) ★★★½

House of Cards

(1993, 108 min, US, Michael Lessac) *Kathleen Turner, Tommy Lee Jones, Park Overall, Shiloh Strong, Esther Rolle.* Utterly engrossing, *House of Cards* is a moving look at the mind of an exceptional child. While living in Mexico, seven-year-old Sally becomes influenced by the legends told to her by a native guide after her father dies in an accident at an archeological dig. Back in the States, Sally withdraws from her family, stops speaking and begins to exhibit spectacular feats of the mind and body, leading doctors to diagnose her as autistic. Sally's mother (Turner) refuses to accept the diagnosis and begins to devise a cure. Besides being a tense and well-acted drama of love and mysticism, *House of Cards* asks tough questions about what's "normal" and the process involved in "curing" a child with a brilliant mind. ★★★½

House of Dark Shadows

(1970, 96 min, US, Dan Curtis) *Jonathan Frid, Joan Bennett, Grayson Hall.* Theatrical version of the popular 1960s daytime horror soap opera, "Dark Shadows." Frid returns as Barnabas Collins, the 18th-century New England aristocrat-turned-vampire, here looking to end his curse. Some good chills, and recommended for fans of the TV show. ★★★ VHS: $19.99

House of Games

(1987, 102 min, US, David Mamet) *Lindsay Crouse, Joe Mantegna, Lilia Skala, J.T. Walsh, Mike Nussbaum, Ricky Jay, William H. Macy, Meshach Taylor.* Playwright Mamet's directorial film debut is this superbly crafted story about an uptight psychiatrist (Crouse) who goes thrill-seeking with a sophisticated con artist (Mantegna). Filled with red herrings and unexpected twists, Mamet's ingenious screenplay imparts a keen sense of psychology doused with a hilarious and wry sense of humor. The acting is outstanding; Crouse is eerily emotion-

House of Sand and Fog

less as the famous shrink and Mantegna is both charming and alluring as the smooth-operating grifter. ★★★½ DVD: $19.99, VHS: $7.99

The House of Mirth

(2000, 140 min, US, Terence Davies) *Gillian Anderson, Eric Stoltz, Dan Aykroyd, Laura Linney, Anthony LaPaglia, Elizabeth McGovern.* Ecclesiastes reads: "The heart of fools is in the house of mirth." The heroine of Edith Wharton's novel of early 20th-century high society, Lily Bart, takes residence there after a heartrending journey. A sumptuous rendering in the same mold as Martin Scorsese's earlier Wharton adaptation, *The Age of Innocence*, but far more successful in its execution, *The House of Mirth* is a sometimes staggering tale of duplicity and loss set against the chillingly repressive atmosphere imposed by Lily's gender and station. While not quite able to elaborate Lily's naïveté, Anderson is nonetheless glimmering as the orphaned society woman in search of a suitable husband (read: rich), all the while in love with a lawyer (Stoltz) of modest means. Marred only by abrupt character introduction, *The House of Mirth* is a superior period piece filled with gorgeous detail and exquisite performances. ★★★½ DVD: $29.99, VHS: $14.99

House of 1,000 Corpses

(2003, 88 min, US, Rob Zombie) *Sid Haig, Karen Black, Michael J. Pollard, Chris Hardwick, Erin Daniels.* Musician — and major horror film freak — Zombie's long-awaited (by fellow horror film freaks, anyway) directorial debut ranks as a major disappointment. While the film seemingly has all the necessary elements (great supporting cast of B-movie character actors, the creepy titular setting and the genuine feel of a '70s drive-in exploitation low-budgeter), the result is much less than the sum of its parts. There's no narrative drive, just a quartet of unappealing jerks screaming and dying for 90 minutes, while the bad guys chomp on the scenery for our attention. Zombie deserves points for attempting a balls-to-the-wall scarefest, especially in this timid age, but his first film is as lifeless as the thousand other corpses in its title. ★½ DVD: $26.99

House of Sand and Fog

(2003, 126 min, US, Vadim Perelman) *Ben Kingsley, Jennifer Connelly, Shohreh Aghdashloo, Ron Eldard, Frances Fisher, Jonathan Ahdout.* In this atmospheric, wrenching adaptation of Andre Dubus III's best-selling novel, tragedy and despair come to those who each has right on their side. In a strong portrayal navigating compassion, greed and pride, Kingsley plays Massoud Amir Behrani, an Iranian immigrant who has relocated to the California coast with his wife and teenaged son. At auction, he purchases the house of Kathy Nicolo (Connelly), a recovering alcoholic who through clerical error has lost her home. As Kathy attempts to use the legal system to reclaim what is properly hers, she and Behrani, who has purchased the house legally, become locked in a battle of wills into who has proper ownership. Their escalating confrontations eventually lead to heartbreaking loss. Kingsley and Connelly, both former Oscar winners, are engaging, etching sympathetic performances even all the while their characters act in unsympathetic ways. It is Iranian-born actress Aghdashloo, however, who delivers the film's most lasting impression, bringing dignity, fear and longing to Behrani's wife who watches the world around her fall to pieces. A haunting, sad but involving story of loss, desperation and misfortune. ★★★½ DVD: $26.99

House of the Dead

(2003, 90 min, US/Canada, Uwe Boll) *Jonathan Cherry, Tyron Leitso, Clint Howard, Jürgen Prochnow.* Derivative, moronic and infuriatingly trendy, this adaptation of the video game sends a group of obnoxious teens to a remote island for a rave party (!), only to have them pitted against a horde of zombies. While the ridiculous, *Matrix*-inspired slo-mo shots of zombie fighting are incongruous (and eradicate whatever horror there might have been), they do become unintentionally funny after the first ten times they're used. Otherwise, there's nothing to recommend here, and horror connoisseurs will be insulted, to boot. A rip-off of Italian zombie flicks while aiming for the video-game crowd at the expense of true terror. ★ DVD: $26.99, VHS: $102.99

The House of the Spirits

(1994, 132 min, US/Sweden, Bille August) *Jeremy Irons, Meryl Streep, Glenn Close, Winona Ryder, Antonio Banderas.* Savagely received by the American film critics but embraced by the European press, this near-epic adaptation of Isabel Allende's acclaimed novel of thwarted love and class distinction fails to fully capture the essence of the original text. But for all its shortcomings, the film possesses a sense of poetry and conviction which counter the heavy dramatics. Set against the backdrop of political upheaval in an unnamed South American country (read: Chile), the story follows the lives of the multi-generational Trueba family: including an oppressive landowner father (Irons); his innocent, clairvoyant wife (Streep); their young daughter (Ryder), who is having an affair with a revolutionary (Banderas); and the family's repressed aunt (the remarkable Close), who has been banished by her unforgiving brother. Awash in mysticism amd romantic symbolism, the film will both intrigue and infuriate with its crystalline emotions and excesses. ★★★ DVD: $9.99

House of Wax

(1953, 88 min, US, Andre de Toth) *Vincent Price, Phyllis Kirk, Charles Bronson, Carolyn Jones.* A smash hit in its day, and originally shown in 3-D, this chiller has long been a horror favorite. Price plays a sculptor who resorts to real subjects to carve after a fire mishap leaves him disfigured. ★★★ DVD: $19.99, VHS: $9.99

The House of Yes

(1997, 90 min, US, Mark S. Waters) *Parker Posey, Josh Hamilton, Tori Spelling, Freddie Prinze, Jr., Geneviève Bujold.* Egregiously ignored in its brief theatrical run, *The House of Yes* is the most wicked comedy-incest-mental illness melodrama of its year. Fans of *Spanking the Monkey* shouldn't miss this sharply written tale of a dysfunctional family get-together. Martin (Hamilton) brings his new fiancée Leslie (Spelling) to his bourgeois home for Thanksgiving. There they must cope with Martin's medicated, Kennedy-obsessed twin Jackie-O (Posey). Jackie-O views Leslie's presence as a very pesky distraction to their sibling bonds of sex and assassination re-enactments, and she berates her with endless biting, offhand remarks about Leslie's poor upbringing and social standing. Posey is fabulous as always, and the rest of the ensemble is splendid. Tori doesn't even suck. ★★★½ DVD: $19.99, VHS: $9.99

The House on Carroll Street

(1988, 100 min, US, Peter Yates) *Kelly McGillis, Jeff Daniels, Mandy Patinkin, Jessica Tandy.* Intriguing thriller set during the McCarthy era as subversive "red" McGillis mixes it up with FBI agent Daniels when she unwittingly uncovers an underground Nazi organization. ★★½ DVD Letterbox: $14.99

House on Chelouche Street

(1973, 120 min, Israel, Moshe Mizrahi) *Gila Almagor, Michal Bat-Adam.* This family drama is set in Tel Aviv during the turbulent period of British rule just before the partition of Palestine. The film successfully captures the excitement and anxiety in a rapidly evolving country. (Hebrew with English subtitles) ★★★ VHS: $19.99

House on Haunted Hill

(1958, 75 min, US, William Castle) *Vincent Price, Carol Ohmart, Richard Long.* Semiclassic haunted house story with Price as an eccentric millionaire who offers a group of strangers $10,000 each to spend a night in his haunted mansion. Good, old-fashioned, eerie fun. (Remade in 1999) ★★★ DVD: $14.99, VHS: $7.99

Gillian Anderson in The House of Mirth

House on Haunted Hill

(1999, 96 min, US, William Malone) *Geoffrey Rush, Famke Janssen, Taye Diggs, Ali Larter, Bridgette Wilson, Peter Gallagher, Chris Kattan, Jeffrey Combs, Max Perlich.* This remake of Vincent Price's 1958 fun ghost story can be lots of fun as well. Never taking itself too seriously, this ghost tale immediately pays homage to the original by naming its lead character Price. He's played by Rush, an amusement park magnate whose trophy wife (Jannsen) convinces him to throw her birthday party at a supposedly haunted, now-abandoned insane asylum. Guests arrive, and all are offered a million dollars if they can live the night. Then things get spooky. It's all red herrings, shadowy figures and what's-around-the-corner boos. But it's done with a certain tongue-in-cheekiness that much of it is hard to resist — on a isn't-it-cheesy, seen-it-before level. ★★½ DVD: $9.99, VHS: $9.99

The House on 92nd Street

(1945, 88 min, US, Henry Hathaway) *William Eythe, Lloyd Nolan, Signe Hasso, Gene Lockhart, Leo G. Carroll.* Based on a real-life spy case during WWII, this exciting, low-keyed thriller is told in a taut semidocumentary style. Nolan stars as an FBI chief who is put in charge of the case of Nazi and Fifth Columnist infiltration after it is discovered the Germans are obtaining secrets about the atom bomb. Eythe is the American double agent setting up the Nazis, and Hasso and Carroll are two of the German agents. Beginning with a shot of J. Edgar Hoover busy at work, the film at times seems to be none-too-subtle propaganda for the government agency, but the story soon takes charge to deliver a well-detailed and crisp espionage adventure. Location footage helps in the film's general feeling of authenticity. ★★★½ VHS: $19.99

House Party

(1989, 96 min, US, Reginald Hudlin) *Christopher Reid, Christopher Martin, Robin Harris, Martin Lawrence, Tisha Campbell.* A refreshingly hip and surprisingly innocent comedy about a day in the life of a group of black suburban teenagers who simply want to throw a party without getting hassled. The story revolves around Kid (Reid, from the rap duo Kid N' Play), who must sneak out of his house and avoid a gang of thugs. Although the plot is thin, this spirited and delightful musical/dance/comedy is even more impressive in that it shows black teens having fun without resorting to the stereotypes of them being druggies, criminals or impoverished. Harris is hilarious as Kid's overprotective, Dolemite-loving father. (Followed by 3 sequels) ★★★ DVD: $14.99, VHS: $9.99

Houseboat

(1958, 110 min, US, Melville Shavelson) *Cary Grant, Sophia Loren, Harry Guardino, Martha Hyer.* Charming romantic comedy starring Grant as an overwhelmed widower who hires Loren as a maid (though she's really a socialite) to take care of his three children and their houseboat. The kind of enjoyable '50s romantic fluff that Grant seemed to have a patent on. Guardino is a scene stealer as the handyman. ★★★ DVD Letterbox: $14.99, VHS: $14.99

Houseguest

(1995, 108 min, US, Randall Miller) *Sinbad, Phil Hartman, Jeffrey Jones, Kim Greist, Stan Shaw.* The premise for this genial comedy is an old one: In order to get away from the thugs looking for him, Sinbad assumes the identity of another; here, the boyhood friend of Hartman. As he is whisked away to the safe confines of suburbia, Sinbad ultimately enriches the lives of these strangers while they do the same for him. While the concept and even the execution is stale, both actors manage to wring whatever comic life is present. *Houseguest* may not be totally unwanted, but it comes dangerously close to overstaying its welcome. ★★ DVD: $14.99, VHS: $9.99

Household Saints

(1993, 124 min, US, Nancy Savoca) *Lili Taylor, Vincent D'Onofrio, Tracey Ullman, Illeana Douglas.* In her previous feature-length outings (*True Love, Dogfight*), director Savoca evidenced an uncanny ability to capture the feel of the films' eras and environments. In *Household Saints*, she adds an element of the surreal which creates the mythic dimension with which we remember our childhoods and the stories our parents and grandparents told us. D'Onofrio and Ullman are winsome as the husband and wife (he wins her in a pinochle game) whose daughter (Taylor) becomes the neighborhood saint in 1950s Brooklyn. The film is delightful, funny and entertaining. ★★★½

The Householder

(1962, 101 min, India, James Ivory) *Shashi Kapoor, Leela Naidu.* The first collaboration between director Ivory, producer Ismail Merchant and writer Ruth Prawer Jhabvala (who would go on to create, among others, *The Remains of the Day*) is this delightful and warmhearted but uneven comedy. Kapoor plays a young teacher who, pushed by his meddlesome mother, enters into an arranged marriage with a woman equally naive and inexperienced. Troubles begin for the couple as they find themselves unprepared for the difficulties of marriage and its financial responsibilities. While not one of the trio's best works, the film provides an interesting background for their future films. ★★½ DVD: $29.99

The Housekeeper

(1986, 106 min, Canada, Ousami Rawi) *Rita Tushingham, Ross Petty, Jackie Burroughs.* Tushingham is excellent in the lead role as a dyslexic cleaning lady who goes on a murderously psychotic jag. Chilling suspense is accented by occasional forays into black humor in this sometimes confusing thriller. ★★½ VHS: $19.99

Housekeeping

(1987, 116 min, US, Bill Forsyth) *Christine Lahti, Sara Walker, Andrea Burchill.* Forsyth's first American film (shot in the Pacific Northwest) is a brilliantly quirky comedy about familial ties and individuality. Lahti gives a sensational performance as vagabond Aunt Sylvie, who comes to stay to look after her recently orphaned nieces (nicely played by Walker and Burchill). The film touchingly examines the close-knit relationship of the two sisters, and the influence Aunt Sylvie has on the two girls: one socially conscious and embarrassed by her aunt, and the other a soulmate. A film of rare sensitivity and character, with a haunting finale. ★★★★

Housesitter

(1992, 102 min, US, Frank Oz) *Steve Martin, Goldie Hawn, Julie Harris, Dana Delany, Donald Moffat, Peter MacNicol.* A funny screwball romp about a woman who, through a web of lies and deceits, squirms her way into the life of an unsuspecting architect with side-splitting results. It's a plot which is vaguely reminiscent of classics like *Bringing Up Baby* and *Ball of Fire*. Of course, Hawn,

admirable a job though she does, can never be compared to the great Kate, and Martin is certainly no Cary Grant; but still, the film's outrageous humor and situations give these two modern-day comics plenty of good material to make for a thoroughly enjoyable laugh fest. ★★★ DVD Letterbox: $14.99

How Green Was My Valley

(1941, 118 min, US, John Ford) *Walter Pidgeon, Maureen O'Hara, Donald Crisp, Roddy McDowall, Anna Lee, Barry Fitzgerald.* This Academy Award winner for Best Picture is a touching, expertly directed saga of a Welsh coal mining family. Crisp won an Oscar for his splendid portrayal of the family patriarch, as did Ford for his outstanding direction. ★★★★ DVD: $14.99, VHS: $9.99

How I Got into College

(1989, 89 min, US, Savage Steve Holland) *Anthony Edwards, Lara Flynn Boyle, Corey Parker, Charles Rocket, Brian Doyle-Murray.* Holland's occasionally funny but predictable and surprisingly lifeless comedy scores about a C-. Told in typical Savage Steve style, wacky characters and situations abound in this not-so-savage farce about the college entrance experience. Some of the jokes fall with a thud — but there are enough truly funny scenes to give this comedy a passing grade. Holland clearly remembers all the anxieties and hopes of the young adult years, but it's about time he grew up a little. ★★½ DVD: $9.99, VHS: $9.99

How I Won the War

(1967, 109 min, GB, Richard Lester) *John Lennon, Michael Crawford, Jack MacGowran, Michael Hordern.* Lennon stars in this funny and surreal portrait of one man's less than Rambo-like military career. This often hilarious presentation of the lives of a ragtag group of WWII soldiers taps into the somewhat naive but joyously nihilistic anti-militarism of the time. The material is certainly "dated," but the heart of the piece is in the right place. ★★★

How Stella Got Her Groove Back

(1998, 121 min, US, Kevin Rodney Sullivan) *Angela Bassett, Whoopi Goldberg, Taye Diggs, Regina King.* Can a 40-year-old woman facing a midlife crisis find happiness in the arms of a handsome 20-year-old? If you believe this well-produced if familiar romantic drama, then the answer is yes. And when the woman is Bassett and the man looks like Diggs, it's not such a totally unappealing proposition. Bassett stars as Stella, a successful San Francisco stock broker and mother who takes an impromptu vacation to Jamaica with lifelong friend Delilah (Goldberg). There she begins a tentative affair with ex-medical student Winston (Diggs). Through some clichéd dramatics and out-of-date dilemmas, Stella faces an uncertain future in the arms of someone 20 years her junior. Bassett gives a competent performance but the script never really gives this terrific actress room to soar. ★★½ DVD: $14.99, VHS: $6.99

How Tasty Was My Little Frenchman

(1973, 80 min, Brazil, Nelson Pereira dos Santos) *Arduino Colasanti, Ana Maria Magalhaes, Ital Natur.* As the French and Portuguese swarm the Brazilian coastline in the mid-1500s, the indigenous Indian tribes align themselves with their would-be conquerers according to their own local conflicts (the friend of my enemy is my enemy). One hapless Frenchman is left to drown by a Portuguese contingent. However, he wades to shore to be found by an

Les Girls (Marilyn, Lauren and Betty) in *How to Marry a Millionaire*

Indian tribe friendly to the French. Unfortunately, they mistake him for a Portuguese, and they are cannibals. Much like colonialism itself, the victim is expected to participate in the ritual of exploitation — he has a speaking part in the cooking ceremony. He is given a wife to help him learn his lines, and is well fed during his period of instruction. He is avidly attentive to his education in tribal ways, hoping to endear himself to his captors. This delightful farce overcomes its low budget and sometimes haphazard construction with droll insight and a wicked sense of humor, courtesy of director dos Santos, a leading proponent of Brazil's Cinema Novo. (French and Tupi with English subtitles) ★★★ VHS: $29.99

How the West Was Won

(1962, 162 min, US, George Marshall, Henry Hathaway, John Ford) *Henry Fonda, John Wayne, James Stewart, Gregory Peck, Richard Widmark, Debbie Reynolds, George Peppard, Robert Preston, Agnes Moorehead.* It took three directors to bring this overblown, epic western to the screen. One of the ultimate "all-star cast" extravaganzas released during the 1960s, this mammoth production was originally shown in 3-strip Cinerama, which is lost on the small screen. The story traces the lives of three generations of a pioneer family. Some outstanding action scenes (the river raft and train sequences in particular). ★★★ DVD Letterbox: $19.99, VHS: $6.99, VHS Letterbox: $6.99

How to Be a Player

(1997, 93 min, US, Lionel C. Martin) *Bill Bellamy, Natalie Desselle, Lark Voorhies.* Anyone who finds minstrel show buffoonery preferable to actual written and staged comedy may enjoy what is yet another treacly entry to the "men are pigs" school of comedy. Bellamy is a "player" whose only objective in life seems to be to make "booty calls" to as many girls as he can without getting caught by his girlfriend (Voorhies). Enter Bellamy's sister (Desselle) who decides to teach him a lesson by inviting all his women to the same party and waiting for the big blowup. Offensive both in its lack of humor and in its assertion that serial infidelity can be both fun and funny (he gets away with it), this is nothing more

than another example of Hollywood throwing a bone to the black community by ridiculing it. ★½ DVD: $9.99, VHS: $9.99

How to Be a Woman and Not Die in the Attempt

(1991, 96 min, Spain, Ana Belén) *Carmen Maura, Antonio Resines, Juanjo Puigcorbé, Carmen Conesa.* An episodic comedy-drama about Carmen (Maura), an Everywoman who deals with a disappointing husband, an underappreciative boss, and some thankless children, *How to Be a Woman* does a great job in setting up the frustrations of its central character, but the expected epiphany never quite arrives. Perhaps director Belén deliberately wants to leave viewers unsatisfied, because several of the story lines introduced remain unanswered. Nevertheless, viewers will care deeply about Carmen — Maura gives an outstanding, expressive performance, radiant one minute and dejected the next — as her character copes with the endless demands of work, home and family life. (Spanish with English subtitles) ★★★ DVD: $24.99

How to Beat the High Cost of Living

(1980, 105 min, US, Robert Scheerer) *Jessica Lange, Jane Curtin, Susan Saint James, Richard Benjamin, Fred Willard, Dabney Coleman.* A trio of housewives embark on a comedic caper to nab some cash from their local shopping mall. Though a good premise, even an agreeable cast can't make sense of this muddled farce. ★½ DVD Pan & Scan: $14.99

How to Get Ahead in Advertising

(1989, 95 min, GB, Bruce Robinson) *Richard E. Grant, Rachel Ward.* A brilliant piece of rowdy leftist propoganda with shades of Monty Python, Kafka and Sigmund Freud. When ace London adman Dennis Bagley (Grant) is unable to concoct that perfect pitch for a pimple remedy, his subconscious kicks in and produces a rapidly growing pimple on his neck. Yet this is no ordinary zit! This one talks and spews a wicked venom, both at Bagley and the viewer. As the pesky pimple grows larger, its rantings on behalf of unbridled materialism become uglier and his urge to take over our hero's body becomes

stronger. Where will it end? The ever shining Ward plays Bagley's wife and is the perfect foil to the boisterous boil's grotesque humor. No adventurous viewer should dare miss this fiendish British satire. ★★★½ DVD Dual: $14.99

How to Lose a Guy in 10 Days

(2003, 98 min, US, Donald Petrie) *Kate Hudson, Matthew McConaughey, Bebe Neuwirth, Adam Goldberg, Michael Michele, Shalom Harlow.* Michael Jordan taking out the trash . . . Paul McCartney doing his taxes . . . Matthew McConaughey and Kate Hudson starring in a formulaic romantic comedy. Great talents have to do grunt work from time to time, but that doesn't make it entertaining. Compounding the problem here is a script based on such deep levels of lies and deceit that love rarely makes an appearance. Advice columnist Hudson is entreated to write a piece on what *not* to do in a relationship, resulting in the film's title; her target is McConaughey, an ad exec who coincidentally (and it's a big one) is trying to prove that he can keep a girl for, yes, 10 days. If it were meaner, this could have been up there with *The War of the Roses* as her boy-torture escalates; but, no, this mall-ready product keeps emphasizing phony sweetness. Is this unearnest duplicity really what America wants in its romantic escapism? ★ DVD Letterbox: $19.99, VHS: $11.99

How to Make a Monster

(2001, 90 min, US, George Huang) *Steven Culp, Clea DuVall, Tyler Mane, Jason Marsden, Karim Prince, Julie Strain.* After the test-marketing disaster of its current "scary" video game, a computer company puts incredible stress on its small group of misfit geniuses to create a terrifying monster in time to make the promised delivery date. They succeed; unfortunately, a power surge causes the game to enter our world. Entertaining and fast-paced silliness, *How to Make a Monster* is given some weight (a bit too much, perhaps) by writer-director Huang, by playing up the cutthroat greed of American business. This is basically a horror variation on the themes explored in Huang's *Swimming with Sharks*, and it works well . . . to a point. While this is overall a fun ride, it goes a bit too far in hammering its "who's-the-real-monster?" theme home, with a somewhat unbelievable, uber-cynical ending leaving a bad taste. ★★½ DVD Dual: $24.99, VHS: $14.99

How to Make an American Quilt

(1995, 109 min, US, Jocelyn Moorhouse) *Winona Ryder, Ellen Burstyn, Anne Bancroft, Maya Angelou, Kate Nelligan, Jean Simmons.* By no means a great film, *How to Make an American Quilt* is probably the most successful of 1995's many female ensemble pieces. Ryder is a college student who spends her summer vacation with her grandmother (the always tangy Bancroft). As the young woman looks to set her romantic and academic lives in order, she becomes enmeshed in Bancroft's quilting circle, a group of mostly older women who all share a past of secrets, pain and camaraderie. With so many stories weaving through the narrative, one or two may not be as dramatically exciting, but each member of the film's terrific cast heartens the tale with a refreshing, robust liveliness. ★★★ DVD: $24.99, VHS: $9.99

How to Marry a Millionaire

(1953, 95 min, US, Jean Negulesco) *Marilyn Monroe, Betty Grable, Lauren Bacall, William Powell, David Wayne, Cameron Mitchell.* Hollywood's first Cinemascope comedy is a witty and stylish soufflé starring Monroe, Grable and Bacall as three Manhattan gold diggers out to trap (and marry) unsuspecting millionaire bachelors. ★★★ DVD: $14.99, VHS: $6.99

H

How to Murder Your Wife

(1965, 118 min, US, Richard Quine) *Jack Lemmon, Virna Lisi, Claire Trevor, Mary Wickes.* Typically funny 1960s sex farce with Lemmon as a happily unmarried cartoonist who awakens one morning to find himself wed to the lovely Lisi. He quickly devises numerous plans to get rid of her. ★★★ DVD Letterbox: $19.99

How to Succeed in Business without Really Trying

(1967, 121 min, US, David Swift) *Robert Morse, Michelle Lee, Rudy Vallee, Anthony Teague.* Delightful screen version of the Tony Award and Pulitzer Prize-winning Broadway musical with Morse re-creating his acclaimed stage role. Morse stars as a mailroom clerk who works his way up the corporate ladder in record time, thanks to the help of a little book and a lot of chutzpah. A terrific farce on big business, with great support from Vallee ("Ground hog!") and Lee. Frank Loesser's classic score includes "Brotherhood of Man" and "I Believe in You." Choreographed by Bob Fosse on stage, only one dance number remains. ★★★ DVD Letterbox: $14.99

How U Like Me Now

(1992, 109 min, US, Darryl Roberts) *Darnell Williams, Salli Richardson, Daniel Gardner.* First-time director Roberts proves to be a talent to be reckoned with with this charming low-budget urban comedy which recounts the professional and romantic struggles of twentysomething friends living in Chicago's South Side. The film tackles many issues, including interracial romance, buppies, back-to-Africa politics and others, without being heavy-handed or alienating like some films of this genre. ★★★

Howard the Duck

(1986, 111 min, US, Willard Huyck) *Lea Thompson, Jeffrey Jones, Tim Robbins.* One of the infamous duds of the 1980s, this comic fantasy isn't the worst movie ever made; however, it is an over-produced mess. Based on the comic book, it's all about an alien duck who travels to Cleveland and is befriended by rock star Thompson. In the immortal words of Groucho: "Why a duck?" ★ VHS: $7.49

Howards End

(1992, 140 min, GB, James Ivory) *Anthony Hopkins, Emma Thompson, Vanessa Redgrave, Helena Bonham Carter, Sam West, Nicola Duffett.* A sumptuous re-creation of E.M. Forster's novel of class struggle in the dying days of the Edwardian era. The story centers around the tragic confluence of three families from London's various social strata. Redgrave and Hopkins personify the upper crust as the Wilcoxes. The Schlegel sisters (Thompson and Bonham Carter) represent the liberal middle class. And Leonard Bast (West), an educated Cockney trying to make his way into the world of business, and his wife (Duffett) embody the lower depths. Filmed with all of the pomp and circumstance one has come to expect of Merchant Ivory productions, and acted with loving attention to both the mannerisms and prose of the era, *Howards End* is a truly marvelous and engaging period piece. Thompson won a well-deserved Oscar for her portrayal of the elder Schlegel, and she is equally matched by Hopkins. ★★★★

The Howling

(1981, 91 min, US, Joe Dante) *Dee Wallace, Patrick MacNee, Dennis Dugan, Christopher Stone, Kevin McCarthy, John Carradine, Slim Pickens.* From the director who loved horror films as a kid (and then never grew up), this werewolf tale is resplendent with in-jokes, character actors and good, scary special effects. Like Dante's other works (*Gremlins 1 & 2, Explorers*), *The Howling* takes off at full gallop and doesn't stop, reflecting his years cutting trailers for Roger Corman. Cowritten by John Sayles. (Followed by 2 sequels) ★★★ DVD Dual Special Edition: $19.99

The Hucksters

(1947, 120 min, US, Jack Conway) *Clark Gable, Ava Gardner, Deborah Kerr, Sydney Greenstreet, Adolphe Menjou, Edward Arnold.* A glossy, satirical look at the business of advertising. Gable is an idealistic go-getter who finds he must virtually sell his soul in order to succeed. Kerr appears in her first American film. ★★★ VHS: $19.99

Hud

(1963, 111 min, US, Martin Ritt) *Paul Newman, Melvyn Douglas, Patricia Neal, Brandon de Wilde.* Newman gives a riveting performance as the disreputable son of Texas cattle rancher Douglas in this outstanding modern-day western. Brilliantly photographed by James Wong Howe, the film centers on Newman's volatile relationships with his estranged father (who is faced with financial ruin), impressionable nephew Brandon de Wilde, and world-weary housekeeper Neal. Oscars deservedly went to Neal as Best Actress and Douglas as Supporting Actor; in fact, the entire ensemble is superb. A film of such grit you can almost taste the dust. Based on a novel by Larry McMurtry ("The Last Picture Show," "Lonesome Dove"). ★★★★ DVD: $19.99, VHS: $14.99

Hudson Hawk

(1991, 95 min, US, Michael Lehmann) *Bruce Willis, Danny Aiello, Andie MacDowell, James Coburn, Sandra Bernhard.* A major disappointment from the director of *Heathers*. Willis stars in this half-hearted comic adventure as a cat burglar who is coerced into committing a series of robberies. MacDowell is the Vatican spy he tangles with, Aiello is his partner, and Coburn is the CIA renegade trying to stop him. In all fairness, the actors try to maintain a degree of wackiness and lightheartedness, but there's too much mugging and winking; the viewer is numbed by a cast going to extremes to show the good time they're (supposed to be) having. Even the always-fun Bernhard appears lost. ★½ DVD: $14.99, VHS: $9.99

The Hudsucker Proxy

(1994, 111 min, US, Joel Coen) *Tim Robbins, Paul Newman, Jennifer Jason Leigh, Charles Durning, John Mahoney, Jim True, Bruce Campbell, Steve Buscemi.* With their usual cinematic aplomb, the Coen Brothers open the floodgates and unleash a torrent of invigorating witticisms and dizzying visuals in this spectacular, over-the-top tribute to the 1940s screwball comedy. Robbins stars as a beamish Midwestern rube working in the Orwellian mailroom of the Hudsucker Corporation, a megalithic industrial powerhouse headed up by a heartless and power-hungry Newman. True to the genre, Robbins soon finds himself on a meteoric rise to power upon which he must learn life's hard lessons. Leigh, as a hard-nosed reporter, rat-a-tat-tats her lines at machine-gun pace while paying splendid homage to Katharine Hepburn, Rosalind Russell and Barbara Stanwyck. ★★★½ DVD: $19.99, VHS: $14.99

Hugo Pool

(1997, 90 min, US, Robert Downey) *Alyssa Milano, Patrick Dempsey, Robert Downey, Jr., Richard Lewis, Malcolm McDowell, Cathy Moriarty, Sean Penn.* Misguided and inept in every department, *Hugo Pool* rivals only the pooch from *As Good as It Gets* as 1997's top dog. Milano is (inexplicably) Hugo, assigned to clean 44 pools in one day. While working her rounds, she encounters an array of "quirky" eccentrics — you know the type, the ones that give quirky a bad name. Given its seizure-inducing dialogue, grating score and career-nadir performances, *Hugo Pool* is an even bigger disappointment given the talented, eclectic cast (with exception of Milano, who has the screen presence of tissue paper). ★ DVD: $24.99, VHS: $14.99

The Hulk

(2003, 138 min, US, Ang Lee) *Eric Bana, Jennifer Connelly, Sam Elliott, Nick Nolte, Josh Lucas.* Marvel Comics' most flawed superhero gets a big-screen adaptation that sets it apart from other comic book adaptations — here you'll find action and effects peppered with angst and introspection, and for the most part it all works. Whilst the character of The Hulk may not have the depth of other comic book heroes, director Lee has created a 21st-century, computer-generated behemoth capable of achieving the kind of excitement-inducing action you wouldn't have seen in the cult TV show — you'd never expect Lou Ferrigno to pick up and hammer-toss a tank before leaping entire chasms with a single bound. Bana is mild-mannered Bruce Banner, whose genetic make-up was altered before birth by his scientist father (bravura, over-the-top Nolte). When a lab accident activates the dormant DNA, Banner discovers that any time he loses his cool he transforms into the not-so-jolly-green-giant. Pitting The Hulk against both the might of the Military and a just-as-powerful nemesis (we won't spoil it for you) gives the story the edge it needed to rise above the two-dimensional. It's a shame that the Batmanesque over-hyping ruined the film for many people, but this translates better to the small screen than the big, anyway. ★★★ DVD Letterbox 2-disc Special Edition: $19.99, DVD Pan & Scan 2-disc Special Edition: $19.99, VHS: $9.99

The Hulk

H

THE DISCERNING FILM LOVER'S GUIDE

Hullabaloo over Georgie and Bonnie's Pictures

(1978, 82 min, India, James Ivory) *Victor Bennerjee, Aparna Sen, Saeed Jaffrey, Peggy Ashcroft.* This film is a lighthearted romp through royal India — a world of princesses, palaces, tourists, precious art objects and the people who wheel and deal with them. What's all the hullabaloo about? Georgie owns a priceless collection of ancient paintings which he loves, but his sister wants more practical objects and wants him to sell. Frantic art dealers are soon in hot pursuit as the royal couple are deluged with people who want to buy. A great double twist ending concludes this exotic film. ★★★ DVD: $29.99

The Human Comedy

(1943, 117 min, US, Clarence Brown) *Mickey Rooney, Frank Morgan, Fay Bainter, James Craig.* Exceptional adaptation of William Saroyan's bestseller about the trials and tribulations of small-town life during WWII. This slice-of-life drama stars Rooney in possibly his best dramatic performance as a sensitive teenager coming of age, and Morgan is terrific in support. ★★★½ VHS: $14.99

Human Condition, Part 1

(1959, 200 min, Japan, Masaki Kobayashi) *Tatsuya Nakadai, Michiyo Aratama.* The Human Condition is an epic chronicle of one man's struggle to retain his humanity as he descends into the hypnotic, distorted reality of war. As Part 1 (*No Greater Love*) opens, production at a mining camp in occupied Manchuria is at a standstill. With a Japan desperate for raw resources for its war machine, Kaji, a pacifist who believes that effective management requires winning the hearts and minds of the workers, is given authority. (Japanese with English subtitles) (Followed by 2 sequels) ★★★ DVD: $29.99, VHS: $59.99

Human Condition, Part 2

(1960, 180 min, Japan, Masaki Kobayashi) *Tatsuya Nakadai, Michiyo Aratama.* Part 2 (*Road to Eternity*) begins with Kaji being tortured by the military police for having treated the Chinese humanely. Allowed one memorable night with his wife, Kaji is then ordered to the front. His records brand him "red" and his superiors mistreat him zealously. (Japanese with English subtitles) ★★★ DVD: $29.99, VHS: $59.99

Human Condition, Part 3

(1961, 190 min, Japan, Masaki Kobayashi) *Tatsuya Nakadia, Michiyo Aratama.* Part 3 (*A Soldier's Prayer*) commences as Kaji awakens to a world in chaos and after the surviving Japanese soldiers savagely retreat from an equally brutal Soviet Army. Kaji's own moral standards are challenged when he is forced to kill to survive. The film's final section, set in a Russian POW camp, has our hero understanding that the socialist ideas that he has championed offer no shield to man's basest tendencies. (Japanese with English subtitles) ★★★ DVD: $29.99, VHS: $59.99

The Human Stain

(2003, 106 min, US, Robert Benton) *Anthony Hopkins, Nicole Kidman, Ed Harris, Gary Sinise, Kerry Washington, Anna Deavere Smith, Wentworth Miller.* Philip Roth's novel dabbles in so many disparate areas that it's surprising that anyone would try to translate it to the screen. But director Benton and screenwriter Nicholas Meyer have given it a nice try and while the result of their efforts is uneven at best, what's on the screen is often compelling. One of the film's most curious aspects is its casting. Hopkins is Coleman Silk, the American-born, British-educated professor who sees his life changing radically after he's accused of using a racial slur. The comment becomes even more pronounced because Silk is, in fact, black, although he's passed for white since he was in college. Kidman plays Faunia Farley, a troubled white-trash custodian who has an unlikely affair with the distinguished Coleman. The tortured past of both characters are revealed in flashbacks and through conversations. In order to accept the film's premise you must buy into the characters essayed by these performers. Unfortunately, despite the fine efforts of all, the stretch is a little too far here. The film tries to get into the various themes of racism, passing-for-white, the plight of Vietnam veterans and coming of age in a novelistic way, but it just doesn't quite click. Well-meaning and sincere, *The Human Stain* is best admired for its serious approach to some pretty heady material. Blame its bumpiness on the excess baggage carried by its characters — and the film's unusual casting decisions. ★★½ DVD: $29.99

Human Traffic

(2000, 84 min, GB, Justin Kerrigan) *John Simm, Lorraine Pilkington, Shaun Parkes, Danny Dyer.* A weekend in the lives of a group of friends, as they take ecstasy, go to raves, have sex, and bitch about their dead-end jobs. First-time director Kerrigan has fashioned an infectious, ultrastylish comedy out of potentially hackneyed material. Spot-on observations on sex, friendship, ambition, family and a slew of other topics are complimented by a fun soundtrack and some big laughs along the way. Even at a scant 84 minutes, *Human Traffic* does lose energy towards the end, but it remains an entertaining, insightful film experience. ★★★ DVD: $14.99, VHS: $9.99

Humanité

(2000, 148 min, France, Bruno Dumont) *Emmanuel Schotté, Séverine Caneele. Philippe Tullier.* Pharaon De Winter (Schotté) is a quietly withdrawn, unremarkable man, a police inspector at times overwhelmed by the stark brutality he encounters in his job. Middle-aged, introspective, he lives with his mother in a small French farming community, more as an observer than a participant in life. The savagely beautiful, uncompromising *Humanité* follows his investigation of a particularly horrific crime through a series of vignettes, each revealing a piece of the puzzle or an aspect of a protagonist's character. Director Dumont has structured a psychological portrait in the manner of *Jeanne Dielman*, a deliberately paced, thoughtfully considered examination of a man who seems sometimes somnambulistic yet is desirous of connection, a man who stands apart yet is much like any other, a decent man capable of acts of humanity. (French with English subtitles) ★★½ DVD: $24.99, VHS: $19.99

Humoresque

(1946, 125 min, US, Jean Negulesco) *Joan Crawford, John Garfield, Oscar Levant.* This superior soap opera stars Crawford as a wealthy society woman becoming romantically involved with a young, talented musician (Garfield). Crawford and Garfield (who each offer an accomplished performance) are engaging together, and the melodramatic story line is consistently entertaining. ★★★ VHS: $19.99

The Hunchback of Notre Dame

(1923, 137 min, US, Wallace Worsley) *Lon Chaney, Patsy Ruth Miller.* Chaney enthralled a generation of filmgoers in this impressive silent film of the Victor Hugo classic about the deformed bell-ringer Quasimodo, and his love for a beautiful Gypsy girl. Chaney's characterization and makeup effects are outstanding. Remade several times, including the 1939 Charles Laughton version (still the best) and even a Disney animated feature. ★★★½ DVD: $24.99, VHS: $24.99

The Hunchback of Notre Dame

(1939, 117 min, US, William Dieterle) *Charles Laughton, Maureen O'Hara, Edmond O'Brien, Cedric Hardwicke, Thomas Mitchell.* Outstanding version of the Victor Hugo classic with Laughton in one of his best performances as the deformed bell-ringer Quasimodo. Told with great style, the film's production values are excellent and the acting first-rate. O'Hara is a lovely Esmeralda. The best of the many screen versions. ★★★★ DVD: $19.99, VHS: $19.99

The Hunchback of Notre Dame

(1996, 95 min, US, Gary Trousdale) *Voices of: Demi Moore, Tom Hulce, Kevin Kline, Jason Alexander, Mary Wickes.* After the high drama and pointed social lessons of the admirable *Pocahontas*, the animators at Disney have taken on an even darker text with this beautifully crafted feature film based on Victor Hugo's classic novel. Changing little of the story but reframing it to reflect Disney's traditional syle of storytelling, *Hunchback* is a brightly colored, fun-filled adaptation that manages to find quite a few laughs in a story not known for having them. Quasimodo (wonderfully voiced by Hulce) is still ugly and deformed, but here he's not quite so grotesque as to frighten little ones, and he's given three gargoyle friends to pal around with. The music by Alan Menken and Stephen Schwartz is capable but not as particularly memorable as other Menken scores. ★★★½ DVD Letterbox: $19.99, VHS: $24.99

A Hungarian Fairy Tale

(1987, 95 min, Hungary, Gyula Gazdag) *David Vermes, Mária Varga, Frantisek Husák, Eszter Csákányi.* Less fairy tale and more political fable, this magical film is a startling video find. Carried away on a cloud of romance after a performance of Mozart's "Magic Flute," a beautiful young woman with a Mona Lisa smile makes love with a handsome stranger. Their union produces a child, who is lovingly raised by the woman until she suddenly dies. The young boy, Andris, lost in the impersonal world of Budapest, begins an odyssey throughout Hungary searching for his father. Told with subtle humor and imbued with poetic beauty, this story of outsiders fleeing the confines of a conformist society is a remarkable achievement. Filmed in vivid black and white, this dreamlike and imaginative story will stay with the viewer long after it is over. (Hungarian with English subtitles) ★★★★

Hunger

(1966, 115 min, Denmark, Henning Carlsen) *Per Oscarsson, Gunnel Lindblom.* Oscarsson won the Best Actor Award at the Cannes Film Festival for his portrayal of a penniless and starving artist in 1890s Norway. This grim yet absorbing drama follows the young man who, despite being physically emaciated from lack of eating and prone to talking to his shoes, as well as to hallucinations, retains hope for his survival and optimism for his success as a writer as he

293

Denzel Washington in *The Hurricane*

tackles his hunger, waning self-respect and an overwhelming loneliness. The film does not have much of a plot, yet Oscarsson's performance keeps the viewer riveted. Based on the first novel by Nobel Laureate Knut Hamsun. (Danish with English subtitles) ★★★

The Hunger

(1983, 99 min, GB, Tony Scott) *Catherine Deneuve, Susan Sarandon, David Bowie, Cliff DeYoung, Willem Dafoe.* Deneuve stars as Miriam, an icy, elegant vampiress, hundreds of years old, who goes on the prowl for a new mate after her 200-year lover (Bowie) quickly ages. Her affections find their way to Sara (Sarandon), a doctor who has written on the subject of accelerated aging. Dripping with cinematic style and chic sexual intrigue, *The Hunger* is both a chilling vampire tale and a sensuous drama of lesbian attraction and desire. The two romp, fall into each other's arms and make love — and, of course, share blood. The two stars create unprecedented sensual sizzle. ★★★½

The Hunt

(1965, 93 min, Spain, Carlos Saura) *Alfredo Mayo, Ismael Merlo.* Under a relentless sun that scorches the parched fields of central Spain, three apparently successful middle-aged men, all veterans of the Spanish Civil War, and a young man set off for a day of rabbit hunting. Fueled by the heat and long simmering tensions, the hunt escalates from petty fighting and bickering into eventual bloodshed as the men's jealousies, obsessions and hatreds rise to the surface. Saura's searing psychological thriller, spare in style, probes man's cruel nature so successfully that its tale should shock the viewer. (Spanish with English subtitles) ★★★½

The Hunt for Red October

(1990, 135 min, US, John McTiernan) *Sean Connery, Alec Baldwin, Scott Glenn, James Earl Jones, Sam Neill, Tim Curry.* Director McTiernan's thrilling adaptation of Tom Clancy's best-seller is a well-paced and gripping Cold War drama filled with intrigue and exciting action. Connery excels as a Soviet submarine skipper who steals a state-of-the-art sub from the Russian fleet and goes AWOL. The question now facing the CIA is this: does he want to defect or is he going to single-handedly plunge the

world into nuclear war? Costar Baldwin is commanding as the CIA bookworm who is convinced of the defection theory. (Sequel: *Patriot Games*) ★★★½ DVD Letterbox Special Collector's Edition: $19.99, VHS: $9.99, VHS Letterbox: $9.99

The Hunted

(1995, 111 min, US, J.F. Lawton) *Christopher Lambert, Joan Chen, John Lone.* This hokey action-er manages lapses of excitement. Lambert stars as an American businessman in Japan who is on the run after witnessing the murder of a beautiful geisha (Chen) by a villainous ninja assassin (Lone). Violent almost to the point of slapstick, Lawton's film is yet another feeble attempt to cash in on the current "Asian cinemania" and as such features decent swordplay and a fast-paced (but ridiculous) script. ★★ DVD: $24.99, VHS: $19.99

The Hunted

(2003, 94 min, US, William Friedkin) *Tommy Lee Jones, Benicio del Toro, Connie Nielsen.* This repellent piece of exploitation does nothing to mute the argument that *French Connection* director Friedkin is permitted to periodically churn out slickly produced but intellectually vacuous action flicks like *The Hunted* only because he's married to the studio chief. Jones stars as a retired Special Forces instructor sought out by the FBI to help track down and kill one of his own trainees (Del Toro), a live-wire who's taken to slaughtering deer hunters in the Pacific Northwest. Though exquisitely photographed by Caleb Deschanel and crisply edited, its brawny machismo and grisly violence are revolting. An obtuse bookend quote about Abraham feebly attempts to infuse the movie with some Biblical subtext, but really it's all about the eventual bloody showdown between two knife-wielding, scowl-wearing men — shamelessly recycled from scoops of previous genre classics, yet handsomely executed. So to speak. ★★ DVD Letterbox: $29.99, VHS: $9.99

Hurlyburly

(1998, 126 min, US, Anthony Drazan) *Sean Penn, Kevin Spacey, Robin Wright Penn, Chazz Palminteri, Garry Shandling, Anna Paquin, Meg Ryan.* David Rabe's 1984 play about drug-addled and emotionally unstable Hollywood almost-players has become something else on-screen. Could be that the cocaine-crazed scene has become passe, or that characters this desperate aren't funny anymore, just pathetic. Too bad, because the performances are all fiery (possibly too fiery for the screen). Spacey comes off best as Mickey, a role he played onstage under Mike Nichols' direction, but there are also surprisingly strong (dramatic) turns by Shandling and a not-as-cute-as-usual Meg Ryan. ★★ DVD: $24.99, VHS: $19.99

The Hurricane

(1937, 102 min, US, John Ford) *Dorothy Lamour, Jon Hall, Mary Astor, Raymond Massey, Thomas Mitchell, John Carradine.* Ford's classic adventure yarn has Lamour (complete with sarong) and Hall as tropical island lovers whose romance is interrupted by a devastating storm and island governor Massey. The film is noted for a spectacular climactic hurricane sequence. ★★★½

The Hurricane

(1999, 146 min, US, Norman Jewison) *Denzel Washington, Vicellous Reon Shannon, Deborah Kara Unger, Liev Schreiber, John Hannah, Rod Steiger, Debbi Morgan, Dan Hedaya, Clancy Brown, David Paymer, Harris Yulin.* With the force of one of

those awesome storms which bear his name, Washington mesmerizes as champion boxer Rubin "Hurricane" Carter in this powerful, moving study of false imprisonment, racial bigotry and belated justice. In the late 1960s, Carter was a middleweight champ when he was framed and sentenced to life for three murders he didn't commit. Though celebrities from all walks of life rallied to his support, he labored in prison with writing his only outlet. In the mid-1980s, a Brooklyn youth (Shannon) stumbles upon Carter's book, setting in motion a series of events to set the boxer free after 22 years behind bars. The film was marred by controversy due to several scenes being historically inaccurate. Despite the dramatic liberties, *The Hurricane* is a gripping reminder of the high cost of personal freedom. ★★★½ DVD: $19.99, VHS: $9.99

Hurricane Streets

(1997, 86 min, US, Morgan J. Freeman) *Brendan Sexton III, Shawn Elliott, L.M. Kit Carson.* This overrated Sundance favorite (isn't every third release a "Sundance Favorite" these days?) does have some decent moments and is an impressive debut by director Freeman (no relation to the actor). *Welcome to the Dollhouse* costar Sexton gives a terrific, wholly real performance in this more accessible, less incendiary cousin to *Kids*. Like that film, *Hurricane Streets* follows a group of ne'er-do-well teens as they commit various crimes and behave like jerks and cause adults to cluck their tongues. To his credit, Freeman coaxes fine portrayals from his cast of mostly young teens and develops strong audience sympathy for his lead character. But the whole thing has the atmosphere of an "Afterschool Special" with gunshots and curse words, and is a bit tiresome for anyone out of their teens. ★★½

The Hurried Man

(1977, 91 min, France, Edouard Molinaro) *Alain Delon, Mireille Darc.* From the director of *La Cage aux Folles* comes this mildly interesting saga of a man driven to live his life in the fast lane. Delon plays a 40-year-old playboy whose carefree lifestyle is threatened when a financial deal becomes more than he bargained for when part of the package includes marriage to a millionaire's daughter (Darc). Delon is delightful as a lifelong bachelor forced into responsibility. ★★

Husbands

(1970, 153 min, US, John Cassavetes) *Ben Gazzara, Peter Falk, John Cassavetes.* Perhaps nothing affects the middle-aged more profoundly than the death of a close contemporary. Director Cassavetes again utilizes his hyper-documentary style to create a reality so sharply focused that it's life mythologized; to offer moments of everyday living so individualistic that they're archetypal. Harry (Gazzara), Archie (Falk) and Gus (Cassavetes) rail at the unnamed anxiety experienced at the death of a close friend. All the cracks and fissures in their relationships manifest during the multiday bender after the funeral. Cassavetes captures the essence of male camaraderie, deliciously choreographing testosterone flare-ups and maudlin introspection as these three embark on a transcontinental road trip. Another brilliant slap in the face from Cassavetes. ★★★½

Husbands and Wives

(1992, 110 min, US, Woody Allen) *Woody Allen, Mia Farrow, Judy Davis, Blythe Danner, Sydney Pollack, Liam Neeson, Juliette Lewis.* In an uncanny example of life imitating art, Allen's last collaboration with Farrow is an often humorous, sometimes relentless examination of disintegrating marriages and fickle attractions between older men and younger women. Made in an almost documentary, cinema verité style (complete with handheld camera work), the film is a kind of eavesdropping on the lives of two couples: Mia & Woody and Pollack & Davis. In the opening scene, Davis and Pollack announce to Farrow and Allen that they've decided to separate and from there, the film, in typical Allen fashion, meanders through all of the intellectual and emotional ramifications of marriage, fidelity and lust. Occasionally using talking head interviews with the characters, Allen probes their thoughts on all of these matrimonial ups and downs. ★★★½ DVD: $24.99, VHS: $19.99

Hush

(1998, 96 min, US, Jonathan Darby) *Gwyneth Paltrow, Jessica Lange, Johnathon Schaech, Nina Foch, Hal Holbrook.* Utterly ridiculous tripe about a manipulating mother (Lange) who will stop at nothing to get her son (Schaech) away from the city and back to the horse farm that is his legacy. Unfortunately, he's quite happy living in New York with his perky new wife (Paltrow). Quicker than you can say "Who put that hole in my diaphragm," Paltrow is pregnant and forced to reconsider life on the farm (especially after being mugged at knifepoint in her own apartment). Then things get really silly! This is the kind of film that relies on impossible actions and improbable reactions to proceed, and still it goes nowhere. Call it faint praise to say that the performances are good; the food on *Titanic* was good, too. ★ DVD: $9.99, VHS: $9.99

Hush . . . Hush, Sweet Charlotte

(1965, 133 min, US, Robert Aldrich) *Bette Davis, Olivia de Havilland, Joseph Cotten, Agnes Moorehead, Mary Astor, Bruce Dern.* Motivated by the success of *Whatever Happened to Baby Jane?*, *Hush . . .* is yet another Grand Guignol thriller which was so common in the 1960s. Originally titled *Whatever Happened to Aunt Charlotte?*, Davis, again in *Baby Jane* territory, stars as a very wealthy victimized hermit, haunted by the memories of a dead lover. Moorehead received an Oscar nomination for her unrecognizable slovenly housekeeper. ★★★ VHS: $19.99

Hustle

(1975, 120 min, US, Robert Aldrich) *Burt Reynolds, Catherine Deneuve, Ben Johnson, Paul Winfield, Eileen Brennan, Eddie Albert, Ernest Borgnine.* Reynolds plays an old-fashioned L.A. cop who spends his days investigating suicides, porn rings and the mob, and spends his nights in the arms of a sexy Parisian call girl (Deneuve). Reynolds is personable, but he's just going through the motions in this below-average police thriller. ★½ VHS: $14.99

The Hustler

(1961, 135 min, US, Robert Rossen) *Paul Newman, Piper Laurie, George C Scott, Jackie Gleason, Myron McCormick, Murray Hamilton.* Newman has never been better than this! His classic portrayal of a disenchanted pool hustler who challenges the champ Minnesota Fats (Gleason) is set against the vivid backdrop of the seedy New York pool hall scene. Also starring Laurie, in an unforgettable peformance as Newman's crippled

girlfriend; and Scott, who gives a brilliant characterization as a gruff promoter. A masterpiece of mood, character study and technique, with sharp direction by Rossen. (Sequel: *The Color of Money*) ★★★★ DVD Special Edition: $14.99, VHS: $6.99

Hustler White

(1996, 81 min, US/Canada, Bruce LaBruce & Rick Castro) *Tony Ward, Bruce LaBruce, Alex Austin, Kevin Kramer, Ron Athey, Wash Westmoreland.* This look into the world of L.A. male prostitutes gleefully criss-crosses the lines between daring and boring; porn and art; and avant-garde satire and obnoxious gross-out. Jurgan Anger (LaBruce) is a prissy German writer who falls hard for Monti Ward (Ward), a street hustler thug. Offering half-hearted homages to such films as *Sunset Boulevard* and *Whatever Happened to Baby Jane?*, the action jerks from this brief outline of a plot to a series of disconnected sexual encounters. The film has a curious lifeless quality, like we're watching a film made by a director who doesn't give a fuck, featuring actors only awkwardly enacting out what they are instructed to do and a plot more interested in simple shock value. ★★ DVD: $29.99, VHS: $29.99

The Hypothesis of the Stolen Painting

(1978, 78 min, France, Râùl Ruiz) *Jean Rougeul, Eva Simonet.* Made for French TV, this intriguing and meditatively intellectual mystery-thriller was directed by the highly original and beguiling avant-garde director Ruiz, a Paris-based, Chilean expatriate. The "detective" story begins with a guide showing an unseen interviewer a series of paintings by Second Empire artist Frederic Tonnerre, in an effort to solve the mystery of a seventh painting. The paintings — actually *tableaux vivants*, live stagings of the works with the people in suspended animation — are only one of the many adventurous techniques used by Ruiz in his playful unraveling of his strange whodunit. A Ruiz short, *Dog's Dialogue*, precedes the feature. (French with English subtitles) ★★★ VHS: $59.99

I, a Woman

(1966, 92 min, Sweden, Mac Ahlberg) *Essy Persson, Jorgen Reenberg, Preben Mahrt.* Unlike the more famous but equally successful *I Am Curious (Yellow)* that hit American shores in 1968, this groundbreaking, sexually explicit drama of a woman's yearning sexuality has survived the sexual revolution quite well. Beautiful blonde Siv (Persson) is an innocent country girl from a deeply religious family who drops her staid (no sex before marriage) boyfriend and the restrictiveness of provincial life to move to the big city and take care of her raging libido. Siv is a refreshing character — a beguilingly attractive temptress, she rejects conventional relationships and their obligations in a pursuit of simple pleasures and freedom. (Swedish with English subtitles) ★★★ DVD: $19.99, VHS: $29.99

I Am a Camera

(1955, 98 min, GB, Henry Cornelius) *Julie Harris, Laurence Harvey, Shelley Winters, Patrick McGoohan.* John van Druten's theatrical interpretation of Christopher Isherwood's "Berlin Diaries" is brought to the screen with intelligence and wit. This marvelously acted piece features Harris as Sally Bowles (a character later made truly famous by Liza Minnelli in Bob Fosse's *Cabaret*). ★★★

I Am a Fugitive from a Chain Gang

(1932, 93 min, US, Mervyn LeRoy) *Paul Muni, Glenda Farrell, Helen Vinson.* The best and most powerful of Warner Brothers' 1930s "social dramas." Muni gives a tour-de-force performance as a WWI veteran unjustly imprisoned and sent to a Southern chain gang. Escaping the brutality of the system, Muni finds himself on the run, and never looking over his shoulder. A daring exposé of criminal injustice, the film was based on the autobiography of Thomas E. Burns. Farrell is impressive in a small part as Muni's fiancée. ★★★★

Paul Muni (l.) in *I Am a Fugitive from a Chain Gang*

I Am Cuba

(1964, 141 min, Cuba/USSR, Mikhail K. Kalatozov) *Luz Maria Collazo, Jose Gallardo*. *I Am Cuba* is a kaleidoscopic exposé of Batista's Cuba, a land of stark, diametric opposites, of great wealth and abject poverty, whose inequalities are flamboyantly juxtaposed by a perpetually moving camera as it reveals the conflicting lifestyles of the monied elite and the barely subsisting underclass. The stark black-and-white cinematography and an unabashed affection for the land are reminiscent of Sergei Eisenstein's *Que Viva Mexico!* The film's political agenda is unapologetic, and within the structure of four short stories of hardship and abuse, it presents the crushing exploitation of Cuba's people and resources, revealing the underlying causes of Castro's revolution. Invigorating, inticing and sometimes brutal, the film shows equal affection to the teeming slums, the entertainment palaces and the fertile countryside. It's lyrical, joyous yet harsh and unwavering. (Spanish and Russian with English subtitles) ★★★★ DVD: $29.99, VHS: $29.99

I Am Curious (Blue)

(1968, 103 min, Sweden, Vilgot Sjoman) With footage shot at the same time as *I Am Curious (Yellow)*, this tepid sequel continues the story of a sociologist's sexual study, though it looks as if *Yellow* features the more "interesting" takes. (Swedish with English subtitles) ★★ VHS: $59.99

I Am Curious (Yellow)

(1967, 120 min, Sweden, Vilgot Sjoman) *Lena Nyman, Peter Lindgren*. Adult film fans seeking titillations from this infamous breakthrough film should reconsider renting this Swedish curiosity. *I Am Curious (Yellow)* spends less time on sex and more in exploring the times and lifestyles of Swedish youth, specifically an adventurous young lady. (Swedish with English subtitles) ★★½ VHS: $59.99

I Am My Own Woman

(1992, 90 min, Germany, Rosa von Praunheim) An inspiring film of one person's determined efforts to be exactly what he wants to be. A documentary with re-created dramatic scenes intercut throughout, the film follows Charlotte von Mahsldorf, born Lother Berfelde, from her teenage years during WWII to operating an East Berlin museum. Despite the repression of the Communists, attacks by skinheads and public scorn, Miss Charlotte retains an amazingly sunny outlook as she freely goes about her life as a woman. Two actors play Charlotte as the young Lother/Charlotte, and Charlotte plays herself in the later years. (German with English subtitles) ★★★½ VHS: $19.99

I Am Sam

(2001, 134 min, US, Jessie Nelson) *Sean Penn, Michelle Pfeiffer, Dianne Wiest, Dakota Fanning, Laura Dern, Richard Schiff, Doug Hutchison, Loretta Devine*. Penn's go-for-broke performance as a mentally challenged father fighting for custody of his seven-year-old daughter can barely compensate for the film's manipulative, sentimental streak. Getting past the idea that Penn's Sam would have gone unnoticed for that long by authorities in raising a child, the story never connects emotionally or truthfully. Pfeiffer's corporate lawyer who's charmed by Sam, ultimately defending him in court, can only be the fiction of an American Bar Association's good will campaign, and Sam's group of friends are clichéd and nearly insulting. The ensemble tries hard, but there are just too many false notes. ★★ DVD Letterbox Platinum Series: $19.99, VHS: $102.99

I Bury the Living

(1958, 77 min, US, Albert Band) *Richard Boone, Theodore Bikel, Peggy Maurer, Herbert Anderson*. A cemetary map has white pins inserted on vacant plots, and black pins inserted on occupied graves. When Boone switches black for white, then live plot owners start dying. Does the owner of the morgue really have supernatural powers? You be the judge. A very creepy little chiller. ★★★ DVD: $14.99, VHS: $6.99

I Can't Sleep

(1995, 110 min, France, Claire Denis) *Alex Descas, Richard Courcet, Line Renaud, Katerina Golubeva*. A provocative, nihilistic French drama based on a true story of two gay "granny" killers. The story is set in the "New France" — not the familiar one of intellectual bourgeoisie contemplating infidelity or the meaning of life, but a France filled with poor immigrants and almost paralyzed by social ills. The story principally follows two brothers from Martinique: Theo (Descas), a hard-working family man, and Camille (Courcet), his strikingly beautiful gay drag queen brother. But Camille harbors a secret other than his sexuality: He and his white French lover (Renaud) have been terrorizing Paris with a series of brutal murders, all on older women. The story is based on Thierry Paulin, who killed more than 20 women between 1984-1987. (French with English subtitles) ★★½ VHS: $29.99

I Come in Peace

(1990, 92 min, US, Craig R. Baxley) *Dolph Lundgren, Brian Benben, Betsy Brantley, Michael J. Pollard*. Lundgren and Benben star in this empty-headed science-fiction action movie as two police officers who must investigate a series of murders they soon discover are being committed by a drug dealer from outer space. Once they discover the exact nature of what the alien is doing and encounter an alien cop tracking the druglord villain, they set out with some extraterrestrial weaponry to kick alien butt. Lundgren is about as good as he ever gets in this by-the-numbers movie, with Benben on hand to provide lukewarm comic relief. The special effects, though good, do not elevate the film above its low-rent feel. Baxley fared much better in 1994 with the highly original *Deep Red*. ★½

I Confess

(1953, 95 min, US, Alfred Hitchcock) *Montgomery Clift, Anne Baxter, Karl Malden, Brian Aherne*. Clift gives a sincere performance as a priest who undergoes a crisis of conscience when he hears a murderer's confession but refuses to divulge any information — either to the police or the Church. Filmed in Quebec, Hitchcock's slow-moving but often compelling moral debate can't quite escape its melodramatic trappings. ★★½

I Could Go on Singing

(1963, 99 min, GB, Ronald Neame) *Judy Garland, Dirk Bogarde, Jack Klugman*. Garland's last movie reveals the legendary singer in commanding voice as a famed entertainer who travels to England to retrieve her son, who is living with his father (Bogarde). The movie is pure melodrama, but Garland's vocal performances are pure magic. ★★½ DVD: $14.99

I Dismember Mama

(1972, 86 min, US, Paul Leder) *Zooey Hall, Joanne Moore Jordan*. Great titles do not great movies make. An escapee from a mental institution falls in love with an 11-year-old and seeks to "purify" his world. ★

I Don't Buy Kisses Anymore

(1992, 112 min, US, Robert Marcarelli) *Jason Alexander, Nia Peeples, Lainie Kazan, Eileen Brennan, Lou Jacobi*. Though its title is quite clever, *I Don't Buy Kisses Anymore* is essentially an updated and rather sluggish *Marty*, without an abundance of that film's insight and wit. Alexander stars as a lonely and overweight thirty-year-old shoe salesman who falls for an attractive psychology student (Peeples). Though not attracted to him, she befriends him and feigns romantic interest for personal gain (for her thesis). Most of the characters are Jewish and Italian caricatures — they're not offensive, just lacking in dimension. Jacobi saves the day with a crackling turn as a colorful family patriarch. Filmed on location in Philadelphia. ★★ VHS: $79.99

I Don't Give a Damn

(1983, 94 min, Israel, Shmuel Imberman) *Ika Sohar, Anat Waxman*. This somber drama deals with the life of Rafi, a young soldier who is paralyzed in a terrorist explosion. Rafi finds that his vibrant, carefree lifestyle is drastically cut short, but he refuses to accept his future life confined to a wheelchair. First in a military hospital and later in his parents' home, his personality changes as he becomes disillusioned, bitter and self-pitying. His despair gradually changes after he becomes interested in photography, accepts his fate and reconciles with his loved ones. (Hebrew with English subtitles) ★★½

I Don't Just Want You to Love Me

(1992, 96 min, Germany, Hans Günther Pflaum) Serious, analytical and dry as the Sahara, this documentary on the life and work of Rainer Werner Fassbinder provides interesting information on the prolific and fast-living director; although in a stifling style that limits its appeal to die-hard fans. Interviewees include fellow German director Volker Schlöndorff, RWF regulars Ingrid Caven, Hanna Schygulla, Harry Baer, Kurt Raab and Fassbinder's mother Lilo Eder. There are also, in a helter-skelter fashion, excerpts from many of his movies. The film sidesteps RWF's homosexuality as well as his drugs and drinking problem. There is a fascinating film to be made about the enfant terrible of German cinema, but this isn't it. ★★

I Don't Want to Talk about It

(1994, 102 min, Argentina, Maria Luisa Bemberg) *Marcello Mastroianni, Luisina Brando, Alejandra Podesta*. This amusing little fantasy stars Mastroianni as an Argentine gentleman who falls in love with a midget. Actually, the story revolves more around the relationship between the wee lady, Podesta, and her mother, Brando, who tries desperately not to let her daughter know she's "different" — hence the film's title, which refers to mama's response whenever anybody mentions her daughter's size. Lusciously filmed with a tinge of magical realism, the film enjoys fine performances and nice characterizations and is, for the most part, mildly enjoyable in spite of a weakened dramatic structure. (Spanish with English subtitles) ★★★

I Hate Blondes

(1981, 89 min, Italy, Giorgio Capitani) *Jean Rochefort*. An unexpectedly funny comedy about a ghostwriter of best-selling detective novels whose work inspires a series of real-life heists. A pretty blonde jewel thief becomes entangled in this web of comic mishaps. ★★★

I Heard the Owl Call My Name

(1973, 79 min, US, Daryl Duke) *Tom Courtenay, Dean Jagger*. A young Anglican priest (Courtenay) is sent by his bishop (Jagger) to live among the Indians of the Northwest, where he gains a new appreciation of human existence. Courtenay delivers a passionate performance in this moving made-for-TV drama. ★★★

I Killed Rasputin

(1967, 85 min, US, Robert Hossein) *Gert Froebe, Peter McEnery, Geraldine Chaplin.* Cult favorite chronicling the life of legendary mystic Rasputin. In 1909 Russia, the mysterious Rasputin wins the favor of Empress Alexandra by saving the life of her son. But wary palace guards distrust the shadowy figure, and secretly plot his demise. ★

I Know What You Did Last Summer

(1997, 100 min, US, Jim Gillespie) *Jennifer Love Hewitt, Sarah Michelle Gellar, Ryan Phillippe, Freddie Prinze, Jr., Johnny Galecki, Anne Heche.* Though it's nothing to *Scream* about, this derivative slasher horror flick does provide a scare or two, but it's really nothing we haven't seen before. Set in coastal North Carolina, the story follows the consequences when four teens run over a man and dump his body after a drunken 4th of July celebration. A year later, when one of them gets a note repeating the film's title, strange occurrences begin and then bodies start piling up. The screenplay is less concerned with plot twists and red herrings and concentrates more on dark shadows and fish hooks gutting young teens. (Sequel: *I Still Know What You Did Last Summer*) ★★½ DVD: $14.99, VHS: $9.99

I Know Where I'm Going!

(1945, 92 min, GB, Emeric Pressburger & Michael Powell) *Wendy Hiller, Roger Livesey, Finlay Currie.* The radiant Hiller plays a wealthy young woman who travels to the Scottish Hebrides to marry an older man, only to have her attentions diverted by a dashing young suitor. Splendid use of the Scottish countryside by directors Powell and Pressburger makes this a lyrically visual treat. ★★★★ DVD Criterion Collection: $39.99

I Like It Like That

(1994, 105 min, US, Darnell Martin) *Lauren Velez, Jon Seda, Rita Moreno, Griffin Dunne.* Director Martin's debut is an explosively funny, poignant and precise look at life in the Bronx. Velez stars as Lisette, a twentysomething Latina with three kids and a jailed husband, Chino (Seda), who thinks his penis is his passport to a woman's heart. Getting her first taste of freedom during his incarceration, and being more than a little put off by his macho posturing upon his return, she kicks him out and is forced to fend for herself. Determined to make it, she lies her way into a job at a record com-

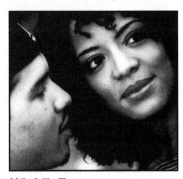

I Like It like That

pany. It's a winning rags-to-a-decent-living story that is as hard-edged as it is likable. Martin shows a strong directorial hand and moves things along at a refreshing pace. Punctuated by pulsing hip-hop, salsa music and colorful camerawork, *I Like It Like That* is a dazzling debut. ★★★½ VHS: $14.99

I Love Trouble

(1994, 120 min, US, Charles Shyer) *Nick Nolte, Julia Roberts, Olympia Dukakis, Robert Loggia, Marsha Mason.* Nancy Myers and Charles Shyer, the husband and wife writer-producer-director team, try to pull off the romantic comedy-action thriller thing (à la *Charade*). As rival reporters who reluctantly team up to crack a big story, Nolte seems to rise above the material, and Roberts returns to *Pretty Woman* mode. One of summer of '94's surprise bombs, this uneven mix of comedy and violence sporting a contrivance-riddled plot is entertaining in spite of itself. ★★½ DVD: $19.99, VHS: $19.99

I Love You

(1982, 104 min, Brazil, Arnaldo Jabor) *Sonia Braga, Paulo Cesar Pereio.* This colorful though pretentious erotic comedy features the stunning Braga as a housewife-cum-hooker drawn into a brief but intense encounter with a bankrupt bra manufacturer. Sparks fly as this whirlwind romance renews the vitality in both their lives. (Portuguese with English subtitles) ★★

I Love You Again

(1940, 99 min, US, W.S. Van Dyke II) *William Powell, Myrna Loy, Frank McHugh, Edmund Lowe.* A joyously screwball romp. Powell plays a con man who discovers he's been a victim of amnesia for nine years and living under the identity of a fuddy-duddy pottery employee. Learning his alter ego has access to great wealth, he concocts a scam with newly acquired partner McHugh. However, when he meets his wife Loy, who's about to divorce him, he plans to rekindle their marriage while setting up the good citizens of his small town. The Powell-Loy magic is ever present, but the lion's share of the laughs belong to Powell as he himself falls victim to a series of sight gags and humiliations. Loy is her usual classy persona. ★★★

I Love You, Alice B. Toklas

(1968, 93 min, US, Hy Averback) *Peter Sellers, Jo Van Fleet, Leigh Taylor-Young, Joyce Van Patten.* Sellers is at his loony best in this dated but hilarious comedy about a middle-aged L.A. lawyer who drops out and turns on. Leaving his bride-to-be at the altar not once, but twice, Sellers loses himself in a haze of drug-dosed cookies and a subsequent whirlwind tour of the hippie subculture. Paul Mazursky cowrote the script. ★★★½ VHS: $14.99

I Love You, I Love You Not

(1997, 80 min, US, Billy Hopkins) *Claire Danes, Jude Law, Jeanne Moreau.* Adapted from a stage play, and it really shows, *I Love You, I Love You Not* stars Moreau as a concentration camp survivor living in Manhattan who takes in her introvert granddaughter (Danes), who's smitten with the class jock (Law). The story deals with issues of anti-Semitism, peer pressure, teen love and self-identity, but with all the subtlety of an "Afterschool Special," and the conflicts and resolutions are so formulaic it's easy to overlook Moreau's graceful performance. Danes has a dual role, too, playing her own grandmother in the WWII flashback sequences. ★★ DVD: $19.99, VHS: $9.99

I Love You Rosa

(1972, 84 min, Israel, Moshe Mizrahi) *Michal Bat-Adam, Gabi Oterman.* This feminist drama and tender love story is set in 1888 Jerusalem, where a childless 20-year-old widow (Bat-Adam) discovers that according to Deuteronomic Law she must marry her husband's brother — with the problem being that he is only 11 years old and determined to fulfill his duties. Rosa, forced to work in a bathhouse and sew for a living, must decide if she should follow the law and wait until the boy is eighteen or break with tradition and find another husband. Sentimental and charming, the story takes an insightful look at religious traditions, love, family and individual freedoms in this Oscar-nominated Best Foreign-Language Film. (Dubbed) ★★★

I Love You to Death

(1990, 96 min, US, Lawrence Kasdan) *Keanu Reeves, Tracey Ullman, Kevin Kline, Joan Plowright, River Phoenix, William Hurt.* Based on a true story, this sometimes funny, hit-or-miss black comedy is about a wife who discovers her husband is cheating on her and attempts to murder him — repeatedly. Kline gives a funny performance as the philandering husband. As the wronged wife, Ullman is given very little to do, and the talented comedienne is wasted. Hurt and Reeves are in alien territory as the hit men. ★★½ DVD Dual: $24.99

I, Madman

(1989, 95 min, US, Tibor Takacs) *Jenny Wright, Clayton Rohner.* Director Takacs shows a flair for combining stop-motion monsters and live-action horror in this deliberately paced, moody mix of film noir and fright flick. Wright stars as a bookseller who unleashes a demon from the pages of a possessed book. Stylish camerawork and a clever script make this film an unusual but effective entry in the all-too-familiar horror lineup. ★★★ DVD Pan & Scan Pan & Scan: $14.99, VHS: $79.99

I Married a Dead Man

(1982, 110 min, France, Robin Davis) *Nathalie Baye, Richard Bohringer.* Baye gives a strong performance as a mysterious woman with a false identity and a threatening past in this romantic suspense thriller. Pregnant, she leaves her abusive husband and travels to the South of France. Her train derails enroute, killing another pregnant woman. The in-laws of the dead woman, whom they have never met, take Baye home, thinking she is their daughter-in-law. Her new life is wonderful until she is threatened by the husband of her past. A compelling, seductive reworking of the 1949 Barbara Stanwyck soaper *No Man of Her Own.* (aka: *I Married a Shadow*) (French with English subtitles) ★★★

I Married a Monster from Outer Space

(1958, 78 min, US, Gene Fowler Jr.) *Tom Tyron, Gloria Talbott, Ty Hardin.* When the major studios saw the grosses that AIP was getting from hot titles like *I Was a Teenage Werewolf* et. al., they decided to play that game too. The surprise is that this is quite a good little film. Atmospheric, effective special effects, a neat-looking bunch of papier-mâché aliens, and a word to young brides everywhere about the dangers of intergalactic miscegenation. ★★½ VHS: $49.99

I Married a Shadow

See: *I Married a Dead Man*

I Married a Strange Person

(1999, 73 min, US, Bill Plympton) A paranormal pustule grows out of the neck of newlywed groom Grant, wrecking havoc on his recent marriage to wife Carrie and eventually threatening world domination via the SmileCorp media conglomerate. The lump allows Grant to actualize his innermost fantasies; from the psychosexual to the banal. Fans of Plympton's *The Toon* will undoubtedly recognize the animator's trademark routines: the literalized hyperboles present in the wacky musical numbers, the visual rebus puzzles that unlock the origins of such biological phenomena as belly-button lint, and the sparse, tongue-in-cheek narration that underscores Grant and Carrie's instructional sex video. The problem here is the abrupt story shift: what begins as a small tale of marital hardship balloons into a madcap, globe-trotting satire on corporate greed and who-knows-what-else, and ends with the shallow moral, "Great sex conquers all." ★★ DVD: $14.99

I Married a Witch

(1942, 77 min, US, René Clair) *Veronica Lake, Fredric March, Susan Hayward, Broderick Crawford.* Entertaining ghost comedy with Lake as a 17th-century Salem witch who comes back to haunt the descendant (March) of the man who had her burned at the stake. Based on a story by Thorne Smith ("Topper"). ★★★

I Never Promised You a Rose Garden

(1977, 96 min, US, Anthony Page) *Kathleen Quinlan, Bibi Andersson, Sylvia Sidney.* Quinlan's astonishing performance as a schizophrenic teenager undergoing treatment highlights this absorbing adaptation of Hannah Green's novel. Andersson ably plays her caring psychiatrist. ★★★

I Never Sang for My Father

(1970, 93 min, US, Gilbert Cates) *Gene Hackman, Melvyn Douglas, Estelle Parsons, Dorothy Stickney.* A sterling version of Robert Anderson's play, with Hackman in a fine performance as the estranged son of Douglas who attempts reconciliation when his father becomes sick and unable to care for himself. Douglas, who in his later years became a brilliant character actor, is superb. ★★★

I.Q.

(1994, 95 min, US, Fred Schepisi) *Walter Matthau, Meg Ryan, Tim Robbins, Gene Saks, Charles Durning, Lou Jacobi, Stephen Fry, Joseph Maher, Frank Whaley.* From director Schepisi, who helmed one of the most beguiling romantic comedies of the 1980s, *Roxanne*, comes an almost equally enchanting confection. Matthau, in a most amusing impersonation, plays Albert Einstein. In a scenario recall-ing the whimsy and appeal of the great 1940s screwball comedies, Einstein plays matchmaker to his brainy but impassioned niece, nicely played by Ryan. Though she's engaged to an egghead researcher (Fry), Uncle Albert coaches a good-natured garage mechanic (Robbins) who has fallen under her spell. And much like the seven professors in *Ball of Fire*, Einstein and his four brainy pals take delight in their romantic experiment to bring the two together. ★★★½ DVD: $14.99, VHS: $14.99

I Remember Mama

(1948, 134 min, US, George Stevens) *Irene Dunne, Barbara Bel Geddes, Oscar Homolka, Ellen Corby, Rudy Vallee.* Dunne gives a captivating performance in this touching drama about an immigrant family living in San Francisco. Thanks to Dunne's sparkling performance and Stevens' delicate direction, the film is sweet and heartfelt without needless sentimentality, and has to it the same flavor as Kazan's *A Tree Grows in Brooklyn*. ★★★½ VHS: $14.99

I Saw What You Did

(1965, 82 min, US, William Castle) *Joan Crawford, John Ireland, Leif Erickson, Andi Garrett, Sarah Lane.* Before *Scream*, before *I Know What You Did Last Summer*, even before *Halloween*, came this first "teen scream" chiller from 1960s horror maven Castle. A very effective thriller, the story follows the consequences of a series of prank calls by two teenaged girls who say, "I saw what you did and I know who you are." When they phone a man who's just murdered his wife, he comes looking for them. Crawford is the murderer's lusty neighbor. After the release of the film, prank calls were all the rage across the country. ★★★

I Sent a Letter to My Love

(1981, 96 min, France, Moshe Mizrahi) *Simone Signoret, Jean Rochefort, Delphine Seyrig.* A perceptive and unusual comedy-drama starring Signoret as a formidable woman who has devoted her life to the care of her crippled brother. Being a bit lonely, she advertises in a personal column. Receiving a reply from a suitor whom she knows to be her brother, she continues the newspaper romance for her brother's sake. Mizrahi also directed Signoret in *Madame Rosa*. ★★★

I Shot Andy Warhol

(1996, 106 min, US, Mary Harron) *Lili Taylor, Jared Harris, Lothaire Bluteau, Martha Plimpton, Stephen Dorff, Craig Chester, Donovan Leitch.* From its opening, which portrays the aftermath of the action of its title, *I Shot Andy Warhol* is a frantically paced and at times gripping chronicle of Valerie Solanas, Warhol's would-be assassin. Solanas (smartly played by Taylor) was a semi-delusional lesbian feminist activist who slummed around Greenwich Village in the early '60s turning tricks to survive. Essentially, Solanas comes off as a born loser, but one with an irrepressible and often brilliant intellect. For the most part, the film hits its mark, despite an overly long party scene at The Factory. With a gritty streetwise demeanor, Taylor delivers rapid-fire speech at a relentless pace, and she's nothing short of first-rate. As Warhol, Harris is an exquisite understatement of ethereal chic. ★★★½ DVD: $19.99, VHS: $14.99

I Spit on Your Grave

(1989, 100 min, US, Meir Zarchi) *Camille Keaton, Eron Tabor.* A young woman takes a writing sabbatical to the country where she is brutally raped and beaten and left for dead. But she survives and exacts bloody revenge. This low-budget exploiter manages to create quite a few suspenseful moments in between scenes of gratuitous violence. ★★ DVD Millennium Edition: $24.99

I Spy

(2002, 110 min, US, Betty Thomas) *Eddie Murphy, Owen Wilson, Famke Janssen, Malcolm McDowell, Gary Cole.* In this by-the-numbers, rather boring remake of the popular 1960s TV series, Murphy plays a profoundly obnoxious professional boxer who's teamed with government agent Wilson to prevent a top-secret military jet from falling into the wrong hands. Once again, Murphy commits the comedy-killing error he's made in a couple of films before this (*Pluto Nash, Showtime*): he confuses strident screaming and braying with comic energy. The end result is the impression of desperation on his part. Faring a little better is Wilson, who merely comes across as a charmless jerk. Watching this poorly written exercise in retro chic, it's difficult to believe that the TV show, starring Bill Cosby and Robert Culp, was any good at all — let alone groundbreaking. ★ DVD: $14.99, VHS: $102.99

I Still Know What You Did Last Summer

(1998, 100 min, US, Danny Cannon) *Jennifer Love Hewitt, Freddie Prinze, Jr., Brandy, Mekhi Phifer, Muse Watson.* More nubile teens get hacked up: what fun. Hewitt returns in this cheesy sequel to the not-quite-as-cheesy hit as the intelligence-impaired heroine. Her lack of world geography somehow lands her and her equally dim chums on an isolated vacation resort. Oh, there's a storm. Oh, there's a killer on the loose. As the secondary characters die around her, Hewitt is promptly stalked by an unstoppable slasher in a raincoat who, frankly, is less frightening than your average Cher impersonator. A howling dud. ★½ DVD: $14.99, VHS: $9.99

I, the Worst of All

(1990, 100 min, Argentina/France, Maria Luisa Bemberg) *Assumpta Serta, Dominique Sanda.* The unconventional story of 17th-century Mexican poet and nun Sor Juana inez de la Cruz. Confined to a prison-like cloister during the Spanish Inquisition, Sister Juana's passionate, philosophical poems become the "rage" amongst both the rich and poor, causing problems for the virtually sealed-off convent and prompting an intimate relationship (though mostly through bars) with a beautiful vicereine (Sanda). The film is elegant and intelligent, though the two women's relationship which is hinted at never goes beyond lingering glances. Based on the novel by Octavio Paz. (Spanish with English subtitles) DVD: $24.99, VHS: $29.99

I Think I Do

(1997, 90 min, US, Brian Sloan) *Alexis Arquette, Christian Maelen, Maddie Corman, Tuc Watkins, Guillermo Diaz, Marianne Hagan, Jamie Harrold, Lauren Velez, Marni Nixon.* The screwball "who will marry who" antics of *The Philadelphia Story* are given a gay update in this romantic and sexy comedy. Bob (Arquette) and Brendan (Maelen) are former college roommates reunited for the marriage of one of their former classmates. Among those in attendance is Brendan's college girlfriend Sarah (Corman), and Bob's handsome but ever-so-dull boyfriend Sterling (Watkins). As everyone parties and consumes just enough booze, libidos are raised and inhibitions lowered. ★★★ DVD: $34.99

I Shot Andy Warhol

THE DISCERNING FILM LOVER'S GUIDE

I Wake Up Screaming
(1941, 82 min, US, Bruce Humberstone) *Betty Grable, Victor Mature, Laird Cregar.* Unusually stylish, this entertaining and moody thriller stars Grable who, after her sister is murdered, teams up with the prime suspect (Mature) to find the real killer. There are plenty of twists to keep the who-dunit experts one body behind. The film features a fine performance by Cregar as a sinister detective relentlessly out for his own form of demented justice. ★★★ VHS: $19.99

I Walked with a Zombie
(1943, 69 min, US, Jacques Tourneur) *Frances Dee, Tom Conway, James Ellison.* Don't let the title fool you — this is a first-rate thriller about a nurse (Dee) who travels to the West Indies to care for a plantation owner's wife. She soon learns the woman is under the spell of a local voodoo priest. Lots of chills and remarkable camerawork and lighting. ★★★

I Wanna Be Your Man
(1994, 97 min, Hong Kong, Chung Chi Shing) *Christy Chung.* A Hong Kong drama that features a sensitive handling of a lesbian policewoman. Police Inspector Susan Wong (Chung) is a beautiful, slightly butch lesbian cop who lives with her petulantly femme girlfriend Ron. The secret of her sexual orientation becomes accidentally known to Luk, an affably mediocre cop who, instead of telling his fellow officers that their boss is a dyke (an action that would ruin her), quickly becomes her friend and confidant. But Ron and Luk soon fall in love, a situation Susan is forced to accept. Better-than-average TV fare made interesting because of its setting and theme. (Cantonese with English subtitles) ★★★ VHS: $79.99

I Wanna Hold Your Hand
(1978, 104 min, US, Robert Zemeckis) *Nancy Allen, Bobby DiCiccio, Marc McClure, Wendy Jo Sperber, Eddie Deezen.* It's 1964 and The Beatles hit New York. The city is thrown into a panic as the Fab Four are to appear on "The Ed Sullivan Show," and everybody scrambles for tickets. With this inspired premise, director Zemeckis lets go with a comic assault about a group of Jersey students who try to crash the show. The film features a fine ensemble of young actors. ★★★ DVD Special Edition: $19.99, VHS: $14.99

I Want to Live!
(1958, 122 min, US, Robert Wise) *Susan Hayward, Simon Oakland, Theodore Bikel.* Hayward won an Oscar for her commanding performance in this true story of prostitute Barbara Graham, who, framed and convicted of murder, was sentenced to death. ★★★ DVD Letterbox: $14.99

I Was a Male War Bride
(1949, 106 min, US, Howard Hawks) *Cary Grant, Marion Marshall, Ann Sheridan, Randy Stuart.* Though not on par with the best of either director Hawks or actor Grant, an abundance of genuine laughs and skillful tomfoolery by its two stars make *I Was a Male War Bride* an appealing wartime comedy. Grant plays a French military attache who is teamed with no-nonsense American WAC Sheridan. While on assignment, the bickering couple fall in love and marry. But complications and Army red tape arise when he tries to accompany his bride to the States — which includes a little transvestism on the part of Grant. ★★★ DVD: $14.99, VHS: $19.99

Cary Grant (in drag) and Ann Sheridan in *I Was a Male War Bride*

I Was a Teenage Werewolf
(1957, 70 min, US, Gene Fowler) *Michael Landon, Whit Bissell, Yvonne Lime.* A youthful Landon plays a juvenile delinquent who's got one on James Dean — he's a werewolf (thanks to mad doc Bissell). This low-budget horror flick is a campy pleasure in spite of the awkward acting and less-than-successful scares. ★★

I Was a Zombie for the FBI
(1986, 105 min, US, Marius Penczner) Aliens plan to steal the formula for the world's most popular cola in order to turn Earth's population into subservient zombies. It's up to two crack FBI agents and a beautiful reporter to save the day. (Did they want a Pepsi or a Coke?) ★

I Went Down
(1997, 111 min, Ireland, Paddy Breathnach) *Brendan Gleeson, Peter McDonald, Peter Caffrey, Tony Doyle.* From its double entendre title to its comedic shoot-outs and its engaging well-defined characters and relationships, *I Went Down* is a nice surprise. McDonald plays Git, a just-released ex-con who lands in trouble with the local mob boss. To set things right, he must accompany an endearingly annoying ne'er-do-well to claim a "package" — a man who owes the boss big time. Along the way, the two men bicker and bond and learn that the package may not be what it seems. Although slight, this buddy/road/gangster flick is quite enjoyable, with bright performances and witty dialogue, and a warm tone and spirit. ★★★ VHS: $102.99

I'll Cry Tomorrow
(1955, 117 min, US, Daniel Mann) *Susan Hayworth, Richard Conte, Eddie Albert, Jo Van Fleet.* Exemplary biography on entertainer Lillian Roth (based on her novel) about the singer's fight with alcoholism. Hayward gives a magnificent performance as Roth, and Van Fleet is fine in support as her mother. ★★★½ VHS: $14.99

I'll Do Anything
(1994, 116 min, US, James L. Brooks) *Nick Nolte, Joely Richardson, Albert Brooks, Julie Kavner, Whitni Wright.* After brilliantly dissecting TV journalisn in *Broadcast News*, writer-director Brooks turns his eye on the movie industry with less-than-satisfying results. Nolte stars as a talented but unemployed actor who unexpectedly gains custody of his bratty six-year-old daughter. While trying to pursue both a coveted film role and a pretty, budding producer (Richardson), he must also get to know his estranged child. When Brooks zeroes in on the moviemaking process, the film is funny and diverting; however, the scenes concerning the reunion of father and daughter are maudlin at best. ★★½ DVD Dual: $19.99, VHS: $9.99

I'll Love You Forever, Tonight
(1992, 76 min, US, Edgar Michael Bravo) *Paul Marius, Jason Adams, David Poynter, Thomas Jane.* Made for under $100,000 by Bravo as his thesis film for UCLA, this somber and searing drama, set in queer twentysomething L.A., revolves around the lives, loves and sexual relations of a group of friends and acquaintances. Serious with occasional flashes of humor, the film delves into the loneliness, self-deception and self-loathing of its several gay male characters with an unflinching realism. Described as "Pinter-on-Fire Island" and "a queer *Big Chill*," this thought-provoking tale, filmed in shadowy black & white and which captures the tensions of today's post-AIDS male youth, is alternately compassionate and gritty but always perceptive. ★★★

I'm All Right, Jack
(1960, 104 min, GB, John Boulting & Roy Boulting) *Peter Sellers, Ian Carmichael, Terry-Thomas, Richard Attenborough, Margaret Rutherford.* No word less than side-splitting will suffice in describing this scathing satire on labor relations in England. The inimitable Sellers stars as a young man caught between the two sides of a bitter labor dispute. The essence of worker-management relations, as practiced in England, are captured with the utmost clarity in this unrelenting farce. ★★★½ DVD Letterbox: $19.99

I'm Almost Not Crazy
(1989, 56 min, US, Michael Ventura) A wonderful look at the life and professional career of maverick filmmaker John Cassavetes. Includes interviews with Cassavetes, his wife Gena Rowlands, Peter Falk and scenes from his films. ★★★

I'm Dancing as Fast as I Can
(1982, 107 min, US, Jack Hofsiss) *Jill Clayburgh, Nicol Williamson, Dianne Wiest, Joe Pesci, Geraldine Page.* Based on Barbara Gordon's memoir, Clayburgh stars as the TV documentary filmmaker who tries to put an end to her valium dependency — with great difficulty. Clayburgh is very good as Gordon, and gets splendid support from ensemble. ★★½ VHS: $7.99

I'm Gonna Git You Sucka
(1988, 87 min, US, Keenan Ivory Wayans) *Keenan Ivory Wayans, Isaac Hayes, Jim Brown, Bernie Casey.* Before he found success with his TV comedy series "In Living Color," Wayans made this good-natured spoof on the blaxploitation flicks of the 1970s. With a fine supporting cast of veterans, the film is about a young, idealistic soldier (Wayans) on leave. He returns home to find that his brother OG'd (died of an overdose of gold chains) and the mob wants to turn his sister to prostitution for some debts left behind by the departed Bro. Our hero, vowing to bring the bad guys to justice, assembles a motley band of "bad" dudes, and with the music of *Shaft* in the background, they battle and kick some butt. ★★★ DVD: $14.99, VHS: $9.99

I'm Losing You

(1998, 103 min, US, Bruce Wagner) *Rosanna Arquette, Frank Langella, Andrew McCarthy, Elizabeth Perkins, Amanda Donohoe, Buck Henry, Gina Gershon, Salome Jens.* Several intertwining story lines, all dealing with an extended family, and all dealing with death and dying, rove their way through the uneven though involving *I'm Losing You.* Langella is the father, a Gene Roddenberry-like TV producer who's just been diagnosed with terminal cancer. McCarthy is his son, a constantly out-of-work actor who falls in love with an HIV-positive beauty (Perkins). Arquette is the adopted daughter, who finds some skeletons in the family closet, and turns to Judaism for comfort. All the stories are interesting, at times gripping, and if Wagner — here adapting and directing his own novel — allows his unfamiliarity with the medium show with some weak pacing and lack of visual flair, the performances and unusually thoughtful, probing nature of the material compensate. ★★½ DVD: $14.99, VHS: $102.99

I'm No Angel

(1933, 88 min, US, Wesley Ruggles) *Mae West, Cary Grant, Edward Arnold.* "It's not the men in your life, it's the life in your men." This is just one of the classic quips made by the one and only West in this sparkling, bawdy pre-Code comedy. The 1930s sex goddess is at her best as a carnival performer who finds it as much a breeze taming the men as she does the lions. Becoming the toast of the town upon her arrival in New York, she crosses paths with businessman Grant, whom she promises, "When I'm good, I'm very good. But when I'm bad, I'm even better." Looking ravishing, West's every other line seems to be a dandy sexual entendre; even when she's not being suggestive, she's suggestive. She has the talk, and she has the walk. Also featuring the famous "grape" line, this is one of two West films that single-handedly saved Paramount Studios from near-bankruptcy in 1933. ★★★½

I'm Not Rappaport

(1996, 135 min, US, Herb Gardner) *Walter Matthau, Ossie Davis, Craig T. Nelson, Martha Plimpton, Amy Irving.* Herb Gardner adapted and directed his Tony Award-winning play about the tender and comic relationship between two disparate New York senior citizens. The stage show was more fluid, but this engaging character piece is buoyed by two endearing performances given by Matthau and Davis. Nat (Matthau) is a rascally 80-year-old Jewish leftist who meets half-blind building custodian Midge (Davis), a black man his same age, during visits to Central Park. Though Midge really wants nothing to do with him, Nat slowly ingratiates himself into Midge's life. The charm of the story is Gardner's wonderful characterizations of Nat and Midge, who most of the time are either feuding, telling jokes, or becoming involved in other people's lives. Through telling moments, Gardner imparts thoughtful observances towards the realities of aging in urban America, producing laughs and poignant moments, alike. ★★★ DVD: $14.99

I'm the One That I Want

(2000, 96 min, US, Lionel Coleman) *Margaret Cho.* A revelatory one-woman show from Margaret Cho, filmed live in San Francisco, that contains enough big laughs, painful truths and poignancy to make it one of the better stand-up concerts captured on film. At first Cho focuses exclusively on her huge gay following, and then mimicks her mother for some easy laughs. But once she details her experiences working on her sitcom "All-American Girl," the film is a fas-

cinating (and extremely funny) look into the inherent racism and beauty-obsession of network television. Scathing, sad and angry, *I'm the One That I Want* is also warm, humorous and ultimately uplifting. ★★★½ DVD: $19.99, VHS: $14.99

I'm the One You're Looking For

(1988, 85 min, Spain, Jaime Chavarri) *Patricia Adrian, Chus Lampreave.* A controversial film that explores the complicated range of feelings generated between a woman (Adrian) and the man who rapes her. The story begins when a beautiful but unhappy model is raped after she stops on a deserted road to help a handsome motorist. The traumatized young woman, fueled by either repulsion or revenge on her attacker or a strange physical attraction to him, becomes obsessed with the young man. With the aid of a ditsy middle-aged housewife and a sexually confused erotic dancer, she begins to hunt for him through the seedy and at times bizarre underworld of Barcelona. Saying things like, "I'll get raped a thousand times in order to find him," young woman's motivations are complex and the viewer's response is certain to be wide-ranged in this absorbing psychological suspense thriller. (Spanish with English subtitles) ★★★

I've Heard the Mermaids Singing

(1987, 81 min, Canada, Patricia Rozema) *Sheila McCarthy, Paule Baillargeon.* McCarthy is nothing short of a revelation in this enchanting comedy. The film itself is cute and whimsical but it is McCarthy as Polly, the day-dreaming romantic Gal Friday, who steals the show as well as our hearts. An avid photographer who dwells in her own fantasy world, Polly secures a job as a temp in the office of an art collector. Her innocence and joie de vivre proves to be a bracing tonic in a world dulled by pretension and greed. A film and a performance that should lift your spirits. ★★★ DVD: $19.99

Ice Age

(2002, 75 min, US, Chris Wedge) *Voices of: Ray Romano, John Leguizamo, Denis Leary, Goran Visnjic, Jack Black, Cedric the Entertainer.* More indebted to Looney Tunes than its more recent predecessors, *Ice Age* is a breezy romp that's entertaining, if awfully thin. After a sabre-toothed tiger raid, a human baby is sent downriver (*Prince of Egypt* style) and rescued by a wisecracking odd couple: a woolly mammoth loner (Romano) and a clumsy, clingy sloth (Leguizamo). Joined by one of the

The computer-generated critters of *Ice Age*

scheming tigers (Leary), they set out, *Land Before Time* style, on a road trip to reunite the baby with its papa. The computer animation is effective, though a lot simpler than Disney's *Dinosaur*, but at least this sucker *moves*. Some bits are nothing new (there's another *Egypt* lift in a hieroglyphic sequence), and some just fall flat (especially when things get poignant). Still, there are some good laughs, with the trek punctuated every so often by a squirrel named Scrat, desperately trying to bury his acorn in the frozen tundra. His throwaway gags, á la Wile E. Coyote, are sorely missed during the rest of the otherwise passable journey. ★★½ DVD 2-disc Special Edition: $19.99, VHS: $12.99

Ice Palace

(1960, 143 min, US, Vincent Sherman) *Richard Burton, Carolyn Jones, Robert Ryan, Shirley Knight.* A sprawling adaptation of Edna Ferber's novel about Alaska's drive toward statehood. Set at the end of WWII, the film casts Burton as a soldier who returns home to Seattle only to find his job has been given away. After roughing up his ex-boss, he heads for Alaska, where he teams up with Ryan and Jones in a fish canning enterprise and an ill-fated love triangle. ★★½ VHS: $19.99

The Ice Pirates

(1984, 93 min, US, Stewart Raffill) *Robert Urich, Anjelica Huston, Mary Crosby.* It is 10,000 years into the future, and an evil empire has gained control of the water supply for the entire universe. It is up to a band of ragtag pirates, led by Urich, to hijack the shipments of frozen ice blocks through space and thwart the evildoers. Mindless and familiar, though occasionally kinda fun. ★★

Ice Station Zebra

(1968, 148 min, US, John Sturges) *Rock Hudson, Patrick McGoohan, Ernest Borgnine, Jim Brown.* Potent Cold War thriller with Hudson as a sub commander whose secret mission to the North Pole sets the stage for a showdown with the Russians. Based on an Alistair McLean novel. ★★½

The Ice Storm

(1997, 113 min, US, Ang Lee) *Kevin Kline, Joan Allen, Sigourney Weaver, Christina Ricci, Elijah Wood, Tobey Maguire.* It's 1973 in Connecticut, and two families are going through some painful adolescences: the children and the parents are discovering their sexualities and learning to express their emotions. Ben (Kline), the head of the Hood family, is lifelessly carrying on with his neighbor Janey Carver, played with gleeful bitchiness by Weaver. This empty affair strains his marriage to Elena (Allen), who is upset about her lot in life but can only express it by emotionally cutting off her husband. Their kids (Maguire, Ricci, Wood) are going through similar situations, but learning and growing instead of falling apart; it is these performances that carry the film. Lee is an obsessively detail-oriented director. Every period detail is just-so, but played for emotional effect rather than comic effect. The details are in the performances, too, as what is said is secondary to what is felt. ★★★½ DVD: $9.99, VHS: $9.99

Iceman

(1984, 99 min, US, Fred Schepisi) *Timothy Hutton, Lindsay Crouse, David Strathairn, John Lone, Danny Glover.* Director Schepisi makes credible and arresting this story of a prehistoric man found frozen in the Arctic and discovered to be still alive by a scientific team. Hutton is one of the researchers who enters into an almost empathic relationship with the Neanderthal, who is remarkably portrayed by Lone. Unusual and surprising. ★★★ VHS: $14.99

The Iceman Cometh

(1960, 210 min, US, Sidney Lumet) *Jason Robards, Myron McCormick, James Broderick, Robert Redford, Tom Pedi, Farrell Pelly, Ronald Radd.* In 1956, the Circle-in-the-Square mounted a production of Eugene O'Neill's 1939 play "The Iceman Cometh" with a little-known actor named Jason Robards in the central part of Hickey. The revival and the actor quickly became part of Broadway legend. Four years later, Robards encored the role in a made-for-TV adaptation, and every brilliant moment has been captured on tape. In a seedy New York saloon pre-WWI, a group of down-and-out alcoholics await the arrival of Hickey, a salesman due for his annual drinking binge. As each character entertains the notion of free drink, they are forced to confront their pipe dreams by a newly on-the-wagon Hickey, determined to impart to his friends an everlasting peace of mind. O'Neill's drama is a harrowing and at times humorous exploration of failed lives and empty hopes, underscored by the author's remarkable prose of recriminations, denial and banter. Robards is simply astonishing as Hickey, the glad-handing barker of delusion and dreams. To watch this performance is to know it is one of the great stage portrayals of the 20th century. How lucky we are to have it preserved forever. (Remade in 1973) ★★★★ DVD 2-disc set: $24.99, VHS: $39.99

The Icicle Thief

(1989, 90 min, Italy, Maurizio Nichetti) *Maurizio Nichetti, Cateria Sylos Labini.* Infectiously funny, this inventive and fast-paced satire on commercial television defies easy plot description. A bungling director (Nichetti himself) is interviewed at a TV station before the screening of his newest film, a black-and-white neorealist drama. The picture, a tender, affectionate tribute to *The Bicycle Thief*, tells the story of the many struggles of an unemployed man (Nichetti again), his beautiful wife and their son, an unbelievably hard-working boy of six. But the family finds that financial hardships are nothing in comparison to the confusion and disruption caused when a scantily clad, English-speaking platinum blonde in full color "falls" out of her bathing suit commercial and into their neorealist lives. With tender humanism and a deft comic touch, Nichetti is a breath of fresh air. (Italian with English subtitles) ★★★½

An Ideal Husband

(1999, 98 min, GB, Oliver Parker) *Rupert Everett, Minnie Driver, Cate Blanchett, Jeremy Northam, Julianne Moore, John Wood, Lindsay Duncan.* Brimming with Wildean witticisms, now familiar bon mots, gorgeous costumes and first-rate acting, this adaptation of one of Oscar Wilde's supposedly lesser plays makes for a delightful film experience if the implausible plotline and the director's unnecessarily lugubrious pacing can be forgiven. Everett is Lord Goring, a foppish young man dedicated to life's pleasures — parties, drinking, clothing, beautiful women, bachelorhood and moneyed friends. His orderly world is complicated when his best friend MP Sir Robert Chiltern's (Northam) political ambitions are put in peril after the conniving Mrs. Cheyeley (Moore) blackmails him with an incriminating letter. What makes the film work is not the story line but Wilde's writing — it's as fresh and entertainingly biting as the day it was written. ★★★ DVD: $19.99, VHS: $9.99

Identity

(2003, 90 min, US, James Mangold) *John Cusack, Ray Liotta, Amanda Peet, John Hawkes, Alfred Molina, Rebecca DeMornay, Clea DuVall, John C. McGinley.* A good, solid suspense film, *Identity* is a nice melding of Agatha Christie, Hitchcock, gimmicky "twist" movie and slasher film. A group of strangers — stranded at an out-of-the-way motel during a ferocious rainstorm — are being picked off one by one by an unknown killer. Fine acting (especially by a well-cast Cusack) and nice turn-of-the-screw direction by Mangold complement Michael Cooney's clever screenplay for the first full hour, until its whopper of a twist is revealed. Here is where viewers will be divided into the "Oh, come on!" camp and the "Cool! Didn't see that coming!" crew. Amazingly, the film keeps going after this seemingly dead-end revelation until its other whopper in the final scene. Surrender yourself to the film, and you'll fully enjoy this tightly wound thriller — a gimmicky flick done right. ★★★ DVD Dual: $19.99, VHS: $102.99

Idi Amin Dada

(1974, 90 min, France, Barbet Schroeder) The repellingly charismatic Idi Amin, brutal dictator of Uganda in the 1970s, secured an almost Hitlerian legacy as a bloodthirsty, power-hungry despot who pillaged the country's treasury and attempted to eliminate all opposition. It was even said that after his overthrow, human remains (presumably for midnight snacks) were found in his refrigerator. From this unlikely subject comes Schroeder's fascinating, funny and shocking documentary that was made with the full cooperation of Idi Amin (although who, after completion, threatened the director with death if certain cuts were not made). We witness a jovial, even likable bully who mugs for the camera, rebuts all of the murderous charges against him and attempts to charm his way into the viewers' hearts and minds. But beneath his friendly posturing, the reality of evil personified seeps through. ★★★ DVD Criterion Collection: $29.99, VHS: $29.99

The Idiot

(1951, 166 min, Japan, Akira Kurosawa) *Toshiro Mifune, Masayuki Mori, Takashi Shimura.* Made immediately after his international success *Rashomon*, Kurosawa faithfully transposed his favorite literary work to the screen with this engrossing adaptation of Fyodor Dostoevsky's complex tale of madness and jealousy. Changing the

time and setting to a snow-battered, postwar Japan, the story follows a kept woman who is wanted for marriage by three different men, including the holy fool Prince Kameda and his raucous friend (Mifune). The video transfer is especially good, highlighting Kurosawa's imaginatively lit black-and-white photography. (Japanese with English subtitles) ★★★½ VHS: $19.99

The Idiots

(2000, 117 min, Denmark, Lars von Trier) *Bodil Jørgensen, Jens Albinus, Anne Louise Hassing, Troels Lyby, Nikolaj Lie Kaas.* Von Trier's entry in the Dogme 95 series is an audacious, ambitious but ultimately pointless work. A group of people decide to shake things up in a staid society by "spazzing," or acting like idiots in public and at family functions. While there is a bit of malicious joy in seeing well-to-do folks shocked and embarrassed by the antics of these "idiots," the interest level flags quickly when one realizes that there really isn't much more to the film. A completely uninhibited orgy spruces things up, but be warned: this domestic release is altered, with black bars blocking out the actors' naughty bits. While the technical and acting credits are accomplished, the whole enterprise feels like a stunt, and a rather hollow one at that. (Danish with English subtitles) ★★½ VHS: $102.99

Idle Hands

(1999, 92 min, US, Rodman Flender) *Devon Sawa, Seth Green, Elden Henson, Jessica Alba, Vivica A. Fox.* Owing more than a bit to *Evil Dead 2* and *The Frighteners*, *Idle Hands* is a derivative but entertaining macabre comedy. Sawa's a high school slacker who doesn't notice for a while that his parents have been murdered by a demon; said demon takes the use of Sawa's right hand. This leads to much *Dr. Strangelove*-esque nonsense where the hand gets randy and murderous. Irreverent, bloody fun, boosted by the amiable Green and Henson as undead stoners. ★★ DVD: $14.99, VHS: $9.99

The Idolmaker

(1980, 119 min, US, Taylor Hackford) *Ray Sharkey, Peter Gallagher, Tovah Feldshuh, Joe Pantoliano, Olympia Dukakis.* Sharkey mesmerizes in this much-overlooked gem about a '50s rock impresario who stops at nothing to insure the success of his teen heartthrob protégés. ★★★ DVD: $14.99

If . . .

(1969, 111 min, GB, Lindsay Anderson) *Malcolm McDowell, David Wood, Arthur Lowe, Mona Washbourne, Simon Ward.* Inspired by Jean Vigo's classic *Zero for Conduct*, this extraordinary allegorical film is set in a repressive public boarding school. McDowell, who made his film debut in this explosive, furiously funny attack on the British establishment, stars as one of three unruly seniors whose refusal to conform ultimately leads to a full-scale student rebellion. Anderson's surreal and manic style seems the perfect cinematic exclamation point to the end of a turbulent decade. The alternating use of color and black-and-white cinematography is not an artistic statement, but more the fact that Anderson, who shot the film out of sequence, ran low on money and was forced to shoot in black and white. ★★★★ VHS: $19.99

If It's Tuesday, This Must Be Belgium

(1969, 99 min, US, Mel Stuart) *Suzanne Pleshette, Mildred Natwick, Murray Hamilton, Peggy Cass, Norman Fell.* Though its humor may be somewhat dated, this congenial comedy about a group of American tourists on the European vacation from hell manages to produce a few hearty laughs. A group of beleaguered travelers visit nine countries in 18 days. And it's the kind of trip — and comedy — where everything that can go wrong will. The film may not always keep time with the slapdash pace it sets for itself, but as a time capsule of swinging '60s mod it's almost invaluable. Donovan sings the dreadful title tune, and appears in a cameo; Hamilton comes off the best from this large cast. ★★½

If Lucy Fell

(1996, 93 min, US, Eric Schaeffer) *Sarah Jessica Parker, Ben Stiller, Eric Schaeffer, Elle Macpherson, James Rebhorn.* An instantly forgettable but relatively painless "love-in-the-'90s" comedy. Parker and Schaeffer star as romantically challenged roomies who've made a pact to throw themselves off the Brooklyn Bridge within one month (Parker's character's 30th birthday) if they haven't found mate material. Wonder what'll happen, eh? Starts off dumb and pseudo-hip, then becomes mildly involving in the middle third, then blows it by making the hugely predictable wrap-up really protracted. Parker is actually half-decent here, but Schaeffer isn't — you don't want him dead real, *real* bad. The kind of film about which two weeks later you'll wonder out loud, "Did I see this?" ★★
DVD: $19.99, VHS: $9.99

If She Says Yes, I Don't Say No

(1983, 95 min, France, Claude Vital & Marcel Julian) *Mireille Darc.* This is certainly a strange title but don't be put off. From the people who gave us the ménage à trois comes this ménage à quatre, a very funny sex comedy about a fiercely independent young woman and the attempts of the three men in her life to please her. Only the French could get away with this one! (French with English subtitles) ★★★

If These Walls Could Talk

(1996, 100 min, US, Cher & Nancy Savoca) *Demi Moore, Sissy Spacek, Anne Heche, Shirley Knight, CCH Pounder, Kevin Cooney, Joanna Gleason, Cher, Lindsay Crouse, Jada Pinkett, Eileen Brennan.* Uneven, tough, cumulatively powerful trio of tales about women dealing with abortion in different time periods in America. Moore wants an abortion in the '50s; Spacek is a pregnant mother in the '70s, indecisive about having another child; and Heche is a '90s woman, pregnant with her married professor's child, who decides to abort it. All three stories have their merits, describing a specific time and political climate contributing to these ladies' choices. Interestingly, while the Moore segment is frustrating, it's the '90s Heche tale that is the scariest and most infuriating. Cher (who also directs) plays a doctor at an abortion clinic beset by vehement protests. This is the most chilling (and, it must be said, sensationalistic) of the three, due in large part to the excellent performances and strong direction, traits which are, to be sure, found in the other two as well. "Walls" is certainly (and predictably) prochoice, but is rather fair to both sides. ★★★ DVD: $9.99

Igby Goes Down

(2002, 97 min, US, Burr Steers) *Kieran Culkin, Susan Sarandon, Ryan Phillippe, Jeff Goldblum, Bill Pullman, Claire Danes, Amanda Peet, Jared Harris.* Inviting comparison to "The Catcher in the Rye" is ballsy at best, and foolhardy at worst. But *Igby Goes Down* is infused with such a savage wit that its attacks on phonies might be as close as we get to having J.D. Salinger's seminal work, or at

Igby (Kieran Culkin) gets down with Sookie (Claire Danes) in *Igby Goes Down*

least its spirit, adapted to the big screen. Culkin stars as Igby, a disaffected prep student on the fast track to Wall Street, who is compelled to rebel against his privilege (personified by Phillippe as his decadently conservative brother) even as he bums around N.Y.C. living off his trust fund. He hangs with characters living under various degrees of artifice: his nutty godfather D.H. (Goldblum), D.H.'s junkie girlfriend (Peet), and kindred spirit/embodiment of ennui Sookie Sapperstein (Danes). It's better than his homelife, where his father (Pullman) has gone mental and his harshly critical mother (Sarandon) is counting the days until her death. First-time director Steers, a nephew of Gore Vidal and apparently no stranger to a life of Riley, knows this motley crowd well, and each scene appears to provide surprising new depth for what seems like archetypes on the surface. Culkin is phenomenal, underplaying the sarcasm while giving his standoffish character an oddly affecting inner beauty. Kieran's brother Rory plays the younger Igby in flashbacks. ★★★★
DVD: $14.99, VHS: $9.99

Ikiru

(1952, 143 min, Japan, Akira Kurosawa) *Takashi Shimura, Nobuo Kaneko.* Kurosawa's most affecting film, *Ikiru (To Live)* salvages great hope from intractable despair. Shimura is both pathetic and radiant as a minor bureaucrat who, about to die of cancer, realizes that he never really meant anything to anyone. The film deals with his attempts to make his existence meaningful. (Japanese with English subtitles) ★★★★ DVD Criterion Collection: $39.99, VHS: $29.99

Illegally Yours

(1988, 102 min, US, Peter Bogdanovich) *Rob Lowe, Colleen Camp, Kenneth Mars.* Bogdanovich made a bold but futile attempt at a comeback with this whimsical but empty-headed romp about a juror (Lowe donning the Ryan O'Neal-*What's Up Doc* persona) who sets out to clear the name of a former high school crush (Camp). ★★ VHS: $14.99

Illtown

(1996, 101 min, US, Nick Gomez) *Michael Rapaport, Lili Taylor, Adam Trese, Kevin Corrigan, Tony Danza, Isaac Hayes.* Rapaport and Taylor head their flourishing family business under siege when a former partner hits town. Since the business is drugs and the town is Miami, the resolution of this conflict involves more than a new ad campaign. Director Gomez fashions a world both somnambulant and acutely brutal, in which the protagonists follow paths of action of their own device, and yet essentially predetermined and out of their control. The players are superb. Taylor and Rapaport deliver

expectedly excellent performances, joining Trese and Corrigan in delivering portrayals simultaneously theatrical and naturalistic. Director Gomez combines a blistering examination of the ground level of a world-wide, multibillion dollar enterprise with a personal story of treachery and betrayal and extinguished hope. ★★★½ VHS: $9.99

Illuminata

(1999, 120 min, US, John Turturro) *Katherine Borowitz, Beverly D'Angelo, Ben Gazzara, Donal McCann, Susan Sarandon, Rufus Sewell, John Turturro, Christopher Walken, Bill Irwin, Leo Bassi.* A sumptuous and lyrical comic romp that explores life, love and lust in the confines of a tightly knit theatre troupe. Vaguely set in turn-of-the-century Italy, the action centers around the megalomaniacal Tuccio (Turturro), a playwright who's searching for his first hit, struggling with his wife and ingénue (Borowitz), and fending off his theatre's owners who want to supplant his work with Ibsen. He smells his big chance when he is approached by the Sarah Bernhard-esque Celimene (Sarandon in a marvelous turn) who wants to woo him away to her own company. A pure delight, full of Shakespearean conceits, sprightly in tone and with a giddy atmosphere that infects the entire ensemble. ★★★½
DVD: $14.99, VHS: $9.99

Illusions Travel by Streetcar (La Illusion en Travnia)

(1953, 90 min, Mexico, Luis Buñuel) *Lilia Prado, Carlos Navarro.* A small, pleasant and surprisingly gentle comedy that revolves aroung two laid-off transit workers in Mexico City who, on learning that it is headed for the scrap heap, commandeer an aging trolley and take it on one final, wild drunken ride. With class-conscious humor, Buñuel pokes gentle fun at the various passengers who board the train and become part of the wildly antic adventures through the city. (Spanish with English subtitles) ★★★ VHS: $59.99

The Image

(1990, 110 min, US, Peter Werner) *John Mahoney, Kathy Baker, Swoosie Kurtz, Marsha Mason, Spalding Gray, Albert Finney.* A successful anchor/reporter for a "60 Minutes"-type news show — played by an engaging Finney — and a wonderfully strong cast strive for hidden truths and higher ratings. Finding that these goals don't often coincide, *The Image* explores TV's role in creating a public's viewpoints and the pitfalls of making oneself a marketable product. A bit of stale New Age music and a somewhat preachy climax are the only drawbacks to this thought-provoking and enjoyably charming HBO production. ★★★ VHS: $9.99

Images

(1972, 101 min, US/Ireland, Robert Altman) *Susannah York, Rene Auberjonois, Marcel Bozzuffi, Hugh Millais.* A challenging, immensely rewarding drama that plays with issues of identity and sanity, based on Susannah York's own story. York won Best Actress at Cannes for her riveting performance. Shot in gorgeous widescreen on location in Ireland. ★★★½ DVD Letterbox: $19.99

Imaginary Crimes

(1994, 106 min, US, Anthony Drazan) *Harvey Keitel, Kelly Lynch, Fairuza Balk, Seymour Cassel, Vincent D'Onofrio.* Keitel delivers an involving and nuanced portrayal of a dreamer and con man whose flights of fancy are borne in silent disappointment by his wife and two daughters. Balk is remarkably powerful as the eldest daughter who assumes the role of family caretaker when her mother (Lynch) dies; the story is told through her eyes. Reminiscent of *This Boy's Life*, *Imaginary Crimes* carefully evokes the same time period of the late '50s and early '60s. Director Drazan has crafted a thoughtful and intimate study of the infinite human capacities for self-delusion and quiet strength. An unexpected surprise, and recommended. ★★★½ DVD: $19.99, VHS: $19.99.

Imitation of Life

(1959, 124 min, US, Douglas Sirk) *Lana Turner, Juanita Moore, John Gavin, Susan Kohler, Sandra Dee.* Arguably the best of the '50s soap-operas, this second screen version of Fanny Hurst's novel stars Turner and Moore as, respectively, an ambitious actress and her self-sacrificing black maid, who each find difficulty in raising their teenage daughters. Dee and Kohner are the troublesome offspring. Moore and Kohner are standouts. A four-hanky tearjerker with the most famous funeral in the movies. DVD: $19.99 (DVD double feature with 1934 original) ★★★½ VHS: $9.99

Immediate Family

(1989, 95 min, US, Jonathan Kaplan) *Glenn Close, James Woods, Mary Stuart Masterson, Kevin Dillon.* Close and Woods are a childless couple who are looking to adopt a baby. Masterson and Dillon are having one, though they are unmarried and unprepared for parenthood. When these four expectant parents get together, the result is a charmingly sweet, innocuous comedy-drama about familial ties and the adoption process. The story, about a privileged couple trying to get to know the parents of their future child, alternates between insightful drama and gentle humor, and director Kaplan handles both with extreme affection. Masterson walks away with the acting honors, giving a sympathetic and intuitive performance as the young mother-to-be. ★★★ DVD: $19.99, VHS: $9.99

El Immigrante Latino

(1972, 89 min, Colombia, Gustavo Nieto Roa) "El Gordo" Lopez, a classical musician from Bogota, decides that the musical opportunities are greater in the United States. So, with his life savings of $1,000, our innocent hero travels to New York on a visitor's visa. His naive hopes to find instant fame and fortune are deflated as he encounters a series of very funny disasters; what we call the "New York Experience." But hope and his good nature prevail as Gordo seeks to find a place in his new world. (Spanish with English subtitles) ★★½

The Immoral Mr. Teas

(1959, 63 min, US, Russ Meyer) *Bill Teas.* The original "nudie-cutie" film that spawned nearly 150 imitations within a year of its release. Starring Russ' army buddy Teas, and a bevy of bosomy beauties. ★★

The Immortal Bachelor

(1979, 94 min, Italy, Marcello Fondato) *Giancarlo Giannini, Monica Vitti, Claudia Cardinale, Vittorio Gassman.* This lusty and altogether enjoyable sex farce stars Giannini as a hot-blooded Italian lover who just can't seem to get enough of the eternal allures of women, one of them the beautiful Vitti. ★★★

Immortal Beloved

(1994, 121 min, GB, Bernard Rose) *Gary Oldman, Jeroen Krabbé, Isabella Rossellini, Valeria Golino, Johanna Ter Steege, Marco Hofschneider, Miriam Margolyes.* Oldman stars as Ludwig van Beethoven in this somewhat trivial examination of the tempestuous composer's life and loves. Beginning with Beethoven's death, the story follows the travails of Beethoven's confidant (Krabbé) who sets out to find the mysterious "Immortal Beloved" named as the composer's beneficiary. His search leads him across war-torn Europe. While all of the actors perform adequately, nothing of real consequence happens. And as the film is structured as a series of flashbacks, there is no foundation of dramatic tension. ★★½ DVD: $19.99, VHS: $14.99

Immortality

(2000, 99 min, GB, Po Chih Leong) *Jude Law, Elina Löwensohn, Timothy Spall, Kerry Fox, Jack Davenport.* What begins as a surreal drama in the vein of *Vampire's Kiss* about a mysterious vampire figure dissolves into a muddled fusion of film styles, none of which is able to totally clarify plot or character. Law stars as a hemophiliac vampire (sort of) looking for love but more in need of blood (and lots of it) to satisfy his carnal cravings. Hampered by lackluster pacing and a cryptic screenplay that isn't able to realize its potential, *Immortality* is nearly saved by its fine sense of atmosphere and the dashing Law. But with no clear direction, the film disintegrates faster than you can say "Count Chocula." ★★ DVD: $19.99, VHS: $9.99

The Importance of Being Earnest

(1952, 95 min, GB, Anthony Asquith) *Michael Redgrave, Dorothy Tutin, Edith Evans, Margaret Rutherford, Joan Greenwood.* An impeccable rendition of Oscar Wilde's classic farce. Wilde's play is certainly one of the hallmarks of British theatre and it represents the height of his genius. He joyously pokes and jabs at the hypocrisy of British society while using the most widely accepted conventions of the stage to present his most radical ideas and social criticisms. Sterling performances from the entire cast make this one of the most outstanding comedies to grace any screen, large or small. (Remade in 2002) ★★★★ DVD Criterion Collection: $29.99

The Importance of Being Earnest

(2002, 94 min, US/GB, Oliver Parker) *Rupert Everett, Colin Firth, Frances O'Connor, Reese Witherspoon, Judi Dench, Tom Wilkinson.* After his successful *An Ideal Husband*, director Parker tackles yet another Oscar Wilde tome, this time the writer's 19th-century masterpiece that was given a classic cinematic interpretation in 1952. However, in trying to underscore the comedy with too-broad playing and a cutesy, laugh-here film score, Parker only occasionally is able to meld Wilde's harmonious elements of farce and social criticism. The story follows the romantic exploits of two friends, Jack Worthing (Firth) and Algy Moncrieff (Everett), who use the imaginary friend Earnest to further their romantic conquests. A great ensemble works hard to mine the sublime comedy inherent in this classic tale, but the way Parker sets up some of the humor, jokes should be followed by a rimshot. Wilde's text is extraordinary, and Parker should have trusted it more — he would have been well served to discover the importance of being subtle. ★★½ DVD: $19.99, VHS: $9.99

Impostor

(2002, 102 min, US, Gary Fleder) *Gary Sinise, Madeleine Stowe, Vincent D'Onofrio, Mekhi Phifer, Tony Shalhoub, Tim Guinee.* Mild-mannered Sinise is yanked from his workplace by sinister D'Onofrio and told that he is actually a walking bomb, designed by enemy forces to assassinate a politician. The "real" Sinise was apparently killed and duplicated while on a camping trip with his wife (Stowe), and this impostor even has the man's memories, so "it" thinks it's real. He escapes custody and the hunt is on. This futuristic riff on *The Fugitive* was originally a short (by Philip K. Dick), part of an abandoned sci-fi anthology film. It feels like exactly what it is: a crackerjack half-hour suspenser, with more than an hour of padding. To its credit it's not always dull, and has a nifty ending, but the whole project just feels forced and protracted. ★★ DVD: $14.99, VHS: $14.99

The Impostors

(1998, 101 min, US, Stanley Tucci) *Stanley Tucci, Oliver Platt, Alfred Molina, Isabella Rossellini, Steve Buscemi, Lili Taylor, Hope Davis, Campbell Scott.* Trying to emulate the madcap, door-slamming, frenetic antics of a Marx Brothers movie, and

Rupert Everett and Dame Judi Dench in *The Importance of Being Earnest*

In America

for the most part, succeeding, *The Impostors* is a decidedly original and off-balanced comedy that is never less than delightful. Con artists and starving actors Tucci and Platt find themselves as stowaways on a cruise ship. For the rest of the voyage, they are forced into a series of impersonations — from crew members to wealthy passengers to bosomy women — to elude detection. A very game cast brings to life this appealing assortment of crazy characters. The look he gives 1930s Depression America evokes memories of those great screwball comedies of the era when evening gowns, art deco and grand ballrooms were accessories to insanity. ★★★½ DVD: $9.99, VHS: $9.99

Impromptu
(1991, 95 min, GB, James Lapine) *Judy Davis, Hugh Grant, Mandy Patinkin, Bernadette Peters, Julian Sands, Ralph Brown, Emma Thompson.* This enchanting and free-spirited romantic period comedy examines the courtship between composer and pianist Frederic Chopin and novelist George Sand. Sand, a liberated woman long before her time, was easily one of the more feisty and bohemian writers of the late 19th century and she set about seducing the reclusive, sickly and fervently chaste Chopin with characteristic wit and charm. Davis is splendid as the vivacious Sand and Grant delivers a wonderfully low key performance as Chopin. The circle of artists and free-spirited souls with whom Sand mingled is played by an excellent supporting cast with Patinkin as her ex-lover, Alfred de Musset; Peters as the scheming Marie d'Agoult; and Sands as composer Franz Liszt. ★★★½ DVD Letterbox: $19.99

Improper Conduct (Mauvaise Conduite)
(1984, 110 min, France, Nestor Almendros & Orlando Jiminez-Leal) This provocative documentary investigates the oppression and abuse faced by Cuba's gay and intellectual populace under the hyper-machismic reign of Castro. Twenty-eight Cuban exiles — homosexuals, poets, artists and former government officials — are interviewed, each detailing their conflicts with a system that suppresses civil rights and considers homosexuality a crime. (English and Spanish with English subtitles) ★★★½ VHS: $19.99

Impulse
(1984, 93 min, US, Graham Baker) *Tim Matheson, Meg Tilly, Hume Cronyn, Bill Paxton, Amy Stryker.* Interesting but inconclusive tale of two young lovers (Matheson and Tilly) who seek answers to the mysteriously erratic behavior of the residents of a small community, who suddenly engage in inexplicable actions for no apparent reason. ★★ DVD: $14.99, VHS: $14.99

Impulse
(1990, 109 min, US, Sondra Locke) *Theresa Russell, Jeff Fahey, George Dzundza, Lynne Thigpen.* Director Locke's second feature is a tough, gritty portrait of a hard-edged undercover vice cop (Russell) who becomes both the number one suspect and next potential victim in a murder case. ★★★ VHS: $19.99

Impure Thoughts
(1985, 87 min, US, Michael Simpson) *Brad Dourif, Lane Davies.* Capturing a period from the filmmaker's experience, Simpson's *Impure Thoughts* is a thoughtful, funny film that both humorously satirizes and seriously reconsiders Catholic parochial education in the '60s and '70s. Flashbacks (confession, nuns with clickers and rulers, illicit lust, cheat sheets, "leaving room for the Holy Ghost" between dance partners) are beautifully integrated by Simpson into his higher purpose of contemplating such issues as life and death, sin, redemption, conscience and the hereafter. ★★★

In a Glass Cage
(1986, 98 min, Spain, Agustin Villaronga) *Gunter Meisner, David Sust, Marisa Paredes.* Although definitely not for the squeamish, this sexually bizarre and violent thriller is a real find for those aficionados of no-holds-barred horror. Set a few years after WWII, the story concerns a former Nazi doctor and child molester who, because of an accident, is confined to an iron lung. The tormentor becomes the tormented after a mysterious young man, employed to be the paralyzed man's nurse, is instead bent on revenge. Mixing the style of *Diva* with the graphic sadomasochism of Pasolini's *Salo*, the film treads on ideas rarely ventured in commercial films. An uncompromising psychosexual drama that is both erotic, painful and terrifying. (Spanish with English subtitles) ★★★ DVD: $24.99

In a Lonely Place
(1950, 91 min, US, Nicholas Ray) *Humphrey Bogart, Gloria Grahame, Frank Lovejoy.* Bogart gives a chilling and complex performance in this terrific and brooding film noir thriller. Bogey plays a mentally unstable Hollywood screenwriter, given to uncontrollable rage, who must clear his own name when he is suspected of murdering a hatcheck girl. Grahame is perfectly cast as a starlet who begins an affair with Bogart, she being his only alibi. The film greatly benefits from Ray's expert, moody direction, and Bogart's strong, atypical portrayal. ★★★½ DVD: $24.99

In a Year of 13 Moons
(1979, 119 min, Germany, Rainer Werner Fassbinder) *Volker Spengler, Ingrid Caven, Eva Mattes, Elisabeth Trissenaar.* A passionate and pessimistic account of the final period in the doomed life of a transsexual named Elvira (ex-Erwin), who underwent a sex change operation on impulse to please a rich eccentric who no longer loves him/her. Now alone, Elvira seeks help from friends and her former wife, only to be repulsed and/or betrayed. *13 Moons* is one of Fassbinder's most chilling and captivating efforts. As with his other films, RFW challenges and disorients the viewer with his sporadic sentimentality and harsh detachment. Spengler excels as Elvira, an innocent sexual casualty in a desperate, and ultimately futile, search of aid. (German with English subtitles) ★★★½ DVD: $24.99

In America
(2003, 105 min, US, Jim Sheridan) *Paddy Considine, Samantha Morton, Djimon Hounsou, Sarah Bolger, Emma Bolger.* A periodically moving memory piece, *In America*, a semiautobiographical tale from director Sheridan written by him and his two daughters Naomi and Kirsten, has moments of quiet beauty that are offset by miscalculated dramatics and surprisingly sloppy homework. Considine and Morton star as Johnny and Sarah, poor Irish immigrants who have brought their family to New York City. It's supposedly the early 1980s, but various shots of Broadway and the camcorder one daughter uses are strictly early 21st century. They find a tenement apartment in Hell's Kitchen, and as the family struggles with poverty and culture clash, they find within themselves the ability to endure. This is clearly personal for Sheridan, and the scenes with the two young daughters (played with abundant charm by the Bolger sisters) resonate with emotion and clarity. But too often the scenes between the adults lack the passion and focus that would have made this a singular achievement. The ensemble is terrific, including Hounsou as a mysterious, sickly neighbor (though his dying to what appears to be AIDS is unbelievable). ★★½ DVD: $27.99

In & Out
(1997, 92 min, US, Frank Oz) *Kevin Kline, Joan Cusack, Matt Dillon, Tom Selleck, Debbie Reynolds, Wilford Brimley, Bob Newhart, Gregory Jbara, Shalom Harlow, Whoopi Goldberg.* "I didn't see *The Birdcage*" schoolteacher Howard Brackett (Kline) tells TV tabloid reporter Peter Malloy (Selleck) after Brackett has been accidentally outed on national TV right before his wedding. Inspired by a Tom Hanks acceptance speech at the Oscars, the very funny *In & Out* skewers gay stereotypes without giving in to them, framing outing and coming out within the scintillating backdrop of a sex farce. It's the kind of comedy Preston Sturges would have made if he could have. Kline is at his very best as the small-town English prof thrust into a frenzied media circus. He's

so good, in fact, that during the film's last 20 minutes when he's hardly on-screen, the film suffers as a result. The hilarious Cusack is splendid as Brackett's finacée, and the well-cast Selleck has never been better. ★★★½ DVD: $19.99, VHS: $9.99

In Cold Blood

(1967, 134 min, US, Richard Brooks) *Robert Blake, Scott Wilson, John Forsythe, Will Geer.* A truly remarkable screen adaptation of Truman Capote's novel. Straightforward presentation in moody black and white avoids sensationalizing the already potent story of random slaughter by two aimless, rootless lost boys (Blake, Wilson). Director Brooks, aided by a masterful script, conveys complex information and muted emotional states with assured skill and humane empathy. Unsettling, discomforting, rewarding. (Remade in 1996) ★★★★ DVD: $24.99, VHS: $19.99

In Country

(1989, 120 min, US, Norman Jewison) *Bruce Willis, Emily Lloyd, Joan Allen, Kevin Anderson, Judith Ivey.* Willis stars as a Vietnam vet whose emotional scars have yet to heal. Lloyd gives a sparkling performance as his spirited niece who harbors her own grief due to the death of her father in combat. Though Willis is top-billed, his is really more of a supporting character, as the film belongs to Lloyd, in both character time and performance. The film, at times, is haunting, but too many scenes seem short-changed dramatically; writer Frank Pierson doesn't fully explore some of the profound themes he has addressed. The film's ending, however, taking place at the Vietnam memorial in Washington, D.C., is extremely moving. ★★½ DVD: $9.99

The In Crowd

(2000, 108 min, US, Mary Lambert) *Susan Ward, Lori Heuring, Matthew Settle, Nathan Bexton, Tess Harper.* A girl from the wrong side of the everything is released from a mental institution; her kindly doctor secures a job for her at a posh resort. While there, she is befriended by one of the In Crowd, a busty beauty who accepts our heroine with open arms. But watch out! We're told the new girl looks just like the busty beauty's sister, who disappeared mysteriously the year before. Somnambulant performances, glacial story telling and zero twists conspire along with a hugely annoying, instantly dated score to drive the viewer to the WB for some wholesome garbage. ★ DVD: $19.99, VHS: $14.99

In Custody

(1994, 123 min, GB, Ismail Merchant) *Shashi Kapoor, Om Puri, Shabana Azmi.* Producer Merchant steps behind the camera for the first time since *The Courtesans of Bombay* with this pleasant comedy of manners set in a small town in northern India. A poor, underappreciated schoolteacher is assigned to interview Nur (played by the wonderful Kapoor), a renowned Urdu poet. The teacher is greeted by a great artist near the end of his life — obese, sickly, cantankerous and confined primarily to his home. The film revolves around a series of aborted interviews (family, friends, food and sex always seem to interrupt.) One suspects that this simple story is actually a pretext for Merchant to offer lively discussions on the fading Urdu culture and language, and to have his actors read from the writings of the great Urdu poet Faiz Ahmad Faiz. ★★★

The In-Laws

(1979, 103 min, US, Arthur Hiller) *Alan Arkin, Peter Falk, Richard Libertini, Nancy Dussault, Rosana De Soto.* Arkin and Falk make an engaging comedy team in this spright comedy about a dentist who becomes involved in the wacky goings-on of his daughter's future father-in-law — a CIA agent. (Remade in 2003) ★★★ DVD: $19.99, VHS: $14.99

The In-Laws

(2003, 98 min, US, Andrew Fleming) *Michael Douglas, Albert Brooks, Robin Tunney, Ryan Reynolds, Candice Bergen.* A remake of the 1979 Peter Falk-Alan Arkin comedy, but without that original film's considerable charms and laughs. Douglas is a CIA agent who gets his future father-in-law, conservative podiatrist Brooks, involved in all sorts of secret agent tomfoolery. Each actor seems to fit his role, but that's part of the problem — there's no chemistry between them as they do their individual schtick. Despite a couple genuine laughs, the film has no rhythm to it — it's merely a collection of skits. A tasteless gay joke that ends the film ruins whatever little good will the film had managed to nuture. ★★ DVD Letterbox: $27.99, DVD Pan & Scan: $27.99, VHS: $6.99

In Love and War

(1987, 96 min, US, Paul Aaron) *James Woods, Jane Alexander, Haing S. Ngor.* Fact-based drama with Woods as a Navy pilot held prisoner for eight years during the Vietnam War. Alexander is his loving wife who organizes other POW wives at home in order to get some straight answers from the government. Both stars offer compelling performances, though the absorbing story isn't quite as powerful as it could have been. ★★½ VHS: $89.99

In Love and War

(1996, 115 min, US, Richard Attenborough) *Sandra Bullock, Chris O'Donnell, Mackenzie Astin, Emilio Bonucci.* Ernest Hemingway's real-life WWI exploits were the inspiration for his classic novel "A Farewell to Arms." Rather than opting to remake a third film version of the classic story, director Attenborough instead adapts the book "Hemingway in Love and War." The result is a languid romantic drama. O'Donnell plays the teenaged Hemingway, who joins the Red Cross and is wounded on the front in Italy. He falls in love with his nurse Agnes von Kurowsky (Bullock). It's a bittersweet May-June romance which later would leave the author emotionally scarred. Bullock gives a flat portrayal; at least O'Donnell captures the enthusiasm of the writer, though not his drive. Attenborough's pacing is sluggish throughout, and for a film about a passionate affair, there's little passion. ★½ DVD: $9.99

In Memoriam

(1977, 89 min, Spain, Enrique Brasso) *Geraldine Chaplin, Jose Luis Gomez.* A somber melodrama about commitment, obsessive love and jealousy. Essentially a three-person play, the film tells the story of a tangled love triangle between Luis, a celebrated novelist; Juan, a struggling writer; and Paulina, the woman they both love. Luis, who is incapable of expressing his deep love of Paulina, finds that he has lost her to the passionate and possessive love of Juan. Chaplin is beguiling as the woman torn between the two men — emotional and personality opposites. A Spanish soap opera that avoids the typical excesses of the genre and delves more into the psychological nuances of the characters. (Spanish with English subtitles) ★★½

In Name Only

(1939, 94 min, US, John Cromwell) *Cary Grant, Carole Lombard, Kay Francis.* Tearjerker starring Grant as a wealthy businessman who is trapped in a loveless marriage to social climber Francis. When Grant falls in love with Lombard and asks for a divorce, scheming wife Francis refuses the request and sets on a ruthless course to foil their affair. A familiar romantic soaper highlighted by Grant and Lombard's affectionate scenes together. ★★★

In Old Chicago

(1938, 96 min, US, Henry King) *Tyrone Power, Don Ameche, Alice Faye, Alice Brady, Brian Donlevy.* With the great success of M-G-M's *San Francisco*, 20th Century-Fox released their own disaster spectacle and the result is a pleasing if fictionalized version of the great Chicago fire of 1871. Power and Ameche play the O'Leary brothers — one a scalawag and the other the mayor. They're the sons of Mrs. O'Leary, who owned that famous cow. Brady won an Oscar for her stalwart but sentimental portrayal of Ma. ★★★ VHS: $19.99

In Praise of Love

(2001, 98 min, France, Jean-Luc Godard) *Bruno Putzulu, Cecile Camp, Jean Davy.* The film opens in black and white as Edgar, a director, is auditioning prospective cast members for his film examining love. He runs into a woman he met three years ago, when she was a law student. At that time, her grandparents, former members of the French Resistance, had asked her to look over a contract offered to them by Hollywood movie people wanting to make a film of their experiences in the war. Now shot in color, *In Praise of Love* moves back to that time three years before, as the grandparents try to decipher the intentions of the Americans. The film is a contemplation of memory and the passage of time, of image and identity and the reclamation of history. In a quintessentially Godardian manner, the film medium is used to conduct a most cerebral discussion. While Godard strikes an effective balance between human emotion and abstract analysis, his lapses into strident anti-Americanism come across as far in excess of any legitimate criticism. Maybe it's post-9/11 sensitivity, but the contention that the United States has no history, no legends of its own seems a tad overbearing. On the other hand, how many other directors could elicit this response with one of their films? (French with English subtitles) ★★★ DVD Letterbox: $29.99, VHS Letterbox: $29.99

In the Army Now

(1994, 91 min, US, Daniel Petrie Jr.) *Pauly Shore, Lori Petty, David Alan Grier, Esai Morales, Lynn Whitfield, Brendan Fraser, Andy Dick.* Following in the military bootsteps of such comic luminaries as Bob Hope, Goldie Hawn, Abbott & Costello and Bill Murray, twentysomething clown Shore joins the service, disproving the slogan "Be all you can be." Toning down his annoying Valley-speak a tad, Shore plays a moronic lad who joins the Army for the financial assistance available after his tour of duty. Once in uniform, of course, he mouths off, makes enemies, tears the place apart and saves the day. This is strictly standard issue, whose few jokes have already been done by those mentioned above. ★★ DVD: $14.99, VHS: $9.99

In the Bedroom

(2001, 138 min, US, Todd Field) *Sissy Spacek, Tom Wilkinson, Marisa Tomei, Nick Stahl, William Mapother, Karen Allen.* Recriminations, unspoken resentments and the festering rage that emerge in the face of tragedy may not be any one family's exclusive domain. But the Fowlers of Maine — the reserved, devastated married couple who inhabit the numbing emotional terrain of the blistering, brilliant drama *In the Bedroom* — can certainly try to lay claim when confronted with unimaginable grief. In performances as raw as they are touching, Wilkinson and Spacek are extraordinary as Matt and Ruth, a doctor and schoolteacer, respectively, whose lives come to a turning point when tragedy strikes. At the heart of the tale, based on Andre Dubus' short story "Killings," is how this once close-knit family handles and reacts to their loss, where guilt and denial are layered like the characters' clothes guarding against a New England winter. Just under the surface, however, is a wrenching story of loss, silence and vengeance, and not always about what it appears. Field, an actor making his directorial debut, captures the cadence of New England life with pacing both lyrical and measured, which is in stark contrast to the tragic, feverish events that transpire. It's a most impressive first film. In support, Tomei is outstanding as a divorced mother attempting to make sense of senselessness. ★★★★ DVD: $19.99, VHS: $14.99

In the Belly of the Dragon

(1989, 100 min, Canada, Yves Simoneau) This plucky little surprise from our northern neighbors is evidence that life is absurd, corporations are out to get you and people are funny all over the world. A young man, in an effort to afford a new pair of cowboy boots, trades the everyday nightmare of his dead-end job distributing circulars door-to-door for the high-tech nightmare of being an experimental subject for biochemical brain research. He begins an odyssey wherein he learns the transient regard for human life, the power of a well-thrown dart and the absolute value of some really good friends. ★★★

In the Company of Men

(1997, 97 min, US, Neil LaBute) *Aaron Eckhart, Stacy Edwards, Matt Malloy.* Sexual politics in the corporate workplace are played out by two mid-America average white boys who consider life to be out of balance whenever they're not on top. Outraged that women no longer appear to be relegated to a subservient role, these two nondescript nonentities set up a cruel game on an unsuspecting victim — a deaf temp new to the office. Consciously equating their own dignity with the willful abasement of another human being, these small, ineffectual, scared men look for any available easy target to bolster their self-esteem. Their myriad frailities and insecurities bubble to boiling as their game turns into a rivalry. The director's script plays well with competent acting and maximum use of modest production values. *In the Company of Men* is a controversial, virulent dark comedy that will undoubtedly offend some by its cavalier manner and intrigue others with both its uncompromising examination of the male psyche and an unnerving, biting comic voice. ★★★ DVD: $27.99

In the Cut

(2003, 119 min, US, Jane Campion) *Meg Ryan, Mark Ruffalo, Jennifer Jason Leigh, Kevin Bacon.* Ryan bares all in this otherwise deadly dull atrocity from art-house favorite Campion. Meg stars as a near-somnambulistic English teacher writing a book on slang, who strikes up a sexual relationship with chauvinistic jerk Ruffalo, a cop investigating a series of serial killings. Their scenes together are unpleasant and unconvincing, rendering the big sex scene interesting solely as a voyeuristic exercise wherein we finally get to see a huge star get naked. Campion allows her overwhelmingly pretentious direction to obliterate any suspense or pulpy enjoyment, determined as she is to make a "statement" about modern male-female relationships while ignoring the audience's desire to stay awake. The camerawork, aiming for edginess, is distracting and annoying, and several subplots are awkward. Ryan and Ruffalo try, and Leigh is terrific as always, but it's all for naught. ★ DVD Unrated: $19.99

In the Gloaming

(1997, 62 min, US, Christopher Reeve) *Glenn Close, Robert Sean Leonard, David Strathairn, Whoopi Goldberg, Bridget Fonda.* In an herculean effort far more inspiring and dramatic than anything offered on the screen, Reeve makes his directorial debut, his first professional outing since his accident. No doubt this story of impending death struck a nerve, and as a director he brings reverence and a fluidity not usually associated with freshman assignments. But this one-hour drama about an estranged young man with AIDS who returns home to die is lacking in passion, and its disjointed screenplay sabotages any chance for true character development. Close is the only exception, giving more depth to the role of the young man's mother than what is really there. ★★½

In the Good Old Summertime

(1949, 102 min, US, Robert Z. Leonard) *Judy Garland, Van Johnson, S.Z. Sakall, Buster Keaton, Spring Byington.* Charming musical remake of Ernst Lubitsch's *The Shop Around the Corner.* Garland and Johnson are the bickering coworkers who unknowingly fall in love via the personals. Though the same story is the basis for the Broadway musical "She Loves Me," this musical and the show have different scores. That's Liza Minnelli as the couple's baby at the end. (Nonmusical remake: *You've Got Mail*) ★★★ DVD: $19.99

In the Heat of the Night

(1967, 109 min, US, Norman Jewison) *Sidney Poitier, Rod Steiger, Lee Grant, William Schallert, Warren Oates.* A Best Picture Oscar went to this exceptional mystery story about a black Philadelphia cop and his experiences with racial bigotry while helping the Sparta, Mississippi, police force solve a murder. Poitier is Virgil Tibbs, a savvy police detective whose assistance to the small town and captain Steiger is ill-rewarded and unappreciated. Both actors are excellent, and Steiger won an Oscar for Best Actor as the racist policeman trying to do right. (Sequel: *They Call Me Mister Tibbs*) ★★★★ DVD: $14.99

In the Land of the War Canoes

(1914, 48 min, US/Canada, Edward S. Curtis) Photographer Edward S. Curtis, best known for his still photographs of Native Americans, spent three years with the Kwakiutl Indians of Vancouver Island in order to capture on film their lifestyle, ceremonial dances and religious rituals. This fascinating documentary is a meticulous re-creation of a tribal society before the invasion of the white man destroyed their culture. ★★★ DVD: $29.99, VHS: $39.99

In the Line of Fire

(1993, 123 min, US, Wolfgang Petersen) *Clint Eastwood, John Malkovich, Rene Russo, Dylan McDermott, Gary Cole, John Mahoney, Patrika Darbo, John Heard.* Petersen follows his underrated *Shattered* with this superior suspense thriller which affords Eastwood a second opportunity to deliver a career performance. Clint plays a seasoned Secret Service agent entangled in a presidential assassination scenario as a routine investigation puts him on the trail of a potential killer, played with great menace by Malkovich. Much of the film's enjoyment lies in the cat-and-mouse relationship Malkovich's would-be assassin nurtures between the agent and himself. For once, Eastwood leaves behind his laconic character, and Jeff Maguire's intelligent screenplay makes it a pleasure to hear the actor form complete sentences. ★★★★ DVD Letterbox: $19.99, VHS: $9.99

In the Mood

(1987, 99 min, US, Phil Alden Robinson) *Patrick Dempsey, Beverly D'Angelo, Talia Balsam.* Amiable comedy based on the real-life experiences of 15-year-old Sonny Wisecarver, who in the 1940s made headlines around the country by having affairs with two older women, one of whom he married. Dempsey is a delight as Carver, who was also known as "The Woo Woo Kid." ★★½ VHS: $14.99

In the Mood for Love

(2000, 98 min, Hong Kong, Wong Kar-Wai) *Tony Leung, Maggie Cheung, Rebecca Pan.* This precious, stylish gem begins in Hong Kong in 1962 and focuses on the forbidden love between two neighbors, Mr. Chow and Mrs. Chan (the dashingly handsome Leung and the mesmerizingly beautiful Cheung). They're both stuck in lonesome marriages to absent mates. In fact, their estranged spouses are so distant we never actually get to see their faces. Propelled by a seductive musical score and rapturous cinematography, the timid pair dares to awaken in each other the tenderness their lonely marriages have long deprived them of. The poignant tragedy of their story is that they can barely acknowledge their love for each other for fear of shaming their families and themselves forever. Leung and Cheung set the screen on fire with their unspoken tension and smoldering sensuality and they both deliver heart-wrenching performances. And director Kar-Wai demonstrates a masterful sense of composition — every shot is exquisite. (Cantonese with English subtitles). ★★★½ DVD Letterbox Criterion Collection: $39.99

In the Mouth of Madness

(1995, 95 min, US, John Carpenter) *Sam Neill, Julie Carmen, Jürgen Prochnow, Charlton Heston, David Warner, John Glover, Bernie Casey.* In this H.P. Lovecraft-based tale, a skeptical insurance investigator (Neill) sets out to prove that the disappearance of best-selling author Sutter Cane (Prochnow) is a publicity stunt. As he digs deeper, he finds out that what Cane has been selling as fiction is actually fact-based memory transmitted by "the dark ones" — and that Cane's final novel will unleash Hell on Earth. What begins as a mature, well-visualized opus into madness and surrealism eventually clashes with the filmmaker's schlocky sense of atmosphere and "boo"-style horror gimmicks, creating a mixed-bag of chills and chuckles. But the film's reflexive ending (not to give anything away) rounds it out nicely, and should leave any viewer just the least bit paranoid. ★★ DVD: $19.99, VHS: $14.99

In the Name of the Father

(1993, 127 min, Ireland, Jim Sheridan) *Daniel Day-Lewis, Emma Thompson, Pete Postlethwaite, John Lynch, Corin Redgrave.* An impassioned scream for justice which dramatizes the real-life plight of Gerry Conlon and his companions, a group

In the Realm of the Senses

of innocents known as the Guilford Four who spent 15 years in a British prison for an IRA bombing. Day-Lewis easily could have won his second Oscar for his fiery portrayal of the emotional Conlon, a petty thief and troublemaker from Belfast who, by sheer coincidence, was caught in the British government's legal net — which also picked up several members of his family and his friends including his father and aunt. And while Day-Lewis' performance sparkles, it is Postlethwaite, in a riveting performance as his steadfastly principled father Giuseppe, who truly carries the film's moral message. Thompson costars as a dedicated lawyer who finally uncovers the truth and helps free them. ★★★★ DVD: $24.99

In the Name of the Pope King

(1977, 105 min, Italy, Luigi Magni) *Nino Manfredi, Danilo Mattei.* Manfredi takes a successful stab at serious acting in this compelling story of intrigue, political conflict and murder. Set in 1867 during a turbulent period of peasant revolt and leftist bombings, the film stars Manfredi as Monsignor Colombo, a magistrate for the conservative papal state. He finds himself immersed in political turmoil when he discovers that his son might be involved in terrorist activity against the state. An interesting companion film to this fascinating political and personal drama is Bertrand Tavernier's similarly themed *The Clockmaker*. (Italian with English subtitles) ★★★ VHS: $59.99

In the Navy

(1941, 85 min, US, Arthur Lubin) *Bud Abbott, Lou Costello, Dick Powell, The Andrews Sisters.* Abbott and Costello are sailors who become involved with the escapades of crooner Powell, who's joined the Navy to escape his adoring fans. This A&C comedy isn't as consistently funny as some of their other romps, especially when the story concentrates on Powell. However, the boys do offer some funny bits (a shell game, proving 7 X 13 = 28), and Lou has a few amusing solo bits as well. Powell and The Andrews Sisters supply the songs, which are mostly forgettable. DVD: $24.99 (DVD includes 7 other Abbott and Costello films) ★★½

In the Presence of Mine Enemies

(1996, 96 min, US, Joan Micklin Silver) *Armin Mueller-Stahl, Charles Dance, Elina Löwensohn, Chad Lowe.* Rod Serling's teleplay is the basis for

this poignant though slow-moving Showtime drama set in the Warsaw ghetto before its eventual extermination. Mueller-Stahl gives a strong, caring portrayal of a rabbi whose determination to keep his family together and provide spiritual guidance to the dwindling number of neighbors — often refusing to acknowledge the horrors surrounding him — causes a crisis of faith and mental breakdown. Dance is the Nazi captain caught in a battle of wills and words with the rabbi, and Lowe is a young soldier whose humanity leads to unexpected redemption and inevitable tragedy. Serling's story pits its characters against each other in moral debate, all trapped in hopeless dilemma; but their voices are often muted and thoughts prone to repetition. ★★½

In the Realm of Passion

(1978, 110 min, Japan, Nagisa Oshima) *Kazuko Yoshiyuki, Takahiro Tamura.* From the director of *Merry Christmas, Mr. Lawrence* comes this erotic ghost story of unremitting passion and impending doom. A young married peasant woman has an affair with another man. Together, they kill her husband; but, twisting the *Ghost* theme on an ominous tilt, the angry husband comes back to haunt the two. Subtle, visually beautiful and a restrained work. (Japanese with English subtitles) (aka: *Empire of Passion*) ★★★ DVD: $19.99, VHS: $14.99

In the Realm of the Senses

(1976, 115 min, Japan, Nagisa Oshima) *Tatsuya Fuji, Eiko Matsuda.* Oshima's most debated work in a career marked by controversy, *In the Realm of the Senses* is an unrelenting journey into the world of passion and eroticism. Oblivious to social restraints and public sentiment, a geisha and her lover engage in a torrid sexual spree, losing themselves in the fervor of their lovemaking and their quest for ultimate ecstasy. The ideology of male dominance and female submission is thoroughly undermined as the obsessed lovers create a closed existence of incessant lovemaking and sadomasochistic experiments. This is an eerily beautiful examination of the intensity of physical desire. (Japanese with English subtitles) ★★★½ DVD Subtitled: $19.99, VHS Subtitled: $14.99, VHS Dubbed: $14.99

In the Soup

(1993, 96 min, US, Alexandre Rockwell) *Steve Buscemi, Seymour Cassel, Jennifer Beals, Jim*

Jarmusch, Carol Kane. Character actor Buscemi is finally given a chance to star in his own film with this enjoyably ragtag independent comedy. Buscemi plays a down-on-his-luck aspiring (but possibly no-talent) filmmaker. His world is turned upside down after an eccentric "businessman" takes him under his dark wing and offers to finance his Tarkovsky/Godard-inspired opus. Strikingly similar to *Mistress*, the film is entertainingly wacky and features great performances by Buscemi as the befuddled loser sucked into a bizarre, criminal world, Cassel as his "savior," and Beals as Buscemi's Puerto Rican *object d'amour*. ★★★

In the Spirit

(1990, 94 min, US, Sandra Seacat) *Marlo Thomas, Elaine May, Peter Falk, Jeannie Berlin, Melanie Griffith, Olympia Dukakis.* A health nut (Thomas) and a socialite (May) stumble into the "date book" of a deceased hooker, and comedic complications ensue. Soon, everyone is after the book. A likable cast rises above the forced material. ★★½ VHS: $89.99

In the White City

(1983, 108 min, Portugal/Switzerland, Alain Tanner) *Bruno Ganz, Teresa Madruga.* A haunting mood piece about a Swiss boat engineer (Ganz) who jumps ship in Lisbon and begins a personal quest of self-discovery. Roaming the streets and frequenting the watering holes, he dives headfirst into the foreignness and unfamiliarity of his new surroundings. Tanner turns this existential odyssey into a fascinating examination of solitude, freedom and self-estrangement as he unravels the psyche of a man's unstructured search for something real. (German and Portuguese with English subtitles) ★★★ VHS: $19.99

In This Our Life

(1942, 97 min, US, John Huston) *Bette Davis, Olivia de Havilland, George Brent, Charles Coburn, Hattie McDaniel, Walter Huston.* Davis lets loose as a neurotic hussy whose tantrums and plottings ruin the lives of sister de Havilland, husband Brent and, finally, herself. Davis gives a commanding performance in this familiar melodrama, though the film suffers somewhat due to director Huston's unfamiliarity with the genre. ★★½

In Which We Serve

(1942, 115 min, GB, David Lean & Noël Coward) *Noël Coward, John Mills, Richard Attenborough, Michael Wilding, Celia Johnson, Kay Walsh, Daniel Massey.* One of the masterpieces of British cinema, *In Which We Serve* provided director/writer/actor/composor Coward with his finest screen hour. Based on the real-life experiences of the British warship *HMS Kelly*, the film recounts — mostly in flashback — the story of the men of a torpedoed destroyer awaiting rescue. Coward brings all the right qualities of leadership and resolve to his role as the ship's captain, and the supporting cast is excellent. Lean's directorial debut. ★★★★

The Incident

(1967, 107 min, US, Larry Peerce) *Martin Sheen, Tony Musante, Beau Bridges, Jack Gilford, Thelma Ritter, Brock Peters, Ruby Dee, Ed McMahon.* A gritty, well-done low-budget thriller set almost exclusively in a New York City subway car. A disparate group of passengers are terrorized by punks Sheen and Musante. Bridges is first-rate as an injured soldier. ★★★ VHS: $59.99

Incident at Map Grid 36-80

(1983, 80 min, USSR, Mikhail Tumanishvili) An interesting premise, sort of a Russian *Hunt for Red October*, and a rare look at Soviet military might help make this a compelling war thriller. While out on routine sea maneuvers, a Soviet squadron receives a distress call from an American submarine that is carrying a secret nuclear arsenal. The Soviets respond to the call but are warned not to approach. Complicating the already tense situation is a malfunctioning computer that sounds the alarm to launch the American sub's cruise missiles. The opposing admirals must decide on the fate of the submarine in a tense stalemate that could possibly trigger WWIII. (Russian with English subtitles) ★★★ VHS: $59.99

Incident at Oglala

(1992, 89 min, US, Michael Apted) This important and long-overdue documentary is about the events that occurred in 1975 on the Sioux Indian reservation in South Dakota. The film asserts that the attack on two FBI agents, which led to the standoff, was an act of self-defense and that those who were punished for it (Leonard Peltier remains the only person jailed in the incident) were innocent. The film also asserts that through a band of violent government cronies known as the "Goon Squads," an atmosphere of brutality and terror was maintained on the reservation, an atmosphere that ultimately led to the fateful confrontation. Robert Redford, who produced the film, also narrates. Apted also directed the fictionalized counterpart, *Thunderheart*, which puts a Hollywood spin on the whole affair. ★★★½ DVD: $14.99, VHS: $19.99

The Incredible Mr. Limpet

(1964, 102 min, US, Arthur Lubin) *Don Knotts, Jack Weston, Carole Cook.* Cute live-action and animated comedy starring Knotts, who falls off a Coney Island pier and becomes a fish — helping the U.S. Navy battle Nazi submarines. ★★½ DVD: $19.99, VHS: $14.99

The Incredible Sarah

(1976, 106 min, GB, Richard Fleischer) *Glenda Jackson, Daniel Massey, Yvonne Mitchell.* An outstanding performance by Jackson breathes life into this otherwise standard biopic on the life of the legendary French stage actress Sarah Bernhardt. ★★½

The Incredible Shrinking Man

(1957, 81 min, US, Jack Arnold) *Grant Williams, Randy Stuart, April Kent.* This existential sci-fi classic written by Richard Matheson has the courage of its convictions in its strange metaphysical climax as an ordinary Joe finds that he is growing smaller every day. Brilliant special effects don't overshadow Williams' performance. ★★★½

The Incredible Shrinking Woman

(1981, 88 min, US, Joel Schumacher) *Lily Tomlin, Charles Grodin, Ned Beatty, Henry Gibson.* A sometimes humorous satire on consumerism and suburbia, Tomlin plays an average American housewife whose exposure to household products causes her to shrink. Great production design and effects highlight the film. ★★½

The Incredibly Strange Creatures Who Stopped Living and Became Mixed-Up Zombies

(1963, 82 min, US, Ray Dennis Steckler) *Cash Flagg, Carolyn Brandt.* A great title highlights this camp gem full of bad acting, a stupid plot, neat zombies and atmospheric camera work thanks to Joe Micelli, Laszlo Kovacs and Vilmos Zsigmond. (aka: *The Teenage Psycho Meets Bloody Mary*) ★

The Incredibly True Adventure of Two Girls in Love

(1995, 95 min, US, Maria Maggenti) *Laurel Holloman, Nicole Parker, Maggie Moore, Kate Stafford.* This thoroughly enjoyable lesbian first love story is a startling film debut by independent filmmaker Maggenti. Randy (Holloman) is a white high school tomboy living with her lesbian aunt. Evie (Parker) is a beautiful and pampered black deb from the right side of the tracks. They meet and love blossoms despite their differences. But trouble brews for the two as both of their families undertake to break the lovers apart. A long-awaited "wholesome lesbian comedy and romance" that ignores queer politics and prejudice and concentrates on the two young women's intense attraction for each other. Not as big city grunge as *Go Fish* nor as jaded as *Bar Girls*, *Two Girls* is a terrifically sweet low-budget romantic comedy. ★★★ DVD: $19.99

Incubus

(1966, 76 min, US, Leslie Stevens) *William Shatner, Allyson Ames, Eloise Hardt.* This one's a real curio: a black-and-white horror film from the '60s, beautifully shot by Conrad Hall, starring a pre-"Star Trek" Shatner, with all dialogue spoken in the "international language" of Esperanto! *Incubus* is basically an enjoyable mix of the moody and atmospheric with the silly and outright laughable (you thought Shatner overacted in English!). A bit too slow and hokey, to be sure, but if you're in the right mood, a good time. ★★½ DVD: $24.99, VHS: $19.99

The Incubus

(1982, 90 min, US, John Hough) *John Cassavetes, Kerrie Keane.* A peaceful New England community is besieged by a series of demonic murders. Cassavetes stars as an investigator who follows the demon's path to a frightened young man whose nightmares may hold the key to the mystery. Boring, confusing and not very exciting. ★

An Indecent Obsession

(1985, 106 min, Australia, Lex Marinos) *Wendy Hughes, Gary Sweet, Richard Moir, Bruno Lawrence.* Adapted from Colleen McCullough's (*The Thorn Birds*) best-selling novel, this hospital drama is set immediately after Japan's surrender in WWII. But for the war-ravaged psychiatric patients of Ward X, the end of the war makes little difference. Their troubled minds and battered spirits, held in check by the beautiful nurse Langtry (Hughes), are soon tested by the appearance of a mysterious man who is admitted into their wing. Vicious currents of lust, homophobia, jealousy, desire and violent death soon undermine them all. A hyperventilating soap opera that squanders its juicy material with a leaden hand; the film ultimately fizzles. ★★

Indecent Proposal

(1993, 118 min, US, Adrian Lyne) *Robert Redford, Demi Moore, Woody Harrelson, Oliver Platt, Seymour Cassel.* Moore and Harrelson are a young married couple experiencing financial troubles. They head to Las Vegas and promptly lose everything. Then, Demi attracts the attention of zillionaire Redford who offers a million dollars to spend the night with her. Aside from the incredulous offer is the disturbing subtheme of "women as chattel." The film really hits bottom, though, after the deed is done. The last hour is dedicated to an unlikable couple whining about everything and Redford acting like a lovesick teenager. A conceit of such calculation it resembles a mathematical equation rather than a movie. ★★ DVD: $14.99, VHS: $14.99

Independence Day

(1983, 110 min, US, Robert Mandel) *Kathleen Quinlan, David Keith, Dianne Wiest, Frances Sternhagen, Cliff De Young, Richard Farnsworth.* A handful of strong performances dominate this telling drama about the day-to-day lives of a small Southwestern town. Quinlan heads the cast as a young woman — involved with mechanic Keith — who longs to escape the confines of her constrictive lifestyle. Wiest is superb as a battered wife. ★★★ VHS: $19.99

Independence Day

(1996, 135 min, US, Roland Emmerich) *Bill Pullman, Will Smith, Jeff Goldblum, Mary McDonnell, Judd Hirsch, Robert Loggia, Margaret Colin, Randy Quaid, Brent Spiner, Harvey Fierstein, Harry Connick, Jr.* Recalling the UFO paranoia/hysteria of those 1950s sci-fi films — the classic and cheesy, alike — in which dastardly aliens set out to destroy our benign planet, *Independence Day* is the ultimate us vs. them sci-fi encounter, boasting great special effects, a plausible story line, good laughs and a cast obviously enjoying themselves. Combining many plots and characters who all come together by story's end, the film's fun starts when several giant spaceships hover over Earth's major cities. As the president, the military and scientists engage in speculation, it soon becomes clear these aliens are no E.T.s. *Star Wars* may be slicker, and *Close Encounters* more visionary, but there's no denying *Independence Day* is a blast. ★★★½ DVD Letterbox Widescreen: $19.99, DVD Basic Edition: $19.99, VHS: $9.99, VHS Letterbox: $9.99

The Indian in the Cupboard

(1995, 96 min, US, Frank Oz) *Hal Scardino, Litefoot, Lindsay Crouse, Richard Jenkins, David Keith.* A family film with just the right amount of fantasy and magic added to a story of childhood friendship and trust. Based on Lynne Reid Banks' book, this charming adaptation stars Scardino as Omri, the youngest of three children in a New York City household. Omri's brother presents him with a cabinet in which Omri places an American Indian figure. The cupboard shakes awaking Omri and when he opens it he is surprised to find the Indian (played by Litefoot) alive. Omri is the personification of wonder and innocence as he learns through his friend to be brave and independent in the rough and troubled world at home and on the streets of New York. ★★★ DVD Dual: $19.99

The Indian Runner

(1991, 127 min, US, Sean Penn) *David Morse, Viggo Mortensen, Charles Bronson, Dennis Hopper, Sandy Dennis, Patricia Arquette, Valeria Golina.* Maverick actor Penn takes his talents behind the camera with this stunningly realized character study centering on the stormy relationship between a highway patrolman (Morse) and his "loose cannon" of a brother (Mortensen). Though short on story, this loving tribute to the filmmaking of the '70s will reward the patient viewer with its detailed attention to time and place. ★★★ DVD Letterbox: $19.99

Indian Summer

(1993, 98 min, US, Mike Binder) *Alan Arkin, Diane Lane, Bill Paxton, Matt Craven, Elizabeth Perkins, Kevin Pollak, Vincent Spano, Julie Warner, Sam Raimi.* This *Big Chill*-like comedy reunites seven old friends who attended Camp Tamakwa during its "golden age" in the early '70s. Invited back to their old stomping grounds by camp owner Arkin, the friends get to work out some of their demons and share old secrets. Especially engaging are Lane as Bethy, a woman whose husband (and camp sweetheart) died in a car crash the year before, and Paxton, who as the rebel of the bunch got kicked out of camp one summer for mysterious reasons. With warmth and humor, *Indian Summer* brings back the sights, sounds, smells and first heartbreaks of summer camp. ★★★ DVD: $9.99

Indiana Jones and the Last Crusade

(1989, 127 min, US, Steven Spielberg) *Harrison Ford, Sean Connery, Denholm Elliott, John Rhys-Davies, River Phoenix.* Indiana Jones and director Spielberg are back in glorious form after the near-fiasco of *Temple of Doom.* Ford is as dashing as ever as Indy, who is off in search of both the Holy Grail and his missing father. Connery is an absolute delight as Indy's dad, a timid scholarly type not really prepared for his son's more dangerous escapades. The humor and the pace are fast and furious and Indy's old enemies — the Nazis — are back to do battle once again. Every bit as enjoyable as the original *Raiders.* Phoenix is great as a young Indy in the film's opening prologue. ★★★½ VHS: $9.99, VHS Letterbox: $9.99

Indiana Jones and the Temple of Doom

(1984, 118 min, US, Steven Spielberg) *Harrison Ford, Kate Capshaw, Ke Huy Quan.* Spielberg attempts to outdo his success with *Raiders of the Lost Ark.* The perils are greater but the plot is weaker. The film is actually a prequel to *Raiders,* following Indy (Ford) and sidekick (Capshaw) in their adventures in the Far East. However disappointing, the opening sequence is worth the price of the rental: Capshaw singing a Mandarin version of "Anything Goes" — leading to a highly exciting and comical nightclub brawl. (Sequel: *Indiana Jones and the Last Crusade*) ★★½ VHS: $9.99, VHS Letterbox: $9.99

Indiscreet

(1958, 100 min, US, Stanley Donen) *Ingrid Bergman, Cary Grant, Phyllis Calvert.* For couples wanting romance, this is the ticket. Bergman plays a ravishing European actress who is courted by an equally ravishing Grant. The fare is at times slow and perhaps even overly romantic, but the film is filled with an engaging sense of wry wit and humor — not to mention a seething sexual tension between its two stars. Bergman and Grant, as the urbane lovers, could not have been better cast. (Letterboxed version) ★★★ DVD: $14.99, VHS: $9.99

Indiscreet

(1998, 101 min, US, Marc Bienstock) *Luke Perry, Gloria Reuben, Adam Baldwin, Peter Coyote.* In this lukearm thriller, Perry is Michael Nash, an ex-cop, ex-alcoholic turned private investigator. Offered a job by a rich lawyer to spy on his unfaithful wife Eve (Reuben), Nash discovers that she is not having an affair, but spending her days alone drinking and skinny dipping. Rescuing Eve from a suicide attempt one afternoon, these two damaged people begin a passionate romance that cools off when her husband is murdered. Of course, Eve is the sole beneficiary of her husband's $75 million will, and Nash, who helped her cover up the crime, is the prime suspect. Although *Indiscreet* is a good-looking production that is filled with as many plot twists as it has plot holes. ★★

Indiscretion of an American Wife

(1954, 72 min, Italy, Vittorio De Sica) *Montgomery Clift, Jennifer Jones, Richard Beymer.* The unusual teaming of American producer David O. Selznick and neorealist Italian director De Sica does not really work. The action centers in Rome's main railroad station and features Jones as an adulterous wife who meets her lover Clift for a final fling. It is no *Brief Encounter* but an interesting try. (aka: *Terminal Station*) ★★ DVD Criterion Collection: $39.99, VHS: $14.99

Indochine

(1992, 155 min, France, Regis Wargnier) *Catherine Deneuve, Linh Dan Pham, Vincent Perez.* An Academy Award winner for Best Foreign-Language Film, *Indochine* is a beautifully photographed and evocative love story set during the French colonization of Indochina. In a rapturous performance, the stunning Deneuve stars as the dowager of a successful rubber plantation. Though a strict foreman, she has an especially loving relationship with her adopted, Indochinese daughter (well played by Pham). Against the backdrop of social upheaval, their worlds collide when they both fall in love with the same man, a handsome French soldier (Perez). A poetic epic that balances romance and politics with equal finesse. (French with English subtitles) ★★★★ DVD: $27.99, VHS: $19.99

Infernal Trio

(1974, 100 min, France, Francis Girod) *Michel Piccoli, Romy Schneider, Mascha Gomska.* While quite shocking and even scandalous in its initial release, time has not been kind to this macabre black comedy about a trio of amoral, larcenous lovers. Piccoli plays a distinguished lawyer who entices two German sisters (Schneider, Gomska) into marrying a series of rich older men. When the husbands die of natural causes or are "encouraged" to leave this life, the three share in the proceeds of the wealth and insurance money. Unevenly paced, the film fluctuates between serious drama, sexy romp and pitch-black comedy. This social satire, which sets out to intentionally shock its unsuspecting nature, delivers an enthusiastically shameless descent into the pleasures and profits of evil. (French with English subtitles) ★★½

Inferno

(1978, 107 min, Italy, Dario Argento) *Eleonora Giorgi, Leigh McCloskey, Gabriele Lavia.* Argento's sequel to *Suspiria* is an almost incomprehensible collection of bizarre images and fantastically realized set piece murders. It lacks a linear narrative, but that does not detract from its overall ambiance of weirdness and terror. A young American poet discovers a book which she believes identifies her ancient New York apartment building as the residence of the Mater Tenebrarum, one of three witches who generate all the misery in the world. *Inferno* is full of stylistic touches which overcome its narrative difficulties. *Suspiria* and *Inferno* are the only two films Argento has made with purely supernatural plots, a fact which gives him the freedom to completely abandon all logic and submerge himself in the stylish, horrifying impulses which make him unique among horror film directors. ★★½ DVD: $29.99, VHS: $14.99

Inferno

(1999, 94 min, US, Harley Cokeliss) *Gloria Reuben, Armin Mueller-Stahl, Ray Liotta, Daniel Kash, Lisa Owen.* Liotta is quite effective in this potent nail-biter

about an even-tempered Average Joe who wakes up in the middle of nowhere with no memory, a fake identity and a dead guy in his bathroom. He then becomes the target of a gang of gun-toting thugs on the trail of a fortune that he may or may not have stolen. A good story line, solid cinematography and well-etched performances make this "desert-noir" surprising entertainment. ★★★ DVD: $24.99

The Infiltrator

(1995, 102 min, US, John MacKenzie) *Oliver Platt, Arliss Howard, Peter Riegert, Alan King.* A powerful HBO film, *The Infiltrator* is based on the book "In Hitler's Shadow," the true-life story of Israeli journalist Yaron Svoray, who while on assignment in Germany went undercover to expose a neo-Nazi group. Platt plays Svoray, a writer living in America who is sent to report on the recent racially motivated attacks by skinheads in Germany. But as Svoray digs deeper, he discovers a well-organized, underground fascist political organization with growing public support. The film — in eye-opening detail — shows the extent of racial hatred permeating in modern Germany. Through the decades we've seen films featuring re-creations of 1940s Germany, but it's doubly unsettling to see it in modern times — it can happen here. ★★★ VHS: $9.99

The Informer

(1935, 91 min, US, John Ford) *Victor McLaglen, Heather Angel, Wallace Ford.* An eerie, dreamlike quality pervades director Ford's film of a dull-witted man who informs on his Irish Republican Army comrade in 1922 Dublin. McLaglen won the Best Actor Oscar for his haunting portrayal of the pathetic misfit; Ford won for Best Director, Dudley Nichols for Best Screenplay and Max Steiner for Best Score. An evocative examination of the human condition. ★★★★

Inherit the Wind

(1960, 127 min, US, Stanley Kramer) *Spencer Tracy, Fredric March, Dick York, Gene Kelly, Florence Eldridge, Harry Morgan.* Tracy and March, possibly America's two greatest film actors, both give tour-de-force performances in this outstanding adaptation of the Lawrence-Lee stage play, based on the infamous Scopes Monkey Trial of 1925. Though the names are changed, Tracy is Clarence Darrow and March is William Jennings Bryan, each on opposite sides of the court when a teacher (York) is arrested and tried for teaching the theories of Darwin. One of the finest, most literate screenplays to grace an American film, the enthralling court sequences are all the more topical today as the battle of separation between Church and State continues. (Remade in 1999) ★★★★ DVD Letterbox: $14.99

Inherit the Wind

(1999, 113 min, US, Daniel Petrie) *Jack Lemmon, George C. Scott, Lane Smith, Tom Everett Scott, Piper Laurie, Beau Bridges.* A made-for-TV remake of the classic Spencer Tracy-Fredric March 1960 drama, this adaptation of the Lawrence-Lee stage play does a fine job in adhering to the original text, but it just misses the mark as great theatre in comparison to the brilliant original. Giving two performances befitting their status as acting giants, Lemmon and Scott essay the roles of two opposing lawyers caught in the middle of the hysteria of the Scopes Trial, in which a teacher in Tennessee is put on trial for teaching the theories of Darwin. A timely and timeless work brought lovingly to the small screen. ★★★

The Inheritance

(1977, 105 min, Italy, Mauro Bolognini) *Anthony Quinn, Dominique Sanda, Fabio Testi.* This well-acted drama, a bit trashy for European standards, features a sexy Sanda as a coolly calculating woman who marries into a wealthy family and begins a steamy affair with her dying father-in-law (Quinn). A titillating and erotic video find. Sanda won the Best Actress Award at the Cannes Film Festival for her role as the money-hungry vixen. ★★½

The Inheritors

(1999, 94 min, Austria/Germany, Stefan Ruzowitzky) *Simon Schwarz, Sophie Rois, Lars Rudolph, Julia Gschnitzer, Ulrich Wildgruber.* A bittersweet fable, *The Inheritors* is a rural period piece about greed and integrity set in 1930s Austria. When a tyrannical farmer dies, he leaves his property to the peasant workers with the decree that they can kill each other fighting over it. While they do struggle among themselves, they ultimately realize that they must work together to keep the village's other landowners from taking their farm away. The story is simple, but it is also quite powerful, as the inheritors defend what they have been given by any means necessary. Bathed in a golden hue, director Ruzowitzky's underdog drama is occasionally slow going, but it is beautifully told nonetheless. (German with English subtitles) ★★★ DVD: $27.99

The Inkwell

(1994, 112 min, US, Matty Rich) *Larenz Tate, Joe Morton, Suzzanne Douglas, Glynn Turman, Mary Alice.* From the director of *Straight Out of Brooklyn* comes this gentle black version of *Summer of '42*. Tate plays Drew, a naïve 16-year-old with a killer smile from the wrongish side of the tracks who comes of age during the summer of '76 when he is visiting his highbrow relatives at a ritzy (and primarily black) beach in Martha's Vineyard. On the arty side of an Afterschool Special, *The Inkwell* is not a particularly original film, but Tate gives such a fresh, guileless performance that one can forgive some of its more artificial moments. The bell-bottoms and mega-Afros are a must for all '70s enthusiasts. ★★½ DVD: $9.99, VHS: $9.99

The Inner Circle

(1991, 139 min, US, Andrei Konchalovsky) *Tom Hulce, Lolita Davidovich, Bob Hoskins.* A fascinating and moody examination of life under Stalin in 1930s Moscow. In this true story, Hulce is a newlywed and loyal party member who is whisked from his home on his wedding day to the great halls of the Kremlin. It is there he begins service to Stalin as his personal projectionist. Politically naïve, it is during this regime that Hulce slowly becomes aware of the corruption and paranoia running rampant within the walls of Russia's party headquarters. The first American film to actually lens at the Kremlin, *The Inner Circle* — which refers to Stalin's elite group of companions — uses its Russian locations to better effect than did *The Russia House*. However, like that film, its locale sometimes seems to dwarf the narrative. ★★★

Innerspace

(1987, 120 min, US, Joe Dante) *Dennis Quaid, Martin Short, Meg Ryan, Kevin McCarthy, Fiona Lewis.* All hell breaks loose when a miniaturized Quaid is accidentally injected into the body of highly manic Short. Hunted down by a pair of evil industrialists (hilariously portrayed by McCarthy and Lewis), the two hit the road where they develop a working relationship: with Quaid giving the orders and Short, the hypochondriac hero, responding with outrageous pratfalls. The film won an Academy Award for Special Effects. ★★★ DVD Letterbox: $19.99, VHS: $9.99

Innocence

(2001, 96 min, Australia, Paul Cox) *Julia Blake, Charles "Bud" Tingwell, Terry Norris, Kristien Van Pellicom, Kenny Aernouts, Norman Kaye.* In this wonderful drama from director Cox, a widowed elderly man rekindles a romance with an old flame, who happens to still be married. When her dullard of a husband senses of the affair, it forces him to reevaluate his marriage — and his entire life — while he ultimately must choose between the men. A heartfelt, dramatically rich love story, *Innocence* provides a fascinating look at one woman's choice between doing the "right thing" (finishing out her years albeit without true love) or follow her heart. It's a fresh surprise to see seniors unabashedly enjoying healthy sex lives on screen for once, without condescending titters, and the acting, editing and writing are across-the-board terrific. Though the finale slightly disappoints, the end result is an emotionally rewarding affair. ★★★½ DVD Letterbox: $29.99, VHS: $102.99

Innocence Unprotected

(1968, 78 min, Yugoslavia, Dusan Makavejev) *Dragoljub Aleksic, Ana Milosavljevic.* This inventive and, at times, hilarious film-within-a-film reunites and interviews the cast of Yugoslavia's first talky: a tacky, ridiculously naïve melodrama. While the stars dreamily reminisce, we watch excerpts from the 1942 film, a story about a seemingly brainless woman saddled with a wicked stepmother and a lecherous older suitor who falls in love with a muscleman/daredevil. Makavejev mischievously inter-mixes footage of the horror of the war with the interviews and the film as he shows the illusion of fame and power. (Serbo-Croatian with English subtitles) ★★★ VHS: $24.99

The Innocent

(1976, 115 min, Italy, Luchino Visconti) *Giancarlo Giannini, Laura Antonelli, Jennifer O'Neill.* Visconti's final masterpiece is set in turn-of-the-century Italy and features a fine cast, sumptuous photography and stunning sets and costumes. Giannini is a chauvinistic aristocrat who ignores his beautiful and loving wife (Antonelli) in order to pursue his adulterous affair with his mistress (O'Neill). Revenge is sweet, however, as the lonely and frustrated wife takes on a lover and turns the tables on her insensitive husband. (Italian with English subtitles) ★★★★

The Innocent

(1995, 119 min, GB, John Schlesinger) *Anthony Hopkins, Isabella Rossellini, Campbell Scott, Hart Bochner, Ronald Nitschke.* In one of director Schlesinger's lesser outings, the historic tearing down of the Berlin Wall sets in motion a bittersweet recollection of Cold War romance and intrigue. Scott plays a British telephone specialist who begins working for the Americans in their attempt to tap into Russian phone lines (by tunneling into East Berlin). Hopkins (bad accent and all) is the brash Yank commander overseeing the project who must contend with possible conspiracy when Scott falls for a local German woman (Rossellini). The espionage aspect of the film is quite compelling, but as a romance the film sags. And though the film features good period design, Schlesinger's sluggish pace helps detract from the story. ★★ DVD: $19.99, VHS: $9.99

Innocent Blood

(1992, 114 min, US, John Landis) *Anne Parillaud, Anthony LaPaglia, Robert Loggia, Don Rickles.* Landis returns to *American Werewolf in London* territory with this anemic comic horror film which could be dubbed *A French Vampire in Pittsburgh*. Parillaud plays a bloodsucker with a social conscience: she attacks only criminals for her blood lust. But when she crosses paths with mob kingpin Loggia and undercover cop LaPaglia, things go awry. As the mobster-turned-vampire, Loggia brings such needed vitality to an otherwise weary film that for a while, it seems he may turn it around. Much of the blame goes to Michael Wolk's thin screenplay; and to the ill pairing of leads Parillaud and LaPaglia — Lily and Herman Munster generated more sparks. There's lots of blood and killings, though. ★★ DVD: $14.99, VHS: $9.99

Innocent Lies

(1995, 88 min, GB, Patrick DeWolfe) *Gabrielle Anwar, Stephen Dorff, Adrian Dunbar, Joanna Lumley.* An absorbing and well-made period piece about a London detective (Dunbar) who is dispatched to a French fishing village, circa WWII, to investigate the mysterious death of his predecessor. He soon becomes entangled in the Freudian affairs of a brother and sister who love each other entirely too much. Boasting a terrific evocation of the times, the film also features a stand-out performance by Lumley as the bitch goddess mother of the incestuous pair. DeWolfe's parable on the price of love weaves its threads of anti-Semitism and incest into an Agatha Christie-like mystery. ★★★

An Innocent Man

(1989, 113 min, US, Peter Yates) *Tom Selleck, F. Murray Abraham, Laila Robins.* In this ordinary, contrived innocent-man-behind-bars prison drama, Selleck is a successful aerospace engineer and loving husband who is framed by two cardboard-cutout dishonest undercover cops. Once incarcerated, he learns, with the kindly help of "lifer" Abraham, that prison can be hell. This sort of thing has been done for decades, and done a helluva lot better. ★ DVD: $9.99

The Innocent Sleep

(1997, 97 min, GB, Scott Michell) *Rupert Graves, Annabella Sciorra, Michael Gambon, Graham Crowden, Franco Nero, John Hannah.* A routine programmer about a homeless man, Alan Terry (Graves), who becomes the hunted when he witnesses a mob hit. Seeing one of the killers in uniform, he tells his story to reporter Billie Hayman (a very mannish Sciorra). As Billie fact-checks his case, Alan learns that her journalism ethics — she believes in revealing her sources — have caused previous informers to commit suicide. Unable to trust anyone, Alan decides to mete out justice himself. Director Michell has all the ingredients for a good B-movie thriller, but this bland film lacks both atmosphere and tension. Only Gambon as one of the killers seems to relish his part, and even he occasionally appears to be sleepwalking. ★★ VHS: $102.99

Innocent Victim

(1988, 89 min, GB, Giles Foster) *Helen Shaver, Lauren Bacall, Colin Firth, Paul McGann.* A dull thriller about a best-selling author (Shaver) whose grief over the loss of her three-year-old son is complicated when her mentally unbalanced mother

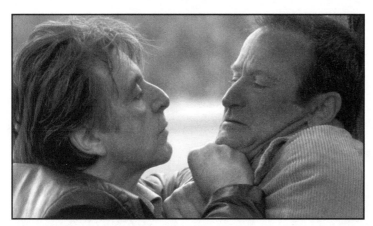

Al Pacino accosts psycho Robin Williams in *Insomnia*

(Bacall) kidnaps a small boy to replace him. Based on a novel by Ruth Rendell. (aka: *Tree of Hands*) ★ VHS: $79.99

Insect Woman

(1963, 123 min, Japan, Shohei Imamura) *Sachiko Hidari, Yitsuko Yoshimura.* The sexual manipulation, subjugation and exploitation of women is the hard-hitting theme in this multiaward-winning film that chronicles 45 years in the harsh life of a woman. Beginning as a child, where she is abused by her stepfather, through her illegitimate pregnancy and finally to her life in a sordid brothel, the film, like the director's *Black Rain*, displays little sentimentality in fleshing out this gripping but somber tale. (Japanese with English subtitles) ★★★

Inserts

(1976, 117 min, US, John Byrum) *Richard Dreyfuss, Bob Hoskins, Jessica Harper, Veronica Cartwright.* Dreyfuss is a fading silent screen star in 1930s Hollywood who turns to making blue movies to supplement his income. Despite its intriguing premise, a lackluster screenplay makes little of the scenario. ★★

Inside

(1996, 94 min, US/GB, Arthur Penn) *Nigel Hawthorne, Eric Stoltz, Louis Gossett, Jr., Ian Roberts.* A claustrophobic prison drama about human rights abuses in South Africa, *Inside* is an intense and at times agonizing viewing experience. The film deals with the lies and transgressions perpetrated by Col. Kruger (Hawthorne), an interrogator who brutalizes Marty (Stoltz), a university professor he suspects of terrorism and treason. Held in a sparse cell, Marty communicates with and observes the prison's other inmates through a peephole while he is tormented physically and mentally. *Inside* also depicts the investigation by one of these prisoners (Gossett) of Kruger's unjust treatment of Marty ten years after his incarceration. Effective and well made, the film tends to suffer from occasional staginess. ★★★

Inside Monkey Zetterland

(1993, 98 min, US, Jefery Levy) *Steven Antin, Patricia Arquette, Sofia Coppola, Sandra Bernhard, Ricki Lake, Rupert Everett, Debi Mazar, Katherine Helmond, Bo Hopkins, Martha Plimpton, Tate Donovan.* With a cast that seems to come straight from the pages of *Details* magazine, *Inside Monkey Zetterland* seems to care more about who is actually in the film rather than telling a story. The film revolves around an ex-child star (writer-producer Antin) whose lesbian sister has left her pregnant lover and moved into his house owned by their soap opera star mother. When radical terrorists come onto the scene, things start getting a little convoluted. It occasionally has a quirky charm, and features a few good performances. ★★

Inside the Third Reich

(1982, 242 min, US, Marvin J. Chomsky) *Rutger Hauer, Derek Jacobi, John Gielgud, Blythe Danner, Ian Holm, Trevor Howard, Viveca Lindfors, Renée Soutendijk.* Superior made-for-TV teledrama based on the autobiography of Hitler's confidant Albert Speer. Hauer stars as the brilliant architect who works his way through the ranks of 1930s Germany to become Hitler's right-hand man. Jacobi is sensational as the maniacal dictator. ★★★½

The Insider

(1999, 157 min, US, Michael Mann) *Al Pacino, Russell Crowe, Christopher Plummer, Diane Venora, Philip Baker Hall, Michael Gambon, Lindsay Crouse, Bruce McGill, Rip Torn, Debi Mazar.* A powerful drama of heroism, corruption and corporate manipulation, *The Insider* is the true story of what led to the airing of the groundbreaking "60 Minutes" story of fraud by the tobacco companies. Reminiscent in both content and execution of *All the President's Men*, the film grabs you by the throat in the very beginning and never lets go. In a sensational performance, Crowe is Jeffrey Wigand, a former top-level scientist for Brown & Williamson tobacco company who blows the whistle on a conspiracy by Big Tobacco to make cigarettes more addictive. Pacino is dynamic as Lowell Bergman, a "60 Minutes" producer who convinces Wigand to put himself on the line for the story of the decade. That CBS isn't there to protect him makes for outstanding drama. Director Mann approaches this more as a detective story to an American tragedy rather than a full-scale attack on tobacco, which would have been too easy a target. *The Insider* is gutsy, stylish, compelling storytelling. ★★★★ DVD: $19.99, VHS Letterboxed: $9.99

Insignificance

(1985, 110 min, GB, Nicolas Roeg) *Gary Busey, Tony Curtis, Theresa Russell, Michael Emil, Will Sampson.* The always adventurous Roeg's apocalyptic farce is a surreal and sexually charged black comedy that records the hot summer night in 1954 that Marilyn Monroe and Albert Einstein spent together. Russell and Emil are the blonde and the brain, Busey and Curtis costar as Joe DiMaggio and Sen. Joe McCarthy, respectively. ★★★ DVD: $14.99

Insomnia

(1997, 97 min, Norway, Erik Skjoldbjærg) *Stellan Skarsgård, Sverre Anker Ousdal, Bjørn Floberg, Gisken Armand.* A crack Swedish detective (Skarsgård) is called to a Norwegian town above the Arctic Circle — where there's no darkness for six months at a time — to investigate the murder of a high school girl. A potentially routine case becomes a languid nightmare for the policeman, as guilt over a major screwup and his insomnia due to the constant sunlight slowly drive him nuts. Moody, stylish, slow-paced but engrossing, *Insomnia* is well directed, with many beautiful, composed shots, creepy moments, and a constant tone of dread and unease. A tense film noir, with psychology and sunlight substituting for shoot-outs and shadows. (In Norwegian and Swedish with English subtitles) (Remade in 2002) ★★★ DVD Criterion Collection: $29.99, VHS: $19.99

Insomnia

(2002, 118 min, US, Christopher Nolan) *Al Pacino, Robin Williams, Hilary Swank, Martin Donovan, Maura Tierney, Paul Dooley, Nicky Katt.* In a picturesque land where there is only daylight, an honored policeman becomes victim to the environment as well as his own momentary lapse of judgment. The eventual, gradual disintegration of his mind and mores form the framework of an exceedingly effective psychological thriller that is every bit as intelligent as it is taut and gripping. Based on the 1997 Norwegian film of the same name, *Insomnia* stars Pacino as L.A. detective Will Dormer, who with his partner (Donovan) travels to the small Alaskan town of Nightmute to aid in the investigation of a possible serial killing. In the pursuit of a suspect, a terrible accident occurs, one which pits an increasingly sleep-deprived Dormer in a relentless game of cat and mouse with the murderer (nicely underplayed by Williams). In his third feature, *Memento* director Nolan leaves little doubt as to his talent as a storyteller and artist. He's maintained the original's sense of atmosphere and psychological collapse, while at the same time incorporating a personal style that is wholly his own. Nolan has also steered Pacino into giving one of the best performances of his career — the actor has rarely been this persuasively subtle, and brings nuance and a tortured resignation to the role. ★★★½ DVD Letterbox: $19.99, DVD Pan & Scan: $19.99, VHS: $14.99

Inspector Gadget

(1999, 78 min, US, David Kellogg) *Mathew Broderick, Rupert Everett, Joely Fisher, Michelle Trachtenberg, Michael G. Hagerty, Chery Oteri, Dabney Coleman, Andy Dick.* A film that seems to be made of the very machinery that embodies the title character, *Inspector Gadget* — based on the cartoon series — plays like an extended trailer that features mere fragments of a real, big-budget movie. Plot covers the death of delivery boy Broderick and his rebirth as Gadget; later, he must fight the evil Claw (a wasted Everett) who has built an evil Gadget clone. The Inspector has the help of a Gadgetmobile, seemingly an annoying relative of Jar-Jar Binks. You'll need the help of aspirin, as the scenes blink by (the film is about 68 minutes until credits roll) interspersed with irritating product placements. A cynical cash-in by Disney. ★ DVD: $19.99, VHS: $14.99

The Inspector General

(1949, 102 min, US, Henry Koster) *Danny Kaye, Walter Slezak, Barbara Bates, Elsa Lanchester.* Kaye lets loose as an inept elixir salesman who is mistaken for the feared Inspector General by a small country village — whose citizens will do anything to please him. Plenty of laughs and Kaye gets to do a patter song or two. ★★★ VHS: $19.99

Inspiration

(1931, 74 min, US, Clarence Brown) *Greta Garbo, Robert Montgomery.* Garbo's third talkie is a minor romantic drama about love and sacrifice. Garbo's in her element as a Parisian artists' model whose past seems to get in the way with her new relationship with student Montgomery. Though not one of her best, even a routine Garbo effort is worth a look. ★★ VHS: $19.99

Instinct

(1999, 120 min, US, Jon Amiel) *Anthony Hopkins, Cuba Gooding, Jr., Donald Sutherland, Maura Tierney, George Dzundza.* Hopkins returns to Hannibal Lecter territory with this hodgepodge of a thriller playing Ethan Powell, a brilliant scientist and primate expert who went psychotic and murdered two park rangers in the wilds of the Rwandan jungle. Gooding is Dr. Theo Caulder, the stateside psychiatrist looking to make a name for himself who is assigned to find out why Powell committed murder. The lethargic pacing is offset by the heroic acting of the two leads, but even these two Academy Award winners can only do so much with a weak script. ★★ DVD: $14.99, VHS: $9.99

Intacto

(2001, 108 min, Spain, Juan Carlos Fresnadillo) *Max von Sydow, Leonardo Sbaraglia, Eusebio Poncela, Mónica López, Antonio Dechent.* Quite a heady experience, *Intacto* has the potential to both engage and confuse with its intricate weblike story and multilayered flights of fancy. Using luck as its central theme, *Intacto*'s lead characters are endowed with the ability to cheat misfortune, stealing luck from those around them. Luck, in and of itself, becomes a commodity, bartered, traded and thieved like cash. One lucky thief, the sole survivor of a very deadly plane crash, gets recruited to join a group of underground players in dangerous games of chance. Russian roulette and blindfolded flights through the woods are involved, creating set pieces that fluctuate between intriguing and absurd. Fresnadillo, with his first feature, shows promise as a moody and haunting director, evoking dread, suspense and thoughtfulness along the way. But the complex, meandering story of *Intacto* sometimes threatens to remain anything *but* intact. (Spanish with English subtitles) ★★★ DVD Subtitled or Dubbed:$24.99

Interiors

(1978, 93 min, US, Woody Allen) *Diane Keaton, Mary Beth Hurt, Geraldine Page, E.G. Marshall, Maureen Stapleton, Kristin Griffith.* Allen's homage to Ingmar Bergman meticulously details the misunderstandings and growing collapse of an upper-middle-class family. Page and Marshall are the repressive parents; Keaton, Hurt and Griffith are the rival siblings; and Stapleton is the "ridiculous" woman who breathes new life into their anguished lives. ★★★½ DVD: $19.99

Intermezzo

(1936, 91 min, Sweden, Gustaf Molander) *Ingrid Bergman, Gosta Ekman, Inga Tidblad.* Bergman is ravishing as an aspiring pianist whose career is interrupted when she falls tragically in love with a world-famous pianist. Despite the fact that he is already married, the two run off together in their interlude of love. Holding up remarkably well over the years, this entertaining love story was seen by producer David O. Selznick, who immediately brought the young Bergman to Hollywood and remade this feature in 1939, the film that launched her international career. (Swedish with English subtitles) ★★★ DVD: $29.99, VHS: $29.99

Intermezzo

(1939, 70 min, US, Gregory Ratoff) *Ingrid Bergman, Leslie Howard, Edna Best.* Bergman repeats the role from the 1936 Swedish romantic drama of the same name, which brought her international acclaim. Bergman plays a musical prodigy involved with her mentor (Howard). A beautifully crafted love story. ★★★ VHS: $14.99

Internal Affairs

(1990, 115 min, US, Mike Figgis) *Richard Gere, Andy Garcia, Laurie Metcalf, William Baldwin.* Brutally realistic violence, potent acting and intense psychological game playing combine to make this tough cop thriller a thoroughly engaging psychological thriller. Gere sinks his teeth into the role of a decorated but menacingly corrupt cop who locks horns with Garcia, an internal affairs officer assigned to investigate wrongdoing on the L.A. police force. Garcia, a tightass "good cop" is teamed up with a lesbian partner (Metcalf) as they attempt to untangle a trail of payoffs, extortion and murder, all leading to the increasingly deranged and dangerous Gere. ★★★ DVD: $24.99, VHS: $9.99

International House

(1933, 72 min, US, Edward Sutherland) *W.C. Fields, Rudy Vallee, George Burns, Gracie Allen, Cab Calloway, Bela Lugosi.* A sometimes hilarious and peculiar episodic comedy that has a Chinese scientist inventing TV, sending a wild assortment of interested buyers to the Orient (including Fields and Burns). ★★★

Interrogation

(1982, 118 min, Poland, Richard Bugajski) *Krystyna Jarda, Janusz Gajos.* Banned for almost eight years by the Polish Communist government, this scathing study of one woman's harassment and torture at the hands of her own government was finally released in 1990 with the star of the film, Jarda, winning the Best Actress Award at Cannes. After a one-night stand with a military officer, a cabaret singer is imprisoned by the secret police, without ever being informed of her alleged crime. For the next five years, she is forced to become a survivor and not a victim in her efforts to maintain her dignity and sanity in the face of an oppressive Stalinist power. (Polish with English subtitles) ★★★½ VHS: $24.99

Intersection

(1994, 98 min, US, Mark Rydell) *Richard Gere, Sharon Stone, Lolita Davidovich, Martin Landau.* Yet another senseless American rehash of a French film, this time Claude Sautet's *Les Choses de la Vie.* Gere plays a whiny architect involved in a car accident. As he looks back at his life, the story concentrates on his relationships with his wife (Stone) and journalist mistress (Davidovich). Though Gere has in recent years acquired a newfound maturity and confidence on-screen, his presence alone does not

warrant a remake. Stone gives the film's best performance as his beautiful but cold wife. ★★ DVD Letterbox: $14.99, VHS: $9.99

The Interview

(1998, 103 min, Australia, Craig Monahan) *Tony Martin, Hugo Weaving.* A sleeping man is rudely awakened by police breaking his door down at five in the morning. He's subsequently brought to an interrogation room at the station, and the majority of the film is the cat-and-mouse interview between the suspect and the police officer. A compelling mystery with a few twists and surprises, *The Interview* is fairly evenhanded in its view of police procedural: on the one hand, the suspect's rights are certainly being violated, but on the other, the officers' strong-arm tactics may be ridding the streets of a vicious serial killer. Who's right? For that you have to wait until the ending. That finale may be a little reactionary, but what comes before it is competent and often clever. ★★★ DVD: $19.99, VHS: $14.99

Interview with the Assassin

(2003, 85 min, US, Neil Burger) *Raymond J. Barry, Dylan Haggerty.* A persuasive mock-documentary, *Interview with the Assassin* purports to be the confession of the second gunman (on the infamous grassy knoll) who shot JFK. Respected character actor Barry finally gets a well-deserved lead role, and he runs with it, giving a restrained, mannered performance that is creepily effective. The film feels at times like *The Blair Witch Project* for JFK-conspiracy buffs; there are many eerie, frightening moments involving suspicious shadows on a home security tape, sinister phone calls and the like, and the whole film maintains an unsettling tone of paranoia. The ending is (perhaps inevitably) a bit of a letdown, but until that point, this is a solid, at times fascinating thriller, with an exceptional performance at its center. ★★★ DVD: $24.99, VHS: $102.99

Interview with the Vampire

(1994, 122 min, US, Neil Jordan) *Tom Cruise, Brad Pitt, Christian Slater, Antonio Banderas, Stephen Rea, Kirsten Dunst.* Rich in atmosphere and bristling with sexual tension and suspense, this highly stylized adaptation of Anne Rice's classic vampire story was the subject of much second guessing before its release. The biggest controversy was the casting of Cruise as Lestat — happily, he acquits himself nicely and is handsomely complimented by the tormented Pitt as Louis. Told in flashback, the story recounts the life of grieving widower and 18th-century plantation owner Louis who bids adieu to his beloved blue sky of morning for the dark shadows of night when Lestat makes him one of his own. As Louis desperately clings to the last vestiges of his humanity, he engages in a battle of conscience and will with his mentor Lestat. Though bloody and violent, the film relies on the psychological makeup of its characters for its power, and detail to time and place is exemplary. ★★★½ DVD: $19.99, VHS: $14.99

Intervista

(1992, 108 min, Italy, Federico Fellini) *Marcello Mastroianni, Anita Ekberg.* Whereas *Amarcord* explores the director's childhood, *8½* his midlife creative crisis and *Fellini's Roma* the city he loves, *Intervista* is the master's nostalgic look at his youthful days at the famed Cinecitta — the film studio where he made all his films. Touchingly evocative and bubbling with magical stories from his past as well as capturing the director at work today, the film is Fellini's valentine to the movies and the filmmak-

I

ing process. Opening with his return to Cinecitta to begin work on his film version of Franz Kafka's "Amerika," a Japanese TV crew doggedly interviews him, prompting the director to recall his life-changing first visit to Cinecitta. That visit, presented as a film-within-a-film, features a wide-eyed Fellini who, on assignment to interview a beautiful star, stumbles across a fantastic film city bustling with excitement, chaos and magic. A joyous celebration — all done in the director's ebullient and seductive style. (Italian with English subtitles) ★★★½ DVD: $24.99, VHS: $9.99

Intimate Relations

(1997, 105 min, GB, Philip Goodhew) *Julie Walters, Rupert Graves, Laura Sadler, Matthew Walker.* "Inspired by a true story," this stylized tragicomedy flows in the same vein as *Heavenly Creatures* and is reminiscent of Mike Leigh's works in its theme of family traps down Britain way. Here a merchant marine (Graves) returns home to his brother's town, and is taken in — in every sense — by an outwardly proper, fiftyish woman, Mrs. Beasley (Walters), who instructs him to call her "mum." Her pubescent daughter and emasculated husband complicate the unusual relationship. The sustained tension comes from wondering exactly what will happen, though the visual symbols point to the general outcome quite clearly. Walters' brilliant, nuanced portrayal of the conflicted predator/victim subtly gets us on her side. *Intimate Relations* sells itself as a black comedy, and the cringe scenes could make even a jaded viewer uncomfortable. ★★★ VHS: $102.99

An Intimate Story

(1983, 95 min, Israel, Nadar Levithan) *Chava Alberstein, Alex Peleg.* Set in the close confines of a kibbutz, this engrossing drama focuses on the problems of a childless couple who have been married for 10 years. Their shattered dreams, as well as the lack of privacy in the "extended family" atmosphere of the kibbutz, force them to reevaluate their relationship. Charming but low-key. (Hebrew with English subtitles) ★★★ VHS: $79.99

Into the Arms of Strangers: Stories of the Kindertransport

(2000, 117 min, US/GB, Mark Jonathan Harris) *Narrated by:, Judi Dench.* With all the various documentaries and narratives that have examined the Holocaust, it would seem there would be little new to convey about this dark chapter in history that hadn't already been told. Remarkably, there is. Combining rare archival footage and poignant remembrances, the Academy Award-winning *Into the Arms of Strangers* is an exemplary documentary that looks at the lives of a few of the more than 10,000 Jewish children who escaped Hitler's grasp. Leaving their families at young ages, these children were (mostly) sent to foster homes in England, where they stayed for the duration of the war. The stories are touching without being sentimentalized, and underscore the breadth and scope of the Nazi threat and the fallout of anti-Semitism. *Into the Arms of Strangers* is a quite powerful, heart-rending experience whose dramas move on a most human scale. ★★★★ DVD: $24.99, VHS: $19.99

Into the Night

(1985, 115 min, US, John Landis) *Jeff Goldblum, Michelle Pfeiffer, David Bowie, Richard Farnsworth, Dan Aykroyd.* Landis' off-center and very engaging comic thriller stars Goldblum as a likable Average Joe who gets tangled with beautiful Pfeiffer and Iranian terrorists. There's a good supporting cast and cameos by 12 noted film directors. ★★★ DVD Letterbox: $14.99, VHS: $9.99

Into the West

(1993, 97 min, Ireland, Mike Newell) *Gabriel Byrne, Ellen Barkin, Colm Meaney.* This harshly realistic and heartwrenching film begins in the urban squalor of Dublin. The story tells the tale of two boys who rescue a mystical white horse from an evil businessman and embark on a journey "into the west" of underdeveloped Ireland. In an almost magical escape, they elude the police across the countryside and come to terms with the death of their mother. Byrne gives a moving performance as the boys' father, a misplaced "traveler," who does his own grieving as he searches for his sons. Although the breathtaking ending leaves some loose ends, each character is spiritually and emotionally matured by their experience. Written by Jim Sheridan. ★★★½ DVD: $19.99

Into the Woods

(1987, 154 min, US, James Lapine) *Bernadette Peters, Joanna Gleason, Chip Zien, Tom Aldredge, Robert Westenberg.* Stephen Sondheim's astute and witty lyrics complement his melodious tunes in this effervescent musical that blends several children's fairy tales to produce one intertwining musical fable. Filmed from a live stage performance, the production features the original Broadway cast bringing to life the stories and characters from "Cinderella," "Jack and the Beanstalk," "Rapunzel" and "Little Red Riding Hood." Gleason (who deservedly won a Tony Award for her vibrant performance) and Zien are a baker and his wife who set out to reverse the spell cast on them by the witch next door (the splendid Peters), thereby meeting other fairy tale characters. Sondheim and author-director Lapine expand on the moralistic and mortality themes inherent in fairy tales creating a sumptuous union of comedy, dancing, music and myth. Deceptively innocent for children but complex and intuitive for adults. ★★★½ DVD: $29.99, VHS: $19.99

Intolerable Cruelty

(2003, 100 min, US, Joel Coen) *George Clooney, Catherine Zeta-Jones, Geoffrey Rush, Cedric the Entertainer, Edward Herrmann, Richard Jenkins, Billy Bob Thornton.* Sort of a companion piece to their screwball farce *O Brother, Where Art Thou?*, the Coen brothers switch gears ever so slightly with this often hilarious, sophisticated screwball romantic comedy. If *Brother* was akin to *Sullivan's Travels*, then this is closer to *The Philadelphia Story* and *The Lady Eve.* Sublime romance and comedy is the result no matter which film inspired it. Clooney (can this guy be any more dashing?) plays Miles Massey, a high-powered divorce attorney who meets his match in the luscious gold-digger Marylin (the gorgeous Zeta-Jones), whose plans for a quick divorce settlement from her rich hubby get somewhat mangled by Massey. Then things really start to get screwy as romance, betrayal, set-ups and hired assassins — all in good and humorous taste — enter the picture. One of the very few post-1960s films to capture the cadence and smarts of the genre (*What's Up, Doc?* remains the bellwether), this is good fun, has great laughs and is a nice reminder that funny can be smart, too. ★★★ DVD: $29.99

Intolerance

(1916, 123 min, US, D.W. Griffith) *Lillian Gish, Mae Marsh, Constance Talmadge.* Griffith's lavish spectacle is a landmark achievement in silent film-making. Following the popular success of *Birth of a Nation*, but stung by charges of racism, Griffith's theme in this classic is man's inhumanity to man. This intolerance and bigotry is illustrated in four interlocking tales from history: transpiring in ancient Babylon, biblical Judea, medieval France and modern America. Innovative film techniques, including the brilliant intercutting of the four stories, create an exciting climax. ★★★★ DVD: $29.99, VHS: $29.99

The Intruder

(1975, 98 min, France, Serge Leroy) *Jean-Louis Trintignant, Mireille Darc, Bernard Fresson.* En route from Rome to Paris, a man and his young stepson are terrorized — for no apparent reason — by an unknown killer who is relentless in his pursuit and lethal to anyone coming between himself and his targets. A Hitchcockian suspense thriller. (French with English subtitles) ★★★

Intruder in the Dust

(1949, 87 min, US, Clarence Brown) *Claude Jarman, Jr., Juano Hernandez, David Brian, Porter Hall.* Released in the same year as *Lost Boundaries* and *Pinky*, two equally acclaimed social dramas examining racial prejudice, this is an exemplary, patient adaptation of William Faulkner's novel. The story is seen through the eyes of a white protagonist — as are films decades later — here a young boy (Jarman) from the South. There's a chilling, business-as-usual tone to the film's opening as the citizens of a small town gather to ceremoniously witness the lynching of accused murderer Hernandez. Only four outcasts, including Jarman, come to his defense as the film balances non-preachy social observations with a crackerjack detective story. Hernandez brings unflinching dignity to the role of the alleged killer. An important cornerstone in the development of American cinema's social conscience. ★★★★ VHS: $19.99

Intruso (The Intruder)

(1993, 90 min, Spain, Vicente Aranda) *Victoria Abril, Antonio Valero, Imanol Arias.* When Luisa

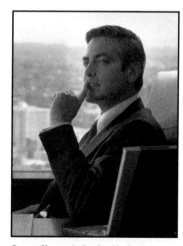

George Clooney in *Intolerable Cruelty*

(Abril) discovers her childhood friend and long-lost first husband Angel (Arias) roaming the streets one day, she takes him home to her family. Angel fascinates Luisa's two children, but her husband Ramiro (Valero) is less thrilled with the intruder's presence. The story, which shifts its focus between Luisa's forbidden desire, Ramiro's increasing jealousy and Angel's obsessive love, is unnecessarily complicated with some metaphysical nonsense about the characters' past and present as well as Angel's impending death. Aranda's film is curiously detached in its examination of these thwarted characters. Despite some steamy love scenes, *Intruso*'s lack of dramatic tension will leave most viewers cold. (Spanish with English subtitles) ★★ VHS: $79.99

Invaders from Mars

(1953, 78 min, US, William Cameron Menzies) *Helena Carter, Arthur Franz.* Slick sci-fi tale about a young boy who witnesses an alien craft land and tries to convince those around him it really exists — those not already possessed by the otherworldly visitors, that is. Lots of fun, and a heck of a sight better than the 1986 remake. ★★★ DVD 50th Anniversary: $24.99

Invaders from Mars

(1986, 102 min, US, Tobe Hooper) *Karen Black, Hunter Carson, Louise Fletcher, Timothy Bottoms, Bud Cort.* Inferior remake of the 1953 classic sci-fi film about a young boy who tries to convince those around him that a Martian attack is under way. Real-life mom and son Black and Carson play mom and son, and Fletcher continues her patented villainous/strange character as a dastardly teacher. ★½ DVD: $14.99

Invasion of the Bee Girls

(1974, 85 min, US, Denis Sanders) *Victoria Vetri, William Smith.* When the men of a small community are dying off due to excessive sexual activity, their wives are brought in for medical experimentation. In the lab, the women are irradiated, covered with bees and cocooned, where they emerge transformed into "Bee Girls." Written by Nicholas Meyer. ★★½

Invasion of the Body Snatchers

(1956, 80 min, US, Don Siegel) *Kevin McCarthy, Dana Wynter, Carolyn Jones, King Donovan.* Classic '50s sci-fi chiller about pod people taking over the bodies of a small California community. Director Siegel's low budget belies the film's extraordinary composition and unrelenting tension. Some at the time saw this as an allegory for Communism in the 1950s, but that notwithstanding, this is great genre filmmaking. (Remade in 1979 and in 1993 as *Body Snatchers*) ★★★★ DVD: $14.99, VHS Black & White: $9.99

Invasion of the Body Snatchers

(1979, 114 min, US, Philip Kaufman) *Donald Sutherland, Brooke Adams, Veronica Cartwright, Jeff Goldblum, Leonard Nimoy.* One of the few instances in which a remake does justice to the original. In this updated and refurbished sci-fi tale, director Kaufman creates an unusually effective sense of dread to chillingly tell the story of pod people taking over the bodies of the citizens of San Francisco. Gutwrenching tension and good performances, especially from Goldblum and the marvelous Cartwright, heighten the enjoyment of this genre masterwork. Just try to forget that haunting

The Ipcress File

(and unsettling) ending. And, yes, that *is* Kevin McCarthy (from the 1956 original) in the beginning. ★★★★ DVD: $14.99

Inventing the Abbotts

(1997, 105 min, US, Pat O'Connor) *Joaquin Phoenix, Liv Tyler, Will Patton, Billy Crudup, Jennifer Connelly, Kathy Baker.* A warm, thoughtful romantic drama whose story of class conflict and small-town pettiness brings to mind those Ross Hunter melodramas of the 1950s (in which this is set). The story is a nicely paced coming-of-age tale that follows the romantic exploits of two brothers from the wrong side of the tracks: Doug (Phoenix), the naïve narrator, and his smoother older brother Jacey (Crudup). Both brothers become involved with the three Abbott daughters, who come from the richest family in town. O'Connor captures the mindset of Eisenhower Americana while allowing his actors to fully explore the compelling characters deftly written by Ken Hixon. Phoenix and Crudup are both splendid, but best of all is Tyler as the youngest Abbott. She's a well-grounded romantic with stars in her eyes, passion to her breath, and purpose to her step. ★★★ DVD: $9.99, VHS: $9.99

Investigation

(1983, 116 min, France, Etienne Perier) *Victor Lanoux, Valerie Mairesse.* This action-packed murder mystery stars Lanoux as a rich, brooding man whose wife refuses his request to divorce him so that he may marry his pregnant mistress. The bloody murder that ensues is powerfully explored, with tantalizing and surprising results. (French with English subtitles) ★★★

The Invisible Man

(1933, 71 min, US, James Whale) *Claude Rains, Gloria Stuart, Una O'Connor, Dwight Frye.* Rains made his debut in Whale's bewitching comic horror tale based on the H.G. Wells novel. Playfully funny and featuring dandy special effects, the film casts Rains as a scientist who has discovered the secret to invisibility — at the cost of his own sanity. As the local snoop, O'Connor proves she can scream with the best of them. (Sequel: *The Invisible Man Returns*) ★★★

Invitation au Voyage

(1982, 95 min, France, Peter Del Monte) *Laurent Malet, Nina Scott.* An incestuous obsession between an introverted young ruffian and his punk rock star sister is rudely interrupted by her tragic death. With hypnotic images of her throbbing in his head, the teenager hits the road for points unknown. A striking rock score punctuates this visually arresting portrait of a young man's descent into dementia. (French with English subtitles) ★★★

Invitation to a Wedding

(1983, 89 min, GB, Joseph Brooks) *Ralph Richardson, John Guilgud, Paul Nicholas.* An American college student flies to England to attend a wedding and, during the dress rehearsal, is accidentally married to the bride by a bumbling country vicar (Richardson). The ensuing farce unfolds at a breakneck pace. Gielgud makes a hilarious appearance as an Englishman turned Southern evangelist. ★★★

The Ipcress File

(1965, 108 min, GB, Sidney J. Furie) *Michael Caine, Nigel Green.* Caine is impressive in his debut as Harry Palmer, an unemotional, Cockney crook turned secret agent. Considered the best of Len Deighton's Harry Palmer series, the film features a tense, complex plot revolving around a group of kidnapped scientists. This high-paced spy thriller is fascinating from start to finish. (Sequel: *Funeral in Berlin*) ★★★½ DVD: $24.99, VHS: $14.99

Iphigenia

(1977, 129 min, Greece, Michael Cacoyannis) *Irene Papas, Costa Kazakos.* Based on Euripides' tragedy, "Iphigenia in the Bay of Aulis," this epic story concerns the fate of man and the demands of the gods. Agamemnon's army, set to sail to war, is immobile because of the lack of winds. In his attempts to appease the gods, he accidentally slays a sacred deer. For this offense, Agamemnon is told to sacrifice his young daughter, Iphigenia. This story of political intrigue unfolds behind the backdrop of Greece's ancient ruins. (Greek with English subtitles) ★★★

Irezumi

(1983, 88 min, Japan, Yokhi Takabayashi) The Japanese art of tattooing is the focal point of this intriguing and erotic contemplation of freedom, commitment and passion. Complying with her lover's demand, a young woman submits to a long and painful procedure in which an intricate tattoo is etched across her entire back. The master illustrator's somewhat unusual technique is to have the woman engage in sexual intercourse with his teenage assistant during the tattooing in order to arouse and prepare the skin. (Japanese with English subtitles) ★★½

Iris

(2001, 90 min, GB, Richard Eyre) *Judi Dench, Jim Broadbent, Kate Winslet, Hugh Bonneville, Penelope Wilton, Juliet Aubrey, Samuel West, Timothy West, Eleanor Bron.* One of England's most prolific and celebrated writers of the 20th century, Iris Murdoch dedicated a lifetime to the written and spoken word, philosophy and education. In her 70s, however, the gifted author was diagnosed with Alzheimer's Disease. In the portrait of the ruthless disintegration of Alzheimer's, and a celebration of a unique, singular spirit, *Iris* gets it remarkably right. Dame Judi gives a superlative performance as Iris, bringing passion, intelligence and ultimately frailty to what undoubtedly was a force of nature. Based on two books by her husband John Bayley, brilliantly played by Oscar winner Broadbent, the film covers two periods in Iris' life: her courtship with the awkward Bayley, and the twilight of their relationship. As a love story it's truthful and vibrant, as a recollection of the passing of a great mind and a great love, it's heartbreaking. Winslet is outstanding as the younger Iris. ★★★½ DVD: $19.99, VHS: $9.99

Iris Blond

(1999, 113 min, Italy, Carlo Verdone) *Carlo Verdone, Claudia Gerini.* A pathetic musician/songwriter believes he's destined to be with gorgeous singer Iris Blond. So he dumps his shrewish, live-in girlfriend and her annoying dog and pursues a professional and personal relationship with the looker. Unfortunately, she's only interested in the former — and who could blame her, when the guy is such a whiny jerk? Alternately dull and cruel, the film's repellent characters and situations are equalled only by a queasy lack of warmth and humor. A depressing experience. (Italian with English subtitles) ★½ DVD: $14.99, VHS: $9.99

The Irishman

(1978, 90 min, Australia, Donald Crombie) *Lou Brown, Michael Craig, Simon Burke, Bryan Brown.* A sweeping tale of a family's futile battle against progress, this gripping frontier drama is set in 1920s North Queensland. The story concerns Paddy Doolan, a proud Irish rancher, whose refusal to accept change and use motorized machinery pits one of his sons against the other. ★★★

Irma la Douce

(1963, 142 min, US, Billy Wilder) *Jack Lemmon, Shirley MacLaine, Lou Jacobi, Herschel Bernardi.* A lively though very broad farce from director Wilder. Lemmon stars as a Parisian policeman who falls for streetwalker MacLaine. Determined to keep her "straight," Lemmon runs a comically ragged course as he doubles as both suitor and, by impersonating British royalty (shades of *The Lady Eve*), her only customer. And then there's the tale of the real British lord, but that's another story. Based on the Broadway musical — *sans* music. ★★★ DVD Letterbox: $19.99

Irma Vep

(1997, 96 min, France, Oliver Assayas) *Maggie Cheung, Jean-Pierre Léaud, Natalie Richard, Bulle Ogier, Arsinée Khanjian.* This winsome, though jumbled, examination of a Parisian film company's chaotic attempt to remake the 10-part, 1915 French silent serial classic *Les Vampires* pokes fun at the absurd intellectualism of the French film industry. Director Assayas prudently offers up this view through the eyes of an outsider, Cheung, who — playing herself — has been asked by the film's high-strung director, René (Leaud), to take on the role of the slinky, latex-clad cat-burglar heroine, Irma Vep. Cheung is a completely appealing character who gamely participates in whatever caprice the filmmakers can send her way. The film's cohesion suffers as it wanders off in a multitude of directions, but its witty, hip attitude more than makes up for its shortcomings. (In English and French with English subtitles) ★★★ DVD: $14.99, VHS: $9.99

Iron and Silk

(1991, 91 min, US, Shirley Sun) *Mark Salzman, Pan Qingfu, Vivian Wu.* Obvious sincerity and knowledge of the subject is not enough to lift this earnest drama about a young man's experience in China above an "Afterschool Special." Based on Salzman's autobiographical book, the film follows Salzman, a handsome American infused with a passion for all things Chinese, who goes to pre-

Tiananmen Square China to study. His experiences in the country — learning to master martial arts, falling in love, attempting to win over the shy people, teaching eager Chinese English — is interesting; but without dramatic conflict, the film seems more a beautifully made travelogue than an insightful drama depicting the differences between East and West. ★★ VHS: $19.99

Iron Eagle

(1986, 117 min, US, Sidney J. Furie) *Jason Gedrick, Louis Gossett, Jr., Tim Thomerson.* Gedrick, with the help of Gossett, flies the unfriendly skies of the Middle East in an attempt for his father being held captive. This tepid *Top Gun* clone lacks that film's technical know-how (and makes it seem good by comparison). (Followed by 3 sequels) ★½ DVD: $9.99, VHS: $9.99

The Iron Giant

(1999, 87 min, US, Brad Bird) *Voices of: Jennifer Aniston, Harry Connick, Jr., Vin Diesel, Cloris Leachman, Christopher MacDonald, John Mahoney.* An excellent family film, this exciting animated feature follows the adventures of a young boy who finds a 50-foot robot (who fell from outer space) and tries to protect his new giant friend from not-so-friendly government forces. Outstanding animation, a good story and some moral lessons combine to make this a classic-in-the-making. ★★★★ VHS: $14.99, VHS Letterbox: $14.99

Iron Maze

(1991, 102 min, US, Hiroaki Yoshida) *Jeff Fahey, Bridget Fonda, J.T. Walsh, Hiroaki Murakami, Gabriel Damon, John Randolph.* A young man in a dying factory town (Fahey) discovers that his old flame (Fonda) is now married to the scion of the Japanese entrepreneur who just bought a decaying industrial complex. The son cannot understand community opposition to turning the site into an amusement park. Coproduced by Oliver Stone, this well-acted and intelligently scripted film examines complex issues from multiple perspectives without stereotyping or condescension. Timely and pertinent, with a *Rashomon*-like style of exposition. ★★★ DVD: $24.99, VHS: $19.99

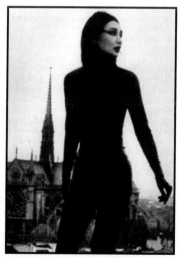

Irma Vep

Iron Monkey

(1993, 86 min, Hong Kong, Yuen Woo-Ping) *Donnie Yen, Yu Rong Guang.* A hugely entertaining Hong Kong martial arts film, *Iron Monkey*, the prequel to the *Once Upon a Time in China* series, is one of the best of its kind. This tale of a "Chinese Robin Hood" is rife with outrageous action (the film is directed and choreographed by *The Matrix*'s Woo-Ping), terrific heroes, evil villains and a large dollop of humor. Its cartoonish violence notwithstanding, *Monkey* is fun for all ages, à la the *Indiana Jones* films, or, indeed, *The Adventures of Robin Hood*. A real treat. By the way, the Iron Monkey's son is actually played by a young girl. ★★★½ DVD: $19.99, VHS Subtitled: $9.99, VHS Dubbed: $9.99

The Iron Triangle

(1988, 94 min, US, Eric Weston) *Beau Bridges, Haing S. Ngor.* A U.S. Army captain (Bridges) leads his men into a bloody battle to capture a Viet Cong stronghold along the Ho Chi Minh trail. A well-meaning if lethargic story which tries to reexamine the conflict of the Vietnam War. ★★

Iron Will

(1994, 104 min, US, Charles Haid) *Mackenzie Astin, Kevin Spacey, David Ogden Stiers, August Schellenberg.* After their success with *White Fang*, Disney is back in the tundra with this equally appealing adventure film. Though heavy on the clichés, the likable story focuses on a teenaged Kansas farm boy, Will (Astin), who enters the big dogsled race of 1917 in place of his deceased father. Competing and holding his own against seasoned adults, the youth quickly becomes a media sensation in his gritty attempt for victory. *Iron Will* has a nice period look to it, and director Haid keeps the action moving at a brisk pace. ★★★ DVD: $19.99, VHS: $9.99

Ironweed

(1987, 144 min, US, Hector Babenco) *Jack Nicholson, Meryl Streep, Carroll Baker, Tom Waits, Michael O'Keefe, Diane Venora, Fred Gwynne, Nathan Lane.* A demanding, rather depressing but expertly acted and brilliant evocation of William Kennedy's Pulitzer Prize-winning novel. Set amongst the squalor of the poor and alcoholic street bums living in late-1930s Albany, the film features two mesmerizing performances by Nicholson and Streep as two part-time lovers living on the skids; each concealing a secret from their past. Though it is certainly downbeat, the tour-de-force portrayals from Jack and Meryl make it a fascinating experience. (Watching Streep sing "She's My Gal" is alternately painful and exhilarating, and is one of the great movie moments of the 1980s.) ★★★

Is It Easy to Be Young

(1986, 85 min, USSR, Yuri Rodniek) Punks in black leather, anesthetized drug addicts and restless youths alienated by an unresponsive government might not seem so out of the ordinary for Americans, but the subject becomes much more interesting when the dissatisfied teens are Russians. With the Soviet Union facing dissolution, this boisterous documentary lends some insight into the thoughts and feelings of the Soviet youth seeking a different way. (Russian with English subtitles) ★★★ VHS: $59.99

Is Paris Burning?

(1968, 172 min, US/France, René Clément) *Jean-Paul Belmondo, Kirk Douglas, Simone Signoret, Charles Boyer, Leslie Caron, Orson Welles, Yves Montand.* An all-star cast highlights this epic WWII film about the liberation of Paris from the Germans and the Nazis' attempt to level the city. Hitler had commanded that the city be destroyed before the Germans left, and the title refers to his constant inquiries as to that order's success. ★★½ DVD: $14.99, VHS: $14.99

Isadora

(1968, 153 min, GB, Karel Reisz) *Vanessa Redgrave, James Fox, Jason Robards, Bessie Love.* Redgrave's bravura performance highlights this gripping biography of dance innovator and free spirit Isadora Duncan. Fox and Robards offer excellent support, but it's Redgrave's show all the way. ★★★

Ishtar

(1987, 107 min, US, Elaine May) *Dustin Hoffman, Warren Beatty, Isabelle Adjani, Charles Grodin.* This megabomb was doomed before it even hit the theatres due to production leaks and trade talk. With a reported cost of over $50 million, it didn't meet anyone's expectations. However, if you can erase all preconceptions, you may find it funny; particularly the intentionally horrendous Hoffman-Beatty duets. A film you either love or hate. ★★

The Island (Hodaka No Shima)

(1962, 96 min, Japan, Kaneto Shindo) *Nobuko Otowa, Taiji Tonoyama.* An unusual work of art, made without dialogue. The story is told only through visuals, sounds and music. Beautifully photographed on a remote and barren island off Japan, the story follows a peasant family's daily struggle for survival. Their precarious existence is continually threatened by nature but the family never ceases its work. An engrossing, visually breathtaking tale told in documentarylike fashion. ★★★½

The Island

(1980, 114 min, US, Michael Ritchie) *Michael Caine, David Warner, Angela Punch McGregor.* Laughable adventure film about modern-day pirates terrorizing the Caribbean. Caine is a journalist investigating area disappearances who is captured by the seagoing bandits. Based on the novel by Peter Benchley ("Jaws"). ★ VHS: $19.99

Island in the Sun

(1957, 119 min, US, Robert Rossen) *James Mason, Dorothy Dandridge, Joan Fontaine, Joan Collins, Michael Rennie, Harry Belafonte, Diana Wynyard, John Williams, Stephen Boyd.* Controversial, popular but not well received in its day, *Island in the Sun* is more of a curio now for its attitudes towards race and sexual relations. Typical of the hoary melodrama of its time, the film isn't as polished or involving as other '50s melodramas like *Imitation of Life* or *Written on the Wind*, despite its then-taboo subject of interracial romance. Set in the serene Caribbean, the film follows four couples: including plantation owner Mason and his wife, who he suspects of infidelity with military man Rennie; Mason's busty sister Collins and buff soldier Boyd; and island politico Belafonte and older Fontaine. The most interesting plots are the Dandridge and Mason story lines. But Belafonte at least gets to sing. ★★

The Island of Dr. Moreau

(1977, 104 min, US, Don Taylor) *Burt Lancaster, Michael York, Nigel Davenport, Barbara Carrere.* This second screen version of H.G. Wells' novel is a mildly entertaining if loopy adaptation. Lancaster plays the demented doc who has created half-human animals. York is the young man who stumbles upon the humanoids. For a more definitive version of the story, see 1932's *Island of Lost Souls*. (Remade in 1996) ★★½ DVD Letterbox: $14.99

The Island of Dr. Moreau

(1996, 96 min, US, John Frankenheimer) *Val Kilmer, Marlon Brando, David Thewlis, Fairuza Balk.* Good and terrible from start to finish, this third version of H.G. Wells' story began with a troubled production history and wound up an incomprehensible mishmash. Thewlis is discovered drifting in the ocean and winds up on Moreau's island, where a brilliant but disgraced scientist conducts experiments into the animal nature of man and vice versa. Kilmer camps it up as Moreau's assistant and eventual successor, Brando throws in a variety of astonishingly stupid bits of business, and Thewlis looks lost. By the end, Kilmer is imitating Brando, Thewlis is throwing his hands up in exasperation and the viewer has wasted an hour and a half. This creation of the mad Dr. Frankenheimer is viewable for camp value only. ★½ DVD: $14.99, VHS: $14.99, VHS Letterbox: $19.99

Island of Lost Souls

(1932, 71 min, US, Erle C. Kenton) *Charles Laughton, Bela Lugosi, Richard Arlen.* This superb adaptation of H.G. Wells' terrifying novel "The Island of Dr. Moreau" was initially banned in many parts of the U.S. because of its horrifying depiction of a man who transforms animals into partial humans through his own form of surgical experimentation. Laughton plays Dr. Moreau, the benign-looking doctor who lives and works on his own private South Seas island. When a shipwreck leaves Edward Parker (Arlen) stranded on the island, he learns of the hideous experiments. Haunting and chilling, *Island of Lost Souls* remains a classic of horror cinema and is one of the most strangely fascinating films ever produced. (Remade in 1977 and 1996 as *The Island of Dr. Moreau*) ★★★½

Islands in the Stream

(1977, 110 min, US, Franklin J. Schaffner) *George C. Scott, Claire Bloom, David Hemmings, Susan Tyrrell.* Scott is most effective as a father reunited with his sons after a self-imposed exile in the Bahamas at the outbreak of World War II. Based on the novel by Ernest Hemingway. ★★½ VHS: $14.99

The Isle

(2001, 89 min, Korea, Kim Ki-Duk) *Suh Jung, Yoosuk Kim.* Contemplating suicide, a young man rents a floating fishing house raft and considers his gun. The young woman who sells bait and coffee to fishermen supplements her income by selling herself. They seem matched in melancholic withdrawal, each isolated and adrift off the eerily fog-bound coast of a verdant, otherworldly island. The floats bobbing on the water's surface are rented for hours, days or months, self-contained modules for living or going through the motions of living; a place to hide out from the wife, the job, the police or, less successfully, oneself. The two leads manifest a haunting eroticism, and the film is imbued in a disturbing prurience and psychosexual tension reminiscent of *In the Realm of the Senses*. While *The Isle* occasionally teeters on the edge of self-indulgent artiness, the gritty portrayals prevent that. Instead, directing us instead to Hee-Jin and Hyun-Shik's descent into mutual dependence, hooking themselves to each other as their world shrinks to the size of a bright yellow house float adrift on an indifferent sea. (Korean with English subtitles) ★★★ DVD Subtitled: $29.99, VHS: $49.99

Isle of the Dead

(1945, 72 min, US, Mark Robson) *Boris Karloff, Ellen Drew.* Karloff gives a passionate portrayal of

a Greek army commander who is trapped, along with several others, on an island hit by plague. This atmospheric chiller bears more than a slight resemblance to Jacques Tourneur's *I Walked with a Zombie* in content and technique, for director Robson worked on that and other Val Lewton classics as editor. ★★★ VHS: $19.99

Isn't She Great

(2000, 93 min, US, Andrew Bergman) *Bette Midler, Nathan Lane, Stockard Channing, David Hyde Pierce, John Cleese, Amanda Peet.* On paper, the idea of the feverishly funny Midler playing flamboyant writer Jacqueline Susann seemed absolutely inspired. A not-so-funny thing happened on the way to the forum. One problem is that Midler plays Susann with such restraint — she should have been bigger than King Kong. Another problem is that the script has turned Susann into a martyr who talks to trees. Adding little zest or comic flair, Bergman's direction is stale and lifeless, leaving a game cast eager to please but having little to do. Anyone who remembers Susann from her talk show appearances in the '60s and '70s knows what a character she was. Unfortunately, no one associated with this film bothered to remember that or care. And one more bitch for the road: Why "cover up" her well-known drug and alcohol use? Cowards! ★ DVD: $9.99

It

(1927, 72 min, US, Clarence Badger) *Clara Bow, Antonio Moreno, William Austin, Gary Cooper.* In her quintessential flapper role, the legendary Bow plays a saucy lingerie salesgirl who sets her sights on the handsome owner of the department store in which she works. Based on a story by Elinor Glyn, *It* is the definitive Jazz Age comedy. Bow, simply stated, certainly had "It." ★★★ DVD: $29.99, VHS: $24.99

It

(1990, 193 min, US, Tommy Lee Wallace) *Richard Thomas, John Ritter, Annette O'Toole, Dennis Christopher, Harry Anderson, Tim Reid.* Frightmaster Stephen King's cheesy but fun made-for-TV tale about a group of childhood friends who reunite as adults to face their own "big chill" — an evil presence that lurks beneath their hometown and manifests as their innermost fear, a demonic killer clown (played by Curry). The horror elements bear the burden of commercial sponsorship and are less than eye-clenching. Still, die-hard scarebears shouldn't be disappointed and the uninitiated will find this one a good place to start. ★★½ DVD: $19.99, VHS: $14.99

It Came from Outer Space

(1953, 81 min, US, Jack Arnold) *Richard Carlson, Barbara Rush, Charles Drake, Russell Johnson.* Based on a short story by Ray Bradbury, *It Came from Outer Space* is one of the quintessential sci-fi films of the 1950s. After a mysterious asteroid crashes in the surrounding desert, a desolate community finds its citizens beginning to act *strangely*. Only amateur astronomer Carlson has a clue to what may be happening — no one will believe him. In one of the first and best 3-D films, genre master Arnold keeps the pacing brisk and the suspense turned up high. (Remade in 1996) ★★★ DVD: $14.99, VHS: $9.99

It Conquered the World

(1956, 71 min, US, Roger Corman) *Peter Graves, Beverly Garland, Lee Van Clef.* Drive-in classic with a creepy monster that releases bloodsucking bats, whose bites reduce people to zombies. This picture is often equated with films from this time period in which the story line mimicks the "Red Scare" that was sweeping 1950s America. ★★

It Could Happen to You

(1994, 101 min, US, Andrew Bergman) *Nicolas Cage, Bridget Fonda, Rosie Perez, Isaac Hayes, Seymour Cassell, Red Buttons, Stanley Tucci.* For all those who bemoan "they don't make them like they used to" comes this gentle romantic comedy. Cage stars as a super-honest New York City cop who gives half of his winning lottery ticket to a perpetually down-on-her-luck waitress (Fonda) as a tip. A charming modern fairy tale without much depth and a Gump-like belief in the triumph of goodness, *It Could Happen to You* relies heavily on the charisma of its two stars, and both deliver affable, slightly kooky performances. Perez, on the other hand, goes completely overboard in a screechingly annoying turn as Cage's money-grubbing wife. ★★★ DVD: $14.99, VHS: $9.99

It Happened Here

(1966, 96 min, GB, Andrew Mollo & Kevin Brownlow) *Pauline Murray, Sebastian Shaw.* Not yet the renown silent film archivist, Brownlow was 18 when he and Mollo began this chilling speculation of what a defeated Britain would be like under Nazi rule. An apolitical nurse, deluded by the optimism that lets her survive, finds that evil lives in the most unassuming corners of the human heart. Shot with a documentary detachment and all the more unnerving for it. Brownlow and Mollo create a cautionary tale that stays with one long after the final image. ★★★½ DVD: $29.99, VHS: $29.99

It Happened in the Park

(1956, 87 min, France/Italy, Gianni Franciolini) Told in a series of vignettes, this simple but affecting drama takes the premise of filming a day in the life of Villa Borghese, the beautiful landscaped park in Rome. The stories revolve mostly around *amore*: budding romances, illicit affairs and bickering lovers. Also included is a touching drama of a teacher revealing to a pupil that he is going blind; and the best episode is the finale, about two warring prostitutes who, on the run from the police, find themselves competing in a Miss Cinema pageant. Please note that the sound is only fair and the subtitles sometimes fall below the screen; but this is the only version currently available. (French with English subtitles) ★★★

It Happened One Night

(1934, 105 min, US, Frank Capra) *Claudette Colbert, Clark Gable, Roscoe Karns, Walter Connolly.* Predicted as a box-office bomb, this hugely entertaining comedy was the smash hit of 1934, not only winning Oscars for almost everyone involved (Best Actor — Gable, Best Actress — Colbert, Best Director — Capra), but also managing to snag the Best Picture Oscar as well; it ushered in a whole new style of Hollywood comedy. This romantic comedy concerns the adventures of a runaway heiress (Colbert) and a newspaperman (Gable) who discovers her identity and helps her by "marrying" her. Full of rapid-fire one-liners and ingenious gags, this enduring classic is every bit as delightful as its reputation suggests. ★★★★ DVD: $24.99

It Happens Every Spring

(1949, 128 min, US, Lloyd Bacon) *Ray Milland, Paul Douglas, Jean Peters, Ed Begley.* Milland plays a scientist who discovers a serum that repels wood. To determine its effectiveness, he tries out as a big-league pitcher — and becomes the major's

new ace. Douglas is terrific as his team's weathered, hen-pecked manager. A lighthearted, funny romp which is one of the semiclassics of the era's many baseball films. ★★★

It Lives Again

(1978, 91 min, US, Larry Cohen) *Frederic Forrest, Kathleen Lloyd, John Marley, John Ryan.* Dreadful sequel to *It's Alive* finds another young couple experiencing the mutant baby syndrome. But this time, the mother gives birth to triplets. (Sequel: *It's Alive III: Island of the Alive*) ★ VHS: $14.99

It Runs in the Family

(2003, 101 min, US, Fred Schepisi) *Michael Douglas, Kirk Douglas, Rory Culkin, Bernadette Peters, Cameron Douglas, Diana Douglas.* Tepid and often badly paced, *It Runs in the Family* takes a look at three generations of a family (Kirk, Michael, and Michael's son, Cameron) each going through personal crises and attempting to reconcile with each other. It starts off terribly, with Cameron an initially unappealing presence (he does get better), followed by some awkward, uncomfortable stabs at humor. Then the film settles down a bit to afford each actor an opportunity to take center stage, though the script doesn't allow any of them to fully explore these two-dimensional characters. Which is too bad, considering this marks the first screen pairing of Michael and Kirk. While it's a minor pleasure seeing them work together, the whole affair is squandered, as they do little beyond taking turns being nasty to each other. The supporting cast is wasted, and the film is tonally unsure — halfhearted comedy one minute, bland TV-movie-level dramatics the next. ★★ DVD: $14.99, VHS: $102.99

It Should Happen to You

(1954, 87 min, US, George Cukor) *Judy Holliday, Jack Lemmon, Peter Lawford.* Charming fluff about a New York City woman, Gladys Glover (Holliday), who rents a Columbus Circle billboard — just to put her name on it; she then receives her 15 minutes of fame. In his film debut, Lemmon plays a filmmaker involved with the wacky Gladys. Holliday, of course, is nothing short of delightful. Written by Ruth Gordon and Garson Kanin. ★★★ DVD: $24.99

It Started in Naples

(1960, 100 min, US, Melville Shavelson) *Clark Gable, Sophia Loren, Vittorio De Sica.* Gable stars as a stuffy Philadelphia attorney who arrives in Italy to bring home his orphaned nephew. But cultures clash when he runs up against the boy's fiery Italian aunt (Loren). A sunny Mediterranean romp. ★★★ VHS: $14.99

It Started with a Kiss

(1959, 104 min, US, George Marshall) *Debbie Reynolds, Glenn Ford, Eva Gabor, Gustavo Rojo, Fred Clark.* Reynolds is the kooky, man-hunting chorine. Ford is the Army sergeant who, after much ado, steals her heart. After one day, they marry, and he is soon transferred to Spain. There they discover the downside of love at first sight, as they try to get to know each other. To make matters worse, she is pursued by handsome matador Rojo; he is pursued by countess Gabor; and colonel Clark is constantly on their case. A fluffy romantic comedy, not without a few chuckles, which tries to be both sexy and innocent. It settles for sappy. For a really good '50s sex farce, check out *Ask Any Girl.* ★★½ VHS: $19.99

It Takes Two

(1995, 101 min, US, Andy Tennant) *Kirstie Alley, Steve Guttenberg, Mary-Kate Olsen, Ashley Olsen, Philip Bosco.* It's contrived, it's cutesy, and, egad, it's the Olsen twins . . . and yet, it has its moments of charm. In this update of *The Prince and the Pauper*, the girls are the identical kids who have grown up under completely different circumstances. One has been raised wealthy and cultured, the daughter of the widowed Guttenberg. The other is an orphan befriended by the unmarried Alley. Once the twins meet each other, they try to bring Kirstie and Steve together. ★★½ DVD: $14.99

It's a Gift

(1934, 68 min, US, Norman Z. McLeod) *W.C. Fields, Baby LeRoy, Kathleen Howard.* One of Fields funniest films, here Bill plays a grocery clerk who goes to California, discovering a funny and wild, wild West. ★★★

It's a Mad, Mad, Mad, Mad World

(1963, 154 min, US, Stanley Kramer) *Spencer Tracy, Mickey Rooney, Sid Caesar, Milton Berle, Phil Silvers, Buddy Hackett, Ethel Merman, Jonathan Winters, Edie Adams, Peter Falk, Eddie Anderson, Terry-Thomas.* One of the top box-office hits of the 1960s, this over-long Cinemascope extravaganza was director Kramer's attempt to revive the silent slapstick comedies of years gone by. For the most part, it works. Tracy, in one of his last screen appearances, heads the truly all-star cast looking for an elusive "W" marking the spot of a buried fortune. The cast is really just second-bananas to a series of hilarious stunts and car chases, though Merman gives a hilarious performance as the mother-in-law from hell. Still good for some genuine laughs, the film is representative of the overblown all-star epics which marked the mid-'60s. ★★★½ DVD Letterbox Basic Edition: $14.99

It's a Wonderful Life

(1946, 130 min, US, Frank Capra) *James Stewart, Donna Reed, Lionel Barrymore, Henry Travers, Thomas Mitchell, Beulah Bondi.* Capra's immortal classic with Stewart as the father who wished he'd never been born — and who gets his wish. Capra as director and Stewart as actor were at the peak of their talents. Travers is moviedom's most endearing angel. ★★★★ DVD: $19.99, VHS Special Edition: $9.99

It's Alive

(1974, 91 min, US, Larry Cohen) *John Ryan, Sharon Farrell, Michael Ansara.* Cult fave about an expectant couple and the birth of their new baby — a hideous mutant killer. (Sequel: *It Lives Again*) ★★½ VHS: $14.99

It's Alive III: Island of the Alive

(1987, 95 min, US, Larry Cohen) *Michael Moriarty, Karen Black, Macdonald Carey.* The *It's Alive* babies are back! This time, more distraught parents have watched the government banish their mutant children to a remote island. Years later, these teenage mutants want to come back to the society that created them. ★★ VHS: $14.99

It's Always Fair Weather

(1955, 102 min, US, Gene Kelly & Stanley Donen) *Gene Kelly, Dan Daily, Cyd Charisse, Michael Kidd, Dolores Gray. Singin' in the Rain* directors Kelly and Donen and writers Betty Comden and Adolph Green reunited for this cheerful, entertaining musical about three former Army buddies who meet 10 years after the end of WWII. There are great dance sequences, a good score, and Kelly, Daily, Charisse, Kidd and Gray are all fine. It's amazing what Kelly can do with a garbage can lid. ★★★½

It's in the Bag

(1945, 87 min, US, Richard Wallace) *Fred Allen, Don Ameche, Rudy Vallee, Jack Benny.* In this funny and crazy romp, popular 1940s radio star Allen is a flea trainer who inherits a small fortune — only the money is hidden in one of five chairs scattered throughout the city. Benny makes a hilarious extended cameo (the entire scene is priceless), and Ameche and Vallee also appear as themselves (as down-on-their-luck cabaret singers!). Similar in plot to Mel Brooks' *The 12 Chairs*. ★★★ VHS: $19.99

It's My Party

(1996, 110 min, US, Randal Kleiser) *Gregory Harrison, Lee Grant, Marlee Matlin, Bronson Pinchot, George Segal, Paul Regina, Eric Roberts, Margaret Cho, Bruce Davison, Roddy McDowall.* Based on the true story of his lover of eight years, director Kleiser has made an emotionally candid, personal AIDS drama which is short of dramatic structure but overpowering in the honest emotions it establishes. Giving a heartfelt performance, Roberts stars as Nick, a gay architect with AIDS who decides to kill himself upon learning he only has a few days to live. But beforehand, he decides to throw a farewell bash — attended by family and friends, and his ex-lover who has crashed the party. The story focuses on Nick's various relationships all the while joking with gallows humor of the inevitable. Though not as polished as *Philadelphia*, *It's My Party* is more aware, and can be sentimental without being maudlin. ★★★ DVD: $19.99

It's Pat: The Movie

(1994, 77 min, US, Adam Bernstein) *Julia Sweeney, David Foley, Charles Rocket, Kathy Najimy.* Sweeney stars in this annoying, one-joke comedy, based on her "Saturday Night Live" sketch, as Pat, an androgynous, bothersome loser who keeps one and all guessing as to his/her gender. Whereas this comic concept inspired a few funny five-minute bits, as a feature-length movie it is interminable. The story has to do with Pat finding love (in the form of an equally androgynous Foley from "The Kids in the Hall") and endlessly searching for the right career. Though the film contains a

number of laughs, it is saved from total abomination by Rocket, who is actually quite good as Pat's neighbor who slowly goes insane trying to determine Pat's sex. ★★½ DVD: $9.99

It's the Rage

(2000, 103 min, US, James D. Stern) *Joan Allen, Josh Brolin, Andre Braugher, Jeff Daniels, Robert Forster, Anna Paquin, Giovanni Ribisi, David Schwimmer, Gary Sinise, Bokeem Woodbine.* A terrific cast is put in the service of a not-so-terrific film. Adapted (oh-so-obviously) from a play, *It's the Rage* follows the cast as they cross paths in L.A.; the connective tissue is guns. See, this is more than just an ensemble drama; it's a treatise on gun control. When the hamfisted political lessons take a back seat, the film is moderately enjoyable, especially for fans of interconnecting stories. The acting (most notably by Allen and the terrific Sinise as an unhinged computer magnate) is good, and the film is well paced. But the end result is hollow and unsatisfying, and the "what happened to them" end title crawl is pathetic — and rather insulting — handwringing hooey. ★★ DVD: $24.99, VHS: $19.99

The Italian Job

(2003, 106 min, US, F. Gary Gray) *Mark Wahlberg, Charlize Theron, Edward Norton, Seth Green, Jason Statham, Mos Def, Donald Sutherland, Franky G.* If it takes a thief to catch a thief, then *The Italian Job*, an enjoyable remake of the 1969 Michael Caine thriller, takes that route five better by providing a quintuple of bad guys, er, good guys, to track down one of their own . . . the bad guy. With most of the action now set in Los Angeles (the original's setting was Italy), the film is a roller-coaster ride of tension and thrills told in a quite efficient style of storytelling. Safecracker Sutherland leads his group to a successful haul, only to be shot by Norton, who leaves the rest of his gang for dead and walks off with $35 million in gold bullion. A year later, Surrogate son Wahlberg convinces real daughter Theron to help exact revenge for her father's murder — and retrieve the money — when they locate their old pal. The plan includes creating a major traffic jam on the streets of L.A. — like anyone would ever notice. The characterizations tend toward stock, and Wahlberg and Theron aren't exactly an electric twosome, but the story never falters in its own sense of logic, Gray's direction is crisp and playful, there's a knockout chase sequence, and the excitement level is always on high. ★★★ DVD Letterbox: $19.99, DVD: $19.99, VHS: $11.99

The Italian Straw Hat

(1927, 101 min, France, René Clair) *Alice Tissat, Paul Oliver.* Clair's madcap comedy based on the Labiche-Michel farce about a groom, minutes before his marriage, who goes on a frantic search for the identical hat his horse has just eaten. The sometimes hilarious escapades are superbly exploited by Clair. (Silent with musical accompaniment) ★★★½ VHS: $39.99

ItalianAmerican/The Big Shave

(1974/78, 54 min, US, Martin Scorsese) *Catherine Scorsese, Charles Scorsese.* Two short films from Scorsese. *ItalianAmerican* features the director's irrespressible mother and father, Catherine and Charles, in an intimate conversation at their Little Italy home in New York. A funny look at one family's ancestry, life and accomplishments. In *The Big Shave*, a young man nicks himself shaving and suddenly, an ordinary morning is transformed into a

frightening religious experience. Scorsese's black humor is much in evidence, even at an early age, and encapsulates his obsessions with religion, suffering and blood. ★★★

The Item

(2000, 100 min, US, Dan Clark) *Dawn Marie Velasquez, Dan Clark, Dave Pressler.* A motley group of criminals take on the (rather vaguely explained) job of delivering an "item" to a client; the item turns out to be a bizarre little creature that likes playing mind games with the gang. This oddball sci-fi/horror/action/satire feels like Tarantino meets Henenlotter, with ridiculously excessive shoot-outs, far-too-clever dialogue complete with impromptu pop-culture symposiums, and a talking puppet monster straight out of *Brain Damage*. Almost equal parts good and bad, the shot-on-video *Item* is far too long and disjointed, but also contains some terrific moments amidst the half-baked ideas. ★★ DVD: $14.99, VHS: $9.99

Ivan and Abraham

(1993, 105 min, France, Yolande Zauberman) *Roma Alexandrovitch, Sacha Iakovlev, Vladimir Machkov, Maria Lipkina.* The poignant and enduring friendship of two adolescent boys — one Jewish and one Christian — makes for a haunting, lyrical coming-of-age tale set against the turbulent backdrop of rising anti-Semitism in 1930s Poland. Beautifully shot in stark black and white, *Ivan & Abraham* is set in a *shtetl*, a small Jewish community. Ivan (Alexandrovitch) is a Catholic youth apprenticing at the home of Abraham (Iakovlev), and the two are inseparable friends. When Abraham's strict grandfather forbids his grandson to see Ivan, the two run away together. With a poetic and focused eye, the film juxtaposes the story of the boys' life on the road; the disturbing, escalating tensions in the village; and the passage of customs for an uncertain future. (Yiddish, Polish, Russian and Gypsy dialect with English subtitles) ★★★½ VHS: $19.99

Ivan the Terrible, Part I

(1943, 100 min, USSR, Sergei Eisenstein) *Nikolai Cherkassov, Ludmila Tselikovskaya.* Eisenstein's epic biography of Ivan Grozny IV, proclaimed Russia's first Czar in the middle of the 16th century. The film, the first of two parts, traces the emperor's coronation, his defeat and his eventual reinstatement. The film features an original score by Sergei Prokofiev. (Russian with English subtitles) ★★★½ DVD: $24.99, VHS: $29.99

Ivan the Terrible, Part II

(1946, 87 min, USSR, Sergei Eisenstein) *Nikolai Cherkassov, Ludmila Tselikovskaya.* Eisenstein's follow-up to his 1943 classic chronicles Ivan's reign in the late 16th century and his revenge on those who had denounced him. (Russian with English subtitles) ★★★½ DVD: $24.99, VHS: $29.99

Ivanhoe

(1952, 106 min, US, Richard Thorpe) *Elizabeth Taylor, Robert Taylor, Joan Fontaine, George Sanders.* A young and absolutely ravishing E. Taylor stars in this rendition of Walter Scott's epic tale of Saxon honor and Norman villainy in middle-age England. R. Taylor stars as Ivanhoe, a young knight torn between the honorable Rowena and the Jewess Rebecca, while at the same time trying to bring the good King Richard back to England. A beautifully filmed historical drama. ★★★

Ivanhoe

(1982, 142 min, GB, Douglas Camfield) *James Mason, Anthony Andrews, Sam Neill, Olivia Hussey, Michael Hordern, John Rhys-Davies.* Lavish version of Walter Scott's classic story of knighthood, love, Richard the Lionhearted, and 12th-century England. Mason heads a good ensemble cast as Isaac of York. ★★★ VHS: $14.99

J'Accuse

(1937, 125 min, France, Abel Gance) *Victor Francen, Jean Max.* A lost masterpiece from the director of *Napoleon*, this, Gance's sound remake of his 1919 film of the same title, is a virulent antiwar film that was originally banned by the French government as being potentially treasonous. An epic of love and the catastrophic effects of war on one man's spirits, this powerful and disturbing cry against man's inhumanity to his fellow man features a particularly chilling sequence where a man calls upon millions of dead soldiers to rise from their graves and march on Paris. (French with English subtitles) ★★★½

J'ai Été au Bal

(1990, 114 min, US, Les Blank) From the sounds of the 1920s and Joe Falcon to the rock 'n' roll beat of Wayne Toups (the Cajun Bruce Springsteen) to the flamboyance of the "King of Zydeco" Clifton Chenier, *J'ai Été au Bal* captures the raw spirit of rural Louisiana through a fascinating blend of archival and current footage. A deeply felt understanding of why and how this infective music has come to be the wonderful gumbo that it is. (French with English subtitles) ★★★ VHS: $49.99

Jabberwocky

(1977, 100 min, GB, Terry Gilliam) *Michael Palin, Eric Idle, Max Wall, Terry Jones.* "T'was brillig and the slithy toves. . ." Gilliam uses the resources of his friends in the Monty Python gang to bring Lewis Carroll's classic poem to the screen with great aplomb. Palin stars in this tale of a medieval kingdom's search for a brave young lad to slay a nasty, scaly beast. Featuring the same bloody absurdities of life as in *Holy Grail.* ★★★ DVD: $24.99, VHS: $14.99

Jabberwocky

Jack

(1996, 113 min, US, Francis Ford Coppola) *Robin Williams, Diane Lane, Brian Kerwin, Bill Cosby, Jennifer Lopez, Fran Drescher.* Jack is a young boy whose body isn't really his own. This didn't happen by wishing, or even the result of an ancient artifact. He's suffering from a disease that makes his body grow four times its normal rate. Which is only one of the missteps with *Jack*, a sullen fable short on magic and humor. Williams plays the title character, a ten-year-old whose body is that of a 40-year-old. Sheltered by his doting mom, Jack eventually makes his way to school and the outside world, where hurt, friends and experience await him. As directed by Coppola, *Jack* is too encompassing in what it tries to accomplish — it's operatic where it should be frolicsome and only occasionally does the story capture the whimsical cadence of childhood. ★★ VHS: $9.99

Jack and Sarah

(1995, 110 min, GB, Tim Sullivan) *Richard E. Grant, Samantha Mathis, Judi Dench, Ian McKellen.* To be fair, a romantic comedy-drama about an unsympathetic yuppie who is suddenly widowed and thrust into single fatherhood is a bit of a hard sell. If such a film had to be made, it probably could have been made better than this stylish but choppy and rarely funny tale. Both the usually engaging Grant as the dad and Mathis as the rookie nanny who find romance seem lost here, stuck in a movie that isn't quite sure of what it wants to be and winds up not being much of anything. Baby care in film is generally good for a few chuckles; but in *Jack and Sarah*, that's about all it adds up to. ★★ DVD Pan & Scan: $19.99

Jack Be Nimble

(1993, 93 min, New Zealand, Garth Maxwell) *Alexis Arquette, Sarah Smuts-Kennedy, Bruno Lawrence.* Creepy "everything-but-the-kitchen-sink" thriller about a young girl (Smuts-Kennedy) who uses her latent psychic powers to find the brother she lost through adoption (played as an adult by Arquette). Of course, this happens just as he murders his abusive adoptive parents and is stalked by his four psycho stepsisters. Eerie photography and a totally twisted story line make this an excellent horror film for the art-house set and a welcome import from the land down under. ★★★

Jack Frost

(1998, 95 min, US, Troy Miller) *Michael Keaton, Kelly Preston, Mark Addy, Joseph Cross.* What would happen if your dad turned into a snowman? Well, if he turned into a snowman as scary looking as this one, we'd say run for the hills. Some of the most repulsive special effects to grace a kids' film, added to a sappy story of parental loss, regret, and bonding, add up to a must-avoid this winter, or any other season. ★ DVD: $14.99, VHS: $9.99

Jack the Bear

(1993, 98 min, US, Marshall Herskowitz) *Danny DeVito, Robert J. Steinmiller, Miko Hughes, Gary Sinise, Julia Louis-Dreyfus.* This is a film with a sneaky left hook. Just when you think you're awash in a mushy "Wonder Years"-for-the-big-screen rip-off, *Jack the Bear* surprises you with some down-to-earth honesty about growing up (and old) with big doses of rage and guilt. DeVito stars as a widowed dad in the early '70s who makes his living as the host of a local TV station's late movie show and who must contend with a possible psycho neighbor. Though it does have a definite sugary "how many times have I seen this before" side, the heart-tugging

performances of DeVito's two sons (Steinmiller, Hughes) make this a definite seven on the tearjerker scale. ★★½

Jack the Giant Killer

(1962, 92 min, US, Nathan Juran) *Kerwin Matthews, Judi Meredith, Torin Thatcher.* After completing Ray Harryhausen's *The Seventh Voyage of Sinbad*, a lot of the same people went to work on this film, which explains why it has the feel of a knockoff. Still, the special effects (by Jim Danforth) are good; featuring a giant, another giant (this one with two heads), a flying dragon, witches, ghouls and a sea monster — in short, the usual Saturday night South Street crowd. ★★ DVD: $14.99

Jack's Back

(1988, 97 min, US, Rowdy Herrington) *James Spader, Cynthia Gibb, Robert Picardo, Chris Mulkey.* Spader gives a solid portrayal of a troubled young man investigating the murder of his twin brother in this very effective update (set in Los Angeles) of the Jack the Ripper tale. A vastly underrated mystery with lots of chills to it. ★★★

The Jackal

(1997, 125 min, US, Michael Caton-Jones) *Bruce Willis, Richard Gere, Sidney Poitier, Diane Venora, Mathilda May, Tess Harper, Stephen Spinella.* An uneven updating of Frederick Forsyth's novel and Fred Zinnemann's film *The Day of the Jackal*. Willis is a mysterious assassin who's been hired by the Russian mob to kill the Director of the FBI. Poitier is the field agent who, working with Russian cop Venora (who's excellent as the tough-as-nails enforcer), must stop the unknown killer. The only lead they have is in the person of IRA sharpshooter Gere, who's serving a life sentence. As the Jackal, using various disguises, gets closer to his target, it becomes a cat-and-mouse game between him and his three hunters. Poitier and Gere bring a conviction to the film, however the script lacks the psychological makeup that made the first film so thrilling. ★★½ DVD Letterbox Collector's Edition: $14.99, DVD DTS sound: $14.99, VHS: $14.99, VHS Letterbox: $14.99

Jackass: The Movie

(2002, 87 min, US, Jeff Tremaine) *Johnny Knoxville, Bam Margera, Steve-O, Henry Rollins, Spike Jonze.* Johnny Knoxville and his pals are a group of postcollege slackers who are still trying to get in touch with their inner frat boys by performing a series of dangerous, sadomasochistic stunts for their own amusement. Their exploits have produced a loyal following on MTV, and now they hit the big screen with gags that were deemed too offensive for television. The difference is about as subtle as urinating on fresh snow, then eating it, and urinating on fresh snow, then eating it while wearing a beanie. Sure, there may be a few laughs to be had with some of their burlesque, but it becomes tiring, repetitive, bullying, stupid and pandering. The Three Stooges made a career in violent stunts, but they also brought wit and comic timing to the table. *Jackass* brings nothing more than the handgrips to further lower the bar on what passes for entertainment, celebrity and comedy. ★ DVD Letterbox: $19.99, DVD Pan & Scan: $19.99, VHS: $22.99

Jackie Brown

(1998, 155 min, US, Quentin Tarantino) *Pam Grier, Robert De Niro, Samuel L. Jackson, Robert Forster, Bridget Fonda, Michael Keaton, Michael Bowen, Chris Tucker.* Tarantino's immensely satis-

Jackie Brown

fying adaptation of Elmore Leonard's "Rum Punch" is less flashy and stylized than his first two films, but with its superb pacing, involving story line, flavorful characters, in-tune acting, and abundant humor and action, this rates as another outstanding effort from the writer-director. Making the most of her best role in years, that glorious '70s action star Grier is Jackie Brown, a down-on-her-luck airline attendant who, caught smuggling money for L.A. gun-runner Ordell Robbie (Jackson), is forced by ATF agents to get the goods on her boss. It's cross, double-cross and who's-scamming-who as Jackie devises her own ingenious plan to rid herself of her meager existence, Ordell and the feds. More character driven than *Dogs* or *Pulp*, the film is helped immeasurably by not only the canny performances by Grier and Jackson, but also by the remarkably nuanced portrayal by Forster as Max Cherry, a city-weary, unflappable bail bondsman who becomes involved with Jackie. In setting up the scam, Tarantino takes his time; thus insuring a maximum payoff for not only Jackie but the viewer as well. ★★★★ DVD Letterbox 2-disc set: $29.99, VHS: $9.99

Jackie Chan's First Strike

(1996, 88 min, Hong Kong, Stanley Tong) *Jackie Chan, Jackson Lou, Chen Chun Wu.* Originally released in Hong Kong as *Police Story 4* (*Supercop* was the third of the series), *First Strike* once again casts Chan as a Hong Kong police officer who must this time travel the globe in order to stop some arms dealers who are in league with the Russian mafia. More a tribute to James Bond films than a traditional Jackie vehicle, the film visits several exotic locales and showcases several large stunt sequences. Only one "traditional" kung fu fight is included in the film, but it is a doozy as Jackie beats up a group of bad guys with a ten-foot aluminum stepladder! *First Strike* is another totally entertaining piece of escapist cinema. (Partially dubbed in English) ★★★ DVD: $9.99, VHS: $9.99, Letterbox: $9.99

Jackie Chan's Project A

See: *Project A*

Jackie Chan's Who Am I?

(1998, 108 min, Hong Kong, Benny Chan & Jackie Chan) *Jackie Chan, Michelle Ferre, Mirai Yamamoto.* Chan's last film produced in Hong Kong, *Who Am I?* is an entertaining, hit-or-miss action fest — typical Chan here. Jackie plays a mercenary who falls into the jungle from a military transport plane during a sabotaged mission. He is rescued and healed by a local tribesman, yet he has no memory whatsoever (hence the title), and sets on

a quest to discover his true identity, pursued by illegal arms dealers and the CIA the whole way. Extremely uneven, silly and pointless, *Who Am I?* is also full of many amusing moments and energetic action sequences. ★★½ DVD Dubbed: $14.99, VHS: $9.99

Jackie Mason on Broadway

(1988, 60 min, US) *Jackie Mason.* A hilarious video presentation of Mason's Tony Award-winning one-man show. Filmed during a Broadway performance, this one-hour comedy routine features Mason's perceptive and unique view of the world, from the differences between Jews and gentiles to politics to Hollywood. Mason, who staged a comeback of sorts with this highly successful show, assaults his audience with a constant barrage of one-liners and anecdotes. Nothing is sacred in the world according to Mason. ★★★½

Jacknife

(1989, 102 min, US, David Jones) *Robert De Niro, Ed Harris, Kathy Baker, Charles S. Dutton.* An extremely compelling drama about two Vietnam vets coming to terms with their tour of duty and the death of an old friend. De Niro visits old Army buddy Harris, together exorcising their demons; De Niro then becomes involved with Harris' sister Bates. The three stars give excellent performances, which makes this oft-told tale seem all the more fresh. ★★★ VHS: $9.99

Jacko and Lise

(1982, 92 min, France, Walter Bal) *Laurent Malet, Annie Girardot.* Jacko and Freddie are inseparable friends whose lives are free of responsibility. Their friendship and their outlook on life change, however, when Jacko falls in love with a young woman and decides to better himself. A story of a young man's growth from a carefree youth into adulthood. (French with English subtitles) ★★½

Jacob's Ladder

(1990, 113 min, US, Adrian Lyne) *Tim Robbins, Danny Aiello, Elizabeth Peña, Jason Alexander, Macaulay Culkin.* From the writer of *Ghost*, Bruce Joel Rubin, and the director of *Fatal Attraction*, Lyne, comes this harrowing, roller-coaster ride about a Vietnam vet terrorized by his own demons. Robbins plays Jacob Singer, who tries to reconcile his past, both as a soldier and as a father devastated by family tragedy. In doing so, he is haunted by freakish hallucinations that threaten both his sanity and his life. A dark, psychological thriller, Lyne's camera gives terror a gruesome yet stylish look. ★★★ DVD Special Edition: $14.99, VHS: $9.99

Jacquot

(1991, 118 min, France, Agnès Varda) *Philippe Maron, Edouard Joubeaud, Laurent Monnier.* Varda's loving tribute to her partner Jacques Demy is a mixture of flashbacks, personal narratives and scenes from his films, which together create a vivid picture of his early interest in film. Varda presents a detailed look at Demy's (nicknamed "Jacquot") experience during the war and especially his early film projects as a youth. The performances are remarkably genuine, especially the three actors who portray Demy. *Jacquot* marks the only collaboration between the two directors, ending with Demy's death in 1990. The film's final scene owes tribute to François Truffaut's *The 400 Blows*. (French with English subtitles) ★★★½

Jade

(1995, 95 min, US, William Friedkin) *Linda Fiorentino, David Caruso, Chazz Palminteri, Richard Crenna, Michael Biehn. Basic Instinct* meets *Jagged Edge* in this worthless and uninspired outing from the author of both better films, Joe Eszterhas. Fiorentino plays the wife of a high-powered defense attorney (Palminteri) who becomes the prime suspect when a wealthy politico is murdered during an act of kinky sex with an unknown femme fatale known only as "Jade." Caruso plays the cop/ex-lover determined to get to the bottom of it all. Friedkin's thriller is a well-mounted but raucous mess, with action sequences that far outshine the ridiculous screenplay. ★½ DVD R-Rated: $19.99, VHS R-Rated: $9.99

Jagged Edge

(1985, 108 min, US, Richard Marquand) *Jeff Bridges, Glenn Close, Peter Coyote, Robert Loggia, Lance Henriksen, Michael Dorn.* An embittered Close defends a charismatic San Francisco newspaper publisher, played with sleek charm by Bridges, in this well-crafted murder mystery/courtroom drama. Coyote almost steals the show as the skeptical D.A. who steadfastly refuses to believe Bridges' protestations of innocence of his wife's murder. Close gives a fine, believable performance in both the courtroom encounters and in her romantic involvement with Bridges. Loggia received an Oscar nomination for his salty-tongued investigator. ★★★ DVD: $14.99

Jail Bait

(1954, 70 min, US, Edward D. Wood, Jr.) *Timothy Farrell, Lyle Talbot, Steve Reeves, Dolores Fuller.* Unlike its title's suggestion, this is not a tale of oversexed, underage teens. Instead, it's a melodrama about small-time crooks in constant run-ins with the law. Wood's notoriously bad film noir piece was shot in four days. ★½ DVD: $24.99, VHS: $9.99

Jailbirds' Vacation

(1965, 125 min, France, Robert Enrico) *Lino Ventura, Marie DuBois.* A middling drama about the desperate lengths a man will go to keep his business afloat. Hector Valentin's financial struggles with his family's sawmill company is greatly helped after he hires two strangers to help operate the factory. On the suggestion of the two, the owner begins to hire several parolees from the local prison only to discover a dark motive behind the scheme. (French with English subtitles) ★★

Jailbreakers

(1994, 76 min, US, William Friedkin) *Shannen Doherty, Antonio Sabato, Jr., Adrienne Barbeau, Adrien Brody, George Gerdes, Vince Edwards.* A fair-to-middling juvenile delinquent flick (produced for Showtime as part of a series of remakes of '50s drive-in flicks by high-profile directors), *Jailbreakers* is helped a great deal by Friedkin's muscular direction. Doherty is the cheerleader gone bad and Sabato her juvey boyfriend-cum-bad influence. Surprisingly straight-faced, this is also a bit leaden in that we don't really give a damn about the two leads (though Brody is charismatic and appealing in an early supporting role). With its short running time, however, it's a palatable time killer, but nothing more. ★★ DVD: $19.99, VHS: $9.99

Jailhouse Rock

(1957, 96 min, US, Richard Thorpe) *Elvis Presley, Judy Tyler, Dean Jones.* Arguably Presley's best musical has the King as a former convict who tries to make it as a rock 'n' roll star — think he succeeds? The musical number "Jailhouse Rock" is a classic. ★★★ DVD: $19.99, VHS: $9.99

Jakob the Liar

(1999, 114 min, US, Peter Kassovitz) *Robin Williams, Alan Arkin, Bob Balaban, Hannah Taylor Gordon, Michael Jeter, Armin Mueller-Stahl, Liev Schreiber, Matthieu Kassovitz.* An American version of the 1977 German film, this earnest, well-acted, downbeat remake will draw comparisons to Roberto Benigni's *Life Is Beautiful.* Both examine the Holocaust with an eye toward humor, though *Jakob* isn't as accomplished as Benigni's masterwork. In the Lodz ghetto during the Nazi Occupation, a widowed ex-café owner (Williams), Jakob, hears on German radio a report of an Allied victory against the Nazis. Telling his neighbors the news, they all assume he has a radio (which is outlawed). In order to give them some hope, he continues the deception — to the point that he puts his own life in jeopardy. The story is moving without being too heavy-handed about the characters' situation, and a subdued Williams and a good ensemble are sincere and effective. ★★½ DVD: $9.99

Jamaica Inn

(1939, 90 min, GB, Alfred Hitchcock) *Charles Laughton, Maureen O'Hara, Leslie Banks, Robert Newton.* This tense, suspenseful melodrama by Hitchcock is based on the best-selling novel by Daphne Du Maurier. The story is set in the 18th century and is about a country squire (Laughton) who is secretly the head of a band of pirates who wreck ships and ransom them. This was Hitchcock's last film in England before he began his "Hollywood period." ★★★ DVD: $29.99, VHS: $19.99

James and the Giant Peach

(1996, 80 min, US, Henry Selick) *Paul Terry, Joanna Lumley, Miriam Margolyes, Pete Postlethwaite, Simon Callow, Richard Dreyfuss, Jane Leeves, Susan Sarandon, David Thewlis.* Roald Dahl's charming children's story makes for an equally charming animated tale, though not quite as inventive as director Selick's debut feature *The Nightmare Before Christmas.* When young James loses his parents, he is forced to live with his two oppressive aunts. That is until a giant peach miraculously appears in their garden, offering James flight across the ocean. Using the same stop-motion animation as in *Nightmare,* Selick and his staff are able to incorporate live-action material, as well, to good effect. Hindered only by an unmemorable score, *James and the Giant Peach* is an affectionate fantasy which is capable of winning the hearts of children and parents alike. ★★★ DVD: $22.99, VHS: $14.99

The James Dean Story

(1957, 80 min, US, George W. George & Robert Altman) Documentary on '50s screen legend James Dean, including interviews with friends, associates and family. A rather one-dimensional portrait, *The James Dean Story* captures neither the mystery nor the power of the actor. For a more complete portrait of Dean, check out *James Dean: The First American Teenager.* ★★ DVD: $14.99, VHS: $12.99

James Joyce's Women

(1986, 91 min, Ireland, Michael Pearce) *Fionnula Flanagan, Timothy E. O'Grady.* Through a series of haunting, often erotically charged vignettes, the remarkable Flanagan offers a true tour de force as she portrays six fascinating women — three from Joyce's writings and three from his life. The film intelligently and successfully captures the spirit of James Joyce and is a one-of-a-kind theatrical experience. ★★★

Jamon Jamon

(1992, 96 min, Spain, Bigas Luna) *Penélope Cruz, Jordi Moll, Javier Bardem, Stephania Sandrelli.* Dripping with Freudian tension, director Luna's loony erotic comedy rips a page of Pedro Almodóvar's book as it delves into the abyss of *l'amour fou.* Set on a lonesome strip of highway in a dusty and deserted Spain, the story begins with a passionate teen tryst between the lower-class Silvia (Cruz) and Jose Luis (Molla), the son of an underwear tycoon. Insisting that he marry within his class, Jose Luis' overbearing mother (a marvelously camp Sandrelli) hires the strapping Raul (Bardem) to lure Silvia away from her son. But her plan backfires when she herself falls prey to Raul's smoldering masculine wiles. Luna's script plays out like an absurdist Greek tragedy, overflowing with sexual jealousies, and some paternal ambiguities for good measure. (Spanish with English subtitles) ★★★

Jane Austen in Manhattan

(1980, 108 min, GB, James Ivory) *Anne Baxter, Robert Powell, Sean Young.* Two rival New York theatre companies vie for the rights to produce a recently unearthed manuscript by Jane Austen. One wants to produce the piece as a period operetta, the other wants to make it an avant-garde performance piece. It's an interesting premise; however, the film is not one of the best to come out of the Merchant Ivory mill. ★★

Jane Eyre

(1944, 96 min, US, Robert Stevenson) *Orson Welles, Joan Fontaine, Elizabeth Taylor, Agnes Moorehead, Margaret O'Brien.* This almost film noirish adaptation of Charlotte Brontë's novel about an unloved orphan girl who grows up to become a governess in a mysterious manor is a shadowy Gothic affair. Fontaine and Welles give such brooding performances, they seem like two Elizabethan actors gone mad. ★★★ VHS: $19.99

Jane Eyre

(1983, 239 min, GB, Julian Amyes) *Timothy Dalton, Zelah Clarke.* Dread not the thought of being tied down for four hours of tedious BBC drama, for this retelling of the Charlotte Brontë classic is a motivating and powerful drama. This rapturous tale of two lovers frustrated by social mores and misty pasts features two superb performances by Dalton and Clarke as the star-crossed lovers. Their portrayals infuse the story with unrivaled immediacy and emotion. ★★★½ VHS: $24.99

The January Man

(1989, 97 min, US, Pat O'Connor) *Kevin Kline, Danny Aiello, Susan Sarandon, Harvey Keitel, Mary Elizabeth Mastrantonio, Alan Rickman, Rod Steiger.* John Patrick Shanley (*Moonstruck*) wrote this mystery-comedy about a serial killer terrorizing New York. Kline is police chief Aiello's brother who helps his sibling solve the case. Though there's a great cast, the story is so muddled, they are mostly wasted. ★★ DVD Dual: $14.99

Jason and the Argonauts

(1963, 104 min, GB, Don Chaffey) *Todd Armstrong, Nancy Kovak, Laurence Naismith, Honor Blackman.* Spectacular special effects by Ray Harryhausen and a beautiful Bernard Herrmann score are the highlights of this otherwise predictable action-adventure fable about Jason's hazardous and monster-filled search for the Golden Fleece. The cast is forgettable; the real stars are Harryhausen's sword-fighting skeletons, multiheaded Hydra, and malevolent Harpies. ★★½ DVD: $27.99, VHS: $14.99

Jason's Lyric

(1994, 120 min, US, Doug McHenry) *Allen Payne, Jada Pinkett, Forest Whitaker, Bokeem Woodbine, Suzanne Douglas.* Smart, hard-working Jason (Payne) and his thuggish malt liquor-swilling sibling Josh (skillfully played by rapper Woodbine) are bonded by the memory of their slain father (Whitaker). But they are also separated by the opposite paths they choose for themselves. When Jason meets Lyric (Pinkett), she inspires him to leave their town and start a peaceful life together; psycho-bro stands between them, dangerous and out of control. Powerful dialogue, fine performances, an intelligent script and eyeglass-fogging lovemaking scenes more than compensate for the occasional cliché. ★★★ DVD: $14.99, VHS: $9.99

Jawbreaker

(1999, 87 min, US, Darren Stein) *Rose McGowan, Rebecca Gayheart, Carol Kane, Pam Grier, William Katt, P.J. Soles, Marilyn Manson.* A prank goes awry and three popular girls accidentally kill one of their best friends. Hmm, where have we heard this one before? Colorful, with great costumes, but even two songs by The Donnas can't save *Jawbreaker* from its limp, unfunny core. ★½ DVD: $9.99, VHS: $9.99

Javier Bardem and Penélope Cruz in *Jamon Jamon*

Jaws

(1975, 120 min, US, Steven Spielberg) *Roy Scheider, Richard Dreyfuss, Robert Shaw, Lorraine Gary, Murray Hamilton.* One of the great box-office hits of all time is also one of the best horror films in the last few decades. Spielberg's classic shark story, based on Peter Benchley's novel, kept millions out of the water during the summer of '75. Scheider, Dreyfuss and the great Shaw go shark hunting off the New England coast and find Melvillian adventure. A classic combination of suspense, effects, editing, cinematography, score and bristling characterizations. (Followed by 3 sequels) ★★★★ DVD Pan & Scan: $14.99, DVD Anniversary Collector's Edition: $14.99, DVD DTS sound: $14.99, VHS Anniversary Collector's Edition: $9.99

Jaws 2

(1978, 117 min, US, Jeannot Szwarc) *Roy Scheider, Lorraine Gary, Murray Hamilton.* Flimsy sequel has a couple of scares to it, but there is absolutely no comparison to the original. Scheider and Gary return (and are much classier than this film deserves) as another great white shark terrorizes Amity Island. On the menu: *teenager du jour.* ★★ DVD Letterbox: $14.99, VHS Special Edition: $9.99

Jaws 3

(1983, 98 min, US, Joe Alves) *Bess Armstrong, Simon MacCorkindale, Louis Gossett, Jr., Dennis Quaid, Lea Thompson.* The action (what there is of it) moves to Florida as now a great white shark terrorizes Sea World. Presented in 3-D in 1983, *Jaws 3* is a mishmash of horror film and disaster film clichés, and the sight of the shark attacking the underwater amusement park is silly rather than scary. ★ DVD Letterbox: $14.99, VHS: $9.99

Jaws: The Revenge

(1987, 91 min, US, Joseph Sargent) *Lorraine Gary, Michael Caine, Lance Guest, Mario Van Peebles, Karen Young, Lynn Whitfield.* In this fourth, ridiculous installment, the shark somehow develops the brain of a serial killer and decides to hunt down Brody's widow. Caine missed picking up his Oscar because he was shooting this — hope the paycheck was worth it. Of note is that the studio recut the film after audiences reacted negatively to Van Peebles becoming lunch. ★ DVD Letterbox: $9.99

Jay and Silent Bob Strike Back

(2001, 104 min, US, Kevin Smith) *Jason Mewes, Kevin Smith, Ben Affleck, Shannon Elizabeth, Will Ferrell, Jason Lee, Chris Rock, Eliza Dushku, Ali Larter.* The two petty weed dealers from New Jersey get their own movie: a road trip, a Hollywood satire, John J. Sullivan's "O Brother, Where Art My Car?" But that's overselling it, as Kevin Smith simply bids a fond and cheeky farewell to his immature characters whom he's carried from *Clerks* to *Dogma.* Mewes again plays himself, that is, Jay, the clueless master of cool and spewer of verbal diarrhea, while Smith lays low as Silent Bob, who is indeed mostly silent but has a tremendously expressive face. They head from Jersey to Hollywood to stop a film about them from being made, and run into characters from all of Smith's films along the way. They also seem to run into a lot of jokes that Smith either cut out from the earlier films, or thought up after the fact. As such, it's a grab bag, alternately extremely funny and uncomfortably flat. It's basically a fetish film for Smith, complete with *Star Wars* references, bad girls in latex (which his real-life wife) and an awful lot of gay jokes. ★★½ DVD Letterbox 2-disc set: $19.99, VHS: $9.99

The Jazz Singer

(1980, 115 min, US, Richard Fleischer) *Neil Diamond, Laurence Olivier, Lucie Arnaz.* Second remake of Al Jolson's "first talkie" about a cantor's son (Diamond) who goes against his father's wishes and becomes a rock star. Pretty bad stuff; even Olivier is embarrassing. ★

Jazzman

(1983, 80 min, USSR, Karen Shakhnazarov) *Igor Sklyar, Alexander Chorny.* With a deft touch and gentle satiric outlook, this pleasant comedy, set in the 1920s, focuses on a musical conservatory student who wants to study jazz. Reacting to the official stance that jazz is a "monstrous product of bourgeois society," our young hero quits school to start his own jazz band. Teaming up with two colorful street musicians and a saxophonist, the young musicians struggle to gain acceptance for this "antirevolutionary" music form. Filled with Dixieland, ragtime and swing sounds, the film joyfully preaches the universality of music. (Russian with English subtitles) ★★★ VHS: $59.99

je tu il elle

(1974, 95 min, Belgium/France, Chantal Akerman) Akerman's first feature is a charming yet demanding, innovative psychodrama. It opens with director/heroine Akerman lying alone and naked in bed eating from a bag of sugar. What follows is a deceptively simple story told in three segments, each containing an element of the traditional depiction of women. Initially she is seen writing a sad letter to an (ex?)lover; another is a brief sexual encounter with a truck driver; and finally, a sexual relationship with another woman. Akerman thinks out ideas such as loss and separation, solitary introspection and voyeurism with startling clarity. (French with English subtitles) ★★★ VHS: $29.99

Jean de Florette

(1986, 122 min, France, Claude Berri) *Gérard Depardieu, Yves Montand, Daniel Auteuil.* Adapted from two of Marcel Pagnol's novels (author of the popular trilogy "Marius," "Fanny" and "César"), this powerful and absorbing tale of greed, betrayal, idealism and love was an art-house hit across the country. Montand gives an unsettling performance as "Papet," an evil old peasant intent on swindling some valuable land from his neighbor. After accidentally killing the original owner of the property, he must now deal with Jean (Depardieu), a city-bred hunchback who optimistically brings his family to the farm and dreams of a new life. (Sequel: *Manon of the Spring*) (French with English subtitles) ★★★★

Jeanne Dielman, 23, Quai du Commerce, 1080 Bruxelles

(1975, 201 min, Belgium/France, Chantal Akerman) *Delphine Seyrig, Jan Decorte.* Widely aclaimed as one of the most important films of the decade, Akerman's monumental saga of a frightfully ritualized existence covers three days in the stifling life of a bourgeois widow (Seyrig) who does household work, takes care of her teenage son and is a part-time prostitute; a tragic figure for whom the acts of cooking, cleaning and intercourse are performed with the same stoic efficiency. This epic exlores the gradual unraveling of a frail human psyche. A bleak and original feminist tragedy and a highly rewardng realization of avant-garde filmmaking aspirations. (French with English subtitles) ★★★★

Jeepers Creepers

(2001, 90 min, US, Victor Salva) *Gina Philips, Justin Long, Jonathan Breck, Eileen Brennan.* A brother and sister, driving down a rural road on the way home from college, spot a sinister dude shoving what looks to be bloody bodies down a sewage pipe in his back yard. Naturally, they decide to go back and investigate. Character motivation is a big problem in this movie, as the kids do some truly moronic things to move the plot along (and having them acknowledge this fact in some *Scream*-like, postmodern observations doesn't make it any more plausible). Director Salva also resorts to the old "the-car-won't-start!" trope a few times too many. Despite these flaws, *Jeepers Creepers* has some very creepy moments, is rather atmospheric, and has a surprisingly bleak (and very effective) ending. Worthwhile for horror fans willing to look beyond its lack of logic. (Sequel: *Jeepers Creepers 2*) ★★½ DVD: $14.99, VHS: $9.99

Jeepers Creepers 2

(2003, 103 min, US, Victor Salva) *Ray Wise, Jonathan Breck, Travis Schiffner, Eric Nenninger.* Follow-up to the sleeper hit of 2001 finds the demonic Creeper terrorizing a broken-down schoolbus of football players and cheerleaders. Writer-director Salva wittily wrings much suspense from the *Lord of the Flies*-like disintegration of civilized behavior among the teens, so that there are no lags between Creeper attacks. Wise is a hoot as a vengeful father on the hunt for the beast after his young son is killed. Like the first film, this does dip now and then into the cheese pool, and there are more than a handful of silly moments. But for horror fans, this is a treat: no stupid one-liners, no wimping out — just straight-ahead, unapologetic horror with only a few, minor missteps. ★★★ DVD Letterbox: $19.99, VHS: $49.99

Jefferson in Paris

(1995, 140 min, GB, James Ivory) *Gwyneth Paltrow, Nick Nolte, Greta Scacchi, Thandie Newton, Simon Callow, James Earl Jones, Jean-Pierre Aumont.* The first Merchant Ivory/Disney collaboration is a lifeless historical epic. Director Ivory and longtime writing partner Ruth Prawer Jhabvala, responsible for the brilliant *The Remains of the Day* among many others, have fashioned a film that is a superior evocation of late-1700s Paris and examines in a dispassionate, casual manner the five-year service of Thomas Jefferson as American ambassador to France. Ivory's works have usually demonstrated extraordinary characterizations, but here the film concentrates on Jefferson's libido while ignoring the essence of a great man living in a troubled time. As Jefferson, Nolte is more lumberjack than patrician; he makes a clever lover but a dubious patriot. Scacchi and Newton are his love interests, and Callow and Paltrow offer good support. ★★½ DVD: $19.99

Jeffrey

(1995, 94 min, US, Christopher Ashley) *Steven Weber, Patrick Stewart, Sigourney Weaver, Michael T. Weiss, Nathan Lane, Kathy Najimy, Bryan Batt, Olympia Dukakis.* Paul Rudnick has adapted his own off-Broadway hit with this witty if slightly flawed comedy. Jeffrey (the chipper Weber), a gay aspiring actor, has come to a momentous decision: In the age of AIDS, he's going to become celibate. Then he meets the devastatingly handsome Steve (Weiss). As these two men tentatively begin a relationship, Jeffrey learns of Steve's HIV-positive status, which only complicates his fear of commitment. The success of Rudnick's play (and to a large degree the film) lies, partially, in creating a comedy centered around the subject of AIDS, and endowing it with an acerbic, even sardonic sense of humor. And when *Jeffrey* is funny, it is very funny. But in the filmization, certain dramatic scenes only magnify their less-than developed emotions. Stewart gloriously camps it up as Jeffrey's rich, designer friend Sterling, bringing unexpected depth to his role. ★★★ DVD: $19.99

Jennifer 8

(1992, 127 min, US, Bruce Robinson) *Andy Garcia, Uma Thurman, Lance Henriksen, Kathy Baker, John Malkovich.* Two good performers get wasted in this muddled thriller. Garcia is a burnt-out L.A. cop who takes a job in a small town only to fall onto the trail of a serial killer. Thurman is a blind schoolteacher who Garcia thinks is going to be the killer's next victim. To give away any of the leaps of logic, or amazing coincidences on which this film relies to unravel its plot, would destroy the little bits of mystery it does manage to create. Suffice to say that you would have to be a lot more than blind not to see this movie killer coming from a mile away. ★★ DVD: $19.99, VHS: $14.99

Jeremiah Johnson

(1972, 117 min, US, Sydney Pollack) *Robert Redford, Will Geer.* Redford is Johnson, the legendary mountain man and trapper who made war on the Blackfoot Indians after they murdered everything he loved. While taking some liberties with the original story, the film is nevertheless an inspired and entertaining tale of a man who cannot abide modern society's rules and restrictions. The film is beautiful testament to the possibility of man's oneness with the natural world and an ode to the indomitable, individual spirit. It is also an uncharacteristic western in a genre which had, at the time it was released, grown tired and repetitive. ★★★ DVD: $19.99, VHS: $9.99, VHS Letterbox: $9.99

The Jerk

(1979, 94 min, US, Carl Reiner) *Steve Martin, Bernadette Peters, Bill Macy, Catlin Adams, Jackie Mason.* Martin had his first starring role and his first big screen success in this very funny and incredibly silly rags-to-riches-to-rags-back-to-riches comedy. Steve plays a hapless schmoe who finds and loses (and finds again?) happiness and Peters. ★★½ DVD: $19.99, VHS: $9.99

The Jerky Boys

(1995, 82 min, US, James Melkonian) *Johnny Brennan, Kamal Ahmed, Alan Arkin, William Hickey.* Having achieved mixed commercial success in the conversion of TV sitcoms, cartoons and comic books to the silver screen, Hollywood once again sets its sights on the recording industry (after the great popularity of Cheech & Chong) and the result is this featherweight comedy featuring the debut of The Jerky Boys. Brennan and Ahmed play a pair of ne'er-do-well phone pranksters who bluff and insult their way into Mafia high society, incurring the wrath of a New York crime boss (Arkin). What may have been funny on their two platinum-selling comedy albums suffers greatly from a skeletal screenplay and a paucity of comic inspiration. ★½

Jerry Maguire

(1996, 139 min, US, Cameron Crowe) *Tom Cruise, Renée Zellweger, Cuba Gooding, Jr., Kelly Preston, Jonathan Lipnicki, Jerry O'Connell, Eric Stoltz,*

Oscar winner Cuba Gooding, Jr. in *Jerry Maguire*

Beau Bridges. An appealing romantic comedy with a thing to two to say about the cutthroat industry that is modern-day sports, *Jerry Maguire* gives Cruise one of his best roles. Jerry Maguire is a sports agent whose night of conscience (and wordy "mission statement" decrying his firm's greediness) casts him into the unknown waters of solo artist. With an admiring accountant (a charming Zellweger) in tow, Maguire takes his one client (Oscar winner Gooding) and attempts to go one-on-one with the big boys. Writer-director Crowe has created likable characters who all get to say and do things within a very romantic framework. His is a smart, lively, funny work. ★★★ DVD Letterbox 2-disc set: $14.99, DVD Special Edition: $27.99, VHS: $9.99

Jersey Girl

(2004, 103 min, US, Kevin Smith) *Ben Affleck, Liv Tyler, George Carlin, Raquel Castro, Jason Biggs, Jennifer Lopez, Stephen Root.* Writer-director Smith continues to expand his horizons with this feel-good flick, but miscalculates with a script that's too smutty for families and too schmaltzy for his fanbase. Affleck is in his romantic element as a widower who cracks and loses his NYC job, relocating to Jersey with his young daughter (the saccharine Castro), who's the Jersey Girl of the title. His broken heart is mended by video clerk Tyler, while fatherly advice is handed down by the acerbic Carlin. There's a whole lot of sex talk, mostly from a carnal Tyler, and some of it shows that old Smith spark. However, the plot machinations are straight from Screenwriting 101, leading to a predictably heart-tugging denouement. Vilmos Zsigmond's cinematography makes for Smith's best-looking film to date, though with such pedestrian material it just makes this disappointment seem even slicker. Infamously, Lopez (Affleck's gal at the time) provides an uncomfortable cameo as his doomed wife. ★★ DVD: $29.99

Jerusalem

(1996, 166 min, Sweden, Bille August) *Max von Sydow, Maria Bonnevie, Ulf Friberg, Olympia Dukakis, Pernilla August.* Director August's spellbinding adaptation of Seim Lagerlöf's novel about religious fervor will lose some of its scope on video, but it is extremely worthwhile, nonetheless. Ingmar (Friberg) and Gertrud (Bonnevie) are villagers in a Swedish community at the turn of the century whose love is divided by their conflicting loyalties. Whereas he hopes to manage his family's farm, she is swayed by a visiting preacher to make a pilgrimage to the Holy Land. *Jerusalem* depicts how the villagers adapt to the tough choices they have made. August pays close attention to detail — both in the physical landscape as well as the expressions of the characters — to create extraordinary emotional depth. Crisply photographed and featuring hypnotic

performances by the leads, *Jerusalem* is an austere but effective drama that resonates long after the credits have rolled. (Swedish with English subtitles) ★★★½ VHS: $29.99

Jesse James

(1939, 105 min, US, Henry King) *Tyrone Power, Henry Fonda, Randolph Scott, Brian Donlevy.* Exciting western focusing on the unlawful exploits of outlaws Jesse and Frank James. Power and Fonda play the brothers. Fonda repeated the role a year later in *The Return of Frank James.* ★★★ VHS: $9.99

Jesus Christ Superstar

(1973, 103 min, US, Norman Jewison) *Ted Neeley, Carl Anderson, Yvonne Elliman, Josh Mostel.* Vibrant screen version of the Andrew Lloyd Webber-Tim Rice rock opera (which appeared on Broadway) about the last days of Jesus Christ. Jewison brings a contemporary flavor to the biblical story. Remastered print. ★★★ DVD Letterbox: $14.99, VHS Letterbox: $9.99

Jesus Christ Superstar

(2000, 112 min, GB, Gale Edwards) *Glenn Carter, Jerome Pradon, Renee Castle, Rik Mayall.* Based on the acclaimed 1996 West End revival, this lively adaptation of the Tim Rice-Andrew Lloyd Webber rock musical stands head and shoulders above the recent Webber video releases (*Cats, Joseph & the Amazing Technicolor Dreamcoat*). Inventive staging, a solid cast and great production values elevate this modern-dress depiction of Christ's last days, aided by one of Webber's best scores and Rice's clever lyrics. Among an exceptional ensemble, Pradon is outstanding as a leather-jacketed Judas. ★★★½ DVD: $19.99

Jesus of Montreal

(1990, 119 min, Canada, Denys Arcand) *Gilles Pelletier, Catherine Wilkening, Lothaire Bluteau, Marie-Christine Barrault.* A serious, intelligent and satiric update of the persecution and crucifixion of Jesus Christ. Set in present-day Montreal, a priest hires a young actor to revamp and modernize his parish's annual Passion Play. Daniel (Bluteau), a serenely intense young man, takes his task quite seriously. With him in the lead as Christ, he and a ragtag collection of his friends present a radical and, in the Church's eyes, scandalous production which soon becomes a hit with the public. Although the story parallels the Bible's account quite closely, the film never sinks to mere rehashing, and offers interesting and, at times, humorous thoughts on spiritualism in the modern world, the function of art, the perils of fame and the struggle to retain one's personal integrity. (French with English subtitles) ★★★½

Jesus' Son

(2000, 109 min, US/Canada, Alison MacLean) *Billy Crudup, Samantha Morton, Will Patton, Denis Leary, Jack Black, Holly Hunter, Dennis Hopper.* In the early '70s, people saw God everywhere, and often thought they saw the god within. *Jesus' Son* has a random and disjointed nature, fitting since it's based on a collection of short stories (by Denis Johnson), fitting since that's much like life. As a young man known only as Fuckhead, Crudup is sweetly spacey as he wanders through his life, bouncing off a collection of demons and oddballs, junkies and miscreants. The story — of a druggie turned small-time thief and of his redemption — folds over itself, nonlinear and episodic, a confluence of happenstance testifying that there's no salvation without sin, no redemption without wretchedness. Maclean's direction is fluid and lyrical, and the ensemble cast work well together to create a heightened alternate reality and deliver a bemused satisfaction. ★★★½ DVD: $14.99

Jew-Boy Levi

(1998, 90 min, Germany, Didi Danquart) *Bruno Cathomas, Caroline Eber, Ulrich Noethen.* The gradual acceptance of the Nazi doctrine by the ordinary citizens of Germany during the 1930s makes for a lethargic but well-intentioned tale of pervading anti-Semitism. Levi is a Jewish merchant making his annual trip to a small village in the Black Forest. Coinciding with his visit is the arrival of a group of Nazi railroad engineers, who begin to rally the villagers against their former friend. Cathomas makes Levi a likable, unsuspecting victim, but the film only occasionally harvests the emotional power to make one really care about his fate. (German with English subtitles) ★★½ DVD: $24.99, VHS: $79.99

The Jewel of the Nile

(1985, 105 min, US, Lewis Teague) *Michael Douglas, Kathleen Turner, Danny DeVito, Avner Eisenberg.* Entertaining if now familiar sequel to *Romancing the Stone* picks up six months later after Douglas and Turner have sailed into the sunset. Douglas once again comes to Turner's rescue after she is held captive by an Arab ruler. Lots of laughs and action and DeVito, as well. ★★½ DVD: $14.99

Jezebel

(1938, 103 min, US, William Wyler) *Bette Davis, Henry Fonda, George Brent, Fay Bainter, Donald Crisp.* Though many believe Davis won her first Oscar (for *Dangerous*) as a consolation prize, there's no doubt whatsoever that she deserved her second one for *Jezebel*. Davis is brilliant as a Southern belle whose flirtations and fickleness drive away boyfriend Fonda; she is then forced to come to terms with her own faults when he returns with a new wife. The ballroom sequence is especially noteworthy. Bainter also won an Oscar as Davis' aunt. ★★★½ DVD: $19.99, VHS: $14.99

JFK

(1991, 189 min, US, Oliver Stone) *Kevin Costner, Tommy Lee Jones, Joe Pesci, Gary Oldman, Donald Sutherland, Sissy Spacek, Jack Lemmon, Walter Matthau, John Candy, Kevin Bacon.* No stranger to controversy, Stone serves up a volatile mix of politics and conspiracy. Technically brilliant and impressively acted, Stone's triumphant speculative drama is based on New Orleans District Attorney Jim Garrison's experience in bringing charges for the murder of John F. Kennedy. Fiercely debated, the film suggests that Lee Harvey Oswald was merely a patsy for others criminally responsible. Whether or not you believe Stone's version of that fateful day's events, there's no denying *JFK* is a labor of love for the director, and he has crafted a fascinating and often spellbinding dissertation. Costner is well-cast as the impassioned D.A. Among a first-rate supporting cast, Jones, Bacon, Oldman and particularly Sutherland are impressive. ★★★★ DVD 2-disc Special Edition: $26.99, VHS Director's Cut: $8.99, VHS Letterbox Director's Cut: $8.99

The Jigsaw Man

(1984, 91 min, GB, Terence Young) *Laurence Olivier, Michael Caine, Susan George, Robert Powell.* The delicious chemistry and edge-of-your seat excitement that arose out of the pairing of Olivier and Caine in *Sleuth* is unfortunately not evident in this effort. Caine plays an ex-British Secret

Service agent who defects to Russia, submits to extensive plastic surgery, and comes back to England for one final mission. Predictable and, sadly, not very exciting. ★★

Jimmy Hollywood

(1994, 110 min, US, Barry Levinson) *Joe Pesci, Christian Slater, Victoria Abril, Jason Beghe.* You can't judge a video by its cover or even its theatrical run, since director Levinson reedited this film for home video viewing. The result is an interesting though not very engaging comedy-drama about a wannabe actor (Pesci) who becomes a vigilante after his girlfriend is mugged on the mean streets of Hollywood. The film tries to examine the power of celebrity criminals, as Pesci's Jimmy Hollywood is partially inspired by the media coverage of his deeds. The surprise of the film is Slater's quirky, low-key performance as Pesci's friend (and henchman) who has lost (and continues to lose) various parts of his memory. ★★½ VHS: $19.99

The Jimmy Show

(2003, 96 min, US, Frank Whaley) *Frank Whaley, Carla Gugino, Ethan Hawke.* Whaley follows his directorial debut *Joe the King* with this minor drama about a loser whose life consists of taking care of his invalid grandmother and working as a stockboy in a supermarket. He also dreams of being a big-time standup comedian; trouble is, he has absolutely no talent. Meanwhile, his high school sweetheart becomes pregnant, and they get married and must live with his grandmother. Though a well-crafted, acted and directed film, *The Jimmy Show* is depressing and hopeless from beginning to end, making it a difficult watch. It's unclear what Whaley was trying to say with this film except that "life sucks." Proceed with caution and a great deal of Prozac. ★★½ DVD: $9.99, VHS: $7.99

Jingle All the Way

(1996, 85 min, US, Brian Levant) *Arnold Schwarzenegger, Sinbad, Phil Hartman, Rita Wilson, Robert Conrad.* If it's holiday cheer you're looking for, you'll have to look elsewhere, for *Jingle All the Way* gets down and dirty. Some of the time, that is — for it's also rather sappy. Its high-concept premise works for awhile: Schwarzenegger is a workaholic father who forgets to buy his son's Christmas present, so he sets out on Christmas Eve for a little last-minute shopping. This scenario, and a rivalry with fellow dad Sinbad on a similar mission, sets in motion some funny physical comedy. But the film soon runs out of steam — and ideas — and turns into a feel-good free-for-all. ★★

Jinxed

(1983, 103 min, US, Don Siegel) *Bette Midler, Ken Wahl, Rip Torn.* This muddled black comedy about blackmail, blackjack and murder stars Midler, in her pre-Touchstone days, as a Las Vegas singer and Wahl as a gambler who hooks up with her. Torn also stars as a dealer, he the "jinxed" of the title. This film is known more for the conflicts on the set than for what is presented on the screen. ★★

Jo Jo Dancer, Your Life Is Calling

(1986, 97 min, US, Richard Pryor) *Richard Pryor, Debbie Allen, Paula Kelly, Wings Hauser, Dennis Farina.* Pryor wrote, directed and stars in this autobiographical story of the rise and fall of a talented black comedian, whose drug habit nearly kills him. Though Pryor commendably opens up some deep

wounds, and the comic's early years are well captured, much of the film suffers from a lack of energy and soul. ★★ DVD Dual: $14.99, VHS: $14.99

Joan of Arc

(1948, 146 min, US, Victor Fleming) *Ingrid Bergman, Jose Ferrer, John Ireland.* Bergman gives a passionate performance as the peasant girl who led the French armies to victory. Based on the Maxwell Anderson play. Ferrer is superb as the Dauphin, future king of France, in this otherwise stagey production. Original theatrical version. ★★½ DVD: $19.99

Joan of Arc

(1999, 140 min, US, Christian Duguay) *Leelee Sobieski, Chad Willett, Jacqueline Bisset, Powers Boothe, Olympia Dukakis, Neil Patrick Harris, Robert Loggia, Maximilian Schell, Peter Strauss, Shirley MacLaine, Peter O'Toole.* It's rare that one can say that a made-for-TV movie outshines its big-screen rival, but that is exactly the case here as this small screen effort completely surpasses the overblown, phantasmagoric *The Messenger*. Newcomer Sobieski is mesmerizing as the "Maid from Lorraine" Jean D'Arc, who, following France's embarrassing loss to Henry V at Agincourt in 1415, almost single-handedly liberated Normandy from the English. Harris is compelling as the French dauphin Charles and O'Toole also stands out as the inquisitor Bishop Cauchon. The battles in *The Messenger* may be more intense, but this *Joan*, by contrast, spares us the martial gore for a far more interesting peek into the political machinations swirling around its hapless young heroine. ★★★½ DVD: $9.99, VHS: $9.99

Joan of Paris

(1942, 91 min, US, Robert Stevenson) *Michèle Morgan, Paul Henreid, Alan Ladd.* Extraordinary "B" WWII drama with Morgan as a young Parisian woman who sacrifices herself so that a group of British pilots can escape the Gestapo in Occupied France. ★★★½

Jock Peterson

(1974, 97 min, Australia, Tim Burstall) *Wendy Hughes, Jack Thompson.* Thompson is an electrician who quits his job and enrolls in college. His education is not limited to books, however, as he soon becomes embroiled in an affair with his English professor's wife (Hughes). An amiable tale with unpredictable appeal, bolstered by Hughes' winning performance. ★★½

Joe

(1970, 90 min, US, John G. Avildsen) *Peter Boyle, Susan Sarandon, Dennis Patrick.* Hard-hitting though dated generation gap drama with Boyle giving a sensational performance as a bigoted New York construction worker (hard hat) whose prejudice leads to tragedy. Sarandon made her debut as his daughter, who becomes involved with a group of "hippies." ★★★ DVD Dual: $19.99

Joe Dirt

(2001, 95 min, US, Dennie Gordon) *David Spade, Dennis Miller, Brittany Daniel, Christopher Walken.* The film walks like a duck, and quacks like a duck, but research indicates that *Joe Dirt* is *not* a lame movie based on a lame "SNL" sketch. So, instead of adding this vehicle to the trash heap with *It's Pat*, add it to the trash heap with other *original* crap from "SNL" stars, like *Billy Madison*. Spade (who cowrote) stars as the titular soil, a white-trash mullethead who's searching for the parents who abandoned him. He tells his life story to a D.J. (Miller, who's annoying in a different way), which sets up a bunch of episodic flashbacks. Dirt is such a pathetic, depressive character (and he knows it) that it's impossible to laugh when he encounters bumps on life's gravel road. Walken is forgettable in an extended cameo, which is really saying something. ★ DVD: $14.99, VHS: $9.99

Joe Gould's Secret

(2000, 110 min, US, Stanley Tucci) *Stanley Tucci, Patricia Clarkson, Hope Davis, Ian Holm, Susan Sarandon.* Based on a true story, Tucci's *Joe Gould's Secret* is an intellectual literary game full of real human drama. Tucci stars as a *New Yorker* writer of human interest stories doing a piece on a New York legend, Joe Gould (Holm). Gould is an eccentric homeless man who has written an oral history that is known all around New York in literary and artistic circles. He camps out in friend's living rooms depositing pieces of his history everywhere. An investigation into the legacy of art ultimately becomes a discovery of our own humanity. Holm and Tucci's performances are sublimely understated in this moving, low-key drama. ★★★ DVD: $19.99

Joe Somebody

(2001, 105 min, US, John Pasquin) *Tim Allen, Julie Bowen, Kelly Lynch, Greg Germann, Jim Belushi.* After losing a fistfight in front of his daughter, meek office worker Joe (Allen) decides to bulk up and teach family audiences dubious lessons in dealing with bullies. Allen's usual Everyman charm is the only thing worth watching in this otherwise lightweight, knockabout comedy. ★½ DVD: $19.99, VHS: $14.99

Joe the King

(1999, 100 min, US, Frank Whaley) *Noah Fleiss, Karen Young, Val Kilmer, Ethan Hawke, John Leguizamo.* This first, semiautobiographical effort from writer-director Whaley succeeds in creating poignant moments in its familiar coming-of-age story, but is undone by an unnecessary sentimental outlook. Fleiss is Joe, a troubled youth growing up poor in a small town. His adolescence is made all the more difficult by an alcoholic father (Kilmer), clueless adults and an indifferent school system. The film follows Joe as he commits a series of petty crimes that graduate to felonious. Whaley gives the film a sharp look, and his actors all give sincere performances (Kilmer is effective as Joe's dad), but this is a case in which sincerity doesn't necessarily make for always involving dramatics. ★★½ DVD: $14.99

Joe Versus the Volcano

(1990, 99 min, US, John Patrick Shanley) *Tom Hanks, Meg Ryan, Lloyd Bridges, Dan Hedaya, Ossie Davis, Amanda Plummer.* Hanks plays Joe, a grim factory worker who learns he is terminally ill. When a tycoon learns of his condition, Joe is given a chance to live like a king for six weeks in exchange for his services as a human sacrifice to a live volcano. En route, he takes up with the tycoon's two daughters (both played exceedingly well by Ryan), and finds true love, adventure and a complete luggage set. The first half of the film is occasionally involving, but the last half is as lost as its hero, adrift at sea with no direction in mind. ★★ DVD: $14.99, VHS: $9.99

Joe's Apartment

(1996, 90 min, US, John Payson) *Jerry O'Connell, Megan Ward, Robert Vaughn, Paul Bartel.* With the exception of *Shinbone Alley*, movies starring singing and dancing cockroaches are rare birds indeed. Unfortunately, the MTV-inspired *Joe's Apartment* — which had the chance to be the *Citizen Kane* of its genre — takes its unusual and potentially camp classic premise and squanders it. O'Connell is Joe, a country bumpkin in the big city. It turns out his New York apartment is overrun by roaches. Only these aren't ordinary bugs — these sing, dance, crack jokes, give romantic advice and party on. Obviously, the film's best moments feature the computer-animated roaches doing their thing. But the filmmakers sharpened their focus on the *Cuca Blattodea* and forgot to flesh out the *Homo Sapiens.* ★★ DVD: $9.99

Joe's Bed-Stuy Barbershop

(1982, 60 min, US, Spike Lee) *Leon Errol, Morris Camovsky.* Lee was still a student at NYU when he made this satirical, slice-of-life tale of bookmaking, murder and trying to make it big; all set at a corner barbershop in the Bed-Stuy section of Brooklyn. ★★★

Joey Breaker

(1993, 92 min, US, Stephen Starr) *Richard Edson, Cedelia Morley, Erik King, Gina Gershon, Philip Seymour Hoffman.* Joey (Edson) is a fast-talking New York talent agent whose pace is slowed down after he meets a Jamaican waitress (Marley). All of the film's characters feel as though they were picked up off a SoHo street corner: a hip-hop comedian, a man infected with AIDS, interracial couples, gay lovers; and the film treats them as the everyday people they are. Edson is charismatic and compelling as

Breaker, and with his flattened-out nose and crooked smile, he proves that you don't have to have movie-star perfect looks to play a romantic lead effectively. *Joey Breaker* is an exuberant and invigorating comedy which dances happily to a reggae beat. ★★★½ VHS: $7.99

John Carpenter's Vampires

(1998, 108 min, US, John Carpenter) *James Woods, Daniel Baldwin, Sheryl Lee, Thomas Ian Griffith, Maximilian Schell.* A slickly made but generic vampire tale, *Vampires* can't hold a stake to *Blade*, and at times seems no more than a rip-off of *From Dusk Till Dawn.* Woods is a vampire hunter hired by the Catholic Church (don't ask) who is roaming the American Southwest looking for covens of bloodsuckers. Carpenter's good premise soon gives way to tired Tarantino-esque humor that doesn't work, Rodriguez-like camerawork/choreographics which lack originality, and some good makeup effects when the thirsty dead get a suntan. Woods is a little too posturing but at least is in on the joke, though Schell as a Catholic bishop looks terribly out of place. ★★ DVD: $19.99, VHS: $9.99

John Grisham's The Rainmaker

(1997, 133 min, US, Francis Ford Coppola) *Matt Damon, Danny DeVito, Jon Voight, Claire Danes, Mary Kay Place, Danny Glover, Teresa Wright, Mickey Rourke, Dean Stockwell, Virginia Madsen.* This John Grisham adaptation is a superior courtroom drama and social commentary that entertains, moves and provokes. Director Coppola establishes a fluid, even-handed tempo throughout which culminates in an absorbing and rewarding finale. In his first starring role, Damon nicely plays Rudy Baylor, an inexperienced, naïve lawyer who takes on a big insurance company (on behalf of a dying leukemia patient denied benefits) for his first case. Partnered with Deck Shifflet (an engaging DeVito), a five-time loser in passing the bar, Rudy balances the high-profile case with a budding romance with an abused wife (Danes), probably the weakest link in this otherwise splendid story. As with most Grisham tales, characters have no moral gray shadings, and this is especially true in the case of the affluent, slimy company attorney smartly played by Voight. ★★★½ DVD: $19.99, VHS: $9.99

John Q

(2002, 110 min, US, Nick Cassavetes) *Denzel Washington, Robert Duvall, James Woods, Anne Heche, Ray Liotta, Kimberly Elise, Eddie Griffin, Shawn Hatosy.* Washington gives a commanding performance as a father who takes a hospital emergency room hostage when his dying son is refused a life-saving operation. There's little else, however, that's exceptional in this bogus story which pretends to examine the health care industry but defaults into a clichéd revenge drama. The plot — which has Washington holding various staff and patients at gunpoint while attempting to gain sympathy — isn't believable at all, and its "HMO-as-villains" message is basically preaching to the choir. A superficial treatise to a complex issue. ★★ DVD Letterbox infinifilm Special Edition: $19.99, VHS: $6.99

Johnny Apollo

(1940, 93 min, US, Henry Hathaway) *Tyrone Power, Dorothy Lamour, Edward Arnold, Lloyd Nolan.* Straight-laced Power turns to a life of crime to help his dad, convicted embezzler/broker Arnold. Lamour is the gangster's moll for whom Power falls hard. ★★★ VHS: $14.99

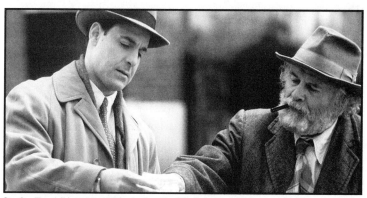
Stanley Tucci (l.) and Ian Holm in *Joe Gould's Secret*

Johnny Be Good

(1988, 84 min, US, Bud Smith) *Robert Downey, Jr., Anthony Michael Hall, Uma Thurman, Seymour Cassel.* Downey once again is the saving grace in an otherwise awful comedy, this one about high school jock Hall being wooed by various colleges. ★ DVD: $14.99, VHS: $9.99

Johnny Belinda

(1948, 103 min, US, Jean Negulesco) *Jane Wyman, Lew Ayres, Charles Bickford, Agnes Moorehead.* Wyman won an Oscar for her sensitive performance as a deaf-mute woman who is taught to communicate by a compassionate doctor (Ayres). Sentimental but stirring entertainment. ★★★½

Johnny Eager

(1941, 107 min, US, Mervyn Taylor) *Robert Taylor, Lana Turner, Van Heflin, Edward Arnold.* Though Taylor and Turner are top billed, it's Heflin's Oscar-winning performance that elevates this standard but glossy underworld melodrama. Taylor plays a heel of a petty crime boss who becomes involved with D.A.'s daughter Turner. It's a contrivance of the plot that we're expected to believe Turner turns a blind eye to Taylor's life of crime. Taking advantage of the only well-crafted role in the film, Heflin revels as Taylor's alcoholic, scholarly, self-pitying friend. ★★ VHS: $14.99

Johnny English

(2003, 88 min, GB, Peter Howitt) *Rowan Atkinson, Natalie Imbruglia, Ben Miller, John Malkovich, Tim Pigott-Smith.* Rowan Atkinson fans should get a small kick out of this ragged spy spoof. Rowan is the title character, a government desk jockey who's promoted to super agent when Britain's top agents are killed. What follows is a series of scenes that are tiny variations on a theme: English screws up, covers his mistakes manfully and is berated by his superiors for being an ass. The formula grows tiresome, and there are some very long stretches with nary a smile. But even when it's not funny, it moves briskly; it's got a catchy Robbie Williams theme song; and a couple hilarious sequences, the best of which comes at the climax, with English singing along to ABBA's "Does Your Mother Know?" Malkovich is also amusing as the French villain, with the goofiest Gallic accent since Inspector Clouseau (though this does open the door for some trendy, unfunny anti-French jokes). ★★ DVD Letterbox: $19.99, DVD Pan & Scan: $19.99, VHS: $14.99

Johnny Got His Gun

(1971, 111 min, US, Dalton Trumbo) *Timothy Bottoms, Jason Robards, Donald Sutherland.* Dalton Trumbo did a disservice to his classic anti-war novel with this sometimes moving but ultimately sluggish adaptation. Bottoms is the severely disabled soldier. ★★½

Johnny Guitar

(1954, 110 min, US, Nicholas Ray) *Joan Crawford, Sterling Hayden, Mercedes McCambridge, Ernest Borgnine.* A true original from Ray, this is the story of a cowboy who carries a guitar instead of a pistol and believes that ". . . when you boil it all down, all a man needs is a good smoke and a cup of coffee." Crawford plays a saloon keeper who enlists Johnny's aid, and McCambridge is incomparable as the local crusader who simply cannot rest until she sees them all hang. Insightful and intoxicating, the film has been cited as a source of inspiration by such contemporaries as Wim Wenders and Jim Jarmusch. ★★★½

Johnny Handsome

(1989, 95 min, US, Walter Hill) *Mickey Rourke, Ellen Barkin, Lance Henriksen, Morgan Freeman, Forest Whitaker.* Rourke stars in this stylish, gritty thriller as a petty thief — whose facial disfiguration has given him the unkindly nickname of "Johnny Handsome" — who is double-crossed by fellow gang members during a robbery. In prison, he undergoes cosmetic surgery, and with a new face and a release from jail, sets out to get revenge. Among the film's supporting cast, Barkin and Henriksen as Rourke's vicious ex-mates, Freeman as a cop not fooled by a pretty face and Whitaker as the doctor who performs the surgery, are all first-rate. ★★★ DVD: $14.99, VHS: $9.99

Johnny Mnemonic

(1995, 98 min, US, Robert Longo) *Keanu Reeves, Dolph Lundgren, Takeshi Kitano, Ice-T, Udo Kier, Barbara Sukowa, Henry Rollins.* It's a meeting of '90s chic and aesthetic: visual artist Robert Longo and cyberpunk William Gibson team on the film adaptation of the latter's technothriller short story. But somehow some computer-generated wires got mighty crossed. Reeves stars as the title character, a high-tech courier working in a bleak future. With a computer-friendly head full of chips and wires, Johnny accepts one final assignment to transport some delicate information. But the ruthless Yakuza are on his trail, and they're after both the data and his head. *Johnny Mnemonic* is set at a lethargic pace, the action scenes are boring, and the story rambles from one pointless predicament to another. ★ DVD Letterbox: $9.99, DVD Letterbox Superbit Edition: $27.99

Johnny 100 Pesos

(1993, 95 min, Spain, Gustavo Graef-Marino) *Armando Araiza, Patricia Rivera, Willy Semler.* A mildly diverting suspense thriller which is based on a true incident. Teenager Johnny Garcia (Araiza) takes part in his first armed robbery with four ex-cons. The plan goes sour, and the five are forced to take hostages. The police are called in, they surround the place, and a media circus unfolds. The film starts off well, with some quirky details and amusing satire. But it soon becomes predictable and rather unexciting. Johnny is uninteresting, and his character rarely goes beyond the "young thug" stage. With little more insight than a newspaper headline, *Johnny 100 Pesos* appears to have stayed close to the actual events, which does not work in its favor. (Spanish with English subtitles) ★★ DVD: $24.99, VHS: $19.99

Johnny Skidmarks

(1998, 97 min, US, John Raffo) *Peter Gallagher, Frances McDormand, John Lithgow, Jack Black.* A plot-driven noir thriller dressed in a character piece's clothing. Johnny Skidmarks is the nickname for police photographer Gallagher, a cold-hearted jerk (the result of his wife having died) who also moonlights as the shutterbug in a blackmail ring. His cronies include his ex-brother-in-law (the always amusing Black), a kindly police officer (Lithgow) and a new tentative love interest (McDormand), none of whom are all that fascinating. When the plot finally kicks in, it's only diverting for a short time before becoming routine. Thoroughly sleazy and unpleasant to boot, *Johnny Skidmarks* is at best a sporadically interesting misfire. ★★ DVD: $22.99

Johnny Stecchino

(1991, 105 min, Italy, Roberto Benigni) *Roberto Benigni, Nicoletta Braschi.* This amiable farce about a bumbling school bus driver who is mistaken for a Mafia leader enjoyed at one time the distinction of being the highest-grossing film in Italian history (now held by director Benigni's own *Life Is Beautiful*). Director, cowriter and star Benigni is the centerpiece of the hilarious tale in which the hopelessly inept Dante (Benigni) is lured to Palermo by the wife of notorious mobster Johnny Stecchino (Benigni again) to be used as his double. Of course, Dante is completely unaware of the deception, which leads him into a hilarious series of misadventures with rival gang members and the police. As an actor, Benigni's comic schtick is almost flawless, while as a director his timing is occasionally suspect. Still, the humor builds throughout, reaching a fever pitch by film's end and leaving those in need of good comedy well sated. (Italian with English subtitles) ★★★

Johnny Suede

(1991, 95 min, US, Tom DiCillo) *Brad Pitt, Calvin Levels, Tina Louise, Nick Cave, Samuel L. Jackson.* A preternaturally coifed Pitt stars in this meandering oddity about a down-and-out, would-be rocker set in Manhattan's lower depths. First-time director DiCillo's tale of postpunk nihilism finds its roots in Susan Seidelman's 1982 *Smithereens* as it follows the insufferably image-conscious Johnny Suede in his vain attempts at relationship, putting together a Rockabilly band and pulling off an armed robbery. These proceedings are precipitated when a pair of suede shoes falls from the sky, providing him the "magical" keys to some unknown subcultural kingdom. Pitt's narcoleptic portrayal of the title character provides most of the amusement in an otherwise static affair. ★★½

johns

(1997, 97 min, US, Scott Silver) *Lukas Haas, David Arquette, Arliss Howard, Keith David, Elliott Gould, Wilson Cruz.* A lyrical, sobering tale of self-respect and friendship amidst L.A.'s seedy underworld of male prostitution. Reminiscent of both *Midnight Cowboy* and *My Own Private Idaho*, *johns* is set on Christmas Eve where 20-year-old John (Arquette) has anxiously anticipated spending the holiday (and his birthday) in a posh hotel. His dream is quashed, however, when his lucky sneakers and the money in them are stolen. Determined to raise the cash, he solicits the help of his pal Donner (Haas), a fellow hustler who is quietly in love with John. Harsh realism merges with dreamy romanticism and quirky humor in this compelling tragidrama that features standout performances from the two leads. ★★★ DVD: $14.99, VHS: $9.99

A Joke of Destiny

(1984, 105 min, Italy, Lina Wertmüller) *Ugo Tognazzi, Piera Degli Esposito, Valeria Golino.* Wertmüller's underrated political satire follows the almost surreal situation of an Italian official's attempts to release a cabinet minister who becomes trapped in his new computerized car. Some really funny moments highlight this subversive little gem. (Italian with English subtitles) ★★★

Jolson Sings Again

(1949, 96 min, US, Henry Levin) *Larry Parks, Barbara Hale, William Demarest.* Sequel to the 1946 monster hit biography on Al Jolson, with Parks repeating his acclaimed incarnation as the legendary singer. With the best material having been covered in the original, this is only occasionally moving. ★★ DVD: $19.99

The Jolson Story

(1946, 128 min, US, Alfred E. Green) *Larry Parks, Evelyn Keyes, William Demarest.* Classic '40s musical of legendary singer Al Jolson, with Parks giving a star-making performance as the showman. Songs (dubbed by Jolson himself) include "Swanee," "April Showers" and "Mammy." One of the biggest hits of the decade. (Sequel: *Jolson Sings Again*) ★★★ DVD: $19.99

Jonah Who Will Be 25 in the Year 2000

(1976, 110 min, Switzerland, Alain Tanner) *Miou-Miou, Jean-Luc Bideau, Myriam Boyer.* Before *The Return of the Secaucus Seven*, *The Big Chill* or even "thirtysomething," there was Tanner's fascinating political comedy which follows a disparate group of post-May '68 "Coke/Marxists" who, each in their own individualistic fashion, must come to grips with a changing political and social scene brought on by the more conservative period of the '70s. The characters all must begin making a living but all the while trying to retain their political commitments in an increasingly repressive environment. The ensemble actors are uniformly excellent, and the dialogue is quick, fascinating and challenging. A remarkably relevant film for any political climate. (French with English subtitles) ★★★★ VHS: $19.99

Joseph and the Amazing Technicolor Dreamcoat

(1999, 78 min, GB, David Mallet & Steven Pimlott) *Donny Osmond, Richard Attenborough, Joan Collins, Maria Friedman, Robert Torti.* A filmed version of Andrew Lloyd Webber and Tim Rice's lively musical, this tacky production ill-advisedly forgoes live performance. Instead, it's presented as an elementary school pageant, and becomes absolutely nauseating when the school children are allowed to join in on some of the songs. Osmond plays Joseph, the biblical hero who is betrayed by his brothers and left for dead, only to become the Pharaoh's governor. Shirtless much of the time, he doesn't make it as a matinee idol. Nevertheless, this is one of Webber's best works, and when the vibrant score is allowed to stand on its own, it outshines the sappy packaging. ★★ DVD: $19.99, VHS: $9.99

Joseph Andrews

(1976, 99 min, GB, Tony Richardson) *Peter Firth, Ann-Margret, Jim Dale, Michale Hordern.* Even if this comedy had been great, which it isn't, director Richardson would have been hard pressed to match the achievements of his earlier excursion into the novels of Henry Fielding (*Tom Jones*). Here, Firth plays a lowly functionary who rejects the advances of the voluptuous Lady Booby (Ann-Margret) in favor of a lowly peasant girl. ★★ DVD Letterbox: $19.99, VHS: $19.99

Joseph Conrad's The Secret Agent

(1996, 94 min, GB, Christopher Hampton) *Bob Hoskins, Patricia Arquette, Gérard Depardieu, George Spelvin, Jim Broadbent, Christian Bale, Robin Williams.* *Joseph Conrad's The Secret Agent* should be awash in high-tension espionage and back-alley intrigue. But this intellectual discourse on politics and morality (or the lack of) never really satisfies with its slow pacing and confusing narrative. Hoskins plays a London shopkeeper and part-time spy for the Russians. When he is ordered to bomb Greenwich Park, it ends in tragedy; this leads to a series of escalating, out-of-control events. Director Hampton creates an effectively enigmatic London,

but the familial drama at the core of a more somber spy tale has difficulty resonating. An uncredited Williams gives the film's best performance as the only true anarchist of the bunch. Conrad's story was the basis for Alfred Hitchcock's far superior 1936 thriller *Sabotage*. ★★ VHS: $102.99

Josepha

(1982, 103 min, France, Christopher Frank) *Claude Brasseur, Miou-Miou.* Set amid the turbulence of the theatre, director and author Frank's intimate psychological drama follows a thespian couple whose marital roles are ones they can't quite master. Following Brasseur's affair with another woman, their union begins a slow and painful disintegration as they are forced to enact a bitter resolution. A glistening portrait of personal triumph, sacrifice and determination that manages both humor and poignancy. ★★★ VHS: $29.99

The Josephine Baker Story

(1991, 120 min, US, Brian Gibson) *Lynn Whitfield, Ruben Blades, Louis Gossett, Jr., David Dukes, Craig T. Nelson.* Whitfield excels in her award-winning performance as the legendary Josephine Baker. The story focuses on the singer's rise to stardom in Paris, her ongoing struggles with racism in America, and two affairs: one with an Italian count (Blades), and the other with orchestra leader Jo Bouillon (Dukes). ★★★ DVD: $14.99, VHS: $9.99

Josie and the Pussycats

(2001, 98 min, US, Deborah Kaplan & Harry Elfont) *Rachael Leigh Cook, Tara Reid, Rosario Dawson, Alan Cumming, Parker Posey, Missi Pyle.* The new word for "cool" is "jerkin," according to subliminal messages disseminated by Posey's evil music empire. So we'll say it: the jerkin' *Josie and the Pussycats* is the new *Clueless*, a slumber party movie for girls that operates on its own subversive level. It's all about teen fads, product placement and staying true to oneself, and not much to do with the "Josie" cartoons and comic books. Cook, Reid and Dawson are winning as the Pussycats, here an unknown garage band launched to stardom by Posey's exec Cumming to replace troublesome boy sensation DuJour. Weighed down by uneven pacing, *Josie* nevertheless has plenty of appeal not just for girls, but for anyone who wonders how the heck these prepackaged bands get so popular. ★★★ DVD PG-13 Rated: $9.99, DVD PG version, "Edited for Family Viewing": $9.99, VHS PG-13 Rated: $9.99, VHS PG version, "Edited for Family Viewing:" $9.99

Favorite Line: "If I could go back in time, I'd meet Snoopy!" —*Tara Reid as Melody*

Jour de Fête

(1949, 70 min, France, Jacques Tati) *Jacques Tati, Guy Decomble.* Tati, France's answer to Chaplin, stars in his first directorial effort. The story concerns the bungling adventures of a small town mailman who, after hearing about the efficiency of the American Postal Service, decides that it is time to do the same. His manic new delivery system, set out to modernize, brings about the opposite result. Great fun in this vintage Tati. (French with English subtitles) ★★★½

Le Jour se Lève

(1939, 85 min, France, Marcel Carné) *Jean Gabin, Jules Berry, Arletty.* From the makers of *Children of Paradise* comes this model of French poetic realism. Gabin is a criminal trapped in an attic. With the police closing in, he flashes back on

the events that drove him to commit murder. A thoughtful, intelligent film. (French with English subtitles) ★★★½ VHS: $14.99

The Journey of August King

(1995, 91 min, US, John Duigan) *Jason Patric, Thandee Newton, Larry Drake, Sam Waterston.* August King (Patric) is a widowed farmer living in North Carolina's Appalachian Mountains in the early 19th century. Grieving over the death of his wife, King lives a lonely existence. As this compelling, leisurely paced film recounts a three-day journey home, August regains his humanity in a humane though illegal act of moral rightness. Newton is Annalees, a runaway slave escaping the brutality of her father/master (Drake). Knowing that death possibly awaits her, King hides Annalees in his wagon as half the county searches for her. Patric gives a beautifully understated performance; as his character blooms, so does this quietly powerful film. Newton is first-rate in bringing to Annalees unfailing determination and a wrenching vulnerability. ★★★ DVD: $19.99, VHS: $19.99

Journey of Hope

(1990, 110 min, Switzerland, Xavier Koller) *Necmettin Cobanoglu, Nur Surer.* Winner of the 1990 Academy Award for Best Foreign-Language Film, *Journey of Hope* is an exquisitely photographed, heartbreakingly tragic yet surprisingly uninvolving tale about a Kurdish family residing in a small mountain village in southeastern Turkey. Unable to provide his family with a decent life, the father decides to uproot the entire clan and journey to Switzerland to join a relative and live in "paradise." Seemingly gleaned from today's headlines, the film bogs down in endless scenes involving harrowing escapes from border patrols and snowbound mountain crossings. While certainly well-meaning, the Academy must have been influenced by the timing of the Gulf War to have chosen this piece over such vastly superior works as Michael Verhoeven's *The Nasty Girl* and Zhang Yimou's *Ju Dou*. (In Kurdish, Turkish, German and Italian with English subtitles) ★★½ VHS: $19.99

The Journey of Natty Gann

(1985, 101 min, US, Jeremy Paul Kagan) *Meredith Salenger, John Cusack, Lainie Kazan, Barry Miller, Scatman Crothers.* This fine, underrated family film follows the adventures of a teenaged girl who travels cross-country during the Depression in search of her father. ★★★ DVD: $14.99, VHS: $9.99

Journey to the Center of the Earth

(1959, 132 min, US, Henry Levin) *James Mason, Pat Boone, Arlene Dahl, Diane Baker.* Entertaining (and old-fashioned) fantasy based on the Jules Verne novel. Mason leads a group of scientists to the Earth's core, where they discover a prehistoric world. ★★★ DVD: $14.99, VHS: $9.99

Joy House (Les Felins)

(1964, 98 min, France, René Clément) *Jane Fonda, Alain Delon, Lola Albright.* A macabre suspense story about the strange happenings in a Riviera villa operated by two American cousins (Fonda, Albright). The women's offer of refuge to the on-the-run Delon seals his fate and slowly turns this "safe house" into an oppressive prison. An interesting, but minor, Clément work. ★★ DVD: $24.99, VHS: $19.99

The Joy Luck Club

(1993, 135 min, US, Wayne Wang) *France Nuyen, Rosalind Chao, Lauren Tom, Kieu Chinh, Tsai Chin,*

Lisa Lu, Ming-Na Wen, Tamlyn Tomita, Andrew McCarthy. Director Wang's absorbing adaptation of the Amy Tan novel is a decidedly emotional affair. Faithfully following Tan's novel, with only a few omissions and changes, the film tells the separate tales of four Chinese-American women and their American-born daughters. The mothers' sagas are the foundation of the film as they relate the misogynist nature of traditional Chinese society and the harrowing journeys that ultimately led them to America. By comparison, the daughters' yuppie, thirtysomething problems may seem meager, but the real aim of both Tan's book and Wang's movie is to examine mothers and daughters with hugely disparate upbringings as they discover common ground. The result is deeply moving and highly effective. ★★★½ DVD: $14.99, VHS: $9.99

Joy of Living

(1938, 90 min, US, Tay Garnett) *Irene Dunne, Douglas Fairbanks, Jr., Lucille Ball, Alice Brady, Guy Kibbee.* Captivating screwball musical comedy with the ever-delightful Dunne as a famous singer being romanced by playboy Fairbanks. (Though it's released as part of the "Lucy Signature" Collection, Lucy really has a supporting role.) ★★★

Joy Ride

(2001, 94 min, US, John Dahl) *Steve Zahn, Paul Walker, Leelee Sobieski, Jessica Bowman.* The open highway provides a sturdy backdrop to terror, but eventually it's the human element of *Joy Ride* that takes it slightly off course. Director Dahl begins the ride with a solid setup, introducing two estranged brothers, Lewis (Walker) and Fuller (Zahn), beginning a cross-country trek to pick up Lewis' girlfriend Venna (Sobieski). Bored on the open road, they play a prank on a trucker with their CB radio: Lewis pretends to be a woman and arranges a rendezvous. However, things take a horrific turn when the trucker shows up and murders the customer staying at the prearranged motel room. Then the jilted would-be lover sets out to exact revenge against the siblings — and Venna. *Joy Ride* keeps its momentum throughout most of the film, maintaining a good amount of suspense for the first hour. Afterwards, though, the film steers its way towards the routine shadings of the slasher genre, unable to fully capitalize on the ingenuity that started it all. (Includes a 29-minute alternate ending) ★★½ DVD Special Edition: $14.99, VHS Special Edition: $9.99

The Joyless Street

(1925, 96 min, Germany, G.W. Pabst) *Greta Garbo, Werner Krauss.* Famous as the film that brought Garbo to international fame, this grimly realistic depiction of the contrasting social conditions in post-war, hyper-inflationary Vienna is also noted for its innovative use of editing and camera work. Pabst films with an unflinching eye to this story about the hunger, destitution and misery of a deteriorating middle class while also showing the moral excesses of the rich. A striking landmark in social realism. Restored with material found in film vaults in Europe, this edition is closer to the original than any version available in the U.S. until now. (Silent) ★★★½ VHS: $29.99

Ju Dou

(1990, 93 min, China, Zhang Yimou) *Gong Li, Li Bao-Tian, Li Wei.* Filmed in striking primary colors, this folktale and political allegory is an erotic tale of tangled passions between two lovers and the bitter consequences of their forbidden love. Set in a small village in 1920s China, a rich and tyrannical middle-aged man operates a cloth dye works. He has just recently married his third wife, Ju Dou, a young beauty who, like the others before her, is brutalized

and degraded by her impotent husband. She soon falls in love with her husband's hardworking but simple nephew. Their illicit affair and illegitimate child soon has the town ablaze with gossip; especially after an accident leaves her husband paralyzed, allowing the couple to take over the factory, silence her incensed husband and brazenly display their affair. But fate is not kind to the obsessed lovers in this dramatic tale of oppression, desire and vengeance. (Chinese with English subtitles) ★★★½

Juarez

(1939, 132 min, US, William Dieterle) *Paul Muni, Bette Davis, Brian Aherne, John Garfield, Claude Rains.* Engrossing, well-produced biography (Hollywood style) of Mexican revolutionary leader Juarez, smartly played by Muni. There's a smashing turn by Rains as Napoleon III. ★★★

Jubilee

(1977, 104 min, GB, Derek Jarman) *Adam Ant, Jenny Runacre, Nell Campbell, Toyah Wilcox, Ian Charleson, Richard O'Brien.* Jarman's wildly inventive, highly personal punk fantasy of a post-apocalyptic future of a dying England takes off where *A Clockwork Orange* ended. The Queen is dead, Buckingham Palace is a recording studio and the police have it off with each other when they're not breaking the heads of young men. In a nod to *Civilization*, Queen Elizabeth I is transported by her astrologer to the close of the 20th century to witness the disintegration of order and the explosion of destruction and chaos. A punk version of "Rule Britannia" is a musical highlight. A fascinating culture shock look at a pre-Thatcherized England. ★★★ DVD Letterbox Criterion Collection: $39.99

Judas Kiss

(1999, 98 min, US, Sebastian Gutierrez) *Emma Thompson, Alan Rickman, Carla Gugino, Gil Bellows, Simon Baker-Denny, Til Schweiger, Hal Holbrook.* An excellent international cast stars in this stylish and offbeat noir set in New Orleans. When a quartet of thieves led by Bellows and Gugino accidentally kill an innocent bystander during a kidnapping, two cops (Thompson and Rickman) try to flush them out of their lair. Meanwhile, the relationship between the gang members fray, and the film becomes a tense game of survival. *Judas Kiss* is especially noteworthy for Thompson's turn as a trash-talking FBI agent — and her playful banter with Rickman is quite enjoyable. Likewise, Gugino is wonderfully tough and sexy as the badass beauty. There are some nice twists in this unexpectedly entertaining film that boasts some great visual flourishes, a fair amount of blood, but, sadly, very little sex. ★★★

Jude

(1996, 123 min, GB, Michael Winterbottom) *Kate Winslet, Christopher Eccleston, Liam Cunningham, Rachel Griffiths.* This somber and austere adaptation of Thomas Hardy's "Jude the Obscure" provides a harrowing vision of an England on the verge of industrial revolution and mired in an unjust class system. Clearly somewhat autobiographical, the story follows Jude (superbly played by Eccleston), an eternally optimistic and socially daring young stonemason who breaks class taboo by pursuing a university education. He further pushes the bounds of societal tolerance when he takes up with his atheist schoolteacher cousin (Winslet), despite his being married. The film's first third is a jumble of vignettes as it appears the filmmakers tried to hurry through a mountain of plot points, and character development suffers as a result. The film's last half provides a much more intricate peek at its protagonists and the social mores of the day. ★★½

Judex

(1963, 100 min, France, Georges Franju) *Channing Pollock, Francine Berge.* A faithful remake of an early French serial that follows the mysterious adventures of the black-cloaked hero/avenger, Judex (The Judge), as he rights wrongs, battles an evil banker and brings the guilty to justice. (French with English subtitles) ★★½

The Judge and the Assassin

(1976, 125 min, France, Bertrand Tavernier) *Philippe Noiret, Michel Galabru, Isabelle Huppert.* This provocative psychological drama, set in 1890s France, follows the lives of two dissimilar men: Judge Rousseau, a respected magistrate from the ruling elite, and a demented ex-army sergeant who roams the countryside indiscriminately raping and killing young women and children. Their lives cross when the crazed killer is arrested and the judge embarks on a frenzied pursuit to prove that the man is sane and guilty. Noiret is perfect as the hell-bent moralizer whose actions, all in the name of justice, are equally repellant as that of the sick killer. (French with English subtitles) ★★★½ VHS: $79.99

Judge Dredd

(1995, 91 min, US, Danny Cannon) *Sylvester Stallone, Armand Assante, Rob Schneider, Jürgen Prochnow, Max von Sydow, Diane Lane, Joan Chen.* Based on the popular British comic book series, *Judge Dredd* is a visually stunning though empty-headed visceral ride into a bleak future. Stallone finds himself in similar territory as his entertaining *Demolition Man* as a good guy who's framed and must battle a wicked villain in a futuristic society. Whereas *Man* was lots of fun thanks to Wesley Snipes' scene-stealing and a good amount of comedy, this trek is a muddled array of action scenes, posturing (by Stallone), lethargic pacing and humorless bits. The production design is terrific, however. Stallone is nothing more than a parody of himself. ★½ DVD Letterbox: $14.99, VHS: $14.99

Judgment

(1990, 89 min, US, Tom Topor) *Blythe Danner, Keith Carradine, David Strathairn, Jack Warden.* The sexual abuse of minors by priests is the delicate issue handled quite effectively in this serious and focused HBO drama. Carradine and Danner star as devout Catholics whose faith in both the law and the Church are shattered when their son reveals that he has been sexually abused by a priest (Strathairn). Along with other parents in the parish, they begin a persistent but painful campaign to remove him and have him prosecuted as a sex offender. An all-too-true and sad story that is given expert handling here, with all of the personalities treated fairly — even the perpetrator is seen as a victim. ★★★

Judgment at Nuremberg

(1961, 179 min, US, Stanley Kramer) *Spencer Tracy, Maximilian Schell, Burt Lancaster, Richard Widmark, Marlene Dietrich, Montgomery Clift, Judy Garland.* Hailed by critics and nominated for a carload of Oscars, Kramer's massive epic on the atrocities committed by the Nazi Third Reich of WWII holds up surprisingly well. A chronicle of the famous Nuremberg trials of war crimes by Nazi officers, the film boasts some terrific performances, namely Schell in an Oscar-winning performance as the German defense attorney. Though unneccesarily overlong (some subplots involving extraneous characters, while certainly historically vital, bog down the film at times), the actual "trials," featuring Tracy as the American judge presiding over the hearings, are mesmerizing. ★★★★

Jules and Jim

Judgment in Berlin

(1988, 92 min, US, Leo Penn) *Martin Sheen, Sam Wanamaker, Max Gail, Sean Penn, Carl Lumbly.* An East German couple hijacks an airliner with a toy gun to defect to the West in this pre-*glasnost* thriller. Sheen stars as the American judge called in to preside over the court case. The compelling scenario is sometimes shortchanged dramatically, but Sheen offers a strong performance, and Penn is terrific in a cameo as a witness. ★★½ DVD Letterbox: $14.99, VHS: $19.99

Judgment Night

(1993, 110 min, US, Stephen Hopkins) *Emilio Estevez, Stephen Dorff, Cuba Gooding, Jr., Denis Leary, Jeremy Piven.* In this lukewarm action thriller, four clean-cut suburbanites decide to venture into the city for an evening of beer drinking, swearing and a boxing match. Quicker than you can say *Grand Canyon*, they find themselves lost in the bad part of town. While trying to find their way home, the boys wreck their vehicle and become involuntary witnesses to a drug hit, spending the rest of the evening being hunted by a wise-cracking psychotic killer (Leary). ★½ DVD Letterbox: $14.99

Juggernaut

(1974, 109 min, GB, Richard Lester) *Richard Harris, Omar Sharif, David Hemmings, Anthony Hopkins, Ian Holm, Shirley Knight, Clifton James, Roy Kinnear.* Incredibly entertaining thriller that, in the end, is a wonderful excuse for director Lester to satirize British mores. Harris and Hemmings are experts hired to find and defuse the bombs placed on a cruise liner, while Hopkins is back in Britain to hunt down the mad bomber dubbed Juggernaut. Lester regular Kinnear gets great comic mileage as the social director who must calm and entertain the possibly doomed vacationers. The defusing scenes, featuring now-clichéd "is it the blue wire or the red wire" tension, are still most effective. ★★★½ DVD: $14.99

Juice

(1992, 95 min, US, Ernest Dickerson) *Omar Epps, Jermaine Hopkins, Tupac Shakur, Samuel L. Jackson.* The directorial debut of Spike Lee's longtime cinematographer, Dickerson, is a moving drama about power, respect and loyalty on the streets of Harlem. The story, which follows the lives of four friends, each with a different set of priorities, is somewhat like a rehashed *Cooley High* for about the first 40 minutes. But it then changes abruptly and becomes an intense examination of the struggle for survival in a decaying urban structure created by an unsympathetic and unaware society. ★★★ DVD: $14.99, VHS: $9.99

Jules and Jim

(1962, 110 min, France, François Truffaut) *Oscar Werner, Jeanne Moreau, Henri Serre.* One of the most beautifully lyrical works in the history of the French cinema, Truffaut's classic saga of an ill-fated ménage à trois captures the sweet melancholia of love's ebb and flow. Moreau gives a performance of stunning grace and power as the tempestuous Catherine, the volatile apex of the love triangle. Werner and Serre star as the two close friends who succumb to Catherine's charms. (French with English subtitles) ★★★★ DVD: $19.99, VHS: $14.99

Julia

(1977, 118 min, US, Fred Zinnemann) *Jane Fonda, Vanessa Redgrave, Jason Robards, Maximilian Schell, Hal Holbrook, Rosemary Murphy, Meryl Streep, John Glover.* A sterling adaptation of author Lillian Hellman's memoir, "Pentimento." Redgrave plays the title role of the WWII Resistance fighter whose friendship involves Hellman (magnificently played by Fonda) in danger and intrigue. Oscars went to Robards, Redgrave and screenwriter Alvin Sargent. ★★★★

Julia and Julia

(1988, 98 min, US, Peter Del Monte) *Kathleen Turner, Gabriel Byrne, Sting.* Set in Italy, this moody, interesting but not quite successful tale is about a woman seemingly losing her grip on reality. Turner is the heroine who is apparently living out two different existences: one in a happy marriage with Byrne and the other involved in a dangerous love affair with a jealous boyfriend, played by Sting. ★★½

Julia Has Two Lovers

(1991, 87 min, US, Bashar Shbib) *Daphna Kastner, David Duchovny, David Charles.* Daphna Kastner cowrote and stars in this offbeat, erotically charged thought talky comedy-drama about a woman on the verge of a convenient marriage to her dull, old-fashioned fiancé (Charles), who is given food for thought via a day-long phone conversation with an amorous wrong number (Duchovny). ★★

Julian Po

(1997, 82 min, US, Alan Wade) *Christian Slater, Robin Tunney, Michael Parks, Allison Janney, Cherry Jones.* Slater is Julian Po, a contemplative bookkeeper who has a profound effect on the residents of a small town he enters. Since everyone suspects this stranger of evil, they are all relieved when Julian announces that he has come to town to kill himself. Almost immediately, he is revered as a prophet, often repeating the phrase "Life is short" to the various citizens who seek his counsel. Rewarded with free meals, clothes, and even a gun to do the deed, Julian is skeptical of his newfound celebrity. He just wants peace, quiet, and the love of Sarah (Tunney), a pretty local girl. Writer-director Wade has crafted an innocuous and unassuming fable, but it is remarkably passionless. ★★ VHS: $19.99

Julien Donkey-Boy

(1999, 94 min, US, Harmony Korine) *Ewen Bremner, Chloë Sevigny, Werner Herzog, Evan Neumann, Joyce Korine, Chrissy Kobylak, Alvin Law.* *Trainspotting*'s Bremner is impressive as the titular Julien, a schizophrenic who is quite a burden on his strange family, including Sevigny as a pregnant wannabe ice skater and Neumann as a reclusive amateur wrestler. Shot on video and grainily transferred to film, this is the first American film to be shot under the auspices of Dogma '95; like its brethren *Breaking the Waves* and *The Celebration*, it's a disturbing slice of a very dysfunctional family life. But without a narrative thread or memorable images, the film is an interminable series of apparently improvised scenes that go nowhere. ★ DVD: $24.99, VHS: $19.99

Juliet of the Spirits

(1965, 142 min, Italy, Federico Fellini) *Guilietta Masina, Valentina Cortese, Sylva Koscina.* A lavishly colorful baroque fantasy with Masina as a middle-aged woman haunted by hallucinations from her past and subconscious. In an effort to prevent her world from crumbling, she confronts these spectres and then is freed from the fantasies that have imprisoned her throughout her life. A richly symbolic work, plunging into the depths of the human psyche. (Italian with English subtitles) ★★★½ DVD Letterbox Criterion Collection: $29.99, VHS: $19.99

Julius Caesar

(1953, 117 min, US, Joseph L. Mankiewicz) *Marlon Brando, James Mason, John Gielgud, Greer Garson, Deborah Kerr, Louis Calhern, Edmond O'Brien.* Classic rendition of Shakespeare's play, with an astonishing cast, including Brando as Marc Antony and Mason as Brutus. To date, the best filmed version of the story. ★★★ VHS: $14.99

Julius Caesar

(1970, 117 min, US, Stuart Burge) *Charlton Heston, Jason Robards, John Gielgud, Diana Rigg, Richard Johnson, Richard Chamberlain, Robert Vaughn.* After parting the Red Sea and proving himself rather adept at chariot racing, Heston tackles the classics with surprisingly satisfactory results. Good performances highlight this version of Shakespeare's classic. (Though the 1953 version is still the definitive production.) ★★★ DVD: $14.99

Jumanji

(1995, 104 min, US, Joe Johnston) *Robin Williams, Bonnie Hunt, Kirsten Dunst, Bradley Pierce, Bebe Neuwirth, David Alan Grier.* Featuring computer graphics special effects of rampaging animals terrorizing its cast, *Jumanji* is heavy on the F/X and light on the execution. A magical board game, Jumanji takes its young players and places them in the center of a jungle adventure, which usually manifests itself in the playing area of its participants. When an adolescent boy disappears into the game, he returns 25 years later (as Williams) when two orphaned children begin play. When not relying too heavily on its many F/X creations, the film has a spirited playfulness and a rather engaging cast. However, *Jumanji* falters when it allows the effects to take center stage at the expense of its human players. ★★½ DVD: $14.99, VHS: $9.99

Jumpin' at the Boneyard

(1992, 107 min, US, Jeff Stanzler) *Tim Roth, Alexis Arquette, Danitra Vance, Samuel L. Jackson, Luis Guzman.* Another in the early '90s string of lower-budget urban dramas, this film stands out as one of the best efforts. Two brothers (outstandingly played by Roth and Arquette) come together after several years apart. One is a drug addict, the other a divorcé. The older one (Roth) tries to get his brother off of drugs by taking him back to their old neighborhood, the Bronx. Not only has the neighborhood changed, but so have they. They relive old memories and try to deal with their own demons. It's a gritty, no-nonsense portrayal, highlighted by realistic dialogue and intense acting. ★★★½ VHS: $29.99

Jumpin' Jack Flash

(1986, 100 min, US, Penny Marshall) *Whoopi Goldberg, Stephen Collins, Carol Kane, Annie Potts, Jon Lovitz, Phil Hartman, John Wood, Jonathan Pryce.* Marshall's directorial debut is an alternately amusing spy comedy with Goldberg as a computer operator who comes to the aid of a British agent held prisoner behind the Iron Curtain. Though Marshall was much more successful with her next film, *Big*, this is nevertheless an enjoyable piece of fluff thanks mostly to Goldberg's comic antics. ★★½ DVD: $14.99

June Bride

(1948, 97 min, US, Bretaigne Windust) *Bette Davis, Robert Montgomery, Fay Bainter, Mary Wickes.* Davis gets to show off her comedic skills in this lively battle-of-the-sexes romantic comedy. Davis plays a magazine editor who is accompanied by ex-lover and writer Montgomery to cover a wedding at an Indiana small town. Montgomery, always at home with a glib remark, and Davis make for a most enjoyable team. ★★★ VHS: $19.99

June Night

(1940, 88 min, Sweden, Per Lindberg) *Ingrid Bergman, Marianne Lofgren.* Bergman plays a promiscuous small-town girl who moves to Stockholm and changes her name after being involved in a shooting. Finding success in her displaced home, she is soon haunted by shadows of the past when the shooting victim and a reporter each threaten to expose her. This routine romancer is highlighted by Bergman's lovely performance. (Swedish with English subtitles) ★★½ DVD: $29.99, VHS: $29.99

The Jungle Book

(1942, 105 min, US, Alexander Korda) *Sabu, Joseph Calleia, Rosemary De Camp.* Beautifully filmed, live-action version of Rudyard Kipling's classic about Mowgli, the jungle boy, who is raised by a pack of wolves after the death of his parents. Sabu plays young Mowgli. ★★★ DVD: $19.99

The Jungle Book

(1967, 78 min, US, Wolfgang Reitherman) *Voices of: Phil Harris, Sebastian Cabot, Louis Prima.* Charming Disney animated feature, based on Kipling's tales, about Mowgli, a young human boy, and his adventures with jungle animals. Wonderful score includes "Bare Necessities" (sung by the great Harris) and "I Wanna Be Like You." ★★★

The Jungle Book

See: *Rudyard Kipling's The Jungle Book*

Jungle Fever

(1991, 132 min, US, Spike Lee) *Wesley Snipes, Annabella Sciorra, John Turturro, Ossie Davis, Ruby Dee, Samuel L. Jackson.* Much like his *Do the Right Thing*, Lee's explosive *Jungle Fever* is a stirring and thought-provoking drama about race relations in modern society. Snipes stars as an aspiring African-American architect who begins an affair with Sciorra, his Italian-American secretary. For Lee, the contentious theme of a mixed-race relationship proves simply to be a springboard for his goal of exploring such divergent topics as tensions within African-American families, drug abuse, the tempestuous relationships between men and women, and the widening social schism between the blacks who attain middle-class "respectability" and the ones left behind. Jackson is riveting in support as Snipes' addict brother. ★★★½ DVD: $14.99, VHS: $9.99

Jungle 2 Jungle

(1997, 105 min, US, John Pasquin) *Tim Allen, Sam Huntington, JoBeth Williams, Lolita Davidovich, Martin Short, David Ogden Stiers.* This tepid and implausible remake of the French film *Little Indian, Big City* stars Allen as a stockbroker who is divorcing his wife in order to marry a flighty designer (Davidovich). Upon finding his wife in the jungle somewhere, he learns he has a 13-year-old son. Allen's arrival coincides with his son's passage into manhood. The tribal chief charges young Mimi-Siku with getting fire from the Statue of Liberty. Thus father and son are off to New York where Mimi's visit is pretty much of a disaster until he saves his dad and a fellow stockbroker from a money-laundering Russian fishmonger. Oh, please. ★★ DVD: $19.99, VHS: $9.99

Junior

(1994, 110 min, US, Ivan Reitman) *Arnold Schwarzenegger, Danny DeVito, Emma Thompson, Frank Langella, Pamela Reed.* Having not learned a lesson with the infamously bad *Rabbit Test*, Hollywood delivers yet another tepid comedy about a man who becomes pregnant. But this time it's not just any man, it's Schwarzenegger. What a concept: *The Terminator* with child. Arnold plays a scientist who impregnates himself with an embryo. With the help of cohort DeVito, he carries to term. And along the way, he falls for fellow researcher Thompson (who seems above all this nonsense). *Junior* isn't without its share of laughs, but the unimaginative screenplay does little to humorously exploit the situation. ★★ DVD: $14.99, VHS: $9.99

Junior Bonner

(1972, 103 min, US, Sam Peckinpah) *Steve McQueen, Robert Preston, Ida Lupino, Ben Johnson.* Peckinpah directed this vibrant western comedy-drama with McQueen as an ex-rodeo star who returns home to enter a local rodeo contest. McQueen has rarely been better, and Preston and Lupino are superb as his estranged parents. ★★★ DVD: $14.99

Jupiter's Thigh

(1981, 96 min, France, Philippe de Broca) *Philippe Noiret, Annie Girardot.* Adventure, romance and comedy mix in this pleasant sequel to *Dear Inspector*. Noiret and Girardot star as honeymooners who stumble upon a rare statue whose missing thigh triggers a humorous chain of wild events. (French with English subtitles) ★★½

Jupiter's Wife

(1994, 78 min, US, Michael Negropont) Filmmaker Negropont spent two years exploring the mystery of Maggie, a schizophrenic homeless woman he finds living in Central Park with her huge family of stray dogs. Fascinated by the intricate mythology that Maggie has built up around herself, Negropont does an outstanding job as both cultural anthropologist and psychological detective as he carefully cajoles ever-more-detailed information from her. Maggie herself is an amazing character and the film's examination of her is at once revelatory and life-affirming and unalterably sad. ★★★½ DVD: $24.99, VHS: $24.99

Le Jupon Rouge

(1987, 90 min, France, Geneviève Lefèbvre) *Marie-Christine Barrault, Alida Valli, Guillemette Groban.* Three women of greatly differing ages and backgrounds engage in a complicated and, at times, contradictory relationship with one another. Manuela (Barrault) has a nominal relationship with her boyfriend, but is actually more committed to her political work. She meets an older woman, Bacha (Valli), a Holocaust survivor and activist, and the two strike up a friendship, which becomes strained when Manuela begins a passionate love affair with another woman. A tender, well-acted drama touching on themes of desire and sensuality in relationships as well as a subtle reminder of the tenuousness of life and love. (French with English subtitles) (aka: *Manuela's Lovers*) ★★★ VHS: $29.99

Jurassic Park

(1993, 125 min, US, Steven Spielberg) *Sam Neill, Laura Dern, Jeff Goldblum, Richard Attenborough.* A spectacular, state-of-the-art fantasy film based on the Michael Crichton best-seller, *Jurassic Park* is a dizzying display of special effects, the likes of which the movies have never seen. Neill and Dern are paleontologists who agree to preview a newly constructed outdoor theme park built by millionaire Attenborough. With mathematician Goldblum along for the ride, all are dazzled by the genetic engineering Attenborough has achieved: dinosaurs have been re-created and are roaming about on his tropical island paradise. However, the thrills begin when the carnivorous dinosaurs escape their confines and pit man against beast. With this scenario, Spielberg has crafted one heart-pounding episode after another, and his film is a high-flying blend of high-tech F/X and nonstop excitement. (Sequel: *The Lost World: Jurassic Park*) ★★★½ DVD Letterbox: $26.99, DVD DTS sound: $26.99, VHS: $9.99

Jurassic Park III

(2001, 92 min, US, Joe Johnston) *Sam Neill, William H. Macy, Téa Leoni, Alessandro Nivola, Trevor Morgan, Michael Jeter, Laura Dern.* Dinosaurs run rampant once more in this third entry. Back is Neill as paleontologist Alan Grant, back are a few edge-of-your-seat thrills, gone is original director Steven Spielberg, and gone is any semblance of a story. Not even the pretense of one. Just dinos stalking humans, and more dinos stalking humans. Dr. Grant accompanies a couple of adventurers (including husband and wife Macy and Leoni) back to the island of the DNA-engineered dinosaurs. When their plane crashlands, Grant and company are in store for a few surprises. Basically, that's it for story, for then it's almost a nonstop chase. Director Johnston creates quite a few exciting chase scenes, but — like riding a roller-coaster for 90 minutes — you need a break between the ups and down once is a while. The dinos, of course, look uncomfortably and menacingly real. ★★½ DVD Letterbox Collector's Edition: $26.99, DVD Pan & Scan Collector's Edition: $26.99, VHS: $9.99

The Juror

(1996, 118 min, US, Brian Gibson) *Demi Moore, Alec Baldwin, Joseph Gordon-Levitt, Anne Heche, Lindsay Crouse, Tony Lo Bianco.* Overbaked, underdeveloped potboiler with Moore as a single mom who gets called for jury duty on a murder case. The accused is a big-time mafioso whose strongarm, played by Baldwin, wants to ensure his boss' acquittal, leading to Moore being threatened and tormented in scene after silly, unpleasant scene. Reminiscent of 1994's equally silly *Trial by Jury*, this is basically a throwaway TV movie with two star names. Though the acting is good, it undistinguished, *The Juror* is over-long and not very exciting — at least the shots are in focus. ★½ DVD: $19.99, VHS: $9.99

Jury Duty

(1995, 86 min, US, John Fortenberry) *Pauly Shore, Tia Carrere, Stanley Tucci, Shelley Winters, Andrew Dice Clay.* Not that his prior films would ever challenge *Some Like It Hot* or *Airplane* in comic stature, but Shore's first three films look like comic masterpieces compared to *Jury Duty*, a horrendous and unbelievably unfunny comedy. Shore stars as a ne'er-do-well who is called for jury duty. Homeless and jobless and assigned to a high-profile case, Shore prolongs the court proceedings to take advantage of the room and board. With a story line and joke cannister equally deficient, *Jury Duty* is guilty of atrocious writing, bad acting and lifeless direction. ★ DVD: $19.99

Just a Gigolo

(1980, 105 min, West Germany, David Hemmings) *David Bowie, Marlene Dietrich, Kim Novak, David Hemmings.* Amid the glittery milieu of decadent post-WWI Germany, Bowie is a debonair "escort" for a host of society women. Novak wants his body, Hemmings wants his body and his soul while Dietrich (in her final film appearance) observes the goings-on while belting out the title tune. ★★½

Just Another Girl on the IRT

(1993, 92 min, US, Leslie Harris) *Ariyan Johnson, Kevin Thigpen, Ebony Jerido, Jerard Washington.* Harris makes her film debut with this low-budget independent drama that, while very rough around the edges, vibrates with energy, tension and humor. Harris has given a strong cinematic voice to a segment of the population long ignored — the black female teenager. And what a voice. Chantel (Johnson, in a dazzling debut) is one of the smartest kids at her Brooklyn high school but she is loud, obnoxious, self-centered and not nearly as mature as she thinks. When the ambitious, promising Chantel finds herself faced with an unwanted pregnancy, a situation too rarely depicted in film, Harris portrays a story as poignant, scary, frustrating and moving as real life. ★★★ DVD: $14.99, VHS: $9.99

Just Another Pretty Face

(1958, 110 min, France, Marc Allégret) *Henri Vidal, Mylene Demongeot, Jean-Paul Belmondo, Alain Delon.* Made right before the cinematic explosion of the French New Wave, this action/melodrama can be seen as typical entertainment fare for France in the 1950s. Vidal stars as a police detective bent on solving a smuggling ring. The situation becomes more difficult when he falls in love with a beautiful member of the smuggling gang. Watch for brief appearances by the very young Belmondo and Delon. (French with English subtitles) ★★½

Just Between Friends

(1986, 120 min, US, Allan Burns) *Mary Tyler Moore, Christine Lahti, Ted Danson, Sam Waterston.* Attractive performances by Moore, Danson and especially Lahti elevate this ordinary romantic comedy-drama about a suburban housewife (Moore) who begins a friendship with the woman having an affair with her husband. ★★½ DVD: $14.99

Just Cause

(1995, 102 min, US, Arne Glimcher) *Sean Connery, Laurence Fishburne, Kate Capshaw, Blair Underwood, Ed Harris, Ruby Dee, Ned Beatty, Chris Sarandon, Lynne Thigpen.* Part social drama and part thriller (without much thrills), *Just Cause* stars Connery as a Harvard law professor who attempts to prove the innocence of a young black man (Underwood) convicted of murder and sentenced to die. When Connery travels to Underwood's small Florida town to investigate, he comes in conflict with the town's redneck black sheriff (Fishburne) who helped put the youth away. Similar to *Malice* insofar that the film starts in one direction and switches gears halfway through, *Just Cause's* change is not for the better: What begins as an involving story of injustice gives way to a ridiculous revenge fantasy. ★★ DVD: $14.99, VHS: $9.99

Just Like a Woman

(1994, 90 min, GB, Christopher Monger) *Julie Walters, Adrian Pasdar, Paul Freeman.* Pasdar stars in this gentle, cross-dressing comedy about an American banker living in London whose penchant for lingerie gets him in trouble with his wife, who thinks he's seeing another woman. She kicks him out, and he winds up lodging with an older woman (Walters) who's just ended a 22-year marriage. After they strike up a relationship, he divulges his secret to her and she helps him fulfill his fantasies. While basically a straight love story, the film nonetheless is an entertaining examination of gender roles in relationships. Based on Monica Jay's book "Geraldine." ★★★

Just Like Weather

(1986, 98 min, Hong Kong, Allen Fong) *Christine Lee, Lee Chi-Keung.* A fascinating independent feature about a couple who, in an effort to save their crumbling marriage, decide to travel to New York for a second honeymoon. What makes the film different is that in the midst of this drama, the director interviews the two about themselves and their worries about their relationship. A thinly veiled allegory about Hong Kong's impending return to the control of Communist China. (Cantonese with English subtitles) ★★★ VHS: $39.99

Just Married

(2003, 90 min, US, Shawn Levy) *Ashton Kutcher, Brittany Murphy, Christian Kane, David Moscow, Thad Luckinbill.* *Just Married* is the kind of impractical, improbable comedy that only Hollywood could seem to muster. Kutcher and Murphy play a lovey-dovey pair that meet when he accidentally hits her in the head with a football (guffaw). It's instant love, captured in two quick scenes, allowing the audience to fill in the gaps. (No time for exposition, we've got cars to crash and heads to bump!) They marry and their subsequent honeymoon is a disaster. But can their love stand the test of time? Aside from the two leads, who do nothing to liven a dead screenplay, every peripheral character is a caricature and every non-American one is a full-blown hackneyed disgrace. The filmmakers have drained the movie of any and all of what little potential there is — a better title for this one may be *Just Marred*. ★ DVD: $19.99

Just Tell Me What You Want

(1980, 114 min, US, Sidney Lumet) *Alan King, Ali MacGraw, Myrna Loy, Keenan Wynn.* A witty comedy with King as an overbearing tycoon who tries to win back the mistress (MacGraw) who walked out on him. King has never been funnier, and Loy has some great moments as his secretary. ★★★ VHS: $14.99

Just the Two of Us

(1970, 82 min, US, Barbara Peters) *Alicia Courtney, Elizabeth Plumb.* Tenderly telling the love story between two married women, *Just the Two of Us* features low production values and sub-par acting, but it rises above these flaws with an engaging pro-lesbian script. Pretty and sensible Denise (Courtney) and the sweetly ditsy blonde Adria (Plumb) are lonely housewives living in suburban L.A. While lunching at a restaurant, they notice two women at another table kissing. Both women are transfixed, and a romance between them ensues. However, what is a fling to one becomes much more to the other. A thoughtful examination of passion and identity. ★★★

Just Visiting

(2001, 88 min, US/France, Jean-Marie Poire) *Jean Reno, Christina Applegate, Christian Clavier, Matthew Ross, Tara Reid, Bridgette Wilson-Sampras, Malcolm McDowell.* After botching a spell that lands a dishonored knight and his faithful peasant in present-day Chicago, a senile wizard travels the corridors of time to get them back. Of course, a lot has changed since the 12th century, but the pair are quickly absorbed by gags involving (mainly) automobiles, indoor plumbing and equal rights. Reno and Clavier are dumbed down a bit further from their roles in the original *The Visitors*, while Applegate and Reid try and soften the blow only to get crushed by this heavy-handed sequel. A tepid mix that eventually saturates every potential subplot into one big blob of cinematic mediocrity. Enter at your own risk. (Filmed in English) ★★ DVD: $14.99, VHS: $9.99

Justine

(1969, 115 min, GB, George Cukor) *Anouk Aimée, Michael York, Dirk Bogarde, Robert Forster, Cliff Gorman.* Interesting character study of a lusty woman (Aimée) who seduces men while helping arm Palestinian Jews poised to revolt against British rule. ★★½ VHS: $59.99

K-9

(1989, 102 min, US, Rod Daniel) *James Belushi, Mel Harris, Ed O'Neill.* Inept man-dog buddy comedy (in the same vein as *Turner and Hooch*), with Belushi as a cop saddled with a mean-tempered German shepherd. You know you're in trouble when one of the film's "best" laughs comes from two dogs doing it. (Sequel: *K911*) ★½ DVD: $19.99, VHS: $14.99

K-Pax

(2001, 120 min, US, Iain Softley) *Kevin Spacey, Jeff Bridges, Mary McCormack, Alfre Woodard, David Patrick Kelly, Conchata Ferrell, Saul Williams.* In *Starman*, Bridges plays an alien visitor hunted by the military. A few years and many terrific performances later, Bridges finds himself on the opposite side of the chase, so to speak, as Dr. Mark Powell, a psychiatrist who races to cure a man who claims he's an alien. As marvelously played by Spacey, that man is Prot, visitor from the distant planet K-Pax. Prot wears sunglasses (our planet is "too bright"), bonds well with his other patients at the hospital where he's been confined and, quite bafflingly, knows things about astronomy and physics that he really shouldn't. *K-Pax* is at its best, which is most of the time, during the compelling scenes between doctor and patient — Prot is as determined and prepared to prove he is an alien as much as Powell is to show he's not. Is he or isn't he? Well, that's where *K-Pax* wants it both ways. And in doing so, it digs a hole for itself in trying to maintain this ambiguity till the very end, stumbling in the process. Fortunately, there are Bridges and Spacey to allow us to forget the incredulities of the appealing if problematic premise. Bridges brings comfort and calm to the role of the caring doc, whose compassion comes at the price of his own family dynamic. Spacey plays Prot with just the right amount of awareness, humor and childlike wonder. Ultimately, *K-Pax* is a little too slowly paced, but it gets by on plenty of heart and two entrancing performances. ★★½ DVD Letterbox Collector's Edition: $14.99, VHS: $9.99

K-19: The Widowmaker

(2002, 138 min, US, Kathryn Bigelow) *Harrison Ford, Liam Neeson, Peter Sarsgaard, Joss Ackland, John Shrapnel.* Though he is uncharacteristically abrasive, Ford nevertheless proves to be a commanding presence in this suspenseful if sometimes aloof submarine thriller that doesn't quite measure up to the daddy of 'em all, *Das Boot*. Directed with competence by ace action helmer Bigelow, the story recalls the true-life tale about a Russian sub that nearly brought about a nuclear nightmare during the height of the Cold War. Ford is Vostrikov, the strict captain who has taken over command of the *K-19*. Neeson is Polenin, the sub's former captain and the man to whom the crew pledge their allegience. When a leak in the sub's cooling system threatens a meltdown, the two men square off against each other in a race to thwart nuclear disaster. The battle for authority eventually becomes secondary to the difficult task at hand: sending their men to almost certain death to repair the leak. Though the conflict between the two captains doesn't quite resonate as it should, Bigelow maintains tension throughout as to who will live, who will die, and — although we know the answer at the outset — will they succeed. ★★★ DVD Letterbox: $19.99, VHS: $9.99

K-2

(1992, 111 min, GB, Franc Roddam) *Michael Biehn, Matt Craven, Patricia Charbonneau.* Biehn and Craven star in this surprisingly engrossing action/drama about a pair of buddies from Seattle who join an expedition to climb one of the Himalayas' most daunting peaks — K2. Based on the award-winning Broadway play by Peter Meyers, the film, shot in breathtaking locations in Pakistan, is filled with exceptionally photographed action sequences which dramatically illustrate the exhilaration and dangers of hard-core mountain-climbing. ★★★

Kaddish

(1984, 92 min, US, Steve Brand) A superb, multi-leveled documentary which details the effects of the Holocaust on a Hungarian survivor and his American-born son. By focusing on the son, Vossi, *Kaddish* enables us to observe a heretofore little examined legacy of the Holocaust: the process by which children come to terms with the parents from whom they've inherited an unimaginable nightmare. It explores how children who were told bedtime stories about concentration camps learn to view a world in which they truly feel that "it can happen here." Filled with unexpected humor, tenderness and a sense of the strength between a father and son, *Kaddish* is a moving portrait of a young man coming to terms with an overwhelming personal and historical tragedy. ★★★½ VHS: $29.99

Kafka

(1992, 88 min, US, Steven Soderbergh) *Jeremy Irons, Theresa Russell, Joel Grey, Ian Holm, Alec Guinness, Armin Mueller-Stahl.* Irons stars as Kafka, a mild-mannered insurance clerk by day and aspiring writer by night, who becomes involved in a complex web of murder and bureaucracy gone wild. While his friends and acquaintances are regularly killed off, Kafka assumes a "Woody Allen-doing-James Bond" persona in his quest to get to the bottom of all the evil. Initially intriguing, but ultimately frustrating, the story has little to do with the writings and life of Franz Kafka and instead becomes a somewhat pedestrian murder mystery. While the film doesn't succeed in attaining its lofty pretentions, its startling, mostly black-and-white cinematography, realistic locales in the brooding city of Prague and several playful surrealistic episodes help keep the story moving (but to where?). ★★½

Kagemusha: The Shadow Warrior

(1980, 160 min, Japan, Akira Kurosawa) *Tatsuya Nakadai, Tsutomu Yamazaki.* Kurosawa's sweeping historical drama weaves elaborate battle sequences with tranquil interior scenes, marvelously displaying the director's artistry. A film of great scope, power and detail. (Japanese with English subtitles) ★★★½

Kalifornia

(1993, 110 min, US, Dominic Sena) *Brad Pitt, Juliette Lewis, David Duchovny, Michelle Forbes.* An unnerving and at times nauseating thriller for the art-house set. Duchovny costars and narrates as a free-lance writer with a fascination for serial killers. Bereft of ideas for his book, he and his photographer girlfriend (Forbes) plan a road trip from Georgia to L.A. visiting the sites of famous murders along the way. Short on cash, they solicit a rideshare and wind up with Pitt and Lewis, the poorest white trash to hit the screen since *Pink Flamingos*. Put these two couples in a '60s Lincoln convertible and you've got the recipe for a nightmarish ride across the Southern heartland. Pitt redefines the term psychopath with his portrayal of a filthy, beer-guzzling, grizzle-faced parolee (for what we never learn). Director Sena creates a cinematic pastiche, straddling the line between hip atmospheric character study and pure quease-inducing terror. ★★★ DVD: $14.99

Kama Sutra

(1996, 117 min, India, Mira Nair) *Indira Varma, Sarita Choudhury, Ramon Tikaram, Naveen Andrews.* Director Nair delves into the pleasures of the flesh with this semi-erotic tale of lust and forbidden love set in precolonial India. But despite a cast that is undeniably pleasing to look at, the film does little to arouse real passion. Newcomer Varma is luminously ravishing as Maya, a young servant girl who steals into the chambers of the princess' groom-to-be and seduces him the day before his wedding. Upon being discovered, she receives a one-way ticket to exile, eventually finding her niche as a student of the famous courtesan Rasa Devi. Sumptuously photographed, awash with exotic olive-tinted flesh, and presented with excellent period detail, *Kama Sutra* would seem to have all the ingredients for a gripping erotic drama, but Nair can't elevate this story above the realm of half-baked melodrama. (Unrated version) ★★ DVD: $24.99

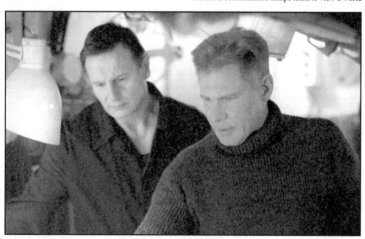

Liam Neeson and Harrison Ford in *K-19: The Widowmaker*

Kameradschaft (Comradeship)

(1930, 89 min, Germany, G.W. Pabst) *Ernst Busch, Alexander Granach.* Although WWI had been over for more than a decade, and Hitler had not yet risen to power, the hostility and tensions between the French and the Germans in 1930 were strained. The melting of this mistrust is the subject of *Kameradschaft*. Tragedy strikes a mining community near the French-German border when a cave-in traps over 400 French miners. Through the efforts of the townspeople and especially the neighboring Germans, disaster is averted and communication is opened. (German with English subtitles) ★★★½

Kamikaze '89

(1982, 106 min, West Germany, Wolf Gremm) *Rainer Werner Fassbinder, Gunther Kaufman, Brigitte Mira, Frank Ripploh, Franco Nero.* This very strange and tense fantasy thriller is based on Per Wahloo's best-selling novel "Murder on the 31st Floor" and features Fassbinder's final screen appearance. He plays a detective who has four days to solve a mystery before a bomb explodes. (German with English subtitles) ★★½

Kanal

(1957, 90 min, Poland, Andrzej Wajda) *Teresa Izewska, Tadeusz Janczar.* Wajda's intense WWII drama is the second of his trilogy which includes *A Generation* and *Ashes and Diamonds*. The story follows the heroic but grim actions of a group of Polish soldiers and patriots who attempt to escape Nazi-occupied Warsaw through the underground sewer system. (Polish with English subtitles) ★★★½ DVD: $29.99, VHS: $24.99

Kandahar

(2001, 85 min, Iran, Mohsen Makhmalbaf) *Niloufar Pazira, Hassan Tantai, Sadou Teymouri.* Below a field of one-legged men running on crutches, a Red Cross helicopter showers prosthetic legs over the barren, dusty landscape. The parachutes float like flower petals. This is Afghanistan. Nafas (Pazira) fled her native land years ago, leaving behind her sister, who has written to Nafas that she will commit suicide at the next solar eclipse. The film opens with the eclipse three days away and Nafas at the Iran-Afghani border. Since women cannot legally travel alone in Afghanistan, Nafas must enter into one subterfuge after another to make her way. Her trek through this land both bizarre and brutally beautiful brings her in contact with a motley assortment of disparate characters. *Kandahar* is a meditation, a state of mind, an indictment; in her incredible odyssey, Nafas returns to all the prisons she escaped before, and again views the world through the tight mesh veil of a burka. (Farsi with English subtitles) ★★★½ DVD Letterbox: $29.99, VHS Letterbox Subtitled: $29.99

Kangaroo

(1986, 105 min, Australia, Tim Burstall) *Colin Friels, Judy Davis, John Walton.* An idealistic English writer and his wife (Friels, Davis) move to Australia in the early 1920s in the hopes of finding a more tolerant world in which to rebuild their lives. However, when the leader of a secret fascist group puts pressure on them to join their ranks, they discover the harmony they thought they had found has given way to the same social and political friction they thought they had left behind. Despite its incendiary theme, the film lacks any emotional spark. Based on D.H. Lawrence's semiautobiographical novel. ★★ VHS: $79.99

Kangaroo Jack

(2003, 88 min, US, David McNally) *Jerry O'Connell, Anthony Anderson, Estella Warren, Christopher Walken, Michael Shannon.* Hollywood should take note: Though they're small in stature, they're large in numbers and will show no mercy in their wrath. Who? Kids, of course. And they, like adults, will only put up with so much crap. Like this moronic "family" comedy that wants to attract the pre-adolescent crowd but is full of sexual innuendo, violent pranks and stupid jokes to cause seven year olds to roll their eyes. O'Connell plays a mob underling who — with best friend Andersen in tow — heads Down Under to deliver a $50,000 payoff. When the titular marsupial runs off with the money, the dunderheaded duo are in hot pursuit. Would it help alleviate the pain of bad writing and terrible direction to have the kangaroo talk? It only adds to the misery of it all. ★ DVD Letterbox: $19.99, DVD Pan & Scan: $19.99, VHS: $6.99

Kansas

(1988, 108 min, US, David Stevens) *Andrew McCarthy, Matt Dillon, Kyra Sedgwick.* An unengaging drama about a mild-mannered drifter (McCarthy) who is tricked into committing a bank robbery by a "friendly" sociopath (Dillon). ★ DVD Letterbox: $14.99

Kansas City

(1996, 110 min, US, Robert Altman) *Jennifer Jason Leigh, Miranda Richardson, Harry Belafonte, Michael Murphy, Dermot Mulroney, Steve Buscemi.* A small-time hood crosses a gangster (an effective Belafonte) in Depression-era Kansas City. The hood's wife (Leigh) wants her husband back after the mob boss' men nab him, so she kidnaps a wealthy, opium-addicted socialite (Richardson) to ensure his release. *Kansas City* may not be anywhere near *Nashville* on the map, but it's certainly no *O.C. and Stiggs* either. The film has the director's visual eye for character detail, as well as his pointed examinations of life's realities and ironies. A jazz background offers a splendid score, and there's a terrific tenor sax duel. ★★½ VHS: $19.99

Kaos

(1984, 188 min, Italy, Paolo & Vittorio Taviani) *Margarita Lozano, Claudio Bigagli.* Set against the stunning backdrop of a sun-bleached, nearly barren Italian landscape, the Taviani brothers' adaptation of five stories by Luigi Pirandello together form a fascinating dramatic quilt. All of the stories, ranging from comedy to tragedy, focus on peasant life in turn-of-the-century Sicily and are stunningly photographed. Never succumbing to maudlin sentimentality, the folk stories are richly told with an embracing celebration of life. (Italian with English subtitles) ★★★★

The Karate Kid

(1984, 126 min, US, John G. Avildsen) *Ralph Macchio, Noriyuki "Pat" Morita, Elisabeth Shue.* A fatherless teenager living in Los Angeles, bullied by the local gang, learns karate from the family handyman. Macchio and Morita are both very likable in this first outing of series. (Followed by 3 sequels) ★★★

The Karate Kid Part II

(1986, 113 min, US, John G. Avildsen) *Ralph Macchio, Noriyuki "Pat" Morita, Danny Kamekona, Tamlyn Tomita, Nobu McCarthy.* Macchio and Morita reprise their roles as student and mentor. In Okinawa, Ralph goes up against a local hood. The first one had charm, this one has counter-charm (but it's not as bad as *III*). ★★ VHS: $9.99

Kandahar

The Karate Kid Part III

(1989, 111 min, US, John G. Avildsen) *Ralph Macchio, Noriyuki "Pat" Morita, Thomas Ian Griffith.* Macchio returns a third time (isn't he a little too old to play a teenager?) to do battle; enough already. ★ VHS: $9.99

Kasaramu Ce (This Land Is Ours)

(1991, 84 min, Nigeria, Saddik Balewa) A political tale of greed and power. Sani, a young farmer, is moved to act when his grandfather is killed by a money-hungry businessman who, finding precious stones throughout a village, tries to buy up all of the property. This film breaks one of the most important elements of a thriller when the mystery of the conspirators is revealed in the first 15 minutes. The lack of female characters provides a glimpse into the powerlessness of women in this Muslim community. The acting is quite natural and the editing keeps the story moving well, despite its predictability. (In English and Hausa with English subtitles) ★★

Katherine

(1975, 98 min, US, Jeremy Paul Kagan) *Sissy Spacek, Henry Winkler, Julie Kavner, Jane Wyatt, Art Carney.* Spacek stars as an overprivileged girl who, rejecting her affluent birthright, transforms from innocent to activist to revolutionary during the turbulent 1960s and early '70s. A compelling drama of conscience and commitment, highlighted by Spacek's compassionate performance. ★★★

The Keep

(1983, 96 min, US, Michael Mann) *Scott Glenn, Jürgen Prochnow, Ian McKellen, Alberta Watson, Robert Prosky, Gabriel Bryne.* From the director of *Manhunter* comes this stylish-looking but empty-headed horror film set during WWII about Nazi soldiers holing up at an ancient site — where a demonic creature has lain dormant. ★½ VHS: $79.99

Keeper of the City

(1992, 96 min, US, Bobby Roth) *Louis Gossett, Jr., Peter Coyote, Anthony LaPaglia, Renée Soutendijk.* Gossett stars as a tough-nosed police detective. Coyote plays a crime reporter. LaPaglia is the son of a deceased Mafia kingpin who can no longer live in the shadow of his father's crooked past and begins murdering the leaders of Mafia families. When the lives of these three men intersect, it makes for an interesting, if familiar, police thriller. ★★½

Keeper of the Flame

(1942, 100 min, US, George Cukor) *Spencer Tracy, Katharine Hepburn, Margaret Wycherly.* Solid performances by Tracy and Hepburn distinguish this intriguing drama about reporter Tracy investigating the life of a deceased politician, only to uncover a dark secret about the man. Kate is the widow. ★★★

333

Keeping the Faith

(2000, 129 min, US, Edward Norton) *Ben Stiller, Jenna Elfman, Edward Norton, Anne Bancroft, Eli Wallach, Ron Rifkin, Milos Forman, Holland Taylor.* A rabbi and a priest walk into a bar. Wait, wait, this ain't no ordinary rabbi and priest joke. Thanks to a winning screenplay, terrific chemistry and an impressive directorial debut by actor Norton, *Keeping the Faith* takes a one-joke premise and charms in totally unexpected ways. Jake (Stiller), Brian (Norton) and Anna (Elfman) were the best of childhood friends. Anna moved away, Jake became a rabbi, and Brian a priest; the latter two remaining close. Years later, Anna returns, only to have both men becoming attracted to her. Norton keeps the pace even and makes sure everything is good-natured. There are plenty of genial laughs, and even when addressing serious subjects such as celibacy and question of faith, it never gets too serious. Stiller, Norton and Elfman have a wonderful rapport with each other, creating warm, endearing characters who do and say funny, endearing things. ★★★ DVD: $19.99, VHS: $9.99

Keetje Tippel

(1975, 104 min, Netherlands, Paul Verhoeven) *Rutger Hauer, Monique Van De Ven.* This early Dutch effort by Verhoeven is a passionate and sensual story of lost innocence. Set in 1880 Amsterdam, the film stars Hauer and centers on the life and struggles of a free-spirited young woman (van de Ven) who is forced into prostitution by her destitute family. A worthy resurrection of early 20th-century social fiction that exhibits wit, detail and conscience. ★★★ DVD Letterbox: $29.99, VHS: $29.99

Kelly's Heroes

(1970, 145 min, US, Brian G. Hutton) *Clint Eastwood, Telly Savalas, Donald Sutherland, Carroll O'Connor, Don Rickles, Harry Dean Stanton.* Though not in the same league as *The Dirty Dozen,* this WWII adventure is nevertheless an entertaining romp with Clint and his Army buddies planning a gold heist behind enemy lines. ★★½ DVD: $19.99, VHS: $9.99

The Kentuckian

(1955, 104 min, US, Burt Lancaster) *Burt Lancaster, Dianne Foster, Walter Matthau, Diana Lynn.* In his only directorial effort, Lancaster wears dual coonskin hats in this dramatically awkward but scenic adventure. Set in Kentucky during the 1820s, the film has Lancaster as a backwoodsman who, with his young son, sets out for Texas and the rugged but rewarding life. On the way, he becomes sidetracked by indentured servant Foster, schoolteacher Lynn, villainous merchant Matthau (in his debut), and two feuding Klansmen on his trail. Director Lancaster is none-too-subtle in the "simple-life-is-better" motif. ★★ DVD: $14.99

The Key

(1958, 121 min, GB, Carol Reed) *William Holden, Sophia Loren, Trevor Howard, Oscar Homolka, Michael Caine.* Based on Jan de Hartog's novel "Stella," this slowly paced though involving romantic drama is set during WWII and follows Loren as she initiates a series of affairs with naval officers, eventually falling in love with Holden. ★★½

The Key

(1983, 106 min, Italy, Tinto Brass) *Frank Finlay.* Soft-core porn for viewers of intellectual pretensions, this Brass production features loads of nudity

as well as the vigorous caressing of bare cheeks, sexy women in black lace and enough kinky sex to give justification to its "X" rating. Set in Venice in 1940, the film stars Finlay as a sexually obsessed aristocrat who chronicles his many exploits and voyeuristic excursions in a diary that is read ravenously by his equally active wife. Accompanied by a lively score by Ennio Morricone, this teasingly erotic tour through the boudoirs of the sexually adventurous is nothing if not tantalizing and just a little bit "dirty." (In English and Italian with English subtitles) ★★ DVD: $29.99, VHS: $19.99

Key Largo

(1948, 101 min, US, John Huston) *Humphrey Bogart, Lauren Bacall, Edward G. Robinson, Claire Trevor, Lionel Barrymore.* An exciting screen version of Maxwell Anderson's hit play. Robinson is the ruthless gangster who takes refuge in an isolated hotel during a storm and terrorizes the patrons and staff, including war veteran Bogey and widow Bacall. Trevor won an Oscar as Robinson's pathetic, alcoholic moll. ★★★½ DVD: $19.99

The Keys of the Kingdom

(1944, 137 min, US, John M. Stahl) *Gregory Peck, Vincent Price, Edmund Gwenn, Thomas Mitchell, Roddy McDowall.* One of Peck's earliest efforts casts him as a priest doing missionary work in 19th-century China in this moving adaptation of A.J. Cronin's novel. Slightly overlong, but compelling nonetheless. ★★★ VHS: $19.99

Keys to Tulsa

(1997, 113 min, US, Leslie Grief) *James Spader, Eric Stoltz, Cameron Diaz, Mary Tyler Moore, James Coburn, Deborah Unger, Michael Rooker, Joanna Going.* A crisp, taut contemporary noir thriller, *Keys to Tulsa* is well-constructed, fast-paced and peppered with trenchant dialogue capably delivered by an eclectic ensemble. Stoltz is the prodigal son who returns to his home town to become quickly ensnarled in murder, blackmail and conflicted loyalties. The convoluted plot is absorbing and punctuated by sharp characterizations: Moore as Stoltz's acerbic society mom; Rooker as a befuddled boy in an angry man's body; Diaz as a poor little rich girl. The intricate web of relationships is revealed as the protagonists play out their roles in the ongoing tragedy, with more than enough guilt to go around. A well-executed exploration of a complexity of soured lives and tarnished expectations. ★★★½ DVD: $14.99, VHS: $14.99

Khartoum

(1966, 136 min, GB, Basil Dearden) *Laurence Olivier, Charlton Heston, Ralph Richardson.* Heston and Olivier square off in this retelling of the 1883 siege at Khartoum, in the British Sudan. Punctuated with magnificently choreographed battle scenes, this epic adventure finds Olivier in peak form as the fanatical Arab leader who incites his people to rise up against the British presence. Heston delivers one of his best performances as the English general who opposes him. ★★★ DVD Letterbox: $14.99

Kicked in the Head

(1997, 86 min, US, Matthew Harrison) *Kevin Corrigan, Linda Fiorentino, Michael Rapaport, James Woods, Lili Taylor, Burt Young.* Redmond (Corrigan) is a manchild on the brink of cosmic change; he thinks he's going through a self-destructive phase, but maybe it's self-revelation. Used as a mule in a really bad drug deal by his sleazy Uncle Sam (Woods), rejected and dismissed by the stew-

ardess (Fiorentino) who may be the guardian angel of his fortune cookie message, and rejecting and dismissive of his very own girl next door (Taylor), Redmond embarks on a personal odyssey more buffeted by outside influences than motivated from within. Corrigan's remarkable performance is well suited to the film's heightened realism and hyperkinetic energy. Wonderfully written, engagingly intelligent, and punctuated with brilliantly staged moments, *Kicked in the Head* is just that. ★★★ DVD: $24.99, VHS: $79.99

Kicking and Screaming

(1995, 96 min, US, Noah Baumbach) *Josh Hamilton, Olivia d'Abo, Eric Stoltz, Christopher Eigeman, Parker Posey, Jason Wiles.* Set in that post-Bachelors' Degree, pre-gainful employment, Twilight Zone time of life, *Kicking and Screaming* follows several newly minted college grads as they haphazardly grapple with deteriorating personal relationships, exacerbating family expectations and a nonexistent job market. No new material here, but director Baumbach crafts an engaging, unpretentious treatment of familiar territory. A sometimes intelligent, sharply observed script and witty performances combine to deliver a fresh entertainment. ★★★

The Kid

(1921, 60 min, US, Charles Chaplin) *Charlie Chaplin, Jackie Coogan.* Chaplin's first true feature-length film tells the saga of an abandoned infant who's adopted by Charlie and, ultimately, becomes his streetwise sidekick. Chaplin expertly mixes slapstick and sentimental melodrama to create a timeless comic experience. Chaplin had defined his Little Tramp role with his priceless performance, and little Coogan could bring you to laughter or tears with just a look. ★★★½ DVD 2-disc set: $29.99

The Kid

(2000, 104 min, US, Jon Turtletaub) *Bruce Willis, Spencer Breslin, Emily Mortimer, Lily Tomlin, Chi McBride.* Bigshot moneymaker Willis finds out just how empty his life is when he runs into himself as an eight-year-old kid (Breslin). The innocent child within has been suppressed, and while the bullies have been left behind, so have his childhood dreams. Breslin makes an impression as the kid, but this touchy-feel-good mush is often too much to take. ★★ DVD: $19.99, VHS Exclusive Video Bonus Edition: $14.99

A Kid for Two Farthings

(1955, 96 min, GB, Carol Reed) *Jonathan Ashmore, Celia Johnson, Diana Dors, Brenda De Benzie.* Reed's heartwarming fable about the hopes and aspirations of an impoverished lad is filled with insights about the human condition. In a play on "Jack and the Beanstalk," the young boy is sent to market where he buys a goat with an odd deformity — a single horn is growing out of its head. Convinced that the kid is a magical, wish-granting unicorn, the boy's head fills with fantasies about ending his family's poverty. ★★★½ DVD: $19.99, VHS: $19.99

The Kid from Brooklyn

(1946, 113 min, US, Norman Z. McLeod) *Danny Kaye, Virginia Mayo, Eve Arden, Fay Bainter.* Kaye is a comic dynamo as a timid milkman who unwittingly becomes a prizefighter. There are plenty of laughs, and Kaye (as usual) is a delight. Mayo also stars. Remake of the Harold Lloyd 1936 comedy, *The Milky Way.* ★★★

The Kid from Spain

(1932, 96 min, US, Leo McCarey) *Eddie Cantor, Lyda Roberti, Robert Young, Ruth Hall.* Busby Berkeley directed the dance sequences in this entertaining musical comedy with Cantor gloriously chewing the scenery when he's mistaken for a famed bullfighter. ★★★

A Kid in King Arthur's Court

(1995, 89 min, US, Michael Gottlieb) *Thomas Ian Nicholas, Joss Ackland, Ron Moody, Art Malik, Kate Winslet.* Mark Twain's classic time travel tale is dusted off for a third time (Will Rogers and Bing Crosby also found medieval adventure) to produce a particularly unimaginative and silly retelling. Nicholas is Calvin, a 20th-century little league player who finds himself hurled back into the 6th century and the court of Camelot. There he finds romance, adventure, intrigue and manages to boost his own sagging self-confidence through a series of lifeless episodes and smirky comedy. Disney once again condescends to its adolescent audience, even toying with the Camelot legend. ★★ DVD: $19.99, VHS: $19.99

The Kid Stays in the Picture

(2002, 91 min, US, Brett Morgen & Nanette Burstein) *Robert Evans.* This engrossing and briskly entertaining documentary about the rise and fall and resurrection of legendary producer Robert Evans contains all the trappings of a sensational tabloid story: money, hubris, sex, drugs, power, betrayal, movie stars, mega-blockbusters, and even a case of murder. The picture traces Evans' rise from obscurity, from his early career as a garment merchant to his brief run as a self-proclaimed bad "B" actor, after which he spring-boarded all the way to the top as head of production at Paramount in the late 1960s and early '70s, then tumbled in the '80s with a string of high-profile duds, a publicly disparaging descent into drugs and a tenuous tie to a mob-related killing, all of which turned the studio's golden boy into an industry whipping post. Evans himself provides the basso narration, and though this might suggest a critical lack of objectivity, his frankness and self-effacing cynicism have rarely been witnessed in a movie about Hollywood and its players. ★★★½ DVD: $27.99, VHS: $8.99

Kidnapped

(1960, 97 min, US, Robert Stevenson) *Peter Finch, James MacArthur, Peter O'Toole.* Disney, after its great success ten years earlier with Robert Louis Stevenson's *Treasure Island,* returns to another Stevenson source with exciting results. Finch and MacArthur are Alan Breck and David Balfour, respectively, the 18th-century adventurer and the young kidnap victim, who join forces to battle pirates and the Redcoats. Not *the* definitive Stevenson adaptation, but entertaining nonetheless. O'Toole's film debut. ★★★ VHS: $9.99

Kids

(1995, 90 min, US, Larry Clark) *Leo Fitzpatrick, Justin Pierce, Chloë Sevigny.* This unrelenting cinema verité look at a group of Manhattan teenagers seems destined to shock even the most hardened sensibilities. The assault begins even before the film's opening shot as we hear two teens ferociously sucking face. The ensuing scene, in which the film's antihero, Telly, talks his way into "fuckin'" a virgin, basically sets the tone for the whole film. As we follow him, his buddy Casper, and a bunch of other delinquents through 18 hours of unbridled hedonism, Telly boasts about previous virginal conquests and plots his next — when he's not suckin' on a 40, smoking a blunt, kicking the shit out of some poor guy or harassing fags. Director Clark employs astounding camerawork and a well-thought out narrative structure to present a disturbingly real picture of these wayward youths. The result is socially compelling though bordering on nauseating to watch and may leave one contemplating a vasectomy or tubal ligation. ★★ DVD: $24.99

Kids in the Hall: Brain Candy

(1996, 89 min, Canada, Kelly Makin) *Scott Thompson, David Foley, Bruce McCullough, Kevin McDonald, Mark McKinney.* Canada's five-man comic arsenal the Kids in the Hall make their big-screen debut in this witty, on-target satire of '90s America. An unscrupulous pharmaceutical company develops a happiness drug and unleashes it on an unsuspecting public. In true Kids fashion, pain and anger are turned into laughter as the Kids skewer America's mindset towards the elderly, drugs, the handicapped, MTV, grunge — and there's a terrific "coming out" song-and-dance number. The cast is great, with everyone playing multiple roles as they did on TV, though with 90 minutes to fill rather than 25, the film doesn't always reach the hilarity level of the show. However, it still packs plenty of laughs. ★★★ DVD Letterbox: $14.99, VHS: $14.99

Kika

(1993, 90 min, Spain, Pedro Almodóvar) *Verónica Forqué, Victoria Abril, Peter Coyote, Alex Casanovas, Rossy De Palma.* Almodóvar's big-budget comedy-drama is filled with outlandish costuming, neon-bright colors and wild characters, all filmed at the director's trademark, frenetic pace. Alternating between farce and an examination of urban crises, the film stars Forqué as Kika, a sweet, sexy makeup artist who is forced to confront urban rape, multiple murders and intrusion of her privacy by the media's prying eyes. When Kiki is raped, it is caught on camera by a neighbor. The tape falls into the clutches of Andrea (Abril), the hostess of Madrid's "Cops"-like TV show called "Today's Worst." And Andrea wants to air the tape on national TV! A sometimes outrageous tale of voyeurism and media manipulation. (Spanish with English subtitles) ★★★

Kill Bill: Vol. 1

(2003, 111 min, US, Quentin Tarantino) *Uma Thurman, Lucy Liu, Vivica A. Fox, Michael Madsen, Daryl Hannah, Sonny Chiba, David Carradine, Michael Parks.* His first film in six years, director Tarantino makes sure the wait is worth the while with this exhilarating mélange of Hong Kong martial arts, Japanese samurai films, anime, spaghetti western and unadulterated cinematic homage. Proving himself to be a pop icon auteur, Tarantino infuses *Kill Bill: Vol. 1* (this was originally one film) with an array of pop tunes, film references, fight sequences and brilliant set pieces that simply astonish. A ravishing and ass-kicking Thurman plays "The Bride," who in the story's beginning is being shot in the head by the unseen Bill; she's the last surviving member of the wedding, and after a four-year coma, sets out to exact revenge against the five-person Deadly Viper Assassination Squad responsible for leaving her to die. Told in various chapters, the film jumps back and forth in time, giving clues and info only when needed, each scene serving as an appetizer for the feast to follow. Tarantino is a master filmmaker, demonstrating prowess where others would falter, fake or forgo; the fact that his characters aren't as fully developed as in his previous three films is incidental, for the hyperventilating action grabs you by the throat and never lets go. The soundtrack is exemplary, from the Nancy Sinatra opening to the strains of Bernard Hermann's "Twisted Nerve." *Kill Bill* is audacious moviemaking, bold and beautiful, a superior tapestry of the films Tarantino grew up on. For all those Tarantino wannabes, the bar has once again been raised. (Sequel: *Kill Bill: Vol. 2*) ★★★★ DVD: $29.99, VHS: $24.99

Favorite Line: "Wiggle your big toe." *—Uma Thurman as The Bride*

Kill Bill: Vol. 2

(2004, 135 min, US, Quentin Tarantino) *Uma Thurman, David Carradine, Michael Madsen, Daryl Hannah, Gordon Liu, Michael Parks, Perla Haney-Jardine.* Other than adding a spoiler/cliffhanger to Vol. 1 and a brief reprise to Vol. 2, this essential second part of the *Kill Bill* saga feels very much a whole with the first. That writer-director Tarantino stages

Uma Thurman is "The Bride" in Quentin Tarantino's *Kill Bill*

K

Daryl Hannah in *Kill Bill: Vol. 2*

completely different fights, wildly tangential trails of dialogue, and cribs from whole new genres of film history should be no surprise, however. In one of the breeziest 2-hours-plus you'll ever see, The Bride (Thurman) completes her checklist (Madsen & Hannah as her feuding ex-squadmates), some emotional backstory is satisfyingly filled in, and the loose ends are wrapped up — leading to an intense showdown with Bill (Carradine) after an epic buildup worthy of Sergio Leone. The film works on so many levels that multiple viewings are required: it's a straight-up revenge tale, a spot-the-references filmgeek fest (check out the breathtaking closing shot from *The Searchers* for starters, or Gordon Liu's Shaw Brothers films to fully understand his exhilarating Pei Mei training scenes), and ultimately a resonatingly emotional tale of two broken hearts. In delightful throwaway bits, Tarantino again shows his skill at resurrecting B-actors: Larry Bishop cameos as a coke-snorting titty-bar owner who humiliates Madsen, and Parks is all but unrecognizable as a slimily charismatic Mexican pimp. ★★★★ DVD: $29.99, VHS: $24.99

Kill Me Again

(1989, 94 min, US, John Dahl) *Val Kilmer, Joanne Whalley-Kilmer, Michael Madsen.* This nifty little thriller is a small, engaging film noir/mystery which bypassed theatrical play. Kilmer plays a private investigator who is hired by femme fatale Whalley to fake her murder — she's being pursued by a boyfriend she's double-crossed. The murder is so convincing that the police now suspect the P.I., and the woman is nowhere to be found. Though one or two of the twists may be predictable to the mystery buff, there's more than enough intrigue and suspense for the rest of us. The love scenes between the future Mr. and Mrs. Kilmer are rather tame, however. ★★★ DVD: $14.99

The Killer

(1983, 110 min, Hong Kong, John Woo) *Chow Yun-Fat, Sally Yeh, Danny Lee.* Fasten your seat belt and get ready to blast off into nonstop action and rip-roaring entertainment in this relentlessly paced and extremely funny tongue-in-cheek exercise in slap-stick violence. The story follows a veteran assassin

(Yun-Fat) who, in the course of performing one last job before retiring, inadvertently blinds a young cabaret singer. Overwrought with guilt, he decides to devote his life to helping her, but the cops and the mob just won't let this killer-with-a-heart-of-gold go straight. Eventually, he teams up with a maverick cop and they embark on an adventure in which bullets fly like popcorn and the hilarity goes to extremes. Director Woo has fashioned a film lover's dream — a perfect blend of art, action and comedy. (Cantonese with English subtitles) ★★★★

Killer: A Journal of Murder

(1996, 90 min, US, Tim Metcalfe) *James Woods, Robert Sean Leonard, Ellen Greene, Cara Buono, Jeffrey De Munn, Lili Taylor, Harold Gould.* Awkwardly narrated, *Killer: A Journal of Murder* is "based" on a true story about a trusting new prison guard (Leonard) at Leavenworth and his misplaced friendship with a sociopathic prisoner (Woods). Produced by Oliver Stone, the movie raises many questions about our penal system without the pretension of trying to answer them. Yet when needed the most, the writing perches on the fence about whether treating these criminals kindly is the act of a fool or a saint. ★★ DVD: $14.99, VHS: $89.99

Killer Condom (Kondom des Grauens)

(1996, 107 min, Germany/Switzerland, Martin Walz) *Udo Samel, Marc Richter.* Based on the comic book by Ralf Konig, this weird horror/mystery satire follows a gay detective's search for the culprit behind a series of grisly deaths. In a seedy New York, detective Luigi Mackeroni (Samel) is assigned the case and what he discovers is that the killers are vicious penis-eating creatures masquerading as innocuous prophylactics. While offering some humorous moments, this cult film remains a lame experience. (German with English subtitles) ★★ DVD: $24.99, VHS: $14.99

The Killer Inside Me

(1975, 99 min, US, Burt Kennedy) *Stacy Keach, Susan Tyrrell, Tisha Sterling.* While not as searing as the Jim Thompson novel on which it is based, *The Killer Inside Me* is still a gripping psychological thriller. Keach stars as the seemingly rock-steady keeper of the law in a small California town whose long-simmering anger caused by a traumatic childhood incident finally explodes. Keach is at his best as the deranged yet sympathetic murderer, and Tyrrell is equally sharp as the white-trash prostitute who triggers his violence. ★★½ VHS: $89.99

The Killer Shrews

(1959, 71 min, US, Ray Kellogg) *James Best, Ken Curtis.* Curtis produced and stars in this tale of shrews the size of dogs — mainly because they *were* dogs, dressed in Pat Nixon's old cloth coat and wearing plastic fangs. Every bit as good as director Kellogg's other feature, *The Giant Gila Monster*, but lacking the sure hand he exhibited in his John Wayne opus *The Green Berets*, where the sun sets in the East (but that's another story for another time). ★

Killer's Kiss

(1955, 67 min, US, Stanley Kubrick) *Frank Silvera, Irene Kane, Jamie Smith.* This early Kubrick curiosity stars Silvera as a farm-bred boxer at the end of a short-lived fighting career. He falls fast and hard for a dance-hall girl. Her job is a self-imposed penance for past "sins," and her sleazy boss' obsessive interest in her results in murder. Kubrick's second feature includes a short but noteworthy night-

mare sequence; not only did he direct, but he co-produced, edited, photographed and wrote the story as well. ★★★ DVD: $14.99

The Killers

(1946, 103 min, US, Robert Siodmak) *Ava Gardner, Burt Lancaster, Edmond O'Brien, Albert Dekker, Sam Levene.* Based on the Ernest Hemingway story, and coscripted by (uncredited) John Huston, this searing crime drama follows the murder of a boxer (Lancaster). The police investigation and story is then told through flashback. Siodmak creates a remarkable atmosphere of tension and mystery in this classic noir. (Remade in 1964) ★★★★

The Killers

(1964, 95 min, US, Don Siegel) *Lee Marvin, Clu Gulager, John Cassavetes, Angie Dickinson, Ronald Reagan.* Marvin and Gulager fulfill the terms of their contract by gunning down Cassavetes. But Marvin needs to know why the doomed man didn't try to run. The killers begin a search for the man who ordered the hit, and uncover several dirty little secrets along the way. Based on a short story by Ernest Hemingway. A reworking of the 1946 noir classic. ★★★ VHS: $14.99

The Killing

(1956, 83 min, US, Stanley Kubrick) *Sterling Hayden, Marie Windsor, Elisha Cook, Jr., Vince Edwards.* Kubrick's first feature film is a taut thriller about an attempted heist at a race track. Filmed in exquisitely noir-ish black-and-white tones, the film stars Hayden as the stone-faced ringleader who pulls together a gang of non-criminals to conspire on the multimillion dollar job. Though not as exuberant as his later works, Kubrick's touches nonetheless permeate this highly stylized tale of human aspiration undone by avarice and deceit. An excellent group of stock supporting actors deliver a conglomeration of superbly melodramatic and emotionally cool performances. ★★★½ DVD: $14.99

Killing Cars

(1986, 104 min, West Germany, Michael Verhoeven) *Jürgen Prochnow, Senta Berger.* Director Verhoeven, who came into American prominence with *The Nasty Girl*, has shown great progress since this mildly interesting action/intrigue

The Killers (1946)

film. Prochnow plays Ralph, an amazingly unlikable hot-rod car designer whose work on a top secret "super car" becomes the target for industrial sabotage and other types of intrigue too numerous to recount. As the plot thickens, our hyperventilating hero (who is a surprisingly inept driver) is forced to confront a roving band of punks, double-crossing lovers and insidious coworkers in his efforts to get his car made. It's all smoke and no fire in this "thinking man's" thriller. ★½

The Killing Fields

(1984, 142 min, GB, Roland Joffé) *Sam Waterston, Haing S. Ngor, Athol Fugard, John Malkovich, Spalding Gray.* This highly emotional and often terrifying examination of Cambodia in the aftermath of the American evacuation stars Waterston as Sidney Schanberg, a Western journalist who stayed behind to witness the takeover of the brutally repressive Khmer Rouge. Ngor (a native of Cambodia who in real life was tortured by the Pol Pot regime) received a much-deserved Oscar for his moving portrayal of Schanberg's translator, Dith Pran. A nightmarish vision of one of history's darkest moments. ★★★★ DVD: $19.99, VHS: $14.99

Killing Heat

(1984, 104 min, Australia, Michael Raeburn) *Karen Black, John Thaw, John Kani.* An intense, provocative version of Doris Lessing's novel "The Grass Is Singing." Black stars as a city girl who marries a farmer, only to find herself unprepared for the rigors of country life. Through her affair with a black farm hand and her husband's violent reaction, director Raeburn is pointedly commenting on the realities of African Colonialism. ★★★

The Killing of a Chinese Bookie

(1976, 109 min, US, John Cassavetes) *Ben Gazzara, Seymour Cassel.* Sure to be the most feared entry at a Gamblers Anonymous Film Festival, *The Killing of a Chinese Bookie* stars Gazzara as Cosmo, the owner/MC of a sleazy nightclub-cum-strip joint whose bad luck at the Mafia-operated poker game throws him into a violent web of extortion, double dealings and contract killings. A tough-talking but oddly moral man, Cosmo finds that his T&A showplace is a church compared to the treachery of organized crime. Director Cassavetes' hand-held camera and seemingly improvised dialogue create a repressively realistic atmosphere where one cannot escape. ★★★ DVD: $24.99, VHS: $14.99

The Killing of Angel Street

(1981, 101 min, Australia, Donald Crombie) *John Hargreaves, Liz Alexander.* Based on actual events, this is the compelling story of corruption and the people who fought against it. A young activist battles to save her neighborhood from developers and becomes embroiled in a web of intrigue. ★★½

The Killing of Sister George

(1968, 138 min, GB, Robert Aldrich) *Beryl Reid, Susannah York, Coral Brown.* One of the most infamous lesbian "breakthrough" films of the 1960s, this story of an aging lesbian who loses her job and her young lover is a shrill, even grotesque exposé on lesbian lifestyles. Reid is magnetic in her portrayal of George, the loud and aggressive, cigar-chomping dyke whose girl-chasing ways (she even accosts a cab full of nuns!) and domineering personality drive away all who care for her. An entertainingly dated tale of love and loneliness that treads a strange line between comedy and sensationalist, perverted drama. Some scenes were shot in the London lesbian bar Getaway Club. ★★

Killing Time

(1997, 91 min, GB, Bharat Nalluri) *Craig Fairbrass, Kendra Torgan.* Frustrated cop Fairbrass, spurred by the killing of his partner by a sicko local crime boss, calls on beautiful Italian assassin-for-hire Torgan to wipe out said criminal and his organization. He also arranges for some thugs to then kill her, once she's done the job, to avoid paying her pricey bill. Things, of course, don't go as planned, and many stylized shoot-outs follow. What begins as a low-rent but stylish and distinctly British thriller quickly degenerates into slick, empty '90s trash. The action scenes are incomprehensible, and while Torgan certainly strikes the right image as a sleek, chic hit lady, she demonstrates all the assassin know-how of a drunk Jerry Lewis. Still, if it's "hot chick with guns" night, *Killing Time* as least lives up to its title. ★★

Killing Zoe

(1994, 96 min, US, Roger Avary) *Eric Stoltz, Jean-Hugues Anglade, Julie Delpy, Gary Kemp, Tai Thai.* Stoltz stars in this Luc Besson-influenced splatter film as an American safecracker who travels to Paris to help his childhood friend (Anglade) knock off a bank. Stoltz soon finds himself trapped in a nightmare that makes Griffin Dunne's wild taxi ride in *After Hours* feel like a sunny stroll through a garden. Delpy plays a call girl whom Stoltz hires his first night in town and who later, it turns out, is a secretary at the targeted bank. All style and no substance, the film has a few entertaining moments, but is ultimately unfulfilling and pointless. ★½ DVD: $14.99, VHS Clearance Price: $9.99

Kim

(1950, 113 min, US, Victor Saville) *Dean Stockwell, Errol Flynn, Paul Lukas, Cecil Kellaway.* Stirring adaptation of Rudyard Kipling's adventure story about a young English boy who becomes involved with a British secret agent in 19th-century India. Stockwell plays the young title character, and Flynn's then-faltering career was saved by his winning portrait of the daring soldier-spy. ★★★ DVD: $19.99, VHS: $19.99

Kind Hearts and Coronets

(1949, 104 min, GB, Robert Hamer) *Alec Guinness, Dennis Price, Valerie Hobson, Joan Greenwood, Hugh Griffith, Arthur Lowe.* Guinness created a sensation with his portrayal of all eight members of an aristocratic family who are eliminated one by one by a wayward relative who's bent on claiming the family's royal title. A delicious Ealing Studio comedy with a droll and macabre worldview. Featuring a zesty costar performance by Price as the ambitious social climber. ★★★★ DVD: $19.99

A Kind of Loving

(1962, 112 min, GB, John Schlesinger) *Alan Bates, June Ritchie, Thora Hird.* Schlesinger's first feature film is a sensitive drama about a young couple who marry because of pregnancy. While the film was unfortunately lost in the shuffle, having been released after its sensational "kitchen sink" counterparts *Room at the Top* and *Saturday Night, Sunday Morning*, it is a nonetheless witty, frank and poignant study of a lust gone awry. Featuring sterling performances by Bates and Ritchie as the young couple. ★★★½

Kindergarten

(1987, 143 min, USSR, Yevgeny Yevtushenko) *Klaus Maria Brandauer.* Poet and neophyte filmmaker Yevtushenko has taken an overused theme — the destructiveness of war as seen through the eyes of a

Alec Guinness in *Kind Hearts and Coronets*

child — and has fashioned from it a completely original and exciting autobiographical work. The setting is 1941 during the evacuation of Moscow. A mother sends her ten-year-old son to the safety of relatives in a Siberian village. En route, however, the youth's train is bombed, and the boy's journey becomes a vivid and harrowing odyssey through a war-charred landscape. The poet emerges from the filmmaker in this sentimental, bombastic and emotional film. (Russian with English subtitles) ★★★½ VHS: $59.99

Kindergarten Cop

(1990, 111 min, US, Ivan Reitman) *Arnold Schwarzenegger, Pamela Reed, Penelope Ann Miller, Linda Hunt, Carroll Baker.* Schwarzenegger mixes comedy and action as a tough Los Angeles cop who is forced to go undercover as a kindergarten teacher in hopes of capturing the criminal father of one of the kids. He goes through the usual comic humilities playing baby-sitter to a group of precocious five-year-olds. The comedy doesn't always work, and the action is less than exciting, but in spite of it all the film maintains a certain level of enjoyment. Arnold is Arnold, which is probably enough to please his fans. Reed, however, as his partner, is the film's biggest asset giving a spirited performance who can make the unbelievable convincing. ★★½ DVD: $14.99

The Kindred

(1987, 92 min, US, Jeffrey Obrow & Stephen Carpenter) *Rod Steiger, Kim Hunter, Amanda Pays.* A mostly entertaining, derivative horror film about a scientific experiment which spawns a half-human sea creature. ★★

The King and I

(1956, 134 min, US, Walter Lang) *Yul Brynner, Deborah Kerr, Rita Moreno.* "Shall We Dance?" That question will be difficult to not ask after viewing this sumptuous film version of Rodgers and Hammerstein's stage classic. Brynner gives an unforgettable and timeless performance as the King of Siam in this story of a proper British schoolteacher who, tutoring the court's children, falls in love with the monarch. Kerr is radiant as the governess, and the great score includes "Getting to Know You" and "Hello Young Lovers." Brynner won a Best Actor Oscar. (Remade twice in 1999) ★★★½ DVD Letterbox: $19.99, VHS: $14.99, VHS Letterbox: $19.99

K

The King of Marvin Gardens

The King and I

(1999, 90 min, US, Richard Rich) When this animated King of Siam asks "Shall we dance?" don't be surprised if the whole family shouts "No!" Terrible animation and lackluster songs will do nothing but leave you thirsting for the Yul Brynner/Deborah Kerr version. ★ DVD: $9.99, VHS: $9.99

King David

(1985, 113 min, US, Bruce Beresford) *Richard Gere, Edward Woodward, Alice Krige.* Gere plays the young David, from the famous fight with Goliath to his time as King. Beresford approaches this with a seriousness which separates it from those lavish 1950s biblical epics; though the first half, featuring Woodward as King Saul, is much more successful than the latter half. ★★½ DVD Letterbox: $19.99, VHS: $9.99

King for a Day

(1980, 88 min, Israel, Asi Dayan) Although Israeli film production is not high in the international filmmaking standards, their films are made for domestic use and are usually fun, light, family entertainment. In *King for a Day*, the story revolves around the return of an older man's daughter to Jerusalem. The problem is that she thinks that he is a rich man so, with the help of his friends, he plays a game of wealth. (Hebrew with English subtitles) ★★½

A King in New York

(1957, 105 min, GB, Charles Chaplin) *Charles Chaplin, Dawn Addams, Michael Chaplin.* Often misunderstood, Chaplin's last starring film is a bittersweet political satire about a deposed European monarch who visits America amidst the McCarthy anti-Communist hysteria. Not at all "anti-American" as its detractors at the time claimed, this somewhat uneven but remarkable stab at social madness is filled with hilarious moments and has much to say about our nuclear and technological insanity. Chaplin's son Michael is featured as a young political malcontent. ★★★ DVD: $29.99, VHS: $19.99

King Kong

(1933, 100 min, US, Ernest B. Schoedsack & Merian C. Cooper) *Fay Wray, Bruce Abbott, Robert Armstrong.* He is billed as "the eighth wonder of the world" and, in the sixty years since the movie's release, animator Willis O'Brien's awesome creature

has all but lived up to that title. There are ample reasons why this parable about the notorious giant ape let loose in New York City has had such an enduring notoriety. As enormous and unwieldy as the whole project is, the simple fable around which the story is built continues to be resonant. As an adventure-fantasy, *King Kong* has yet to be outdone. (Sequel: *Son of Kong*) (Remade in 1976) ★★★★

King Kong

(1976, 134 min, US, John Guillerman) *Jeff Bridges, Jessica Lange, Charles Grodin, Rene Auberjonois.* Perhaps the most hyped film of the 1970s, especially for its supposedly spectacular mechanical effects. Despite winning an honorary Oscar, the effects are anything but special. Whatever possessed producer Dino De Laurentiis, the king of the bloated epic, to remake the 1933 classic is beyond human (or simian) comprehension. The only redeeming factor of this remake is the launching of Lange's career and the end of De Laurentiis'. ★ DVD: $19.99, VHS: $14.99

King Lear

(1971, 137 min, GB, Peter Brook) *Paul Scofield, Irene Worth, Alec McCowan, Cyril Cusack, Patrick Magee.* Stark black-and-white cinematography and a somber Danish landscape underscore director Brook's heavy treatment of the Shakespeare tragedy. Scofield makes for a magnificent Lear, and receives excellent support from the great ensemble. ★★★½

King Lear

(1984, 158 min, GB, Michael Elliot) *Laurence Olivier, Diana Rigg, Anna Calder-Marshall, Dorothy Tutin, Leo McKern, John Hurt, Robert Lindsay.* Who better to play Lear than Olivier in his later life? This Emmy Award-winning production is one of the finest versions of Shakespeare's play available. ★★★★ VHS: $29.99

King Lear

(1987, 90 min, US/Switzerland, Jean-Luc Godard) *Molly Ringwald, Woody Allen, Peter Sellers, Burgess Meredith, Norman Mailer.* Even for hard-core Godardians, this incomprehensible version of Shakespeare's classic might prove to be tough going, the end result sadly suggesting that perhaps we already have seen all of the exciting filmic

innovations from France's most innovative director. The oddball cast meander through the various scenes with Godard himself starring as a crazed professor with a penchant for strange headgear. ★½

The King of Comedy

(1983, 139 min, US, Martin Scorsese) *Robert De Niro, Jerry Lewis, Sandra Bernhard, Tony Randall, Diahnne Abbott, Shelley Hack, Fred De Cordova.* De Niro is Rupert Pupkin, an aspiring but psychotic comedian, who schemes his way onto network TV and instant celebrity. Scorsese directs a finely tuned cast, including Lewis as a cynical dean of the airwaves and Bernhard as Pupkin's rubber-faced accomplice. ★★★ DVD Letterbox: $14.99, VHS: $9.99

King of Hearts

(1967, 102 min, France, Philippe de Broca) *Alan Bates, Geneviève Bujold, Adolfo Celi.* A perennial favorite at TLA, De Broca's classic comedy is a moving celebration of the triumph of innocence. Bates stars as a Scottish soldier dispatched to a small French village where the only remaining inhabitants are the inmates of the local asylum. (English and French with English subtitles) ★★★½ DVD: $19.99

King of Kings

(1961, 174 min, US, Nicholas Ray) *Jeffrey Hunter, Siobhan McKenna, Robert Ryan, Rip Torn.* Ray, an accomplished veteran of noir and mysteries, turned his talents to the story of Christ in this beautifully filmed religious epic. Hunter plays Jesus. A better spectacle and far more successful in its storytelling than 1965's similarly themed *The Greatest Story Ever Told.* ★★★½ DVD: $19.99

The King of Marvin Gardens

(1972, 104 min, US, Bob Rafelson) *Jack Nicholson, Ellen Burstyn, Bruce Dern, Julia Anne Robinson, Scatman Crothers.* An enthralling drama fueled by a poignant story of the American Dream lost and the dynamic acting of Nicholson, Dern and especially Burstyn. Nicholson is David Stabler, a quiet, almost mousy late night Philly D.J. who is pulled out of his staid life when his volatile, always-in-trouble brother (Dern) calls from an Atlantic City jail. Traveling to an off-season, geriatric-filled pre-casino A.C., David is sucked into his brother's grandiose scheme of easy money, willing women and ownership of a small Hawaiian island. Nicholson ably plays off his boisterous image as the shy loser given one last chance. Dern is maniacal as the naïve dreamer/crook and Burstyn, in perhaps her most affecting role, plays a wacked-out, aging beauty queen. Another star of the film is Atlantic City itself, a seedy, forlorn dead end at the edge of a cold, empty ocean. One of the most underrated and accomplished films of the 1970s. ★★★★ DVD: $24.99, VHS: $19.99

The King of Masks

(1999, 101 min, China, Wu Tianming) *Chu Yuk, Chao Yim Yin, Zhang Riuyang.* An elderly street performer, a master of the dying art of mask making and performance, wishes to pass on his knowledge. According to tradition, the heir to the secrets of the art must be male, so the old man buys an eight-year-old boy from a homeless father. The boy and the old man become close, until the boy's secret — he is a girl — is revealed, and their relationship as well as the old man's traditional values are severely tested. Well-paced and ultimately moving, *The King of Masks* is enhanced greatly by the two leads' assured performances, and an intelligent script that avoids sentimentality. (Mandarin with English subtitles) ★★★½ DVD: $27.99, VHS: $21.99

King of New York

(1990, 106 min, US, Abel Ferrara) *Christopher Walken, David Caruso, Laurence Fishburne, Giancarlo Esposito, Wesley Snipes.* Walken stars in this savage exposé of a ruthless drug kingpin who fancies himself a modern day Robin Hood. Upon his release from prison, Walken begins a campaign, using a veil of moral superiority, to eliminate all of the "bad" elements from the drug trade. Ferrara's film, intensely gratuitous in its violence, has an undeniable power in its examination of corruption and betrayal. ★★★ DVD Dual 2-disc Special Edition: $19.99

King of the Gypsies

(1978, 112 min, US, Frank Pierson) *Susan Sarandon, Judd Hirsch, Sterling Hayden, Annette O'Toole, Shelley Winters, Eric Roberts.* Roberts takes over leadership of his Gypsy tribe when his grandfather dies; which doesn't sit too well with Roberts' father Hirsch. Sarandon is Hirsch's wife who defies her husband and gives her support to her son. ★★½ VHS: $14.99

King of the Hill

(1993, 115 min, US, Steven Soderbergh) *Jesse Bradford, Jeroen Krabe, Lisa Eichhorn, Karen Allen, Spalding Gray, Elizabeth McGovern.* Set in Depression-era St. Louis, *King of the Hill* is based on the memoirs of A.E. Hotchner and tells the tale of a boy who is essentially abandoned by well-meaning but desperate parents. While not ignoring the realities of the period, director Soderbergh manages to pick out the story's joyous moments without ever getting sentimental. Much credit has to go to 13-year-old Bradford who stars as Aaron, a boy who begins to lose everything but always keeps his sense of fairness, fun and dignity. Bradford's soulful eyes reveal his thoughts with a subtlety that's remarkable for an actor of any age. With an impeccable eye, Soderbergh has taken a small story and given it quiet, resonant power. ★★★½

King, Queen, Knave

(1972, 92 min, GB, Jerzy Skolimowski) *Gina Lollobrigida, David Niven, John Moulder-Brown.* Undeservedly maligned by critics, this surreal adaptation of Victor Nabokov's novel is filled with stinging black humor. The story concerns an impish young lad who falls in love with his aunt (Lollobrigida); and together they plot to murder her husband (Niven). ★★★

King Ralph

(1991, 97 min, US, David S. Ward) *John Goodman, Peter O'Toole, Joely Richardson, John Hurt.* In this lightweight but engaging comedy, Goodman plays a Las Vegas lounge singer (who does a mean Little Richard) who, after an accident wipes out the entire royal family, becomes the King of England. Most of the comedy centers on the big guy's "fish out of water" comedy of errors. O'Toole also stars as the royal secretary who acts as baby-sitter and cultural guide to King Ralph. ★★½ DVD: $14.99

King Rat

(1965, 133 min, US, Bryan Forbes) *James Fox, Tom Courtenay, Denholm Elliott, George Segal, John Mills.* A gritty, first-rate drama, based on James Clavell's novel. Set at a POW camp in Malaysia during WWII, the story focuses on the rigors of captivity facing Allied prisoners, and the high cost they pay for their dignity and survival. Segal stars as a mercenary American G.I. financially benefiting from the hunger and sickness around him; and Fox is terrific as his principled, British right-hand man. ★★★½ VHS: $19.99

King Solomon's Mines

(1937, 80 min, GB, Robert Stevenson) *Paul Robeson, Cedric Hardwicke, Roland Young.* This exciting adventure story tells of the search for a legendary diamond mine deep in the heart of Africa. The robust and legendary Robeson fills the screen with star quality as a mysterious African chieftan. Based on a novel by H. Rider Haggard. (Remade in 1950 and 1985) ★★★ DVD: $14.99

King's Row

(1942, 127 min, US, Sam Wood) *Ann Sheridan, Robert Cummings, Ronald Reagan, Betty Field.* This gripping and well-made drama features Reagan's best performance (excluding his portrayal of the "I can't remember" president). Set in a small Midwestern town, the story follows the friendship of Sheridan, Cummings and Reagan from childhood to young adulthood — as Cummings studies medicine overseas, Sheridan and Reagan stay behind, with tragedy in store for Reagan. Sheridan and Field (as a reclusive childhood friend) excel. ★★★½ VHS: $19.99

The King's Whore

(1992, 111 min, US/Italy/West Germany, Axel Corti) *Timothy Dalton, Valeria Golino.* "Masterpiece Theatre" meets Danielle Steele in this lavishly produced variation on the "Dangerous Liaisons" theme. Dalton stars as a 19th-century Italian king who stops at nothing in the pursuit of his chancellor's wife (Golino). The film is surprisingly well-made and entertaining to the end, and definitely qualifies as a "guilty pleasure." ★★½ VHS: $19.99

The Kingdom

(1994, 279 min, Denmark, Lars von Trier) *Ernst-Hugo Jaregard, Kirsten Rolffes, Udo Kier.* You may have your "E.R.," America, but look away: *The Kingdom*, a joyfully creepy and surrealistic Danish medical thriller/satire, is full of jaded New Age practices, a crying for mother Casper, a nationalistic neurologist longing for his homeland through binoculars, and more information about voodoo than one would expect in a waiting room. Jaregard stars as the new staff member to a Copenhagen hospital, where patients and doctors, alike, engage in totally unexpected behavior. Though comparisons have been made to "E.R." and "Twin Peaks," *The Kingdom* is a singular effort. At four-and-a-half hours, the film is hardly dull or repetitive, and if expectations are put on hold, von Trier's stylistic smorgasbord can be as compelling and visually hypnotic as his earlier work *Zentropa*. (Danish with English subtitles) ★★★½ VHS: $9.99

Kingdom Come

(2001, 92 min, US, Doug McHenry) *LL Cool J, Jada Pinkett Smith, Whoopi Goldberg, Vivica A. Fox, Loretta Devine, Anthony Anderson, Toni Braxton, Cedric the Entertainer.* With its all-star cast and promise of laughs and warmth, *Kingdom Come* rarely delivers either, making it all the more disappointing resulting its potential. Based on the play "Dearly Departed" by David Dean Bottrell and Jessie Jones (who wrote the screenplay adaptation), the story follows a family's get-together when their surly patriarch passes away. Those left behind include widow Mama Ray (Goldberg), her two sons (Cool J, Anderson) and overweight daughter, and his holy-roller sister (Devine). As each family member mourns, they must also deal with their own disastrous life, as well, culminating in a family showdown. The ensemble performs admirably, but no one person is really given the chance to establish

anything but perfunctory characters as the story often jumps from one to another without benefit of shading or depth. It is, however, all wrapped up with love and a song. ★★ DVD: $14.99, VHS: $6.99

Kingpin

(1996, 113 min, US, Bobby Farrelly & Peter Farrelly) *Woody Harrelson, Randy Quaid, Bill Murray, Vanessa Angel, Chris Elliott, Richard Tyson.* A one-handed bowling wiz takes a moronic Amish farmer and tries to turn him into the next champion. What sounds like a pitch from *The Player* actually turns out to be an unexpectedly funny, dark-edged entry from the "dumb" school of comedy filmmaking. Harrelson plays a potential champion bowler whose brush with rival Murray ends up with his bowling hand being cut off. Years later and now an alcoholic grifter, Harrelson stumbles upon Quaid, a talented Amish bowler. With just the sparest of double talk, Harrelson and Quaid are on the road to Reno to enter the national championship. Not wallowing in its silliness, *Kingpin* is very cynical, and much as you may, you can't help but laugh. *Kingpin*'s also of note for three prominent stars having desperately bad hair days. ★★★ DVD: $14.99, VHS R-Rated: $9.99

Kings Go Forth

(1958, 109 min, US, Delmer Daves) *Frank Sinatra, Tony Curtis, Natalie Wood.* An intriguing war story that explores racial bigotry. Sinatra and Curtis are American G.I.s fighting in France during WWII who both fall in love with Wood. When they discover she is half black, their prejudices come to the fore, forcing them to face and examine their bigotry. All three stars give fine performances in this penetrating melodrama. ★★★ DVD: $14.99

Kings of the Road

(1976, 176 min, West Germany, Wim Wenders) *Rudiger Vogler, Hans Zischler.* This early Wenders masterpiece is a somber tale of a projector repairman and a friend who slowly thread through the barren landscape of the border regions of West and East Germany visiting shattered movie theatres, listening to rock ?n' roll and encountering strangers with strange stories. The "New" Germany that Wenders paints is one of a vast and underpopulated hinterland which proves to be both empty and imprisoning. (German with English subtitles) ★★★½

Kipperbang

(1982, 80 min, GB, Michael Apted) *John Albasiny, Abigail Cruttenden, Alison Steadman.* This lightweight comedy details the romantic fantasies of a group of young teens and their teachers in 1948 Britain. *Kipperbang* evokes the mood of a Bill Forsyth film, but lacks resonance and sense of direction. ★★½

Kipps

(1941, 82 min, GB, Carol Reed) *Michael Redgrave, Phyllis Calvert, Michael Wilding.* Redgrave puts in a solid performance as Mr. Kipps, a shopkeeper who, upon inheriting a fortune, attempts to enter into high society. Sidney Gilliat's screenplay is faithfully adapted from the H.G. Wells novel. (Made into the Broadway musical "Half a Sixpence.") ★★★½

Kiss Me Deadly

(1955, 105 min, US, Robert Aldrich) *Ralph Meeker, Albert Dekker, Cloris Leachman, Strother Martin.* With the despairing plea "Remember me" from a soon-to-be-dead dame echoing in his head, private eye Mike Hammer (Meeker) becomes involved in a

Kiss Me Guido

convoluted case of torture, murder and a stolen, white-hot Pandora's box. Hammer, a sometimes sadistic and violent man, attempts to find the killers of a frantic, near-naked woman (Leachman) whom he picks up in his car one night. A great, fast-moving plot, loads of unforgettable characters and creative photography contribute in making this Mickey Spillane detective story (and Cold War allegory) a classic of late film noir. ★★★½ DVD: $14.99

Kiss Me Guido

(1997, 91 min, US, Tony Vitale) *Nick Scotti, Anthony Barrile, Craig Chester, Anthony DeSando.* When he discovers his girlfriend having sex with his brother, Frankie (Scotti) decides to leave the Bronx for Manhattan. But where to stay? Looking in the personals, he notices "GWM." And thinking it "Guy with Money," he heads to the Village and the apartment of gay actor Warren (Barrile), who's in desperate need of this month's rent. Such is the premise of this slight though disarming independent comedy which finds its humor in gay and straight stereotypes, though the film can't overcome a pedestrian screenplay and the laughs aren't as frequent as they should be. But what the film lacks in creativity it makes up for in spirit, and the eager cast does try to sustain a degree of lightheartedness. (The basis for a short-lived TV show) ★★½ DVD: $29.99, VHS: $14.99

Kiss Me Kate

(1953, 119 min, US, George Sidney) *Howard Keel, Kathryn Grayson, Ann Miller, Bob Fosse, Tommy Rall, Keenan Wynn, James Whitmore.* One of Cole Porter's best scores highlights this vibrant adaptation of the Broadway musical about a divorced theatrical couple who are reunited for a performance of Shakespeare's "The Taming of the Shrew." Keel and Grayson are wonderful as the estranged husband and wife; and the dance sequences are terrific. ★★★½ DVD: $19.99

Kiss Me, Stupid

(1964, 126 min, US, Billy Wilder) *Dean Martin, Kim Novak, Ray Walston.* A rollicking sex farce unfairly maligned on its initial release, this wicked comedy offers many a nasty swipe at sexual politics. Martin plays a successful, womanizing singer ending a tour. En route through a small Nevada town, Martin is "shanghaied" by struggling composer Walston, who will do anything to have Dino hear his music — including hiring prostitute Novak to masquerade as his wife, hoping Dean will take a fancy to her. ★★★ DVD Letterbox: $19.99

Kiss of Death

(1947, 98 min, US, Henry Hathaway) *Victor Mature, Richard Widmark, Anne Grey, Brian Donlevy, Karl Malden.* Mature, in his best role, is Nick Bianco, a hard-luck crook who turns state's evidence only to find himself stalked by a vengeful hoodlum. Widmark, in his screen debut, steals the show as a sadistic, psycho hood with a demonic giggle and a propensity for throwing old ladies in wheelchairs down flights of stairs. (Remade in 1995) ★★★½

Kiss of Death

(1971, 80 min, GB, Mike Leigh) *David Threlfall, John Wheatley, Kay Adshead.* A minor film from the early career of director Leigh, *Kiss of Death* is essentially the dead-end story about the dead-end life of Trevor, a pathetic and slightly sociopathic Manchester youth. Trevor hangs out with his best friend, makes a half-hearted and mean-spirited stab at dating, and keeps up his work as a mortuary assistant. As slice-of-life and character study, the film exhibits Leigh's innate talents, but its story goes nowhere and lacks any shred of motivating interest. ★★ VHS: $29.99

Kiss of Death

(1995, 101 min, US, Barbet Schroeder) *David Caruso, Samuel L. Jackson, Nicolas Cage, Helen Hunt, Kathryn Erbe, Stanley Tucci, Michael Rapaport, Ving Rhames.* An accomplished, intense and satisfying crime thriller, director Schroeder's gritty updating of the 1947 film noir classic is a high-octane ride through New York City's underworld. Caruso makes a credible, satisfying leading man debut as a Queens ex-con trying to stay legit but who's pulled back into crime out of a misguided sense of loyalty. Much like Victor Mature's imprisoned jewel thief in the original, Caruso's Jimmy Kilmartin wants nothing to do with the assistant D.A.; that is until his family is directly affected by his partners-in-crime. Turning on them in an ingenious manner, he infiltrates a gang led by low-level mob figure Junior Brown (Cage), while at the same time coping with a cop with a grudge (Jackson). ★★★½ DVD: $14.99, VHS: $9.99

Kiss of the Dragon

(2001, 98 min, US/France, Chris Nahon) *Jet Li, Bridget Fonda, Tcheky Karyo.* Li stars as a Chinese detective assigned to a case in Paris that goes terribly wrong. Turns out he's been set up by a corrupt Parisian cop, with hooker Fonda caught in the middle. Plotwise, this is tepid stuff, but *Kiss of the Dragon* is graced with Li's charisma and fighting skills. This could have been a bit less mean-spirited, and Fonda certainly could have been given something more to do, but more often than not, the film attempts to deliver, and it's got a very hissable villain to boot (the over-the-top Karyo). But, ultimately, there's got to be more to it than Jet Li kicking and punching a lot. ★★½ DVD Pan & Scan: $14.99, DVD: $14.99, VHS: $9.99

Kiss of the Spider Woman

(1985, 120 min, Brazil, Hector Babenco) *Raul Julia, William Hurt, Sonia Braga.* Babenco's spellbinding meditation on political idealism and self-delusion stars Hurt (who won a Best Actor Oscar) and Julia, who portray two dramatically opposite inmates thrown together in a dungeon-like cell somewhere in South America. Julia, a cold political realist and activist, is forced to endure the fantasies of Hurt, a hopelessly romantic and politically naïve homosexual. An exotic Braga plays both Julia's one-time lover and Hurt's imagined heroine. (Made into a Broadway musical) (Filmed in English) ★★★½

Kiss or Kill

(1997, 97 min, Australia, Bill Bennett) *Frances O'Connor, Matt Day, Chris Haywood, Barry Otto.* As Al and Nikki, Day and O'Connor run neck-and-neck with Micky and Mallory as the most sympathetic sociopaths since Bonnie and Clyde. A sucker-punch opening sequence catapults us into this frenetically paced, twisted road movie. During a standard scam which results in an unexpected homicide, our antiheroes inadvertently get the goods on Zipper Doyle (Langrishe), a retired major sports figure now an institution in the community. As the cats and mice hopscotch all over the vast expanses of the arid Australian wasteland, the parties involved indulge in the human predilection for base behavior and mystical confabulation. This movie is like Australian wine: You've had plenty of it before, but the peppery afterbite takes you by surprise. ★★★ VHS: $9.99

Kiss the Girls

(1997, 120 min, US, Gary Fleder) *Morgan Freeman, Ashley Judd, Cary Elwes, Tony Goldwyn, Jay O. Sanders, Bill Nunn, Jeremy Piven, Alex McArthur, Gina Ravera.* Borrowing liberally from *Seven* and *The Silence of the Lambs*, *Kiss the Girls* is a modest, entertaining, seen-it-before variation of the serial-killer thriller which gets its main strength from its two leads. Freeman is a psychiatrist for the Washington, D.C. police department. When his niece is kidnapped by a serial killer in North Carolina, he takes matters in his own hands and begins a private investigation. He hooks up with doctor Judd, another kidnap victim who just barely escaped the killer's desolate hideout. Together they try to track down the killer before it's too late for the rest of the captives. *Kiss the Girls* does manage some good moments of suspense, and it's very absorbing as a police procedural when Freeman is doing his Sherlock Holmes bit. (Sequel: *Along Came a Spider*) ★★½ DVD: $14.99, VHS: $9.99

Kiss Tomorrow Goodbye

(1950, 102 min, US, Gordon Douglas) *James Cagney, Barbara Payton, Ward Bond.* A cold-blooded mobster (Cagney) escapes from prison and embarks on a crime spree with his love-struck gun moll. But when he murders her brother and dumps her for a classy debutante, Cagney learns the hard way that hell hath no fury like a gun moll scorned. ★★★ DVD: $14.99

Kissed

(1997, 75 min, Canada, Lynne Stopkewich) *Molly Parker, Peter Outerbridge, Jay Brazeau.* You would think that a movie about a necrophiliac woman working as an embalmer would be fairly shocking. This may be true with a poorly executed, low-budget horror film like *Nekromantik*, but it is unfortunately not the case with this glossier production based on a short story from a book of women's erotica. Parker stars as a curious young woman who happens to be sexually attracted to youthful, fresh male corpses. While in embalming school, she meets a med student (Outerbridge) who becomes attracted to her obsession and eventually begins to share her compulsion for cadavers. Fairly tame and placid, the film attempts to explore its subject obliquely, without showing too much in the way of sex and gore. Too bad, because this restraint works against the movie, since the ability of the first-time filmmakers is not up to the challenge of conveying an uncomfortable point without graphically showing it. ★★½

K

Kissing a Fool

(1998, 94 min, US, Doug Ellin) *David Schwimmer, Jason Lee, Mili Avital, Bonnie Hunt.* Schwimmer works against type as a dunderheaded slimeball, as opposed to the sweet dunderhead on "Friends." Here he plays an egomaniacal sports anchor who, engaged to Avital, gets cold feet. He convinces old college chum Lee to try to seduce her. There are more complications than necessary for a 90-minute film, none of which will surprise. Lee does his usual inspired schtick, giving each line reading a gusto that clashes with the rest of the flat movie. Schwimmer fails to make a difference between an annoying character and an annoying performance. Blame for the film's failure must rest with him, since he also executive produced and helped Ellin to write and direct. ★½ DVD: $9.99, VHS: $7.49

Kissing Jessica Stein

(2002, 96 min, US, Charles Herman-Wurmfeld) *Jennifer Westfeldt, Heather Juergensen, Scott Cohen, Tovah Feldshuh.* Copy editor Jessica Stein has high expectations with every guy she attempts to date. Jaded by constant disappointment with men, she answers a singles ad under the "women seeking women" section. She meets art dealer Helen Cooper, who is equally tired of her mundane routine in which she has a different gent for various sexual needs. What happens when these two formidable women get together forms the core of a most charming romantic comedy. Romance in the new millenium isn't made any easier for Jessica as she must contend with her overzealous Jewish mother (Feldshuh in a marvelous performance), helpful friends and coworkers all the while wanting to take her newfound relationship *slowly* with the patient yet horny Helen. Look beyond its feel-good sentimentality and *Kissing Jessica Stein* is a witty and smart confection that's as good-humored and personable as Jessica herself. ★★★½ DVD Letterbox: $19.99, VHS: $14.99

The Kitchen Toto

(1988, 96 min, GB, Harry Hook) *Edwin Mahinda, Bob Peck, Phyllis Logan.* Offering an uncompromising child's eye view of 1950s Kenya, when that state was still very much a colony of Great Britain, *The Kitchen Toto* is a mesmerizing and at times harrowing examination of a land imprisoned by the boundaries of cultural and racial alienation. The title refers to a kitchen helper, in this case Mwangi (Mahinda), a young Kenyan of the Kikuyu tribe who leaves his widowed mother to work in the house of the British chief of police. Scorned by both colonialist and tribesmen, Mwangi tries peacefully to find his way through a turbulent world where violence is the norm. ★★★½ VHS: $19.99

Kissing Jessica Stein

Kitty and the Bagman

(1982, 95 min, Australia, Donald Crombie) *Liddy Clark.* The glory days of the Warner Brothers back lot are revived in this colorful Aussie Roaring Twenties comedy, full of flappers, gamblers and an earnest interest in the dishonestly earned dollar. Set in Sydney, it follows a beautiful innocent young bride, Kitty O'Rourke, who turns to the oldest profession in order to spring her small-time hood husband from jail. ★★½

Kitty Foyle

(1940, 105 min, US, Sam Wood) *Ginger Rogers, Dennis Morgan, James Craig.* Rogers won an Oscar (beating Katharine Hepburn in *The Philadelphia Story*!) for her strong portrait of a career woman torn between two men of different social backgrounds. Dalton Trumbo adapted the screenplay from Christopher Morley's novel. ★★★ VHS: $14.99

The Klansman

(1974, 112 min, US, Terence Young) *Richard Burton, Lee Marvin, Cameron Mitchell, O.J. Simpson.* With a cast including Burton and Marvin, a script cowritten by Samuel Fuller and a topic as important as race relations in the deep South, one would expect something from this film. Don't. It's almost impossible to convey the disappointment of this embarrassingly trashy and exploitative little oddity. Fuller was set to direct, but took an early walk. ★ VHS: $14.99

Klondike Annie

(1936, 77 min, US, Raoul Walsh) *Mae West, Victor McLaglen, Helen Jerome Eddy.* West adapted her own stage play and stars in this unusual comedy-drama and morality tale. West plays an entertainer who murders her possessive lover and escapes on a steamer bound for Alaska. On board, she meets love-struck captain McLaglen and missionary Eddy. With the police hot on her trail, and Eddy dying at sea, West changes identities with the dead woman and, on arrival in Alaska, is forced to continue the charade. Though Mae still manages to knock off a few "West-ern" zingers, the film's do-good, sentimental attitude doesn't altogether mix with La West's brazen character. ★★

Klute

(1971, 114 min, US, Alan J. Pakula) *Jane Fonda, Donald Sutherland, Roy Scheider, Charles Cioffi.* Fonda won an Academy Award for her mesmerizing portrayal of a high-priced New York call girl in this psychological thriller. Sutherland stars in the title role of an out-of-town cop on the trail of a missing husband who may have been a client of Fonda's. An outstanding use of sound and editing, along with the sexual frankness of the script, make this one of the landmark films of the '70s. ★★★★ DVD Letterbox: $19.99, VHS: $14.99, VHS Letterbox: $14.99

Knife in the Head

(1978, 108 min, Germany, Reinhard Huff) *Bruno Ganz, Angela Winkler.* Ganz stars in this well-paced mystery as Hoffman, a scientist who is shot in the head at a local radical hangout while searching for his estranged wife. The injury leaves him partially paralyzed and causes him to lose much of his memory. As Hoffman tries to uncover the truth about the shooting, he is caught between the radicals and police who each want to exploit him for their own purposes. Brilliant acting and a great script make this a top-notch thriller. (German with English subtitles) ★★★ VHS: $19.99

Kitty Foyle

Knife in the Water

(1962, 95 min, Poland, Roman Polanski) *Leon Niemczyk, Jolanta Umecka, Zygmunt Malandowicz.* Polanski's extraordinary study of three characters interacting on a small boat and how an innocent yachting weekend is transformed into a journey of mistrust and adultery. Polanski's first film, a fascinating study of sexual obsession, is riveting in its narrative, and creates a tension-filled atmosphere throughout. (Polish with English subtitles) ★★★★ DVD Criterion Collection: $39.99, VHS: $29.99

Knight Moves

(1992, 90 min, US, Carl Schenkel) *Christopher Lambert, Tom Skerritt, Diane Lane, Daniel Baldwin.* This psycho-thriller is an effective, bone-chilling mystery about a serial killer who gives clues to an international chess master about where and when his next victim will die because he wants to play against the best. Lambert is very convincing as the champion and Skerritt, in a sturdy performance, is the local police chief who both suspects and helps him. The standard thriller ending doesn't detract from the film; in fact, it's very intense despite its predictability. If you can figure out who the killer is before he's revealed, you're a bit of a chess master yourself. ★★★ DVD: $14.99, VHS: $9.99

Knight without Armour

(1937, 107 min, GB, Jacques Feyder) *Marlene Dietrich, Robert Donat.* This cross-cultural oddity was produced by British movie mogul Alexander Korda, directed by Frenchman Feyder, and takes place in Russia. The story concerns an aristocratic Russian woman (Dietrich) who is rescued from the Bolshevik Revolution by a British undercover agent (Donat). Based on a novel by James Hilton, the film is imbued with sumptuous production values, charismatic acting and lots of romance and atmosphere. ★★★

A Knight's Tale

(2001, 125 min, US, Brian Helgeland) *Heath Ledger, Mark Addy, Rufus Sewell, Shannyn Sossamon, Paul Bettany, Alan Tudyk, Roger Ashton-Griffiths.* It's the 1300s, and a peasant named William (Ledger) is about to take the place of his master in a jousting match. In an instant, the crowd is on its feet and singing "We Will Rock You!" This little bit of anachronistic tomfoolery sets the tone for a most entertaining comic adventure that's funny, romantic and full of action. Ledger brings a natural charm to William, who masquerades as a nobleman named Ulrich to compete in knight-errantry: specifically the sporting matches occuring throughout Europe. Accompanied by two valets and a budding writer named Geoffrey Chaucer, William makes a

K

name for himself while finding romance and rivalry. Adding to the merriment of all this is the score: modern classics used to underscore the story's delectable chain of events. Among a quite appealing cast, Bettany steals the show as the golden-tongued Chaucer. ★★★ DVD Letterbox Superbit Edition: $27.99, DVD Special Edition: $14.99, VHS: $14.99

Knightriders

(1981, 145 min, US, George Romero) *Ed Harris, Gary Lahti, Tom Savini, John Amplas.* This nonhorror feature from Romero is a deeply personal, idealistic but perhaps naïve moral tale about the difficulties of remaining true to one's personal beliefs. King Billy (Harris) and his troop of knights travel around the country putting on motorcycle-jousting competitions and medieval fairs. The members of the group follow Billy and live this lifestyle because they want a respite from the pressures and temptations of the modern world. Ironically, their growing popularity brings these same pressures to bear upon their group, fragmenting it in the process. Harris is terrific in an early, pre-star performance, and a huge cast of supporting players lend authenticity. A rousing action-adventure. ★★★ DVD: $29.99, VHS: $19.99

Knights

(1993, 89 min, US, Albert Pyun) *Kris Kristofferson, Lance Henriksen, Kathy Long.* It's cyborg vs. man in yet another predictable sci-fi actioner. With the usual ravaged wasteland serving as a backdrop, cyborg leader Kristofferson has discovered that enemy robo (Henriksen) has a new source of fuel: human blood. Hero Kris teams up with a vengeance-seeking human (Long) in a disjointed frenzy of kickboxing chaos. ★ VHS: $14.99

Knock Off

(1998, 91 min, US, Tsui Hark) *Jean-Claude Van Damme, Rob Schneider, Lela Rochon, Paul Sorvino.* *Rip Off* is more like it. In this visually impressive though terrible actioner, Jean-Claude teams up with Schneider as a pair of jeans manufacturers in Hong Kong who discover that their product is comprised of "knock offs" — inferior imitations. Not only that, but these jeans contain tiny explosives in place of buttons to be used as terrorist devices when they reach the U.S. (we're not making this up). *Maybe* this could have worked as an outrageously satirical action sendup, but it's all deadpan. ★ DVD: $14.99, VHS: $9.99

Knockaround Guys

(2002, 93 min, US, Brian Koppelman & David Levien) *Barry Pepper, Vin Diesel, Seth Green, Dennis Hopper, John Malkovich.* A run-of-the-mill mob flick, *Knockaround Guys* is given a slight boost by its star power and atmospheric direction. Pepper, in an effort to prove himself worthy to his mob boss pop (Hopper), takes charge of an extremely important package delivery for the family business. In the incompetent hands of screwup cohort Green, things inevitably go wrong, and Pepper and pals have to make things right. A formulaic story line, standard characters and some inept dialogue explain why the studio kept this on the shelf (that is until costar Diesel hit it big). However, Pepper, Diesel and Green are able to rise above the script, each giving an intriguing performance. ★★ DVD: $19.99, VHS: $6.99

Knockout

(1999, 100 min, US, Lorenzo Doumani) *Sophia Adella-Hernandez, Eduardo Yañez, Maria Conchita Alonso, Paul Winfield, William McNamara, Tony*

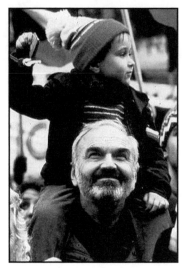

Kolya

Plana. A young girl, raised by her ex-boxer dad and homily spouting, ultra-supportive mom, decides to pursue boxing as her career, despite the inherent obstacles. This unremarkable "Afterschool Special"-like drama boasts a typically strong performance from Alonso, but little else. There's nary a convincing moment in the bland script or direction, and all but the most desperate-for-something-to-watch will have tuned out before the denouement. *Knockout* is destined for "also-ran" status alongside the similarly themed *Girlfight*. ★½ DVD: $24.99, VHS: $99.99

Kojiro

(1967, 152 min, Japan, Hiroshi Inagaki) *Kikunosuke Onoe, Tatsuya Nakadai.* Kojiro is a young man with an attitude. Taken into a home as a foundling, he chafes under the rough authority of the family's son, Hyosuké, with whom he has been raised as a brother. He gains Hyosuké's mortal enmity when he runs off with his sister, Toné. Hyosuké pursues his sister and our hero, even though Toma, Toné's fiancé and Kojiro's best friend, refuses to do so, wanting only Toné's happiness. With Hyosuké in hot pursuit, Kojiro vows to Toné to become famous and secure their position in society. To do this, he challenges a martial arts school, and wins by flying in the face of tradition. A late-night indulgence of flying fists, flashing swords, bruised egos and flailing passions, where the characters are either tributes to order and decorum or totally at the mercy of their emotions. Warning: inferior subtitles. But don't worry; you'll get the idea without getting all the text. (Japanese with English subtitles) ★★½ VHS: $49.99

Koko: A Talking Gorilla

(1978, 81 min, France, Barbet Schroeder) This fascinating documentary has director Schroeder and cinematographer Nestor Almendros traveling to laboratories at Stanford University to take a close look at Koko, a female gorilla that has been taught to talk through sign language. The film also probes the controversial techniques used by the scientists and captures the excitement of this rare breakthrough in communication. (In English and French with English subtitles) ★★★ VHS: $19.99

Kolya

(1996, 111 min, Czechoslovakia, Jan Sverak) *Zdenek Sverak, Andrej Chalimon, Libuse Safrankova.* This Academy Award winner for Best Foreign Language Film is a sweetly rendered fable about a washed-up, middle-aged classical cellist and compulsive womanizer who's struggling to make ends meet in 1988 Prague. Having been booted off the state Philharmonia for having too many close relatives who've "immigrated" to the West, Frantisek Louka (Sverak) ekes out a living by playing funerals and touching up gravestones. Out of desperation, he agrees to a fake marriage to a Russian émigré for a substantial sum of money. Louka finds himself up a tree, however, when she splits town leaving him with her 5-year-old boy, Kolya (Chalimon), and a suspicious police inspector who seems determined to lock him up. Ultimately, the film avoids the maudlin trap and delivers a tender and subtly profound look at the latter days of Communism and Soviet occupation in the Czech Republic. (Czech with English subtitles) ★★★½ DVD: $19.99, VHS: $9.99

Komodo

(2000, 90 min, US, Michael Lantieri) *Jill Hennessy, Billy Burke, Kevin Zegers, Paul Gleeson.* Several komodo dragon eggs are chucked into a field on a remote island. By chance (as is in films like these), the island also houses a toxic chemical plant. Years later, mutant komodos kill a boy's parents (and, in the movie's one good scare, his cute dog). Emotionally scarred, his therapist takes him back to the island for confrontational therapy. *Komodo* is stupid, silly, cheesy and a lot more entertaining than you might expect. The effects run the gamut from hideous to pretty damned convincing, though this is the epitome of formula filmmaking. A hoot if you're in the right frame of mind. ★★ DVD: $29.99, VHS: $102.99

Korczak

(1990, 118 min, Poland, Andrzej Wajda) *Wojtec Pszoniak, Ewa Dalkowska.* Wajda returns to his roots with this haunting story of Janusz Korczak, a well-known Jewish doctor and poet who ran an orphanage for 200 children in the Warsaw ghetto. Realizing that his wards would surely be sent to the camps, he vowed to stay with them until the end, despite repeated efforts by members of Poland's intelligentsia to convince him to run to freedom. Stylistically the film resembles Wajda's 1950s classics *Ashes and Diamonds* and *Kanal*, including shadowy black-and-white camera work by Robby Müller and the scratchy sound quality. The screenplay by Agnieska Holland is heavy-handed at times, but is nonetheless powerful in conveying the overwhelming love which Korzcak gave to his children. (Polish with English subtitles) ★★★★ VHS: $29.99

Kostas

(1986, 88 min, Australia, Paul Cox) *Wendy Hughes, Takis Emmanuel.* A Greek immigrant taxi driver and a wealthy socialite fall in love. When pressure from friends and family threaten their relationship, they must decide whether to live by the rules or by their hearts. Hughes' passionate performance highlights this otherwise standard star-crossed romantic drama. ★★½ VHS: $69.99

Koyaanisqatsi

(1983, 90 min, US, Godfrey Reggio) A remarkable and riveting cinematic poem that astonishes the viewer with its aural and visual splendor. This nonconventional, non-narrative feature is a mesmerizing compilation of images; a study of awesome natural and man-made landscapes observed and presented in an invigorating fashion through the use of speeded-up, time-lapse and slow-motion photography. Few films have offered such a rich integration of sounds, ideas and images. Composer Philip Glass has provided a hypnotic score which serves as an amplification of the visuals' power. ★★★½ DVD Letterbox: $19.99

Kramer vs. Kramer

(1979, 104 min, US, Robert Benton) *Dustin Hoffman, Justin Henry, Meryl Streep, Jane Alexander, JoBeth Williams.* Hollywood takes a movie-of-the-week "topical" subject — Mom takes off to find herself and Dad is left with the kid — and with solid performances, beautiful cinematography and competent scripting and direction from Benton, transforms it into a compassionate study of urban life and family ties, not to mention a media sensation. Oscars for Best Picture, Best Direction, Best Actor, Best Supporting Actress and Best Screenplay. ★★★★ DVD: $24.99, VHS: $9.99

The Krays

(1990, 119 min, GB, Peter Medak) *Gary Kemp, Martin Kemp, Billie Whitelaw.* A highly original and haunting account of the true-life rise to power of two of England's most notorious thugs — the Kray twins. Under the loving care of their tough-as-nails mum (played with a down-to-earth forcefulness by Whitelaw), the brothers ride a wave of unthinkable violence and terror, becoming the most feared men in the ganglands of 1960s London. Filmed with an eerie and atmospheric sense of the surreal, director Medak's vision of the Krays' sadistic reign offers a fascinating psychological profile of these ruthless killers. Despite their differing sexual orientations, they are ultimately bound to each other and to their mother. ★★★½

Krippendorf's Tribe

(1998, 96 min, US, Todd Holland) *Richard Dreyfuss, Jenna Elfman, Lily Tomlin, Natasha Lyonne.* This insipid family comedy of anthropological fraud features Dreyfuss as the washed-up Professor James Krippendorf. To save his job and family, he claims to have discovered a lost tribe in New Guinea: the Shelmikedmu. Smelling a hoax, Krippendorf's adversary Ruth Allen (Tomlin) demands film footage of the tribe. The resulting home movies are bizarre at best. Highlighted intermittently with jokes about farting monkeys, *Krippendorf's Tribe* is a hackneyed offering fraught with cheap product placement and even cheaper phallic humor. Ask for it by name: Krippendorf's Tripe. ★★ DVD: $14.99, VHS: $9.99

Kronos

(1957, 78 min, US, Kurt Neumann) *Jeff Morrow, Barbara Lawrence.* An alien arrives on Earth to steal her natural resources, and becomes larger and more destructive as it absorbs more and more energy. Any good? While it's understatement to say it was hampered by a modest production budget, it's not bad for its decade. ★★½ DVD: $14.99

Krush Groove

(1988, 97 min, US, Michael Schultz) *Blair Underwood, Joseph Simmons, Sheila E., Fat Boys.* Although saddled with a formula plot, this infectious hip-hop and rap musical still has a fresh, exciting feel mostly as a result of the spirited music of Sheila E., the Fat Boys and Kurtis Blow. The story centers around some ambitious but naïve renegades who want to set up their own record label dedicated to the sounds of the inner city, but who soon find themselves immersed in the loansharking and drug underworld. The Fat Boys are funny in their Three Stooges-like comedy relief. ★★½ DVD Letterbox: $14.99, VHS: $14.99

Kuffs

(1992, 102 min, US, Bruce A. Evans) *Christian Slater, Tony Goldwyn, Milla Jovovich.* Slater plays the brother of a San Francisco Police Patrol captain who inherits the security agency business after his sibling is murdered. Partnered with suspended cop Goldwyn, Slater takes on the killer and the slimy businessman he works for. The film is reminiscent of *Beverly Hills Cop*, especially in pacing, editing and musical score. And, like Eddie Murphy's hit, mixes action, suspense and lots of comedy; though not as successfully. ★★ DVD Letterbox: $14.99

Kull the Conqueror

(1997, 96 min, US, John Nicolella) *Kevin Sorbo, Tia Carrera, Karina Lombard, Litefoot, Harvey Fierstein, Thomas Ian Griffith.* TV's "Hercules" Sorbo's straight-faced and sincere delivery is a pleasant surprise as the "man who would be king" of mythical Valusia — if he can break the curse of a 3000-year-old sorceress (Carrere) with a plunging neckline and a taste for pyrotechnics. To do this, he borrows the ship and crew of an old pirate buddy (Fierstein!) for a quest to find the one thing that can end Akivasha's rule — the Breath of Valka. Nicolella's well-meaning but uneventful direction combines with unambitious

special effects (not the least of which are Carrere's breasts) to make this a fun movie for anyone not expecting anything. ★★ DVD: $9.99

Kundun

(1997, 132 min, US, Martin Scorsese) *Tenzin Thuthob Tsarong, Gyurme Tethong, Kunga Tenzin.* A low-key yet impassioned historical epic, *Kundun* tells the story of the 14th Dalai Lama, from his discovery as a toddler in a Tibetan village to his escape from Chinese-occupied Tibet as a young man. *Kundun* is sumptuously photographed and features gorgeous production design and costumes, but director Scorsese wisely opts to take a simple approach for much of the film — with minimal editing and camera showmanship — resulting in an austere yet quietly powerful work. Those looking for a history lesson may be disappointed; Scorsese shows the period's events solely through the eyes of the Dalai Lama, and the story provides only a medium of political and historical exposition. But as a story of one remarkable man — and, by extension, a remarkable people — the film succeeds admirably. ★★★½ DVD Letterbox: $9.99, VHS: $9.99, VHS Letterbox: $9.99

Kung Pow: Enter the Fist

(2002, 81 min, US, Steve Oedekerk) *Steve Oedekerk, Jennifer Tung, Leo Lee.* Idiocy auteur Oedekerk (*Ace Ventura: When Nature Calls*) seemed to have found a niche with short internet parodies like *Thumbtanic* and *Thumb Wars*, where the low humor and groaner puns are at least over with quickly. But when the running time exceeds the IQ — watch out. *Kung Pow* takes the *What's Up, Tiger Lily?* concept of redubbing a bad movie (in this case, obscure kung-fu flick *The Savage Killers*) and goes one step further, digitally inserting Oedekerk into the action as a pasty Caucasian hero. Despite the technology involved, the whole affair is amateurish, full of fratboy in-jokes that don't work, and embarrassing slapstick that will amuse only the very young or the very drunk. ★½ DVD The Chosen Edition: $14.99, VHS: $9.99

Kurt and Courtney

(1998, 95 min, US, Nick Broomfield) A surprisingly good documentary, considering its incendiary subject matter, *Kurt and Courtney* (which was banned from Sundance) is actually a rather even-sided investigation into the circumstances leading to rocker Kurt Cobain's death, focusing especially on his relationship with wife Courtney Love. Director Broomfield casts himself in the detective role, complete with voice-over, as he interviews family, ex-girlfriends and ex-boyfriends, nannies and old junkie mates of K & C. While most of these talks yield minimal valuable info, they're all fascinating insights into an array of oddball characters. ★★★ DVD: $14.99, VHS: $14.99

Kwaidan

(1964, 164 min, Japan, Masaki Kobayashi) *Michiyo Aratama, Rentaro Mikuni, Takashi Shimura.* This legendary Japanese film is a superb anthology of four terrifying tales of the supernatural. Filmed with exquisite visual sensitivity, this distinctive work of art is filled with dreamlike settings, elaborately stylized action and haunting sound effects. (Japanese with English subtitles) ★★★½ DVD Criterion Collection: $29.99, VHS: $29.99

Kundun

K

343

L.627

(1992, 145 min, France, Bertrand Tavernier) *Didier Bezace, Jean-Paul Comart, Cecile Garcia-Fogel.* A gritty, semidocumentary-like look at the day-to-day lives of undercover narcotic agents in a Paris most tourists will never see, *L.627* is a disturbing, overlong and possibly racist examination which despite its flaws still manages to be compelling. Capably directed by Tavernier, the film centers on a rogue cop named Lulu (Bezace), who has been transferred to an overworked precinct. The story's power is accumulative in the relationship of the officers and Lulu's personal and professional life. However, it is difficult to determine if the film panders to racial stereotypes as all of the dealers are either black or Arab — which is defended by Tavernier as what he saw when accompanying real police officers on assignment. (French with English subtitles) ★★★ VHS: $24.99

L.A. Confidential

(1997, 137 min, US, Curtis Hanson) *Kevin Spacey, Russell Crowe, David Strathairn, Guy Pearce, Kim Basinger, James Cromwell, Danny DeVito.* An engrossing, rock-'em-sock-'em study of cops, corruption, racism and romance in 1950s Los Angeles, Hanson's marvelous adaptation of James Ellroy's densely written multicharacter novel is a thriller with blood, sweat and guts. The film follows three distinctly different cops on the LAPD: Crowe, a brooding, tough-as-nails vet; Spacey, a cop who moonlights as an advisor for a reality-based TV show; and Pearce, a determined college grad. This trio of crime-stoppers are stirred into a batch of police brutality, Hollywood sleaze and political hoi-polloi after a group of people are massacred at a downtown eatery. As Pearce digs deeper into the case, he unites the three cops to uncover the truth. Showcasing terrific period design, stylish visuals and a crackerjack adaptation of difficult material, the film looks and sounds great. ★★★★ DVD Letterbox: $19.99, VHS: $12.99, VHS Letterbox: $12.99

L.A. Story

(1991, 95 min, US, Mick Jackson) *Steve Martin, Victoria Tennant, Sarah Jessica Parker, Richard E. Grant, Marilu Henner, Kevin Pollack.* Martin wrote the screenplay for stars in this fabulously entertaining and witty satire on life in Los Angeles' fast lane. Martin plays a wacked-out TV weatherman who loses his job, and begins affairs with two dissimilar women: Valley girl Parker (in a wonderfully comic turn) and British reporter Tennant. Martin's screenplay is full of on-target jabs, lively slapstick and metaphysical revelations (our favorite: the two very different lines at an Automatic Teller Machine). Martin's best work since *Roxanne*, and a pure delight. ★★★½ DVD: $14.99, VHS: $9.99

L.I.E.

(2001, 97 min, US, Michael Cuesta) *Brian Cox, Paul Franklin Dano, Billy Kay, Bruce Altman, James Costa.* Set in suburban Long Island, the controversial and quite compelling *L.I.E.* (*Long Island Expressway*) is a sensational look at the relationship between a gay teen and a middle-aged pedophile —

L.A. Confidential

without the sensationalism. Howie (Dano) is a fifteen year old whose life is going nowhere fast. When he and his friend Gary break into the home of Big John (Cox), a gregarious ex-Marine and client of part-time hustler Gary, a delicate, surrogate father-son relationship begins between the troubled teen and unapologetic Big John. An incendiary subject matter is handled with sensitivity and clarity — director Cuesta is interested in neither condemnation nor advocacy. Rather, *L.I.E.* is a frank, mature study of sexuality, alienation, coming-of-age and disappointment, framed in nonexploitative fashion within the unsettling arena of teen sex-for-hire. The ensemble is uniformly excellent, especially veteran character actor Cox as Big John, who brings unexpected depth and compassion to a role that could have been caricature. Although the film received an NC17-rating, there is no nudity or actual sex depicted. It was clearly given for the subject alone. ★★★½ DVD Uncut: $29.99, VHS Uncut: $19.99

Labyrinth

(1986, 101 min, US, Jim Henson) *David Bowie, Jennifer Connelly, Toby Froud.* George Lucas combined his talents with the magical puppet artistry of Jim Henson to create this imaginative fantasy. A young girl (Connelly), searching for her kidnapped brother, is forced to weave her way through a treacherous maze where she encounters the deliciously maniacal elfin-like Bowie. This *Wizard of Oz*-like odyssey features adorable puppetry, catchy tunes, and a rather complex story line which only slightly detracts from its whimsical tone. ★★★ DVD Letterbox Superbit: $26.99, DVD: $19.99, DVD Collector's Edition Box Set: $49.99, VHS: $14.99

Labyrinth of Passion

(1982, 100 min, Spain, Pedro Almodóvar) *Antonio Banderas, Imanol Arias, Cecilia Roth.* Almodóvar's second feature film is a dazzling display of a great future talent in its rawest form. The story centers around both Riza Niro, the son of a deposed Middle Eastern tyrant who likes to hang around with Madrid's sleazier denizens, and Sexi, an aspiring rock singer and unabashed nymphomaniac. The two fall for each other and decide to run away, but first they must deal with their respective rock groups, a group of terrorists who are bent on kidnapping Riza, and a whole host of other outrageous plot twists. Bristling with loony humor, the film lacks the visual punch and flawless timing of his later works, but still it is a frantic, if somewhat uneven, portrait of Almodóvar's explosive potential. (Spanish with English subtitles) ★★½

The Lacemaker

(1977, 108 min, France, Claude Goretta) *Isabelle Huppert, Yves Beneyton.* A very young Huppert stars as an inexperienced shopgirl who meets a bourgeois student on the deserted beaches of an off-season Normandy resort. They return to Paris where their romance strains under the weight of class and intellectual differences. Huppert is breathtakingly beautiful and gives a tender portrait of love. Lovingly filmed by Goretta. (French with English subtitles) ★★★½ VHS: $29.99

Ladies of the Chorus

(1949, 61 min, US, Phil Karlson) *Adele Jergens, Marilyn Monroe, Rand Brooks.* Though Marilyn gets star billing on the video box, she really has a secondary role in this, her second film. MM is a burlesque dancer who's looking for a ticket out; and if a wealthy bachelor can help, so be it. Jergens plays her mother who has been there before and tries to help her daughter not make the same mistakes. Marilyn sings some songs, and looks great, but it's a minor vehicle nonetheless. ★★

Ladies on the Rocks

(1983, 100 min, Denmark, Christian Braad Thomsen) *Helle Ryslinge, Anne Marie Helger.* Two women — Misha, stuck with a good-for-nothing boyfriend, and Laura, married with kids — decide to chuck the domestic scene and join forces, become a cabaret comedy team and take their act on the road. This Danish "*Thelma and Louise*-meets-*Punchline*" follows the aspiring comediennes as they fine-tune their revue in the small clubs which dot rural Denmark. The two women, who also cowrote the script, center their strange but amusing schtick on stereotypically pre-feminist obsessions: their far-from-perfect bodies, men, love and more about men. An unusual comedy-drama about two self-determined women. (Danish with English subtitles) ★★½ VHS: $29.99

Lady and the Tramp

(1955, 75 min, US, Hamilton Luske) Beloved Disney classic rates as one of the studio's top animated features. Who can forget the spaghetti scene, which is more romantic than most modern "love stories." ★★★★

Lady by Choice

(1934, 77 min, US, David Burton) *Carole Lombard, May Robson.* In a role similar to her brilliant success a year earlier in *Lady for a Day*, Robson encores as a cantankerous, scraggy old lady who gets the once-over. Lombard is a fan dancer looking to cool her image. So her press agent gets the idea to "adopt a mother," and guess who gets chosen. This is a bright, appealing comedy, and Lombard and Robson work extremely well together. ★★★

Lady Chatterley's Lover

(1955, 102 min, France, Marc Allégret) *Danielle Darrieux, Erno Crisa.* Darrieux stars as the repressed Lady Chatterley who enjoys a sexual awakening and personal freedom when she meets a handsome, muscular workman in this fine French version of D.H. Lawrence's classic novel. Although when viewed today the film is quite tasteful, it caused a storm in the U.S. in the 1950s and was banned by the New York State Board of Censors. (French with English subtitles) ★★½

The Lady Eve

(1941, 93 min, US, Preston Sturges) *Barbara Stanwyck, Henry Fonda, Charles Coburn, William Demarest, Eugene Pallette.* Sturges, the most prolific and arguably the greatest comic filmmaker of the 1940s, wrote and directed this hilarious screwball comedy, one of the director's finest achievements. Stanwyck, in a great comic performance, is a card-sharp who sets out to hook gullible millionaire Fonda. They fall in love, but when he gets wise she gets dumped, and Stanwyck devises a scheme to get him back — by impersonating royalty. Among a first-rate supporting cast, Pallette is very funny as Fonda's exasperated father. ★★★★ DVD Criterion Collection: $39.99

Lady for a Day

(1933, 96 min, US, Frank Capra) *May Robson, Warren William, Guy Kibbee, Glenda Farrell.* Capra's enchanting comedy based on Damon Runyon's story "Madame La Gimp," about a group of Broadway denizens who come together to help an old apple seller. Character actress Robson has her greatest screen role as "Annie," and she makes the most of it. Capra's deft touch helps immeasurably in the film's enjoyment. Capra remade the story in 1961 as *A Pocketful of Miracles*. ★★★½ DVD: $24.99

The Lady from Shanghai

(1948, 87 min, US, Orson Welles) *Orson Welles, Rita Hayworth, Everett Sloane.* Hayworth is the scorching femme fatale with a heavenly body and a devilish mind in this fascinating murder mystery. Welles himself plays her prime victim who, with a skull as thick as his Irish brogue, steps right into her trap. ★★★ DVD: $24.99, VHS: $19.99

Lady in a Cage

(1964, 93 min, US, Walter Grauman) *Olivia de Havilland, James Caan, Jeff Corey, Ann Sothern, Scatman Crothers.* Caan's first starring role. He plays the sadistic leader of a vicious gang of thieves who trap de Havilland in her own home. This fast-paced, lurid melodrama really delivers in the finale. ★★½

Lady in Cement

(1968, 93 min, US, Gordon Douglas) *Frank Sinatra, Raquel Welch, Dan Blocker.* Sinatra is back in this sequel to *Tony Rome* as the titular detective, investigating the death of a nude woman who went swimming wearing only cement overshoes. Sinatra could play this role in his sleep — which he looks like he's doing throughout. Few thrills punctuate this standard mystery. ★★ VHS: $59.99

The Lady in the Lake

(1946, 104 min, US, Robert Montgomery) *Robert Montgomery, Audrey Totter, Lloyd Nolan, Jayne Meadows.* Montgomery stars as private dick Phillip Marlowe searching for a missing wife and discovering a different woman's corpse floating in a mountain lake. Montgomery, who also directed, uses first person camera angles from Marlowe's point of view. Complete with Raymond Chandler's standards of gritty dialogue between troublesome cops and L.A. lowlifes. ★★★

Lady in White

(1988, 112 min, US, Frank LaLoggia) *Lukas Haas, Alex Rocco, Len Cariou, Katherine Helmond.* A real find. Young Haas gets locked in school overnight and uncovers — with the help of a young girl's spirit — the mystery of the legendary "Lady in White"; not to mention the identity of the girl's murderer. An extremely accomplished ghost story, with a great visual style. Though some may guess who the killer is before the denouement, it detracts nothing from the suspense and total enjoyment of this first-rate sleeper. ★★★½

The Lady Is Willing

(1942, 92 min, US, Mitchell Leisen) *Marlene Dietrich, Fred MacMurray, Aline MacMahon.* Pleasant comedy-drama with Dietrich as a stage siren who marries baby doc MacMurray just so she can adopt a tot. The film's breezy pacing is brought to a halt near the end with a heavy-handed tragic turn of events. ★★★

Lady Jane

(1985, 141 min, GB, Trevor Nunn) *Helena Bonham Carter, Cary Elwes, Sara Kestelman, Michael Hordern, Joss Ackland, Patrick Stewart.* Overlooked in its initial release, this elegant and absorbing romance is about the real-life adolescent aristocrat Lady Jane, who ascended to the British throne for a brief and tragic nine days. A bittersweet historical drama. ★★★ DVD Letterbox: $14.99, VHS: $14.99

Lady of Burlesque

(1943, 91 min, US, William Wellman) *Barbara Stanwyck, Michael O'Shea, Pinky Lee.* Stanwyck brings plenty of pizzazz to this sassy and enjoyable comic mystery based on Gypsy Rose Lee's "The G-String Murders." Stanwyck plays a burlesque dancer who sets out to solve who's killing her fellow strippers. ★★★ VHS: $14.99

Lady on the Bus

(1978, 102 min, Brazil, Neville D'Almeida) *Sonia Braga.* In this spicy romp, Sonia plays a frigid young married woman who can't seem to make it with her new husband. Seeking a cure, our heroine seeks sexual help of her husband's male friends and even strangers in her determined efforts to loosen up. Why not? A charming and entertaining diversion. ★★½

Lady Sings the Blues

(1972, 144 min, US, Sidney J. Furie) *Diana Ross, Billy Dee Williams, Richard Pryor, James Callahan.* Ross makes a sensational film debut as the legendary blues singer Billie Holiday. The film has all the dramatic trappings of a standard Hollywood biography; Ross, however, is in great voice. Pryor is a standout as Ross' piano player. ★★★ VHS: $14.99

The Lady Vanishes

(1938, 97 min, GB, Alfred Hitchcock) *Michael Redgrave, Margaret Lockwood, Dame Mae Whitty, Paul Lukas.* The quintessential train murder mystery with Redgrave and Lockwood as a pair of travelers who undertake a search for a missing passenger — a diminutive old woman who holds secrects of international espionage. Upon vanishing, only a name on a window and a haunting melody serve as proof of her existence. (Remade in 1979) ★★★★ DVD Criterion Collection: $39.99, VHS: $24.99

The Lady with the Dog

(1960, 89 min, USSR, Josef Heifitz) *Iya Savvina, Alexei Batalov.* Thought to be one of the few films to capture the essence of Anton Chekov, this much admired romantic yet bittersweet love story is set in turn-of-the-century Russia. While vacationing at a resort in Yalta, a married, middle-aged banker meets a beautiful but sad young woman who, having left her husband behind in the city, has come on holiday accompanied only by her little dog. Attracted to one another, they begin an affair and eventu-

ally fall in love. Resolving to continue their affair after the holiday, they meet for years clandestinely in Moscow, but knowing full well that their love and relationship is doomed. (Russian with English subtitles) ★★★ VHS: $29.99

Ladybird, Ladybird

(1994, 102 min, GB, Ken Loach) *Crissy Rock, Vladimir Vega, Ray Winstone, Sandie Lavelle.* A disarming, well-wrought drama based on a true story. Rock is unerringly authentic as a young mother who loses several children to state care — a woman whose pick of men mirrors her abusive childhood and whose love of her children is outstripped by bad choices, circumstances and a social welfare system which loses the human element in a sea of categorization. A cycle of childbirth, beatings and stays in women's refuges is broken by a chance encounter with a Paraguayan political refugee (portrayed with quiet passion by Vega), a victim of an even more repressive state. ★★★½

Ladybugs

(1992, 89 min, US, Sidney J. Furie) *Rodney Dangerfield, Jackee, Jonathan Brandis, Ilene Graff.* Mr. No Respect finds himself as the coach of a girls' soccer team in this distant cousin of *The Bad News Bears*, where all the stereotypes and clichés are firmly in place. This often silly though somewhat entertaining and moralizing film showcases a kinder, gentler Rodney (the film is rated PG-13), but parents should be warned that there are some naughty words, risque innuendos and a dream sequence that borderlines on tastelessness. ★★ VHS: $14.99

Ladyhawke

(1985, 121 min, US, Richard Donner) *Rutger Hauer, Matthew Broderick, Michelle Pfeiffer, John Wood, Leo McKern, Alfred Molina.* An entertaining medieval fantasy which combines adventure, romance and magic to produce an exciting story. Hauer stars as a knight deeply in love with a beautiful maiden (Pfeiffer), but the two are cursed by an evil bishop with a terrible spell. The lovers are eternally separated — for in the day, the young woman

The Lady Eve

345

The Ladykillers

is turned into a hawk and in the night, when she is transformed back into human form, he is changed into a wolf. It takes a young pickpocket (a delightfully funny Broderick) to assist them in breaking the curse. ★★★ DVD: $14.99

The Ladykillers

(1955, 90 min, GB, Alexander MacKendrick) *Alec Guinness, Katie Johnson, Peter Sellers, Herbert Lom, Cecil Parker, Danny Green.* Another mordant comedy classic from the Ealing Studios with Guinness leading a group of maladroit thieves whose plans are undone by a sweetly obtuse little old lady (superbly portrayed by Johnson). The other members of this bumbling gang of hoods are played by an impressive and well-seasoned cast. (Remade in 2004) ★★★★ DVD Letterbox: $19.99

Lagaan: Once Upon a Time in India

(2001, 224 min, India, Ashutosh Gowariker) *Aamir Khan, Gracy Singh, Rachel Shelley, Paul Blackthorne, Suhasini Mulay.* At the end of the 19th century, British imperialists in India demand lagaan (tax in the form of food from crops) from the small villages. Due to lack of rain, the crops are small, and the villagers will surely starve if lagaan isn't relaxed. Instead, a priggish Brit demands double lagaan from the villagers, just to show them who's boss, but he'll waive lagaan for three years if a ragtag team of villagers can beat his crack cricket team in a match. If the villagers lose, however, they must pay triple lagaan, which would spell their death. This terrific entertainment, wonderfully acted, directed and written, is a perfectly paced (even at four hours, it never drags for a second), extremely compelling melodrama, a great David and Goliath story. The cricket match itself, which takes up nearly half the running time of the film, is intense, and makes wonderful use of its many varied characters. With its gorgeous widescreen photography, seamlessly integrated musical numbers, and an almost unbearably nerve-wracking finale, *Lagaan* is not to be missed. (In English and Hindi with English subtitles) ★★★★ DVD Letterbox: $27.99, VHS: $24.99

The Lair of the White Worm

(1988, 94 min, GB, Ken Russell) *Amanda Donohoe, Hugh Grant, Peter Capaldi, Sammi Davis, Catherine Oxenberg.* Russell's intoxicating adaptation of Bram Stoker's final work is a tongue-in-cheek romp into the world of Gothic horror. Donohoe offers up a truly kinky performance as a mysterious snake lady who slithers her way into modern England in search of virgins to feed to her giant worm god. Russell's flair isn't lost as this slimy tale of rampant vampirism oozes with an abundance of camp humor, serpentine symbolism, and just about every daft snake joke in the book — oh, and let's not forget those requisite Russellian hallucinations. ★★★½ DVD: $14.99

Lake Consequence

(1992, 90 min, US, Rafael Eiseman) *Billy Zane, Joan Severance, May Kurasun.* "Hey honey, did you catch any fish?" is undoubtedly the most memorable line in *Lake Consequence*, though you'll have to watch the film to figure out why. But this is not a movie that's counting on its witty repartee to capture the viewer's interest; it's a plain and simple *9½ Weeks*/Zalman King/soft-core erotica portrayal of a woman's plunge into sexual abandon. The cast includes some blindingly attractive performers: Zane is the drifter, Severance is the requisite repressed housewife, and Karasun is the requisite bisexual exhibitionist. ★★

Lake Placid

(1999, 82 min, US, Steve Miner) *Bill Pullman, Bridget Fonda, Oliver Platt, Brendan Gleeson, Betty White.* TV's golden boy David E. Kelley ("Ally McBeal," "The Practice") wrote the screenplay for this tired horror send-up. Judging by this, he'd better stick to the small screen. A giant crocodile is terrorizing a peaceful lakeside community in Maine. Pullman is the fish-and-game warden, Fonda is the scientist, Gleeson the glib sheriff, and Platt the eccentric croc expert all investigating a series of deaths. The characters spend the entire film yelling at each other, in between the unfunny barbs. Kelley's story is neither scary nor funny, only head-scratchingly mediocre. Though the giant croc is kinda fun, the only truly scary thing in the movie is Betty White's vocabulary. ★½ DVD Pan & Scan: $14.99, DVD: $14.99, VHS: $9.99

Lakki: The Boy Who Grew Wings

(1992, 104 min, Norway, Svend Wam) Wam's film about a troubled youth's struggle towards spiritual ascent is about as obvious as the mysterious wings that grow on young Lakki's back. Yes, the film actually depicts scenes of sprouting feathers and dreams of flight as Lakki tries to come to grips with his parents' separation, his father's new fiancée, his mother's flagrant sexual behavior, and perhaps his own sexual orientation. The symbolism is so heavy-handed that it almost becomes insulting, but the cinematography itself merits the film a look. (Norwegian with English subtitles) ★★

Lamerica

(1995, 116 min, Italy, Gianni Amelio) *Enrico Lo Verso, Michele Placido, Carmelo Di Mazzarelli.* Amelio's nightmare vision of post-Communist Albania should serve as a shocking wakeup call to the European community about a festering wound in their backyard. Italians especially should be jarred from political inaction as theirs are the shores receiving the flood of refugees from Albania's chaos. Gino (Lo Verso) and Fiorre (Placido) are a pair of carpetbagging Italians who are poised to set up a phoney corporation in Albania, presumably as a front to launder lire. But first they must find an Albanian lackey to pose as their CEO. They pluck a withered old man, Spiro (Di Mazzarelli), from a hellish labor camp and name their chairman. But disaster strikes when Spiro disappears forcing Gino to search for the old codger in the perilous anarchy of the Albanian countryside — and the picture Amelio paints of this ravaged landscape is inconceivably bleak. Visually arresting tale of moral conflict and the journey that leads to atonement. (Italian with English subtitles) ★★★½ DVD Letterbox: $34.99, VHS: $14.99

Lancelot of the Lake

(1974, 80 min, France, Robert Bresson) *Luc Simon, Laura Duke Condominas, Humbert Balsan, Vladimir Antolek-Oresek.* Hailed in its day as a magnificent cinematic achievement, this austere examination of the end of chivalry and the dissolution of King Arthur's Court is more a curious relic from a bygone cinematic era. Stark and somber in atmosphere, the film follows Lancelot as he returns empty-handed from his quest for the Holy Grail filled with foreboding that his failure is linked to his illicit love for Queen Guinevere. Bresson's approach is stylistically minimal to the extreme as the film features barren dialogue and severely restrained performances which, though seemingly wooden, disguise a bristling subtext. It's of a style that was all the rage in the art-houses of the era, but the success of its translation to the small screen some decades later is less than certain. (French with English subtitles) ★★½ DVD Letterbox: $29.99, VHS: $14.99

Land and Freedom

(1995, 109 min, GB, Ken Loach) *Ian Hart, Rosana Pastor, Iciar Bollain.* Loach offers a powerful and heartrending look at the Spanish Civil War as seen through the eyes of an earnest young Liverpudlian. Through flashback, the story focuses on his involvement as a youth in the volunteer brigades in Spain. Young David (portrayed with engaging sincerity by Hart) begins his journey as an ardent unionist and card-carrying member of the Communist Party. Upon his arrival in Spain, he is swept up into the POUM movement, a rather freely organized and highly egalitarian sector of the Resistance, and graduates to a front-line "militia" where he and his group make occasional incursions into Francoista territory and liberate villages. Ever the left-wing agitator, Loach once again has created a brilliant blend of personal history and political treatise that is riveting and intellectually fascinating. ★★★★

The Land Before Time

(1988, 66 min, US, Don Bluth) This rather short but charming animated feature should entertain younger children with its story of a baby dinosaur, Littlefoot, who becomes separated from his parents. Like the director's previous animated film, *An American Tail*,

Amanda Donohoe in
The Lair of the White Worm

the story centers on the little lost hero's search for home. The animation, though less than superlative, is fine for the film's simplistic story and the plotline should be easy for young ones to follow. (Followed by 8 sequels) ★★★ DVD: $24.99, VHS: $14.99

The Land Girls

(1998, 110 min, GB, David Leland) *Catherine McCormack, Rachel Weisz, Anne Friel, Steven Mackintosh.* A good old-fashioned British wartime drama, *The Land Girls* may be unremarkable, but that is precisely what makes it special. Three young women, Stella (McCormack), Ag (Weisz) and Pru (Friel), do their bit for the war effort by working as farmhands. Their trials and tribulations include all of the genre staples of heroism and heartbreak as they bond together through hard work and romance. Written and directed with a sure hand by Leland (he adapted Angela Huth's novel), *The Land Girls* could have been corny and sentimental, but its earnestness sees it through. The striking performances by the attractive leads, the gorgeous cinematography, and fine period detail also lend the film class. ★★★ VHS: $14.99

The Land of Faraway

(1988, 95 min, Norway/Sweden, Vladimir Grammatikov) *Timothy Bottoms, Susannah York, Christopher Lee, Christian Bale.* A young boy in Stockholm is whisked away by a friendly spirit to meet the father he has never known — the King of the Land of Faraway. Soon, the boy is embroiled in a desperate bid to save the children of Faraway from an evil knight who has kidnapped them. ★★½

Land of Look Behind

(1982, 88 min, US/Jamaica, Alan Greenberg) The lush sensuality of Jamaica, the Rastafarian faith and the mystical fervor of reggae are the subjects of this impressionistic documentary. Director Greenberg journeys into the hearts and minds of the island people and chronicles their cultural and religious beliefs. This magical meditation on Jamaican life evolved from a planned documentary on Bob Marley's funeral, and includes the music of Marley, performances by Gregory Isaacs and Lui Lepki and dub poet Mutaburuka. ★★★

The Langoliers

(1995, 150 min, US, Tom Holland) *Dean Stockwell, David Morse, Bronson Pinchot.* There's an unusually effective eeriness to the opening of *The Langoliers*, a made-for-TV adaptation of Stephen King's story. A select group of passengers on a red-eye from Los Angeles to Boston awaken mid-flight to discover their fellow passengers and the crew have literally disappeared into thin air. What follows is a silly, lethargic story of parallel universes and cartoon monsters from the subconscious out to eat everything in sight. ★★ DVD: $14.99, VHS: $14.99

Lantana

(2001, 120 min, Australia, Ray Lawrence) *Anthony LaPaglia, Geoffrey Rush, Barbara Hershey, Kerry Armstrong, Rachael Blake.* In the opening moments of this skilled mystery-drama, the camera moves gracefully through a lantana bush to reveal a dead body, recalling *Blue Velvet* as it coyly undermines the tranquility of a peaceful suburban landscape. Who this dead person is and how they got there will be addressed soon enough. For director Lawrence and writer Andrew Bovell (adapting his own play "Speaking in Tongues") take their time filling in all the pieces, setting in motion a gripping character study in which the lives of several strangers ulti-

Lantana

mately intersect. LaPaglia (a native Australian, let's not forget) is terrific as a Sydney police detective who — between his rocky marriage and unfulfilling extramarital affair — is emotionally numb. Across town, another married couple is experiencing marital woes, as well. Hershey plays a noted psychiatrist who begins to suspect that her husband (Rush) may be gay. That these lives will soon converge is of no surprise. However, by carefully examining what drives each character and by allowing the viewer to digest the small, telling moments as well as the big ones, the film gradually builds to a powerful, raw conclusion. ★★★½ DVD: $24.99

Lara Croft Tomb Raider

(2001, 105 min, US, Simon West) *Angelina Jolie, Jon Voight, Iain Glen, Noah Taylor, Daniel Craig.* Have they yet to make a good film based on a video game? No doubt the filmmakers of *Lara Croft: Tomb Raider* thought they could break the jinx by making this a female *Indiana Jones* for the postadolescence set. They just forgot a few things: like story, character and thrills. Looking the best she's ever been on-screen, Jolie flies, somersaults, kicks, punches and teases her way through the role of Lara Croft, ace adventuress/archeologist/orphan. She finds herself in a complex web of intrigue when an ancient sect vies for an artifact left to her by her recently deceased father. It's a convoluted race when they steal it from her and she sets out to retrieve it. The series of fights and action scenes, though well staged, lack an energy and originality to set it apart from countless other action films. Jolie tries her best, though, and is game for anything the screenwriters can imagine for her. It's just they didn't come up with a whole helluva lot. (Sequel: *Lara Croft Tomb Raider: The Cradle of Life*) ★★ DVD Letterbox Special Edition: $14.99, VHS Special Edition: $9.99

Larger Than Life

(1996, 93 min, US, Howard Franklin) *Bill Murray, Janeane Garofalo, Matthew McConaughey, Linda Fiorentino, Jeremy Piven, Lois Smith.* Murray inherits an elephant from the father he never knew, then must decide whether to sell her to Fiorentino's sexy but unscrupulous animal talent agent or allow sensible zoologist Garofalo to take her to Sri Lanka to be in her natural habitat. Have no idea what'll happen? Then you must see *Larger Than Life*. Otherwise, there isn't much to recommend, although the film — save for some goopy sentimentality — is painless enough. The elephant has its requisite cutesy/funny moments,

and even a slumming Murray is still entertaining, though Garofalo is once again underused. You can't help wonder: What were the makers (and especially Murray) thinking? ★★ DVD Pan & Scan: $14.99

Larks on a String

(1968, 96 min, Czechoslovakia, Jiri Menzel) *Vera Kresadlova, Vaclav Neckar.* From the director of *Closely Watched Trains* comes this surprisingly timely, playfully subversive allegory on the crumbling of the Communist State. Made in 1968 immediately after the Soviet invasion of Czechoslovakia, the film was promptly banned and not made available until 23 years later. Set in an almost surreal scrap heap, the story follows the work, thoughts and loves of a group of prisoners — professors, musicians, union organizers and Jews — who are caught in the crackdown, believed to pose a "threat to the state." Although thoroughly political, the satire retains a light, almost joyful stance, taking particular delight in the love interest between two prisoners — a simple boy and a pretty young woman. (Czechoslovakian with English subtitles) ★★★½ VHS: $19.99

Las Vegas Hillbillys

(1966, 90 min, US, Arthur C. Pierce) *Jayne Mansfield, Mamie Van Doren.* Mansfield and Van Doren need plenty of support in this story about a busted Las Vegas bar invigorated when it is inherited by a hayseed who starts booking it with country acts. Musical performances by Bill Anderson, Sonny James and Del Reeves. ★ DVD: $19.99

Laserman

(1990, 92 min, US, Peter Wang) *Marc Hayashi, Peter Wang, Tony Leung, Sally Yeh.* Intelligent, eccentric multicultural comedy-thriller about a Chinese-American scientist who accidentally kills his lab assistant in an experiment, resulting in the loss of his job. His "grifting" brother-in-law convinces him to sell his new laser device to some "business associates" — actually hit men for a terrorist organization. All the while, police inspector Lu is on their trail as the hero reluctantly enters the black market of high-tech weapons, mistaken identities, telepathic orgasms and more! ★★★ VHS: $19.99

Lassiter

(1984, 100 min, US, Roger Young) *Tom Selleck, Bob Hoskins, Lauren Hutton, Jane Seymour.* Selleck tries his hand at *Bond*age in this slick if derivative spy thriller about a notorious 1930s cat burglar pressed into service by the British government to steal a cache of diamonds from the Nazis. The usual thrills and chills abound. ★★½

Last Action Hero

(1993, 130 min, US, John McTiernan) *Arnold Schwarzenegger, Mercedes Ruehl, Art Carney, Anthony Quinn, Charles Dance, F. Murray Abraham, Joan Plowright, Ian McKellen, Robert Prosky.* Schwarzenegger finally bombed with this disappointing action-parody, sort of a *Purple Rose of Cairo* meets *Lethal Weapon.* A 12-year-old kid is magically transported by a magical movie ticket into the celluloid world of his favorite film hero, Jack Slater. The trouble really starts, however, when they both emerge in the real world on this side of the screen. The film is an endless barrage of gags referring to the insipidness of many Hollywood actioners: hundreds of smashing cars; tons of insufficient back-up officers; Arnold Schwarzenegger. Suffering from lackluster direction, *Last Action Hero* is a good joke with a really awful punchline. ★★ DVD Letterbox: $9.99, VHS: $12.99

The Last American Hero

(1973, 100 min, US, Lamont Johnson) *Jeff Bridges, Valerie Perrine, Gary Busey, Geraldine Fitzgerald.* Bridges gives a commanding performance as stock car champion Junior Jackson in this vibrant racing drama based on a series of articles by Tom Wolfe. The story follows backwoods moonshiner Jackson from his running whiskey to his determined bid for the championship on the independent circuit. Bridges brings to mind a young Paul Newman with an icy cool portrayal of swaggering confidence. On par with another splendid racing feature, *Heart Like a Wheel.* ★★★½

The Last Boy Scout

(1991, 105 min, US, Tony Scott) *Bruce Willis, Damon Wayans, Halle Berry.* Here's another live-action cartoon from the *Lethal Weapon/Die Hard* factory. Willis is a Secret Service agent turned private investigator who teams up with a burned-out former football star (Wayans). Together they take on a gang of well-dressed bad guys conspiring to . . . posturing does feature some slam-bang action sequences. Easily offended law enforcement officers, African-Americans, athletes, homosexuals, pacifists, women and others may need to take this one with a grain or two of salt. ★★ DVD: $14.99, VHS: $9.99

The Last Butterfly

(1993, 106 min, GB, Karel Kachyna) *Tom Courtenay, Brigitte Fossey, Freddie Jones.* In a sincere and moving performance, Courtenay plays a renowned Parisian mime artist who is coerced by the Nazis to perform at Terezin, Czechoslavakia, or "city of the Jews" — a propaganda community established by the Germans. A virtual prisoner himself, the apolitical performer soon discovers the truth about the town (it's a midway point for the camps). Unable to communicate with the visiting Red Cross, he tries to alert them the best way he knows how: through his art. These final scenes, a harrowing, updated adaptation of "Hansel and Gretel," are mesmerizing and give the film its emotional power. (In English) ★★★ VHS: $19.99

Last Call at Maud's

(1993, 75 min, US, Paris Poirier) The 1989 closing of Maud's Study, a lesbian bar and institution in San Francisco since 1966, propelled filmmaker Poirier to explore the 23-year life of the bar and its patrons as well as offer a fascinating minihistory of recent (post-WWII) lesbian life and the role that lesbian bars played in it. Many longtime patrons of Maud's offer a lively and informative account of lesbian life from the 1940s to the present, with stories of the many raids and police harassment of "queer" bars. An engaging and informative documentary which provides an essential chapter in the social and political history of lesbians. ★★★ DVD: $29.99, VHS: $29.99

The Last Castle

(2001, 120 min, US, Rod Lurie) *Robert Redford, James Gandolfini, Mark Ruffalo, Delroy Lindo, Clifton Collins, Jr., Steve Burton.* Sense of duty and sense of honor, which may not always go hand in hand, collide head-on in director Lurie's stylish though familiar prison drama that plays like *Les Misérables* behind bars. Redford stars as General Irwin, an esteemed Army commander who is sentenced to military prison for disobeying orders. He immediately comes in conflict with the warden, Col. Winter (Gandolfini), a martinet who is in awe of his new prisoner. Though Irwin states that he wants to "serve my time and go home," he sets out to try to right the injustices the prisoners are suffering at the hands of Winter, leading to a showdown and prison takeover. Lurie, whose first two films *The Contender* and *Deterrence* also examined the climate of political crises, is quite adept at setting up the action scenes and the fallout that follows, but the screen-

play only occasionally rises above the clichés of the prison drama. In military terms, *The Last Castle* is standard issue, but it manages to compel when concentrating on the rather unmilitary revolt that pits a man of discipline against a man of action. ★★½ DVD Letterbox: $14.99

The Last Days

(1998, 87 min, US, James Moll) A wrenching documentary, executive produced by Steven Spielberg, this is a must. Director Moll juxtaposes archival footage with interviews with five survivors of Hitler's Final Solution in Hungary, at a time when Germany knew they would lose WWII, but refused to lose the war on the Jews. The five people chosen each have fascinating remembrances, and their separate stories complement each other well for a full portrait of this time and place. Difficult to watch at times, to be sure, but incredibly moving and powerful as well. You won't soon forget these tough survivors revisiting their hometowns and even the death camps for the first time since the war, or many of their incredible observations. This is well-deserving of 1998's Oscar for Best Documentary. ★★★★ DVD: $19.99, VHS: $19.99

The Last Days of Chez Nous

(1992, 96 min, Australia, Gillian Armstrong) *Lisa Harrow, Bruno Ganz, Miranda Otto, Kerry Fox.* A charming character study of a dysfunctional Sydney family. Beth (Harrow) is an underpaid novelist and the unofficial matron of Chez Nous, a household comprised of her, her French husband J.P. (Ganz) and her teenage daughter, Anna (Otto). Into the soup comes her carefree sister and a gawky young male boarder. What follows is a fundamentally plotless, but nevertheless engaging and entertaining examination of the ways that people fail to communicate in spite of their desire for human contact — hmmm, could be a Wim Wenders film. ★★★ VHS: $19.99

The Last Days of Disco

(1998, 114 min, US, Whit Stillman) *Chloë Sevigny, Kate Beckinsale, Chris Eigeman, Mackenzie Astin, Matt Keeslar, Robert Sean Leonard, Jennifer Beals.* Though reminiscent of his first two films, there's still a lot to like about this look at the thoughts and loves of a group of friends during the last days of the disco era. Using the waning days of the dance craze as a backdrop to more worldly discussions, Stillman has assembled a good-looking, articulate and successful group who work all day to party all night. Sevigny stars as Alice, a literary agent who shares an apartment with the acid-tongued Charlotte (Beckinsale in a great turn), each becoming involved with a couple of potential Mr. Rights. As would be expected, Stillman is much more interested in the thoughts and deeds of his characters rather than a more narrative-driven story line. And he's written some remarkable and funny observations about love, relationships, career and, of course, disco. But he's got to move on or he'll become a relic of his time — does K.C. and the Sunshine Band ring a bell? ★★★

The Last Detail

(1973, 105 min, US, Hal Ashby) *Jack Nicholson, Otis Young, Randy Quaid, Michael Moriarty, Carol Kane, Nancy Allen.* Nicholson received an Academy Award nomination for his portrayal of "Bad Ass" Buddusky, one of two "lifer" sailors who are given the detail of escorting a young recruit convicted of stealing to Portsmouth Naval Prison. Ashby's direction and Michael Chapman's cinematography give this film a gritty look that complements its cynical, uncompromising atmosphere. One of Nicholson's most fully realized characterizations. ★★★½ DVD: $24.99

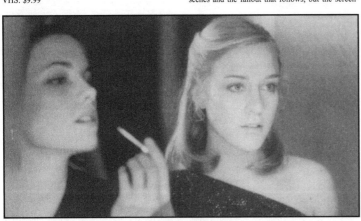

Kate Beckinsale (l.) and Chloë Sevigny in *The Last Dasy of Disco*

Last Embrace

(1979, 102 min, US, Jonathan Demme) *Roy Scheider, Christopher Walken, Janet Margolin, John Glover.* Engaging thriller à la Hitchcock about a CIA agent (Scheider) who, believing himself to be a target for assassination after his wife is murdered, finds himself entrapped in the mystery of his own identity. To say more would give the show away. The climax is a shocker. ★★★

The Last Emperor

(1987, 162 min, US/Italy, Bernardo Bertolucci) *John Lone, Joan Chen, Peter O'Toole.* Winner of nine Academy Awards, this sweeping historical epic chronicles the turbulent life and times of China's last emperor, Pu Yi. John Lone is mesmerizing as the weak-willed monarch, a man ascended to the Dragon Throne at the age of three, only to abdicate at six and then coerced to spend his early life within the opulent walls of China's Forbidden City. His story — from "Lord of 10,000 years" to playboy, prisoner, political puppet and finally common gardener — is told by Bertolucci in the grandest of cinematic traditions. An enthralling and extravagant story of one rather simple man engulfed by the events of his times. (Filmed in English) ★★★★ DVD Director's Cut: $14.99, VHS: $9.99

Last Exit to Brooklyn

(1990, 103 min, US/Germany, Uli Edel) *Jennifer Jason Leigh, Stephen Lang, Alexis Arquette, Burt Young, Ricki Lake, Jerry Orbach, Stephen Baldwin, Peter Dobson, Jason Andrews.* This German production of Hubert Selby, Jr.'s 1957 underground classic is a hard-hitting, no-holds-barred look at life in hell along the docks of Brooklyn in the early '50s. This isn't just Ozzie and Harriet in reverse; it's an all-out indictment of the American experience as seen through the eyes of Brooklyn's lower depths. It's not pretty — it is, however, a gripping and undeniably overwhelming drama. Lang is excellent as a bewildered union leader who is painfully forced to come to grips with his repressed homosexuality. Leigh is dazzling as the teenage hooker Tralala who enforces her womanhood at the end of the film in one of the most disturbing scenes ever filmed. (Filmed in English) ★★★½

The Last Five Days

(1982, 112 min, West Germany, Percy Adlon) *Lena Stoltz, Irm Hermann.* Belying his trademark playful touch, Adlon goes for much weightier subject matter in telling the shattering true story of a young girl and her brother who were executed by the Nazis for distributing anti-fascist propaganda. Stoltze plays Sophie Scholl, the woman compelled to almost suicidal political action against the Nazis in 1943 in this restrained, precise film of crushing emotional impact. (German with English subtitles) ★★★ VHS: $79.99

Last House on the Left

(1972, 91 min, US, Wes Craven) *David Hess, Lucy Grantham, Sandra Cassel, Marc Scheffler.* Two young women are abducted and brutalized by some buffoonish escaped convicts in this economic but severely dated horror outing which launched the careers of both Craven and Sean S. Cunningham (*Friday the 13th*). Whether or not this appeals to you depends on your tolerance for corny humor and amateurish acting. ★ DVD Dual: $14.99

The Last Hurrah

(1958, 121 min, US, John Ford) *Spencer Tracy, Jeffrey Hunter, Basil Rathbone, Pat O'Brien, James Gleason, Donald Crisp.* Tracy gives an outstanding performance in this absorbing and stellar version of Edwin O'Connor's novel about the last days of a political boss. Great supporting cast. ★★★½ DVD: $27.99, VHS: $19.99

Last Hurrah for Chivalry

(1978, 108 min, Hong Kong, John Woo) *Damian Lau, Wei Pai.* Just before he reinvented the gangster movie with his phenomenally successful *A Better Tomorrow*, writer-director Woo bid farewell to the "heroic swordplay" movies with which he began his career with this fun, well-written story of two killers-for-hire who foreshadow the honorable criminals of his modern blood operas. Lau and Pai are master swordsmen who have no allegiances and adhere strictly to the code of their personal art. When they both decide to help out a wealthy local who is seeking revenge against an evil kung fu master, they discover that few hold honor, duty and friendship in the same high esteem. The film features some exciting, traditional swordfights interspersed with its themes of male bonding and righteous sacrifice. (Cantonese with English subtitles) ★★★ DVD: $29.99, VHS: $19.99

The Last Kiss

(2001, 114 min, Italy, Gabriele Muccino) *Stefano Accorsi, Giovanna Mezzogiorno, Stefania Sandrelli.* Maintaining a pace that matches the ongoing convolutions in the frenetic lives of its characters, *The Last Kiss* is an engaging, funny and unerringly perceptive examination of the interlocking relationships in a multigenerational group of friends, relatives and acquaintances. The film centers on Carlo and Giulia, a beautiful young couple who find out they're about to become parents. Their parents expect them to marry, but they're not sure; especially Carlo, who feels a noose tightening around him. Carlo and Giulia are surrounded by people in various stages of transition, or, more to the point, people looking for change from perceived entrapment. Director Muccino's hyperkinetic camera never loses sight of the human element, and through a witty, grown-up script related by a superb ensemble he has fashioned a totally engaging and entertaining study of the human condition. (Italian with English subtitles) ★★★½ DVD: $29.99, VHS: $102.99

The Last Klezmer

(1994, 84 min, US/Poland, Yale Strom) Leopold Kozlowski, a teacher of music and klezmer musician, returns home for the first time in fifty years to his home town in Poland. This intimate portrait and homecoming documentary is poignant in its sincerity and insightful in director Strom's focus on Kozlowski's passion for teaching the art of klezmer to opera and piano students. Absence of klezmer music — which has been called "Jewish jazz" — is apparent in the stark landscape of post-WWII and post-Communist Poland, and it is this vacancy which serves to underscore the messages of both Kozlowski and the filmmaker. (In English and Polish, Yiddish & Russian with English subtitles) ★★★ VHS: $29.99

The Last Laugh

(1924, 73 min, Germany, F.W. Murnau) *Emil Jannings, Maly Delshaft.* One of the classics from Germany's "Golden Era," *The Last Laugh* features the great Jannings as a proud doorman of a luxury hotel who is demoted to washroom attendant. Once envied and respected by his neighbors, the baffled old man sees his world and status crumble; but in a surprising ending, he still gets the last laugh. (Silent) ★★★★ DVD: $29.99, VHS: $24.99

Last Man Standing

(1996, 100 min, US, Walter Hill) *Bruce Willis, Christopher Walken, Bruce Dern, Alexandra Powers, William Sanderson.* Combining the gangster and western genres and using a ghost town during the rough-and-tumble 1930s as its setting, *Last Man Standing* is a particularly stylish reworking of *Yojimbo* whose narrative isn't quite as accomplished as its visuals. As the perennial Man-with-No-Name, Willis is a mysterious drifter who arrives in a near-deserted Texas town and immediately gets caught between two feuding mob factions. The golden-hued cinematography nicely captures the dusty landscape, and the gunfight sequences are well staged. But the drama nestled in-between the fights and shootouts are slowly paced. ★★½ DVD Letterbox: $14.99, VHS: $9.99, VHS Letterbox: $9.99

The Last Metro

(1980, 135 min, France, François Truffaut) *Catherine Deneuve, Gérard Depardieu, Jean-Louis Richard.* Truffaut's poignant account of Parisian theatre under the Nazi thumb stars Deneuve and Depardieu as members of an acting troupe struggling through the Occupation. Heinz Bennett plays Deneuve's husband and stage director, forced underground because of his Jewish heritage. (French with English subtitles) ★★★ DVD: $19.99, VHS: $14.99

The Last Movie

(1971, 110 min, US, Dennis Hopper) *Peter Fonda, Michelle Phillips, Dean Stockwell, Sam Fuller.* After his phenomenal success with *Easy Rider*, the powers-that-be in Hollywood believed that they had found the voice of the young, restless America in Hopper. Universal Pictures bankrolled the neophyte director's next project and gave him carte blanche to produce his next "blockbuster" — an "artsy," possibly drug-induced and complicated (some said incomprehensible) mess. The film revolves around the happenings of an American movie crew filming a western in a small Peruvian village. ★★

Last Night

(1999, 95 min, Canada, Don McKellar) *Don McKellar, Sandra Oh, David Cronenberg, Tracy Wright, Geneviève Bujold, Roberta Maxwell, Sarah Polley, Callum Keith Rennie.* It's evening in Toronto, and the world will be ending at midnight. No explanation is given, but the news stations keep mentioning it, so it's apparently sunk in for the residents. How do the various citizens react when faced with their own premature mortality? This is the intriguing premise behind writer-director McKellar's *Last Night*, which goes beyond the usual apocalyptic drama to satirize our worker-colony cities and provide a darkly uplifting portrait of what some people are capable of when they let their emotions free. The poignancy comes when least expected, for the audience and for the characters alike, in this restrained, deeply satisfying portrait of intellectual armageddon. ★★★½ DVD: $14.99, VHS: $9.99

The Last of England

(1988, 87 min, GB, Derek Jarman) Uncompromising in its vision, *The Last of England* is a beautifully photographed fragmented poem structured within a series of cross-cutting vignettes. Filled with homoerotic images, the film deals with the destruction of our physical and emotional world by the ravages of Thatcherism and the callousness of Man. Accompanied by Nigel Terry's baleful narration, the visuals include shots of Jarman, male prostitutes and scenes of urban squalor and decay. It's a baffling but interesting work, reminiscent of Jean Cocteau. ★★★

The Last of His Tribe

(1992, 90 min, US, Harry Hook) *Graham Greene, Jon Voight, Anne Archer, David Odgen Stiers.* This made-for-HBO drama stars Greene as Ishi, the last known survivor of the Yahi people. His tribe having been wiped out in the slaughter of California's natives (a decimation which brought the total Indian population of the state from 300,000 in 1800 to 20,000 in 1900), Ishi is discovered by the "civilized" world in 1911. Voight plays the eager anthropologist who ventures to save the Yahi ways and traditions for posterity. ★★½ VHS: $19.99

The Last of Mrs. Cheyney

(1937, 98 min, US, Richard Boleslawski) *Joan Crawford, William Powell, Robert Montgomery.* Crawford had one of her biggest hits of the 1930s with this fairly entertaining remake of the 1929 Norma Shearer success. Crawford is in her element as an American jewel thief working her way through the cream of British high society. What she finds besides stolen gems is love. ★★½ VHS: $19.99

The Last of Phillip Banter

(1986, 100 min, US/Spain, Herve Hachuel) *Tony Curtis, Greg Henry.* This limp thriller about a man's mental breakup lacks both tension and complexity. Set in Madrid, the story centers on Phillip Banter, a world-weary drunk whose marriage to the boss' daughter is deteriorating. Is this handsome but self-pitying bore really losing his marbles or is there a conspiracy out? By the time the viewer discovers the truth, it's too late — you'll be sound asleep. Curtis seems surprised to be in this film. ★ VHS: $79.99

The Last of Sheila

(1973, 120 min, US, Herbert Ross) *James Coburn, James Mason, Dyan Cannon, Richard Benjamin, Joan Hackett, Raquel Welch, Ian McShane.* Entertainingly puzzling to the very end, this star-studded murder-mystery features Coburn as a game-obsessed film producer who invites six of his Hollywood jet-set "friends" on a cruise in the Mediterranean where a mean-spirited game, begun by him and designed to expose a dark secret of each member, backfires. Twists and turns abound in this plexus murder mystery written by Anthony Perkins and Stephen Sondheim. ★★★ DVD Letterbox: $19.99, VHS: $14.99

The Last of the Finest

(1990, 97 min, US, John MacKenzie) *Brian Dennehy, Bill Paxton, Jeff Fahey, Joe Pantoliano.* Though its title may be a little too self-congratulatory, this is a surprisingly effective and taut police adventure. Dennehy stars as the leader of a special police unit who accidentally stumbles upon a drug operation with ties to high-ranking officials. Taken off the case when they get too close, Dennehy and his partners continue the unwanted investigation after one of their own is killed. ★★★ VHS: $14.99

The Last of the Mohicans

(1992, 112 min, US, Michael Mann) *Daniel Day-Lewis, Madeleine Stowe, Jodhi May, Russell Means, Wes Studi, Colm Meaney.* James Fenimore Cooper's novel of Colonial America makes for an efficient, exciting romantic adventure. Day-Lewis is cast as Indian scout Hawkeye, and he so immerses himself in the part it's easy to forget he's not really an American. It's Day-Lewis' determined portrayal, well-staged action sequences, astonishing camerawork and a splendid re-creation of pre-Revolutionary times which make *Mohicans* the lump-in-your-throat adventure that it is. And it's bloody romantic, too. Stowe plays a British major's daughter, whom Hawkeye escorts through the wilderness and eventually falls in love with. Especially good in support is May as Stowe's younger and ultimately brave sister. ★★★½ DVD Letterbox: $19.99, VHS: $9.99

Last of the Red Hot Lovers

(1972, 98 min, US, Gene Saks) *Alan Arkin, Sally Kellerman, Paula Prentiss, Renee Taylor.* Minor screen adaptation of Neil Simon's play with Arkin as a restaurant owner desperately trying for an extramarital affair. ★★ DVD: $19.99, VHS: $14.99

Last Orders

(2002, 109 min, GB, Fred Schepisi) *Michael Caine, Tom Courtenay, David Hemmings, Bob Hoskins, Helen Mirren, Ray Winstone.* A group of old friends gather to remember their deceased comrade and set off on a bittersweet journey across the English countryside to scatter his ashes. Based on Graham Swift's Booker Prize-winning novel, *Last Orders* is a beautifully told, touching story of memories, friendship and new beginnings, poignantly brought to life by a marvelous ensemble. ★★★½ DVD: $24.99, VHS: $14.99

The Last Picture Show

(1971, 118 min, US, Peter Bogdanovich) *Jeff Bridges, Joseph Bottoms, Cybill Shepherd, Cloris Leachman, Ben Johnson, Eileen Brennan, Randy Quaid.* Bogdanovich's brilliant adaptation of Larry McMurtry's novel is regarded as one of the definitive coming-of-age sagas: not only in its depiction of the "end of innocence" for its characters, but for an entire way of life. Set in a one-horse town in 1950s Texas, the film stars Bottoms and Bridges as heat-struck teens sweltering in the dustbowl of their own lives. Leachman and Johnson won Oscars for their gutsy portrayals. Bogdanovich's eye for the period and place paints a picture of a ghost town more chilling than any horror movie. (Sequel: *Texasville*) ★★★★ DVD: $19.99

The Last Remake of Beau Geste

(1977, 85 min, US, Marty Feldman) *Marty Feldman, Michael York, Ann-Margret, James Earl Jones, Peter Ustinov.* Feldman directed, wrote and stars in this uneven though sometimes funny spoof on Foreign Legion movies — *Beau Geste* in particular. York plays Marty's twin brother (and Arnold and Danny thought they had an original idea) who accompanies his sibling to the legendary French outpost in Morocco. ★★

Tom Cruise in *The Last Samurai*

The Last Samurai

(2003, 154 min, US, Edward Zwick) *Tom Cruise, Ken Watanabe, Timothy Spall, Billy Connelly, Tony Goldwyn, Hiroyuki Sanada, William Atherton.* Cruise control radiates through this impressive, large-scale historical adventure saga. The actor plays Nathan Algren, a washed-up former Civil War hero eeking out a living in the 1870s at Wild West shows. An expert at weapons, languages and fighting, Algren is recruited to go to the Far East, where he's to train a young Japanese emperor's troops in preparation for a war against the antiquated samurai populace of the country. But Cruise is soon captured by the samurai and their no-nonsense leader Katsumoto (Watanabe), where he learns to relish the discipline and ancient fighting methods of the warriors, eventually joining their side to lead them against the emperor. Director Zwick does a commendable job delivering the action along the way, mounting a thinking man's epic that succeeds on many levels. Aided by an expert script, the film offers food for thought in its examination of the struggle of a country willing to sacrifice their traditions for economic reasons, as the New World seeks to obliterate the values of the old. Sumptuously photographed, *The Last Samurai* is a wonder to watch, filled with gorgeous landscapes, authentic period detail and expertly staged battle sequences. At the center of the picture is Cruise, and he turns in one of his best performances, really getting under the skin of the character and has you rooting for him in his struggle. Oscar-nominated Watanabe is magnificent as the calm, charismatic samurai who teaches the old Tom some new tricks. ★★★½ DVD Letterbox 2-disc Special Edition, Widescreen: $29.99, DVD 2-disc Special Edition, Full-Frame: $29.99

The Last Seduction

(1994, 110 min, US, John Dahl) *Linda Fiorentino, Peter Berg, J.T. Walsh, Bill Pullman, Bill Nunn.* Fiorentino is in nightmarishly good form as Bridget Gregory, the ultimate femme fatale. When her New York med-school husband (Pullman) comes home with the proceeds of a major drug deal, she scampers with the loot and heads upstate. And oh, you boys upstate better beware! Filled with delightful twists and turns, *The Last Seduction* follows Bridget as she sets up shop in a sleepy little burg where she gets Mike (Berg) in her talons. Mike is a perfect rube for Bridget. He's so bent on getting out of small town life, that he falls squarely into every trap she sets. Fiorentino is incredibly sharp as Bridget. Ultimately, what makes this film so seductive is Bridget's completely unapologetic nature: she's the woman who's been wronged by men and is going to take everything she can to make up for it. And what makes it all so much fun is that we're rooting for *her.* ★★★★ DVD: $9.99, VHS: $14.99

The Last September

(1999, 104 min, GB, Deborah Warner) *Maggie Smith, Michael Gambon, Jane Birkin, Fiona Shaw, Lambert Wilson, Keeley Hawes.* Set in County Cork, Ireland, in 1920, this sumptuous though uninspiring adaptation of Elizabeth Brown's novel traces the end of an era for the aristocratic Anglo-Irish Naylor family, and, in effect, the end of Anglo-Irish aristocracy in Ireland. The fight for Irish independence arrives on the Naylor's front door when their young daughter is torn between a British soldier and a freedom fighter in hiding. The good ensemble (especially Shaw) helps keep interest but the film lacks full dramatic tension and only intermittently is able to keep pace with its ambitious story. ★★½ DVD: $24.99

The Last Starfighter

(1984, 100 min, US, Nick Castle) *Robert Preston, Lance Guest, Barbara Bosson, Catherine Mary Stewart, Wil Wheaton.* Amiable sci-fi adventure with Guest as a small-town youth who yearns for excitement — and finds it when he is recruited by a space promoter (Preston) to help in the fight against an evil conquerer. Preston is tops in a slight variation of his *Music Man* con man. ★★½ DVD: $14.99, VHS: $7.49

Last Summer

(1969, 97 min, US, Frank Perry) *Barbara Hershey, Bruce Davison, Richard Thomas, Cathy Burns.* Poignant coming-of-age drama about three restless teenagers and their summer of discovery at a private beach. Oscar-nominee Burns is a stand-out in support. Stunning photography by Gerald Hirschfield. ★★★

Last Summer in the Hamptons

(1995, 108 min, US, Henry Jaglom) *Victoria Foyt, Viveca Lindfors, Jon Robin Baitz, Roddy McDowall, Martha Plimpton, Roscoe Lee Browne, Andre Gregory, Ron Rifkin.* Jaglom's story centers around a famous theatrical family holding their last summer production before they sell their country house. The elegant matriarch, Helena (the great Lindfors), holds court while the various guests attempt awkward seductions with each other. Jaglom's own *Smiles of a Summer Night* employs his meandering, relaxed style to film this encounter session with equal amounts of insight, bickering, humor and pretention. The debate about stage versus cinema is interesting and observant, but the same can't be said for rather bad concentration exercises in which one of the family members "interprets" various animals. Like the

characters, some of the actors fare better than others. *Last Summer in the Hamptons* can be affectionate and appealing when not being downright irritating. ★★★ DVD: $14.99

The Last Supper

(1976, 110 min, Cuba, Tomás Gutiérrez Alea) *Nelson Villagra, Silvano Rey.* Reminiscent of Buñuel's delightfully vicious *Viridiana*, this sardonic political allegory is about a pious slaveholder at the turn of the century who, feeling the pangs of guilt, tries to cleanse his soul in front of God by staging a re-enactment of the Last Supper. Asking his slaves to forget their shackles for a night, the plantation owner "enlists" twelve of them to play the apostles. Told with caustic wit and blasphemous irony, this dazzling tour de force features a powerful black cast and a not-so-subtle preaching of imminent political revolt. (Spanish with English subtitles) ★★★½ VHS: $19.99

The Last Supper

(1995, 94 min, US, Stacy Title) *Cameron Diaz, Ron Eldard, Annabeth Gish, Jonathan Penner, Courtney B. Vance, Bill Paxton, Jason Alexander.* An unexpected murder over Sunday dinner leads a group of five grad students to a unique course of political action. They alter their weekly ritual of inviting a sixth person for dinner and conversation by choosing as their guest someone they believe the world would be better off without. As the freshly dug mounds of earth in their backyard steadily increase in number, the members of the group go through disconcerting changes of their own, each finding that final solutions have fearsome effects on the perpetrators as well as the victims. While the film raises some intriguing questions, its potency is undercut by uneven performances and inconsistent plot developments. Still, it might be just the thing the next time you have the gang over for Sunday dinner. ★★½ DVD Letterbox: $24.99, VHS: $14.99

Last Tango in Paris

(1973, 129 min, Italy, Bernardo Bertolucci) *Marlon Brando, Maria Schneider, Jean-Pierre Léaud.* An aging expatriate (Brando) becomes involved in a doomed sexual liaison with a young French woman (Schneider). A landmark film which lays bare the primal nature of man. Brando equals his greatest performances as a seeker of truth, seething with sexual anger and drunk with self-loathing and contempt. (In English and French with English subtitles) ★★★★ DVD: $19.99

The Last Temptation of Christ

(1988, 164 min, US, Martin Scorsese) *Willem Dafoe, Harvey Keitel, Barbara Hershey, Harry Dean Stanton, David Bowie, Andre Gregory, Verna Bloom.* Scorsese's adaptation of the Nikos Kazantzakis novel is a controversial telling of the Christ story, but for many a believer and non-believer alike this epic exploration of the man behind the myth has proven to be a true article of faith. Dafoe delivers a stylistically brilliant portrayal of a Jesus who, uncertain whether the voices he hears are from God or Satan, is locked in an agonizing battle with his own destiny. Scorsese has succeeded in crafting a truly elegant and thought-provoking treatise on spirituality and existence — clearly a labor of love. ★★★★ DVD Criterion Collection: $39.99

The Last Time I Committed Suicide

(1997, 93 min, US, Stephen Kay) *Keanu Reeves, Thomas Jane, Adrien Brody, Claire Forlani.* According to many who knew him, beatnik Neal

Cassady was a genius of sorts, but the only impression we get from this film about his life is that he was a mildly intelligent, womanizing slacker. This is an uninvolving, annoying wisp of a movie that tries to compensate for the lack of a script (and a point) with an empty, clichéd music video technique. Director Kay most likely was excited by the parallels between Cassady's lifestyle and Generation X's perceived "attitude"; but like most twentysomething films, this is condescending and vapid. ★½

The Last Time I Saw Paris

(1954, 116 min, US, Richard Brooks) *Elizabeth Taylor, Van Johnson, Donna Reed, Walter Pidgeon.* Romance blossoms between a young Army writer (Johnson) and a fun-loving socialite (Taylor) in post-war Paris. This uneven drama is enhanced by slick production values and Taylor's charm and beauty. Based on the novel "Babylon Revisited" by F. Scott Fitzgerald. ★★ DVD: $9.99, VHS: $19.99

The Last Tycoon

(1976, 123 min, US, Elia Kazan) *Robert De Niro, Tony Curtis, Robert Mitchum, Jeanne Moreau, Jack Nicholson.* This screen version of F. Scott Fitzgerald's unfinished novel is an accomplished film for its acting alone, but it still seems unfinished, although Harold Pinter's script does the best it can. Worth seeing if only for De Niro's performance. Nicholson has a memorable small part as a scriptwriter trying to start a union. ★★½ DVD Letterbox: $19.99, VHS: $14.99

The Last Waltz

(1978, 117 min, US, Martin Scorsese) *The Band, Bob Dylan, Neil Young, Ringo Starr, Eric Clapton, Van Morrison, Joni Mitchell, Emmylou Harris, Dr. John, Ron Wood, Ronnie Hawkins, Pops Staples, Mavis Staples, Paul Butterfield, Muddy Waters.* Scorsese's dazzling documentation of The Band's momentous farewell performance on Thanksgiving Day, 1976. Concluding over a decade and a half of playing together, the group is joined on stage by a wealth of guest artists: Bob Dylan, Eric Clapton, Neil Young, Van Morrison and many others. Songs include "The Weight," "Up on Cripple Creek" and "The Night They Drove Old Dixie Down." The first film to fully utilize the Dolby stereo surround process. ★★★½ DVD Letterbox Special Edition: $24.99

The Last Wave

(1978, 106 min, Australia, Peter Weir) *Richard Chamberlain, Olivia Hamnett.* Chamberlain plays a Sydney lawyer who, while defending a group of Aborigines accused of murder, becomes entangled in the labyrinthine world of ancient tribal magic, rituals and spiritualism. Atmospheric and moody, Weir's cerebral exercise in psychological horror is sometimes too ambitious but nevertheless has an ingenuity which heralded the director as a major player in the Australian film community. ★★★ DVD Letterbox Criterion Collection: $29.99, VHS: $19.99

The Last Winter

(1984, 92 min, Israel, Riki Shelach) *Kathleen Quinlan, Yona Elian.* A patriotic Israeli living in America returns to his homeland to fight in the Yom-Kippur War of 1973. After he is reported missing in action, his distraught American wife flies to Tel Aviv in search of answers. Her friendship with another MIA wife helps alleviate the pain and frustration of her wait. A serious, thoughtful and absorbing drama. (Filmed in English) ★★★

Late Chrysanthemums

Last Year at Marienbad

(1961, 93 min, France, Alain Resnais) *Delphine Seyrig, Giorgio Albertazzi.* At the spa in Marienbad a man (X) confronts a woman (A) with the conviction that they had an affair the previous year. Resnais transcends the limits of spatial and temporal storytelling rules. A classic of innovative cinema. Scripted by Alain Robbes-Grillet. (French and Italian with English subtitles) ★★★½

Latcho Drom

(1993, 103 min, France, Tony Gatlif) A pulsating musical and visual odyssey, this ode to the Gypsy life initially chronicles Europe's modern vagabonds who began their journey westward 1,000 years ago as a nomadic tribe from the north of India. It then launches into a series of MTV-inspired segments of ethnic music and dance — with stops in Egypt, Turkey, Romania, Hungary, Slovakia and Spain. As a kind of cultural travelogue mapping the source of musical inspiration from Asia to Europe — and linking those continents — the film is fascinating. But as the film's focus ventures westward, its outlook becomes as bleak, ultimately disintegrating into shameless and maudlin political propaganda bemoaning the plight of Europe's migratory underclass. ★★½ VHS: $19.99

Late Bloomers

(1997, 104 min, US, Gretchen Dyer & Julia Dyer) *Connie Nelson, Dee Hennigan, Gary Carter, Lisa Peterson, Val Lumpkin.* A delightfully romantic lesbian coming-out love story, this comedy-drama is set in Eleanor Roosevelt High School where Dinah, a gangly fortysomething math teacher and basketball coach, becomes friends with the cute but doughy Carly, a married school secretary and mother of two. What begins as innocent friendship soon becomes much more. As the two become more demonstrative in their affection, those around them become increasingly troubled. But romance triumphs over all adversities as the two women throw caution to the wind and fall passionately in love with each other. A bit too sugary (and fantastically unrealistic) for some, but sweetness and fantasy have their place. ★★★ DVD: $29.99

Late Chrysanthemums

(1954, 101 min, Japan, Mikio Naruse) *Haruko Sugimura, Chkako Hosokawa.* This moving portrait of three retired geishas and their struggle to earn a living and retain respect long after the bloom of youth has gone is a detailed and poignant tragicom-edy. Adapted from three Fumiko Hayashi stories, director Naruse masterfully depicts the subtle nuances of the women's emotionally intertwined relationships. Despite their meager living conditions and declining years, they determinedly fight for their dignity. (Japanese with English subtitles) ★★★½ VHS: $19.99

Late for Dinner

(1991, 92 min, US, W.D. Richter) *Brian Wimmer, Peter Berg, Marcia Gay Harden, Peter Gallagher.* Director Richter followed up *The Adventures of Buckaroo Banzai* (seven years later) with this subtly moving tale that mixes science fiction, romance and comedy to produce one of 1991's great films that nobody saw. Wimmer and Berg play best buddies who wind up "frozen" by a scientist as they run from the law in 1962. When the pair are thawed out nearly thirty years later, they have to contend with a society that has left them behind. More significantly, they have to rediscover and reconcile with the people they love. We've all seen this Rip Van Winkle, *Back to the Future* stuff before, but rarely has it been done with such sensitivity and soul. ★★★½

Late Marriage

(2002, 102 min, Israel, Dover Koshashvili) *Lior Ashkenazi, Ronit Elkabetz, Moni Moshonov.* Zaza is a 31-year-old Doctor of Philosophy student at Tel Aviv University. He contemplates the nature of existence and lives a comfortable lifestyle on his daddy's credit card. In despair of his unmarried status, his parents seek the efforts of a matchmaker and enlist the support of the extended family to find a suitable mate for their handsome, Peter Pan-syndrome son. Zaza goes through the motions of the matchmaking process, enduring awkward meeting after awkward meeting. At the end of another evening, he returns to the arms of the ravishingly beautiful Judith, his longtime girlfriend, who is divorced with children and three years older than Zaza, all of which removes her from consideration in the Zaza marriage sweepstakes in the eyes of his family. Ashkenazi and Elkabetz smolder on screen as the star-crossed Zaza and Judith; but their passionate attraction and shared ardor meet fierce resistance of surprising strength from the bonds of tradition and familial expectation. *Late Marriage* is intriguing, involving and in many ways disturbing; it's intelligent and rewards the viewer's attention even as it confronts our 21st-century preconceptions. (Georgian and Hebrew with English subtitles) ★★★ DVD: $29.99, VHS: $29.99

The Late Show

(1977, 94 min, US, Robert Benton) *Art Carney, Lily Tomlin, Bill Macy, Joanna Cassidy.* Two superior performances by Carney and Tomlin highlight this winning mystery comedy written and directed by Benton. Carney plays an aging private eye who is thrown together with slightly daffy Tomlin as he investigates the death of his partner. Thoroughly enjoyable and a terrific homage to those great detective mysteries of the 1940s. ★★★½ DVD Letterbox: $19.99, VHS: $14.99

Late Spring

(1949, 108 min, Japan, Yasujiro Ozu) *Chishu Ryu, Setsuko Hara, Hakuro Sugimura.* Director Ozu brings great subtlety and elegance to this beautifully crafted film about a young woman with an unhealthy attachment to her aging, widowed father. Fearful that she will become an old maid on his account, the old man pretends that he himself is going to wed and tricks her into marriage. Unfortunately, the grandeur of Ozu's exquisite but slow-paced style does not translate well to video — much of the beauty of Ozu's films come from his discerning eye for black-and-white imagery. Still, his finely drawn characters and meticulous study of familial relations make this unequalled viewing for lovers of great drama. (Japanese with English subtitles) ★★★★

Late Summer Blues

(1987, 101 min, Israel, Renen Schorr) *Dor Zweigenbom, Shahar Segal.* Set in 1970 during the War of Attrition at the Suez Canal, this moving drama chronicles the bittersweet dilemma facing a group of seven teenage students who, just finishing their final exams and high school, face impending induction into the Israeli armed forces. Sobered by the gruesome realities of war, the film focuses on the enthusiastic innocence and idealism of these youths as they are thrust into adulthood. (Hebrew with English subtitles) ★★★ VHS: $29.99

The Lathe of Heaven

(1979, 100 min, Canada, David Loxton & Fred Barzyk) *Bruce Davison, Kevin Conway, Margaret Avery.* Based on the popular novel by Ursula K. Le Guin, this near-stunning sci-fi tale stars Davison as George Orr, a young man whose haunted dreams become reality. Conway is the psychiatrist who sees Orr's special powers as the answer to the world's bleak troubles. An intelligent, gripping piece of science fiction that balances the social and the fantastic. (Remade in 2002) ★★★½ DVD: $24.99, VHS: $24.99

Laugh for Joy

(1954, 106 min, Italy, Mario Monicelli) *Anna Magnani, Ben Gazzara.* Magnani, in one of the best performances of her career, stars in this moving and bitter drama as a movie extra in Rome's Cinecitta Studio who becomes entangled in a messy relationship with two men: an American executive (Gazzara) and a crafty con man. (Italian with English subtitles) ★★★ VHS: $59.99

Laughing Sinners

(1931, 72 min, US, Harry Beaumont) *Joan Crawford, Clark Gable, Neil Hamilton, Guy Kibbee, Roscoe Karns.* Top-billed Crawford and Gable appear for the first time together in this predictable pre-Hays melodrama, based on the romantic Broadway play "Torch Song." Joan plays a nightclub singer who tries to commit suicide when she gets dumped by Hamilton. She's saved by Salvation

L

Army preacher Gable. Just when it seems Joan has found happiness, back into her life comes Hamilton . . . and temptation. This morality tale is a little rough around the edges, but is nonetheless appealing for its antiquated posture. ★★½ VHS: $19.99

Laura

(1944, 85 min, US, Otto Preminger) *Gene Tierney, Clifton Webb, Dana Andrews, Vincent Price, Judith Anderson.* With the question of "Who killed Laura?" (and *not* Palmer), Preminger sets the stage for a complex, riveting and one-of-a-kind murder mystery. Andrews plays a police detective investigating the murder of successful businesswoman Laura Hunt (the beautiful Tierney). Through a series of flashbacks, cynical columnist Waldo Lydecker (Webb) recalls Laura's life up to the murder. Featuring extraordinary photography, a haunting score, unexpected twists, remarkable performances and a scalpel-sharp wit, *Laura* is not to be missed. Webb gives a quintessential performance as the acerbic Lydecker, and Tierney is simply exquisite. ★★★★

Favorite Line: "I don't use a pen. I write with a goose quill dipped in venom." —*Clifton Webb as Waldo Lydecke*

Laurel Canyon

(2003, 103 min, US, Lisa Cholodenko) *Frances McDormand, Christian Bale, Kate Beckinsale, Natascha McElhone, Alessandro Nivola.* Laurel Canyon is one of those mystical California enclaves populated by the kindred spirits of Peter Pan and the Lost Boys; a place where personal freedom and artistic expression are de rigeur; a place where, when a young man wants to rebel against his music industry mom, he goes to Boston to study medicine. Sam (Bale) and his fiancée Alex (Beckinsale) visit his mom Jane (McDormand) when the betrothed couple moves to La La Land to complete their studies. The plan is to live with Mom until they find an apartment. But this is Alex's first taste of freedom and her counterculture enchantments are Sam's bad memories. Mom Jane is muse and nemesis, and for all her surface flakiness, the glue that holds the house together. McDormand, who could gather Oscar

Frances McDormand in *Laurel Canyon*

attention for a recitation of the phone book, delivers a deceptively guileless performance as the charmingly flawed earth mother/industry executive/sensualist whose basic core of strength and decency resolves all turbulence and even facilitates reconciliation with her resistant yet always-loving son. ★★★ DVD: $19.99, VHS: $14.99

The Lavender Hill Mob

(1951, 82 min, GB, Charles Crichton) *Alec Guinness, Stanley Holloway, Sidney James, Alfie Bass.* Yet another of the Ealing Studio greats, this mischievous comedy features a stand-up performance by Guinness as a mild-mannered bank employee who dreams up what he thinks is a foolproof plan to steal one million British pounds in gold from the Bank of England. Winner of a Best Screenplay Oscar, this zany comedy climaxes with a madcap chase and features Audrey Hepburn in a bit part. ★★★★ DVD: $19.99

Law Breakers
(Les Assassins de L'Ordre)

(1971, 107 min, France, Marcel Carné) *Jacques Brel, Catherine Rouvel, Michael Lonsdale, Charles Denner.* An engrossing and sobering exploration into police corruption in the French judicial system. A burglary suspect is brought in for questioning, but hours later, is found dead in his cell. All the officials in the prison deny any misconduct and the case seems unsolvable until the judge (Brel) assigned to the case takes a special interest in bringing the guilty to justice, even at the expense of his friends and his personal safety. (French with English subtitles) ★★★

Law of Desire

(1987, 100 min, Spain, Pedro Almodóvar) *Carmen Maura, Antonio Banderas, Eusebio Poncela, Bibi Andersson, Rossy De Palma.* Almodóvar's foray into sexual obsession is a wonderfully overheated sexual melodrama which basks in its farcical intentions. The story revolves around Pablo, a popular gay filmmaker, and his sister Tina (Maura), who used to be his brother until he changed his sex in order to please his lover — their father! Banderas is the darkly handsome but demented fan who attempts to win the director's heart by any means possible. Their loves, passions and wild adventures are splashed on the screen with the uninhibited eroticism, camp and outlandish wit that one would expect from the Spanish equivalent to Warhol. (Spanish with English subtitles) ★★★½

Lawman

(1971, 95 min, US, Michael Winner) *Burt Lancaster, Robert Ryan, Lee J. Cobb, Robert Duvall.* Lancaster heads a first-rate cast in this solid, leisurely paced western as a marshal who travels to a neighboring town to bring in seven cowpokes on a charge of murder. As Lancaster tracks the mostly law-abiding men, he battles with vigilante citizens, and comes to question his inflexible allegiance to the letter of the law — much like Javert in "Les Misérables." Ryan plays the impotent town sheriff who reluctantly aids Lancaster. ★★★½ DVD Letterbox: $19.99

Lawn Dogs

(1998, 100 min, US, John Duigan) *Kathleen Quinlan, Sam Rockwell, Christopher McDonald.* Sexy trailer trash Rockwell mows lawns for the snooty residents of a cloistered neighborhood complex. Another misfit, the very imaginative ten-year-old daughter of a well-to-do couple in this suburban hell, has no friends and takes a shining to Rockwell,

Peter O'Toole as *Lawrence of Arabia*

and after a fair amount of her pestering, they become unlikely friends. Predictably, the community misunderstands this strong, though innocent and platonic relationship. Though it has a low-key fairy-tale atmosphere, the entire movie is negated with a completely wrong-headed final act that piles on the contrivances and ridiculous events and motivations, until a ludicrous finale. ★★ DVD: $19.99

The Lawnmower Man

(1992, 132 min, US, Brett Leonard) *Pierce Brosnan, Jeff Fahey, Jenny Wright.* Originally released in theatres under the banner *Stephen King's Lawnmower Man*, this virtual reality, sci-fi thriller was in fact only based in small part of one of the horror maven's stories. King went to court and got his name removed from the title and it's easy to see why. Though the film features some outstanding computer-generated special effects, the story is incredibly thin. Brosnan stars as a scientist who uses his dim-witted gardener (Fahey) as a guinea pig in a virtual reality-based experiment aimed at expanding mental capacity. This release is the director's cut containing 34 extra minutes, making it slightly more coherent than its theatrical release. ★½ DVD: $9.99, VHS: $14.99

Lawnmower Man 2: Jobe's War

(1995, 93 min, US, Farhad Mann) *Patrick Bergen, Matt Frewer, Ely Pouget, Austin O'Brien.* Having little connection with the first film, this awful sequel begins as Jobe (Frewer) survives the cataclysmic destruction of the virtual reality labs where he has been given superhuman intelligence and powers. He's now an honest, caring human being who becomes dependent upon electronic technology because of physical handicaps. He teams up with Ben (Bergen), the creator of a new kind of microchip which (of course) will revolutionize computer technology. An embarrassment for all involved. ★

Lawrence of Arabia

(1962, 222 min, GB, David Lean) *Peter O'Toole, Omar Sharif, Alec Guinness, Claude Rains, Jack Hawkins, Jose Ferrer.* O'Toole is possessed as T.E. Lawrence in this biography of a man who almost single-handedly helped the Arabs to escape their Turkish bondage in a brilliant saga of courage, sun and sand. The breathtaking Cinemascope photography is sadly lost on the small screen, but Lean's brilliant direction and a peerless ensemble will quickly put this out of mind. Winner of 7 Academy Awards including Best Picture and Director. ★★★★ DVD Letterbox Basic Edition: $19.99, VHS Pan & Scan: $19.99

Laws of Gravity

(1992, 100 min, US, Nick Gomez) *Peter Greene, Adam Trese.* Director Gomez makes a startling debut with this high-voltage independent film that bears more than a passing resemblance to *Mean Streets* as it tracks the ups and downs of a group of small-time Brooklyn hoods whose immaturity gets in the way of the big score. Greene stars as an aging "reservoir pup" whose day-to-day dealings in "the hood" collide with keeping his hot-headed, gun-running buddy (Trese) out of hot water. Gomez's deft mixture of surefooted performances from a cast of unknowns, a blisteringly improvisational script and frenetic camerawork that defies all laws of gravity suggest the arrival of a new screenwise master. ★★★½

Le Corbeau

(1943, 92 min, France, Henri-Georges Clouzot) *Pierre Fresnay, Ginette Leclerc.* An extremely dark and tense thriller about a small town in France besieged by paranoia in the wake of a mysterious, poisonous letter campaign written by "The Raven" and addressed to the town's physician. The uncompromising depiction of the French middle class caused quite a storm when the film was released because it was made with the assistance of the Germans and was viewed by many as anti-French propaganda. (French with English subtitles) ★★★½ DVD Criterion Collection: $29.99

The Leading Man

(1998, 96 min, GB, John Duigan) *Jon Bon Jovi, Anna Galiena, Lambert Wilson, Thandie Newton, Barry Humphries, Patricia Hodge, David Warner.* Backstage bedhopping and backstabbing make up *The Leading Man*, a guilty pleasure that has beautiful people seducing each other for fun and profit. Felix Webb (Wilson) is a successful West End playwright bedding Hilary (Newton), a ravishing talent seeking a plum role in his new play. When his gorgeous wife Elena (Galiena) discovers the affair, Felix conspires with the play's star, Hollywood hunk Robin Grange (Jovi), to seduce Elena and cure her malaise. Complications, of course, ensue. As directed by Duigan and written by his sister Virginia, the film never quite establishes the right tone. The material is a bit thin, but the actors seem to relish their juicy parts. ★★½ DVD: $9.99, VHS: $9.99

The League of Gentlemen

(1960, 115 min, GB, Basil Dearden) *Jack Hawkins, Nigel Patrick, Richard Attenborough, Roger Livesey.* An exciting and briskly paced escapade about a group of ex-army officers who use their military talents to rob a bank. Imbued with a light sense of humor, the film is peppered with classic British witticisms. ★★★½ VHS: $19.99

A League of Their Own

(1992, 127 min, US, Penny Marshall) *Geena Davis, Lori Petty, David Strathairn, Tom Hanks, Madonna, Rosie O'Donnell, Jon Lovitz, Bill Pullman.* A marvelously entertaining baseball comedy, *A League of Their Own* is inspired by the real-life antics of the all-girls baseball league founded in 1943. Davis and Petty star as country-girl sisters who are discovered by ever-acerbic scout Lovitz. Whisked off to Chicago, they join the Rockford Peaches under the watchful bloodshot eyes of the team's over-the-hill, boozing manager (Hanks, who gives one of his richest characterizations). As the sisters whose sibling rivalry would make Joan Fontaine and Olivia de Havilland blush, Davis and Petty offer splendid performances. And it doesn't hurt that they look good in uniform and can handle a ball and glove. Director Marshall has a wonderful sense of comic timing, and she has crafted a sweet and funny valentine of a film. ★★★½ DVD: $14.99, DVD 2-disc Special Edition: $24.99, VHS: $9.99

Lean on Me

(1989, 104 min, US, John G. Avildsen) *Morgan Freeman, Beverly Todd, Robert Guillaume, Lynne Thigpen, Michael Beach.* Director Avildsen (*Rocky*) takes his "go for it" attitude and puts it in the classroom with mostly unsatisfactory results. Freeman gives a powerhouse performance as real-life principal Joe Clark, who took control of a Paterson, New Jersey, high school overrun by drugs, violence and apathy. You want to root for him, but when he starts bullying those around him and violates city and fire ordinances — and lies about doing so — he is clearly not the kind of hero who warrants such an idealized tribute. The film is at its best when it is not lionizing Clark as crusader, but rather showing his earnest commitment to his students. ★★ DVD: $14.99, VHS: $9.99

Leap of Faith

(1992, 107 min, US, Richard Pearce) *Steve Martin, Debra Winger, Liam Neeson, Lukas Haas, Lolita Davidovich, Meat Loaf, Philip Seymour Hoffman.* Despite the immeasurable comedic talents of Martin and a perfect premise for skewering evangelical preachers, this dramatic comedy falls short of its mark. When their bus breaks down, Martin (doing his best Jim Bakker) and company set up shop in a depressed farming community. The town's crops are being devastated by drought, and its inhabitants are primed for Martin's promises of divine intervention. Despite this ideal setup, Martin never really clicks, mainly because it's hard to believe someone so smarmy could convince anyone he's on God's side. The most interesting thing about *Leap of Faith* is its behind-the-scenes look at how preachers make those miracles. ★★½ DVD: $19.99, VHS: $14.99

The Leather Boys

(1963, 105 min, GB, Sidney J. Furie) *Rita Tushingham, Dudley Sutton, Colin Campbell.* Tushingham stars as a woman trapped in an incompatible marriage to a motorcycle-loving mechanic in this compelling and uncompromising study of compulsive behavior. Focusing on their opposing viewpoints and sleazy environment, the film chronicles the ever-widening rift which leads to infidelity and unhappiness. ★★★ DVD: $24.99, VHS: $19.99

Leather Jackets

(1992, 90 min, US, Lee Drysdale) *Bridget Fonda, D.B. Sweeney, Cary Elwes.* Even the buoyant presence of Fonda can't keep this inane thriller from drowning under the weight of its attitude-heavy, cliché-ridden plot. Writer-director Drysdale aims low and misses with a shopworn tale of two former friends, one of whom (Sweeney) is a reformed petty thief. The other (Elwes), however, still enjoys a life of crime until he finds himself on the run from a gang whose leader he has just killed. ★½ VHS: $79.99

Leave It to Beaver

(1997, 88 min, US, Andy Cadiff) *Christopher McDonald, Janine Turner, Cameron Finley, Erik von Detten, Adam Zolotin.* In bringing TV's semi-cultural institution to the big screen, the filmmakers could have gone the *Brady Bunch* route and spoofed the show's wholesomeness. They didn't. They could have gone the *Addams Family* route and played up the original's comic sensibilities. They didn't. They could have exaggerated the show's sentimentality without supplying any sustained laughs. They did. Turner is wasted as June, who's barely on-screen; Ward is a sports buff pushing his children; and the Beav and Wally are homogenized '90s kids who could feel at home on any stupid contemporary sitcom. ★½ DVD: $14.99, VHS: $9.99

Leaving Las Vegas

(1995, 112 min, US, Mike Figgis) *Nicolas Cage, Elisabeth Shue, Julian Sands, Richard Lewis, Steven Weber, Valeria Golino, Laurie Metcalf, R. Lee Ermey, Julian Lennon, Xander Berkeley.* In bringing John O'Brien's decidedly downbeat novel about a man bent on suicide through alcohol to the screen, director Figgis and company took a huge cinematic risk that pays off in spades. This sultry and sometimes subversively funny examination of a self-declared loser (Cage) and the proverbial "hooker with a heart of gold" (Shue) who befriends him is on the one hand as depressing a film as has been made and on the other remarkably refreshing and engrossing for its undaunted emotional honesty. Cage plays Ben, a self-destructive minor Hollywood player who heads for a final showdown with the bottle in Vegas. Once there, he takes up with Sera (Shue), a buff streetwalker who takes him in — on the condition that she never try to convert him. Cage won a highly deserved Oscar for his unflinching portrayal, and Shue delivers a nuanced, rock solid performance. ★★★★ DVD: $19.99

Leaving Normal

(1992, 110 min, US, Edward Zwick) *Christine Lahti, Meg Tilly, Lenny Von Dohlen, Patrika Darbo.* The first of the *Thelma and Louise* "clones," *Leaving Normal* is a quirky, affectionate if uneven road movie about two uncertain women coming to terms with themselves. Featuring two sumptuous performances by Lahti and Tilly, the film follows the misadventures taken by Darly (Lahti), a quick-witted cocktail waitress and Marianne (Tilly), a waifish divorcee, who cross paths and decide to set out together on the road to Alaska. In contrast to *T & L*, most of the characters they encounter are comic foils, someone for the two lead characters to react to rather than gain any personal or interpersonal insight. Darbo is splendid as a waitress named 66. ★★½ VHS: $14.99

La Lectrice (The Reader)

(1988, 98 min, France, Michel Deville) *Miou-Miou, Christian Ruche.* Miou-Miou is enchanting in this labyrinthine tale of a woman who reads to her husband the story of a woman who reads to those who can't read for themselves. While not nearly as confusing as it sounds, director Deville's choices of the texts of Tolstoy, Beaudelaire, de Maupassant and Carroll tend to render this a trying (albeit welcome) challenge for even the most literate filmgoer. However, the mixture of humor and pathos, and the general zaniness of the characters and situations, make it as much fun as curling up with a good book. (French with English subtitles) ★★★ VHS: $19.99

The Left Hand of God

(1955, 87 min, US, Edward Dmytryk) *Humphrey Bogart, Gene Tierney, Lee J. Cobb, E.G. Marshall, Agnes Moorehead.* Bogart stars as a downed WWII pilot who enters a Catholic mission posing as a priest to escape a vengeful Chinese warlord (Cobb). Tierney costars as the beautiful missionary whose heart sees through his disguise. ★★½

The Left-Handed Gun

(1958, 102 min, US, Arthur Penn) *Paul Newman, James Best, James Congdon.* Penn's directorial debut is a stylistic, provocative if not totally successful adaptation of Gore Vidal's story about Billy the Kid. The depiction of Billy by the intensely handsome Newman is that of a pensive, misunderstood but hot-headed loner — a tormented youth in the fashion of James Dean and Hamlet. After his boss is murdered, Billy and his two best friends, Tom (Best) and Charlie (Congdon), become obsessed with gunning down the man's killer. Penn's emphasis is more on psychological development rather than the traditional western good guys vs. bad guys, bringing an originality rarely seen to the time-honored genre. ★★½ VHS: $14.99

Left Luggage

(1998, 100 min, US/Netherlands, Jeroen Krabbé) *Isabella Rossellini, Maximilian Schell, Marianne Sägebrecht, Laura Fraser, Chaim Topol.* Chaja (Fraser) is a 20-year-old philosophy student in 1972 Antwerp, caught up in the spontaneous rebellion and heady revolutionary fervor of the time. She finds no relevance in her Jewish heritage; her father's (Schell) obsession to find two suitcases he buried in flight during the war is just a baffling idiosyncrasy to her. She's brought back to her father's world when she becomes nanny to the Kalmans, a family of Hassidic Jews. Initially in conflict with the strict household rules, she stays to form a supportive bond with the mother (Rossellini) and a loving affection for the quiet, four-year-old Simcha. In bringing Simcha out of his shell, Chaja develops a deeper connection to her roots; and she experiences a profound loss that deepens her understanding of her father and his luggage. This is actor Krabbé's first directorial effort, and it is quite successful, evidencing a warm humanity and a supple ease with the filmmaking process. ★★★ DVD: $14.99, VHS: $14.99

The Legacy

(1979, 100 min, US, Richard Marquand) *Katharine Ross, Sam Elliott, Roger Daltrey.* Six strangers are invited to a remote English mansion when they suddenly begin dying off. A supernatural presence is in the air and is using the process of elimination to select an heir. This *Omen*-inspired horror tale lacks suspense or a plot but tries to make up for it with gore and nonsense. ★★ DVD: $14.99

Legal Eagles

(1986, 116 min, US, Ivan Reitman) *Robert Redford, Debra Winger, Daryl Hannah, Brian Dennehy, Terence Stamp.* Earnest performances save this genial though disappointing comedy. Redford and Winger play, respectively, a successful district attorney and an eccentric lawyer who team to defend a SoHo performance artist (Hannah) accused of murder. It's not really all that bad, but with that cast, it doesn't meet expectations. ★★½ DVD, VHS: $7.49

Legally Blonde

(2001, 96 min, US, Robert Luketic) *Reese Witherspoon, Luke Wilson, Selma Blair, Matthew Davis, Victor Garber, Jennifer Coolidge, Ali Larter, Holland Taylor.* Witherspoon absolutely enchants in this funny, crowd-pleasing comedy that's in the mold of *Clueless* and is as light as air. Reese plays Elle Woods, a materialistic blonde who's not exactly dumb, but is smart in all matters *Vogue*. When her Kennedyesque boyfriend dumps her (because she's *too* blonde) instead of proposing and then heads off to attend Harvard Law School, she pulls all her

resources together and follows him there to win him back. She eventually finds a world outside of *Vogue*, becomes a whirlwind in the courtroom and sets the heart of a third-year law student (Wilson) all aflutter. The movie's simple, to be sure, but damn if Reese doesn't keep you smiling through it all. Special mention goes to Coolidge as a blue-collar nail technician whom Elle befriends. (Sequel: *Legally Blonde 2: Red, White & Blonde*) ★★★ DVD: $14.99, VHS: $9.99

Legally Blonde 2: Red, White & Blonde

(2003, 95 min, US, Charles Herman-Wurmfeld) *Reese Witherspoon, Sally Field, Bob Newhart, Luke Wilson, Bruce McGill, Dana Ivey, Jennifer Coolidge.* After she's fired from her high-powered law firm for objecting to a client's animal testing practice, our heroine decides to use her formidable talents to change the law itself. Yep, it's *Ms. Woods Goes to Washington* — Capra's classic is even shown on a TV set, which should give you an idea of the subtlety of this second outing. What was fresh and cute in the original *Blonde* is tired and unfunny here. Witherspoon is fine, as usual, but old pros like Field and Newhart look understandably bored. McGill has his moments as a political conservative whose eyes are opened a bit when he discovers his beloved, manly dog is gay, and there are a smattering of smiles throughout. But coming from Reese and the director of the witty sleeper *Kissing Jessica Stein*, this should've had more snap — not to mention laughs. ★★ DVD Special Edition: $19.99, VHS Special Edition: $14.99

Legend

(1985, 89 min, GB, Ridley Scott) *Tom Cruise, Mia Sara, Tim Curry, David Bennent, Billy Barty.* Sexual undercurrents abound in this lavishly mounted and incredibly handsome fantasy about the Devil's attempts to gain control over a young girl. The film has its moments as a modern rendition of Grimm's Fairy Tales. It is symptomatic, however, of Scott's post-*Alien* inability to provide a forceful, powerful narrative in addition to his typical wealth of visual detail. ★★½ DVD Letterbox Ultimate Edition: $19.99, VHS: $9.99

The Legend

(1993, 100 min, Hong Kong, Corey Yuen) *Jet Li.* Another Jet Li vehicle comes to U.S. video in hobbled form. An inferior score, bad dubbing and choppy editing only accentuate this lesser Li entry's considerable flaws. In its original, widescreen, uncut and subtitled incarnation, *The Legend of Fong Sai-Yuk* (its Hong Kong title) is still a threadbare, overly silly story with some knockout action scenes. But this release is merely irritating, and Li fails to engage. However, the fight scenes are still here in all their glory, and — like a porn film or a clichéd musical — they're worth watching with index finger at the ready on the fast forward button. ★★ DVD Letterbox: $19.99, VHS: $9.99

The Legend of Bagger Vance

(2000, 125 min, US, Robert Redford) *Will Smith, Matt Damon, Charlize Theron.* An elegant but slow-moving period piece, director Redford's *The Legend of Bagger Vance* has all the romanticism of a wistful memory, but is unable to establish full-rounded characterizations or make their actions as compelling as they should be. Damon plays Rannulph Junuh, a golf prodigy who has hit the skids. He is given a second chance when a mystical, kindly stranger Bagger Vance (Smith) suddenly appears to guide him to the championships. Smith brings charm to the role of the

mysterious Vance, but the film can't make its mind up as to exactly who he is: vagabond, mystic, con man, apparition? It is this uncertainty that denies the film the magical realism it seeks. The acting is enchanting down to the smallest role, and Redford's pacing is elegiac and leisurely. ★★½ DVD: $19.99

The Legend of Dolemite: Bigger & Badder

(1994, 75 min, US, Foster Corder) *Rudy Ray Moore.* The Godfather of Rap, the black Lenny Bruce and the inspiration for comedians Richard Pryor and Eddie Murphy, recording artist, satirist/comedian and film star Moore is surprisingly unknown outside his nadir group of fans. With a tongue filthier than Richard Nixon on a bad day, Rudy Ray (aka Dolemite) has parlayed his macho urban braggadocio to a hilarious art form. This low-budget video, while technically below average, does feature interviews with Rudy Ray, scenes from his nightclub act (not to be missed is a disgustingly funny joke about Bill and Hillary Clinton), interviews with admirers (Ice-T, Eazy-E) and clips from his now-classic 1970s blaxploitation films. For fans a must; for neophytes, a coarse but entertaining eye-opener. ★★½ DVD: $14.99, VHS: $19.99

The Legend of Drunken Master

See: *Drunken Master II*

The Legend of Hell House

(1973, 95 min, GB, John Hough) *Roddy McDowall, Clive Revill, Pamela Franklin.* Four psychics agree to spend a week at a haunted mansion to discover why their colleagues, conducting experiments at the house years earlier, were murdered. One of the best of its genre, this is quite suspenseful and the scares are many. ★★★ DVD: $14.99, VHS: $9.99

The Legend of Suriyothai

(2003, 142 min, Thailand, Chatri Chalerm Yukol) *M.L. Piyapas Bhirombhakdi, Johnny Anfone, Sarunyu Wongkrachang, Mai Charoenpura.* A lavishly re-created historical drama of Thailand's queen Suriyothai and (get out your textbook!) account of the political intrigue, insider murders and bloody territorial battles that plagued 16th-century Thailand. With some truly gruesome battle scenes, *The Legend of Suriyothai* is a grand spectacle, but one which makes no concessions to those who go into the film without a thorough knowledge of Thai history. Thailand is still a loose collection of city-states, ruled over by whatever local king is strong enough to keep his enemies at bay. Our heroine Suriyothai is a minor princess in the court of the dominant city-state Ayudthaya. No less than three kings are murdered until Suriyothai becomes queen, risking her life in battle to defend her country. You can't help but be impressed by the beauty of the scenery, the exoticism of the film, the detail of the re-enactments and the graphic nature of the battles. But with a script that's heavy on plot and low on emotion, together with wooden acting, director Yukol (himself a member of the Thai royal family) concentrates more on cramming every detail of Thai history into the film, giving the impression it was made more to glorify the ancestors of Thailand's ruling family than to entertain a modern audience. (Thai with English subtitles) ★★½ DVD: $29.99

Jean Reno as *Léon: The Professional*

The Legend of the Suram Fortress

(1985, 87 min, USSR, Sergei Paradjanov) *Levan Outchanechvili, Zourab Kipchidze.* Based on ancient Georgian legend and dedicated to all Georgian warriors killed in defense of the Motherland, this unique, but for most viewers inscrutable, tale has minimal dialogue and dazzling visuals. When a newly built Georgian fortress mysteriously collapses, the townspeople are at a loss and vulnerable to attack. An aging soothsayer claims that the only way to keep the walls standing is to have the son of the lover who jilted her buried alive inside the walls. (Georgian with English subtitles) ★★★ DVD: $34.99, VHS: $59.99

The Legend of the Swordsman

(1991, 102 min, Hong Kong, Siu-Tung Ching & Stanley Tong) *Jet Li, Brigitte Lin, Michelle Reis.* A domestic release of the Hong Kong actioner *Swordsman II*, this is a near-bastardization of its source. Cut (seemingly arbitrarily) by eight minutes, terribly dubbed, and with a merely so-so transfer, *Legend of the Swordsman* nevertheless manages to be entertaining in its current form. Never a perfect film to begin with, the original doesn't compare to classics of the genre like *Iron Monkey* or *Chinese Ghost Story*, but this somewhat unwieldy supernatural action film still has a lot to recommend it, namely its exciting fight scenes. The convoluted story, about Li doing battle with a martial arts master out to control the world, is even more troublesome with the cuts and lousy dubbing, but Li fans should still enjoy it. Die-hard Li fans, however, should seek out the original Hong Kong release. ★★½ DVD: $19.99, VHS: $9.99

Legends of the Fall

(1994, 134 min, US, Edward Zwick) *Brad Pitt, Anthony Hopkins, Aidan Quinn, Henry Thomas, Julia Ormand, Tantoo Cardinal.* Like those fondly remembered soapers of the 1940s, *Legends of the Fall* is an old-fashioned melodrama which, while occasionally overdone in its dramatic construction, never fails to entertain. Beginning just before the start of WWI, the film stars Pitt as one of three sons of a stalwart Montana rancher (Hopkins). When their youngest brother (Thomas) returns home with a beautiful fiancée (Ormond), siblings Pitt and Quinn nuture romantic feelings for her. Thus sets in motion an encompassing story of love, betrayal, war and familial ties. Director Zwick allows his actors full range of emotions, and however good the ensemble is, all are upstaged by the sprawling locales and the film's gorgeous cinematography. ★★★½ DVD Letterbox: $14.99, DVD Letterbox Superbit Edition: $26.99, VHS Special Edition: $9.99

Legion of the Dead

(2000, 84 min, US/Germany, Olaf Ittenbach) *Michael Carr, Russell Friedenberg, Kimberly Liebe, Matthias Hues. Legion of the Dead* is an inept gore comedy from director Ittenbach (who became so incensed at a recent film festival audience's derisive comments about this film, he uttered one final expletive and stormed offstage). While the film aims for the heights of a *Re-Animator* or *Dead/Alive*, it falls *waaaay* short of those classics, and the rampant gore and extreme violence end up being painfully monotonous, unfunny, unscary and certainly not entertaining. Even with a group of rowdy friends and some mind-altering substances, *Legion* just plain stinks. ★ DVD: $24.99, VHS: $79.99

Legionnaire

(1998, 95 min, US, Peter MacDonald) *Jean-Claude Van Damme, Daniel Caltagirone, Nicholas Farrell, Steven Berkoff, Adewale Akinnuoye-Agbaje.* This Van Damme vehicle may be the first $35 million direct-to-video action flick. While it's easy to see why this dramatically flat adventure was overlooked for theatrical release, it's still leagues better than Van Damme's more recent efforts. This is an unabashedly old-fashioned adventure yarn in the mold of '30s & '40s serials, with nary a roundhouse kick in sight. Set in the 1920s, the film casts Jean-Claude as a French boxer who joins the Foreign Legion to escape the gangster he double-crossed. The film's pace is brisk, and the action is well-handled, and Van Damme is actually kind of appealing. The script is pure hokum, however. This is a mixed bag, but a nice change of pace for the Muscles from Brussels. ★★½ DVD: $14.99, VHS: $9.99

The Lemon Sisters

(1990, 93 min, US, Joyce Chopra) *Diane Keaton, Carol Kane, Kathryn Grody, Elliott Gould, Aidan Quinn, Ruben Blades.* A pleasant, low-key comedy with an accent on characterizations more than story, with Keaton, Kane and Grody as three childhood pals who are members of a singing group known as the Lemon Sisters; they're looking to make their mark in the nightclubs of Atlantic City. The performances are fine, though Kane steals the film with her delightful portrayal of the wacky and hopelessly mediocre singer (her solo performance is a highlight). ★★½ DVD: $24.99, VHS: $14.99

Leningrad Cowboys Go America

(1990, 80 min, Finland, Aki Kaurismäki) *Matti Pellonpaa, Kari Väänänen, Jim Jarmusch, Nicky Tesco.* Infused with his trademark droll sense of humor and peopled by an arresting cast of weirdos sporting gravity-defying hair and razor-sharp shoes, this Finnish comedy is a successful, albeit one-note, cultural satire. Beginning in the frozen tundra of Finland, a group of aspiring but not very good rock musicians decide to tour America seeking fame and fortune. An inopportune death, gigs in seedy Louisiana bars, and dumbfounded or bored-to-tears audiences prove to be little deterrence to these beer-guzzling aliens bent on becoming an overnight American success. Told with little dialogue and in neat vignettes, this misfits-on-the-road movie will prove to be a grinning delight for adventurous videophiles. ★★★

Lenny

(1974, 112 min, US, Bob Fosse) *Dustin Hoffman, Valerie Perrine, Jan Miner.* Adapted from Julian Barry's play, *Lenny* is a powerful and often touching portrait of the troubled and controversial comedian Lenny Bruce. Filmed in a richly textured black and white, *Lenny* features superb performances by Hoffman as the comic and Perrine as his wife, stripper Honey Harlowe. ★★★½ DVD Dual: $19.99

Léolo

(1992, 115 min, Canada, Jean-Claude Lauzon) *Maxime Collin, Ginette Reno, Roland Blouin.* A wonderful and rather bizarre coming-of-age tale, about an imaginative 12-year-old boy who believes he is the offspring of a Sicilian tomato (yes, the fruit). A clever mixture of reality and imagination, the film follows the exploits of young Léolo and his dysfunctional family: his parents who are obsessed with bowel movements; a dim-witted weight lifting brother; and a sister calmed only by her secret bug collection. The imagery is haunting, beautiful, disgusting and often hysterical, and the film is enhanced by beautiful cinematography and a soundtrack featuring Tom Waits and The Rolling Stones. (French with English subtitles) ★★★½

Léon: The Professional

(1994, 133 min, US/France, Luc Besson) *Gary Oldman, Jean Reno, Natalie Portman, Danny Aiello, Ellen Greene.* Besson retools his art-house hit *La Femme Nikita* for an American audience, expanding the role of "Victor the Cleaner" into that of a cuddly, lovable hit man who becomes the reluctant guardian and mentor of a precocious 12-year-old (Portman) when her family is executed by a psychotic, drug-dealing cop (Oldman in a role so over-the-top that Nicolas Cage probably fired his agent for not getting him the part). The twist comes when, hellbent for revenge, she asks him to teach her to kill. This director's cut of *The Professional* substantially expands the relationship between the two assassins (including more of the girl's desire to be violent and sexual, which was presumably too distasteful for prudish American audiences). ★★★½ DVD: $29.99

Léon Morin, Priest

(1961, 118 min, France, Jean-Pierre Melville) *Jean-Paul Belmondo, Emmanuelle Riva.* A lonely young widow (Riva) with anticlerical, atheist and Communist views meets and befriends a handsome young priest (Belmondo). Their lively exchange of ideas on religion and life soon results — almost against her will — in an "invasion by God" into her soul, and the process of conversion into Catholicism begins. Set during the German and Italian Occupation and the beginning days of the Liberation, this austere, intense lesson of independence, love and faith is reminiscent of Robert Bresson's works. While Belmondo's role as the almost saintly priest is glazed over, it is Riva's Barny — a determinedly independent, opinionated woman — that is quite memorable in this moving religious, political and allegorical drama. (French with English subtitles) ★★★

Leon the Pig Farmer

(1993, 98 min, GB, Gary Sinyor & Vadim Jean) *Mark Frankel, Janet Suzman, Brian Glover, Connie Booth.* A witty take on the Jewish mother syndrome, but this time from the British. Having just been fired from his job, the unmarried Leon takes a job with his mother's kosher catering service. While on a delivery to a local fertility clinic, he happens to find out that he was conceived by artificial insemination. What's a nice Jewish boy to do when he discovers that his father is in reality a pig farmer from a small English hamlet? Why, get to know his newly discovered parent, of course. The film features plenty of laughs, and Frankel is wonderful as Leon. ★★★

The Leopard

(1963, 185 min, Italy, Luchino Visconti) *Burt Lancaster, Claudia Cardinale, Alain Delon.* A meticulous, atmospheric epic about 19th-century Italian nobility with Lancaster in the title role as the Leopard, price Fabrizio de Salina, an aging aristocrat whose elegant world undergoes a dramatic upheaval during the social turbulence of the 1860s. Delon is his opportunistic nephew who siezes the chance to become a prominent officer in the revolutionary regime. Cardinale costars as Delon's ill-bred fiancée. A sumptuous portrait of a vanquished age featuring sparkling performances and a lavish Nino Rota score. ★★★½ DVD Criterion Collection 3-Disc Set: $49.99

The Leopard Man

(1943, 66 min, US, Jacques Tourneur) *Jean Brooks, Isabel Jewell, Dennis O'Keefe, Margo.* Val Lewton's follow-up to his highly successful *Cat People* is another first-rate, low-budget chiller, also directed by Tourneur. Set in a small New Mexico town, the search is on for an escaped leopard, which may be responsible for a series of gruesome killings. ★★★

Leprechaun

(1990, 91 min, US, Mark Jones) *Warwick Davis, Jennifer Aniston, Ken Olandt.* A playfully sadistic munchkin wreaks havoc when his personal possessions are threatened. No, it's not the latest entry in the *Home Alone* series. A leprechaun (Davis) from Ireland goes on killing spree to reclaim his stolen bag of gold. Having sat on the shelf for three years before its gratuitous theatrical release, the strictly rudimentary "insert fiend here" screenplay bears the

distinction of being quite possibly the only horror movie to be set in rural North Dakota. Oooh, scary? (Followed by 3 sequels) ★

Les Girls

(1957, 114 min, US, George Cukor) *Gene Kelly, Mitzi Gaynor, Kay Kendall, Tiana Elg.* Three showgirls take their former dancing partner to court; but during testimony, can't agree as to what really happened. A joyously entertaining musical with Kelly in good form as the hoofer. ★★★ DVD: $19.99, VHS: $14.99

Les Misérables

(1935, 108 min, US, Richard Boleslawski) *Fredric March, Charles Laughton, Cedric Hardwicke, Florence Eldridge.* Excellent adaptation of Victor Hugo's classic novel with March and Laughton giving great performances as, respectively, petty thief Valjean and relentless police inspector Javert. Remade several times, including as a Broadway musical. ★★★½ VHS: $9.99

Les Misérables

(1995, 174 min, France, Claude Lelouch) *Jean-Paul Belmondo, Michel Boujenah, Alessandra Martines, Clementine Celarie.* Victor Hugo's classic treatise on social injustice gets a radical updating by director Lelouch. His invigorating and spellbinding three-hour epic begins at the turn of the century as Fortin (Belmondo), a chauffeur, serves time in prison for his employer. Jumping many years forward to the Nazi Occupation, the story revolves around Fortin, Jr. (again Belmondo), who is helping a Jewish family make a run for the Swiss border. Fortin, an illiterate, has become fascinated with the parallels between himself and Hugo's hero Jean Valjean, and so he has his Jewish riders read the novel out loud for him. Lelouch then enacts these readings (with Belmondo playing Valjean) and draws the obvious analogies between Hugo's characters and those of Vichy France. Belmondo revels in his multiple roles, and his rich performance combined with Lelouch's ingenious screenplay makes for a one-of-a-kind classic. (French with English subtitles) ★★★★ VHS: $29.99

Les Misérables

(1998, 129 min, GB, Bille August) *Liam Neeson, Geoffrey Rush, Uma Thurman, Claire Danes, Hans Matheson.* A good cast breathes life into this solemn version of Victor Hugo's classic novel

which doesn't quite compare with the 1935 Fredric March-Charles Laughton version, but is rather a straightforward, condensed interpretation that tries to flesh out some of the more main characters. It's a good primer for those unfamiliar with the story. Neeson is properly stoic as Jean Valjean, a poor Frenchman who stole a loaf of bread and spent 19 years in prison for it. Rush is good at conveying the inner demons of Inspector Javert, the relentless policeman on Valjean's trail. The film is staged in an efficient if none-too-exciting manner, and the settings and costumes are evocative without being unduly opulent. ★★★ DVD: $19.99, VHS: $14.99

Less than Zero

(1987, 96 min, US, Marek Kanievska) *Andrew McCarthy, Jami Gertz, Robert Downey, Jr., James Spader, Tony Bill, Nicholas Pryor.* Never has a title more aptly fit its film. A creative void by all concerned has made this limp attempt to be the *Easy Rider* of the '80s alienated teen pic nothing more than a sad curiousity piece. Purging the ennui, drug taking and bisexuality of the novel for cheap moralistic posturing, the film is almost an antithesis of the Bret Easton Ellis best-seller. Downey is the only cast member with an active pulse while McCarthy and Gertz listlessly cruise the highways of L.A. as zombies in search of motivation, direction and characterization. ★ DVD: $14.99, VHS: $9.99

A Lesson in Love

(1954, 95 min, Sweden, Ingmar Bergman) *Eva Dahlbeck, Gunnar Björnstrand, Yvonne Lombard, Harriet Andersson.* This Bergman romantic comedy, lightweight but nonetheless satisfying, details the marital tensions and break up of a middle-aged gynecologist who, although happily married for 15 years, has a short affair with a patient. His wife finds out and abruptly leaves him to live with her former lover, his best friend. (Swedish with English subtitles) ★★★ VHS: $29.99

Lessons at the End of Spring

(1989, 75 min, Russia, Oleg Kavan) The triumph of the human spirit over repression and injustice is the theme of this emotionally powerful drama set in a Krushchev-era Soviet Union. A 13-year-old boy is mistakenly thrown into an adult prison where begins a harrowing odyssey in which inhuman treatment of the prisoners is the norm. Despite this, our young hero retains, throughout, his naive sense of justice as well as his defiant survival instincts. Not only great

Les Misérables (1995)

storytelling, but startling in its unflinching criticism of the Soviet state. (Russian with English subtitles) ★★★½ VHS: $59.99

Let Him Have It

(1991, 115 min, GB, Peter Medak) *Christopher Eccleston, Paul Reynolds, Tom Courtenay.* This chilling and engrossing drama is based on an actual incident which led Great Britain to reevaluate, and eventually abolish, its death penalty. Set in the '50s, amidst the ruins of a bombed-out London still recovering from the war, the story follows the demise of a quiet, learning-disabled and epileptic young man who naïvely falls in with a group of Hollywood gangster-influenced, would-be thugs. When a bungled robbery attempt leads to the cold-blooded killing of a policeman, he finds himself not only implicated in the murder, but also subject to the wrath of a vengeful society seeking blood. ★★★½ VHS: $14.99

Let It Be

(1970, 80 min, GB, Michael Lindsay-Hogg) A fascinating look at the final days of the world's most famous rock group, punctuated by the Beatles' great songs and the legendary "rooftop" concert sequence. It is a wistful film, full of portentous glances, asides and remarks. It captures the group at the moment before the end, and is important viewing for all music fans. ★★★

Let It Ride

(1989, 91 min, US, Joe Pytka) *Richard Dreyfuss, Teri Garr, Jennifer Tilly, Robbie Coltrane, David Johansen.* A surprisingly appealing lark. Dreyfuss is a winner as a race track gambler whose wish for a "great day" comes true when he becomes privy to a hot tip. Garr has some nice moments as his long-suffering wife, Tilly is her usual delightful self as a gambler's gal and Coltrane is a scene-stealer as a track cashier. ★★★ DVD Letterbox: $19.99, VHS: $14.99

Let the Devil Wear Black

(1999, 95 min, US, Stacy Title) *Jonathan Penner, Mary-Louise Parker, Jacqueline Bisset, Philip Baker Hall, Jamey Sheridan, Chris Sarandon.* If Quentin Tarantino had ever decided to update and desecrate Shakespeare's "Hamlet," he might have come up with this relentlessly irreverent black comedy about a fresh-out-of-rehab L.A. rich kid (Penner) haunted by the idea that his uncle (Sheridan) may have killed his father and now plans to marry his not-so-grief-stricken mother (Bisset). But in order to take revenge, he must survive a night populated by L.A. gangbangers, drug-dealing best friends, and an unknown assassin hired by his uncle to kill him. The script (cowritten by the star and the director) is so venomously witty, you'll forget it's Shakespeare. ★★★

Let's Dance

(1950, 112 min, US, Norman Z. McLeod) *Fred Astaire, Betty Hutton, Roland Young.* Astaire is the song-and-dance man who helps ex-partner Hutton battle her deceased husband's grandmother for custody of her young son. Some good dance sequences get lost in the sentimental story. ★★ VHS: $14.99

Let's Do It Again

(1975, 112 min, US, Sidney Poitier) *Sidney Poitier, Bill Cosby, Jimmie Walker, John Amos, Ossie Davis, Denise Nicholas, Calvin Lockhart.* Poitier and Cosby are back together again in this very funny sequel to *Uptown Saturday Night.* This time around, Poitier and Cosby scheme to turn neophyte Walker into a champion boxer — through hypnosis — in order to save their lodge. High-spirited and lots of fun. ★★★ DVD: $19.99

Let's Get Lost

(1987, 119 min, US, Bruce Weber) *Chet Baker, Chris Isaak, Andy Minsker, Lisa Marie.* The life and music of jazz great Chet Baker is the subject of this poignant, fascinating documentary by noted photographer Weber. In fact, Weber's roots show to tremendous effect as this examination of a tortured artist's genius and self-destruction looks every bit as handsome as its subject in his early years. Weber splendidly intercuts rare recording sessions, interviews with family and friends, and even includes clips from Baker's short-lived movie career in the 1950s. The scenes of Baker's later years are heartbreakingly sad as the ravages of drug addiction had clearly taken its toll on this legendary trumpeter. ★★★½

Let's Make Love

(1960, 118 min, US, George Cukor) *Marilyn Monroe, Yves Montand, Tony Randall.* A well-intentioned misfire, this sporadically amusing musical stars Montand as a millionaire who learns he is to be parodied in an off-Broadway show. He becomes intent on closing the show until he sees leading lady Marilyn, and, well, you know the rest. This could have been a lot more palatable had anyone other than Montand starred as the millionaire. ★★ DVD: $14.99, VHS: $6.99

Let's Talk about Sex

(1998, 82 min, US, Troy Beyer) *Troy Beyer, Paget Brewster, Randi Ingerman, Joseph C. Phillips.* Director Beyer stars as Jasmine, an ambitious young woman putting together a demo tape for a proposed TV show. She selects potential interviewees from students at that staunch bastion of intellectual pursuit, the University of Miami, to discuss — guess what? — their sex lives. The film spends much of its time basking in the hormonal splendor of the beach and bar scene, which is considerable. For much of the time, the film is crappy, soft-core sexploitation. While occasionally attempting forays into the insightful and sensitive, it depends way too much on faux gravity and tacky titillation. There are a few authentic moments (Michelle and her mom, Jasmine's secret) which unfortunately occur way too deep into the film, way too little too late. An earnest, film school, South Beach attempt. ★ VHS: $19.99

Lethal Weapon

(1987, 110 min, US, Richard Donner) *Mel Gibson, Danny Glover, Gary Busey, Mitchell Ryan, Darlene Love.* Gibson unleashes a charismatically explosive action persona in this rousing and violent cop vs. druggies movie. He plays an emotionally off-balanced undercover cop with Glover costarring as his stable, family man partner; and together, they become embroiled in a series of tense and exciting situations. Combining humor, action and more action to great advantage, this started a whole new buddy pic genre — this remains one of the best of its kind. (Followed by 3 sequels) ★★★½ DVD Letterbox: $19.99, VHS Director's Cut: $9.99, VHS Letterbox Director's Cut: $9.99

Lethal Weapon 2

(1989, 113 min, US, Richard Donner) *Mel Gibson, Danny Glover, Joe Pesci, Joss Ackland, Patsy Kensit, Darlene Love.* Mel and Danny are back, and as the old movie ads used to say, they're bigger and better than ever. As in the original, Gibson and Glover have redefined the genre with a spontaneous, fresh repartee which is as entertaining as it is humorous. Plot really takes a back seat to the fast, frantic action scenes and the delectable rapport between the two stars. But for the record, Roger and Martin find themselves up against a ruthless South African

diplomat, who happens to be a part-time drug dealer. Pesci does the impossible by stealing the show as a loquacious, ingratiating accountant being protected by Mel and Danny. ★★★½ DVD Letterbox: $19.99, VHS Director's Cut: $9.99, VHS Letterbox Director's Cut: $9.99

Lethal Weapon 3

(1992, 118 min, US, Richard Donner) *Mel Gibson, Danny Glover, Joe Pesci, Rene Russo, Stuart Wilson, Darlene Love.* In this average third installment, Roger (Glover) and Martin (Gibson) uncover a scheme to steal high-powered weaponry from police storage, with the prime suspect being a corrupt ex-cop. Along the way they are investigated by a sexy Internal Affairs officer (Russo) who conveniently winds up with the hots for Riggs. Pesci reprises his role as low-life Leo Getz and delivers some of the film's best one-liners. Despite a screenplay which resists all logic, director Donner's flair for humor and chase scenes, along with Gibson and Glover's charisma and on-screen chemistry, makes for a mindless though entertaining ride. ★★½ DVD Letterbox: $19.99, VHS Director's Cut: $9.99, VHS Letterbox Director's Cut: $9.99

Lethal Weapon 4

(1998, 120 min, US, Richard Donner) *Mel Gibson, Danny Glover, Rene Russo, Joe Pesci, Chris Rock, Jet Li, Darlene Love.* Warner Brothers may be going to the well once too often with this fourth installment in the series. Unnecessary though mildly entertaining, the film gets by with what made the original such a memorable actioner: the terrific rapport between Gibson and Glover. Though gone is Gibson's angst-ridden characteristics of Martin Riggs (he's found love, you know), the two stars know these guys awfully well, and it is their portrayals which make *4* watchable. This time around, Riggs and Murtaugh take on members of a Chinese syndicate. There's a couple of good action scenes, but the film is offset by a nonchalance in tone, scenes and jokes which go on too long. ★★½ DVD Letterbox: $19.99, VHS: $9.99, VHS Letterbox: $14.99

The Letter

(1940, 95 min, US, William Wyler) *Bette Davis, Herbert Marshall, James Stephenson, Gale Sondergaard.* Davis and director Wyler's second film together (after their success with *Jezebel*) is a knockout adaptation (and second screen version) of W. Somerset Maugham's novel about a tycoon's wife who murders her lover and claims self-defense; only to be a victim of blackmail when "the letter" proves otherwise. ★★★½

Letter from an Unknown Woman

(1948, 90 min, US, Max Ophüls) *Joan Fontaine, Louis Jourdan, Mady Christians.* Lush romantic drama with Fontaine suffering from cinema's worst case of unrequited love as she is obsessed with musician Jourdan. A film of visual splendor; and one that, thanks to director Ophüls' sturdy direction, avoids the clichés usually found in melodramas. ★★★

Letter to Brezhnev

(1985, 94 min, GB, Chris Bernard) *Peter Firth, Alfred Molina, Alexander Prigg, Margi Clarke.* A bawdy, low-budget comedy about two Liverpool girls, looking for sex and romance, who chance upon two Soviet sailors in a local disco. It offers a vibrant, gritty portrait of young people in the harsh industrial wasteland of northern England as they look for love and dream of escape from their dreary daily lives. ★★★

A Letter to Three Wives

(1949, 103 min, US, Joseph L. Mankiewicz) *Ann Sothern, Jeanne Crain, Linda Darnell, Kirk Douglas, Paul Douglas, Thelma Ritter, Jeffrey Lynn.* A year before he would write and direct the classic *All About Eve*, Mankiewicz won two Oscars for both writing and directing this scintillating and extremely witty comedy-drama which dissects and devours, among other things, marriage, education, consumerism and social strata. Three suburban matrons learn that one of their husbands has run off with another woman. Told in three flashbacks, the story focuses on each couple's shaky marital history while giving clues as to whom the dastardly Addie (who is never seen) betrayed. Sothern runs away with the picture as the socially ambitious wife of teacher K. Douglas. P. Douglas makes a terrific film debut as another husband. ★★★★ VHS: $19.99

Letters from My Windmill

(1954, 134 min, France, Marcel Pagnol) *Henri Velbert, Yvonne Gamy.* Pagnol's splendid trilogy of short tales. "Three Low Masses": The Devil takes over the body of a dunce and torments a priest. "The Elixer of Father Gaushet": Brother Gauchier inherits some home-made brew and begins to sell the wine for charitable purposes. "The Secret of Master Cornielle": A sentimental story of an ancient miller who for 18 years had been pretending to compete with a modern steam mill. (French with English subtitles) ★★★ VHS: $59.99

Letters from the Park

(1988, 85 min, Cuba, Tomás Gutiérrez Alea) *Victor Laplace, Ivonne Lopez.* Adapted from a Gabriel García Márquez short story, this elegant tale of innocence, romance and forbidden love is set in turn-of-the-century Cuba. Shy young lovers Juan and Maria are attracted to one another, but find it impossible to articulate their feelings. They each enlist an older man to compose beautifully poetic love letters to the other, letters that eventually bring the two together. Problems arise after the poet, swept away with their romance and his own repressed feelings, falls in love with the young woman but is forced to keep his feelings silent. This Spanish "Cyrano de Bergerac" — without the nose — is a wonderfully enchanting, dreamy and seemingly universal story. (Spanish with English subtitles) ★★★

Leviathan

(1989, 98 min, US, George Pan Cosmatos) *Peter Weller, Richard Crenna, Ernie Hudson, Amanda Pays, Daniel Stern.* The director's in over his head and the actors out of their depth trying to pump life into this tale about a monster terrorizing an undersea community. ★ DVD: $14.99

Lewis & Clark & George

(1996, 90 min, US, Rod McCall) *Rose McGowan, Salvator Xuereb, Dan Gunther, Art LeFleur, Paul Bartel, James Brolin.* On an exploration for a gold mine, ex-convicts Lewis (Xuereb) and Clark (Gunther) meet George (McGowan), a mute woman who is also on the lam. As this trio ride a bullet-paved path through the Southwest, friendship is tested, love blossoms, and betrayal rears its ugly head. *Lewis & Clark & George* offers nothing new in its depiction of greed prompting a killing spree, but writer-director McCall does employ some arty storytelling techniques as the bodies pile up. The three leads are attractive, but their characters are unlikable, and it becomes difficult to care who will survive and if the gold will ever be found. ★★ DVD: $9.99, VHS: $9.99

Li'l Abner

(1959, 113 min, US, Melvin Frank) *Peter Palmer, Leslie Parrish, Stubby Kaye, Julie Newmar.* Colorful screen version of the hit Broadway musical, based on Al Capp's comic strip, about the eccentric citizens of Dogpatch, USA. The story follows Li'l Abner, a muscle-bound loafer, and his romantic near-misses with beautiful girlfriend Daisy Mae. The story and lyrics are as witty and sardonic as Capp's strip often was. Songs include the politically astute "The Country's in the Very Best of Hands." ★★★ VHS: $14.99

Les Liaisons Dangereuses

(1960, 111 min, France, Roger Vadim) *Jeanne Moreau, Gerard Philip, Jean-Louis Trintignant.* Vadim's riveting version of Choderlos De Laclos' decadent tale of the sexual games of the morally bankrupt is set within the chic and smoky jazz clubs of modern-day Paris. Moreau and Philip are the wealthy couple in a marriage where adultery and deceit are allowed and even encouraged just as long as love is absent. Philip's Valmont is a debonair, mysterious manipulator whose conquests are recounted to, and equalled by, Moreau — his wickedly duplicitous wife Juliette. The film, possibly Vadim's best, pulsates with sexual energy and excitement with its cool mood enhanced by a sultry jazz score by Thelonious Monk with Art Blakey and the Jazz Messengers. "C'est la guerre." "Tres bien, la guerre!" (French with English subtitles) (Remade in 1988 as *Dangerous Liaisons* and in 1999 as *Cruel Intentions*) ★★★½ DVD: $24.99, VHS: $79.99, VHS: $19.99

Liam

(2001, 91 min, GB, Stephen Frears) *Ian Hart, Claire Hackett, Anthony Borrows, Anne Reid, David Hart, Megan Burns.* An intimate, heartfelt drama from director Frears, who returns to the more personal kind of filmmaking that defined his early career, *Liam* is a captivating, lyrical portrait of one family's struggle against poverty and, sometimes, themselves. Set in 1930s Liverpool, the story is seen through the eyes of the adorable eight-year-old Liam (Borrows), an impish, wide-eyed heartbreaker who is too distracted by his upcoming First Communion to initially notice all the family tension caused by his father's unemployment. But notice it he will, as the family gradually disintegrates when his father (I. Hart) looks for salvation with a group of fascists. Unlike the similarly themed and set *Angela's Ashes*, an undercurrent of humor is used to offset the tragic events happening around them, bringing more definition to all the characters. Like its namesake, *Liam* sees a most difficult world and approaches it with charm, resilience and promise. ★★★½ DVD: $24.99

Lianna

(1982, 113 min, US, John Sayles) *Linda Griffiths, Jo Henderson, Jane Hallaren, Jessica Wight MacDonald, Jon DeVries, John Sayles, Maggie Renzi.* Director-writer Sayles' exceptional and humorous exploration of the coming out of the "good wife" offers a compassionate view of lesbianism, self-determination and unrest. Lianna (Griffiths) confronts her husband's infidelity, falls in love with her graduate instructor and sets out on her own. Sayles directs with a sensitive hand, and his perceptive screenplay contains many vulnerable and tender moments examining one woman's budding lesbian self-realization. ★★★ DVD: $19.99

Liar, Liar

(1997, 87 min, US, Tom Shadyac) *Jim Carrey, Maura Tierney, Swoosie Kurtz, Jennifer Tilly, Cary Elwes, Justin Cooper.* In this often hilarious but frequently mawkish comedy, Carrey plays a divorced father and unscrupulous lawyer; unfortunately for his adoring five-year-old son, not in that order. Making a birthday wish, young Cooper wishes his father could go one day without telling a lie. This starts a terrific premise which is realized most of the time. Watching Carrey blurt out the truth at the most inopportune times is truly funny. And his boardroom rant is classic. However, most of the scenes with his son and ex-wife are maudlin; you expect Carrey to skewer this kind of sap, not embrace it. ★★½ DVD Letterbox Collector's Edition: $19.99, DVD Pan & Scan: $19.99, DVD DTS sound: $19.99, VHS: $9.99, VHS Letterbox: $19.99

Liar's Moon

(1983, 106 min, US, David Fisher) *Matt Dillon, Cindy Fisher, Yvonne DeCarlo, Susan Tyrrell, Hoyt Axton, Broderick Crawford.* A teen from the wrong side of the tracks (Dillon) falls for the richest girl in town (Fisher), much against the wishes of both families, who carry a dark secret that could ruin the lovers' chance at happiness. Dillon's passionate performance elevates this otherwise familiar, star-crossed lovers romantic drama. ★★ DVD: $9.99

Libeled Lady

(1936, 98 min, US, Jack Conway) *Spencer Tracy, William Powell, Myrna Loy, Jean Harlow, Walter Connolly, Hattie McDaniel.* Classic screwball comedy featuring an impeccable cast. Tracy is a scheming newspaper editor looking for a story; he hires Powell (a hilarious performance and what a great fisherman!) to implicate heiress Loy in a romantic scandal. Harlow rounds out the powerhouse cast as Tracy's long-suffering fiancée. ★★★½ VHS: $19.99

The Liberation of L.B. Jones

(1969, 101 min, US, William Wyler) *Lee J. Cobb, Barbara Hershey, Roscoe Lee Browne, Lola Falana, Anthony Zerbe, Yaphet Kotto.* A race-conscious town in Tennessee is divided over the scandalous divorce of a black lawyer and his adulterous wife, who has been having an affair with a white cop. Wyler deftly demonstrates the sexual and racial passions boiling over in the tiny town, but the screenplay can't overcome its melodramatic roots. ★★½

Liberty Heights

(1999, 128 min, US, Barry Levinson) *Adrien Brody, Bebe Neuwirth, Joe Mantegna, Ben Foster.* Another autobiographical, Baltimore-based Levinson film (in the spirit of *Diner* and *Avalon*), which is where his strengths lie. Brody and Foster play Jewish boys growing up in 1950s Baltimore, standing up to the anti-Semitic (and racist, snobby) community while discovering cross-cultural romance. Mantegna plays their father, who balances his time between the burlesque house he runs and a gambling operation. Plenty of smart comedy within a touching, serious framework. ★★★½ DVD: $9.99, VHS: $14.99

Liberty Stands Still

(2002, 96 min, US/Canada, Kari Skogland) *Wesley Snipes, Linda Fiorentino, Oliver Platt.* The fact that Liberty is actually Fiorentino's gun-manufacturing-magnate character's name, and she must not move from her spot in a public park or an unseen sniper will kill her (with one of her company's top-sellers, to boot), should tip you off to how subtle this film is. Despite its heavy-handedness, however, it does have a decent, pulpy premise (nearly identical to the Larry Cohen-scripted *Phone Booth*), and a good, marquee-friendly cast, though it never becomes the smart diatribe on gun control it so wants to be. Several suspenseful sequences and excellent turns by Fiorentino and Snipes nearly compensate for an unsatisfying wrap-up and a plot hole or two. ★★½ DVD: $24.99

Licence to Kill

(1989, 133 min, GB, John Glen) *Timothy Dalton, Robert Davi, Talisa Soto, Carey Lowell.* Dalton makes his second appearance as agent 007, and while he may not make anyone forget the one and only Sean Connery, he proves once and for all that Moore is less. In this exciting and well-paced adventure, set mostly in Miami and Central America, Bond loses his "licence to kill" when he sets out to avenge the murder of his friend's wife. There are, to be sure, hair-raising action scenes and the trademark Bond humor, plus two beautiful costars in Soto and Lowell — the latter demonstrating that Bond women have finally grown up and can definitely hold their own with the big guys. (Sequel: *Goldeneye*) ★★★ DVD: $19.99

Lie Down with Dogs

(1995, 84 min, US, Wally White) *Wally White, Bash Halow, Randy Becker, James Sexton, Darren Dryden.* Though this low-budget comedy does have its share of laughs, it's saddled with poor acting and a plot line you couldn't hang your Calvin Kleins on. A relentlessly grinning Tommie (writer-director White) decides to chuck his job in sweaty New York for three months of pleasure in gay mecca Provincetown. He tries to find a job as a houseboy ("In Provincetown, you don't apply, you audition!"), and quickly dives into a series of sexual escapades. The film's most interesting character is that of Tom, a handsome, Brazilian mooch (played by Becker) — possibly because Becker is the only one that can act. ★★ DVD: $19.99

Liebelei

(1932, 83 min, Germany, Max Ophüls) *Wolfgang Liebeneiner, Magda Schneider.* Suppressed by the Nazis for years and subsequently rarely seen, *Liebelei* finds Ophüls' visual style yet to exhibit the long, languid tracking shots of his later works such as *La Ronde* or *The Earrings of Madame de...*, though it shares with them a common theme. This, his first big success, is another of his meditation on the nature of love — here a love blocked not so much by class strata, but by class custom. In late 19th-century Vienna, a philandering lieutenant vows to mend his ways when he falls for a woman of a more modest station. Unfortunately, he soon becomes the victim of his past. Though *Liebelei* is not remarkable in either story or storytelling, Ophüls' unsteady but promising directorial hand allows this somber love story to be of historical interest. (German with English subtitles) ★★½ VHS: $24.99

Liebestraum

(1991, 105 min, US, Mike Figgis) *Kevin Anderson, Kim Novak, Bill Pullman, Max Perlich, Catherine Hicks.* An absorbing, noir-influenced thriller which skillfully merges two violent, obsessive love triangles, 40 years apart. Anderson is an architectural journalist who, while on a visit to his home town to see his dying mother (Novak in a wonderful supporting role), meets an old friend, Paul (Pullman). Paul is a real estate developer in the process of tearing down a main street department store which has been shuttered for 40 years after the gruesome double murder of its owner and his mistress. The

writer's interest in the building and its mysterious past causes him to become romantically involved with Paul's wife, who is photographing the building's destruction. The result is a torrid tale of lust and jealousy. This is the director's cut, seven minutes longer than the theatrical version. ★★★ DVD Letterbox: $19.99

Lies

(1999, 115 min, Korea, Jang Sun Woo) *Lee Sang Hyun, Kim Tae Yeon.* In the surprisingly compelling sexual drama *Lies*, a married 38 year old begins an obsessive, S&M affair with an 18-year-old virgin. Containing graphic sex (ranging from steamy to disturbing), the film boasts nearly every position imaginable, as well as paddles, rubber hoses — you get the picture. To the film's credit, this is one of the few sex-themed films where the sex is the drama; it isn't just used as titillating filler à la your typical "erotic thriller." There is also the sporadically used (but effective) technique of the actors commenting on their roles, and the director reflecting on the banned novel on which the film is based. An original if sometimes unsettling exercise in sexual dynamics and excess. (Korean with English subtitles) ★★★ DVD: $24.99, VHS: $14.99

Life

(1999, 108 min, US, Ted Demme) *Eddie Murphy, Martin Lawrence, Obba Babatunde, Ned Beatty, Bokeem Woodbine, Nick Cassavetes, Clarence Williams III, R. Lee Ermey, Rick James.* Murphy and Lawrence make a solid comic team in this unexpectedly dramatic comedy spanning 55 years in the lives of two convicts. Con man Ray (Murphy) and law-abiding Claude (Lawrence) meet when both run afoul of bootlegger Spanky (James). They immediately don't hit it off. Things go from bad to worse when they are both sent to prison for a murder they didn't commit. That the filmmakers can derive any comedy from this premise is a marvel, but they have two top comedians with Murphy and Lawrence, who both have a field day with the material. Their constant bickering is cause for many a laugh, and when this aims to be funny, it is. But there's a serious subtext to the story, and though it may not be handled with total sensitivity, it makes for compelling dramatics. ★★★ DVD Letterbox: $14.99, VHS: $14.99

The Life and Death of Colonel Blimp

(1943, 115 min, GB, Emeric Pressburger & Michael Powell) *Roger Livesey, Deborah Kerr, Anton Wolbrook.* A memorable British wartime classic which follows the long and eventful life of a prosperous, old-fashioned officer of the British Army. At 115 minutes, the video version of this tale, which winds its way through several wars and four different women (all played by Kerr!), is regrettably a full 48 minutes shorter than the theatrical cut. ★★★★ DVD Criterion Collection: $39.99

Life and Nothing But

(1990, 135 min, France, Bertrand Tavernier) *Philippe Noiret, Sabine Azéma, Françoise Perrot.* Tavernier's film is a somber, meditative yet romantic exploration of war, loneliness and love. Noiret stars as a cynical army officer assigned to catalogue the dead, injured and missing French soldiers at the end of WWI. The story revolves around two women, one an elegant lady and the other a young waitress, who both travel to the rain-drenched and battle-scarred fields of the front and solicit the aid of Noiret in finding their missing husbands. A thoughtful film on the emotional healing process. (French with English subtitles) ★★★½

The Life and Times of Allen Ginsberg

(1993, 83 min, US, Jerry Aronson) *William Burroughs, Jack Kerouac, Allen Ginsberg.* Enlightening and highly entertaining, this intimate portrait of visionary Beat poet and self-proclaimed "faggot and individualist" Allen Ginsberg seeks to venture beyond his fame and controversy to explore the man who has dedicated his work and life "to ease the pain of living." Through photos and interviews with relatives, friends and Ginsberg himself, the film begins with his influential childhood and follows him to his Greenwich Village days and initial success as a poet (and his friendship with Beat poets Jack Kerouac and William Burroughs). The film also touches upon his anti-Vietnam War activities, and the mellower years which followed. ★★★

The Life and Times of Hank Greenberg

(2000, 95 min, US, Aviva Kempner) *Hank Greenberg, Ira Berkow, Bob Feller, Walter Matthau, Alan Dershowitz, Charlie Gehringer, Senator Carl Levin, Congressman Sander Levin, Michael Moriarty, Ralph Kiner.* It's been said that baseball is slow and documentaries are boring. So what happens when you make a documentary about baseball? In the case of the fascinating *The Life and Times of Hank Greenberg*, both clichés get smashed like a Greenberg home run. With thoughtful interviews of family, friends and fans interspersed with newsreel footage of the time, director Kempner presents a detailed account not only about the life of baseball legend Greenberg, but what the Jewish superstar meant to his community, especially during Hitler's reign, and how rampant anti-Semitism in the 1930s and '40s affected the game. Kempner coaxes heartfelt and spirited accounts of Greenberg's legend, and makes exciting the ballplayer's chase of Babe Ruth's home run record (before Roger, Mark, Sammy, Barry) in 1938 when Greenberg hit 58 round trippers. Having led the Detroit Tigers to two World Series championships, what impresses most about Greenberg is — a few years before Jackie Robinson would endure the same — how he withstood the racial taunts from fans and players, alike; always carrying himself with dignity and class. A fitting tribute to a heroic figure of the 20th century. ★★★★ DVD: $9.99, VHS: $9.99

The Life and Times of Judge Roy Bean

(1972, 120 min, US, John Huston) *Paul Newman, Anthony Perkins, Ned Beatty, Victoria Principal, Jacqueline Bisset, Tab Hunter, Roddy McDowall, Ava Gardner, John Huston, Stacy Keach.* Newman plays the legendary outlaw in this not-quite-a-western. It's an interesting, unusually self-aware but slightly uneven film, with a star-studded cast. ★★½ DVD: $19.99, VHS: $14.99

Life Begins for Andy Hardy

(1941, 102 min, US, George B. Seitz) *Mickey Rooney, Judy Garland, Lewis Stone.* In this 11th Andy Hardy outing, Rooney is off to take a bite out of the Big Apple, but finds the big city can be tough on a small-town boy. Garland is the perky Betsy Booth. This entry in the popular series is easier going and has less of a sentimental quota than most of the earlier films. ★★½ VHS: $19.99

A Life in the Theatre

(1993, 78 min, US, Gregory Mosher) *Jack Lemmon, Matthew Broderick.* Lemmon and Broderick offer fine performances in this very capable made-for-cable adaptation of David Mamet's play. The comedic piece is more of an excuse for Mamet to offer a portrait of actors fretting their hour upon the stage rather than a conventional story. Here, more so than in most of Mamet's film works, it is clearly the rhythm of his dialogue that is the real star. Though plot and characterization are very subtle here, both stars appear proficient and quite comfortable with Mamet-speak (even allowing themselves to be upstaged by it), which only further elevates the production. ★★★

Life Is a Long Quiet River

(1987, 89 min, France, Etienne Chatiliez) *Benoit Magimel, Helene Vincent.* The Quesnoys are a well-bred, bourgeois Catholic family living in France. Everything is wonderful and polite in their lives until one fateful day when they discover that, in the delivery room twelve years prior, their doctor had switched their son with the daughter of the Groseille family, a sordid group of low-income slobs from The Other Side of Town. What ensues is an entertaining farce as the Groseilles attempt to get every penny they can out of the "accident" and the Quesnoys struggle to keep their family values intact. A comic and often caustic commentary on social classes and the family unit. (French with English subtitles) ★★★½ VHS: $29.99

Life Is Beautiful

(1981, 102 min, Italy, Grigorig Ciukhrai) *Giancarlo Giannini, Ornella Muti.* The title of this tense and electrifying drama is purely ironic. Set during the politically unstable situation in pre-revolutionary Lisbon, the story concerns itself with the false arrest of a man. He is beaten, imprisoned and kept away from his wife and family. His political neutrality and personal sanity are severely tested by his abusive jailers. ★★★

Life Is Beautiful

(1998, 114 min, Italy, Roberto Benigni) *Roberto Benigni, Nicoletta Braschi, Giorgio Cantarini, Giustino Durano, Horst Buchholz.* Recalling the physical grace and comic timing of Chaplin, Benigni takes the subject of the Holocaust and makes a personal and extraordinary fable about one dedicated father. In 1939, Guido (Benigni) falls in love with schoolteacher Dora (Braschi). He courts her with laughter, humor and heart; and the two marry. It's several years later, and they have a wonderful son, Joshua (Cantarini), and a happy marriage. But Italy is now under fascist rule, and the Jewish Guido and his family are sent to a concentration camp. Desperate to keep the horrific reality of their situation from his son, Guido devises a series of charades and stories to make Joshua think they are in an elaborate game (the winner gets a real tank!). *Life Is Beautiful* is an astonishing comedy, and a heartrending story of sacrifice and, ultimately, love. Winner of 3 Oscars, including Best Actor and Foreign Film. (Italian with English subtitles) ★★★★ DVD: $19.99, VHS Subtitled: $9.99, VHS Dubbed: $9.99

Life Is Sweet

(1991, 102 min, GB, Mike Leigh) *Alison Steadman, Jim Broadbent, Jane Horrocks, Claire Skinner, Timothy Spall.* Leigh follows his wickedly satirical *High Hopes* with this mirthful and touching slice of middle-class life set in the English Midlands. Taking on the notion of family dysfunctionality, the film fol-lows the daily trials of a middle-aged couple (Steadman, Broadbent) and their twentysomething twin daughters — one an aspiring plumber (Skinner), the other an aspiring radical feminist (Horrocks). The common obsession in the film is food. Dad's a chef in a hotel kitchen, family friend Aubrey (Spall) is gonzo over the gourmet restaurant he's opening and Horrocks is an anorexic/bulimic. Leigh masterfully takes this soap opera situation and creates a wry, witty comedy filled with social commentary and a surprising amount of tender moments. ★★★½

Life Is to Whistle

(1998, 106 min, Cuba, Fernando Perez) *Luis Alberto Garcia, Isabel Santos, Coralia Veloz.* Director Pérez has weaved a tribute to life in Havana admirably blending humor, music, sex and a touch of magical realism. Our tour guide of Cuba is the (literally) underwater narrator, Bebe, who tells the tale of three orphans: Elpidio, a musician lamenting his absent mother (not too subtly named "Cuba"); Julia, a woman who faints whenever she hears the word "sex"; and Marianna, a man-loving dancer who vows celibacy to God in exchange for the lead role in an upcoming ballet. Pérez shows the vitality, color and beauty of life in Havana without omitting the poverty, political and social strife of its people. The sentimental film is both funny and touching, but at times is marred by obvious symbolism and an overly fairy tale-esque ending that neatly ties the three tales together. (Spanish with English subtitles) ★★½ DVD: $19.99, VHS: $29.99

A Life Less Ordinary

(1997, 103 min, US, Danny Boyle) *Ewan McGregor, Cameron Diaz, Holly Hunter, Delroy Lindo, Ian Holm, Stanley Tucci, Tony Shalhoub, Dan Hedaya, Judith Ivey.* After the brilliant success of *Shallow Grave* and especially *Trainspotting*, the third film in the "bag-of-money" trilogy from director Boyle is a curious misfire. Despite a beautifully realized opening sequence which confirms that the filmmakers have talent to waste, this romantic-comedy-action-musical-fantasy tries to pay homage to just about every genre imaginable. The story involves two angels (Hunter, Lindo) who are given the thankless task of uniting heiress Diaz and ex-janitor-turned-kidnapper McGregor — or else. While the outcome is obvious, getting there is no picnic.

Life Is Beautiful (1998)

Viewers will have to endure a schizophrenic pastiche which features both a *Road Warrior* tribute and a knock-out karaoke number. A clumsy piece of whimsy. ★★½ DVD: $9.99, VHS: $9.99

The Life of Emile Zola

(1937, 116 min, US, William Dieterle) *Paul Muni, Gale Sondergaard, Joseph Schildkraut, Gloria Holden.* In one of the best of the 1930s Hollywood biographies, Muni gives a remarkably controlled performance as the famed French author. Gale Sondergaard is well-cast as his wife, and Schildkraut won a supporting Oscar as the wrongly accused Captain Dreyfus, for whom Zola intervened. Winner of 3 Academy Awards including Best Picture. ★★★★

A Life of Her Own

(1950, 108 min, US, George Cukor) *Lana Turner, Ray Milland, Tom Ewell, Louis Calhern, Ann Dvorak, Jean Hagen.* Lana plays a Midwestern girl who moves to New York to start a career in modeling. In no time, she's on all the magazine covers. She also becomes involved with married tycoon Milland, with whom there can be no happy ending. The film's beginning sizzles as it peeks behind the scenes of the Big Apple's modeling circles, but it quickly changes gears and fizzles into another routine other-woman melodrama. Dvorak nearly steals the show as an aging model who briefly takes Turner under her wing — she leaves the story all too quickly. ★★½ VHS: $19.99

The Life of Jesus

(1997, 96 min, France, Bruno Dumont) *Sébastien Bailleul, Samuel Boidin, Kader Chaatouf, Geneviève Cottreel, Marjorie Cottreel.* Young epileptic slacker Freddie (Bailleul) spends his time hanging out with his motorcycle buddies and fooling around with his pretty girlfriend. When an Arab teen begins pursuing her, Freddy's buried rage — about his epilepsy, being unemployed, his best friend dying of AIDS — comes to the surface. With his debut film, hot new French director Dumont has no qualms about halting the action to admire a beautiful landscape or linger on a well-composed shot. And though it does test the patience now and then, *Life of Jesus* remains quite powerful and moving. The widescreen photography is sumptuous, and the acting is persuasive. The story of alienated youth has been done before, and even better, but the film is easy on the eyes, offers a credible look at "the angry young man," and has for its protagonist an interesting and ultimately sympathetic antihero. (French with English subtitles) ★★★ DVD: $14.99, VHS: $9.99

Life of Oharu

(1952, 137 min, Japan, Kenji Mizoguchi) *Toshiro Mifune, Kinuyo Tanaka.* One of the most enduring masterpieces of world cinema, this is an exquisitely rendered portrait of a woman who is tragically victimized by the brutal strictures of 17th-century feudal Japanese society. The director shows remarkable insight into the psychology of his female protagonist and fills the screen with hauntingly beautiful camera work. (Japanese with English subtitles) ★★★★ VHS: $29.99

Life of Sin

(1990, 112 min, US, Efrin Lopez Neris) *Raul Julia, Miriam Colón, Jose Ferrer.* The short, stationary shots in the opening sequence of *Life of Sin* establish a moody, almost dreamlike quality which permeates the rest of the film. Colón is engrossing as the peasant woman who gains fame and fortune during an unhappy and unfulfilled life. In a role which could easily have engendered histrionics, her understated and measured portrayal is all the more powerful. Julia is strong in support as Colón's lifelong friend, whose loyalty is unquestioning until a tragic, unnecessary confrontation. An interesting study of hypocrisy and societal double standards, though somewhat marred by an unclear resolution. ★★½

Life Stinks

(1991, 95 min, US, Mel Brooks) *Mel Brooks, Leslie Ann Warren, Jeffrey Tambor, Howard Morris.* Brooks hits rock bottom with this comedy — a sad, humorless and offensive parody of homelessness and big business. Brooks plays a multimillionaire who bets he can live penniless and homeless on the streets of Los Angeles for one month. Once there, director-writer Brooks lets loose an incredible array of comic vulgarities, none of which are the least bit amusing or original. *Sullivan's Travels* it's not. ★ DVD: $14.99

Life with Judy Garland: Me & My Shadows

(2001, 170 min, US, Robert Allan Ackerman) *Judy Davis, Victor Garber, Hugh Laurie, Tammy Blanchard, Marsha Mason, John Benjamin Hickey.* Made-for-TV biographies aren't especially known for their artistic merits unless they happen to be, of late, from HBO. Network movies tend to be glossy, homogenized trite — which makes this extraordinary biography of legendary singer/actress Judy Garland all the more startling. Perhaps being based on daughter Lorna Luft's memoirs gives it the authenticity and vitality that sets it apart. Perhaps it's Davis's virtuoso, Emmy Award-winning performance as Judy. The film traces the rise of Judy from child star to one of Hollywood's biggest movie stars, and her various, often rocky relationships with her five husbands. Whether phoning JFK at the White House for a little spiritual pick-me-up, or "singing them all" at Carnegie Hall, Davis has the moves, the voice, the temperament, the attitude; everything, in fact, that defined America's first multimedium diva. ★★★★ DVD: $14.99, VHS: $9.99

Life with Mikey

(1993, 91 min, US, James Lapine) *Michael J. Fox, Christina Vidal, Nathan Lane, Cyndi Lauper, Ruben Blades.* Fox stars as an ex-child actor who opens his own kiddie talent agency. The biggest belly laughs in this lazy comedy come when Fox holds open auditions to find the next Macaulay Culkin and ends up with tiny tots spouting *The Odd Couple*, baton twirlers and Ethel Merman's bastard daughter. The movie gets mired down in its own plot about a street-smart kid (Vidal) who, by the sheer force of her uninhibited charm, nabs a major cookie commercial and saves the agency from impending doom. Her lifeless performance mixed with Fox's affable but lackluster performance turns this into pure mush. Lane, at least, is good in support as Fox's business partner. ★★ DVD: $14.99

Life without Dick

(2001, 97 min, US, Bix Skahill) *Sarah Jessica Parker, Harry Connick, Jr., Johnny Knoxville, Teri Garr, Ever Carradine, Craig Ferguson.* A neo-Elvis movie with Connick in the King's spot as a hapless would-be hit man who aspires to a life as an Irish balladeer. The female foil, phoned in by Parker, is a flaky painter-type with a crack shot, who mistakenly offs her boorish beau, a private dick played by "Jackass" Knoxville. Life gets wacky for both of them when they meet, fall in love, and liberally crack wise with thousands of tired "dick" jokes. It

turns out Connick has somehow committed to five contract killings with an Irish mob kingpin, and — inept as a murderer — has Parker finish his dirty work. A surefire laugh riot for the sensibility-impaired. ★★ DVD Dual: $19.99, VHS: $14.99

Lifeboat

(1944, 96 min, US, Alfred Hitchcock) *Tallulah Bankhead, John Hodiak, William Bendix, Canada Lee, Walter Slezak, Hume Cronyn.* After an ocean liner is torpedoed by a German sub, a handful of disparate survivors are left adrift in a cramped lifeboat. When a final castaway appears, one of the Nazi crew members and the only individual aboard with any navigational skill, the group is caught in an equally cramped moral dilemma. A cinematically daring work which, though confined to a single setting, is never claustrophobic, and is suspenseful and intriguing throughout. John Steinbeck wrote the screenplay. Acting awards went to Bankhead for her only truly satisfying screen appearance. ★★★★ VHS: $14.99

Lifeforce

(1985, 100 min, US, Tobe Hooper) *Steve Railsback, Peter Firth, Mathilda May, Patrick Stewart.* Some elaborate special effects can't hide the silliness of the plot and ineffectiveness of Hooper's direction. Space vampires are terrorizing London. An intriguing premise gone sour. ★ DVD: $14.99

The Lift

(1985, 95 min, Netherlands, Dick Maas) *Huub Stapel, Willeke van Ammelrooy.* A Dutch thriller about an elevator in a high-tech office building with a murderous mind of its own. The highlight of this film was probably the ad which said: "Take the stairs! Take the stairs! For God's sake, take the stairs!" Great premise that holds up for a while, but when it comes to horror and splatter films, nothing beats the Americans. ★★

Light of Day

(1987, 107 min, US, Paul Schrader) *Michael J. Fox, Gena Rowlands, Joan Jett, Jason Miller, Michael Rooker.* Fox and Jett play a brother and sister who perform together in a local Cleveland rock band, trying to make it big time. Rowlands is their dying mother, at odds with her carefree daughter. Full of clichés in both its family drama and trying-to-get-ahead show business story. ★★

Light Sleeper

(1992, 103 min, US, Paul Schrader) *David Spade, Willem Dafoe, Susan Sarandon, James Clennon, Dana Delany, Mary Beth Hurt, Victor Garber.* Despite the heavy-handedness of Schrader's direction and its unsatisfying sugarcoated ending, *Light Sleeper* is an engrossing and intriguing drama. Essentially the story of the midlife crisis of alienated 40-year-old drug runner John LeTour (Dafoe), the story is punched up by an entertainingly frantic, amphetamine-driven performance by Sarandon as the brains and balls behind a high-class New York drug ring. LeTour is a loyal and decent but slumberous man who, after years of delivering the goods to the yuppies, posers and rich lowlifes, begins to question it all. Under Schrader's direction, the denizens of this seedy world of drug pushers, users and abusers become a metaphor for the world at large. A serious, arty, flawed yet entertaining drama. ★★★ DVD: $14.99, VHS: $9.99

Light Years

(1987, 80 min, US, Renée Laloux) *Glenn Close, Christopher Plummer.* "In a thousand years,

Gandahar was destroyed. A thousand years ago, Gandahar will be saved." With this intriguing mathematical paradox, acclaimed director Laloux (*Fantastic Planet*) and master science fiction writer Isaac Asimov combine their formidable talents to produce a captivating and truly original animated sci-fi adventure. This rewarding odyssey of sight and sound tips its hat to some of the great animated classics before it, from *Yellow Submarine* to *Lord of the Rings*. ★★★

The Lighthorsemen

(1988, 115 min, Australia, Simon Wincer) *Jon Blake, Peter Phelps, Bill Kerr, Sigrid Thornton.* The thrilling true story of the Australian Light Brigade's military exploits during World War I, and especially their assault on thousands of German and Turkish troops in Beersheba, is the focus of this sweeping saga. Wincer impressively directs the elaborately staged battle sequences, although some of the widescreen spectacle will be lost on video. While the characters are all too simply drawn and its heavy-handed clichés of "war is hell" get tiring, fans of military adventure films will overlook this and become absorbed in the sweeping action of this epic. ★★½

Lightning Jack

(1994, 101 min, US, Simon Wincer) *Paul Hogan, Cuba Gooding, Jr., Beverly D'Angelo.* An insipid comedy set in the Old West. Hogan plays Lightning Jack Kane, an aging outlaw who teams up with a deaf and mute Gooding to knock off a few banks. Gooding tries to liven things up with his physical schtick, and he might have succeeded had his material been elevated anywhere above insulting. Hogan makes us yearn for the less-nauseating "Crocodile" Dundee, and D'Angelo is embarrassing as the virtuous whore who pines for him. This is Muzak filmmaking — the film's cheesy humor and fluffy plot line leave one with that kind of hollow feeling otherwise found only in elevators and supermarkets. ★ DVD: $14.99, VHS: $9.99

Lightning over Water

(1980/81, 91 min, US, Nicholas Ray & Wim Wenders) While not a documentary, this unusual film chronicles the last days of famed director Ray who was dying of cancer. While visiting Ray in his SoHo loft, Wenders listens to a story Ray would like to film. They decide to film that story, as it is being lived. The result is a film about friendship as well as a rather unfocused look at a man attempting to finish his life and work with the help of those around him. ★★★ DVD: $24.99

The Lightship

(1985, 89 min, US, Jerzy Skolimowski) *Robert Duvall, Klaus Maria Brandauer, William Forsythe, Arliss Howard.* What might have been a standard good vs. evil allegory is elevated to a B-grade suspense thriller starring the chameleonic Duvall as an effeminate bank robber who, along with two sadistic partners, escapes from the law by hijacking a lightship piloted by a pacifist captain (Brandauer). Duvall's excessively flamboyant performance makes this worthwhile viewing. ★★½ VHS: $79.99

Like Father, Like Son

(1987, 98 min, US, Ron Daniel) *Dudley Moore, Kirk Cameron, Catherine Hicks, Sean Astin.* One of the least successful of the "body switching" comedies, with harried surgeon Moore and teenage son Cameron switching bodies thanks to an ancient potion. ★★ DVD: $19.99, VHS: $9.99

Lilo & Stitch

Like Water for Chocolate

(1992, 105 min, Mexico, Alfonso Arau) *Lumi Cavazos, Marco Leonardi, Regina Torne.* An immensely satisfying cinematic experience in every regard, this runaway art-house hit is at the same time whimsical, romantic, comic, tragic, sensuous and, above all, pure in spirit. In the grandest Latin American tradition of magical realism, the film tells the tale of Tita, a young woman who is condemned to a lonely and passionless life by her family's cruel tradition that the youngest daughter must care for her mother until she dies. Denied her one true love, Pedro, and forced into servitude, she responds by pouring her emotions into the recipes she is forced to cook for the family, resulting in witches' brews that have a profound effect on all who partake. It's mouth-watering good fun, sprinkled with intrigue and a heavy dash of passion. (Spanish with English subtitles) ★★★★ DVD: $14.99, VHS: $9.99

Lili

(1953, 87 min, US, Charles Walters) *Leslie Caron, Jean-Pierre Aumont, Mel Ferrer, Zsa Zsa Gabor.* An absolute delight! Caron gives an enchanting performance as a 16-year-old French orphan who joins a traveling carnival. There she falls in love with the magician (Aumont), and is given a valuable lesson in life and love from a crippled puppeteer (Ferrer), who uses his small creatures to cheer the sorrowful Lili. Oscar-winning score includes the wonderful "Hi-Lili, Hi-Lo." ★★★★

Lilies of the Field

(1963, 95 min, US, Ralph Nelson) *Sidney Poitier, Lilia Skala, Lisa Mann.* Poitier won an Oscar for Best Actor with his portrayal of a carpenter who reluctantly becomes involved in helping a group of German nuns. Poitier meets the nuns by chance after his car breaks down in front of their decaying convent. The sisters take this as a sign from God that he is the one who will save their home and build them a new chapel. Poitier's performance is full of charm and Skala is wonderful as the mother superior. A good, lighthearted film that is as inspiring as it is entertaining. ★★★½ DVD: $14.99

Lilo & Stitch

(2002, 89 min, US, Chris Sanders & Dean Deblois) *Voices of: Chris Sanders, Daveigh Chase, Tia Carrere, Ving Rhames, David Ogden Stiers, Kevin McDonald, Jason Scott Lee, Zoe Caldwell.* With computer animation threatening to take over the world, Disney's *Lilo & Stitch* bucks the trend: it's

a two-dimensional treasure that is worthy of its studio's pedigree. Lilo is perhaps Disney's most fiery heroine, a one-girl tsunami that her guardian sister can't contain. Booted from camp for beating up a classmate, Lilo's lonely ostracism is a perfect match for space alien Stitch, a likably evil dog-monster who's programmed for chaos. Stitch lands in Lilo's Hawaiian neighborhood, and they share growing pains, language barriers and an irresistible Elvis fetish. Of course, there's good in both of their hearts, but before the fuzzy ending there are fist-fights, bad attitudes and outer-space gunplay — refreshingly different stuff for Disney. The animation is top-notch, and Rhames is a treat as a hulking yet sympathetic social worker named Bubbles. ★★★½ DVD: $29.99, VHS: $24.99

Lily in Love

(1985, 104 min, GB, Karoly Makk) *Maggie Smith, Christopher Plummer, Elke Sommer.* Engaging performances highlight this minor though enjoyable update of Molnar's comedy "The Guardsman." Plummer plays an aging classical actor who disguises himself as a younger man to get the lead in a film written by his wife (Smith). When he lands the role, his wife becomes attracted to the "young man," unaware of his true identity. ★★½

Limbo

(1999, 127 min, US, John Sayles) *Mary Elizabeth Mastrantonio, David Strathairn, Vanessa Martinez, Kris Kristofferson, Casey Siemaszko.* The beautiful, perilous Alaskan landscape provides a striking balance between the harmony and discord amid a group of citizens of a small coastal town in writer-director Sayles' efficient, smartly acted drama/thriller. Donna (Mastrantonio), a struggling singer, and Joe (Strathairn), a reclusive handyman, begin a tentative affair. Sayles examines these and the town's other characters with his usual discerning, compassionate eye for human frailty and the need for emotional contact. However, the film takes an unexpected turn when romance gives way to a survival adventure, where Joe, Donna and her teenaged daughter find themselves in both a physical and spiritual state of uncertainty. A compelling character study offering noteworthy performances, good local color and a story that isn't afraid to take its time. ★★★ DVD: $24.99, VHS: $19.99

Limelight

(1952, 145 min, US, Charles Chaplin) *Charles Chaplin, Claire Bloom, Buster Keaton.* In this, his last American film, Chaplin returned to the London music halls of his childhood. This bittersweet tale tells the story of an aging performer who triumphs over his own foibles (declining popularity and his own mortality) and "passes the torch," so to speak, by curing a young, aspiring ballet dancer of her paralysis and thus launching her career (and ending his). The film is certainly overlong and, at times, sluggishly paced; but even this Chaplin "failure" is still a moving tribute to those with whom Chaplin has always sympathized: the underprivileged. ★★★ DVD Chaplin Collection - 2 disc set: $29.99, VHS: $19.99

The Limey

(1999, 89 min, US, Steven Soderbergh) *Terence Stamp, Peter Fonda, Lesley Ann Warren, Luis Guzman.* In director Soderbergh's near-perfect action/thriller, Stamp excels as a father who travels from his native England to Los Angeles to search for the person responsible for his estranged daughter's death. It's a simple plot from which Soderbergh is

able to create unrelenting tension — literally from start to finish. As Stamp arrives in L.A. greeted by unwelcome arms, Soderbergh ingeniously utilizes flashbacks and forwards to give bits and pieces of information which become whole by the story's end. The non-linear editing only enhances Soderbergh's taut direction, and underscores a mean, lean screenplay without an out of fat. The use of film clips from Stamp's 1967 British film *Poor Cow* helps in shading the character, and even helps in making this an homage to a couple of '60s icons. One of those, Fonda, is excellent as the shady record producer who may have been responsible for the young woman's death. ★★★½ DVD: $14.99, VHS: $9.99

The Line King: The Al Hirschfeld Story

(1997, 86 min, US, Susan Dryfoos) Anyone who has ever seen an issue of Sunday's *New York Times* will undoubtedly recognize the work of the late Al Hirschfeld, the newspaper's beloved caricaturist. For over sixty years, the bearded, introspective Hirschfeld captured Broadway's best on the *Times* pages with his distinctive pen-and-ink drawings. This loving, Oscar-nominated documentary, coproduced by the *Times*, chronicles the artist's life by letting him and his work do most of the talking. Of course, there's also coverage of "Nina" his daughter whose name has been hidden throughout his drawings since she was born. ★★★½ DVD: $24.99

The Linguini Incident

(1992, 100 min, US, Richard Shepard) *David Bowie, Rosanna Arquette, Eszter Balint, Buck Henry, Andre Greogry, Marlee Matlin, Viveca Lindfors.* Monty (Bowie), the new British bartender at the latest New York theme park restaurant (a palace of trend), needs to marry to get a green card. Or so it seems in this giddy, convoluted and very entertaining foray into the world of Manhattan's super-rich, super-chic and wannabes. Escape artistry, Mrs. Houdini's wedding ring and some very serious wagers are a few of the backdrops to tell the tale of deception, survival and monetary gain in a place where robbery becomes performance art if you're wearing the right bra. ★★★

The Lion in Winter

(1968, 135 min, GB, Anthony Harvey) *Peter O'Toole, Katharine Hepburn, Anthony Hopkins, Nigel Terry, John Castle, Timothy Dalton, Jane Merrow.* Hepburn and O'Toole are both at their fiery best as Eleanor of Aquitaine and King Henry II of England. With undaunted ferocity, the two engage in a bitter battle over who will be the successor to the throne while their children surreptitiously battle each other for the position. Unparalleled performances in the supporting roles make this an overall acting gem. Based on James Goldman's Broadway play. (Remade in 2004) ★★★★ DVD: $19.99

A Lion Is in the Streets

(1953, 88 min, US, Raoul Walsh) *James Cagney, Barbara Hale, Anne Francis.* Cagney's brisk performance brings unexpected life to this interesting but otherwise average political potboiler. Cagney plays a drifter from the Deep South who becomes a favorite son and runs for Governor. As he gains power and influence, he becomes more corrupt and ruthless, which sets the stage for a final showdown. ★★ VHS: $19.99

The Lion King

(1994, 84 min, US, Rob Minkoff & Roger Allers) *Voices of: Jeremy Irons, Matthew Broderick, James Earl Jones, Whoopi Goldberg, Nathan Lane.* Highly

Liquid Sky

overrated and the subject of much undeserving ballyhoo, *The Lion King* revolves around young Simba, the crown Prince of Pride Rock, where all of the beasts live in peace and harmony under the benevolent dictatorship of his father, Mufasa. When the King's evil brother Scar conspires to murder his royal sibling, Mufasa's son Simba, thinking himself responsible for the inevitable tragedy, goes into self-imposed exile, only to return when the kingdom is on the verge of ecological ruin. Its weak plot aside, what really makes *The Lion King* disappointing is its score. Elton John and Tim Rice's sappy pop musical numbers are completely lacking the razzmatazz and good-natured fun of their forebears Alan Menken and Howard Ashman. ★★½ DVD 2-disc set: $29.99, VHS: $24.99

Lionheart

(1991, 115 min, US, Sheldon Lettich) *Jean-Claude Van Damme, Harrison Page.* Van Damme plays a member of the French Foreign Legion who travels to America when he learns his brother is dying. En route, he becomes involved in the financially lucrative but deadly sport of streetfighting, where he is champion and in great demand. Typical Van Damme actioner: lots of fights and little sense. ★★ DVD: $14.99

Lipstick

(1976, 89 min, US, Lamont Johnson) *Margaux Hemingway, Chris Sarandon, Mariel Hemingway, Anne Bancroft, Perry King, Inga Swenson.* Inferior revenge film and ridiculous social drama with Margaux taking on rapist Sarandon. Mariel is her little sister; Bancroft plays an attorney. ★ DVD: $14.99, VHS: $9.99

Lipstick on Your Collar

(1993, 180 min, GB, Renny Rye) *Giles Thomas, Louise Germaine, Ewan McGregor, Peter Jeffrey.* As with Dennis Potter's *The Singing Detective* and *Pennies from Heaven*, *Lipstick on Your Collar* is a multilayered, intricately structured exploration of the human psyche. At the height of Cold War, military intelligence officers spend their 9 to 5 days decoding information about Russian troop movements in bureaucratic isolation. Their personal lives are spent in a threadbare England still recovering from WWII. These private and professional worlds collide when the newest member of the intelligence group, a naïve private, finds himself living in the same building as his corporal — and his corporal's

beautiful, ill-treated wife. Dull, utter normalcy is bizarrely juxtaposed with outbursts of pop tunes, sublimely choreographed under saturated lighting: the subconscious made manifest. Potter has delivered another adventurous examination of the human condition. ★★★★

Liquid Sky

(1983, 112 min, US, Slava Tsukerman) *Anne Carlisle, Paula Sheppard.* Flying saucers, fatal orgasms, rampant androgyny and relentless nihilism make *Liquid Sky* a most original and hallucinatory film. Coauthor Carlisle stars in dual roles as Jimmy, a snarling junkie, and Margaret, his female nemesis, a languid model with an unusual kiss of death. Perched atop Margaret's penthouse terrace are mite-sized aliens who crave the sensation of a heroin rush, which, it seems, is duplicated organically during human orgasm. A stunning cultural collage that offers an alien's-eye view of Manhattan's lurid clubs, majestic skyline and jaded populace. ★★★

Lisbon Story

(1994, 100 min, Germany, Wim Wenders) *Rüdiger Vogler, Patrick Bauchau, Teresa Salgueiro, Madredeus.* Director Wenders takes us on another odyssey of discovery, revelation and everyday miracles. Sound engineer Philip Winter (Volger) gets a postcard from a director friend of his, emphatically requesting Winter's immediate presence in Lisbon. Winter obligingly jumps into his car, which dies en route loaded with sound equipment. Winter and his gear make it to the Lisbon address, an apartment empty of his friend but with film without sound on an editing table. Waiting for his friend to appear, our protagonist decides to record sound for the film he's discovered; through which activity he connects with the lives of the city's inhabitants. As in *Wings of Desire*, the mundane is transmogrified by magical realism, and the banal seems touched by the divine. Wenders' consummate humanism is again the informing catalyst in this sweet, uplifting movie from that genre's master. (English, Portuguese and German with English subtitles) ★★★ VHS: $19.99

The List of Adrian Messenger

(1963, 98 min, US, John Huston) *George C. Scott, Kirk Douglas, Burt Lancaster, Dana Wynter, Tony Curtis, Robert Mitchum, Frank Sinatra.* Scott heads an all-star cast in this potent Agatha Christie-like murder mystery about a maniac (and master of disguise) who is killing off potential heirs to a family fortune. Scott plays the detective on the case. ★★★

Lisztomania

(1975, 104 min, GB, Ken Russell) *Roger Daltrey, Sara Kestelman, Paul Nicholas, Ringo Starr, Nell Campbell.* Franz Liszt, classical composer, gets the full treatment from Russell in this outlandish visual and sexual assault on historical accuracy and biographical detail. The presumption is that Liszt was a precursor to the rock superstars of today and in unabashed Russell fashion, he turns this into a garish, psychosexual extravaganza. Daltrey brings a certain Adonis-like quality to his role as Liszt, but Starr as the Pope is heresy in anyone's book. ★★

Little Big League

(1994, 119 min, US, Andrew Scheinman) *Luke Edwards, Timothy Busfield, John Ashton, Ashley Crow, Jason Robards, Kevin Dunn, Jonathan Silverman, Dennis Farina.* Little Big League is equal parts *Rookie of the Year* and *The Kid from Left Field*,

and despite its lack of originality it still manages to produce a certain charm all its own. An 11-year-old baseball fanatic inherits the Minnesota Twins when his beloved grandfather dies. The youth quickly appoints himself manager, and must rally his players towards the inevitable championship showdown. Though the kid is a boorish walking baseball encyclopedia, you can't help rooting for him; and he's surrounded by some entertaining and zany players, most of whom seem to be *Major League* rejects. ★★★ DVD: $9.99, VHS: $14.99

Little Big Man

(1970, 139 min, US, Arthur Penn) *Dustin Hoffman, Faye Dunaway, Chief Dan George, Richard Mulligan, Martin Balsam, Jeff Corey.* Hoffman stars as the 121-year-old Jack Crabbe, who recounts his experiences with General Custer, Wild Bill Hickok, Indians and medicine show con men. An epic comedy, with touches of drama and a perfect cast. ★★★½ DVD: $14.99, VHS: $9.99

Little Boy Blue

(1998, 104 min, US, Antonio Tibaldi) *Ryan Phillippe, Nastassja Kinski, John Savage, Shirley Knight, Tyrin Turner.* A creaky melodrama about a Texas family harboring some painful secrets, *Little Boy Blue* slowly approaches its finale, but when it does come, it packs a wallop. Jimmy West (Phillippe) is about to go away to college with his girlfriend and pursue a baseball career, but he really wants to stay home to care for his two small brothers. Actually, Jimmy in hoping to rescue them and their mom (Kinski) from their sadistic dad Ray (Savage), a vet who is dealing with some pretty serious issues. Director Tibaldi's gritty film does not hold much in the way of drama, but its characterizations are well done. ★★½ VHS: $14.99

Little Buddha

(1994, 123 min, US, Bernardo Bertolucci) *Bridget Fonda, Keanu Reeves, Chris Isaak, Ying Ruocheng, Alex Wiesendanger.* Beautifully photographed and emotionally uplifting, Bertolucci's surprisingly accessible story of spiritual enlightenment has the grand sweep of his *The Last Emperor* but on a smaller scale. Interweaving the modern-day story of a young boy who may or may not be the reincarnation of the Dalai Lama, and the ravishing telling of the origins and tenets of Buddhism and specifically the coming-of-age of the prophet Siddhartha, the film is insightful throughout and amazingly balances both worlds with equal artistry. The real treat here is Reeves as the young Indian prince Siddhartha — and while traces of his California upbringing are present, he nevertheless is believable . . . and he looks great in mascara, too. ★★★½ DVD: $19.99, VHS: $9.99

Little Caesar

(1930, 80 min, US, Mervyn LeRoy) *Edward G. Robinson, Glenda Farrell, Douglas Fairbanks, Jr., Sidney Blackmer.* Robinson gives a live-wire performance as Caesar Enrico Bandella, one of moviedom's most infamous and ruthless criminals. Robinson has been caricatured as this persona so often that it takes a while to realize how subtle his performance really is. Rico is as classless, cold-blooded and blindly ambitious as the real gangsters we read about; and the film, the first of the 1930s crime movies, traces his bloody rise and bloody fall. ★★★★

L

Little Dorrit: Pts I & II

(1988, 178 min, GB, Christine Edzard) *Derek Jacobi, Sarah Pickering, Alec Guinness, Joan Greenwood, Miriam Margolyes.* A magnificent two-part adaptation of Charles Dickens' classic novel, released in two separate volumes (it is recommended that they be viewed in their correct order). The film, set in early 19th-century London, tells the story of the Dorrit family: from their internment in debtor's prison to their eventual rescue and financial security, and of their relationship with the rich Clennam family, in particular the family's idealistic son, Arthur. Part One, *Nobody's Fault*, is told through the eyes of Arthur, and Part Two, *Little Dorrit's Story*, is seen through the eyes of young Amy, the title character. The film abounds with remarkable performances. ★★★½

The Little Drummer Girl

(1984, 130 min, US, George Roy Hill) *Diane Keaton, Klaus Kinski, Sami Frey.* A stirring if over-long political thriller, based on John Le Carre's novel, exploring the volatile situation in the Middle East, the complexities of personal allegiance and one woman's emotional dismantling as the result of her involvement with sparring terrorist forces. Keaton gives a splendid performance as an actress who is "hired" to pose as an agent, thrusting her into political intrigue. ★★★

The Little Foxes

(1941, 116 min, US, William Wyler) *Bette Davis, Herbert Marshall, Patricia Collinge, Teresa Wright.* Terrific screen version of Lillian Hellman's Broadway smash. Davis is at her bitchy best as Regina, the matriarch of a bickering Southern clan facing financial ruin. Collinge gives a heartbreaking performance as the kind-hearted aunt. ★★★½ DVD: $14.99

Little Fugitive

(1953, 75 min, US, Morris Engel, Ray Ashley, Ruth Orkin) *Richie Andrusco, Rickie Brewster, Winifred Cushing, Will Lee.* One of the first American independent films, Little Fugitive is a wonderful mix of cinema verité, funny observations of youth, and touching reflections of familial relationships. Shot on location on the streets of New York City, Little Fugitive follows two adventurous days of Joey (Andrusco), a seven-year-old Brooklyn youth and constantly harassed little brother. When his older brother Lennie (Brewster) and friends make Joey believe he's killed Lennie, Joey runs away to Coney Island where he's left to fend for himself. Andrusco is a marvel; the youngster is so at ease in front of the camera the film appears more documentary than fictional. Little Joey's escapades are certain to enthrall, to the point that the significant contributions of *Little Fugitive* to the birth of American independent filmmaking are easily overlooked. ★★★½ DVD: $29.99, VHS: $19.99

Little Giants

(1994, 106 min, US, DuWayne Dunham) *Rick Moranis, Ed O'Neill, Shawna Waldron.* Moranis and O'Neill play highly competitive brothers — one can't play sports and the other is a little league football coach. While Moranis may have no athletic ability, his daughter (nicknamed Icebox) is a natural but is rejected for uncle O'Neill's team solely because she's a girl. Eventually a team of other outcasts is born, with Moranis as its coach. While the ending is predictable, there are some laughs along the way. ★★½ DVD: $19.99, VHS: $19.99

Little Man Tate

(1991, 99 min, US, Jodie Foster) *Jodie Foster, Dianne Weist, Adam Hann-Byrd, Harry Connick, Jr., Debi Mazar.* Foster's impressive directorial debut is a quirky, entertaining comedy/melodrama about a seven-year-old genius who gets caught in a tug-of-war between his working-class mom (Foster) and a determined educator (Weist). The story centers around young Fred Tate's lack of social skills (a trait invariably attached to child prodigies), and his leaving his mother to study at an academy for gifted children living under Weist's supervision. Both Foster and Weist give strong performances and newcomer Hann-Byrd is affecting as Fred. ★★★ DVD Letterbox: $14.99

The Little Mermaid

(1989, 82 min, US, John Musker & Ron Clements) *Voices of: Jodi Benson, Christopher Daniel Barnes, Pat Carroll, Buddy Hackett, Nancy Cartwright.* From the masters at Disney studios comes the company's best film since *Mary Poppins*, and the finest full-length animated feature since *Cinderella*. Howard Ashman and Alan Menken have written a joyously tuneful score to tell the tale of a young mermaid who falls in love with a handsome human prince, much to the chargrin of her father. The film features outstanding animation, a witty, thoroughly enjoyable story, the delightful Oscar-winning song "Under the Sea," and a bewitching cast of characters. *The Little Mermaid* will come to be cherished for years as *Snow White*, *Bambi* and *Pinocchio* have before it: it is certainly as accomplished. ★★★★

The Little Minister

(1934, 110 min, US, Richard Wallace) *Katharine Hepburn, John Beal, Alan Hale, Donald Crisp.* Hepburn is in prime form as a Gypsy girl in 1840 who falls in love with a conservative Scottish minister, shocking his conservative congregation. ★★★

Little Monsters

(1989, 103 min, US, Richard Alan Greenberg) *Fred Savage, Howie Mandel, Daniel Stern, Margaret Whitton, Frank Whaley.* The movie that proves there really are monsters under our beds! Savage meets Maurice (Mandel), a zany monster that lives under *his* bed, and wacky misadventures ensue. Not as cute as the premise suggests, the cast tries hard to overcome a pedestrian screenplay. ★★ DVD: $14.99

Little Murders

(1971, 110 min, US, Alan Arkin) *Alan Arkin, Elliott Gould, Marcia Rodd, Donald Sutherland, Vincent Gardenia, Elizabeth Wilson.* Arkin directed this blackest of black comedies about urban decay, both physical and moral. Gould is the catatonic photographer; Gardenia, his paranoid father-in-law; Sutherland, the hippie priest; and Arkin, the schizophrenic detective in a frighteningly funny vision of a not-so-distant present. ★★★ DVD: $9.99

Little Nicky

(2000, 84 min, US, Steven Brill) *Adam Sandler, Patricia Arquette, Harvey Keitel, Rhys Ifans, Rodney Dangerfield, Tom 'Tiny' Lister, Jr., Reese Witherspoon, Jon Lovitz, Jackie Titone.* Sandler, who last appeared in the terrible *Waterboy* and *Big Daddy*, sinks to a new low even by his "standards." The posterboy for pubescent silliness plays Nicky, the Devil's dimwitted youngest son, who must venture to Earth to retrieve his two brothers causing havoc throughout New York City. Armed with a bad lisp and awful jokes, Nicky sets out to capture his siblings and falls in love with a mortal in the process. There could have been a mediocre movie somewhere in all this, but the screenplay ruins every single comedic possibility, making this comedy abortion truly one of the worst film comedies of all time. ★ DVD: $14.99, VHS: $14.99

A Little Night Music

(1978, 124 min, US, Harold Prince) *Elizabeth Taylor, Len Cariou, Diana Rigg, Hermione Gingold, Lawrence Guittard.* A rather mediocre adaptation of the brilliant Tony Award-winning musical written by Stephen Sondheim (which was based on Ingmar Bergman's *Smiles of a Summer's Night*). Taylor is miscast as Desiree, the actress who re-enters the life of newly married Cariou (repeating his stage role). Rigg steals the show as the wife of soldier Guittard, who is having an affair with Taylor. The film captures none of the magic which made the Bergman film and the stage play great hits. Though "A Weekend in the Country" is performed quite admirably. ★½

Little Nikita

(1988, 98 min, US, Richard Benjamin) *Sidney Poitier, River Phoenix, Richard Bradford.* Mommie's a Commie (and Daddy, too) in this contrived thriller with young Phoenix unaware of his parents' political sympathies; all of them under investigation by FBI agent Poitier. Both Phoenix and Poitier deliver strong performances but the muddled screenplay takes its time setting up the bare-bones action. ★★ VHS: $9.99

Little Odessa

(1995, 98 min, US, James Gray) *Tim Roth, Edward Furlong, Moira Kelly, Vanessa Redgrave, Maximilian Schell.* This brooding, pungent exploration of familial loyalties and personal isolation is Gray's astonishing directorial debut. Roth is arresting as Joshua, hit man for the Russian mafia, whose profession has estranged him from his Russian Jewish family; particularly his father (Schell), who is watching his wife (Redgrave) die of a brain tumor. Like his brother, the younger son Reuben (Furlong) is caught between ancestral custom and assimilation into American culture; and Joshua, who kills without thought or hesitation, is in some ways an icon of that assimilation. Thoughtful and deliberate direction guides uniformly remarkable performances through this haunting examination of the painful human longing to make contact. ★★★★ DVD: $14.99, VHS: $9.99

Little Caesar

The Little Prince

(1974, 88 min, GB, Stanley Donen) *Richard Kiley, Gene Wilder, Bob Fosse, Joss Ackland, Donna McKechnie.* Antoine de Saint-Exupery's magical book had all the trappings of a great film and you'd think that by putting Donen (*Singin' in the Rain*) in the director's chair, assembling an eclectic cast, and adding a musical score by Lerner and Loewe that you'd have a winner. But the film is a disappointment. The story of a neurotic aviator who counsels a young boy from outer space about such Earthly matters as love and life is presented coyly and lacks affection. ★★ DVD Letterbox: $14.99, VHS: $14.99

A Little Princess

(1995, 100 min, US, Alfonso Cuaron) *Eleanor Bron, Liam Cunningham, Liesel Matthews.* Based on the novel by Frances Hodgson Burnett, which was filmed once before in 1939 as *The Little Princess* with Shirley Temple, *A Little Princess* is an excellent adaptation embracing the themes of loneliness and courage. A young girl, Sara, is moved from her home in India to the same private girls' school in New York City attended by her deceased mother when her doting father joins the military ranks of WWI. Her fairytale existence is abruptly ended when he is pronounced killed in action and all of his assets are seized by the British government, leaving Sara penniless. The headmistress, played with delicious disdain by Bron, forces her to become a serving girl. Sara learns to keep her faith in miracles and inspires the other girls along the way until the wonderful tear-laden ending. ★★★½ DVD: $14.99, VHS: $9.99

A Little Princess

The Little Rascals

(1994, 83 min, US, Penelope Spheeris) *Bug Hall, Travis Tedford, Brittany Ashton Jones, Daryl Hannah, Lea Thompson, Whoopi Goldberg, Mel Brooks.* Coaxing charming performances from an almost all-child cast, Spheeris has made a most entertaining and updated big-screen version of the *Our Gang* comedies. With no real plot to speak of, the story centers on the antics of the "He Man Womun Haters Club," and the fateful day when one of their own (Alfalfa) falls in love...with a girl. A pint-sized "battle of the sexes" comedy, *Little Rascals*'s amusing screenplay gives the children ample opportunity to mug, flirt, sing, dance, race go-carts, blow bubbles and act like little big people — all of which they do with an endearing quality. ★★★ DVD Letterbox: $14.99, VHS: $14.99

A Little Romance

(1979, 108 min, US, George Roy Hill) *Laurence Olivier, Diane Lane, Thelonious Bernard, Sally Kellerman.* Charming coming-of-age tale about the budding romance between an American girl (Lane)

living in Paris and a young French boy (Bernard). The two of them run away to Venice together, under the eye of kindly con man Olivier. ★★★ DVD Letterbox: $19.99, VHS: $14.99

Little Shop of Horrors

(1960, 70 min, US, Roger Corman) *Jonathan Haze, Jackie Joseph, Mel Welles, Dick Miller, Jack Nicholson.* This cult comedy, shot in a mind-boggling two-and-a-half days, is a delightful grab bag of goofy gags and kooky characters. Welles is the skid row florist, Nicholson is the masochistic dentist's patient and Audrey, Jr. is the bizarre begonia with a diet of human blood. (Remade in 1986) ★★★ DVD 3-D Version: $19.99, VHS: $19.99

Little Shop of Horrors

(1986, 88 min, US, Frank Oz) *Rick Moranis, Ellen Greene, Steve Martin, Bill Murray, Vincent Gardenia, John Candy, Christopher Guest, James Belushi, Levi Stubbs.* "He's a mean, green mother from outer space and he's bad!" Science fiction, comedy and musical doo-wop blend wonderfully in this screen version of the hit off-Broadway musical, itself based on Roger Corman's 1960 exploitation cult classic. Audrey II, the alien Venus Flytrap with an appetite for human blood, befriends a nerdish Moranis in its fiendish plot to take over. The many show-stopping scenes include a great production number, "Downtown," and a maniacal Martin as a sadistic dentist who meets his match in Murray's hilariously masochistic patient. ★★★½ DVD: $19.99, VHS: $9.99

The Little Theatre of Jean Renoir

(1968, 100 min, France, Jean Renoir) *Jeanne Moreau, Jean Renoir, Fernand Sardou.* Renoir's final film is a lovely gem told in three episodes with each story recalling Renoir's favorite themes and styles and introduced by the filmmaker himself. The first episode, "The Last Christmas Dinner," follows a tramp looking for a Christmas dinner. The second, "The Electric Floor Polisher," is an amusing tale of a woman in love with a home appliance and her two husbands who object. The concluding segment, "The Virtue of Tolerance," is about an elderly man who must accept the affairs of his wife. Moreau makes a memorable appearance as a solemnly untalented music hall performer. (French with English subtitles) ★★★½ VHS: $24.99

The Little Vampire

(2000, 94 min, US, Uli Edel) *Jonathan Lipnicki, Richard E. Grant, Rollo Weeks.* Harmless hijinks abound when a nine-year-old American boy (Lipnicki) living in Scotland befriends a kid his same age — who's a vampire. Kids probably won't care that there's too-few laughs; they'll just enjoy the silly set-up and kids-take-charge attitude. ★★½ DVD: $12.99

Little Vera

(1987, 109 min, USSR, Vasily Pichul) *Natalya Negoda, Andrei Sokolov.* Hailed as a breakthrough film, *Little Vera* is one of the first Soviet movies to show nudity as well as expose the internal problems confronting the working class in the USSR. Negoda is wonderful as Vera, a pouty, sultry and restless teenager who falls in love with an older student. Problems erupt after he moves in with Vera, her nervous mother and alcoholic father. This is a fascinating work, showing a Russia not bent on the destruction of the capitalist world, but one embroiled in ethnic strife, where rebellious, Western-influenced

teens seek a new life and where the family unit is threatened by the freedoms and sexual promiscuity of the free world. (Russian with English subtitles) ★★★ DVD: $29.99, VHS: $29.99

Little Voice

(1998, 96 min, GB, Mark Herman) *Michael Caine, Brenda Blethyn, Jane Horrocks, Ewan McGregor, Jim Broadbent.* Judy Garland, Marilyn Monroe and Shirley Bassey all come to miraculous life in the person of a pint-sized impersonator named Little Voice, superbly played by Horrocks. Unfortunately, this uneven adaptation of Jim Cartwright's hit London play spotlights L.V. in the first half, leaving the story nowhere to go but down. A way-over-the-top Blethyn plays Mari, L.V.'s mussy mother whose current beau, Ray (Caine), is a down-on-his-heels talent agent. When he hears L.V. singing one night, he begins seeing dollar signs. Only one drawback: L.V. is painfully shy and has no desire to be a star. The story then follows Ray's efforts to get L.V. to the show on time. Once L.V. has performed, however, the film loses its momentum; how could it possibly sustain that kind of energy level. It gave its finale at intermission. The rest of the film is loud, obnoxious people behaving badly. The ensemble saves the film from tedium: Horrocks is amazing in her many voices, Caine oozes slime, Blethyn snaps her one-liners with slingshot precision. ★★½ DVD: $14.99, VHS: $9.99

Little Women

(1933, 115 min, US, George Cukor) *Katharine Hepburn, Joan Bennett, Paul Lukas, Edna May Oliver, Frances Dee, Spring Byington.* A thoughtful, and very faithful adaptation of Louisa May Alcott's classic book, with a wonderful performance by Hepburn as Jo, one of four sisters growing up in pre-Civil War New England. An impeccable production with superb direction from Cukor. ★★★★ DVD: $19.99

Little Women

(1994, 118 min, US, Gillian Armstrong) *Winona Ryder, Susan Sarandon, Gabriel Byrne, Trini Alvarado, Samantha Mathis, Kirsten Dunst, Christian Bale, Eric Stoltz.* Ryder stars in this winsome adaptation of the Louisa May Alcott classic that, though bearing little resemblance, compares favorably to George Cukor's 1933 classic starring Katharine Hepburn. Indeed, under the keen direction of Armstrong, and with various liberties taken in Robert Swicord's excellent screenplay, the film becomes more autobiographical in nature than Alcott's book ever was. The result is masterful as the film not only tells the familiar tale of Little Jo, her three sisters and their Marmee, it becomes an examination of the roots of "liberalism" as experienced by Alcott, who grew up imbued in the Transcendentalist movement of Walden Pond. For her part, Ryder makes a wonderful Jo, though period acting still seems a stretch for her, and Sarandon is a powerful presence as Marmee, a feminist mom way before her time. ★★★★ DVD: $19.99, VHS: $9.99

Live and Let Die

(1973, 121 min, GB, Guy Hamilton) *Roger Moore, Yaphet Kotto, Jane Seymour.* Moore's first outing as 007 takes us on an excursion to the Caribbean where he unearths a heroin ring masterminded by Kotto. The tropical climate allows for ample unveiling of female décolletage, principally Seymour, and the usual bevy of would-be starlets. Perhaps not the best of the Bond series, but certainly worth a look for anyone interested in a capable action-adventure flick. (Sequel: *The Man with the Golden Gun*) ★★½

L

Jane Horrocks in *Little Voice*

Live Flesh

(1997, 101 min, Spain, Pedro Almodóvar) *Javier Bardem, Francesca Neri, Liberto Rabal, Angela Molina, Jose Sancho.* Telling a good story rather than get carried away with plotting, Almodóvar deliberately paces this sexy thriller to allow the audience to get inside the heads of the characters and understand their crazy behavior. Victor (Rabal) is a handsome jailbird who reunites with the people who had him wrongly incarcerated. He falls into bed with Clara (Molina), the wife of Sancho (Sancho), whose old partner is David (Bardem), the cop crippled on the night Victor's fate was sealed. As Victor tries to exact revenge, naturally, all hell breaks loose. Although the plot could function as a bedroom farce, Almodóvar wisely milks it for its palpable sex and suspense. The result is a more mature work that may disappoint the bad-boy director's hard-core fans, but will also earn him new ones. (Spanish with English subtitles) ★★★ DVD: $19.99, VHS: $19.99

Live Wire

(1992, 87 min, US, Christian Duguay) *Pierce Brosnan, Ron Silver, Ben Cross.* Brosnan is the renegade cop, Silver the slimy U.S. senator and Cross the obsessed terrorist in this formulaic but mindlessly entertaining action-thriller. The explosive *du jour* is a colorless, tasteless liquid, convenient for single servings or punch bowls, which leaves no trace in the scattered remains of its victims. Washington D.C. is the natural setting for this slick and cynical commentary on the abuse of position and privilege, and the disastrous consequences of unbridled greed. ★★ DVD: $19.99, VHS: $14.99

Lives of a Bengal Lancer

(1935, 109 min, US, Henry Hathaway) *Gary Cooper, Franchot Tone, Richard Cromwell.* A rousing adventure film comparable with the similarly themed *Gunga Din* and *Beau Geste*. Cooper stars as a Canadian serving in the British army in the parched desert of colonial India. Excitement and danger await him and fellow officer Tone as they serve under a cold-hearted commander, attempt to reconcile their leader and his naïve son, and battle the crafty enemy. Good action sequences are offset by well-etched characterizations, unexpected comedy and a fair amount of suspense, all of which are under the tight direction of Hathaway. ★★★½

Livin' Large

(1991, 96 min, US, Michael Schultz) *Terrence "T.C." Carson, Lisa Arrindell.* What begins as a surprisingly amusing satire on racial relationships and television journalism quickly deteriorates into a questionable and misogynist sitcom. Carson brings a lot of life to his role of a young black man being

groomed to be the next superstar reporter for an Atlanta TV station. He soon finds that his success comes with a price, however, which includes ignoring his own cultural identity. The film's creators sabotage their efforts with their less-than-congenial depiction of the only two white women in the cast, whose "crime" is wanting to succeed in a "white man's world." From the film's distorted viewpoint, it doesn't matter if you're black or white, as long as you're male. ★★ DVD Dual: $14.99, VHS: $9.99

The Living Daylights

(1987, 130 min, GB, John Glen) *Timothy Dalton, Maryam d'Abo, Jeroen Krabbé, John-Rhys Davies.* Dalton takes over the reigns as super British agent 007. James Bond is up against a KGB defector who's really a double agent, and an American arms dealer. Dalton is a fabulous choice for Bond, bringing a sophistication to the part Roger Moore never dreamed of — more in line with Sean Connery's interpretation. Lots of great action and stunts, coupled with Dalton's dashing presence, make this one of the best of the Bonds. (Sequel: *Licence to Kill*) ★★★

The Living End

(1992, 84 min, US, Gregg Araki) *Mike Dytri, Craig Gilmore, Mary Woronov, Paul Bartel.* With its opening close-up shot of a bumper sticker that reads "Choose Death," one can rest assured that this self-described "irresponsible" black comedy about two HIV-positive men who set out on a lawless road adventure will not hesitate to provoke. Produced on a miniscule budget, the film presents an in-your-face reaction to society's disregard for the plight of HIV-positive people. Jon is a whiny, urban gay — a film writer and critic — who happens into a relationship with fellow "positive" Luke, a free-spirited and rageful drifter who precipitates their angst-driven journey into anarchy. It's best to ignore the film's thinly written script, awkward scenes and less-than-professional acting and concentrate instead on its irresistable "Yeah, I'm HIV-positive and I blame society!" message; for despite its faults, it's a totally entertaining effort. ★★★

Living in Oblivion

(1995, 91 min, US, Tom DiCillo) *Steve Buscemi, Dermot Mulroney, Catherine Keener, Danielle Von Zerneck, James LeGros, Rica Martens.* A delightful and ingenious comedy that chronicles a disastrous three-day period on the set of an independent film production. Buscemi is perfectly cast as Nick, the high-strung director who desperately tries to tie down all the loose ends of his latest movie. His accomplices include the hilarious Mulroney as the hulking cinematographer; and Keener as the leading lady who can't remember the simplest of lines. The capper, however, is LeGros, who blows onto the set as one-time indie hack, newfound Hollywood darling, Chad Palomino — an inspired caricature of Brad Pitt (who starred in DiCillo's first film, *Johnny Suede*). DiCillo's inventive script is filled with fantastical — almost Pirendellian — surprise twists, bristling humor and plenty of good-natured skewering of the film industry. ★★★½ DVD Letterbox: $29.99

Living on Toyko Time

(1987, 83 min, US, Steve Okazaki) *Minako Ohashi, Ken Nakagawa.* Offbeat and charming romantic comedy about a Japanese girl who marries — to stay stateside — a Japanese-American rock musician, who has little interest in anything but rock 'n' roll and a vegetative lifestyle. ★★★

Living Out Loud

(1998, 99 min, US, Richard LaGravenese) *Holly Hunter, Danny DeVito, Queen Latifah, Martin Donovan, Richard Schiff, Elias Koteas.* Re-creating the charm and quirkiness of *The Fisher King*, which he wrote, LaGravenese's debut film as director is a beguiling romantic comedy with a decidedly impish view of romance that is underscored by a touching story of self-examination. In a particularly smart portrayal, Hunter plays Judith, a 40-ish recent divorcée who is having difficulty trying to move on after her break-up. When Judith befriends Pat (DeVito), her building's elevator operator (with whom she becomes romantically involved), and Liz (Latifah), a sultry cabaret singer, she begins to awaken from the stagnant, lonely existence she had been living. LaGravenese nicely balances Judith's sexual and personal explorations, and never allows Judith's wonderfully executed fantasy sequences to detract from the story. ★★★ DVD: $19.99, VHS: $14.99

Loaded

(1996, 105 min, New Zealand, Anna Campion) *Oliver Millburn, Nick Patrick, Thandie Newton, Catherine McCormick.* Jane Campion's little sister Anna makes an inauspicious directorial debut with this dreary psychological thriller, an uneventful discourse whose one-dimensional characters substitute pretense with pretension. With its film-within-a-film backdrop, the story centers on a group of friends who weekend at a country mansion to make a horror movie. As the dynamics and romantic couplings of the group change, a death underscores the participants' anxieties and uncertain allegiances. Unfortunately for director Campion, she's working from her own flat screenplay. It's one of those stories in which the viewer impatiently waits for *something* to happen. It doesn't. A tripping scene is the only sequence of interest. ★½ DVD: $14.99, VHS: $9.99

Loaded Weapon 1

(1993, 82 min, US, Gene Quintano) *Emilio Estevez, Samuel L. Jackson, William Shatner, Tim Curry, Jon Lovitz, Charlie Sheen, Bill Nunn, F. Murray Abraham, Denis Leary, J.T. Walsh.* Looks like a case of an older brother trying to keep up with a younger sibling. After Charlie Sheen's spoofing of Tom Cruise in *Hot Shots*, Estevez takes on the lighter side of Mel Gibson in this amiable spoof. Jackson joins him as the other half of the *Lethal Weapon* team. The film is perhaps a little too self-aware and does not have the rapid fire-delivery of some of the more successful films in this genre, like *The Naked Gun* series. However, even though it doesn't go far enough, the film does provide some serious chuckles at the expense of the Gibson/Glover team. (aka: *National Lampoon's Loaded Weapon 1*) ★★½ DVD: $14.99

Living in Oblivion

Local Hero

(1983, 111 min, Scotland, Bill Forsyth) *Burt Lancaster, Peter Reigert, Denis Lawson, Jenny Seagrove, Peter Capaldi.* Forsyth's enchanting comedy stars Peter Reigert as a reluctant Texas oil company executive who is sent overseas to purchase an idyllic Scottish village. Almost to his chagrin, the townsfolk, one of the strangest assortment of oddballs ever to hit the screen, seem all too eager to sell. All but one, that is. Burt Lancaster makes a commanding appearance as the company's owner who gets helicoptered in to take over the negotiations. This clever concoction offers a gentle treatise on the continuing march of progress and what we stand to lose by it. ★★★★ DVD: $14.99

Lock, Stock and Two Smoking Barrels

(1999, 106 min, GB, Guy Ritchie) *Jason Flemyng, Dexter Fletcher, Nick Moran, Jason Statham, Steven Mackintosh, Sting.* A jolt of lightning, director Ritchie's comic crime caper is from the *Reservoir Dogs* and *Trainspotting* school, but firmly stands on its own as fresh and original. Ritchie has a terrific eye and employs a whole bag of visual gimmicks (grainy sepia, jerky freeze-frame, slo-mo) to lend considerable style to this hectic story of four London pals embroiled in a complex but highly satisfying stew of cheating cardplayers, double-crossing losers, porn paraphernalia, a bag of stolen loot, a forest of ganja and various underworld types. The young cast strikes the right note of nervous energy and tough-guy moxie, and the script is chock-full of snappy one-liners. Ritchie's assured direction elevates this familiar stuff far above other wannabes; the film's over-the-top visual kineticism is perfectly matched with the material. It's a slap-happy acknowledgment of and tribute to all the great underworld classics that paved the way for it, but with an energetic sensibility that somehow seems entirely new. ★★★½ DVD Letterbox: $14.99, VHS: $9.99

Lock Up

(1989, 106 min, US, John Flynn) *Sylvester Stallone, Donald Sutherland, John Amos.* Even Stallone has rarely sunk this low. Stallone plays a convict who is transferred to a new prison, run by mean warden Sutherland — who's got a grudge to settle with Sly. ★ DVD: $14.99, VHS: $9.99

The Locusts

(1997, 125 min, US, John Patrick Kelly) *Kate Capshaw, Jeremy Davies, Vince Vaughn, Paul Rudd, Daniel Meyer, Ashley Judd.* Vaughn is the catalyst of this lethargic drama about a drifter whose flight from justice lands him smack in the middle of "black widow" Capshaw's stud ranch. But, instead of yielding to her sultry poses and constant offers to drink scotch and light her cigarettes, he befriends her repressed son (Davies) and sets in motion a tragedy of Oedipal proportions. Kelly's surefooted screenplay recalls the boozy, summertime tales of Williams and Inge, but Capshaw steps into shoes much better worn by Stanwyck and Crawford (as a vamp Capshaw packs all the punch of June Cleaver after a bad PTA meeting). ★★½ DVD Letterbox: $14.99

The Lodger

(1926, 75 min, GB, Alfred Hitchcock) *Ivor Novello, Marie Ault.* Hitchcock's mastery of narrative and atmosphere is stylishly evident in this silent thriller about a mysterious rooming house tenant who is suspected of being Jack the Ripper. Although not his first film, *The Lodger* ostensibly begins the

Lock, Stock and Two Smoking Barrels

Hitchcock oeuvre, for it was his first commercial success, first thriller, first cameo appearance and the first use of his favorite "innocent man falsely accused" plot line. ★★★ VHS: $12.99

Logan's Run

(1976, 120 min, US, Michael Anderson) *Michael York, Jenny Agutter, Richard Jordan, Peter Ustinov, Farrah Fawcett.* York plays Logan, a man with a problem: He's a 29-year-old bounty hunter who collects the people who didn't submit to state mandated euthanasia when they hit the age of 30 — and tomorrow is *his* birthday. Large futuristic sets, great special effects and Ustinov highlight this episodic, intriguing vision of the near future. ★★★ VHS: $9.99

Lola

(1960, 91 min, France, Jacques Demy) *Anouk Aimée, Marc Michel.* With its breezy tone, distinctive editing and innovative cinematography (thanks to Raoul Coutard), this New Wave-influenced fairy tale proved to be an audacious debut for Demy, a director who, with the exception of *The Umbrellas of Cherbourg*, never achieved his potential. Owing much to *On the Town* and the works of Max Ophüls (to whom it is dedicated), this fanciful love story stars Aimée as a free-spirited nightclub singer who is faced with the enviable dilemma of choosing between a trio of lovers. Framed within a series of coincidences and chance encounters and offering the notion that love is transient, the story never bogs down in "realities" and takes the wonderfully innocent approach that love conquers all. (French with English subtitles) ★★★½ DVD Letterbox: $24.99, VHS: $24.99

Lola

(1969, 98 min, GB/Italy, Richard Donner) *Charles Bronson, Susan George, Trevor Howard, Honor Blackman, Robert Morley.* Bronson stars as a 40-something American porno writer who has a tempestuous affair with a liberated 16-year-old girl (George as the irrepressible young Lola). Not as provocative as it would like to be, though the two stars offer appealing performances. ★★

Lola Montes

(1955, 110 min, France, Max Ophüls) *Martine Carol, Peter Ustinov, Anton Wolbrook, Oskar Werner.* In a 19th-century circus in Vienna, the famous Lola Montes, fleeing scandal, is reduced to living out the highlights of her exotic life for the pleasure of the masses and at the urging of a forceful ringmaster. Ophüls' first film is a scintillating tale of excess and regret, and is beautifully photographed. (French with English subtitles) ★★★½ DVD: $14.99, VHS: $9.99

Lolita

(1962, 152 min, GB, Stanley Kubrick) *James Mason, Peter Sellers, Shelley Winters, Sue Lyons.* Kubrick's screen adaptation of Vladimir Nabokov's

provocative novel, though not a complete success, effectively captures the author's sense of black humor and features outlandish performances by Sellers and Winters. Mason is a college professor who marries a lonely widow only for the opportunity it offers to seduce the sexually precocious Lyons. This peculiar tale of murder and lust is an example of earlier Kubrick efforts where powerful and eccentric characters ruled the screen. (Remade in 1998) ★★★ DVD: $19.99, VHS: $19.99

Lolita

(1998, 137 min, GB, Adrian Lyne) *Jeremy Irons, Melanie Griffith, Frank Langella, Dominique Swain.* A surprisingly erotic — but not exploitative — adaptation of the Nabokov classic, director Lyne actually scores with this sensual telling of the controversial story. As the lecherous Humbert Humbert who marries the shrill Charlotte Haze (Griffith) only so he can be close to her pre-teen daughter Lolita (Swain), Irons is magnificent in the lead role, giving weight and meaning to Stephen Schiff's thoughtful screenplay. Irons maintains a good rapport with the appealing Swain, and even Langella seems well cast as the goofy, flamboyant Clare Quilty. While this whole project could have been a disaster, Lyne's tasteful and literate *Lolita* brilliantly creates a sexually charged atmosphere without being offensive on any level. Fans of the novel, or even Kubrick's earlier screen treatment, might not be overly impressed, but the filmmakers really did do an admirable job in bringing Nabokov's masterpiece to the screen. ★★★½ DVD Signature Series: $14.99

London Kills Me

(1992, 107 min, GB, Hanif Kureishi) *Justin Chadwick, Steven Mackintosh, Roshan Seth, Fiona Shaw, Brad Dourif, Gordon Warnecke.* A humorous exploration of life on the fringe unhibably of a post-punk, beyond-hope society. The story follows Clint, a pale, emaciated 20-year-old who, despite being mired in a seemingly hopeless world of drugs, homelessness and prostitution, retains a cheery optimism. Hope springs eternal after an exasperated owner of an upscale Portabello Road restaurant promises the bedraggled Clint a job if he comes in the following week with a new pair of shoes. Clint's odyssey, following this promise of respectability, becomes his repeated and increasingly frantic attempts to acquire this elusive pair of shoes. A fascinating yet flawed comedy-drama that despite a tagged-on happy ending that borders on the bizarre is fun nonetheless and vividly captures this part of London. ★★★½

Lone Star

(1996, 135 min, US, John Sayles) *Chris Cooper, Kris Kristofferson, Elizabeth Peña, Joe Morton, Matthew McConaughey, Ron Canada, Clifton James, Miriam Colon, Frances McDormand.* Lone Star, possibly Sayles' best film to date, is a brilliantly conceived, gripping mystery-thriller with so many simmering emotions under its surface that it's in constant threat of either self-destructing or losing its way. Thankfully, it does neither. Cooper plays Sam Deeds, a low-keyed sheriff in a small Texas town investigating some skeletal remains and a lawman's rusty badge found in the desert. The son of Buddy Deeds, a much-revered sheriff, Sam believes his father (played in flashbacks by McConaughey) may have had something to do with the findings. He soon discovers that the more digging he does, the more skeletons he finds. Moving fluidly from the past to the present, *Lone Star* is a compelling, quietly powerful work that stays with you long after its stunning but daringly conceived secret is revealed. This is stirring stuff from a filmmaker who would have it no other way. ★★★★ DVD: $19.99, VHS: $19.99

Lone Wolf and Child series

Based on a popular Japanese comic book or manga by Kazuo Koike and Goseki Kojima, this incredible series tells the ongoing tale of Itto Ogami (Tomisaburo Wakayama), the Shogun's official executioner, who is disgraced by a rival family's plot and forced to walk "the road to Hell" with his young son after the murder of his wife and ostracism of his entire clan. Ogami becomes an assassin for hire, wheeling young Daigoro (Akihiro Tomikawa) around in a wooden cart, which is accessorized with a multitude of weapons (and which has given the films the alternate title of the "Baby Cart" series) and selling his formidable swordplay skills. Always on the lookout for enemy ninja, the films tell the stories of Ogami's encounters with various characters in feudal Japanese life and his usually heroic adventures, all the while teaching Daigoro the meaning of courage and sacrifice. The films were first introduced to American audiences in the re-edit *Shogun Assassin*, which emphasized some of the campiness and cult value of the story. The Japanese originals, however, are deadly serious. They tell a tale of honor surviving through disgrace and redemption made possible only through wholesale slaughter. Each individual film is a masterpiece of the samurai genre, and together they form a collection which ranks as one of the best film series in world cinema.

Lone Wolf and Cub: Sword of Vengeance

(1972, 83 min, Japan, Kenji Misumi) *Tomisaburo Wakayama, Fumio Watanabe, Shigeru Tsuyuguchi, Yunosuke Ito, Tomoko Mayama.* The first film tells the origin story of the Lone Wolf and of his expulsion from his home at the hands of the duplicitous Yagyu clan. After his wife is murdered, Ogami, one of the Shogun's most loyal servants, is falsely accused of conspiring against his Lord and is ordered to commit *harakiri.* Refusing to comply with the royal decree, he becomes a "demon on the road to Hell," with no future and no hope for escape from his chosen fate. Along for the ride is his infant son Daigoro. Its beautiful widescreen photography is filled with dazzling visuals and breathtaking colors, but are rather staid compared to the wild carnage which is to come. (Japanese with English subtitles) ★★★★ DVD: $29.99

Lone Wolf and Cub: Baby Cart at the River Styx

(1972, 81 min, Japan, Kenji Misumi) *Tomisaburo Wakayama, Kayo Matsuo, Minoru Ohki.* This time around, Ogami faces two of the most colorful villains of the entire series. The first is a clan of female ninja, sent to kill Ogami. The second villains, however, are even better: the three "Gods of Death" whom John Carpenter paid homage to in his *Big Trouble in Little China.* Assigned to protect an official whom Ogami has been hired to kill, each wields his own hand-to-hand weapon with fearsome skill and is a master killer in his own right; together they are unbeatable, until they meet Lone Wolf and Child. Again featuring the trademark geysers of blood which distinguishes the series, *Lone Wolf 2* features even more action than its predecessor, and is possibly the best entry in the series. (Japanese with English subtitles) ★★★★ DVD: $29.99

Lone Wolf and Cub: Baby Cart to Hades

(1972, 89 min, Japan, Kenji Misumi) *Tomisaburo Wakayama, Go Kato, Yuko Hama.* The third film in the blood-filled samurai series finds Ogami paralleled with a disgraced ronin warrior who has become a thug-for-hire in order to make a living. Both are shown as men trying to act within their codes of honor, having been made outcasts by society at large. After he gets involved in a dispute between two rival clans, the climax of the film finds Itto fighting a veritable army of soldiers, some armed with early firearms. But the Lone Wolf's accessorized baby cart holds a few more surprises for the unsuspecting foe! One of the more philosophically complex episodes of the series. Originally released in the U.S. in a dubbed version called both *Lightning Swords of Death* and *Lupine Wolf.* (Japanese with English subtitles) ★★★★

Lone Wolf and Cub: Baby Cart in Peril

(1973, 81 min, Japan, Buichi Saito) *Tomisaburo Wakayama, Yoichi Hayashi, Michi Azuma, So Yamamura.* This enthralling entry's main villain is both beautiful and deadly: the tattooed female assassin Oyuki. Hired to kill her early in the film, Ogami later learns that, far from being a bloodthirsty killer, Oyuki is a desperate woman who has been severely wronged — raped and betrayed by her teacher — and began life as an assassin only because she was forced to. Sympathizing with her, Ogami must nevertheless carry out his assignment: his code of *bushido* requires it. But before he does so, he allows Oyuki revenge against those who had previously despoiled her. (Japanese with English subtitles) ★★★★ DVD: $29.99

Lone Wolf and Cub: Baby Cart in the Land of Demons

(1973, 89 min, Japan, Kenji Misumi) *Tomisaburo Wakayama, Akihiro Tomikawa.* A series of messengers, each with a part of the final orders to hire Ogami, confront the Lone Wolf as he makes his way across the landscape. Killing each of them, he pieces his mission together and, along with the viewer, slowly learns the entire story: an insane local samurai has substituted his young daughter, raised as a boy, as the clan's legitimate heir. Ogami has been hired to kill the clan leaders and prevent such an unconventional transfer of power from occurring. Ogami's reaction is also highly dramatic, and contrary to what many Western viewers would expect. One of the more complex episodes of the series. (Japanese with English subtitles) ★★★★ DVD: $29.99

Lone Wolf and Cub: White Heaven in Hell

(1974, 85 min, Japan, Yoshiyuki Kuroda) *Tomisaburo Wakayama, Junko Hitomi, Isao Kimura, Minoru Ooki, Akihiro Tomikawa.* This final episode, unfortunately, does not feature any major confrontation between Ogami and his archenemy Retsudo Yagyu, but that does not prevent it from being as entertaining as the five preceding it. Yagyu has sent two of his remaining children to kill Ogami, one of whom is a bastard child who spurns any connection to his father, instead preferring to kill Ogami for his own glorification. With the assistance of three supernatural warriors, he dogs Ogami's heels, killing any innocent people Lone Wolf and Child come in contact with, thus assuring his complete isolation from the rest of humanity. Ogami retreats to the frozen wastelands, where a gigantic battle between him and what remains of the Yagyu clan is staged. An exciting fight on skis (with the baby cart on a sled!) follows, where the white of the snow is stained by the series' ever-present crimson blood. A fine end to a fantastic series. (Japanese with English subtitles) ★★★★ DVD: $29.99

Lonely Are the Brave

(1962, 107 min, US, David Miller) *Kirk Douglas, Walter Matthau, Gena Rowlands, Carroll O'Connor, George Kennedy.* A riveting modern-day western with cowboy and escaped prisoner Douglas on the lam, pursued by a relentless sheriff's department. ★★★

The Lonely Guy

(1984, 90 min, US, Arthur Hiller) *Steve Martin, Charles Grodin, Judith Ivey.* When Martin is dumped by his girlfriend, he takes up with similarly fated Grodin, who introduces him to the wonderful world of bachelorhood. Based on the book by Bruce Jay Friedman, and adapted by Neil Simon, this offbeat, low-keyed comedy offers some comic insights into romance but is a little too introverted for its own good. ★★½ DVD: $24.99, VHS: $9.99

The Lonely Lady

(1983, 92 min, US, Peter Sasdy) *Pia Zadora, Lloyd Bochner, Ray Liotta.* Tacky, tasteless and completely satisfying only in a campy way, this Hollywood exposé, adapted from the Harold Robbins novel, was made to showcase the talent and body of the spunky Zadora. The story begins with young Pia, a high school virgin (now that's great acting), being raped by a garden hose wielded by a Hollywood brat. On recovery, she is determined to become a successful writer in the sleazy world of show business. Sleeping her way to the top, our chipmunk-faced Pia achieves the success she sought, only to find emptiness and remorse. Champagne bottles are popped, lesbianism is hinted, breasts are bared and phallic images abound in this Zadora-ized "star" vehicle. ★

The Lonely Man

(1957, 87 min, US, Henry Levin) *Jack Palance, Anthony Perkins, Neville Brand, Robert Middleton, Elaine Aiken.* Palance grimaces and clenches his jaw through most of this lean western as a retired gunfighter trying to make peace. Emulating Henry King's outstanding *The Gunfighter,* though with only partially satisfying results, the story centers on aging Palance who wants to forget his "triggering" days and reconcile with his estranged son Perkins. The Law of the West and his son's hatred won't allow either. It's almost funny to hear Perkins spout a Norman Bates-like devotion to his mother, and Palance lassoing and hog-tying Perkins has got to be seen to be believed. ★★½ DVD: $14.99, VHS: $14.99

The Lonely Passion of Judith Hearne

(1987, 116 min, GB, Jack Clayton) *Maggie Smith, Bob Hoskins, Wendy Hiller.* Brian Moore's 1955 novel is brought to the screen with a pair of outstanding performances. Smith stars as the title character, a crestfallen middle-aged woman who suffers because of her undying and somewhat misplaced faith in the church and whose life is stalled in run-down boarding houses. Hoskins is superb as her self-effacing suitor. ★★★

Lonelyhearts

(1958, 101 min, US, Vincent J. Donehue) *Montgomery Clift, Robert Ryan, Myrna Loy, Maureen Stapleton.* Good performances highlight this occasionally moving Nathanael West story with Clift taking over the "Miss Lonelyhearts" newspaper column, becoming involved with the lives of his readers. ★★½ VHS: $19.99

Long Ago Tomorrow

(1971, 111 min, GB, Bryan Forbes) *Malcolm McDowell, Nanette Newman, Bernard Lee.* Filmgoers used to McDowell's screen persona as a virile, sometimes violent, young man, will be surprised by this subdued melodrama in which he plays a paraplegic involved in a love affair with another disabled person. Surprisingly engaging with powerful performances from both McDowell and Newman. ★★★

The Long Day Closes

(1992, 83 min, GB, Terence Davies) *Leigh McCormack, Marjorie Yates, Anthony Watson.* Somber, melancholy and haunting, this restrained drama of a young boy's maturation is a very effective mood piece recalling director Davies' childhood. Filmed in a leisurely, almost floating style and obviously autobiographical, the story concerns Bud (McCormack), a pre-adolescent boy living with his close-knit family in 1950s Liverpool. A thoughtful but shy boy with few friends, Bud immerses himself in escapist Hollywood musicals and develops an especially close relationship with his mother. There's surprisingly little dialogue, and not much happens in the way of dramatic excitement or tension. Yet this poetic style of filmmaking is both entrancing and pensive. ★★★½

Long Day's Journey into Night

(1962, 180 min, US, Sidney Lumet) *Katharine Hepburn, Ralph Richardson, Jason Robards, Dean Stockwell.* A staggering adaptation of Eugene O'Neill's classic autobiographical play detailing his explosive homelife in early 1900s New England. In a tour de force performance, Hepburn plays O'Neill's drug-addicted mother whose grasp on reality slowly dissipates to the helpless horror of those around her. Richardson masterfully portrays the patriarch of the family — an aging, alcoholic actor who'd rather reminisce on a glorious past than face the truths of the present. As their sons, Stockwell plays the youngest brother stricken with TB, and Robards is a powerful presence as the troubled author witnessing his family's decay. ★★★★ DVD: $14.99

Long Day's Journey into Night

(1987, 169 min, US, Jonathan Miller) *Jack Lemmon, Bethel Leslie, Peter Gallagher, Kevin Spacey.* Lemmon re-creates his acclaimed performance from the Broadway revival in this expert production of Eugene O'Neill's classic drama. Leslie is outstanding as Lemmon's drug-addicted wife, and Gallagher and a pre-stardom Spacey are excellent as their sons. ★★★

Long Gone

(1987, 110 min, US, Martin Davidson) *William L. Petersen, Virginia Madsen, Henry Gibson.* A wonderful made-for-cable production, an offshoot of *Bull Durham*, about the manager of a minor league team whipping his players into shape for a run at the championship. Petersen deftly plays the manager, and Madsen is the beauty queen with an eye for marriage. A delightful suprise. ★★★ VHS: $14.99

The Long Good Friday

(1980, 105 min, GB, John MacKenzie) *Bob Hoskins, Helen Mirren, Eddie Constantine, Pierce Brosnan.* A powerful English mobster suddenly finds himself and his empire victims of a bloody battle decree and desperately seeks its source. This taut gangster saga stars Hoskins as the besieged underworld head, Mirren as his sturdy mistress and Constantine as an influential American investor. ★★★½ DVD: $29.99

The Long Goodbye

(1973, 112 min, US, Robert Altman) *Elliott Gould, Nina Van Pallandt, Sterling Hayden, Henry Gibson, Mark Rydell, Jim Bouton.* Gould gives his best performance as a burned-out Philip Marlowe out to find out if and why he was framed by a good friend (Bouton) for a woman's murder. Altman takes the tired, used-up detective film genre and fills it with quirky, nasty characters and bizarre humor. Look for *On Golden Pond* director Rydell as an incredibly sadistic, dry-witted gangster who can injure his loved ones just to show what he can do to people he hates. ★★★½ DVD Letterbox: $19.99

The Long, Hot Summer

(1958, 117 min, US, Martin Ritt) *Paul Newman, Joanne Woodward, Orson Welles, Lee Remick, Anthony Franciosa, Angela Lansbury.* Ritt directed this engaging film, a successful translation of William Faulkner's story. Newman became a star thanks to his stand-out performance as Ben Quick, a wandering farmhand who becomes involved with the Varner family, headed by a domineering father (Welles). From first encounter, Ben takes a shine to the elegant but aloof Varner daughter (Woodward), which suits Daddy just fine, since he's hankerin' for plenty of Varner heirs. Whether under the scorching sun or the shade of the front porch, this all-star cast deliver fiery performances, especially Newman as the lusty opportunist. ★★★½ DVD: $14.99, VHS: $6.99

The Long Kiss Goodnight

(1996, 120 min, US, Renny Harlin) *Geena Davis, Samuel L. Jackson, Patrick Malahide, Craig Bierko, David Morse.* After the mishap of *Cutthroat Island*, husband and wife Davis and Harlin are back in good form with this entertaining and always unpredictable (if farfetched) mystery/suspenser. In this rollercoaster ride of intrigue, Davis stars as a mild-mannered housewife who suffers from amnesia. When she is involved in a car accident, bits of memory begin to surface — like how to accurately throw a knife and an alter ego named Charlie. When a private investigator (Jackson) she had previously hired stumbles across a clue to her identity, the two set out to uncover the truth, with some very nasty secret agents on their trail. We may not always believe what Harlin asks us to, but what fun we have trying. ★★★ DVD Letterbox: $14.99, VHS: $14.99, VHS Letterbox: $14.99

The Long, Long Trailer

(1954, 103 min, US, Vincente Minnelli) *Lucille Ball, Desi Arnaz, Marjorie Main, Keenan Wynn.* Released at the height of their TV popularity, Lucy and Desi star in this comic romp about a newly married couple's adventures on the road in the titular vehicle. Lots of fun. ★★★

The Long Night

(1947, 97 min, US, Anatole Litvak) *Henry Fonda, Barbara Bel Geddes, Vincent Price, Ann Dvorak, Elisha Cook, Jr.* Too strong meat for Hollywood, yet they still decided to remake Marcel Carne's French masterpiece *Le Jour Se Lève* about love and murder among the working class. When gunshots fell a dapper man in a drab boarding house, police quickly trap the killer (a miscast Fonda) in his third floor room. As the night wanes the killer remembers how things came to such a deadly impasse. Bowdlerized

with an unconvincing Hollywood ending, *The Long Night* offers no compelling reason to watch it over *Le Jour Se Lève*. ★★ DVD: $29.99, VHS: $24.99

The Long Riders

(1980, 100 min, US, Walter Hill) *Stacy Keach, David Carradine, Christopher Guest, Dennis Quaid, Nicholas Guest, James Keach, Keith Carradine, Robert Carradine, Randy Quaid.* Sometimes stunt casting works, as in this film which features the Keach Brothers as the outlaws The James Brothers; the Carradine Brothers as The Younger Brothers; the Quaid Brothers as the brothers Miller; and the Guest Brothers as the Fords. Director Hill captures the melancholy in the passing of the Old West, while not ignoring the shoot-outs and chases as The James Gang face the penalty for one withdrawal too many. ★★★ DVD Letterbox: $19.99, VHS: $9.99

The Long Voyage Home

(1940, 104 min, US, John Ford) *John Wayne, Thomas Mitchell, Ian Hunter, Barry Fitzgerald.* Director Ford's slightly stagey but brilliantly cinematic rendering of four Eugene O'Neill one-acts depicts life on a merchant ship, following the day-to-day affairs of a group of seamen whose loneliness and frustrations give way to suspicion and the off-shore frivolities which bring about tragedy. Wayne, in a very uncharacteristic portrayal, plays a naïve Swede; and Mitchell is unforgettable as a seasoned old salt. Outstanding black-and-white cinematography by Gregg Toland (*Citizen Kane*). ★★★½ VHS: $14.99

The Long Way Home

(1997, 120 min, US, Mark Jonathan Harris) Narrated by *Morgan Freeman, Featuring the voices of: Ed Asner, Sean Astin, Martin Landau, Miriam Margoyles, David Paymer, Nina Siemaszko, Helen Slater, Michael York.* Whereas most documentaries dealing with the Holocaust examine the devastating years during the second world war, this harrowing film recounts the struggle of the Jewish camp survivors after their liberation, which for many was only marginally better than their captivity by the Nazis. Through astonishing archival footage, *The Long Way Home* details exactly that — the arduous path taken from the camps to the newly found state of Israel. With reminiscences from survivors and U.S. military personnel, the film often shocks in its revelations, such as that many Jews were housed by the U.S. Army in "Displaced Person" settlements on the very same sights as the Nazi death camps, and that they were treated in the same, militaristic manner in which the Germans had treated them. A thoughtful, illuminating and often anguished look at a people's history and a world's shame. ★★★★

The Longest Day

(1962, 169 min, US, Andrew Marton, Bernhard Wicki, Ken Annakin) *Henry Fonda, John Wayne, Richard Burton, Sean Connery, Red Buttons, Robert Mitchum, Robert Ryan, Rod Steiger, Kenneth More, Sal Mineo, Roddy McDowall.* Classic WWII epic which accounts the Allied invasion of Normandy. One might think that at nearly three hours in length this could be a tedious affair, but the action here is carried at a brisk pace and with great attention to detail. The all-star cast delivers a plethora of strong performances. One of the best WWII dramas ever made. ★★★★ DVD: $14.99, VHS: $9.99, VHS Letterbox: $19.99

The Longest Yard

(1974, 123 min, US, Robert Aldrich) *Burt Reynolds, Eddie Albert, Ed Lauter, Bernadette Peters.* Former pro Reynolds gets incarcerated and heads the prison football team to victory. Some good laughs and lots of action in this forceful comedy. ★★★ DVD: $19.99, VHS: $9.99

Longtime Companion

(1990, 96 min, US, Norman René) *Campbell Scott, Bruce Davison, Dermot Mulroney, Stephen Caffrey, Patrick Cassidy, Brian Cousins, Mary-Louise Parker, Michael Schoeffling.* One of the first American films to address the AIDS crisis, *Longtime Companion* is an exceptional look into the lives of a group of gay friends, and how the disease affects them, both collectively and singularly. Director René and writer Craig Lucas succeed in creating full-dimensioned characters and the film is rich in sharp observations and keen wit. There is a terrific ensemble cast, but Davison must be given a special mention for his superlative portrayal of the lover who slowly watches his longtime companion succumb. ★★★½ DVD: $19.99, VHS: $19.99

Look Back in Anger

(1958, 99 min, GB, Tony Richardson) *Richard Burton, Claire Bloom, Mary Ure, Donald Pleasence.* John Osborne's play made theatre history in England as a rebellious attack against the rigidity of the English establishment. Bristling with heated dialogue, the story represents the first signs of postwar dissatisfaction with the social immobility of life in a dying Empire. A trend-setting "angry young man" drama that is exceptionally acted and remarkably written. ★★★½ DVD Letterbox: $19.99

Look Back in Anger

(1980, 101 min, GB, Lindsay Anderson) *Malcolm McDowell, Lisa Barnes.* McDowell once again teams up with Anderson in this compelling remake of John Osborne's explosive "angry young man" play. McDowell offers a passionate performance as Jimmy Porter, and Anderson deftly directs the action. ★★★

Look Back in Anger

(1990, 114 min, GB, David Jones) *Kenneth Branagh, Emma Thompson, Gerard Horan.* Branagh stars in this version of John Osborne's powerful "kitchen sink" drama based on Judi Dench's West End revival. Branagh re-creates the role made famous by Richard Burton as Jimmy Porter, a young man whose poor position in life results in a simmering rage that is directed towards both his wife (nicely played by Thompson) and to the indifferent world that surrounds him. Branagh's excellent performance is the core of the piece offering a blistering portrayal of frustration and passion. ★★★ VHS: $19.99

Look Who's Talking

(1989, 90 min, US, Amy Heckerling) *John Travolta, Kirstie Alley, Olympia Dukakis, Bruce Willis, George Segal.* The surprise hit of 1989, this mostly amusing comedy is charming due partially to two great gimmicks: a talking baby whose thoughts are heard on screen, and the ever-glib Willis as the vocal incarnation of the little tyke, Mikey. Alley is Mikey's mom, a single accountant having an affair with married business associate Segal. While waiting for him to leave his wife, she ignores the attentions of a helpful and obviously made-for-each-other taxi driver. Travolta delivers a wonderful comic performance as the cabbie. (Followed by 2 sequels) ★★½ DVD: $19.99, VHS: $9.99, VHS Letterbox: $19.99

Looker

(1981, 94 min, US, Michael Crichton) *Albert Finney, James Coburn, Susan Dey, Leigh Taylor-Young, Dorian Harewood.* From the creator of *Coma* and *Westworld* comes this sci-fi satire about beautiful models who are murdered and then reconstituted by a computer hoping to produce the perfect spokesperson. (No, this is *not* the Vanna White story.) With Dey as the model out for vengeance, Finney as the plastic surgeon going out of business and Coburn as the C.E.O. ★★½ VHS: $14.99

Looking for Langston

(1989, 45 min, GB, Isaac Julien) This pensive yet celebratory meditation on black poet Langston Hughes is an original work. Stylish and sexy, the film incorporates the lyrical poetry of Essex Hemphill and Bruce Nugent with archival footage of the Harlem Renaissance of the 1920s. Re-enacted Cotton Club scenes, romantic shots of two intertwined lovers, Robert Mapplethorpe's photographs of beautiful black men and the pounding disco beat of "Can You Feel It" are also used in telling the story of black consciousness in a culturally evolving America. ★★★½ VHS: $29.99

Looking for Mr. Goodbar

(1977, 136 min, US, Richard Brooks) *Diane Keaton, Richard Gere, William Atherton, Tuesday Weld, Richard Kiley.* Keaton's terrific performance isn't enough to sustain this horrid adaptation of Judith Rossner's best-seller about a repressed schoolteacher who turns to nightly bar-hopping for sexual and personal fulfillment. ★

Looking for Richard

(1996, 118 min, US, Al Pacino) *Al Pacino, Alec Baldwin, Winona Ryder, Aidan Quinn, Estelle Parsons, Kevin Spacey, Penelope Allen, Kenneth Branagh, Kevin Kline, James Earl Jones, Derek Jacobi.* It's long been a presumption that Yanks can't do Shakespeare; American actors have carried that on their shoulders with the foreboding of Hamlet's ghost. The debunking and playful spoofing of this theatrical myth is only one of the delicious treats in store in *Looking for Richard*, a scintillating peek into the soul of Shakespeare's evil prince, Richard III. Making an assured directorial debut, Pacino leads his crew (and audience) on an odyssey to discover the inner workings of "Richard III," both the play and the character. Intercutting actual scenes, the actor talks to everyone from an American Average Joe to some of England's acting royalty to come to an understanding of the Bard. Comical and always fascinating, the film actually makes Shakespeare accessible. ★★★½ VHS: $29.99

Loose Cannons

(1990, 94 min, US, Bob Clark) *Gene Hackman, Dan Aykroyd, Dom DeLuise, Ronny Cox.* Hackman makes so many movies a year, the odds are that occasionally a clinker is going to get through. This is one of them. Mis-matched cops (now *there's* an original idea) Hackman and Aykroyd are up against modern-day Nazis in Washington D.C. ★ DVD Letterbox: $24.99, VHS: $14.99

Loose Connections

(1983, 90 min, GB, Richard Eyre) *Lindsay Duncan, Stephen Rea, Robbie Coltrane.* A delightful little road comedy about a dedicated feminist who decides to drive across Europe to attend a women's conference in Munich. She winds up with Harry, a less-than-savory traveling companion whose outright chauvinism tests her nerve all the way down the Autobahn. ★★★

Loot

(1972, 101 min, GB, Silvio Narizzano) *Lee Remick, Roy Holder, Hywell Bennett, Milo O'Shea.* Joe Orton's frantically paced, door slamming farce/black comedy — by far one of the most original and uproarious plays ever to grace the British stage — is presented here with all the outrageousness it deserves. The story concerns a pair of misguided youths who, having knocked over a bank, hide the swag in mom's coffin. All hell breaks loose as the distraught duo tries to retrieve their booty. Inspired performances abound from a crackerjack cast. ★★★

Lord Jim

(1965, 154 min, GB, Richard Brooks) *Peter O'Toole, James Mason, Curt Jurgens, Eli Wallach, Jack Hawkins.* O'Toole is Jim, a romantic young English seaman whose life is irrevocably altered when he violates his personal code of honor by a single act of cowardice. In subsequent attempts to erase his guilt, he finds himself in the middle of a massive Indonesian labor dispute and incipient rebellion. O'Toole gives an outstanding performance under the direction of Brooks, who scripted from the Joseph Conrad novel. ★★★ VHS: $19.99

Lord Love a Duck

(1966, 104 min, US, George Axelrod) *Roddy McDowall, Tuesday Weld, Lola Albright, Martin West, Ruth Gordon, Harvey Korman.* Though better known for his brilliant screenplays (from *The Seven Year Itch* to *The Manchurian Candidate*), Axelrod proved himself to be an inspired director with this rather insane black comedy about a nutty high schooler (McDowall) who lets his fantasy life overwhelm reality — though '60s California ends up seeming even crazier! The sequence where Tuesday Weld models different colored sweaters for her disturbingly approving dad is a riot. ★★★½ DVD Letterbox: $14.99, VHS: $14.99

Lord of Illusions

(1995, 121 min, US, Clive Barker) *Scott Bakula, Kevin J. O'Connor, Famke Janssen, Vincent Schiavelli.* Barker's third film as director is a tale of magic and illusion, cults and murder. Originally released theatrically in a heavily edited 108-minute version, this director's cut rectifies its confusion and abruptness. Bakula stars as Harry D'Amour, a private investigator who becomes embroiled in a bizarre series of murders involving an illusionist whose high-profile act turns out to be supported by real magic. Harry follows the trail through its twists and turns until he learns the truth: the illusionist Swann was the disciple and eventual murderer of an evil magician named Nix, whose resurrection is being engineered by a murderous cult. Adapted from Barker's superb short story "The Last Illusion," the basic premise itself is promising and original. Still radically different from most horror films, it was perhaps too far ahead of its time to please the studio powers-that-be. ★★½ DVD: $14.99

Lord of the Flies

(1963, 91 min, GB, Peter Brook) *James Aubrey, Tom Chapin.* A haunting and powerful adaptation of William Golding's novel brought to the screen by the incomparably daring British stage director Brook. Unlike his masterful *Marat/Sade*, which exploded on the screen with theatrical brilliance, here the "theatre" tends to slightly overshadow the strength of the story. However, this allegory of English schoolboys who slowly revert to brutal savagery when stranded on an island is still a fascinating and disturbing film in its own right. (Remade in 1990) ★★★ DVD: $39.99, VHS: $29.99

Lord of the Flies

(1990, 90 min, GB, Harry Hook) *Balthazar Getty, Danuel Pipoly, Chris Furrh, Badgett Dale, Andrew Taft, Gary Rule.* Deep greens and beautiful forests dominate the frames of this remake, complete with yowling children and war paint. Director Hook displays his true forte, cinematography, paying more attention to picture than content. Detailing the regression of shipwrecked boys from an ordered existence into primitive, warring factions, this slightly updated version of William Golding's allegorical novel makes it to the screen with little change, except that the boys run around with glows-sticks instead of torches. ★★½ DVD Letterbox: $14.99

Lord of the Rings

(1978, 133 min, US, Ralph Bakshi) Bakshi's ambitious adaptation of J.R.R. Tolkien's classic fantasy trilogy covers only one-half of the series. Filmed in rotoscope (live-action enhanced with animation — a technique better utilized in his later work *American Pop*), *Lord of the Rings* tells of the War of the Rings within the mystical land, Middle Earth. Despite any shortcomings for the book's enthusiasts, it's a joy to see Tolkien's creations, such as Frodo and Gollum, on film. (Remade in 2001) ★★★ DVD: $12.99, VHS: $9.99

The Lord of the Rings: The Fellowship of the Ring

(2001, 178 min, US/New Zealand, Peter Jackson) *Elijah Wood, Ian McKellen, Viggo Mortensen, Sean Astin, Sean Bean, Ian Holm, Liv Tyler, Cate Blanchett, Christopher Lee, John Rhys-Davies, Hugo Weaving, Billy Boyd, Dominic Monaghan, Orlando Bloom, Andy Serkis.* Some of the most lyrical, transcendent images to ever appear on screen are married with balls-to-the-wall filmmaking in the intense and glorious first installment of J.R.R. Tolkien's "Lord of the Rings." And it's important to note that this is just the first part, because after sharing three hours of the glorious quest of hobbit Frodo Baggins (Wood), it can be frustrating to have no climax or resolution to the plot threads. In this installment, Frodo discovers the terrible history of the One Ring, and joined by an elite group of different races, most notably wizard Gandalf (a majestic McKellen) and warrior Aragorn (Mortensen), he sets across Middle-earth to find the one location where the Ring can be destroyed. Tolkien basically created the fantasy genre, and here director Jackson creates a new standard for the fantasy film, the first of its kind to be so seamlessly immersed in its world. The adventure is wondrous and often terrifying, a road trip with many sharply rendered villains both external and internal. Best of all, Jackson doesn't pander to any audience, hoping to bring the lowest common denominator up to his high level. (Sequel: *The Lord of the Rings: The Two Towers*) ★★★★ DVD Letterbox 2-disc set: $29.99, DVD Pan & Scan 2-disc set: $29.99, DVD 5-disc Collector's Gift Set: $79.99, DVD 4-disc Extended Director's Edition: $39.99, VHS: $6.99, VHS Letterbox Extended Director's Edition: $24.99

The Lord of the Rings: The Two Towers

(2002, 179 min, US/New Zealand, Peter Jackson) *Elijah Wood, Viggo Mortensen, Ian McKellen, Sean Astin, John Rhys-Davies, Andy Serkis, Bernard Hill, Miranda Otto, Liv Tyler, Christopher Lee, Billy Boyd, Dominic Monaghan, Brad Dourif, Cate Blanchett, Hugo Weaving.* While *The Fellowship of the Ring* played like a road movie, this ambitious sequel seamlessly follows several simultaneous story lines. Hobbits Frodo and Sam are sidetracked on their quest by the tortured Gollum, a beautifully fleshed-out CGI character that's voiced by Serkis (who also served as the model). Saruman (Lee) is raising his army, while Gandalf (McKellen) has been resurrected as a glorious white wizard. Pippin and Merry, on their way back to the shire, run into a race of slow, wizened treefolk — it's daunting to make a believable walking and talking tree, yet the effects are tremendous, and the trees' plight even becomes, dare we say it, moving. And most incredible is the DeMille/Griffith-sized spectacle of the battle at Helm's Deep: a few hundred humans, including hero Aragorn (the terrifically charismatic Mortensen), taking on an army of ten thousand monstrous orcs. Such scale could lead to chaos, but Jackson makes sense of it all, expertly showing all the smaller clashes while keeping an eye on the bigger picture. For anyone who laments that movies just aren't the same as during the golden era, this second installment of Jackson's mindbending trilogy is how they used to make 'em. All of 'em, all at once. And it is breathtaking. (Sequel: *The Lord of the Rings: The Return of the King*) ★★★★ DVD Letterbox 2-disc set: $29.99, DVD Letterbox 5-disc Collector's Gift Set: $79.99, DVD Letterbox 4-disc Extended Director's Edition: $39.99, DVD Pan & Scan 2-disc set: $29.99, VHS: $6.99, VHS Extended Director's Edition: $24.99

The Lord of the Rings: The Return of the King

(2003, 201 min, US/New Zealand, Peter Jackson) *Elijah Wood, Ian McKellen, Viggo Mortensen, Sean Astin, Orlando Bloom, Andy Serkis, John Rhys-Davies, Bernard Hill, Billy Boyd, Dominic Monaghan, Liv Tyler, Cate Blanchett, Hugo Weaving.* In movies, at least, good things rarely come in threes. From *Godfather*s to *Matrix*es, the final acts of cinematic trilogies are often crushing disappointments. Leave it to the remarkable *Lord of the Rings* trilogy to create a third installment that not only succeeds, but is indeed the best of the three and one of the best adventure films ever made. Deftly

Elijah Wood in *The Lord of the Rings: The Return of the King*

wrapping up ten hours of loose ends while inventing dozens of new creatures and countless stunning special effects, *The Return of the King* follows Frodo, Sam and Gollum's final steps to Mordor, Aragorn's ascent to the throne, and Gandalf's rousing of an entire Middle-earth army. A gripping seige at the midpoint escalates from sword and arrow play to the felling of ten-story mastodons to the summoning of an undead army. It might all be computer effects, but director Jackson uses technology as a necessary tool to create the seamless, large-scale excitement. The actors, as always, are terrifically engaging, and in an extended epilogue are given a quiet chance to really expand their chops. It's incredibly sad to part with these delightful hobbits, elves, dwarves and men — a surprisingly resonant emotion coming from the fantasy realm, but one that is earned by the care, enthusiasm and daring that went into the electrifying whole. Winner of 11 Academy Awards, including Best Picture and Director. ★★★★ DVD Letterbox 2-disc set: $29.99, DVD Pan & Scan 2-disc set: $29.99, VHS 2-tape set: $24.99

Favorite Line: "My friends, you bow to no one." — *Viggo Mortensen as Aragorn*

The Lords of Discipline

(1983, 102 min, US, Franc Roddam) *David Keith, Mark Breland, Michael Biehn, Bill Paxton, Judge Reinhold, Rick Rossovich, Matt Frewer.* A sensationalistic thriller about a senior (Keith) at a 1964 South Carolina military academy charged with protecting the school's first black student (Breland) from a mysterious hazing organization known as "The Ten." Based on Pat Conroy's semiautobiographical novel. ★★½ VHS: $14.99

Lorenzo's Oil

(1992, 135 min, US, George Miller) *Nick Nolte, Susan Sarandon, Peter Ustinov, Kathleen Wilhoite.* A stirring adaptation of the real-life story of Michaela and Agusto Odone, whose son Lorenzo was stricken by an incurable, and fatal, disease known as ALD. Rising above its mushy "disease-of-the-week" roots, *Lorenzo's Oil* is more riveting scientific detective story than melodrama as it follows the Odones in their relentless search for a scintilla of hope while battling a complacent medical establishment. Both Sarandon and Nolte offer superb performances as the beleaguered parents whose love for their son drives them to feverishly search for their own cure. ★★★½ DVD Letterbox: $14.99

Lorna

(1964, 78 min, US, Russ Meyer) *Lorna Maitland.* The first film in which Russ added violence to spice up the sex. Maitland is a sexually frustrated housewife who becomes involved with an escaped convict. The first of Russ' black and whites. ★★ DVD: $39.99

Losing Chase

(1996, 93 min, US, Kevin Bacon) *Helen Mirren, Kyra Sedgwick, Beau Bridges.* An accomplished, made-for-cable directorial debut from actor Bacon, *Losing Chase* is a well-acted, if slightly uneven character study of two women who form an intense bond over the course of a summer. After suffering a nervous breakdown, Chase (the magnificent Mirren) returns to her family's summer home on Martha's Vineyard. A sensitive young woman (Sedgwick) is hired to be a "mother's helper" for the suspicious and unwelcoming Chase. Soon, the two women discover they have a lot in common, perhaps more than do Chase and her well-meaning but ineffectual husband. The first half of the film is especially compelling, as the two women's relationship blossoms. ★★★

Losing Isaiah

(1995, 108 min, US, Stephen Gyllenhaal) *Jessica Lange, Halle Berry, David Strathairn, Cuba Gooding, Jr., Samuel L. Jackson.* With its made-for-TV premise of a child custody battle, the compelling *Losing Isaiah* tugs at the heart while prodding the mind. Berry, in an exceptionally fine performance, plays a crack-addicted mother who throws her newborn baby in the trash (later thinking him dead). Lange, in a passionate portrayal, plays a hospital social worker who adopts the child. Four years later, however, after Berry has gone through rehab, she discovers the baby is alive, and takes Lange to court to obtain custody. In addressing the contentious social issues of interracial adoption, the film smartly and effectively acknowledges that no easy or even correct answers are readily available. ★★★ DVD: $19.99, VHS: $9.99

The Loss of Sexual Innocence

(1999, 106 min, GB, Mike Figgis) *Julian Sands, Saffron Burrows, Hanne Klintoe, Femi Ogumbanjo, Jonathan Rhys-Meyers.* One of the most pretentious titles ever to grace a feature-length film should be enough warning, but just in case the wildly hot-and-cold Figgis name piques some interest, here are the facts: *The Loss of Sexual Innocence* is an almost unwatchable treatise on sexual growth and emotional immaturity that makes *The Blue Lagoon* look like an Oscar contender. The non-linear, non-sensical plot follows the life of a film director through various stages, including affairs, an unhappy marriage and murder. (Didn't Truffaut do this better with his Antoine Doinel cycle?) An overly grave tone, a heavyhanded jazz score by Figgis, and a decided lack of drama add to the mess. ★ DVD: $27.99, VHS: $14.99

Lost and Found

(1979, 112 min, US, Melvin Frank) *Glenda Jackson, Maureen Stapleton, George Segal.* Attempting to capitalize on their success in *A Touch of Class*, Jackson and Segal pair up once again for this mordant comedy on married life. While not quite as funny or lively as the first go-round, Jackson and Segal do have a certain screen chemistry which makes this worthwhile viewing. ★★½

Lost & Found

(1999, 99 min, US, Jeff Pollack) *David Spade, Sophie Marceau, Patrick Bruel, Artie Lange, Mitchell Whitfield, Martin Sheen, Jon Lovitz.* Spade takes his wise-ass dweeb to new lows in this unfunny piece of tedium which makes the mistake in thinking wisecracks make a comedy make. Spade plays a restaurant owner who falls for his beautiful new neighbor (Marceau). He concocts a plan to steal her dog, thus being able to spend time with her pretending to look for it. Spade spends most of the film whining and throwing out one-liners, very few of which are even worthy of a smirk. He's paired, for a short time anyway, with another overweight guy (in the absence of Chris Farley), but there are no sparks here. At least the dog's kinda cute. ★½ DVD: $19.99, VHS: $14.99

Lost Boundaries

(1949, 105 min, US, Alfred L. Werker) *Mel Ferrer, Beatrice Pearson, Richard Hylton, Susan Douglas, Canada Lee.* A post-war social drama made at a time when American cinema was rediscovering its political voice, *Lost Boundaries* is the affecting, if slightly slow-moving story of racial intolerance in rural America. In his debut, Ferrer plays a dedicated light-skinned black doctor who, with his wife, "passes" for white in order to accept the lucrative position of town physician in an all-white New Hampshire town. Based on a true story, the film recounts the couple's dilemma as they must deny their cultural heritage but are afforded the opportunity to give their children a privileged upbringing. The film is directed at an even pace throughout, but there are times one would wish for the action to move a bit more briskly. ★★★ VHS: $19.99

The Lost Boys

(1987, 98 min, US, Joel Schumacher) *Jason Patric, Kiefer Sutherland, Dianne Wiest, Corey Haim, Barnard Hughes, Corey Feldman, Edward Herrmann, Jami Gertz, Billy Wirth, Alex Winter.* Hip vampire tale about a family moving to a small California coastal town, and discovering the city is populated with teenage vampires. Patric and Haim are the brothers battling bloodsuckers Sutherland and friends. Wiest is the boys' supermom, and Hughes is the coolest grandfather this side of Grandpa Munster. (Even if it did bring together "the Coreys," it's still good fun.) ★★★ DVD Letterbox 2-disc Special Edition: $26.99, DVD: $14.99, VHS: $9.99

Favorite Line: "You're a creature of the night, Michael . . . Wait 'til Mom hears about this!" — *Corey Haim as Sam Emerson*

The Lost Continent

(1968, 97 min, GB, Michael Carreras) *Eric Porter, Hildegard Knef, Suzanna Leigh.* Based very loosely on Dennis Wheatley's novel "Uncharted Seas," this enjoyable piece of Hammer Studios hokum is about a small group of passengers aboard a tramp steamer who, after a few adventures in love and danger, find themselves adrift in the Sargasso Sea. After being attacked by some intelligent seaweed, our motley crew discover the existence of a cult of modern-day Spanish conquistadors. As if all this weren't enough, there are also giant man-eating mollusks to contend with! Shot entirely within a studio, the film has an artificial look which works to its advantage, given its fantastic story line. ★★½ VHS: $14.99

Lost Highway

(1997, 134 min, US, David Lynch) *Bill Pullman, Patricia Arquette, Robert Blake, Balthazar Getty, Robert Loggia, Richard Pryor, Jack Nance, Henry Rollins.* Making the excesses and narrative of *Blue Velvet* seem the model of restraint by comparison, Lynch's *Lost Highway* is eerie, scary, enigmatic, weird and provocative. Sometimes the film is all of these at once, when it's in high gear; and sometimes it just tries too hard to evoke just one of those moods, stalling in its tracks. Graced by beautiful cinematography by Peter Deming, *Lost Highway* is the bizarre, often incomprehensible but nevertheless hypnotic story of a murder, a jazz musician and his wife, a youth in over his head, and the ability to phone someone while standing right next to them without being on the phone. Story coherency is of little consequence in *Lost Highway*; Lynch and cowriter Barry Gifford go out of their way to give bits of traditional narrative structure and then rub your face in it the very next minute. Blake gives an effectively creepy portrayal. ★★½ VHS: $14.99

The Two Roberts: Blake and Loggia in David Lynch's *Lost Highway*

The Lost Honor of Katharina Blum

(1975, 95 min, Germany, Margarethe von Trotta & Volker Schlöndorff) *Angela Winkler, Mario Adorf, Jürgen Prochnow.* A political thriller which examines the havoc wrought by West Germany's yellow journalism. A woman is victimized and traumatized by the relentless press coverage of an evening she spent with a suspected terrorist. Directed by the husband-wife team of Schlöndorff (*The Tin Drum*) and von Trotta. (German with English subtitles) ★★★ DVD Letterbox Criterion Collection: $29.99, VHS: $19.99

Lost Horizon

(1937, 132 min, US, Frank Capra) *Ronald Colman, Sam Jaffe, Jane Wyatt, Edward Everet Horton.* The restoration of Capra's exotic fantasy about the fabled kingdom of Shangri-La is in itself an epic of sorts: a 13-year search of worldwide archives to locate some 20 minutes of lost footage, cut following the film's original 1937 release. Capra, then at the peak of his fame and very much the Spielberg of his day, had a staggering budget of $4 million to re-create James Hilton's utopian novel about a noted British diplomat (Colman) who is abducted so that he can succeed a dying High Lama (Jaffe) at a remote Himalayan paradise. ★★★★ DVD: $27.99, VHS: $19.99

Lost in a Harem

(1944, 89 min, US, Charles Riesner) *Bud Abbott, Lou Costello, Marilyn Maxwell, Douglas Dumbrille.* It's hijinks aplenty as Abbott and Costello run amok in the Middle East with some occasionally funny results. Bud and Lou are magicians stranded in the desert who become involved with sultan Dumbrille and harem beauty Maxwell. Mideast relations have never been the same. Also with the Jimmy Dorsey Orchestra. ★★½ VHS: $14.99

Lost in America

(1985, 91 min, US, Albert Brooks) *Albert Brooks, Julie Haggerty, Garry Marshall.* Brooks hilariously stars as an upwardly mobile young ad executive who loses a big promotion and decides to turn his back on yuppiedom to discover the "real" America (in a $40,000 Winnebago). Hagerty is his accepting wife in this sharply detailed comedy on the American Dream/Nightmare. ★★★½ DVD: $19.99

Lost in Space

(1998, 131 min, US, Stephen Hopkins) *William Hurt, Gary Oldman, Mimi Rogers, Matt LeBlanc, Heather Graham, Jack Johnson, Lacey Chabert, Jared Harris, Mark Goddard, Cameos by: June Lockhart, Angela Cartwright, Marta Kristen.* A slick, confusing, effects-laden version of the 1960s sci-fi TV show, which was pure camp at best. Though far-too serious for out-and-out, lost-in-the-stars fun, this *Lost in Space* does try to be more cerebral than its TV prototype — and that's both a good thing and a bad thing. Hurt and Rogers are Don and Maureen, head of the Robinson clan, who've all been '90s-fied (though this is set in 2058). Also on board is the nefarious Dr. Smith, played with hand-wringing glee by Oldman. The action scenes are familiar though competent, the effects are well-done though not remarkable, and the ending is too convoluted for its own good. ★★ DVD Letterbox Platinum Edition: $14.99, VHS: $9.99, VHS Letterbox: $14.99

Lost in Translation

(2003, 102 min, US, Sofia Coppola) *Bill Murray, Scarlett Johansson, Giovanni Ribisi, Anna Faris, Fumihiro Hayashi.* Even at his most manic, there's a melancholic, Emmett Kelly undercurrent in every Bill Murray performance (yes, even *Caddyshack*). That ephemeral sadness comes to the fore in *Lost in Translation*, an unexpectedly poignant exploration of the vagaries of fame and the impact of personal crisis at any stage of life. Murray is Bob Harris, American movie star, in Japan to do a whiskey commercial. He's disoriented in Asia, suffering profound jet lag, in the hands of smiling handlers and a director who wants to imbue the commercial with the intensity of (ahem) *Apocalypse Now*. In the eternal Tokyo nightlife, he meets Charlotte (Johansson), young, attractive, intelligent, who's accompanying her photographer husband on a shoot. Bob and Charlotte are both adrift, clinging to the international refuge of the insomniac — TV — and aching for one iota of purpose and connection. This May-December odd couple lends each other enough camaraderie and mutual commiseration to buffer the incomprehensible differences of an alien environment; this frees them to see the astonishing similarities that unite us all across any generational or cultural divide. Writer-director Coppola adroitly shifts between manic activity and beautifully quiet moments, playing to her performers' strengths and offering arresting visual imagery. But whether careening through the neon-infused hyperactivity of downtown Tokyo or golfing in the serene shadow of Mt. Fuji, the camera returns to Murray. The actor delivers a seminal performance and Coppola crafts a sparkling jewel in telling this affecting tale of two people who share the exquisite and transcendent experience of mutual understanding. ★★★★ DVD Letterbox: $19.99, DVD Pan & Scan: $19.99, VHS: $9.99

Bill Murray and Scarlett Johansson in *Lost in Translation*

Lost in Yonkers

(1993, 112 min, US, Martha Coolidge) *Mercedes Ruehl, Irene Worth, David Strathairn, Richard Dreyfuss, Brad Stoll, Mike Damus.* Neil Simon's Pulitzer Prize-winning and Tony Award-winning play loses some of its luster in this appealing if uneven adaptation. Two adolescent brothers go to live with their stern grandmother (Worth) and endearing, slow-witted aunt (Ruehl). As a childhood remembrance, the film is funny and sweet, with Stoll and Damus as very likable youths. Halfway through, however, the film runs out of energy, and even a canister of Simon one-liners is not sufficient to give it a full recharge. Worth gives a gallant characterization, but she's such a one-note holy terror, the film plays like *Throw Grandmamma from the Train* whenever she's on screen. Ruehl gives an earnest performance as Aunt Bella, whose child-like innocence endows her with pathos and charm. ★★½ DVD Letterbox: $24.99

The Lost Language of Cranes

(1992, 90 min, GB, Nigel Finch) *Corey Parker, John Schlesinger, Rene Auberjonois, Eileen Atkins, Brian Cox, Angus McFayden, Cathy Tyson.* David Leavitt's critically acclaimed novel about a troubled family's crisis with homosexuality is powerfully adapted for the screen. Phillip, a young gay man, falls in love and begins to feel the need to tell his parents about his true sexual self. The twist is that Phillip's father is also gay/bisexual but keeps his yearning closeted from his wife and family. The parallel stories of these two men and the emotionally distraught wife and mother caught in-between results in an undeniably painful melodrama that is exceptionally sensitive to the issues of homosexuality, bisexuality, coming out and familial miscommunication. ★★★½ VHS: $19.99

The Lost Moment

(1947, 88 min, US, Martin Gabel) *Robert Cummings, Susan Hayward, Agnes Moorehead.* An involving drama based on Henry James' "The Aspern Papers," with Cummings as an American publisher in Venice looking for a deceased writer's lost love letters, finding the woman he sent them to (Moorehead) and becoming involved with her niece (Hayward). ★★★

The Lost Patrol

(1934, 74 min, US, John Ford) *Victor McLaglen, Boris Karloff, Wallace Ford, Alan Hale.* Ford's rousing adventure film about a small British army unit, lost in the Mesopotamian desert, which comes under attack by Arab forces. McLaglen stars as the unit's commander, and Karloff has a field day as a religious fanatic. ★★★½

Lost Souls

(2000, 98 min, US, Janusz Kaminski) *Winona Ryder, Ben Chaplin, John Hurt, Philip Baker Hall, Elias Koteas.* Betraying a splendid visual style, this convoluted occult thriller lacks excitement, scares or characters to care about. An *Exorcist* knock-off, *Lost Souls* is the murky story of a young woman (Ryder) who must convince a crime journalist that he is Satan's chosen body for human reincarnation. Exorcisms, dark streets and religious mumbo-jumbo populate director Kaminski's unoriginal horror tale, in which very little will come as a surprise to anyone who's ever seen a film from this overcrowded genre. ★½ DVD: $19.99, VHS: $9.99

The Lost Weekend

(1945, 101 min, US, Billy Wilder) *Ray Milland, Jane Wyman, Howard da Silva, Frank Faylen.* Wilder's uncompromising and devastating social drama on alcoholism startled audiences in its day with its brutally honest depiction of life on the bottle. Milland won a much-deserved Oscar for his intense performance as a writer whose two-day alcoholic binge becomes a descent into hell. Da Silva is a stand out as a disapproving bartender. Winner of 4 Academy Awards including Best Picture and Best Director. ★★★★ DVD: $14.99

The Lost World

(1960, 98 min, US, Irwin Allen) *Michael Rennie, Jill St. John, Claude Rains, David Hedison, Fernando Lamas, Richard Haydn.* Campy and at times cheesy sci-fi fun courtesy of '60s cheese manufacturer Allen. Professor Rains and chums go exploring beneath an inactive volcano and discover a lost world full of prehistoric monsters, danger and a fortune in jewels. This remake of the 1925 classic silent (itself based on Arthur Conan Doyle's story) really doesn't compare to the original (the effects here are only marginally better), and characters do and say ridiculous things every 15 minutes, but the cast is engaging, never taking themselves too seriously. ★★½

The Lost World: Jurassic Park

(1997, 134 min, US, Steven Spielberg) *Jeff Goldblum, Julianne Moore, Pete Postlethwaite, Arliss Howard, Richard Attenborough, Vince Vaughn.* In Spielberg's frenzied, hard-edged sequel to *Jurassic Park*, claws are definitely sharper, teeth have more of a bite, and the horror is more horrific. Displaying even more impressive effects than in the first film, but lacking a developed story line and having a Swiss cheese-like plot, *The Lost World* finds Dr. Ian Malcolm (Goldblum) returning to take on those deadly prehistoric beasts. It seems there was another island populated by the dinosaurs, and there are those who would capture them and bring them to the U.S. (didn't they see *King Kong*?). That's all the plot that's needed to produce great scares (including a classic, hold-your-breath scene in a camper) and greater visuals. (Sequel: *Jurassic Park 3*) ★★★ DVD Letterbox: $26.99, DVD Pan & Scan: $26.99, DVD DTS sound: $26.99, VHS: $9.99

Louisiana

(1984, 208 min, US, Philippe de Broca) *Margot Kidder, Ian Charleson, Len Cariou.* In 1836, a young woman (Kidder) returns to Louisiana after 11 years in Paris, expecting great wealth from her father's estate. She finds that the bank has foreclosed, the land and slaves have been sold and all that's left are a house badly in need of repair and one spectacular necklace. Her response to her circumstances is played out against the realities of a slave economy and a brutally enforced caste system. It's possible that director de Broca wanted this film to comment on the slave trade as *King of Hearts* commented on WWI; unfortunately, it misses the mark. The simplicity and broadly drawn characters are an embarrassment, and at times almost trivialize the profound subject matter. ★★

Louisiana Purchase

(1941, 98 min, US, Irving Cummings) *Bob Hope, Victor Moore.* Politics takes it on the chin in this mildly entertaining Hope comedy. Bob plays an elected official who takes the rap for illegal goings-on by his associates. A senator is sent to investigate, and Hope and pals will try anything to save their skins. Hope is in his element as a wise-cracking dupe, but it's Moore's marvelous stint as the visiting senator which saves this comedy from the ordinary. Hope's filibuster is a particular highlight. ★★½ DVD Double Feature: $14.99

Louisiana Story

(1948, 77 min, US, Robert J. Flaherty) Produced by Standard Oil on a "no-strings-attached" policy, Flaherty's final film focuses on the story of a young Cajun boy who watches his Bayou sanctuary being invaded when an oil rig begins drilling in the swamp. Filming in an almost poetic style, Flaherty captures the mysterious appeal of the pristine paradise and offers a stirring tribute to the Bayou people. This beautiful and heartfelt semidocumentary was shot by Richard Leacock with a Pulitzer award-winning score by Virgil Thompson. ★★★½ DVD: $29.99, VHS: $19.99

LouLou

(1980, 110 min, France, Maurice Pialat) *Gérard Depardieu, Isabelle Huppert, Guy Marchant.* An engrossing look at a wife who spurns the comforts of bourgeois security for the pleasures of a bohemian lifestyle with a dangerously charming, drunken and chain-smoking womanizer. Depardieu is LouLou and Huppert is Nelly, the bright but bored wife of the sappy Marchant, whose demure behavior unravels in the face of the unabashed sexual excesses offered by LouLou. Riding a sexual and emotional rollercoaster, the incongruous pair slowly discover real love and affection. A rambling road movie that captures life on the edge, yet all the while, never leaving the streets of Paris. (French with English subtitles) ★★★ DVD: $19.99, VHS: $14.99

Love

(1971, 92 min, Hungary, Karoly Makk) *Lili Darvas, Mari Torocsik.* Legendary Hungarian actress Darvas, in her final film, is mesmerizing in this funny, touching and politically astute Academy Award nominee. After her husband is imprisoned on political charges, his wife keeps his memory alive and his sick elderly mother happy by telling the woman that her son had emigrated to America. The daughter-in-law continues the illusion by faking letters from her husband about America, as well as his fabulous success there as a movie director, and sending them to the old woman, who is kept alive by the excitement and happiness of her son. The film is about both personal and political falsehoods as well as a family's love and compassion. (Hungarian with English subtitles) ★★★★

Love Actually

(2003, 129 min, GB, Richard Curtis) *Hugh Grant, Liam Neeson, Emma Thompson, Colin Firth, Laura Linney, Alan Rickman, Keira Knightley, Martine McCutcheon, Bill Nighy, Rowan Atkinson.* Allen had Keaton, Truffaut had Léaud, Ford had Wayne, Bergman had Ullmann, writer and now-director Curtis has Grant. Okay, so maybe the latter's output doesn't exactly ante up to the formers' collaborative works, but even in the lighter genre in which they operate it is no less important of a relationship. After writing such solid romances as *Four Weddings and a Funeral* and *Notting Hill*, which both featured Grant quite effectively, Curtis makes his directorial debut with this equally appealing, equally funny if somewhat overly ambitious romantic comedy: At least nine subplots populate the film, and that's about two too many. Grant plays the Prime Minister who finds romance with his secretary; Thompson and Rickman are a married couple coping with his wandering eye;

Neeson is a widower raising his young son; Firth is a successful writer who falls for his housekeeper; best of the lot is Nighy as an aging rock star looking for a comeback. With these and more to give time to, Curtis shortshrifts his characters a bit, but fortunately what he has given them to do and say makes up for it. The story is charming throughout, the laughs are consistent, the ensemble is in fine form, and the romance just sort of sneaks up on you and catches you by surprise. ★★★ DVD: $26.99, VHS: $22.99

Love Affair

(1939, 87 min, US, Leo McCarey) *Irene Dunne, Charles Boyer, Maria Ouspenskaya.* The irresistible Dunne finds shipboard romance with suave Boyer, even though each is already engaged. They agree to meet six months later, only fate has other plans. The first half of the film is played more as a comedy, which can be very funny; the second half is a more traditional romantic drama, but it's all very lovely. (Remade in 1957 as *An Affair to Remember* and in 1994 as *Love Affair*) ★★★½

Love Affair

(1994, 108 min, US, Glenn Gordon Caron) *Warren Beatty, Annette Bening, Katharine Hepburn, Garry Shandling, Chloe Webb, Pierce Brosnan, Brenda Vacarro.* Third time's almost a charm. Robert Towne wrote the screenplay for this easy-going remake of the 1939 classic *Love Affair*, which itself was remade in 1957 as *An Affair to Remember*. Though moderately updated, the plot is basically the same with Beatty and Bening, both engaged to other partners, meeting and ultimately enjoying a shipboard romance. The two stars' relaxed and natural delivery give the film a pleasant edge, though they are a sometime victim to a glib screenplay which clearly tries too hard to be hip. As Beatty's beloved aunt, Hepburn makes a memorable appearance, looking frail but resolute; and there's a movie first as Kate utters the "f" word. ★★½ DVD Letterbox: $19.99, VHS: $9.99

Love Affair: Or, The Case of the Missing Switchboard Operator

(1967, 70 min, Yugoslavia, Dusan Makavejev) *Eva Ras, Slobodan Aligrudic.* A bizarre and unpredictable curiosity from Yugoslavia's greatest filmmaker. The story, both an unusual love story and a political parable, follows the budding relationship of a vivacious young woman and her rat-exterminating boyfriend. All is well until she allows herself to be seduced by a man of higher means. A daring work. (Serbo-Croatian with English subtitles) ★★★ VHS: $24.99

Love Among the Ruins

(1975, 100 min, US, George Cukor) *Katharine Hepburn, Laurence Olivier, Colin Blakely.* An exceptional TV movie starring film legends Hepburn and Olivier at their regal best as former lovers reunited years later when barrister Olivier defends aging actress Hepburn in court. A delightful and totally grand romantic comedy, directed with panache by Cukor. ★★★½

Love and a .45

(1994, 90 min, US, C.M. Talkington) *Renée Zellweger, Gil Bellows, Rory Cochrane, Jeffrey Combs, Jack Nance, Peter Fonda, Ann Wedgeworth.* Aiming for sardonic, hip commentary on today's modern world and life on the edge, *Love and a .45* never quite escapes its derivative origins and unoriginal execution. Some interesting people pop up, but the viewer is never moved from mild interest to involvement. This ain't no *True Romance*, but if you're into the genre, you might want to check out

William Powell (l.) is ready to rumble in *Love Crazy*

the random assortment of marginal characters who flit in and out of the precarious lives of this would-be Bonnie and Clyde team. ★★ DVD: $24.99

Love & Anarchy

(1973, 100 min, Italy, Lina Wertmüller) *Giancarlo Giannini, Mariangela Melato.* An enormously powerful political drama about Italian Fascism during the 1930s, brilliantly written and directed by Wertmüller. Giannini stars as a Venetian peasant who takes up residence in a brothel as he awaits his opportunity to assassinate Mussolini. Music by Nino Rota. (Italian with English subtitles) ★★★½ DVD: $19.99, VHS: $14.99

Love & Basketball

(2000, 127 min, US, Gina Prince-Bythewood) *Omar Epps, Sanaa Lathan, Dennis Haysbert, Debbie Morgan, Alfre Woodard.* Uneven but definitely worthwhile, *Love & Basketball* follows two friends from their first meeting as eleven-year-olds, through their tumultuous dating period, to being lovers in college and pursuing careers in the NBA. Both aspire to be brilliant basketball players, and struggle to reconcile their ambition with their relationship. The film begins awkwardly, and, unfortunately, doesn't really get a foothold until the two get to college, when our rooting interest deepens considerably. The two leads are quite good, and there's a terrific supporting cast led by Haysbert and Woodard. For all its flaws (overlength being another), *Love & Basketball* still manages to be entertaining and satisfying. ★★½ DVD: $19.99, VHS: $9.99

Love and Death

(1975, 82 min, US, Woody Allen) *Woody Allen, Diane Keaton, Harold Gould.* Tolstoy, Dostoevsky, Bergman (Ingmar) and the history books take a beating in Allen's hilarious comedic assault on 1800s Russia. Woody romances Diane, and they both try to assassinate Napoleon. ★★★½ DVD: $19.99, VHS: $14.99

Love and Death on Long Island

(1997, 103 min, GB, Richard Kwietniowski) *John Hurt, Jason Priestley, Fiona Loewi, Sheila Hancock, Maury Chaykin.* Funny, endearing, wise and invigorating, this tale of an older man's fixation on a younger man is nominally based on the Thomas Mann novella and the Luchino Visconti screen adaptation *Death in Venice.* Giles De'Ath (Hurt in a wonderful portrayal) is an acclaimed writer who accidentally

sees the sex comedy *Hot Pants College II* and is immediately struck by Ronnie Bostwick (Priestley), one of the film's stars. With the fervor of a teeny-bopper in love, Giles becomes obsessed with his object of perfection, and eventually travels to the United States in search of his "love." There he stalks the actor and eventually befriends him, making a quite unlikely pair. ★★★½ DVD: $14.99, VHS: $9.99

Love and Faith

(1978, 154 min, Japan, Kei Kumai) *Toshiro Mifune, Takashi Shimura.* This moving Japanese period drama stars Mifune and Takashi Shimura. The rise of Christianity in 16th-century Japan is used as a backdrop for a tragic romance involving the beautiful stepdaughter of Japan's leading tea master, whose love for a young Christian lord precipitates a conflict with vile warlord Mifune. (Japanese with English subtitles) ★★★

Love and Human Remains

(1993, 100 min, Canada, Denys Arcand) *Ruth Marshall, Cameron Bancroft, Thomas Gibson, Mia Kirshner, Rick Roberts, Joanne Vannicola, Matthew Ferguson.* Adapted from Brad Fraser's play "Unidentified Human Remains and the True Nature of Love," this somber drama might also be titled "Sex and Human Alienation." The story takes place in a nameless Canadian city populated by attractive, sexually active but world-weary young people of all sorts of sexual orientations. There is the gay David (Gibson), a sexually active waiter. His roommate is Candy (Marshall), a pretty and intelligent young woman who soon gets involved with both a straight man and an especially intense lesbian schoolteacher (Vannicola). Ladies' man Bernie (Bancroft) is the troubled yuppie, and Kane (Ferguson) is a sexually confused teenager fixated on the older David. Weaving its tale of souls emotionally adrift, Arcand's first English-language film effectively goes from one character to another charting their collective ennui and their valiant attempts to use sex as a facilitator towards intimacy, fulfillment and happiness. ★★★

Love and Other Catastrophes

(1996, 90 min, Australia, Emma-Kate Croghan) *Alice Garner, Frances O'Connor, Matthew Dyktynski.* Funky and hip from the very start, this amusing little Australian screwball comedy follows one mixed-up day in the life of a group of grad students in Melbourne. At the center are Alice (Garner),

a sprightly young woman who is four years late with her dissertation on "Doris Day as Feminist Warrior," and her lesbian roommate Mia (O'Connor), who finds herself caught in the bureaucratic nightmare of trying to change her department. The film zips around through their respective day while introducing a slew of supporting oddballs, especially in regards to their search for a new, third roommate. Director and cowriter Croghan demonstrates a marvelous sense of character while delivering occasionally cracking dialogue, and Garner and O'Connor both make thoroughly engaging protagonists. ★★★

Love at First Bite

(1979, 96 min, US, Stan Dragoti) *George Hamilton, Susan Saint James.* Very enjoyable take-off on the Dracula legend with Hamilton as the Count searching New York City for new victims — finding Saint James. Lots of laughs in this parody which isn't afraid to use every bat joke in the book. ★★★

Love at Large

(1990, 97 min, US, Alan Rudolph) *Tom Berenger, Elizabeth Perkins, Anne Archer, Kate Capshaw, Annette O'Toole.* For the first 60 minutes, this stylish homage to '40s film noir is nearly perfect: Berenger is a wonderfully befuddled and rumpled detective; there is a labyrinthine and duplicitous plot; and enough femme fatales to enrapture a slew of Sam Spades. Regrettably, however, this Rudolph-scripted mystery cannot sustain its initial high level and slowly unravels near the end. Gravel-voiced P.I. Harry Dobbs (Berenger) is hired to tail a possibly two-timing husband, but follows the wrong person — a man who leads the private eye into an increasingly sordid mess of murder, bigamy and deception. ★★½ DVD: $14.99

Love Crazy

(1941, 99 min, US, Jack Conway) *William Powell, Myrna Loy, Gail Patrick, Jack Carson.* A lively and zany screwball comedy, the story follows the merry exploits of Powell and Loy on their fourth anniversary. When she gets jealous over hubby's former girlfriend moving in upstairs, Loy files for divorce. Concocting a loony plan to get her back, Powell feigns insanity...and he's so convincing she has him committed. But we've already given away too much. Powell and Loy are, of course, terrific. Powell suffers almost every indignity (the elevator scene is a hoot) with his customary élan. ★★★

Love Crimes

(1992, 90 min, US, Lizzie Borden) *Sean Young, Patrick Bergen, Arnetia Walker.* Young stars as an unorthodox District Attorney trying to build a case against a mysterious man who is impersonating a well-known photographer and is taking advantage of a number of unsuspecting and vulnerable women. Bergin plays yet another deranged and sadistic villain. Overall, independent feminist filmmaker Borden's (*Working Girls*) attempt to enter the mainstream, while slightly perplexing and uneven, is an interesting and watchable thriller. Unrated version. ★★

Love Field

(1992, 104 min, US, Jonathan Kaplan) *Michelle Pfeiffer, Dennis Haysbert, Stephanie McFadden, Brian Kerwin.* Pfeiffer's sincere performance more than redeems the few plot holes in this otherwise endearing drama. She plays Lurene, a Dallas housewife who, upon the assassination of JFK, buses to Washington for his funeral. Enroute, she inadvertently involves a fellow passenger, a black man (Haysbert), with the police. Traveling with his young

L

daughter, the father and child hit the back roads to elude the authorities, accompanied by the naïve, good-intentioned Lurene. What follows is a charming road movie with touches of whimsy, romance and history lessons on racial attitudes, 1960s-style. ★★★ DVD: $14.99

Love Film

(1970, 130 min, Hungary, István Szabó) *Andras Balint, Judit Halasz.* Although unknown by most American audiences, this poignant human drama, political allegory and romantic love story is considered a pivotal film in Hungary's postwar cinema. Jancsi boards a train in Budapest on a journey to be reunited with his childhood sweetheart, Kata, who fled after the 1956 uprising. The trip also proves to be a journey into his pain-filled past — of innocent childhood moments, romantic rendezvous, as well as haunting images of WWII airraids, Communist youth rallies and the suffering caused by the Russian suppression of the Budapest Spring. (Hungarian with English subtitles) ★★★½ DVD Letterbox: $29.99, VHS: $24.99

Love Finds Andy Hardy

(1938, 92 min, US, George B. Seitz) *Mickey Rooney, Judy Garland, Lana Turner, Ann Rutherford.* Rooney finds himself with two dates for the big Christmas Dance — steady girlfriend Rutherford and voluptuous Turner. Then, a new girl moves in next door (Garland). Geez! What's a poor guy to do? One of the best of the Andy Hardy series with Mickey and Judy in good form. ★★★ DVD: $19.99, VHS: $19.99

Love from a Stranger

(1947, 81 min, US, Richard Whorf) *Sylvia Sidney, John Hodiak.* Newly married Sidney marries wholesome Hodiak, only to begin to suspect he may be a killer — and she may be his next victim. Based on an Agatha Christie story, which bears a resemblance to Alfred Hitchcock's *Suspicion.* It's a familiar story line with a degree of suspense. An earlier version was made in Great Britain in 1937 with Ann Harding and Basil Rathbone. ★★½ VHS: $14.99

Love Happy

(1949, 91 min, US, David Miller) *Groucho Marx, Harpo Marx, Chico Marx, Ilona Massey, Vera-Ellen, Raymond Burr, Marilyn Monroe.* Some swell kids want to put on a show, but the money's run out. But wait — the spectacular Romanov diamonds are in the can of sardines that the cat is dining on... Chico and Harpo track down the gems as Groucho tracks down the sullen but fabulously wealthy Massey, who's also after the loot. Vera-Ellen and Burr dance up a storm (yes, Raymond Burr), and Marilyn has a walk-on that makes up in intensity what it lacks in length. Ben Hecht was one of the scriptwriters for this occasionally funny Marx Brothers romp. ★★½ DVD: $14.99

Love Hurts

(1989, 110 min, US, Bud Yorkin) *Jeff Daniels, Cynthia Sikes, John Mahoney, Cloris Leachman, Judith Ivey.* A beguiling if familiar comedy-drama about a family coming together for a weekend wedding. Daniels heads a fine cast as a newly divorced insurance agent who returns home for his sister's nuptials. Complicating the visit are his ex-wife (Sikes) and children, who have just moved in. The story focuses on Daniels' various relationships with his family, including his estranged young daughter, drunken father and wary ex-wife. As in his excellent family drama *Twice in a Lifetime*, director Yorkin

handles familial trauma, rich characters and warm humor all with equal command. Mahoney and Leachman are extremely appealing as Daniels' colorful parents. ★★★ VHS: $14.99

Love in a Fallen City

(1984, 97 min, Hong Kong, Ann Hui) This compelling romantic wartime drama centers on the troubled love affair between a young divorcée and a rich, Westernized playboy right at the time of Hong Kong's fall to the Japanese in 1941. (Cantonese with English subtitles) ★★½

A Love in Germany

(1984, 110 min, West Germany, Andrzej Wajda) *Hanna Schygulla, Piotr Lysak, Armin Mueller-Stahl.* Amid the sweeping crush of the Nazi terror, a German shopkeeper (Schygulla) falls in love with a Polish POW and suffers the grave consequences of the illicit affair. Director Wajda conveys the poignance of personal tragedy overshadowed by the grand obscenity of war. (German with English subtitles) ★★★½

Love in the Afternoon

(1957, 130 min, US, Billy Wilder) *Gary Cooper, Audrey Hepburn, Maurice Chevalier, John McGiver.* Hepburn is captivating as a young Parisian artist whose curiosity and romanticism leads to romance in Wilder's enchanting and sardonic comedy. Chevalier is a private eye who is hired to tail American playboy Cooper, who is having an affair with a married woman. Starry-eyed Audrey hears that the cuckold husband may resort to firearms, and sets out to warn the Casanova. Romance ensues as the innocent Audrey gets philandering Gary to change his ways. Wilder casts a sarcastic eye towards romance and relationships while ultimately creating a sweetly caring one between Hepburn and Cooper. Here, Chevalier reminds one why he was one of France's biggest stars, and who could forget the wonderful train sequence? ★★★½ DVD Letterbox: $19.99, VHS: $14.99

Love in the City

(1953, 90 min, Italy, Various) *Ugo Tognazzi, Maresa Gallo.* This six-episode film is based on a very interesting idea: the director of each segment is "sent off" to capture, cinema verité style, an aspect of love and romance in the Eternal City. This hidden camera technique has each director act as a secret reporter out to explore typical Italian life. The Michelangelo Antonioni and Federico Fellini segments provide a fascinating hint to their future filmmaking careers. Other directors include Cesare Zavattini, Dino Risi, Alberto Lattuada and Francesco Maselli. (English narration) ★★★

Love in the Time of Money

(2001, 90 min, US, Peter Mattei) *Vera Farmiga, Domenick Lombardozzi, Jill Hennessy, Malcolm Gets, Steve Buscemi, Rosario Dawson, Adrian Grenier, Carol Kane.* A great cast is wasted in an ensemble piece that apes the structure of *Slacker* and *Twenty Bucks.* Those films had a comic tone and a sharp point of view, and were well-suited to the brief but insightful vignettes. In this dour drama, the limited time spent with each character just lends a vague, depressing monotony to the film. It's hardly believable, and only intermittently involving (Buscemi and Kane command our attention and make us care about their characters, despite the weak writing and direction). By the time the muddled, contrived, pessimistic denouement arrives, one is likely to feel ripped off. ★½ DVD: $29.99, VHS: $103.99

Love Is a Many Splendored Thing

(1956, 102 min, US, Henry King) *William Holden, Jennifer Jones, Torin Thatcher.* Based on the autobiographical best-seller by Han Suyin, this slick but hokey romantic drama is, at best, a partially splendored thing. Set in Hong Kong before the start of the Korean War, the film stars Jones as an Eurasian doctor involved in an affair with married American correspondent Holden. Jones and Holden both offer tender, captivating performances, but the film is slow moving, and John Patrick's dialogue, in trying to capture the mysticism and beauty of Chinese culture, borders on the clichéd; though a line such as "Let us have tea and talk of absurdities" is hard to resist. ★★½ DVD: $14.99, VHS: $9.99

Love Is Colder Than Death

(1969, 85 min, Germany, Rainer Werner Fassbinder) *Ulli Lommel, Hanna Schygulla.* Fassbinder's first film is a somber, stylized gangster drama inspired by American B-movies and the works of Sam Fuller and early Godard. Lommel is a trench-coated mobster who befriends a disheveled pimp (Fassbinder) and his prostitute girlfriend (Schygulla). The two men get in over their heads when they plan to eliminate a rival pimp. This black-and-white noir manages to rise above its low budget, poor sound quality and uneven pacing with bristling characterizations, an unpredictable story and a nice sense of atmosphere. (German with English subtitles) ★★½ DVD: $24.99, VHS: $19.99

Love Jones

(1997, 101 min, US, Theodore Witcher) *Larenz Tate, Nia Long, Isaiah Washington, Lisa Nicole Carson, Bill Bellamy.* Flavorful, romantic and funny, *Love Jones* is a real sleeper of a comedy. A very sexy photographer (Long) falls for the persistent charms of a budding novelist/poet (Tate), despite having given up on love after a failed marriage engagement. The film follows their relationship through all the usual obstacles — career, jealousy, pride, insecurity, etc. While the story is certainly tried and true, *Love Jones* has a funky, distinctive feel; for every aspect of the film that is clichéd or simplistic, there are many that are truthful and engaging. Despite its minor flaws — and an oddly unsatisfying ending — *Love Jones* is a winner. ★★★ DVD: $14.99, VHS: $9.99

The Love Letter

(1999, 88 min, US, Peter Ho-Sun Chan) *Kate Capshaw, Tom Selleck, Ellen Degeneres, Blythe Danner, Tom Everett Scott, Gloria Stuart, Geraldine McEwan, Julianne Nicholson.* A charming, low-keyed romantic comedy with Capshaw as a bookstore owner who finds an unsigned love letter and thinks it's meant for her. But who sent it? Complications arise when the letter finds its way into the hands of others in her small New England coastal town, each thinking it's meant for them as well. DeGeneres is a natural sidekick as the store's manager, and Selleck is quite appealing as the local fire chief in love with Capshaw. ★★★ DVD: $14.99

Love Me or Leave Me

(1955, 122 min, US, Charles Vidor) *James Cagney, Doris Day, Cameron Mitchell.* Cagney and Day (in her best film role) both give terrific performances in this musical biography of 1920s torch singer Ruth Etting. Cagney plays her gangster boyfriend. Score includes "Ten Cents a Dance" and "Shaking the Blues Away." ★★★½

Love Me Tender

(1956, 89 min, US, Robert D. Webb) *Elvis Presley, Debra Pagent, Richard Egan.* Presley's film debut is an acceptable Civil War drama about a Southern family taking different sides in the conflict. Elvis sings the title tune and "Let Me," among others. ★★½ DVD: $19.99, VHS: $9.99

Love Meetings

(1964, 90 min, Italy, Pier Paolo Pasolini) *Love Meetings* is a gritty, cinema verité-style investigation of sex in Italy. The film includes appearances by author Alberto Moravia and noted psychologist Cesare Musatti. Pasolini appears as the interviewer and asks a wide range of individuals to share their tales of love — including their thoughts on prostitution, homosexuality, marital and nonmarital liaisons. (Italian with English subtitles) ★★★ DVD: $29.99, VHS: $29.99

Love on the Run

(1979, 93 min, France, François Truffaut) *Jean-Pierre Léaud, Marie-France Pisier, Claude Jade.* Léaud makes his final appearance as Antoine Doinel in Truffaut's complex, bittersweet concluding installment of the Doinel saga. Through a marvelous sequence of flashbacks from earlier films, Truffaut documents Doinel's rocky road to adulthood. (French with English subtitles) ★★★ DVD: $19.99, VHS: $14.99

Love Potion #9

(1992, 90 min, US, Dale Launer) *Tate Donovan, Sandra Bullock, Anne Bancroft.* This lightweight fluff written and directed by the creator of *My Cousin Vinny* and *Ruthless People* is a far cry from the classic screwball comedies it wants most desperately to be — but then any movie that takes its inspiration from a '60s pop tune can't hope for much. Hormonal hijinks ensue when a pair of nerdy scientists (Donovan, Bullock) accidentally discover a love potion. While utterly predictable from start to finish, the film is redeemed somewhat by director Launer's hip take on the subject matter. ★★ DVD Letterbox: $14.99, VHS: $6.99

Love Serenade

(1997, 101 min, Australia, Shirley Barrett) *Miranda Otto, Rebecca Frith, George Shevtsov.* A witty, bizarre and very Australian take on love, sibling rivalry, Barry White and fish. In tiny Sunray, Australia, two quirky (to say the least) sisters have their humdrum lives turned upside-down when famed big-city DJ Ken Sherry (a terrifically droll Shevtsov) moves in next door. Unusual and funny, *Love Serenade* is brightly written and directed by Barrett, with spot-on performances by both Otto and Frith as the sisters, and especially Shevtsov, whose Ken Sherry is quite an imaginative character. Until an admittedly unique though abrupt and unsatisfying end, *Love Serenade* is a truly odd, enjoyable comedy. ★★★ DVD: $14.99, VHS: $9.99

Love Songs

(1986, 107 min, France, Elie Chouraqui) *Catherine Deneuve, Richard Anconina, Christopher Lambert, Nick Mancuso.* Deneuve and Lambert are enticingly matched as the ill-fated lovers in this entertaining and perceptive drama set in the rock music world of Paris. Deneuve is a successful talent agent, married to an American writer for 12 years and mother of two children, who reluctantly succumbs to a persistent and alluringly charming client, rock singer Lambert. The film's appeal could rest solely on the sexually charged love affair, but director Chouraqui also focuses on the people affected by the relationship. ★★★

Love Stinks

(1999, 94 min, US, Jeff Franklin) *French Stewart, Bridgette Wilson, Tyra Banks, Bill Bellamy.* A low-rent comic take-off on *Fatal Attraction*, this silly story stars Stewart (of TV's "3rd Rock from the Sun") as dorky sitcom writer who wins the heart of a beautiful woman (Wilson). Now get ready. . . The big joke is that she will stop at nothing to get him to walk down the aisle. Their ensuing battle of the sexes does produce a chuckle or two, but it's all of the chuckle-headed variety. Love may not stink, but it's certainly not worth the effort. ★★ DVD: $14.99

Love Story

(1970, 99 min, US, Arthur Hiller) *Ryan O'Neal, Ali McGraw, Ray Milland, John Marley, Tommy Lee Jones.* This box-office success is either classic romantic drama or ridiculous foolishness — depending on your tastes. O'Neal is the guy from the right side of the tracks, in love with McGraw, who's from the wrong side of town and has a fatal disease. (Sequel: *Oliver's Story*) ★★½ DVD: $14.99, VHS: $9.99

Love, Strange Love

(1982, 120 min, Brazil, Walter Khouri) *Vera Fischer, Mauro Mendonea.* This controversial film, about a young boy's sexual awakening in a brothel, caused quite a storm several years back when it played the film festival circuit. Possibly because of its subject matter, it never was released theatrically in the U.S., but is now on video in a complete unedited version. The story follows the development and growth of a young boy who is sent to live at his aunt's brothel. The enticing girls prove too much for the curious boy as he adjusts to this strange world. ★★½

Love Streams

(1986, 122 min, US, John Cassavetes) *John Cassavetes, Gena Rowlands, Diahnne Abbott, Seymour Cassel.* Two offbeat siblings, both desperate for some kind of happiness in their lonely existences, address their erratic ways in this examination of contemporary lifestyles. Cassavetes also appears as the hedonistic brother; Rowlands is the overly loving sister. Both Cassavetes and Rowlands are compelling in this insightful glimpse into two slightly neurotic romantic psyches. ★★★

Love! Valour! Compassion!

(1997, 115 min, US, Joe Mantello) *Jason Alexander, John Glover, Randy Becker, Stephen Spinella, Stephen Bogardus, Justin Kirk, John Benjamin Hickey.* Terrence McNally's Tony Award-winning play, trimmed from its three-hour running time, makes for an affecting, low-keyed tragicomedy which offers alternately insightful, heartrending and funny moments, but this film adaptation misses in capturing the play's greatness. A group of gay friends from New York spend their summer holiday weekends in the country at the beautiful lakeside estate of two lovers. With a discerning eye and ear, McNally explores the bonds and boundaries of friendships and romantic relationships which is perceptive drama no matter what sexual orientation characters may be. All but Alexander starred in the Broadway production, and he effortlessly fits in giving a tender, funny portrait. Glover is exceptional as twin brothers, one a sweet-natured, flamboyant PWA. ★★★ DVD Widescreen: $19.99

Love Walked In

(1998, 91 min, US, Juan J. Campanella) *Denis Leary, Terence Stamp, Aitana Sánchez-Gijón, Danny Nucci, Michael Badalucco.* An intriguing noir mystery, *Love Walked In* is a stylish and sexy story of deception and betrayal. Leary stars as a second-rate piano player married to the beautiful Sánchez-Gijón. When their small town's richest businessman takes a fancy to her, they plot to extort money from him. But *Love Walked In* goes in different directions than its premise suggests. There are a couple of nifty twists, and all three leads are quite good. Some of the story's set-up is familiar, but director Campanella's sustains interest throughout thanks to some snappy dialogue and a nice visual style. ★★★

Love with the Proper Stranger

(1963, 100 min, US, Robert Mulligan) *Natalie Wood, Steve McQueen, Edie Adams, Tom Bosley.* Wood and McQueen's impassioned performances dominate this hearty romantic comedy-drama about the love affair between shopgirl Wood and musician McQueen. ★★★ VHS: $19.99

Love without Pity

(1990, 95 min, France, Eric Rachont) *Hippolyte Girarodt, Mireille Perrier.* A delightfully witty drama of romantic love in the land of existentialism. Hippo — young, handsome, and with a seductive Belmondo-cool attitude — leads a carefree bohemian life; living with friends, bumming money and casually picking up women, only to drop them when his interest flags. A sexist pig certainly, but a charming one. But his "love 'em and leave 'em" attitude towards women comes back to haunt him when he meets a professional woman who does not immediately succumb to his charms. Intrigued by this evasive victim, he goes all out, only to find himself smitten with love, jealousy and obsession, all traits that mean nothing to the young lady. (French with English subtitles) ★★★ VHS: $19.99

Love's Labour's Lost

(2000, 93 min, GB, Kenneth Branagh) *Alessandro Nivola, Alicia Silverstone, Natascha McElhone, Kenneth Branagh, Carmen Ejogo, Matthew Lillard, Adrian Lester, Emily Mortimer, Nathan Lane.* Branagh may be the reigning screenwriter laureate of Shakespeare's plays, adapting the greater themes and gentler nuances to such works as *Hamlet*, *Henry V* and *Much Ado about Nothing*. In this condensation of *Love's Labour's Lost*, he especially proves to be an adroit handler of Shakespeare's gentle side, lending natural, playful readings to the trippingly delightful dialogue. But this comedy is saddled with an awkward, labeled conceit, as the story (placed somewhere in the 1930s) is constantly interrupted by musical numbers in the style (and with music) of that era. It's hard to tell whether the numbers would be entertaining in a different film, but here they are so unwelcome as to tarnish the scenes that surround them. ★★ DVD: $14.99, VHS: $9.99

The Loved One

(1965, 116 min, US, Tony Richardson) *Robert Morse, John Gielgud, Rod Steiger, Tab Hunter, Liberace, Jonathan Winters, Roddy McDowall.* Evelyn Waugh's audacious satire on the Southern California way of life (and death) was adapted for the screen by Terry Southern and Christopher Isherwood ("I Am a Camera"). This classic black comedy, which was billed as "the film with something to offend everyone," follows the sometimes surreal journey of a young man as he makes his way through studio intrigue, romance and a mystical

L

funeral parlor. Morse is the Candide-like nephew who travels to L.A. to visit his uncle; Steiger is the Oedipal Mr. Joyboy; and Liberace is a fastidious casket salesman. A refreshing slap in the face to both normality and eccentricity. ★★★½

Lovely & Amazing

(2002, 91 min, US, Nicole Holofcener) *Catherine Keener, Brenda Blethyn, Emily Mortimer, Jake Gyllenhaal, Raven Goodwin, Dermot Mulroney, James LeGros, Aunjanue Ellis, Michael Nouri.* The Marks women deal in various ways with the unfulfilled promise of life in present-day Los Angeles. Mom Jane (Blethyn) has adopted an at-risk inner-city child, and is undergoing liposuction for a flat stomach and the new relationship that is expected to result from the surgical procedure. Elizabeth (Mortimer) exacerbates her deeply ingrained insecurities by being an actress, with every callback a fresh opportunity for rejection and negative self-evaluation. Michelle (Keener, in a stand-out performance) is the bitter, caustic ex-homecoming queen in a barely functioning marriage, who plays at being an artist making miniature chairs out of twigs and responds to almost everything with a dispirited "fuck you." Adopted daughter Annie (Goodwin, in a notable film debut) watches them all with clear eyes, fondly nursing her own neuroses while observing the professional neurotics she now calls family. The characters are all adroitly delineated by the smartly cast ensemble, and director Holofcener is wry and effective in capturing the sights and sounds of contemporary urban living. A slice-of-life snapshot that shows warts and all, yet manages to leave the audience with a grudging affection for the Marks clan and all their foibles. ★★★½ DVD Signature Series: $14.99

The Lover

(1992, 119 min, France, Jean-Jacques Annaud) *Jane March, Tony Leung, Jeanne Moreau.* Set in Vietnam in 1929, this adaptation of Marguerite Duras' story about a French schoolgirl is a sensual feast for the eyes and ears. The girl, struggling to gain independence from her difficult family life and trying to understand her own sexual awakening, begins a torrid and illicit affair with a wealthy Chinese man. Although they don't really approve of the affair, her family tries to manipulate the situation for their own benefit. Annaud captures the tension-filled colonial setting that serves as a backdrop for these displaced persons, and the film is aided by gorgeous cinematography. (Filmed in English) ★★½ DVD Letterbox Unrated: $19.99

Lover Come Back

(1962, 107 min, US, Delbert Mann) *Tony Randall, Doris Day, Rock Hudson, Edie Adams, Jack Oakie.* Hudson and Day reteamed after their 1959 smash *Pillow Talk*, and the result is every bit as successful. In this genuinely funny satire on Madison Avenue, Doris plays an ad exec determined to land the account of scientist Rock's new invention — only he's really a rival ad exec, and, of course, there is no new invention. Love is what he's after. Lively '60s fun. ★★★½ DVD Letterbox: $14.99, VHS: $9.99

Loverboy

(1989, 98 min, US, Joan Micklin Silver) *Patrick Dempsey, Kate Jackson, Kirstie Alley, Robert Ginty.* After her tremendous success with *Crossing Delancey*, Silver's irresponsible and unfunny sex farce rates as a major disappointment. Dempsey plays a teenager who becomes the romantic idol of a group of older women — jumping in and out of bed with each of them. ★★ DVD: $24.99

Catherine Keener in *Lovely & Amazing*

Lovers (Amantes)

(1991, 105 min, Spain, Vicente Aranda) *Victoria Abril, Jorge Sanz.* In a story that makes the films of Pedro Almodóvar seem innocuously tame, this sexually charged, hyperventilating melodrama is a lurid tale of love triangle gone dangerously awry. Fresh from a stint in the military, the broodingly handsome Paco finds his well-planned life with his prim and virginal fiancée shattered when his sultry, widowed landlady seduces him. Luisa (Abril), the luscious "older woman," proves to be a seasoned sexual dynamo and a tough opponent for Trini, Paco's inexperienced girlfriend. But faced with losing him, she decides that, "if you can't beat 'em, join 'em" and begins her own assault to capture the heart and loins of our young hero. What self-respecting foreign film lover would miss a film seething with a plethora of out-of-control Latino passions, sexual deception, bloody revenge and a fist-clenching scene with a strategically stuffed handkerchief? (Spanish with English subtitles) ★★★½

The Lovers

(1958, 89 min, France, Louis Malle) *Jeanne Moreau, Alain Cuny.* Boasting a casual view of adultery, this early Malle melodrama became famous mostly for censorship problems and court cases on its initial United States release. Moreau stars as a restless woman, bored by the privileges of her Pernod-and-caviar provincial life and trapped in a loveless marriage. Weekly sojourns into the elegant world of Parisian society produce some diversion until one day she meets an unpretentious young student who offers her sexual fulfillment and temporary relief from her emptiness. Moreau, with her sad, sultry beauty, was made an international star by the film. (French with English subtitles) ★★★

Lovers and Liars

(1981, 93 min, Italy, Mario Monice) *Goldie Hawn, Giancarlo Giannini, Laura Betti.* A disappointing black comedy about the ill-fated and calamity-prone romance of American tourist Hawn and married businessman Giannini. The two make an interesting couple as they wind their way through a series of comic disasters and arguments on the way to true love, but neither have much to work with. ★★

Loves of a Blonde

(1965, 88 min, Czechoslovakia, Milos Forman) *Jana Brejchova, Josef Sebanek.* Years before his international success with such films as *Amadeus, Cuckoo's Nest* and *Ragtime*, Forman directed a series of quirky, funny films from his Eastern European homeland. This film depicts life in a small factory town near Prague with a curious social injustice: the women outnumber the men ten to one. A visit by a group of army reservists allows Anduka, the blonde in question, to enjoy a welcomed but bittersweet respite. (Czechoslovakian with English subtitles) ★★★½ DVD Criterion Collection: $29.99, VHS: $29.99

The Loves of Carmen

(1948, 99 min, US, Charles Vidor) *Rita Hayworth, Glenn Ford.* Bizet's famous opera about a soldier who becomes obsessed with a comely Gypsy woman is so flamboyant and loaded with such sensuous music that one must wonder why anyone would want to turn it into a nonmusical drama. This rendition of the tragic tale will leave one wondering. On the up side, however, Hayworth's dazzling beauty is enough to make this easy viewing. ★★½ DVD: $27.99

Lovin' Molly

(1974, 98 min, US, Sidney Lumet) *Beau Bridges, Anthony Perkins, Blythe Danner, Susan Sarandon.* This atmospheric if slowly paced film version of Larry McMurtry's novel "Leaving Cheyenne" is sort of a western *Jules and Jim*. Spanning over 40 years, the story centers on Texas farmboys and brothers Bridges and Perkins who spend a lifetime lovin' Molly (exceptionally played by Danner). An often charming, quirky film with three splendid performances from the three leads. ★★★

A Low Down Dirty Shame

(1994, 110 min, US, Keenan Ivory Wayans) *Keenan Ivory Wayans, Jada Pinkett, Salli Richardson, Charles S. Dutton.* Those expecting an action-packed tribute to the blaxploitation films of the '70s will surely be disappointed by this mind-numbing disaster. Director-writer-actor Wayans plays a former cop-turned-private investigator who is hired by ex-partner Dutton to take on a nefarious drug lord. Those who are brave enough to sit through this are sure to feel that it's a low down dirty shame a film this bad was made in the first place. ★½ DVD: $9.99, VHS: $9.99

The Low Life

(1996, 98 min, US, George Hickenlooper) *Rory Cochran, Kyra Sedgwick, Sean Astin, Christian Meoli, Ron Livingston, James LeGros, J.T. Walsh.* Partially based on the director's own experiences after graduating from Yale, *The Low Life* follows a recent grad and aspiring writer (Cochran) through demeaning temp jobs and a frustrating relationship with a manic-depressive Southern belle beauty (Sedgwick doing her best in a basically unplayable role). And this being a GenX movie, there are obligatory bar scenes with Cochran and cohorts discussing pop culture, philosophy and life's injustices. Cochran is good in an extremely low-key role, and Astin is great as Cochran's annoying but ultimately sympathetic roommate. *The Low Life* has many flaws, but it's moving and insightful and doesn't condescend. ★★½

Ludwig

The Lower Depths

(1957, 125 min, Japan, Akira Kurosawa) *Toshiro Mifune, Isuzu Yamada.* Kurosawa's compelling adaptation of Maxim Gorky's classic play. The story concerns a group of peasants living in absolute squalor. Crammed in on top of each other, the tenants are locked in a constant battle of wits: some clinging desperately to their broken dreams while others viciously shoot them down. This truly touching tale features an exceptional ensemble cast headed by the incomparable Mifune. (Japanese with English subtitles) ★★★ DVD Criterion Collection 2-Disc Set: $39.99, VHS: $29.99

Lucas

(1986, 100 min, US, David Seltzer) *Corey Haim, Charlie Sheen, Winona Ryder.* A pleasant surprise, this charming teen comedy follows the romantic misadventures of a love-struck 14-year-old (played with wide-eyed innocence by Haim) who falls for the new girl in town, a newly acquainted friend who has set her sights on the football team captain (Sheen). Haim, before he had his 15 minutes of fame as one of the two Coreys, is wonderful; and Ryder shows that, even before she hit it big, she had star quality. ★★★ DVD: $14.99, VHS: $6.99

Lucia Lucia

(2003, 108 min, Mexico, Antonio Serrano) *Cecilia Roth.* Riding the new wave in Mexican cinema, Serrano has directed a heartfelt tale of love, sadness and reawakening. Lucia's husband has just been kidnapped by a band of violent Marxists. With the help of her wise elderly neighbor, Felix, and a nubile young musician, Adrian, Lucia embarks upon a life-changing journey in search of truth, meaning and her missing spouse. Clever editing sequences take the viewer inside Lucia's fertile imagination, while the plot weaves together the lives of disparate characters who share hidden desires and deep losses. Based upon Rosa Montera's novel "La Hija Del Canibal" ("The Cannibal's Daughter"), *Lucia Lucia* boasts strong characterizations and a richly realized script. (Spanish with English subtitles) ★★★ DVD: $14.99, VHS: $102.99

Lucie Aubrac

(1997, 116 min, France, Claude Berri) *Carole Bouquet, Daniel Auteuil, Patrice Chéreau.* A gripping drama of determination and the inexhaustible power of love, Berri's exquisite WWII film tells the true story of a French woman, Lucie Aubrac (marvelously played by Bouquet), a schoolteacher and mother who risks all for the safety of her husband. Auteuil is Monsieur Aubrac, a Resistance member fighting the Nazis in Lyons. When he and other partisans are captured by the Germans, his wife joins the Resistance and plans and executes a daring escape. Berri, who directed Auteuil in the masterful *Jean de Florette* and *Manon of the Spring*, maintains tension throughout the film as the outcome is never a given. *Lucie Aubrac* is also a fascinating peek into the anatomy of a group of freedom fighters who placed themselves in harm's way every single day. (French with English subtitles) ★★★½ VHS: $102.99

Lucky Numbers

(2000, 105 min, US, Nora Ephron) *John Travolta, Lisa Kudrow, Tim Roth, Ed O'Neill, Michael Rapaport, Bill Pullman, Michael Moore, Richard Schiff.* Suggested by an actual incident which happened in the 1980s, *Lucky Numbers* is a peculiar, ultimately unsuccessful blend of screwball and dark comedy that never quite finds its groove. Set in Harrisburg, Pennsylvania, the story follows colorful TV weatherman Travolta and lotto ball-girl Kudrow, who in-between their romantic trysts concoct a scheme to rig the state lottery. Director Ephron and writer Adam Resnick attempt to milk greed, betrayals and killings for wacky laughs, but unappealing characters and uneven pacing only weigh down what little amusing moments the film has. ★★ DVD: $19.99, VHS: $14.99

Lucrezia Borgia

(1935/1923/1916, 93/31/14 min, France, Abel Gance) Along with the short films "Au Secours!" and "La Folie du Docteur Tube," this is a fascinating, rarely seen work by silent film pioneer Gance. The shorts veer towards the experimental, with avant garde tendencies that are more aggressive than Gance used in his features. *Lucrezia Borgia* is an opulent portrait of one of history's most ambitious families. Pity the girl; historians now agree that the tales of vice and corruption levied against Lucrezia were greatly exaggerated. Gance paints her more to be pitied than scorned, made victim by a father renowned as the deliciously corrupt Pope Alexander VI. When your film is narrated Niccolo Machiavelli, reveling at each melodramatic turn, it is difficult to miss. ★★★ DVD: $24.99, VHS: $19.99

Ludwig

(1972, 231 min, Italy, Luchino Visconti) *Helmut Berger, Romy Schneider, Trevor Howard, Silvana Mangano, Helmut Griem, Gert Frobe.* Through a series of talking heads, each of accusation, the downfall of one of Europe's most tragic and historically enigmatic figures is brought into director Visconti's realm of neorealism in this full-length version not previously seen in the United States. Berger is "the mad king of Bavaria," who saw himself as a poet and architect of dreams through the construction of Gothic castles for his people's destiny of happiness, and who, ironically as he was slowly going mad, secluded himself in his self-made "prison." Politically naïve, King Ludwig found solace as a patron of the arts. His friendships with Wagner and other artists eventually became a vampire on the Bavarian state's gold vein, which ultimately created enemies within the walls of his reluctant empire who would later have him committed. Visconti's characters are often too cold to allow for sympathy, but his vision opens the realities of a world more too often intolerant of anything in quest of personified passion. It may be overlong, but *Ludwig* is sumptuous and stately. (Italian with English subtitles) ★★★½ VHS: $24.99

Lulu in Berlin

(1985, 50 min, US, Richard Leacock & Susan Woll) *Louise Brooks.* Louise Brooks' life and film work, which took her from Hollywood to pre-Hitler Germany and 1930s France, was exciting and controversial. Her remarkable career is recounted in this absorbing documentary that features the only filmed interview with Ms. Brooks as well as clips from several of her films. The filmmakers, renowned documentarians, capture the radiance of this articulate, seductive and beguiling woman. ★★★½

Lulu on the Bridge

(1999, 103 min, US, Paul Auster) *Harvey Keitel, Mira Sorvino, Willem Dafoe, Gina Gersho, Mandy Patinkin, Vanessa Redgrave.* A rock found in a briefcase has mysterious powers over all who touch it, including a disabled sax player (Keitel) and an aspiring actress (Sorvino). The title refers to Lulu from *Pandora's Box*. A strange, even sentimental thriller from Auster, who makes his solo directing debut after writing *Smoke* and codirecting *Blue in the Face*. ★★½ DVD: $24.99

Lumiere

(1976, 95 min, France, Jeanne Moreau) *Jeanne Moreau, Bruno Ganz, François Simon.* Moreau's warm and endearing directorial debut chronicles the lives, loves, careers and friendships of four women of different ages all living in Paris. The film's affectionate yet insightful look at these people produces a wonderful human drama. (French with English subtitles) ★★★

Lumiere & Company

(1995, 88 min, Claude Lelouch, Constantin Costa-Gavras, David Lynch, Hugh Hudson, Ismail Merchant, Jacques Rivette, James Ivory, John Boorman, Lasse Hallström, Liv Ullmann, Peter Greenaway, Spike Lee, Theo Angelopoulos, Wim Wenders, Zhang Yimou) *Spike Lee, François Mitterrand, Liam Neeson, Sven Nykvist, Aidan Quinn, Stephen Rea, Alan Rickman, Max von Sydow, Bruno Ganz, Lena Olin, Liv Ullmann, Pernilla August, Isabelle Huppert, John Boorman, Spike Lee, David Lynch, Peter Greenaway, Zhang Yimou.* A fascinating collection of 40 short films by 40 filmmakers from around the world. All the films are 52 seconds in length, and shot with the original camera built by the Lumière Brothers at the turn of the century. It's a terrific challenge, and exciting to see how the various directors use the very brief running time and primitive technology to their advantage. The results range from the dull and uninspired, to the brilliant and beautiful. The best efforts seem to come from expected sources — John Boorman, Claude Lelouch, and especially Zhang Yimou and David Lynch. Some of the lesser-known directors contribute strong pieces as well. An absolute must for serious film buffs. ★★★½ DVD: $24.99, VHS: $19.99

Luna Park

(1993, 108 min, Russia, Pavel Lounguine) *Oleg Borisov, Andrei Goutine.* Employing the same herky-jerky, low-budget look of his earlier *Taxi Blues*, director Lounguine has created a gritty, nightmarish and all-too-real treatise on Russia's seemingly inevitable slide into total social chaos. The story follows Andrei, a neo-Nazi thug who hangs with a loosely organized band in a Moscow amusement park. Upon learning that he is half Jewish, he begins a desperate search for his Semitic father, finally landing upon Naoum, an aging intellectual, songwriter and esthete. As Andrei struggles with his emotions (should he murder Naoum or embrace him as his father?), Lounguine evokes a terrifying image of Russia on the edge where class differences, deep-rooted anti-Semitism, xenophobia, and a complete lack of state control are giving rise to unspeakable violence. (Russian with English subtitles) ★★★ VHS: $29.99

Lupo

(1970, 100 min, Israel, Menahem Golan) *Yuda Barkan, Gabi Armoni.* Fifty-year-old Lupo, widower and neighborhood character, stands up to city hall when his dilapidated but beloved community is threatened with demolition. A zesty, unpredictable comedy. (Filmed in English) ★★★ VHS: $59.99

Lust for Life

(1956, 122 min, US, Vincente Minnelli) *Kirk Douglas, Anthony Quinn, Pamela Brown.* Douglas gives possibly his best performance as painter Vincent Van Gogh in this riveting drama about the artist's tortured life. Quinn won an Oscar as Van Gogh's compadre, Paul Gauguin. Minnelli's film avoids the clichés of the artist at work, and succinctly presents the tale with subtlety and a narrative coherency. ★★★½

Lust in the Dust

(1985, 85 min, US, Paul Bartel) *Tab Hunter, Divine, Lainie Kazan, Geoffrey Lewis, Cesar Romero.* Gold lies somewhere in the squalid town of Chile Verde and the person who can line up the asses of Divine and Kazan will be able to follow the map tattooed thereon (half a map per cheek) to the treasure's whereabouts. A wildly funny spoof of westerns. ★★★ DVD: $19.99

The Luzhin Defence

(2001, 106 min, GB, Marleen Gorris) *John Turturro, Emily Watson, Geraldine James, Stuart Wilson, Christopher Thompson.* Turturro's penchant for imbuing his characters with smoldering, manic intensity is well used in his portrayal of Alexander Luzhin, a driven chess genius focused on the game to the exclusion of all else. His obsessive concentration has successfully blocked out those aspects of his life that he is ill-equipped to handle; but this protective bulwark is dangerously weakened by a sudden, unexpected arousal of the heart. Young Natalie is a lady of society, of means and expectations, whose family seeks a suitable marriage for her, in keeping with the rigid structural guidelines of the pre-WWI European elite. The disheveled, distracted Luzhin does not at all meet their standards. As Luzhin faces the chess match of his life, he must deal not only with the withering objections of Natalie's family, but the machinations of his former mentor and exploiter, who has arrived at the tournament to sabotage the pupil who has surpassed him. Director Gorriss has once again vividly re-created an historic era while delineating distinct personalities and communicating oblique states of mind and unspoken social mores. A wonderfully developed and involving drama, based on the Nabokov novel. ★★★½ DVD: $29.99, VHS: $21.99

Luzia

(1987, 112 min, Brazil, Fabio Barreto) *Claudia Ohana, Thales Pan Chacon.* Substituting for Sonia Braga in the saucy, sensuous and beguiling role, Ohana (one of Brazil's biggest stars) more than fills her place in this exciting Brazilian western. Ohana is a rodeo cowgirl caught in a clash between squatters and the powerful ranch owners. (Portuguese with English subtitles) ★★½

M

(1931, 106 min, Germany, Fritz Lang) *Peter Lorre, Ellen Widmann, Inge Landgut.* After a decade of making hugely popular fantasy, sci-fi and spy movies, Lang made his own undisputable masterpiece, *M*, scripted by his wife, Thea von Harbou, a Nazi sympathizer. Working on a tighter budget and a shorter schedule that he was used to, Lang brilliantly synthesized his expressionistic tendencies with the torn-from-today's-headlines style that typified his later Hollywood work. Lorre, in one of his earliest film roles, finds the pathos in this nondescript Everyman whose psyche has been so poisoned that he is driven to raping and murdering little girls. The terrified city wants action: swift, decisive, effective. But when the State is found to be impotent, the metagovernment — organized crime — sets up a dangerous option for a nation ill-prepared to select wisely. A harrowing psychological drama inspired by an actual 1929 Dusseldorf incident. This is the remastered, longer (by seven minutes) version, which includes the original German ending. (German with English subtitles) ★★★★ DVD Criterion Collection: $29.99, VHS: $19.99

M. Butterfly

(1993, 100 min, US, David Cronenberg) *Jeremy Irons, John Lone, Ian Richardson, Barbara Sukowa.* The much-anticipated screen version of David Henry Hwang's hit play is something of a letdown. Inspired by a true story, the tragic tale is about a man's self-delusional love for and betrayal by an alluring Chinese woman who is actually a man. A deer-in-the-headlights-like Irons stars as Rene Gallimard, a nebbish accountant at the French Embassy who falls in love with an opera singer, Song Liling (Lone). As the two begin an affair, Gallimard rises in rank at the embassy, unknowingly disseminating government secrets. The action unfolds slowly and the film's emotional level never seems to rise above the simmering point of grand tragedy. ★★½

Mr. Hulot's Holiday

(1953, 86 min, France, Jacques Tati) *Jacques Tati, Nathalie Pascaud.* Tati, one of the greatest mime and

Ma Vie en Rose

Peter Lorre in *M*

visual artists since Chaplin and Keaton, stars as Mr. Hulot, that charming and totally naive fool who creates disorder wherever he wanders. A French seaside resort is the setting for the Hulot pratfalls in this captivating comedy classic. ★★★★ DVD: $29.99

Ma Vie en Rose

(1998, 89 min, Belgium, Alain Berliner) *Michèle Laroque, Jean-Philippe Ecoffey, Hélène Vincent, George du Fresne.* A precious Belgian film about a little boy who wants to be a little girl, *Ma Vie en Rose* is a fantastic story about being true to one's self. Ludovic (du Fresne) delights in wearing dresses and makeup, even at inopportune moments like his family's "welcome to the neighborhood" party. While his antics are dismissed as a childish phase, Ludo knows better. An embarrassment to his family, Ludo perseveres with his desires, unwavered by shame. While there are several painful scenes of Ludo being harassed, rejected, and ridiculed (his aunt is supportive), Ludo's courage is inspirational. Director Berliner's unusual film is extremely enjoyable not just for its central concept, but also for its incredibly fluid camerawork and candy-colored set design. It's a tenderhearted, remarkably affecting film. (French with English subtitles) ★★★½ DVD: $27.99

Mac

(1993, 120 min, US, John Turturro) *John Turturro, Michael Badalucco, Carl Capotorto, Katherine Borowitz, Ellen Barkin.* Actor Turturro makes an extremely impressive directorial debut with this drama about three Italian-American brothers who start their own construction company. Set in mid-1950s Queens, the film tells of the enterprising brothers' struggle against rival developers, procedural setbacks and most often each other. Turturro (who also coscripted the film) plays the eldest — the trio's inspiration and ultimately their leader. Meticulously crafted and carefully photographed, the film's tight-knit ensemble of actors provide outstanding, rich and multilayered characterizations. As a director, Turturro shows a strong, clear vision as he keeps the pace lively and tells his story with precision. ★★★★ DVD: $24.99

Macao

(1952, 81 min, US, Josef von Sternberg) *Robert Mitchum, Ava Gardner, William Bendix.* In the notorious Far East, a mysterious American adventurer helps a detective hunt down an elusive gangster. A seedy atmosphere and a fair amount of tension heightens this noirish tale. ★★★ VHS: $14.99

Macario

(1960, 91 min, Mexico, Roberto Gavaldon) A poetic fairy tale, the story follows Macario, an impoverished woodcutter who, with his young wife and four children, struggles to eke out an existence in rural Mexico. Plagued by a sense of failure, our hero vows not to eat again until he can have a turkey all for himself. On the Day of the Dead, his wife steals a bird, cooks it and gives it to him as he goes into the forest to work, where he is confronted by the Devil, God and Death, all asking him to share his prized meal. He eventually chooses Death, and in return receives magical powers to heal the sick and dying. His life changes as he accumulates wealth and possessions, all the while attracting the attention of the Church's local inquisition. Based on a story by B. Traven (author of "The Treasure of the Sierra Madre"). ★★★

Macaroni

(1985, 104 min, Italy, Ettore Scola) *Jack Lemmon, Marcello Mastroianni.* Lemmon plays a weary business executive who returns to Naples for the first time since WWII. There he is reunited with a wartime acquaintance (Mastroianni), who has been sending his own sister forged letters from the serviceman since the war ended. The two stars overcome an intriguing story which is only half-heartedly explored. (Filmed in English) ★★½ VHS: $7.99

MacArthur

(1977, 130 min, US, Joseph Sargent) *Gregory Peck, Dan O'Herlihy, Ed Flanders.* In an attempt to reproduce the sweep and historical significance of *Patton*, the filmmakers set their sights on another controversial military leader of WWII: General Douglas MacArthur. Even with an actor of Peck's caliber in the title role, the film is only mildly interesting. The story covers in episodic, sometimes melodramatic fashion, the career of the general from the 1940s thru Korea. Peck gives a compelling performance, but lacks the necessary panache befitting the larger-than-life commander. Flanders is quite good, however, as President Truman. ★★½ DVD Letterbox: $24.99

MacArthur's Children

(1985, 115 min, Japan, Masahiro Shinoda) *Masako Natsume, Shima Iwashita, Juzo Itami.* The effects of America's victory over Japan and subsequent occupation and cultural domination of this proud nation are the themes of Shinoda's poignant and funny film. Set in a small fishing village immediately after WWII, the film explores the relationship and attitudes of the townspeople to their foreign "rulers." The film is not a biting indictment against Americans, but rather a loving remembrance of these strange people who came and changed Japan forever. (Japanese with English subtitles) ★★★

Macbeth

(1948, 112 min, US, Orson Welles) *Orson Welles, Jeanette Nolan, Dan O'Herlihy, Roddy McDowall.* A presentiment of evil overshadows every frame of Welles' *Macbeth*. A most faithful adaptation, both to Shakespeare's writing and to the historical era depicted. Welles makes optimum use of lighting and set design, and he is as much Macbeth as he was Kane. Nolan epitomizes the woman whose desire for power can be exercised only through her husband. ★★★½

Macbeth

(1971, 140 min, GB, Roman Polanski) *Jon Finch, Nicholas Selby, Francesca Annis, Martin Shaw.* Who knows what evil lurked in the heart of the Bard when he penned this murderous tale of treachery and violence? In any case, Polanski's grim and gory conception of Shakespeare's bloody drama is not only one of his greatest films, but is one of the truest renditions of this sordid tale. Gripping and highly atmospheric, the film was greeted by an uproar fueled by its extreme (but not unwarranted) violence, a speech by Lady Macbeth in the nude, and problems in Polanski's personal life. ★★★½ DVD Letterbox: $29.99, VHS: $19.99

The Machine (La Machine)

(1994, 96 min, France, François Dupeyron) *Gérard Depardieu, Nathalie Baye, Didier Bourdon.* A slumming Depardieu plays a psychiatrist, fascinated with psychosis, who invents a machine which enables him to switch minds with an institutionalized psychotic killer. Thus, the killer (in the doctor's body) goes home to the wife and kid, while the doctor (in the killer's body) goes back to the padded cell. This could have been an interesting examination of identity, the nature of evil or other philosophical goodies. It settles for formulaic plotting, goofy dialogue and the occasional dark thrill. ★★ VHS: $9.99

Macho Dancer

(1988, 136 min, Philippines, Lino Brocka) *Jacklyn Jose, Daniel Fernando, Princess Punzalan, Alan Paule, William Lorenzo.* The eternal tale of the naïve country boy who is seduced and corrupted by the evils of the big city is played out in this fascinating and erotic drama. Paul, a somnambulistic teenage beauty, is drawn to Manila after his American lover and supporter of his family returns to the U.S. Paul is enamored by the city's notorious gay bars and nightclubs and is seduced into a world of prostitution, sexually explicit dancing and "brown slavery." The film offers a voyeuristic glimpse into the tacky yet lascivious gay underground where sexual acts are performed on stage and then bought and sold off stage. (Tagalog with English subtitles) ★★★ DVD: $29.99

The Mack

(1973, 110 min, US, Michael Campus) *Max Julien, Richard Pryor, Don Gordon.* One of the most popular of the '70s blaxploitation flicks, this gritty, misogynous actioner is the story of Goldie, a likable but sleazy ex-convict who aspires and attains his lofty goal of being a superpimp — the meanest 'mack' in town." With an envious stable of fine 'hos, plenty of muscle and a cutthroat business attitude, our hero soon discovers that pimping's profitable but, "what gains a man to win the world and lose his own soul." Heavy, man. ★★ DVD Platinum Edition: $19.99, VHS: $9.99

Mack the Knife

(1989, 122 min, GB, Menahem Golan) *Raul Julia, Richard Harris, Julie Walters, Roger Daltrey.* A misbegotten version of "The Threepenny Opera," about the numerous, unsuccessful attempts of London's street people to keep England's most notorious criminal behind bars. ★½

The Mackintosh Man

(1973, 105 min, GB, John Huston) *Paul Newman, James Mason, Dominique Sanda, Harry Andrews, Ian Bannen.* Newman and Mason are on opposite sides of the fence in this derivative though enjoyable spy thriller about a freelance agent (Newman) who must ferret out a Communist traitor high in the ranks of the British government. ★★½ VHS: $14.99

Mad City

(1997, 114 min, US, Constantin Costa-Gavras) *Dustin Hoffman, John Travolta, Alan Alda, Blythe Danner, Mia Kirshner, Robert Prosky, William Atherton, Ted Levine.* Hoffman is a weasily TV anchorman who is inadvertently caught in the story of his life when a disgruntled museum security guard (Travolta, doing his best in an underrealized role) blows a head-gasket and takes hostages. As the event becomes a media three-ring circus, the film dives into the muddled water of ethics vs. ratings, news vs. sensationalism, truth vs. manipulation. Not as bitingly satiric as it could have been, *Mad City* charges along on a fever pitch for about an hour, but soon the film settles into a more predictable groove and degenerates into a sanctimonious morality tale. ★★½ DVD: $14.99, VHS: $14.99

Mad Dog and Glory

(1993, 96 min, US, John McNaughton) *Robert De Niro, Bill Murray, Uma Thurman, David Caruso, Kathy Baker.* De Niro stars as an extremely mild-mannered police photographer who, after he saves the life of mobster/stand-up comic Murray, is given — as a little "thank you" — the service of Thurman for one week. This amiable comedy-drama finds its niche as a character study, focusing on how the harsh world can bring very different people together. De Niro and Thurman are both endearing and funny, in a clumsy sort of way, and Murray puts an oddly menacing (if not fully believable) air. Caruso, before his one-year-wonder stint on TV's "N.Y.P.D. Blue," is especially good as De Niro's police buddy. ★★★ DVD: $14.99

Mad Dog Morgan

(1978, 93 min, Australia, Philippe Mora) *Dennis Hopper, David Gulpilil.* Hopper, a few years before he was accepted back in the Hollywood fraternity with *Blue Velvet*, traveled Down Under to make a few bucks in this explosively violent "western" saga. Playing the role with maniacal intensity, Hopper's Morgan is a man who, after killing a police chief, becomes an outlaw on the run and famous throughout the land for his daring and improbable escapes from the noose. An unusual but exciting actioner with Hopper in good form. ★★★ VHS: $14.99

Mad Love

(1995, 99 min, US, Antonia Bird) *Drew Barrymore, Chris O'Donnell, Joan Allen, Jude Ciccolella, Kevin Dunn, Matthew Lillard.* This could have been a fun-loving teen rebel romp across the American West, but instead it's a tedious, soppy melodrama that makes a half-hearted attempt to address mental illness. O'Donnell plays the grade-A high school senior who helps his single dad keep the family together. Barrymore is the rebellious new kid in town. It's not hard to guess that O'Donnell falls for her and forsakes his comfy life for the dangerous female newcomer. Add to this time-honored contrivance an oh-too-trendy Seattle backdrop and a relentless grunge soundtrack and you get the feeling that the producers threw this together with tired formulas and scotch tape. ★ DVD: $9.99, VHS: $9.99

Mad Max

(1979, 93 min, Australia, George Miller) *Mel Gibson, Joanne Samuel.* The original adventures of Max, the Road Warrior, valiant law enforcer combatting the deranged highway marauders of a not-too-distant future. Gibson stars in this nerve-bending classic of automotive madness. (Dubbed from Australian English into "American") (Sequel: *The*

Mad Max Beyond Thunderdome

Road Warrior) ★★★ DVD Special Edition: $19.99

Mad Max Beyond Thunderdome

(1985, 106 min, Australia, George Miller & George Ogilvie) *Mel Gibson, Tina Turner, Bruce Spence, Angelo Rossitto.* The last and least of the *Mad Max* trilogy, this movie still delivers some exciting action sequences, or at least half of it does. Directed in two parts by two different directors, the lines of division and talent show very clearly. While the first half of the film, directed by series veteran Miller, is along the lines of the previous two, with an angry Max (Gibson) trying to survive an authoritarian community called Bartertown, it later drags to a crawl when Max goes off into the desert and encounters a band of post-apocalyptic children awaiting the appearance of a savior, who turns out to look a lot like Max. The fun of the first half of the movie is fueled by the presence of Turner in her wildly overblown performance as Auntie Entity. ★★½ DVD: $14.99, VHS: $9.99

The Mad Miss Manton

(1938, 80 min, US, Leigh Jason) *Barbara Stanwyck, Henry Fonda, Hattie McDaniel.* Stanwyck and Fonda appeared together for the first time (they were reunited in *You Belong to Me* and Preston Sturges' marvelous *The Lady Eve*) in this madcap mystery-screwball comedy. Stanwyck plays a zany socialite who, along with a group of friends, investigates a murder. Lots of fun. ★★★

Mad Monster Party

(1967, 94 min, US, Jules Bass) *Boris Karloff, Phyllis Diller.* This off-the-wall oddity defies categorization: it's a tongue-in-cheek musical monster movie done in stop-motion animation. Dr. Frankenstien (appropriately vocalized by Karloff) has decided to retire and invites all the monsters under his leadership to a convention where he will announce an heir to his evil throne. The cast, such as it is, includes the Mummy, Dracula, the Frankenstein monster and his mate (hilariously rendered by Diller), the Werewolf and others. The plot is paper thin, but the one-liners and take-offs are witty and amusing. ★★★ DVD: $19.99, VHS: $9.99

Madadayo

(1992, 134 min, Japan, Akira Kurosawa) *Kyoko Kagawa, Tatsuo Matsumura.* Kurosawa caps a long and distinguished career with this revelatory examination of a respected, elderly teacher. The film opens in 1943, when Hyakken Uchida, at 60, decides to retire from teaching to write. The full devastation of the war has not yet hit Japan as his loyal students begin a yearly ritual of a birthday party tribute to him. During it, they ask him, "Mahda-kai?" ("Are you ready?"); he responds, "Madadayo" ("Not yet"). The children's game takes on a different meaning for the teacher. For years, Hyakken remains a guiding force for his students, imparting wisdom and compassion with humor and good will. Kurosawa again imparts intimate human moments against larger historic events, conveying a sense of that particular moment with shared universal experience. One suspects Kurosawa's own last years were as replete with respect and admiration. (Japanese with English subtitles) ★★★ DVD: $24.99, VHS: $19.99

Madagascar Skin

(1995, 93 min, GB, Christian Newby) *John Hannah, Bernard Hill.* Newby makes his feature film debut with this unusual and often engaging love story between two outsiders. In a gay world where beauty is paramount, Harry (Hannah) is a man ostracized because of a large facial birthmark the color of port wine and in the shape of the island of Madagascar. Rejected and with no one to embrace, he finally runs away, resurfacing on a beach where he saves the life of Flint (Hill), a gruff older man found beaten and buried in the sand. With neither one of them having a place to turn, they set up house in an abandoned cottage. There, their friendship soon turns into love. The film begins unrelentingly bleak, but as the offbeat tale unfolds the dry humor and cynical charm of the story begins to surface to create a unique, compelling change-of-pace romance. ★★★ DVD: $29.99, VHS: $39.99

Madame Bovary

(1934, 117 min, France, Jean Renoir) *Valentine Tessier, Pierre Renoir.* While not considered one of Renoir's best works, this faithful retelling of Gustave Flaubert's novel is still of interest for fans of both artists. In 1840, a young woman, eager to escape her dreary provincial life, marries a dull country doctor. As her situation becomes more desperate, however, she begins a series of affairs with other men; actions that cause her to become a tragic victim of her own romantic illusions. Tessier in the title role is overly dramatic and too old for the part. (French with English subtitles) ★★½ VHS: $59.99

Madame Bovary

(1949, 115 min, US, Vincente Minnelli) *Jennifer Jones, James Mason, Van Helfin, Louis Jourdan, Gladys Cooper.* Lavish screen version of Flaubert's novel about a 19th-century French woman whose lust for social and financial power brings on her own doom. Jones makes an alluring Bovary. ★★★ VHS: $19.99

Madame Bovary

(1991, 130 min, France, Claude Chabrol) *Isabelle Huppert, Jean-François Balmer, Jean Yanne.* A lushly photographed yet starkly realized adaptation of Gustave Flaubert's classic. Huppert delivers a restrained performance as Emma Bovary, a 19th-century woman whose lust for self-fulfillment sets her against a hypocritically pietistic society amd ultimately leads her to adultery. Her character is filled with contradictions, sometimes cold, calculating and intensely materialistic; other times convivial, passionate and vulnerable. Filmed in the countryside surrounding Rouen, the film convincingly captures the mood of Flaubert's France. (French with English subtitles) ★★½ DVD Letterbox: $19.99

Madame Butterfly

(1995, 129 min, France, Frédéric Mitterrand) *Ying Huang, Richard Troxell, Ning Liang, Richard Cowan.* A sumptuous, wrenching filmization of Puccini's heartbreaking opera. Philadelphia's own Troxell is quite good as that slime, Lt. Pinkerton, a horny jerk who buys a gorgeous fifteen-year-old geisha's hand in marriage, only to abandon her. Mitterrand's camera direction is a bit uninspired in the early scenes, allowing only the beautiful exteriors and editing to tell us this ain't no stage version. But the film is more assured and stylish as it progresses, becoming a rich, cinematic jewel of a film. Huang is wonderful in the title role. She has a stunning voice, but she's not of the plant-my-feet-and-belt-it-out school of opera performance. She gives a full-blown, dramatic portrayal, and if you find yourself scrambling for a tissue by film's end, she's to blame. (Italian with English subtitles) ★★★½

Madame Rosa

(1977, 105 min, France, Moshe Mizrahi) *Simone Signoret, Samy Ben Youb, Claude Dauphin, Constantin Costa-Gavras, Michal Bat-Adam.* The touching story of a loving relationship between an aging Holocaust victim and former prostitute (Signoret) and a young Arab boy she tends. Academy Award-winning Best Foreign Film. ★★★½ VHS: $24.99

Madame Satan

(1930, 116 min, US, Cecil B. DeMille) *Kay Johnson, Reginald Denny, Roland Young, Lillian Roth.* Not entirely successful in some of its parts, *Madame Satan* is a fascinating excursion into '30s cinema. Rather than displaying director DeMille's characteristically heavy touches, the film is reminiscent of Ernst Lubitsch, Noël Coward, Busby Berkeley and Alfred Hitchcock! Johnson plays a wife who learns of her husband's (Denny) unfaithfulness. She soon is masquerading as the mysterious Madame Satan to get him back. After viewing a spectacular musical production number taking place en route and aboard a high-flying zeppelin, one would think they've seen it all. But DeMille has another wild card up his sleeve for an unbelievable finale. A pre-Code production,

Vince Vaughn and Jon Favreau in *Made*

the film's themes of sexuality and adultery would have assured it could not have been made as is after 1934. ★★★½ VHS: $19.99

Madame Sin

(1971, 90 min, US, David Greene) *Bette Davis, Robert Wagner, Denholm Elliott.* Davis has the title role in this made-for-TV espionage flick à la James Bond. Wagner plays a former CIA agent deluded into assisting the evil Madame Sin in the theft of a Polaris submarine. Production design and sets nearly rival those of the Bond films and, for a change, good doesn't triumph over evil. ★★½ VHS: $9.99

Madame Sousatzka

(1988, 122 min, GB, John Schlesinger) *Shirley MacLaine, Peggy Ashcroft, Navin Chowdhry, Twiggy.* MacLaine gives a spirited performance as an eccentric and demanding piano teacher who dedicates herself to her new student — a gifted 15-year-old Indian boy. A lovely, lyrical film directed by Schlesinger with great sensitivity. ★★★ VHS: $9.99

Madame X

(1966, 100 min, US, David Lowell Rich) *Lana Turner, John Forsythe, Keir Dullea, Ricardo Montalban, Burgess Meredith.* Sixth screen version of the weepy chestnut, this time around with Turner as the woman with a past who sacrifices all for the sake of her son. Dullea plays her offspring, a lawyer who unknowingly defends his mother. ★★

Mädchen in Uniform

(1931, 89 min, Germany, Leontine Sagan) *Hertha Thiele, Dorothea Wieck.* This landmark film dealing with a lesbian relationship between a sensitive student and her teacher still retains both its timeliness and power in dealing with this controversial subject. Written by Christa Winsloe, this legendary film is a sympathetically handled account of one girl's rebellion against suffocating discipline and sexual repression in a Prussian boarding school. (German with English subtitles) ★★★½ VHS: $24.99

Made

(2001, 94 min, US, Jon Favreau) *Jon Favreau, Vince Vaughn, Famke Janssen, Sean Combs, Peter Falk, Faizon Love.* Bobby (Favreau) and Ricky (Vaughn) have, in their way, been made since high school; Bobby the serious, plodding loser with heart; Ricky the pain-in-the-rear screw-up who would

never have a job if Bobby didn't make himself a two-for-one deal. The film opens at a dismal boxing ring as the two — sweating, overweight, out of shape and out of breath — lumber and jab at each other to a draw. As Bobby contemplates the future of his boxing career, he continues doing construction work by day and chauffeuring his live-in girlfriend to her lap dances at night, parties that are part of local capo Max's (Falk) operations. Max taps Bobby for a higher-echelon job, from driver to muscle, sending him to New York City to oversee a drop. Of course, Ricky comes along on the journey, adding unnecessary and often dangerous complications at every turn. Director (and screenwriter) Favreau maintains a frenetic pace, painting numerous character portraits with swift, deft strokes, and underlying the action with timeless rat pack tunes, music to delineate the clueless duo lost in time and space. *Made* is edgy, wry, self-knowing, with an unexpected jolt of authentic emotion buried in the phony cool. ★★★½ DVD Special Edition: $14.99

Made for Each Other

(1939, 85 min, US, John Cromwell) *James Stewart, Carole Lombard, Charles Coburn, Lucille Watson, Lousie Beavers.* Sentimental, heartwarming melodrama with Stewart and Lombard as newlyweds battling illness, poverty and a meddling mother-in-law (Watson). ★★½ VHS: $14.99

Made in America

(1993, 110 min, US, Richard Benjamin) *Whoopi Goldberg, Ted Danson, Nia Long, Will Smith, Paul Rodriguez, Jennifer Tilly.* Thanks to a couple of winning performances from Danson and Goldberg, what might easily have been just another insipid comedy from the Hollywood mill is instead a fun-loving, briskly paced romp. When Goldberg's daughter, Zora (Long), discovers that she is the result of artificial insemination, she investigates only to discover that not only is her father white, but worse, he's Hal Jackson, the obnoxious, egotistical car dealer whose insane TV advertisements plague the local airwaves. She quickly goes to confront him with the fact and the hilarity begins. Of course, Danson and Goldberg slowly warm to each other and . . . well, you can guess the rest — life really did imitate art (for awhile, anyway). ★★★ DVD: $14.99, VHS: $9.99

Made in Heaven

(1987, 103 min, US, Alan Rudolph) *Timothy Hutton, Kelly McGillis, Maureen Stapleton, Mare Winningham, Amanda Plummer.* Sweetly romantic fantasy about a young man (Hutton) who dies, goes to Heaven, and falls in love with a new spirit (McGillis), who is about to be sent to Earth. Unbalanced but interesting handling of the subject of predestination from the director of *Choose Me* and *Trouble in Mind.* Watch for cameos by Debra Winger and Ellen Barkin. ★★½

Madeline

(1998, 90 min, US, Daisy von Scherler Mayer) *Frances McDormand, Nigel Hawthorne, Hatty Jones, Ben Daniels.* Aided in large part with warm performances from McDormand as Miss Clavell and Jones as Madeline, this live-action version of the beloved children's classic is only moderately entertaining. It takes three different plots to concoct a coherent tale, creating nice but unconnected pleasant moments. Madeline meets her school's benefactress just before her death. Her husband, devastated by her loss, plans to close the school. The Spanish ambassador moves next door and his wild young son, Pepito, becomes both a friend and an

adversary to the girls. Add to this a kidnapping plot by the boy's tutor and you have a lot of story to handle in 90 minutes. ★★½ DVD: $19.99

Mademoiselle

(1966, 105 min, France/GB, Tony Richardson) *Jeanne Moreau, Ettore Manni.* Jean Genet is credited with the scenario for this atmospheric drama although reportedly several others were involved (including Richardson) at some point. The story unfolds in a French farming village which has seen its tranquility upset by a series of floods, fires and poisoning of animals. No one suspects the real culprit — the sexually repressed and emotionally disturbed spinster schoolteacher (Moreau). The townspeople come, instead, to suspect a virile, pleasant Italian woodcutter (Manni) who is also the object to Moreau's sexual scheming and bridled lust. A quietly brooding tale of evil and the suffering of the innocent. (French with English subtitles) ★★★ DVD Letterbox: $19.99

Madhouse

(1990, 90 min, US, Tom Ropelewski) *Kirstie Alley, John Larroquette, Alison La Placa.* A paltry black comedy about a married couple whose lives are turned upside-down by visiting relatives, neighbors, etc. There are about 15 minutes in the middle of this film which are funny, but the rest of the film is as uninviting as Alley and Larroquette's pain-in-the-ass houseguests. ★½

The Madness of King George

(1994, 105 min, GB, Nicholas Hytner) *Nigel Hawthorne, Helen Mirren, Ian Holm, Rupert Everett, Amanda Donohoe, Rupert Graves, John Wood.* In one of the most entertaining, witty and literate history lessons one will ever encounter, author Alan Bennett's adaptation of his stage hit "The Madness of George III" is a sumptuously filmed and costumed historical epic which royally details the madness of a king, backstage power struggles, and the frivolity of ceremony. Hawthorne excels as George III, the British monarch who has just lost the American colonies and who is about to lose his mind. As the king succumbs to increasingly bizarre behavior under the watchful eye of his doctor (Holm), a bemused court looks on, ambitious princes plot, and the faithful Queen Charlotte (the wonderful Mirren) performs 18th-century damage control. Hytner has a sharp eye for pageant and is meticulous in forging the relationships of his characters while simultaneously exposing Bennett's sardonic edge. ★★★★ DVD: $19.99

Madonna: Truth or Dare

(1991, 118 min, US, Alek Keshishian) *Madonna, Warren Beatty, Sandra Bernhard, Kevin Costner, Niki Harris, Donna DeLory, Antonio Banderas, Pedro Almodovar, Carlton Wilborn.* Though not technically a documentary, this fascinating behind-the-scenes look at pop icon Madonna's worldwide "Blonde Ambition" tour seeks to reveal the singer in on- and offstage actions and interactions. And though she is the executive producer, therefore with much at stake, Madonna is to be credited with "opening up" and revealing much about herself in front of the camera — calculated as that may be. ★★★½ DVD: $14.99

The Madwoman of Chaillot

(1969, 132 min, US, Bryan Forbes) *Katharine Hepburn, Charles Boyer, Yul Brynner, Richard Chamberlain, Danny Kaye, Edith Evans, Guiletta Masina, Paul Henreid, Margaret Leighton.* Hepburn heads an all-star cast in this hokey adaptation of the Jean Giradoux play. Kate is an eccentric "countess" no longer able to cope with the world's loss of inno-

M

cence. With her streetpeople cohorts, she concocts a plan to get even with the corporate world. You really want to like it, but the film's good intentions get in its way — but oh, what a cast! The basis for the Broadway musical "Dear World." ★★ VHS: $19.99

Mafia!

(1998, 84 min, US, Jim Abrahams) *Jay Mohr, Billy Burke, Christina Applegate, Lloyd Bridges, Olympia Dukakis, Pamela Gidley.* From some of the folks who brought us *Airplane* comes this sporadically funny spoof on *The Godfather* that also manages to get some digs in on *Casino, Showgirls* and *Goodfellas*. In his last role, Bridges plays an elderly Don who finds sons Mohr and Burke in competition for his underworld throne. With that, director Abrahams moves the action all over the place — from New York to Las Vegas, and — in flashbacks — to Salmonella, Italy. All of this is briskly handled for an hour; then, with a series of gross-out sequences, one gets the idea the well ran dry. (aka: *Jane Austen's Mafia!*) ★★ DVD: $14.99, VHS: $9.99

The Magdalene Sisters

(2003, 119 min, Ireland, Peter Mullan) *Geraldine McEwan, Anne-Marie Duff, Nora-Jane Noone, Dorothy Duffy, Peter Mullan.* Operating at full strength through the 1970s, the Irish Catholic church sanctioned homes for wayward girls in the hope to redeem their souls sufficiently to get them into heaven. But the homes were little more than laundry-processing sweatshops operated like a prison, and the girls' offenses ranged from single motherhood to simply being pretty and flirting. There is no way to get out unless a family member (who has often disowned the girl completely) comes in, no way to communicate the conditions with the outside world. Sadly, the girls often end up committing more egregious sins inside just to survive. While the Vatican was quick to condemn this movie, there has been no apology forthcoming from the church for the fact-based events depicted within. However, with the constant and often sexual humliations, *The Magdalene Sisters* has trouble escaping the feel of a women-in-prison exploitation movie. If watching girls suffer for two hours qualifies as feminist filmmaking, then Rocco Siffredi is Gloria-fucking-Steinem. Mullan compensates with a dour tone that makes the events even harder to take. Yet his visual style is bracing, using crushing telephoto lenses to accentuate the girls' sense of isolation, and ultimately making this gripping story a must to be told. ★★★ DVD: $29.99

The Magic Christian

(1970, 95 min, GB, Joseph McGrath) *Peter Sellers, Ringo Starr, Raquel Welch, Yul Brynner, Christopher Lee, Roman Polanski.* The hilarious escapades of Sellers as the world's wealthiest man, and Starr as his handpicked messiah, as they embark on a zany scheme to expose society's corruptibility. This scathing indictment of avarice and the lust for power is dated in style, but not in substance. ★★★ DVD: $14.99

The Magic Flute

(1974, 134 min, Sweden, Ingmar Bergman) This lavish production of Mozart's last opera, considered by many to be his greatest, is a delicious dreamlike fairy tale mixing German folk elements with French orchestrations and Italian humor. Featuring the Gewandhaus Orchester of Leipzig with a cast of Germany's great opera stars. ★★★★ DVD Criterion Collection: $29.99, VHS: $29.99

Magic in the Water

(1995, 101 min, US, Rick Stevenson) *Mark Harmon, Sarah Wayne, Joshua Jackson, Harley Jane Kozak.* An underwater *E.T.*, this girl-meets-lake monster tale replaces Reeses Pieces with Oreos, substitutes the divorced mom with a divorced dad, and saves a lot of special effects money by hardly ever showing the creature. While on vacation in Canada, two kids and their dad encounter a mysterious underwater serpent who helps heal some family wounds and who exposes illegal toxic dumping at the same time. ★★

The Magic Sword

(1962, 80 min, US, Bert I. Gordon) *Gary Lockwood, Ed Wood, Jr., Vampira, Basil Rathbone.* Loosely based on the story of St. George and the dragon, this romantic fairy tale unfolds when a young knight (Lockwood) vows to rescue a damsel in distress. Armed with a magic sword, he begins a dangerous journey through an enchanted forest where seven deadly curses await him. ★★

Magic Town

(1947, 103 min, US, William Wellman) *James Stewart, Jane Wyman, Kent Smith.* Director Wellman invades Frank Capra's territory in this story of a pollster who finds a small, quiet town the perfect barometer for national polls. That is, until the town's notoriety changes everyone's outlook. ★★★ VHS: $19.99

Magical Mystery Tour

(1967, 60 min, GB, The Beatles) *John Lennon, Paul McCartney, George Harrison, Ringo Starr.* Sometimes called a rock *Un Chien Andalou*, The Fab Four's charmingly surreal musical chronicles their escapades on a psychedelic bus trip. Songs include "The Fool on the Hill," "I Am the Walrus" and the title tune.

The Magician

(1959, 102 min, Sweden, Ingmar Bergman) *Max von Sydow, Ingrid Thulin, Gunnar Björnstrand.* Set in 19th-century Sweden, this richly Gothic and visually exciting "thinking man's horror film" follows the supernatural exploits of a magician (von Sydow) and his troupe who are detained in a small village when his magical powers are disbelieved. The clash between truth and illusion, reality versus the supernatural and the dramatic contrasting the comic all contribute to make *The Magician* a landmark in film history. (Swedish with English subtitles) ★★★½ VHS: $29.99

The Magnificent Ambersons

(1942, 88 min, US, Orson Welles) *Joseph Cotten, Tim Holt, Anne Baxter, Agnes Moorehead.* Welles' follow-up to *Citizen Kane* is a shattering adaptation of Booth Tarkington's novel about the self-destruction of a turn-of-the-century aristocratic family. Moorehead gives a mesmerizing performance as Holt's maiden aunt in this butchered masterpiece (the studio edited 20 minutes from Welles' final cut). ★★★★ VHS: $19.99

Magnificent Obsession

(1954, 108 min, US, Douglas Sirk) *Rock Hudson, Jane Wyman, Agnes Moorehead, Barbara Rush.* One of the best of the '50s soap operas, and the first Ross Hunter-Douglas Sirk collaboration. Hudson, in the role which made him a star, gives a strong portrayal of a careless playboy whose wastrel ways lead to an auto accident that blinds Wyman. Dedicating his life to a "magnificent obsession," Hudson becomes a

surgeon determined to restore Wyman's sight. Remake of the 1935 Irene Dunne-Robert Taylor tearjerker. ★★★

The Magnificent Seven

(1960, 128 min, US, John Sturges) *Yul Brynner, Steve McQueen, Eli Wallack, James Coburn, Charles Bronson, Robert Vaughn, Horst Buchholz, Brad Dexter.* A terrific and exciting American remake of Akira Kurosawa's *The Seven Samurai*. There's action aplenty as seven American gunslingers come to the aid of a small Mexican village being terrorized by bandits (led by Wallach). Crisp direction by Sturges and a memorable score by Elmer Bernstein. ★★★½ DVD Letterbox: $14.99, VHS: $9.99

Le Magnifique

(1974, 86 min, France, Philippe de Broca) *Jean-Paul Belmondo, Jacqueline Bisset.* Belmondo plays a double role as both a hapless hack novelist and his macho fictional alter ego in this action-filled spoof of the super-spy genre. Bisset is his glamourous assistant with whom he falls in love. It's not art, and it isn't even *That Man from Rio*, but it is a fun adventure comedy. ★★½ DVD Letterbox: $24.99

Magnolia

(1999, 189 min, US, Paul Thomas Anderson) *Jeremy Blackman, Tom Cruise, Melinda Dillon, Philip Baker Hall, Philip Seymour Hoffman, William H. Macy, Julianne Moore, John C. Reilly, Jason Robards, Melora Walters, Henry Gibson.* L.A. does strange things to people, especially fictional ones. Anderson's unbelievably ambitious *Magnolia* brings together dark pairs of people: a

The Magnificent Ambersons

young TV quiz whiz (Blackman) and an over-the-hill one (Macy), a dying producer (Robards) and a dying TV game show host (Hall), along with other related Angeleans at crisis points in their lives, and then puts them in the midst of the strangest weather pattern in recorded history. The framework is reminiscent of Altman, the long, free-flowing scenes could be Cassavetes, but the well-schooled young director makes an exhilarating concoction out of his parts, the whole being not a plot but dozens of moments of redemption that have deep personal meaning in a random and coincidental city. Cruise stands out as a woman-hating self-help guru. The movie's length and obsession with detail will alienate a few; most, however, will be left with mouths agape and emotions swelled. ★★★★ DVD: $26.99

Magnum Force

(1973, 124 min, US, Ted Post) *Clint Eastwood, Hal Holbrook, Mitchell Ryan, Felton Perry, David Soul, Robert Urich.* Eastwood returns in this second Dirty Harry film, trying to uncover a conspiracy within the San Francisco police department involving a group of vigilante officers who execute notorious criminal suspects. Holbrook is Harry's superior, who disagrees with Harry's unorthodox methods. While nothing could match the power and intensity of Don Siegel's original *Dirty Harry*, this sequel nevertheless works as an entertaining, average action film. The film's most interesting point is its distinction between the work of the vigilantes and the violent work of Harry himself — a fine line indeed — and seems to be an attempt to explain the subtleties of the first film to its critics. (Sequel: *The Enforcer*) ★★½ DVD Letterbox: $14.99, VHS: $9.99

The Mahabharata

(1989, 318 min, GB, Peter Brook) Brook's epic undertaking of the Mahabharata, the Hindu story of the origins of the world, a massive tome which is over 15 times longer than the Bible. The result is nothing less than what we've come to expect from Brook: a brilliantly acted and thoughtfully directed epic with an ensemble cast from over 19 different countries and every continent. The running time of close to six hours — short considering the subject — has been broken down into three separate stories for the video release: "The Game of Dice" (97 min), "Exile in the Forest" (111 min) and "The War" (110 min). ★★★½ DVD 2-disc set: $39.99, VHS Edited version: $49.99, VHS: $99.99

Mahler

(1974, 115 min, GB, Ken Russell) *Robert Powell, Georgina Hale, Richard Morant.* Russell kept his normal excesses to a minimum in this sumptuously filmed and costumed biography of the famed Swedish composer Gustav Mahler. The film is a dazzling evocation of the loves, moods and music of the artist. Through flashbacks and beautiful dream imagery, it focuses on the tormented life and turbulent relationship he endured with his wife. Such Russellisms as a dream sequence with a Nazi Pope (a Nazi Pope?) do sneak through. On the whole, however, this is Russell in a mellow mood. ★★★ DVD: $24.99, VHS: $19.99

Mahogany

(1975, 109 min, US, Berry Gordy) *Diana Ross, Billy Dee Williams, Anthony Perkins, Jean-Pierre Aumont, Beah Richards, Nina Foch.* An inferior, even ridiculous drama set in the fashion world with Ross making it big as a model. Williams is her boyfriend, a community activist who disapproves of her profession. Looking like a fey Bernard Goetz, Perkins plays the photographer who discovers her

and then goes all bitchy and neurotic when she rebukes his romantic overtures. Pure trash and not even fun on a camp level. ★ VHS: $14.99

Maid in Manhattan

(2002, 110 min, US, Wayne Wang) *Jennifer Lopez, Ralph Fiennes, Natasha Richardson, Stanley Tucci, Bob Hoskins, Tyler Garcia Posey, Frances Conroy, Chris Eigeman.* Having made Julia Roberts a full-fledged movie star in *Pretty Woman*, the "Cinderella" formula is once again at work, this time attempting to make J-Lo a superstar. The result, *Maid in Manhattan*, an innocuous romantic comedy, is no more or no less satisfying than that Roberts-Gere box-office hit. Lopez plays Marisa, a single mom who is a maid at a four-star Manhattan hotel. By mistaken identity barely believable by Hollywood's standards, she is thought to be a socialite by handsome, too-good-to-be-true Christopher Marshall (Fiennes), a politician as bland as his name. Sparks fly, she continues the charade until the inevitable "moment of truth." The screenplay by Kevin Wade doesn't allow for too many humorous lines or moments, which is a shame because there's a workable chemistry between Lopez and Fiennes, only it's buried somewhere beneath the clichés. ★★ DVD Dual: $19.99, VHS: $14.99

Maid to Order

(1987, 92 min, US, Amy Jones) *Ally Sheedy, Beverly D'Angelo, Michael Ontkean, Tom Skerritt, Valerie Perrine.* Agreeable Cinderella comedy with Sheedy as a pampered rich girl whose father wishes she had never been born — and with the help of fairy godmother D'Angelo, it comes true. Kinda cute if you don't think about it too much. ★★ VHS: $9.99

The Main Event

(1979, 109 min, US, Howard Zieff) *Barbra Streisand, Ryan O'Neal, Paul Sand.* Tired comedy about a bankrupt perfume manufacturer who inherits the contract of a retired boxer. Not very funny, implausible with none of the chemistry between the two stars in their earlier outing, this is tough going even for die-hard Streisand fans. ★½ DVD: $19.99, VHS: $9.99

Maitresse

(1976, 112 min, France, Barbet Schroeder) *Gérard Depardieu, Bulle Ogier.* The kinky underground world of sadomasochism is revealed in this enjoyably shocking drama that will remind many of the sexual outlandishness of *Last Tango in Paris*. Depardieu stars as a burglar who breaks into the flat of Ogier, a professional sadist who, as a leather-clad, whip-snapping dominatrix, rules over her compliant stable of wealthy clients. A wickedly tantalizing fable about the darker side of love. An interesting item about the film is that the featured customers (all masked) are real Parisian masochists who paid to be in the film. (French with English subtitles) ★★★ DVD Letterbox Criterion Collection: $29.99, VHS: $29.99

The Major and the Minor

(1942, 101 min, US, Billy Wilder) *Ray Milland, Ginger Rogers, Rita Johnson, Robert Benchley, Diana Lynn.* Terrific screwball comedy with Rogers masquerading as a 12-year-old to get half-price train fare, then being taken under the wing of military academy teacher Milland. Wilder's script is sharp and funny, his leads are in good form, and the "Veronica Lake" scene is classic. ★★★½

Major Barbara

(1941, 131 min, GB, Gabriel Pascal) *Wendy Hiller, Rex Harrison, Robert Newton, Robert Morley, Deborah Kerr.* George Bernard Shaw collaborated with director Pascal on this superb rendition of his poignant social comedy. Hiller is excellent as the daughter of a wealthy munitions manufacturer who, disillusioned with her father's world, joins the Salvation Army. Filled with Shaw's unswerving and razor-sharp commentary. ★★★★ VHS: $29.99

Major League

(1989, 107 min, US, David S. Ward) *Tom Berenger, Charlie Sheen, Corbin Bernsen, Margaret Whitton, Wesley Snipes, Rene Russo, Dennis Haysbert.* Contrived though amiable baseball comedy with a few well-placed laughs about the new owner of the Cleveland Indians (Whitton) purposely making her team lose so she can move the team to Florida. (Followed by 2 sequels) ★★½ DVD Letterbox: $14.99, VHS: $9.99

Major Payne

(1995, 97 min, US, Nick Castle) *Damon Wayans, Karyn Parsons, William Hickey.* About as funny as a night in war-torn Bosnia, *Major Payne* is a pointless remake of the so-so 1955 Charlton Heston military comedy *The Private War of Major Benson.* An insipid Payne is a seemingly slow-witted career soldier who is booted out of the Army and sent to command a group of junior ROTC cadets. The story follows his mean-spirited efforts to help them win a military competition. Coauthor Wayans gives a tedious and irritating performance, and his script? At one point, Payne attempts to literally break the fingers of a five-year-old. Such wit. ★ DVD: $19.99, VHS: $14.99

A Majority of One

(1962, 149 min, US, Mervyn LeRoy) *Rosalind Russell, Alec Guinness, Mae Questel, Marc Marno.* An intimate stage piece, this schmaltzy but nevertheless beguiling comedy-drama only slightly misses its mark in the screen adaptation. Russell plays Mrs. Jacoby, a Jewish widow from Brooklyn who accompanies her daughter and diplomat son-in-law to Japan, where she is romanced by a high-ranking Japanese businessman (played by Guinness). It's distracting having Anglo thespian Guinness (as good as he may be) playing an Asian, but the film's observations on love, culture clashes and bigotry compensate. In support, Questel and Marno repeat their stage roles, with Marno very appealing as Eddie, a hipster servant. ★★½ VHS: $19.99

Make Mine Mink

(1960, 101 min, GB, Robert Asher) *Terry-Thomas, Billie Whitelaw.* Terry-Thomas stars in this often hilarious farce about a retired army officer who becomes the leader of a philanthropic band of fur thieves. ★★★½

Make Room for Tomorrow

(1981, 106 min, France, Peter Kassovitz) *Jane Birkin, Victor Lanoux.* The generation gap is explored in this comedy-drama about four generations of a family who gather to celebrate the birthday of their great-grandfather. At the reunion, the eccentricities of each seem just a little more outrageous than the last. (French with English subtitles) ★★★

The Maker

(1997, 98 min, US, Tim Hunter) *Matthew Modine, Mary-Louise Parker, Jonathan Rhys Meyers, Fairuza Balk, Michael Madsen.* An orphaned slack-

Denzel Washington as *Malcolm X*

er, on the cusp of heading off to college, has his life irrevocably transformed when his long-lost brother (Modine) shows up on his doorstep on his 18th birthday. The younger sibling is then told the truth about his parents' deaths, while being schooled in the art of pulling "tricks" and the importance of being "the maker." While *The Maker* is never dull, it's never really excites either, and the clichéd drama of the young man's choice is far from compelling. ★★½

Making Love

(1982, 113 min, US, Arthur Hiller) *Michael Ontkean, Kate Jackson, Harry Hamlin, Wendy Hiller, Arthur Hill.* Sort of a breakthrough for American films, this slick but superficial romantic drama features Ontkean as a successful doctor who leaves his wife (Jackson) for a handsome writer (Hamlin). One of the first Hollywood films to feature well-adjusted gay characters in nonsupporting roles, and to show two men kissing. With all its "good intentions," the story is at times soap operaish, but involving nonetheless. Good performances from its three lead players. ★★½

Making Mr. Right

(1987, 95 min, US, Susan Seidelman) *John Malkovich, Ann Magnuson.* The ingredients for this film sure seemed right: Malkovich and offbeat comic Magnuson starring in Seidelman's follow-up to *Desperately Seeking Susan;* what could go wrong? Well, just about everything, but the real tragedy here is the script. Magnuson plays a P.R. expert who is hired to help develop a human image for Chemtech Corporation's new android (Malkovich), but ends up clashing with the android's creator (also Malkovich) when she falls in love with the machine. ★ DVD Dual: $14.99

The Makioka Sisters

(1983, 110 min, Japan, Kon Ichikawa) *Keiko Kishi, Yoshiko Sakuma.* Director Ichikawa breathtakingly adapted Junichiro Tanizaki's best-selling novel about the lives and loves of four sisters in 1930s Osaka. Brilliantly photographed, the film explores the sisters' efforts to sustain and come to terms with the passing of their proud customs, which have slowly slipped away — victims to encroaching Westernization in the ever-changing days of pre-war Japan. The story follows the two married sisters' valiant attempts to find a suitable husband for the third sister while the youngest one, rebelliously promiscuous, discovers and embraces the new freedoms available. (Japanese with English subtitles) ★★★★

Malcolm

(1986, 86 min, Australia, Nadia Tass) *Colin Friels, John Hargreaves, Chris Haywood.* This refreshingly funny Aussie import follows the madcap antics of part-time inventor Malcolm (played with elfish charm by Friels), a naive young man who, after teaming up with a bank robber and his moll, uses his technical wizardry to pull off a series of hilarious heists. ★★★

Malcolm X

(1992, 205 min, US, Spike Lee) *Denzel Washington, Angela Basset, Albert Hall, Al Freeman, Jr., Delroy Lindo, Spike Lee, Theresa Randle, Lonette McKee, Giancarlo Esposito.* An intense and highly accomplished biography of the slain religious and community leader. Featuring a tour de force performance by Washington as Malcolm, the film traces his life from his zoot suited-youth in the 1940s; to his imprisonment, where he was first introduced to the Muslim faith; to his rise as a disciple of Elijah Muhammad, the Supreme Minister of the Nation of Islam; to his tragic assassination. Lee's film succinctly examines these stages of Malcolm's life, creating a fluid transition from each period to the next. As a storyteller, Lee has never been more focused, capturing Malcolm's conviction and the unrest of the era while viewing Malcolm's evolutionary process with unexpected objectivity. Lee's big, complex and powerful film befits the life and legend of such a complicated and fervent man. ★★★★ DVD: $19.99, VHS: $19.99

Male and Female

(1919, 117 min, US, Cecil B. DeMille) *Gloria Swanson, Thomas Meighan, Raymond Hatton, Lila Lee.* A wealthy, pampered young woman and her snobbish family are shipwrecked on a desert island along with "the help" — their long-suffering butler and maid. In order to survive, the socialite must turn to the butler, Crichton (Meighan), for help, while the formerly derisive young lady begins to fall for him. Based on J.M. Barrie's "The Admirable Crichton," the social and class comedy-drama *Male and Female* is certainly dated in its attitudes. But DeMille's storytelling skills are sharp. With strong acting (especially a quietly powerful performance by Meighan), lavish sets, and an outrageously over-the-top, non sequiter sequence featuring Swanson and Meighan in Babylonian times, *Male and Female* is DeMille at his most DeMille. ★★★½ DVD: $24.99, VHS: $29.99

Male of the Century

(1979, 101 min, France, Claude Berri) *Claude Berri.* Berri, the Renaissance man of "French Cinema Souffle," directed, wrote and stars in this pleasant comedy. It is the story of a befuddled chauvinist whose liberated wife is kidnapped by bank robbers. Taken from an idea by Milos Forman. (French with English subtitles) ★★½

Maléna

(2000, 92 min, Italy, Giuseppe Tornatore) *Monica Bellucci, Giuseppe Sulfaro.* Like director Tornatore's *Cinema Paradiso, Maléna* tells a story of WWII Italy through the eyes of a young boy. But *Maléna,* while containing many comedic moments, is a starker tale of resentment, jealousy and loss, revealing a darker side of human nature. Twelve-year-old Renato is one of the many males (of a wide range of ages) in a small Sicilian village with a schoolboy crush on Maléna, an outsider from another province who married a local man who is now off at war. Her beauty and grace illicit lust, fantasy and incessant gossip. The hardships of the continuing war bring out the worst in many. The report of Maléna's husband's

death marks her as fair game for the lecherous and an object of hatred for the hypocritically pious. As Maléna's position in the community worsens, Renato grows beyond his immature obsession with her to recognize and appreciate her as a human being, a person suffering isolation in a sea of envy and prejudice. A superb re-creation of the era effectively underscores this affecting drama of one woman's struggle to survive hostile forces. (Italian with English subtitles) ★★★½ DVD: $19.99, VHS: $9.99

Malice

(1993, 107 min, US, Harold Becker) *Alec Baldwin, Gwyneth Paltrow, Nicole Kidman, Bill Pullman, Anne Bancroft, Bebe Neuwirth, George C. Scott, Peter Gallagher.* Baldwin plays a brilliant surgeon newly arrived to a small New England town. He rents a room from married couple Kidman and college professor Pullman. In a nasty series of events, Baldwin unnecessarily operates on Kidman, initiating a multimillion dollar lawsuit. But this is only half of it. And what begins as a slow-paced melodrama quickly blossoms into a cagey psychological thriller complete with figure-eight plot twists and baffling detective work. In the *Body Heat* mold, the film takes wicked delight in its crafty composition. Pullman ties the film together with his sleuthing academic. ★★★ DVD: $14.99

Malicious

(1973, 97 min, Italy, Salvatore Samperi) *Laura Antonelli, Turi Ferro.* Antonelli stars in this spicy though abrasive sex comedy as a housekeeper hired by a widower to look after him and his three sons. But she soon becomes the object of desire for all the men in the house, including the youngest, a 14-year-old coming of age, and the father, with his own plans for courtship and marriage. ★★½

Mallrats

(1995, 96 min, US, Kevin Smith) *Jeremy London, Jason Lee, Shannon Doherty, Claire Forlani, Ben Affleck.* Director Smith's follow-up to his witty *Clerks* is a disappointing but not entirely unentertaining entry into the disaffected youth genre. The action is moved from Hell's shopping strip to Hell's suburban shopping mall, from black and white to color reminiscent of colorization. The film opens as the two central characters, Brodie and T.S. (London, Lee), are dumped by their respective girlfriends Rene and Brandi (Doherty, Forlani). Our protagonists would get on with their lives if they had any. That not being the case, they speed to their local mall, where fate, chance and an odd assortment of characters (many in exile from *Clerks*) provide our antiheroes with the means of retribution and reconciliation. The film opens flatly and often feels forced. ★★ DVD Collector's Edition: $19.99

Malou

(1983, 94 min, West Germany, Jeanine Meerapfel) *Ingrid Caven, Helmut Griem.* Hannah lives with her husband in West Germany. Her life and marriage are affected, however, by her obsession with her dead mother, Malou, whose frantic life included a marriage to a Jew during Hitler's reign and her efforts to save him. Told through flashbacks, the film explores the relationship between the two women's lives and how Hannah deals with her present condition. The slow pacing and obvious dramatics rarely live up to its promising premise. (German with English subtitles) ★★

The Maltese Falcon

(1941, 100 min, US, John Huston) Humphrey Bogart, Mary Astor, Sydney Greenstreet, Peter Lorre, Elisha Cook, Jr., Gladys George. Huston made his impressive directorial debut with this classic mystery and third screen version of Dashiell Hammett's novel. Bogart stars as Sam Spade, tough-guy private eye whose investigation into the death of his partner leads him to tangle with femme fatale Brigid O'Shaughnessy (the ravishing Astor) and underworld art collector Kasper Gutman (Greenstreet in his Oscar-nominated film debut). Huston's film is awash in shadowy black and white which only heightens the tension brought about by the mysterious goings-on in the search for the elusive black bird, a jewel-encrusted statuette which leaves a trail of corpses in its wake. One of the first films of the budding noir genre, and one of the best. ★★★★ DVD: $19.99, VHS: $14.99

Mama, There's a Man in Your Bed

(1989, 111 min, France, Coline Serreau) Daniel Auteuil, Firmine Richard. Released theatrically under its less wieldy French title, *Romuald et Juliette*, this engaging social comedy is the story of a very unlikely love between a CEO from the "white" side of the tracks and a poor black cleaning lady with five kids (all from different husbands). Cuckolded by his wife and ousted from his executive position in a yogurt company, our privileged young man finds comfort, sympathy and a comrade-in-arms with the charming black woman. Their alliance soon blossoms into romantic love in this sweet, surprisingly entertaining farce that features several spirited performances and a fine blues soundtrack. (French with English subtitles) ★★★

Mama Turns 100

(1978, 100 min, Spain, Carlos Saura) Geraldine Chaplin, Fernando Gomez. Wildly imaginative, this sly black comedy is set in a cavernous house in rural Spain where a family prepares to celebrate the 100th birthday of their elderly matriarch. But this familial celebration is not as innocent as one might expect: the wacky children are bent on making this birthday her last, but the eccentric and shrewd Mama has her own devious plans. A circuitous tale of greed, power and money. (Spanish with English subtitles) ★★★ VHS: $59.99

The Mambo Kings

(1992, 104 min, US, Arne Glimcher) Armand Assante, Antonio Banderas, Cathy Moriarty, Roscoe Lee Browne. Set to the pulsating rhythms of a Latin beat, *The Mambo Kings* opens like gangbusters and rarely lets go. Based on the Pulitzer Prize-winning novel "The Mambo Kings Play Songs of Love," by Oscar Hijuelos, this stirring film adaptation has the look and feel of a 1950s musical, which only enhances its style. Assante and Banderas are musician brothers from Cuba who flee their homeland and venture to the uncertainty of New York City's nightclubs and ballrooms. Most of the film centers on the brothers' attempts to get ahead, which culminates into a lucky break: an appearance on "I Love Lucy." If the film falters at all, it's during the last half hour, which echoes tragic melodramatic moments from musicals past. ★★★½ VHS: $14.99

Mambo Mouth

(1992, 60 min, US, Thomas Schlamme) John Leguizamo. With razor-sharp satire and hilariously inspired portrayals of the diverse personas of the American Latino, Leguizamo proves that he is a talent to be reckoned with in this hugely entertaining video adapted from his off-Broadway show. A skilled

The Maltese Falcon: "The stuff that dreams are made of"

critic, Leguizamo creates six different aspects of the Latino — from the sexual bravura of a misogynist macho male, to a goofy 14-year-old homeboy's first sexual experience with a prostitute, as well as an acid-tongued, hip-swiveling prostitute. A wonderfully revealing commentary on the self-image and perceptions of the Latino in America. ★★★ VHS: $19.99

Mame

(1974, 131 min, US, Gene Saks) Lucille Ball, Robert Preston, Bea Arthur, Jaen Connell, Bruce Davison. The Broadway musical "Mame" is one of the most endearing of all stage shows — which benefitted greatly from Angela Lansbury's immortal performance. Unfortunately, there's little magic to this flat screen verison, with Ball miscast as Auntie Mame. Preston makes a good Beau, and Arthur and Connell repeat their roles as, respectively, Vera and Agnes Gooch. Another instance in which Hollywood outsmarted itself by replacing the star of a stage hit. ★½

Mamma Roma

(1962, 110 min, Italy, Pier Paolo Pasolini) Anna Magnani, Ettore Garofolo, Franco Citti, Silvana Corsini. Magnani is a heartrending revelation in this intensely moving neorealist urban drama. Magnani plays a poor but tenacious individualist who, despite her sad eyes and an arduous life, never loses her vitality, her hearty laugh nor the passionate love she has for her son. A former prostitute, she longs for a middle-class existence for her long estranged teenaged son, but when a former pimp threatens to expose her past, she is forced back on the streets. A disquieting tale set amidst the gloom of a crime- and poverty-plagued modern high-rised Rome. A tough, uncompromising though well-crafted film. (Italian with English subtitles) ★★★½ DVD Criterion Collection 2-Disc Set: $39.99, VHS: $29.99

A Man, a Woman and a Killer

(1975, 95 min, US, Rick Schmidt & Wayne Wang) Ed Nylund, Dick Richardson, Carolyn Zaremba. This collaboration with northern California filmmaker Schmidt and Wang is a beguiling, Godard-influenced meditation of a film about the making of the film. Essentially a two-character story, the film explores the relationship, both within the story as well as the rehearsals, between a paranoid man, his girlfriend and his imagined assassin. The pacing is slow and the "cut and paste" narrative style will agitate some, but overall the film is an interesting primer for Wang's future films. ★★ VHS: $59.99

A Man and a Woman

(1966, 102 min, France, Claude Lelouch) Anouk Aimée, Jean-Louis Trintignant. This Oscar-winning film is a joy to watch and a must for all people in love. Aimée and Trintignant are wonderful as a widow and widower who meet at a boarding school for their children. A simple and heartwarming contemporary love story. (French with English subtitles) ★★★½ DVD Letterbox: $19.99, VHS Dubbed: $14.99

A Man and a Woman: 20 Years Later

(1986, 120 min, France, Claude Lelouch) Anouk Aimée, Jean-Louis Trintignant. Aimée and Trintignant reprise their wonderful characters from Lelouch's classic love story, *A Man and a Woman*. But the 20 years have both dimmed their attractiveness as well as the ability and even sanity of the director. The two ex-lovers are reunited in an attempt to make a film about their long-gone love affair. Throw in an escaped mental patient, a murder and a desert scene and you end up with a true mess. (French with English subtitles) ★½ VHS: $14.99

Man Bites Dog

(1992, 96 min, Belgium, André Bonzel, Benôt Poelvoorde, Rémy Belvaux) Benôt Poelvoorde, Rémy Belvaux, Jenny Drye. Morbidly funny is probably the best way to describe this amoral mockumentary about a poetry-reciting serial killer with a heart of gold whose sadistic exploits are recorded by a film crew. While finding themselves both repulsed and fascinated, the filmmakers in this "cinema veritasteless" spoof are drawn into the likable maniac's perverse pastime. Some viewers may be put off by the film's excruciatingly slow pace, but it seems a necessary device for the filmmakers to capture the rhythm of this maniac's life. A brutal, vulgar, repellent open sore of a film that pushes its NC-17 rating to the furthest. (French with English subtitles) ★★★ DVD Letterbox Criterion Collection: $29.99

A Man Called Horse

(1970, 114 min, US, Elliot Silverstein) Richard Harris, Judith Anderson, Jean Gascon, Manu Tupou, Dub Taylor. Harris goes Native in this gripping western adventure as an English aristocrat who is captured by the Sioux Indians and undergoes a series of physical tests. (Sequel: *Return of a Man Called Horse*) ★★★ DVD: $19.99, VHS: $9.99

A Man Called Peter

(1955, 119 min, US, Henry Koster) *Richard Todd, Jean Peters, Marjorie Rambeau.* A remarkable performance by Todd highlights this sensitive biography of Peter Marshall, a Scottish minister who became chaplain to the U.S. Senate. ★★★ VHS: $19.99

A Man Escaped

(1956, 102 min, France, Robert Bresson) *François Leterrier, Charles Le Clainche, Maurice Beerblock.* A riveting drama set almost entirely within a prison cell, *A Man Escaped* stars Leterrier as a Resistance fighter who is captured and imprisoned by the Nazis and is sentenced to be executed. As he charts his plans for escape, a young boy is placed in his cell, and the man must decide whether to trust the youth or kill him as a possible spy. Rather than resorting to artificial film devices to create tension (music, editing), the film successfully relies entirely on the central character and his studied actions. Based on a true story. (French with English subtitles) ★★★½ DVD: $29.99, VHS: $14.99

Man Facing Southeast

(1987, 108 min, Argentina, Elisio Subiela) *Lorenzo Quinteros, Hugo Soto.* A fascinating sci-fi drama exploring the role of psychiatry in the modern world and the struggle of the individual vs. society. At a Buenos Aires mental institution, a man mysteriously appears, claiming he is from another planet. Though not officially a patient, he is regarded as just another delirious paranoid by his psychiatrist and the staff. It is only after a series of intellectual verbal sparrings between patient and doctor, and an otherworldly spiritual calm he casts on the other inmates, that the doctor begins to suspect that his story could very well be true. A compassionate, grown-up fairy tale. (Spanish with English subtitles) ★★★

A Man for All Seasons

(1966, 120 min, GB, Fred Zinnemann) *Paul Scofield, Robert Shaw, Wendy Hiller, Orson Welles, Susannah York, John Hurt.* This splendid film version of Robert Bolt's play about the conflict between Sir Thomas More and King Henry VIII is one of the outstanding films of its decade. Scofield gives a mesmerizing, Oscar-winning performance as More, and is brilliantly supported by Shaw as Henry, Welles as Cardinal Wolsey and Hiller as More's devoted wife. The film was awarded six Oscars and is a must for all those interested in rich, historical dramas. (Remade in 1988) ★★★★ DVD: $19.99

The Man from Elysian Fields

(2001, 106 min, US, George Hickenlooper) *Andy Garcia, Mick Jagger, Julianna Margulies, James Coburn, Olivia Williams.* Dejected writer Byron Tiller (Garcia), struggling to provide for his family, strikes a Faustian bargain with Luthor Fox (Jagger), a suave Continental operating a high-class escort service. Tiller gets absorbed in an odd trilateral affair with a lonely beauty (Williams) and her dying husband (Coburn), a three-time Pulitzer Prize-winning author whom Tiller happens to idolize. When the hired stud isn't working on the alienated wife in the boudoir, he's off in the study collaborating with his hero and sudden best friend on a new novel. Alas, Tiller's oblivious wife (Margulies) soon gets wise and their marriage is thrown into a predictable tizzy, just as his own bought emotions for his wealthy clients come to a searing head. This finely polished curio contains sporadic sparks of wit and some classy performers, but never quite rises above its melodrama-of-the-week trappings. ★★½ DVD: $29.99, VHS: $14.99

The Man from Nowhere (L'Homme de Nulle Part)

(1937, 98 min, France, Pierre Chenal) *Pierre Blanchar, Ginette Leclerc.* This unjustly forgotten black comedy deftly combines elements of Pagnol's rural tales like "The Fanny Trilogy" with Carné's satirical bent in *Bizarre, Bizarre.* When a quiet young man, married to an unforgiving wife and henpecked by his shrewish mother, is mistaken for being dead, he decides to remain in that state and start life anew in Rome. Unfortunately with his new identity comes new problems. Adapted from Luigi Pirandello's only novel and filmed entirely in Italy. (French with English subtitles) ★★★ VHS: $59.99

The Man from Snowy River

(1982, 115 min, Australia, George Miller) *Kirk Douglas, Tom Burlinson, Sigrid Thornton, Jack Thompson.* Based on a beloved Australian poem, Miller's splendid adventure film spins the tale of a young mountain horseman who faces the challenge of snaring a valuable runaway colt. An inspirational paean to the majesty of the Australian landscape and the ruggedness of its inhabitants. (Sequel: *Return to Snowy River*) ★★★ DVD: $14.99, VHS: $6.99

A Man in Love

(1987, 108 min, France, Diane Kurys) *Peter Coyote, Greta Scacchi, Jamie Lee Curtis.* Kurys' long anticipated follow-up to her critically acclaimed *Entre Nous* is a mildly disappointing but interesting love story set within the filming of a movie in Italy. This film-within-a-film stars Coyote as a married American actor who falls in love with Scacchi, his on-screen lover. Kurys creates a romantic and sensual world where the fantasies of film overtake reality. (Filmed in English) ★★½

The Man in the Gray Flannel Suit

(1956, 153 min, US, Nunnally Johnson) *Gregory Peck, Jennifer Jones, Fredric March, Lee J. Cobb, Marisa Pavan.* Extremely competent film version of Sloan Wilson's novel examining Madison Avenue mores, as seen through the eyes of go-getter Peck. ★★★ VHS: $39.99

The Man in the Iron Mask

(1939, 119 min, US, James Whale) *Louis Hayward, Joseph Schildkraut, Joan Bennett.* Alexander Dumas' swashbuckling tale of sibling rivalry between France's King Louis XIV and his twin brother, raised by the Three Musketeers, makes for high-spirited adventure. Whale directs with a sure hand, making the production both exciting and smart. ★★★

The Man in the Iron Mask

(1998, 132 min, US, Randall Wallace) *Leonardo DiCaprio, Jeremy Irons, John Malkovich, Gérard Depardieu, Gabriel Byrne.* This overlong swashbuckler has very little swash to it, no thanks to Wallace's sluggish, unimaginative directorial debut. The setting is 1660, and all but one of the infamous Musketeers are retired. The one remaining Musketeer serves the cruel and arrogant young snit of a king, Louis XIV (DiCaprio), who's intent on letting his people starve to death. DiCaprio also plays Louis' secret twin, Philippe, who's been imprisoned in the Bastille and hidden in an iron mask to conceal his identity. To save their nation, the Musketeers reunite for a daring plot to kidnap the king and replace him with his mysterious twin. The prestigious foursome is a joy to behold, but there's little else to recommend. ★★½ DVD: $14.99

The Man in the Moon

(1991, 99 min, US, Robert Mulligan) *Sam Waterston, Tess Harper, Reese Witherspoon, Emily Warfield, Jason London.* With the same locale, tone and youthful themes explored in his classic *To Kill a Mockingbird*, Mulligan's thoroughly satisfying coming-of-age tale centers on two sisters growing up in the 1950s. As the two siblings who fall in love with the same boy-next-door, Witherspoon and Warfield give glowing portrayals of teenage uncertainty and familial anxiety. Waterston gives a passionately intense performance as their father. A gentle, sweet-natured family drama. ★★★ DVD Letterbox: $14.99

The Man in the Silk Hat

(1983, 96 min, France, Maud Linder) *Max Linder,* France's most popular comedian of the silent era, is lovingly remembered in this funny and insightful documentary made by his 50-year-old daughter, Maud. Through numerous excerpts from his two-reelers and features, we rediscover Linder's comic genius and enjoy his infectious humor. From his slapstick antics and pratfalls to his work behind the camera, we learn of a man of whom Charles Chaplin once said, "He was my professor." (Narrated in English) ★★★ VHS: $24.99

The Man in the White Suit

(1952, 84 min, GB, Alexander MacKendrick) *Alec Guinness, Joan Greenwood.* Another one of Guinness' peerless '50s comedies. Here he stars as an unassuming lab assistant who invents a miracle fabric that can be woven into indestructible cloth. The potential catastrophe that this poses for clothing manufacturers pits Guinness against the industry in a Chaplinesque battle which serves as a witty and incisive chastisement against the greed of capitalism. ★★★★ DVD: $19.99

The Man Inside

(1990, 93 min, US, Bobby Roth) *Jürgen Prochnow, Peter Coyote, Nathalie Baye, Philip Anglim.* Intriguing political thriller with Prochnow as a German reporter who goes undercover at a right-wing tabloid to expose its unethical operating practices. Coyote costars as an embittered veteran who takes Prochnow under his wing. ★★★ VHS: $19.99

Man Is Not a Bird

(1965, 80 min, Yugoslavia, Dusan Makavejev) *Eva Ras, Milena Dravic.* The *enfant terrible* of Eastern European cinema, this, Makavejev's first feature, is a delirious satire on the state of Communism as well as a humorous celebration of guiltless eroticism (a theme which runs throughout all his works). An engineer gets a job in a bleak industrial town and there, meets and falls in love with his landlord's daughter. The young woman, a carefree and impetuous individual, proves to be the undoing of the man. An amusing highpoint in all of the wild proceedings is the crosscutting of Beethoven's "Ode to Joy" being performed in a factory with our heroes frantically making love. (Serbian with English subtitles) ★★★½ VHS: $24.99

A Man Like Eva

(1983, 89 min, Germany, Radu Gabrea) *Eva Mattes, Elizabeth Kreuzer.* Mattes turns in a startling opposite-gender performance as a thinly disguised R.W. Fassbinder-like film director who loves, dominates and even terrorizes his cast and crew. This absorbing drama charts the inevitable self-destruction of an artist who longed for love but could not receive it. (German with English subtitles) ★★½ VHS: $39.99

Man of a Thousand Faces

(1957, 122 min, US, Joseph Pevney) *James Cagney, Dorothy Malone, Jane Greer.* Cagney scores another triumph in a biographical role, this time as silent screen star Lon Chaney. The film divides its time between Chaney's personal life and his career: effectively re-creating some of Chaney's best-known roles; and, somewhat melodramatically, detailing his two marriages. Malone plays his first, troubled wife; and Greer is his beloved second wife. Like Cagney's *Yankee Doodle Dandy*, this film is an affectionate tribute to its subject. ★★★ DVD: $24.99

Man of Aran

(1934, 77 min, US, Robert J. Flaherty) Flaherty's lifelong cinematic interest in documenting the resilient efforts of man in his battle against a hostile enviornment continues in this brilliant chronicle set in the barren wind- and surf-swept islands of Aran — situated off the western coast of Ireland. Two years in the making, the film dramatically captures the constant struggle of the independently minded people who must conquer the rough forces of nature to insure their simple survival. ★★★★ DVD: $29.99

Man of Flowers

(1984, 110 min, Australia, Paul Cox) *Norman Kaye, Alyson Best, Chris Haywood, Werner Herzog.* An unusual Australian black comedy. Kaye stars as a sexually repressed lover of art and flowers who, each Wednesday, pays a beautiful artist's model to perform an impassioned striptease to the strains of classical music. His lonely life, caused by childhood sexual traumas, is enlivened and upset as he reluctantly becomes involved with her tumultuous personal life. Weirdly funny, with a hypnotic, ever-present classical score. ★★★ DVD: $24.99

Man of Iron

(1981, 140 min, Poland, Andrzej Wajda) *Lech Walesa, Jerzy Radziwilowicz, Krystyna Janda, Marian Opania.* Seamlessly weaving documentary and fictional footage alike, director Wajda has given crated a portrait of the Polish Solidarity strike in 1980 that will not soon be forgotten. Wajda tells his story through the eyes of an alcoholic TV journalist who is ordered to smear a key Solidarity figure, the "man of iron." His investigation shows in flashbacks the abortive 1968 and 1970 strikes through rare footage. Lech Walesa makes appearances both in the dramatic and documentary footage. (Polish with English subtitles) ★★★

Man of La Mancha

(1972, 130 min, US, Arthur Hiller) *Peter O'Toole, Sophia Loren, James Coco, Harry Andrews, John Castle, Brian Blessed.* Another in a long line of dreadful screen adaptations of classic Broadway musicals. In the same league as *Mame, A Chorus Line* and *A Little Night Music*, this is probably the worst offender, as a brilliant theatre piece has been reduced to a deadened bore. O'Toole, who was so good in the musical *Goodbye, Mr. Chips*, is embarrassingly bad as Don Quixote; though not half as embarrassing as Loren as Dulcinea. Only Coco as Sancho captures the spirit of the stage production. Where, oh where, was Richard Kiley? ★ DVD: $14.99

Man of Marble

(1977, 160 min, Poland, Andrzej Wajda) *Krystyna Janda, Jerzy Radziwilowicz.* Made just before the emergence of the Solidarity movement, Wajda's look at the fate of the worker in Communist Poland was slightly ahead of its time. Employing a documentary-like style, Wajda follows a young filmmak-

er as she unearths the history of Radziwilowicz, a bricklayer who, in the Stalinist 1950s, was exalted to the lionized stature of worker-hero only to be later crushed as an enemy of the state. A fascinating look into the machinations of the Polish bureaucracy, the film suffers a bit from its weighty running time. (Polish with English subtitles) ★★★½ DVD: $29.99

A Man of No Importance

(1994, 98 min, GB/Ireland, Suri Krishnamma) *Albert Finney, Rufus Sewell, Brenda Fricker, Tara Fitzgerald, Michael Gambon.* Finney shines in this slender but engrossing drama as Alfie Byrne, a seemingly happy-go-lucky bus conductor who undergoes a late midlife crisis and reawakening. Set in Dublin in the early 1960s, the story follows bachelor and deeply closeted gay man Alfie, who quietly lives with his sister (Fricker), keeps his passengers amused with poetry readings, and harbors a crush for Bobby (Sewell), a handsome coworker. Alfie's life takes a turn when he organizes a community theatre presentation of Oscar Wilde's "Salome," which ultimately inspires him to confront his true sexual desires. A character study of limited insight which celebrates life and individuality, *A Man of No Importance* manages to succeed in spite of its dramatic shortcomings by the sheer force of Finney's acting prowess. ★★½

Man of the House

(1995, 98 min, US, James Orr) *Chevy Chase, Jonathan Taylor Thomas, Farrah Fawcett, George Wendt.* Attempting a film comeback, Chase abandons his smart-aleck screen persona and instead goes the Disney route appearing as yet another adult upstaged and outsmarted by a precocious adolescent. Teen idol *du jour* Thomas plays 12-year-old son to Fawcett's divorced mom. Their years of togetherness is intruded upon when U.S. Attorney Chase moves in with hopes of marrying Fawcett. But Thomas has other plans, which includes keeping the adults in separate beds and forcing Chevy to join a father-son Indian scout troop to further humiliate him. With only a few laughs scattered about, the film isn't helped by Thomas' whining or flat direction by Orr. ★★ DVD: $19.99, VHS: $9.99

Man on Fire

(1987, 92 min, US, Elie Chouraqui) *Scott Glenn, Brooke Adams, Danny Aiello, Joe Pesci, Jonathan Pryce.* Italy is under siege by terrorists, and Glenn, a cynical ex-CIA agent, is out to rescue a 12-year-old girl kidnapped by the merciless bunch. Boring and pointless. ★ VHS: $79.99

Man on Fire

(2004, 145 min, US, Tony Scott) *Denzel Washington, Dakota Fanning, Christopher Walken, Mickey Rourke, Giancarlo Giannini, Radha Mitchell, Marc Anthony, Rachel Ticotin.* This second adaptation of the A.J. Quinnell novel (the first being a forgotten 1987 clunker with Scott Glenn) features Washington as Creasy, an alcoholic haunted by his past — as a Black Ops soldier. He gets a shot at redemption by working as a bodyguard to the young daughter of a well-to-do couple in Mexico City. Creasy has his icy resistance broken by her persistence and charm, and when she is kidnapped, he goes on a vengeful rampage to get to the head honcho, known only as "The Voice." Despite being slightly miscast, Denzel gives his usual strong performance, and brings a vicious, cold intensity to the very brutal revenge scenes. However, potentially powerful and suspenseful sequences are nearly destroyed by director Scott's insistence on multiple

Jim Carrey as Andy Kaufman in *Man on the Moon*

exposures, unnecessary subtitles, headache-inducing camerawork and an intrusive, very loud soundtrack. Though the film is much too long, Washington's and Fanning's excellent performances, and the seductive, sleazy pull of the story line assure that it is at least of interest. ★★½ DVD: $29.99

The Man on the Eiffel Tower

(1949, 85 min, US, Burgess Meredith) *Charles Laughton, Franchot Tone, Burgess Meredith.* A highly suspenseful psychological thriller about a police inspector (Laughton) playing mental cat-and-mouse games with a suspected murderer (Tone). Filmed in Paris. ★★★½ DVD: $7.99

Man on the Moon

(1999, 119 min, US, Milos Forman) *Jim Carrey, Danny DeVito, Courtney Love, Paul Giamatti.* Carrey excels as eccentric comedian Andy Kaufman in this hit-or-miss biography. More of a collection of episodes from Kaufman's life (mostly his comedy pieces) rather than a look inside the mind of a man who may have been a comedy genius, *Man on the Moon* traces Andy's life in brief skits from childhood to his rise as a comedy club and TV performer to his untimely death. With a brilliant opening that would have no doubt pleased the late comedian, the film works best when Carrey is bringing to life Andy's own, unique brand of performance comedy. Less successful are the personal moments; the filmmakers bring little depth into the psyche of the comedian. No matter, it is Carrey's show, and he doesn't disappoint on any level. ★★½ DVD: $14.99

The Man on the Roof

(1976, 110 min, Sweden, Bo Widerberg) *Carl Gustav Lindstedt, Sven Wollter, Thomas Hellberg.* The Sidney Lumet-style cop thriller gets a sedate arthouse treatment in director Widerberg's mannered film. When a corrupt inspector is stabbed to death in his hospital bed, it's up to Martin Beck (Lindstedt) and an ensemble of police to find the killer and the motives. The questions of why cops go bad has apparently never been raised in this city, so there is a lot of philosophizing in-between the action scenes. Widerberg is more interested in the day-to-day procedures of the police than their heroism; it's surprising to see screen time devoted to paperwork, car travel, and routine questioning. It's not boring, but it's not particularly compelling storytelling, either. Still, *The Man on the Roof* has style to spare, making the situations seem immediate without ever feeling fake. (Swedish with English subtitles) ★★½ VHS: $79.99

Man Trouble

(1992, 90 min, US, Bob Rafelson) *Jack Nicholson, Ellen Barkin, Beverly D'Angelo, Harry Dean Stanton, Veronica Cartwright.* Check your expectations at the door for this romantic comedy that heralds the reunion of superstar Nicholson and director Rafelson. Nicholson stars as a dog trainer who becomes involved with a prima donna (Barkin) caught up in underworld affairs. Though critically lambasted upon its theatrical release, the film is not so much bad as it is disappointing; it simply cannot sustain the burden of being a "minor" movie with major talent. ★★ VHS: $9.99

Man Wanted

(1995, 92 min, Hong Kong, Benny Chan) *Simon Yam, Yu Rong Guang, Christy Chung.* A by-the-numbers "undercover cop with conflicted loyalties" movie that benefits from the presence of charismatic HK actor Yam but suffers from an overreliance on music video-style sequences and Cantopop tunes to sustain its mood. Yam is a cop who has spent two years infiltrating the gang of local crime boss Yu. When the time comes to make the bust, he is betrayed by an overambitious police lieutenant and seriously injured. His target, who has become his unlikely friend, is apparently killed. Flash forward several months, and Yu reappears on the scene, alive and with vengeance in mind. It's all a soap opera, with neon-lit, rain-slicked streets providing most of the atmosphere. (Cantonese with English subtitles) ★★½ DVD: $19.99, VHS: $59.99

The Man Who Came to Dinner

(1941, 112 min, US, William Keighley) *Monty Wooley, Bette Davis, Ann Sheridan, Billie Burke, Jimmy Durante, Mary Wickes.* Woolley re-creates his acclaimed stage role in this gloriously funny adaptation of the Kaufman and Hart stage hit. Woolley is at his acerbic best as a famed critic who visits the small-town home of Burke and family and is forced to stay after an accident makes him immobile. The epitome of the unwanted house guest, he proceeds to run everyone's life and sends the household into hysteria. Davis took a supporting role as Woolley's secretary, but this is Woolley's show all the way, and it is one of the funniest performances of the 1940s. ★★★½

The Man Who Captured Eichmann

(1996, 96 min, US, William A. Graham) *Robert Duvall, Arliss Howard, Jeffrey Tambor, Joel Brooks.* The true story of the Israeli *Mossad* agent who led the operation to capture infamous Nazi war criminal Adolf Eichmann makes for a thrilling and thought-provoking made-for-cable movie. After a concentration camp survivor reports meeting someone who may be Eichmann at a cafe, a commando squad is sent to Buenos Aires to kidnap him and bring him back to Israel to stand trial. Equally divided between action and dialogue, the first half of the film concerns the mechanics of grabbing the Nazi while the second half examines the team's wait for an opportunity to leave the country. A fascinating look at the banality of evil. Duvall is terrific as Eichmann. ★★★½ VHS: $19.99

The Man Who Could Work Miracles

(1937, 86 min, US, Lothar Mendes) *Roland Young, Ralph Richardson, Joan Gardner.* Enchanting adaptation of H.G. Wells' story about an "ordinary little fellow" endowed with the power to work miracles. Young (best known as *Topper*) is engaging as the mild-mannered miracle man. ★★★

The Man Who Cried

(2001, 100 min, GB, Sally Potter) *Christina Ricci, Cate Blanchett, John Turturro, Johnny Depp, Harry Dean Stanton.* Ricci plays Suzie, a Russian Jew abandoned by her father in 1930s Europe. She crosses the continent, landing in Paris and befriending a showgirl (Blanchett), an opera singer (Turturro) and a gypsy (Depp). Potter's overwrought drama plays like a 1930s melodrama, with trial on top of tribulation on top of tragedy. It's absurd and exhausting, and undermines the pleasures of the attractive cast and the elaborate camerawork. ★★ DVD Letterbox: $29.99, VHS: $14.99

The Man Who Fell to Earth

(1976, 140 min, GB, Nicolas Roeg) *David Bowie, Candy Clark, Buck Henry, Rip Torn.* Bowie stars as the frail and mysterious visitor from another planet who unknowingly threatens American industry with his powers. A tremendously original sci-fi drama presented with the surreal and mind-boggling sensitivities of director Roeg. ★★★ DVD Letterbox Restored and Uncut: $29.99

The Man Who Knew Too Little

(1997, 94 min, US/GB, Jon Amiel) *Bill Murray, Peter Gallagher, Joanne Whalley, Alfred Molina, Richard Wilson.* With its playful titular nod to Hitchcock and a very engaging premise, this spy spoof isn't as much fun as it could have been. Though producing a fair amount of laughs, many of the jokes are stifled. Murray plays an American visiting his hotshot businessman brother (Gallagher) in London. To get rid of him for the evening, Gallagher buys his sibling the hottest theatre ticket in town: "Theatre of Life," in which the audience member becomes part of the play in an unknown, acted-out scenario. Then, Murray is mistaken for a spy, though he thinks it's all part of the show. As the video stars from Des Moines, Murray is not at his best; but fault must lie with director Amiel, who gives the film a sluggish pace and is unable to excite or inspire his cast. ★★ DVD: $14.99, VHS: $9.99

The Man Who Knew Too Much

(1934, 75 min, GB, Alfred Hitchcock) *Leslie Banks, Peter Lorre, Edna Best.* Based on a Bulldog Drummond story, this fast-paced thriller stars a villainous Lorre (in his first English-speaking role) as a

kidnapper who snares an innocent couple's child in order to insure their silence about a planned political assassination. Film historians have long argued the comparative merits of this version versus its 1956 remake; see for yourself the different approaches Hitchcock took at varied points in his career. ★★★ VHS: $12.99

The Man Who Knew Too Much

(1956, 120 min, US, Alfred Hitchcock) *James Stewart, Doris Day, Brenda de Banzie, Bernard Miles, Carolyn Jones.* While vacationing in French Morocco, doctor Stewart and wife Day become embroiled in a case of international intrigue, and with the kidnapping of their youngest son, are thrust into the very heart of a dangerously murderous scheme. An invigorating and suspenseful remake of Hitchcock's own 1934 thriller. Stewart and Day offer typically endearing performances which add to the flavor of this slick bag of tricks. Doris sings "Que Sera, Sera." ★★★½ DVD: $19.99, VHS: $14.99

The Man Who Loved Women

(1978, 119 min, France, François Truffaut) *Charles Denner, Leslie Caron, Brigitte Fossey, Nathalie Baye.* This bittersweet comedy, the inspiration for the American remake (remember, the one with Burt Reynolds?), is most aptly served by Truffaut. Gallic enchantment as the female of the species plagues Denner, the continually tempted skirt-chaser who seeks to transcribe his romantic legacy. (French with English subtitles) ★★★ DVD: $19.99

The Man Who Shot Liberty Valance

(1962, 122 min, US, John Ford) *James Stewart, John Wayne, Lee Marvin, Vera Miles, Edmond O'Brien, Woody Strode, Strother Martin, Andy Devine, Lee Van Cleef.* A classic study of the character of man and the nature of convenient truths. Stewart is catapulted into political prominence when he's credited with ridding a frontier town of a murderous villain. Stewart and Wayne represent different codes of honor; Marvin is the common evil, to be dealt with as conscience dictates; and Miles is the woman sought as helpmate and prize. There's a strong supporting cast, and excellent direction by Ford. ★★★★ DVD: $14.99, VHS: $9.99

The Man Who Wasn't There

(2001, 116 min, US, Joel Coen) *Billy Bob Thornton, Frances McDormand, James Gandolfini, Michael Badalucco, Richard Jenkins, Scarlett Johansson, Jon Polito, Tony Shalhoub, Katherine Borowitz.* The Coens continue their slash and burn through film history with this moody and sly black-and-white film noir. Thornton gives a crafty performance as Ed, a barber who, if not for his constant plumes of cigarette smoke, would hardly be noticed as he slinks quietly through life. His wife (McDormand) is a ball of fire, working her way up through the Nerdlinger's department store empire with the adulterous help of boss Big Dave (Gandolfini). In typical noir fashion, Ed finds himself knee-deep in circumstances beyond his control, a murderous web of murder and mistaken identity. But this is the Coen brothers after all, so there's plenty of humor present, often at the expense of their expansive palette of dim-witted characters. Jenkins is a particular standout, among a terrific cast, as the local lawyer who drinks just a little too much. Roger Deakins' cinematography is the only truly reverent aspect of the film, invoking a moodiness that clashes knowingly with the winkingly improbable story. But please, for once, could the Coens write a character who's as smart as they are? ★★★ DVD: $14.99, VHS: $9.99

The Man Who Wasn't There

The Man Who Would Be King

(1975, 127 min, US, John Huston) *Sean Connery, Michael Caine, Christopher Plummer, Saeed Jaffrey.* Rudyard Kipling's exhilarating yarn of the daring exploits of two English soldiers in colonial India. Connery and Caine star as the ambitious explorers who attempt to infiltrate an ancient land and establish themselves as deities. Exotic locales, hair-raising adventures and deft direction make this one of Huston's finest. ★★★½ DVD Letterbox: $19.99, VHS: $14.99, VHS Letterbox: $14.99

Man with a Cross

(1943, 88 min, Italy, Roberto Rossellini) Made under Fascist control and later rejected by Rossellini, this drama deals with the Italian expeditionary forces on the Russian Front during the summer of 1942. The story focuses on a saintly chaplain who tends to both the spiritual and physical needs of the Italian soldiers, as well as to the peasants during a Russian artillery bombing. (Italian with English subtitles) ★★½ VHS: $59.99

Man with a Movie Camera

(1928, 90 min, USSR, Dziga Vertov) A seminal and still controversial film which attempts to create a cinematic reality by "simply" depicting a day in the life of Moscow. But director Vertov, fascinated by the possibilities of the medium, utilizes editing, fast/slow motion, split screen and superimposition to distort the very reality he seeks to represent. An exciting, surreal compendium which explores the relation between cinema, actuality and history. ★★★½ DVD Michael Nyman Score: $29.99, VHS: $24.99

The Man with Bogart's Face

(1980, 111 min, US, Robert Day) *Robert Sacchi, Franco Nero, Michelle Phillips, Olivia Hussey, Sybil Danning.* Bogie look-alike Sacchi stars as a fledgling private eye whose business increases dramatically due to his unique chiseled features. Soon, he finds himself deluged with requests to locate a pair of priceless blue sapphires in a *Maltese Falcon*-esque caper. A pleasant if inconsequential mystery comedy which playfully acknowledges its noir roots. ★★½ DVD: $24.99, VHS: $9.99

The Man with One Red Shoe

(1985, 100 min, US, Stan Dragoti) *Tom Hanks, Lori Singer, Jim Belushi, Carrie Fisher.* One of the least successful of the many American adaptations of French comedies — in this instance, *The Tall Blond Man with One Black Shoe*. Hanks plays a violinist mistaken for a secret agent. ★½ VHS: $9.99

The Man with the Golden Arm

(1955, 119 min, US, Otto Preminger) *Frank Sinatra, Eleanor Parker, Kim Novak, Darren McGavin.* Sinatra received an Oscar nomination for his powerful performance as a drug addict trying to go straight. Preminger's stirring drama pulls no punches. Parker is terrific as Sinatra's handicapped wife. ★★★ VHS: $9.99

The Man with the Golden Gun

(1974, 125 min, GB, Guy Hamilton) *Roger Moore, Christopher Lee, Herve Villechaize, Britt Ekland.* Moore's second outing as 007 finds him a little more comfortable in the role that he soon got *too* comfortable with. A distant cousin of Bond creator Ian Fleming, Lee, plays the titular character, a paid assassin named Scaramanga, abetted in no small

way by his major domo Nick Nack (Villechaize). (Sequel: *The Spy Who Loved Me*) ★★½ DVD: $19.99, VHS: $9.99

The Man with Two Brains

(1983, 90 min, US, Carl Reiner) *Steve Martin, Kathleen Turner, David Warner, Sissy Spacek.* Martin and Reiner struck comic gold a third time in this improbable but hilarious spoof with Martin as a scientist who falls in love with a brain in a jar, and begins the search for the perfect body to harbor it. Turner also stars as Martin's faithless wife, and Spacek gives voice to the brain. ★★★ DVD: $9.99, VHS: $7.99

The Man without a Face

(1993, 125 min, US, Mel Gibson) *Mel Gibson, Nick Stahl, Margaret Whitton, Gaby Hoffman, Richard Masur.* In an unusual choice to make his directorial debut, Gibson stars in this involving, surprisingly downbeat adaptation of Isabelle Holland's novel. Gibson plays a disfigured loner whose life and appearance are a mystery to his New England neighbors. When young Stahl learns of Gibson's possible past as a teacher, he lobbies him for private tutoring. Gibson agrees, and a friendship soon develops between the two. Gibson serves as a commendable mentor and friend until news of previous child molestation charges begin to surface. Gibson gives an earnest performance as the compassionate tutor, but the film, though competently produced, is sometimes as evasive as its titular character. ★★½ DVD Letterbox: $19.99

The Man without a Past

(2002, 97 min, Finland, Aki Kaurismäki) *Markku Peltola, Kati Outinen, Annikki Tahti.* A typically deadpan comedy-drama from director Kaurismäki, *The Man without a Past* tells the tale of the titular character, beaten almost to death by some thugs in a park, who awakens to find he has no memory of his identity or past. The episodic film follows his path to make a new life for himself, which proves quite difficult. At times, a bit too difficult — no one in a position of power believes his story (and are extremely cruel), and his constant passivity in the face of this grows a bit wearisome and frustrating. That caveat aside, the film is as amusing and even joyful as other Kaurismäki films. And, of course, the man who brought us *Leningrad Cowboys Go America* must have some oddball musical numbers, and they're fun and unobtrusive here. The film is also valuable as a (perhaps overstated) look at day-to-day life among the lower class in Finland, and the simple joys they experience together. (Finnish with English subtitles) ★★★ DVD: $29.99, VHS: $79.99

Man's Best Friend

(1993, 87 min, US, John Lafia) *Ally Sheedy, Lance Henricksen, Robert Costanzo.* One of the best "killer animal" movies since *Jaws*, this extremely well-mounted sci-fi shocker stars Sheedy as an ambitious TV reporter who goes after an exclusive on a suspected animal rights violator (Henricksen) and winds up in the possession of his prize experiment: a genetically altered superdog with a psychotic streak and a short fuse. ★★★ DVD: $19.99, VHS: $14.99

Man's Favorite Sport

(1963, 121 min, US, Howard Hawks) *Rock Hudson, Paula Prentiss, Charlene Holt, John McGiver.* Hudson stars in this entertaining, amusing comedy as a renowned fishing expert who really can't stand the sport or the great outdoors. When he agrees to make an appearance at a fishing tournament, public relations director Prentiss has her hands

full making Rock an outdoorsman. An amusing spoof on sports and manhood with many well-placed jabs. ★★★ DVD Letterbox: $14.99

The Manchurian Candidate

(1962, 126 min, US, John Frankenheimer) *Frank Sinatra, Laurence Harvey, Janet Leigh, Angela Lansbury, Henry Silva.* Richard Condon's best-seller about a brainwashed Korean War vet out to do our country dirt is superbly brought to the screen by Frankenheimer, who would explore similar territory two years later with *Seven Days in May*. Among a first-rate cast, Lansbury is exceptional, giving a most chilling portrayal of deception and betrayal. (Remade in 2004) ★★★★ DVD Letterbox Special Edition: $14.99

Mandela

(1987, 135 min, US, Philip Saville) *Danny Glover, Alfre Woodard, John Matshikiza.* Gripping, first-rate made-for-cable production about the life of South African leader Nelson Mandela. Glover brilliantly portrays the jailed activist, whose lifelong battle against Apartheid served as a rallying cry around the world. Woodard is remarkable as Nelson's wife, Winnie. ★★★

Mandela and deKlerk

(1997, 114 min, US, Joseph Sargent) *Sidney Poitier, Michael Caine, Tina Lifford.* This made-for-cable drama documents Nelson Mandela's 30-year odyssey as radical protestor, political prisoner, peace negotiator and, finally, president of South Africa, in his undying dedication to end Apartheid. Caine portrays F.W. deKlerk, the moderate minister who replaced ousted conservative P.W. Botha as president and eventually freed Mandela from prison to further a free, democratic South Africa. Poitier is excellent, embodying Mandela's strength, resolve and dignity; Caine is equal, capturing the conflicting emotions of a man determined to do the right thing. While *Mandela and deKlerk* is only middling as drama (facts don't always conform to satisfying story structure), it's completely absorbing as history. ★★★ VHS: $9.99

Mandingo

(1975, 127 min, US, Richard Fleischer) *James Mason, Ken Norton, Susan George.* A steamy love story set on a slave breeding plantation. It's just like *Gone with the Wind*, only all the characters are in heat. Trashy, awful and a definite guilty pleasure. ★

The Mangler

(1995, 95 min, US, Tobe Hooper) *Robert Englund, Red Levine.* An atmospheric misfire (based on yet another Stephen King short story) about a sweatshop bedsheet folding machine that develops a taste for human flesh when an accidental combination of circumstances awakens the demon residing within. It's as silly as it sounds. Englund's campy performance as the Scrooge-like caretaker of The Mangler, and director Hooper's Grand Guignol treatment of the subject matter, along with some really grotesque death sequences, almost compensate for the skimpy screenplay and poor performances. ★★ VHS: $14.99

The Mango Tree

(1982, 92 min, Australia, Kevin Dobson) *Geraldine Fitzgerald, Robert Helpmann.* A story of a young man's coming-of-age as he, his family, and his friends experience the tumultuous changes of the early 1900s in a small Australian town. Sweetly done but not out of the ordinary. ★★½ VHS: $69.99

Diane Keaton (l.) and Woody Allen in *Manhattan*

Manhattan

(1979, 93 min, US, Woody Allen) *Woody Allen, Diane Keaton, Mariel Hemingway, Michael Murphy, Meryl Streep, Wallace Shawn, Karen Ludwig.* Allen is at his most insightful with this valentine of a film which pays tribute to his favorite city, romance, Gershwin, neuroses and bungled love affairs. Arguably his best film (some would say *Annie Hall*), *Manhattan* follows the jagged course of love taken by a group of New York sophisticates. Shot in a romanticized black and white, the film is both deliriously comic and assuredly dramatic while exploring romantic indiscretions, misjudgments and betrayals. Allen plays a TV writer who is involved with high schooler Hemingway. His married best friend Murphy is involved with pseudo-intellectual magazine editor Keaton. As these romantics crisscross and grapple with the frailties of relationships, Allen succinctly addresses the nature of romance and its tenacious grip on us all. ★★★★ DVD: $19.99

Manhattan Melodrama

(1934, 93 min, US, W.S. Van Dyke) *Clark Gable, William Powell, Myrna Loy, Leo Carrillo.* Though best known as the movie John Dillinger saw before being gunned down, this crime saga is actually quite good (it won an Oscar for Best Screenplay). Gable and Powell are childhood pals who find themselves on opposite sides of the law. And they're both in love with Loy. Yeah, it's a familiar theme, but this was one of the first films to use it. One of Gable's better '30s outings, and the first pairing of Powell and Loy. ★★★ VHS: $14.99

Manhattan Murder Mystery

(1993, 108 min, US, Woody Allen) *Woody Allen, Diane Keaton, Alan Alda, Anjelica Huston, Ron Rifkin.* In his first post-Mia production, Allen reteams with his old partner Keaton to bring about this engaging and genuinely funny whodunit in the tradition of *The Thin Man*. Allen and Keaton play a calcified middle-aged couple who befriend the seemingly blissful older couple down the hall. But when the wife suddenly drops dead of a heart attack, Keaton suspects her husband of murder and takes it on herself to uncover the truth, setting off a hilarious and, at times, tense mystery. Alda costars as a friend who plays along with Keaton's theory while Allen thinks she's just deranged. Throughout, Allen serves up his usual repertoire of quips and one-liners and they consistently amuse. *Manhattan* is an enjoyable

affair that does Nick and Nora Charles proud, albeit without the 15 martinis per scene. ★★★½ DVD: $29.99, VHS: $19.99

The Manhattan Project

(1986, 117 min, US, Marshall Brickman) *John Lithgow, Christopher Collet, Cynthia Nixon, John Mahoney.* Quirky sci-fi comedy about a teenager (Collet) who builds an atomic bomb in hopes of exposing a secret nuclear plant in his neighborhood. Lithgow plays a scientist who befriends the youngster. ★★½ DVD Dual: $14.99, VHS: $14.99

Manhunter

(1986, 119 min, US, Michael Mann) *William L. Petersen, Kim Greist, Brian Cox, Dennis Farina.* Stylish, gritty police thriller based on Thomas Harris' "Red Dragon." Petersen stars as an unorthodox ex-FBI agent — he is able to think exactly like a criminal and thereby deduce his next move — who comes out of retirement to track down a serial killer. The character of Dr. Hannibal Lecter, played by Cox, would surface a few years later as the psychopath in *The Silence of the Lambs*, played by Anthony Hopkins. (Remade in 2002 as *Red Dragon*) ★★★ DVD Theatrical Cut: $14.99, DVD Director's Cut: $19.99

Maniac

(1962, 86 min, GB, Michael Carreras) *Kerwin Matthews, Nadia Gray.* Hammer Studio head Carreras takes a turn as director in this stylish knock-off of *Psycho*, about an American (Matthews) in Paris who runs into problems with his girlfriend's family. Fairly suspenseful and rather coherent considering its derivative roots. ★★★

Maniac

(1980, 87 min, US, William Lustig) *Joe Spinell, Caroline Munro, Tom Savini.* A terrifying and extremely gross film with Spinell as a schizophrenic who takes to the streets at night to kill at random. The horror of the killings is intensified by Spinell's sympathetic portrayal of the killer. Recommended for gore fans only. ★ DVD Letterbox Limited Edition Collector's Tin: $39.99, DVD: $24.99

Maniac Cop

(1988, 92 min, US, William Lustig) *Tom Atkins, Bruce Campbell, Richard Roundtree, Sheree North.* New York is being terrorized by a series of mutilation murders, and the public breaks out in a panic when the killer is discovered to be a police officer.

Bloody and violent, this horror tale is slightly elevated by its intriguing premise and few scares. Written and produced by cult fave Larry Cohen. ★★ VHS: $14.99

Mannequin

(1938, 95 min, US, Frank Borzage) *Joan Crawford, Spencer Tracy, Alan Curtis, Leo Gorcey.* An extremely competent performance by Crawford is the main attraction of this otherwise ordinary romantic drama. Joan is a working girl from a Hester Street tenement in New York who marries ne'er-do-well Curtis to escape her poverty. At her wedding party, she meets wealthy shipping magnate Tracy, who immediately falls for her. Though she loves her husband, she's torn between both men — that is until Curtis gets a nasty idea to frame Tracy. In support, Gorcey has some good scenes as Crawford's younger brother. ★★ VHS: $19.99

Mannequin

(1987, 89 min, US, Michael Gottlieb) *Andrew McCarthy, Kim Cattrall, Meshach Taylor, James Spader.* Set at Wanamaker's department store in Philadelphia, this lifeless comedy stars McCarthy as a store employee who discovers that a mannequin (Cattrall) has come to life — but only he can see her. That's about the calibre of the jokes, if you don't include Taylor's caricature of a lisping, limp-wristed flamboyantly gay window dresser. (Sequel: *Mannequin 2: On the Move*) ★ DVD Dual: $14.99

Manny & Lo

(1996, 90 min, US, Lisa Krueger) *Mary Kay Place, Scarlett Johansson, Aleska Palladino.* A mesmerizing fairy tale of two sisters on the run which is brought to life by three enthralling performances. Living in different foster homes, the pregnant Lo (Palladino) rescues her sister Manny (Johansson) from the household who had her sleeping in the garage. They take to the road in their deceased mom's car, shoplifting what they need. When Lo is ready to give birth, they kidnap a clerk (Place) from a children's store to aid them in the delivery. Director Krueger has constructed a wryly observant film illuminated by insightful moments in which a person's life is delineated in a few words or a chance gesture. A remarkable film with unexpected warmth and humor, and a loving respect for its three protagonists. ★★★½ DVD Letterbox: $24.99

Manon of the Spring

(1986, 112 min, France, Claude Berri) *Yves Montand, Daniel Auteuil, Emmanuelle Béart.* Set 10 years after the conclusion of *Jean de Florette*, this sequel unfolds with César and his nephew Ugolin now tilling the soil they stole from Jean de Florette. Manon, Jean's daughter, has grown into a beautiful, untamed woman who roams the countryside tending goats. The drama concerns Manon's efforts to reclaim the land and renounce the men who were responsible for her father's demise. The conclusion to this epic of revenge and treachery is riveting drama and is a superlative finale to two exquisite stories. (French with English subtitles) ★★★★

Mansfield Park

(1999, 112 min, GB, Patricia Rozema) *Frances O'Connor, Jonny Lee Miller, Alessandro Nivola, Embeth Davidtz, Harold Pinter, James Purefoy.* Director Rozema's revisionist version of Jane Austen's novel, *Mansfield Park* is a comic feminist delight — a truly sweet, romantic film. Like all of Austen's stories, this one revolves around a family, their unwed daughters and marrying them off. The

Frances O'Connor in *Mansfield Park*

plucky heroine Fanny Price (a superlative O'Connor), from poor beginnings and now living on the stately Bertram family estate, is being courted by a rake, Henry Crawford (Nivola). She has been in love since childhood with her cousin Edmond (Miller), who is now engaged to Henry's worldly sister Mary. Not to worry, for by the end of the film the proper couplings will be made. Though there are a few liberties taken by Rozema the film possesses a magical quality and remains true to Austen's spirit. ★★★½ DVD: $19.99, VHS: $9.99

The Manster

(1959, 91 min, Japan, George P. Breakstone & Kenneth B. Crane) It took two directors to make this movie about an American reporter in Japan who is given an injection by mad Dr. Suzuki. When an eyeball appears on his shoulder, he looks the other way. But things soon come to a head when an entire face forms and starts growing in his ear! So they decide to split up and go their separate ways. ★ VHS: $9.99

Manufacturing Consent: Noam Chomsky and the Media

(1993, 166 min, Canada, Mark Achbar & Peter Wintonick) Noam Chomsky, probably one of the greatest thinkers of the late 20th century, is examined, discussed, explored and even ridiculed in this engrossing, well-paced and humorous documentary. The film chronicles Chomsky's rise to fame as well as his fall from grace as a controversial author and professor of linguistics, and examines the inequities in American television journalism and the problems with the medium of television itself. In interviews, Chomsky covers everything from World War II to sports to basic communication theories. This film stands as a wonderful testament to a truly thought-provoking and incredibly astute political and philosophical thinker. ★★★★ DVD: $29.99, VHS: $30.99

The Manxman

(1929, 90 min, GB, Alfred Hitchcock) *Carl Brisson, Anny Ondra.* Hitchcock's last silent film is an appealing romantic melodrama about a rich lawyer and an indigent fisherman in love with the same woman. ★★★ VHS: $49.99

Map of the Human Heart

(1993, 109 min, Canada/Australia, Vincent Ward) *Jason Scott Lee, Anne Parillaud, Patrick Bergin,*

John Cusack, Jeanne Moreau. Director Ward has crafted a dense web of dusky, beautiful images in this story of a love affair that spans 30 years and three continents. Arvik, a half-Inuit boy suffering from tuberculosis, is whisked away from the Arctic by a visiting mapmaker who takes him to a Catholic orphanage in Canada. There, Arvik befriends a young girl of mixed Native American and French Canadian heritage. Many years later as adults (played by Lee and Parillaud) they meet in WWII London, where both are engaged in the fight against Germany. The film's expansiveness of time and place unfortunately results in a distancing of the characters, yet Ward succeeds in provoking thought on the people, places and events that shape one's life. ★★★ DVD Letterbox: $19.99, VHS: $9.99

A Map of the World

(1999, 128 min, US, Scott Elliott) *Sigourney Weaver, Julianne Moore, David Strathairn, Chloë Sevigny, Louise Fletcher, Arliss Howard.* Alice Goodwin (Weaver) lives on a struggling dairy farm in Wisconsin with her husband and two daughters. Her best friend is Theresa, who also has two daughters. When one of them drowns under the supervision of Alice, the young girl's death causes Alice to suffer a breakdown, which sets the stage for a tragic turn of events. Based on Jane Hamilton's moving best-seller, this downbeat adaptation finds its biggest strength in Weaver, who is excellent as the physically strong but emotionally fragile Alice. But in spite of a good ensemble and some tearjerking dramatics, the film only occasionally involves, offering instead a series of somber moments which fail to truly come together as a whole. ★★½ DVD: $19.99, VHS: $14.99

Marat Sade

(1967, 118 min, GB, Peter Brook) *Patrick Magee, Glenda Jackson, Clifford Rose, Ian Richardson.* Peter Weiss' play (the full title of which is "The Persecution and Assassination of Jean-Paul Marat as Performed by the Inmates of the Asylum of Charenton Under the Direction of the Marquis de Sade") is brought to the screen with lurid intensity by the Royal Shakespeare Company. The play is, as its title says, the story of the manipulation of the inmates by the Marquis in order to destroy his most hated political enemy: Marat. Jackson is stunning in her film debut as Charlotte Corday (the unwitting tool of Magee's truly maniacal de Sade). This dark and disturbing film is a powerful allegory of the cruelty and abuse inherent in the wielding of political power. ★★★½

Marathon Man

(1976, 125 min, US, John Schlesinger) *Laurence Olivier, Dustin Hoffman, Roy Scheider, Marthe Keller, William Devane.* Nail-biting thriller with Hoffman as a Columbia University student who unwittingly becomes involved with the CIA, Nazi war criminals and the beautiful Keller. Olivier is chilling as one of the screen's most vicious villains. Does for dentists what *Psycho* did for showers. Based on the William Goldman novel. ★★★½ DVD Letterbox: $14.99, VHS: $14.99

March of the Wooden Soldiers

(1934, 73 min, US, Gus Meins) *Stan Laurel, Oliver Hardy.* Laurel and Hardy's classic musical comedy is based on the Victor Herbert operetta "Babes in Toyland." Stan and Ollie are Santa's hapless helpers, who help save Toyland with their giant wooden soldiers. ★★★ DVD: $9.99

Il Mare (The Sea)

(1962, 104 min, Italy, Giuseppe Patroni Griffi) With its sweeping camera capturing the desolate beauty of off-season Capri, *Il Mare* is a beguiling and enveloping drama that depicts the constantly shifting relationships between two men and a woman. A man wanders around and becomes the object of desire for both a young woman and a male teen. This sexual and psychological melodrama evokes the atmosphere and deep sexual longing of Visconti's *Death in Venice* (filmed several years later). A romantic, drunken, sensual and often violent tale of sexual tension and unrequited love. (Italian with English subtitles) ★★★

Margarita Happy Hour

(2001, 98 min, US, Ilya Chaiken) *Eleanor Hutchins, Larry Fessenden, Holly Ramos.* A group of women friends, approaching 30 and with children now, meet every week for margarita happy hour at their favorite watering hole. Some of them still cling to the bohemian lifestyle of the N.Y.C. underground art and music scene, but they all have made sacrifices in becoming mothers, and find it difficult, if not impossible, to devote the same energy to their way of life as they used to. Writer-director Chaiken focuses on Zelda (sexy and talented Hutchins) and her alcoholic poet boyfriend Max (another strong acting turn by director Fessenden) and digs up a lot of painful truths about parenting, ambitions and friendship. Several scenes don't work as well as others, and the ending is almost a brush-off, but *Margarita Happy Hour* transcends its Lifetime Channel Special Film for Former Punk Girls possibilities to become a stylish, probing drama. ★★★ DVD: $14.99, VHS: $9.99

Maria Chapdelaine

(1984, 108 min, Canada, Gilles Carle) *Nick Mancuso, Carole Laure.* A family's hardships and determined pioneering spirit against the stark, brutal wilderness of North Canada is the theme of this lyrical drama based on the novel that has become a literary cornerstone of French-Canadian culture. Set against the breathtaking backdrop of the unspoiled beauty of Quebec's upper Gatineau region, the lovely Maria is the object of affection of two young men, one of whom offers escape from the difficult life in the snow-covered north. Remake of a 1934 French film. (French with English subtitles) ★★★

El Mariachi

(1992, 81 min, US, Robert Rodriguez) *Carlos Gallardo, Consuelo Gomez.* While the story of the funding for this $7,000 film is almost legendary, it cannot prepare one for the exciting, inventive and entertaining fun that first-time director Rodriguez creates. Displaying dazzling visual virtuosity and a playful, almost mocking approach, *El Mariachi* tells the tale of a congenial mariachi singer who, with his beloved guitar in hand, arrives in a dusty, nameless Mexican town seeking a place to sing. But, before he can even quench his thirst and strum his first note, he is mistaken for a gun-toting, vengence-seeking criminal and is thrown into the midst of an unbelievably bloody battle between warring gangs. Acrobatic gunfights and flailing bodies are never far away, as he slugs it out (and more than holds his own) with the bad guys. A thrilling western that belies its low budget in delivering an exhilarating and often hilarious film. (Spanish with English subtitles) ★★★½ DVD Special Edition: $19.99

Marianela
(1972, 108 min, Spain, Angelino Fons) Based on the novel by Benito-Perez Galdos, this touching story, set in late-19th-century Spain, tells of a young disfigured woman whose only solace is to serve as guide to a young, handsome blind man. However, when his eyesight is restored, her fragile world is shattered. (Spanish with English subtitles) ★★½

Marie
(1985, 112 min, US, Roger Donaldson) *Sissy Spacek, Jeff Daniels, Morgan Freeman, Fred Thompson.* Spacek gives a fine performance in this true story of Marie Ragghianti, a divorced mother who becomes the chairman of the Tennessee State Board of Pardons and Paroles, and whose exposure of political corruption led to the ousting of a governor. Ragghianti's real-life lawyer, Thompson, appears as himself. ★★★ VHS: $79.99

Marie Antoinette
(1938, 149 min, US, W.S. Van Dyke II) *Norma Shearer, Tyrone Power, John Barrymore, Gladys George, Robert Morley.* Grand M-G-M costumer about the life of the doomed 18th-century French queen. Shearer plays the title role, and Morley is outstanding as Louis XVI. ★★★

Marie Baie des Anges
(1998, 90 min, France, Manuel Pradal) *Vahina Giocante, Frederic Malgras, Nicolas Welbers.* Stunning hand-held cinematography and a cast of gorgeous sun-drenched youths make *Marie Baie des Anges* beautiful to watch, but director Pradal's debut film lacks true emotion. The story line is elliptical — it begins and ends with the same confusing sequence — but there are episodes in between that are riveting. Orso (Malgras) is a handsome young thief who drifts into a casual relationship with the luscious Marie (Giocante) only to face dire consequences. There is tremendous sexual tension throughout the film, but there is little payoff to all the teasing. While the film's visuals will keep viewers interested — particularly the focus on shirtless boys and provocative girls — this is still pretension masquerading as style. (French with English subtitles) ★★½

Marius
(1931, 123 min, France, Alexander Korda) *Raimu, Pierre Fresnay, Charpin.* This first film of the legendary Pagnol Trilogy introduces Marseilles cafe owner César and his son Marius. Marius loves Fanny but leaves her for a life at sea. Shortly afterwards, Fanny finds herself pregnant. The joy and hardship of the simple people of Provence are splendidly captured. This is followed by *Fanny* and *César*. ★★★★ VHS: $24.99

Mark of the Devil
(1970, 90 min, GB/West Germany, Michael Armstrong) *Herbert Lom, Olivera Vuco, Udo Kier.* During the 18th century, a corrupt, impotent witch hunter has his way with women in more grotesque ways than can be imagined. This once *cause célèbre* is really much ado about nothing, as it offers gross instead of scares. ★ VHS: $14.99

Mark of the Vampire
(1935, 61 min, US, Tod Browning) *Lionel Barrymore, Bela Lugosi, Lionel Atwill.* An eerie horror tale by *Dracula* director Browning about vampire expert Barrymore and police detective Atwill investigating a series of attacks in a small rural village. ★★★ VHS: $19.99

The Mark of Zorro
(1920, 90 min, US, Fred Niblo) *Douglas Fairbanks, Marguerite de la Motte.* Fairbanks in another of his patented swashbuckling roles. Lots of great sword fights, lots of great sets and lots of people running around a lot. ★★★ DVD Double Feature: $29.99, VHS: $24.99

The Mark of Zorro
(1940, 93 min, US, Rouben Mamoulian) *Tyrone Power, Basil Rathbone, Linda Darnell, Eugene Pallette.* Power's first attempt at swashbuckling, and he proves himself quite adept at it. Returning to his home in 1800s California after studying abroad, Power discovers his father has been forcably replaced as Alcalde of Los Angeles, and that the new mayor is corrupt. Though a master swordsman, Power plays the fop while secretly fighting the powers that be as the heroic Zorro. Rathbone is, once again, a worthy opponent in this exciting and well-made adventure tale. ★★★ DVD: $14.99

Marked for Death
(1990, 93 min, US, Dwight H. Little) *Steven Seagal, Joanna Pacula.* It's voodoo and violence as Seagal plays a tough DEA agent who finds he and his family are targets of a vicious drug lord. Needless to say, martial arts action ensues. The little bit of action can't compensate for the ridiculous story or Seagal's awful acting. ★ DVD: $14.99, VHS: $9.99

Marked Woman
(1937, 97 min, US, Lloyd Bacon) *Bette Davis, Humphrey Bogart.* Loosely based on the trial of New York crime boss "Lucky" Luciano, this taut gangster drama stars Davis as a clip joint hostess who is persuaded by D.A. Bogart to testify against the racketeer boss responsible for her sister's disappearance. Davis is terrific in this crisp tale which is as enthralling as it is cynical. ★★★ VHS: $19.99

Marlene
(1986, 91 min, Germany, Maximilian Schell) *Marlene Dietrich.* Marlene Dietrich, screen legend and public recluse, is the subject of this fascinating, amusing and insightful portrait. Miss Dietrich agreed to make the film with the unusual stipulation that director Schell not film her. So with only microphone in hand, the resourceful Schell interviews, confronts, compliments and does battle with this tough yet vulnerable lady. An unconventional portrait of one of Hollywood's greatest stars. (Filmed mostly in English) ★★★½ DVD: $24.99, VHS: $14.99

Marlowe
(1969, 95 min, US, Paul Bogart) *James Garner, Rita Moreno, Jackie Coogan, Carroll O'Connor, Bruce Lee.* A director named Bogart (no relation) brings famed detective Philip Marlowe to the 1960s in this neat little thriller. The plot has something to do with Marlowe (Garner) investigating the disappearance of a young man. Lee makes kindling out of Marlowe's office. ★★★ VHS: $14.99

Marnie
(1964, 129 min, US, Alfred Hitchcock) *Sean Connery, Tippi Hedren, Bruce Dern, Diane Baker.* Initially misunderstood, *Marnie* has been reevaluated as a continued exploration of the themes explicated in *Vertigo*: sexual inhibition and anxiety, the complex network of communication between men and women, and the tyranny of the past over the present. Hedren essays the man-hating heroine and Connery is her prey and predator. ★★★ DVD: $19.99, VHS: $14.99

Marooned
(1969, 134 min, US, John Sturges) *Gregory Peck, Richard Crenna, Gene Hackman, James Franciscus, Lee Grant.* Low-key sci-fi adventure with Peck as a panicky aerospace chief trying to get three stranded astronauts back to Earth. Oscar for Best Special Effects. ★★½ DVD: $24.99, VHS: $9.99

Marooned in Iraq
(2002, 97 min, Iran, Bahman Ghobadi) *Shahab Ebrahimi, Iran Ghobadi.* A revered, elderly Iranian musician cajoles his two sons into accompanying him on a journey through post-gulf War Iraq upon hearing his ex-wife (who had run off with his best friend years ago) may be in trouble. Affecting and surprisingly fast-paced, this serio-comic road movie is thoroughly entertaining, despite its sometimes depressing subject matter. The three leads all give memorable performances, and stage some great musical sequences; there's a particularly well-crafted comic suspense scene that involves an impromptu wedding song by the men, a man buried up to his neck in the sand, and the father of the bride's threats against the groom. There are many other terrific scenes throughout, and a supremely satisfying wrap-up is the icing on the cake. An intelligent, warm, funny yet emotionally powerful film that shouldn't be missed. (Farsi with English subtitles) ★★★½ DVD: $24.99, VHS: $24.99

Marquis
(1990, 80 min, France, Henru Xhonneux) Sort of an X-rated Ren & Stimpy-visit-the-French Revolution, this bizarre tale tells of the Marquis de Sade's imprisonment in the Bastille during the upheaval of 1789 — with the twist being that all of the cast play out their roles in grotesque animal costumes. Devilishly witty and shockingly vulgar, this bestial satire's cast includes, in a leading role, Colin, de Sade's frisky and dialectically opinionated penis; the Marquis himself (a horny but pensive hound-faced intellectual); a lusty prison guard in love with the Marquis who is intent on being buggered by him; and a whip-wielding, horse-faced dominatrix who flails at the flanks of the decadent rulers. Despite being bogged down by the intricate 18th-century French politics, this will certainly shock some, and entertain, amuse and titillate others. (French with English subtitles) ★★★½ VHS: $29.99

The Marriage of Maria Braun

The Marriage of Maria Braun

(1978, 120 min, Germany, Rainer Werner Fassbinder) *Hanna Schygulla, Ivan Desny, Klaus Lowitsch, Gisela Uhlen, Elisabeth Trissenaar.* Fassbinder's superb mixture of historical epic, offbeat comedy and social commentary stars Schygulla as the enterprising heroine who rises from the ashes of post-war Germany to become a captain of industry. (German with English subtitles) ★★★★ VHS: $19.99

Married to It!

(1993, 112 min, US, Arthur Hiller) *Beau Bridges, Stockard Channing, Ron Silver, Cybill Shepherd, Mary Stuart Masterson, Robert Sean Leonard.* If *Married to It!* were a person, it would never get asked to the prom. It's whiny, pretentious and tries way too hard to be popular. With "something for everyone," the story revolves around three couples: rich and materialistic Silver and Shepherd; socially conscious, old hippies Bridges and Channing; and newlyweds Leonard and Masterson. Like a Woody Allen film with all of the complaining but none of the insights, *Married to It!* is redeemed only by the buoyant presence of Masterson. ★★ DVD: $14.99, VHS: $6.99

Married to the Mob

(1988, 105 min, US, Jonathan Demme) *Michelle Pfeiffer, Matthew Modine, Dean Stockwell, Mercedes Ruehl, Alec Baldwin, Joan Cusack.* A vibrant and colorful comedy awash with trendy pop music, cool ethnic types and hip American iconography. The very engaging Pfeiffer stars as a "mob" widow who sets out to leave "the family" behind her. But her late husband's boss has other ideas about it, and goes to great lengths to let her know it. Into her life comes FBI agent Modine, who thinks she has yet to sever the umbilical, and sees a chance to nab the nefarious don — by romancing the frustrated widow. Stockwell gives a hilariously sleazy performance as the don and Ruehl is terrific as Stockwell's manically jealous wife. ★★★ DVD: $14.99

A Married Woman
(Une Femme Mariée)

(1964, 94 min, France, Jean-Luc Godard) *Véronique Duval, Jean-Luc Godard, Margaret Le Van, Roger Leenhardt.* A Married Woman is a fine example of Godard's wild experimentation with narrative, sound usage, editing, and literary allusions. Subtitled, "Fragments of a Film Shot in 1964," the film begins with a concern for woman's role in society but he is really much more interested in ideas of memory, the present and intelligence. (French with English subtitles) ★★★½

Marry Me! Marry Me!

(1968, 96 min, France, Claude Berri) *Elisabeth Wiener, Regine, Claude Berri.* A charming romantic comedy produced, directed, written by and starring Berri. It's an offbeat story about European Jewish families, and follows Claude, a Jewish encyclopedia salesman in Paris, as he inconveniently falls in love with a pregnant Belgian girl. Berri unfolds the story with gentle, perceptive humor. ★★★

The Marrying Man

(1991, 115 min, US, Jerry Rees) *Alec Baldwin, Kim Basinger, Elisabeth Shue, Paul Reiser.* Plagued by controversy, this Neil Simon-scripted comedy misses the mark as an affectionate tribute to the screwball comedies of the '30s and '40s. Groom-to-be Baldwin is caught philandering with Basinger by her gangster beau. Forced to marry her, Baldwin's engagement to heiress Shue is cancelled and he's left distraught . . . until he's re-engaged to Shue and meets Basinger again. Baldwin is competent, but Basinger appears to be imitating Michelle Pfeiffer in *The Fabulous Baker Boys*, especially in her musical numbers. ★★ DVD: $9.99

Mars Attacks!

(1996, 103 min, US, Tim Burton) *Jack Nicholson, Tom Jones, Glenn Close, Annette Bening, Pierce Brosnan, Danny DeVito, Michael J. Fox, Sarah Jessica Parker, Lukas Haas, Jim Brown, Pam Grier, Martin Short, Rod Steiger, Natalie Portman, Lisa Marie, Sylvia Sidney, Christina Applegate, Paul Winfield.* Combining some gleefully twisted black humor with plenty of homages and references to schlocky (and not-so-schlocky) alien invasion and sci-fi flicks of the 1950s and '60s, director Burton's magnum opus is the perfect companion piece to his eloquent, intimate masterwork *Ed Wood*. A parody of the kind of movie Ed Wood only wishes he could have afforded to make, *Mars Attacks!* is the story of some funny-looking but terribly ill-tempered aliens who declare war on the Earth. Why? Because it's there! An all-star cast plays various hapless Earthlings, most of whom deserve their fate. Great special effects, deliberately designed to evoke memories of afternoon sci-fi matinees, an outstanding score by Danny Elfman and campy, wild-eyed performances by everyone involved all add up to an "A" budget "B" movie. ★★★½ DVD Letterbox: $14.99, VHS: $9.99, VHS Letterbox: $9.99

La Marseillaise

(1937, 130 min, France, Jean Renoir) *Pierre Renoir, Lise Delamare.* This grand epic chronicles the events of the French Revolution of 1789. This is a stirring account of the events which led to the uprising, and Renoir has filmed it in a episodic, tense fashion. (French with English subtitles) ★★★ VHS: $59.99

Martha & Ethel

(1995, 80 min, US, Jyll Johnstone) *Martha Kniefel, Ethel Edwards, Jyll Johnstone, Barbara Ettinger.* A highly personalized labor of love, this endearing documentary offers two radically different portraits of the filmmakers' childhood nannies. Director Johnstone and producer Ettinger examine each of their families' interactions with their paid child rearers and uncover a fascinating study of family dynamics as well as an entertaining exposé on the lives of the wealthy. Martha (of the Johnstone family), a cranky 87-year-old German immigrant, is a stern disciplinarian who was feared by the children. Ethel is an extraordinarily resilient and graceful 92-year-old daughter of South Carolina sharecroppers. Though the stories of these two remarkable women have little in common, their differing styles and the clearly divergent attitudes of their employers make this captivating viewing. ★★★½

Martin

(1978, 95 min, US, George Romero) *John Amplas, Lincoln Maazel, Tom Savini.* A witty and sardonic updating of the Dracula legend about a young man with a troublesome fondness for blood. What distinguishes Romero's work is an ability to maintain an atmosphere of terror and suspense while simultaneously indulging in a most kinky sense of humor. ★★★

Marty

(1955, 91 min, US, Delbert Mann) *Ernest Borgnine, Betsy Blair, Joe Mantell, Esther Minciotti.* Oscar-winning Best Picture about a shy butcher who finds true love, and a glimpse into the lives of two ordinary, lonely people who meet by chance in a dance hall. Borgnine won an Oscar for his poignant portrayal of the title character, a hapless Everyman, and is given solid support by Blair and Mantell. Screenplay by Paddy Chayefsky (Best Screenplay Award). ★★★★ DVD: $14.99

Marvin and Tige

(1982, 104 min, US, Eric Weston) *John Cassavetes, Billy Dee Williams, Gibran Brown.* Cassavetes stars as an alcoholic ad exec who meets an embittered, streetwise 11-year-old contemplating suicide because of his mother's recent death. Cassavetes takes an interest in the child, and tries to reunite him with his estranged father (Williams). A film which wears its heart on its sleeve in its well-meaning examination of racial intolerance. ★★½

Marvin's Room

(1996, 105 min, US, Jerry Zaks) *Meryl Streep, Diane Keaton, Robert De Niro, Leonardo DiCaprio, Gwen Verdon, Hume Cronyn, Dan Hedaya.* Keaton and Streep are sisters estranged for 20 years, brought together by Keaton's onset of leukemia after a lifetime as family caretaker. The younger Lee (Streep) jumped ship when she refused responsibilities for ailing relatives; the older Bessie's (Keaton) life is defined by the illnesses of others. From the first awkward reacquaintance of the two sisters, the uncanny symbiosis of familial interrelationships ameliorates the harsh edges of conflict, imparting a blessed balance to both sisters and both brothers. This actors' vehicle suffers somewhat from stage director Zaks' unfamiliarity with the medium and a curiously toned-down script. But the strength and honesty of the ensemble portrayals rise above these failings with unexpected humor and warmth of emotion without artifice. ★★★ DVD: $14.99, VHS: $9.99

Martha & Ethel

Mary My Dearest
(Maria de Mi Corazón)

(1983, 100 min, Mexico, Jaime Humberto Hermosillo) *Maria Rojo, Hector Bonilla.* This Mexican soap opera, adapted from a story by Gabriel García Márquez, is a moderately interesting black comedy of ill-fated love, produced independently by one of Mexico's most popular directors. After a mysterious eight-year absence, Maria, a beautiful young magician, returns to the home of small-time crook Hector. The couple fall in love for a second time, but are soon separated when Maria, in a bizarre mix-up, is placed in an insane asylum and can't get out. (Spanish with English subtitles) ★★½ VHS: $29.99

Mary Poppins

(1964, 140 min, US, Robert Stevenson) *Julie Andrews, Dick Van Dyke, Glynis Johns, David Tomlinson, Ed Wynn.* "In every job that must be done, there is an element of fun." And there could be no greater fun than Walt Disney's classic live-action and animated musical. Andrews won an Oscar for her delightful performance as everyone's favorite magical nanny, Mary Poppins, who arrives at the Banks household to oversee two young children. The film features a wonderful supporting cast. Quick — can you say supercalifragilisticexpialidocious backwards? ★★★★

Mary, Queen of Scots

(1971, 128 min, GB, Charles Jarrott) *Vanessa Redgrave, Glenda Jackson, Patrick McGoohan, Timothy Dalton, Nigel Davenport, Trevor Howard, Daniel Massey, Iam Holm.* Lavish costume drama about the power struggle between Queen Elizabeth (a forceful Jackson) and her cousin Mary (a luminous Redgrave). ★★★

Mary Reilly

(1996, 118 min, GB, Stephen Frears) *Julia Roberts, John Malkovich, George Cole, Glenn Close, Michael Gambon.* Director Frears' disjointed adaptation of the tale of Dr. Jekyll and Mr. Hyde uses the intriguing premise of following the action from the point of view of the good doctor's maidservant, Mary Reilly (Roberts). The film eventually becomes a claustrophobic and uninteresting spine-tingler along the lines of another British Gothic film, *The Turn of the Screw*. Also primary to the film's laconic pace is Malkovich's stoic performance as Jekyll and Hyde. Roberts, usually the one to pick on critically, gives an able performance, mildly believable Irish accent and all. ★★ DVD: $9.99, VHS: $9.99

Mary Shelley's Frankenstein

(1994, 123 min, GB, Kenneth Branagh) *Kenneth Branagh, Robert De Niro, Helena Bonham Carter, Ian Holm, Tom Hulce, Aidan Quinn, John Cleese.* Branagh sets his sights away from Shakespeare and onto less fanciful fare with this egocentric and grisly adaptation of the time-honored tale which takes the notion "the sins of the father . . . " to a truly horrific level. Returning to the original source and the central theme that man was not meant to play God, Branagh delivers an emotionally complex portrayal of Dr. Frankenstein as a man who creates life and then turns his back on it, thus setting the stage for a Gothic tragedy of Shakespearean proportions. There are, of course, Branagh's trademark histrionics — dizzying, non-stop camerwork, a booming and somewhat distracting score, and some shameless overacting by the director-star. De Niro is an un-Karloff monster. ★★★ DVD: $14.99, VHS: $9.99

Masala

(1993, 100 min, Canada, Srinivas Krishna) *Srinivas Krishna, Saeed Jaffrey.* Krishna's ingenious feature debut is this wildly entertaining brew which examines the difficulties of assimilation for Indian immigrants in North America. Krishna himself stars as a thuggish young hunk who dabbles in drugs and petty crime. When his entire family is killed in a plane crash, he moves to Toronto to live with his ruthlessly greedy uncle (Jaffrey). He strikes up a relationship with the daughter of a financially strapped postman (Jaffrey in a multiple role), whose mother has candid conversations with her favorite deity Krishna (Jaffrey again) through her VCR. The film is a tasty mélange of spicy subplots, twists and characters. Colorful and wild, *Masala* presents a wholly original take on the struggles of Indian immigrants to retain their cultural identity. ★★★½ VHS: $19.99

Mascara

(1987, 99 min, Belgium, Patrick Conrad) *Derek De Lint, Michael Sarrazin, Charlotte Rampling.* The Crying Game owes a debt to this stylishly shot psychosexual thriller about a sexually repressed police inspector on the brink of murderous insanity triggered by a particularly pretty dress he fancies. Sarrazin stars as the inspector and Rampling costars as his sister and the object of his incestuous desires. Filled with themes of lust, love, transvestism and transexuality, the film features some scenes in a kinky after hours club which are worthy of one of Ken Russell's fevered dream sequences. (Filmed in English) ★★★ VHS: $19.99

Masculin-Feminin

(1966, 103 min, France, Jean-Luc Godard) *Jean-Pierre Léaud, Brigitte Bardot.* Starting from a Du Maupassant short story, Godard fashions a remarkable portrait of French youth in the '60s — "the children of Marx and Coca-Cola." A blending of experimental fiction with documentary segments aims to drive the "political truth" home to the workers. Léaud is an aimless revolutionary who wants answers but sees nothing in the political turmoil that surrounds him. Godard's "fifteen precise facts" on the problems of the younger generation. (French with English subtitles) ★★★½ VHS: $29.99

M*A*S*H

(1970, 116 min, US, Robert Altman) *Elliott Gould, Donald Sutherland, Tom Skerritt, Sally Kellerman, Robert Duvall, Gary Burghoff, Bud Cort, Fred Williamson, Rene Auberjonois.* One of the most devastating black comedies and potent antiwar films ever to hit the screen, Altman's blisteringly funny, anarchic romp rocketed him to stardom and set the tone for a generation of irreverent filmmakers. Set during the Korean War, the film stars Gould (back when he had screen presence) and Sutherland as two hotshot, unconventional doctors assigned to a Mobile Army Surgical Hospital. In between the blood and death of war and surgery, they let loose in binges marked by drinking, sex, disobedience and other flagrant actions of nonmilitary behavior. Kellerman is terrfic as "Hot Lips" Houlihan, and the rest of the supporting cast is first-rate. The film was made into a successful TV series which only partially retained the film's hard edge and biting cynicism. ★★★★ DVD Letterbox Five Star Collection: $26.99, VHS Special Edition: $9.99

Mask

(1985, 120 min, US, Peter Bogdanovich) *Cher, Eric Stoltz, Sam Elliott, Laura Dern, Estelle Getty.* Cher gives a stirring performance as the mother of

Antonio Banderas in *The Mask of Zorro*

Rocky Dennis, a teenager afflicted with a disfiguring congenital condition. Director Bogdanovich effectively paints a sympathetic portrait of the young man's life, and Stoltz gives a commendable performance as Dennis. ★★★ DVD Special Edition: $19.99, VHS: $7.49

The Mask

(1994, 102 min, US, Charles Russell) *Jim Carrey, Cameron Diaz, Richard Jeni, Peter Riegert.* Rubber-faced Carrey gets totally bent out of shape (with the help of F/X meister Greg Cannom) in this enjoyable follow-up to his debut *Ace Ventura*. The one-dimensional story, which is really an excuse to get from one special effect to another, is the standard "underdog has his day" scenario, with Carrey as a beleaguered nebbish who finds an ancient mask that turns him into a green-faced, zoot-suited, whacked-out super-hormonal superhero. But under the direction of Russell, what amazing effects they are. Carrey's world becomes a Tex Avery-style cartoon replete with side-splitting computer-generated F/X and technicolored, show-stopping musical numbers. ★★★ DVD: $14.99, VHS PG-13 Rated: $9.99, VHS Letterbox PG-13 Rated: $9.99

The Mask of Fu Manchu

(1932, 72 min, US, Charles Babin) *Boris Karloff, Lewis Stone, Myrna Loy.* Considered to be the best movie adapted from the Fu Manchu novels, this very fun adventure yarn stars Karloff as the evil mastermind intent on world domination and Stone as the hero dedicated to stopping him. The film moves along at a good pace and is highlighted by a stupendous pyrotechnic show as Fu tries to determine the authenticity of a powerful sword brought to him. Archaic racial stereotypes notwithstanding, Karloff's performance is the real treat here — he obviously relishes playing such a juicy role of mad genius and diabolical villain rolled into one. Dated and old-fashioned, but enjoyable nonetheless. ★★½ VHS: $19.99

The Mask of Zorro

(1998, 135 min, US, Martin Campbell) *Antonio Banderas, Anthony Hopkins, Catherine Zeta-Jones, Stuart Wilson, Matt Letscher.* Banderas proves he can swash with the best of them in this very entertaining, big-hearted comic adventure which is a fun throwback to the Errol Flynn swashbucklers of the '30s and '40s. Giving the production a bit of added

M

class, Hopkins is the masked avenger in the film's beginning. But years later, he's just getting a little too old for this line of work, and passes the mask onto ne'er-do-well Banderas — though not without a lesson or two. Eventually, they take on a ruthless governor who is exploiting local peasants. There's lots of swordsplay and action, and quite a bit of comedy which is well-placed. Banderas cuts a fine romantic figure, as does the gorgeous Zeta-Jones who plays Hopkins' daughter, abducted and raised by the first Zorro's adversary. ★★★ DVD Special Edition: $19.99, VHS: $9.99

Masque of the Red Death

(1991, 83 min, US, Alan Birkinshaw) *Herbert Lom, Brenda Vaccaro, Frank Stallone.* In this minor, updated version of Edgar Allan Poe's short story, Lom plays a dying patriarch who throws one last grand ball — if he's gotta go he's determined to take his friends along with him. Vaccaro as a foul-mouthed matron, and Stallone, one of her men in arms, are just two of the guests who would rather not accompany him. ★★ VHS: $79.99

Mass Appeal

(1984, 99 min, US, Glenn Jordan) *Jack Lemmon, Zeljko Ivanek, Charles Durning.* Lemmon gives a commanding performance in this appealing adaptation of the Broadway comedy-drama about the clash of wills between a well-to-do priest (Lemmon) and an outspoken seminarian (Ivanek). The film touches upon clashes between the old Church and the younger ideology — some of it is superficial and some of it is surprisingly thorough. ★★½

Massacre at Central High

(1976, 87 min, US, Renee Daalder) *Andrew Stevens, Robert Carradine, Kimberly Beck.* Cult favorite with Stevens as the new kid in school who begins a one-man campaign of terror against a brutal student gang. ★★½

Master and Commander: The Far Side of the World

(2003, 139 min, US, Peter Weir) *Russell Crowe, Paul Bettany, James D'Arcy, Edward Woodall, Chris Larkin, Max Pirkis.* With a storytelling style so visceral you'll need to towel off after the storm sequences, director Weir attempts his most ambitious undertaking — that of translating two of Patrick O'Brian's "Jack Aubrey" novels for one big-screen epic adventure. Its unexpected success can be measured not so much by the rousing action scenes or sumptuous cinematography or even the bracing tale of men at sea, but ultimately by the dedication of craft exhibited by director, writer, star and crew. Crowe is well within his element as Aubrey, the heroic captain of *HMS Surprise*, a British warship assigned the daunting task of stopping the superior and deadly French ship *Acheron* during the Napoleonic wars. A crafty game of cat and mouse ensues as Aubrey uses the wiles of each and every crew member to outwit an enemy clearly holding the advantage. On the heels of *Pirates of the Caribbean*, with which it shares nothing more than ships and swordplay, *Master and Commander* both embraces and expands the conventions of the genre, thus creating a singular achievement whose attention to action and spectacle is as every bit as developed as a character's thought and deed. The ensemble is uniformly good, though Bettany is especially memorable as the ship's doctor and Aubrey's friend/moral compass. *Far Side of the World* presents a smart, thrilling ride into history that explodes with excitement and vigor. ★★★★ DVD Single-disc Version: $29.99, DVD 2-disc Special Collector's Edition: $39.99

Master Harold and the Boys

(1985, 105 min, US/GB, Michael Lindsay-Hogg) *Matthew Broderick, Zakes Mokae, Jon Kani.* This powerful film written by South Africa's eminent playwright, Athol Fugard, concerns a South African white youth whose "special friendship" with two black men is adversely affected by the return of his father to the family-owned tea room. The youth's uncovered, heretofore unrecognized racism helps us understand the difficulty in escaping the values that surround us as we grow to personhood. ★★★½ VHS: $19.99

The Master of Disguise

(2002, 80 min, US, Perry Andelin Blake) *Dana Carvey, Brent Spiner, Jennifer Esposito, James Brolin, Harold Gould.* Carvey plays multiple roles in this family comedy about a waiter who learns he hails from a family of secret agents who can morph into various disguises. When his father is kidnapped, he must use quite a few of them to rescue him. You'd think Carvey impersonating different characters would produce many a chuckle. Instead, it's excruciating to see this talented comic resort to such a low. As Dad, Brolin looks absolutely embarrassed by the whole affair; only Gould as wise Grandfather seems to know exactly what he's doing. Too bad no one else does. ★ DVD: $14.99, VHS: $14.99

Master of the World

(1961, 104 min, US, Roger Corman) *Vincent Price, Charles Bronson, Henry Hull.* One of Corman's most entertaining and effective films. Price plays Robur the Conquerer in this Jules Verne story about a peace activist out to destroy the armies of the world from his flying ship. ★★★

Mastergate

(1992, 90 min, US, Michael Engler) *Richard Kiley, David Ogden Stiers, James Coburn, Ed Begley, Jr., Jerry Orbach, Darren McGavin, Bruno Kirby, Burgess Meredith.* With the subheading "A Play on Words," writer Larry Gelbart's hilarious political farce is just that, a wondrous whirlwind of words, doublespeak and raillery. Taking aim at network news, Washington, the military and Hollywood, *Mastergate* asks the seemingly familiar question, "What did the President know — and did he have any idea that he knew it?" The story centers on a Congressional hearing into illegal arms delivered to Central American rebels funded through a movie's $1.3 billion budget. Though the satire is obvious, it is Gelbart's scintillating dialogue — which easily could have been penned by Stoppard or Chayefsky — which propels the film, creating an uproarious verbal confrontation of half-truths and evasions. Though enjoyable on any level, this is a must for politicos. ★★★½

Masterminds

(1997, 120 min, US, Roger Christian) *Patrick Stewart, Vincent Kartheiser, Brenda Fricker.* In this sillier, high-tech version of *Toy Soldiers*, a computer genius with a grudge (Stewart) takes over a private school with the help of some armed terrorist friends. Instead of a group of misfit cadets, here there's only one misfit cadet who happens to be a computer whiz. It's hacker vs. hacker as the youth tries to sabotage the terrorist's every move. ★½ VHS: $19.99

Masters of the Universe

(1987, 106 min, US, Gary Goddard) *Dolph Lundgren, Frank Langella, Meg Foster, Courtney Cox.* Lundgren flexes his muscles as a space-age warrior whose battle with evil lord Langella brings him to Earth. Pretty inept in all departments. ★½ DVD: $12.99, VHS: $9.99

Mata Hari

(1931, 100 min, US, George Fitzmaurice) *Greta Garbo, Lionel Barrymore, Ramon Navarro.* Garbo rarely looked lovelier than as the famed WWI spy whose exotic looks seduced every male she met. Navarro and Barrymore are just two who fall victim to this woman's wiles. Navarro utters the famous line, "What's the matter, Mata?" ★★★ VHS: $19.98

Matador

(1988, 102 min, Spain, Pedro Almodóvar) *Assumpta Serna, Antonio Banderas, Carmen Maura.* This wickedly satiric romp is a decidely twisted and thoroughly amusing wallow in the world of sexual desires. A series of bizarre sexual murders are baffling the police in Madrid until young Angel — the son of an ultra-right-wing, religiously obsessive mother — turns himself in to the police. The problem is that he is innocent and has been experiencing the killings clairvoyantly. His femme-fatale attorney is aware of his innocence, as is his bullfighting instructor: for they are each responsible for the grisly murders. Director Almodóvar rips away the facade of human behavior and reveals a hilarious, sometimes frightening, subterranean view of a world ruled by passion and death. (Spanish with English subtitles) ★★★½

Russell Crowe in *Master and Commander: The Far Side of the World*

The Match Factory Girl

(1989, 70 min, Finland, Aki Kaurismäki) *Kati Outinen, Elina Salo.* A bleak little saga about a mousy factory worker whose dreary life includes living at home with her mother and stepfather while desperately seeking male companionship despite her bland looks and nondescript personality. Kaurismäki's film is every bit as personality-less as its main character. What is so perplexing is that the film contains not one scintilla of emotion, not even a blip — granted, life in Helsinki may be unbearably innocuous at times, especially for the underprivileged proletariat, but it is hard to fathom life on the level Kaurismäki presents it. Even so, the film lacks the director's subtle sense of humor and incisive commentary usually found in his other works; it only displays an effective use of minimalism. (Finnish with English subtitles) ★★ VHS: $79.99

The Matchmaker

(1958, 101 min, US, Joseph Anthony) *Shirley Booth, Paul Ford, Shirley MacLaine, Anthony Perkins, Robert Morse.* Enjoyable screen version of Thornton Wilder's play, with Booth giving a wonderful performance as turn-of-the-century matchmaker Dolly Levi. As Horace Vandergelder, one of her clients and romantic interest, Ford is in good form. The basis for the musical *Hello, Dolly.* ★★★ VHS: $14.99

The Matchmaker

(1997, 97 min, US/Ireland, Joseph Anthony) *Janeane Garofalo, David O'Hara, Milo O'Shea, Denis Leary, Jay O. Sanders.* Typical American fish-out-of-water plot is greatly enlivened by winning performances, beautiful scenery and a script that walks the fine line between rustic charm and heavy-handed sentimentality. Garofalo plays a senator's aide sent to Ireland to find some long-lost relatives. What happens next has been a cliché since before "Brigadoon" was on Broadway: cynical American goes to a small foreign village, at first can't fathom the conditions she must live under and how incredibly barbaric the locals are. And then the gorgeous landscapes and the quaint charm take over with the help of a particularly cute local (in this case, O'Hara) and the cynicism melts away. It's all here: the local eccentrics, lovesick teenagers and, of course, lots of Whiskey, Guiness & Singing. But the charm only rarely seems forced and there are some genuine moments of sweetness. ★★★ DVD: $9.99

La Maternelle

(1933, 83 min, France, Jean Benoit-Levy & Maria Epstein) A society girl down on her luck becomes a maid in "la maternelle," a kindergarten which provides a temporary refuge for the poor children of a Parisian slum. The compassionate young woman befriends and mothers the children, many of them victims of abuse, and takes into her home a lonely waif abandoned by her "working girl" mother. An affectionate and heartwarming, yet grimly realistic drama. (French with English subtitles) ★★★ VHS: $29.99

Matewan

(1987, 132 min, US, John Sayles) *Chris Cooper, James Earl Jones, David Strathairn, Mary McDonnell, Will Oldham.* The dramatic retelling of a 1920s coal strike in West Virginia has been sensitively written and directed by Sayles and beautifully photographed by Haskell Wexler. This compelling story of solidarity and martyrdom amidst the grime and dust of the coal town features fine performances from the entire cast. ★★★½ DVD: $44.99

Matilda

(1996, 90 min, US, Danny DeVito) *Mara Wilson, Rhea Perlman, Danny DeVito, Embeth Davidtz.* Matilda is a little girl with serious problems: Her parents never wanted her in the first place and treat her with great disdain. After refusing to let her go to school (someone has to stay home and accept the boxes of illegal car parts!), they finally send her to a school where the principal loves to torment the students. Luckily, Matilda has discovered she has telekinetic powers that allow her to exact a very satisfying revenge on the adults who mistreated her. Wilson is adorable as Matilda, acting with both a maturity and innocence that is utterly endearing. The story is told with style and humor. ★★★

Matinee

(1993, 107 min, US, Joe Dante) *John Goodman, Simon Fenton, Cathy Moriarty, Kevin McCarthy, John Sayles, Dick Miller, Jesse White, William Schallert.* Dante shows just where he cut his teeth as a youthful movie fan with this playful homage to '60s schlock films. Set during the Cuban Missile Crisis, the story revolves around a teenager (Fenton), an avid creature feature fan, who becomes assistant to John Goodman's big-hearted film director — part Alfred Hitchcock, part William Castle. Goodman has come to the youth's small Florida town to screen his newest, grade-Z creation, *Mant* (Half Man, Half Ant, All Terror!). Dante and writers Charlie Haas and Jerico clearly are enjoying their sometimes hilarious send-ups of the dreadful matinee horror films of decades yore, and their film-within-a-film has some delectable scenes. ★★★

The Mating Game

(1959, 96 min, US, George Marshall) *Debbie Reynolds, Tony Randall, Paul Douglas, Una Merkel.* Anyone wishing for an old-fashioned comic confection should appreciate this homespun romantic comedy. All others, however, beware: insulin shock ahead. Reynolds is the red-blooded, eldest daughter of farmer/trader Douglas' Maryland brood. When IRS agent Randall comes to investigate Douglas' 20-year nonpayment of taxes, her parents do their darndest to match Reynolds and their educated visitor. There's no shortage of good spirits, but it's all so damn cute this was probably corn when released in 1959. ★★½ VHS: $19.99

The Matrix

(1999, 136 min, US, Andy Wachowski & Larry Wachowski) *Keanu Reeves, Laurence Fishburne, Carrie-Anne Moss, Hugo Weaving, Joe Pantoliano, Gloria Foster, Marcus Chong, Julian Arahanga.* Kung fu without gravity, machine guns with unlimited ammo and ultra smooth heroes who have all the right moves form the entirety of *The Matrix*, the Wachowski brothers' big-budget follow-up to *Bound.* Supercool right down to the omnipresent blue-grey hues, this is the rare action film to slowly build its ideas and technologies to a truly mind-blowing climactic showdown. Keanu is Neo, a hacker who learns that his fellow humans are at the mercy of computers. He may or may not be "the One" to enter the virtual world of the Matrix to save humankind. The convoluted plot is merely a vehicle for Fishburne, Moss and Reeves to kick ass against an impressive Weaving (as a neo-fascist enforcer). Visually stunning, *The Matrix* uses its arsenal of visual effects for maximum impact. (Sequel: *The Matrix Reloaded*) ★★★½ DVD Letterbox: $19.99, VHS: $6.99, VHS Letterbox: $6.99

Laurence Fishburne in *The Matrix Reloaded*

The Matrix Reloaded

(2003, 138 min, US, Andy Wachowski & Larry Wachowski) *Keanu Reeves, Laurence Fishburne, Carrie-Anne Moss, Hugo Weaving, Jada Pinkett-Smith, Gloria Foster.* If the original was a series of fantastic revelations exploring the world of the Matrix, this sequel, less ambitious plotwise but tremendously exciting in terms of pure action, at least proves that it's a terrific world in which to play. Neo (Reeves) is The One, and he sets out on a quest to find the keymaster, who can unlock the door to the mainframe, which can . . . oh hell, this thing isn't about story. It's about badass battles, like when Neo must take on a gaggle of cloned Agent Smiths (Weaving) in a glorious fight set in a virtual playground. Or a massive car chase, with cars and trucks flipping while our heroes use kung fu at 70 mph. The philosophy spouted by Morpheus (Fishburne) is appropriately grave, while vague enough to appeal to everyone in the audience — as are the multiracial cast, the blossoming romance between Neo and Trinity (Moss), and even a closing song that mixes hippie pop and techno. Maybe it's calculated to please, maybe it's all 1s and 0s, but for those who want to plug in, it's a real blast. (Sequel: *The Matrix Revolutions*) ★★★ DVD Letterbox: $19.99, DVD Pan & Scan: $19.99, VHS: $8.99

The Matrix Revolutions

(2003, 129 min, US, Andy Wachowski & Larry Wachowski) *Keanu Reeves, Laurence Fishburne, Carrie-Anne Moss, Hugo Weaving, Mary Alice, Jada Pinkett-Smith.* Shot at the same time as *The Matrix Reloaded*, this final chapter of the *Matrix* trilogy shares many of the aspects of its predecessor, but makes a fatal miscalculation. While the plugged-in world of *The Matrix* is a glorious hyperreality allowing for incredible pyrotechnic martial arts, the reality of Zion and Earth is a gloomy electro-world populated by villianous robots without personality. *Revolutions* is rooted in this world, and it sucks the fun out of the franchise. The film's centerpiece is a 30-minute battle with an endless stream of robots invading Zion's core, and an equally endless stream of bullets fired by the humans. Not even the spectac-

Neo (Keanu Reeves) strikes a stupefied pose in *The Matrix Revolutions*

ular effects can keep this section from being a downright bore. Several big plot developments, including a protracted death scene, fall emotionally flat, as does an early shootout inside The Matrix that seems a mere copy of the first film. The whole shebang is almost redeemed by the climactic duel (in The Matrix, thankfully) between Agent Smith (Weaving) and Neo (Reeves) — a high-wire punchout in the pouring rain. But what is Neo saving, really? That dreary world below the earth that was such a chore to sit through earlier? Screw that! Bring back The Matrix — and next time, don't wake us up. ★★ DVD Letterbox 2-disc set: $29.99

A Matter of Taste

(2000, 90 min, France, Bernard Rapp) *Charles Berling, Florence Thomassin, Jean-Pierre Léaud, Bernard Giraurdeau, Jean-Pierre Lorit, Artus De Penguem.* A deliciously twisted affair, *A Matter of Taste* is a psychological thriller of the highest order. Adapted from Philippe Balland's novel, the film drives a sharp skewer through class issues and social order. Nicolas (Lorit) works as a waiter in a posh Parisian restaurant. One day he serves lunch to wealthy, high-profile executive Frédéric (Giraurdeau) who professes a sensitivity to certain ingredients. Asking Nicolas to taste his food for him, Frédéric discovers the young man's ability to identify every ingredient precisely and, smitten by his charms to boot, hires him as personal food taster. As the pair slowly become close, Frédéric begins resorting to cunning schemes to tailor Nicolas' culinary preferences, lifestyle and moral values more precisely to his own tastes. This gels an obsessive codependency between the two, and leads to worsening games of cruelty and escalating domination and questionable intents. A sly, tasteful dish, regardless of the bitter aftertaste it can leave in your mouth. (French with English subtitles) ★★★★ DVD: $19.99, VHS: $14.99

Maurice

(1987, 140 min, GB, James Ivory) *James Wilby, Hugh Grant, Rupert Graves, Ben Kingsley, Billie Whitelaw, Denholm Elliott, Simon Callow, Helena Bonham Carter.* With the same reverence and regal authority he brought to *A Room with a View*, director Ivory has created a personal triumph with this exquisite adaptation of E. M. Forster's semiautobiography. Set in pre-WWI England, the film examines the social and sexual repression of the era in this story of the emotional conflict facing a college student coming to terms with his homosexuality. Wilby is perfectly cast in the title role, Grant gives a precise

performance as his platonic lover who transforms from free spirit to social prig, and Graves is splendid as the handsome gardener who awakens Maurice's dormant feelings. ★★★★ DVD 2-disc set: $29.99

Mauvaise Graine

(1933, 77 min, France, Alexander Esway & Billy Wilder) *Pierre Mingand, Danielle Darrieux, Raymond Galle.* When his rich, indulgent daddy takes the roadster away, spoiled, amoral Henry (Mingand) gets himself mixed up with a fast woman (Darrieux) and a ring of car thieves. Shot on location in and around a Paris of the early Thirties, *Mauvaise Graine* captures a city at the height of its beauty and a career about to burst into bloom. Like many, screenwriter and director Wilder had to leave a Germany about to go insane. Exhibiting many of the narrative touches that would become Wilder's trademarks, the film is fast-paced and action-packed, recklessly driven along by a jazzy score from Franz Waxman (like Wilder himself, to be bound for Hollywood). (French with English subtitles) ★★★ DVD: $24.99, VHS: $24.99

Maverick

(1994, 120 min, US, Richard Donner) *Mel Gibson, Jodie Foster, James Garner, Graham Greene, James Coburn, Danny Glover, Alfred Molina.* In their initial meeting, Foster — as an alluring con artist — sums up her impression of dashing gambler Bret Maverick, played by Gibson: "Irritating and likable." This also ably describes this pleasant if inconsistent big screen version of the popular 1960s TV series. Gibson takes over the James Garner role, and he gives an amiable account of the rascal/cardsharp who only wants to play in the big poker tournament but who gets sidetracked at every turn. Foster is uncharacteristically breezy as Maverick's equally roguish partner. Both are eclipsed, however, by Garner, who appears as a crusty lawman. The actor's effortless charm is a reminder of what distinguished the TV show. *Maverick* may not totally capture the effervescence of its prototype, but it does contain many enjoyable moments of nonsensical whimsy. ★★★ DVD: $14.99, VHS: $9.99, VHS Letterbox: $9.99

The Maverick Queen

(1956, 92 min, US, Joseph Kane) *Barbara Stanwyck, Barry Sullivan, Wallace Ford, Jim Davis.* Faithful screen version of a Zane Grey novel with Stanwyck as a lady bandit who falls in love with the Pinkerton detective (Sullivan) sent to track her down. ★★½

Max

(2002, 106 min, Canada/Germany/GB/Hungary, Menno Meyjes) *John Cusack, Noah Taylor, Leelee Sobieski, Molly Parker.* A serious attempt to gauge the political climate of post-WWI Germany and examine what would eventually push a young Adolf Hitler towards the dispicable acts of anti-Semitism that would come to shape the Nazi regime, the bold but ultimately shallow *Max* is a difficult watch. Cusack, who's in fine form here, plays Max Rothman, a disabled veteran of WWI whose art career evaporated when he lost his right arm in battle. Now an art promoter specializing in Modernism, he comes across struggling artist Hitler (Taylor), a corporal with strong conservative views. With Rothman acting as his mentor, Hitler's artistic aspirations collide with those of his army commander, who sees in the young man leadership potential in a growing anti-Jewish movement. The theme of Hitler being torn between art and politics and two surrogate fathers is a bit heavy-handed, marked by disturbing diatribes on Aryan supremacy. ★★ DVD: $24.99

Max Dugan Returns

(1983, 98 min, US, Herbert Ross) *Jason Robards, Marsha Mason, Mathew Broderick, Donald Sutherland, Kiefer Sutherland.* Amiable Neil Simon comedy with Robards, as Mason's long-lost father, who reenters his daughter's life. Broderick debuts as Mason's teenage son. ★★½ VHS: $59.99

Max Mon Amour

(1986, 97 min, US/France, Nagisa Oshima) *Charlotte Rampling, Anthony Higgens.* The attention-grabbing premise of this film — that a sophisticated Parisian woman falls in love with a chimpanzee — should generate some interest in this unusual satire from Oshima. Margaret (Rampling) and English diplomat Peter (Higgens) are an unhappy couple opulently living in Paris. Their marriage is strained when the husband discovers that his wife is having an affair not with another man, but with a chimpanzee. Even with its premise, the film disappoints; for after Max is introduced, there is nothing more to shock, and every time the story approaches a surreal level, it steps back, embracing conventionality. (In English and French with English subtitles) ★★ VHS: $29.99

Maxie

(1985, 98 min, US, Paul Aaron) *Glenn Close, Mandy Patinkin, Ruth Gordon, Barnard Hughes, Harry Hamlin.* The considerable talents of Close and Patinkin are not enough to save this mediocre ghost comedy. Close and Patinkin play a married couple whose lives are interrupted when the spirit of a flapper — murdered in the 1920s — inhabits the body of the former. It's nice to see Close let down her hair, but the flimsy screenplay just doesn't give her enough to do. The last film of the great Gordon. ★½

Maximum Overdrive

(1986, 97 min, US, Stephen King) *Emilio Estevez, Pat Hingle, Laura Harrington.* Author King stepped behind the camera for the first time to direct his story of rampaging trucks — and this is so bad it may be some time before he steps there again. Estevez, Hingle and Harrington are some of the people trapped in a cafe terrorized by those murderous 18-wheelers. (Remade in 1998 as *Trucks*) ★ DVD: $24.99, VHS: $9.99

Maximum Risk

(1996, 101 min, US, Ringo Lam) *Jean-Claude Van Damme, Natasha Henstridge.* The Van Damme curse continues for former Hong Kong directors as ace action auteur Lam (*City on Fire*) is brought low by the Muscles from Brussels. Van Damme stars in this lame, brainless chase picture about a former French soldier who discovers he had a twin brother involved in some shady dealings with the Russian mob. Another surprise awaits Jean-Claude when he meets his bro's girlfriend (Henstridge), who turns out to be very resourceful at avoiding professional killers. Not even stylishly shot, it displays none of the talent or promise which probably got its director the job in the first place. ★ DVD: $14.99, VHS: $9.99

May

(2003, 90 min, US, Lucky McKee) *Angela Bettis, Jeremy Sisto, Anna Faris, James Duval.* Creepy and disturbing, *May* is a character study with shades of horror elements. Bettis is excellent as the title character, an oddball loner whose best friend is a porcelain doll given to her by her mother. Sisto is also quite good as the hunky budding filmmaker whose hands capture May's attention. Director McKee builds tension nicely as May's grip on reality loosens, leading to an extremely intense and gory wrap-up. The film never quite cuts loose, and it's not in the same league as other mad-protagonist character pieces like *Spider* or *The Tenant*. It is, however, a good, solid, visceral drama, and Bettis is a talent to watch. ★★★ DVD: $24.99

May Fools

(1990, 108 min, France, Louis Malle) *Michel Piccoli, Miou-Miou, Dominique Blanc.* A mildly entertaining comedy of manners about the family squabbles of a petit bourgeois clan. Set against the backdrop of the 1968 student uprising in Paris (an event which toppled the government of Charles de Gaulle), the film follows the Vieusacs as they converge on their ancestral country mansion to pick through the possessions of a recently deceased matriarch. Piccoli stars as Milou, the hopelessly romantic father of the remaining kin, and the only family member who opposes the sale of the house and surrounding vineyard. Malle shows the family bickering as a microcosm of the era's social turmoil with Milou's idealism and joie de vivre representing the country's heart and soul. The results are mixed, but Piccoli's performance is pure gold. ★★

Maybe . . . Maybe Not

(1996, 98 min, Germany, Sonke Wertman) *Til Schweiger, Katja Reimann, Joachim Krol.* This slick sex comedy follows the frenzied antics of Axel, a hunky, womanizing young man who, after burning all of his heterosexual bridges, moves in with Norbert, a gay man who quickly falls in (one-sided) love with his new roomie. The comedy rests on the confusion Axel creates by his friendship with Norbert and his gay friends — a perplexing situation for Axel's still interested girlfriend. A funny, enjoyable and non-demanding sex comedy. (German with English subtitles) ★★★ VHS Subtitled: $24.99

Mayerling

(1935, 91 min, France, Anatole Litvak) *Charles Boyer, Danielle Darrieux.* The passion and agony of two doomed lovers is explored in this sumptuous true story which stars Boyer as the Crown Prince Rudolph of Austria who falls under the trance of the stunningly beautiful Darrieux. A shimmering romance that sadly, yet inevitably, leads to tragedy. (French with English subtitles) ★★★ VHS: $29.99

McCabe and Mrs. Miller

(1971, 121 min, US, Robert Altman) *Warren Beatty, Julie Christie, William Devane, Keith Carradine, Shelley Duvall.* One of Altman's best, *McCabe and Mrs. Miller* is a wonderfully poignant drama which explores ambition, greed, love and alienation, all within a decidedly quirky western setting. Beatty is the cocky McCabe, a naively optimistic gambler who builds a town and hires Christie to set up a high-class brothel. Featured is a haunting Leonard Cohen soundtrack. ★★★½ DVD Letterbox: $19.99; VHS: $14.99

The McGuffin

(1985, 95 min, GB, Colin Bucksey) *Charles Dance, Ritza Brown, Phyllis Logan, Anna Massey.* This tribute to Hitchcock's *Rear Window* derives its title from the phrase coined by the late mystery master. The story concerns a film critic whose nagging curiosity leads him to become embroiled in a murder plot being perpetrated by his neighbors. The film lacks a cohesiveness and delivers few thrills. ★★

McHale's Navy

(1997, 108 min, US, Brian Spicer) *Tom Arnold, Tim Curry, Dean Stockwell, David Alan Grier, Bruce Campbell, French Stewart, Ernest Borgnine.* With *McHale's Navy*, the popular TV comedy about a group of conniving WWII sailors, there's yet another casualty in the long line of small-to-big screen transfers. Arnold, in a surprisingly amiable performance, takes over the title role, though it's wasted; as is a talented group of cohorts who aren't given anything to do. Grier's Ensign Parker only reminds us how funny Tim Conway was in the show. The writers of this seasick voyage have forgotten what made the TV show mindless fun — now it's only mindless. ★ DVD: $14.99, VHS: $7.49

McVicar

(1980, 111 min, GB, Tom Clegg) *Roger Daltrey, Adam Faith, Ian Hendry.* The Who Films presents this portrayal of John McVicar (Daltrey), whose real-life escape from the high-security wing of a British prison led to his being dubbed "Public Enemy No.1" by the British press. This tough and tense prison drama won the critics' raves, but failed to find a crossover audience in the U.S. ★★★

Me and Him

(1989, 94 min, US, Doris Dorrie) *Griffin Dunne, Carey Lowell, Craig T. Nelson, Ellen Greene, Mark Linn-Baker.* An up-and-coming architect (Dunne) finds his life turned upside-down when he wakes up one morning and finds his penis starts talking to him. An ironically tame film despite its controversial nature. ★★

Me, Myself & Irene

(2000, 116 min, US, Bobby Farrelly & Peter Farrelly) *Jim Carrey, Renée Zellweger, Robert Forster, Chris Cooper, Richard Jenkins.* Wherever the thin line exists between funny silliness and unfunny silliness, the Farrelly brothers have crossed it and then back again. In this humorless retread, Carrey is in moron mode as Charlie, a schizophrenic Rhode Island state trooper whose wife has left him with three black children. Getting no respect from his small town, a maniacal alter ego named Hank appears, getting Charlie into all sorts of trouble. Zellweger plays Irene, a motorist who must be escorted by Charlie/Hank back to her native New York. This could have been riotous, but the filmmakers seem content to have Carrey mug endlessly. Yes, he does produce a couple laughs, but the long periods of time spent between these laughs only magnify an inferior script and aimless direction. ★★ DVD Special Edition: $14.99, VHS: $9.99

Me Myself I

(2000, 104 min, Australia, Pip Karmel) *Rachel Griffiths, David Roberts, Sandy Winton.* Pamela (Griffiths) enters her 30s with a fair degree of professional success but wondering about the high school sweetheart who got away. She literally runs into herself while crossing the street and finds she's in the alternate life she did not choose in her youth. Her travels down the rabbit hole of self-discovery are highlighted by sparkling portrayals describing circumstances at once extreme and recognizable. The peformances are uniformly intelligent and good-humored, and this contemporary fantasy is a witty mixture of most satisfactory entertainment with wry social commentary and the unsettling contemplation that our choices inform our identities for better *and* worse. These underlying themes are more resonant through this comedy than the suddenly serious turns of *Sliding Doors*. ★★★ DVD: $29.99

Me without You

(2002, 107 min, Germany/GB, Sandra Goldbacher) *Michelle Williams, Anna Friel, Oliver Milburn, Trudie Styler, Kyle MacLachlan.* Though its running time is relatively brief, Goldbacher's piercing drama covers much ground and has plenty to say

Me without You

about relationships, rivalries and the contradictory bonds of friendship. Marina and Holly are childhood friends who have remained together through the best and worst of times. Tracing their lives through three eras makes for an ambitious journey, but the film jumps the hurdles of this kind of storytelling with strong lead performances and a story that stings with the pleasure, pain and even competition that true friendship brings. Goldbacher gets the feel of each decade just right without letting design or costumes get in the way of her characters' development. And Williams proves there is life beyond "Dawson's Creek" with her tempered, nuanced performance. ★★★ DVD: $24.99, VHS: $102.99

Me You Them

(2000, 106 min, Brazil, Andrucha Waddington) *Regina Case, Lima Duarte, Stênio Garcia, Luís Carlos Vasconcelos, Nilda Spencer.* Casé brings a sumptuous earthiness to her portrayal of Darlene, a young woman who returns to the Bahian cane fields in northeastern Brazil with a young son in tow. She marries Osias, a house-proud older man who soon puts his right up, taking to rest upon her unremitting hard work. As time progresses, more children follow, and Darlene exhibits an amazing facility for balancing backbreaking work, four sons and three de facto husbands. These developing living arrangements actually seem to make supreme sense in view of the harsh, difficult farm life; but a toll is being taken on Osias, whose pride is further wounded with each new wrinkle in Darlene's familial configurations. The film balances with deceptive ease the hardships of working the land, the stinging pain of jealousy, and the pure joy of family affection. Strong, natural performances allow a complete acceptance of the characters in this involving story of a most unusual domestic arrangement. (Portuguese with English subtitles) ★★★ DVD: $29.99, VHS: $21.99

Mean Girls

(2004, 97 min, US, Mark S. Waters) *Lindsay Lohan, Rachel McAdams, Tim Meadows, Tina Fey, Ana Gasteyer, Amy Poehler, Lizzy Caplan, Daniel Franzese.* Watch out Heathers, there's a new clique in town, and they're taking no prisoners. They're called the Plastics, and they embody everything good and everything evil about such young girls who wield such power in the hallways of American high schools. Taking its cue from *Clueless* and *Heathers*, the charmingly funny, often rude but never tasteless *Mean Girls* is based on Rosalind Wiseman's book "Queen Bees and Wannabes." With a sharp, funny screenplay adaptation from Tina Fey ("Saturday Night Live"), the story focuses on young Cady Heron (Lohan), who at 16 is attending school for the first time. Pretty, intelligent and quickly befriending the school misfits, Cady is taken in by the Plastics and groomed to be one of their own. Only she's doing it get the dirt on them . . . that is until she starts to like being a queen bee, not a wannabe. Lohan, who is reunited with *Freaky Friday* director Waters, is absolutely captivating. The ensemble is first-rate, and fortunately they all have some delicious dialogue to repeat. Like Cady or Lindsay herself, *Mean Girls* is a cut above the rest. It's a smart look at the social strata of contemporary teens, and presents it in a thoroughly entertaining and humorous fashion. ★★★½ DVD: $29.99

The Mean Season

(1985, 106 min, US, Phillip Borsos) *Kurt Russell, Mariel Hemingway, Richard Jordan, Andy Garcia, Joe Pantoliano, Richard Masur.* Intriguing mystery thriller with Russell as a Miami newspaper reporter who becomes involved with a serial killer when the latter offers him an "exclusive" story. This puts both the reporter and his girlfriend (Hemingway) in danger. ★★½ DVD: $14.99

Mean Streets

(1973, 110 min, US, Martin Scorsese) *Harvey Keitel, Robert De Niro, Amy Robinson, David Proval.* Scorsese's early masterpiece, set in New York's Little Italy, features a tremendous cast headed by Keitel and De Niro. Keitel, an aspiring mobster, finds his Catholic background, his love for a young woman and his attachment to an irresponsible friend hindering his fledgling Mafia career. Well integrated into the story is a superlative '60s soundtrack. Scorsese's gritty portrayal of gangland life and his superlative photographic and editing techniques have made this bristling drama often imitated but rarely equalled. ★★★★ DVD: $19.99

Meantime

(1983, 103 min, GB, Mike Leigh) *Tim Roth, Marion Bailey, Phil Daniels, Pam Ferris, Gary Oldman, Alfred Molina.* Among uniformly solid performances, Roth executes a subtle, compelling portrait of the achingly befuddled younger son of a contentious East End family, working class without work, without hope, without future. Daily petty frustrations and standard sibling rivalries are exacerbated by mind-numbing boredom and total lack of purpose. *Meantime* describes a brief observation of lives lived in abeyance, whole lifetimes spent in the no-man's land of a meantime with no end in sight. Director Leigh offers scattershot glimpses at familial antagonisms and societal prohibitions explored with more polish and in more depth in *Secrets and Lies*; yet, though more roughly cut, *Meantime* still offers flashes of revelation, in which a history is alluded to in a sidelong glance, a secret revealed in an unguarded word. ★★★ DVD: $14.99, VHS: $14.99

Meatballs

(1979, 94 min, Canada, Ivan Reitman) *Bill Murray, Harvey Atkin, Kate Lynch.* Murray's first hit comedy. Alternately funny and ridiculous, the film follows the comic exploits of counselor Murray at summer camp. (Followed by 3 sequels) ★★½

The Mechanic

(1972, 100 min, US, Michael Winner) *Charles Bronson, Jan-Michael Vincent, Keenan Wynn, Jill Ireland.* This average Bronson suspense/action film casts the stone-faced actor as an aging hit man who reluctantly takes on an apprentice (Vincent) in order to pass on his bloody craft. Bronson's confident muttering and quiet strength make his cookie-cutter character more interesting than it ought to be, which keeps the viewer's attention riveted to his performance and diverts it from Vincent's hyperactive hit man wannabe. Winner is also able to sustain a sufficient level of tension throughout the film's slow points, ending the movie with a literal bang and a surprise which will satisfy even the most charitable viewer's thirst for revenge. ★★½ DVD Dual: $14.99

Medicine Man

(1992, 104 min, US, John McTiernan) *Sean Connery, Lorraine Bracco, Jose Wilker.* Director McTiernan sets out to save the Venezuelan rain forest, but after this mess, he'll be lucky to salvage his career. Connery, looking great in ponytail, plays an eccentric botanist who retreats into the jungle and discovers the cure for cancer. Enter Bracco, Brooklyn scientist, who's been sent to find him. There, they exchange barbs, lose the cancer cure, befriend the natives, battle greedy land developers destroying the forests and fall in love. Sad to say, even Connery's ever-commanding presence isn't enough to make this worthwhile. And Bracco is sorely miscast. Though the story has a good premise, *Medicine Man* is one doc whose license should be revoked. ★★ DVD: $9.99, VHS: $9.99

Mean Girls

Mediterraneo

(1991, 92 min, Italy, Gabriele Salvatores) *Diego Abatantuono, Giuseppe Cederna.* Catering unashamedly to the saccharin-loving moviegoer, this winner of the Academy Award for Best Foreign-Language Film takes Hollywood's penchant for "feel good" movies, throws in some exotic locales and produces an entertaining but mindlessly unrealistic comedy-drama. Early in WWII, a bungling platoon of Italian military misfits become stranded on a beautiful Greek island. Cut off from the war, this motley assortment of Italian stereotypes find themselves not in battle, but in an idyllic land. Greek-Italian relations have never been closer than in this "cultural fantasy." (Italian with English subtitles) ★★½ VHS: $9.99

Medium Cool

(1969, 110 min, US, Haskell Wexler) *Robert Forster, Verna Bloom, Peter Bonerz, Marianna Hill, Peter Boyle.* Acclaimed cinematographer Wexler directed this fascinating political drama set against the turbulent backdrop of the 1968 Chicago Democratic Convention. A TV news cameraman (Forster) finds that the dispassion by which he covers his news stories is beginning to be the way he deals with his personal life. A unique blend of fictionalized narrative juxtaposed with the real world. ★★★★ DVD Letterbox: $29.99, VHS: $14.99

Meet Joe Black

(1998, 180 min, US, Martin Brest) *Brad Pitt, Anthony Hopkins, Claire Forlani, Jake Weber, Marcia Gay Harden.* Death has angst, and really wants a break from it all. Maybe he'll use his free time to taste peanut butter, to smell perfume, even to find love (few people respond to Death's personals). So when a minor character who looks just like Brad Pitt dies, Death opportunistically takes his body, names it Joe, and proceeds to use those handsome features to woo a rich woman (Forlani), learn about peanut butter (possible sequel: *Death Needs a Zagat's*), and putter around Hopkins' estate. This, in essence, is what happens in this overly long, slick, self-important remake of the 1934 classic *Death Takes a Holiday*. Frustratingly, there's a good 110-minute movie in here somewhere. At least the cast looks great. Hopkins does his best in a thankless role as Death's chaperone. ★★ DVD: $14.99, VHS: $9.99

Meet John Doe

(1941, 123 min, US, Frank Capra) *Barbara Stanwyck, Gary Cooper, Edward Arnold, Walter Brennan, James Gleason.* Capra's social drama stars Stanwyck as a newspaper reporter who turns hayseed drifter Cooper into a national hero. Arnold offers his usual strong support as a corrupt politician benefitting from Stanwyck's mock grassroots campaign. Capra offers his usual "common man vs. the corporate mindset" in a most capable setting, and the two stars certainly help. ★★★ DVD: $19.99, VHS: $9.99

Favorite Line: "I don't read no papers, and I don't listen to radios either. I know the world's been shaved by a drunken barber, and I don't have to read it." —*Walter Brennan as The Colonel*

Meet Me in St. Louis

(1944, 114 min, US, Vincente Minnelli) *Judy Garland, Mary Astor, Leon Ames, Margaret O'Brien, Marjorie Main, June Lockhart.* Garland had one of her biggest hits with this charmingly old-fashioned, sentimental musical — a loving reminiscence of turn-of-the-century family life. Astor and Ames are Judy's parents, and little O'Brien as her sister demonstrates rare and extraordinary emotion for a five-year-old. Judy sings "The Trolley Song" and "Have Yourself a Merry Little Christmas." ★★★★ DVD 2-disc Special Edition: $26.99

Meet the Feebles

(1992, 92 min, New Zealand, Peter Jackson) If you've ever wondered what becomes of Muppets when they go bad, then this determinedly disgusting (but unfunny) comedy reveals all. Marketed as "one of the sickest movies ever made," this drug, sex and bodily fluid-immersed backstage tale includes such characters as lovelorn Heidi Hippo (a big-titted serial-killing Miss Piggy); a drug-addicted, knife-throwing frog; a promiscuous bunny who contracts AIDS; a fey gay fox who belts out a musical number called "Sodomy"; and many other animal grotesques. A film to offend just about everyone which wallows in its own distastefulness. ★ DVD: $24.99

Meet the Parents

(2000, 108 min, US, Jay Roach) *Robert De Niro, Ben Stiller, Teri Polo, Blythe Danner, Owen Wilson, Jon Abrahams, James Rebhorn.* Greg Focker (Stiller) certainly has his work cut out for him. He's on his way to meet the parents of his intended fiancée Pam (Polo). He wants to ask permission for Pam's hand in marriage from her strict dad, and everything has to go right. It's to our enjoyment that nothing goes right for Greg, and the worse things get for him, the funnier things get for us. Combining some nifty one-liners with uproarious sight gags, *Meet the Parents* once again demonstrates (after *Analyze This*) the golden comic talents of De Niro, here at his gruffest comic best as Jack, Pam's doting father. Director Roach basically brings the same anarchic comic sensibility he brought to *Austin Powers*, though the film rarely approaches the nastier comic regions which could have set it apart. Stiller is a terrific foil, and he and De Niro have great chemistry. ★★★ DVD Collector's Edition: $19.99, VHS: $9.99

Meet Wally Sparks

(1997, 105 min, US, Peter Baldwin) *Rodney Dangerfield, Debi Mazar, Cindy Williams, Burt Reynolds, David Ogden Stiers.* Igniting very few comic sparks, this scattershot comedy has Dangerfield as a controversial TV talk show host who tries to push the limits of FCC regulations. When threatened with cancellation, he sets out to interview the conservative Governor of Georgia (Stiers) and winds up being a most unwelcome house guest. In this updated *The Man Who Came to Dinner*, Dangerfield can't overcome the stilted material and general foolishness, even if every other word out of his mouth is a double entendre. Sure Rodney's inimitable delivery can cause a chuckle or two, but this is strictly for die-hard fans of the "no-respect" comedian. ★★ DVD: $24.99

Meeting Venus

(1991, 124 min, US/GB, István Szabó) *Glenn Close, Niels Arestrup, Erland Josephson.* Hungarian director Szabó, highly acclaimed for his German trilogy of human nature (*Colonel Redl*, the Academy Award-winning *Mephisto* and *Hanussen*), changes his tune with this romantic drama about the efforts of a world-renowned conductor (Arestrup) to mount a multinational production of Wagner's "Tannhauser" while maintaining an amorous affair with his temperamental diva (Close). While there are a few great moments of tenderness and passion between the leads, Close's character is otherwise wooden and the dubbing of her operatic performances (actually performed by Kiri Te Kanawa) is obvious. ★★½ VHS: $19.99

Meetings with Remarkable Men

(1979, 107 min, GB, Peter Brook) *Terence Stamp, Dragan Maksimovic.* The astounding tale of G.I. Gurdjieff, a man driven by a quest for knowledge and the answers to the meaning of existence. Beautifully photographed on location in the mountains of Afghanistan. An illuminating vision. ★★★ VHS: $69.99

Mein Kampf

(1961, 117 min, Sweden, Tore Sjoberg) The rise and fall of Hitler and Nazi Germany is graphically detailed in this powerful documentary. Unusually restrained, the film relies less on sermonizing and allows the images, culled from newsreels and from the extensive footage shot by the Nazis, to speak for themselves. An effective historical foray into the nature of evil, *Mein Kampf* is an invaluable primer for those interested in World War II. ★★★ VHS: $39.99

Meltdown

(1995, 101 min, Hong Kong, Wong Jing) *Jet Li, Jackie Cheung, Yau Shuk Ching, Charlie Young.* Li plays a government agent who botches a rescue when his wife and a busload of schoolchildren are killed by a terrorist's bomb. Li gets his chance for revenge when the same terrorist attempts to steal a valuable jewel from a hi-rise. This highly entertaining actioner (despite the domestic VHS release's atrocious dubbing and poor, trendy musical score) boasts some terrific setpieces and a very funny Jackie Chan parody in the form of Cheung's egomaniac Hong Kong film star, who claims to do all his own stunts, but clearly does not. Li proves to be a great comic straight man to the mugging Cheung, as well as, of course, kicking serious butt. Director Jing and Li also collaborated on the excellent *New Legend of Shaolin*. (aka: *High Risk*) ★★★½ DVD Letterbox Dubbed: $19.99, VHS Letterbox Subtitled: $19.99, VHS Pan & Scan Dubbed: $14.99

Melvin and Howard

(1980, 95 min, US, Jonathan Demme) *Paul Le Mat, Jason Robards, Mary Steenburgen, Jack Kehoe, Pamela Reed, Dabney Coleman.* A "slice of life" film that looks so spontaneous it borders on voyeurism. A sweet-natured study of Melvin Dummar, who claimed to have given a ride to Howard Hughes one night; later he's mentioned as one of Hughes' heirs for his effort. Le Mat gives a sturdy performance as Melvin, and Steenburgen won an Oscar as his mostly estranged wife. Robards is Howard Hughes. ★★★★ DVD: $14.99, VHS: $14.99

Memento

(2001, 113 min, US, Christopher Nolan) *Guy Pearce, Carrie-Anne Moss, Joe Pantoliano, Stephen Tobolowsky.* If you chance to meet Leonard Shelby (Pearce), a wiry, intense man sporting tattoos all over his body, he'll probably tell you about his "condition." In fact, you can count on it. Shelby suffers

M

from short-term memory loss. Within minutes, he'll forget where he is, how he got there, or exactly what it is he's doing. Shelby may have a problem with memory, but anyone lucky enough to see this lean, inventive noir won't soon forget one of the most fascinating experiments with narrative since *Pulp Fiction*. Pearce gives a tough, supple performance as Shelby, who has gathered enough pieces of the puzzle to determine the identity of the man who killed his wife. In snippets of drama that last about as long as Shelby's own memory, the film flashes back — in near-literal reverse — to track the investigation of this amnemonic sleuth. Writer-director Nolan delights in the gimmickry of this sleight of hand to produce an edgy, hypnotic puzzle. ★★★★ DVD Letterbox: $24.99, DVD Limited Edition 2-disc set: $27.99, VHS: $9.99

Memoirs of an Invisible Man

(1992, 95 min, US, John Carpenter) *Chevy Chase, Sam Neill, Daryl Hannah, Michael McKean.* You'd think Hollywood would have learned by now. There hasn't been a really good "invisible man" movie since the original Claude Rains thriller in 1933. Chase stars as a San Francisco businessman who falls asleep during a business meeting and thanks to a neighboring nuclear fusion accident, wakes up invisible. And to make matters worse, he's got CIA heavy Neill after him. Some good special effects and visual humor help hide a transparent plot, though director Carpenter seems more interested in playing politics than creating a definitive "invisible" comedy. ★½ DVD: $19.99, VHS: $9.99

Memories of a Marriage

(1989, 90 min, Denmark, Kaspar Rostrup) *Ghita Norby, Frits Helmuth.* Nominated for an Academy Award for Best Foreign Film, this romantic drama is a love story which depicts the joys, sorrows and conflicts of a love affair which lasted a lifetime. Sort of a mix between Bergman's *Scenes of a Marriage* and Merchant Ivory's *Mr. and Mrs. Bridge*, the film's star Norby won Denmark's Best Actress Award for her performance. The film itself won the "Film of the Year" award in Germany. (Danish with English subtitles) ★★★

Memories of Me

(1988, 105 min, US, Henry Winkler) *Alan King, Billy Crystal, JoBeth Williams.* King's flamboyant performance highlights this pleasant comedy-drama about a heart surgeon (Crystal) who tries to mend the severed relationship with his father (King). ★★★ DVD: $14.99, VHS: $9.99

Memories of Underdevelopment

(1968, 97 min, Cuba, Tomás Gutiérrez Alea) *Sergio Corrieri, Daisy Granados.* The first film from post-revolutionary Cuba to be released in the United States, this wise and fascinating tale of a man finding himself a stranger in his own land was produced by the Cuban Film Institute, but does not contain the doctrinal politicking one would expect from a film sponsored by a young Communist country. The story, set in 1961, revolves around a young man from a bourgeois Europeanized family who, instead of fleeing to Miami with the rest of his family, decides to stay and come to terms with the revolution. Wanting to adapt to the new society, the man, however, finds himself incapable of shedding his bad capitalistic habits and turning over a new socialist leaf. (Spanish with English subtitles) ★★★½ VHS: $19.99

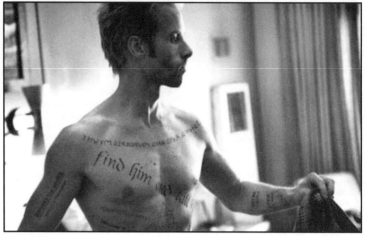

Guy Pearce in *Memento*

Memphis Belle

(1990, 101 min, GB, Michael Caton-Jones) *Matthew Modine, Eric Stoltz, David Strathairn, Harry Connick, Jr., Tate Donovan, D.B. Sweeney, Billy Zane, Sean Astin, John Lithgow, Jane Horrocks.* Suggested by the real-life experiences of the crew of the WWII B-17 fighter-bomber *Memphis Belle* and, in part, on the 1944 documentary of the same name, this old-fashioned war film manages to entertain in spite of all the clichés. A good cast is featured as each crew member is introduced before the plane's historic bombing raid. ★★½ DVD: $19.99, VHS: $9.99

Men . . .

(1985, 99 min, Germany, Doris Dorrie) *Heiner Lauterbach, Uwe Ochsenknecht.* A shrewdly comic satire about an advertising man who loses his wife to a surly young bohemian. In order to discover where he went wrong, he moves in with his wife's new beau (unbeknownst to her) and thus sets the stage for this scintillating behavioral comedy. The lively script is loaded with outrageous comic asides and intelligent wit. (German with English subtitles) ★★★½ VHS: $29.99

The Men

(1950, 85 min, US, Fred Zinnemann) *Marlon Brando, Teresa Wright, Jack Webb, Everett Sloane, Richard Erdman.* Brando's screen presence is immediately evident in this, his debut film performance. He's a WWII vet battling the consequences of a wartime injury. Solid acting all around. ★★★½ DVD: $14.99

Men Don't Leave

(1990, 113 min, US, Paul Brickman) *Jessica Lange, Arliss Howard, Joan Cusack, Chris O'Donnell, Charlie Korsmo, Tom Mason, Kathy Bates.* After her husband's accidental death, suburban mother Lange is forced to sell her home and, with her two sons (O'Donnell, Mason), she moves to Baltimore for a better-paying job. All three endure their own adjustment to the unfamiliar urban environment, via a parade of teenaged video pirates, elementary school rip-off artists, bitchy gourmet shop owners, one very strange nurse (a quirky charcterization by Cusack) and a "professional musician" (Howard). Brickman's direction seems a bit diffuse early on, but tightens up as the story progresses to a satisfying, believable con-

clusion. Life does go on, with or without a fairy-tale white knight. (Based on the French film *La Vie Continue*) ★★★ VHS: $19.99

Men in Black

(1997, 95 min, US, Barry Sonnenfeld) *Tommy Lee Jones, Will Smith, Linda Fiorentino, Rip Torn, Vincent D'Onofrio, Tony Shalhoub.* In this uproariously entertaining sci-fi comedy, Smith and Jones play government agents whose task it is is to monitor illegal aliens — as in the extra-terrestrial kind. When a nasty alien assassin (a giant bug who literally takes the form of D'Onofrio) arrives to murder an alien dignitary living incognito in New York, our men in black hunt him down like the pesky cockroach he is. Sonnenfeld crams lots of humor, excitement and terrific effects into the film's efficiently brisk 95-minute running time. *MIB* is funny, hip and a technical wonder. It also nicely explains how and why certain celebrities in our culture achieved their success. That's the *real* scary part. (Sequel: *Men in Black II*) ★★★½ DVD: $19.99, DVD Deluxe Edition: $24.99, DVD DTS sound: $29.99, VHS: $9.99

Men in Black II

(2002, 82 min, US, Barry Sonnenfeld) *Tommy Lee Jones, Will Smith, Rip Torn, Lara Flynn Boyle, Rosario Dawson, Tony Shalhoub, Johnny Knoxville, Patrick Warburton.* The freshness may be gone, but the chemistry between its two leads and an assortment of good laughs still remain in this broad sequel that manages to be fun in spite of a little self-referential backslapping. Smith returns as Jay, the slick MIB agent who's having some trouble finding a suitable replacement for his ex-partner Kay (Jones), whose memory was, of course, "neuralized" in the first film. When slimy alien Serleena (Boyle) arrives in search of the all-powerful Light of Zartha, Jay tracks down Kay to have him reprogrammed to join the fight. It's all an excuse for a series of familiar, often silly but funny set pieces, most of them accentuated by skilled makeup and special effects. Being basically a rehash of the first film, there's few surprises and the humor doesn't cut as deep. But thanks to the playing of Jones and Smith, some good-humored jokes and a scene-stealing talking pug, you won't remember how formulaic it all is, only that it strives for nothing but to entertain — and mostly succeeds. ★★½ DVD Letterbox 2-disc set: $28.99, DVD Pan & Scan 2-disc set: $28.99, VHS: $24.99

Men of Honor

(2000, 128 min, US, George Tillman Jr.) *Robert De Niro, Cuba Gooding, Jr., Charlize Theron, Aunjanue Ellis, Hal Holbrook, Michael Rapaport, Powers Boothe.* Based on the heroic life of Carl Brashear, the Navy's first African-American master chief diver, *Men of Honor* breaks no new ground in the military drama genre, but does offer a sincere, honorable account of one man's determination in pursuing his dreams in the face of racial intolerance. Gooding is well cast as Brashear, the son of a Kentucky share-cropper, who is accepted to the Navy's diving school. As the first black student enrolled there, he becomes the victim of rampant discrimination. On his case the most is his alcoholic instructor, Billy Sunday (De Niro), who plants a series of obstacles in the young man's path. More inspiring than dramatic, the story follows Brashear's struggle to overcome a stacked deck. Gooding and De Niro make the most of a by-the-books screenplay that nevertheless stirs the emotions. ★★★ DVD Pan & Scan: $14.99, DVD Letterboxed: $14.99, VHS: $9.99

Men of Respect

(1991, 113 min, US, William Reilly) *John Turturro, Katherine Borowitz, Peter Boyle, Rod Steiger.* Reilly's directorial debut is this stunning take on Shakespeare's "Macbeth," a frenzied gangland tragedy about the bloody rise and fall of a self-destructive and ambitious young man. The film is uneven at times, but has a visceral intensity that should be savored. Turturro is possessed in the lead role and his real-life wife, Borowitz, is alluringly deadly as the Lady Macbeth character. ★★½ DVD: $19.99

The Men Who Tread on the Tiger's Tail

(1945, 60 min, Japan, Akira Kurosawa) *Denjiro Okochi, Susumu Fujita, Masayuki Mori, Suho Nishina.* Based on a traditional Kabuki theatre piece, this early Kurosawa fable in set in late 12th-century feudal Japan. Having led the Genji Army to victory in battle, Yoshitsune returns home only to incur the wrath of his jealous Shogun brother. With a price on his head, Yoshitsune and his faithful bodyguard/monk Benkei engage a group of warriors to help Yoshitsune regain his lordly stature. Thus begins Kurosawa's short (one-hour) though engaging film which follows Yoshitsune's trek across the stylized Japanese countryside to return to his city, now under guard. But there are no battles here. Kurosawa revels in the power of the spoken word, eschewing action for the dynamics of personal conflict. Simplistic in its storytelling, *Men* produces a tension and lyricism through cunning and myth. (Japanese with English subtitles) ★★★ VHS: $39.99

Men with Guns

(1998, 128 min, US, John Sayles) *Federico Luppi, Dan Riviera Gonzales, Damian Delgado, Damian Alcazar, Tania Cruz, Mandy Patinkin, Kathryn Grody.* Chameleon-like independent maverick Sayles goes happily against the grain again with this haunting tale of political rumbles in the jungle. Shot almost entirely in Spanish and Indian dialects, this unsettling fable centers on an aging, widowed physician who decides in the twilight of his life to take a journey into the jungles of his anonymous Latin American country to find a group of medical students he once taught. The students were sent as "ambassadors of health" to remote Indian villages, but as the film unfolds, the doctor discovers his legacy has become more frightening than he could ever imagine. Like Sayles' masterful *Lone Star*, *Men with Guns* is concerned with the small tragedies endured by common people, whom we get to know intimately by film's end. As the doctor who discovers the heart of darkness that lies beyond the comfortable confines of his city practice, Luppi is exceptional as Dr. Fuentes — another in a long line of fascinatingly noble Sayles figures. (In English and Spanish and Indian dialects with English subtitles) ★★★½ DVD: $24.99, VHS: $102.99

The Men's Club

(1986, 100 min, US, Peter Medak) *Roy Scheider, Treat Williams, Frank Langella, Harvey Keitel, Jennifer Jason Leigh, Richard Jordan, Stockard Channing, Craig Wasson, Ann Wedgeworth.* A group of middle-aged men gather for an evening to discuss their lives, and end up at a whorehouse. Mediocre version of Leonard Michael's novel. Even a high-profile cast can't help matters. ★

Menace II Society

(1993, 90 min, US, The Hughes Brothers) *Tyrin Turner, Larenz Tate, Jada Pinket, Samuel L. Jackson, Charles S. Dutton, Bill Duke.* A gripping and unapologetic view of life on the mean streets of L.A.'s Compton. The film centers on Caine, an archetypal, disenfranchised '90s urban youth who follows the street's kill-or-be-killed code with an eerily dispassionate degree of stoicism — it all seems to be beyond his scope of caring, or as his homey O-Dog puts it, "I'm America's nightmare: young, black and I don't give a fuck." Featuring superb ensemble acting and a seamless visual acumen, the film may indeed prove frightening to some as it gives witness to the brutality which shapes young lives without so much as a hint of judgment: There are no heroes or villains in this story, just average people living average lives. A scary thought, perhaps, but it is what gives the film its brilliance. ★★★★ DVD: $19.99, VHS: $14.99

Ménage

(1986, 84 min, France, Bertrand Blier) *Gérard Depardieu, Miou-Miou, Michel Blanc.* Family values are turned inside-out in this outrageously wacky sexual farce that takes demonic delight in its vulgarity, misogyny and demented sexual mores. Life changes abruptly for the feuding, poverty stricken couple Antoine (Blanc) and his wife Monique (Miou-Miou) after they meet the bombastic and dangerously exciting Bob (Depardieu), who showers them with money and promises of the good life — made possible by inviting them to his nightly burglary raids of rich homes. But soon the burly Bob falls passionately in love with, no, not the sexy Monique, but the bald, mousy and frantically tight-lipped Antoine! Watching Depardieu wax poetic and become all girlish in front of the bewildered Antoine is a hilariously priceless moment in French cinema. (French with English subtitles) ★★★½

Mephisto

(1981, 135 min, West Germany, István Szabó) *Klaus Maria Brandauer, Krystyna Janda.* A riveting portrait of the artist as opportunist. Brandauer turns in a breathtaking performance as an actor whose burning ambition leads him to compromise his artistry, relationships and well-being. Director Szabó captures the grand spectacle and subtle nuances of a man obsessed. ★★★½

The Mephisto Waltz

(1971, 108 min, US, Paul Wendkos) *Alan Alda, Curt Jurgens, Jacqueline Bisset, Barbara Perkins.* Very effective satanic chiller with Alda as a journalist who experiences changes after interviewing dying musician Jurgens. ★★★ VHS: $59.99

The Merchant of Four Seasons

(1972, 88 min, Germany, Rainer Werner Fassbinder) *Hans Hirschmuller, Irm Hermann, Hanna Schygulla.* Fassbinder's first widely recognized film concerns the life struggle of Hans: a born loser who is rejected by his bourgeois family, spurned by his "one true love," married to an unfaithful wife, cheated by his friends and reduced to peddling fruit to sustain a meager existence. A superb mixture of black humor, melodrama and satire with an unforgettable and haunting ending. (German with English subtitles) ★★★★ DVD: $29.99, VHS: $19.99

Merci pour le Chocolat

(2000, 99 min, France, Claude Chabrol) *Isabelle Huppert, Jacques Dutronc, Anna Mouglalis, Rodolphe Pauly.* A sublimely entertaining thriller told with the authority of a master craftsman. The intricate story begins with the remarriage of Mika (the riveting Huppert) and Claude, a widower whose second wife died under mysterious circumstances. Mika runs a chocolate factory and Claude is a concert pianist, though his son Guillaume doesn't seem to share the family gene. It could have something to do with a mix-up at birth, if Jeanne — who has tracked down her possible father Claude — is to be believed. This sets in motion misgivings, betrayals, alliances and a case of murder, informed with subtle suggestion and cunning observation. Chabrol, like Hitchcock, knows how to mine suspense from the most common of actions — in this instance a nightly cup of hot chocolate (like that glass of milk in *Notorious*) can become a catalyst for suspicion and doubt. (French with English subtitles) ★★★½ DVD Subtitled: $24.99, VHS: $19.99

Mercury Rising

(1998, 112 min, US, Brian Grazer) *Bruce Willis, Alec Baldwin, Miko Hughes, Chi McBride, Kim Dickens.* Willis stars as grizzled and disgruntled FBI agent Art Jeffries, who has been relegated to a future of deskwork. But when the "most sophisticated code the world has ever known" is broken by a prepubescent crossword savant, it's up to Jeffies to rescue the boy and protect the country from its own worst enemy; the NSA (that's National Security Agency for you neophytes). Enter Baldwin as a super badass agent. The clunky script is riddled with hyperbolic technobabble, all of which serves to make this all the less enjoyable. File under: Cheesy Espionage Thriller with Saccharine Human Interest Bent. ★½ DVD Letterbox: $14.99, DVD DTS sound: $14.99

Mere Jeevan Saathi (My Life Partner)

(1965, 126 min, India, Ravee Nagaich) Although India produces hundreds of films each year, the very few that ever reach our shores are almost exclusively limited to the works of Satyajit Ray. And while the vast majority of these releases are produced solely for domestic viewing, there are many that can be enjoyed by an international audience. *Mere Jeevan Saathi*, an exuberant romance/comedy/musical which details a businessman's sudden rise and fall, is a good example of modern Indian filmmaking. (Hindi with English subtitles) ★★★

Meridian

(1990, 91 min, US, Charles Band) *Sherilyn Fenn, Malcolm Jamieson.* Sexy Fenn stars as an artist who returns to her family's ancestral estate in Italy, where she finds and falls in love with a gentle yet hideous creature. Soon, she learns that the castle is under the spell of an ancient curse that only she can dispel. ★★½

Merlin

(1998, 140 min, US, Steve Barron) *Sam Neill, Miranda Richardson, Isabella Rossellini, Helena Bonham Carter, John Gielgud, Rutger Hauer, Martin Short.* An excellent made-for-TV movie, *Merlin* has strong performances, a fast pace, nifty special effects, and has style to spare. As directed by veteran music video helmer Barron, it never rests for a second — due in large part to its editing, which keeps the eye riveted even when the story (very occasionally) flags. Neill is outstanding as Merlin, playing him with sly wit. All the players here — even comic Short — play it straight, but not *too* seriously; allowing for the perfect tone of a potentially goofy tale made compelling yet leavened with knowing humor. Purists may quibble, but *Merlin* takes fewer liberties than most adaptations, and provides the sweep and magic that most in the genre lack. ★★★½ DVD: $14.99, DVD Special Edition: $19.99, VHS: $9.99

Mermaids

(1990, 115 min, US, Richard Benjamin) *Cher, Winona Ryder, Bob Hoskins, Christina Ricci, Michael Schoeffling, Jan Miner.* A pair of winning performances from Cher and Ryder punctuate this pleasantly quirky coming-of-age comedy-drama about a thoroughly unconventional single mother and her abundantly confused and zealously pious teenage daughter. Along with baby sister Kate (Ricci), they uproot and move to a small New England town, circa 1963, where neighbors duly observe that they are not the typical nuclear family. Ryder's saturnine portrayal of adolescence is quickly becoming a thing of legend and her ability to deliver sullen, dead-pan one-liners transforms *Mermaids* from potentially gooey family melodrama to often hilarious, sometimes heartwarming comedy. ★★★ DVD: $14.99

Merrill's Marauders

(1962, 98 min, US, Samuel Fuller) *Jeff Chandler, Ty Hardin, Peter Brown, Andrew Duggan, Will Hutchins.* Director Fuller delivers another solid WWII actioner set in the Pacific Theatre. Chandler leads a war-weary battalion in the Burmese jungle on an arduous trek through hostile terrain populated by deadly, well-concealed Japanese troops. Based on the actual exploits of Brigadier General Frank D. Merrill. ★★★ VHS: $9.99

Merry Christmas, Mr. Lawrence

(1983, 122 min, GB/Japan, Nagisa Oshima) *Tom Conti, David Bowie, Ryuichi Sakamoto, Takeshi, Jack Thompson.* Oshima's mesmerizing drama studies the conflicting cultures of East and West, which surface within the confines of a WWII POW camp. Bowie is a captured New Zealander whose stiff-lipped bravery and rebellious nature perplex his Japanese guards and intrigue the compound's commanding officer, who is gravely smitten by Bowie's allure. (Filmed in English) ★★★ VHS: $9.99

A Merry War

(1998, 101 min, GB, Robert Bierman) *Richard E. Grant, Helena Bonham Carter.* Grant and Bonham Carter sparkle in this wry and witty tale of a promising young copywriter who spurns promotion to write poetry. Seeking a garret and his muse, Gordon Comstock (Grant) quits his advertising agency and scoffs at bourgeoise convention to wrestle with the creative process. A precipitous financial descent accompanies a raging ennui. Comstock's friends — especially girlfriend Rosemary (Bonham Carter) —

attempt to keep him afloat as he seeks redemption in poverty. Based on George Orwell's "Keep the Aspidistra Flying," the film is intelligent and urbane while skewering the infinite layers of the British class system. ★★★

The Merry Widow

(1934, 99 min, US, Ernst Lubitsch) *Maurice Chevalier, Jeanette MacDonald, Una Merkel, Edward Everett Horton.* The great Lubitsch had the right "touch" with this delightfully sophisticated, tongue-in-cheek adaptation of the Franz Lehar operetta. Chevalier is at his best as the dashing nobleman who tries to woo a rich widow (MacDonald) from Paris to her homeland where the bankrupt country is in desperate need of her funds. ★★★½ VHS: $14.99

Mesmer

(1994, 107 min, GB, Roger Spottiswoode) *Alan Rickman, Amanda Ooms.* Rickman is certainly in his element as Franz Anton Mesmer, 18th-century charlatan/saint, part visionary, part revival tent preacher. His search for harmony and balance through the conscious utilization of "animal magnetism" seems a beacon of scientific sanity against the tortures that masquerade as the medicine of his age. His encounter with a young, blind pianist (Ooms) reveals the nobler motivations of his egomania, and speaks against a formalized society whose myriad hysterias roil just beneath the surface. The film is an elegant expression of human anguish, incomparably scripted by Dennis Potter, and delivered with brutal sensitivity by director Spottiswoode. ★★★½ DVD: $9.99, VHS: $9.99

Message in a Bottle

(1999, 132 min, US, Luis Mandoki) *Kevin Costner, Robin Wright Penn, Paul Newman, John Savage, Illeana Douglas, Robbie Coltrane.* Chicago reporter Wright Penn finds a love letter in a bottle and is intrigued to the point that she tries to track down its author. It turns out to be North Carolina widower and boatmaker Costner. She heads there and promptly falls in love. The premise doesn't quite add up, but the cast seems not to care as they attack this with sincerity. To no one's surprise, Newman comes off best as Kevin's cantankerous father. As romantic drama, most of this works; but as credible storytelling, this glossy, muddled film doesn't hit the right notes. ★★½ DVD: $14.99, VHS: $9.99, VHS Letterbox: $14.99

The Messenger: The Story of Joan of Arc

(1999, 158 min, France, Luc Besson) *Milla Jovovich, John Malkovich, Faye Dunaway, Dustin Hoffman, Tcheky Karyo, Pascal Greggory.* Fresh from saving the universe in *The Fifth Element*, director Besson and actor Jovovich here reunite to merely save France. Jovovich is creditable as Joan, Maid of Orleans, spritely and fired with youthful charisma. Her voices direct her to battle the brutal English invaders as they attempt to wrest control of a disunited Gaulle from the hands of the disaffected Dauphin (Malkovich). Her heavenly communications should have given her better information about the political theatre in which she is only a pawn. The film attempts to sustain some discussion of religious belief and the nature of conscience, but is too disjointed and unfocused in its efforts to contemporize the story for a modern audience. ★★ DVD: $14.99, VHS: $14.99

Meteor

(1979, 105 min, US, Ronald Neame) *Sean Connery, Natalie Wood, Henry Fonda, Brian Keith, Karl Malden.* The worst special effects you've ever seen highlight this strangely intriguing disaster film, one of the last in the line of buildings, ships, killer quakes and other forces of nature. Connery brings unexpected humor to this mishmash as a scientist who has six days to prevent a giant meteor from destroying most of Earth. Keith, as Connery's Soviet counterpart, also rises above the script and direction to give a funny performance. ★★ DVD: $14.99

Favorite Line: "What do you want me to do? Stick a broom up my arse and sweep the floor on my way out?" —*Sean Connery as Dr. Paul Bradley*

Meteor Man

(1993, 100 min, US, Robert Townsend) *Robert Townsend, Marla Gibbs, Eddie Griffin, Don Cheadle, Robert Guillaume, James Earl Jones, Sinbad.* Absolute silliness from actor-director Townsend, who stars as a young urban idealist who believes in a better life for his ghetto community. Opportunity comes knocking one day when he is hit by a meteor and given the supernatural powers needed to rid his neighborhood of drug dealers. Hokey beyond reckoning, the film is not without its endearing moments and occasionally Townsend's comic genius shines through — a particularly hilarious moment finds Townsend and his nemesis doing battle on the streets using runway modeling moves. ★★ DVD: $14.99

Metro

(1997, 117 min, US, Thomas Carter) *Eddie Murphy, Michael Rapaport, Michael Wincott.* At the heart of this Murphy action/comedy is a terrific car chase down the precarious streets of San Francisco. Logic and crashed cars alike are tossed through the air like matchbox toys in this hyperkinetic, over-the-top piece of Hollywood stunt craftsmanship — and excess. But as *Metro* zooms along, it feels more like the film was written "around" this spectacular chase scene. Murphy plays a police hostage negotiator who runs afoul of a vicious killer after a botched robbery. Rapaport is his new trainee, who merely turns up whenever Murphy needs an extra pair of eyes or a sharpshooter or a lipreader (don't ask). Ultimately, *Metro* is a by-the-numbers police thriller. ★★ DVD: $9.99, VHS: $9.99

Metroland

(1997, 102 min, GB, Philip Saville) *Christian Bale, Emily Watson, Lee Ross, Elsa Zylberstein.* Chris (Bale) used to be a dreamer, an artist, a Parisian even, but after meeting Marion (Watson) he moved back to England in the '70s to settle down. Seemingly happy, he reexamines all the major decisions in his life when his old punk friend (Ross) pays him a visit. Did he really throw away the love of his life (Zylberstein) in Paris, or is the more pragmatic Marion his soulmate? Remarkably, even in delving into the sexual affairs of all four characters, *Metroland* remains cold and distant, a mistake when dealing with affairs of the heart. Bale has tremendous presence, and Watson plays a difficult role with charm. But the sexual liberation and the ensuing sexual boredom are both explored with the same unenthusiastic calculation. ★★ DVD: $14.99, VHS: $9.99

Metropolis

(1926, 120 min, Germany, Fritz Lang) *Brigette Helm, Alfred Abel.* Lang's spectacularly stunning vision of a world ruled by machines and controlled by Big Brother is one of the most important works to come out of the German Expressionist Film Movement in the 1920s. Its continued popular appeal lies in the fact that so many of Lang's images of future society still capture our imagination. Picture quality is very good (remastered from a 35mm print), and is accompanied by a classical music soundtrack. ★★★★ DVD: $29.99, VHS: $29.99

Metropolis

(2001, 106 min, Japan, Katsuhiro Otomo & Rintaro) Not a remake of the Fritz Lang silent classic, this anime still has much in common with that earlier sci-fi film — visual splendor being the most obvious. The plight of the urban downtrodden is another trait both films share, and both are equally simplistic in their views, really. Animation buffs (especially anime fanatics) won't give a hoot about this film's few drawbacks, considering how gorgeous and detailed the backgrounds are. An absolute must for students of animation; casual viewers willing to overlook some lazy writing will still find much to like here as well, as it's terrific eye candy, to be sure. Based on the comic by Tezuka Osamu. ★★★ DVD 2-disc set: $27.99, VHS: $102.99

Metropolitan

(1990, 108 min, US, Whit Stillman) Edward Clements, Carolyn Farina, Christopher Eigeman, Taylor Nichols. A cast of unknowns breathes life into first-time writer-director Stillman's Oscar nominated screenplay about a preppie "divorce orphan," from the less-than-fashionable Upper West Side, who falls in with the right crowd for a season of meaningless social events. He mocks their empty lifestyle with a refreshing no-holds-barred honesty, which, while not comedic in content, transforms Metropolitan into hilarious social satire. ★★★½

The Mexican

(2001, 123 min, US, Gore Verbinski) Brad Pitt, Julia Roberts, James Gandolfini, Bob Balaban, David Krumholtz, Gene Hackman. Roberts and Pitt, two contemporary heartthrobs and bona fide movie stars, appear together for the first time but aren't able to fully generate the kind of excitement one would hope for. A convoluted screenplay and a lazy tempo certainly don't help, compounded by the fact that the two stars are only together on-screen for a few scenes. Pitt is a hapless mob underling assigned to retrieve a valuable gun called "The Mexican" waiting for him across the border. Roberts is his girlfriend, who is kidnapped by hired gun Gandolfini to assure Pitt's success. Of course, things go wrong, and Pitt has his hands full trying to make everything right, while Roberts is on the road against her will. There are a few intermittently amusing scenes, but unfortunately there just isn't enough for any of the leads to do to really make an impression. ★★ DVD Letterbox: $14.99

Mexican Bus Ride

(1951, 73 min, Mexico, Luis Buñuel) Lilia Prado, Esteban Marquez. The misadventures of an innocent young man who is sent to the mountains to fetch the family lawyer to his dying mother is delightfully brought to the screen by the always mischievous, irreverent and surrealistic Buñuel. (aka: Ascent to Heaven) ★★★

Mexico City

(2000, 95 min, US, Richard Shepard) Stacy Edwards, Robert Patrick, Jorge Robles, Johnny Zander. Mitch (Edwards), a single mother who has just lost her two children in a car accident, travels to the title locale, with her irresponsible but loving brother, to get away. When he doesn't come back to the hotel after a night of bar-hopping, she begins to suspect foul play and starts a search for him with the help of an American consul (Patrick). The missing relative in a hostile foreign land premise is a nearly fail-safe story hook, and it carries this moderately intriguing film for quite a while. Unfortunately, Mexico City never really catches fire, and without the political anger of a Missing or the pulpy suspense of a Frantic, this is merely a decent time killer with good performances, nice location work, and a weak ending. ★★½ DVD: $19.99, VHS: $9.99

Mi Vida Loca (My Crazy Life)

(1994, 92 min, US, Allison Anders) Angel Aviles, Seidy Lopez, Nelida Lopez. Writer-director Anders' follow-up to her hit art-house film Gas Food Lodging is an insightful look into the lives of young Latino gangsters living in Echo Park, Los Angeles. The film is divided into three main segments that intertwine to tell the story of a gangland community from the perspective of the main characters. Differing from the usual gang picture in that it is told from a primarily female vantage point, Mi Vida Loca centers around two best friends, Sad Girl and Mousey, and the man they both love, Ernesto. The well-written script emotionally portrays the struggle of gangland females to raise children in a place where most fathers are dead or in jail by adulthood. It's all done with well-written dialogue, an interesting story and excellent acting. ★★★★ VHS: $19.99

Miami Blues

(1990, 97 min, US, George Armitage) Fred Ward, Alec Bladwin, Jennifer Jason Leigh, Nora Dunn. Baldwin, sporting a crew cut and oftentimes a topless torso, stars in this offbeat, funny and wildly enjoyable comedy-thriller as a recently paroled killer

and pathological liar who poses as a cop to save crime victims before he himself rips them off. He soon meets a gullible young prostitute, Leigh, and together they play house, with Leigh cooking and cleaning and Baldwin leaving in the morning for his day of crime. Ward also stars as the slovenly cop, who, after losing his gun and false teeth to Baldwin, is determined to bring him to justice. All have fun with their roles, but Leigh is almost too good for the film, bringing heartbreaking depth in an unusually moving performance. ★★★½ DVD Dual: $14.99

Miami Rhapsody

(1995, 95 min, US, David Frankel) Sarah Jessica Parker, Mia Farrow, Antonio Banderas, Paul Mazursky, Kevin Pollak, Jeremy Piven. Farrow appears in this fluffy romantic comedy which is about as close to a Woody Allen film as one can get without having Allen's name on the credits. But that's not to suggest that Miami Rhapsody bears a resemblance either artistic or comical to the Woodman: This is most definitely "Woody Lite." Trying to act more sophisticated than she really is, Parker plays a twentysomething writer whose impending marriage opens her eyes to the failings of the relationships of those around her. These include her mother Farrow, father Mazursky and brother Pollak. There are some amusing moments and one-liners to this Rhapsody, but the characters' and story's lack of development makes it all seem half-a-beat off. ★★½ DVD: $9.99, VHS: $9.99

Michael

(1996, 105 min, US, Nora Ephron) John Travolta, William Hurt, Andie MacDowell, Robert Pastorelli, Bob Hoskins, Jean Stapleton, Teri Garr. As if his otherworldly role in Phenomenon wasn't enough, Travolta now takes on the part of an angel — a wisecracking, crotch-scratching, barhopping one at that — in this sloppy romantic comedy. Three reporters for a supermarket tabloid respond to Iowa housewife Stapleton's letter about her angel houseguest Michael (Travolta). Low and behold, he's the real thing. As they set out to return to their Chicago offices with Michael in tow, all are affected in one way or another by their heavenly traveling companion. Travolta once again proves that he's such an engaging presence on-screen that he can rise above such drivel, and he alone is the saving grace of this inexplicable box office hit. ★★ DVD: $14.99, VHS: $14.99

Michael Collins

(1996, 127 min, GB/Ireland, Neil Jordan) Liam Neeson, Aidan Quinn, Julia Roberts, Alan Rickman, Stephen Rea, Ian Hart, Charles Dance. In a role befitting his larger-than-life screen presence, Neeson gives his best performance since Schindler's List playing another real-life character who overcomes odds to carve a niche for himself in history. Michael Collins is the passionate, remarkably detailed story of the Irish revolutionary who sought to seek Ireland's independence from British rule. With the complex political issues of the formation of the Irish Republican Army at its core, the film traces the rise of Collins as a party official whose legend and determination led to brief peace and an Ireland which still exists today. An impressive achievement on all levels, Michael Collins is stirring as both history and cinema. ★★★★ DVD Letterbox: $19.99, VHS: $14.99, VHS Letterbox: $19.99

Mickey Blue Eyes

(1999, 102 min, US, Kelly Makin) *Hugh Grant, James Caan, Jeanne Tripplehorn, Burt Young, James Fox, Joe Viterelli.* Grant is as engaging as ever in this feather-lite comedy about Cockneys and mobsters. He plays Michael Felgate, the manager of a struggling New York auction house who's rushing into an engagement with the daughter, he soon finds out, of a notable mafiaso (Caan, smug as ever). Tripplehorn plays the fiancée, who desperately wants to protect Michael from the ever-grasping clutches of her family. Complications ensue when the art world and the underworld collide. The movie has fun with the notion of what happens when someone refuses an offer they shouldn't refuse, and gives some familiar gangster-movie faces the opportunity to toy with their own tough-guy personas. Nothing monumental here, but an innocuous romp played to the hilt by a likable cast. ★★½ DVD: $19.99, VHS: $9.99

Microcosmos

(1996, 75 min, France, Claude Nuridsany & Marie Perennou) Bugs! Those are the stars of this enthralling French nature production which takes an extremely up-close look at what lurks in the woods behind your house. But rather than going for a *Life on Earth*-style narrated documentary which explains the sex life of snails, *Microcosmos* simply shows it, with amplified sound effects and minimal musical accompaniment. The result is truly mesmerizing; getting closer than you imaged a camera could, the details and complexity of creatures we ordinarily step on are impossible to look away from, even though some of the images border on the grotesque. The camerawork and patience put into the miniscule production are herculean in scale and the film is appropriate for all ages even though, yes, you do get to see that snail sex, very up close and personal. ★★★½ VHS: $9.99

Midaq Alley

(1995, 140 min, Mexico, Jorge Fons) *Ernesto Gómez Cruz, Salma Hayek, Bruno Bichir, Claudio Obregón.* This episodic drama, based on a novel by Naguib Mahfouz, delves into three different tales of mismatched lovers, family bitterness and betrayal in a small street in Mexico City. The first story is a startlingly gay-themed one. Mr. Ru (Cruz) is a restaurateur who has just come out, which causes strife with his macho son and frustrated wife. Tensions boil for father and son when Mr. Ru becomes involved with a younger man. Meanwhile, his neighbor Mr. Fidel (Obregón) pursues the sexy young Alma (Hayek), while her mother yearns for Fidel. Alma, however, has promised herself to Abel the barber, who is leaving for the U.S. to earn money for them to marry. Can she wait for his return? Fans of odd couples in the cinema will enjoy this melodramatic mix of sex, longing and obsession. (Spanish with English subtitles) ★★★ DVD: $19.99, VHS: $19.99

The Midas Touch

(1989, 100 min, Hungary, Geza Beremenyi) Winner of the 1990 European Film Award for Best Director, this involving political drama unfolds in Budapest in the early 1950s. Monori is a quick-thinking merchant with a penchant for making a quick profit — from the sale of anything from apples to lentils. His schemes and techniques are severely tested with the approaching turmoil of 1956. (Hungarian with English subtitles) ★★★ VHS: $79.99

Midnight

(1939, 94 min, US, Mitchell Leisen) *Claudette Colbert, Don Ameche, John Barrymore, Mary Astor.* "Every Cinderella has her midnight" says imposter Colbert, and in trying to escape hers a breezy, sophis-

ticated romp is born. Cleverly written by Billy Wilder and Charles Brackett, this effervescent romantic comedy stars Colbert as a penniless showgirl newly arrived to Paris. She befriends cabbie Ameche, who soon falls for her. But true love must wait when Colbert is hired by baron Barrymore (in a spirited comeback performance) to impersonate a countess — it seems his wife Astor is involved in a romantic indiscretion with a playboy, and it's up to Colbert to come between them. Director Leisen sets a brisk pace, though the film's theme of mistaken identity and the screenplay's sexual innuendo is pure Wilder. Colbert, as usual, is a delight. ★★★★ VHS: $14.99

Favorite Line: "From the moment you looked at me I had an idea you had an idea." —*Claudette Colbert as Eve Peabody*

A Midnight Clear

(1992, 107 min, US, Keith Gordon) *Ethan Hawke, Peter Berg, Gary Sinise, Kevin Dillon, Frank Whaley, Arye Gross.* Gordon's second directorial feature is a vigorous and very polished antiwar drama, and a much more assured piece of filmmaking than his debut *The Chocolate War.* Set during the last months of WWII, the story traces the emotional toll taken on a group of weary, young G.I.s at the front line who come in contact with a group of German soldiers. The equally tired enemy soon makes clear their desire for surrender. As each side cautiously builds to a ceasefire, both armies enjoy a respite from the hell around them. But for how long? Gordon handles his young cast very well. ★★★½

Midnight Cowboy

(1969, 113 min, US, John Schlesinger) *Dustin Hoffman, Jon Voight, Brenda Vaccaro, Sylvia Miles, John McGiver, Bob Balaban, Barnard Hughes.* No longer the shocking tale it was when first released, this classic slice of pop culture has evolved into a somewhat nostalgic reminder of the '60s mindset, capturing the naiveté and upheaval of a society enduring growing pains. Voight and Hoffman create a pair of legendary screen losers: Joe Buck, the aspiring stud-for-hire; and Ratso Rizzo, his rodent-like mentor. Winner of 3 Academy Awards, including Best Picture. ★★★★ DVD: $19.99

Midnight Crossing

(1988, 104 min, US, Roger Holzberg) *Faye Dunaway, Daniel J. Travanti, Kim Cattrall, Ned Beatty.* Tedious thriller with Dunaway and Travanti as a husband and wife who are searching for buried loot he had stashed away years before. ★

Midnight Dancers

(1994, 100 min, Philippines, Mel Chionglo) *Lawrence David, Gandong Cervantes, Alex Del Rosario, Soxy Topacio.* This eye-opening but over-the-top mess of melodramatic excess explores the tumultuous life and unconventional loves of "macho dancers" — male prostitutes who work as dancers and hustlers in Manila's gay bars. A more chaste and unrefined take on these young men than Lino Brocka's luridly watchable *Macho Dancers,* the tale begins when young country-bred Sonny (David) rejoins his family in Manila. He learns that his two brothers both earn a living dancing and prostituting themselves. Sonny becomes intrigued by the scene and begins to work there, ultimately beginning an affair with a sultry transvestite. The film's simple story lacks dramatic tension or focus; though despite the awkward handling of the many social themes it explores, the drama proves to be impassioned, sexy and involving. (Filipino with English subtitles) ★★½ DVD: $29.99, VHS: $29.99

Midnight Express

(1978, 121 min, US, Alan Parker) *Brad Davis, Randy Quaid, John Hurt, Bo Hopkins.* Based on the autobiography of Billy Hayes, this intense film explores the hellish years Hayes spent in a Turkish prison for drug smuggling. Violent, raw and powerful, *Midnight Express* works on both an emotional level as Hayes witnesses, experiences and fights back against the brutality of the prison staff, and as an exposé on corruption and examination of camaraderie. The film does contain one false note, however, as in real life Hayes was lovers with a fellow prisoner, but here he is politely brushed aside. Oscar-winning screenplay by Oliver Stone. Davis gives a remarkably complex performance as Hayes, and Hurt is outstanding as a drugged-out fellow prisoner. ★★★½ DVD: $14.99

Midnight in the Garden of Good and Evil

(1997, 154 min, US, Clint Eastwood) *Kevin Spacey, John Cusack, Jack Thompson, Alison Eastwood, The Lady Chablis, Irma P. Hall, Jude Law, Dorothy Loudon.* With this ambitious though not entirely successful adaptation of John Berendt's based-on-fact best-seller, director Eastwood takes a walk on the wild side — Southern style. Cusack is John Kelso, a New York writer assigned to cover an exclusive society party in Savannah. Agendas change, however, when Jim Williams (Spacey), the party's host, is arrested that night for shooting his hustler boyfriend (Law). Was it self-defense or premeditated? Eastwood is able to convey the rhythms of Southern culture and attitudes with a leisurely tempo, though at 154 minutes the film is just too long. Also, there's a startling addition of a romantic interest for Kelso,

Kevin Spacey evokes Southern charm in Clint Eastwood's *Midnight in the Garden of Good and Evil*

which only contradicts the sexual tension between Kelso and Williams. But the film can be fascinating and surprisingly funny, as mannered and charismatic as Williams himself. Playing herself, The Lady Chablis steals every scene she's in. ★★★ DVD Letterbox: $9.99, VHS Letterbox: $14.99

Midnight Madness

(1980, 110 min, Michael Nankin & David Wechter) *David Naughton, Debra Klinger, David Damas, Michael J. Fox, Stephen Furst, Andy Tennant, Paul Reubens.* Perfectly awful re-hash of *Scavenger Hunt* (which was itself perfectly awful), as stereotypical coeds ransack L.A.'s mini-golf courses and penny arcades, looking for clues that lead to: a buffet! Notable for early appearances by Fox and Reubens, and for prominent Pabst product placement in a Disney film. ★½ DVD: $14.99

Midnight Run

(1988, 122 min, US, Martin Brest) *Robert De Niro, Charles Grodin, Yaphet Kotto, Dennis Farina, Joe Pantoliano.* De Niro stars as a modern-day bounty hunter who is hired to escort mob accountant Grodin from New York to Los Angeles to stand trial. What begins as a simple plane ride turns into a no-holds-barred cross-country free-for-all involving the FBI, the Mafia, hit men and rival bounty hunters. Highlighted by well-staged shootouts and chase scenes, and quite humorous and delightfully venomous sparring between the two stars. ★★★ DVD: $14.99, VHS: $7.49

A Midsummer Night's Dream

(1935, 117 min, US, Max Reinhardt) *James Cagney, Mickey Rooney, Dick Powell, Olivia de Havilland, Joe E. Brown, Mickey Rooney.* Famed theatre director Reinhardt based this captivating version of Shakespeare's classic on his acclaimed stage production he made the year before. An all-star cast is featured, including Cagney (as Bottom) and Rooney, who steals the show as Puck. ★★★ VHS: $14.99

A Midsummer Night's Dream

(1968, 124 min, GB, Peter Hall) *Diana Rigg, David Warner, Ian Richardson, Ian Holm, Judi Dench.* Shakespeare goes Mod! The Royal Shakespeare Company's frolicking rendition of the Bard's masterful farce is indeed a daring departure from the norm, but is in every way true to the author's intent. A must for fans of theatre. ★★★ VHS: $24.99

A Midsummer Night's Dream

See: *William Shakespeare's A Midsummer Night's Dream*

A Midsummer Night's Sex Comedy

(1982, 88 min, US, Woody Allen) *Woody Allen, Mia Farrow, Tony Roberts, Mary Steenburgen, Jose Ferrer, Julie Hagerty.* Allen ponders the foibles of sex, love and courtship in this whimsical period piece. Six couples engage in a romantic roundelay during an idyllic country outing. ★★★ DVD: $19.99

A Midwinter's Tale

(1995, 98 min, GB, Kenneth Branagh) *Michael Maloney, John Sessions, Richard Briers, Julia Sawalha, Nicholas Farrell, Joan Collins, Celia Imrie.* Lovers of theatre will rejoice in this uproarious and frenetic look at the inner-workings of a haphazardly slapped together theatre troupe and their attempt to mount a Christmas Eve production of "Hamlet." *A Midwinter's Tale* opens with a perky rendition of Noël Coward singing his "Why Must the Show Go On?" which immediately sets an irreverent tone. The madness begins when out-of-work

actor-director Joe Harper (Maloney) begs his agent (Collins) for some money to stage "Hamlet." He quickly assembles a cast of theatre rejects that includes Sessions as a drag queen Gertrude and in a hilarious turn, Imrie as a designer so ethereal, her concept doesn't occur to her until opening night. With just two weeks to rehearse, the question becomes "how can the show possibly go on?" Branagh's cast does a crackling job exploring the tenuous relations of so many superegos, and the film becomes increasingly riveting as their collective cool breaks down. ★★★½ VHS: $14.99

Mifune

(1999, 102 min, Denmark, Søren Kragh-Jacobson) *Iben Hjejle, Anders W. Berthelsen, Jesper Asholt, Susanne Storm.* The third in the Dogme95 films is by far the most conventional. It's more palatable than Lars Von Trier's entry, *The Idiots*, but it's infinitely less daring; and *Mifune* can't hold a candle to the brilliant and bracing *The Celebration*. The film is basically a romantic comedy, as contrived and predictable as the latest Meg Ryan vehicle: after his estranged father dies, a self-involved yuppie (Berthelsen) must go to the family farm to take care of his mentally challenged brother. He enlists the help of a hooker-with-a-heart-of-gold (the lovely Hjejle) as housekeeper. It's interesting enough to see the Dogme technique (available light only, no music score, handheld camera) in the service of a formula film, and the Dogme style is integrated so well it ceases to call attention to itself, but this is still just a well-acted, nicely directed piece of fluff. There are some terrific moments —especially in the first half — but it becomes less and less involving as it reaches its foregone conclusion. (Danish with English subtitles) ★★½ DVD: $29.99, VHS: $21.99

The Mighty

(1998, 100 min, US, Peter Chelsom) *Kieran Culkin, Sharon Stone, Elden Henson, Gena Rowlands, Harry Dean Stanton, Gillian Anderson, James Gandolfini.* Max (Henson) is a hulking, quiet lad, straddling childhood and young adulthood, who reacts to constant taunting by turning ever inward. Kevin (Culkin), exceptionally bright and verbally adroit, is victim to his crutches and his increasingly curving spine. They are trapped together in a big city public school system, joined by their deficiencies and strengthened by their union; their friendship forms a whole greater than the sum of its parts. Remarkable performances from the two young leads lift the familiar story line to produce a film of some achievement and great heart. *Not* a Sharon Stone movie. ★★½ DVD: $14.99, VHS: $9.99

Mighty Aphrodite

(1995, 95 min, US, Woody Allen) *Woody Allen, Helena Bonham Carter, Mira Sorvino, F. Murray Abraham, Michael Rapaport, Claire Bloom, Olympia Dukakis, Peter Weller, Jack Warden.* Not as complex in character and narrative as Allen's former films, this is nevertheless consistently funny and thoroughly entertaining. Allen plays a sports writer married to an ambitious art gallery employee (Bonham Carter). They decide to adopt, and as the exceptional child grows, Allen becomes determined to locate the real mother. All his preconceptions about familial lineage and genes are smashed when he meets a ditzy prostitute/porn actress (marvelously played by Oscar winner Sorvino), and then becomes involved in her life. Many of Allen's signature themes — neurosis, infidelity and upper-class New York anxieties — are on display; they may not cut as deep, but they run wild just the same. ★★★ DVD: $14.99, VHS: $9.99

The Mighty Ducks

(1992, 104 min, US, Stephen Herek) *Emilio Estevez, Joss Ackland, Lane Smith.* This amiable Disney farce stars Estevez as Gordon Bombay, a high-powered schmuck of a lawyer who is sentenced to community service as the coach of a public league hockey team in Minneapolis' poorest neighborhood. Of course, this is the perfect setup for the type-A, egomaniacal Gordon to come to terms with his fall from grace as a child hockey star and learn the traditional virtue that "winning isn't everything." Purely formulaic, *The Mighty Ducks* goes out of its way to be predictable schmaltz and nonetheless, if one suspends one's normal critical faculties for an hour-and-a-half, the film is enjoyable and contains all of the right elements to thoroughly entertain the kids — which it did in droves in its theatrical run. Ackland appears as a hockey shop owner and Gordon's childhood mentor. (Followed by two sequels) ★★½ DVD: $14.99, VHS: $9.99

Mighty Joe Young

(1949, 94 min, US, Ernest B. Schoedsack) *Robert Armstrong, Terry Moore, Ben Johnson.* Schoedsack and Armstrong, the director and star of *King Kong* and *Son of Kong*, are back together; yet again sharing the spotlight with an ape. This cult favorite, which features good special effects, is about a young girl and her pet gorilla. Lots of fun. (Remade in 1998) ★★★ VHS: $14.99

Mighty Joe Young

(1998, 114 min, US, Ron Underwood) *Charlize Theron, Bill Paxton, Rade Serbedzija, Peter Firth, David Paymer.* This lackluster remake of the 1949 RKO favorite pairs chemistry-free Theron and Paxton as a couple protecting giant gorilla Joe by moving him from his jungle home to a California preserve. But, wouldn't you know it, the evil poacher who killed both Theron and Joe's moms when they were tots is back. The connect-the-dots screenplay will barely please small ones; this is very much a calculated piece of Hollywood product. Joe can't hold a candle to Willis O'Brien and Ray Harryhausen's original stop-motion animation. The only real thrill of this '90s update is seeing the RKO Pictures logo. ★½ DVD: $14.99, VHS: $9.99

Mighty Peking Man

(1977, 90 min, Hong Kong, Meng-Hwa Ho) *Evelyne Kraft, Danny Lee.* Hilariously bad HK "King Kong" rip-off from the '70s has been released to video thanks to Quentin Tarantino's Rolling Thunder distribution. Hero Lee (later to play the cop in John Woo's *The Killer*) captures fabled giant ape with help of scantily clad (and lip-glossed) jungle girl. They fall in love, and cavort in slo-mo through the jungle with her pet leopard to the strains of a hideous love ballad (this scene is sidesplitting). When Mighty Peking Man is taken to civilization, however, many obvious stunt doubles and fake miniatures get trampled. Almost painfully funny at times, *Mighty Peking Man* is the perfect party tape; so blatantly bad, no "Mystery Science Theater 3000"-esque comments are remotely necessary. It's camp that works. ★★★ DVD: $14.99, VHS: $9.99

The Mighty Quinn

(1989, 98 min, US, Carl Shenkel) *Denzel Washington, Robert Townsend, James Fox, Mimi Rogers, M. Emmet Walsh, Sheryl Lee Ralph.* Here's a film which, while it's not going to win any awards, will provide the viewer with a mildly entertaining evening of mystery and fun. Washington stars as Xavier Quinn, a police chief on a small Carribean island. Determined to clear the name of his child-hood friend — now a somewhat notorious local criminal (Townsend) — Quinn tenaciously probes the murder of a white businessman on the island. In a somewhat predictable twist, he runs into a lot of opposition from some of the island's more presti-gious constituents. ★★½ DVD: $14.99

A Mighty Wind

(2003, 92 min, US, Christopher Guest) *Christopher Guest, Michael McKean, Fred Willard, Catherine O'Hara, Eugene Levy, Bob Balaban, Parker Posey, Harry Shearer.* Cowriters Guest and Levy reunite once again for another mockumentary, *A Mighty Wind*, a riotous cornball caricature of the mid-'60s folk movement. Balaban plays a worry-wart producer hastily orga-nizing a folk reunion concert in homage to his late father, a folk music impresario. The bill features three reformed folk bands: The Folksmen (Shearer, McKean and Guest as a cracker-barrel trio plucking shanty rhythms with barnyard cho-ruses); The New Main Street Singers, a smiling, commercial, nine-piece combo of white-bread lads and lasses; and finally Mitch & Mickey, poster children-lovers reunited. Levy plays the emotionally stunted Mitch, O'Hara the fragile peacenik-past-her-expiration-date. With only two weeks to prepare, the groups pull off the event, despite in-fighting and last-minute fiascos. It is these "uncomfortable" moments emerging from an otherwise deadpan delivery where laughter becomes the stopgap. Much like the best Coen brothers works, Guest and Levy have a knack for presenting unconventional character types recog-nizable to all. Yet they take things several notches further, disarming us with dollops of pure absurdi-ty and leaving us in utter stitches. ★★★½ DVD: $19.99, VHS: $8.99

Mikey and Nicky

(1976, 105 min, US, Elaine May) *John Cassavetes, Peter Falk, Ned Beatty, William Hickey, Joyce Van Patten, M. Emmet Walsh.* This acclaimed drama written and directed by May (which was re-released ten years after its initial run to critical praise) stars Cassavetes and Falk as two small-time hoods who try to avoid a mob hit man (Beatty). Quirky and very appealing. ★★★

Mildred Pierce

(1945, 111 min, US, Michael Curtiz) *Joan Crawford, Ann Blyth, Jack Carson, Eve Arden, Zachary Scott, Butterfly McQueen.* An Oscar-win-ning performance by Crawford highlights this high-gloss soaper about a long-suffering mom who com-petes with her ungrateful little minx of a daughter for the affections of the same man. Blyth is wonderfully rotten as daughter Vida, and the always reliable Arden is a scene-stealer as Joan's best friend. ★★★½ DVD: $19.99

Milk Money

(1994, 110 min, US, Richard Benjamin) *Ed Harris, Melanie Griffith, Malcolm McDowell, Michael Patrick Carter, Casey Siemaszko.* Part *Pretty Woman* and part adolescent coming-of-age fantasy, *Milk Money* is an innocuous comedy about prostitution, suburbia, Grace Kelly and parenthood. Carter plays a 12-year-old boy who goes searching for a prosti-tute in the big city. There he meets good-hearted Griffith who, through a series of circumstances, comes to stay at his place in the burbs, prompting the youth to try to set her up with his widowed father (Harris). The film is a little too grown up for kids

Eugene Levy and Catherine O'Hara in *A Mighty Wind*

and too childish for adults, and there's its problem. Harris' goofy, lighthearted absent-minded dad pro-vides a few smiles. ★★ DVD: $14.99, VHS: $14.99

The Milky Way

(1936, 89 min, US, Leo McCarey) *Harold Lloyd, Adolphe Menjou, Verree Teasdale, Helen Mack.* Lloyd's best talkie has the silent clown as a mild-mannered milkman who becomes an unlikely boxing sensation when he accidentally knocks out the champ. Lots of laughs. (Remade in 1946 as *The Kid from Brooklyn*) ★★★

The Milky Way

(1969, 102 min, France, Luis Buñuel) *Laurent Terzieff, Paul Frankeur, Delphine Seyrig.* The reli-gious pilgrimage of two tramps traveling from France to Spain is the pretense of a plot in this sav-agely funny and continually imaginative heretical assault on organized religion. The folly of man's continual adherence to the insanities of Church dogma are portrayed through the tramps' surrealistic encounters with the Virgin Mary and Jesus Christ, as well as the Marquis de Sade. (French with English subtitles) ★★★★

The Mill on the Floss

(1997, 120 min, GB, Graham Theakston) *Emily Watson, Cheryl Campbell, James Frain, Bernard Hill, Ifan Meredith.* A Masterpiece Theatre adapta-tion of the George Eliot novel, this handsomely mounted saga of the Tulliver family and their river mill is absorbing, if unremarkable. The headstrong Maggie (Watson) cares deeply for both her father (Hill) and her brother Tom (Meredith), but she stirs up trouble when she falls in love with Philip (Frain), the son of her father's arch rival. As Maggie strug-gles for her free will, Tom tries to regain financial control of the mill. The bonds forged between the characters are heartfelt, particularly Tom and Maggie's devotion to each other; yet the story, which concerns tolerance and forgiveness, only truly engages the emotions when tragedy strikes. Nevertheless, the attention to period details, cos-tumes, and the beautiful British countryside, make this a lovely looking film, and Watson demonstrates extraordinary range. ★★★ VHS: $19.99

Mille Bolle Blu

(1993, 83 min, Italy, Leone Pompucci) *Stefano Dionisi, Claudio Bigagli.* Like a palimpsest used once too often, this breezy little comedy is marred by a faded familiarity that comes from having seen this all before. It is 1961. All Rome awaits the projected solar eclipse. The summer's warmth forces open the win-dows and doors on an archtypical street in the heart of the city. Imagine, if you will, Alfred Hitchcock's *Rear Window* with lots of yelling and gesticulation; no one has any secrets for long, and everyone has a colorful story. Someone dies. Someone marries. Characters are drawn with Fellini-esque broad strokes: endear-ing, entertaining, and as flat and as fleeting as the color comics section on Sunday. (Italian with English subtitles) ★★½ VHS: $19.99

Millennium

(1989, 95 min, US, Michael Anderson) *Cheryl Ladd, Kris Kristofferson, Daniel J. Travanti, Robert Joy, Brent Carver.* An intriguing concept for a sci-ence-fiction adventure — about a group of aliens who rescue passengers of airplanes right before they crash — is given an uneven treatment in this occa-sionally entertaining thriller. Ladd stars as a benign extraterrestrial from an underpopulated, dying plan-et whose scientists keep track of crashes, whisking away the doomed passengers to help repopulate their own world. ★★½ VHS: $9.99

Miller's Crossing

(1990, 115 min, US, Joel Coen) *Gabriel Byrne, John Turturro, Marcia Gay Harden, Albert Finney, Jon Polito, J.E. Freeman, Steve Buscemi, Michael Jeter, Mike Starr.* This thoroughly engrossing and brilliantly produced gangland sendup overflows with sardonic wit, bristling dialogue and operatic vio-lence. Byrne heads an excellent cast as Tom, a mob insider whose endless scheming provides the plot with an abundance of unexpected twists, double-crosses and red herrings. The story follows a fight for control of City Hall between Tom's boss, Leo (confidently portrayed by Finney), and an arch-rival. In the midst of the fray is Bernie Bernbaum, a weasely small-time hood who's trying to muscle in on both men's numbers racket. As Bernie, Turturro delivers a tantalizingly over-the-top performance. In her cinematic debut, Harden is superb as the hard-as-nails Verna, who is both Bernie's sister and Leo's girlfriend. ★★★★ DVD: $19.99

Millhouse: A White Comedy

(1971, 92 min, US, Emile de Antonio) Richard Milhous Nixon gets the De Antonio treatment in this biting "documentary" satire that exposes, through creative use of newsreel footage and interviews, the abominations of our 37th president. Made before the Watergate scandal, we view a calculating, opportunistic and amoral Nixon who, on occasion, has advocated the death penalty for drug dealers and a nuclear assault on Southeast Asia. A funny but sobering view of an American megalomaniac. ★★★ VHS: $39.99

Le Million

(1931, 85 min, France, René Clair) *Annabella, Rene Lefevre.* A finely tuned musical comedy which follows the wild adventures of a penniless and creditor-hounded painter who wins a million francs in a lottery but loses the winning ticket in a pair of pants he had pawned. His hurried attempts to retrieve the ticket, while keeping just one step ahead of his creditors, make this a delightful film. (French with English subtitles) ★★★½ DVD: $29.99, VHS: $29.99

The Million Dollar Hotel

(2000, 122 min, US, Wim Wenders) *Jeremy Davies, Mel Gibson, Milla Jovovich, Jimmy Smits, Peter Stormare, Amanda Plummer, Gloria Stuart, Tim Roth.* Film-school pretentiousness, Bukowski-esque outcasts and beautiful imagery all smack into each other with the subtlety of a freight train at *The Million Dollar Hotel.* At this seedy last chance for a group of down-and-out Los Angelenos, a young man is killed from a fall off the roof. Was it suicide or murder? That's what FBI agent Skinner (Gibson) wants to know. As written by Nicholas Klein, from a story idea by U2's Bono, the film is a collection of talky episodes in which the insane are enobled and the sane unenlightened. It's a message told with a heavy hand. Wenders' jump into the abyss is a fascinating fiasco. ★½ DVD: $24.99

Millionaire's Express

(1986, 107 min, Hong Kong, Sammo Hung) *Sammo Hung, Rosamund Kwan, Yuen Biao, Richard Norton, Yukari Oshima, Cynthia Rothrock.* Hanshui Town was a peaceful little villa along the rail line connecting Shanghai with the interior of China. That is, until several bands of outlaws decided to make their fortunes by robbing the "Millionaire's Express" train (named for its wealthy passengers) while it was

stopped at Hanshui. Madcap action ensues, and lots of it — this is part Keystone Cops, part "spaghetti western," but most definitely a Hong Kong action comedy. Gatling guns, striped prisoners in chains, kung fu battles on rooftops, romantic liaisons, explosions, horse chases, naked stove dances for Russian soldiers, Japanese spies and just about every Hong Kong star working for Golden Harvest Studios at the time (except Jackie Chan) combine to make an irresistable concoction of laughs and gasps. The comedy may prove a bit much for the hard-core action fan, but the film has so much charm it is sure to win over every other viewer. (Cantonese with English subtitles) ★★★½ DVD Widescreen: $29.99, VHS Subtitled: $19.99, VHS Dubbed: $19.99

Mimic

(1997, 105 min, US, Guillermo del Toro) *Mira Sorvino, Jeremy Northam, Josh Brolin, Giancarlo Giannini, F. Murray Abraham, Charles S. Dutton.* Bringing the same stylish chills he brought to *Cronos,* director Del Toro unleashes a steady stream of scares in this very good-looking, level-headed horror tale. Due to an untreatable virus passed on by cockroaches, the children of New York City are dying in increased numbers. Entomologist Sorvino creates a mutated roach that eventually kills them off. But a few years later, the genetically engineered bug has evolved into a human-sized, deadly adversary. *Mimic* takes a group of scientists and bystanders and pits them, in a confined space, against an unknown and elusive monster, here terrorizing the catacombs of the New York City subway system. Unlike many a horror film, children and pets aren't off limits — they too become roach food. ★★★ DVD Letterbox: $14.99, VHS: $9.99

Min and Bill

(1930, 66 min, US, George Hill) *Marie Dressler, Wallace Beery, Marjorie Rambeau.* Dressler won an Oscar for her heartbreaking performance as a feisty waterfront hotel proprietress who fights to keep the abandoned girl, whom she has raised as her own, from being taken away. In one of the big hits of the 1930s, Dressler and Beery make a great team. ★★★ VHS: $14.99

Mina Tannenbaum

(1994, 128 min, France, Martine Dugowson) *Romane Bohringer, Elsa Zylberstein, Florence Thomassin.* A rich, layered film, *Mina Tannenbaum* charts the winding path of a relationship between two women. Mina, a rebellious painter (Bohringer), meets Ethel (Zylberstein) in dance class at age seven. Alongside their relational development, the film conquers such issues as ethnic identity, mental illness and the power of familial history. In addition, the two women must resolve their struggles with art and feminism in face of a dominant and conformist culture. Though thematically the film bites off more than it can chew, each of these issues is handled with subtlety and sensitivity. (French with English subtitles) ★★★ VHS: $29.99

Minbo (Or the Gentle Art of Japanese Extortion)

(1994, 123 min, Japan, Juzo Itami) *Nobuko Miyamoto, Akira Takarada.* When a high-class hotel comes under siege from the Yakuza, it takes the savvy of a strong-willed woman to face them down. Beginning as a whimsical comedy that slowly turns into an intense exposé on the wiliness of the criminal world, this biting satire makes for spirited and entertaining fun. The Hotel Europa and its employees become the object of elaborate extortion plots from

cartoonish thugs, despite the efforts of the meek accountant-turned-security head. Help arrives in the form of Mahiru Inoue, a small, well-dressed young woman and attorney-at-law who goes to battle with nothing more than her devilish grin, disarming wit and tons of *chutzpa.* While some of the film's reliance on the Japanese honor code might distance some viewers, this daring film should intrigue most. Director Itami was attacked and injured by outraged Yakuzas during its making yet he finished the film and it became one of Japan's highest-grossing films. (Japanese with English subtitles) ★★★ VHS: $79.99

Mindwalk

(1991, 110 min, US, Bernt Capra) *Liv Ullmann, Sam Waterston, John Heard.* Written by theoretical physicist Fritjof Capra ("The Tao of Physics") and directed by his brother Bernt, this intriguing environmental talk-fest is certainly no masterpiece of drama, but for lovers of "Nova" and other PBS science programs, as well as environmentalists and New Age adherents, this will undoubtedly prove to be both fascinating and entertaining. Waterston is a liberal politician who, having just lost a bid for the White House, travels to France to visit his old '60s buddy, poet Heard. As they walk aroung the medieval Iles de St. Michel, they happen upon Ullmann, a semi-retired Norwegian quantum physicist. This chance meeting gives way to what can best be described as *My Dinner with Andre* meets *A Brief History of Time* as Ullmann lectures the two men on the history of physics and how Cartesian and Newtonian mechanical thinking has led us to our current environmental crisis. ★★½ VHS: $19.99

The Miniver Story

(1950, 104 min, US, H.C. Potter) *Greer Garson, Walter Pidgeon, John Hodiak, James Fox.* Released eight years after the classic *Mrs. Miniver,* this decidedly inferior sequel begins on VE-Day, following the postwar life of Mrs. Miniver as she welcomes back her husband and family separated during the war. Mr. M., unlike other postwar film characters, has no difficulty adjusting to civilian life — it's as if he's been on an extended fishing trip. Whereas the original explored war-time issues with intelligence, this postwar saga is artificial and meandering. ★★ VHS: $19.99

Minnie and Moskowitz

(1971, 115 min, US, John Cassavetes) *Gena Rowlands, Seymour Cassel, Val Avery, Timothy Carey, Katherine Cassavetes.* Rowlands and Cassel give marvelous performances in this offbeat, very appealing Cassavetes comedy. Rowlands is Minnie, a museum curator involved with a married man, who meets Moskowitz (Cassel), a down-to-earth parking lot attendant. A most wonderful romance follows. ★★★½ DVD: $24.99

Minority Report

(2002, 144 min, US, Steven Spielberg) *Tom Cruise, Colin Farrell, Samantha Morton, Max von Sydow, Lois Smith, Peter Stormare, Tim Blake Nelson.* Maybe working with Kubrick on *A.I.* rubbed off. Maybe it's the source material. Or maybe, just maybe, it's a case in which one of Hollywood's most successful directors continues to mature. Whatever the reason, Spielberg has taken cult writer Philip K. Dick's short story and turned it into a mesmerizing and intelligent sci-fi adventure. Darker than anything Spielberg has done before, *Minority Report* casts Cruise as John Anderton, a top cop for the elite Pre-Crime unit. It seems in the year 2054, psychics can pre-

Zachary Scott and Joan Crawford in *Mildred Pierce*

dict murder before it happens and the guilty are arrested before they can commit the crime. Events spiral out of control for Anderton when he is marked as a would-be killer, sending him on a quest to prove his innocence of a crime he hasn't committed against a man he doesn't even know. Farrell impresses as a government observer looking for flaws in the system, and Morton also registers as one of the psychics who holds the key to a long-buried secret. Despite an ending bordering on the cliché, *Minority Report* is an imaginative epic whose state-of-the-art effects are never allowed to overshadow its compelling, thoughtful characters. This illustrious marriage of humanity, vision and technique is what makes *Minority Report* an original and most entertaining experience. ★★★★ DVD Letterbox 2-disc set: $29.99, DVD Letterbox Basic Edition: $19.99, VHS: $9.99

The Minus Man

(1999, 111 min, US, Hampton Fancher) *Janeane Garofalo, Owen Wilson, Brian Cox, Dwight Yoakam.* After the grand-slam publicity campaign for *The Blair Witch Project*, perhaps the second-best ad campaign of 1999 was for *The Minus Man*. The enigmatic posters ("Don't bring a dumb date!") and trailer hinted at some sort of paranoid, Orwellian thriller. Actually, the film is an understated noir psychodrama set in Small Town, U.S.A. Wilson stars as Van Siegert, an affable chap who happens to be a serial killer. The film follows Van as he travels the lonesome back roads of America, befriending lost and lonely folks like himself — and eventually offing them. Fancher's direction is sluggish and he never generates enough tension or momentum to keep the story hurtling forward. Despite an eclectic cast, the performances are as dry as the pace. ★★ DVD: $14.99, VHS: $9.99

Miracle

(2004, 135 min, US, Gavin O'Connor) *Kurt Russell, Patricia Clarkson, Noah Emmerich, Sean McCann, Kenneth Welsh.* The potential for this story — about the 1980 U.S. Olympic hockey team pulling off one of the greatest upsets in American sports — to be an overdone, schmaltzy mess is obvious, but director O'Connor adeptly sidesteps the pitfalls to deliver an engaging and uplifting film history. *Miracle* succeeds due in large part to its authenticity. More than just about the details, the film firmly establishes the feeling in America during the late 1970s. America was struggling emotionally, and needed to recapture some of its past glory; the Olympic Games at Lake Placid served as the unlikely stage for this. In addition to these palpable undercurrents, there are first-rate performances, most notably by Russell as Herb Brooks. His portrayal of the hard-nosed coach, with a relentless determination to sculpt the young athletes into Olympic champions is subtle and convincing, and he brings depth to a role that could very easily become one-dimensional. *Miracle* has great sports action, with moments that are truly moving and inspirational. The best part about it is that someone understands that some stories don't need embellishment — sometimes the truth is exciting. ★★★ DVD 2-disc set: $29.99, VHS: $24.99

Miracle Down Under

(1987, 106 min, Australia, George Miller) *Dee Wallace Stone, John Waters, Bill Kerr.* From director Miller (*The Man from Snowy River*, not *Mad Max*), this compelling Australian drama follows the adventures and personal conflicts of a group of settlers exploring new uncharted southeastern Australian territory in the late 1800s. ★★★

Miracle in Milan

(1951, 96 min, Italy, Vittorio De Sica) *Francesco Golisano, Brunella Bova.* Merging his trademark style of Neorealism with an enchanting urban fable, De Sica succeeds in creating a politically charged yet endearing poetic tale. The story begins when a poor old lady finds a baby abandoned in a cabbage field. The orphan, Toto, grows up a smiling, accepting and generous young man, despite the abject poverty that surrounds him in war-ravaged Milan. Toto, with the help of the city's homeless, constructs a squatter city, only to see it threatened by greedy developers. Hope is not lost, however, for with the aid of a magical dove given to him by his departed stepmother, he tries to save their beloved home town. A humorous story of survival told without bitterness, from one of Italy's greatest filmmakers. (Italian with English subtitles) ★★★½ VHS: $29.99

Miracle in Rome

(1989, 76 min, Colombia, Lisandro Duque Naranjo) *Frank Ramirez, Gerardo Arellano.* This wonderfully tender and heart-rending story of faith, hope and love is set in a small town in Colombia. A man's seven-year-old daughter, Evelia, dies suddenly in his arms. She is buried, but 12 years later the man, Margarito, is forced to exhume the body. To his amazement, her body is just as he left it, with Evelia seemingly only asleep. The town soon claims a miracle and declares her a saint. Margarito goes off to Rome, with the girl's body in tow, to plead his case for beatification to the Pope; only to be greeted by indifference and a labyrinthine religious bureaucracy. But his faith and love for his child keep him resolute as he soon realizes that a miracle of a different order is needed. Adapted from a story by Gabriel Garcia Marquez. (Spanish with English subtitles) ★★★

Miracle Mile

(1989, 102 min, US, Steve DeJarnatt) *Anthony Edwards, Mare Winningham, Denise Crosby.* An off-the-wall, strangely upbeat (not to mention offbeat) and thoroughly entertaining nuclear annihilation yarn about a pair of young lovers caught in the madness of the final few hours before the dawn of the Mad Max Millenium. DeJarnatt's madcap vision of impending doom takes off when Edwards picks up a ringing pay phone only to hear what seems to be the frantic voice of an Air Force silo operator who is desperately trying to reach his father and warn him that the unthinkable has been made real. The ensuing whirlwind of mayhem is brimming with acerbic wit and hilarious black comedy, and offers a refreshing perspective on what things may be like as we sink back into the primordial ooze. ★★★½ DVD: $14.99

The Miracle of Morgan's Creek

(1944, 99 min, US, Preston Sturges) *Betty Hutton, Eddie Bracken, William Demarest, Diana Lynn.* Writer-director Sturges had a field day with this brilliantly funny farce. Hutton gets impregnated by a G.I. leaving for overseas, and the unwed mother-to-be can't remember who the soldier was. It was a miracle that Sturges got this past the censors. ★★★★ VHS: $14.99

Miracle on 34th Street

(1947, 97 min, US, George Seaton) *Maureen O'Hara, John Payne, Edmund Gwenn, Natalie Wood.* Classic Christmas story about a Macy's Santa Claus who insists he's the real Kris Kringle — sending New York City into a frenzy. Gwenn deservedly won an Oscar for his delightful and definitive portrayal of Santa, and nine-year-old Wood is charming as a disbelieving youngster who is befriended by St. Nick. (Remade in 1994) ★★★½ DVD: $19.99, VHS: $9.99

Miracle on 34th Street

(1994, 114 min, US, Les Mayfield) *Richard Attenborough, Elizabeth Perkins, Dylan McDermott, Mara Wilson, J.T. Walsh, Robert Prosky.* With exception to Attenborough's lively interpretation of Santa Claus, and a charming performance by Wilson as the youngster who under his guidance learns to believe, there's little else to recommend about this updated remake of George Seaton's 1947 holiday classic. New York's 34th Street is still the setting for this tale of a department store Santa who insists he's the genuine article, but now the competing stores are fictional, which sets the tone for a story devoid of real emotion. ★★ DVD: $19.99, VHS: $9.99

Tom Cruise and Samantha Morton share a psychic moment in Steven Spielberg's *Minority Report*

The Miracle Worker

(1962, 107 min, US, Arthur Penn) *Anne Bancroft, Patty Duke, Victor Jory, Inga Swenson.* Brilliant screen version of William Gibson's acclaimed play which heartbreakingly details Helen Keller's fight to speak. Bancroft gives a stunning performance as Annie Sullivan, the half-blind teacher whose guidance enables the young Helen to communicate. Duke as Helen matches Bancroft all the way, and both actresses deservedly won Oscars. (Remade in 1979 with Duke playing Sullivan and in 2001) ★★★★ DVD: $14.99

Miracles

(1989, 127 min, Hong Kong, Jackie Chan) *Jackie Chan, Anita Mui.* A solid Chan vehicle, *Miracles* combines the feel (and plotline) of a 1930s gangster melodrama with Chan's typical self-effacing humor and terrific action; this is one of his more satisfying films. While this American release thankfully has kept the goofy but infectious original music score, it has replaced the Chinese language track with some idiotic dubbing (one bad guy sounds like a bad Edward G. Robinson impression, another is a poorman's Peter Lorre) that detracts a bit from the fun. Still, *Miracles* — while a bit long in the tooth — is highly enjoyable, and contains some of Jackie's most astonishing action setpieces. And he looks pretty damned sharp in those period get-ups! Based on Frank Capra's *A Pocketful of Miracles.* (aka: *Mr. Canton and Lady Rose*) ★★★

Mirage

(1965, 109 min, US, Edward Dmytryk) *Gregory Peck, Walter Matthau, Kevin McCarthy, Jack Weston, Diane Baker.* Intriguing Hitchcockian thriller with Peck as an amnesia victim who becomes entangled in a murder mystery while trying to regain his memory. ★★★

Miranda

(2002, 95 min, US, Marc Munden) *Christina Ricci, Kyle MacLachlan, John Hurt.* An uneven noirish romantic comedy, *Miranda* finds dorky Simm falling for comely Ricci, whom he discovers is under the thumb of not-so-nice-guy Hurt. Semi-witty, borderline interesting developments follow. Simm (who was quite appealing in *Human Traffic* and *Wonderland*) is well-cast, and Ricci (who seems a bit distracted and under duress here) is cute as always, but poor MacLachlan continues to be (mis)cast in smallish, weak roles. Ricci-philes will certainly enjoy her sexy wardrobe and sassy demeanor, and fans of noir will most likely be mildly amused, but the film never lives up to the promise of its fun, retro opening titles. ★★ DVD: $24.99, VHS: $59.99

The Mirror

(1974, 106 min, USSR, Andrei Tarkovsky) *Margarita Terekhova, Philip Yankovsky.* Fusing personal memories of his childhood as a wartime exile with fragments of his adult life and reflecting on his mother's experience with political terror, Tarkovsky has fashioned a haunting dreamlike puzzler that might best be described as an autobiographical poem. The director reflects on three generations of his family, as well as the painful experience of his parents' marital breakup, in making this deeply moving, powerful and challenging film. An intense and very personal film. (Russian with English subtitles) ★★★½ DVD: $29.99, VHS: $19.99

The Mirror Crack'd

(1980, 105 min, GB, Guy Hamilton) *Angela Lansbury, Elizabeth Taylor, Kim Novak, Rock Hudson, Tony Curtis, Edward Fox, Geraldine Chaplin, Pierce Brosnan.* Before she went sleuthing in "Murder She Wrote," Lansbury appeared as Agatha Christie's crack sleuth Miss Marple in this enjoyable, if slight, mystery. Miss Marple becomes involved with show people when Taylor is almost murdered. Taylor and Novak are well-cast as rival and catty movie queens. ★★ DVD: $14.99, VHS: $9.99

The Mirror Has Two Faces

(1996, 126 min, US, Barbra Streisand) *Barbra Streisand, Jeff Bridges, Lauren Bacall, Pierce Brosnan, George Segal, Mimi Rogers, Brenda Vacarro.* A sometimes giddy, sometimes overbearing romantic comedy. Streisand plays a supposedly unattractive college professor. Bridges, in an extremely likable performance, is a fellow professor looking for an asexual relationship. So he searches for a plain Jane. He finds Babs, and, of course, she falls in love with him; he fixes herself up; he falls in love with her; mix-ups and hijinks ensue. There are quite a few appealing comedic moments to the film, and Streisand is a congenial professor and mate. But the whole setup of the movie doesn't work, which magnifies not only Streisand's ego (her refusal to look really "bad") but the often fluffy, routine comedy as well. ★★½ DVD: $19.99, VHS: $9.99, VHS Letterbox: $19.99

The Misadventures of Mr. Wilt

(1990, 84 min, GB, Michael Tuchner) *Griff Rhys Jones, Mel Smith, Alison Steadman.* Although not nearly as funny as the wildly absurd Tom Sharpe novel, "Wilt," from which it is based, this frantic comedy still has its moments. Henry Wilt spends his days teaching English Lit in a second-rate community college and his nights fantasizing about elaborate ways to kill his fad-obsessed wife. When she disappears, he learns the police suspect *him* of doing her in. Sinking him further into the mess are Wilt's doings on the night of the disappearance which include a much-witnessed sexual tryst with a full-sized anatomically correct doll. Rhys Jones is perfect as the hapless Wilt in this rollicking black comedy. ★★★ VHS: $89.99

Misery

(1990, 107 min, US, Rob Reiner) *James Caan, Kathy Bates, Lauren Bacall, Richard Farnsworth, Frances Sternhagen.* Director Reiner returns to Stephen King territory (after the wonderful *Stand by Me*) leading Bates to a Best Actress Oscar for her creepy portrayal of a schizophrenic fan who first rescues, then imprisons her favorite author (Caan) when he kills off her favorite romance novel character. Reiner once again demonstrates that horror need not be all blood and guts. ★★★ DVD: $14.99

The Misfits

(1961, 124 min, US, John Huston) *Clark Gable, Marilyn Monroe, Montgomery Clift, Thelma Ritter, Eli Wallach.* A stark, poignant film with Gable, Clift and Wallach as modern-day cowboys, and Marilyn as a delicate divorcée entangled in their games of camaraderie and machismo. Scripted largely for Monroe by husband Arthur Miller, *The Misfits* marked her and Gable's final screen roles. ★★★ DVD: $9.99

Mishima: A Life in Four Chapters

(1985, 121 min, US/Japan, Paul Schrader) *Ken Ogata, Kenji Sawada.* Yukio Mishima, Japan's most celebrated novelist, stunned his country in 1970 when, after a bizarre attempt at a political overthrow, he committed *seppuku* (ritual suicide). With this puzzling event at its center, Schrader has created a daring film that tries to understand the man through his writings. With the final day of Mishima's life as the background, the film is intercut with three stylized episodes from his novels. A fascinating look at an obsessed artist. (Japanese with English subtitles) ★★★ DVD Letterbox: $19.99, VHS: $79.99

Miss Congeniality

(2000, 105 min, US, Donald Petrie) *Sandra Bullock, Michael Caine, Benjamin Bratt, Candice Bergen, William Shatner, Ernie Hudson.* An FBI agent who can't follow rules; an FBI agent who goes undercover; an underdog FBI agent who ultimately saves the day. These familiar elements are what you get in the formula comedy *Miss Congeniality*, whose one hook is that it's a female FBI agent, played with comic zest by Bullock. She and partner Bratt head to San Antonio for the Miss USA beauty pageant, where a serial bomber will strike next. The tomboyish agent gets a makeover (a fussy Caine is her Henry Higgins) and becomes a contestant. The usual jokes — unable to walk in heels, wearing falsies, dumb fellow contestants — follow. ★★ DVD: $14.99, VHS: $6.99

Miss Firecracker

(1989, 102 min, US, Thomas Schlamme) *Holly Hunter, Mary Steenburgen, Tim Robbins, Alfre Woodard, Scott Glenn, Ann Wedgeworth, Christine Lahti.* Welcome to Yazoo City, Mississippi. What more likely setting for playwright Beth Henley to serve up this thoroughly charming piece of American pie filled with a cast of characteristically odder-than-odd characters. A crackerjack ensemble of actors is headed by Hunter as a slightly eccentric "girl with a past," whose one dream in life is to win the annual Miss Firecracker Beauty Pageant. Sparks fly when her rapacious cousins Steenburgen and Robbins descend on her fragile ego with a ferocity that only family members can muster. Woodard adds comic zip as Hunter's daffy seamstress with a penchant for hearing voices through her eyeballs. ★★★ DVD Letterbox: $9.99, VHS: $7.99

Miss Julie

(1985, 90 min, Sweden, Alf Sloberg) *Anita Bjork, Ulf Palme.* This dazzling adaptation of Strindberg's riveting play concerns one woman's social and sexual domination. Miss Julie, a noblewoman, allows her butler to seduce her after her engagement is broken. Her actions then lead to a haunting and unremitting exploration of how the woman's disgrace begins to destroy her. Outstanding performances and magnificent cinematography enhance the intensity of this story. (Swedish with English subtitles) ★★★

Miss Rose White

(1991, 95 min, US, Joseph Sargent) *Kyra Sedgwick, Amanda Plummer, Maximilian Schell, Maureen Stapleton.* This Emmy Award winner is a sensitive tale of a young Jewish immigrant who must come to terms with her ethnicity when her sister, a Holocaust survivor, comes to join her and her father in America just after WWII. Sedgwick is marvelous as the title character and Schell boasts a strong supporting performance as her father, as does the always wonderful Plummer as her sister. Based on the off-Broadway play "A Shayna Maidel" by Barbara Lebow. ★★★½ VHS: $14.99

Rita Hayworth knocks 'em dead in *Miss Sadie Thompson*

Miss Sadie Thompson

(1953, 93 min, US, Curtis Bernhardt) *Rita Hayworth, Jose Ferrer, Aldo Ray, Charles Bronson.* Although Hayworth's Sadie Thompson won't make anyone forget *Gilda*, she nevertheless gives a sparkling performance in this musical remake of W. Somerset Maugham's story "Rain" (the 1932 version starred Joan Crawford). Rita plays a "good time" entertainer who, while stranded on a tropical island during WWII, becomes involved with a brawny G.I. (Ray) and a hypocritical minister (Ferrer) whose obsession with Sadie's salvation cloaks other desires. (Timely, isn't it?) ★★★

Missing

(1982, 122 min, US, Constantin Costa-Gavras) *Jack Lemmon, Sissy Spacek, John Shea, Melanie Mayron, David Clennon.* Costa-Gavras' award-winning thriller probes the mysterious disappearance of a young American writer during the bloody political upheaval in Chile. Spacek and Lemmon star as the wife and father whose persistent search uncovers some frightening facts on U.S. involvement in South America. ★★★½ VHS: $9.99

The Missing

(2003, 135 min, US, Ron Howard) *Tommy Lee Jones, Cate Blanchett, Evan Rachel Wood, Jenna Boyd, Eric Schweig, Aaron Eckhart, Jay Tavare, Val Kilmer.* A girl is kidnapped by Indians and a grizzled frontiersman rides to her rescue. No, this isn't *The Searchers*, but the film version of Thomas Eidson's novel "The Last Ride." In attempting the same western subgenre as the great John Ford, director Howard may appear to be treading on hallowed ground, but thankfully Howard's somber, raw film — while not on the level of Ford's classic — serves as a reminder on the pleasures of the western and the perils of the Old West. In a tough portrayal that sometimes strays towards the two-dimensional (the film's weakest link is Ken Kaufman's generic adaptation), Blanchett plays Maggie, a taciturn healer and mother of two girls. When her eldest daughter is kidnapped by Apache renegades, she must reluctantly rely on her estranged father Samuel (Jones), who has spent the last few decades living with the Apaches, to lead them on a rescue mission. Even with *Apollo 13* and *A Beautiful Mind* to his credit, Howard has crafted his darkest film to date, his characters residing in a near-barren landscape in which hope is as fleeting as sand in a duststorm. Jones is at his best with his turn as the father searching for redemption at any price. Overlong at 135 minutes, *The Missing* nevertheless engages, allowing the viewer to forget some of the genre's conventions and wade instead in the grit and grime of such a treacherous, often exciting journey. ★★★ DVD Letterbox 2-disc Special Edition: $28.99, DVD Pan & Scan 2-disc Special Edition: $28.99, VHS: $14.99

The Mission

(1986, 125 min, GB, Roland Joffé) *Jeremy Irons, Robert De Niro, Ray McAnally, Aidan Quinn, Philip Bosco, Liam Neeson.* A Best Picture nomination went to this acclaimed, based-on-fact historical drama, set in 18th-century South America. Irons stars as a Jesuit priest who leads a tribe of native Indians in a revolt against mercenary colonialists. De Niro is a soldier whose social conscience leads him to become involved on behalf of Irons and his cause — an act which draws him into an insurmountable challenge and inevitable tragedy. Gorgeous Oscar-winning cinematography. ★★★½ DVD Letterbox 2-disc set: $26.99, VHS: $14.99

Mission: Impossible

(1996, 111 min, US, Brian De Palma) *Tom Cruise, Jon Voight, Emmanuelle Béart, Jean Reno, Ving Rhames, Henry Czerny, Vanessa Redgrave, Emilio Estevez, Kristin Scott Thomas.* The popular 1960s TV drama "Mission: Impossible" gets a '90s facelift with this exciting, well executed though somewhat dense thriller. Serving as producer and star, Cruise plays Ethan Hunt, a member of the elite undercover team. Voight plays Jim Phelps, the team's leader and a carryover character from the TV series. On a mission Mr. Phelps decides to accept, most of the members are killed, with Hunt the only likely survivor. It soon becomes apparent that they were set up, and Hunt — who is now the number one suspect — goes underground to discover the identity of the mole. Maybe it's a little too intricate for its own good, but the twists are unpredictable, the action plentiful; and among several terrific sequences, there's a hold-your-breath ending. (Sequel: *Mission: Impossible II*) ★★★ DVD Letterbox: $14.99, VHS: $9.99, VHS Letterbox: $9.99

Mission: Impossible II

(2000, 124 min, US, John Woo) *Tom Cruise, Thandie Newton, Dougray Scott, Ving Rhames, Anthony Hopkins.* Perhaps Cruise's *Mission* series will follow the lines of the *Alien* movies, with each sequel radically unlike the previous. Unfortunately, instead of *Aliens* for a second film, Woo has given us *Mission: Resurrection*. This stylish misfire at least has a comprehensible plot, as our hero Ethan Hunt (Cruise) tracks down a deadly virus being exploited for cash (or stock) by villianous entrepeneur Scott. Hunt's pilferous recruit Newton provides a romantic complication for both. Woo provides his usual operatic grandeur, but his moves (and the nascent franchise) have become so predictable that even the villain knows what will happen during a would-be set piece. It all just seems too over-the-top. ★★ DVD: $14.99, VHS: $9.99

Mission: Kashmir

(2000, 157 min, India, Vidhu Vinod Chopra) *Sanjay Dutt, Hrithik Roshan, Preity Zinta, Jackie Shroff.* When a hard-nosed policeman accidentally massacres a terrorist's family, he is unable to find treatment for his own dying son, due to the terrorist organization's threat to kill anyone who helps the policeman in any way. The grieving policeman and his wife decide to adopt the only surviving member of the massacre: the terrorist's son. Trouble ensues when the young boy finds out the truth, pitting father against adopted son. *Mission: Kashmir* is a terrific Bollywood melodrama with exciting action scenes, superb performances and, of course, musical numbers. The music may be the stumbling block for many Western viewers, but they're rarely intrusive; in fact, there is one unbearably suspenseful musical number that resembles something Hitchcock would have done if forced to direct a song-and-dance scene. This film has it all: tough drama, tear-jerking heartbreak, romance, topicality. Only the end feels like a concession to commerciality; it's easily forgiven. (Hindi with English subtitles) ★★★★ DVD: $24.99

Mission to Mars

(2000, 112 min, US, Brian De Palma) *Gary Sinise, Tim Robbins, Connie Nielsen, Don Cheadle, Jerry O'Connell, Kim Delaney, Armin Mueller-Stahl.* After losing the signal to their friends on Mars, a second mission is sent to rescue them. This lackluster, clichéd, cornball would-be sci-fi epic is salvaged somewhat by director DePalma's always interesting visual direction, an able cast and Ennio Morricone's pleasingly eclectic score. But this is hardly the rousing, fascinating (if obviously derivative) spectacle suggested by the trailers. Still, there's an amazing 20-30 minute chunk of pure suspense cinema halfway through the film that culminates in an emotionally resonant climax; it's one of DePalma's best setpieces (despite rampant product placement). Sadly, the film lumbers along for 40 more minutes after that, to a decidedly anticlimax. An interesting misfire. ★★½ DVD: $14.99, VHS: $9.99

The Missionary

(1982, 93 min, GB, Richard Loncraine) *Michael Palin, Maggie Smith, Trevor Howard, Denholm Elliott.* Monty Pythonite Palin stars in this eccentric comedy-drama as a naïve English missionary just returned from Africa and assigned to rehabilitate the fallen women of Edwardian London. Smith costars as his lascivious benefactor in this refined satire. ★★★½ DVD: $14.99

Mississippi Blues

(1983, 96 min, US/France, Bertrand Tavernier & Robert Parrish) French director Tavernier and Georgia-born independent filmmaker Parrish combine their talents in approaching the people and music of the Mississippi Delta. This charming, affable film explores the ever-shifting landscape, the lives of the people in the river towns, their customs and most wonderfully, their musical traditions of Delta Blues and gospel. ★★★ VHS: $19.99

Mississippi Burning

(1988, 125 min, US, Alan Parker) *Gene Hackman, Willem Dafoe, Frances McDormand, Brad Dourif, R. Lee Ermey, Stephen Tobolowsky, Michael Rooker, Pruitt Taylor Vince, Frankie Faison.* This gutwrenching masterwork is one of the most powerful American films to date to explore racial prejudice. Based on the actual 1964 murders of three civil rights workers, the film presents a fictionalized account of the investigation. Hackman and Dafoe are the FBI agents assigned to the case. At odds with each other from the start, together the two men confront a hostile white community either unwilling or unable to cooperate, and an oppressed black community impregnated with fear of reprisal at the hands of the ruthless white bigots controlling the town. Dafoe is very good as the conventional FBI man, but it is Hackman's virtuoso performance which forms the core of the film. ★★★★ DVD: $14.99

Mississippi Masala

(1992, 118 min, US, Mira Nair) *Denzel Washington, Sarita Choudhury, Roshan Seth.* Director Nair sets her sights on the subtleties of insidious racism in this affecting modern-day "Romeo and Juliet" set in the deep South. The story follows the forbidden love that blossoms between a young Indian woman (Choudhury), whose family fled Idi Amin's Uganda, and an African-American carpet cleaner (Washington). Nair expertly exposes the unspoken and unacknowledged racism that permeates the Indian community. Washington and newcomer Choudhury give heartfelt performances and Nair puts their stunning looks to good use. Seth delivers yet another superb supporting performance as Choudhury's lawyer father who yearns to return to Uganda. ★★★ DVD: $19.99

Mississippi Mermaid

(1969, 123 min, France, François Truffaut) *Catherine Deneuve, Jean-Paul Belmondo.* This intriguing but tame romantic thriller was one of the director's few certifiable flops, despite the superstar casting of Belmondo and Deneuve. The story concerns a tobacco plant owner (Belmondo) on an African island who gets more than he bargained for after the arrival of his mysterious mail-order bride (Deneuve). The Hitchcock-inspired plot is elaborately presented, but the film lacks needed tension and fails to reach its intended suspense. (French with English subtitles) ★★ DVD: $19.99, VHS: $19.99

The Missouri Breaks

(1976, 126 min, US, Arthur Penn) *Marlon Brando, Jack Nicholson, Randy Quaid, Kathleen Lloyd, Harry Dean Stanton, Frederic Forrest.* Brando plays a sadistic gunslinger hired to kill horse thief Nicholson and his gang (Quaid, Stanton). Set in the late 1880s in Montana hill country, where Brando and Nicholson play a deadly game of cat-and-mouse, this bizarre western was a financial disappointment upon release. It has, over the years, taken on cult status thanks to its two stars. ★★

Mr. and Mrs. Bridge

(1990, 105 min, US, James Ivory) *Paul Newman, Joanne Woodward, Kyra Sedgwick, Blythe Danner, Robert Sean Leonard, Simon Callow.* A leisurely, fine character study highlighted by two bravura performances from Newman and especially Woodward as an upper-middle-class Kansas City husband and wife. Based on two Evan S. Connell novels, "Mr. Bridge" and "Mrs. Bridge," the film, set in the years between the two World Wars, examines with razor-sharp intensity and formidible wit the couple's everyday, and even mundane, existence. A series of continuing and perfectly constructed stories, the film's most memorable scenes include Newman's "battle" with a tornado and Woodward's astonishing reaction at her son's Boy Scout meeting. ★★★½ DVD: $19.99

Mr. and Mrs. Smith

(1941, 95 min, US, Alfred Hitchcock) *Carole Lombard, Robert Montgomery.* Amusing, fast-paced comedy, a real change of pace for Hitchcock, that has husband and wife Montgomery and Lombard finding out that, due to a technicality, they aren't really married. ★★★

Mr. Arkadin

See: *Confidential Report*

Mr. Baseball

(1992, 108 min, US, Fred Schepisi) *Tom Selleck, Ken Takakura, Aya Takanashi, Dennis Haysbert.* A lackluster confection about a bad-boy baseballer (Selleck) whose losing streak and outfield antics get him traded to Japan. There he becomes involved in the obligatory misunderstandings, misadventures, romance and culture clashes. Schepisi's sure-footed direction is the saving grace of this mediocre addition to the "stranger in a strange land" body of filmmaking. Also starring is Ken Takakura, Japan's answer to . . . well . . . Tom Selleck. ★★ DVD Letterbox: $14.99

Mr. Blandings Builds His Dream House

(1948, 94 min, US, H.C. Potter) *Cary Grant, Myrna Loy, Melvyn Douglas.* In this delightful screwball comedy, Grant is Mr. Blandings, a city-bred man who yearns for the "good life" — to be a country boy, with a big, old country house in the idyllic Connecticut countryside. But Mr. Blandings soon discovers that the "good life" isn't quite what he expected... and the fun begins. Forget the remake with Tom Hanks and Shelley Long, *The Money Pit*; this is the real thing. ★★★ DVD: $19.99

Mr. Death: The Rise and Fall of Fred A. Leuchter, Jr.

(1999, 91 min, US, Errol Morris) Fred A. Leuchter, Jr. began tinkering with design modifications for the electric chair in his young adulthood. In the forefront of the industry, he became known as a consultant, branching out into gas chambers and lethal injection. Leuchter's self-contained and relatively harmless world explodes when he is called in as an expert on death machines by revisionist historians seeking to dispute the occurrence of the Holocaust. His examination of Auschwitz reveals the limitations of his science; his inability to see a larger picture reveals his limitations as a man. Director Morris has again organized and communicated complex and detailed information with outstanding clarity and precision. ★★★★ DVD: $14.99, VHS: $9.99

Mr. Deeds

(2002, 96 min, US, Steven Brill) *Adam Sandler, Winona Ryder, Peter Gallagher, John Turturro, Erick Avari, Conchata Ferrell, Steve Buscemi.* After Sandler's notorious flop *Little Nicky*, one would have assumed that he would have paid slightly more attention to his next film's creative input/output. Well, attention was *not* paid. Sandler reunites with *Nicky* director Brill and screenwriter Tim Herlihy for a remake of Frank Capra's 1936 classic *Mr. Deeds Goes to Town*, and the result is truly awful. Sandler takes over the Gary Cooper role, now a small-town pizza shop owner who inherits $40 billion. This sends him to the big city and catapults him into the spotlight. Ryder is the reporter (unbeknownst to him) who befriends him for the scoop. Sloppily directed and edited, *Mr. Deeds* is so unfunny and undisciplined that it's almost as if Sandler were testing his audience to see exactly how much bad writing and acting they could take. The only stench of spontaneity comes from Turturro as a quick-footed butler, but it alone is not enough to make this even barely tolerable. ★ DVD Letterbox Special Edition: $14.99, DVD Pan & Scan Special Edition: $14.99, VHS: $14.99

Mr. Deeds Goes to Town

(1936, 115 min, US, Frank Capra) *Gary Cooper, Jean Arthur, Lionel Stander, H.B. Warner.* One of director Capra's great achievements, this delightfully entertaining and "pixilated" social comedy stars Cooper as Longfellow Deeds, a small-town boy who becomes heir to a fortune; when he decides to give it away to the needy, he goes on trial for insanity. Arthur, in the first of her three Capra films, shines as a newspaper reporter who gets the first scoop on Mr. Deeds. One of Cooper's best and most endearing performances. (Remade in 2002 as *Mr. Deeds*) ★★★★ DVD: $19.99, VHS: $14.99

Mr. Destiny

(1990, 105 min, US, James Orr) *Michael Caine, James Belushi, Linda Hamilton, Jon Lovitz, Bill McCutcheon, Hart Bochner, Rene Russo, Courtney Cox.* This modern-day *It's a Wonderful Life* stars Belushi as Larry Burrows, a 35-year-old Average Joe who's down on his luck. Along comes Mr. Destiny (Caine) in the guise of a bartender with an attentive ear. He slips Larry a magic potion which allows him to see how his life would have turned out if he'd managed to hit the ball in that fateful little league game 20 years earlier — in reality he had struck out, of course. Despite its total predictability, the film still holds a certain charm and is mildly entertaining. ★★ DVD: $9.99

Mr. Frost

(1989, 92 min, GB, Philip Setbon) *Jeff Goldblum, Alan Bates, Kathy Baker, Jean-Pierre Cassel.* Goldblum plays an icy killer who hasn't spoken in two years. Bates is the cop out to find his true identity and Baker is the psychiatrist caught in the middle. In trying to create uncertainty in Mr. Frost's identity, the film only manages to occasionally intrigue with its slow pace and strange occurrences. ★★

Mr. Hobbs Takes a Vacation

(1962, 116 min, US, Henry Koster) *James Stewart, Maureen O'Hara, Fabian, John Saxon.* Stewart brings considerable charm to this genial comedy about Stewart and wife O'Hara taking the kids on vacation, where nothing turns out the way they expect. ★★½ VHS: $19.99

Mr. Holland's Opus

(1995, 142 min, US, Stephen Herek) *Richard Dreyfuss, Glenne Headly, Jay Thomas, Olympia Dukakis, William H. Macy, Alicia Witt, Joanna Gleason.* Though movies featuring dedicated teachers are most assuredly a dime a dozen, and most of them, including *Mr. Holland's Opus*, frequently languish in sentimentality, it's Dreyfuss' solid portrayal which distinguishes this alternately clichéd and absorbing drama. The story follows 30 years in the career of Mr. Holland (Dreyfuss), a budding composer who accepts a seemingly temporary position as a high school music teacher. Flashing through several time periods, the film examines both the extraordinary effect Mr. Holland has on his many students, and his sometimes rocky home life. Dreyfuss ages in the part quite effectively; Headly as Mr. Holland's wife is slyly understated. ★★½ DVD: $19.99, VHS: $9.99

Mister Johnson

(1991, 100 min, GB, Bruce Beresford) *Pierce Brosnan, Edward Woodward, Maynard Eziashi, Denis Quilley.* A well-intentioned but disappointing adaptation of Joyce Cary's novel about colonial Africa. Set in the African bush in the 1920s, the film tells the story of Mr. Johnson, a mischievous black clerk who, in his zealousness to be accepted as an Englishman, manipulates, lies and steals. Despite some strong performances, Beresford's vision seems blurred and it's unclear whether he is making a film about a man who turns his back on his people, the diabolical nature of British colonialism, or the incumbent tragedy in the forced modernization of tribal cultures. Whatever his intent, the result is a bleak and almost misanthropic muddle. ★★ VHS: $14.99

Mr. Jones

(1993, 114 min, US, Mike Figgis) *Richard Gere, Lena Olin, Bill Pullman, Anne Bancroft, Tom Irwin, Lauren Tom, Delroy Lindo.* In a highly flamboyant role, Gere gives an appropriately over-the-top performance as a charming manic-depressive; but even the star's energetic bravado can't elevate this standard romantic drama. Following a suicide attempt, Gere is hospitalized and placed under the care of psychiatrist Olin. As she attempts to treat his neurosis, the two become romantically involved. The implications of a doctor-patient relationship is glossed over in favor of two wayward lovers at odds with the world — which only negates the power of a potentially involving drama. ★★½ DVD: $19.99

Mr. Klein

(1977, 124 min, France, Joseph Losey) *Alain Delon, Jeanne Moreau, Michel Lonsdale.* A disturbing mystery-drama about a self-centered, amoral man (Delon) in Nazi-occupied Paris. He takes advantage of the sweeping anti-Semitism until his world is suddenly shattered when he is mistaken for another — a Jewish Klein. A powerful indictment well-acted and thoughtfully directed. (French with English subtitles) ★★★ DVD: $19.99

Mr. Lucky

(1943, 99 min, US, H.C. Potter) *Cary Grant, Laraine Day, Charles Bickford, Gladys Cooper.* Grant stars in this romantic comedy-drama as the owner of a gambling ship who sets out to sting Day, but ends up falling in love with her and trying to go straight instead. Not one of Grant's better efforts, but mildly entertaining. ★★½

Mr. Magoo

(1997, 85 min, US, Stanley Tong) *Leslie Nielsen, Kelly Lynch, Matt Keeslar, Ernie Hudson, Malcolm McDowell, Miguel Ferrer.* Not that it was a classic to begin with, but the one-joke "Mr. Magoo" cartoon was an intermittently amusing series which found its humor at the expense of a half-blind old codger; Jim Backus voicing the character was the best thing about it. That it has found its way to the big screen in a live-action version is not only puzzling but probable cause to re-examine the collected brain power of Hollywood studios execs but yet again. Nielsen is totally wasted as Magoo, who here gets involved with jewel thieves, bumbling FBI and CIA agents, and a beautiful assassin (Lynch). With no verbal wit at all, it's a collection of tired pratfalls and hoary knockabout shenanigans. ★ DVD: $14.99, VHS: $9.99

Mr. Majestyk

(1974, 104 min, US, Richard Fleischer) *Charles Bronson, Linda Cristal, Lee Purcell.* Surprisingly flavorful Bronson actioner about an ex-con trying to run a straight business, but is pushed too far by local corrupt law enforcers and a sinister Mafia hit man. Elmore Leonard penned the script. ★★½ DVD Dual: $14.99

Mr. Mom

(1983, 92 min, US, Stan Dragoti) *Michael Keaton, Teri Garr, Christopher Lloyd, Martin Mull.* Written by John Hughes, this amiable comedy stars Keaton as a brand new househusband who must contend with housework and wife Garr working 9 to 5. Yes, it's been done before, though Keaton's comic finesse makes most of this familiar territory seem fresh. ★★½ DVD: $14.99

Mr. Nice Guy

(1998, 87 min, Hong Kong, Sammo Hung) *Jackie Chan, Richard Norton.* A lesser Chan vehicle, but even mediocre Jackie is better than most Hollywood action films. As in most of his films, Jackie plays a wide-eyed innocent (in this case, a popular TV chef) who is unwittingly caught up in a battle with drug lords for possession of an incriminating videotape. Once again, plot matters little in these films — it's the action that counts, and *Mr. Nice Guy* has its share of exciting moments (though not enough of them, to be honest). The film is surprisingly sloppy and stupid, considering director Hung's films have included some truly sharp filmmaking, and like *Rumble in the Bronx*, the clunky (anti-)climax has a big vehicle (here, a *gigantic* construction truck) causing the destruction instead of Chan's fists and feet. Still, it's a breezy 87 minutes. ★★½ DVD: $9.99, VHS: $9.99

Mr. North

(1988, 92 min, US, Danny Huston) *Anthony Edwards, Robert Mitchum, Lauren Bacall, Anjelica Huston, Mary Stuart Masterson, Harry Dean Stanton.* John Huston's son Danny took over the reigns of this quirky comedy when his legendary father died just before the start of production. Edwards plays the ingratiating title character, who warms himself to the flaky citizens of Newport's upper class. A real charmer. Based on Thornton Wilder's "Theophilus North." ★★★ DVD Dual: $14.99

Mr. Reliable

(1996, 110 min, Australia, Nadia Tass) *Colin Friels, Jacqueline McKenzie.* Based on a true story, *Mr. Reliable* is an undistinguished Australian comedy which could have been a sleeper but turns out to be more of a snore. Friels stars as Wally, an ex-con who unexpectedly stages a hostage crisis during a nasty heatwave in the summer of 1968. Director Tass strives for whimsy by making the police buffoons and the various neighbors "lovable" eccentrics. But these characters — like Wally himself and his "hostage" Beryl (McKenzie) — are a one-dimensional bunch. *Mr. Reliable* only becomes diverting during the final third, when the temperature rises, tempers flare and actions are taken. ★½ VHS: $9.99

Mister Roberts

(1955, 140 min, US, John Ford & Mervyn Le Roy) *Henry Fonda, James Cagney, Jack Lemmon, William Powell, Betsy Palmer, Nick Adams.* Classic film version of Thomas Heggen and Joshua Logan's Broadway smash about life aboard a military cargo ship during WWII. Fonda, in one of his best roles, plays the title character, a dedicated naval officer who yearns for combat duty. Cagney is terrific as the small-minded ship's captain who's more concerned with his treasured palm tree than with the anxieties of his men. Lemmon won an Oscar for his memorable comic turn as Ensign Pulver, the ship's laundry and morale officer. ★★★★ DVD Letterbox: $19.99, VHS: $14.99, VHS Letterbox: $14.99

Mr. Saturday Night

(1992, 114 min, US, Billy Crystal) *Billy Crystal, David Paymer, Julie Warner, Helen Hunt, Ron Silver, Jerry Lewis.* Crystal makes his directorial debut with this disappointing comedy of a Catskills comedian who flirts with stardom. Reminiscent of Neil Simon's *The Sunshine Boys*, the story follows the tumultuous personal life and career of fictional stand-up comic Buddy Young, Jr. (whose catchphrase "Don't get me started" is as catchy as it is annoying). As played by Crystal, Young is a self-destructive one-man arsenal of one-liners who can no more handle personal relationships than he can the success he spends a lifetime trying to achieve. Though there are funny lines, most of *Mr. Saturday Night* is an overly ambitious and shallow examination of Young's offstage life. ★★ DVD: $9.99

Mr. Skeffington

(1944, 146 min, US, Vincent Sherman) *Bette Davis, Claude Rains, Walter Abel.* A sensational Davis performance is the heart of this grand soap opera with Davis in rare form as a youthful beauty who marries Rains for money and position circa mid-1910s. The film, spanning several decades, follows Davis as she ages and discovers the true meaning of love and loyalty. Rains is terrific as her devoted spouse. ★★★

Mr. Smith Goes to Washington

(1939, 129 min, US, Frank Capra) *James Stewart, Jean Arthur, Claude Rains, Edward Arnold, Thomas Mitchell, Harry Carey, Jr., Beulah Bondi, Eugene Pallette, Guy Kibbee, Jack Carson.* Fresh from the success the year before in *You Can't Take It with You*, director Capra and Stewart reteamed to create, arguably, their finest achievement. Stewart gives a superb performance as an idealistic, newly appointed U.S. Senator and political dupe to Rains (terrific as a corrupt senator) and Arnold (a powerful characterization as boss Taylor). Once there, he uncovers — with more than a little help from secretary Arthur — political wrongdoings, and sets out to expose them. Though Capra is known to be somewhat excessive in patriotic zeal and sentimentality, here they work to his advantage as his characters act according to their moral dictates. This Capra masterpiece features one of the finest ensemble casts ever assembled. ★★★★ DVD: $27.99, VHS: $14.99

Mr. Stitch

(1995, 90 min, US, Roger Avary) *Rutger Hauer, Nia Peeples, Wil Wheaton.* Originally meant to be a TV movie, this direct-to-video release is an ambitious, intelligent sci-fi thriller which adapts the Frankenstein myth to a near-future setting and adds an interesting wrinkle to it. Hauer is a scientist who creates a composite human being from the parts of corpses. His creation (Wheaton), who names himself Lazarus, is superior to a normal human in both intellect and strength, but is wracked by nightmares. Under the supervision of a psychiatrist (Peeples), Lazarus becomes obsessed with determining the cause of his nightmares and discovering what lies beyond the doors of his white-walled cell. *Mr. Stitch* does succumb late in its story to a clichéd showdown between science and the military. But the cast works well together, the design is breathtaking, and Avary truly makes the viewer care about Lazarus' plight. ★★★ VHS: $89.99

Mr. Wrong

(1996, 92 min, US, Nick Castle) *Ellen Degeneres, Bill Pullman, Joan Cusack, Dean Stockwell, Joan Plowright, Robert Goulet.* Making her big screen starring debut, DeGeneres manages to utilize the waifish charm she demonstrates on her TV sitcom, but unfortunately her smiles, grimaces and rolling eyes can't sustain a lackluster screenplay. Ellen plays a successful TV producer who meets whom she thinks is Mr. Right (Pullman). But as he shows his true and obnoxious colors, she is unsuccessful in getting rid of him or getting him to understand the meaning of "it's over." There are few laughs to be had, and the story meanders from mediocre to bad; though the two stars do occasionally generate a degree of compatibility. ★★ DVD: $14.99, VHS: $9.99

Mistress

(1992, 109 min, US, Barry Primus) *Robert De Niro, Robert Wuhl, Martin Landau, Eli Wallach, Danny Aiello, Laurie Metcalf, Sheryl Lee Ralph, Christopher Walken.* Where Robert Altman's *The Player* relentlessly lampooned the world of Hollywood's movers and shakers, Primus' low-budget, independent *Mistress* pokes lighthearted fun at the making of low-budget, independent films. Wuhl stars as a washed-up writer-director who one day receives a call from retired studio hack Landau, who has unearthed one of Wuhl's old scripts. Together, they take the script and run the gauntlet of potential money brokers (De Niro, Aiello and Wallach), each of whom, of course, has a mistress they want in the film. Directed with care and wit by first-timer Primus, the film astutely delves into the challenges facing would-be filmmakers who want to maintain the artistic integrity of their scripts. All of this is done with a good dose of humor and an earnest sense of moral vision. ★★★½

The Mistress

(1953, 106 min, Japan, Shiro Toyoda) *Hideko Takamine, Hiroshi Akutagawa.* This deeply affecting film is not only a beautiful cinematic work, but also an exceptional study of female psychology. A woman believes that she is married to a prosperous man, but discovers that he is already married and that she is no more than his mistress. Set in a period when Japan was moving toward industrialization, *The Mistress* explores the conflict between the demands of society and individual freedom. (Japanese with English subtitles) (aka: *Wild Geese*) ★★★

Mixed Blood

(1985, 97 min, US, Paul Morrissey) *Marilia Pera, Richard Ulacia, Linda Kerridge.* A jet-black comedy from director Morrissey set in New York's notorious Alphabet City about a gang of drug-running youths, under the guidance of a Fagan-like protector and her hunkish son, who set out to control the neighborhood drug trade. ★★★

Mixed Nuts

(1994, 98 min, US, Nora Ephron) *Steve Martin, Madeline Kahn, Juliette Lewis, Anthony LaPaglia, Rob Reiner, Adam Sandler, Garry Shandling.* A contender for the worst film of 1994. Martin headlines this so-called comedy about the wacky (and grim) happenings that befall a band of miserable misfits at a suicide prevention center on Christmas Eve. Considering the cast, one can't but wonder what blackmail-worthy dirt director Ephron may have had on everyone involved to get this "nightmare before Christmas" made. Boring and unsightly, these *Mixed Nuts* should have stayed in the can. ★ DVD Pan & Scan: $9.99, VHS: $9.99

Mo' Better Blues

(1990, 135 min, US, Spike Lee) *Denzel Washington, Giancarlo Esposito, Spike Lee, Joie Lee, Wesley Snipes, Cynda Williams, Bill Nunn, John Turturro, Samuel L. Jackson.* Despite the engaging presence of Washington and a catchy jazz score by Bill Lee and Branford Marsalis, Lee's story of jazz musicians is a disapointment. Saddled with an uninvolving script, Spike fails to capture the creative spark and passion of the jazz world and its habitués. Washington plays Bleek Gilliam, a moderately successful trumpet player and singer who, to the detriment of the plot, is a really "nice guy" whose only flaw seems to be his inability to settle down with just one girlfriend. Don't be completely turned off by this criticism, however, for even Lee's failures are more interesting and enjoyable than most of the stuff that comes out of Hollywood. The one truly inexcusable aspect of the movie is Lee's heinously anti-Semitic depiction of the exploitive Jewish club owners. ★★ DVD: $14.99, VHS: $9.99

Mo' Money

(1992, 91 min, US, Peter MacDonald) *Damon Wayans, Marlon Wayans, Stacey Dash, Joe Santos.* With the success of many "Saturday Night Live" spin-offs, it would follow that giving big-screen treatment to the lovably dysfunctional characters created by "In Loving Color"'s Wayans would produce a natural hit. Unfortunately, the forced insertion of the comic crazies into a cut-and-paste action plot proves to be more "ho-hum" than "ha-ha." Wayans stars (along with brother Marlon) as a con man whose first legitimate job lands him smack in the middle of a major credit card scam. As with most middle-of-the-road productions of this kind, this action-comedy is neither funny enough, nor exciting enough to garner anything more than the occasional bemused chuckle. ★★ DVD Pan & Scan: $24.99, VHS: $9.99

Mobsters

(1991, 104 min, US, Michael Karbelnikoff) *Christian Slater, Patrick Dempsey, Richard Grieco, Costas Mandylor, F. Murray Abraham, Michael Gambon, Anthony Quinn, Lara Flynn Boyle, Christopher Penn.* A stylishly made but flat underworld crime saga riddled with uneven characterizations and lots of bullets. The story follows the beginnings of the youthful partners-in-crime "Lucky" Luciano (Slater), Meyer Lansky (Dempsey) and "Bugsy" Siegel (Grieco). Ostensibly about the birth of a national organized crime syndicate, the film is content to be merely a glossy, bloody shoot 'em up. Even with an admirable re-creation of 1920s New York, *Mobsters* is recommended only for those who can't get enough of gangster stories. ★★ VHS: $7.49

Moby Dick

(1956, 116 min, US, John Huston) *Gregory Peck, Richard Basehart, Orson Welles.* It is generally agreed that Peck was miscast in the role of Captain Ahab, but his performance detracts nothing from Huston's masterful interpretation of Herman Melville's classic novel. Extraordinary action scenes abound in this immortal sea epic. (Remade in 1998) ★★★½ DVD: $14.99

Moby Dick

(1998, 145 min, US, Franc Roddam) *Patrick Stewart, Henry Thomas, Ted Levine, Gregory Peck.* With all good intention the folks at USA network endevoured to put some modern heart and soul into the Herman Melville classic that was so eloquently committed to film by John Huston in 1958. The result, however, falls like a poorly cast harpoon catching nothing but water and leaving its prey unscathed. As the lugubrious and vengeful Captain Ahab, Stewart can't get his thespian engines started as he resorts mainly to fits of loud ranting completely lacking in subtlety. Even at 145 minutes, the whole affair seems rushed and jumbled, and lost is the stoic, almost mystical sense of dread that pervades the original. ★½ DVD: $19.99, VHS: $9.99

The Mod Squad

(1999, 95 min, US, Scott Silver) *Claire Danes, Giovanni Ribisi, Omar Epps, Dennis Farina, Steve Harris, Josh Brolin, Michael Lerner.* Though it really wants to please, this big-screen version of the early 1970s TV show about three young adults (all with records) going undercover for the police misses the mark. The writers have basically reinvented the TV characters (and for the worse): Julie (Danes) is a softie who can be hurt by romance; Pete (Ribisi) is now a lovable screw-up; and Linc (Epps) is, well, kinda bland. They uncover some sort of police corruption scheme we've seen a million times before. There are nods to the era, like a musical cue from *Car Wash*, '70s zooms, and sayings like "right on," but in the end, *The Mod Squad* is nothing more than a conventional '90s cop flick. ★½ DVD: $9.99, VHS: $9.99

Modern Problems

(1981, 91 min, US, Ken Shapiro) *Chevy Chase, Patti D'Arbanville, Mary Kay Place, Nell Carter, Dabney Coleman.* Chase lets loose as an air traffic controller who acquires telekinetic powers after exposure to nuclear waste. Some funny bits thanks to Chase's mugging, but very silly. ★★ VHS: $9.99

Modern Romance

(1980, 100 min, US, Albert Brooks) *Albert Brooks, Kathryn Harrold, Bruno Kirby, James L. Brooks.* An insightful and playfully funny therapeutic comedy session written and directed by A. Brooks. He plays a highly neurotic film editor looking for romance, but obsessively drawn to Harrold. As with most Brooks films, his deadpan though manic observations are not for everyone; but he has such a unique view of the world, it's hard to resist his charms. ★★★

Modern Times

(1936, 89 min, US, Charles Chaplin) *Charles Chaplin, Paulette Goddard.* When the backers of Rene Clair's *À Nous la Liberté* prepared to sue Chaplin over the similarities they found in *Modern Times*, Clair wouldn't hear of it, as he was honored by the homage — though over the years Chaplin did find himself in hot water over the film's supposed Commie leanings. At any rate, this extraordinary silent comedy (Chaplin's last silent) is a wildly funny and touching social satire. Victimized by the machine age, Chaplin goes berserk and inadvertently leads a factory riot. The radiant Goddard plays the orphan waif with whom he falls in love. ★★★★ DVD Chaplin Collection - 2 disc set: $29.99, VHS: $19.99

Modern Vampires

(1999, 95 min, US, Richard Elfman) *Casper Van Dien, Kim Cattrall, Natasha Gregson Wagner, Natasha Lyonne, Rod Steiger.* A comic horror movie that is neither funny nor scary, *Modern Vampires* still has plenty of skin and gore galore to keep it from being a complete waste of time. This updated version of Dracula has Dallas (Van Dien, who coproduced) returning to present-day Los Angeles to recruit fresh young newcomer Nico (Wagner) into bloodletting, and stop Professor Van Helsing (Steiger) from making a killing. This cheaply made production seems to have spent its entire budget on the buckets of blood, but director Elfman forgot to make any of the antics interesting. ★★½ DVD: $14.99, VHS: $102.99

The Moderns

(1988, 128 min, US, Alan Rudolph) *Keith Carradine, Linda Fiorentino, Geneviève Bujold, John Lone, Kevin J. O'Connor.* An exquisite-looking period drama set against the backdrop of the Paris art scene of the 1920s. Carradine, Fiorentino and Lone are American expatriates who become involved in romantic intrigue as well as an art forgery scam. Bujold steals the film as an art dealer, and O'Connor makes a splendid Hemingway. ★★★ DVD Letterbox: $19.99

Mogambo

(1953, 115 min, US, John Ford) *Clark Gable, Ava Gardner, Grace Kelly, Donald Sinden.* Solid remake of 1932's *Red Dust*, with Gable repeating his role from that film as a hunter in the wilds of Africa who's involved with both earthy Gardner and society girl Kelly. Gardner is especially good as the brassy showgirl. ★★★

The Mole People

(1956, 78 min, US, Virgil Vogel) *John Agar, Hugh Beaumont.* 1950s B-film thespian Agar and Beaumont (Beaver's dad) star as explorers who climb down a hole in Asia and find a lost underground civilization of albino Sumerians, who have the half-human Mole People as their slaves. But their minions revolt and save our brave captive heroes from the surface. ★½

Moll Flanders

(1996, 123 min, US, Pen Densham) *Robin Wright, Morgan Freeman, Stockard Channing, John Lynch, Brenda Fricker, Geraldine James.* Daniel Defoe's classic novel has been dumbed-down so that every man, woman, child or frog in the audience can understand it. Badly paced, this updating awkwardly stumbles around the story of an orphaned young woman doing her best to survive in 18th-century London. Potentially potent material is pureed into an insipid source for cheers of "You go, girl" from the Oprah crowd. A popcorn-muncher like *Mission: Impossible* has more to say about an innocent trying to survive in a corrupt, cynical world than this "important" film. Freeman and Wright give their best to undeserving material. ★½ DVD: $9.99

Molly

(1999, 87 min, US, John Duigan) *Elisabeth Shue, Aaron Eckhart, Jill Hennessy, D.W. Moffett.* Shue plays an autistic woman who becomes quite a handful for her upwardly mobile brother when he must take care of her. Wacky misadventures ensue (oh, those crazy autistics!) until she undergoes experimental surgery and becomes "normal." But will the change be too sudden and too great? This wretched amalgam/ripoff of *Rain Man* and *Charly* begins as a wholly insulting, drastically unfunny "comedy," then predictably shifts gears to tug the heartstrings. Shue and Eckhart both overact, and the direction by Duigan is uninspired. ★ DVD: $14.99, VHS: $6.99

The Molly Maguires

(1970, 123 min, US, Martin Ritt) *Sean Connery, Richard Harris, Samantha Eggar.* Connery and Harris give earnest performances in this gritty drama of clashing coal miners in Pennsylvania during the 1870s. Solid direction by Ritt. ★★★ DVD Letterbox: $14.99, VHS: $14.99

Mom and Dad Save the World

(1992, 88 min, US, Greg Beeman) *Teri Garr, Jeffrey Jones, Jon Lovitz, Thalmus Rasulala, Wallace Shawn, Eric Idle.* Some nice special effects can't help this mildy amusing sci-fi adventure/spoof. Garr and Jones are celebrating 20 years of marriage with a weekend getaway when the evil Lovitz, petty dictator of a far-away planet, kidnaps them with the intent to marry Garr. As it turns out, his planet is inhabited by imbeciles (the screenwriters must hail from there, too), so Mom and Dad's job is markedly easier than it might have been. ★★ VHS: $9.99

Mommie Dearest

(1981, 129 min, US, Frank Perry) *Faye Dunaway, Diana Scarwid, Steve Forrest, Howard da Silva.* The campy, spirited version of Christine Crawford's novel detailing her abused childhood as the adopted daughter of actress Joan Crawford. Dunaway pulls out all the stops in a no-holds-barred portrayal of the movie queen. (Ironically, Crawford herself remarked that if her life story were ever filmed, she wanted Dunaway to play her.) The film which immortalized the line, "No wire hangers!" ★★★ DVD Letterbox: $14.99, VHS: $14.99

Mon Oncle

(1958, 116 min, France, Jacques Tati) *Jacques Tati, Jeanne-Pierre Zola.* Tati's bumbling M. Hulot confronts modern architecture in this hilarious pratfall comedy. Without relying on dialogue, Tati has created a true classic in visual farce. ★★★★ DVD: $29.99

Mon Oncle D'Amerique

(1980, 123 min, France, Alain Resnais) *Gérard Depardieu, Nicole Garcia.* A brilliant and witty contemporary comedy on the human condition. The title refers to the proverbial French uncle who, fortune made, will return with his riches to solve every problem. A comedy about the drama of life that weaves its way through a metaphysical maze in its attempt to understand the motivations, ambitions and frustrations of man. (French with English subtitles) ★★★★ DVD: $19.99, VHS: $14.99

Mona Lisa

(1986, 104 min, GB, Neil Jordan) *Bob Hoskins, Michael Caine, Cathy Tyson, Robbie Coltrane, Sammi Davis.* Hoskins won international acclaim for his searing performance as a dim-witted Cockney thug who falls hopelessly in love with a beautiful prostitute (Tyson). Initially hired as her chauffeur, a warm relationship develops between the two, and the ex-con moonlights as detective to track down her missing girlfriend. Caine also stars as a slimy crime boss. A film bristling with sardonic humor and unnerving suspense. ★★★½ DVD: $39.99

Mondo

(1996, 80 min, France, Tony Gatlif) *Ovidiu Balan, Philippe Petit, Pierrette Fesch.* Writer-director Gatlif's charming and poignant adventure of a young Gypsy boy, *Mondo* is exquisitely photographed and beautifully performed. This natural, impressionistic film concerns the 10-year-old Mondo (Balan), who wanders around Nice asking various individuals to take him home with them. While some people ignore his request, others offer him temporary companionship. Each stranger, however, touches his life in some remarkable way. Offering a rare glimpse of the world through the eyes of this curious child, *Mondo* is absorbing and quietly powerful. Gatlif admires the innocent yet streetwise Gypsy lifestyle, and he coaxes a highly affecting performance from Balan. (French with English subtitles) ★★★ VHS: $29.99

Charlie Chaplin takes on technology in *Modern Times*

Mondo New York

(1988, 83 min, US, Harvey Keith) Lock up the children, throw away your inhibitions and most of all, hide your pet mice before you descend into the rotten core of the Big Apple in this bustling tour of New York's entertainment underbelly. Amusing, nauseating yet always fascinating, first-time director Keith takes us on a voyeuristic journey to the clubs and back-alley downtown venues to observe performance artists and other assorted nocturnal denizens perform their bizarre, twisted and scandalous acts to appreciative audiences. The extraordinaire Dean and the Weenies will have you rushing to the rewind control to listen again to their infamous post-punk anthem, "Fuck You!" Let the weak of stomach be warned — this ain't Kansas, Dorothy! ★★★

Mondo Topless

(1966, 60 min, US, Russ Meyer) A documentary on the topless craze of the Sixties. Meyer's trademark deep-voiced narration is truly hilarious. With a cast of cantilevered cuties including big-busted Babette Bardot, capaciously domed Darla Paris and the "buxotic" Darlene Grey. ★★

Mondo Trasho

(1969, 95 min, US, John Waters) *Divine, Mary Vivian Pearce.* This celluloid atrocity by America's Father of Filth, Waters, is visual assault and battery, laying waste an already crumbling civilization. Explore a world oozing with sex, violence and overwhelming seaminess. It's just another day in the life of a 300-pound transvestite. Divine, in skin-tight, gold lamé Capri pants, runs over Pearce in a 1959 Cadillac and commits other acts of mayhem. There's also sightings of the Virgin Mary, drug-addicted doctors, nasty 1950s rock tunes, nods to *The Wizard of Oz* and *Freaks*, and the requisite dismemberment of feet and hands. ★★

Money for Nothing

(1993, 90 min, US, Ramon Menendez) *John Cusack, Benicio del Toro, Debi Mazar, Michael Madsen, Michael Rapaport, Philip Seymour Hoffman.* Based on the amazingly true story of Joey Coyle (played by Cusack), a Philadelphia Average Joe who stumbles upon mountains of cash, *Money for Nothing* totally ignores the fact that in real life, Joey had a history of drug and psychological problems — an explanation needed as to why Joey totally goes off kilter when money becomes no object. Even without the subtext, however, this comedy-drama still fails — its attempts to extricate humor from Joey's moral dilemma come off pathetic rather than farcical. ★½ DVD: $9.99, VHS: $19.99

The Money Pit

(1986, 91 min, US, Richard Benjamin) *Tom Hanks, Shelley Long, Alexander Godunov, Maureen Stapleton.* A modern reworking of the Cary Grant comedy *Mr. Blandings Builds His Dream House.* Hanks and Long buy a suburban New York home real cheap, and after moving in and starting remodeling, discover why the low cost. Very few of the gags work here; most of this is predictable, unfunny and terribly over-produced. Stick to the original. ★½ DVD: $14.99, VHS: $7.49

Money Talks

(1997, 92 min, US, Brett Ratner) *Chris Tucker, Charlie Sheen, Heather Locklear, Paul Sorvino, Veronica Cartwright, David Warner.* Loud, abrasive, and just not that funny, *Money Talks*, like its high-pitched, squeaky-voiced star Tucker, tries to be a lot more than what it really is. It wants to be *48 HRS.*

What's up on the screen is altogether a different matter. As annoying as he is animated, Tucker plays a small-time hustler who's set up by ambitious reporter Sheen. En route to prison, Tucker is framed for the murders of police guards and fellow prisoners. Tucker eventually enlists the aid of Sheen. Then they're both suspected of a series of murders, and they must clear their names. For a comedy, there's an alarmingly high body count. ★½ DVD: $14.99, VHS: $9.99

Money Train

(1995, 110 min, US, Joseph Ruben) *Wesley Snipes, Woody Harrelson, Jennifer Lopez, Robert Blake, Bill Nunn.* *Money Train* is an actioner/heist movie which doesn't deliver on either aspect. With a contrived screenplay which rarely makes sense, mugging from its two stars, and a misrepresented plot development, about the only thing this has going for it is its impressive location shooting and the occasional chemistry of Misters Snipes and Harrelson. They play transit cops (and foster brothers) who work for the New York City transit system. In between their undercover assignments, they talk of robbing the "money train" (the payroll car), and the plans for such are set in motion. The two actors demonstrate none of the comic zing from *White Men Can't Jump*, though due in large part to the silly dialogue they are forced to scream at one another. ★★ DVD: $19.99, VHS: $9.99

Monika

(1952, 82 min, Sweden, Ingmar Bergman) *Harriet Andersson, Lars Ekborg.* A sultry, irresponsible teenager (Andersson) from a working-class district in Stockholm spends an idyllic summer with a shy and poetic boy on the tranquil islands off the Swedish coast. Basking in the sun and living for the moment, the two lovers explore their emotions and sensuality until the cold winds of autumn sweep away their innocent dreams and force them back to the city where Monika, saddled with an unwanted pregnancy, is forced to marry and settle down. This early Bergman effort is a tender yet unsentimental look at a love affair extinguished all too suddenly. (Swedish with English subtitles) ★★★ VHS: $29.99

Monkey Business

(1931, 77 min, US, Norman Z. McLeod) *Groucho Marx, Harpo Marx, Chico Marx, Zeppo Marx, Thelma Todd.* Those wild and zany Marx Brothers

The Marx Brothers are a barrel of laughs in *Monkey Business*

start out as stowaways on an ocean liner and end up rescuing a kidnapped damsel in distress in a run-down barn, all the while spewing out some of their best lines of anarchistic, iconoclastic chatter. The first of their movies written directly for the screen is a sheer delight, with gun-toting tough guys, disgruntled molls, befuddled shipboard officers and a bevy of beauties who live to be chased by the ever-lecherous Harpo. Zeppo exudes warmth and charm as a man in love; Groucho and Chico exhibit a physical agility matched only by the running of their mouths. A fine madness. ★★★½ VHS: $14.99

Monkey Business

(1952, 97 min, US, Howard Hawks) *Cary Grant, Ginger Rogers, Marilyn Monroe, Charles Coburn.* Grant is the archetypal absent-minded professor searching for the drug of eternal youth. Both he and wife Rogers give the elixir a test spin, along with their new roadster; youth is fleeting, and mercifully so. Marilyn is the secretary of every corporate executive's dream — like the boss says, anybody can type. Director Hawks has great fun with this happy exercise in regression. ★★★ DVD: $14.99

Monkey Grip

(1982, 101 min, Australia, Ken Cameron) *Noni Hazlehurst, Colin Friels.* The story of Nora (Hazlehurst), an independent, strong-willed woman trying to raise a daughter alone amidst the underground world of musicians, actors and writers. The film follows unconventional Nora as she becomes involved with a brooding, sexually volcanic man (Friels) whose fascination with her becomes dangerously obsessive. Good performances by Hazlehurst and Friels help gloss over the story's melodramatics. ★★½

Monkey Trouble

(1994, 93 min, US, Franco Amurri) *Thora Birch, Mimi Rogers, Christopher McDonald, Harvey Keitel.* A nice family film, *Monkey Trouble* follows Dodger, a kleptomaniac simian, who runs away from owner Keitel and a life of crime and straight into the arms of Birch, a young girl who longs for a pet. She soon discovers the primate's propensity for pick-pocketing and retrains him. Keitel is determined to get Dodger back and get even, with often funny results. ★★★ DVD: $12.99, VHS: $9.99

M

Monkeybone

(2001, 87 min, US, Henry Selick) *Brendan Fraser, Bridget Fonda, Whoopi Goldberg, Chris Kattan, Giancarlo Esposito, Rose McGowan, Dave Foley, Megan Mullally, Voice of: John Turturro.* There are moments in *Monkeybone* that are so unbelievably bad, you can't take your eyes off the screen lest you miss something even worse. Fraser plays a self-deprecating cartoonist who falls into a coma and awakes in a freakish fantasyland of collected dreams and nightmares. Director Selick proved himself capable of macabre fantasy with *The Nightmare Before Christmas*, but the animated sequences here are leaden and joyless. They feel like they're part of another movie, bracketed by a half-baked love story between Fraser and Fonda and a subplot that has Fraser's eternally horny alter ego — an annoyingly animated monkey — assuming his body. The film neglects to develop several promising ideas introduced early on, and looks to have been sliced-and-diced in the editing room. ★½ DVD Letterbox Special Edition: $9.99, VHS: $9.99

Monsieur Beaucaire

(1946, 93 min, US, George Marshall) *Bob Hope, Joan Caulfield, Patric Knowles, Cecil Kellaway.* Booth Tarkington's novel of court intrigue gets the Hope treatment, and the result is a consistently funny romp. Set in 18th-century Europe, the story has Bob playing a barber who is forced to impersonate royalty, much against his will. And, of course, the charade puts him in constant danger. At this point in his career, Hope could do this sort of comedy in his sleep. But to his credit, he gives an engaging comic performance, and he gets to recite some dandy one-liners. ★★★ DVD Double Feature: $14.99, VHS: $9.99

Monsieur Hire

(1989, 81 min, France, Patrice Leconte) *Michel Blanc, Sandrine Bonnaire, Luc Thuillier.* Blanc delivers an exquisitely understated performance as the voyeuristic anti-hero in this haunting thriller. Suspected of murdering a young woman, Blanc's favorite pastime is to spy on his attractive neighbor, Alice (Bonnaire). She soon becomes aware of his fixation and, much to his horror, tries to befriend him. Alice's boyfriend, Emile (Thuillier), seems to have no objection to her flirtations, for reasons which become obvious only at the film's clever conclusion. Director Leconte exhibits a fine sense of detail and imbues the film with a compellingly eerie atmosphere. Based on a 1933 novel by George Simenon, which was first adapted for the screen in Julien Duvivier's 1946 *Panique*. (French with English subtitles) ★★★

Monsieur Verdoux

(1947, 128 min, US, Charles Chaplin) *Charles Chaplin, Martha Raye.* From an idea suggested by Orson Welles, Chaplin fashioned Hollywood's first black comedy about a wife murderer who feels amateurish compared to what the governments of the world were doing. Chaplin took a long time to make talkies; but when he did, he made certain that they talked. Fortunately the long passages of philosophical digressions, while obvious, are interesting and make a nice binder 'twixt the comedy set pieces. Raye holds her own against the acknowledged master of physical comedy as he tries many ways to murder her. ★★★½ DVD 2-disc set: $24.99

Monsieur Vincent

(1947, 112 min, France, Leon Carre) *Pierre Fresnay, Lise Delamare.* This excellent biography of

Christina Ricci (l.) and Charlize Theron in *Monster*

St. Vincent de Paul, who gave up his worldly possessions and devoted his life to the poor, preaching charity and understanding, won an Oscar for Best Foreign Film of 1948. Set in 17th-century France, the film successfully avoids the sententious piety which permeates most religious bios, weaving instead with quiet fervor and ineffable grace a story of a saintly hero with the courage of his convictions. Fresnay portrays the title role with a masterful performance. (French with English subtitles) ★★★½ VHS: $24.99

Monsoon Wedding

(2002, 114 min, US/India, Mira Nair) *Naseeruddin Shah, Lillete Dubey, Shefali Shetty, Vijay Raaz, Tilotama Shome, Vasundhara Das, Kulbhushan Kharbanda.* The colorful pageantry of a traditional four-day wedding ceremony is the backdrop for this sublimely intoxicating celebration of family, tradition, love and life in New Delhi. As an entire extended family converges for an arranged marriage, perceptions are challenged, temptations mount, secrets are revealed and relationships become as stormy as the weather. The pathos is laid on pretty thick, but the intimacy with which director Nair examines her characters makes for an exuberant comedy of manners. Nair's documentary roots are evident in the vibrant, guerrilla-style sequences that show the bustling enormity of the city, a contrasting motif for her recurring theme of class separation. Inadvertent similarities to an inexplicably popular film about a Greek family of eccentrics might prompt some to label this one *My Big Fat Hindi Wedding*, but don't let that scare you. (English and Hindi and Punjabi with English subtitles) ★★★½ DVD: $14.99, VHS: $9.99

The Monster (Il Mostro)

(1996, 111 min, Italy, Roberto Benigni) *Roberto Benigni, Nicoletta Braschi, Michel Blanc.* As a physical comedian, the versatile Benigni is like a Jacques Tati with a raging libido, or a Jim Carrey properly potty trained. His unique predilection for plot lines would usually be thought of as inappropriate for this kind of buffoonery. In *The Monster*, he plays a small-time shoplifter mistaken for a sex fiend who has been murdering and mutilating the town's female population for the last 18 years. When policewoman Braschi volunteers to use her wiles to entrap him, she soon discovers that while he is guilty of many things, murder is not among them. Once again Benigni manages to get a lot of mileage out of some pretty tired sex jokes by sheer force of will, physical grace and outright silliness. (Italian with English subtitles) ★★½ DVD: $24.99

Monster

(2003, 109 min, US, Patty Jenkins) *Charlize Theron, Christina Ricci, Bruce Dern, Scott Wilson, Pruitt Taylor Vince, Lee Tergesen, Annie Corley.* In a performance that is nothing short of a revelation, Theron is stunning as real-life serial killer Aileen Wuornos, a prostitute who murdered several of her johns along the cold, deserted roads intersecting the Florida interstate. In her feature film debut, director Jenkins has created an unforgettable portrait of this woman, framed in an impressive tableau of desire, oppression and violence. A victim of sexual abuse as a child and forced into prostitution at age 13, Wuornos is an embittered, hard-edged, suicidal adult who bounces from one bad relationship to another. When she meets young lesbian Selby (Ricci in an uncharacteristically awkward performance), and though not gay, Wuornos responds to the woman's kindness and compassion — the two beginning a tentative relationship with Aileen taking the traditional "husband" role in looking after her girlfriend. Finding roadblocks at every turn for employment because of her past, Aileen turns to the only work she knows. But when a trick turns violent, she kills him in self-defense, setting in motion an almost cathartic series of murders. There are times one feels genuine pity for Wuornos, thanks to Jenkins' anguished storytelling and Oscar winner Theron's bravura portrayal, but neither lets the viewer forget that this is foremost a tale of a killer. Jenkins downplays the inherent sociopolitical aspect of a story of a woman raging against men, and finds at its core a bittersweet love story of two lonely misfits. At times difficult and not always fluid as it should be, *Monster* is also mesmerizing, a bold and hypnotic film that thankfully suggests in this tragic case there was no black or white. ★★★½ DVD: $26.99

Monster from Green Hell

(1957, 71 min, US, Kenneth Crane) *Jim Davis, Robert Griffin.* A cheapie B-movie about a government rocket that crashes in the Congo, spawning mutant insects. To keep production costs down, director Crane actually lifted some scenes straight from his past films. ★ VHS: $14.99

Monster in a Box

(1992, 96 min, US, Nick Broomfield) *Spalding Gray.* Renowned storyteller/actor Gray returns to the screen to perform yet another of his insightful and hilarious monologues (the uninitiated should most definitely see *Swimming to Cambodia*). Sitting in front of a live audience, Gray engagingly prattles on about the difficulties he encountered over the past several years while trotting around the globe in a desperate attempt to escape his "monster in a box," a monolithic 1,800-page autobiographical manuscript which has, lurking in its pages, the death of his mother. In his typical fashion, Gray intricately weaves his tales of joy and woe, along the way evoking in his audience a myriad of emotional responses ranging from outright hilarity to somber reflection. ★★★

Monster's Ball

(2001, 111 min, US, Marc Forster) *Billy Bob Thornton, Halle Berry, Peter Boyle, Heath Ledger, Sean Combs, Mos Def.* Somewhat overshadowed by Berry's historic win as the first African-American woman to win an Academy Award for Best Actress is the fact that she's sensational in this compelling drama, itself a penetrating look at loneliness, racism and loss. Halle plays a working mother whose husband has been executed. Thornton (who should have been in award contention himself but was shutout) is the white guard who oversaw the execution. How these two emotionally distant, fragile souls come together forms the core of an often sexy, always moving story. Though the film is given to possibly one-too-many tragedies, it's potent viewing. ★★★ DVD Lions Gate Signature Series: $19.99

Monsters, Inc.

(2001, 88 min, US, Pete Docter, Lee Unkrich, David Silverman) *Voices of: John Goodman, Billy Crystal, Steve Buscemi, Mary Gibbs, James Coburn, Jennifer Tilly, John Ratzenberger.* "You won't believe your eye" reads the ads for Disney and Pixar's entertaining animated comedy. And, for the most part, you won't. For *Monsters, Inc.* is a funny, cheerful and imaginative look at what goes on on the other side of the closet door where children often think monsters lurk. The teeming city of Monstropolis gets its source of power by collecting the screams of children. And there's none better at his job than Sullivan (nicely voiced by Goodman), a big, hairy creature who could be third cousin to the Abominable Snowman (who happens to make a cameo appearance). When a three-year-old human girl accidentally enters this forbidden land, Sullivan and his one-eyed sidekick Mike (Crystal) have their hands full in trying to return her back beyond the closet door. The animation is superb, and the two lead characters make quite an appealing pair. However, *Monsters, Inc.* does occasionally falter due to a sentimental streak pulsing throughout the film. No matter, it's full of good cheer and prankish laughs, enough to keep any adult or child captivated. ★★★½ DVD 2-disc set: $29.99, VHS With new animated short: $24.99

Monte Walsh

(1970, 100 min, US, William A. Fraker) *Lee Marvin, Jack Palance, Jeanne Moreau, Jim Davis.* Aging cowboys Marvin and Palance watch the West they knew being bought up by Eastern conglomerates and trivialized in traveling Wild West shows. As the open ranges get fenced in, some give up and settle down, some become outlaws and some just hang on. Perceptive characterizations and stunning location photography combine to deliver a bittersweet ode to a dying way of life. ★★★

Montenegro

(1981, 98 min, Sweden, Dusan Makavejev) *Susan Anspach, Erland Jospehson.* This marvelously anarchic and subversive black comedy stars Anspach as a sexually frustrated housewife who is lured away from her beautiful home and family and tumbles into the Zanzibar, a Yugoslavian bar filled with a carnival world of misfits and twisted characters. Filmed in Sweden by a Yugoslavian director in the English language. ★★★ DVD: $14.99, VHS: $14.99

A Month by the Lake

(1995, 92 min, GB, John Irvin) *Vanessa Redgrave, James Fox, Uma Thurman, Alida Valli, Alessandro Gassman.* As a genre, tales of hapless Brits seeking solar solace in the Italian countryside have provided some gems; this tiresome comedy isn't one of them. Redgrave plays Miss Bentley, a single, middle-aged woman who, during the spring of 1937, travels to the Lake Como resort of her youth. There she meets the distinctly unlikable and rather pompous Major Wilshaw (Fox) and inexplicably chases after him with the chutzpah of a schoolgirl. Thurman comes on the scene as the American nanny of a boisterous Italian family and she immediately bedazzles Wilshaw. The film's inept script and awkward direction attempt to make broad comedy out of the gener-

ational rivalry between Redgrave and Thurman, but the result is mostly silly, irksome and embarrassing. ★½ DVD: $19.99

A Month in the Country

(1988, 96 min, GB, Pat O'Connor) *Colin Firth, Kenneth Branagh, Natasha Richardson.* A beautifully filmed, sensitive adaptation of J.L. Carr's novel about two WWI veterans who, emotionally ravaged by their wartime experiences, come to terms with their past during an idyllic summer in the English countryside. Firth and Branagh both offer outstanding performances as the men; Richardson is the daughter of the local vicar who falls in love with Firth. ★★★½

Monty Python and the Holy Grail

(1974, 90 min, GB, Terry Gilliam & Terry Jones) *Graham Chapman, John Cleese, Terry Gilliam, Eric Idle, Terry Jones, Michael Palin.* The Python troupe takes on King Arthur in this insane farce set amongst the castles, lochs and moors of Scotland. Like the early works of Woody Allen, this is a scattershot affair with gags flying at every turn; miraculously, most hit their mark. The result is a hilarious and inspired excursion into knighthood, medieval pagentry, religious sentiment and transvestism. ★★★½ DVD 2-disc set: $29.99, DVD Collector's Edition: $49.99, VHS: $14.99

Monty Python Live at the Hollywood Bowl

(1982, 78 min, GB, Terry Hughes) *Graham Chapman, John Cleese, Terry Gilliam, Eric Idle, Terry Jones, Michael Palin, Carol Cleveland.* Britain's premiere loonies invade Los Angeles with this madcap series of sketches and routines. All of their favorite concerns, including God, death, and life in heaven, are hilariously explored. A must for Python fans. ★★★ VHS Out of Print: $9.99

Monty Python's Life of Brian

(1979, 93 min, GB, Terry Jones) *Graham Chapman, John Cleese, Terry Gilliam, Eric Idle, Terry Jones, Michael Palin.* The Gospel According to Monty Python! This side-splitting spoof lampoons 2,000 years of religious thought and mankind's hysterical hankering for a good Messiah. Perhaps Python's best

feature. Just remember — always look on the bright side of life. ★★★½ DVD Letterbox Criterion Collection: $39.99, DVD: $14.99, VHS: $9.99

Monty Python's the Meaning of Life

(1983, 101 min, GB, Terry Jones) *Graham Chapman, John Cleese, Terry Gilliam, Terry Jones, Michael Palin, Carol Cleveland, Matt Frewer.* This effort from the Python troupe is a wild collection of vignettes on the humorous aspects of existence — from conception through demise. Included are the educational song and dance production, "Every Sperm Is Sacred," and an unforgettable restaurant retching sketch. ★★★ DVD Letterbox Special Edition: $14.99, VHS Special Edition: $9.99

Monument Ave.

(1998, 93 min, US, Ted Demme) *Denis Leary, Jason Barry, Billy Crudup, John Diehl, Greg Dulli, Noah Emmerich, Ian Hart, Famke Janssen, Colm Meaney, Martin Sheen, Jeanne Tripplehorn.* Leary is Bobby O'Grady, the nominal head of a bunch of neighborhood guys, some of the working class, still young but much too old to be getting their kicks from setting yuppie car alarms. One night, they witness an execution. Neighborhood boss Jacky (Meany) can count on everyone's collective amnesia. What Jacky doesn't get is Bobby's barely controlled rage, incited through the pain of self-recognition and reflected through the eyes of his visiting Irish cousin. A desperate act, an attempt at freedom and the apparent moral rectitude of a cop mirror the inherent conflict of the law of the street vs. our communally held illusions as to how we govern ourselves. A thoughtfully directed, well-constructed film, highlighted by a uniformly excellent ensemble. (aka: *Snitch*) ★★★ DVD: $14.99, VHS: $9.99

Moon 44

(1989, 102 min, US/Germany, Roland Emmerich) *Michael Paré, Malcolm McDowell, Lisa Eichhorn, Stephen Geoffreys, Roscoe Lee Browne.* Paré headlines this outer space actioner about yet another corporate conspiracy in a future where profit is the bottom line and the workers are expendable. Light years better than anyone would expect it to be, with serious performances and a wholehearted attempt at special effects. Not just another money-making *Star Wars* clone. ★★½ DVD: $14.99

The Monty Python troupe ridicules pompous Biblical epics in *Monty Python's Life of Brian*

The Moon in the Gutter

(1983, 126 min, France, Jean-Jacques Beineix) *Nastassja Kinski, Gérard Depardieu, Victoria Abril, Dominique Pinon.* After the incredible promise of *Diva*, Beineix's eerie follow-up was greeted with puzzled shrugs by the most sympathetic critics. Its reputation aside, however, this sordid tale of obsession is bristling with technical wizardry and sinuous noirism. A fascinating failure. (French with English subtitles) ★★

Moon over Broadway

(1999, 98 min, US, Chris Hegedus & D.A. Pennebaker) *Carol Burnett, Philip Bosco.* A fascinating behind-the-scenes look at the making of the Broadway comedy "Moon over Broadway," which marked Burnett's return to the New York stage after a 30-year absence. The production is followed from first rehearsals to opening night to closing as directors Pennebaker and Hegedus succinctly capture the many faces of the creative process at work. ★★★½ DVD: $29.99, VHS: $24.99

Moon over Miami

(1941, 91 min, US, Walter Lang) *Betty Grable, Carole Landis, Don Ameche, Robert Cummings, Jack Haley, Charlotte Greenwood.* Enjoyable Grable musical about two sisters (Grable, Landis) who go millionaire hunting in Miami. They find Ameche, Cummings and Haley. Greenwood is a particular delight as Grable's cohort who joins Betty and her sister on their quest. ★★½

Moon over Parador

(1988, 105 min, US, Paul Mazursky) *Richard Dreyfuss, Sonia Braga, Raul Julia, Jonathan Winters, Fernando Rey, Ed Asner, Dick Cavett.* Energetic though silly comedy from Mazursky set in the small (fictional) Latin American country of Parador whose hated dictator dies, and is replaced by a look-alike — an American actor. Dreyfuss has a field day as the politically naive actor who gets a quick lesson in politics and love when he impersonates the country's ruler. ★★½ DVD: $14.99

Moondance

(1995, 92 min, Germany/Ireland, Dagmar Hirtz) *Ruaidhri Conroy, Ian Shaw, Julia Brendler, Marianne Faithfull.* Two Irish brothers — wacky ne'er-do-wells who "live by their own rules" — share a strong bond, an unshakable familial love that can't be tainted; except by a sexy young thing, of course. When their aunt complains that the younger sibling must go to school instead of galavanting around the Irish countryside all day, her teenage companion — a pretty, bright lass — offers to tutor the irrepressible lad. The close-knit bros are soon embroiled in a web of jealousy and lust of a strictly juvenile bent. Clichéd, hackneyed, lightly annoying drama plays like a Gaelic "Dawson's Creek" — if you like airy teen angst, you may get some enjoyment out of this piffle. ★★ DVD: $19.99, VHS: $9.99

Moonlight and Valentino

(1995, 105 min, US, David Anspaugh) *Elizabeth Perkins, Gwyneth Paltrow, Whoopi Goldberg, Kathleen Turner, Jon Bon Jovi.* A familiar story of a woman coming to terms with the death of her husband and of her relationship with her supportive friends and family, *Moonlight and Valentino* is a congenial female buddy movie which is more heart than soul, more emotion than depth. Perkins' husband is killed in a morning jog. As her sister (Paltrow), best friend (Goldberg) and stepmother (Turner) gather to give her comfort, she has a degree

of difficulty in trying to get on with her life. Written by Ellen Simon (Neil's daughter), the film exhibits a genuine bond between the women, and they're given some good dialogue to recite. Jovi makes an impressive debut as Perkins' hunky house painter. ★★½ DVD: $14.99

Moonlight Mile

(2002, 117 min, US, Brad Silberling) *Jake Gyllenhaal, Dustin Hoffman, Susan Sarandon, Holly Hunter, Ellen Pompeo, Dabney Coleman.* Based on experiences in his own life, writer-director Silberling examines the devastating effect the death of a young woman has on her parents and fiancé. However, in the shadow of such emotionally honest, similarly themed films as *In the Bedroom* and *The Son's Room*, *Moonlight Mile*'s superficiality only ends up sabotaging occasionally moving scenes of loss and grief inherit in the story. Diana and Joe were engaged to be married, but days before the wedding Diana was shot to death. Joe and Diana's grief-stricken parents, JoJo and Ben, console each other in small acts of solace, but are unable to communicate or acknowledge the pain they are feeling. Silberling's story follows what it takes for each survivor to move on, though the path to recovery isn't as fully explored as it could have been, and as a result certain story lines become muted and trivial. Despite the film's shortcomings, the acting is terrific and many scenes resonate, ensuring that *Moonlight Mile* is nothing less than compelling. ★★½ DVD: $19.99, VHS: $9.99

Moonlighting

(1982, 97 min, GB, Jerzy Skolimowski) *Jeremy Irons, Eugene Lipinski.* Working illegally in London, a group of Polish laborers are brutally cut off from home and family when martial law is declared in their country. Skolimowski's moving and imaginative parable of the Polish struggle stars Irons as the only member of the group who can speak English. ★★★½

Moonraker

(1979, 126 min, GB, Lewis Gilbert) *Roger Moore, Michael Lonsdale, Richard Kiel, Lois Chiles.* In this, the 11th outing of agent 007, Moore is on the trail of a wealthy industrialist (Lonsdale) who plans to poison the human race from the safety of his own private space station. Jaws (Kiel) returns, and Chiles is Dr. Holly Goodhead. Gimmicky but still fun. (Sequel: *For Your Eyes Only*) ★★★ VHS: $9.99

Moonrise

(1948, 90 min, US, Frank Borzage) *Dane Clark, Lloyd Bridges, Ethel Barrymore.* This grim psychological melodrama is a brooding tale of a young man who, after years of being taunted about things from his and his father's past, accidentally kills a banker's son. A rural drama of violence, insanity and revenge. ★★★ VHS: $19.99

Moonstruck

(1987, 102 min, US, Norman Jewison) *Cher, Nicolas Cage, Olympia Dukakis, Danny Aiello, Vincent Gardenia, John Mahoney.* Cher won an Oscar for her performance as a young Italian-American widow in this loopy tale about the power of love over reason. Cage delivers an inspired over-the-top performance as her misfit brother-in-law-to-be to whom she is inextricably attracted. Jewison's direction of John Patrick Shanley's Oscar-winning screenplay "hits your eye like a big pizza pie!" Dukakis also won an Oscar in support as Cher's no-nonsense mother. ★★★½ DVD: $14.99

More

(1969, 110 min, Barbet Schroeder) *Mimsy Farmer, Klaus Grunberg.* The energy, excitement, innocence and eventual demise of the hippie/youth movement of the '60s is wonderfully captured in Schroeder's first film. The story is a tender tale of a West German student who travels across Europe — from the cafes of Paris to the sun-drenched beaches of Ibiza — searching for love and adventure. Schroeder provides a definitive image of this improbable era where peace, revolt, sex, drugs and rock 'n' roll reign supreme. The soundtrack features great music by Pink Floyd. (English and French, German and Spanish with English subtitles) ★★★½ VHS: $29.99

More Tales of the City

(1998, 330 min, US, Pierre Gang) *Olympia Dukakis, Laura Linney, Colin Ferguson, Thomas Gibson, William Campbell, Swoosie Kurtz, Barbara Garrick, Jackie Burroughs, Nina Siemaszko, Paul Bartel.* The stories of 28 Barbary Lane continue with more laughs, more sex and more mysteries with Armistead Maupin's *More Tales of the City*, a six-part miniseries (available on 3 tapes) follow-up to the highly successful *Tales of the City*. Picking up where the original left off, Anna Madrigal (Dukakis) is still keeping watch over her tenants Mary Ann (Linney), who finds love with the mysterious Burke (Ferguson), and Michael "Mouse" Tolliver (Hopkins, replacing Marcus D'Amico), who falls hard for the dreamy Dr. Fielding (Campbell). Meanwhile, Mona (Siemaszko replacing Chloe Webb) heads off in search of her birth mother; and Beauchamp (Gibson) deals with his wife Dede (Garrick) impending motherhood. *More Tales* is just as enjoyable as the original, and since there is less time introducing the characters, there's more time spent with them and developing them. Tensions about showing nudity and depicting homosexuality, which caused a controversy with the first production, have been lessened, making the sequel more relaxed. As before, the series captures 1970s San Francisco in all its glory, featuring fabulous period details in the clothes, music and fads of the era. It's like reuniting with long-lost old friends. ★★★½

The More the Merrier

(1943, 104 min, US, George Stevens) *Jean Arthur, Joel McCrea, Charles Coburn.* A sparkling comedy from director Stevens. In overcrowded, wartime Washington D.C., Arthur shares her small, one-bedroom apartment with McCrea and Coburn; the latter playing matchmaker. Coburn deservedly won a Best Supporting Oscar as the lovable Mr. Dingle; Arthur (though a nominee) probably should have won Best Actress for her captivating portrayal. Stevens also won an Oscar as Best Director. ★★★★ VHS: $19.99

Morgan!

(1966, 92 min, GB, Karel Reisz) *David Warner, Vanessa Redgrave, Robert Stephens, Graham Crowden, Edward Fox.* One of the finest and funniest black comedies ever to hail from the shores of Great Britain, *Morgan!* stars Warner as an artist teetering on the precipice of total insanity. After his wife (Redgrave) divorces him, he sets out on a series of lunatic escapades in an effort to reconcile himself to his new status. Filled with truth and pathos, this is a very funny look at the process of "breaking up." ★★★★ DVD: $19.99

Morgan Stewart's Coming Home

(1987, 96 min, US, Alan Smithee) *Jon Cryer, Lynn Redgrave, Nicholas Pryor.* Maybe he should have stayed where he was. . . he might have had better luck. The usually reliable Cryer gives it the old college try playing a student who returns home to aid his father's election bid — turning the campaign upside down. Director Paul Aaron took his name off the film, replacing it with "Alan Smithee," the industry moniker for such occasions. ★½

Morituri

(1965, 128 min, US, Bernhard Wicki) *Marlon Brando, Yul Brynner, Trevor Howard, Janet Margolin, Wally Cox.* One of Brando's more fascinating failures from the 1960s (a decade in which the star took many chances in his film roles — most of which foundered). Brando plays an anti-Nazi German demolitions expert who is "recruited" by the British to help them seize a German freighter which is booby-trapped to explode upon capture. Brynner also stars as the ship's captain. (aka: *The Saboteur* and *The Saboteur, Code Name Morituri*) ★★ DVD: $14.99, VHS: $19.99

The Morning After

(1986, 103 min, US, Sidney Lumet) *Jane Fonda, Jeff Bridges, Raul Julia, Diane Salinger, Kathy Bates.* Fonda's bravura performance as an alcoholic actress on the skids highlights this predictable though gritty mystery thriller. Fonda awakes one morning to discover a corpse beside her — and she can't remember anything about the night before. Bridges helps her find out the truth. ★★½ VHS: $9.99

Morning Glory

(1933, 73 min, US, Lowell Sherman) *Katharine Hepburn, Douglas Fairbanks, Jr., Adolphe Menjou.* Hepburn won her first Oscar for her glorious performance as a starstruck actress determined to succeed on the New York stage. In a role similar to the one she would play in *Stage Door* a few years later, Hepburn shines in this compelling theatrical drama as Eva Lovelace, a small-town girl with stars in her eyes, and enough determination and talent to make sure her dreams come true. ★★★

Morocco

(1930, 92 min, US, Josef von Sternberg) *Gary Cooper, Marlene Dietrich, Adolphe Menjou.* The impossibly seductive Dietrich made her American film debut as a cabaret singer in Morocco, torn between Foreign Legionnaire Cooper and wealthy Menjou. Romantic and very interesting. ★★★½

Morons from Outer Space

(1985, 87 min, GB, Mike Hodges) *Griff Rhys Jones, Mel Smith, James B. Sikking.* They came, they saw, they did a little shopping. The title says it all: four not-quite-right-in-the-head humanoids from the planet Blob crash Earth, where these pinheads are treated as media heroes and eventually become successful rock stars. The trousers of the well-known British reserve are ceremoniously dropped in this daffy sci-fi comedy. ★★½ DVD Letterbox: $14.99

Mortal Kombat

(1995, 101 min, US, Paul Anderson) *Christopher Lambert, Robin Shou, Talisa Soto.* One of the more successful video game-to-film transfers, this movie is a fun ride through strange worlds and raucous martial arts competitions which wisely abandons any aspirations to plot or character development; everything in this movie is at the service of its action scenes. These scenes, therefore, are well-staged and exciting, pitting three human heroes against a variety of evil humans, monsters and sorcerers. The outcome: the future of our world. Spectacular computer effects highlight its fight scenes, and the set design, also computer-aided, is impressive. Sequel: *Mortal Kombat 2: Annihilation*) ★★½ DVD: $19.99, VHS: Letterbox: $9.99

The Mortal Storm

(1940, 100 min, US, Frank Borzage) *James Stewart, Frank Morgan, Margaret Sullavan, Robert Young, Robert Stack.* A moving, powerful adaptation of Phyllis Bottome's novel about life in pre-WWII Germany. Lovers Stewart and Sullavan are risk it all to leave the country as Nazism tears their families apart. Morgan is terrific as Sullavan's father, a professor whose humanistic beliefs become his undoing. ★★★½

Mortal Thoughts

(1991, 102 min, US, Alan Rudolph) *Demi Moore, Glenne Headly, Harvey Keitel, Bruce Willis.* A stylish, gripping psychological thriller dripping in atmosphere and tension. Moore and Headley are lifelong friends and business partners; the latter is married to abusive Willis (thankfully underplaying his role). In an accident, he dies and the two cover up his death. But was it an accident? And who really did it? Keitel is the police detective grilling Moore for the answers — reliving the story through flashbacks right up to the unexpected ending. Though Moore's screen work here is possibly her best, Headly steals the show with a hypnotic performance as the suspected murderess. ★★★ DVD: $9.99, VHS: $9.99

Moscow Does Not Believe in Tears

(1980, 152 min, USSR, Vladimir Menshov) *Vera Alentova, Irina Muravyova, Raisa Ryazanova.* This surprise Oscar winner of 1981 is a light and charming look into contemporary Soviet life. The story concerns three young provincial girls' move to Moscow and their search for work, love and marriage. Can it really just well be a *How to Marry a Millionaire* — Soviet style! (Russian with English subtitles) ★★★ DVD: $29.99, VHS: $24.99

Moscow on the Hudson

(1984, 115 min, US, Paul Mazursky) *Robin Williams, Maria Conchita Alonso, Cleavant Derricks.* Williams gives an endearingly sweet performance as a Russian musician who defects to America in the middle of Bloomingdale's. Writer-director Mazursky fills this benign satire with interesting eccentrics and amusing anecdotes as the befuddled defector suffers some severe culture shock. A totally winning social comedy. ★★★½ DVD: $19.99

The Mosquito Coast

(1986, 119 min, US, Peter Weir) *Harrison Ford, River Phoenix, Helen Mirren, Martha Plimpton, Andre Gregory, Butterfly McQueen, Jason Alexander.* Ford is well cast as Pennsylvania inventor Allie Fox, whose disgust with the direction of American culture prompts him to upheave his family to a primitive Central American island to start a utopian society. But for Fox there is no escaping civilization. Once they reach their paradise, the society left behind begins to rear its ugly head, sending the father into a paranoic state, and eventually madness. Phoenix gives a powerful performance as the teenage son who must protect his family when their paradise turns hellish. Paul Schrader's screenplay digs deep into a man's psyche and the nature of our modern existence. ★★★ DVD: $9.99

Most Wanted

(1997, 99 min, US, David Glenn Hogan) *Keenen Ivory Wayans, Jon Voight, Jill Hennessy, Paul Sorvino, Robert Culp, Eric Roberts.* Looking as if he's trying to emulate Steven Seagal (and not the likable *Under Siege* persona, either), Wayans plays a Marine (sentenced to die after accidentally killing a superior officer) who is recruited into a secret government organization. But since most of the story in this derivative, formulaic actioner we've seen before, we know that when he's hired to assassinate a target, and the First Lady is killed instead, he'll be blamed, he'll set out expose the conspiracy. Director Hogan gives the film a good look, though his action scenes are routine. ★★ DVD: $9.99, VHS: $9.99

Mostly Martha

(2001, 106 min, Germany, Sandra Nettelbeck) *Martina Gedeck, Sergio Castellitto, Maxime Foerste, August Zirner, Ulrich Thomsen.* Martha spends her weekly 50 minutes of analysis rhapsodically reciting recipes to her therapist. When he asks why she sees him, she matter-of-factly says that her boss would fire her if she didn't. Martha is the chef at a posh gourmet restaurant. She's a driven perfectionist who will not hesitate to tell a boorish patron that he's a boor. Compromise and accommodation are not in her lexicon until tragic circumstances make her the caretaker of her eight-year-old niece. Added to this is the arrival of a new cook, who establishes a strong, warm presence where she had ruled with grim determination. On the surface the familiar story of the compulsive career woman who gradually awakens to her feminine side, *Mostly Martha* is expressive, poignant, deeply touching and wryly funny, a cautionary tale that instructs us that there are no foolproof recipes for living life. Gedeck's ability to communicate complexity with a minimum of dialogue is well utilized by the director, and Castellitto effortlessly enters and dominates the screen as well as the kitchen. (German with English subtitles) ★★★½ DVD: $19.99

Mostly Martha

Motel Hell

(1980, 92 min, US, Kevin Connor) *Rory Calhoun, Nancy Parsons.* This spoofy horror film brings new meaning to the term "tongue-in-cheek." A country sausage king has a secret ingredient for his delicious product: the guests staying at his backwoods motel. ★½ DVD Letterbox Double Feature: $14.99

Mother

(1926, 90 min, Russia, Vsevolod Pudovkin) *Vera Baranovskaya, Nikolai Batalov.* Set during the unsuccessful workers' rebellion of 1905, Pudovkin's engrossing story is about one family's hardships under the cruel czarist regime. A technically impressive allegory for Russia's conversion to Communism. (Silent with musical soundtrack) ★★★ DVD: $24.99

Mother

(1996, 104 min, US, Albert Brooks) *Albert Brooks, Debbie Reynolds, Rob Morrow, Lisa Kudrow, John C. McGinley.* Brooks sets out to prove that even though she may not wear Army boots, there's still plenty to fear from that dear old materfamilias, especially when you're a middle-aged divorcé caught in the throes of depression. Brooks is in his element as an author of cheap sci-fi thrillers that nobody reads who decides that the only way to get his life back in gear is to move back in with his mother. Reynolds is superb as his put-upon mom who just can't understand what all his fussing is about anyway. Brooks' script does a fine job skewering mother-son stereotypes, delivering several big laughs at the expense of just about everybody from cheap pop psychologists to mom herself. With this wonderful lark, Brooks proves *Mother* knows best. ★★★½ DVD: $29.99, VHS: $9.99

The Mother and the Whore

(1973, 215 min, France, Jean Eustache) *Bernadette Lafont, Jean-Pierre Léaud, Françoise Lebrun.* A 3-hour, 35-minute Gaullic exploraton of the perverse, dichotomous delineation of woman, aptly summed up by the film's title. As he served so ably for Truffaut, one gets the impression that Léaud functions as director Eustache's alter ego. Léaud is Alexandre; a man whose intellectual pretensions provide the unending polemic of his objectification of women — woman as object of desire, disdain, faux adoration; woman as only a reflection of man's desire. Under the pretense of an open relationship with two of his several female lovers, Alexandre requires commitment, offering none in return. The women are complicit in the underlying belief system, even as it engenders deep unhappiness. Fittingly, there is no resolution. A radical exposition in its time, the film now plays as a cultural relic; yet easily remains an item of interest to both cinephiles and Francophiles. (French with English subtitles) ★★★ VHS: $29.99

Mother Kusters Goes to Heaven

(1976, 108 min, Germany, Rainer Werner Fassbinder) *Brigitte Mira, Ingrid Caven, Margit Carstensen.* Mira is outstanding as Mother Küsters, an older woman whose sedate, ordinary life is thrown into turmoil when her husband goes mad at work, killing the paymaster, and then committing suicide. As she struggles to understand what happened to her husband, the emotional poverty of her life is revealed in her casual comments regarding her husband's lack of communication, her daughter's ability to turn the media attention to career advantage and her son's inability to counter his wife's desire to distance herself from the embarrassment. As the media vultures descend, the facts of her prosaic life are twisted and

sensationalized to sell papers. Mira's entirely believable performance and Fassbinder's unerring cynical eye deliver a powerful treatise on the human propensity toward exploitation. (German with English subtitles) ★★★½ DVD: $24.99, VHS: $19.99

Mother Night

(1996, 113 min, US, Keith Gordon) *Nick Nolte, John Goodman, Sheryl Lee, Alan Arkin, David Strathairn, Kirsten Dunst, Arye Gross, Henry Gibson.* A wonderfully wry and unexpectedly romantic adaptation of Kurt Vonnegut's 1974 novel, *Mother Night* marks another successful behind-the-camera turn for actor-turned-director Gordon. Using flashback to recall the life of an American double agent living in Nazi Germany, the story begins with Howard Campbell (Nolte) serving time in an Israeli prison. Traveling back and forth in time (much like Vonnegut's *Slaughterhouse-Five*), the film focuses on Campbell's post-war life as a desolate, lonely widower in New York whose name perversely comes before the public once more. All during the story, Vonnegut takes a moral dilemma and devours it, spitting out chunks of ambiguity and the bizarre with devilish delight. ★★★½ DVD: $24.99, VHS: $19.99

Mother's Boys

(1994, 95 min, US, Yves Simoneau) *Jamie Lee Curtis, Peter Gallagher, Joanne Whalley-Kilmer, Vanessa Redgrave, Joss Ackland.* A Freudian suspenser about a well-bred sociopath who, having abandoned her husband (Gallagher) and children years earlier, tries to reclaim them using her eldest son as leverage. Curtis is suitably creepy as a woman who will stop at nothing — even sexual intimidation — to win back her family. However, the film ultimately deteriorates into standard shock fare. ★★½ DVD: $9.99

The Mothman Prophecies

(2002, 119 min, US, Mark Pellington) *Richard Gere, Laura Linney, Will Patton, Debra Messing, Alan Bates, Lucinda Jenney.* A creepily effective chiller, *The Mothman Prophecies* is well-directed by Pellington (*Arlington Road*), and features solid performances by Gere, Linney and Patton. Journalist Gere, recently widowed, investigates sightings of a large, moth-like creature in a small West Virginia

Nicole Kidman and Ewan McGregor in Baz Luhrmann's *Moulin Rouge*

town — a creature his wife claims to have seen just before her death. There's very little action per se, and special effects buffs will be disappointed by the mere glimpses of the monster, but fans of suggestive horror should eat this one up. Pellington sets up an atmosphere of unease that hardly lets up, with many eerie moments along the way, punctuated by an impressive score by tomandandy. ★★★ DVD: $14.99, VHS: $14.99

Mothra

(1962, 100 min, Japan, Inoshiro Honda) *Yumi Ito, Frankie Sakai.* The director of the first *Godzilla* movie created this cute fairy tale about two twin six-inch princesses kidnapped from their throne on Infant Island and exhibited on Tokyo television singing their siren song — a song that calls their giant moth to come and save them, at the city's expense. ★★

Motor Psycho

(1965, 65 min, US, Russ Meyer) Three bikers, led by a crazed Vietnam vet, go on an unstoppable orgy of rape and murder, until a vengeful husband gets on their trail and forces a showdown. Made between *Mudhoney* and *Faster, Pussycat, Kill! Kill!* and featuring the alluring Haji, *Motor Psycho* is Meyer's entry into the biker genre and presages *Faster, Pussycat*'s theme of rampaging maniacs in the desert terrorizing hapless strangers. ★★ VHS: $79.99

Mouchette

(1966, 90 min, France, Robert Bresson) *Nadine Nortier, Maria Cardinal.* The last 24 hours in the life of a 14-year-old peasant girl is starkly presented without pity and without offering a single glimmer of hope. This moving story of humiliation and defeat traces the experiences of Mouchette, a bewildered youngster who is victimized at home by her drunken father, alienated at school, isolated from a hostile world and who is finally driven to suicide. A simply told, overwhelming story whose strong narrative and technical virtuosity transcends the unrelentingly grim dramatics. (French with English subtitles) ★★★½ VHS: $24.99

Moulin Rouge

(1952, 123 min, US, John Huston) *Jose Ferrer, Zsa Zsa Gabor, Christopher Lee, Peter Cushing, Colette Marchand.* A fascinating film biography, rich in color and detail, about the life of 19th-century French painter Henri de Toulouse-Lautrec. Ferrer gives a stunning portrayal of the troubled artist, whose growth impediment was impetus to his flagrant lifestyle and art. ★★★½ DVD: $14.99

Moulin Rouge

(2001, 126 min, Australia, Baz Luhrmann) *Nicole Kidman, Ewan McGregor, John Leguizamo, Jim Broadbent, Richard Roxburgh, Jacek Koman.* Audacious, energetic and off-the-wall, *Moulin Rouge* moves at the speed of sound as it nearly reinvents the movie musical with bursts of color, frenetic pacing and a whole new way to look at musical scoring. Director Luhrmann's story of the quest for "truth, beauty, freedom, but above all things, love," is often stunning to behold. Incorporating contemporary songs (from Madonna to *The Sound of Music*) into a Paris at the turn of the century is a risky undertaking, but it works thanks to some fancy editing and an assault of the senses. Displaying a fine voice, McGregor plays a naïve writer who falls for the most beautiful courtesan (Kidman) at the Moulin Rouge. She would like to return his love, but she's promised to another. Thus begins this Orphean descent into heartbreak and tragedy. Dizzying musical numbers, lush costumes and sets, and nods to opera, Comédie-Française and Bollywood all combine to make this a real kick in the pantaloons. ★★★★ DVD Letterbox: $14.99, DVD 2-disc Special Edition: $26.99, VHS Special Edition: $6.99

The Mountain

(1956, 105 min, US, Edward Dmytryk) *Spencer Tracy, Robert Wagner, Claire Trevor, William Demarest, E.G. Marshall.* Tracy and Wagner are two brothers at odds while climbing a treacherous peak to reach an aircraft that crashed. Tracy's sincere performance highlights this familiar tale of familial conflict. ★★½ VHS: $14.99

Mountains of the Moon

(1990, 135 min, US, Bob Rafelson) *Patrick Bergin, Iain Glen, Fiona Shaw, Bernard Hill, Richard E. Grant, Roger Rees, Delroy Lindo, Roshan Seth.* Inspired by the journals of 19th-century explorers Richard Burton and Jack Speke, this is a stirring account of the torturous and famous expedition taken by the two adventurers to discover the source of the Nile. Rafelson meticulously re-creates the worlds of privileged Britain and small-tribe Africa, and has fashioned an exhilarating adventure film of the highest order. Bergin and Glen give outstanding performances as Burton and Speke, respectively, whose sometimes perilous and always enlightening journey began in 1854, and ended many years and thousands of miles later in betrayal and death. ★★★★ DVD: $14.99, VHS: $9.99

The Mouse on the Moon

(1963, 85 min, GB, Richard Lester) *Margaret Rutherford, Bernard Cribbins, Ron Moody, Terry-Thomas, Michael Crawford.* Very funny sequel to *The Mouse That Roared* has the tiny country of Duchy of Grand Feswick entering the space race. Rutherford steals the show as the Grand Duchess. ★★★½ DVD: $19.99

The Mouse That Roared

(1959, 83 min, GB, Jack Arnold) *Peter Sellers, Jean Seberg, Leo McKern.* This hilarious satire on the idiocies of foreign policy involves the miniscule Grand Duchy of Fenwick which declares war on the United States with the intention of losing in order to receive foreign aid. This is a film which could have only been made in the pre-Vietnam era, when America was still basking in its Marshall Plan glow. Featuring Sellers in three amusing roles, and a pre-opening sequence which ranks as a classic. ★★★½ DVD Letterbox: $24.99, VHS: $19.99

Mousehunt

(1997, 97 min, US, Gore Verbinski) *Nathan Lane, Lee Evans, Christopher Walken, Vicki Lewis, Michael Jeter.* A very funny slapstick family comedy which is fun for all ages, *Mousehunt* is a live-action Road Runner cartoon, with two hapless brothers as the coyote, and one clever, little mouse as the object of their disaffection. Brothers Lane and Evans inherit a not-so-profitable string factory and a runned-down mansion. Circumstances dictate that they both stay at their new home, which is deteriorated beyond belief and beset by a pesky rodent. In some finely detailed broad comedy that *The Money Pit* could have used, *Mousehunt* depicts the merry destruction which ensues at the hands of the brothers in their quest to get rid of the mouse. Lane and Evans are a couple of inspired lunatics, and their succession of pratfalls, one-liners and comic humiliations keep this rodenticide safari a consistently entertaining journey. ★★★ DVD: $14.99, DVD DTS sound: $14.99, VHS: $14.99

Mouth to Mouth

(1995, 96 min, Spain, Manuel Gomez Pereira) *Javier Bardem, Aitana Sanchez-Gijon, Josep Maria Flotats.* A strained Spanish sex farce, *Mouth to Mouth* concerns Victor (Bardem), an out-of-work actor who reluctantly takes a job as a phone sex operator while awaiting his big break. Although he becomes the favorite of a male client, Victor is straight, and he is soon seduced by a caller named Amanda (Sanchez-Gijon), whom he arranges to meet on the side. When Amanda involves Victor in a blackmail scheme which backfires, his personal and professional worlds begin to collide. *Mouth to Mouth* does have some madcap moments which brings together all of the film's "wacky" characters, but ultimately the film plays its comedy too broadly. Despite Bardem's wholesome sex appeal and energetic performance, his desperation is just not very amusing. ★★ DVD: $19.99, VHS: $9.99

Move over, Darling

(1963, 103 min, US, Michael Gordon) *Doris Day, James Garner, Polly Bergen, Thelma Ritter, Chuck Connors, Don Knotts, John Astin.* Remake of *My Favorite Wife* with Doris stranded on a desert island for seven years with hunk Chuck, then returning home to husband James, who's just been remarried. Some cute laughs, though not as consistently funny as the original. This was originally intended to star Marilyn Monroe and Dean Martin under the title *Something's Got to Give*, but Marilyn died after shooting only a few scenes. ★★½ VHS: $14.99

Movie Movie

(1979, 107 min, US, Stanley Donen) *George C. Scott, Trish Van Devere, Harry Hamlin, Eli Wallach, Red Buttons, Barbara Harris, Barry Bostwick, Art Carney.* A joyous tribute to 1930s and '40s filmmaking, this "double feature" offers two stories (and a trailer) that affectionately poke fun at the conventions and clichés of particular genre films from that era. "Dynamite Hands" is first, a black-and-white boxing tale with Scott as a grizzled manager and Hamlin as a raw youth who makes good; the second story is "Baxter's Beauties of 1933, " a color spoof of Busby Berkeley musicals. ★★★½

Moving

(1988, 89 min, US, Alan Metter) *Richard Pryor, Beverly Todd, Randy Quaid, Dana Carvey, Stacey Dash, Rodney Dangerfield.* New Jerseyites Pryor and family pack up and move to Idaho when Dad lands a great job. Most of this is of the predictable sort, but Pryor's manic reactions and character make it tolerable. ★★

Moving the Mountain

(1995, 83 min, US/China, Michael Apted) Director Apted has made an insightful exploration of the human condition with this powerful documentary. Chronicling several people in leadership positions during the Tiananmen Square protests, the film recounts their involvement and gives a history of the events which led to the killing of thousands and the reawakening of an undercurrent of change within China. The empassioned Li Lu, one of the student leaders, is profiled with reenactments of his life from childhood and actual news footage of the events surrounding the protests. *Moving the Mountain* is a sobering view of these now-exiled students, and the film is enhanced by stylish editing, engaging principals, and inspirational stories. ★★★½

The Mozart Brothers

(1986, 98 min, Sweden, Suzanne Osten) *Etienne Glaser, Philip Zanden.* An often hilarious view of the artistic process choosing to draw upon the Marx Brothers' *A Night at the Opera* for inspiration. The story concerns a radically innovative production of Mozart's "Don Giovanni" as done by a Stockholm opera company. We are given a profound look at the trials of Walter, the fanatically avant-garde theatre director, whose attempts to win the hearts of the intransigent singers often result in some of the film's funniest moments. In a somewhat Bergman-esque touch, the ghost of Mozart offers Walter encouragement and advice through nocturnal visitations. For fans of opera, theatre and music alike, this is a wonderful flight of fancy which will surely not disappoint. (Swedish with English subtitles) ★★★ VHS: $24.99

Mr.

See: *Mister*

Mr. Wonderful

(1993, 98 min, US, Anthony Minghella) *Matt Dillon, Annabella Sciorra, William Hurt, Mary Louise Parker, Vincent D'Onofrio.* A pleasant though insubstantial comedy, Minghella's second film casts Dillon as a working-class divorcé whose alimony payments stand between him and a happy new life. Evoking the spirits of films afar afield as *The Awful Truth* and *Send Me No Flowers*, Dillon begins an exhaustive search for his ex's (Sciorra) perfect match. ★★½ DVD: $9.99, VHS: $9.99

Mrs. Brown

(1997, 103 min, GB, John Madden) *Judi Dench, Billy Connolly, Antony Sher.* With eyes of icy steel and manner fixed and regal, Dench gives a superlative portrayal of England's Queen Victoria in this handsome historical drama about her 20-year relationship with her servant/confidant John Brown. It is 1864, and the queen is still mourning the death of her beloved Albert, prompting all to walk gently in her presence. That is until the arrival of Brown (Connolly), Albert's former footman. At first, his loyalty and candor bring him to favor with the queen. But gradually she learns to depend only on him, which sends shock waves around the court and rumors of a romantic nature all over England — hence the queen's new nickname, Mrs. Brown. Director Madden gives

M

the film a splendid look, effortlessly evoking the time and place of 19th-century court. But it is Dench's performance which really distinguishs the film — it's a revelation, rich in subtlety and fervor. ★★★ DVD: $19.99, VHS: $9.99

Mrs. Brown, You've Got a Lovely Daughter

(1968, 110 min, GB, Saul Swimmer) *Herman's Hermits, Mona Washbourne, Stanley Holloway.* A lightweight vehicle for '60s pop group Herman's Hermits. The band, of course, sings the title song along with their other hit, "There's a Kind of Hush." This jump on the Beatles' *A Hard Day's Night* bandwagon is only intermittently entertaining. ★★

Mrs. Dalloway

(1998, 98 min, GB, Marleen Gorris) *Vanessa Redgrave, Natascha McElhone, Rupert Graves, Michael Kitchen.* On a perfect day in 1923, memories of her youth course through the day's events as Mrs. Dalloway (Redgrave) prepares for another of her elaborate parties. In an ordered English garden, a young veteran makes his own peace with the ravages of shell shock; at a nearby bench, Mrs. Dalloway's rejected suitor of decades past indulges his own reminiscences. Director Gorris has captured Virginia Woolf's novel of that society of manners, a complex social structure unaware of its impending demise; juxtaposing it against the oncoming realities of the modern age. An intricately crafted film sparkled with superb portrayals, *Mrs. Dalloway* unerringly evokes a time recently, irrevocably past. ★★★½ DVD: $9.99, VHS: $7.99

Mrs. Doubtfire

(1993, 105 min, US, Chris Columbus) *Robin Williams, Sally Field, Pierce Brosnan, Harvey Fierstein, Robert Prosky, Polly Holliday, Scott Capurro.* Heavy on the laughter as well as the sentiment, *Mrs. Doubtfire* is an appealing comedy in spite of its sprinkling of Afterschool Special schmaltz. Featuring a very funny performance by Williams, this genuinely entertaining, high-concept comedy casts Williams as a recently divorced actor. Losing a custody battle over his three children, Williams takes advantage of his ex-wife Field's search for a housekeeper — and impersonates a sixty-ish British nanny. It takes a half-hour for the beguiling Mrs. Doubtfire to make her appearance, but when she does, Williams and the film become nearly inspired. Often recalling *Tootsie, Mrs. Doubtfire* isn't on that film's level, but it does firmly stand on its own two orthopedic pumps. ★★★ VHS: $9.99

Mrs. Miniver

(1942, 134 min, US, William Wyler) *Greer Garson, Walter Pidgeon, Teresa Wright, Dame May Whitty, Henry Travers, Peter Lawford.* A beautifully filmed, exceptionally acted drama of a British family facing the rigors of WWII. Garson won a Best Actress Oscar as the title character, a formidable wife and mother who does her best to keep her family together in the wake of separation and tragedy. Pidgeon is just fine as Mr. Miniver, and Wright is lovely as their daughter-in-law. Winner of seven Oscars, including Film and Director. (Sequel: *The Miniver Story*) ★★★½ DVD: $19.99

Mrs. Parker and the Vicious Circle

(1994, 123 min, US, Alan Rudolph) *Gwyneth Paltrow, Jennifer Jason Leigh, Campbell Scott, Matthew Broderick, Andrew McCarthy, Peter Gallagher, Martha Plimpton, Stephen Baldwin, Jennifer Beals, Lili Taylor, James LeGros.* Leigh

gives a tour de force performance as Algonquin wit and writer Dorothy Parker. In this extremely humorous though slightly downbeat examination of a troubled soul, director Rudolph has brilliantly reconstructed 1920s New York — a time when a select group of Manhattan's literary set convened to sling the next bon mot. In a series of flashbacks, the story follows Parker's rise as an author, her relationships with humorist Robert Benchley (Scott) and playwright Charles MacArthur (Broderick), and the formation of the legendary Algonquin Round Table. Leigh inhabits Parker as if possessed, conveying an eerie worldliness and heartbreaking vulnerability. ★★★½ VHS: $19.99

Mrs. Parkington

(1944, 124 min, US, Tay Garnett) *Greer Garson, Walter Pidgeon, Agnes Moorehead, Edward Arnold.* A dedicated cast enlivens this compelling soap opera. Spanning the course of 60 years in the life of the title character, the film features Garson as a wealthy New York family matriarch who is faced with a familial crisis. Remembering the past for guidance, Mrs. Parkington recalls her life and marriage to her "scoundrel" industrialist husband, played by Pidgeon. Although the dramatics is routine, it is the earnest performances from the entire cast which elevate it. Moorehead gives a splendid characterization as Pidgeon's wise ex-mistress. ★★½ VHS: $19.99

Mrs. Soffel

(1985, 110 min, US, Gillian Armstrong) *Diane Keaton, Mel Gibson, Mathew Modine, Edward Herrmann.* Keaton is the sheltered wife of a stern prison warden who surrenders to the powerful attraction of a death-row convict (Gibson); both become the object of a massive hunt when she helps him escape and they run away together. The attractive pairing of Keaton and Gibson and a good evocation of the period aren't sufficient enough to mask a dreary story and a passionless directorial style. ★★ VHS: $14.99, VHS Letterbox: $14.99

Ms. Don Juan

(1973, 87 min, France, Roger Vadim) *Brigitte Bardot, Maurice Ronet, Jane Birkin.* Vadim, mediocre filmmaker but successful promotor of such sex sirens as Jane Fonda, Brigette Bardot and Catherine Deneuve, directed this half-baked tale of murder and passion. BB stars as an evil seductress with an insatiable sexual appetite and hypnotic charms who devours and destroys everyone in sight. A sexual switch of the Don Juan story. ★★

Ms. 45

(1981, 84 min, US, Abel Ferrara) *Zoe Tamerlis, Steve Singer.* A Freudian, feminist revenge fantasy. Tamerlis is riveting as a victimized deaf-mute who adopts the Charles Bronson method of street sanitation and wages a war against the male scum population. (aka: *Angel of Vengeance*) ★★★ DVD: $24.99, VHS: $19.99

Much Ado about Nothing

(1993, 110 min, GB, Kenneth Branagh) *Denzel Washington, Keanu Reeves, Kenneth Branagh, Emma Thompson, Michael Keaton, Robert Sean Leonard, Brian Blessed, Richard Briers.* Returning to the familiar soil of Shakespeare, actor-director Branagh springs forth with a delightfully giddy and frantic romp set in the sundrenched fields of Tuscany. Shakespeare's bawdy comic tale of love torn assunder casts Branagh and Thompson as the sharp-witted, acerbic would-be

lovers Benedick and Beatrice, whose course of true love is not a tranquil one. Branagh and Thompson, radiant together, elevate the Bard's prose to resplendent levels of ecstasy. Featuring a splendid ensemble cast, the film is peppered with brilliant comic timing and seasoned with moments of overwhelming romanticism. *Much Ado* is truly a to do: a joyous celebration of unbridled passions. ★★★★ DVD Letterbox: $14.99

Mudhoney

(1965, 92 min, US, Russ Meyer) A black-and-white profile of rural Missouri lowlife in the '30s, which rails against American morality and religious hypocrisy. Stars Lorna Maitland, Rena Horten ("the embodiment of the body") and the buxom Lee Ballard. ★½ DVD: $39.99

Mulan

(1998, 88 min, US, Barry Cook & Tony Bancroft) *Voices of: Ming-Na Wen, Eddie Murphy, B.D. Wong, Lea Salonga, Donny Osmond, Harvey Fierstein, Miguel Ferrer.* The Disney machine has cranked out yet another sumptuous animated treat, this one a sprawling samurai epic with a cross-dressing heroine who defies family and tradition by secretly going off to war in the place of her father — dressed as a boy. Building on the timeless themes of honor and loyalty, of adolescent rebellion and seeking out your own destiny, the storytellers have found the right material to adapt into a musical. However, the songs themselves lack the jubilant spirit of the tunes from better Disney classics. The animation is glorious, despite the fact that Disney has become far-too-reliant on computers to generate complex, eye-popping vistas. *Mulan* is hardly worthy of comparisons to the jewels in the Disney crown, but remains a fast-paced, high-spirited entertainment. ★★★½ DVD Letterbox 2-disc Special Edition, Widescreen: $29.99, VHS: $24.99

Mulholland Drive

(2001, 146 min, US, David Lynch) *Naomi Watts, Laura Elena Harring, Justin Theroux, Ann Miller, Robert Forster, Dan Hedaya, Chad Everett.* Lynch has made a career of exploring the dark side of Americana, and what could be more American than the Hollywood dream? Wide-eyed Betty (Watts), a naïve, aspiring actress (aren't they all?), gets off the plane at LAX and into her apartment, only to find "Rita" (Harring) hiding there, an amnesiac fatale with a purse full of money. They bond and, like Rivette's Celine and Julie, try to unravel a mystery to which they hold only a tenuous connection. Or something like that. With its genesis as a TV pilot (which ABC rightly figured the masses were not ready for), there are enough characters and plot threads for several seasons. Lynch expanded the pilot to include generous helpings of sex and violence (with a particularly hot scene between the two leads), and a whopper of an ending that turns everything inside out and, incidentally, makes no sense at all. But you know that going in: this is Lynch's hypnotic and darkly beautiful dream world, full of monsters, desires and fantasies that no one in the real America could touch. Scene follows colorful scene, mixing high emotion and quirky humor masterfully, unlike the herky jerky attempts of *Lost Highway*. *Mulholland Drive* is Lynch in full REM state, America as imagined by *Eraserhead*'s lady in the radiator. ★★★★ DVD Letterbox: $14.99, VHS: $9.99

Mulholland Falls

(1996, 107 min, US, Lee Tamahori) *Nick Nolte, Melanie Griffith, Chazz Palminteri, Michael Madsen, Chris Penn, John Malkovich, Treat Williams, Jennifer Connelly, Andrew McCarthy.* In 1950s Los Angeles, a renegade group of cops known as the "Hat Squad" implemented their own individual brand of justice against criminals with an unlawful but patriotic zeal. Had they ever seen this muddled though frequently exciting exposé of vigilantism and cover-up suggested by their real-life exploits, the filmmakers may have been next to be "escorted" out of town. Nolte heads the cast as Max Hoover, one of the four elite cops who become entangled in a complex mystery which ultimately leads to military conspiracy. This excellent evocation of post-war L.A. is unfortunately a bargain basement *Chinatown*, which only belies its original premise. Tamahori has a great feel for time and place but isn't able to jump start a contrived script. ★★½

Multiple Maniacs

(1971, 94 min, US, John Waters) *Divine, Mink Stole.* The film Waters claimed "flushed religion out of my system" is so irredeemable that even describing it offends public standards of morality. But we'll try. A traveling carnival called "Lady Divine's Cavalcade of Perversions" lands in Baltimore and disrupts the lives of the creeps living there. We're treated to a junkie shooting up on a church altar, bearded transvestites, the semi-classic scene of Divine being raped by a 15-foot lobster, Stole's rosary beads, cannibalism, Kate Smith's rendition of "God Bless America" and, perhaps most disturbing of all, shots of downtown Baltimore. ★★★

Multiplicity

(1996, 110 min, US, Harold Ramis) *Michael Keaton, Andie MacDowell, Richard Masur, Harris Yulin, Eugene Levy, Brian Doyle-Murray.* Keaton gets cloned and essentially plays with himself in this amiable though lackluster comedy whose cute premise is never fully realized. Keaton plays a harried construction foreman who, after a chance meeting with a scientist, is cloned, enabling the original to spend more quality time with the wife (MacDowell) and kids while the "xerox copy" shows up at work. In time, there are four Keatons running around on the screen, engaging in predictable shenanigans. The special effects are terrific, and Keaton creates distinct personalities for his four

Naomi Watts and Laura Elena Harring in David Lynch's *Mulholland Drive*

"Dougs." But the screenplay doesn't come close to the film's F/X wizardry, and the laugh quotient is surprisingly low. ★★ DVD: $14.99, VHS: $9.99

The Mummy

(1932, 72 min, US, Karl Freund) *Boris Karloff, Zita Johann, David Manners.* Noted cinematographer Freund (*Metropolis, Dracula*) made his directorial debut in Karloff's second greatest horror role. Buried alive for trying to restore life to his great love, it is he who is accidentally revived by an overeager archaeologist. Moody and foreboding, this tragic tale of love lost over the centuries moves ceaselessly forward towards its inevitable destiny. ★★★½ VHS: $9.99

The Mummy

(1959, 86 min, GB, Terence Fisher) *Christopher Lee, Peter Cushing, Yvonne Furneaux.* Journeyman director Fisher brings his usual panache to the remake of the Karloff classic based on an early draft for that film. Lee is the resurrected avenger out for archaeologist Cushing's blood in this, one of Hammer Films' most stylish efforts. ★★★ DVD Letterbox: $19.99, VHS: $9.99

The Mummy

(1999, 124 min, US, Stephen Sommers) *Brendan Fraser, Rachel Weisz, John Hannah, Arnold Vosloo, Kevin J. O'Connor.* Don't expect to be frightened out of your wits with an unrelenting barrage of horror sequences. Sommers' *Mummy* doesn't go there. Borrowing a little derring-do from *Raiders of the Lost Ark* and some off-hand humor from *Gunga Din*, this update of the 1930s chestnut is cheesy fun, down to its hackneyed screenplay, great special effects and mix of humor, action and scares. In the lost city of Hamunaptra, Fraser, Weisz and Hannah unwittingly let loose the spirit of a 3,000-year-old mummy, who plans to conquer the world as soon as he regenerates. It's the sort of film in which every 10 minutes or so our hapless heroes find themselves in another inescapable predicament. It's fun to watch them weasle out of them. (Sequel: *The Mummy Returns*) ★★★ DVD Letterbox: $19.99, VHS: $9.99, VHS Letterbox: $9.99

The Mummy Returns

(2001, 125 min, US, Stephen Sommers) *Brendan Fraser, Rachel Weisz, John Hannah, Arnold Vosloo, Oded Fehr, The Rock, Adewale Akinnuoye-Agbaje.* The mummy returns, indeed. Not quite a promise as it is a threat, this sequel to 1999's enjoyable surprise hit is much more of the same — emphasis on same. Fraser returns as the derring-do adventurer; so do Weisz and Hannah. Vosloo is back, too, as the 3,000-year-old mummy whose name you can't pronounce. Back are the terrific special effects, cheesy story and mix of humor and action. The Rock is new. Don't count on anything else new, however. This rehash isn't as fun as the original, and the characters are secondary to the stunning effects. There's always something going on, some predicament to get out of, but it just isn't quite the same. Oh, wait, yes it is. (Prequel: *The Scorpion King*) ★★½ DVD Letterbox: $19.99, DVD Pan & Scan: $19.99, VHS: $9.99

The Mummy's Hand

(1940, 67 min, US, Christy Cabanne) *Dick Foran, Wallace Ford, Peggy Moran, Tom Tyler, Cecil Kellaway.* Before passing the role to Lon Chaney, Tyler starred as Kharis, the mummy, in this first of a series. The action takes place at an archaeological dig where explorers find the sacred tomb of an Egyptian princess still guarded by Kharis. Excellent set design and good acting combine to make this a classic from

the golden age of horror films. Trivia buffs take note: look for ten minutes of footage from Karloff's *The Mummy*, used here as flashback. ★★★

The Muppet Christmas Carol

(1992, 85 min, US, Brian Henson) *Kermit, Miss Piggy, Fozzie, Michael Caine.* Jim Henson may be gone, but his legacy continues through his son Brian in this latest adaptation of the Dickens classic. Caine (looking very well, thank you) stars as Ebenezer Scrooge, and Kermit and Miss Piggy star as Bob and Emily Crachit. This could easily become a perennial family favorite with the familiar characters intact, but toned down just slightly for the younger set. Narration by Gonzo as Dickens himself helps introduce the plot lines and add some background. It's funny, touching and, of course, a technical marvel, seamlessly blending Muppet characters with the humans. ★★★½ DVD: $19.99, VHS: $9.99

The Muppet Movie

(1979, 94 min, US, James Frawley) *Kermit, Miss Piggy, Fozzie, Cameos: Steve Martin, Carol Kane, Orson Welles, Milton Berle, Mel Brooks, Madeline Kahn, Bob Hope.* The first of the Muppet films, this sweet, entertaining children's film follows the trail of Kermit the Frog on his way to stardom. Miss Piggy, Fozzie, Gonzo and the rest of the gang tag along. There's a charming musical score by Paul Williams. ★★★ DVD Dual: $19.99, VHS: $9.99

Muppet Treasure Island

(1996, 99 min, US, Brian Henson) *Kermit, Miss Piggy, Gonzo, Rizzo, Fozzie Bear, Tim Curry, Kevin Bishop, Jennifer Saunders, Billy Connelly.* The always-welcome Muppets return in an energetic retelling of the Stevenson classic. Gonzo and Rizzo the Rat take center stage joined by Muppet faves Kermit, Miss Piggy and Fozzie (playing a lunatic whose best friend lives in his index finger); Curry, Bishop and Connelly lend human support. This is a wholly entertaining lark, thanks to both the kooky antics in which the characters engage, and the fact that the creators play the story straight (as they did in the even better *Muppet Christmas Carol*). Not without its slow moments, the film nevertheless has wondrous bits, such as a Carmen Miranda-inspired free-for-all performed by pirates and Muppets in drag. ★★★ DVD: $14.99, VHS: $9.99

The Muppets Take Manhattan

(1984, 94 min, US, Frank Oz) *Kermit, Miss Piggy, Fozzie, Cameos: Sandra Bernhard, James Coco, Joan Rivers, Liza Minnelli, Gregory Hines, Art Carney.* The title is more than lived up to as Kermit, Miss Piggy and the rest of the gang head to New York to put on a Broadway musical. Lots of fun. ★★★ DVD Dual: $19.99, VHS: $9.99

Murder

(1930, 92 min, GB, Alfred Hitchcock) *Herbert Marshall, Norah Baring.* A fast-paced and inventive whodunit about a juror in an actress' murder trial who becomes convinced of the woman's innocence and sets out for some amateur sleuthing. The bizarre truth is ultimately revealed with an extraordinary twist. ★★★ VHS: $12.99

Murder at 1600

(1997, 107 min, US, Dwight H. Little) *Wesley Snipes, Diane Lane, Daniel Benzali, Alan Alda, Ronny Cox.* A by-the-books but competently made thriller which suggests that there's more shenanigans going on in the White House than seances and shredding parties. Snipes plays a D.C. homicide detective investigating a murder in the White House who is up against constant interference from Secret Service chief Benzali and staff, including Lane — who eventually becomes Snipes' ally. There are a couple of unpredictable twists and a few red herrings, but director Little seems more concerned with chases and the rudiments of the action film than laying the foundation for a good mystery. ★★½ DVD: $14.99, VHS: $9.99

Murder by Death

(1976, 94 min, US, Robert Moore) *Peter Falk, David Niven, Peter Sellers, Maggie Smith, Alec Guinness, Elsa Lanchester, James Coco, James Cromwell, Nancy Walker, Truman Capote.* Neil Simon wrote the screenplay for this delightfully zany spoof on movie detectives; with an all-star cast doing a number on Nick and Nora Charles (Niven, Smith), Miss Marple (Lanchester), Charlie Chan (Sellers), Hercule Poirot (Coco) and Sam Spade (Falk). Plenty of laughs and lots of fun. ★★★ DVD Dual: $24.99

Murder by Decree

(1979, 121 min, Canada/GB, Bob Clark) *Christopher Plummer, James Mason, Candy Clark, Geneviève Bujold, Donald Sutherland, John Gielgud.* A superior, dark-edged Sherlock Holmes mystery with Plummer as the famous sleuth, and Mason as Dr. Watson. An investigation into the murders of Jack the Ripper suggest involvement by a member of the Royal family. Plummer makes a most convincing Holmes, and Mason is a wondrous Watson. ★★★½ DVD Letterbox: $19.99

Murder by Numbers

(2002, 118 min, US, Barbet Schroeder) *Sandra Bullock, Ben Chaplin, Ryan Gosling, Michael Pitt, Agnes Bruckner, Chris Penn.* You have to hand it to Sandra Bullock — after the ripping she received playing an FBI agent in *Miss Congeniality*, she's bounces back to yet again wear a badge. This time out she plays a small-town police detective, and maybe not playing it for laughs is the way to go for she gives a commendable performance. Involving if rather familiar, *Murder by Numbers* follows Bullock's seasoned, weary policewoman who, with a new partner, investigates the murder of a woman killed by two high school students who committed the crime just for kicks (comparisons to Leopold and Loeb are obviously intentional). It then becomes a game of cat and mouse as she sets out to trap them. When director Schroeder concentrates more on the relationships of the two boys (which hints at but never commits to the homoerotic) and the two cops, the film is the more compelling for it. It falls short, however, in providing genuine thrills and keeping consistent pacing that would have elevated it above standard genre entertainment. ★★½ DVD Letterbox: $14.99, DVD Pan & Scan: $14.99, VHS: $9.99

Murder in the First

(1994, 122 min, US, Marc Rocco) *Kevin Bacon, Christian Slater, Gary Oldman, Kyra Sedgwick, Embeth Davidtz, Brad Dourif.* Bacon shines in this somber and tragic slice of history about Henri Young who, in 1937, after a botched escape attempt lands him three years naked and freezing in the bowels of Alcatraz, murders in plain sight the stool pigeon who turned him in. Slater is the fledgling public defender who turns a simple open-and-shut case into an indictment against the prison system and Alcatraz itself. Director Rocco enhances what would normally be deemed "made-for-TV" fare with gripping scenes of prison brutality. This violence is characterized by yet another showy performance from Oldman as the sadistic associate warden. ★★★ DVD: $14.99, VHS: $9.99

Murder, My Sweet

(1944, 95 min, US, Edward Dmytryk) *Dick Powell, Claire Trevor, Anne Shirley, Otto Kruger, Mike Mazurki.* One of the classics of film noir, this adaptation of Raymond Chandler's "Farewell, My Lovely" is a raw but exhilarating murder mystery where hard-boiled, wise-cracking detective Phillip Marlowe (Powell) becomes immersed in a duplicitous world of evil where everyone is a suspect and no one should be trusted. After taking on the case of finding ex-con Moose Malloy's missing girlfriend Velma, Marlowe soon is over his head in a sordid and ever more confusing maze of kidnappers, liars and ruthless killers. Superb dialogue and a great story highlight this stylish, trend-setting mystery. ★★★½ DVD: $19.99

Murder on the Bayou

(1987, 91 min, US, Volker Schlöndorff) *Holly Hunter, Louis Gossett, Jr., Richard Widmark, Woody Strode, Will Patton, Papa John Creach.* Written by Charles Fuller, this is a powerful drama of racial tensions in the New South. Set amidst the sugar cane fields of a searingly hot Louisiana, the film stars Hunter as a liberal plantation owner who galvanizes a group of long down-trodden black farmers and fishermen to militantly defend a fellow black man who claims that he killed a white man in self-defense. Impressive acting from the ensemble of elderly 38 men and a deft touch from German director Schlöndorff highlight this absorbing story of unity and courage. (aka: *A Gathering of Old Men*) ★★★½

Murder on the Orient Express

(1974, 127 min, GB, Sidney Lumet) *Albert Finney, Ingrid Bergman, Lauren Bacall, Sean Connery, Jacqueline Bisset, Vanessa Redgrave, Anthony Perkins, Richard Widmark, John Gielgud, Wendy Hiller, Michael York, Martin Balsam, Rachel Roberts.* Agatha Christie's popular novel makes for a sumptuous ride on the Orient Express in this big-budget, large-scaled, all-star murder mystery. Finney, obviously enjoying himself, stars as Hercule Poirot, that famed Belgian detective who finds himself investigating the murder of an American industrialist (Widmark) while a passenger on the famed luxury train. With more than enough suspects to go around, Poirot systematically interrogates and eliminates until the final and very surprising conclusion. A truly impressive cast. Lumet's pace is even throughout, which doesn't give rise to too many overly exciting scenes, but he keeps the whodunit aspect absolutely entrancing. ★★★½ VHS: $14.99

Murder, She Said

(1962, 87 min, GB, George Pollock) *Margaret Rutherford, Arthur Kennedy.* While dozing on a train, Miss Jane Marple awakens to witness a murder on a passing train. The police don't believe her. We, however, know better. Rutherford made her debut as Agatha Christie's famous sleuth. ★★★

Murderers Are Among Us

(1946, 85 min, Germany, Wolfgang Stoudte) *Hildegard Knef, Ernst Wilhelm Borchert.* Filmed in the rubble of Berlin at the end of WWII, *Murderers Are Among Us* is both a casebook example of the neorealist style and an unsettling historical document. A young woman recently released from a concentration camp returns to her apartment to find it occupied by a surgeon traumatized and embittered by his war experiences. Her stalwart resolve to begin life anew is in diametric opposition to his disillusionment: He who once saved lives no longer believes mankind worth saving. He encounters his former superior officer, a butcher of a man thriving in the devastation and at no loss for new opportunities for exploitation. The surgeon sees this encounter as a chance for retribution, and finds redemption instead. A startling and revelatory piece of filmmaking, and a testament to the human ability to salvage hope from utter desolation. (German with English subtitles) ★★★ DVD: $29.99, VHS: $24.99

Muriel

(1963, 111 min, France/Italy, Alain Resnais) *Delphine Seyrig, Jean-Pierre Kerien.* Resnais continues his exploration of the theme of the relationship between present and past in this serious film about the concrete realities of everyday life. Helen, a 40-year-old antique dealer, disillusioned with her situation, attempts to relive her past be renewing a relationship with a lover of 20 years before. (French with English subtitles) ★★★ VHS: $19.99

Muriel's Wedding

(1995, 105 min, Australia, P.J. Hogan) *Toni Collette, Bill Hunter, Rachel Griffiths, Daniel Lapaine, Jeane Drynan.* Collette gives a magical performance as the overweight, unemployed Muriel who desperately wants to fit in with the popular girls from high school. Her obsession with the clique prompts to steal from her father. When the theft is discovered, she leaves her family home in Porpoise Spit, Australia, for the big city life of Sydney. There she reaquaints herself with high school buddy Rhonda (brilliantly played by Griffiths), and tries to realize her life-long dream of marriage. The sometimes despairing events in Muriel's life are played out against extremely funny and often cynical comedy, humor which seems to take the sting out of her forlorn life. And as with other "ugly duckling" tales, the release of the swan inside allows for both humor and pathos. ★★★½ DVD: $14.99, VHS: $9.99

Murmur of the Heart

(1971, 118 min, France, Louis Malle) *Benoit Ferreux, Lea Massari.* Although tame by today's standards, Malle's infectious comedy about a boy's sexual coming-of-age and his relationship with his carelessly sensual mother caused quite a stir in 1971. Set in France in 1954, the story follows the day-to-day lives of a bourgeois family and especially Laurent, a precocious 14-year-old boy whose interests lie mainly in the jazz music of Charlie Parker and attempting to lose his virginity. His success in love takes an unexpected turn when he, accompanied by his free-spirited mother, is sent to a spa to recover from rheumatic fever. A tender and funny film which affectionately satirizes familial relationships. (French with English subtitles) ★★★½

Murphy's Romance

(1985, 107 min, US, Martin Ritt) *James Garner, Sally Field, Brian Kerwin, Corey Haim.* Garner received an Oscar nomination for his delightful performance in this simple and charming romantic comedy. Garner plays a small-town pharmacist who romances a recently divorced mother (Field), much to the dismay of her ne'er-do-well ex-husband (Kerwin). ★★★ DVD: $14.99, VHS: $9.99

Murphy's War

(1971, 106 min, GB, Peter Yates) *Peter O'Toole, Philippe Noiret, Sian Phillips.* When a British merchant ship is sunk by German torpedoes off the coast of Venezuela at the end of WWII, O'Toole finds himself in the unenviable position of being the sole survivor. For the remainder of the film, he dedicates himself to hunting down and destroying the U-boat responsible for the tragedy. Superbly staged action sequences and O'Toole's formidable presence make this a highly entertaining adventure film. ★★★ DVD: $14.99, VHS: $9.99

The Muse

(1999, 97 min, US, Albert Brooks) *Albert Brooks, Sharon Stone, Jeff Bridges, Andie MacDowell.* Brooks wrote, directed and stars in this often funny though a little too self-indulgent comedy as a successful screenwriter who is suffering from writer's block. Into his life stumbles Sarah (a luminous Stone), a descendent from Zeus and one of the nine Muses. As he tries to bang out a hit script, she takes control of not only his life but his family's life as well. Brooks manages some friendly and not-so-friendly jabs at the Hollywood filmmaking community, and when his jokes hit their targets, *The Muse* charms as it produces its laughs. But there's often too much time waiting for the next punchline, however expertly they are delivered by the good ensemble. ★★½ DVD: $19.99

Music Box

(1989, 128 min, US, Constantin Costa-Gavras) *Jessica Lange, Armin Mueller-Stahl, Frederic Forrest, Lukas Haas, Donald Moffat.* Director Costa-Gavras delivers another taut political thriller based on co-producer Joe Esterhas' finely drawn script. Lawyer Lange takes on her Hungarian-émigré father's case when he is accused of Nazi collaboration and heinous atrocities during WWII. Her firm belief that her father is innocent, however, gradually erodes as the evidence against him accumulates. A suspenseful, thoughtful exploration of the conflict between familial devotion and the strength of ethical belief. Fine ensemble acting is highlighted by the performances of Oscar-nominee Lange, Mueller-Stahl as her father, and Forrest as the prosecuting attorney. ★★★ VHS: $14.99

Music from Another Room

(1997, 104 min, US, Charlie Peters) *Gretchen Mol, Jude Law, Jennifer Tilly, Martha Plimpton, Brenda Blethyn.* Although it is a far-fetched romance, *Music from Another Room* does feature some pretty sweet and sentimental moments. Danny (Law) is a mosaic tiler who reunites with the Swan family he knew briefly 25 years before. As a young boy, Danny helped deliver Anna Swan, and swore he would one day marry her. Now an uptight adult, Anna (Mol) is alternately drawn to and annoyed by this mysterious suitor who transforms the rest of her highly dysfunctional family. While the central romance between the good-looking leads nearly sinks the film (Mol is miscast and Law lacks charisma), the episodes involving Anna's blind sister Nina (Tilly) are endearing. Writer-director Peters has made a noble effort, but the themes of kismet and taking chances are diluted by some painfully obvious clichés. ★★ DVD Pan & Scan: $9.99

The Music Lovers

(1971, 122 min, GB, Ken Russell) *Glenda Jackson, Richard Chamberlain, Christopher Gable, Max Adrian.* This extravagant account of the life of Tchaikovsky is classic Russell — wonderfully over-acted and filled with wildly overstated imagery. Chamberlain stars as the tortured, repressed homosexual composer; Gable is his clinging blond boyfriend; and Jackson, in a ferocious performance, plays his mad, nymphomaniac wife. Set in turn-of-the-century Russia, the film is impressively costumed and feverishly presented — with the hilarious, phallic and symbolism-laden "1812 Overture" dream sequence a particular highlight. ★★★

The Music Man

(1962, 177 min, US, Morton Da Costa) *Robert Preston, Shirley Jones, Buddy Hackett, Paul Ford, Hermione Gingold, Ron Howard.* This outstanding adaptation of Meredith Willson's Broadway smash is one of the great American musicals. Preston reprised his triumphant stage role to give the performance of his career as turn-of-the-century con man Prof. Harold Hill, who comes to River City, Iowa, to form a boys' band. Classic score includes "Trouble," "76 Trombones" and "Till There Was You." Jones is in good voice as Marion the Librarian. (Remade in 2003) ★★★★ DVD Letterbox: $19.99, VHS: $19.99, VHS Letterbox: $19.99

The Music of Chance

(1993, 98 min, US, Philip Haas) *James Spader, Mandy Patinkin, Charles Durning, Joel Grey, M. Emmet Walsh, Samantha Mathis, Christopher Penn.* With the intricacies of a good symphony and the eerie mystery of a good campfire story, *The Music of Chance*, based on the Paul Auster novel, is a complex and superbly acted tale of happenstance. Spader plays a polyester-clad cardsharp who is plucked from the mouth of despair by a drifter of another sort, Patinkin. The two embark on a road trip to a card game where Spader has set up two rich marks, Grey and Durning. When Spader and Patinkin arrive at the remote mansion of the eccentric billionaires, their lives are set on a dangerous and ludicrous path. Spader occasionally goes a little over-the-top in his weasel-like performance, but Patinkin, as a man of morals set adrift in a world of skewed honor, has a depth of character that anchors the ephemeral story. ★★★½

Music of the Heart

(1999, 123 min, US, Wes Craven) *Meryl Streep, Aidan Quinn, Angela Bassett, Gloria Estefan, Cloris Leachman, Jane Leeves, Jay O. Sanders.* Based on the documentary *Small Wonders*, this moving, life-affirming drama looks at the true-life experiences of music teacher Roberta Guaspari, who taught the violin to grade schoolers in East Harlem, and who made — with her students — a momentous trip to Carnegie Hall. Playing her role with verve and grit, Steep is excellent as the divorced mom of two who, with her own 50 violins goes about teaching kids in the economically depressed East Harlem school district. In no-nonsense fashion, director Craven follows Roberta's struggles as teacher, mom and lover in well-constructed episodes that don't always flow as well as they should but are involving nonetheless. *Music of the Heart* benefits from Roberta's own measured outlook, and Streep's unsentimental way of bringing it to the screen. ★★★ DVD: $14.99, VHS: $9.99

The Music Teacher

(1989, 100 min, Belgium, Gerard Corbiau) *Jose van Dam, Anne Roussel.* This opulent yet winsome drama is set in turn-of-the-century France where a world renowned opera singer suddenly announces his departure from the stage and retires to his estate in the countryside. It is there that he establishes a private school and selects two aspiring singers to be his pupils. The aspiring singers, a shy young woman and a poor but proud thief, are tutored by the older man, all in an effort to be ready for a singing competition hosted by the maestro's long-time enemy. Infused with humor, pathos and an innocently blossoming love story, this charming story features musical excerpts from Mahler, Verdi, Mozart, Schubert and Puccini. (French with English subtitles) ★★★

Musica Proibita (Forbidden Music)

(1943, 93 min, Italy, Carlo Camogalliani) *Tito Gobbi, Maria Mercader.* This interesting find was a typical example of the filmmaking style in Italy before the arrival of Neorealism in the late 1940s. The melodrama is set in the world of Italian opera and tells the haunting story of the love affair between a young conductor and the woman he loves. But their relationship is forbidden by the girl's grandmother when she learns of the identity of the man's father. An explosive tale of romance, murder, revenge and passion. (Italian with English subtitles) ★★½

The Musketeer

(2001, 106 min, US, Peter Hyams) *Justin Chambers, Catherine Deneuve, Tim Roth, Mena Suvari, Stephen Rea.* The swashbuckling tales of Alexandre Dumas' Three Musketeers are so inherently exciting that it would probably take a genius to make them seem boring and trivial. Alas, director Hyams and screenwriter Gene Quintano have accomplished just that — we'll refrain, however, from calling them geniuses just yet. A monotone Chambers is D'Artagnan, the famous fourth musketeer, who here sets out to avenge the murder of his parents. He tangles with a villainous commander (Roth) and Cardinal Richelieu (Rea), while saving the queen and, oh yeah, re-energizing the guard. He should have re-energized the script. The *raison d'être* for this remake is the choreography by martial arts master Xin-Xin Xiong, but even that fails to excite. *The Musketeer* falls flat with *un grand thud*. ★ DVD Letterbox Collector's Edition: $14.99, VHS: $9.99

Mussolini and I

(1985, 130 min, US/Italy, Alberto Negrin) *Bob Hoskins, Anthony Hopkins, Susan Sarandon, Annie Girardot, Fabio Testi, Kurt Raab.* An international cast spotlights this made-for-cable treatment of the conflicts between Mussolini (Hoskins) and his son-in-law Count Galeazzo Ciano, Minister of Foreign Affairs (Hopkins). Sarandon plays Benito's daughter in this sumptuously photographed and enjoyably overblown escapist entertainment. Cut down from a TV running time of 192 minutes, the film was originally titled *Mussolini: The Decline and Fall*. ★★½ DVD 2-disc set: $29.99, VHS 2-tape set: $29.99

Mute Witness

(1995, 92 min, US, Anthony Waller) *Mary Sudina, Fay Ripley, Evan Richards, Oleg Jankowskij, Alec Guinness.* A mute American F/X artist working on a low-budget slasher film in Russia witnesses her coworkers seemingly making an after-hours snuff film and is accidentally locked in the studio with them. She is then stalked through the hallways in a brilliantly conceived, tension-laden extended chase sequence which is unrelenting in its suspense. First-time director Waller, in an obvious though unacknowledged homage, infuses the film with the nail-biting suspense and horrific violence of De Palma and Argento to create a highly stylized and visceral thriller. The film's second half, however, becomes needlessly convoluted as an attempt to add humor puts it starkly at odds with the constant terror which comes before it. ★★★

Mutiny on the Bounty

(1935, 132 min, US, Frank Lloyd) *Charles Laughton, Clark Gable, Franchot Tone, Donal Crisp.* The first, and best, of the three *Bounty* pictures about the tyrannical Captain Bligh, his 18th-century voyage to Tahiti, and the events leading up the the notorious mutiny, led by First Officer Mister

Christian. Laughton gives a tour de force performance as the severe Bligh, and Gable is well-cast as Christian. Oscar for Best Picture. (Remade in 1962 and in 1984 as *The Bounty*) ★★★★ DVD: $19.99

Mutiny on the Bounty

(1962, 179 min, US, Lewis Milestone) *Marlon Brando, Trevor Howard, Richard Harris, Hugh Griffith, Richard Haydn.* This grandiose, self-important, often ludicrous remake manages to be thoroughly entertaining almost in spite of itself. Lush tropical locations help as does Brando's campy, bemused performance. Howard plays the sadistic Capt. Bligh with tremendous relish. The two stars reportedly disliked each other, leading to on-set confrontations that rivaled those aboard the Bounty. ★★½ VHS: $24.99, VHS Letterbox: $24.99

My American Cousin

(1985, 95 min, Canada, Sandy Wilson) *Margaret Langrick, John Wildman.* The time and setting for this enjoyable story is 1959 in the quiet outback of western Canada, where rock 'n' roll, hot rods and James Dean-influenced teens are still American phenomena. It's home, however, for Sandy, a precocious 12-year-old whose life takes a heated turn when Butch, her hip, handsome teenage cousin from America, visits. A humorous coming-of-age drama that explores first love as well as the dreams and frustrations of two very different people. (Sequel: *American Boyfriends*) ★★★

My Baby's Daddy

(2004, 86 min, US, Cheryl Dunye) *Eddie Griffin, Anthony Anderson, Michael Imperioli, Method Man, John Amos, Bai Ling, Marsha Thomason.* Three lifelong friends become fathers at almost exactly the same time, and need to put aside their adolescent ways. Set (laughably) in Philadelphia, but obviously mostly shot nowhere near the city, this at-times appalling comedy is unrelentingly infantile. It offers no insights, other than men should help take care of their kids, and provides no more than one or two laughs, and a boatload of ill will and borderline offensive, desperate material. A Chinese woman stops her boyfriend mid-apology to exclaim, "You had me with herro," while, in an astonishingly tasteless drunken fantasy scene, Griffin's character imagines the babies — via horrific CGI-enhancement — egging him on to bed a woman in the lewdest language possible. Who was this movie made for? The always-reliable Amos manages a chuckle or two, but this is otherwise an embarrassment. ★ DVD: $29.99

My Beautiful Laundrette

(1985, 98 min, GB, Stephen Frears) *Daniel Day-Lewis, Gordon Warnecke, Saeed Jaffrey, Roshan Seth, Shirley Ann Field.* An unpredictable and charming social comedy which follows the unlikely success story of a young English-born Pakistani and budding capitalist (Warnecke) and his punk lover (Day-Lewis). Together they brave the ugly spectre of racism and transform a dingy East End laundrette into a glitzy and profitable laundry emporium. ★★★★ DVD: $19.99

My Best Friend's Girl

(1984, 110 min, France, Bertrand Blier) *Isabelle Huppert, Thierry L'Hermitte, Coluche.* Huppert gives an erotically charged performance in Blier's whimsical look at male-bonding set around the ski resorts of Switzerland. Coluche costars with sexy ski-shop proprietor L'hermitte as the fast friends who share an enthusiasm for femme fatale Huppert. (French with English subtitles) ★★½

My Best Friend's Wedding

(1997, 105 min, US, P.J. Hogan) *Julia Roberts, Dermot Mulroney, Rupert Everett, Cameron Diaz, Philip Bosco, Rachel Griffiths, M. Emmet Walsh.* Roberts plays off the sweet character she's played for nearly ten years to give a bristling portrayal of a former lover out to stop the wedding of her ex — at any cost. Recalling Irene Dunne in *The Awful Truth* rather than Glenn Close in *Fatal Attraction*, Julia is Julianne, a successful food critic who has been best friends with Michael (Mulroney) since they broke up several years ago. Harboring a crush but never admitting it, her feelings for Michael are realized when he announces he's in love with another woman. She then sets in motion a plan to sabotage their relationship. One of the strengths of the film is that not all the humor is dependant upon Julianne's schemes, for the film is filled with delightful off-the-wall and totally unexpected comedic moments. As Julianne's gay confidant, Everett gives a smashing performance and one only wishes he had more screen time. ★★★ DVD Special Edition: $19.99, VHS: $9.99

My Big Fat Greek Wedding

(2002, 95 min, US, Joel Zwick) *Nia Vardalos, John Corbett, Lainie Kazan, Michael Constantine, Andrea Martin, Joey Fatone, Gia Carides, Louis Mandylor.* Dark-haired, pudgy Toula (Vardalos) dutifully carried her plastic container of moussaka to the school cafeteria even though she wanted the white-bread sandwiches the blonde girls had. Years later, 30 and unmarried, still dutiful, she works at Dancing Zorba's, the family restaurant. The rest of Toula's life seems mapped out, until a chance encounter with a young man (Corbett) first noticed in the restaurant takes Toula down a path very different from that envisioned by her very demonstrative, very Greek family. Small changes have a cumulative effect. Vardalos brings her one-woman play to the screen and, refreshingly, presents Toula's metamorphosis as gradual and believable, creating a strong female with native intelligence under surface naïveté. Sometimes the personalities are broadly drawn, frequently more caricature than character; but there's warmth and sweetness and a lot of heart without too much mawkishness. The cast is effective, demonstrating a true affection for their characters. Vardalos know-

My Big Fat Greek Wedding

ingly explores the effects of cultural isolation and the resolution of family constraints in her portrayal of Toula as she travels from frump to self-possessed, changing profoundly yet never leaving her roots. ★★★ DVD: $27.99, VHS: $22.99

My Blue Heaven

(1990, 95 min, US, Herbert Ross) *Steve Martin, Rick Moranis, Joan Cusack, Melanie Mayron, Bill Irwin, Carol Kane.* This funny though uneven look at the witness protection program run amok may be considered the demented "what-if" sequel to *GoodFellas*. Martin is an ex-gangster with a new identity relocated to suburbia and Moranis is a G-Man who has to keep an eye on him. Good idea. Good cast. So what happened? We think director Ross should leave the dopey high-concept comedies to Ivan Reitman and John Hughes. ★★ DVD: $14.99, VHS: $14.99

My Bodyguard

(1980, 96 min, US, Tony Bill) *Chris Makepeace, Adam Baldwin, Martin Mull, Ruth Gordon, Matt Dillon, John Houseman, Joan Cusack.* A youngster (Makepeace) hires the biggest kid in his class (Baldwin) as his bodyguard to protect him from a gang of bullies. Mull plays the little guy's dad, Gordon his grandmom, and Dillon is one of the toughs. ★★½ DVD Letterbox: $14.99, VHS: $6.99

My Brilliant Career

(1979, 101 min, Australia, Gillian Armstrong) *Judy Davis, Sam Neill, Wendy Hughes.* A radiant Davis stars in this period drama about a young woman in Australian outback at the turn of the century who is torn between marrying a local landowner (Neill) and pursuing her career as a writer. Lovingly photographed and directed by director Armstrong, the film is a marvelously understated look at a Victorian woman's struggle with the constraints of her social position. ★★★½

My Cousin Vinny

(1992, 119 min, US, Jonathan Lynn) *Joe Pesci, Marisa Tomei, Ralph Macchio, Fred Gwynne.* Pesci plays a fish-out-of-water in this good-natured comedy about a smallfry Brooklyn lawyer who travels to a backwoods Southern town to save his cousin (perpetual teenager Macchio) from a murder rap. Tomei's Oscar-winning, over-the-top performance as Pesci's gum-popping girlfriend easily outshines the rest of the goings-on in this small movie that acquits itself nicely. Gwynne has some fun as the incredulous judge. ★★★ DVD: $14.99

My Darling Clementine

(1946, 97 min, US, John Ford) *Henry Fonda, Victor Mature, Linda Darnell, Walter Brennan.* The often-told tale of Wyatt Earp, the Clanton Gang and the infamous fight at the O.K. Corral. This western is blessed with the sure hand of director Ford, who imbues his story with such a visual splendor and poetic grace it ranks among his finest works. Fonda is the famed marshall who, with Doc Holliday (Mature), cleans up the town of Tombstone. ★★★★ DVD: $14.99, VHS: $9.99

My Dinner with Andre

(1981, 110 min, US, Louis Malle) *Andre Gregory, Wallace Shawn.* Malle serves up a delectable duet by the quest-crazed Gregory (former artistic director of TLA) and the pragmatic Shawn. A supremely intelligent film which asks the question, "Is there any more reality on the top of Mount Everest than there is in the cigar shop next door?" ★★★½ DVD: $19.99, VHS: $29.99

My Dog Skip

(2000, 95 min, US, Jay Russell) *Frankie Muniz, Diane Lane, Luke Wilson, Kevin Bacon, Narrated by: Harry Connick, Jr.* Evoking the kind of memories each and everyone of us would be lucky to share, this heartwarming, inspiring memory piece is that rarity: a family film rich in emotion and spirit. Based on the book by Willie Morris, the gentle and funny *My Dog Skip* recalls young Willie growing up in a small Mississippi town during the second world war, and the special relationship he has with — you guessed it — his dog Skip. Muniz makes an especially appealing young hero, an outcast who learns to blossom with a little help from his canine friend. Lane, as Willie's mom, and Bacon, as his war-scarred father, each hit just the right note. An enchanting, make-you-smile reminiscence not to be missed. ★★★½ DVD: $14.99, VHS: $9.99

My Fair Lady

(1964, 171 min, US, George Cukor) *Audrey Hepburn, Rex Harrison, Stanley Holloway, Wilfred Hyde-White, Gladys Cooper, Theodore Bikel, Mona Washbourne.* Although much will be lost in watching this enchanting musical extravaganza on the little screen, *My Fair Lady* still dazzles the viewer with spectacular sets and costumes, an inspired Lerner & Loewe score and wonderful performances by Harrison and Hepburn. Winner of eight Academy Awards, this musical version of George Bernard Shaw's "Pygmalion" tells the now familiar tale of Professor Henry Higgins, an arrogant linguist, who takes Cockney flower waif Eliza Doolittle under his wing on a bet that he can transform her into a lady. ★★★★ DVD Letterbox: $19.99, DVD Letterbox 2-disc Special Edition: $26.99, VHS: $9.99

My Family (Mi Familia)

(1995, 125 min, US, Gregory Nava) *Jimmy Smits, Edward James Olmos, Esai Morales, Elpidia Carrillo.* A sometimes engrossing but ultimately unfocused three-generational family saga, this failed attempt at a Mexican-American *Godfather* was produced by Francis Ford Coppola and pays homage to his epic. Following an immigrant's life from his arrival in Los Angeles until the time his last grandchild leaves his household, the film tries to show the strength of its characters through heartbreaking tragedy, inflicting upon them one horrible event after another. The weepy story is at its best when it balances the heavy drama with a lighter tone, supplied by Olmos as narrator. *My Family* vividly captures several decades in a period East Los Angeles, the dust of which contrasts sharply with the art deco of a white West L.A. ★★½ DVD: $19.99

My Father Is Coming

(1991, 82 min, US/Germany, Monika Treut) *Alfred Edel, Shelley Kastner, Annie Sprinkle.* A comical story of sexual confusion, sexual awakening and self-discovery. Vicky, an aspiring actress and struggling waitress, is involved with both a man and a woman at the same time her German father arrives for a visit. Haven given the impression that she is a successful actress and happily married, Vicky vainly tries to impress her father and demanding pop, even resorting to getting a gay friend to play her husband. But papa doesn't get a chance to complain for he is immediately swept up in a whirlwind of romance, TV commercials and kinky sex — an odyssey which eventually leads to the bed of a lovely sex guru (played by Sprinkle.) The many characters in this charming comedy cover the spectrum of sexuality,

Wallace Shawn (l.) and Andre Gregory in *My Dinner with Andre*

and the result is an exuberant slice-of-life tale. (Filmed in English with some German with English subtitles) ★★★ VHS: $14.99

My Father's Glory

(1991, 110 min, France, Yves Robert) *Philippe Caubere, Nathalie Roussel.* The cherished childhood memories of author Marcel Pagnol are tenderly told in this enchanting and romantic tale set in turn-of-the-century Marseilles and Provence. The story follows Marcel, an 11-year-old boy who, along with his loving mother, schoolteacher father and other relatives, spends an idyllic summer in the rugged but beautiful terrain of southern France. It is there, amidst the tranquil hills, that the boy begins to learn about nature, friendship and life. A deceptively simple film, with great insights into familial relationships set in an era long ago lost to progress. The story continues in *My Mother's Castle*. (French with English subtitles) ★★★½

My Favorite Blonde

(1942, 78 min, US, Sidney Lanfield) *Bob Hope, Madeleine Carroll, Gale Sondergaard.* In his old radio show, Hope made so many compliments about Carroll it was almost a running gag. How appropriate, then, that he costars with her in this very funny spy comedy which pays homage to Carroll's classic thriller *The 39 Steps.* Hope stars as a second-rate entertainer (his partner, a penguin, has far more talent) who becomes involved with British agent Carroll, who must transport secret bombing information cross-country. And, of course, the enemy is in hot pursuit. Clever one-liners, non-stop adventure and a breezy pace all contribute to make this arguably Hope's best comedy outside of the *Road* series. ★★★½ DVD Double Feature: $14.99

My Favorite Brunette

(1947, 87 min, US, Elliott Nugent) *Bob Hope, Dorothy Lamour, Peter Lorre, Lon Chaney, Jr.* A funny romp with Bob as a baby photographer who really wants to be a private eye; and through mistaken identity, gets his chance. In-joke cameos include Alan Ladd and Der Bingle. ★★★

My Favorite Martian

(1998, 95 min, US, Donald Petrie) *Christopher Lloyd, Jeff Daniels, Elizabeth Hurley, Daryl Hannah, Wallace Shawn, Christine Ebersole,*

Michael Lerner, Ray Walston. The 1960s TV sitcom "My Favorite Martian" had a respectable three-year run on CBS, was often very cute, and was lucky enough to have Ray Walston in the lead as a Martian stranded on Earth. Its silly situations and genial laughs make it seem like "Frasier" compared to the big-screen remake — this is an absolute mess. An over-the-top Lloyd is now Uncle Martin, who is taken in by reporter Tim O'Hara (Daniels). Martin just wants to get back home, while Tim wants an exclusive for his paper. Nuttiness of the most boring kind ensues. Lloyd and Daniels are sabotaged by a poor script and careless direction. Too bad that a whole generation will only know this version. ★½ DVD: $14.99, VHS: $9.99

My Favorite Season (Ma Saison Préférée)

(1993, 124 min, France, André Téchiné) *Catherine Deneuve, Daniel Auteuil, Chiara Mastroianni, Marthe Villalonga.* A highly accomplished examination of three generations of a family, *My Favorite Season* deals with the guilt and regrets that surface between parent and children, siblings and spouses. The film concerns Emilie (Deneuve) and Antoine (Auteuil), a brother and sister who resume their fragile relationship when they are forced to care for their ailing mother (Villalonga). Téchiné gradually develops — or breaks — the bonds between the characters, most notably in the suggestion that Antoine harbors incestuous longing for his sister. As Emilie strives late in her life for personal growth and understanding, she comes to some difficult realizations. As is the director's style, the dramatic focus shifts back and forth to allow his themes on love and honesty to resonate clearly. Radiant as ever, Deneuve makes Emilie a sympathetic heroine, while Auteuil lends fine support as the boorish Antoine. (French with English subtitles) ★★★½ DVD: $19.99, VHS: $9.99

My Favorite Wife

(1940, 88 min, US, Garson Kanin) *Cary Grant, Irene Dunne, Randolph Scott, Gail Patrick.* In this fabulously funny comedy, Grant and Dunne appear in their second of three films together. Dunne returns home after seven years lost at sea to discover husband Grant has just remarried. Scott is the handsome hunk who was marooned with Dunne, much to Grant's chagrin. A joy from beginning to end. (Remade in 1963 as *Move Over, Darling*) ★★★½ DVD: $19.99

My Favorite Year

My Favorite Year

(1982, 92 min, US, Richard Benjamin) *Peter O'Toole, Mark Linn-Baker, Jessica Harper, Joseph Bologna, Lainie Kazan, Bill Macy, Anne DeSalvo.* A delightful comedic reflection on the early years of television. O'Toole runs wild as a swashbuckling celluloid hero (patterned after Errol Flynn) brought to his knees by the prospect of a live TV appearance. Sparkling support by Bologna as an ersatz Sid Caesar and Linn-Baker as O'Toole's impressionable escort. O'Toole has probably never been funnier, and the screenplay offers hilarious observations on stardom and the grind of behind-the-scenes TV. ★★★★ DVD Letterbox: $19.99, VHS: $14.99

My Fellow Americans

(1996, 101 min, US, Peter Segal) *Jack Lemmon, James Garner, Dan Aykroyd, John Heard, Sela Ward, Wilford Brimley, Lauren Bacall.* Call it what you may: *Grumpy Old Presidents* or *In the Line of Fire of Grumpy Old Men*; but *My Fellow Americans*, a predictable, puerile comedy about two feuding, ex-presidents on the run, manages to produce a few laughs in spite of itself. Lemmon and Garner rely on their invaluable comedic instincts to play former commander-in-chiefs (and opponents) who, having individually discovered a cover-up by the current president (Aykroyd), flee together when they are almost assassinated by the Secret Service. Most of the film consists of them bickering as they try to elude the hit men, and each handles the one-liners and put-downs with charm and ease. For those who found enjoyment in the *Grumpy Old Men* series. ★★½ DVD: $9.99

My First Mister

(2001, 109 min, US, Christine Lahti) *Albert Brooks, Leelee Sobieski, Desmond Harrington, Carol Kane.* *Ghost World* meets *Harold and Maude*, and youthful alienation meets middle-aged despondency in this accomplished directorial turn by Lahti. Goth Jennifer (Sobieski) is suffering an unwilling and unprepared-for entry into post-high school extended adolescence. Looking for subsistence wages in retail, she finds her aging reverse image in the studiously buttoned-down Randall (Brooks), the manager of a conservative men's clothing store. It's portly vs. pierced, practiced conformity vs. studied anarchism, as the two mismatched antagonists become each other's sounding boards and second chances; they break down each other's self-con-

structed barriers, opening up to the possibilities surrounding them. Sobieski and Brooks perfectly complement each other, projecting their characters in synchronicity and with intelligence. Refreshing in its contemplation of reconciliation, closure and inauguration, *My First Mister* is a compassionate examination of the paths we choose in life, and the startling redemptive power of human interaction. ★★★½ DVD Letterbox: $29.99, VHS: $14.99

My First Wife

(1984, 89 min, Australia, Paul Cox) *John Hargreaves, Wendy Hughes.* Hargreaves and Hughes give powerful, anguished performances in Cox's award-winning drama about the disintegration of a ten-year marriage. Told from "the man's point of view," this portrait of the disemboweling of their union is gutty and emotionally involving. ★★★

My Forbidden Past

(1951, 72 min, US, Robert Stevenson) *Robert Mitchum, Ava Gardner, Melvyn Douglas.* Gardner seeks to marry a promising young doctor, but family members disrupt her nuptial plans. When Ava later attempts to rekindle the affair, she finds her lover has since married. Mitchum and Douglas are the men in her life. An uninvolving soaper which barely rises above its melodramatic story line. ★★ VHS: $19.99

My Giant

(1998, 104 min, US, Michael Lehmann) *Billy Crystal, Kathleen Quinlan, Joanna Pacula, Gheorghe Muresan, Steven Seagal.* Crystal plays Sammy, a super-slick talent agent in a slump who makes a gigantic discovery while on location in Romania. Max, a seven-foot-seven-inches tall countryman who's lived his entire adult life in a monastary. In this gentle giant Sammy sees a star and vows to put him in movies. The film relies heavily on the visual sight gag of Max assimilating to the hustle-and-bustle of city life, and one goofy sequence has Max fending off seven dwarfs in a bizarre wrestling match. Besides the obligatory size jokes, there's nothing new here to add to the "mismatched-buddy-flick" genre. Stunningly, some of the biggest laughs come from Seagal, who pokes fun at himself. His self-deprecating humor is the only element which gives the film any personality. ★★ DVD: $14.99, VHS: $9.99

My Girl

(1991, 102 min, US, Howard Zieff) *Anna Chlumsky, Dan Aykroyd, Macaulay Culkin, Jamie Lee Curtis, Richard Masur, Griffin Dunne.* Alternating between comedy and drama, *My Girl* is an ever-so-cute, very sentimental "kids" movie" (from its marketing advertising) which may prove to be too intense for particularly young viewers. One scene in question is the death of the Culkin character; which, though handled awkwardly in dramatic terms, is sensitively portrayed. Chlumsky is an 11-year-old girl living with her father (Aykroyd), a funeral director. The story follows her summer vacation, where she befriends Culkin, reluctantly witnesses her father fall in love with Curtis. There are a few laughs to be had, though this is more dramatic than the ads suggest. (Sequel: *My Girl 2*) ★★½ DVD: $14.99, VHS: $14.99

My Girl 2

(1994, 99 min, US, Howard Zieff) *Anna Chlumsky, Dan Aykroyd, Jamie Lee Curtis.* What might have been an affecting tale of a young girl's quest to discover the history of her deceased mother is instead overwhelmed by heavy-handed sentimentality and a mawkish sensibility which makes the frequently saccharine original seem like something from Abel Ferrara by comparison. Aykroyd and Curtis sleepwalk through their reprised roles as "My Girl" Vada's (Chlumsky) parents. The film's only redeeming quality is that it avoids attacking those who don't fit into the Quayle Family Values it so heartily celebrates. ★½

My Girlfriend's Boyfriend

(1998, 81 min, US, Kenneth Schapiro) *Valerie Perrine, Deborah Gibson, Chris Bruno, Linda Larkin, Jill Elizabeth Novick, Sean Runnette.* Valiantly attempting a screwball comedy, this lame gay comedy fails on most counts. To further his career, soap opera hunk Cliff (Bruno) plans to marry sweet society gal Cory but Cliff is secretly gay (he's lovers with the best man). All hell breaks loose on the wedding day when Cory's best friend Liberty arrives with her lanky boyfriend and the question of who is gay, who is straight, and who is going to marry who looms in the air. One could overlook its low-budget roots, but the tired plot, repetitive pratfalls that are not funny, flat acting and stagnant photography make this film more of a chore than a pleasure. ★★

My Heroes Have Always Been Cowboys

(1991, 106 min, US, Stuart Rosenberg) *Scott Glenn, Kate Capshaw, Ben Johnson, Tess Harper, Gary Busey.* Glenn plays an aging rodeo circuit bullrider who returns to his small Texas home town for the first time in 20 years after an accident leaves him injured. There, he picks up the pieces he left behind, taking care of his invalid father, rebuilding the family's deserted ranch and renewing a romance with an old flame. Glenn is particularly good in this involving though choppy tale of familial conflict and loyalty. ★★½

My Left Foot

(1989, 103 min, Ireland, Jim Sheridan) *Daniel Day-Lewis, Brenda Fricker, Hugh O'Connor, Ray McAnally, Fiona Shaw, Adrian Dunbar.* It came as no surprise when Day-Lewis walked away with an Oscar for Best Actor for his portrayal of the severely handicapped Irish painter/author Christy Brown. Born with cerebral palsy, Brown never gained the use of his limbs except for his left foot, with which he brushed canvases so stunning they earned him recognition as an acclaimed artist. With acute sensitivity, Day-Lewis depicts Brown as an intense, brooding, complicated and restless soul with a zest for life far beyond that of most people. Fine support comes from Fricker, who also won a much-deserved Oscar for her gutsy performance as Christy's resilient mother. A stunning portrait both passionate and intelligent. ★★★★

My Life

(1993, 112 min, US, Bruce Joel Rubin) *Michael Keaton, Nicole Kidman, Haing S. Ngor, Queen Latifah.* With the screenplays for both *Ghost* and *Jacob's Ladder* to his credit, Rubin, making his directorial debut, is in familiar waters with this emotional and surprisingly persuasive drama about life and death. Keaton stars as a successful L.A. executive dying of cancer. About to become a first-time parent, he decides to leave a video autobiography for his child, whom he will probably not live to meet. As he and his wife (Kidman) anticipate the birth of their new baby, each must come to terms with Keaton's impending demise. Although a little too steeped in ancient mysticism for its own good, Rubin's text is moving and probably has more to say about the dying process than the high-profile *Philadelphia.* Keaton's performance is uncommonly good. ★★★ DVD: $9.99

My Life and Times with Antonin Artaud

(1993, 98 min, France, Gérard Mordillat) *Sami Frey, Marc Barbé, Julie Jezequel, Valerie Jeannet.* Based on the diaries of Parisian poet Jacques Prevel, this fictionalized account follows a young Prevel (Barbé) as he develops a tentative relationship with theatre innovator Antonin Artaud (Frey). Prevel himself is a piece of work, a down-and-out philanderer who spends most of his time in a flophouse with his emotionally strung-out girlfriend and occasionally spending time with his inexplicably devoted wife. When he hears of Artaud's release from an insane asylum, he finagles an introduction in hopes of developing fame by association. Filmed in black and white, the film does a fine job of evoking a sumptuous post-war imagery and has a stylish, Euro-chic appeal. But it is a sadly inappropriate memorial to Artaud to present his final days so harmlessly — no suffering in the fires of his own internal hell here. It's just too safe. (French with English subtitles) ★★½

My Life as a Dog

(1985, 101 min, Sweden, Lasse Hallström) *Anton Glanzelius, Manfred Serner, Anki Lidén, Melinda Kinnaman, Tomas von Brömssen, Ing-Marie Carlsson.* A captivating and heartwarming look at the trials and tribulations of a 12-year-old boy who, in the wake of his mother's death, is shipped off to live with his uncle in a rural Swedish village in the 1950s. Touching drama is sprinkled with poignant comedy as the boy battles his feelings of self-abasement and despair. A truly winning insight into the joys and sorrows of childhood which features outstanding performances from its two child stars. (Swedish with English subtitles) ★★★★ DVD Criterion Collection: $39.99

My Life So Far

(1999, 95 min, GB/Scotland, Hugh Hudson) *Colin Firth, Mary Elizabeth Mastrantonio, Malcolm McDowall, Robbie Norman, Iréne Jacob, Rosemary Harris.* A sweet, and at times sentimental portrait of a young boy growing up in Scotland in the 1930s, director Hudson's modest film is a pleasant coming-of-age tale. When Morris (McDowell) and Edward (Firth) quibble over the estate of matriarch Gamma Macintosh (Harris), family tensions escalate. As seen through the eyes of 10-year old Fraser (Norman), the situation really stems from the arrival of Morris' new wife Heloise (Jacob), who becomes the object of Edward's misplaced affections. Although the drama is a little stiff, *My Life So Far* is really quite charming and uplifting. ★★★ DVD: $19.99, VHS: $9.99

My Life to Live (Vivre sa Vie)

(1962, 85 min, France, Jean-Luc Godard) *Anna Karina, Saddy Rebbot.* Godard's detached and at times analytical approach to his subjects continues in this richly paradoxical tale of a young shop assistant (Karina) who turns to prostitution but who "gives her body to keep her soul." Set up in 12 tableaux segments, Godard has said that this film was "not a new departure, but an arrival." (French with English subtitles) ★★★ DVD: $14.99, VHS: $9.99

My Life without Me

(2003, 106 min, Canada/Spain, Isabel Coixet) *Sarah Polley, Amanda Plummer, Scott Speedman, Leonor Watling, Deborah Harry, Maria de Medeiros, Mark Ruffalo.* Polley is fine as usual playing a young, happily married mother of two who learns she only has weeks to live. She decides to tell no one, and makes a list of things she wants to do before she dies. An interesting premise is overshadowed a bit by the lead character's selfishness; of course, she has the right to do what she wishes with her last weeks on earth, and no one could entirely begrudge her for focusing on herself. But by blocking her family completely from her feelings she becomes a rather alienating character, and it's only Polley's talent and charm that holds the film together. A near-miss, *My Life without Me* is also buoyed by nice supporting turns by Harry as Polley's mom and Richings as her squeamish yet sympathetic doctor. ★★½ DVD Letterbox: $24.99, VHS: $102.99

My Life's in Turnaround

(1994, 84 min, US, Donal Lardner Ward & Eric Schaeffer) *Eric Schaeffer, Donal Lardner Ward, Dana Wheeler Nicholson, Phoebe Cates, Martha Plimpton, John Sayles, Casey Seimaszko.* With this ultra no-budget impromptu, actor/writer/producer/directors Schaeffer and Ward really had no idea what to make a film about, so they made a film about exactly that — two burnt-out denizens of lower Manhattan's grunge art scene searching to make a film deal. It's a contrivance that on face value is not the least bit clever, but in this duo's hands it somehow becomes ingenious. Think of it, these guys make an asset out of their dearth of creative inspiration! What makes it all work is their infectious personalities and the hilarious and incessant banter between them — what develops is actually a thoughtful look at their friendship. ★★★ DVD: $9.99, VHS: $14.99

My Little Chickadee

(1940, 83 min, US, Eddie Cline) *W.C. Fields, Mae West, Margaret Hamilton.* Fields was an alcoholic; West practiced abstinence. The two did not get along. Fields wrote his scenes; she hers. Count the

number of times they're in the same shot together. Perhaps it was this animosity that goaded them to do some of their best work in this tale of a woman of easy virtue entering into a marriage of convenience with a con man. It is in this film that Fields says that the only thing worse than being in Philadelphia is being hanged. ★★★

My Little Girl

(1986, 118 min, US, Connie Kaiserman) *Mary Stuart Masterson, Geraldine Page, James Earl Jones, Anne Meara, Peter Gallagher.* Masterson gives a touching performance in this absorbing drama of an overprivileged miss who tries to make a difference by working with disadvantaged young girls. Page is used to good advantage as her supportive grandmother. Portions filmed in the Main Line area of Philadelphia. ★★★

My Lucky Stars

(1985, 99 min, Hong Kong, Sammo Hung) *Jackie Chan, Yuen Biao, Sammo Hung.* Amiable sequel to *Winners and Sinners* reteams Jackie, Samo and Biao in a wildly uneven, though always entertaining action/comedy. Biao is captured by the bad guys, and Jackie and Samo have to save him; that's all the plot you need for this film, which, after a fun opening chase in an amusement park, settles down into silly comedy mode for perhaps a bit too long, then delivers the action — the highlight of which is an infamous catfight. Never as tough or fast-paced as you want it to be, *My Lucky Stars* is best approached as a silly, Hong Kong hodgepodge, and on that level, is fun stuff indeed. (Cantonese with English subtitles) ★★★ DVD: $9.99, VHS: $39.99

My Man

(1997, 95 min, France, Bertrand Blier) *Anouk Grinberg, Gérard Lanvin, Olivier Martinez, Mathieu Kassovitz.* Though audacious, writer-director Blier's *My Man*, which addresses how people are transformed by love and money, is ultimately an unfulfilling sex comedy. Marie (Grinberg) is a high-class prostitute who encounters Jeannot (Lanvin), a homeless stranger. She takes him in and falls madly in love. In the film's most fascinating sequence, Marie seduces Jeannot, and asks him to be her pimp. The main problem with the film is that although these changes may speak volumes about the characters, they are not credible within the framework Blier has established. (French with English subtitles) ★★½ VHS: $29.99

My Man Godfrey

(1936, 96 min, US, Gregory La Cava) *William Powell, Carole Lombard, Alice Brady, Eugene Pallette, Mischa Auer, Franklin Pangborn.* Classic screwball comedy with Lombard giving a priceless performance as a daffy heiress who meets a hobo on a scavenger hunt, and hires him as the family butler, unaware that he is actually a successful businessman. Powell is dapper as ever as the title character, and there's great comic support from Pallette, Brady and the hilarious Auer, who earned an Oscar nomination for, among other things, imitating a monkey. (Remade in 1957) ★★★★ DVD Criterion Collection: $39.99, VHS: $9.99

My Michael

(1975, 95 min, Israel, Dan Wolman) *Efrat Lavie, Oded Kotler.* Two intelligent young adults find each other and marry in a divided Jerusalem in the late 1950s. Michael, a responsible and hard-working scientist, is comfortable in the arrangement, in contrast to Hanna, who finds herself unfulfilled by the petit-bourgeois life she is leading. Loneliness and fantasy take over in this gentle, yet controversial rendering of the Amos Oz novel. (Hebrew with English subtitles) ★★★ VHS: $79.99

My Mother's Castle

(1991, 98 min, France, Yves Robert) *Julien Caimaca, Philippe Caubere, Nathalie Roussel.* The childhood remembrances of young Marcel continue in this captivating story which begins where *My Father's Glory* ends. Marcel's family returns to the city after their magical summer in Provence, only to decide later to make their country cottage a weekend and holiday retreat. It is there, in the barren, parched hills, that Marcel discovers the joy and pain of first love as well as a deep affection for and understanding of his loving parents. Possibly a bit too saccharine for hardened existential French videophiles, this unpretentious, heartwarming drama should prove to be a treasured delight for others. (French with English subtitles) ★★★

My Name Is Bill W.

(1989, 118 min, US, Daniel Petrie) *James Woods, James Garner, JoBeth Williams, Fritz Weaver, Gary Sinise.* Woods gives one of his trademark on-target performances as Bill Wilson, cofounder of Alcoholics Anonymous. An intensely driven businessman and alcoholic, Wilson is literally kept alive by his wife (Williams) until he finds treatment which handles his condition as a disease, not a lack of will. By chance he meets Dr. Robert Smith (Garner), fellow drunk; together they formulate what will develop into the 12-step program. This TV production has a fine eye for period detail and enjoys good performances from the entire cast. ★★★

My Name Is Ivan

(1966, 84 min, USSR, Andrei Tarkovsky) *Kolya Burlaiev, Valentin Zubkov.* The first film by this visionary Russian director is a poetic, sad story of a young boy caught up in World War II. Following the death of his mother during the early days of the war, 12-year-old Ivan's childhood is quickly ended when he joins the ranks of youths working as intelligence scouts for the army. The film is made in a style which moves from terrifying realism to lyrical impressionism. A haunting film experience. (Russian with English subtitles) ★★★½

My Name Is Joe

(1999, 105 min, Scotland, Ken Loach) *Peter Mullan, Louise Goodall, David McKay, Anne-Marie Kennedy, David Hayman.* Loach's second film, following *Carla's Song*, about the lower class in Glasgow, is a riveting character study which earned Mullan the best actor prize at Cannes. Mullan's Joe is a recovering alcoholic, trying to set his life straight while on the dole. His main interest is his soccer team; he has a framed newspaper clipping of their sole victory. One of the players, Liam (McKay), is in trouble with the local drug kingpin (Hayman); in this community, everyone helps each other out, and Joe's affinity for Liam and desire to see him set things right sends him back into the world he is trying to escape. Complicating things is Joe's relationship with a social worker (Goodall); never mind that his 12-step program advises against finding new love so soon. Joe's struggles are poignant, funny and heartbreaking, and watching Mullan wrestle with them is unforgettable. This English-language film is helpfully subtitled in English. ★★★½ VHS: $102.99

My Neighbor Totoro

(1994, 87 min, Japan, Hayao Miyazaki) This superbly animated tale is both an enchanting story and a terrific look at Japanese life in the country. Two young girls move out of the city with their father while their mother recuperates from a long illness in a distant hospital. In their new home they meet two large, furry and lovable totoros, creatures visible only to the children. When the youngest girl mistakenly starts to fear that her mother is going to die, she runs away to find the mystical and is rescued by the totoros. ★★★½ DVD: $9.99, VHS Dubbed: $9.99

My New Gun

(1992, 99 min, US, Stacy Cochran) *Diane Lane, James LeGros, Stephen Collins, Tess Harper, Philip Seymour Hoffman.* Lane stars in this quirky comedy as a yuppie, suburban housewife who doesn't know how to react when her husband (Collins) gives her a .38 revolver for protection — so she gives it to her wacky new neighbor (LeGros). LeGros, with *Drugstore Cowboy* and *Gun Crazy* behind him, inches ever closer to being awarded a patent for his emotionless, zoned-out drifter character, who in this case purports to need a gun to protect his mother. Brimming with suspicion, and a possible infatuation, Lane starts to snoop around his house in search of clues about his real motives. Is he a drug dealer? A Mafia hit man? What she finds only confuses her more. First-time director Cochran keeps the action moving at a snappy pace and gives the film just the right amount of skewed humor to make it most refreshing viewing. ★★★

My New Partner

(1985, 104 min, France, Claude Zidi) *Philippe Noiret, Thierry L'Hermitte, Regina.* A delightful French farce about the antics of a charmingly amoral cop. Noiret stars as the veteran "flic" who must teach the ways of the world to his new partner, a scrupulously innocent rookie. Noiret and L'hermitte offer engaging performances. (French with English subtitles) ★★★

My Night at Maud's

(1970, 105 min, France, Eric Rohmer) *Jean-Louis Trintignant, Françoise Fabian, Marie-Christine Barrault.* Scintillating conversation on life, love and morality forms the bedroom talk in Rohmer's witty and fascinating comedy of manners. Trintignant plays the staunch Catholic who finds his principles tested when he is invited by the charming but free-spirited Maud (Fabian) to spend the night in her nonexistent spare room. The focus is not how they get together, but rather, how they manage not to. The third of Rohmer's Six Moral Tales and one of the director's most captivating works. (French with English subtitles) ★★★½ DVD: $14.99, VHS: $9.99

My Other Husband

(1985, 110 min, France, Georges Lautner) *Miou-Miou, Rachid Ferrache.* This story, about a frantic woman who has a husband and child in Paris and a lover and two children in the country, has the potential of being just another *comédie soufflé*. But happily, coupled with a funny script, some great supporting characters and the exhilarating presence of Miou-Miou in the starring role, the film rises above the situation comedy and becomes not only a successfully zany farce but also a sensitive feminist look at one woman's life. (French with English subtitles) ★★★ VHS: $59.99

My Own Private Idaho

(1991, 105 min, US, Gus Van Sant) *River Phoenix, Keanu Reeves, Udo Kier, William Richert, James Russo, Flea, Rodney Harvey.* With his third film, Van Sant has proven himself one of the most daring, innovative and accomplished directors of the day. Phoenix's portrayal of Mike, a solitary, narcoleptic street hustler searching for his long-lost mother is brilliant. Van Sant deftly weaves in a subplot based on Shakespeare's "Henry IV, Pt II," even borrowing a smattering of the Bard's dialogue. Reeves gives strong support as Mike's Prince Hal-like friend and Richert is superb as the Falstaff-derived Bob Pigeon. Dreamily photographed, with mood ranging from hilarious to tragic to highly erotic, *Idaho* is a modern classic. ★★★★ VHS: $19.99

My Science Project

(1985, 95 min, US, Jonathan Betuel) *John Stockwell, Fisher Stevens, Dennis Hopper,*

River Phoenix (l.) and Keanu Reeves in *My Own Private Idaho*

THE DISCERNING FILM LOVER'S GUIDE

Danielle Von Zerneck. A high school senior working on a class project creates a device which can alter time and space. It's not really as fun as it sounds. ★½ VHS: $14.99

My Sex Life
(Or How I Got into an Argument)
(1996, 178 min, France, Arnaud Desplechin) *Mathieu Amalric, Emmanuelle Devos, Emmanuel Salinger, Chiara Mastroianni.* A philosophical romance about the sexual and professional escapades among a group of graduate students, *My Sex Life* is overlong and underwhelming. Paul (Amalric) is unhappy; not only is he unmotivated to complete his thesis, but he is in the process of ending his relationship with his long-term girlfriend. Coasting through his routine, Paul becomes infatuated with a number of women, and these dalliances, combined with a series of humiliations by a professional rival, force him to re-examine his behavior. While the second half of *My Sex Life,* which chronicles Paul's increasing despair, offers more interest than the tedious beginning, the film's main problem is that the protagonist simply lacks charm. Since little actually happens in the film, there's no real payoff when any drama does come to a head. Ultimately, *My Sex Life* is largely unsatisfying. (French with English subtitles) ★★ DVD: $24.99, VHS: $19.99

My Sister Eileen
(1955, 108 min, US, Richard Quine) *Betty Garrett, Janet Leigh, Jack Lemmon, Bob Fosse, Dick York, Tommy Rall.* In 1942, Rosalind Russell starred in *My Sister Eileen,* a film comedy based on Ruth McKinney's stage hit. Eleven years later, Russell reprised her role in the Broadway musical adaptation, retitled "Wonderful Town." However, a new musical score was written when the story returned to the screen in this musical form in 1955. Though the music is not on par with "Wonderful Town," it's nevertheless snappy and engaging. Garrett and Leigh play sisters from Ohio who move to Greenwich Village, hoping to find fame and fortune. They find Lemmon and Fosse. Fosse choreographed the film, and his fledgling trademark movements are in evidence. ★★★

My Son the Fanatic
(1999, 87 min, GB, Udayan Prasad) *Om Puri, Akbar Kurtha, Rachel Griffiths, Gopi Desai, Stella Skarsgård.* Hanif Kureishi (*My Beautiful Laundrette*) wrote this look at the immigrant community experience in contemporary Britain. Puri stars as the troubled father of a young man (Kurtha) who's utterly alienated. Kureishi's genius here is to switch the expected generation-gap conflict: father wants assimilation and marriage into the white world for son, while son rejects his white fiancée and embraces radical Islam. The script continues to surprise, with Puri getting involved with a local prostitute, further complicating this family melodrama. There's gentle humor, frank observations and warm characters, who are brought to life through appealing performances. ★★★ DVD: $14.99, VHS: $9.99

My Summer Story
(1994, 85 min, US, Bob Clark) *Charles Grodin, Mary Steenburgen, Kieran Culkin, Christian Culkin.* Jean Shepherd's childhood reminiscences are continued the summer following the delightful *A Christmas Story.* Unfortunately, the results aren't nearly as lively or inspired. This time around, family members (here portrayed by Grodin, Steenburgen, and two more Culkins: Kieran and

Christian) each have a personal quest. The eldest son wants to find the perfect killer top. Mom wants to collect a complete set of movie theatre giveaway china. And Dad sets out to vanquish an obscenely extended family of miscreant neighbors. This effort lacks the consummate charm and whimsy of *Christmas*; the characters are too broadly drawn, and lack the warmth and accessibility which make the first film a perennial favorite. ★★

My Teacher's Wife
(1995, 92 min, US, Bruce Leddy) *Tia Carrere, Christpher McDonald, Jason London, Jeffrey Tambor, Alexondra Lee, Zak Orth.* Boy falls in love with tutor, who just happens to be the wife of his vile math teacher. A tired formula to be sure, but a fun and likable cast makes *My Teacher's Wife* rather upbeat. There are a few love stories to one's interest, as London leaves his girlfriend in the lurch as he figures out what he wants out of love and life. Though the events are predictable, the characters seem genuine in getting there. ★★½ DVD: $24.99

My Twentieth Century
(1989, 104 min, Hungary, Ildiko Enyedi) *Dorothea Segda, Oleg Jankowsky.* Crisscrossing confusion and strange coincidence propel this lighthearted fairy tale about twin sisters, separated at birth, who are reunited years later. Set against the tumultuous chaos of turn-of-the-century Hungary, as well as many other exotic locales throughout Europe, the story has the twins meeting once again on the Orient Express — one, a wealthy courtesan; the other, an anarchist carrying explosives. While unknown to one another, each woman is having an affair with the same man. (Hungarian with English subtitles) ★★★ VHS: $19.99

My Wife Is an Actress
(2002, 95 min, France, Yvan Attal) *Charlotte Gainsbourg, Yvan Attal, Terence Stamp, Noemie Lvovsky, Laurent Bateau.* Real-life partners Attal and Gainsbourg imitate life through art in this entertaining bit of Gaullic whimsy that marks Attal's directorial debut. Sportswriter Yvan (Attal) and film star Charlotte (Gainsbourg) enjoy the comfort of the fast-paced lives of the affluent and famous, even if Charlotte's notoriety occasionally bruises Yvan's ego. But Yvan finds his personal security shaken when Charlotte's new costar (Stamp) turns out to be an older, sexy, world-renown ladies' man. This comedy of manners plays out beautifully against the lush elegance of Paris and London, as Yvan bounces back and forth between them, trying to keep tabs on his wife and her leading man. Attal and Gainsbourg's conjugal affinity is right up on the screen, and despite a few first-time-director indulgences, Attal keeps the action moving, making good use of the sparkling cast and the stunning locations. A welcome bit of fluff in these highly stressed times, this is 95 minutes of harmless escapist entertainment. (French with English subtitles) ★★★ DVD Letterbox: $29.99

Myra Breckinridge
(1970, 94 min, US, Michael Sarne) *Raquel Welch, Rex Reed, John Huston, Farrah Fawcett, Mae West, Roger Herren, Tom Selleck.* An outrageous X-rated version of Gore Vidal's "scandalously" satiric transsexual novel that has taken on mythic proportions for being such a bomb. Reed and Welch are the male and female embodiment of the same person — before and after the operation. Huston, West and Fawcett are just some of the casting oddities. Combine them with a talentless director, and a

screenplay imbued with a slap-dash '60s mentality, and the result had critics running to their thesauruses looking for stronger words than "atrocious." Yes, it's bad. But in a campy, smirky, hipper-than-fag sort of way. Why, either the lesbian scene between Welch and Fawcett or the tasteless sequence in which Welch rapes a strapping stud of a cowboy (Herren) is worth the price of rental. It really has to be seen to be believed. (★★★★ Camp Value) ★ DVD: $14.99

Mysteries
(1978, 93 min, Netherlands, Paul de Lussanet) *Rutger Hauer, Sylvia Kristel, Rita Tushingham.* Hauer stars in this rather stiff but absorbing film version of Nobel Prize-winning Knut Hamsun's novel. On the Isle of Man late in the 19th century, a mysterious, lonely, and possibly insane young stranger (Hauer) arrives in a small coastal community and begins to upset the townspeople's well-ordered lives. Kristel and Tushingham play the unattainable women he falls in love with. A bit muddled in execution, the film successfully creates an eerie, somber world where love and understanding prove to be tantalizingly elusive. ★★

Mysterious Island
(1961, 101 min, GB, Cy Endfield) *Michael Craig, Joan Greenwood, Michael Callan, Gary Merrill, Herbert Lom.* Ray Harryhausen created some of his best work in this adaptation of the Jules Verne novel about Confederate prisoners whose escape attempt leaves them stranded on an island infested with giant animals. Bernard Herrmann's score is outstanding. Lots of fun. ★★★ DVD Letterbox: $24.99

Mystery, Alaska
(1999, 119 min, US, Jay Roach) *Russell Crowe, Hank Azaria, Lolita Davidovich, Ron Eldard, Mary McCormack, Burt Reynolds.* Written by workaholic David E. Kelley ("Ally McBeal"), this genial hockey flick concerns the tiny titular town — where hockey is a religion — that sports a team good enough to take on the pros. At least, that's what Azaria writes in *Sports Illustrated.* Led by Crowe, the team must graduate from its weekly hockey games to the national spotlight . . . and the New York Rangers. A good ensemble makes the most of a familiar but benign sports story, where the underdogs rally to take on the reigning champs. Crowe is very believable as the small-town sheriff, and Reynolds is in his element as the town's crusty judge. ★★½ DVD: $14.99, VHS: $9.99

Mystery Date
(1991, 98 min, US, Jonathan Wacks) *Ethan Hawke, Brian McNamara, Teri Polo, Fisher Stevens, B.D. Wong.* When a young man on his dream date finds himself mistaken for his older brother, sparks fly and his world is turned upside down. The film is filled with implausibilities so common to the teen comedy, but there's actually a few laughs to be had. ★★ DVD Dual: $14.99, VHS: $6.99

Mystery Men
(1999, 122 min, US, Kinka Usher) *Janeane Garofalo, Ben Stiller, Hank Azaria, William H. Macy, Greg Kinnear, Geoffrey Rush, Paul Reubens, Eddie Izzard, Kel Mitchell, Claire Forlani, Lena Olin, Wes Studi, Tom Waits.* How many superheroes does it take to make you laugh? Evidently as many as are on-screen in this energetic, funny romp based on the popular comic book. Kinnear is Captain Amazing, superhero extraordinaire of Chapagne City. But things have been a little slow lately in the crime-fighting business because he's put all the

Janeane Garofalo and her dead dad in *Mystery Men*

criminals in jail. When he allows his super arch-enemy Casanova Frankenstein (Rush) to escape to liven things up, he's captured by the evil genius. Who is there to come to the rescue? Why, a ragtag team of superhero wannabes. There's quite a few laughs at hand when these bunglers set out to free Captain Amazing — thanks to an extremely wily cast who know how to have a good time. It's not rocket science; but, hey, what is. ★★★ DVD: $14.99, VHS: $14.99

The Mystery of Alexina

(1985, 84 min, France, René Feret) *Vuillemin, Valeri Stroh.* This literate, beautifully photographed film, based on a mid-19th-century memoir, tells the tale of a convent-bred teacher at a girls' elementary school. She falls in love with another girl, but soon discovers that she herself is a man. This fascinating love story poses intriguing questions of identity and character in a romantic, stylish setting. Screenplay by Jean Gruault (*Jules and Jim, The Wild Child*). (French with English subtitles) ★★★

The Mystery of Picasso

(1956, 77 min, France, Henri-Georges Clouzot) Declared a national treasure by the French government, this fascinating documentary features Pablo Picasso at work, creating over 15 works before the camera's eyes. The paintings were destroyed after the filming so this is the only opportunity to view them. An absorbing look at one of the greatest artists of the 20th century as well as a study of an artist's vision and its physical results. Picasso's mind and artistic motivations are wonderfully and forever on view. (French with English subtitles) ★★★★ DVD: $29.99, VHS: $29.99

The Mystery of Rampo

(1995, 100 min, Japan, Kazuyoshi Okuyama) *Masahiro Motoki, Naoto Takenaka, Michiko Hada.* A challenging contemporary Japanese film which explores the connections between fiction and reality, *The Mystery of Rampo* tells the story of a well-known but misunderstood writer, Rampo. In a beautiful animated segment, we see one of his stories come to life: An invalid father accidentally locks himself in a lacquer cabinet, and when his wife discovers him and urges him to suffocate. Although the story is never published, Rampo learns that a real-life situation has mirrored his story. Rampo becomes obsessed with the wife. Fascinating, thought-pro-

voking, and even an absorbing mystery, *Rampo* is a feast for the senses. (Japanese with English subtitles) ★★★½ DVD: $19.99

Mystery Train

(1989, 113 min, US, Jim Jarmusch) *Masatoshi Nagase, Youki Kudoh, Screamin' Jay Hawkins, Cinque Lee, Nicoletta Braschi, Elizabeth Bracco, Joe Strummer, Steve Buscemi, Rockets Redglare.* Jarmusch continues to explore the theme of strangers in even stranger lands. This time out he uses Memphis, Tennessee, as the backdrop for three interwoven stories which collide in a rundown hotel in the sleazy part of town. The episodes follow a young and very hip Japanese couple who have come to pray at the temple of rock ?n' roll; three Memphis low-lifes on a drunken, brawling and murderous night of debauchery; and a young Italian woman, stranded by the death of her husband and waiting to accompany his coffin back to Italy. Jarmusch delights in the oddball quirkiness of his characters. ★★★ DVD: $19.99, VHS: $14.99

Mystic Pizza

(1988, 102 min, US, Donald Petrie) *Julia Roberts, Annabeth Gish, Lili Taylor, Vincent D'Onofrio, Conchata Ferrell, Matt Damon.* This fresh and winning romantic comedy-drama follows the ups and downs of three young waitresses trying to come to terms with their impending adulthood. Along the way, they fall in love, play some pool, and even pass out at their own weddings — all the while serving the best damn pizza in the state of Connecticut. ★★★ DVD: $14.99

Mystic River

(2003, 137 min, US, Clint Eastwood) *Sean Penn, Kevin Bacon, Tim Robbins, Laurence Fishburne, Marcia Gay Harden, Laura Linney, Kevin Chapman, Thomas Guiry.* Lyrical, haunting and steadfast, *Mystic River* is an epic tragedy of Shakespearean proportions, the kind of which American cinema hasn't seen since Tennessee Williams or Arthur Miller. Based on the novel by Dennis Lahane, the film starts ostensibly as a police mystery. Returning to the working-class Boston neighborhood of his youth to investigate a murder, detective Sean Devine (Bacon) unlocks the ghosts of his past when the deceased turns out to be the daughter of a childhood friend, Jimmy Markum (Penn). Jimmy and Sean share in common the memory of the kidnapping and

molestation of their pal Dave (Robbins) 30 years ago. As the grief-stricken father looks for answers, and possibly revenge, Sean begins the painstaking hunt for a killer, the clues of which point to Dave. Director Eastwood has done a stunning job in articulating the myriad of emotions and conflicts besetting these tragic figures, thanks to remarkably composed pacing, an unflinching honesty to character, and an exhilarating ensemble. Penn has simply never been better, imparting the unimaginable sorrow of losing one's child with an intensity that is only rivaled by his resolve for vengeance. Robbins is a revelation as the sadly tortured Dave, a father himself haunted by a terrible past and left for emotional dead. *Mystic River* is a tough, brutal work, exacting and spare, but one of beauty and scope, power and restraint. Both Penn and Robbins won much-deserved Academy Awards. ★★★★ DVD Letterbox Widescreen: $27.99, DVD Fullscreen: $27.99, DVD 2-DVD plus 1 CD Special Edition: $39.99

The Myth of Fingerprints

(1997, 91 min, US, Bart Freundlich) *Julianne Moore, Noah Wyle, Blythe Danner, Roy Scheider, Hope Davis, Michael Vartan, Brian Kerwin, James LeGros.* Rookie director Freundlich serves up a lukewarm slice of home-for-the-holidays pie that is fraught with dysfunction and unendurable ennui — for the audience, that is. Wyle stars as the prodigal son who returns to his Ethan Allen-esque New England home for Thanksgiving to confront his father (an impenetrable Scheider) and try to rekindle a past flame with his ex-sweetie. What ensues is a whole bunch of bitchiness with his siblings which are framed between long stretches of wispy but meaningless tableaus. Freundlich attempts to cover up his characters' intrinsic vapidity with an off-kilter sense of quirkiness that really only serves to render the film all the more incomprehensible. ★★ DVD: $27.99

Sean Penn in Clint Eastwood's *Mystic River*

Nadine

(1987, 83 min, US, Robert Benton) *Jeff Bridges, Kim Basinger, Rip Torn, Gwen Verdon, Glenne Headly.* Sweet-natured comic thriller set in 1954 Texas starring Bridges and Basinger as a separated husband and wife who unwittingly become involved with a local gangster when Basinger witnesses a murder and mistakenly takes possession of secret documents. Torn is a most spirited villain. ★★★

Nadja

(1995, 92 min, US, Michael Almereyda) *Elina Löwensohn, Peter Fonda, Galazy Craze, Martin Donovan, Suzy Amis, Jared Harris, David Lynch.* This bloodless, art-house vampire film aspires to be innovative in both its narrative and its cinematography, but is not completely successful in either respect. Nadja (the cadaverous Löwensohn), a Romanian vampire transplanted to New York City, lives a life of coffeehouse ennui and predatory hunting. She begins a lesbian relationship with a similarly disaffected twentysomething burnout married to a likable but dimwitted amateur boxer, who just happens to be the nephew of the vampire-hunter who slew Nadja's father! The film's tone veers wildly from angst-ridden to campy humor, and attempts to create a sort of "vampire-vision" fragments the picture. Though the production design is very good, *Nadja* ultimately is too pretentious for its own good. ★★

Naked

(1993, 126 min, GB, Mike Leigh) *David Thewlis, Lesley Sharp, Katrin Cartlidge.* A brilliant, terrifying and undeniably real vision of the welfare state. Leigh takes us on a picaresque journey following Johnny (Thewlis in a stunning performance), our 27-year-old protagonist (or is that antagonist?), an embittered, overly loquacious ne'er-do-well who spews forth a relentlessly nihilistic tirade against man, God and society. After sexually assaulting a woman in Manchester, he flees to London and insinuates himself on his former girlfriend, Louise, and immediately beds her roommate, Sophie. Quickly tiring of their company, he hits the streets for a midnight sojourn, on which he waxes eloquent with every stranger about his apocalyptic philosophies. Leigh does a brilliant job of framing Johnny's rage against a backdrop of urban decay. ★★★★

The Naked and the Dead

(1958, 131 min, US, Raoul Walsh) *Aldo Ray, Cliff Robertson, Raymond Massey, Joey Bishop.* A tough and gritty film version of Norman Mailer's novel about a group of WWII soldiers stationed in the Pacific; though its familiar, disparate characters have surfaced in just about every "platoon" film. ★★½

Naked City

(1948, 96 min, US, Jules Dassin) *Barry Fitzgerald, Don Taylor, Howard Duff.* In a trendsetting, "just the facts, ma'am," semidocumentary style seen in countless films and TV shows since, this gripping crime thriller follows a police investigation's probe into the brutal murder of a beautiful young model. Fitzgerald plays the folksy, pipe-smoking Lieutenant Muldoon who, along with his strikingly handsome assistant

(Taylor), combs the classy veneer of Upper West Side society in an attempt to crack open the case. Noteworthy and quite fascinating is the film's entirely on location shooting in old New York, a rarity at a time when Hollywood stuck with studio sets. ★★★ VHS: $19.99

The Naked Civil Servant

(1980, 80 min, GB, Jack Gold) *John Hurt.* Based on the autobiography of Quentin Crisp, this is a witty examination of the process of growing up gay in the repressive England of the 1930s and '40s. Hurt's portrayal of Crisp is nothing less than superb as he fights back against society's intolerance, ostracism and violence with pointed, razor-sharp humor. ★★★½ VHS: $19.99

The Naked Country

(1985, 90 min, Australia, Tim Burstall) *John Stanton, Rebecca Gilling.* Forget the box art picturing a scantily clad woman baking in the Australian sun, for rather than cheesy erotica this is nothing more than a run-of-the-mill action/melodrama set in the Australian Outback. The story centers around a white rancher who has come into conflict with the local tribe of Aborigines over grazing rights. It all culminates in a showdown between rancher and natives which unsuccessfully aspires to the magical imagery of *The Last Wave.* ★★

The Naked Edge

(1961, 97 min, GB, Michael Anderson) *Gary Cooper, Deborah Kerr, Eric Portman, Diane Cilento, Hermione Gingold, Peter Cushing.* Cooper's last film is a disappointing psychological thriller borrowing much from Hitchcock's *Suspicion.* Kerr costars as Cooper's wife, who slowly begins to suspect her husband is a murderer. It seems Cooper's testimony about his employer's murder sent a coworker to prison; and now it looks like the wrong man may have been incarcerated. Despite a few stylish touches, this is kinda sluggish and the twists are unexciting. ★★

The Naked Gun

(1988, 85 min, US, David Zucker) *Leslie Nielsen, George Kennedy, Priscilla Presley, Ricardo Montalban, O.J. Simpson.* From the makers of *Airplane!* and "Police Squad," comes this zany, irreverent and anarchistic comedy. Stonefaced Nielsen is Lt. Drebin — a hilarious mixture of the bungling innocence of Mr. Magoo and Maxwell Smart with the ruthlessness and often sadistic crimefighting tactics of a Philly cop (no letters please!). Here we find Lt. Drebin investigating a plot to assassinate the Queen of England while she is on a visit to America. The story line, however, serves simply as a backdrop for the wild cavalcades of silly, sick and stupid jokes that we have come to expect from the Zucker/Abrahams/Zucker team. (Followed by 2 sequels) ★★★ DVD: $14.99, VHS: $14.99

The Naked Gun 2½: The Smell of Fear

(1991, 85 min, US, David Zucker) *Leslie Nielsen, Priscilla Presley, George*

Kennedy, Robert Goulet, O.J. Simpson. Nielsen returns as that lethal weapon Lt. Frank Drebin in this consistently funny sequel. Lt. Drebin is on the case in Washington, D.C. and he's up against greedy industrialists determined to sabotage our nation's antipollution measures. Though the film is not as hilarious as the original *Naked Gun* or *Airplane!* — both films seem to produce a never-ending stream of guffaws — 2½ is nevertheless a constant pleasure. And its White House opening scene is priceless. Who needs the Democrats for Bush-bashing when Drebin is around? ★★★ DVD: $14.99, VHS: $14.99

The Naked Gun 33⅓: The Final Insult

(1994, 83 min, US, Peter Segal) *Leslie Nielsen, Priscilla Presley, George Kennedy, Fred Ward, O.J. Simpson, Ellen Greene, Pia Zadora, Kathleen Freeman.* Nielsen and company are back for another side-splitting round of slapstick hijinks and stupid puns in this third *Naked Gun* film cowritten by David Zucker and Pat Proft and helmed by first-time director Segal. Frank Drebin, now enjoying the bliss of retirement with his wife (Presley) goes to work, is persuaded by old pal Kennedy to help him on a case. This leads Drebin to prison where he befriends a terrorist and he eventually helps save the Academy Awards. As would be expected, the laughs are fast and furious, and Nielsen's comic timing and mugging is priceless. ★★★ DVD: $14.99, VHS: $14.99

Naked in New York

(1994, 91 min, US, Dan Algrant) *Eric Stoltz, Mary Louise Parker, Ralph Macchio, Jill Clayburgh, Timothy Dalton, Kathleen Turner, Whoopi Goldberg, Tony Curtis, Quentin Crisp.* The story of a young writer's rites of passage, *Naked in New York* is appealing only in a dilapidated, disorganized sort of way. Stoltz stars as a bohemian Jewish New York playwright who meets a WASPy photographer (Parker) while in college and proceeds to set up housekeeping. Billed as a romantic comedy, this lacks the focus to be much of anything but a series of amusingly eclectic scenes tied together by Stoltz's artsy, philosophical angst. However, Turner steals the movie with her exuberant portrait of a boozy, pot-smoking seductress/actress. ★★½

Naked Gun 33⅓: The Final Insult

Peter Weller plays William Burroughs' literary alter ego in *Naked Lunch*

The Naked Jungle

(1954, 95 min, US, Byron Haskin) *Charlton Heston, Eleanor Parker, William Conrad.* This is the one with the ants! Plantation owner Heston tries to make a go of it in South America; he loses to the elements and Parker. Though silly at times, it's a lot of fun and even manages to offer some high moments of jungle adventure. ★★½ VHS: $19.99

The Naked Kiss

(1965, 90 min, US, Samuel Fuller) *Constance Towers, Anthony Eisley.* From its electrifying opening sequence — in which an enraged bald-headed prostitute (Towers) beats a man senseless with a telephone — through its exposé of corruption and vice in "Small Town, USA," this torrid melodrama never lets up. Towers is Kelly, a hip-swinging, eye-flirting floozy who "escapes" to a bucolic backwater town to begin life anew as a nurse to handicapped children. But an unforgiving and hypocritical society hounds her and just won't let a bad girl go good. Fuller fans won't be able to supress a smile throughout this deliciously enjoyable cult potboiler. ★★★½ DVD: $29.99, VHS: $19.99

Naked Lunch

(1991, 115 min, US, David Cronenberg) *Peter Weller, Judy Davis, Julian Sands, Ian Holm, Roy Scheider, Monique Mercure, Nicholas Campbell.* William Burroughs' 1950s free-form classic, with its nonlinear narration and shocking imagery, had long been thought "unfilmable." Director Cronenberg has done the impossible, for this hallucinatory horror/sci-fi/comedy/drama is a witty and imaginative interpretation. Weller stars as Burroughs' monosyllabic alter ego, Bill Lee, a bug exterminator who, along with his sharp-tongued wife (the amazing Davis), gets hooked on his own bug powder. Lee, swimming in a narcotics-induced paranoia, sees his Remington typewriter come alive in the form of a slimy, bug-shaped creature who informs him that he is really an underground agent on a mission to fight a worldwide "Interzone" conspiracy. An audacious and demanding foray into the psyche of a drug-addicted artist that will prove for some to be disgusting and incompre-

hensible — a response that would have delighted Burroughs. ★★★★ DVD Letterbox Criterion Collection: $39.99, VHS: $29.99

The Naked Prey

(1966, 94 min, US, Cornel Wilde) *Cornel Wilde, Gert Van Der Berger.* Rather exciting action film with Wilde as an African safari guide who becomes human prey to a group of tribal hunters. ★★★ VHS: $19.99

The Naked Spur

(1952, 93 min, US, Anthony Mann) *James Stewart, Robert Ryan, Janet Leigh.* Flavorful, exciting western with Stewart as a bounty hunter obsessed with tracking down outlaw Ryan and his companion Leigh. ★★★ VHS: $19.99

Naked Tango

(1991, 90 min, US, Leonard Schrader) *Esai Morales, Vincent D'Onofrio, Mathilda May.* Set in 1924, this surreal thriller set in Buenos Aires stars ravishing May as a scheming woman who unwittingly becomes involved with two feuding brothers (Morales and the sensually brutal D'Onofrio), both of whom are stylishly murderous criminals. Boasting lush camerawork, stunning production design and the erotic world of the Tango, this sexually charged though slow-moving thriller is a treat. ★★★

Naked Youth

(1959, 80 min, US, John F. Schreyer) *Carol Ohmart, Robert Hutton.* Three teens bust out of their juvenile detention center and head south of the border, where they encounter "dangerous drugs, thugs, gun molls, dope dolls and bad guys." ★ VHS: $9.99

The Name of the Rose

(1986, 128 min, France/Italy/West Germany, Jean-Jacques Annaud) *Sean Connery, F. Murray Abraham, Christian Slater, Ron Perlman, William Hickey.* A visually rich medieval murder mystery set in a remote monastary. A monk falls from a high tower: was it suicide or murder? As other brothers are found dead, visiting monk Connery investigates the series of bizarre deaths. Full of tongue-in-cheek allusions to Sherlock Holmes (Connery's sleuthing monk is named William of Baskerville), this film may be a

disappointment to those who have read the novel; but the film perfectly captures the atmosphere of the era and maintains a sufficient amount of suspense. (Filmed in English) ★★★ DVD Letterbox: $19.99

Nana

(1980, 92 min, Italy, Don Walman) *Katya Berger, Jean-Pierre Aumont.* Emile Zola's classic erotic novel about a Parisian streetwalker who, by seducing the rich and powerful, becomes the toast of Parisian society, is successfully brought to the screen. The sensuous Berger plays the lusty and ambitious woman with Aumont also starring as her most ardent and long-suffering lover. ★★½

Nanook of the North

(1922, 79 min, US, Robert J. Flaherty) The first and possibly the finest of Flaherty's social documentaries, this simply constructed but trailblazing film is set in the frozen vastness of the Hudson Bay region of Canada. The story follows Inuit Nanook's heartrending daily struggle for survival as he and his family battle nature for only the barest essentials of life. An absorbing classic that has been restored to its original condition and graced with a new musical score. A sad note to this film is that Nanook died of hunger shortly after the film was released. ★★★★ DVD: $29.99, VHS: $24.99

Napoleon

(1927, 235 min, France, Abel Gance) *Antonin Artaud, Albert Dieudonne.* Gance's overwhelming historical saga charts the French leader's youth, rise to power and triumphant Italian campaign. Meticulously reconstructed over the years, this silent classic remains a monument of technical innovation and virtuosity. ★★★★

Narc

(2003, 105 min, US, Joe Carnahan) *Jason Patric, Ray Liotta, Busta Rhymes, Chi McBride.* Shamed undercover cop Patric is paired with burned-out veteran Liotta to find a cop killer. A fairly straightforward policier, *Narc* is given weight and authority by two excellent, surprisingly sensitive lead performances, and the gritty, stylish direction. The film's opening is explosive and sets just the right tone, but nothing that follows can equal the intensity of the first few minutes. Director Carnahan uses some interesting throwbacks to '70s-era filmmaking (there's a nicely handled split-screen sequence that condenses potentially tedious footwork exposition into a snappy montage), and his script is complete with odd, amusing moments in addition to many affecting conversations between the two cops. Though it never reaches greatness after the opening, *Narc* is most worthwhile, especially for the much-lauded Liotta and often-overlooked Patric. ★★★ DVD Pan & Scan: $14.99, DVD: $14.99, VHS: $9.99

Jason Patric in *Narc*

The Narrow Margin

(1952, 70 min, US, Richard Fleischer) *Charles McGraw, Marie Windsor.* Well-acted, well-paced thriller about a detective (McGraw) assigned to protect a mobster's widow traveling by train from a gang of hoods who want her dead. Windsor costars as the targeted woman under McGraw's wing. (Remade in 1990) ★★★

Narrow Margin

(1990, 97 min, US, Peter Hyams) *Gene Hackman, Anne Archer, James B. Sikking, M. Emmet Walsh, J.T. Walsh.* This remake of the 1952 thriller of the same name bears all of the action and suspense associated with some of director Hyams' earlier films (*Outland*), but lacks the substance. Hackman stars as an FBI agent assigned to escort the reluctant eyewitness of a mob killing (Archer) from Canada to Los Angeles in safety. With hit men hot on their trail, the two board a train and — the rest you can guess. The film carries a fair number of thrills and the interplay between the characters is enjoyable enough, but there's nothing new here. ★★½ DVD: $14.99, VHS: $9.99

Nashville

(1975, 160 min, US, Robert Altman) *Keith Carradine, Lily Tomlin, Ronee Blakely, Henry Gibson, Barbara Harris, Barbara Baxley, Allen Garfield, Geraldine Chaplin, Lauren Hutton, Shelley Duvall, Michael Murphy, Ned Beatty, Jeff Goldblum.* Altman's masterful, multilayered mosaic of 1970s Americana. A wonderful ensemble of 24 characters interact at a Tennessee political rally resulting in comedic and often poignant vignettes. One of the greatest achievements of the decade, with a stellar ensemble. Carradine won an Oscar for his song, "I'm Easy." ★★★★ DVD: $14.99, VHS: $14.99

The Nasty Girl

(1990, 95 min, Germany, Michael Verhoeven) *Lena Stolze, Monika Baumgartner.* Teasing the viewer into thinking that this is a simple, modern-day Bavarian fairy tale, Verhoeven's hugely enjoyable satire soon becomes much more. The story begins with sweet-faced Sonja, the daughter of a nice middle-class couple, entering an essay contest proposing as her theme "My Town in the Third Reich." The seemingly tranquil community's guilty memory is jolted and, faced with an exposition of their fascist-collaborative past, begin efforts, including threats of violence and a firebombing, to stop the determined young lady's goal of uncovering the truth. An invigorating mixture of comedy, investigative journalism, history lesson and moral heroism; all done in a lilting and audacious style of filmmaking. (German with English subtitles) ★★★½

Nasty Habits

(1976, 91 min, GB, Michael Lindsay-Hogg) *Glenda Jackson, Sandy Dennis, Anne Meara, Geraldine Page, Anne Jackson, Melina Mercouri, Edith Evans.* This odd comic allegory transposes Nixon and his Watergate cronies to a Philadelphia convent and was produced and distributed by Brut Productions (yes, the perfume company). It stars a fine comic cast with Jackson as Nixon, Dennis as John Dean, Meara as Gerald Ford, and Page as Robert Haldeman. It's an offbeat affair with some good laughs, but not enough for a feature film. ★★

National Lampoon's Animal House

(1978, 109 min, US, John Landis) *John Belushi, Tim Matheson, Tom Hulce, Peter Riegert, Karen Allen, Stephen Furst, Kevin Bacon, Donald Sutherland, Verna Bloom.* Belushi made the most of his film debut, giving a truly funny performance, in this raucous, sophomoric comedy about an anarchic college fraternity's comic exploits. A good cast of then-youthful performers. ★★★ DVD Letterbox Double Secret Probation Edition: $19.99, DVD Pan & Scan Double Secret Probation Edition: $19.99

National Lampoon's Christmas Vacation

(1989, 97 min, US, Jeremiah Chechik) *Chevy Chase, Beverly D'Angelo, Randy Quaid, Diane Ladd, Julia Louis-Dreyfus, Juliette Lewis, Johnny Galecki.* This third entry of the *National Lampoon Vacation* series, continuing the saga of the hapless Griswold family, finds Clark, Ellen and family home for the holidays. The laughs are surprisingly plentiful as they prepare for a family gathering where, of course, nothing goes right. Returning as patriarch Clark is Chase, a master of pratfall and schtick, and the comedian has some good sightgags here. (Sequel: *Vegas Vacation*) ★★★ DVD Special Edition: $19.99, VHS: $6.99

National Lampoon's European Vacation

(1985, 94 min, US, Amy Heckerling) *Chevy Chase, Beverly D'Angelo, Jason Lively, Dana Hill, Eric Idle, Victor Lanoux, John Astin, Paul Bartel, Mel Smith, Robbie Coltrane.* The Griswald family head to Europe for their second vacation in this disappointing, unfunny sequel. (Sequel: *National Lampoon's Christmas Vacation*) ★½ DVD Letterbox: $14.99, VHS: $9.99

National Lampoon's Vacation

(1983, 98 min, US, Harold Ramis) *Chevy Chase, Beverly D'Angelo, Randy Quaid, Dana Barron, Anthony Michael Hall, Imogene Coca, Eddie Bracken, John Candy.* The first, best and funniest of the *National Lampoon's Vacation* series. The Griswald family, accompanied by their miserly aunt (Coca), head off to Wally World (read Disney anybody?) and family bliss. What they get is another story. Lots of laughs, some sick, some sicker. Quaid is hilarious as distant cousin. (Sequel: *National Lampoon's European Vacation*) ★★★ DVD 20th Anniversary: $19.99, VHS: $9.99

National Lampoon's Van Wilder

(2002, 95 min, US, Walt Becker) *Ryan Reynolds, Tara Reid, Teck Holmes, Kal Penn, Tim Matheson.* Van Wilder (Reynolds) is a student forever matriculating, a BMOC by virtue of seniority and the ability to throw terrific parties. Is that a plot? Guess so. Reynolds is actually good in the lead, treading the line between laid-back cool and aloof feyness. But the closest *Van Wilder* comes to its *Animal House* aspirations is the appearance of Tim Matheson as Wilder's monkey jacketed dad. The movie's most notable feature is actually on the DVD, which features "topless menus." So now, for the first time, you don't even have to watch the movie to get the best parts. ★★ DVD Unrated: $14.99, DVD R-Rated: $14.99, VHS R-Rated: $14.99, VHS Unrated: $14.99

National Security

(2003, 90 min, US, Dennis Dugan) *Martin Lawrence, Steve Zahn, Colm Feore, Bill Duke, Eric Roberts.* Will someone *please* write Martin Lawrence a funny script. The affable comedian is cast, yet again, as a humorless fast-talker in yet another witless comedy. This time, he plays a police academy reject who, while trying to break into his own locked car, is stopped by police offi-

Abel Gance's *Napoleon*

cer Zahn. A scuffle between the two men is captured on videotape, which looks as if Zahn is beating Lawrence, when in reality he is swatting away a bee. Zahn serves time for the "offense," and is hired by a security firm where — hey, folks, this is where it gets really funny — Lawrence is employed. They eventually team to stop a burglary ring, but not before executing every action comedy cliché of the last 20 years. This is by far Lawrence's least-likable on-screen character, and the usually reliable Zahn looks like he's wondering where his career went. ★½ DVD: $19.99, VHS Special Edition: $14.99

National Velvet

(1944, 125 min, US, Clarence Brown) *Elizabeth Taylor, Mickey Rooney, Anne Revere, Donald Crisp, Angela Lansbury.* Lovely family drama with Taylor and Rooney training their horses for the Grand National Steeplechase competition. Terrific entertainment. ★★★★ DVD: $9.99, VHS: $9.99

Native Son

(1986, 112 min, US, Jerold Freedman) *Victor Love, Matt Dillon, Elizabeth McGovern, Geraldine Page, Oprah Winfrey.* This second film version of Richard Wright's best-seller is a capable production made by "American Playhouse." The story is about a poor black youth living in 1930s Chicago who accidentally kills a rich white girl and is sentenced to death. Love plays Bigger Thomas, the embittered youth. Filmed in 1951 with author Wright as Thomas. ★★★

The Natural

(1984, 134 min, US, Barry Levinson) *Robert Redford, Glenn Close, Wilford Brimley, Richard Farnsworth, Robert Duvall, Kim Basinger, Barbara Hershey.* Astonishing cinematography highlights this affecting fantasy drama with Redford as a mystical 1930s ballplayer; his career is cut short in his youth and he returns to the game later in life. A grand supporting cast. ★★½ DVD: $14.99, VHS: $9.99

439

Natural Born Killers

(1994, 118 min, US, Oliver Stone) *Woody Harrelson, Juliette Lewis, Robert Downey, Jr., Tommy Lee Jones, Tom Sizemore, Rodney Dangerfield.* Stone's hallucinatory roller-coaster ride follows a pair of unrepentant serial killers (Harrelson, Lewis) on a cross-country spree of wanton carnage and mind-bending schizoid dementia. Ultimately joining them is Downey as the Aussie-accented host of a sensationalist TV tabloid show who is determined to get their story at any cost. Quentin Tarantino's inventive script has the two homicidal lovebirds consummating their relationship with the murder of her abusive father (Dangerfield) in a bizarre and hilarious skit that parodies TV sitcoms. But Stone has trouble finding the humor in the rest of Tarantino's tale and the result is yet another exercise in bashing the audience over the head — this time about our culture's love affair with violence and the media's mercenary job of feeding that appetite. This is the director's cut which includes 3 additional minutes. ★★½ DVD Theatrical Cut: $24.99, DVD Director's Cut: $24.99, VHS: $19.99, VHS Director's Cut: $19.99

The Natural History of Parking Lots

(1990, 92 min, US, Everett Lewis) *Charlie Bean, B. Wyatt.* The title is probably the most intriguing aspect of this independent black-and-white film. Dripping "L.A. cool" attitude, the drama revolves around the relationship of two troubled brothers — the boyish Chris (Bean) and the elder, hunky Lance (Wyatt). The two live together in an opulent home without their divorced parents and occupy their time languidly laying about on their jockeys, teasing each other in a troubling, pseudo-homosexual incestuous fashion — but nothing comes of this fleshy posturing (if it did, then there might have been a plot). ★★ VHS: $29.99

Naughty Girl (Mam'zelle Pigale)

(1958, 77 min, France, Michel J. Boisrond) *Brigitte Bardot, Jean Bretonniere, Françoise Fabian.* Bardot, in a role that plays against her bombshell image, stars as an innocent but klutzy schoolgirl who finds herself the unwitting pawn in a cat-and-mouse chase between the police, a ring of counterfeiters and her ex-con father. Scantily clad in either a tight-fitting tennis outfit, a flimsy bikini, a bath towel or even, for a time, a Roman tunic, young Brigitte is both disarmingly likable and sexy in this minor but amusing film which features more than its fair share of tacky musical numbers. (French with English subtitles) (aka: *That Naughty Girl*) ★★ DVD: $29.99, VHS: $14.99

Naughty Marietta

(1935, 106 min, US, W.S. Van Dyke) *Jeanette MacDonald, Frank Morgan, Nelson Eddy, Elsa Lanchester.* MacDonald and Eddy's first film together is a sappy musical with the two falling in love in the American wilderness. Score includes "Tramp, Tramp, Tramp" and "Ah, Sweet Mystery of Life." MacDonald and Eddy make an appealing romantic and singing duo, though the story is overly sentimental. (And she's not *that* naughty!) ★★½

The Naughty Nineties

(1945, 76 min, US, Jean Yarbrough) *Bud Abbott, Lou Costello, Henry Travers.* The classic skit "Who's on First" highlights this otherwise average Abbott and Costello romp, with the boys trying their luck as Mississippi gamblers. ★★ VHS: $14.99

The Navigator, The Boat & The Love Nest

(1921, 102 min, US, Buster Keaton, Donald Crisp, Eddie Cline) *Buster Keaton, Kathryn McGuire.* A collection of three Buster Keaton comedies. *The Navigator* (1924, 60 min) is a masterful comedy directed by Keaton and Donald Crisp. Featuring exceptional comic visuals, great running gags and inventive plot twists, the film casts Keaton as a rich slacker who finds himself stranded on an ocean liner with the woman (McGuire) who has jilted him. Adrift at sea, the two are beset by problems ranging from making morning breakfast to finding suitable sleeping accomodations. One remarkable scene finds Keaton underwater fighting with swordfish and an octopus, and, as usual, Keaton's stunts are without peer. This is classic comedy. (★★★★) *The Boat* (1921, 23 min) continues the volume's nautical theme, with Keaton and family losing home, car and dignity to live on their homemade houseboat the Damfino). Clever slapstick and funny vignettes combine to make this a delight. (★★★½) *The Love Nest* (1923, 20 min) is a cute high seas comedy with Keaton being rescued by a tyrannical captain and turning his ship upside-down with uninhibited buffoonery. (★★★) DVD: $29.99, VHS: $29.99

The Navigator

(1989, 92 min, New Zealand, Vincent Ward) *Hamish McFarlane, Bruce Lyons, Chris Haywood.* A thinking person's fantasy is a rare breed, indeed; which makes this totally original and captivating time travel odyssey all the more praiseworthy. Set in the 14th century besieged by the Black Plague, a small village free of the disease fears that it too will succumb. Its only hope lies in a young boy with psychic powers who, accompanied by his older brother and four villagers, makes a perilous trek across his land to fulfill a vision — only to find himself in modern-day New Zealand. This accomplished production belies its low budget, featuring splendid photography and an impressive first-rate cast and technical know-how. ★★★½ DVD: $24.99, VHS: $19.99

Navy SEALS

(1990, 113 min, US, Lewis Teague) *Charlie Sheen, Michael Biehn, Joanne Whalley-Kilmer, Bill Paxton, Rick Rossovich.* A Navy SEAL team (SEa, Air, Land) on a mission to free U.S. hostages in the Middle East discovers a terrorist's arsenal of missiles. Mindless, even confusing, action adventure with cardboard caricatures in uniforms performing derring-do in combat. ★½ DVD: $14.99

Nazarin

(1958, 91 min, Mexico, Luis Buñuel) *Francesco Rabal, Rita Macedo.* Religious hypocrisy is the theme in this, one of Buñuel's most powerful, realistic and yet often overlooked films. An eccentric young priest, imbued with the teachings of Christ, sets out to live a life of purity outside the confines of the church. Yet his journey through the land is met with hostility, indifference and confusion by those he encounters. For (in the Buñuelian world) the idealistic precepts of love and simplicity are no match in a world dominated by physical needs and limitations. (Spanish with English subtitles) ★★★★

Near Dark

(1987, 95 min, US, Kathryn Bigelow) *Adrian Pasdar, Jenny Wright, Lance Henriksen, Bill Paxton, Jenette Goldstein, Tim Thomerson, Joshua Miller.* This stylish, gritty vampire tale is one of the better horror films of the 1980s. Young Pasdar falls for Wright, who's part of a traveling group of night-stalkers — including Henriksen, Paxton and Goldstein (who all worked together in *Aliens*). When he gets bitten, he joins them on their reign of terror throughout the West. Though the film takes some liberties with the vampire legend, it's one of the most intense shockers of the genre. ★★★½ DVD Letterbox 2-disc set: $29.99

Necessary Roughness

(1991, 108 min, US, Stan Dragoti) *Scott Bakula, Hector Elizondo, Robert Loggia, Larry Miller, Sinbad, Rob Schneider.* It's *Back to School* meets *Semi-Tough* as a misfit college football team attempts to win a game. Bakula is a 37-year-old farmer and former high school football star who enrolls at a Texas university to become their quarterback. Under the guidance of new, straight-arrow coach Elizondo and assistant Loggia, the team learns to band together for what, of course, will be the big game at the finale. The film shares much with the baseball farce *Major League*. ★★½ DVD: $19.99, VHS: $9.99

Necronomicon: The Book of the Dead

(1996, 90 min, US, Brian Yuzna, Christophe Gans, Shusuke Kaneko) *David Warner, Jeffrey Combs, Bruce Payne, Belinda Bauer, Dennis Christopher.* This triptych of episodes based on stories by H.P. Lovecraft can be classified along with most other attempts to bring his highly imaginative works to the big screen, as a nice try. Fans of Lovecraftian lore will either be overjoyed or outraged, and more casual viewers will probably be mildly entertained. ★★

Ned Kelly

(1970, 100 min, GB, Tony Richardson) *Mick Jagger, Clarissa Kaye.* Set in 19th-century Australia, this ambitious Outback western features the screen acting debut of Jagger. He plays Ned Kelly, Australia's most notorious outlaw, who with his band of fellow Irishmen does battle against the repressive British authorities. Jagger, much better used as the decadent rock star in *Performance*, is out of place in this film. A bit too scrawny for the role, he does not possess the needed screen presence and his painful attempt at an Irish brogue doesn't help either. (Remade in 2004) ★★½ DVD: $14.99

Needful Things

(1993, 120 min, US, Fraser C. Heston) *Max von Sydow, Amanda Plummer, Ed Harris, Bonnie Bedelia, J.T. Walsh.* Heston's quasioperatic adaptation of Stephen King's story boasts a knock-'em-dead performance by von Sydow as Leland Gaunt, a satanic salesman whose curio shop, Needful Things, springs up out of nowhere causing all hell to break loose in the small New England town of Castle Rock. Kudos also to Plummer as a downtrodden spinster who becomes enmeshed in the soul-stealing machinations of the demonic Mr. Gaunt. ★★½ DVD: $14.99

Negatives

(1968, 90 min, GB, Peter Medak) *Glenda Jackson, Peter McEnery, Diane Cilento.* Medak's directorial debut is a macabre and erotic tale about a young couple with a somewhat more than kinky sexual bent. They encounter a glamorous photographer with an equally warped sense of bedroom play and enter an even stranger world of sexual fantasy. A stylish and unusual film. ★★★

The Negotiator

(1998, 138 min, US, F. Gary Gray) *Samuel L. Jackson, Kevin Spacey, David Morse, Ron Rifkin, J.T. Walsh, John Spencer.* A tense, exciting and intelligent police hostage drama with the good guy as the hostage taker, *The Negotiator* casts Jackson as Danny Roman, a well-respected Chicago cop who excels at his job as police negotiator in hostage situations. When his partner is murdered and Danny is framed, Danny takes a group of office workers hostage himself (in an effort to clear his name). Enter Chris Sabian (Spacey), another well-respected police negotiator. Thus begins a cat-and-mouse game of words and deeds between the two. In addition to the smart dramatics, another feather in this film's cap is the dynamic pairing of Jackson and Spacey; each actor brings an intensity and flavor to his role. The ensemble cast is equally adept, especially the late Walsh in one of his final roles. ★★★ DVD Letterbox: $14.99, VHS: $14.99, VHS Letterbox: $14.99

Neighbors

(1981, 91 min, US, John G. Avildsen) *John Belushi, Dan Aykroyd, Kathryn Walker, Cathy Moriarty.* Belushi's last film finds him the straight man as Aykroyd, for once, gets a chance to cut loose as the maniac who moves in next door and makes life a living hell. This reverse casting is indicative of the chances this film was willing to take, especially in the decision to maintain the novel's dark and unrelenting tone. While it provides comedic moments of dark-edged humor, the overall effect is one of a tired, overambitious project. ★★

Nell

(1994, 113 min, US, Michael Apted) *Jodie Foster, Liam Neeson, Natasha Richardson, Richard Libertini.* Foster's remarkably nuanced performance highlights this otherwise dispassionate, ordinary tale of a "wild child" discovered in the backwoods of North Carolina. Neeson costars as a caring physician who has his hands full when Foster is found living wild and speaking a language no one understands. Though the dramatics lead to tender moments between the two characters, the film is strangely devoid of emotion. However, the mystery of Foster's condition and the actress' unearthly inhabitation of the title character make *Nell* at the very least a compelling watch. ★★½ DVD: $14.99

Nelly and Monsieur Arnaud

(1995, 103 min, France, Claude Sautet) *Emmanuelle Béart, Michel Serrault, Jean-Hugues Anglade.* A talky though quietly powerful examination of unspoken desire, *Nelly and Monsieur Arnaud* concerns the relationship between a despondent young woman and a wealthy older man. Nelly (Béart) is a young Parisian who owes six months back rent and is trapped in a loveless marriage. A friend introduces her to Monsieur Arnaud (Serrault), a judge who needs help writing his memoirs. Meeting on a daily basis, a power struggle masquerading as a flirtation develops. As these characters move closer to realizing their destinies, their jealousies come into bold relief. The performances by both leads are quite moving. Sautet has crafted an intelligent French chamber drama that aches with the resonance of heartbreak. (French with English subtitles) ★★★½ DVD Letterbox: $19.99, VHS: $14.99

Nenette and Boni

(1997, 103 min, France, Claire Denis) *Gregoire Colin, Alice Houri, Valeria Bruni-Tedeschi, Vincent Gallo.* There are many dreamlike images in *Nenette and Boni*, a wistful rumination on two troubled adolescents, but little drama. In this artfully photographed film about the shiftless Boni (Colin) reuniting with his pregnant sister Nenette (Houri), director Denis proves that she has an uncanny eye for visuals, but can not tell a story. Denis constructs a sensuous mood, filming Boni's frequently shirtless physique like a canvas, but there is no depth beyond the surface of these disenfranchised youths. Alienation can be fascinating, but in *Nenette and Boni* it is woefully tedious. (French with English subtitles) ★½ VHS: $29.99

The Neon Bible

(1995, 92 min, GB, Terence Davies) *Gena Rowlands, Denis Leary, Diana Scarwid, Drake Bell, Jacob Tierney.* Based on a story by John Kennedy O'Toole, the film is one which is of obvious attraction to director Davies: A coming-of-age tale of a sensitive teenage boy brought up in a household dominated by loving women. Set in 1940s Georgia, the story centers on David, who is brought up in a stifling Christian Fundamentalist household headed by his father (a very effective Leary). His only real communication comes when his big city aunt (Rowlands) — a former showgirl — comes for an extended visit. Not much happens as the strangely friendless, sad-eyed David floats from one incident to another developing a longing for something different. Davies films in his trademark haunting style, but the meandering story ultimately produces a less-than-successful film. ★★ DVD: $9.99, VHS: $9.99

The Nest

(1980, 109 min, Spain, Jaime de Arminan) *Ana Torrent, Hector Alterio.* A passionate and haunting film that depicts the complex relationship between a lonely 60-year-old widower and a captivating and intelligent 12-year-old girl. A moody, sensitive portrait about the meaning of friendship and love as he follows this relationship to its inevitable, tragic conclusion. (Spanish with English subtitles) ★★★

The Nest

(1987, 89 min, US, Terence H. Winkless) *Robert Lansing, Lisa Langlois.* A genetic experiment goes awry and turns ordinary cockroaches into bloodthirsty carnivores. The creepy bugs will definitely make one's skin crawl, and the film, while giving in to horror genre clichés, uses its mutilegged stars to good effect. Get out the industrial-strength Raid! ★★

The Net

(1995, 118 min, US, Irwin Winkler) *Sandra Bullock, Jeremy Northam, Dennis Miller, Wendy Gazelle, Diane Baker, Ken Howard.* The considerable charm of its leading lady Bullock is barely enough to keep this muddled computer-age thriller afloat. *The Net* consists of lots of computer talk, computer gadgets and hackers lovingly doting on their computers, but what it doesn't have is a well-developed screenplay or memorable suspense. Bullock plays a lonely computer whiz who becomes involved in a high-tech conspiracy when she gets hold of a disc able to enter any system. After the bad guys erase her identity in a particularly eerie sequence, she spends the rest of the film trying to elude them. ★★ DVD Letterbox Special Edition: $19.99, DVD Basic Edition: $14.99

Network

(1976, 121 min, US, Sidney Lumet) *Peter Finch, Faye Dunaway, William Holden, Robert Duvall, Beatrice Straight, Ned Beatty.* A boisterous, brilliantly savage satire on television, America's fickle viewing habits and the corporate mentality. Paddy Chayevsky's scathing script is given extraordinary life by a remarkable cast to tell the story of the rise of a fourth network. Finch won an Oscar as the weary newsman who loses his sanity and becomes a guru; Dunaway also won an Oscar as the ruthless news department head whose aphrodisiac is high ratings. Holden gives a tremendous performance as the ex-department chief, who impotently witnesses the craziness around him. Straight won a Supporting Oscar as Holden's neglected wife. An original and breathtaking masterwork. ★★★★ DVD: $19.99, VHS: $14.99

Neurosia: Who Shot Rosa von Praunheim?

(1995, 93 min, Germany, Rosa von Praunheim) *Desiree Nick, Rosa von Praunheim.* Part murder mystery, part self-critical autobiography and all satire, this is a delightfully candid film. It begins in a cinema, where a pompous von Praunheim is shot by someone in a crowd. The mystery begins when his body disappears from the stage. Gesine (Nick), a homophobic tabloid TV journalist, is assigned the task of digging up dirt on the controversial politico and filmmaker. *Neurosia* wanders all through von Praunheim's life, but the final ten minutes brings it all together in an inventively funny and self-deprecating fashion. (aka: *Neurosia: Fifty Years of Perversity*) (German with English subtitles) ★★★ VHS: $14.99

Nevada

(1998, 109 min, US, Gary Tieche) *Amy Brenneman, Kirstie Alley, Gabrielle Anwar, Saffron Burrows, Kathy Najimy, Dee Wallace Stone.* Brenneman plays a sexy drifter first seen walking on a hot desert highway with only a suitcase and a bottle of water. Refusing a ride from a very interested guy from the nearest town, she obviously doesn't crave human contact. She gets it anyway when, barely across the town line, she answers a young boy's plea for help — his mother's having a baby. Brenneman delivers the baby and raises the curiosity and ire of the paranoid local woman. This sluggish, uneventful drama boasts a story that is completely without interest, same for the marginally compelling "mysterious past" of Brenneman's character that goofy flashbacks intermittently show glimpses of. ★★

Nevada Smith

(1966, 130 min, US, Henry Hathaway) *Steve McQueen, Karl Malden, Brian Keith, Arthur Kennedy, Suzanne Pleshette.* Exciting western with McQueen in the title role based on a character from Harold Robbins' "The Carpetbaggers" — as a cowboy who tracks down the gang who murdered his parents. ★★★ DVD: $19.99, VHS: $9.99

Never Been Kissed

(1999, 107 min, US, Raja Gosnell) *Drew Barrymore, David Arquette, Michael Vartan, Molly Shannon, John C. Reilly, Garry Marshall, Leelee Sobieski.* The ever-engaging Barrymore plays a gawky reporter who goes undercover and finds herself back in high school hell in this misdirected romantic comedy. Josie Geller (Barrymore) is a newspaper copy editor who gets her first assignment: pose as a high school student. This brings back painful memories for Josie, but not nearly as painful for those watching her, and that doesn't refer to the office staff who's viewing her escapades through closed-circuit TV. Director Gosnell takes a high-concept, intriguing idea and drops the ball, giving the film a sluggish pace and too many boo-hoo moments. The screenwriters have concocted a few cute scenes, but Gosnell is out of his league in bringing to life the joys of romantic comedy. ★★ DVD: $14.99, VHS: $6.99

Never Cry Wolf

(1983, 105 min, US, Carroll Ballard) *Charles Martin Smith, Brian Dennehy.* Farley Mowat's stirring novel about his trek through the Canadian tundra to study the Arctic wolf is brought beautifully to the screen in this Disney production. The film capitalizes on the book's romantic vision of the frozen wilderness through breathtaking landscapes and a sense of daring high adventure. ★★★½ DVD: $24.99, VHS: $14.99

Never Give a Sucker an Even Break

(1941, 71 min, US, Edward Cline) *W.C. Fields, Margaret Dumont, Franklin Pangborn.* Fields' last starring film, with a script reportedly written on the back of an envelope, is a sometimes hilarious collection of gags, with Fields playing himself. ★★★½

Never on Sunday

(1959, 97 min, Greece, Jules Dassin) *Melina Mercouri, Jules Dassin, Titos Vandis.* This Greek *Pygmalion* was a huge international hit when first released and was considered quite daring in its day. Mercouri is unforgettable as an exuberant and carefree prostitute who meets up with an American tourist (Dassin) who falls in love with her and attempts to educate her to the finer things in life. Mercouri won the Best Actress Award at Cannes and the film won an Academy Award for Best Song. A thoroughly entertaining romp with wonderful location shooting in Piraeus and the Greek countryside. (Filmed in English) ★★★½ DVD Letterbox: $19.99

Never Say Never Again

(1983, 137 min, GB, Irvin Kershner) *Sean Connery, Klaus Maria Brandauer, Max von Sydow, Barbara Carrera, Kim Basinger.* Connery will never say never to Bond, James Bond. . . He's back after 12 years and dives into this remake of *Thunderball.* If you missed this exciting spy adventure, see it; Connery is as suave and debonair as ever. ★★★ DVD: $14.99

Never Talk to Strangers

(1995, 86 min, US, Peter Hall) *Rebecca De Mornay, Antonio Banderas, Dennis Miller, Len Cariou, Harry Dean Stanton.* De Mornay plays a psychiatrist who specializes in multiple personality disorder. While treating a serial killer (Stanton), she meets and begins an affair with a mysterious and sexy surveillance specialist (Banderas). And while her upstairs neighbor (Miller) pines away for her, she becomes the target for a series of deadly threats from an anonymous source. This "erotic thriller" is both predictable and tame, offering few chills and only one steamy encounter of note. De Mornay acts as if she were on tranquilizers. ★★ DVD: $14.99

The Neverending Story

(1984, 92 min, GB, Wolfgang Petersen) *Barret Oliver, Noah Hathaway.* Petersen's first English-language film is a near-classic fairy tale about a young boy who becomes so immersed in the book he's reading that he is magically drawn into the story and must help save the tale's world from destruction. Wonderful children's fare, perhaps a bit scary for the wee-est of tykes, but filled with good special effects and an earnest young hero. Only a slight clumsiness and not-too-subtle allegorical message keep this from the highest pantheon of children's film. (Followed by 2 sequels) ★★★½ DVD: $19.99, VHS: $9.99

Neverwhere

(1996, 180 min, GB, Dewi Humphreys) *Gary Bakewell, Laura Fraser, Hywel Bennett, Clive Russell.* Gaiman's miniseries is, at best, a mixed blessing. Richard Mayhew, a dull man with a dull life, befriends a young woman named Door (who looks suspiciously like Gaiman's character Death from his "Sandman" comic book), whom he finds bleeding in the street. The next day, he finds that his life no longer exists, as he becomes introduced to Door's world, known as London Below. Gaiman's script is inventive, imaginative and exciting. Unfortunately, it falls victim to sloppy direction, over-the-top acting and low production values, which is a shame considering the magic within the pages of Gaiman's book of the same title. The series seems to represent all of the intense action scenes found in the book, but omits any of the tender moments in-between, leaving most characters rather lifeless (or just annoying, like the god-awful Marquis). Still, underneath all the bombastic diatribes, there's a fantastic story lurking somewhere, though it may only be worthwhile to Gaiman's fans. ★★½ DVD 2-disc set: $39.99

The New Age

(1994, 110 min, US, Michael Tolkin) *Judy Davis, Peter Weller, Patrick Bauchau, Rachel Rosenthal, Adam West, Samuel L. Jackson.* Davis and Weller are well-suited in their roles as a pair of wanton yuppies whose comfortable material world comes crashing down around them. Their marriage is too hip for words, they live in a multi-zillion dollar house in the hills, and hobnob with the rich and famous. But it all falls apart and they are forced to search for some deeper meaning to their lives, leading them to new sex partners and a succession of New Age gurus who can only pose more questions than answers. Writer-director Tolkin evokes the same eerie atmosphere of his earlier work, *The Rapture*, as he unfolds this tale of spiritual emptiness in a world of decadence and consumption. ★★★ VHS: $19.99

The New Centurians

(1972, 103 min, US, Richard Fleischer) *George C. Scott, Stacy Keach, Jane Alexander, Rosalind Cash, Scott Wilson.* Stinging depiction of cop life: Scott is a veteran officer who dreads retiring; Keach is a young cop whose work comes before everything, including his wife. Based on the novel by Joseph Wambaugh. ★★★

New Fists of Fury

(1984, 120 min, Hong Kong, Lo Wei) *Jackie Chan.* Chan plays a former pickpocket during WWII who is forced to fight for his life when his fiancée's school is destroyed and its master savagely murdered. With her help, he learns a new and deadly fighting art and together they exact vengeance for the death of her master. A brutal ballet of martial arts mayhem. ★★★ DVD Letterbox Dubbed: $19.99, VHS: $9.99

New Jack City

(1991, 101 min, US, Mario Van Peebles) *Wesley Snipes, Ice T, Judd Nelson, Mario Van Peebles, Chris Rock, Allen Payne, Vanessa Williams, Bill Nunn.* Pulsating with the music, life and ever-present violence of a drug-infested inner city, this tough gangster thriller, ostensibly a black *Scarface*, should keep even the most taciturn viewer riveted to his seat. The city is New York, where a vicious crack dealer (villainously played by Snipes) is driving his way to the top of the drug underworld. It takes two renegade cops (Ice T, Nelson) to try to bring him and his sordid empire down. Van Peebles' first film is a tough, exciting and impressive work that successfully straddles the fine line of glorifying the drug culture while also presenting a stringent anti-drug message. ★★★ DVD: $14.99, VHS: $9.99

New Jersey Drive

(1995, 98 min, US, Nick Gomez) *Sharron Corley, Gabriel Casseus, Christine Baranski.* Based on a true story of police corruption in Newark, New Jersey, this Spike Lee-produced tale centers around a young "boy in the hood" (Corley) who finds himself thrust into the middle of a turf war between his car thief friends and the law when one of them steals a policeman's private car. Gomez's violent, flashy and somewhat predictable second effort falls short of his gritty debut *Laws of Gravity*, weakened by stock characters, flashy MTV-style camerawork and overbearing rap music soundtrack. ★★

A New Leaf

(1971, 102 min, US, Elaine May) *Walter Matthau, Elaine May, Jack Weston, George Rose, William Redfield, James Coco.* May wrote, directed and stars in this comedy about a rich but clumsy woman (May) who is courted by a bankrupt playboy (Matthau), who's only after her money. Both stars are in good form, and the film offers many a well-placed laugh. ★★★ VHS: $14.99

A New Life

(1988, 104 min, US, Alan Alda) *Alan Alda, Ann-Margret, Hal Linden, John Shea, Veronica Hamel.* Alda goes through middle-aged angst as he and wife Ann-Margret divorce and find new loves. Alda retreads familiar territory here, but he and a good cast wring some life out of the unremarkable material. ★★½ VHS: $14.99

New Rose Hotel

(1999, 92 min, US, Abel Ferrara) *Christopher Walken, Willem Dafoe, Asia Argento.* Despite its gorgeous, sleek visuals, Ferrara's *New Rose Hotel* is a vacant exercise. Two partners, Fox (Walken) and X (Dafoe), offer one million dollars to Sandii (Argento), an Italian hooker, to lure a Japanese businessman to another company. X falls in love with Sandii, and a series of double crosses ensue. Ferrara, who is adapting a William Gibson short story, eschews narrative convention, making much of the plotting incomprehensible. Walken does his patented emoting and Dafoe feigns cool detachment, but the film has no pulse and no point. ★½ DVD: $14.99, VHS: $102.99

New Wave (Nouvelle Vague)

(1990, 89 min, France, Jean-Luc Godard) *Alain Delon.* The eternal war between the sexes and the classes is given the Godard treatment in this dense, meandering and ultimately enigmatic drama/thriller. A befuddled Delon is almost run over by the wealthy daughter of an industrialist. She picks him up and takes him home, but is it love or does she have something else in mind for him? Never simply content to tell a singular story, Godard infuses the film's soundtrack with layers of overlapping dialogue, poetry and music while the camera roams, circles and pans during each scene. While the earnest film enthusiast might see "art" and meaning, others, including casual viewers and the more cynical cinéaste, will conclude that the master has run out of new ideas. (French with English subtitles) ★★

New Year's Day

(1990, 89 min, US, Henry Jaglom) *Henry Jaglom, Gwen Welles, Maggie Jakobson, David Duchovny, Milos Forman.* While the films of Jaglom are not everyone's idea of entertainment and fun, there is an unwavering flock of devotees who actually enjoy his personal style of angst-ridden filmmaking. Jaglom appears as a recently divorced Los Angelino who flees to New York on New Year's day. His new apartment, however, is still occupied by the old tenants, three young women who invite him to stay while they pack and throw a farewell party. At the party, peopled by a diverse assortment of oddball New Yorkers, our lecherous and unsympathetic hero views the proceedings with a detached air as he dispenses advice and tries to pick up women. While the caliber of the acting varies, Welles is especially affecting as the fragile Anne. Awkward at times, repetitive and something of a vanity production, the film nevertheless holds one's attention. ★★★ VHS: $79.99

New York, New York

(1977, 164 min, US, Martin Scorsese) *Liza Minnelli, Robert De Niro, Lionel Stander, Mary Kay Place, Diahnne Abbott, Larry Kert.* Minnelli and De Niro meet at a WWII victory party; the innocent pop singer and volatile jazz musician wed. As she reaches stardom, his fortunes decline, further straining an already combative marriage. The potent performances are ably underscored by a superb evocation of the era, though the story line is at times predictable and given to backstage clichés. Another dark look at human relations from director Scorsese. ★★½

New York Stories

(1989, 123 min, US, Francis Coppola, Martin Scorsese, Woody Allen) *Nick Nolte, Rosanna Arquette, Woody Allen, Mae Questel, Mia Farrow, Julie Kavner, Heather McComb, Talia Shire, Giancarlo Giannini, Patrick O'Neal, Jesse Borrego, Steve Buscemi, Illeana Douglas, Deborah Harry, Peter Gabriel.* Three-part film by New York directors Scorsese, Coppola and Allen. Scorsese's *Life Lessons* stars Nolte as a moody and talented painter tormented by the end of his relationship with his apprentice/lover Arquette. The second segment, Coppola's *Life without Zoe*, is a cold story of a bratty child's indulgent birthday party. The final film, Allen's *Oedipus Wrecks*, is the lifesaver of the three, and one of Allen's funniest works. Allen stars as a successful lawyer who is haunted, nagged and criticized by his ever-present mother, wonderfully portrayed by Questel. Not wholly successful, but still an interesting venture. ★★½ DVD: $14.99

News from Home

(1976, 85 min, Belgium/France, Chantal Akerman) Avant-gardist Akerman has produced in this static, repetitive exercise her own unique filmic symphony to New York City. Attempting to explore the differences between European myths of the city against its gritty reality, cinematographer Babette Mangolte captures the strangely stark beauty of an alienated, lifeless world while offscreen Akerman occasionally reads, in a monotone voice, letters from a Belgian mother to her daughter living in New York. A demanding, abstract work of art. (French with English subtitles) ★★½ VHS: $24.99

Newsfront

(1978, 110 min, Australia, Phillip Noyce) *Bryan Brown, Bill Hunter, Wendy Hughes, Gerard Kennedy, Angela Punch.* This much celebrated and award-winning film vividly re-creates the glory days of newsreels and the men who captured the turbulent war years of the 1940s. Director Noyce intercuts a fictional story with actual news events to create this spirited true-life adventure. ★★★

Newsies

(1992, 121 min, US, Kenny Ortega) *Christian Bale, Bill Pullman, Robert Duvall, Ann-Margret, Michael Lerner, Max Casella.* This Disney musical about a group of newsboys who strike against a corrupt newspaper mogul boasts a wonderful cast of young talent, but unfortunately the story drags between musical numbers leaving the viewer mostly dispassionate. Even the always magnetic screen presences of Duvall and A-M can't liven up this one. ★½ DVD: $19.99, VHS: $14.99

The Newton Boys

(1998, 122 min, US, Richard Linklater) *Matthew McConaughey, Ethan Hawke, Skeet Ulrich, Vincent D'Onofrio, Julianna Margulies, Dwight Yoakam.* It's period-piece dress-up time in Linklater's dud. *The Newton Boys* is a Prohibition era western about brazen, cocky bank robbers; it has little violence, little blood, little excitement — three ingredients usually associated with the genre. Based on a true story, the film follows four brothers who grew up as farmers to become the most successful bank robbers in American history. The tone of the films suggests *Johnny Dangerously* meets *Young Guns*, and although the banjo and fiddle score spells comedy, there's nothing particularly humorous (or dramatic for that matter) on the screen. ★½ DVD: $9.99, VHS: $9.99

The Next Best Thing

(2000, 108 min, US, John Schlesinger) *Rupert Everett, Madonna, Michael Vartan, Lynn Redgrave, Josef Sommer, Neil Patrick Harris, Illeana Douglas, Benjamin Bratt.* Gay cinema may not have come as far as it could have by the year 2000, but the comedy-drama *The Next Best Thing* does prove that a story revolving around gay characters can be as pointless as stories about straight ones. After a drunken roll in the sack with gay best friend Robert (Everett), single mom Abbie (Madonna) decides she's keeping her baby. The two raise the child together — which they do with great success and little fuss. That is until Abbie meets Mr. Right (Bratt), and the story takes a weird twist into *Kramer vs. Kramer* territory. Everett is especially good as Robert, but he and a good cast aren't enough to compensate for a scatter-shot screenplay — admittedly funny in the first half — that ends up not taking one road at the fork, but all the roads. ★★ DVD: $19.99, VHS: $14.99

Next Friday

(2000, 98 min, US, James Carr) *Ice Cube, Mike Epps, John Witherspoon, Tom 'Tiny' Lister, Jr.* Debo, the giant villain from the first *Friday*, escapes from prison, so Ice Cube's dad decides Cube should stay with his uncle and cousin in the 'burbs for a while and lay low. Stupid, potentially offensive (not the most charitable view of Latinos on display here) and sloppy as hell, *Next Friday* can be funny, anchored by another appealing performance by Cube. To be sure, Chris Tucker is sorely missed from the first film, and this whole affair is pretty pointless, but *Next Friday* is a more entertaining than anyone has a right to expect. ★★½ DVD: $14.99, VHS: $14.99

The Next Karate Kid

(1994, 104 min, US, Christopher Cain) *Noriyuki "Pat" Morita, Hilary Swank, Michael Ironside.* Originality and reality are sorely missing in this blatant rip-off of all the other *Karate Kid* movies. Yes, they did replace Ralph Macchio with Swank, but many of the lines are lifted directly out of the first film. The excesses are beyond belief. ★ DVD: $19.99, VHS: $9.99

Next of Kin

(1984, 72 min, Canada, Atom Egoyan) *Patrick Tierney.* Egoyan's fascination with family relations and the effects of electronic media on one's life are explored in this sly, off-the-wall comedy-drama. Peter, in most respects a normal young man, finds his relationship with his tyrannical WASP family to be unbearable. After a session of video therapy, he sees a video about a troubled Armenian family that had lost a baby to adoption 20 years before. Deciding that a new family is in order, he acts out the role of their long-lost son. Inspired lunacy reigns in this brilliant and original directorial debut that explores not only family tensions but ideas of displacement, cultural stereotypes and role playing. ★★★½ VHS: $79.99

Next Stop, Greenwich Village

(1976, 109 min, US, Paul Mazursky) *Lenny Baker, Ellen Greene, Shelley Winters, Dori Brenner, Lois Smith, Christopher Walken, Antonio Fargas, Jeff Goldblum, Lou Jacobi.* Mazursky's excellent semi-

Next Stop, Greenwich Village

autobiographical account of his early adulthood in 1950s Greenwich Village is one of the first American films in which a writer-director looks back at his youth. Baker gives a rich characterization as an aspiring actor who leaves his Brooklyn home for the unknown wilds of the Village. There, he befriends an eccentric group while waiting for his big break. Mazursky sees the era as a magical time, and his affection shows. The director's evocation of an almost mythical period is first-rate; it's as if Marty McFly grabbed a camera and took the DeLorean for another ride. There's a strong supporting cast, but the acting honors go to Winters for her hilarious turn as Baker's quintessential overprotective mom. Though not as well known as some of his other films, *Next Stop, Greenwich Village* is possibly Mazursky's best. ★★★★ VHS: $29.99

Next Stop Wonderland

(1998, 96 min, US, Brad Anderson) *Hope Davis, Alan Gelfant, Victor Argo, Holland Taylor, Robert Klein, Phillip Seymour Hoffman.* Indy doyenne Davis plays a night nurse at a Boston hospital who tries to make the best of a bad situation when her live-in lover Hoffman decides to dump her. Yenta mother Taylor decides to help by placing a personal ad, and soon a host of loser bachelors are coming out of the woodworks. Not one of them is Gelfant, a hard-working plumber who's studying to be a marine biologist. Writer-director Anderson peppers his film with nice location work, a moody bossa-nova soundtrack and engagingly quirky characters. While Gelfant is downright likable, it's Davis who holds this Beantown chowder together. ★★★ DVD: $19.99, VHS: $9.99

Next Summer

(1986, 100 min, France, Nadine Trintignant) *Fanny Ardant, Philippe Noiret, Jean-Louis Trintignant, Claudia Cardinale.* An all-star cast sadly cannot save this pretentious drivel which claims to give a penetrating humanistic insight into familial relationships. In a rambling country house, the extended family of patriarch Noiret live, love, argue and reconcile (and all within 100 minutes). French fluff at its most nauseating. (French with English subtitles) ★★ VHS: $69.99

The Next Voice You Hear

(1950, 83 min, US, William Wellman) *James Whitmore, Nancy Davis.* An odd drama about the voice of God being heard on the radio and the effect it has on the residents of a small town. The execution is not quite up to the premise, yet the film is strangely moving if one releases all cynical thoughts. ★★½

Next Year If All Goes Well

(1983, 97 min, France, Jean-Loup Hubert) *Isabelle Adjani, Thierry L'Hermitte.* A whimsical romantic comedy about a modern couple involved in an ambivalent affair. While Adjani, a pragmatic career woman, longs for a comfortable domestic life, L'hermitte, a boyish cartoonist, quakes at the mere mention of parenthood and retreats to the safer realm of his outer space comic strip. A megahit in France, *Next Year...* is an often riotous glimpse at marriage and infidelity. ★★★ VHS: $69.99

Niagara

(1953, 89 min, US, Henry Hathaway) *Joseph Cotten, Marilyn Monroe, Jean Peters, Casey Adams, Don Wilson.* The turning point in Monroe's career, this taut suspenser gave Marilyn her first big break towards stardom, and hinted at the legendary persona which would soon emerge. While vaca-

tioning at Niagara Falls, a faithless wife (MM) plots to murder her husband (Cotten) and run off with her lover; but when the distraught husband gets wise, he has other ideas. The importance of this film in MM's career usually overshadows the fact that this is quite an accomplished thriller. ★★★ DVD: $14.99, VHS: $6.99

Niagara, Niagara

(1997, 93 min, US, Bob Gosse) *Robin Tunney, Henry Thomas, Michael Parks, Stephen Lang.* Tunney gives a mesmerizing performance as a young woman isolated by Tourette's Syndrome. Through a chance encounter, she instantly bonds with a young man (Thomas, who is equally remarkable) whose own isolation is a function of his father's casual brutality. Their shared lack of connection overrides their differing circumstances, uniting them against a harsh and uncaring outside world. They embark on a road trip to Canada encountering little except staunch hostility, with one exception: an equally isolated old man (Parks in a stand-out performance) who takes them into his home. Their odyssey to Toronto is beautifully crafted by director Gosse with keen observation of human frailties and a refreshing lack of saccharine sentimentality. ★★★

Nicholas and Alexandra

(1971, 184 min, GB, Franklin J. Schaffner) *Michael Jayston, Janet Suzman, Tom Baker, Laurence Olivier, Michael Redgrave.* This lavish chronicle of the Russian Revolution is rich with scenery, costumery, and even some good acting, though at a three-hour running time it's a little on the long side. The film offers a sprawling and often interesting look at the Russian monarchy during the 14 years leading to the revolution which proved its undoing. Jayston and Suzman (an Oscar nominee) are both splendid, and Baker appears as Rasputin. ★★★ DVD: $24.99, VHS: $29.99

Nicholas Nickleby

(1947, 95 min, GB, Alberto Cavalcanti) *Derek Bond, Cedric Hardwicke, Stanley Holloway.* Charles Dickens' classic story follows a young man's struggle to protect himself and his family from a scheming and miserly uncle. It's a story full of resonance and emotional power and the film stands as a faithful rendition. (Remade in 2002) ★★★ VHS: $14.99

Nicholas Nickleby

(2002, 132 min, GB, Douglas McGrath) *Charlie Hunnam, Jamie Bell, Christopher Plummer, Anne Hathaway, Jim Broadbent, Nathan Lane, Dame Edna (Barry Humphries), Juliet Stevenson, Alan Cumming, Tom Courtenay.* A seasoned cast and spectacular sets, costumes and cinematography highlight this trimmed-down but rewarding adaptation of Charles Dickens' lengthy novel that nicely balances both the comic and tragic elements of the story. Hunnam makes an appealing Nickleby, who travels to London for gainful employment. His heartless rich uncle (Plummer in a tasty performance) sends him to teach at a repressive, run-down school, where he befriends the crippled caretaker Smike (a poignant Bell). Eventually, they both escape and hit the road for adventure. This includes a short stint for a traveling theatrical troupe, with Lane and Dame Edna in great form as director and star, respectively. Director McGrath envisions this tale with humor, pathos and splendor, if not much restraint. A wonderfully entertaining interpretation of an oft-told classic. ★★★½ DVD Special Edition: $14.99

Nick of Time

(1995, 89 min, US, John Badham) *Johnny Depp, Christopher Walken, Charles S. Dutton, Courtenay Chase, Roma Maffia, Marsha Mason.* Filmed in the gimmicky fashion of real time, *Nick of Time* is a not-so-plausible but nevertheless intriguing political thriller which manages to offer a few thrills along the way. Depp plays a father whose daughter (Chase) is abducted upon arriving by train to Los Angeles. Walken and Moffia are the kidnappers, assassins who have been hired to kill the incumbent governor of California (Mason). As they hold his daughter captive, Depp is coerced to pull the trigger with a maniacal Walken following his every move. The film sets up an interesting dilemma for the loving father, which it only occasionally explores. ★★½ DVD: $29.99, VHS: $14.99

Nico and Dani

(2000, 90 min, Spain, Cesc Gay) *Fernando Ramallo, Jordi Vilches, Marieta Orozco, Esther Nubiola, Chisco Amado, Ana Gracia.* Adapted from a popular Spanish play entitled "Krampack," the witty, fresh and funny *Nico and Dani* is a welcome addition to the "gay teen coming-of-age" canon. Teen best buds Nico (Vilches) and Dani (Ramallo) spend another seaside summer together. But rather than go hunting, skinny-dipping or exchange "krampacks" (sexual favors) like achingly gay Dani wishes, Nico prefers to chase girls. Soon, an older gay man and a young sassy girl enter the picture, affording distraction for both boys. The leads are completely believable in their awkward adolescent manner, which only heightens the film's tension and realsim. Director Gay's shrewdly bittersweet ending adds a refreshing, honest final touch to this *muy* beautiful thing. (Spanish with English subtitles) ★★★★ DVD: $29.99, VHS Unrated: $19.99

Nico Icon

(1995, 67 min, US/Germany, Susanne Ofteringer) *Nico, Andy Warhol, Viva, Lou Reed, Paul Morrissey, John Cale, Jackson Browne.* Nico Icon is director Ofteringer's brief but fascinating documentary about the goddess/pop star/junkie/icon known as Nico (Christa Paffgen). A high-profile model in Germany who went to Paris and then to New York, Nico became part of Andy Warhol's Factory in the 1960s. Chronicling Nico's assorted personal and professional affairs, Ofteringer eschews a descriptive voice-over, relying instead on archival footage and on-camera monologues by family, friends and lovers to unravel the Nico mystique — whose "detached elegance" epitomized cool for a generation. (In English and German and French with English subtitles) ★★★½

Night after Night

(1932, 73 min, US, Archie Mayo) *George Raft, Mae West, Constance Cummings, Louis Calhern.* West appears in her film debut, and though she's only on screen for about 15 minutes, it's easy to see why she became a star. A young, Valentino-looking Raft gets star billing in this light underworld comedy-drama as a speakeasy owner who has his hands full with rival gangs and old girlfriends. West plays a former girlfriend, and when she steps on screen, an otherwise pedestrian film suddenly comes alive with energy and humor. West, who had yet to fully hone her campy, staccato delivery and "Diamond Lil" persona, says her archetypical line "Goodness had nothing to do with it, dearie." ★★½

Night and Day

(1946, 128 min, US, Michael Curtiz) *Cary Grant, Alexis Smith, Monty Woolley, Jane Wyman, Eve Arden, Mary Martin.* As Hollywood fiction, this is pretty entertaining stuff; but as the true biography of legendary songwriter Cole Porter, it's laughably inaccurate. And though no one ever complained about seeing Grant in a film, he's not exactly the perfect choice to play the composer. Woolley plays himself as Cole's best friend. Martin has a small scene singing "My Heart Belongs to Daddy." Of course, a film made in 1946 would never have even hinted at Porter's well-known homosexuality. ★★½ DVD: $19.99

Night & Day

(1991, 90 min, Belgium/France, Chantal Akerman) A breezy, post-feminist comedy about a woman's loving relationship with two men, *Night & Day* is a deceptively simple blending of Eric Rohmer's obsession with talky young lovers and the filmic exuberance of early Jean-Luc Godard. Julie and Jack live and love in blissful isolation. He drives a taxi in the evening, and during the day they make love. The arrangement is altered but not upset after Julie meets Joseph, a fellow taxi-driving young man. Erotic, stylish and unconventional. (French with English subtitles) ★★★ VHS: $19.99

Night and Fog

(1956, 32 min, France, Alain Resnais) One is tempted to look at Resnais' Holocaust documentary *Night and Fog* in light of his later works, but to do so is to denigrate the history it so powerfully records. "Records" is not accurate either, for this is not mere documentation, this is an indictment; not of Germans, or even Nazis, but of humanity. Color footage of a placid countryside oddly framed with barb wire gives way to the grays of Auschwitz. The dry, flat narration is brittle from withholding the rage that does not express itself with words. Details record this yesterday to remind us that history exists only when it is remembered. A disturbing and haunting film experience. ★★★★ DVD Criterion Collection: $14.99, VHS: $19.99

Night and the City

(1950, 101 min, US, Jules Dassin) *Richard Widmark, Gene Tierney, Googie Withers, Hugh Marlowe, Herbert Lom.* Widmark is unnerving as a small-time hustler scouring the rubble of a decimated London barely recovered form the ravages of WWII. He facilitates small cons, setting up traveling businessmen for the benefit of his objectionable bar-owning boss. He thinks he sees a way out. With blind frenzy, he steals from the woman (Tierney) who loves him, connives the woman who would provide him with a lucrative set-up, and betrays the employer who supports him. Widmark scurries like a rat over London's bombed-out remains with an enthralling, hyperkinetic desperation used to great effect by director Dassin. (Remade in 1992) ★★★½

Night and the City

(1992, 104 min, US, Irwin Winkler) *Robert De Niro, Jessica Lange, Cliff Gorman, Jack Weston, Alan King.* Winkler's visceral, punchy direction propels outstanding performances from the cast through Richard Price's frenetic screenplay. This is a slick and clever update of the 1950 Richard Widmark classic which captures the feel of contemporary urban noir. D Niro is Harry Fabian, the quintessential street-smart, fast-talking hustler — the *Mean Streets* wise guy all grown up. After a lifetime of tak-

ing the money and running, he decides to go for the big score in the fight game. In going up against the major players, he enters an unfamiliar world with rules he barely understands and unwittingly disrupts an uneasy truce in a decades-old familial conflict. As the married woman who becomes involved with Fabian, Lange is luminous, portraying just the right balance of big-city knowing and innocent naïveté. ★★★½ VHS: $9.99

The Night and the Moment

(1994, 90 min, France/GB/Italy, Anna Maria Tatò) *Willem Dafoe, Lena Olin, Miranda Richardson, Jean Claude Carrière.* A third-rate *Dangerous Liaisons, The Night and the Moment* casts Dafoe as a fop trying to bed a willful Olin by relating past sexual conquests and other stories. This dull, lifeless trash aims for *Tom Jones*-like sophisticated ribaldry, but ends up only as an episodic mishmash. Dafoe seems more desperate and disturbed than calculatedly malicious, and Olin is a letdown. Though several of Dafoe's anecdotes are of mild interest (a detailed description of the usage of an outmoded torture device has a macabre charm), these scenes are separated by long-winded, would-be witty word play, and lackluster story telling. ★½ DVD: $19.99, VHS: $9.99

A Night at the Opera

(1935, 92 min, US, Sam Wood) *Groucho Marx, Harpo Marx, Chico Marx, Margaret Dumont, Allan Jones, Kitty Carlisle.* Groucho is Otis B. Driftwood, con artist extraordinaire and Dumont's financial advisor. He hooks up with an opera company on its way from Italy to America via luxury liner. Complete with young lovers, scurrilous cads, pompous fools, stowaways Chico and Harpo, and the often imitated but never duplicated stateroom scene. ★★★½ DVD: $19.99

Night Crossing

(1981, 106 min, GB, Delbert Mann) *Beau Bridges, John Hurt, Jane Alexander, Glynnis O'Connor.* Fairly entertaining true story about two families who plan an escape from East Berlin by hot-air balloon. ★★ DVD: $19.99

Night Falls on Manhattan

(1997, 113 min, US, Sidney Lumet) *Andy Garcia, Lena Olin, Ian Holm, Ron Leibman, Richard Dreyfuss, James Gandolfini, Colm Feore.* Returning to the city and theme in which he has previously excelled, Lumet has crafted an intoxicating police procedural and courtroom drama. Assistant D.A. Garcia is given his first case — prosecuting the drug lord responsible for the shooting of his policeman father (Holm). The court case is the only thing that's cut-and-dry in the story, for Lumet has more in mind than just a routine trial. His screenplay (based on Robert Daley's "Tainted Evidence") explores the subtleties of racial stereotype, the duplicity of familial and professional loyalties, and the accepted boundaries of duty and corruption. Holm excels as Garcia's father, and Leibman makes a most spirited district attorney who's wiser than he acts. The only false note is Olin's rather contrived romance with Garcia. ★★★½ DVD: $29.99, VHS: $14.99

The Night Flier

(1996, 100 min, US, Mark Pavia) *Julie Entwisle, Dan Monahan, Miguel Ferrer.* This diverting Stephen King adaptation builds slowly, but ends with a bang. Ferrer is perfectly cast as a weasely tabloid reporter with zero scruples in pursuit of the notorious "Night Flier" — a serial killer who finds his victims

at the airport wherever he lands his small plane. Ferrer has competition in the new hungry young buck, a female reporter who dogs his every step. Based on a short story, *The Night Flier* does feel a bit padded out, and the first two thirds — while interspersed with some creepy moments — are somewhat lackluster, held together mainly by Ferrer's spot-on performance. The last half hour or so really picks up steam, with a climax that is genuinely frightening. ★★½ DVD: $14.99, VHS: $9.99

A Night Full of Rain

(1978, 104 min, Italy, Lina Wertmüller) *Giancarlo Giannini, Candice Bergen, Anne Byrne.* In this Italian battle-of-the-sexes drama, Giannini stars as an Italian Communist journalist trapped in a rocky marriage to Bergen, an American photographer and feminist. Director Wertmüller attempts to wring life out of the clash between an old-world chauvinist intent on keeping his wife in check and a liberated woman equally determined to continue her career. Set in Italy and San Francisco, the film has moments of visual spectacle, insight and humor, but the confused plot undermines it all. The full title is *The End of the World in Our Usual Bed in a Night Full of Rain.* (Italian with English subtitles) ★★½ VHS: $19.99

A Night in Casablanca

(1946, 85 min, US, Archie Mayo) *Groucho Marx, Harpo Marx, Chico Marx, Charles Drake, Sig Ruman.* Groucho, Chico and Harpo battle Nazis and uncover stolen loot in the exotic if seedy Hotel Casablanca. There's a young couple in love, a femme fatale, a dastardly villain, some bungling idiots and the usual suspects. Not on par with the Marx Brothers' earlier works, but entertaining just the same. ★★½ DVD: $19.99

A Night in the Life of Jimmy Reardon

(1988, 90 min, US, William Richert) *River Phoenix, Ann Magnuson, Ione Skye, Meredith Salenger.* Young Phoenix explores his sexuality with various women as he decides between college and his girlfriend. An irresponsible sexual coming-of-age comedy which alternates between near-kiddie porn and adult romantic comedy. ★★ DVD: $24.99, VHS: $19.99

Night Is My Future

(1947, 87 min, Sweden, Ingmar Bergman) *Mai Zetterling, Birger Malmsten.* An upper-class pianist is blinded in an accident on a firing range and is cared for by his maid, with whom he falls in love. This little-known Bergman film is done with craftsmanship and taste, and contains a powerful dream/nightmare sequence. (Swedish with English subtitles) ★★½

The Night Larry Kramer Kissed Me

(2000, 90 min, US, Tim Kirkman) *David Drake.* With this striking concert film, David Drake brings his captivating one-man show to the screen. This semiautobiographical performance piece contains several poignant stories about growing up gay in the '90s. From his brilliant opening monologue describing the impact playwright Larry Kramer's "The Normal Heart" had on him to his amusing riff on "Why I Go to the Gym," Drake gives a fierce, full-bodied performance. With rhythmic storytelling and wry observations on gay life, *The Night Larry Kramer Kissed Me* is a funny, knowing and ultimately powerful collection of vignettes. ★★★½ DVD Letterbox: $19.99, VHS: $14.99

Night Mother

(1986, 97 min, US, Tom Moore) *Sissy Spacek, Anne Bancroft.* Spacek and Bancroft offer good performances as mother and daughter in this adaptation of Marsha Norman's Pulitzer Prize-winning play. Spacek plays a troubled woman intent on committing suicide; Bancroft plays her mother who desperately tries to talk her out of it. The film can't overcome its depressing theme, but the two actresses make the drama involving. ★★½ VHS: $14.99

Night Moves

(1975, 95 min, US, Arthur Penn) *Gene Hackman, Susan Clark, Jennifer Warren, Melanie Griffith, James Woods.* Hackman excels in this gripping psycho-thriller from the pen of Alan Sharp. Hackman plays an emotionally on-the-edge private detective who is hired to track down a wayward daughter (Griffith) in Florida. Penn provides able direction in this pessimistic film which captures the sanguine mood of post-Watergate America. ★★★ VHS: $19.99

Night of the Comet

(1984, 95 min, US, Thom Eberhardt) *Catherine Mary Stweart, Kelli Maroney, Robert Beltran.* Entertaining, clever "B" sci-fi comedy about two Valley Girls who seem to be the last survivors of a killer comet. After an exhausting shopping spree at the local mall, however, they soon realize they are not alone: zombies! ★★½

The Night of the Following Day

(1969, 93 min, US, Hubert Cornfield) *Marlon Brando, Rita Moreno, Richard Boone, Pamela Franklin.* A dated but intriguing drama about four professional criminals and their "foolproof" kidnapping scheme that goes horribly wrong when fate and human nature conspire against them. As the leader of the group, Brando (obviously in the middle of a bad hair day) drinks heavily from the method acting well, and is outshined by Boone, who gives a splendid performance as a sadistic psychopath. ★★½ DVD: $14.99

The Night of the Generals

(1966, 148 min, GB, Anatole Litvak) *Peter O'Toole, Omar Sharif, Tom Courtenay, Donald Pleasence, Philippe Noiret.* This WWII thriller follows a Nazi intelligence officer hot on the trail of a psychotic general suspected of murdering prostitutes. Over-the-top performance by O'Toole makes a laughable script interesting. ★★

The Night of the Hunter

(1955, 93 min, US, Charles Laughton) *Robert Mitchum, Shelley Winters, Lillian Gish, Peter Graves.* This enigmatic suspense thriller is the distinguished actor Laughton's sole directorial effort; and he succeeds magnificently. A dreamlike, disturbing fable in which two children are pursued by a madman, *The Night of the Hunter* is full of haunting images. The psychotic preacher with L-O-V-E and H-A-T-E tattooed on his knuckles is chillingly portrayed by Mitchum and the black-and-white cinematography is incredibly lyrical. ★★★★ DVD: $14.99

Night of the Iguana

(1964, 118 min, US, John Huston) *Richard Burton, Ava Gardner, Deborah Kerr, Grayson Hall, Sue Lyon.* In this expertly acted film version of Tennessee Williams's steamy Broadway play, Burton, Gardner and Kerr give stellar performances as participants in a love triangle in a small Mexican resort town. Burton plays a defrocked priest-turned-bus tour guide who becomes involved with young nymphette Lyon, sexually repressed Kerr and fiery hotel proprietor Gardner (who is stunning in possibly her best screen portrayal). ★★★

Night of the Living Dead

(1968, 96 min, US, George A. Romero) *Judith O'Dea, Duane Jones.* The foremost fright film ever. On a ghoulish night in Pittsburgh, decomposing corpses return to life to devour the living. Graphically gruesome and morosely funny, this black-and-white gem established director Romero as a master of the genre. (Remade in 1990) ★★★★ DVD Millennium Edition: $24.99, DVD Basic Edition: $14.99, VHS: $6.99

Night of the Living Dead

(1990, 95 min, US, Tom Savini) *Tony Todd, Patricia Tallman.* Makeup master Savini directs this color remake of George Romero's black-and-white horror classic. It's virtually shot-for-shot. The only difference is that Barbara, the catatonic female lead from the original, is now in the Sigourney Weaver-Linda Hamilton school of film heroines. Ironically, the film loses some of its tension in color; but nevertheless delivers the goods. ★★½ DVD: $19.99, VHS: $9.99

The Night of the Shooting Stars

(1982, 106 min, Italy, Paolo & Vittorio Taviani) *Omero Antonutti, Margarita Lozano.* A fascinating probe into the collective consciousness of post-war Italy. Filtered through the memory of a woman whose childhood was spent during the period, it is the tale of the war's closing days in a small Italian town. Poetic, enthralling and magnificently crafted. (Italian with English subtitles) ★★★½ DVD: $19.99

Night on Earth

(1991, 125 min, US, Jim Jarmusch) *Gena Rowlands, Winona Ryder, Armin Mueller-Stahl, Giancarlo Esposito, Rosie Perez, Béatrice Dalle, Isaach de Bankolé, Robert Benigni, Paolo Bonacelli, Paolo Bonacelli, Matti Pellonpää, Kari Väänänen, Sakari Kousmanen.* Director Jarmusch explores the subculture of the taxi cab with this enchanting series of five offbeat vignettes set respectively in Los Angeles, New York, Paris, Rome and Helsinki; each centering around a cabbie and their fare(s). The includes Rowlands and Ryder (L.A.); Mueller-Stahl, Esposito and Perez (N.Y.); Dalle and de Bankolé (Paris); Benigni and Bonacelli (Rome); and Pellonpää, Väänänen and Kousmanen in Helsinki. While each of the stories is entertaining, the standouts are Mueller-Stahl and Esposito's hilarious cultural collision in the New York episode and Benigni's outrageous portrayal of a loopy Italian who speeds around Rome in the middle of the night while wearing dark sunglasses and entertaining himself with an endless series of one-liners. (Filmed in English, French, Italian and Finnish with English subtitles) ★★★½

The Night Porter

(1973, 118 min, Italy, Liliana Cavani) *Dirk Bogarde, Charlotte Rampling.* Few films equal the unrelenting intensity of Cavani's disturbing drama. Years after surviving sexual imprisonment under a Nazi stormtrooper, a woman inadvertently encounters her former torturer/lover working as a night porter at a Viennese hotel. Despite their reversed positions of power, they ultimately reenact their sadomasochistic roles in a gruesomely lecherous dance of death. (Filmed in English) ★★ DVD: $29.99, VHS: $19.99

Night Shift

(1982, 106 min, US, Ron Howard) *Michael Keaton, Henry Winkler, Shelley Long, Kevin Costner.* Howard's directorial debut produced this funny comedy about a fast-talking city morgue assistant (Keaton in his debut) who turns his workplace into a bordello. ★★★ DVD: $9.99, VHS: $7.99

The Night Stalker

(1971, 73 min, US, John Llewellyn Moxey) *Darren McGavin, Carol Lynley, Simon Oakland, Ralph Meeker, Claude Akins.* An immensely enjoyable made-for-TV vampire tale (the pilot for the short-lived TV series) with McGavin as a hard-boiled investigative reporter who unearths a story about a modern-day bloodsucker terrorizing Las Vegas. The film successfully combines the style of a 1940s noir mystery with comedy and horror; and McGavin is tops as the cynical journalist. ★★★

The Night They Raided Minsky's

(1968, 99 min, US, William Friedkin) *Jason Robards, Britt Ekland, Norman Wisdom, Bert Lahr, Elliott Gould, Denholm Elliott.* A fine comic romp heralding the infamous days of Burlesque, with Robards as a vaudeville comic who becomes involved with Pennsylvania Dutch girl Ekland. The film captures the flavor of the bawdy comics and comely strippers, and provides a fascinating glimpse of life both on- and offstage during this bygone era. Wisdom is especially good as a stage comic. ★★★½

Night Tide

(1963, 84 min, US, Curtis Harrington) *Dennis Hopper, Luana Anders, Bruno Ve Sota, Linda Lawson, Gavin Muir, Tom Dillon, Marjorie Eaton.* Inspired by Val Lewton's *Cat People*, this surreal fantasy tells the story of a young sailor (a baby-faced Hopper) who falls in love with a strange woman posing as a mermaid in a seafront carnival. She believes herself to be a descendant of the "sea people" who must kill during the full moon. This moody chiller features a fine supporting cast, and a special cameo by Ed Wood, Jr.'s rubber octopus from *Bride of the Monster.* ★★★ DVD: $29.99, VHS: $29.99

A Night to Remember

(1958, 123 min, GB, Roy Baker) *Kenneth More, Honor Blackman, David McCallum, George Rose, Alec McCowan.* A first-rate drama about the infamous night the luxury liner Titanic hit an iceberg and sank in the freezing waters of the Atlantic, killing over 1,500 passengers and crew. More, exceptional as the ship's captain, heads a highly competent cast. A riveting, meticulous production told in semidocumentary style, which only adds to the overall authority of the film. ★★★★ DVD: $39.99

Night Train to Munich

(1940, 95 min, GB, Carol Reed) *Rex Harrison, Margaret Lockwood, Paul Henreid, Basil Radford, Naunton Wayne.* Reed's thrilling reworking of Hitchcock's *The Lady Vanishes* is a pleasure to watch. A spy/chase thriller of the highest order, it tells the story of a pair of undercover agents (Harrison and Henried) who are both after a prominent industrialist and his daughter (Lockwood). Bouncing back and forth from Germany to England and in-between, the plot is full of captures, escapes and recaptures. Most movies are content with one or two nail-biting sequences: this is full of them. Even the somewhat dated comic relief of a pair of English comics (Radford and Wayne) is welcome. ★★★★ VHS: $24.99

Night Train to Venice

(1993, 98 min, Germany/Italy, Carlo U. Quinterio) *Hugh Grant, Malcolm McDowell, Tahnee Welch.* Trying to pass itself off as stylish through a mishmash (nay, a cacophony!) of images, *Night Train to Venice* assaults the viewer with an endless parade of meaningless drivel about a group of skinheads terrorizing the Orient Express on its way to Venice. McDowell tries to keep a straight face portraying a thinly veiled Mephistopheles. ★

The Night Walker

(1964, 86 min, US, William Castle) *Barbara Stanwyck, Robert Taylor, Lloyd Bochner.* Stanwyck plays a wealthy widow who has strange recurring dreams about her lost husband. The $1.99 special effects during the dream sequences and *Psycho* author Robert Bloch's mind-numbing screenplay help to do for Barbara what *Trog* did for Joan Crawford, which easily could explain her quick leap to TV and "The Big Valley." The film does have its moments, though. ★★ VHS: $14.99

The Night We Never Met

(1993, 99 min, US, Warren Leight) *Annabella Sciorra, Matthew Broderick, Kevin Anderson, Louis Lasser, Jeanne Tripplehorn, Garry Shandling, Bill Campbell.* The comings and goings of three strangers who time-share a New York apartment without meeting sets the stage for an amiable comedy of convenient coincidence — i.e., light on convincing plot, heavy on funny lines and scenes. Broderick delivers a droll yet engaging performance as a heartbroken would-be gourmet chef. Sciorra as a semi-happily married dental hygenist, and Anderson as a loutish, immature stockbroker are his roommates. ★★½ VHS: $9.99

Night Zoo

(1987, 117 min, Canada, Jean-Claude Lauzon) *Roger Lebel, Gilles Maheu.* A schizophrenic film if there ever was one — is it a darkly violent crime thriller or a heartwarming human drama of the rapprochement of a man with his father? The film focuses on both themes and suffers for it. After being released from prison, Marcel, an angry punk of questionable sexuality, tries to readjust to life on the outside but his efforts are thwarted by two sleazy gay cops. Set in a dark and dangerous Montreal, the film's action sequences are exciting, but generally the film bogs down when it deals with the sappy familial angle. (French with English subtitles) ★★½

Nightbreaker

(1989, 100 min, US, Peter Markle) *Martin Sheen, Emilio Estevez, Lea Thompson, Melinda Dillon.* A gripping thriller about lethal government testing. Sheen and son Estevez play the same character — in the 1950s and the 1980s — a doctor who was involved in atomic experiments in the Nevada desert using — and endangering — American military personnel. ★★★

Nightbreed

(1990, 93 min, GB, Clive Barker) *Craig Sheffer, Anne Bobby, David Cronenberg, Charles Haid.* Barker's second feature, based on his novella "Cabal," is ambitious but falls short in its execution. Hidden away in a deserted cemetery is a mythical civilization of ghoulish outcasts. A young man, Boone (Sheffer), has horrific visions of these creatures and in an act of poor judgment seeks treatment from a creepy psychiatrist (Cronenberg), who frames Boone for a series of killings he himself is committing. Boone is killed and then reincarnated as one of

the Nightbreed, a race of underground monsters who are readying themselves for battle against their human oppressors. Though Barker's intentions are good, the film is sluggish and meandering, and the director fails to create any palpable suspense. ★★ DVD Letterbox: $19.99, VHS: $14.99

The Nightcomers

(1972, 96 min, US, Michael Winner) *Marlon Brando, Stephanie Beacham, Harry Andrews.* Tired thriller which attempts to hint at why the children of Henry James' "The Turn of the Screw" became the way they did. Brando is a sadistic and sexually abusive gardener who serves as perverse mentor; Beacham is the governess involved in a kinky relationship with Brando. The sexual aspect of the film predates the similarly themed Brando film *Last Tango in Paris*, but lacks that classic's detailed character development or cinematic stylization. ★★

Nighthawks

(1978, 113 min, GB, Paul Hallam & Ron Peck) *Ken Robertson.* London's gay scene, and one man's search for belonging in it, are explored in this sensitive and intelligent drama which was Britain's first independent gay-themed film. Robertson plays a quiet teacher who divides his time between the classroom and the closet and evenings spent aimlessly cruising the city's gay bars and discos. Using mostly unprofessional actors, this gritty, heartfelt drama has surprising depth despite the lack of any discernable plot, as it sympathetically portrays one man's homosexual lifestyle without resorting to theatrics and stereotyping. ★★★ VHS: $39.99

Nighthawks

(1981, 99 min, US, Bruce Malmuth) *Sylvester Stallone, Billy Dee Williams, Rutger Hauer, Persis Khambatta, Lindsay Wagner.* The suspense is riveting in this little-seen police thriller starring Stallone and Williams as a pair of New York cops on the trail of a ruthless international terrorist. Hauer shines as the terrorist Wulfgar, in a role which prefigures his sadistic killer in *The Hitcher* five years later. Even Stallone's presence can't ruin this gem of a film. ★★★ DVD: $14.99

The Nightmare Before Christmas

(1993, 74 min, US, Henry Selick) *Voices of: Danny Elfman, Chris Sarandon, Catherine O'Hara, William Hickey, Ken Page, Paul Reubens.* This enchanting animated musical bears the trademark of its producer Tim Burton, for it's a daring and imaginative entertainment. Made in cooperation with and released by Disney studios, *Nightmare* features the best in stop-motion animation to tell the tale of Jack Skellington and his fellow inhabitants of Halloweentown who band together to bring their own special ghoulish flavor to Christmas. Kidnapping Santa Claus, Jack takes over the reins of Santa's sleigh and delivers a holiday to remember. Determinedly dark and decidedly funny, *Nightmare* boasts a devilishly playful score by Danny Elfman. ★★★½ DVD Special Edition: $22.99, VHS Special Edition: $14.99

A Nightmare on Elm Street

(1984, 91 min, US, Wes Craven) *John Saxon, Ronee Blakely, Heather Langenkamp, Amanda Wyss, Johnny Depp, Robert Englund.* When the psychosexual desires of young girls come out in their dreams, the result is a blood-crazed apparition with razor sharp, phallic-like talons. This is surely one of the most frightening films of the 1980s, due primarily to

its inventive premise of this villain literally escaping from the victims' minds, rather than from the local insane asylum. (Followed by 6 sequels) ★★★ DVD: $14.99, VHS: $9.99, VHS Letterbox: $9.99

A Nightmare on Elm Street Part 2: Freddy's Revenge

(1985, 87 min, US, Jack Sholder) *Mark Patton, Kim Myers, Robert Rusler, Clu Gulager, Hope Lange, Marshall Bell, Robert Englund.* The second entry in the *Elm Street* series is the least successful of the series. It's five years later, and Freddy is back trying to possess a teenage boy in order to continue his murderous ways. H½ DVD: $14.99, VHS: $9.99

A Nightmare on Elm Street 3: Dream Warriors

(1987, 96 min, US, Chuck Russell) *Robert Englund, Heather Langenkamp, Laurence Fishburne, Craig Wasson, Dick Cavett, Zsa Zsa Gabor.* One of the most popular of the *Nightmare* series, this imaginative and sometimes wickedly funny sequel has Freddy back tormenting more hapless teens, here being cared for by Langenkamp from the original. ★★★ DVD: $14.99, VHS: $9.99

A Nightmare on Elm Street 4: The Dream Master

(1988, 92 min, US, Renny Harlin) *Robert Englund, Rodney Eastman, Danny Hassel, Andras Jones.* You can't keep a good mass-murderer-from-beyond-the-grave down. Freddy returns once again to wreak havoc on poor, unsuspecting teenagers. Very stylish, with a few good scares. Director Harlin would go on to direct the explosive *Die Hard 2*. ★★½ DVD: $14.99, VHS: $9.99

A Nightmare on Elm Street 5: The Dream Child

(1989, 89 min, US, Stephen Hopkins) *Robert Englund, Lisa Wilcox, Kelly Jo Minter, Danny Hassel, Whitby Hertford.* Freddy Krueger goes surreal. Freddy teams up with an unborn child to continue his murderous ways. Good visuals but not much more. ★★ DVD: $14.99, VHS: $9.99

Freddy's Dead: The Final Nightmare

(1991, 96 min, US, Rachel Talalay) *Robert Englund, Lisa Zane, Yaphet Kotto, Roseanne, Tom Arnold, Johnny Depp.* Freddy Krueger (Englund) camps it up again in this inane, effects-heavy sequel. Zane plays a child psychologist who leads a group of troubled teens into their dream worlds to get to the bottom of their recurring nightmares — all starring Freddy! ★ DVD: $14.99, VHS: $9.99

Wes Craven's New Nightmare

(1994, 112 min, US, Wes Craven) *Heather Langenkamp, John Saxon, Robert Englund.* This inventive movie within a dream within a movie turns on the interesting premise that the power of the cult following of the previous six *Nightmare* films has served to bring Freddy Krueger to life in the real world. Scary nightmare sequences, a good script and an even more menacing Freddy are put to good use, but for all this Craven cannot restore the series' original luster. ★★½ DVD: $14.99, VHS: $9.99

Nine Queens

Nights of Cabiria

(1957, 117 min, Italy, Federico Fellini) *Giulietta Masina, François Perier.* This Academy Award-winning film is a grim but very moving drama from Fellini's early career. The film lacks the flash and fantasy of the director's later films but has a power and intensity that is sadly lacking in his final works. This is a poignant tale of a naïve prostitute who searches for love and fulfillment in every man she meets. The waifish streetwalker is wonderfully portrayed by Masina. The story would form the basis for the musical *Sweet Charity.* This is the full-length version, including a previously banned 7-minute sequence. (Italian with English subtitles) ★★★★ DVD: $39.99, VHS: $29.99

Nightwatch

(1998, 101 min, US, Ole Bornedal) *Ewan McGregor, Nick Nolte, Patricia Arquette, Josh Brolin, John C. Reilly.* McGregor stars in this tepid thriller as a law student moonlighting as a security guard at a morgue. Meanwhile, a vicious serial killer is prowling the city, preying on prostitutes, whose bodies keep crowding the morgue. Is McGregor the killer? The answer, unfortunately, is fairly obvious. Director Bornedal (who cowrote with Steven Soderbergh) here remakes his own overrated 1994 Danish chiller *Nattevagten,* and sadly, delivers a carbon copy of that film, carrying its same flaws — an illogical plot, a slack pace, and most damaging, extremely unlikable characters and needlessly unpleasant situations. ★½ DVD: $9.99, VHS: $9.99

Nijinsky

(1980, 125 min, GB, Herbert Ross) *George de la Pena, Alan Bates, Jeremy Irons, Leslie Brown, Colin Blakely, Janet Suzman, Alan Badel.* Ross, who scored a major triumph with *The Turning Point,* once again turns to the world of ballet with this expertly acted, rather melodramatic but intriguing biography about the legendary dancer Nijinsky (de la Pena) and his professional and private relationship with his

mentor/lover Sergei Diaghilev (impressively played by Bates). Badel gives an outstanding performance as a wealthy patron of the arts. ★★½ VHS: $14.99

Nil by Mouth

(1998, 128 min, GB, Gary Oldman) *Kathy Burke, Charlie Creed-Miles, Edna Dore, Lalia Morse, Ray Winstone.* A stunner of a film from actor Oldman, making his debut as writer and director. Loosely based on his own family, Oldman's raw, intense drama examines a lower-class London family with an unflinching eye. The superb cast delivers incredibly rich, nuanced performances and the jittery, you-are-there cinematography captures the documentary look intended without becoming artificial. The film is bleak, to be sure, but by the end, we've seen a terrific, wholly real confrontation between put-upon wife Burke (a Best Actress winner at Cannes for her performance) and her bully husband — and a satisfying, believable ending. ★★★★ DVD: $29.99

9½ Weeks

(1986, 113 min, US, Adrian Lyne) *Mickey Rourke, Kim Basinger, Margarte Whitton.* Rourke and Basinger star as two SoHo yuppies who meet by chance and quickly find themselves entangled in a highly erotic sadomasochistic relationship. Rourke is well-cast as the domineering, slightly sinister commodities broker who draws Basinger, a sexy art dealer, into a series of kinky, sex-for-sex's-sake adventures. Whether in a back alley or a clock tower, the heat from these attractive actors is enough to make the screen sweat, though not enough to produce a totally comprehensible film. ★★½ DVD: $19.99

Nine Months

(1995, 102 min, US, Chris Columbus) *Hugh Grant, Julianne Moore, Tom Arnold, Joan Cusack, Jeff Goldblum, Robin Williams.* This occasionally funny but always obvious comedy stars Grant as a reluctant father-to-be who loses the woman he loves (Moore) before realizing that, damn it, there's nothing better than "family values." Director Columbus offers little humor or style, and the pacing rarely catches on in this cloying tribute to masculinity. ★★ DVD: $9.99

Nine Queens

(2002, 115 min, Argentina, Fabian Bielinsky) *Ricardo Darín, Gaston Pauls, Leticia Bredice, Tomas Fonzi.* A thoroughly engaging Mamet-like shell game, *Nine Queens* is two full hours of fun from debut director Bielinsky. A seasoned, soulless con man saves a greenhorn from going to jail after flubbing a "trick" in a gas station market. He then offers to teach him the ropes for a day. The two eventually have the opportunity of a lifetime fall into their lap, involving some highly valuable stamps: the Nine Queens. The real pleasure here is that the main characters aren't fools; their guard is always up, even when they're convinced everything might be on the level. We don't feel (as in many films in the subgenre) that a character has to be gullible for a certain twist to be effective. The spot-on acting certainly helps pull this off, of course, including Darín, who was also quite impressive in *Son of the Bride.* A solid, entertaining film that would keep Mamet himself on the edge of his seat. (Spanish with English subtitles) ★★★ DVD Letterbox: $29.99, VHS: $102.99

976-Evil

(1988, 89 min, US, Robert Englund) *Stephen Geoffreys, Sandy Dennis.* Robert Englund (alias Freddy Krueger) directed this effective horror outing about an outcast teenager (Geoffreys) who acquires demonic powers thanks to a 976 phone number. ★★½ DVD: $19.99, VHS: $9.99

9 to 5

(1980, 110 min, US, Colin Higgins) *Jane Fonda, Lily Tomlin, Dolly Parton, Dabney Coleman, Sterling Hayden.* Fonda, Tomlin and Parton proved to be a formidable team in this amusing and topical hit comedy. Three secretaries get even with their sexist, insensitive boss (Coleman); and raise office efficiency and productivity to new highs in his absence. Tomlin's cartoon fantasy sequence is a hilarious highlight. ★★½ DVD: $14.99, VHS: $9.99

1918

(1985, 89 min, US, Ken Harrison) *Matthew Broderick, William Converse-Roberts, Hallie Foote.* Two-time Academy Award-winning screenwriter Horton Foote (*To Kill a Mockingbird, Tender Mercies*) adapted his own play about the frustrations and loss of innocence of a small Texas town during the final months of WWI. Extremely well-acted, this somber story is a little too leisurely paced, which sometimes distracts from the heartfelt dramatics. (Sequel: *Valentine's Day*) ★★½ DVD: $19.99

1984

(1984, 115 min, GB, Michael Bradford) *John Hurt, Richard Burton, Suzanna Hamilton.* After watching this excruciating, but unequalled, version of George Orwell's classic novel, one may well be expected to seek counseling. Gripping performances by Hurt, Burton (in his last screen appearance) and Hamilton along with impressive production design and grainy, muted cinematography, power this overwhelming and gloomy depiction of Orwell's futuristic nightmare world. A harrowing film experience. ★★★ DVD: $19.99

1941

(1979, 146 min, US, Steven Spielberg) *John Belushi, Dan Aykroyd, Treat Williams, Lorraine Gary, Ned Beatty, Nancy Allen, Tim Matheson, Christopher Lee, Robert Stack, Wendie Jo Sperber, John Candy.* Although labeled as Spielberg's first "flop," this epic WWII comedy is definitely not the

N

dud it was proclaimed to be. Over-produced as it may be (it's the *It's a Mad, Mad, Mad, Mad World* of the '70s), there are some very funny sequences in this story of wartime hysteria in Los Angeles. The film is highlighted by great special effects, and features a solid all-star cast. This is the Director's Cut, which includes 28 minutes of footage not in the theatrical release. ★★ DVD Letterbox Collector's Edition: $14.99

1900

(1977, 235 min, Italy, Bernardo Bertolucci) *Robert De Niro, Gérard Depardieu, Dominique Sanda, Donald Sutherland, Burt Lancaster.* Bertolucci examines the intertwined lives of De Niro and Depardieu, both born on the same day at the turn of the century; one to a landowner, one to a peasant household. This grand, sweeping yet personal epic follows them through the rise of Fascism in Italy, and beyond. Studded with exceptional performances. (Filmed in English) ★★★½ VHS: $14.99

1969

(1988, 93 min, US, Ernest Thompson) *Kiefer Sutherland, Robert Downey, Jr., Winona Ryder, Bruce Dern, Joanna Cassidy.* A good cast is mostly the reason to see this sincere though dramatically impotent teen drama set against the backdrop of the '60s anti-war protests. ★★ DVD Dual: $14.99

90° South

(1933, 70 min, GB, Herbert G. Ponting) A spellbinding chronicle of Captain Robert Scott's heroic but ultimately tragic race for the South Pole — not only did Norwegian explorer Amundsen reach the goal first, but Scott and his entire expedition died on the trip. Originally released in 1913, photographer Herbert G. Ponting remade the film in 1933, adding narration taken from the journal found next to Captain Scott's frozen body. ★★★ DVD: $29.99, VHS: $39.99

92 in the Shade

(1976, 91 min, US, Thomas McGuane) *Peter Fonda, Warren Oates, Margot Kidder, Burgess Meredith, Harry Dean Stanton.* McGuane (*Cold Feet*) adapted and directed this flavorful version of his acclaimed novel. Fonda plays a fishing boat captain who finds romance and rivalry in the Florida Keys. ★★★ VHS: $59.99

Ninotchka

(1939, 110 min, US, Ernst Lubitsch) *Greta Garbo, Melvyn Douglas, Sig Ruman, Ina Claire, Bela Lugosi.* The ads read "Garbo laughs," and so she does in Lubitsch's witty and captivating comedy. As a rigid Russian agent, Comrade Greta risks honor and career when she falls for Paris and playboy Douglas. Impeccable direction from Lubitsch, and scintillating dialogue cowritten by Billy Wilder. (Musical remake: *Silk Stockings*) ★★★★ VHS: $19.99

The Ninth Configuration

(1979, 115 min, US, William Peter Blatty) *Stacy Keach, Scott Wilson, Jason Miller, Ed Flanders, Moses Gunn, Robert Loggia.* Before he retreated back to familiar territory with *The Exorcist III*, author Blatty made an impressive directorial debut with this creepy, surrealistic adaptation of his novel "Twinkle, Twinkle, Killer Kane" (the film's alternate title). Keach plays a psychiatrist treating a group of military outcasts at an isolated mental hospital. A sometimes funny and very disturbing psychothriller. ★★★ DVD Letterbox: $19.99, VHS: $14.99

The Ninth Gate

(2000, 133 min, GB, Roman Polanski) *Johnny Depp, Lena Olin, Frank Langella, Emmanuelle Seigner.* Depp stars in this atmospheric, but ultimately silly supernatural mystery about an unethical rare book dealer whose assignment to retrieve three copies of an arcane tome brings him into contact with haughty aristocrats, psycho satanists and murder. Polanski's second foray into the supernatural features the same patient and detailed storytelling as his earlier works (*Rosemary's Baby*), but with a far less interesting denouement. ★★ DVD: $14.99, VHS: $9.99

Nixon

(1995, 192 min, US, Oliver Stone) *Anthony Hopkins, Joan Allen, Paul Sorvino, James Woods, Ed Harris, Bob Hoskins, Powers Boothe, Mary Steenburgen, David Paymer, E.G. Marshall.* If moviemaking is this century's conveyance of contemporary folklore, *Nixon* mythologizes a historical figure deeply imbedded over decades in the American consciousness. And few personalities elicit such polar extremes of reaction as President Richard Milhous Nixon, a deeply conflicted man with true world vision yet bogged down in consuming, petty hatreds and beset by driving personal demons. Hopkins approaches the formidable task of portraying a public figure with a consummate actor's creation of a multilayered, contradictory and often baffling personality. Stone's technical filmmaking expertise exploits the innermost soul of an individual against the backdrop of a nation's psyche; if you hold his political interpretation as indulgence, you must allow an auteur's sure hand at his medium. In support, Allen stands out as Pat Nixon, the one person who saw it all yet was least seen by the public eye. ★★★½ DVD Letterbox Collector's Edition: $19.99, VHS Exclusive Video Bonus Edition: $9.99

No Escape

(1994, 118 min, US, Martin Campbell) *Lance Henriksen, Ray Liotta, Stuart Wilson, Kevin Dillon, Kevin J. O'Connor, Michael Lerner, Ernie Hudson.* A slumming Liotta stars in this futuristic action-thriller, sort of *Escape from New York* meets *Lord of the Flies*. After killing his superior officer, ex-soldier Liotta is sent to a secret island prison where he's caught between two warring factions. He reluctantly joins forces with Henrikson and the more "civilized" prisoners in their fight against Wilson (playing a flamboyantly evil leader) and his band of cutthroats. Gory and not without a few thrills, *No Escape* is a by-the-book adventure story. ★★½ DVD: $14.99, VHS: $9.99, VHS Letterbox: $14.99

No Fear, No Die

(1992, 97 min, France, Claire Denis) *Alex Descas, Isaach de Bankolé, Jean-Claude Brialy, Solveig Dommartin.* A gritty, ugly and surprisingly slow-moving tale of the underground world of cockfighting. Dah and Jocelyn are two trainers who work for a sleazy club owner and his wife. What ensues is a tangled web of deceit and greed between the four characters. Unfortunately, the film spends too much time depicting disturbingly graphic scenes of cockfighting and not enough time developing the relationships between the characters and the metaphorical values of the cock-fights. An excellent cast and great cinematography cannot overcome the underdeveloped script. (French with English subtitles) ★★ VHS: $14.99

No Good Deed

(2003, 97 min, US, Bob Rafelson) *Samuel L. Jackson, Milla Jovovich, Stellan Skarsgård, Doug Hutchison, Joss Ackland, Grace Zabriskie.* Director Rafelson has been on autopilot for about a decade now, and that doesn't change with this by-the-books noir adapted from a Dashiell Hammett story ("The House on Turk Street"). Jackson is never believable in his role as a cop who, searching for a missing girl, instead stumbles upon a gang of thieves plotting to steal $10 million from a bank. He's taken hostage and moll Jovovich kinda falls for him, while she also manipulates ringleader Skarsgård and temperamental thug Hutchison. The twists are mild (though at least they're plot-driven), the romance understated, and the violence is sudden and fierce. But at the same time the noir touches feel forced, and Jackson's character development is limited to his diabetes and cello playing. It says something when the most notable directorial touch is the incongruous appearance of the song "I'm Not Your Stepping Stone," a reminder of Rafelson's hand in creating The Monkees. ★★ DVD: $19.99, VHS: $14.99

No Highway in the Sky

(1951, 98 min, GB, Henry Koster) *James Stewart, Marlene Dietrich, Glynis Johns, Jack Hawkins, Kenneth More.* Stewart is in top form as an absent-minded scientist whose investigation into the structural weaknesses of a new airplane turns him into a one-man crusader. As he tries to convince his superiors that a crash is imminent, he finds himself on one of the doomed aircraft. The film nicely balances benign comic episodes with a story both suspenseful and gripping. Dietrich costars in a part not unlike herself, that of a cynical, famous movie actress — she's made-to-order and nearly defines the word glamorous. ★★★ VHS: $19.99

No, I Have No Regrets

(1973, 75 min, GB, Michael Houldey) The indomitable spirit and mesmeric talents of the legendary French singer and songwriter Edith Piaf are showcased in this captivating musical biography. From her beginning singing on the back streets of Pigalle through her rise to international stardom, Piaf's life was anything but ordinary. The film features many performances as well as exploring the diminutive Piaf's tumultuous private life which entranced the people of France for over 20 years. Interviewed are several of her friends (Eddie Constantine) as well as a former husband (Yves Montand) who all recount anecdotes on the beloved pop songstress. ★★★½

No Looking Back

(1998, 96 min, US, Edward Burns) *Lauren Holly, Edward Burns, Jon Bon Jovi, Blythe Danner, Connie Britton, Jennifer Esposito.* With his third film, writer-director Burns again casts himself as the lead, a slacker who left girlfriend Holly alone and waiting for an abortion three years ago. Now he's back to his grey, depressing New York beach resort hometown and she's living with best friend Bon Jovi. Will restless Holly leave the dead-end town to get back with her ex-beau? That's the premise. As an actor, the scratchy voiced Burns has turned smug and annoying. He's not helped by Holly, either, who seems to be in no short supply of attention-getting facial expressions. Burns keeps dishing out the same stuff. He's a talented guy, but he's got to start learning something from his titles. ★½

No Man of Her Own

(1950, 98 min, US, Mitchell Leisen) *Barbara Stanwyck, John Lund, Phyllis Thaxter.* Stanwyck's gripping performance distinguishes this seductive, moody noir melodrama. Surviving a train crash and on the lam, Stanwyck assumes the identity of a woman who, about to meet her deceased husband's family for the first time, is killed in the accident. Taken in by the family, Stanwyck's newfound happiness is short-lived, however, as a blackmailing ex-boyfriend enters the picture. Though the plot and execution of the drama is pure soap opera, Stanwyck's gutsy portrayal makes it all the more involving. (Remade as the French film *I Married a Shadow*) ★★★

No Man's Land

(1987, 107 min, US, Peter Werner) *Charlie Sheen, D.B. Sweeney.* An undercover rookie cop (Sweeney) investigates a charming high-class car thief (Sheen) and finds himself being seduced by the deadly, fast-paced world of money, power and corruption. ★★ DVD Pan & Scan: $14.99

No Mercy

(1986, 105 min, US, Richard Pearce) *Richard Gere, Kim Basinger, Jeroen Krabbé, Ray Sharkey.* Routine police thriller benefitting from the teaming of Gere and Basinger. Gere plays an undercover cop who investigates the murder of his partner, leading him to the sultry, mysterious Basinger. ★★ DVD: $9.99

No Regrets for Our Youth

(1946, 111 min, Japan, Akira Kurosawa) *Setsuko Hara.* This, the master's first major work, an epic drama of feminist self-discovery, is set in 1930s Japan — a time of growing nationalism and right-wing militarism. Yukie, a vivacious young woman, falls in love with her father's most outspoken left-wing law student. She gives up a life of ease to move to Tokyo and support his dangerous antiwar activities, only to see him executed for espionage. Her own life undergoes an amazing transformation after his death as she retreats to the countryside of her ancestors to begin a new life, alone. (Japanese with English subtitles) ★★★½ VHS: $19.99

No Skin off My Ass

(1990, 85 min, Canada, Bruce LaBruce) *Bruce LaBruce, G.B. Jones, Caroline Azar, Laurel Purvis, Kate Ashley, Nicholas Davies, Klaus von Buecker, Gloria B. Jones.* A wry, low-budget and sexually explicit comedy about a punkish hairdresser who becomes obsessed with a tough-looking but shy skinhead. Filmed in grainy black and white and blown up from Super-8, the story opens when the coiffeur (who also narrates) invites the seemingly lost, baby-faced skinhead home. Sort of a fag version of the beautiful and near-catatonic Joe Dallesandro in *Trash*, the skinhead passively and diffidently accepts his offers of a bubblebath and a place to live. While the gay sex is hardcore at times, it is also romantic. ★★★ VHS: $29.99

No Such Thing

(2001, 103 min, US/Iceland, Hal Hartley) *Sarah Polley, Robert John Burke, Helen Mirren, Julie Christie.* Hal Hartley films are an acquired taste like fennel or curry — lots of flavor but certainly not for everyone. When Hartley is at his best, his odd flavorings and off timings are charming and poetic. However, when he is at his worst, these charms wear thin. *No Such Thing* falls somewhere in between. In a postmodern take on "Beauty and the Beast," Burke plays "the Monster" as an alcoholic misanthrope

who terrorizes a small Icelandic village because he is disgusted with human stupidity. Polley is the young journalist who unwittingly turns him into the media sensation of the moment. Hartley's moral that in our media-obsessed "society of spectacle" we have all become shallow, soulless monsters may be admirable but is heavy-handed and simplistic at best. ★★½ DVD Letterbox: $14.99

No Surrender

(1986, 100 min, GB, Peter Smith) *Ray McAnally, Micahel Angelis, Joanne Whalley, Elvis Costello, Bernard Hill.* This no-holds-barred satire examines (and skewers) the political and religious passions that are rife in today's England. Three busloads of senior citizens descend on a seedy Liverpool nightclub for their New Year's Eve celebration. They add to the already volatile mix of Irish Protestant loyalists, Irish Catholics, punks and an inept magician (Costello) to make the laconic manager's evening a nightmare. The film hilariously dives into the fray and observes the pitiful state of human relations. ★★★½

No Telling

(1991, 93 min, US, Larry Fessenden) *Miriam Healy-Louie, Stephen Ramsey, David van Tieghem.* Fessenden's debut film is a heartfelt, personal twist on the Frankenstein myth. Medical researcher and his voluptuous wife head to the country, the better for him to conduct his experiments on animals in private. While he spends more and more hours in the lab, she becomes attracted to a local hunk. Fessenden certainly wears his heart on his sleeve in this one; yet, except for one rather hamfisted dinner table conversation, in which the characters' political leanings are explicitly expressed, *No Telling*'s views are rooted in compelling drama. Healy-Louie is quite good as the increasingly suspicious wife, and there's a memorable, sickening image near the end that will give even non-animal lovers pause. A well-crafted, creepy, original little movie, well worth checking out. ★★★ DVD: $29.99, VHS: $19.99

No Time for Sergeants

(1958, 119 min, US, Mervyn LeRoy) *Andy Griffith, Murray Hamilton, Nick Adams, Don Knotts.* Griffith, repeating the acclaimed stage role which

Sarah Polley in Hal Hartley's *No Such Thing*

brought him prominence, gives a wonderful performance as bumpkin Will Stockdale, the Georgia farmboy who takes the U.S. Air Force (after Will gets finished that's U.S. Air Farce) by surprise. Full of down-home, folksy humor, the story revolves around the series of misadventures which befall Will and his cohorts. Knotts, who would team with Griffith a few years later on TV, repeats his stage role with a funny turn as the camp psychiatrist. ★★★ VHS: $14.99

No Way Home

(1996, 101 min, US, Buddy Giovinazzo) *Tim Roth, Deborah Kara Unger, James Russo.* A heavy-handed drama about an ex-con trying to adjust to his freedom, *No Way Home* boasts edgy performances, but not much else. The film's first half, in which Joey (Roth) returns home to his lowlife brother Tommy (Russo) and his brother's wife (Unger), is extremely slow moving and unremarkable. Things pick up a bit when Tommy's mounting debts plunge him into a vortex of violence that may cost his brother his newfound freedom. The relationship that is forged between the long-suffering Lorraine and the shy Joey is better realized than the one between the brothers, yet the emotional core of the film is overwhelmed by some intense bloodletting. ★★ VHS: $9.99

No Way Out

(1950, 106 min, US, Joseph L. Mankiewicz) *Richard Widmark, Sidney Poitier, Linda Darnell, Ossie Davis, Ruby Dee, Stephen McNally. No Way Out* is an exceptionally made, tense drama which succeeds both as medical soap opera and social thriller. In his debut role, Poitier is very good as a talented young doctor in a metropolitan hospital. When mobsters Widmark and his brother are brought in wounded, Poitier's life is forever changed when the brother dies and Widmark holds Poitier responsible. Widmark begins a hatred campaign solely based on race, which soon escalates into racial hostility in the city. Widmark is exceptional as the explosive gangster, and also making strong debuts are Dee and Davis. ★★★½ VHS: $14.99

No Way Out

(1987, 116 min, US, Roger Donaldson) *Kevin Costner, Gene Hackman, Sean Young, Bill Paxton, George Dzundza.* Complex political thriller starring Costner as a naval officer who is assigned to the Pentagon. There he becomes involved with his boss' mistress, leading to murder and political cover-up. Remake of the 1948 film noir classic *The Big Clock*. ★★½ DVD: $14.99

No Way to Treat a Lady

(1968, 108 min, US, Jack Smight) *Rod Steiger, Lee Remick, Eileen Heckart, George Segal.* Steiger gives a bravura performance in this extremely well-done thriller as a psychopath who uses various impersonations to make contact with his victims. Segal is the cop on the case, and Remick is caught between them. ★★★½ DVD Letterbox: $14.99, VHS: $14.99

Noa at Seventeen

(1982, 86 min, Israel, Isaac Yeshurun) *Dalia Shimko, Idit Zur.* It is 1951, and Noa, a 17-year-old girl, struggles for autonomy as the ideological debate over the future of kibbutz socialism tears her family apart. Should she finish high school or follow her youth movement friends to kibbutz? Will Israel's labor movement follow Moscow blindly or turn its attention to the West? This sophisticated allegory penetrates the very essence of the bond which fused the personal and political in the early years of the state. (Hebrew with English subtitles) ★★ VHS: $79.99

Nobody

(1999, 100 min, Japan, Shundo Ohkawa) *Masaya Katoh, Jimpachi Nezu, Riki Takeuchi.* When a trio of Japanese yuppie businessmen innocently criticize the attire of another group of men in a bar one night, the stage is set for a thriller of Hitchcockian proportions as they are stalked and brutalized by the men whose identity remains a mystery. This strange and violent Japanese noir mixes Kafkaesque paranoia with Woo-like ballistics. (Japanese with English subtitles) ★★★½ DVD: $19.99, VHS: $19.99

Nobody's Daughter

(1976, 90 min, Hungary, Laszlo Ranody) *Zsuzsi Czinokoczi.* Csore is an eight-year-old orphaned girl who is adopted by a poor farming family. However, her chance for happiness is thwarted as the family is only interested in their government allocation. Running away from their cruelty to search for her real mother, Csore finds herself, once again, back at the orphanage. When she is adopted by a rich family, she is treated even worse. It is young Csore's struggle to overcome the odds against her which makes for a poignant, heartbreaking tale of courage and resilience. (Hungarian with English subtitles) ★★★

Nobody's Fool

(1994, 101 min, US, Robert Benton) *Paul Newman, Melanie Griffith, Jessica Tandy, Bruce Willis, Dylan Walsh, Elizabeth Wilson, Gene Saks, Philip Seymour Hoffman.* Newman's superlative performance distinguishes this excellent and at times humorous character study of an aging rambler who tries to piece together the loose ends of his life. In one of his most accomplished screen portrayals, Newman plays Sully, a sixty-ish handyman with a bum leg who lives in a small New York town. Divorced and estranged from his family, this lothario who refuses to acknowledge the passing of time has been seemingly content with both odd jobs thrown his way and his own meager existence. But when he is reunited with his son and forced to reexamine his life, Sully's soul-searching leads to magnificent, introspective dramatics. Based on Richard Russo's novel and skillfully adapted by director Benton, *Nobody's Fool* is a grand, intimate day-in-the-life. ★★★★ DVD: $19.99, VHS: $9.99

Noises Off!

(1992, 101 min, US, Peter Bogdanovich) *Michael Caine, Christopher Reeve, Carol Burnett, John Ritter, Marilu Henner, Denholm Elliott, Nicollette Sheridan, Julie Hagerty, Mark-Linn Baker.* Bogdanovich must have been sure that this screen adaptation of Michael Frayn's hilarious, Tony Award-winning farce was going to fire up his directorial comeback. And by all rights it should have, but for some reason audiences stayed away from this superbly directed, well-acted and screamingly funny romp. Caine is the director of an incestuous touring company of an English drawing room farce. Following Frayn's script nearly to the letter, the action proceeds through three acts in which we see the play first at rehearsal, then a side-splitting view of a performance from backstage and finally a full performance in which all of the company's foibles and sexual trysts result in complete utter confusion. ★★★½ DVD: $14.99

Nomads

(1986, 95 min, US, John McTiernan) *Pierce Brosnan, Leslie-Anne Down, Adam Ant.* From the director of *Die Hard* comes this imaginative but flat chiller with Brosnan as the inevitable victim of ghoulish phantoms; Down is the psychiatrist who tries to help him, only to experience first-hand his ordeal. ★★ DVD Dual: $14.99

None But the Brave

(1965, 106 min, US, Frank Sinatra) *Frank Sinatra, Clint Walker, Tommy Sands, Tony Bill.* Ol' Blue Eyes directs and stars in this tale of two enemy platoons, one American and one Japanese, who find themselves stranded on a remote island in the Pacific at the height of World War II. Lots of war film clichés, though Sinatra gives an especially appealing performance. ★★ VHS: $9.99

None But the Lonely Heart

(1944, 113 min, US, Clifford Odets) *Cary Grant, Ethel Barrymore, Barry Fitzgerald, Jane Wyatt.* It is ironic that Grant, a peerless comedian whose impeccable comic timing would create upteen comedy classics, received his only two Oscar nominations for dramas. One of these is Clifford Odets' moody melodrama set in the 1930s about a Cockney drifter who returns home to look after his dying mother. Barrymore won an Oscar as Grant's mum. ★★★ VHS: $14.99

Norma Rae

(1979, 113 min, US, Martin Ritt) *Sally Field, Ron Liebman, Beau Bridges, Pat Hingle.* Field won an Oscar (and newfound respect) for her triumphant portrayal of a Southern mother and textile worker who defies the abusive management of her company and organizes a union. Liebman plays the New York labor organizer who introduces Field to the idea, and Bridges is her husband who feels the neglect and ostracism of his wife's activism. Based on a true story. ★★★½ DVD: $9.99, VHS: $9.99

Normal Life

(1996, 108 min, US, John MacNaughton) *Luke Perry, Ashley Judd.* A fact-based crime drama about a white-trash couple who turn to crime to solve their financial and marital woes. Perry's surprisingly persuasive performance and Judd's dead-on, energetic portrayal go a long way toward making these unappealing characters sympathetic. The screenplay is less successful, offering spotty characterizations and obvious satire. ★★½ VHS: $19.99

Norman, Is That You?

(1976, 92 min, US, George Schlatter) *Redd Foxx, Michael Warren, Dennis Dugan, Pearl Bailey, Wayland Flowers.* This gay sex farce tries to have it both ways — making fun of faggots while espousing a what-will-be-will-be sexual philosophy. The story revolves around Norman (Warren), a handsome black man who lives with Garson (Dugan), his cute, swishy white lover in West Hollywood. Trouble brews when Norman's father, and eventually his mother (Foxx, Bailey), land at the doorstep of their presumably straight son. The film's dialogue is at time funny despite some lame jokes, stupid stereotypes and a regular lexicon of innocuous gay name-calling. Flowers and his sassy puppet Madam add to the campy humor. ★★½

Norman Loves Rose

(1982, 98 min, Australia, Henri Safran) *Carol Kane, Tony Owen.* Kane is very good as the wildly attractive sister-in-law of a 14-year-old boy who

The classic crop-dusting scene in *North by Northwest*

develops a tremendous crush on her. A little fooling around was nice, but problems arise when Kane becomes pregnant — and the father is not her husband! ★★½

North

(1994, 87 min, US, Rob Reiner) *Elijah Wood, Dan Aykroyd, Kathy Bates, Bruce Willis, Jon Lovitz, Jason Alexander. North,* the story of a child who "divorces" his parents and searches for new ones, is too close in theme to *Irreconcilable Differences* to be original. And its execution is part sentimental and part *Naked Gun,* and the two don't mix. Evidently it was doomed from the start. Wood plays North, whose search takes him around the world. Much like Dorothy in *The Wizard of Oz,* he soon realizes he was better off at home but has difficulty getting there. Though the reason for North leaving France is hilarious, the film is a misfire no matter where on Earth it's set. ★½ VHS: $9.99

North by Northwest

(1959, 137 min, US, Alfred Hitchcock) *Cary Grant, Eva Marie Saint, James Mason, Martin Landau, Leo G. Carroll.* Hitchcock returns to his favorite theme of an innocent man falsely accused in this terrifically exciting, funny and suspenseful thriller. Grant is the epitome of cool sophistication as a Madison Avenue ad executive mistaken for a spy. Mason is a perfect villain and Saint is the perennial icy blonde beauty. Classic Hitchcock touches include the crop-dusting scene and the Mt. Rushmore finale. ★★★★ DVD: $19.99, VHS: $12.99, VHS Letterbox Special Edition: $12.99

Favorite Line: "No. No, Mother, I have not been drinking. No. No. These two men, they poured a whole bottle of bourbon into me. No, they didn't give me a chaser." —*Cary Grant as Roger Thornhill*

North Dallas Forty

(1979, 119 min, US, Ted Kotcheff) *Nick Nolte, Mac Davis, Charles Durning, John Matuszak, Bo Svenson, Dabney Coleman.* An entertaining, perceptive football comedy following the careers (on and off the field) of NFL players Nolte and Davis, who makes an impressive screen debut. ★★★ DVD: $19.99

The North Star

(1943, 106 min, US, Lewis Milestone) *Dana Andrews, Anne Baxter, Walter Huston, Erich Von Stroheim.* Involving WWII drama about the efforts of a small Eastern Russian village who fight off the invading Nazis. Written by Lillian Hellman. ★★★ VHS: $39.99

North to Alaska

(1960, 122 min, US, Henry Hathaway) *John Wayne, Stewart Granger, Ernie Kovacs, Fabian, Capucine.* Sprawling comic western with Wayne and friends prospecting for gold in our northernmost state. Kovacs is particularly good as a con man out to fleece partners Wayne and Granger. ★★★ DVD: $14.99, VHS: $6.99

Northern Pursuit

(1943, 94 min, US, Raoul Walsh) *Errol Flynn, Helmut Dantine, Gene Lockhart.* Flynn does his part as a Canadian Mountie who hunts a crashed Nazi pilot through the wilderness. Exciting in places, but nothing out of the ordinary. ★★½ VHS: $19.99

Nosferatu

(1922, 84 min, Germany, F.W. Murnau) *Max Schreck, Gustav Von Wagenheim, Greta Schroeder, Alexander Granach.* Murnau's "symphony of horror" was the first, and most macabre, of the film versions of the legendary vampire, Count Dracula. Max Schreck's loathsome count, with his bald head, rodent face, long pointed ears, skeleton-like frame and talons will chill the most callous viewer. (Silent with musical soundtrack) An alternative version is also available which features a soundtrack by Type O Negative. From the Bram Stoker novel. ★★★½ DVD: $24.99, VHS: $24.99

Nosferatu the Vampyre

(1979, 107 min, Germany, Werner Herzog) *Klaus Kinski, Isabelle Adjani, Bruno Ganz, Roland Topor.* Director Herzog's classic interpretation of the vampire myth. It is 1850 in the beautiful town of Wismar. Jonathan Harker (Ganz) is about to leave on a long journey, leaving behind his wife Lucy (Adjani). Upon his departure, he is greeted by a pale, wraith-like figure who identifies himself as Count Dracula (Kinski). As the town succumbs to plague and death, Harker

The incomparable Max Schreck in *Nosferatu*

and his wife become convinced there is a vampire in their midst, and they soon realize that they, too, are in danger. A haunting, hypnotic and beautifully rendered film, Herzog elevates the horror tale to a new level. (German with English subtitles) ★★★½ DVD 2-disc set: $29.99, VHS Dubbed: $9.99

Nostalghia

(1983, 120 min, Italy/USSR, Andrei Tarkovsky) *Oleg Yankovsky, Erland Josephson.* Tarkovsky traveled to Italy to make this haunting and fascinating film on one man's mystical odyssey through his past, and his attempt to deal with his cultural and philosophical alienation. Yankovsky plays Gorchakov, a Russian poet doing research in rural Italy on an expatriate composer. Accompanied by Eugenia, his beautiful interpreter, his journey takes him to a Tuscan village, shrouded by mists and enveloped in an eerie silence. Here, Gorchikov confronts his past, his Russian family and an impending spiritual and midlife crisis. Tarkovsky dares to test the confines of the filmmaking process, and in doing so has crafted a film as exhilarating in thought and deed as it is beautiful in design and detail. (Italian with English subtitles) ★★★★

Nostradamus

(1994, 118 min, US, Roger Christian) *Tcheky Karyo, Amanda Plummer, Julia Ormond, Rutger Hauer, F. Murray Abraham.* Born into a Europe ravaged by plague and the persecution of the Inquisition, physician Michel de Nostradame garnered a reputation as a mystic and seer. The rabid suppression of knowledge by the establishment religion necessitated that information be passed in secrecy, under sworn oaths of silence. This workmanlike exposition of Nostradamus' life and times is enhanced by beautiful cinematography and exquisitely detailed period costume. Though the film opens slowly, it's worth a bit of patience; the viewer is amply rewarded. ★★★ VHS: $14.99

Not Another Teen Movie

(2001, 82 min, US, Joel Gallen) *Jaime Pressly, Mia Kirshner, Randy Quaid, Chyler Leigh, Chris Evans, Mr. T, Molly Ringwald, Paul Gleason.* The title *Not Another Teen Movie* can be pronounced with either excitement or exasperation, and that largely depends on your tolerance for the genre itself. Same goes for the entire movie, a spoof that needles the clichés of the John Hughes/Freddie Prinze, Jr. comedies while also falling prey to the vulgar traps of *American Pie* and *Scary Movie*. Half the fun is picking up the references, and a cameo at the end by everyone's favorite redhead (Molly, not Lucy) seals the deal. But there are also plenty of uncomfortable gross-out gags (and you have to get *very* crude to parody *Scary Movie 2*) that grind the laughter to a halt. ★★½ DVD Special Edition: $19.99, VHS: $9.99

Not for Publication

(1984, 87 min, US, Paul Bartel) *Nancy Allen, David Naughton, Laurence*

Luckenbill, Alice Ghostley. Cult favorite Bartel takes on the tabloids in this offbeat tale of muckraking journalism and political scandal. Allen is a moonlighting reporter who discovers her boss, the incumbent mayor of New York, at an orgy she is assigned to cover. ★★½ DVD Letterbox: $19.99

Not One Less

(1999, 102 min, China, Zhang Yimou) *Wei Minzhi, Zhang Huike.* Director Zhang has crafted a gentle, poignant parable of sacrifice and poverty. Wei Minzhi (playing herself) is a 13-year-old girl who becomes the substitute teacher for her remote mountain village. Determined to keep the small class together (otherwise she won't be paid), she has her hands full coping with the children's lively spirits and the school's nonexistent budget. When one of her students (Zhang Huike) flees to the big city, she sets out alone to return him to school. Young Wei, a nonprofessional, is a natural, a heartbreaker with a killer smile and attitude to spare. *Not One Less* may appear simple in scope, but it charms and moves us in not-so-simple ways. (Mandarin with English subtitles) ★★★ DVD: $29.99

Not Wanted

(1949, 94 min, US, Elmer Clifton & Ida Lupino) *Sally Forrest, Keefe Brasselle, Leo Penn, Rita Lupino.* Though Clifton is credited as director for this compelling '40s melodrama, Lupino finished the film after he died three days into shooting. As a result, the film may have acquired more of a sympathy towards the lead character than what may have originally been there. *Not Wanted* is a concise, neo-realist tale about a teenager (Forrest) who, as a result of "hanging out with the wrong crowd," becomes pregnant after a one-night stand with a troubled but talented pianist (Penn) who has already dumped her. The story is rather routine in the relationship between the starstruck youngster and the embittered musician; however, Lupino (who also cowrote the screenplay) finds power in the teen's subsequent relationship with a slightly handicapped vet (Brasselle). ★★★ VHS: $24.99

Not without My Daughter

(1991, 117 min, US, Brian Gilbert) *Sally Field, Alfred Molina, Roshan Seth.* An American woman, married to an Iranian husband, becomes trapped in Iran when they visit his family for a two-week vacation. Two years later, after being forced to endure the oppressive Islamic life, she tries to escape with her daughter back to America. Based on a true story, the film nevertheless indulges cultural stereotypes, though Field gives an impassioned performance which heightens the story's intrigue. ★★ DVD Letterbox: $14.99

Notebook on Cities and Clothes

(1990, 80 min, France, Wim Wenders) Ostensibly a documentary about Japanese fashion designer Yohji Yamamoto, this Wenders film is really a reflection on art and the creative process. Filmed in and around Paris, the filmmaker and designer engage the viewer in contemplation about the nature of visual communication and the creation of images. The opening sequence establishes the nature of the inquiry with narration which ponders the believability of photographs and other images in the digital age. ★★★ DVD: $24.99

Notes for an African Orestes

(1970, 75 min, Italy, Pier Paolo Pasolini) This fascinating look at the artistic process of one of the world's most daring and creative filmmakers is, simply put, a cinematic notebook. We follow Pasolini as he treks around East Africa scouring remote villages and crowded marketplaces for raw footage and discusses all of the possibilities for what he hoped would be a production of Aeschylus' "The Orestia." For fans of Pasolini, this will prove to be a mesmerizing and poetic view of underdevelopment and the quest for modernization which plagues the Third World today. ★★★½

Nothing in Common

(1986, 130 min, US, Garry Marshall) *Tom Hanks, Jackie Gleason, Eva Marie Saint, Bess Armstrong.* Bittersweet comedy-drama with Hanks as an advertising exec caught in the middle of his parents' separation. Gleason gives a terrific performance as Hanks' gruff father, and Saint nicely plays his mom. ★★★ DVD Dual: $19.99

Nothing Sacred

(1937, 75 min, US, William Wellman) *Carole Lombard, Fredric March, Walter Connolly.* The delightful Lombard, a small town girl, thinks she's dying of a rare disease and is turned into the "Sweetheart of New York" by scheming reporter March. This riotous and cynical battle-of-the-sexes classic was written by Ben Hecht. Presented in three-strip Technicolor for the first time on video, and digitally remastered from archive prints. ★★★½ VHS: $24.99

Nothing to Lose

(1997, 97 min, US, Steve Oedekerk) *Martin Lawrence, Tim Robbins, John C. McGinley, Giancarlo Esposito, Kelly Preston, Michael McKean, Irma P. Hall.* The premise of the black con and uptight white guy coming together for a series of misadventures is already becoming passé, but the amiable if familiar *Nothing to Lose* manages to entertain in spite of its clichéd roots and predictable plot. Upon discovering his wife in bed with his boss, a distraught Robbins drives aimlessly throughout the city. Things go from bad to worse when Lawrence attempts to hijack his car. With nothing to lose, the captive becomes the captor as Robbins turns the tables and takes Lawrence prisoner, taking him on the wildest ride of his life. Robbins is a delight as the sad-sack husband; Lawrence adds just the right amount of urban cool and wry delivery to give a funny, even restrained performance. If only the screenplay were as consistent and fresh as the two stars. ★★½ DVD: $14.99, VHS: $9.99

Notorious

(1946, 101 min, US, Alfred Hitchcock) *Ingrid Bergman, Cary Grant, Claude Rains, Louis Calhern.* Romance and intrigue are the ingredients in this Hitchcock thriller set in post-war Brazil. American secret agent Bergman marries an elderly spy (Rains) to gain information on Nazi activity. Grant is her contact in Rio and her partner in a seething love affair. Grant and Bergman are ravishing, but it is Rains who steals the show. ★★★½ DVD: $39.99

La Notte

(1961, 120 min, Italy/West Germany, Michelangelo Antonioni) *Jeanne Moreau, Marcello Mastroianni.* Antonioni's exploration of noncommunication, boredom and inpenetrable loneliness features Moreau and Mastroianni as a troubled married couple who have stopped understanding each other and themselves. Set in one night in Milan, this unforgettable mood piece is classic Antonioni. (Italian with English subtitles) ★★★ DVD: $24.99, VHS: $19.99

Notting Hill

(1999, 123 min, GB, Roger Michell) *Julia Roberts, Hugh Grant, Hugh Bonneville, Emma Chambers, Rhys Ifans.* "You're Beverly Hills, I'm Notting Hill," Grant's bewildered bookseller tells Roberts' big-time actress, trying to convince both of them they're not right for each other. And, in essence, he's correct. Roberts' Anna is closer to, well, Julia Roberts, and Grant's William is right out of *Four Weddings and a Funeral.* But damn it all, it all works. Screenwriter Richard Curtis has concocted a charmer of a romantic comedy, a delicious fairy-tale romance that is played to the hilt by its two personable stars. Grant and Roberts have a wonderful chemistry together, and both are given some great lines to recite. *Notting Hill* is funny, endearing and very romantic. ★★★ DVD Collector's Edition: $14.99, VHS Special Edition: $9.99

Nous N'Irons Plus au Bois

(1982, 88 min, France, George Dumoulin) *Marie France Pisier, Siegfried Rauch.* During the Spring of the 1944 in a Nazi-occupied forest in northern France, a Resistance group of several Frenchmen hold out. Their unity and purpose are put to the test when they come upon several German deserters. The group is divided on whether they are indeed deserters, and if they are, what should they do with them? (French with English subtitles) ★★★

November Moon

(1984, 107 min, Germany, Alexandra von Grote) *Gabriele Osburg, Danièle Delorme, Stéphane Garcin, Louise Martini, Christine Millet.* This ambitious WWII drama from director Von Grote stars Osburg as November, a plucky Jewish lesbian whose flight from the Nazis leads her to Paris and freedom. But when Occupation forces enter the city, she is again threatened. Her Parisian lover, Ferial, at grave risk, poses as a collaborator in an attempt to save the life of the woman she loves. A moving film experience that reaches beyond the horrors of WWII as it speaks out against violence, war and the persecution of all minorities. (German with English subtitles) ★★★ DVD: $24.99, VHS: $24.99

Novocaine

(2001, 95 min, US, David Atkins) *Steve Martin, Helena Bonham Carter, Laura Dern, Scott Caan, Elias Koteas, Keith David, Lynne Thigpen.* In *Little Shop of Horrors,* Steve Martin demonstrated a comic brilliance in his cameo as a sadistic dentist. Unfortunately, none of that comic inspiration be found in *Novocaine,* a tired black comedy with Martin once again playing a dentist. Here he's Frank Sangster, a successful doc who's engaged to his attractive nurse (Dern). He then gets caught in a scam perpetrated by an alluring new patient (Bonham Carter). Instead of putting a stop to it all, he goes with it until he almost loses everything. *Novocaine* wants to be an edgy comic thriller, but the jokes aren't funny or dark enough, and the plot never gives way to anything even remotely thrilling. Martin's perseverance in making Frank a likable Hitchcock-like Everyman/Wrong Man gives the film what very little appeal it has. ★★ DVD: $24.99, VHS: $102.99

Now and Then

(1995, 96 min, US, Lesli Linka Glatter) *Christina Ricci, Thora Birch, Gaby Hoffmann, Ashleigh Aston Moore, Demi Moore, Melanie Griffith, Rosie O'Donnell, Rita Wilson.* Essentially a derivative, inferior female *Stand by Me, Now and Then* features four

inseparable friends who obsess over a dead body, with all of this set against an (obtrusive) oldies soundtrack. Four friends get together for the birth of Wilson's baby; this is the cue for the flashback to the childhood summer which cemented their friendship. The basic plot is the girls' determined efforts to get to the mystery of a deceased boy, whose spirit they think they've brought back to life. *Now and Then* only offers the infrequent but admittedly amusing observation of adolescence. ★★ DVD: $14.99, VHS: $9.99

Now, Voyager

(1942, 117 min, US, Irving Rapper) *Bette Davis, Claude Rains, Paul Henreid, Gladys Cooper.* Davis received a Best Actress nomination for her portrayal of a lonely spinster who, with the help of a caring analyst, changes from an ugly duckling to a high-flying swan. Rains and Henreid also star as the doctor and love interest, respectively. Bette's stunning transformation, memorable dialogue and a lush Max Steiner score highlight this classic tearjerker. ★★★½ DVD: $19.99

Nowhere

(1996, 82 min, US, Gregg Araki) *James Duval, Rachel True, Nathan Bexton, Chiara Mastroianni, Debi Mazar, Christina Applegate, Kathleen Robertson, Guillermo Diaz, Ryan Phillippe.* One could easily be tempted to call *Nowhere,* Araki's angst-fest of masturbation, bondage, drugs, murder and alien abduction, his *Pink Velvet.* He captures entertainingly weird Lynch moments and an oddly fascinating outlook on '90s life, but ultimately the film does go nowhere. Araki regular Duval and an eclectic young cast are pessimistic high schoolers mired in pop culture hell as they ditch class and kill an afternoon with sex, deep thoughts and black forest cake while waiting for a party that evening. It's there everybody gets wasted and awaits the Apocalypse. Throbbing to a great soundtrack, *Nowhere* is mesmerizingly shallow, and its director is focused on individual parts and pays less attention to the cohesive whole. As a result, the film is only somewhat wild at heart. ★★½ VHS: $19.99

Nowhere in Africa

(2003, 141 min, Germany, Caroline Link) *Juliane Kohler, Merab Ninidze, Sidede Onyulo, Matthias Habich.* Remembrance is often paid for with one-too-many emotional air-raids. Caroline Link's *Nowhere in Africa* is not without its dour moments, but does offer an entirely different angle on the WWII Jewish plight, and, ultimately, a hopeful message. It is the true story of a German Jewish family encamped in interior Africa as bwana, or farmers, under British colonial rule. Through sprawling terrain and bustling ports-of-call we experience the cultural uprootedness and realities of enemy aliens staying afloat in the agri-business complex of the British Empire. Walter (Nindze) is struggling through wartime internment and slippery employment, while his wife Jettel (Kohler) gradually balances new language and culture with old. The film relates the detached but no-less-horrific feeling of unfolding war front news and the fate of distant relatives, a tenuous link with the outer world through long-awaited letters. Lensed here are some spectacular scenes of life on the Kenyan plains, conveying wisdom and attunement with the native culture; and an acute eye cast on the experiences linking family ever tighter to the land — bad news from abroad, doubts about German repatriation. Superbly acted, this film is remarkable for both its story and aesthetic value. (German with English subtitles) ★★★½ DVD Special Edition: $29.99

Nowhere to Run

(1992, 95 min, US, Robert Harmon) *Jean-Claude Van Damme, Rosanna Arquette, Kieran Culkin, Ted Levine, Joss Ackland.* Van Damme attempts to do something different in this film: act. Trying to show off his sensitive side as an escaped convict, he befriends a family being coerced by evil land developers into selling their land. Arquette plays the lonely widowed mother and Culkin (Macaulay's younger brother) is actually quite good as her son. The film starts off well enough, but suffers from extreme predictability and dull action sequences. ★½ DVD: $14.99, VHS: $9.99

Nueba Yol

(1996, 104 min, Dominican Republic, Angel Muñiz) *Luisito Martí, Caridad Ravelo.* Never certain why, a recent widower feels compelled to leave behind the comforts of his friends and home in the Dominican Republic to make a success of himself in New York City. Needless to say, a workable definition of "success" is not to be learned on *those* mean streets. Warm and funny, *Nueba Yol* is also honest and real, recalling the best cinema can be: full of life in all its joyfulness and sorrow. Like Renoir or Ozu, director Muñiz lets the camera quietly eavesdrop on people too genuine to be giving performances, a rarity these days when too much of world cinema looks to emulate the latest from a Hollywood grown out of touch. (Spanish with English subtitles) ★★★½ VHS: $19.99

La Nuit de Varennes

(1982, 133 min, France/Italy, Ettore Scola) *Marcello Mastroianni, Hanna Schygulla, Jean-Louis Barrault, Harvey Keitel.* Scola's brilliant historical drama is set in 1791 on the night of Louis XVI and Marie Antoinette's flight from Paris. First-hand witnesses to the revolution against the ancient regime include the ribald Restif (Barrault), the aging Casanova (Mastroianni), Thomas Paine (Keitel) and a lady-in-waiting (Schugulla). (French with English subtitles) ★★★½

Number Seventeen

(1932, 83 min, GB, Alfred Hitchcock) *Leon M. Lion, Anne Grey.* This strange and entertaining comedy-thriller about jewel thieves is first set in a spooky abandoned house and concludes with an exciting cross-country chase involving a hijacked train, a bus, a ferry and lots of water. ★★★ VHS: $12.99

The Nun (La Religieuse)

(1965, 140 min, France, Jacques Rivette) *Anna Karina, Micheline Presle.* An intensely somber drama about a young woman who suffers physical and psychological anguish at the hands of her family, a religious order and society. Set in 18th-century France, the film stars the beautiful Karina as Suzanne, who is sent unwillingly to a convent. Lacking a calling for the religious life, Suzanne stubbornly refuses to take her vows which results in her being beaten and semistarved. She eventually escapes, but she soon finds that her new freedom leads only to more suffering. Banned by the French government for its "anti-clerical" stance, this unsentimental film is uncompromising in presenting a world bereft of compassion and understanding. (French with English subtitles) ★★★

The Nun

The Nun's Story

(1959, 149 min, US, Fred Zinnemann) *Audrey Hepburn, Peter Finch, Edith Evans, Peggy Ashcroft, Dean Jagger, Mildred Dunnock, Beatrice Straight, Colleen Dewhurst.* Excellent adaptation of the Kathryn Hulme novel following the life of a young novice from the convent to service in the Belgian Congo. Hepburn is simply magnificent as the dedicated nun, who endures great hardships working with doctor Finch (in an admirable performance) in the jungle. ★★★★ VHS: $14.99

Nuns on the Run

(1990, 90 min, GB, Jonathan Lynn) *Eric Idle, Robbie Coltrane, Janet Suzman.* Two entry-level gangsters find themselves wanted by both the police and the mob. After they are set up and marked for murder by "Mr. Big," they turn the tables and run off with the mob's ill-gotten booty; and in the process cross a rival gang, as well. Where do the boys choose to hide out? In the nearest convent, naturally. Donning habit and attitude, they masquerade as two novices, and proceed to turn the well-ordered order upside-down. Lighthearted, mindless fun. ★★½ VHS: $19.99

Nurse Betty

(2000, 110 min, US, Neil LaBute) *Renée Zellweger, Morgan Freeman, Chris Rock, Greg Kinnear, Aaron Eckhart, Crispin Glover, Pruitt Taylor Vance.* Zellweger brings charm to spare to this modest comedy that can't quite deliver on the ambitious, edgy goals it sets for itself. Betty (Zellweger) is a mousy waitress who witnesses her husband's murder at the hands of two hit men. She then loses her grip on reality and heads out to California to meet the man of her dreams: a doctor on a TV soap she thinks is a real person. On her trail: the two hit men determined to silence her. Director LaBute mixes brutality, screwball humor and quirky characters to tell this original but not fully realized tale of fantasy and reality colliding. Though there are several scenes that are gloriously rendered, the whole doesn't come together as it should. Freeman is excellent as one of the hit men, whose heart and conscience sends him in a surprising direction. ★★½ DVD: $14.99, VHS: $9.99

Nuts

(1987, 116 min, US, Martin Ritt) *Barbra Streisand, Richard Dreyfuss, Maureen Stapleton, Eli Wallach, James Whitmore, Karl Malden.* Based on Tom Topor's stage hit, this highly successful courtroom drama features one of Streisand's most accomplished dramatic performances. Streisand plays a high-priced prostitute on trial for murdering a john; however, while she insists it was self-defense, her family petitions to have her certified mentally incompetent. Dreyfuss is terrific as the laywer who defends Streisand's right to a trial. ★★★ DVD: $19.99

Nuts in May

(1976, 84 min, GB, Mike Leigh) *Alison Steadman, Roger Showman.* A young couple — a pair of highly compulsive, vegetarian neatniks — on holiday in East Anglia check into a campground for some communing with nature. They immediately come into conflict with their neighbors. The film lazily meanders with them as their well-planned holiday slowly unravels. ★★ DVD: $29.99, VHS: $29.99

The Nutty Professor

(1963, 107 min, US, Jerry Lewis) *Jerry Lewis, Stella Stevens, Howard Morris, Kathleen Freeman.* Fifty million Frenchmen can't be wrong. This is *the* Jerry Lewis film for those who don't like Jerry Lewis (let's see those hands). Mild-mannered professor Lewis becomes lounge lizard Buddy Love thanks to a potion he quaffs accidentally. Lots of brilliant sight gags and a good use of color give proof that this is a director in control of his medium. (Remade in 1996) ★★★ DVD: $14.99, DVD Special Collector's Edition: $19.99, VHS: $9.99

The Nutty Professor

(1996, 95 min, US, Tom Shadyac) *Eddie Murphy, Jada Pinkett, Larry Miller, James Coburn, Dave Chappelle.* This hilarious remake of the 1963 Jerry Lewis semiclassic is a twofold success: Murphy has finally delivered on his comic promise, and — a rarity — a remake is worthy of (and possibly better than) the original. Murphy plays Sherman Klump, a brilliant, 400-pound chemistry professor. Sherman is supervising a DNA experiment to curb obesity which he tries on himself. Sherman's Mr. Hyde turns out to be Buddy Love, a slim, attractive, testosterone-driven alter ego who is so over the top Murphy almost seems to be doing a self-parody of his own image. *The Nutty Professor* is consistently funny complete with humorous sight gags, snappy dialogue and good special effects. Murphy is splendid, playing seven parts including four family members at a convulsive dinner. (Sequel: *Nutty Professor II: The Klumps*) ★★★ DVD: $19.99, DVD DTS sound: $19.99, VHS: $9.99

Nutty Professor II: The Klumps

(2000, 107 min, US, Peter Segal) *Eddie Murphy, Janet Jackson, Larry Miller.* Bigger isn't always necessarily better; this loud, only occasionally funny sequel to the hilarious 1996 remake certainly proves that point. Murphy returns as: Sherman Klump, that endearing overweight college professor; Buddy Love, his on-the-make alter ego; and the entire Klump family. Murphy is a marvel creating such distinct characters; too bad the screenplay is nothing more than a collection of toilet humor and sex jokes. ★★ DVD Letterbox PG-13 Rated: $14.99, DVD Letterbox Uncensored Director's Cut: $14.99, VHS PG-13 Rated: $9.99, VHS Pan & Scan Uncensored Director's Cut: $9.99

O

"O"

(2001, 91 min, US, Tim Blake Nelson) *Mekhi Phifer, Josh Hartnett, Julia Stiles, Martin Sheen, Elden Henson, John Heard, Andrew Keegan, Rain Phoenix.* Once again, mature Shakespearean drama is fodder for teenage angst and tomfoolery as the Bard's "Othello" is transferred to the world of high school basketball. Hartnett plays Hugo (a rather clumsy modernization of the name Iago), who's terribly jealous of the attention his father (Sheen, as the coach) lavishes upon star player "O" (Phifer). If you know the original play, you know what happens next: Hugo fools "O" into believing horrible lies about his girlfriend Desi (Stiles), and the downward spiral begins. Though there are several involving scenes, the movie ultimately feels pointless: Iago's motivation was courtly (as in royal) power plays. Screenwriter Brad Kaaya fails to give Hugo motivation for his wretched deeds other than Daddy doesn't pay attention. The central theme of blind ambition is gone, with only deceit and betrayal at the core. It's just not quite enough to pull it off. Phifer is most impressive as the wronged "O." ★★½ DVD Letterbox Lions Gate Signature Series: $19.99

O Brother, Where Art Thou?

(2000, 103 min, US, Joel Coen) *George Clooney, John Goodman, John Turturro, Tim Blake Nelson, Holly Hunter, Charles Durning, Stephen Root, Chris Thomas King.* Leave it to the Coen brothers to combine Preston Sturges' *Sullivan's Travels* and Homer's "The Odyssey" and produce one of its year's most entertaining and funniest films. A screwball comedy in the best style of Sturges, *O Brother, Where Art Thou?* (which gets its name from the film *Sullivan's* director wanted to make) transcribes Homer's mythic epic to the rural South during the Great Depression. Clooney is Ulysses McGill, one of three chain-gang convicts on the run from their Mississippi captors and in search of untold treasure. En route, they meet a gallery of eccentric characters

and fanciful adventure. Lighter in tone than some of their former works, this is nonetheless one of the Coens' best films. The casting for this wholly original excursion into madcap hijinks is on-target down the line. Clooney looks like he stepped out of a 1930s film, Nelson is hilarious as a dim-witted farm boy, and Root gets a special mention as a partially blind radio station manager. Add to this intoxicating mix a superb bluegrass/folk soundtrack, and it's easy to reason the Coens have done it again — they're bona fide. ★★★★ DVD: $19.99, VHS: $14.99

O Lucky Man!

(1973, 174 min, GB, Lindsay Anderson) *Malcolm McDowell, Arthur Lowe, Ralph Richardson, Rachel Roberts, Alan Price, Helen Mirren, Mona Washbourne.* Anderson's mammoth and brilliant allegory stars McDowell as a latter-day Candide, buoyed by optimism in a sea of sham and corruption. A young coffee salesman pushes his way to the top only to fall and rise and fall yet again. A tremendous score is provided by Alan Price. ★★★★ VHS: $24.99

The Object of Beauty

(1991, 101 min, US/GB, Michael Lindsay-Hogg) *John Malkovich, Andie MacDowell, Joss Ackland, Lolita Davidovich.* Malkovich and MacDowell are an American couple living at an expensive London hotel. Their financial crunch leads them to an insurance swindle — only before they are able to institute the hoax, someone beats them to it. A very low-key comedy with few laughs, and two rather annoying people as the principal characters. ★★½ DVD: $9.99, VHS: $9.99

The Object of My Affection

(1998, 112 min, US, Nicholas Hytner) *Jennifer Aniston, Paul Rudd, John Pankow, Nigel Hawthorne, Alan Alda, Tim Daly, Allison Janney.* A romantic comedy of unrequited love with a '90s, gay twist, *The Object of My Affection* is a pleasant if lightweight tale which is at its best when not trying too hard to be the cutting-edge romp it only occasionally is. Aniston is extremely engaging as Nina, a Brooklyn social worker who invites gay teacher George (Rudd) to move in with her. Acting more like girlfriends, the two become close with Nina falling in love with the unattainable George. To further complicate matters, Nina learns she is pregnant and decides to dump her boyfriend, hoping that George

will act as surrogate father. Very matter-of-fact in its gayness for a Hollywood film, *The Object of My Affection* is alternately insightful and artificial. Hawthorne brings a quiet dignity to the role of an aging critic. ★★½ DVD: $14.99, VHS: $6.99

Objective: Burma!

(1945, 142 min, US, Raoul Walsh) *Errol Flynn, George Tobias.* Flynn leads a familiar ragtag team of soldiers into the Burmese jungle to destroy a Japanese stronghold. The film scored well with wartime American audiences as a rather suspenseful first-rate morale booster. But across the sea, our British allies were less-than-enthusiastic as the film ignores the contributions of the Allied forces, including the long-suffering British 14th Army, which had spearheaded the Burmese campaign. Still, a well-made, if jingoistic, war story. ★★★ DVD: $19.99

Oblomov

(1979, 140 min, USSR, Nikita Mikhalkov) *Oleg Tabakov, Elena Solovel.* This delightful social satire and sensitive character study of a likable but lazy aristocrat was adapted from the 1859 Russian novel by Ivan Goncharov. Oblomov, a good-natured and indolent landowner in Czarist Russia who has never worked a day in his life, decides that he has no reason for getting out of bed and finds himself in a melancholy stupor and paralyzed with lethargy. While a procession of friends fail to change his slothful ways, it is his passionate love for a woman named Olga that energizes him and gives the man a new lease on life. (Russian with English subtitles) ★★★ DVD Letterbox: $29.99, VHS: $24.99

Obsession

(1976, 104 min, US, Brian De Palma) *Cliff Robertson, Geneviève Bujold, John Lithgow.* De Palma's elegant thriller is one of the most underrated films of the 1970s, largely because it is always unjustly relegated to the category of "Hitchcock rip-off." Robertson stars as a man who feels responsible for the death of his wife in a kidnapping tragedy and seeks to resurrect her in the form of another woman (Bujold, in a dual role). Sound familiar? Don't be misled. True, the film owes a great deal to Hitchcock's *Vertigo*, but its strength lies in its ability to work independently as a mystery on its own merits. Magnificent score by Bernard Herrmann. ★★★½ DVD: $24.99

O.C. and Stiggs

(1987, 95 min, US, Robert Altman) *Daniel H. Jenkins, Neill Barry, Paul Dooley, Jane Curtin, Jon Cryer, Ray Walston, Tina Louise, Martin Mull, Dennis Hopper, Melvin Van Peebles.* Altman attempts the teen comedy. The spirit of revolution runs deep in this one, folks, but Altman's flourish can't save this meaningless yarn about a couple of kids whose passion in life is to humiliate a wealthy insurance tycoon and his family while skipping to the beat of King Sunny Ade. ★★

Ocean's 11

(1960, 127 min, US, Lewis Milestone) *Frank Sinatra, Dean Martin, Sammy Davis, Jr., Peter Lawford, Joey Bishop, Angie Dickinson, Cesar Romero.* The "Rat Pack" is in full bloom in this enjoyable caper comedy. Frank, Dino, Sammy and pals come up with a foolproof plan to rob five Las Vegas casinos — at the same time! (Remade in 2001) ★★★ DVD Letterbox: $19.99, VHS: $9.99

O Brother, Where Art Thou?

Ocean's Eleven

(2001, 110 min, US, Steven Soderbergh) *George Clooney, Brad Pitt, Julia Roberts, Matt Damon, Andy Garcia, Don Cheadle, Casey Affleck, Scott Caan, Elliott Gould, Carl Reiner, Bernie Mac, Eddie Jemison, Shaobo Qin.* The 1960 version of *Ocean's 11* stood for a generation as the epitome of cool. Alas, the old must make way for the new. How mightily the reins have been handed. In the hands of Soderbergh, this breezy remake is consistently entertaining from beginning to end and, ultimately, is more satisfying than the original. Wisely not having Clooney and company "echo" the Frank, Dean, etc. roles, screenwriter Ted Griffin reinterprets the story for today, giving the film a modern sensibility while able to maintain the sleek, nostalgic cool of the first film. The ever-agreeable Clooney is Danny Ocean, just released from prison, who masterminds the robbery of three casinos in Las Vegas. Pitt is his #2 guy, and Roberts is Danny's ex, now involved with the owner (Garcia) of the three casinos Danny has targeted. Obviously, there's more to this caper than just money. And there's more to this movie than just its impressive line-up of stars (of which, Reiner and Gould nearly steal the show). Soderbergh demonstrates such a pleasing storytelling ability that he's liable to con you into thinking there's less here than there really is. Don't be fooled — this is the genuine article; a splashy, smart heist film that may not set out to reinvent the genre, but succeeds on charm, wit, a little bit of suspense and a great, big, wonderful cast. (Sequel: *Ocean's Twelve*) ★★★★ DVD Letterbox: $19.99, DVD Pan & Scan: $19.99, VHS: $6.99

October
(Ten Days That Shook the World)

(1928, 99 min, USSR, Sergei Eisenstein) Commissioned to celebrate the tenth anniversary of the revolution, this stirring portrait of an entire nation set on the edge of change is taken from American John Reed's writings. Director Eisenstein had endless resources to make the film and with the virtual absence of any footage of the real events of 1917, this powerful epic is elevated into the realm of historical importance. (Silent with musical soundtrack) ★★★★ DVD: $24.99

October Sky

(1999, 108 min, US, Joe Johnston) *Jake Gyllenhaal, Chris Cooper, Laura Dern, Chris Owen, William Lee Scott, Chad Lindberg, Natalie Canderday.* The inspirational, warm-hearted real-life story of making one's dreams come true against insurmountable odds, *October Sky* is quiet, powerful storytelling. Set in 1957 in the small coal mining town of Coalwood, West Virginia, the tale follows high schooler Homer (Gyllenhaal) who teams with three friends to build a working rocket and enter it into the science fair. More than a way out of the coal mines, the "rocket boys" begin their quest. That the viewer is immediately drawn into this simple story speaks volumes about Lewis Colick's fluid adaptation of Homer Hickam's novel and Johnston's level-headed, graceful direction. Cooper stands out as Homer's strict father, with whom Homer is continually at odds. Poignant, involving and extremely well-crafted, *October Sky* goes about its small, unheralded task with unassuming but unqualified success. ★★★½ DVD: $14.99

Octopussy

(1983, 130 min, GB, John Glen) *Roger Moore, Maud Adams, Louis Jourdan.* The 13th Broccoli Bond production found itself up against itself as

Connery returned to the role in the competing project *Never Say Never Again*. Moore is confronted with several villains including the title character, played by Adams, who may or may not be working for any one side at any moment. This isn't one of the better films in the series; though the stunts are adequate, and the customary tongue-in-cheek humor is considerably low-brow. (Sequel: *A View to a Kill*) ★★½

The Odd Couple

(1968, 106 min, US, Gene Saks) *Jack Lemmon, Walter Matthau, Herb Edelman, John Fiedler.* The laughs are plentiful in this first-class adaptation of Neil Simon's Broadway hit. Lemmon and Matthau are in great form as Felix and Oscar, the two most unlikely and mismatched roommates in New York City. (Sequel: *The Odd Couple II*) ★★★½ DVD: $19.99, VHS: $9.99

The Odd Couple II

(1998, 97 min, US, Howard Deutch) *Jack Lemmon, Walter Matthau, Christine Baranski, Barnard Hughes, Jonathan Silverman, Jean Smart.* Returning to the source in which they are arguably most identifiable as a team, Lemmon and Matthau reprise their 1968 roles of Felix Unger and Oscar Madison in this sporadically funny though over-the-hill sequel penned by Neil Simon. Felix and Oscar come together for the marriage of Felix's daughter to Oscar's son. The bickering begins immediately, and soon they are lost on the road to the wedding. The chemistry between the two stars is still evident, and there are quite a few zingy one-liners and humorous scenes, but Simon has taken the joy out of Felix and Oscar, and that's what keeps this from being anything but *Grumpy Old Men 3*. ★★ DVD: $19.99, VHS: $14.99

Odd Man Out

(1947, 113 min, GB, Carol Reed) *James Mason, Kathleen Ryan, Robert Newton, Dan O'Herlihy.* Under cover after escaping from prison, Mason plans a payroll heist to finance IRA operations. During its execution, he kills a man. In the process of escaping the scene of the crime, he briefly enters the lives of many people, eliciting a gamut of reactions and exposing a wide range of human idiosyncrasies. A perceptive examination of values and morality, incisively directed by Reed and with excellent performances. (Remade as *The Lost Man*) ★★★★ DVD: $24.99

Odd Obsession

(1960, 96 min, Japan, Kon Ichikawa) *Machiko Kyo, Ganjiro Nakamura, Junko Kano, Tatsuya Nakadai.* Director Ichikawa's disturbing drama about the strained marital relations between an ex-beauty queen and her elderly husband who keeps himself going sexually with injections, jealousy and by taking photos of his nude, sleeping wife. The couple's twisted story has a surprise ending. Remastered print. (aka: *The Key*) (Japanese with English subtitles) ★★★ VHS: $29.99

Ode to Billy Joe

(1976, 106 min, US, Max Baer) *Robby Benson, Glynnis O'Connor.* A wonderful example of why more Top 40 hit songs are not adapted for the screen. Robby Benson is the teen Billy Joe McAllister who mysteriously jumps off the Tallahatchie Bridge? Glynnis O'Connor is his confused girlfriend. Over-emotionalized, although it does offer a fine recreation of 1950s-'60s rural southern life, the film misses more than it hits. Want to save a few bucks and some time? Billy Joe jumped because he had sex with a man! Lordy! ★★

The Odessa File

(1974, 128 min, GB, Ronald Neame) *Jon Voight, Maximilian Schell, Derek Jacobi, Maria Schell.* Frederick Forsyth's best-seller comes to the big screen with Voight as a German journalist who is on the track of Nazis in the early 1960s. Voight gives a solid performance which single-handedly elevates an otherwise muddled mystery. ★★½ DVD: $14.99, VHS: $9.99

The Odyssey

(1997, 165 min, US, Andrei Konchalovsky) *Armand Assante, Greta Scacchi, Isabella Rossellini, Vanessa L. Williams, Bernadette Peters, Geraldine Chaplin, Eric Roberts, Jeroen Krabbé, Irene Papas, Roger Ashton-Griffiths.* An admirable attempt to put one of the greatest adventures ever told onto film, *The Odyssey* includes most of the high points of the story while never sacrificing its characters or morals for entertainment value. After a long, drawn-out war and on the eve of heading home, Greek captain Odysseus accidentally offends Poseidon, God of the Sea. So begins Odysseus' decades-long wandering. Managing to be both educational and entertaining, this *Odyssey* is worth devoting some time to. ★★★

Oedipus Rex

(1967, 110 min, Italy, Pier Paolo Pasolini) *Franco Citti, Silvana Mangano.* Filmed in and around an awesome, 15th-century adobe city in the Moroccan desert, Pasolini's version of the Oedipus legend retain's the basic elements of Sophocles' classic tragedy. A young man, abandoned at birth by his parents, is foretold of his doomed fate by an oracle; nonetheless, he unknowingly murders his father and marries his mother. This tragic story of a man's intractable road to his destiny shimmers with lavish costumes, bloody sword fights, sun-drenched locales and expressive performances. (Italian with English subtitles) ★★★ DVD: $29.99, VHS: $29.99

Of Human Bondage

(1934, 83 min, US, John Cromwell) *Bette Davis, Leslie Howard, Frances Dee.* This low-key treatment of the W. Somerset Maugham novel is enlivened by the striking presence of a truly luminous and effectively trashy Davis. Howard is his usual earnest self as a failed artist turned medical student who becomes obsessed with Davis' aloof, uncaring waitress. A scandal ensued when Davis was overlooked as a Best Actress nominee — causing a massive write-in campaign and, some say, a consolation Oscar for Bette the following year. (Remade in 1964) ★★★ VHS: $19.99

Of Human Bondage

(1964, 100 min, US, Ken Hughes) *Kim Novak, Laurence Harvey, Robert Morley, Roger Livesey.* W. Somerset Maugham's celebrated novel of a doctor (Harvey) whose passion for a crude waitress (Novak) leads to tragedy is given inferior treatment in this third screen adaptation. Stick to the 1934 Bette Davis version (unless you're really a Novak or Harvey fan). ★★ VHS: $24.99

Of Mice and Men

(1939, 106 min, US, Lewis Milestone) *Burgess Meredith, Lon Chaney, Jr., Betty Field, Charles Bickford.* In top-drawer Hollywood style, Milestone's terse, idiomatic treatment of John Steinbeck's melancholy classic wrings charged melodrama, tension and sex from the tragic tale of two California farm laborers' descent into a Depression-era maelstrom. Top-drawer Hollywood casting delivers indelible performances from Chaney as the mentally slow, physically lumbering giant

Office Space

who crushes the creatures he loves and Meredith as the overburdened friend who must be his protector and, ultimately, his judge. Field smolders as the treacherous farmer's wife whose role emphasizes the material's desperate carnality and endemic sexism. All in all, the film represents the type of prototypically dark Americana that only an émigré from Odessa (like Milestone) could conjure. (Remade in 1992) ★★★★ DVD: $19.99, VHS: $29.99

Of Mice and Men
(1992, 110 min, US, Gary Sinise) *Gary Sinise, John Malkovich, Ray Walston, Sherilyn Fenn, Joe Morton, Casey Siemaszko.* Coproducer, costar and director Sinise's retelling of John Steinbeck's classic novel is an absorbing, brilliantly acted film. Sinise stars as the world-weary drifter George, opposite Malkovich's thoroughly convincing portrayal of the helpless man-child Lenny. Horton Foote's literary screenplay beautifully translates the novel to film. Heightened by marvelous supporting performances. ★★★½ DVD Letterbox: $19.99, DVD Special Edition: $19.99

Off Beat
(1986, 92 min, US, Michael Dinner) *Judge Reinhold, Meg Tilly, Cleavant Derricks, Fred Gwynne, John Turturro.* Reinhold, who played the young officer in *Beverly Hills Cop*, is back in uniform — but with little success — as a New York library clerk who masquerades as a police officer to win the affection of policewoman Tilly. ★★

Off Limits
(1988, 102 min, US, Christopher Crowe) *Willem Dafoe, Gregory Hines, Fred Ward, Scott Glenn, Amanda Pays.* Senseless actioner with Dafoe and Hines as two military policemen looking for a murderer in 1968 Saigon. ★ VHS: $14.99

Off the Menu:
The Last Days of Chasen's
(1998, 90 min, US, Robert Pulcini & Shari Springer Berman) A strange picture emerges from *Off the Menu: The Last Days of Chasen's.* At once, it's an oddly affectionate look at this classically styled resto, right in the heart of Tinseltown. We're all supposed to get rather teary-eyed (and we do) over the fact that this joint is closing. Many stars, of both

today and yesteryear, show up to pay their respects to the terminal institution. The best bits involve profiles of those who actually work there. *Off the Menu* becomes a strange contradiction in its own right; on the one hand, it's a loving ode to the people who made this famous resto work. On the other, it's a stinging testimony to the rather sleazy side of Hollywood. After all, it was only after this resto announced that it was going to fold that business suddenly picked up. Did Hollywood types feel genuine sentiment or simply sense an opportunity for a solid photo op? You be the judge. ★★★ VHS: $24.99

Office Killer
(1998, 83 min, US, Cindy Sherman) *Carol Kane, Molly Ringwald, Jeanne Tripplehorn. Michael Imperioli.* Photographer Cindy Sherman made her artistic reputation with her "Untitled Film Stills" series. With her directorial debut, however, Sherman proves that while she has an eye for composition, she has no clue about *moving* pictures. *Office Killer* is a static film that is unfunny as a black comedy and suspenseless as a thriller. The story line involves the meek Doreen Douglass (Kane) offing her coworkers and then storing the bodies in her basement. While there is some unpleasant gore, the film's cheesy effects are a greater drawback. ★½ DVD: $14.99, VHS: $9.99

Office Space
(1999, 90 min, US, Mike Judge) *Ron Livingston, Jennifer Aniston, Stephen Root, Gary Cole.* Beavis and Butt-head creator Judge brings his "Milton" shorts to life in this often very funny comedy that goes further than Dilbert in lampooning the idiocy of office work. Livingston is the charmingly bland hero, who undergoes a funky hypnosis and begins rebelling against his corporation; somehow this is interpreted as brilliance and he ascends the ranks of his company. Root steals the show as Milton, the nebbish supporting character who can't fend for himself; Cole is just right as the monotoned supervisor. Unfortunately, the film bogs down in a lame romantic subplot involving Aniston, but before it gets there, *Office Space* provides many a laugh for anyone who's ever encountered a copying machine. ★★★ DVD Pan & Scan: $19.99, DVD: $19.99, VHS: $9.99

Favorite Line: ". . . but then they switched from the Swingline to the Boston stapler, but I kept my

Swingline stapler because it didn't bind up as much, and I kept the staples for the Swingline stapler and it's not okay because if they take my stapler then I'll set the building on fire." —*Stephen Root as Milton*

An Officer and a Gentleman
(1982, 126 min, US, Taylor Hackford) *Richard Gere, Debra Winger, Louis Gossett, Jr., David Keith, Lisa Blount, Robert Loggia, David Caruso.* Three outstanding performances by Gere, Winger and Gossett highlight this compelling romantic drama about a naval officer who begins an affair with a girl from the wrong side of the tracks. Gossett won an Oscar for his tough-as-nails performance as Gere's drill instructor. ★★★ DVD: $14.99, VHS: $9.99

The Official Story
(1985, 112 min, Argentina, Luis Puenzo) *Norma Aleandro, Hector Alterio.* 1985's Academy Award winner is a politically explosive and emotionally draining drama set in the tumultuous period after the Falklands debacle. Aleandro is mesmerizing as a comfortably middle-class woman who is determined to find out the truth about "los desaparecidos," the many people who disappeared during the military dictatorship. (Spanish with English subtitles) ★★★★ DVD: $19.99

Oh Dad, Poor Dad,
Mama's Hung You in the
Closet and I'm Feeling So Sad
(1966, 86 min, US, Richard Quine) *Rosalind Russell, Robert Morse, Barbara Harris, Jonathan Winters, Hugh Griffith.* Zany black comedy about a "typical" American family: a domineering mother, two man-eating piranhas, several Venus flytraps, a weirdo baby-faced son, a lecherous baby sitter, and a father who happens to be a stuffed corpse hanging in the closet. ★★½

Oh, God!
(1977, 98 min, US, Carl Reiner) *George Burns, John Denver, Teri Garr.* Pleasant family comedy with Burns as The Almighty visiting Earth and summoning supermarket manager Denver to spread His word. (Followed by 2 sequels) ★★½ DVD Letterbox: $12.99, VHS: $14.99

Oh! My Three Guys
(1994, 96 min, Hong Kong, Chiu Sung Kee) This touching comedy/melodrama goes one step further than the standard HK film by singularly focusing on the lives and loves of three young gay men who live together as roommates. Their stories involve spurned male lovers, AIDS, suicide, drag queens and a woman determined to change one of them. A shrill but entertaining and sensitive melodrama. (Cantonese with English subtitles) ★★½

Oklahoma!
(1955, 145 min, US, Fred Zinnemann) *Gordon MacRae, Shirley Jones, Rod Steiger, Charlotte Greenwood, Gloria Graham, Eddie Albert.* Sprawling though unremarkable film version of the landmark Rodgers and Hammerstein Broadway musical. MacRae and Jones are the youthful lovers; their romance interrupted by hired hand Steiger. A great score complements the immortal Agnes de Mille dance sequences. Good supporting cast includes the always-fine Greenwood and Graham as Ado Annie. ★★★ DVD Letterbox: $19.99

Okoge

(1992, 120 min, Japan, Takehiro Nakajima) *Misa Shimizu, Takehiro Murata, Takeo Nakahara.* Japan's teeming if still underground gay life is explored and celebrated in this pleasant story of the relationship between two gay lovers and the effervescent woman who befriends them. The story revolves around Goh, a young, self-employed man, and Tochi, an older married corporate worker. Their inability to find a suitable location for their lovemaking is solved by Sayoko, a naive young woman who inexplicably finds herself drawn to gay men. She offers her small apartment as a convenient love-pad. Funny but deceptively lighthearted, the film addresses the serious theme of homophobia which is pervading Japan. (Japanese with English subtitles) ★★★ DVD: $29.99, VHS: $39.99

Old Boyfriends

(1977, 103 min, US, Joan Tewkesbury) *Talia Shire, Richard Jordan, Keith Carradine, John Belushi, John Houseman, Buck Henry.* Shire stars in this bittersweet story of a woman who seeks out her past lovers in an attempt to learn more about herself. A mixed bag of romance and identity which is ambitious but not always successful. ★★

The Old Dark House

(1932, 72 min, US, James Whale) *Boris Karloff, Charles Laughton, Melvyn Douglas, Gloria Stuart, Raymond Massey, Ernest Thesiger, Eva Moore.* It was a dark and stormy night . . . Five weary travelers are stranded in the ancestral home of the Femm family. Horace Femm (Thesiger) is an athiest so frightened of God that he trembles at every thunderbolt. His sister Rebecca (Moore) taunts him and their unwanted company with sermons against the sins of the flesh. Morgan (Karloff), their mute and malevolent butler, is either their protector or prisoner, depending on his intake of gin. Whale has fashioned a sardonic comic essay on rot and decay, as intricate and delicate as a fugue. The film cunningly balances cheap thrills against metaphysical chills; Whale looks into the abyss, forces a laugh, and hides his anguish behind a witty bon mot. ★★★½ DVD: $29.99, VHS: $19.99

Old Enough

(1984, 91 min, US, Marisa Silver) *Sarah Boyd, Rainbow Harvest, Danny Aiello.* A coming-of-age drama about two New York City girls, one from Park Avenue and the other from Brooklyn, who befriend each other. A meandering look at adolescence which can't overcome — despite accurate moments of insight — its stereotypes. ★★

Old Gringo

(1989, 141 min, US, Luis Puenzo) *Jane Fonda, Gregory Peck, Jimmy Smits.* A period romance set against the backdrop of Pancho Villa's Mexican uprising in 1913. Fonda plays a spinster who travels south of the border, where she becomes involved with revolutionary Smits and writer Ambrose Bierce (played with perfection by Peck). Though the story lacks a coherent structure, it has an undeniable emotional power; and the chemistry between the three leads is palatable. Peck's soliloquy on love is a reminder of the power and excitement of great acting. ★★½ DVD Dual: $19.99, VHS: $9.99

The Old Gun

(1980, 141 min, France, Robert Enrico) *Philippe Noiret, Romy Schneider.* Winner of three César Awards, this riveting drama is set in World War II France where a Frenchman's huge estate is taken over by the Germans. The brutality of the Nazis result in his wife and child being murdered. Noiret's quiet life is forever destroyed which results in his methodical vengence against the killers. ★★★

Old Ironsides

(1926, 111 min, US, James Cruze) *Wallace Beery, Esther Ralston, Boris Karloff.* Beery is as hammy as ever in this silent tale about Merchant Marines battling pirates in the early 1800s. Great action and great fun. ★★★ VHS: $7.99

The Old Maid

(1939, 95 min, US, Edmund Goulding) *Bette Davis, Miriam Hopkins, George Brent, Jane Bryan.* Davis plays to the hilt the role of an unwed mother who, after her boyfriend is killed in the Civil War, gives up her child to be raised by her cousin (Hopkins). It's an acting tour de force as Davis and Hopkins battle it out with each other over daughter Bryan. ★★★

The Old Man and the Sea

(1958, 86 min, US, John Sturges) *Spencer Tracy, Felipe Pazos, Harry Bellaver.* Tracy delivers a remarkably moving performance as an aging fisherman struggling against Nature in this thoughtful adaptation of Ernest Hemingway's novel. (Remade in 1990) ★★★ DVD: $19.99

Old School

(2003, 90 min, US, Todd Phillips) *Luke Wilson, Vince Vaughn, Will Ferrell, Ellen Pompeo, Jeremy Piven, Juliette Lewis.* Director Phillips, after *Road Trip* and the documentary *Frat House* a veritable Greek auteur, goes to the well one time too many in this flat throwback. Old buddies ("old" meaning thirtysomething and settled) Wilson, Vaughn and Ferrell find themselves forced to convert Wilson's house into a frat when evil Dean Pritchard (Piven) rezones the land. Party scenes ensue. The one bright spot is an energetic Ferrell as Frank "The Tank," a hard-living vision of what *Animal House*'s Bluto might look like after attempting marriage. However, Wilson and Vaughn are lifeless straight men, and Piven's dean is so despicable as to be a real buzzkill. The ample star wattage attests Phillips' reputation, but like the three protagonists, it's time to kiss college goodbye, buddy. ★½ DVD Letterbox Unrated: $19.99, DVD Pan & Scan Unrated: $19.99, VHS: $14.99

Old Yeller

(1957, 83 min, US, Robert Stevenson) *Tommy Kirk, Fess Parker, Dorothy McGuire.* Life on a Texas farm, circa 1859, highlights this popular Disney tale of a boy and his dog, based on Fred Gipson's well-liked novel. ★★★ DVD 2-disc set: $22.99, VHS: $19.99

The Oldest Profession

(1967, 97 min, France/Italy/West Germany, Various) *Jeanne Moreau, Raquel Welch, Anna Karina, Jean-Claude Brialy.* Six chronological stories, all directed and starring different artists, humorously probe the history of prostitution from prehistoric times to the present and beyond. The final segment, "Anticipation," by Jean-Luc Godard, is an especially good short film that speculates on aliens from outer space and their Parisian sex habits. ★★½

Oleanna

(1994, 101 min, US, David Mamet) *William H. Macy, Deborah Eisenstadt.* Granted, a play by Mamet about sexual harassment is kind of like letting the fox guard the chickens, but that's not what makes this examination of campus politics a failure. The problem is more dramatic in nature. Mamet's patented dialogue, brash and stacatto to the extreme, is usually what makes his plays so dynamic, but in this two-actor setting, it falls flat, ultimately rendering his characters unbelievable. The first act finds John (Macy), an arrogant, self-serving college professor who is up for tenure, locking horns with Carol (Eisenstadt), a student who wants to know why she has failed his class. His career is put in peril in act two when she submits a scathing letter to the tenure review board full of accusations of impropriety. ★½ DVD Letterbox: $19.99

Oliver!

(1968, 153 min, GB, Carol Reed) *Ron Moody, Mark Lester, Oliver Reed, Jack Wild, Shanni Wallis.* This elaborate musical rendition of the Charles Dickens tale about a young boy swept into a gang of thieves is as close to flawless as a movie can get. Its frolicking score, splendid re-creation of 1830s London and an unforgettable performance by Moody as the scurrilous Fagin helped win it five Oscars, including Best Picture and Best Director. A trifle long, the film nonetheless holds the attention of even young viewers throughout. ★★★★ DVD: $27.99

Oliver & Company

(1988, 72 min, US, George Scribner) *Voices of: Bette Midler, Joey Lawrence, Billy Joel, Roscoe Lee Browne, Robert Loggia, Dom DeLuise.* While *Oliver & Company* won't acquire the classic status of so many Disney animated films, it is an enjoyable entry into the family film arena. Loosely based on Dickens' "Oliver Twist," this version features Oliver as a tabby kitten lost in New York City. He is befriended by a gang of dogs engaged in working scams on behalf of Einstein, their bumbling human owner who is indebted to a villainous loan shark. Enlivened by the music of Billy Joel, the film benefits from a good ensemble, though Midler steals the show as the snooty French poodle Georgette. ★★★ DVD: $29.99, VHS: $22.99

Oliver Twist

(1948, 116 min, GB, David Lean) *Alec Guinness, Anthony Newley, Robert Newton, Francis L. Sullivan, Kay Walsh.* This brilliant adaptation of Charles Dickens' classic novel stands as the finest cinematic treatment of all the screen versions to tell Dickens' story of a young orphan's adventures in 18th-century London. Guinness gives a captivating performance as Fagin; and there's a remarkable supporting cast, including a young Newley as the Artful Dodger. (Remade as a musical in 1968) ★★★★ DVD: $39.99

Olivier, Olivier

(1991, 109 min, France, Agnieszka Holland) *François Cluzet, Brigitte Rouan, Grégoire Stevenin.* Olivier, a precocious nine-year-old coddled by his doting mother, one day mysteriously disappears without a trace. His family is torn apart by the loss, but are reunited six years later when a 15-year-old homosexual prostitute claims to be their long-lost son. The family, especially the mother, desperately wants to believe that this savvy teen is indeed the innocent of years past. As in the similarly themed *Return of Martin Guerre*, doubts soon emerge as to the true identity of the youth. This engrossing drama creates suspense as to why he disappeared, and tenderly unfolds a tale of a boy learning about love and trust. (French with English subtitles) ★★★

Los Olvidados
(The Young and the Damned)
(1950, 88 min, Mexico, Luis Buñuel) *Alfonso Mejias, Roberto Cobo.* Buñuel's social protest film is set in a Mexico populated by juvenile delinquents, beggers, cripples and other physically and/or socially deformed characters. The story centers around a particular boy as he learns the skills of survival within an oppressive society. (Spanish with English subtitles) ★★★★

Olympia, Pts 1 & 2
(1936, 220 min, Germany, Leni Riefenstahl) This magnificent account of the Berlin Olympic Games of 1936 transcends a typical documentary of a sporting event. Through imaginative use of editing and camera movement, as well as spectacular photography, Riefenstahl's film achieves its goal of being a Nazi propaganda film but more importantly, it is a graceful, nonpolitical look at the majestic beauty of the athletes. (German with English subtitles) ★★★★ VHS Parts 1 & 2: $49.99, VHS Part 1: $29.99, VHS Part 2: $29.99

The Omega Code
(1999, 100 min, US, Robert Marcarelli) *Michael York, Casper Van Dien, Catherine Oxenberg, Michael Ironside.* A truly laughable experience financed by the Trinity Broadcasting Network. An obnoxious, Tony Robbins-like motivational speaker (the consistently awful Van Dien) preaches his belief in the prescience of a mathematical interpretation of "The Bible," dubbed the Bible Code. As a result, he finds himself embroiled in some listless, amateur-nite espionage. An unremarkable story hook is given a by-the-numbers treatment, while the characters and dialogue wouldn't pass muster in a Sunday School pageant (well, maybe just). There's a "family values" subplot that only adds to the preaching-to-the-converted feel of this nonsense. (Sequel: *Megiddo: Omega Code 2*) ★ DVD: $14.99, VHS: $9.99

The Omega Man
(1971, 98 min, US, Boris Sagal) *Charlton Heston, Rosalind Cash, Anthony Zerbe.* Updated version of Vincent Price's *The Last Man on Earth* (itself based on Richard Matheson's story "I Am Legend"), now with Heston as the stalwart survivor of germ warfare who takes on a band of mutants. Director Sagal gives the film a great look, and there's some exciting scenes throughout, though the languid pacing sometimes sabotages an interesting story. Heston watching *Woodstock* over and over again is so ludicrous it's camp. ★★½ DVD: $19.99, VHS: $14.99

The Omen
(1976, 111 min, US, Richard Donner) *Gregory Peck, Lee Remick, Billie Whitelaw, David Warner, Harvey Stephens.* This blockbuster thriller set the trend in horror films for years to come. Peck and Remick play the newly appointed American ambassador to England and his wife, who unwittingly become the parents of the Antichrist, Damien. Whitelaw is chilling as the nanny who stops at nothing to protect her charge. Definitely not for the squeamish. (Followed by 2 sequels) ★★★ DVD: $14.99, VHS: $9.99

On a Clear Day You Can See Forever
(1970, 129 min, US, Vincente Minnelli) *Barbra Streisand, Yves Montand, Bob Newhart, Larry Blyden, Jack Nicholson.* Based on the Broadway musical, this splashy if occasionally muddled adaptation stars Streisand as a woman who learns of a

Los Olvidados

past life when under hypnosis. Montand is her psychiatrist, who falls in love with her — only the woman she was, not the woman she is. Streisand gives a good performance in the "dual" role, though Montand is woefully miscast. Nicholson is Barbra's guitar-playing brother. Score by Alan Jay Lerner and Burton Lane. ★★½ VHS: $14.99

On Borrowed Time
(1939, 99 min, US, Harold S. Bucquet) *Lionel Barrymore, Cedric Hardwicke, Beulah Bondi.* This sentimental variation of *Death Takes a Holiday* is pure '30s corn, but underneath the folksy interplay there's a thoroughly intriguing fantasy at work. Death (played by Hardwicke) has just taken a married couple. And now he's set his sights on the rest of the family. But Grandpa Barrymore has a trick or two in store for the Grim Reaper when he comes to call. ★★★

On Dangerous Ground
(1951, 82 min, US, Nicholas Ray) *Robert Ryan, Ida Lupino, Ward Bond.* Ray's second collaboration with producer John Houseman is this brilliant exposé of a tough, inner-city policeman (Ryan) who falls prey to the violence of the urban jungle. So much so, that he is sent for a cooling off period to upstate New York where the real intrigue begins when he falls in with a blind woman (Lupino) and her mentally retarded brother. Bernard Hermann's score was reportedly his favorite. ★★★½

On Deadly Ground
(1994, 100 min, US, Steven Seagal) *Steven Seagal, Michael Caine, Joan Chen.* In this pretentious, ridiculous eco-thriller, Seagal's P.C. action hero asks several questions, such as "What is the essence of a man?" and "How much wealth is enough?" He should have been inquiring how to make a movie. In his directorial debut, Seagal plays a born-again environmentalist who takes on his former boss, an evil oil magnate (Caine). One-dimensional heroes, cardboard villains and a predictable story line punctuate this turkey. As an actor, Seagal couldn't be more wooden if he were a totem pole. ★ DVD: $14.99, VHS: $9.99

On Golden Pond
(1981, 109 min, US, Mark Rydell) *Henry Fonda, Katharine Hepburn, Jane Fonda, Dabney Coleman, Doug McKeon.* Both Kate and Henry received Oscars for their affecting, expansive performances in

this thoughtful, sentimental comedy-drama. Fonda stars as Norman Thayer, an 80-year-old retired teacher preoccupied with death, whose birthday celebration only triggers his fear of old age and dying. Hepburn is Ethel, Norman's devoted wife, who dutifully contends with her husband's cantankerous moods and encompassing anxiety. Jane, in her only film appearance with her father, plays the couple's alienated daughter vying for her father's affection. ★★★ DVD Letterbox Special Edition: $19.99, VHS: $9.99, VHS Letterbox: $14.99

On Her Majesty's Secret Service
(1969, 140 min, GB, Peter Hunt) *George Lazenby, Diana Rigg, Telly Savalas.* Despite the fact that Lazenby was an unimpressive, and very temporary, James Bond, incredible action and location photography make this one of the finest and most exciting entries in the series. The usual mayhem is given an unusual twist as Bond marries a Spanish contessa (Rigg). (Sequel: *Diamonds Are Forever*) ★★★

On Moonlight Bay
(1951, 95 min, US, Roy Del Ruth) *Doris Day, Gordon MacRea, Leon Ames, Rosemary De Camp, Mary Wickes.* Comparisons to *Meet Me in St. Louis* are inevitable as this bright, wholesome musical has the same folksy (corny?) charm as that Judy Garland classic. It also has Ames as a father whose decision to move has disrupted his loving family. Day plays a tomboy who acquires feminine ways when she meets new neighbor MacRea. Their course of true love is a rocky one, but it is tuneful. Gray does a nice turn on the mischievous youth, and Wickes, as a wise-cracking maid, is a welcome addition to any household. It's sappy, but it's fun. ★★★

On the Beach
(1959, 134 min, US, Stanley Kramer) *Gregory Peck, Ava Gardner, Fred Astaire, Anthony Perkins, Donna Anderson.* One of the first films to seriously address the issues of a nuclear apocalypse, this first-rate adaptation of Nevile Shute's novel tells the tale of an American submarine crew who find themselves in Australia awaiting the fallout with the rest of the inhabitants. (Remade in 2000) ★★★½ DVD: $14.99

On the Town
(1949, 98 min, US, Gene Kelly & Stanley Donen) *Gene Kelly, Frank Sinatra, Jules Munchin, Vera-Ellen, Betty Garrett, Ann Miller.* A grand, energetic and immensely enjoyable adaptation of the popular Broadway musical. With a score by Leonard Bernstein and a book by Betty Comden & Adolphe Greene, directors Kelly and Donen have opened up, with location shooting, this exuberant tale about three sailors on a 24-hour pass, and of their romantic adventures in New York City. Kelly, Sinatra and Munchin are the men in uniform; and Vera-Ellen, Garrett and Miller are the women with whom they meet and fall in love. ★★★★ DVD: $19.99, VHS: $9.99

On the Waterfront
(1954, 108 min, US, Elia Kazan) *Marlon Brando, Rod Steiger, Lee J. Cobb, Karl Malden, Eva Marie Saint.* Brando became a legitimate contender with

this textbook study of Method acting. After he sings to the law about dockside corruption, the union mob comes down hard on him. Cobb is the waterfront godfather, Malden is the street-smart priest, Steiger is Brando's spineless brother and Saint is the troubled girlfriend. A rare combination of a superlative ensemble, exact direction, topical story line and a brilliantly structured screenplay played out in a singular vision. ★★★★ DVD: $24.99

On Top of the Whale

(1982, 93 min, Netherlands, Râùl Ruiz) Chilean expatriate Ruiz's unusual film is a demanding, complex and imaginatively photographed film, both invigorating and a challenging entertainment. The bare bones plot outline is as follows: a Dutch anthropologist and his girlfriend meet up with Narcisso, an eccentric millionaire who claims to have the last survivors of a lost Indian tribe in his summer home in Patagonia. The three, along with the woman's daughter, travel to this bleak country house and there the anthropologist attempts to understand the Indians' bizarre language, a language consisting of one word, spoken with different inflections. With all of the characters arbitrarily switching from English, French, Spanish, German, Dutch and the cryptic Indian dialect, Ruiz has made an amusing exercise on the mysteries of language and communication. ★★★ VHS: $59.99

On Valentine's Day

(1986, 105 min, US, Ken Harrison) Hallie Foote, Matthew Broderick, Michael Higgins, Steven Hill. Writer Horton Foote's satisfactory prequel to 1918. Set in a small texas town one year earlier, the film traces the emotional struggle and reconciliation of young Elizabeth (Foote), disowned by her family for marrying against their wishes. Broderick reprises his role as Elizabeth's brother. ★★½

Once a Thief

(1991, 90 min, Hong Kong, John Woo) Chow Yun-Fat, Leslie Cheung, Cherie Chung. Fans of Woo won't want to miss this over-the-top comedy about a trio of Chinese art thieves. The action follows Fat, Cheung and Chung as sophisticated larcenists of European art treasures. The film's first hour, filmed on location in Paris, is at times uneven — one senses that Woo and his crew weren't well-suited to the demands of location shooting. But the action explodes about halfway through when Chow and Cheung botch a job and wind up in a dizzyingly exciting chase scene, ultimately leading them back to Hong Kong where Woo turns to his patented knack for turning gut-wrenchingly violent action sequences into side-splitting laugh fests. (Cantonese with English subtitles) ★★★½ DVD Dual: $24.99, VHS: $9.99

Once Around

(1991, 115 min, US, Lasse Hallström) Richard Dreyfuss, Holly Hunter, Danny Aiello, Gena Rowlands, Laura San Giacomo. From the director of My Life as a Dog comes this endearing and offbeat romantic comedy, with Dreyfuss and Hunter reteaming after Always as mismatched lovers who marry and settle down. Aiello and Rowlands play Hunter's exasperated parents, at odds with their decidedly different, and same-age, son-in-law. Good performances help compensate occasional lapses in the script. ★★½

Once Bitten

(1985, 93 min, US, Howard Storm) Jim Carrey, Lauren Hutton, Cleavon Little. Atrocious comedy with vampire Hutton on the lookout for a virgin in present-day Los Angeles — having trouble finding one. ★ DVD Letterbox: $14.99

Once Upon a Honeymoon

(1942, 116 min, US, Leo McCarey) Cary Grant, Ginger Rogers, Walter Slezak. Ex-burlesque queen Rogers marries Nazi spy Slezak — only she's not aware of his true identity. However, reporter Grant is, and he pursues them on their honeymoon to expose the German agent and rescue Rogers from possible assassination. A curious mix of adventure, drama and comedy from director McCarey. ★★½

Once Upon a Time in America

(1984, 227 min, US, Sergio Leone) Robert De Niro, James Woods, Elizabeth McGovern, Treat Williams, Tuesday Weld. Leone's epic is a fascinating analysis of unyielding ambition, moral decay and the predatory nature of the past. Through an opium-induced haze, De Niro traces the events of a lifetime led on the wrong side of the law. ★★★½ DVD 2-disc Special Edition: $26.99, VHS: $29.99

Once Upon a Time in China

(1991, 100 min, Hong Kong, Tsui Hark) Jet Li. Arguably Li's best film from his early career is a martial-arts epic focusing on the (entirely fictional) exploits of real-life Chinese hero, Wong Fei-Hung. While the film is a bit too long and leisurely paced, Once Upon a Time does feature stylish direction from Hark and terrific fight choreography. If you're a martial arts fan, you must see this film; do try to see it in its widescreen, English-subtitled version at its original 134-minutes running time (available on DVD). (Followed by 5 sequels) ★★★½ DVD: $24.99, VHS: $14.99

Once Upon a Time in China Part 2

(1993, 113 min, Hong Kong, Tsui Hark) Jet Li. In this second entry in the series, Wong Fei-Hung (Li) arrives in Canton to deliver a lecture on acupuncture at a medical conference. Unfortunately, the xenophobic, isolationist White Lotus Clan is attempting to cut off Canton from all outside influence — by any means necessary. Li joins in the fight against them, of course. Slightly lesser than its predecessor, this is still fun stuff, with several slam-bang action sequences to make up for some uneven pacing. ★★★ DVD: $24.99, VHS Dubbed: $14.99

Once Upon a Time in China Part 3

(1993, 112 min, Hong Kong, Tsui Hark) Jet Li. Li is about the only reason to watch this lackluster entry in the series. An overly complicated, confusing, sub-plot-laden story line combined with awkward dramatics make Part 3 tough going. The film is attractively shot, but even the fight scenes have lost their spark. There's a great setup for an action setpiece wherein Li and his enemies must do battle while in cumbersome dragon costumes during a raucous celebration, but even this unique bit is marred by lackadaisical editing. Casual viewers should skip to Once Upon a Time in China and America, which is a great deal more fun. ★★ DVD: $24.99, VHS Dubbed: $14.99

Once Upon a Time in Mexico

(2003, 101 min, US, Robert Rodriguez) Antonio Banderas, Salma Hayek, Johnny Depp, Mickey Rourke, Eva Mendes, Willem Dafoe, Ruben Blades, Cheech Marin. The prolific and talented Rodriguez completes his El Mariachi trilogy with this surprisingly cold, hugely uneven pseudo-epic. Banderas is back, this time known simply as "El," and he's been recruited by a renegade CIA agent (Depp) to assassinate the (supposedly corrupt) President of Mexico. El has his own mission as well: to avenge the death of his wife and child. Good premise for an action-

Once Upon a Time in America

packed film; but, for better and worse, Rodriguez feels the need to add several more subplots and a host of other characters. This reduces El to a secondary lead in his own sequel, which, since that leaves the always-inventive Depp as the main attraction, isn't such a terrible thing. It also leaves room for great turns by Blades and Rourke, and some terrific little asides. The action runs the gamut from routine to rousing, but there's so much of it, that it's hard to complain. Mexico never quite comes together — and it has a real nasty streak that at times is off-putting — but its considerable qualities almost outweigh its missteps. ★★½ DVD: $19.99, VHS: $14.99

Favorite Line: "Are you a Mexican or a Mexican'?" —Johnny Depp as Agent Sands

Once Upon a Time in the West

(1969, 165 min, Italy, Sergio Leone) Charles Bronson, Henry Fonda, Claudia Cardinale, Jason Robards, Jack Elam, Woody Strode, Keenan Wynn. Expanding upon the plot line of Johnny Guitar, Leone and story collaborators Dario Argento and Bernardo Bertolucci produce a polemic that is stunning in its grandeur, funny in its cynical sense of humor — using the horse opera as a metaphor for all that is wrong with the American capitalist system. Fonda had one of his greatest roles as one of the most cold-blooded killers in westerns ("I never trust a man who wears a belt with suspenders"). Bronson is in fine form as "The Man with the Harmonica" out for revenge. Another brilliant score by Ennio Morricone. ★★★★ DVD 2-disc Collector's Edition (Widescreen): $14.99, VHS: $14.99

Once Upon a Time . . . When We Were Colored

(1996, 112 min, US, Tim Reid) Al Freeman, Jr., Phylicia Rashad, Leon, Paula Kelly, Richard Roundtree, Salli Richardson, Polly Bergen, Bernie Casey, Isaac Hayes, Taj Mahal. First-time director Reid has crafted an affectionate and richly textured portrait of life in a black community in 1940s Mississippi. At a time when the dominate white society provided no legal or moral recourse for prejudice and brutality, African-Americans bonded to nurture and protect themselves. Seen through the eyes of a boy on the cusp of manhood, the film is remarkable in its ability to convey the internal reality of its protagonists, to enable the viewer to see these people as they see themselves and the world around them. This warmly told story of strength and solidarity captures the special intonations of a particular time and place, with compassionate understanding of the people who inhabited it. ★★★½ DVD: $14.99, VHS: $14.99

Once Were Warriors

(1995, 102 min, New Zealand, Lee Tamahori) *Rena Owen, Temuera Morrison, Mamaengaroa Kerr-Bell, Julian Arahanga.* At once searingly brutal and lyrically poetic, *Once Were Warriors* is an unflinching examination of one exceptionally strong woman's struggle to keep her family whole while battling a husband mired in drink and violence. In an unforgiving urban wasteland, the young still attempt to forge identities with purpose and dignity, despite all restrictions of class, race and economics. The performances are so vital and authentic that the film seems more documentary than drama. Director Tamahori has crafted a potent and volatile exploration of one family's survival in an environment devoid of hope or expectation — as alien as Maori tattooing and as familiar as the exhaust fumes outside your window. ★★★★ DVD: $19.99

The One

(2001, 80 min, US, James Wong) *Jet Li, Delroy Lindo, Carla Gugino, Jason Statham.* From a rather awkward prologue we learn that ours is not the only universe; there is a multiverse, with many versions of our "selves" throughout. Li plays several of these selves, one of whom is traveling between worlds to destroy his other selves, absorbing their power along the way, thereby becoming "The One." Li also appears as the last self standing in this villain's way. Got that? Contrived, silly premise could have been handled in a more exploratory, interesting way. That said, however, this is a little better than you'd expect, with exciting action scenes (that are actually enhanced with CGI effects, instead of ruined by them), a witty sense of humor, and the always-welcome Lindo. Li has fun as both villain and hero, and the final Li vs. Li fight is a doozy. ★★½ DVD Special Edition: $14.99, VHS: $102.99

One Crazy Summer

(1986, 94 min, US, Savage Steve Holland) *John Cusack, Demi Moore, Bobcat Goldthwait, Curtis Armstrong.* Though not as successful as his hilarious *Better Off Dead*, this crazy comedy is nonetheless an entertaining if uneven spoof with Cusack as a teenager spending summer vacation in Nantucket — surrounded by a gang of wackos. ★★½ DVD Letterbox: $14.99, VHS: $9.99

One Day in September

(1999, 94 min, US, Kevin MacDonald) *Narrated by: Michael Douglas.* The compelling *One Day in September* covers the '72 Munich Olympics' terrorist assault in a detailed, nearly hour-by-hour manner: eight armed Palestinians hold eleven Israeli athletes and coaches hostage until their demands are met. Though there are too many filler montages, and too little time spent is on the Palestinians' motivations, *September* is a gripping experience. It offers a chance to listen to the only surviving terrorist speak for the very first time about his involvement, and details the criminal bumbling of the German authorities. Not quite as powerful as *4 Little Girls*, the film it beat at the Oscars, *September* is potent documentary filmmaking. ★★★ DVD: $29.99, VHS: $14.99

One Day in the Life of Ivan Denisovich

(1971, 100 min, GB, Caspar Wrede) *Tom Courtenay, Alfred Burke.* An earnest, literate adaptation of Alexander Solzhenitsyn's epic novel about life in a Siberian labor camp during the early 1950s. Though a difficult book to translate to film, director Wrede has crafted a mesmerizing look at the hardships of a prisoner serving the last years of a ten-year sentence. In the title role, Courtenay is nothing short of brilliant. Beautiful cinematography by Sven Nykvist. ★★★½

187

(1997, 119 min, US, Kevin Reynolds) *Samuel L. Jackson, Kelly Rowan, John Heard, Clifton Gonzalez Gonzalez, Tony Plana, Karina Arroyave.* Few films about teachers have been as downbeat and hopeless as *187*, a determined, single-minded drama which casts a sad light on lower-class, urban education. Written by Scott Yagemann, a L.A. teacher for seven years, *187* follows Trevor Garfield (Jackson), a committed science teacher who moves to Los Angeles. He is not greeted by a group of students long forgotten by the system and who have given up on themselves. Jackson gives a tremendous portrayal of a man both in love with and fearful of his job, a good teacher possibly pushed too far. This is difficult medicine to digest, and the film's ending may take too many liberties, but the loss of passion and innocence is movingly told. ★★★ DVD: $14.99, VHS: $9.99

One-Eyed Jacks

(1961, 141 min, US, Marlon Brando) *Marlon Brando, Karl Malden, Slim Pickens, Pina Pellicer, Ben Johnson.* Brando's only directorial effort pits him as an outlaw against sheriff Malden in a psychological tug-of-war. An unusual, intriguing western morality tale. ★★★ VHS: $9.99

One False Move

(1992, 105 min, US, Carl Franklin) *Bill Paxton, Billy Bob Thornton, Cynda Williams, Michael Beach.* This film's opening 10 minutes are so violently disturbing that it's enough to make one stop viewing it. However, stick with this one for *One False Move* is an intense, original thriller. The story follows a gang of three ruthless Los Angeles drug dealers who, having raided their rivals, make off with a bag full of cash and hit the road for Arkansas in search of a place to lie low. Waiting at the other end are Dale "Hurricane" Dixon (Paxton), the country "Bumpkin" local sheriff in Star City, Ark., and a couple of L.A. cops who have reason to believe the bad guys are headed their way. While the tension mounts, the filmmakers use the situation to deftly probe the underbelly of American life, from racial tensions to the inherent conflict between rural and urban values. ★★★½ DVD: $27.99, VHS: $14.99

One Fine Day

(1996, 100 min, US, Michael Hoffman) *Michelle Pfeiffer, George Clooney, Mae Whitman, Alex D. Linz, Charles Durning, Holland Taylor, Ellen Greene.* Though they exude great charm and have a wonderful chemistry between them, Pfeiffer and Clooney just aren't able to give an added boost to this convoluted romantic comedy which is short on both romance and comedy. They play divorced parents who come together when their children miss the class trip. Each having a professional crisis looming, they take turns babysitting both kids. Of course, they're antagonistic in the beginning, but soon they succumb to each other's magnetism. manipulation. They'd probably be better matched the next time Catwoman and Batman meet. ★★ DVD: $14.99, VHS: $6.99

One Flew Over the Cuckoo's Nest

(1975, 133 min, US, Milos Forman) *Jack Nicholson, Louise Fletcher, Brad Dourif, Will Sampson, William Redfield, Danny DeVito, Christopher Lloyd, Scatman Crothers, Vincent Schiavelli.* Nicholson gives a triumphant performance as the dangerously sane McMurphy, the feisty ringleader of an asylum's inmates. Forman adapts Ken Kesey's eloquent novel with boundless zeal and multi-award-winning results. Fletcher won an Oscar (as did Nicholson) for her unforgettably adversarial head nurse whose unwavering strictness leads to defiance and tragedy. Winner of 5 Academy Awards, including Best Picture. ★★★★ DVD: $19.99, DVD 2-disc set: $26.99, VHS: $6.99

One from the Heart

(1982, 100 min, US, Francis Ford Coppola) *Frederic Forrest, Teri Garr, Raul Julia, Nastassja Kinski.* Coppola's celebrated bomb (costing some $25 million) stars Forrest and Garr as lovers who split after five years. They find new lovers, only to realize they were really meant for each other. Nothing more than a stylized, full-length music video which lacks any dramatic structure. Music by Tom Waits. ★★ DVD 2-disc set: $29.99

One Good Cop

(1991, 114 min, US, Heywood Gould) *Michael Keaton, Rene Russo, Anthony LaPaglia, Kevin Conway, Rachel Ticotin.* Keaton gives a competent performance in a relatively lackluster treatment of the good-cop-loses-partner-and-has-a-crisis-of-faith formula. The occasional sparks generated by the cast can't quite compensate for the flat, predictable script and mundane direction. ★★ DVD: $14.99

One Hour Photo

(2002, 95 min, US, Mark Romanek) *Robin Williams, Connie Nielsen, Michael Vartan, Dylan Smith, Erin Daniels, Eriq LaSalle, Gary Cole.* Williams is haunting in his understated performance as Seymour "Sy" Parrish. An exacting, precise man, his concerted efforts to control a small corner of the

Robin Williams in *One Hour Photo*

world begin to fray under the strain of continued repression and the emergence of imperfection in his fantasy life. Sy (the photo guy) has been developing the photos of the Yorkin family since son Jakob was a fetus. He's come to see himself as a member of the clan, uncle Sy, running off duplicates of their snapshots for the walls of his antiseptic apartment. Sy learns a lot about all of his regular customers through the images they bring to him. When he detects deception in his surrogate family just as his own circumstances start to deteriorate, this sad, emotionally isolated man feels his intricately constructed, stringent sense of order dissolve into terrorizing chaos. Effective counterbalance to Williams' portrayal is offered by Nielsen as mom Nina and Smith as son Jakob, the child Sy was never allowed to be. A thoughtful, involving study of the many forms of abuse people inflict on each other, and the lingering effects they can elicit. ★★★½ DVD Letterbox: $14.99, DVD Pan & Scan: $14.99, VHS: $12.99

101 Dalmatians

(1961, 80 min, US, Clyde Geronimi, H.S. Luske, Wolfgang Reitherman) An enchanting Disney classic, this animated tale follows the adventures of a faithful dalmatian, Pongo, and his mate as they attempt to stop one of Disney's best villains, Cruella DeVil, from kidnapping a truckload of pups and turning them into fur coats. The animation is splendid, and the comical story is one of Disney's best. (Remade as live-action film in 1996) ★★★★

101 Dalmatians

(1996, 103 min, US, Stephen Herek) *Glenn Close, Jeff Daniels, Joely Richardson, Joan Plowright, Hugh Laurie.* The names are the same and so essentially is the story. But wait! The lively animated characters, mean, colorful villainess and cuddly spotted canines have been replaced by real people. So who can fault the suits at Disney for taking this golden marketing opportunity by the tail and racing with it. Close gives a dazzling grand-old-dame turn as flamboyantly dressed "über-bitch" Cruella. But Disney handed the writing and producing bone to John Hughes. Blame him for the insipid slapstick humor that eventually turns this puppy into *Dog Home Alone.* (Sequel: *102 Dalmatians*) ★★

102 Dalmatians

(2000, 100 min, US, Kevin Lima) *Glenn Close, Gérard Depardieu, Alice Evans, Ioan Gruffudd, Eric Idle.* In this cartoonish sequel to the 1996 live-action remake of the beloved 1961 animated film, Cruella DeVil is released from prison presumably reformed. However, her old self reappears and she's back on her quest for a new mink coat. Close is in great form, once again (it's amazing the kind of indignities she suffers), and the costumes are smashing, but this dog-eared franchise is getting doggone tired already. It's overplayed, over-the-hill, and, well, we're just over it. ★★ DVD Pan & Scan: $19.99, DVD: $19.99, VHS: $14.99

One Magic Christmas

(1985, 100 min, US, Phillip Borsos) *Mary Steenburgen, Harry Dean Stanton, Arthur Hill.* This poignant family fantasy draws much of its inspiration from both *It's a Wonderful Life* and *A Christmas Carol.* Steenburgen stars as a housewife whose lost Christmas spirit is found with the help of an unlikely guardian angel, played by Stanton. ★★★ VHS: $9.99

One Million Years B.C.

(1966, 100 min, GB, Don Chaffey) *Raquel Welch, John Richardson.* Hammer Films made this campy remake of the 1939 adventure with Welch in her star-making role of scantily clad cavewoman fighting off man and beast. Special effects by Ray Harryhausen are a plus, as is Welch. ★★½ DVD: $14.99, VHS: $9.99

One Night at McCool's

(2001, 93 min, US, Harald Zwart) *Liv Tyler, Matt Dillon, Paul Reiser, John Goodman, Michael Douglas, Reba McIntire. One Night at McCool's* is a veritable squirm-fest, with each character taking full advantage of a multitude of opportunities to embarrass himself. That is, except for Jewell (Tyler), the sultry focal point of a love triangle that is unfavorably reminiscent of *There's Something about Mary.* But whereas Cameron Diaz's Mary was the epitome of virtue, Tyler's Jewel is a Marilynesque vixen who would be innocent if she weren't so darn guilty all the time. She manipulates the heartstrings of her town's unfortunate men to feed her need for home furnishings and consumer electronics. The *Rashomon*-like multiperspective narrative is a neat gimmick that breathes some added life into an otherwise formulaic outing, but too many antics smack of desperation. ★★ DVD: $19.99, VHS Bonus Edition: $14.99

One Night of Love

(1934, 80 min, US, Victor Schertzinger) *Grace Moore, Tullio Carminati.* A captivating musical with Moore in a wonderful performance as an American opera singer who studies and falls in love with Italian maestro Carminati. ★★★

One Night Stand

(1997, 104 min, US, Mike Figgis) *Wesley Snipes, Nastassja Kinski, Robert Downey, Jr., Ming Na-Wen, Kyle MacLachlan.* In this awkwardly constructed, unsatisfying but fitfully interesting infidelity drama, Snipes plays a happily married director who has a one night stand with yummy Kinski. The first half sets up the fling, and shows its effects on Snipes' personal and professional life. The film takes a radical right turn when Snipes visits his best friend from college (Downey) who is dying of AIDS, and then picks up the adultery story line for a truly goofy wrap-up. The ending, while silly and unbelievable, actually does mirror events in original screenwriter Joe Eszterhas' personal life. ★★ DVD: $24.99, VHS: $19.99

One Sings, the Other Doesn't

(1977, 90 min, France, Agnès Varda) *Therese Leotard, Valerie Mairesse.* Varda's feminist triumph follows the friendship and developing self-fulfillment of two young women in Paris from 1962 to 1976. Pauline is a free-spirited singer while Susanne becomes an organizer in a family planning clinic and both succeed through the love and support of each other. This warm and thoughtful film blends fact, fiction and feeling to sing its song in praise of women. (French with English subtitles) ★★★

One Touch of Venus

(1948, 81 min, US, William A. Seiter) *Ava Gardner, Robert Walker, Eve Arden.* Long before *Mannequin* came this charming musical comedy with Gardner as a department store statue who magically comes to life and is romanced by window dresser Walker. ★★★

One Trick Pony

(1980, 98 min, US, Robert M. Young) *Paul Simon, Blair Brown, Rip Torn, Joan Hackett, Lou Reed.* A bittersweet, unfulfilled story of an aging rock star trying to salvage his marriage and his flagging career. Simon also wrote the script. ★★ VHS: $14.99

Onibaba

One True Thing

(1998, 128 min, US, Carl Franklin) *Meryl Streep, Renée Zellweger, William Hurt, Tom Everett Scott, Lauren Graham.* The poignant relationship between mother and daughter is at the heart of this articulate, compelling drama which tenderly examines the tenuous threads of familial ties and the emotions and deeds which bind them. Streep is Kate, a housewife and mother who is newly diagnosed with cancer. Her daughter Ellen (Zellweger), a promising writer in New York, reluctantly returns to the small town of her youth to look after her mother. The story concentrates on the family unit, but its strength lies in the bond between Kate and Ellen. Streep is miraculous in giving multilayered shadings to Kate, a woman whose talents and loves were hidden to her daughter. Zellweger more than holds her own with Streep, making Ellen more than just an inconvenienced daughter. ★★★ DVD: $14.99

One, Two, Three

(1961, 110 min, US, Billy Wilder) *James Cagney, Arlene Francis, Horst Buchholz, Pamela Tiffin.* A hilarious, lightning-paced (this may be the fastest comedy since Howard Hawks' *His Girl Friday*) political farce from director Wilder, made during the heyday of the Cold War. Cagney — who would not make another film for 20 years — is in top form as the harried Coca-Cola executive stationed in West Berlin who must contend with card-carrying Commies, ex-Nazis and Southern belles when the boss' daughter secretly marries a young Communist. All this and Pepsi-Cola, too. ★★★★ DVD Dual: $19.99

One Wild Moment

(1977, 88 min, France, Claude Berri) *Victor Lanoux, Jean-Pierre Marielle.* An engaging French farce that follows the adventures of a recently divorced 44-year-old man who goes on vacation in the hope of having an affair with some beautiful young girl. His fantasy comes true, but he then realizes that the young beauty that seduced him is the daughter of his best friend. (American remake: *Blame It on Rio*) (French with English subtitles) ★★½

One Woman or Two

(1986, 97 min, France, Daniel Vigne) *Gérard Depardieu, Sigourney Weaver, Ruth Westheimer.* A curious international cast of team in this silly, occasionally funny remake of the classic *Bringing Up Baby.* Depardieu plays a foggy paleontologist who finds what he thinks to be the fossilized remains of the first Frenchwoman. Weaver is the opportunistic ad exec who wants to market the discovery in a perfume advertising campaign. And if this wasn't enough, Dr. Ruth plays an American philanthropist . . . maybe she should stick to just giving out sexual advice. (French with English subtitles) ★★

Onibaba

(1965, 103 min, Japan, Kaneto Shindo) *Nobuko Otowa, Yitsuko Yoshimura.* This exotic and macabre story is set in medieval Japan, a land ravaged by bloody battles between powerful warlords and where suffering peasants grow desperate in the struggle to survive. An elderly woman and her son's wife eke out their existence by searching for wounded soldiers, killing them — if necessary — and stripping them of their armor which they exchange for food. When a friend returns from the war with news of her son's death, the old lady becomes suspicious, both of the returning soldier and of her daughter-in-law — neither of whom seem in the least upset by his untimely demise. When the two begin a passionate affair, the old lady calls upon the demons and spirits to help her punish her daughter-in-law. *Onibaba* is a disturbing tale of deceit and survival. (Letterboxed version) (Japanese with English subtitles) ★★★½ DVD Criterion Collection: $29.99, VHS: $29.99

The Onion Field

(1979, 122 min, US, Harold Becker) *James Woods, John Savage, Ted Danson, Franklyn Seales, Ronny Cox.* Powerful film version of Joseph Wambaugh's fact-based novel about the killing of a policeman and his partner's eventual breakdown. Woods' electrifying performance as the psychopathic hood brought him international acclaim. ★★★ DVD Letterbox: $19.99

Only Angels Have Wings

(1939, 121 min, US, Howard Hawks) *Cary Grant, Jean Arthur, Thomas Mitchell, Rita Hayworth, Richard Barthelmess.* Top-flight adventure with pilot Grant running a small airline in the South American jungle, resisting the considerable charms of the ever-charming Arthur. Good support from Mitchell and a young Hayworth; solid direction from Hawks. ★★★½ DVD: $29.99, VHS: $19.99

Only One Night

(1939, 90 min, Sweden, Gustaf Molander) *Ingrid Bergman.* This intense melodrama stars Bergman as a repressed young woman, who, in order to please her father, becomes involved with a rich, philandering older man. (Swedish with English subtitles) ★★½ VHS: $19.99

Only the Lonely

(1991, 102 min, US, Chris Columbus) *John Candy, Ally Sheedy, Maureen O'Hara, Anthony Quinn, James Belushi, Milo O'Shea.* Candy gives possibly his best performance in this low-keyed comedy-drama. Effectively underplaying his part, he stars as a thirtysomething, single Chicago cop, still living at home with his mother, who falls in love with Sheedy: only problem is he just can't break away from mom. In her first screen appearance in 20 years, O'Hara returns as Candy's feisty mother. Much credit goes to O'Hara for her solid portrayal of the basically unlikable, prejudiced and outspoken Rose; she creates a three-dimensional, totally complex woman. ★★½

Only Two Can Play

(1962, 106 min, GB, Sidney Gilliat) *Peter Sellers, Mai Zetterling, Richard Attenborough, Virginia Maskell.* This highly entertaining sex comedy is a wonderful example of early '60s British cinema. Sellers stars as a Welsh librarian who has soured on married life and spends his days dreaming of naughty affairs with other women. When he gets his wish in the form of a vivacious socialite, Zetterling, he finds it might be more than he can handle. Both Sellers and Zetterling deliver wonderful performances. ★★★

Only When I Laugh

(1981, 120 min, US, Glenn Jordan) *Marsha Mason, Kristy McNichol, James Coco, Joan Hackett.* Neil Simon's screenplay, based on his play "The Gingerbread Lady," rates as one of his best and most underrated. Mason excels in this serio-comic gem as an alcoholic actress, just released from a sanitarium, who tries to stay off the bottle. McNichol is her teenage daughter; and Coco and Hackett both give outstanding performances in support as, respectively, a struggling gay actor and a mentally unstable socialite. ★★★½

Only You

(1994, 108 min, US, Norman Jewison) *Marisa Tomei, Robert Downey, Jr., Bonnie Hunt, Joaquin DeAlmeida, Fisher Stevens, Billy Zane.* A young woman (Tomei) who, ten days before her wedding, takes off for Italy to find the man who she thinks is her ultimate destiny. Once abroad, she engages in a series of misadventures searching for Mr. Right, while roguish American Downey pursues her under false pretenses. Though Tomei can occasionally step on the line between endearing and cloying, Downey has a sparkling charm and ease. Cynics may wonder if Tomei would really have such an extensive ready-to-travel wardrobe in her meager closet; others will just bask in the film's witty dialogue and warm Italian sunshine. ★★★ DVD: $14.99, VHS: $9.99

Open City

(1946, 105 min, Italy, Roberto Rossellini) *Anna Magnani, Aldo Fabrizi.* Rossellini's classic, which marked the beginning of Italian Neorealism, is about the underground movement operating in Rome during the Nazi occupation. The brilliant performance by Magnani brought her international acclaim. Coscripted by Federico Fellini. (Italian with English subtitles) (aka: *Rome, Open City*) ★★★★ VHS: $19.99

Open Doors

(1990, 109 min, Italy, Gianni Amelio) *Gian Maria Volonte, Ennio Fantastichini.* Exactingly paced, this psychological drama on the nature of justice is a thoughtful film which is quite similar in theme to Bertrand Tavernier's *The Judge and the Assassin*. Set in 1937, the film begins with a man going to a government office and calmly killing his former boss, his seemingly supportive successor, and later, raping and killing his wife. He is arrested, says little, shows no regret and simply awaits his punishment. One of the judges assigned to the case, an older, wealthy patrician, becomes intrigued by the man and, risking his reputation and against the wishes of the defendant, tries to find out what caused the man to resort to such violence. The title refers to the Fascist promise that with their harsh penal code, people would be able to sleep with their doors open. (Italian with English subtitles) ★★★

Open Range

(2003, 135 min, US, Kevin Costner) *Robert Duvall, Kevin Costner, Annette Bening, Michael Gambon, Michael Jeter, Diego Luna, James Russo.* Director-star Costner marks a nice return to form after a few bloated vanity projects with this well-tempered, highly enjoyable western. He and Duvall (they make a very appealing team) play veteran free grazers who must take up arms when one of their group is murdered and the other is badly wounded by the hench-men of slimy rancher Gambon. A classic good guys vs. bad guys battle begins, culminating in a long, terrifically exciting shoot-out that'll have horse opera fans cheering. Unlike revisionist westerns from the likes of Sam Peckinpah and Clint Eastwood, *Open Range* finds its strengths in the traditional — a leisurely pace, heroes you root for and villains you hate, moral men dictated by a code of ethics. Beautifully shot, elegantly directed and extremely well-acted (especially by the always-great Duvall), the film does have its share of hokum, but that's really part of this anachronistic film's charm. These attributes, along with a touching if compone romance subplot involving Costner's wooing of Bening ("I reckon you're the handsomest woman I ever laid eyes on") make this a welcome addition to the genre. ★★★½ DVD 2-disc set: $29.99, VHS: $24.99

Open Your Eyes (Abre los Ojos)

(1997, 117 min, Spain, Alejandro Amenábar) *Eduardo Noriega, Penélope Cruz, Chete Lera, Fele Martínez, Gérard Barray, Pepe Navarro.* This hypnotic thriller — both sexy and beautifully filmed — takes a European approach to the idea of virtual reality. Carlos (Noriega) has a problem: he has turned up in a psychiatric hospital wanted for murder after one of his girlfriends tried to kill him. Does Sofia (the luscious Cruz), the woman he may truly love, hold the answer? Director Amenabar keeps the audience guessing as the plots flash back, forward, and eventually intertwine before the satisfying ending. Noriega is terrific in the main role, a smug ladies' man who discovers the unexpected truth while Cruz smolders as the femme fatale. The film's stylish visuals are dazzling, though it falls prey to a few too many plot twists. (American remake: *Vanilla Sky*) (Spanish with English subtitles) ★★★ DVD: $14.99

Opening Night

(1977, 144 min, US, John Cassavetes) *Gena Rowlands, John Cassavetes, Ben Gazzara, Joan Blondell.* Complex, emotional, disquieting and at times exasperating, *Opening Night* is a none-too-subtle but riveting drama of the midlife crisis of an aging actress (Rowlands) as she works in a play about a woman quite like herself. As the star Rowlands is a talented but high-strung alcoholic who teeters on the verge of a nervous breakdown while costar and ex Cassavetes, harried director Gazzara and sympathetic but tough playwright Blondell helplessly watch. The theatre world provide an ideal location for Cassavetes' exploration of a woman facing middle age in a profession that idolizes youth and discards the "old." The acting is superb, from Rowlands' intense emoting to Gazzara's subtle nuances and taut facial expressions. ★★★ DVD: $24.99, VHS: $14.99

Opera do Malandro

(1986, 105 min, Brazil, Ruy Guerra) *Edson Celulari, Claudia Ohana.* This Brazilian reworking of "Three Penny Opera" is set in the slums of Rio in 1942 and is a highly stylized, tango-influenced homage to the splashy M-G-M musicals of the '50s. Our hero is Max Oversees, a charming scoundrel whose heart is divided between his longtime ex-prostitute lover and a young, convent-trained beauty who is also the daughter of the local crime boss. Guerra (*Erendira*) directed this exuberant and highly enjoyable musical; the highlights of which include a flamenco-style duel (read: cat fight) between the two leading ladies and an imaginative musical number set amidst the urinals in a nightclub's men' room. (Portuguese with English subtitles) ★★★

Operation Condor

(1991, 95 min, Hong Kong, Jackie Chan) *Jackie Chan, Carol "Dodo" Cheng, Eva Cobo Garcia, Shoko Ikeda.* This is actually the sequel to Chan's previous *Armour of God*, which was his first appearance as the Indiana Jones-like adventurer, the "Asian Hawk." This time around, Jackie is hired to find a secret cache of gold left in the desert after WWII by the fleeing German army. Along for the ride are an expert on desert travel (Cheng), the granddaughter of one of the German soldiers (Garcia) and a Japanese vagabond (Ikeda), not to mention a variety of bad guys who dog his every step. The film is virtually a nonstop chase scene, with Chan and cohorts looking for the gold, and everyone else either trying to beat him to it or kill him before he gets it! Some of the best sequences include a motorcycle and car chase through the Barcelona seaport, and the famous end fight scene, in which Chan fights two of the bad guy's henchmen in a wind tunnel. One of Chan's best films. ★★★½ DVD: $14.99, VHS: $9.99

Operation Condor 2: Armour of the Gods

(1990, 80 min, Hong Kong, Jackie Chan) *Jackie Chan, Alan Tam, Rosamund Kwan, Lola Forner.* This is actually the 1990 film *Armour of God*, which was followed by *Operation Condor: Armour of God 2* in 1991. But since the latter was released first in the U.S., the former is now being marketed as the sequel! Regardless, there's no reason to feel bamboozled: this is classic Jackie, in Indiana Jones mode (just like its predecessor/follow-up), with a slew of terrific stunts, exciting action scenes and riotous comedy. Highlights include an exhilarating fight with four leather-clad, tough-as-nails women, and the *de rigueur* end-credits outtakes, where we witness the stunt-gone-wrong which almost cost Chan his life. Nicely directed by Jackie, this is one of his best, an extremely accomplished crowd-pleaser. ★★★½ DVD: $14.99, VHS: $14.99

Operation Dumbo Drop

(1995, 108 min, US, Simon Wincer) *Danny Glover, Denis Leary, Ray Liotta, Doug E. Doug, Corin Nemec.* Disney offers this cardboard paste-up of a Vietnam War film which plays like "*The Absent-Minded Professor Goes to War*." And though it's based on a true story, a screenplay stuck in neutral and eye-rolling shenanigans keep this from attaining much comic mileage. The story centers on a group of Green Berets stationed in Vietnam who are assigned to transport an elephant from the jungle to a friendly village. Of course, things go awry, tempers flair, and

The Opposite of Sex

eventually they succeed. The film relies too heavily on obvious elephant jokes, and rarely gives its human actors anything equally amusing to say or do. ★★ DVD: $14.99

Operation Petticoat

(1959, 120 min, US, Blake Edwards) *Cary Grant, Tony Curtis, Joan O'Brien, Arthur O'Connell, Dina Merrill.* This sometimes hilarious comedy, which was one of the box-office smashes of the 1950s, stars Grant as the captain of a crippled WWII submarine who has his hands full not only making his ship seaworthy but also looking after five nurses rescued at sea. Directed with flair by Edwards. ★★★½ DVD: $14.99, VHS: $9.99

Opportunity Knocks

(1990, 105 min, US, Donald Petrie) *Dana Carvey, Robert Loggia, Todd Graff, Milo O'Shea.* Opportunity wasn't knocking too loud for Carvey's starring debut. His mastery of mimicry and sketch comedy isn't well-served in this story of a con man who ingratiates himself into the family of a wealthy industrialist. ★★ DVD: $9.99, VHS: $7.49

The Opposite of Sex

(1998, 100 min, US, Don Roos) *Christina Ricci, Martin Donovan, Lisa Kudrow, Lyle Lovett, Johnny Galecki, Ivan Sergei.* A deliciously subversive comedy. Never before has one character (and a teenage girl at that) wreaked more havoc on tranquil lives than in this hilariously mean-spirited comedy. Dedee (Ricci) is a 16-year-old, bad-to-the-bone, white-trash gal eager to sow her wild oats. She leaves her Louisiana life for an extended visit to her gay half-brother Bill (Donovan), a placid and altogether nice guy living with his dumb-as-a-doornail but sexy younger boyfriend Matt (Sergei). And before she has a chance to unpack her bags, she's seduced Matt and has convinced him to go off together. And there begins the action in this razor-sharp satire that skewers the filmic conventions of a bad girl who really wants to do good. Kudrow is priceless as the sister of Bill's deceased lover who can't help interfering in his and everyone else's life. Anyone numbed by predictable gay love stories or sensitive coming-out tales should thoroughly enjoy this wicked comedy. ★★★★ DVD: $27.99

The Opposite Sex

(1956, 117 min, US, David Miller) *June Allyson, Joan Collins, Ann Sheridan, Ann Miller, Joan Blondell, Agnes Moorehead, Jim Backus.* Musical updating of *The Women* (with men in this version). The film, which lacks the supreme artistry of the original, does possess a charm all its own, and the performers all appear to be in their element. ★★★

Orange County

(2002, 83 min, US, Jake Kasdan) *Colin Hanks, Jack Black, Catherine O'Hara, Schuyler Fisk, John Lithgow, Lily Tomlin, George Murdock, Kevin Kline.* Kasdan's (son of Lawrence) follow-up to his impressive *Zero Effect* is a real mixed-bag of familial blessings. Based on a screenplay by Mike White (who wrote the highly original *Chuck and Buck*), *Orange County* is equal parts annoying teen yukfest, half-baked satire and showcase for its high-profile cast. A very thin plot — Hanks (son of Tom) really, really wants to go to Stanford to study under his idol (a brilliant writer) and become a novelist himself — can't even sustain the brief running time. But direction that occasionally borders on the stylish and that cast keep things afloat, and there are more laughs than there should be. An appealing Fisk (daughter of

Sissy Spacek) and a nice last-minute cameo by a Kasdan, Sr. regular also help. Black is his usual love-him-or-hate-him self. ★★ DVD Letterbox: $14.99, VHS: $9.99

Oranges Are Not the Only Fruit

(1989, 165 min, GB, Beeban Kidron) *Geraldine McEwan, Charlotte Coleman.* Adapted for BBC-TV by Jeanette Winterson from her novel of the same name, director Kidron's three-part production chronicles the coming-of-age of a young British lesbian, Jess (McEwan). In her turbulent struggles with her domineering evangelist mother (Coleman), Jess grows up to be a fiercely independent young woman. This poignant story features a marvelous ensemble cast and charming performances from its two leads. ★★★½ VHS: $29.99

Orchestra Rehearsal

(1979, 72 min, Italy, Federico Fellini) As only the great Federico could, Fellini transforms this 72-minute mockumentary about an orchestra rehearsal into a frenzied, riotous excoriation of the Italian political spectrum. Commissioned by Italian state television to make a modest observance of an orchestra at work, Fellini instead served up this little Molotov cocktail that was championed and denounced with equal vigor at the time of its release. Filmed from the perspective of a television film crew, the film is mainly comprised of a series of interviews with the various orchestra members, stage hands and, of course, the maestro as they practice in a medieval Roman chapel. Order slowly begins to break down as the class tensions between fiercely unionist musicians and the conductor (read: management) reach a anarchic crescendo. Filled with Fellini's trademark vulgarity and outrageous humor. (Italian with English subtitles) ★★★ DVD: $19.99, VHS: $9.99

Ordeal by Innocence

(1984, 87 min, GB, Desmond Davis) *Donald Sutherland, Christopher Plummer, Faye Dunaway, Sarah Miles.* A good cast barely manage to salvage this marginal Agatha Christie mystery from the video junk heap. Sutherland stars as an American who sleuths his way about a 1950s English hamlet. See it for the cast, but don't expect much more. ★★ VHS: $79.99

The Order

(2003, 127 min, US, Brian Helgeland) *Heath Ledger, Shannyn Sossamon, Mark Addy, Peter Weller, Benno Fürmann.* Ledger and Addy play the last of an ancient order of Catholic priests whose goal is the pursuit of knowledge through forbidden texts. When their mentor dies of an apparent suicide, they begin to suspect the involvement of the mythical Sin Eater, a centuries-old man with the ability to absorb people's sins, thus absolving them. This minor film went through some major casting, marketing and post-production woes before undergoing a title change (the original one being the more appropriate *Sin Eater*) and being released eight months after schedule. It's easy to see the studio's trepidation: it has the look and premise of a horror film, but plays like a low-key drama about faith and morality — not exactly Saturday night at the multiplex fare. A lack of vitality and some ill-advised CGI effects are balanced by a few good performances, but don't expect *The Exorcist*. Hell, don't expect *Exorcist II*. ★★ DVD: $19.99

Ordet

(1954, 126 min, Denmark, Carl Dreyer) *Henrik Malberg.* A gripping, award-winning drama about two families, separated by religious beliefs, who must come to terms with their children's love for each other. (Danish with English subtitles) ★★★½ VHS: $29.99

Ordinary People

(1980, 123 min, US, Robert Redford) *Timothy Hutton, Donald Sutherland, Mary Tyler Moore, Judd Hirsch, Elizabeth McGovern, M. Emmet Walsh.* A collection of great performances are featured in this gripping, Oscar-winning Best Picture exploring a family's disintegration in the wake of their eldest son's death. Hutton won an Oscar for his sensitive portrayal of a teenager coming to terms with his brother's passing. Moore and Sutherland have never been better as the parents; and Hirsch is outstanding as Hutton's caring psychiatrist. Redford's directorial debut is remarkably assured. ★★★★ DVD: $14.99, VHS: $14.99

The Organization

(1971, 107 min, US, Don Medford) *Sidney Poitier, Raul Julia, Allen Garfield, Ron O'Neal, Daniel J. Travanti, Demond Wilson.* Poitier appears for a third time as Virgil Tibbs, the quick-witted police detective he first introduced in *In the Heat of the Night.* Set in San Francisco, the story centers on Tibbs' investigation of a group of kidnappers-vigilantes, who have concocted an elaborate plan to bring down drug-peddling underworld figures. There's a really good ten-minute opening robbery sequence, and the film, though it does lag in certain scenes, is peppered with exciting chases and a few twists. ★★★ DVD: $14.99

Organized Crime and Triad Bureau

(1993, 91 min, Hong Kong, Kirk Wong) *Danny Lee, Cecilia Yip, Anthony Wong.* A combination of a John Woo-style "heroic bloodshed" film and an American police procedural, this semi-sequel to Jackie Chan's *Crime Story* follows an unconventional cop (Lee) who relentlessly pursues an underworld gang leader (Wong) and his moll (Yip). After several battles, escapes and legal loopholes, Lee corners Wong on a small island. A massive search ensues, in which the criminal becomes as much of a victim as the people he's blackmailed and killed. An interesting variation of the crime thriller, *Bureau* is an original and entertaining by-the-numbers story of cops and criminals. (Cantonese with English subtitles) ★★★½ DVD: $19.99, VHS: $19.99

Orgazmo

(1997, 94 min, US, Trey Parker) *Trey Parker, Dian Bachar, Robyn Lynne Raab, Michael Dean Jacobs, Matt Stone, Ron Jeremy.* "South Park" creator Parker stars as a Mor(m)on who gets sucked into the world of porno. His old cronies Bachar (as Choda Boy) and Stone are there to help bring the humor down to an aggressively dumb level. It's very raunchy, with the funniest scene involving Choda Boy's Orgazmorator, a machine that produces big Os at a distance (not even Hasidim are safe). Yet it's also as tame and fun as *Austin Powers,* with nothing more than bare butts and dildos on-screen. There are plenty of laughs to be had, but they're undermined by uneven direction, some sloppy timing and an unfortunate fascination with kung-fu that prove this stuff is funnier when it's animated. (Unrated version) ★★

Orgy of the Dead

(1966, 90 min, US, Edward D. Wood, Jr.) *Criswell, Fawn Silver.* Just when you thought it was safe to be dead comes this campy mess of zombie girls and tortured teens in bondage. Filmed in "Astravision" and "Sexicolor." From the creator of *Plan 9 from Outer Space,* which says it all. ★ VHS: $9.99

Oriana

(1984, 88 min, France/Venezuela, Fina Torres) *Daniela Silvero, Doris Wells, Rafael Briceño.* First-time director Torres' beautiful and hauntingly romantic film studies the relationship between a young woman and her deceased aunt through a series of mesmerizing flashbacks and surrealistic fantasy. The story follows Marie, who must venture through the jungle and other wilderness to arrive at the remote hacienda which she has just inherited from her aunt, Oriane. As she rummages through all of the relics and artifacts in the house, memories are stirred within her and slowly, a mysterious family secret comes to the fore. (Spanish with English subtitles) ★★★ DVD: $29.99

Original Gangstas

(1996, 98 min, US, Larry Cohen) *Fred Williamson, Jim Brown, Pam Grier, Paul Winfield, Richard Roundtree, Ron O'Neal, Isabel Sanford, Wings Hauser.* A very nasty gang, the Rebels, is taking over the dying town of Gary, Indiana. The police and city hall are powerless, so it's up to the founders of the Rebels — now in their fifties — to put an end to this nonsense! Yeah, you'll be cheerin' on Williamson and the gang as they whip some ragamuffin butt in this entertaining throwback to the '70s blaxploitation films. Cohen uses his cast to full advantage, allowing everyone to strut their tuff-ass moment. Subtle it's not — this is a B-movie through and through. But it's fast-paced fun, and while they may be past their prime, these original gangstas put most of the newer crop of action stars to shame. ★★★ DVD: $14.99, VHS: $4.99

The Original Kings of Comedy

(2000, 111 min, US, Spike Lee) *Steve Harvey, D.L. Hughley, Cedric the Entertainer, Bernie Mac.* While the true original king might be Richard Pryor, the title refers to a smash arena tour featuring these four comedians. This Charlotte, N.C., stop has been preserved by Spike Lee for the wider audience that it deserves. Harvey is the most old school here (and proud of it), radiating pride that seems to be lost in the age of rap. He also comes, introducing the quietly raging Hughley, the physically fluid and aptly named Cedric the Entertainer, and the thisclosetotheedge Mac. Each has his own profane view of race relations, love and sex, and family, and it's all wildly hilarious. Except for familiar racial themes, you wouldn't know this was a Spike Lee joint; he excercises directorial restraint and lets the four jesters ascend to the throne. ★★★½ DVD: $14.99, VHS Special Edition: $9.99

Orlando

(1993, 93 min, GB, Sally Porter) *Tilda Swinton, Billy Zane, Lothaire Bluteau, Quentin Crisp, John Wood, Jimmy Somerville.* Adapted from Virginia Woolf's 1928 modernist novel, this is a wholly

Tilda Swinton is *Orlando*

original, stunningly filmed comedy of sexual mores, attitudes and gender switching. The tale begins in 1600, when the bewitchingly androgynous Orlando captures the eye of the aging Queen Elizabeth I (regally played to the hilt by Crisp), who promises the nobleman the deed to his family's estate on the condition that he retain his beauty and does not age. As the centuries roll by, the immortal Orlando strolls through the elaborate pageant of English history. During this quest for love and self-discovery, Orlando changes sexes while still retaining her/his personality, independence, kind heart and droll sense of humor. Spectacularly staged and costumed, this witty, enchanting film is infused with wry jokes and emotional truths and is a thrilling odyssey that should not be missed. ★★★★ DVD: $29.99, VHS: $19.99

Orphans

(1965, 105 min, USSR, Nikolai Gubenko) Winner of the Special Jury Prize at Cannes, this tender and revealing film is set in a boys' boarding school and follows the growth, education and budding sexuality of a young boy. (Russian with English subtitles) ★★★

Orphans

(1987, 115 min, US, Alan J. Pakula) *Matthew Modine, Kevin Anderson, Albert Finney.* This extremely well-acted drama tells the story of two orphaned brothers, on the edge of society, who live in a broken-down house in Newark and survive through petty thievery. Their lives are dramatically transformed when their plan to rob a drunk goes haywire. That drunk, a wealthy gangster, superbly played by Finney, is intrigued by the two youths and turns the tables a bit by developing a close father-son relationship with the boys. Based on Lyle Kessler's successful stage play. A unique, rewarding film experience. ★★★

Orphans of the Storm

(1921, 126 min, US, D.W. Griffith) *Dorothy Gish, Lillian Gish.* This powerful melodrama about two girls caught up in the French Revolution stars real-life sisters Dorothy and Lillian, playing two sisters in Paris in search of a cure for one's blindness. A classic from the silent era, from the director of *Birth of a Nation.* ★★★★ DVD: $29.99, VHS: $24.99

Orpheus

(1949, 95 min, France, Jean Cocteau) *Jean Marais, Francois Perier.* Cocteau's allegorical update of the Orpheus myth is a mesmerizing blend of the natural and the fantastic, poetry and science fiction. Marais stars as the successful poet who becomes enamored with the Princess Death — who travels between this world and the next via chauffeur-driven Rolls Royce. The director's major achievement in cinema. (French with English subtitles) ★★★★ DVD: $79.99, VHS: $29.99

Orpheus Descending

(1990, 117 min, GB, Peter Hall) *Vanessa Redgrave, Kevin Anderson, Anne Twomey, Miriam Margolyes.* A searing screen adaptation of Tennessee Williams' drama about a forbidden love in a sleepy Southern town. Redgrave stars as Lady Torrence, a very unhappily married woman whose repressed sexual passions erupt when she encounters a mysterious, young drifter (Anderson). As the two revel in their tryst, her tyrannical, bedridden husband plots his revenge. ★★★ VHS: $79.99

Osaka Elegy

(1936, 71 min, Japan, Kenji Mizoguchi) *Isuzu Yamada.* One of the earliest surviving films from Mizoguchi's early film career, this drama is a subtle examination of Japanese cultural mores and a indictment of the country's mistreatment of women. Told in realistic fashion, the story follows the travails of Ayako, a good-hearted young woman who, in order to repay the debt of her drunken father and support her school-age brother, reluctantly becomes involved with her boss, a henpecked and unsavory lout. She eventually sinks into prostitution and is both exploited and condemned by society. (Japanese with English subtitles) ★★★½ VHS: $39.99

Oscar and Lucinda

(1997, 135 min, Australia/GB, Gillian Armstrong) *Ralph Fiennes, Cate Blanchett, Ciaran Hinds, Tom Wilkinson, Richard Roxburgh.* Using the gorgeous Australian Outback as her canvas, director Armstrong has created a sumptuous tapestry blending the fabric of romance with the colors of eccentricity. Based on the Peter Carey novel, *Oscar and Lucinda* is a charming, often amusing and certainly unconventional romantic drama about the relationship between two outcasts who find each other through their love of gambling. Fiennes is Oscar, a much-too serious divinity student who happens to like to play the ponies. Blanchett is Lucinda, an heiress and rebellious spirit who can't resist a good game of cards. Their story takes an unusual bent when they decide to float a glass church to the heart of Aborigine country. Armstrong has given the film a beautiful look, all shimmering and robust, and her two leads offer distinctively strong performances. ★★★½ VHS: $29.99

Osmosis Jones

(2001, 90 min, US, Bobby Farrelly, Peter Farrelly, Piet Kroon, Tom Sito) *Bill Murray, Molly Shannon, Chris Elliott, Elena Franklin, Voices of: Chris Rock, Laurence Fishburne, David Hyde Pierce, William Shatner.* Murray plays a slob of a zookeeper who follows the 10-second rule (if a hard-boiled egg falls on the ground, it's okay to eat if it's picked up within ten seconds) and pays the price, coming down with a particularly nasty virus. His live-action scenes, directed by the Farrelly brothers, are remarkably repulsive, but also leaden and unfunny. Thank goodness the bulk of this film is animated in classic Warner Brothers style, a Friz Freleng fever dream courtesy of animation directors Kroon and Sito. Theirs is a fantastic voyage inside Murray's body, where a white blood cell (voiced by Rock) teams up with a time-release capsule (Pierce) to fight the invading virus (Fishburne). There are puns aplenty, and enough visual gags to warrant multiple viewings for Looney fans of all ages. The pace and energy are truly infectious. ★★★ DVD: $19.99, VHS: $14.99

Ossessione

(1942, 135 min, Italy, Luchino Visconti) *Massimo Girotti, Clara Calamai.* For this, his first feature film, Visconti adapted James M. Cain's powerful tale of ill-fated love, "The Postman Always Rings Twice," and transplanted it to wartime rural Italy. Gino, a virile young drifter, meets and falls in love with Giovanna, a beautiful yet desperately unhappy woman who is trapped in a loveless marriage with an older man. The two begin a doomed affair, conceived in passion and lust, but ending in greed, murder and recrimination. This remarkable neorealist debut was banned by Mussolini during the war, and because it was an unauthorized version of the Cain novel, it was not permitted into the United States until 1975. (Italian with English subtitles) ★★★½ DVD: $24.99

The Osterman Weekend

(1983, 102 min, US, Sam Peckinpah) *Rutger Hauer, John Hurt, Burt Lancaster, Craig T. Nelson, Dennis Hopper, Chris Sarandon, Meg Foster.* Peckinpah's final film is a sometimes intriguing but rather confusing thriller about a TV reporter (Hauer) who is used by CIA agent Hurt to spy on three of his friends — suspected Soviet agents. ★★½ DVD 2-disc Collector's Edition (Widescreen): $29.99

Otello

(1986, 123 min, Italy, Franco Zeffirelli) *Placido Domingo.* The dark treacheries and intense passions of Shakespeare's classic is vividly brought to the operatic screen with visual splendor by director Zeffirelli. Set in an unreal Mediterranean locale, this soaring and lavish production features a strong performance by Domingo as the tragic, crazed king. (Sung in Italian with English subtitles) ★★★½ DVD: $19.99, VHS: $24.99

Othello

(1952, 107 min, US, Orson Welles) *Orson Welles, Suzanne Cloutier, Michael MacLiammor, Robert Coote.* Welles' masterful interpretation of Shakespeare's tale of murder, jealousy, betrayal and racism was thought to have been lost forever. Thanks to the determination of his daughter Beatrice Welles-Smith, however, the film's negatives were unearthed in a New Jersey vault, restored, and seen by audiences in 1992 for the first time since 1955. Extremely stylish in production and exquisitely filmed in highly contrasted black-and-white cinematography, the film has the feel of an Eisenstein epic, an effect which is enhanced by the poor sound quality — apparently, when found, the negatives were in excellent condition, but the soundtrack was not. Welles himself stars as the Moor of Venice who ill-advisedly allows his evil sidekick, Iago (MacLiammor), to convince him that his newlywed wife, Desdemona (Cloutier), is unfaithful. Tragic in every detail, Welles portrays the deceived lover with bravado. ★★★½ DVD: $24.99

Othello

(1995, 124 min, GB, Oliver Parker) *Kenneth Branagh, Laurence Fishburne, Iréne Jacob.* Parker's brooding, sexy adaptation of one of Shakespeare's most enduring works bares the distinction of being the first theatrical film version to use an African-American actor (Fishburne) in the role of the Moorish general. The story, of course, centers on Othello's manipulation by the power-hungry lieutenant Iago (Branagh), who makes Othello believe his new bride (Jacob) is guilty of infidelity and, ultimately, drives him to madness. This is an enthralling reworking which gives power to Shakespeare's written word and the emotions they harness. Fishburne givesba tense, emotional portrayal; Branagh, who obviously slid from the womb quoting the Bard, is mesmerizing as the evil Iago. The story centuries later resonates and has lost none of its universality. ★★★½ DVD: $19.99, VHS: $19.99

The Other

(1972, 100 min, US, Robert Mulligan) *Uta Hagen, Diana Muldaur, Chris Udvarnoky, Martin Udvarnoky.* A sleepy New England town in 1935 is the setting for this first-rate psychological thriller about two twin boys, one of whom is a murderer. Based on Thomas Tryon's best-seller. ★★★ VHS: $29.99

Laurence Fishburne (l.) and Kenneth Branagh in *Othello*

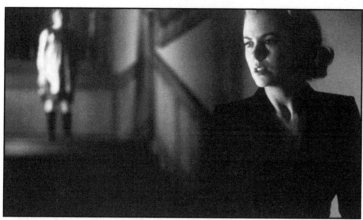

Nicole Kidman in *The Others*

Other People's Money

(1991, 115 min, US, Norman Jewison) *Danny DeVito, Gregory Peck, Penelope Ann Miller, Piper Laurie.* DeVito delights as Larry "The Liquidator" Garfield, a heartless, greed-driven corporate raider who is the centerpiece of this amusing adaptation of Jerry Sterner's off-Broadway hit. The latest subject of Larry's insatiable takeover fancies is the New England Wire & Cable Company, a small "mom & pop" factory run by a paternal Peck. Jewison's direction uses the showdown between small-time family capitalist and Wall Street power-broker to deliver a predictably Capra-esque message, but the film does have one surprisingly candid moment when DeVito delivers an impassioned speech to the stockholders of the little company. ★★½ VHS: $14.99

The Other Side of Midnight

(1977, 165 min, US, Charles Jarrott) *Marie-France Pisier, John Beck, Susan Sarandon, Raf Vallone.* Trashy melodrama based on Sidney Sheldon's novel. Set before, during and after WWII, the story centers on a steamy love affair between an American pilot and a married French actress, and the deadly revenge exacted on them by her husband. ★½ VHS: $59.99

The Other Sister

(1999, 129 min, US, Garry Marshall) *Juliette Lewis, Diane Keaton, Giovanni Ribisi, Tom Skerritt, Hector Elizondo, Juliet Mills.* There was *Gigot, Charly,* and Leonardo DiCaprio in *What's Eating Gilbert Grape* as some of screendom's best and worst mentally challenged characters. But nothing any of them did on-screen is enough to prepare for the sentimental outburst of bombast exhibited by this aren't-we-sensitive-and-funny-at-the-same-time comedy-drama. Lewis plays Carla, who comes home after years in a special school and ready to tackle the world. She enrolls in community college, and meets fellow spirit Danny (Ribisi). They fall in love, but must withstand interference and prejudice around them. Director Marshall is in overkill mode with this unsubtle story, and the screenplay offers little of the sensitivity it pretends to contain. ★½ DVD: $14.99, VHS: $9.99

The Others

(2001, 104 min, US/GB/Spain, Alejandro Amenábar) *Nicole Kidman, Fionnula Flanagan, Christopher Eccleston, Alakina Mann, James Bentley, Elaine Cassidy, Eric Sykes.* Creating atmosphere so thick you could cut it with a scream, Spanish director Amenábar travels the lonely, haunted hallways of *The Innocents* and *The Turn of the Screw* with this mannered though stylish, effective ghost story, his first English-language film. In the last days of WWII, Grace (Kidman), a war widow, lives on the isolated Isle of Jersey with her two children hoping against hope that her MIA husband will return home. The servants have left without word, creating positions for the newly arrived, mysterious trio of domestics seeking work. As it becomes apparent the servants have an unknown agenda, the children soon report sightings of a child from the other world. Kidman gives a controlled, passionate performance as the reserved Grace, attempting to find normality in surroundings bereft of it. Her composure (and its eventual loss) is in smart sync with director Amenábar's deliberate pacing, in which details are economically given. Mysteries soon give way to chills, which become overpowering until the turn of the last screw — an ingenious twist no one should see coming. ★★★½ DVD 2-disc set: $19.99, VHS Bonus Edition: $14.99

Our Daily Bread

(1934, 73 min, US, King Vidor) *Karen Morley, Tom George, John Qualen.* When no Hollywood studio would make this paean to communal living, Vidor risked his own money and made it himself. While as a socialist tract it's embarrassingly simplistic, to audiences suffering under the full wallop of the Depression it must have been as uplifting as a Berkeley musical number. An unemployed laborer and his wife are given a second chance when a rich uncle lets them squat on a bankrupt farm. They soon turn it into a cooperative, recruiting other victims of the crash. Vidor brings all his dramatist skills to the meager plot, setting off his striking visuals with a dynamic montage style right out of Eisenstein. ★★★½ DVD: $29.99

Our Hospitality & Sherlock Jr.

(1923, 119 min, US, Buster Keaton, John Blystone, Keaton) *Buster Keaton.* A collection of two Keaton comedies. In *Sherlock, Jr.* (1924, 44 min), Keaton is less concerned with physical schtick and slapstick (though there is certainly enough to go around) and concentrates more on the possibilities of the medium of film. He plays a projectionist and amateur sleuth whose daydreaming puts him in the film he is projecting. There's a brilliant sequence in which Keaton is trapped on-screen as the film changes from one scene to another. And even better is the finale in which he rides driverless on the handlebars of a motorcycle through crowded streets and open countryside. (★★★★) *Our Hospitality* (1923, 75 min) is the winning story of Keaton returning to his Southern hometown and becoming involved in an on-going family feud. The story is more complex than most, there's an abundance of wonderful sight gags, and Keaton's stunts atop a waterfall are awe-inspiring. (★★★½) DVD: $29.99, VHS: $29.99

Our Lady of the Assassins

(2001, 98 min, Colombia, Barbet Schroeder) *German Jaramillo, Anderson Ballesteros, Juan David Restrepo, Manuel Busquets.* A raw, unapologetic account of a writer returning to his Colombian hometown to die, *Our Lady of the Assassins* is an unpleasant story that is told with haunting imagery and unnerving immediacy. Poverty-stricken and drug-infested Medellin may be the murder capital of the world, or at least it appears that way from the amount of violence gripping the city (a sign requesting "Do Not Dump Corpses Here" underlines this). Having left the city 30 years earlier, Fernando — now a celebrated writer and in his 50s — returns. Sullen and ready to die, Fernando meets Alexis, a young male hustler and begins an affair with the handsome youth, who teaches him life is cheap in this violent society. As a result of being shot in high-definition video, the film has a gritty look befitting this hellish environment, but the heavy-handed love story meanders between pretension and insight. (Spanish with English subtitles) ★★½ DVD Widescreen: $29.99, VHS: $14.99

Our Man Flint

(1965, 108 min, US, Daniel Mann) *James Coburn, Lee J. Cobb, Gila Golan.* A smugly charming Coburn karate-chops his way to an island paradise, to save the world from climate-controlling evil scientists. *Flint* seems less goofy in retrospect, given Roger Moore's sillier Bond films, but it's still fun, especially when viewed as the kitschy American answer to 007. (Sequel: *In Like Flint*) ★★½ DVD Letterbox: $14.99, VHS: $9.99

Our Miss Fred

(1975, 96 min, GB, Bob Kellett) *Danny LaRue.* This guilty, campy pleasure stars female impersonator LaRue as a soldier who, during WWII, is caught in drag just when the Germans invade France. The admittedly ridiculous story follows his inventive attempts to get through Nazi-infested lands (under the *nom de guerre* of Frederika) without the Germans catching on to his identity — sort of a slapstick/drag version of *Europa, Europa*. Our heroine traipses through the countryside dazzling the enemy (and even a few horny Frenchmen) with her fabulously outrageous frocks, wigs and sharp-tongued wit. (aka: *Operation Fred*) ★★★

Our Sons

(1991, 100 min, US, John Erman) *Julie Andrews, Ann-Margret, Hugh Grant, Zeljko Ivanek.* From the director of *An Early Frost* comes this moving made-for-TV AIDS drama. Andrews and Ann-Margret star as the respective mothers of gay lovers Grant and Ivanek. Andrews is a wealthy businesswoman who remained close to her son after he came out, while A-M, a barmaid from Arkansas, refuses to accept her son's sexuality and rejects him. When Ivanek becomes sick, Andrews is persuaded by her son to meet his lover's mother and try to get the two to reunite. A serious, straightforward story which, while suffering a bit from a talking heads-style of filmmaking, remains compelling and compassionate. ★★★

Our Town

(1940, 90 min, US, Sam Wood) *William Holden, Martha Scott.* One of the greats of 20th-century American theatre makes for an equally majestic on-screen experience as director Wood creates a stunning look at small-time American life, based on Thornton Wilder's Pulitzer Prize-winning play. Holden and Scott (in a remarkable debut reprising her stage role) are the young neighbors who marry, the story following their joys and tragedies over a 12-year period. ★★★ DVD: $14.99

Our Vines Have Tender Grapes

(1945, 105 min, US, Roy Rowland) *Edward G. Robinson, Agnes Moorehead, Margaret O'Brien.* This earnest, folksy drama does not hold up quite as well as other similarly themed films — *Our Town* or *The Human Comedy* for instance — which bestow blessings upon the virtues of American small-town life. Robinson plays a kindly Norwegian farmer living with wife Moorehead and daughter O'Brien. Though not much really happens, the story follows one year in the lives of the family, mostly centering on seven-year-old O'Brien (whose cheerfulness would put Pollyanna to shame). Adapted by soon-to-be blacklisted writer Dalton Trumbo, who paints Americana with broad, sentimental strokes. ★★½

Out Cold

(1989, 92 min, US, Malcolm Mowbray) *Teri Garr, John Lithgow, Randy Quaid.* This delightfully sick comedy stars Garr as a slightly demented housewife who, after finding out that husband Ernie is cheating on her, locks him in his butcher shop's freezer. Her frenzied attempts to get rid of her frozen hubbie entangles Lithgow, the nerdish partner of Ernie as well as a bungling private eye (Quaid). ★★★

Out of Africa

(1985, 160 min, US, Sydney Pollack) *Meryl Streep, Robert Redford, Klaus Maria Brandauer, Michael Kitchen, Graham Crowden, Iman, Donal McCann.* Gorgeous cinematography by David Watkin, a tremendous performance by Streep, a moving score by John Barry, and subtle direction by Pollack make this film worthy of its several Academy Awards. Based on the life and works of Isak Dinesen, it's the story of a Danish woman, Karen Blixen (Streep), who moves to Nairobi with her aristocratic husband. There, she falls in love with Africa and with a handsome British explorer (Redford thankfully minus the accent). A beautiful film. ★★★★ DVD Letterbox Collector's Edition: $14.99, VHS: $9.99

Out of Bounds

(1986, 93 min, US, Richard Tuggle) *Anthony Michael Hall, Jenny Wright.* Inept thriller with Hall as an Iowa farmboy who unwittingly becomes involved with drug pushers on his first visit to Los Angeles. ★

Out of Order

(1985, 90 min, Netherlands, Carl Schenkel) *Renée Soutendijk.* When two films about killer elevators (the other being *The Lift*) are released from the same country in the same year, it would be prudent to avoid entering tall buildings while visiting that land. Anyway, this intense thriller is miles ahead in terror than *The Lift*. The story is set in a deserted office building where four people discover, to their horror, that the lift is *out of order*. ★★★

Out of Sight

(1998, 120 min, US, Steven Soderbergh) *George Clooney, Jennifer Lopez, Ving Rhames, Don Cheadle, Albert Brooks, Luis Guzman, Steve Zahn, Dennis Farina, Catherine Keener, Isaiah Washington, Nancy Allen.* Clooney is quite charismatic playing a convicted bank robber who escapes from prison only to collide with a tough, sexy Marshal (Lopez). Sparks fly, temperatures rise and before they both know it, they're disregarding priorities and duty respectively, only to pursue their improbable mutual attraction. The plot unfolds in hectic flash-back-and-forth fashion and shifts from Miami to Detroit to two different prisons, but director Soderbergh manages a minor coup by keeping the plot streamlined and cohesive, and giving the film a visual panache. Soderbergh knows how to create and maintain suspense and allow a running joke to build momentum before perfectly timing its pay-off. *Out of Sight* is sure-fire, lightning-fast excitement, and it'll keep you guessing right up till its great ending. Based on Elmore Leonard's novel. ★★★★ DVD Letterbox Collector's Edition: $14.99, VHS: $9.99, VHS Letterbox: $14.99

Out of the Blue

(1947, 86 min, US, Leigh Jason) *George Brent, Ann Dvorak.* Enjoyable screwball comedy with Brent as a hen-pecked husband who has some explaining to do when wacky Dvorak is found unconscious in his apartment. ★★½

Out of the Blue

(1980, 93 min, US, Dennis Hopper) *Linda Manz, Dennis Hopper, Sharon Farrell.* Before Hopper burst back onto the Hollywood scene, he made this gritty and extraordinarily low-budget feature about a nihilistic, punked-out teenager. With an alcoholic truck driver (Hopper) for a dad and a junkie mom (Farrell), the young girl (Manz) gets all of her life experience in seedy roadhouses and various watering holes. Excellent performances make this a harrowing experience of the emptiness of life on the edge. ★★★½ VHS: $14.99

Out of the Past

(1947, 97 min, US, Jacques Tourneur) *Robert Mitchum, Kirk Douglas, Jane Greer.* Mitchum is memorable as a retired private eye, living as a gas station owner, who is lured back to his old job by gangster Douglas (wonderfully greasy) to find his dame who ran off with his heart as well as his money. Our fated hero's sleuthing leads him to Mexico where he not only finds his prey (Greer, cunningly seductive as the femme fatale), but falls in love with her as well. A riveting drama of double dealings, *amour mort* and pervasive corruption. A '40s film noir classic. (Remade in 1984 as *Against All Odds*.) ★★★½ DVD: $19.99

Out of Time

(2003, 105 min, US, Carl Franklin) *Denzel Washington, Eva Mendes, Sanaa Lathan, Dean Cain. Devil in a Blue Dress* director Franklin and star Washington reunite for this slight but thoroughly entertaining noir. Denzel is quite good as Matt Whitlock, a Florida small-town police chief who swipes some drug money being held as evidence to help a dying friend. When she dies in a suspicious fire, Matt becomes the number one suspect. Of course, things spiral out of control, and the last hour of the film is pure suspense as Whitlock attempts to elude both the feds and his soon-to-be ex-wife Alex (Mendes), who's investigating the arson case, while trying to figure out exactly what's going on. Scaled-back with only a few action scenes and twists, *Out of Time* is nevertheless a lean thriller that's never less

The Out-of-Towners (1970)

than involving and will keep you on the edge of your seat for most of its running time. ★★★ DVD Letterbox Special Edition: $14.99

The Out-of-Towners

(1970, 97 min, US, Arthur Hiller) *Jack Lemmon, Sandy Dennis, Anne Meara.* The laughs are plentiful (and very close to home) in this Neil Simon romp with Lemmon and Dennis as the title couple, an Ohio exec and his wife visiting New York City, where they encounter one disaster after another. (Remade in 1999) ★★★ DVD: $19.99, VHS: $14.99

The Out-of-Towners

(1999, 91 min, US, Sam Weisman) *Steve Martin, Goldie Hawn, John Cleese, Mark McKinney.* This lackluster remake, even with Martin and Hawn taking over for Jack Lemmon and Sandy Dennis, can't overcome impotent direction and a lifeless, brand new updated script. The story is basically the same. Martin heads to NYC for a job interview accompanied by wife Hawn. They lose luggage, miss planes and trains, get mugged (the "identity" of the culprit is kinda funny), go hungry, get arrested — all the fun things that happen to tourists in New York. But the film lacks an inspired comic energy. Cleese saves the day with a funny bit as a snooty hotel manager. ★★ DVD: $19.99, VHS: $14.99

Out on a Limb

(1992, 82 min, US, Francis Veber) *Jeffrey Jones, Matthew Broderick, John C. Reilly.* An awful screwball comedy from the director of *Three Fugitives.* Broderick is miscast as a hotshot Manhattan stockbroker who pays a visit to his hometown en route to complete a multimillion dollar deal and runs afoul of the murderous activities of his stepfather. Director Veber's interesting use of narration and flashback adds nothing to the mundane plot. ★

Out to Sea

(1997, 107 min, US, Martha Coolidge) *Jack Lemmon, Walter Matthau, Dyan Cannon, Brent Spiner, Gloria De Haven, Hal Linden, Donald O'Connor, Elaine Stritch.* As close to a big-screen version of "The Love Boat" as one is likely to see, *Out to Sea* takes the considerable talents of those two comic treasures, Lemmon and Matthau, and stretches their comic resolve with this amiable, lightweight comedy. Matthau plays a con artist who convinces brother-in-law and widower Lemmon to join him on a holiday cruise. What Lemmon doesn't know is that they're both signed on as dance hosts, and Matthau — who's looking for a rich widow — can't dance a step. There are a few laughs, though Lemmon and Matthau's seasoned timing and a bright supporting cast gloss over the rough spots. ★★ DVD: $14.99

Outbreak

(1995, 127 min, US, Wolfgang Petersen) *Dustin Hoffman, Rene Russo, Morgan Freeman, Donald Sutherland, Cuba Gooding, Jr., Kevin Spacey, Patrick Dempsey, J.T. Walsh.* Hoffman stars in this exciting topical thriller as a cantankerous Army doctor who, along with his ex-wife (Russo), a newly appointed bigwig at the CDC, races against time (and a top-level military conspiracy) to stop the spread of a highly infectious mutant virus that kills within 24 hours of contact. While short on characterization and guilty of eventually deteriorating into a standard "good guys vs. bad guys" actioner, the film displays director Petersen's knack for mixing tension, claustrophobia and doom. As such, it's quite successful in its gruesome depiction of the ultimate end-of-the-world scenario. ★★★ DVD: $14.99, VHS: $9.99

Outcasts

(1986, 102 min, Taiwan, Yu Kan Ping) After being caught having sex with another student, young Ah Ching is both expelled from school and beaten out of his home by his father. Befriended by a middle-aged photographer as well as by other young gays, Ah rebuilds his life with the help of his new surrogate family and begins to explore his own sexuality. The first film from Taiwan with a gay theme, *Outcasts* is, at times, unintentionally funny in its heavy-handed melodramatic excesses, but is nonetheless a powerful and sensual look at youth finding a place in an uncaring and insensitive world. (Mandarin with English subtitles) ★★★ VHS: $49.99

Outland

(1981, 109 min, US, Peter Hyams) *Sean Connery, Peter Boyle, Frances Sternhagen, James B. Sikking.* Connery gives one of his best performances in this taut sci-fi thriller as a lone cop determined to smash a drug ring on Io, the ninth moon of Jupiter. Boyle is the slimy, corrupt executive who wants to buy his badge. Director Hyams presents an isolated world where law is practically extinct and capitalism reigns supreme. This underrated jewel was affectionately dubbed "*High Noon*" in Space" by critics upon its theatrical release. ★★★ DVD: $14.99, VHS: $9.99

The Outlaw

(1943, 117 min, US, Howard Hawks) *Jane Russell, Walter Huston, Thomas Mitchell, Jack Buetel.* Russell made a notorious film debut (though the film was shot in 1941) in this legendary (and at the time scandalous) western adventure about Billy the Kid and his girlfriend. Though most of the attention over the years has been focused on Russell's ample bosom, not to be overlooked is Huston's showy turn as Billy. ★★★ VHS: $19.99

The Outlaw and His Wife

(1918, 73 min, Sweden, Victor Sjostrom) *Victor Sjostrom, Edith Erastoff.* Sjostrom directed and stars in this superbly acted and visually stunning drama which gave Sweden its breakthrough after WWI. The setting is Iceland in the 19th century where a farmer and his wife are being hunted by the police for a petty crime. Fleeing to the mountains and fjord hills to escape detection, they soon succumb to the brutal forces of nature. Color tinted, this video version features a full orchestral score and was beautifully restored in 1986 by the Swedish Film Institute. ★★★½ VHS: $24.99

The Outlaw Josey Wales

(1976, 135 min, US, Clint Eastwood) *Clint Eastwood, Chief Dan George, Sondra Locke.*

Exciting post-Civil War adventure about a Confederate renegade (Eastwood) on a trail of vengeance against the Union soldiers who murdered his wife and son. ★★★½ DVD: $19.99, VHS: $14.99, VHS Letterbox: $14.99

Outrage

(1994, 108 min, Spain, Carlos Saura) *Francesca Neri, Antonio Banderas.* Don't believe the hype — this is not some sex-drenched, exotic shoot-'em-up which could be misinterpreted, but a thoughtful, moderately paced examination of a young woman's reaction to a brutal violation. Neri is compelling as a circus sharpshooter, the victim of three young thugs whose advances she rejects. Banderas delivers an effective, subdued performance as a reporter captivated by the vivacious woman. In physical and emotional shock from the severity of the attack on her, she turns instinctively to a familiar weapon, near at hand, to execute her act of vengeance. Certainly not a great film, but compassionate in its depiction of one woman's response to an act of carnage that shatters her life. (Spanish with English subtitles) ★★½ DVD: $9.99, VHS: $14.99

Outrageous Fortune

(1987, 92 min, US, Arthur Hiller) *Bette Midler, Shelley Long, Peter Coyote, George Carlin.* One of the most hilarious films of the 1980s, *Outrageous Fortune* finds its success in the ingenious pairing of pretty, prim and proper bitch Long with flamboyant, aggressive floozy Midler (and, as with Olivier's *Hamlet*, a role the Divine Miss M was born to play). The fireworks given off by these two are priceless. The truly outrageous plot finds the female odd couple searching for a "missing" boyfriend; they become involved with the CIA, Russian agents, biochemical warfare, and Indian guide Carlin. ★★★½ DVD: $14.99, VHS: $9.99

Outrageous!

(1977, 97 min, Canada, Richard Benner) *Craig Russell, Hollis McLaren, Richard Easley, Helen Shaver.* One of the earliest North American gay-themed films to receive theatrical distribution, *Outrageous!* is a funny and affecting film about a female impersonator and his touching friendship with a schizophrenic girl. Russell plays a gay hairdresser and star-wannabe who does flawless impressions of Barbra Streisand, Judy Garland, Bette Midler, Mae West and others. And while the musical segments are fun, the film best succeeds in his friendship with Liza (McLaren), a troubled young woman who checks herself out of a mental hospital but who becomes frightened and confused when her family and doctors want her to return to the institution. A tender story of ambitions, eccentricity and the courage of being oneself. (Sequel: *Too Outrageous!*) ★★★½ VHS: $29.99

The Outside Chance of Maximilian Glick

(1989, 95 min, Canada, Allan A. Goldstein) *Noam Zylberman, Jan Rubes, Saul Rubinek.* This low-budget Canadian film set in 1960 is a charming coming-of-age comedy which plays as sort of a "Jewish Wonder Years." Making an impressive film debut, Zylberman stars as a 13-year-old boy who is readying for his bar mitzvah. The film follows the days before, when Max experiences first love with a pretty gentile girl; befriends the new, unorthodox, Orthodox rabbi; and for the first time rebels against his family. Rubinek is a total delight as the new rabbi whose candor and sense of humor turns an entire town on its ear. ★★★

The Outside Man

(1973, 104 min, US, Jacques Deray) *Roy Scheider, Ann-Margret, Angie Dickinson, Jean-Louis Trintignant.* It's killer vs. killer in this dated actioner about a sad-eyed assassin (Trintignant) who finds himself at the wrong end of a gun when his latest employer (Dickinson) embraces the philosophy that "dead men tell no tales." Scheider gives another surefire performance as the hit man whose credo is "there's no honor among thieves," and Ann-Margret is on target as the helpful floosie whose philosophy is "leave it to cleavage." ★★½

Outside Ozona

(1998, 99 min, US, J.S. Cardone) *Robert Forster, Kevin Pollak, Sherilyn Fenn, David Paymer, Penelope Ann Miller, Swoosie Kurtz, Taj Mahal, Meat Loaf, Lucy Webb, Beth Ann Styne.* All roads lead to Ozona in this occasionally though retread psychodrama about a various group of people whose lives become intertwined at day's end while traveling on the dusty roads of Texas. Forster is great as a truck driver recovering from the death of his wife. He befriends Native American Webb and her dying grandmother for the film's strongest plot line. The weakest is bickering sisters Fenn and Styne traveling to their father's funeral. Somewhere in there is angst-ridden clown Pollak and his stripper wife Miller; D.J. Mahal and his nervous boss Meat Loaf; and an unknown serial killer. The high-profile cast performs admirably, but the film tends to drag in places; its pacing uneven and the screenplay hit and miss. ★★

Outside Providence

(1999, 96 min, US, Michael Corrente) *Shawn Hatosy, Amy Smart, Alec Baldwin, George Wendt, Jon Abrahams.* With a screenplay cowritten by Peter and Bobby Farrelly and based on Peter's novel, this alternately poignant and comic coming-of-age tale doesn't share much in common comedically with their gross-out comedies. But not to worry — this is a smart, funny, touching even mature work. Hatosy is very appealing as Tim, the oldest son from a working-class family in a small Rhode Island town. Being raised by his widowed, gruff father (Baldwin who is especially good), Tim is sent to prep school after a run-in with the police. It is there the young man discovers first love and his inner voice against the pot-smoking haze of the early '70s. Director Corrente nicely balances comedy and poignancy in telling Tim's story of youthful shenanigans and eventual growing up. ★★★ DVD: $19.99, VHS: $9.99

The Outsiders

(1983, 91 min, US, Francis Ford Coppola) *Matt Dillon, Patrick Swayze, Emilio Estevez, Tom Cruise, C. Thomas Howell, Ralph Macchio, Rob Lowe, Diane Lane, Leif Garrett.* S.E. Hinton's best-selling teen novel about kids from the wrong side of the tracks in the early 1960s is transformed into a stylish if familiar coming-of-age tale by director Coppola. The cast is interesting to watch — it includes several well-knowns before they hit it big. ★★½ DVD: $14.99

Over the Brooklyn Bridge

(1983, 108 min, US, Menahem Golan) *Elliott Gould, Sid Caesar, Margaux Hemingway, Carol Kane, Shelley Winters, Burt Young.* A Brooklyn luncheonette owner (Gould) needs to borrow money to open a posh Manhattan eatery. His uncle (Caesar) is willing to loan him the cash — if he drops his current Christian girl (Hemingway) and settles down with a nice Jewish girl (Kane). Unmemorable and not all that funny, either. ★½

Over the Edge

(1979, 95 min, US, Jonathan Kaplan) *Matt Dillon, Michael Kramer, Pamela Ludwig, Vincent Spano.* Aimless violence is the result of the frustration and alienation of suburban youths in director Kaplan's dynamic youth-in-revolt film. The hard-rock soundtrack with Cheap Trick, The Ramones and Jimi Hendrix heightens the tension in this powerful sleeper. ★★★

Overboard

(1987, 112 min, US, Garry Marshall) *Goldie Hawn, Kurt Russell, Roddy McDowall, Katherine Helmond, Edward Herrmann.* Pleasant Hawn comedy with Goldie as an obnoxious society woman who gets amnesia and is convinced by workman Russell that she is his wife and the mother of his three wild children. One of Goldie's better comedies with a fair share of laughs. ★★★ DVD: $14.99, VHS: $9.99

The Overcoat (Shinel)

(1959, 73 min, USSR, Aleksei Batalov) *Rolan Bykov.* This faithful adaptation of Nikolai Gogol's tragicomic story follows a beleaguered clerk, whose dreams of a glorious new coat are not only realized, but change his destiny. The setting is 19th-century czarist St. Petersberg in this simple yet moving story. (Russian with English subtitles) ★★★½ VHS: $59.99

Overindulgence

(1987, 95 min, GB, Ross Devenish) This retelling of the scandalous murder trial of a wealthy British expatriate in 1941 colonial East Africa has its moments, but it can't compare to *White Mischief*, which is based on the same incident. ★★

The Owl and the Pussycat

(1970, 95 min, US, Herbert Ross) *Barbra Streisand, Robert Klein, Allen Garfield, George Segal.* Streisand and Segal are terrific together in this raucous and very funny screen version of Bill Manoff's Broadway play. Streisand, in sensational form, plays a hooker who is kicked out of her apartment after complaints made by neighboring writer Segal; so she moves in with him. ★★★½ DVD: $19.99

Owning Mahowny

(2003, 107 min, US, Richard Kwietniowski) *Philip Seymour Hoffman, Minnie Driver, Maury Chaykin, John Hurt.* Hoffman shines in this true tale about the fall of Dan Mahowny, a Toronto bank manager who taps company coffers to feed a gambling addiction. His savvy of the system is absent on visits to Atlantic City, where a persistence for beating the odds leaves him sleepless and ever deeper in the red. Wife Belinda (Driver) offers dubious support of her husband, as further signs of his vice come to light. We share Mahowny's pallor as mammoth sums are frittered away. Soon revealed is the quiet torment of a man capable of little judgment and even fewer emotions. The film is well-nuanced with the gaming industry's phony hospitality — even the casino manager can manage to personally hand Mahowny his cold spare ribs and coke to go, wishing him farewell after losing 9 million. But all of this dour weight yields little clues toward what is behind Mahoney's compulsions, as the film hits a slow stride. However, the pathetic complexity of Hoffman's portrayal compensates for the story's uneven patches. ★★½ DVD: $24.99

The Ox

(1992, 91 min, Sweden, Sven Nykvist) *Stellan Skarsgård, Ewa Froling, Max von Sydow.* Ingmar Bergman's longtime cinematographer Nykvist made his directorial debut with this grim parable about the day-to-day struggles for life in 1860s famine-stricken Sweden. The film's opening scene introduces Helge (Skarsgård), a destitute tenant farmer who, in a fit of desperation over his family's poverty, brutally bludgeons one of his landlord's two remaining oxen, quickly butchering the animal and hiding the evidence. Of course, Helge and his wife Elfrida (Froling, looking remarkably like a young Liv Ullmann) go on to suffer the guilt that their devious act, coupled with the austere piety of Nordic Christianity, must inevitably bring to bear. Based on a true incident, the film is yet another example of the life-is-so-grim-above-the-Arctic-Circle school of Swedish filmmaking which here is mildly unengaging. Von Sydow brings a small breath of life to the film as the town's humanistic vicar. (Swedish with English subtitles) ★★

The Ox-Bow Incident

(1943, 75 min, US, William Wellman) *Henry Fonda, Henry Morgan, Anthony Quinn, Dana Andrews.* A classic western morality play. Fonda and Morgan ride into town just in time to experience the formation of a lynch mob. The scene in which they question the "rustlers" who are one wrong answer from a hangman's noose is suitably tense. ★★★★ DVD: $14.99, VHS: $9.99

Oxford Blues

(1984, 97 min, US, Robert Boris) *Rob Lowe, Ally Sheedy, Amanda Pays, Julian Sands, Cary Elwes.* Updated, sloppy version of the 1938 hit *A Yank at Oxford*, with Lowe (in the Robert Taylor role) as an American rower enrolled at Oxford and in love with Pays. ★½

P.S. Your Cat Is Dead!

(2002, 88 min, US, Steve Guttenberg) *Steve Guttenberg, Lombardo Boyar, Cynthia Watros, A.J. Benza, Shirley Knight.* An often engaging character piece based on James Kirkwood's cult novel, *P.S. Your Cat Is Dead!* marks actor Guttenberg's director-ial debut. In this sweet-and-sour comedy, Guttenberg plays Jimmy Zoole, who is having one bad day. It's New Year's Eve, and his girlfriend has left him, he's lost his job, and he's just come home to find a burglar in his apartment. Nearing the emotional breaking point, he finds an outlet when he ties the luckless intruder to the kitchen counter. What ensues is a New Year's celebration unlike any other as an unlikely relationship develops between Jimmy and the gay thief. Despite some uneven pacing and not being as edgy as it could have been, the film is compelling throughout, and the two lead characters always keep our interest. ★★★ DVD: $29.99, VHS: $39.99

Pacific Heights

(1990, 102 min, US, John Schlesinger) *Michael Keaton, Matthew Modine, Melanie Griffith, Mako, Nobu McCarthy, Laurie Matcalf.* A "yupwardly mobile" couple (Modine, Griffith) renovate a large Victorian home in an upscale San Francisco neighborhood. Enter Keaton as sociopath Carter Hayes, a tenant from hell who seems to know that a lodger can do just about anything to his landlords and not be evicted — including nonpayment of rent and cockroach breeding. An infuriating blend of "who says life is fair anyway" legal procedures and sweaty-palm psychological warfare, and the film really doesn't work on either level. ★★ DVD: $14.99, VHS: $9.99

The Package

(1989, 108 min, US, Andrew Davis) *Gene Hackman, Tommy Lee Jones, Joanna Cassidy, Dennis Franz, Pam Grier.* This taut political thriller stars the ideally cast Hackman as an Army Security specialist stationed in Germany who is assigned to escort a wayward soldier (Jones) back to the United States for a court-martial. This apparently routine mission comes unglued when his "package" gives him the slip. As Hackman sets out on the trail of his charge, he is framed and becomes the subject of a murder investigation forcing the on-the-lam officer to hunt down Jones himself. Cassidy is tops as Hackman's estranged wife who winds up joining him in his adventure. ★★★ DVD: $14.99, VHS: $9.99

Padre Nuestro

(1986, 90 min, Spain, Francisco Rabal) *Fernando Rey, Victoria Abril.* Rey stars as a powerful Vatican Cardinal who, upon learning he has only one year to live, returns to the village of his youth in order to set-

Preston Sturges (c.) leads his cast of *The Palm Beach Story*

tle the errors of his mischievous childhood. Thus is set in motion a series of richly comic confrontations with the people of his past: his sexually repressed brother, his domineering mother, the peasant woman who 30 years earlier bore his illegitimate child, and his prostitute daughter, "La Cardenala," portrayed with unabashed sensual zeal by Abril. Director Rabal has painted a colorful portrait of Spanish society that exposes the country's struggles with the demands of the church, the flesh and the aristocracy. (Spanish with English subtitles) ★★★

Padre Padrone

(1977, 117 min, Italy, Paolo Taviani & Vittorio) *Omero Antonutti, Marcella Michalangeli.* The moving struggles of an illiterate shepherd who overcomes hardships to become a successful scholar are wonderfully recounted in this Taviani brothers classic. Autobiographical in nature, the story revolves around the relationship of a young man who has a yearning for knowledge and the brutalizations inflicted on him by his tyrannical father who fears both education and civilization. (Italian with English subtitles) ★★★½ DVD: $19.99, VHS: $9.99

The Pagemaster

(1994, 85 min, US, Joe Johnston & Maurice Hunt) *Macaulay Culkin, Christopher Lloyd, Whoopi Goldberg, Patrick Stewart, Leonard Nimoy.* An able cast, respectable animation and an enjoyable story line all work together to create a pleasant children's tale which mixes live-action and animation. Culkin stars as an overly timid boy who, after getting caught in a rainstorm, takes shelter in a library. There he is transformed into a cartoon character thereupon meeting The Pagemaster (Lloyd). His mission: to find his way out of the library and through the plots of several well-known novels with the help of some engaging, talking books. ★★★ DVD: $19.99, VHS: $9.99

A Pain in the A—

(1974, 90 min, France/Italy, Edouard Molinaro) *Jacques Brel, Caroline Cellier.* A hilarious story of a hired killer who crosses paths with a suicidal shirt salesman. An odd friendship ensues as the contract killer attempts to protect the hapless salesman from his attempts at self-destruction. Music by Brel. (American remake: *Buddy Buddy*) (French with English subtitles) ★★★ VHS: $29.99

Paint It Black

(1989, 101 min, US, Tim Hunter) *Rick Rossovich, Sally Kirkland, Martin Landau, Julie Carmen, Doug Savant.* A hunky sculptor (Rossovich) is "discovered" by a sexy gallery owner (Kirkland) who has more on her mind than art. However, obsession soon escalates into a web of intrigue and murder. A rather effective thriller buoyed by a good performance by Kirkland and a nicely written screenplay. ★★★ VHS: $79.99

The Paint Job

(1992, 90 min, US, Michael Taav) *Bebe Neuwirth, Will Patton, Robert Pastorelli.* Patton is Wesley, a lonely man who falls in love with his neighbor's wife (Neuwirth). The problem is she's married to his boss and best friend Willy (Pastorelli). The dark past of one of these central characters mixes with primal urges, leading to deadly consequences boiling to a violent climax. An average psychological thriller which offers a couple of jolts and an unexpected plot twist. ★★½

Paint Your Wagon

(1969, 166 min, US, Joshua Logan) *Lee Marvin, Clint Eastwood, Jean Seberg, Harve Presnell.* Marvin and Eastwood (two unlikely musical stars but certainly at home with the western) play a pair of California gold prospectors in the Old West, both involved with Seberg and looking for a fortune. Presnell gets the plaudits for his singing (including the standard "They Call the Wind Maria") in this sturdy adaptation of the Broadway musical. ★★★ DVD: $14.99, VHS: $19.99

Paisan

(1946, 90 min, Italy, Roberto Rossellini) *Maria Michi, Carmela Sazio.* Written by Rossellini and Federico Fellini, this gritty, neorealist classic is set up in six vignettes, all dealing with the relationship between the Americans and Italians during the liberation of Italy in WWII. Rossellini used mostly nonprofessional actors for the roles and he presents the stories in a style reminiscent of a wartime documentary. (Italian with English subtitles) ★★★★ VHS: $24.99

The Pajama Game

(1957, 101 min, US, George Abbott & Stanley Donen) *Doris Day, John Raitt, Eddie Foy, Jr., Carol Haney, Rita Shaw.* Snappy choreography from Bob Fosse is only one of the highlights of this effervescent musical starring Day, whose love-hate relationship with Raitt is mirrored by labor unrest between the workers and managers of a pajama factory. Songs include Haney's knockout "Steam Heat," and the standards "Hernando's Hideaway" and "Hey, There." One of the better stage-to-screen adaptations of a Broadway musical. ★★★½ DVD: $19.99, VHS: $14.99

Pal Joey

(1957, 109 min, US, George Sidney) *Frank Sinatra, Rita Hayworth, Kim Novak.* Lively film version of the Rodgers and Hart musical with Sinatra as a cabaret entertainer involved with socialite Hayworth and dancer Novak. Songs include "The Lady is a Tramp" and "Bewitched, Bothered and Bewildered." ★★★ DVD: $19.99, VHS: $19.99

Pale Rider

(1985, 116 min, US, Clint Eastwood) *Clint Eastwood, Michael Moriarty, Carrie Snodgress, Sydney Penny, Richard Dysart, Christopher Penn.* Eastwood wears two hats as director and actor in this first-rate western adventure, Eastwood's homage to *Shane.* Clint stars as the mysterious stranger who comes to the aid of a gold prospecting community being harassed by an unscrupulous land baron. A gorgeously photographed film. ★★★ DVD: $14.99

The Paleface

(1948, 91 min, US, Norman Z. McLeod) *Bob Hope, Jane Russell, Robert Armstrong.* The one-and-only Hope plays a cowardly dentist out West who becomes involved with sharpshooter Russell. Loaded with very funny gags. An even funnier sequel followed in 1952, *Son of Paleface.* ★★★ DVD Basic Edition: $14.99, DVD Double Feature: $14.99, VHS: $9.99

The Pallbearer

(1996, 97 min, US, Matt Reeves) *David Schwimmer, Gwyneth Paltrow, Barbara Hershey, Michael Rapaport, Toni Collette, Carol Kane.* Only intermittently funny with a suspect comic intuition, *The Pallbearer* will do little to repair the image of the Generation X'er as a slacker and a whiner. In

what could have been a "Friends" plot line, Schwimmer is invited to be a pallbearer — and then give the eulogy — for a former classmate he can't remember. He soon becomes romantically involved with the deceased man's grieving mother (Hershey) while at the same time trying to initiate a relationship with a younger woman (Paltrow). Besides the absence of much humor, the screenplay's handling of Hershey as the "older woman" is insensitive; and though sometimes personable, Schwimmer's act soon grows tiresome. ★★ DVD: $9.99, VHS: $9.99

The Palm Beach Story

(1942, 90 min, US, Preston Sturges) *Claudette Colbert, Joel McCrea, Mary Astor, Rudy Vallee, William Demarest, Franklin Pangborn.* Colbert decides that her beloved inventor husband McCrea would be better off without a wife to support; she skips down to Palm Beach to divorce him and find a millionaire husband who can finance his inventions. On the train . . . But before we get to the train, keep your eyes open during the opening credits, where more happens than during the entirety of some contemporary films. Of course, so much else happens that you may forget the beginning until the end, when everything is resolved. Or is it? A great cast contributes to this madness, written and directed by — who else? — Sturges. ★★★★

Favorite Line: "That's one of the tragedies of this life - that the men who are most in need of a beating up are always enormous." —*Rudy Vallee as John D. Hackensacker III*

Palmetto

(1998, 113 min, US, Volker Schlöndorff) *Woody Harrelson, Elisabeth Shue, Gina Gershon, Chloë Sevigny.* Heat rises from director Schlöndorff's steamy noir thriller. Harrelson plays a certified loser who becomes enmeshed in a loony kidnapping scheme that is out of control and over his head. Released after serving two years on a framed-up conviction, he heads back to Palmetto, the backwater site of his earlier misfortune. Then he meets Shue. Earthy and sensual and willing to forgive his attempt to lift her wad of cash, she offers him a job: to be a threatening phone voice, one element in a plan to extort big bucks from her husband by staging her co-conspirator stepdaughter's abduction. Complications ensue. Harrelson is a man with no anchor, and his precipitous descent into this ill-conceived quagmire is related with amusement and wry observation of the baser human foibles. ★★★ DVD: $19.99, VHS: $9.99

Palookaville

(1996, 92 min, US, Alan Taylor) *William Forsythe, Vincent Gallo, Adam Trese, Gareth Williams, Lisa Gay Hamilton, Frances McDormand.* Three losers try to better their financial situations by staging an armored car robbery in this adequate low-budget, independent comedy. A botched jewelry store heist and an abortive attempt to start a private cab company are only the latest in a string of failures for three friends. After saving the life of an armored car driver who suffers a heart attack on the road, they later get the idea to rob the same company in what passes for a master criminal plan. Almost annoyingly quirky, the film still has its merits. A hesitant romance between Forsythe's shlump and a down-on-her-luck clothing store clerk is the sweetest and most satisfying part of the film. ★★½ DVD Dual: $14.99

The Panama Deception

(1992, 91 min, US, Barbara Trent) This well-crafted, meticulously researched and tightly structured documentary is a clear and lucid presentation of a complex analysis of the U.S. invasion of Panama and the press coverage which was made available to the American people. On December 19, 1989, 20,000 U.S. troops launched a midnight attack. The official story of that incursion is juxtaposed with testimony from eyewitness Panamanian citizens, various analysts and the camera's evidence. U.S. media had no coverage of the thousands of civilians killed or the continued use of overwhelming deadly force after stated objectives were achieved. This is an important and fascinating eposé, and required viewing for anyone interested in an independent press and a responsible military. ★★★★ VHS: $29.99

Pandora's Box

(1928, 110 min, Germany, G.W. Pabst) *Louise Brooks, Fritz Kortner.* This expressionistic classic from Pabst features a luminous Brooks, with her haunting beauty, sexual mystique and trademark helmet of black bobbed hair, as the sexually insatiable Lulu, a prostitute who ensnares a series of men (and one woman) with her fetching beauty and beguiling indifference. Lulu's cavalier approach to love results in a self-destructive path — but not before she unwittingly destroys all who come close to her. (Silent) ★★★★ VHS: $24.99

Panic

(2000, 93 min, US, Henry Bromell) *William H. Macy, Neve Campbell, Tracey Ullman, Donald Sutherland, John Ritter.* This somewhat moody crime drama features Macy as Alex, a hit man with a heart of gold who considers getting out of the business, much to the consternation of his mentor and boss — his father (Sutherland). Despite his profession, he's a somewhat mild-mannered mid-lifer who seeks the help of a therapist (Ritter). In the waiting room he meets Sarah (Campbell), a free-spirited youngster that sets his middle-aged heart aflutter and sends his life into deeper turmoil. Director Bromell sets everything on edge and a slightly surreal *Stepford Wives* tone permeates, which at times feels just right and at others feels off. Sutherland gives another one of his grand, patronly performances as an overbearing dad who may have gone just one step too far with junior. ★★½ DVD: $24.99, VHS: $89.99

Panic Room

Panic in the Streets

(1950, 93 min, US, Elia Kazan) *Richard Widmark, Jack Palance, Barbara Bel Geddes, Paul Douglas, Zero Mostel.* When a corpse in New Orleans is found to be carrying the plague, a desperate search begins to track down its source. Widmark is terrific as a health official supervising the hunt, and Palance is memorable as an edgy psychopath who unwittingly holds the key to the mystery. A superb film noir thriller, directed in crisp, crackling fashion by Kazan. ★★★★

Panic in Year Zero

(1962, 95 min, US, Ray Milland) *Ray Milland, Jean Hagen, Frankie Avalon.* Milland is both director and star of this low-budget but surprisingly effective post-Apocalypse chiller. Milland, wife Hagen and family take a vacation in the mountains. While there, a nuclear bomb strikes the city, and as they attempt to return to civilization, they stumble upon a newly ravaged society. Milland is stiff upper-lipped as the heroic father, and his direction is equally rigid. But the film's premise, setting, cast of characters and cheesy cinematography and score all combine to make this a real panic. ★★★

Panic Room

(2002, 108 min, US, David Fincher) *Jodie Foster, Forest Whitaker, Kristen Stewart, Dwight Yoakam, Jared Leto.* In *Panic Room*, director Fincher's stylish, intense thriller, the terror of home intrusion and one family's fight for survival isn't as fully realized as it could have been, but what's on the screen will surely get the adrenaline racing. Foster plays a well-to-do, recently divorced mother who moves into a new Manhattan townhouse with her teenage daughter. What should be the start of a joyous new life quickly dissipates when a group of thieves — thinking the house is empty — break in to steal a fortune hidden in the "panic room," an enclosed room that is secure from the outside. It is also where mother and daughter find themselves trapped when that menacing visitors make themselves known. That two main characters spend most of the film locked in a room is more of a challenge and less a gimmick to writer David Koepp, and he maintains suspense but not at the cost of characterization. Director Fincher, given limited breathing room here, gives his camera a life of its own as he finds new and often ingenious ways to move from one room to another. ★★★ DVD Letterbox Superbit Edition: $14.99, DVD 3-disc Special Edition: $39.99, VHS: $14.99

Panique (Panic)

(1946, 82 min, France, Julien Duvivier) *Michel Simon, Viviane Romance.* From the novel by Georges Simenon, France's master of suspense, this clever study of mob psychology is set in the slums of Paris during the aftermath of WWII. Two lovers frame a stranger for a murder, but is the plan as perfect as they think? (French with English subtitles) ★★★½

Panther

(1995, 124 min, US, Mario Van Peebles) *Kadeem Hardison, Bokeem Woodbine, Courtney B. Vance, Marcus Chong, Chris Rock, James Russo, M. Emmet Walsh, Mario Van Peebles.* Denounced by real-life Panther Bobby Seale for its shameless inaccuracies, this clichéd melodrama not only manages to rewrite history, it also reduces a revolutionary group's actions to the level of a common street gang. Even the group's positive activities are handled as an afterthought. In spite of the terrific performances by Chong as Huey Newton and Vance as Bobby Seale, *Panther* only occasionally hits its mark as it unevenly presents its social and political thoughts. ★★

The Paper

(1994, 112 min, US, Ron Howard) *Michael Keaton, Robert Duvall, Glenn Close, Marisa Tomei, Randy Quaid, Jason Robards, Spalding Gray, Catherine O'Hara.* A solid ensemble cast helps bring to life this otherwise ordinary but involving newspaper comedy-drama. In this a-day-in-the-life-of-a-journalist, Keaton stars as the city editor of a New York daily tabloid who is caught in a dilemma when his managing editor (the wonderfully steely Close) wants to publish a story proclaiming two black youths guilty of murder when there's a chance they might be innocent. It becomes a battle of business vs. ethics when the two literally butt it out. Quaid has some funny scenes as a paranoid photographer who may not be that paranoid after all. ★★½ DVD: $14.99, VHS: $9.99

The Paper Chase

(1973, 111 min, US, James Bridges) *Timothy Bottoms, John Houseman, Lindsay Wagner, Edward Herrmann, James Naughton.* Exceptional study of academia with Bottoms as a Harvard Law student and Houseman (in his brilliant Oscar-winning performance) as his professor and adversary. ★★★½ DVD: $14.99

Paper Moon

(1973, 103 min, US, Peter Bogdanovich) *Ryan O'Neal, Tatum O'Neal, Madeline Kahn, P.J. Johnson, John Hillerman.* Bogdanovich's triumphant follow-up to *The Last Picture Show* and *What's Up Doc*, his other two classics, is, unfortunately, his last great work. One of the most charming comedies of the 1970s, Papa Ryan and Oscar winner Tatum star as Depression-era Bible-selling grifters working their way through the Midwest. Excellent support from Kahn, Johnson and Hillerman. ★★★★ DVD Letterbox: $14.99, VHS: $14.99, VHS Letterbox Director's Cut: $19.99

A Paper Wedding

(1991, 90 min, Canada, Michel Brault) *Geneviève Bujold, Manuel Aranguiz.* A Canuck *Green Card*, this predictable but nevertheless charming drama features a deceptively impassive performance by Bujold. She plays an unmarried university professor who, in order to help her immigration lawyer-sister, agrees to a marriage of convenience with a Chilean dissident who hopes to avoid deportation. The paper wedding becomes complicated, however, after immigration officials begin an investigation, forcing the unlikely couple to live together. Is love just around the bend? (French with English subtitles) ★★★ VHS: $79.99

Paperhouse

(1989, 92 min, GB, Bernard Rose) *Charotte Burke, Elliott Spiers, Glenne Headly, Ben Cross.* First-time director Rose has fashioned an engrossing, surreal and frightening psychological horror film about an 11-year-old girl whose vivid imagination propels her from the safety of her bedroom to an eerie world conjured up by her own subconscious fears. Confined to bed because of recurring fainting spells, Anna spends her time drawing and becomes especially interested in finishing her sketch of a lonely house. But when she is asleep, she is transported to this house to find a paralyzed young boy and an

Louise Brooks in *Pandora's Box*

unseen yet palpable evil. Vivid images, ominous landscapes and an ending to rattle even the most impassive viewer. ★★★

Papillon
(1973, 150 min, US, Franklin J. Schaffner) *Steve McQueen, Dustin Hoffman, Victor Jory, Anthony Zerbe.* McQueen gives what may be his best performance as the Devil's Island convict who is determined to escape, no matter what the cost. Easily one of the best "escape" films ever made. Hoffman gives magnificent support as a wise and easily contented prisoner. An intense and beautiful film. ★★★★ DVD Letterbox: $19.99, VHS Letterbox: $19.99

Parade
(1973, 88 min, France, Jacques Tati) *Jacques Tati.* Newly rediscovered and restored, Tati's final film was shot on video and was originally made for Swedish television. While not ranking with his best work, the film features many gloriously funny visual gags as Tati takes us through the many acts of a circus troupe who perform for an appreciative audience of two small children. This celebration of innocence and simple entertainment has clowns, magicians, acrobats and mimes who all take center stage for a time. A witty and humorously entertaining film with minimal dialogue and maximum enjoyment. ★★★ VHS: $19.99

The Paradine Case
(1948, 116 min, US, Alfred Hitchcock) *Gregory Peck, Ethel Barrymore, Charles Laughton, Ann Todd, Louis Jourdan, Charles Coburn, Leo G. Carroll.* Attorney Peck risks his marriage and profession when he falls in love with the enigmatic Mrs. Paradine, on trial for murdering her rich, blind husband. This talky but fascinating did-she-or-didn't-she also features Laughton as the delightfully lascivious judge. ★★★

Paradise
(1991, 115 min, US, Mary Agnes Donoghue) *Don Johnson, Melanie Griffith, Elijah Wood, Thora Birch.* A surprisingly effective remake of the French

hit *Le Grand Chemin*. Johnson and Griffith play a troubled rural couple who take care of a friend's young son for the summer. The shy, sheltered youth (well played by Wood) befriends a young tomboy (Birch), who helps the boy emerge from his shell. And, in turn, the youth helps the couple come to terms with the death of their baby. A low-key, rather sweet coming-of-age tale. ★★★

Paradise Alley
(1978, 109 min, US, Sylvester Stallone) *Sylvester Stallone, Anne Archer, Armand Assante.* Stallone wrote, directed and stars in this gritty though contrived story of three brothers from Hell's Kitchen who enter the world of wrestling to escape their New York City ghetto environment. ★★

Paradise Lost: The Child Murders at Robin Hood Hill
(1996, 150 min, US, Bruce Sinofsky & Joe Berlinger) Picking up where they left off with *My Brother's Keeper*, directors Berlinger & Sinofsky once again travel to small-town America to cover a sensational murder trial. In this case, the locale is West Memphis, Arkansas, and the trial is that of three teens who are accused of the brutal satanic ritual murder of three 8-year-old boys. The film's excessive running time will seem all-too-brief as Berlinger and Sinofsky do a brilliant job of presenting the myriad points of view and stringing them together into a riveting narrative. Sure to leave the viewer wondering — did they or didn't they? ★★★★ VHS: $9.99

Paradise Road
(1997, 113 min, US/GB, Bruce Beresford) *Glenn Close, Frances McDormand, Pauline Collins, Cate Blanchett, Jennifer Ehle, Julianna Marguiles, Wendy Hughes, Clyde Kusatsu.* Based on actual incidents that occured in a Japanese POW camp during WWII, this is the affecting, hard-hitting story of a group of female Allied prisoners who for nearly three years suffered at the hands of the often brutal Japanese. Under the leadership of Close, the women form a "vocal orchestra" to show the enemy "they still have life to them." And it is through their music that the prisoners retain their faith and will to survive. Though it sometimes approaches sappy and clichéd waters, it is quite touching and affirming. Close's stirring performance is the film's center of gravity, and Collins as a missionary excels in support. ★★★ DVD: $9.99

The Parallax View
(1974, 102 min, US, Alan J. Pakula) *Warren Beatty, Paula Prentiss, William Daniels, Hume Cronyn.* Complicated and fascinating political thriller with Beatty as a newspaper reporter investigating the assassination of a senator. As he digs further into the story, his own life and the lives of witnesses and those around him become increasingly in danger. ★★★½ DVD: $29.99, VHS: $14.99

Pardon Mon Affaire
(1977, 105 min, France, Yves Robert) *Jean Rochefort, Claude Brasseur, Guy Bedos, Victor Lanoux.* Miserably remade by Gene Wilder as *The Woman in Red*, this lovely, wry French boudoir comedy follows four buddies who undergo a series of complicated comic adventures through the streets and bedrooms of Paris. Rochefort stars in a wonderful comic performance as the ringleader and chief erotic provocateur. (Sequel: *Pardon Mon Affaire, Too*) ★★★

Pardon Mon Affaire, Too
(1977, 110 min, France, Yves Robert) *Jean Rochefort, Claude Brasseur, Guy Bedos, Victor Lanoux.* A film that pokes fun at marriage, fidelity, love and friendship, is a zestful continuation of the extramarital affairs of Rochefort and his middle-aged friends. Their appetites for inflated fantasies and faded dreams are insightfully explored in this gently satiric farce. ★★½

Pardon My Trunk (Buongiorno, Elefante!)
(1952, 85 min, Italy, Gianni Franciolini) *Vittorio De Sica, Sabu.* De Sica turns in a fine performance in this wild though uneven satire of a Italian schoolteacher who receives an unwanted gift of an elephant from a wealthy prince. His efforts to rid himself of the bulky present set off a series of comic vignettes. ★★½

The Parent Trap
(1961, 127 min, US, David Swift) *Hayley Mills, Brian Keith, Maureen O'Hara.* Cute though sentimental Disney comedy with Mills doubling as long-lost twin sisters who meet at summer camp and devise a plan to reunite their divorced parents Keith and O'Hara. (Remade in 1998) ★★½ DVD 2-disc set: $22.99, VHS: $19.99

The Parent Trap
(1998, 128 min, US, Nancy Meyers) *Natasha Richardson, Lindsay Lohan, Dennis Quaid.* Separated-at-birth twins meet at camp, and decide to try to reunite their parents in this ceaselessly optimistic remake of the 1961 hit. All the right emotional buttons are hit: sisterhood, reunions with never-before-seen parents, unwanted evil stepparents, and of course the desire to see divorced parents together, in love, again. It's fun and sweet, and hard to not get sucked in, even if you're the parent and not the kid. ★★★ VHS: $14.99

Parenthood
(1989, 124 min, US, Ron Howard) *Keanu Reeves, Steve Martin, Jason Robards, Mary Steenburgen, Dianne Wiest, Rick Moranis, Tom Hulce, Martha Plimpton.* An all-star cast shines in Howard's charming and very funny family comedy. Howard and cowriters Lowell Ganz and Babaloo Mandel examine American middle-class family life as seen through the not-so-ordinary eyes of the multigenerational Buckman clan. Martin stars as Gil, a worrisome father who is ever-aware of personal shortcomings with his own father and is determined not to repeat the same with his troubled son. ★★★ VHS: $9.99

Parents
(1989, 90 min, US, Bob Balaban) *Bryan Madorsky, Randy Quaid, Sandy Dennis, Mary Beth Hurt.* First-time director Balaban serves up a wild postmodern feast that may leave you with a bad taste in your mouth but a grin on your face. Young Madorsky discovers his Ozzie and Harriet parents have a terrible secret and it's hardly appetizing. Not for everyone, but if you prefer your filmmaking adventurous, give it a nibble. ★★★

Les Parents Terribles
(1948, 98 min, France, Jean Cocteau) *Jean Marais, Josette Day, Yvonne deBray.* This adaptation of Cocteau's play, considered by many to be his finest work, is a riveting psychological tragicomedy about the complicated tangle of sexuality, parental rivalry and jealousy within a troubled family. Cocteau creates a claustrophobic intimacy (only two

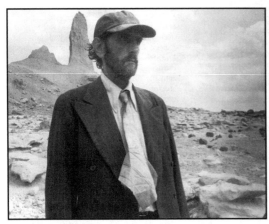

Harry Dean Stanton in *Paris, Texas*

sets, static camera, many close-ups, no exteriors) as this incestuously close family bares its soul. DeBray is wonderful as the domineering mother, Marais plays the son, and Day is the woman he (and his father) loves. (French with English subtitles) ★★★★ VHS: $29.99

Paris Belongs to Us

(1959, 138 min, France, Jacques Rivette) *Jean-Claude Brialy, Betty Schneider, Cameos: Jean-Luc Godard, Claude Chabrol, Jacuqes Demy.* New Wave director Rivette's first feature is this low-budget drama. The story is set in a near-deserted Paris one summer where a group of enthusiastic young amateurs get together in an effort to present a production of Shakespeare's "Pericles." But the death of the composer, suicide of the producer and mounting political and sexual tensions between the actors undermine their efforts. A spare and moody tale of optimism and doom. (French with English subtitles) ★★★

Paris Blues

(1961, 98 min, US, Martin Ritt) *Paul Newman, Sidney Poitier, Joanne Woodward, Diahann Carroll, Louis Armstrong.* Jazz and romance in the City of Lights, as musicians Newman and Poitier court Woodward and Carroll. The film makes good use of a fine Duke Ellington score. Entertaining and well done. ★★★

Paris Express

(1953, 80 min, GB, Harold French) *Claude Rains, Anouk Aimée, Herbert Lom.* Rains stars as a low-level clerk who embezzles from his business in hopes of going on extended holiday, but instead finds himself lured by a femme fatale into a web of robbery, murder and intrigue. Rains' good performance and a moody atmosphere compensate for the sometimes muddled narrative. ★★½

Paris, France

(1993, 96 min, Canada, Gérard Ciccoritti) *Leslie Hope, Victor Ertmanis, Dan Left, Peter Outerbrige.* Deliriously paced and entertainingly saturated with numerous and inventively diverse sexual couplings, this tale of mid-life crisis, regret, longing and sexual repression is anything but your standard melodrama. Set in Toronto, the story involves the three owners of a small publishing company: a married couple, Lucy and Michael, and their business partner, William. The stability of their lives is thrown into an emo-

tional maelstrom with the arrival of Sloan, a former boxer turned writer. Beyond the steamy sex scenes is the uninhibited notion of exploring all of one's many sexual needs. (French with English subtitles) ★★★ DVD: $9.99, VHS: $9.99

Paris Is Burning

(1990, 78 min, US, Jennie Livingston) *Dorian Corey, Pepper LaBeija, Willi Ninja, Freddie Pendavis, Kim Pendavis, Octavia St. Laurent, Junior LaBeija, Venus Xtravaganza.* Welcome to the world of the Ball, where everyone is Cinderella. The balls in question are the voguing and drag-balls of Harlem, the subject of director Livingston's entertaining documentary. Voguing, an underground dance invented by black and Latino queers, burst upon the pop scene when Madonna "took" voguing for herself and popularized it. But it's the originators of the form who are the film's subject. Voguers, or "ball walkers," affiliate themselves with "Houses," the equivalent of nonviolent gay street gangs, and compete for trophies at the late-nite balls. Livingston uses sensitivity and compassion in documenting her stars. ★★★★

Paris, Texas

(1984, 150 min, US, Wim Wenders) *Harry Dean Stanton, Nastassja Kinski, Dean Stockwell.* Wenders' understated exploration of human loneliness and vulnerability features Stanton as a near-catatonic wanderer who is somewhat snapped out of his stupor by his brother (Stockwell). Upon reuniting with his young son, he and the boy set off in search of their long-lost wife and mother, Kinski. Sam Shepard's screenplay and Robby Müller's camera keenly map out the desert of the human soul as set against the bleak Texas landscape; Ry Cooder's haunting slide guitar finishes off the effect. ★★★

Paris Trout

(1991, 100 min, US, Stephen Gyllenhaal) *Dennis Hopper, Barbara Hershey, Ed Harris, Tina Lifford.* A stunning made-for-cable adaptation of Pete Dexter's award-winning novel. Hopper is outstanding as the title character, a racist 1940s Southern storekeeper who kills a young black girl, the sister of a man Trout cheated in a car sale, and who now stands trial for murder. Hershey is terrific as Hopper's abused wife, whose moral outrage to her husband's actions sends her into the arms of lawyer Harris (in a wonderful characterization). ★★★★ VHS: $19.99

Paris When It Sizzles

(1964, 110 min, US, Richard Quine) *Audrey Hepburn, William Holden, Cameos: Fred Astaire, Frank Sinatra, Noël Coward, Marlene Dietrich, Tony Curtis.* Despite an engaging premise and a first-rate cast, this forced comedy offers little in laughs or enjoyment. Screenwriter Holden and secretary Hepburn romp around Paris in a series of fantasies acting out his new script. ★½ DVD: $14.99, VHS: $14.99

Parsifal

(1982, 26 min, West Germany, Hans-Jurgen Syberberg) *Michael Kutter, Karen Krick.* Syberberg, director of *Our Hitler*, has created a spectacular and provocative film experience with this version of Richard Wagner's splendid opera. The eternal drama of the search for the Holy Grail is imaginatively enacted within the crevices and crannies of a mammoth replica of Wagner's death mask, with the character of Parsifal portrayed by both a man (Kutter) and a woman (Krick). The film, while a note-complete performance of the opera, is anything but conventional and is a must for all opera fans and adventurous film enthusiasts. ★★★½ DVD: $39.99, VHS: $29.99

Parting Glances

(1986, 90 min, US, Bill Sherwood) *Richard Ganoung, John Bolger, Steve Buscemi, Adam Nathan.* A wonderfully rich and seductively appealing independent production that definitely rates as one of the best of all gay-themed films. The action takes place in a 24-hour period and centers around Michael (Ganoung) and Robert (Bolger), a gay New York couple who are about to temporarily separate as Robert is transferred overseas. Their attempts to keep the relationship strong and to understand each other is the core of this simple but wise comedy-drama. Buscemi who steals the film with a bravado performance as Nick, a rock singer and Michael's ex-lover who's dying of AIDS. Produced on a low budget, the film's strengths lie in its simple and honest moments — a loving embrace or a telling confession. A joyful, knowing gay love story. ★★★★ DVD: $29.99, VHS: $29.99

Partisans of Vilna

(1986, 130 min, France, Josh Waletzky) This stirring documentary examines the Jewish resistance during WWII. Interspersing interviews with former freedom fighters from around the world with rare archival footage from the war years, the film spellbindingly introduces us to the Jewish youths who organized an underground resistance in the Vilna ghetto and fought as partisans against the Nazis. A powerful, heartrending tribute to courage in the face of unrelenting adversity. (In English and French, Hebrew and Yiddish with English subtitles) ★★★½

Partner

(1968, 112 min, Italy, Bernardo Bertolucci) *Pierre Clementi.* Madness, romanticism, theatre and politics are the theme in *Partner*, a surprisingly noncommercial film director Bertolucci now repudiates. Greatly influenced by the 1968 student rebellions which swept Europe as well as the political cinema of Jean-Luc Godard and the theatrical devices developed by Julian Beck's Living Theatre, the film is a free adaptation of Dostoevsky's "The Double." Clementi stars as a repressed art teacher who is possessed and ultimately driven mad by his alter ego, a political revolutionary. A beautiful but off-setting film that is a must for fans of Bertolucci and followers of political cinema. (Italian with English subtitles) ★★★½

Partners

(1982, 98 min, US, James Burrows) *Ryan O'Neal, John Hurt, Kenneth McMillan.* An odious cop comedy with a "fag" angle, this has to be one of the most offensive gay-themed films ever made. O'Neal plays a straight detective who teams up with effeminate, in-the-closet desk cop Hurt to go undercover as gay lovers to investigate a gay serial killer. The film indulges every conceivable homophobic stereotype.

P

Dressed entirely in pink and lilac, Hurt is seen as a scared, helpless femme while O'Neal is the leather-clad man. Watch it and wince! ★

The Party

(1968, 99 min, US, Blake Edwards) *Peter Sellers, Claudine Longet.* Sellers gives one of his funniest performances as a clumsy Indian actor invited to a private Hollywood party. Edwards directs with the same comic assurance that he exercised in the *Pink Panther* series: inventive sight gags and crazy comedy abound. ★★★½ DVD Letterbox: $19.99

Favorite Line: "Num-num. Num-num. Birdie num-num." —*Peter Sellers as Hrundi V. Bakshi, lost in translation with the parrot*

Party Girl

(1994, 90 min, US, Daisy von Scherler Mayer) *Parker Posey, Anthony DeSando, Guillermo Diaz, Donna Mitchell, Liev Schreiber, Omar Townsend, Sasha Von Scherler.* The joys of capitalism and social conformity are the hidden agendas in this scattershot comedy which ostensibly celebrates bohemian/alternative life in New York's East Village. The story revolves around 24-year-old Mary (Posey) who undergoes a transformation from mindless "party girl" to being a prim and proper librarian. We've seen it all before, but it's a harmless romp. ★★ DVD Pan & Scan: $24.99

Pascali's Island

(1988, 104 min, GB, James Dearden) *Ben Kingsley, Charles Dance, Helen Mirren.* Kingsley gives an admirable performance in this rather slowly paced drama set on a small Greek island during the last days of the fading Ottoman Empire. Kingsley plays a local eccentric and Turkish spy who unwittingly becomes involved with a suave British archeologist (Dance) and his plot to steal a precious artifact from the isle. Also caught up in the intrigue is an Austrian expatriate (Mirren in a captivating performance), a lonely artist who falls in love with the handsome adventurer with tragic results. The film is highlighted by sumptuous cinematography and beautiful locales. ★★

A Passage to India

(1984, 164 min, GB, David Lean) *Judy Davis, Victor Banerjee, Peggy Ashcroft, James Fox, Alec Guinness.* Master filmmaker Lean proves himself capable of pulling yet another beautifully crafted "big" picture out of his hat with this meticulous adaptation of the E. M. Forster novel about the clash between British and Indian cultures and classes in the colonial India of the 1920s. A superlative cast plays against the brilliance of Lean's craft, with which he imbues each and every backdrop with flavor and nuance. Very satisfying. ★★★★ DVD: $29.99

Passage to Marseille

(1944, 109 min, US, Michael Curtiz) *Humphrey Bogart, Claude Rains, Sidney Greenstreet, Peter Lorre.* Curtiz, the director of *Casablanca*, reteamed with that film's star, Bogart for this acceptable WWII adventure about escaped Devil's Island convicts who join the Free French in the fight against the Nazis. Confusing flashbacks-within-flashbacks keep this film from being the first-rate production Curtiz and company had hoped. ★★½ VHS: $19.99

La Passante

(1982, 106 min, France, Jacques Rouffio) *Michel Piccoli, Romy Schneider.* Schneider is wonderful in a dual role in this, her final film. It is the story of two lovers who are mysteriously compelled for political actions to become involved in the assassination of a South American ambassador who may have been a former Nazi leader. (French with English subtitles) ★★½

The Passenger

(1975, 123 min, Italy, Michelangelo Antonioni) *Jack Nicholson, Maria Schneider, Ian Hendry.* Nicholson stars in this hypnotic thriller as a discontented reporter who changes his identity for a dead man. A brilliant portrayal of alienation's pangs and the barren landscape of one man's soul. ★★★½

Passenger 57

(1992, 84 min, US, Kevin Hooks) *Wesley Snipes, Tom Sizemore, Bruce Payne, Bruce Greenwood, Elizabeth Hurley.* A *Die Hard* clone, Hooks' cartoonish action film has the friendly skies substituting for the skyscraper as the backdrop for the act of terrorism. Snipes stars as an ex-secret service agent-turned-airline security consultant who battles a group of deadly international skyjackers. While the script is laughably illogical at points, Snipes shows what a good actor can do with a bland script. ★★ DVD: $14.99, VHS: $9.99

Passion

(1995, 114 min, US, James Lapine) *Donna Murphy, Jere Shea, Marin Mazzie, Gregg Edelman.* Stephen Sondheim's Tony Award-winning musical has been filmed live with the original Broadway cast. Based on the Ettore Scola film *Passione d'Amore*, the story follows Giorgio (Shea), a heroic army captain, who receives a military transfer. At his new post lives the cousin of his superior officer, Fosca (Murphy), an unattractive, psychologically wounded young woman who becomes obsessed with the handsome captain. Though *Passion* debuted to less than enthusiastic response, especially with Sondheim devotees, time appears to have aged the musical nicely (much like his "Merrily We Roll Along"). Though a case can be made that this is lesser (and warmed-over) Sondheim, *Passion* is inventive, involving and, yes, passionate; its lyrics often witty, its score characteristic but effective, and its book economically good. ★★★½ DVD: $24.99, VHS: $19.99

Passion Fish

(1992, 136 min, US, John Sayles) *Mary McDonnell, Alfre Woodard, David Strathairn, Angela Bassett, Nora Dunn, Vondie Curtis-Hall.* Sayles' upbeat comic melodrama explores the rigors of adjusting to life as a paraplegic. McDonnell stars as May-Alice, a soap opera star who, after being crippled by a New York taxi, returns to her home town on the Louisiana bayou to wallow in self-pity and heap abuse on a succession of house nurses. She finally meets her match, however, when the agency sends her the equally uncompromising Chantelle (Woodard). Sayles wrings every ounce of humanity and wry humor from the clash of these two emotional tyrants as they slowly warm to each other. Marvelously photographed on location, the film sports a trio of splendid performances from McDonnell, Woodard and Strathairn as a local Cajun handyman who takes an obvious shine to McDonnell. ★★★½ DVD: $24.99, VHS: $9.99

Passion for Life

(1948, 89 min, France, Jean-Paul Chanois) *Bernard Blier, Julliette Faber.* A sincere young teacher (Blier), impassioned with progressive ideas, comes to a provincial village where he meets opposition from the stodgy parents. Predating *Dead Poets* Society and *Stand and Deliver* by many decades, this sincere though sentimental tale follows the teacher as he must not only prove his worth but his methods as well after he promises that every one of the students in his class will pass a national test. (French with English subtitles) ★★½ VHS: $59.99

The Passion of Anna

(1969, 100 min, Sweden, Ingmar Bergman) *Liv Ullmann, Max von Sydow, Erland Josephson, Bibi Andersson.* Bergman continues with the recurring theme of a couple (or couples) isolated from society yet under attack from either, or both, outside forces as well as within their own selves. In this deeply textured psychological drama, von Sydow moves to a sparsely populated island where he meets a widowed young woman (the remarkable Ullmann) and an architect (Josephson) and his wife (Andersson). Complex emotional and spiritual fears are brought to the surface as the four develop revealing relationships that lay bare their despair and protective self-deceptions. (Swedish with English subtitles) ★★★★ DVD: $24.99, VHS: $19.99

The Passion of Joan of Arc

(1928, 82 min, France, Carl Dreyer) *Maria Falconetti, Eugena Sylvaw.* Based on the actual transcripts of the historical trial and using innovative close-ups that have made film history, Dreyer's extraordinary film of the Inquisition, trial and death of Joan of Arc remains as fresh and powerful today as it was over 70 years ago. This is director Dreyer's original cut, recently found and remastered. (Silent with musical accompaniment) ★★★★ DVD: $39.99, VHS: $29.99

Passion of Mind

(2000, 105 min, US, Alain Berliner) *Demi Moore, Stellan Skarsgård, William Fichtner.* Treading similar ground as *Sliding Doors* and *Me Myself I*, *Passion of Mind* is a serious drama of Marie (Moore), a widowed Parisian who dreams that she is Marty, a single career woman in New York. Or is it the other way around? When romances bloom in both lives simultaneously, she fears confronting the fact that, perhaps, only one of them can be real. Demi's return to acting, after a post-*G.I. Jane* hiatus, only serves to prove that too often, Moore is less. This rather arty fever-dream, the first English-language feature from Berliner, relies on Moore to carry every scene, and she's not up to the task. ★★½ DVD: $29.99, VHS: $14.99

The Passion of the Christ

(2004, 126 min, US, Mel Gibson) *Jim Caviezel, Monica Bellucci, Claudia Gerini, Maia Morgenstern.* The polar opposite of the traditional Biblical epic, Gibson's deeply personal pet project expands a line from the Gospels ("Then Pilate therefore took Jesus, and scourged him" - *John 19:1*) into twelve minutes of speculative horror as the centerpiece of this controversial, undeniably powerful *Passion* play. It's possibly the first mainstream splatter film, an *I Spit on Your Grave* without revenge or catharsis. The balance of the film plays like Jesus' greatest hits, as Gibson and cowriter Benedict Fitzgerald pick and choose segments from the four Gospels. It's not subtle, to say the least, but neither is the source material. As for the many complaints of anti-Semitism, it's no more or less anti-Semitic than the Gospels themselves, which is to say very. The various Gospels place the blame for Jesus' crucifixion squarely on the Jews, and Gibson repeats this bias in varying ways. On one hand, he distills many of the crowds' sentiments into one character (the high priest Caiaphas), rendering one authority responsible rather than an entire people; on the other, Caiaphas screams the notoriously racist line from Matthew ("His blood be on us, and on our children" *Matthew 27:25*) — which Gibson neglects to subtitle for American audiences. The Romans, meanwhile, are merely apolitical sadists. Yet as a work of art, however hateful, it's impossible to ignore the breathtaking way that Gibson puts it all together, especially the stunning cinematography by Caleb Deschanel. But one can't help but wonder why Gibson concentrated solely on Jesus' suffering and totally ignored His beliefs and His message that would change a world. If you're looking for spirituality, look elsewhere; this is blood-and-guts religion. (Latin and Aramaic with English subtitles) ★★ DVD Letterbox: $29.99, DVD Pan & Scan: $29.99

The Passionate Thief

(1962, 100 min, Italy, Mario Monicello) *Toto, Ben Gazzara, Anna Magnani.* The director of *Big Deal on Madonna Street* brings his comedic talents to this entertaining story of larceny and love. Italian favorite Toto is a small-time bit player who repeatedly thwarts the efforts of a pickpocket (Gazzara) to earn his living one New Year's Eve night. A minor, but worthwhile comedy of errors. (Italian with English subtitles) ★★½ VHS: $19.99

Passione d'Amore

(1982, 117 min, Italy, Ettore Scola) *Laura Antonelli.* A handsome and witty tale about the ironies and intricacies of love and beauty. In 19th-century Italy, a dashing young cavalry officer engages in an adulterous affair with a voluptuous woman only to become involved with his commanding officer's homely, cantankerous cousin. This sardonic, dark comedy received a special jury prize at the Cannes Film Festival. (The basis for the Stephen Sondheim musical "Passion") ★★★½

Passport to Pimlico

(1948, 85 min, GB, Henry Cornelius) *Stanley Holloway, Basil Radford, Margaret Rutherford.* This wonderful little British comedy has an anarchic "little man battling the establishment" attitude. A fish store proprietor unearths an ancient treaty that establishes Pimlico as a part of Burgundy, instead of London, thus releasing store owners from both the postwar rationing and British licensing laws. A wonderful parody of the post-war state of Europe. ★★★½

Pastime

(1991, 95 min, US, Robin B. Armstrong) *William Russ, Glenn Plummer, Scott Plank.* Tucked in between the theatrical releases of *Field of Dreams* and *A League of Their Own*, this small-scaled, bittersweet drama is not in the same league as those two gems, but is nevertheless an appealing, carefully rendered character study. Russ gives a gorgeous turn as a veteran minor league ballplayer at the end of his career. Having had a brief stint in the majors, and after twenty years in the minors, Russ is now the butt of his teammates' jokes, not fully aware of his own shortcomings and still hoping to make it back to "the Bigs." When he befriends a young, talented pitcher, both men strike a friendship to help each other face their uncertain futures. ★★½ DVD: $19.99, VHS: $14.99

Pat and Mike

(1952, 95 min, US, George Cukor) *Katharine Hepburn, Spencer Tracy, Aldo Ray, Jim Backus.* This enjoyable sports comedy is a pleasant tale with

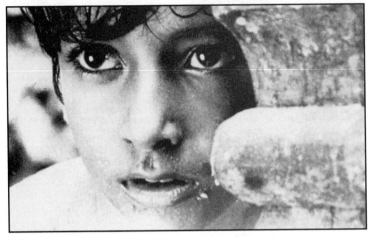

Pather Panchali

Kate as a sports pro and Spencer as her manager. It's here Tracy says the line, "There's not much meat on her, but what there is is cherce." Written by Ruth Gordon and Garson Kanin. ★★★ DVD: $19.99, VHS: $14.99

Pat Garrett and Billy the Kid

(1973, 122 min, US, Sam Peckinpah) *James Coburn, Kris Kristofferson, Jason Robards, Slim Pickens, Rita Coolidge, Bob Dylan.* Outlaw-turned-lawman Pat Garrett (Coburn) stalks Billy the Kid (Kristofferson) across the New Mexican desert in this vivid Peckinpah western. Dylan makes his acting debut. ★★½

Patch Adams

(1998, 116 min, US, Tom Shadyac) *Robin Williams, Monica Potter, Daniel London, Philip Seymour Hoffman, Bob Gunton, Irma P. Hall.* Doctor Williams, wanted in overkill. Playing a physician for what seems like the upteenth time, Williams is certainly at home in this overly sentimental, crowd-pleasing comedy (based on a true story) which gives the actor the chance to both mug and tug (at the heart). He plays Patch Adams, a sanitorium inmate who decides to go to medical school; his unique, irreverent humor and outlook make him a hit with patients and other students, but not so with school administration. Eventually, he opens his own makeshift clinic for the poor, which is still in operation today. Williams is able to milk some laughs thanks to Patch's schtick, but the story goes way overboard in the syrup department, and patches in Adams' life are glossed over which gives the film a jagged feel. ★★ DVD Letterbox Ultimate Edition: $14.99, DVD Pan & Scan: $14.99, DVD DTS sound: $14.99, VHS: $9.99

A Patch of Blue

(1965, 105 min, US, Guy Green) *Sidney Poitier, Elizabeth Hartman, Shelley Winters, Wallace Ford, Ivan Dixon.* A moving, sensitive drama of a blind white woman (Hartman) falling in love with a black man (Poitier). Fine acting accentuates this story; Winters won an Oscar as Hartman's overbearing mother. ★★★ DVD Letterbox: $19.99, VHS: $9.99, VHS Letterbox: $9.99

Pather Panchali

(1955, 115 min, India, Satyajit Ray) *Kanu Banerjee, Karuna Banerjee.* This first film of Ray's widely acclaimed Apu Trilogy tells of Apu's childhood as a member of a poverty-stricken family in a Bengali village. The film is grippingly realistic and, although the locales are exotic, the human situation it portrays is shattering. (Bengali with English subtitles) (Sequel: *Aparajito*) ★★★★ DVD: $29.99, VHS: $19.99

Pathfinder

(1988, 88 min, Norway, Nils Gaup) *Mikkel Gaup, Nils Utsi.* Set in the bitter cold and snow-covered tundra of northern Finland, this exciting, violent and emotional adventure story, taken from a 1,000-year-old legend, concerns an unusually dramatic coming-of-age of a teenage boy whose family is massacred by a rampaging band of thieves. Young Aigin flees to another village but finds that the killers are on his trail. He must decide whether to flee with the others, stand and fight a hopeless battle or join forces with the village's elderly but still powerful "pathfinder." Infused with the cultural mysticism and superstitions of the nomadic Lapp people, this Academy Award-nominated tale tells of the eternal battle of man against his own forces of evil. (Lapp with English subtitles) ★★★½ VHS: $19.99

Paths of Glory

(1957, 86 min, GB, Stanley Kubrick) *Kirk Douglas, Ralph Meeker, Adolphe Menjou, George Macready.* Kubrick's first true masterpiece combines superb direction with outstanding performances and remains one of the most shattering studies of the insanity of war to date. During WWI, a French general orders his men on a futile mission. When they return in failure, he picks three soldiers to be tried and executed for cowardice. This scathing attack on the hypocrisies of war is, so far as we know, still banned in France. ★★★★ DVD: $14.99

The Patriot

(2000, 165 min, US, Roland Emmerich) *Mel Gibson, Heath Ledger, Joely Richardson, Jason Isaacs, Chris Cooper, Tcheky Karyo, Tom Wilkinson, Rene Auberjonois.* An often rousing, often sentimental actioner, *The Patriot* is an old-fashioned Revolutionary War story told with outstanding cinematography and elegant production design. Gibson

P

is Benjamin Martin, a father and widower who would rather use diplomacy than guns for American independence. When a particularly nasty British colonel (Isaacs) murders one of his children, Martin spearheads the local militia in the bloody, deadly fight against the British. This is not subtle storytelling — Isaacs' military monster is a Nazi bad guy dressed in a red coat. But at the heart of the story is a compelling, even stirring re-creation of the birth of a nation, and the determination of a father to keep his family together. Based on a real-life character who was also the inspiration for the 1950s TV show "Swamp Fox." ★★★ DVD Letterbox Superbit Deluxe Edition: $29.00, DVD Special Edition: $19.99, VHS: $9.99

Patriot Games

(1992, 118 min, US, Philip Noyce) *Harrison Ford, Anne Archer, Patrick Bergen, Sean Bean, Richard Harris, James Earl Jones, Samuel L. Jackson.* A very capable sequel to the hit thriller *The Hunt for Red October*, with Ford taking over the role of CIA agent Jack Ryan first introduced by Alec Baldwin. While on a lecture tour in London, Ryan thwarts an attempted Royal Family assassination, killing one of the terrorists in the process. This makes him and his family a target of the dead man's brother. Punctuated by a series of well-mounted and exciting action scenes, the film is marred only by a hastily tacked-on ending. Whereas Baldwin's Jack Ryan was a protagonist driven by rational thought, Ford's Ryan is a reluctant but nevertheless visceral hero to be reckoned with. (Sequel: *Clear and Present Danger*) ★★★ DVD Letterbox Special Collector's Edition: $19.99, VHS: $9.99, VHS Letterbox: $9.99

Pattes Blanches

(1949, 92 min, France, Jean Grémillon) *Suzy Delair, Fernand Ledoux.* Set against lovingly rendered Breton landscapes, this perverse melodrama of obsessive rivalry is a twisted mesh of sexual jealousies, intrigues, violence and revenge. Director Grémillon, best known for his documentaries and for presiding over the Cinémathèque, fills his film with strange scenes and a wonderful trick ending. The film follows the sordid story of two sons who fight for the love of a pretty but vicious innkeeper's mistress. The title refers to the white spats worn by a reclusive aristocrat who is ridiculed and loathed by the villagers. (French with English subtitles) ★★½ VHS: $59.99

Patti Rocks

(1988, 105 min, US, David Burton Morris) *Chris Mulkey, John Jennings, Karen Landry.* An original and quite controversial dissection of the attitudes and misconceptions of what some men feel about women. Billy (Mulkey), a 30-year-old married dock worker, convinces his old friend Eddie (Jennings) to accompany him on a long ride to Billy's pregnant girlfriend's house, to help him break off their relationship. The first half of the film is the car ride, as the two men exchange their conflicting views on women and life in vivid, locker-room talk. The second-half takes place at Patti's apartment, where the men discover an independent and compassionate woman who has her own ideas on her future with Billy and the baby. ★★★

Patton

(1970, 170 min, US, Franklin J. Schaffner) *George C. Scott, Karl Malden, Stephen Young.* Scott won (and refused) an Oscar for his powerhouse performance of the controversial WWII commander, General George Patton, in this superior wartime

biography. The film, which won seven Oscars including Best Picture, follows Patton's campaign in Europe and Northern Africa. ★★★★ DVD Basic Edition: $14.99, VHS: $9.99

Patty Hearst

(1988, 108 min, US, Paul Schrader) *Natasha Richardson, William Forsythe, Ving Rhames, Frances Fisher, Dana Delany.* Richardson plays the title role in this dark, gritty version of Patty Hearst's story about the young heiress being kidnapped and brainwashed by the Symbionese Liberation Army; then being forced to participate in a series of bank robberies. ★★½

Paul Robeson

(1978, 118 min, US, Lloyd Richards) *James Earl Jones.* Jones, accompanied only by Burt Wallace on piano, holds the stage for nearly two hours as Paul Robeson, recounting a remarkable life in a mesmerizing performance. Jones adeptly shifts mood and tone from episode to episode as Robeson responds to indignity and prejudice with good humor and a well-justified anger tempered by a towering intellect. Written by Phillip Hayes Dean, the story's first act covers Robeson's undergraduate days at Rutgers to his rise as a star in the London production of "Showboat." In Act Two, his career dissolves as the rise of Fascism alters the face of Europe. He returns home only to face racism and the House Un-American Activities Committee. This complex, courageous man of integrity is given full voice with Jones' vital, stirring portrayal; and this play on film is satisfying both dramatically and as history. ★★★½ VHS: $59.99

Pauline at the Beach

(1983, 94 min, France, Eric Rohmer) *Amanda Langlet, Arielle Dombasle.* This effervescent sex farce follows the amorous escapades of a precocious young girl, her stunningly beautiful cousin, an adventurous rogue and a beleaguered beachcomber. A witty meditation on the folly of love and the quest for romance. (French with English subtitles) ★★★ DVD: $19.99

The Pawnbroker

(1965, 116 min, US, Sidney Lumet) *Rod Steiger, Geraldine Fitzgerald, Brock Peters.* Gripping drama of a New York pawnbroker haunted by the memory of his imprisonment in a Nazi camp during WWII. Steiger gives a virtuoso performance as the embittered Holocaust survivor. Remarkably realized by director Lumet. ★★★★ DVD: $14.99

Pay It Forward

(2000, 122 min, US, Mimi Leder) *Kevin Spacey, Helen Hunt, Haley Joel Osment, Jay Mohr, James Caviezel, Angie Dickinson, Jon Bon Jovi.* In this promising fable that is both heart-warming and overly dramatic, an outcast schoolboy named Trevor (Osment) invents "pay it forward" as a school project. What that means is you do something nice for someone, and they do something nice for 3 people, and they each do something nice for 3 other people, and so on. One of Trevor's own acts is to play matchmaker for his waitress mom (Hunt) and disfigured schoolteacher (Spacey), an unlikely romance that is one of the weaker links in this uneven chain. Osment gives a full-blooded portrayal of an adolescent wise beyond his years. There are scenes in *Pay It Forward* that genuinely touch the heart, and others that will turn the stomach; but the film could have come together as a whole had it not been for its awful ending. ★★½ DVD: $14.99, VHS: $9.99

Payback

(1999, 110 min, US, Brian Helgeland) *Mel Gibson, Gregg Henry, Maria Bello, David Paymer, Kris Kristofferson, James Coburn, William Devane, Deborah Kara Unger, Bill Duke, John Glover.* "That's just mean, man," Coburn's exasperated gangster chief declares as Gibson's determined thief bent on revenge shoots his expensive alligator luggage. That also ably describes this sadistic, loud and violent thriller which is competently made but doesn't know when enough is enough. *Payback* is based on Richard Stark's "The Hunter," the same source material for 1967's *Point Blank*. But it is there similarities end. Gibson is double-crossed and left for dead. He returns to get even and get money owed to him. Helgeland keeps the film rolling at a brisk pace, but its stylized shootings, torture and explosions become numbing after awhile. ★★ DVD: $14.99, VHS Special Edition: $9.99

Paycheck

(2003, 110 min, US, John Woo) *Ben Affleck, Uma Thurman, Aaron Eckhart, Michael C. Hall, Joe Morton, Paul Giamatti, Colm Feore.* Michael Jennings (Affleck), a callow computer genius, agrees to an intensive, top-secret, three-year-long gig for which he'll be paid $90 million. The catch is that those three years will be completely erased from his memory. Upon attempting to collect his paycheck, he discovers that he forfeited his money and mailed himself a collection of banal, everyday objects — which turn out to be clues as to why everyone seems to want him dead. An intriguing premise (courtesy of famed sci-fi writer Philip K. Dick) is sabotaged by some ridiculous plot holes, a lightweight lead and a protracted last third. Director Woo does provide a couple of delicious flourishes (incongruous slow motion, operatic meet-cute introduction of Thurman's character), but he can't overcome the script's inadequacies, and should have brought a harder edge to the film. It doesn't say much for a thriller about a man running for his life that we never feel the main character is in any real danger. ★★ DVD Collector's Edition: $29.99

PCU

(1994, 85 min, US, Hart Bochner) *David Spade, Jeremy Piven, Chris Young, Jon Favreau, Megan Ward, Jessica Walter, Jake Busey.* A lot funnier than it has a right to be, this *Animal House* rip-off for the '90s follows to the letter the rules of the campus comedy (especially pitting uptight students and administration against fun-loving misfits), which

Paths of Glory

Pee-wee's Big Adventure

makes *PCU* just another teenage comedy clone. However, that's only half the story. For as a satire on political correctness, this is a surprisingly funny, predictably sophomoric romp which takes pot shots at all of the sacred cows of the 1990s. It could even bring a smile or two to PCers (with a sense of humor). ★★½ DVD: $14.99

The Peacemaker

(1997, 122 min, US, Mimi Leder) *George Clooney, Nicole Kidman, Armin Mueller-Stahl, Marcel Lures.* A highly entertaining, kick-ass thriller, *The Peacemaker* marks a very credible directorial debut for Leder as she mixes action, suspense and drama to produce quite a few heart-pounding scenes filmed from all over the globe. A terrific opening sequence introduces a group of Russian terrorists hijacking a trainload of nuclear missiles. Enter nuclear physicist Kidman and military agent Clooney as they try to track the terrorists, missiles and their eventual destination. Leder keeps the action going at a steady clip, and the finale set on the crowded streets of New York City is quite suspenseful. ★★★ DVD Letterbox: $14.99, DVD DTS sound: $14.99, VHS: $9.99

Pearl Harbor

(2001, 180 min, US, Michael Bay) *Ben Affleck, Josh Hartnett, Kate Beckinsale, Cuba Gooding, Jr., Tom Sizemore, Ewen Bremner, William Lee Scott, Alec Baldwin, Jon Voight, Dan Aykroyd, Colm Feore, Mako.* It would be easy to dismiss the epic *Pearl Harbor* were it not for the amount of attention heaped upon it by the filmmakers and an anxious public. In restaging the surprise attack on Pearl Harbor, director Bay has lavished outstanding state-of-the-art special effects upon a film that is more often than not devoid of human drama. In essence a three-act play, *Pearl Harbor* begins with pilots/best friends Affleck and Hartnett both falling for nurse Beckinsale in revoltingly cutesy fashion. The middle section is the extremely well-crafted attack sequence; the final third tries to find a compelling rhythm but, unfortunately, it's too little too late. Screenwriter Randall Wallace plays fast and loose with historical accuracy, but what's more irritating is the umpteenth war film in which buddies fall for the same girl in a long, drawn-out plot. The superb re-creation of the attack is the attraction here, but *what* it takes to get there! *Pearl Harbor*, like its many good-looking characters, is spectacular to

look at but rather empty inside. ★★ DVD PG-13 Rated: $19.99, DVD Vista Series: $39.99, DVD Gift Set: $49.99, VHS Double Cassette: $14.99, VHS Gift Set: $39.99, VHS Letterbox Double Cassette: $14.99

Pecker

(1998, 86 min, US, John Waters) *Edward Furlong, Christina Ricci, Bess Armstrong, Mary Kay Place, Martha Plimpton, Brendan Sexton III, Mink Stole, Lili Taylor, Lauren Hulsey, Jean Schertler, Patricia Hearst.* Writer-director Waters returns to his subversive comedic grabbag for *Pecker*, a restrained though amusing comedy which combines the director's penchant for shock comedy and a more accessible filmmaking style he honed after *Hairspray*. Set in Baltimore (where else?), the story follows the rise of young Pecker (Furlong), a fledgling photographer whose pictures of his slightly dysfunctional family and working-class neighborhood capture the attention of the New York art scene. It's trash vs. flash when these worlds collide, and Waters milks some good laughs at the expense of one and all involved. Furlong has an agreeable comic air about him, though it's up to everyone else around him to offer the titillating laughs. We've seen John down and dirtier, but he's in an awfully good mood. ★★★

The Pedestrian

(1974, 97 min, West Germany, Maximilian Schell) *Maximilian Schell, Peggy Ashcroft.* An excellent drama examining the guilt of Nazi crimes against humanity and their effects on German society 45 years later. A wealthy industrialist is involved in a car accident in which his son is killed. The ensuing publicity brings out a story that he might have participated in the slaughter of a Greek village during the war. The circumstantial evidence linking him to the crimes and the country's reaction to the news combine to indict the man. But is he guilty? ★★★½

Pee-wee's Big Adventure

(1985, 90 min, US, Tim Burton) *Paul Reubens, Elizabeth Daly, Mark Holton, Jan Hooks, Morgan Fairchild, James Brolin.* There are things about him you wouldn't understand, there are things you couldn't understand, things you shouldn't understand. He's Pee-wee Herman, loner and rebel. Reubens' triumphant characterization is the ultimate child of the Eighties. Follow Pee-wee as he desperately searches for his most prized possession: his recently stolen bicycle. Anti-intelligence was never so brilliant. ★★★½ DVD: $19.99

Peeping Tom

(1960, 101 min, GB, Michael Powell) *Karl-Heinz Boehm, Moira Shearer, Anna Massey, Shirley Anne Field, Nigel Davenport.* Powell's long-suppressed masterpiece is a lucid, slyly witty thriller about a deranged cameraman's obsession with photographing beautiful women as he murders them. So hostilely received at the time of its release, this film virtually ended this great director's career. ★★★½ DVD: $39.99, VHS: $19.99

Peggy Sue Got Married

(1986, 104 min, US, Francis Coppola) *Kathleen Turner, Nicolas Cage, Joan Allen, Jim Carrey, Barry Miller, Barbara Harris, Don Murray, Kevin J. O'Connor, Helen Hunt.* A separated 43-year-old mother (Turner) travels back in time to her senior year in high school — where she attempts to set the future right. Cage is her once and future husband. A sweet-natured blend of fantasy, comedy and drama, which, for the most part, works beautifully. Turner is most engaging. ★★★ DVD: $9.99, VHS: $9.99

Peking Opera Blues

(1986, 104 min, Hong Kong, Tsui Hark) This entertaining satirical adventure film features stunning set design, gold-digging dames, plots and counterplots, assassinations, singers and soldiers, all coming together in furiously paced, breathlessly choreographed action sequences. Set in 1913, the frenetic comedy features three young women who become enmeshed in dangerous intrigue involving efforts to topple a general. Director Tsui has been quoted as saying that the film is a satire on "Chinese ignorance of Democracy," but it doesn't stop the fun in this tongue-in-cheek farce. (Cantonese with English subtitles) ★★★½

The Pelican Brief

(1993, 125 min, US, Alan J. Pakula) *Denzel Washington, Julia Roberts, Sam Shepard, John Heard, Stanley Tucci, Tony Goldwyn.* Roberts is a law student who uncovers the diabolical plot behind the assassination of two Supreme Court justices. Jokingly — but accurately — called a Nancy Drew for the '90s, this slick but lackadaisical film version of John Grisham's best-seller lacks the excitement and tension which made his other '93 movie adaptation, *The Firm*, so enjoyable. Washington costars as a journalist who helps Roberts stay alive after her savvy detective work puts her life in peril. ★★½ DVD: $19.99, VHS: $9.99

Pelle the Conqueror

(1988, 160 min, Denmark, Bille August) *Max von Sydow, Pelle Hvengaard.* Winner of the Academy Award for Best Foreign Picture, this epic drama about human resilience stars the hypnotic von Sydow as a poor, but never downtrodden widower who emigrates with his young son from the economically depressed Sweden to Denmark at the turn of the century. His illusory quest for the good life leads only to a straw bed in the cold barn of a brutally insensitive farmer. The story centers around the close relationship between the father and son as they attempt to eke out a happy life amid crushing oppression. (Danish and Swedish with English subtitles) ★★★ DVD: $14.99, VHS: $14.99

Pennies from Heaven

(1981, 107 min, US, Herbert Ross) *Steve Martin, Bernadette Peters, Christopher Walken, Jessica Harper.* Martin had long wanted to do this transplanted version of Dennis Potter's tale of a Depression-era sheet music salesman whose dreary life is in stark contrast to the cheerful songs he sells. With the original recordings of the songs of the era acting as a Greek chorus, Potter's world remains every bit as bleak here as in his other works ("The Singing Detective," "Dreamchild"). Beautifully photographed by Gordon Willis, on stylized sets designed by Ken Adams. And Walken's dance sequence is a show-stopper. ★★★½ DVD Letterbox: $19.99, VHS: $19.99

P

Penny Serenade

(1941, 95 min, US, George Stevens) *Cary Grant, Irene Dunne, Beulah Bondi, Edgar Buchanan.* Grant and Dunne give compelling performances in this first-rate tearjerker as a couple whose attempts to adopt after the death of their baby brings about tragedy. A three-hankier. Fine support from Bondi as a sympathetic adoption official and Buchanan as the couple's best friend. ★★★ VHS: $9.99

The People That Time Forgot

(1977, 90 min, US, Kevin Connor) *Patrick Wayne, Doug McClure, Sarah Douglas.* Our heroes battle prehistoric monsters and savage tribespeople while searching for a lost adventurer. This sequel to *The Land That Time Forgot* is forgettable though silly fun. Based on a story by Edgar Rice Burroughs. ★★ DVD Letterbox: $14.99, VHS: $9.99

The People under the Stairs

(1991, 102 min, US, Wes Craven) *Brandon Adams, Everett McGill, Wendy Robie, Ving Rhames.* Weird horror tale about a young boy, hoping to prevent his family's eviction from their ghetto apartment, who becomes terrorized by his crazed landlords. A big mess of a film — and not at all suspenseful — that aims to be socially relevant but only succeeds as being boring. ★½ DVD Letterbox: $14.99, VHS: $9.99

The People vs. Larry Flynt

(1996, 128 min, US, Milos Forman) *Woody Harrelson, Courtney Love, Edward Norton, Brett Harrelson, James Cromwell, Crispin Glover, Donna Hanover, James Carville.* This is a film full of surprises — from the caliber of its acting to the agility and energy of its storytelling. As unlikely a hero to the Constitution as any in modern America, Larry Flynt started as publisher of *Hustler* magazine. Tasteless and exploitative, the magazine brought him notoriety and many brushes with the law. As the film succinctly recalls, one of these brushes landed him in front of the Supreme Court in a historic case. Director Forman and writers Scott Alexander and Larry Karaszewski never lionize Flynt; it's balanced writing and Flynt is no more than a sleazy publisher who happened to make a significant social contribution. But the beauty of the film is that the story is always appealing. As Flynt, Harrelson has never been more effective, and Love is absolutely riveting as his wife. Forman has crafted a cunning biography, timely political fable, and, most surprisingly, a crushing story of romantic loss. ★★★★ DVD Special Edition: $24.99

The People vs. Paul Crump

(1968, 60 min, US, William Friedkin) Originally made for TV, this powerful criminal investigative documentary was made by a young Friedkin decades before Errol Morris' similarly themed *The Thin Blue Line.* The film investigates the crime and prosecution of Paul Crump, a black man convicted of murder and sentenced to die in the electric chair. Reenacting the crime and murder in dramatic fashion, in which $20,000 was stolen and a security guard killed, action returns to Crump in jail, where even his jailers acknowledge that he is a rehabilitated man. The film is less concerned about his involvement in the murder and more on the man himself, the function of prison and a possible conspiracy by officials to continue to seek his death. ★★★ VHS: $39.99

Pépé le Moko

(1936, 86 min, France, Julien Duvivier) *Jean Gabin, Mirielle Balin.* Set in the Algerian Casbah, this sumptuously photographed, *tres* complex, fascinating story follows a hardened gangster's (Gabin) successful ploy to elude the police. The melodramatic story observes his attraction to a beautiful femme fatale (Balin) who eventually causes his undoing. (French with English subtitles) ★★★½ DVD Criterion Collection: $29.99, VHS: $14.99

Pepi, Luci, Bom y otras Chicas del Montón

(1980, 86 min, Spain, Pedro Almodóvar) *Carmen Maura, Eva Siva, Olvido Gara, Julieta Serrano.* Spanish bad-boy director Almodóvar's 1980 feature debut, a mock-pornographic farce, is rude, funny and *very* nasty. The inimitable Maura plays the heiress Pepi, who seeks revenge on the cop who deflowered her by becoming involved with his masochistic wife Luci and her lesbian rock-star friend Bom. Replete with drugs, erection-measuring parties, beatings and body fluids, this low-budget, raw and crude camp piece lacks the frenetic pace and lush panoramic color scheme of his later works; but as a curio, it is a must for Almodóvar fans. (Spanish with English subtitles) ★★

Peppermint Soda

(1977, 94 min, France, Diane Kurys) *Eléonore Klarwein, Odile Michel.* An art-house favorite for years, this engaging comedy about growing up is set in Paris in the early 1960s. The story follows the lives of two spirited sisters, 12-year-old Anne and 15-year-old Frederique. Writer-director Kurys manages to examine those often explored topics of teendom (first loves, strict parents, fascist teachers and "becoming a woman") with a freshness and honesty that is an absolute delight. Especially good is Klarwein, who as Anne has a kind of sulky, impertinent charm and a devastatingly impish smile. (French with English subtitles) ★★★½

The Perez Family

(1995, 112 min, US, Mira Nair) *Marisa Tomei, Anjelica Huston, Alfred Molina, Chazz Palminteri, Trini Alvarado.* This sensual and hypnotic comedy of errors and culture clash is set during the 1980 Mariel boat-lift (during which thousands of Cuban political prisoners were released and placed in American holding centers to await citizenship). Tomei stars as Dorita Perez, a sultry Cuban floosy who tries to scam her way out of the American internment camp by claiming to be the wife of Juan Raul Perez (Molina), a once dapper, now bedraggled wreck who wants to be reunited with his wife of 20 years, Carmela (Huston), who doesn't even know he's been released. An intoxicating blend of humor, irony and romance enhanced by gorgeous cinematography but marred only by the distracting but effective use of non-Hispanic actors in the lead roles. ★★★ DVD Dual: $14.99

Perfect

(1985, 120 min, US, James Bridges) *John Travolta, Jamie Lee Curtis, Marilu Henner, Carly Simon.* Travolta plays a *Rolling Stone* reporter who is writing an exposé on Los Angeles health clubs and becomes infatuated with a club owner (Curtis). A real stinker. ★ DVD: $9.99

A Perfect Murder

(1998, 108 min, US, Andrew Davis) *Gwyneth Paltrow, Michael Douglas, Viggo Mortensen, David Suchet, Sarita Choudhury.* A slick, uneven, updated version of Alfred Hitchcock's *Dial M for Murder,*

itself a lesser film from the Master of Suspense. While director Davis and writer Patrick Smith Kelly do add a few twists of their own, they aren't enough to make this new version stand on its own. Douglas plays a smarmy business exec who, upon hearing he's nearly broke, decides to murder his wife (Paltrow) for her vast family fortune. He hires her obnoxious, duplicitous lover (Mortensen) to do the job. There's no subtext or resonance here — this is strictly by-the-numbers. ★★ DVD: $14.99, VHS Collector's Edition: $9.99, VHS Letterbox Collector's Edition: $9.99

The Perfect Storm

(2000, 129 min, US, Wolfgang Petersen) *George Clooney, Mark Wahlberg, Diane Lane, Mary Elizabeth Mastrantonio, John C. Reilly, William Fichtner, John Hawkes, Allen Payne, Karen Allen, Bob Gunton, Cherry Jones.* Outstanding special effects combine with a story that's not as clichéd as it could have been to make for a rip-roaring, action-flavored entertainment. Based on a true incident that occurred in 1991, the story follows a group of Gloucester, Massachusetts, fishermen who head to sea during one of the worst storms of the century. Clooney is the captain of the swordfishing boat *Andrea Gail,* whose crew of six sets sail for a final outing of the season. There's no arguing that the special effects are the main attraction here. But *The Perfect Storm* is more than *Twister* at sea. The screenplay, though lacking in subtlety, manages to create sympathetic characters with some depth to them, and sustains credible tension throughout. A good ensemble and a keen sense of atmosphere go a long way in making the viewer forget the occasional lapse in narrative. ★★★ DVD Letterbox Special Edition: $14.99, VHS: $19.99, VHS Letterbox: $19.99

A Perfect World

(1993, 137 min, US, Clint Eastwood) *Kevin Costner, Clint Eastwood, Laura Dern, T.J. Lowther.* An unusual and worthy follow-up to the director's Oscar-winning *Unforgiven.* In an electric and atypically malevolent performance, Costner plays an escaped prisoner who kidnaps an eight-year-old boy and holds him hostage as he tries to outrun the police. Eastwood and Dern play a Texas lawman and criminologist, respectively, tracking them across the state. The film has a dark edge to it, and Eastwood's deliberate pacing only accentuates the tension produced by both the examination of the symbiotic relationship which develops between captive and convict and an unnerving fifteen-minute attempted murder sequence. ★★★½ DVD Letterbox: $19.99, VHS: $14.99

Peppermint Soda

Perfectly Normal

(1991, 106 min, Canada, Yves Simoneau) *Robbie Coltrane, Michael Riley.* British laughmeister Coltrane stars in this quirky sleeper about an opera-loving brewery worker (Riley) who is conned by Coltrane into using his inheritance to open a restaurant staffed by aria-singing waiters. Imaginative visuals by Alain Dotsie. ★★★

Performance

(1970, 106 min, GB, Donald Cammell & Nicolas Roeg) *Mick Jagger, James Fox, Anita Pallenberg.* Fox is a gangster on the run drawn into the richly decadent, hallucinatory and erotic life of a retired rock idol — portrayed by Jagger with androgynous glee. Using this alien world for refuge, he finds himself surrounded by an atmosphere of sex and violence which puts even his hardened senses on edge. A fascinating, yet repellent, visual experience. ★★★ VHS: $19.99

Peril

(1985, 100 min, France, Michel Deville) *Michel Piccoli, Richard Bohringer.* A provocative, erotic thriller about a wealthy industrialist family who hires a musician to give lessons to their precocious daughter. The plot thickens as the wife of the industrialist seduces the young man and uses him as a pawn in a deadly, mysterious game of lust. An enigmatic tale of sexual duplicity. (French with English subtitles) ★★★

Period of Adjustment

(1962, 111 min, US, George Roy Hill) *Jane Fonda, Jim Hutton, Anthony Franciosa, Lois Nettleton.* Hill made his directorial debut in this lively film version of Tennessee Williams' successful stage comedy. In one of her first starring roles, Fonda plays the newlywed wife of war veteran Hutton. However, en route to Miami, their honeymoon trip is anything but sweet. Constantly at odds with each other, they stop at the home of Hutton's war buddy Franciosa, himself experiencing marital difficulties with wife Nettleton. What follows is a comic and tender exploration of love, marriage, male bravado and sexual compatibility. ★★★ VHS: $19.99

Permanent Midnight

(1997, 85 min, US, David Veloz) *Ben Stiller, Elizabeth Hurley, Maria Bello, Owen Wilson.* Based on Stahl's autobiography, *Permanent Midnight* follows Stahl's rise and fall as a writer for various TV shows (such as "Alf"), his "arranged" marriage to a comely TV exec (Hurley) and his near-total collapse from heroin addiction. Stiller gets to contort his face a lot, and look really crappy, but this just isn't the serious breakthrough role he was probably hoping for. Perhaps in this age of "heroin chic," we could use a powerful antidote, but *Permanent Midnight* is just too tedious and facetious to fit the bill. ★★ DVD: $14.99, VHS: $9.99

Permanent Record

(1988, 92 min, US, Marisa Silver) *Keanu Reeves, Alan Boyce, Barry Corbin, Michelle Meyrink, Kathy Baker.* Reeves delivers a compelling performance in this moving, sensitive drama as a tormented youth who can't figure out why his best friend killed himself. ★★★ DVD Letterbox: $14.99, VHS: $7.99

Permanent Vacation

(1980, 87 min, US, Jim Jarmusch) *Chris Parker.* The aimlessness and ennui of the "post-punk generation" is the theme of Jarmusch's first feature film. Drawing from the now-familiar world of the Lower East Side, the film follows the dreamlike odyssey of a 16-year-old (Parker of The Blank Generation) as he looks for meaning in his surroundings and his relationships with his girlfriend, acquaintances and parents. Utilizing the logic of a walking dream, Jarmusch has created a gritty, oppressive yet fascinating world. The film features a jazzy score by John Lurie. ★★★

Permission to Kill

(1975, 96 min, GB, Cyril Frankel) *Dirk Bogarde, Bekim Fehmiu, Ava Gardner, Timothy Dalton, Frederic Forrest.* International intrigue abounds in this complex spy thriller. Bogarde stars as the world-weary head of a spy consortium who must prevent a political expatriate (Fehmiu) from returning to his fascist homeland where certain death awaits. ★★★

Persona

(1966, 83 min, Sweden, Ingmar Bergman) *Liv Ullmann, Bibi Andersson.* Bergman probes the depths of human psychology in this absorbing study of spiritual anguish. Ullmann plays an actress who suffers a nervous breakdown and falls mute. A young nurse (Andersson) is employed to help, but instead, a deep emotional attachment is formed between the two as Andersson tries to bring her out of her silence and back into the world. This fascinating, complex film is erotically charged and remarkably intuitive, and beautifully shot in black and white. Ullmann gives a stunning, haunting performance without uttering one word. (Swedish with English subtitles) ★★★★ DVD: $24.99

Personal Best

(1982, 124 min, US, Robert Towne) *Mariel Hemingway, Patrice Donnelly, Scott Glenn.* Two women become friends and lovers during tryouts for the Olympics. Hemingway plays the fast but feckless Chris who gets a chance to make the team through her involvement with Tori (Donnelly). They become romantically involved, even though Chris denies the true nature of their romance, which only exasperates Tori. Their jealous, bitter coach (Glenn) adds to their relationship's problems by eventually pitting them against each other personally and professionally. The film runs a bit too long and the cinematography is unimpressive with too many lingering group shower scenes and crotch close-ups, though the relationship between the two women is sensitively handled. ★★★ VHS: $14.99

Personal Velocity

(2002, 86 min, US, Rebecca Miller) *Kyra Sedgwick, Parker Posey, Fairuza Balk, John Ventimiglia, Tim Guinee, Wallace Shawn, Ron Leibman.* In this film adaptation of Miller's novel, the right talent, the right prose and the right direction come together seamlessly to paint three powerful portraits of women in transition. Sedgwick gives one of her best performances as an abused wife and mother who learns to reclaim her power. Posey pulls from a place deep within for her portrayal of a woman whose advancing career and painful family history force her to reevaluate her stagnant marriage. And Balk makes waves as a hip, Goth girl who is brought face-to-face with the troubles of her past. Truly magical is the film's ability to create characters with histories, the kind whose every experience is reflected in their present. It's a testament to Miller's detailed screenplay and actresses who understand how to live inside a role. ★★★½ DVD: $14.99

Persuasion

(1995, 103 min, GB, Roger Michell) *Amanda Root, Ciaran Hinds, Susan Fleetwood, Corin Redgrave, Phoebe Nichols, Fiona Shaw, John Woodvine.* A superlative though admittedly modest production, this Jane Austen adaptation is enchanced by an unfaltering cast that delivers performances both sincere and charming. The story revolves around the failing fortunes of the Elliot family and specifically of their as yet unmarried daughter Anne (Root). Shortly after the family has given up its manor, Anne is reunited with her one former true love, Frederick Wentworth (Hinds). Romance follows and, oh, does it make for a swooning good time. Root and Hinds are not your typical screen beauties, and that is precisely what makes them so appealing — their radiance comes from within and it infects the entire film. Furthering the film's charm is its gritty, mud-strewn look at life in the English countryside circa 1810. ★★★★ DVD: $27.99, VHS: $19.99

The Pest

(1997, 90 min, US, Paul Miller) *John Leguizamo, Jeffrey Jones, Edoardo Ballerini.* In his first starring role, Leguizamo is so over the top he often makes Jim Carrey appear subtle by comparison. In this updated, '90s comic version of *The Most Dangerous Game,* Leguizamo plays a small-time con artist who agrees to be hunted by big-game hunter Jeffrey Jones for $50,000. This premise is all Leguizamo needs to offer a hyperventilating series of impersonations, jokes and pratfalls which rarely offer a punch line. Leguizamo is a comic whirlwind, a human Tasmanian Devil, but ultimately *The Pest* is about as substantial as hot air. ★½ DVD: $14.99

Pet Sematary

(1989, 102 min, US, Mary Lambert) *Dale Midkiff, Fred Gwynne, Denise Crosby.* One of Stephen King's scariest books makes for one of his least successful screen adaptations. When his young son is accidentally killed, a grieving father uses a magical graveyard to bring him back to life, though he's not the same fun kid he used to be. (Sequel: *Pet Sematary II*) ★★ DVD: $19.99, VHS: $9.99

Pete Kelly's Blues

(1955, 95 min, US, Jack Webb) *Jack Webb, Lee Marvin, Janet Leigh, Martin Milner, Peggy Lee, Ella Fitzgerald.* Webb and Marvin play Roaring '20s jazz musicians trying to keep ahead of the mob. This beautiful looking film is as stiff as Webb's demeanor; however, it is still worth a look for both a rare and wonderful dramatic performance by Lee as a doomed lounge singer, and two numbers by Fitzgerald. ★★½ VHS: $14.99

Pete 'n' Tillie

(1973, 100 min, US, Martin Ritt) *Walter Matthau, Carol Burnett, Geraldine Page, Rene Auberjonois.* Low-key though very engaging comedy-drama about the courtship and marriage of unlikely partners Matthau and Burnett. Page is terrific in support as Burnett's bitchy friend (she received an Oscar nomination). ★★½ VHS: $14.99

Pete's Dragon

(1977, 129 min, US, Don Chaffey) *Helen Reddy, Jim Dale, Mickey Rooney, Charlie Callas.* Charming live-action and animated Disney musical about an orphaned boy and his friendship with Elliott, the magic dragon. ★★★ DVD: $29.99, VHS: $22.99

Peter Pan

(1953, 78 min, US, Walt Disney) Even by today's standards of super-techno-FX and computer-generated wizardry, Disney's classic *Peter Pan* maintains its stature as an acme in animation technique. And the story is equally dazzling. The airborne hero takes Wendy and her brothers to Never-never Land, an island beyond space and frozen in time; where a determined, ticking crocodile stalks the nefarious Captain Hook, who in turn stalks the boy who will never grow up. How joyful to return to a time and place where — if we believe, and think happy thoughts — we can fly, we can fly, we can fly. ★★★★

Peter Pan

(1960, 100 min, US, Vincent J. Donohue) *Mary Martin, Cyril Ritchard.* Martin's timeless performance highlights this 1955 Emmy Award-winning television broadcast of the Broadway musical. Martin sparkles as the young boy determined never to grow up, and Ritchard is on-hand as the troublesome Captain Hook. Favorite songs inclde "I Won't Grow Up," "Never Never Land" and, of course, "I'm Flying." ★★★½

Peter's Friends

(1992, 102 min, GB, Kenneth Branagh) *Kenneth Branagh, Emma Thompson, Rita Rudner, Stephen Fry, Hugh Laurie.* Attempting to be a British *Big Chill* meets *The Rules of the Game*, the film is set in a large English manor where six old university friends meet for a ten-year reunion. This cast of "wacky" stock characters includes director-star Branagh as a talented writer who sells out; his vulgar, loud-mouthed wife Rudner (the film's cowriter); Fry as the lumbering host harboring a "secret"; and Thompson (who outshines them all) as a gawky, eccentric woman trying desperately to change. Infused with admittedly funny, even witty one-liners, the film suffers from an all-too-familiar sitcom feel. The film's final "revelation" that the bisexual Peter is infected with HIV is a cheap, exploitative device aimed at triggering sappy, liberal sympathies. ★½

Le Petit Amour

(1987, 80 min, France, Agnès Varda) *Jane Birkin, Mathieu Demy, Charlotte Gainsbourg.* Varda's sad tale of a 40-year-old divorcée who takes comfort in the innocent arms of her daughter's best friend, even though he is only fifteen. Aware that the relationship is doomed from the beginning ("I know you won't be around when you start shaving," she tells him), she finds herself unable to resist the charms of what should have been an uncomplicated fling. (French with English subtitles) ★★½ VHS: $79.99

Petit Con

(1984, 90 min, France, Gérard Lauzier) *Guy Marchand, Bernard Brieux.* Whereas most teenage comedies worship their young protagonists, *Petit Con* offers welcome relief with its pungent ironic humor that sends up both its adolescent hero and the values he blithely adheres to. Brieux gives a painfully acute performance as Michel, an 18-year-old cauldron of horniness, oversensitivity and naïve politics who tries to find his niche amongst the charlatans, hoods and weirdos of Paris. A Feifferesque observation of post-Sixties culture. (French with English subtitles) ★★★

La Petite Bande

(1984, 91 min, France, Michel Deville) This delightfully cheery romp follows the fantastic adventures of a group of English school children who play mass hooky and sneak off to France. Their travels take them through towns and countryside. All the while, they are an elusive target for the police who are intent on sending them home. (No dialogue — music and sound effects) ★★★ VHS: $59.99

La Petite Sirene (The Little Mermaid)

(1980, 104 min, France, Roger Andrieux) *Philippe Leotard, Laura Alexis.* They're at it again! More sexual encounters between adults and teenagers are morally forbidden fruit in the States, for French filmmakers, it's almost a way of life. And this tantalizing Nabokovian drama, infused with engaging humor, is no exception. Leotard stars as a middle-aged auto mechanic who becomes the befuddled object of desire to a rich, spoiled 14-year-old obsessed with a fairy tale, "The Little Mermaid." (French with English subtitles) ★★½ VHS: $19.99

Petits Frères

(1999, 92 min, France, Jacques Doillon) *Stéphanie Touly, Iliès Sefraoui.* Doillon's plot-sparse glimpse into contemporary, poor French kids' lives follows thirteen-year-old Talia, who flees her abusive Parisian home for the projects of nearby Pantin. There, a group of Arab and black kids clandestinely steal her only possession, her beloved pitbull named Kim, with designs on selling it. Steaming mad and unaware of the betrayal, Talia relentlessly hunts for Kim while her little clique of new "friends" play innocent and pretend to help. As days pass, a group of older boys enroll Kim in dog fights for their own gain, while Talia gets hold of a firearm, determined to right some wrongs. With *frères* like these . . . Doillon portrays a tragic food chain of screwing-over that begins with adults and, near the bottom, adolescents hungrily waiting to step up. Still, much sympathy for these young subjects, and many unpreachy messages, shine through this highly naturalistic, touching exercise. (French with English subtitles) ★★★ DVD: $29.99, VHS: $19.99

The Petrified Forest

(1936, 83 min, US, Archie Mayo) *Bette Davis, Leslie Howard, Humphrey Bogart.* Davis shines as an Arizona cafe waitress who meets up with English drifter and poet Howard. There at the café, they and a small party are held hostage by escaped felon Bogart. A sterling adaptation of Robert Sherwood's hit play. ★★★½ VHS: $19.99

Petulia

(1968, 105 min, US, Richard Lester) *Julie Christie, George C. Scott, Richard Chamberlain, Shirley Knight, Arthur Hill, The Grateful Dead, Big Brother, and the Holding Company.* Psychedelic San Francisco comes alive in this scintillating romantic drama, one of the great films of the 1960s. Scott is mesmerizing as a staid, recently divorced doctor who begins a bittersweet affair with unhappily married, free spirit Christie. Based on the novel "Me and the Arch Kook Petulia" by John Haase, the film offers a sometimes scathing view of '60s pop and mainstream cultures, though shimmers with a grown-up romanticism. Christie is excellent as the kooky Petulia, but it is Scott and Knight, as Scott's ex-wife, who walk away with the acting honors. ★★★★ VHS: $14.99

Peyton Place

(1957, 157 min, US, Mark Robson) *Lana Turner, Hope Lange, Lloyd Nolan, Arthur Kennedy, Russ Tamblyn.* This box-office smash (which served as the basis for the popular TV series) is a well-made screen version of the Grace Metalious novel. A quintessential soap opera, the story follows the lives of the citizens of a small New England town. ★★★ DVD: $14.99, VHS: $14.99

Phantasm

(1979, 87 min, US, Don Coscarelli) *Michael Baldwin, Bill Thornbury, Angus Scrimm.* Watch out for that flying silver ball! Two brothers decide to investigate the strange goings-on at a mausoleum and become the prey of a demonic figure. Gory, inventive and very unusual. Contains four minutes of outtakes and a deleted scene not included in the original release. (Followed by 3 sequels) ★★★

The Phantom of Liberty

(1974, 104 min, France, Luis Buñuel) *Jean-Claude Brialy, Adolfo Celi, Michel Piccoli, Monica Vitti.* Well into his 70s, Buñuel continued to cinematically pinch our noses with his playful surreal satires on the middle class, democracy and love. "I am fed up with symmetry." So says a character early on in this montage of episodes, dreams and nightmares — each of which makes fun of man's idealistic notions of freedom. Filmed in an almost stream-of-consciousness style, this subversive little comedy is a delight. (French with English subtitles) ★★★½

The Phantom of the Opera

(1925, 90 min, US, Rupert Julian) *Lon Chaney, Mary Philbin.* One of the greatest of all silent films, this chillingly atmospheric adaptation of the classic horror tale stars Chaney in a tour de force performance as the masked composer haunting a Parisian opera house. ★★★½ DVD Milestone Collection: $24.99, VHS: $24.99

The Phantom of the Opera

(1943, 93 min, US, Arthur Lubin) *Claude Rains, Suzanna Foster, Nelson Eddy.* Good remake of the classic silent film. Rains gives a fine performance as the masked phantom living in the sewers beneath the Paris Opera House. ★★★ VHS: $9.99

Phantom of the Opera

(1990, 90 min, US, Dwight H. Little) *Robert Englund, Jill Schoelen.* Slice-n-dice remake of the

Lon Chaney in *Phantom of the Opera*

The Philadelphia Story

delivers a strong emotional punch despite suffering from some procedural flaws, including underdeveloped relationships between characters. Additionally, the film's courtroom scenes are lacking in the expected drama. However, the result is a very moving experience. ★★★ DVD: $14.99, VHS: $9.99

The Philadelphia Experiment

(1984, 102 min, US, Stewart Raffill) *Michael Paré, Nancy Allen, Bobby Di Cicco, Eric Christmas.* Intriguing sci-fi thriller about two WWII sailors who are catapulted into the 1980s. Allen brings a nice no-nonsense sensibility to the modern girl who befriends time travelers Paré and Di Cicco. (Sequel: *The Philadelphia Experiment 2*) ★★½ DVD: $24.99

The Philadelphia Story

(1940, 112 min, US, George Cukor) *Katharine Hepburn, James Stewart, Cary Grant, Ruth Hussey, Roland Young, John Howard.* Cukor's dedication to character, Philip Barry's delicious dialogue, and three of the most enchanting lead performances ever to grace the screen all combine to create the wittiest and most sophisticated comedy of the 1940s. Hepburn repeats her stage role as the Philadelphia socialite faced with a dilemma on her wedding day: who to marry. Stewart won an Oscar for his delightful performance as a reporter covering Hepburn's wedding; and Grant is the essence of charm as Kate's ex-husband. ★★★★ DVD: $19.99

Favorite Line: "The prettiest sight in this fine pretty world is the privileged class enjoying its privileges." —*James Stewart as Macaulay Connor*

Phobia

(1980, 91 min, US, John Huston) *Paul Michael Glaser, Susan Hogan.* The phobia-ridden patients of a psychiatrist are being murdered one by one. The problem is — everyone appears guilty. Glaser stars. It's hard to believe this mess was directed by the great Huston. ★ VHS: $7.99

Phoenix

(1998, 107 min, US, Danny Cannon) *Anthony LaPaglia, Daniel Baldwin, Ray Liotta, Jeremy Piven, Anjelica Huston, Giancarlo Esposito, Tom Noonan, Giovanni Ribisi.* A quartet of crooked Arizona cops are the central characters in this unpleasant but not uninteresting crime drama. Harry (Liotta) is a cop who is also a compulsive gambler. Although he won't welsh on a bet, Harry is not against ripping off a loan shark with his colleagues. Ironically, he is the moral center of director Cannon's misguided film. *Phoenix* spends half its running time setting up a robbery, and by then the coincidences and double crosses have strained credibility. While the performances by the four leads are intensely macho, it is the supporting players — Noonan, Esposito and Ribisi — that make the best impressions. No matter how hard the film wants to rise from its ashes, it can't help but self-destruct. ★★ DVD: $14.99

The Phoenix

(1978, 137 min, Japan, Kon Ichikawa) Set thousands of years ago, this mystical and exciting film tells the story of the quest by an aging queen for the blood of the elusive phoenix, which she believes will give her eternal life. A fantasy-adventure combining live action and animation by world-famous cartoonist Osamu Tezuka. (Japanese with English subtitles) ★★★ VHS: $79.99

horror classic about the cursed opera house dweller and his lady love. Englund (aka Freddy Krueger) barely changes his makeup. Has *no* relation to the Broadway version. ★½

The Phantom of the Paradise

(1974, 92 min, US, Brian De Palma) *William Finley, Paul Williams, Jessica Harper, Gerritt Graham.* The first Faust-influenced horror, rock-musical comedy. A thwarted songwriter sells his soul to the Devil (an astute casting of Williams) for rock 'n' roll success and Harper. A witty satire on at least a dozen different films and genres. De Palma directs many memorable scenes and performers including Beef, a hilarious rock superstar parody played by Graham. ★★★ DVD: $14.99, VHS: $9.99

Phantoms

(1997, 91 min, US, Joe Chappelle) *Ben Affleck, Liev Schreiber, Peter O'Toole, Rose McGowan, Joanna Going.* This Dean Koontz adaptation has a delicious opening: two estranged sisters arrive in their hometown to vist their mother but discover the town is nearly deserted (save for a few fresh corpses). *Phantoms* has some damaging flaws — with the exception of O'Toole (surprisingly effective in what is basically the Peter Cushing role), everyone is cast way too young. And little things like character development, subtlety and dramatic tension are jettisoned completely. Not a bad try, though. ★★ DVD: $14.99, VHS: $9.99

Phar Lap

(1983, 108 min, Australia, Simon Wincer) *Ron Leibman, Tom Burlison, Martin Vaughn.* An inspirational and entertaining account of the rise and fall of one of history's most phenomenal race horses, Phar Lap, who became a Depression-era hero to the Australian people. Liebman stars as the Jewish-American owner who does battle with the high-brow, anti-Semitic Aussie racing elite. ★★★

Phase IV

(1974, 86 min, US, Saul Bass) *Nigel Davenport, Michael Murphy.* Famed title designer Bass (he did a lot of work with Preminger and Hitchcock) directed this cerebral sci-fi tale about a colony of ants that learn the power of their numbers as they fight man for supremacy of the planet. ★★½

Phedre

(1968, 92 min, France, Pierre Jourdan) *Marie Bell.* Jean Racine's Greek tragedy was first staged in Paris in 1677. This film version was theatrically filmed and powerfully presents the sad story of the consuming passion of Phedre, who falls in love with her stepson Hippolyte. Torn with remorse, she is compelled to confess her love to her husband. ★★★

Phenomena

(1984, 110 min, Italy, Dario Argento) *Jennifer Connelly, Donald Pleasence.* A deranged killer stalks a young girl through the grounds of her boarding school, but little does he know this girl can communicate telepathically with all species of insects. Now, she and her allegiant minions have a bone to pick. Uncut European release. (aka: *Creepers*) ★★½ DVD: $29.99

Phenomenon

(1996, 117 min, US, Jon Turtletaub) *John Travolta, Kyra Sedgwick, Forest Whitaker, Robert Duvall, Richard Kiley, Jeffrey DeMunn, Brent Spiner.* Travolta goes the *Charly* route with mixed results. He plays George, an auto mechanic with not much going for him but who's very likable. When he sees what appears to be an extraterrestrial light in the sky, he is infused with a super intelligence and powers of telepathy. As a fantasy, *Phenomenon* beguiles. It's as personable as George himself — yes, he could be smarter but you kinda like what you see. But the romance between George and a divorced mom drags, and the ending is a cheat, a cop-out. *Phenomenon* tries to be magical but ultimately settles for common. ★★½ DVD: $14.99, VHS: $9.99

Philadelphia

(1993, 120 min, US, Jonathan Demme) *Denzel Washington, Tom Hanks, Antonio Banderas, Joanne Woodward, Jason Robards, Mary Steenburgen, Quentin Crisp.* Hanks won a Best Actor Oscar for his performance as a high-powered gay lawyer at a prestigious Philadelphia law firm who is stricken with AIDS. When his employers catch wind of this, they sabotage his work and fire him on false pretense. He retaliates with a lawsuit, soliciting a homophobic ambulance chaser (Washington) to represent him. The first Hollywood film about AIDS, *Philadelphia*

P

Phone Booth

(2003, 81 min, US, Joel Schumacher) *Colin Farrell, Forest Whitaker, Katie Holmes, Kiefer Sutherland, Radha Mitchell.* An 82-minute film in which the main character does nothing more than talk on the phone? Sheer folly even by Hollywood's standards. Or so you'd think. Solid direction from Schumacher and a fierce performance by Farrell transform screenwriter Larry Cohen's gimmicky story into a tense, suspenseful thriller that may have even amused Hitchcock. Farrell plays Stu Shepard, a cocky, shallow New York publicist who hasn't quite lost his soul . . . yet. In between juggling clients, Stu answers a ringing phone on the street, and is told by the person on the other end that if he hangs up he'll be shot. To prove the point, the mysterious caller shoots a troublesome pimp, precipitating a police standoff, TV news coverage and life-threatening demands when everyone thinks it was Stu who pulled the trigger. Schumacher keeps the pacing quick, and flashy cinematography and editing conspire to give the impression that the film is more active than it really is. However, it's to Farrell's credit that *Phone Booth* always appears in motion — residue from a high-velocity performance that assures an improbable scenario is never anything but believable, compelling and wholly enjoyable. ★★★ DVD: $19.99

Phone Call from a Stranger

(1952, 96 min, US, Jean Negulesco) *Bette Davis, Gary Merrill, Shelley Winters, Keenan Wynn, Michael Rennie.* A survivor of a plane crash (Merrill) visits the families of various victims, and receives understanding from a kindly, invalid widow, played by Davis. Involving melodrama. ★★★ VHS: $19.99

Photographing Fairies

(1997, 107 min, GB, Nick Willing) *Toby Stephens, Ben Kingsley, Emily Woof.* Traversing the same territory as *Fairy Tale — A True Story*, this British film takes a more sober view of the subject. Charles Castle (Stevens) is a photographer in 1912 whose life is undone by two obsessions. After he loses his wife on their honeymoon, Charles experiences terrible grief. His despair is further complicated when he becomes aware of the existence of fairies, and is determined to find proof. The truth, however, is a secret that may be best left undiscovered. Director Willing's odd film blends fantasy and reality with decidedly mixed results. The film is ambiguous at best, and the tone shifts uneasily between supernatural mystery and tragic romance. ★★ VHS: $14.99

Physical Evidence

(1989, 99 min, US, Michael Crichton) *Burt Reynolds, Theresa Russell, Ned Beatty.* Reynolds plays a suspended, washed-up cop, awash in booze and self-pity, who is the prime suspect in the murder of an old criminal adversary. Prospects look grim when the defender's office assigns the neophyte "little rich girl" Russell as his lawyer. Did he kill during a drunken fury or was he set up? You may know the answer long before the final resolution, but the film's deft action and Reynolds' always-present self-deprecating humor helps gloss over the film's inconsistencies with plot to produce a mindless escapist entertainment. ★★½ VHS: $14.99

Pi

(1998, 85 min, US, Darren Aronofsky) *Sean Gullette, Mark Margolis, Ben Shenkman, Pamela Hart.* While owing a certain debt to Kafka and *Eraserhead*, *Pi* is an original paranoia story about, well, numbers. Gullette plays Max, a math genius who for two decades has been trying to find a pattern in the stock market. He may have stumbled onto a key number that holds the answers to many problems. But can he handle this knowledge? Max is also prone to headaches and hallucinations that allow this film to be marketed as a thriller. Full of intense music and a bracingly fast black-and-white camera, *Pi* effectively captures a state of mind where a little too much is going on. Detracting from the brilliance are some familiar freshman flaws by director Aronofsky, including an inconsistent pace and an excessive voiceover. When *Pi* settles into its groove, however, it is something to behold. ★★★ DVD: $14.99

Piaf

(1981, 115 min, US, Howard Davies) *Jane LaPortaire.* LaPortaire won a Tony Award for her touching portrayal of the legendary French songstress Edith Piaf. Ballads are woven closely together to re-create the bittersweet life of the woman who so captivated the world with her voice and life. Written by Pam Gems. ★★★

The Pianist

(2002, 148 min, France/Poland, Roman Polanski) *Adrien Brody, Emilia Fox, Thomas Kretschmann, Frank Finlay, Maureen Lipman.* There's a moment a third of the way through *The Pianist*, Polanski's devastating story of survival, in which Wladyslaw Szpilman, a pianist for Polish radio, runs through the ravaged streets of the Warsaw Ghetto having just escaped a train ride to certain death. It is an indelible picture of solitude, of one man's tortured conscience, of a heartbreaking, interrupted farewell. To this scene, as he does to all those before and after it, director Polanski brings an emotional power as to make the heart ache as he captures moments of his own childhood in Nazi-occupied Poland to tell the true story of another afflicted survivor. Academy Award winner Brody is miraculous as Szpilman, who slowly watches his family and fellow Jewish neighbors suffer indignity upon indignity under Nazi rule. As one by one those around him are sent to the death camps, Szpilman must summon all his courage in order to survive. Though *The Pianist* doesn't back away from showing the myriad of hateful Nazi acts, the film's focus is on what acts Szpilman must do and endure to live. This is not a story of a heroic underground fighter, but of a witness to actrocity, a hero by merit of his own survival. *The Pianist* is Polanski's best film in decades, and through craft and cunning and awakened demons of his own, he has composed a singular testament to the struggle of not just one man, but all men. ★★★★ DVD Letterbox: $19.99, DVD Pan & Scan: $19.99, VHS: $9.99

The Piano

(1993, 121 min, New Zealand, Jane Campion) *Holly Hunter, Sam Neill, Harvey Keitel, Anna Paquin, Genevieve Lemon.* Set in 19th-century New Zealand, this is a sumptuously photographed and atmospheric tale of repressed passions. Oscar winner Hunter is Ada, a mute Scottish woman who is forced into an arranged marriage. She and her illegitimate daughter, Flora (the Puck-like Paquin, who also won an Oscar), arrive at their new home with their worldly possessions — including Ada's prized piano. However, Ada's pious new husband, Stewart (Neill), refuses to carry the instrument through the bush, and abandons it on the beach. He then sells the piano to an illiterate settler (Keitel), who in turn agrees to sell it back to Ada in exchange for lessons. His true intentions, however, involve Ada in a bizarre but passionate affair. Campion masterfully uses the power struggles between all of the characters to explore the various themes of colonialism and the plight of women while sketching a mesmerizing and emotionally involving story. ★★★★ DVD: $14.99, VHS: $9.99

The Piano Lesson

(1995, 99 min, US, Lloyd Richards) *Alfre Woodard, Charles S. Dutton, Carl Gordon, Courtney B. Vance.* August Wilson's Pulitzer Prize-winning Broadway drama is given an excellent realization in this made-for-TV adaptation. Re-creating his acclaimed stage role, Dutton stars as Boy Willie, a 1930s black sharecropper with dreams of buying the land his family had once worked as slaves. He travels to Pittsburgh to convince his sister Berniece (Woodard) to sell the family's prized piano to pay for the farm. Thus sets in motion a passionate, heartfelt series of soul-searching and familial confrontations and reminiscences. Wilson's dialogue conjures another time and place, evoking through hearty though poetic anecdotes and conversations the history of a family. As Boy Willie, Dutton gives an outstanding performance, balanced by Woodard's superbly underplayed Berniece. ★★★★ DVD: $19.99, VHS: $14.99

The Piano Teacher

(2001, 125 min, Austria/France, Michael Haneke) *Isabelle Huppert, Benoit Magimel.* Huppert delivers the most compelling portrayal of profound emotional disintegration since Jeanne Dielman as Erika, a well-respected professor of music and teacher of a master class in piano. Erika lives with her domineering, overbearing mother (Girardot); her claustrophobic existence is both ameliorated and exacerbated by the control she exercises over her students and her uncompromising, obsessional relationship with the music to which she's devoted. Enter Walter (Magimel), a young, vigorous sciences student with the audacity to audition for Erika's master class as an elective. Confrontation is inevitable, and her secret vices and self-imposed penances are no longer adequate release. Haneke's effective, arresting direction delivers a covert evocation of Erika's indefatigable inner demons, allowing full expression to Huppert's commanding and forceful creation. *The Piano Teacher* manifests a palpable anxiety as it shows the prosaic commonplaces of day-to-day life interspersed with the intellectual and sensual stimulation of magnificent music — as the ridiculous often mixes with the divine. (French with English subtitles) ★★★★ DVD Letterbox Unrated: $29.99, VHS Unrated: $24.99

Adrien Brody in *The Pianist*

The Pick-Up Artist

(1987, 81 min, US, James Toback) *Robert Downey, Jr., Molly Ringwald, Dennis Hopper, Danny Aiello, Harvey Keitel, Mildred Dunnock.* A good cast valiantly tries to bring some life to this otherwise lifeless drama. Downey is the title character, setting his sights on Ringwald. ★★ DVD: $9.99, VHS: $9.99

The Pickle

(1993, 103 min, US, Paul Mazursky) *Danny Aiello, Dyan Cannon, Shelley Winters, Barry Miller, Chris Penn, Ally Sheedy, Isabella Rossellini, Dudley Moore.* Since Mazursky has dabbled with autobiographical material in the past, and had a flop with *Scenes from a Mall*, the obvious question is whether this comedy springs from some personal experience. Aiello effectively assumes the role of Harry Stone, the hedonistic yet weary director who reluctantly checks his integrity and accepts a job at the helm of a movie about a giant pickle from outer space. Though *The Pickle* is a curious mix of genuine drama and broad sitcom humor that never quite gels, it is entertaining and more than holds its own amidst the crowded giant vegetable genre. ★★½

Pickpocket

(1959, 75 min, France, Robert Bresson) *Martin LaSalle, Marika Green, Jean Pelegri, Pierre Leymaire.* Director Bresson paints a picture of self-conscious obsession in *Pickpocket*, an unadorned and spare examination of a haunted young man (LaSalle) who schools himself in light-fingered theft. The film employs a quasi-documentary style as the thief Michel roams the subterranean concourses of the Paris Metro, looking for easy marks, or casing fat handbags at the races. At once determined and conflicted, Michel seeks philosophic justification for his actions in discussions at coffee bars, yet cannot visit his ailing mother to face her concerns for him. In only 75 minutes, the emotionally riveting *Pickpocket* provides a multilayered character study within a tale of personal despair and ultimate redemption, creating an in-depth portrait with a minimal of brush strokes. (French with English subtitles) ★★★½ VHS: $19.99

Pickup on South Street

(1953, 81 min, US, Samuel Fuller) *Richard Widmark, Jean Peters, Thelma Ritter.* Widmark stars in this classic film noir spy thriller as a small-time pickpocket whose latest sting unwittingly involves him in political espionage. Director Fuller expertly extorts maximum tension from its novel premise; and Ritter gives a sensational performance as the pathetic, streetwise fence. ★★★½ DVD Criterion Collection: $29.99, VHS: $19.99

Picnic

(1955, 115 min, US, Joshua Logan) *William Holden, Kim Novak, Cliff Robertson, Rosalind Russell.* Riveting film version of William Inge's play about the sexual frustrations and longings in a small Kansas town. Holden is the beefy drifter who sets hearts aflutter; Robertson is his old college friend; Novak is Robertson's girlfriend who prefers Holden; and Russell gives an electrifying performance as a spinster schoolteacher. ★★★★ DVD: $24.99

Picnic at Hanging Rock

(1977, 115 min, Australia, Peter Weir) *Rachel Roberts, Helen Morse, Dominic Guard, Margaret Nelson.* This dreamlike puzzle revolves around the disappearance of three schoolgirls and their teacher on an afternoon outing. Imbued with a swooning atmosphere of sexual mystery and ominous desire. ★★★½ DVD Criterion Collection: $29.99, VHS: $19.99

Picnic on the Grass

(1959, 95 min, France, Jean Renoir) *Paul Meurisse, Catherine Rouvel.* Set near the ancestral home of his painter father, Auguste, and filmed in an impressionistic style, Renoir has made a "filmed poem" to the mystery and power of nature. The story centers on a hardened biologist and candidate for President of the United States of Europe whose dedication to genetic engineering and the power of science is broken by the love of a peasant girl. (French with English subtitles) ★★★ VHS: $59.99

Picture Bride

(1995, 101 min, US, Kayo Hatta) *Toshiro Mifune, Youki Kudoh, Akira Takayama, Tamlyn Tomita.* A subtle, deliberately paced and seductively involving portrait of one young woman's long, protracted journey across land, oceans and the terrain of the heart. Kudoh is luminous as Riyo, one of the more than 26,000 Asian women who in the early 1900s traveled to Hawaii to marry men farming the cane fields. The couples were known to each other only by photos and letters, and both Riyo and her new husband Matsuji (played with earthiness by Takayama) had concealed secrets from each other in their communications. Meticulously produced, lushly photographed and told with love and heart, the film leaves the viewer with a sense of the warmth of fond memory. ★★★ DVD: $19.99, VHS: $9.99

Picture Perfect

(1997, 100 min, US, Glenn Gordon Caron) *Jennifer Aniston, Kevin Bacon, Jay Mohr, Olympia Dukakis, Illeana Douglas.* Aniston is Kate, a career-driven employee at an upscale advertising company who gets passed over for a promotion because she's single. Instead of pursuing legal action, Kate agrees to a faux fiancé, Nick (Mohr). Even though Kate has only met Nick once, she offers to pay him to join in the charade, unaware that Nick wants more than a business proposition from her. The cast is attractive, and there's some low-key chemistry amongst the principals. But several genuine laughs and the thankfully brisk pacing are hampered by a too-cutesy climax and the unremarkable, contrived scenario. A watchable, amiable, easy-to-swallow time killer whose title is wishful thinking. ★★½ DVD: $14.99, VHS: $6.99

Pie in the Sky

(1996, 94 min, US, Bryan Gordon) *Josh Charles, Anne Heche, John Goodman, Peter Riegert, Christine Ebersole, Christine Lahti.* Charles plays a young man with two obsessions: his childhood love, Amy (Heche), and traffic. Conceived while his parents were stuck in a traffic jam, he feels it's his life work, and he dreams of meeting his idol, traffic reporter Alan Davenport (Goodman). Meanwhile, he and Amy have an on-again, off-again romance. A mildly enjoyable romantic comedy, *Pie in the Sky* isn't as whimsical or romantic as it wants to be, nor as edgy or energetic as it should be, but the traffic-obsession angle lends it a nice, quirky feel. ★★½ DVD Letterbox: $19.99

A Piece of the Action

(1977, 135 min, US, Sidney Poitier) *Sidney Poitier, Bill Cosby, James Earl Jones, Denise Nicholas, Hope Clarke, Eric Laneuville, Sheryl Lee Ralph.* Con men Poitier and Cosby do their best to help a group of ghetto children. Overlong film mixes the crazy criminal antics of Cosby and Poitier with the social drama of life in the ghetto. For the most part, it doesn't work. ★★ DVD: $19.99, VHS: $14.99

Pieces of April

(2003, 81 min, US, Peter Hedges) *Katie Holmes, Patricia Clarkson, Oliver Platt, Derek Luke, Sean Hayes, Alison Pill.* April Burns is having a hard time pulling herself up from the mattress on the floor of her East Village apartment. It's Thanksgiving Day, and she's invited her estranged, quintessentially suburban family to dinner. The family is as reticent as she, but all trudge inexorably to the expected seasonal horror of making small talk while eating way too much food with people you avoid the rest of the year. As the film bounces between April's adventures in cooking and the Burns family road trip, random, painful memories reemerge on both sides of the lifestyle divide, dropping clues to the family dynamics — whether the family of birth or the family of choice. Making a skillful directorial debut, writer Hedges (*What's Eating Gilbert Grape?*) juxtaposes wildly divergent moods, careening between laugh-out-loud comedy and solemn pathos with the unexpected quickness found during actual family dinners. The remarkable cast is fearless in its emotional exposure and accomplished in the execution of character portrayals. This is, of course, expected from trusted veterans Clarkson and Platt; but Holmes as April brings an intelligent complexity to her role which belies her youth. Hedges' remarkable control of the medium and the energetic flow of the film, the ensemble's dead-on-target and often improvisational performances, a maximum use of location and a refreshingly quick-witted script coalesce into an entertainment with surprising emotional impact. ★★★½ DVD: $14.99, VHS: $39.99

Pierrot le Fou

(1965, 110 min, France, Jean-Luc Godard) *Jean-Paul Belmondo, Anna Karina.* Godard's ebullience for life and his fascination with the possibilities of film are wonderfully displayed in this frantic and stylized tale of love, intrigue and betrayal. Belmondo and Karina star as two young lovers who involve themselves in a murder and begin an idyllic flight from justice. Filming without a script, Godard embellishes his story of doomed romantic love with splashy colors, exotic settings in the south of France, his trademark use of jump-cuts, classical music and literary references. (French with English subtitles) ★★★½

The Pillow Book

(1997, 126 min, GB, Peter Greenaway) *Ewan McGregor, Vivian Wu, Ken Ogata.* Director Greenaway achieves new levels of cinematic outlandishness with this visually sumptuous, kaleidoscopic panoply of fetishism and sexual degradation as set against the world of literature and poetry. Wu stars as Nagiko, a young Japanese woman who is obsessed with two childhood rituals: one in which her father (Ogata) wrote on her neck and forehead, the other being read to from the 1000-year-old "Pillow Book" of an imperial courtesan. This manifests in her adult life as a fixation for having her lovers write all over her body. When she meets McGregor, a translator who immediately takes to her lust for erotic penmanship and encourages her to publish her own "Pillow Book." Greenaway, never one to shy away from on-screen flesh, provides plenty of it here including full frontals of both McGregor and Wu. Some viewers might be little more than bewildered by Greenaway's overarching intellectualism (his references *are* obscure) and his opulent visual sense, but this is nothing less than a masterful addition to his opus. (In English and Japanese, Mandarin and Cantonese with English subtitles) ★★★★ DVD: $27.99

Pillow Talk

(1959, 105 min, US, Michael Gordon) *Rock Hudson, Doris Day, Tony Randall, Thelma Ritter.* A box-office sensation in 1959, this delightful sex farce teamed Hudson and Day in the first and best of their "battle of the sexes." Though they can't stand each other in person, Rock and Doris unknowingly fall in love on their party line. Great support from Randall and the always reliable Ritter. ★★★½ DVD: $14.99, VHS: $9.99

Piñero

(2001, 94 min, US, Leon Ichaso) *Benjamin Bratt, Giancarlo Esposito, Talisa Soto, Nelson Vasquez, Michael Wright, Michael Irby, Jaime Sanchez, Mandy Patinkin, Rita Moreno.* A fragmented, often compelling biography of the late Puerto Rican poet/playwright Miguel Piñero, that much like his life is a fractured, free-form jazz poem that wanders all over the place. The handsome Bratt has been prettied-down to play Piñero, a junkie and ex-con torn between drugs and his genius. The story follows the writer's rise to success, his battle with drugs and other demons, and his various relationships (though his bisexuality is almost ignored). Director Ichaso employs a sometimes irritating, jagged color/black-and-white style that's supposed to echo Piñero's chaotic existence. He relies too heavily on flashbacks and fidgety camerawork, but has provoked a terrific performance from Bratt who brings the writer's words to life. ★★½ DVD Director's Cut: $19.99, VHS: $9.99

Ping Pong

(1987, 95 min, GB, Po Chih Liong) *David Yip, Lucy Sheen.* From the mysterious nocturnal streets of London's Chinatown comes this exotic, noirish comedy-thriller about a young Anglo-Chinese law student who is whisked into the tantalizingly complex task of executing a traditional Chinese will. Simple at first, but because of an intricate web of conditions and bequests, it falls to a vivacious young woman to piece together some unresolved mysteries. A richly textured and often comical portrait of a transplanted society caught between tradition and transition, flavored with a striking visual flair and moments of magic and fantasy. ★★★

Pink Cadillac

(1989, 122 min, US, Buddy Van Horn) *Clint Eastwood, Jim Carrey, Bernadette Peters, Geoffrey Lewis.* This change-of-pace comedy is a misfire for director Eastwood. He plays a bail-bond bounty hunter who becomes unlikely partners with the wife (Peters) of one of his prey. Not as abysmal as some critics have complained, there are some entertaining

moments in the film — especiallly when Eastwood is afforded the chance to masquerade as various characters. But those hoping for a "make-my-day" Clint or rock'em-sock'em action would do better to look elsewhere. ★★ DVD: $19.99, VHS: $14.99

Pink Flamingos

(1972, 95 min, US, John Waters) *Divine, Edith Massey, Danny Mils, Mink Stole, David Lochary.* The sleazo-porn-trash extravaganza that made the fabulous Divine a household word and Waters an object of fear, awe and nausea all over the world. In one of the most disgusting and perversely funny films ever made, zaftig matriarch Babs Johnson (Divine) and her family of egg-adoring Mom (Massey) and chicken-loving son (Mils) battle the repugnant Connie and Raymond Marble (Mink Stole and Lochary) for the title of "filthiest person alive." Restored version with additional footage. ★★★★ VHS: $19.99

Pink Floyd: The Wall

(1982, 99 min, GB, Alan Parker) *Bob Geldof, Christine Hargreaves, Bob Hoskins.* Pink Floyd's mammoth rock 'n' roll allegory is vividly brought to the screen by Alan Parker in this visually impressive and sonically explosive epic. Geldof (Mr. Live Aid) is the embodiment of a frazzled rock idol as the down and out Pink. ★★★ DVD: $31.99, VHS: $19.99

The Pink Panther

(1964, 113 min, GB, Blake Edwards) *Peter Sellers, Herbert Lom, David Niven, Robert Wagner, Claudia Cardinale.* This delightful comedy caper introduced Sellers' now-famous characterization of the bumbling Inspector Clouseau. While not the best of the Pink Panther series (that honor goes to its sequel *A Shot in the Dark*), this is still a zesty and sophisticated farce with many of the "trademarks" of Sellers' unsurpassed comic ability. ★★★½ DVD: $19.99

The Pink Panther Strikes Again

(1976, 103 min, GB, Blake Edwards) *Peter Sellers, Herbert Lom, Leslie Anne Down, Burt Kwouk.* This hilarious fourth installment in the *Pink Panther* series is one of the best of the bunch. The Inspector's former boss, chief Dreyfuss (Lom), has gone off the deep end and will stop at nothing, including holding the entire world hostage with a giant death ray, to see Clouseau dead. Sellers, as always, is hysterical, especially in the Munich Octoberfest scene. (Sequel: *Revenge of the Pink Panther*) ★★★½ DVD: $19.99

Favorite Line: Peter Sellers as Inspector Clouseau, after being asked what kind of a bomb was set off: "The exploding kind."

Pinky

(1949, 102 min, US, Elia Kazan) *Jeanne Crain, Ethel Waters, Ethel Barrymore, Nina Mae McKinney, William Lundigan.* Crain stars as a Southern black woman who passes for white when she leaves her home to live in the big city, finds work as a nurse and becomes romantically involved with a white doctor. After her mother (Waters) takes ill, she returns home to care for her and is confronted with racism and her own personal identity crisis. Tightly directed by Kazan and featuring standout performances by Oscar nominees Crain, Waters and Barrymore, this melodramatic masterpiece is a must-see for those seeking drama that hits hard and doesn't let up until the last Kleenex is used. ★★★★ VHS: $19.99

Jeanne Crain and Ethel Waters in *Pinky*

Pinocchio

(1940, 88 min, US, Ben Sharpsteen & Hamilton Luske) Disney's second animated feature is filled with fantastical imagery and a wild carnival-like atmosphere as Geppetto's little wooden boy goes on an almost picaresque journey toward a more fleshy existence. While the film is guaranteed to inspire delight (let us not forget Jiminy Cricket), the story's invective morality along with Disney's at times horrific representation of killer whales and an underwater purgatory for little boys who lie may prove a tad frightening for many a tot. Still, as with all vintage Disney, this is a must-see. ★★★★

Pippin

(1981, 120 min, US, David Sheehan) *Ben Vereen, William Katt, Eric Berry, Chita Rivera, Martha Raye.* First-rate production of Bob Fosse's Tony Award-winning musical. One of Fosse's greatest stage triumphs, "Pippin" is a jubilant, colorful and tuneful look at Pippin, son of King Charlamagne, and his search for fulfillment and love. Vereen recreates his award-winning role as the Narrator. Fosse's dance numbers are outstanding, and Stephen Schwartz's score is earthy, witty and vibrant. ★★★½ DVD: $19.99

Piranha

(1978, 92 min, US, Joe Dante) *Bradford Dillman, Heather Menzies, Kevin McCarthy, Barbara Steele, Dick Miller.* Director Dante and writer John Sayles teamed for the first time (they encored with *The Howling*) for this engaging horror spoof. You'll regret it if you pass up this biting tale of mutant, man-eating fish making julienne fries of beach-loving teens. Promises lots of laughs and chills, and contains the immortal line, "Excuse me sir, the fish are eating the guests." (Sequel: *Piranha: The Spawning*) ★★★ DVD: $14.99, VHS: $14.99

Piranha II: The Spawning

(1981, 88 min, US, James Cameron) *Lance Henriksen, Tricia O'Neill.* This sequel to *Piranha* takes its stylistic cues from *Wolfen*, mixes in a bunch of Roger Corman camp and resembles *Jaws* in substance. Put it all together and you have an amazingly silly but enjoyable horror movie . . . and, yes, it was directed by *that* James Cameron. He shows nothing of the greatness which would follow. ★★ DVD Pan & Scan: $19.99, VHS: $14.99

The Pirate

(1948, 102 min, US, Vincente Minnelli) *Gene Kelly, Judy Garland, The Nicholas Brothers.* Kelly's thrilling dance numbers highlight this charming musical about traveling acrobat Kelly being mistaken for a notorious pirate by love-struck Garland. Cole Porter's score includes "Be a Clown" and the Nicholas Brothers are sensational in support. ★★★

Pirates

(1986, 124 min, US/France, Roman Polanski) *Walter Matthau, Charlotte Lewis, Cris Campion.* A fun if convoluted pirate comedy with Matthau in good form as a ruthless scalawag in search of a famed treasure. ★★½

The Pirates of Penzance

(1983, 112 min, US, Wilford Leach) *Kevin Kline, Rex Smith, Angela Lansbury, Linda Rondstadt, George Rose.* All of the exuberance and rollicking sense of fun of the 1980s hit Broadway revival of Gilbert and Sullivan's operetta has been joyously captured on screen in this vastly underrated musical. Kline repeats his Tony Award-winning role as the

Johnny Depp in *Pirates of the Caribbean: The Curse of the Black Pearl*

Pirate King, with Smith as the "slave to duty" pirate apprentice, Lansbury as his guardian, the wonderful Rose as "the very model of a modern major general." Kline is in terrific form, both as singer and physical comedian; and the colorful sets are a major asset. ★★★½

Pirates of the Caribbean: The Curse of the Black Pearl

(2003, 133 min, US, Gore Verbinski) *Johnny Depp, Geoffrey Rush, Orlando Bloom, Keira Knightley, Jonathan Pryce, Jack Davenport.* Throughout his career, producer Jerry Bruckheimer has packaged some processed movie junk that has screamed "concept" — but making a movie based on a Disneyland attraction? Sheer folly, if not downright the end of civilization as we know it, right? Well, a funny thing happened on the way to the road of ruin: a long-dead film genre is reborn, a Hollywood rebel hits the mainstream big time, and the movie summer of '03 has one of its biggest — and most deserved — hits. Not since Errol Flynn and Burt Lancaster buckled their swash has a pirate adventure delivered the goods. In a wonderfully comic performance that combines the attitude of Keith Richards, the timing of Jack Benny and the swagger of Lauren Bacall, Depp shines as the notorious Captain Jack Sparrow, a pirate commander who has lost his ship, the *Black Pearl*. It's been stolen by the nasty Captain Barbossa (a devilishly sly Rush), whose crew has attacked the Caribbean port town Port Royal and kidnapped the governor's feisty daughter Elizabeth (Knightley). The unlikely tag team of Jack Sparrow and heroic blacksmith Will Turner (Bloom) sail to her rescue, setting in motion high-seas adventure with supernatural spirits, black-hearted pirates and the British navy. Director Verbinski, who brought just the right amount of suspense to *The Ring*, nicely balances comedy, intrigue, swordplay and special effects (which aren't allowed to overshadow the story), ensuring that while no one will take it too seriously, all will be mightily entertained. ★★★½ DVD Letterbox 2-disc set: $29.99, VHS: $24.99

The Pit and the Pendulum

(1991, 97 min, US, Stuart Gordon) *Lance Henriksen, Jeffrey Combs.* From the director of the cult classic *Re-Animator* comes this stylishly sadistic remake of the Edgar Allan Poe horror classic. Henriksen stars as Torquemada, the mad monk of the

Spanish Inquisition, who goes to extreme lengths to suppress his awakening sexual desires for a beautiful peasant girl. Director Gordon sacrifices atmosphere for hard-core shocks with surprisingly effective results. ★★½ VHS: $79.99

Pitch Black

(2000, 109 min, US, David Twohy) *Vin Diesel, Radha Mitchell, Cole Hauser, Keith David.* Marooned on a seemingly lifeless planet, a group of desperate passengers turn to a convicted murderer for help when they discover that the planet is inhabited by an army of deadly alien creatures. Good special effects, better-than-average action scenes and a nice sense of atmosphere go a long way to compensate for a familiar story line and stock characters. *Pitch Black* may be derivative, and you may know every film from which its borrowing, but it's also a lot of fun, something few sci-fi films have been recently. ★★½ DVD Unrated: $26.99, DVD R-Rated: $26.99, VHS Unrated: $9.99, VHS R-Rated: $9.99

The Pitfall

(1948, 86 min, US, Andre de Toth) *Dick Powell, Jane Wyatt, Raymond Burr, Lizabeth Scott.* The Great American Dream gone sour is the theme of this intriguing moral tale. Powell — the bored husband of Wyatt — forgets his idyllic suburban family to enjoy a brief fling with a sexy siren (Scott) — an action that soon brings violence, deceit, tragedy and sudden death. Burr is memorable as the hulking private eye. ★★★

Pixote

(1981, 127 min, Brazil, Hector Babenco) *Fernando Ramos da Silva, Marilla Pera, Gilberto Moura, Edilson Lino.* A brilliant, disturbing film about a band of youths who escape a brutal juvenile detention center to resume their desperate lives of petty crime in the slums of São Paulo and blaze a trail of violence. Our hero Pixote (da Silva), a gun-toting 10-year-old outcast, and his youthful friends get involved in a drug smuggling scheme and soon befriend an aging alcoholic prostitute (the riveting Pera), who offers them a brief respite of tenderness as a mother figure and a lover. Pixote, a desperate boy in a winless situation, struggles against the hardships of an environment deprived of hope and ruled by casual brutality. From a novel by Jose Louzeiro. (Portuguese with English subtitles) ★★★★ DVD: $29.99

A Place in the Sun

(1951, 122 min, US, George Stevens) *Montgomery Clift, Elizabeth Taylor, Shelley Winters, Raymond Burr, Anne Revere.* An ambitious effort, and one of the few movies of its day to address the subject of class conflict in America. Clift gives a great performance as a young man content to climb the social ladder by ordinary means. That is, until he meets rich society girl Taylor. Although occasionally heavy and slow-moving, and the impending tragedy is perhaps all too inevitable, this is still poignant material, and Clift and Taylor express genuine tenderness and passion. Winters is memorable as the girlfriend who Clift wishes would vanish. Based on Theodore Dreiser's "An American Tragedy." ★★★½ DVD: $14.99, VHS: $14.99

A Place in the World

(1992, 120 min, Argentina, Adolfo Aristarain) *Federico Luppi, Jose Sacristan, Cecilia Roth, Leonor Benedetto.* This remarkably moving coming-of-age "western" from Argentina is an extended flashback depicting the trials and tribulations that help teenager Ernesto (Batyi) find a place in the world. The son of schoolteacher Mario (Luppi) and

doctor Ana (Roth), Ernesto lives in the commune of San Luis, a small farming village near Buenos Aries. Writer-director Aristarain uses the arrival of an outsider — a geologist (Sacristan) — to explore the lives and values of the townspeople as their rural world is slowly transformed by industry. *A Place in the World* is one from the heart: for its respect for the characters and their choices are both heartwarming and heartbreaking. The powerful message of this simple, eloquent film will have a lasting impact. (Spanish with English subtitles) ★★★½

A Place of Weeping

(1986, 88 min, South Africa, Darrell James Roodt) *James Whylie, Geini Mhlophe.* A powerful human drama of one woman's personal fight for freedom and her battles against the hatred and resentment of a people, as well as the oppressive hand of the Apartheid system. A heroic story of her bravery and emotional traumas against undignified abuse. ★★★

Places in the Heart

(1984, 113 min, US, Robert Benton) *Sally Field, Danny Glover, John Malkovich, Ed Harris, Lindsay Crouse, Amy Madigan.* Outstanding autobiographical drama from director Benton with Field in her (second) Oscar-winning role as a stalwart widow, raising her young son in Depression-era Texas, who partners with a black transient (the terrific Glover) to raise cotton. The film features a superb supporting cast. ★★★½ DVD Dual: $19.99, VHS: $14.99

Plague

(1991, 105 min, Argentina/France/GB, Luis Puenzo) *William Hurt, Robert Duvall, Raul Julia, Sandrine Bonnaire, Jean-Marc Barr.* Albert Camus' haunting novel of the anarchy, suffering and isolation that befalls a city when the plague resurfaces is brought to the screen in this serious, well-intentioned effort. The film focuses more on personal traumas and human nobility than Camus' greater existential thought. The film tries hard not to be too grim, concentrating instead on the human interests of the people whose courage and selflessness shine during the tragedy. A worthy attempt to translate such a distressing story to the screen. ★★★

Plague of the Zombies

(1966, 90 min, GB, John Gilling) *Andre Morrell, Diane Clare, John Carson.* Extremely atmospheric and highly chilling, this overlooked gem from Hammer Films introduced zombies to moviegoers two years before *Night of the Living Dead*. While not the flesh-eating kind, the *Plague* zombies are still

Pixote

quite terrifying: silent, staring, mindless servants who are virtually unstoppable. A voodoo cult has sprung up in a small Cornish village, terrorizing its inhabitants and preying on the young people of the town. A recently arrived London doctor uncovers the sinister goings-on and sets about to destroy the unholy coven. Beautifully photographed, the film contains a remarkable, classic cemetery resurrection scene which must be seen to be believed. ★★★½ VHS: $14.99

Le Plaisir

(1951, 96 min, France, Max Ophüls) *Simone Simon, Claude Dauphin.* These three stories from Guy De Maupassant all deal with man's eternal search for pleasure. The first story contrasts pleasure and old age, the second pleasure and purity, and the third pleasure and marriage. Ophüls' stylish, brilliant film, set in 1890s France, playfully speculates on man's alternating natures and conventions. (French with English subtitles) ★★★½ VHS: $14.99

Plan 9 from Outer Space

(1959, 79 min, US, Edward D. Wood, Jr.) *Bela Lugosi, Criswell.* As TV psychic Criswell admits, "There comes a time in every man's life when he just can't believe his eyes." Rent this and your time has come. Based on sworn testimony, this opus, often considered the worst movie ever made, tells about some silly suited space alien's latest attempt at taking over the world after failing the eight previous tries (makes you wonder why we even bother to keep watching the skies). Lugosi died shortly after shooting commenced, so a chiropractor half his age and twice his size acted as his stand-in, disguising himself by holding a cape over his face the whole time. We could go on . . . . ★ DVD: $14.99, VHS: $9.99

Planes, Trains and Automobiles

(1987, 93 min, US, John Hughes) *Steve Martin, John Candy, Edie McClurg.* Teenmeister Hughes wrote and directed this funny tale of uptight businessman Martin trying to get home to Chicago for Thanksgiving, only to face disaster at every attempt. Candy is endearing as a bumbling chatterbox who becomes Martin's unwanted traveling companion. ★★★ DVD: $19.99, VHS: $9.99

Planet of the Apes

(1968, 112 min, US, Franklin J. Schaffner) *Charlton Heston, Roddy McDowall, Kim Hunter, Maurice Evans.* Classic sci-fi adventure with Heston as a modern-day astronaut hurled centuries into the future to a planet where apes rule and man is hunted for sport. McDowall, Hunter and Evans, all under some incredible makeup effects, appear as adversarial and not-so-adversarial simians. (Sequel: *Beneath the Planet of the Apes*) (Remade in 2001) ★★★½ DVD Letterbox 35th Anniversary: $26.99, DVD Pan & Scan 35th Anniversary: $26.99, VHS: $9.99

Planet of the Apes

(2001, 120 min, US, Tim Burton) *Mark Wahlberg, Tim Roth, Helena Bonham Carter, Michael Clarke Duncan, Paul Giamatti, Cary-Hiroyuki Tagawa, Kris Kristofferson, David Warner, Charlton Heston.* Those "damn dirty apes" are back, a lot more dirtier and virulent than last seen in the five-film series from the 1960s and '70s. This slicker, effects-centric "reinterpretation" of the 1968 classic moves at a swifter pace, but comes up a little short in the sheer thrills-and-fun department. Maybe it has to do with the rather bland lead, stoically but humorlessly played by Wahlberg, an Air Force captain from the year 2029 who finds himself thrust onto a futuristic planet ruled by apes. Gone are such affable charac-

ters as Cornelius and Zira; they've been replaced by a ruthless general (a nimble Roth) and various militaristic gorillas. But some of the complications (some parallel the original, some don't) in which the writers place the characters can be thrilling, nicely captured by cinematographer Philippe Rousselot. Director Burton has certainly stamped his own, unique vision on Pierre Boulle's novel, but while being a visual accomplishment, it is curiously absent of passion and humor. ★★½ DVD Letterbox 2-disc set: $19.99, VHS Special Edition: $9.99

Planet of the Vampires

(1965, 86 min, Italy, Mario Bava) *Barry Sullivan, Norman Bengell.* The crew of an interplanetary spacecraft crash land on a mysterious planet and must defend themselves from a race of formless creatures determined to take over their bodies. Mindless schlock that only occasionally delivers the horror goods. ★★ DVD Letterbox: $14.99, VHS: $14.99

Platinum Blonde

(1931, 86 min, US, Frank Capra) *Jean Harlow, Loretta Young, Robert Williams.* Capra's bright comedy may be stagey but never fails to entertain. Harlow stars as an heiress who decides to do Pygmalion one better by marrying her subject — down-to-earth newspaper reporter Williams. She vows to make him a gentleman, but finds her work cut out for her. Though Harlow's delightful performance would make her a full-fledged star (her nickname "platinum blonde" would stick till her untimely death), it is Williams who is the main attraction. With his Will Rogers-like plainness, Williams has a natural screen presence. ★★★ DVD: $24.99

Platoon

(1986, 120 min, US, Oliver Stone) *Charlie Sheen, Willem Dafoe, Tom Berenger, Forest Whitaker, John C. McGinley, Kevin Dillon, Johnny Depp.* Stone's numbing Vietnam War drama is one of the finest war films ever made, and is the best film made about the experiences of American infantrymen in that war. Sheen plays a young recruit torn between sergeants Dafoe and Berenger. Stone won an Oscar for this masterful achievement, and he would win another one for his equally brilliant companion piece, *Born on the Fourth of July.* Winner of 4 Academy Awards including Best Picture. ★★★★ DVD Special Edition: $19.99, VHS: $9.99

Play It Again, Sam

(1982, 84 min, US, Herbert Ross) *Woody Allen, Diane Keaton, Tony Roberts, Susan Anspach, Jerry Lacy.* Allen is a hapless girl chaser who depends on the ghost of his hero, Humphrey Bogart, to guide him in matters of the heart. And he needs all the help he can get! Scripted by Allen. ★★★½ DVD Letterbox: $19.99, VHS: $14.99

Play It to the Bone

(1999, 100 min, US, Ron Shelton) *Woody Harrelson, Antonio Banderas, Lolita Davidovich.* Shelton, the writer-director of *Bull Durham,* delivers a boxing comedy that's just plain bull. Harrelson and Banderas play two aging pugilist buddies who are convinced to go on a road trip to Vegas, where they will fight each other for a shot at the title. *Play It to the Bone* is raunchy without being funny, violent without being exciting. ★★ DVD: $9.99, VHS: $9.99

Play Misty for Me

(1971, 102 min, US, Clint Eastwood) *Clint Eastwood, Jessica Walter, Donna Mills.* Eastwood's directorial debut is an accomplished thriller about a

Jean Harlow in *Platinum Blonde*

California D.J. (Eastwood) and his number one fan (Walter), who loves the song "Misty" and whose fatal attraction for the radio jock puts him and those around him in danger. Lots of chills; Walter is terrific as the obsessed fan. ★★★ DVD 30th Anniversary: $14.99

Playboy of the Western World

(1962, 100 min, Ireland, Brian Desmond Hurst) *Siobhan McKenna, Gary Raymond.* This is a beautiful and lyrical film version of J.M. Synge's classic Irish play about a boyish young man who captivates a small village with his tale of how he did in his dad. Synge's soaring poetry is faithfully translated to the screen and the film is inestimably aided by a transcendent performance by McKenna — one of the great Irish actresses of her day. ★★★½

The Playboys

(1992, 110 min, Ireland, Gillies MacKennon) *Aidan Quinn, Robin Wright, Milo O'Shea, Adrian Dunbar, Albert Finney.* This sweet comic fable stars the ever-luminous Wright as the strong-willed Tara, a young woman who defies her small Irish town by having a baby out of wedlock. Determined not to let a man influence her life, Tara nevertheless finds herself drawn to one of the vaudevillians in an Irish acting group. The man (strongly played by handsome Quinn) vies for Tara's attention along with the local heavy-drinking constable (Finney), whose obsession with Tara leads to a series of tragic circumstances. The film suffers from some sappy dialogue and the main plot point can be seen a mile away. But it does offer sumptuous settings (circa 1957) and a truly awe-inspiring performance from Finney. ★★★ DVD: $14.99, VHS: $14.99

The Player

(1992, 123 min, US, Robert Altman) *Tim Robbins, Greta Scacchi, Fred Ward, Whoopi Goldberg, Peter Gallagher, Brion James, Cynthia Stevenson, Vincent D'Onofrio, Dean Stockwell.* *The Player* is a trenchant black comedy about a young film studio executive named Griffin Mill (played with unnerving restraint by Robbins) who finds his fax-filled, mineral water-drinking, Range Rover-driving life coming apart after he receives death threats from a screenwriter he has shunned. As he dives deeper into paranoia, we learn more and more about an industry that thrives on schmoozing, back-stabbing and green-lighting multimillion dollar projects that are pitched in 25 words or less. With a brilliant, pointedly satiric script by Michael Tolkin, who adapted his own cult novel, *The Player* marks the return to power of its iconoclast director Altman. There's also the miraculous supporting cast, and then there are the cameos too numerous, and too revealing to name. A sublime movie-going experience, *The Player* is filled with cinematic jazz riffs that transcend all expectations. ★★★★ DVD: $19.99

The Players Club

(1998, 103 min, US, Ice Cube) *Ice Cube, Jamie Foxx, Bernie Mac, Monica Calhoun, A.J. Johnson, Alex Thomas, LisaRaye, John Amos.* The Players Club marks a disappointing directorial debut from rapper/actor Cube. The story, what little there is, centers around Diamond (LisaRaye) and her experiences at The Players Club, a Florida strip joint where she works as a dancer in order to pay for college and support her young son. Cube proves that as a director he is visually competent and knows how to keep the action moving at a swift pace, but he is sabotaged by a misogynistic, homophobic script full of one-dimensional caricatures and inane dialogue. ★½ DVD: $14.99, VHS: $6.99

Playing Away

(1986, 102 min, GB, Horace Ove) *Norman Beaton, Robert Urquhart.* Lightweight though amiable "culture-shock" comedy about a country village's attempts to prove its liberalness by challenging a rough-and-tumble Jamaican cricket team from Brixton in honor of their "Third World Week." ★★½

Playing by Heart

(1998, 121 min, US, Willard Carroll) *Gillian Anderson, Ellen Burstyn, Sean Connery, Anthony Edwards, Angelina Jolie, Dennis Quaid, Jay Mohr, Ryan Phillippe, Gena Rowlands, Jon Stewart, Madeleine Stowe.* Episodic look at matters of the heart through different couples, from enduring to maternal to puppy love. With so many different storylines, it's hard not to play favorites, and here Phillippe and Jolie's mutual seduction is a standout, with his brooding fiercely complemented by her vibrancy (note to actors: you'll always be upstaged by dogs, babies, and Angelina Jolie). It's so much fun to see these actors at work (and in such brief bursts) that it's easy to overlook how soapy and unimportant it all is. ★★½ DVD: $19.99, VHS: $9.99

Playing for Time

(1980, 150 min, GB, Daniel Mann) *Vanessa Redgrave, Jane Alexander, Maud Adams, Verna Bloom, Melanie Mayron.* A brutally honest account of the real-life story of Fania Fanelon (Redgrave), a survivor of the Auschwitz death camp. Redgrave, Alexander and playwright Arthur Miller (who scripted this American production) won Emmy Awards for their contributions to this unusually powerful telemovie. ★★★★

Playing God

(1997, 94 min, US, Andy Wilson) *David Duchovny, Timothy Hutton, Angelina Jolie, Michael Massee, Peter Stormare. Playing God*, a big-screen vehicle for TV star Duchovny, is in desperate need of repair. He plays a former doctor who lost his license when he lost a patient who doped up. Acquiring his stash one night, Duchovny saves the life of a shooting victim who turns out to be a henchman of local crime boss Hutton, who hires

Duchovny as his gang's full-time doc. This premise could have made an interesting thriller, but the plot just drunkedly stumbles along, piling up clichés (soft-boiled, monotonous voice-overs; technoesque soundtrack; pointlessly artsy cinematography) while its story line rambles on. Duchovny has no charisma, and Hutton is about as menacing as a squirt gun. ★ DVD: $14.99, VHS: $9.99

Playtime

(1967, 119 min, France, Jacques Tati) *Jacques Tati.* Monsieur Hulot returns, with his simple life meeting modern Paris head-on, from a labyrinthine airport to a haywire supper club. This is Tati's astonishing comic masterpiece, giving his themes of history (and innocence) lost a grand, 70mm canvas on which to play. The filmed metropolis is actually an elaborate set (dubbed Tativille at the time); real Parisian landmarks are winkingly glimpsed in reflections. ★★★★

Plaza Suite

(1971, 115 min, US, Arthur Hiller) *Walter Matthau, Barbara Harris, Lee Grant, Maureen Stapleton.* Matthau plays the roles of three different men in this engaging Neil Simon comedy, based on his stage play. Matthau plays a businessman, a Hollywood producer and the father of a would-be bride. ★★★ DVD: $19.99, VHS: $14.99

Pleasantville

(1998, 124 min, US, Gary Ross) *Tobey Maguire, Reese Witherspoon, Jeff Daniels, Joan Allen, William H. Macy, J.T. Walsh, Don Knotts.* An enchanting comedy, endearing fantasy and subtle social commentary, *Pleasantville* marks the directorial debut of writer Ross (*Dave, Big*), who once again has created a wondrous fish-out-of-water story. David and Jennifer (Maguire and Witherspoon in charming performances) are typical '90s siblings — that is, until they are literally zapped into a 1950s sitcom, "Pleasantville." Now living out episodes in black and white, they proceed to raise consciousness (and havoc) by bringing real-life issues into this perfect, Ozzie and Harriet world. As characters begin to turn to color, issues of prejudice and individuality are soon brought to the forefront. Gorgeous art direction and special effects enhance the smart story, and Ross never allows the remarkable production values to overshadow the tale at hand. ★★★½ DVD Letterbox: $14.99, VHS With extra footage: $9.99, VHS Letterbox With extra footage: $9.99

The Pledge

(2001, 123 min, US, Sean Penn) *Jack Nicholson, Robin Wright Penn, Aaron Eckhart, Benicio del Toro, Helen Mirren, Vanessa Redgrave, Sam Shepard.* Disturbing, moody and complex, Penn's raw, edgy mystery takes you on a road you're not sure you want to travel, but it turns out to be a fascinating journey. In a tortured, haunting performance, Nicholson is Jerry Black, a Nevada police detective on the eve of retirement. When his going-away party is interrupted by the brutal murder of a young girl, he joins the investigation, which quickly produces a likely suspect. But Jerry isn't so sure. That doubt and a pledge he makes to the dead girl's mother sends Jerry on an obsessive search for the real killer. Based on the novel by Friedrich Dürrenmatt, the film explores the conflicting emotions Jerry experiences as he adjusts to a new town, new job, new relationships, old instincts. As Jerry's behavior becomes all the more consumed, Penn skillfully shifts between police procedural, romantic melodrama and arty psychological treatise. A daring, rewarding, uncompromising film whose subject matter may make this tough going for more sensitive viewers. ★★★½ DVD Letterbox: $14.99, VHS: $9.99

Plenty

(1985, 119 min, US, Fred Schepisi) *Meryl Streep, Sam Neill, Sting, John Gielgud, Tracey Ullman.* Schepisi brings an elegant directorial style to David Hare's acidic drama about England after WWII. As Susan Traherne, a complex woman whose psychological breakdown mirrors Britain's own post-war decay, Streep is riveting. ★★★ DVD: $19.99, VHS: $9.99

The Plot Against Harry

(1969/1990, 80 min, US, Michael Roemer) *Martin Priest, Ben Lange, Maxine Woods.* Made by NYU film professor Roemer, this witty and amazingly insightful social comedy was originally shot in 1969, but money problems kept it in the can until 1990 when Roemer reedited the film. The result is a joyous, cooly observed and, at times, hilarious story about the tales of woe that befall Harry Plotnick, a modern-day Job and small-time Jewish gangster. Roemer's direction, sort of pre-Jarmusch Jarmusch, is astute; especially his uncanny eye for capturing '60s kitsch as well as the impending changes brought on New York by drugs and violence. ★★★½ VHS: $29.99

The Ploughman's Lunch

(1983, 100 min, GB, Richard Eyre) *Jonathan Pryce, Tim Curry, Rosemary Harris.* This cutting inquiry into the devious opportunism of a BBC journalist scans the subconscious mood of Britain behind the false huzzahs of the Thatcher brigade. Pryce is the cold-hearted protagonist who will stop at no romantic treachery or professional hypocrisy in his claw up the social ladder. ★★★

Plucking the Daisy

(1956, 99 min, France, Marc Allégret) *Brigitte Bardot, Robert Hirsch.* This amusing Bardot romp has our buxom beauty as the daughter of a French official who seems to get into all kinds of trouble. First, she enters an amateur striptease contest and then becomes involved in the theft of a rare book from the Balzac museum. The film will not strain your mental capacity, but it's an enjoyable vehicle for BB fans. (French with English subtitles) (aka: *Mademoiselle Striptease* and *Please Mr. Balzac*) ★★½ DVD Letterbox: $29.99, VHS: $19.99

The Plumber

(1980, 76 min, Australia, Peter Weir) *Judy Morris, Ivar Kants.* A sinister comedy-drama that presents the case of an unexpected and unknown visitor, a manipulative plumber, who invades the home of a medical researcher and his wife and instigates emotional turmoil. A darkly funny thriller. ★★★

Plunkett & Macleane

(1999, 102 min, GB, Jake Scott) *Robert Carlyle, Alan Cumming, Jonny Lee Miller, Liv Tyler, Michael Gambon.* A visually striking 18th-century adventure that pays more attention to look than story. But what a look for this tale of two highwaymen who team to rob London's aristocracy. Carlyle and Miller are Plunkett & Macleane, who meet in prison and eventually make the rounds of society functions, with the grungy Plunkett posing as the dapper Macleane's servant. Scott maintains a lively pace and endows the film with gorgeous production design, but he can't always sustain tension as the story occasionally meanders and loses the energy that the well-staged robberies and charades produce. ★★½

THE DISCERNING FILM LOVER'S GUIDE

Pocahontas

(1995, 80 min, US, Eric Goldberg & Mike Gabriel) *Mel Gibson, Irene Bedard, Judy Kuhn, David Odgen Stiers, Russell Means, Christian Bale, Linda Hunt.* A Disney film that is serious in tone but satisfying in story and execution. Disney's first animated feature based on real-life characters recalls the tale of the young, feisty Indian princess Pocahontas who falls in love with British explorer John Smith. This mythic "Romeo and Juliet" romance is set in the New World's colony of Virginia, where a greedy English governor has arrived intent on wiping out the Algonquin nation in his search for treasure. Less comedic than other Disney films, *Pocahontas* through story and song relays powerful messages of prejudice, avarice, spirituality and environmental concerns. ★★★ DVD: $29.99, VHS: $22.99

Pocket Money

(1972, 102 min, US, Stuart Rosenberg) *Lee Marvin, Paul Newman, Strother Martin, Wayne Rogers, Hector Elizondo.* Two marginal, modern-day cowpokes go for the big score with a larcenous cattle deal in this sardonic, existential western. Newman and Marvin are particularly delicious in this Terrence Malick-scripted fable about the quest for salvation (read: "big money"). Fine cinematography by Lazlo Kovacs. ★★★ VHS: $14.99

Pocketful of Miracles

(1961, 136 min, US, Frank Capra) *Bette Davis, Glenn Ford, Peter Falk, Glenn Ford, Hope Lange, Ann-Margret.* Entertaining remake of director Capra's own 1934 hit *Lady for a Day*. Davis chews much scenery as Apple Annie, the poor, old apple seller who masquerades as a rich matron — with a little help from her friends — for the sake of her daughter (Ann-Margret in her film debut). Oscar-nominee Falk is a scene-stealer. ★★★ DVD Letterbox: $14.99

Poetic Justice

(1993, 108 min, US, John Singleton) *Janet Jackson, Tupac Shakur, Tyra Ferrell, Regina King.* Singleton follows his sizzling debut, *Boyz N the Hood*, with this disappointing drama starring Jackson as a hairdresser and part-time poet who is wooed by tough guy Shakur. Though hampered by an anemic plot, Singleton gets some nice work out of both Jackson and Shakur (whose easy-going demeanor belies his real-life character). Sadly, though, Jackson fails to breathe adequate life into her screen persona's poetry, written in real life by Maya Angelou. ★★ DVD: $14.99, VHS: $9.99

Point Blank

(1967, 92 min, US, John Boorman) *Lee Marvin, Angie Dickinson, Keenan Wynn, Carroll O'Connor.* Director Boorman creates a stylish new form of film noir using wide screen and color in this cynical thriller. Marvin is at his meanest as a man shot and left for dead by his unfaithful wife and her mobster lover. Now he's back and out for revenge against the businessmen and mobsters who did him wrong. ★★★½ VHS: $19.99

Point Break

(1991, 122 min, US, Kathryn Bigelow) *Keanu Reeves, Patrick Swayze, Gary Busey, Lori Petty, John C. McGinley, James LeGros, Anthony Kiedis, Lee Tergesen.* An action-packed and incredibly silly adventure film. Reeves plays a novice FBI agent who goes undercover on the Southern California beaches to infiltrate a group of surfers suspected of being The Ex-Presidents — a highly successful gang of bank robbers whose masks feature the likenesses of President Bush's four predecessors. Swayze is the philosophy-quoting, mystical gang leader whose series of macho stunts of one-upmanship with Reeves creates several astonishing action scenes — including a hold-your-breath, how-did-they-do-that sky jumping scene, a prolonged but impressive surfing sequence and a lengthy chase scene amid the back alleys of Los Angeles. ★★½ DVD Letterboxed: $14.99

Point of No Return

(1993, 109 min, US, John Badham) *Bridget Fonda, Gabriel Byrne, Dermot Mulroney, Anne Bancroft, Harvey Keitel, Miguel Ferrer.* For those who saw Luc Besson's dazzling *La Femme Nikita*, it is difficult to recommend this faithful remake. Though the film copies the original nearly shot-for-shot, it lacks its predecessor's visual panache and chilling neo-pop style. Still, the film fared well at the box office, and standing on its own, it is not an unworthy effort. Fonda is fine in the lead role of a societal throwaway who is saved from the executioner by a shadowy government official who wants to make a super assassin out of her. It's yet another case of Hollywood not being able to leave well enough alone. ★★½ DVD: $9.99, VHS: $6.99

The Pointsman

(1987, 95 min, Netherlands, Jos Stelling) *Jim Van Der Woude, Stephane Excoffier.* In the dead of winter, a beautiful, fashionably attired French woman accidentally gets off a train in the remote Scottish Highlands where she encounters a strange recluse who lives and works at the desolate train station. In this "artsy," quirky and complex story, the two, neither speaking the other's language, begin a strange relationship. This unconventional tale is a visually stunning mood piece which, for those with the patience, proves to be an absorbing and thoughtful treatise on the vagrancies of love and communication. ★★★

Poison

(1991, 85 min, US, Todd Haynes) This amazingly self-assured first feature by director Haynes interweaves three seemingly unconnected stories, each with its own individual filmmaking style. *Hero* is told in a semidocumentary form, recounting a young boy's killing of his abusive father and his miraculous flight away. *Horror*, filmed in a '50s sci-fi horror flick manner, follows the tragedy that strikes a scientist after he successfully isolates the human sex drive in liquid form. The final tale, adapted from the writings of Jean Genet, *Homo*, an intensely sensual and lyrical story of obsessive, unrequited love set in a prison. *Poison* is a wholly original, provocative, unsettling and intelligent film that is a must-see for adventurous videophiles. ★★★½ DVD: $14.99, VHS: $9.99

Poison Ivy

(1992, 89 min, US, Katt Shea Ruben) *Drew Barrymore, Sara Gilbert, Tom Skerritt, Cheryl Ladd.* Barrymore stars as the mysterious, seductive, possibly naughty Ivy, who insinuates herself into the dysfunctional family of an awkward and angry classmate, Sylvie, played convincingly by Gilbert. A familiar battle for identity ensues as the two outcasts venture to see if a slut and an intellectual can maintain a friendship. Ivy soon manipulates her way into Sylvie's wealthy family and sets her sights on seducing dad (Skerritt), whose wife (Ladd) is dying of emphysema. *Poison Ivy* may be melodramatic, predictable and based on many unfortunate stereotypes, but it sure makes for amusing trash. (Followed by 2 sequels) ★★ DVD: $19.99

Pola X

(2000, 134 min, France, Leos Carax) *Guillaume Depardieu, Katerina Golubeva, Catherine Deneuve.* After his first two critically acclaimed films, director Carax fell into disfavor with the critics and public, alike, with his next film *Lovers on the Bridge*. In choosing Herman Melville's obscure 1852 novel "Pierre, or the Ambiguities" (itself a critical and commercial disaster) for his next film, Carax may have seen a camaraderie with a fellow artist suffering disappointment. *Pola X* is the story of a young literary sensation, Pierre (Depardieu), who lives a life of wealth and privilege. He is engaged to the lovely Lucie (Chaillot), but his life begins to spiral out of control when he meets the mysterious Isabelle (Golubeva), who claims to be his half-sister. Pierre and Isabelle abruptly run off together to a ramshackle industrial flat in Paris, where Pierre begins work on his new literary masterpiece while consumating a relationship with Isabelle and an ever-quickening descent into the depths of madness. Carax's direction is heavy handed at times, but it is always audacious and provocative. The absolutely stunning cinematography recalls both the rich textures of German Expressionism and the spontaneity of the French New Wave. (French with English subtitles) ★★★ DVD: $24.99, VHS: $19.99, VHS Letterbox: $19.99

Police

(1984, 113 min, France, Maurice Pialat) *Gérard Depardieu, Sophie Marceau, Sandrine Bonnaire.* On the surface, Pialat's tensely exciting "policier" is about a brutal Paris cop's (Depardieu) efforts to break up a North African drug ring. But Pialat, who combines ferocious rawness with pristine formality, goes further than anyone before him in establishing the policeman's physical, moral and emotional intimacy with the criminals he interrogates and brutalizes. Depardieu is at the top of his form as the course, crude cop. A film of stunningly vivid temperment that is less a typical, action-packed thriller and more a psychological probe done with exacting realism. (French with English subtitles) ★★★½ VHS: $29.99

Police Academy

(1984, 97 min, US, Hugh Wilson) *Steve Guttenberg, Bubba Smith, Kim Cattrall, George Gaynes.* An insipidly funny slapstick comedy about zany misfit police cadets being let loose on an unsuspecting public. This combination of low-brow hijinks and sophomoric schtick does contain a few laughs, but this imitative romp is years behind other "dumb" comedies such as *Airplane!* (Followed by 6 sequels) ★★½ DVD Letterbox Special Edition: $19.99; DVD: $14.99, VHS: $14.99

Police Story

(1985, 92 min, Hong Kong, Jackie Chan) *Jackie Chan, Bridget Lin, Maggie Cheung, Cho Yuen, Bill Tung, Kenneth Tong.* *Police Story* is certain to amaze, delight and entertain. The plot has Jackie as a policeman on the trail of drug smugglers, but story matters little for it is the action-comedy sequences, with Jackie doing all of his own death-defying stunts, that capture one's attention. From dangling on a runaway bus with only an umbrella handle to his balletic dance on speed boats, Jackie Chan's stunts should excite even the most jaded action fan. (aka: *Jackie Chan's Police Force*) ★★★½ VHS: $29.99

Ponette

Polish Wedding

(1998, 105 min, US, Theresa Connelly) *Claire Danes, Gabriel Byrne, Lena Olin, Jon Bradford, Mili Avital.* Set in Detroit at an indeterminate time, *Polish Wedding* is a muddled and disjointed though earnest effort by writer-director Connelly. Byrne and Olin are a husband and wife whose lives barely intersect. He bakes bread, she makes babies: 7 children, 5 living, 4 sons. Danes is the roving daughter, who is named to lead the procession of the Virgin just before she finds out she's pregnant. At times a meditation on procreation and fecundity, sometimes an exploration of working-class travails, the film is too long and awkwardly structured; its attempt at hyperrealism is inauthentic and flat. Slapstick is no substitute for charm, or melodrama for profundity. ★½ DVD: $9.99, VHS: $9.99

Pollock

(2001, 122 min, US, Ed Harris) *Ed Harris, Marcia Gay Harden, Amy Madigan, Val Kilmer, Jennifer Connelly, John Heard, Bud Cort, Jeffrey Tambor.* One of the more difficult accomplishments in film is to capture the creative process at work. Artist, author, actor, composer, they all seem to be painted with the same broad brush stroke. There are, to be sure, a few exceptions, such as *Pollock*, an intense, challenging portrait of noted 20th-century painter Jackson Pollock. Directed with competence but acted with brilliance by Harris, the film isn't able to fully flesh out Pollock as a man, but Harris has superbly conveyed the drive, frustration, technique and evolution of an artistic genius. The story follows Pollock's struggling early years in New York's 1940s art scene, to his romance and marriage to artist Lee Krasner (Harden), to his eventual celebrity, all the while given to bouts of alcoholic binges and self-destructive behavior. As the guiding force in Pollock's life, Oscar winner Harden excels as the supportive Krasner, whose belief in her husband's ability never waivers. An invigorating glimpse at a most unconventional man. ★★★ DVD: $24.99, VHS: $14.99

Pollyanna

(1960, 134 min, US, David Swift) *Hayley Mills, Jane Wyman, Agnes Moorehead.* Cute children's tale about a beguiling young girl (Mills) who captures the hearts of an entire New England town with her warm and sunny disposition. ★★★ DVD 2-disc set: $22.99, VHS: $19.99

Poltergeist

(1982, 114 min, US, Tobe Hooper) *Craig T. Nelson, JoBeth Williams, Beatrice Straight, Heather O'Rourke, Dominique Dunne, Zelda Rubenstein,* Oliver Robins, James Karen. A classic horror story from director Hooper, this film owes much to its writer and producer, Steven Spielberg. When spirits from the "other side" kidnap their young daughter (the adorable O'Rourke), an ordinary suburban family goes through Heaven and Hell to get her back. Williams and Nelson offer the right blend of playfulness and seriousness as the hapless parents, and Straight and Rubinstein are the best ghostbusters yet. This is the finest ghost story since *The Haunting*, and the special effects are terrific. (Followed by 2 sequels) ★★★★ DVD Letterbox: $14.99, VHS: $9.99, VHS Letterbox: $14.99

Polyester

(1981, 86 min, US, John Waters) *Divine, Tab Hunter, Edith Massey, Mink Stole.* In this odorized ode to suburban decay, Divine is a campy delight as Baltimore housewife Francine Fishpaw, who experiences her own private hell when hubby-with-a-bad-toupee has an affair, her daughter turns out to be a slut, and her revered son is cited as the notorious foot-stomper. Then, Golden Boy Tab Tomorrow (Hunter) comes into her life. Waters tones down the crudeness to win new fans and succeeds. Waters' gimmick of offering Odorama cards to cinema patrons (number two on the scratch-and-sniff card is a doozy) works wonderfully, but sadly, unless you kept yours from 1981, they are not available for the video. ★★★

Ponette

(1997, 97 min, France, Jacques Doillon) *Victoire Thivisol, Matiaz Caton, Xavier Beauvois, Delphine Schiltz, Marie Trintignant.* An intimate and moving portrait of a 4-year-old girl coping with the death of her mother, *Ponette* is astonishing in its utter simplicity. Writer-director Doillon's poignant film builds inexoribly to a powerful conclusion as it examines the mourning of a young girl. Capturing both the innocence and cruelty of children, the film examines Ponette's every emotion as she is advised, taunted and given "trials" by other classmates following her tragedy. What drives Ponette, however, is her unfailing belief that God will allow her to reunite with her mother not only in her dreams, but in life as well. Doillon's grasp of childhood trauma is heartbreaking, and his shooting much of the film from Ponette's point of view is very effective. The large cast of children here are cute, but never cloying, making the emotional impact of the story realistic, without being melodramatic. (French with English subtitles) ★★★½ DVD: $19.99, VHS: $14.99

Pool Hustlers

(1984, 101 min, Italy, Maurizio Ponzi) *Francesco Nuti, Gulliano de Sio.* The smoke-filled rooms of pool halls provide the unlikely backdrop to this charming comedy-drama. Francesco, a poor man's Pierre Richard, is a mop-headed amateur billiards wizard who gets himself hustled out of thousands of dollars by an unscrupulous champion. His efforts to pay off the debt, first by stealing and second by competing in a high-stakes billiards contest, is the basic plot. But it is our bungling hero's endearing personality that gives the film its appeal. (Italian with English subtitles) ★★★ VHS: $24.99

Poolhall Junkies

(2003, 99 min, US, Mars Callahan) *Mars Callahan, Chazz Palminteri, Rod Steiger, Christopher Walken, Michael Rosenbaum, Rick Schroder, Alison Eastwood.* Walking the line of mediocrity, the conventional *Poolhall Junkies* involves a hotshot pool hustler who struggles to go legit, but is inevitably drawn back into his old ways due to circumstances beyond his control. Johnny (Callahan) is a pool natural who after screwing his shady mentor (Palminteri), tries to get a real job to appease his well-to-do law student girlfriend, Tara (Eastwood). Naturally, it doesn't last long and before you know it, Johnny is locked into a high-stakes game with his former mentor's new hired gun (Schroder). It's an all-too-familiar premise told in an all-too-familiar way. However, the ensemble is terrific, giving more dimension than what's on the written page. Walken, in particular, shines in his two tragically brief appearances as a wealthy lawyer who takes a liking to the young pool hustler. ★★ DVD: $26.99, VHS: $49.99

Poor White Trash

(1962, 84 min, US, Harold Daniels) *Peter Graves, Tim Carey.* Cajun camp starring Graves as a self-righteous city slicker, and Carey (the sharpshooter in Kubrick's *The Killing*) as a bayou bully. So controversial upon its release that armed guards were posted at the drive-ins to keep out minors! ★

Pootie Tang

(2001, 81 min, US, Louis C.K.) *Lance Crouther, Wanda Sykes, Chris Rock, Jennifer Coolidge, Robert Vaughn.* Yet another skit-turned-feature film (based on an act from "The Chris Rock Show"), *Pootie Tang* promises to be better than the pack with a very funny first 15 minutes or so. The central joke, Pootie speaks in his own unintelligible language and everyone seems to get what he's saying, gets old after a while. And, like most skit/features, it wears out its welcome looooong before the end credits. Still, there are some hilarious moments (the nature of Pootie's hit single being one of them), and the blaxploitation fight scene parodies are well done, making the acceptable *Pootie Tang* indeed better than the recent skit comedies which came before it. A backhanded compliment, sure, but a compliment just the same. ★★½ DVD: $19.99, VHS: $9.99

Popcorn

(1990, 93 min, US, Mark Herrier) *Jill Schoelen, Tom Villard, Dee Wallace Stone, Ray Walston, Tony Roberts.* Nice twist to the "crazed killer" genre, where a horror film festival is the setting for a killer stalking members of the audience who believe his escapades are all just a part of the show. ★★½ DVD Letterbox: $24.99

The Pope Must Die(t)

(1991, 89 min, GB, Peter Richardson) *Robbie Coltrane, Paul Bartel, Beverly D'Angelo.* A rollicking poke at the Catholic Church, the Vatican and the men who occupy its hallowed halls. Coltrane plays a this-close-to-being-defrocked priest who, through a misspelling made by a near-deaf dictation clerk, is accidentally catapulted into the Papacy. What follows is a sometimes hilarious commentary on the role of the Church in late-20th-century life as this new Pope promulgates his liberal philosophies on birth control, abortion and the use of Vatican money. ★★★

The Pope of Greenwich Village

(1984, 120 min, US, Stuart Rosenberg) *Mickey Rourke, Geraldine Page, Daryl Hannah, Eric Roberts.* A tough, gritty crime drama with Rourke and Roberts as two small-time hoods trying to make a name for themselves in New York Mafioso territory. Rourke and Roberts are very good, as is Page in a sensational supporting role as a crooked cop's slovenly mother. ★★★ DVD: $19.99, VHS: $9.99

P

Popeye

(1980, 113 min, US, Robert Altman) *Robin Williams, Shelley Duvall, Ray Walston, Paul Dooley, Bill Irwin.* Though this musical based on the famous comic strip and cartoon is not without its momentary enjoyments, the story of Popeye the Sailor, his "goil" friend Olive Oyl and lifelong nemesis Bluto is mostly an overblown extravaganza. Williams gets "A" for effort for his daring performance as Popeye, and Duvall is a perfect Olive, but Harry Nilsson's forgettable score and Altman's clumsy direction offer little to recommend. ★★ DVD: $14.99, VHS: $9.99

Porcile (Pigsty)

(1968, 99 min, France/Italy, Pier Paolo Pasolini) *Pierre Clementi, Franco Citti, Jean-Pierre Léaud, Ugo Tognozzi.* Two contrasting stories are interwoven in a single narrative in Pasolini's biting satire on society's darker nature and the entrenched powers that be who are compelled to squash it. One tale, set in a barren, mountainous land in medieval times, features Clementi as a wandering soldier who descends into cannibalism, eventually recruiting a cult of followers. The contrasting story, set in modern times, stars Léaud as the bourgeois son of a former Nazi, now a wealthy industrialist, who is politically and sexually confused — so confused as to prefer the sexual companionship of his neighboring peasants' pigs. While not as explicitly outrageous as *Salo: 120 Days of Sodom*, this brutal allegory of savage "innocents" and their threat to organized society is intense and involving. (Italian with English subtitles) ★★★ DVD: $29.99, VHS: $29.99

Porky's

(1981, 94 min, US/Canada, Bob Clark) *Dan Monahan, Kim Cattrall, Wyatt Knight.* Sophomoric sex comedy manages a few laughs but is mostly lamebrained. Set in 1954 Florida, the story tells of a group of high school teenagers who play practical jokes and try to get laid. (Followed by 2 sequels) ★★ DVD: $14.99

Porn Star: The Legend of Ron Jeremy

(2002, 76 min, US, Scott J. Gill) *Ron Jeremy, William Margold, Al Goldstein, Seymore Butts, Sharon Mitchell, Larry Flynt, Tabitha Stevens, Veronica Hart.* To look at Ron Jeremy, one wouldn't immediately peg him for one of the world's most popular and prolific porn stars. Affectionately dubbed the "Hedgehog," Ron's atypical schlubiness is a jolly rebuke to the buff, waxed, pretty-boy image of what women ostensibly find sexy. In an industry notorious for its savage narcissism, Ron is an anomaly, unlikely and shameless proof that even Average Joes — notably generously endowed ones — can get laid. This illuminating and often hilarious get-to-know-him documentary doesn't offer up any vicious dirt on the porn industry, but rather paints a likable everyman portrait of the guy who's starred in about 1,700 films in the past 21 years, becoming not only a cult legend, but recognized and celebrated around the globe. He comes off as one of the most doggedly driven actors in show biz, not to mention one of the luckiest, too. ★★★ DVD R-Rated: $26.99, DVD Uncut and Unrated Version: $26.99, VHS Uncut and Unrated Version: $26.99, VHS R-Rated: $26.99

The Pornographers

(1966, 128 min, Japan, Shohei Imamura) *Shoichi Ozawa, Massaomi Konda.* Imamura's wonderful black comedy focuses on a group of diligent 8mm porno filmmakers, struggling with the high risks and low production values inherent to Japan's booming underground sex trade. Imbued with Imamura's mordant philosophical sensibility, and populated with his stock company of misfits, the film is a hilarious and scathing look at modern Japanese society. (Japanese with English subtitles) ★★★½ DVD Letterbox Criterion Collection: $29.99, VHS: $29.99

Port of Call

(1948, 100 min, Sweden, Ingmar Bergman) *Ivine-Christine Jonsson, Bengt Eklund.* A minor Bergman drama of morality, love and self-awareness which is significant as one of the director's first attempts at Neorealism. The story traces — in an almost documentary fashion — the relationship between a bitter, resigned "experienced" woman and the sailor who falls in love with her. (Swedish with English subtitles) ★★

Portnoy's Complaint

(1972, 101 min, US, Ernest Lehman) *Richard Benjamin, Lee Grant, Jack Somach, Karen Black, Jill Clayburgh, Jeannie Berlin.* Benjamin is a discontented Jewish boy whose doting parents (Grant, Somach) refuse to let him grow up. This cinematic atrocity is based on Philip Roth's best-seller. ★ VHS: $14.99

The Portrait of a Lady

(1996, 144 min, US/GB, Jane Campion) *Nicole Kidman, John Malkovich, Barbara Hershey, Mary-Louise Parker, Martin Donovan, Shelley Winters, Richard E. Grant, Shelley Duvall, Christian Bale.* Director Campion's adaptation of Henry James' 19th-century novel opens with a black screen accompanied by voiceovers of modern young women talking about love and sex. Right away, we know that Campion has more in mind than a straightforward read on James' tale of the willful young American Isabel Archer, a woman who sets out to rise above the conventions of her day only to suffer at the hands of her own naïveté. Having rejected two suitable suitors on the grounds of wanting to explore life, Isabel sets out on a transcontinental trek only to embrace the advances of slithering malcontent Gilbert Osmand (Malkovich). Kidman is at once compelling and enigmatic, but Malkovich's performance is tired. Hershey is outstanding as Madame Serena Merle, a dangerously alluring friend of Osmand's. ★★★

Portrait of a Woman, Nude (Nudo di Donna)

(1983, 112 min, Italy, Nino Manfredi) *Nino Manfredi.* Manfredi directed and stars in this erotically charged comedy of sexual illusions and delusions. Set against an incomparable Venice, the film casts Manfredi as a husband who suspects that his wife is the model for a life-size portrait in a photographer's palazzo. His torments, as he struggles for the truth, are a marvel of sexual paranoia and comic energy. (Italian with English subtitles) ★★★

Portrait of Jennie

(1948, 86 min, US, William Dieterle) *Jennifer Jones, Joseph Cotten, Ethel Barrymore, Lillian Gish, Cecil Kellaway, David Wayne.* A beautifully filmed romantic fantasy with the lovely Jones inspiring struggling artist Cotten; the latter believing she may be the spirit of a deceased woman. ★★★

Portrait of Teresa

(1979, 115 min, Cuba, Pastor Vega) *Daisy Granados.* Perhaps one of the most controversial films to emerge from post-revolutionary Cuba, this cinema verité drama centers around the life of Teresa, a housewife and mother who works in a textile factory by day and attends political and cultural meetings in the evenings. With compassion and authenticity, the film probes the problems of her household, as her husband becomes increasingly frustrated and resentful towards his nontraditional wife. A revealing look into sexism and women's struggles in the face of ingrained traditions of machismo in a country that boldly proclaims their liberation. (Spanish with English subtitles) ★★★ VHS: $19.99

A Portrait of the Artist as a Young Man

(1977, 93 min, GB, Joseph Strick) *Bosco Hogan, John Gielgud.* This beautifully filmed slow-moving adaptation of James Joyce's autobiographical novel stars Hogan as Stephen Dedalus, a young man who is forced to question and confront his Irish Catholic upbringing before he sets out on life's journey. Age-old issues such as sexual guilt, familial repression and Church oppression are met with rebellion by the young man. Gielgud provides a highlight (and should wake up the nappers) with his spirited hellfire speech from the pulpit. ★★½ DVD: $29.99, VHS: $19.99

The Poseidon Adventure

(1972, 117 min, US, Ronald Neame) *Gene Hackman, Ernest Borgnine, Shelley Winters, Carol Lynley, Stella Stevens, Red Buttons, Jack Albertson.* One of the more enjoyable entries of the 1970s disaster films. New Year's Eve partiers go on an upside-down tour of their luxury liner when a tidal wave capsizes the ship. Great sets. ★★½ DVD Letterbox: $9.99, VHS: $9.99, VHS Letterbox: $19.99

Positive I.D.

(1987, 95 min, US, Andy Anderson) *Stephanie Rascoe, John Davies.* On a shoestring budget, director Anderson has fashioned a complex and fascinating thriller about a Texas woman whose rage leads her to live a second life — with a new identity and all. The film's look is clearly low-budget, but the story, twists and directorial style are first-rate. ★★★

Posse

(1975, 94 min, US, Kirk Douglas) *Kirk Douglas, Bruce Dern, Bo Hopkins, James Stacy.* Douglas produced, directed and stars in this amiable tale of a U.S. cavalry marshall out to nab a vicious criminal — not for justice's sake, but so he can get elected to the Senate. ★★½ DVD Letterbox: $14.99, VHS: $9.99

Posse

(1993, 113 min, US, Mario Van Peebles) *Mario Van Peebles, Stephen Baldwin, Charles Lane, Big Daddy Kane, Billy Zane.* On the heels of Kevin Costner and Clint Eastwood's Oscar-winning, revisionist westerns comes director Van Peebles' distinctive, anachronistic updating of the genre. Van Peebles stars as a "mysterious drifter" who leads a down 'n' dirty posse of Army deserters in escaping from a renegade colonel (Zane) and engaging in a quest for stolen gold. And while the film historically acknowledges the presence of black cowboys on the American frontier in much the same way *Glory* did for the Civil War, it is most effective when viewed as Hollywood escapist fare. ★★★ DVD: $14.99

P

Possessed

(1931, 77 min, US, Clarence Brown) *Joan Crawford, Clark Gable.* Crawford, in one of her patented tough-gal roles, plays an ambitious factory worker who dreams of a better life. Gable is an influential New York lawyer with an aversion to marriage who can give her the life she wants. Lots of snappy dialogue. ★★★ VHS: $19.99

Possession

(2002, 103 min, US, Neil LaBute) *Gwyneth Paltrow, Aaron Eckhart, Jeremy Northam, Jennifer Ehle, Lena Headey.* As beautiful but shrewlike literary scholar Maud Bailey, Paltrow once again showcases her well-practiced British accent. And the play of Paltrow's steely British resolve against Eckhart's American J. Crew whimsy is the friction that drives this heated centuries-spanning romance. Director LaBute shoots auteur theory to shit and dips his feet in Merchant Ivory waters, registering much higher on the energy scale than many of those period dramas while displaying an unfettered romantic heart. LaBute regular Eckhart plays a research assistant who uncovers some handwritten love letters from misogynistic 19th-century poet Randolph Henry Ash (a swoonworthy Northam). He and Paltrow embark on a journey to uncover intense details about the married poet and his secret lover, a writer (Ehle) who was involved in a lesbian relationship at the time. It's a bit predictable and pat, but so seductively absorbing that it's easy to trade the disbelief for a box of hankies. LaBute, clearly possessing a writer's mind, evokes the passion of the written word, and through his able actors, translates it elegantly to film. ★★★½ DVD Dual: $14.99, VHS: $9.99

Postcards from the Edge

(1990, 101 min, US, Mike Nichols) *Meryl Streep, Shirley MacLaine, Gene Hackman, Dennis Quaid, Richard Dreyfuss, Mary Wickes, Annette Bening.* Actress Carrie Fisher's first attempt at screenwriting is this breezy comedy based on her true-life battle

with alchohol and drug abuse. Streep and MacLaine are fabulously funny as the struggling Hollywood daughter and her aging celebrity mom. Fisher's screenplay deftly confronts the serious side of substance abuse while not straying from her comedic intent. ★★★ DVD: $9.99

Il Postino (The Postman)

(1993, 108 min, Italy, Michael Radford) *Massimo Troisi, Philippe Noiret, Maria Grazia Cucinotta, Linda Moretti.* A sublime divertimento about a simple-minded Italian postman and his budding relationship with the exiled Chilean poet and socialist Pablo Neruda. Noiret plays Neruda, who seeks political refuge on a tiny Mediterranean island. Mario (Troisi) is the postman whose sole purpose is to deliver Neruda's mail. Ultimately, Mario approaches "Don Pablo" seeking advice about his unrequited love for the local barmaid, Beatrice (Cucinotta). Carefully avoiding becoming Mario's Cyrano, Neruda gently mentors him in the ways of both love and "metaphors." Noiret logs another unflappable performance that is beautifully complemented by Troisi's shy and awkward Mario. (Italian with English subtitles) ★★★½ DVD Collector's Edition: $19.99, VHS: $9.99

The Postman

(1997, 178 min, US, Kevin Costner) *Kevin Costner, Will Patton, Larenz Tate, Olivia Williams, James Russo.* Directed in the same style as his Oscar-winning *Dances with Wolves*, Costner gets sanctimonious once again, but this time with a screenplay so laughably inane you don't dare take any of it to heart. He plays a drifter in postapocalyptic middle-America, a land now devoid of government and torn by gangs and renegade armies. When Costner steals the uniform from a dead postman (and takes his mail bag), he unintentionally becomes a beacon of hope for a gaggle of survivors (he represents the restoration of the government back East). The image of the mailman as savior of the new frontier — and as heroic action figure, period — is so ridiculous that the movie borders on sheer camp. ★ DVD: $14.99, VHS: $19.99

The Postman Always Rings Twice

(1946, 113 min, US, Tay Garnett) *Lana Turner, John Garfield, Cecil Kellaway, Hume Cronyn.* Both Garfield and Turner had rough-and-tumble lives off-camera: Garfield spent his childhood in various Bronx gangs and Turner landed in Hollywood as a 16-year-old orphan. Perhaps it was the reflection of their real-life dramas that smolders in their definitive portrayals of the ultimate drifter and the unhappily married woman whose passions lead to betrayal and murder. James M. Cain's book inspired four films, but not even Jack Nicholson and Jessica Lange, in the most recent remake, were able to give it the gritty intensity captured in this classic film noir. (Remade in 1981) ★★★★ DVD: $19.99

Lana Turner and John Garfield:
The Postman Always Rings Twice

The Postman Always Rings Twice

(1981, 123 min, US, Bob Rafelson) *Jack Nicholson, Jessica Lange, John Colicos, Anjelica Huston.* A loner on the skids (Nicholson) and a suacy waitresss (Lange) become a sexually ravenous pair driven to murder in Rafelson's sexy if uneven adaptation of the James M. Cain novel — both give impassioned portrayals of lust-blinded lovers with fogged-up moral compasses. ★★½ DVD: $14.99, VHS: $14.99

Powaqqatsi

(1988, 99 min, US, Godfrey Reggio) Following the phenomenal success of their art-house hit *Koyaanisqatsi*, director Reggio and cinematographers Leonidas Zourdoumis and Graham Berry reconvened to create this whirlwind vision of life in the Third World. Employing the same time-lapse photography techniques and yet another dazzling score from composer Philip Glass, the filmmakers delve into the myriad issues affecting developing countries as the forces of international capitalism forever change the quality and pace of life for the people. ★★★ DVD Letterbox: $19.99

Powder

(1995, 108 min, US, Victor Salva) *Mary Steenburgen, Sean Patrick Flanery, Lance Henriksen, Jeff Goldblum, Susan Tyrrell.* With a social outcast theme at its core, *Powder* is an affecting, sentimental fantasy about a teenager afflicted with an unusually severe albinotic disorder. When his grandfather dies, Jeremy (Flanery), nicknamed "Powder," is taken to a state home. As he assimilates into society, Jeremy endures the pain of ostracism and physical abuse. But it soon becomes clear that Jeremy has other qualities which separate him from others. It is these special powers which give *Powder* its magical feel. Overshadowing the film is the disclosure of director Salva's conviction of child molestation. It brings a different perspective to the subtly homoerotic film which magnifies Powder's alienation and ostracism. ★★½ DVD: $14.99, VHS: $9.99

Power

(1986, 111 min, US, Sidney Lumet) *Denzel Washington, Richard Gere, Gene Hackman, Julie Christie, Kate Capshaw.* Gere stars as a hotshot political consultant in this muddled exposé of politics and the media. Christie plays his ex-wife, Hackman is his former partner. ★★½ DVD: $9.99, VHS: $9.99

The Power of One

(1992, 111 min, US, John G. Avildsen) *Morgan Freeman, Stephen Dorff, John Gielgud, Armin Mueller-Stahl.* During the early days of Apartheid, PK, a young boy (Dorff) of English descent, is sent to an Afrikaner boarding school. Witnessing racial injustice, this "Great White Hope" takes it upon himself to battle oppression and right the wrongs of the world via native music and boxing! (Why not?) Directed by Avildsen with about as much subtlety as his *Karate Kid* movies, this is pretentious, dull and even slightly racist. ★½ DVD: $14.99, VHS: $14.99

Powwow Highway

(1988, 91 min, US, Jonathan Wacks) *Gary Farmer, A. Martinez, Graham Greene.* A delightful, heartfelt and poignant examination of the problems facing Native Americans today. A lumbering Cheyenne buys a battered Buick from the local junkyard and, with a buddy (a radical Indian Rights activist) in tow, sets out on a modern-day "vision quest." As the two wayfarers stray farther and farther from the safety of their reservation, the film exposes not only the distrust and racial hatred they encounter, but also the deep rifts in their own community. ★★★ VHS: $14.99

Practical Magic

(1997, 103 min, US, Griffin Dunne) *Sandra Bullock, Nicole Kidman, Dianne Weist, Stockard Channing, Adian Quinn.* Once again Hollywood takes a good book and reduces it to a saccharine assemblage of MTV moments. Neither Kidman nor Bullock is at the height of her acting ability as sisters, the present-day recipients of a 300-year-old legacy. Made outcasts by a curse and a family tradition of witchcraft, the quiet and conforming sister (Bullock) loses love through happiness; the rebellious, wild sister (Kidman) by bad choices. When the two sisters unite for an unwise application of a powerful magic spell, the result is a nemesis beyond either sisters' ability to control. The book-to-film conversion turns the unsettling and disquieting into the formulaic and bland. And the tone is so lighthearted that the film can't successfully shift gears in moments of threat and menace. ★ DVD: $14.99, VHS: $14.99, VHS Letterbox: $14.99

Practice Makes Perfect
(Le Cavaleur)

(1980, 105 min, France, Philippe de Broca) *Jean Rochefort, Annie Girardot.* Rochefort's comic talents are put to fine use in this wry, graceful comedy about a philandering concert pianist. The journey to his inevitable comeuppance is filled with lustful encounters with present and former wives, agents, mistresses, and daughters of former girlfriends. (French with English subtitles) ★★★

Prancer

(1989, 103 min, US, John Hancock) *Sam Elliott, Cloris Leachman, Abe Vigoda, Rebecca Harrell.* A nice holiday film for the kiddies with a hopeful message and some sweet spirit. It's the story of a young girl who finds a wounded reindeer in the woods and, believing it's Prancer, nurses it back to health so she can return it to Santa. Cute, old-fashioned and a welcome change of pace from all that drivel the kids watch on Saturday mornings. ★★½ DVD Letterbox: $14.99, VHS: $9.99

A Prayer for the Dying

(1987, 107 min, GB, Mike Hodges) *Mickey Rourke, Bob Hoskins, Alan Bates, Sammi Davis, Liam Neeson.* Rourke delivers a subdued performance as a guilt-ridden IRA assassin in Hodges' adaptation of Jack Higgins' novel. With their usual skill, Hoskins, as a feisty priest, and Bates, as a cold-blooded racketeer, lend strong support. Though not as thrilling as its source, the film offers insight into the power of forgiveness and man's atonement for his sins. ★★½ DVD Dual: $14.99

The Preacher's Wife

(1996, 124 min, US, Penny Marshall) *Denzel Washington, Whitney Houston, Courtney B. Vance, Jenifer Lewis, Gregory Hines, Loretta Devine.* In this update of the 1947 classic *The Bishop's Wife*, Washington takes over the Cary Grant role as an angel who is sent to aid a minister having a crisis of faith. Denzel is charismatic, debonair and effortlessly romantic. But unfortunately Washington's presence alone isn't enough to make *The Preacher's Wife* a wholehearted success. It's endearing, rather uneven and rather sentimental. Houston is the title character, and after a few starring roles, she still is stiff on camera. Maybe the biggest liability is changing the magical aspect of the film. Denzel is an angel who isn't afforded many opportunities to strut his stuff. But the film does boast a fine supporting cast, and the inherent charm of the original story is still evident. ★★½ DVD: $14.99, VHS: $9.99

Predator

(1987, 107 min, US, John McTiernan) *Arnold Schwarzenegger, Carl Weathers, Elpidia Carrillo.* Gory science-fiction thriller with Arnold as the leader of an elite government fighting unit whose mission to rescue political prisoners from the jungles of South America turns deadly when they are stalked by a lethal, unseen enemy. (Sequel: *Predator 2*) ★★★ DVD Letterbox 2-disc Collector's Edition (Widescreen): $26.99, DVD 2-disc Collector's Edition: $26.99

Predator 2

(1990, 108 min, US, Stephen Hopkins) *Danny Glover, Ruben Blades, Maria Conchita Alonso, Gary Busey.* An extraterrestial lands in L.A. in the future and is confronted by a jungle far different than that of the original *Predator*. Glover is a police officer who, forced to take time out from his busy drug war schedule, finds himself pitted against something slightly more destructive than a Jamaican with an Uzi. Though the story is very thin, the film is saved by some good action sequences. ★★ DVD Letterbox: $14.99, VHS: $9.99

Prefontaine

(1997, 107 min, US, Steve James) *Jared Leto, R. Lee Ermey, Ed O'Neill, Breckin Meyer, Lindsay Crouse, Kurtwood Smith.* Leto is Steve Prefontaine, celebrated runner and Olympic contender who was a shining star in the 1970s until a fatal car crash cut him down in his prime. The film follows "Pre" from his childhood as a frustrated athlete with thwarted ambitions, to the '72 Olympics in Munich, to his untimely death. As directed by James of *Hoop Dreams* fame, *Prefontaine* starts awkwardly, mixing conventional docudrama with faux-documentary interviews with the cast in old-age makeup. But the film soon gains its footing, however, and becomes a fairly engrossing — if minor — portrait of a short, passionate life. ★★½ DVD: $9.99

Prelude to a Kiss

(1992, 110 min, US, Norman René) *Alec Baldwin, Meg Ryan, Sydney Walker, Patty Duke, Kathy Bates, Ned Beatty, Stanley Tucci.* Based on the Tony Award-nominated play, this opened-up film version loses very little of the passion and charm of the original stage production. Baldwin (reprising his Broadway role) and Ryan star as a couple who meet, fall in love and marry. However, on their wedding day, the souls of Ryan and an uninvited guest, a seventy-year-old man (played with high spirits by Walker), are transposed. As this AIDS allegory continues, Baldwin suddenly finds his mate, once young and healthy, now sickly and old virtually overnight. But how to get them to switch? Adapting his own play for the screen, Craig Lucas imbues this tale with great good humor, and gives thoughtful testament to the responsibility, resilience and consummate power of love. ★★★ DVD: $14.99

Premonition

(1978, 83 min, US, Alan Rudolph) Director Rudolph makes his debut with this largely unknown "glorified" student film about a musician whose nightmares of his own death cause him to question his hedonistic life and his sanity. Though Rudolph, an acknowledged protégé of Robert Altman, has become known as one of our more liberal directors, this somehow winds up being a "Say No to Drugs" treatise rather than the supernatural thriller the box promises. ★★½

The President's Analyst

(1967, 104 min, US, Theodore J. Flicker) *James Coburn, Godfrey Cambridge, Severn Dardern.* Supremely entertaining political romp with Coburn as the title character deciding he no longer wants the position; eluding various American and world-wide government agents who either want to kill him or want to know the chief executive's inner-most secrets. Cambridge and Dardern are particularly funny in support as a CIA agent and his Russian counterpart. ★★★½ DVD Letterbox: $14.99

The Presidio

(1988, 97 min, US, Peter Hyams) *Sean Connery, Mark Harmon, Meg Ryan, Jack Warden.* San Francisco cop Harmon squares off against military base commander Connery over the policeman's murder investigation and Connery's daughter Ryan, with whom Harmon is romantically involved. Few sparks, though Connery is, as usual, commanding. ★★½ DVD: $14.99, VHS: $14.99

Pressure Point

(1962, 88 min, US, Hubert Cornfield) *Sidney Poitier, Bobby Darin, Peter Falk.* After their great success with *The Defiant Ones*, producer Stanley Kramer and Poitier reteamed for this stimulating and hard-hitting psychological drama. Set during WWII, Poitier plays a prison psychiatrist who treats American Nazi Darin, jailed for sedition. As Poitier tries to get to the root of Darin's chronic sleeping disorder, the black doctor must contend with his white patient's continual racial and ethnic assaults. Darin gives a subtle, chilling performance. ★★★ DVD: $14.99

Presumed Innocent

(1990, 127 min, US, Alan J. Pakula) *Harrison Ford, Brian Dennehy, Raul Julia, Bonnie Bedelia, Greta Scacchi.* In this taut thriller, Ford plays a veteran prosecutor whose life is abruptly shattered when he is accused of brutally raping and murdering a colleague. Against an avalanche of damning evidence, Ford proclaims his innocence only to discover that the judicial process, in which he so steadfastly believed, is rife with corruption and political intrigue. Ford's portrayal, filled with anxiety and pathos, will keep the viewer guessing from beginning to end as to his guilt. ★★★½ DVD: $14.99, VHS: $9.99

Pretty Baby

(1978, 109 min, US, Louis Malle) *Brooke Shields, Susan Sarandon, Keith Carradine, Barbara Steele, Diana Scarwid.* Malle's controversial film is a sensitively handled story of a 12-year-old girl (Shields) born and raised in Storyville, New Orleans' old whorehouse district. Carradine, in one of his most effective performances, plays the photographer who becomes obsessed with her. Malle's impressive evocation of WWI Louisiana is complemented by a remarkably textured examination of sexual proclivity. Sarandon is especially good as Shields' floozy mother. ★★★½ DVD Letterbox: $19.99

Pretty Boy

(1993, 86 min, Denmark, Carsten Sonder) *Christian Tafdrup.* This dark, kinky and violent tale of one youth's tough coming-of-age takes place amidst the lurid world of teenage male prostitution. Nick (Tafdrup) is a handsome and innocent 13-year-old runaway who quickly falls in with the wrong crowd when he arrives in Amsterdam. Befriended by a hardened, violence-prone gang of teen hustlers, Nick is soon immersed in a world where sex is performed only for money and love rarely comes into play. (Danish with English subtitles) ★★½

Pretty in Pink

(1986, 96 min, US, Howard Deutch) *Molly Ringwald, Jon Cryer, Harry Dean Stanton, James Spader, Annie Potts.* Ringwald — John Hughes' Liv Ullmann? — stars in this witty comedy-drama scripted by Hughes as a girl from the "other side of the tracks" who braces the taunts of her snobby classmates and lets herself be wooed by class dreamboat McCarthy. Cryer is a standout as Ringwald's wacky cohort. ★★★ DVD Letterbox: $14.99, VHS: $9.99

Pretty Village, Pretty Flame

(1997, 125 min, Yugoslavia, Srdjan Dragojevic) *Dragan Bjelogrlic, Nikola Kojo, Zoran Cvijanovic.* A very droll and beautifully filmed opening — wry, sarcastic and lyrical in expression — frames this often powerful, well-intentioned antiwar film which, while losing some of its bite in midsection, manages to end with the same great spiteful, grotesque humor with which it began. The nucleus of the film is the friendship between childhood pals Milan, a Serbian, and Halil, a Muslim, which lasts until the onset of war in 1992. From a hospital ward where soldiers Milan and Halil are recovering, the story of how they were wounded is told through flashback. (Serbo-Creatian with English subtitles) ★★★ DVD: $14.99, VHS: $9.99

Pretty Woman

(1990, 117 min, US, Garry Marshall) *Julia Roberts, Richard Gere, Hector Elizondo.* This Cinderella story about a Los Angeles hooker-with-a-heart-of-gold who becomes involved with a repressed New York tycoon borrows much from better films before it. But few of them featured as charming a performance as that of Roberts. As the businessman, Gere reacts nicely and looks quite handsome with his greying hair, but his role is simply a foil for the enchanting Ms. Roberts. ★★½ DVD 10th Anniversary: $19.99, VHS: $14.99

A Price above Rubies

(1998, 117 min, US, Boaz Yakin) *Renée Zellweger, Christopher Eccleston, Allen Payne, Glenn Fitzgerald, Julianna Margulies.* Zellweger plays a young Jewish woman who marries a Hasidic scholar and slowly realizes that her spirit and sexuality are being crushed by her strict, cloistered surroundings. We feel for the woman's plight, but her character, as written by director Yakin and portrayed by a squinty, pouting Zellweger, is more petulant brat than stifled spirit. The fanciful device of Zellweger periodically chatting with her long-dead childhood friend is clunky and unrevealing, and many scenes are cloying, pandering or just dull. *Rubies* does have the occasional dramatic moment, but it's all topped off with a dippy, featherweight music score. ★★ DVD: $19.99, VHS: $9.99

Prick Up Your Ears

(1987, 108 min, GB, Stephen Frears) *Gary Oldman, Alfred Molina, Vanessa Redgrave, Julie Walters, Wallace Shawn, Lindsay Duncan.* This chilling and graphic portrayal of the life and death of British playwright Joe Orton is a masterful tribute to a man who fearlessly attacked English morals and custom. Cut down in his prime, Orton's legacy is well remembered here through scathingly witty dialogue and stand-out performances by Oldman (as Orton) and Molina (as Kenneth Halliwell, Orton's tormented lover who brutally murdered him in 1967). A brilliantly candid look at the gay scene in London during the late '50s and early '60s. ★★★★ DVD: $14.99

Pride and Prejudice

(1940, 118 min, US, Robert Z. Leonard) *Laurence Olivier, Greer Garson, Edna May Oliver, Edmund Gwenn, Mary Boland, Maureen O'Sullivan.* Exquisite comedy of manners based on Jane Austen's classic novel about five sisters' search for husbands. Olivier and Garson are splendid as young lovers, and the film features a fine evocation of 19th-century England. ★★★½

Pride and Prejudice

(1995, 226 min, GB, Simon Langton) *Colin Firth, Jennifer Ehle, Alison Steadman.* An absolutely charming BBC adaptation of Jane Austen's classic. Ehle is enchanting as Elizabeth Bennet who, with her three sisters, suffers a mixed social standing because their father married low. As always with Austen, the central paradox is how to marry off these undesireables while at the same time skewering the very class snobbery that makes their chance at marriage so precarious. An enjoyable and engrossing romantic drama that may occasionally show its low-born roots but is really as flawless as its upper-crust, recent cousins. ★★★★ DVD 2-disc set: $39.99, VHS: $59.99

The Pride and the Passion

(1957, 132 min, US, Stanley Kramer) *Cary Grant, Sophia Loren, Frank Sinatra.* Not even the talents of the cast can elevate this laughable war epic. Set in Spain after Napoleon's conquest of that country, the story follows the efforts of a group of Spanish peasants, led by Sinatra, to transport a cannon to a French occupied town. Grant is a British officer who helps them. Loren is there to look lovely, which she does; and on those dusty roads, she never gets dirty, either. The film offers some impressive battle sequences, but little else. ★½ DVD Letterbox: $14.99

The Pride of St. Louis

(1952, 93 min, US, Harmon Jones) *Dan Dailey, Joanne Dru, Richard Crenna.* The professional and personal life of St. Louis pitching great Dizzy Dean is given the Hollywood treatment in this very likable baseball biography. Dailey had one of his best roles as the famous pitcher, who created a stir whether on the field or in the radio booth. ★★½ VHS: $19.99

The Pride of the Yankees

(1942, 127 min, US, Sam Wood) *Gary Cooper, Teresa Wright, Walter Brennan, Babe Ruth, Dan Duryea.* The best of all the baseball biographies, and — until *Field of Dreams* came along — the best of all sports-themed films. Cooper gives a terrific performance as New York Yankees legend Lou Gehrig, whose remarkable career was ended by sickness. Ruth appears as himself. ★★★★ DVD: $14.99

Priest

(1995, 97 min, GB, Antonia Bird) *Linus Roache, Tom Wilkinson, Cathy Tyson, Robert Carlyle.* Not quite as incendiary as its theme would suggest, *Priest* is the moving, provocative story of one clergyman's struggle for sexual identity and religious idealism. Roache gives a stirring performance as Father Greg, a newly transferred priest assigned to a parish in a working-class neighborhood of Liverpool. As he comes in conflict with the liberal Father Matthew (Wilkinson in a terrific portrayal), who is having an affair with the housekeeper (Tyson), Father Greg tries to come to terms with his emerging gay sexuality. At the heart of the film, however, is the touching story of a sexually abused teen who confides in Father Greg, thus engaging him in a crisis of conscience. A remarkably compelling

debate on religious dogma, one intended to provoke thought as it stirs one's emotions. ★★★★ DVD: $14.99, VHS: $9.99

Priest of Love

(1981, 125 min, GB, Christopher Miles) *Ian McKellen, Janet Suzman, John Gielgud, Ava Gardner, Sara Miles.* An elegantly photographed biography of D.H. Lawrence's final days. Detailed are the author's self-exile to New Mexico, his sojourn to Italy to write "Lady Chatterley's Lover," and the tempestuous relationship with his Frieda (Suzman). McKellen gives a stirring portrait of the author. ★★★

Primal Fear

(1996, 130 min, US, Gregory Hoblit) *Richard Gere, Laura Linney, Edward Norton, Andre Braugher, John Mahoney, Frances McDormand.* Gere gives a high-voltage portrayal of a cocky, glory-seeking defense attorney who bites off more than he can chew when he finagles his way into the case of a backwoods, "butter-wouldn't-melt-in-his-mouth" altar boy (Norton) accused of murdering a beloved archbishop. Hoblit's complex whodunit combines compelling courtroom drama with a stellar supporting cast, but this is clearly a showcase for newcomer Norton whose character navigates the film's ever-increasing maze of plot twists to its shocking conclusion. ★★★ DVD: $14.99, VHS: $9.99

Primary

(1960, 53 min, US, Robert Drew) Drew and his small crew followed JFK for a week at the height of his primary run against Hubert Humphrey, resulting in this riveting look at not only Kennedy's persona, but the tension of any political campaign on election night. Credited as the first documentary to use a portable camera with sync sound, and thus ushering in the cinema verité style that is the standard today. D.A. Pennebaker and Albert Maysles were among the crew, further attesting to *Primary's* influence. ★★★★ DVD: $24.99, VHS: $24.99

Primary Colors

(1998, 104 min, US, Mike Nichols) *John Travolta, Emma Thompson, Billy Bob Thornton, Kathy Bates, Adrian Lester, Maura Tierney, Paul Guilfoyle, Larry Hagman.* This peppy political comedy based on the best-selling book, an examination of a "fictional" presidential candidate from Arkansas, makes for zippy, exceptionally well-acted and highly entertaining storytelling. The action unfolds from the per-

Primary Colors

P

spective of Henry Burton (Lester), a young "buppy" political consultant who's brought onto Gov. Jack Stanton's campaign for the presidency (Travolta makes the perfect choice for the Clinton stand-in). Thompson, as Mrs. Gov. Stanton, struggles to nail her "American" accent but is nonetheless solid. But it's Bates who steals the show as Libby Holden, a ruthless, unapologetically leftwing political muck-racker who's called on to dig up some dirt. So despite being part and parcel of all those headlines about Clinton and his intern (remember Monica?), *Primary Colors* proves to be just the right antidote for the politically jaded. ★★★★ DVD: $14.99, DVD DTS sound: $14.99

Prime Cut

(1972, 86 min, US, Michael Ritchie) *Lee Marvin, Gene Hackman, Sissy Spacek.* Marvin and Hackman make the most of this gritty, tongue-in-cheek gang-land drama about a Kansas City mobster in deep trouble when an enforcer from Chicago is sent to collect a debt. Spacek makes her film debut. ★★★

The Prime of Miss Jean Brodie

(1969, 116 min, GB, Ronald Neame) *Maggie Smith, Celia Johnson, Pamela Franklin, Jane Carr.* Smith won a much-deserved Best Actress Oscar (edging out Jane Fonda's staggering portrayal in *They Shoot Horses, Don't They*) for her magnificent performance as an eccentric schoolteacher in 1930s Edinburgh. Based on Muriel Spark's novel, the story centers on the schoolmistress' life in and out of the classroom, where she exerts an enormous influence on her young, impressionable girls. A sincere and absorbing character study. ★★★½ DVD Letterbox: $14.99, VHS: $19.99

Prime Suspect 1

(1992, 208 min, GB, Christopher Menaul) *Helen Mirren, John Benfield, Tom Bell, Zoe Wanamaker, Tom Wilkinson.* A deserved Emmy Award winner for Best Miniseries, "Prime Suspect" is a tremendous, gripping tale which combines mystery and the poli-tics of gender. Mirren gives an outstanding perfor-mance as Detective Chief Inspector Jane Tennison, a policewoman who is able to confront rampant sex-ism in the police department when she is given the opportunity to head the search for a serial killer ter-rorizing London. An intelligent, suspenseful and extremely well-acted film. (Followed by 6 sequels) ★★★★ DVD 2-disc set: $29.99

The Primrose Path

(1940, 93 min, US, Gregory La Cava) *Ginger Rogers, Joel McCrea, Marjorie Rambeau.* Rogers stars in this involving comedy-drama as a girl from the "wrong side of the tracks" and a family of pros-titutes, who falls in love with straight-arrow propri-etor McCrea. Rambeau is splendid as Rogers' moth-er. ★★★

The Prince and the Pauper

(1937, 120 min, US, William Keighley) *Errol Flynn, Claude Rains, Billy Mauch, Bobby Mauch, Alan Hale.* The classic Mark Twain novel is given royal treatment in this story about a young prince and a look-alike peasant boy trading places. ★★★ DVD: $19.99, VHS: $14.99

The Prince and the Pauper

(1978, 113 min, GB, Richard Fleischer) *Mark Lester, Oliver Reed, Raquel Welch, George C. Scott, Charlton Heston, Ernest Borgnine, Rex Harrison.* An all-star cast highlights this uninspiring version of the Mark Twain classic, with Lester in the dual role of a poor British boy who impersonates the prince. (aka: *Crossed Swords*) ★★ VHS: $14.99

The Prince and the Showgirl

(1957, 117 min, GB, Laurence Olivier) *Laurence Olivier, Marilyn Monroe, Sybil Thorndike.* By all reports, there was no love lost between Olivier and Monroe on the set of this light romantic comedy. There was nothing lost on the screen, however. As a pair, they work magnificently together with Marilyn playing an American chorus girl who is courted by Olivier's Balkan prince at the coronation of King George V in London. Terrence Rattigan provides a vivacious script based on his hit play "The Sleeping Prince." ★★★ DVD: $19.99, VHS: $14.99

Prince of Central Park

(1999, 110 min, US, John Leekley) *Kathleen Turner, Danny Aiello, Harvey Keitel, Frankie Nasso, Cathy Moriarty, Paul Sorvino.* A young boy runs away from his abusive foster mother to live in Central Park. There he encounters a homeless man (Keitel) and an estranged couple (Aiello and Turner), who may turn out to be the answer to his prayers. Well-meaning but mawkish, *Prince of Central Park* has "Afterschool Special" written all over it, with corny flashbacks and fantasy scenes, against-all-odds personal triumphs for the young protagonist, and nary an honest, dramatic moment to be found. ★½ DVD: $24.99

Prince of Darkness

(1987, 110 min, US, John Carpenter) *Donald Pleasence, Lisa Blount.* Priest Pleasence is up against Satan in the form of an icky goo; he, a col-lege professor and his students are out to stop the demon's return to earth. Director Carpenter has cer-tainly done better. ★½ DVD Letterbox: $14.99, VHS: $14.99

The Prince of Egypt

(1998, 97 min, US, Brenda Chapman, Simon Wells, Steve Hickner) *Voices of: Val Kilmer, Ralph Fiennes, Michelle Pfeiffer, Sandra Bullock, Jeff Goldblum, Danny Glover, Patrick Stewart, Helen Mirren, Steve Martin, Martin Short.* The biblical epic is back, spectacular and hollow as ever, in Dreamworks' first animated film. The look is per-fect, with thousands of "extras," huge pyramids, and rich sandy tones evoking an Egypt that is appropri-ately larger-than-life. There's even a thrilling set-piece involving a chariot race. But this rendition of Exodus is strangely uninvolving, lumbering from plot point to song to action sequence with little heart. The parting of the Red Sea is breathtaking to the eye, but it will inspire more awe regarding the animation rather than Moses himself. ★★★ DVD: $19.99, DVD DTS sound: $19.99, VHS: $9.99

The Prince of Homburg

(1997, 89 min, Italy, Marco Bellocchio) *Andrea Di Stefano, Barbara Bobulova, Toni Bertorelli.* Leading actors Di Stefano and Bertorelli bring grace and poise to this Italian adaptation of playwright Heinrich von Kleist's "The Prince of Homburg." Set amidst the Prussian-Swedish battles of the 1700s, the film offers both a bleak message about morality in wartime and a hopeful one about the valor of love. Moved by an allegorical dream of victory, the prince hastily decides to breach his commander's orders on the field. Despite great heroism, he is condemned to death, which he ultimately accepts in observance of honor. Through its dimly lit gauze, the film success-fully conveys the emotional detachment of mili-tarism, and, in its quiet nocturnal moments, the inner turmoil and solitude of a death sentence. Steeped in

period detail and with the intimacy of stage play, this is recommended viewing for those with a passion for period dramas. ★★★ DVD: $29.99, VHS: $29.99

The Prince of Pennsylvania

(1988, 93 min, US, Ron Nyswaner) *Fred Ward, Keanu Reeves, Bonnie Bedelia, Amy Madigan.* An offbeat dude (Reeves) wants to avoid following in his blue-collar father's footsteps, so he kidnaps his pop and holds him for ransom. The problem? No one wants him back. Director Nyswaner also wrote the cult hit *Smithereens*. ★★½ VHS: $14.99

Prince of the City

(1981, 167 min, US, Sidney Lumet) *Treat Williams, Jerry Orbach, Lindsay Crouse.* Director Lumet returns to *Serpico* territory in this riveting, epic police drama which is based on a true story. Williams gives a truly remarkable performance as a New York City narcotics officer who risks his job, friendships and safety when he reports widespread department corruption. Orbach is terrific in support as Williams' friend and fellow cop. ★★★½ VHS: $24.99

The Prince of Tides

(1991, 132 min, US, Barbra Streisand) *Barbra Streisand, Nick Nolte, Kate Nelligan, Blythe Danner, George Carlin, Melinda Dillon, Jeroen Krabbé.* Streisand's second directorial effort is a lush, excep-tional-looking film version of Pat Conroy's novel. Nolte is outstanding as a married, Southern high school coach who travels to New York when his sis-ter is admitted to a psychiatric hospital. There he meets her doctor (Streisand), and the two begin a brief affair. Though Streisand's character was less conspicuous in the book, here the doctor has a greater presence — which is one of the few disser-vices to this otherwise laudatory adaptation. A touching romance and a rather harrowing childhood memory piece. Nelligan excels in support as Nolte's mother. ★★★½ DVD: $24.99, VHS: $14.99

The Princess and the Pirate

(1944, 94 min, US, David Butler) *Bob Hope, Virginia Mayo, Walter Brennan, Walter Slezak, Victor McLaglen.* One of Hope's funniest films *sans* Bing, this hilarious pirate spoof stars Bob as a traveling entertainer who becomes mixed up with a runaway princess (Mayo) and a band of cutthroat pirates. The laughs seem to come about every 15 seconds, and a highlight has Bob dressing up as an old hag, being romantically pursued by Brennan! And that's not to mention the typical Hope barrage of puns, double-entendres and silly one-liners. ★★★½

The Princess and the Warrior

(2001, 130 min, Germany, Tom Tykwer) *Franka Potente, Benno Fürmann, Joachim Krol.* The film establishes its otherworldly, mythic persona as it opens with a pensive woman writing a letter (not e-mailing!) in a small cottage at the very edge of a large ocean. The letter requests a favor from her friend Sissi (Potente), a waif of a woman whose life is defined by the mental institution she works in. Saving the life of another, Sissi is struck down, pinned under a huge truck, unable to breathe. A wounded, tragic hero literally breathes life into her, then disappears, wanting no thanks or recognition. When she recovers, she's consumed by the desire, the need, to find him. Entering a morality play defined by elements of fantasy, she becomes totally submersed in her quest, an odyssey in which lives overlap and intertwine. The film uses with mesmer-izing effectiveness recurring images, re-echoing themes, and unexpected connections; it imparts a

Princess Mononoke

sense of a blithe inevitability of redemption in the most horrible of circumstances. In the end, it crystallizes those rare, blessed moments when we watch ourselves move past an outworn version of ourselves, when we realize our capability to see life through fresh eyes. (German with English subtitles) ★★★½ DVD Letterbox: $27.99, VHS: $19.99

The Princess Bride

(1987, 98 min, US, Rob Reiner) *Cary Elwes, Robin Wright, Mandy Patinkin, Christopher Guest, Chris Sarandon, Wallace Shawn, Peter Falk, Billy Crystal, Carol Kane.* Reiner faithfully adapts William Goldman's fairy tale of love and swashbuckling adventure with style, wit and just the right amount of "mushy stuff." Elwes stars as a stable boy; Wright is the beauty in love with him. As with most fairy tales, the course of true love does not run smooth until story's end. Patinkin steals the show as a swordsman out to avenge his father's death. ★★★½ DVD Special Edition: $19.99, VHS: $9.99

Favorite Line: "You only *think* I guessed wrong — that's what's so funny. I switched glasses when your back was turned. You fell victim to one of the classic blunders, the most famous of which is 'Never get involved in a land war in Asia,' but only slightly less well known is this: '*Never* go in against a Sicilian, when *death* is on the line!'" —*Wallace Shawn as Vizzini*

Princess Caraboo

(1994, 96 min, GB, Michael Austin) *Phoebe Cates, Kevin Kline, John Lithgow, Jim Broadbent, Wendy Hughes, Stephen Rea.* Cates stars in this picturesque but uneven swipe at aristocratic hypocrisy that might best be described as *Anastasia*-lite. Cates plays an enigmatic beauty found wandering the English countryside and, speaking no English, is taken in by a social-climbing couple (Hughes, Broadbent) who assume her to be foreign royalty. Rea is an inquisitive journalist enchanted by her innocence but intent on solving the mystery of her identity. A based-on-fact story. ★★ DVD: $19.99

Princess Mononoke

(1999, 133 min, Japan, Hayao Miyazaki) *Voices of: Claire Danes, Billy Crudup, Minnie Driver, Gillian Anderson, Jada Pinkett, Billy Bob Thornton.* A young warrior, dying from a wound received during a fight with a terrifying beast, is sent away by his village elders. On his journeys, he discovers an industrial village, which is at odds with the surrounding nature, and whose conflict results in epic violence. Epic is a good word for this amazing piece of animation that, while perhaps a bit too long, is still mesmerizing throughout. An unusually thoughtful work, allowing all sides of a conflict their say. A feast for the eyes and mind, this is terrific entertainment for children and adults alike. ★★★½ DVD: $22.99, VHS: $14.99

Princess Tam Tam

(1935, 80 min, France, Edmond Greville) *Josephine Baker, Albert Prejean.* It's a musical Parisian Pygmalion! A French novelist travels to North Africa seeking inspiration but instead finds himself becoming steadily more infatuated and entranced by a native girl (Baker). She accompanies him back to Paris where, to everyone's amazement, she is the toast of the town. (French with English subtitles) ★★★ VHS: $29.99

Princess Yang Kwei Fei

(1955, 91 min, Japan, Kenji Mizoguchi) *Machiko Kyo, Masayuki Mori.* An eighth-century Chinese Cinderella story, *Princess Yang Kwei Fei* tells the tale of an unspoiled stepsister who is unwittingly used by an ambitious gentleman who wants to get in with the emperor. Soon the emperor himself becomes enchanted by this beautiful and talented woman and makes her his wife. Featuring beautiful sets and stunning visuals, this historical love story's slow pace may lose some viewers; but for lovers of Mizoguchi's meticulous style, the leisurely pace proves to be a virtue. (Japanese with English subtitles) ★★★ VHS: $29.99

The Principal

(1987, 109 min, US, Christopher Cain) *James Belushi, Louis Gossett, Jr., Rae Dawn Chong, Esai Morales.* New inner-city high school principal Belushi goes head to head with the bad dudes in his school. Belushi and Gossett play well off each other in this effort to make a difference, but the script is full of high school-thug clichés and an inconsistent mix of comedy and drama. ★★ DVD: $9.99, VHS: $9.99

Prison

(1988, 102 min, US, Renny Harlin) *Lane Smith, Viggo Mortensen, Chelsea Field.* There's quite a few chills in this stylish horror film. The spirit of a prisoner wrongfully executed two decades before comes back to get even with his former guard (Smith) — who's now the warden. ★★½

Prisoner of Honor

(1991, 88 min, US, Ken Russell) *Richard Dreyfuss, Oliver Reed, Peter Firth, Brian Blessed, Lindsay Anderson.* Russell is unusually restrained in this made-for-HBO retelling of "The Dreyfus Affair," a scandalous incident of anti-Semitism in 19th-century France. Dreyfuss stars as an officer who refuses to allow his army to betray its honor by framing an innocent Jewish officer for treason. A good companion piece to *The Life of Emile Zola.* ★★★ VHS: $9.99

The Prisoner of Second Avenue

(1975, 105 min, US, Melvin Frank) *Jack Lemmon, Anne Bancroft, Gene Saks, Elizabeth Wilson, Sylvester Stallone.* One of the best of the Neil Simon stage-to-screen adaptations, this gloriously funny and, at times, bittersweet comedy benefits greatly from two superlative performances from Lemmon and Bancroft. Lemmon plays a recently unemployed exec who suffers a breakdown, which prompts wife Bancroft back into the workplace. All the while, they contend with noisy neighbors, robberies, attempted muggings, a 14th-floor walk-up, picky cab drivers, trash, and the sweltering summer heat; everything, in fact, which makes living in New York a singular experience. A treat from beginning to end. ★★★½ DVD: $19.99, VHS: $14.99

Prisoner of the Mountains

(1996, 99 min, Russia, Sergei Bodrov) *Oleg Menshikov, Sergei Bodrov, Jr., Jemal Sikharulidze.* This gritty adaptation of Tolstoy's "Prisoner of the Caucasus" is a stirring antiwar drama that offers Western audiences an unprecedented and incredibly lucid look into the little-seen world of the Caucasus Mountain region. The story follows two Russian soldiers (Menshikov, Bodrov) who are captured by a local Muslim patriarch (Sikharulidze). Hoping to cut a deal to get his son out of a Russian prison, the father steadfastly resists the relentless pressure from his townspeople to execute his charges. Bleak beyond imagination and yet unparalleled in grandeur. Director Bodrov, Sr. never misses a beat in delivering his heart-rending message on the insanity of war. (Russian with English subtitles) ★★★½ DVD Letterbox: $19.99

The Prisoner of Zenda

(1937, 101 min, US, John Cromwell) *Ronald Colman, Madeleine Carroll, Mary Astor, Douglas Fairbanks, Jr., David Niven.* This third of many screen versions of Anthony Hope's celebrated novel is by far the best of the bunch. Colman had one of his most popular roles as both the King of Ruritania and his look-alike cousin, who impersonates H.R.M. when the ruler is kidnapped. A good cast is featured in this exciting adventure film. ★★★½

The Prisoner of Zenda

(1952, 101 min, US, Richard Thorpe) *Stewart Granger, Deborah Kerr, James Mason, Louis Calhern.* Not as exciting as the 1937 Ronald Colman version, this extravagant though lifeless remake stars Granger as the commoner who doubles for the King. ★★½ VHS: $19.99

The Prisoner of Zenda

(1979, 108 min, US, Richard Quine) *Peter Sellers, Jeremy Kemp.* Even Sellers' comic mastery can't save this farcical remake about a king's double who is forced to step into the royal shoes when his highness is kidnapped. Not a career high point for Sellers. ★

Prisoners of Inertia

(1989, 92 min, US, J. Noyes Scher) *Amanda Plummer, Christopher Rich, John C. McGinley.* What starts out as a simple Sunday brunch date deteriorates into an *After Hours*-style nightmare for a young Manhattan couple (Plummer, Rich) in this mildly amusing independent film. ★★½ VHS: $79.99

Private Benjamin

(1980, 110 min, US, Howard Zieff) *Goldie Hawn, Eileen Brennan, Armand Assante, Albert Brooks.* Hawn's effervescent performance highlights this hit comedy about a pampered "Jewish American Princess" who enlists in the Army — only to find it wasn't what she expected. Brennan gives a solid comic turn as Hawn's ever-suffering captain. ★★★ DVD: $9.99, VHS: $9.99

A Private Function

(1985, 93 min, GB, Malcolm Mowbray) *Michael Palin, Maggie Smith, Denholm Elliott, Liz Smith.* Class snobbery, petty vice and social climbing are given a sharp satiric examination in this grand British black comedy. Set in post-war England, the film stars Palin and Smith as a couple who kidnap a pig earmarked for the nuptials of Princess Elizabeth and Prince Phillip. ★★★½ DVD Dual: $14.99

Private Life

(1982, 102 min, USSR, Yuli Raizman) Reminiscent of Arthur Miller's "Death of a Salesman," this sensitive drama of an older man forced to reevaluate his life values after being unexpectedly dismissed from his lifelong job, was made by 80-year-old Soviet director Raizman. Sergei, a taciturn manager of a large factory, finds himself baffled by his enforced retirement and at a loss regarding what to do with his "endless string of Sundays." Quickly, he realizes that he was insensitive to the importance in his life of his wife, relatives and friends. Symbolic of Russia at the time, the man begins a personal awakening to both the joys of life and of human relations. Nominated for the 1983 Foreign Film Oscar. (Russian with English subtitles) ★★★ VHS: $59.99

The Private Life of Henry VIII

(1933, 97 min, GB, Alexander Korda) *Charles Laughton, Elsa Lanchester, Binnie Barnes, Robert Donat, Merle Oberon.* This sweeping historical chronicle of the 16th-century British monarch features a robust performance by Laughton as the ever-hitchable king. The film had a major impact on the image of British cinema around the world as it featured then-unexpected tongue-in-cheek humor which set it apart from the usual dour historical drama. ★★★★ DVD: $19.99, VHS: $13.99

The Private Life of Sherlock Holmes

(1970, 126 min, US, Billy Wilder) *Robert Stephens, Colin Blakely, Geneviéve Page.* Thoroughly engaging film about, well, the title says it all. When a famous Russian ballerina wants Holmes to be the father of her child, he cleverly sidesteps her invitation by suggesting that he and Dr. Watson are more than just roommates. A convenient lie or the truth? You decide. To complicate matters, there's the mystery of the Belgian amnesiac, her missing husband and the Loch Ness monster. Served up as only Wilder can. ★★★ DVD Letterbox: $19.99

Private Lives

(1931, 84 min, US, Sidney Franklin) *Norma Shearer, Robert Montgomery, Reginald Denny, Una Merkel.* One of Noël Coward's most delightful stage comedies is given sparkling treatment in this very funny screen adaptation. Shearer and Montgomery are a divorced couple who meet each other on their respective second-marriage honeymoons. In a flash, they leave their spouses and run off to rekindle their relationship — and their bickering. The film is ripe with those scintillating Coward witticisms, and if Shearer and Montgomery aren't the Lunts, they nevertheless handle this sophisticated hilarity with great charm. ★★★★ VHS: $19.99

The Private Lives of Elizabeth and Essex

(1939, 106 min, US, Michael Curtiz) *Bette Davis, Errol Flynn, Olivia de Havilland, Vincent Price.* A must-see for fans of Davis, this screen version of Maxwell Anderson's play may be short on historical accuracy, but it remains an excellent period costume drama. Davis is superb as Queen Elizabeth I whose love for the dashing Earl of Essex (Flynn) is put to rest by political neccessity. ★★★

A Private Matter

(1992, 100 min, US, Joan Micklin Silver) *Sissy Spacek, Aidan Quinn, Estelle Parsons.* Director Silver tackles the true story of an abortion case that gained national attention in 1964. Spacek delivers a strong, measured portrayal of the mother who, while pregnant with her fifth child, weighs the option of abortion when the effects of Thalidomide on fetuses begins to be disclosed. As she and her husband (Quinn) are catapulted into the national spotlight, their personal lives become political fodder. A powerful examination of an issue that has lost none of its potency in the intervening 40 years. A noteworthy HBO production. ★★★½ VHS: $9.99

Private Parts

(1997, 111 min, US, Betty Thomas) *Howard Stern, Robin Quivers, Mary McCormack, Fred Norris, Paul Giamatti.* Controversial radio and TV shock jock Stern acquits himself rather nicely in this film "bio" of his rise to fame, based on his best-seller. After several directors took a stab at it, *Private Parts* finally landed in the capable hands of Thomas, who keeps the pace brisk, wrangles quite a few laughs and gets a winning performance from Stern, who's just as good at his patented "offensive" schtick as he is as a romantic lead! Not all of *Private Parts* clicks, but it's nevertheless a funny, entertaining comedy which can be enjoyed even by those who aren't fans of his radio show. ★★★ DVD: $14.99, VHS: $9.99

Privates on Parade

(1984, 95 min, GB, Michael Blakemore) *John Cleese, Denis Quilley, Simon Jones, Julian Sands.* Alternately hilarious and heartwarming, this romp covers the comic adventures of a theatrical troupe of British soldiers tap-dancing their way through WWII. Cleese stars as the commander of this motley crew and Quilley is ferociously funny as the director whose productions would make a USO show look like Shakespeare-in-the-Park. Don't miss the uproarious closing credits sequence. ★★★ DVD Letterbox: $14.99

Prix de Beaute

(1931, 93 min, France, Augusto Genina) *Louise Brooks, Jean Bradin.* Brooks' final starring vehicle, and her only film made in France, has her as a bored young office worker who, against the wishes of her boyfriend, seeks fame and fortune by becoming an entrant in the Miss Europa beauty contest. A standard melodrama that is highlighted by another luminous performance by the enigmatic international star. The film, coscripted by director Genina and René Clair, features the voice of Edith Piaf who sings for Ms. Brooks. (French with English subtitles) ★★ VHS: $24.99

The Prize

(1963, 135 min, US, Mark Robson) *Paul Newman, Edward G. Robinson, Elke Sommer, Leo G. Carroll, Diane Baker.* An entertaining Cold War spy thriller, *The Prize* is the sort of fun, mindless romp typical of the halycon days of the mid-1960s. Newman plays a Nobel Prize-winning author who becomes entangled in international intrigue when he attends the Nobel ceremonies in Stockholm. He suspects that kindly nuclear physicist Robinson has been kidnapped and replaced with an imposter. Anyone who's seen *Foreign Correspondent* knows it's the truth. ★★★

Prizzi's Honor

(1985, 129 min, US, John Huston) *Jack Nicholson, Kathleen Turner, Anjelica Huston, Robert Loggia, William Hickey, CCH Pounder.* Nicholson stars as Charlie Pantana, a lonely and confused hit man who falls hopelessly in love with mysterious and alluring femme fatale Turner. Huston won the Oscar for Best Supporting Actress as Nicholson's once-betrothed. Director Huston infuses this wry black comedy with his characteristic joie de vivre. ★★★★ DVD Dual: $14.99

The Private Life of Henry VIII

Problem Child

(1990, 81 min, US, Dennis Dugan) *John Ritter, Michael Oliver, Jack Warden, Amy Yasbeck, Gilbert Gottfried, Michael Richards.* Bastard precursor to *Home Alone*, about an adopted seven-year-old who tortures his new parents after they whisk him away to the suburbs from an orphanage thrilled to see him gone. Ritter is the oh-so-happy dad who believes his psycho-loving son is just in need of affection. The movie's tone is surprisingly mean-spirited; however, there are a number of slapstick laughs. (Sequel: *Problem Child 2*) ★★ DVD: $19.99

The Producers

(1968, 88 min, US, Mel Brooks) *Zero Mostel, Gene Wilder, Kenneth Mars, Christopher Hewett, Dick Shawn.* Brooks' hysterical farce is certainly one of the funniest films of all time. Mostel gloriously chews the scenery, the furniture and whatever else is in sight as a Broadway producer aching for a hit. He schemes with meek accountant Wilder to produce a flop and make a fortune. They happen upon "Springtime for Hitler" and its crazed Nazi author (Mars). The rest, as they say, is history. (The basis for the hit Broadway musical) ★★★★ DVD Basic Edition: $14.99

The Professional

See: *Léon: The Professional*

The Professionals

(1966, 117 min, US, Richard Brooks) *Burt Lancaster, Lee Marvin, Robert Ryan, Ralph Bellamy, Woody Strode, Jack Palance, Claudia Cardinale.* A rollicking adventure tale expertly directed by Brooks. Lancaster heads the cast as a soldier who is hired to rescue the kidnapped wife of millionaire rancher Bellamy. Palance is the villain holding Cardinale captive. ★★★½ DVD: $24.99

Profumo di Donna
(Scent of a Woman)

(1975, 103 min, Italy, Dino Risi) *Vittorio Gassman.* Gassman was winner of the Best Actor Award at Cannes for his portrayal of a blind, one-armed ex-army captain who resourcefully uses his other senses to savor the beguiling attractions of the other sex. With a young army cadet acting as his eyes, our pleasure-seeking hero travels to Naples in search of love. An Italian farce with undercurrents of drama as well as a decidedly chauvinist attitude to women and relationships. (American remake: *Scent of a Woman*) (Italian with English subtitles) ★★★

The Program

(1993, 114 min, US, David S. Ward) *James Caan, Halle Berry, Omar Epps, Craig Sheffer, Kristy Swanson, Joey Lauren Adams.* Writer-director Ward makes a serious attempt to tackle the highly charged subject of collegiate football but winds up fumbling the ball. The potential to depict a fascinating behind-the-scenes drama disappears in the first quarter, giving way to a haphazard series of clichés and bad calls. Notorious for its controversial scene of characters playing chicken on a busy road, which was eventually cut from the film when several real-life copy-cat pranks resulted in deaths. ★½ DVD: $9.99, VHS: $9.99

Project A

(1983, 83 min, Hong Kong, Jackie Chan) *Jackie Chan, Sammo Hung.* This classic Chan film from the mid-'80s is a hoot. Period piece finds Jackie getting involved in pirate shenanigans, but the plot doesn't matter at all — just sit back and revel in the terrific slapstick and amazing stuntwork and fights. It's all here — the hilarious Buster Keaton-inspired bicycle chase, the infamous fall from the clocktower, and the eye-popping barroom brawl. If you love Jackie, you can't miss this one; Jackie at his most entertaining, jaw-dropping best. (Sequel: *Project A 2*) ★★★½ DVD: $14.99, VHS: $9.99

Project A2

(1987, 104 min, Hong Kong, Jackie Chan) *Jackie Chan, Maggie Cheung, Rosamund Kwan.* Like the first *Project A*, this is a throwback to simpler, slapsticky times, right down to a very obvious Buster Keaton homage. Chan again plays Dragon Ma, who is assigned to the police force. He finds himself caught between the government and revolutionaries. This sets the stage for plenty of stunts, which are all pretty good, though the pace tends to lag in comparison with the original. (Cantonese with English subtitles) ★★★ DVD: $19.99, VHS Dubbed: $9.99

Prom Night

(1980, 91 min, Canada, Paul Lynch) *Jamie Lee Curtis, Leslie Nielsen.* A group of teenagers readying for the high school prom are stalked by a mysterious killer in this run-of-the-mill slasher pick. Curtis continued her reign as scream queen of the '80s. Also with Leslie Nielsen, who plays it relatively straight here. (Followed by 3 sequels) ★★

La Promesse

(1996, 93 min, Belgium, Jean-Pierre Dardenne & Luc Dardenne) *Jeremie Renier, Olivier Gourmet, Assita Ouedraogo, Rasmané Ouedraogo.* A riveting Belgian film, *La Promesse* is raw, gritty and unforgettable. Igor (Renier) is a wise beyond his years teenager, who helps his father Roger (Gourmet) smuggle illegal immigrants into his Antwerp housing project. Roger exploits these aliens after they get settled, and Igor turns a blind eye because this arrangement provides his livelihood. One day, however, an immigrant worker, Hamidu, is fatally injured. Before Roger gets Igor to help him dispose of the body, the boy has made a secret promise that he would take care of Hamidu's wife Assita (Ouedraogo) and their child. As Igor shifts his loyalties back and forth between the father and Assita, the boy realizes he must make a difficult, if not impossible, choice. The film's quiet power stems from Igor's realization that there is no simple solution to his conflict. The film's abrupt ending only slightly mars this otherwise flawless feature. (French with English subtitles) ★★★★ DVD: $19.99, VHS: $14.99

The Promise

(1995, 115 min, France/Germany, Margarethe von Trotta) *Corinna Harfouch, August Zirner.* Von Trotta's misguided love story is nothing more than a melodramatic tale of love between cement slabs that made up the Berlin Wall. Accompanying his girlfriend Sophie and several friends, teenager Konrad is torn apart when he trips and misses his chance for escape to West Germany. Left behind, Konrad years later becomes a scientist who is kept under the thumb of the government, while Sophie becomes a tour guide of historic buildings. Through the years and several chance meetings, their love is tested, stretched, rekindled and finally quashed under the weight of the opposing countries. Though their romance occasionally moves, the soap opera pacing, contrived plot developments and wooden acting make this all the more disappointing. (German with English subtitles) ★★ VHS: $79.99

Promises! Promises!

(1963, 90 min, US, King Donovan) *Jayne Mansfield, Marie McDonald, Tommy Noonan, Mickey Hargitay.* Mansfield plays a happy housewife who takes an ocean cruise with her overworked husband, hoping to get pregnant. Notable for Mansfield's bathtub nude scene, which caused a stir during the film's original release. ★

The Promoter

(1952, 89 min, GB, Ronald Neame) *Alec Guinness, Glynis Johns, Petula Clark.* An engaging comedy about a young man who climbs out of his lowly social rank and rises to the pinnacle of power in his small town. (aka: *The Card*) ★★★

Proof

(1991, 91 min, Australia, Jocelyn Moorhouse) *Russell Crowe, Genevieve Picot, Hugo Weaving.* This spellbinding, pleasant surprise from Australia tells the twisted tale of Martin, a neurotic, blind photographer — no, that's not a typo — who's convinced that everyone lies to him about his surroundings. He snaps off photos as physical evidence that he hopes will one day expose this alleged deceit. When he befriends a young man named Andy, he finds a companion to whom he entrusts the job of describing photographs. But his housekeeper Celia, an obsessive woman who is secretly in love with him, does every-

La Promesse

Janet Leigh in Hitchcock's immortal classic *Psycho*

thing in her power to sabotage their friendship. Director Moorhouse gets great performances from her ensemble in this fascinating, taut and well-made psychological examination of trust, perceived childhood wounds and sexual obsession. ★★★★

Proof of Life

(2000, 135 min, US, Taylor Hackford) *Russell Crowe, Meg Ryan, David Morse, David Caruso, Pamela Reed, Anthony Heald.* An exciting and efficiently directed actioner, *Proof of Life* may be more noted for its pairing of Ryan and Crowe, who had a brief, headline-making fling. Thankfully, their real-life chemistry comes through, only adding to the many pleasures of this solid adventure tale. Ryan plays Alice, the wife of Peter (Morse), an American engineer who is supervising the building of a dam in a fictional South American country. When he is kidnapped by rebels, expert K&R (kidnap and ranson) negotiator Terry Thorne (Crowe) enters the picture. As Terry bargains for Peter's life and plans for a possible rescue, he and Alice become attracted to each other. It's *Casablanca* revisited as a wife is torn between her husband and the man who could save his life. But unlike many rip-offs of that classic film, *Proof of Life* has its own identity and features characters who you really care about. ★★★ DVD Letterbox: $14.99, VHS: $14.99

Prophecy

(1979, 95 min, US, John Frankenheimer) *Robert Foxworth, Talia Shire, Armand Assante.* An ecological horror film with more emphasis on the eco than logical. Nuclear pollutants are turning our freshwater friends into oversized and very upset monsters. ★★ DVD Letterbox: $14.99, VHS: $19.99

The Prophecy

(1995, 95 min, US, Gregory Widen) *Christopher Walken, Eric Stoltz, Virginia Madsen, Viggo Mortensen.* This very original horror film about a second war in Heaven stars Walken as the archangel Gabriel, who has come to Earth to enlist help in a war he and other renegade angels are waging against God. Stoltz plays a lesser angel who has to stop Gabriel. The film's low-budget origins prevent its grand premise from being realized, and a confusing ending makes it all frustrating. (Followed by 2 sequels) ★★ DVD: $19.99, VHS: $9.99

The Proposition

(1998, 115 min, US, Lesli Linka Glatter) *William Hurt, Madeleine Stowe, Kenneth Branagh, Frank Loggia, Neil Patrick Harris.* Painfully dull and extremely slow moving, *The Proposition* wastes a talented cast in a film so bad, its greatest shame is that it is not unintentionally funny. Told in flashback by Father Mike McKinnon (Branagh), the story concerns the ongoing efforts of a sterile businessman named Arthur (Hurt) to have his wife Eleanor (Stowe) impregnated by young stud Roger (Harris). Once Eleanor does become pregnant, she miscarries and seeks solace in Father Mike, and an unlikely affair ensues. *The Proposition* is awash in bad plot twists, clunky symbolism and awkward mouthfuls of dialogue. ★ VHS: $14.99

Prospero's Books

(1991, 129 min, GB/Netherlands, Peter Greenaway) *John Gielgud, Michael Clark, Michel Blanc, Erland Josephson.* Greenaway's kaleidoscopic, hallucinatory spin on Shakespeare's "The Tempest." Gielgud not only stars as Prospero but also gives voice to every other character in the film. While the film sketchily follows the narrative, Greenaway pays more attention to the thematic content of the Bard's work and plays it up as an allegory for the conquering of the magical New World (read: the Americas). For adventurous viewers of cinema, this is a must, but be warned that a knowledge of "The Tempest" is extremely helpful in one's comprehension of the film. ★★★½

Protocol

(1984, 96 min, US, Herbert Ross) *Goldie Hawn, Chris Sarandon, Andre Gregory.* Hawn's endearing charm elevates this average comedy about a Washington waitress who saves the life of a diplomat and becomes involved in international diplomacy and intrigue. ★★½ DVD: $14.99, VHS: $14.99

Providence

(1977, 104 min, France, Alain Resnais) *John Gielgud, Dirk Bogarde, Ellen Burstyn, David Warner.* Gielgud creates a vivid character in the person of Clive Langham, a noted elderly author, in this fascinating story on creativity and imagination. In a superlative portrayal, Gielgud plays the often drunk, foul-mouthed old man, who despite suffering from a fatal disease, spends a night hallucinating about members of his family while trying to plot out his next novel. Fact, fantasy and his unconscious thoughts and feelings as well as his growing senility are incorporated into the fabric of his tale. (Filmed in English) ★★★

Provincial Actors

(1980, 104 min, Poland, Agnieszka Holland) *Tadeusz Huk, Halina Labonarska.* In her debut feature, director Holland takes the trials and tribulations of a rural theatre troupe and politicizes in a meandering fashion their attempt to produce a play. Christopher, the leading actor of the troupe, is a dedicated artist — to the extent he ignores his impatient wife Anna, herself a former actress but now relegated to children's puppet shows. In the course of rehearsals and performances, Christopher experiences marital problems and a near-mental breakdown. Holland demonstrates little of the dramatic structure or a fluent style evident in her later

works, but the film does offer an interesting glimpse into the mind and the relationship of the artist. (Polish with English subtitles) ★★ VHS: $29.99

Psycho

(1960, 109 min, US, Alfred Hitchcock) *Anthony Perkins, Janet Leigh, Vera Miles, John Gavin, Martin Balsam.* What more can be said about this classic shocker that has forever altered the sanctity of the shower (not to mention tainted the reputations of taxidermists and loving sons)? Perkins made his mark with the jagged-edged portrait of mild-mannered hotel proprietor Norman Bates. A masterpiece of both suspense and narrative form, *Psycho* is Hitchcock at his best. (Remade in 1998) (Followed by 3 sequels) ★★★★ DVD Letterbox: $29.99

Psycho

(1998, 104 min, US, Gus Van Sant) *Vince Vaughn, Anne Heche, Julianne Moore, William H. Macy, Viggo Mortensen, Robert Forster, Philip Baker Hall, Chad Everett, James Remar, James LeGros, Flea.* Remakes should serve several purposes. Amongst them are updating an entirely dated work for modern audiences, or stamping source material with another auteur's distinctive ring. Van Sant does neither with his remake of Alfred Hitchcock's classic thriller, a nifty-in-theory experiment which should have been relegated to film school. A miscast Vaughn sullies the character of Norman Bates, now a fey masturbator. Basically, Van Sant's own directorial output includes some technically sophisticated shots, color and a few weird edits (Macy sees blurred visions of cows when stabbed!). This remake is totally uncalled for. ★★ DVD Collector's Edition: $14.99

Psycho II

(1983, 113 min, US, Richard Franklin) *Anthony Perkins, Vera Miles, Meg Tilly, Robert Loggia.* Perkins returns as Norman Bates. It's 20 years later, and Norman has been released from the asylum, trying to keep his hands (not to mention the shower) clean. ★★½ DVD: $19.99, VHS: $14.99

Psycho III

(1986, 96 min, US, Anthony Perkins) *Anthony Perkins, Diana Scarwid, Jeff Fahey.* The Bates Motel is open for business once more. Perkins returns as Norman, who here becomes attracted to Scarwid, his new assistant manager, who bears a striking resemblance to the ill-fated Marion Crane. Some scenes are played strictly for laughs. ★★ DVD: $19.99, VHS: $14.99

Anne Heche in Gus Van Sant's ill-conceived remake of *Psycho*

Puberty Blues

(1981, 86 min, Australia, Bruce Beresford) *Neil Schofield, Jad Capelja.* Beresford's comic, risqué look at the coming-of-age of two teenage girls around the surfing beaches outside Sydney. It offers an insightful look at adolescent rites of passage, told from the female point of view. ★★½ VHS: $14.99

Public Access

(1992, 86 min, US, Bryan Singer) *Ron Marquette, Dina Brooks, Burt Williams, Larry Maxwell.* An intriguing but ultimately unfulfilled thriller, *Public Access* is the promising first feature film by director Singer and writer Christopher McQuarrie (*The Usual Suspects*). The slickly handsome Marquette is Whiley Pritcher, an enigmatic stranger who comes to the sleepy town of Brewster. He buys time on the local public access channel, hosting a show called "Our Town," and asks the question, "What's wrong with Brewster?" Soon a bevy of semi-lunatic callers tell on their neighbors, threatening to uncover a scandal lurking beneath Brewster's surface. Though Singer and McQuarrie fail to find a satisfying resolution to the questions they pose, the ending is nevertheless thought-provoking and unique. ★★½ DVD: $24.99, VHS: $19.99

Public Enemy

(1931, 83 min, US, William Wellman) *James Cagney, Jean Harlow, Joan Blondell.* Classic 1930s gangster film with Cagney giving a star-making performance as a slum kid who rises to the top of the underworld. First-rate cast includes Clarke, who was the recipient of that famous grapefruit. ★★★½ VHS: $19.99

The Public Eye

(1992, 99 min, US, Howard Franklin) *Joe Pesci, Barbara Hershey, Stanley Tucci.* Fireball Pesci reveals a seldom-seen sensitivity in this atmospheric biography based on the life of '40s tabloid photographer Leon Bernstein. Pesci is "The Great Bernzini," a papparazzi prototype whose photojournalistic aspirations get him embroiled with the cops, the mob and a sultry femme fatale (Hershey). While the "beauty and the beast" angle wears thin at times, Peter Suschitzky's dead-on mixture of black-and-white photography with color cinematography captures the gritty milieu of the 1940s New York underworld. (Not to be confused with the 1972 Mia Farrow romantic comedy of the same name.) ★★½ VHS: $19.99

Pulp Fiction

(1994, 153 min, US, Quentin Tarantino) *John Travolta, Samuel L. Jackson, Bruce Willis, Uma Thurman, Harvey Keitel, Tim Roth, Amanda Plummer, Eric Stoltz, Maria de Medeiros, Peter Greene, Ving Rhames, Rosanna Arquette, Alexis Arquette, Quentin Tarantino, Christopher Walken, Julia Sweeney, Frank Whaley, Steve Buscemi.* Tarantino's audacious arthouse actioner is perhaps the only American film so story-intensive that it deserves the title "the *Gone with the Wind* of action movies." Travolta and Jackson give exceptional performances as a pair of gregarious hit men whose day-to-day activities take them through an interlocking series of darkly comic and horrific scenarios ranging from an accidental drug overdose to a graphic rape sequence. Tarantino introduces a rogue's gallery of well-drawn characters into a labyrinthine story line, playing with perspective, time and place. Lengthy without ever being boring, this gritty walk on the wild side features an astounding ensemble. ★★★★ DVD Letterbox Special Edition: $29.99, VHS: $9.99

Pump Up the Volume

(1990, 100 min, US, Allan Moyle) *Christian Slater, Ellen Greene, Samantha Mathis, Annie Ross.* Slater dons the troubled youth persona and is dead-on target in capturing teenage disillusionment in the land of "white bread." Slater plays a shy high school student who lets go and "talks hard" as Harry Hard-on, an irreverent pirate D.J. His voice in tune to both the misfits and the hip of his school, Harry soon becomes an unwilling guru to his classmates, and a "threat" to school and local authorities. *Pump Up the Volume* is brimming with great dialogue and an excellent musical score. ★★★ DVD: $14.99, VHS: $9.99

Pumping Iron

(1977, 85 min, US, George Butler & Robert Fiore) *Arnold Schwarzenegger, Lou Ferrigno.* A sometimes mesmerizing glimpse into the little-dissected world of bodybuilding, this part-adulatory, part-voyeuristic documentary centers on the Mr. Olympia contest and on its two main competitors — Schwarzenegger and Ferrigno. There's lots of scenes of bulging biceps and sweaty faces as the directors interview the men in and out of the gym, and cinematically eavesdrop on conversations and workouts. ★★★ DVD 25th Anniversary Special Edition: $19.99

Pumping Iron II: The Women

(1985, 107 min, US, George Butler) Butler returns to the gyms in this engaging look at female bodybuilding. As the camera ogles the bronzed women pumping up, champions Rachel McLish, Bev Francis and a dozen others discuss their commitment to the sport and demonstrate their physical prowess. ★★★ DVD: $19.99, VHS: $19.99

Pumpkin

(2002, 117 min, US, Adam Larson Broder & Anthony Abrams) *Christina Ricci, Hank Harris, Brenda Blethyn, Dominique Swain, Marisa Coughlan.* Ricci is cast against type as a peppy sorority girl/cheerleader who, to her surprise, falls for a physically and mentally handicapped teenager named Pumpkin — much to the horror of her fellow cheerleaders. A very strange mix of black comedy, outrageously offensive situations and politically correct life lessons, *Pumpkin* desperately tries to produce the humor and hip quotient of *Heathers*, but is overlong and wildly uneven. ★★ DVD Dual: $14.99

Pumpkinhead

(1988, 87 min, US, Stan Winston) *Lance Henriksen, Jeff East.* This Gothic-like horror film, a cut above the typical teen slasher film, provides creepy fun which relies more on suspense than gore (although the film does have its share). A group of city kids go "wilding" in the country and accidentally kill one of the young locals. The dead child's father (Henriksen) wants revenge and summons a mythical demon, which comes to life and inhabits the surrounding mountains. ★★½ DVD: $14.99

Punch-Drunk Love

(2002, 89 min, US, Paul Thomas Anderson) *Adam Sandler, Emily Watson, Philip Seymour Hoffman, Luis Guzman, Mary Lynn Rajskub.* This unlikely pairing of actor and director brings out the best in both, and a wonderful surprise for romantic cinephiles. Sandler is at home in his usual role — a likable, shy guy with a violent temper — here a toilet plunger entrepreneur with seven viciously judgmental sisters. Insecure and lonely to the point of dialing a shady phone-sex line, and odd enough to wrangle frequent flier miles by buying pallets of pudding, he's nonetheless cautiously pursued by cute Brit Watson. Is there a reason for them to fall for

each other? Not really, but isn't that how love works? There's attraction, a connection, and pillow talk like "I love you so much I want to rip out your eyeballs and suck on them" that simultaneously sounds funny, passionate and *just right* for these two. Director Anderson completely drops his cynical guard to create, in a purely cinematic language, a whimsical and exhilarating expression of puppy love. ★★★½ DVD Letterbox 2-disc Superbit Edition: $28.99, DVD: $19.99, VHS: $102.99

Punchline

(1988, 128 min, US, David Seltzer) *Sally Field, John Goodman, Tom Hanks, Mary Rydell, Damon Wayans.* This intriguing and often hilarious comedy-drama stars Hanks (in an unusual departure from his other film roles) as a self-centered medical student drop-out determined to make it in the world of stand-up comedy. Field nicely plays a New Jersey housewife (patterned on Roseanne?) who yearns to make people laugh. The film entertainingly explores both the milieu of the comic and the touching story of the friendship and ill-fated romance between Hanks and Field. ★★★ DVD Dual: $9.99, VHS: $9.99

The Puppet Masters

(1994, 95 min, US, Stuart Orme) *Donald Sutherland, Eric Thal, Julie Warner, Yaphet Kotto.* Sci-fi visionary Robert A. Heinlein's gripping cold war parable about alien possession is updated and streamlined into this tense if derivative chiller with more than a passing resemblance to *Invasion of the Body Snatchers*. This time out the alien is a parasite that attaches itself to the spinal cord of its victim and drills into the brain. Though we've seen it all before, the film benefits from a fast-paced script, good special effects and a commanding performance by Sutherland as the resident know-it-all science expert called in to stem the tide of alien domination. ★★★ DVD: $9.99

Pups

(1999, 100 min, US, Ash) *Cameron Van Hoy, Marsha Barton, Burt Reynolds, Kurt Loder.* Two young kids find one of their parents' handguns and decide to rob a bank on the way to school. They're forced to take hostages, and a media circus soon develops. This *Kids*-lite meets *Dog Day Afternoon* would've made a decent short, but as a feature it doesn't feel fully developed. Reynolds (almost literally) phones in his performance, while the two kids are allowed to flounder in long, faux-Cassavetes, seemingly improvised scenes. While moderately suspenseful at times, the film also makes mincemeat out of its already obvious, "big-whoop" social observations, complete with predictable, hollow, tragic ending. ★★½ DVD: $19.99, VHS: $102.99

A Pure Formality

(1994, 108 min, France/Italy, Giuseppe Tornatore) *Gérard Depardieu, Roman Polanski, Sergio Rubini.* An arresting opening sequence of murder and flight begins an intricately constructed battle of intellect and will between two formidable opponents. As the prime suspect, a rain-soaked and disheveled Depardieu emits a raw intensity reminiscent of his performance in *Going Places*. As Police Inspector Bogart, Polanski seems to carry the burden of his personal experiences with police procedures. The conflict between these evenly matched protagonists is a sly game of cat and mouse. Tornatore keeps a tight ship, deftly utilizing all the materials at his disposal — not the least of which is Ennio Morricone's score. The film's resolution is satisfying in its ambiguity, a wry treatise on the many-layered nature of reality. (French with English subtitles) ★★★½

Pure Luck

(1991, 96 min, US, Nadia Tass) *Martin Short, Danny Glover, Harry Shearer, Scott Wilson.* This limp remake of the hilarious French comedy *La Chevre* falls decidedly flat. When the accident-prone daughter of a wealthy industrialist disappears at a Mexican resort, the only person capable of finding her is the equally maladroit and bumbling Short. Glover is the company detective who reluctantly accepts him as a partner in the search. The pairing doesn't seem like a bad one, but this comic duo simply can't match the sidesplitting slapstick achieved by Gérard Depardieu and Pierre Richard in the original. ★★ VHS: $9.99

Purlie Victorious

(1963, 105 min, US, Nicholas Webster) *Ossie Davis, Ruby Dee, Alan Alda, Godfrey Cambridge, Sorrell Booke.* Leisurely film version of Ossie Davis' Broadway satire about a free-wheeling preacher (Davis) who goes up against an oppressive, bigoted landowner (Booke). The basis for the award-winning musical "Purlie." (aka: *Gone Are the Days*) ★★★

The Purple Heart

(1944, 99 min, US, Lewis Milestone) *Dana Andrews, Farley Granger, Richard Conte, Sam Levene.* This WWII drama doubles as a fascinating piece of war-time propaganda and an interesting examination of individual heroism. A group of U.S. pilots captured and held prisoner by the Japanese Army. ★★★

Purple Noon

(1960, 118 min, France, René Clément) *Alain Delon, Marie Laforet, Maurice Ronet.* This stylish, gorgeously photographed and sexy thriller is far from being dated and is possibly more impressive when viewed today. Set amidst the opulent, sun-drenched locales of the Mediterranean, the film's serpentine plot involves the tangled affairs of three young "beautiful people." Delon is the stunningly handsome Tom, a friend and hanger-on to Phillip (Ronet), a brattily rich American playboy cruising the warm blue waters in his sailboat with his long-suffering girlfriend (Laforet) and Tom. But this surface beauty and tranquility only masks a deadly scheme of revenge and murder as Tom concocts a plot to take over his friend's life and love. Hitchcockian in detail and twists, *Purple Noon*, adapted from Patricia Highsmith's "The Talented Mr. Ripley," is certain to enthrall. (French and Italian with English subtitles) ★★★½ DVD Letterbox: $19.99, VHS: $9.99

Purple Rain

(1984, 111 min, US, Albert Magnoli) *Prince, Apollonia Kotero, Morris Day, Olga Karlatos, Clarence Williams III.* Prince makes an prodigous film debut as The Kid, a young band leader with an alcoholic father, an uptight attitude and problems with women. Filled with outrageous production numbers and pulsating music by Prince and the Revolution as well as Morris Day and the Time. The film's treatment of women is suspect, but the question arises, is it unmitigated misogyny or a comment on the ravages of spousal abuse? You decide. (Sequel: *Graffiti Bridge*) ★★½ DVD: $14.99, VHS: $9.99

The Purple Rose of Cairo

(1985, 82 min, US, Woody Allen) *Mia Farrow, Jeff Daniels, Danny Aiello, Dianne Wiest, Edward Herrmann, Glenne Headly.* Farrow stars as a waifish Depression-era waitress who is swept off her feet by Daniels, the star of her favorite movie. The catch, of course, is that he literally walks off the movie screen to get to her! A delicious concept, done full justice by Allen. "I'm in love with a wonderful man — he's fictional, but you can't have everything." ★★★★ DVD: $19.99

The Purple Taxi

(1977, 107 min, France/Italy/Ireland, Yves Boisset) *Charlotte Rampling, Philippe Noiret, Fred Astaire, Peter Ustinov.* An unusual French drama with an international cast about a group of expatriates who live in Ireland and are involved in a complicated ménage of relationships. (Filmed in English) ★★

The Pursuit of D.B. Cooper

(1981, 100 min, US, Roger Spottiswoode) *Robert Duvall, Treat Williams, Kathryn Harrold.* A fictionalized account of a real-life event, this appealing caper comedy tries to speculate what "really" happened to infamous hijacker D.B. Cooper in 1971. Williams is the thief, and Duvall is the policeman hot on his trail. ★★½

Pushing Hands

(1992, 100 min, US, Ang Lee) *Sihung Lung, Bo Z. Wang, Deb Snyder, Haan Lee, Lai Wang.* Pushing Hands is a Tai Chi exercise of ebb and flow, accomodation and imposition, a physical manifestation of the quest for balance. In director Lee's first film, the balance of the Chu household is disrupted when Alex (B. Wang) brings his father (Lung), a Tai chi master in China, to New York to live with him, his Caucasian wife and their child where circumstances exacerbate generational and cultural differences. Master Chu embarks on a solo journey into this strange new world, and his quest is delicately considered with compassion and sharp observance by the director. A small gem of a film whose resolution offers warmth without naiveté. (In English and Mandarin with English subtitles) ★★★

Pushing Tin

(1999, 123 min, US, Mike Newell) *John Cusack, Billy Bob Thornton, Cate Blanchett, Angelina Jolie, Jake Weber, Vicki Lewis.* Cusack thinks he's the best air traffic controller, until hotshot Thornton comes to the tower; thus begins a bitter rivalry that inevitably leads to respect and friendship. The high-stress environment in which they work makes for very entertaining scenes, but director Newell loses focus of what makes these people interesting and instead *Pushing Tin* drifts into an average domestic drama, with adultery and other mundane subplots that were more interesting in hundreds of earlier movies. As would be expected, the cast is fine, with Blanchett underplaying her unhappy New Jersey wife. But the TV-movie mechanics are a major disappointment. ★★½ DVD: $14.99, VHS: $9.99

Putney Swope

(1969, 88 min, US, Robert Downey) *Arnold Johnson, Laura Greene.* While the liberal wing of Hollywood was making a big show out of inviting Sidney Poitier home to dinner, Downey was preaching true equality when he argued that given half the chance blacks could be every bit as corrupt as whites. Downey sets his fable in the milieu he knew well — Madison Avenue advertising. When token black Swope is accidentally elected the agency's new president, change is in the air. First up, a corporate make over, starting with the name. Now called "Truth & Soul," the company vows not to accept any politically incorrect clients — until the cash flow gets tight. Downey mixes faux commercials with a wild narrative style that influenced mainstream movies for years to come. ★★★ DVD: $19.99, VHS: $19.99

Pygmalion

(1938, 96 min, GB, Anthony Asquith & Leslie Howard) *Leslie Howard, Wendy Hiller.* George Bernard Shaw helped write the screenplay for this first real expert film translation of one of his plays. Hiller is captivating as Eliza Doolittle, the guttersnipe flower seller who is transformed into a proper socialite by the efforts of Professor Henry Higgins (Howard). Unfortunately lost in the shuffle since the international success of the musical "My Fair Lady" on which it is based, this earlier, more modest, version is exemplary of classic British cinema. ★★★★ DVD Criterion Collection: $29.99, VHS: $24.99

A Pyromaniac's Love Story

(1995, 96 min, US, Joshua Brand) *William Baldwin, John Leguizamo, Sadie Frost, Erika Eleniak, Michael Lerner, Joan Plowright, Armin Mueller-Stahl.* A cloying comedy of errors about a poor schlub (Leguizamo) who takes the blame for setting a fire he didn't commit in exchange for the $20,000 he needs to run away with his beloved (Frost) who'll now have nothing to do with him. Enter the real culprit (Baldwin) who set the fire as a tribute to his beloved (Eleniak) and now wants proper credit! Part O'Henry and part Wilde, without the flair of either, Brand's quirky and miscast mishmash relies on the kinetic energy of Leguizamo to sustain it, though the screenplay doesn't make it worth the effort. ★★ DVD: $14.99, VHS: $19.99

Python

(1999, 95 min, US, Richard Clabaugh) *Casper Van Dien, Robert Englund, Wil Wheaton, Jenny McCarthy.* A giant, genetically engineered python survives a plane crash and kills lotsa people. That's it for plot — well, actually, that should be it, but the filmmakers seem to be operating under the mistaken impression that we need weak, overlong comic interludes and loads of dull "character development." Still, the snake scenes are fake but fun, and any movie with Van Dien struggling with a ridiculous Southern accent while scolding Robert Englund for creating a giant killer snake can't be all bad. (Sequel: *Python II*) ★★ DVD: $9.99, VHS: $9.99

Adam Sandler in *Punch-Drunk Love*

Q (The Winged Serpent)

(1982, 92 min, US, Larry Cohen) *Michael Moriarty, Candy Clark, David Carradine, Richard Roundtree.* From the fertile mind of Cohen comes this very exciting half monster movie/half cop story about an ancient winged creature that's alive and well and living atop the Chrysler Building. Moriarty is great as a two-bit loser who discovers the nest and then blackmails the city for millions to divulge the location. Pure fun and actually suspenseful at times. ★★★ DVD: $19.99, VHS: $14.99

Q & A

(1990, 132 min, US, Sidney Lumet) *Nick Nolte, Timothy Hutton, Armand Assante, Patrick O'Neal, Charles S. Dutton.* Director Lumet scrutinizes the mean streets of New York City in this powerful but insensitive urban drama. In a forceful and maniacal performance, Nolte stars as a racist cop whose murder of a suspect is being investigated by young assistant D.A. Hutton, who uncovers a web of political corruption. Assante is commanding as a gangster being investigated by Hutton. As unflinching as the drama is in its examination of bigotry, *Q & A* is shockingly callous in its depiction of gays. ★★½ DVD: $9.99, VHS: $9.99

Quackser Fortune Has a Cousin in the Bronx

(1970, 90 min, Ireland, Waris Hussein) *Gene Wilder, Margot Kidder.* Wilder delivers an exceptionally subdued performance as a man who follows horses around the streets of Dublin and sells their manure for gardening. A charming and offbeat comic love story which also stars Kidder as an American coed who becomes the center of Wilder's amorous attentions. ★★★ DVD: $14.99, VHS: $14.99

Quadrophenia

(1979, 115 min, GB, Franc Roddam) *Phil Daniels, Mark Wingett, Sting.* It's Mods versus Rockers in The Who's gripping portrait of teenage anguish and anger played out in '60s Britain amid pill-popping, gang warfare and rock 'n' roll. This vibrantly-paced film is filled with great music and features the momentous film debut of Sting as an ace face. ★★★½ DVD: $24.99, VHS: $14.99

Quality Street

(1937, 84 min, US, George Stevens) *Katharine Hepburn, Franchot Tone, Fay Bainter.* Fanciful screen version of James Barrie's whimsical play of mistaken identity and romantic trickery. Hepburn stars as a beautiful society girl whose fiancé goes off to the Napoleonic Wars. When he returns 10 years later, he doesn't recognize his former girlfriend, whose beauty has somewhat faded. So she masquerades as her own high-spirited niece to win him back. ★★★

Quartet

(1948, 120 min, GB, Ken Annakin) *Dirk Bogarde, Mai Zetterling, Honor Blackman.* First-rate episodic drama featuring four W. Somerset Maugham short stories, which are introduced by the author himself. The stories are: *The Facts of Life*, *The Alien Corn*, *The Kite* and *The Colonel's Lady*. ★★★½

Quartet

(1981, 101 min, France/GB, James Ivory) *Alan Bates, Maggie Smith, Isabelle Adjani.* In this adaptation of Jean Rhys' novel, Adjani plays a young woman who, upon being stranded in Paris, falls prey to a beguiling British couple (Bates, Smith). Excellent performances and Ivory's steady hand at the helm make this tale of hedonism and treachery a spine-tingling treat. ★★★ VHS: $19.99

Quatermass and the Pit

(1968, 98 min, GB, Roy Ward Baker) *Andrew Keir, James Donald, Barbara Shelley, Julian Glover.* The third of the "Quatermass" films from Hammer Studios and screenwriter Nigel Kneale is arguably the best one, successfully bringing together the odd combination of common sci-fi elements and more heady philosophical issues. Keir is rocket scientist Quatermass, called to the site of a strange discovery: an eons-old spacecraft buried beneath a London subway station is unleashing energy causing more susceptible Londoners to turn on their less-fortunate neighbors. Chaos ensues and Quatermass and company barely save the day, in one of the most downbeat and mind-numbingly powerful climaxes of any sci-fi film of the 1960s. (aka: *Five Million Years to Earth*) ★★★½ DVD: $29.99, VHS: $14.99

Que Viva Mexico!

(1930/1984, 90 min, Mexico/USSR, Sergei Eisenstein) This famous aborted project has endured a long, rocky history. In 1930, Eisenstein traveled to Mexico in an effort to make a film on that country. The project was suspended after a dispute with his producer, the writer Upton Sinclair. With filming only partially completed, Eisenstein left for the Soviet Union expecting the rushes to be sent to him for completion; but they never arrived and the project languished for over 40 years until Grigory Alexandrov, his former editor, obtained the rushes and constructed a version Eisenstein might have done. The result is a glorious and compelling vision of a mystical Mexico. Told in five segments, Eisenstein explores different aspects of Indian life as well as their plight after the Spanish conquest and Catholic indoctrination. Strikingly photographed, this poetic and vivid film explores both the beauty and the underlying tragedy of this fascinating country. (Russian with English subtitles) ★★★ DVD: $29.99, VHS: $24.99

The Queen

(1968, 80 min, US, Frank Simon) This outlandish behind-the-scenes look at the drag Miss All-American Beauty Pageant of 1967 has only improved with age, offering a fascinating and humorous peek into the world of drag and a glimpse at one aspect of pre-Stonewall gay life. Staged in New York, the film captures the frantic days of preparation for the elaborately staged finals as the 40 regional contestants arrive, rehearse their stage entrance and dance numbers, and exchange makeup, fashion and beauty secrets. The pageant itself is a glamorous, sensational affair which gives center stage to these beauties, especially Philadelphia's Harlow. After the crowning of the new queen, many of the attitude-throwing, jealous losers bare their sharp claws and venomous tongues. A camp delight and finger-snapping fun. ★★★ VHS: $29.99

Queen Bee

(1955, 95 min, US, Ranald MacDougall) *Joan Crawford, Barry Sullivan, Betsy Palmer, Fay Wray.* Crawford is at her fire-breathing best in this soaper about the machinations of the manipulative matri-

Quadrophenia

arch of a dysfunctional Southern family who destroys the lives of those around her (in between costume changes). More fashion show than film, *Queen Bee* sparkles with the cattiest dialogue this side of *All about Eve*. ★★★ DVD Letterbox: $24.99

Queen Christina

(1933, 97 min, US, Rouben Mamoulian) *Greta Garbo, John Gilbert, Lewis Stone*. In one of her most intoxicating performances, Garbo radiates sensuality and regal authority as the lonely but compassionate 17th-century Swedish monarch — who renounced her throne rather than be forced to wed and produce an heir. Exquisitely photographed, the film also features Gilbert as her intended, who can't understand her reluctance and constant wearing of men's trousers. Mamoulian's classic works as both historical epic and examination of individual expression, and Garbo posed sphinx-like at the bow of a ship is unforgettable. ★★★★

Queen Kelly

(1929, 101 min, US, Erich von Stroheim) *Gloria Swanson, Walter Byron*. Let's dish some dirt! Even though von Stroheim was supposed to be nothing more than her bimbo director, he still managed to make this Swanson vehicle into something of his own before the plug was pulled. A handsome prince falls for a cute little convent girl, only to lose her when she is shipped off to an East African brothel run by her aunt. It's Cinderella with a few kinks; but the film was never really completed after Swanson had a snit about a scene where a syphilitic cripple drools tobacco juice on her in bed. Needless to say, it's the kind of fun only von Stroheim could create. Some scenes cropped up in Billy Wilder's *Sunset Boulevard* twenty years later. ★★★½ DVD Deluxe Collector's Edition: $29.99, VHS: $24.99

Queen Margot

(1994, 140 min, France, Patrice Chereau) *Isabelle Adjani, Jean-Hugues Anglade, Virna Lisi, Daniel Auteuil, Vincent Perez, Dominique Blanc*. This lavishly produced French epic, based on a novel by Alexandre Dumas, examines the bloody history of the struggle between France's Catholics and Protestants in the late 16th century. Opening with the marriage of the Catholic Margot (the unbelievably radiant Adjani) to the Protestant Henri of Navarre (Auteuil), the film details the events leading up to and following the St. Bartholomew's Day massacre in Paris, when the Catholic guard slaughtered over 6,000 Huguenots. Brimming with more palace intrigue than the best of Shakespeare, the story's central villainess is the Queen Mother, Catherine de Medici (Lisi), who is constantly hatching plots to dispatch poor Henri and keep her three sons in power. A superb costume drama that is filled with graphic images of brutal violence. (French with English subtitles) ★★★½ DVD: $19.99, VHS: $9.99

Queen of Hearts

(1989, 112 min, GB, Jon Amiel) *Anita Zagaria, Joseph Long*. Wonderfully wacky tale from the director of *The Singing Detective* about an Italian couple who elope to London to escape an arranged marriage, only to be tracked down by the vengeful would-be groom. Director Amiel ably mixes whimsical ideas with dead-on characterizations. ★★★½

The Queen of Spades

(1948, 95 min, GB, Thorold Dickinson) *Edith Evans, Anton Walbrook*. Walbrook stars as a young Russian officer who is consumed by an obsession to learn the secret of winning at cards from a dia-

bolical old countess (a bravura performance by Evans). Based on a story by Alexander Pushkin, the film is infused with an eerie atmosphere of the macabre. ★★★

Queen of the Damned

(2002, 100 min, US, Michael Rymer) *Stuart Townsend, Aaliyah, Vincent Perez, Lena Olin, Marguerite Moreau*. In this sequel to *Interview with the Vampire*, Lestat is awakened from his decades-long slumber by some lame Goth music, and decides to become an international rock superstar. This rankles the rest of the vampire population, because Lestat has effectively "outed" them. Some intriguing ideas and lush sets and costumes can't make up for the overall tone of amateurishness here: this seems more like a quickie straight-to-video knockoff than a high-profile sequel. Flashy but wholly empty direction, choppy storytelling, and an OK-at-best performance by Townsend (who took over from Tom Cruise) as Lestat are further debits. The late Aaliyah is rather good as the Queen, but — despite the film's title and her top-billing — she only has about fifteen minutes of screen time. ★½ DVD Letterbox: $14.99, DVD Pan & Scan: $14.99, VHS: $14.99

Queens Logic

(1991, 116 min, US, Steve Rash) *Joe Mantegna, Kevin Bacon, Linda Fiorentino, John Malkovich, Jamie Lee Curtis, Ken Olin, Chloe Webb*. A remarkable ensemble cast breathes life into this *Big Chill*-like, thought-provoking examination of growing up and growing apart. A group of friends return to the old neighborhood for a wedding which may or may not happen. As events accelerate toward a fateful bachelor party, the childhood friends discover how the world has changed, and how they've remained the same. ★★½ DVD: $14.99

Querelle

(1982, 106 min, West Germany, Rainer Werner Fassbinder) *Brad Davis, Burkhard Driest, Franco Nero, Jeanne Moreau*. Some say that Fassbinder was past the point of dissipation as he worked on Jean Genet's homoerotic story of lust and murder. There is no denying that the final result lacks the cohesion of the director's greatest works. But its ominously dark and determinedly artificial sets and the stylized acting all gel to create a brooding, melancholy mood quite fitting with the classic novel. Davis is Querelle, a ruggedly handsome, narcissistic and sexually confused sailor who exploits and even kills the ones who lust after him. Nero is perfect as the commander who secretly worships him while Moreau is completely miscast as Querelle's part-time lover and brothel madam. (English language version) ★★½ DVD: $24.99

The Quest

(1996, 95 min, US, Jean-Claude Van Damme) *Jean-Claude Van Damme, Roger Moore, James Remar*. Van Damme proves that he can be as bad a director as he is an actor in this, his debut behind the camera. He stars in this period tale as the leader of a group of kiddie thieves who becomes entangled with a debonair pirate (Moore). He's then sold into slavery and then becomes a martial arts master. All that hooey only serves to bring the slow-moving story to the final competition, which is actually staged rather well. ★★ DVD: $9.99, VHS: $9.99

Quest for Fire

(1982, 97 min, Canada/France, Jean-Jacques Annaud) *Rae Dawn Chong, Everett McGill, Ron Perlman*. An enthralling supposition on the evolution of mankind, skillfully and imaginatively crafted by Annaud. Novelist Anthony Burgess and Desmond Morris collaborated to create the original language and body movement of prehistoric man in this unique mesh of fantasy and pop-archaeology. ★★★½ DVD: $14.99

A Question of Silence

(1983, 92 min, Netherlands, Marleen Gorris) This production is surely one of the most controversial and provocative films released in some time. Ostensibly a feminist thriller, the film chronicles the seemingly unmotivated murder of a male shopkeeper by three middle-aged women who had never met before and did not know their victim. A woman psychologist tries to piece together the puzzle of why they killed the man. Was it senseless murder or a political act — the rage of women against a male dominated society? (Dutch with English subtitles) ★★★ VHS: $29.99

The Quick and the Dead

(1995, 103 min, US, Sam Raimi) *Sharon Stone, Gene Hackman, Leonardo DiCaprio, Russell Crowe, Gary Sinise, Lance Henriksen*. A deglamorized Stone stars as a vengeful gunslinger who rides into the dustball town of Redemption (no symbolism there) looking for the man responsible for her father's murder. She winds up smack-dab in the middle of the annual "Fastest Gun in the West" contest. Hackman gives an over-the-top performance as the sadistic town overlord who, until now, has won the contest hands down. Needless to say, he's the man she's looking for. Though it's mostly predictable fun, what distinguishes the film is director Raimi's patented inventive technical prowess; he deftly meshes gruesome violence with side-splitting humor. It's a visual and darkly comic feast. ★★★ DVD: $14.99, VHS: $9.99

Quick Change

(1990, 88 min, US, Bill Murray & Howard Franklin) *Bill Murray, Geena Davis, Jason Robards, Randy Quaid, Phillip Bosco*. Likable caper comedy with Murray, Davis and Quaid pulling off a perfect bank robbery — but their troubles begin when they try to make it out of New York City. Robards is the cop assigned to the case, and veteran stage actor Bosco has some good moments as a fastidious bus driver. ★★½

Quicksilver

(1986, 106 min, US, Tom Donnelly) *Kevin Bacon, Jami Gertz, Laurence Fishburne*. Routine youth pic with Bacon as a burned-out stockbroker who takes a job with a bicycle messenger service, unwittingly becoming involved with drug dealers. ★½

Quiet Days in Hollywood

(1998, 95 min, US, Josef Rusnak) *Hilary Swank, Bill Cusack, Peter Dobson, Natasha Gregson Wagner, Chad Lowe, Daryl Mitchell*. *Quiet Days in Hollywood* tells a series of interlocking stories, few of which are actually compelling. In the first piece, Swank is a foulmouthed hooker. By the film's end she is connecting with a closeted actor (Dobson). The most interesting episode is about a corporate attorney (Lowe) who is having an affair with his boss' wife. A mixed bag, to be sure, *Quiet Days in Hollywood* will barely pass the time on a very slow night. ★★ DVD: $9.99, VHS: $9.99

The Quiet Earth

(1985, 110 min, New Zealand, Geoff Murphy) *Bruno Lawrence, Alison Routledge.* Lawrence stars in this thought-provoking sci-fi tale as a scientist who awakens one morning to find himself the last person on earth. An imaginative film with an ending as haunting as that of *2001, The Quiet Earth* has much to say about man's race towards self-destruction. ★★★

The Quiet Man

(1952, 129 min, US, John Ford) *John Wayne, Maureen O'Hara, Victor McLaglen, Barry Fitzgerald.* You will be amazed by Wayne's nuanced performance as *The Quiet Man*, the Irishman returning home to Inisfree after years in Pittsburgh steel mills. The entire cast is a delight, and the camera caresses the Irish countryside. Ford won a Best Director Oscar for this one. ★★★★ DVD Collector's Edition: $14.99, VHS: $14.99

The Quiet Room

(1996, 91 min, Australia, Rolf de Heer) *Celine O'Leary, Paul Blackwell, Chloe Ferguson, Phoebe Ferguson.* A remarkable film of shattering perception, *The Quiet Room* uniquely conveys the absolute certainty of childhood perceptions. C. Ferguson delivers an affecting and unaffected performance as the seven-year-old daughter who responds to her parents' constant contentiousness by retreating into silence and fantasy wish fulfillment and forays back into earlier times of childhood happiness. Writer-director de Heer employs compassion and understanding in crafting this involving exploration into the effects of parental discord on a child. This is a film which moves fluidly and adroitly touches on the basic truths of the strengths and frailties of family life. ★★★ VHS: $19.99

Quigley Down Under

(1990, 120 min, US, Simon Wincer) *Tom Selleck, Alan Rickman, Laura San Giocomo, Chris Haywood.* Selleck stars in this appealing western as an American cowboy who travels to mid-19th century Australia to work for ruthless ranch owner Rickman. When Selleck refuses to be a paid assassin, he's left for dead in the Outback and extracts vengence against his former boss. ★★★ DVD Letterbox: $14.99, VHS: $9.99

The Quiller Memorandum

(1966, 105 min, GB, Michael Anderson) *Alec Guinness, Max von Sydow, George Segal.* Harold Pinter provided an entertaining though not particularly suspenseful screenplay for this espionage thriller about an American operative rooting out neo-Nazis in modern-day Berlin. ★★½ VHS: $59.99

Quills

(2000, 120 min, GB, Philip Kaufman) *Geoffrey Rush, Kate Winslet, Joaquin Phoenix, Michael Caine, Billie Whitelaw.* Setting the stage for outlandish humor, scintillating dialogue and a no-holds-barred battle for artistic expression, the devilish and delightful *Quills* wallows in its own ingeniously twisted embrace of madness and sex. Adapting his own stage play, Doug Wright's feverish, witty story in essence details the last years of the imprisoned Marquis de Sade at the Charenton Insane Asylum. But at the core of this blistering satire is the age-old conflict between art and censorship. Rush is delectable as the mad de Sade, whose sexually candid works have turned him into the artist *du jour* in 1790s Paris. De Sade's increasingly graphic output sends the pious, repressive Dr. Royer-Collard (Caine) to oversee the asylum, setting in motion a fight to the finish to see who has the last word. Rush's glorious interpretation that balances depravity, defiance and desire. ★★★★ DVD Letterbox: $9.99, VHS: $9.99

Quilombo

(1984, 120 min, Brazil, Carlos Diegues) *Vera Fischer, Antonio Pompeo.* Diegues' historical saga is a stirring fusion of folklore, political impact and dynamic storytelling. Based on historical fact, the setting is 17th-century Brazil where groups of runaway black slaves escaped into the jungle where they formed self-governing communities. Set on the border line between history and legend, between mountains and the sky, *Quilombo* is a powerful vision of paradise — sensual and alive, with exotic scenery and spectacular blood-and-thunder battles, all touched with a bit of the mystical and surreal. (Portuguese with English subtitles) ★★★ VHS: $29.99

Quintet

(1979, 110 min, US, Robert Altman) *Paul Newman, Vittorio Gassman, Fernando Rey.* Atmospheric but confusing fantasy about the survivors of a new ice age who pass the time playing Quintet, a game where all the losers end up dead and there is only one winner. ★★ VHS: $19.99

Quitting

(2002, 112 min, China, Zhang Yang) *Hongshen Jia, Xiuling Chai, Fengsen Jia, Tong Wang.* A penetrating if unusual autobiographical account of one

Quilombo

man's true-life experiences with drug addiction and rehab. Director Zhang (*Shower*), using many actual participants (including family, friends, doctor and mental asylum inmates), shows restraint and sensitivity in the story of popular Chinese actor Jia Hongshen (playing himself), who struggled for four years with a heroin addiction. Much of the film's power comes from Hongshen's parents, who helplessly sit by and watch their son succumb but are always there to offer emotional support. (Mandarin with English subtitles) ★★★ DVD Subtitled: $29.99

Quiz Show

(1994, 130 min, US, Robert Redford) *Ralph Fiennes, John Turturro, Rob Morrow, Paul Scofield, David Paymer, Hank Azaria, Elizabeth Wilson, Martin Scorsese.* It's 1958, and "Twenty-One" is the most popular game show on TV. Herb Stempel (Turturro) is its long-running champion; that is until he is forced to "take a dive," making handsome challenger Charles Van Doren (Fiennes) its newest winner. Initially unaware of any wrongdoing, Van Doren slowly learns of the show's fix but succumbs to the easy winnings. This forces Stempel to go public and brings Congressional investigator Richard Goodwin (Morrow) onto the scene. In adapting the real-life story of the quiz show scandal to the screen, director Redford has fashioned an immaculate, evocative drama of self-delusion, investigation and conspiracy and superbly juxtaposes it with a stinging allegory of America's loss of innocence. As Van Doren, Fiennes is extraordinary in capturing the moral dilemma of an honest man caught in the claws of bribery and adulation. ★★★★ DVD: $9.99

Quo Vadis

(1951, 171 min, US, Mervyn LeRoy) *Robert Taylor, Deborah Kerr, Peter Ustinov.* Epic M-G-M production about the love affair between a Roman soldier (Taylor) and a Christian woman (Kerr). Ustinov gives a great performance as Roman emperor Nero. Everything about this box-office smash is done on a grand scale, from its art direction and costumes to its story and screenplay which manages to rise above religious film clichés. ★★★½

Kate Winslet with Geoffrey Rush as the Marquis de Sade in *Quills*

Rabbit-Proof Fence

(2002, 94 min, Australia, Philip Noyce) *Everlyn Sampi, Tianna Sansbury, Kenneth Branagh, Laura Monaghan.* In 1931, the Aborigines Act of the State of Western Australia allows the legal abduction of half-caste children, sending them to camps where they received "the benefits" of white culture. Sisters Molly and Daisy and their cousin Gracie are pulled from their loving mothers' arms and taken to a barracks half a continent away. Children from all over the Western State are stripped of their native identity, forbidden to speak their own language and taught Christian hymns. Led by the indomitable Molly, Daisy and Gracie escape to trek an unforgiven landscape to return to their mothers. With help from hunters and farmers along the way, the three come to use as a signpost the 1,500-mile rabbit-proof fence erected to protect farm land. Well-shot and with nimble pacing, *Rabbit-Proof Fence* adroitly involves the audience in this tale of three children's intrepid odyssey across 1,000 miles of open, inhospitable ground. Absolutely remarkable performances from the ensemble, especially Sampi as Molly. Based on the book written by Doris Pilkington Garimara, Molly's daughter. ★★★½ DVD: $19.99, VHS: $9.99

Rabbit Test

(1978, 86 min, US, Joan Rivers) *Billy Crystal, Roddy McDowall, Imogene Coca, Paul Lynde, Alice Ghostley.* Occasionally tasteless, episodic comedy with Crystal as the world's first pregnant man. Rivers, who also cowrote the screenplay, extracts one or two amusing scenarios from this premise, but most of it is abysmal. ★½

Rabid

(1972, 90 min, Canada, David Cronenberg) *Marilyn Chambers, Frank Moore, Joe Silver.* Porn queen Chambers stars as a young woman who undergoes experimental skin-graft surgery after a motorcycle accident. One month later, she emerges from a coma with an insatiable appetite for blood which she obtains though the use of a spiked organ growing out of very sexual-looking orifice in her armpit. Less cerebral and more reliant on standard shocks for its success, *Rabid* is nevertheless a highly original exploration of the familiar vampire and living dead genres. ★★½ DVD Special Edition: $24.99, VHS: $14.99

The Rachel Papers

(1989, 92 min, GB, Damian Harris) *Dexter Fletcher, Ione Skye, Jonathan Pryce, James Spader.* Charles Highway (Fletcher) can have any girl he chooses, guided by his customized computer program, "Conquests and Techniques," an assortment of enticing props including appropriate clothing and home decor, and sensitive poetic quotations. But when he meets Rachel Noyce (Skye), all his irresistible schemes fail; Charles must reveal his true self to win her. *The Rachel Papers* is candid, funny and touching, a charming story of young lust and love with a remarkably grown-up sensibility. ★★★ DVD: $14.99, VHS: $9.99

Rachel, Rachel

(1968, 101 min, US, Paul Newman) *Joanne Woodward, Estelle Parsons, James Olson, Geraldine Fitzgerald.* An intensely somber but affecting drama of a woman who, after years of self-imposed fear, decides to experience life. Woodward, in a poignant and carefully realized performance, plays Rachel, a 35-year-old schoolteacher and walking tinderbox of repressed emotions and sexual frustration. Newman's directorial debut is a film of great subtlety and beauty. Parsons gives a tender portrait of a closeted lesbian in love with Rachel. ★★★★ VHS: $19.99

Racing with the Moon

(1984, 108 min, US, Richard Benjamin) *Sean Penn, Nicolas Cage, Elizabeth McGovern, Crispin Glover, Michael Madsen, Dana Carvey, Carol Kae.* Benjamin's bittersweet tale of youthful yearnings and indecision boasts strong performances by Penn and Cage as a pair of buddies biding their freedom on the eve of military duty. McGovern is beguiling as a young woman involved with Penn. Ripe with the gentle air of innocence and a warmhearted sense of humor. ★★★ DVD Letterbox: $14.99, VHS: $14.99

The Racket

(1951, 88 min, US, John Cromwell) *Robert Ryan, Robert Mitchum, Lizabeth Scott.* The professional and personal battle between two former friends now on opposing sides of the law is the story in this hard-hitting crime drama. Mitchum is a tough-as-nails precinct captain determined to keep his turf clean from the likes of Ryan, his old chum who stops at nothing in his quest for expansion of his crime kingdom. Some scenes were directed by Nicholas Ray. ★★★

Radio Days

(1986, 85 min, US, Woody Allen) *Mia Farrow, Seth Green, Julie Kavner, Josh Mostel, Michael Tucker, Dianne Wiest, Wallace Shawn, Danny Aiello, Jeff Daniels, Tony Roberts, Diane Keaton.* Allen's loosely structured but powerfully envisioned series of fables and vignettes takes us back to the halcyon days of radio. Through a series of hilarious, and often magical, reminiscences about his childhood, Allen eavesdrops on the lives of actors, singers, talk show hosts, and even the cigarette girl who made good. As usual, Allen deftly utilizes an extraordinary company of actors. ★★★★ DVD: $19.99

Radio Flyer

(1992, 114 min, US, Richard Donner) *Elijah Wood, Joseph Mazzello, Lorraine Bracco, John Heard, Adam Baldwin, Narrated by: Tom Hanks.* Radio Flyer has the look of an affectionate childhood memory piece — but these reminiscences are sweetened with bitter recollections. Wood and Mazzello play two brothers whose divorced mom (Bracco) remarries. Unbeknownst to her, the kids' new stepdad turns out to be a child abuser, and the boys devise a plan to escape his brutality: to take flight by making their red radio flyer wagon airworthy. The underlying child abuse theme is clearly out of place in this otherwise Spielberg-esque fantasy. ★★½

Radio Inside

(1994, 102 min, US, Jeffrey Bell) *William McNamara, Elisabeth Shue, Dylan Walsh.* Though the story line is virtually nonexistent (a love triangle involving two radically different brothers), *Radio Inside* has a nonchalant quirkiness that ultimately makes it watchable. Take for instance the way the one brother (McNamara), an un-career oriented, guilt-ridden artist, off-handedly calls up Jesus (yes, that Jesus) on a pay phone to get advice when he falls for the girlfriend (Shue) of his yuppie sibling (Walsh). An idiosyncratic look at relationships, both romantic and familial. ★★½ VHS: $19.99

Radioland Murders

(1994, 112 min, US, Mel Smith) *Brian Benben, Mary Stuart Masterson, Ned Beatty, George Burns, Anita Morris, Christopher Lloyd.* An unstable, frenzied comedy set against the backdrop of radio during the late 1930s. Masterson plays a secretary/manager of a new radio network. As they prepare for their opening night, she must contend with an estranged husband (Benben) seeking reconciliation, inept cast members and technicians, and a series of murders. The film tries to achieve the madness and quick pace of a Marx Brothers movie, but the actors have little to work with, and the film doesn't capture the excitement and popularity that was live radio. ★★ VHS: $9.99

Kenneth Branagh in *Rabbit-Proof Fence*

Rage

(1972, 100 min, US, George C. Scott) *George C. Scott, Martin Sheen, Richard Basehart, Barnard Hughes.* Scott, in a respectable first-time directing effort, stars as a Wyoming rancher who, with his son, is victim of a fatal dose of experimental nerve gas discharged in an accident. The nearby military installation initiates an immediate cover-up, inciting the dying man to acts of enraged vengeance. ★★½ VHS: $14.99

The Rage: Carrie 2

(1999, 101 min, US, Katt Shea) *Emily Bergl, Jason London, Dyland Bruno, J. Smith-Cameron, Amy Irving.* A pointless, unnecessary sequel, this is very tenuously linked to the original — though it's really just a stripped-down, '90s-ized rehash. Bergl is the put-upon outsider (though suffers in comparison to Sissy Spacek's seminal performance) with the powers of telekinesis. Only her guidance counselor (Irving, the only holdover from the original, in a ridiculous role) and new boyfriend from the in-crowd understand her, but can they stop her from using her powers for revenge against the cruel snobs and jocks? The villains are one-dimensional, so there's little fun in them being massacred in a brutal, gory revenge climax. ★½ DVD: $14.99

A Rage in Harlem

(1991, 115 min, US, Bill Duke) *Forest Whitaker, Robin Givens, Gregory Hines, Danny Glover, Zakes Mokae.* A fine cast brings unexpected life to this boisterous and funny crime comedy set in 1950s Harlem. Whitaker is well cast as a naive, religious virgin who becomes involved with luscious swindler Givens after she arrives in New York with a shipment of gold from a Southern robbery. Her appearance sets off a wild series of events as seemingly everyone in the Big Apple is after the booty. In a surprising comic turn, Givens gives a wonderfully controlled and vampish performance as the foxy femme fatale. A colorful version of a Chester Himes story, and every bit as successful as the author's *Cotton Comes to Harlem.* ★★★ DVD: $19.99

The Raggedy Rawney

(1987, 95 min, GB, Bob Hoskins) *Bob Hoskins, Dexter Fletcher.* Actor Hoskins throws his hat into the directorial ring with this offbeat tale of a wartime deserter (Fletcher) who disguises himself as a woman to escape his vindictive superior. Hoskins also stars as the head of a Gypsy camp who mistakenly thinks Fletcher is a witch — a "rawney." Not completely successful, but a welcome change for the adventurous viewer. ★★½ DVD: $14.99

Raging Bull

(1980, 128 min, US, Martin Scorsese) *Robert De Niro, Joe Pesci, Cathy Moriarty, Frank Vincent.* De Niro is nothing short of astonishing as boxing champion Jake La Motta, who struck it rich in the ring then squandered his fortune and alienated his family and friends. Scorsese's most brooding work (and that's saying something), shot in vibrant tones of black and white, is a masterpiece of technical brilliance, excrutiatingly observant dialogue and almost mythical boxing sequences. Stand-out support by Pesci and Moriarty. ★★★★

Ragtime

(1981, 155 min, US, Milos Forman) *Harold E. Rollins, Jr., James Cagney, Elizabeth McGovern, Mary Steenburgen, Maureen Stapleton, Mandy Patinkin, Kenneth McMillan.* Forman, a director

Harrison Ford makes the switch in *Raiders of the Lost Ark*

who can take the most difficult source material and create masterworks, has done it again with this remarkable screen version of E.L. Doctorow's complex novel. Set in New York City in the turbulent early 1900s, the story follows black musician Coalhouse Walker, Jr. (Rollins, in an outstanding performance) and his quest for justice after being the victim of a racial attack. After a 20-year absence in film, Cagney returned to the screen to play the Police Commissioner. *Ragtime* features a superb ensemble. (The basis for the Broadway musical) ★★★½ DVD Letterbox: $14.99

Raiders of the Lost Ark

(1981, 115 min, US, Steven Spielberg) *Harrison Ford, Karen Allen, Denholm Elliott, John Rhys-Davies.* From South American jungles to the mountains of Nepal to the North African desert, our hero, archeology prof and world-class adventurer Indiana Jones (Ford), deciphers mystical symbols in search of the Ark of the Covenant, battling scurrilous Nazis with an intrepid, hard-drinking helpmate (Allen). Strong story line, solid performances and state-of-the-art moviemaking potently combine in a fast-paced, most enjoyable and intelligent action-adventure film. Written by Lawrence Kasdan from a story by George Lucas and Philip Kaufman. (Sequel: *Indiana Jones and the Temple of Doom*) DVD: $49.99 for the trilogy. ★★★★ VHS: $9.99, VHS Letterbox: $9.99

Railroaded

(1947, 74 min, US, Anthony Mann) *John Ireland, Sheila Ryan, Hugh Beaumont.* In the dark, crime-ridden jungle of an inner city where mobsters rule, a lone police detective begins a search for a killer on the lam from the police, who, in a desperate fight for survival, involves an innocent youth. Ireland stars as a ruthless gangster in this taut, suspenseful, low-budget crime melodrama. ★★★ DVD: $29.99, VHS: $19.99

The Railway Children

(1970, 104 min, GB, Lionel Jeffries) *Jenny Agutter, William Mervyn, Bernard Cribbins.* Distinguished character actor Jeffries directed this engaging film version of the Edwardian children's classic about three young kids who are determined to clear their father's name. A vivid and heartwarming look at turn-of-the-century British life filmed in

the beautiful countryside of Yorkshire and filled with youthful determination. ★★★ DVD Letterbox: $19.99

Rain

(1932, 95 min, US, Lewis Milestone) *Joan Crawford, Walter Huston.* Freewheeling passion collides with hypocritical self-righteousness on a primitive South Seas island to the rhythms of hot jazz records and the steady beat of the falling rain. Based on Somerset Maugham's short story about a puritanical missionary determined to convert a wanton woman, *Rain* is a fascinating film, far ahead of its time in its depiction of human frailties. ★★★ DVD: $19.99, VHS: $14.99

Rain Man

(1988, 140 min, US, Barry Levinson) *Dustin Hoffman, Tom Cruise, Valeria Golino.* Hoffman gives a remarkable performance as an "idiot savant" who is virtually kidnapped by his younger brother (Cruise) and taken on a cross-country trip. From beginning to end, the film is an emotionally overpowering experience told in a surprisingly stylish and entertaining fashion. Hoffman won all sorts of kudos for his portrayal, but not to be overlooked is the terrific contribution by young Cruise, who more than holds his own. ★★★½ DVD Letterbox Special Edition: $19.99

The Rain People

(1969, 102 min, US, Francis Ford Coppola) *Shirley Knight, James Caan, Robert Duvall.* This sensitive drama tells the compassionate story of a pregnant woman who leaves her husband in search of self-fulfillment. Knight, in a beautifully restrained performance, is the young voyager who sets out on the road, befriending dim-witted Caan along the way. An intimate work exploring one woman's social awakening and personal independence. ★★★ VHS: $19.99

The Rainbow

(1989, 104 min, GB, Ken Russell) *Sammi Davis, Amada Donohoe, Glenda Jackson, Christopher Gable.* An unusually restrained "classic" adaptation of D.H. Lawrence's novel. The setting is early 20th-century England and follows the sexual and spiritual liberation of young Ursula, the Jennie Linden character in *Women in Love*. Davis is great as the earnest and doe-eyed young woman whose sexuality and desires erupt, all the while yearning for true love, self-respect and independence in a society which frowns on all three. Donohoe is delightfully decadent as Ursula's gym instructor, seductress and mentor. ★★½

Raining Stones

(1993, 90 min, GB, Ken Loach) *Bruce Jones, Julie Brown.* Loach has drummed up a veritable masterpiece of agitprop with this engaging tale of an out-of-work laborer who hatches a hundred lame-brained schemes to make ends meet. Through the comedic escapades of Bob (Jones), Loach sternly disabuses us all of the notion that the underclass are a bunch of boozing loafers uninterested in a hard day's work. A devout Catholic, Bob desperately needs money to buy his daughter a new outfit for her first communion. But rather than let Bob's conundrum stand merely as a condemnation of the Church, Loach passionately and with great force of conviction shows the Church also as his only shred of hope — it is the only thing that keeps Bob going. This conflict is at the heart of Loach's film and it is what gives it its beauty, helping it rise above simple dialectical materialism and touch on notions of spirit. ★★★★

The Rainmaker

(1956, 121 min, US, Joseph Anthony) *Burt Lancaster, Katharine Hepburn, Lloyd Bridges, Wendell Corey.* Lancaster and Hepburn offer terrific performances in this fine adaptation of the N. Richard Nash play. Set in 1913, the film casts Lancaster as con man who promises a small drought-ridden Kansas town he can deliver much-needed rain. Kate is the spinster-ish farm girl who falls for the charming grifter. ★★★ VHS: $14.99

The Rainmaker

See: *John Grisham's The Rainmaker*

Raintree County

(1957, 188 min, US, Edward Dmytryk) *Elizabeth Taylor, Montgomery Clift, Lee Marvin, Eva Marie Saint, Agnes Moorehead, Rod Taylor.* Fanciful costume drama set during the Civil War with Taylor as a Southern belle and Clift as her lover. M-G-M tried, but did not succeed in creating another *Gone with the Wind* — though there is much that is praiseworthy about this mammoth production. (Original roadshow version) ★★½ VHS: $19.99, VHS Letterbox: $19.99

Raise the Red Lantern

(1991, 125 min, China, Zhang Yimou) *Gong Li, Ma Jingwu.* A lyrically haunting tale about a young educated woman who is sold into marriage against her will, becoming the newest of four concubines kept by a wealthy man. Immediately at odds with her three predecessors and bewildered by her strict and mysterious master, she reacts to her new situation with a mixture of rebellion and resignation. Director Zhang imbues the film with an extraordinary attention to detail, filming from the perspective of the fledgling concubine, giving the viewer a unique appreciation for the character's existential loneliness. Additionally, the film's understated dialogue and bewitching visual style amplify Zhang's compelling tale of the subjugation of women in feudal China. Gong is spellbinding as the young woman who finds herself trapped in the jaws of a regimented and unforgiving patriarchy. (Mandarin with English subtitles) ★★★★

A Raisin in the Sun

(1961, 128 min, US, Daniel Petrie) *Sidney Poitier, Ruby Dee, Claudia McNeil, Diana Sands, Ivan Dixon, Louis Gossett, Jr., John Fielder.* Poitier stars as Walter Lee Yonger, a young African-American man struggling with his place in a white dominated society. Lena (McNeil), Walter's mother, receives a $10,000 insurance check and the family must decide how the money should be spent. Walter wants to invest with a friend in a liquor store, Lena wants to use the money to buy a house in a better neighborhood, while her daughter (Dee) wants to use the money to finish medical school. A powerful tale of a poor, proud family living in a 1950s Chicago ghetto facing the truth of the limited opportunities for blacks in society. Based on the play by Lorraine Hansbury. (Remade in 1989) ★★★★ DVD: $24.99

A Raisin in the Sun

(1989, 120 min, US, Bill Duke) *Danny Glover, Esther Rolle, Kim Yancy.* Remake of the classic 1961 screen version of Lorraine Hansbury's play, and every bit as accomplished as that earlier adaptation. Glover gives a tremendous performance as Walter Lee Younger; and as his recently widowed mother, Rolle is wonderfully down to earth. A remarkable work. ★★★½ DVD: $19.99, VHS: $19.99

Raising Arizona

(1986, 94 min, US, Joel Coen) *Nicolas Cage, Holly Hunter, John Goodman, William Forsythe, Trey Wilson, Frances McDormand.* The Coen Brothers unleash a veritable grab bag of tricks and surprises as they unspool the hilarious tale of H.I. and Ed McDonough, would-be-parents who baby-nap a youngster from a recent batch of quintuplets in order to fulfill their parental urges. This truly off-beat, supremely comic film is loaded with crazy characters, wild chase scenes and inexhaustible energy. Cage and Hunter give antic yet touching performances as the barren but determined couple. ★★★★ DVD: $19.99, VHS: $9.99

Raising Cain

(1992, 91 min, US, Brian De Palma) *John Lithgow, Lolita Davidovich, Frances Sternhagen, Steven Bauer.* Lithgow stars in this hodge-podge of every other De Palma film (and some Hitchcock, of course) about a schizophrenic child psychologist who moonlights as a sociopathic baby-stealer. While nowhere near the caliber of filmmaking displayed in *Carrie* or *Dressed to Kill*, *Raising Cain* holds up fairly well when viewed as a black comedy rather than as the nail-biter it pretends to be. Features a scene-stealing performance by Sternhagen. ★★½ DVD Letterbox: $9.99, VHS: $19.99

Raising Victor Vargas

(2003, 88 min, US, Peter Sollett) *Victor Rasuk, Judy Marte, Melonie Diaz, Altragracia Guzman, Silvestre Rasuk.* Complex, vibrant and realistic lives are being lived inside Sollett's urban film landscape and it's a refreshing thing to see. *Raising Victor Vargas* allows its audience the opportunity to experience a young man and his family through the most naturalistic of details: the grandmother as concerned matriarch, the four-person unit packed tightly inside a two-bedroom apartment, the summer heat, the buzz of a community, the energy of a non-whitewashed life. This is the world of Victor Vargas, a headstrong teenage boy who is learning each day the responsibilities of growing up. His primary occupation this

summer is Judy (Marte), a girl for whom he pines while playing it cool in front of his friends. But Judy has some of her own interests in mind and a relationship blossoms in untraditional ways between the two. Sollett used much improv in his writing and work with his actors, giving the performances a Mike Leigh-like documentary feel. This smartly crafted, heartfelt coming-of-age film contains life lessons that become as important to its audience as they are to its characters. ★★★½

Rambling Rose

(1991, 112 min, US, Martha Coolidge) *Laura Dern, Robert Duvall, Diane Ladd, Lukas Haas.* Dern earned a well-deserved Oscar nomination for her portrayal of Rose, a Depression-era orphan who is taken as a live-in maid by a respectable Southern family in 1930s Georgia. Her sexual energy bursting at the seams, Rose turns the family's traditional values upside down and precipitates a dispute between Mom (Ladd) and Dad (Duvall) as to how best to deal with her. Ladd, Dern's real-life mom, was also an Oscar nominee for her splendid work as Rose's matronly advocate. Charmingly humanistic in tone, the film is imbued with a wonderful sense of mirth. ★★★½ DVD: $14.99, VHS: $9.99

Rambo: First Blood Part II

(1985, 93 min, US, George P. Cosmatos) *Sylvester Stallone, Richard Crenna.* Stallone's sequel to *First Blood* is a ridiculous war film by any standards, but it did introduce an idiom (or is that idiot?) into our vocabulary and culture. For the record, Johnny Rambo returns to Vietnam to locate American POWs. ★½ VHS: $9.99

Rambo III

(1988, 101 min, US, Peter MacDonald) *Sylvester Stallone, Richard Crenna, Kurtwood Smith.* More inane and implausible action scenes from Stallone as Superman Johnny Rambo. Rambo sets out to rescue captured Crenna from behind enemy lines. ★ VHS: $9.99

Rampage

(1992, 97 min, US, William Friedkin) *Michael Biehn, Alex McArthur, Grace Zabriskie, Deborah van Valkenburgh.* Biehn stars as a liberal D.A. recovering from the accidental death of his young daughter in this often tense but grim courtroom drama about the capture and sentencing of a serial murderer (McArthur). While the film shows the murders with luridly vivid detail, it deals more with the inner workings of our not always perfect judicial system. A gnawing film that's not for everyone. (Made in 1987 but not released until five years later.) ★★½ VHS: $14.99

Raining Stones

R

Ramparts of Clay

(1971, 85 min, Algeria/France, Jean-Louis Bertucelli) Against the hauntingly beautiful setting of an isolated Tunisian village, this stunning, visually breathtaking fictional documentary portrays the struggles of a young woman to liberate herself from the subservient role her people's ancient customs demand. Her participation in a strike-like action against a local entrepreneur allows her a glimpse of life outside her rigidly structured village. (Berber with English subtitles) ★★★½

Ran

(1985, 160 min, Japan, Akira Kurosawa) *Tatsuya Nakadai, Akira Terao.* Seventy-five-year-old Kurosawa has reached the culmination of his brilliant career with this majestic free-telling of Shakespeare's "King Lear." Set in the 16th century, the epic thunders with breathtaking scenery, boldly staged battle sequences and the tragic story of an old man's war with his sons. The love, death and treachery between both friends and adversaries is universal in theme and provides the human backdrop for this classic. (Japanese with English subtitles) ★★★★ DVD Letterbox Masterworks Edition: $34.99, DVD: $24.99, VHS: $19.99

Rancho Deluxe

(1974, 93 min, US, Frank Perry) *Jeff Bridges, Sam Waterston, Harry Dean Stanton, Elizabeth Ashley, Slim Pickens.* Bridges and Waterston star as two petty grifters; New West cowboys who decide to go after the big score. With intent to rustle some cattle, they team up with Stanton, hired hand to a couple of Easterners for whom the West is little more than a commodity. Sweeping Montana vistas offer mute witness to a delightful display of human foibles and crackling idiosyncracies as the crew sets about their business. Director Perry adeptly guides Tom McGuane's multilayered, sardonic and witty screenplay. ★★★½ DVD: $19.99

Rancho Notorious

(1952, 89 min, US, Fritz Lang) *Marlene Dietrich, Mel Ferrer, Arthur Kennedy.* Frontier love triangle develops between a breathy saloon songstress (Dietrich), a once-great gunslinger (Ferrer) and a revenge-seeking cowpoke (Kennedy). An unusual and invigorating western which concentrates as much on character development as it does with the genre's other staples. ★★★½

Random Harvest

(1942, 124 min, US, Mervyn LeRoy) *Ronald Colman, Greer Garson, Susan Peters, Henry Travers.* A grand, lush soap opera of the highest order with Colman as a shell-shock and amnesiac WWI veteran who marries dance-hall girl Garson. When he regains his memory, he returns to his old life but has no memory of his wife; who has now become his secretary in the hopes that he'll remember. Colman and Garson's compelling performances should capture the hearts of even the most cynical. ★★★½

Random Hearts

(1999, 133 min, US, Sydney Pollack) *Harrison Ford, Kristin Scott Thomas, Charles S. Dutton, Bonnie Hunt, Dennis Haysbert.* Ford plays an Internal Affairs officer whose wife dies in an airplane crash. He soon discovers that she was involved in an extramarital affair, with the husband of a congresswoman (Scott Thomas). The two surviving spouses then begin an affair themselves. There's nothing romantic about this story, which mostly consists of Ford dogging Scott Thomas at every turn. And the subplot of Ford investigating a dirty cop goes nowhere. Given a smart look by director Pollack, *Random Hearts* is a cheap gift wrapped in pretty packaging. ★★ DVD: $14.99, VHS: $9.99, VHS Previously Viewed: $9.99

Ransom

(1996, 120 min, US, Ron Howard) *Mel Gibson, Rene Russo, Gary Sinise, Delroy Lindo, Lili Taylor, Brawley Nolte, Dan Hedaya, Liev Schreiber.* The nightmare of a child's kidnapping has been turned into a slick, calculated thriller which intermittently conveys the pain and suspense of losing one's child. Gibson plays a wealthy airline owner whose nine-year-old son is kidnapped. The story then focuses on the parents and FBI's attempts to deal with the criminals, and the conflict growing within the group of kidnappers. The screenplay (based on a 1956 Glenn Ford film) doesn't take much time setting things up as the kidnapping (a taut scene) occurs rather quickly. Unfortunately, the best plot point in the film had already been given away in the film's trailers. ★★½ DVD Letterbox: $29.99, VHS: $9.99, VHS Letterbox: $19.99

Raoni: The Fight for the Amazon

(1979, 82 min, Brazil/France, Jean-Pierre Dutilleux) The Amazon Indians' fight against the Brazilian government's genocidal land policies is the center of this engrossing film. With civilization rapidly encroaching into their isolated and simple lives, the many Indian tribes who populate the Amazonian rainforest are forced to either drastically change their lifestyle or fight. The filmmaker focuses his attention on one tribe, the Mekranotis, and is especially taken in by their charismatic and forceful chief, Raoni. With ethnographic footage of their village, we see the tribe's attempts to stop the decimation of the rainforest. An exhilarating adventure into a previously unseen world and a cautionary environmental tale. ★★★½ VHS: $29.99

Rapa Nui

(1994, 107 min, US, Kevin Reynolds) *Jason Scott Lee, Esai Morales, Sandrine Holt.* Lee stars in this well-intentioned but ultimately disappointing "ecological message movie" about the demise of the natives of Easter Island. Call it a loinclothed "Romeo and Juliet" as Lee, a member of the "Long Ear" clan hotly pursues Holt, a member of the subservient "Short Ears," much to the chagrin of Lee's childhood chum and now rival in love. Hokey in the extreme, the film does have its entertaining moments and, hey, with the entire cast parading around nearly stark naked, it can't be all bad. ★★½ VHS: $19.99

Rape of Love

(1977, 117 min, France, Yannick Bellon) *Nathalie Nell, Alain Foures.* A disturbing film with Nell as a nurse who is ruthlessly raped by four drunkards. Tragically, she discovers this is only the beginning of her ordeal. A poignant account of insensitivity and injustice. (French with English subtitles) ★★½

Rapid Fire

(1992, 90 min, US, Dwight H. Little) *Brandon Lee, Powers Boothe, Nick Mancuso.* Lee chops his way into the "B-movie" arena with this extremely mindless actioner that might just as easily been called *Vapid Fire.* Lee plays a peace-loving student who must fight for his life when he becomes a witness to some Mafia activity. Lee provides his own comic relief with a "valley girl" delivery guaranteed to leave the bad guys unsure whether to fight him or fuck him. ★★ DVD: $14.99, VHS: $9.99

The Rapture

(1991, 100 min, US, Michael Tolkin) *Mimi Rogers, David Duchovny, Will Patton, Patrick Bauchau.* A startling philosophical drama, *The Rapture* brings to light such weighty issues as religious zealousness, life after death and the search for faith. Rogers stars as a woman with a mind-numbing job as an L.A. telephone operator who seeks release from her existential emptiness in alcohol, drugs and sex. Her life changes dramatically, however, after she discovers God through a religious awakening. Her newly inspired faith is put to the test in a series of Job-like trials culminating in a vision to go to the desert and await the Second Coming. A thought-provoking film that offers many angles to the religious issues and an ending which forces viewers to decide for themselves. ★★★½

The Rascals

(1981, 93 min, France, Bernard Revon) *Thomas Chabrol.* The French have been making films about the sexual awakening of young people years before the births of the American directors who are obsessed with the same theme. Rather than titillate the viewer with cheap sex jokes, the films usually focus more on the psychological and emotional problems of budding adulthood. This film, a thoroughly delightful comedy about the coming-of-age of an irrepressible boy in a Catholic school, deals with his first relationship with an older girl. (French with English subtitles) ★★★

Rashomon

(1951, 88 min, Japan, Akira Kurosawa) *Toshiro Mifune, Machiko Kyo.* The film which opened the West to Japanese cinema, Kurosawa's brilliantly conceived Academy Award-winning classic delves into the mysteries of truth, reality and illusion, telling the story of a murder and rape through the conflicting testimony of all those involved: the "murdered" man, his ravished wife, the murderer, the arresting officer and a "neutral" bystander. The result is five completely different versions of the story. (Japanese with English subtitles) ★★★★ DVD Criterion Collection: $39.99, VHS: $29.99

Rashomon

Rasputin

(1978, 104 min, USSR, Elem Klimov) *Alexei Petrenko, Anatoly Romashin.* The demonic rise and bloody fall of Gregori Rasputin is explored in this fascinating and elaborate period piece. Although certainly not history, this Russian version of the Rasputin legend seems to be the definitive exposé of a man whose hypnotic spell over the royal family hastened their downfall. The story follows Rasputin, a religious fanatic who not only craved power, but women and booze as well. Was he the only hope for the Russian aristocracy or was he simply a madman bent on self-destruction? Both sides of the man are explored in this mesmerizing melodrama. (Russian with English subtitles) ★★★½ VHS: $24.99

Rasputin and the Empress

(1933, 123 min, US, Richard Boleslawski) *Lionel Barrymore, John Barrymore, Ethel Barrymore, Diana Wynyard, Edward Arnold.* The legendary Barrymores made only one film together: and the result is a static, well-acted and affecting historical drama of the Romanoffs. Set in Russia just before the Revolution, the film examines the calamitous reign as "the power behind the throne" of the notorious Rasputin, who contributed to the fall of the royal dynasty. Ethel plays Alexandra with a regal authority, and brother John is a chivalrous Colonel of the Guards. But it's Lionel's crafty portrayal of Rasputin that elevates the film. He's cunning and vile, and is exact in bringing to life a character who's "like a man-eating shark with a bible under his fin." ★★★ VHS: $19.99

Rat

(2000, 91 min, GB, Steve Barron) *Pete Postlethwaite, Imelda Staunton, Frank Kelly, David Wilmot.* Think "Metamorphosis" with rat instead of cockroach. Hapless Irish Everyman Hubert Flynn (Postlethwaite) is the man who becomes a rat and gains a greater humanity. The dictates of our inner natures are revealed as the Flynn family processes through their dysfunctional dynamic the price of fame and the prodding of avarice, contemplating considerations from the financial (can a rat apply for unemployment?) to the theological (can the son of a man who turned into a rat become a priest?). While the family attempts some semblance or normailty, they contemplate how best to accommodate their new circumstances. The ensemble delivers captivating performances, with special mention to the rat, provided by the Jim Henson Company. *Rat* is steeped in quixotic charm and strange whimsy, alternating broad humor and sly observation with delightful glee. ★★★ DVD: $9.99, VHS: $14.99

Rat Race

(2001, 112 min, US, Jerry Zucker) *Whoopi Goldberg, John Cleese, Cuba Gooding, Jr., Rowan Atkinson, Jon Lovitz, Kathy Najimy, Seth Green, Breckin Meyer, Amy Smart, Vince Vieluf, Lanai Chapman, Kathy Bates.* Don't expect witty bon mots. Don't expect amusing banter between well-drawn characters. Don't even expect a collection of puns and toilet jokes to make you groan. What you get with *Rat Race*, director Zucker and writer Andy Breckman's broad, extravagant, did-we-mention-over-the-top reworking of *It's a Mad, Mad, Mad, Mad World* is laughs. The premise is basically the same: A group of strangers come together to locate a small fortune in cash; the ensuing race spells disaster for all. Among the cast are Goldberg as a mother reuniting with her daughter; Gooding as a football referee trying to escape a bad call; Green and the hilarious Vieluf as con artist brothers; Cleese as the

hotel owner who instigates it all; and Najimy and Lovitz as a married couple on vacation with the kids. Breckman's screenplay isn't as fluid as it could be, and a lot of this borders on the ridiculous-to-stupid end of the comedy scale, but he's created some of the funniest set pieces to be seen in a movie in years. Whether it's the hysterical scene of Lovitz and Hitler's car or Gooding coping with a busload of Lucy imitators, *Rat Race* has only one purpose in mind: to make you laugh. And boy does it succeed. ★★★½ DVD Letterbox: $14.99, VHS: $9.99

The Raven

(1963, 86 min, US, Roger Corman) *Vincent Price, Boris Karloff, Peter Lorre, Jack Nicholson.* Set in 15th-century England, this satiric version of the Edgar Allan Poe work pits two magicians (Price, Lorre) against a master sorcerer (Karloff), who has absconded with Price's wife. (DVD double feature with *The Comedy of Terrors*) ★★★ DVD Letterbox: $14.99

Ravenous

(1999, 100 min, US, Antonia Bird) *Guy Pearce, Robert Carlyle, Jeremy Davies, Jeffrey Jones, David Arquette.* Cowardly Captain John Boyd (Pearce) is transferred to a chilly, remote post during the Mexican-American war. He finds himself among a small army of misfits and the legend of Wendigo, a cannibal spirit that moves from man to man through the ingestion of flesh. Part black comedy, part gruesome horror and part '70s-style western, *Ravenous* has many interesting elements but is quite unsatisfying, especially as the mysterious plot threads find themselves resolved too literally. Carlyle is wonderfully menacing as the outsider who first discovers the joys of flesh, and the musical score by Michael Nyman and Blur's Damon Albarn is stunning and fresh. Too bad Bird never finds a consistent tone to help ground this very bizarre story. ★★½ DVD: $9.99, VHS: $9.99

The Ravishing Idiot

(1965, 99 min, France, Edouard Molinaro) *Anthony Perkins, Brigitte Bardot.* Perkins stars in this slapstick caper comedy as a bungling bank clerk who, with walking disaster area Bardot, unwittingly becomes involved with a Soviet spy ring. ★★½

Raw Deal

(1948, 80 min, US, Anthony Mann) *Dennis O'Keefe, Claire Trevor, Marsha Hunt, Raymond Burr, John Ireland.* With tough-talking guys, hard-boiled dames, plenty of cross and double-cross and a hero so gruff you almost expect to hear his street-smart moll call him a "lug," *Raw Deal* is a startling good noir thriller which doesn't pinch on action or characterization. O'Keefe is a prisoner ready for break. He took the rap for his creepy, sadistic boss Burr, who's helping in the escape. Only Burr doesn't want to see him succeed. To complicate matters, O'Keefe, accompanied by flame Trevor, has taken his lawyer Hunt hostage, and he's soon torn between the two women. Sexual tensions simmer, jealousies erupt and the line between right and wrong becomes blurred. Mann directs in a crisp, no-nonsense fashion, and the dialogue is priceless. ★★★½ VHS: $19.99

Raw Deal

(1986, 106 min, US, John Irvin) *Arnold Schwarzenegger, Kathryn Harrold.* This violent and tongue-in-cheek thriller has Arnold as a small-town sheriff (and former FBI agent) who single-handedly takes on the Chicago mob. A below-average effort. ★★ DVD Letterbox: $14.99, VHS: $9.99

The Razor's Edge

(1946, 146 min, US, Edmund Goulding) *Tyrone Power, Anne Baxter, Clifton Webb, Herbert Marshall.* Fine adaptation of W. Somerset Maugham's acclaimed novel with Power going through heaven and hell in his search for spiritual truth. Baxter won an Oscar for her heartbreaking alcoholic, and Webb should have won one as the cynical Elliott Templeton. (Remade in 1984) ★★★ VHS: $19.99

The Razor's Edge

(1984, 129 min, US, John Byrum) *Bill Murray, Theresa Russell, Denholm Elliott.* Murray, in his dramatic debut, plays a disillusioned WWI vet who rejects his materialistic lifestyle and retreats to the Himalayas in search of truth. An inferior remake of the 1946 classic which doesn't work on any level. ★ DVD Letterbox: $24.99

Ready to Rumble

(2000, 106 min, US, Brian Robbins) *David Arquette, Oliver Platt, Scott Caan, Rose McGowan, Joe Pantoliano, Ahmet Zappa.* The presence of WCW stars instead of the more popular WWF is the first sign that this comedy about pro wrestlers and their dunderheaded fans might not reach its (low) potential. Doughy Platt is woefully miscast as Jimmy King, the greatest wrestler in the world. When the King is suspiciously dethroned, his two most ardent fans (Arquette and Caan, doing a redneck Bill & Ted shtick) look to set things right. The film is a victim of laugh-free writing, and an indecision whether to satirize grapplers and their fans or to revel in their low humor. ★½ DVD: $14.99, VHS: $14.99

Ready to Wear (Prêt-a-Porter)

(1994, 132 min, US, Robert Altman) *Lauren Bacall, Kim Basinger, Julia Roberts, Tim Robbins, Sophia Loren, Marcello Mastroianni, Stephen Rea, Rupert Everett, Anouk Aimée, Rossy De Palma, Lili Taylor, Ute Lemper, Forest Whitaker, Richard E. Grant, Lyle Lovett, Tracey Ullman, Sally Kellerman, Linda Hunt, Teri Garr, Danny Aiello, Jean Rochefort, Michel Blanc, François Cluzet, Christy Turlington, Jean-Paul Gaultier, Naomi Campbell, Linda Evangelista.* Altman's take on the Paris fashion world rates as a disappointment in spite of being intermittently fascinating. Assembling (once again) an amazing all-star cast, Altman sets out to both satirize and demystify the carnival-like atmosphere of the *prêt-a-porter* fashion shows, but sabotages himself by presenting too many players, the majority of which are dramatically shortchanged. However, some characters stand out, including Robbins as an American sports writer, Roberts as a rival reporter, Mastroianni and Loren as ex-flames, and Basinger, who nearly steals the film as a hilariously inept TV reporter. ★★½ DVD: $19.99, VHS: $9.99

The Real Blonde

(1998, 107 min, US, Tom DiCillo) *Matthew Modine, Catherine Keener, Kathleen Turner, Maxwell Caulfield, Daryl Hannah, Christopher Lloyd, Marlo Thomas, Elizabeth Berkley.* Director DiCillo lampoons the entertainment industry in this light-hearted comedy about women and men, how they perceive themselves and each other in a society preoccupied with beauty, sex and perfection. Modine and Keener play a couple whose personal and professional lives are at a crossroads. Modine, an actor, can't get his career off the ground; Keener, a makeup artist, has become frustrated with what her life represents. Caulfield is Modine's friend and

R

Joan Fontaine (l.) is tormented by Judith Anderson in *Rebecca*

fellow actor, a man obsessed with one thing — finding a real (read: natural) blonde. DiCillo creates some original and often funny situations, but this is just another film about love and sex in the '90s. ★★½ DVD: $29.99, VHS: $14.99

Real Genius

(1985, 108 min, US, Martha Coolidge) *Val Kilmer, Gabe Jarret, Michelle Meyrink, William Atherton, Patti D'Arbanville.* Diverting teen comedy with Kilmer as a member of a group of super-intelligent teenagers who create a sophisticated laser system for a class project. However, when they discover that they have been working on a military secret, they devise an elaborate scheme to get revenge. ★★½ DVD Dual: $24.99

The Real Glory

(1939, 95 min, US, Henry Hathaway) *Gary Cooper, David Niven, Andrea Leeds.* An exciting adventure film which bears more than just a little resemblance to *Gunga Din.* Cooper and Niven are soldiers of fortune who assist the American Army in their battle against a guerrilla uprising in the Philippines just after the Spanish-American War. Director Hathaway excels at this type of filmmaking, and the action scenes are terrific. ★★★

Real Life

(1979, 99 min, US, Albert Brooks) *Albert Brooks, Charles Grodin.* Director/writer/star Brooks attacks such suspect documentaries like PBS did to the Louds in "An American Family." Every bit as biting and as funny as *This Is Spinal Tap,* Brooks plays a very egocentric documentary filmmaker who, after invading Grodin's home, will stop at nothing to make this "reality" as interesting as possible. ★★★ DVD: $29.99, VHS: $14.99

Real Women Have Curves

(2002, 90 min, US, Patricia Cardoso) *America Ferrera, Lupe Ontiveros, Ingrid Oliu, George Lopez, Brian Sites.* Rare is it that full-figured girls grace the screen with pride and joy, which makes Cardoso's comedy a wonderful breath of fresh air. The film tells the story of Ana (Ferrera), a high school senior at the cusp of adulthood. As she approaches graduation, a number of opportunities come her way, including the possibility of a prestigious college education. But she is bound by the chains of her over-bearing mother (Ontiveros) who constantly tells her she's too big and needs to join her sister in the sewing shop where they make high quality dresses for low quality wages. The film follows Ana through a variety of awakenings, including a sense of self-acceptance and pride in her curvy body, good looks and intelligence. Both a smart coming-of-age tale and joyous feminist statement, *Real Women Have Curves* only amplifies the shortage of both ethnic and women's films currently being made. This little gem should help pave the way for more. ★★★½ DVD: $26.99

Reality Bites

(1994, 99 min, US, Ben Stiller) *Winona Ryder, Ben Stiller, Ethan Hawke, Janeane Garofalo, Steve Zahn.* A whimsical film that looks at some of life's more monumental choices, like who to love, what low-pay, low-reward job to take and which psychic hot line to call. Ryder is splendid as a recent college grad whose life is thrown into a depressed frenzy when she has to find a new job and is confronted with one too many romantic decisions. Both Hawke and Stiller make charming leading men as Ryder's bi-polar love interests, and Garofalo almost steals the show as her ironic, '70s obsessed apartment mate. With cultural and "generational" references jammed into every corner, *Reality Bites* is an intriguing look at the way that some people under 30 deal with life, but it has an even more captivating and witty take on the way many people deal with love. ★★★ DVD 10th Anniversary: $19.99, VHS: $9.99

Re-Animator

(1985, 86 min, US, Stuart Gordon) *Jeffrey Combs, Bruce Abbott.* H.P. Lovecraft would turn over in his grave if: a) he took some of the re-animation serum developed by the mad scientist in this nifty film; or b) he saw the liberties taken with his story. This film proves that director Gordon would beat George Romero hands down in a gross-out contest, as a decapitated body gives head both figuratively and literally. (Answer to the question: both.) Unrated version. ★★★½ DVD Millennium Edition: $29.99

Rear Window

(1954, 112 min, US, Alfred Hitchcock) *James Stewart, Grace Kelly, Thelma Ritter.* Hitchcock confronts the manifold by-products of voyeurism with this splendid study of a murder's detection. Stewart is superlative as the intrusive observer who reflects our own sometimes dangerous desires. An uncommonly carnal Kelly is his eager accomplice. (Remade in 1998) ★★★★ DVD: $19.99, VHS: $14.99

Rebecca

(1940, 115 min, US, Alfred Hitchcock) *Laurence Olivier, Joan Fontaine, Judith Anderson, George Sanders.* Hitchcock's first Hollywood movie is a Gothic masterpiece based on the book by Daphne Du Maurier. Fontaine plays a passive and awkward paid companion for the snooty dowager Mrs. Van Hopper. While on vacation at Monte Carlo, she falls in love with the ominous and rich Maxim de Winter (Olivier) who whisks her off to his mansion. However, his mysterious attachment to his deceased first wife wreaks havoc upon their marriage. The most durable performance comes from Anderson as the creepy Mrs. Danvers, the fanatically devoted housekeeper (paramour?) of the first Mrs. de Winter. A chilling script and superb acting and direction won *Rebecca* an Oscar for Best Picture. ★★★★ DVD Criterion Collection: $39.99

Rebel

(1985, 93 min, Australia, Michael Jenkins) *Bryan Brown, Matt Dillon.* Dillon stars as a U.S. Marine stationed in Sydney and on the run from the military police. Complications arise when he falls in love with a nightclub singer. Brown is the stranger who offers a solution . . . for a price. ★★

Rebel Rousers

(1967, 78 min, US, Martin B. Cohen) *Bruce Dern, Cameron Mitchell, Jack Nicholson, Harry Dean Stanton.* Dern is the philosophising leader of a pack of motley motorcyclists; he's the kind of guy who takes his hog everywhere — including into the cantina of the small Mexican town where he meets old high school buddy Mitchell. Mitchell is having paternity problems and looks about 20 years older than Dern. A biker flick typical of the era. ★★ VHS: $9.99

Rebel without a Cause

(1955, 111 min, US, Nicholas Ray) *James Dean, Natalie Wood, Sal Mineo, Jim Backus.* A testament to adolescent angst with Dean as the prototypical angry young man at odds with his parents, himself and the future. A brooding film that cemented the Dean legend. In her first adult role, Wood offers an incandescent performance as a soul mate; and Mineo is especially touching as Plato, a friendless youth who is secretly in love with Dean's charismatic character Jim. ★★★½ DVD: $19.99

Reckless

(1995, 100 min, US, Norman René) *Mia Farrow, Scott Glenn, Mary-Louise Parker, Tony Goldwyn, Eileen Brennan, Giancarlo Esposito, Stephen Dorff.* Farrow is a howling delight in this wacky and inventive Christmas-themed fairy tale based on the play by Craig Lucas. Farrow plays Rachel, an idiotically sweet chatterbox housewife and mother who is forced out of her home on Christmas Eve when she discovers that her husband has put a contract out on her life. She is rescued by the superficially nice social worker Lucas (Glenn) and his deaf paraplegic wife Pooty (Parker). But for poor Rachel, her new-found happiness proves to be short-lived as poisoned champagne, dark secrets and a drunken Santa Claus test the limits of sanity. A droll, warped romp of self-discovery infused with purposefully cheesy special effects, oddball cameos and an intoxicating mix of comedy, fantasy and surreal nightmare. ★★★

Record of a Tenement Gentleman

(1947, 73 min, Japan, Yasujiro Ozu) *Choko Iida, Hohi Aoki.* A charming, melancholy portrait of life in Japan after the war, director Ozu's inspirational tale examines the alternately heartfelt and comic exploits of a young boy abandoned by his parents. Discovering the youth and feeling sorry for him, a tenement dweller brings him home only to find his flatmate will not allow him to keep the child in the apartment. After straws are drawn to see who takes care of the child among the neighbors, an older widow grudgingly ends up with him. Against the odds, a close relationship soon develops between them nurtured by mutual understanding and respect. The film holds true as a wonderful story of enriched lives and community living during a difficult time in history. (Japanese with English subtitles) ★★★★

The Recruit

(2003, 113 min, US, Roger Donaldson) *Al Pacino, Colin Farrell, Bridget Moynahan, Gabriel Macht.* Handsome James Clayton (Farrell) is an MIT computer whiz who has a difficult choice to make: stay the course and become rich in computer programming, or accept the offer of becoming a spy from very persistent CIA recruiter Walter Burke (Pacino). Since Burke has hinted that Clayton's dead father may have been an agent, his decision is made all the more easier. It's the fallout that follows — from training school to field work — that sets the stage for an alternately exciting and bombastic espionage yarn that's as gritty as it is implausible. Pacino fits nicely into the role of the grizzled mentor, and the magnetic Farrell gives an intense, vigorous performance. Director Donaldson's pacing is even and sure, and he maintains credibility in the film's first half. It's the finale of *The Recruit*, given to one too many twists, where things begin to unravel, turning what had been enjoyable into something of a head-scratcher. ★★½ DVD: $19.99, VHS: $14.99

Red

(1994, 98 min, France, Krzysztof Kieslowski) *Jean-Louis Trintignant, Irène Jacob.* The last of director Kieslowski's "color" trilogy (following *Blue* and *White*) is a sumptuous finale, and the most satisfying of the three films. A beautiful Jacob stars as a model preparing a trip to reunite and reconcile with her boyfriend. But events and emotions are skewed when she runs over a dog and seeks out the animal's owner. Who she eventually finds is Trintignant, a burned-out, bitter ex-judge who spends his spare time spying on his neighbors. An unusual relationship develops between the two, culminating in an act of self-examination and moral responsibility. Kieslowski weaves a compelling and haunting tale of communication, emotion and love gone awry, and it's all enhanced by a seductive, mysterious atmosphere. (French with English subtitles) ★★★½ DVD Subtitled: $19.99, VHS: $9.99

The Red and the White

(1967, 92 min, Hungary/USSR, Miklós Jancsó) *Tatyana Konyukova, Krystyna Mikolajewska.* Hungary's premiere director Jancsó sets this haunting antiwar drama in central Russia during the Civil War of 1918, in which the Red Army tangled with a counterrevolutionary threat from the Whites in the hills along the Volga River. The action centers around a monastery where a group of nurses do their

best to conceal the identities of the wounded and administer equal care to all. Employing remarkable visuals, Jancsó forges a compelling treatise on the absurdity of war and the humiliation of mechanical slaughter. (Hungarian with English subtitles) ★★★½ DVD: $29.99, VHS: $24.99

The Red Balloon

(1956, 38 min, France, Albert Lamorisse) *Pascal Lamousse.* This highly acclaimed short film is a fantasy guaranteed to appeal to both adults and children. It tells the story of Pascal, a lonely French boy who befriends a wondrous red balloon which follows him everywhere and fills his need for friendship. This beautiful film maintains a true sense of childish wonder and has much to say about the need for love. (No dialogue) ★★★★ VHS: $14.99

Red Beard

(1965, 185 min, Japan, Akira Kurosawa) *Toshiro Mifune, Yuzo Kayama.* Mifune is the wise, pragmatic doctor who guides a young intern through the trials and frustrations of the profession. The humanistic education changes him from a conceited technician to a humble man who values each of his patients as a whole person. (Japanese with English subtitles) ★★★½ DVD Criterion Collection: $39.99, VHS: $39.99

Red Cherry

(1996, 120 min, China, Ye Ying) *Guo Ke-Yu, Xu Xiaoli.* An unsettling account of two orphaned Chinese friends living during WWII. Chuchu and Luo Xiaoman are orphaned, Communist Chinese youths who are brought to Moscow in the winter of 1940. Refugees from Chairman Mao's revolution, they eventually settle into their new environment and find respect among their peers. All seems well until their world is uprooted by unpredictable, life-changing events brought on by the war. A disturbing look at a side of the war few Americans may have considered, *Red Cherry* reminds how violence can bleed itself into beautiful nightmares. (Mandarin with English subtitles) ★★★ DVD: $14.99, VHS: $14.99

Red Corner

(1997, 119 min, US, Jon Avnet) *Richard Gere, Bai Ling, Tsai Chin.* Gere plays Jack, a smug, cocksure lawyer — the type of guy you know is careening towards a serious crisis of conscience and attitude. In the midst of business negotiations with the Chinese government, Jack is arrested for the murder of a dancer he met in a nightclub.

Abandoned by his American colleagues and the American Embassy, he must try to acquaint himself with the intricacies of the Chinese judicial system and learn to trust his beautiful court-appointed defense advocate (Ling). It's difficult to say which is more frustrating: the legal entanglements depicted in the Chinese judicial system or the predictable plot trajectory of the movie itself. The romantic subplot between Gere and Chin is a clumsy afterthought at best. ★★ DVD: $14.99

Red Dawn

(1984, 110 min, US, John Milius) *Patrick Swayze, C. Thomas Howell, Charlie Sheen, Lea Thompson, Jennifer Grey.* Contrived (and often ridiculous) political action-adventure film about a group of teenage resistance fighters who do battle with the Communist invaders who have taken over their small town. ★½ DVD: $14.99, VHS: $9.99

Red Desert

(1965, 116 min, Italy, Michelangelo Antonioni) *Richard Harris, Monica Vitti.* Antonioni's first color film is an intriguing study of the alienation of man. Against the backdrop of a sterilized, impersonal industrial landscape, a love affair is enacted out. The film deals with the impossibility of real communication between people entrapped in this modern, hostile environment and longs for a return to a more innocent era. (Italian with English subtitles) ★★★

Red Dragon

(2002, 124 min, US, Brett Ratner) *Anthony Hopkins, Edward Norton, Ralph Fiennes, Emily Watson, Harvey Keitel, Mary-Louise Parker, Philip Seymour Hoffman.* Sir Anthony sups with diabolical relish for a third time as Hannibal Lecter, and he's the sole *raison d'être* for this efficient but needless remake of Thomas Harris' first Lecter novel, previously adapted in 1986 by Michael Mann as *Manhunter*. Set before the events of *The Silence of the Lambs*, the good doctor is called upon by the man who caught him, FBI agent Will Graham (Norton), to help profile and snare a vicious serial killer (Fiennes, wonderfully, frightfully freaky). Though top-loaded with A-list talent and gleaming with all the spit and polish of a sleek, big-budget production, *Red Dragon* is surprisingly devoid of urgency. Director Ratner wisely steers clear of the Gothic excess of Ridley Scott's *Hannibal* and manages to capture the tone of seething malevolence that made *Silence* so unnerving, though the film doesn't cut as deeply into the tortured souls of its

Edward Norton and Anthony Hopkins do a little of the ol' *quid pro quo* in *Red Dragon*

inhabitants as it could have. ★★★ DVD Letterbox Collector's Edition: $14.99, DVD Pan & Scan Collector's Edition: $14.99, DVD 2-disc Director's Edition: $34.99, VHS: $9.99

Red Dust

(1932, 83 min, US, Victor Fleming) *Clark Gable, Jean Harlow, Mary Astor.* Gable stars as a rubber plantation worker in Indochina who romances good-time girl Harlow and a coworker's wife, Astor. A pre-Code production simmering with sexuality and with its fair share of laughs for the usually rigid adventure genre. Gable and Harlow are particularly appealing together. Gable also appeared in the 1953 remake, *Mogambo*. ★★★½ VHS: $19.99

Red Firecracker, Green Firecracker

(1994, 111 min, China, He Ping) *Ning Jing, Wu Gang, Zhao Xiaorui.* Director He's third feature is weakened by his inability to bring anything new to the overly familiar territory of the Chinese New Wave. Set against the country's transition into the 20th century, *Red Firecracker* is an epic lovers' triangle that, while being visually rewarding, is unfortunately emotionally hollow. Female child Chun Zhi (Ning) is raised male in order to inherit the family fireworks business. But these years of repression melt with the arrival of Nie Bao (Wu), an itinerant painter hired to help decorate the home for the New Year's holiday. Taking umbrage at this interloper is Man Dihong (Zhao), the house foreman who sees his long cherished dream of winning "the master's" hand turn quickly into a nightmare. As in other, better films (*To Live*, *The Blue Kite*), there are epic landscapes, but their use here as emotional correlatives is too obvious to be effective. (Mandarin with English subtitles) ★★½

Red-Headed Woman

(1932, 81 min, US, Jack Conway) *Jean Harlow, Chester Morris, Charles Boyer.* Harlow is a sexy siren out to get the man she loves — her boss (Morris). Look for an aspiring Boyer in the small role of the chauffeur who befriends her. Vintage Harlow. ★★★ VHS: $19.99

Red Heat

(1985, 104 min, US/Germany, Robert Collector) *Linda Blair, Sylvia Kristel, Gina Gershon.* A pedestrian Cold War women-in-prison flick set in a nameless Communist country. Blair, an American innocent, is captured by Communists after inadvertently witnessing the abduction of a political dissident. She is sent to a hellhole women's prison which seems to be run by a lesbian prisoner (a campy Kristel). The lifeless film contains the requisite hair-pulling-in-their-underwear fights and snippets of gratuitous nudity. Barely enjoyable on a camp level. ★½

Red Heat

(1988, 106 min, US, Walter Hill) *Arnold Schwarzenegger, James Belushi.* A tepid buddy cop action flick. Arnold is a rigid Russian officer teaming with free-wheeling Chicago cop Belushi to search for a Soviet drug dealer. ★★ DVD: $9.99

Red King, White Knight

(1989, 106 min, GB, Geoff Murphy) *Tom Skerritt, Max von Sydow, Helen Mirren.* Skerritt is a seasoned CIA veteran who is sent into the Soviet Union to thwart a hardline general's planned assasination of Mikhail Gorbachev. He joins forces with his one-time nemesis, KGB agent Szaz (von Sydow), and together they hunt down the conspirators. An exciting post-*glasnost* political thriller. ★★★ VHS: $19.99

Red Kiss (Rouge Baiser)

(1986, 100 min, France, Vera Belmont) *Charlotte Valandrey, Marthe Keller.* Exploring the budding sexuality of teenagers, this sincere, charming and intelligent drama is punctuated by both its background setting (the turbulent political times in 1952 France) and its star, Valandrey — a beguiling, dark-eyed beauty of fifteen. Committing as much time to championing the French Communist Party as she does carousing in a graveyard with friends, young Nadia's life begins to change when she meets a handsome apolitical fashion photographer. This young man's world of beautiful women and "cool" Gauloise-filled jazz clubs confuses and entices Nadia as her ardently idealistic beliefs clash with those of the real world. (French with English subtitles) ★★★

Red Lion

(1969, 115 min, Japan, Kihachi Okamoto) *Toshiro Mifune, Shima Iwashita.* Mifune gives a bravura performance as the scarlet-maned bumbler who returns to his village after a ten-year absence, only to discover that he is to be the one to liberate his villagers from their deceitful, oppressive government. The pace of the film changes from a humorous beginning to an action-packed violent ending, with much exciting swordplay. (Japanese with English subtitles) ★★★ VHS: $29.99

Red Planet

(2000, 100 min, US, Antony Hoffman) *Val Kilmer, Carrie-Anne Moss, Tom Sizemore, Terence Stamp, Simon Baker, Benjamin Bratt.* It's 2056 and Earth lays devastated by pollution. A group of space-traveling scientists head off to Mars to determine if it's inhabitable. The stock characters are offset by an intriguing story, some good visuals and a few exciting scenes. Moss encores her tough-as-nails soldier from *The Matrix* to good effect, though the supporting characters aren't given much to do. About on par with 2000's other Mars epic, *Mission to Mars*. ★★½ DVD: $19.99, VHS: $9.99

Red Pomegranate

(1969, 75 min, USSR, Sergei Paradjanov) The powerful works of 17th-century Armenian poet Arutuin Sayadian are captured in this exotic mosaic of a film. Essentially a tribute to his life as well as to his dedication to the Armenian people, the film is divided into eight sections each depicting, from childhood to death, a period of the poet's life. Filled with oblique, symbolic imagery, this film is definitely only for specialized tastes and those devotees who have a knowledge of the poet and of Armenia. (Armenian with English subtitles) ★★★

Red River

(1948, 133 min, US, Howard Hawks) *John Wayne, Montgomery Clift, Walter Brennan, Joanne Dru.* Hawks' epic western rates as one of the finest of the genre. Wayne, in an unsympathetic role, plays a rancher who heads a strenuous cattle drive along the Chisolm Trail. As the journey wears on, the other men, including his foster son Clift, begin to question his ability as a leader, prompting a collision course between father and son. An astonishing accomplishment featuring gorgeous cinematography and brilliant direction by Hawks. (Remastered director's cut) ★★★★ DVD: $14.99, VHS: $9.99

The Red Shoes

Red Rock West

(1993, 98 min, US, John Dahl) *Nicolas Cage, Lara Flynn Boyle, Dennis Hopper, J.T. Walsh.* A *Blood Simple*-esque thriller that offers more twists than a Philadelphia soft pretzel. Cage is as an out-of-work wildcatter with a gimpy leg, a heart of gold and a pocketful of lint who sees dollar signs when a small-town bar owner (Walsh) mistakes him for the hit man he just hired to kill his wife (Boyle). Then the real killer (perennial ham Hopper) shows up. Perhaps the only film ever to go from cable to video to a successful theatrical run, this sleeper is an expertly plotted game of cat-and-mouse and a well-studied tribute to the film noir era. ★★★½ DVD: $24.99, VHS: $19.99

The Red Shoes

(1948, 133 min, GB, Emeric Pressburger & Michael Powell) *Moira Shearer, Anton Walbrook.* This lavishly breathtaking realization of the classic fairy tale is a glorious ode to the wonders of dance and the pursuit of artistic and personal fulfillment. Shearer gives an exquisite performance. ★★★★ DVD: $39.99

Red Sonja

(1985, 89 min, US, Richard Fleischer) *Arnold Schwarzenegger, Brigitte Nielsen.* Schwarzenegger takes a back seat to Nielsen in this sword and sorcery adventure with Nielsen as the fearless female warrior. Unmemorable action scenes and wooden acting only accentuate the laughable story line. ★ DVD Letterbox: $14.99

Red Sorghum

(1988, 92 min, China, Zhang Yimou) *Gong Li, Jiang Wen.* A breathtaking epic of peasant life by first-time director Zhang. Visually stunning, the film revolves around the reminiscences of a young man for his grandparents — peasants who lived in a remote section of northwestern China during the 1920s and '30s. Nine (the remarkable Gong) is a young beauty who, immediately prior to her arranged marriage with a leper, is saved by a heroic servant. They both fall in love and their ensuing relationship, through personal turmoils as well as Japan's invasion of their area, is dazzlingly dramatized. This visually stunning folk tale that celebrates the vitality and endurance of the peasant people. (Chinese with English subtitles) ★★★½ VHS: $29.99

R

The Red Squirrel (La Ardilla Roja)

(1993, 104 min, Spain, Julio Medem) *Emma Suarez, Nancho Novo, Maria Barranco.* Novo plays a rock star who takes advantage of a beautiful woman's amnesia — brought on by a motorcycle accident — to create another dream lover now that his songwriting days are over. But is this dream lover (Suarez) dreaming, too? Like some antipodal Hitchcock film — most obviously *Vertigo* — director Medem tightens the psychological threads until they are just about to break, then he begins to weave a tapestry that, while dark, is not bereft of life. Unfortunately, the white subtitles get lost during some of the lighter passages. (Spanish with English subtitles) ★★½ VHS: $79.99

The Red Tent

(1969, 121 min, Italy/USSR, Mikhail K. Kalatozov) *Sean Connery, Claudia Cardinale, Hardy Kruger, Peter Finch.* An international all-star cast highlights this exciting adventure film detailing General Nobile's ill-fated 1928 Arctic expedition, where the survivors of a crashed dirigible struggle against nature and the odds while waiting to be rescued. Finch as Italian explorer Nobile. Similar in theme to Jan Troell's memorable *Flight of the Eagle*. (Filmed in English) ★★★ VHS: $19.99

The Red Violin

(1998, 132 min, GB, François Girard) *Samuel L. Jackson, Greta Scacchi, Jason Flemyng, Don McKellar, Colm Feore.* An eloquent journey through time and across continents, *The Red Violin* is a tale of cursed love and obsession. A renowned 17th-century artist crafts the titular instrument, the most acoustically perfect musical apparatus ever fashioned. The film traces the 300-year life of the violin as it's passed on through generations. Lost, stolen, damaged, resurrected, the mysterious violin seems to harbor the secrets and souls of each of its former owners and, as told through a contemporary framing device, becomes a priceless treasure that men would fight — perhaps even kill — for. Compelling, if a bit episodic, the film is a feast for the eyes and ears with a sumptuous production design and a haunting musical score. ★★★ DVD: $14.99

Reds

(1981, 201 min, US, Warren Beatty) *Warren Beatty, Diane Keaton, Jack Nicholson, Maureen Stapleton, Gene Hackman, Edward Herrmann.* Beatty won a Best Director Oscar for this epic drama about the last years of John Reed, the American journalist who becomes involved in the Russian Revolution. Keaton, in a finely controlled performance, is Louise Bryant, his wife. This long but interesting film serves as both lush romantic drama and political exposé. Nicholson, as a heartbroken Eugene O'Neill, steals every scene he's in. Stapleton also won an Oscar as Best Supporting Actress. ★★★★ VHS: $19.99

Redwood Curtain

(1995, 99 min, US, John Korty) *Jeff Daniels, Lea Salonga, John Lithgow.* Playwright Lanford Wilson demonstrates a remarkable ability to decipher and communicate the frailties of relationships and the need for human contact by characters on the fringe in this extremely poignant made-for-TV adaptation of his play. Salonga gives a touching portrayal of an adopted Vietnamese teen who, after the death of her troubled but adoring adoptive father (Lithgow), sets out to find her biological parents. Director Korty's pacing is deliberate and absorptive, underscoring the fragile and uncertain search of the young girl. Daniels nicely handles the difficult role of a disturbed Vietnam vet who may hold the answer to the puzzle. ★★★½ VHS: $14.99

Reefer Madness

(1936, 68 min, US, Louis Gasnier) The evils of marijuana exposed! Bill was a happy all-American high school student until that fatal puff of the deadly weed. The effects: wild parties, violence, sex and . . . insanity! Is it worth it? (Camp Value: ★★★★) ★ DVD: $14.99, VHS: $19.99

The Ref

(1994, 92 min, US, Ted Demme) *Denis Leary, Judy Davis, Kevin Spacey, Glynis Johns.* Sporting a wit as nasty as its star Leary's devil-may-care grin, *The Ref* is a refreshingly funny and resourceful slant on *Desperate Hours*-type films. Leary stars as a hapless thief who kidnaps bickering married couple Davis and Spacey and hides out in their not-so-sweet home. However, nothing this streetwise criminal has seen in or out of prison can prepare him for the fireworks that erupt when the feuding husband and wife go at it. The characters may be in a near-constant state of screeching, but fortunately most of the wickedly delightful dialogue is worth hearing. The performances from the three leads are as energetic as they are funny, and Johns is just right as the mother-in-law you love to hate. ★★★ DVD: $9.99, VHS: $9.99

The Reflecting Skin

(1990, 98 min, Canada, Philip Ridley) *Viggo Mortensen, Lindsay Duncan.* This bizarre, independently produced horror movie owes more to Luis Buñuel than to Wes Craven. A young boy growing up in the Midwest must contend with a father who *may* be a child molester, a beautiful neighbor who *may* be a vampire, dead children, exploding frogs, a hidden human fetus and a mysterious black Cadillac. The film goes over the top at times, but it is consistently interesting and offers more than a few good jolts. ★★½

Reflections in a Golden Eye

(1967, 108 min, US, John Huston) *Marlon Brando, Elizabeth Taylor, Robert Forster, Brian Keith Julie Harris, Zorro David.* Sexual repression abounds in this kinky version of Carson McCullers' novel. Brando is the latent homosexual Army officer and Taylor is his unsatisfied, contemptuous wife. Forster is the hunky object of Brando's affection, and David is a fey houseboy. Not totally successful, the performances, however, make it slightly interesting. Unfortunately, the film suffers from being made at a time when there was a budding sexual freedom for all but gay characters; which made it impossible to fully explore Brando's character and sexual yearnings. The right director could make a helluva remake. ★★½ VHS: $19.99

Reform School Girls

(1986, 94 min, US, Tom DeSimone) *Wendy O. Williams, Sybil Danning, Linda Carol, Pat Ast.* Definitely one of the best and most outlandish films of the women-in-prison flicks. Innocent Jenny (Carol) finds herself sent to Pridemore, a hellish reformatory/prison supervised by lecherous female guards and ruled over by Head Matron Edna, a cartoonishly evil dyke. Oh yes, they're bad! There is plenty of nudity, riots, cat fights and breakouts to keep any fan entranced. The title song says it all, "So Young, So Bad, So What." ★★ DVD: $9.99, VHS: $9.99

Regarding Henry

(1991, 107 min, US, Mike Nichols) *Harrison Ford, Annette Bening, Bill Nunn, Elizabeth Wilson, John Leguizamo.* Ford plays a very nasty corporate lawyer who is shot in a holdup, thereby drastically changing his life. Forced to undergo a lengthy healing and therapy process, Ford is changed "for the better" when he returns to his ignored wife (Bening) and neglected adolescent daughter. Though clearly a "yuppie fantasy" for the '90s (no matter how ruthlessly or insensitively one acts, one can be redeemed in the end), there is much satisfaction in seeing Ford's transformation. And to his credit, Ford's beguiling performance as the child-like family man makes the most of the manipulative screenplay. ★★★ DVD: $14.99, VHS: $14.99

Reign of Fire

(2002, 101 min, US, Rob Bowman) *Matthew McConaughey, Christian Bale, Izabella Scorupco, Gerald Butler, Scott James Moutter, Alice Krige.* Fire-breathing dragons take over the Earth, and it's up to a fearful Bale and a gung-ho McConaughey to reclaim the planet. Don't let the enticing poster fool you: we never get to see the all-out battle between a huge army and hundreds of dragons. The film is much more low-key than that. But taken on its own Saturday matinee terms, *Reign of Fire* can be good fun. There may be not enough dragons here, but when they show up, they don't disappoint. Bale is properly intense throughout, and McConaughey leaves no location, prop or actor unchewed. Some silly dialogue, uneven pacing and a curiously anti-climactic last fight (despite a rousing buildup) do detract from the fun, but this is a little more enjoyable than what you'd expect. ★★½ DVD Letterbox: $19.99, VHS: $9.99

Reilly: Ace of Spies

(1984, 80 min, GB, Jim Goddard) *Sam Neill, Leo McKern, Jeanne Crowley.* This short but thrilling spy caper stars Neill as Reilly, the poor man's James Bond — an international scoundrel and womanizing superspy. It's a story of Eastern European intrigue, Russian oil and beautiful women. Watch it despite the fact that the director's next project was the disastrous Madonna-Sean Penn flop, *Shanghai Surprise.* ★★★ VHS: $14.99

The Reincarnation of Golden Lotus

(1989, 99 min, China, Clara Law) *Joi Wong, Eric Tsang, Lam Chun Yen.* This tale of ill-fated love and the objectification of women is a kind of Chinese *Dead Again* without the whodunit subplot. Starting in Mainland China during the Cultural Revolution, the story follows a young Chinese woman who turns out to be the incarnation of the Golden Lotus, the wife of a wealthy landowner in feudal China. She is swept away to modern-day Hong Kong by a rich baker where she falls into the same traps of her previous life. Director Law skillfully shows the parallels between the mistreatment of women under Communism, in old Imperial China and in colonial Hong Kong. (Mandarin with English subtitles) ★★★ VHS: $79.99

Reindeer Games

(2000, 105 min, US, John Frankenheimer) *Ben Affleck, Charlize Theron, Gary Sinise, Dennis Farina, Clarence Williams III, Donal Logue.* Screenwriter Ehren Kruger has apparently bought a *Usual Suspects*-brand Mad Libs, filling in clichés for the blanks and spitting out this arbitrary thriller. Affleck plays Rudy (get it?), a car thief who gets out

R

of jail and hooks up with his late-cellmate's girlfriend (Theron) and is trapped into a scheme to rob a casino with her evil brother (Sinise). It's hard to say more, since the twists are so convoluted, yet dozing off for a few minutes won't hamper your ability to keep up. The plot's machinations are driven by a need to have twists, rather than out of any logic or character. If Affleck ever becomes a top action star, then the Apocalypse may well be nigh. ★ DVD Exclusive Director's Cut: $14.99, VHS Exclusive Director's Cut: $9.99, VHS Theatrical Cut: $9.99

The Reivers

(1969, 107 min, US, Mark Rydell) *Steve McQueen, Mitch Vogel, Rupert Crosse.* Totally charming screen version of William Faulkner's story set in the early 1900s about an adventurous 12-year-old boy (Vogel) who travels from Mississippi to Tennessee with carefree McQueen and pal Crosse by motorcar. ★★★

Relentless

(1989, 92 min, US, William Lustig) *Judd Nelson, Robert Loggia, Meg Foster, Leo Rossi.* Nelson turns psycho in this often effective thriller written by one Jack T.D. Robinson, better known as Phil Alden Robinson (the director of *Field of Dreams*). Nelson sinks his teeth into the role of a Los Angeles serial killer who delights in showing up the baffled police. Loggia is the seasoned detective assigned to the case. ★★½

The Relic

(1997, 110 min, US, Peter Hyams) *Penelope Ann Miller, Tom Sizemore, Linda Hunt, James Whitmore.* Based on the novel by Douglas Preston and Lincoln Child, this big-budget production boasts great special effects and an original and terrifying monster. What it doesn't have in abundance is originality, but that's all right because its effective shocks and high level of suspense make up for any feeling of having seen it all before. Miller is the brains and Sizemore the brawn in a battle with a bizarre new life form accidentally brought back to the Chicago Museum of Natural History from the Amazon jungle. Leave it to the management to hold a gala reception one dark and stormy night while the creature is loose in the building. It's up to our heroes to stop the beast. Lotsa fun. ★★★ DVD: $14.99, VHS: $9.99

The Reluctant Debutante

(1958, 94 min, US, Vincente Minnelli) *Rex Harrsion, Kay Kendall, Sandra Dee, Angela Lansbury.* Harrison and Kendall bring a degree of respectability to this mildly amusing drawing-room comedy. A British couple ready their daughter (Dee), schooled in the States, for her society debut. A rather sappy and dated family film, rescued by the two stars' earnest performances. ★★

The Remains of the Day

(1993, 137 min, GB, James Ivory) *Anthony Hopkins, Emma Thompson, Christopher Reeve, Hugh Grant, James Fox.* The unequivocal masterpiece of producer Ismail Merchant and director Ivory. Spare in plot yet devastatingly powerful in its theme of repressed emotions, the deceptively simple story simmers with complex, unexpressed passions by its main characters. Adapted from Kazuo Ishiguro's novel, the story is set in a stately English manor with action being intercut from its 1930s heyday to its faded glory in the 1950s. In a magnificent performance, Hopkins stars as Stevens, the manor's longtime butler. With an unswerving and unquestioned devotion to his employer, Lord Darlington (Fox), Stevens sacrifices any semblance of a personal life — including an unconsummated relationship with the estate's vivacious housekeeper, charmingly played by Thompson. Devoid of heavy-handedness, the film is witty and entertaining, and is beautifully composed — its characters create almost unbearable tension and joy. ★★★★ DVD Special Edition: $29.99

Rembrandt

(1936, 84 min, GB, Alexander Korda) *Charles Laughton, Elsa Lanchester, Gertrude Lawrence.* Laughton delivers an inspired and moving performance as the renowned Dutch painter. He portrays Rembrandt as a complex and multifaceted egotist whose deep religious faith drove him to ignore poverty and lack of sponsorship in pursuit of his art. Korda's direction imbues the screen with a plethora of stunning tableaux. ★★★½ DVD: $19.99

Remember the Titans

(2000, 114 min, US, Boaz Yakin) *Denzel Washington, Will Patton, Wood Harris, Ryan Hurst, Donald Faison.* Bringing great determination and strength of character to the part of a football coach thrown into the political and social maelstrom of the early 1970s, Washington delivers a tough, compassionate performance to stand along side his best work. In this involving true story, director Yakin explores race relations on a human scale and how adversity in any game can be overcome. Much to the dismay of the white establishment of Alexandria, Virginia, the newly integrated T.C. Williams High School gets its first black coach, Herman Boone (Washington). The heartened story follows the struggles of players, faculty and townspeople as they all come to grips with the adolescence of the Civil Rights movement. Using the gridiron as a stand-in for the American mindset, the film captures these tentative first steps under the guise of a familiar but stirring underdog tale. ★★★ DVD Pan & Scan: $19.99, DVD Letterboxed: $22.99, VHS: $9.99

Remo Williams

(1985, 121 min, US, Guy Hamilton) *Fred Ward, Joel Grey, Wilford Brimley.* A New York policeman (Ward) becomes a highly trained, top-secret government agent, with a little help from an elderly Korean master (played by Grey). This entertaining adventure features well-staged action sequences, including a hold-your-breath fight atop the Statue of Liberty. ★★★ DVD: $14.99, VHS: $9.99

Renaissance Man

(1994, 129 min, US, Penny Marshall) *Danny DeVito, Gregory Hines, Cliff Robertson, James Remar, Mark Wahlberg, Lillo Brancato, Jr., Kadeem Hardison.* This sappy service comedy stars DeVito as a hapless, unemployed teacher who accepts an Army position to have his life changed for the better. DeVito takes charge of a group of military rejects, ultimately allowing his students to discover their own self-respect and at the same time putting his own life in order. There are some pleasurable moments to the film, but Marshall goes over the top with its sentimental message. The big surprise of the film is the effective performance given by Wahlberg as a backwoods G.I. ★★½ DVD: $14.99

Rendez-Vous

(1985, 83 min, France, André Téchiné) *Juliette Binoche, Lambert Wilson, Wadek Stanczak, Jean-Louis Trintignant.* This stylish melodrama stars Binoche as a naive 18-year-old girl who moves from the provinces to Paris in order to seek independence and establish an acting career. She soon becomes entangled in two love affairs; one with an overly idealistic young man (Stanczak) and another with a self-destructive youth (Wilson). A chic, well-cast study of opposing forces in life and fate. (French with English subtitles) ★★★ VHS: $29.99

Les Rendez-Vous d'Anna

(1978, 122 min, Belgium/France, Chantal Akerman) *Aurore Clement, Lea Massari, Helmut Griem, Jean-Pierre Cassel.* Filmed in a minimalist style, this quietly moving drama of alienation features a young Belgian director, Anna, who travels by train through Europe publicizing her newest film. Along the way, she meets a stream of characters: friends, lovers, relatives and strangers. The pervading malaise enveloping Anna is brought out by Akerman's trademark style of static camera shots, understated images, monologues and silence. A grim portrait of one woman adrift as well as a vision of an insensate Europe. (French with English subtitles) ★★½ VHS: $29.99

Rendezvous in Paris

(1995, 100 min, France, Eric Rohmer) *Mathias Megaro, Clara Bellar, Judith Chancel, Antoine Basler.* A trio of heartbreaking tales from director Rohmer. All of the films tackle themes of fidelity and trust, chance and coincidence, but none as well

The Remains of the Day

as the opening piece, *A 7 pm Rendezvous*. When a young woman learns that her boyfriend may be cheating on her, she arranges a meeting with a stranger in order to get at the truth. The second film, *The Benches of Paris*, depicts a romantic tug-of-war between a man who craves the affections of a woman who is merely using him to get back at her cheating husband. The last tale, *Mother and Child 1907*, tells of the improper seduction of an art student by a pick-up artist in the Picasso Museum. Driven by dialogue, each of these mini-films showcase attractive performers and, as always, Rohmer's graceful romantic touch. (French with English subtitles) ★★★ VHS: $19.99

Renegades

(1989, 106 min, US, Jack Sholder) *Lou Diamond Phillips, Kiefer Sutherland, Jami Gertz.* Labored police thriller with Sutherland as an undercover cop who teams with Lakota Indian Phillips to track down killers who stole a sacred Indian artifact. Supposedly set in Philadelphia, but most of the scenes will be unrecognizable to natives. ★½ DVD: $14.99

Repentance

(1983, 153 min, Russia, Tengiz Abuladze) *Avtandil Makharadze, Zeinab Botsvadze.* A savage, outrageous satire, this is a nightmarish political allegory about the excesses of the Stalinist era. A mysterious old woman defies the law and repeatedly exhumes the body of a recently deceased local chieftain. In a series of flashbacks, we learn that the much loved Georgian mayor was actually a despotic ruler, a Stalinist bully — with the gestures of Mussolini and the mustache of Hitler — who was content only with power, no matter the cost. An important, thought-provoking film. (Russian with English subtitles) ★★★ DVD Subtitled: $29.99

The Replacement Killers

(1998, 88 min, US, Antoine Fuqua) *Chow Yun-Fat, Mira Sorvino, Michael Rooker, Jürgen Prochnow.* The American film debut of prodigious Hong Kong superstar Chow-Yun Fat is a far cry from the movies that won him a following in the West. Chow's hit man — ordered by his employer to murder a cop's young son as revenge for the drug bust death of his own slimy dealer son — has a last-second change of heart, and spends the rest of the film trying to protect his initial hit. Chow is his usual ultra-cool self, and even Sorvino is fun as the streetwise tough who reluctantly assists him. But director Fuqua's style is all attitude and posturing, vapidly aping Woo and Lam, but possessing none of their passion or artistry. An entertaining though empty action flick. ★★½ DVD Letterbox Special Edition: $24.99, DVD: $14.99, VHS: $9.99

The Replacements

(2000, 118 min, US, Howard Deutch) *Keanu Reeves, Gene Hackman, Jon Favreau, Orlando Jones, Rhys Ifans.* Reeves plays a disgraced ex-star of the college gridiron, who blew a crucial play in a bowl game. When the pro players go on strike, Reeves and a motley group of stereotypes are called upon to be . . . The Replacements! Or scabs, really — a political issue this movie sidesteps by making the pros a bunch of pampered jackasses. It's hard not to get a little riled during the Big Game and root for the underdogs, but the road to the game is a rough one: wretched comedy, moronic dialogue, with only the always-professional Hackman to get you by. ★½ DVD: $14.99, VHS: $9.99

Replicant

(2000, 100 min, US, Ringo Lam) *Jean-Claude Van Damme, Michael Rooker, Catherine Dent.* Van Damme plays a sadistic serial killer who burns his victims, as well as the killer's clone, created by a government agency for military purposes, but used by cop Rooker to track down the psycho. Stupid, goofy and cheesy, *Replicant* is one of Van Damme's better films (which, admittedly, isn't saying a lot), with a fun performance by Rooker. After a protracted start, *Replicant* becomes fast-moving fun, with nifty Van Damme vs. Van Damme fights courtesy of Hong Kong action director Lam. ★★½ DVD: $9.99, VHS: $9.99

Repo Man

(1983, 92 min, US, Alex Cox) *Emilio Estevez, Harry Dean Stanton.* Scorned, feared and ruthless . . . he's a breed apart . . . he's a repo man. This raunchy romp sideswipes white dopes on punk, life in the 'burbs, hot-blooded Puerto Ricans and alien-in-the-car flicks. 'Nuff said? ★★★½ DVD Letterbox: $14.99

Report to the Commissioner

(1975, 112 min, US, Milton Katselas) *Michael Moriarty, Yaphet Kotto, Richard Gere.* A high-tension police drama with Moriarty as a rookie cop who accidentally kills an undercover policewoman, resulting in a departmental cover-up. ★★★ VHS: $29.99

Repulsion

(1965, 105 min, GB, Roman Polanski) *Catherine Deneuve, Yvonne Furneaux, Ian Hendry.* An eerie, kaleidoscope profile of a troubled young girl, imprisoned by her sexual fears and splintered by her shattered psyche. When her sister leaves her alone for the weekend, she is thrust into a world of mental deterioration and hallucinatory nightmares. Polanski directs a profoundly moving performance by Deneuve as the demure manicurist plagued by frightening visions. ★★★★ VHS: $19.99

Requiem for a Dream

(2000, 102 min, US, Darren Aronofsky) *Ellen Burstyn, Jared Leto, Jennifer Connelly, Marlon Wayans, Christopher McDonald, Louise Lasser, Sean Gullette.* In his hallucinatory, hypnotic second feature, director Aronofsky (who cowrote the screenplay with the author of the novel, Hubert Selby) has made a mind-numbing exploration of a mother and son's disparate, gradual descent into the abyss of drug addiction. Not content to simply make a "just-say-no" treatise, Aronofsky delves into the mindset and routine of his characters in astonishingly filmic set pieces, allowing facts and attitudes to speak for themselves without hyperbole or agenda. A very effective Leto is Harry, a small-time dealer and full-time user. His mother, Sara (Burstyn), is happy just to dream about being a contestant on her favorite TV show. When it appears Sara will be a contestant, she begins a harrowing weight reduction program, aided by diet pills. As both mother and son attempt the realization of their dreams (he's trying to raise money for his girlfriend's dress shop), each becomes ensnared in an out-of-control spiral. Burstyn grounds the film with a startling, immensely moving performance of a woman slowly losing control. ★★★★ DVD Director's Cut: $14.99

Michael Madsen in *Reservoir Dogs*

Requiem for Dominic

(1990, 88 min, US/Germany, Robert Dornhelm) *Felix Mitterer, Viktoria Schubert.* Set amidst the December 1989 Romanian uprising which toppled Ceaucescu, this docudrama combines feature film sequences along with shocking and sometimes brutal documentary-style footage of the revolution with unrelenting realism. The story follows the true-life story of Dominic Paraschiv, a political activist wrongly accused of murdering 80 of his colleagues. A childhood friend returns from exile to champion his cause. Director Dornhelm delivers a potent and harrowing tale of political upheaval. (German with English subtitles) ★★★ VHS: $79.99

The Rescuers

(1977, 79 min, US, Art Stevens, John Lounsberry, Wolfgang Reitherman) *Voices of: Eva Gabor, Bob Newhart, Geraldine Page.* A group of mice named the Rescue Aid Society find a bottle with an SOS from a little girl named Penny. They must save her from the evil Madame Medusa and her creepy crocodiles who plan to use Penny to retrieve a valuable diamond from a small cave. As usual, Disney's animation and musical score are excellent. ★★★ DVD: $29.99, VHS: $22.99

The Rescuers Down Under

(1990, 109 min, US, Hendel Butoy) *Eva Gabor, Bob Newhart.* This appealing sequel to Disney's The Rescuers finds mice Bernard and Miss Bianca traveling to Australia to rescue a young boy and a near-extinct eagle. ★★★ DVD: $29.99, VHS: $22.99

Reservoir Dogs

(1992, 100 min, US, Quentin Tarantino) *Harvey Keitel, Tim Roth, Steve Buscemi, Michael Madsen, Christopher Penn, Lawrence Tierney, Quentin Tarantino.* With one of the most intense and original directing debuts in memory, Tarantino manages with great success to add a new tier to the gangster film genre. The film opens with the bloody aftermath of a failed jewelry heist during which the surviving thieves go to extreme lengths to root out the "rat" in their midst. Bolstered by an excellent ensemble, Tarantino effectively presents his story in an exciting and unique non-linear style. With gritty dialogue and a level of realistic violence which borders on pornographic, the film gives the viewer an unusual fly-on-the-wall perspective of a desperado lifestyle. ★★★★ DVD Special Edition: $14.99, VHS Basic Edition: $9.99, VHS Special Edition: $14.99

The Return of Martin Guerre

R

Resident Evil

(2002, 100 min, US, Paul W.S. Anderson) *Milla Jovovich, Michelle Rodriguez, Eric Mabius, James Purefoy, Martin Crewes.* Based on the extremely popular (and extremely violent) video game, *Resident Evil* should have been gory, scary fun. It's merely gory. Jovovich plays an amnesiac corporate agent who must do battle with zombified office workers when an experimental drug is released in an underground lab. The zombies aren't very scary or cool, the characters are nil, the CGI effects are unconvincing, and the film is derivative in the extreme. Okay, zombie movies tend to be moronic, but they occasionally are fun. This one doesn't come close. Has the feel of watching someone else play a video game. ★½ DVD Special Edition: $19.99, VHS: $102.99

The Respectful Prostitute

(1955, 75 min, France, Charles Brabant & Marcel Pagliero) *Ivan Desny, Barbara Laage.* The seething racial hatred of America's Deep South is the theme in this surprisingly hard-hitting melodrama adapted from a play by Jean-Paul Sartre. When a drunken white man, a senator's son, kills an innocent black bystander on a train, the police conspire to call it self-defense and begin a manhunt for the dead man's black friend. The only witness to the killing is a white woman who is embroiled in the controversy when the law resorts to bribes, blackmail and violence in an effort to get her to recant her testimony and save the killer. Years ahead of its time, this fascinating story is a powerful and terribly disturbing look into the soulless void of man. ★★★ VHS: $19.99

Restoration

(1995, 118 min, GB, Michael Hoffman) *Robert Downey, Jr., Sam Neill, David Thewlis, Meg Ryan, Polly Walker, Ian McKellen, Hugh Grant, Roger Ashton-Griffiths, Ian McDiarmid.* An unexpected and lavish period drama, *Restoration* is an impressively mounted production rich in character and tone. It's mid-1600s England, a time when that country embraced the passions of the intellect and the sensuous. Young doctor Robert Merivel (Downey) balances his energies between hedonistic pursuits and his profession. A chance meeting with Charles II (Neill) elevates the buffoonish Merivel to court physician, thus setting Merivel on a com-pelling and at times fascinating odyssey through the course of English history which restores his and a country's humanity. Despite its change of gears from frothy to serious (or maybe because of it), *Restoration* engages as it provokes, and is consistent in its irradiative vision. ★★★½ VHS: $9.99

The Resurrected

(1991, 108 min, US, Dan O'Bannon) *Chris Sarandon, John Terry.* Screenwriter Dan O'Bannon *(Alien)* tries a rather successful hand at directing this ghastly H.P. Lovecraft tale of a scientist (Sarandon) who goes too far in his attempts to revive the dead. While a little too slow in getting started, the film is revitalized by some gruesome special effects. ★★½

Resurrection

(1980, 103 min, US, Daniel Petrie) *Ellen Burstyn, Sam Shepard, Eva Legallienne, Roberts Blossom, Lois Smith, Richard Farnsworth.* Burstyn gives a powerful performance as a woman who survives a near-fatal car accident, endowing her with the powers of spiritual healing and making her a target of religious fanatics. A graceful, beautiful drama, one of the most underrated films of the 1980s. Shepard is splendid as Burstyn's youthful lover, and stage legend Legallienne is heartbreaking as her wise grandmother. ★★★★

Return from Witch Mountain

(1978, 95 min, US, John Hough) *Bette Davis, Christopher Lee.* Good special effects highlight this amiable sequel to *Escape to Witch Mountain* as Davis and Lee kidnap two psychic alien children to use them in robbing a museum (how does one kidnap a psychic, anyhow?). ★★½ DVD: $24.99

The Return of Frank James

(1940, 92 min, US, Fritz Lang) *Henry Fonda, Gene Tierney.* Fonda reprises his role as Jesse James is this excellent sequel which was nicely directed by Lang. This time he's out to get the man who shot his brother in the back. ★★★½ VHS: $9.99

The Return of Martin Guerre

(1983, 111 min, France, Daniel Vigne) *Gérard Depardieu, Nathalie Baye.* Depardieu and Baye star in this sensuous saga of truth, desire and devotion. After a long absence, Martin Guerre returns to the village of his youth, and to a warm reception from its townspeople. However, his life takes an unexpected turn when his identity comes into question and he is brought to trial. An unabashedly romantic, yet never trite, statement on the strength of love. (American remake: *Sommersby*) (French with English subtitles) ★★★½ DVD: $29.99, VHS: $14.99

Return of the Jedi

(1983, 133 min, US, Richard Marquand) *Harrison Ford, Mark Hamill, Carrie Fisher, Billy Dee Williams.* The sixth and final chapter in George Lucas' *Star Wars* series lives up to its expectations as a nail-biting battle for the galaxy, but does not surpass *Star Wars* or *The Empire Strikes Back.* Featuring great special effects, it is also unfortunately the most commercial. The film begins with our heroes attempting to repair the damage of the Empire's strike back, by rescuing Han from the abode of the gangster-slug Jabba the Hut and getting Luke a new hand and a completion to his Jedi training with Yoda. The story then shifts to the Rebellion's grand plan: to destroy the new Death Star, the Emperor and Darth Vader in one final assault. A bit sappy, perhaps, but the audience of the original *Star Wars* grew up between the first and third movies, and was not the target audience of *Jedi.* (Sequel: *Star Wars: Episode 1 — The Phantom Menace*) ★★★½ Available in a DVD Letterboxed Trilogy-pack for $69.99

Return of the Living Dead

(1985, 90 min, US, Dan O'Bannon) *James Karen, Thom Mathews.* Funny and gory horror spoof of "living dead" zombie movies. The dead are ready to party when a secret military chemical brings them back to life. The film which introduced those immortal words: "Send more cops!" (Followed by 2 sequels) ★★½ DVD Dual: $14.99

The Return of the Pink Panther

(1975, 113 min, GB, Blake Edwards) *Peter Sellers, Herbert Lom, Christopher Plummer.* After a six-year hiatus, Sellers returns to the screen as the hilariously inept Inspector Clouseau. Like many of the post-*Shot in the Dark* sequels, Edwards tends to concentrate too heavily on big, violent sight gags and Sellers' peerless knack for slapstick and pratfalls. Still, this is one of those films that will keep you laughing throughout. (Sequel: *The Pink Panther Strikes Again*) ★★★ DVD: $14.99, VHS: $9.99

The Return of the Secaucus 7

(1980, 100 min, US, John Sayles) *Mark Arnott, Maggie Cousineau, David Strathairn, Gordon Clapp.* What happens when seven former activists get together for a reunion is the focus of Sayles' first directorial work. Ten years after being jailed for a night on trumped-up protesting charges, these friends reminisce about the causes, concerns and convictions of their youth. Emotions flow as the weekend turns into a series of bittersweet realizations regarding the group's goals and accomplishments. ★★★★ DVD Director's Edition: $19.99

The Return of the Soldier

(1985, 101 min, GB, Alan Bridges) *Alan Bates, Glenda Jackson, Julie Christie, Ann-Margret, Ian Holm.* A powerhouse cast highlights this riveting psychological drama adapted from Rebecca West's first novel. During WWI, a soldier (Bates) experiences shell shock and amnesia and returns to his country estate without the memory of his past 20 years. His only recollections are of a bucolic childhood and a youthful love affair. Christie is wonderful as the pampered wife who is only familiar to her husband "like any other guest in the same hotel." A subtle, handsomely mounted and involving production. ★★★½

Return of the Tall Blonde Man with One Black Shoe

(1974, 84 min, France, Yves Robert) *Pierre Richard, Jean Rochefort.* Richard revives his role as the incredibly clutzy and bumbling musician who accidentally stumbles into international intrigue. A hilarious spoof of spy movies. ★★★

The Return of the Vampire

(1943, 69 min, US, Lew Landers) *Bela Lugosi.* Columbia Studios tried to sneak into Universal's demi-monde with this atmospheric tale of a caped vampire named Armand Tesla, stalking the ruins of war-torn London. No matter what name you give the character, when Lugosi plays a vampire, it's Dracula. ★★ DVD: $19.99

Return to Me

(2000, 116 min, US, Bonnie Hunt) *David Duchovny, Minnie Driver, Carroll O'Connor, Robert Loggia, David Alan Grier, Bonnie Hunt, Joely Richardson, James Belushi.* In this heartwarming romantic comedy, Duchovny plays a widower who learns that his deceased wife's heart has been used in a transplant operation. He befriends the recipient (Driver) and falls in love all over again. Comedianne Hunt makes an effective directorial debut, nicely capturing the flavor of her native Chicago. Far-fetched but winsome. ★★★ DVD: $14.99, VHS: $9.99

Return to Oz

(1985, 110 min, US, Walter Murch) *Fairuza Balk, Nicol Williamson, Jean Marsh, Piper Laurie.* Dark and rather depressing sequel to the classic *The Wizard of Oz*, with Dorothy returning to Oz (after a bout in a sanitarium) but finding things changed for the worst. ★★ DVD: $19.99

Return to Paradise

(1998, 109 min, US, Joseph Ruben) *Vince Vaughn, Anne Heche, Joaquin Phoenix, David Conrad, Jada Pinkett.* A good idea in search of a good script, *Return to Paradise* stars Vaughn as Sheriff, a limo driver who, three years earlier, had enjoyed a boisterous, pot-fueled trek through Malaysia with two casual acquaintances. While working one night, he finds Beth (Heche) in the back seat, who informs him that one of those buddies has been arrested for drug dealing and is sentenced to die in a week. The conviction will be reversed if he goes back, takes equal blame, and serves time voluntarily. Amid the soul searching, Sheriff changes his mind everyday, but considering the film's title, there's not much doubt or dramatic suspense to the outcome. *Return to Paradise* is in need of more narrative drive, suspense, and momentum. ★★ DVD: $14.99

Return to Salem's Lot

(1987, 96 min, US, Larry Cohen) *Michael Moriarty, Samuel Fuller, Addison Reed.* Entertaining theatrical sequel to Stephen King's acclaimed TV miniseries. Moriarty plays an anthropologist who, with his young son, travels to the small Northeastern town, overrun by vampires. ★★★ VHS: $14.99

Return to Snowy River

(1988, 97 min, Australia, Geoff Burrowes) *Brian Dennehy, Tom Burlinson.* While not as good as the original *Man from Snowy River*, this drama of romance and ambition set against a backdrop of a horse ranch proves to be diverting, highlighted by lush photography of galloping horses and a nicely

drawn villain in Dennehy. The story follows the love affair between young ranchhand Jim (Burlinson) and Jessica, the lovely daughter of the ranch. Once again, Jim must prove his worth in order to win the young woman's hand. ★★½ VHS: $9.99

The Returner

(2002, 117 min, Japan, Takashi Yamazaki) *Takeshi Kaneshiro, Anne Suzuki, Goro Kishitani, Kirin Kiki.* A girl from a war-ravaged future comes back in time to the present to kill an alien that apparently started a world war against humans. She teams up with a former street punk seeking revenge on a peroxided baddie who murdered his childhood friend. Many *Matrix/Terminator*-inspired antics ensue. Overlong, unoriginal, and mostly tedious, *The Returner* received a lot of hype in the genre press when released theatrically overseas. It turns out to be merely hype, unfortunately, as even the action scenes (despite a handful of clever moments and gags) grow wearisome rather quickly. The villain is a clichéd, juvenile bore, and the heroes aren't much more thrilling. Most of the effects (with the glaring exception of the cheesy aliens) are well-done, however, and sci-fi action junkies may want to check it out for its fleeting glimpses of quality. ★★ DVD: $24.99

Reuben, Reuben

(1983, 101 min, US, Robert Ellis Miller) *Tom Conti, Kelly McGillis, Roberts Blossom, Lois Smith.* A wonderfully witty character study with the superb Conti as a recklessly amorous, casually amoral and usually inebriated Scottish poet. Though his last verses were conjured long ago, he suffers no lack of charm as he takes a New England college town by storm. ★★★

Revenge

(1990, 124 min, US, Tony Scott) *Kevin Costner, Anthony Quinn, Madeleine Stowe, Miguel Ferrer.* This tepid romantic thriller stars Costner as a former pilot who travels to Mexico to visit millionaire gangster Quinn. Once there, the hotshot flyboy promptly falls in love with his host's beautiful, bored wife (Stowe). As passions ignite, Quinn quickly learns of the couple's affair, and he initiates a near-fatal beating of the two (Revenge #1); then there's the Revenge of the Revenge, and so on and so on. Director Scott is an accomplished visual stylist, but plot and characterization are not his forte. ★ DVD: $14.99, VHS: $9.99

Revenge of the Nerds

(1984, 90 min, US, Jeff Kanew) *Robert Carradine, Anthony Edwards, Curtis Armstrong, Ted McGinley, Julie Montgomery.* One of the more engaging of the silly teen sex comedies, with Carradine and Edwards leading fellow campus nerds to form their own fraternity. (Followed by 3 sequels) ★★½ VHS: $9.99

Revenge of the Pink Panther

(1978, 99 min, GB, Blake Edwards) *Peter Sellers, Dyan Cannon.* Director Edwards had clearly run out of ideas by the time of this last Sellers go-round as Inspector Clouseau. The film is barely redeemed by the usual pratfalls and a fine performance from Cannon. Quite unfortunately, Sellers gives a sloppy and ill-timed performance as even his comic genius is not able to save Edwards' lackluster material. (Sequel: *Trail of the Pink Panther*) ★★ DVD: $19.99

Reversal of Fortune

(1990, 120 min, US, Barbet Schroeder) *Jeremy Irons, Ron Silver, Glenn Close, Annabella Sciorra, Uta Hagen.* Irons won an Oscar for his stunning portrayal of Claus von Bulow in this remarkable satire on greed and the upper class, based on the novel by von Bulow's lawyer, Alan Dershowitz. Accused of trying to murder his wife, Sunny, von Bulow was tried, convicted and then eventually acquitted. The film details in fascinating fashion the events leading up to this; all told with a dark and sometimes hilarious sense of humor. Close, who spends most of the film in a coma, is splendid as Sunny; and Silver is terrific as Dershowitz, whose passionate defense for the unlikable von Bulow led to his release. Irons' masterful and cynical portrait distinguishes this classic comedy of manners. ★★★★ DVD: $19.99, VHS: $14.99

The Revolt of Job

(1983, 97 min, Hungary, Imre Gyongyossy) *Fereno Zenthe, Hedi Tenessy.* Autobiographical in nature, this touching, compassonate film follows the actions of an elderly Jewish couple who, having lost all seven of their children during Nazi occupation, become determined to retain and pass on their proud heritage. They do so by illegally adopting a gentile boy. Their love and understanding for the boy helps him see the world not as an ugly place, but one in which nature, religion and love are one. (Hungarian with English subtitles) ★★★

Revolution

(1985, 125 min, US, Hugh Hudson) *Al Pacino, Donald Sutherland, Nastassja Kinski, Joan Plowright.* Almost legendary bomb with Pacino as an illiterate trapper who becomes involved in the Revolutionary War when his 14-year-old son joins in the fight against the British. Stick to *1776* if you want to know the story. ★ VHS: $9.99

Rhapsody in August

(1991, 98 min, Japan, Akira Kurosawa) *Sachiko Murase, Richard Gere.* Japanese grand master Kurosawa's eloquent examination of the nuclear holocaust in Nagasaki — as seen through the eyes of a survivor and her four grandchildren 44 years later — is a highly emotional and engrossing drama. Sprinkled throughout with touches of wry humor, the film follows the four youngsters who, deposited by their parents with Grandma for the summer, constantly needle her for more information about the war and the bomb, allowing us to discover the grisly details through their innocent eyes. Ultimately, it is the old lady who takes center stage, however, as she falls into despair over the loss of her husband in the blast as its anniversary draws near. Gere makes an effective appearance as an Amerasian relative from Hawaii who comes to visit. This understated film is a beautifully crafted and heartfelt requiem. (Japanese with English subtitles) ★★★½ DVD Letterbox: $19.99

Rhapsody in Blue

(1945, 139 min, US, Irving Rapper) *Robert Alda, Joan Leslie, Alexis Smith.* As with 1946's *Night and Day*, this biography of musical genius George Gershwin is a fictionalized account of an American icon's life. Alda plays Gershwin, and the film's main interest is the great composer's classic music. Not as much fun as the Porter bio. ★★

Rich and Famous

(1981, 117 min, US, George Cukor) *Candice Bergen, Jacqueline Bisset, David Selby, Hart Bochner, Meg Ryan.* Cukor's last film is a likable, updated remake of *Old Aquaintance*, with Bisset and Bergen taking over the Bette Davis-Miriam Hopkins roles as college friends and rivals. Both novelists, Bisset is the "serious" and single writer who careens from one sexual encounter to another, while Bergen is the housewife who finds acclaim, but loses a husband, by writing low-brow fiction. ★★★

Rich and Famous

(1987, 104 min, Hong Kong, Taylor Wong) *Chow Yun-Fat, Alex Man, Andy Lau, Carina Lau, Alan Tam.* Raised as brothers in abject poverty, two young men seek help with a gambling debt from a local boss (Yun-Fat). They are poorly prepared for the world they've entered, an escalating conflict between warring crime lords played out with seething violence and deliberate cruelty. While not very polished and hampered by a pedestrian story and uneven pacing, *Rich and Famous* at least spotlights Chow's screen charisma and the region's breaknek filmmaking style. (Sequel: *Tragic Hero*) (Cantonese with English subtitles) ★★ DVD: $29.99, VHS: $19.99

Rich and Strange

(1934, 92 min, GB, Alfred Hitchcock) *Henry Kendall, Joan Barry.* Hitchcock's favorite film from his British period is a suprisingly funny yarn about a bored couple who inherit a large sum of money and embark on a journey around the world. Their "idyllic" vacation is enlivened by adulteries, swindles, a shipwreck and a tasty meal that turns out to be a fried cat. ★★★ VHS: $9.99

The Rich Man's Wife

(1996, 100 min, US, Amy Holden Jones) *Halle Berry, Christopher McDonald, Peter Greene, Clive Owen.* Derivative, unbelievable and about as thrilling as looking for Iowa license plates on the L.A. Freeway, Berry is having marital problems with her rich husband (McDonald); while vacationing in the mountains, she meets one of the relatives from *Deliverance*. Then her husband ends up dead. If you really need noir thrills, rewatch *Body Heat* and *Mortal Thoughts* — just two of the many good films this borrows from. ★ DVD: $14.99, VHS: $9.99

Richard Pryor Live! In Concert

(1979, 78 min, US, Jeff Margolis) This concert film, showing the comic at the very peak of his talent, succeeds where most other "live" perfomance documentaries fall short. Many comedians have flashes of brilliance, but only Pryor's comic tour de force lasts the entire length of the film. Re-creating everything from his heart attack to his pet monkey's sex drive, Pryor's act is, of course, excruciatingly funny. At the same time, the intimacy with which he discusses painful real-life experiences makes this a cathartic experience. ★★★½ DVD: $24.99, VHS: $19.99

Richard III

(1995, 106 min, GB, Richard Loncraine) *Ian McKellen, Annette Bening, Jim Broadbent, Maggie Smith, Nigel Hawthorne, Robert Downey, Jr., Kristin Scott Thomas, John Wood, Adrian Dunbar.* McKellen wrote the screenplay adaptation and stars in this virbrant, often thrilling updating of Shakespeare's classic tragedy of betrayal and ambition, now set in the 1930s. The story traces the rise of Richard (McKellen in a hypnotic performance), the ruthless prince who plots and kills his way to the throne. McKellen and director Loncraine have created a Nazi-like society which Richard commands, and Shakespeare's story and dialogue superbly underscore Richard's oppressive regime and fascist roots. Smith is simply great as Richard's mother who can barely conceal the contempt she holds for her son. The outstanding production design complements the rampant hysteria of Richard's new order, which has been brilliantly maneuvered by Richard and envisioned by McKellen. ★★★★ DVD: $19.99, VHS: $14.99

Richard III

(1955, 158 min, GB, Laurence Olivier) *Laurence Olivier, Ralph Richardon, Claire Bloom, John Gielgud, Cedric Hardwicke.* Olivier leads a dream cast as the physically grotesque and completely villainous Richard III, King of England. Sir Larry seems to revel in his part as the vile and fiendish hellhound who slices his way into conquest on the battlefield and in the boudoir. Outstanding on every level. ★★★★ DVD Letterbox Criterion Collection 2-Disc Set: $39.99, VHS: $24.99

Richard's Things

(1980, 104 min, GB, Anthony Harvey) *Liv Ullmann, Amanda Redman, Tim Pigott-Smith, Elizabeth Spriggs, Michael Maloney.* This made-for-TV drama wallows in somber pretentiousness and is unusually stagnant for its subject matter. Ullmann stars as a widow who is seduced by her late husband's girlfriend. A relationship develops, and the two women fall in love. A good premise, but sexual seduction never looked so dreary as Ullmann goes through the film as if in the frozen existential wasteland of Bergmania. ★½

Richie Rich

(1994, 95 min, US, Donald Petrie) *Macaulay Culkin, Edward Herrmann, Christine Ebersole, John Larroquette.* Based on the popular comic book, *Richie Rich* is weak on plot and heavy on the gimmicks, but it's also surprisingly entertaining. Culkin is unusually understated as the richest kid in the world, Richie Rich, who has everything he could want but friends. The story follows his attempts to befriend a group of neighborhood kids, and foil bad guy Larroquette who has stolen the family fortune. ★★½ VHS: $14.99

Ricochet

(1991, 97 min, US, Russell Mulcahy) *Denzel Washington, John Lithgow, Ice T, Kevin Pollak.* A stylized action film starring Lithgow as a crazed serial killer who plots the downfall of a politically ambitious buppie cop (Washington) who sends him to prison. The film is packed with enough non-stop action to please any fan of the genre. Ice-T offers strong support as a hip-hop crack-dealing revolutionary. ★★½ DVD: $14.99, VHS: $9.99

Riddance

(1973, 84 min, Hungary, Márta Mészáros) A factory worker pretends to be a student when she meets a handsome scholar at the university. However, after they fall in love, she confesses her working-class background. Though caring little about her class, he will only introduce her to his parents as a fellow student. As she comes closer to acceptance, she realizes that she cannot live under false pretenses and chooses independence over social position. (Hungarian with English subtitles) ★★½ VHS: $69.99

The Riddle of the Dead Sea Scrolls

(1990, 80 min, GB, Richard Cassidy) The Dead Sea Scrolls were hidden during the Maccabean Wars by the Essenes. Their discovery by a shepherd in 1947 provided the world-wide academic community an unparalleled opportunity to examine 2,000-year-old documents with this amount of writing intact and in such good condition. At first dated roughly 150 years before the birth of Christ, later examination questions that. This fascinating documentary explores the implications inherent in the discrepancy between the two schools of thought regarding the dating of the scrolls. *Riddle* is a well-considered exploration of issues which have archeological, historical and religious implications. ★★★ VHS: $24.99

The Riddle of the Sands

(1979, 102 min, GB, Tony Maylan) *Michael York, Jenny Aguter, Simon MacCorkindale.* A rousing thinking-man's adventure film set in the early part of the 1900s which follows the fantastic adventures of two young British yachtsmen who, while on a pleasure cruise on the North Sea, stumble upon a German plot to invade England. Our daring heroes do what is expected of them — stop the nefarious Germans! ★★★

Ian McKellen makes a most malevolent *Richard III*

Ride the High Country

(1962, 94 min, US, Sam Peckinpah) *Randolph Scott, Joel McCrea, Mariette Hartley.* Peckinpah's first masterwork and one of the great, classic westerns. Scott and McCrea (who must have at least 50 westerns between them) are two aging ex-lawmen who have helped tame the West that no longer has a place for them. McCrea is hired to transport gold from a mining community; he hires Scott and a young cowboy to help, unaware the two men are conspiring to steal the shipment. The literate script, beautiful locations and touching performances make this melancholy western linger in one's memory. ★★★½

Ride with the Devil

(1999, 138 min, US, Ang Lee) *Tobey Maguire, Skeet Ulrich, Jewel, Jeffrey Wright, Simon Baker, James Caviezel, Jonathan Rhys Meyers, Thomas Guiry, Tom Wilkinson, Mark Ruffalo.* This Civil War adventure covers an especially fractious segment: southern Bushwhackers in Missouri waging a guerrilla war against northern Jayhawkers. The Bushwhackers here include Maguire as the son of an immigrant northern sympathizer, his buddy Ulrich and a freed slave (Wright). Jewel is a young widow who provides them with shelter during a dangerous winter. The complicated connections lead to some appropriately chaotic battles, but director Lee generally fails to translate these action scenes dramatically. However, the cinematography is majestic and the compelling story comes complete with rustically poetic dialogue (the screenplay is by longtime collaborator James Schamus) and natural performances by the ensemble cast. ★★★ DVD: $14.99, VHS: $9.99

Rider on the Rain

(1970, 119 min, France, René Clément) *Marlene Jobert, Charles Bronson, Jill Ireland.* A surprisingly good, nail-biting thriller. Bronson is Harry Dobbs, a police inspector in a small French village who unwittingly becomes involved in a bizarre murder mystery involving a mysterious drifter, rape and revenge. In a genre that all too often sinks to insipid levels, this intelligent and taut Hitchcockian puzzler is a refreshing alternative. ★★★

Riders of the Storm

(1986, 92 min, GB, Maurice Philips) *Dennis Hopper, Michael J. Pollard.* Offbeat comedy about a group of high-flying Vietnam vets who set out to sabotage the presidential campaign of a conservative female candidate. ★★½

Riders to the Sea

(1987, 45 min, Ireland, Ronan O'Leary) *Geraldine Page, Amanda Plummer, Sachi Parker.* Page stars (in her final performance) in this powerful rendition of J.M. Synge's classic one-act play about three women waiting in quiet desperation for word of a son who has disappeared at sea. ★★★

Ridicule

(1996, 102 min, France, Patrice Leconte) *Charles Berling, Jean Rochefort, Fanny Ardant.* With a barrage of pomp and circumstance and a pocketful of wit, this extravagant and delightful period piece follows the travails of an overly eager and naïvely optimistic young viscount, Ponceludon (Berling), who sets out for the court of Louis XVI to petition the king to build a series of canals. Of course, he is regarded as nothing more than a country bumpkin and soon learns that the greatest currency in the palace is repartee. To achieve any hope of audience with the king, one must be a master of the rejoinder.

He excels, of course, but this only brings the notice of Ardant, an influential countess whose friendship is as much a hazard as it is a help. Director Leconte is very much at home in the regalia of costume spectacle. (French with English subtitles) ★★★½ DVD: $19.99, VHS: $9.99

Riding in Cars with Boys

(2001, 132 min, US, Penny Marshall) *Drew Barrymore, Steve Zahn, Brittany Murphy, Adam Garcia, Sara Gilbert, James Woods, Lorraine Bracco, Maggie Gyllenhaal.* Mismarketed as a laugh-out-loud comedy with dramatic overtones, the extremely downbeat *Riding in Cars with Boys* is actually a rather heavy drama with some occasional comic relief. The film, based on Beverly D'Onofrio's autobiography, stars Drew as a teenage girl who gets pregnant and marries slacker (and eventual junkie) Zahn, thus dashing her dreams of being a writer. We follow her through the years, suffering one heartbreak and crushed hope after another, until she reaches a small level of peace by film's end. Director Marshall paints the film with broad strokes of sentimentality and slapdash comedy. Ultimately, *Riding in Cars with Boys* is too episodic and haphazardly structured to fully engage. Barrymore tries to give Beverly a shading but the screenplay doesn't always allow her to do so. Zahn, however, is terrific as her alcoholic husband, giving dimension to a difficult role. ★★½ DVD Special Edition: $14.99

Riff Raff

(1992, 94 min, GB, Ken Loach) *Robert Carlyle, Emer McCourt.* This is guerrilla filmmaking at its finest. Loach's ultra-realistic, documentary-style peek into the lives of lower-class British construction workers is a marvelously subversive skewering of England's collapsing welfare state. The action centers around a young Glaswegian drifter named Stevie who arrives at a London construction site and is taken in by the regulars of the crew. Peppered with moments of deep insight as well as hilarious comedy, the film's fly-on-the-wall perspective offers a remarkably personal and unapologetic view of the people buried beneath the ashes of the British Empire. Featuring thick dialects from all over the U.K., the film's gritty dialogue is subtitled for American audiences. ★★★★ VHS: $19.99

Rififi

(1955, 116 min, France, Jules Dassin) *Jean Servais, Carl Mohner, Jules Dassin.* The archetypical heist flick, this delightful movie concerns itself with four sleazy Montmartre jewel thieves who plan and execute a daring robbery but soon find that their fellow gangsters are more dangerous than the police. Director Dassin, who moved to France after being blacklisted in the States during the McCarthy era, meticulously enacts the robbery in a daring and wonderfully tense 25-minute sequence filmed in total silence. (French with English subtitles) ★★★★ DVD: $29.99, VHS: $29.99

The Right Stuff

(1983, 193 min, US, Philip Kaufman) *Sam Shepard, Ed Harris, Scott Glenn, Dennis Quaid, Fred Ward, Kathy Baker, Barbara Hershey, Veronica Cartwright.* All involved with this mammoth, sensational adaptation of Tom Wolfe's bestseller about the early days of America's space program certainly have the right stuff, too. A fabulous cast including Shepard as pioneer pilot Chuck Yeager, and Harris, Glenn, Quaid and Ward as our

Dennis Quaid as "Gordo" Cooper in *The Right Stuff*

first astronauts are all mesmerizing in their depiction of the men whose courage and skill began our exploration into space. The film, which is over three hours long, seems half that running time thanks to exceptional editing and photography, a well-defined screenplay, enthralling aerospace sequences, and director Kaufman's keen eye for pacing and detail. ★★★★ DVD Letterbox: $19.99, DVD 2-disc Special Edition: $26.99, VHS: $19.99, VHS Letterbox: $19.99

Rikisha-Man

(1958, 105 min, Japan, Hiroshi Inagaki) *Toshiro Mifune.* This Venice Film Festival Grand Prix winner is a classic story of unrequited love. Mifune stars as a feisty rikisha cart-puller who helps a lost boy home, where he falls hopelessly in love with the boy's beautiful mother. The cultural differences between the two preclude any relationship in this sad and unforgettable story. (Japanese with English subtitles) ★★★

Rikki and Pete

(1988, 107 min, Australia, Nadia Tass) *Nina Landis, Stephen Kearney, Bruce Spence, Bruno Lawrence.* From the director and writer (David Parker) of *Malcolm* comes this gadget-laden follow-up about an off-the-wall inventor and his geologist sister who escape the local sheriff by fleeing to the Outback. Suffice it to say, chaos ensues in this humorous though lightweight "Les Miserables Down Under." ★★½

Rikyu

(1991, 116 min, Japan, Hiroshi Teshigahara) *Rantaro Mikuni, Tsutomu Yamazaki.* From the director of *Woman in the Dunes* comes this intelligent drama on the strained relationship between the art of politics and the politics of art. Set in the 16th century, a power-hungry peasant rises to leadership after a powerful warlord is killed. Ignorant of the traditions of higher Japanese culture, he appoints Hideyoshi, a wise and elderly tea master, to teach him the Zen approach to Ikebana (flower arranging) as well as the delicate and mysterious tea ceremony. However, social and spiritual instruction soon evolve into political advice, a turn of events unforeseen by the taciturn old teacher. (Japanese with English subtitles) ★★★ DVD: $19.99, VHS: $79.99

R

The Ring

(2002, 109 min, US, Gore Verbinski) *Naomi Watts, Martin Henderson, David Dorfman, Brian Cox, Jane Alexander, Lindsay Frost.* Scary, atmospheric and — amazingly — pretty damn smart for a supernatural thriller, *The Ring* is based on the cult Japanese chiller *Ringu.* Equally as frightening as the original, the film is still basically the story of a teenaged folk legend, spruced up for an American audience without losing any of its freshness or effectiveness. Watts plays Rachel, a Seattle newspaper reporter who investigates the mysterious death of her niece. It seems it all started with a creepy video, which will bring about the gruesome death of anyone who watches it. Watching the video herself, Rachel has only seven days to get to the heart of the mystery. Watts brings a believability to the film that rarely makes you question the other-worldly goings-on. Director Verbinksi maintains good pacing throughout, and cannily creates suspense and scares without having to rely on gore, tricky editing or flashy effects. ★★★½ DVD Widescreen: $19.99, VHS: $14.99

Ringmaster

(1998, 90 min, US, Neil Abramson) *Jerry Springer, Jaime Pressly, Molly Hagan, William McNamara, Michael Dudikoff.* Take all the excitement of a real Jerry Springer TV show, then remove the drama of having actual people airing their dirty laundry in public, and you get this pointless film. Jerry himself is reduced to cameo status as the film focuses on two stories: one a white-trash family that features a stepfather-stepdaughter coupling; and a black-trash trio of girlfriends who all hate one two-timing (three-timing, four-timing) man. Hair-pulling, breast-baring, mother-cursing just isn't as much fun when you know it's scripted, like the day you found out professional wrestling isn't real. ★½ DVD: $14.99, VHS: $9.99

Ringu

(1998, 96 min, Japan, Hideo Nakata) *Nanako Matsushima, Miki Nakatami, Hiroyuki Sanada, Rie Inou.* It has the trappings of an urban legend: there's a mysterious tape out there that looks like a Bergman kabuki film; after watching it, you get a frightening phone call and have but one week to live. But some kids have watched it and died of fright, sending the reporter aunt of one victim, ex-husband in tow, to get to the bottom of it all. Naturally, they watch the tape and get the call, giving them seven days to lift the curse. This extremely effective horror film relies on a constant atmosphere of dread, and the suspense builds with each viewing of the tape, which seems to run a little longer as the days progress. The mood is punctuated by occasional violent shocks, which are far removed from the false scares in most American horror films, and the ultimate climax is unforgettable. Incidentally, this is the rare film that's scarier if you watch it on tape instead of DVD. (American remake: *The Ring*) (Japanese with English subtitles) ★★★½ DVD Letterbox: $19.99, VHS Letterboxed: $9.99

Rio Bravo

(1959, 141 min, US, Howard Hawks) *John Wayne, Dean Martin, Angie Dickinson, Ricky Nelson, Walter Brennan.* Hawks' classic western with Wayne as a small town sheriff determined to keep a killer confined to his jail, despite a limited source of man-power in the town. Flavorful direction from Hawks. (The basis for *Assault on Precinct 13*) ★★★½ DVD: $19.99, VHS: $14.99

Rio Grande

(1950, 105 min, US, John Ford) *John Wayne, Maureen O'Hara, Ben Johnson, Victor McLaglen, Claude Jarman, Jr., Harry Carey, Jr., Chill Wills.* The third entry in director Ford's cavalry trilogy (*Fort Apache* and *She Wore a Yellow Ribbon* came before it) is another compelling western, here centering on the conflict between commander Wayne and his estranged son (Jarman), who he has not seen in 15 years. O'Hara is Wayne's ex-wife, determined to come between them. ★★★ DVD Collector's Edition: $19.99, VHS: $14.99

Riot

(1969, 97 min, US, Buzz Kulik) *Gene Hackman, Jim Brown, Gerald S. O'Laughlin.* Brown reluctantly helps fellow jailbird Hackman start a riot to cover their prison breakout in this stereotyped, extremely violent jailhouse romp. Wonderfully clichéd performances, hard-boiled dialogue and the prison's (Arizona State Penitentiary) real warden, personnel and inmates as performers combine to make this film an exploitative, entertaining treat. ★★½

Riot in Cell Block 11

(1954, 80 min, US, Don Siegel) *Neville Brand, Leo Gordon.* A collection of cutthroats seize control of their cellblock in this hardboiled crime flick. A gritty, early entry from the director of *Dirty Harry.* ★★★ VHS: $19.99

The Rise to Power of Louis XIV

(1966, 100 min, France, Roberto Rossellini) *Jean-Marie Patte, Raymond Jourdan.* Rossellini's first in his series of historical dramas tells the story of Louis XIV's rise to power as well as his decline. Includes a memorable scene where he forces his court to watch him devour a 14-course meal. Made in only 23 days for French television, this is one of Rossellini's most important and influential works. (French with English subtitles) ★★★½

Rising Sun

(1993, 126 min, US, Philip Kaufman) *Sean Connery, Wesley Snipes, Harvey Keitel, Mako, Stan Shaw, Tia Carrere, Steve Buscemi.* Michael Crichton's adaptation of his Japan-bashing, high-tech best-seller is a tedious tale of corporate espionage. Connery and Snipes are an unlikely duo as a pair of L.A.P.D. liaison officers sent to investigate a murder at the boardroom of a major Japanese multinational. Of course, their search for the killer leads them right into the middle of the trade wars between Japan and the United States. Ultimately, the film can't decide whether it wants to be a full-fledged action-thriller or an overly worded primer on Japanese business treachery. ★★ DVD: $14.99

Risky Business

(1983, 99 min, US, Paul Brickman) *Tom Cruise, Rebecca DeMornay, Joe Pantoliano, Curtis Armstrong, Bronson Pinchot, Nicholas Pryor, Janet Carroll, Richard Masur.* Cruise created a small sensation in his first starring role as a college-bound teenager who turns his upper-class Chicago home into a bordello while his parents are out of town. There are plenty of laughs and a good, youthful supporting cast. ★★★ DVD: $14.99, VHS: $9.99

Rita, Sue and Bob Too

(1986, 93 min, GB, Alan Clarke) *Siobhan Finneran, Michelle Holmes, George Costigan.* This interesting sex comedy with a dark edge features Finneran and Holmes as Rita and Sue, two lower-class teenagers who baby-sit for nouveau riche yuppie Bob (Costigan). Bob initiates both girls sexually in very quick succession and everything moves along quite happily until Rita becomes pregnant, signaling a turn for the worse for all parties concerned. The film captures the gritty hopelessness of the industrial midlands of England quite well, and is marred only slightly by a trite ending. ★★★

The Rite

(1969, 75 min, Sweden, Ingmar Bergman) *Ingrid Thulin, Gunnar Björnstrand, Anders Ek, Eric Hell.* Bergman's claustrophic treatise on censorship and the arts pits three members of a successul cabaret act against a Kafka-esque magistrate (Hell) who must determine whether a piece of their show is "obscene." The troupe is comprised of Thulin, her husband Björnstrand and Ek, with whom she is having a torrid affair. As the judge individually interrogates them, their stories unravel along with all of their interpersonal foibles and neuroses. The film culminates, naturally, with their performing the offending piece for the astonished judge. The opressive sense of ennui may prove too much to bear, even considering the film's graciously short running time. (Swedish with English subtitles) ★★½ VHS: $29.99

The Ritz

(1976, 91 min, US, Richard Lester) *Jack Weston, Rita Moreno, Treat Williams, F. Murray Abraham, Kaye Ballard, Jerry Stiller.* Lester's riotous farce stars Weston as a Cleveland garbage collector on the lam in a gay bathhouse. There he encounters entertainer Moreno ("You thought I was a drag queen?"), detective Williams ("You madicon hump!"), the Andrews Sisters and the ever-popular steam room. Not as hilarious or as refined as the Broadway production (written by Terrence McNally), but very entertaining nonetheless. ★★★

The River

(1951, 99 min, India, Jean Renoir) *Patricia Walters, Adrienne Corri.* In 1949 and 1950, Renoir traveled to Bengal to make his first color film, the story of a large British family living on the banks of the Ganges River. Though it has never attained the classic status of many of his earlier works, it remains one of Renoir's loveliest, drollest and most pleasing films. The film features outstanding cinematography by Jean's brother Claude. Also of special note is Renoir's assistant director for the production: Satyajit Ray. ★★★★

The River

(1984, 124 min, US, Mark Rydell) *Mel Gibson, Sissy Spacek, Shane Bailey, Becky Jo Lynch, Scott Glenn.* Gibson and Spacek play a farm couple struggling against nature and business interests to hold on to their home. Good production values (including lush cinematography by Vilmos Zsigmond) and earnest performances from the two leads can't make up for dramatic inconsistencies. The least of the trilogy of "farm films" released in 1984 (including *Places in the Heart* and *Country*). ★★ DVD: $14.99

River of No Return

(1954, 91 min, US, Otto Preminger) *Robert Mitchum, Marilyn Monroe, Rory Calhoun, Tommy Rettig.* A big, sprawling western (shot in Cinemascope, which means some of the spectacular cinematography will be lost on the small screen) with Mitchum as a farmer who is double-crossed by gambler Calhoun and sets out, with his young son and saloon singer Monroe, to even the score. There's explosive chemistry between Marilyn and Mitchum which propels the film well beyond the usual western adventure. ★★★ DVD: $14.99, VHS: $6.99

R

The River Rat

(1984, 93 min, US, Tom Rickman) *Tommy Lee Jones, Martha Plimpton, Brian Dennehy.* A semi-involving, if not completely successful tale of a wrongly convicted man (Jones) paroled from prison attempting to establish a relationship with the daughter (Plimpton) he's never known. Jones and Plimpton give solid performances, but the film strays off into a subplot about a hidden fortune and an evil prison psychiatrist (Dennehy) which is never as gripping as the genuine moments between father and daughter. ★★½ VHS: $14.99

A River Runs Through It

(1992, 123 min, US, Robert Redford) *Brad Pitt, Craig Sheffer, Tom Skerritt, Emily Lloyd, Brenda Blethyn.* A meticulous and beautifully rendered adaptation of Norman MacLean's autobiographical novella, with a romanticized view of aw-shucks country living and astonishing picturesque backdrops. The story follows the relationship between young MacLean (Sheffer), a straight-laced scholar and his wilder, younger brother, Paul (Pitt). Though opposites in temperament, it is their reverence for fly-fishing which bonds them. As Norman travels to the East to attend college, Paul stays behind in Montana and lives the life of a boozing, cynical journalist. As the brothers are reuinted, MacLean's text is movingly realized: "It is those we live with and love and should know who elude us." Pitt's star-making performance anchors the film. ★★★½ DVD: $14.99, VHS: $9.99

The River Wild

(1994, 108 min, US, Curtis Hanson) *Meryl Streep, Kevin Bacon, David Strathairn, John C. Reilly, Joseph Mazzello.* Streep tackles the action adventure movie with often rip-roaring results. Streep, husband Strathairn and young son Mazzello go on a white water rafting vacation. Unbeknowst to any of them, neighboring rafter Bacon and his companions are actually escaped criminals on a getaway. And when the latter's guide "unexplainedly" vanishes, Streep and family are ultimately terrorized into helping with their escape. Hanson keeps the film afloat with hair-raising action scenes, most of which have Streep doing her own stunts. Her performance propels the film, making it easy to gloss over any inconsistencies. Bacon makes a most effective heavy. ★★★ DVD Letterbox: $14.99, DVD DTS sound: $14.99, VHS: $9.99, VHS Letterbox: $14.99

River's Edge

(1986, 99 min, US, Tim Hunter) *Keanu Reeves, Ione Skye, Crispin Glover, Dennis Hopper, Daniel Roebuck.* A perfect counterpoint to Rob Reiner's *Stand by Me*, released the same year, *River's Edge* is the disturbing story of a group of burned-out '80s teens who find the body of a friend killed by a classmate, greeting the discovery with a lack of emotion or concern. A gripping story of youthful alienation and hopelessness. Hopper is effective as a half-crazed ex-biker and, interestingly, is the film's moral center. Based on an actual incident. ★★★ DVD: $14.99, VHS: $14.99

Road Games

(1982, 100 min, Australia, Richard Franklin) *Stacy Keach, Jamie Lee Curtis.* This early entry from the director of *Psycho II* deals with an Aussie psycho-killer and the trucker (Keach) who sets out to bring him in. Curtis is a hitchhiker who finds herself in the middle of this "road game." Director Franklin, who at one time studied under Alfred Hitchcock, tries hard to deliver the same shocks and is not entirely unsuccessful. All in all, a decent thriller. ★★½

The Road Home

(1999, 89 min, China, Zhang Yimou) *Zhang Ziyi, Honglei Sun, Hao Zheng.* His father's death brings a young man home from the city to the small village of his birth. His journey is a catalyst for memory, as he recalls oft-told stories of his parents' initial meeting, when his father came from the city decades earlier to become the village schoolteacher. Through unwanted separations resulting from the political upheavals of the time, his parents' courtship lasts several years, taxing but never breaking their commitment. His mother's profound grief and her insistence on following traditional burial rites highlight the generational distance between mother and son. Lyrcial and tender, *The Road Home* is a deceptively simple story; one of two people inextricably bound together in the face of massive historical forces and thousand-year-old traditions, who seem to unite solely through a force of will. (Mandarin wih English subtitles) ★★★½ DVD: $29.99, VHS: $14.99

Road House

(1948, 95 min, US, Jean Negulesco) *Richard Widmark, Ida Lupino, Cornel Wilde.* A torrid melodrama with Widmark and Wilde as partners in a roadside bar who begin feuding when Widmark hires alluring singer Lupino, only to have her fall in love with Wilde. From there, passions and jealousies erupt, leading to betrayal and murder. A solid noir rife with sexual tension, and featuring a slam-bang ending. Lupino is terrific as the raspy-voiced entertainer. ★★★½ VHS: $19.99

Road House

(1989, 114 min, US, Rowdy Herrington) *Patrick Swayze, Ben Gazzara, Sam Elliott, Kelly Lynch, Kevin Tighe, John Doe, Kathleen Wilhoite.* Swayze plays a tough philosopher who takes a job as a bouncer at a rough 'n' tumble Midwest bar; he comes in conflict with crooked Gazzara. About as dramatically plausible as a philosophy major who doubles as a bouncer, and given to random violence which most assuredly would have upset its hero under any other circumstances. ★ DVD Dual: $14.99, VHS: $9.99

Road Scholar

(1993, 75 min, US, Roger Wesberg) *Andrei Codrescu.* A definite must-see for lovers of Romanian-born poet Codrescu's National Public Radio commentaries. Part documentary, part flight of fancy, the film is basically an extended series of observations by Codrescu on American culture as he motors in a huge Cadillac convertible across the country. First, he has to learn how to drive, an amusing episode in itself. On his journey across the continent, Codrescu finds an assortment of oddballs to interview including New Age "channelers," Las Vegas wedding vendors and the inhabitants of Biosphere Two, among others. ★★★

The Road to El Dorado

(2000, 89 min, US, Bibo Bergeron, Don Paul, Will Finn) *Voices of: Kevin Kline, Kenneth Branagh, Armand Assante, Edward James Olmos, Rosie Perez.* The appropriately titled *Road to El Dorado* (Hope and Crosby would have felt right at home in this wacky musical comedy) is a delightful animated buddy movie. Kline and Branagh supply the voices for a couple of partners-in-crime, who search for the fabled lost city of gold. After all, they have the map. They find adventure, silly shenanigans, and Dorothy Lamour . . . no, make that a feisty village girl (voiced by Perez).

The animation is first-rate, the jokes funny, though the songs are kinda forgettable. ★★★ DVD: $19.99, VHS: $9.99

Road to Morocco

(1942, 83 min, US, David Butler) *Bob Hope, Bing Crosby, Dorothy Lamour, Anthony Quinn.* "We're off on the road to Morocco" Bing and Bob sing as they gallop across the desert on camelback. It's more hilarious one-liners, funny sight gags and sticky situations as Bing sells Bob to a slave trader for a good meal, and both adore Lamour. Second only to *Road to Utopia* (which was next in the series) in the laughs department. ★★★ DVD: $14.99, VHS: $9.99

Road to Perdition

(2002, 116 min, US, Sam Mendes) *Tom Hanks, Paul Newman, Jude Law, Jennifer Jason Leigh, Tyler Hoechlin, Stanley Tucci, Daniel Craig, Dylan Baker.* The sins of the father needn't be visited upon the son, but as illustrated in director Mendes' brilliant follow-up to *American Beauty*, there is an inordinately high price to insure such an outcome. This is, at least, what young Michael Sullivan, Jr. can deduce after the brutal series of events that he and his father experience in a Depression-era Midwest. Hanks is extraordinary as Michael Sr., a low-keyed though accomplished hit man for the Irish mob. More of a son to John Rooney (Newman in an outstanding portrayal), the local boss, than Rooney's own, troubled offspring Connor (Craig), Michael soon finds himself and his own son in peril when the boy witnesses a gangland execution. Thus begins Sullivan's travels to save his son and redeem himself in the process. Not an easy task, as Sullivan must match wits with an expert assassin (a terrific Law) hired to eliminate them both. Mendes has crafted a powerful story of loyalty, conflict and revenge, performed by an ensemble that is in total synchronization with the director's measured pacing and superior evocation. Based on a graphic novel by Max Allan Collins and Richard Piers Rayner, *Road to Perdition* is smart, intense filmmaking, and reminds us that there can be more to a father's legacy than just wealth or wisdom — sometimes it can be the gift of life itself. ★★★★ DVD DTS sound: $19.99, VHS: $9.99

Tom Hanks in *Road to Perdition*

R

Road to Rio

(1947, 100 min, US, Norman Z. McLeod) *Bob Hope, Bing Crosby, Dorothy Lamour, The Andrews Sisters, Gale Sondergaard.* One of the funnier Hope-Crosby-Lamour "Road" pictures, with the boys as stowaways arriving in Rio, forming an "authentic" American jazz band, and helping Dorothy escape the influence of her evil aunt. (Sequel: *Road to Bali*) ★★★ VHS: $14.99

Road to Utopia

(1945, 90 min, US, Hal Walker) *Bob Hope, Bing Crosby, Dorothy Lamour, Robert Benchley.* A nonstop barrage of hilarity, *Utopia* is probably the best of the seven "Road" pictures. Hope, Crosby and Lamour are off on the road to Alaska in search of gold and romance. What they find are outlaws, talking fish, scheming showgirls and lots of snow. The plot of Bob and Bing helping Dorothy retrieve her stolen gold mine plays a back seat to the crazy collection of one-liners, impersonations, schtick and in-jokes. (Sequel: *Road to Rio*) ★★★½ DVD: $14.99

The Road to Wellville

(1994, 120 min, US, Alan Parker) *Anthony Hopkins, Matthew Broderick, Bridget Fonda, John Cusack, Dana Carvey, Colm Meaney.* Part Bugs Bunny and part John Huston, Hopkins stars as Dr. John Harvey Kellogg, he of the cereal fame who later in life ran the spa/hospital Battle Creek Sanitorium. Kellogg's principles were based on the philosophy of "no meat and no sex," and that the key to good health lies in the constant cleansing of the bowels. With this premise, director Parker takes an outrageous journey down the halls of the sanitorium, where enemas both become a part of the daily routine and form the core of the humor of the film, whose cheap flatulation jokes become redundant. It's a shame an engaging cast is forced to make personal hygiene funny. ★★

Road Trip

(2000, 94 min, US, Todd Phillips) *Breckin Meyer, Seann William Scott, Amy Smart, Tom Green, Paulo Costanzo, Anthony Rapp, Fred Ward, DJ Qualls, Andy Dick.* Executive producer Ivan Reitman revisits his *Animal House* formula over two decades later and, darned, if it doesn't still work. Combining the gross with the sweet, Phillips directs a group of dormmates who set off from New York to Texas on the most important mission of their lives: to retrieve a sex tape mistakenly sent to one of their girlfriends. Green holds down the fort at the dorm with such amiable schtick as tasting a mouse before feeding it to a pet snake. But he can't steal the show from the winning cast and their bizarre adventures — that task goes to scrawny and pasty Qualls, who goes from nerd to hero when he learns to let loose. *Road Trip* is no classic, but it's sure to emerge from the gross-out renaissance's ashes unscathed. ★★★ DVD Unrated: $19.99

The Road Warrior

(1982, 94 min, Australia, George Miller) *Mel Gibson, Bruce Spence, Kjell Nilsson.* He roams the barren plains of a post-apocalyptic wasteland, a tight-lipped, leather clad loner, living only for the ever-precious petrol. Gibson writes the book on existential cool in Miller's violent vision of a fuelless future. Suspenseful throughout, this boasts great action sequences and a stunning, futuristic look. (Sequel: *Mad Max Beyond Thunderdome*) ★★★½ DVD: $14.99, VHS Special Edition: $9.99, VHS Letterbox Special Edition: $9.99

Roadracers

(1994, 93 min, US, Robert Rodriguez) *David Arquette, Salma Hayek, William Sadler, Jason Wiles.* Quirky to the extreme, this made-for-cable movie was part of a series of remakes of vintage AIP exploitation movies. Director Rodriguez is obviously right at home in the genre, and he revels in having a rocking good time. A young punk (Arquette) feels out of place in his small town life. Onto the scene comes a local tough guy who has it in for our hero. Rodriguez throws in enough twists to make the film transcend its cable and genre limitations, and his signature mobile camerawork helps to keep things lively. ★★★ VHS: $9.99

Roads to the South

(1978, 100 min, France, Joseph Losey) *Yves Montand, Miou-Miou.* With cool directorial elegance and subtle perception, Losey creates a complex portrait of a man grappling with deep personal conflicts. Montand plays an exiled Spanish revolutionary who, after establishing himself as a successful screenwriter abroad, returns to his homeland to fight Fascism; but instead he's forced to deal with a lifetime of personal deceptions, illusions and hypocrisies. (French with English subtitles) ★★★ VHS: $29.99

Roadside Prophets

(1992, 96 min, US, Abbe Wool) *John Doe, Adam Horovitz, John Cusack, Arlo Guthrie, David Carradine, Timothy Leary.* Wool's directorial debut is a disappointing attempt at '90s hip. Doe teams with Horovitz for this story of two reluctant heroes without a clear destination. Set against the motorcycle subculture and the lure of the open road, the film tries to blend the idealism of the '60s with the unanswered promises of the '90s. In their travels, the protagonists encounter assorted visionaries, freaks and philosophers. With no memorable dramatics, *Roadside Prophets* at least features a great soundtrack. ★½

The Roaring Twenties

(1939, 106 min, US, Raoul Walsh) *James Cagney, Humphrey Bogart, Jeffrey Lynn, Priscilla Lane.* Cagney stars as a WWI veteran who returns home to New York, becoming an underworld kingpin.

The Road Warrior

Bogart and Lynn are Cagney's war buddies who become his associates. One of the last of the great Warner Brothers gangster films. ★★★½

Rob Roy

(1995, 139 min, GB, Michael Caton-Jones) *Liam Neeson, Jessica Lange, Tim Roth, John Hurt, Eric Stoltz.* Neeson dons the historical kilt of 18th-century Scottish hero Robert Roy MacGregor. And, though the film suggested by his life lacks a particular warmth and narrative strength, *Rob Roy's* skirt lifts Neeson like a glove. As the almost saint-like leader of the Clan MacGregor, Rob Roy must rescue hearth and home from the nefarious clutches of the British, represented here by dishonest nobleman Hurt and the scene-stealing Roth as a dastardly dandy. Director Caton-Jones displays a flair for evocation and inducing richly textured performances from his cast, though the film's screenplay is in need of the necessary swash that generally makes these adventures so enduring. ★★½ DVD: $14.99

The Robe

(1953, 135 min, US, Henry Koster) *Richard Burton, Victor Mature, Jean Simmons, Michael Rennie.* Extravagant, if over-produced, biblical epic with Burton as a Roman guard overseeing Christ's Crucifixion who becomes haunted by his deed. The first Cinemascope film. ★★½ DVD Letterbox: $14.99, VHS: $6.99, VHS Letterbox: $9.99

Robert et Robert

(1979, 105 min, France, Claude Lelouch) *Charles Denner, Jacques Villeret, Jean-Claude Brialy.* Lelouch's humorous, affecting portrait of two lonely men: a middle-aged, hot-headed cab driver, and a bumbling rookie patrolman. Stood up at a dating service, they quickly develop a fast relationship. (French with English subtitles) ★★★

Roberta

(1935, 105 min, US, William A. Seiter) *Irene Dunne, Fred Astaire, Ginger Rogers, Lucille Ball, Randolph Scott.* Jerome Kern-Otto Harbach musical with Dunne as a young heiress, Astaire as a band leader, and Rogers masquerading as a countess. The story, to be honest, is fluffy even by '30s standards, but the sublime teaming of Astaire and Rogers elevates it — giving it a degree of unexpected charm. Songs include "Smoke Gets in Your Eyes" and "I Won't Dance." ★★★

Robin and Marian

(1976, 112 min, GB, Richard Lester) *Sean Connery, Audrey Hepburn, Robert Shaw, Ian Holm, Richard Harris, Nicol Williamson, Denholm Elliott.* A genuinely touching and affecting love story which offers a revisionist view of medieval history and our legendary friends from Sherwood Forest. Connery and Hepburn are a magical pairing as the aging Robin Hood and Maid Marian in this telling of Robin's return to Sherwood after years of exile. ★★★ VHS: $14.99

Robin and the 7 Hoods

(1964, 123 min, US, Gordon Douglas) *Frank Sinatra, Dean Martin, Bing Crosby, Sammy Davis, Jr., Peter Falk, Edward G. Robinson.* The Rat Pack is back (in their final outing) in this fairly entertaining comic romp about 1920s Chicago hoods. ★★½ DVD Letterbox: $19.99

Robin Hood

(1973, 83 min, US, Wolfgang Reitherman) *Voices of: Brian Bedford, Pat Buttram, Andy Devine, Phil Harris, Terry-Thomas, Peter Ustinov.* Walt Disney's animated version of the Robin Hood legend, with the Bandit of Sherwood Forest as a cunning fox. Cute and well done. ★★★ DVD: $29.99, VHS: $22.99

Robin Hood

(1991, 104 min, US, John Irvin) *Patrick Bergin, Jürgen Prochnow, Jeroen Crabbe, Edward Fox, Uma Thurman.* Swashbuckling adventure with one of 1991's "Robin Hood" adaptations. In this version, Bergin plays the nobleman-turned-outlaw who robs from the rich and gives to the poor. Exciting and darker than previous versions. ★★★ DVD: $14.99

Robin Hood: Men in Tights

(1993, 103 min, US, Mel Brooks) *Cary Elwes, Richard Lewis, Roger Rees, Amy Yasbeck, Tracey Ullman, Mel Brooks, Dom DeLuise, Isaac Hayes.* The once brilliant Brooks provides further proof that his comedic well ran dry long ago with this inane skewering of the legend of Sherwood Forest. Despite rolling out a barrel of half-decent one-liners and sight gags, the film clumsily plods from joke to joke, with very little of interest in between. Elwes does his jolly best to add a spark as Robin of Loxley, but he generally hams things up beyond all proportion. ★★

Robin Hood: Prince of Thieves

(1991, 145 min, US, Kevin Reynolds) *Kevin Costner, Alan Rickman, Morgan Freeman, Mary Elizabeth Mastrantonio, Christian Slater.* A big-hearted retelling of the Robin Hood legend with a whole new story to convey. Costner is the new Robin, lacking the accent and sophistication we have all come to expect of the Bandit of Sherwood Forest, but compelling nonetheless. The story pits Robin against the evil Sheriff of Nottingham, who attempts to seize control of the throne of England in King Richard's absence. Rickman gives a hysterical, over-the-top portrayal of the Sheriff — he takes a role which Basil Rathbone had owned for nearly six decades and creates an equally memorable, singular villain. ★★★ DVD Letterbox: $19.99, DVD 2-disc Special Edition: $26.99, VHS: $6.99, VHS Letterbox: $6.99

Robocop

(1987, 103 min, US, Paul Verhoeven) *Peter Weller, Nancy Allen, Dan O'Herlihy, Ronny Cox, Kurtwood Smith, Miguel Ferrer.* When officer Murphy (Weller) of the Detroit Police Department (its services now subcontracted out to a large, faceless conglomerate) is brutally executed in the line of duty, his brain and other body bits become the unwitting components for a new kind of law enforcement robot. Director Verhoeven marshals an exciting array of stunning special effects, exciting action sequences and a razor sharp wit in delivering this scathingly funny, yet nightmarishly believable, parable of corporate capitalism run amok. (Followed by 2 sequels) ★★★½ DVD Letterbox: $14.99

Robocop 2

(1990, 118 min, US, Irvin Kershner) *Peter Weller, Nancy Allen, Dan O'Herlihy.* This follow-up to Verhoeven's brilliant original lacks the insightful political commentary and wit of the first film. On top of that, the film is excessively

Sean Connery in *The Rock*

violent — to the point of mean-spiritedness. The special effects are excellent, particularly the animated face of the villainous Robocop 2, and the action moves at a spirited pace. ★★ DVD: $14.99, VHS: $9.99

Robocop 3

(1993, 95 min, US, Fred Dekker) *Robert Burke, Nancy Allen, Rip Torn, CCH Pounder.* It's "half-man/half-machine" and all drivel in this rusty retread about the cyborg cop caught in the crossfire between a militaristic police force, a renegade group of freedom fighters and a ninja! The creaky screenplay (copenned by the director and comic book scribe Frank Miller) could have used a stiff injection of WD40 oil. ★½ DVD: $14.99

Robot Monster

(1953, 63 min, US, Phil Tucker) *George Nader, Claudia Barrett.* Notoriously bad sci-fi horror film. This is the one where the monster has a diving helmet head and a gorilla-suit body. P.U. ★ DVD: $14.99

Rocco and His Brothers

(1960, 180 min, Italy, Luchino Visconti) *Alain Delon, Renato Salvatori, Claudia Cardinale, Annie Girardot, Katina Paxinou.* An epic tale of five peasant brothers and their widowed mother who migrate from the impoverished south to northern Italy only to find their dreams of happiness shattered when they confront the mean streets of industrial Milan. This neorealist melodrama chronicles the family's struggle in their new world. Told in four episodes, the story centers on Rocco (Delon), the gentle and withdrawn brother who tragically falls in love with Nadia (Girardot), the girlfriend of his thuggish boxer brother. The escalating tensions between the two, fueled by the repressions and frustrations of an unfeeling land, build to a climax of rape and murder. A powerful operatic drama about opposing cultures, lust, greed and the will to survive. (Italian with English subtitles) ★★★½ DVD Letterbox: $29.99

The Rock

(1996, 131 min, US, Michael Bay) *Sean Connery, Nicolas Cage, Ed Harris, Michael Biehn, John C. McGinley, Bokeem Woodbine, William Forsythe, David Morse.* Connery helps agent Cage break in to Alcatraz and in doing so helps create a cracking good, crackerjack action thriller — plot holes and all. When military man Harris takes control of the defunct prison — holding hostages and threatening nuclear attacks on the city of San Francisco — FBI agent Cage enlists the help of longtime con Connery, who's the only man ever to have escaped from the notorious prison. *The Rock* has humor, suspense and the good sense to give its three very personable stars the text and breathing room to do what they do best. ★★★ DVD: $19.99, DVD Criterion Collection: $39.99, VHS: $9.99, VHS Letterbox: $9.99

Rock Baby, Rock It

(1957, 80 min, US, Murray Douglas Sporup) *Kay Wheeler, John Carroll.* All the cool cats and slick chicks band together to save their local rock club from the mob. The ludicrous script is equalled by appalling performances and shoddy direction, though it certainly does qualify as top-of-the-list late-nite cult status. ★ VHS: $9.99

Rock Hudson's Home Movies

(1992, 63 min, US, Mark Rappaport) *Eric Farr, Rock Hudson.* Often hilarious, highly original and utterly convincing, this revisionist interpretation of Rock Hudson's film career and life seeks to discover the "real" Hudson through his "reel" persona. Was this Hollywood hunk completely out of touch with his secreted sexuality, or did he throughout his career offer subtle — or not so subtle — hints at his homosexuality. Exploring this idea, Rappaport's insightful and unconventional biography cleverly dissects — through freeze-frame, slo-mo and replays — Hudson's films, seeking clues and overtly gay signals. ★★★ DVD: $29.99, VHS: $29.99

Rock 'N Roll High School

(1979, 87 min, US, Allan Arkush) *P.J. Soles, Vincent Van Patten, The Ramones, Clint Howard, Paul Bartel, Mary Woronov.* 1970s jail-bait beauty P.J. Soles is the blonde student who wants to have the straggly punk band The Ramones play at their high school dance. But uptight authorities will hear nothing of it. What to do? Invite them anyway, listen to wild music and see the students go berserk and burn the school down! Kids just wanna have fun. A late night treat. ★★★ DVD Special Edition: $14.99, VHS Special Edition: $9.99

Rock Star

(2001, 105 min, US, Stephen Herek) *Mark Wahlberg, Jennifer Aniston, Jason Flemyng, Timothy Olyphant, Timothy Spall, Dominic West.* Wahlberg plays Chris Cole, a Pittsburgh copy machine repairman who moonlights as the lead singer in a "tribute band" to his favorite headbanging group, Steel Dragon. Fate is on his side when fate idols spot Chris in a video and want him to replace the lead singer they just dumped. What follows is a dream come true: headlining his favorite band on tour. Loosely based on the true story of Tim "Ripper" Owens, who replaced Judas Priest lead singer Rob Halford, *Rock Star* is a harmless, unremarkable morality tale that isn't as bad as it is mundane. Occasionally amusing in a most superficial way, the film runs into trouble when it tries to teach us a lesson about what's important. Yawn. Wahlberg tries his best, but can't overcome the one-note screenplay. ★★ DVD: $14.99, VHS: $9.99

R

Rocket Gilbraltar

(1988, 100 min, US, Daniel Petrie) *Burt Lancaster, Macaulay Culkin, Suzy Amis, John Glover, Bill Pullman, Kevin Spacey.* Lancaster's commanding presence distinguishes this moving tale about a family coming together to celebrate their dying patriarch's birthday. The film focuses on his special relationship with his young grandchildren who help him realize his last wish. Culkin makes a good impression as one of Lancaster's grandkids. ★★★ DVD: $19.99, VHS: $9.99

The Rocketeer

(1991, 108 min, US, Joe Johnston) *Bill Campbell, Timothy Dalton, Jennifer Connelly, Alan Arkin.* Some great special effects highlight this lightweight though enjoyable family adventure. Set in 1930s Hollywood, the story follows the beginnings of a comic book-like hero, The Rocketeer, who helps fight off the Nazis in Los Angeles (yes, they were there, too). Dalton seems to be having the most fun, playing a Hollywood superstar and Nazi spy, clearly patterned after Errol Flynn. Though the flying sequences are excellent, the script is no more than an ordinary good guys vs. bad guys scenario. Based on Dave Steven's '80s comic book. ★★½ DVD: $14.99, VHS: $9.99

Rocketship X-M

(1950, 77 min, US, Kurt Neuman) *Lloyd Bridges, Hugh O'Brien.* Even though Irving Block was only trying to capitalize on George Pal's publicity for *Destination Moon, Rocket Ship X-M,* while no match for *Moon,* holds up quite well as the Saturday matinee programmer it was intended to be. Bridges and O'Brien are the astronauts headed for the moon who accidentally overshoot it and end up on Mars, partying with the radiation mutants. ★★½ DVD: $14.99, VHS: $19.99

The Rocking Horse Winner

(1950, 91 min, GB, Anthony Pelissier) *John Mills, Valerie Hobson, John Howard Davies.* Moody though very successful adaptation of the D.H. Lawrence fable about a young boy who discovers that he can predict the winners of horse races by riding his rocking horse. ★★★½ DVD: $39.99

Rocky

(1976, 119 min, US, John G. Avildsen) *Sylvester Stallone, Talia Shire, Burgess Meredith, Carl Weathers, Burt Young.* Sequels aside, let us not forget that this Oscar-winning, Capra-esque boxing drama is quite good, and introduced Stallone to a wide audience, not to mention his popular creation: South Philly boxer Rocky Balboa. Rocky goes after the title against champion Apollo Creed (Weathers); he's aided by trainer Meredith. Shire is quite good as Stallone's plain-Jane girlfriend. (Followed by 4 sequels) ★★★½ DVD Special Edition: $14.99

Rocky II

(1979, 119 min, US, Sylvester Stallone) *Sylvester Stallone, Talia Shire, Burgess Meredith, Burt Young, Carl Weathers.* Stallone returns as Rocky Balboa in this sequel to the Oscar-winning original. Rocky goes after yet another championship. Nothing new here, and not nearly as good as the first film. Though the film shows a new route to get from the Spectrum to a South Philadelphia hospital which should amuse locals. ★★

Rocky III

(1982, 99 min, US, Sylvester Stallone) *Sylvester Stallone, Talia Shite, Burt Young, Carl Weathers, Burgess Meredith, Mr. T.* Rocky now takes on Mr. T in the third *Rocky* film. Here he's under the tutelege of former opponent Weathers — whatever happened to old Meredith, you may ask (we won't tell). ★★

Rocky IV

(1985, 91 min, US, Sylvester Stallone) *Sylvester Stallone, Talia Shire, Dolph Lundgren, Brigitte Nielsen.* The fourth in the series, and probably the most ludicrous. Stallone wraps himself in the flag as Rocky takes on a Russian superhuman competitor (played by Lundgren). ★

Rocky V

(1990, 103 min, US, John G. Avildsen) *Sylvester Stallone, Talia Shire, Sage Stallone, Tom Morrison.* Stallone stars with his own son Sage in this story pitting Rocky, now punch-drunk, penniless and back in his South Philly beginnings, against his former, youthful protégé, whom Rocky had been training. Shire returns, yet again, as Mrs. Rocky. ★★

The Rocky Horror Picture Show

(1975, 95 min, GB, Jim Sharman) *Tim Curry, Susan Sarandon, Barry Bostwick, Meat Loaf, Little Nell, Patricia Quinn, Richard O'Brien.* "Come up to the lab, and see what's on the slab." In the cult-midnight show attraction, scientist, alien and bisexual transvestite Dr. Frank N. Furter is visited by average Americans Brad and Janet; the latter two giving themselves over to "absolute pleasure." A wacked-out, spoofy, goofy, hip and campy one-of-a-kind musical. Curry is the Doc, with Sarandon as Janet, Bostwick as Brad, and writer/lyricist/composer O'Brien as the hunchback valet Riff-Raff. Based on the British stage musical. (Sequel: *Shock Treatment*) ★★★½ DVD Letterbox: $19.99, VHS: $9.99

Rodan

(1957, 70 min, Japan, Inoshiro Honda) This cousin to *Godzilla* is filled with the usual images of crumbling cities, people running and screaming, and out-of-synch dubbing. As such, it's a very entertaining post-war atomic paranoia fest featuring a giant pterodactyl who, after being hatched from an egg, dines on giant bugs in a mine, causing amazing amounts of destruction and more. ★★★

Roe vs. Wade

(1989, 100 min, US, Gregory Hoblit) *Holly Hunter, Amy Madigan, Terry O'Quinn, Kathy Bates.* Two moving performances by Hunter and Madigan highlight this absorbing made-for-TV drama about the controversial Supreme Court battle concerning a woman's right to abortion, and the events which led to the historic decision. ★★★ VHS: $14.99

Roger & Me

(1989, 90 min, US, Michael Moore) Moore's hilarious "documentary" about the relationship between General Motors and the people of his hometown, Flint, Michigan, and the subsequent slow death of that town, is a highly personal statement of frustration in the face of the unyielding greed of America's megacorporations. The theme which ties the film together is Moore's relentless effort to get an interview with Roger Smith, the chairman of G.M. Along the way he settles for the townsfolk, assorted "native" celebrities like Bob Eubanks and other players in the plant closing game, many of whom provide mockeries of themselves or the situation in general. The film is rounded by Moore's narration, which he delivers in an unerring deadpan and adds all the more comic spice to the brew. ★★★★ DVD: $19.99, VHS: $14.99

Roger Dodger

(2002, 104 min, US, Dylan Kidd) *Campbell Scott, Jesse Eisenberg, Isabella Rossellini, Elizabeth Berkley, Jennifer Beals.* Roger Swanson (Scott) is quite a talker. Able to pull anyone into his web with crafty conversation and analysis, people will listen to him spout off about anything. They'll even stick around a bit to let him debase them in public. When Roger (nicknamed "Roger Dodger" for his ability to talk his way out of difficult situations) finds a relationship ending that words can't save, he reaches his lowest and most vulnerable state. Enter his nephew Nick (Eisenberg) for a surprise visit, seeking girl advice from the uncle he admires. What follows is a caustic journey through Manhattan hangouts with a

The Rocky Horror Picture Show — "Come up to the lab and see what's on the slab. . ."

newly broken-hearted Roger teaching his nephew the sultry ways of women. Scott gives the most complex performance of his career and newcomer Eisenberg plays Nick with such natural grace that we feel his adolescent frustrations as if they were our own. A film that is constantly revealing new layers, *Roger Dodger* peels away the surface of chauvinism to expose the pained feelings beneath. ★★★ DVD Letterbox: $14.99, VHS: $59.99

Rollerball

(1975, 123 min, US, Norman Jewison) *James Caan, Maud Adams, Ralph Richardson, Moses Gunn.* Slick though violent and empty-headed sci-fi adventure, set in the 21st century, where man has eliminated crime, pollution and other social ills. Now, a violent form of entertainment is sought by the masses — a deadly physical contact sport called Rollerball. (Remade in 2002) ★★ DVD: $14.99

Rollerball

(2002, 98 min, US, John McTiernan) *Chris Klein, LL Cool J, Jean Reno, Rebecca Romijn-Stamos.* Words are inadequate when it comes to describing exactly how bad this remake actually is. This could have been fun; the Norman Jewison original had a neat premise, but watered it down with portentous dialogue and glacial pacing. At least it had an effective ending, and the game sequences were good. This disaster waters the premise down even further, making the film a vague, supremely dated statement against greed for TV ratings. How daring! Action fans could have forgiven the lack of substance, the wretched acting, the tired direction, the risible dialogue and maybe even the Cuisinart editing, if the game sequences were enjoyable. They're decidedly not, like everything else associated with this mess. ★ DVD R-Rated: $14.99, VHS R-Rated: $9.99

Rollercoaster

(1977, 119 min, US, James Goldstone) *George Segal, Richard Widmark, Timothy Bottoms, Henry Fonda, Harry Guardino, Susan Strasberg, Helen Hunt.* One of the worst "disaster movies" (and that's saying something), *Rollercoaster* stars Segal as a grumpy cop frustrated by a bland mad bomber (Bottoms), who's rigged explosives in an amusement park. Notable for its rumbling Sensurround, the fact that Hunt hasn't aged since she was a teenager, and extensive product placement for the world's first looping steel coaster, which looks pretty tame today. ★ DVD: $14.99

Roman Holiday

(1953, 119 min, US, William Wyler) *Audrey Hepburn, Gregory Peck, Eddie Albert.* Captivating romantic comedy featuring Hepburn's magical Oscar-winning starring debut. Hepburn plays a princess whose unofficial tour of Rome is aided by newsman Peck, who's after a hot story, but finds romance instead. Hepburn and Peck are simply wonderful together, and Albert ably supports them as Peck's quick-fingered photographer. ★★★★ DVD Special Collector's Edition: $14.99, VHS: $9.99

Roman Scandals

(1933, 92 min, US, Frank Tuttle) *Eddie Cantor, Gloria Stuart, Ruth Etting, Edward Arnold.* One of the unsung heroes of 1930s comedy, Cantor is a delight in this funny musical romp about Cantor finding himself back in Roman times. Busby Berkeley choreographed the dance sequences. ★★★

The Roman Spring of Mrs. Stone

(1961, 104 min, US, Jose Quintero) *Vivien Leigh, Warren Beatty, Lotte Lenya, Bessie Love.* Leigh is Karen Stone, a middle-aged widowed actress who retires and settles in Rome to live in peace and solitude. Through a vulgar procuress (Lenya, in a terrific performance), Mrs. Stone meets a swarthy young stud, Paolo (Beatty). Before long, Mrs. Stone succumbs to the suave gigolo's chicanery, and she soon finds herself losing both her money and her self-respect. Beatty's accent may cause a chuckle or two, but the film, based on a Tennessee Williams novella, does come off, thanks to Leigh's tender portrayal. (Remade in 2003) ★★★

Romance

(1930, 76 min, US, Clarence Brown) *Greta Garbo, Lewis Stone, Gavin Gordon.* Garbo's second talkie is a stagey but compelling romantic melodrama with the diva as an opera star involved in an affair with young clergyman Gordon. Stone is particularly good as Gordon's best friend, who also becomes involved with Garbo. ★★½ VHS: $19.99

Romance

(1999, 98 min, France, Catherine Breillat) *Caroline Trousselard, Sagamore Stévenin, François Berléand, Rocco Siffredi.* Pornography as art, *Romance* is writer-director Breillat's daring, explicit and often remarkable meditation on the division between sex and love. Marie (Trousselard) is a young woman with a handsome boyfriend, Paul (Stevenin), who can not get aroused when she fellates him. While Marie avers that she truly madly deeply loves Paul with all her mind, she insists on having to satisfy her physical needs elsewhere. Embarking on a series of trysts, Marie tries to separate the idea of love from the act of love. While some may find the film pretentious, it does, in fact, pack a wallop. Trousselard gives a full-bodied performance trying to show how Marie's affairs intensify and consume her. (French with English subtitles) ★★★ DVD Unrated (Theatrical Version): $14.99

Romancing the Stone

(1984, 106 min, US, Robert Zemeckis) *Kathleen Turner, Michael Douglas, Danny DeVito, Ron Silver.* Frenetic comic adventure starring Turner as a romance novelist whose fantasies come true when she travels to South America to rescue her kidnapped sister and meets a daring adventurer (Douglas). Though Turner and Douglas play well off each other, Turner's wonderfully comic turn is the core of this entertaining comedy. (Sequel: *The Jewel of the Nile*) ★★★ DVD: $14.99

Romantic Comedy

(1983, 103 min, US, Arthur Hiller) *Dudley Moore, Mary Steenburgen, Frances Sternhagen.* Stilted adaptation of Bernard Slade's play about two playwriting partners who share successes, flops and repressed love. Moore and Steenburgen do their best to carry it off, but in all, marginally romantic and not all that funny. ★★ DVD Letterbox: $14.99

The Romantic Englishwoman

(1975, 115 min, GB, Joseph Losey) *Michael Caine, Glenda Jackson, Helmut Berger, Kate Nelligan.* Caine and Jackson star as a novelist and his wife who invite Berger into their home with the hopes that he will both share their bed and help Caine with his new novel. This elegant and underrated comedy-drama candidly explores many of our modern neuroses. Written by Tom Stoppard and Thomas Wiseman. ★★★½

Romeo and Juliet

(1936, 126 min, US, George Cukor) *Norma Shearer, Leslie Howard, John Barrymore, Basil Rathbone, Edna May Oliver.* Though leads Shearer and Howard are much too old for the parts of star-crossed teenagers Romeo and Juliet, this is nevertheless an excellent screen version of Shakespeare's tragedy. Cukor directs with a sublime understanding of the text and a delicate eye for time and place. Great supporting cast, especially Barrymore as Mercutio. ★★★½ VHS: $19.99

Romeo and Juliet

(1954, 138 min, GB, Renato Castellani) *Laurence Harvey, Susan Shentall, Flora Robson, John Gielgud.* This popular and beautifully filmed version of Shakespeare's tragic tale of star-crossed lovers unfortunately falls victim to to miscasting in the lead roles. Harvey and Shentall, like the 1936 pairing of Norma Shearer and Leslie Howard, are too old for their parts. Nevertheless, they both give admirable performances. The film features sumptuous cinematography, and magically re-creates the atmosphere of Renaissance Verona. ★★★½

Romeo and Juliet

(1968, 138 min, GB, Franco Zeffirelli) *Olivia Hussey, Leonard Whiting, Milo O'Shea, Michael York.* With an eye for romantic detail that is almost unsurpassed in the film industry, director Zeffirelli brings Shakespeare's immortal masterpiece to the screen with a flourish. Hussey and Whiting are youthfully cast as the ill-fated lovers, and O'Shea brings his mature wisdom to this visually ravishing production. ★★★★ DVD Letterbox: $14.99, VHS: $9.99, VHS Letterbox: $9.99

Romeo and Juliet

See: *William Shakespeare's Romeo and Juliet*

Romeo Is Bleeding

(1994, 110 min, US, Peter Medak) *Gary Oldman, Lena Olin, Will Patton, Annabella Sciorra, Juliette Lewis, Roy Scheider.* *Romeo Is Bleeding* has all the right elements: a nifty script about greed, corruption and sex; a grimy film noir feel that's tinged with a hallucinatory edge; a haunting jazz soundtrack; and a great cast that includes the always intriguing Oldman as a crooked cop on the take from the mob, Sciorra as his good wife and Olin as a devil-in-disguise cop killer. Unfortunately, the film lacks an overall cohesiveness as the disparate elements go on their merry way without ever really connecting to each other. Ultimately, *Romeo* leaves one entertained but unsatisfied. ★★½ DVD Letterbox: $14.99

Romeo Must Die

(2000, 115 min, US, Andrzej Bartkowiak) *Jet Li, Aaliyah, Isaiah Washington, Delroy Lindo, Russell Wong, DMX.* Martial arts superstar Li gets his first Hollywood starring vehicle, and, despite some good actions scenes, this convoluted actioner doesn't capture the excitement of his Hong Kong works. Li is a gangster's son who falls for a rival gangster's daughter (Aaliyah) and gets caught up in gangland rivalries on the Oakland docks. Way too long, *Romeo Must Die* is packed with lesser hip hop and R&B music, making it just a trendy time-killer. Li's stuntwork is amazing, but the wirework is obvious and badly used. For die-hard Li fans only. ★½ DVD: $19.99, VHS: $9.99

Romper Stomper

Romper Stomper

(1992, 92 min, Australia, Geoffrey Wright) *Russell Crowe, Jacqueline McKenzie, Daniel Pollock. Romper Stomper* impacts like a smartly landed fist, using the unbridled fury of its protagonists to propel this story of disenfranchised adolescents lost in a squalid urban wasteland, as abandoned as the empty factories in which they squat. The film opens with a horrific gang war scene, as Hando (Crowe) takes his cronies to stomp a group of young Vietnamese in a subway station. The violence is its own reward, getting it as gratifying as giving it. The introduction of a poor little rich girl (McKenzie) into the group, and especially her impact on the relationship between Hando and his lieutenant Davey (Pollock), occupies much of the later story line; but the film will be remembered for the emotional toll it demands of the viewer. A remarkable piece of filmmaking. ★★★ DVD Dual Basic Edition: $14.99

Romy and Michele's High School Reunion

(1997, 91 min, US, David Mirkin) *Mira Sorvino, Lisa Kudrow, Janeane Garofalo, Alan Cumming.* Sorvino and Kudrow go the dumbed-down comedic route as two joined-at-the-hip, totally airheaded, underemployed, fashion-victim space cadets preparing for their tenth anniversary high school reunion. Now living in L.A., they plan their assault on their middle-America home town, hoping to prove to their adolescent nemeses that they are no longer losers. The characters are too broadly drawn and the film too self-consciously sardonic to elicit any real emotional response. It is, however, marginally saved by some warm moments and biting insights. Check out Garofalo in support as the hostile, bitter, intellectual chick. ★★½ DVD: $19.99, VHS: $9.99

La Ronde

(1950, 97 min, France, Max Ophüls) *Anton Walbrook, Simone Signoret, Simone Simon, Danielle Darrieux, Jean-Louis Barrault.* Ophüls directs a stellar group of French actors in this witty, elaborate satire on sexual behavior. Ten sketches are presented, in which an interconnecting group of lovers change partners until their liaisons come full circle. A bemused view of affairs of the heart. (French with English subtitles) ★★★½ VHS: $29.99

Ronin

(1998, 121 min, US, John Frankenheimer) *Robert De Niro, Jean Reno, Natascha McElhone, Stellan Skarsgård, Jonathan Pryce, Sean Bean.* Three intense car chases highlight this thrilling action tale which manages to maintain interest even between all the well-staged automotive mayhem. With a style reminiscent of 1970s adventure films, *Ronin* is a thinking man's thriller about a group of hired mercenaries ("ronin") who come together to steal the suitcase and its highly secret contents of a mysterious attache. There's cross, double-cross and enough high-speed chases through Paris, Nice and the countryside to populate five action films. Director Frankenheimer isn't merely content to let the chases speak for the film, as the relationships between his characters form the real core of *Ronin*. A bristling, unrelenting and smart roller-coaster ride. ★★★½ DVD: $14.99

The Roof

(1956, 98 min, Italy, Vittorio De Sica) *Gabriella Pallotti, Giorgio Listuzzi.* De Sica's realistic and gentle drama follows a poverty-striken young couple who must overcome red tape in trying to find a home and happiness in post-war Rome. (Italian with English subtitles) ★★★

The Rookie

(1990, 121 min, US, Clint Eastwood) *Clint Eastwood, Charlie Sheen, Raul Julia, Sonia Braga.* A formulaic thriller directed by and starring Eastwood about a hardened veteran of the L.A.P.D. who is assigned a rookie partner. Following all of the guidelines for the good cop/bad cop buddy movie, *The Rookie* riddles the screen with bullets, car chases and blazing pyrotechnics. The film enjoys its share of wry, self-effacing humor and the pace is brisk. ★★½ DVD: $19.99, VHS: $14.99

The Rookie

(2002, 127 min, US, John Lee Hancock) *Dennis Quaid, Rachel Griffiths, Brian Cox, Jay Hernandez, Beth Grant.* An inspiring true story, *The Rookie* is the emotionally satisfying, always compelling biography of Jim Morris, a popular Texas schoolteacher/coach and aspiring ballplayer who at the age of 35 realized a lifelong dream and became a major league pitcher. Quaid is excellent as Morris, who tried out for the majors at the insistence of his students. It's an unlikely road Morris travels, but director Hancock makes sure it's always a compelling journey as Morris defies the odds to become the oldest player to make his major league debut. Heartwarming without the sap, *The Rookie* benefits from a stirring story, good storytelling and a first-rate ensemble. ★★★ DVD Letterbox: $19.99, DVD Pan & Scan: $19.99, VHS: $14.99

Rookie of the Year

(1993, 103 min, US, Daniel Stern) *Thomas Ian Nicholas, Gary Busey, Albert Hall, Amy Morton, Daniel Stern.* A delightful baseball comedy for the whole family. When young Nicholas breaks his arm, he discovers he has the newly acquired ability to throw a 90 m.p.h. fastball. Which is good news for his home town team, the struggling Chicago Cubs (this is before the arrival of Sammy Sosa, of course). The youth finds himself thrust into the spotlight, with predictable but good-natured comic results. ★★★ DVD Letterbox: $14.99, VHS: $6.99

Room at the Top

(1959, 115 min, GB, Jack Clayton) *Laurence Harvey, Simone Signoret, Heather Sears, Hermione Baddeley.* This effervescent story about a low-born Brit's ruthless drive to reach the top of the ladder in a northern industrial town is powered by the gutsy performances by Harvey and Signoret (who won an Oscar). An unhappily married French woman falls desperately in love with the determined young man. Considered a far-reaching, seminal work, the use of and attitude towards sex and language paved the way for the ultra-realistic "kitchen sink" school of British drama. ★★★★ DVD: $14.99

Room Service

(1938, 78 min, US, William A. Seiter) *Groucho Marx, Harpo Marx, Chico Marx, Lucille Ball, Ann Miller, Jack Albertson.* Groucho is a struggling producer with a potential hit show on his hands — all he needs is money. Which wouldn't hurt his hotel bill, either. Chico and Harpo add their usual dazzle, and Ball and Miller are the love interests. The film is interesting in that, in addition to the trademark absurdist humor, there are definite indications of Groucho's acting potential, which was never fully utilized by Hollywood. Script by Morrie Ryskind. (Remade in 1944 as a musical, *Step Lively*) (DVD only available in a seven-film pack for $59.99) ★★★ VHS: $19.99

A Room with a View

(1985, 115 min, GB, James Ivory) *Helena Bonham Carter, Julian Sands, Maggie Smith, Denholm Elliott, Daniel Day-Lewis, Judi Dench, Simon Callow, Rupert Graves.* E.M. Forster's classic novel of the sexual awakening of a young woman amidst the emotional repression of Victorian England is brilliantly captured in this comedy of manners. During a trip to Florence, the girl's simmering sensuality is exposed when she meets and falls in love with a free-spirited and handsome young man. The struggle between this love and the expectations of a "proper society" features outstanding performances by the entire ensemble, though Smith and Elliott do steal the show. ★★★★ DVD 2-disc Special Edition: $26.99

R

Roommates

(1995, 109 min, US, Peter Yates) *Peter Falk, D.B. Sweeney, Julianne Moore, Ellen Burstyn, Jan Rubes.* A sweet, old-fashioned though uneven examination of a grandfather and grandson's enduring relationship, *Roommates* gives Falk one his best film roles. He plays Rocky, who at 75 years of age raises his young grandson Michael after the youth loses his parents. Their years together are spent happily until Michael, now an adult (played by Sweeney), is on his own. The two reunite when Rocky is evicted and moves in with his grandson. Much of the comedy stems from their Felix and Oscar shenanigans. But the film also wallows in its unpleasantness, and after a charming first half the story loses its good humor for a succession of tragedies which are clumsily handled. ★★½ DVD: $9.99

Rope

(1948, 80 min, US, Alfred Hitchcock) *James Stewart, Farley Granger, John Dall.* The Master of Suspense's audacious experimentation with real time and ten-minute takes gives this murder-thriller both a kinetic and claustrophobic atmosphere. Suggested by the Leopold-Loeb case, the story concerns two friends (played by Granger and Dall) who murder an old schoolmate for the thrill of it, stuff his corpse in an old chest, and then proceed to hold a party around the makeshift casket with attendees including the victim's father and fiancée. (The Leopold-Loeb story has also been told in *Compulsion* and *Swoon*) ★★★½ DVD: $29.99

Rorret

(1987, 105 min, Italy, Fulvio Wetzl) *Lou Castel, Anna Galiena.* Inspired by the films of Alfred Hitchcock, this creepy thriller centers on a reclusive and voyeuristic owner of a cinema specializing in horror films who goes on a killing rampage whenever he gets "excited" by terror. Although needlessly talky, the film has moments of tension and intrigue with the highlight being the film-within-a-film homages (re-creations) to famous horror sequences from *Peeping Tom, Strangers on a Train, Psycho* and *Dial M for Murder.* (Italian with English subtitles) ★★ VHS: $29.99

La Rosa Blanca

(1960, 100 min, Mexico, Roberto Gavaldon) Based on the controversial novel by B. Traven ("Treasure of the Sierra Madre"), this compelling and impassioned film tells the story of the armed struggle that ensues between the land-thirsty Condor Oil Company and Don Jacinto, owner of the hacienda "La Rosa Blanca," an oil-rich land the company wants to expropriate. Contrasting the peasant's spiritualism and reverence for the land with the malfeasance and greed of the multinational, the film obviously takes sides but is very good drama nonetheless. (Spanish with English subtitles) ★★★

Rosa Luxemburg

(1986, 122 min, Germany, Margarethe von Trotta) *Daniel Olbrychski, Otto Sander, Barbara Sukowa.* Von Trotta has created a mesmerizing epic on the personal and political life of Rosa Luxemburg, one of the most dynamic and passionate leaders of the socialist democracy in Germany. Sukowa gives a truly amazing performance as "Red Rosa," whose life is chronicled from her emergence in the Social Democratic Party to her loss of faith after WWI. A wonderfully produced portrait, the film has a starkness befitting a war picture which is juxtaposed with a realism rare to what are usually overblown period pieces. (German with English subtitles) ★★★★ VHS: $29.99

Rosalie Goes Shopping

(1990, 94 min, US, Percy Adlon) *Marianne Sagebrecht, Brad Davis, Judge Reinhold, Alex Winter.* Director Adlon teams with *Sugarbaby* star Sagebrecht to produce this pleasant but disappointingly thin satire on America's obsession with consumerism. Determined to provide everything "money" can buy for her children and loving husband (Davis), Rosalie, our devoted and increasingly frenetic housewife, soon finds herself juggling 37 credit cards, several mortgage payments and writing out worthless checks. With the wolf soon baying at her comfortable suburban door, our intrepid consumer devises more and more ingenious ways to stay a few steps ahead in her great pursuit of the American Dream. ★★

The Rosary Murders

(1987, 105 min, US, Fred Walton) *Donald Sutherland, Charles Durning, Belinda Bauer.* Slow but interesting tale of a parish priest (Sutherland) who hears the confession of a serial killer preying on priests and nuns, and finds himself torn between his sacred vows and the pursuit of justice. ★★

The Rose

(1979, 134 min, US, Mark Rydell) *Bette Midler, Alan Bates, Frederic Forrest, Harry Dean Stanton, Sylvester, Sandra McCabe, Barry Primus, David Keith, Michael Greer.* Midler makes an impressive film debut as a hard-drinking, fast-living rock chanteuse — suggested by the life of Janis Joplin — struggling against the pressures of success. Bates is her mean-spirited manager and Forrest is her on-again, off-again lover. The film's musical numbers contain a raw energy thanks to the conviction of the Divine Miss M, and her earthy performance avoids the usual industry clichés. ★★★ DVD: $14.99

The Rose Garden

(1989, 152 min, US/West Germany, Fons Rademakers) *Liv Ullmann, Maximilian Schell, Peter Fonda.* This gripping drama, which exposes the latent anti-Semitism in modern-day Germany, stars Ullmann as a tenacious lawyer who is hired to defend a man (Schell) accused of committing a seemingly unprovoked attack on an elderly businessman. As the drama unfolds, Ullmann uncovers the fact that the old man was a commandant of a Nazi concentration camp and presided over the death of many Jews and children. A serious, compassionate psychological drama that features fine performances by both Ullmann and Schell as well as an oddly cast but effective Fonda. (Filmed in English) ★★★ VHS: $79.99

The Rose Tattoo

(1955, 117 min, US, Daniel Mann) *Burt Lancaster, Anna Magnani, Marisa Pavan.* Magnani gives an extraordinary performance in this riveting adaptation of Tennessee Williams' play as a widow, still obsessed with the memory of her late husband, who begins an affair with trucker Lancaster. Magnani won the Oscar for her portrayal, and is matched all the way by Lancaster. ★★★½ DVD Letterbox: $14.99, VHS: $14.99

Roseland

(1977, 103 min, US, James Ivory) *Lilia Skala, Christopher Walken, Joan Copeland, Helen Gallagher, Geraldine Chaplin, Teresa Wright.* Set in the famed New York dance hall, *Roseland* is a collection of three captivating short character vignettes studying the tattered lives of the people who gravitate to the club. Exceptional performances from the cast. ★★★

Rosemary's Baby

(1968, 136 min, US, Roman Polanski) *Mia Farrow, John Cassavetes, Ruth Gordon, Sidney Blackmer, Maurice Evans.* Classic chiller from Polanski with newlyweds Farrow and Cassavetes unwittingly befriending devil worshippers Gordon and Blackmer in modern-day New York. Gordon won an Oscar for her performance, and the film contains many frightening moments. ★★★★ DVD: $14.99, VHS: $9.99

Rosencrantz and Guildenstern Are Dead

(1991, 119 min, GB, Tom Stoppard) *Gary Oldman, Tim Roth, Richard Dreyfuss, Iain Glen.* Adapting and directing his own play for the screen might have been too much for the talented Stoppard, but although the film is a bit stage-bound, it still proves to be an exhilarating mental exercise with Stoppard toying with the English language in this witty, intellectual comedy. The story takes the ingenious ploy of changing the focus of "Hamlet" from the brooding Dane to two minor flunkies, Rosencrantz and Guildenstern. Roth and Oldman are scintillating as the lost and, at times, pathetic duo who are forced by circumstances to pontificate on their seemingly predetermined fate. Though he sometimes can be annoying in certain film roles, Dreyfuss is a delight here as the Player King. All told, an audacious, verbally duelling metaphysical comedy. ★★★½

Mia Farrow and John Cassavetes in *Rosemary's Baby*

Rosetta

(1999, 95 min, France, Jean-Pierre Dardenne & Luc) *Émilie Dequenne, Fabrizio Rongione, Anne Yernaux.* Rosetta is emotion exploded, a driven, angry, obsessive, fiercely independent teenager who can never stop moving in her quest to keep herself and her drunken whore mother no further in the gutter than they've already sunk. The hyperactive pace matches the protagonist's frenetic energy; the camera follows her closely as she attempts to exert some control over her tenuous existence by squirrelling away random objects in bizarre hiding places. She unceasingly seeks normalcy: a job, a friend, a secure roof over her head. Her desperation to get a job leads to a conflict with the one person who has reached out to her, a conflict she is ill-equipped to handle. Dequenne is remarkable, delivering an almost feral performance. This harsh, unrelenting film ends ambiguously, yet is as uniquely satisfying as it is emotionally exhausting. (French with English subtitles) ★★★★

Rosewood

(1997, 139 min, US, John Singleton) *Ving Rhames, Jon Voight, Bruce McGill, Don Cheadle, Michael Rooker, Esther Rolle, Loren Dean.* The story of a real-life tragedy is told with sledgehammer subtlety by director Singleton, who sacrifices ambiguity, character development and moral conflict for the sake of a shallow, easy political statement. Rhames stars as an enigmatic WWI veteran who comes to Rosewood, Florida — a town built and populated almost entirely by black Americans — to buy some land and begin a peaceful life. Instead, a case of mistaken identity brings a mob of angry whites from a neighboring, poorer town to wreak a violent vengeance and retribution on Rosewood. Unfortunately, the film neglects historical drama in favor of crowd-pleasing sentiment and simplicity. Singleton has taken a fascinating, important and tragic story and made a terrible, albeit good-looking movie out of it. ★★ DVD: $14.99, VHS: $9.99, VHS Letterbox: $9.99

Rouge

(1988, 93 min, Hong Kong, Stanley Kwan) With stunning visuals and a great story, this supernatural love story alternates between the brothels and theatres of an opium-hazed 1930s Hong Kong and the sophisticated, bustling world of the present-day city. A courtesan, who died in a love-induced suicide, returns to earth years later seeking out her lover after he fails to join her in Heaven. A terrifically stylish movie. (Cantonese with English subtitles) ★★★½ DVD: $49.99, VHS: $19.99

Rough Magic

(1997, 105 min, GB, Clare Peploe) *Bridget Fonda, Russell Crowe, Jim Broadbent, D. W. Moffett, Kenneth Mars, Paul Rodriguez.* Fonda treads water in this picaresque soufflé from the director of *High Season* about a gold-digging magician's assistant (circa 1950) who skips out on her engagement to a wealthy industrialist. Enter Crowe as the hardboiled gumshoe sent to track her to a small Mexican town where magic, destiny and romance await. Adapted from James Hadley's novel "Miss Shumway Waves a Wand," this charming misfire mixes elements of film noir, romantic adventure and mystical mumbo jumbo with a willing and able cast, but the results are somewhat lackluster and the "love conquers all" resolution feels strained rather than uplifting. ★★ DVD: $19.99, VHS: $19.99

Round Midnight

(1986, 130 min, US/France, Bertrand Tavernier) *Dexter Gordon, Lonette McKee, François Cluzet, Herbie Hancock.* Gordon gives a painfully touching performance as Dale Turner, a raspy-voiced saxophone player ravaged by drugs and booze, but who nonetheless retains his dignity and possesses the "elegant soul of a poet." Tavernier creates a moody and authentic world of American jazz exiles and the habitués of the smokey Parisian jazz clubs of the '50s. Wonderful music performed by Gordon, Herbie Hancock, Ron Carter, Tony Williams and John McLaughlin. ★★★½ DVD: $19.99, VHS: $14.99

The Round Up

(1965, 89 min, Hungary, Miklós Jancsó) *János Görbe, Tibor Molnár.* A Hungarian film masterpiece that paints an unflinching portrait of fear, torture and oppression. Set in the mid-19th century after the establishment of the Austro-Hungarian empire, the camera acts as an unseen observer as several hundred Hungarian peasants, outlaws and herdsmen are rounded up, imprisoned and tortured by the Austrian authorities in an effort to uncover and crush the remaining rebel stronghold. The men are forced to confess and identify other freedom fighters before they themselves are eliminated. A harsh, disturbing chronicle of a demonic police state told with little dialogue and set in a timeless, bleak plain where routine terror reigns. (Hungarian with English subtitles) ★★★★ VHS: $59.99

Rounders

(1998, 102 min, US, John Dahl) *Gretchen Mol, Matt Damon, Edward Norton, John Turturro, Martin Landau, John Malkovich.* Slick and sleazy at the same time, *Rounders* is a testosterone-heavy variation on classic gambling movies *The Cincinnati Kid* and *The Hustler.* Fresh-faced, poker-playing law student Damon comes to the rescue when pal Norton gets out of the slammer carrying heavy debts from seedy underworld types. But Norton keeps playing and losing; leading Damon to a showdown with the hammy Malkovich, playing an Oreo-chomping Russian hood. While the story meanders all over the place, director Dahl finds fas-

cination with his gallery of idiosyncratic characters. Damon, however, is too bland as the lead. Ultimately, the jokers may be wild here, but the main characters aren't wild enough. ★★½ DVD: $19.99, VHS: $9.99

Roustabout

(1964, 100 min, US, John Rich) *Elvis Presley, Barbara Stanwyck, Raquel Welch.* Presley joins the carnival, run by none other than Stanwyck. Look quick for Welch as a college coed. Though not one of Elvis' best, it's kinda cute in that isn't-Elvis-the-living-end sort of way. Elvis sings "Hard Knocks," "It's a Wonderful World" and "Big Love, Big Heartache." ★★½ DVD: $14.99, VHS: $9.99

Route 666

(2001, 90 min, US, William Wesley) *Lou Diamond Phillips, Lori Petty, Steven Williams, L.Q. Jones.* Phillips and Petty must bring mob witness Williams to trial as soon as humanly possible, so they decide to take a shortcut on the closed-down "Route 666," so named because a chain gang was killed there in an accident years ago, and now the road is supposedly haunted. Turns out the rumors are true, and one of the zombie convicts is Phillips' departed dad. Stupid, silly, wholly unscary flick is also kinda fun, more due to the three leads' easy banter and some witty lines than the shaky-cam killings, which are rather tame. Jones brings his usual, appealingly laconic attitude to the film. ★★ DVD: $19.99, VHS: $89.99

Rover Dangerfield

(1991, 74 min, US, Bob Seeley & Jim George) *Rodney Dangerfield.* Dangerfield's entry into the world of animation (he wrote the screenplay and cowrote the songs with Harold Ramis) is surprisingly entertaining and well done. Some jokes will soar over the kids' heads, but they should enjoy the songs and story of the cynical city dog transported to the country, where he finds love and a family. ★★½

Roxanne

(1987, 107 min, US, Fred Schepisi) *Steve Martin, Daryl Hannah, Rick Rossovich, Shelley Duvall, Michael J. Pollard, Damon Wayans.* Martin's comic tour de force performance highlights this breathless-

The Royal Tenenbaums

ly funny updating of "Cyrano de Bergerac." Martin plays a small Northwestern town's fire chief whose elongated nose has kept him from romantic entanglements; that is, until he falls in love with beautiful astronomy student Hannah. Rossovich is the handsome but vacuous hunk — himself terrified of romantic repartee — who speaks Martin's heartfelt words of love. Duvall offers wonderful support as Martin's confidant. Martin's "20 insults" is a classic. (Though Michael Douglas won the Oscar that year for *Wall Street*, Martin's performance was by far and away the year's best.) ★★★½ DVD: $14.99

Royal Deceit

(1997, 85 min, GB, Gabriel Axel) *Gabriel Byrne, Helen Mirren, Christian Bale.* What a waste. An excellent cast, along with a capable director, fail to enliven this D.O.A. version of Hamlet, the mad prince of Denmark (based on the folk tales, not the Shakespeare play). Bale hardly registers as the surprisingly decisive lad who fakes madness upon learning his uncle (a somnambulistic Byrne) has murdered his father. Maddeningly choppy, with all the good parts cut out, *Royal Deceit* plays like a late-night Cinemax version of *Hamlet* with rampant gratuitous nudity, boring dialogue and clunky action that strains to be artsy-retro. ★ DVD: $19.99, VHS: $9.99

The Royal Family

(1977, 112 min, US, Kirk Browning & Ellis Rabb) *Rosemary Harris, Eva Le Gallienne, Ellis Rabb, Sam Levene, Keene Curtis.* Rabb received a Tony Award as Best Director for this effervescent, sublimely witty revival of the 1927 George S. Kaufman-Edna Ferber stage hit that simultaneously pokes fun and pays homage to an eminent and eccentric acting dynasty that's about as close to the Barrymores as you could possibly get. Harris brings great theatricality and grace to the role of Julie Cavendish, a Broadway legend who's flirting with retirement. Director Rabb dons his best John Barrymore as her brother Tony, a stage legend-turned Hollywood matinee idol. A presentation of Great Performances. ★★★★ DVD: $24.99, VHS: $29.99

The Royal Tenenbaums

(2001, 109 min, US, Wes Anderson) *Gene Hackman, Anjelica Huston, Ben Stiller, Gwyneth Paltrow, Luke Wilson, Owen Wilson, Danny Glover, Bill Murray.* Writers Wes Anderson and Owen Wilson return to the narrative and visual style of *Rushmore*, all bright colors and studied compositions, for this clever comic portrait of a most dysfunctional family. Having grown up geniuses, the Tenenbaum kids (Stiller, Paltrow and Luke Wilson) have wilted in adulthood, and find themselves drifting back to the Manhattan mansion of their mother (Huston), as does Huston's separated husband, Royal Tenenbaum (Hackman). There's a surprising amount of pathos at work as the family confronts their failures, simultaneously broadening the scope of Anderson's direction and revealing his limitations. He's most at home with quirky irony, such as the two carbon-copy sons of Stiller's obsessive businessman, or the way that Luke Wilson's retired tennis pro still wears his headband 24/7. Hackman is fiercely funny as the returning patriarch who can only connect with others through emotional maniuplation. ★★★½ DVD Criterion Collection: $29.99, VHS: $9.99

Royal Warriors

(1986, 95 min, Hong Kong, David Chung & Yuen Kwai) *Michelle Yeoh, Henry Sanada, Michael Wong.* Early in her career, Yeoh made a series of films for then-husband Dickson Poon's D & B Films. This is one of the best of them, a vengeance-minded action tale pitting her against a quartet of bad guys, each sworn to avenge the death of his brother. Michelle plays a Hong Kong cop who foils a highjacking attempt aboard a jet, with the help of an airline security agent (Wong) and a vacationing Japanese cop (the awesome Sanada). Once back home, the trio are marked by the remaining pair of killers. With plenty of fight sequences (both gun battles and kung fu bouts) and a killer ending, film is sure to please fans of Yeoh. (Cantonese with English subtitles) ★★★ DVD: $9.99, VHS: $19.99

Royal Wedding

(1951, 93 min, US, Stanley Donen) *Fred Astaire, Jane Powell, Peter Lawford.* Light-hearted musical with Fred and Powell as a famous brother-and-sister act who travel to England to perform their show, coinciding with the marriage of Queen Elizabeth II. (Fred dances on the ceiling in this one.) ★★½ VHS: $19.99

Rubin and Ed

(1991, 90 min, US, Trent Harris) *Howard Hesseman, Crispin Glover, Karen Black.* Ed (Hesseman), a middle-aged, leisure-suited failure at life, must bring a new recruit to his highly charged motivational real estate seminar or face expulsion and the loss of promised riches, self-esteem and inner peace. His search leads him to Rubin (Glover), an oddly dressed malcontent under the thumb of an overbearing mom, who agrees to go to the seminar if Ed will help him bury his dead cat. Hesseman and Glover bounce off each other with just the right amount of manic energy to make this delightfully quirky road-trip saga (a post-Reagan era exploration of the latest wrinkle in the American Dream) an audacious romp. ★★★

Ruby

(1977, 84 min, US, Curtis Harrington) *Piper Laurie, Stuart Whitman.* After her success in *Carrie*, Laurie encored with another horror opus, though with considerable less results. The spirit of a murdered 1930s gangster returns to haunt the descendants of those responsible. A few thrills in this derivative chiller. ★★

Ruby

(1992, 100 min, US, John MacKenzie) *Danny Aiello, Sherilyn Fenn, Arliss Howard.* Aiello stars as Jack Ruby, the Dallas nightclub owner who shot Lee Harvey Oswald, in this intriguing though needlessly complex underworld look at the J.F.K. assassination. Following on the heels of Oliver Stone's *JFK*, *Ruby* details the events leading up to that fateful day in Dallas from Ruby's point of view, all the while portraying him as a small-time gangster who got in over his head. ★★½ DVD: $24.99, VHS: $14.99

Ruby in Paradise

(1993, 115 min, US, Victor Nunez) *Ashley Judd, Todd Field, Bentley Mitchum, Allison Dean, Dorothy Lyman.* Writer-director Nunez presents the simple story of Ruby, a young woman who flees a desolate life in rural Tennessee and settles on the Gulf Coast of Florida. Judd is a revelation as Ruby, who explores who she is while happily working in a tacky seaside gift shop. Her graceful performance is one of subtlety and nuance which, combined with Nunez' gentle direction, elevates what could have

been a run-of-the-mill outing. Despite some minor screenplay contrivances, this is the kind of work that gives independent filmmaking its good name. ★★★½ VHS: $9.99

Rude

(1995, 90 min, Canada, Clément Virgo) *Sharon M. Lewis, Richard Chevolleau, Rachel Crawford.* This hard-hitting independent film delves beneath the surface of problem-plagued inner city life to explore the personal lives of those who are forced to live there. Virgo's feature film debut tells three stories all set on an Easter Sunday and all dealing with personal redemption and the struggle to survive and love in a tough world. The first is about an older black man and former drug dealer attempting to adjust to life after release from prison. The second looks at the loneliness of a young woman who, abandoned by her boyfriend, contemplates an abortion. The third tale follows a handsome young boxer who must face the truth about himself and his own sexuality after participating in a gay-bashing. ★★★ DVD: $9.99, VHS: $9.99

Rude Awakening

(1989, 100 min, US, Aaron Russo & David Greenwalt) *Cheech Marin, Julie Hagerty, Robert Carradine, Buck Henry, Louise Lasser, Cindy Williams, Eric Roberts.* Two hippies in hiding since the 1960s reemerge and find their old friends have become materialistic yuppies. A good premise isn't fully realized in this only occasionally funny comedy. ★★

Rudy

(1993, 112 min, US, David Anspaugh) *Sean Astin, Ned Beatty, Charles S. Dutton, Robert Prosky, Lili Taylor.* From the director of *Hoosiers* comes this likable *Knute Rockne* for the '90s. Nearly pouring on the sentiment as much as its 1940s counterpart, the film stars Astin as Rudy, a mill worker who has dreamed his whole life of entering Notre Dame and playing for their football team. This based-on-fact story follows his attempts to realize both dreams, despite being short in stature and dyslexic. Astin's Rudy eventually wins you over by the end credits. ★★½ DVD Special Edition: $14.99, DVD Deluxe Edition: $24.99, VHS: $9.99

Rudyard Kipling's The Jungle Book

(1994, 108 min, US, Stephen Sommers) *Jason Scott Lee, Cary Elwes, Lena Headey, Sam Neill, John Cleese.* A smashing live-action adaptation of Rudyard Kipling's classic tale, this Disney-produced adventure yarn is one of the most entertaining version of the story to date. A loin-clothed and extremely fit Lee portrays Mowgli, the Indian boy who becomes lost in the jungle and is raised by animals. His carefree existence is shattered when he meets the humans he once knew as a child. Director Sommers blissfully mixes Indian lore and Indiana Jones-type antics, all set against beautifully designed backgrounds of tropics, English pageantry and lost treasure. A high-flying adventure both smart and thrilling. ★★★½ DVD: $19.99, VHS: $9.99

Ruggles of Red Gap

(1935, 92 min, US, Leo McCarey) *Charles Laughton, Charlie Ruggles, Mary Boland, ZaSu Pitts, Roland Young.* Laughton is priceless in this absolutely delightful comedy. He plays a proper English butler who heads to the American West to work for an unconventional family. Ruggles and Boland offer terrific support as his new employers. (Remade as *Fancy Pants*) ★★★★

The Rules of Attraction

(2002, 110 min, US, Roger Avary) *James Van Der Beek, Shannyn Sossamon, Ian Somerhalder, Kip Pardue, Jessica Biel, Thomas Ian Nicholas, Swoosie Kurtz, Faye Dunaway.* Van Der Beek goes a long way to thwart his wholesome TV image (gay sex, masturbating, drugs, you name it), but it's not enough to salvage this undisciplined adaptation of Bret Easton Ellis' novel of campus sexual hijinks. However, much like the book on which it is based, the film disguises lack of substance with a polished sheen. The story takes place at a northeastern university (whose attendees are rich and self absorbed) and focuses on the lives of three students. Van Der Beek's Sean is a drug dealer who lusts after the virginal Lauren (Sossamon) while at the same time teasing bi-boy Paul (Somerhalder). There's not much studying going on, but there is plenty of sex. There's a virtuoso sequence of a European vacation, a truly amazing mise-en-scène, but unfortunately most of the rest of the film lacks its energy and finesse. ★★ DVD: $14.99

Rules of Engagement

(1999, 127 min, US, William Friedkin) *Tommy Lee Jones, Samuel L. Jackson, Guy Pearce, Bruce Greenwood, Anne Archer, Ben Kingsley, Blair Underwood, Philip Baker Hall.* In the passable but stuffy *Rules of Engagement*, military stratagem meets courtroom drama. Supposedly in the tradition of *A Few Good Men*, but lacking that film's structured screenplay and taut direction, Friedkin's well-acted, busy melodrama is ultimately at cross-purposes: It wants to be a kick-ass combat film and a hard-edged examination of military bureaucracy. Jackson plays a Marine colonel who is put on trial after his troops kill civilians in an embassy evacuation in Yemen. Jones is a military lawyer and old friend who defends him. Gutsy performances help sustain interest, but flat supporting characterizations and contrived plot developments work against it. ★★ DVD: $14.99, VHS: $9.99

Rules of the Game

(1939, 110 min, France, Jean Renoir) *Marcel Dalio, Jean Renoir.* Renoir's grand comedy of manners is a sublime study of social codes and crum-bling morals. Within the confines of a lavish country estate, the intricate lives of the aristocracy and their servants undergo a dramatic unravelling. A marvel of ensemble acting and a perennial contender as one of the greatest films of all time. (French with English subtitles) ★★★★ DVD Criterion Collection: $39.99, VHS: $29.99

The Ruling Class

(1971, 139 min, GB, Peter Medak) *Peter O'Toole, Alastair Sim, Arthur Lowe, Coral Browne.* O'Toole gives a comically possessed performance as Jack, the 14th Earl of Guerney, who insists he's Jesus Christ. This irreverent and boisterous black comedy overflows with madness as people burst into song and assume whacked-out characters at the drop of a hat. Great support from Sim as a befuddled bishop and Lowe as a bolshevik butler. ★★★½ DVD Letterbox Criterion Collection: $39.99, VHS: $39.99

Rumble Fish

(1983, 94 min, US, Francis Coppola) *Matt Dillon, Mickey Rourke, Dennis Hopper, Diane Lane, Nicolas Cage.* Coppola's film adaptation of S.E. Hinton's novel was a financial and critical failure. Unlike his version of *The Outsiders*, this film lacks Coppola's usual glossiness. Rourke stars as "The Motorcycle Boy," who returns to his home town to try to stop his brother (Dillon) from following in his legendary, wandering footsteps. This is a film which viewers will find either a pretentious bore or a rewarding film experience. (We find it the former.) Shot in black and white. ★½

Rumble in the Bronx

(1994, 90 min, Hong Kong, Stanley Tong) *Jackie Chan, Anita Mui, Francoise Yip, Bill Tung.* In this story-light, action-heavy, redubbed romp through Vancouver that still manages to charm, Chan plays Keung, who runs afoul of a local multiethnic biker gang, who beat him up and trash his uncle's store. After making amends with the gang leader's girl-friend (Yip), both Chan and the gang must bury the hatchet in the face of a bigger threat: a group of homicidal mobsters searching for a bag of stolen diamonds. The martial arts and comedy scenes more than make up for any other deficiencies. As the amazing action scenes prove, Chan is the real thing; he's a charismatic superstar who can do his own stunts and perform successful physical comedy. ★★½ DVD Letterbox: $9.99, VHS: $9.99, VHS Letterbox: $9.99

A Rumor of War

(1980, 106 min, US, Richard T. Heffron) *Brad Davis, Brian Dennehy, Keith Carradine, Stacy Keach, Michael O'Keefe.* Davis heads a good cast in this outstanding made-for-TV Vietnam War drama. In a compelling and rich performance, Davis plays a newly arrived G.I. whose — like that of Tom Cruise in *Born on the Fourth of July* some nine years later — unblinking support of the war gives way to self-doubt and tragedy. ★★★½

Run Lola Run

(1999, 81 min, Germany, Tom Tykwer) *Franka Potente, Moritz Bleibtreu, Herbert Knaup, Nina Petri.* Lola's boyfriend Manni has left 100,000 marks on a subway, and he'll be dead if he doesn't get it to his gangster boss in 20 minutes. Good thing he has a strong woman behind him. As played by Potente, Lola is so powerful that she breaks glass when she screams, can heal the dying, and won't even let the movie end until everything is right. Director Tykwer has fashioned a massive, kinetic music video (he also cowrote all the music) that also stops long enough to enrich each character, adding layers as the story is revisited. He also relentlessly toys with the medium, including giving flash-forward life-stories to mere extras and running the credits backwards. Tremendous fun, in a serious, German sort of way. (German with English subtitles) ★★★½ DVD: $19.99, VHS: $9.99

The Run of the Country

(1995, 116 min, Ireland, Peter Yates) *Albert Finney, Matt Keeslar, Victoria Smurfit, Anthony Brophy.* This charming coming-of-age tale is set in the breathtaking Irish countryside, populated with believable characters and describing that tenuous time of life when children must separate from home before they can find a true connection with it. Keeslar is authentic in his description of Danny, the bereaved young man whose recent loss of his mother is the traumatic catalyst to monumental changes in his life. Finney is expectedly captivating as the domineering father whose own loss makes him even less receptive to his son's state of mind. A touching story of loss and reconciliation with the wit to avoid the maudlin and the warmth to heal the heart. ★★★ VHS: $19.99

Runaway

(1984, 100 min, US, Michael Crichton) *Tom Selleck, Gene Simmons, Kirstie Alley, Cynthia Rhodes.* Futuristic thriller with Selleck as a bounty hunter tracking down defective, murderous robots. Crichton's story is a miss on practically all levels. ★★ DVD: $24.99

Runaway Bride

(1999, 116 min, US, Garry Marshall) *Julia Roberts, Richard Gere, Joan Cusack, Hector Elizondo, Rita Wilson, Paul Dooley.* Roberts and Gere reunite for this splashy if formulaic romantic comedy. Gere plays a reporter who travels to a small Maryland town to do research on the woman (Roberts) who has stood up three fiancés at the altar. And she's set to walk down the aisle once more. Of course, the antagonists soon become attracted to each other. Roberts looks great, and her performance

The Ruling Class

Gene Hackman oozes sleaze in *Runaway Jury*

is beguiling, though she's not afforded an opportunity to bring some shadings to her character. Gere looks great, as well, and is actually quite funny, but neither he nor his enchanting costar are fully able to bring sizzle to a script which is operating at only half-flame. ★★½ DVD: $19.99, VHS: $9.99

Runaway Jury

(2003, 125 min, US, Gary Fleder) *John Cusack, Gene Hackman, Dustin Hoffman, Rachel Weisz, Bruce Davison, Bruce McGill, Jeremy Piven.* John Grisham takes on the gun manufacturers in this sly, slick courtroom drama that's as entertaining as it is occasionally implausible. Grisham, in his novel of the same name, actually took on big tobacco, but the switch here for the screen surprisingly doesn't hurt it. Cusack plays a reluctant juror on a big case in New Orleans — a widow is suing a gun company after the murder of her husband. Hackman oozes sleaze from every pore as the hired gun for the defense whose expertise as a jury consultant — and whose hi-tech privacy-invasion techniques — is second to none. Hoffman is restrained and effective as the idealistic lawyer representing the young widow. As the case begins, it soon becomes apparent that there is more than one person out to sway the jury's decision and thwart justice, assuring a verdict to the highest bidder. That some of the characters could get away with what they do tests the boundaries of credibility, but the entire package is wrapped in such an appealing fabric of mystery and suspense, that the improbable can be quickly accepted or at least ignored. The courtroom scenes have an effecient tempo to them, Hackman's state-of-the-art survellience operation is often fascinating, each making up for the familiar drama and types which make up the jury and deliberation process. ★★★ DVD: $27.99

Runaway Train

(1985, 107 min, US, Andrei Konchalovsky) *Jon Voight, Rebecca DeMornay, Kenneth McMillan, Eric Roberts.* High-voltage action film, based on a screenplay by Akira Kurosawa, with Voight and Roberts as two escaped prisoners who become trapped on a runaway train in the frozen wasteland of the Northwest. Voight and Roberts both received Oscar nominations — unusual for an action film. ★★★½ DVD: $14.99

The Rundown

(2003, 102 min, US, Peter Berg) *The Rock, Seann William Scott, Christopher Walken, Rosario Dawson, Ewen Bremner.* Berg's second feature film is an action-packed ride through the jungle, with some amazing acrobatic sequences and enough pyrotechnics to more than satisfy fans of the genre. What sets *The Rundown* apart from other Hollywood action films (think *XXX*) is none other than its star. In addition to his well-known physical talents, The Rock displays a wonderful sense of comedic timing as Beck, the retrieval expert "hired" to go and get the son (Scott) of a wealthy, crime boss from the clutches of a sleazy despot (Walken) who rules the jungle. He relishes the opportunity to poke fun at his tough-guy image, and succeeds in doing so without compromising the action of the film or his place as its able-bodied star. He's surprisingly good, and quite enjoyable to watch. Scott, who endures several "smack-downs" before finally finding his heart, complements the comedy of the film quite well, while also providing the buddy element to the Rock's Beck. A fun, adrenaline-fueled film, *The Rundown* is sure to please. ★★★ DVD: $26.99, VHS: $22.99

The Runner Stumbles

(1979, 109 min, US, Stanley Kramer) *Dick Van Dyke, Kathleen Quinlan, Maureen Stapleton, Beau Bridges.* In a small Washington mining town during the 1920s, a priest (Van Dyke) is accused of murdering a young nun. Considering the volatile subject matter, this is pretty tame stuff. ★★

The Running Man

(1987, 100 min, US, Paul Michael Glaser) *Arnold Schwarzenegger.* Futuristic actioner with Arnold Schwarzenegger as a condemned prisoner whose one chance of hope lies in a torturous and deadly televised game where contestants are pitted against brutal opponents and impossible obstacles. Richard Dawson is well cast as the game show host. ★★½ DVD Dual Special Edition: $19.99, DVD: $14.99, VHS: $9.99

Running Mates

(1992, 85 min, US, Michael Lindsay-Hogg) *Ed Harris, Diane Keaton.* A bittersweet comedy about love and loyalty in the whirlwind of a political campaign. The exceptionally photogenic Harris stars as Hugh Hathaway, the senator stud bucking for a presidential nomination. Keaton is Aggie Shaw, a charmingly kooky author who wins his heart. However, the spin doctors aren't sure if Aggie is First Lady material, what with her outspoken demeanor and questionable past. Winning performances by both Harris and Keaton makes this love-conquers-all story a delight. ★★★ VHS: $9.99

Running on Empty

(1988, 116 min, US, Sidney Lumet) *Christine Lahti, Judd Hirsch, River Phoenix, Martha Plimpton, Steven Hill.* An exceptional cast highlights this powerful and perceptive drama about a family's struggle to stay together. Lahti and Hirsch portray former '60s radicals wanted by the FBI who have been living underground for two decades. Borrowing the names of the deceased and able to move their family at a moment's notice, they must face the extra burden of separation when their eldest son, a gifted musician, applies for college — which would bring the boy into the open and guarantee his not seeing his parents again. Phoenix is exceptional as the devoted son faced with the possibility of not seeing his family again, and the reunion scene between Lahti and Hill is simply astonishing. A tour de force from all involved. ★★★★ DVD: $9.99, VHS: $14.99

Running Scared

(1986, 106 min, US, Peter Hyams) *Gregory Hines, Billy Crystal, Jimmy Smits.* Hines and Crystal work well together in this effective police thriller as two streetwise undercover Chicago cops on the trail of a drug kingpin. The film is highlighted by funny dialogue and an exciting (if improbable) chase scene on the elevated line. ★★½ DVD Letterbox: $14.99

Running Wild

(1928, 68 min, US, Eddie Cline) *W.C. Fields.* Even in this hilarious silent film, you can hear every word Fields is muttering under his breath. Once again sporting that sleazy little dab of a mustache that he seemed to favor in his silent films, Fields is a mere milquetoast of a man, emboldened by a chance encounter with a hypnotist. ★★★½ VHS: $7.99

Rush

(1991, 120 min, US, Lili Fini Zanuck) *Jason Patric, Jennifer Jason Leigh, Gregg Allman, Max Perlich, William Sadler.* A dark, intense look at undercover cops in 1970s Texas, *Rush* has an unrelentingly grim outlook which, though obstensibly about agents becoming lost in another world, comes off more as a "just-say-no" parable. Leigh stars as a novice police officer who is teamed with brooding Patric to snare alleged drug kingpin Allman. As the two officers introduce themselves to the denizens of the underworld, they slowly become what they're hunting. It's a point, though well made, which would have been used to better dramatic effect if not for the blatant moralizing. ★★½ DVD Letterbox: $14.99

Rush Hour

(1998, 97 min, US, Brett Ratner) *Jackie Chan, Chris Tucker, Tom Wilkinson, Chris Penn, Elizabeth Peña.* Bringing together two unlikely screen personalities with unexpected comic results, *Rush Hour* is a funny, energetic and exciting comic cop adventure. Tucker plays a maverick, wisecracking L.A. cop who is "recruited" into

Franka Potente in *Run Lola Run*

babysitting Hong Kong detective Chan who is investigating the kidnapping of the daughter of the Chinese consul. Since their assistance isn't wanted by the FBI agents on the case, the two team up to track down the kidnappers themselves. Of course, a lot of the humor comes from Chan's fish-out-of-water, but there's much more to offer here. Chan is a marvel performing his own stunts, Tucker's delivery of some very funny lines is terrific, and their rapport is marvelous. (Sequel: *Rush Hour 2*) ★★★ DVD Letterbox: $14.99, VHS: $6.99, VHS Letterbox: $6.99

Rush Hour 2

(2001, 90 min, US, Brett Ratner) *Jackie Chan, Chris Tucker, John Lone, Zhang Ziyi, Roselyn Sanchez, Harris Yulin, Alan King.* Entertaining sequel to the highly entertaining 1998 hit is more of the same, but just as good. The "plot" — Chan and Tucker team up to fight more criminals — is almost negligible, and that's just fine. This isn't a movie that's meant for film school symposiums; it's a fast-paced, frequently hilarious crowd-pleaser with some surprisingly exciting, agile fights (considering Chan's age), amusing cameos, and plenty of hysterical yammering from Tucker. As always with Chan's films, some of the best bits come during the end credits, with some very funny outtakes and bloopers. Good fun. ★★★ DVD Letterbox infinifilm Special Edition: $19.99, VHS: $6.99

Rushmore

(1998, 93 min, US, Wes Anderson) *Jason Schwartzman, Bill Murray, Olivia Williams, Seymour Cassel, Brian Cox, Mason Gamble.* This outlandish, hilarious and inventive comedy delights in its irreverent examination of the vicious underbelly of adolescence and the dark and twisted side of puppy love. Schwartzman stars as 15-year-old Max Fischer, a brilliant intellect and academic underachiever who is *the* body politic of Rushmore. After forging an alliance with one of Rushmore's wealthiest benefactors, Herman Blume (Murray), his institutional confidence becomes undermined when he meets the newest first grade teacher, Rosemary Cross (Williams), and is instantly overcome by an

obsessive love that only increases when his good friend Herman joins the fight for her attentions. The ensuing rivalry stays firmly ensconced in its own wacky brand of delightfully subversive, Salinger-esque humor. Schwartzman is stellar in his film debut as the crafty and vindictive pubescent, and Murray delivers a career performance as a befuddled and lonely millionaire teetering on the verge of his midlife crisis. ★★★★ DVD Criterion Collection: $39.99, DVD Basic Edition: $19.99, VHS: $9.99

The Russia House

(1990, 123 min, US, Fred Schepisi) *Sean Connery, Michelle Pfeiffer, Roy Scheider, James Fox, John Mahoney.* An intriguing espionage thriller, based on John Le Carré's novel. Connery plays a down-on-his-heels London publisher who is unwittingly thrust into political intrigue when a top secret Russian manuscript is sent to him. Connery travels to Moscow to uncover the story and its writer. Pfeiffer (complete with accent) ably plays the Russian liaison with whom the reluctant spy falls in love. As a spy story, *The Russia House* is at its best; but the romantic angle between Connery and Pfeiffer, though handsome, is not always believable. ★★½ DVD Letterbox: $14.99

Russian Ark

(2002, 96 min, Russia, Alexander Sokurov) *Sergei Dreiden, Maria Kuznetsova.* A Russian man from the present day wakes up to find himself in the Hermitage in St. Petersburg, an invisible witness to events within its confines from the early 1700s to the early twentieth century. He wanders from room to room, scenario to scenario, often in discussion with a 19th-century French diplomat. This singular experience engenders friendly debates between the two observers on philosophy and art and the Russian character, all imbued with quintessential Russian melancholy and spiritualism. *Russian Ark* is both a uniquely cerebral filmic exploration and a unique experiment in filmmaking. Director Sokurov took months of preparation, and well over a thousand people to shoot this lavish costumed period piece

Rushmore

in a single day. The Hermitage does indeed become an ark of Russian consciousness afloat in a spectral sea, and *Russian Ark* is a lyrical visual poem, a whimsical fusion of intellectual abstraction and sensory stimulation. ★★★½ DVD Masterworks Edition: $29.99, VHS: $29.99

The Russians Are Coming, the Russians Are Coming!

(1966, 135 min, US, Norman Jewison) *Alan Arkin, Brian Keith, Jonathan Winters, Carl Reiner, Eva Marie Saint.* Hysteria breaks out in a small New England coastal town when a Russian submarine runs aground on their beach. Some hilarious moments from an inspired cast, including Oscar nominee Arkin as a Russian sailor and Winters as a gun-toting local, make this one of the biggest pleasures of all 1960s comedies. ★★★½ DVD Letterbox: $19.99

Ruthless People

(1986, 93 min, US, David Zucker, Jerry Zucker, Jim Abrahams) *Bette Midler, Danny DeVito, Judge Reinhold, Helen Slater, Anita Morris, Bill Pullman.* Larceny, infidelity and murder among California's nouveau riche form the core of this hilarious comedy. DeVito plays an unfaithful husband who plots to kill his overbearing wife, Midler, who, fortunately for him, has been kidnapped by a not-so-ruthless couple whom DeVito swindled. Reinhold and Slater are the hapless couple. A hip, modern retelling of O. Henry's celebrated short story, "The Ransom of Red Chief." ★★★½ DVD: $14.99, VHS: $9.99

Ryan's Daughter

(1970, 177 min, GB, David Lean) *Robert Mitchum, Sarah Miles, Christopher Jones, John Mills, Trevor Howard.* This unabashedly sentimental, wildly cinematic story was filmed in Northern Ireland and features Miles as a young girl who marries a simple, plodding schoolteacher (Mitchum) only to have an affair with a British soldier (Jones). As directed by Lean, the film is brisk and stylish, but the simplicity of the story doesn't support the elephantine production values that Lean heaped upon it. Mills owns an Oscar for his touching portrayal of the town idiot. ★★★

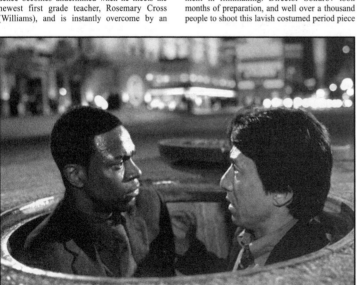

Chris Tucker (l.) and Jackie Chan in *Rush Hour 2*

S.F.W.

(1995, 92 min, US, Jefery Levy) *Stephen Dorff, Reese Witherspoon, Jake Busey.* Dorff and Witherspoon are the two surviving hostages of a 36-day incarceration at a Fun Stop convenience store, held captive by the terrorist group Split Image — a group savvy enough to bring video equipment but with no apparent message. *S.F.W.*, which stands for "So Fucking What," takes a swipe at every element of the machinery that turns a news story into a prime time event: the packaging of TV movies, instant analysis from "Nightline," psychobabble from shrinks, and groupies eager to bask in other people's 15 minutes of fame. While the film could be easily written off as a *Natural Born Killers* clone with B-movie execution, it does manage to juxtapose the horror of hostage taking with the banality of media hype. Uneven and awkward. ★★ DVD: $14.99

S.O.B.

(1981, 121 min, US, Blake Edwards) *William Holden, Robert Preston, Julie Andrews, Robert Mulligan, Robert Webber, Shelley Winters, Robert Vaughn, Rosanna Arquette.* Edwards' brilliant, scathing indictment of Hollywood and the men and women behind and in front of the cameras. Holden gives a sterling performance as a jaded director with a predilection for teenaged girls. Preston is exceptional as a wise-cracking doc, Andrews as a superstar who bares all, and Mulligan is Edwards' alter ego who discovers exactly what it takes to make a hit. One of the most underrated and misunderstood films of its decade. ★★★½ DVD: $19.99, VHS: $14.99

S.W.A.T.

(2003, 117 min, US, Clark Johnson) *Samuel L. Jackson, Colin Farrell, Michelle Rodriguez, LL Cool J, Josh Charles, Olivier Martinez.* A terrible police action film, the surprise box-office hit *S.W.A.T.* is an overblown spectacle with outlandish action scenes and heroes performing superhuman feats. Farrell, Jackson, Rodriguez et al play S.W.A.T. team members who train to the strains of bad hip-hop and fight the worst of the bad guys. That's truly it for story — and forget characters; these cardboard cutouts have no motivations other than those the screenwriters deem acceptable from scene to scene. And, depending on your political leanings, *S.W.A.T.* is potentially offensive, as well: liberals, the French and — in one particularly gratuitous scene — vegetarians are all derided, without irony, in a seemingly desperate attempt to accrue yahoo "cred." Whatever their politics, action fans won't forgive the flaws, considering the boring action scenes on display here. ★ DVD Letterbox: $19.99, DVD Pan & Scan: $19.99, VHS: $14.99

Sabotage

(1936, 76 min, GB, Alfred Hitchcock) *Sylvia Sidney, Oscar Homolka.* Freely adapted from Joseph Conrad's "Secret Agent," this elaborately detailed and disquieting film concerns a kindly movie theater manager who doubles as a dangerous foreign agent. The man's wife (Sidney), after her younger brother is killed by a bomb, begins to develop suspicions and then has a little trouble carving the roast that evening. (Remade as *Joseph Conrad's The Secret Agent*) ★★★

Saboteur

(1942, 108 min, US, Alfred Hitchcock) *Robert Cummings, Priscilla Lane, Norman Lloyd.* Cummings is charged with the wartime sabotage of a munitions factory and forced into a hurried flight from misguided justice. Racing across the country, he pursues the true culprit, an elusive individual named Fry, and eventually confronts him atop the Statue of Liberty. One of Hitchcock's lesser-known works, this nonetheless is a tense, exciting spy story with many scenes which bear the Master's touch. ★★★½ DVD: $29.99

Sabrina

(1954, 113 min, US, Billy Wilder) *Audrey Hepburn, Humphrey Bogart, William Holden, John Williams.* Charming romantic comedy featuring an impeccable cast. Holden is a rich playboy smitten with chauffeur's daughter Hepburn; but older brother Bogey steps in to separate the pair and falls in love with her himself. Based on Samuel Taylor's play "Sabrina Fair." (Remade in 1995) ★★★½ DVD: $14.99, VHS: $9.99

Sabrina

(1995, 127 min, US, Sydney Pollack) *Harrison Ford, Julia Ormond, Greg Kinnear, Nancy Marchand, John Wood, Richard Crenna.* One of the joys of Billy Wilder's 1954 romantic comedy *Sabrina* is the enchanting performance by Audrey Hepburn as the chauffeur's daughter who becomes involved with her father's employer. In taking over her role, no one expected Ormand to be another Hepburn. But in Pollack's tranquil remake, sadly, the magic is just not there. Not without its own modest charms, though, including a charismatic performance by Ford, *Sabrina* is an appealing though unnecessary remake. ★★½ DVD Letterbox: $14.99, VHS: $9.99

Sacco and Vanzetti

(1971, 120 min, France/Italy, Giuliano Montaldo) *Gian Marie Volonte, Riccardo Cucciolla, Milo O'Shea, Cyril Cusack.* Told in pseudo-documentary style, this exposé of the famous 1920 trial of two Italian anarchists who were unjustly accused of crimes is a classic look at the American injustice system and the American penchant for mass political hysteria when it suits its leaders. A realistic and moving account with Joan Baez singing the title song. ★★★ DVD: $14.99, VHS: $19.99

El Sacerdote (The Priest)

(1977, 100 min, Spain, Eloy de la Iglesia) *Simon Andreu.* Set during the repressive Franco regime (which acts as a symbol of the equally repressive Catholic Church), this involving drama follows the tortured life of a 36-year-old priest as he struggles with his vow of celibacy. Father Miguel (Andreu) is a conservative priest who becomes troubled with his raging and unspent libido. Unable to find solace in either Christ or the arms of a married woman, the tormented man resorts to a horrible act in an attempt to solve his problems. Similar in tone and theme to 1994's *Priest*, this film stays more focused on the dilemma of a sincere man who must fight the conflicting forces of his religious calling and the calling of physical desire. (Spanish with English subtitles) ★★★ VHS: $59.99

The Sacrifice

(1986, 145 min, Sweden/USSR, Andrei Tarkovsky) *Erland Josephson, Susan Fleetwood.* Alexander's family is gathered to celebrate his 70th birthday. A quiet tension fills the air. When an uneasy silence is shattered by an emergency broadcast which reports an impending nuclear attack, they begin to fall apart. Alexander then learns of a way the disaster can be prevented . . . but is the world worth saving? In this, his final film, Tarkovsky forms a powerful vision of the future which will haunt the memory. (Swedish with English subtitles) ★★★½ DVD: $39.99

Sadie McKee

(1934, 90 min, US, Clarence Brown) *Joan Crawford, Edward Arnold, Franchot Tone, Gene Raymond.* Crawford is in good form in this three-hanky weeper as a maid involved, at various times, with millionaire Arnold, ne'er-do-well Raymond and employer Tone. ★★★ VHS: $19.99

Sadie Thompson

(1928, 97 min, US, Raoul Walsh) *Gloria Swanson, Lionel Barrymore, Raoul Walsh.* W. Somerset Maugham's "Rain" gets a good workout as Swanson plays a whore in Pago Pago who takes up with reformer Barrymore. Director Walsh has fun on both sides of the camera playing the sailor who really loves her. Seldom seen, until the recent reconstruction of the lost last reel using surviving production stills and frame enlargements. (Remade in 1932 as *Rain* and in 1953 as *Miss Sadie Thompson*) ★★★½ DVD: $29.99, VHS: $24.99

Safe

(1995, 121 min, US, Todd Haynes) *Julianne Moore, Xander Berkeley, Peter Friedman, James LeGros, Jessica Harper.* Restrained but emotionally involving, this is a harrowing tale of a woman who physically suffers at the hands of "progress." The deceptively simple story follows Carol White (the remarkable Moore), a Stepford Wife-like Southern California housewife who finds her body slowly ravaged by allergic reactions to everyday chemicals, fragrances and fumes. Her doctors cannot find anything physically wrong with her, so Carol sets off to New Mexico for answers and a cure at a New Age-style spa/convalescence resort. With a bold yet austere visual style, Haynes chillingly explores suburban complacency and existential alienation. Ultimately, *Safe* is anything but and is thought-provoking and quietly disturbing. ★★★½ DVD: $29.99

Safe Men

(1998, 89 min, US, John Hamburg) *Steve Zahn, Sam Rockwell, Harvey Fierstein, Michael Lerner, Paul Giamatti.* An overlooked indie gem, *Safe Men* is a very funny comic caper in which two really lousy lounge singers, Sam and Eddie (Zahn, Rockwell), are mistaken for safecrackers by Veal Chop (Giamatti), a henchman for the local Jewish Mafia. Asked to retrieve a "cup" for Big Fat Bernie Gayle (Lerner), a Jewish gangster, the luckless duo get in over their heads and into a rivalry with Big Fat's nemesis Good Stuff Leo (Fierstein). The jokes range from broad to subtle, and the pairing of Zahn and Rockwell is inspired. Director Hamburg has some really good ideas going on here — perhaps too many; the film could have been sharpened slightly — but most of the targets he hits are a bull's eye. ★★★

Safe Passage

(1994, 97 min, US, Robert Allan Ackerman) *Susan Sarandon, Sam Shepard, Nick Stahl, Sean Astin, Robert Sean Leonard, Marcia Gay Harden, Jason London.* Sarandon plays mother to seven sons, one of whom is a soldier stationed in the Middle East. When word comes that his barracks has been bombed, the entire family comes together for the requisite tears and laughter, revelations and recriminations. Though there's nothing overtly original in either the film's plot line or execution, it's the conviction of the ensemble, headed by the radiant Sarandon, which gives *Safe Passage* its emotion. ★★★ DVD: $19.99

The Sailor Who Fell from Grace with the Sea

(1976, 104 min, GB, Lewis John Carlino) *Sarah Miles, Kris Kristofferson, Jonathan Kahn.* This striking and erotic drama centers itself with a group of young schoolboys who commit a ritual murder upon a visiting sailor. Miles plays a lonely widow who falls in love with the sailor (Kristofferson) before his unfortunate demise. Filled with steamy love scenes (featured in *Playboy* at the time), this unusual and beautifully photographed film is based on a novella by Yukio Mishima. ★★★ DVD Letterbox: $19.99

The Saint

(1997, 115 min, US, Phillip Noyce) *Val Kilmer, Elisabeth Shue, Rade Serbedzija.* Simon Templar, aka The Saint, has been around for a long time. The hero of over 50 books, a film series in the 1940s and a popular 1960s TV show, this guy has seen a lot of action. And while there's a bit of action, as well, in this update starring Kilmer as Templar, its formulaic and convoluted story keeps it from ever becoming a truly satisfying espionage adventure. Templar is hired to locate and steal the cold-fusion formula of scientist Shue. Natch, he falls for her during the execution of his duties. There's a couple competent action scenes and a few laughs along the way, but *The Saint* never gets as flavorful and fun as its predecessors. ★★ DVD: $14.99, VHS: $9.99

Saint Clara

(1995, 85 min, Israel, Ari Folman & Uri Sivan) *Lucy Dubinchik.* It's the class of 1999, Israel — and this ain't no Breakfast Club: This is an Israeli apocalyptic sci-fi surf movie without the beach! What

Val Kilmer in *The Salton Sea*

concerns the students at Golda Meir Junior High School are the Richter scale, what pills to take, Edith Piaf, revolution and a mysterious classmate from Russia named Clara, who has clairvoyant powers. Clara's powers are used to challenge the school's authorities when she uses them on a math test and everyone in the class gets perfect scores. Soon everyone in town knows about the girl with the prophecies, the girl who comes from "the zone" in Russia where the gift runs in the family. Directors Folman and Sivan have created a beguiling, funny and irreverent tale. (Hebrew with English subtitles) ★★★ VHS: $24.99

St. Elmo's Fire

(1985, 110 min, US, Joel Schumacher) *Emilio Estevez, Rob Lowe, Andrew McCarthy, Demi Moore, Ally Sheedy, Mare Winningham.* Though it wants to be more, this drama of post-college grads struggling in Washington D.C. is nothing more than "The Little Chill." A who's-who cast of 1980s teen celebs is featured. ★★ DVD: $14.99

The St. Francisville Experiment

(2000, 76 min, US, Ted Nicolaou) *Tim Baldini, Madison Charap.* Shot in the same faux documentary-like style of *The Blair Witch Project*, this low-budget rip-off follows four strangers who investigate a legendary haunted house. The director assures us that what we are about to see is real — like a series of clumsily staged ghostly occurences, awful acting and laughable plot developments. Has all the grace of an elephant tap dancing through a minefield. ★ DVD: $24.99

Saint Jack

(1979, 112 min, US, Peter Bogdanovich) *Ben Gazzara, Denholm Elliott, George Lazenby.* An American businessman in Singapore (Gazzara) aims to run the classiest whorehouse in town, but runs afoul of the Chinese mafia. A well-played tale set against the seedier side of small-time operations. ★★★ DVD: $19.99, VHS: $14.99

St. Martin's Lane

(1938, 85 min, GB, Tim Whelan) *Charles Laughton, Vivien Leigh, Rex Harrison, Larry Adler.* Incorporating a Warner Brothers backstage musical with a British class melodrama, this touching and lively rags-to-riches tale is a bittersweet look at

ambition and romance. The story follows the rise of a street gamine (Leigh) who is at first taken under the wing of a mediocre busker, marvelously played by Laughton. Under his supervision, her natural talent blossoms. She eventually becomes the toast of the town, while her former mentor flounders. Leigh creates a totally sympathetic character who does many unsympathetic things, and in an early role, Harrison gives a nuanced performance as the sophisticated songwriter who spirits her away to fame, fortune, and his penthouse. ★★★ VHS: $24.99

St. Michael Had a Rooster

(1971, 87 min, Italy, Paolo & Vittorio Taviani) *Giulio Brogi, Renato Scarpa, Vittorio Fantoni, Cinzia Bruno.* This black comedy from the brothers Taviani, as dry and tart as well-aged sherry, is based on a short story by Leo Tolstoy, here reset in the chaotic Italy of the late 1800s. After taking over the town hall while the citizens of its tiny city are at Sunday services, "internationalist" Giukio Manieri (Brogi) is surprised when the local population fail to throw off their shackles and join the uprising. Indeed, the whole revolution is quickly quelled by the authorities, not through the use of violence, but through a far more ruinous weapon: indifference. Deemed not even worth executing, he is imprisoned for ten years only to emerge more out of touch than ever with the people he wanted to liberate, the new subversives he had hoped to inspire, and, all too tragically, with himself. (Italian with English subtitles) ★★★ VHS: $19.99

The Saint of Fort Washington

(1993, 107 min, US, Tim Hunter) *Matt Dillon, Danny Glover, Rick Aviles, Nina Siemaszko, Ving Rhames, Joe Seneca.* A poignant if familiar character study examining the friendship between two homeless men. Dillon plays a schizophrenic photographer newly homeless. At the prison-like shelter Fort Washington, he is befriended by Vietnam vet Glover, who takes him under his wing. The two confront an uncaring, suspicious and hostile society in their battle to survive on the streets. Both actors give strong performances, and the film succeeds in putting a face to the faceless army of the homeless; though its important message of "they're not criminals" is at times heavy-handed. ★★½ VHS: $19.99

Salaam Bombay!

(1988, 114 min, France/India, Mira Nair) *Shafiq Syed, Hansa Vithal.* A spectacular directorial debut for Nair, this shockingly graphic yet compassionate tale chronicles the wretched but ever resourceful life of 10-year-old Krishna, a boy thrown out from his house and forced to fend for himself. Initially scared and alienated, Krishna soon befriends the prostitutes, drug dealers and fellow street urchins of the red-light district and eventually becomes part of their milieu of exploitation, squalor and survival. Vividly drawn, using many non-professional actors and filming on the teeming streets of Bombay, this revelation avoids being preachy or heavy-handed in telling its realistic tale. (Hindi with English subtitles) ★★★ DVD Special Edition: $24.99

Salem's Lot: The Miniseries

(1979, 184 min, US, Tobe Hooper) *David Soul, James Mason, Lance Kerwin, Bonnie Bedelia.* Though still missing 16 minutes from the original miniseries telecast, this restored adaptation of the Stephen King novel easily qualifies as one of the scariest horror movies ever made for television. Soul stars as a successful novelist who returns to his small New England home town. Unfortunately, his arrival coincides with that of a worldly antique dealer (Mason in a superbly sinister performance) who has earmarked the inhabitants as "fang fodder" — vampires, that is. Also available in the more violent 112-minute "European" version. ★★★½ DVD: $14.99, VHS: $19.99

Sallah

(1963, 110 min, Israel, Ephraim Kishon) *Chaim Topol, Geula Noni.* One of the best Israeli films ever made, *Sallah* was an Academy Award nominee for Best Foreign Film and won First Prize in the San Francisco International Film Festival. Topol stars as the head of an immigrant family from North Africa who encounter nothing but frustration and disappointment during their period of transition in the Promised Land. (Hebrew with English subtitles) ★★★★ VHS: $79.99

Salo: 120 Days of Sodom

(1975, 115 min, Italy, Pier Paolo Pasolini) *Giorgio Cataldi, Umberto P. Quinavalle.* Pasolini's last film is an unbelievably bleak and depressing vision of the human condition which shocked audiences with its brutally graphic scenes of sexual degradation and oppressive violence. The director transposes the Marquis de Sade's novel about the debauching of the four pillars of 18th century French Society to World War II Italy. A group of older Fascists (men and women) bring together a group of teenagers of both sexes and subject them to all kinds of sexual, mental and physical degradation. (Italian with English subtitles) ★★★½

Salome

(1922, 35 min, US, Alla Nazimova (Charles Bryant)) *Nazimova, Mitchell Lewis.* Nazimova directed (under her husband's name) this extravagant version of the Oscar Wilde play, with stylized sets and costumes by Rudolph Valentino's wife Natasha Rambova (she based her work on the drawings of Aubrey Bearsley). Sensual and wildly eccentric, the story of Herod's vixen stepdaughter who danced for the head of John the Baptist is even more outrageous than Ken Russell's over-the-top *Salome's Last Dance.* ★★★ DVD: $24.99

Salome

(1953, 103 min, US, William Dieterle) *Rita Hayworth, Charles Laughton, Judith Anderson, Stewart Granger.* Hayworth's lustrous beauty shines in this liberal retelling of the biblical story of Salome — daughter to Queen Herodia of Galilee — who offered herself to spare John the Baptist. Laughton stars as King Herod who cannot bring himself to silence the good Baptist despite the prodding of his wicked queen (Anderson). Palace intrigue abounds. While extremely well-acted and often entertaining, the film suffers from a heavy-handed treatment of its religious themes. ★★½

Salome's Last Dance

(1988, 87 min, GB, Ken Russell) *Glenda Jackson, Stratford Johns, Nickolas Grace, Imogen Millais-Scott.* With his usual flair for decadence and depravity, Russell crafted this brilliant tribute to the literary genius of Oscar Wilde. The film follows Wilde to a male brothel where he is entertained by an "illegal" performance of his banned play, "Salome." The play itself represents Wilde's twisted vision of the fateful biblical encounter between Salome (daughter of King Herod) and John the Baptist. Here re-enacted full of pulsating sexual innuendo, Russell eagerly sinks his teeth into Wilde's poetry and renders the play, in its entirety, at a frenetic pace. Jackson is nothing short of perfect as the steely, evil Queen Herodias. ★★★

Salon Kitty

(1975, 133 min, West Germany, Tinto Brass) *Ingrid Thulin, Helmut Berger.* Made in the "grand" tradition of *Caligula, The Damned* and *The Night Porter,* this exploitative, sexually graphic shocker features a crazed Berger as a powerful SS officer who will do anything to get the dirt on his fellow Nazis and their wives. An erotic and, at times, disturbing probe into the sickness of man. (aka: *Madam Kitty*) ★★½ DVD Letterbox: $29.99

Salsa: The Motion Picture

(1988, 97 min, US, Boaz Davidson) *Bobby Rosa.* Horrendously — but at least laughably — bad, this misguided attempt to cash in during the "salsa craze" of the late 1980s features ex-Menudo star Rosa as a grease monkey with a twitch in his hips, an itch in his crotch and stars in his eyes. Rosa, with a chiseled body but a squeaky, Michael Jackson voice; but that alone can't save this insipid *Saturday Night Fever/Dirty Dancing* rip-off. ★ DVD: $14.99

Salt of the Earth

(1953, 94 min, US, Herbert Biberman) *Will Geer, Rosaura Revueltas.* One of the classics of American independent filmmaking, this impassioned, pro-feminist drama chronicles the events in a bitter strike by Chicano zinc miners in New Mexico. When an injunction is issued against the workers, the wives of the strikers take to the picket line. Seemingly incomprehensible even in today's conservative climate, the film was boycotted by most cinemas on its release; with director Biberman, actor Geer, producer Paul Jarrico and screenwriter Michael Wilson all subsequently blacklisted for their part in its production. ★★★½ VHS: $29.99

The Salton Sea

(2002, 103 min, US, D.J. Caruso) *Val Kilmer, Vincent D'Onofrio, Adam Goldberg, Luis Guzman, Doug Hutchison, Anthony La Paglia, Peter Sarsgaard, Deborah Kara Unger.* In the spirit of the leading lights of the neo-noir genre, director Caruso's debut alternates deliberately between the absurd comedy of drug culture and that culture's attendant misery. *The Salton Sea* renders this duality explicitly, providing its protagonist (Kilmer) with two identities: Danny Parker, a speed junkie, and Tom Van Allen, a jazz trumpeter — one propelled by vengeance for the murder of his wife, the other decidedly not propelled by anything. We meet a panoply of scumbags and outcasts, and it becomes clear that Caruso and writer Tony Gayton owe a great debt to the kind of "loserspeak" dialogue laced with pop culture references that Quentin Tarantino single-handedly made an indie trend. The film's pleasures lie in appreciating the craft of an effective genre study; its success stemming not from its innovation, but from its studied execution. ★★★ DVD Letterbox: $19.99, VHS: $14.99

Salut L'Artiste

(1973, 96 min, France, Yves Robert) *Marcello Mastroianni, Françoise Fabian.* Mastroianni's extraordinary talent to portray the "naïve oaf" comes fully to life in this captivating and witty modern farce about a fumbling bit actor trying to live two lives at once. His mistress finally leaves him and so he sheepishly returns home to his wife only to discover that she is carrying someone else's child. Full of pratfalls and pitfalls, this engaging and sardonic comedy sparkles with effervescence. (French with English subtitles) ★★★

Salvador

(1986, 123 min, US, Oliver Stone) *James Woods, James Belushi, John Savage, Michael Murphy.* Released the same year as his classic *Platoon,* Stone wrote and directed this taut, hard-hitting political drama based on American photojournalist Richard Boyle's experiences in El Salvador in 1980. Woods gives what may be his finest performance as Boyle, and Belushi has certainly never been better as Boyle's sidekick just along for the ride. ★★★½ DVD Special Edition: $14.99, VHS: $14.99

Samantha

(1992, 101 min, US, Stephen La Rocque) *Martha Plimpton, Dermot Mulroney, Hector Elizondo, Ione Skye, Mary Kay Place.* When Samantha is informed by her parents that they found her on their doorstep 21 years earlier, she locks herself in her room and booby traps herself in a comedy. Plimpton is Samantha, a young woman in search of her own identity in this comedy that tries too hard to be offbeat. However, Plimpton gives an edgy, headstrong performance, and the charming relationship between Samantha and her best friend Henry (Mulroney) nearly makes up for the often ridiculous screenplay. ★½ VHS: $79.99

Same Time, Next Year

(1978, 119 min, US, Robert Mulligan) *Alan Alda, Ellen Burstyn.* Two engaging performances by Alda and Burstyn highlight this appealing film adaptation of Bernard Slade's hit Broadway play. Combining comedy, romance and drama, the story follows the 20-year extramarital affair of George and Doris, who meet once a year for a romantic reunion. ★★★ DVD Letterbox: $14.99, VHS: $9.99

Sammy and Rosie Get Laid

(1987, 100 min, GB, Stephen Frears) *Ayub Kahn Din, Frances Barber, Shashi Kapoor, Claire Bloom.* Director Frears and writer Hanif Kureishi reunite after their triumphant *My Beautiful Laundrette* to fashion another brilliantly scathing portrait of present-day London. Sammy (Din), the son of a right-wing Pakistani politician, is involved with a sexually liberated English woman (Barber). When his father, fleeing political enemies, comes to live with them, their informal relationship begins to mirror the mounting social unrest in the streets outside their window. ★★★½

Le Samouraï

(1967, 95 min, France, Jean-Pierre Melville) *Alain Delon, Nathalie Delon, François Périer, Cathy Rosier.* Melville's stylish thriller, admittedly influenced by 1930s gangster flicks and film noir of the 1940s, is a taut tale circling around the life of a professional hit man. Graced with an icy beauty, A. Delon stars as Jef Costello, a solitary, grim-faced killer-for-hire whose methodically ordered (and idealistic) code of behavior becomes unraveled when the police begin to track him down after a hit. Especially appealing in this nearly wordless film are the women in his life: N. Delon as the woman who loves him and Rosier as a sultry nightclub singer. A masterwork of evocation, atmosphere and narrative. (French with English subtitles) ★★★★ VHS: $29.99

Samson and Delilah

(1949, 128 min, US, Cecil B. DeMille) *Hedy Lamarr, Victor Mature, Angela Lansbury, George Sanders.* Lamarr is ready for her close-up as the seductive Delilah in this typically lush DeMille biblical drama. Mature is quite good as strongman Samson who gets the "cut" from rejected lover Delilah. ★★★ VHS: $14.99

Samurai I: Musashi Miyamoto

(1954, 92 min, Japan, Hiroshi Inagaki) *Toshiro Mifune.* Scintillating thrills and excitement are promised for fans of samurai and adventure films with this rousing trio called the "Samurai Trilogy," which is based upon the real-life adventures of legendary swordsman Miyamoto Musashi. The great Mifune is the peasant who trains to become a master swordsman and protector of his people. This, the first part, introduces the aspiring samurai and examines his arduous training and indoctrination. (Japanese with English subtitles) ★★★ DVD: $29.99, VHS: $19.99

Samurai II: Duel at Ichijoji Temple

(1955, 102 min, Japan, Hiroshi Inagaki) *Toshiro Mifune.* Part two of the "Samurai Trilogy" deals with the developing skills of samurai Mifune and centers around a bloody duel with a particularly mean warrior. (Japanese with English subtitles) ★★★ DVD: $29.99, VHS: $19.99

Samurai III: Duel at Ganryu Island

(1956, 102 min, Japan, Hiroshi Inagaki) *Toshiro Mifune.* In this, the concluding chapter of the "Samurai Trilogy," we follow our hero's romantic interlude as well as his defense of a village from a marauding horde. We also witness the inevitable showdown with his arch nemesis, Kojiro. Please note: Although the three films in the "Samurai Trilogy" follow a chronology, each film can be enjoyed and understood independently of each other. (Japanese with English subtitles) ★★★ DVD: $29.99, VHS: $19.99

San Francisco

(1936, 116 min, US, W.S. Van Dyke) *Clark Gable, Spencer Tracy, Jeanette MacDonald, Jack Holt.* One of the most popular films of the 1930s, this early disaster film stars Gable as a saloon owner and MacDonald as a singer who fall in love — all set

right before the big earthquake of 1905. Tracy is excellent in support as Gable's best pal, and the special effects are quite good. ★★★

Sand and Blood

(1987, 101 min, France, Jeanne Labrune) *Sami Frey, Andre Dussollier.* Coming on the heels of Pedro Almodóvar's exploration of sex and violence in the bullring with *Matador* comes this more thoughtful yet equally provocative, erotically charged drama. An upcoming matador from "the wrong side of the tracks" meets and befriends a wealthy doctor who is morally opposed to the violence of the bullfight. Their unlikely relationship affects both their lives and their families as together they confront their hidden secrets and fears. (French with English subtitles) ★★★

The Sand Pebbles

(1966, 179 min, US, Robert Wise) *Steve McQueen, Richard Attenborough, Candice Bergen, Mako, Richard Crenna.* This beautifully photographed, compelling drama features a splendid performance by McQueen as a jaded sailor on an American gunboat on the Yangtze River in 1926. His increasing awareness of the volitile political situation contributes to his escalating confrontation with his superiors. A sprawling combination of action, romance and subtextual editorial comment. ★★★½ DVD: $14.99, VHS: $14.99

Sandakan No. 8

(1974, 121 min, Japan, Kei Kumai) *Kinuyo Tanaka, Yoko Takakashi.* This heartrending drama follows a female journalist who befriends an impoverished old lady who recounts her anguished life as a prostitute in a brothel in Borneo in the early 1900s. (Japanese with English subtitles) ★★★½

Sanders of the River

(1935, 98 min, GB, Zoltan Korda) *Paul Robeson, Leslie Banks.* This outmoded adventure tale about the captain of a river patrol in colonial Africa is filled with caricature and offers little insight into the colonial mindset. Still, the film is made interesting by its early use of location shooting and the dominating screen presence of Robeson. ★★½ VHS: $19.99

The Sandlot

(1993, 101 min, US, David Mickey Evans) *Tom Guiry, Mike Vitar, Denis Leary, Karen Allen, James Earl Jones, Arliss Howard, Brooke Adams.* It's the 1960s, and soon-to-be fifth grader Scotty Smalls is the new kid in town. An avid baseball fan, Scotty is befriended by a baseball-loving group of kids who all spend an idyllic summer playing our national pastime. Things are going great until Scotty's dad's prized baseball, autographed by Babe Ruth, lands in a junkyard guarded by a ferocious dog. How to get it back? This heartwarming family film is a wonderful coming-of-age tale which should entertain both child and adult. ★★★ DVD Letterbox: $14.99, VHS: $6.99

Sanjuro

(1962, 96 min, Japan, Akira Kurosawa) *Toshiro Mifune, Tatsuya Nakadai.* Mifune is at his scruffy, steely-eyed best as the leader of young revolutionaries. An action-packed adventure film, sequel to *Yojimbo.* (Japanese with English subtitles) ★★★ DVD: $29.99, VHS: $29.99

Sankofa

(1993, 125 min, US, Haile Gerima) *Oyafunmike Ogunlano, Kofi Ghanaba, Alexandra Duah, Mutabaruka.* In this successful, thought-provoking "issue" film, a modern-day, African-American model is unexplainably transported back in time to experience life as a slave. The film is all the more remarkable for avoiding polemic and for refusing to pander. After a heavy-handed opening, *Sankofa* finds its rhythm to become an extremely intense, harrowing yet dramatically rich study of a repugnant time in American history. The title says it all: "Sankofa" is an Akan word meaning "one must return to the past in order to move forward." A highly rewarding independent film. ★★★½

Sanshiro Sugata

(1943, 80 min, Japan, Akira Kurosawa) *Denjiro Okochi, Yikiko Todoroki.* Made under the watchful eye of censors, this first film by a 33-year-old Kurosawa helped establish him as a major director. Set in the late 19th century, the story revolves around Sanshiro Sugata, an eager student looking for a master to teach him the martial art of Judo. With explosive martial arts choreography, this understated philosophical film features the theme that runs throughout Kurosawa's work; that of a man who champions a principle despite an often hostile established order. (Japanese with English subtitles) ★★★ VHS: $19.99

Sansho the Baliff

(1954, 125 min, Japan, Kenji Mizoguchi) *Kinuyo Tanaka, Yoshiaki Hanayagi.* Set in the 11th century, this epic drama begins in a land ruled by a kind-hearted provincial governor who is overthrown and exiled. His wife is reduced to prostitution while his children are kidnapped and sent into slavery. One of the children escapes and vows to establish a group of followers and return to his land in force. This sweeping drama, while played on a grand scale, retains the human quality in unfolding this sad yet beautiful tale. (Japanese with English subtitles) ★★★½ VHS: $39.99

Santa Claus: The Movie

(1985, 104 min, US, Jeannot Szwarc) *Dudley Moore, John Lithgow, David Huddleston.* Big-budget, clumsy but harmless children's story about one of Santa's elves falling prey to an evil toymaker, who may use "elfin" magic to control Christmas. Huddleston is an appropriately larger-than-life Santa; however, most of the cast appear very embarrassed by what's going on. ★★ VHS: $9.99

The Santa Clause

(1994, 95 min, US, John Pasquin) *Tim Allen, Judge Reinhold, Wendy Crewson, Eric Lloyd, Peter Boyle.* A satisfactory family comedy which is in need of a lot more laughs, *The Santa Clause* rarely demonstrates the caliber of humor suggested by its catchy title. Allen plays a divorced dad who on Christmas Eve knocks Santa off the roof. Taking over Kris Kringle's holiday obligations, Allen learns in doing so he is now the new Santa — hence the Santa Clause. While the story does occasionally live up to its enjoyable premise, the film never really ignites sparks in the laughs department, depending instead on F/X wizardry and the odd wink at the audience. (Sequel: *The Santa Clause 2*) ★★½ DVD Pan & Scan Special Edition: $29.99, DVD Special Edition: $29.99, VHS Special Edition: $9.99

Santa Sangre

(1990, 120 min, Italy/Mexico, Alejandro Jodorowsky) *Axel Jodorowsky, Sabrina Dennison, Guy Stockwell.* In the furiously imaginative tradition of Jodorowsky's '70s cult classic *El Topo* comes this violent, bizarre and mystifying parable of a young man's ultimate Oedipal complex. Set in Mexico, the story begins in a circus where a young boy is witness to his mother's dismemberment and his father's suicide. Understandably affected, the neurotic boy spends his adolescence in an insane asylum, but soon escapes (or does he?) and is reunited with his armless mom. Together, they begin a killing rampage against any woman who comes close to him. Plot matters little here, for it is Jodorowsky's intense visuals, like a hallucinogenic Fellini spectacle, that assaults the viewer leaving one both exhausted and exalted by this nighmarish vision. (English language) ★★★ VHS R-Rated: $9.99

The Saphead/
The High Sign/One Week

(1920, 118 min, US, Buster Keaton, Eddie Cline, Herbert Blanche) *Buster Keaton.* A collection of three Buster Keaton comedies. *The Saphead* (1920, 78 min) features Keaton as the title character, a Wall Street heir oblivious to life around him. The creaky plot has to do with Keaton's brother-in-law trying to steal the family fortune. Keaton shines in a lengthy, well-staged sequence about a run on the stock exchange. (★★½) *One Week* (1921, 19 min) was Keaton's first short as director and writer (with Cline). It's a truly inventive, hilarious slapstick comedy about Keaton and his newlywed wife trying to build their pre-fab honeymoon home. Performing his own stunts, Keaton is a marvel. (★★★★) *The High Sign* (1921, 21 min) is a humorous story of Keaton becoming involved with a gang of cutthroats. What makes this short memorable is an unbelievable finale in which Keaton takes on the gang with the help of a booby-trapped mansion. (★★★) DVD: $29.99, VHS: $29.99

Sarafina!

(1992, 99 min, US/South Africa, Darrell James Roodt) *Whoopi Goldberg, John Kani, Leleti Khumalo, Miriam Makeba.* Mbogeni Ngema's powerful musical play about the struggle for freedom amongst South Africa's black school children receives mixed results. The young Khumalo is superb in the title role of Sarafina, a teenage girl whose ambition is to play Nelson Mandela in the school play but instead finds herself caught up in vicious conflagration of hatred. The film suffers from an almost schizophrenic vacillation between moments of profound emotional impact and almost trivial song-and-dance routines. Still, by its end the film imparts a potent message on the destructive nature of hatred. ★★½ DVD: $14.99, VHS: $9.99

Satan Met a Lady

(1936, 75 min, US, William Dieterle) *Bette Davis, Warren William.* Second screen version of Dashiell Hammet's "The Maltese Falcon" — the first was filmed in 1931 — and not on par with John Huston's 1941 classic. William plays the private eye, and Davis is the mystery woman. ★★ VHS: $19.99

Satan's Brew

(1976, 112 min, Germany, Rainer Werner Fassbinder) *Kurt Raab, Ingrid Caven.* RFW's first comedy is a weird, vulgar and perverse story of the adventures of Walter Kranz (Raab), a "revolutionary" poet who imagines himself to be the 19th-century homosexual poet Stefan George. The film, shot in a black comedic slapstick style, boasts among its peculiar characters Kranz's butch wife (Caven), a retarded brother, a wart-faced admirer and a troupe of prostitutes. (German with English subtitles) ★★½ DVD: $24.99, VHS: $19.99

Saturday Night and Sunday Morning

(1960, 89 min, GB, Karel Reisz) *Albert Finney, Shirley Anne Field, Rachel Roberts.* With a savage comic perspective, this biting drama is a classic of the "angry young man" genre. A youthful and handsome Finney is mesmerizing as a Nottingham factory worker whose rebellious nature is neatly summarized by his opening narration, "What I want is a good time. The remainder is all propaganda." The story follows Finney as he lets off steam on the weekends through his drinking binges and two romantic affairs — one of them with a married woman (a magnificent Roberts). Though no Alfie, Finney doesn't tread lightly with his depiction of a likable cad; and he and director Reisz take care in attention to time and place. A remarkable, insightful work both honest and daring. ★★★★ DVD Letterbox: $14.99

Saturday Night Fever

(1977, 118 min, US, John Badham) *John Travolta, Karen Lynn Gorney, Donna Pescow, Barry Miller, Joseph Cali.* Travolta created a cultural phenomenon as a Brooklyn youth who uses the disco dance floors to escape the tedium of his home and social life. Pescow is exceptional as a local girl in love with Travolta. A tune-filled, trendsetting time capsule both compelling and hoary. Musical score by the Bee Gees. ★★★ DVD Letterbox: $19.99, VHS R-Rated: $9.99

Saturn 3

(1980, 88 min, GB, Stanley Donen) *Kirk Douglas, Farrah Fawcett, Harvey Keitel.* From the director of *Charade* comes this odd little sci-fi parable. Space-aged, hydroponic gardeners Douglas and Fawcett find their little astro-Eden no longer a lovely, verdant garden after that snake Keitel shows up with his psycho-robot Hector. ★★

Savage Messiah

(1972, 100 min, GB, Ken Russell) *Dorothy Tutin, Scott Antony, Helen Mirren, Lindsay Kemp.* Early 20th-century French sculptor Henri Gaudier-Brzeska (Antony) and his four-year affair with the older Sophie Brzeska (Tutin) is told in this fierce, energetic if fragmented drama. A bawdy celebration of life, love and art in London's pre-WWI avant-garde art scene. ★★½

Savage Nights (Les Nuite Fauves)

(1992, 126 min, France, Cyril Collard) *Cyril Collard, Romane Bohringer, Carlos Lopez.* Possibly the most personal and controversial of all the films dealing with AIDS, *Savage Nights* is a startlingly semiautobiographical melodrama by former rock star Collard (who died from AIDS just four days before his film swept the César Awards). Collard stars as Jean, a high-living bisexual photographer who discovers he is HIV-positive. He becomes involved with both lovesick 17-year-old Laura (Bohringer) and S&M obsessed, neo-Nazi soccer player Sami (Lopez). With its jagged feel, the film effectively and unapologetically delves into the life of a nonhero and his personal response to coping with AIDS. (French with English subtitles) ★★★

The Savage Woman

(1991, 100 min, Canada, Léa Pool) *Patricia Tulasne, Matthias Habich.* After her suicide attempt fails, Marianne wanders the French wilderness avoiding contact with people and slowly losing her civilized self. She is eventually befriended by Elyseé, a lonely engineer working nearby at a dam, who nurses her back to health. The unlikely couple, seemingly against their will, soon fall in love. But their deepening relationship is strained by Marianne's secret: she's wanted by the police for murder. A taut melodrama kept interesting right until the surprise ending. (French with English subtitles) ★★★ VHS: $39.99

Savages

(1972, 106 min, GB, James Ivory) *Lewis J. Stadlen, Anne Francine, Thayer David, Sam Waterston.* By far the most offbeat result from Ivory and Ismail Merchant, this is the story of a group of clay covered savages who stumble across an abandoned mansion. Bit by bit, they assume the roles of the former, more civilized, inhabitants until finally they have constructed their own little microcosm of the landed gentry. This strange and hypnotic film evokes images of *King of Hearts* and *The Emerald Forest*. ★★½ DVD Letterbox: $29.99, VHS: $29.99

Saturday Night and Sunday Morning

Save the Last Dance

(2001, 112 min, US, Thomas Carter) *Julia Stiles, Sean Patrick Thomas, Terry Kinney, Fredro Starr, Bianca Lawson. Save the Last Dance* may be tepid, pandering teen-film garbage, but at least it has a positive message. A surprisingly weak Stiles is a dance student who moves to Chicago to live with her deadbeat dad. She attends a mostly black inner-city high school, and goes through all the usual clichés, ending up falling for Thomas. Numbingly predictable and glacially paced to boot. Rent *Flashdance* or *Dirty Dancing*, instead, and save yourself from this last dance. ★½ DVD Letterbox: $14.99, VHS: $9.99

Save the Tiger

(1973, 101 min, US, John G. Avildsen) *Jack Lemmon, Jack Gilford, Laurie Heineman, Patricia Smith, Thayer David, Lara Parker.* Lemmon's outstanding Academy Award-winning performance punctuates this often gripping account of one man's journey towards a moral divide. He plays an L.A. garment manufacturer whose business is near financial ruin. He must resort to more corrupt means for a quick financial fix. Steve Shagan's screenplay is a searing commentary on consumerism and a country's lost direction during a volatile time. In support, Gilford excels as Lemmon's ethical business partner. ★★★ VHS: $14.99

Saving Grace

(1986, 112 min, US, Robert M. Young) *Tom Conti, Giancarlo Giannini, Erland Josephson, Edward James Olmos.* With a tip of the hat to *Roman Holiday,* this muddled comedy stars Conti as the Pope who, tiring of his rigid regime, unceremoniously leaves the Vatican to spend time with the common folk. ★★

Saving Grace

(2000, 100 min, GB, Nigel Cole) *Brenda Blethyn, Craig Ferguson.* Small-town eccentrics once again populate a humorous, low-keyed British comedy, but they've done so with a new twist. The sparkling Blethyn stars as Grace, a recent widow whose husband has left her nothing but debt. Looking for financial salvation, she teams with her gardener (Ferguson) to grow marijuana in her greenhouse. Little by little, the townspeople become involved in one way or another, prompting some obvious but funny jokes. A weak ending slightly mars this otherwise winning comedy that is able to see beyond the inherent pot humor for a few sharp observations on human behavior. ★★★ DVD: $24.99

Saving Private Ryan

(1998, 170 min, US, Steven Spielberg) *Tom Hanks, Tom Sizemore, Edward Burns, Matt Damon, Jeremy Davies, Giovanni Ribisi, Adam Goldberg, Barry Pepper, Vin Diesel, Ted Danson.* D-Day, June 1944. American troops prepare to invade the beaches at Normandy. This would be the singular defining moment of WWII. The first 25 minutes of the astonishingly powerful *Saving Private Ryan,* an unflinching look of this pivotal battle, is crafted with such raw emotion and technical superiority that it nearly redefines a genre with the consummate brush stroke. What follows during the next 145 minutes is just as riveting. Hanks plays an Army sergeant who must lead an eight-man unit through enemy territory to search for and rescue a G.I., Private Ryan (Damon), whose three brothers have all been killed in combat and who now has a pass home. Spielberg has certainly done his home-

work. His re-creations of WWII battles, the camaraderie of the men, the threat of death around the corner flow in a narrative logic rarely captured on film. The ensemble is extraordinary, with Sizemore, Burns and Davies (who silently steals the film with his tortured coward) most memorable. *Saving Private Ryan* is Spielberg at his best, and, for that matter, American cinema at its best. ★★★★ DVD Letterbox: $19.99, DVD Letterbox D-Day 60th Anniversary Commemorative Edition: $26.99, VHS: $14.99, VHS Letterbox: $14.99

Saving Silverman

(2001, 92 min, US, Dennis Dugan) *Jason Biggs, Jack Black, Steve Zahn, Amanda Peet, R. Lee Ermey.* Wayne (Zahn) and J.D. (Black), lifelong friends of the titular Silverman (Biggs), feel compelled to wrest him from the clutches of his evil, obnoxious fiancée (Peet). A mix of the humorous and the annoying, *Saving Silverman* does have its pluses: a Neil Diamond is worth a few laughs, Zahn and Black are a good team, and any movie where Ermey plants a wet kiss on Jack Black's lips is worth a look. Unfortunately, Biggs is blandness itself, and Peet is almost unwatchable. However, in the end, the film's few laughs aren't enough to overcome uneven pacing, stupid human tricks and questionable shenanigans. ★★ DVD R-Rated: $14.99, DVD PG-13 Rated: $14.99, VHS PG-13 Rated: $9.99

Sawdust and Tinsel

(1953, 95 min, Sweden, Ingmar Bergman) *Harriet Andersson, Ake Gronberg.* Bergman's powerful classic is set in the circus milieu and deals with the fluctuating love allegiances between a circus owner, his wife, his mistress and her other lover. For sheer spectacle, psychological accuracy and richness of composition, this dazzling film is unrivaled. (aka: *Naked Light*) (Swedish with English subtitles) ★★★½ VHS: $29.99

Say Anything

(1989, 100 min, US, Cameron Crowe) *John Cusack, Ione Skye, John Mahoney, Joan Cusack, Lili Taylor, Bebe Neuwirth, Eric Stoltz.* Cusack stars in this intelligent, insightful and entertaining teen comedy as a high school grad who falls in love with the class valedictorian. Skye is lovely as the class queen, and Mahoney gives a stunning portrayal of her doting father. Credit writer and first-time director Crowe for making a "wrong side of the tracks" romance imbued with blithe observations on young adulthood and on the complexities of relationships — whether they be romantic or otherwise. ★★★½ DVD: $14.99, VHS: $6.99

Say It Isn't So

(2001, 97 min, US, J.B. Rogers) *Heather Graham, Chris Klein, Sally Field, Orlando Jones, Richard Jenkins.* A strained, tired farce, *Say It Isn't So* offers more bawdy foolishness from the producers of *There's Something about Mary,* grafted onto a semisweet romantic melodrama. Likable orphan hunk (Klein) falls deliriously in love with angelic chick (Graham) . . . who turns out to be his long-lost sister. Field camps it up as Graham's money-hungry, trailer-

trash mama, whose scheme for her daughter to marry a cute millionaire scumbag necessitates all sorts of connivery against hapless Klein. Here you'll find crude incest humor and merciless jibes at the disabled and deformed. Most of the laughs have the discernable whiff of previous Farrelly Brothers movie moments. ★½ DVD: $14.99, VHS: $9.99

Sayonara

(1957, 147 min, US, Joshua Logan) *Marlon Brando, Red Buttons, Miyoshi Umeki, Miiko Taka.* Immensely popular upon its release, this romantic drama benefits from a commanding performance from Brando as an American pilot stationed in post-WWII Tokyo who falls in love with a Japanese woman (Taka). Buttons and Umeki both won Oscars for their moving portrayals of ill-fated lovers. ★★★½ DVD Letterbox: $19.99

The Scalphunters

(1968, 102 min, US, Sydney Pollack) *Burt Lancaster, Ossie Davis, Shelley Winters, Telly Savalas, Dabney Coleman.* Rollicking comic western with Lancaster as a fur trapper who teams with educated slave Davis when his furs are stolen. ★★★

Scandal

(1989, 114 min, GB, Michael Caton-Jones) *John Hurt, Jeroen Krabbé, Joanne Whaley-Kilmer, Ian McKellen.* First-time director Caton-Jones' vivid enactment of the incredible sex scandal that brought a conservative British government to its knees in 1963. Whaley-Kilmer sparkles as Christine Keeler, a nightclub showgirl whose sexual dealings with the then-Minister of War, John Profumo (stoically portrayed by McKellen), and a Soviet Naval Attache (Krabbé) sparked what is still the biggest scandal in British political history. Hurt is extraordinary as Stephen Ward, the socialite and sexual provocateur whose manipulations brought about what came to be known as "The Profumo Affair." ★★★½ DVD: $14.99, VHS: $9.99

John Cusack in *Say Anything*

THE DISCERNING FILM LOVER'S GUIDE

A Scandal in Paris

(1946, 100 min, US, Douglas Sirk) *George Sanders, Signe Hasso, Akim Tamiroff, Carole Landis.* An excellent script distinguishes this early treasure from director Sirk, his first American film. Sanders' droll magnificence is well served as the legendary (and reportedly real-life) 18th-century French rogue, Eugene François Vidocq, who realized that the best way to make crime pay was to become the chief of police. But, as fate (and artistic license) would have it, he is ultimately undone by love. (aka: *Thieves' Holiday*) ★★★ DVD: $24.99, VHS: $24.99

Scandal Man

(1972, 86 min, France, Richard Balducci) *Maurice Ronet, Vittirio de Sica.* The sordid world of yellow journalism is explored in this riveting, sometimes violent look at a photojournalist working in a Parisian version of the *New York Post*. The reporter, no stranger to sensationalistic coverage, finds himself in hot water when he creates a scandal by photographing a black man kissing a white American woman, who is the daughter of a leading Ku Klux Klan member. Conspiracy, murder and intrigue follow in this rarely seen crime drama. (French with English subtitles) ★★★

Scanners

(1981, 102 min, Canada, David Cronenberg) *Patrick McGoohan, Jennifer O'Neill, Stephen Lack.* Cronenberg first achieved wide notoriety with this tense horror film about amoral scientist McGoohan who keeps track of pharmaceutically created mutants who can read your mind or make your head explode. Warning: Not for the squeamish. (Followed by 4 sequels) ★★★ DVD Letterbox: $14.99

The Scar

(1948, 82 min, US, Steve Sekely) *Paul Henreid, Joan Bennett.* Henreid is a fugitive who kills his look-alike psychiatrist and assumes his identity to see his plan backfire when the dead man's own crimes begin to surface and implicate him. An interesting low-budget thriller. (aka: *Hollow Triumph*) ★★★ VHS: $19.99

Scarecrow

(1973, 115 min, US, Jerry Schatzberg) *Al Pacino, Gene Hackman, Eileen Brennan, Ann Wedgeworth, Dorothy Tristan.* Two towering performances by Hackman and Pacino dominate this unusual but fascinating buddy film with Gene and Al as drifters who team up together and head out on the road. ★★★ VHS: $14.99

Scarecrow

(1983, 130 min, USSR, Roland Bykov) This extraordinary and haunting drama centers around the pretty Lena, a 12-year-old girl who moves to a small city on the outskirts of Moscow. Although teased by her fellow sixth graders and nicknamed "Scarecrow," Lena good-naturedly accepts it. But the pestering soon becomes mean and vicious after a school trip is cancelled and the blame is mistakenly directed at Lena. Reminiscent of *Lord of the Flies*, this powerful film is a chilling group portrait of the incredible tyranny and torment of which children are capable, as well as the strength of the individual against it. (Russian with English subtitles) ★★★½ VHS: $59.99

Scarface

(1932, 93 min, US, Howard Hawks) *Paul Muni, Ann Dvorak, George Raft, Boris Karloff.* Hawks' classic crime drama is the definitive gangster film of the 1930s. Unrelenting in its delineation of a ruthless crime lord, Muni excels as Tony Carmonte (loosely based on Al Capone), an ambitious hood who "climbs" his way to the top of the Chicago underworld in the 1920s. Expert direction by Hawks. (Remade in 1983) ★★★★ VHS: $19.99

Scarface

(1983, 170 min, US, Brian De Palma) *Al Pacino, Michelle Pfeiffer, Steven Bauer, Robert Loggia, F. Murray Abraham, Mary Elizabeth Mastrantonio, Richard Belzer.* Pacino is Tony Montana, a particularly vicious thug in the Cuban Mafia, who, fueled by a perverse vision of the American Dream, rises to the top of the drug world. Director DePalma's controversial updating of the 1932 classic is excessive, bloody, lurid and lacking even a hint of subtlety. Yet it is also visually exciting, delivering salacious fun and complete enjoyment on a gut level. ★★½ DVD Letterbox Anniversary Edition: $26.99, DVD Pan & Scan Anniversary Edition: $26.99, DVD Deluxe Gift Set: $59.99, VHS: $22.99

The Scarlet Empress

(1934, 104 min, US, Josef von Sternberg) *Marlene Dietrich.* Visually extravagant and narratively bizarre, von Sternberg's feast is unforgettable. Dietrich portrays Princess Sophia, who is transformed into sexual libertine Catherine the Great through her forced marriage to Russia's Grand Duke. ★★★ DVD: $29.99, VHS: $14.99

The Scarlet Letter

(1995, 135 min, US, Roland Joffé) *Demi Moore, Gary Oldman, Robert Duvall, Joan Plowright, Robert Prosky, Dana Ivey, Roy Dotrice.* Nathaniel Hawthorne's classic novel of romance, witchcraft and betrayal in colonial America is given a definite Cliffs Notes reworking in Joffé's muddled though handsome adaptation. A one-dimensional Moore is Hester Prynne, the noble heroine who falls in love with the local pastor (Oldman), bears a child out of wedlock, is forced to wear a scarlet "A" (for adultery) and must contend with her long-thought-dead husband (a hammy Duvall) bent on revenge. Joffé's film, while looking authentic in design and costumes, has an irritating, disjointed feel to it and most of the actors look embarrassed. ★★ DVD: $14.99, VHS: $9.99

The Scarlet Pimpernel

(1934, 95 min, GB, Harold Young) *Leslie Howard, Merle Oberon, Raymond Massey.* A stiff-lipped adventure classic with Howard, perfectly cast, as the elusive pimpernel who aids innocent victims of the French revolution while posing as a foppish member of British society. ★★★½

Scarlet Street

(1945, 102 min, US, Fritz Lang) *Edward G. Robinson, Joan Bennett, Dan Duryea.* Originally judged to be immoral here in the United States, this Lang remake of Jean Renoir's *La Chienne* moves the action from Paris to Greenwich Village, as its story of obsession, manipulation and tortuous fate unfolds. Robinson is a meek middle-aged cashier who becomes fatally attracted to the seductive charms of prostitute/actress Bennett. Egged on by the deceptive but sexy vixen, Robinson is driven to embezzlement and certain tragedy. Lang's darkest film is an expressionist moral tale and a fine example of psychological film noir. ★★★½ VHS: $19.99

Al Pacino in *Scarface* (1983)

Scary Movie

(2000, 88 min, US, Keenen Ivory Wayans) *Anna Faris, Marlon Wayans, Shawn Wayans, Carmen Electra, Jon Abrahams, Shannon Elizabeth, Cheri Oteri, Regina Hall.* Scary Movie tweaks and makes fun of all the self-serious postmodern horror flicks like *Scream* and *I Know What You Did Last Summer* that revitalized the long-dead slasher genre. But those flicks themselves were send-ups of the genre, poking playful fun at the very cinematic clichés and conventions that the characters (and the audience members) were consciously weaned on. Like any pop-cultural shooting gallery, the film fires away with goofy sight gags, double entendres and frat-boy raunchiness. Some of the jokes work, some of them fall flat with a thud. (Followed by 2 sequels) ★★½ DVD: $19.99, VHS: $9.99

Scary Movie 2

(2001, 82 min, US, Keenan Ivory Wayans) *Shawn Wayans, Marlon Wayans, Anna Faris, Regina Hall, Chris Masterson, James Woods, Tim Curry, Tori Spelling.* The Wayans brothers continue to stretch the limits of the R rating with this rather foul sequel. Insipid parodies, offensive handicapped jokes and just plain disgusting bodily fluid gags compete with the occasional good laugh. The pre-credits *Exorcist* parody is rather amusing and there's a hilarious ad for a hip-hop Christmas album. Otherwise, this is thin stuff, wasting everyone's comedic talents and displaying some true desperation on the part of the Wayans. This ends up being more depressing than funny. ★½ DVD: $19.99, VHS: $14.99

Scary Movie 3

(2003, 84 min, US, David Zucker) *Anna Faris, Anthony Anderson, Simon Rex, Leslie Nielsen, Camryn Manheim, Queen Latifah, Charlie Sheen, Eddie Griffin, Denise Richards, Regina Hall, George Carlin.* At least a step up from the last entry, *Scary Movie 3* still isn't exactly Nöel Coward, but when it's funny — which is not often enough — it's very funny. Basically a double parody of *The Ring* and *Signs* (with many other references, of course, including a Michael Jackson bit), the film moves quickly, isn't nearly as mean-spirited as its predecessors (though it does have a nasty and laughless funeral scene), and has a hilarious extended cameo by the king of these types of comedies, Leslie Nielsen. He's able to wring laughs from some weak gags, and even gets to do an in-joke about his *Airplane!* character (no big shock, since director Zucker was a codirector of that film). Unfortunately, long moments of the film go by without even producing a smile, but when you do laugh, you might find yourself laughing harder than you expected. ★★ DVD Pan & Scan: $29.99, DVD: $29.99, VHS: $24.99

Scene of the Crime

(1986, 90 min, France, André Téchiné) *Catherine Deneuve, Danielle Darrieux, Victor Lanoux.* Deneuve delivers a wonderfully multilayered performance as a divorced woman living in the French countryside. Her frustrated dreams of love and fantasy become real when she meets up with a handsome young man, recently escaped from prison, who lures her into a passionate love affair and provides a way out of the deadening provincial life. A taut, well-structured suspense thriller. (French with English subtitles) ★★★

Scenes from a Mall

(1991, 87 min, US, Paul Mazursky) *Woody Allen, Bette Midler, Bill Irwin.* The casting of Allen and Midler as a married couple was inspired — on paper. And indeed, they work well together, but this lightweight farce, set against the glitz and glamour of the Beverly Mall is basically dull and flat. She's a high-powered psychologist and he's a major promoter. They wend their way through the seemingly endless mall and go through a series of petty fights, major revelations and other assorted marital spats. Director Mazursky tries to squeeze some life out of the bone-dry script, but if it weren't for the talents of Allen and Midler, this film would be only slightly less boring than going to the mall on a Saturday night. ★★ DVD: $9.99

Scenes from a Marriage

(1973, 168 min, Sweden, Ingmar Bergman) *Liv Ullmann, Joseph Erlandson, Bibi Andersson.* The long and prolific filmmaking career of Bergman is highlighted by many classics; this film, originally a five-hour Swedish television special, must certainly count as one of his best. The film examines the decay and disintegration of a marriage. An intimate and painful look at a couple's arguments, misunderstandings, and lovemaking, as well as their eventual divorce, ending with a new post-divorce friendship. Ullmann and Erlandson excel as the wife and husband. A passionate and fascinating look at human relations. (Swedish with English subtitles) (DVD includes the film and the TV series) ★★★★ DVD Criterion Collection 3-Disc Set: $49.99, VHS: $29.99

Scenes from the Class Struggle in Beverly Hills

(1989, 95 min, US, Paul Bartel) *Jacqueline Bisset, Paul Mazursky, Ed Begley, Jr., Wallace Shawn, Paul Bartel, Ray Sharkey.* Director Bartel stays true to his slap-dash style of comedy in this often funny, sometimes outlandish and always entertaining drawing-room farce. Bisset stars as a Beverly Hills widow who mourns the loss of her husband by plotting the sexual conquest of her Chicano male-servant . . . who has a bet with another servant on who can seduce the other's employer first . . . get the picture? The stage is set for a no-holds-barred explosion of comedy in which everyone is trying to get into bed with someone. Sharkey steals the show as a bisexual butler. ★★★

Scent of a Woman

(1992, 157 min, US, Martin Brest) *Al Pacino, Chris O'Donnell, Gabrielle Anwar, Philip Seymour Hoffman.* Pacino's Oscar-winning performance is the heart and soul of this overlong and manipulative but nevertheless wickedly funny, touching comedy-drama based on the 1974 Italian comedy *Profumo di Donna.* O'Donnell is a college student who is hired to watch cantankerous, blind vet Pacino for the

Ben Kingsley in *Schindler's List*

weekend. What should be an uneventful stay at home gives way to a whirlwind tour of New York City as Pacino dupes his companion into accompanying him for a razzle-dazzle three-day getaway. The success of the film lies in Pacino's cynical, hard-bitten military man; and the actor sinks his teeth into one of the juiciest roles of his career. ★★★½ DVD Letterbox: $19.99, VHS: $9.99, VHS Letterbox: $9.99

The Scent of Green Papaya

(1993, 104 min, Vietnam, Tran Anh Hung) *Tran Nu Yen Khe, Truong Thi Loc.* An exquisite portrait of domestic life in Saigon seen through the eyes of a young Vietnamese country girl. Divided into two parts, the first and far more interesting segment shows the arrival of ten-year-old servant girl Mui. There is an internal strife amongst the family in which the innocent Mui becomes a part. The second part takes place ten years later. Mui has a new master with whom she has fallen in love, and the story concentrates on their romance. Though the film features beautiful cinematography throughout, the last half doesn't have the tension or joy of discovery which makes the first half so successful. Still, the film is a rare look into a culture and people, and its feelings of family and love are transcendent. (Vietnamese with English subtitles) ★★★ DVD: $29.99

Schindler's List

(1993, 185 min, US, Steven Spielberg) *Liam Neeson, Ben Kingsley, Ralph Fiennes, Embeth Davidtz.* In his boldest attempt to create a "cinematic masterpiece" and finally get noticed by a stubbornly disinterested Academy, Spielberg bypasses the heart and goes right for the jugular in this drama on the Holocaust. Undeniably driven by sincerity, Spielberg's Oscar-winning Best Picture is alternately impressive, maudlin, focused and well acted. Shot in black and white, the film deals with the Nazi extermination of Polish Jews and how one man, Oskar Schindler, transformed from a philandering opportunist (and Nazi profiteer) to a capitalist savior to 1,200 imprisoned Jews. With fluid camera-work, Spielberg re-creates life for Krakow's Jews during Nazi occupation. Spielberg's scenes of Nazi atrocities are emotionally wrenching, but the film's pacing, the director's trademark sentimentality and

an artificial ending keep *Schindler's List* from being the classic the director so fervently strived for. ★★★ DVD Letterbox Collector's DVD Gift Set: $34.99, DVD Pan & Scan: $26.99, DVD Widescreen: $26.99, VHS Pan & Scan: $22.99

Schizopolis

(1996, 96 min, US, Steven Soderbergh) *Steven Soderbergh, Betsy Brantley, David Jensen.* Soderbergh's experimental, witty take on contemporary middle-class values, corporate life and relationships, like his other films, is far from uplifting and is low-key to the extreme. The story, such as it is, deals with a dull mid-level executive with a stagnant marriage who, midway through the film, suddenly "turns into" a different character. The new character, it turns out, is having an affair with the exec's wife. Even more bizarre than it sounds, *Schizopolis* is an entertaining, unconventional surprise. ★★★ DVD Criterion Collection: $39.99, VHS: $19.99

School Daze

(1988, 114 min, US, Spike Lee) *Laurence Fishburne, Ossie Davis, Spike Lee, Giancarlo Esposito, Tisha Campbell, Samuel L. Jackson.* Lee's bold but ultimately unsatisfying social comedy-drama set at a black university centers on the friction between two cliques: the "wanna-bees" and the "jigaboos." Lee sets out to examine racial identity and self-discrimination in the black community; but his heavy-handed approach makes for little interest. The best scene is a musical fantasy number, which is alive with an energy unfortunately missing from the rest of the film. ★★½ DVD: $9.99

The School of Flesh
(L'Ecole de la chair)

(1998, 102 min, France, Benoît Jacquot) *Isabelle Huppert, Vincent Martinez, François Berleand, Marthe Keller.* Huppert is mesmerizing as Dominique, a fashion executive whose life becomes unraveled after she begins an affair with a thuggish bisexual hustler/bartender. Dominique's successful but romantically empty life is thrown into a whirlwind after she visits a gay bar and is inextricably attracted to the handsome bartender Quentin (Vincent Martinez). She plays the aggressor to the younger man with the two eventually entering into a turbulent relationship. Their economic, educational and age differences begin to tear at their fragile domesticity — especially when he begins a relationship with a daughter of one of Dominique's friends. Huppert is breathtaking to watch in this cool, subtle sexual drama that was adapted from a story by Yukio Mishima. (French with English subtitles) ★★★

School of Rock

(2003, 108 min, US, Richard Linklater) *Jack Black, Joan Cusack, Mike White, Sarah Silverman.* Black captures the lovable slobbery of John Belushi, the wacky irreverence of Bill Murray and the ill-focused rebelliousness of every marginally talented rock star wannabe looking for the ultimate backstage pass in *School of Rock,* a wickedly funny tribute to sticking it to the man through rock 'n' roll. The story has all the familiar elements: Dewey Finn (Black) just got kicked out of the band he founded and is about to get kicked out of his friend Ned's pad. Ned (White, who also scripted) is a substitute teacher. Dewey gets the phone call summoning Ned to a job which Dewey takes. Dewey transforms the class into a band so he can enter the Battle of the Bands and show his old band mates a thing or two . . . you get the idea. Stop rolling your eyes; while this may not have the depth of *The Commitments*, it definitely has the energy and exuberance of any rock 'n' roll band flick you can name. It nods briefly to a few teen angst staples, but was probably wise not to try to delve too deeply. Chances are excellent that you will watch this with a shit-eating grin on your face and indulge in some air guitar and screaming vocals shortly after. Needless to say, it's all about the music, man! ★★★ DVD Special Collector's Edition: $29.99, VHS: $11.99

School Ties

(1992, 107 min, US, Robert Mandel) *Brendan Fraser, Matt Damon, Chris O'Donnell, Ben Affleck, Anthony Rapp.* It is the 1950s and David Green (Fraser), a lower-middle-class kid from Scranton is recruited by the exclusive St. Matthews School to help break their three-year losing streak in football. David is quickly embraced by the school elite. But he's also forced to hide his Jewish heritage from his new anti-Semitic friends. The underlying theme of what parts of ourselves we are willing to give up in order to fit in and "be a part of things" gives this film its punch. *School Ties* is a heartfelt story with just the right amount of nostalgia and sentimentality. ★★★ DVD: $19.99, VHS: $14.99

Scooby-Doo

(2002, 80 min, US, Raja Gosnell) *Freddie Prinze, Jr., Sarah Michelle Gellar, Matthew Lillard, Linda Cardellini, Rowan Atkinson.* Scooby-Doo, where are you? You're nowhere to be found in this ramshackle, live-action version of your popular animated TV series. Where's the humor that produced joyous, endless groans from those bad puns; where's the spooky fun that came from investigating the supernatural. And why do you look so funny? Is it because you're not drawn, but a horrible CGI effect? Why is the plot about you and the gang splitting up and then reuniting so bad and the action scenes of you guys taking on zombies so poorly conceived as to make any of the TV shows seem Shakespearean in comparison? And Scoob, why is it that only Lillard even remotely captures his character Shaggy, while everyone else acts lost in limbo? Scooby, better get in touch with your agent . . . and

maybe a lawyer. (Sequel: *Scooby-Doo 2: Monsters Unleashed*) ★ DVD Letterbox: $19.99, DVD Pan & Scan: $19.99, VHS: $14.99

The Score

(2001, 124 min, US, Frank Oz) *Robert De Niro, Edward Norton, Marlon Brando, Angela Bassett, James Harrold, Gary Farmer.* Nick Wells, played with a hypnotic world-weariness by the ever dazzling De Niro, is a master thief who doesn't like to take chances. That's all about to change when he hooks up with Jack (Norton), a young, cocky protégé for an impossible score in this taut, clever heist film. When Nick is approached by his old friend Max (Brando as sort of a gay godfather) to break into the tightly guarded Customs House to retrieve a priceless scepter, he's at first reluctant. But the offer of four million dollars is quite an incentive, even if he has to pair with the inexperienced Jack. In *The Score*, as with Nick, the beauty is in the detail, and the filmmakers revel in the planning as much as the hold-your-breath execution of the crime. Director Oz creates great tension in the relationships of the three men, but not so with Nick's girlfriend Diane (Bassett), an underwritten, throwaway part. Up until its surprise ending, *The Score* is a consistently entertaining, unpredictable ride. ★★★½ DVD Letterbox: $14.99, VHS Special Edition with Behind-the-scenes Featurette: $9.99

Scorpio

(1972, 114 min, US, Michael Winner) *Burt Lancaster, Alain Delon, Paul Scofield.* Delon is a CIA assassin who is contracted by the Agency to kill his one-time partner (Lancaster) who they say is selling secrets to the Soviets. The acting in this film is, for the most part, wooden, with the exception of Scofield's portrayal of a last-of-his-breed Russian superspy living in Vienna. There are too many loose ends left hanging at the conclusion of the film, but there's a few neat non-weapons-related spy tricks to keep your mind off the hokiness of this thrill-less thriller. ★★ DVD: $14.99

The Scorpion King

(2002, 88 min, US, Chuck Russell) *The Rock, Michael Clarke Duncan, Kelly Hu, Bernard Hill, Grant Heslov, Peter Facinelli.* Macaroni and

cheese. Extra cheese pizza. Cheese-whiz. Cheesy-poofs. They're all amateurs compared to the fromage output of director Russell's silly but action-flavored sand-and-sandals adventure. Technically a prequel to the two Brendan Fraser *Mummy* movies, *The Scorpion King* brings back The Rock from *Mummy Returns*, where he played a half-human scorpion bad guy. Here, he's not quite yet icky, but a muscular mercenary out to stop the local conqueror. Eye-rolling dialogue, plenty of battle scenes (most too quickly edited to fully appreciate) and lots of ham to go with the cheese punctuate an action film that was never meant to be taken too seriously anyway. So you were expecting Shakespeare? ★★ DVD Letterbox Collector's Edition: $14.99, DVD Pan & Scan: $14.99, DVD Limited Edition with CD Soundtrack: $39.99, VHS: $9.99

The Scorpion Woman

(1989, 95 min, Austria, Susanne Zanke) *Angelica Domrose, Fritz Hammel.* The often scandalous yet strangely mesmeric theme of an older woman's relationship with a much younger man is explored once again in this interesting drama. Lisa, a 44-year-old magistrate living in Vienna, takes up with a legal assistant twenty years her junior. This relationship soon affects her professional life after she is assigned a case in which an older woman, accused of assault on a young man, is found to have been romantically involved with the victim. (German with English subtitles) ★★½ VHS: $59.99

La Scorta

(1993, 92 min, Italy, Ricky Tognazzi) *Claudio Amendola, Enrico Lo Verso, Carlo Cecchi, Ricky Memphis, Ugo Conti.* Loosely based on the real-life account of an Italian prosecutor and his crusade againt La Cosa Nostra in Sicily, *La Scorta* follows the intensely anxious lives of Judge De Francesco (Cecchi) and his "escort" of four bodyguards as they zip from meeting to meeting in rundown Alfa Romeos. New to the region, the judge quickly picks up the thread of his assassinated predecessor and thus finds himself the recipient of increasing threats. *La Scorta* concentrates very little on the actual violence or details of the investigations, but instead adeptly zeroes in on the intense bonding between the judge and his guardians. Ennio Morricone provides slightly too bombastic a soundtrack. (Italian with English subtitles) ★★★

Scotland, PA

(2001, 104 min, US, Billy Morrissette) *James LeGros, Maura Tierney, Christopher Walken, Kevin Corrigan, James Rebhorn, Tom Guiry, Andy Dick, Amy Smart.* A clever, modern update on Shakespeare's "Macbeth" set in a '70s fast-food restaurant called Duncan's, *Scotland, PA* is a quirky black comedy that can be a lot of fun even when it's not entirely hitting all its intended marks. Norm Duncan (Rebhorn) has been peddling fast food for what seems like an eternity. His employees jockey for power and are robbing him blind. Slighted when he is overlooked to be manager, Joe McBeth (LeGros) plots with his wife (Tierney) to murder Duncan. A frying pan and a vat of cooking grease takes care of him. His two sons inherit the business, but neither one of them wants to follow in Dad's footsteps. They sell to the McBeth's, who start a drive-in and must contend with Ernie McDuff (Walken), a shuffling TV-style cop investigating the mysterious fat-fryer murder case. With great '70s haircuts, clothing, sets and a classic rock score, *Scotland, PA* revels in its own peculiar invention. ★★★ DVD: $19.99, VHS: $79.99

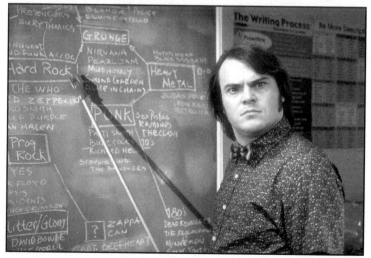

Jack Black in *School of Rock*

The Scout

(1994, 100 min, US, Michael Ritchie) *Albert Brooks, Brendan Fraser, Dianne Wiest, Lane Smith.* An occasionally funny, improbable and mawkish baseball tale. Brooks is a scout for the New York Yankees. Sent to Mexico, he discovers phenom Fraser. And before the film looks like another fish out of water comedy, Brooks brings him back to the States. That's when his and the film's problems begin. Fraser turns out to be mentally unstable, and Brooks and shrink Wiest attempt to get to the root of the problem. The film's beginning has a charm to it, thanks to Brooks' underplaying, and Fraser gives an appealing performance. But the last half is painfully bad, underscored by an incredulous ending. ★★ DVD: $9.99, VHS: $9.99

Scream

(1996, 110 min, US, Wes Craven) *Neve Campbell, Skeet Ulrich, Drew Barrymore, David Arquette, Courteney Cox, Rose McGowan, Matthew Lillard, Jamie Kennedy, Liev Schreiber.* Full of in-jokes and references to countless splatter movies from the 1980s, *Scream* works as homage, spoof and as one scary horror film. Beginning as a slasher movie, the story soon becomes a murder mystery with plenty of red herrings. A masked killer is terrorizing the town, slowly working his (or her?) way to the traumatized daughter (Campbell) of another local murder victim. The remaining teens gather at a big house in the woods to watch horror movies, drink and get laid. The killer, of course, is there and all hell breaks loose. Destined to become a postmodern horror movie classic which will eventually be ranked along with *Halloween* and *Dawn of the Dead*. (Followed by 2 sequels) ★★★½ DVD Letterbox Collector's Edition: $14.99, VHS: $9.99, VHS Letterbox: $9.99

Scream 2

(1997, 120 min, US, Wes Craven) *Neve Campbell, Courteney Cox, David Arquette, Sarah Michelle Gellar, Jada Pinkett, Jerry O'Connell, Liev Schreiber, Laurie Metcalf, Omar Epps, Heather Graham, David Warner.* A solid follow-up, *Scream 2* takes place two years after the events of the first film, as Sidney (Campbell) is attending a Midwestern college. A handful of copycat murders coincide with the release of the film *Stab*, based on the events from the first film. While not as scary as the original, this is just as suspenseful and full of surprises. Good performances, crisp photography and an effective score complement Craven's stylish direction and Kevin Williamson's well-crafted screenplay. Although a protracted climax does detract a bit from the fun, this is almost on par with the original. ★★★ DVD Collector's Edition: $19.99, VHS: $9.99, VHS Letterbox: $14.99

Scream 3

(2000, 117 min, US, Wes Craven) *Neve Campbell, Courteney Cox, David Arquette, Lance Henriksen, Jenny McCarthy, Parker Posey, Carrie Fisher, Kelly Rutherford, Liev Schreiber.* This could be dubbed *Return of the Law of Diminishing Returns*. After the enjoyable first two films, it appears the gang has just run out of ideas and is cashing in. Sidney, now a recluse living under a pseudonym, works as a phone counselor, while *Stab 3*, the newest installment of the film-within-a-film series is being shot in Hollywood. The opening is good, and there's an amusing chase through a soundstage mockup of Sidney's original house, but Craven's bored direction and a shockingly unshocking climax are more indicative of the desperation of this enterprise. Please, no *Scream 4*! ★★ DVD Collector's Edition: $19.99, VHS: $9.99

Scream of Stone

(1990, 105 min, Canada/West Germany, Werner Herzog) *Donald Sutherland, Brad Dourif.* In this, one of his most disciplined films, Herzog has again found his emotional correlative in nature: a monolith of a mountain in Argentina, a "scream of stone." Sutherland has been hired to produce a live TV program as two of the world's greatest mountain climbers try to conquer unknown territory — both external and internal. Dourif gives a rich performance as the one climber who has come to peace with The Mountain having tried to conquer it to win the affections of (the late) Mae West. ★★★

Screamers

(1996, 100 min, US, Christian Duguay) *Peter Weller, Roy Dupuis, Jennifer Rubin.* Weller stars as a beleaguered colonel in this not uninteresting adaptation of a short story by Philip K. Dick (*Blade Runner*). Weller's laconic character commands a small group of soldiers stationed on a distant mining planet at war with biochemical entities known as "Screamers." The story focuses on Weller's attempts to cross the planet's wasteland to broker a truce. Not very original nor particularly good, though the limited special effects can be entertaining. ★★ DVD: $19.99

Screw Loose

(2000, 85 min, US/Italy, Ezio Greggio) *Mel Brooks, Ezio Greggio, Julie Condra.* Greggio plays a much-put-upon son, whose father's dying wish is to thank the American G.I. who saved his life in WWII. Since Papa only has two weeks to live, Greggio hurriedly flies to the U.S. to find the man. He turns out to be . . . wacky Mel Brooks, who resides in a mental institution. While Greggio and company obviously aim for the old-school comedy style of Buster Keaton and Jacques Tati, they fall well below the mark. Painful one-liners, sloppy slapstick and zero comic timing sink this quickly. ★ DVD: $24.99, VHS: $19.99

Scrooge

(1970, 114 min, GB, Ronald Neame) *Alec Guinness, Edith Evans, Kenneth Moore, Albert Finney.* Though it won't replace Alastair Sim's 1951 *A Christmas Carol* as the definitive screen version of Dickens' novel, there's a lot to like in this musical adaptation. Finney makes an appropriately cantankerous Ebenezer Scrooge, the miser and all-around-humbug who is visited by three spirits on Christmas Eve. A pleasant if uninspired score by Leslie Bricusse. ★★★ DVD: $14.99, VHS: $14.99

Scrooged

(1988, 101 min, US, Richard Donner) *Bill Murray, Karen Allen, Carol Kane, Bobcat Goldthwait, Alfre Woodard, Robert Mitchum, Buddy Hackett.* A mildly entertaining updating of Dickens' "A Christmas Carol" with Murray taking over the role of Scrooge, here as a heartless TV executive. It's not as funny as it could have been, but there are some good moments: especially Kane as a whacked-out Ghost of Christmas Present and Goldthwait as a 1980s Bob Cratchet. ★★½ DVD: $19.99, VHS: $9.99

Scrubbers

(1982, 90 min, GB, Mai Zetterling) *Amanda York, Chrissie Cotterill.* A comic and tragic tale about a tough crop of women inmates at a dingy British borstal. From the black lesbian lovers to the mute anorexic, the leather-jacketed tough girl and the baby-faced heroine, the performers are feisty and unforgettably human. ★★★

Scum

(1980, 98 min, GB, Alan Clarke) *Phil Daniels, Ray Winstone, Mick Ford.* This harrowing British drama explores the physical, sexual and psychological violence in a borstal (prison) for youthful offenders. A powerful and disturbing tale. The film could have used a more palatable title for its commercial release. ★★★

The Sea Hawk

(1940, 127 min, US, Michael Curtiz) *Errol Flynn, Claude Rains, Donald Crisp, Flora Robson, Alan Hale.* Classic sea adventure with Flynn swashing-many-a-buck on the high seas as a pirate captain taking on the Spaniards in the name of England and Queen Elizabeth I. Outstanding score by Erich Wolfgang Korngold. ★★★½

Sea of Grass

(1947, 131 min, US, Elia Kazan) *Spencer Tracy, Katharine Hepburn, Melvyn Douglas, Robert Walker.* Unusual western based on a Conrad Richter story about New Mexico grasslands and the fight to preserve them. The film features a good cast, but much of this is heavy going. ★★½

Sea of Love

(1989, 112 min, US, Harold Becker) *Al Pacino, Ellen Barkin, John Goodman, Michael Rooker.* Pacino gives a solid performance as a veteran New York City detective assigned to catch a serial killer who makes contact through the personals. Placing an ad, Pacino goes undercover, setting up a rendezvous under the watchful eye of partner Goodman. There he meets sexy prime suspect Barkin. The two begin a passionate affair; all the while clues point to her guilt. ★★★ DVD Collector's Edition: $14.99, VHS: $9.99

The Sea Wolf

(1941, 90 min, US, Michael Curtiz) *Edward G. Robinson, Ida Lupino, John Garfield, Alexander Knox.* Jack London's exciting tale of the sea makes for a riveting, atmospheric high-seas adventure. Adapted for the screen by Robert Rossen, the story plots the course of three civilians who find themselves on board the aptly-named schooner *Ghost*, helmed by the tyrannical Cpt. Wolf Larsen. Robinson is dynamic as the hardened captain; a lovely Lupino and a handsome Garfield are both fugitives from the law; and Knox is an idealistic writer forced to face the barbaric side of human nature. A rip-roaring action film which gives berth to both high adventure and intelligent characterizations. (Remade in 1997) ★★★½ VHS: $19.99

The Sea Wolves

(1980, 120 min, US/GB, Andrew V. McLaglen) *Gregory Peck, Roger Moore, David Niven, Trevor Howard, Patrick MacNee.* An engaging WWII adventure about a group of ex-British cavalry soldiers doing their part against the Nazis. They go after a German radio transmitter with some suspenseful and funny results. ★★★ DVD: $9.99, VHS: $14.99

Seabiscuit

(2003, 145 min, US, Gary Ross) *Tobey Maguire, Jeff Bridges, Chris Cooper, William H. Macy, Elizabeth Banks, Gary Stevens.* In an era when sports legends such as Babe Ruth, Joe Louis and Don Budge were front-page news, it's hard to imagine that in 1937 they were all eclipsed by a ragged, undersized race horse. Adapted from Laura Hillenbrand's best-seller, *Seabiscuit* tells the

Tobey Maguire astride *Seabiscuit*

improbable but true tale of how a tattered, weary steed weathered all to become champion. An old-fashioned entertainment that is stirring though occasionally distant, the film traces the lives of the three men who brought Seabiscuit to its legacy. The ever-reliable Bridges is Charles Howard, a successful car dealer who buys Seabiscuit at the urging of trainer Tom Smith (Cooper in mystical mode). Down-on-his-luck jockey John Pollard (Maguire) is hired to ride the horse, establishing a bond with both surrogate father Howard and the once-abandoned animal. Writer-director Ross spends a lot (possibly too much) time in establishing the characters, though each one's story is compelling and nicely told. When Seabiscuit finally makes his entrance, the film picks up steam and gains momentum, establishing a good pace, exhibiting exciting racing scenes, and exploring moving dynamics between the characters. Though never as great as it should have been, *Seabiscuit* is a handsome crowd-pleaser that effortlessly evokes 1930s America and its mindset which turned three outcasts and a broken-down horse into national heroes. ★★★ DVD Letterbox Limited Edition Gift Set: $49.99, DVD Letterbox: $26.99, DVD Pan & Scan: $26.99, VHS: $14.99

Séance on a Wet Afternoon

(1964, 116 min, GB, Bryan Forbes) *Kim Stanley, Richard Attenborough, Margaret Lacey.* This enthralling psychological thriller breathes with an atmosphere of ever-building suspense that is unrelentingly sustained. A pair of superb performances are offered by Stanley and Attenborough as a medium and her husband who kidnap a child in order to publicize her clairvoyant skills. Written and directed by Forbes, it stands as one of the best and most unusual British films of the '60s. ★★★½ DVD Letterbox: $29.99

The Search

(1948, 104 min, US, Fred Zinnemann) *Montgomery Clift, Aline MacMahon, Ivan Jandl.* A touching story, sensitive direction and a sobering theme all contribute to make this a classic post-war drama. Clift gives a fine performance as an American soldier stationed in war-ravaged

Germany who takes in a young Czech boy — a concentration camp survivor — when he finds the youth alone on the streets. Meanwhile, the boy's mother searches for her son from camp to camp. Filmed on location in Berlin amid the bombed out buildings, which only serves to enhance the poignant narrative. Little Jandl is a heartbreaker as the boy. ★★★★

Search and Destroy

(1995, 90 min, US, David Salle) *Griffin Dunne, Dennis Hopper, John Turturro, Christopher Walken, Illeana Douglas, Rosanna Arquette, Ethan Hawke, Martin Scorsese.* Dunne heads a cast of Hollywood's coolest in this self-consciously hip adaptation of the Broadway play about a Florida film producer, at odds with the IRS, who tries to orchestrate a movie deal based on the writings of an eccentric New Age guru (Hopper). Possessed by moments of articulate insights, painter-turned-artist Salle's work is not altogether successful, relying too much on the gratuitously weird nature of the characters and situations to sustain it. He should have allowed his marvelous ensemble to breathe life into it. ★★½

The Search for One-Eye Jimmy

(1996, 86 min, US, Sam Henry Kass) *Steve Buscemi, Samuel L. Jackson, Jennifer Beals, John Turturro, Ray Mancini, Michael Badalucco, Nicholas Turturro, Anne Meara. Sherman's March* meets *The Third Man*? Not quite. A film student returns to his Brooklyn neighborhood to make a documentary about it and becomes wrapped up in a missing persons case — with the camera rolling, of course. Kass' lifeless direction sabotages his subtle screenplay, and bits that should have worked just aren't that funny. A few big names in small parts add a little life, but this one gets filed under "promising fiasco." ★½

The Search for Signs of Intelligent Life in the Universe

(1991, 120 min, US, Jane Wagner) *Lily Tomlin.* This delightful and engaging Tony Award-winning two-hour, one-woman show can easily be considered Tomlin's magnum opus. The show centers

around Trudy the Bag Lady as she escorts a group of visiting aliens from outer space and attempts to enlighten them on human idiosyncracies. Using this premise, Lily jumps from one character to another amazingly giving life — without benefit of makeup or costume — to a host of wonderful characters. ★★★½ VHS: $29.99

The Searchers

(1956, 155 min, US, John Ford) *John Wayne, Jeffrey Hunter, Natalie Wood, Vera Miles, Ward Bond.* In a career rich with milestones, Ford achieved one of his greatest artistic triumphs with this beautifully filmed western. Wayne had one of his most complex characters — possibly wanted by the law and consumed with racial hatred — as Ethan Edwards, who after his brother and sister-in-law are murdered by Indians, sets out to locate his kidnapped niece (played by Wood). Hunter is Wood's brother who accompanies Wayne on his relentless, years-long search. ★★★★ DVD: $19.99, VHS: $14.99, VHS Letterbox: $14.99

Searching for Bobby Fischer

(1993, 110 min, US, Steven Zaillian) *Max Pomerance, Joe Mantegna, Laurence Fishburne, Joan Allen, Ben Kingsley.* Every competitive endeavor, whether baseball, figure skating or chess, contains at its core artistry and purity. It's remarkable for a film to capture the passionate involvement of an activity's participants; even more so when the activity is as internal as that of chess. *Searching for Bobby Fisher* is profoundly successful in this. The story of a young boy's initiation into a glorious obsession with chess is intercut with an almost mythologized recounting of the career of Bobby Fisher. Pomeranc is mesmerizing as Josh, the 10-year-old whose intuitive grasp of the game thrusts him into a world of rivalry, clashing egos and immense satisfactions. ★★★★ DVD: $19.99, VHS: $9.99

Season of the Witch

(1972, 89 min, US, George A. Romero) *Jan White, Ray Laine, Anne Muffly.* The director of *Night of the Living Dead* takes on witchcraft with this boring tale of a young woman grappling to hang onto her sanity as she becomes enmeshed with members of a witches' coven. ★½ VHS: $14.99

Sebastiane

(1976, 85 min, GB, Derek Jarman & Paul Humfress) *Leonardo Treviglio, Neil Kennedy, Barney James, Richard Warwick.* Jarman's sensual, lushly photographed, highly erotic (and homoerotic) vision of the legend of St. Sebastian is filled with beautiful images of male bodies and graphic scenes of sex and torture. The lives of few saints are as shrouded in mystery as that of the celebrated martyr Sebastian, whose arrow-pierced body has become one of the most familiar images in Christian iconography. In this film, he is perceived as a Christian sympathizer who, sent into exile by the Emperor Diocletian, becomes involved in a sadomasochistic intrigue which ultimately results in his death. Music by Brian Eno. (Latin with English subtitles) ★★★ DVD Letterboxed: $29.99, VHS: $24.99

The Second Awakening of Christina Klages

(1977, 93 min, Germany, Margarethe von Trotta) *Tina Engel, Sylvia Reize, Katharina Thalbach, Peter Schneider, Marius Müller-Westernhagen.* In von Trotta's intriguing debut, Christa (Engel) is a frustrated day care worker who robs a bank with her

Kate Maberly and Andrew Knott in Agnieszka Holland's *The Secret Garden* (1993)

lover Werner (Müller-Westernhagen) to insure its continued operation. As the police try to track the criminals down, Christa and Werner seek refuge with her friend Ingrid (Reize), a beautician. Meanwhile, another woman, Lena (Thalbach), who was a hostage in the robbery, is searching for the thieves for her own reasons. Von Trotta's film is a lyrical and passionate story that builds to a powerful conclusion. In the title role, Engel gives a riveting performance. (German with English subtitles) ★★★ VHS: $39.99

Second Best

(1994, 105 min, GB, Chris Menges) *William Hurt, Chris Cleary Miles, Keith Allen, John Hurt, Jane Horrocks, Prunella Scales.* A harrowing and at times bleak story of father-son relationships. Hurt is an introverted Welsh postmaster who petitions to adopt a troubled ten-year-old. The story, which has as much to do with the adoption process as with interpersonal relationships, follows the rocky road on which Hurt must gain the trust and ultimately the affection of his young charge, who still envisions a reunion with his gaoled father. Hurt and young Miles help smooth over some of the more choppy dramatics. ★★½ VHS: $19.99

Second Chance

(1953, 81 min, US, Rudolph Maté) *Robert Mitchum, Linda Darnell, Jack Palance.* Potent mystery thriller with Mitchum as an ex-boxer who helps gangster's girlfriend Darnell elude contract killer Palance in Mexico. ★★½

Second Chorus

(1940, 83 min, US, H.C. Potter) *Fred Astaire, Paulette Goddard, Burgess Meredith.* Astaire and Meredith are fellow musicians who set their sights on their lovely manager, Goddard. Not without its charms, but by no means one of Fred's better musicals. ★★½ VHS: $19.99

Second Skin

(1999, 104 min, Spain, Gerardo Vera) *Javier Bardem, Jordi Moll, Ariadna Gil, Cecilia Roth.* A bisexual affair won't always guarantee provocative drama, as evidenced by this sullen potboiler which nearly makes ménage à trois look boring. Alberto is a successful, married businessman who spends much of his time on the road. His wife, Elena, has her hands full as an artist and mother — she has no

time to think about if her husband is cheating on her. Which, as it turns out, he is — with another man. Bardem is Diego, a handsome surgeon who is unaware that his new boyfriend, Alberto, is married. Thus is set in motion a soap operatic chain of events to please only lovers of "One Life to Live." Bardem is actually quite good as the lover who has difficulty grasping why his amorous mate can't stay overnight, and while Diego's scenes with Alberto crackle with sexual tension, Molla is less successful in conveying Alberto's turmoil over his sexual identity. (Spanish with English subtitles) ★★ DVD Unrated: $29.99, VHS Unrated: $29.99

Seconds

(1966, 106 min, US, John Frankenheimer) *Rock Hudson, Salome Jens, John Randolph, Will Geer.* Hudson stars, in arguably his best screen performance, as the "after" part of a bizarre transformational experiment. A middle-aged businessman goes to a mysterious organization which promises to give him a second chance. After extensive surgery, he wakes up with a new face and identity. Settling into his new life, he eventually realizes that he will never find the happiness that he thought was waiting around the corner. So he returns to the organization for another try, with unfortunate results. This bizarre but simple story is itself transformed into a masterpiece of paranoia and horror by Frankenheimer's taut direction and James Wong Howe's dazzling, canted-angled, black-and-white cinematography. Disturbing but brilliant, *Seconds* always remains plausible, its proposition desirable enough to make it seem very real. ★★★½ DVD Letterbox: $14.99, VHS: $9.99

Secret Admirer

(1985, 98 min, US, David Greenwalt) *C. Thomas Howell, Lori Laughlin, Kelly Preston, Fred Ward, Dee Wallace Stone.* An intriguing premise can't sustain this uneven sex comedy about a teenager (Howell) who wrongly assumes the identity of the sender of an anonymous love letter. When the letter falls into the hands of parents and neighbors, further complications arise. ★★ DVD Dual: $14.99

The Secret Agent

(1935, 86 min, GB, Alfred Hitchcock) *John Gielgud, Madeleine Carroll, Peter Lorre, Robert Young, Lilli Palmer, Michael Redgrave.* Taken from an episode in "Ashenden," a W. Somerset Maugham

novel, this gripping story follows agent Gielgud, dispatched to Switzerland to terminate a spy whose identity he doesn't know. Director Hitchcock creates maximun suspense with his usual flair. Lorre is great in support as a Russian agent who certainly likes his vodka. ★★★ VHS: $24.99

The Secret Agent

See: *Joseph Conrad's The Secret Agent*

Secret Ceremony

(1968, 109 min, US, Joseph Losey) *Elizabeth Taylor, Mia Farrow, Robert Mitchum, Peggy Ashcroft, Pamela Brown.* This campy psychological thriller stars Taylor as a middle-aged tart who becomes involved in a strange relationship with a mentally unbalanced rich orphan (Farrow). Taylor's character, still in mourning over the loss of a young daughter, finds her emotional and financial needs answered with "poor little doc" Mia. They play mommy and daughter, yet with interesting lesbian undertones. Soon, Farrow's sexually abusive stepfather (Mitchum) returns unexpectedly, prompting a dramatic escalation of tensions. ★★

The Secret Garden

(1993, 101 min, US, Agnieszka Holland) *Kate Maberly, Heydon Prowse, Andrew Knott, Maggie Smith, Iréne Jacob.* Holland makes her English-language debut with this superlative adaptation of Frances Hodgson Burnett's 1909 children's classic, crating what must be the definitive screen translation of this oft-adapted tale. Ten-year-old Mary Lennox is sent to live in the gloomy estate of her uncle, Lord Craven. There she is chastened by the manor's obdurate housekeeper Mrs. Medlock (stonily portrayed by Smith) not to snoop which, of course, she immediately does. Emotionally and visually rich in every detail, Holland's film probes the psychological aspects of the story as young Mary (flawlessly portrayed by Maberly) uncovers the house's secrets and befriends both its sickly young master and a local farm boy with an affinity for animals. ★★★★ DVD: $14.99, VHS: $9.99

Secret Honor

(1984, 90 min, US, Robert Altman) *Philip Baker Hall.* Hall gives a bravura performance in this lacerating Altman adaptation of an original screenplay about the political and personal demise of Richard Nixon. The action transpires in Nixon's private office, sometime after his resignation. Embittered by his political fortunes, brimming with hatred and vengeance, he launches into a ferocious monologue about his obsessions and regrets. Throughout, we are given a sometimes touching, often repugnant look at a frighteningly complex man. ★★★½

The Secret Life of Walter Mitty

(1947, 110 min, US, Norman Z. McLeod) *Danny Kaye, Virginia Mayo, Boris Karloff.* One of Kaye's most popular films, this funny adaptation of James Thurber's comedy has Danny as the timid, daydreaming hero whose constant fantasies get him involved in real-life adventures. Kaye's constant costar Mayo is as lovely as ever, and Karloff has an amusing supporting role as a psychiatrist. ★★★

The Secret of My Success

(1987, 110 min, US, Herbert Ross) *Michael J. Fox, Helen Slater, Richard Jordan, Margaret Whitton.* There are echoes of *How to Succeed in Business* in this amiable though lowbrow comedy with Fox coming to the big city and moving up the corporate ladder thanks to a little chicanery. Fox is the main attraction here. ★★½ DVD Letterbox: $14.99, VHS: $7.49

The Secret of N*I*M*H

(1982, 84 min, US, Don Bluth) *Voices of: Dom DeLuise, Derek Jacobi, Peter Strauss.* Charming, low-keyed animated tale, based on Robert C. O'Brien's award-winning children's book, about a mother mouse who tries to save her home from being destroyed with the aid of her wacky animal friends. ★★★ DVD: $14.99, VHS: $9.99

The Secret of Roan Inish

(1995, 103 min, US, John Sayles) *Jeni Courtney, Mick Lally, Eileen Colgan.* Sayles has created a lyrical and enchanting Irish fairy tale based on the novel "Secret of Ron Mor Skerry" by Rosallie K. Fry. Young Fiona Coneelly (Courtney) is sent to live with her grandparents on Ireland's rugged and forbidding northwestern coast. Unperturbed by her change of scene, Fiona begins to pursue her murky family history and long-lost baby brother. His mystery revolves around a remote island called Roan Inish, the ancestral stomping grounds of the Coneelly clan and home to Selkies, mystical half-seal and half-human sea creatures. With the help of cinematographer Haskel Wexler's haunting imagery, Sayles presents a flawless piece of storytelling that is as heartwarming as it is foreboding. Sayles pays brilliant homage to oral traditions. ★★★★ DVD: $24.99

Secret Places

(1985, 96 min, GB, Zelda Barron) *Maria Therese Relin, Tara MacGowan, Jenny Agutter.* Set in an English boarding school during WWII, this warm, often moving drama follows two schoolgirls from very different backgrounds who form an ill-fated friendship. A poignant and sensitive exposé of the chasms between social classes featuring a youthful dialogue on love, sex, philosophy and patriotism. ★★★ VHS: $79.99

The Secret Rapture

(1994, 96 min, GB, Howard Davies) *Juliet Stevenson, Joanne Whalley-Kilmer, Penelope Wilson, Neil Pearson, Alan Howard.* David Hare's masterful screen adaptation of his original play is this study of a young woman (Stevenson) who must reevaluate her life when her father's death leaves her in the care of his manipulative, alcoholic widow (Whalley-Kilmer). The film is at once intimate and powerful and, flawed fourth act notwithstanding, is consistently gripping. Stevenon goves a remarkably textured performance that is sorrowful and triumphant. ★★★½

Secretary

(2002, 111 min, US, Steven Shainberg) *James Spader, Maggie Gyllenhaal, Jeremy Davies, Lesley Ann Warren, Stephen McHattie.* Even for those who don't like being spanked, *Secretary* has something intensely rewarding to offer. The film is anchored by Gyllenhaal's breakthrough performance as Lee, a shy young woman who has only recently been released from a mental institution. Her history has been to resolve problems by cutting herself, which makes sharp blades, band aids and iodine essential accessories in her makeup bag. When Lee answers a lawyer's ad for a secretarial position, all seems to be on the up and up. But she soon finds this is no ordinary lawyer, and before you can say fax machine, the employer/employee relationship is given a *spanking* new definition. While playful and even a bit humorous in its kinkiness, *Secretary* still takes its characters seriously. *Secretary* makes for a nice alternative love story that transcends the lovey-dovey romance of many lesser films. ★★★½ DVD: $14.99, VHS: $49.99

Secrets & Lies

(1996, 143 min, GB, Mike Leigh) *Brenda Blethyn, Marianne Jean-Baptiste, Timothy Spall, Phyllis Logan, Claire Rushbrook.* Director Leigh brilliantly communicates two decades of one family's secrets and lies brought to light by one woman's search for her birth mother. Jean-Baptiste gives one of several superlative performances from the ensemble as Hortense, the daughter given up for adoption. Her quest to discover her biological mother injects Hortense into another family's intricate obfuscations and smoldering resentments. As her birth mother Cynthia, Blethyn perfectly embodies a woman at sea in the world, buffeted by circumstance, imbued with defeat and helplessness. Cynthia, who is white, is at first overwhelmed by the arrival of Hortense, who is black. But before long, the shock transforms to catharsis as Hortense invites Cynthia to participate in a happier world. *Secrets & Lies* utilizes the grinding minutiae of daily living to underscore raw emotion and numbing

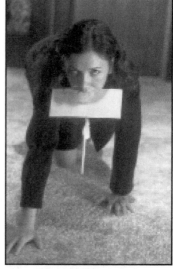

Maggie Gyllenhaal in *Secretary*

regret, and yet acknowledges with joyous tribute the indomitable human spirit. ★★★★ VHS: $9.99

Secrets of Women

(1952, 108 min, Sweden, Ingmar Bergman) *Jarl Kulle, Anita Bjork.* This early Bergman comedy is a thought-provoking and witty story of the indiscretions and foibles of man. Set in a summer home, three women confide in one another about their relationships with their husbands. Their extramarital affairs and the rapprochements with their men make for interesting conversation with amusing insights into the human condition. (Swedish with English subtitles) ★★★ VHS: $29.99

Seduced and Abandoned

(1964, 118 min, Italy, Pietro Germi) *Saro Urzi, Stefania Sandrelli.* This witty yet bitter film studies the inequalities and injustices of the Sicilian moral code. A young woman is befriended and seduced by the fiancé of her sister. His denial of any responsibility and his abandonment destroys her. The film alternates between a bedroom farce and social realism and is a successful follow-up to the director's *Divorce, Italian Style.* (Italian with English subtitles) ★★★

The Seduction of Mimi

(1974, 89 min, Italy, Lina Wertmüller) *Giancarlo Giannini, Mariangela Melato, Turi Ferro, Agostina Belli, Elena Fiore.* A boisterous farce on machismo Italian-style. On one level, a socio-politicial satire, the film also gives stunning portrayals of passion, revenge and paranoia. Sicilian metalworker Mimi (Giannini) won't support the local Mafia candidate in an election. Forced to move north, he falls in love with Fiore (Melato), a Trotskyite with a penchant for knitting. Wertmüller's surgically sharp satire earned her a reputation on the international scene. (American remake: *Which Way Is Up*) (Italian with English subtitles) ★★★½ DVD: $14.99, VHS: $29.99

The Seduction of Mimi

Seduction: The Cruel Woman

(1985, 84 min, Germany, Monika Treut & Elfie Mikesch) *Mechthild Grossmann, Sheila McLaughlin.* Treut and Mikesch's highly stylized and dreamlike exploration of sado-masochism stars Grossmann as Wanda — a glamorous dominatrix and proprietor of the local "gallery" of bondage. As she moves from relationship to relationship, the film plumbs the depths of the dark side of sexual desire. A slick, visual fantasy which is inspired as much by the photography of Helmut Newton as by Leopold Sacher-Masoch's 1869 work, "Venus in Furs." (German with English subtitles) ★★★ DVD: $24.99, VHS: $29.99

See No Evil, Hear No Evil

(1989, 103 min, US, Arthur Hiller) *Richard Pryor, Gene Wilder, Joan Severance.* Pryor and Wilder team for a third time in this amiable and often funny comedy. The comics play two mismatched, prospective coworkers — the catch is that Pryor is blind and Wilder is deaf — who become suspects in a murder which they (sort of) witness. The film is mostly one long chase as the two try to elude the police while they try to track down the real killers. *See No Evil* has questionable taste in a couple of its gags, but it's enlivened by two comic princes. ★★½ DVD: $19.99, VHS: $9.99

See Spot Run

(2001, 94 min, US, John Whitesell) *David Arquette, Michael Clarke Duncan, Leslie Bibb, Paul Sorvino, Anthony Anderson.* There are some things that parents will never understand: the Pokémon phenomena, the prevalence of mega-sour candy, and the enduring appeal of poopy. *See Spot Run* is an aggressively stupid comedy, in which a cute dog (he's also an FBI agent) upstages a buffoon (Arquette) and charms a kid; in other words, it's a formula that preteens will love. And there's plenty of doody to go around. So trust us, your kids will eat this up. Trust us also that while they're laughing their heads off and you're wondering where you went wrong, they *will* grow out of it (unless they're named David Arquette). ★½ DVD: $14.99, VHS: $14.99

See You in the Morning

(1989, 119 min, US, Alan J. Pakula) *Jeff Bridges, Alice Krige, Farrah Fawcett, Linda Lavin, Drew Barrymore, Lukas Haas.* Bridges and Krige star in this uneven romantic comedy-drama as a middle-aged couple struggling with issues of parenthood and past spouses. A slightly disappointing effort from Pakula. ★★ VHS: $14.99

See You Monday

(1979, 100 min, Canada, Maurice Dugowson) *Miou-Miou, David Birney.* With possibly the worst title song ever recorded for a motion picture, this French-Canadian coproduction starts off on the wrong foot and never recovers. Miou-Miou costars with '70s cute TV personality Birney in this middle-of-the-road soap opera made in Montreal. Miou-Miou is a saccharine-sweet redhead who, along with her friend, realize that they are tired of getting involved with married men and become determined to change their ways. An oddity, and a poor one at that. ★

Seems Like Old Times

(1980, 121 min, US, Jay Sandrich) *Chevy Chase, Goldie Hawn, Charles Grodin, Robert Guillaume.* Hawn and Chase reteam after their successful *Foul Play* in this bright, funny Neil Simon comedy. Goldie plays a lawyer whose ex-husband (Chase) reenters the scene, much to the chagrin of new husband Grodin. ★★★ DVD Dual: $24.99

Seize the Day

(1986, 105 min, US, Fielder Cook) *Robin Williams, Glenne Headly, Joseph Wiseman, Jerry Stiller.* Compelling adaptation of Saul Bellow's novel starring Williams in a fine dramatic performance as an unemployed 40-year-old divorcée who moves to New York City to begin life anew. There he is greeted by the brutality and corruption of the corporate world. ★★★ DVD: $19.99, VHS: $19.99

Seizure

(1974, 93 min, Canada, Oliver Stone) *Jonathan Frid, Troy Donahue, Mary Woronov.* A horror novelist (Frid) invites several friends to his home for the weekend, where his sinister dreams come to life to torment his guests. This ordinary thriller marks Stone's first feature — he has done better since. ★★

Selena

(1997, 127 min, US, Gregory Nava) *Jennifer Lopez, Edward James Olmos, Jon Seda, Constance Marie.* Lopez headlines this biopic of the ill-fated Mexican-American singing sensation Selena, whose young life was tragically cut short by an over-zealous fanatic's bullet in 1995. Unfortunately, this tepid film does neither the doomed singer nor the actress full justice. Olmos plays Selena's father and manager, who helps the teenaged singer break down racial barriers to become a crossover star. *Selena* is pretty much in the same vein as *La Bamba* and *The Buddy Holly Story*, two better dramatic musical biographies, but other than some energetic and snappily edited concert sequences, this plays like a routine TV movie-of-the-week. ★★ DVD: $14.99, VHS: $6.99, VHS Letterbox: $6.99

A Self-Made Hero

(1997, 105 min, France, Jacques Audiard) *Mathieu Kassovitz, Anouk Grinberg, Sandrine Kiberlain, Jean-Louis Trintignant.* A wondrous blend of reality and fiction, this French comedy tackles such weighty issues as identity, ambition and desire as its protagonist struggles to find his place in history. Albert Dehousse (Kassovitz) wants so desperately to become a member of the Resistance that he inveigles himself into the party as a war hero. Celebrated for the accomplishments he never achieved, Albert quickly moves up in rank despite the fact that he was unable to serve. Using a significant period in history to explore one man's ordinary life, director Audiard has created a marvelous parable about the price of deception. (French with English subtitles) ★★★ VHS: $29.99

Semi-Tough

(1977, 108 min, Michael Ritchie) *Burt Reynolds, Kris Kristofferson, Jill Clayburgh, Robert Preston, Lotte Lenya, Bert Convy, Carl Weathers, Brian Dennehy.* A pleasant, often funny look at professional sports, this eager-to-please comedy follows the happy exploits of two football players (Reynolds, Kristofferson) and their mutual relationship with the daughter (Clayburgh) of the team's owner (Preston). A weird subplot about self-help analysis takes the film in a dicey direction, but this remains one of the more entertaining sports films. Great rapport between the three leads. ★★★ DVD: $14.99

The Senator Was Indiscreet

(1947, 81 min, US, George S. Kaufman) *William Powell, Ella Raines.* In the great playwright George S. Kaufman's only directorial effort, Powell is perfect as an incompetent, foolhardy senator who decides to run for president (that could never happen in *real* life); Powell's candidacy is sabotaged by a personal diary. An effervescent political satire. ★★★ VHS: $19.99

Send Me No Flowers

(1964, 100 min, US, Norman Jewison) *Rock Hudson, Doris Day, Tony Randall, Paul Lynde.* Breezy marital mix-ups abound with Rock as a hypochondriac who mistakenly believes he is going to die. He sets out to find a suitable new husband for wife Doris. Their last film together. ★★★

The Sender

(1982, 92 min, GB, Roger Christian) *Zeljko Ivanek, Kathryn Harrold, Shirley Knight, Paul Freeman.* A suicidal mental patient (Ivanek) turns his horrific nightmares into reality by choosing receivers for his demented thoughts. Some good chills in this unexpected thriller. ★★½ VHS: $19.99

Sense and Sensibility

(1986, 174 min, GB, Rodney Bennett) *Irene Richard, Tracey Childs.* This excellent TV version of Jane Austen's first novel is a charming tale about two sisters — one well mannered and restrained and the other outspoken and impetuous — who are looking for love and happiness amidst the rigid social mores of 18th-century England. Imbued with a lighthearted and amorous humor, the story follows their initial attempts at husband hunting and their ensuing disappointments. ★★★½ DVD: $14.99

Sense and Sensibility

(1995, 135 min, GB, Ang Lee) *Emma Thompson, Kate Winslet, Alan Rickman, Hugh Grant, Greg Wise, Gemma Jones, Hugh Laurie.* Thompson produced and wrote the adaptation, and then hired the masterful Taiwanese director Lee to helm — together they have made as seemly a rendering of Jane Austen as one is likely to see. Thompson and Winslet play the two Dashwood sisters who, legally unable to be the rightful heirs of their father's will, are forced out of their impressive estate (and "polite" society). Their dilemma, of course, is how to marry. Hence, the story revolves around their conundrum as they pin their hopes on a handful of suitors. Though essentially a drama, Thompson's playful screenplay, in the hands of Lee, finds a great deal of good humor in Austen's story and makes the most of it. Awash with excellent performances, the film exhibits an economy of manners that would do Austen proud. ★★★★ DVD: $19.99, VHS: $9.99

Sense and Sensibility (1995)

THE DISCERNING FILM LOVER'S GUIDE

A Sense of Freedom
(1978, 85 min, Scotland, John MacKenzie) *David Hayman, Alex Norton.* Based on an autobiographical novel by Jimmy Boyle, an inveterate Glasgow gangster whose activities earned him a life sentence for homicide and whose violent disposition hardly abated once behind bars. Filmed for Scottish television, it features an intense, hard-edged performance by Hayman as the pugilistic Boyle who revels in antagonizing prisoners and guards alike. ★★★

A Sense of Loss
(1978, 105 min, France, Marcel Ophüls) *Bernadette Devlin, Ian Paisley.* Ophüls, the director of *The Sorrow and the Pity*, made this searing but balanced documentary about the neverending conflict in Northern Ireland. The film reveals how this ageless tragedy creates a nightmarish society of hatred and violence. ★★★

Senseless
(1997, 88 min, US, Penelope Spheeris) *David Spade, Marlon Wayans, Matthew Lillard, Brad Dourif, Tamara Taylor, Rip Torn.* A very silly slapstick comedy, *Senseless* stars Wayans as a desperate-for-cash business major who agrees to take an experimental drug for $3,000. The drug enhances the five senses tenfold, thus giving Wayans an extra edge in attaining a competitive job at a high-powered finance firm. While the premise *is* clever and some of the gags work, the story is weak, clichéd and dull, and the jokes become more desperate as the film goes on. ★★ DVD: $9.99, VHS: $9.99

Senso
(1954, 117 min, Italy, Luchino Visconti) *Alida Valli, Farley Granger.* A lavish and tragic tale of love and war and one of the landmarks of post-war Italian cinema. The story concerns the careless actions of an aristocratic woman (Valli) who sacrifices her marriage and security for a handsome but cowardly soldier (Granger). This lavishly romantic story is set in Venice in 1866 on the eve of the great conflict between Venice and Austria. (aka: *Wanton Countess*) (Italian with English subtitles) ★★★½ VHS: $29.99

Sensual Man
(1974, 90 min, Italy, Marco Vicario) *Giancarlo Giannini.* The ubiquitous Giannini, the Gérard Depardieu of Italian films, stars as a lusty, irresponsible playboy whose life consists of a series of sexual episodes which include a relationship with the former mistress of Mussolini as well as a Communist member of Parliament. His fantasy-filled life ends when he falls in love and marries: his wife suffers from a psychological block which prevents her from consummating the marriage. ★★

The Sentinel
(1977, 92 min, US, Michael Winner) *Christina Raines, Chris Sarandon, Ava Gardner, Burgess Meredith.* A young model (Raines) moves into a Brooklyn Heights brownstone, which happens to be the gateway to Hell. This hilariously hyperventilating mix of *The Exorcist* and *Rosemary's Baby* is enjoyably bizarre trash. ★★ DVD: $14.99, VHS: $14.99

La Sentinelle
(1992, 139 min, France, Arnaud Desplechin) *Emmanuel Salinger, Thibault de Montalembert, Jean-Louis Richard, Valérie Dréville.* An intriguing psychological mystery, *La Sentinelle* tells the story of Mathias (Salinger), a handsome French patholo-gy student who finds a head in his luggage and decides to determine the identity of its owner. It seems the French secret police have a hand in the matter, and here begins Mathias' trouble. This long but absorbing European thriller places less emphasis on action than it does on the hero's obsession, which is shown in painstaking detail. Director Desplechin makes the presentation of medical tests, the tension between Mathias and his roommate (de Montalembert) and his increasing fear that the authorities are after him very palpable, but the film's cool tone will test the patience of viewers looking for thrills and excitement. Its unpleasant subject matter makes this one for discriminating viewers. (French with English subtitles) ★★★ DVD: $19.99, VHS: $14.99

A Separate Peace
(1972, 104 min, US, Larry Peerce) *Parker Stevenson, John Heyl.* John Knowles' best-selling novel makes a not-altogether successful transition to film in this sun-splashed teenage drama of friendship, initiation and betrayal. At a prep school at the beginning of WWII, two roommates develop a friendship. Stevenson is the freshly scrubbed narrator Gene who falls under the charismatic power of the athletic and domineering Finny (Heyl). Their friendship is tested after a freak accident injures Finny. The ensuing strain on their relationship forces the two to grow up and begin to face the harsh reality of the world outside the school's protective gates. While pretty to look at, the film slows to an aimless crawl after the accident. ★★

Separate Tables
(1958, 98 min, US, Delbert Mann) *Burt Lancaster, Rita Hayworth, David Niven, Deborah Kerr, Wendy Hiller.* A superlative adaptation of two Terence Rattigan one-act plays, combined in one telling, about a group of vacationers at an English seaside resort. A miraculous ensemble includes Lancaster and Hayworth as a divorced couple; Niven (in his Oscar-winning role) as an ex-military hero who may or may not be a fraud; Kerr as a lonely spinster; and Oscar winner Hiller as Lancaster's long-suffering mistress. Though the entire cast is praiseworthy, it is Niven, Kerr and Hiller who walk away with the acting honors. ★★★★ DVD Letterbox: $19.99

Separate Tables
(1983, 112 min, GB, John Schlesinger) *Alan Bates, Julie Christie, Claire Bloom, Irene Worth.* An accomplished retelling of Terence Rattigan's pair of playlets, which had been previously told in the 1958 classic. In "Table by the Window," Christie plays an aging fashion model who travels to a seaside resort in the hopes of rekindling a relationship with her ex-husband (Bates). In "Table Number Seven," Christie plays a woman who holds a secret love for an army major (Bates) who is embroiled in a public scandal. Both Christie and Bates offer superb performances, and there's an excellent supporting cast. ★★★½

La Séparation
(1994, 88 min, France, Christian Vincent) *Isabelle Huppert, Daniel Auteuil, Jérôme Deschamps, Karin Viard.* Two striking performances by the extraordinary Huppert as Anne and the somber Auteuil as Pierre make the difficult *La Séparation* immensely watchable. This tough domestic drama, about a couple initiating a break-up, is heartbreaking to endure yet so fiercely acted, it still fascinates. The cause for the separation is that Anne is in love with another (faceless) man. Pierre tries to accept this harsh fact and the film charts his efforts to come to terms with his feelings. The grayness of fault and blame is closely examined by director-cowriter Vincent in an intimate and intelligent manner. *La Separation* is talky but it also packs a powerful punch. (French with English subtitles) ★★★ DVD: $19.99, VHS: $14.99

September
(1987, 82 min, US, Woody Allen) *Denholm Elliott, Mia Farrow, Elaine Stritch, Sam Waterston, Jack Warden, Dianne Wiest.* Venturing into his *Interiors* ouvre, Allen's yuckless, Chekhovian chamber piece concerns a group of six successful people who vent their frustrations, angst and regrets during a weekend retreat in Vermont. A seriously flawed work by Allen which is probably his least accomplished film. ★★ DVD: $19.99, VHS: $14.99

September 30, 1955
(1977, 107 min, US, James Bridges) *Richard Thomas, Lisa Blount, Tom Hulce, Dennis Christopher, Dennis Quaid, Deborah Benson.* Thomas heads a terrific youthful cast in this intriguing character study. The title refers to the day actor James Dean died, and the film traces the effect Dean's death has on an idolizing college student (Thomas) and his fellow classmates. The film alternates between the merry exploits of teenage hijinks and the drama of *East of Eden*-like soul-searching. Leonard Rosenman's score from that film is used here to good effect, and writer-director Bridges has created compelling characters in this semiautobiography. Thomas successfully captures the essence of teenage alienation. ★★★

Serendipity
(2001, 95 min, US, Peter Chelsom) *John Cusack, Kate Beckinsale, Molly Shannon, Jeremy Piven, Eugene Levy, Bridget Moynahan.* *Serendipity* is pure cotton-candy fluff, with Cusack and Beckinsale playing an adorable pair of strangers who meet cute and, through a series of happy accidents, become convinced they're destined to be together. As chance would have it, they're both otherwise involved, so they tempt fate by parting ways, each leaving the other a clue that might one day reunite them. Flash forward a few years and both are engaged to other people, but they can't stop thinking about their one night together. Just days before his wedding, our boy John races across the country to find his soulmate, who herself has her own plans to find him. The appeal of this sweet confection isn't so much in the outcome but in the many comical diversions the story invents to trip them up along the way. Charming performances and a magical, snowy Manhattan backdrop heighten the romantic flavor. ★★★ DVD Letterbox: $19.99, VHS: $9.99

Sgt. Bilko
(1996, 94 min, US, Jonathan Lynn) *Steve Martin, Dan Aykroyd, Phil Hartman, Glenne Headly, Chris Rock, Max Casella.* If this occasionally funny version of the classic TV series doesn't sustain a consistent comic level, it does make up for it by an engaging cast who perform with unswerving energy. Taking over the role created by the immortal Phil Silvers, Martin has big shoes to fill as Sgt. Bilko, military con man and bull artist extraordinaire. The story — what there is of it — has to do with Bilko and his gang facing the wrath of a visiting major, played to the hilt by Hartman. Impersonations, pratfalls, silly sight gags and double speak are the order of the day. Though the big-screen *Sgt. Bilko* lacks the lightning-fast pace of the show, there's still laughs to be found. ★★½ DVD: $14.99, VHS: $7.49

Sergeant Rutledge

(1960, 118 min, US, John Ford) *Jeffrey Hunter, Woody Strode, Billie Burke, Juano Hernandez.* Ford's tale of an African-American sergeant in the U.S. Cavalry standing trial for rape and murder. Ford's attempts to comment on racism are marred by the fact that the story is a muddled mix of the Old West and contemporary politics, and that the story really focuses on Hunter, the white lieutenant who defends Sergeant Rutledge. Strode's quiet performance as the title character is engaging, but in the end is nothing more than a cliché. ★★½ VHS: $14.99

Sergeant York

(1941, 134 min, US, Howard Hawks) *Gary Cooper, Joan Leslie, Walter Brennan, George Tobias.* Cooper won the first of his two Oscars for his stirring performance in this fact-based story of backwoodsman Alvin York, a pacifist drafted during World War I whose mental anguish and soul-searching leads him to reconcile his conflicting convictions, becoming a war hero on the battlefields of France. Expert direction by Hawks. ★★★★

Serial Mom

(1994, 95 min, US, John Waters) *Kathleen Turner, Sam Waterston, Ricki Lake, Mink Stole, Traci Lords, Patricia Hearst, Matthew Lillard.* Waters has a wonderfully executed satire on suburbia, sex and violence, and our obsession with celebrity criminals. Turner is delicious as Beverly Sutphin, a June Cleaver-ish housewife who cooks, cleans, listens to Barry Manilow, and even recycles; oh, she's also a serial killer! But this deadly vixen is no ordinary murderer, for this bloody mama only kills to protect family and hearth. As husband and kids begin to realize the truth and the police close in, Waters lets loose a series of comic salvos which both tantalize and underscore his topical burlesque. You know you're in familiar Waters when Turner kills a victim with a leg of lamb while the score to *Annie* blares in the background. ★★★½ DVD: $14.99

Series 7

(2001, 86 min, US, Daniel Minahan) *Brooke Smith, Marylouise Burke, Glenn Fitzgerald, Michael Kaycheck, Richard Venture.* An exceptional satire of reality shows, *Series 7* is by turns hilarious, gut-punch intense and even a little disturbing, often in the same scene. The movie is set up as a marathon of a reality show called "The Contenders," in which people are chosen by lottery to take part in a game in which they must kill each other until there's only one left alive. Reigning champion Smith, who is eight months pregnant, must survive only one more round, and she's free. *Series 7* works both as a scathing, dead-on satire (of an admittedly easy target) and as a particularly involving, more intense variation of shows like "Survivor." The basic premise has been tackled before (*The Tenth Victim, The Running Man*), but never with such ferocity. A real sleeper. ★★★½

The Serpent's Egg

(1978, 120 min, US/West Germany, Ingmar Bergman) *Liv Ullmann, David Carradine, Gert Frobe, James Whitmore.* Bergman's troubled and frightening drama about survival in the dawn of Nazi Germany. Set in 1933 Berlin, the film is about a Jewish-American trapeze artist (Carradine) and his sister-in-law (Ullmann), threatened by a mad doctor who portends the Nazi catastrophe that is soon to befall Germany. (Filmed in English) ★★½ DVD: $24.99

Brad Pitt and Morgan Freeman in *Se7en*

Serpico

(1973, 129 min, US, Sidney Lumet) *Al Pacino, John Randolph Jack Kehoe, F. Murray Abraham.* Pacino gives a sterling performance in this based-on-fact story about a non-conformist New York City undercover cop who is ostracized by his fellow officers when he reports widespread police corruption. Director Lumet's first of his "corruption" films (followed by *Prince of the City, Q & A* and *Night Falls on Manhattan*) is a hard-hitting and exemplary look at one man's personal courage. Fine location shooting helps in the authenticity of the story. Based on Peter Maas' best-seller. ★★★½ DVD: $14.99, VHS: $9.99

The Servant

(1963, 115 min, GB, Joseph Losey) *Dirk Bogarde, Sarah Miles, James Fox.* One of director Losey's most tantalizing and complex films. Taken from Harold Pinter's first screenplay and based on a short story by Robin Maugham, the film is about the developing role reversal between a pampered, aristocratic weakling (Fox) and his manipulative and domineering manservant (Bogarde). An unnerving study of class struggle and sexual repression. ★★★½ DVD: $19.99

Servants of Twilight

(1991, 96 min, US, Jeffrey Obrow) *Bruce Greenwood, Belinda Bauer, Grace Zabriskie, Carel Struycken.* A mother and her young son are accosted by a wild-eyed, disheveled woman in a parking garage who claims that the son is the child of Satan and must be destroyed. Frustrated by police inaction, the mother hires a private investigator to protect the boy from murderous attacks by crazed cult members. The action moves through various twists and turns as the viewer is guided to a quite unexpected denouement. Zabriskie and Struycken are especially good as two of the lunatic cult members. Based on a best-seller by Dean R. Koontz. ★★½ DVD: $14.99

Session 9

(2001, 100 min, US, Brad Anderson) *Peter Mullan, Paul Guilfoyle, David Caruso, Brendan Sexton III.* While renovating an old asylum on a very tight schedule, a handful of workers experience some bizarre phenomena that point to the possibility that the place is haunted. Effective, creepy, at times downright scary, *Session 9* benefits from good performances by all (with another nice supporting turn from Caruso) and a methodical, though never too slow pace. Director Anderson creates an eerie, foreboding atmosphere that rarely lets up, and has a keen, fetishistic eye for unsettling detail, both aural and visual. The denouement is disappointing, perhaps, but up until the finale, *Session 9* is a surprisingly worthwhile horror effort. ★★★ DVD: $26.99, VHS: $14.99

Set It Off

(1996, 120 min, US, F. Gary Gray) *Jada Pinkett, Queen Latifah, Vivica A. Fox, Kimberly Elise, John C. McGinley, Blair Underwood.* Four black women, close friends and sick and tired of being screwed by the system, decide to turn the tables by robbing some banks. An enjoyable caper film, *Set It Off* is never believable, but energetic and pulpy enough to satisfy. The social commentary is obvious, and the circumstances leading up to the ladies' fateful decision is as heavy-handed and generic as a stock gangster film from the '30s. Once you can get past the "it's society's fault" exposition, however, *Set It Off* becomes a genuinely entertaining crime film which manages a few kinetic action scenes along the way. Latifah steals the show as a kick-ass lesbian tough. ★★★ DVD: $14.99, VHS: $9.99

The Set-Up

(1949, 72 min, US, Robert Wise) *Robert Ryan, Audrey Totter, George Tobias.* Ryan is splendid as a washed-up boxer who, instead of throwing a big fight, rescues his pride but incures the wrath of mobsters. A stirring drama of rampant corruption and personal redemption. ★★★ DVD: $19.99

Se7en

(1995, 125 min, US, David Fincher) *Brad Pitt, Gwyneth Paltrow, Morgan Freeman, Kevin Spacey, R. Lee Ermey, Richard Roundtree, John C. McGinley.* Seven is a plummeting descent into the ink-black recesses of the human soul — and one human soul in particular so revolted by his fellow creatures that he devises a series of intricate and carefully produced executions/passion plays/performance pieces to express his revulsion. He re-creates each of the seven deadly sins in tableaux of rare irony and brutal torture. The police on his trail (Freeman, world-weary and bone tired; Pitt, young and eager and newly transferred) are dogged and determined, but there is no moral redemption here. While the film at first seems textbook in its element — grizzled veteran, frisky new guy, crazed serial killer — the formula resolution is rejected for a darker vision. Freeman's performance is a study of nuance. A remarkable execution of extremely unsettling material. ★★★½ DVD Letterbox: $19.99, DVD Box Set: $29.99

Seven Beauties

(1976, 115 min, Italy, Lina Wertmüller) *Giancarlo Giannini, Fernando Rey, Shirley Stoler.* Giannini is superb as Wertmüller's Everyman who lives through the horrors of WWII and the concentration camps. A film of stunning accomplishment and staggering foibles. Arguably her greatest achievement. (Italian with English subtitles) ★★★★ DVD: $19.99, VHS Subtitled: $14.99

Seven Brides for Seven Brothers

(1954, 103 min, US, Stanley Donen) *Howard Keel, Jane Powell, Russ Tamblyn, Tommy Rall, Julie Newmar.* A classic M-G-M musical. Keel plays the eldest of seven brothers who marries, prompting the other six to take wives — by kidnapping them. Superb dance sequences choreographed by Michael Kidd. ★★★★ DVD Letterbox: $19.99, VHS: $14.99, VHS Letterbox: $14.99

Seven Chances, Neighbors & The Balloonatic

(1920, 96 min, US, Buster Keaton & Eddie Cline) *Buster Keaton, Virginia Fox.* A collection of three Keaton comedies. Seven Chances (1925, 56 min) is a buoyant romp with Keaton as a sad sack who will inherit seven million dollars — but only if he weds by 7:00 PM that evening. Thus begins a wild scramble to find a willing wife. The film is highlighted by a hilarious prolonged chase sequence in which Keaton is pursued by hundreds of women through back alleys, city streets and across the countryside. (★★★★) *Neighbors* (1920, 18 min), written and directed by Keaton and Eddie Cline, is a delightful comedy with Keaton involved in a "Romeo and Juliet"-type romance with neighbor Fox. The film's accent is on physical stunts, and all are remarkable. (★★★½) *The Balloonatic* (1923, 22 min) finds Keaton adrift in a hot air balloon, eventually crashing to earth and finding love and misadventures. (★★★) DVD: $29.99, VHS: $29.99

Seven Days in May

(1964, 118 min, US, John Frankenheimer) *Burt Lancaster, Fredric March, Kirk Douglas, Edmond O'Brien, Ava Gardner.* This flawless political thriller is so frightening because it is so possible. Lancaster is the Chairman of the Joint Chiefs of Staff planning a military coup if the president (March) goes ahead and signs a nuclear disarmament treaty with the Russians. A taut script from Rod Serling is accentuated by fine direction from Frankenheimer and terrific performances the cast. ★★★★ DVD: $19.99, VHS: $14.99

The Seven Deadly Sins

(1953, 113 min, France, Various) An enjoyable moral comedy devoted to man's seven deadly sins — Avarice, Anger, Sloth, Lust, Envy, Gluttony and Pride. This omnibus is fashioned episodically, with each of the dangerously alluring vices made by a different director, including: Yves Allegret ("Lust"), Claude Autant-Lara ("Pride"), Eduardo De Filippo ("Avarice" and "Anger"), Jean Dréville ("Sloth"), Georges Lacombe ("The Eighth Sin"), Carlo Rim ("Gluttony") and Roberto Rossellini ("Envy"). Surprisingly ribald, this is a delightfully irreverent peek into man's baser nature. (French with English subtitles) ★★★

7 Faces of Dr. Lao

(1964, 100 min, US, George Pal) *Tony Randall, Barbara Eden, Arthur O'Connell.* Pal's fanciful fantasy with Randall giving a tour de force performance as the proprietor of a traveling circus. Randall plays seven roles. Oscar-winner for Makeup Effects. ★★★ DVD: $24.99, VHS: $14.99

The Seven Percent Solution

(1976, 113 min, US, Herbert Ross) *Nicol Williamson, Robert Duvall, Alan Arkin, Vanessa Redgrave, Laurence Olivier, Joel Grey.* Sherlock Holmes' coke paranoia has gotten so bad that Dr. Watson (Duvall) concocts a scheme, with the help of Prof. Moriarty (Olivier), to get Holmes (Williamson) to see Dr. Sigmund Freud (Arkin) and take the cure. While in Vienna, he might as well solve a few mysteries while he's at it. Engrossing, smart fun from the pen of Nicholas Meyer, directed with panache by Ross. ★★★½

Seven Samurai

(1954, 200 min, Japan, Akira Kurosawa) *Toshiro Mifune, Takashi Shimura.* A passionate, exhilarating epic that stands alone in the realm of adventure films. To defend a flock of villagers, a small band of mighty warriors combat a horde of invading bandits. Kurosawa studies the intricate code of honor among the fighting men and their uneasy alliance with the downtrodden farmers. The complete, uncut version. (American remake: *The Magnificent Seven*) (Japanese with English subtitles) ★★★★ DVD Criterion Collection: $39.99, VHS: $34.99

Seven Thieves

(1960, 102 min, US, Henry Hathaway) *Edward G. Robinson, Rod Steiger, Joan Collins, Eli Wallach, Sebastian Cabot.* A brilliant thief (Robinson) gathers a crew of criminal cronies to help him pull off his final crowning heist: robbing the casino vault at Monte Carlo. Tension-filled with good characterizations. ★★★ VHS: $39.99

The Seven Year Itch

(1955, 105 min, US, Billy Wilder) *Tom Ewell, Marilyn Monroe, Evelyn Keyes.* Wilder's witty and zany romp exposes the sexual fantasies of the middle-aged married man. Marilyn is the unintending temptress upstairs who becomes the object of Ewell's Walter Mitty-ish, philandering escapades. ★★★½ DVD: $14.99, VHS: $6.99

Seven Years in Tibet

(1997, 136 min, US, Jean-Jacques Annaud) *Brad Pitt, David Thewlis, B.D. Wong, Mako, Jamyang Jamtsho Wangchuk, Victor Wong.* Visually stunning and dramatically compelling, Seven Years in Tibet is a sometimes breathtaking journey into the heart of a people and a glossy adventure tale of redemption and hope. Pitt is well cast as Heinrich Harrer, an arrogant Austrian mountain climber whose attempt to scale the Himalayas in 1939 eventually lands him in the company of the young Dalai Lama. Thus begins a journey of self-discovery as he soon becomes a tutor to the young religious leader. Director Annaud's pacing is deliberate if occasionally slow, though his attention to detail is exemplary. Seven Years in Tibet thankfully avoids sentimentality, and replaces it with honest emotions regarding faith, love, and soul-searching. ★★★½ DVD Letterbox Superbit Edition: $26.99, DVD: $19.99, VHS: $9.99

1776

(1972, 166 min, US, Peter H. Hunt) *William Daniels, Howard da Silva, Ken Howard, Blythe Danner, John Cullum.* A sparkling version of the Tony Award-winning Broadway musical about the events leading up to the signing of the Declaration of Independence. Far from a detail-ridden history lesson, this rousing entertainment is a witty, clever and significant glance at the framing of a country. Most of the original stage stars repeat their roles, with Daniels in his finest hour as the antagonistic lobbyist for independence, John Adams; he's smartly supported by the wonderful da Silva as Ben Franklin, Howard as Thomas Jefferson, and the golden-voiced Cullum as Edward Rutledge. ★★★½ DVD Letterbox Director's Cut: $29.99

The Seventh Cross

(1944, 112 min, US, Fred Zinnemann) *Spencer Tracy, Signe Hasso, Hume Cronyn, Agnes Moorehead, Jessica Tandy.* A superb melodrama with Tracy escaping from a Nazi concentration camp accompanied by six others. On the run, they do their best to elude their captors, who have marked seven graves with crosses for their return. ★★★½ VHS: $19.99

Seven Samurai

The famous game of chess in *The Seventh Seal*

The Seventh Seal

(1956, 96 min, Sweden, Ingmar Bergman) *Max von Sydow, Bibi Andersson.* Plague stalks 14th-century Sweden in this mystical classic, as a war-weary knight (von Sydow) encounters Death by the seaside and challenges him to a perilous chess match with his life in the balance. Unquestionably one of Bergman's greatest. (Swedish with English subtitles) ★★★★ DVD: $39.99, VHS: $29.99

The Seventh Sign

(1988, 98 min, US, Carl Schultz) *Demi Moore, Michael Biehn.* The premise of this occult thriller says the Bible foretells the destruction of the planet by seven warning signs. No matter how close you look in the Old or New Testaments, you won't find any warnings about bad horror films such as this. Moore is the pregnant woman privy to the apocalyptic prophecies. ★ DVD: $14.99, VHS: $9.99

The Seventh Victim

(1943, 71 min, US, Mark Robson) *Kim Hunter, Tom Conway, Hugh Beaumont.* Exceptionally eerie occult thriller produces many a chill in this story of a woman (Hunter) who unwittingly becomes involved with a satanic cult while searching for her missing sister in New York's Greenwich Village. One of producer Val Lewton's best films; the screenplay was written by Lewton under the pseudonym "Carlos Keith." ★★★

The 7th Voyage of Sinbad

(1958, 87 min, US, Nathan Juran) *Kerwin Matthews, Kathryn Grant.* Though a little creaky around the edges, good special effects make this one of the more enjoyable of the Ray Harryhausen films. Hero Sinbad battles an evil magician to restore his girlfriend — who has been shrunk only inches tall — to her normal size. Bernard Herrmann did the score. ★★½ DVD: $19.99

Severed Ties

(1992, 95 min, US, Damon Santostefano) *Billy Morrissette, Elke Sommer, Oliver Reed, Garrett Morris.* Severed Ties tries to be part *Basket Case*, part *Street Trash*, part *Dead Alive*, but fails to be as witty, scary or gory as any of them. A young scientist tries to perfect a formula for a plasma replacement which will allow spontaneous regeneration of any wounded limb or organ. It's put to the test after he loses his arm. There are a few interesting effects, but the performances by Sommer as the doc's evil mother and Reed as her cohort are overdone. ★½

Sex and Zen

(1993, 99 min, Hong Kong, Michael Mak) *Lawrence Ng, Amy Yip, Kent Cheng, Isabella Chow.* An oddball sex comedy-drama from Hong Kong, *Sex and Zen* features a horny stud who grafts a certain appendage from a horse onto his own body. That's about it for plot as our hero hops in and out of bed with various women until a goofy, melodramatic denouement. For those unfamiliar with Hong Kong films, *Sex and Zen* will be almost impenetrable (so to speak), with its stilted, Ed Wood-esque dialogue and drastic cultural differences in perspective and taste. This is tough going — it has unlikable characters, a dull story and scenes straining so hard to be "outrageous" that they end up being neither funny nor shocking. (Cantonese with English subtitles) ★★ DVD Widescreen: $19.99

Sex Is . . .

(1992, 81 min, US, Lawrence Helman & Marc Huestis) Contemporary gay men's preoccupation with sex and its side and after effects (love, relationship, AIDS) is entertainingly explored in this verbally and visually graphic documentary. Essentially a film of talking heads with some additional footage (mostly hard-core sex scenes) added, the film records the thoughts and opinions of various gay men who recount their childhood sexual obsessions, fantasies, proclivities and dislikes. Raunchy, blunt and unapologetic, *Sex Is . . .* is an important testimony to gay men and their sexual lives before and during the age of AIDS. ★★★ DVD: $29.99, VHS: $29.99

sex, lies and videotape

(1989, 100 min, US, Steven Soderbergh) *James Spader, Andie MacDowell, Peter Gallagher, Laura San Giacomo.* Soderbergh's debut film is an emotionally powerful and darkly comic examination of infidelity, honesty and the darker side of human sensuality. John (Gallagher) and Ann Dellany (MacDowell) are the perfect young American couple: he's a new partner in a successful law firm; she's a squeaky-clean and somewhat prudish housewife; and he's having a torrid affair with her sister (lustily played by the ravishing San Giacomo). Into the fray comes John's old roommate Graham (played with a quiet brilliance by Spader), an austere and strangely pious wanderer who is returning home after years on the road. An eruption of hidden passions and untold secrets follow as the four move inevitably towards a final confrontation. The entire ensemble in this would-be love quadrangle is superb and Soderbergh's script and direction are bold, new and refreshing. ★★★★ DVD: $14.99

The Sex of the Stars

(1993, 100 min, Canada, Paule Baillargeon) *Denis Mercier.* This preachy Canadian melodrama details the difficult relationship between an adolescent girl and her estranged father, who returns into her life a transsexual woman. Intent on rekindling, however awkwardly, their relationship, Camille accepts the obvious — that her father is now a woman called Marie-Pierre — but refuses to alter any of the traditional father-daughter dynamics that. The film tries to be "feel good" in spirit, but it ultimately reinforces the notion that deviant homosexuality is a sad, violent and unfulfilling world whose characters must pay the price for living a grotesque lifestyle. (French with English subtitles) ★★

Le Sex Shop

(1973, 92 min, France, Claude Berri) *Claude Berri, Juliet Berto.* This congenial French satire wittily explores our modern preoccupation with sex, and our changing sexual mores. Claude, the owner of a sexual paraphernalia shop, decides to keep his own marriage in high gear by testing his merchandise "firsthand." Taking advice from his own manuals, he attempts to introduce his wife to swing clubs and a ménage à trois. ★★½

Sextette

(1978, 91 min, US, Ken Hughes) *Mae West, Timothy Dalton, Ringo Starr, Tony Curtis, George Hamilton, Alice Cooper.* Four on the floor is standard equipment with this classic beauty, as West returns to the showroom after an absence of nearly 40 years, loaded with options and ready for action. Her turbo-charged headers make it clear that this is one body built to go the distance in this camp classic about a vixen whose honeymoon keeps getting interrupted by her many ex-husbands. A pre-James Bond Dalton faces his most dangerous challenge as Mae requires more servicing than a Buick Skylark. Starr, Curtis and Hamilton are just a few who take her out for a spin after a quick look under the hood. ★½ DVD: $9.99, VHS: $19.99

Sexy Beast

(2001, 88 min, GB, Jonathan Glazer) *Ray Winstone, Ben Kingsley, Ian McShane, Amanda Redman, James Fox.* Ah, to be a retired British gangster on a Spanish villa, where your only concern is the boulder that fell in your swimming pool. Alas, this bliss doesn't last long enough for Gal (Winstone), who is visited by his old boss Don Logan (Kingsley) who wants Gal for "one last job" back in rainy old London. A battle of wills ensues between the two men, forming the core of a taut thriller/caper film that breathlessly uses tension, humor, suspense and a whole lot of menace to fan the fires of intimidation and murder. Kingsley is astonishing as the maniacal Logan, a torrent of brutality who at any moment could explode, only needing the slightest of reasons to do so. And Gal's reluctance to join him for a trip back to England could just do the trick. Winstone strikes the proper balance to Kingsley's volcanic gangster. ★★★½ DVD: $19.99, VHS: $9.99

Shack Out on 101

(1955, 80 min, US, Edward Dein) *Lee Marvin, Keenan Wynn, Terry Moore.* Hyperventilating Red paranoia at its most entertaining! Marvin is Slob, a trouble-making hash-slinger (with a hidden agenda) in a remote greasy spoon operated by lug Wynn. Set almost entirely in the ramshackle beanery, the story features a great cast of oddball characters with the Marilyn Monroe-like Moore as the saucy but determined blonde who uncovers a nefarious ring of traitors. ★★★ VHS: $19.99

Shades of Fear

(1997, 93 min, GB, Beeban Kidron) *John Hurt, Vanessa Redgrave, Jonathan Pryce, Rakie Ayola, Dorothy Tutin.* Originally called *Great Moments in Aviation*, the equally misnamed *Shades of Fear* isn't some third-rate, quick-paycheck hack job mystery which the advertising suggests. It's an unusual, rewarding drama revolving around a handful of passengers on a cruise to England and of their respective secrets. Well written by Jeanette Winterson (*Oranges Are Not the Only Fruit*) and directed with just the right amount of sensitivity and humor by Kidron, *Shades of Fear* also boasts a stellar cast of British stalwarts and a radiant newcomer, Ayola. ★★★ DVD: $19.99, VHS: $9.99

Shadey

(1987, 90 min, GB, Philip Saville) *Antony Sher, Billie Whitelaw, Patrick MacNee, Katherine Helmond.* Offbeat espionage spoof with Sher as a garage mechanic who agrees to use his special powers — the ability to read minds and project those images onto film — to finance his sex-change operation. An irreverent comedy. ★★½

The Shadow

(1994, 112 min, US, Russell Mulcahy) *Alec Baldwin, Penelope Ann Miller, Tim Curry, Ian McKellen, John Lone, Peter Boyle, Jonathan Winters, Andre Gregory.* Based on the popular 1930s radio program, this lifeless cartoon "adventure" tale stars a grim Baldwin as the avenging hero/bad guy Lamont Cranston, aka The Shadow. Borrowing the set design ideas of *Batman* without any of its excitement, the film is a series of awkward battle scenes and comic vignettes as The Shadow takes on a mystical madman (Lone) bent on world domination. ★ DVD Pan & Scan DTS Edition: $14.99, DVD: $14.99, VHS: $14.99

The Shadow Box

(1980, 100 min, US, Paul Newman) *Joanne Woodward, Christopher Plummer, Valerie Harper, Sylvia Sidney, James Broderick, Melinda Dillon.* A well-made and sensitive version of Michael Cristofer's Tony Award- and Pulitzer Prize-winning play. The story follows the lives of three terminally ill patients as they and their families spend a day at an experimental retreat in the California mountains. Woodward gives a beautifully controlled performance, and Plummer is equally splendid as her gay ex-husband. ★★★

Willem Dafoe in *Shadow of the Vampire*

Shadow Catcher

(1974, 90 min, US, T.C. McLuhan) This engaging documentary details Edward Curtis in his life and work among the Native Americans of the Northwest during the early 1900s. Curtis' incredible passion for his craft and his commitment to his subject are described through journal entries, correspondence and, above all, his photographs. A special treat is Curtis' own film, shown in fragments, called *Life Among the Headhunters*, which is unique for both its artistic and historical content. ★★★ VHS: $29.99

Shadow Hunter

(1992, 98 min, US, J.S. Cardone) *Scott Glenn, Angela Alvarado, Robert Beltran, Benjamin Bratt.* Glenn is a burnt-out L.A. cop sent to Arizona to pick up a Native American wanted for murder. When Twobear (Bratt in a chilling performance) escapes from his custody, Glenn enters into an odyssey in which his survival may well depend on the strength of his soul. A well-paced combination of psychological thriller and action/adventure, sprinkled with elements of Native American mysticism. The spectacular Arizona desert is beautifully captured. ★★½

Shadow Magic

(1999, 115 min, US/China, Ann Hu) *Jared Harris, Yu Xia, Liu Peiqi.* Capturing the wonder and magical possibilities of cinema in much the same way that distinguished *Cinema Paradiso*, this enchanting Chinese-American coproduction is the story of China's first movie house as seen through the eyes of a wide-eyed photographer. Liu is a young apprentice for Peking's most prestigious photography studio. Intrigued by Western technology, Liu is the first to respond when a British "show man" opens Peking's first movie house. Now working at the theater and the studio, Liu soon finds himself caught between two conflicting cultures: one steeped in tradition and the other certain to bring about change. A joyful celebration of the mystique of movies prevails in director Hu's valentine to not only the birth of Chinese cinema but true love as well. (Mandarin with English subtitles) ★★★½ DVD: $29.99, VHS: $21.99

Shadow of a Doubt

(1943, 108 min, US, Alfred Hitchcock) *Joseph Cotten, Teresa Wright, Patricia Collinge, Hume Cronyn, Henry Travers.* Cited by Hitchcock as one of his personal favorites, this cat-and-mouse, spellbinding psychological thriller stars Cotten as an apparently ordinary fellow who visits his small-town kin. However, his diabolical past gradually becomes evident, and threatening, to his suspicious young niece (wonderfully played by a wide-eyed and innocent Wright). ★★★★ DVD: $19.99, VHS: $14.99

Shadow of the Vampire

(2000, 93 min, US, E. Elias Merhige) *John Malkovich, Willem Dafoe, Cary Elwes, Aden Gillett, Eddie Izzard, Udo Kier, Catherine McCormack, Ronan Vibert.* Here's a terrific what-if: What if the classic vampire film *Nosferatu* had an actual vampire playing the part of the legendary bloodsucker? Director Merhige and screenwriter Steven Katz take this intriguing premise and are only able to deliver on it in short bursts of creativity. Malkovich is German director F. W. Murnau, who is preparing an adaptation of Bram Stoker's "Dracula." However, there's an air of mystery concerning the enigmatic actor Max Schreck (Dafoe). The cast thinks him an obsessive method actor; but the man playing a vampire could be one himself. And if he is, what peril awaits the cast? *Shadow of the Vampire* comes alive whenever the remarkable Dafoe is on-screen — he essays menace with mocking glee. But when he's not featured, the film is unfocused and lethargic, and there are a few plot inconsistencies that can't be overlooked. ★★½ DVD Letterbox: $14.99

A Shadow You Soon Will Be (Una Sombra Ya Pronto Seras)

(1994, 105 min, Argentina, Hector Olivera) *Miguel Angel Sola.* Olivera explores the state of post-democratic Argentinian society through the means of allegory and metaphor. Based on a novel by Osvaldo Soriano, *A Shadow You Soon Will Be* follows the meanderings of an unemployed computer programmer (Sola) through an eerily barren countryside. Our hero's travels lead him not towards any one particular fate (despite an intriguing run-in with a fortune teller), but rather towards an understanding of exactly how he has landed where he is. Not technically proficient, *Shadow* provides an ironic, amusing exploration of the "journey" for those philosophically inclined. (Spanish with English subtitles) ★★★ VHS: $29.99

Shadowlands

(1987, 73 min, GB, Norman Stone) *Joss Ackland, Claire Bloom.* A West End and Broadway hit, this moving love story stars Ackland as writer C.S. Lewis, who finds that his ordered Don's life at Oxford is thrown into turmoil after he meets and falls in love with American poet Joy Gresham (Bloom). Winner of two British Academy Awards. ★★★

Shadowlands

(1993, 130 min, GB, Richard Attenborough) *Anthony Hopkins, Debra Winger, John Wood.* Attenborough brings unexpected poignancy to this captivating romantic drama about the real-life love affair between author C.S. Lewis and writer Joy Gresham. Based on William Nicholson's hit stage play, the film stars Hopkins as Lewis, a proper British professor/lecturer whose ordered life takes a turn when American Gresham (Winger) arrives on his doorstep. As she insinuates herself into his life, they marry in order for Gresham to stay in the country — and ultimately and inevitably fall in love. This is unexpectedly funny, beautifully told, exceptionally written, and features two remarkable performances. ★★★★ DVD: $9.99, VHS: $9.99

Shadows

(1960, 87 min, US, John Cassavetes) *Hugh Herd, Lelia Goldini, Ben Carruthers, Anthony Ray, Rupert Crosse.* Cassavetes' directorial debut is a roughhewn improvisation pulsating with hyperkinetic energy. The grainy black-and-white cinematography and Charlie Mingus score augment the quasi-documentary intimacy delivered by the competent cast. Goldini is a naïve 20-year-old black woman living with her two brothers, one a ne'er-do-well (Carruthers) and the other a struggling jazz musician (Herd). The complexities of racism are explored from their perspectives, as the brothers deal with the underside of the entertainment industry, and their light-skinned sister handles the emotional upheaval of a relationship with a Caucasian man who does not know she is an African-American. The low-budget production values are reminiscent of the British "kitchen sink" dramas of that time. Riveting and involving, and quintessential Cassavetes. ★★★ DVD: $24.99

Shadows and Fog

(1992, 86 min, US, Woody Allen) *Woody Allen, Mia Farrow, John Malkovich, Jodie Foster, Lily Tomlin, Kathy Bates, John Cusack, Madonna, Kate Nelligan, Wallace Shawn, Robert Joy.* Lost amid the controversy surrounding the breakup of Allen and Farrow, this minor addition to Allen's filmography is nonetheless an entertaining and often amusing ode to early German cinema. Based on Allen's stage play "Death," the story centers on Woody's hapless nebbish who becomes the object of a lynch mob's hunt for a serial killer. The action takes place in an archetypal pre-WWII European city on a foggy night and is shot in a stark black and white which is filled with visual references to German Expressionist classics. In addition to an impressive supporting cast, there's the superb soundtrack composed of a delightful mélange of Kurt Weill cabaret tunes. ★★★ DVD: $19.99, VHS: $14.99

Shadows of Forgotten Ancestors

(1964, 99 min, USSR, Sergei Paradjanov) *Ivan Micholaichuk, Larisa Kadochnikova.* The historical pageantry and epic legends of medieval times are enacted in this visually and musically vibrant love story. Set in 19th-century Ukraine, the drama centers around a young man who is trapped in a loveless marriage and haunted by his true but dead sweetheart. But make no mistake about its simple plot, for the film is a wonderful compendium of folk dances, religious zealousness and witchcraft. It is filmed in a psychedelic rampage and has more spectacular effects, spectacular camera movements, wild experiments with color and bizarre musical scenes than anyone would imagine in one film. (Ukrainian with English subtitles) ★★★★ VHS: $29.99

Shadrach

(1998, 86 min, US, Susanna Styron) *Harvey Keitel, Andie MacDowell, John Franklin Sawyer, Scott Terra, Daniel Treat.* A slow-moving but evocative tale from William Styron and directed by the author's daughter, *Shadrach* offers a look at Virginia 1935 as seen through the eyes of a ten-year old boy. Paul (Terra) is a well-to-do Southerner, whose best friend is Little Mole Dabney (Treat), the youngest son of a family hit hard by the Depression. While things like money and racial segregation rarely enter into the mind's of these two boys, with the arrival of Shadrach (Sawyer), a 99-year-old for-

mer slave, they soon learn some valuable facts about life. Although the drama is slight, the mood is flavorful thanks to Styron's sure hand. Terra and Treat are natural talents, and Sawyer is beguiling in the title role. ★★★ DVD: $29.99

Shaft

(1971, 106 min, US, Gordon Parks) *Richard Roundtree, Moses Gunn.* With Isaac Hayes' rhythmic score in the background, this sexy and violent (always a great combo in blaxploitation) crime story stars Roundtree as John Shaft, a mean and resourceful private dick. Essentially a black *French Connection*, the story has Shaft hired by a ruthless drug lord (Gunn) to find his daughter, who was kidnapped by the white Mafia. Slick, action-packed urban fun. (Followed by 2 sequels) (Remade in 2000) ★★★ DVD: $14.99, VHS: $9.99

Shaft

(2000, 99 min, US, John Singleton) *Samuel L. Jackson, Vanessa L. Williams, Jeffrey Wright, Christian Bale, Busta Rhymes, Dan Hedaya, Toni Collette, Richard Roundtree.* Jackson is certainly in his element as that suave private eye John Shaft in this flavorful remake of the 1971 action fave. Updated to reflect a millennium mindset, the slam-bang story follows police detective Shaft — nephew to the original Shaft played by Roundtree, who turns up here as "Uncle John" — and his investigation into a racially motivated murder. Bale is the snotty, rich white kid who killed a black youth in cold blood. When it looks as if he may get away with it, it's up to Shaft to make sure the creep does his time. Wright steals the show as a neighborhood drug lord whose path both Shaft and the racist killer cross. Director Singleton keeps the action moving at a swift pace and there are a couple of great set pieces. A hip, defiantly entertaining mix of action, humor and police procedural. And, yes, Isaac Hayes' classic theme song returns. ★★★ DVD: $14.99, VHS Special Edition: $9.99

Shaft in Africa

(1973, 111 min, US, John Guillermin) *Richard Roundtree, Vonetta McGee.* Shaft (Roundtree) goes undercover in Africa to expose a new slave trade. He does some badass espionage using just his mouth, his fists, and his attitude. Theme song "Are You Bad Enough" performed by the Four Tops. Good action scenes highlight this exciting, tough film. ★★★ DVD: $9.99, VHS: $9.99

Shaft's Big Score!

(1972, 105 min, US, Gordon Parks) *Richard Roundtree, Moses Gunn.* The baddest mutha in town is back, in this well-paced, action-packed sequel. While investigating the murder of a friend by an underworld crime figure, hero Shaft (Roundtree) discovers that the money he was going to use to pay off his pal's gambling debt is missing. He then makes a deal with crime boss Stumpy (Gunn) and makes the same deal with another boss, putting himself in the middle of an intense war. Stylish and never boring. ★★★ DVD: $9.99, VHS: $9.99

Shakedown

(1988, 90 min, US, James Glickenhaus) *Peter Weller, Sam Elliott, Patricia Charbonneau.* Weller and Elliott are the mismatched partners in this routine actioner about a public defender (Weller) and a burned-out undercover cop (Elliott) who go after some corrupt policemen. Some good action scenes, but the plot makes little sense. ★★ DVD: $14.99

Shakes the Clown

(1991, 87 min, US, Bobcat Goldthwait) *Bobcat Goldthwait, Julie Brown, Robin Williams, Adam Sandler.* Written, directed and starring Goldthwait, this story of a drunken, down-on-his-luck clown drags a bit, but delivers some good laughs. Set in a semi-surrealistic town populated by all types of unemployed, has-been clowns, Goldthwait is a "good clown" whose love of booze eventually complicates him in a murder. Yes, the story itself is not very interesting nor well constructed, and some of the scenes and main characters are decidedly unfunny. But overall, a funny little oddity. Williams steals the film as a fey yet militaristic mime instructor. ★★½ DVD: $24.99

Shakespeare in Love

(1998, 122 min, GB, John Madden) *Gwyneth Paltrow, Joseph Fiennes, Geoffrey Rush, Judi Dench, Ben Affleck, Colin Firth, Tom Wilkinson, Antony Sher, Rupert Everett, Simon Callow.* Gloriously romantic comedy of manners about what happened in the life of young William Shakespeare which inspired him to write "Romeo and Juliet" — or as he *was* going to call it, "Romeo and Ethel, the Pirate's Daughter." The dashing Fiennes is Will, England's up-and-coming playwright of the late 16th century. Oscar winner Paltrow is luminous as Viola, a high-born, stagestruck lady who poses as a man and tries out for Will's new production. From there, romance of an extraordinary kind blossoms. The writers and director Madden have done a terrific job taking slices of text from "Romeo and Juliet" and incorporating them into the plot, which becomes more ingenious as it moves along. The ensemble is superb, but it's Oscar winner Dench who steals the show in her few scenes as Queen Elizabeth. *Shakespeare in Love* is that rarity — an intelligent, funny and captivating romantic entertainment. Winner of 7 Academy Awards, including Best Picture. ★★★★ DVD Collector's Edition: $19.99, VHS: $9.99

Shakespeare Wallah

(1965, 122 min, India, James Ivory) *Laura Liddell, Geoffrey Kendal, Felicity Kendal, Shashi Kapoor.* The setting is India during the last days of the British Raj when the struggling nation was trying to free itself of colonial imperialism and cultural saturation by the British. Amidst all of this turmoil, an English Shakespearean acting troupe

Colin Firth and Dame Judi Dench (in her Academy Award-winning role) in *Shakespeare in Love*

S

valiantly tours the countryside. The story concerns the budding love affair between the daughter of one of the actors and a young Indian. Their infatuation and innocence and persistence amidst the changes help make this a charming and delightful tale. ★★★ DVD Letterbox: $29.99

Shall We Dance

(1937, 116 min, US, Mark Sandrich) *Fred Astaire, Ginger Rogers, Edward Everett Horton.* Captivating Astaire-Rogers musical with Fred and Ginger as a dance team pretending to be married; of course, they fall in love. Needless to say, there are great dance numbers, and the Gershwins' score includes "Let's Call the Whole Thing Off," "They All Laughed" and "They Can't Take That Away from Me." ★★★½ VHS: $14.99

Shall We Dance

(1997, 119 min, Japan, Masayuki Suo) *Koji Yakusho, Tamiyo Kusakari, Naoto Takenaka, Reiko Kusamura.* Recalling the exhilaration of *Strictly Ballroom*, the wonderfully comic and bittersweet *Shall We Dance* also manages to evoke the whimsy of that film as well. Shohei (Yakusho) is a weary Japanese office worker who decides to enroll in a ballroom dance class — though he keeps it from his wife and coworkers. Gradually, he gains self-confidence and enters the big contest at the finale. Though not as elaborate as in *Strictly Ballroom*, the dance sequences are engagingly performed by an appealing cast of characters, and director Suo is able to effectively balance their lightheartedness with the more serious clash of romanticism and culture. A delightful, often giddy affair. (Japanese with English subtitles) ★★★½ VHS: $14.99

Shallow Grave

(1994, 92 min, Scotland, Danny Boyle) *Ewan McGregor, Kerry Fox, Christopher Eccleston, Keith Allen.* This grisly Scottish black comedy tells an all-too familiar tale of greed-conquers-all, but an eccentric sense of style and some truly shocking twists make it a surprising and riveting thriller. The film follows three unlikable roommates: Alex (McGregor), David (Eccleston) and Juliet (Fox). Looking for a flatmate, they decide on a shady character (Allen) whose irascible nature feeds their misanthropic appetites. Things unravel when he dies and leaves them with a suitcase full of cash. They immediately go about hatching schemes to keep the money and dispose of the body and ultimately begin an inexorable descent into madness and greed. Debut director Boyle shows great promise; his visual prowess and sprightly script keep the tension building right up to the excruciating climax. ★★★½ DVD: $14.99

Shallow Hal

(2001, 114 min, US, Bobby Farrelly & Peter Farrelly) *Gwyneth Paltrow, Jack Black, Jason Alexander, Joe Viterelli, Susan Ward.* Remove the teeth from a shark and without its bite it probably won't prove to be too much of a threat. The same can be said of the Farrelly brothers, if their bland comedy *Shallow Hal* is any indication. They've softened their humor, even getting sentimental and all warm and fuzzy. The result is akin to being gummed to death by that toothless shark. Black is Hal, a superficial womanizer who judges women only on their looks. After a meeting with self-help guru Robbins (playing himself), he begins to see the inner beauty of people and falls for the overweight Rosemary, who he sees as looking like Gwyneth Paltrow. A series of fat jokes follow,

Shall We Dance: Will the real Ginger Rogers please step forward?

mostly from Hal's equally shallow friend Mauricio (Alexander). In downplaying the edgy comedy for misplaced sensitivity, the Farrellys have no room to expand upon the premise, ultimately never establishing a rhythm or being able to develop the tame comic set-ups that leave them no place to go. ★½ DVD: $14.99

Shame

(1968, 103 min, Sweden, Ingmar Bergman) *Max von Sydow, Liv Ullmann.* The personal horrors of war are explored in this intense story of a couple caught up in a senselessly violent civil war. The setting is 1971, when a seemingly happy but quarrelsome couple (von Sydow, Ullmann) have fled to a secluded farmhouse to escape the unexplained war. Both orchestra musicians, von Sydow is a self-absorbed, emotionally fragile man and Ullmann his strong-willed wife. The war and its horrific violence soon spills into their world, trapping them and then brutally stripping them of their dignity as they desperately struggle for survival. Very powerful acting by von Sydow and Ullmann and a gripping, action-filled story make this powerful drama one of Bergman's best. (Swedish with English subtitles) ★★★★ DVD: $24.99, VHS: $19.99

Shame

(1988, 90 min, Australia, Steve Jodrell) *Deborra-Lee Furness, Tony Barry.* A taut, violent story of rape, murder and oppression. A woman, traveling alone on a motorcycle, encounters engine trouble and seeks help from the citizens of a small, out-of-the-way town. Instead, she discovers a conspiracy of violence directed against many of the town's young women. Confronted with this terror, our heroine chooses to stay and fight. The ensuing sexual battle is told in the best Rambo-like style as this riveting film not only delivers potent doses of action, but also explores the tumultuous relationship between the sexes. ★★★

The Shameless Old Lady

(1966, 94 min, France, René Allio) *Sylvie, Malka Ribovska.* Sylvie, a French character actress for almost 50 years, is finally the star in this touching and delightful film based on a Brecht short story. A

70-year-old widow, after devoting herself to her family during a drab, uneventful life, decides to change her ways and boisterously enjoy her remaining years. Shocking her children and neighbors, she buys a *Deux Chevaux*, joins a political group, befriends a prostitute and goes on holiday. (French with English subtitles) ★★★½

Shampoo

(1975, 112 min, US, Hal Ashby) *Warren Beatty, Julie Christie, Lee Grant, Goldie Hawn, Jack Warden, Carrie Fisher.* Potent sexual and social comedy about the romantic exploits of a bed-hopping Beverly Hills hairdresser (Beatty). A first-rate cast includes Oscar winner Grant. ★★★ DVD Dual: $19.99, VHS: $9.99

Shane

(1953, 118 min, US, George Stevens) *Alan Ladd, Jean Arthur, Jack Palance, Van Heflin, Brandon deWilde.* Director Stevens' classic western stars Ladd as a mysterious gunfighter who comes to the aid of a homesteading family (Heflin, Arthur), and is idolized by their young son (De Wilde). Palance is a most memorable villian. ★★★★ DVD: $14.99, VHS: $9.99

Shanghai Blues

(1984, 108 min, Hong Kong, Tsui Hark) Belying one's preconceived notions of Hong Kong's cinema, this gleefully anachronistic, gag-filled screwball comedy, set in 1937 and 1947 Shanghai, has a not-too-ordinary plot — boy meets girl, boy loses girl, boy and girl wind up as fueding neighbors without recognizing each other. A pretty cast and imaginatively wacky ideas fuel this enjoyable oddity. (Cantonese with English subtitles) ★★★

Shanghai Knights

(2003, 107 min, US, David Dobkin) *Jackie Chan, Owen Wilson, Fann Wong, Donnie Yen, Aidan Gillen.* In this mildly entertaining sequel to *Shanghai Noon*, our mismatched heroes are now in London, searching for a stolen Great Seal of China, and avenging the murder of Chan's estranged father. Jackie's beautiful sister tags along as well, catching the eye of anachronistic surfer-dude Wilson. Even more featherweight than its predecessor, *Knights* is by no means a classic action film; it is, however, buoyed by the chemistry of its stars, and some amusing (if less than spectacular) fight scenes. The film's *Forrest Gump*-isms (the pair run into Arthur Conan Doyle and Charlie Chaplin, among other celebrities-to-be) and tired put-downs of Britain will most likely result in more groans than giggles, and the pace does flag occasionally. ★★★ DVD: $29.99, VHS: $24.99

Shanghai Noon

(2000, 110 min, US, **Tom Dey**) Jackie Chan, Lucy Liu, Brandon Merrill, Owen Wilson, Roger Yuan, Xander Berkeley. Jackie teams up with the perpetually laid-back Wilson for an amusing if unremarkable action-comedy. When a Chinese princess (Liu) is kidnapped and taken to the American West, ne'er-do-well Chan accompanies his uncle and several royal warriors to retrieve her. Of course, in the end, it's up to Jackie — and newfound, reluctant partner Wilson — to save her. Though there's much less action than the typical Jackie vehicle, he and Wilson have good chemistry together, though they aren't as funny a pair as Chan and Chris Tucker (in *Rush Hour*). ★★½ DVD: $19.99, VHS: $9.99

Shanghai Surprise

(1986, 97 min, US, **Jim Goddard**) Sean Penn, Madonna, Paul Freeman. One of the candidates for Worst Film of the Decade, this laughable adventure film teamed then-husband and wife Penn and Madonna in the story of a missionary in 1930s China who enlists the aid of a down-and-out adventurer to track a missing opium shipment. Just dreadful on every level. ★ DVD: $14.99, VHS: $14.99

Shanghai Triad

(1995, 108 min, China, **Zhang Yimou**) Gong Li, Li Boatian, Li Xuejian, Shun Chin, Wang Xiao Xiao. At times entrancing and at others simply tediously trance-enducing, this 1930s crime period piece follows the first several days in the apprenticeship of young Tang Shuisheng, a 14-year-old "country bumpkin." Thanks to his uncle Liu's influence, Shuisheng is to be the personal servant of Bijou (Gong), the extravagant moll of triad boss Mr. Tang. The film meanders through its first half, suffering from a sonambulistic editing pace and overly long singing numbers in which Bijou entertains at the Boss' nightclub. The film finally finds a narrative pace as it explores Bijou's process of personal transformation. Still, the film ultimately fails to provide the crystal clear social commentary that is so evident in all of Zhang's other films, which might have been OK had it served up the action-packed crime drama that it might have. (Mandarin with English subtitles) ★★½ DVD: $29.99

The Shape of Things

(2003, 97 min, US, **Neil LaBute**) Rachel Weisz, Paul Rudd, Gretchen Mol, Fred Weller. Director LaBute (*In the Company of Men*) adapts his own Broadway success and returns to the big screen with a top-notch, squirm-in-your-seat film about such light topics as the meaning of art and cruelty in relationships. The film opens on a chance meeting between a part-time museum guard, Adam (Rudd), and a dedicated art-student, Evelyn (Weisz), who vaguely defines her Master's Thesis as a "sculpture-thingy," as she is about to deface a nude museum piece that had been modified by those who were only concerned with the surface of it — the shape of things. It is at this chance meeting that Evelyn suggests to the vulnerable Adam that he could be cute

with some work, and thus their relationship is begun. True to his own previous works of art, LaBute's film is another brilliant story about the malice and utter disregard humans can have for one another where matters of the heart are concerned. The story is a compact tale of a relationship filled with issues of trust, insecurities and, of course, LeBute's trademark of betrayal. The cast is wonderful in reprising their Broadway roles on the big screen, with Weller giving a particularly convincing performance as the consummate jerk you love to hate. The film does suffer once or twice from its occasional stage-like atmosphere, which is present in some scene blocking and delivery of dialog early on. Although one can feel that it was written originally for the stage, it does translate very well to the screen and ultimately succeeds with an ending that makes the viewer want to tear out his own heart. Another victory for LeBute — this one has both shape and substance. ★★★ DVD Letterbox: $14.99, VHS: $9.99

Sharky's Machine

(1981, 119 min, US, **Burt Reynolds**) Burt Reynolds, Rachel Ward, Vittorio Gassman, Brian Keith, Charles Durning. A bit overlong but nevertheless a flavorful police thriller with police detective Reynolds taking on sleazeball Gassman. ★★½ DVD: $14.99, VHS: $14.99

Sharma and Beyond

(1984, 85 min, GB, **Brian Gilbert**) Suzanne Burden, Robert Urquhart. This installment of David Putnam's "First Love Series" is a winning and poignant exploration of the complex relationship that develops between a father, a daughter and her suitor. The young woman, recently wounded in love, is not at all sure whether this new young man, an aspiring sci-fi writer, is more interested in her, or in her father who is a famous author. ★★★

Shattered

(1991, 97 min, US, **Wolfgang Petersen**) Tom Berenger, Greta Scacchi, Bob Hoskins, Corbin Bernsen, Joanne Whalley-Kilmer. A postmodern whodunit whose psychological complexities, which sometimes obscure the action, probably doomed this inventive, very exciting thriller at the box office. Berenger is left an amnesiac after a near-fatal accident and there are twists aplenty as he tries to get some idea of who he used to be, who he is now and who he can trust to tell him the truth. Scacchi is his loving wife (or is she?), and Hoskins is the private detective trying to solve Berenger's intricate puzzle. A film rich in suspense and overflowing with atmosphere and style. ★★★½ DVD Dual: $14.99

Shattered Glass

(2003, 103 min, US, **Billy Ray**) Hayden Christensen, Peter Sarsgaard, Chloë Sevigny, Rosario Dawson, Melanie Lynskey, Steve Zahn, Hank Azaria. A fascinating account of a real-life story that itself plays like a scintillating journalism investigative story, *Shattered Glass* recounts the events leading up to the exposure of reporter Stephen Glass of *The New Republic*, who fabricated over 25 stories in that magazine. As played by Christensen, whose magnetic portrayal makes up for his wooden *Star Wars* appearances, Glass is a good-looking, charming manipulator who easily ingratiates himself with most of the magazine's staff. One of those coworkers not immediately taken in is his new editor, Chuck Lane (Sarsgaard), who begins to suspect something's not right when an online reporter contacts him about checking certain

Helen Gahagan in *She* ('35)

facts in Glass' latest story. This leads to an investigation that soon tears apart the office and places in jeopardy a once-promising journalistic career. Sarsgaard is outstanding as the idealistic Lane, giving a controlled, even-tempered performance that underscores the growing suspicion of chicanery. ★★★½ DVD Letterbox: $26.99

Shattered Image

(1998, 103 min, US, **Raúl Ruiz**) Anne Parillaud, William Baldwin, Graham Greene. Ruiz is in an unusually muted mood with this intermittently involving English-language thriller of a woman haunted by troubling dreams and a split identity. Parillaud plays two aspects of the same character — is she the professional killer paid to kill antique storeowner Baldwin or is she the beautiful but somnambulistic bride to the seemingly loving Baldwin? These two personas clash during what is either the couple's Caribbean honeymoon or when she is stalking her prey. At its best, Ruiz creates a beguiling puzzle infused with fear, deception, violence and eventually murder. But this psychological mystery-drama is Ruiz-lite and seems to be a thinly veiled rip-off of Hitchcock's *Vertigo*. Exotic settings and steamy sex scenes are offset by Parillaud's monotone, French-accented English and Ruiz's clunky approach. ★★½ DVD: $14.99

The Shawshank Redemption

(1994, 142 min, US, **Frank Darabont**) Tim Robbins, Morgan Freeman, Bob Gunton, James Whitmore, William Sadler. An emotionally moving and satisfying adaptation of a Stephen King novella, this is the story of Andy Dufresne (Robbins), a banker given life imprisonment for the murder of his wife. Sentenced to Shawshank Prison, Andy is brutalized regularly when not staying to himself. Life turns around for him when he befriends Red (Oscar nominee Freeman), a lifer with connections, and becomes financial broker for the crooked warden and his guards. As Andy serves his life sentence, he manages to sustain a hopefulness which affects the other prisoners as well. Director Darabont makes a very assured feature debut, the cinematography and other technical aspects are first-rate and the ensemble is remarkable. ★★★★ DVD Letterbox: $19.99, VHS: $9.99, VHS Letterbox: $9.99

She

(1935, 94 min, US, Irving Pichel & Lansing Holden) *Helen Gahagen, Randolph Scott, Helen Mack, Nigel Bruce.* Deep within an Arctic glacier is the unknown land of Kor. With a hot temper and a colder heart, an ancient queen (Gahagen) rules over this subterranean land while pining still for her long dead lover. She keeps at bay the ravages of the centuries by bathing in a fountain of flames. Finally her Romeo does return — reincarnated as Scott. Produced by the same team that made *King Kong*, *She* is a marvelous mélange of matinee-movie dialogue, kitschy costumes and campy art deco sets. ★★★ DVD: $29.99, VHS: $19.99

She

(1965, 106 min, GB, Robert Day) *Ursula Andress, John Richardson, Peter Cushing.* Great, campy, lost-world fun is to be had in this Hammer Films retelling of the old H. Rider Haggard story about a lost city, a doomed hero, slave sacrifices, an ancient cult and a beautiful, immortal queen. Explorer Richardson and scholar Cushing discover a lost city which at first seems a paradise but becomes a prison when the beautiful queen (Andress) is revealed to be ageless. As it turns out, Richardson is the reincarnation of her lost love, who long ago betrayed her. Will he walk into the Eternal Flame for everlasting life? A pleasure-seeking eternity with Andress? Where do you sign? ★★★ VHS: $19.99

She Creature

(2001, 89 min, Sebastian Gutierrez) *Rufus Sewell, Carla Gugino, Jim Piddock, Reno Wilson, Gil Bellows.* One of a series of low-budget horror remakes made for Showtime, *She Creature* is the best of the lot. Carny con man Sewell and his cronies have been duping small-town folk with their faux freaks, with ex-prostitute Gugino pretending to be a mermaid, among other frauds. When a seemingly senile old man shows them a real mermaid he has kept captive, Sewell steals the creature, and the carnival sets sail. If only they'd listened to the old man's warnings about this diabolical beast. Director Gutierrez has made an enjoyably old-fashioned, atmospheric chiller, eschewing the many camp possibilities of the premise in favor of suspense and goosebumps, with a nifty monster (by Stan Winston) to boot. ★★★ DVD Dual Creature Feature Series: $24.99, VHS: $79.99

She-Devil

(1989, 99 min, US, Susan Seidelman) *Roseanne Barr, Meryl Streep, Ed Begley, Jr., Linda Hunt.* What's a slovenly, socially inept suburban housewife to do when her accountant husband starts a passionate affair with his favorite glamorous and achingly beautiful romance novelist? Take revenge . . . what else? When Roseanne dumps the kids and the dog on wandering hubby Begley and soft-focus sweetie Streep, she begins her metamorphosis from frump to take-charge woman (hear her roar). Streep reveals an unexplored panache for comedic understatement and Barr serves her role well. ★★½ DVD Letterbox: $14.99

She-Devils on Wheels

(1968, 83 min, US, Hershell Gordon Lewis) Lewis' stab at the biker genre, about a violent female motorcycle gang with "guts as hard as the steel of their hogs!" The girls wage war with a rival (male) bike gang, pick their men from a "stud line" and have an all-around "real bad time!" ★ DVD: $24.99, VHS: $19.99

She Done Him Wrong

(1933, 66 min, US, Lowell Sherman) *Mae West, Cary Grant.* West coauthored this classic gay '90s spoof based on her stage hit "Diamond Lil." La West is at her buxom best as Lady Lou, diamond collector and man snatcher — which came first? Grant is the next-door missionary bent on saving her soul — or is he? Mae says it best — "Why don't you come up sometime and see me?" ★★★★

She Must Be Seeing Things

(1988, 85 min, US, Sheila McLaughlin) *Sheila Dabney, Lois Weaver.* McLaughlin's lesbian love story explores the complex sexual and emotional commitment of two women professionals. The love story follows the rocky relationship of Agatha, a New York lawyer, and Jo, a filmmaker. While Jo is out of town, Agatha comes upon her diary and photos which suggest that she is developing an interest in men and may be unfaithful to her. Agatha's attempts to keep her wavering lover interested result in her donning men's clothing and spying on her unsuspecting partner. The drama is a bit stilted and not entirely successful, but there are moments of great insight and fine acting. ★★½ VHS: $29.99

She Wore a Yellow Ribbon

(1949, 103 min, US, John Ford) *John Wayne, Joanne Dru, John Agar, Ben Johnson, Victor McLaglen.* The second (and more successful) film in director Ford's cavalry trilogy. Wayne gives a commanding performance as an officer about to retire, experiencing emotional conflict in doing so. Oscar-winning cinematography. ★★★★ DVD: $19.99, VHS: $9.99

She'll Be Wearing Pink Pyjamas

(1985, 90 min, GB, John Goldschmidt) *Julie Walters, Anthony Higgins.* Walters is a delight in this amiable comic adventure about a group of professional women who volunteer to spend a week at a survival training camp. ★★½

She's All That

(1999, 95 min, US, Robert Iscove) *Freddie Prinze, Jr., Rachael Leigh Cook, Matthew Lillard, Kevin Pollak, Kieran Culkin, Anna Paquin.* When BMOC Zach (Prinze) gets dumped by his beautiful girlfriend, he finds the biggest loser to turn into a prom queen in order to massage his ego in this derivative update of *Pygmalion*. He decides on Laney, an arty wallflower (the personality-less Cook). Of course, all it takes is a set of contacts and a clingy skirt to complete the transformation. Unlike other versions of the story, our heroine has other concerns than wanting just to fit in. Despite the attractive leads, there's not much here that hasn't been seen before, but it does supply a laugh or two. ★★½ DVD: $14.99, VHS: $9.99

She's Gotta Have It

(1986, 84 min, US, Spike Lee) *Tracy Camilla Johns, Tommy Redmond Hicks, John Canada Terrell, Spike Lee.* Lee's inspired and raucous comedy about Nola Darling and her three boyfriends: Mars — "Please baby, please baby, baby, baby, please"; Jamie — "Wherever you want to go, I'll go, whatever you want to do, I'll do"; Greer — "Am I not beautiful darling?" This miraculous cinematic achievement was put together on a shoestring budget and shot over a period of 11 days in a two-square block area of Brooklyn, and yet it stands as one of the funniest and most poignant statements to date on a woman's sexual freedom and how it affects the men in her life. ★★★½

She's Having a Baby

(1988, 106 min, US, John Hughes) *Kevin Bacon, Elizabeth McGovern, Alec Baldwin, William Windom.* Bacon and McGovern fall in love and marry, set up house and prepare for the blessed event; all the while contending with the rigors of married life. Hughes brings about as much character development to this stilted "adult" comedy-drama as he does to his lesser teen flicks. ★★ DVD: $14.99, VHS: $14.99

She's So Lovely

(1997, 100 min, US, Nick Cassavetes) *Sean Penn, Robin Wright Penn, John Travolta, Harry Dean Stanton, Gena Rowlands.* Wright's revelatory performance anchors a sterling collection of finely drawn portrayals in Cassavetes' powerfully crafted exploration of an unwavering true love prevailing in the most desperate of circumstances. Penn and Wright are man and wife in an environment so steeped in violence that escalating menace goes unremarked. After the attack of his wife by a neighbor, Penn almost commits murder and is sentenced to a mental institution. Ten years later, he returns to her — even though she has remarried a rough-hewn contractor (Travolta) and is living the good suburban life. Directing his father John Cassavetes' unproduced screenplay, Nick is his father's son in his unblinking, unflinching exposure of the human condition — stark yet imbued with compassion. ★★★½ DVD: $14.99, VHS: $9.99

She's the One

(1996, 96 min, US, Edward Burns) *Jennifer Aniston, Maxine Bahns, Edward Burns, Cameron Diaz, John Mahoney, Mike McGlone.* A testosterone-centric examination of familial bonding and sibling rivalry, this is a sometimes contrived but entertaining tale of two dissimilar brothers, one crusty dad and the women in their lives. Francis (McGlone) works on Wall Street and possesses a beautiful wife (Aniston) and the morals of pond scum. Mickey (Burns) drives a cab and lives in a ratty flat with a broken heart. Dad (the endearingly cantankerous Mahoney) runs his waterfront dwelling as part boot camp and part locker room. This lively tale of miscommunication and erroneous assumptions is precipitated by Mickey's marriage to an intriguing stranger (Bahns) 24 hours after she flags his cab. He then crosses paths with his ex-

John Richardson and Ursula Andress in *She* ('65)

fiancée (Diaz); setting in motion events which uncover a web of jealousies, secrets and lies. Lots of fun topped off with a sweet resolution. ★★★ DVD: $9.99, VHS: $9.99

The Sheep Has Five Legs

(1954, 95 min, France, Henri Verneuil) *Fernandel, Louis De Funes.* Fernandel, in a role that brought him international recognition, is both hilarious and believable in this comedy in which he plays six different roles. A town seeking publicity decides to reunite its oldest resident with his long-estranged quintuplet grandsons. Fernandel plays both the old man and all five sons — from a salty sea captain to an arrogant hair dresser. Bringing to mind (and equally as talented) the masters of multiple personalities, Peter Sellers and Alec Guinness, the manic Fernandel is a marvel of comic deftness. (French with English subtitles) ★★★½ VHS: $39.99

The Sheltering Sky

(1990, 138 min, GB/Italy, Bernardo Bertolucci) *John Malkovich, Debra Winger, Campbell Scott, Timothy Spall.* Against the vast backdrop of the sweltering heat and punishing sky of Northern Africa, Bertolucci's intimate epic (adapted from Paul Bowles' classic novel) follows the lives of three American travelers during the early 1950s. A husband and wife (Malkovich, Winger) and their traveling companion (Scott) embark from Tangier in search of the "real" Morocco. Slow moving but with sumptuous photography, this is a sun-drenched existential journey that should enthrall the patient viewer. Malkovich is perfect as the arrogant and unfeeling husband who is overwhelmed by culture shock, and Winger's performance as a complacent woman who undergoes a radical transformation is mesmerizing. ★★★½ DVD Letterbox: $19.99, VHS: $14.99

Shenandoah

(1965, 105 min, US, Andrew V. McLaglen) *James Stewart, Doug McClure, Glenn Corbett, Patrick Wayne, Katharine Ross.* An enormously satisfying Civil War drama blessed with one of Stewart's most moving performances. He plays a Virginia patriarch whose family is ripped apart by the conflict. The basis for the Broadway musical of the same name. ★★★ DVD: $14.99, VHS: $9.99

Sherman's March

(1985, 156 min, US, Ross McElwee) What begins as a documentary chronicling the destruction and after-effects of General Sherman's march through the South during the Civil War soon turns into the director's own destructive Southern quest: a quest not of war but of love and romance. In this engaging non-fiction film, we follow McElwee, an energetic, self-indulgent optimist as he cuts a swath through the affluent New South to find not the smoldering remains of the war but a formidable array of extravagant Southern belles. These women constantly distract, bewilder and ultimately conquer our intrepid hero during his disastrously hilarious search for romance, love and meaning. An entertaining and original film. ★★★½ DVD: $29.99, VHS: $29.99

Shine

(1996, 105 min, Australia, Scott Hicks) *Geoffrey Rush, Noah Taylor, Armin Mueller-Stahl, Lynn Redgrave, Alex Rafalowicz, John Gielgud, Googie Withers.* Two parts biopic and one part fairy tale, this real-life drama about Australian pianist David Helfgott's triumph over a lifetime of mental illness is as inspiring as it is well crafted. Told as flashback, the film's narrative walks through the three stages of Helfgott's life: A young prodigy (Rafalowicz) driven by his stern Holocaust survivor father (Mueller-Stahl); a troubled but brilliant teen (Taylor); and finally the broken adult (Rush) who has fallen into a mental collapse that includes endless rapid-fire mumbling. While *Shine* necessarily walks the fine clichéd line of the typical victory-over-adversity tale, Taylor and Oscar winner Rush's dazzling portrayals, director Hicks' acute attention to detail and the rousing use of Rachmaninov's "Piano Concerto No. 3" make this an emotionally satisfying winner. ★★★★ DVD: $24.99, VHS: $19.99, VHS Letterbox: $19.99

Shiner

(2000, 100 min, GB, John Irvin) *Michael Caine, Martin Landau, Frances Barber, Frank Harper, Andy Serkis.* Caine gives a searing performance in this tense, terse but ultimately downbeat drama. A two-bit boxing promoter (Caine) gets his one last shot at the big time when his son is matched against a rival American promoter's best boxer. When things go awry, Caine goes on a rampage, not willing to rest until he's had his revenge. At times intriguing, *Shiner* is undone a bit by its depressing wrap-up — and while it can be argued that the ending is inevitable, it still doesn't cast much more light on character than we've already seen. Still, Caine is so good — and is matched, in a much smaller role, by Landau — that any quibbles with the script don't matter much in the end. He's consistently fascinating to watch, and makes *Shiner* compelling viewing. ★★★ DVD: $19.99, VHS: $9.99

The Shining

(1980, 142 min, GB, Stanley Kubrick) *Jack Nicholson, Shelly Duvall, Scatman Crothers, Danny Lloyd.* Nicholson is at his absolute lunatic best as a once loving father who slips deeper and deeper into homicidal frenzy. His family is contracted to care for a snow-bound, and decidedly sinister, hotel and the descent into madness begins. For those who have read Stephen King's masterpiece of horror and suspense, Kubrick's treatment may be disappointing, but the film is worth a look for Nicholson's inspired ravings and for Garret Brown's stunning Steadicam photography. (Remade in 1997) ★★★ DVD: $19.99, VHS: $8.99

The Shining Hour

(1938, 80 min, US, Frank Borzage) *Joan Crawford, Melvyn Douglas, Robert Young, Margaret Sullavan.* A good cast is featured in this appealing romantic drama. Crawford is at the center of a family crisis as a nightclub dancer who comes between two brothers when she becomes engaged to one of them. Douglas and Young are the feuding siblings. ★★★ VHS: $19.99

Shining Through

(1992, 127 min, US, David Seltzer) *Michael Douglas, Melanie Griffith, Liam Neeson, Joely Richardson, John Gielgud.* Those nasty Nazis are back and this time they're up against America's *Working Girl.* Griffith encores the role of a secretary who wants more in life than just to take dictation. Here, she speaks German and can make a wicked strudel. Of course, these two qualifications are enough to send her off to Germany in the middle of WWII to obtain secret information. Just for good measure, she's in love with her boss, secret agent Douglas. There are some good moments to this slick but silly spy thriller, especially when Neeson as a Nazi official is on screen. ★★½

Ship of Fools

(1965, 149 min, US, Stanley Kramer) *Simone Signoret, Oskar Werner, Vivien Leigh, Lee Marvin, George Segal, Jose Ferrer, Elizabeth Ashley, Michael Dunn.* Absorbing, well-made drama examining the lives of a group of shipboard passengers traveling from Mexico to Germany right before the start of WWII. Powerful performances from a great cast. ★★★½ DVD: $24.99

Shipwrecked

(1990, 93 min, US, Nils Gaup) *Gabriel Byrne, Stian Smestad.* High-spirited adventure yarn about a young boy stranded on a tropical island, fighting for survival while trying to outwit a vicious gang of pirates. From the director of *Pathfinder.* ★★★

Shiri

(1999, 125 min, Korea, Je-gyu Kang) *Suk-kyu Han, Min-sik Choi, Kang-ho Song.* Shiri opens with a stunning, insanely brutal training montage during which North Korean military elite hone their skills on hapless prisoners. The toughest of this lot is Hee, a kick-ass female soldier who is an exceptional, prolific assassin. After a series of vicious murders, two South Korean cops discover that Hee is involved in a terrorist plot to bring about the unification of the two Koreas and sets out to stop her. An exciting cop thriller, *Shiri* never actually matches the sheer intensity of that opening, but remains engrossing due as much to the characters' relationships as its first-rate action scenes. (Korean with English subtitles) ★★★ DVD Letterbox: $24.99, VHS: $89.99

Shirley Valentine

(1989, 108 min, GB, Lewis Gilbert) *Pauline Collins, Tom Conti, Alison Steadman, Joanna Lumley, Bernard Hill.* Collins re-creates her award-winning West End and Broadway role as a London housewife who leaves her family in search of self-fulfillment. In an enchanting performance, Collins is Shirley, the vivacious homemaker whose outlook on life is as entertaining as the one-liners she joy-

Here's Johnny! Jack Nicholson in *The Shining*

ously delivers to the camera. If the idea of a woman fleeing husband and hearth to gain her own independence is not exactly original, writer Willy Russell imbues both the story and its heroine with such a delightful sense of humor that it all seems as new and refreshing as Shirley's near-idyllic Greek island getaway. ★★★ VHS: $14.99

Shivers

(1975, 110 min, Canada, David Cronenberg) *Barbara Steele, Paul Hampton, Joe Silver, Lynn Lowry.* Cronenberg's bizarre and immensely effective horror film is about deadly parasites which infect a high-rise apartment building, causing its victims to commit exaggerated acts of sex and violence. Director's cut. (aka: *They Came from Within*) ★★★ DVD: $14.99, VHS: $9.99

Shoah

(1985, 563 min, Israel, Claude Lanzmann) Lanzmann brings the unspeakable reality of the Holocaust down to human scale in this monumental epic that explores this deplorable page of human history through an examination of the particular physical details and specifics of mass genocide. In *Shoah*, Lanzmann rejects the notion that the Holocaust was a result of impersonal historical forces and grimly examines the harsher reality of it as being the actions of men against men. A landmark effort. (French, German, Yiddish, Italian and Polish with English subtitles) ★★★★ DVD Letterbox 4-Disc Boxed Set: $149.99, VHS: $74.99

Shock Corridor

(1963, 101 min, US, Samuel Fuller) *Peter Brock, Constance Towers.* In this wonderfully entertaining and over-the-top melodrama, Brock stars as a Pulitzer Prize-hunting reporter who fakes madness in order to be admitted into an insane asylum and uncover the perpetrator of an unsolved murder. In the hospital, where the inmates represent a microcosm of a sick and violent society, his investigation bogs down as he himself slowly sinks into dementia. Towers is terrific as his apprehensive stripper girlfriend. A gripping story told with frenzied fervor. ★★★½ DVD: $29.99, VHS: $19.99

A Shock to the System

(1990, 87 min, US, Jan Egleson) *Michael Caine, Peter Riegert, Will Patton, Swoosie Kurtz, Elizabeth McGovern.* Caine shines in this pitch black comedy. When his long overdue promotion is unexpectedly handed to a smarmy young hot shot, Caine is incensed. When he accidentally discovers the convenience and simplicity of murder, Caine is inspired. Director Egleson's tilted angles and off-beat camera movement serve the story well, depicting Caine's skewed view of a world in which he casually knocks off those who get in his way. A scathing indictment of the corporate sensibility, the film is fueled by an insightful, razor-sharp wit which in turn is contrasted with several moments of bone-chilling terror. ★★★½ DVD Letterbox: $9.99, VHS: $7.99

Shock Treatment

(1981, 90 min, US, Jim Sharman) *Richard O'Brien, Cliff De Young, Jessica Harper.* This musical-comedy sequel to *The Rocky Horror Picture Show* finds Brad and Janet (now palyed by De Young and Harper) prisoners in demented Denton, home of happiness and TV game shows. O'Brien leads the proceedings as a mentally suspect medic in this twisted satire on The American Way (greed, lust, media-manipulation and skimpy attire). ★★★ VHS: $14.99

Shocker

(1989, 110 min, US, Wes Craven) *Michael Murphy, Peter Berg.* Director Craven only manages a few sparks in this grisly tale about a mass murderer who comes back from the grave to get even with the psychic teenager who helped fry him. Special effects are good, story is ridiculous and there's an amazing surrealistic chase scene which takes place inside a television set. At least it has more scares and a better look to it than the inferior, similarly themed *The Horror Show*. ★★ DVD: $14.99

The Shoes of the Fisherman

(1968, 152 min, US, Michael Anderson) *Anthony Quinn, Laurence Olivier, John Gielgud, David Jannsen, Leo McKern, Oskar Werner.* Quinn heads an all-star cast in this labored epic as the first Russian-born Pope who tries to bring about world peace. ★★

Shoeshine

(1946, 92 min, Italy, Vittorio De Sica) *Rinaldo Smerdoni, Franco Interlenghi.* This brutal but brilliantly conceived story about two boys surviving in the squalid conditions of post-war Italy is told in a tragic, neorealist style. Giuseppe and Pasquale are two shoeshine boys whose goal is to pool their savings and buy a horse. Their plans are interrupted, however, when they run afoul of the law and end up in a repressive reform school. Their friendship becomes strained and tragedy strikes as the desensitized adult world crushes their youthful innocence. (Italian with English subtitles) ★★★★

Shoot Loud, Louder I Don't Understand!

(1966, 100 min, Italy, Eduardo De Filippo) *Marcello Mastroianni, Raquel Welch.* Not to be confused with "great art," this Italian screwball comedy stars Mastroianni as an eccentric artist with an even stranger uncle, who together become involved in a series of zany escapades which result in seductions, fireworks and eventual betrayal and murder. Written and directed by Italy's best known playwright, De Filippo (*Marriage Italian Style*), this wild romp features the music of Nino Rota. ★★½

Shoot the Moon

(1982, 123 min, US, Alan Parker) *Albert Finney, Diane Keaton, Peter Weller, Karen Allen, Dana Hill, Tracey Gold, Tina Yothers.* Parker's brutally honest film about the breakup of a Marin County family was a disappointment at the box office, which is a tragedy because it features impeccable performances by Finney and Keaton as the couple, and young Hill as their daughter. Not an "escapist" film by any means, its ending will send you reeling. ★★★½

Shoot the Piano Player

(1962, 85 min, France, François Truffaut) *Charles Aznavour, Marie DuBois.* Aznavour is a timid pianist in a second-rate Parisian bistro who accidentally becomes entangled with the mob. Truffaut cavalierly mixes comedic element with a film noir tone in what is surely his quirkiest masterpiece. (French with English subtitles) ★★★★ DVD: $19.99, VHS: $14.99

Shoot to Kill

(1988, 110 min, US, Roger Spottiswoode) *Sidney Poitier, Tom Berenger, Kirstie Alley, Clancy Brown, Richard Masur.* Suspenseful thriller with Poitier on the trail of a ruthless killer, who is hiding out amid a mountain tour group. Berenger is the mountain guide who teams with Poitier when it turns out his girlfriend Alley is leading the group. ★★★ DVD: $14.99

The Shooting

(1967, 82 min, US, Monte Hellman) *Jack Nicholson, Warren Oates, Millie Perkins.* Nicholson and Oates are in uncomfortable alliance as the woman with no name (Perkins) follows a trail and keeps her own counsel in this Old West tale of vengeance and morality. Gritty and atmospheric; you can feel the heat of the Southwestern desert. Nicholson also coproduced. ★★½ DVD: $29.99, VHS: $14.99

Shooting Fish

(1997, 109 min, GB, Stefan Schwartz) *Dan Futterman, Stuart Townsend, Kate Beckinsale.* A frothy comedy about con artists, *Shooting Fish* features a trio of good-looking characters who embark on some routine mischief. Jez (Townsend) and Dylan (Futterman) are orphans who prey upon wealthy victims. The boys' assistant, Georgie (Beckinsale), is even generally amused by her bosses, whose charm is infectious. They, in return, are both smitten with her, even though she is engaged to someone else. The romantic antics of these carefree souls plays out to the music of Burt Bacharach, which gives this contemporary film a bit of a retro feel. Although the outcome is never in doubt — which is the film's only drawback — *Shooting Fish* is an undemanding, entertaining romp. ★★★ DVD: $9.99

The Shooting Party

(1977, 105 min, Russia, Emil Loteanu) *Galina Belyayeva.* A sumptuous realization of Anton Chekhov's early novella of the same name. This tale of passion, set amidst the absurd excesses of pre-Czarist Russian nobility, tells the story of a local magistrate who falls in love with a young woodsman's daughter (Belyayeva). It's a gripping story of unrequited love, murder and the injustices of fate. (Russian with English subtitles) ★★★ VHS: $29.99

The Shooting Party

(1985, 108 min, GB, Alan Bridges) *James Mason, John Gielgud, James Fox, Dorothy Tutin.* Set on a great English estate in the autumn of 1913, this entertaining and highly acclaimed film casts a slightly jaded eye towards both the landed gentry of an Edwardian England on the brink of WWI, and the irrevocable changes that it produced. It marvelously identifies the petty ceremonies and traditions of a declining ruling class and is filled with crisp conversations of a cast of well-defined, idiosyncratic individuals. ★★★½

The Shootist

(1976, 99 min, US, Don Siegel) *John Wayne, Lauren Bacall, James Stewart, Ron Howard.* Wayne's final film is an exemplary western tale set at the turn of the century with the Duke as a famed ex-gunfighter who learns he is dying of cancer. In this touching allegory for the death of the Old West, Wayne sets out to put his affairs in order, but is constantly haunted by his past. ★★★½ DVD: $14.99, VHS: $9.99, VHS Letterbox: $9.99

The Shop Around the Corner

(1940, 97 min, US, Ernst Lubitsch) *James Stewart, Margaret Sullavan, Frank Morgan.* Very charming romantic comedy with Stewart and Sullavan as feuding coworkers in a Budapest shop who unknowingly fall in love with each other when they begin corresponding after answering a lonelyhearts ad. (Remade as *In the Good Old Summertime* and *You've Got Mail*) ★★★½ DVD: $19.99, VHS: $19.99

The Shop on Main Street

(1966, 128 min, Czechoslovakia, Jan Kadar) *Ida Kaminsky, Josef Kroner.* This heartbreaking story follows the tragic relationship between an elderly Jewish woman and the Slovak man assigned by the Nazis to watch over her. This Academy Award?winning Best Foreign Film is not only a moving story but also an impassioned and heartrending plea for peace and understanding. (Czechoslovakian with English subtitles) ★★★★ DVD Criterion Collection: $29.99, VHS: $29.99

Shopping

(1993, 100 min, GB, Paul Anderson) *Jude Law, Sadie Frost, Sean Pertwee, Jonathan Pryce, Marianne Faithful.* A hip, slick and colorful debut film, *Shopping* takes an unsentimental look at the life of Billy (Law), a young adrenaline junkie recently released from prison. Abandoned by both parents and society, he spends his time stealing cars and robbing shops with his friends. At odds with the police (in the person of Pryce) and a jealous chieftan (Pertwee in a terrific and intense performance), Billy careens along his collision course with arrest and/or death with reckless abandon. Anderson brings a remarkable visual artistry to the film, imbuing it with equal parts MTV fast-cuts and Terry Gilliamesque urban British waste-scape. ★★★ VHS: $89.99

Short Circuit

(1986, 98 min, US, John Badham) *Steve Guttenberg, Ally Sheedy, Fisher Stevens.* Pleasant sci-fi comedy about a state-of-the-art robot who escapes from the lab and teams up with a free-spirited artist (Sheedy). (Sequel: *Short Circuit 2*) ★★½ DVD: $14.99

Short Cuts

(1993, 189 min, US, Robert Altman) *Andie MacDowell, Matthew Modine, Bruce Davison, Jack Lemmon, Lily Tomlin, Tim Robbins, Jennifer Jason Leigh, Robert Downey, Jr., Madeleine Stowe.* Based on nine short stories and a poem by Raymond Carver, *Short Cuts* immediately calls to mind one of Altman's masterpieces from the '70s, *Nashville*. But where *Nashville* is centered around a single event, *Short Cuts* examines the comings and goings of 22 characters connected simply by being part of the sprawl that is suburban Los Angeles, a microcosm of contemporary America. Altman explores the everyday lives of these characters with a cynical bite. He also has managed to put together an impressive ensemble. A tremendous slice of life, *Short Cuts* is brilliant, audacious filmmaking. ★★★★ VHS Letterbox: $19.99

Short Eyes

(1977, 104 min, US, Robert M. Young) *Bruce Davison, Luis Guzmán, Miguel Piñero, Curtis Mayfield, Freddie Fender, Willie Hernandez.* Miguel Piñero's powerhouse play, scripted during his stint in Sing-Sing, is a gritty, nerve-rattling glimpse of life behind bars. The prison is peopled by Muslim zealots, angry blacks, knife-wielding Latinos and a smaller group of tough but cautious whites, all of whom hate each other. Casual brutality and violent lust are the norm. But racial tensions dissolve as the prisoners unite in their hatred of Clark Davis (Davison), a white, first-time offender who, after they discover that he is a child abuser ("short eyes"), becomes the target of an onslaught of threats and bloody violence. ★★★ DVD: $24.99, VHS: $19.99

Short Time

(1990, 100 min, US, Gregg Champion) *Dabney Coleman, Matt Frewer, Teri Garr, Barry Corbin, Joe Pantoliano.* Amiable comedy about how a mixed-up medical test has mistakenly convinced a police officer (Coleman) that he's dying. In order for his family to collect on his insurance policy, he's got to be killed in the line of duty. Now, he has become a "super cop," tracking down all sorts of vicious bad guys in an effort to get someone, anyone, to bump him off . . . quickly. ★★½

A Shot in the Dark

(1964, 101 min, GB, Blake Edwards) *Peter Sellers, Elke Sommer, George Sanders, Herbert Lom.* Edwards and Sellers hit the mark with this hysterical "Pink Panther" masterpiece. Arguably the best of the series, the film is inundated with hilarious comedy, great stars, and an undaunted performance by Sellers. Inspector Clouseau ineptly sets out to prove that the ravishing Sommer is innocent of murder despite all evidence to the contrary. When you come down with a bout of Pink Panther-itis, this is the one to rent! (Sequel: *The Return of the Pink Panther*) ★★★★ DVD: $19.99

The Shout

(1978, 87 min, GB, Jerzy Skolimowski) *Alan Bates, John Hurt, Susannah York, Tim Curry.* Bates plays a mysterious intruder in an English couple's household. York is the woman who succumbs to his emotional and sexual domination in this chilling tale of overwhelming menace and aggression. Hurt also stars as the high-strung husband in this adaptation of Robert Graves' ("I, Claudius") short story. ★★★

Shout at the Devil

(1976, 148 min, GB, Peter Hunt) *Lee Marvin, Roger Moore, Barbara Perkins.* Set in Mozambique at the outset of WWI, this over-long, but occasionally exciting, action film features the unlikely pairing of Marvin and Moore as an elephant poacher and an expatriate Englishman. Together, with Marvin's daughter (Perkins) in tow, they set out to sink a German battleship. ★★½

Show Boat

(1936, 113 min, US, James Whale) *Irene Dunne, Paul Robeson, Allan Jones, Charles Winninger, Helen Morgan.* This second of three film versions of the Kern-Hammerstein perennial is the best of the bunch thanks to Whale's sensitive yet firm direction and a superb evocation of 1880s America. In unforgettable voice, Morgan sings "Bill," and Robeson gives a staggering vocal performance of "Ol' Man River." ★★★½ VHS: $19.99

Show Boat

(1951, 107 min, US, George Sidney) *Kathryn Grayson, Ava Gardner, Howard Keel, Joe E. Brown, Agnes Moorehead.* Colorful version of the Kern-Hammerstein musical, though the 1936 version is by far the better of the two. Good cast, though. ★★★ DVD: $19.99

Show Business

(1944, 92 min, US, Edwin L. Marin) *Eddie Cantor, Joan Davis.* The inestimable comedic talents of the great Cantor and the hilarious Davis are combined in this quite entertaining comedy with the two stars as vaudeville performers. ★★★

A Show of Force

(1990, 93 min, US, Bruno Barreto) *Robert Duvall, Andy Garcia, Lou Diamond Phillips, Kevin Spacey, Amy Irving.* An intriguing political thriller about a crusading TV journalist (Irving) investigating one of Puerto Rico's biggest scandals: the brutal 1987 killing of two young men atop a mountainous broadcast tower. Were they terrorists, as the government claims, or were they student activists lured to their deaths by the FBI? ★★½ DVD Letterbox: $14.99, VHS: $14.99

Margaret Sullavan, Frank Morgan and James Stewart in *The Shop Around the Corner*

THE DISCERNING FILM LOVER'S GUIDE

Show People
(1928, 81 min, US, King Vidor) *Marion Davies, William Haines.* Davies stars in this wonderful silent comedy as a country girl who comes to Hollywood to be a "serious" actress, but finds unexpected success as a comedy star. ★★★ VHS: $29.99

Showdown in Little Tokyo
(1991, 79 min, US, Mark L. Lester) *Dolph Lundgren, Brandon Lee, Tia Carrere.* Heads roll and fingers fly as L.A. cop Lundgren teams up with Lee to stop evil, tattooed Japanese druglords from smuggling "ice" into the country, and to avenge the hideous murder of Dolph's parents. No ponderous moral messages in this one, just a lot of mindless action, despicable villains and a rocket-speed chase. ★★ DVD: $9.99, VHS: $4.99

Shower
(2000, 94 min, China, Zhang Yang) *Zhu Xu, Pu Cunxin, Jiang Wu.* A remarkable story of familial bonds and emotional healing, the wondrous Chinese film *Shower* speaks volumes about the resilience of the human spirit. Thinking his father has died, the successful Da Ming returns to the family business, a popular bathhouse. Though all are healthy there, including his estranged elderly father and mentally challenged younger brother, Da Ming stays to repair the wounds of his long absence. In doing so, he comes to enjoy the familiar and see his father in an altogether new light. Director Zhang delights in the old traditions and the daily routines, creating an atmosphere of camaraderie, joviality and accord. A beautiful meditation on life's most important ingredients, and what it takes to recognize them. (Mandarin with English subtitles) ★★★½ DVD: $29.99, VHS: $21.99

Showgirls
(1995, 131 min, US, Paul Verhoeven) *Elizabeth Berkley, Gina Gershon, Kyle MacLachlan, Glenn Plummer, Robert Davi, Alan Rachins, Gina Ravera.* Damned by critics, condemned by conservatives and ignored by the public, this relentlessly bad and wildly camp extravaganza is one of the most cheesily entertaining films to come out of Hollywood since *Myra Breckinridge* and *Beyond the Valley of the Dolls.* The rags-to-nipple clamps tale (and raunchy update of *All about Eve*) centers around the tough-talking white trash Nomi (Berkley), a brain-dead bleached blonde Barbie doll who is lured to the bright lights, fast living and tacky lifestyle of Las Vegas. Blessed with spunk, a curvaceous body and piston-gyrating hips, Nomi steadily claws up the greased pole of success, going from trailer trash tramp to glittery star. Hearing lines like, "It must be weird not having anyone coming on you," Nomi knows she's made it to the top. (★★★★ Camp Rating) ★ DVD: $14.99, DVD V.I.P. Edition: $39.99

Shrek
(2001, 89 min, US, Andrew Adamson & Vicky Jenson) *Voices of: Mike Myers, Eddie Murphy, Cameron Diaz, John Lithgow.* In the opening moments of the gleefully irreverent *Shrek*, a calm-voiced narrator reads a story from an engraved children's book. Seconds later, a page is torn and used as a paper substitute for a certain outhouse activity. This ain't your mother's animated fairy tale. Bordering on the naughty that children will no doubt love, this wildly funny tale based on William Steig's book has as its hero an irascible ogre named Shrek (Myers), who teams with a chatty talking donkey (a hilarious Murphy) to search for a princess

Shrek makes nice with Puss in Boots in *Shrek 2*

(Diaz) imprisoned in a forbidding castle. Lovestruck dragons, magic spells and some twisted jokes await these mismatched adventurers. A marvelous, one-of-a-kind children's classic. (Sequel: *Shrek 2*) ★★★★ DVD Pan & Scan Basic Edition: $19.99, DVD 2-disc set: $26.99, VHS With Extended Ending: $14.99

Shrek 2
(2004, 92 min, US, Andrew Adamson, Kelly Asbury, Conrad Vernon) *Voices of: Mike Myers, Eddie Murphy, Cameron Diaz, Julie Andrews, Antonio Banderas, John Cleese, Rupert Everett, Jennifer Saunders.* There are only a handful of sequels that it can be said truly live up to the original — thankfully, *Shrek 2*, the hilarious sequel to the 2001 animated hit, is one of them. And boy does it deliver. Stunning animation, great humor and delightful characters caught in delightful predicaments go a long way into making this an irresistible joy. Shrek and Fiona are on their honeymoon when Fiona's royal parents summon her to the land of Far Far Away (which looks just like Hollywood). This begins the avalanche of visual and verbal jokes that once again distinguish this franchise from all the others. Donkey returns as well, but now is fighting for attention/scene-stealing from a wily cat named Puss in Boots, wonderfully voiced by Banderas. It's all here: the naughty humor that's okay for the little ones to see or hear; the witty puns only adults could savor; the jabs at our sacred cows; and (our personal favorite) the ton of movie takeoffs. Who could ask for more? *Shrek 2* is unabashed fun. ★★★★

Shy People
(1987, 119 min, US, Andrei Konchalovsky) *Jill Clayburgh, Barbara Hershey, Martha Plimpton, Mare Winningham.* Clayburgh is a street-smart New York magazine writer working on an article about long-lost relatives who live deep within the Louisiana bayou. Hershey is the fierce marshland matriarch sheltering her brood from the outside world. Together, they clash big time. ★★ VHS: $19.99

Siberiade
(1979, 206 min, Russia, Andrei Konchalovsky) *Vladimir Samoilov, Vitaly Solomin, Nikita Mikhalkov.* The tumultuous events in Russia's 60-year history from 1900 to the 1960s provide the

backdrop for this lavishly photographed and lyrically poetic saga of three generations of two families in a Siberian hamlet. The film follows the day-to-day events of the poor Ustyuzhanin and the middle-class Solomin families, both virtually untouched by 19th-century progress. Feuds, affairs, murder and revenge transpire amid the social upheaval in this microcosm of a peasant Russia forced into the 20th century. Despite its length, *Siberiade* is a fast-moving and touching drama of the universal story of humanity caught in the turbulence of sweeping development. (Russian with English subtitles) ★★★★ VHS: $29.99

Siberian Lady Macbeth
(1962, 93 min, Yugoslavia, Andrzej Wajda) *Olivera Markovic, Ljuba Tadic.* This lusty, bombastic melodrama is great pre-"Dynasty" fun. Set in turn-of-the-century Russia, the story focuses on Katarina, a beautiful but bored wife of an often out-of-town merchant whose life takes a decidedly tumultuous and erotic turn after she meets a boisterous wanderer. In a very short time, she dispatches her tyrannical father-in-law (with rat poison), takes her compliant peasant as a live-in lover and plots to kill her soon-to-return husband — it's all in a week's fun in this passion-fueled tale of murder, sex, madness and violence. (aka: *Fury Is a Woman*) (Serbo-Croatian with English subtitles) ★★★ DVD Letterbox: $29.99, VHS: $24.99

Sibling Rivalry
(1990, 88 min, US, Carl Reiner) *Kirstie Alley, Scott Bakula, Bill Pullman, Carrie Fisher, Sam Elliott.* Alley brings some life to this sometimes amusing black comedy as a doctor's wife whose sexual frustration leads to an affair. However, things go from bad to worse when her lover dies in bed and she learns his true identity. Bakula plays her hapless husband. ★★½ DVD Dual: $14.99

The Sicilian
(1987, 146 min, US, Michael Cimino) *Christopher Lambert, Terence Stamp, John Turturro.* A gangster takes on the mob by robbing the rich and distributing the wealth among the peasants in post-WWII Sicily. Needless to say, the Mafia is not happy. A misguided and lethargic crime saga. ★ DVD: $14.99

559

Sid & Nancy

(1986, 111 min, US, Alex Cox) *Gary Oldman, Chloe Webb, Courtney Love.* Cox takes the story of two self-destructive junkies, Sid Vicious of the Sex Pistols and Nancy Spungen, and sparks it up with savage energy and sardonic wit. It's no easy feat to romanticize, yet not idealize, these flamboyantly adolescent creatures. In spectacular performances, Oldman and Webb bring a ferociousness to their roles that draws us to this doomed pair, if only to be repelled by their self-absorbed stupidity. ★★★½ DVD: $19.99

Sideburns

(1990, 110 min, Russia, Yuri Mamin) Uncannily timely for a post-Communist Russia and a post-unification Germany, this exuberantly wacky yet cautionary political satire is a seriously funny film that, with its antic filmic style, is reminiscent of Dusan Makavejev's early works. Two geeks dressed in turn-of-the-century waistcoats arrive in a backwater Russian city and begin winning adherents with their reactionary, Nazi-tinged political philosophy that idolizes poet Alexander Pushkin and seems to be against all change. The first target of their violent rampage for social conformity is the hippy-dippy "Children of Perestroika," but soon other reactionary groups spring up to vie for power and it takes the really bad guys (the Communists) to restore "order" to the land. (Russian with English subtitles) ★★½ VHS: $59.99

Sidewalks of New York

(2001, 107 min, US, Edward Burns) *Edward Burns, Rosario Dawson, Dennis Farina, Heather Graham, David Krumholtz, Brittany Murphy, Stanley Tucci.* Writer-director Burns borrows just a little too heavily from the pages of Woody Allen for this somewhat pretentious romantic comedy that nevertheless offers a witty look at love, marriage and sex in modern New York City. *Sidewalks of New York* is strident at first, with nearly everyone coming across as terribly self-absorbed. But, like the film, they soon grow on you and become a bit more complex. In a story of the love lives of six Manhattanites whose lives intertwine, Burns plays a TV producer who is romantically involved with two women, each of them bringing some emotional baggage into the relationship. As writer, Burns does cop-out in a few of the stories, but *Sidewalks of New York* still manages to be an involving, amusing film with good performances to detract from the overall familiarity. ★★½ DVD Letterbox: $19.99, VHS: $14.99

The Siege

(1998, 116 min, US, Edward Zwick) *Denzel Washington, Annette Bening, Bruce Willis, Tony Shalhoub, Sami Bouajila.* In this muddled thriller, Washington plays an FBI agent investigating a rash of bombings. Bening is the mysterious government operative who definitely knows more than she's letting on to. The implausible story soon has renegade general Willis taking control and turning Brooklyn into a fascist state. With Arab terrorists, torture, mass murder and military men run amok, the only villainous element missing from the story is Nazis. Bening is the only one to carve some meat from this lean bone, which wants to be both action film and social commentary. Spread too thin, it isn't fully developed as either. Willis' one-note performance certainly doesn't help. ★★ DVD: $19.99, VHS: $9.99

Mel Gibson in M. Night Shyamalan's *Signs*

Siesta

(1987, 105 min, US, Mary Lambert) *Ellen Barkin, Gabriel Byrne, Jodie Foster, Martin Sheen, Isabella Rossellini, Grace Jones, Julian Sands, Alexei Sayles.* Barkin is Claire, a professional daredevil who suddenly awakens to find herself lying on an airport runway covered in blood. Unable to recall her last three days and mystified by the origins of the blood, which is not her own, she begins an erotic and hallucinatory odyssey through a sun-bleached Spain where she encounters a menacingly horny cabbie, her now indifferent ex-lover and an eccentric group of intoxicated British "artists." This feature film debut by Lambert is a refreshingly complex, frenzied and enigmatic mystery-drama. Music by Miles Davis. ★★★ VHS: $14.99

The Sign of the Cross

(1932, 124 min, US, Cecil B. DeMille) *Fredric March, Elissa Landi, Claudette Colbert, Charles Laughton.* DeMille's religious opus is a stylistically extravagant tale that mixes religious dogma with scenes of Roman excesses of sex and violence. Roman bigwig March falls in love with Christian do-gooder Landi. Then he spends the rest of the story trying to keep her from being lion bait. Far more interesting are Laughton, as an effeminate Nero, and Colbert, who is a cunning and sexy Poppaea. DeMille overplays the religious aspect but outdoes himself depicting the many torturous deaths in the arena (by elephant, alligator, gorilla) and with a sizzling lesbian seduction. ★★★

Signal 7

(1983, 92 min, US, Rob Nilsson) *Bill Ackridge, Dan Leegant.* A rambling but sensitive portrayal of two middle-aged cab drivers who are going nowhere fast. Shot on videotape on a shoestring budget, this largely improvised drama can be uncomfortably revealing during its soul-baring scenes, reminding one of the early works of John Cassavetes, to whom the film is dedicated. ★★½ VHS: $79.99

La Signora di Tutti

(1934, 94 min, Italy, Max Ophüls) *Isa Miranda.* Ophüls' only Italian film, this sublime and powerful melodrama features Miranda as Gaby Doriot, an aging film star who, at the top of her professional career but in the depths of despair in her private life, attempts suicide. Under anesthesia on the operating table, her sordid past, one of great excesses, ambitions and painful loves, is relived in her thoughts. (Italian with English subtitles) ★★★ VHS: $29.99

Signs

(2002, 108 min, US, M. Night Shyamalan) *Mel Gibson, Joaquin Phoenix, Cherry Jones, Rory Culkin, Abigail Breslin, M. Night Shyamalan.* "I can't even imagine (what's happening out there)" says Graham Hess, a Pennsylvania farmer and former minister, as his family comes under attack from unseen forces. Through a savvy bit of filmmaking prowess, one watching writer-director Shyamalan's tense, eerie sci-fi psychological thriller could ponder that aloud, too, as we only see what the characters see. Consequently, the fear of the unknown is taken to the next degree of the horrific as the *Sixth Sense* creator comes up with another original and effective way to creep us out. Gibson is Hess, a widower with two children and a question of faith. When strange happenings occur on his farm, beginning with a huge crop circle in his corn field, it becomes apparent he and the rest of the world are being visited by extraterrestrials. Recalling Hitchcock rather than Spielberg, Shyamalan maintains a deliberate, steady pace, offering only little bits of information that give rise to several highly suspenseful set pieces. *Signs* isn't showy, but by way of its spare filmmaking style, it quietly, almost subversively, creates chills of quite the scary kind. ★★★½ DVD Vista Series: $19.99, VHS: $14.99

Signs of Life (Lebenszeichen)

(1968, 90 min, Germany, Werner Herzog) *Peter Brogle, Wolfgang Reichmann, Athina Zacharopoulou.* This early Herzog feature exhibits many of the director's signature touches, albeit sometimes haltingly utilized. During WWII, a wounded German soldier is billeted to an occupied Greek island to recuperate in the company of his Greek wife and two other German soldiers. At first seemingly idyllic, their lives bog down in tedium, heat and boredom. The young man unravels, his mental deterioriation leading to the munitions dump in an attempt to shake his fist at God. The director's trademark static shots are not as effective in their conveyance of existential anguish as they would become in his later films; but the film is a valuable glimpse into the early development of a major filmmaker. (German with English subtitles) ★★½ VHS: $29.99

Signs of Life

(1989, 91 min, US, John David Coles) *Arthur Kennedy, Kevin J. O'Connor, Vincent D'Onofrio, Michael Lewis, Kate Reid, Beau Bridges.* An extremely talented cast highlights this personal and touching drama about the final days of a boat-building business and how the closing affects those around it. Kennedy is remarkable as the patriarchal owner who refuses to accept the inevitable. O'Connor and D'Onofrio are both fine as the two young workers planning to leave their small town at the expense of a loved one. Though these types of films are usually described as "small," there is nothing miniature in the scope or achievement of this "little" gem. ★★★½ VHS: $14.99

The Silence

(1963, 95 min, Sweden, Ingmar Bergman) *Ingrid Thulin, Gunnel Lindstrom.* An intense story of two sisters, emotionally and physically united since childhood, who, while traveling together, begin the struggle of separation. The younger woman seeks freedom from her embittered sister by entering into a relationship with a stranger. Last of Bergman's trilogy on faith which includes *Through a Glass Darkly* and *Winter Light.* (Swedish with English subtitles) ★★★ VHS: $24.99

The Silence of Neto

(1994, 106 min, Guatemala, Luis Argueta) *Eva Tamargo Lemus, Oscar Javier Almengor, Herbert Meneses, Julio Díaz.* Guatemala's first film to achieve international notice, *The Silence of Neto* is set within a forgotten instance of American/Latin relations. In 1954, under the guise of fighting the scourge of Communism, the U.S. bombed Guatemala and replaced its government with a puppet regime. The film begins as young Neto mourns the death of his beloved uncle. In flashbacks, we see his affections are directed towards his dashing but mostly absent Uncle Ernesto. With tastes of magical realism, particularly surrounding the uncle's unexpected comings and goings while living and dead, Uncle Ernesto and Neto share imaginative fantasies. First love, loss and fantasy round out the roster in this quiet coming-of-ager. (Spanish with English subtitles) ★★★

The Silence of the Lambs

(1991, 118 min, US, Jonathan Demme) *Jodie Foster, Anthony Hopkins, Scott Glenn, Ted Levine, Anthony Heald, Frankie Faison, Kasi Lemmons, Brooke Smith, Tracey Walter, Roger Corman, Ron Vawter, Charles Napier, Kenneth Utt.* Demme's nerve-racking psychological chiller based on the novel by Thomas Harris stars Foster as Clarice Starling, a fledgling FBI agent who is assigned the daunting task of interviewing convicted psycho-killer, Dr. Hannibal Lecter (Hopkins) in the hopes that he can help her develop a profile of "Buffalo Bill" — a mass murderer who likes to skin his victims. Hopkins' portrayal of the maniacally twisted Lecter is sheer terrifying brilliance. For her part, Foster is equally stellar. Her Clarice is an intricate and subtly drawn character who finds herself in a dangerous pas de deux with Lecter. Their scenes are riveting. Demme's direction throughout is superb. Winner of 5 Academy Awards including Best

Picture, Director, Actress (Foster) and Actor (Hopkins). (Sequel: *Hannibal*) ★★★★ DVD Letterbox: $19.99, DVD Pan & Scan: $19.99, DVD Theatrical Cut: $14.99, VHS: $9.99

Silent Fall

(1994, 100 min, US, Bruce Beresford) *Richard Dreyfuss, Linda Hamilton, Ben Faulkner, Liv Tyler, John Lithgow, J.T. Walsh.* Dreyfuss stars as a noted psychiatrist who battles his own demons while helping a child come to terms with his. Faulkner plays a ten-year-old autistic youth who is the sole witness to the murder of his parents. Dreyfuss is reluctantly called into the investigation to try to reach the boy, made more difficult by the child's silence, an interfering doctor (Lithgow) and an impatient sheriff (Walsh). Beresford's subtle direction creates a suspenseful mood throughout. ★★★ DVD: $9.99, VHS: $14.99

Silent Movie

(1976, 86 min, US, Mel Brooks) *Mel Brooks, Dom DeLuise, Marty Feldman, Bernadette Peters, Ron Carey.* Although this Brooks spoof on Hollywood filmmaking is not on the comic level with his best works, it is nonetheless an enjoyable lark. Brooks plays a has-been producer who attempts a comeback by making a silent movie. All this, of course, is set within a silent film, more than living up to its title. Cameos include Anne Bancroft, Paul Newman and Liza Minnelli. ★★★

The Silent Partner

(1978, 103 min, Canada, Daryl Duke) *Christopher Plummer, Elliott Gould, Susannah York, John Candy.* Plummer teams with Gould in this original and riveting suspense thriller. Gould plays a bank teller who figures out Plummer's plan to rob his bank, turning the tables on him. However, when the psychotic would-be robber figures out the double-cross, he sets out after Gould and the loot. ★★★

Silent Running

(1971, 89 min, US, Douglas Trumbull) *Bruce Dern, Cliff Potts.* Special effects master Trumbull (*2001*) directed this inventive though leisurely sci-fi/environmental tale with Dern tending a space garden when Earth has become barren, losing control when the powers that be decide to shut it down. Written by Michael Cimino, Steven Bochco and Deric Washburn. ★★★ DVD Letterbox: $14.99

Silent Shakespeare

(1899-1911, 88 min, GB) Shakespeare without spoken words? Folly perhaps on the part of these early filmmakers, but no less of a stretch than the recent mining of the Bard's work by Hollywood. One of the most intriguing points to this assemblage of rare footage from the British Film Institute is the international mix. From the U.S., "A Midsummer Night's Dream," 1909; and "Twelfth Night," 1910. From the U.K. "King John," 1899; "The Tempest," 1908; and "Richard III," 1911. From Italy (these are the only films with hand-stenciled color), "King Lear," 1910; and "The Merchant of Venice," 1910, apparently filmed in Venice. Fragmentary and damaged, the films act as documentary material about the early cinemas of three nations. And if you look closely, you can even see nuanced variances in how these cultures interpret the Bard. ★★★ DVD: $29.99, VHS: $29.99

Silent Tongue

(1994, 98 min, US, Sam Shepard) *River Phoenix, Alan Bates, Richard Harris, Dermot Mulroney, Tantoo Cardinal.* The final theatrical release of Phoenix, this involving though labored ghost story is slightly odd, but it achieves a poetic, mystical tone. Set in the Old West, the film casts Bates as a slimy sideshow owner who traded his Indian daughter to pioneer Harris for his son (Phoenix) to marry. However, after the woman dies in childbirth, Harris returns to negotiate for Bates' remaining daughter to comfort his near-mad, grieving son — whose refusal to bury his wife causes her spirit to return to seek vengeance. *Silent Tongue* is an unusual, slowly paced but nevertheless gripping treatise on 19th-century Western culture. ★★½

The Silent Touch

(1992, 92 min, Denmark/GB/Poland, Krzysztof Zanussi) *Max von Sydow, Sarah Miles, Lothaire Bluteau, Sofie Grabol.* Von Sydow perfectly balances emotional extremes in his intensely involving portrayal of a world-renowned composer whose forty-year silence is broken by the silent touch of a young music student. The composer is a gruff bear in continuous hibernation, literally lashing out at whoever dares to approach his lair. Miles endows a modern, practical saintliness to her portrayal of the composer's supportive, caretaking wife. The quality of the performances elevates the film above the lapses in the script, as the film explores myriad contradictions of human existence. A delicate, considered film, revealing that the past is always with us, and the future is ours to create. ★★★ VHS: $79.99

The Silk Road

(1988, 99 min, Japan, Junya Sato) A "sukiyaki western" in the best sense of the term, this spectacular saga of love, heroism and war is set on the Silk Road (the ancient 5,000-mile trade route that stretches through the Asian desert). The story follows the adventures of a reluctant warrior, Zhao, a young man who rescues a captured princess but finds that his reward is only to be hunted down by a vengeful crown prince intent on killing both of them. This exhilarating romantic adventure should not be confused with the similarly packaged, but somewhat less satisfying battle-filled epic, *Heaven and Earth.* (Japanese with English subtitles) ★★★½ VHS: $9.99

Silk Stockings

(1957, 117 min, US, Rouben Mamoulian) *Fred Astaire, Cyd Charisse, Janis Paige, Peter Lorre, George Tobias.* Charming musical remake of Ernst Lubitsch's *Ninotchka,* with Astaire in the Melvyn Douglas role as a movie producer, and the lovely Charisse in the Garbo role as the Russian envoy. Score by Cole Porter. ★★★ DVD Letterbox: $19.99

Silkwood

(1983, 128 min, US, Mike Nichols) *Meryl Streep, Kurt Russell, Cher, David Strathairn, Diana Scarwid, Fred Ward, Ron Silver.* In yet another remarkable performance, Streep stars as Karen Silkwood, the nuclear plant worker who died under mysterious circumstances after uncovering damaging information against the plant for which she worked. Russell as her boyfriend and Cher as her lesbian roommate both offer strong support in Nichols' tense, harrowing and compelling drama. ★★★½ DVD: $14.99

Silver Bullet

(1985, 95 min, US, Daniel Attias) *Gary Busey, Corey Haim, Megan Follows.* Stylish version of Stephen King's story about a small town being terrorized by a werewolf, with Busey and young Haim determined to put a stop to it. ★★½ DVD: $14.99, VHS: $9.99

Silver Streak

(1976, 113 min, US, Arthur Hiller) *Richard Pryor, Gene Wilder, Jill Clayburgh, Patrick McGoohan, Ned Beatty, Ray Walston, Scatman Crothers.* Wilder and Pryor team for the first time in this engaging and often hilarious comedy which tips its hat to Hitchcock and the mystery-aboard-a-train films. Passenger Wilder gets himself mixed up with Clayburgh, FBI agents, murder, con artist Pryor and spies as he travels from Los Angeles to Chicago. Pryor is a standout. ★★★

Silverado

(1985, 132 min, US, Lawrence Kasdan) *Kevin Costner, Kevin Kline, Danny Glover, Scott Glenn, Brian Dennehy, Jeff Goldblum, Rosanna Arquette.* Entertaining and very stylish western adventure with the "two Kevins" — Kline and Costner — and Glover and Glenn as four drifters who team up to battle a crooked town sheriff and the gang who controls him. ★★★ DVD Letterbox Collector's Edition: $14.99, VHS: $9.99

Silverlake Life: The View from Here

(1992, 99 min, US, Peter Friedman & Tom Joslin) Arguably the most harrowing vision of death and dying ever recorded, this emotionally devastating video diary of two lovers living with and dying from AIDS is far from a morbid recording of one's own death. Rather, it's a celebration of life and of the enduring love the two men had for each other. The camera follows them as they visit the doctor, buy medicine and herbal "cures" and other activities, but stays primarily in their apartment in the Silverlake section of Los Angeles. One's immediate feeling — after the sadness of their story — is an acknowledgement of their overriding commitment to each other, making this personal diary an astonishing love story. ★★★★ DVD 10th Anniversary: $24.99, VHS: $19.99

Simon Birch

(1998, 114 min, US, Mark Steven Johnson) *Ian Michael Smith, Jim Carrey, Joseph Mazzello, David Strathairn, Oliver Platt, Ashley Judd, Dana Ivey.* Suggested (not based) on John Irving's novel "A Prayer for Owen Meany," *Simon Birch* uses only the first third of Irving's book. Gone are the boyhood adolescent talks, masturbation sessions, college; gone, in fact, is much of the spirit. Writer-director Johnson has, instead, fashioned a shamefully manipulative family drama defined by tragic acts, rather than a black comedy touched by tragedy. Set in 1964, the story centers on the friendship of 12-year-olds Joe (Mazzello) and Simon (Smith), the two town outcasts (Joe's illegitimate, Simon was born with dwarfism). Johnson concentrates on the sap, forgetting that the original story is laced with irony and humor. He manages a few good touches, but most of it is sledgehammer subtle. ★★ DVD: $14.99, VHS: $9.99

Simon of the Desert

(1965, 45 min, Mexico, Luis Buñuel) *Claudio Brook, Silvia Pinal.* This comic and surreal attack on the Church is drawn from the life of Saint Simeon Stylites who, in order to lead the "correct Christian life," resided atop a pillar. Vain, self-important and sexually repressed, our hero soon finds that he is tempting prey for the cunning Devil. (Spanish with English subtitles) ★★★½ VHS: $29.99

Simone

(2002, 117 min, US, Andrew Niccol) *Al Pacino, Catherine Keener, Pruitt Taylor Vance, Jay Mohr, Rachel Roberts (II), Elias Koteas, Jason Schwartzman, Winona Ryder.* Alfred Hitchcock always denied saying the infamous "actors are cattle" line. Though after seeing what writer-director Niccol thinks of them in his tame Hollywood satire *Simone*, Hitch shouldn't have worried about a thing. Walking through a role like he's never done before, Pacino plays Viktor Taransky, a Hollywood director on the verge of ruin when his leading lady (Ryder) walks out of his picture. When all seems lost, he runs into a computer programmer who has the answer: a computer-generated actress. Named Simone, she becomes an overnight hit, and Taransky goes to crazy lengths in trying to keep the public from learning the truth. There's a scintillating Hollywood satire somewhere in here, but as realized by Niccol the film has no bite, only sitcom predicaments and canned-laugh jokes. ★★ DVD Dual: $14.99, VHS: $9.99

Simpatico

(1999, 97 min, US, Matthew Warchus) *Nick Nolte, Sharon Stone, Jeff Bridges, Catherine Keener, Shawn Hatosy, Kimberly Williams, Albert Finney.* Wealthy horse ranch owner Bridges is about to close a multimillion dollar racehorse sale when he receives a call from old friend Nolte. It seems Nolte is about to be arrested, and is afraid he'll spill the beans about their shady past. Meanwhile, Bridges' wife (Stone) whiles her miserable days away in a drunken haze. Adapted from a lesser Sam Shepard play, *Simpatico* is inert, muted and saddled with awkward flashback scenes. The chief reason to watch this — and it's reason enough — is the terrific cast. It's a joy to see two of our greatest actors, Bridges and Nolte, share the screen for the first time. Though the story gets sillier and murkier as it goes along, *Simpatico* is still reasonably compelling material given urgency by strong performances. ★★½ DVD: $9.99, VHS: $4.99

Simple Men

(1992, 105 min, US, Hal Hartley) *Robert Burke, Karen Sillas, William Sage.* Where other than in a Hartley film would you find such characters as a brawling, chain-smoking nun, a French-speaking, grunge-rocking gas-station attendant, and a beautiful Romanian epileptic? However, *Simple Men* lacks the cohesion of his more successful efforts. The story follows Bill, a petty criminal, and his kid brother Daniel, on their search for their escaped-con dad, who may or may not have bombed the Pentagon 20 years earlier. Their quest leads them to the little town of Sagapownac, Long Island, where each man, buoyed by Jim Beam and long-winded philosophical chitchat, realizes his destiny. The film suffers mainly from its somewhat meandering pace and a few too many incidental characters. ★★½ DVD Letterbox: $14.99, VHS: $19.99

A Simple Plan

(1998, 120 min, US, Sam Raimi) *Bill Paxton, Billy Bob Thornton, Bridget Fonda, Brent Briscoe, Chelcie Ross, Gary Cole.* Recalling the style and achievement of former collaborators Joel and Ethan Coen, director Raimi's striking psychological thriller is a nerve-racking, thought-provoking morality tale played out as American tragedy. Based on Scott Smith's best-seller, the story begins as two brothers, the respectable Hank and the slow-witted Jacob (Paxton and Thornton), unearth a downed plane hiding a duffel bag containing millions in cash. Immediately, Smith (who adapted his novel) and Raimi set in motion a moral dilemma as they try to decide what to do with the money. As each layer of the characters' moral fiber is slowly stripped away, the men struggle not to lose their humanity as the inevitable chaos of paranoia and greed engulf their lives. Often wickedly funny and always riveting, this features an excellent ensemble, none more effective than Thornton. As the dimmer sibling, he brings unexpected complexity and compassion to Jacob. ★★★★ DVD: $19.99, VHS: $14.99

A Simple Story

(1978, 110 min, France, Claude Sautet) *Romy Schneider, Bruno Cremer.* Schneider is an unalloyed pleasure in this subtle, incisive look at a woman's mid-life crisis. Though she's a successful designer with a teenage son and a sympathetic circle of friends, Schneider is plagued by doubts and fears about the path she has chosen, and can't figure out how to change things. Schneider won a French Academy Award for her gripping performance. (French with English subtitles) ★★★ VHS: $29.99

A Simple Twist of Fate

(1994, 106 min, US, Gillies MacKinnon) *Steve Martin, Gabriel Byrne, Laura Linney, Catherine O'Hara, Stephen Baldwin.* Mistakenly billed as a comedy, this drama inspired by "Silas Marner" follows one hard-luck and heartbreaking story after another. Martin finds out that the child his wife is expecting isn't his; then he moves to a small town where his fortune in gold coins is stolen; then a hero-in addict dies in the snow outside his house. Only after the woman's young daughter wanders into Martin's home and life does the film lighten up. He adopts her and things are fine for years, until her real father (Byrne) decides to take her back, leading to an emotional ending. ★★½ DVD: $9.99, VHS: $14.99

A Simple Wish

(1997, 89 min, US, Michael Ritchie) *Martin Short, Mara Wilson, Robert Pastorelli, Amanda Plummer, Kathleen Turner, Ruby Dee.* Wilson is Anabel, a daughter desperate for her dad (Pastorelli) to get the lead role in a Broadway musical. She wishes for a fairy godmother. She gets Murray, played by an overacting Short. He then bungles every aspect of Anabel's wish. Meanwhile, Turner, a fairy godmother turned evil witch, is complicating matters by stealing all the godmother wands at the national godmother convention. Murray, Anabel and her brother must retrieve the wands in order to undo the incorrect fairy godmother wishes, leading to a lackluster climax. ★★ VHS: $9.99

Simply Irresistible

(1999, 100 min, US, Mark Tarlov) *Sarah Michelle Gellar, Sean Patrick Flanery, Patricia Clarkson, Dylan Baker, Christopher Durang.* Gellar is the chef for a tiny restaurant in TriBeCa that is on the verge of closing because she's an awful cook. But at the farmer's market, she runs into a creepy guy who gives her a guardian crab which looks over her shoulder and puts magic into her recipes. Someone call the FDA! Her concoctions make rival and budding restaurateur Flanery fall for her while babbling about her delicious eclairs. Sorry to say, but the magic here is more forced than Doug Hennings', and the result is simply embarrassing. Between the fog that comes out of the peach dessert and the cut-aways to the crab during romantic conversations, it's hard to pay attention to the characters. All in all, the worst romantic comedy since *Mandingo*. ★ DVD: $9.99, VHS: $9.99

The Sin of Harold Diddlebock

(1947, 90 min, US, Preston Sturges) *Harold Lloyd, Margaret Hamilton, Rudy Vallee, Franklin Pangborn.* Sturges and Lloyd share the dubious distinction of being two of America's most undervalued treasures. Writer-director Sturges is witty, hilarious, touching and intelligent; Lloyd's capable synthesis of subtle characterization and side-splitting slapstick is unmatched. The plot involves an ex-football star who, after 20 years in a dead-end job, uses his life savings to make a fortune at the track only to lose it at the circus. At the circus? Just watch it — you won't regret it. (aka: *Mad Wednesday*) ★★★ DVD: $19.99

The Sin of Madelon Claudet

(1931, 73 min, US, Edgar Selwyn) *Helen Hayes, Lewis Stone, Robert Young.* Hayes, the First Lady of the American Theatre, makes one of her rare screen appearances in this superb soap opera, and she won an Oscar for it. In the tradition of *Stella Dallas* and *Madame X*, Hayes, in a glorious performance, plays a mother who sacrifices all for the sake of her son. Sure it's been done before, even back then, but Hayes' portrayal and the sharp directorial style make it all the more refreshing. ★★★ VHS: $14.99

Sinbad and the Eye of the Tiger

(1977, 113 min, GB, Sam Wanamaker) *Patrick Wayne, Jane Seymour.* The weakest of the whole Harryhausen/Sinbad series is saddled with a predictable plot, anemic characters, and (most surprisingly) less than spectacular special effects. For the record, the plot concerns Sinbad's quest to help a prince who's been transformed into a baboon by a sorceress' evil spell. ★½ DVD: $19.99, VHS: $14.99

Since You Went Away

(1944, 172 min, US, John Cromwell) *Claudette Colbert, Shirley Temple, Jennifer Jones, Joseph Cotten, Monty Woolley, Hattie McDaniel, Agnes Moorehead.* A tremendous cast brings life to this compelling and first-rate WWII soaper, a huge hit back in 1944. Sort of *Mrs. Miniver* with an American family, the story follows the struggles and daily lives of those on the homefront. Colbert shines as the mother and wife keeping a stiff upper lip while her husband is fighting overseas. ★★★½ VHS: $29.99

Sincerely Charlotte

(1986, 92 min, France, Caroline Huppert) *Isabelle Huppert, Niels Arestrup.* Huppert camps it up as a beguiling nightclub singer who is on the lam for the suspected murder of her boyfriend. With the net closing, and in desperation, she reenters the life of her old boyfriend, now married. Smitten with the alluring Huppert, the man's attention is divided between his quiet domestic life and the carefree, dangerous but exciting world of his ex. Huppert is wonderful as the femme fatale; part innocent, part liar and bitch. (French with English subtitles) ★★★

Un Singe en Hiver (Monkey in Winter)

(1962, 105 min, France, Henri Verneuil) *Jean Gabin, Jean-Paul Belmondo.* In theme and acting prowess, *Un Singe en Hiver* can be favorably compared to *The Color of Money*. Crusty old-timer Gabin is wasting his days away in a small town. His life is reinvigorated when a young man (Belmondo) moves into town, for Gabin sees in this wild drinker and dreamer fragments of his own vibrant youth. They join together for a few unforgettable adventures. (French with English subtitles) ★★½

Singin' in the Rain

(1952, 102 min, US, Gene Kelly & Stanley Donen) *Gene Kelly, Debbie Reynolds, Donald O'Connor, Jean Hagen, Cyd Charisse, Rita Moreno.* Movie musicals just don't come any better than this. A collection of superbly creative talents are at their peak with this spoof on 1920s Hollywood, with directors Kelly and Donen and writers Betty Comden and Adolph Green combining forces after their success with *On the Town*. Kelly, who also choreographed, plays a popular silent screen star faced with the advent of "talkies" and salvaging his new film. Reynolds is perfectly cast as the pert chorine romanced by the actor; O'Connor is priceless as Kelly's childhood pal; and Hagen's Lina Lamont is one of the great "dumb blondes" in movie history. It's hard to pinpoint just one highlight in a film rich in magical moments, but O'Connor's "Make 'Em Laugh" and Kelly's "Broadway Ballet" certainly stand out. ★★★★ DVD: $19.99, DVD 2-disc set: $26.99, VHS: $14.99

Favorite Line: "I make more money than Calvin Coolidge . . . put together!" —*Jean Hagen as Lina Lamont*

The Singing Detective

(1986, 415 min, GB, Jon Amiel) *Michael Gambon, Janet Suzman, Joanne Whalley.* With this richest of oeuvres, writer Dennis Potter has created the most textured and densest of "autobiography" ever to be concocted since Proust chowed down on those tea-soaked madeleines. Produced for the BBC, *The Singing Detective* is a murder mystery in-the-composing as its author, one Philip Marlow (Gambon), assumes the title role as he lies in his hospital bed, racked. His hallucinations interweave personal memories with those of the hero of his novel "The Singing Detective" which weaves the convoluted tale of a sleuth who moonlights with a big band. Arguably the best film/miniseries ever produced for television. ★★★★ DVD: $59.99, VHS: $59.99

The Singing Detective

(2003, 109 min, US, Keith Gordon) *Robert Downey, Jr., Robin Wright Penn, Mel Gibson, Jeremy Northam, Katie Holmes, Adrien Brody, Alfre Woodard.* A well-intentioned adaptation of the classic Dennis Potter-scripted BBC miniseries, this American version just doesn't cut it, despite a strong lead performance and a screenplay by Potter himself. Downey portrays Dan Dark, a pulp mystery novelist spending time in a hospital receiving treatment for a terrible skin disease. He ruminates about his childhood, his relationships and his fiction, which — in his psychological tender state — begin to intertwine in his mind. While the film is watchable enough, it never approaches the level of sophistication or power of the masterful original, and ends up feeling like a neutered Cliffs Notes version — one which is borderline incoherent. Even the musical numbers (so good — and so relevant — in the original) don't work, save for a too-short dance between Downey and Gibson that is kind of touching. Fans of the original will wish they were viewing it instead, and newcomers most likely won't be able to follow this one — which leaves Downey terrific turn the only reason to watch. ★★ DVD Letterbox: $29.99, VHS: $29.99

What a Glorious Feeling

SINGIN' IN THE RAIN

MGM's *TECHNICOLOR* MUSICAL TREASURE!

GENE KELLY
DONALD O'CONNOR
DEBBIE REYNOLDS

JEAN HAGEN · MILLARD MITCHELL · CYD CHARISSE
BETTY COMDEN · ADOLPH GREEN

Singing the Blues in Red

(1987, 110 min, GB/West Germany, Ken Loach) *Gerulf Pannach, Fabienne Babe.* An acerbic, flawed yet stimulating look at East-West relationships as seen through the unblinking eyes of a wary political émigré. Klaus, a celebrated political songwriter/singer from East Berlin, is kicked out of East Germany but is enthusiastically welcomed into the capitalist arms of the West. Klaus soon finds his worst fears of the West confirmed and feels no compunction about biting the corrupt hands that feed him. Loach pulls no punches as he explores the disillusionment of the socialist dream as well as the myths and contradictions inherent in the "Free World." (English and German with English subtitles) ★★½

A Single Girl

(1996, 90 min, France, Benoît Jacquot) *Virginie Ledoyen, Benoît Magimel.* A small, uneventful story that somehow could be applied to anyone's life, *A Single Girl* is a brief glimpse into an hour of one anonymous woman's life. Valerie (Ledoyen) is uncertain whether to meet her boyfriend Remi (Magimel) to tell him that she is pregnant. She gives the matter some thought on the first day of her new job as a room service waitress. At work, she encounters an array of personality types which subtly influences her decision. Shot in real time, the film shows both how brief encounters with strangers can alter their lives, and that any given period in one's own life may be involving to someone else. Never boring but never truly inspired, *A Single Girl* is well acted and often intriguing. (French with English subtitles) ★★½ DVD: $24.99, VHS: $19.99

Single Room Furnished

(1968, 93 min, US, Matteo Ottaviano) *Jayne Mansfield.* Mansfield's last film features her as a tenement resident desperately looking for love after being deserted by the two men she cared for. ★ VHS: $19.99

Single White Female

(1992, 107 min, US, Barbet Schroeder) *Bridget Fonda, Jennifer Jason Leigh, Steven Weber.* Schroeder jumps on the Hollywood Formula bandwagon and almost comes up with a potent psycho-

S

Bridget Fonda (l.) and Matt Dillon in *Singles*

logical suspenser. Leigh answers Fonda's ad to share her New York apartment. A mousy woman with no discernable personality of her own, Leigh becomes infatuated with the hipness of Fonda's breezy demeanor. This "crush," however, soon gives way to jealousy when Fonda reenters the dating game. Though lacking the stylish trappings of a *Fatal Attraction*, or even that film's narrative strengths, it is Leigh's and Fonda's strong performances which slightly elevate this tale above the ordinary. ★★½ DVD: $19.99, VHS: $9.99

Singles

(1992, 100 min, US, Cameron Crowe) *Matt Dillon, Bridget Fonda, Campbell Scott, Kyra Sedgwick, Bill Pullman.* A post-Brat Pack ensemble cast is featured as a group of Seattle MTV spawn trying to cope with their disillusionment about life and, more importantly, dating. Crowe's humorous coverage of their adventures splashing around in the dating pool redeems what might have been yet another whiny, self-centered product of the "new enlightenment." ★★★ DVD: $9.99, VHS: $9.99

The Sinister Urge

(1962, 75 min, US, Edward D. Wood, Jr.) *Jean Fontaine.* More schlock from the man who gave us *Glen or Glenda.* Here, a police officer investigates a series of porn star murders. Look out for the ruthless, evil, over-acting Mrs. Big (Fontaine). Title could be used for a Wood bio on his ability to make awful films. ★ VHS: $19.99

Sink the Bismarck

(1960, 97 min, GB, Lewis Gilbert) *Kenneth More, Dana Wynter.* The British Navy launches an all-out effort to destroy the pride of Hitler's fleet. Excellent special effects help this well-made WWII action-drama. ★★★ DVD: $14.99, VHS: $9.99

Sirens

(1994, 94 min, Australia/GB, John Duigan) *Hugh Grant, Sam Neill, Tara Fitzgerald, Elle Macpherson.* Filled with sun, sea, wine, sex and just the right amount of stimulating conversation, *Sirens* is like the perfect mini-vacation: not too taxing but very refreshing. Grant is an uptight preacher in the 1920s who must try to convince erotic painter Neill to withdraw one of his "shocking" pictures from an

exhibition. To achieve his task, Grant, accompanied by his wife Fitzgerald, visits Neill and his lusty models, who do their best to get the couple to take the plunge into hedonism. Witty and nicely photographed, *Sirens* is eye candy for the Merchant Ivory set. ★★★ DVD: $9.99, VHS: $9.99

Sirocco

(1951, 98 min, US, Curtis Bernhardt) *Humphrey Bogart, Lee J. Cobb, Zero Mostel, Marta Toren.* Bogart stars as a cynical, unscrupulous businessman and black marketeer without political convictions in French-occupied Syria (sound familiar?). Cobb is the French Lt. Colonel in charge of an investigation to discover who is supplying the Arab resistance with arms. Not one of Bogie's best, but he has a good world-weary presence. ★★ DVD: $24.99

Sister Act

(1992, 101 min, US, Emile Ardolino) *Whoopi Goldberg, Maggie Smith, Harvey Keitel, Kathy Najimy, Mary Wickes, Bill Nunn.* Goldberg is a comic delight as a Reno lounge singer who, upon witnessing a gangland murder, is sent to hide out at a San Francisco convent run by the inestimable Smith. Captivating the order one by one, Whoopi does anything but lay low when she takes control of the church's choir and turns them into an overnight sensation. Of course, a lot of the humor stems from the nuns engaging in very un-nun-like behavior. But most of the comedy is sharper than that suggests. And though the premise is strictly formulaic, it's one Hollywood formula which works. Najimy steals every scene she's in as an unbelievably perky sister. (Sequel: *Sister Act 2: Back in the Habit*) ★★★½ DVD Letterbox: $19.99, VHS: $9.99

Sister Act 2: Back in the Habit

(1993, 112 min, US, Bill Duke) *Whoopi Goldberg, Maggie Smith, Kathy Najimy, Michael Jeter.* Goldberg is back as lounge singer Deloris Van Cartier; but this time, instead of having to save a bunch of nuns, she has to turn a rag-tag Catholic School music class into something resembling a choir. The charm of the first film was watching the nuns coming out of their shells; but how many times have we seen sassy, underachieving kids learn the meaning of self-respect because of a dedicated

teacher. Najimy and the impish Jeter do add some holy spirit to this rather unimaginative if harmless sequel. ★★ DVD: $14.99, VHS: $9.99

Sister, My Sister

(1994, 85 min, GB, Nancy Meckler) *Joely Richardson, Jodhi May, Julie Walters.* Inspired by Jean Genet's "The Maids," this provocative and polished drama is set in 1930s France and stars Richardson and May as two repressed sisters who work as servants to an obsessively demanding madam (Walters) who rules her house with a velvet-gloved iron fist. Held virtual prisoners in the claustrophobic house, the two young women soon become incestously involved with each other and their hot passions soon unravel their facade of orderliness. A highly sensual, intense, at times funny but ultimately unsettling tale. ★★★ DVD: $24.99, VHS: $24.99

Sisters

(1973, 93 min, US, Brian De Palma) *Margot Kidder, Jennifer Salt, Charles Durning, Barnard Hughes.* The beginning of director De Palma's sometimes overwhelming display of technical wizardry, this (dare we say it?) Hitchcockian tale follows the crisscrossing path of twin sisters (one good, one evil, both played by Kidder) and a reporter (Salt), who thinks she has witnessed a murder (shades of *Rear Window*). Scathing in its treatment of society as a breeding ground of thrill-seeking voyeurs, this appetizing but deadly serving of sibling rivalry is more than just another "evil twin" hors d'oeuvre. ★★★ DVD: $29.99, VHS: $19.99

Sisters, or the Balance of Happiness

(1979, 96 min, Germany, Margarethe von Trotta) *Jutta Lampe, Gudrun Gabriel, Jessica Frueh, Rainer Delventhal.* Director von Trotta's extraordinarily accomplished *Sisters* explores the symbiotic relationship between two very close but vastly different siblings. A severe, no-nonsense executive secretary, Maria (Lampe) provides financial and emotional support for her distracted younger sister, Anna (Gabriel), a student. When Maria begins to break out of her shell, Anna has a breakdown that prompts Maria to re-examine her life. *Sisters* brilliantly captures the angst of these characters. In demanding roles, the actresses give powerhouse performances. Visually haunting, and extremely moving, *Sisters* confirms Trotta's place as a masterful feminist filmmaker. (German with English subtitles) ★★★★ VHS: $39.99

Sitcom

(1998, 80 min, France, François Ozon) *Évelyne Dandry, François Marthouret, Marina de Van, Stéphane Rideau, Antoine Fischer. Sitcom* is outrageous black comedy that mercilessly skewers the superficial refinement of the French bourgeois. Ozon introduces us to a perfectly happy upper-class family whose members include hard-working dad, the doting and attractive mom and their two wonderful children. But deep within this apparently harmonious household are the seeds of destruction. And those seeds come in the form of a cute white rat Dad brings home one day as the home's new pet. One by one, each family member gets close to the rat and after their encounter, release all of their pent-up anger, sexual desires and secret perversions. Every taboo — homosexuality, incest, S&M, violence — befalls this loving family and it's all filmed in the familiar sitcom format. A no-holds-barred satire. (French with English subtitles) ★★★½ DVD: $29.99, VHS: $14.99

Sitting Ducks

(1978, 90 min, US, Henry Jaglom) *Michael Emil, Zack Norman.* Emil and Norman are the zany and querulous odd couple in this delightfully wacky road comedy. After the whiny and fastidious Emil steals $750,000 from his employer, he and his cohort Norman go on the road to Florida and from there Costa Rica. But along the way, these clashing nebbishes meet, befriend and take along for the ride a strange assortment of characters. Improvised dialogue and Jaglom's sympathetic eye and ear for misfits heighten an entertaining road movie. ★★★ DVD: $24.99, VHS: $19.99

Sitting Pretty

(1948, 84 min, US, Walter Lang) *Clifton Webb, Robert Young, Maureen O'Hara, Richard Haydn.* Webb received an Oscar nomination for his hilariously finicky performance as babysitter/housekeeper extraordinaire Lynn Belvedere. Webb milks every laugh there's to be had in this funny family comedy. The basis for the sitcom "Mr. Belvedere." (Sequel: *Mr. Belvedere Goes to College*) ★★★½ VHS: $14.99

Six Days, Seven Nights

(1998, 100 min, US, Ivan Reitman) *Harrison Ford, Anne Heche, David Schwimmer, Jacqueline Obradors, Temuera Morrison, Allison Janney.* An old-fashioned romantic comedy with good laughs but caught in a "what-do-we-do-next" conundrum, *Six Days, Seven Nights* is a pleasant diversion with not much substance. Heche plays Robin, a successful New York magazine editor on vacation with her fiancé (Schwimmer). Called away on assignment, she hires Quinn (Ford), a craggy pilot, to fly her there. En route, they crash land on a deserted island during a storm. There the two mismatched castaways struggle against the elements and each other before falling in love. Ford and Heche are very agreeable here, making this at least a trip not wasted. ★★½ DVD: $19.99, VHS: $9.99

Six Degrees of Separation

(1993, 112 min, US, Fred Schepisi) *Stockard Channing, Will Smith, Donald Sutherland, Ian McKellen, Bruce Davison, Mary Beth Hurt, Richard Masur, Anthony Michael Hall, Eric Thal, Heather Graham, Anthony Rapp, Catherine Kellner.* Based on John Guare's acclaimed Broadway play, which itself was inspired by a strange but true story, this witty and involving exploration of self-deception is an exhilarating comedy. The charismatic Smith plays a gay con man who ingratiates himself into the households of several rich New Yorkers by claiming to be the son of Sidney Poitier. One of those scammed is art dealer Sutherland and his wife Channing (brilliantly re-creating her award-winning stage role). As they recount their experiences in a series of anecdotal flashbacks, they play detective, ultimately learning the truth about their charming hoaxster. Guare, who wrote his own screenplay adaptation, has fashioned a modern masterwork. ★★★★ DVD: $19.99

Six Ways to Sunday

(1999, 97 min, US, Adam Bernstein) *Isaac Hayes, Deborah Harry, Adrien Brody, Norman Reedus, Elina Löwensohn.* Alternately dull and annoying, this hip/cult flick wanna-be wastes an interesting cast. A pathetic teenage boy is inducted into the local mob after displaying some useful violent tendencies. The last thing the world needs is another small-time crook/gangster movie, and the very last thing the world needs is one that is also badly directed and unnecessarily uncomfortable. Harry is let

down by the ill-conceived role of a manipulative mother with incestuous designs on her own son. In every way a botch. ★ DVD: $9.99

Sixteen Candles

(1984, 93 min, US, John Hughes) *Molly Ringwald, Justin Henry, Anthony Michael Hall, Paul Dooley, Michael Schoeffling, John Cusack, Gedde Watanabe, Jami Gertz.* Charming, often funny and affecting coming-of-age tale with Ringwald as a perplexed teen beseiged by creepy freshmen, spoiled siblings, confused parents and rampant hormones. ★★★ DVD Letterbox: $19.99, VHS: $9.99

The 6th Day

(2000, 124 min, US, Roger Spottiswoode) *Arnold Schwarzenegger, Robert Duvall, Tony Goldwyn, Michael Rooker, Sarah Wynter, Michael Rapaport.* Schwarzenegger is in familiar territory with this futuristic thriller that pits man vs. technology. Much like Arnold himself, the film gets by being competent without covering any new ground. In the not-too-distant future, cars drive themselves and scientists have cloned pets and human organs. Human cloning, however, is illegal, but nevertheless performed. When pilot Schwarzenegger finds that he's been cloned, he sets out to reclaim his former life. Good visuals and a few exciting scenes enhance this otherwise ordinary actioner. ★★½ DVD 2-disc Special Edition: $24.99, VHS: $9.99

The 6th Man

(1997, 108 min, US, Randall Miller) *Marlon Wayans, Kadeem Hardison.* It's *Ghost* meets *Blue Chips* in this slight comedy about a deceased basketball player who returns to Earth to help his younger brother. Hardison and Wayans star as Antoine and Kenny, siblings who grow up dreaming of basketball stardom. Antoine is killed just before they make it, and returns to help Kenny come to terms with his brother's death and aid in a little courtside action. *The 6th Man* is mostly predictable stuff, though fans of the sport may find some amusement in the otherworldly shenanigans. ★★ DVD: $9.99, VHS: $9.99

The Sixth Sense

(1999, 107 min, US, M. Night Shyamalan) *Bruce Willis, Haley Joel Osment, Toni Collette, Olivia Williams, Donnie Wahlberg.* With a child's eerie pronouncement of "I see dead people," writer-director Shyamalan's suspenseful psychological thriller enters into the realm of the supernatural and never falters in delivering credible, unnerving chills. Willis is Dr. Malcolm Crowe, a renowned child psychologist who begins counseling a troubled nine-year-old, Cole (Osment), who initially refuses to open up about his painful secret: He can communicate with the dead. As the two engage in soul-searching conversation, Crowe soon discovers that Cole may be telling the truth. Shyamalan doesn't resort to bootype scares to get the pulse racing and hairs standing on end. His is a thinking man's horror tale, one that finds its scares in the possibilities of the unknown. Osment brings a world-weary sadness to Cole; it's a remarkably nuanced and subtle portrayal, as potent as the unpredictable and surprise ending. ★★★★ DVD Letterbox Basic Edition: $19.99, DVD Vista Series: $29.99, VHS: $9.99

Skin Deep

(1989, 101 min, US, Blake Edwards) *John Ritter, Vincent Gardenia, Julianne Phillips.* Minor Edwards comedy with a few laughs, but mostly a disappointment for the writer-director. Ritter is a writer who can't keep his mind off women. ★½ DVD: $14.99, VHS: $14.99

Skin Game

(1971, 102 min, US, Paul Bogart) *James Garner, Louis Gossett, Jr., Susan Clark, Ed Asner.* Extremely likable comedy set pre-Civil War with Garner as a con man teaming with runaway slave Gossett, the two posing as master and servant. ★★★ VHS: $14.99

Skins

(2002, 87 min, US, Chris Eyre) *Graham Greene, Eric Schweig, Noah Watts, Gary Farmer.* Haunting images of a sedentary culture long marginalized by a neglectful country underscore director Eyre's (*Smoke Signals*) moving adaptation of Adrian C. Louis' novel about two Native-American brothers. In Pine Ridge, South Dakota, alcoholism and despair are the town's cottage industry, inherited from a sorrowful past that most inhabitants have been unable to overcome. Rudy (Schweig), a hulking Indian police officer, is reminded of his people's painful legacy nightly when he locks up the drunks and disorderlies — his older brother Mogie (Greene), an embittered veteran, among them. Rudy's frustration to his own impotence in making a difference leads to an act of unlawfulness — which has dire consequences on both Mogie and himself. Though *Skins* is slowly paced, Eyre's unerring eye towards the realities of Native-American life on the reservation, the intense lead performances and the poignant story of two siblings desperately trying to connect paint an enduring picture of family, a people and one's heritage. ★★★ DVD: $14.99, VHS: $9.99

The Skull

(1965, 83 min, GB, Freddie Francis) *Christopher Lee, Peter Cushing, Jill Bennett.* A collector of the occult who obtains the skull of the Marquis de Sade descends into a nightmare of murder and madness in this Amicus production. Cushing plays the skeptical collector, who realizes too late the evil influence the skull is having on him. Lee plays a fellow collector whose help and warnings Cushing ignores until they can no longer do him any good. The film is properly atmospheric and tense but is hindered somewhat by lackluster special effects involving the skull. ★★★ VHS: $9.99

The Skulls

(2000, 107 min, US, Rob Cohen) *Joshua Jackson, Paul Walker, Hill Harper, Leslie Bibb, Craig T. Nelson, William Petersen, Christopher MacDonald, Steve Harris.* An underprivileged but brilliant ivy-leaguer (Jackson) is given the opportunity to join an

Haley Joel Osment in *The Sixth Sense*

elite, secret campus society — the Skulls — which would afford him untold power and wealth. But he must follow the rules, or else. Ridiculous beyond belief, *The Skulls* unravels immediately following a decent setup that promises a minor but suspenseful little thriller. Instead, *The Skulls* feels like nothing so much as a lackluster "Dawson's Creek" episode; there is no suspense, no drama and zero paranoia, which is the raison d'être of these movies. (Sequel: *The Skulls 2*) (Why?) ★ DVD Collector's Edition: $14.99, VHS Special Edition: $14.99

The Sky Above, The Mud Below

(1962, 92 min, France, Pierre-Dominique Gaisseau) This extraordinary documentary charts the enthralling yet dangerous expedition of a group of anthropologists through the jungles of Dutch New Guinea and into man's savage and violent past. Their endurance was tested daily as they encountered cannibals, headhunters and wild animals, as well as disease and death. Academy Award for Best Documentary Feature. (Narrated in English) ★★★★

The Sky's the Limit

(1943, 89 min, US, Edward H. Griffith) *Fred Astaire, Joan Leslie, Robert Benchley.* Fred is a war hero on leave in New York, falling in love with photographer Leslie. Fred's dancing is the tops. ★★★ VHS: $14.99

Skyline

(1985, 84 min, Spain, Fernando Colomo) *Antonio Resines.* A witty, droll depiction of the adventures of a Spanish photographer who comes to Manhattan seeking fame and fortune. The problems he encounters, including an extremely competitive job market, the fast-track lifestyle, and the incomprehensible language of the natives, drive him into the company of the few Spanish friends he has in the city. The film is a fine comic study of one immigrant's problems in the land of opportunity. (English and Spanish with English subtitles) ★★★ VHS: $39.99

Skyscraper Souls

(1932, 99 min, US, Edgar Selwyn) *Warren William, Maureen O'Sullivan.* Big business, middle class and working class are all struggling to strike it rich, or at least hold on to what they've got. Set in a skyscraper, the ultimate symbol of America in the '30s, the film follows the lives of several "souls" that live and work there. William plays a sly and ruthless businessman, trying to gain total ownership of the building. A young O'Sullivan is the innocent secretary who is tempted by him. Underneath the story, there is a darker, cynical side reflecting the mood of the times. Great art direction exquisitely captures the era of geometrics and chrome. ★★★

Slacker

(1991, 97 min, US, Richard Linklater) First-time director Linklater takes us on a kaleidoscopic journey through the neo-beatnik scene of Austin, Texas. Using an interesting cinematic device, Linklater introduces the viewer to a series of random characters, following each one until some other interesting person pops up. The film literally weaves its way from one to the next without ever looking back. Starting with Linklater himself, we meet a seamless string of vagabonds, pseudo-intellectuals, conspiracy theorists and even a woman hawking what she claims is a Madonna Pap smear. Filled with hilarious moments, the film is a fascinating document of a generation of would-be philosophers with nowhere to go and nothing to do. ★★★ VHS: $14.99

Slam

(1998, 103 min, US, Marc Levin) *Saul Williams, Sonja Sohn, Bonz Malone, Beau Sia, Lawrence Wilson.* A solid indie effort, *Slam* boasts strong acting, believable situations and some excellent writing in this story of an African-American poet/rap artist (Williams) who is busted for marijuana possession and sent to jail. While there, he refuses to choose a gang to join (thereby losing "protection"); instead he chooses to fight violence with his "slam" poetry. What may sound like earnest hokum and preachy sincerity is actually a powerful representation of the strength of art in the face of chaos. The poetry performances are riveting and moving and reflect the characters' difficult choices. A subplot of fighting the possession charge dramatizes the injustice of his plight, and is done with a minimum of histrionics. ★★★½ DVD: $14.99

Slamdance

(1987, 100 min, US, Wayne Wang) *Tom Hulce, Mary Elizabeth Mastrantonio, Virginia Madsen, Harry Dean Stanton.* Hulce plays an artist who is suspected of murdering club-hopper Madsen. Director Wang offers a splash of style to the filmmaking, but can't save the muddled story. A moody attempt at modern film noir. ★★½ DVD Dual: $14.99

Slap Shot

(1977, 122 min, US, George Roy Hill) *Paul Newman, Michael Ontkean, Lindsay Crouse, Jerry Houser, Melinda Dillon.* Racy comedy with Newman as a hockey player on a losing minor league team. When they start playing rough, they find attendance booms, and they win as well. This is a very funny film, though the language is quite strong — those offended by such dialogue should take note. ★★★ DVD 25th Anniversary: $14.99, VHS: $9.99

Slate, Wyn & Me

(1987, 90 min, Australia, Don McLennan) *Sigrid Thornton, Simon Burke.* Borrowing heavily on such American "mixed up, violent but attractive young people on the lam from the law" flicks as *Bonnie and Clyde* and *Badlands*, this mindless Aussie road movie has moments of interest but is generally a below-average import. The story begins suspiciously with two bungling brothers who rob a bank, kill a cop and then kidnap a witness. A meandering drama filled with a rock 'n' roll soundtrack and countless car chases. ★★

Michael Sacks and Valerie Perrine on the planet Tralfamadore in *Slaughterhouse-Five*

Slaughter of the Innocents

(1994, 104 min, US, James Glickenhaus) *Scott Glenn, Jesse Cameron-Glickenhaus.* A gripping FBI procedural about a serial child rapist/killer. Glenn stars as a special agent thrust into the path of a maniac when his precocious, computer prodigy son makes a startling connection linking a recent killing to a 15-year-old series of grisly child slayings. Warning: Weak stomachs need not apply. ★★★ DVD: $9.99, VHS: $14.99

Slaughterhouse-Five

(1972, 104 min, US, George Roy Hill) *Michael Sacks, Valerie Perrine, Ron Liebman, Eugene Roche, Sharon Gans.* Kurt Vonnegut's hero Billy Pilgrim becomes unstuck in time — between his war experiences in Dresden, his life as an optometrist in '70s suburbia and as a member of a select zoo on the planet Tralfamadore. This very faithful adaptation is a visually stunning and emotionally satisfying trek in time which captures Vonnegut's irreverence, novelty and irony. ★★★½ DVD: $14.99

A Slave of Love

(1978, 94 min, USSR, Nikita Mikhalkov) *Elena Solovel, Rodion Nakhapetov.* A dazzling, imaginative tale set in 1919 concerning a White Russian film crew's trials and tribulations in completing a romantic melodrama amid the rising tide of the revolution. The stunning Solovel, as the naïve leading lady, is a revelation. (Russian with English subtitles) ★★★½

Slaves of New York

(1989, 125 min, US, James Ivory) *Bernadette Peters, Chris Sarandon, Mary Beth Hurt, Mercedes Ruehl, Madeleine Potter, Adam Coleman Howard, Michael Schoeffling, Steve Buscemi, Charles McCaughan, Nick Corri.* Disappointing screen version of Tama Janowitz's best-selling novel about the trendy New York art scene, with Peters as a struggling hat designer involved with a self-centered artist. ★★

SLC Punk

(1999, 97 min, US, James Merendino) *Matthew Lillard, Michael A. Goorjian, Annabeth Gish, Jennifer Lien, Christopher McDonald, Devon Sawa, Jason Segel, Summer Phoenix, James Duval.* Set in Salt Lake City in the Reagan era 1985, this hyperventilating tale of outsiders, losers, rebels and nonconformists plays a bit like an American-lite version of *Trainspotting*. Stevo (Lillard) is a blue-haired punk who drops out of his Mormon-infused childhood for a brief dance on the dark side. With his Mohawked best bud Heroin Bob (Goorjian), the two spend their days and nights fucking off, beating up strangers, taking drugs and having sex. The film has a quick, jarring visual style, some pulse-pounding music and an array of beautiful losers, but eventually, you know the scene all too well and their naïve rebel-rousing begins to feel hollow. ★★½ DVD: $19.99

Sleep with Me

(1994, 85 min, US, Rory Kelly) *Eric Stoltz, Meg Tilly, Craig Sheffer, Todd Field, Quentin Tarantino, June Lockhart, Lewis Arquette, Thomas Gibson, Parker Posey, Joey Lauren Adams, Vanessa Angel, Adrienne Shelly.* A loosely scripted tale of two best friends (Stoltz, Sheffer) and the woman (Tilly) they both love. With Tilly sputtering her lines in confused sentences and Stoltz sighing and smoking heavily while philosophizing irrationally, *Sleep with Me* takes on its own unusual rhythms. Add to that an eclectic supporting cast and a beguilingly shy performance by Sheffer and this film almost begins to make up for its complete lack of control. Check out Quentin Tarantino as a party guest attempting to explain why *Top Gun* is homoerotic. ★★½ DVD: $14.99

Sleeper

(1973, 88 min, US, Woody Allen) *Woody Allen, Diane Keaton, John Beck, Howard Cosell.* Allen enters the hospital in 1973 for treatment of an ulcer and, because of "complications," reawakens after cryogenic sleep in the year 2173. Our hapless hero and latter-day Lazarus directs his wit to the future and his body to the orgasmitron. Consistently hilarious, and Allen and Keaton make a perfect comedic team. ★★★½ DVD: $19.99

Favorite Line: "Sex and death. Two things that come once in a lifetime. But at least after death you're not nauseous." —*Woody Allen as Miles Monroe*

Sleepers

(1996, 152 min, US, Barry Levinson) *Brad Pitt, Robert De Niro, Jason Patric, Kevin Bacon, Dustin Hoffman, Joe Perrino, Brad Renfro, Minnie Driver, Vittorio Gassman, Billy Crudup, Ron Eldard.* Despite its talented high-profile cast and excellent evocation of 1960s New York, *Sleepers*, a supposedly "true" story about torture, revenge and the loss of innocence, never overcomes the trappings of a gangster-themed dime novel. Four boyhood friends from Hell's Kitchen are sent to reform school where their life is a living hell. The story picks up years later when two of them kill one of their former attackers (Bacon) and are prosecuted by one of their old buddies (Pitt). The biggest controversy of *Sleepers* isn't its surprising homophobia but the fact that original author Lorenzo Carcaterra claimed this was a biography — it later came to light that nothing in the story could be proved. As fact *Sleepers* is tragic history; as fiction it's an adolescent revenge fantasy. ★★½ DVD Letterbox: $14.99, VHS: $9.99, VHS Letterbox: $9.99

Sleeping Beauty

(1959, 75 min, US, Clyde Geronimi) *Voices of: Mary Costa, Bill Shirley.* Charming Disney animated feature based on the fairy tale classic about the beautiful Princess Aurora who falls into an enchanted slumber when the evil Maleficent casts a spell on her. Prince Phillip, who must contend with dragons and the wicked fairy, comes to her rescue. ★★★ DVD 2-disc set: $29.99, VHS: $24.99

Sleeping Dogs

(1977, 107 min, New Zealand, Roger Donaldson) *Sam Neill, Warren Oates.* This political chase thriller is a suspenseful tale of paranoia, repression of freedom and one man's resistance. Neill stars as Smith, a man who flees domestic trouble and finds solace on a quiet coastal island. His newfound peace is shattered when the right-wing government declares martial law and begins a crackdown on dissidents. Smith is jailed on trumped-up charges, escapes and begins a new life as a reluctant insurgent. ★★★ VHS: $19.99

Sleeping with the Enemy

(1991, 99 min, US, Joseph Ruben) *Julia Roberts, Patrick Bergin, Kevin Anderson.* Roberts brings a lot of energy to this ordinary thriller. She plays a mistreated wife, married to neurotic Bergin. Instead of divorce, she stages her own death, and moves to another town under a new identity. But her husband finds out the truth, and goes looking for her, stalking his spouse and planning his revenge. Short on thrills and credibility. ★★ DVD: $14.99, VHS: $9.99

Sleepless in Seattle

(1993, 100 min, US, Nora Ephron) *Tom Hanks, Meg Ryan, Bill Pullman, Ross Malinger, Rosie O'Donnell, Rob Reiner, Gaby Hoffmann.* Basking in the romantic tradition of our cinematic past, Ephron has created her quintessential comedy — warts and all — with just a little help from *An Affair to Remember*. Hanks plays a Seattle widower who's still not over his wife's death. His young son (the likable Malinger) calls a national radio talk show, forcing his dad to talk on the air. Ryan, meanwhile, lives in Baltimore and though engaged, she realizes there's something missing in her life. When she hears Hanks, she thinks she's found it. The next 90 minutes is an appealing comedy in which these misplaced spirits try to connect. Thanks to Hanks' and Ryan's enchanting performances, the film seems breezier and more substantial than it really is. ★★★ DVD 10th Anniversary: $19.99, VHS: $9.99

Sleepwalk

(1987, 90 min, US, Sara Driver) A lyrical and witty feature debut for director Driver, *Sleepwalk* has the logic and landscape of a dream, an open-ended fairy tale set in the margins of an imaginary New York. The theft of an ancient and sacred manuscript, one which a young woman is translating, leads to strange happenings — her fingers begin to bleed, the woman's roommate becomes bald, and a woman is killed just as the mysteries of the book are about to be solved. Driver has a sharp eye for color and light and imbues the film with a lively, humorous style. ★★★

Sleepy Hollow

(1999, 105 min, US, Tim Burton) *Johnny Depp, Christina Ricci, Miranda Richardson, Michael Gambon, Casper Van Dien, Jeffrey Jones, Richard Griffiths, Christopher Walken, Christopher Lee, Ian McDiarmid, Michael Gough, Lisa Marie, Steven*

Waddington, Claire Skinner. Director Burton rides once more into the fantastic with this gorgeous-looking, atmospheric and often spine-tingling adaptation of Washington Irving's perennial "Legend of Sleepy Hollow." Depp is Ichabod Crane, here a young police inspector who comes to the small, quiet village of Sleepy Hollow to investigate several murders by beheading — and comes face to face with the infamous Headless Horseman. Burton and company have meticulously re-created 1790s New England, though their inspiration has come in the many terrific effects — from the beheadings to the nightmarish Horseman who literally gallops from a tree. If this tale of yore has more of a 1990s accent to it than it should, it's a minor intrusion worth bearing; for Burton's end result is one of eerie beauty and irresistible chills. ★★★ DVD: $14.99, VHS: $9.99

The Slender Thread

(1966, 98 min, US, Sydney Pollack) *Sidney Poitier, Anne Bancroft, Telly Savalas. Steven Hill.* Sincere performances elevate this compelling drama. Poitier plays a college student who is a volunteer at a Seattle crisis center. What looks to be a slow night becomes a fight for survival when he gets a call from Bancroft — who's just taken an overdose of pills. As Poitier desperately tries to get Bancroft to reveal her location, the events leading to her suicide attempt are told in flashback. These scenes are rather routine, but the sequences involving Poitier's verbal rescue attempt are enthralling. Pollack's directorial debut. ★★½ VHS: $14.99

Sleuth

(1972, 138 min, GB, Joseph L. Mankiewicz) *Laurence Olivier, Michael Caine.* Olivier is an eccentric upper-class English cuckold who plans a confrontation with Caine, the man who has not only stolen his wife's affections, but has the effrontery to be the wrong class. Both Olivier and Caine give knockout performances in this royal battle of wit and wills. Screenplay by Anthony Shaffer from his play. Eclectic direction from Mankiewicz makes maximum use of a limited setting. ★★★½ DVD: $14.99

Johnny Depp in *Sleepy Hollow*

Sliding Doors

Sliding Doors

(1998, 99 min, GB, Peter Howitt) *Gwyneth Paltrow, John Hannah, John Lynch, Jeanne Tripplehorn.* Paltrow gives a winsome performance in this engaging romantic fantasy that explores the path less traveled. She plays Helen, a London marketing executive who's just been sacked. Heading dejectedly home, she rushes for the subway only to have the train doors close in her face. But just at that moment, the film diverges onto a parallel path, the one where she *does* catch the train and director Howitt deftly weaves back and forth between these two separately unfolding universes. *Sliding Doors* only occasionally strays too far afield into the land of cutesy, but for the most part is an edifying look at the alternate destinies that are governed by our decisions. ★★★½ DVD: $29.99, VHS: $14.99

A Slightly Pregnant Man

(1973, 92 min, France, Jacques Demy) *Marcello Mastroianni, Catherine Deneuve.* A daffy, gender-bending comedy that features Mastroianni and Deneuve as a loving but childless couple whose lives are upturned when Marcello discovers that he is in the family way. Their exploitation of the notorious birth-to-be and the changing ways Catherine treats the pregnant and irritable Marcello are the ingredients for this enjoyable farce. ★★½

Sling Blade

(1996, 135 min, US, Billy Bob Thornton) *Billy Bob Thornton, Natalie Canerday, Lucas Black, Dwight Yoakam, John Ritter, J.T. Walsh.* Writer-director Thornton crafts an unforgettable character in his portrayal of Carl Childers, a slightly retarded 37-year-old man newly released from a mental institution. He reenters his small Arkansas home town with a repairman's job and a cot in a tool room and a new friend, young Frank Wheatley (played with amazing presence by Black). The details of Carl's history are revealed as he gets closer to Frank and his mom, Linda (Canerday), suggesting parallels and similarities, especially regarding Doyle (Yoakam), Linda's boyfriend and Frank's nemesis. In this unfolding drama of decent, unassuming people defending themselves in a hostile world, Carl becomes increasingly sane by comparison. A superb, Oscar-winning screenplay, an effective minimalist musical score and a sure directorial hand describe this involving, heartfelt tale. ★★★★ VHS: $9.99

The Slingshot

(1994, 102 min, Sweden, Ake Sandgren) *Jesper Salen, Stellan Skarsgård.* How many times must one be punched, hit, kicked and verbally abused before your resiliency of optimism is gone? You'll have to watch this abusive and not-so-happy coming-of-age film to find out. If you've seen *A Christmas Story*, *Leolo* and *My Life as a Dog*, you've caught all of the nuances of this film. Set in Sweden in the 1930s, the story centers on Roland, a precocious youngster who will do anything to get enough money for a bicycle, even sell slingshots made of contraband condoms. Great artistic design and good acting can't hide a lackluster film that can't deliver the final punch. (Swedish in English subtitles) ★★

The Slipper and the Rose

(1976, 143 min, GB, Bryan Forbes) *Richard Chamberlain, Gemma Craven, Annette Crosbie, Edith Evans, Christopher Gable, Michael Hordern, Margaret Lockwood, Kenneth More.* A sumptuous musical version of the Cinderella story. Chamberlain makes a dashing Prince, and Craven is a lovely Cinderella. Music by Richard and Robert Sherman (*Mary Poppins*). ★★★ DVD: $24.99, VHS: $19.99

Sliver

(1993, 106 min, US, Phillip Noyce) *Sharon Stone, William Baldwin, Tom Berenger, Colleen Camp, Martin Landau, CCH Pounder.* No, the title doesn't refer to the amount of logic within the plot, but to a Manhattan luxury high-rise apartment building plagued by a series of unexplained deaths. Stone plays a recently divorced book editor who moves into the "horror high-rise" where romance and terror await in the form of Baldwin and Berenger. As penned by Joe Eszterhas and directed by Noyce, what might have been a trenchant study of voyeurism and social responsibility is reduced to a slick, trashy and befuddled whodunit with a dime-store resolution. ★★½ VHS: $14.99

Slow Burn

(2000, 97 min, US, Christian Ford) *Minnie Driver, James Spader, Josh Brolin, Stuart Wilson.* A well-wrought "drama of errors" about a young woman (Driver) fighting for survival in the Mexican desert against two escaped convicts (Spader and Brolin) who accidentally find the fortune in diamonds she's spent her life searching for. Well-tuned performances and a mature script make this familiar though suspenseful tale a worthwhile character study as well as an agreeable actioner. ★★½ DVD: $14.99, VHS: $14.99

Slumber Party Massacre

(1982, 78 min, US, Amy Jones) *Brinke Stevens, Michelle Michaels.* Novelist Rita Mae Brown ("Rubyfruit Jungle") penned this horrific lampoon of mad-slasher films. If its tongue weren't firmly planted in cheek, it would probably get lopped off. (Followed by 2 sequels) ★★ DVD: $9.99, VHS: $9.99

Slums of Beverly Hills

(1998, 91 min, US, Tamara Jenkins) *Natasha Lyonne, Alan Arkin, Marisa Tomei, David Krumholtz, Kevin Corrigan, Jessica Walter, Carl Reiner, Rita Moreno.* Writer-director Jenkins' debut feature is a refreshing, funny and offbeat coming-of-age tale told through the eyes of a budding 15-year-old. Both amusing and tender, the film follows Vivian (the very appealing Lyonne), who lives with her unemployed, single dad (Arkin) and two broth-ers. Though Dad is on hard financial times, he's always made sure that the kids have a Beverly Hills address, thereby assuring they can attend school in the prestigious B.H. district. Things pick up when cousin Rita (a delightful Tomei) arrives from rehab. Jenkins peppers her film with wry and knowing observations on growing up and familial ties, and includes one helluva self-stimulation scene. It's often unexpectedly poignant. ★★★ DVD: $9.99, VHS: $102.99

Small Change

(1976, 104 min, France, François Truffaut) Truffaut's buoyant visual soufflé is a winning observation of youthful resiliency. Set in a tiny French town, *Small Change* follows a group of school children through their daily endeavors. (French with English subtitles) ★★★½ DVD: $19.99, VHS: $19.99

Small Faces

(1996, 113 min, Scotland, Gillies MacKinnon) *Iain Robertson, Joseph McFadden, J.S. Duffy, Laura Fraser, Kevin McKidd.* The incongruous glint of gunmetal in a heather-dappled, wooded lane belies the apparent tranquility of pastoral Glasgow, and serves as an emblem of the underlying tensions of gang affiliations that allow no neutrality and broker no dissent. Set in 1968, the story is told through the eyes of 13-year-old Lex (Robertson), the youngest of three brothers, who is sucked into a vortex of conflicting allegiances. Events unfold quickly and inexoribly, leaving the adults to watch in stunned incomprehension and bitter helplessness, equally shocked by the acts of brutality and by the young ones' ease of adaptability to this new world. Director MacKinnon adeptly utilizes a strong cast to explore one family's response to crisis and loss. ★★★½

Small Soldiers

(1998, 105 min, US, Joe Dante) *Kirsten Dunst, Phil Hartman, Gregory Smith, Jay Mohr, Denis Leary, Tommy Lee Jones, Frank Langella, Ernest Borgnine, Jim Brown, Sarah Michelle Gellar, Christina Ricci.* Both live-action and animated, *Small Soldiers* tells the cautionary tale of what happens when a new state-of-the-art toy line, manufactured with a microprocessor chip used in defense department hardware, comes to life. The toys — two warring factions — are programmed to fight each other, but their chips allow for advanced functions. This is the high-concept gimmick of *Small Soldiers*, much like the "toys come to life" hook of Disney's *Toy Story*. But this is more violent (in a comic book sort of way). It may not be for younger ones. Director Dante has a flair for bizarre sight gags, and his film has the feel of an old Warner Brothers' Tazmanian Devil cartoon, but the human element is inconsistent. ★★½ DVD Letterbox Signature Selection: $14.99, DVD DTS sound: $14.99

Small Time Crooks

(2000, 95 min, US, Woody Allen) *Woody Allen, Tracey Ullman, Elaine May, Hugh Grant, Elaine Stritch, Jon Lovitz, Michael Rapaport, George Grizzard, Tony Darrow.* Recalling both *Take the Money and Run* and *Broadway Danny Rose* in a story of bumbling crooks, Allen's appealing comedy may tell us that crime does not pay and there's no changing a leopard's spots, but, ultimately, nothing beats a good cookie recipe. A funny, feather-light caper comedy, *Small Time Crooks* follows the misadventures of Ray (Allen) and his misfit assortment of cohorts as they plan a bank heist. Things go wrong, of course, but their cover — a cookie shop run by Ray's wife Frenchy (Ullman) — becomes an overnight success. Suddenly it's the Kramdens hit Park Avenue. Woody has given himself and Ullman endearing parts, and they have a nice rapport and some wonderful one-liners. May is a standout as Frenchy's wafty cousin who's always saying the wrong thing at the right time. ★★★ DVD: $14.99

Small Wonders

(1996, 80 min, US, Allan Miller) One of the most disarming films about children since Truffaut's *Small Change*, Miller's modest but jubilant sleeper examines a divorced mother of two who teaches violin to Harlem elementary school kids. This straight-ahead, no frills, shot-on-video documentary may sound like a sappy, dull "Afterschool Special," but *Small Wonders* is anything but. The film follows Roberta Guaspari-Tzavaras and her students from first meeting to their sold-out concert at Carnegie Hall. A superb argument for the continued support of music and art in our public school systems. (Meryl Streep stars in the 1999 film *Music of the Heart* based on the same story) ★★★½ VHS: $9.99

The Smallest Show on Earth

(1957, 81 min, GB, Basil Dearden) *Peter Sellers, Margaret Rutherford, Bill Travers, Virginia McKenna.* This highly amusing little British comedy tells the tale of a young couple who inherit a run-down movie theatre. Travers and McKenna are charming as the pair who are thrust against their will into the cinema business. Sellers, as the drunken, near-sighted projectionist, and Rutherford, as the slow-moving octogenarian cashier, play two of the ancient employees who come along with the theatre — both are magnificent as always. Filled with joie de vivre, the film imparts an alluring sense of nostalgia for anyone who considers themselves a dyed-in-the-wool cinema buff. ★★★ DVD Letterbox: $19.99, VHS: $9.99

Smash Palace

(1981, 100 min, New Zealand, Roger Donaldson) *Bruno Lawrence, Anna Jemison.* This highly acclaimed work by Donaldson is a compelling drama set in the cities and countryside of New Zealand. It is a powerful tale of a marriage jeopardized by a man's obsession with auto racing and a woman's overriding need for love and affection. ★★★½

Smash-Up

(1947, 103 min, US, Stuart Heisler) *Susan Hayward, Lee Bowman, Eddie Albert.* Hayward shines in an Oscar-nominated role as a nightclub singer who turns to the bottle after giving up her career for marriage. Dramatically it's familiar territory but Hayward's performance more than compensates. (aka: *Smash-Up, the Story of a Woman*) ★★½

Smile

(1975, 113 min, US, Michael Ritchie) *Bruce Dern, Barbara Feldon, Melanie Griffith, Annette O'Toole.* Ritchie's best film is this hilariously biting satire of Americana. Dern is a small-town California car salesman who, with his perky and maniacally organized wife (Feldon), helps organize the Young Miss Beauty contest. The "behind the scenes" peek at the pretty contestants, their amazingly talentless talent and the lascivious judges are only a few of the highlights of this perceptive and witty film. ★★★½ VHS: $14.99

A Smile Like Yours

(1997, 99 min, US, Keith Samples) *Greg Kinnear, Lauren Holly, Joan Cusack, Jay Thomas, Jill Hennessy, Christopher McDonald.* Possessing limited charms, *A Smile Like Yours* will amuse only those viewers who find humor in frequent visits to fertility clinics. Since cowriters Kevin Meyer and director Samples seem to be the only ones, everyone else can admire the low-watt dynamics of Danny (Kinnear) and Jennifer (Holly) as they try to make a baby. The poorly conceived film follows Danny's unfunny impotence episodes with a lame story line about each partner suspecting the other of having an extramarital affair. The leads offer little in the way of sparks. ★★ DVD Letterbox: $14.99, VHS: $14.99

Smiles of a Summer Night

(1955, 108 min, Sweden, Ingmar Bergman) *Eva Dahlbeck, Harriet Andersson, Jarl Krulle.* An exquisite carnal comedy about eight people who become four couples in turn-of-the-century Sweden. Bergman's witty treatise on changing partners under the midnight sun is filled with delightfully ironic humor. The basis for the Tony Award-winning musical "A Little Night Music," which was poorly adapted to film. (Swedish with English subtitles) ★★★★ DVD Criterion Collection: $29.99, VHS: $29.99

Smilla's Sense of Snow

(1997, 121 min, Denmark/Germany/Sweden, Bille August) *Julia Ormand, Gabrial Byrne, Richard Harris, Vanessea Redgrave, Robert Loggia, Jim Broadbent.* This very disappointing adaptation of Peter Høeg's best-selling thriller stars Ormond as the titular character, a half Dane, half Greenlander scientist whose obsession with the "accidental" death of a young boy leads her deeper into a web of murder and deception. Instead of a fascinating journey into the convoluted workings of Smilla's personality all we get is the icy exterior, a shortcoming that only makes her more perplexing. August shows that he's more at home directing smaller, more personal movies although his locations and sense of mis-en-scène provide the film's best evocation of the book. ★★ DVD: $9.99, VHS: $9.99

Smithereens

(1982, 93 min, US, Susan Seidelman) *Susan Berman.* Wren is a legend in her own mind — a self-assured, narcissistic New Wave hanger-on with a yen for the big time. This gritty Greenwich Village odyssey is a distinctly modern version of the American Dream. ★★★ VHS: $29.99

Smoke

(1995, 113 min, US, Paul Auster & Wayne Wang) *Harvey Keitel, William Hurt, Stockard Channing, Forest Whitaker, Harold Perrineau, Jr., Giancarlo Esposito, Ashley Judd.* The divergent rhythms of New York come alive in the guise of this immensely satisfying slice-of-life comedy-drama centered around the habitués of a tobacco shop in the heart of Brooklyn. Keitel is Joe, who becomes involved in the lives of some of his customers. As one of them, Hurt exhibits the right amount of ennui and melancholy as a widowed WASPy author who befriends a black youth (nicely played by Perrineau) whose fabrications mask deep familial hurts. These stories effortlessly coalesce into a deeply affecting tale defined by rich characterizations and buoyant comedy — the least of which explains Keitel's passion for photography. Followed by an anti-sequel, *Blue in the Face*. ★★★★ DVD: $19.99, VHS: $9.99

Smoke Signals

(1998, 89 min, US, Chris Eyre) *Adam Beach, Evan Adams, Gary Farmer, Tantoo Cardinal, Irene Bedard.* The first film starring, written, directed and produced solely by Native Americans, *Smoke Signals* is a truly original and thoroughly charming independent whose themes and truths happen to transcend cultures. At once a coming-of-age tale, road movie and social comedy, the story concerns Victor (Beach), a troubled though good-hearted teen who has been affected by the absence of his father. When the family receives news of the father's death, Victor, accompanied by his nerdy, storytelling childhood friend Thomas (a remarkable Adams), travels from his Idaho reservation to Phoenix to collect his father's ashes. Though Sherman Alexie's screenplay (based on his collection of short stories "The Lone Ranger and Tonto Fistfight in Heaven") examines life that is particular to American Indians, it's his observations on the human psyche which propel the story. None better is Thomas' stories of history and folklore — Alexie's talent for language is commanding, and his bent for comedy is persuasive. An enchanting film experience. ★★★★ DVD: $19.99, VHS: $9.99

Smokey and the Bandit

(1977, 96 min, US, Hal Needham) *Burt Reynolds, Sally Field, Jerry Reed, Mike Henry, Paul Williams, Pat McCormick.* Burt mugs up a storm in this mindlessly enjoyable action-comedy that's actually one long car chase. Burt's wanted by lawman Gleason; runaway bride Field's along for the ride. (Followed by 2 sequels) ★★½ DVD: $14.99, VHS: $9.99

Smooth Talk

(1985, 91 min, US, Joyce Chopra) *Laura Dern, Treat Williams.* Based on Joyce Carol Oates' short story "Where Are You Going, Where Have You Been," this compelling, gutsy coming-of-age drama explores a 15-year-old California girl's sexual awakening. Dern is excellent as the budding teen, and Williams exudes charm and malevolence as her seducer. ★★★

Snake and Crane Arts of Shaolin

(1978, 95 min, Hong Kong, Chen Chi Hwa) *Jackie Chan.* After nearly being killed a dozen times while trying to learn an ancient fighting technique developed by a group of Shaolin masters, student Hsu Yin Fung (Chan) is unjustly accused of killing the masters and destroying all records of their dead-

Smoke Signals

ly art. When his girlfriend is murdered, he seeks the help of another master who finally teaches him the form which he in turn uses in his search for the true killer. Brisk kung fu chaos, enlivened by Chan's trademark stunt-laden style. ★★½ DVD Letterbox Dubbed: $19.99, VHS: $19.99

Snake Eyes

(1998, 100 min, US, Brian De Palma) *Nicolas Cage, Gary Sinise, Carla Gugino, John Heard, Stan Shaw, Kevin Dunn, Luis Guzman.* An animated Cage stars as Ricky Santoro, an Atlantic City cop who's about to settle in and enjoy the big fight. But when a government official is murdered ringside, the journey Santoro and the audience are taken on in De Palma's stylish, loopy thriller is anything but tranquil. With a constantly moving camera and tennis-match editing, *Snake Eyes* follows Santoro has he tries to solve a murder committed before 14,000 people. Relatively early on, the bad guy is revealed, so the story concentrates on Santoro's police investigation. De Palma certainly keeps things moving, but no matter how fast the pace, it can't hide a cheesy story. At least it looks good. ★★½ DVD: $14.99, VHS: $9.99

Snake in the Eagle's Shadow

(1978, 94 min, Hong Kong, Yuen Woo-Ping) *Jackie Chan, Siu Tien Yeun, Yuen Hsiao Tieng, Huang Cheng Li.* This early Chan vehicle bears all the clichés and ridiculous dialogue ("Your snake fist style is no match for my eagle's claw style!") of the worst of the '70s chopsocky groaners, but *Shadow* is so energetic and, in the person of Jackie, charismatic, that it transcends its inherent flaws. Chan plays a much put-upon "punching bag" at a well-regarded martial arts school whose kindness toward an old man results in the stranger's teaching Chan the dying art of the Snake Fist. Meanwhile, an evil practitioner of the Eagle's Claw is obsessed with killing off all Snake Fist experts. Not remotely as polished as other Woo-Ping-choreographed films, *Shadow* is still a very enjoyable, fast-paced outing, with some lowbrow slapstick. (aka: *The Eagle's Shadow*) ★★★ DVD Letterbox: $24.99, VHS Dubbed: $14.99

The Snake Pit

(1948, 108 min, US, Anatole Litvak) *Olivia de Havilland, Mark Stevens, Leo Genn, Celeste Holm.* An intelligent, fascinating drama about a young woman who experiences a nervous breakdown and is committed to a mental institution. It's a disturbing look into the life inside of a mental institution and even more chilling considering when the film was made. The film features some fantastic camerawork and a brilliant performance from de Havilland. ★★★★ DVD: $14.99, VHS: $19.99

The Snapper

(1993, 95 min, Ireland, Stephen Frears) *Colm Meaney, Ruth McCabe, Tina Kellegher.* A wonderful character study full of laughs and tears. Kellegher is the strong-willed daughter of an Irish working-class family who becomes pregnant and refuses to reveal who is the father of the baby. Meaney is outstanding as her good-hearted father and McCabe stands out as the loving mother who keeps her family together through it all. Marvelous acting and a humorous and insightful screenplay make this film a rare treat. Director Frears is in a playfully droll mood. (Sequel: *The Van*) ★★★★ DVD Letterbox: $19.99, VHS: $9.99

Snatch

(2000, 103 min, GB, Guy Ritchie) *Brad Pitt, Jason Statham, Vinnie Jones, Dennis Farina, Benicio del Toro, Rade Sherbedgia, Alan Ford, Jason Flemyng, Stephen Graham, Ewen Bremner, Mike Reid.* With his second feature, director Ritchie is back in the same territory as his high-energy debut *Lock, Stock and Two Smoking Barrels*: colorful gangsters, fast-paced action, jet-black humor, lightning-quick editing and lots of gun play. And while one could complain that *Snatch* is a carbon copy of Ritchie's first film, that doesn't take away from the sheer fun of this knock-'em-dead heist tale. The story follows what happens when Franky Four Fingers (Del Toro) stops off in London on his way to New York to deliver a stolen 84-carat diamond. Soon, an Irish boxer (Pitt) who you can't understand, a boxing promoter (Statham) just trying to stay alive, and a crazed Russian gangster (Sherbedgia) all enter the picture to further complicate and amuse. Ritchie knows how to sustain action at a fast clip, and the film moves at remarkable speed. ★★★ DVD Dual 2-disc Special Edition: $27.99, DVD Letterbox Superbit Edition: $26.99, DVD: $19.99, VHS: $14.99

Sneakers

(1992, 105 min, US, Phil Alden Robinson) *Robert Redford, Sidney Poitier, Dan Aykroyd, David Strathairn, Ben Kingsley, Mary McDonnell, River Phoenix, James Earl Jones.* A clever, humorous and complex computer-age thriller, the story centers on a group of professional thieves and computer hackers who are coerced by the U.S. government to steal a mysterious black box. Once it is in their possession, they learn the box is really the ultimate code breaker, able to decipher any computer program in the world. And now there are some very dangerous people out to retrieve it at any cost. While not in the same class as *Topkapi* or *The Sting*, which it at times recalls, *Sneakers* is nevertheless exuberant and fun. ★★★ DVD Letterbox Collector's Edition: $14.99, VHS: $14.99

Snow Country

(1957, 134 min, Japan, Shiro Toyoda) *Ryo Ikebe, Keiko Kishi.* Based on the novel by Yasunari Kawabata, this passionate love story tells of the budding relationship between two people and the nagging cultural differences that pull them apart. Shimamura, an artist in Tokyo, escapes to the tranquil rural Honshu region in the northwestern part of the country for relaxation. There he meets and falls in love with Kumako, a charming young woman from the snow-covered village. The disparities in their upbringing as well as the antagonism of the townsfolk kind of make this a Japanese "Romeo and Juliet." (Japanese with English subtitles) ★★★ VHS: $59.99

Snow Falling on Cedars

(1999, 128 min, US, Scott Hicks) *Ethan Hawke, James Cromwell, Richard Jenkins, Youki Kudoh, Max von Sydow, Sam Shepard, Rick Yune.* Using flashbacks and forwards in much the same way as his award-winning *Shine*, director Hicks' follow-up to that film isn't quite as successful in imparting bits and pieces to create a whole. However, a compelling story and beautiful cinematography contribute to make this a moving look at racial distrust, small-town politics and the bond to overcome them both. A reporter (Hawke) investigates the story of a Japanese-American man accused of killing an American fisherman. The fact that the man is the brother of the girl he loved as a youth complicates matters as much as the small Pacific Northwest town's resentment towards the defendant. Based on David Guterson's best-selling novel, *Snow Falling on Cedars* only lightly tackles the incendiary theme of the treatment of Asian-American citizens during WWII, using it instead as a backdrop to romance and courtroom drama. ★★★ DVD: $14.99, VHS: $14.99

Snow White and the Seven Dwarfs

(1937, 83 min, US, Ben Sharpsteen) Arguably Disney's finest achievement (and his first feature-length animated film), *Snow White* is the perfect blend of animation, story and character utilizing charming songs and good humor. A huge smash at the box office in 1937, the film, of course, follows the adventures of Snow White, who does battle with an evil, jealous witch and who finds her prince, all the while living in the forest with seven adorable little men. Tamer than any cartoon made today, the film still captivates — it is one of the authentic masterpieces of American cinema. ★★★★

So Fine

(1981, 91 min, US, Andrew Bergman) *Ryan O'Neal, Jack Warden, Mariangela Melato.* O'Neal plays a mild-mannered professor who accidentally creates a fashion sensation for his father, a clothing manufacturer: see-through pants. Warden's spirited portrayal of O'Neal's father is the bright spot of this see-through comedy. ★★ VHS: $19.99

So I Married an Axe Murderer

(1993, 93 min, US, Thomas Schlamme) *Michael Myers, Nancy Travis, Anthony LaPaglia, Amanda Plummer, Brenda Fricker, Phil Hartman.* Myers should be axed from the comedy register for this insultingly inept follow-up to *Wayne's World*. Myers headlines as a so-bad-he's-good coffeehouse poet whose fear of marriage ends when he weds the quirky but beautiful owner (Travis) of the local butcher shop despite his mounting fears that she may be (drum roll, please) an axe murderer. ★½ DVD: $19.99, VHS: $9.99

So Proudly We Hail

(1943, 126 min, US, Mark Sandrich) *Claudette Colbert, Paulette Goddard, Veronica Lake, George Reeves, Sonny Tufts.* One of the few WWII films to be seen through the eyes of women, this gallant, terse drama follows the sometimes heartbreaking role of nurses in combat. The sublime Colbert stars as an Army head nurse who, at the film's start, is catatonic and on her way home. The story then traces her path on the many battlefields of WWII, where romance, tragedy and camaraderie shape her life. Excellent in support are Goddard as Colbert's right-hand gal and Tufts as a soldier who "never gets killed." Though high in 1940s and wartime sentiment, this is a no-nonsense, pleasurable melodrama. ★★★½

The Snapper

Ethan Hawke in *Snow Falling on Cedars*

Soapdish

(1991, 95 min, US, Michael Hoffman) *Sally Field, Kevin Kline, Whoopi Goldberg, Robert Downey, Jr., Cathy Moriarty, Elisabeth Shue, Garry Marshall, Kathy Najimy.* A terrific comic cast makes the most of this funny spoof of soap operas. Field is the reigning Queen of the Soaps. Goldberg is her writer and longtime friend. Kline is Field's ex-beau, who returns to the airwaves after a 20-year absence to be reunited with Sally — both on-screen and off. Downey is the inefficient producer, more worried about bedding actress Moriarty than his show's quality. And Shue rounds out the cast as Field's niece who, unbeknownst to her aunt, has signed on with the show. The film's tempo is played as grand farce, and though not all of the humor works, it's a joyously loony romp. ★★★ DVD Letterbox: $19.99, VHS: $14.99

Sofie

(1993, 145 min, Sweden, Liv Ullmann) *Karen-Lise Mynster, Erland Josephson.* Ullmann debuts behind the camera with this affecting if somewhat overlong saga about the life of an unassuming Jewish woman in turn-of-the-century Sweden. Early on, the film hinges on her choice between an affair with a Christian painter or an arranged marriage to a dour Jewish man from the countryside. As she spends much of her time with her three spinster aunts, the film examines her struggle between virtue and spiritual freedom. Benefitting from a host of fine performances, the film often captures the whimsical nature of Bergman's *Fanny and Alexander*, but at 145 minutes, the film too often overstays its welcome. (Swedish with English subtitles) ★★½ DVD: $19.99, VHS: $14.99

The Soft Skin

(1964, 118 min, France, François Truffaut) *Jean Desailly, Françoise Dorleac.* A mature, underrated work by Truffaut that explores the ill-fated fling with infidelity by a successful publisher and a pretty airline stewardess. Truffaut focuses on their day-to-day life in this precisely-told examination of a catastrophe-prone situation. (French with English subtitles) ★★★ DVD: $19.99, VHS: $14.99

Solaris

(1972, 165 min, USSR, Andrei Tarkovsky) *Donatas Banionis, Natalya Bondarchuk.* Hailed by its admirers as a visionary, philosophical work and by others (especially sci-fi fans) as difficult, if not turgid, Tarkovsky's best-known film adapts the popular science-fiction theme of men lost in space to his own idiosyncratic style of filmmaking. Eschewing high-tech gimmickry and special effects, the story centers on a psychologist who is sent to investigate a series of unexplained deaths on a Russian space station. There he finds that the killers are not aliens but rather phantoms materialized from the cosmonauts' guilty past. Admittedly heavy going, it's also an imaginative, serious work about man's limits as well as his barely concealed fears and self-destructive nature. (Russian with English subtitles) (Remade in 2002) ★★★½ DVD Letterbox Criterion Collection: $39.99

Solaris

(2002, 99 min, US, Steven Soderbergh) *George Clooney, Natascha McElhone, Jeremy Davies, Viola Davis, Ulrich Tukur.* Director Soderbergh remakes Andrei Tarkovsky's 1972 Russian art-house masterpiece (based on Stanislaw Lem's novel) about a doctor whose mission to rescue inhabitants of a space station brings about a metaphysical self-examination when his deceased wife suddenly appears. With this eerie and meditative exploration, Soderbergh decides to take the Kubrick route to sci-fi, more of a moody unsettling love story about a man who has lost, yet aches to find again. Clooney is solid as the sullen psychiatrist, who knows that this isn't his wife but is helpless to act otherwise. McElhone is the woman who "returns from the dead," and her chemistry with Clooney is palpable. Not as solemn but equally as retrospective as the original, *Solaris* is an intelligent, observant film on human relations and regrets, told against a traditional backdrop of science fiction that is anything but traditional. ★★★½ DVD Letterbox: $29.99

Soldat Duroc

(1975, 85 min, France, Michel Gerard) *Pierre Tornade.* In September 1944, a few days after the liberation of Paris, a young French soldier secretly crosses the German lines in the middle of the night to rejoin his fiancée in Senlis, a small town still occupied by the German Army. His plans become unraveled, however, when he is captured by two soldiers, one American and the other French, who were sent by General Patton to help liberate the Nazi-held village. An absorbing and nicely told war drama. (French with English subtitles) ★★★

Soldier

(1998, 99 min, US, Paul Anderson) *Kurt Russell, Jason Scott Lee, Connie Nielsen, Michael Chiklis, Gary Busey.* The future's bleak in this tired sci-fi adventure that offers about as much thrills as the director's previous yawner, *Event Horizon*. Having a good look but even a lesser story than *Horizon*, *Soldier* manages to make the usually engaging Russell nothing more than a Stallone-clone, playing a monosyllabic futuristic warrior who helps a stranded space colony when they come under attack by militaristic forces (who were the ones who left him to die on the supposedly empty planet). What a waste of an intriguing idea. ★½ DVD: $9.99

Soldier in the Rain

(1963, 88 min, US, Ralph Nelson) *Jackie Gleason, Steve McQueen.* Blake Edwards adapted William Goldman's novel for this touching story about the friendship between a wheeling-dealing Army sergeant (Gleason) and his young sidekick (McQueen). ★★★

Soldier of Orange

(1979, 165 min, Netherlands, Paul Verhoeven) *Rutger Hauer, Jeroen Krabbé, Edward Fox.* The title of this intelligent and engrossing adventure story refers to the House of Orange, The Netherlands' Royal Government which was put in exile after the Nazi invasion of their country. Verhoeven demonstrates his ability to both re-create an era pregnant with fear and danger as well as tell a hypnotic war story. Hauer and Krabbé are aristocratic students who are caught up in the war effort and become dangerously involved in the Dutch resistance. (Dutch with English subtitles) ★★★½ DVD Letterbox: $29.99, VHS Letterbox: $14.99

Natascha McElhone haunts *Solaris* (2002)

A Soldier's Daughter Never Cries

(1998, 128 min, US, James Ivory) *Kris Kristofferson, Barbara Hershey, Leelee Sobieski, Jane Birkin, Dominique Blanc, Jesse Bradford, Bob Swaim, Luisa Conlon.* One sublime characteristic of Merchant Ivory productions is that as they tell a story, they also capture a mood, a time, a frame of mind. Kristofferson plays Bill Willis, an American writer in Paris, an ex-soldier living in affluence with his wife (Hershey) and daughter and writing about the burgeoning war in Vietnam. They adopt a young French child and bring him into their loving if eccentric fold. The actors impart presence and sensitivity to their roles, especially the two talents who portray the daughter Channe (Conlon plays her at age 7; Sobieski at 14 up), who is arguably the film's pivotal character. Stages of life pass like seasons of the year, momentous events marked by definitive statements expressed in the smallest gestures. A remarkable film describing an arc in one family's life, bearing witness to the fact that our history is always with us. ★★★½ VHS: $14.99

A Soldier's Story

(1984, 102 min, US, Norman Jewison) *Denzel Washington, Howard E. Rollins, Jr., Adolphe Caesar, Dennis Lipscomb, Patti LaBelle, Robert Townsend.* Crackling with racial tension, Jewison's searing murder mystery probes the multifaceted dilemma of black advancement in a predominantly white man's Army. Brilliantly acted with power and grace, Philadelphian Charles Fuller's Pulitzer Prize-winning play is a rare triumph of the stage to screen process. Caesar was Oscar nominated for his powerful portrayal of a much-disliked drill sergeant. ★★★★ DVD: $14.99, VHS: $9.99

The Solid Gold Cadillac

(1956, 99 min, US, Richard Quine) *Judy Holliday, Paul Douglas, Fred Clark, John Williams, Arthur O'Connell, Narrated by: George Burns.* That divine blithe spirit Holliday is impeccably funny as a daffy blonde who takes on the corporate world. She stars as a minor shareholder in one of those giant, faceless New York corporations. When she learns of wrongdoing on the company's board, she sets out to straighten things up. The film is a continuing series of gentle swipes at big business framed by delightful comic vignettes with Judy at her best. Douglas is in fine form as one of the board members who falls under Judy's luminous spell. ★★★½ DVD: $19.99

Solo

(1996, 106 min, US, Norberto Barba) *Mario Van Peebles, William Sadler, Barry Corbin, Adrien Brody.* With Hollywood's mega-action stars becoming as aged as some pungent French cheese, there exists a great opportunity for a young studling to emerge and take center stage. No, Mario, get off the pedestal; you're not the one. Despite an impressive set of pecs, Van Peebles just can't pull it off in this tediously flaccid sci-fi actioner. He plays an android who discovers that his maker, the U.S. Army, is using him for something *really* bad. The deadly pacing and bad acting complement the hackeneyed story. ★ DVD: $14.99, VHS: $9.99

Solomon & Gaenor

(2000, 100 min, Wales, Paul Morrison) *Ioan Gruffudd, Nia Roberts.* Evoking the simple yet stirring discovery of first love in a grand cinematic gesture, this sweetly romantic Welsh film was deservedly nominated for an Academy Award for Best Foreign-Language Film. In a poor Welsh village in 1911, a young coal miner's daughter and a Jewish youth begin a clandestine affair. His faith

Some Like It Hot

unbeknownst to her, the lovers attempt to forge a future all the while growing anti-Semitism grips the town. Director Morrison is masterful in capturing the pangs and delights of falling in love, and the two stars have a wonderful chemistry. (Welsh with English subtitles) ★★★½ DVD: $29.99, VHS: $21.99

Some Came Running

(1958, 136 min, US, Vincente Minnelli) *Frank Sinatra, Shirley MacLaine, Dean Martin, Martha Hyer.* Sinatra stars as an author who stirs things up in his sleepy hometown after several years away. Disillusioned, Sinatra steps off a bus with a good-natured floozy (MacLaine) in tow, and contrary to his family's wishes, manages to run into trouble at every turn. Martin also stars as Sinatra's buddy, who accompanies the ex-G.I. on his self-destructive binges. Though the film has a few slow stretches, the first-rate performances and the stunning conclusion make it all worthwhile. ★★★

Some Girls

(1988, 94 min, US, Michael Hoffman) *Patrick Dempsey, Jennifer Connelly, Andre Gregory, Lila Kedrova.* This refreshingly offbeat youth comedy stars a hilariously deadpan Dempsey as a lovesick college student who visits his girlfriend (Connelly) and her family during Christmas break. Dempsey expects a jolly good time, but gets more than he bargained for when he discovers that her family is more than a little eccentric. It's *You Can't Take It with You* meets *Risky Business*, and to director Hoffman and writer Rupert Walters' credit, the majority of the film's many gags score exceedingly well. ★★★

Some Kind of Hero

(1982, 97 min, US, Michael Pressman) *Richard Pryor, Margot Kidder, Ray Sharkey.* Based on James Kirkwood's novel, this disappointing adaptation stars Pryor as a former Vietnam POW returning home after six years in captivity who finds trouble adjusting to civilian life. ★★ VHS: $14.99

Some Kind of Wonderful

(1987, 93 min, US, Howard Deutch) *Eric Stoltz, Lea Thompson, Mary Stuart Masterson.* More teenage angst courtesy of John Hughes, with Stoltz in love with Thompson; Masterson in love with Stoltz. Hughes' bucket from the well must be worn out by now. ★★ DVD Letterbox: $14.99, VHS: $14.99

Some Like It Hot

(1959, 122 min, US, Billy Wilder) *Jack Lemmon, Tony Curtis, Marilyn Monroe, Joe E. Brown, George Raft, Pat O'Brien.* Director Wilder's masterpiece rates as one of the funniest American comedies of all time, and it only gets better with age. Lemmon and Curtis, at their comic best, star as down-and-out musicians in 1920s Chicago who, upon witnessing the St. Valentine's Day Massacre, don wig and dress and join an all-female band to escape the murderous thugs looking for them. Marilyn is Sugar Kane, the band's beautiful blonde singer who the boys are enraptured by. Curtis romances MM (out of drag, of course) and Lemmon is courted by millionaire Brown ("Well, nobody's perfect"). They just don't come any better than this. ★★★★ DVD: $14.99, DVD Special Edition: $19.99, VHS: $9.99

Favorite Line: "Look how she moves. That's just like Jell-O on springs. Must have some sort of built-in motor or something." —*Jack Lemmon as Daphne*

Some Mother's Son

(1996, 112 min, Ireland, Terry George) *Helen Mirren, Fionnula Flanagan, Aidan Gillen, David O'Hara, John Lynch.* A poignant glimpse into Northern Ireland politics. As seen through the eyes of two mothers whose sons have been imprisoned as IRA terrorists, *Some Mother's Son* explores the divergent viewpoints and impassioned partisanship dividing that country. Mirren gives an excellent performance as Kathleen, an apolitical schoolteacher whose life is torn apart when her teenaged son is arrested. Despite differences in education, class and politics, she befriends Annie (a terrific Flanagan), the plain-spoken, IRA-supporting mother of another teen arrested with Kathleen's son. As good as the Irish characterizations are, they are offset by one-dimensional depictions of the British, which only diminishes the film's authority and structure. ★★★ VHS: $19.99

Somebody Up There Likes Me

(1956, 113 min, US, Robert Wise) *Paul Newman, Steve McQueen, Robert Loggia, Pier Angeli, Sal Mineo.* Newman's fine performance as boxer Rocky Graziano highlights this sturdy biography, tracing the fighter's life from youth to champion. ★★★

Someone Like You

(2001, 95 min, US, Tony Goldwyn) *Ashley Judd, Hugh Jackman, Greg Kinnear, Ellen Barkin, Marisa Tomei.* Sandra Bullock watch your back; Ashley Judd is trying hard to capture your share of the romantic comedy market. Actually, trying *too* hard, as she overacts, overemotes and overcutes in an attempt to bring some life into a character which is underwritten. Based on Laura Zigman's acerbic novel "Animal Husbandry," characters disappear within the massive yet predictable plot, where Judd's talk-show coordinator finds her personal man-as-bull theories attracting a national audience amid her desperate romantic life. Jackman proves a good foil in a subdued role, while Kinnear plays a typical two-dimensional male ass. Snippets of scenes shine but overall, like a wax bottle candy, there's not enough sweetness in the center of this confection. ★★ DVD: $14.99, VHS: $6.99

Someone to Love

(1987, 109 min, US, Henry Jaglom) *Henry Jaglom, Orson Welles, Sally Kellerman.* Jaglom hosts a party inviting all acquaintances who would find themselves alone on Valentine's Day. Desperately driven to understand why successful and attractive people find true love elusive, he "circulates" among the guests, probing their lives. Welles, in his final screen appearance, hypnotizes the audience with his controversial views on the affairs of the heart. ★★★ VHS: $7.99

Someone to Watch over Me

(1987, 113 min, US, Ridley Scott) *Tom Berenger, Mimi Rogers, Lorraine Bracco, Jerry Orbach.* The director of *Alien* and *Thelma and Louise* brings his hyperbolic visual sense to this tension-filled love story about a cop from Queens (Berenger) who falls in love with the socialite-turned-mob informer (Rogers) he's been assigned to protect. Between the mobsters and his wife (the splendid Bracco), his life is in constant jeopardy. ★★★ DVD: $9.99

Something for Everyone

(1970, 112 min, GB, Harold Prince) *Michael York, Angela Lansbury, Anthony Corlan, Jane Carr.* Prince's directorial film debut is this witty black comedy that stars a seductive York as a cunning, amoral opportunist who insinuates himself into the household of the flamboyant Countess von Ornstein of Bavaria (Lansbury). Once inside, he proceeds to infiltrate the bedrooms of both her and her son. Lansbury camps it up wonderfully, acting as though she were a drag queen on stage at a New York fashion show. Corlan plays Helmut, the countess' gay teenage son, whose dark and sullen good looks prove to be a nice contrast to York's fair complexion. Carr plays Lansbury's corpulent daughter who has the last laugh. Sly fun and sophistication abound in this charming gem. ★★★½

Something of Value

(1957, 113 min, US, Richard Brooks) *Rock Hudson, Sidney Poitier, Wendy Hiller.* Compelling screen version of Robert C. Ruark's best-selling novel about the Mau Mau uprising in Kenya and the effect it has on two friends, one black, one white. ★★★

Something to Talk About

(1995, 101 min, US, Lasse Hallström) *Julia Roberts, Robert Duvall, Kyra Sedgwick, Dennis Quaid, Gena Rowlands.* Roberts demonstrates a certain charm but neither she nor a rather capable cast are able to gloss over a rather contrived and pedestrian screenplay. She plays a well-to-do wife who discovers her husband (Quaid) is having an affair. She retreats to the horse ranch run by her stoic father (Duvall). The film centers on her state of indecision and her husband's attempts to win her back, and throws in a subplot of her good-natured mother (Rowlands) discovering her father's past philandering for extra measure. Written by Callie Khouri (*Thelma and Louise*), the film tries to be a serious if comedic examination of adultery and reconciliation but can only address its concerns in superficial, episodic skits. ★★ DVD: $14.99, VHS: $9.99

Something Wicked This Way Comes

(1983, 94 min, US, Jack Clayton) *Jason Robards, Jonathan Pryce, Pam Grier.* Ray Bradbury wrote the screenplay based on his own novel about a mysterious carnival's visit to a turn-of-the-century Midwestern town. Full of wonderfully magic moments, redolent with evil, this film captures the essence of a young boy's imagination — one who thinks the carnival's proprietor may have demonic origins. ★★★ DVD: $24.99

Something Wild

(1986, 113 min, US, Jonathan Demme) *Melanie Griffith, Jeff Daniels, Ray Liotta, Margaret Colin.* The screwball comedy is given a violent twist by director Demme. When businessman Daniels skips out on a lunch bill, he encounters sexy, wild

Griffith, who proceeds to abduct him and take him on the ride of his life. Liotta is a standout as Griffith's psychotic ex-husband. A totally original road movie which is something of a cross between *Bringing Up Baby* and *Blue Velvet*. ★★★½ DVD: $14.99, VHS: $7.99

Something's Gotta Give

(2003, 128 min, US, Nancy Meyers) *Jack Nicholson, Diane Keaton, Keanu Reeves, Amanda Peet, Frances McDormand, Jon Favreau.* Keanu Reeves as a doctor . . . a 57-year-old Diane Keaton doing a nude scene . . . Jack Nicholson having, um, dysfunctional problems . . . these and other seemingly absurd plot points are on display in writer-director Meyers' engaging romantic comedy. That any of this would work is heresy; that it all works is just part of the fun, and though the story is often lightweight, the acting and enjoyment level is not. Keaton plays Erica Barry, a successful playwrite and an irresistible force. Jack is Harry Sanborn, a sixtyish record producer and an old immovable object. He's dating her daughter, but when these two get together, you can bet as sure as you live . . . well, you know the rest. To further complicate problems, Reeves' too-good-to-be-true doctor is also smitten with Erica, and as delightfully played by Keaton. . . who wouldn't be? This is a major acting triumph for the actress, shading Erica with the kind of charm and humor and sophistication usually associated with 1930s screen goddesses. And she's matched by Jack word for word, smile for smile. When these two are on the screen, which is most of the time, you forget the impotence and menopause and old age jokes. Instead, you relish the chemistry and experience and the occasional smart, funny line and savor two late-20th-century masters at work in a decidedly non-21st-century romance. ★★★ DVD Letterbox: $28.99

Sometimes a Great Notion

(1971, 114 min, US, Paul Newman) *Henry Fonda, Paul Newman, Richard Jaeckel, Michael Sarrazin, Lee Remick.* A first-rate cast distinguishes the absorbing drama set in the Oregon woodlands about a logging family, headed by patriarch Fonda, whose decision to ignore a local strike brings about tragedy. Jaeckel received a well-deserved Oscar nomination, due mostly to an amazing drowning scene. (aka: *Never Give an Inch*) ★★★

Sometimes Aunt Martha Does Dreadful Things

(1971, 95 min, US, Thomas Casey) Unintentional laughs abound in this little-known camp classic about a fugitive killer who both hides from the law and lives "in sin" with his young male lover by parading around in drag pretending to be the boy's aunt. As bad as it sounds, the film certainly gives in to gay stereotyping (and much more); but it's good for a laugh. ★

Somewhere I'll Find You

(1942, 117 min, US, Wesley Ruggles) *Clark Gable, Lana Turner.* Full of crackling dialogue, this handsome romantic adventure features its two stars in larger-than-life form in the story of correspondent Gable falling for reporter Turner, but who ignores his true feelings because his younger brother is also in love with her. All three find themselves hurried from the safety of pre-Pearl Harbor America into the thick of war-torn Indochina. The abrasive ending befits the mindset of an America at war. ★★★ VHS: $19.99

Somewhere in Time

(1980, 103 min, US, Jeannot Szwarc) *Christopher Reeve, Jane Seymour, Christopher Plummer, Teresa Wright.* Old-fashioned romantic fantasy with Reeve as a contemporary playwright who falls in love with a turn-of-the-century actress (Seymour) he sees in a portrait, and wills himself back in time. The film never quite delivers on its intriguing premise, though John Barry's beautiful score and the attractive scenery help. ★★½ DVD Collector's Edition: $14.99, VHS: $14.99

Sommersby

(1993, 117 min, US, Jon Amiel) *Richard Gere, Jodie Foster, Bill Pullman, James Earl Jones, William Windom.* This sweeping post-Civil War adaptation of *The Return of Martin Guerre* is a pleasant Hollywood rarity: an American remake that lives up to the original. Gere plays Jack Sommersby, a wealthy Confederate landowner who returns to his little valley several years after the war. Long thought dead, he is greeted with a mixture of disbelief, distrust and cautious joy by both the townsfolk and his wife, marvelously portrayed by Foster. Ultimately, Gere's Sommersby is so uncharacteris-

Something Wild

tic that finally the question is raised: Is he who he claims to be? Director Amiel superbly re-creates the antebellum South, but what makes it all worthwhile is the dazzling on-screen magnetism between Foster and Gere. ★★★½ DVD: $14.99, VHS: $9.99

Son of Dracula

(1943, 78 min, US, Robert Siodmak) *Lon Chaney, Jr., Evelyn Ankers.* Chaney takes over for Bela Lugosi in this successful and very atmospheric sequel with Dracula now terrorizing the American South. ★★★ VHS: $14.99

Son of Frankenstein

(1939, 99 min, US, Rowland V. Lee) *Boris Karloff, Bela Lugosi, Basil Rathbone.* Karloff would appear as "The Monster" for the last time in this genuinely eerie chiller, the third in the *Frankenstein* series. Rathbone is the chip off the old block who tries to make the monster "good" and clear the family name. Like father, like son, and things go awry. In an unexpected and effective performance, Lugosi plays Ygor. (Sequel: *Ghost of Frankenstein*) ★★★

Son of Godzilla

(1967, 86 min, Japan, Joh Fukuda) When Godzilla lays an egg in this movie, out pops another living butane lighter, this one called Minya. Godzilla and son decide to tear up the town in celebration of Jr.'s coming out party — even though Allstate doesn't cover acts of Godzilla. ★½

Son of Kong

(1933, 70 min, US, Ernest B. Schoedsack) *Robert Armstrong, Helen Mack, Victor Wong.* When *King Kong* became a hit, RKO rushed this sequel out the same year — but it's still lots of fun. Carl Denham (Armstrong), hounded by lawsuits for all the damages that big old ape did, flees New York for the solitude of Skull Island, only to run into Kong, Jr. Master animator Willis O'Brien continued his best work with lots of battles with giant animals of one era or another (some of it left over from the first film), with a heartrending ending accentuated by a fine Max Steiner score. ★★★

Son of Paleface

(1952, 95 min, US, Frank Tashlin) *Bob Hope, Jane Russell, Roy Rogers.* This very funny sequel to the Hope-Russell hit comedy, *The Paleface*, tops the original. Bob plays a timid Harvard graduate who heads West to claim an inheritance and tangles with outlaws, Rogers, Trigger and gorgeous showgirl Jane. ★★★½ DVD: $14.99, VHS: $14.99

Son of the Shark

(1995, 85 min, France, Agnes Merlet) *Ludovic Vandendaele, Erick Da Silva.* Imagine if you will a kiddie version of *A Clockwork Orange.* Maybe a little *The 400 Blows*, just to be considered an homage. Getting a clear picture yet? If you have one, you've got the story of Martin and Simon, two brothers abandoned by their mother, abused by their father and split up by the state because they are too dangerous together. The film is powerful and gritty, and the photography is as dark as much of their life must be. These kids hold the whole town at bay while they watch movies at the local theatre, with one projecting the film while the other watches it eating popcorn. It must be tough to be a French parent these days. (French with English subtitles) ★★★

A Song Is Born

(1948, 113 min, US, Howard Hawks) *Danny Kaye, Virginia Mayo, Hugh Herbert, Steve Cochran, Benny Goodman, Louis Armstrong, Lionel Hampton, Tommy Dorsey.* Director Hawks remade his 1942 classic *Ball of Fire*, this time as a musical, with Kaye taking over for Gary Cooper. And though Danny and a fine jazz score are commendable, the film doesn't reach the original's inspired comic heights. But there are laughs to be found. And what a treat to see such '40s music greats as Armstrong, Goodman, Dorsey and Hampton all in one movie. Danny's constant costar, Mayo, is attractive but lacks the snap Barbara Stanwyck brought to the first film. ★★½

The Song of Bernadette

(1943, 159 min, US, Henry King) *Jennifer Jones, William Eythe, Charles Bickford, Vincent Price, Lee J. Cobb, Anne Revere, Gladys Cooper.* Jones won an Oscar for her moving performance in this sentimental but well-crafted drama as the young French girl who sees a vision of the Virgin Mary, which inspires her to become a nun and causes her small town to turn against her. ★★★ DVD: $14.99, VHS: $9.99

Song of Love

(1947, 119 min, US, Clarence Brown) *Katharine Hepburn, Paul Henried, Robert Walker.* A glossy though dramatically uneven biography of Robert and Clara Schuman (Henreid, Hepburn) and their friendship with young composer Johannes Brahms (Walker). ★★½ VHS: $19.99

Song of the Loon

(1970, 90 min, US, Andrew Herbert) *Jon Iverson, Morgan Royce, Lancer Ward.* Long considered a classic of independent gay filmmaking, *Song of the Loon* is an earnest tale of love and brotherhood among men as well as a naturalist's delight. Set in northern California in the 1870s, the story follows the odyssey of Ephraim McKeever, a young man in search of love and happiness. By using non-professional actors, not showing hard-core sex scenes and featuring such silly lines as "Dammit, you're beautiful," the film is at times awkward and dated, but it is also a welcome change from the normal X-rated fare that abounds. ★★

A Song to Remember

(1945, 112 min, US, Charles Vidor) *Cornel Wilde, Merle Oberon, Paul Muni.* The life of famed composer Frederic Chopin — his music and his love affair with author George Sand. Wilde stars as Chopin, Oberon makes a lovely Sand, and Muni appears as Chopin's mentor. Good acting can't elevate this above the ordinary. ★★½ VHS: $19.99

Songcatcher

(2000, 109 min, US, Maggie Greenwald) *Janet McTeer, Aidan Quinn, Pat Carroll, Jane Adams, Emmy Rossum, Taj Mahal.* McTeer is a perfect combination of steely determination and awed enthusiasm as Lily Penleric, a respected musicologist who is once again passed over for a tenured position at her school. She leaves at the summer break to visit her sister in the Appalachian Mountains. There, she discovers that the Scottish and English ballads she's sung to her own piano accompaniment in her classroom have been sung in these mountains for hundreds of years with strong, unfamiliar vocalizations and accompanied by banjo, fiddle and guitar. Knowing that she's made an important discovery, she travels the area, recording and transcribing this music. Lily's involvement in the community opens up challenging and joyous possibil-

ities in her own life; the harsh land holds unexpected, idiosyncratic beauty, yet suffers the same dangers and prejudices one can find anywhere. *Songcatcher* is an unexpected pleasure; images of undulating forests underscored by heartrendingly pure vocalizations remain long after the film is over. ★★★½ DVD Signature Series: $19.99

Sonny Boy

(1990, 96 min, US, Martin Carroll) *David Carradine, Paul L. Smith, Brad Dourif.* This extremely weird film features a family that would feel right at home in John Waters' Mortville. A dark tale of family love gone berserk, *Sonny Boy* features Smith as a 300-pound psychotic crook who with his wife, Pearl, raises an orphan boy to become an animal-like killing machine to advance their criminal enterprise. The role of the sweet, loving mother Pearl is played oddly enough by Carradine, who plays the part entirely as a woman. As they go about their murderous ways, all involved ignore the fact that Pearl is a transvestite, which only adds to the pleasure of this mean-spirited oddity. ★★½ VHS: $89.99

The Sons of Katie Elder

(1965, 122 min, US, Henry Hathaway) *John Wayne, Dean Martin, Michael Anderson, Jr., Earl Holliman.* Solid western action with Wayne, Martin, Anderson and Holliman as the title characters, out to avenge their mother's murder. ★★★ DVD: $14.99, VHS: $9.99

Sons of the Desert

(1933, 69 min, US, William A. Seiter) *Stan Laurel, Oliver Hardy.* Henpecked Laurel and Hardy want to go to the national convention of their lodge, The Sons of the Desert, but their wives won't let them. So like little boys are wont to do, they sneak off anyway, only to get caught when Stanley ends up in a newsreel. The title of this Laurel and Hardy masterpiece is also the name of their fan club — still in existence today! (DVD includes 4 shorts) ★★★½ DVD: $19.99

Sophie's Choice

(1982, 157 min, US, Alan J. Pakula) *Meryl Streep, Kevin Kline, Peter MacNicol.* A tour-de-force, Academy Award-winning performance by Streep distinguishes this powerful adaptation of William Styron's sweeping novel. Kline is Streep's volatile lover, who learns the horrid secret of Sophie's Auschwitz survival. MacNicol is Stingo, a young author who falls in love with Sophie. The film is divided between Sophie's harrowing life at Auschwitz and her postwar years as a guilt-ridden survivor living in Brooklyn. Both time frames offer heartrending, compassionate drama, and in bringing Sophie to life in the two time periods, Streep delivers a portrayal of such nuance and emotion that it certainly ranks as one of the greatest performances in American cinema. ★★★½ DVD: $14.99

Sorcerer

(1977, 122 min, US, William Friedkin) *Roy Scheider, Bruno Cremer.* From the director of *The French Connection* comes this expensive remake of H.G. Clouzot's classic *Wages of Fear.* Just as spine-tingling but not nearly as involving as the original. Scheider plays one of four desperate hoods now in hiding in a seedy Latin American town trying to buy their way out. Their only hope: help extinguish a raging oil fire by driving their trucks loaded with nitroglycerine on a suicide run over almost impassable roads. ★★½ DVD: $24.99, VHS: $19.99

Sorceress

(1989, 98 min, France, Suzanne Schiffman) *Christine Boisson, Tcheky Karyo.* Though this is only her first film, Schiffman has made a decidedly self-assured and moving drama of religious beliefs, hypocrisy and persecution. Set in a peasant village during the 13th century, a young monk, sent by the Church to ferret out heretics, comes in conflict with a mysterious young woman who lives in the forest, who tends to the health of the villagers by making and administering herbal potions. This is a moving, complex drama that explores not only religious themes but also the role and persecution of women during the Middle Ages. ★★★ VHS Subtitled: $19.99, VHS Dubbed: $19.99

Sordid Lives

(2000, 111 min, US, Del Shores) *Beau Bridges, Bonnie Bedelia, Delta Burke, Ann Walker, Leslie Jordan, Olivia Newton-John, Kirk Geiger, Beth Grant.* Lovers of white-trash camp may get a kick in the ass from this loopy if forced comedy of family dysfunctionalism, Southern style. The story centers on the extended family of Texas rednecks who've come together for the funeral of their adulterous matriarch. This gives way to much wailing and flailing about for the survivors, including her ever-squabbling, big-haired daughters LaVonda (Walker) and Latrelle (Bedelia). Even of more concern is getting their drag queen brother Earl (Jordan) out of the institution and to the service. The story is told through the eyes of Ty (Geiger), Latrelle's estranged gay son, and the film loses whatever momentum it had gained when he's center stage. However, there's a few good lines and Jordan is a force unto himself as brother Earl, giving a hilarious performance as the Tammy Wynette-obsessed, acid-tongued transvestite who thankfully gets the last laugh. ★★½ DVD: $14.99, VHS: $9.99

The Sorrow and the Pity

(1970, 261 min, France, Marcel Ophüls) A landmark film in cinema history, one of the most brilliant and shattering films ever made. Ophüls creates a sense of living history as he examines France's occupation by Germany during WWII, and France's complicity in the virulent racial and religious bigotry that defined the Third Reich. ★★★★ DVD: $49.99, VHS: $94.99

Sorry, Wrong Number

(1948, 89 min, US, Anatole Litvak) *Barbara Stanwyck, Burt Lancaster, Wendell Corey.* Based on the acclaimed radio program (which starred Agnes Moorehead), this stylized thriller features Stanwyck in an electrifying performance as a bedridden wife who overhears a murder plot on her phone's party line — unaware that she is the intended victim. Lancaster plays her scheming husband. (Remade in 1989) ★★★ DVD: $14.99, VHS: $14.99

Sotto Sotto

(1984, 104 min, Italy, Lina Wertmüller) *Enrico Montesano, Veronica Lario, Luisa de Santis.* The prototypical machismo-obsessed Italian male must come to grips with the sexual freedoms and diversity of the late 20th century in this wild sexual comedy that is both illuminating and troubling in its depiction of two women in love with each other. Set in Naples, the story revolves around Ester and Adele, two friends who witness two women kissing. This initiates a revelation, and the two fall in (unconsummated) love. Then Ester's husband discovers his wife is in love with someone else, and sets out to discover who. (Italian with English subtitles) ★★½

Soul Food

(1997, 114 min, US, George Tillman Jr.) *Vanessa L. Williams, Vivica A. Fox, Nia Long, Michael Beach, Mekhi Phifer, Irma P. Hall, Brandon Hammond, Gina Ravera.* Don't let *Soul Food*'s "Afterschool Special" mushiness put you off. Yes, it's maudlin, but this story about the trials and tribulations of a black family struggling for the good life in Chicago is refreshing, funny and well-paced entertainment. Williams (a high-powered lawyer), Fox (a stay-at-home mom) and Long (a salon owner) star as the three female offspring of a powerful but aging matriarch (the fabulous Hall). The story unfolds from the point-of-view of Fox's young son Ahmed (Hammond), who provides the narration and beholds his grandmother (known as Mother Joe) with reverential awe. The soap opera really heats up when Mother Joe goes into the hospital for surgery and in the absence of her traditional Sunday meals family unity begins to crumble. Chock full of effervescent humor. ★★★ DVD Director's Edition: $14.99, VHS: $6.99

Soul Man

(1986, 101 min, US, Steve Miner) *C. Thomas Howell, Rae Dawn Chong, James Earl Jones.* Ineffectual social satire with Howell as a white student masquerading as an African-American in order to qualify for a scholarship to Harvard Law School. Chong is Howell's girlfriend fooled by the charade. ★★ DVD Letterbox: $9.99

Soul Survivors

(2001, 85 min, US, Steve Carpenter) *Casey Affleck, Wes Bentley, Eliza Dushku, Angela Featherstone, Melissa Sagemiller, Luke Wilson.* Sagemiller and Affleck play college sweethearts who are in a terrible car accident with their friends. Affleck dies in the accident . . . or does he? Sagemiller keeps seeing him around campus, as well as other mysterious visions. What is happening? Who will give a crap? It's all bland and boring, and everyone (with exception to the energetic Dushku) looks distracted or half-asleep, and you will be, too. ★ DVD Killer Cut: $14.99, VHS Killer Cut: $14.99

The Sound of Music

(1965, 172 min, US, Robert Wise) *Julie Andrews, Christopher Plummer, Eleanor Parker, Richard Hadyn, Angela Cartwright.* This classic adaptation of Rodgers and Hammerstein's Broadway musical has long been a family favorite — and one of the most popular films of all time. Based on the true experiences of the Von Trapp family, the film stars Andrews as Maria, an Austrian novice who becomes governess to seven children during the onset of WWII. A sentimental concoction of schmaltz and over-kill which still manages to work in spite of it all. The R&H score includes "Do Re Mi" and "Climb Every Mountain." Winner of 4 Academy Awards, including Best Picture. ★★★★ DVD Letterbox 2-disc Special Edition: $26.99, DVD Pan & Scan Basic Edition: $19.99, DVD Basic Edition: $19.99, VHS: $9.99

Sounder

(1972, 105 min, US, Martin Ritt) *Cicely Tyson, Paul Winfield, Kevin Hooks, Taj Mahal.* Tyson and Winfield both received much-deserved Oscar nominations for their superlative performances in this sensitive and beautifully crafted drama about a black sharecropping family's struggle in the early 1930s. As their young son, Hooks is outstanding. Also nominated for Best Picture. (Remade in 2003) ★★★★

Sour Grapes

(1998, 91 min, US, Larry David) *Steven Weber, Craig Bierko, Karen Sillas, Matt Keeslar.* Writer David flogs his dead "Seinfeld" horse in his disappointing directing debut. While David's usual sharp (and exceedingly bitter) dialogue and situations are present, the pacing is leaden and poor timing makes the jokes crash and burn. Weber mimics Seinfeld as he and Bierko do their best to be as unlikable as possible. The creaky premise involves slot machine winnings and much coincidence; David seems to be taking funny situations and desperately trying to cram them into a plot. ★½ DVD: $9.99, VHS: $14.99

South Central

(1991, 99 min, US, Steve Anderson) *Glenn Plummer, Carl Lumbly.* Set in 1981, this wildly violent and highly entertaining history of crack and L.A. street gangs is based on the real-life story of West Coast drug dealing gangsters, the Crips. The film's coke-addled hero, Bobby Johnson (Plummer), soon learns that killing rival pimps, freebasing, smoking angel dust and blow-

Soul Food

South Park: Bigger, Longer & Uncut

ing out a deceitful woman's private parts with a .44 magnum isn't as cool as quietly reading Muslim literature and "rejecting the circle of hate that society inflicts on the black man." Covers much of the same ground nearly as effectively as *Boyz n the Hood*. ★★★ DVD: $14.99, VHS: $9.99

South of Heaven, West of Hell

(2000, 104 min, US, Dwight Yoakam) *Vince Vaughn, Dwight Yoakam, Bridget Fonda, Billy Bob Thornton, Paul Reubens, Peter Fonda, Michael Jeter, Bud Cort.* What a shameful waste of a terrific cast. Just the thought of seeing these actors in a western should have guaranteed this film would be at the very least watchable. Alas, with Yoakam performing an anti-hat trick as star, director and cowriter, *South of Heaven, West of Hell* is a complete washout. Dull and painfully self-indulgent, this boring story of a marshal taking on his outlaw family aims to be allegorical and revisionist but fails on all counts. If you sit through this mess, keep in mind that the theatrical cut was twenty minutes longer. That version is now playing on a movie screen in Hell, not west of it. ★ DVD Theatrical Cut: $19.99

South Pacific

(1958, 150 min, US, Joshua Logan) *Mitzi Gaynor, Rossano Brazzi, John Kerr, France Nuyen, Juanita Hall, Ray Walston.* Rodgers and Hammerstein's landmark Broadway musical is given the royal treatment in this lush adaptation. Gaynor (in the Mary Martin role) plays an American nurse who finds love while stationed in the South Seas during WWII. Hall sings the haunting "Bali H'ai." (Remade in 2001) ★★★ DVD: $19.99, VHS: $14.99

South Pacific

(2001, 135 min, US, Richard Pearce) *Glenn Close, Harry Connick, Jr., Rade Sherbedgia, Jack Thompson, Lori Tan Chinn, Ilene Graff, Natalie Mendoza, Simon Burke, Steve Bastoni, Kimberley Davies, Robert Pastorelli.* A reverent if subdued made-for-TV remake of the more theatrical 1958 film hit of Rodgers & Hammerstein's classic stage musical. In good voice, Close nicely dons the uniform of Nellie Forbush, a Navy nurse stationed in the South Pacific during WWII. Emblematic of the production, Connick is quite reserved as a young Marine, sent to track Japanese aircraft, who falls for a native girl. ★★½ DVD: $14.99, VHS: $9.99

South Park: Bigger, Longer & Uncut

(1999, 80 min, US, Trey Parker) *Voices of: Trey Parker, Matt Stone, Mary Kay Bergman, Isaac Hayes, George Clooney, Brent Spiner, Minnie Driver, Dave Foley, Eric Idle.* Irreverent, tasteless and a brilliant social satire for added good measure, *South Park: Bigger, Longer & Uncut* is one of the funniest and most shrewdly observed comedies in years. Yes, a lot of its humor is scatological, and the animation is less-than-stellar, and it appears "fuck" is uttered every twenty seconds or so. But beyond the juvenile façade of toilet humor and sex jokes is a scintillating satire of contemporary mores and, in particular, an appropriately timely jab at censorship, the MPAA, and societal and parental responsibility. The story — told in numerous, upbeat musical production numbers which should have Broadway taking notice — follows the consequences when Stan, Kyle, Cartman and Kenny go to see their favorite TV characters, Terrance and Phillip, in their new theatrical release not meant for kids. The parallels are delicious. And though this *South Park* is definitely not for kids, its humor is fast, furious, ferocious, fresh, flip, foul . . . you know, all the "f" words. ★★★★ DVD: $14.99, VHS: $9.99

Favorite Line: "You don't have to spend your life addicted to smack, homeless on the streets giving hand jobs for crack." —*Trey Parker as Mr. Mackey*

South Riding

(1938, 85 min, GB, Victor Saville) *Ralph Richardson, Edna Best, Glynis Johns, Edmund Gwenn, John Clements, Ann Todd.* Trying to condense Winifred Holtby's sprawling tale of local political and social intrigue into a mere 85 minutes, *South Riding* moves along at a furious clip, setting up and then forgetting plot lines, suggesting others, painting in broad strokes this "typical" British community. As an examination of the British class system, it is a little naïve, but thanks to a quorum of fine performances, the film comes alive like some incipient episode of "Masterpiece Theatre." Richardson heads the cast as a husband who is land rich and cash poor, drained by an institutionalized wife (Todd) and a daughter (a spirited Johns) in dreadful need of public schooling. ★★★ VHS: $24.99

Southern Comfort

(1981, 106 min, US, Walter Hill) *Keith Carradine, Powers Boothe, Fred Ward, Peter Coyote, Franklin Seales.* Competent action film (reminiscent of *Deliverance*) about a group of National Guardsmen who are forced to fight for their lives in the Louisiana swamps when gun-toting Cajuns come their way. ★★½ DVD: $14.99

A Southern Yankee

(1948, 90 min, US, Edward Sedgwick) *Red Skelton, Arlene Dahl, Brian Donlevy.* The ever-hilarious Skelton stars in this Civil War comedy about a buffoonish bellhop who is accidentally recruited to spy for the Union Army. Along the way, he falls for a Southern belle (Dahl), inadvertently foils the Rebels and immortalizes the line, "My, it's so nice to be among the magnolias again." ★★★ VHS: $19.99

The Southerner

(1945, 91 min, US, Jean Renoir) *Zachary Scott, Beulah Bondi, Betty Field, Norman Lloyd, Percy Kilbride, J. Carrol Naish.* A naturalistic portrayal of one family's struggle to start a farm in South. Tied to the land for better or worse, the Tuckers endure poverty, disease, and flood with dignity, humor, and a deep store of hope. Though not credited, novelist

William Faulkner contributed to Renoir's sparse, authentic sounding dialogue. Great performances from the cast. ★★★★ DVD: $19.99, VHS: $19.99

Southie

(1998, 95 min, US, John Shea) *Donnie Wahlberg, Rose McGowan, Anne Meara, Jimmy Cummings, Amanda Peet, Will Arnett, Lawrence Tierney.* A fairly routine entry in the criminal-gone-legit-gets-sucked-back-into-his-old-ways subgenre. Wahlberg's nice performance anchors this too laid-back crime drama that also has decent turns by McGowan as Wahlberg's sister and Meara as his mom. Donnie's a former alcoholic and punk who comes back to South Boston for a wedding. After being refused legitimate union work because of a misunderstanding, and seeing his mother's escalating medical bills, Donnie reluctantly enters into a shady deal with some former cronies. Vaguely TV movie-ish, this underwhelming film still manages to make one care about the characters despite all the rough edges. ★★ DVD: $14.99, VHS: $102.99

Soviet Spy

(1961, 130 min, France, Yves Ciampi) *Thomas Holtzman.* This docudrama presents the case of Richard Sorge, a German journalist covering WWII in Japan. Official records show that Sorge was hanged as a Soviet spy in 1944. The film explores this mystery man's life, beginning with conflicting opinions by his associates on his alleged espionage activities and then moving up to a reenactment of the events that led to his capture. A very interesting exploration into the life and role of a possible Soviet spy. (French with English subtitles) ★★★

Soylent Green

(1973, 97 min, US, Richard Fleischer) *Charlton Heston, Edward G. Robinson, Leigh Taylor-Young, Chuck Connors.* This frighteningly prescient sci-fi tale about the dangers of the "greenhouse effect" was made long before the term became a popular buzzword. Heston plays a hardened New York cop who stumbles onto the secret of Soylent Green, a nutritional wafer used to feed the masses. Robinson is excellent in his final role as Heston's aging roommate who can remember the halcyon days of Earth when it was still green. ★★½ DVD: $19.99, VHS: $14.99

Space Cowboys

(2000, 129 min, US, Clint Eastwood) *Clint Eastwood, Tommy Lee Jones, James Garner, Donald Sutherland, James Cromwell, Marcia Gay Harden, William Devane, Courtney B. Vance.* Director Eastwood leaves the wide open spaces of his beloved West for the last frontier of space to tell an entertaining tale of heroism and friendship. A highly enjoyable comic adventure, the story follows four former test pilots who train for a space mission even though they've all been retired for years — and have never been into space. Eastwood is the laconic leader of the group, an engineer whose knowledge of a crippled satellite makes him essential to its rescue. When he demands that his old crew (Jones, Garner, Sutherland) accompany him, they have a chance to realize a 40-year-old dream. Eastwood is in a lighter, breezier mood here, making the most of some genuinely funny moments that are performed by a relaxed, in-charge ensemble. ★★★ DVD: $14.99, VHS: $9.99

S

Space Jam

(1996, 87 min, US, Joe Pytka) *Michael Jordan, Wayne Knight, Bill Murray, Bugs Bunny, Daffy Duck.* Falling far short of its intended "Pro basketball meets *Roger Rabbit*" aspirations, Jordan's debut does not bode well for his future success as a movie star. Jordan teams up with a plethora of Looney Tunes characters in a game of intergalactic and multidimensional basketball when some evil (but very lovable) aliens try to kidnap Bugs Bunny and company. Though the animation is good, the humor is forced and the film is padded out to feature length with some boring montage sequences. ★★ DVD: $19.99, DVD Special Edition: $26.99, VHS: $14.99

Spaceballs

(1987, 96 min, US, Mel Brooks) *Mel Brooks, John Candy, Rick Moranis, Bill Pullman.* A misfire for Brooks, this lame and untimely parody of George Lucas' *Star Wars* series features the usual Brooks assault of visual and verbal puns, which more often than not fail to hit their desired target. Die-hard "Star-heads" may be amused, but *Hardware Wars* did it better and earlier. The best scene of the film is an on-target takeoff on *Alien* and the classic Warner Brothers cartoon "One Froggy Evening." ★★ DVD: $14.99, VHS: $9.99

Spacecamp

(1986, 108 min, US, Harry Winer) *Kate Capshaw, Lea Thompson, Kelly Preston, Joaquin Phoenix, Tom Skerritt.* A group of teenagers attending a NASA summer camp are accidentally launched into space, where they're on their own to get back to Earth. A very ordinary teen adventure. ★★ DVD: $14.99

Spaghetti House

(1982, 102 min, GB/Italy, Guilio Pardisi) *Nino Manfredi, Rita Tushingham.* Manfredi, Italy's master of film comedy, abandons his usual persona to star in this drama of a bungled robbery attempt which results in a tense hostage situation. He plays an unspoken Italian waiter in London who, along with four of his compatriots, is held hostage by three desperate black men. Although this film falls occasionally into depicting easy stereotypes, it also explores race relations, prejudices and the common oppression suffered by both immigrants and blacks in lily-white England. ★★½

The Spanish Prisoner

(1998, 110 min, US, David Mamet) *Campbell Scott, Steve Martin, Ben Gazzara, Felicity Huffman, Ricky Jay, Rebecca Pidgeon.* Scott is a perfect foil in this quintessential Mamet labyrinth of misleading appearances, misplaced trust and superbly executed duplicity. He plays Joe Ross, brilliant at his job, whose innate decency and courtesy make him an easy target. Creator of a process which is expected to garner huge profits for his company, he is perturbed by his superior's (Gazzara) reticence in discussing profit sharing. He meets a man (a marvelously underplayed Martin) of apparent wealth and worldliness, who advises young Ross to protect his interests; and plummets into a byzantine abyss in which he is the prime suspect of theft and murder. Layers unfold and red herrings abound in this intriguing puzzle which plays on the viewer's own preconceptions and sustains suspense until the final scene. ★★★½ DVD: $19.99

Spanking the Monkey

(1994, 106 min, US, David O. Russell) *Jeremy Davies, Alberta Watson, Benjamin Hendrickson.* Don't let the title fool you. Russell's film is an insightful and offbeat look at love, sexuality and incest. Davies is convincing as a college freshman student, Ray, who must stay home on his summer vacation to take care of his bedridden mother instead of taking a prestigious internship. The relationship between the two becomes increasingly convoluted as the mother looks towards her son to fill the void left by a traveling husband, and Ray's sexual frustrations grow. *Monkey* boasts first-rate acting and a well-written script. ★★★ VHS: $19.99

Sparkle

(1976, 98 min, US, Sam O'Steen) *Philip Michael Thomas, Lonette McKee, Irene Cara, Dwan Smith, Mary Alice.* The trials and tribulations of stardom, as experienced by three sisters during the 1950s rock era. Curtis Mayfield's rousing score highlights this sometimes clichéd story made all the more appealing by its musical numbers and sincere performances. Written by the director Joel Schumacher. ★★½

Sparkler

(1999, 90 min, US, Darren Stein) *Freddie Prinze, Jr., Jaime Kennedy, Park Overall, Veronica Cartwright.* Overall is quite appealing as a trailerpark wife who catches her loutish husband in bed with a friend. She decides to head to Vegas to look up a high school classmate and forget her troubles for a while, and keeps crossing paths with three young men. Meanwhile, her scummy hubby is hot on her trail. This slight but likable comedy-drama is harmed by trailer trash-bashing and iffy direction, but Overall and Kennedy and just enough warmth offset the sleaze and cheese. Far better than Stein's *Jawbreaker*, and where else will you get to see Cartwright do a lewd striptease? ★★

Sparrows

(1926, 84 min, US, William Beaudine) *Mary Pickford.* A gaggle of orphans, a quicksand-infested swamp, a Lindbergh-like kidnapping and 'gators. Fine fixin's for a melodrama. Pickford, racing through her '30s, plays a waif half her age trying to get her brood out of the Bayou alive. One of the classics of the silent era, which the kids will love as much as the adults. ★★★½ DVD: $29.99, VHS: $24.99

Spartacus

(1960, 184 min, US, Stanley Kubrick) *Kirk Douglas, Peter Ustinov, Laurence Olivier, Jean Simmons, John Gavin, Tony Curtis, Charles Laughton.* This epic adventure is highlighted by remarkable action sequences and strongly developed characterizations, all set against the visual spectacle of Kubrick's discerning eye for locale and cinematic tone. Douglas stars in the title role as a rebel slave who leads the revolt against the Roman Republic. Featuring a cast of (literally) thousands! Music by Alex North. ★★★★ DVD Criterion Collection: $49.99, VHS: $14.99, VHS Letterbox: $14.99

Spawn

(1997, 97 min, US, Mark A.Z. Dippe) *Michael Jai White, John Leguizamo, Martin Sheen, Theresa Randle, Nicol Williamson.* Todd McFarlane's *Spawn* is an immensely popular comic book series, but a lousy live-action film. White stars as Al Simmons, a government assassin working for mega-evil Jason Wynn (Sheen). When Wynn double-crosses Simmons and has him murdered, Simmons is resurrected as Spawn, a sort of superhero from Hell. It seems that Al was so good at his job that Satan wants to use him as the General of one of his armies. But Spawn begins to use his newly acquired powers on the part of good, sort of. Leguizamo is very good as one of Satan's clown-like emissaries, but the direction and the script are weak. (Followed by 2 sequels) ★★ DVD: $14.99, VHS PG-13 Rated: $9.99, VHS Letterbox R-Rated: $9.99, VHS Pan & Scan R-Rated: $9.99

Speaking Parts

(1989, 93 min, Canada, Atom Egoyan) *Michael McManus, Arsinée Khanjian.* Similar in theme to *sex, lies, and videotape*, this perceptive look at the delicate balance between love and sex in the age of video features the entangled lives of three young people. Lance, a part-time actor and full-time bedchanger at a hotel, becomes the object of desire for both Clara, a scriptwriter intrigued by the physical similarities between Lance and her dead brother, and Lisa, a shy hotel maid who obsessively watches his minor appearances as an extra in films she rents on video. This quietly stylized drama is a dark glimpse into the way people act and how they show themselves to others. ★★★ DVD: $29.99, VHS Out of Print: $9.99

Special Bulletin

(1983, 105 min, US, Edward Zwick) *Ed Flanders, Kathryn Walker, Rosalind Cash, Roxanne Hart, David Clennon, David Rasche.* Outstanding made-for-TV drama about a group of nuclear protestors who, holding a TV reporter and cameraman hostage, threaten to detonate nuclear bombs if warheads in Charleston, South Carolina, are not disarmed. Like Orson Welles' "War of the Worlds," the film is presented as if it were a live news broadcast. Intelligently written, expertly acted and directed. ★★★½ VHS: $19.99

A Special Day

(1977, 110 min, Italy, Ettore Scola) *Marcello Mastroianni, Sophia Loren.* The day Hitler arrives in Rome to meet with Mussolini is the time setting for this touching drama of an oppressed housewife (Loren) who meets and befriends a troubled homosexual (Mastroianni). Fine performances from the two as well as Scola's realistic treatment make this a memorable film. ★★★

Special Effects

(1985, 90 min, US, Larry Cohen) *Eric Bogosian, Zoe Tamerlis.* Intriguing, top-notch Grade-B thriller with Bogosian as a maniacal movie director who murders an actress, and then hires a look-alike and makes a movie about the killing. Tamerlis plays both actresses. ★★½ DVD: $14.99

The Specialist

(1994, 115 min, US, Luis Llosa) *Sharon Stone, Sylvester Stallone, James Woods, Rod Steiger, Eric Roberts.* Llosa is far better directing explosions than people with this hormone-driven soap opera that pleases the eye as it insults the intelligence. Stallone plays an ex-CIA operative and explosives expert who is hired by hypersexy Stone to wipe out the men responsible for her parents' death. But there's a hitch: The bad guys have hired Sly's vengeful ex-partner (the scene-stealing Woods) as their security chief. The steamy shower scene between Stallone and Stone is a sight to behold. ★★ DVD: $14.99, VHS: $9.99

Ingrid Bergman and Gregory Peck in *Spellbound*

Species

(1995, 111 min, US, Roger Donaldson) *Ben Kingsley, Michael Madsen, Alfred Molina, Forest Whitaker, Narg Helgenberger, Natasha Henstridge.* An unintentionally funny horror film about a half-human, half-*Alien* creature whose attempts at perpetuating her own species by mating with a human male is hampered by a ragtag team of experts. Donaldson's first foray into the field of horror is sabotaged by an incredibly clichéd script, hokey dialogue and lackluster performances. *Species* does feature first-rate special effects, including H.R. Giger's déjà vu alien design. (Sequel: *Species II*) ★½ VHS: $9.99

Species II

(1998, 93 min, US, Peter Medak) *Michael Madsen, Natasha Henstridge, Marg Helgenberger, Mykelti Williamson, George Dzundza.* Henstridge returns, this time as Eve, a good half-alien who is the subject of a government research project. But the film's real story concerns as astronaut who contracted deadly alien blood. When he returns to Earth to spread bad DNA through violent sex, it's only a matter of time until he and Eve meet and mate. *Speces II* gives cheesy alien sex and violence a bad name. ★½ DVD: $14.99, VHS: $4.99

Speechless

(1994, 98 min, US, Ron Underwood) *Geena Davis, Michael Keaton, Christopher Reeve, Bonnie Bedelia, Ernie Hudson.* This frothy, lightweight battle-of-the-sexes comedy casts Keaton and Davis as rival candidate speechwriters who become romantically involved. Both suffering from insomnia, they meet cutesy late one night, though unaware of each other's political association. It's difficult to fully appreciate a romantic comedy whose political observations are subtler and more compelling than the love story. As the two love birds, Keaton and Davis rattle off some funny exchanges, but their chemistry is lacking. ★★½ DVD Dual: $14.99

Speed

(1994, 120 min, US, Jan De Bont) *Keanu Reeves, Sandra Bullock, Dennis Hopper, Joe Morton, Jeff Daniels, Alan Ruck.* Reeves stars as a rough-and-ready member of an elite LAPD SWAT team that specializes in disarming the handiwork of even the wiliest of terrorists. Here it's Hopper, who does himself proud as the film's mad bomber. He brews up a brilliant scheme to extort money from the good citizens of L.A. by rigging a bus to blow sky-high if it slows down below 50 mph. Once Reeves boards the ill-fated vehicle and the winning Bullock, a courgeous passenger, takes the wheel, the race is on and the action never slows for a second. Despite several sequences that push the boundaries of believability, the film is an entertaining and often amusing diversion. (Sequel: *Speed 2*) ★★★ DVD Five Star Collection: $26.99, VHS: $9.99, VHS Letterbox: $19.99

Speed 2: Cruise Control

(1997, 121 min, US, Jan De Bont) *Sandra Bullock, Jason Patric, Willem Dafoe, Temuera Morrison, Colleen Camp, Lois Chiles, Tim Conway.* Keanu Reeves smartly said "no" to reprising the role of Jack Traven from *Speed* for its sequel. Bullock, however, returns in this waterlogged, empty-headed encore, this time set on a cruise ship. She's got a new boyfriend (Patric) and once again crosses paths with a mad bomber (the bug-eyed Dafoe). Everything there was to like about the original is absent this second time around. Director De Bont had too much money, too much control and too few ideas. ★ DVD Letterbox: $19.99

Speedway Junky

(1999, 102 min, US, Nickolas Perry) *Jesse Bradford, Jordan Brower, Jonathan Taylor Thomas, Daryl Hannah, Patsy Kensit, Tiffani-Amber Thiessen.* The story of a naïve youth who ventures to the big city and discovers a newfound maturity, though usually at a cost, has long been a favorite of novelists and filmmakers. Few, however, will resort to so many clichés, acts of coincidence and melodramatic devices as writer-director Perry and company do with *Speedway Junky*. Bradford stars as Johnny, a 19-year-old runaway who arrives penniless in Las Vegas and is immediately befriended by a group of polysexual street kids/prostitutes. This includes Eric, a gay orphan who falls for Johnny, and Steven (Thomas), a cocky cynic who tries to get Johnny involved in the business. Perry gives this hard-edged film a slick look that would befit a story about life on the streets, but any visual accomplishment is severely undermined by a screenplay lacking in depth or believability. Thomas tries to smash his TV "Home Improvement" wholesome image, which he does in spite of a rather one-dimensional portrait. ★½ DVD Letterboxed: $24.99

Spellbound

(1945, 111 min, US, Alfred Hitchcock) *Gregory Peck, Ingrid Bergman, Leo G. Carroll.* Peck stars as the victim of a troubling mental paralysis and Bergman is the analyst determined to unlock the door to his mysterious past. An intriguing, trendsetting work with a dazzling dream sequence designed by Salvador Dalí. ★★★½ VHS: $9.99

Spetters

(1981, 123 min, Netherlands, Paul Verhoeven) *Renée Soutendijk, Rutger Hauer.* Three Dutch youths find themselves at the crossroads of adulthood in this arresting drama. Seeking to escape their working-class destinies, they dream of fame and fortune racing motorcycles, but are sidetracked by the fateful intervention of a scheming hash-slinger (the sultry Soutendijk). A penetrating slice-of-life which incorporates first love, youthful shenanigans, teen suicide, coming out and comaraderie. The European version has never been seen theatrically in the United States. (Dutch with English subtitles) ★★★ DVD Unrated Director's Cut: $19.99

Sphere

(1998, 124 min, US, Barry Levinson) *Dustin Hoffman, Sharon Stone, Samuel L. Jackson, Peter Coyote, Liev Schreiber, Queen Latifah.* Based on the Michael Crichton novel, this imaginative if jumbled sci-fi tale is well served by its high-profile cast and excellent production values, which often mask the rambling narrative and confusing scenario. Hoffman, Jackson and Stone are elite scientists who are summoned when a mysterious craft is discovered on the floor of the Pacific Ocean. Setting up home on the sea's bottom, they set out to investigate the ship, which now has a large, shining sphere protecting it. *Sphere* borrows from *The Abyss* and *Forbidden Planet*, though it's the relationships — not the sci-fi element — that provides the most interesting story lines of the film. ★★½ DVD: $14.99, VHS: $14.99, VHS Letterbox: $14.99

Ralph Fiennes in *Spider*

THE DISCERNING FILM LOVER'S GUIDE

Spice World

(1998, 93 min, GB, Bob Spiers) *The Spice Girls, Alan Cumming, Richard E. Grant, George Wendt, Mark McKinney, Roger Moore, Meat Loaf.* A virtual DNA splicing of *A Hard Day's Night* and *Wayne's World*, the campily fun *Spice World* chronicles life on the road with the saucy quintet (Posh, Baby, Scary, Sporty and Ginger). Watch as the Spice Girls crisscross England in their fabulous tour bus to attend cheesy photo sessions and press parties. Cheer as the Spice Girls perform live. Giggle uncontrollably to their pure, unironically humorous sketches and some fairly acute one-liners. Never mind the uneven pacing, the static direction or characters as deep as a puddle of leftover syrup after a pancake breakfast; just shamefully revel in the overall Spice Girls persona. Surprisingly watchable, *Spice World* is absolutely bubblelicious. ★★★ DVD: $14.99, VHS: $9.99

Spices

(1986, 98 min, India, Ketan Mehta) Set in 1940s British-controlled India, this engaging melodrama deals with the beginnings of the nationalistic rumblings of the colony and specifically one community's reaction to the plight of an oppressed woman. Sanbai, a young, defiant beauty, spurns the advances of a sudebar, the military-backed tax collection force, and is forced to take refuge against his wrath. Initially fearful and reluctant to help, the men and women of the village must make a stand against the injustice and tyranny of a belligerent oppressor. (Hindi with English subtitles) ★★★ VHS: $29.99

Spider

(2003, 98 min, Canada, David Cronenberg) *Ralph Fiennes, Miranda Richardson, Gabriel Byrne, Lynn Redgrave, Bradley Hall, John Neville.* A fascinating, subtly disturbing drama, *Spider* ranks with Cronenberg's and Fiennes' best work. Fiennes is Spider, a just-released mental patient who's been locked up for 20 years. The halfway house he's been assigned is, unfortunately, in his old neighborhood, thus stirring up painful childhood memories. These scenes (flashbacks? fabrications?) are superbly realized, with the older Spider observing himself as a child (played by the amazing Hall). Cronenberg's visualization of Spider's tortured memories and dawning self-realization are enhanced greatly by spot-on art direction and another terrific score by Howard Shore. Fiennes — mumbling semi-coherently, doodling indecipherably in his notebook — is wholly convincing, and he's matched by Byrne and the wonderful Richardson in three roles. *Spider*'s view of schizophrenia won't bring to mind *A Beautiful Mind*'s symmetry, but it weaves a rich, haunting examination of the fragility of the human mind all the same. ★★★★ DVD: $19.99

Spider-Man

(2002, 121 min, US, Sam Raimi) *Tobey Maguire, Kirsten Dunst, Willem Dafoe, James Franco, Cliff Robertson, Rosemary Harris, J.K. Simmons, Bill Nunn, Bruce Campbell.* Mild-mannered high schooler-cum-newspaper photographer Peter Parker (Maguire) is bit by a mutant spider, enabling him to climb walls, beat up bullies and swing from buildings with his sticky web. This happens just in time, too, as scientist Norman Osborne (Dafoe) has gone a bit nuts, ready to destroy New York City via his alter ego

Kirsten Dunst greets "your friendly neighborhood" *Spider-Man* (Tobey Maguire)

Green Goblin. And, oh yes, Peter's in danger of never winning the heart of his high school crush, Mary Jane (Dunst). Ultimately, all superheros have some similarities; so *Spider-Man* can be forgiven for some familiarity. Focusing on the familial relationships and the coming-of-age of the young (and surprisingly sexually charged) characters, the film's big selling point, of course, is the web-slinging and swinging. A beefed-up Maguire is able to carry both the strength of Spider-Man and the meekness of Peter Parker, and Dafoe is just enough over-the-top to be able to emote from behind the Green Goblin's mask. As a whole, it does the trick, popcorn-ready summer entertainment and the foundation for a franchise that's long overdue. (Sequel: *Spider-Man 2*) ★★★ DVD Letterbox 2-disc set: $19.99, DVD Letterbox Limited Edition 2-disc Deluxe Version: $24.99, DVD Pan & Scan 2-disc Special Edition: $19.99, VHS: $24.99

The Spider's Stratagem

(1970, 97 min, Italy, Bernardo Bertolucci) *Giulio Brogi, Alida Valli.* This stylish and intelligent political thriller, taken from a Jorge Luis Borges short story, follows a young man's journey to the village of his youth. There he finds the statue of his father (a hero killed 30 years earlier by anti-fascists) has been defaced and the townsfolk mysteriously hostile. While attempting to discover the truth about his father, he soon finds himself entangled in an increasingly complex web of lies, mysteries and omens. Magnificently staged by director Bertolucci. (Italian with English subtitles) ★★★★ VHS: $29.99

Spiders

(1919, 137 min, Germany, Fritz Lang) Planned as the first installment of a four-part adventure serial, Lang produced only this one entry, a wildly exotic forerunner to the *Indiana Jones* trilogy. With tongue-in-cheek humor, our hero must battle the arch-criminal Lio-Shar and his unsavory gang, the Spiders, as they search for lost Inca treasure. Filled with scenes of lost civilizations, human sacrifice and pirates, this big-budget action silent is very interesting and one of the ear-

liest surviving films of the great German filmmaker. (Silent with musical soundtrack) ★★★ DVD: $29.99, VHS: $24.99

Spiders

(2000, 94 min, US, Gary Jones) *Lana Parrilla, Oliver Macready, Josh Green.* Crazy military men inject spiders with alien DNA to create the one-billionth movie "ultimate biological weapon." Shockingly, things go awry, and a mutated spider escapes. Moronic, badly acted cheese is pretty slow for a good half hour, but once the spiders show up, it becomes an entertaining (though still moronic and badly acted) *Aliens* rip-off with better-than-average effects for a low-budget horror flick, plenty of action and a sizable "yecch!" factor. ★★½ DVD: $24.99

Spies

(1928, 88 min, Germany, Fritz Lang) Lang's fascination with futuristic technology, expressionistic design and sweeping adventure reaches a high point in this enthralling spy thriller featuring an evil criminal mastermind and agent #326, a suave super agent. (Silent) ★★★ DVD: $19.99

Spies Like Us

(1985, 103 min, US, John Landis) *Chevy Chase, Dan Akyroyd, Bruce Davison.* Until *Nothing But Trouble* came along, this inferior spy comedy was at the bottom of the film pile for Chase and Aykroyd. The guys play bumbling CIA agents who, let loose in the Middle East to serve as decoys, nearly start WWIII. ★½ DVD: $14.99, VHS: $14.99

Spike of Bensonhurst

(1988, 100 min, US, Paul Morrissey) *Sasha Mitchell, Ernest Borgnine, Geraldine Smith, Sylvia Miles.* Written and directed by ex-Warholite Morrissey, this mob comedy stars Mitchell as Spike Fumo, an ambitiously arrogant yet charming two-bit boxer who, on sheer chutzpa, tries to climb his way to the top. Borgnine is great as the befuddled neighborhood don who must contend with Spike after his WASPy daughter falls under his seductively dangerous charms. Miles steals a few scenes as a coke-sniffing congresswoman. ★★★

579

Spin the Bottle

(1999, 83 min, US, Jamie Yerkes) *Jessica Faller, Heather Goldenhersh, Mitchell Riggs, Kim Winter, Holter Graham.* What begins as a pleasant reunion of five childhood friends at a remote lakeside lodge soon escalates into a weekend of tense emotions, sexual hijinks and subtle but effective revenge. This engaging if somewhat underdeveloped comedy-drama brings together the recently engaged Ted (Riggs) and Bev (Winter); the vampish Alex (Faller); the comically co-dependent/manic depressive Rachel (Goldenhersch); and Jonah (Graham) the former wimp now grown into a hunk. When the chickens come home to roost, an innocent game of Spin the Bottle unleashes sexual secrets, brings about frantic bed hopping and allows one person to get some long-awaited retribution. Good acting, some bitchy dialogue and a personable cast help elevate this above the generic twentysomething tale. ★★½ DVD: $14.99, VHS: $9.99

The Spiral Staircase

(1946, 83 min, US, Robert Siodmak) *Dorothy McGuire, George Brent, Ethel Barrymore, Kent Smith, Rhonda Fleming, Elsa Lanchester.* McGuire gives a superlative performance as a mute servant in this eerie psychological thriller based on the novel "Some Must Watch" by Ethel Lina White. Helen Capel (McGuire), who has not spoken since childhood, is housekeeper for the rich Mrs. Warren (Barrymore) and her family. Helen's life is soon put in danger when a series of murders target the disabled — and strange occurrences begin happening at the Warren household. Atmospheric, suspenseful and marvelously acted. (Remade in 1975) ★★★½

Spirit of '76

(1991, 82 min, US, Lucas Reiner) *David Cassidy, Olivia d'Abo, Julie Brown, Tommy Chong, Carl Reiner, Rob Reiner.* Time machine inventor Cassidy sets sail back through time to the year 1776 to retrieve the Constitution of the United States — and other remnants of our past — with the hopes of saving Earth from a cold, grey future. By mistake, however, our traveler winds up in the year 1976 where he encounters a world of Pop Rocks, disco and mood rings. Lightweight with the occasional laugh, the film features a good supporting cast that has more familiar faces than a "Love Boat" episode. ★★ DVD Letterbox: $19.99

The Spirit of St. Louis

(1957, 138 min, US, Billy Wilder) *James Stewart, Patricia Smith.* Stewart's absorbing portrayal of aviator Charles Lindbergh highlights this interesting though overlong look at the flyer's early years and his historic, transatlantic flight. ★★½

Spirit of the Beehive

(1973, 95 min, Spain, Victor Erice) *Fernando Gomez, Teresa Gimpera, Ana Torrent.* An unforgettable and hypnotic drama by first-time director Erice, and one that features moving performances by two young girls, both nonprofessional actors. In a remote Castilian village, two children watching *Frankenstein* at a traveling film show become entranced by the image of the monster. The younger girl, a sensitive eight-year-old, believing that he is the spirit of the monster, discovers and befriends a fugitive soldier just before he is captured. A haunting and poetic mood piece. (Spanish with English subtitles) ★★★½ VHS: $29.99

Spirited Away

(2002, 124 min, Japan, Hayao Miyazaki) Japanese filmmaker Miyazaki is telling some of the most creative stories in contemporary animated cinema. And with *Spirited Away*, he transports viewers into an even deeper realm of imagination than his previous work, *Princess Mononoke*. When a vacationing family comes across a mysterious cave in the woods, the parents stop to explore. To their daughter's dismay, the parents discover a ghost town and indulge in lavish feasts mysteriously set before them. What happens next starts the daughter on a magical and bizarre journey through a spirit land to help resolve her parent's missteps. The colors are rich, the animation detailed and the characters are truly imaginative. A film about one's connection to roots and family and the importance of those elements, *Spirited Away* makes for one richly rewarding animated experience. ★★★★ DVD 2-disc set: $29.99, VHS Dubbed: $19.99

Spirits of the Dead (Histoires Extraordinaires)

(1967, 117 min, France, Federico Fellini, Louis Malle, Roger Vadim) *Jane Fonda, Peter Fonda, Alain Delon, Terence Stamp, Brigitte Bardot.* An anthology film nominally based on three short stories by Edgar Allan Poe, this mélange of '60s-style, Felliniesque grotesquerie and soft-core eroticism

only lives up to its title in its final segment. Fonda is the object of Vadim obsession in the first story, *Metzengerstein*, about a young countess who believes that her dead cousin has been reincarnated as a magnificent black horse. The second story, *William Wilson*, by Malle, stars Delon as a young libertine whose debaucheries are continually foiled by a mysterious doppelganger. The third story, *Toby Dammit*, directed by Fellini, is the best. Stamp is an alcoholic and egocentric English actor haunted by the vision of a young girl playing with a bouncing ball. Only Fellini's segment captures the true spirit of Poe. (French with English subtitles) ★★½ DVD: $19.99, VHS: $19.99

Spitfire

(1934, 94 min, US, John Cromwell) *Katharine Hepburn, Robert Young, Ralph Bellamy.* Hepburn plays an uninhibited South Carolina mountain woman who evokes the wrath of the local townsfolk when she kidnaps a baby from its mother because she feels it's not being properly cared for. Unusual and occasionally compelling. ★★½

The Spitfire Grill

(1996, 111 min, US, Lee David Zlotoff) *Alison Elliott, Ellen Burstyn, Will Patton, Marcia Gay Harden, Kieran Mulroney.* Sentimental and deliberately paced, *The Spitfire Grill* is a heartwarming though manipulative tearjerker about an ex-con and her profound impact on a small town in Maine. The multiple story lines of determined women trying to establish their place in the world is right out of *Fried Green Tomatoes*, but the film at least distinguishes itself with solid female bonding, homespun wisdom and beautiful scenery. Elliott is a marvel as Percy, a stranger with a secret who acts as catalyst to unlock the mysteries of the town's most prominent residents. She can be moving even in the hokiest of scenes. There's an absorbing drama at work here if you can get past the melodramatic excess and contrived ending. ★★½ DVD: $14.99

Spitting Image

(1987, 60 min, GB, Graham C. Williams) Few American political satires are as scathing, astute or plain darned funny as Britain's *Spitting Image*, the now-famous puppet show which uses grotesque caricatures of prominent public figures to lampoon their policies and pretensions. The programs are filled with fantastic images, rapid-fire dialogue and outrageous musical numbers. Each of the music video shorts hits its target squarely. Keep your eye on the screen — it moves fast. ★★★½ VHS: $24.99

Splash

(1984, 109 min, US, Ron Howard) *Tom Hanks, Daryl Hannah, John Candy, Eugene Levy.* Director Howard and stars Hanks and Hannah hit it big with this charming comedy about a businessman (Hanks) who falls in love with a mermaid (Hannah). Candy has some amusing scenes as Hank's cohort. ★★★ DVD 20th Anniversary: $29.99, VHS: $9.99

Splendor in the Grass

(1961, 124 min, US, Elia Kazan) *Natalie Wood, Warren Beatty, Sandy Dennis, Phyllis Diller.* Beginning with screendom's first French kiss, this lyrical and delicate examination of youthful love and the heartache and joy that accompanies it is somewhat sentimental, but after nearly 40 years it's still a heartbreaking and timeless story. Wood, in her most accomplished performance, and Beatty, in his screen debut, star as young lovers in 1920s Kansas who are hopelessly trapped by overbearing parents,

Hayao Miyazaki's *Spirited Away*

social class lines and the boundaries of first love. Director Kazan handles his actors and story with great sensitivity, and William Inge won an Oscar for his insightful screenplay. ★★★½ DVD: $19.99

Split Decisions

(1988, 95 min, US, David Drury) *Gene Hackman, Jeff Fahey, Craig Sheffer.* Heavy-handed boxing drama about three generations of fighters, with a *Rocky* slant, as the youngest takes to the ring to avenge his brother's death. ★★ VHS: $14.99

Split Image

(1982, 111 min, US, Ted Kotcheff) *James Woods, Michael O'Keefe, Dennis Hopper, Brian Dennehy, Karen Allen.* A well-acted drama with college student O'Keefe joining Hopper's cult to be with Allen. Dad Dennehy hires deprogrammer Woods to get him back. Good performances accentuate this compelling story. ★★★

Split Second

(1992, 90 min, GB, Tony Maylam) *Rutger Hauer, Kim Cattrall, Neil Duncan, Pete Postlethwaite.* London in the year 2008 is the setting for this *Lethal Weapon*-meets-*Alien* rip-off which, while woefully unoriginal, winds up being entertaining and, at times, very funny. A potbellied Hauer continually growls, grimaces and "lives on anxiety, caffeine and chocolate" in his pursuit of a serial killer. Duncan is Hauer's overeducated new partner. Two questions: Why does the Dutch actor playing a British cop have an American accent and what is "Nights in White Satin" doing all over the soundtrack? ★★½

Splitting Heirs

(1993, 86 min, US/GB, Robert Young) *Eric Edle, Rick Moranis, Barbara Hershey, John Cleese.* Idle stars as a poor Cockney schlub who discovers one fateful day that he is the true heir to a vast dukedom and that the Pakistani family that raised him since infancy is not his real family (gasp!). Such is the level of humor in this execrable attempt at cross-breeding Monty Python with "The Corsican Brothers." Moranis is the cretinous American yuppie who, having been switched at birth with the unfortunate heir, has usurped Idle's rightful title as "Duke of Something-or-Other" and is none too willing to return it. ★ VHS: $9.99

Spring Forward

(1999, 110 min, US, Tom Gilroy) *Ned Beatty, Liev Schreiber, Campbell Scott, Ian Hart, Peri Gilpin, Bill Raymond, Catherine Kellner.* A terrific little gem, *Spring Forward* is a simple, low-key, wonderfully acted drama that displays a healthy dose of humor. Ex-con Schreiber and near-retiree Beatty (both superb) play Parks and Recreation workers who form an unlikely friendship over the course of a year. Though that's it for plot, it matters little for this is about the two men's relationship, and it's a joy to see these underused actors rise to the occasion. They have real chemistry together, so that by its quietly moving ending, the film has earned its emotions, not manufactured them. Filled with great moments and scenes and some excellent cameos. ★★★½ DVD Dual: $14.99

Spring Symphony

(1984, 102 min, Germany, Peter Schamoni) *Nastassja Kinski, Rolf Hoppe.* The passionate life and musical genius of German composer Robert Schumann is featured in this interesting if familiar drama. While a student, Schumann becomes violently involved with his teacher's daughter, pianist Clare Wieck (Kinski). Their affair threatens the teacher who becomes jealous and forces young Kinski to choose between family, love of her music and desire. (Filmed in English) ★★½ DVD: $24.99, VHS: $19.99

Springtime in the Rockies

(1942, 91 min, US, Irving Cummings) *Betty Grable, John Payne, Carmen Miranda, Charlotte Greenwood, Cesar Romero, Edward Everett Horton, Jackie Gleason.* Grable is at her best in this blithe musical comedy about a bickering theatrical couple at a mountain resort. Miranda is as delightful as ever. ★★★ VHS: $19.99

Der Sprinter

(1985, 90 min, Germany, Christoph Böll) *Wieland Samolak.* A witty social satire about a young closeted gay man who, in order to please his mother, decides to be "normal." Samolak portrays our confused hero, a pale, wide-eyed young man with expressionistic silent film star looks and a charming comedic touch. He chooses sports, specifically running, as his entrance into the straight world. His attempts at sports produce little until he meets and falls in love with a buxom butch female shot putter. (German with English subtitles) ★★★

Sprung

(1997, 108 min, US, Rusty Cundieff) *Tisha Campbell, Rusty Cundieff, Paula Jay Parker, Joe Torry.* A repellent, unfunny comedy about gold-digging women and shallow, sex-obsessed men. There's no plot, no laughs, just four jerks flailing through a series of completely illogical, annoying situations. After his very funny *Fear of a Black Hat* and the stylish *Tales from the Hood*, director Cundieff definitely takes a major step backwards with this one. It's really a shame that while African-Americans have a larger role (relatively speaking) in studio film production in the '90s, most of the output is either gangsta violence or lame sex comedies like *Sprung.* And this one's worse than most. ★ DVD: $9.99

Spun

(2002, 101 min, US, Jonas Akerlund) *John Leguizamo, Jason Schwartzman, Mena Suvari, Brittany Murphy, Patrick Fugit, Mickey Rourke, Alexis Arquette, Deborah Harry, Eric Roberts, Peter Stormare.* A movie on speed about kids on speed, *Spun* starts out in high gear and keeps on truckin'. Following four days in the life of Ross (Schwartzman), who has flittered away a relationship with his beautiful girlfriend by getting hooked on methamphetamines, the film is both cautionary and comically caustic in its approach. Akerlund's carnival ride is filled to the brim with quirky characters including strippers, drug-addicted cops, lesbian neighbors and various sleazy hangers-on. But it centers around Ross and the people he meets when he heads to his dealer's house to score more speed. Akerlund has made a scarringly sexy, revved-up look at drug users that doesn't dig too deep below the surface but also does little to glamorize its characters' lives. It's kind of a fun roller coaster ride, getting under your skin with its screwball feel, its speed-induced dream sequences and its low-budget subversiveness. Yes, much of this has been done before (see the better *Trainspotting*), but that doesn't keep this story from being a thrilling enterprise. ★★★ DVD Unrated Director's Cut: $19.99, VHS R-rated Edited Version: $14.99

Spy Game

(2001, 127 min, US, Tony Scott) *Robert Redford, Brad Pitt, Catherine McCormack, Stephen Dillane, Larry Bryggman, Marianne Jean-Baptiste, David Hemmings, Charlotte Rampling.* Director Scott makes the most of this exciting espionage thriller whose tight, compelling screenplay is smartly performed and often shrewdly observed. Back in form in a role reminiscent of his *Three Days of the Condor*, Redford plays Nathan Muir, a CIA operative whose retirement is put on hold when he learns his protégé Tom Bishop (Pitt) has been captured in China and sentenced to death. With few resources and from across the globe, Muir has 24 hours to set in motion a plan to save Bishop and fend off the agency who wants nothing to do with the captured spy. The complex tale also flashbacks to when the two men first met, and Bishop's eventual tutoring under Muir. The story flows easily from past to present and back again, enabling the viewer to savor all the intrigue from the back alleys of foreign lands to the round tables of Washington, D.C. ★★★ DVD Letterbox Collector's Edition: $14.99, DVD Pan & Scan Collector's Edition: $14.99, VHS: $9.99

Spy Hard

(1996, 81 min, US, Rick Friedberg) *Leslie Nielsen, Nicollette Sheridan, Charles Durning, Andy Griffith.* This *really* stupid comedy, executive-produced by its star Nielsen, doesn't come close in duplicating the hilarity level of the *Naked Gun* films. Nielsen plays Agent WD-40 (har har), assigned to stop his arch-nemesis (Griffith) from blowing up the world. En route, the film lampoons almost every hit of the 1990s. There are a few laughs to be had, but even the best of these would only be middling fare in a *Naked Gun* comedy. Nielsen tries hard, but the writers let him down. ★★ DVD: $14.99, VHS: $9.99

The Spy in Black

(1939, 82 min, GB, Michael Powell) *Conrad Veidt, Valerie Hobson.* Veidt plays a German naval officer and spy in this intriguing tale of espionage set amidst the moors of Scotland during WWI. Legendary director Powell adds his spice with a series of ingenious plot-twists and a keen eye for romance. ★★★

Spy Kids

(2001, 88 min, Robert Rodriguez) *Antonio Banderas, Carla Gugino, Alexa Vega, Daryl Sabara, Alan Cumming, Teri Hatcher, Cheech Marin, Danny Trejo, Robert Patrick, Tony Shalhoub.* Nothing like parenthood to turn a bloodshed-loving individual into a sanguine family man. And so we find *Desperado*'s director and star infiltrating the kiddie market with the high-powered family values flick *Spy Kids*. Full of James Bond-style gadgets, big chases and bloodless action scenes, there's plenty here to keep young and old engaged for the concise running time. Banderas and Gugino play retired, married spies who go on one last mission. When they're kidnapped, it's up to their two children to rescue them. Positive messages abound, sure to unite such disparate groups as Latinos and conservatives in their praise. Yet Rodriguez's breathtaking and efficient camera trickery is evident in every frame, giving film buffs plenty to cheer about as well. (Sequel: *Spy Kids 2: The Island of Lost Dreams*) ★★★ DVD: $19.99, VHS Letterbox: $14.99, VHS Pan & Scan: $14.99

William Holden in *Stalag 17*

Spy Kids 2: The Island of Lost Dreams

(2002, 100 min, US, Robert Rodriguez) *Antonio Banderas, Carla Gugino, Alexa Vega, Daryl Sabara, Mike Judge, Ricardo Montalban, Cheech Marin, Steve Buscemi, Danny Trejo, Alan Cumming, Tony Shalhoub.* With more emphasis on the kids and less on Mom and Dad, this sequel finds the intrepid siblings gadgeting their way around an island lair ruled by . . . gasp! Buscemi. He plays an evil scientist whose new invention could destroy the world, and it's up to two precocious, underage spies to stop him. *Spy Kids 2* is more fun for the whole family, and hip enough for adults, too. (Sequel: *Spy Kids 3-D: Game Over*) ★★★ DVD Letterbox Collector's Series: $14.99, VHS: $22.99

The Spy Who Came in from the Cold

(1965, 112 min, US, Martin Ritt) *Richard Burton, Claire Bloom, Oskar Werner.* This adaptation of John LeCarre's novel is every bit as cold as the Cold War intrigue it chronicles — and that's what makes it so good. Burton is an embittered agent who's as much a sacrificial pawn as anything — and he knows it. Bloom is the woman who can still see him through his alcoholic haze, only to be tragically betrayed. One of Burton's best performances. ★★★½ DVD Letterbox: $14.99

The Spy Who Loved Me

(1977, 125 min, GB, Lewis Gilbert) *Roger Moore, Barbara Bach, Richard Kiel.* One of the best of the Moore Bond films, this scintillating spy thriller pairs 007 with a seductive Russian agent (Bach) to quash an arch-villain's plans for world destruction — does he ever do anything else? Kiel is featured as the seven-foot henchman Jaws. (Sequel: *Moonraker*) ★★★

Square Dance

(1987, 112 min, US, Daniel Petrie) *Winona Ryder, Jane Alexander, Jason Robards, Rob Lowe.* Well-acted drama about a young farm girl's coming of age when she runs away from home to live with her estranged mother in the city. Ryder gives a superb performance as the young girl, as does Alexander as her mom, and Robards as her grandfather. Lowe gives a surprisingly effective portrayal of a young retarded man. ★★★ DVD Letterbox: $9.99

Squeeze

(1997, 89 min, US, Robert Patton-Spruill) *Tyrone Burton, Eddie Cutanda, Phuong Duong, Russell G. Jones.* An earnest melodrama about a trio of Boston kids who must choose between dealing drugs or living a crime-free life, *Squeeze* marks the impressive debut of writer-director Patton-Spruill. As Ty (Burton), a 14-year-old black youth, and his crew, Hector (Cutanda), a Puerto Rican, and Bao (Duong), a Vietnamese, try to earn money by pumping gas, they are taunted by Tommy (Jones), a gang leader who forces them to make some tough decisions about their futures. The sweeping camerawork and nervy acting by the three leads contribute to the overall grittiness of this hard-hitting film. ★★★ DVD Letterbox: $19.99, VHS: $9.99

The Squeeze

(1987, 102 min, US, Roger Young) *Michael Keaton, Rae Dawn Chong.* Inferior comedy with Keaton as a down-on-his-luck con man who joins forces with an aspiring detective (Chong) to investigate a murder which implicates Keaton's ex-wife. ★½ VHS: $14.99

Stage Door

(1937, 92 min, US, Gregory La Cava) *Katharine Hepburn, Ginger Rogers, Andrea Leeds, Lucille Ball, Eve Arden, Ann Miller, Adolphe Menjou.* Hepburn and Rogers are just two of the inhabitants of the Footlights Club, a boarding house for aspiring starlets. Fast, witty repartee and uniformly fine performances highlight this story of a wealthy newcomer (Hepburn) trying to break into show business and gain acceptance from her new companions. Menjou is superb as a suave and lecherous producer. Based on the play by Edna Ferber and George S. Kaufman. ★★★★

Favorite Line: "The calla lilies are in bloom again. Such a strange flower, suitable to any occasion. I carried them on my wedding day and now I place them here in memory of something that has died." —*Katharine Hepburn as Terry Randall*

Stage Struck

(1958, 95 min, US, Sidney Lumet) *Henry Fonda, Susan Strasberg, Joan Greenwood, Christopher Plummer.* Mild remake of *Morning Glory*, suffering most from Strasberg's less-than-inspired performance as a struggling actress determined to become a star. ★★

Stagecoach

(1939, 97 min, US, John Ford) *John Wayne, Claire Trevor, John Carradine, Andy Devine, Thomas Mitchell.* Director Ford, with one masterful stroke, took the western, heretofore a "B" programmer, and with sweeping panoramas, landmark use of camera and editing techniques, superlative action sequences and strong character development, elevated the genre to a singular American art form. Wayne heads a consummate cast in this story of a group of disparate travelers heading west by stagecoach, besieged by Indian attacks and internal conflict. Mitchell won an Oscar for his stirring portrayal of a drunken doctor. (Remade in 1966) ★★★★ DVD: $19.99, VHS: $9.99

Stairway to Heaven

(1946, 104 min, GB, Emeric Pressburger & Michael Powell) *David Niven, Kim Hunter, Raymond Massey, Roger Livesey, Richard Attenborough.* Classic WWII film which brilliantly balances reality and fantasy with Niven as a downed pilot who goes before a Heavenly court to argue he was taken before his time. (aka: *A Matter of Life and Death*) ★★★★

Stakeout

(1987, 115 min, US, John Badham) *Richard Dreyfuss, Emilio Estevez, Madeline Stowe, Aidan Quinn.* Dreyfuss and Estevez team up as a pair of cops assigned to keep an eye on a beautiful woman (Stowe) whose ex-boyfriend (Quinn) escaped from jail, leaving a trail of bodies behind him. Complications arise when Dreyfuss falls in love with their subject. Dreyfuss and Estevez have a wonderful chemistry which heightens the enjoyment of this entertaining comic thriller. (Sequel: *Another Stakeout*) ★★★ DVD: $14.99, VHS: $9.99

Stalag 17

(1953, 120 min, US, Billy Wilder) *William Holden, Don Taylor, Otto Preminger, Robert Strauss, Harvey Lembeck, Peter Graves, Sig Ruman.* The quintessential POW film. Holden deservedly won an Oscar for his knockout performance as a cynical prisoner of war suspected of leaking secrets to his German captors. Alternately funny and suspenseful, director Wilder keeps the action moving at a remarkable pace, and allows the viewer to feel the confines of the barracks without a moment of claustrophobia. ★★★★ DVD: $14.99, VHS: $9.99

Stalingrad

(1993, 150 min, Germany, Joseph Vilsmaier) *Dominique Horwitz, Thomas Kretschmann, Jochen Nickel, Sebastian Rudolph.* This stunning German production follows a group of soldiers from Italy to the snowy steppes of Russia in their futile attempt to capture the city of Stalingrad in what was one of the bloodiest battles of WWII. Much like *Das Boot* or *Cross of Iron*, the film's narrative features some unlikely heroes: German soldiers. Vividly and authentically drawn, with a diversity of motivations and moralities, the script avoids making each character a cliché. (German with English subtitles) ★★★½ DVD: $34.99, VHS Subtitled: $29.99

Stalker

(1979, 160 min, Russia, Andrei Tarkovsky) *Alexander Kaidanovsky, Nikolai Grinko, Anatoli Solonitsin, Alice Friendlich.* A stark, hallucinatory work that formulates a tormented vision of postapocalyptic existence. The film revolves around a mysterious, government-restricted "Zone" where a meteor shower has altered the rules of nature. Rumor abounds that within the Zone is a "Room" which holds the "Truth" and can fulfill one's deepest desires, but it is only with the aid of a physically gifted guide, or "Stalker," that the dangerous, forbidden area can be reached. What this nightmarish sci-fi film lacks in pacing is made up in its startling, psychedelic imagery. (Russian with English subtitles) ★★★★ DVD 2-disc set: $49.99, VHS: $19.99

The Stalking Moon

(1969, 109 min, US, Robert Mulligan) *Gregory Peck, Eva Marie Saint, Robert Forster.* Peck plays an Army scout who escorts Saint, captured years before by the Indians, and her young half-breed son home — with the boy's father in pursuit. The story's good premise is only occasionally realized, though the two stars work well together. ★★½ VHS: $14.99

The Stand

(1994, 360 min, US, Mick Garris) *Gary Sinise, Rob Lowe, Ruby Dee, Ossie Davis, Laura San Giacomo, Ray Walston, Miguel Ferrer.* Based on the best-seller by Stephen King, this epic six-hour made-for-TV adaptation is typical King: fascinating, excessive, fantastical, impulsive and imaginative, with its fair share of slow moments. Set in modern times, the story begins as a virus wipes out 99% of the planet's population. While some survivors (mostly white) are spiritually drawn to a kindly, psychic old black woman (wonderfully played by Dee), others answer the calling of the devil incarnate. ★★★ DVD: $19.99, VHS: $14.99

Stand and Deliver

(1987, 105 min, US, Ramon Menendez) *Edward James Olmos, Lou Diamond Phillips, Rosana De Soto, Andy Garcia.* Olmos gives an outstanding performance as a strict public school math teacher who commits himself to his East L.A. students as they prepare for a difficult mathematics test. He is ultimately able to instill a pride and confidence in the previously unrecognized. Moving tribute to the tenacity of Jaime Escalante, the real-life teacher on whom the story is based. ★★★ DVD: $9.99

Stand by Me

(1986, 87 min, US, Rob Reiner) *Wil Wheaton, River Phoenix, Corey Feldman, Jerry O'Connell, Kiefer Sutherland, Richard Dreyfuss.* This sweet-natured reminiscence is set in the late 1950s and concerns the misadventures of four pubescent boys who set out in search of the body of a young boy killed in a train accident. Based on the Stephen King novella, "The Body." Reiner's enchanting observation on the predilection of (specifically male) youth is winsome, articulate and refreshingly entertaining. ★★★½ DVD Special Edition: $19.99

Stand-In

(1937, 91 min, US, Tay Garnett) *Humphrey Bogart, Leslie Howard, Joan Blondell.* In this amusing show-biz comedy, Howard plays an efficiency expert who is dispatched to Hollywood to save a studio from financial ruin. Not knowing the business, he enlists the aid of former child star Blondell and boozy producer Bogart. Bogie is surprisingly funny in his first comedic role, and Blondell is, as always, sassy and smart. ★★★

Stand-Off

(1989, 97 min, Hungary, Gyula Gazdag) *Ary Beri, Gabor Svidrony, István Szabó.* Filmed in documentary-like fashion, this suspenseful thriller recounts the actions of an 18-year-old Hungarian youth who, along with his younger brother, enters a student dormitory near the Hungarian border and holds 16 girls hostage. Their demands: a flight out of Budapest, $1,000,000 and eventual freedom in the West. (Hungarian with English subtitles) ★★★ VHS: $79.99

Standing in the Shadows of Motown

(2002, 116 min, US, Paul Justman) *Richard 'Pistol' Allen, Jack Ashford, Bob Babbitt, Benny 'Papa Zita', Eddie 'Bongo' Brown, Johnnie Griffith, Bootsy Collins, Ben Harper.* In the 1960s, Motown Records ruled the pop radio airwaves. Their stars were/are household names, though the musicians who played on their records went largely uncredited. That is until now. In this fascinating documentary that is as informative as it is entertaining, The Funk Brothers — the dynamic house band for Motown who collaborated with every big name from The Supremes to Stevie Wonder to The

Temptations — finally get their due. These guys had a rythym section that resembled in depth of sound a symphony orchestra rather than a rock 'n' roll band. The stories recalled are compelling, funny and historic, but it's the performances by the now-aged group that will get your feet tapping, memories rushing and spirits soaring. An exhilarating, fitting tribute to a group of musical legends. ★★★½ DVD 2-disc set: $14.99, VHS: $14.99

Stanley & Iris

(1990, 103 min, US, Martin Ritt) *Jane Fonda, Robert De Niro, Swoosie Kurtz, Martha Plimpton.* The title protagonists have monotonous, dead-end factory jobs; Iris (Fonda) on one of the production lines, Stanley (De Niro) in the company kitchen. She's a widow raising two children. He's trying to function in the world while hiding his illiteracy. The film develops a nice rhythm as the details of their separate lives start to intertwine and mesh, changing midway to an almost fairy-tale conclusion. ★★★ DVD: $14.99

Stanley and Livingstone

(1939, 101 min, US, Henry King) *Spencer Tracy, Cedric Hardwicke, Nancy Kelly, Walter Brennan.* Tracy gives a stirring performance as Stanley searching for missionary Livingstone (Hardwicke) lost in darkest Africa at the turn of the century. A vastly entertaining '30s biopic. ★★★

The Star

(1952, 89 min, US, Stuart Heisler) *Bette Davis, Sterling Hayden, Natalie Wood.* A ninth Oscar nomination for Best Actress went to Davis for her solid portrayal of a fading movie queen in this vitriolic Hollywood melodrama. Though Davis herself was at the time experiencing sort of a "comeback," there is no real parallel between the legendary actress and her character of Margaret Elliott, though certain similarities are open to interpretation. ★★★ VHS: $19.99

The Star Chamber

(1983, 109 min, US, Peter Hyams) *Michael Douglas, Hal Holbrook, Yaphet Kotto, Sharon Gless.* Douglas is a judge frustrated at the number of lowlifes our judicial system lets free on mere technicalities. What will he do when he finds himself invited to join a clandestine organization of like-minded litigants? An intriguing premise is half-heartedly explored making this a thinking man's thriller without a lot of smarts to it. ★★½ VHS: $9.99

Star 80

(1983, 102 min, US, Bob Fosse) *Mariel Hemingway, Cliff Robertson, Eric Roberts.* Never one to avoid controversy, Fosse picks apart the trappings of the American Dream in this unsettling account of a fantasy gone haywire. Hemingway portrays Dorothy Stratten, the peaches-and-cream Canadian girl whose taste of stardom was all too brief. The film's greatest strength lies in the performance of Roberts, whose calculating swagger and coiled intensity are frightfully ominous. ★★★½ DVD: $14.99, VHS: $14.99

A Star Is Born

(1937, 111 min, US, William Wellman) *Janet Gaynor, Fredric March, Adolphe Menjou, May Robson.* The original of the story of Esther Blodgett, an aspiring actress who marries matinee idol Norman Maine: her career takes off, his career fizzles. Gaynor had one of her best roles as Blodgett, bringing freshness and charm to the role, and March is outstanding as the fading star Maine. Dorothy

Parker and Alan Campbell were two of the writers. Digitally remastered from an archives print. (Remade in 1954 and in 1976) ★★★½ DVD: $29.99, VHS: $24.99

A Star Is Born

(1954, 175 min, US, George Cukor) *Judy Garland, James Mason, Jack Carson, Tom Noonan, Charles Bickford.* Director Cukor often referred to *A Star Is Born* as his "butchered masterpiece" because the studio cut nearly 30 minutes from the finished film just weeks after its successful opening in 1954. After years of painstaking research and compilation, the film was restored to its original release length. The immortal Garland gives her finest performance, both vocally and dramatically, as Vicki Lester, the young songstress who rockets to stardom upon discovery by matinee idol Mason. Mason is equally brilliant as Norman Maine, the fading star who falls in love with Judy. One of the many songs is the unforgettable "The Man That Got Away." ★★★★ DVD Letterbox: $19.99

A Star Is Born

(1976, 140 min, US, Frank Pierson) *Barbra Streisand, Kris Kristofferson, Paul Mazursky, Gary Busey, Sally Kirkland.* Though this second remake of the classic romance was dubbed by those-less-kind as "A Bore Is Starred," it's not *quite* as bad as that suggests. Streisand takes over the Janet Gaynor/Judy Garland role as an aspiring singer whose romance with a faltering rock star leads to tragedy. Kristofferson is the fading star. The least successful of the three screen versions. ★★½ VHS: $14.99

The Star Maker

(1995, 113 min, Italy, Giuseppe Tornatore) *Sergio Castellitto, Tiziana Lodato, Franco Scaldati.* Director Tornatore (*Cinema Paradiso*) returns to the theme of the magic of the cinema with this often wry fable. Castellitto stars as Morelli, a con man making his way through 1950s Sicily. For a nominal fee, he films any and all with the promise of sending these screen tests to the cinematic giants of Italian filmmaking. Of course, the tests go no further than the back of his dilapidated truck which trumpets his arrival in each town. Unmoved by the various, funny and sometimes touching stories he is told, it is too late when he realizes the special power he and the camera holds. Tornatore captures the flavor of the times with the same accuracy he demonstrated in *Paradiso*, though this morality tale is not the sophisticated romp the box art suggests. (Italian with English subtitles) ★★★ DVD Subtitled: $14.99, VHS: $89.99

Star Maps

(1997, 93 min, US, Miguel Arteta) *Douglas Spain, Efrain Figueroa, Kandeyce Jorden, Martha Velez.* Funny, controversial and sexy, this melodramatic independent drama makes for absorbing viewing. Baby-faced but tough-minded Carlos (Spain) returns to L.A. and his unconventional family after a two-year absence in Mexico. Only 18 years old, he dreams of making it big as a Latino movie star. His weasel of a dad recruits him into the family business: selling maps to the homes of the stars, a front for a prostitution ring made up primarily of young Hispanic men who service both men and women. But Carlos has his sights set much higher than just peddling his flesh — and when a beautiful soap actress takes him under her wing, Carlos' tyrannical, violence-prone father has other thoughts about his son's future. ★★★½

S

583

Star Trek: The Motion Picture

(1979, 143 min, US, Robert Wise) *William Shatner, Leonard Nimoy, DeForest Kelley, James Doohan, Nichelle Nichols, Walter Keonig, George Takei.* The first theatrical outing for the crew of the Starship Enterprise. Captain Kirk and friends are sent to stop a deadly energy field heading towards Earth. Not as exciting as its sequels, some good special effects help compensate for its extremely long running time. Still, if you're a "Star Trek" fan, you gotta love it. This is the extended edition, with 11 minutes added to the theatrical version. ★★½ DVD Letterbox 2-disc set: $24.99, VHS: $9.99

Star Trek II: The Wrath of Khan

(1982, 113 min, US, Nicholas Meyer) *William Shatner, Leonard Nimoy, DeForest Kelley, Ricardo Montalban, Kirstie Alley.* The crew of the Starship Enterprise battle their old foe Khan (see "Star Trek" TV episode "Space Seed"), who is determined to get revenge against Captain Kirk for . . . (you have to see the TV show). *II* is a gloriously entertaining sci-fi adventure, containing splendid special effects. Montalban nicely plays Khan. ★★★½ DVD Director's Edition: $19.99, VHS: $9.99, VHS Letterbox: $14.99

Star Trek III: The Search for Spock

(1984, 105 min, US, Leonard Nimoy) *William Shatner, Leonard Nimoy, DeForest Kelley, John Larroquette, Judith Anderson, Chrisopher Lloyd.* With the possibility of Spock being regenerated on the fast-disintegrating planet Genesis, Admiral Kirk and company hijack their old ship and go out after their friend — no matter what he may have evolved into. Intriguing sci-fi notions and a fast-paced story make this an enjoyable yarn. ★★★ DVD Special Collector's Edition: $24.99, VHS: $9.99

Star Trek IV: The Voyage Home

(1986, 119 min, US, Leonard Nimoy) *William Shatner, Leonard Nimoy, DeForest Kelley, James Doohan, Catherine Hicks.* This fourth film in the *Star Trek* movie series is possibly the best of the bunch. The crew of the Starship Enterprise, on their way home for criminal prosecution, are diverted to 1980s San Francisco to prevent the destruction of Earth in the 23rd century — by saving the whales. Good special effects and terrific humor highlight this top science-fiction adventure. ★★★½ DVD: $29.99, DVD Special Collector's Edition: 2-Disc Set: $24.99, VHS: $9.99

Star Trek V: The Final Frontier

(1989, 106 min, US, William Shatner) *William Shatner, Leonard Nimoy, DeForest Kelley, Laurence Luckinbill, David Warner.* This fifth entry was savaged by the critics and overlooked by audiences because of the ludicrous plot line (the Enterprise must travel through the allegedly awesome Great Barrier in search of God — the great and powerful Oz was more ominous) and the corniness of Luckinbill as a Vulcan with a heart of gold. But it's also humorous and often touching. Director Shatner may have some problems parlaying action scenes to the screen, but nobody knows the crew of the Enterprise better than he and for that, we can thank him. ★★½ DVD 2-disc Special Collector's Edition: $24.99, VHS: $9.99

Casper Van Dien in *Starship Troopers*

Star Trek VI: The Undiscovered Country

(1991, 110 min, US, Nicholas Meyer) *William Shatner, Kim Cattrall, Leonard Nimoy, DeForest Kelley, Christopher Plummer, David Warner.* Not wanting to end on a down note after the disappointment of *Star Trek V*, the aging crew of the Enterprise are back in this winning adventure. Faced with a dwindling supply of oxygen on their home planet, the Klingons decide to make peace with the rest of the galaxy. Fittingly, Capt. Kirk is chosen as the emissary to negotiate this "new universal order." But there are powerful forces at work on both sides which don't want to see an end to their warring ways. The entire cast has a blast with this clearcut allegory for our current international climate. ★★★ DVD Special Collector's Edition: 2-Disc Set: $19.99, DVD: $24.99, VHS: $9.99

Star Trek: Generations

(1994, 118 min, US, David Carson) *Patrick Stewart, William Shatner, Whoopi Goldberg, Malcolm McDowell, Jonathan Frakes, Brent Spiner, Levar Burton.* A new crew takes control of the Starship Enterprise's theatrical adventures, and as James T. Kirk passes the captain's chair to Jean-Luc Picard, *Generations* brings both men together in an enjoyably familiar sci-fi tale. The story begins with the mysterious death of Kirk, and then skips ahead three-quarters of a century where Picard and his able crew answer an SOS, rescuing, among others, loony scientist McDowell, who spells trouble for all. As would be expected, the plot consists of lots of techno-babble, alternate universes and devious Klingons. Data (Spiner) gets the best share of the laughs as he finally acquires long-elusive human emotions, and there's a show-stopping crash scene worth seeing twice. ★★★ DVD Letterbox: $24.99, DVD Letterbox Special Collector's Edition: 2-Disc Set: $19.99

Star Trek: First Contact

(1996, 110 min, US, Jonathan Frakes) *Patrick Stewart, Jonathan Frakes, Brent Spiner, Levar Burton, Michael Dorn, Gates McFadden, Marina Sirtis, Alfre Woodard, James Cromwell, Alice Krige.* Exciting, darker than expected and still funny when you need it to be, *First Contact* reunites Captain Picard (Stewart) with the Borg, those ominous alien beings who a few years earlier had nearly "assimilated" the good captain on a fine two-part TV episode. To take the Borg on, the filmmakers take a cue from *Star Trek IV* and travel back in time to save Earth in the "present." The Borg are a terrific foil for Picard and company — dangerous, unpredictable and almost undefeatable — exactly what we have come to expect from good villains. Technical credits are commendable, and there are a couple of cameos to bring on a smile. Director Frakes has done a yeoman's job. ★★★ DVD Letterbox: $24.99

Star Trek: Insurrection

(1998, 103 min, US, Jonathan Frakes) *Patrick Stewart, Brett Spiner, Levar Burton, Jonathan Frakes, F. Murray Abraham, Donna Murphy.* This would probably have made a great hour-long TV show. But stretched to feature length, this third voyage of the "Next Generation" crew is an enjoyable though listless ride. Capt. Picard and company come to the rescue of the Ba'ku, who live a utopian existence on an uncharted planet. It seems the peace-loving folks are literally sitting on a fountain of youth, and those ruthless outcasts, the Son'a, want it all for themselves. *Insurrection* is like a family reunion: not a lot exciting happens but it's certainly good to see everyone again. But the story is full of New Age babble and contains little of the universe-shaking fights and dilemmas which makes the series fun. ★★½ DVD Letterbox: $24.99, VHS: $9.99

Star Trek: Nemesis

(2002, 116 min, US, Stuart Baird) *Patrick Stewart, Jonathan Frakes, Brent Spiner, Levar Burton, Michael Dorn, Gates McFadden, Marina Sirtis, Tom Hardy, Ron Perlman.* It may be time to consider retiring Captain Picard and his crew if this fourth "Next Generation" film is any indication of the future of the franchise. While it's always nice to see the entire cast together again voyaging on the *Enterprise*, their mission fails to fully excite. *Nemesis* pits Picard against his evil clone Shinzon (Hardy), who has joined forces with a renegade group of Romulans. As Picard comes face to face with his darker side, the rest of the gang ready for a galactic showdown to determine the fate of the universe. Director Baird supplies competent action sequences, and the Picard/Shinzon face-off is quite entertaining, but the film lacks a good story and isn't quite as fun as it should be — a sign that this series is in need of either a transfusion or its plug pulled. ★★½ DVD Letterbox: $19.99, DVD Pan & Scan: $19.99, VHS: $9.99

S

THE DISCERNING FILM LOVER'S GUIDE

Star Wars

(1977, 121 min, US, George Lucas) *Mark Hamill, Harrison Ford, Carrie Fisher, Alec Guinness, James Earl Jones.* A little while ago and not too far away, a man nearly reinvented the American film industry. Dialogue, characters and situations from Lucas' trilogy have crept into the American psyche since this blockbuster first appeared on movie screens. One reason for this influence is the fact that Lucas himself was drawing on the myths and fables present in American film throughout its history, particularly in early serials and later Hollywood westerns. A group of motley adventurers must rescue a princess from the clutches of an evil tyrant, and then rally their forces to destroy his empire. Lucas combines a primal story line with dazzling special effects, sound, production design and an otherworldly galaxy of alien characters, thus making it appealing to everyone with a taste for adventure, fantasy, romance or fable. (Sequel: *The Empire Strikes Back*) ★★★★ Available in a DVD Letterboxed Trilogy-pack for $69.99

Star Wars: Episode I — The Phantom Menace

(1999, 132 min, US, George Lucas) *Liam Neeson, Ewan McGregor, Natalie Portman, Jake Lloyd, Ian McDiarmid, Pernilla August, Samuel L. Jackson.* Lucas lets loose his imagination and creates a fully realized universe in the first part of his trilogy prequel. *Episode 1* follows Jedi master Qui-Gon Jinn (Neeson) and his young apprentice Obi-Wan Kenobi (McGregor) through many lands and fights for the federation, where they also discover Anakin Skywalker (Lloyd), the future Darth Vader. Planets are rendered with such detail that multiple viewings, as with all *Star Wars* films, are mandatory. However, as the title "Episode One" suggests, it's very much in the style of an old cliffhanger, complete with wooden characterizations, overplotting and only occasional action sequences to break the monotony. The simple, mythic elements of the previous films are missing here, replaced by rote superheroism, even as the art direction and effects set new standards. (Sequel: *Star Wars: Episode II — Attack of the Clones*) ★★½ VHS: $14.99, VHS Letterbox: $29.99

Star Wars: Episode II — Attack of the Clones

(2002, 143 min, US, George Lucas) *Ewan McGregor, Natalie Portman, Hayden Christensen, Samuel L. Jackson, Christopher Lee, Ian McDiarmid, Pernilla August, Jimmy Smits, Jack Thompson, Frank Oz, Temuera Morrison.* To paraphrase his THX tagline, Mr. Lucas is listening: Jar-Jar is out (almost), Yoda with a lightsaber is in, and Boba Fett gets a really cool dad. The silly plot (about a big vote) takes a backseat, as it should, and instead propels the characters from planet to planet, with confrontations at many steps of the way. Young Anakin has grown up; he's not yet Darth Vader, but he's getting there. However, Christensen plays him like a rebel without a cause: all James Dean method acting in a King's English world. McGregor (as Obi-Wan), however, has this thing down, reading the serial's lines with the reverence of Shakespeare. The effects are terrific, and will likely look even better on DVD, since the entire film was shot digitally. Yoda is now completely computer generated and not a muppet, which is a letdown until a climactic showdown where he shows what The Force is *really* made of. Despite all this good stuff, Anakin and Amidala's affair takes

up entirely too much time and is very flat. Still, it's a step up for the series, perhaps setting the stage for a final installment that will be completely, unabashedly worthy of the *Star Wars* name. ★★★

Stardom

(2000, 103 min, Canada, Denys Arcand) *Jessica Paré, Dan Aykroyd, Charles Berling, Thomas Gibson, Robert Lepage, Camilla Rutherford, Frank Langella.* A beautiful Canadian hockey player is transformed overnight into a supermodel/celebrity, and almost as quickly disappears from the spotlight. Director Arcand's pretentious satire is fairly redundant and obvious: the fact that many models are vacuous, many older men are obsessed with young women, and that the media are bastards is hardly news. Even the format of the film — told almost exclusively through entertainment shows and mock-umentaries — is old hat. Barely worth seeing for its fleeting moments. ★★ DVD: $14.99, VHS: $9.99

Stardust Memories

(1980, 88 min, US, Woody Allen) *Woody Allen, Charlotte Rampling, Marie-Christine Barrault, Jessica Harper.* Allen's autobiographical statement is a daring if rambling film which pits the artist against his audience. Allen plays a comedian/writer/director whose growing legion of fans crave more comedies while he is preoccupied with human suffering. ★★½ DVD: $19.99, VHS: $14.99

Stargate

(1994, 125 min, US, Roland Emmerich) *Kurt Russell, James Spader, Jaye Davidson, Viveca Lindfors.* This entertaining if lightweight sci-fi thriller plays like *Star Wars* meets *Indiana Jones.* Russell and the ever-engaging Spader are a military burnout and nerdy Egyptologist, respectively, who are assigned to decipher the markings on an ancient discovery. When it turns out it's a galactic gateway, they travel to the other side where peace-loving desert tribes are enslaved by an evil, skin-shedding alien (Davidson). Though the story line is lackluster, the film is greatly benefited by an intriguing premise and good special effects. ★★½ DVD Letterbox Ultimate Edition Director's Cut: $19.99

Starlight Hotel

(1987, 94 min, New Zealand, Sam Pillsbury) *Greer Robson, Peter Phelps.* Fine family fare about a 12-year-old waif who sets off across the New Zealand countryside in search of her father, and instead finds herself on the run with a fugitive from the law. Though lacking the panache of *The Journey of Natty Gann*, it nonetheless stands on its own as an interesting variation of the buddy-road movie. ★★★

Starman

(1984, 115 min, US, John Carpenter) *Jeff Bridges, Karen Allen, Charles Martin Smith, Richard Jaeckel.* Bridges' captivating performance highlights this good-natured and extremely satisfying Carpenter sci-fi adventure about an alien on the run from the authorities. Allen plays a widow who is at first kidnapped by the extraterrestrial (who has taken on the form of her late husband), but who later helps and befriends him. ★★★½ DVD: $14.99, VHS: $9.99

Stars and Bars

(1988, 94 min, US, Pat O'Connor) *Daniel Day-Lewis, Harry Dean Stanton, Martha Plimpton, Joan Cusack, Steven Wright, Laurie Metcalf, Glenne Headly.* Wacky and offbeat comedy with Day-Lewis as a British art dealer who travels to the American

South to purchase a prized painting and is introduced to one of the craziest families this side of the Vanderhoffs. ★★

The Stars Fell on Henrietta

(1995, 110 min, US, James Keach) *Robert Duvall, Aidan Quinn, Frances Fisher, Brian Dennehy.* Set in Depression-era Texas, this nostalgic if colorless character study gives Duvall another chance to deliver a sterling portrayal of a gruff but lovable curmudgeon. He plays Mr. Cox, an aging wildcatter who happens upon the struggling farm of Mr. and Mrs. Day (Quinn, Fisher) and begins claiming there's oil on their property. Mr. Cox sets about to raise the money as Mr. Day falls under the spell cast by the self-proclaimed "oil man" and begins drilling, risking his farm in the process. A listless pace is offest by a strong ensemble, good period design and lovely cinematography. ★★½

The Stars Look Down

(1939, 110 min, GB, Carol Reed) *Michael Redgrave, Margaret Lockwood, Emlyn Williams.* Exquisite performances by Redgrave and Lockwood highlight this searing film adaptation of A.J. Cronin's novel about a poor Welsh mining family's struggles and their son's resolution to run for public office. ★★★★ VHS: $14.99

Starship Troopers

(1997, 130 min, US, Paul Verhoeven) *Casper Van Dien, Dina Meyer, Denise Richards, Jake Busey, Neil Patrick Harris, Patrick Muldoon, Michael Ironside.* Director Verhoeven returns to *Robocop*-form with this scathingly satirical futuristic sci-fi thriller that plays like "Archie and Veronica Go to War!" A bunch of giant space bugs have taken to lobbing killer asteroids at Earth from their side of the galaxy, and a group of young heroes must gamely venture out to the alien home world for a preemptive strike. The film's first hour is positively goofy (in the best way) as it introduces these youthful cadets. This gives way to blood-and-guts destruction, a cinematic orgy of human and insect insides splashed on the screen with abandon. The special effects are top-notch and the action is riveting. ★★★½ DVD Special Edition: $27.99

Starstruck

(1982, 95 min, Australia, Gillian Armstrong) *Jo Kennedy, Ross O'Donovan.* A zesty, new-wave musical brimming with infectious tunes, inspired choreography and enchanting performances. Jackie, a winsome waitress at the family pub in Sydney, has a hankering for stardom; and, with the help of her mite-sized manager/cousin, sets out to launch her singing career. Armstrong directed this ebullient Australian comedy with an abundance of flair and originality. ★★★½

Starstruck

585

Start the Revolution without Me

(1970, 91 min, US, Bud Yorkin) *Gene Wilder, Donald Sutherland, Orson Welles, Billie Whitelaw.* Engaging spoof set during the French Revolution with Wilder and Sutherland chewing the scenery as two pairs of twins separated at birth; reunited years later resulting in cases of mistaken identity between the aristocracy and peasantry. ★★★ DVD: $19.99, VHS: $14.99

Startup.com

(2001, 103 min, US, Chris Hegedus & Jehane Noujaim) *Tom Herman, Kaleil Isaza Tuzman.* *Startup.com* tracks the rise and fall of govWorks.com, one of the many startup internet companies that littered the market durint the '90s. Kaleil and Tom envision a web site that facilitates interactions between local governments and their constituents. Starting out with eight employees and a few laptops, the company experiences rapid growth. But it's a house of cards; 20-hour days and continuing personal sacrifices ultimately fail against ongoing internal conflict, suspected corporate sabotage and the vicissitudes of the market. The entire trip takes 19 months. A fascinating look at a recent — and continuing — episode in modern financial history. Kaliel and Tom have since started another startup . . . this one to advise troubled dot.coms. ★★★ DVD: $14.99, VHS: $9.99

State and Main

(2000, 102 min, US, David Mamet) *William H. Macy, Alec Baldwin, Rebecca Pidgeon, Philip Seymour Hoffman, Sarah Jessica Parker, David Paymer, Julia Stiles, Charles Durning, Patti LuPone, Clark Gregg.* From writer-director Mamet comes this winning comedy about a film company invading a peaceful Vermont community. As Hollywood and small-town America clash, careers are nearly ruined, engagements broken and alliances shifted. Macy is terrific as the cool-headed but acerbic director desperately trying to maintain order; Hoffman is the insecure writer who may have found paradise; best of all is Pidgeon as the local bookstore owner and theatre director who always seems to be one-up on everyone. Mamet has great fun at both poking fun at the system while showing exactly what it takes to get a movie made. It's not always pretty, but it can be damn funny. ★★★½ DVD Dual: $24.99, VHS: $14.99

State of Grace

(1990, 130 min, US, Phil Joanou) *Gary Oldman, Sean Penn, Ed Harris, Robin Wright Penn, John Turturro.* A *Mean Streets*-like vision of the inner workings of Manhattan's Irish-American mob. Based on journalistic accounts of the "Westies," a real-life Hell's Kitchen band of thugs known for their brutal savagery, the film accurately depicts the erratic and unpredictable violence which rules the streets of New York. Oldman is stellar as Jackie Flannery, a dangerously loose cannon in the gang. Penn is a childhood friend who returns to the neighborhood after a long absence. Highly stylized, *State of Grace* centers on the attempted union of the "Westies" with the Italian mafia in the mid-'70s. ★★★ DVD Letterbox: $14.99

State of Siege

(1973, 120 min, France, Constantin Costa-Gavras) *Yves Montand, Renato Salvatori.* This tense drama of the kidnapping of a U.S. "special advisor" provides the background for the uncovering of the United States' true role in the internal affairs of Latin America. (French with English subtitles) ★★★

State of the Union

(1948, 122 min, US, Frank Capra) *Spencer Tracy, Katharine Hepburn, Angela Lansbury, Van Johnson, Adolphe Menjou.* A well-scripted political comedy based on the Pulitzer Prize-winning play by Howard Lindsay and Russell Crouse. Tracy gives a commanding performance as an idealistic industrialist who is drafted as a presidential nominee. Hepburn is the estranged wife who returns to her husband for the sake of the campaign, where the candidate is torn between his ambition for office and the integrity of his wife's uncompromising and outspoken views. Lansbury is especially noteworthy as Tracy's rich sponsor. ★★★

The State of Things

(1982, 110 min, US/West Germany, Wim Wenders) *Samuel Fuller, Roger Corman, Viva, Paul Getty III.* Wenders' 8½ is an imaginative and engrossing picture dealing with the condition of the European art film and its corrupting nemesis: Hollywood. The story concerns the crew and cast of a film who find themselves marooned in Portugal and their production money and film stock depleted. The crew, waiting for more money, must kill time. A compelling meditation on the inertia of the moviemaking process, creative impasses and the impossibility of telling stories anymore. (Filmed in English) ★★★

Static

(1985, 93 min, US, Mark Romanek) *Keith Gordon, Amanda Plummer, Bob Gunton.* A young inventor (Gordon) prepares to launch his earth-shattering new creation (a TV which gets pictures of Heaven) with the aid of his new-wave friend and his ex-Green Beret evangelist cousin. Gordon cowrote the uneven though imaginative script. ★★

The Station

(1992, 92 min, Italy, Sergio Rubini) *Margherita Buy, Ennio Fantastichini.* Charming, romantic and quintessentially European, *The Station* tells of an unlikely love between a nerdy railway station attendant and an elegant young woman. The fastidious young man finds his order coming to an end after the mysterious woman, seemingly on the run, enters the station in the middle of the night to wait for the morning train. Their relationship, first as a typical clerk to an indifferent customer, develops into more after trouble descends on the station and the man is forced to take drastic action to defend them. Deliberate in pacing, but rich in nuance and emotion, this quiet, gentle love story is a real delight. (Italian with English subtitles) ★★★½ VHS: $19.99

The Station Agent

(2003, 88 min, US, Tom McCarthy) *Peter Dinklage, Patricia Clarkson, Bobby Cannavale, Raven Goodwin, Paul Benjamin, Michelle Williams.* Finbar McBride, a handsome dwarf, is the co-owner of a train/hobby shop in Hoboken, New Jersey. He's soft-spoken, introspective and reclusive — it's not necessarily his size but more his personality that makes it a bit difficult for him to warm up to strangers. He just prefers to keep his distance. When his partner passes away, Fin inherits and relocates to an abandoned train station in the Jersey countryside. Little did Fin or anyone watching this funny, glorious character study know what immense pleasure would come from such a move. With his debut as writer-director, McCarthy has fashioned a charming, quirky story of three outsiders who come together in spite of themselves to form an endearing bond of unconditional friendship. Dinklage is extraordinary as Fin, who combines vulnerability, resolve and a world-weariness well beyond Fin's years; Clarkson continues to demonstrate she's one of the leading actresses of American independent cinema with a ferocious but touching portrayal of a woman a little too close to the edge; and Cannavale rounds out this appealing trio as a gregarious hot dog stand vendor looking after his dying father. An enchanting, superior story of comaraderie and acceptance, loneliness and the ability to defeat it. ★★★★ DVD: $29.99

The Stationmaster's Wife (Bolwiessar)

(1977, 111 min, West Germany, Rainer Werner Fassbinder) *Kurt Raab, Elisabeth Trissenaar.* Originally a two-part TV series running 200 minutes, this shorter version is Fassbinder's take on "Madame Bovary" in a Nazi Germany rotting from within. Raab is the sheepish, masochistic stationmaster who suspects his wife's infidelities. But not wanting to risk losing the small luxuries to which he has become accustomed, he chooses not to act upon his suspicions. Trissenaar gives a mesmerizing performance as a woman in love with her carnal desires and the power they give her. Fassbinder's visual style is rich, gorgeous, and suffocating, mirroring their bourgeois lifestyle. (German with English subtitles) ★★★

Stavisky

(1974, 117 min, France, Alain Resnais) *Jean-Paul Belmondo, Charles Boyer.* Starting off with the details from a real 1930s French political scandal, Resnais adroitly blends facts — from the real case with Leon Trotsky's arrival in exile — with fiction in presenting this absorbing drama about moral degeneracy and political corruption. Belmondo plays Serge Alexandre (nee Sacha Stavisky), a suave, elegantly-attired con man who concocts a financial swindle that soon involves powerful government officials and high-ranking police. Resnais creates a visually breathtaking and chilling allegory of France's political situation on the eve of fascist aggression. (French with English subtitles) ★★★½ DVD Letterbox: $24.99, VHS: $19.99

Stay Hungry

(1976, 103 min, US, Bob Rafelson) *Jeff Bridges, Sally Field, Arnold Schwarzenegger.* Bridges stars as a Southern pre-yuppie who buys a gym as part of a business deal, only to gain an appreciation for the people he exploits while learning something about himself as well. Schwarzenegger appears in his first major acting role. ★★½ DVD: $14.99

Stay Tuned

(1992, 89 min, US, Peter Hyams) *John Ritter, Pam Dawber, Jeffrey Jones.* The irony is delicious: Ritter and Dawber finally make the transition to the big screen only to be sucked back into the "television from Hell" in this boob tube spoof. Ritter plays a video addict whose ritual TV watching is given a twist when Satan's helper (Jones) offers him 666 channels of the ultimate in interactive television. Though not as consistently savage as it might have been, *Stay Tuned* does offer some funny parodies — especially of "Three's Company" and an animated segment by Chuck Jones. ★★ DVD: $9.99, VHS: $6.99

Stealing Beauty

(1996, 119 min, GB/Italy, Bernardo Bertolucci) *Jeremy Irons, Liv Tyler, Donal McCann, Sinéad Cusack.* One might expect this tale of sexual awakening in the sun-drenched hills of Tuscany to be no more than a panderous exercise in lechery. And to some degree this is true, *Stealing Beauty* is also a touching examination of the young woman's innocent, oddly chaste desire for sexual initiation. The story revolves around a 19-year-old American staying with family friends at their homestead. Clearly out of her element and surrounded by middle-aged adults, she turns to an ailing houseguest (Irons) for solace and comfort. More style than substance, the film is a very satisfying and refreshing look at romance amongst the privileged artist class. Delivering a marvelously natural performance, newcomer Tyler proves herself a worthy lead. ★★★ DVD: $14.99, VHS: $6.99

Stealing Harvard

(2002, 83 min, US, Bruce McCulloch) *Tom Green, Jason Lee, Leslie Mann, Megan Mullally, Dennis Farina, Richard Jenkins.* While an integral (and still very funny) member of the Kids in the Hall, Bruce McCulloch continues to come up empty on his own as a director. Witness this paceless, obvious and formulaic comedy that manages to render the usually endearing Lee unwatchable. After being confronted with a videotaped promise to pay for the college education of his niece (who the hell was taping it, anyway?), Lee realizes he must steal the thirty grand to make good. Enter immature buddy Green (in his usual role), and a series of schemes that not only go horribly wrong but fall comically flat. And in what would normally be an admirable development, Green stays largely under control, denying the movie its only chance at gaining energy. ★ DVD Letterbox: $27.99, VHS: $9.99

Stealing Heaven

(1988, 108 min, GB, Clive Donner) *Peter de Lint, Kim Thomson, Denholm Elliott.* De Lint stars as Peter Abelard, a 12th-century French philosopher and churchman who broke taboo and secretly married one of his students, Heloise (Thomson). Elliott is her wrathful father in this passionate tale of forbidden love. ★★★

Stealing Home

(1988, 98 min, US, Steven Kampmann) *Mark Harmon, Jodie Foster, William McNamara, Blair Brown, Helen Hunt.* America's two favorite pastimes, baseball and sex, take it on the chin in this uneven though well-acted comedy-drama. Harmon stars as a down-and-out ballplayer who, upon hearing of the death of a childhood friend, reminisces and reflects upon their relationship two decades earlier. Partially told in flashback, the film is equally divided between the present and past, and is far more successful in the scenes involving the latter. Foster gives a wonderful performance as Harmon's free-spirited mentor. ★★½ DVD: $9.99, VHS: $9.99

Steamboat Bill, Jr.

(1927, 71 min, US, Charles Riesner) *Buster Keaton.* One of Keaton's finest comedies casts him as a returning college graduate who must prove himself to his burly father, Steamboat Bill, Sr. The cyclone at the climax gives Keaton the chance to reconcile with his father and demonstrate the comic genius of one of the all-time great physical comedians. ★★★★ DVD: $29.99, VHS: $29.99

Steaming

(1985, 95 min, GB, Joseph Losey) *Vanessa Redgrave, Sarah Miles, Pati Love, Diana Dors.* Losey's last film is an adaptation of the critically acclaimed play by Neal Dunn which features a stellar female cast. Set on "ladies' day" at a London bathhouse, we find six women, of wildly divergent backgrounds, coming together to discuss their intimate secrets and commiserate about their place in the world. The production is perhaps a bit over-stagey, but it is carried by first-rate performances. ★★½

Steel

(1997, 97 min, US, Kenneth Johnson) *Shaquille O'Neal, Harvey Silver, Annabeth Gish, Judd Nelson, Richard Roundtree, Irma P. Hall.* A laughable attempt to start a new superhero franchise for kids, *Steel*, based on the DC comic book, is a bland time waster. We are then introduced to our tree trunk hero (Shaq) and oily villain (Nelson) as they test a new sonic weapon for the Army. After a tragic mishap, Shaq quits the Army and becomes a well-armored vigilante in his old 'hood, while Nelson graduates to supervillain status. ★ VHS: $14.99

Steel Magnolias

(1989, 115 min, US, Herbert Ross) *Sally Field, Shirley MacLaine, Olympia Dukakis, Julia Roberts, Dolly Parton, Daryl Hannah, Tom Skerritt, Dylan McDermott, Sam Shepard, Kevin J. O'Connor.* A fine ensemble cast is featured in this heartrending, sentimental comedy-drama. The story centers on the friendship of six women in a small Louisiana town who meet periodically at the local beauty shop. Field heads this terrific cast as mother of newlywed Roberts, whose marriage is much of the focus of the film. MacLaine is hilarious as the town curmudgeon; and Dukakis is splendid as the gossipy town matriarch. The first half of the film suffers from sloppy editing, and sometimes the characters seem interchangeable with other Southern-themed works, but the performances are so captivating the film's flaws can be overlooked. ★★½ DVD Special Edition: $19.99, VHS: $9.99

Steelyard Blues

(1973, 93 min, US, Alan Myerson) *Jane Fonda, Donald Sutherland, Peter Boyle.* A group of misfits band together to restore a vintage airplane, hoping to fly away to paradise. Amiable counterculture hijinks. Written by David S. Ward (*The Sting*). ★★½ VHS: $19.99

Stella

(1990, 109 min, US, John Erman) *Bette Midler, John Goodman, Trini Alvarado.* Even the great Midler can strike out on occasion, as proved by this turgid remake of the perennial classic. Bette plays the sacrificing and (supposedly) slovenly mother of teenager Alvarado; but she's more schizophrenic as one moment she's wise and creative and the next crude with no fashion sense. It just doesn't work in the 1990s. Stick with Barbara Stanwyck's 1937 version, *Stella Dallas*. ★½ DVD: $14.99

Stella Dallas

(1937, 111 min, US, King Vidor) *Barbara Stanwyck, Anne Shirley, John Boles.* Stanwyck gives a stellar performance in this classic tearjerker as a mother who sacrifices all for the sake of her daughter (Shirley). (Remade as *Stella*) ★★★½

Step into Liquid

(2003, 87 min, US, Dana Brown) Wave-worshippers and landlubbers alike will be mesmerized by this engaging documentary from Brown, a surfer/filmmaker whose father Bruce made the seminal surfing flick *The Endless Summer*. Intercut with insightful interviews of world-renown surfers are awesome and visually seductive sequences of them conquering some truly humongous waves all over the globe: from the jagged shores of Hawaii and Australia to the swells of Lake Michigan and Vietnam; from the icy coast of Ireland to the tropical remotes of Rapa Nui; from riding the wake of super-tankers in Texas to braving "The Cortes Bank" — a frightful spot 100 miles off San Diego where the most daring surfers ride the most mind-bogglingly tall waves ever churned. A spectacular feast for the senses, though the soothing hypnotic imagery is somewhat undercut by an obstreperous music score and by Brown's own dry narration. ★★★½ DVD Letterbox 2-disc set: $24.99

Step Lively

(1944, 88 min, US, Tim Whelan) *Frank Sinatra, George Murphy, Gloria De Haven.* A fast-paced musical version of the Marx Brothers' *Room Service*. Murphy plays the part of a Broadway producer who, despite no financial resources, schemes to put on a show. ★★★ VHS: $9.99

The Stepfather

(1987, 98 min, US, Joseph Ruben) *Terry O'Quinn, Shelley Hack.* This frightening thriller gets most of its chills because it could so easily be true. O'Quinn is a meek family guy who wants a perfect family and home, and by damn, *he's going to have it* — no matter what the cost or who gets killed in the process. (Followed by 2 sequels) ★★★½

The Stepford Wives

(1975, 115 min, US, Bryan Forbes) *Katharine Ross, Paula Prentiss, Peter Masterson, Tina Louise, Patrick O'Neal.* Ross stars as an aspiring photographer who moves to a seemingly perfect planned community with her hotshot lawyer husband. She soon sticks out amongst the apron-clad hausfraus who smilingly serve their husband's every need and whim. Digging a little deeper beneath the happy surface of Stepford, she and her equally independent best friend (a wonderful Prentiss) discover the horrifying secret of the Stepford Mens' Association and their man-made paradise. Perhaps a bit slow to begin with, the film delivers quite a few good shocks in its final reel. (Remade in 2004) ★★★ DVD: $14.99

Stephen King's Thinner

(1996, 92 min, US, Tom Holland) *Robert John Burke, Joe Mantegna, Al Ruggiero.* A selfish lawyer accidentally but recklessly runs down the daughter of an ancient gypsy mystic and becomes the object of a sinister curse in this adaptation of a Stephen King story. Extremely overweight, the lawyer (Burke) suddenly finds himself losing fat at an alarming rate. Pleased at first, he realizes the horror of his situation when he cannot stop his wasting away. He must confront the old gypsy and persuade him to lift the curse. Competently acted and produced, it's satisfying while it lasts but leaves no lasting impression. ★★½ DVD Letterbox: $14.99, VHS: $9.99, VHS Letterbox: $14.99

Stepmom

(1998, 124 min, US, Chris Columbus) *Susan Sarandon, Julia Roberts, Ed Harris, Jena Malone, Lynn Whitfield.* With oh-so sincerity and jerking of tears, this mawkish mess of manipulation uses its good cast to try to hide a sappy story of two moms, two kids and two rivalries that becomes all-two much. Sarandon and Harris are a divorced couple with two kids. Dad has a new girlfriend (Roberts), setting the stage for a continuing battle of the divas as Roberts and Harris marry, pitting mom against step-mom for control of the kids. And wouldn't you know it, just when it looks like they might actually get along, tragedy strikes. The performances all around are good, but it's all for naught. We've all been down this well-traveled road, and there's nothing new on the horizon. ★★ DVD: $14.99, VHS: $9.99

The Sterile Cuckoo

(1969, 107 min, US, Alan J. Pakula) *Liza Minnelli, Wendell Burton.* Minnelli gives a heartrending performance as a lonely and eccentric college student searching for love and acceptance. She finds the former in the unlikely person of shy Burton. A perceptive and touching look at first love. ★★★½ VHS: $7.99

Stevie

(1978, 102 min, GB, Robert Enders) *Glenda Jackson, Mona Washbourne, Alec McCowen.* Jackson stars in this wonderful character study of British poetess Stevie Smith. Adapted from Hugh Whitemore's hit London play, the film celebrates love, family, and Stevie's own fascination with the English language. Jackson and Washbourne both offer exquisite performances. ★★★★

The Stickup

(2001, 97 min, US, Rowdy Herrington) *James Spader, Leslie Stefanson, David Keith, John Livingston.* is what your typical, straight-to-video suspense flick should be: unassuming, unremarkable, yet completely engaging. Spader plays a suspended cop who is wanted in a small town for holding up a bank. He gets involved with the local sheriff's ex while trying to clear his name. Very much a B-movie (the epitome of what used to be called "programmers"), *The Stickup* is an efficient, slick, unpretentious piece of entertainment, with good acting, a decent screenplay, and just the right amount of humor. It's truly nothing special, and certainly unmemorable, but it's fun while it lasts. ★★½ DVD: $9.99

Sticky Fingers

(1988, 97 min, US, Catlin Adams) *Helen Slater, Melanie Mayron, Loretta Devine.* Two dizzy roommates "borrow" from the stash of cash they're holding for a friend (Devine), and go overboard. The film tries for the slap-dash energy of the crazy romps of yore, but it's mostly wasted in unfunny and contrived situations. ★½

Stigmata

(1999, 102 min, US, Rupert Wainwright) *Gabriel Byrne, Patricia Arquette, Jonathan Pryce, Portia de Rossi, Nia Long.* An intriguing story of supernatural possession and religious conflict is turned into a boring, atmospheric merry-go-round ride. Byrne plays a Vatican priest who is sent to Pittsburgh to investigate a young woman (Arquette) who is experiencing signs of the stigmata, or unexplained wounds mirroring those suffered by Christ. With one-too-many jump cuts and not-nearly enough scares, the story follows the good reverend as he tries to protect his lonely charge — but from what? The film's good look can't hide a silly screenplay and uninvolving direction. ★½ DVD: $14.99, VHS: $9.99

Still Crazy

(1999, 95 min, GB, Brian Gibson) *Stephen Rea, Billy Connolly, Jimmy Nail, Timothy Spall, Bill Nighy, Bruce Robinson.* Seeking to combine the Baby Boomer humor of *This Is Spinal Tap* with the plight of the working-class dramedy (*The Full Monty*, e.g.), *Still Crazy* is thoroughly inconsequential but still enjoyable. Rea is the keyboardist for Strange Fruit, a rock band that was apparently huge in the '70s, and he wants to experience that magic again. But the band is full of petty conflicts that hamper a reunion. No matter, when they get together to play punk dives they naturally discover love, friendship and the dangers of farting in a trailer. Wildly uneven but always light and enjoyable. ★★½ DVD: $29.99, VHS: $21.99

Still of the Night

(1982, 91 min, US, Robert Benton) *Roy Scheider, Meryl Streep, Jessica Tandy.* Hitchcockian murder mystery about a psychiatrist (Scheider) who tries to solve the murder of one of his patients, falling in love with the prime suspect (Streep) in the process. Streep chain-smokes and chews the scenery in this somewhat involved thriller which, like most Hitchcock imitations, fails to measure up to the master. ★★½ VHS: $9.99

The Stilts (Los Zancos)

(1984, 95 min, Spain, Carlos Saura) *Laura del Sol.* Director Saura returns to the familiar surroundings of theatrical life and sexual obsession. An aging, recently widowed professor initiates an affair with his beautiful neighbor, who is married to the charismatic leader of a local theatre company. In an attempt to retain her affection, the professor writes a play for the troupe, which is performed on stilts. Against this backdrop, the trio play out an anguished and explosive scenario infused with unrestrained desires and emotional manipulation. (Spanish with English subtitles) ★★★

The Sting

(1973, 129 min, US, George Roy Hill) *Paul Newman, Robert Redford, Robert Shaw, Eileen Brennan, Ray Walston, Harold Gould.* Delightful comedy set in 1930s Chicago with Newman and Redford as con artists out to "sting" gangster Shaw. There's so many twists you won't know what's what or who's who. Winner of seven Oscars, including Best Picture and one for David S. Ward's first-rate screenplay. There's an impeccable supporting cast and terrific costumes and sets. ★★★★ DVD: $19.99, VHS: $9.99

Stir Crazy

(1980, 111 min, US, Sidney Poitier) *Gene Wilder, Richard Pryor, JoBeth Williams, Georg Stanford Brown, Craig T. Nelson.* The second and most popular of the Wilder-Pryor comedies, and it's very funny. The guys are two bungling thieves who are sent to prison, and are quite ill-prepared for life behind bars. ★★★ DVD: $14.99, VHS: $9.99

Stir of Echoes

(1999, 94 min, US, David Koepp) *Kevin Bacon, Kathryn Erbe, Illeana Douglas, Kevin Dunn.* This often intense psychological thriller which falls apart by story's end is sure to draw comparisons to the superior *The Sixth Sense.* A family man (Bacon) is haunted by the spirit of a recently murdered woman. So she may rest in peace, he must bring to justice those responsible for her death. The film is at its best when delving into the supernatural, effectively creating a few chilling set pieces. But it is the human element which is underdeveloped, and by the end of the film, there's nothing up its sleeve but a *Death Wish*-type ending. Bacon tries a little too hard to convey mannerisms of an Average Joe, though Douglas is quite good as his sister-in-law who first unlocks this window to the other world. ★★½ DVD: $14.99, VHS: $9.99, VHS Previously Viewed: $102.99

Stolen Kisses

(1968, 90 min, France, François Truffaut) *Jean-Pierre Léaud, Delphine Seyrig.* The third episode in the Antoine Doinel series finds Léaud, our inept but lovable hero, doing what he must to stay on the furtive heels of love and romance. A poignant and comic look at the foibles of romance. (French with English subtitles) ★★★½ DVD: $19.99, VHS: $14.99

A Stolen Life

(1946, 107 min, US, Curtis Bernhardt) *Bette Davis, Glenn Ford, Walter Brennan.* Davis lets loose as a set of twins, one of whom takes the other's place in marriage to the man they both loved when her sibling dies in a boating accident. Not Bette's best, but more than interesting thanks to La Davis' histrionics. ★★½ VHS: $19.99

The Stone Boy

(1984, 93 min, US, Christopher Cain) *Jason Pressman, Robert Duvall, Glenn Close, Wilford Brimley, Frederic Forrest.* Duvall and Close star as the confused parents of a young boy who kills his older brother in a hunting accident. Exceptionally portrayed by Presson, the boy goes into shock and is unable to explain the circumstances leading up to the shooting, and sinks deep within a grim-faced exterior. Duvall delivers an understated performance as a Montana rancher caught in a situation beyond his understanding but compelled to muster the strength needed to heal his family and reconcile with his son. Powerful and true and beautiful. ★★★ VHS: $59.99

Stonebrook

(1999, 90 min, US, Byron W. Thompson) *Seth Green, Brad Rowe, Zoe McLellan, William Mesnik, Stanley Kamel.* Predating a sorry wave of behind-the-Ivy-curtain thrillers (*The Skulls, Gossip*) but certainly no better, this minor thriller falls into clichéd traps that the protagonists should have seen coming. Rowe plays Erik, a working-class outcast at wealthy Stonebrook U; when he loses his scholarship, he needs to scrape up some cash. Enter Green and his plans to swindle the local underworld. The schemes become a random series of who's-playing-who twists in a plot too complicated for its own good. ★½ DVD: $9.99

Stonewall

(1996, 93 min, GB, Nigel Finch) *Guillermo Diaz, Frederick Weller, Brendan Corbalis, Duane Boutte, Bruce MacVittie, Peter Ratray, Dwight Ewell, Luis Guzmán, Candis Cayne.* Far from being a dry, fictionalized account of the people involved in the 1969 Stonewall Riots, this adaptation of Martin Duberman's book is instead a rollicking musical drama that successfully blends gay history and queer fabulousness to wonderful effect. Matty (Weller), a studly country boy, arrives in New York City and almost immediately becomes involved with a rambunctious group of black, white and Latino drag queens. A passionate, spirited tale — torn from gay history — that is alternately funny, touching, upsetting and even a bit educational. ★★★ DVD: $14.99

Stop Making Sense

(1984, 99 min, US, Jonathan Demme) *Talking Heads, David Byrne.* Visual wit and dynamic rhythms faithfully and inventively convey the near-religious fervor of a Talking Heads concert. Demme's rockumentary won laurels for being a new breed of performance film, one which showcases a band's unique personality rather than the director's pyrotechnics. Shunning clips of frothing crowds and backstage doodlings, Demme and fig-ure-Head David Byrne have constructed a film which builds to a rousing crescendo as additional performers join the stage with each successive song. Truly a scintillating celebration of rock 'n' roll. ★★★★ DVD Letterbox: $29.99, VHS: $19.99, VHS Letterbox: $19.99

Stop! or My Mom Will Shoot

(1992, 87 min, US, Roger Spottiswoode) *Sylvester Stallone, Estelle Getty, JoBeth Williams, Roger Rees.* In this flat and predictable high-concept comedy, a Los Angeles police sergeant (and here's the concept, folks) teams up with his sixtysomething mom. While visiting her son, she witnesses a murder and demands to be part of the investigation. ★½ DVD Letterbox: $14.99, VHS: $9.99

Stop the World I Want to Get Off

(1966, 98 min, GB, Philip Saville) *Tony Tanner, Millicent Martin.* This lively film adaptation of Anthony Newley-Leslie Bricusse's smash London/Broadway musical is filmed directly from a staged performance, inexplicably minus its star Newley. Tanner takes over the role of Littlechap, a British Everyman who, through song (and what classics they are), observes his life — including courtship, marriage and infidelity. This was one of the groundbreaking stage musicals of its era, and the film version nicely captures the play's originality and vitality. Songs include "What Kind of Fool Am I" and "Gonna Build a Mountain." ★★★ VHS: $19.99

Stormy Monday

(1988, 93 min, GB, Mike Figgis) *Melanie Griffith, Sting, Tommy Lee Jones, Sean Bean.* A moody and atmospheric mystery-thriller set in the dreary city of Newcastle. Jones plays an American businessman who is trying to take advantage of the town's depressed economy by snatching up real estate, including Sting's jazz club. ★★★ DVD Dual: $14.99

Stormy Weather

(1943, 77 min, US, Andrew L. Stone) *Lena Horne, Bill Robinson, Cab Calloway, Fats Waller, The Nicholas Brothers.* A dazzling, high-spirited tribute to the legendary Bill "Bojangles" Robinson. Tunes include "Ain't Misbehavin'" and Lena's sultry version of the title number. ★★★

The Story of a Three Day Pass

(1967, 87 min, France, Melvin Van Peebles) *Harry Baird, Nicole Berger.* This tale of an African-American soldier's affair with a French woman while on leave in Paris in the 1960s is an entertaining love story. The two principals, Baird and Berger, act as conduits on a surreal journey exploring race relations in the military and how some American mores become irrational in other societies. While at times flawed, van Peebles' cut and camerawork stand out as he pays homage to Luis Buñuel and Jean Cocteau. ★★½ VHS: $19.99

The Story of Adele H.

(1975, 97 min, France, François Truffaut) *Isabelle Adjani, Bruce Robinson.* Adjani portrays the young heroine whose obsessive attachment to an uncaring scoundrel in the military drives her to the brink of madness . . . and beyond. An exceptionally told and acted drama based on the memoirs of the daughter of French literary giant Victor Hugo. (French with English subtitles) ★★★★ DVD: $19.99, VHS: $19.99

The Story of Boys and Girls

(1991, 92 min, Italy, Pupi Avati) *Lucrezia Lante della Rovere, Massimo Bonetti.* A sumptuously filmed parable about two disparate Italian families coming together for a nuptual banquet signifying the joining of the clans. Set for the most part on a small Italian farm, the film details the fabulous 20-course feast over which these two families (one of the intellectual city class, the other of rural peasant stock) meet for the first time. Filled with some wonderfully mirthful moments, the film uses the festivities as the platform for some time-honored commentary on class differences as well as the occasional amorous roll in the hay. (Italian with English subtitles) ★★★

The Story of G.I. Joe

(1945, 108 min, US, William Wellman) *Burgess Meredith, Robert Mitchum, Freddie Steele, Wally Cassell, Jimmy Lloyd.* Based on a series of articles by Pulitzer Prize-winning war correspondent Ernie Pyle, this gripping, unsentimental war WWII film follows Pyle and the men of Company C of the 18th Infantry as they advance from North Africa to Italy. Meredith is outstanding as Pyle, and Mitchum — in his first major role — received an Oscar nomination for his dynamic portrayal of the company's captain. Unquestionably one of the best of all war-themed films produced during America's war years. ★★★★ DVD: $24.99, VHS: $19.99

The Story of Louis Pasteur

(1936, 85 min, US, William Dieterle) *Paul Muni, Josephine Hutchinson.* Muni won an Oscar for his detailed performance as French scientist Louis Pasteur. Hollywood storytelling and scientific heroics mesh perfectly in this first-rate biography. ★★★★ VHS: $14.99

The Story of Qiu Ju

(1992, 100 min, China, Zhang Yimou) *Gong Li, Lei Lao Sheng.* This collaboration between Zhang and actress Gong bears little resemblance to their previous period dramas such as *Raise the Red Lantern* and *Ju Dou.* Unlike those examinations of feudal China, *Qiu Ju* is an almost upbeat and decidedly proletarian look at one woman's crusade for justice. When her husband is severly beaten by the local party boss, Qiu Ju, a poor peasant woman, demands an apology. Upon his repeated refusals, she takes her case to ever-higher courts and encounters every stone wall the byzantine Chinese bureaucracy can put in her way. *Qiu Ju* is remarkable in its simplicity; Zhang has stripped his cinematic style to the bare minimum, eschewing the luxurious mise-en-scène and stunning photography of his other works. (Chinese with English subtitles) ★★★½

Story of Sin

(1975, 128 min, Poland, Walerian Borowczyk) An elegant, full-bodied melodrama, set in turn-of-the-century Poland, tracing the life of a young girl, strictly raised, whose downfall is presaged when she opens her heart and soul to a married man. Misfortunes befall our innocent heroine as she becomes pregnant, is forced to get rid of the baby and slinks into degrading prostitution. Adopting the position that love has no place in an immoral, exploitative world, the harrowing drama takes an erotic, albeit sluggish, angle on *amour fou.* (Polish with English subtitles) ★★★

The Story of the Last Chrysanthemum

(1939, 145 min, Japan, Kenji Mizoguchi) *Shotaro Hanayagi, Kakuko Mori, Gonjuro Kawarazaki.* Bristling with passion and filmed with startling imagery, this poignant tale chronicles the life of a Kabuki actor in 1880s Tokyo. The young man, Kikunosuke, despondent after being ridiculed by other members of his father's famous troupe, returns home and begins an affair with a servant girl and, on his father's insistence, sets out on his own. The responsibility for both their survival and his eventual rise as a celebrated actor rests with his wife, Okoku, who sacrifices everything, even her health, for his success. This heartbreaker borders on over-sentimentality but is still a fascinating classic of doomed love. (Japanese with English subtitles) ★★★½ VHS: $29.99

The Story of Us

(1999, 120 min, US, Rob Reiner) *Bruce Willis, Michelle Pfeiffer, Rob Reiner, Rita Wilson, Colleen Rennison, Jake Sandvig, Tim Matheson, Julie Hagerty, Paul Reiser.* It seems we've been down this road before. The characters look familiar, as well as the conversations, the story, the outcome. Wasn't it Woody Allen? Or was it Nora Ephron? In this *Snippets from a Marriage,* a husband and wife, Ben (Willis) and Katie (Pfeiffer), narrate the route to their current break-up. The story follows through numerous flashbacks their meeting, marriage, parenthood, careers, friends, misunderstandings; all of which pit them against each other on the road to divorce. Willis and Pfeiffer give sincere performances, but the writing is sparse and the bittersweet film never delivers when it should. Despite a few laughs, this is all the fun of going through one's own separation. ★★ DVD: $9.99, VHS: $9.99

The Story of Vernon and Irene Castle

(1939, 93 min, US, H.C. Potter) *Fred Astaire, Ginger Rogers, Edna May Oliver, Walter Brennan.* The last of the Astaire-Rogers 1930s musicals for RKO is an appealing bio of the early 20th-century dancing team. Fred and Ginger's dancing is up to par, but it certainly doesn't rate with their other 1930s classics. ★★½ VHS: $14.99

Story of Women

(1988, 110 min, France, Claude Chabrol) *Isabelle Huppert, François Cluzet.* In this chilling and thought-provoking drama set in Vichy, France, Huppert is extraordinary as a wife whose husband is away at the front. She is persuaded to perform an abortion on a distraught neighbor. In a desperate attempt to support herself, she begins offering the service to others; but she is soon arrested by the fascist officials. The drama, based on a real-life criminal case, recounts the story without sentiment and flawlessly evokes the tense mood of an occupied people. But it is Huppert's spellbinding portrayal of an independent, vunerable and, at times, unsympathetic character which gives the film its lasting power. (French with English subtitles) ★★★½ VHS: $19.99

5

Storyville

(1992, 112 min, US, Mark Frost) *James Spader, Joanne Whalley-Kilmer, Jason Robards, Piper Laurie.* Spader plays an ambitious young man running for the Senate position recently vacated by the indictment, and later death, of his father. Robards is Spader's more ambitious, self-serving and unscrupulous uncle, using his own private agenda as he guides the candidate's career. The campaign runs into trouble when Spader becomes involved in a murder investigation that threatens to expose more deep secrets than he could imagine. An involving romantic courtroom mystery with a little gratuitous sex and violence thrown in. ★★½ DVD: $19.99

Stowaway in the Sky

(1962, 82 min, France, Albert Lamorisse) *Andre Gille, Maurice Baquet, Pascal Lamorisse, Narrated by:, Jack Lemmon.* This enchanting fable is a terrific companion piece to director Lamorisse's *The Red Balloon* and will delight children as well as adults as it presents an aerial tour of Europe from the cockpit of a hot air balloon. Pascal climbs aboard his grandfather's magical flying machine for an unforgettable journey. From the streets of Paris to the tip of Mont Blanc and the Canary Islands, this exhilarating ride features spectacular cinematography of Paris and the French countryside. Scenes of a stag hunt and flamingos in flight are breathtaking, and director Lamorisse punctuates the "action" with some slapstick comic moments courtesy of a clumsy mechanic. ★★★½ VHS: $19.99

La Strada

(1954, 115 min, Italy, Federico Fellini) *Anthony Quinn, Guilietta Masina, Richard Basehart.* Fellini's tender and haunting tale of a brutish circus strongman (Quinn) and his sidekick (Masina) whose loneliness and solitude bind them together in a tenuous relationship. A truly poetic classic and an Academy Award winner, with stunning portrayals from both Masina and Quinn. (Italian with English subtitles) ★★★★ DVD Criterion Collection: $39.99, VHS: $29.99

Straight for the Heart

(1988, 92 min, Canada, Léa Pool) *Matthias Habich.* Returning from a harrowing trip to Nicaragua, where he has witnessed and photographed the horrors of war, prize-winning photojournalist Pierre returns home to Montreal only to find that Sarah and David, his lovers in a ten-year ménage à trois, have both left him. This absorbing drama, unusual for its matter-of-fact approach to bisexuality, explores the man's devastated life — from his futile attempts to reunite the threesome, to his wanderings through the city photographing urban decay. An intriguing, melancholy love story and quiet study of a man's emotional void, reminiscent in part of Alain Tanner's *In the White City*. (French with English subtitles) ★★★ VHS: $39.99

Straight Out of Brooklyn

(1991, 91 min, US, Matty Rich) *George T. Odom, Ann D. Sanders, Lawrence Gilliard, Matty Rich.* Nineteen-year-old Rich wrote and directed this remarkable and highly personal exposé of life in the projects. The story follows Dennis, a teenager who thinks of nothing but getting out of the ghetto. Plagued by his savagely alcoholic father, and with nowhere to go, he ultimately concocts an outrageous and ill-advised scheme to rob a drug dealer. While lacking the power and sophistication of *Boyz n the Hood*, this is nevertheless a gritty and hard-hitting film. ★★★ DVD Dual: $14.99, VHS: $9.99

Guilietta Masina (l.) and Anthony Quinn in Fellini's classic *La Strada*

The Straight Story

(1999, 115 min, US, David Lynch) *Richard Farnsworth, Sissy Spacek, Jane Galloway Heitz, James Cada, Everett McGill, Harry Dean Stanton.* In a quiet, commanding portrayal, Farnsworth gives a career performance as Alvin Straight, an Iowa widower who lives with his speech-impaired daughter (Spacek). Having suffered a stroke which now requires him to walk with two canes, Alvin sets out on an impossible trek when he learns that his estranged brother is gravely ill: journey 250 miles to Wisconsin to see him — traveling on a lawnmower. Lynch embraces the American Heartland without his signature cinematic touches. Having pushed the envelope with his previous films, Lynch retreats in the opposite direction and finds artistry in the traditional. He tells this simple, affecting true story with precision and exquisite grace. Thankfully, no one's in a hurry, and the film's deliberate pacing befits Alvin's slow, determined, fascinating trip. On his way, Alvin meets some interesting people, demonstrates his resolve, and finds meaning in ordinary endeavors. And we're all the richer for it. ★★★★ DVD: $19.99, VHS: $14.99

Straight Talk

(1992, 91 min, US, Barnet Kellman) *Dolly Parton, James Woods, Griffin Dunne, Michael Madsen, John Sayles, Jerry Orbach.* A mildly entertaining comedy about a good-hearted country girl (Parton) who moves to Chicago and manages to get herself a job as a telephone operator at a radio station. On her first day, she searches for the bathroom and ends up in the control room where she's mistaken for the new on-air psychologist. Of course, she's a hit with the listeners, a profitable problem for the station manager (Dunne) and the subject of an investigation from cynical newspaper reporter Woods, who is completely out-of-sync with the rest of the cast. ★★ DVD: $9.99

Straight Time

(1977, 114 min, US, Ulu Grosbard) *Dustin Hoffman, Theresa Russell, Gary Busey, Harry Dean Stanton.* A recently released con (Hoffman) finds himself trapped between an indifferent criminal system and his own unconscious bent toward self-destruction. A provocative if ambitious drama helped by a strong supporting cast. ★★½ VHS: $14.99

Straight to Hell

(1987, 86 min, US, Alex Cox) *Sy Richardson, Joe Strummer, Dick Rude, Courtney Love, Dennis Hopper, Elvis Costello, Grace Jones, Jim Jarmusch.* Director Cox takes on the spaghetti western, as the bizarre citizens of a desert hamlet find themselves at the mercy of two rival gangs. Only partially successful, it's pretentious though occasionally amusing. ★★ DVD Letterbox: $24.99

Strait-Jacket

(1964, 89 min, US, William Castle) *Joan Crawford, Leif Erickson.* "Have Ax Will Travel" as Crawford plays an ax murderer recently released from prison. She moves to a community where it seems she's up to her old tricks. Crawford's Gothic horror follow-up to *Baby Jane* is alternately campy and occasionally effective — though its little success obviously is in the star's hammy playing. ★★½ DVD Letterbox: $24.99, VHS: $19.99

The Strange Affair of Uncle Harry

(1945, 80 min, US, Robert Siodmak) *George Sanders, Geraldine Fitzgerald.* Sanders is affecting as a shy man who must take drastic steps to get out of the domineering psychological grip of his two scheming sisters in this impressive Hitchcockian small-town thriller. A gripping and intelligent drama of obsession, hypochondria and the recuperative powers of love. ★★★ VHS: $19.99

Strange Behavior

(1981, 98 min, New Zealand, Michael Laughlin) *Louise Fletcher, Michael Murphy, Fionna Lewis.* A small college town is rocked by a series of brutal murders, which appear to be strangely linked to a psychology class experiment with an auto-suggestive drug. Laughlin sustains an eerie mood throughout, but the film loses some steam in the final half. ★★½ DVD Letterbox: $19.99

Strange Days

(1995, 145 min, US, Kathryn Bigelow) *Ralph Fiennes, Angela Bassett, Juliette Lewis, Tom Sizemore, Vincent D'Onofrio.* Full of visceral thrills, this slam-bang, hallucinatory thriller set on the eve of the new millennium stars Fiennes as Lenny, a former policeman who peddles virtual reality discs containing the experiences of others. However, when one of his clients is murdered, Lenny becomes involved in an out-of-control pursuit to find her murderer, track a serial killer, and expose a police cover-up of a racially motivated murder. Bassett is Mace, a bodyguard and friend who helps Lenny, and occasionally acts as moral compass. Their performances help immeasurably in giving the film an intelligence that clearly elevates it above teh standard actioner.Bigelow's direction assures one exciting scene is followed by another. There is, however, a brutal rape sequence which could offend many viewers. Written by James Cameron. ★★★½ DVD Letterbox: $9.99, VHS: $9.99, VHS Letterbox: $19.99

Strange Impersonation

(1946, 68 min, US, Anthony Mann) *Brenda Marshall, William Gargan, Hillary Brooke, Lyle Talbot.* Just on the brink of her greatest discovery, scientist Marshall has her experimental new anesthetic — and her love life — stolen by her ruthless assistant. Horribly disfigured in a lab fire, she melds out revenge undercover of a new face against all those who have wronged her. Hyperbolic and hypnotic, this tearjerker twists and turns like a sports car on a mountain road, frantic fun and one wild ride. ★★★ DVD: $29.99, VHS: $24.99

Strange Interlude

(1932, 111 min, US, Robert Z. Leonard) *Norma Shearer, Clark Gable, May Robson, Maureen O'Sullivan.* Eugene O'Neill's powerful Pulitzer Prize-winning play of deceit and unrequited love gets a poignant and sturdy film adaptation — surprising considering the film retains O'Neill's innovative theatrical device of characters speaking their innermost thoughts. Shearer rises to the demands of her most challenging role, playing a woman who is haunted by the death of her fiancé. Though condensed, the film still manages to capture the essence of O'Neill's complex work. ★★★½ VHS: $19.99

Strange Invaders

(1983, 94 min, US, Michael Laughlin) *Paul LeMat, Nancy Allen, Louise Fletcher, June Lockhart, Kenneth Tobey.* When a small town gets taken over by aliens that look just like you and me, how can anybody tell? And does it make any difference? Fifties icons Tobey and Lockhart show a cast of young turks how one went about vanquishing spacemen back in the old days. A generally entertaining spoof. ★★★ DVD Letterbox: $14.99

The Strange Love of Martha Ivers

(1946, 117 min, US, Lewis Milestone) *Barbara Stanwyck, Kirk Douglas, Van Heflin.* Though its title suggests a '40s "B" potboiler, this gritty melodrama is anything but. Stanwyck gives a smashing performance as a wealthy, neurotic wife who is haunted by a murder in her past. Douglas makes a fine film debut as her spineless husband. Their lives come apart when old friend Heflin returns to town, digging up the past. ★★★ DVD: $19.99, VHS: $19.99

The Strange One

(1957, 100 min, US, Jack Garfein) *Ben Gazarra, George Peppard, Pat Hingle, James Olson.* Gazarra is riveting in a star-making performance as Jocko DeParis, a senior cadet at a Southern military college whose sadistic bullying and cocky manipulations pave the way for his downfall. He, along with his less self-assured roommate (Hingle), take pleasure in intimidating two freshman and later in concocting a scheme that ends in a beating. Cadets caught in the crossfire are forced to choose between silence (and staying in the school) or telling the truth (and face expulsion). A taut, sweaty drama that features excellent acting and an intense screenplay by Calder Willingham. ★★★

Strangeland

(1998, 90 min, US, John Pieplow) *Dee Snider, Kevin Gage, Elizabeth Peña, Brett Harrelson, Robert Englund.* In this ugly, incredibly amateurish feature, former Twisted Sister lead singer Snider makes his writing and acting debut as a deranged "modern primitive" who kidnaps and tortures people to "free" them with body piercing and the like. He lures his victims by posing as a rad teen in teen chat rooms on the internet. There's none of the over-the-top fun of the old Twisted Sister music videos on display here, just insipid horror. ★ DVD: $14.99, VHS: $9.99

The Stranger

(1946, 95 min, US, Orson Welles) *Edward G. Robinson, Orson Welles, Loretta Young.* Well-crafted thriller with Robinson as a government agent who is sent to a small college town in Connecticut to track down an escaped Nazi war criminal. Welles, as the feared German, is the embodiment of evil. Young is Welles' unsuspecting fiancée. ★★★½ VHS: $19.99

The Stranger

(1967, 104 min, France/Italy, Luchino Visconti) *Marcello Mastroianni.* A faithful, hypnotic adaptation of Albert Camus' existential treatise, this involving drama stars Mastroianni as Mersault, an individual seized by emptiness and isolated from society. Against the languid backdrop of Algiers, his detachment from existence abruptly ends when he commits a senseless murder and stands trial. Imprisoned and stripped of his physical freedom, Mersault experiences a liberating resignation as he surrenders to the "benign indifference of the universe." A quietly powerful and unsettling work. (Italian with English subtitles) ★★★

The Stranger

(1988, 93 min, US, Adolfo Aristarian) *Bonnie Bedelia, Peter Reigert.* A woman (Bedelia) stricken with amnesia slowly realizes she is the only witness to a series of brutal murders and must piece together the mystery before the killer can find her. An intriguing premise is well played, though it's not as suspenseful as it could have been. ★★½

The Stranger

(1991, 120 min, India, Satyajit Ray) *Depankar De, Mamata Shankar, Bikram Bannerjee, Utpal Dutt.* Ray's swan song is a wonderful and fitting tribute to the artist's legacy — using simple cinematic jestures to tell a simple tale while delivering ample emotional, spiritual and narrative clout. The film opens when Anila (Shankar) — a prototypical Indian middle-class housewife — receives a letter from her long-lost uncle (Dutt) announcing that he will be in Calcutta and wishes to visit. Filled with suspicion that he is not who he says, but an imposter attempting to freeload, she and her family become obsessed with verifying his true identity. The enchanting, enigmatic uncle — all the while playing cat and mouse with the family's suspicions — gently guides them towards some inner-awakening. (Bengali with English subtitles) ★★★★ VHS: $29.99

A Stranger Among Us

(1992, 109 min, US, Sidney Lumet) *Melanie Griffith, Eric Thal.* This Lumet dramatic thriller so resembles Peter Weir's *Witness* that it has been dubbed *Vitness.* Griffith is a New York undercover cop sent into Brooklyn's Hasidic community to root out a jewel thief/killer. Of course, all of her coarse, unladylike behavior is transformed by the gentle, loving touch of this quaint people, but not before she tries her best to lead the Rabbi's son to temptation. The film can't overcome its formulaic shallowness and fails to rise above its gushy, adoring view of the Hasidim. ★★ DVD: $9.99

Stranger on the Third Floor

(1940, 64 min, US, Boris Ingster) *Peter Lorre, Elisha Cook, Jr., John McGuire.* Thanks to the stunning art direction by Van Nest Polglase (whose next project would be *Citizen Kane*), this little sleeper is considered by many to be the first true film noir. Taxi driver Cook is sentenced to the chair for a rather brutal murder on the testimony of press reporter McGuire. Now the reporter is having some doubts. Lorre as the titular character gives his best performance since *M*. ★★★

Stranger than Paradise

(1984, 90 min, US, Jim Jarmusch) *John Lurie, Eszter Balint, Richard Edson.* From the scroungy anomie of New York's Lower East Side to the snowy desolation of Cleveland to the sunny listlessness of Florida, this poker-faced neo-comedy follows the stillborn adventures of three amiable misfits in search of a natural habitat. Director Jarmusch's cool shaggy-dog minimalism is absurdly funny and boldly original. ★★★★ DVD: $19.99

Stranger Than Paradise

Strangers in Good Company

(1990, 101 min, Canada, Cynthia Scott) *Alice Diabo, Mary Meigs.* This spirited, low-budget gem documents the travails of eight elderly women who become stranded in the wilderness when their tour bus breaks down. Using their resources, they find an abandoned house and begin foraging for food. Tremendously diverse in character and background, they each have a story to tell and the film allows them to do just that. Filmed entirely on location with an ensemble of non-actors who essentially play themselves, *Strangers in Good Company* is a wonderfully heartwarming homage to the spirit of these women, and to the wondrous application of one's continual self-discovery. ★★★½ DVD: $29.99, VHS: $19.99

Strangers on a Train

(1951, 103 min, US/GB, Alfred Hitchcock) *Farley Granger, Robert Walker, Ruth Roman, Leo G. Carroll, Marion Lorne.* Hitchcock's slick psycogical thriller tackles blackmail, murder and latent homosexuality as Granger meets Walker on a train and soon becomes an unwilling partner in crime. A superior effort that features a knockout ending which is exemplary of the unrelenting tension the Master of Suspense could create. The basis for the spoof *Throw Momma from the Train.* (Includes two minutes not shown in the American theatrical release) ★★★★ DVD Double Feature: $19.99, VHS Hollywood Version: $14.99, VHS British Version: $14.99

Strapless

(1989, 103 min, GB, David Hare) *Blair Brown, Bridget Fonda, Bruno Ganz.* With lush settings and a dreamy score (including Nat King Cole's "When I Fall in Love"), writer-director Hare sets a romantic tone in this unconventional film. Brown (Hare's wife) portrays an American physician living in Britain who discovers love and confusion in both her carefree sister (Fonda) and an enigmatic businessman (Ganz). Hare's direction is fluent, his dialogue graceful; Brown beautifully depicts a woman on the uneasy path to self-discovery. ★★★ DVD: $14.99, VHS: $9.99

Straw Dogs

(1972, 118 min, GB, Sam Peckinpah) *Dustin Hoffman, Susan George, David Warner.* Hoffman is the meek mathematician who, when his wife and home are attacked, finds catharsis and renewed masculinity in a violent, bloody confrontation. A film of incredible tension masterfully directed and conceived by Peckinpah. Includes footage not shown in the American theatrical print. ★★★½ DVD Letterbox Criterion Collection: $39.99

Strawberry & Chocolate

(1993, 110 min, Cuba, Juan Carlos Tabío & Tomás Gutiérrez Alea) *Jorge Perugorria, Vladimir Cruz, Marta Ibarra.* This Oscar nominee is both a delightful comedy of friendship and love as well as a surprisingly critical political drama. Set in 1979 Havana, the story centers on the unlikely friendship between David (Cruz), a shy, straight and lost soul who blindly believes in the righteousness of the Revolution, and Diego (Perugorria), a swishy but intelligent, witty and opinionated gay man. Diego seduces David — not through sex but by his free-thinking appreciation of life, art and by an effervescent personality. A celebration of individuality in the face of conformity. (Spanish with English subtitles) ★★★½ DVD: $19.99, VHS: $9.99

Stray Dog

Strawberry Blonde

(1941, 97 min, US, Raoul Walsh) *James Cagney, Rita Hayworth, Olivia de Havilland.* Cagney is terrific as a young dentist whose life becomes a chaotic, emotional maze when he falls for a ravishing gold-digger (Hayworth) only to marry a more proper de Havilland. Director Walsh offers up a timely blend of laughter, nostalgia, action and romance. ★★★ VHS: $19.99

The Strawberry Statement

(1970, 109 min, US, Stuart Haggman) *Bruce Davison, Kim Darby.* Dated but interesting version of James Kunen's novel of '60s campus protest. Davison stars as a college jock who becomes involved with Darby and a campus strike. Featuring an outstanding soundtrack containing many '60s rock standards. ★★★ VHS: $69.99

Stray Dog

(1949, 122 min, Japan, Akira Kurosawa) *Toshiro Mifune, Takashi Shimura.* This stylized, non-samurai work from Kurosawa is an intense police thriller set in a seamy, war-ravaged Tokyo. Mifune plays a rookie detective who loses his gun to a pickpocket and, fearing the pistol will fall into the hands of a killer, begins a desperate search through the underworld in an attempt to find the pistol and the thief. An under-appreciated murder mystery from the master of Japanese cinema. (Japanese with English subtitles) ★★★ DVD Criterion Collection: $39.99, VHS: $29.99

Streamers

(1983, 118 min, US, Robert Altman) *David Alan Grier, Matthew Modine, Mitchell Lichtenstein, Michael Wright.* Altman utilizes the intensity of the theatrical experience with the opportunities offered through film in this adaptation of David Rabe's award-winning play. *Streamers* is an ensemble piece, set in a claustrophobic Army barracks, featuring four ill-assorted young soldiers waiting for assignments to Vietnam. Hidden fears and prejudices generate sexual intolerance, racial distrust and a misunderstanding which leads to violence. ★★★

Street Fighter

(1994, 95 min, US, Steven E. deSouza) *Jean-Claude Van Damme, Raul Julia, Wes Studi, Simon Callow, Roshan Seth.* Van Damme stars as the head of an elite military unit whose mission in life is to stop the nefarious General Bison (Julia), a dictator bent on global domination. With the help of martial arts experts who would look more at home broadcasting the weather on CNN, Van Damme plays a boring game of cat and mouse with his adversary until a prolonged and surprisingly unexciting fight finale. ★ DVD Collector's Edition: $9.99

Street Kid

(1990, 89 min, Germany, Peter Kern) Fourteen-year-old Axel prowls the mean streets of Dusseldorf selling his body to pederasts — all of whom are out to taste forbidden fruit. Similar to *Christiane F.* in depicting the gritty and harsh life of teenagers on the streets, the film's sardonic humor keeps it from being somber as it follows the bisexual Axel who, despite abusive parents (his own father rapes him at one point), possesses a fun-loving and tender attitude. Life takes an unexpected change for the boy after he meets an unhappily married man twice his age who falls in love with him. (German with English subtitles) ★★★ VHS: $49.99

Street Music

(1981, 88 min, US, Jenny Bowen) *Elizabeth Daily, Larry Breeding.* An ambitious street musician/singer (Daily) and her bus driver boyfriend (Breeding) find themselves unlikely champions of the elderly when the run-down hotel in which they all live is about to be torn down. An intriguing mixture of social responsibility and musical aspiration that occasionally manages to rise above the clichés and its unusual scenario. ★★½ VHS: $69.99

Street of Shame

(1956, 88 min, Japan, Kenji Mizoguchi) *Machiko Kyo, Aiko Mimasu.* Mizoguchi's final film is set in 1956 in a Tokyo brothel and explores the lives, dreams and hardships facing a group of prostitutes. This stirring portrait of the women delves not only into brothel life but follows them into the harsh streets of the city and into their homes. A penetrating study of love and sex and a powerful cinematic vision. (Japanese with English subtitles) ★★★½ VHS: $29.99

Street Smart

(1987, 95 min, US, Jerry Schatzberg) *Morgan Freeman, Christopher Reeve, Kathy Baker.* Freeman's blistering portrait of a ruthless pimp highlights this gritty urban drama about a newspaper reporter (Reeve in a change-of-pace role) who fabricates a story about the private life of a pimp — which turns out to be all too close to that of Freeman. Baker is exceptional as one of Freeman's working girls. ★★★ DVD Dual: $14.99

Street Trash

(1987, 90 min, US, Jim Muro) Totally disgusting, *Street Trash* is not more than one step up from a student film, though it is competently made and has good production values considering its setting. The minimal story is about a toxic brand of cheap liquor which melts its imbibers from the inside out. The movie has a guilty pleasure feel about it, from its well-done and completely disgusting special make-up effects to its gallows humor to its depiction of life in the seediest part of town. ★★ VHS: $79.99

The Street with No Name

(1948, 91 min, US, William Keighley) *Richard Widmark, Mark Stevens, Lloyd Nolan.* An exciting crime thriller with a chilling performance by Widmark as an up-and-coming crime boss who targets an FBI agent for death when the feds get too close to his gang's operations. ★★★ VHS: $19.99

A Streetcar Named Desire

(1951, 122 min, US, Elia Kazan) *Marlon Brando, Vivien Leigh, Karl Malden, Kim Hunter.* Brando is the brutish Stanley Kowalski, who psychologically strips his fragile sister-in-law Blanche (Leigh) until her breakdown is complete. Tennessee Williams' masterpiece is layered with sexual symbolism and haunting imagery, and features fine support from Malden as a well-intentioned suitor and Hunter as Stanley's beleaguered wife. Brando and Oscar winner Leigh's performances have over time become part of our cinematic heritage. (Includes additional footage not in the American theatrical release) ★★★★ DVD: $19.99

The Streetfighter

(1975, 91 min, Japan, Seiji Ozawa) *Sonny Chiba.* An entertaining, slightly cheesy 1970s martial arts film. Presented in its original, uncut version, the film is awash in brutal violence. Terry Tsurugi (Chiba) is a killer-for-hire who helps rescue Junjo, an important gang member, from prison. After killing Junjo's associate during a double-cross attempt, Terry finds himself pursued by the criminals who hired him. Great martial arts fun is available in megadoses here. ★★★ VHS: $19.99

Streets of Fire

(1984, 93 min, US, Walter Hill) *Michael Paré, Willem Dafoe, Diane Lane, Rick Moranis, Amy Madigan.* Kinda hip and fun rock 'n' roll fable with Paré as a soldier of fortune who returns to his old neighborhood to rescue his ex-girlfriend from the clutches of a vicious motorcycle gang. ★★★ DVD: $14.99

Streets of Gold

(1986, 95 min, US, Joe Roth) *Klaus Maria Brandauer, Wesley Snipes, Adrian Pasdar.* A sincere performance from Brandauer elevates this ordinary

boxing drama about a Russian fighter, now living in Brooklyn as a dishwasher, who trains two youths (Pasdar, Snipes) for the American team — in the hopes of competing against his former coach. ★★½

Streetwise

(1985, 92 min, US, Martin Bell) An extraordinary documentary which chronicles the lives of nine young runaways, ages 13 to 19, who survive in the drug and tenderloin district of Seattle and support themselves by prostitution, pimping, panhandling and petty thievery. It's a bleak picture, but one that also captures sweet flirtatious moments and times of shared humor and experience as these kids try to create a niche for themselves. Oscar nominee for Best Documentary. ★★★★

Strictly Ballroom

(1992, 94 min, Australia, Baz Luhrmann) *Paul Mercurio, Tara Morice, Bill Hunter, Barry Otto.* Tapping into the Fred and Ginger in all of us, Luhrmann has crafted a glorious take on the elegant world of ballroom dancing. Mercurio is a bad-boy hoofer whose innovative technique flies in the face of tradition, making him an outcast in a dance community where "ballroom" has been elevated to a religion. With a nod to *Dirty Dancing*, he takes up with an awkward dance student (Morice) and the two set out to win the big dance competition. As by-the-books as it sounds, a laugh-out-loud, zany and enjoyable musical is born. ★★★½ DVD Letterbox: $19.99, VHS: $9.99

Strictly Business

(1991, 83 min, US, Kevin Hooks) *Jospeh C. Phillips, Tommy Davidson, Halle Berry, Samuel L. Jackson.* Hooks has fashioned a warm comedy about a dyed-in-the-wool "buppie" (Phillips) who enlists the aid of a mailroom clerk (Davidson) to help him meet the girl of his dreams (Berry). While yet another "message" movie from the black community for the black community, this one manages to mix a little sugar with the medicine, making its theme of unity and racial harmony an enjoyable pill to swallow. ★★½ VHS: $19.99

Strike

(1924, 82 min, USSR, Sergei Eisenstein) *Maxim Shtraukh, Grigori Alexandrov.* In a remarkable directorial debut, Eisenstein introduced radical innovations in editing, montage and camera work in presenting this impassioned film about the struggles of workers embroiled in a violent strike at a Moscow factory, set before the Revolution. He recounts the workers' hardships and exploitation as well as the devastating strike itself — the resulting hunger, the presence of predatory infiltrators and ultimately the bloody massacre by the militia. (Silent with music by the Alloy Orchestra) ★★★★ DVD: $24.99, VHS: $19.99

Strike!

(1999, 97 min, US, Sarah Kernochan) *Kirsten Dunst, Gaby Hoffman.* The most attractive cast of young women outside of the horror genre is unfortunately dumped into this confused movie about a girls' school. Godard's School for Girls is out of money and going co-ed, unless the girls can stop the merger. *Strike!* tries to be a sweet coming-of-age film of female bonding, but any sincerity is sorely tested by a climax that involves a choir of boys vomiting on everything. Despite the eye candy of Dunst, Hoffman and Cook, this *Strike* couldn't end any sooner. (aka: *All I Wanna Do*) ★½

Striking Distance

(1993, 102 min, US, Rowdy Herrington) *Bruce Willis, Sarah Jessica Parker, Dennis Farina, Tom Sizemore, John Mahoney.* A by-the-books thriller about a by-the-books cop whose demotion to the Pittsburgh River patrol comes in handy when his ex-girlfriends start turning up as fishbait courtesy of a serial killer with an inside knowledge of police procedure. ★★½ DVD: $14.99, VHS: $9.99

Stripes

(1981, 106 min, US, Ivan Reitman) *Bill Murray, Harold Ramis, P.J. Soles, Warren Oates, John Candy.* Murray and Ramis team up with director Reitman in this mildly successful, pre-*Ghostbusters* comedy spoof on life in the Army. Murray and Ramis play a couple of losers who join under the assumption that life in the forces will be an easy overseas holiday. Along the way, they hoodwink their superiors and become inadvertent heroes. Goofy and sophomoric, Murray's charm and the spirited performances of the supporting cast provide this military farce with "a few good laughs." ★★½ DVD: $14.99, VHS: $9.99

The Stripper

(1963, 95 min, US, Franklin J. Schaffner) *Joanne Woodward, Richard Beymer, Claire Trevor, Gypsy Rose Lee.* Woodward's competent performance saves this William Inge melodrama about an aging stripper and her affair with a young man. ★★½

Striptease

(1996, 115 min, US, Andrew Bergman) *Demi Moore, Burt Reynolds, Armand Assante, Ving Rhames, Robert Patrick.* Carl Hiaasen's cunning satirical novel has been stripped of its bite and wit. When she loses custody of her child to her slimy husband, Moore takes a high-paying job at a Fort Lauderdale strip club to earn enough money to reopen the case. Becoming its star attraction, Moore becomes the unwilling object of lust from a local congressman (Reynolds) which leads to murder and run-ins with the mob. Bergman is unable to capture the flavor of the book or convey the energy and tempo of good satirical comedy. And he's not helped

Striptease

by a sullen Moore. Reynolds, on the other hand, appears to fully understand the nuances of farce, and gives a most pleasurable performance. ★½ DVD Unrated: $19.99

Stromboli

(1950, 81 min, Italy, Roberto Rossellini) *Ingrid Bergman.* This neorealist Rossellini drama stars Bergman as a woman who escapes an internment camp only to marry an unresponsive fisherman and live on a barren, bleak island confronting poverty and a spiritual sort of prison. Although the film received excellent reviews, the Bergman/Rossellini extramarital affair during the time of the release doomed the picture commercially. (Filmed in English) ★★★ VHS: $29.99

Stroszek

(1977, 108 min, Germany, Werner Herzog) *Bruno S., Eva Mattes.* Three German misfits — a whore, a former mental patient and an eccentric old man — confront the American Dream in one of Herzog's funniest and most accessible films. Fleeing Berlin, the trio's wanderings lead them to the barren bleakness of Railroad Flats, Wisconsin. Setting up house in a mobile home bought on credit, they attempt to come to terms with the dubious splendors of American culture: TV, football, dancing chickens, and other oddball bits of Americana. A lyrical, perceptive and bittersweet comedy. (German with English subtitles) ★★★½

Stuart Little

(1999, 85 min, US, Rob Minkoff) *Geena Davis, Hugh Laurie, Jonathan Lipnicki, Michael J. Fox, Nathan Lane.* The perfectly strange Little couple (Davis and Laurie) head to the orphanage. In E.B. White's fanciful world (and to their son Lipnicki's consternation), the fact that they adopt a mouse named Stuart is really no big deal, just another happy little quirk in their two-story townhouse overlooking Manhattan's Central Park. Computer effects and Fox's permapubescent voice blend seamlessly to create this new family member, who experiences the same pains as anyone entering a new home. Though things get too frenetic at the end, the comedy within the family is grandly entertaining, with plenty of imagination for kids and grownups alike. (Sequel: *Stuart Little 2*) ★★★ DVD Deluxe Edition: $19.99, VHS: $14.99

Sugar Cane Alley

Stuart Saves His Family

(1995, 97 min, US, Harold Ramis) *Al Franken, Laura San Giacomo, Vincent D'Onofrio.* Based on his "S.N.L." skit, Franken stars as the nebbishly New Age talk show host who's "good enough and smart enough . . . " until the cancellation of his cable-access show forces him to come to terms with his own dysfunctional family. Alternately funny and tired, Franken's screenplay pokes fun at the New Age and 12-step programs while also trying to reach a catharsis from their application, though he is more successful in his spoofing than the sometimes dreadful pathos. ★★ DVD: $29.99, VHS: $19.99

The Student Prince at Old Heidelberg

(1927, 105 min, US, Ernst Lubitsch) *Ramon Novarro, Norma Shearer.* This silent film version doesn't really miss the music of Romberg's operetta, with its breezy charm that became known as the "Lubitsch Touch." Novarro is effervescent as the heir to the throne getting to cut loose for the first time now that he's away from college. Everything would have been fine if he hadn't fallen in love with bar-frau Shearer at the fraternity beer bash. ★★★½ VHS: $29.99

The Stuff

(1985, 93 min, US, Larry Cohen) *Michael Moriarty, Andrea Marcovicci, Garrett Morris, Paul Sorvino, Danny Aiello.* Playfully satiric horror film about a mysterious goo — the newest culinary fad — which turns those who eat it into zombies with an appetite. ★★

The Stunt Man

(1980, 129 min, US, Richard Rush) *Peter O'Toole, Steve Railsback, Barbara Hershey.* O'Toole is the maniacal film director who befriends then dominates a young man (Railsback) on the run from the police. A frenetically paced, tautly edited story about paranoia and illusion versus reality. ★★★★ DVD Letterbox: $19.99, DVD Limited Edition: $29.99, VHS Letterboxed: $9.99

The Subject Was Roses

(1968, 107 min, US, Ulu Grosbard) *Patricia Neal, Martin Sheen, Jack Albertson.* Reprising their acclaimed stage roles from the Pulitzer Prize-winning play by Frank D. Gilroy, Sheen and Oscar winner Albertson offer heartfelt performances in this story of a troubled WWII vet returning to his Bronx home. Neal, however, is the heart and soul of this moving film, giving a shimmering portrait of a mother trying to establish communication with those around her, and by returning to the screen after an almost career-ending stroke. ★★★ VHS: $14.99

The Substance of Fire

(1996, 101 min, US, Daniel Sullivan) *Ron Rifkin, Sarah Jessica Parker, Tony Goldwyn, Timothy Hutton, Ronny Graham, Eric Bogosian, Debra Monk.* A father-son relationship is the central theme to this story of a publisher and his sons as they disagree on the direction of the family business. Based on the successful off-Broadway play, with Rifkin reprising his role of the headstrong patriarch. Intense performances from the whole cast, especially Rifkin as the publisher/father. ★★★ DVD: $19.99

The Substitute

(1996, 114 min, US, Robert Mandel) *Tom Berenger, Ernie Hudson, Diane Venora, Marc Anthony, Glenn Plummer, Cliff De Young, William Forsythe.* Berenger's patented sensitive tough guy is this time an unemployed covert op. He assumes

the cover of substitute teacher, replacing his on-again, off-again lover (Venora) when her leg is broken by the school's reigning gang leader. Within a few days, this warrior-with-a-gentle-heart uncovers a nasty little secret on school grounds and enlists his mercenary buddies to help take on the gang. (Followed by 2 sequels) ★★ DVD Double Feature: $9.99, VHS: $9.99

Suburban Roulette

(1967, 70 min, US, Hershell Gordon Lewis) *Tom Wood.* Although best known for his gore films, director Lewis also made a number of cheap exploitation flicks. In this one, Wood stars as the father of the new family in suburbia, where the wives are swapping more than just recipes. ★ VHS: $12.99

The Suburbans

(1999, 81 min, US, Donal Lardner Ward) *Jennifer Love Hewitt, Craig Bierko, Amy Brenneman, Will Ferrell, Donal Lardner Ward, Tony Guma, Robert Loggia.* A feeble rock 'n' roll fable, *The Suburbans* is an alleged comedy about an '80s one-hit-wonder band trying to make a comeback eighteen years later. Cowritten, directed by, and starring Ward, the film fails on all three counts as the jokes are unfunny, the staging is uninspired, and most of the cast mimics Ward's wry deadpan delivery to ill effect. Hewitt stars an a record exec trying to generate interest in a now middle-aged pop band. ★ DVD: $9.99, VHS: $9.99

Suburbia

(1984, 96 min, US, Penelope Spheeris) *Chris Pederson, Bill Coyne, Jennifer Clay.* This archly funny anthem to punk nihilism captures the spirit of anomie rampant on the Mellow Coast. If only there were more social clubs, these kids wouldn't be going around ransacking neighborhood garages. (aka: *The Wild Side*) ★★½ DVD: $19.99, VHS: $14.99

SubUrbia

(1997, 117 min, US, Richard Linklater) *Giovanni Ribisi, Steve Zahn, Amie Corey, Parker Posey, Nicky Katt, Jayce Partak, Dina Spybey, Ajay Naidu.* Eric Bogosian's off-Broadway play about youthful alienation, which the author has adapted for the screen, makes a most hearty and funny film. A terrific ensemble brings to life a cast of engaging characters who, though familiar in their appearance and deed, are individualists who speak for no one but themselves. A "night in the life of," *SubUrbia* eavesdrops on a group of "misfit" friends who gather, drink beer, have sex and philosophize at the local convenience store. Their routine is interrupted one night when a former classmate and promising rock star returns after performing at a local arena. Among the talented cast, Zahn wonderfully plays the group clown, and Posey gives a smart, sensuous performance as a spirited publicist. ★★★

Subway

(1985, 103 min, France, Luc Besson) *Christopher Lambert, Isabelle Adjani, Jean-Hugues Anglade, Jean Reno.* Tuxedoed punks, mondo body-builders, roller-skating purse snatchers and roving musicians stylishly adorn Besson's glimpse at Paris underground life. A brilliantly choreographed car chase romps and roars its way into the Paris Metro, where Lambert eludes his pursuers. Amidst the labyrinthine corridors and twisted passage ways of the cavernous underground, a wonderfully colorful world of outrageous misfits springs into bloom, highlighted by a luminously attired Adjani. ★★★½ DVD: $24.99, VHS Dubbed: $14.99

Subway to the Stars

(1987, 103 min, Brazil, Carlos Diegues) *Guilherme Fontes, Milton Goncalves.* An enchanting fable that is a modernization of the Orpheus legend. The story revolves around the young Vinicius, an innocent sax-ophonist who embarks on an odyssey through the seedy and sleazy underworld of Rio de Janeiro in search of his missing girlfriend. His journey brings him in contact with cops and bandits, slum dwellers and dreamers, prostitutes and poets. Although the settings are grim and his task seemingly endless, our young hero, as well as the demimondes of the slum, retains an optimistic and dreamy attitude. (Portuguese with English subtitles) ★★★

Success Is the Best Revenge

(1984, 90 min, GB, Jerzy Skolimowski) *Michael York, Michel Piccoli, John Hurt, Anouk Aimée.* Director Skolimowski's follow-up to his widely successful *Moonlighting* continues to explore the plight of Polish immigrants in foreign lands. This time his view is slightly more autobiographical as he tells the tale of a Polish filmmaker (York) living in exile in London. As he works feverishly to make a film about the growing unrest in his homeland, he becomes estranged from his rebellious teenage son. ★★★ VHS: $9.99

Sudden Death

(1995, 110 min, US, Peter Hyams) *Jean-Claude Van Damme, Powers Boothe, Ross Malinger, Whittni Wright, Dorian Harewood.* More pre-dictable action with Van Damme, this time as an ex-firefighter who, having been unable to rescue a little girl from a burning building in the film's opening, sees a chance for redemption when terrorists take his daughter — and the Vice-President — hostage at the Stanley Cup finals. There's some fast-paced action and elaborate stuntwork, but the story starts to grow thin. ★★ DVD: $14.99

Sudden Fear

(1952, 110 min, US, David Miller) *Joan Crawford, Jack Palance, Gloria Grahame, Bruce Bennett, Virginia Huston, Mike Connors.* Crawford's face wore emotion as liberally as lipstick; here it is paired with the icy mug of Palance in an elegant romantic thriller that turns on images of inhuman faces: a clock's, a toy dog's, Palance's. As the actor fired by hit playwright Crawford for being too sin-ister-looking to play a romantic lead, Palance ener-getically charms as the film's own romantic lead — until the truth emerges, and he turns sinister, prov-ing a Hollywood Truth: appearances are everything. The film overflows with much of what made '50s noir fun: moody cinematography, a tough, tightly twisted Lenore Coffee script, an atmospheric, jazzy Elmer Bernstein score, along with the unparalleled vision of its diva star dashing up the hills of San Francisco in high heels and furs. ★★★½ DVD: $29.99, VHS: $19.99

Sudden Impact

(1983, 117 min, US, Clint Eastwood) *Clint Eastwood, Sondra Locke, Pat Hingle.* Eastwood's fourth go-round as San Francisco detective "Dirty" Harry Callahan puts him on the trail of a woman (Locke) who is getting revenge against the gang who raped her and her sister years before. The series is starting to show its age, but director Eastwood still manages to bring some life to the familiar tale. (Sequel: *The Dead Pool*) ★★½ DVD Letterbox: $14.99, VHS: $9.99

Suddenly

(1954, 77 min, US, Lewis Allen) *Frank Sinatra, Sterling Hayden, James Gleason.* Sinatra, in sort of a precursor to *The Manchurian Candidate*, plays the leader of a group of assassins in this suspenseful thriller. Little-seen for many years after the Kennedy assassination, the story concerns a group of gunmen who take over a house in a small town where the president is due. ★★★ DVD: $19.99, VHS: $19.99

Suddenly, Last Summer

(1959, 114 min, US, Joseph L. Mankiewicz) *Elizabeth Taylor, Montgomery Clift, Katharine Hepburn, Mercedes McCambridge.* A blistering Tennessee Williams drama (co-scripted by Gore Vidal) about psychiatrist Clift investigating what caused Taylor to crack while on summer vacation with Hepburn's son Sebastian. Terrific performances by Taylor and Hepburn. (Remade in 1992) ★★★

Suffering Bastards

(1990, 90 min, US, Bernard McWilliams) *John C. McGinley, David Warshofsky, Eric Bogosian.* Independent low-budget comedy about a pair of born-loser brothers (McGinley, Warshofsky) who rip off their low-life boss (Bogosian) and use the money to buy back their dead mother's Atlantic City night club, revitalizing their lounge-singing careers. Unusual, uneven but not without an abundance of quirky charm. ★★★ VHS: $89.99

Sugar & Spice

(2001, 81 min, US, Francine McDougall) *Marla Sokoloff, Marley Shelton, Melissa George, Mena Suvari, Rachel Blanchard, James Marsden.* There's not much nice with *Sugar & Spice*, a brainless satire about a cheerleading squad that robs a bank. Shelton, playing the pregnant squad captain who initiates the robbery idea, makes for a blank lead, and the rest of the cast seem similarly ill-at-ease. Check out *Bring It On* for a witty, clever cheerlead-ing satire. ★ DVD Dual Extended version: $24.99, VHS Extended version: $14.99

Sugar Cane Alley

(1984, 104 min, Martinique, Euzhan Palcy) *Gerry Cadenet.* This bittersweet Third World tale about French colonial exploitation during the 1930s focus-es on Jose, a young boy who manages to escape shantytown poverty through intellectual pursuit and the aid of his indomitable grandmother. (French with English subtitles) ★★★ VHS: $29.99

Sugar Hill

(1994, 125 min, US, Leon Ichaso) *Wesley Snipes, Michael Wright, Theresa Randle.* Director Ichaso's sometimes grisly yet gripping character study owes more to the works of William Shakespeare than to its gangster roots. Snipes stars as a Harlem drug lord who, having seen both his parents destroyed by heroin, finally decides to get out, much to the dis-may of his firebrand brother (Wright in a typically drugged-out performance). While action fans may find this a little too talky, it is nonetheless extreme-ly well acted and a worthy addition to the gangster canon. ★★★ VHS: $9.99

Sugarbaby (Zuckerbaby)

(1985, 108 min, West Germany, Percy Adlon) *Marianne Sagerbrecht, Eisi Gulp.* This tender and endearing comedy stars Sagerbrecht as a sad, over-weight mortuary attendant helplessly smitten with a slim blond subway conductor. The film radiates a fine erotic warmth as Marianne, taking leave of both her job and her senses, stalks and then captures her

Suddenly, Last Summer

prey. An unusual and compassionate essay on the power of love and will. (American remake: *Baby Cakes*) (German with English subtitles) ★★★

The Sugarland Express

(1974, 109 min, US, Steven Spielberg) *Goldie Hawn, William Atherton, Michael Sacks, Ben Johnson.* Based on a true story, Spielberg's theatri-cal debut is a vastly entertaining comedy-drama. In one of her best performances, Hawn plays a mother who helps her husband escape jail, and together they plan to kidnap their own baby, now a ward of the state. In the ensuing confusion, they take a state trooper hostage, and have the entire Texas police force on their trail as they attempt to retrieve their child. ★★★½

Suicide Kings

(1988, 103 min, US, Peter O'Fallon) *Christopher Walken, Denis Leary, Henry Thomas, Sean Patrick Flanery, Johnny Galecki, Jay Mohr, Jeremy Sisto, Laura San Giacomo, Cliff DeYoung.* Four children of privilege kidnap Charles Barrett (Walken), a man of wealth, in an attempt to pay a ransom for another kidnapping victim, the sister of one of the four. Barrett is thought to have contacts who can aid in the sister's rescue. What Barrett has without ques-tion is an unerring ability to read human nature; and as the conspirators' alliance splinters under the stress of unforeseen contingencies, Barrett exploits the schisms festering in their personal relationships. The ensemble delivers well-portrayed character studies in this ably constructed battle of wit and will. ★★★ DVD: $9.99, VHS: $9.99

Suite 16

(1994, 109 min, GB/Netherlands, Dominique Deruddere) *Pete Postlethwaite, Antoine Kamerling.* Psychological and sexual games run amok on the Côte D'Azur in this intriguingly sick English-language drama. Chris (Kamerling) is a handsome, self-assured German blond con man who finds temporary refuge in the opulent suite/apart-ment of Glover (Postlethwaite), a rich but wheel-chair-bound paraplegic. After a menacing first night, tables are turned as captor becomes captive when Glover offers the young man a lucrative offer to stay and have sex with women and allow him to watch. Chris becomes comfortable with the arrange-ment, until Glover hires a thuggish, muscle-bound leather man to bring a new dimension to the sexual shenanigans. This kinky tale palpitates in homo-eroticism as its story of humiliation, greed, abuse and ultimately love unfolds. ★★★

S

The Suitors

(1989, 106 min, US/GB, Ghasem Ebrahimian) This unpredictable and outrageous dark comedy tells the story of an Iranian woman, newly married and arrived in New York City. Mariyum arrives in the U.S. with her rich husband, Haji. But during a celebration, a friend's landlord mistakes a religious feast (in which a sheep is sacrificed) for a terrorist act, and a SWAT team accidentally shoots Haji, leaving the young émigré a widow. Alone in a strange land, and having tested some of the freedoms belonging to American women, Mariyum is courted by her late husband's four friends, who prove to be as relentless in their romantic attentions as they are in their desire for Mariyum to return to traditional Islamic values. ★★★ VHS: $29.99

Sullivan's Travels

(1941, 91 min, US, Preston Sturges) Joel McCrea, Veronica Lake, William Demarest, Franklin Pangborn. One of director Sturges' many great comedies of the 1940s, this brilliant probe into the psyche of a comedy filmmaker — decades before Woody Allen or Blake Edwards found success with the theme — is his most personal film and a classic road movie. McCrea stars as a successful movie director who longs to direct a "serious" film — so he sets out on the road, dressed as a hobo, to see the "real world." He befriends Lake, an actress wannabe about to head back home, and learns a few valuable lessons on the resilience of man and the power of laughter. A masterful combination of razor-sharp satire and sentimentality. ★★★★ DVD Criterion Collection: $39.99, VHS: $14.99

The Sum of All Fears

(2002, 118 min, US, Phil Alden Robinson) Ben Affleck, Morgan Freeman, James Cromwell, Liev Schreiber, Alan Bates, Bridget Moynahan, Philip Baker Hall, Ron Rifkin, Bruce McGill, Ciaran Hinds, Colm Feore. In this fourth installment of Tom Clancy's Jack Ryan series, logic and history crash head-on with pyrotechnics and narrative, making for a slickly made thriller that is never quite as involving as it should have been. Affleck gives a "gee-whiz, I'm-a-spy" performance as Ryan, a CIA operative who finds himself — besides much younger than his previous screen incarnations — embroiled in Cold War-style intrigue when three Russian scientists go missing. It all leads up to scheming Nazis and a stolen nuclear bomb. Director Robinson maintains tense pacing throughout and has crafted some exceptional scenes of political machinations, but much is lost by the underplaying of Affleck. He doesn't offer a glimpse of the cerebral man-of-action that is to come. His frat-boy overachiever is a distraction, and diminishes an otherwise extremely competent, often gripping thriller that, because of its miscast star, plays like "A Hardy Boy joins the CIA." ★★½ DVD Letterbox Special Collector's Edition: $19.99, VHS: $9.99

The Sum of Us

(1994, 100 min, Australia, Geoff Burton & Kevin Dowling) Jack Thompson, Russell Crowe, John Polson, Deborah Kennedy, Joss Moroney, Mitch Matthews. From the 1991 off-Broadway play comes this endearing family comedy-drama about the unusual relationship between a father and son. Set in a working-class area of Sydney, the story centers on the widowed but fun-loving Harry (Thompson) and his football-playing son Jeff (Crowe). What makes their story so different is that Dad not only knows that his son is gay, but is quite accepting of it — hoping that Jeff will eventually find Mr. Right. With great wit and charm, the two men's home life is explored. Funny, tender though slightly maudlin towards the end, The Sum of Us breaks many sexual stereotypes. Thompson and Crowe endow Harry and Jeff with humor, sympathy and sensibility. ★★★½ DVD: $19.99

Summer

(1986, 99 min, France, Eric Rohmer) Marie Riviere, Lisa Heredia. Rohmer's illuminating and moving exploration of loneliness stands as one of his most accomplished works to date. An independent but melancholy Parisian secretary, recently separated from her boyfriend, seems unwilling, even incapable, of enjoying her two-week holiday. Her loneliness and frustrations are compounded by her shyness as well as a strong will that refuses to compromise. Rohmer paints a vivid portrait of this woman and her efforts to connect and enjoy life. (French with English subtitles) ★★★½ DVD: $19.99, VHS: $14.99

Summer and Smoke

(1961, 118 min, US, Peter Glenville) Geraldine Page, Laurence Harvey, Una Merkel, Rita Moreno, Earl Holliman. Page repeats her acclaimed stage role in Tennessee Williams' searing drama, and is dazzling. She plays a sexually repressed minister's daughter who falls in love with dashing playboy Harvey. Set in a small Mississippi town in 1916, the story is a sensitive treatise on unrequited love and ignored passion. ★★★½ VHS: $14.99

Summer Catch

(2001, 100 min, US, Mike Tollin) Freddie Prinze, Jr., Jessica Biel, Matthew Lillard, Brian Dennehy, Brittany Murphy, Bruce Davison, Fred Ward, Jason Gedrick. With accent more on the Bull than Durham, this awful romantic comedy with a baseball backdrop desperately tries to rekindle the sex and laughs of that Kevin Costner-Susan Sarandon classic. The result is merely desperate. In another in a long line of poorly chosen film roles, Prinze plays a promising though self-destructive pitcher playing for a Cape Cod league in which talented college players and amateurs perform for major league scouts. Forget the fact that nearly every baseball cliché is trotted out, or the characters act in moronic fashion; this is just plain boring. Summer Catch is a mindless sex comedy that confuses idiocy as our national pastime. ★ DVD Letterbox: $14.99, VHS: $14.99

Summer City

(1976, 83 min, Australia, Christopher Frazer) Mel Gibson. A very young Gibson stars in this little known Australian sex comedy about the final free-for-all fling of four students who are on the prowl for girls, thrills and surf. Set in the early Sixties, this routine teen hijinks comedy is of interest for Gibson's film debut. ★★½

Summer Fling

(1997, 103 min, US, David Keating) Catherine O'Hara, Jared Leto, Christina Ricci, Gabriel Byrne, Amanda Shun, Stephen Rea, Colm Meany. Yet another bland comedy-drama about those quirky Irish. This one gets another mark on the trendy check list for taking place in the '70s. An affable but underachieving, slightly withdrawn lad (Leto) spends the summer before starting college avoiding work, looking for girls and sweating the results of his senior finals. His wacky, eccentric family, led by flamboyant stage actor Da (Byrne) — and raging stereotype, scream-at-ya-cuz-I-love-ya Ma (O'Hara), drive him batty, while a visiting American girl arrives to flirt with him. ★★ DVD: $19.99, VHS: $9.99

The Summer House

(1993, 85 min, GB, Waris Hussein) Jeanne Moreau, Joan Plowright, Julie Walters, Lena Headey, John Wood. This enchanting British comedy unites two of the grande dames of international cinema: Moreau and Plowright. Giving one of the most sparkling performances of her long career, Moreau plays the hard-drinking, high-spirited childhood friend of Walters, who's preparing her daughter's marriage. When Moreau arrives for the wedding, she's shocked to discover that the intended groom is a boorish mama's boy. So entering into a mischievous coconspiracy with the cantankerous mother of the groom, royally played by Plowright, she sets out to prevent the marriage from ever taking place. ★★★

Summer Interlude

(1950, 94 min, Sweden, Ingmar Bergman) Maj-Britt Nilson, Birger Nilsson. This early Bergman romantic drama, an affecting story told with the director's usual able hand but lacking in his visual expertise, is a bittersweet tale about a famed ballerina (Nilson) who chances upon a deceased lover's diary, triggering memories of first love, happier days and tragic circumstance. (aka: Illicit Interlude) (Swedish with English subtitles) ★★★ VHS: $29.99

Summer Lovers

(1982, 98 min, US, Randal Kleiser) Peter Gallagher, Daryl Hannah, Valerie Quennessen. This exotic eye-pleaser, from the director of The Blue Lagoon, focuses on how three young people (Gallagher, Hannah and Quennessen) spend their summer vacation. Not a lot of substance, but any movie about a ménage à trois in the Greek islands can't be all bad. ★★½ DVD Pan & Scan: $14.99

Summer Night

(1987, 94 min, Italy, Lina Wertmüller) Mariangelo Melato, Michele Placido. Director Wertmüller returns to the familiar terrain of sexual and political conflict in this enjoyably erotic comedy, reminiscent in many ways to her 1975 hit Swept Away. That film's star Melato plays a bitchy millionairess who has the tables turned on a notorious terrorist responsible for a series of kidnappings. She kidnaps him and holds him captive on her isolated Mediterranean isle, where the two become locked in a lusty battle of the sexes — Wertmüller style. The handsome Placido plays the befuddled kidnapper. ★★★

Summer of '42

(1971, 102 min, US, Robert Mulligan) Gary Grimes, Jennifer O'Neill, Jerry Houser. A captivating coming-of-age tale which concentrates more on character and emotion than sentimentality. Set in 1942, the film stars Grimes as a teenager vacationing in New England who falls in love with beautiful and married O'Neill, whose husband is overseas. What follows are blithe observations on first love and the teen years which should have anyone who's been through it smiling in recognition. (Sequel: Class of '44) ★★★ DVD Letterbox: $19.99

The Summer of Miss Forbes

(1988, 87 min, Mexico, Jaime Humberto Hermosillo) *Hanna Schygulla, Alexis Castanares.* A luminous Schygulla stars as a sexually repressed governess in this erotic, beautifully photographed but ultimately silly melodrama scripted by Gabriel García Márquez. In a lush sea resort, a frenzied couple goes on a six-week cruise and hires Miss Forbes (Schygulla), a stern Prussian schoolteacher, to instill manners and discipline into their two chubby, calculating sons. Matronly dressed and militarily tough by day, Miss Forbes harbors another personality — for at night, she becomes a tequila-guzzling, cake-stuffing floozy. While enjoyable, the film never completely works, with Ms. Schygulla miscast as the barely concealed basket case. (Spanish with English subtitles) ★★½

Summer of Sam

(1999, 142 min, US, Spike Lee) *John Leguizamo, Mira Sorvino, Adrien Brody, Jennifer Esposito, Anthony LaPaglia, Ben Gazzara.* Serial-killer buffs beware: *Summer of Sam* deals with the famed Son of Sam mostly on the periphery. The main focus of the film is the atmosphere of fear, paranoia and rage that he helped instill in that summer of 1977 in New York City. A handful of excellent performances — most notably Leguizamo as a weak-willed adulterer and Brody as a punk outsider — and Lee's customary stylish visuals inject a bristling energy into this overlong, and at times meandering, drama. Though it can be somewhat uneven, as an evocation of a specific time and place, *Summer of Sam* is quite successful. ★★★ DVD: $14.99, VHS: $9.99

Summer School

(1987, 98 min, US, Carl Reiner) *Mark Harmon, Kirstie Alley.* Director Reiner manages to produce a few laughs in this otherwise ordinary comedy with Harmon as a summer school teacher who'd rather be elsewhere. ★★ DVD: $14.99, VHS: $14.99

Summer Stock

(1950, 109 min, US, Charles Walters) *Judy Garland, Gene Kelly, Eddie Bracken, Phil Silvers, Marjorie Main.* Judy sings "Get Happy" in this entertaining musical about a theatrical troupe, including dancer Gene, who plan to turn her farm's barn into a theatre. A good supporting cast is featured. ★★★

Summer Stock

A Summer to Remember

(1960, 78 min, USSR, G. Danelia & I. Talankin) *Sergey Bondarchuk.* Based on a young child's view and acceptance of the atmosphere that surrounds him, this film focuses on a six-year-old boy's relationship with his mother and stepfather. The stepfather is brilliantly played by Bondarchuk (director of *War and Peace*). (Russian with English subtitles) ★★★

Summer Vacation 1999

(1988, 90 min, Japan, Shusuke Kaneko) A provocative and lushly photographed tale of budding sexuality and the loss of innocence that owes more to French cinema than that of Japanese filmmaking. Four teenage boys (all intriguingly played by young girls) are left behind in their boarding school during the summer where their idyllic world will be forever changed. By using women to play the leads, the film takes on an interestingly androgynous angle while at the same time hauntingly exploring the fragile period in time when youth is suspended between innocence and experience, uncomplicated friendships and the initial pangs of romantic love and sexual awareness. (Japanese with English subtitles) ★★★ VHS: $29.99

Summer Wishes, Winter Dreams

(1973, 95 min, US, Gilbert Cates) *Joanne Woodward, Martin Balsam, Sylvia Sidney.* A trio of outstanding performances by Woodward, Balsam and Sidney is the heart of this compelling drama about a housewife facing a midlife crisis. Both Woodward and Sidney received well-deserved Oscar nominations. ★★★

A Summer's Tale

(1999, 113 min, France, Eric Rohmer) *Melvil Poupaud, Amanda Langlet, Gwenaëlle Simon.* More Gaullic relationship fluff from a master of the genre. Rohmer manages to transform standard fare into adult diversion with the help of beautiful people spouting pretentious dialogue against fabulous scenery. In *A Summer's Tale*, the third entry in the director's "Tales of the Four Seasons" series, a tousled-haired, guitar-playing graduate student comes to a picturesque seaside resort with indefinite plans to meet his sort-of-girlfriend. As he confides to the ethnologist waitress he meets, he knows there is no real love between them. You expect a triangle to form at this point, but yet another woman enters the equation, complicating the permutations in this comedy of manners and precipitating endless analyses and discussions and revelations and pensive gazes and thoughtful silences. It's neurosis and young adult angst served on a silver platter with fine champagne. Sometimes the ambience does make the meal. (French with English subtitles) ★★½ DVD: $19.99, VHS: $14.99

Summertime

(1955, 99 min, US, David Lean) *Katharine Hepburn, Rossano Brazzi.* Extraordinarily beautiful, captivating romantic drama with Hepburn as a highstrung, lonely American spinster from Akron, Ohio, looking for romance in extremely photogenic Venice. Fortunately, Brazzi is nearby. ★★★½ DVD: $29.99, VHS: $24.99

Sun Valley Serenade

(1941, 86 min, US, Bruce Humberstone) *Sonja Henie, John Payne, Milton Berle, The Nicholas Brothers.* A lively musical about a Norwegian war refugee given shelter at the Idaho resort; but the main attraction is Glenn Miller and His Orchestra, and Berle as their manager. Songs include "Chattanooga Choo-Choo" and "It Happened in Sun Valley." ★★★ VHS: $19.99

Sunchaser

(1996, 122 min, US, Michael Cimino) *Woody Harrelson, Jon Seda, Anne Bancroft.* Director Cimino's career is still on hold with this weak entry in the "soulless-yuppie-finds-himself" subgenre starring Harrelson as a wealthy oncologist who's carjacked by Seda, a terminally ill juvenile delinquent. They embark on a spiritual journey to a sacred mountain to cure Seda's cancer. Along the way, the disparate men find a shared humanity and learn "to get along." It's as hokey as it sounds. The concept is sentimental and unrealistic and the execution artificial and preachy. ★½ VHS: $19.99

Sunday

(1997, 93 min, US, Jonathan Nossiter) *David Suchet, Lisa Harrow, Jared Harris, Larry Pine.* So this is what Skid Row feels like. First-time director Nossiter pushes us closer than feels comfortable to the lower depths in this haunting and disturbing look at a case of mistaken identity that brings two hapless souls together. It is Sunday. For Oliver (Suchet) leaves his men's shelter environs and sets out to wander the streets of Queens, when suddenly a beautiful woman (Harrow) mistakes him for a film director. As she rushes over to renew their acquaintance, a certainly less-than-ordinary Sunday begins for both of them. Nossiter, who coscripted the film, unfolds the details of these two unlucky lives with striking clarity while making great use of the Queens locales. Though the film does have a few dead spots, Suchet's and Harrow's stirring portrayals of these drifting, joyless souls are riveting. ★★★½ VHS: $89.99

Sunday, Bloody Sunday

(1971, 110 min, GB, John Schlesinger) *Glenda Jackson, Peter Finch, Murray Head, Daniel Day-Lewis.* Jackson and Finch are sparkling in this landmark work. A *cause célèbre* in the early 1970s, this moving drama centers around the troubled participants in a bisexual triangle. The kiss between Finch and Head aroused an audible gasp from the audience of the day. Marvelously directed by Schlesinger. ★★★★ DVD: $19.99

A Sunday in the Country

(1984, 94 min, France, Bertrand Tavernier) *Louis Ducreux, Sabine Azéma.* An illuminating, visually ravishing tale which centers around an elderly painter and the weekend visit paid to him by his children. Many primal issues of life are delicately handled in this subtle, masterfully crafted drama. (French with English subtitles) ★★★★ DVD: $29.99, VHS: $24.99

Sunday in the Park with George

(1984, 147 min, US, James Lapine) *Mandy Patinkin, Bernadette Peters, Charles Kimbrough, Dana Ivey.* Stephen Sondheim's Pulitzer Prize-winning Broadway musical, filmed directly from the stage, about the life of 19th-century French artist Georges Seurat, and his painting of the masterpiece "Sunday Afternoon on the Island of La Grand Jette." The original Broadway cast is featured in this superb production. ★★★★ DVD: $29.99

Sunday Too Far Away

(1975, 95 min, Australia, Ken Hannam) *Jack Thompson, John Ewart.* A simple yet solid drama about the dangerous rivalries between the members of a group of macho sheep shearers. Thompson is especially good as one of the group's hardened leaders. ★★★

TLA VIDEO AND DVD GUIDE • 2005

Gloria Swanson is ready for her close-up in *Sunset Boulevard*

Sunday's Children

(1994, 94 min, Sweden, Daniel Bergman) *Henrik Linnros, Thommy Berggren, Per Myrberg.* Daniel, the son of Ingmar Bergman, makes his directorial debut with this heartfelt, magical memory piece. An autobiography written by the elder Bergman, the story centers on the life of the eight-year-old Ingmar, here called Pu (played by the sullen Linnros), and the relationship with his distant but loving father (Berggren). As the story flashes from the past to the present, Pu must come to terms with his dying father while being haunted by images and recollections from his childhood. Though Ingmar's script is fragmented, *Sunday's Children* is a beautifully crafted, eloquent and bittersweet stroll with one's ghosts and demons. (Swedish with English subtitles) ★★★ VHS: $29.99

Sundays and Cybele

(1962, 110 min, France, Serge Bourguignon) *Hardy Kruger, Nicole Courcel.* An intelligent and touching story of the developing relationship between an amnesiac man and a young orphan girl whom he befriends by telling her that he is her father. (French with English subtitles) ★★★★ VHS: $29.99

The Sundowners

(1960, 133 min, US, Fred Zinnemann) *Robert Mitchum, Deborah Kerr, Peter Ustinov, Glynis Johns.* Exceptional adaptation of Jon Cleary's best-seller about a 1920s Australian sheepherding family. Mitchum and Kerr give excellent performances, and the film features stunning cinematography. ★★★★ VHS: $14.99

Sunrise

(1927, 95 min, US, F. W. Murnau) *George O'Brien, Janet Gaynor, Margaret Livingston, J. Farrell MacDonald.* In his first U.S. film, director Murnau curtailed the usual heaviness of German Expressionism, evoking a deceptively Amercian sort of soufflé that foreshadowed the transparent narrative style of the talkies. Considered the apex of the art of silent filmmaking, the haunting *Sunrise* tells the unnervingly bleak tale of a married farmer (O'Brien) who is led astray by a heartless vamp (Livingston). The film won three Academy Awards in the first year Oscars were handed out, including one for Gaynor as Best Actress who is unforgettable as the wronged wife. ★★★★

Sunrise at Campobello

(1960, 144 min, US, Vincent J. Donehue) *Ralph Bellamy, Greer Garson, Hume Cronyn.* Bellamy's tour-de-force performance accentuates this compelling look at the early life of President Franklin D. Roosevelt. The story focuses on Roosevelt's infancy in politics and his devastating battle against polio. Garson is equally as impressive as Eleanor Roosevelt. Though Roosevelt's years as president aren't covered, there's more than enough potent drama here. ★★★ VHS: $19.99

Sunset

(1988, 107 min, US, Blake Edwards) *James Garner, Bruce Willis, Malcolm McDowell, Mariel Hamingway, Kathleen Quinlan.* This Edwards mystery comedy set in 1920s Hollywood is short on laughs but does contain considerable charm thanks entirely to Garner's delectable turn as Wyatt Earp. The famous lawman helps investigate a bordello murder and crosses paths with Tom Mix (played by Willis) and a nefarious silent screen star obviously based on Charlie Chaplin. ★★½ DVD: $14.99, VHS: $9.99

Sunset Boulevard

(1950, 110 min, US, Billy Wilder) *William Holden, Gloria Swanson, Erich Von Stroheim, Nancy Olson, Jack Webb, Buster Keaton.* Arguably the most vitriolic and macabre statement yet on the movie-making capital. Wilder uncovers the fractured dreams, withered ambitions and gruesome neuroses of Tinseltown's denizens. Holden is the two-bit hack writer nursing a case of self-disgust and Swanson, in an astonishing performance, is the aging film queen secluded with her bitterness in a Gothic mansion. ★★★★ DVD Special Collector's Edition: $14.99, VHS: $9.99

Sunset Park

(1996, 100 min, US, Steve Gomer) *Rhea Perlman, Fredro Starr, Carol Kane, Terrence DaShon Howard.* A middle-class white schoolteacher picks up an extra gig coaching her inner city's high school basketball team. Initially unaccepted in a hostile environment, she eventually makes contact with her alienated charges, learning from them as she instructs them, and leads them to the city championship game. "Seen it," you say? Well, yes, you have, though it somehow avoids being as bad as could be expected. Perlman delivers just enough earthy believability to an otherwise soft-focused effort. ★★½ DVD Pan & Scan: $24.99, VHS: $9.99

Sunshine

(2000, 180 min, US, István Szabó) *Ralph Fiennes, Jennifer Ehle, Rosemary Harris, Rachel Weisz, David De Keyser, Miriam Margolyes, James Frain, William Hurt, Deborah Kara Unger.* An epic story of three generations of a Hungarian Jewish family, *Sunshine* is a sweeping historical drama that explores the loss of identity set against the backdrop of the two world wars, the carnage of Communism and the 20th century's rising tide of anti-Semitism. In the late 1800s, the Sonnenschein family, headed by the gentlemanly Emmanuel, makes its fortune from the family recipe for medicinal tonic. During the course of the next half a century, the Sonnenscheins endure the hardships of a nation and more as each generation struggles to free itself from emotional and physical restraints both self-inflicted and imposed. Fiennes is excellent portraying three generations of Sonnenscheins. He is matched by Ehle and her real-life mother Harris, who play the same character as youth and matriarch. *Sunshine* is masterful storytelling, a richly textured, intimate saga that delineates a family and a world in turmoil. ★★★½ DVD: $29.99, VHS: $102.99

The Sunshine Boys

(1975, 111 min, US, Herbert Ross) *George Burns, Walter Matthau, Richard Benjamin, F. Murray Abraham.* After an absence from the big screen of over 30 years, Burns returned to join up with Matthau as the famous vaudevillians, The Sunshine Boys, who broke up decades before. Now a big producer would like to have them do one of their classic routines on a television special. Burns received an Oscar for his performance in this engaging adaptation of Neil Simon's hit Broadway play. (Remade in 1995) ★★★ DVD: $19.99

Sunshine State

(2002, 141 min, US, John Sayles) *Angela Bassett, Edie Falco, James McDaniel, Mary Alice, Timothy Hutton, Mary Steenburgen, Bill Cobbs, Ralph Waite, Jane Alexander, Alan King, Miguel Ferrer.* Writer-director Sayles, with his usual command of character, language and ensemble, casts a decisive eye on the state of affairs both social and political on a diverse group of Floridians affected by a real estate takeover in a fractured coastal community. Heading a terrific cast are Bassett and Falco, each superlative in delineating a fragile character whose vulnerability is offset by sheer tenacity. Bassett is Desiree, who has returned home for the first time in nearly 20 years to mend fences with her mother (an outstanding Alice); Falco is Marly, who is about to tear down a fence, in this case the family restaurant that she has single-handedly run since her father (a very touching Waite) went blind. The interconnecting lives who cross both women's paths are the fabric that shape a compassionate, intelligent tapestry of greed, unfulfilled dreams, betrayal, romance, family, racial identity and reconciliation. Sayles' pacing isn't quite as efficient as his masterpiece *Lone Star*, and the film does meander when it should snap, but *Sunshine State* is overflowing with fascinating characters, smart writing and a social conscience that is sorely missing in contemporary American cinema. ★★★½ DVD Letterbox: $24.99, VHS: $102.99

The Super

(1991, 90 min, US, Rod Daniel) *Joe Pesci, Vincent Gardenia, Ruben Blades.* By the sheer force of his personality, Pesci saves this lightweight, formulaic comedy from the video junkpile. He plays a bigot-

598

ed, unscrupulous New York ghetto landlord who is forced by the courts to live in one of his own ramshackle buildings. Of course, the misunderstood realtor comes to respect his tenants, each of whom discovers newfound compassion for him. Another '90s redemption story, the film's characters are pure stereotypes, and the ending would have made Frank Capra squirm. ★★ DVD: $14.99

Super Mario Brothers

(1993, 104 min, US, Rocky Morton) *Bob Hoskins, John Leguizamo, Dennis Hopper, Samantha Mathis, Fisher Stevens, Fiona Shaw, Lance Henriksen.* The Mario Brothers are just two average plumbers from Brooklyn who find themselves defending the Earth against a bunch of humanoid dinosaur descendants from another dimension. The story is as flimsy as you would expect a movie based on a video game to be, but the dialogue has a nice, quirky style. This live-action comic book is an oddly entertaining if ridiculous action-comedy. ★★ DVD: $9.99

Super Troopers

(2002, 100 min, US, Jay Chandrasekhar) *Kevin Heffernan, Jay Chandrasekhar, Steve Lemme, Paul Soter, Erik Stolhanske, Brian Cox.* The comedy troupe Broken Lizard is responsible for this insane, often funny chronicle of Vermont State Troopers who play pranks on speeders and have syrup-guzzling competitions to alleviate the boredom. A series of silly skits, haphazardly strewn together, *Super Troopers* manages to milk some inventive laughs underneath the familiar *Police Academy* trappings. ★★½ DVD: $26.99, VHS: $14.99

Supercop

(1996, 93 min, Hong Kong, Stanley Tong) *Jackie Chan, Michelle Yeoh, Maggie Cheung.* Chan's masterful *Police Story 3* has been redubbed, reedited and renamed to serve as his follow-up to *Rumble in the Bronx* — it's a better movie, more accurately depicting the combination of action and humor which made Chan an international star. Jackie is a Hong Kong police officer sent undercover into Mainland China to spring a mobster from a prison camp and follow him back to Hong Kong, where Jackie can dismantle the crime organization from the inside. Things go well until his girlfriend (Cheung) is kidnapped and Jackie must blow his cover to save the day. The climax of Jackie hanging from a ladder suspended beneath an airborne helicopter as it flies over Kuala Lumpur should satisfy even the most jaded American action movie fan. And if it doesn't, check your pulse. ★★★½ DVD: $14.99, VHS: $9.99

Supercop 2

(1999, 94 min, Hong Kong, Stanley Tong) *Michelle Yeoh, Yu Rong Guang, Jackie Chan.* This is actually a semi-sequel to *Supercop*, originally titled *Project S*, with Yeoh (*Heroic Trio*) reprising her role as a beautiful, tough-as-nails cop, here on the trail of a band of thieves, led (unbeknownst to her) by her ex-boyfriend. A routine (even derivative) story line is enlivened greatly by exciting action scenes, and the miraculous Yeoh. Doing all her own stunts (à la Jackie Chan), she's a joy to watch, though one greedily wishes for more martial arts and less shoot-outs here. Also, the film is hurt by a terribly awkward, abrupt ending. Still, a good time overall, with a very silly though amusing cameo by Jackie in drag! ★★½ DVD: $14.99, VHS: $9.99

Superfly

(1972, 98 min, US, Gordon Parks, Jr.) *Ron O'Neal, Shelia Frazier.* Picketed by blacks for its glorification of the drug underworld, *Superfly* was nonetheless a huge popular success. New York City is an urban wasteland which provides the gritty backdrop to this tawdry tale of one tough-talking, coke-sniffing pusher (O'Neal) who plots for one final megadeal before retiring. With a hypnotic Curtis Mayfield score in the background, the film captures the drug dealing world and, unlike most films of this type, takes no moral high ground. ★★ DVD: $19.99

Superfly T.N.T.

(1973, 87 min, US, Ron O'Neal) *Ron O'Neal, Roscoe Lee Browne, Sheila Frazier, Robert Guillaume.* O'Neal returns as the super-slick, super-bad hustler Priest in this inept sequel. This time, Priest, retired and trying to clear his head in Rome, is enlisted into service by a freedom fighter from Africa to assist in a gun-running mission. The soundtrack is composed and performed by obscure 1970s funk supergroup Osibisa. ★½ VHS: $19.99

Supergirl

(1984, 114 min, GB, Jeannot Szwarc) *Faye Dunaway, Helen Slater, Peter O'Toole, Mia Farrow.* This juvenile fantasy about Superman's comic book cousin is barely saved from complete mediocrity by Dunaway's ultra-campy portrayal of the arch villainess. Slater is cute but shallow as the superhero, and the film really never gets off the ground. ★★ DVD: $24.99, VHS: $14.99

The Supergrass

(1987, 105 min, GB, Peter Richardson) *Adrian Edmondson, Jennifer Saunders, Nigel Planer, Alexi Sayle.* Outrageous, silly comedy about a young man who pretends to be a drug smuggler to impress his girlfriend, becoming involved with real smugglers and the police — who believe him to be a drug kingpin. The cast includes regulars from "The Young Ones." ★★½

Superman: The Movie

(1978, 143 min, US, Richard Donner) *Christopher Reeve, Gene Hackman, Marlon Brando, Margot Kidder, Ned Beatty, Valerie Perrine.* In a style reminiscent of a Spielberg or a Lucas, director Donner retells the Superman myth in a grand, often gaudy epic. Spectacular special effects, garish set design, an all-star cast and the obligatory John Williams score highlight this box-office smash. The film follows Superman (Reeve) from his origins on Planet Krypton to his adolescence in Smallville to his heroics in Metropolis. (Followed by 3 sequels) ★★★ DVD: $19.99, VHS: $14.99

Superman II

(1981, 127 min, US, Richard Lester) *Christopher Reeve, Gene Hackman, Margot Kidder, Terence Stamp, Ned Beatty, Valerie Perrine.* Reeve returns as the Man of Steel in this rollicking sequel. Three fugitives from Krypton travel to Earth, and give Superman a great big headache. Hackman returns as Lex Luthor, and he's as funny as he was in the original adventure. ★★★ DVD: $19.99

Superman III

(1983, 123 min, US, Richard Lester) *Christopher Reeve, Richard Pryor, Robert Vaughn.* Reeve is back once more as the man from Krypton in this comedic Superman outing with Pryor fronting for villain Vaughn, out to defeat Clark Kent's alter ego.

Some of this is funny, but mostly it's just laughable. (Where's Hackman when you need him?) ★★ DVD: $19.99, VHS: $9.99

Superman IV: The Quest for Peace

(1987, 90 min, US, Sidney J. Furie) *Christopher Reeve, Gene Hackman, Jon Cryer, Margot Kidder.* Superman decides to rid the world of its nuclear weapons; but his good deed backfires as Lex Luthor appropriates the warheads for an elaborate arms deal. A middling adventure with a timely message. ★★ DVD: $19.99, VHS: $9.99

Supernova

(2000, 91 min, US, Walter Hill) *James Spader, Angela Bassett, Robert Forster, Lou Diamond Phillips, Peter Facinelli, Robin Tunney, Wilson Cruz.* Spader and Bassett makes an unlikely but attractive couple in this otherwise turgid and choppy space opera. A space vessel receives a distress call and discovers a lone survivor: a mysterious young man with a connection to Bassett. A typical but potentially cool premise is dragged out interminably, despite the strong efforts of the cast. Original director Hill was replaced immediately after production by Jack Sholder, who was replaced in the editing room by Francis Ford Coppola. As would be expected, the result is a jumble. Apparently, there's 20 minutes missing from Hill's original vision, and the whole affair ends with a perversely romantic wrap-up. ★★ DVD: $14.99

SuperPhan

(1998, 80 min, US, Alex Weinress & Vince Mola) *Vince Mola, Mike Missanelli, Frank DiLeo.* This engaging shot-on-video about the "ultimate" football fan uses the medium so well, it's entirely conceivable that unsuspecting victims could mistake the film as "real." Indeed, lead actor-codirector Mola — as SuperPhan — appears in character on Philadelphia's Channel 10 News, outside Veteran's Stadium and (most amusingly) at a college hockey game, where he tries in vain to pump up the somnambulant crowd. If you're from Philly — or any big sports town, for that matter — you've known someone like SuperPhan, and Mola plays the character to the hilt. In fact, it's the disturbing aspect of the humor that makes *SuperPhan* so compelling and realistic, and so much more than the regional in-joke it could have been. ★★★

Superstar

(1999, 82 min, US, Bruce McCulloch) *Molly Shannon, Will Ferrell, Harland Williams.* Yet another "S.N.L." skit unwisely stretched out to feature length, *Superstar* leaves both Shannon and Ferrell stranded and flailing. The story has Shannon's popular character, Mary Catherine Gallagher — the accident-prone Catholic high school girl — pining for two things: a kiss from school stud Ferrell and superstardom. *Superstar* is mostly a downbeat experience, directed with little inspiration or style. ★½ DVD: $14.99, VHS: $9.99

Supervixens

(1975, 106 min, US, Russ Meyer) *Shari Eubank, Charles Napier.* The story of a young man who, wrongfully accused of having killed a woman, is running from the policeman who actually commited the murder (Napier). Scenes such as the placing of a stick of dynamite between a bound Supervixen's spread legs marks Meyer's return to his tried and true mixture of sex and violence. ★★ DVD: $39.99

Support Your Local Gunfighter

(1971, 92 min, US, Burt Kennedy) *James Garner, Suzanne Pleshette, Joan Blondell, Harry Morgan, Jack Elam, Dub Taylor.* An amiable follow-up to *Support Your Local Sheriff.* On the lam, con man Garner chooses the small Western mining town of Purgatory to hide out. The locals think he is a notorious gunslinger, involving him in a war between two mining factions. There's a lot of good humor, and familiar character actors aid in the film's overall enjoyment. ★★½ DVD: $14.99

Support Your Local Sheriff

(1969, 93 min, US, Burt Kennedy) *James Garner, Joan Hackett, Walter Brennan, Harry Morgan, Bruce Dern, Jack Elam.* Wonderful western spoof with Garner a delight as a town's sheriff up against a lawless breed when gold is found in them thar hills. (Sequel: *Support Your Local Gunfighter*) ★★★ DVD: $14.99

Sure Fire

(1993, 86 min, US, Jon Jost) *Tom Blair, Kristi Hager.* Trouble is brewing in a small Southwestern town and mounting tensions erupt with tragic results. Unfortunately, the real trouble might have been on the other side of the camera, because it feels like the filmmakers could not strike a balance between art film and thriller. Although Jost may have had some comment on the human condition in mind here, and he certainly has a way with imagery, a slower, more monotonous 86-minute film would be hard to find. ★ DVD Letterbox: $29.99, VHS: $19.99

The Sure Thing

(1985, 94 min, US, Rob Reiner) *John Cusack, Daphne Zuniga, Anthony Edwards, Nicolette Sheridan, Tim Robbins.* Reiner's impressive follow-up to *This Is Spinal Tap* is an intelligent and fresh look at adolescent romance. It offers a distinct alternative to most youth-oriented comedies by presenting teenagers that are hip, witty and even sensitive. Sort of a modern reworking of *It Happened One Night.* Cusack is terrific in one of his first starring roles. ★★★½ DVD Special Edition: $14.99

Surrender

(1987, 95 min, US, Jerry Belson) *Sally Field, Michael Caine, Steve Guttenberg, Peter Boyle, Julie Kavner.* Flat romantic comedy with Field trying to choose between a caring but seemingly impoverished writer (Caine) and a wealthy yuppie attorney (Guttenberg). ★★ DVD: $24.99, VHS: $14.99

Surrender Dorothy

(1998, 87 min, US, Kevin DiNovis) *Peter Pryor, Kevin DiNovis, Jason Centeno, Elizabeth Casey, Marcos Muniz, Keri Merboth.* A bold and compelling psychosexual, cross-dressing drama that offers a decidedly controversial twist in its treatment of same-sex relationships. *Apartment Zero* meets *Blue Velvet* through the eyes of Harold Pinter in this low-budget, black-and-white tale that is infused with moments of both intense drama and black comedy. The story focuses on two young men: 26-year-old Trevor (Pryor), an angry, sexually confused busboy, and Lanh (director DiNovis), a heroin addict who needs a place to crash. But what begins as a simple house-sharing arrangement quickly escalates into a frenzied battle of manipulation, co-dependency and gender-bending submission as the emboldened Trevor lures Lanh, with the promise of drugs, into becoming Dorothy, Trevor's demented concept of his ideal girlfriend. ★★★ DVD: $14.99, VHS: $9.99

Surviving Picasso

Surviving Picasso

(1996, 123 min, GB, James Ivory) *Anthony Hopkins, Natascha McElhone, Julianne Moore, Joan Plowright, Joss Ackland.* Genius, lover, sexist, bully, egotist, artist: legendary painter Pablo Picasso is perfectly brought to life by Hopkins. But his riveting portrayal is not quite enough to overcome director Ivory's static account of the final years of the artist's life and his love affairs. Suggested by the novel "Picasso: Creator and Destroyer," *Surviving Picasso* is narrated by Picasso's longtime lover Francoise Gilot (nicely played by McElhone), mother to two of his children. The film almost ignores Picasso the artist in favor of his relationships with Gilot and others. Hopkins at least makes sure that Picasso is always center stage and cognizant of his place in the world. ★★½

Surviving the Game

(1994, 94 min, US, Ernest Dickerson) *Ice-T, Rutger Hauer, Charles S. Dutton, Gary Busey, F. Murray Abraham, John C. McGinley.* Ice-T stars as a bum . . . er, residentially challenged person . . . who is recruited by an urban missionary (Dutton) to lead a hunting party through the Northwest wilderness, only to find that he is the prey. Dickerson adds nothing new to this shopworn premise — introduced in 1932 as *The Most Dangerous Game* — that has been tried by everyone from Robert Wise to John Woo and even on "Gilligan's Island." What the film lacks in story is more than compensated for in violence and hammy performances. ★★ DVD: $9.99, VHS: $14.99

Susan and God

(1940, 117 min, US, George Cukor) *Joan Crawford, Fredric March, Ruth Hussey, Rita Hayworth.* Anita Loos (*The Women, Gentlemen Prefer Blondes*) adapted Rachel Crothers' stage hit, a curious blend of sophisticated comedy and family drama. Crawford gives an atypical daffy performance as a flighty socialite who finds religion; she begins preaching love and God and interferes with her society friends' lives. March is Crawford's alcoholic and estranged husband who does not benefit from his wife's new spiritual awakening. ★★½ VHS: $19.99

Susan Lenox: Her Fall and Rise

(1931, 77 min, US, Robert Z. Leonard) *Greta Garbo, Clark Gable, Jean Hersholt.* The only pairing of screen legends Garbo and Gable is this blustery melodrama with Garbo as a poor farm girl forced to marry a brutish neighbor. She runs away, straight into the arms of a tall, handsome engineer (Gable). However, fate seems destined to keep the lovers apart. ★★½ VHS: $19.99

Susan Slept Here

(1954, 98 min, US, Frank Tashlin) *Debbie Reynolds, Dick Powell, Anne Francis.* A young troublemaker (Reynolds) finds herself the unlikely guest of a man-about-town writer (Powell) and proceeds to complicate his bachelor existence. Francis plays Powell's society beauty sweetheart. Kinda cute. ★★½

Susana

(1951, 82 min, Mexico, Luis Buñuel) *Rosita Quintana, Fernando Soler, Victor Manuel Mendoza.* A mischievous Buñuel focuses this subversive melodrama on a born-bad sexpot who escapes from prison and finds refuge in a hacienda with a kindly family. From the moment she enters the house, the wanton vamp does nothing but wreak havoc, sending just about every man within 20 miles to the brink of sexual frenzy. In a truly kinky ending, our heroine's bedeviling force is brought under control by the lady of the ranch with the aid of a studded riding crop. Brimming with sly humor and trademark touches, *Susana* is delicious fun for all Buñuel lovers. (Spanish with English subtitles) ★★★

Suspect

(1987, 122 min, US, Peter Yates) *Cher, Liam Neeson, John Mahoney, Dennis Quaid.* This taut courtroom thriller stars Cher as a public defender who takes on the difficult case of a deaf derelict (Neeson) who has been charged with murder. When a juror (Quaid) approaches her with helpful evidence, she finds herself not only facing an ethical dilemma, but is also drawn into a whirlwind of Hitchcockian intrigue. ★★★ DVD: $19.99, VHS: $9.99

The Suspect

(1998, 108 min, Hong Kong, Ringo Lam) *Louis Koo, Julian Cheung.* In this standard Hong Kong actioner, Cheung is an ex-con who's just served a ten-year prison sentence. His old crime boss immediately demands he assassinate a political figure. When he refuses, the chase is on from both the cops (he's been framed for the murder anyway) and the bad guys. There's a strong been-there, done-that feel to the film, and though it's a bounce back from Lam's *Maximum Risk*, it can't compare with his earlier, more passionate works. Still, it is entertaining, and while there's little action per se, it's never less than involving. (Cantonese with English subtitles) ★★½ DVD: $29.99, VHS: $19.90

Suspicion

(1941, 99 min, US, Alfred Hitchcock) *Joan Fontaine, Cary Grant, Nigel Bruce.* Fontaine won a belated Oscar as a shy girl who enters a hasty marriage with the charming but sinister (?) Grant, and begins to believe that he could be a murderer — with her as his next victim. Of interest: the studio changed the ending to fit Grant's image, fearing the public would not accept the writer's original conclusion. Crisp direction from Hitchcock. ★★★

Suspiria

(1976, 97 min, Italy, Dario Argento) *Jessica Harper, Joan Bennett.* Argento's classic horror film features mayhem galore at a swank private school in Europe complete with stormy nights, psychopaths and a frenzied soundtrack. Argento's plot is barely skin deep, but his highly stylized camerawork and editing, and the edge-of-your-seat suspense will leave one gasping. Look for a particularly effective homage to the French surreal masterpiece *Un Chien Andalou*. (Sequel: *Inferno*) (Filmed in English) ★★★ DVD Letterbox: $19.99, DVD Limited Edition: $29.99, VHS: $9.99

Suture

(1994, 96 min, US, David Siegel & Scott McGehee) *Dennis Haysbert, Michael Harris, Mel Harris, Sab Shimono.* Unscrupulous patricidal Victor Towers (Harris) sets up his long-lost, almost identical half-brother Clay Arlington (Haysbert), attempting to murder him and have it look as though he himself has been killed. But Clay survives, disfigured and amnesiac, and is accepted as Victor, who is now under suspicion for their father's murder. Adding a special dimension to this exploration of identity and self-knowing is that Clay is played by Haysbert, who is black, and Victor by Harris, who is white. Shot in stark black and white, and employing a pared-down but effective soundtrack, *Suture* is an interesting premise with an intriguing execution. ★★★ DVD: $19.99

Swamp Thing

(1982, 91 min, US, Wes Craven) *Louis Jourdan, Adrienne Barbeau.* Tongue-in-cheek monster movie with a scientist transformed into a half-man/half-vegetable when one of his experiments goes awry. Jourdan camps it up as a fellow scientist, and Barbeau is the woman Swamp Thing loves. ★★½

The Swan

(1956, 109 min, US, Charles Vidor) *Grace Kelly, Alec Guinness, Louis Jourdan, Agnes Moorehead, Leo G. Carroll.* This beguiling comedy of manners begins as a European matriarch seeks to reverse her family's declining fortunes by marrying off her only daughter (Kelly) to the country's crown prince (Guinness). Jourdan plays the young woman's tutor, who is disappointed to see that she is actually smitten with the prince. ★★★ VHS: $19.99

Swann in Love

(1984, 115 min, France, Volker Schlöndorff) *Jeremy Irons, Ornella Muti, Alain Delon, Fanny Ardant, Marie-Christine Barrault.* Schlöndorff beautifully renders the emotional intricacies and period flavor of Marcel Proust's illustrious "Swann's Way." Irons is the dashing, cultivated Charles Swann who loses his heart and esteem in a passionate tryst with a pouting courtesan (Muti). A sparkling ensemble of supporting players. (Filmed in English) ★★★ DVD Letterbox: $19.99

The Swap

(1979, 90 min, US, John C. Broderick & John Shade) *Robert De Niro, Jennifer Warren, Lisa Blount, Sybil Danning.* An ambitious young filmmaker learns the power and perils of his medium when his homemade pornos of powerful friends are used for political blackmail. Originally filmed in 1969, reedited and rereleased in 1979. ★★½

The Swashbuckler

(1979, 101 min, France, Jean-Paul Rappeneau) *Jean-Paul Belmondo, Laura Antonelli.* It is a shame that so many of Belmondo's films never make it over to these shores because generally you can count on them being action-packed and full of adventure. However, the film distribution system being what it is, few of his recent efforts have received showings in the U.S. *The Swashbuckler* is a fun comedy/adventure that features the charismatic rogue as a man-on-the-run who gets involved in fighting in the American War for Independence. (French with English subtitles) ★★★

Swedenhielms

(1935, 88 min, Sweden, Gustaf Molander) *Ingrid Bergman.* Bergman plays a young woman engaged to the son of a renowned aristocrat in line to win the Nobel Prize. When it becomes apparent, however, that the father will not be awarded the prestigious prize, the family is thrown into an emotional and financial crisis, affecting each family member, and the young Bergman, in disparate ways. (Swedish with English subtitles) ★★½ VHS: $19.99

Sweeney Todd: The Demon Barber of Fleet Street

(1984, 140 min, US, Harold Prince & Terry Hughes) *Angela Lansbury, George Hearn, Cris Groenendaal, Sara Woods, Edmund Lyndeck, Calvin Remsberg.* Live performance of Stephen Sondheim's Tony Award-winning musical. Magnificently re-created for video, Lansbury (also a Tony Award winner) and Hearn repeat their stage roles as, respectively, the evil Mrs. Lovett and the demonic barber Sweeney, who together conspired to murder his customers and serve them up in her meat pies. An unusual topic for a musical, to be sure, but the genius of Sondheim's music and lyrics and Harold Prince's original staging combine to create a musical masterpiece. Lansbury and Hearn give two of the greatest performances to be seen in the theatre in recent memory. An unforgettable theatre piece, and not to be missed. ★★★★ DVD: $24.99

Sweet and Lowdown

(1999, 95 min, US, Woody Allen) *Gretchen Mol, Sean Penn, Samantha Morton, Uma Thurman, Anthony LaPaglia, Brian Markinson, John Waters.* Penn received an Oscar nomination for his scintillatingly complex performance as Emmet Ray, the "second greatest jazz guitarist" of the 1930s. In this fictional biography, writer-director Allen has crafted an engaging comedy-drama that — maybe in reference to his own life — attempts to separate the artist from the man. Morton also garnered an Oscar nomination for her touching portrayal of a mute woman involved with the misanthropic but talented musician. A great jazz score punctuates Allen's snappy story. ★★★½ DVD: $29.99, VHS: $21.99

Sweet Bird of Youth

(1962, 120 min, US, Richard Brooks) *Geraldine Page, Paul Newman, Ed Begley, Rip Torn.* An expert adaptation of Tennesse Williams' critically acclaimed play. Page excels as a former movie queen whose career has given way to achohol and compromise. Searching for seclusion, she arrives in a small Southern town accompanied by ne'er-do-well hometown boy Newman. Begley won an Oscar for his powerful portrayal of the town's corrupt boss who has it in for Newman. (Remade in 1989) ★★★½ VHS: $14.99

Sweet Charity

(1969, 133 min, US, Bob Fosse) *Shirley MacLaine, John McMartin, Chita Rivera, Stubby Kaye, Paula Kelly, Ricardo Montalban, Barbara Bouchet, Sammy Davis, Jr., Alan Hewitt, Ben Vereen.* Fosse's first film as director is based on his hit Broadway musical, itself based on Fellini's *Nights of Cabiria*. MacLaine is at her best as dance hall hostess Charity Hope Valentine, the quintessential hooker with a heart of gold. Forever having her heart broken by Mr. Wrong, Charity finds solace in her never-ending optimism and joie de vivre while confronting a series of romantic adventures. Fosse's storytelling is highly stylized, with special emphasis on editing, and features memorable musical numbers. ★★★½ DVD: $14.99

Sweet Country

(1987, 150 min, US, Michael Cacoyannis) *Jane Alexander, John Cullum, Irene Papas, Carole Laurie, Franco Nero.* Some good actors can't save this unfortunate political thriller about an American couple who move to Chile after the Allende assassination, becoming involved in a Marxist underground movement. ★½

Paula Kelly (l.), Shirley MacLaine (c.) and Chita Rivera in *Sweet Charity*

Sweet Dreams

(1985, 115 min, US, Karel Reisz) *Jessica Lange, Ed Harris, Ann Wedgeworth, David Clennon.* Lange gives an affecting performance as country superstar Patsy Cline in this moving portrait of the singer's vibrant life, her climb to stardom and her untimely death. Harris costars as Cline's husband Charley Dick, and Wedgeworth is stirring as her mother. ★★★ DVD: $9.99, VHS: $9.99

Sweet Hearts Dance

(1988, 101 min, US, Robert Greenwald) *Susan Sarandon, Don Johnson, Jeff Daniels, Elizabeth Perkins, Justin Henry.* A good cast adds some sparkle to this routine romantic comedy as husband and wife Johnson and Sarandon decide to split; while friend Daniels begins an affair with Perkins. ★★½ DVD Pan & Scan: $24.99, VHS: $9.99

The Sweet Hereafter

(1997, 112 min, Canada, Atom Egoyan) *Maury Chaykin, Sarah Polley, Bruce Greenwood, Ian Holm, Gabrielle Rose, Arsinée Khanjian.* Low-key and desolate in tone, Egoyan's adaptation of the Russell Banks novel is a profound and intimate portrait of a small town reeling from tragedy. Holm is impenetrably brilliant as Mitchell Stephens, an ambulance-chasing lawyer who descends on the inhabitants of Sam Dent, a community nestled in the Canadian Rockies, in the hopes of convincing them to join a class-action suit concerning a deadly school bus accident. As he is digging deep into the town's collective sorrow, he is also uncovering his own disjointed sense of loss. Egoyan masterfully flashes back to the months and moments leading up to the calamity, and seamlessly snakes the film's timeline back and forth. And, as with all of Egoyan's films, the characters' inner struggles take center stage. Polley excels as a teenager who survives but who pays a terrible price. ★★★★ DVD Letterbox: $24.99, VHS: $19.99, VHS Letterbox: $19.99

Sweet Home Alabama

(2002, 102 min, US, Andy Tennant) *Reese Witherspoon, Josh Lucas, Patrick Dempsey, Ethan Embry, Candice Bergen, Fred Ward, Mary Kay Place, Jean Smart.* "People need a passport to come down here" New York designer Melanie (Witherspoon) chirps, commenting on the disparity between the North and the South. It also underscores exactly how much Melanie — born and raised in the small Alabama town she is visiting — feels disconnected to her roots. However, the premise to get her back home, and its comic followthrough, is so counterfeit the U.S. Treasury should investigate. As engagingly played by Witherspoon, Melanie is a throwback to the '30s screwball heroine. Charming, kooky but smart when she needs to be, Melanie is engaged to the most eligible bachelor in N.Y.C. Only her hunky husband back home stands in her way, so she sets south to finalize the divorce. Of course, seven years later, he still pines for her, and refuses to sign hoping to win her back. Gee, ya think he will? There's precious little that's funny in this implausible romantic comedy, which mistakes caricature and cliché for depth. Embry is memorable as the gay best friend. ★★ DVD Letterbox: $19.99, VHS: $14.99

Sweet Jane

(1998, 83 min, US, Joe Gayton) *Joseph Gordon-Levitt, Samantha Mathis, William McNamara, Bud Cort, Mary Woronov.* Mathis is Jane, a streetwise junkie, jaded survivor of many ODs. Gordon-Levitt is Tony, a child of the streets, survivor of abandonment and abuse. Each turns in a remarkable performance as two marginal characters existing below society's radar, both angry, afraid, alone. Jane's latest OD lands her in a clinic, where she finds out that she's HIV-positive, and where she crosses paths with Tony, who follows her and cares for her despite her protestations. They eventually form a bond in mutual desperation that comes to be stronger than either of them has previously known. The authentic performances more than compensate for the script's occasional lapses into predictability, and writer-director Gayton constructs an involving tale at once allegoric and neorealist. ★★★ DVD: $19.99, VHS: $19.99

Sweet Liberty

(1986, 107 min, US, Alan Alda) *Alan Alda, Michael Caine, Bob Hoskins, Michelle Pfeiffer, Lillian Gish.* The films of Alda are either hit (*The Four Seasons*) or miss (*A New Life*), but this pleasant comedy sits comfortably towards the former. Alda is a college professor whose book on American history is being made into a movie — and a wild assortment of film types descend upon his peaceful and unprepared town. ★★★ VHS: $9.99

Sweet Lorraine

(1987, 91 min, US, Steve Gomer) *Maureen Stapleton, Lee Richardson, Trini Alvarado, Giancarlo Esposito, Todd Graff.* Charming, bittersweet comedy-drama about the last days of an 80-year-old Catskills Mountain hotel. Stapleton gives a winning performance as the hotel's matriarchal owner. ★★★ VHS: $7.99

Sweet Movie

(1974, 105 min, Canada/France/West Germany, Dusan Makavejev) *Carole Laure, Pierre Clementi, Sami Frey.* One woman's sexual initiation and her descent into the liberating pleasures of the flesh is just one of the stories in this bizarre and sensual celebration of political and sexual anarchism. Makavejev, a sort of Serbo-socialist John Waters, fuses several stories in trying to answer the question, "Is there life after birth?" The main story revolves around a virginal Miss World who, after fending off the lustful advances of her new husband, the richest man in the world and his black muscle-building bodyguard, finally finds her libido liberation on the top of the Eiffel Tower with a singing mariachi star. A wildly outrageous and original film. (In English, French, Dutch, German and Serbo-Croatian with English subtitles) ★★★ VHS: $24.99

Sweet Nothing

(1996, 90 min, US, Gary Winick) *Michael Imperioli, Mira Sorvino, Paul Calderon.* A depressing but well-intentioned look into the life and mind of a Bronx crackhead, *Sweet Nothing* is based on diaries found in a New York apartment. The first (and weaker) half of this low-budget film depicts how Angelo (Imperioli) gets caught in the vicious cycle of drug addiction. When he finally decides to kick the habit, the film — like its protagonist — begins to recover. Suddenly, the clichés disappear and Angelo's downward spiral starts earning the viewer's sympathy. Offering an unromanticized view of addiction and recovery, *Sweet Nothing* sometimes misfires, but at least maintains the courage of its convictions. ★★½ VHS: $19.99

Sweet November

(2001, 120 min, US, Pat O'Connor) *Keanu Reeves, Charlize Theron, Jason Isaacs, Greg Germann, Frank Langella.* Mistaking quirkiness for character, glibness for intellect, this pointless remake of the Sandy Dennis-Anthony Newley 1968 romantic drama desperately tries to be relevant but winds up only being desperate. In one of his worst performances, Reeves plays Nelson, a high-powered ad exec who meets in horribly cutesy fashion the kooky Sarah (Theron), a woman who inexplicably lives with a man for one month to boost his "confidence," and then moves on to the next a month later. Nelson is Mr. November. You don't need a crystal ball to predict that the materialistic Nelson falls for this bohemian girl, ready to renounce his capitalist ways all for true love. The premise absolutely creaks. Lost in all this is a sly turn by Isaacs as Sarah's neighbor, an even more high-powered ad exec/drag queen. ★ DVD Letterbox: $14.99, VHS: $9.99

Sweet Revenge

(1998, 90 min, GB, Malcolm Mowbray) *Sam Neill, Helena Bonham Carter, Kristin Scott Thomas, Rupert Graves, Martin Clunes.* A rather lukewarm British comedy with a decent cast, *Sweet Revenge* revolves around the revenge fantasies of two potential suicides. Neill and Scott Thomas meet each other on the Tower Bridge. They agree to set up their respective partners, who have set them on the road to ruin. Bonham Carter plays Thomas' nemesis, the wife of the man with whom she has been having an affair. A simple premise goes terribly awry when Neill falls in love with the woman he is supposed to victimize, while Scott Thomas ends up taking the "game" all too seriously. The film is effective in creating some mild laughs although falling well short of utilizing the full talent of the cast. (aka: *The Revengers' Comedies*) ★★ DVD: $19.99, VHS: $9.99

Sweet Smell of Success

(1957, 96 min, US, Alexander MacKendrick) *Burt Lancaster, Tony Curtis, Martin Milner.* Lancaster is J.J. Hunsecker, N.Y.C.'s most popular gossip columnist. Curtis is the weaselly press agent who will do anything to keep his favor. Screenwriters Clifford Odets and Ernest Lehman worked overtime on the dialogue as each character spits words like knives in an attempt to get the "one up" on the next guy. Everyone gets their just deserts in this cynical masterwork. (The basis for the Broadway musical) ★★★★ DVD: $14.99

Sweet Sweetback's Baadasssss Song

(1971, 97 min, US, Melvin Van Peebles) *Melvin Van Peebles, Rhetta Hughes, Simon Chuckster, John Amos.* Van Peebles wrote, directed and stars in this trendsetting work — which initiated the "blaxploitation" film cycle of the 1970s — about an African-American on the run from "the Man." Violent and told with a discernable rage, the film is in some ways rather dated, with its long montages of Sweetback running and running (complete with split-screen, super-impositions and freeze frame), wall-to-wall, loud '70s jazz, and some stereotypes of its own (mostly women and gays). But the film has lost little of its power in depicting the brutal effects of racism, and even the film's dated score and technical aspects add to *Sweetback's* nightmarish quality. ★★★ DVD: $19.99, VHS: $19.99

Sweet William

(1980, 92 min, GB, Claude Whatham) *Sam Waterston, Jenny Agutter, Anna Massey, Arthur Lowe.* Practically unseen in the U.S., this charming and sexy comedy features Waterston as a promiscuous young playwright who becomes involved with a

S

woman who refuses to accept his compulsive philandering. Waterston is beguiling and raffish, and is ably assisted by the strong supporting cast. ★★★

The Sweetest Thing

(2002, 84 min, US, Roger Kumble) *Cameron Diaz, Christina Applegate, Thomas Jane, Selma Blair, Jason Bateman, Parker Posey, Georgia Engel.* Attempting to combine the gross-out hijinks of *There's Something about Mary* and the sexual politics of "Sex and the City," writer Nancy M. Pimenthal and director Kumble demonstrate little comic flair in this story of a manizing beauty (Diaz) who meets Mr. Right (the handsome Jane), but has trouble connecting. Along the way, she commiserates with her best friend (Applegate) about being single, in between various jokes that lack punch or punchline. *The Sweetest Thing* is bad not because of its tastelessness, but because it fails to either set up or follow through on a joke. Gross and stupid aren't funny in themselves. At least Applegate can finally say goodbye to her "Married with Children" persona. ★½ DVD Dual Unrated: $14.99, DVD Dual R-Rated: $14.99, VHS R-Rated: $14.99

Sweetie

(1990, 97 min, Australia, Jane Campion) *Karen Colsten, Tom Lycos, Genevieve Lemon.* First-time director Campion's spellbinding drama follows the story of Kay (Colsten), a highly superstitious and emotionally repressed cafeteria worker whose once-blissful but slowly disintegrating relationship with a handsome coworker is further rattled when her unpredictable sister Sweetie shows up on her doorstep. Mentally unstable and possibly schizophrenic, the ill-tempered Sweetie destroys Kay's routine; and when their parents show up, it's a virtual free-for-all. As Sweetie, Lemon gives a devastating performance. ★★★½

Swept Away

(1975, 116 min, Italy, Lina Wertmüller) *Giancarlo Giannini, Mariangela Melato.* A swarthy sailor and his beautiful, wealthy employer are cast adrift on the hot sands of a Mediterranean island. The sweeping blue waves and the blazing August sun thrust them together in a steamy, passionate affair. The battle of the sexes and class struggles are played out in this handsomely photographed drama. (Remade in 2002) (Italian with English subtitles) ★★★★

Swept Away

(2002, 89 min, GB/Italy, Guy Ritchie) *Madonna, Adriano Giannini, Jeanne Tripplehorn, Bruce Greenwood.* Let's all give thanks to Guy Ritchie, for proving that it's not just Americans who can remake classic films into putrid garbage. Madonna stars as the stuck-up wife of a businessman, who ends up stranded on a deserted island with one of the deck-boys (Giannini, son of the original's Giancarlo). The roles reverse, in a satiric taming of the shrew that just doesn't work, now that women's status as societal equals is inarguable. It's hard to tell whether Ritchie really loves his wife (for casting the notorious non-actress in the lead) or hates her (for subjecting her to a two-note role as a harpy-cum-submissive slave). Where original director Lina Wertmüller pushed buttons in the original, Ritchie merely seems to be punching the clock. ★ DVD: $19.99, VHS: $14.99

Swept from the Sea

(1998, 114 min, US, Beeban Kidron) *Vincent Perez, Rachel Weisz, Ian McKellen, Joss Ackland, Kathy Bates.* Based on Joseph Conrad's short story "Amy Foster," this waterlogged period romantic spectacle tells the story of a shipwrecked immigrant (Perez) who falls in love with a town outcast (Weisz) whom some fear is a witch. The first-rate production design is undermined by a cast with no chemistry (despite the presence of such pros as McKellen and Bates), and a screenplay with no soul. The cinematography is beautiful, and the sweeping romantic score by John Barry is worth mention, but Kidron's rigid direction makes it hard to care when she starts plucking the heartstrings. ★★ DVD: $14.99

Swimfan

(2002, 85 min, US, John Polson) *Jesse Bradford, Erika Christensen, Shiri Appleby, Kate Burton, Dan Hedaya.* The Stamford University swim team scouts are 8 days away, and Ben needs to concentrate on his performance for their scrutiny. He's got it all: looks, brains, ability, good friends, loving girlfriend, supportive mom. Enter Madison, new girl at school, replete with pouty lips and golden curls, who's staying with her cousin, the high school's creepy guy. Acquaintance leads to flirtation leads to seduction and entrapment and jealousy and obsession and stalking and accusation and hostile retaliation. You'll see most of it coming; it's a high school *Basic Instinct* with cute, affluent teenagers sporting nice bods and big cars and perfect hair. The film is slightly elevated by competent performances, especially Bradford as the beleaguered Ben. ★½ DVD Dual: $14.99, VHS: $12.99

The Swimmer

(1968, 94 min, US, Frank Perry) *Burt Lancaster, Janice Rule, Kim Hunter.* Lancaster is splendid in this unusual but rewarding film as a businessman whose disgust for his middle-class life prompts him to, one afternoon, swim his way home from one pool to another, reflecting upon his life. ★★★ DVD Letterbox: $19.99

Swimming

(2000, 98 min, US, Robert J. Siegel) *Lauren Ambrose, Joelle Carter, Jennifer Dundas Lowe, Jamie Harrold.* In a Hollywood wasteland of starved starlets and plastic-surgery queens, the voluptuous Ambrose is a true original. With *Swimming*, the "Six Feet Under" star pumps up the frump factor as boyish-girl Frankie, a misfit in overalls who goes all but ignored by the endless stream of young boys on vacation in Myrtle Beach. Frankie spends most of her time working at a diner and hanging with her sassy and unclassy best friend Nicola (Lowe) until bombshell Josee (Carter) comes to town and opens Frankie's eyes to a world of possibility. The relationship Frankie and Josee build is definitely tinged with sexual energy, but the film doesn't take things too far down that road. In a flash of subtle beauty, Ambrose imbues her character with the awkwardness and self-awakening that so accurately reflects life at this age, and *Swimming* becomes a metaphor for how to stay afloat in the rocky waves of adolescence. ★★★½ DVD: $24.99, VHS: $79.99

Swimming Pool

(2003, 103 min, France/GB, François Ozon) *Charlotte Rampling, Ludivine Sagnier, Charles Dance.* An enigmatic psychosexual thriller, director Ozon's *Swimming Pool* is a stunning story of a woman who rediscovers her passion and her voice. Rampling is simply ravishing as Sarah Morton, an uptight English mystery writer who has lost all passion for her life and her work. She buttons her blouses up to the top and wears a permanent, thin-lipped grimace on her face. In an uncharacteristically impulsive move, she agrees to spend a few weeks at her publisher's summer home in France. It is there she meets Julie (the gorgeous Sagnier), her publisher's daughter, a free-spirited and sexually ravenous girl who beds almost every man she meets. Sagnier is terrific as Julie, the polar opposite to Sarah, who also becomes the author's muse as Sarah slowly loosens the buttons on her life with each exposure to Julie's world. Director Ozon, who makes a subtle use of wardrobe to reflect Sarah's self-discovery, masterfully juxtaposes repression and expression, and ultimately makes you unsure as to what is real and what is not. An entertaining and thoughtful thriller that is sexy and terribly smart. (In English and French with English subtitles) ★★★½ DVD Unrated: $19.99, VHS Letterbox Unrated: $9.99

Ludivine Sagnier in *Swimming Pool*

Swimming to Cambodia

(1987, 85 min, US, Jonathan Demme) *Spalding Gray.* A unique fusion of stage and film, Gray's theatrical monologue about his experiences in Cambodia while filming a small role in *The Killing Fields*, makes for captivating and enlightening entertainment. Director Demme, who had already directed the quintessential live concert film *Stop Making Sense*, unleashes an attentive camera on Gray, who, in brilliantly comic and cerebral morsels of insight, hypnotically weaves a tale of life, the war, and the search for the perfect moment. ★★★★

Swimming with Sharks

(1995, 93 min, US, George Huang) *Kevin Spacey, Benicio del Toro, Frank Whaley, Michelle Forbes.* "The fastest way to get to the top is to work with someone already there." This is the advice taken to heart by ambitious but naïve writer Guy (Whaley) when he accepts the job as assistant to Buddy Ackerman (Spacey), the abusive V.P. of Production of Keystone Pictures. But daily dosages of insults take their toll as Guy takes Buddy hostage. And through a series of flashbacks, *Swimming with Sharks* tells the story of what drove Guy to this act and to possibly commit murder. Writer-director Huang's black comedy is of the darkest shade, a numbing satire whose venom penetrates to the bone. Spacey gives a dazzling portrayal of the acid-tongued, demanding exec; it's at once vile, funny, brutal and remarkably controlled. "Shut up, listen, and learn." ★★★ DVD: $19.99

The Swindle

(1999, 105 min, France, Claude Chabrol) *Isabelle Huppert, Michel Serrault, François Cluzet.* What happens when long-time practitioners of the short con attempt one last, big score with the long con? Although their precise relationship is never explicitly stated, Huppert and Serrault bicker like a long-married couple, tag-team tricksters who trawl for conventioneers in big, impersonal hotels. Their lives are amazingly routine, essentially bourgeoise, until he discovers the man behind her increasingly frequent absences, and the couple is drawn into a pool of deception and greed far in excess of their experience. The film evidences touches of Chabrol's early blithe insouisance, and fancies itself a jaundiced commentary on society's inherent hypocrisy. But it's really just a caper film, a confection, an amusing Gallic diversion. (French with English subtitles) ★★½ VHS: $19.99

Swing

(1999, 97 min, GB, Nick Mead) *Hugo Spear, Lisa Stansfield, Tom Bell, Danny McCall, Alexei Sayle, Rita Tushingham, Clarence Clemons.* Surely if they were going to make a film to cash in on the Swing craze, they could come up with a better one than this British import. Speer stars as Martin, an ex-con whose ex-girlfriend Joan (Stansfield) has married his arresting officer. During his incarceration, Martin is taught the saxophone by his cell mate (Clemons, who does all the sax music in the film). Putting together a swing band, Martin deals with his devious brother, a group of high-strung fellow musicians and Joan's jealous husband. *Swing* only cooks when the band is on stage. ★½ VHS: $19.99

Swing Kids

(1993, 112 min, US, Thomas Carter) *Robert Sean Leonard, Christian Bale, Frank Whaley, Barbara Hershey, Kenneth Branagh.* A truly disappointing, even awful story of individualism, Nazism and

swing music. Leonard plays a German teenager who is part of a youthful clique that includes Whaley and Bale. They spend their nights dancing to American swing and days avoiding the Hitler Youth. But these 1930s hipsters soon discover the Nazis are formidable foes as one by one they either join the movement or perish. Screenwriter Jonathan Marc Feldman gives characters no moral dance steps to go along with their jitterbug, or any emotional depth as they try to sidestep the Nazis. ★½ DVD: $9.99

Swing Shift

(1984, 100 min, US, Jonathan Demme) *Goldie Hawn, Christine Lahti, Ed Harris, Christine Lahti.* When America's men left to fight WWII, her women took their places on the job, altering the structure of the family and women's self-expectations. The film's uneveness is perhaps due to reported disagreements between Demme and Hawn as to her character's personality; it is nonetheless well-worth watching. Lahti is outstanding as one of those women on the job. ★★★ DVD Letterbox: $14.99

Swing Time

(1936, 103 min, US, George Stevens) *Fred Astaire, Ginger Rogers, Helen Broderick, Eric Blore.* One of the best of the Astaire and Rogers musicals, with Fred and Ginger as a dance team in a romantic predicament — he's engaged to the girl back home. Extraordinary dance numbers, and the fine score includes "The Way You Look Tonight" and "Pick Yourself Up." ★★★★ VHS: $14.99

Swingers

(1996, 96 min, US, Doug Liman) *Jon Favreau, Vince Vaughn, Ron Livingston, Patrick Van Horn, Heather Graham.* In *Swingers*, men wear retro clothing, emulate Frank Sinatra and his Rat Pack crew, and worship at the altar of Tarantino, Travolta and Scorsese. Mixing retro 'tude with contemporary guy predicaments, Liman's second feature is an upbeat, winning look at the romantic and social entanglements of a group of hepcat Los Angeles lounge lizards. The focus is on Mike (Favreau, who also scripted), a New Yorker who has come to L.A. to try to make it as a comic. He joins ultra-slick Trent (Vaughn) and some other pals for after-hour prowls of area clubs. Eventually, Mike realizes he's longing for a real relationship. But can he find it with a martini in one hand and a bossa nova record in the

Swingers

other? With dialogue that jives and characters that cook, you often feel like you're watching a documentary about the cool, cool world it depicts. This is one happy-and-a-half hour worth checking out. ★★★½ DVD Collector's Edition: $14.99, VHS: $9.99

Swiss Family Robinson

(1960, 126 min, US, Ken Annakin) *John Mills, Dorothy McGuire, James MacArthur.* Disney's exciting version of the classic adventure story about a family shipwrecked on a deserted island. ★★★ DVD 2-disc set: $22.99, VHS: $19.99

Switch

(1991, 103 min, US, Blake Edwards) *Ellen Barkin, Jimmy Smits, JoBeth Williams, Perry King, Lorraine Bracco.* Edwards wrote and directed this occasionally amusing though ordinary body-switching comedy. Barkin single-handedly saves the picture with a vibrant portrayal of a sexist philanderer who is murdered and comes back as a beautiful blonde. King is what she used to look like; Smits is his partner who is now attracted to his associate. In view of Edwards' brilliant sex farce *Victor/Victoria*, *Switch* is all the more disappointing. ★★ DVD: $9.99, VHS: $9.99

Switchback

(1997, 118 min, US, Jeb Stuart) *Danny Glover, Jared Leto, R. Lee Ermey, Dennis Quaid, Ted Levine, William Fichtner.* So-so thriller with several intriguing elements, featuring a very glum Quaid as an FBI agent on the trail of a serial killer, with the help of a small-town sheriff (Ermey). The pursuit, it turns out, is quite personal — the killer has kidnapped Quaid's young son. Meanwhile, in a parallel thread, Glover gives hitchhiker Leto a ride to Utah . . . could one of them be the killer? Conventional for most of its running time, *Switchback* does occasionally spark to life in its details. There's not a great deal of action, only a modicum of suspense. ★★ DVD: $14.99, VHS: $9.99

Switchblade Sisters

(1975, 91 min, US, Jack Hill) *Robbie Lee, Joanne Nail.* Worth its weight in gold as a cultural artifact of an unfortunate time in American cinematic history, *Switchblade Sisters* will undoubtedly entertain those audience members who are already in love with its dubious endowments: babes, bikers and blades. And no amount of argument from any one will convince them that the movie really is trash. The story is simple: teenage gang debutantes fight enemies within and without in a series of brawls, rape sequences and prison scenes. ★ DVD: $14.99, VHS: $9.99

Switching Channels

(1988, 105 min, US, Ted Kotcheff) *Burt Reynolds, Kathleen Turner, Christopher Reeve, Ned Beatty.* A bargain-basement remake of the classic *His Girl Friday*, with Reynolds and Turner in the Cary Grant and Rosalind Russell roles. The characters have been changed from newspaper to TV reporters. ★½

Swoon

(1992, 95 min, US, Tom Kalin) *Craig Chester, Daniel Schlachet.* The scandalous 1924 murder trial of Nathan Leopold and Richard Loeb for the inexplicable murder of a young boy is given a slightly tilted, definitely New Queer Cinema treatment in this intriguing independent black-and-white feature that will fascinate some and upset others. Lovers Leopold and Loeb bungle a scheme to kidnap a boy, resulting in the youth's cold-blooded killing. The two are eventually tracked down by the police, arrested, tried and sentenced to life in prison. But director Kalin's real interest lies less in the horrendous act of the unlikely criminals and more with the lovers' secretive, intense and self-destructive relationship. Other films adapted from the notorious murder are *Rope* and *Compulsion*. ★★★

The Sword & the Rose

(1953, 91 min, GB, Ken Annakin) *Richard Todd, Glynis Johns, Michael Gough.* Flavorful Disney adventure. Mary Tudor, unhappily betrothed to King Louis XII of France, falls for the dashing Palace Captain of the Guard. This incurs the wrath of the evil Duke of Buckingham, who stops at nothing to destroy the romance. (aka: *When Knighthood Was in Flower*) ★★★

The Sword and the Sorcerer

(1982, 100 min, US, Albert Pyun) *Lee Horsley, Kathleen Beller, Simon MacCorkindale.* A ruthless king summons a long-dormant sorcerer to aid him in his evil-doings, but a young prince (Horsley) aims to stop him. Unexciting combination of adventure and sorcery. ★★ DVD Letterbox: $19.99, VHS: $9.99

The Sword in the Stone

(1963, 79 min, US, Wolfgang Reitherman) Amiable Disney animated feature based on the Arthurian legend about young Arthur's search for the famed sword and his adventures with Merlin. Highlighted by bouncy songs and a great wizard duel between Merlin and Mad Madam Mim. ★★½ DVD: $29.99, VHS: $14.99

Sword of Doom

(1967, 120 min, Japan, Kihachi Okamoto) *Tatsuya Nakadai, Toshiro Mifune.* Nakadai stars as an amoral, disaffected young samurai who shifts between moods of brooding nihilism and outbursts of extreme and random violence. After accidentally killing an opponent in a tournament duel, he leaves his village in disgrace and wanders the countryside in a seemingly pointless search to find an opponent worthy of his deadly swordplay skills. He is pursued by the vengeance-seeking brother of the man he killed, who has since become the student of a master swordsman (Mifune). Beautifully filmed in stark widescreen black and white, the film is a dark exploration of the violent and base natures of humanity. (Japanese with English subtitles) ★★★½ VHS: $29.99

Sword of Fury I

(1973, 90 min, Japan, Tai Kato) This dazzling film follows the exciting life of Japan's most famous swordsman of the 17th century, Musashi Miyamoto. It features almost unbelievable displays of swordsmanship and easily made Miyamoto one of Japan's most famous samurai. (Japanese with English subtitles) ★★★½

Sword of Fury II

(1973, 77 min, Japan, Tai Kato) *Hideki Takahashi, Jiro Tamiya.* This sequel follows samurai Musashi in his preparation for the battle against the notorious Kojiro to be Japan's premiere swordsman. (Japanese with English subtitles) ★★★

Sylvia and the Phantom

Sword of the Valiant

(1984, 102 min, GB, Stephen Weeks) *Miles O'Keefe, Sean Connery.* Connery's brief but commanding presence is about the only reason to see this sword-and-sorcery adventure. O'Keefe plays a knight (Sir Gawain) who goes up against the infamous Green Knight. ★★ DVD: $14.99

Swordfish

(2001, 99 min, US, Dominic Sena) *John Travolta, Hugh Jackman, Halle Berry, Don Cheadle, Vinnie Jones, Sam Shepard.* Travolta hams it up as the suave, conceited leader of a gang of cyber-crooks who blackmail hunky ex-con Jackman into committing a dastardly hack job, all as a ruse to distract the cops from their true objective. An infuriatingly slow, unnecessarily talky crime thriller, *Swordfish* is notable for an explosive opening, a spectacularly silly chase involving an airborne city bus, some crackling sexual tension between Jackman and Berry and for the surprisingly protracted shot of Berry's bodacious, bared boobs. Producer Joel Silver has delivered some hardcore testosterone-pumped hits before (*Matrix, Die Hard*), and director Seña managed to make parts of *Gone in 60 Seconds* fun. Yet, somehow, in collaborating on a seemingly sure-fire connect-the-dots formula flick like this, they've spawned a cold, limp fish indeed. ★★ DVD: $14.99, VHS With two additional scenes not seen in theaters: $14.99

Sybil

(1976, 198 min, US, Daniel Petrie) *Sally Field, Joanne Woodward, Brad Davis.* Field gives a virtuoso performance in this haunting and technically superior made-for-TV movie about a young woman's multiple personality disorder. Field left behind the ghost of "The Flying Nun" forever when she tackled this demanding and career-making role. Woodward is splendid as the psychiatrist trying to help the suffering Sybil. ★★★★

Sylvia

(1986, 99 min, New Zealand, Michael Firth) *Eleanor David, Tom Wilkinson, Nigel Terry.* A teacher's unorthodox yet highly successful methods meet strong opposition from local authorities. David stars as the revolutionary educator Sylvia Ashton-Warner in this moving fact-based drama. ★★★ VHS: $79.99

Sylvia and the Phantom

(1950, 97 min, France, Claude Autant-Lara) *Jacques Tati.* An enchanting supernatural comedy. The story is set in a haunted castle where Tati and his 16-year-old daughter live. Trouble brews when his daughter falls in love with the ghost of her grandmother's long-deceased lover. Not your typical French film. (French with English subtitles) ★★★ VHS: $24.99

Sylvia Scarlett

(1936, 94 min, US, George Cukor) *Katharine Hepburn, Cary Grant, Edmund Gwenn.* A rakish thief and his daughter (Gwenn) are on the run from the law, so Kate becomes a "he," and the pair hooks up with con artist Grant. All the while, Kate maintains her secret identity, until she falls in love and must make a fateful decision. This is one of Cukor's fascinating misfires, which was crucified when released. Over the years, it has taken on cult status for its unusual premise and stylish tone. ★★½

Sympathy for the Devil (One Plus One)

(1969-70, 110 min, France, Jean-Luc Godard) This fascinating "song of revolution" intercuts The Rolling Stones rehearsing "Sympathy for the Devil" while the always controversial Godard wanders among them with occasional interruptions, car crashes, political diatribes as well as a visit to a porn store as he attempts to expose a society in collapse. A whirling attack on and an examination of politics, society and cinema. (English and French with English subtitles) ★★★ DVD: $19.99, VHS: $29.99

T-Men

(1948, 92 min, US, Anthony Mann) *Dennis O'Keefe, Alfred Ryder, June Lockhart, Wallace Ford.* Return with us now to those thrilling days of yesteryear, when all government agents were square-jawed, clean-living, right-thinking white men fighting the evil nemesis of non-Anglo minorities washing upon our shores like scum in a bathtub. Two stalwart protectors of our nation's security infiltrate a loosely knit organization of counterfeiters. Earnest orchestrations alternate with ingratiatingly banal incidental music to accompany images shot in extreme noir and with a penchant for highly reflective surfaces. A nostalgic reminder of a time when most people actually trusted the government. ★★½ VHS: $19.99

Tabu

(1931, 82 min, US, F.W. Murnau) Filmed entirely on the seemingly idyllic island of Tahiti, and made through the unusual collaboration between directors Murnau and Robert Flaherty, *Tabu* is an early, rarely seen masterpiece. Set amidst the glistening sun and fine sand beaches of the island, the film tells the tragic tale of two young lovers, forced to separate after a tribal edict calls the girl "tabu" to all the men of the village. The video transfer is taken from a strikingly beautiful print that was restored at the UCLA film archives. ★★★★ DVD: $29.99, VHS: $39.99

Tadpole

(2002, 78 min, US, Gary Winick) *Aaron Stanford, Sigourney Weaver, John Ritter, Bebe Neuwirth.* Newcomer Stanford plays the title character, a cultured, Voltaire-loving 15-year-old (going-on-40) schoolboy. Over the course of one Thanksgiving weekend, Tadpole returns from private school to spend the holiday in Manhattan with his dad (Ritter) and his stepmother Eve (Weaver). His feelings for Eve are stronger than that of most stepsons, which

leads to both tender and tensely comic moments between the two. Stanford makes a fine debut, striking a pleasant balance between both Tadpole's maturity and naivety within the very grown-up situations he finds himself in. And Weaver gives a heartfelt performance as the woman in the middle of an awkward situation. But the film's real scene-stealer is the hilarious Neuwirth. Playing Eve's best friend Diane, a jaded, bored 40-year-old with her own uses for Tadpole, Neuwirth creates comic magic in a few key scenes. A clever, breezy comedy with keen insight into the different packages in which love comes, *Tadpole* swims nicely. ★★★ DVD Letterbox: $29.99, VHS: $14.99

Taffin

(1988, 96 min, GB, Francis Megahy) *Pierce Brosnan, Ray McAnally, Patrick Bergin.* Brosnan stars as a reclusive heavy in a small Irish coastal town who makes his living collecting bills — it's no wonder that he's not well-liked by the townsfolk. But when big business attempts to build a chemical plant in their backyard, the natives come begging for him to put up a fight. It's a fairly simple premise, but the inventive ways in which Brosnan and the locals beat up on the corporate big boys offer some amusing moments and satisfy some sense of social justice. ★★ DVD: $9.99

The Tailor of Panama

(2001, 109 min, GB, John Boorman) *Pierce Brosnan, Geoffrey Rush, Jamie Lee Curtis, Brendan Gleeson, Catherine McCormack, Harold Pinter.* Just as John le Carré is not your typical writer of spy tales, *The Tailor of Panama*, based on his novel and coadapted by the author, is not your typical le Carré espionage tale. Sophisticated with more wit than one would expect, this disarming story of an expatriate tailor and a disgraced agent in search of redemption makes for a fanciful, polished excursion into the back alleys of espionage's players and wannabes. In a smashing turn, Rush is Harry Pendel, a tailor to Panama's political bigwigs. Harry is recruited by British agent Andy Osnard (Brosnan, who revels in his smart-ass antihero) to keep an ear open for news about the current administration. Things get a little out of control, however, when Harry begins to fabricate stories to stay on the payroll and placate the ambitious, relentless Andy.

Director Boorman's canny eye for location shooting (captured beautifully by cinematographer Philippe Rousselot) and detail is served well here, as Panama itself becomes an important character to a complex piece immersed in culture and intrigue. ★★★½ DVD Special Edition: $14.99, VHS: $14.99

Take Me Out to the Ball Game

(1949, 93 min, US, Busby Berkeley) *Gene Kelly, Frank Sinatra, Esther Williams, Betty Garrett.* Though it doesn't really rank with the best of the Kelly-Sinatra musicals, there's a lot to like in this flavorful romp with Gene and Frank as ball players greeting the new owner of their club: the aquatic Williams. ★★★ DVD: $19.99

Take the Money and Run

(1969, 85 min, US, Woody Allen) *Woody Allen, Janet Margolin, Louise Lasser.* Allen's first film as writer and director uses a documentary-like format, which he would use again in his later *Zelig*. This hilarious odyssey follows the misadventures of Virgil Starkwell, a bumbling thief who can't even write a holdup note without messing up (Gub? What's a gub?). A nonstop verbal assault featuring some of Allen's funniest sight gags. ★★★½ DVD: $14.99

Taking Care of Business

(1990, 108 min, US, Arthur Hiller) *James Belushi, Charles Grodin, Anne DeSalvo, Hector Elizondo, Gates McFadden.* Escaped con Belushi assumes the identity of rich businessman Grodin when the former finds the latter's appointment book/wallet, or filofax, and carries off the charade while enjoying the sweet life. There are a few laughs to be found in this genial comedy, though it's mostly predictable stuff. ★★ DVD: $14.99, VHS: $9.99

The Taking of Pelham One Two Three

(1974, 104 min, US, Joseph Sargent) *Walter Matthau, Robert Shaw, Martin Balsam, Hector Elizondo, Jerry Stiller.* It's a mystery why this incredibly suspenseful thriller wasn't a box-office hit when released in the theatres. Shaw heads a four-man gang who hijack a New York City subway car at rush hour and demand one million dollars in ransom — to be delivered in one hour. Matthau is the transit inspector on the case, Balsam is one of the gang members, and Shaw is at his malevolent best as the leader. Filmed on location, *One Two Three* is superb entertainment. ★★★½ DVD: $14.99

A Tale of Springtime

(1990, 107 min, France, Eric Rohmer) *Anne Teyssedre, Hugues Quester.* With the completion of his "Six Comedies and Proverbs," Rohmer's new series "Tales of the Four Seasons" begins auspiciously with this engaging, sophisticated drama starring his usual coterie of attractive, young intellectual Parisians. Jenny, a philosophy graduate is befriended by Natasha, a chatty young piano student. Jealous of her divorced father's girlfriend (the same age as she), Natasha manipulates, in a none-too-subtle maneuvering, to make her father and Jenny a couple, resulting in a rather awkward weekend of shifting allegiances. A deceptively simple and entertaining story, brought to thought-provoking complexity through Rohmer's elegant style and his perceptive approach to human relations. (French with English subtitles) ★★★½ DVD Letterbox: $19.99

Jamie Lee Curtis and Pierce Brosnan in *The Tailor of Panama*

A Tale of Two Cities

(1935, 121 min, US, Jack Conway) *Ronald Colman, Elizabeth Allen, Edna May Oliver, Basil Rathbone.* The best of the many screen versions of the Charles Dickens classic set during the French Revolution, which was " . . . the best of times, the worst of times." Colman is in fine form as the lawyer who does " . . . a far, far better thing than I have ever done before." ★★★½

A Tale of Two Cities

(1958, 117 min, GB, Ralph Thomas) *Dirk Bogarde, Dorothy Tutin, Cecil Parker, Donald Pleasance.* One of seven film versions of Charles Dickens' immortal classic about the French Revolution, this faithful adaptation falls just short of the 1935 version. A terrific cast makes this a still worthwhile endeavor. ★★★

A Tale of Winter

(1994, 114 min, France, Eric Rohmer) *Charlotte Very, Frederic Van Dren Driessche.* Told in his trademark spare style, Rohmer's deceptively simple story of the search for love varies from his usual talky, philosophical dramas by featuring a protagonist who lives through emotions, not by intellectual reason. Felicie (Very) spends an idyllic summer in a passionate romance with Charles (Driessche). Through an accidental mix-up, however, they are separated and never see each other again. Five years pass with Felicie still yearning for him — a passion kept alive by her feeling that they will be reunited. The film is held together by the wonderful creation that is Felicie, a vacillating but determined romantic whose ambition lies not in understanding the complexities of desire or emptiness but to simply be happy. An endearing *Sleepless in Seattle* for the Francophile set. (French with English subtitles) ★★★ VHS: $19.99

Talent for the Game

(1991, 91 min, US, Robert M. Young) *Edward James Olmos, Lorraine Bracco, Jeff Corbett.* Olmos brings much sincerity to the role of a veteran major league scout who happens upon a gifted, Midwestern pitcher. The focus of the story follows the young ball player's introduction into the majors and his exploitation at the hands of the team's new owner. The film is one long, predictable cliché, but Olmos and costar Bracco, as Olmos' longtime girlfriend, are likable characters and director Young fills his film with beguiling, personal moments. ★★½ DVD: $14.99, VHS: $14.99

The Talented Mr. Ripley

(1999, 139 min, US, Anthony Minghella) *Gwyneth Paltrow, Matt Damon, Jude Law, Cate Blanchett, Philip Seymour Hoffman, James Rebhorn, Philip Baker Hall.* Minghella's succulent dramatic thriller is one of the best Alfred Hitchcock films *not* made by the Master of Suspense. Based on the novel by Patricia Highsmith (whose "Strangers on a Train" was adapted by Hitchcock), and filmed once before in 1960 as *Purple Noon*, this devious exercise in deception is a twisted little tale much like its young hero — handsome trappings masking more sinister intent. Damon is excellent as Tom Ripley, who accepts a job from a shipping magnate to try to convince his wastrel son Dickie, who is living it up in Italy, to return to the States. Once there, Tom is enamored not only by Dickie's way of life but by Dickie as well. But accidents do happen, and soon Tom finds himself spiraling down an egregious path with no salvation. Giving a dazzling performance

Gwyneth Paltrow, Jude Law and Matt Damon in *The Talented Mr. Ripley*

which should cement him as a leading man, Law exudes sensuality and charm, leaving little doubt as to why Tom's senses would be impaired. ★★★★ DVD: $14.99

Tales from the Crypt

(1972, 92 min, GB, Freddie Francis) *Ralph Richardson, Joan Collins, Patrick Magee, Ian Hendry, Richard Greene.* A chilling anthology of five frightening tales of deceit, mayhem, and treachery as experienced by five people lost in a catacomb. Five wayward souls who are shown their futures by a mysterious and evil monk (Richardson). ★★★ VHS: $9.99

Tales from the Darkside: The Movie

(1990, 95 min, US, John Harrison) *Deborah Harry, Christian Slater, Rae Dawn Chong, David Johansen.* Sporting a versatile cast and stories by George Romero and Stephen King, among others, *Tales from the Darkside: The Movie* leaves behind the familiar, bloody turf covered by the likes of Freddy Krueger and Jason and instead calls upon evil housewives, gargoyles, mummies and a black cat to keep its audience on the edge of its seat. It's all good fun, but occasionally stumbles when it swings from a serious mood to tongue-in-cheek horror and back again. ★★★ DVD Letterbox: $14.99, VHS: $9.99

Tales from the Gimli Hospital

(1989, 72 min, Canada, Guy Maddin) *Kyle McCulloch, Michael Gottli.* Maddin's ferociously funny Gothic creation is set during the turn of the century in the small Icelandic village of Gimli during a smallpox epidemic. Filmed in an eerie black and white and featuring minimal dialogue, the film tells the story of two hospitalized patients, Einar and Gunnar, who battle each other over everything from telling the perfect story to winning the attentions of their Louise Brooks-look-alike nurses. Wildly impressionistic and surreal, the film will elicit the same kind of astonished chuckles and gasps as another cult classic, *Eraserhead.* ★★★ DVD: $29.99, VHS: $24.99

Tales from the Hood

(1995, 97 min, US, Rusty Cundieff) *Clarence Williams III, Rosalind Cash, Corbin Bernsen, David Allen Grier, Rusty Cundieff.* With the same irreverence and stylish flourishes he brought to *Fear of a Black Hat*, director Cundieff has fashioned possibly the first horror anthology film with a social conscience. Not having to rely on monsters for his horrific tales, Cundieff uses the realities of life in the

'90s — drug abuse, domestic violence, gang warfare, black-on-black crime, dishonest cops and racism — to create four ironic tales from the supernatural. A devilishly bug-eyed Williams is the storyteller, whose audience of three drug-dealing youths listen impatiently to his scary yarns. Mixing chills with ills, Cundieff's *Hood* is fun for all. ★★★ DVD: $14.99, VHS: $9.99, VHS Letterbox: $9.99

The Tales of Hoffmann

(1951, 125 min, GB, Emeric Pressburger & Michael Powell) *Robert Rounseville, Robert Helpmann, Moira Shearer.* This Powell and Pressburger follow-up to *The Red Shoes* has been given special treatment in its transfer to video, highlighting its lurid Technicolor. During intermission at the Nuremberg Opera House, a group of students gather in the *bierkeller* to drink, smoke and listen to the acclaimed poet Hoffman spin tales of love, loss, mystery and evil. Located somewhere between the poetic surrealism of Jean Cocteau and the highly stylized works of Peter Greenaway, this film version of Offenbach's operatic fantasy will appeal to music lovers and the casual viewer alike. (Filmed in English) ★★★ VHS: $29.99

Tales of Ordinary Madness

(1983, 107 min, Marco Ferreri) *Ben Gazzara, Ornella Muti.* Italian director Ferreri provokes every reaction but boredom, and with a scenario launched from the sordid musings of cult poet Charles Bukowski, he has perhaps found the vehicle best suited for his iconoclastic style. A grizzled Gazzara is the derelict author stumbling through adventures in a sickeningly sun-drenched L.A. The tauntingly beautiful Muti adds a new dimension to screen masochism. ★★★ DVD: $24.99, VHS: $19.99

Tales of Terror

(1963, 90 min, US, Roger Corman) *Vincent Price, Peter Lorre, Basil Rathbone, Debra Pagent.* In this portmanteau movie, Corman fashions four of Edgar Allan Poe's short stories into three episodes, each featuring Price. Vincent's daughter gets a strange mother's day surprise; Rathbone is an evil mesmerist whose sultry looks turn Vincent to putty; and, in a comedic segment, Lorre quells a wine taster before his time. ★★★ DVD: $14.99, VHS: $9.99

Tales of the City

(1993, 360 min, US/GB, Alastair Reid) *Olympia Dukakis, Chloe Webb, Marcus D'Amico, Laura Linney, Donald Moffat, Bill Campbell, Thomas Gibson, Barbara Garrick, Parker Posey, Ian*

McKellen, Country Joe McDonald, Cynda Williams, Paul Bartel, Mary Kay Place, Vaginal Davis, Don Novello, Rod Steiger, Karen Black, Lance Loud. Taken from Armistead Maupin's endearing and popular novel, this boldly original and faithful adaptation follows the interconnected lives of a group of San Francisco eccentrics (both gay and straight) during the halcyon 1970s. This six-part miniseries centers around exotic Earth Mother Anna Madrigal (Dukakis), landlady of 28 Barbary Lane. Her colorful extended family of tenants includes innocent Mary Ann (Linney), a recent arrival from Cincinnati; bisexual/fag hag Mona (Webb); and Michael (D'Amico), a hopeless romantic eternally searching for Mr. Right. The lives of these people and others come together in an amazingly complex series of eye-opening episodes that involve marital infidelity, ribald sexuality, recreational drug use and scenes of the emerging gay lifestyle. *Tales* is funny, provocative and totally unpredictable. (Sequel: *More Tales of the City*) ★★★★ DVD: $59.99, VHS: $59.99

Talk of Angels

(1998, 96 min, US, Nick Hamm) *Polly Walker, Vincent Pérez, Franco Nero, Marisa Paredes, Frances McDormand.* A dreadfully dull, annoyingly "tasteful" Merchant Ivory wannabe, *Talk of Angels* follows the story of a woman (Walker) who becomes the new nanny to the young girls of a wealthy family in Spain. At first considered too young to be a proper governess, Walker is soon accepted and respected by all; then she initiates a torrid affair with Latin hunk Pérez. Bliss is interrupted by that pesky Spanish Civil War. Boredom ensues. There is no drama to speak of, the acting is wooden (even by Walker and a slumming McDormand), and the "triumphant moments" clichéd and artificial. ★ DVD: $19.99, VHS: $9.99

The Talk of the Town

(1942, 118 min, US, George Stevens) *Cary Grant, Jean Arthur, Ronald Colman, Rex Ingram, Edgar Buchanan.* When discussing the movie career of Grant, other films will undoubtedly spring to mind before *Talk of the Town*, but this little-known Stevens comedy is unquestionably one of the actor's best efforts. Grant stars as an escaped convict (framed, naturally) who hides out in the house of an old friend, the captivating Arthur. But she has just rented it to Supreme Court nominee Colman. While Grant poses as the gardener, Arthur and an unsuspecting Colman attempt to prove Cary's innocence. Of course, both men fall in love with her, and Arthur herself is torn between them. Sparkling romantic comedy and potent social commentary as well. ★★★★ DVD: $29.99

Talk Radio

(1988, 119 min, US, Oliver Stone) *Eric Bogosian, Ellen Greene, Alec Baldwin, John C. McGinley.* A hard-hitting, explosive look at the world of talk radio, public opinion and social intolerance that is loosely based on slain talk show host Alan Berg. Bogosian gives a dazzling performance as Barry Champlain, a popular late-nite radio host whose verbal sparrings with his audience, not to mention his unapologetic views spoken in rapid-fire delivery, keep his listeners coming back for more. Through a series of flashbacks chronicling his success on the air, the film examines Champlain's complex psychological makeup and his volatile relationships, both in the present and the past, with those closest to him. ★★★½ DVD: $26.99, VHS: $14.99

Talk to Her

(2002, 112 min, Spain, Pedro Almodóvar) *Javier Camara, Dario Grandinetti, Leonor Watling, Rosario Flores, Geraldine Chaplin.* After a series of relatively lighthearted movies about women, Almodóvar dives deeply and darkly into men's passions in this moving masterwork. Tabloid reporter Marco (Grandinetti) is going after a sordid story about an unlucky-in-love bullfighter (Flores), but just as he falls for her, she's gored and finds herself in a coma. The hospital's adjoining room houses a gorgeous dancer (Watling), comatose for years, who's cared for by obsessive nurse Benigno (Camara). The two men share an unrequited love for their unconscious women, with Benigno's expressions of amor being uncomfortably disturbing and, in Almodóvar's cunning way, blackly comic. His ravishing visual flair continues unabated, especially in the recurring dancing scenes that break up the melodrama, and an unforgettable silent-film fantasy about a little lover willing to go to uncharted depths to please his woman. What's ultimately stunning is the empathy that Almodóvar conveys for such tragically flawed, easily demonized characters. Pushing the envelope while invoking compassion — it's a triumph that only Almodóvar could achieve. (Spanish with English subtitles) ★★★★ DVD Subtitled: $26.99

Talkin' Dirty After Dark

(1991, 86 min, US, Topper Carew) *Martin Lawrence.* Talkin' Dirty After Dark takes a look at the lives of struggling black comics in Los Angeles. Lawrence does some excellent stand-up, but for the most part, the material is substandard. One might get the impression that the only things black comics make fun of is sex, what white folks do, sex, what brothers do, and . . . more sex. ★★ DVD Letterbox: $14.99, VHS: $9.99

The Tall Blond Man with One Black Shoe

(1972, 90 min, France, Yves Robert) *Pierre Richard, Bernard Blier.* A bungling young violinist unwittingly becomes involved with a bunch of would-be James Bonds and sets off a madcap chase of agents and assassins in this hilarious French farce. (French with English subtitles) (Sequel: *Return of the Tall Blond Man with One Black Shoe*) (American remake: *The Man with One Red Shoe*) ★★★

The Tall Guy

(1990, 92 min, GB, Mel Smith) *Jeff Goldblum, Emma Thompson, Rowan Atkinson.* Essentially a one-joke affair, the film follows Dexter King (Goldblum), an expatriate American stage actor living in London. Because of his above-average height, he is constantly cast in humiliating "fool" roles. Demonstrating a flair for physical comedy, Goldblum is at his best in the movie's real show-stopper — a musical version of "The Elephant Man," one of the most tasteless and undeniably funny sequences ever put to film. ★★½ DVD Letterbox: $14.99, VHS: $9.99

Tall Tale: The Unbelievable Adventures of Pecos Bill

(1995, 96 min, US, Jeremiah Chechik) *Patrick Swayze, Oliver Platt, Nick Stahl, Scott Glenn.* Not to be confused with Shelley's Duvall's Tall Tales productions, this Disney adventure starring Swayze as Pecos Bill is a heartwarming coming-of-age story featuring old-time Western mythic heroes. When his

Rosario Flores in *Talk to Her*

family's farm and the nearby town are threatened by a ruthless railroad baron (played with maliciousness by Glenn), a young boy (Stahl) turns to Pecos Bill, Paul Bunyon and John Henry for help. Along the way, he learns the power of his own faith and commitment in the face of adversity. ★★★

Tamango

(1958, 98 min, France, John Berry) *Dorothy Dandridge, Curt Jurgens, Alex Cressan.* This standard seafaring yarn is rescued from certain obscurity by its theme of African slave-trading, black revolt and a "steamy" interracial love story. Jurgens plays a ruthless sea captain of a Dutch slave ship in the 1820s who falls in love with a beautiful black slave (Dandridge). Revolt simmers when one strong-willed and resourceful slave, and former warrior (Cressan), attempts to break his chains and lead a rebellion. Despite poor English dubbing of some minor characters and Dandridge's strange, Hollywood diva-ish acting style, the film holds great interest with its depiction of a proud but enslaved village. ★★½ VHS: $19.99

The Tamarind Seed

(1974, 123 min, GB, Blake Edwards) *Julie Andrews, Omar Sharif, Anthony Quayle.* Edwards makes an infrequent foray into the world of drama with this espionage/romancer. The material isn't strong, but the locations (London, Paris and Barbados) are wonderful and Andrews and Sharif have some fine moments as the Cold War Romeo and Juliet. ★★

The Taming of the Shrew

(1967, 126 min, GB/Italy, Franco Zeffirelli) *Elizabeth Taylor, Richard Burton, Michael York, Cyril Cusack.* Sumptuous screen version of Shakespeare's classic comedy with rich characterizations from Taylor and Burton as the feuding couple; she an unmarried "wildcat" and he the only man in Padua willing to court her. The story, of course, is the basis for the Cole Porter musical "Kiss Me Kate." ★★★½ DVD: $19.99

Tampopo

(1987, 114 min, Japan, Juzo Itami) *Ken Watanabe, Tsotomu Yamazaki.* One of the most inspired and zaniest comedies to be released in years, this Japanese satire on food and sex is a delectable send-up of American westerns. A widow, who operates a noodle restaurant in Tokyo, is befriended by a transient truck driver. Together, in the search for the perfect noodle, they recruit a ragtag team of social misfits to aid them in their quest. This appetizing comedy of epic proportions presents a world where the power of sex is second only to the power — you've guessed it — the noodle! (Japanese with English subtitles) ★★★★ DVD: $19.99, VHS: $19.99

Tango

(1998, 105 min, Spain, Carlos Saura) *Miguel Ángel Sola, Cecilia Narova, Mia Maestro, Juan Carlos Copes.* Sola plays a director whose wife has left him; while making a documentary about Tango dancing, he falls for a dancer. The story is there only to make room for spectacular and romantic dancing sequences, stunningly photographed by Vittorio Storaro. A fine companion piece to Saura's *Flamenco.* ★★★½ DVD: $27.99, VHS: $21.99

Tango and Cash

(1989, 105 min, US, Andrei Konchalovsky) *Sylvester Stallone, Kurt Russell, Jack Palance.* Stallone and Russell star in this slick, formulaic police thriller framed by a megalomaniac drug dealer. Skipping the standard love interest (or are the two stars the love interest?), the film includes enough car crashes to keep Detroit in the black for another five years. The money combination of a mangy and volatile Russell with a well-dressed, bespectacled Stallone allows both actors to play with their screen images and made the latter likable for the first time since *Rocky.* ★★½ DVD: $9.99, VHS: $9.99

The Tango Lesson

(1997, 101 min, Argentina/France/GB, Sally Potter) *Sally Potter, Pablo Veron.* Writer-director Potter stars as a fictionalized version of herself in this lyrical and mesmerizing contemplation of love, seduction, power and the Argentine tango. Potter plays "Sally," a British filmmaker who, while scouting Paris for her upcoming film, wanders aimlessly into a theatre and is instantly absorbed into a live tango exhibition starring Veron. She gamely introduces herself to the maestro and entreats him to

tutor her, offering to put him in a film in return. This transaction in *Tango Lesson* represents a real-life event, but to what degree the ensuing entanglement on-screen represents the depth of Potter and Veron's offscreen relationship is unclear. With the help of Robby Müller's exquisite sepia-toned cinematography and Potter's haunting score, the film's dance sequences are as pure a delight as we've gotten since the era of Fred and Ginger. ★★★★

Tank Girl

(1995, 104 min, US, Rachel Talalay) *Lori Petty, Ice-T, Malcolm McDowell, Naomi Watts.* Petty is the title character, a buzz-cut grunge girl with a slightly phallic passion for tanks. Along for the ride is Watts as her sidekick Jet Girl. Together they join forces with the Rippers (a mutant band of half-human, half-kangaroo renegades) and battle the powerful Water and Power overlords (led by McDowell) in the year 2033. Though as visually bombastic as the worst of MTV, this mishmash *might* prove fun for the less-discriminating viewer looking for a mindless yuk. ★★ DVD: $14.99

Tanner '88, Vols 1-3

(1988, 120 ea. min, US, Robert Altman) *Michael Murphy, Pamela Reed, Kevin J. O'Connor, Veronica Cartwright, Jeff Daniels, Rebecca DeMornay.* In 1988, director Altman created a fictional Democratic presidential candidate and used the actual primary process as location shooting. Murphy as Jack Tanner hits the campaign trail, shaking hands with Bob Dole, Gary Hart and Pat Robertson, who may or may not know it's only a movie. Tanner's flashes of brilliance in a quagmire of mediocrity (sometimes his own) are packaged for media consumption by his campaign staff. It's a cynical, intelligent and sardonic look at the photo ops, pollsters, spin doctors, petty sabotage, backbiting and pure chance that comprise the modern American political system. Written by Garry Trudeau, with Sidney Blumenthal as a political consultant. ★★★½ VHS: $79.99

The Tao of Steve

(2000, 87 min, US, Jenniphr Goodman) *Donal Logue, Greer Goodman, Kimo Wills.* How is it that overweight, perpetually stoned slacker Dex (a perfectly cast Logue) beds so many attractive women?

He lives according to the "Tao of Steve," a homemade philosophy made up of equal parts Lao Tzu and Steve McQueen, which seems to work like a charm on the ladies. Dex's supremely laid-back attitude towards women and life in general is put to the test when a conquest from college (whom Dex can't even remember) comes to town for a short-term job — and Dex finds himself falling in love. Winning performances (especially from Logue), great moments of insight and some hilarious discussions of philosophy and sex that beat anything from Mars or Venus more than make up for a too-cute tone. ★★★ DVD: $24.99

Tap

(1989, 110 min, US, Nick Castle) *Gregory Hines, Suzanne Douglas, Sammy Davis, Jr., Joe Morton, Savion Glover, Paul Nicholas.* A frenzied celebration of dance set against an urban backdrop, as a disillusioned tap dancer (Hines) is torn between his craft and a lucrative living as a thief. As would be expected, there are some great tap sequences. ★★★

Tape

(2001, 83 min, US, Richard Linklater) *Ethan Hawke, Robert Sean Leonard, Uma Thurman.* An intriguing, shot-on-digital-video chamber piece, *Tape* is based on Stephen Belber's stage play and takes place entirely in one setting: a Lansing, Michigan, hotel room. Vince (Hawke), an Oakland drug dealer not above distorting the truth about himself, has returned from a reunion with boyhood friend and now budding film director Johnny (Leonard). As they reminisce about old times and old friends, including high school pal Amy (Thurman), alcohol, drugs and repressed rage soon bring dirty secrets to the surface. Minimal but powerfully intimate and very involving, *Tape* is mainly about the performances, and all three actors excel in their roles. To his credit, director Linklater keeps things brisk with well-chosen compositions and snappy editing preventing the single locale from becoming too claustrophobic. ★★★ DVD: $14.99

Tapeheads

(1988, 97 min, US, Bill Fishman) *John Cusack, Tim Robbins, Susan Tyrrell.* An exhilaratingly original and innovative spoof which will not disappoint. The film's story follows the unusual road to fame taken by two misfits: the deliciously sleazy Cusack and the constantly bewildered Robbins. They join forces and set up an independent video production company. Stymied by their failure to make rock videos, they subside on the fringe, making living (and not so living) wills as well as taping funerals until their big break comes. The film is crammed with crazy comedy and peppered with unforgettable lines. There's some wild musical numbers and both Cusack and Robbins are wonderful farceurs — and if that's not enough, Junior Walker and Sam Moore appear as "The Swanky Modes." ★★★½ DVD: $9.99, VHS: $9.99

Taps

(1981, 124 min, US, Harold Becker) *George C. Scott, Timothy Hutton, Sean Penn, Tom Cruise, Ronny Cox, Giancarlo Esposito, Brendan Ward, Donald Kimmel.* Military cadets seize control of their military academy when outside forces threaten to shut it down. Some of this is by-the-books, and slow going, but its young cast is enthusiastic. ★★ DVD: $14.99

Ethan Hawke in *Tape*

Tarantula

(1955, 80 min, US, Jack Arnold) *Leo G. Carroll, John Agar, Clint Eastwood.* Carroll stars as a scientist whose secret growth formula works a little too well, resulting in a mutated spider which chews up the countryside and anything else that gets in its way. One of the best of the many 1950s giant/mutant schlock films, *Tarantula* features a credible story and great F/X. Highly entertaining. ("I knew Leo G. Carroll was over a barrel when *Tarantula* took to the hills.") ★★★

Target

(1985, 117 min, US, Arthur Penn) *Gene Hackman, Matt Dillon, Gayle Hunnicutt.* Director Penn and actor Hackman are reunited for a third time in this satisfactory espionage thriller. Hackman plays a former CIA agent who, with son Dillon, sets out to rescue his wife, kidnapped by enemy agents out for revenge. ★★½

Targets

(1968, 90 min, US, Peter Bogdanovich) *Boris Karloff, James Brown.* Karloff had his last great role as an aging horror film star who decides to retire because events in the real world have rendered his talents superfluous. As if to underscore the point, a soldier just back from Vietnam begins a rampage of killing which leads him to a drive-in, where the old star is making a public appearance. ★★★ DVD Letterbox: $9.99, VHS: $14.99

Tart

(2001, 94 min, US, Christina Wayne) *Dominique Swain, Brad Renfro, Bijou Phillips, Mischa Barton, Lacey Chabert, Melanie Griffith, Scott Thompson.* An exclusive Manhattan prep school is the home to a handful of clichéd students: the bad girl (Phillips), the cute druggie (Renfro), the uptight Brit (Barton) and, of course, the personality-free protagonist (Swain) who gets upstaged by her costars. Ostensibly a drama about fitting in and growing up, *Tart* eventually takes a sharp right turn into overwrought thriller territory, with a healthy dose of homophobia to boot. True to its title, *Tart* will leave a sour taste in your mouth. ★½ DVD Letterbox: $24.99

Tartuffe

(1984, 140 min, France, Gérard Depardieu) *Gérard Depardieu, Elizabeth Depardieu, François Perier.* Depardieu makes his directorial debut with this version of Moliere's classic stage play about religious and sexual hypocrisy. The story revolves around a rich merchant who, with his wife, comes under the manipulative spell of a cunning charismatic religious zealot. He is threatened with exposure after the husband discovers that the rascal that made love to his young, attractive wife. Similar to *Cyrano de Bergerac* in its use of poetic dialogue, this satire exposing man's greed and delusions is a skillfully faithful adaptation. (French with English subtitles) ★★★

Tarzan

(1999, 88 min, US, Chris Buck & Kevin Lima) *Voices of: Tony Goldwyn, Minnie Driver, Glenn Close, Rosie O'Donnell, Nigel Hawthorne.* Though falling victim to the curse of Disney's last few animated features of having a less-than inspiring score, this flavorful animated film is a thorough delight. Excellent animation, a colorful story line and winning vocal characterizations all contribute to make this another in a long lone of splendid Disney family films. The tale of a young boy raised by the apes

seems a natural for the studio, and the filmmakers have wonderfully brought to life the monkeys, elephants and even humans who drive the story. If the film has a weakness, it is Phil Collins' unexceptional musical score. Fans of the singer/songwriter may appreciate him singing each song, but it becomes tiresome after awhile. ★★★½

Tarzan and the Lost City

(1998, 84 min, US, Carl Schenkel) *Casper Van Dien, Jane March.* This latest entry adds little to the Tarzan series. Van Dien has the act of glowering down to a science but is fairly wooden unless swinging from vine to vine. A band of mercenaries searching for the treasures of a lost city are terrorizing the natives and capturing animals for sale to finance their expedition. Tarzan, soon to be married, leaves England and returns to the jungle. His fiancée, realizing that she must stand by her (ape) man, soon joins him. Together, Tarzan, Jane, the natives, some ole jungle magic and some guys in really bad ape costumes save the sacred city. ★★ DVD: $9.99, VHS: $8.99

Tarzan the Ape Man

(1932, 99 min, US, W.S. Van Dyke) *Johnny Weissmuller, Maureen O'Sullivan.* The first of the Weissmuller Tarzan pictures, with the Olympic swimmer as the definitive Ape Man, and O'Sullivan as a lovely Jane. Very entertaining adventure film. ★★★ VHS: $19.99

Tarzan the Ape Man

(1981, 90 min, US, John Derek) *Bo Derek, Miles O'Keefe, Richard Harris, John Philip Law.* Bo Derek fever was at its height when hubby John directed this jiggle-filled quickie. Yes, she's naked, but there's no plot to speak of, and this high-profile disaster helped kill her career prematurely. Oh, O'Keefe is Tarzan . . . like anyone cared. ★

Taste of Cherry

(1997, 95 min, Iran, Abbas Kiarostami) *Homayon Ershadi, Abdolrahman Bagheri, Afshin Khorshid.* A troubled Iranian man in a Range Rover rides through the outskirts of Tehran looking for an accomplice to return to a designated location at 6:00 the next morning to shovel 20 spadefuls of dirt on his suicidal grave. Profoundly alienated, he

Robert De Niro in *Taxi Driver*

is the displaced person among the Kurds, Afghanis and Turks whom he encounters in his quest. His request elicits various responses — fear, religious counseling. But the man who agrees to perform the task offers a story of his own flirtation with suicidal intent born of despair. *Taste of Cherry* is rich in stark imagery, stunningly used to evoke at once existential angst and the inexhaustive human will to survive. It's marred only slightly by the inexplicable addition of a "filmmakers at work" coda. (Farsi with English subtitles) ★★★ DVD: $29.99, VHS: $29.99

A Taste of Honey

(1962, 100 min, GB, Tony Richardson) *Rita Tushingham, Robert Stephens, Dora Bryan.* This lovely, heartbreaking film is a "minor" masterpiece. Tushingham stars in this earthy tale about a group of social rejects in Britain's bleak, industrial North. A poetic saga, which is aided by top-notch performances, and transcends lower-class cliché. ★★★½

Taste the Blood of Dracula

(1970, 95 min, GB, Peter Sasdy) *Christopher Lee, Geoffrey Keen, Gwen Watford, Roy Kinnear.* The fourth in the Hammer vampire stories. Dracula seeks vengeance against three Victorian thrill-seekers whose cowardice causes the death of a magician trying to resurrect the Prince of Darkness. More campy, hokey fun with Lee as the evil bloodsucker. ★★½ DVD: $19.99

Tatie Danielle

(1990, 100 min, France, Etienne Chatiliez) *Tsilla Chelton, Catherine Jacob.* The supposed dignity of one's "golden years" is the target of this sharply satirical black comedy. Seemingly innocent and helpless, our sinister heroine Tatie Danielle is, in actuality, a bitter, calculating old lady who receives sick pleasure out of hurting all who try to help her. Tatie meets her match one day when an equally manipulative young nurse arrives on the scene. The film, to its detriment, ignores the motives for Auntie's meanness, and instead takes devious delight in simply chronicling her often hilariously terroristic antics. (French with English subtitles) ★★½

The Tavern

(1999, 88 min, US, Walter Foote) *Cameron Dye, Kevin Geer, Carlo Alban, Margaret Cho.* Two down-on-their-luck lifelong friends (one, a career bartender, the other, an assistant manager at a department store) attempt to fulfill their dream of owning a bar/restaurant, unaware of and unprepared for the brutal reality of keeping it running. Writer-director Foote (son of playwright Horton Foote) has a real knack for naturalistic dialogue, and draws expert performances from his cast. Dye and Geer are especially good, and extremely likable, which makes their hardships all the more painful. This is an utterly believable, completely involving film, aided by an appealing song score by The Saw Doctors; just don't expect to feel all warm and fuzzy once it's over. ★★★ DVD: $14.99, VHS: $14.99

Taxi Blues

(1990, 110 min, France/Russia, Pavel Lounguine) *Piotr Mamonov, Piotr Zaitchenko.* This superbly rendered street-level saga about a unique friendship between a rough-hewn Moscow cab driver and an alcoholic saxophone player is a brutal but moving testament to the arduous process of change in the former Soviet Union. Filmed in the early-morning emptiness of Moscow's mean streets, the film uses these two characters to symbolize the faces of the new Russian psyche (the black marketeer and the newly freed intellectual). It is a sometimes humorous, often upsetting and uniformly bleak look at the hardships facing the common people as they struggle to move out of decades of stagnation. (Russian with English subtitles) ★★★★ VHS: $29.99

Taxi Driver

(1976, 113 min, US, Martin Scorsese) *Robert De Niro, Jodie Foster, Cybill Shepherd, Harvey Keitel, Albert Brooks, Peter Boyle.* De Niro is Travis Bickle, a lonely cab driver obsessed with the squalor and decay of New York City. He sets out on a one-man mission to clean the streets of its underworld of pimps, junkies and hookers. Scorsese directs this sordid and haunting film featuring Foster in the tragic and memorable role of a teenage prostitute. De Niro's quintessential performance, Scorsese's sardonic view of American urban life, and a mesmerizing and unsettling use of non-exploitative violence propels this masterwork to the forefront of American cinema. ★★★★ DVD Letterbox: $19.99, VHS: $14.99

Taxi zum Klo

(1980, 92 min, Germany, Frank Ripploh) *Frank Ripploh, Orpha Termin, Bernd Broaderup, Peter Fahrni, Dieter Godde.* Ripploh's witty autobiographical social/sexual comedy offers an illuminating portrait one man's gay lifestyle, his conflicting image in a straight-laced profession and his relationship with a monogamous lover, who disapproves of his hedonistic promiscuity. Funny, charming and unflinchingly honest. (German with English subtitles) ★★★ DVD: $29.99, VHS: $39.99

A Taxing Woman

(1988, 127 min, Japan, Juzo Itami) *Nobuko Miyamoto, Tsutomu Yamazaki.* The Japanese post-Kurosawa New Wave continues in this sexy and whimsical comedy from the director of *Tampopo*. The story follows Ryoko (Miyamoto), a diligent and resourceful female tax inspector who tackles the ever-ingenious tax evading efforts of the citizens. Her greatest challenge is presented by Gondo, a suave operator of "love hotels" whom she suspects is underreporting massive amounts of money. Her impassioned efforts to catch him in the act and his equally feverish schemes to evade detection bring this unlikely pair together in this highly charged comedy. (Japanese with English subtitles) ★★★½ VHS: $19.99

A Taxing Woman's Return

(1988, 127 min, Japan, Juzo Itami) *Nobuko Miyamoto, Rentaro Mikuni.* This irreverent and free-wheeling comedy about the ingenious efforts of the Japanese to evade taxes and the tenacious tax collectors who are equally determined to ferret out every hidden taxable yen is a welcome follow-up to the hugely successful *A Taxing Woman*. Miyamoto is again the charming tax inspector who this time investigates a corrupt fundamentalist religious order which might be a front for a real estate racket. While not as fresh as the original, this scathing satire is, nevertheless, still a joy to watch. (Japanese with English subtitles) ★★★ VHS: $29.99

Tchaikovsky

(1970, 153 min, US/Russia, Igor Tlaankin) *Innokenti Smoktunovsky.* Though nominated for a Best Foreign-Language Oscar, this is a disappointing, standard bio of composer Pyotr Ilyich Tchaikovsky. The film suffers from a below-aver-

Cher in *Tea with Mussolini*

age musical soundtrack — a sin for a film infused with classical music. The story examines Tchaikovsky's life (from his tortured childhood to his struggles with loneliness and despair to his eventual renown) with an ice-cold austerity which gives little insight into the studious, intense and taciturn composer. Tchaikovsky's homosexuality has been completely ignored, omitting a vital element explaining his rocky romances and disastrous marriage. The film begs for the excesses of Ken Russell's *The Music Lovers*. (Russian with English subtitles) ★½ VHS: $24.99

Tchao Pantin

(1985, 94 min, France, Claude Berri) *Richard Anconina, Coluch, Philippe Leotard.* Berri, a director noted for his light comedies (*Le Sex Shop, Male of the Century*), leaves behind his safe stories to probe the back alleys, sleazy bars and tenements of the Parisian underbelly. A darkly somber and intensely moving thriller about the relationship between an alienated old man, retired from everything around him, and a lonely punk youth. An exciting tale of survival in a heartless world. Winner of 5 Césars. (French with English subtitles) ★★★

Tea and Sympathy

(1956, 123 min, US, Vincente Minnelli) *John Kerr, Deborah Kerr, Leif Erickson.* Adapted (and watered down) by Robert Anderson from his own Broadway play, this tale of a sensitive teen at a New England boarding school who is accused of being a homosexual is both involving and curiously tame. J. Kerr plays the youth, who is suspected by his classmates of being a "sister boy." D. Kerr is the understanding wife of the headmaster who befriends the confused teen and who eventually exorcises any latent homosexual desires. ★★★ VHS: $19.99

Tea with Mussolini

(1999, 117 min, GB/Italy, Franco Zeffirelli) *Joan Plowright, Maggie Smith, Judi Dench, Cher, Lily Tomlin, Charlie Lucas, Baird Wallace.* Based on a chapter from director Zeffirelli's autobiography, this old-fashioned, nostalgic memory piece lacks a cer-

tain cinematic flourish, but makes up for it with both a great cast in great form and a beguiling coming-of-age story. In mid-1930s Florence, young Luca is raised by a group of elderly English expatriate women, known as "the Scarpioni" (for their biting wit). Each instills in Luca a love for the arts, theatre and life. However, their worlds change when Fascism grips Italy — sending all on different roads but never separated in spirit. Zeffirelli pays great respect to these women with his heartfelt tale, and they have been marvelously brought to life by a once-in-a-lifetime ensemble. It's their conviction that overcomes the sometimes dramatically short-changed story to produce a wistful recollection that is graced with heart, wit and admiration. ★★★ DVD: $14.99, VHS: $14.99

Teacher's Pet

(1958, 120 min, US, George Stevens) *Clark Gable, Doris Day, Gig Young, Nick Adams.* Entertaining romantic farce with Gable as a newspaperman and Day as a teacher. Both come together when he takes her writing course. ★★★ VHS: $14.99

Teachers

(1984, 106 min, US, Arthur Hiller) *Nick Nolte, JoBeth Williams, Judd Hirsch, Morgan Freeman, Ralph Macchio, Laura Dern.* A good cast is mostly wasted in this story of the everyday ups and downs of an urban high school. ★★

Teaching Mrs. Tingle

(1999, 96 min, US, Kevin Williamson) *Helen Mirren, Katie Holmes, Barry Watson, Jeffrey Tambor, Molly Ringwald, Vivica A. Fox.* Scream scribe Williamson makes a disappointing directorial debut. Technically more of a black comedy than a horror film, *Teaching Mrs. Tingle* tells the tale of a straight-A student (Holmes) who is in danger of losing her academic scholarship if her hated history teacher — Mrs. Tingle — gives her the F she's threatened to. Holmes ends up holding the evil educator hostage until she changes her mind. A not-bad premise is chucked in favor of juvenile dramatics and pandering humor. ★½ DVD: $19.99, VHS: $9.99

The Teahouse of the August Moon

(1956, 124 min, US, Daniel Mann) *Marlon Brando, Glenn Ford, Eddie Albert.* A mild-mannered Army captain (Ford) is left in charge of an occupied village in 1946 Okinawa, and wacky results ensue. Brando plays a wily Asian interpreter. ★★★

Teaserama

(1955, 75 min, US, Irving Klaw) Fabulous '50s pin-up queen Betty Page and busty glamazon Tempest Storm are featured in this truly amazing burlesque presentation. Performances by pin-up faves Honey Baer, Trudy Wayne, Chris LaChris and Cherry Knight, campy comic routines by famed vaudeville player Joe E. Ross ("Sgt. Bilko," "Car 54, Where Are You?"), and a great dance/striptease by female impersonator Vicky Lynn combine to make this film a "Burly-Q" classic. ★★★ DVD: $19.99

Teen Wolf

(1985, 90 min, US, Rod Daniel) *Michael J. Fox, James Hampton.* Though *Back to the Future* was released several months before it, this harmless teen comedy was Fox's film debut. He plays a teenager who discovers he's really a werewolf. To its credit, there are a few laughs. (Sequel: *Teen Wolf Too*) ★★½ DVD Letterbox Double Feature: $14.99

Teenage Caveman

(2001, 100 min, US, Larry Clark) *Andrew Keegan, Tara Subkoff, Richard Hillman, Tiffany Limos, Stephen Jasso, Shan Elliot.* Or, *Kids* goes sci-fi. The increasingly sleazy Clark has fashioned a truly lame story as an excuse to (yet again) ogle a group of naked young teens. In the postapocalyptic future, kids are still doing nasty drugs and having lots of sex and beating each other up. Yawn. This is (aside from the aforementioned ogling factor, if that's your bag) absolutely pointless and, since there's really no story, utterly dull. Horribly shot, *Teenage Caveman* has tacky dialogue and unconvincing performances to boot. Easily the worst of the Creature Features series. ★ DVD Dual: $14.99

Teenage Mutant Ninja Turtles

(1990, 93 min, US, Steve Barron) Long popular on video in cartoon form, these live-action Teenage Mutant Ninja Turtles proved to be just as popular on the big screen in this hokey but crowd-pleasing (if you're under 15) adventure-comedy. Here the TMNT find themselves up against a group of teenagers under the evil influence of a Japanese gangster. Cowabunga, dude. Though a bit sluggish throughout, there's still enough action to appeal to the younger set, and Jim Henson's full-size costumes are terrific. (Followed by two sequels.) ★★ DVD: $14.99

Telefon

(1977, 100 min, US, Don Siegel) *Charles Bronson, Donald Pleasence, Lee Remick, Tyne Daly, Patrick Magee.* Exciting espionage thriller with Bronson playing a Russian agent sent to the U.S. to preserve detente by stopping a psychotic defector (Pleasence) from activating scores of hypnotized saboteurs. ★★★

Tell Me Something

(2000, 116 min, Korea, Chang Youn-Hyun) *Han Suk-gyu, Shim Eun-ha.* Large plastic garbage bags filled with bloody body parts (not always from the same person) begin turning up in odd places around the city. A troubled police detective discovers that all the victims had a relationship with the same woman. What's the connection? Is she the killer? A diverting (and fairly gory) Korean serial-killer thriller, *Tell Me Something* has some good suspense scenes and an accomplished, foreboding atmosphere. What it doesn't have is a particularly satisfying ending, leaving a somewhat bad taste. Until that point, however, this is a nice addition to a well-worn subgenre. (Korean with English subtitles) ★★★ DVD: $29.99, VHS Subtitled: $24.99, VHS Dubbed: $24.99

Tell Them Willie Boy Is Here

(1969, 96 min, US, Abraham Polonsky) *Robert Redford, Katharine Ross, Robert Blake, Susan Clark, Barry Sullivan.* Blake stars as Willie Boy, an American Indian who becomes the object of a massive hunting party and a political scapegoat during the early 1900s. Set in the arid deserts of Southern California, the film begins with a drunken pool room fight involving Willie Boy and a white patron. From there, events start to snowball as Willie Boy kills the father of his girlfriend (a tanned Ross), and the two go on the run with a disinterested sheriff (Redford) and a blood-thirsty posse on their trail.

Director Polonsky sets an ominous tone as he effectively tells a tale of injustice and hysteria and juxtaposes it with an exciting chase story. ★★★

Telling Lies in America

(1997, 101 min, US, Guy Ferland) *Kevin Bacon, Brad Renfro, Calista Flockhart, Maximilian Schell, Paul Dooley.* Screenwriter Joe Eszterhas' semiautobiographical coming-of-age tale finds the writer in a less bombastic, more reflective mood. Ably conveying the inner turmoil of youth at the crossroads, Eszterhas has written a memory piece that is a little too self-serving but can be compelling all the same. Renfro is Karchy, a Hungarian immigrant living in early 1960s Cleveland with his father (Schell). When Karchy lands the job as assistant to a hotshot and shady local D.J. (Bacon, in a very effective portrayal), his learning experience encompasses betrayal, deceit, unrequited love and discovering the little inequities of his newfound land. The film has a lively soundtrack, including an entertaining song, "Medium Rare," written by Bacon. ★★½

The Temp

(1993, 99 min, US, Tom Holland) *Timothy Hutton, Lara Flynn Boyle, Faye Dunaway, Dwight Schultz, Oliver Platt, Steven Weber.* Hutton, an upwardly mobile marketing executive with a penchant for paranoia, is blown away by the skills of his new temporary secretary, played by Boyle. She files, she types, and, unfortunately, she also may be bumping off most of Hutton's competition in the dog-eat-dog world of cookie manufacturing. The main problem with *The Temp* is that Boyle is so blatantly obvious in her manipulations of Hutton that the film loses its tension early on. ★★ DVD: $14.99, VHS: $9.99

The Tempest

(1979, 95 min, GB, Derek Jarman) *Elisabeth Welch, Heathcote Williams, Jack Birkett.* Shakespeare gets the Jarman treatment in this lighthearted, visually eclectic and idiosyncratic version of the Bard's final play. Quite funny, outlandish and campy, the film includes singing, dancing, exotic and erotic visuals and Welch's rendition of "Stormy Weather." ★★★ DVD: $29.99, VHS: $24.99

The Tempest

(1982, 140 min, US, Paul Mazursky) *John Cassavetes, Gena Rowlands, Susan Sarandon, Raul Julia, Molly Ringwald.* Mazursky's contemporary treatment of Shakespeare's drama has Cassavetes attempting to resolve his midlife crisis by abandoning his successful Manhattan existence to search for truth and beauty in the Greek isles. Beautiful location shooting and engaging performances compensate for weaknesses in the script. ★★½ VHS: $9.99

Temptation of a Monk

(1994, 118 min, Hong Kong, Clara Law) *Joan Chen, Wu Hsinkuo.* While stylishly filmed, this tale of a betrayed general who must seek refuge in a temple is slow-moving and confusing. Chen stars as the siren princess who tempts a general of a royal family's army as he tries to atone for his errors in being accused a traitor. Lavish costumes, open landscapes and period music abound. The actors leave a good impression on a poorly written script. Though director Law has exhibited a fine edge with her prior works, she is unable to overcome a taxing story line and laborious characters in this well-intentioned but misguided effort. (Mandarin with English subtitles) ★★½

Temptress Moon

(1997, 115 min, China, Chen Kaige) *Leslie Cheung, Gong Li, Kevin Lin, He Saifei.* Cheung and Gong are radiant as ill-fated lovers in this overly tragic jumble. It's the tale of Yu Zhongliang (Cheung) and Pang Ruyi (Gong), who were raised together as youths in Ruyi's ancestral home. Zhongliang eventually winds up in Shanghai where he becomes the favorite of a local crime boss and acts as a gigolo/con man. Then he's instructed to return to the Pang household and put the con on Ruyi and thus is born a setup for tragedy. The film is lushly photographed and features fine performances from its brooding leads, but sadly its arcane plot has incomprehensible moments that muddle the film's message. (Mandarin with English subtitles) ★★ DVD: $14.99, VHS: $9.99

10

(1979, 121 min, US, Blake Edwards) *Dudley Moore, Julie Andrews, Bo Derek, Robert Webber, Brian Dennehy.* Edwards wrote and directed this hit comedy about a famed composer (Moore) who becomes obsessed by a woman (Derek) he rates a perfect "10." Moore is good at playing Edwards' slapstick, and Andrews and Dennehy offer good support. Webber's self-pitying gay composer is a bit much, though. ★★★ DVD: $14.99

Ten Benny

(1998, 98 min, US, Eric Bross) *Adrien Brody, Michael Gallagher, Sybil Temchen, Tony Gillian, Frank Vincent.* Growing up in the milieu of low-level mob action in Bloomfield, N.J., Ray (a very engaging Brody) rests his future on a bet on the ponies, financed by loan sharks and fueled by a hot tip. Eager to quit his job in a shoe store, buy an engagement ring for his beloved and set up shop in a prime storefront location, he bets $10,000 on a horse that can't lose. Guess what? It does. Ray, once calm, easy-going and in control, devolves into just another mark, just another neighborhood guy with big ideas and lowered expectations. He is transformed from a decent guy whom everyone likes to a desperate man who alienates those closest to him. *Ten Benny* is a small, thoughtful exploration of the decisions people make, the paths they take, and the true meaning of loss. ★★½ DVD: $9.99, VHS: $9.99

The Ten Commandments

(1923, 146 min, US, Cecil B. DeMille) Unfortunately DeMille never heeded the eleventh commandment which is: Thou shalt not make epic movies out of "The Bible" pandering to people's prurient interests. The first portion of this sprawling mess violates that edict, then goes on to tell a contemporary tale of two brothers — one good, one evil — and how the Word saves their souls. Great camp fun with two-strip Technicolor sequences. DeMille would try his hand at the story again in 1956. ★★½ VHS: $19.99

The Ten Commandments

(1956, 220 min, US, Cecil B. DeMille) *Charlton Heston, Yul Brynner, Anne Baxter, Edward G. Robinson, Vincent Price, John Saxon.* Mammoth epic from DeMille, based on his silent classic. Heston dons beard and robe to portray Moses, leading the Jews out of Egypt. A spectacular production, though some scenes may cause a few smirks. Even with today's state-of-the-art special effects, the parting of the Red Sea is still impressive. ★★★ DVD Letterbox: $19.99, DVD Letterbox Special Collector's Edition: 2-Disc Set: $19.99, VHS: $14.99, VHS Letterbox: $14.99

Ten Days' Wonder

(1972, 105 min, France, Claude Chabrol) *Anthony Perkins, Orson Welles, Marlene Jobert.* Although not well received in its initial release in 1971, this oddity is a distinctly original work that fans of Chabrol and of the avant-garde should enjoy. Adapted from an Ellery Queen story, the film stars Perkins as a mentally and emotionally disturbed young man who falls in love with his father's (Welles) child bride. A bewildering mystery of madness, adultery and blackmail. (Filmed in English) ★★½ DVD: $19.99

Ten from Your Show of Shows

(1973, 92 min, US, Max Liebman) *Sid Caesar, Imogene Coca, Carl Reiner, Howard Morris.* For those of you who remember the classic TV comedy show of the 1950s, "Your Show of Shows," no more additional information is needed other than that this is a collection of their most hilarious routines. For those not familiar, these examples of the very best of TV sketch comedy, performed live each week, are not to be missed. Starring the madcap team of Caesar, Coca and Reiner, and with many skits written by Mel Brooks, the film concludes with a painfully funny parody of "This Is Your Life." ★★★★

Ten Little Indians

(1974, 98 min, GB, Peter Collinson) *Oliver Reed, Elke Sommer, Richard Attenborough, Gert Frobe.* Second remake of the Agatha Christie mystery "And Then There Were None," this time set in a remote desert inn, where ten strangers are gathered and then murdered one by one. Lackluster pacing adds nothing new to this oft-told tale. ★★

10 Rillington Place

(1971, 111 min, GB, Richard Fleischer) *Richard Attenborough, John Hurt, Judy Geeson.* This gripping psychological thriller is another true-life murder case brought to the screen by director Fleischer (*Compulsion, The Boston Strangler*). The story centers on notorious mass-murderer John Christie (Attenborough) and his unwitting pawn Timothy Evans (Hurt). Sometimes too clinical to be completely successful as a thriller, the film manages to remain interesting nonetheless. ★★★

10 Things I Hate about You

(1999, 97 min, US, Gil Junger) *Heath Ledger, Julia Stiles, Joseph Gordon-Levitt, Larisa Oleynik, David Krumholtz, Larry Miller.* Extremely loose adaptation of "The Taming of the Shrew," with teens, high school and, of course, a climactic prom. Frighteningly overprotective dad Miller won't let his popular daughter Oleynik go to the prom unless his unpopular shrew daughter Stiles goes too. She is conned into a date with outcast Ledger, then finds out about a wager about the date, but he's fallen for her? Oh, why bother explaining? It's an old story but it has equal parts charm and bile, making it hard not to get swept up. Fun performances by all the kids make this a diverting treat, even if the writers can't tell Shakespeare from Elizabeth Barrett Browning. ★★½ DVD: $19.99, VHS: $9.99

Ten Violent Women

(1979, 97 min, US, Ted V. Mikels) *Sherri Vernon, Dixie Lauren, Sally Alice Gamble.* Bored with their jobs, ten female coal miners attempt to increase their income through a jewelry heist and by dealing cocaine. This lands them in prison, which is headed by a butch dyke and populated by curvaceous gals. A terrible women-in-prison flick that makes for hilarious fun. ★ DVD: $24.99

The Tenant

(1976, 125 min, US/France, Roman Polanski) *Roman Polanski, Isabelle Adjani, Melvyn Douglas, Shelley Winters.* Polanski himself stars in this dark and eerie film noir about a social misfit who moves into a Parisian apartment and begins a bizarre descent into madness. Filled with paranoia and foreboding, the film takes on its own twisted logic as it makes its way towards a truly outrageous denouement. ★★★ DVD: $9.99, VHS: $19.99

Tender Mercies

(1982, 89 min, US, Bruce Beresford) *Robert Duvall, Tess Harper, Betty Buckley, Ellen Barkin, Wilford Brimley.* Duvall delivers a powerful, Oscar-winning performance as a country singer on the skids who is rescued from despair and the bottle by the quiet strength and sensitivity of a young widow. Australian Beresford makes his American directorial debut with this humanistic drama. ★★★★ DVD Letterbox: $19.99, VHS: $9.99

The Tender Trap

(1955, 111 min, US, Charles Walters) *Frank Sinatra, Debbie Reynolds, Celeste Holm, David Wayne, Carolyn Jones.* Sinatra stars in this engaging comedy about an insufferably unattached bachelor who falls for sweet young-and-innocent Broadway hopeful Reynolds and gets more than he bargained for. One of the better "sophisticated" comedies to come out of the '50s, this adaptation of the Max Schulman/Robert Paul Smith play features a bunch of winning musical numbers (especially the Cahn-Van Heusen title tune). ★★★½

Tenderness of the Wolves

(1973, 86 min, Germany, Ulli Lommel) *Kurt Raab, Jeff Roden, Margit Carstensen, Rainer Werner Fassbinder.* Produced by Rainer Werner Fassbinder, this creepy low-budget shocker is suggested by the infamous murder case which inspired Fritz Lang's classic *M*, though now updated to postwar Germany. Raab plays the sleazy predator — now a vampire — who lures young boys to his attic lair and has his way sexually with them before sucking their blood. He then sells their body parts as meat to unsuspecting buyers. Filmed with a tantalizing mix of titillation, gore and black comedy, this grisly gem is both disturbing and oddly entertaining. (German with English subtitles) ★★★ DVD: $29.99, VHS: $14.99

Tendres Cousines

(1980, 90 min, France, David Hamilton) *Thierry Tevini, Anja Shute.* A funny, tender coming-of-age film which follows the sexual antics of a 14-year-old boy and his beautiful cousin. Master erotic photographer Hamilton (*Bilitis*) presents this romp of unrequited love amidst the haylofts of rural France. (French with English subtitles) ★★½

Tenebre

(1984, 101 min, Italy, Dario Argento) *Anthony Franciosa, John Saxon, Daria Nicolodi.* Franciosa plays Peter Neal, a popular American writer who comes to Rome for a publicity tour. He soon learns that a killer is using his book as inspiration for a series of murders. Neal and his secretary begin to help the police in their search for the killer and, like all good Argento heroes, eventually set off on their own to solve the mystery. *Tenebre* is remarkably strong in narrative content for an Argento film, and the film is brilliantly lit and shot, including one absolutely terrifying shot at the very end as the killer is revealed. The full-length director's cut. (aka: *Unsane*) ★★★ DVD: $29.99, VHS: $14.99

The Tenth Man

(1988, 100 min, GB, Jack Gold) *Anthony Hopkins, Kristin Scott Thomas, Derek Jacobi.* Written by Graham Greene in 1944 while under contract to M-G-M, the manuscript for this riveting thriller, about a man's cowardly act and eventual redemption, languished in the studio archives until it was rediscovered in 1983. The setting is Occupied France, 1941. Wealthy lawyer Jean-Louis Chavel (Hopkins) is imprisoned in a Nazi roundup. When he is chosen to be executed, he trades places with another man, offering his substantial fortune to his family. Years later, a penniless Chavel returns to his former chateau, now home to the dead man's lovely family. Assuming a new identity, he becomes their gardener and friend, his secret shame hidden until one day a stranger arrives claiming that *he* is Chavel. ★★★★

The Tenth Victim

(1965, 92 min, Italy, Elio Petre) *Marcello Mastroianni, Ursula Andress.* A macabre yet compelling sci-fi tale set in the 21st century where killing has been ritualized in a sport where men and women pursue each other in a deadly game. This nightmarish thriller blends just the right amount of satire in its exploration of the uneasy relationship between the individual and society. Miss Andress' bullet-firing brassiere is worth the price of the rental alone! ★★★ DVD Letterbox Subtitled: $24.99, VHS Subtitled: $14.99

Teorema (Theorem)

(1968, 93 min, Italy, Pier Paolo Pasolini) *Terence Stamp, Silvano Magnano, Massimo Girotti.* Pasolini's fusion of Marxism, sex and religion stars a very young and attractive Stamp as a divine stranger who enters the household of a bourgeois family and profoundly affects their lives when he seduces the mother, father, son, daughter and maid. A surreal and sensual allegory with the Pasolini postulation that the ruling class can be undermined and destroyed by the one thing that it cannot control — sex. Despite winning the Grand Prix at the Venice Film Festival in 1968, the film was publicly denounced by Pope Paul VI and banned as obscene in Italy. Pasolini was arrested, but in a celebrated trial he was acquitted of all charges. (Italian with English subtitles) ★★★

Tequila Sunrise

(1988, 116 min, US, Robert Towne) *Michelle Pfeiffer, Kurt Russell, Mel Gibson, Raul Julia, Arliss Howard, Arye Gross, J.T. Walsh.* An uneven but gorgeous-looking romantic thriller which tries to and occasionally succeeds in capturing the mood of *Chinatown*, which Towne wrote. Gibson stars as a former drug dealer trying to go straight, but is about to be busted by his high school chum Russell. The two men become embroiled in a game of cat-and-mouse as both fall in love with a beautiful restaurant owner, Pfeiffer. The three stars give earnest performances, but are unable to hide some of the contrivances of the script. ★★ DVD: $19.99, VHS: $9.99

Teresa Venerdi

(1941, 90 min, Italy, Vittorio De Sica) *Vittorio De Sica, Anna Magnani.* A delectable comedy directed by and starring De Sica as a young physician working in an orphanage who finds himself innocently involved with three women. The magnificent Magnani is a doctor's assistant who sets out to win the doctor herself. Filled with action, intrigue and jealousy. (aka: *Doctor Beware*) (Italian with English subtitles) ★★★

Terminal Bliss

(1992, 91 min, US, Jordan Allan) *Luke Perry, Timothy Owen, Alexis Arquette.* Before shooting to fame as a moody California rich kid on TV's "Beverly Hills 90210," teen heartthrob Perry played a moody California rich kid in this pointless tale of adolescent decadence. While the sex and drugs sequences during the first 15 minutes offer generous helpings of delicious B-movie juvenile delinquency, the aimless, episodic structure of the film eventually grows tiresome. Who needs plot, depth and style when you can hear lines like, "Mom, I'm going out to kill myself now. I'll be home late." ★ VHS: $19.99

The Terminal Man

(1974, 107 min, US, Mike Hodges) *Joan Hackett, Jill Clayburgh, George Segal.* Interesting if flawed thriller based on Michael Crichton's novel with Segal as a scientist who becomes controlled by a computer. ★★ VHS: $14.99

Terminal Velocity

(1994, 102 min, US, Deran Sarafian) *Charlie Sheen, Nastassja Kinski.* This high-flying actioner starring Sheen as a devil-may-care sky diver and Kinski as a Russian agent who lures him into helping her beat the bad guys is filled with implausibilities, bad dialogue, wretched acting and is still somehow fun. There are plenty of fist fights, gunplay, explosions (there's even a tribute to *Die Harder*) and general chaos. ★★½ DVD: $14.99, VHS: $9.99

The Terminator

(1984, 108 min, US, James Cameron) *Arnold Schwarzenegger, Linda Hamilton, Michael Biehn, Paul Winfield, Bill Paxton, Lance Henriksen.* Director Cameron and actor Schwarzenegger both burst on the action scene with this explosively entertaining and taut sci-fi thriller. Arnold plays a cyborg sent from the future to present-day Los Angeles to terminate the mother (Hamilton) of a revolutionary. Biehn is the soldier also from the future sent to eliminate Arnold. (Followed by 2 sequels) ★★★½ DVD: $14.99, VHS: $9.99

Terminator 2: Judgment Day

(1991, 135 min, US, James Cameron) *Arnold Schwarzenegger, Linda Hamilton, Edward Furlong, Joe Morton, Robert Patrick.* The $100 million price tag on this impressive sci-fi sequel made a lot of jaws drop, but that's nothing compared to what the rip-roaring, non-stop action and eye-popping special effects do. The year is 1997. The evil cyborgs have sent the new, improved T-1000 terminator unit back through time on a mission to eliminate the future leader of the human resistance — a typical Southern California adolescent named John Connor (nicely played by Furlong). But into the fray comes a second killing machine (guess who), reprogrammed by the humans and sent back to protect the lad. Together, they liberate his mom (a buff

Terminator 3: Rise of the Machines

Hamilton), who's been institutionalized for her babblings about robots from the future, and the relentless chase begins. (Sequel: *Terminator 3: Rise of the Machines*) ★★★½ DVD Extreme DVD: $19.99, VHS: $9.99

Terminator 3: Rise of the Machines

(2003, 110 min, US, Jonathan Mostow) *Arnold Schwarzenegger, Nick Stahl, Claire Danes, Kristanna Loken, David Andrews.* Totally unnecessary but surprisingly entertaining, this sequel finds Arnold fighting a female (or female-shaped, anyway) enemy, while still protecting John Connor. Sarah (played by Linda Hamilton) is sorely missed this time, and the whole thing has a somewhat strained, contrived "sequelitis" feel to it. The good news is that the film has a good sense of humor about itself (Arnold's de rigeur search for clothing — especially his sunglasses — is a real hoot), and the action is great, most notably the first big chase, which is nothing short of terrific. There's also a witty cameo from a veteran of the first two films, and an unexpected ending. Schwarzeneggar and Danes are quite good, though Stahl (standing in for Furlong as John Connor) seems a bit ill at ease. Director Mostow is no James Cameron, but he's no slouch, either; the film moves at a fast clip, and, all things considered, is pretty darned good. As science fiction, *Terminator 3* is marginal at best; as a dumbfun action flick, however, you could do a helluva lot worse. ★★★ DVD Letterbox 2-disc set: $19.99, DVD Pan & Scan 2-disc set: $19.99, VHS Pan & Scan: $22.99

Terms of Endearment

(1983, 132 min, US, James L. Brooks) *Shirley MacLaine, Debra Winger, Jack Nicholson, Jeff Daniels, John Lithgow, Danny DeVito, Lisa Hart Carroll, Huckleberry Fox, Troy Bishop.* A sensitive, funny and deeply touching examination of the tumultuous relationship between a mother and daughter. *Terms* virtually monopolized the Oscar ceremony, taking Best Picture and Best Director honors as well as (finally) acknowledging MacLaine for her crackling conception of a rigid matriarch. Winger is sensational as her spunky daughter and Nicholson rises to the occasion as the ex-astronaut next door with the wrong stuff. (Sequel: *The Evening Star*) ★★★½ DVD Letterboxed: $14.99, VHS: $9.99

Terra em Transe

(1966, 105 min, Brazil, Glauber Rocha) *Terra em Transe*, about the disillusionment and death of a young poet and journalist who is persuaded to become involved in the politics of his country, is a landmark of political cinema and a vivid example of Brazil's Cinema Novo movement. A powerful and quite personal film which was denounced by the Right as incendiary propaganda, hailed by the Left as an impassioned exposé, and banned by the government for some time. (Portuguese with English subtitles) ★★★½ VHS: $69.99

La Terra Trema

(1948, 160 min, Italy, Luchino Visconti) Initially setting off to make a Communist Party-financed short documentary on the conditions of the peasants in poverty-stricken Sicily, Visconti soon abandoned this idea to work on an epic focusing on the harsh conditions of southern Italy's fishermen, factory workers and miners. He finished only this segment, "Episodes del Mare" — and the result is a neorealist masterpiece. Filmed on location with nonprofessional actors, the story tells of the conditions and struggles of an exploited fisherman's family and the unsuccessful revolt by them and others against insurmountable odds. Startlingly beautiful images and a simple narrative combine to make this one of Visconti's best works. (Italian with English subtitles) ★★★★ DVD: $24.99

The Terror

(1963, 81 min, US, Roger Corman) *Boris Karloff, Jack Nicholson, Dick Miller.* Effective Corman cheapie about an injured soldier from Napoleon's army recovering at an eerie castle with strange goings-on. ★★½ VHS: $9.99

The Terror Within

(1988, 89 min, US, Thierry Notz) *George Kennedy, Andrew Stevens.* A chemically induced plague has ravaged the Earth and its remaining survivors are trapped in a laboratory 500 feet below the Mojave Desert. When a pregnant woman is found, the group soon learns that the baby she is carrying is an embryonic mutant. Just a little bit spooky, though its good premise isn't thoroughly realized. ★★ VHS: $14.99

The Terrorist

(2000, 100 min, India, Santosh Sivan) *Ayesha Dharkar.* An exceptional Indian film, *The Terrorist* is the impressive directorial debut of noted cinematographer Sivan. The film is ravishing, providing a rich contrast to a story of a voluntary martyr. With her gigantic, gorgeous eyes and looking much like a forgotten silent film star, Dharkar plays a serene but ruthless zealot willing to give her life in an assassination plot. Kernels of doubt are planted in her mind, however, building quite a bit of suspense as to whether she will or won't at the crucial moment. A powerful character study with a stunning lead performance. (Tamil with English subtitles) ★★★½ DVD: $24.99, VHS: $19.99

The Terrornauts

(1967, 75 min, GB, Montgomery Tully) *Simon Oates, Zena Marshall.* Mysterious alien forces kidnap an entire building containing research scientists and transport them to another planet. There, a robot takes the Earthlings to yet another planet, where little green men show them the fate of Earth. Fun, low-budget British sci-fi based on the novel "The Wailing Asteroid." ★★

Tess

(1979, 180 min, France/GB, Roman Polanski) *Nastassia Kinski, Peter Firth, Leigh Lawson.* Polanski's Academy Award-winning interpretation of Thomas Hardy's novel features breathtaking cinematography and a strong, eloquent performance by Kinski as a peasant girl who ruins and is ruined by two men. Polanski precisely and memorably portrays the moral rigidity of Victorian England and brilliantly moves this story to its inexorable climax. (Filmed in English) ★★★½

Testament

(1983, 89 min, US, Lynne Littman) *Jane Alexander, William Devane, Lukas Haas, Mako, Kevin Costner.* The devastation of a nuclear attack is powerfully conveyed via personal relationships rather than elaborate special effects in Littman's staggering drama. Alexander gives a virtuoso performance as a housewife who helplessly watches the demise of family and friends. An extremely intense film which resists strident advocacy, opting for sensitivity and restraint in its warning of a nuclear nightmare. ★★★½ DVD Letterbox: $14.99, VHS: $14.99

The Testament of Dr. Mabuse

(1933, 120 min, Germany, Fritz Lang) *Rudolph Klein-Rogge.* Banned in Germany soon after its release, Lang's brilliant thriller is a trenchant allegory on the rise of Nazism, as well as the thinking of its crazed leader. In this follow-up to Lang's 1922 silent classic *Dr. Mabuse: Der Spieler (The Gambler)*, Klein-Rogge returns as the now lunatic underworld crime lord imprisoned in an insane asylum, spending his final days writing diabolical plans to create "an abyss of terror" in Germany. From his cell, these plans are carried out, much to the consternation of the police, even after his death. (German with English subtitles) ★★★½ DVD Criterion Collection 2-Disc Set: $39.99, VHS: $24.99

The Testament of Orpheus

(1959, 83 min, France, Jean Cocteau) *Jean Cocteau, Jean Marais, Pablo Picasso, Yul Brynner, Charles Aznavour.* "I shall present a striptease in which I shed my body to expose my soul." With this statement, Cocteau opens his final film, a farewell celebration to art. Cocteau himself takes the lead in this private diary which explores the relationship between the artist, his work and his dreams. An arresting piece with an eclectic cast. (French with English subtitles) ★★★½ DVD: $79.99, VHS: $29.99

Tevye

(1939, 96 min, US, Maurice Schwartz) *Maurice Schwartz.* Taken from the famous Sholom Aleichem story from which *Fiddler on the Roof* is based, this moving human drama set in Czarist Russia (yet filmed on Long Island) will remind viewers less of the famous musical play and more of the works of such directors as Pagnol, Renoir and Bresson. Director and Yiddish stage actor Schwartz stars as Tevye, a deeply religious man thrown into a conflict between the rules of his religion and his love for his family after he discovers that his daughter Khave has fallen in love with a Gentile and plans to marry him. (Yiddish with English subtitles) ★★★

Tex

(1982, 103 min, US, Tim Hunter) *Matt Dillon, Meg Tilly, Ben Johnson, Emilio Estevez.* A young Dillon gives a sensitive performance as a teenager on the verge of adulthood. Abandoned by their father, he and his brother struggle with responsibili-

ty and indecision. Based on S.E. Hinton's novel (Francis Ford Coppola would find limited success with two other Hinton novels, *The Outsiders* and *Rumble Fish*). Hunter directs with clarity. ★★★ DVD: $24.99, VHS: $14.99

Texas

(1941, 94 min, US, George Marshall) *William Holden, Glenn Ford, Claire Trevor.* Solid western with Holden and Ford as two drifters in search of love and fortune in the wilds of Texas. They find Trevor. ★★★ DVD: $19.99

The Texas Chainsaw Massacre

(1974, 81 min, US, Tobe Hooper) *Marilyn Burns, Allen Danzinger.* Hooper directed this horrific tale about the gruesome slaughter of a group of innocent youngsters by a family of maniacs, headed by "Leatherface." This much-imitated gorefest has yet to be equaled for its sheer terror and shocking but surprisingly non-bloody depictions of violence. You have been warned. (Followed by 3 sequels) (Remade in 2003) ★★★ DVD: $19.99, VHS: $19.99

The Texas Chainsaw Massacre

(2003, 98 min, US, Marcus Nispel) *Jessica Biel, Jonathan Tucker, Eric Balfour.* Misanthropic, pointless and sleazy (and not in a fun way), this remake of Tobe Hooper's seminal '70s horror classic is just plain awful. Biel (who's, quite honestly, distractingly easy on the eyes) takes the heroine role here, and her character does things so brainless you may find yourself cheering on the film's killer Leatherface by film's end. The crazy family here is unappealing and stereotypical, and the usually reliable Ermey is disgusting and abrasive, and is no match for the original's blackly comic, frightening Jim Siedow. There's no subtext here (as in the original's hippies vs. hicks tension), no extra layers, which in itself isn't really a flaw: there's nothing wrong with a movie that just wants to say, *Boo!!* Unfortunately, director Nispel, producer Michael Bay and the rest have no clue as to what is scary, only what is violent and looks "cool." ★ DVD Letterbox Basic Edition: $27.99, DVD Letterbox 2-disc Platinum Series Special Edition: $39.99, VHS: $22.99

The Texas Chainsaw Massacre (2003)

Texasville

(1990, 125 min, US, Peter Bogdanovich) *Jeff Bridges, Cybill Shepherd, Annie Potts, Cloris Leachman, Timothy Bottoms, Eileen Brennan, Randy Quaid.* Sad to report that as good as *The Last Picture Show* is, its sequel, *Texasville*, is as bad. In a small, dusty town in 1970s Texas, frumpy and double-chinned Bridges is in the throes of midlife crisis: he's disillusioned and broke, married to an unresponsive, verbally abusive Potts and attracted to the returning "look but don't touch" Shepherd. Strangely, the plot is lifeless, uninvolving and tepid, especially in light of the film's intended goal of being a torrid Southern sexual comedy. ★½ DVD Letterbox: $19.99

Thank Your Lucky Stars

(1943, 130 min, US, David Butler) *Eddie Cantor, Bette Davis, Errol Flynn, Ida Lupino, Olivia de Havilland, Humphrey Bogart, John Garfield.* Warner Brothers' entry into the all-star musical which the studio released during WWII to help the war effort. Cantor plays dual roles as himself and a show business hopeful, and there's plenty of 1940s stars: Davis sings "They're Either Too Young or Too Old," Flynn sings "That's What You Jolly Well Get" and Lupino and de Havilland jitterbug! ★★★ VHS: $29.99

That Championship Season

(1982, 110 min, US, Jason Miller) *Robert Mitchum, Bruce Dern, Paul Sorvino, Stacy Keach, Martin Sheen.* A well-acted but static adaptation of the Pulitzer Prize-winning Broadway drama about the reunion of a championship high school basketball team. Mitchum is their coach. (Remade in 1999) ★★½ DVD: $14.99

That Cold Day in the Park

(1969, 113 min, US, Robert Altman) *Sandy Dennis, Michael Burns, Michael Murphy.* Dennis stars as a 32-year-old virgin who is attracted to a handsome young mute (Burns) she meets in the park. However, when she takes him home to care for him, a sly psychological game begins between the sexually repressed woman and the prankish drifter. An occasionally unfocused though unsettling drama. ★★½ VHS: $14.99

That Darn Cat

(1965, 116 min, US, Robert Stevenson) *Dean Jones, Hayley Mills, Dorothy Provine.* Cute Disney comedy about a cat who helps solve a kidnapping mystery. (Remade in 1997) ★★½

That Darn Cat

(1997, 100 min, US, Bob Spiers) *Christina Ricci, Doug E. Doug, Dyan Cannon, Dean Jones.* This remake of Disney's popular 1965 family comedy retains very little of the appeal of the original. Even the presence of the usually adorable Ricci can't bring to life the story of a cute feline which helps solve a kidnapping. Slow, rarely funny, and ultimately a pointless retread. ★½ DVD: $14.99, VHS: $9.99

That Hamilton Woman

(1941, 125 min, US, Alexander Korda) *Laurence Olivier, Vivien Leigh, Gladys Cooper.* Good performances highlight this story of the ill-fated romance between Lord Admiral Nelson and Lady Emma Hamilton. The best of the three films made by then-husband and wife Olivier and Leigh. (aka: *Lady Hamilton*) ★★★

That Obscure Object of Desire

That Obscure Object of Desire

(1977, 103 min, France, Luis Buñuel) *Fernando Rey, Carole Bouquet, Angela Molina.* Buñuel's surreal comedy of the sexes stars Rey as an aging aristocrat who falls obsessively in love with a beguiling but unapproachable woman, played by two different actresses: the detached Bouquet and the voluptuous Molina. Buñuel's final film takes us mischievously through the enigma of human passion. (French with English subtitles) ★★★½ DVD Letterbox Criterion Collection: $29.99, VHS: $29.99

That Old Feeling

(1997, 107 min, US, Carl Reiner) *Bette Midler, Dennis Farina, Paula Marshall, Danny Nucci, David Rasche, Gail O'Grady.* An old-fashioned and funny battle-of-the-sexes comedy. Divorced for 15 loathing years, Midler and Farina reunite for their daughter's wedding. However, neither could have anticipated the reunion in store when old resentments give way to uncontrollable lust and they run away together. With his most entertaining film since *All of Me*, director Reiner wisely lets his wonderful cast cut loose. Midler is a master of the one-liner, and Farina is a marvelous comic presence. Though some of the story loses its balance when it concentrates too much on the daughter, Midler and Farina make any old feeling seem new again. ★★★ DVD: $9.99

That Sinking Feeling

(1979, 82 min, Scotland, Bill Forsyth) *Gordon John Sinclair, Robert Buchanan.* This first feature by gifted Scottish director Forsyth only came to America after the successes of *Local Hero* and *Gregory's Girl*. In his characteristic way, Forsyth imbues this tale with amiable but lunatic teenagers and a host of daft adults. The story involves a gang of Glasgow youths who concoct a scheme to rob a warehouse full of stainless steel sinks. ★★★

That Thing You Do!

(1996, 110 min, US, Tom Hanks) *Tom Everett Scott, Liv Tyler, Johnathan Schaech, Steve Zahn, Ethan Embry, Tom Hanks, Kevin Pollak.* It should come as no surprise that the first film Hanks has written and directed is a witty, nice, beguilingly old-fashioned movie-movie. After all, double Oscar-winner Hanks is a witty, nice, old-fashioned movie star. What may come as a surprise is that Hanks has made a well-crafted and toe-tapping charmer. *That*

Thing You Do! chronicles the rise, quick star status and even quicker slide of a pop band in 1964. With Necco-wafer colored cinematography and lovingly rendered period detail, the film moves at a rapid clip tracking the group's roots in smalltown America and their ascension to the top of the charts. With *That Thing You Do!*, Hanks seems to know that sometimes it's hip to be square, and he's proud of it. ★★★ DVD: $19.99, VHS: $9.99

That Touch of Mink

(1962, 99 min, US, Delbert Mann) *Doris Day, Cary Grant, Gig Young, Audrey Meadows, John Astin.* Day made two "sex" comedies in 1962: this one costarring Grant; and *Lover Come Back*, with Rock Hudson. Though *That Touch of Mink* is not nearly as funny as *Lover Come Back*, it is nevertheless a pleasant enough nostalgia course for an era when women (nice girls, anyway) did everything possible to keep their virginity, and men did everything they could to dissuade them. Tame stuff compared to today, but it did manage to curl a few lips "way back" in '62. ★★½ DVD: $14.99, VHS: $9.99

That Uncertain Feeling

(1941, 84 min, US, Ernst Lubitsch) *Merle Oberon, Melvyn Douglas, Burgess Meredith.* Sophisticated if lightweight romp from the great Lubitsch about a married couple's dilemma when the wife gets the hiccups. Oberon and Douglas give appealing performances as the husband and wife, and Meredith steals the show as their pianist neighbor. ★★½ DVD: $24.99, VHS: $19.99

That Was Then . . . This Is Now

(1985, 101 min, US, Christopher Cain) *Emilio Estevez, Craig Sheffer, Kim Delaney, Morgan Freeman.* Estevez stars in and adapted this routine version of S.E. Hinton's novel about a troubled teen's coming-of-age. ★★ DVD: $14.99, VHS: $9.99

That'll Be the Day

(1974, 90 min, GB, Claude Whatham) *David Essex, Ringo Starr, Keith Moon, Robert Lindsay.* An underrated and compelling drama of a British working-class youth (Essex), and would-be rock 'n' roller, as he moves through adolescence to adulthood. This down-to-earth story of musical aspiration is set in the 1950s. (Sequel: *Stardust*) ★★★ DVD: $24.99, VHS: $9.99

That's Entertainment!

(1974, 132 min, US, Jack Haley Jr.) Compilation of some of M-G-M's best musical moments. Includes clips from *The Wizard of Oz*, *Gigi* and *Singin' in the Rain*, among many others. Hosts include Fred Astaire, Gene Kelly, James Stewart and Elizabeth Taylor. The musical sequences that were chosen and the wealth of wonderful stars who appear combine to make this a delightfully nostalgic musical experience. (Followed by 2 sequels) ★★★½

That's Life!

(1986, 102 min, US, Blake Edwards) *Jack Lemmon, Julie Andrews, Sally Kellerman, Robert Loggia.* Edwards wrote and directed this absorbing drama starring Lemmon in a remarkable performance as a successful architect facing emotional crisis as his 60th birthday nears. Andrews gives a solid portrayal as his wife. ★★★

Theatre of Blood

(1973, 105 min, GB, Douglas Hickox) *Vincent Price, Diana Rigg, Robert Morley, Jack Hawkins.* Though its joke wears thin, this is nevertheless an entertaining horror film about a demented Shakespearean actor (Price) who takes a bloody revenge against the eight theatre critics who gave him "thumbs down." ★★★ DVD Letterbox: $14.99

Thelma & Louise

(1991, 120 min, US, Ridley Scott) *Susan Sarandon, Geena Davis, Harvey Keitel, Michael Madsen, Brad Pitt, Christopher McDonald, Stephen Tobolowsky, Jason Beghe.* A wildly entertaining and remarkably accomplished road movie which features uncharacteristically sensitive and intuitive direction from Scott. Sarandon and Davis are the title characters, two friends who leave their male counterparts and head for a leisurely weekend getaway. En route, however, their trek turns deadly and they find themselves on the run from the police. Stylish and witty, Callie Khouri's Oscar-winning screenplay follows their series of escalating criminal adventures as the two women break away from the confines of a male-dominated society, searching for their own identity and independence. Sarandon and Davis create enormously appealing, substantial and distinct characters. ★★★★ DVD Letterbox Special Edition: $24.99

Them!

(1954, 94 min, US, Gordon Douglas) *James Whitmore, Edmund Gwenn, James Arness, Joan Weldon.* A horror favorite for years, this is the one with the giant ants. Humongous insects are spotted in the desert, and they're working their way to Los Angeles. Lots of good old-fashioned chills. ★★★½ DVD: $19.99, VHS: $14.99

Theme

(1979, 108 min, Russia, Gleb Panfilov) *Mikhail Ulyanov, Inna Churikova.* Once banned by Russian censors, the most fascinating thing about this otherwise very standard drama is that anyone would ever find it worthy of suppression. The film's action centers around a 54-year-old poet who is thoroughly under the wing of the Soviet bureaucracy. While vacationing in the country, he is confronted by an alluring young woman who accuses him of selling out his artistic integrity to the state. Naturally, he finds himself smitten by both her and her uncompromising views and sets out to reform himself. While not particularly successful in its condemnation of Soviet artistic bureaucracy, the film is more interesting as a study of one man's struggle for artistic integrity. (Russian with English subtitles) ★★½

Theodora Goes Wild

(1936, 94 min, US, Richard Boleslawski) *Irene Dunne, Melvyn Douglas, Thomas Mitchell, Spring Byington.* A delightful and at times hilarious escapade with Dunne at her best. She plays a religious-bred New England woman who unbeknowst to her family and small town is actually the popular writer of a series of racy women's novels. Douglas, exuding great charm, plays the ne'er-do-well who thinks Dunne to be as provocative as the women in her novels, and who helps let her secret out when he comes a-courtin'. The laughs are plentiful, and the film even manages a friendly swipe or two at puritanism. This was Dunne's first real chance to play comedy, and she proved herself to be a peerless comedienne. ★★★½ VHS: $19.99

The Theory of Flight

(1998, 98 min, GB, Paul Greengrass) *Helena Bonham Carter, Kenneth Branagh, Gemma Jones, Holly Aird.* A man's attempt to soar off the roof of a London bank earns him a term of community service, through which he meets a young woman slowly dying in a wheelchair. Bonham Carter is creditable as she assays *My Left Foot* territory, as is Branagh as an artist whose canvases no longer engage his attention except as materials with which to test theories of flight. They are both outsiders, initially as separate from each other as they each are from the world that surrounds them; yet over time are bonded in mutual support and acceptance. While the actors delineate their characters with wit and sensitivity and a thankful absence of saccharine sentimentality, the film often lapses into MTVitis and predictability. Based on a true story. ★★ VHS: $19.99

There Goes My Baby

(1994, 95 min, US, Floyd Mutrux) *Dermot Mulroney, Rick Schroder, Noah Wyle, Kelli Williams, Seymour Cassel.* It's the early 1960s: The Vietnam War is still called a police action, the hippies are just gathering in San Francisco, Watts is on fire and the class of '65 is spending their last night together. Mulroney, Schroder and Wyle are a group of friends who must deal with their impending separation and the changes both they and their country are experiencing. Poignant and achingly nostalgic but flawed by the familiarity of the material. ★★ DVD Pan & Scan: $14.99

There's Something about Mary . . . and her hair gel

There Was a Crooked Man

(1970, 123 min, US, Joseph L. Mankiewicz) *Kirk Douglas, Henry Fonda, Hume Cronyn, Warren Oates, Burgess Meredith, Lee Grant.* Outrageous comedy-western adventure with Douglas as a prisoner who matches wits with his incorruptible warden (Fonda). ★★★ VHS: $14.99

There's No Business Like Show Business

(1954, 117 min, US, Walter Lang) *Ethel Merman, Dan Dailey, Donald O'Connor, Mitzi Gaynor, Marilyn Monroe, Johnny Ray.* This Irving Berlin song fest is a particularly sentimental but entertaining musical about the professional and personal ups and downs of a theatrical family. Merman and Dailey are the parents, with kids O'Connor, Ray and Gaynor joining the act. Marilyn is an aspiring singer, and she gets to sing "Heat Wave." Sure it's sappy, but who can resist Merman and O'Connor's onstage reconciliation. ★★½ DVD: $14.99, VHS: $6.99

There's Something about Mary

(1998, 119 min, US, Bobby Farrelly & Peter Farrelly) *Cameron Diaz, Ben Stiller, Matt Dillon, Chris Elliott, Lee Evans.* The Farrelly brothers take comic absurdity to new, hilarious heights. Their humor may be over-the-top, and some of the film lags between jokes, but there's no denying that there's something about this comedy which is flat-out hysterical. Stiller is wonderfully droll as Ted, a nerdy high schooler whose prom date with his dream girl, Mary (the bewitchingly beautiful Diaz), results in disaster. Thirteen years later, he's still obsessed with her. He hires Pat (Dillon), a smarmy detective, to track her down. This sets the stage for uproarious cases of mistaken identity, double cross, impersonation, animal cruelty, human cruelty, masturbation jokes, gay jokes, handicapped jokes and the old fishhook-caught-in-the-mouth gag. There's obviously nothing sacred to the Farrelly brothers, but their un-PC, scatological toilet humor and burlesque bits work. ★★★½ DVD Letterbox 2-disc Collector's Edition: $19.99, DVD 2-disc Collector's Edition: $19.99, VHS: $9.99

Theremin: An Electronic Odyssey

(1995, 84 min, US, Steven M. Martin) An interesting if incomplete documentary about the grandfather of electronic music, Russian-born Leon Theremin. Theremin was an inventor and all-electronics mastermind who created the first all-electronic musical instrument, a wooden box with two metal probes protruding from it. This instrument, which bears his name, generates a magnetic field and is played when a person's hands interfere with the field, manipulating musical pitch. Theremin and his instrument were the toast of New York society during the '30s until an unexpected political incident completely changed his life and influence. ★★★

Therese

(1986, 90 min, France, Alain Cavalier) *Catherine Mouchet, Aurore Prieto.* This radiantly beautiful, impeccably crafted film recounts the life of St. Therese — the Little Flower — a teenage girl whose devotion to the Church is surpassed only by her love for Christ. Therese, who died in 1897, was canonized in 1925. Mouchet shines in the title role. Based on Therese's famous diaries. (French with English subtitles) ★★★½ DVD: $24.99, VHS: $19.99

Susan Sarandon (l.) and Geena Davis in *Thelma & Louise*

Therese and Isabelle

(1968, 118 min, France, Radley Metzger) *Essy Persson, Anna Gael, Barbara Laage, Anne Vernon.* Set in an all-girls' Catholic boarding school, this milestone film is a tender glimpse at the erotic affair of two young women. Unlike many other works of the period, this provocative drama offers a non-exploitative picture of budding female sexuality, some very hot love scenes and lots of schoolgirl emotional tension. With voice-over narration taken directly from Viloette Leduc's autobiographical novel, the film is genuinely sweet in spite of a lingering Euro soft-porn atmosphere. (French with English subtitles) ★★★ VHS: $19.99

These Three

(1936, 93 min, US, William Wyler) *Miriam Hopkins, Merle Oberon, Joel McCrea, Bonita Granville.* Lillian Hellman's controversial play, "The Children's Hour," about two women's lives torn apart by rumors of lesbianism, is toned down considerably — the play's "scandalous" relationship is now a heterosexual triangle — in this well-crafted and thoughtfully acted drama. Karen (Oberon) and Martha (Hopkins) run a school for girls. Trouble begins when a student falsely accuses Martha and Joe (McCrea), Karen's fiancé, of having an affair. Hellman's text is strong commentary on the destructive power of gossip and the so-called innocence of youth. Director Wyler remade the film, under the play's original title and theme, in 1962 with Shirley MacLaine and Audrey Hepburn. ★★★

Thesis

(1996, 121 min, Spain, Alejandro Amenábar) *Ana Torrent, Fele Martínez, Eduardo Noriega.* The film debut of director Amenábar is basically *8mm* done right. A beautiful grad student seeks help from her professor in acquiring extremely violent videos for her thesis on violence in the media. When he dies of a heart attack watching one of these tapes, she steals the tape and discovers it's a snuff film. Then she begins to investigate. Amenábar not only tightens the screws with great finesse, he neatly avoids cheap exploitation and preachiness. This is a good, solid suspenseful mystery, that (only in retrospect) may be a shade too long. Winner of six Goya awards (Spain's Oscars) including Best Picture. (Spanish with English subtitles) ★★★½ DVD Special Edition: $19.99, VHS: $14.99

They

(2002, 89 min, US, Robert Harmon) *Laura Regan, Marc Blucas, Ethan Embry, Dagmar Dominczyk.* Strikingly similar in many ways to the concurrently released *Darkness Falls, They* follows several young adults who, as children, suffered "night terrors" — and they seem to be starting again. Sporting some nifty monsters and a chillingly downbeat ending, *They* has some quality ingredients. Unfortunately, much of the film feels like padding — and rather bland padding at that. A disappointment coming from director Harmon, who handled a simple horror script with far more aplomb with *The Hitcher*. (aka: *Wes Craven's They*) ★★ DVD: $29.99, VHS: $14.99

They All Laughed

(1981, 115 min, US, Peter Bogdanovich) *Audrey Hepburn, John Ritter, Ben Gazzara, Colleen Camp, Dorothy Stratten.* Charming, low-key comedy about a team of detectives and their romantic adventures. Director Bogdanovich extracts pleasant performances from the cast. ★★★ VHS: $9.99

They Call Me Mr. Tibbs!

(1970, 108 min, US, Gordon Douglas) *Sidney Poitier, Barbara McNair, Martin Landau, Juano Hernandez.* Poitier repeats his acclaimed role as Detective Virgil Tibbs from the Oscar-winning *In the Heat of the Night*. In this ordinary sequel, Tibbs has moved to San Francisco and is involved in a murder investigation in which the main suspect is a local priest (Landau). (Sequel: *The Organization*) ★★ DVD: $14.99

They Came to Cordura

(1959, 123 min, US, Robert Rossen) *Gary Cooper, Rita Hayworth, Van Heflin, Tab Hunter, Richard Conte.* Cooper heads a good cast in this handsomely photographed western about an Army major (Cooper) who, believing himself guilty of cowardice, is relieved of his command and assigned to locate five potential Medal of Honor candidates. In the wilds of a desert region, he finds the five heroes, a torturous struggle against the elements, and Hayworth. ★★½ VHS: $14.99

They Died with Their Boots On

(1941, 138 min, US, Raoul Walsh) *Errol Flynn, Olivia de Havilland, Arthur Kennedy, Anthony Quinn.* Expedient adventure with Flynn as a heroic General Custer. The film traces his rise in the military ranks to the legendary Battle of the Little Bighorn. What the film lacks in authenticity it makes up for in flavor and entertainment. ★★★ VHS: $19.99

They Drive by Night

(1940, 97 min, US, Raoul Walsh) *George Raft, Ann Sheridan, Ida Lupino, Humphrey Bogart.* Bogart took a back seat to stars Raft, Sheridan and Lupino in this riveting trucking drama — but he didn't stay there for long as *The Maltese Falcon* was released a year later. Raft plays a wildcat trucker who, with brother Bogie, unwittingly becomes involved with the mob while trying to keep his truck from repossession. A good cast in a crisp, solid 1940s entertainment. ★★★ DVD: $19.99, VHS: $19.99

They Got Me Covered

(1943, 95 min, US, David Butler) *Bob Hope, Dorothy Lamour, Lenore Aubert, Otto Preminger.* There are a few laughs to be found in this otherwise standard-issue Hope espionage spoof. Bob and Dorothy are journalists who go after foreign spies based in Washington, D.C. ★★½

They Live

(1988, 87 min, US, John Carpenter) *Roddy Piper, Keith David, Meg Foster.* Professional wrestler Piper stars in Carpenter's allegorical sci-fi action-adventure about the fateful day when we discover that aliens are among us, and they are hardly benevolent ETs. Carpenter has a great scenario but is unable to thoroughly deliver the goods. ★★½ DVD Letterbox: $14.99

They Live by Night

(1949, 95 min, US, Nicholas Ray) *Farley Granger, Cathy O'Donnell, Howard da Silva.* Ray's directorial debut pairs Granger and O'Donnell as young innocents who find themselves on the wrong side of the law. Da Silva turns in a chilling performance as their corruptor. Ray's sense of atmosphere is remarkable, and the performances and diligent screenplay elevate what should have been a "B" programmer. (Remade as *Thieves Like Us*) ★★★½

They Made Me a Criminal

(1939, 92 min, US, Busby Berkeley) *John Garfield, Claude Rains, May Robson, Dead End Kids.* Intriguing crime drama with Garfield as a young boxer who takes refuge at a Western ranch when he thinks he's killed an opponent. ★★★ VHS: $19.99

They Might Be Giants

(1971, 98 min, US, Anthony Harvey) *George C. Scott, Joanne Woodward, Jack Gilford, Rue McClanahan, Oliver Clark, Eugene Roche, F. Murray Abraham.* Charming adaptation of James Goldman's play about a former judge who thinks he's Sherlock Holmes — and is treated by a psychiatrist named Dr. Watson. Scott plays his part with great panache and Woodward is a spirited cohort. A wonderful supporting cast populates the film, featuring a most appealing collection of eccentrics. ★★★ DVD: $24.99

They Saved Hitler's Brain

(1963, 81 min, US, David Bradley) *Walter Stocker.* A fanatical band of Nazis (is there any other kind?) give life to Hitler's brain and kidnap an American scientist to help them conquer the world. Le bad cinema. ★ DVD: $14.99, VHS: $9.99

They Shoot Horses, Don't They?

(1969, 121 min, US, Sydney Pollack) *Jane Fonda, Michael Sarrazin, Gig Young, Susannah York, Red Buttons, Bonnie Bedelia, Bruce Dern.* Few films in the 1960s were able to capture such raw power and unrelenting emotional tension as this devastating adaptation of Horace McCoy's novel of Depression-era America. With a dance marathon serving as metaphor for a crippled nation, the story centers on a disparate group of unemployed hopefuls who come together to win the "big" jackpot. No one's prepared for the gruelling, exhaustive, deadly competition that follows — all for the enjoyment of a few paying spectators. Fonda gives an extraordinary performance as a woman at road's end; it signaled her arrival as her generation's premiere actress. Young won an Oscar as the unscrupulous M.C. The dance sequences as staged by Pollack are riveting. ★★★★

They Were Expendable

(1945, 135 min, US, John Ford) *Robert Montgomery, John Wayne, Donna Reed.* Rousing WWII drama about an American PT boat crew fighting in the Pacific. One of the best of all the war films produced during WWII. ★★★★ DVD: $19.99, VHS: $14.99

They Were Ten

(1961, 105 min, Israel, Baruch Dienar) *Ninette, Oded Teomi.* The first feature-length film made entirely by Israelis sensitively re-creates the establishment of a 19th-century settlement in Palestine by 10 Russian Jews. These early pioneers not only undertook the tremendous task of building the land, but also had to contend with Arab resentment and the Turkish military. (Hebrew with English subtitles) ★★★

They Won't Believe Me

(1947, 95 min, US, Irving Pichel) *Robert Young, Susan Hayward, Jane Greer, Rita Johnson.* Startling noir thriller starring Young as a man who wakes up after a car accident with a scheme for the perfect crime. He is subsequently lured by two temptresses (Hayward and Greer) from his wife (Johnson). ★★★

Thief

(1981, 122 min, US, Michael Mann) *James Caan, Tuesday Weld, Willie Nelson.* An extremely stylish drama from first-time director Mann, with Caan in a splendid performance as a professional thief caught between corrupt cops and a malevolent crime boss. ★★★½ DVD Director's Cut: $14.99

After the Thin Man

The Thief

(1998, 93 min, Russia, Pavel Chukhrai) *Ekaterina Rednikova, Misha Philipchuk, Vladimir Mashkov.* A dazzling Russian film, *The Thief* features three vulnerable characters and the tenuous bonds that form between them as they struggle for survival under Stalin's regime. Writer-director Chukhrai has crafted a throwback to the melodramas of early Soviet cinema. Yet *The Thief* is never cloying or sentimental; its realism and solid performances are its strengths. Katya (Rednikova) is a young woman travelling by train with her six-year-old son Sanya (Philipchuk). When they meet Toljan (Mashkov), a soldier, Katya instantly falls in love, and Sanya is thrilled to get a father figure. However, Toljan soon reveals himself to be a thief, and perceptions change within this makeshift family. Despite its heavy subject matter, the film still has moments of real humor and charm. But don't be fooled, *The Thief* ultimately packs an emotional wallop. ★★★★

The Thief and the Cobbler

(1995, 73 min, US, Richard Williams) *Jennifer Beals, Matthew Broderick, Vincent Price, Jonathan Winters.* Featuring a distinctive animation style with Escher-like effects that go far beyond the typical cartoon, *The Thief and the Cobbler* follows the adventures of a hapless cobbler (nicely voiced by Broderick) who falls in love with and saves the Princess Yum-Yum (Beals). Though the story occasionally falters, the film is of high quality and very imaginative. ★★★

The Thief of Bagdad

(1924, 140 min, US, Raoul Walsh) *Douglas Fairbanks, Jr., Anna May Wong.* Classic silent film with Fairbanks as a swashbuckling thief who falls in love with a beautiful princess. Fairbanks is at his rousing best, and the film is nonstop excitement. ★★★½ DVD: $29.99

The Thief of Bagdad

(1940, 106 min, GB, Ludwig Berger, Michael Powell, Tim Whelan) *Sabu, Conrad Veidt, Rex Ingram.* This Arabian Nights tale is classic entertainment, enhanced by gorgeous cinematography. Sabu stars as the native boy who battles an evil magician, played by Veidt. Ingram makes a terrific genie. Great special effects. ★★★★ DVD: $19.99

Thieves (Les Voleurs)

(1996, 117 min, France, André Téchiné) *Catherine Deneuve, Daniel Auteuil, Laurence Côte.* A luminous and impossibly youthful Deneuve and a gruffly attractive Auteuil are lovers of Côte, a young student in over her head in a scheme that comes to involve murder. Deneuve, a professor of philosophy, and Auteuil, a police inspector, are drawn together in their concern for the young woman, who begins to unravel under the pressure of her destructive associations. The film is at once hyperventilating and elegantly structured, seasoned with staccato dialogue that propels the convoluted plot with wit, awareness and just the right touch of Gallic pretense. Concisely drawn characters add depth of understanding to the rapidly developed story line; director Téchiné's command of the film is complete and admirable. An intelligent, adult mystery-thriller that makes optimum use of all its components. (French with English subtitles) ★★★½

Thieves Like Us

(1974, 123 min, US, Robert Altman) *Keith Carradine, Shelley Duvall, John Schuck, Louise Fletcher, Bert Remsen, Tom Skerritt.* Altman's brooding, atmospheric remake of *They Live By Night*, based on Edward Anderson's novel. Carradine and Schuck play prison escapees who go on a robbing spree across 1930s Depression America. Duvall plays the small-town girl who becomes involved with Carradine. ★★★½

The Thin Blue Line

(1988, 106 min, US, Errol Morris) Part documentary, part murder investigation, this highly acclaimed and original film investigates the "truth" surrounding the 1976 murder of Dallas policeman Robert Wood — who was gunned down at point blank range after stopping a car for a minor infraction. Randall Adams, the man arrested and sentenced to life in prison for the murder, claimed innocence and, indeed, through mesmerizing reconstructions of the crime from the point-of-view of investigators, witnesses, Wood's partner as well as a suspect cleared of all wrongdoing, the "facts" become all the more blurred as we begin to see that justice might well have been blind as well as perverted. ★★★★

The Thin Man Series

In the 10 years that elapsed between its first and last entries, the *Thin Man* series straddled two decades, reflecting America's mores and attitudes from her recovery from the Depression thru WWII. As personified by William Powell and Myrna Loy, Nick and Nora Charles are urbane, suave, witty and rich. They have a relationship in their marriage that most would envy today; they even raise a kid without being too damned cute about it. And they know how to handle their dog, the estimable Asta. Their friends and relatives represent a range of societal classes and reflect a diversity of lifestyles seldom found in today's homogenized entertainment. The plots are well-crafted, the wardrobe is dashing and everybody gets good lines. Other constants: He never wants the case, she always wants him to take the case and everyone else thinks he's already on the case. Nora's always assuring someone that it's all right, they're married; and their consumption of alcohol is considerable and greatly enjoyed. The supporting cast's characterizations are consistently on target, the story lines satisfyingly intricate and the black-and-white cinematography deliciously noir, especially those graced with James Wong Howe's exemplary expertise. ★★★★

The Thin Man

(1934, 93 min, US, W.S. Van Dyke II) *William Powell, Myrna Loy, Maureen O'Sullivan.* "Come on, kid. Shed the chapeau." The original, and the best. An eccentric, wealthy inventor disappears and, before too long, corpses start piling up. The inventor is actually the thin man in question, but the title became inextricably linked to Powell. Based on a Dashiell Hammett story. ★★★★ DVD: $19.99

After the Thin Man

(1936, 113 min, US, W.S. Van Dyke II) *William Powell, Myrna Loy, James Stewart.* "Look at him prancing around with that clue in him." Nick's relation with Nora's (S)Nob Hill family is an element in this tale of a rich wife cheated by a gigolo husband, and a thwarted love twisted into a crime of passion. ★★★½ VHS: $19.99

Song of the Thin Man

Another Thin Man

(1939, 105 min, US, W.S. Van Dyke II) *William Powell, Myrna Loy, Virginia Grey.* "Colonel MacFay — the swimming pool's on fire." Nick and Nora were starting on an extended trip and Nora announced her pregnancy at the end of *After the Thin Man*. *Another Thin Man* opens with their return from their travels, and with an infant. Nora's uncle is being hounded by a blackmailer with ominous dreams and a penchant for melodramatic warnings; the curmudgeon uncle seems deserving of this treatment. ★★★ VHS: $19.99

Shadow of the Thin Man

(1941, 97 min, US, W.S. Van Dyke II) *William Powell, Myrna Loy, Barry Nelson, Donna Reed.* "Funny how I meet you at all my homicides." A jockey is accused of throwing the race and is dead the next day, an apparent suicide. His death is convenient for the gambling syndicate, not so convenient for the crusading young reporter. Little Nicky, Jr. has his own Army uniform (he''s an officer, of course) and calls his dad "Nick." There's a great restaurant fight scene, and the writing's by Dashiell Hammett. ★★★

The Thin Man Goes Home

(1944, 100 min, US, Richard Thorpe) *William Powell, Myrna Loy, Gloria De Haven.* "You just pick out anybody at all, and I put 'em in jail for life." The effects of WWII are evidenced during Nick and Nora's train ride to Sycamore Springs, Nick's hometown. Nick resolves a case of wartime industrial espionage, as well as his relationship with his father. Cinematography by Karl Freund, and another Dashiell Hammett script. ★★★

Song of the Thin Man

(1947, 86 min, US, Edward Buzzell) *William Powell, Myrna Loy, Keenan Wynn.* "The dust don't start rising 'til deuce o' bells." Wynn is the hep cat clarinet player who gives Nick and Nora a guided tour through the netherworld of jazz musicians, high society, heavy gamblers and murderous jealousies. "And now Nick Charles is going to retire." ★★★

The Thin Red Line

(1998, 170 min, US, Terrence Malick) *Sean Penn, Jim Caviezel, Elias Koteas, Nick Nolte, Ben Chaplin, Woody Harrelson, John Cusack, Adrien Brody, John Savage, John Travolta, George Clooney, Jared Leto.* With his first film in 20 years, director Malick returns to filmmaking with this gorgeous-looking, philosophical adaptation of James Jones' novel about the bloody fight for Guadacanal during WWII. *The Thin Red Line* is a bracing look at the machinations of combat and of the inner turmoil of the soldiers, the latter somberly recalled by dry, almost tedious narration which nearly grinds the film to a halt. But Malick's battle sequences are unquestionably powerful, and the director has created some gut-wrenching moments staged with a visionary's eye. The large cast services the story well, though often characters begin to look alike and it's difficult to tell them apart. Of the large supporting cast, Nolte is most memorable, giving a chilling performance as a colonel prepared to win at any cost. Though the film feels heavily edited, the final result is a poetic, ethereal though slightly flawed epic which marks a long-overdue return for a singular artist. ★★★½ DVD Letterbox: $14.99, VHS: $9.99, VHS Letterbox: $14.99

The Thing

(1951, 80 min, US, Christian Nyby) *James Arness, Kenneth Tobey.* Classic '50s horror film produced by Howard Hawks. An Arctic expedition is forced to fight for their lives when they dig up an alien creature frozen in the ice. The chills are rampant as the basic ingredients of sci-fi faultlessly meld with hold-your-breath terror. (Remade in 1982.) ★★★★ DVD: $19.99, VHS: $14.99

The Thing

(1982, 108 min, US, John Carpenter) *Kurt Russell, Wilford Brimley, Keith David.* A gruesome and terrifying tale of a hideous, metamorphic monster which torments the crew of an Antarctic outpost. Carpenter's new version of the short story (which inspired the 1950s classic produced by Howard Hawks) is highlighted by realistic and horrifying special effects. ★★★½ DVD Letterbox Collector's Edition: $19.99

The Thing Called Love

(1993, 116 min, US, Peter Bogdanovich) *Samantha Mathis, River Phoenix, Dermot Mulroney, Sandra Bullock.* Mathis stars as an East Coast gal who travels to Nashville determined to become a country music star. Upon her arrival, she immediately, and literally, bumps into a brooding, bad-boy musician (Phoenix). A love-hate relationship ensues. Also onto the scene ambles Mulroney, a displaced Connecticut cowboy, and Bullock as a new kind of Southern belle. Though *The Thing Called Love* seems to have lost something in the editing process, its odd country-grunge quality, the interplay between the young actors and the fun they have with the music, saves this film from being a hackneyed, hayseed version of *A Star Is Born*. ★★★ DVD Letterbox: $14.99, VHS: $19.99

Things Change

(1988, 100 min, US, David Mamet) *Joe Mantegna, Don Ameche, Robert Prosky, J.T. Walsh.* Ameche's subtle yet complex portrait of an Italian shoe repairman caught in a high stakes impersonation of a Mafia don is a delight. Writer-director Mamet's social comedy does not deliver the visceral thrills of his previous film, *House of Games*, but nonetheless is a sly comedy which explores the honor among thieves and the deadly temptations that money and power offer. The always fascinating Mantegna is a low-level hood who is responsible for the weekend safety of Ameche. But what starts as a simple job of baby-sitting, ends in a comedy of errors as the reticent Ameche is mistaken for a Mafia kingpin. A thinking person's comedy and one that is highly recommended. ★★★½ DVD: $27.99

Things to Come

(1936, 96 min, GB, William Cameron Menzies) *Raymond Massey, Ralph Richardson.* This stunning visualization of H.G. Wells' visionary novel features Menzies' intriguing, ultra-modern sets and a sonorous score by Arthur Bliss. Massey stars as the leader of the new world opposite Richardson as a despotic and belligerent ruler. An interesting film from a sociological standpoint as it represents the mindset of the '30s as people looked to the future. ★★★ VHS: $19.99

Things to Do in Denver When You're Dead

(1995, 114 min, US, Gary Fleder) *Andy Garcia, Treat Williams, Christopher Walken, Gabrielle Anwar, Christopher Lloyd, William Forsythe, Bill Nunn, Jack Warden, Steve Buscemi.* First-time director Fleder puts a new spin on a tried-and-true gangster formula (former hood is pulled back into the game). Garcia stars as Jimmy the Saint, an expetty criminal who has gone legit. Soon after happening upon the woman of his dreams, Jimmy is summoned to the ghostly mansion of a quadriplegic crime lord (Walken) who bids him to do one more bit of service for him. Jimmy assembles the old gang one last time, and when the job is botched, the crew finds themselves on a hit list with a master hit man (Buscemi) on their trail. Some plot logic is sacrificed to further the style, but what style it has. ★★★ DVD: $9.99, VHS: $14.99

3rd Degree Burn

(1989, 97 min, US, Roger Spottiswoode) *Treat Williams, Virginia Madsen.* Steamy though familiar made-for-cable thriller with Williams as a down-and-out detective who is hired by a millionaire to watch his sexy wife. However, things get complicated when they meet, have an affair, and Williams is framed for his client's murder. ★★ VHS: $14.99

The Third Man

(1950, 100 min, GB, Carol Reed) *Orson Welles, Joseph Cotten, Alida Valli, Trevor Howard.* Based on an original screenplay by Graham Greene, this Reed classic epitomizes the aesthetics of film noir. Amid the lurid decadence of a shell-shocked, postwar Vienna, a lonely American (Cotten) searches for his maligned friend, a mysterious "third man" in a city of rampant deceit and corruption. A haunting score, shadowy cinematography and top-notch performances (notably Welles as the utterly immoral Harry Lime) make this one of the memorable tales of intrigue in film history. ★★★★ DVD: $39.99, VHS: $29.99

The Third Miracle

(2000, 118 min, US, Agnieszka Holland) *Ed Harris, Anne Heche, Armin Mueller-Stahl, Charles Haid.* *The Third Miracle* is a haunting spiritual journey led by Holland into the political and sometimes not-so-spiritual process of sainthood. Father Frank Harris (a terrific Harris) is a disillusioned priest living in a Chicago flophouse who is called back into service by the Church looking for him to debunk the "myth" of a crying statue of Virgin Mary. He investigates his faith and his chastity through the process when he meets Roxanne (Heche), the potential saint's daughter, and falls in love with her. Issues of church politics, faith, celibacy and just plain passion rule this smart, candid film. ★★★ DVD: $29.99, VHS: $21.99

The Third Sex/Vapors

(1958, 102 min, US/Germany, Frank Winterstein & Gerald Jackson) *The Third Sex* (1958, 77 min, Germany, Frank Winterstein) is intriguingly contemporary, especially for its time and place (West Germany in the mid-1950s). This historically important potboiler melodrama centers on a parents' efforts to make their gay son "normal." The film is rather extraordinary in its depiction of gays, society's extremist reaction to them and the clash between the old Germany and the new. (German with English subtitles) Also includes a 25-minute short, *Vapors*, set in the notorious St. Mark's Bathhouse. ★★★

Thirteen

(2003, 100 min, US, Catherine Hardwicke) *Evan Rachel Wood, Nikki Reed, Holly Hunter, Jeremy Sisto, Deborah Kara Unger, Brady Corbet.* Nothing matches the explosive potential of a 13-year-old girl's energy level mixed with a lack of focus and the absolute certainty that she understands the world completely. Tracy (Wood, in a sterling performance) asserts her independence with rage and disdain, watches her mother Melanie repeat her favorite mistakes, misses the father who has moved on. Melanie (the always remarkable Hunter) makes ends meet for her son and daughter by operating a beauty salon in her home. That she dresses much like her daughter makes Tracy's requisite rebellion more difficult. Honor student, sensitive poet, she one day hooks up with bad girl Evie (Reed, who cowrote the script based on her own experiences). Evie, master manipulator and foster child, soon controls both mother and daughter until she overplays her hand. Director Hardwicke makes palpable the emotional vicissitudes, the layers of frustration and nuances of violence, as a hyperkinetic camera follows a careening Tracy from one self-induced crisis to another. *Thirteen* is a breathtaking surprise, both exhausting and exhilarating. It successfully captures the rabid hell of adolescence and the laidback anxiety of the lost California dream. ★★★½ DVD Dual: $19.99, VHS: $9.99

Holly Hunter in *Thirteen*

13 Conversations about One Thing

(2002, 102 min, US, Jill Sprecher) *Matthew McConaughey, Alan Arkin, John Turturro, Clea DuVall, Amy Irving, Barbara Sukowa, Tia Texada.* Director and cowriter Sprecher constructs an intricate, interwoven set of connected stories, relating telling details much as they are revealed in everyday life: disjointedly and out of sequence. As this cerebral yet emotionally evocative tale unfolds, the viewer makes belated connections and recognizes causalities after the fact, rearranging the pieces of this jigsaw puzzle of disparate lives to form a larger picture. Each member of the superlative cast deftly captures the essence of the protagonists; the innocent naturalism of the serenely optimistic housekeeper (DuVall); the rigid condescension of the stilted and formal university professor (Turturro); the submerged guilt of the smoothly ambitious attorney (McConaughey); the sad resignation of the betrayed wife (Irving); the condemnatory spite of the bitter businessman (Arkin). The film plays with the quixotic nature of chance as it induces permutations on the inexorable inevitability dictated by each individual soul, as they collide into each other like molecules of air in a gust of wind. *13 Conversations* balances thoughtful meditation with wry humor in a contemporary treatment of timeless issues. ★★★★ DVD Letterbox: $24.99, VHS: $102.99

Thirteen Days

(2000, 147 min, US, Roger Donaldson) *Kevin Costner, Bruce Greenwood, Steven Culp, Dylan Baker.* An intense drama about the true story of the Cuban Missile Crisis that shook America and the world in 1962, this is an exhilarating entertainment masquerading as part history lesson and part heart pounder. *Thirteen Days* is seen through the eyes of JFK's presidential aide Kenneth P. O'Donnell (nicely played by Costner), whose memoirs are the source material for David Self's assured screenplay adaptation. Director Donaldson brings a you-are-there feel to this gripping profile in courage that documents the showdown between President Kennedy and the Soviet Union over Soviet missiles in Cuba that could have ended in nuclear war. Greenwood is excellent as JFK, endowing him with emotion and depth, while Culp is pinpoint as Bobby Kennedy. Complex, articulate and often nerve-racking, *Thirteen Days* is an intelligent, enthralling exercise in social studies and storytelling. ★★★★ DVD Letterbox infinifilm Special Edition: $19.99, VHS: $14.99

13 Ghosts

(1960, 88 min, US, William Castle) *Rosemary DeCamp, Martin Milner, Margaret Hamilton.* Cute ghost mystery about a family who inherit a house, complete with buried treasure and — count 'em — 13 ghosts. (Remade in 2001) ★★½ DVD Letterbox: $14.99, VHS: $9.99

13 Rue Madeleine

(1947, 95 min, US, Henry Hathaway) *James Cagney, Annabella, Richard Conte.* Told in an almost semidocumentary style, this absorbing spy thriller stars a rigid but forceful Cagney as an OSS operative who trains youthful candidates. The intrigue really starts when he discovers a Nazi spy among his cadets, and is then forced to use the double agent on a dangerous mission in Germany. Perhaps too calculating in its efforts to present a realistic portrait of the spy game, the film nevertheless is gripping and Cagney gives a no-nonsense portrayal. ★★★ DVD: $14.99, VHS: $9.99

The Thirteenth Floor

(1999, 100 min, US, Josef Rusnak) *Craig Bierko, Gretchen Mol, Armin Mueller-Stahl, Vincent D'Onofrio.* Slow pacing and an unfulfilled screenplay dampen an initially arresting idea about identity and our place in the world. Sort of a noir murder-mystery, the film follows Bierko as he investigates the murder of his boss (Mueller-Stahl). The answer could lie in his computer invention — a virtual reality creation of 1930s Los Angeles. The re-creation of yesteryear is quite good, but the film offers few thrills as Bierko travels back and forth from his own reality to the created one — ultimately coming to question which reality is real and which is fabricated. Few sci-fi effects. ★★ DVD: $19.99

The Thirteenth Warrior

(1999, 103 min, US, John McTiernan) *Antonio Banderas, Omar Sharif, Diane Venora, Dennis Storhoi.* A 10th-century Arab aristocrat (Banderas) reluctantly joins a dozen Vikings in their quest to destroy a tribe of cannibalistic "monsters" that is terrorizing local villages. That's the entire plot, with nary a surprise or twist or dramatic revelation in the film's entire running time. The cannibals are at first — when only glimpsed — rather frightening, but in the second half become standard villains, and, despite a nice buildup, the final battle is anticlimactic. A sporadically rousing if silly and thin adventure. ★★ DVD: $19.99, VHS: $9.99

38: Vienna Before the Fall

(1989, 97 min, Austria, Wolfgang Glück) *Tobias Engel, Sunnyi Melles, Heinz Trixner.* Nominated for Best Foreign Film (the first such nominee from Austria), this elegant but impassioned drama is set a few months before Hitler's annexation of Austria and deals with such themes as political apathy, the roots of anti-Semitism and the Holocaust. Set against the deceptively beautiful backdrop of pre-war Vienna, the drama centers around two lovers, a Jewish playwright and a popular Aryan actress, who are blissfully blind to the escalating inhumanity which surrounds them. A powerful film experience. (German with English subtitles) ★★★½

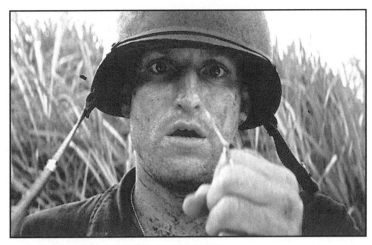

Woody Harrelson in Terrence Malick's *The Thin Red Line*

35 Up

(1991, 127 min, GB, Michael Apted) Director Apted continues his seven-year study of a group of British children from childhood through adulthood, which he began with *7 Up.* Having offered their hopes and dreams on-camera as children in the earlier films, it can be heart-wrenching to see adults rationalizing why they haven't realized their dreams. Though *35 Up* suffers from the fact that the changes that occur between 28 and 35 are less perceptive than the dramatic swings between the other earlier ages, this series remains one of the most revealing looks at life and the aging process ever to be captured on film. ★★★½

Thirty Is a Dangerous Age, Cynthia

(1968, 85 min, GB, Joseph McGrath) *Dudley Moore, Suzy Kendall.* Moore stars in this eccentric comedy as a nightclub pianist fast approaching his 30th birthday. Overwrought by the angst of reaching this milestone without having ever married or produced a hit song, he sets out to achieve both these goals in a six-week period. Moore cowrote the script and scores high marks with this offbeat comedy which casts a jaundiced eye at the absurdities of sex and marriage. ★★★

The 39 Steps

(1935, 89 min, GB, Alfred Hitchcock) *Robert Donat, Madeleine Carroll, Peggy Ashcroft.* Donat stars as an innocent man on the lam, handcuffed to Carroll, linked with a spy ring, pursued by a villain with a severed finger and chased through the Scottish highlands. A vintage thriller which is thick with intrigue and colored with Hitchcock's droll humor. (Remade in 1959 and 1979) ★★★★ DVD Criterion Collection: $39.99

Thirty Seconds over Tokyo

(1944, 138 min, US, Mervyn LeRoy) *Spencer Tracy, Robert Mitchum, Van Johnson, Phyllis Thaxter.* One of the top box-office hits of the 1940s, this exciting WWII drama details the first aerial attack on mainland Japan by American forces and is enhanced by a solid cast. A good companion piece is *Destination Tokyo*, the 1943 Cary Grant drama which tells the same story from the point of view of the submarine crew which made the air strike possible. ★★★ VHS: $14.99

36 Fillette

(1988, 88 min, France, Catherine Breillat) *Delphine Zentout, Jean-Pierre Léaud.* Heralded by many as a refreshing tale of a precocious girl's rite of sexual passage told from a woman's point of view and reviled by others for its wanton depiction of a manipulating, selfish brat, this saucy Gallic comedy will leave few viewers without a strong opinion. Lili, a pouty, sexy 14-year-old who is literally bursting out of her children's sizes, decides to lose her virginity while on vacation with her family. Her first choice for the despoiler is Maurice, a middle-aged playboy and musician, but our heroine soon finds that losing her viriginity is not such an easy decision. (French with English subtitles) ★★½ DVD: $14.99, VHS: $14.99

36 Hours

(1964, 115 min, US, George Seaton) *James Garner, Rod Taylor, Eva Marie Saint, Werner Peters, John Banner.* Based on the novel "Beware of the Dog" by Roald Dahl, this intriguing suspenser, though taking its time getting there, offers a few twists and turns getting to its exciting climax. Garner is a U.S. major with intimate knowledge of the impending D-Day invasion. With only 36 hours left, the Germans kidnap him, drug him, and make him believe it's five years later and the war is over — all in order to get the vital information. Taylor is a German psychiatrist, and Saint is the housekeeper in on the charade. It's talky but suspenseful and well done. ★★★ VHS: $19.99

32 Short Films about Glenn Gould

(1994, 94 min, Canada, François Girard) *Colm Feore, Derek Keuvorst, Katya Lada.* Director Girard has constructed a kaleidoscopic exploration of the eccentric life of world-renowned concert pianist Glenn Gould, engagingly portrayed by Feore. Gould left the concert stage at age 32 at the height of his career. Searching for an ideal performance arena, he intended to communicate with the audience solely through media. Passionately obsessed with music, this justifiably egomaniacal perfectionist lived in sound, cadence and tone in a consuming vortex of self-absorbed creativity. The 32 short films include interviews with family, friends and other artists; selected performances of his compositions and radio programs; and dramatized biographical episodes. ★★★½ DVD: $29.99

This Boy's Life

(1993, 115 min, US, Michael Caton-Jones) *Robert De Niro, Ellen Barkin, Leonardo DiCaprio, Jonah Blechman.* Based on the autobiography of writer Tobias Wolff, this intensely moving coming-of-age drama is a courageous tale examining the hopes and desperation of an unsettled youth. DiCaprio plays a troubled teen who, with his newly married mother (Barkin), moves to a small town in Washington state to live with her new stepfather (De Niro). But what had promised to be a fresh start — an emotional rebirth for mother and son — quickly degenerates into an oppressive and claustrophobic lifestyle neither is able to protest or divorce. Wolff's illuminating process of self-discovery and self-determination raises *This Boy's Life* well above the pack of a crowded genre. The acting from the three leads is exemplary. ★★★★ DVD: $19.99

This Could Be the Night

(1957, 105 min, US, Robert Wise) *Jean Simmons, Anthony Franciosa, Paul Douglas, Joan Blondell.* Simmons shines as a schoolteacher who takes a part-time job at a New York nightclub, thus furthering her own education in matters romantic. Playboy Franciosa and lovably gruff Douglas are her bosses, who both fall under the spell of Simmons' naïve charm. This risqué, colorful comedy features splashy musical numbers, and extracts cheerful performances from its entire cast. ★★★ VHS: $19.99

This Gun for Hire

(1942, 80 min, US, Frank Tuttle) *Alan Ladd, Veronica Lake, Robert Preston.* Taken from a Graham Greene novel, this gripping crime drama stars Ladd as Raven, a tight-lipped paid assassin who, after he is double-crossed by an "employer," seeks revenge. The alluring Lake is a sultry "singing magician" who gets innocently involved and good guy Preston is the detective on the trail. Above-average thriller with wonderfully complex twists and chance encounters. With an oil company as the real bad guy, the film was ahead of its time. ★★★½

This Happy Breed

(1944, 114 min, GB, David Lean) *Robert Newton, Celia Johnson, John Mills, Kay Walsh.* Noël Coward's keen adaptation of his own hit play about the affairs of a lower middle-class family was immensely popular in its day. Set between the two World Wars, the film delves into the petty bickerings and small triumphs of the Gibbons clan as they grapple with the difficulties of a world ravaged by social strife and war. Director Lean makes excellent use of Ronald Neame's penetrating camerawork. ★★★½

This Is My Life

(1992, 94 min, US, Nora Ephron) *Julie Kavner, Samantha Mathis, Gaby Hoffman, Carrie Fisher, Dan Aykroyd, Kathy Najimy.* Ephron makes her directorial debut with this lightweight comedy-drama not without a certain charm. Kavner gives an enchanting performance as a single mother who tries to make it big in show biz. As her star slowly but assuredly ascends, it is her two daughters who are most affected by their mother's new-found success as it demands more and more of her time. Though Ephron doesn't fully explore many of the scenarios she introduces, she manages to infuse in the film a fair amount of good humor. ★★½ VHS: $19.99

This Is Spinal Tap

(1984, 82 min, US, Rob Reiner) *Rob Reiner, Michael McKean, Christopher Guest, Harry Shearer, Fran Drescher.* Reiner's riotous, razor-sharp satire is a pseudo-rockumentary on Britain's loudest band, Spinal Tap. Captured during a swan-song U.S. tour, these over-the-hill, heavy metal moptops offer their sentiments on life in the fast lane, the merits of their "Smell the Glove" LP and the mysterious deaths of their past 35 drummers. ★★★★ DVD: $19.99

Favorite Line: "Have a good time, all the time." —David Kaff as Viv Savage

This Is the Sea

(1998, 104 min, Ireland, Mary McGuckian) *Samantha Morton, John Lynch, Richard Harris, Ross McDade, Gabriel Byrne.* A sweet, but fated romance between the Protestant Hazel (Morton) and the Catholic Malachy (McDade) is the centerpiece of this otherwise toothless drama about the 1994 cease-fire in Belfast. Writer-director McGuckian strives for melodrama, but the intriguing subplot about a car bombing that implicates the lovers and their families is underwhelming. The

Alan Ladd and Veronica Lake in *This Gun for Hire*

Irish countryside is quite beautiful, but the film's lack of tension keeps *This Is the Sea* from being anything truly special. Morton, who was remarkable in *Under the Skin*, gives another sterling performance, while McDade is winning as her suitor. ★★½ VHS: $59.99

This Island Earth

(1954, 86 min, US, Joseph Newman) *Jeff Morrow, Faith Domergue, Rex Reason, Russell Johnson.* A group of scientists are kidnapped by aliens, who need them to help defend their planet. This clever outer space tale is one of the most popular of the '50s sci-fi films. Features good special effects. (The film used for the theatrical debut for *Mystery Science Theatre 3000*.) ★★½

This Man Must Die

(1969, 110 min, France/Italy, Claude Chabrol) *Michael Duchaussoy, Caroline Cellier.* One of Chabrol's finest films, this first-rate thriller concerns the father of a boy who was a hit-and-run victim and his obsessive and unrelenting need to track down his son's killer and extract his vengeance. This Hitchcockian tale has plot twists that will keep you guessing until the startling conclusion. (French with English subtitles) ★★★½ DVD: $19.99

This Property Is Condemned

(1966, 110 min, US, Sydney Pollack) *Robert Redford, Natalie Wood, Charles Bronson, Kate Reid, Dabney Coleman.* This reworking of the Tennessee Williams tragedy stars Wood as a Southern belle who longs for out-of-towner Redford to sweep her away to the big city and help her escape the family boarding house. Pollack directs and Francis Ford Coppola helped write the screenplay. ★★ DVD: $19.99, VHS: $19.99

This Sporting Life

(1963, 129 min, GB, Lindsay Anderson) *Richard Harris, Rachel Roberts, Alan Badel, Colin Blakely, Arthur Lowe.* Harris gives a career performance as Frank Machin, a Yorkshire lad who tries to escape the restrictions of his working-class background and his personal limitations by becoming a star on the city rugby team. Gritty and stark, peopled with great performances. Screenplay by David Storey based on his book; produced by Karel Reisz and perceptively directed by Anderson. ★★★½ DVD: $24.99

This Sweet Sickness

(1977, 105 min, France, Claude Miller) *Gérard Depardieu, Miou-Miou.* Forget *Boxing Helena*: For this thriller, based on the novel by Patricia Highsmith ("Strangers on a Train"), is one of the most chilling and strangest portraits of obsessive love. Depardieu gives a compelling performance as David, a man so obsessed with his former lover, Lise, that his life becomes one of deceit and delusion. And David isn't dissuaded in his obsession by the fact that Lise is now remarried and that his neighbor (Miou-Miou) has fallen in love with him. Tension builds as the characters' lives become further entangled, ultimately resulting in tragedy. (French with English subtitles) ★★★½ VHS: $24.99

This World, Then the Fireworks

(1997, 100 min, US, Michael Oblowitz) *Billy Zane, Gina Gershon, Sheryl Lee.* A stylish adaptation of Jim Thompson's story, this film noir oozes sex and violence in heavy doses. Marty (Zane) and Carol (Gershon) are incestuous twins bent on bad behavior. He has a vicious temper; she is a heartless hooker who leaves a trail of poisoned bodies in her wake. Their fragile bond, which stems from an ugly childhood incident, holds the clues, yet somehow the parts are much greater than the whole. Director Oblowitz has a keen ear for dialogue and a great eye for detail, but moody atmosphere can only camouflage the lack of plot for so long — the film goes nowhere slowly. ★★½

The Thomas Crown Affair

(1968, 102 min, US, Norman Jewison) *Steve McQueen, Faye Dunaway, Paul Burke, Jack Weston, Yaphet Kotto.* A solid heist adventure with the ever-cool McQueen masterminding an ingenious bank robbery and becoming involved with equally cool insurance investigator Dunaway. (Remade in 1999) ★★★ DVD: $14.99

The Thomas Crown Affair

(1999, 113 min, US, John McTiernan) *Pierce Brosnan, Rene Russo, Faye Dunaway, Denis Leary.* A straightforward, no-frills remake of the 1968 Steve McQueen-Faye Dunaway thriller, this adequate update abandons style for slickness and substitutes lukewarm in place of cool. Brosnan stars as the thrill-seeking, art-thief billionaire who becomes involved with the insurance investigator (Russo) on his trail. There's little sexual tension between the two stars, though individually each is admirable. Dunaway turns up as Russo's psychiatrist — a reminder of a more glorious past. ★★½ DVD: $14.99, VHS: $9.99

Thoroughly Modern Millie

(1967, 138 min, US, George Roy Hill) *Julie Andrews, Mary Tyler Moore, Carol Channing, James Fox, Beatrice Lillie.* Delightfully entertaining musical spoof with Andrews as the title character, a husband-hunting secretary during the Roaring '20s. Moore also stars as an orphaned ingenue who comes to the big city and is befriended by Millie. Channing received an Oscar nomination for her spirited performance as a daffy and lovable socialite. Memorable Oscar-winning score by Elmer Bernstein and André Previn. (The basis for the Tony Award-winning Broadway musical) ★★★ DVD: $14.99, VHS: $14.99

Those Who Love Me Can Take the Train (Ceux qui m'aiment prendront le train)

(1998, 122 min, France, Patrice Chereau) *Jean-Louis Trintignant, Valeria Bruno-Tedeschi, Vincent Perez, Pascal Gregory, Dominique Blanc, Vincent Ward.* Director Chereau has created an intensely emotional multicharacter drama set primarily on a moving train. A bisexual Parisian painter, Jean-Baptiste (Trintignant), dies and his body is to be buried in his hometown of Limoges. As dictated by the diseased, the funeral mourners all board a train for the ride south. On board are a collection of divergent people all of whom were involved with the tyrannical yet charming artist. Here they meet, talk, argue and make love. Involving, darkly convoluted and wonderfully observant of human foibles, the film won three Césars (including Best Director). ★★★ DVD: $29.99, VHS: $24.99

A Thousand Acres

(1997, 105 min, US, Jocelyn Moorhouse) *Jessica Lange, Michelle Pfeiffer, Jason Robards, Jennifer Jason Leigh, Keith Carradine, Colin Firth, Kevin Anderson.* A Thousand Acres is a well-acted, occasionally moving drama of family conflict which unfortunately isn't quite as involving as it promises to be. Based on Jane Smiley's Pulitzer Prize-winning novel, the story concerns an Iowa farming family and the ramifications which occur when patriarch Robards decides to divide his homestead between his three daughters. This sets in motion a series of soul-searching and emotional confrontations which ultimately shed light on dark family secrets. The wonderful performances of Lange and Pfeiffer go far to gloss over the sometimes slow pacing and dispassionate feel director Moorhouse gives the film. ★★½ DVD: $14.99, VHS: $9.99

1,000 Eyes of Dr. Mabuse

(1960, 103 min, West Germany, Fritz Lang) *Gert Frobe.* He's back! The arch supervillain who foreshadowed Hitler's Germany returns from beyond the grave, now a scientist whose headquarters is a large hotel full of secret panels, peep holes and dungeons. The Mabuse series was a clear inspiration for the James Bond movies, and this one — Lang's last film — even stars Frobe who went on to play the title role of "Goldfinger" a few years later. ★★ DVD: $29.99, VHS: $19.99

Thousand Pieces of Gold

(1991, 105 min, US, Nancy Kelly) *Rosalind Chao, Dennis Dun, Chris Cooper.* A startlingly good independent film, this impressive historical drama centers on the harsh fate of a fiercely defiant woman thrown into the rough-and-tumble world of Gold Rush fever in the 1880s American West. Lalu, a Chinese woman in her twenties, is sold by her famine-stricken father and eventually brought to San Francisco, where she is auctioned off to an obnoxious saloon keeper in a dismal Idaho town. Refusing to succumb to forced prostitution and virtual slavehood, Lalu must overcome insurmountable odds in preserving her dignity and gaining independence. Based on a true story, this western epic is filmed in a simple, straightforward fashion by Kelly. Chao is unforgettable as the determined Lalu. (In English and Cantonese with English subtitles) ★★★½

Threads

(1985, 110 min, GB, Mick Jackson) *Karen Meagher, Rita May.* One of the best of the "day after" nuclear dramas, this powerful, uncompromising BBC production examines the devastating aftermath of global nuclear war on present-day London. Presented in pseudo-documentary style, the film is uncomfortably realistic in its portrayal of a nuclear nightmare. ★★★½

Three Ages, The Goat & My Wife's Relations

(1921/22, 111 min, US, Buster Keaton, Eddie Cline, Mal St. Clair) *Buster Keaton, Margaret Leahy, Wallace Beery.* A collection of three Keaton comedies. *Three Ages* (1923, 63 min) pokes fun at Griffith's *Intolerance*, telling three stories from different ages — The Stone Age, the Roman Empire and "Modern Times." In all three, Keaton plays the lovable schnook in love with Leahy — but Beery stands in his way. Highlights include a funny chariot race and a wedding ceremony which looks to be the precursor of *The Graduate.* (★★★) *The Goat* (1921, 23 min) is the highly amusing story of Keaton being mistaken for a notorious gangster. The short features inventive visuals and a hilarious, prolonged chase scene. (★★★½) *My Wife's Relations* (1922, 25 min) has Keaton mistakenly married and moving in with ne'er-do-well relations. (★★½) DVD: $29.99, VHS: $29.99

Three Amigos!

(1986, 105 min, US, John Landis) *Steve Martin, Chevy Chase, Martin Short, Joe Mantegna.* Occasionally amusing spoof of westerns and *The Magnificent Seven* in particular. Martin, Chase and Short play unemployed silent western stars who, thought to be real cowboys, are summoned to save a small Mexican town terrorized by desperadoes. Hijinks ensue. ★★ DVD: $14.99, VHS: $9.99

Three Brothers

(1980, 111 min, Italy, Francesco Rossi) *Philippe Noiret, Michele Placido, Charles Vanel.* A vivid and affecting portrait of three very different brothers who return to the village of their youth for their mother's funeral. Political and social concerns as well as their strained relationships are probed in this extraordinary film. (Italian with English subtitles) ★★★½ DVD: $29.99, VHS: $29.99

Three Came Home

(1950, 106 min, US, Jean Negulesco) *Claudette Colbert, Sessue Hayakawa, Patric Knowles.* A superlative performance by Colbert highlights this absorbing and powerful drama based on Agnes Keith's novel detailing her experiences in a Japanese internment camp in Borneo. Separated from their husbands, American Colbert and a group of British women endure the hardships of imprisonment and the cruelties of their captors. ★★★½ VHS: $14.99

Three Cases of Murder

(1954, 99 min, GB, David Eady, George O'Ferrall, Wendy Toye) *Orson Welles, Alan Badel.* The title says it all with this nicely executed trilogy of murder and the supernatural. The first short, *In the Picture*, is an effectively eerie chiller about a deceased artist who comes back to life to perfect his masterpiece. The second, *You Killed Elizabeth*, is the least successful of the three. It's the story of a ménage à trois which ends in murder. The last piece, *Lord Mountdrago*, features an extraordinary Welles as an ambitious, callous Foreign Secretary serving in Parliament who is haunted by the man whom he has ruined. Based on a short story of W. Somerset Maugham, it's a fascinating, humorous tale. ★★★ VHS: $39.99

Three Comrades

(1938, 98 min, US, Frank Borzage) *Margaret Sullavan, Robert Taylor, Robert Young, Franchot Tone.* Coscripted by F. Scott Fitzgerald and based on an Erich Maria Remarque novel, this tender, lushly romantic tearjerker has the beguiling Sullavan in her best performance, a timeless portrait of love and sacrifice. Set in post-WWI Germany, the story follows the close relationship of three soldiers (Taylor, Tone and Young), and their devotion to ailing, former aristocrat Sullavan after she and Taylor wed. The rise of Fascism in Germany is its backdrop, and the film effortlessly extracts the best of Fitzgerald and Remarque in the marriage of love story and political study. ★★★½ VHS: $19.99

Three Days of the Condor

(1975, 117 min, US, Sydney Pollack) *Robert Redford, Faye Dunaway, Cliff Robertson, Max von Sydow, John Houseman.* Pollack's exciting espionage thriller stars Redford as a CIA researcher working in a Manhattan think tank. When all of his coworkers are brutally assassinated, he suddenly finds himself on the run and not knowing whom to trust. Good performances come from Dunaway, as a civilian who is kidnapped by Redford and coerced to help him. ★★★½ DVD: $19.99, VHS: $14.99

The Three Faces of Eve

(1957, 91 min, US, Nunnally Johnson) *Joanne Woodward, Lee J. Cobb, David Wayne.* Woodward won a deserved Academy Award for her stunning performance as a woman with a multiple personality disorder. Told in an almost documentary style (complete with narration from Alistair Cooke), the film begins as dreary Georgia housewife Eve White visits a psychiatrist (Cobb) because of headaches and blackouts. It's soon discovered, however, she is harboring a second and third personality: Eve Black, a sexy flirt, and a sensible "normal" Jane who may be Eve's real identity. Cobb is especially sincere as her doctor. Based on an actual case. ★★★ VHS: $19.99

Three Fugitives

(1989, 93 min, US, Francis Veber) *Nick Nolte, Martin Short, Sarah Rowland Doroff, James Earl Jones.* Disarming remake of the French comedy *Les Fugitifs*, with Nolte as a paroled bankrobber who is taken hostage by inept Short, who's committing his first hold-up. Some good slapstick in an otherwise sentimental comic tale. ★★ DVD: $14.99, VHS: $9.99

3 Godfathers

(1948, 105 min, US, John Ford) *John Wayne, Ward Bond, Harry Carey, Jr., Pedro Armendariz.* Director Ford is in a sentimental mood with this glossy remake of Peter B. Kyne's popular story about three outlaws who find a baby while crossing the desert and take charge of it. Wonderful cinematography highlights this Wayne tale. Filmed five times before this one (two versions with Carey, Sr.), and since then as a Jack Palance TV movie. ★★★ VHS: $14.99

317th Platoon

(1965, 94 min, France, Pierre Schoendoerffer) *Bruno Crémer, Pierre Fabre, Jacques Perrin.* Capturing both the horrors of battle and the anguish and solitude each soldier endures, this realistic war drama describes, with wrenching clarity, the final bloody days of an army platoon. Set in 1954 during the last days of the French involvement in Southeast Asia (and filmed entirely in the jungles of Cambodia), the story follows the frantic retreat from the front lines of the 317th platoon, made up of 41 Laotians and four Frenchmen. The director and cinematographer Raoul Coutard (both veterans of the French Vietnam war) focus intimately on these ordinary young men as they, through enemy ambushes, disease and fatigue, are slowly annihilated. (French with English subtitles) ★★★½

Three in the Attic

(1968, 92 min, US, Richard Wilson) *Christopher Jones, Yvette Mimieux.* Jones stars in this playful if silly 1960s sex comedy as a college student whose three girlfriends give him a lesson in fidelity when they kidnap him, lock him in an attic and literally try to fuck him to death. ★★

Three Kings

(1999, 114 min, US, David O. Russell) *George Clooney, Mark Wahlberg, Ice Cube, Spike Jonze, Nora Dunn.* After tackling Oedipal incest (*Spanking the Monkey*) and road-movie farce (*Flirting with Disaster*), director Russell heads into the Persian Gulf war to make a heist film. Clooney again proves his magnetism as he leads his three cronies (Wahlberg, Cube, Jonze) through an absurd theater of war to steal Saddam's secret stash of gold. An exciting, inventive adventure/comedy/caper film

with as much brains as brawn. ★★★½ DVD: $19.99, VHS Collector's Edition: $9.99, VHS Letterbox Collector's Edition: $9.99

Three Little Words

(1950, 102 min, US, Richard Thorpe) *Fred Astaire, Red Skelton, Vera-Ellen, Debbie Reynolds.* Astaire and Skelton make a nice team in this appealing, Hollywoodized biography of songwriters Bert Kalmer and Harry Ruby, whose songs include "I Wanna Be Loved by You," "Who's Sorry Now" and the title tune. ★★★ VHS: $19.99

Three Men and a Baby

(1987, 102 min, US, Leonard Nimoy) *Tom Selleck, Ted Danson, Steve Guttenberg.* A box-office smash, this amiable and sometimes funny remake of the French hit *Three Men and a Cradle* stars Selleck, Danson and Guttenberg as three bachelor roommates who find themselves playing daddy to an adorable baby when the infant's mother drops the child on their doorsteps. (Sequel: *Three Men and a Little Lady*) ★★½ DVD: $14.99, VHS: $9.99

Three Men and a Cradle

(1985, 100 min, France, Coline Serreau) *Roland Giraud, Michel Boujenah, Andre Dussollier.* Similar to American "concept" pictures, the story line is simple: Three swinging bachelors wake up one morning and suddenly find a baby at their door, none of them the father. The antics of the novice fathers as they tend the child are predictable but also hilariously funny. (American remake: *Three Men and a Baby*) (French with English subtitles) ★★★ VHS: $14.99

Three Men and a Little Lady

(1990, 100 min, US, Emile Ardolino) *Ted Danson, Steve Guttenberg, Tom Selleck, Nancy Travis, Fiona Shaw.* While mildly entertaining, this sugar-coated sequel fails to live up to the original and is badly hampered by its utterly predictable ending. The thin story follows Selleck's snail-paced realization that he loves the little lady's mother. This is more aptly titled *Three Men and a Lot of Hokum.* ★½ DVD: $14.99, VHS: $9.99

Three Men on a Horse

(1936, 87 min, US, Mervyn LeRoy) *Frank McHugh, Joan Blondell, Sam Levene, Teddy Hart.* There's a Damon Runyon flavor to this zesty film adaptation of George Abbott's stage comedy. Character actor McHugh had his finest hour as the hen-pecked greeting card writer who becomes involved with small-time gambler Levene and his gang. It seems McHugh can accurately predict the ponies, which makes him very popular. There's quite an abundance of wonderfully funny lines, and silliness is the order of the day. Special mention goes to Hart for his priceless turn as a bug-eyed, gravel-voiced stooge. One of the better kept secrets of 1930s comedies. ★★★ VHS: $19.99

The Three Musketeers

(1949, 125 min, US, George Sidney) *Gene Kelly, Frank Morgan, Lana Turner, Angela Lansbury, Vincent Price.* One of the ten screen versions of the Alexander Dumas classic is a colorful swashbuckler with a mostly appealing cast. But it's not quite up to par with Richard Lester's wonderful 1974 romp. ★★½ VHS: $19.99

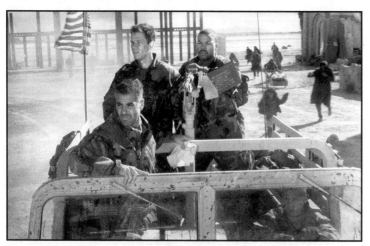

George Clooney, Mark Wahlberg and Ice Cube in David O. Russell's *Three Kings*

The Three Musketeers

(1973, 107 min, GB, Richard Lester) *Richard Chamberlain, Oliver Reed, Michael York, Raquel Welch, Charlton Heston, Faye Dunaway.* From the director of *A Hard Day's Night* comes this delightful, tongue-in-cheek version of the Dumas classic. York is at his best as the young D'Artagnan in this artful mix of swashbuckling adventure, romance and uproarious slapstick comedy. Among a great cast, Welch (in her finest hour) excels as Constance. Arguably the best sound version of the famous story. (Sequel: *The Four Musketeers*) ★★★½ VHS: $9.99

The Three Musketeers

(1993, 105 min, US, Stephen Herek) *Charlie Sheen, Kiefer Sutherland, Chris O'Donnell, Tim Curry, Rebecca DeMornay, Oliver Platt, Gabrielle Anwar.* It would take a lot of panache to equal Richard Lester's classic 1974 treatment of the Dumas novel. Unfortunately, neither director Herek nor his Frat Pack cast are up to the challenge — the result being an enjoyable if inconsequential retelling. Wise-cracking incarnations of Athos, Aramis and Porthos are joined D'Artagnan as they take on Cardinal Richelieu (a lively Curry). The duel scenes have a certain verve, and the costumes are splashy, but most of the sets look like throwaways from "The Pirates of the Caribbean" (the ride, not the movie). ★★½ DVD: $14.99, VHS: $9.99

3 Ninjas

(1992, 81 min, US, Jon Turtletaub) *Victor Wong, Michael Treanor.* The *Karate Kid* meets the Three Stooges in this obvious yet somewhat entertaining kids' action comedy. Three blond-haired, blue-eyed Asian-American (!) brothers receive martial arts training from their sensei grandfather, once a powerful ninja. When their FBI-agent dad gets on the wrong side of an international arms merchant, the kids get their chance to prove their mettle. It's hokey and formulaic, and trivializes violence in a big way. (Followed by 3 sequels) ★★½ DVD: $9.99, VHS: $9.99

3 Nuts in Search of a Bolt

(1964, 78 min, US, Tommy Noonan) *Paul Gilbert, John Crinin, Mamie Van Doren.* Three madcap loonies, each too poor to seek help on their own, pool their funds and their neuroses to send an unemployed actor to a world-famous psychiatrist hoping to receive a cure. The results? Blackmail, movie offers, big money and Van Doren in a bathtub full of beer! ★

Three O'Clock High

(1987, 101 min, US, Phil Joanou) *Casey Siemaszko, Anne Ryan, Richard Tyson.* Thanks to an engaging cast and some remarkable cinematography, this teenage comedy manages to rise above the norm of the genre. Siemaszko is quite appealing as a student bookstore manager who accidentally "touches" the school bully. This sends the youth into a day-long hysteria when the antisocial thug (Tyson) challenges him to a fight after school. ★★★ DVD Letterbox: $14.99

Three of Hearts

(1993, 101 min, US, Yurek Bogayevicz) *Sherilyn Fenn, Kelly Lynch, William Baldwin, Joe Pantoliano.* Stung by her sudden breakup with Ellen (Fenn), the love-lorn Connie (Lynch) concocts a wild plan to get revenge by hiring a male hustler (Baldwin) to trap her ex into falling in love with him, only to have him break her heart which in turn would hopefully have Ellen running back to her lov-

ing embrace. But the plan backfires when Joey, the streetwise prostitute with a heart of gold and now a roommate and friend of Connie, inadvertently falls in love with the charming university teacher. A lighthearted, charming romantic comedy with a ménage à trois twist. ★★★ DVD: $19.99

Three Seasons

(1999, 110 min, US/Vietnam, Tony Bui) *Don Duong, Nguyen Ngoc Hiep, Manh Cuong Tran, Harvey Keitel, Zoe Bui, Nguyen Huu Duoc.* The first American film to be shot in Vietnam since the war, this exquisitely photographed, poetic drama explores the diverse, interconnecting lives of a group of disparate people in modern Saigon. Writer-director Bui has made an impressive debut about the clash between the old and the new Vietnams, even if its politics are muted and stories sometimes familiar. Hai (Duong) is a good-hearted cyclo driver who falls for a bitter prostitute, Lan (Z. Bui), while taxiing her around the city night after night. Ken An (Hiep) is a flower seller newly arrived to the city who forms a bond with her reclusive employer. Into this mix comes James (Keitel), an American ex-G.I. searching for his daughter. Bui is able to imbue the film with fable-like romanticism to fully incorporate the themes of the passing of the old, the coming of the new, and a country on the road to reconciliation. That it looks so good makes it all the more striking. (In English and Vietnamese with English subtitles) ★★★½ VHS: $14.99

Three Strange Loves

(1949, 88 min, Sweden, Ingmar Bergman) *Eva Henning, Brigit Tengroth.* This early Bergman psychological drama is set on a train trip from Germany to Sweden during which the lives of a dry scholar, his wife and his former wife all reach an impasse. (Swedish with English subtitles) ★★½

Three Strikes

(2000, 82 min, US, DJ Pooh) *Brian Hooks, N'Bushe Wright, Faizon Love, David Alan Grier.* A young ne'er-do-well is released from prison — after a term for his second offense — and spends a wacky first-day-out desperately trying to avoid committing a third crime, which would land him an automatic twenty years in jail. Writer-director Pooh cowrote and produced the funny comedy *Friday*, but none of the talent demonstrated in that film is on display here. Instead, he trots out infantile, laughless gags and stock characters. ★ DVD: $14.99, VHS: $9.99

3:10 to Yuma

(1957, 92 min, US, Delmer Daves) *Van Heflin, Glenn Ford.* Very suspenseful western with farmer Heflin agreeing to guard prisoner Ford, but losing a battle of wits while waiting for the train to take him away. A classic western adventure, one of the best of the genre. Based on an Elmore Leonard story. ★★★½ DVD: $19.99

Three the Hard Way

(1974, 93 min, US, Gordon Parks, Jr.) *Jim Brown, Fred Williamson, Jim Kelly.* Three superstars of blaxploitation team up in this pulsating, yet unusually nonviolent thriller about a white supremacist who plans to inject a deadly serum — which kills off blacks but is harmless to whites — into the water supply. ★★½

3,000 Miles to Graceland

(2001, 121 min, US, Demian Lichtenstein) *Kurt Russell, Kevin Costner, Courtney Cox, Christian Slater, Kevin Pollak, David Arquette, Bokeem*

Woodbine, Jon Lovitz. Russell and Costner are two ex-cons who pull off the daring robbery of a Las Vegas casino — dressed as Elvis impersonators. From this juncture, the plot could have gone in any one of several promising directions, but instead the filmmakers steer down the much-traveled road of the vengeful-psycho-killer-with-an-arsenal chasing after the bag of loot. Costner has fun playing an irascible badass who, it's hinted at, may be the King's illegitimate son. Russell's got the swaggering hero stuff down pat and plays off Costner rather well. But there's indeed trouble in Graceland: the project is derailed by an inferior screenplay, inadequate direction, hectic over-editing and needless hyper-violence. ★★ DVD Letterbox: $14.99, VHS: $14.99

Three to Tango

(1999, 98 min, US, Damon Santostefano) *Matthew Perry, Neve Campbell, Dylan McDermott, Oliver Platt, John C. McGinley.* Gay activists, in response to the statement that gays actually choose their lifestyles, often quote the line, "Who would *want* to be gay in a homophobic society?" *Three to Tango*, comic drivel of nearly epic proportions, attempts to show the who, what, where and why of "who." Perry plays an architect whose zillionaire client (McDermott) thinks he's gay (but he's not), so Perry's asked to keep on eye on the mogul's "wild" girlfriend (Campbell). Think they eventually fall in love? This probably would have been funny if it was made in the 1960s; but alas, it's nothing more than a series of stereotypes and hoary comic situations. ★½ DVD: $9.99, VHS: $14.99

Three Wishes

(1995, 107 min, US, Martha Coolidge) *Patrick Swayze, Mary Elizabeth Mastrantonio, Joseph Mazzello, Seth Mumy, Michael O'Keefe, Diane Venora.* This flashback-framed fantasy/drama is an enjoyable diversion for the family, but it never quite catches fire or makes the most of its premise. Swayze plays a mysterious drifter who is taken in by Mastrantonio and her two young sons after they accidentally hit him with the car. He brings a bit of male companionship to the widowed mother and acts as a father figure to young Mazzello, much to the chagrin of the well-to-do neighbors. Little is made of the fantasy elements in the story, and the expected big, emotional ending is a piffle and, to be frank, a cop-out. ★★½ DVD: $9.99, VHS: $9.99

301 / 302

(1995, 92 min, Korea, Chul-Soo Park) *Eun-jin Banh, Sin-Hye Hwang.* An odd pastiche that blends a squeaky clean Asian high-tech look with the sensibilities of Juenet y Caro, this sometimes amusing black comedy involves two neighbors in a very chi-chi apartment block for affluent single women. When the woman in apartment 302 goes missing, the police interview 301 trying to dig up clues, setting in motion a series of flashbacks that retell the two women's lives. (Korean with English subtitles) ★★½ VHS: $79.99

The Threepenny Opera

(1931, 114 min, Germany, G.W. Pabst) *Lotte Lenya, Rudolph Forster.* Pabst's wild and eerie adaptation of the Bertolt Brecht/Kurt Weill "beggar's opera" captures the play's marvelous milieu of 19th-century underworld and features the magical performances of Lenya as Jenny and Forster as the infamous Mack the Knife. (German with English subtitles) ★★★ VHS: $19.99

Threesome

(1994, 93 min, US, Andrew Fleming) *Stephen Baldwin, Lara Flynn Boyle, Josh Charles, Alexis Arquette.* This often funny story revolves around the friendship and evolving sexual relations between three college students sharing the same dorm. Baldwin is Stuart, a sex-obsessed jock. Eddy (Charles) is the "sexually ambivalent" (read: gay) narrator/roommate, and Alex (Boyle) is the sexually aggressive woman mistakenly assigned to their room. Complications arise when lust rears its ugly head. Sure it's "high concept," but what saves the film from being tiresome and predictable (no surprises, though) is a witty script. ★★★ DVD: $19.99

The Thrill of It All

(1963, 108 min, US, Norman Jewison) *James Garner, Doris Day, Arlene Francis, Edward Andrews, Carl Reiner.* This delightful spoof is very typical of the good-natured, family-oriented comedies Day and Universal were releasing at the time. Day stars as a housewife who becomes a celebrity spokesperson, much to the dismay of husband Garner. Though at times the film seems to advocate feminist principles, in the end Doris' place is in the home (evidently in 1963 she couldn't have it all). ★★★ DVD: $14.99, VHS: $14.99

Throne of Blood

(1957, 110 min, Japan, Akira Kurosawa) *Toshiro Mifune, Isuzu Yamada.* Shakespeare's "Macbeth" is superbly adapted to the screen in this gripping tragedy of a samurai warrior who is spurred by his ambitious wife and an old witch to kill his lord. Amidst an atmosphere of obsessive madness, and utilizing aspects of Noh theatre, Kurosawa concludes his film with an unforgettable and graphic depiction of Mifune's bloody death by arrows. (Japanese with English subtitles) ★★★½ DVD Criterion Collection: $39.99, VHS: $29.99

Through a Glass Darkly

(1961, 91 min, Sweden, Ingmar Bergman) *Harriet Andersson, Max von Sydow.* Andersson is mesmerizing as a recently released mental patient who, while vacationing on a remote island with her husband, brother and father, relapses into schizophrenia. This Oscar winner is one of Bergman's most intense and riveting films. (Swedish with English subtitles) ★★★½ VHS: $29.99

Throw Momma from the Train

(1987, 88 min, US, Danny DeVito) *Danny DeVito, Billy Crystal, Anne Ramsey.* A hilariously dark black comedy, with its inspiration coming from Hitchcock's classic *Strangers on a Train.* Crystal stars as a teacher who gets mixed-up with one of his students, DeVito, who is determined to get rid of his overbearing, mean-spirited mother. Ramsey steals the film with an over-the-top, one-of-a-kind portrayal of DeVito's wicked Mom. ★★★ DVD: $14.99

Thunder Road

(1958, 92 min, US, Arthur Ripley) *Robert Mitchum, Gene Barry.* The ideal picture to watch while passing around a jug of White Lightning. This lively potboiler has interesting behind-the-scenes glimpses of Kentucky moonshiners and a fun backwoods milieu. When a big-city operation tries to muscle in, bootlegger Mitchum vows to stop them while at the same time attempting to elude the ceaseless pursuit of government agents. ★★★ DVD: $14.99

Thunderball

(1965, 132 min, GB, Terence Young) *Sean Connery, Claudine Auger, Adolfo Celi.* Connery has tongue firmly in cheek in this fourth James Bond outing. 007 is up against Emilio Largo (Celi), who has masterminded the greatest nuclear hijacking of all time. Excellent underwater photography highlights this glorious Bond adventure, which won an Oscar for Best Special Effects. (Sequel: *You Only Live Twice*) ★★★

Thunderbolt and Lightfoot

(1974, 115 min, US, Michael Cimino) *Clint Eastwood, Jeff Bridges.* Eastwood stars as a master thief who teams up with a wise-cracking drifter (Bridges) to search for stolen money from a previous robbery. Bridges received an Oscar nomination for his spirited performance (not to mention his drag routine). ★★★ DVD: $14.99

Thundercrack!

(1975, 130 min, US, Curt McDowell) *George Kuchar.* A very funny and outrageously sexy spoof of all those horror films in which a group of strangers is forced to spend a stormy night in an old dark house full of eerie sounds, creepy happenings and, in this case, inhabited by a sexually active gorilla. Greeting the stranded motorists at her decaying mansion is a crazed hostess who initiates her unwitting guests in a series of increasingly bizarre sexual trysts. A sexually graphic camp classic that is a titillating scream. ★★★

Thunderheart

(1992, 118 min, US, Michael Apted) *Val Kilmer, Graham Greene, Sam Shepard, Fred Ward.* Kilmer stars in this fictionalized look at the conflict between the American Indian movement and the Bureau of Indian Affairs on the Sioux reservation in South Dakota. Kilmer plays a half-native FBI agent who is sent to sort things out. He takes the assignment reluctantly at first, but as he gets to know life on the reservation, he finds that perhaps he is on the wrong side. Apted lets the action loose at the appropriate moments, but doesn't hesitate to meditate on the mystical ways of his Native American subjects. ★★★ DVD: $19.99, VHS: $19.99

THX-1138

(1971, 88 min, US, George Lucas) *Robert Duvall, Donald Pleasence.* Before he revitalized the sci-fi genre with *Star Wars*, Lucas directed this chilling tale set in a 1984-like society where computers regulate the subterranean populace with mind-controlling drugs. This is a feature-length version of his award-winning short film. ★★★ DVD The George Lucas Director's Cut: $26.99, VHS: $14.99

The Tic Code

(2000, 90 min, US, Gary Winick) *Gregory Hines, Polly Draper, Christopher George Marquette, Bill Nunn, Tony Shalhoub.* Set against the East Village jazz scene, this often compelling drama is elevated beyond its movie-of-the-week pedigree thanks to some fine acting and dedication of character. Twelve-year-old pianist Miles (Marquette) is a child prodigy with Tourette's syndrome. An outcast at school, Miles finds comfort at a local jazz club, where he feels connected to his absent father, a successful musician living in Hollywood. When he is befriended by Tyrone (Hines), an accomplished saxophonist also with Tourette's, both Miles and Tyrone come to find peace within themselves. Draper (she wrote the sensitive screenplay) is smart as Miles' supportive mother, who begins an affair with Tyrone. ★★★ DVD: $14.99, VHS: $9.99

Ticket to Heaven

(1981, 107 min, Canada, Ralph L. Thomas) *Nick Mancuso, Meg Foster, Saul Rubinek.* Made a year before the equally riveting, similarly themed *Split Image*, this psychological drama stars Mancuso as a teacher who comes under the influence of a religious cult, robbing the educator of his will and spirit. When friends and family finally locate him, it's a desperate struggle to "deprogram" him to the way he was. ★★★

Tie-Died

(1995, 89 min, US, Andrew Behar) Behar spent a summer on the road with the world's most fanatic fans, the Grateful Dead followers. For some of them, it's a way of life; for others, extended weekends several times a year (the reservists?). Parking lots are transformed into small mobile communities, an extended gypsy family espousing antimaterialism, environmental consciousness and a tribal spirituality. *Tie-Died* is a sometimes fascinating look at a quintessentially American subculture, made accessible to even the nonfan civilian. ★★★ DVD: $24.99, VHS: $14.99

Tie Me Up! Tie Me Down!

(1990, 101 min, Spain, Pedro Almodóvar) *Antonio Banderas, Victoria Abril, Julieta Serrano, Maria Barranco, Rossy De Palma.* This Almodóvar comedy may not satisfy those people who were won over by *Women on the Verge*, but for lovers of Pedro and his outrageous style, this will be a pure delight. A released mental patient (Banderas) kidnaps a heroin addicted porn star (Abril) and professes his love for her. Surprisingly sentimental for Almodóvar, this is an often hilarious tale of love and bondage which features a truly steamy sex scene and a water toy with a penchant for swimming into the nether regions of the female anatomy. (Spanish with English subtitles) ★★★ DVD Letterboxed: $29.99, VHS Letterboxed: $14.99

The Tie That Binds

(1995, 98 min, US, Wesley Strick) *Keith Carradine, Daryl Hannah, Vincent Spano, Moira Kelly.* This wreck of a movie attempts to make a statement about contemporary child-rearing but succeeds only in being a lesson in how to make a terrible film. Spano and Kelly adopt a mysterious little girl. When they decide to check into her birth parents' background, they discover Carradine and Hannah, a part-time serial killer and his psychotic white-trash/hymn-singing wife. The plot rehashes every "psychotic (nanny-policeman-tenant) from hell" movie, and the dialogue is ludicrous. ★ DVD: $9.99

Tieta of Agreste

(1996, 115 min, Brazil, Carlos Diegues) *Sonia Braga, Marilia Pera, Chino Anisio.* Based on the Jorge Amado novel, this story that "may have no moral" follows Tieta (the sultry Braga), who as a young girl left her hometown in shame but has returned a rich and powerful businesswoman. She becomes the town's benefactor, and fulfills the financial — and in some cases sexual — desires of her family and the townspeople. Yet when Tieta gives everyone what they want, they really end up getting what they deserve. Director Diegues has created a joyful comedy about sex, greed, and politics that pulses to the bouyant sounds of Caetano Veloso's bossa nova. (Portuguese with English subtitles) ★★★½ DVD: $14.99, VHS: $14.99

Tiger Bay

(1959, 105 min, GB, J. Lee Thompson) *Hayley Mills, John Mills, Horst Buchholz.* This morality play disguised as a suspense thriller stars H. Mills (in her debut) as a friendless girl who witnesses a murder, then shelters the murderer (Buchholz) from the investigating detective (J. Mills). A sensitive study of the power of loneliness, desperation and the need to be loved, which makes this not just another "cops & robbers" story. The scenes between young Hayley and Buchholz are unforgettable. ★★★ DVD: $24.99

A Tiger's Tale

(1987, 97 min, US, Peter Douglas) *C. Thomas Howell, Ann-Margret, Charles Durning.* Pleasant but aimless comedy about a high school senior (Howell) who becomes romantically involved with his girlfriend's mother (Ann-Margret). Director Douglas is one of Kirk's sons. ★★

Tigerland

(2000, 100 min, US, Joel Schumacher) *Colin Farrell, Matthew Davis, Clifton Collins, Jr., Tom Guiry, Shea Whigham, Russell Richardson.* This gritty, involving antiwar film is set at a boot camp in the early 1970s where soldiers are being hastily trained for a quick flight to Vietnam. Amongst the ranks is Bozz (Farrell), a pacifist rebel who only wants out of the Army. During the grueling weeks of training, that end with simulated combat at a makeshift jungle called Tigerland, Bozz comes to have a palpable effect on his fellow soldiers — and reclaims a little of his own humanity in the process. *Tigerland* transcends the clichés of the war film not only through compelling dramatics but bristling characterizations as well. At the eye of this storm is a force of great intensity, Irish actor Farrell — his tempered, riveting portrayal provides a stark balance to circumstances that are out of control. ★★★ DVD: $9.99, VHS: $9.99

Tigers in Lipstick

(1978, 85 min, Italy, Luigi Zampa) *Laura Antonelli, Monica Vitti, Ursula Andress, Sylvia Kristel.* Four of the sexiest sirens of 1970s Europe star in this tame but cute series of vignettes. Taking their inspiration from O. Henry, these humorous tales with a sexual bent all focus on the fatally seductive charms of the female sex. All feature our femme fatales as beautiful and aggressive manhandlers whose task is made all that much easier by the wide-eyed and horny complacency of their oh-so-willing victims. ★★

Tightrope

(1984, 114 min, US, Richard Tuggle) *Clint Eastwood, Geneviève Bujold, Dan Hedaya.* Eastwood stars as a New Orleans cop who, while hunting down a vicious rapist, suffers his own descent into sexual darkness. This razor-sharp crime thriller is a gripping examination of the twisted mind of the sexual criminal. ★★★ DVD: $19.99, VHS: $14.99

Tigrero: A Film That Was Never Made

(1995, 75 min, US, Mika Kaurismäki) *Samuel Fuller, Jim Jarmusch, The Karaj.* Forty years after his initial trip up the Amazon to scout locations, director Samuel Fuller returns, with Jim Jarmusch in tow, to the land of the Karajá Indian tribe. The tribe has survived myriad incursions from the outside over the intervening years, their culture amaz-

Matthew Davis and Colin Farrell in *Tigerland*

ingly intact despite wars, power politics and that eternal nemesis, progress. Fuller and Jarmusch sometime seem like just another annoyance in the villagers' lives; but there is one scene in which Fuller holds a screening for the tribe — a screening of some of the footage which sat in his closet for those 40 years. The Karajá watch with awe and wonder and recognition, remembering friends and relatives long dead. It's a moment that speaks to the magic of the medium. ★★★ VHS: $79.99

'Til There Was You

(1997, 114 min, US, Scott Winant) *Jeanne Tripplehorn, Sarah Jessica Parker, Dylan McDermott, Jennifer Aniston, Steve Antin.* In this New Age variation of *Sleepless in Seattle*, things cutely fall out windows, trendy sculptures exhibited in trendier restaurants knock customers on the head in obvious burlesque bits, and everyone seems so attractive and successful. So why isn't anyone smiling? Tripplehorn and McDermott are separated childhood friends and supposed soul mates. What it takes to bring these two together forms the core of this overly cute, minor romantic comedy-drama. ★★ DVD Letterbox: $29.99, VHS: $14.99

Tilaï

(1990, 81 min, Burkina Faso, Idrissa Ouedraogo) Director Ouedraogo's haunting and starkly realized tale of forbidden love and tribal law is a masterfully crafted African take on Greek tragedy. The story follows Saga, who returns to his home village after a many years' absence only to find that his father, a powerful village elder, has stolen and married *his* fiancée, Nogma. His hands are tied by the strict code of law that governs the village. Ultimately, he goes into exile, but stays close enough to the village to have an illicit affair with Nogma. Ouedraogo's excellent sense of storytelling is nicely complimented by an well-honed script and exceptional performances to make this a superisingly compelling and thoughtful Oedipal spin on forbidden passion. ★★★½ VHS: $79.99

Till Marriage Do Us Part

(1976, 97 min, Italy, Luigi Comencini) *Laura Antonelli, Michele Placido.* Set in the early 20th century, this funny bedroom farce features Antonelli as a naive and virginal beauty who, on the night of her wedding, discovers that she has married her illegitimate brother. Unable to consummate the marriage, our enterprising heroine is determined to discover and explore the "mysteries of the flesh." A delightful and bawdy romp. (Italian with English subtitles) ★★★

Till the Clouds Roll By

(1946, 137 min, US, Richard Whorf) *Robert Walker, Van Heflin, Judy Garland, Frank Sinatra, Lena Horne.* By-the-books musical biography of songwriter Jerome Kern, with Walker playing the gifted composer. An all-star cast appears in supporting roles and cameos. ★★½ VHS: $9.99

Tillie's Punctured Romance

(1914, 73 min, US, Mack Sennett) *Charles Chaplin, Mabel Normand.* Shot in 1914, this delightful Chaplin silent comedy was made at producer Mack Sennett's famous Keystone Pictures studio. The film is basically a slapstick love story, replete with Chaplin's brilliant trademark physical comedy. This was the only full-length feature Chaplin made for Keystone, and was the film where Chaplin refined his character that would later become his world-famous "Little Tramp." ★★★★ VHS: $19.99

Tim

(1979, 108 min, Australia, Michael Pate) *Mel Gibson, Piper Laurie.* A sensitive and compassionate story of the developing love between a handsome, slightly retarded young man (Gibson) and an older career woman (Laurie). After meeting by chance, the two find themselves bound by a deep affection and a tender sensuous longing. Based on the novel by Colleen McCullough. ★★½

Time After Time

(1979, 112 min, US, Nicholas Meyer) *Malcolm McDowell, David Warner, Mary Steenburgen.* An exhilarating sci-fi murder mystery written and directed by Meyer. In Victorian England, writer H.G. Wells (MacDowell) learns the identity of Jack the Ripper, but the infamous murderer uses Wells' newly invented time machine to transport himself to current-day San Francisco, an environment where he's "just an amateur." Wells follows him into the future, where he is assisted by bank clerk Steenburgen. Warner makes an appropriately demented Jack. Though a bit gory, it's a thrill a minute. ★★★½ DVD Letterbox: $19.99, VHS: $9.99

Time and Tide

(2000, 113 min, Hong Kong, Tsui Hark) *Nicholas Tse, Wu Bai, Anthony Wong, Joventino Couto Remotigue, Candy Lo, Cathy Chui.* Okay, *Time and Tide* has good guys and bad guys. Once you figure out who's who, just go with it, for this features one of the most convoluted, confusing narratives ever contrived for an action film. But its characters are recognizably human and interesting, and the action is spectacular. There are some terrific stunts and fights, but the "story" is a problem, and the action would have certainly been more effective and dramatic if we knew exactly what was happening. (Cantonese with English subtitles) ★★½ DVD Dual: $24.99, VHS Subtitled: $14.99

Time Bandits

(1981, 116 min, GB, Terry Gilliam) *John Cleese, Sean Connery, Shelley Duvall, Ian Holm, Katherine Helmond, Michael Palin, Ralph Richardson, David Warner.* A young boy is abducted by time-traveling midgets, who, assisted by the Supreme Being (Richardson), take him on a harrowing journey through time where they encounter Robin Hood, a giant ogre (and his lovely wife), the *Titanic*, and much, much more. A funny and frolicking fantasy. ★★★ DVD Letterbox 2-disc Special Edition: $14.99, DVD Criterion Collection: $39.99, VHS: $9.99

Time Code

(2000, 97 min, US, Mike Figgis) *Saffron Burrows, Salma Hayek, Stellan Skarsgård, Jeanne Tripplehorn, Kyle MacLachlan, Steven Weber, Julian Sands, Xander Berkeley, Glenne Headly, Holly Hunter.* Figgis' experimental film takes some getting used to, but it tells a unique story of the film business and relationships in crises. *Time Code* uses a four-part split screen with four different scenes going simultaneously showing different aspects of the same story. The actors were supplied a scenario and all the dialogue was improvised. Most of the action takes place in and around the offices of a film production company, where nearly everyone is snorting coke or drinking and trying to make business decisions during a morning of break-ups, liaisons and earthquakes. Once you get used to the spilt screens, the acting and the tale can be quite compelling. For the record, the finished product is take 15. ★★★ DVD: $24.99

Time Cop

(1994, 98 min, US, Peter Hyams) *Jean-Claude Van Damme, Ron Silver, Mia Sara, Bruce McGill.* Van Damme is in *Terminator* territory with this action-flavored time travel adventure which mixes predictable heroics and villainy with a few spiffy twists on time tripping. Van Damme plays a special forces cop from the future who retrieves those in the past who are changing history. He meets his match, however, in the person of ruthless presidential candidate Silver, who is trying to alter the course of human events for his own political gain. ★★½

Time for Revenge

(1983, 112 min, Argentina, Adolfo Aristarain) *Federico Luppi, Haydee Padilla.* This gripping thriller tells the story of one man's struggle against a corrupt system. In an effort to publicize the unsafe working conditions at a demolition site, our hero fakes an industrial accident in order to blackmail the ruthless company. The scam, however, backfires — resulting in the death of a coworker. The man continues with his scheme by claiming that he was struck speechless in the explosion. The company, knowing that something is up, gets desperate in their attempt to break his silence. A compelling story of oppression and distrust. (Spanish with English subtitles) ★★★½ VHS: $24.99

Time Indefinite

(1993, 117 min, US, Ross McElwee) Self-reflexive documentarian McElwee follows up his art-house hit *Sherman's March* by going a few steps further down the road of introspection, offering this kind of cradle-to-grave examination of his own family. McElwee's wry wit and intelligent commentaries are in evidence right from the start in which he and fellow documentarian Marilyn Levine film themselves announcing their engagement at his family reunion. He then wends his way through the next couple of years of his life, documenting all of the joys and sorrows. *Time Indefinite* is a fascinating, revealing and highly entertaining journey that explores some of life's universal questions. ★★★½ VHS: $29.99

The Time Machine

(1960, 103 min, US, George Pal) *Rod Taylor, Yvette Mimieux, Alan Young, Sebastian Cabot, Whit Bissell.* Special effects master Pal expertly brings to the big screen another of H.G. Wells' writings (Pal did *The War of the Worlds* earlier), this time retaining the novel's Victorian setting. On his way to year 802,701, Taylor witnesses our atomic Armageddon of 1966 (you remember *that* one, don't you?) and the rise of the Morlock domination of the Eloi. One of the best screen adaptations of Wells' work. (Remade in 2002) ★★★½ DVD: $19.99, VHS: $9.99

The Time Machine

(2002, 96 min, US, Simon Wells) *Guy Pearce, Samantha Mumba, Orlando Jones, Mark Addy, Jeremy Irons, Sienna Guillory, Phyllida Law, Alan Young.* Since the debut in 1960 of George Pal's *The Time Machine*, the first screen adaptation of H.G. Wells' novel, visual effects have improved tenfold. By comparison, the effects in Pal's endearing time-travel adventure appear creaky. But it has one or two things on director Wells' (great-grandson of H.G.) own peculiar life. The renowned author, on his deathbed, looks back at his life in a series of fragmented memories, which become the formation for characters and events in this final book of "Remembrance of Things Past." A dense, compelling film, quite comparable to reading Proust. (French with English subtitles) ★★★ DVD: $29.99, VHS: $19.99

A Time of Destiny

(1988, 118 min, US, Gregory Nava) *William Hurt, Timothy Hutton, Stockard Channing.* It should be a comfort both to Hurt and his fans that he'll probably never make a movie as bad as this contrived and confusing WWII drama about revenge and obsession. Hutton and Channing can probably find solace, also. ★

Time of the Gypsies

(1989, 115 min, Yugoslavia, Emir Kusturica) *Davor Dujmovic, Sinolicka Trpkova.* Sort of a Serbian version of *The Godfather II*, the story is set in a Gypsy village where a young boy, gifted with kinetic powers, grows up. His innocence and love for his mother, girlfriend and pet chicken are soon replaced by a soulless love of money, bright polyester clothing and life in the fast lane after he joins up with a gang of petty thieves. Visually hallucinatory and imbued with much humor, the director used non-professional actors and real Gypsies for most of the roles, giving the film an authentic yet eccentric feel. (Serbian with English subtitles) ★★★

The Time of Their Lives

(1946, 82 min, US, Charles Barton) *Bud Abbott, Lou Costello, Marjorie Reynolds.* Extremely entertaining Abbott and Costello romp about a couple killed during Revolutionary times (Costello and Reynolds) whose spirits reappear in the 20th century to haunt Bud, just moving into his new country home. ★★★

Time Out

(2002, 128 min, France, Laurent Cantet) *Aurélien Recoing, Karin Viard, Serge Livrozet.* At a stage in history where the words "job" and "security" don't often go together, *Time Out* is a film of urgent sig-

nificance. Vincent (Recoing), corporate mover and shaker as well as family man, has been fired. But since his job has so shaped his self-worth and dignity, he can't bring himself to tell his family (or himself) that he's unemployed. He crafts a web of stories and lies about his new, imagined employment and almost makes himself believe it. His days are spent driving around the city and hanging out in office building lobbies aching to be a part of that world again. Recoing does a stellar job at painting this damaged character. A moving film made better by its sense of restraint, *Time Out* dutifully explores the notion of how to keep one's humanity and sanity in the midst of painful life changes. (French with English subtitles) ★★★½ DVD Subtitled: $29.99, VHS Subtitled: $14.99

Time Regained

(1999, 158 min, France, Râúl Ruiz) *Catherine Deneuve, Emmanuelle Béart, John Malkovich, Vincent Perez.* An existential, surreal-like drama loosely suggested by Proust's last novel "In Search of Lost Time" and the many details of his own peculiar life. The renowned author, on his deathbed, looks back at his life in a series of fragmented memories, which become the formation for characters and events in this final book of "Remembrance of Things Past." A dense, compelling film, quite comparable to reading Proust. (French with English subtitles) ★★★ DVD: $29.99, VHS: $19.99

Time Stands Still

(1981, 99 min, Hungary, Peter Gothar) *Istvan Znamenak, Henrik Pauer.* This witty and richly composed film is a compassionate coming-of-age drama set amid the debris of post-war Hungary, with its tightening grip of repression. It follows a group of friends — two brothers abandoned by their father, an enticing nymphette and a stylish rogue — as they encounter the hardships of growing up. A brilliant, seductive film seething with sexual tension, confused violence and the foreshadow of the rock 'n' roll culture. (Hungarian with English subtitles) ★★★½

A Time to Kill

(1996, 150 min, US, Joel Schumacher) *Matthew McConaughey, Samuel L. Jackson, Sandra Bullock, Kevin Spacey, Brenda Fricker, Oliver Platt, Charles S. Dutton, Ashley Judd, Kiefer Sutherland.* Strong performances and a compelling, textured story line combine to make this the best screen adaptation of a John Grisham novel to date. In this powerful examination of race relations, McConaughey plays a white Southern lawyer who defends a black man (Jackson) on trial for murdering the men who raped his ten-year-old daughter. The story focuses on the culpability of a prejudiced society and the morality of the crime — all under the guise of exciting and even eloquent courtroom drama. Heading a good ensemble cast, McConaughey is splendid in his first starring role; Jackson gives a finely layered portrait of rage and decency. This is very nearly great filmmaking — only director Schumacher's less-than-fluid transitions mar an otherwise terrific endeavor. ★★★½ DVD: $19.99, VHS: $9.99, VHS Letterbox: $9.99

Time without Pity

(1957, 88 min, GB, Joseph Losey) *Michael Redgrave, Ann Todd, Leo McKern, Alec McCowen, Peter Cushing, Joan Plowright.* His first film made under his own name after being blacklisted during the McCarthy era, Losey's melodrama is a tense, overmannered but engaging thriller. Less of a whodunit (the murderer is revealed in the first scene) and more of a how-will-he-do-it, the film stars Redgrave as the alcoholic father of a convicted murderer (McCowen) sentenced to die. Having only 24 hours, Redgrave sets out to prove his son's innocence — if he can stay off the bottle. Losey's anti-capital punishment story is played broadly but effectively. ★★★ DVD: $19.99, VHS: $39.99

The Times of Harvey Milk

(1984, 87 min, US, Richard Schmiechen & Robert Epstein) This extraordinary, compelling portrait of the slain San Francisco supervisor won a much deserved Academy Award for Best Documentary. Few films pack such a powerful wallop as it documents the true-life story of Harvey Milk, a Castro Street camera shop owner who became the country's first openly gay elected official. His rise to power and success as a leader of minorities was abruptly ended in 1978 when he and Mayor George Moscone were assassinated by Dan White, an antigay former colleague of Milk's on the Board of Supervisors and a former police officer. The film follows the searing episode of injustice as White is given a light sentence — using the infamous "Twinkie defense" — which sent thousands of outraged citizens into the streets of San Francisco. ★★★★ DVD 2-disc set: $29.99, VHS: $39.99

Times to Come

(1981, 98 min, Argentina, Gustavo Mosquera) *Hugo Soto, Juan Leyrado.* This amazingly adventurous surrealist drama takes its title from the Argentinian saying, "It'll even be worse in times to come." In the ruined urban landscape of Buenos Aires, a young man is shot by a policeman during an antigovernment demonstration. He falls into a coma in the hospital but his brain is fully functioning. The policeman responsible for the shooting is an unpredictable and violent man who is in turn hounded by a mysterious caller bent on punishing him. An angry film that successfully combines political fervor with daring camera work and imaginative storytelling. (Spanish with English subtitles) ★★★ VHS: $39.99

Tin Cup

(1996, 130 min, US, Ron Shelton) *Kevin Costner, Rene Russo, Don Johnson, Cheech Marin, Linda Hart. Bull Durham* star and director reunite for this easygoing, enjoyable sports comedy set against the world of golf. Displaying the rustic charm he demonstrated in *Durham*, Costner plays a golf pro relegated to giving lessons for beer money. He becomes attracted to a new student (Russo), who turns out to be the girlfriend of an arrogant ex-golf partner (Johnson) who has hit the big time. To woo her, he readies himself for the U.S. Open — it may only happen in the movies, but here it's actually fun to watch. While lacking the red-hot chemistry of *Durham*'s Costner-Sarandon coupling, *Tin Cup* is as amiable as its hapless hero: wide-eyed and determined to please in spite of itself. ★★★ DVD: $14.99, VHS: $9.99, VHS Letterbox: $9.99

The Tin Drum

(1979, 142 min, France/Germany, Volker Schlöndorff) *David Bennent, Charles Aznavour, Mario Adorf, Angela Winkler, Katharina Thalbach.* This powerful adaptation of Gunter Grass' masterpiece is about a young boy, disgusted by the rising tide of Nazism, who wills himself to stop growing. A mesmerizing "realistic fantasy" with an extraordinary piece of acting by 12-year-old Bennent as the determined dwarf. (German with English subtitles) ★★★★ DVD Criterion Collection 2-Disc Set: $39.99

Tin Men

(1987, 112 min, US, Barry Levinson) *Richard Dreyfuss, Danny DeVito, Barbara Hershey, Bruno Kirby, John Mahoney.* Director Levinson is quite at home with this second entry in his "Baltimore" trilogy (*Diner, Avalon*). Dreyfuss and DeVito are both exceptional as feuding salesmen in early 1960s Baltimore. A small fender-bender escalates into full war, as each tries to outdo the other in retaliation, including Dreyfuss seducing DeVito's wife. Hershey is splendid as the woman innocently caught between them. An outstanding comedy-drama with an exemplary supporting cast. ★★★½ DVD: $14.99, VHS: $9.99

Tinseltown

(1997, 85 min, US, Tony Spiridakis) *Arye Gross, Ron Perlman, Kristy Swanson, Joe Pantoliano, Tom Wood.* A tired mix of serial-killer kitsch and Hollywood satire, *Tinseltown* is brightened only by a good cast. Two hack screenwriters stumble upon the celebrated "costume killer" and decide to make his story into a movie, pleasing low-rent producer Pantoliano. While the satire is moldy by this point, and the serial-killer angle is thin (at times, the film threatens to become *Man Gums Dog*), the performers are enthusiastic and the denouement has a surprise or two. ★★ VHS: $14.99

'Tis Pity She's a Whore

(1971, 109 min, Italy, Guiseppi Patrone Griffi) *Charlotte Rampling, Oliver Tobias, Fabio Testi.* Freely adapted from John Ford's Elizabethan tragedy, this surprisingly absorbing film about a scandalous, incestuous affair has the beauty of Zeffirelli's *Romeo and Juliet* combined with the poetically perverse sensuality of Cocteau's *Les Enfants Terribles.* Giovanni, an intensely handsome young man, is troubled by his passionate love for his sister, Annabella (Rampling). The two, vowing undying love and commitment towards each other, are soon torn apart by their father who forces Annabella to marry an arrogant young nobleman — all the while pregnant with Giovanni's baby. Lushly photographed with several steamy sex scenes, this absorbing drama has a shocking, overpowering finale. (Filmed in English) ★★★

Titan A.E.

(2000, 94 min, US, Don Bluth & Gary Goldman) *Voices of: Matt Damon, Drew Barrymore, Nathan Lane, John Leguizamo, Tone Loc.* Awesome computer and hand-painted animation more than compensate for overused sci-fi clichés in this entertaining animated fantasy. Borrowing from just about every genre flick, this amicable toon is a feast for the eyes, showcasing some imaginative visuals. The story begins when the Drej, a vicious alien species, destroys Earth, leaving a band of survivors to fend for themselves in a lone spaceship as they search for

a secret map that will lead them to Dryland, er, to Earth 2. Vocal contributions are well cast, especially Damon and Barrymore as a pair of teenaged lovers literally star-crossed. ★★★ DVD: $9.99, VHS: $6.99

Titanic

(1953, 98 min, US, Jean Negulesco) *Barbara Stanwyck, Clifton Webb, Robert Wagner, Richard Basehart, Thelma Ritter.* Stanwyck and Webb offer accomplished performances in this luxuriously melodramatic retelling of the sinking of the *Titanic.* As opposed to the excellent British drama *A Night to Remember,* which tells its story via ship's personnel, this glossy Hollywoodization is seen through the eyes of ship's passengers, with married couple Stanwyck and Webb its main focus. And even if *Night* is more authentic, this *Titanic* is soap opera of the first order, thanks to an Academy Award-winning screenplay and a marvelous ensemble. (The story of *Titanic* was also told in 1996 and 1997) ★★★ DVD: $14.99, VHS: $9.99

Titanic

(1997, 197 min, US, James Cameron) *Leonardo DiCaprio, Kate Winslet, Billy Zane, Kathy Bates, Gloria Stuart, Bill Paxton, Frances Fisher, David Warner, Bernard Hill, Victor Garber, Danny Nucci.* As mammoth an undertaking as the big ship itself, Cameron's epic story of the sinking of the *Titanic* is moviemaking on the grandest of scales. The story of the fateful night of April 14, 1912, has been told before, but never like this. The story begins in the present when artifacts of the sunken ship are recovered. A *Titanic* survivor, 101-year-old Rose (played with great charm by Stuart), identifies them and is whisked away to the North Atlantic. There she recounts the story of decades past, and her romance as a youth (Winslet as a 17-year-old Rose) with an adventurous, penniless artist named Jack (DiCaprio). She gets around to the sinking, eventually, too. Though three hours-plus, Cameron's film is tightly edited and paced, and though the dialogue isn't always the best, everything else is first-class. The handsome DiCaprio is romantic and heroic, and the beautiful Winslet shades Rose with intelligence and verve. *Titanic* is a marvel of popular mainstream filmmaking. Winner of a record 11 Academy Awards, including Picture and Director. ★★★★ DVD Letterbox: $14.99, VHS: $12.99, VHS Collector's Edition: $39.99, VHS Letterbox: $12.99

Titus

(1999, 162 min, US, Julie Taymor) *Anthony Hopkins, Alan Cumming, Jessica Lange, Jonathan Rhys Meyers, Matthew Rhys, Colm Feore.* Shakespeare's tragedy "Titus Andronicus" is regarded as a minor work, more interested in grotesqueries than the bright writing of his later masterpieces. So director Taymor glosses over the material and lets loose a visual panoply of sets, settings and costumes that span the eras (from Elizabethan to modern), using tanks, the Popemobile, what-have-you to enhance the bloody melodrama. Lange's performance as ladder-climbing Goth Queen Tamora is especially pulpy, while Cumming camps it up as the spoilt king. It's certainly not *Romeo and Juliet,* but it may be the best possible adaptation of this particular work. ★★★★ DVD 2-disc set: $24.99

Carole Lombard (c.) is not one to toy with in this scene from *To Be or Not to Be*

To Be or Not to Be

(1942, 99 min, US, Ernst Lubitsch) *Jack Benny, Carole Lombard, Robert Stack, Sig Ruman.* With the involvement of America in WWII, most audiences didn't know what to make of Lubitsch's hilarious and biting war comedy. With the advantage of the decades, however, this black farce has taken on legendary status, and deservedly so. Lombard (in her final role) and Benny are a husband and wife acting team in Occupied Poland. When they cross paths with a double agent, they devise a plan — with the help of their acting troupe — to expose the spy and flee to safety. Lombard was an exceptional comedienne and farceur, and her performance is radiant; and Benny gives a truly funny performance as "that great, great actor" Joseph Tura. (Remade in 1983) ★★★★ VHS: $14.99

Favorite Line: "What a husband doesn't know won't hurt his wife." —*Maude Eburne as Anna*

To Be or Not to Be

(1983, 108 min, US, Alan Johnson) *Mel Brooks, Anne Bancroft, Tim Matheson, Charles Durning, Jose Ferrer.* Inferior, somewhat entertaining remake of the 1942 Ernst Lubitsch classic with Brooks (who wrote but did not direct) and Bancroft as the bickering thespian couple played by Jack Benny and Carole Lombard. The story is of a Polish theatre troupe who outwit the Nazis in Occupied Warsaw. Brooks adds a slightly misplaced but certainly well-intentioned update by introducing a gay character (who's swishy as hell) who also suffers under Nazi rule. ★★½ VHS: $9.99

To Catch a Killer

(1991, 95 min, Canada, Eric Till) *Brian Dennehy, Michael Riley, Margot Kidder.* The police investigation and arrest of serial killer John Wayne Gacy is the subject of this crime drama which has been edited from its original miniseries length. Rather than being cheap, sensationalistic exploitation, the film is actually quite suspenseful. Dennehy is believable as the demented Gacy, a stocky construction contractor who was eventually sent to death row for kidnapping, sexually torturing and killing at least 33 teenage boys and then burying their bodies in the dirt basement of his Illinois home. Without the mys-

tery of whodunit, the film instead focuses on the police's frantic efforts in tracking him down. Sad, creepy and riveting. ★★★ DVD: $29.99

To Catch a Thief

(1955, 97 min, US, Alfred Hitchcock) *Cary Grant, Grace Kelly, Jesse Royce Landis, John Williams.* This fast-paced romantic thriller features glorious Rivera settings, sparkling comic touches and the sizzling sexual chemistry between Kelly and Grant. Grant plays a reformed jewel thief who may be up to his old tricks; Kelly may be his intended victim. ★★★ DVD Letterbox: $14.99, VHS: $9.99

To Die For

(1995, 100 min, US, Gus Van Sant) *Nicole Kidman, Matt Dillon, Joaquin Phoenix, Casey Affleck, George Segal, Illeana Douglas, Dan Hedaya, Kurtwood Smith.* Kidman offers a scintillating performance in this stylish and hilarious social satire that attacks America's media-obsession with razor-sharp precision. Kidman is a model of icy effervescence as Suzanne Stone, a small-town New Hampshire girl who is determined to make a name in television, at any cost. Working at the local cable station, she begins a video documentary about the wasted lives of three local teens, including a perfectly cast Pheonix as her unlikely paramour. When her husband (Dillon) begins making demands for marital bliss, Suzanne, determined to stay the course, enlists the youths to help rid her of her domestic distraction. Based in part on a real incident, Buck Henry's masterful script finds itself in good hands with Van Sant. Douglas is captivating in support as Dillon's sister, who also acts to some degree as the film's Greek chorus. ★★★½ DVD: $14.99

To Each His Own

(1946, 122 min, US, Mitchell Leisen) *Olivia de Havilland, John Lund, Mary Anderson, Roland Culver.* De Havilland won the first of her two Oscars, giving a splendid portrayal of a small-town girl who bears a child out of wedlock, and is forced to give it up. She watches from afar as the baby grows from infancy to childhood to manhood. Leisen elevates this soap opera by offering sensitive direction which bypasses the usual melodramatic pitfalls; and de Havilland creates a three-dimensional character one can't help but care about. ★★★

To Forget Venice

(1979, 110 min, Italy, Franco Brusati) *Mariangela Melato, Erland Josephson.* Brusati has fashioned a sensitive and refined story of a group of people (two gay men and two lesbians) who visit together at an old country estate. The film explores the important events of their past, their first sexual encounters and their worried looks to the future. A good film, but one in which many will debate the accuracy of the film's sexual politics. ★★★

To Gillian on Her 37th Birthday

(1996, 93 min, US, Michael Pressman) *Michelle Pfeiffer, Peter Gallagher, Claire Danes, Kathy Baker.* Based on the off-Broadway play, this comedy-drama of a deceased wife returning from the grave has a certain charm to it but there's nothing special about the dialogue or the story line — *Ghost* and *Truly, Madly, Deeply* did it better. Gallagher gives an earnest performance as a husband still mourning the loss of his wife. Pfeiffer plays the ghost who returns to console and romp on the beach with her husband. As his family and friends start to think him mad, they gather for a weekend of memories and therapy. The film never ignites and takes off the way it should, despite some appealing performances. *Gillian* has laughs and tears, but this ghost story gets caught somewhere in limbo. ★★½ DVD Pan & Scan: $9.99, VHS: $14.99

To Have and Have Not

(1944, 101 min, US, Howard Hawks) *Humphrey Bogart, Lauren Bacall, Walter Brennan, Hoagy Carmichael.* This polished Hawks production is usually remembered more as the film in which Bogart and Bacall first met than for any artistic accomplishment, which is a disservice to its stars, director and writers. Bogie plays a hardboiled American charter boat captain who becomes involved with French freedom fighters, Nazis and, of course, Bacall; who, among other things, teaches Bogie how to whistle. Brennan is terrific in support as their boozing compadre. ★★★½ DVD: $19.99, VHS: $14.99

To Joy

(1950, 93 min, Sweden, Ingmar Bergman) *Britt Nilsson.* Taking its title from Beethoven's "Ode to Joy," *To Joy* marks Bergman's creative passage from films depicting the darkness of evil forces to films that celebrate the light of affirmation. This intensely moving, sensitive film focuses on the life of a talented violinist who must come to grips with the fact that his young wife was killed. Through despair and introspection, he discovers that his love for his son and for music gives him the strength to continue. ★★★

To Kill a Mockingbird

(1962, 131 min, US, Robert Mulligan) *Gregory Peck, Mary Badham, Philip Alford, Brock Peters, John Megna, Robert Duvall, Rosemary Murphy, Paul Fix, William Windom, Alice Ghostley, Narrated by: Kim Stanley.* Peck won an Oscar for his brilliant performance as Southern lawyer Atticus Finch in this brilliantly realized courtroom drama and memory piece. Based on the best-selling novel by Harper Lee, the film is seen through the eyes of Finch's young daughter, Scout (Badham), and recounts her days as a youth in 1930s Georgia as well as following her father's court case in which he defends a black man accused of rape. One of the greatest of all American films. ★★★★ DVD Letterbox: $19.99, VHS Letterbox: $9.99

To Kill a Priest

(1989, 116 min, France, Agnieszka Holland) *Christopher Lambert, Ed Harris, Tim Roth, Joanne Whalley, Pete Postlethwaite.* This fictionalized account of an actual murder of a Polish priest stars Lambert as the martyred clergyman whose campaign for Solidarity disfavors him with the military authorities. Harris costars as a midlevel officer with the security police who engineers, and executes, the assassination plot. Exiled Polish director Holland finds great human drama in the priest's dedication to his beliefs, but unwisely concentrates more on the dilemma of the Communist officer, whose zeal for the good of the party contradicts his own moral being. (Filmed in English) ★★½

To Live

(1994, 135 min, China, Zhang Yimou) *Gong Li, Ge You.* Though pulling at the heartstrings, this two-hour-plus melodrama about the harrowing journey of a Chinese family (from the end of the Nationalist reign to the Cultural Revolution) revels in its visual splendor and exceptional dramatics. Ge stars as a wealthy landlord who loses his entire estate gambling, only to be ironically spared the rod when the Reds crack down on their former oppressors. Gong plays his strong-spirited and, at times, estranged wife. Together, with their rambunctious son and deaf daughter, they wend their way through life, suffering all of the conceivable outrages that a country at war with itself can throw their way. Ge and Gong are both superb — creating characterizations that inexorably draw the viewer into the urgencies of their harrowed lives. Perhaps Zhang's best work to date. (Mandarin with English subtitles) ★★★★ DVD Letterbox: $19.99

To Live and Die in L.A.

(1985, 116 min, US, William Friedkin) *William Petersen, Willem Dafoe, Dean Stockwell, John Turturro.* Gritty, fast-paced police thriller with Petersen as a Secret Service agent who will stop at nothing to capture the counterfeiter who murdered his partner. Dafoe is a particularly villainous heavy. Made at the height of popularity of TV's "Miami

Wesley Snipes in *To Wong Foo . . .*

Vice," director Friedkin gives this bloody cops and robbers tale a similar, slick look. ★★★ DVD Special Edition: $14.99

To See Paris and Die

(1993, 110 min, Russia, Alexander Proshkin) *Tatyana Vasilyeva, Dimitri Malikov, Ekaterina Semenova.* It's the Soviet Union in the 1960s, and what's a Jewish mother to do? For the widowed Elena, the only hope is escaping with her son to Paris by having him entered in a piano competition there. This is, of course, easier said than done, and forces Elena down a road of deceit and degradation. She needs to conceal her son Yuri's (and her own) Jewish heritage in order to make the competition. She also needs to suck up to a bureaucrat involved in the decision making process. It's not hard to empathize with Elena's plight, and the drabness of everday Russian life is essayed extremely well, but *To See Paris and Die* lacks the dramatic tension that would allow the effect of the increasing humiliation to be greater than the sum of its parts. The inability for the film to find its emotional chord undermines its ability to disturb, enrage and provoke. (Russian with English subtitles) ★★ VHS: $79.99

To Sir, with Love

(1966, 105 min, GB, James Clavell) *Sidney Poitier, Lulu, Judy Geeson, Suzy Kendall.* Poitier plays an inexperienced schoolteacher, Mr. Thackeray, who's assigned a class of rowdy, headstrong and undisciplined Mods in London's East End. The students of the graduating class are determined to break Thackeray's will, but he surprises them all by giving the students respect while commanding and getting it from them. Poitier is excellent in this compelling and refreshing teacher-student drama, and he's supported by a fine group of young actors. Lulu sings the hit title song. ★★★½ DVD: $24.99, VHS: $14.99

To Sleep with Anger

(1990, 95 min, US, Charles Burnett) *Danny Glover, Sheryl Lee Ralph, Mary Alice, Carl Lumbly, Richard Brooks.* A chilling independent production by maverick director Burnett. Glover plays an "old family friend" from the South who arrives at the doorstep of an upwardly mobile black family and insinuates his way into their home, wreaking havoc on the family unit by preying on their individual weaknesses. Mixing myth, metaphor and an offbeat sense of humor, director Burnett shows that progress made over shakey ground is sometimes no progress at all. ★★★½

To the Devil a Daughter

(1976, 95 min, GB, Peter Sykes) *Nastassja Kinski, Christopher Lee, Denholm Elliott, Richard Widmark.* The legendary Hammer Studios brought forth this satanic horror story about a defrocked priest (Lee) who earmarks Kinski for selection as the Devil's daughter on her 18th birthday. Kinski's distraught father (Elliott) enlists the aid of an expert occultist (Widmark) and the fun begins. A kinky adventure into the unknown. ★★½ DVD Letterbox: $19.99

To the Lighthouse

(1985, 115 min, GB, Colin Gregg) *Rosemary Harris, Michael Gough, Kenneth Branagh.* Virginia Woolf's tale of family turmoil is set in a lush Cornwall resort at the outset of WWI where the towering lighthouse comes to symbolize the spirit of reconciliation and hope for the future. A touching drama. ★★★ DVD: $14.99

To Wong Foo, Thanks for Everything! Julie Newmar

(1995, 108 min, US, Beeban Kidron) *Patrick Swayze, Wesley Snipes, John Leguizamo, Blythe Danner, Stockard Channing, Arliss Howard, Chris Penn, Jason London, Robin Williams, Quentin Crisp.* Destined to be forever referred to as the "American *Priscilla*," this bit of cross-dressing whimsy lacks that film's exhilaration and sharp character definition, but ultimately pleases with its good humor and spirited performances. Swayze and Snipes get in touch with their feminine side as they don sequins and high heels as two New York drag queens who win a preliminary drag contest and ride off towards Hollywood for the finals. Along for the ride is Latina spitfire Leguizamo. En route, they run afoul of the law, and are stranded in a small Midwestern town which provides most of the story. Though the gay characters are positively portrayed, they are virtually sexless fairy godmothers who who help the hapless heterosexuals with no fashion sense. This is so tame you can watch it with your mom. Leguizamo steals the show as the fiery Chi Chi. ★★★ DVD Letterbox: $14.99, VHS: $9.99

Tobruk

(1967, 110 min, US, Arthur Hiller) *Rock Hudson, George Peppard, Nigel Green, Guy Stockwell.* Routine WWII adventure with Rock and George out to destroy Rommel's fuel supply at the Mediterranean stronghold. ★★½

The Todd Killings

(1971, 93 min, US, Barry Shear) *Robert F. Lyons, Richard Thomas, Barbara Bel Geddes, Ed Asner.* Lyons is a kill-for-thrills psycho in this tense and atmospheric drama. Based on real-life accounts, and predating *River's Edge*, the film offers a look into the twisted mind of a killer who provides drugs and parties to a group of alienated teens who in turn protect him from the law. ★★★ VHS: $19.99

Der Todesking

(1989, 80 min, West Germany, Jörg Buttgereit) Bathtub suicide, castration, neighbors on a killing rampage, rotting corpses and Nazi torture are just some of the "highlights" in this angst-ridden splatter film. Espousing diatribes such as "the motiveless mass murderer is the martyrdom of post-modernism," this deliberately shocking low-budgeter features a series of segments about sad, lonely, frustrated people who decide to end it all, with the finale being a cinema verité murder rampage. (German with English subtitles) ★½

Together

(2003, 116 min, China, Chen Kaige) *Tang Yun, Liu Peiqi, Wang Zhiwen, Chen Hong, Chen Kaige.* Sometimes a piece of music will start out deceptively simple, with a pleasant enough but uninspiring tune; as it progresses, melodious complexities are introduced, resulting in surprising emotional affect. Director Chen's *Together* takes this path. Xiaochun (Tang) is a remarkably gifted young violinist in a small town; his father Cheng (Liu) is singularly, selflessly devoted to Xiaochun's full realization of his gift. Father and son travel to Beijing, embarking on an odyssey of discovery and revelation. They enter an unfamiliar world and encounter both duplicity and heartfelt friendship in unexpected places. *Together* is emersed in superlative music; indeed, the soundtrack makes as full a contribution as any other in the solid ensemble. The standout is Tang, whose extraordinary artistry on the violin combines with an engaging screen presence. Liu is just as effective as Cheng, the man who engenders sympathy but not pity, who can be ingratiating but never without dignity. *Together* culminates in a powerful finale, as two children find resolution with the two men who raised them. An enchanting, warmhearted story that explores the essential nature of family. (Mandarin with English subtitles) ★★★½ DVD Letterbox: $29.99, VHS: $49.99

The Toilers and the Wayfarers

(1996, 75 min, US, Keith Froelich) *Matt Klemp, Andrew Woodhouse, Ralf Schirg, Joan Wheeler, Jerome Samuelson.* A tender coming out drama, *The Toilers and the Wayfarers* is modest on budget (nicely shot in black and white) but compelling and highly original nonetheless. Sixteen-year-olds Phillip (Woodhouse) and Dieter (Klemp) are best friends; that is, until Phillip reveals that he is gay. Dieter spurns his friend, unwilling to admit the same about himself. Phillip runs away to Minneapolis, eventually followed by Dieter. The film takes a less interesting turn there, where the two boys turn to prostitution to survive. Quietly ambitious, the drama succeeds despite its notch-below-professional acting and flimsy plot. ★★★ DVD: $24.99, VHS: $49.99

Tokyo Decadence

(1991, 112 min, Japan, Ryu Murakami) *Sayoko Amano, Yayoi Kusama, Sayoko Maekawa, Hiroshi Mikami.* This controversial, fiercely original and visually shocking portrait of a young Japanese call girl's quest for ecstasy is adapted from director Murakami's novel "Topaz." Plunging headfirst into the steamy world of S&M, drugs and depravity, the story revolves around Ai, who as the film opens seeks beatitude through the advice of a fortune teller. While the film bathes the viewer in a sea of heroin abuse, cocaine snorting, floggings and humiliations, these uncomfortable images are necessary to show how the successful and powerful businessmen clients seek these bizarre pleasures to further quench their thirst for power. A darkly powerful film that's clearly not for all tastes, but a challenging experience for open-minded viewers. (Japanese with English subtitles) ★★★

Tokyo Drifter

(1966, 83 min, Japan, Seijun Suzuki) *Tetsuya Watari, Chieko Matsubara, Hideaki Nitani.* A deadpan but wildly visual and stylish gangster tale, *Tokyo Drifter* is an amalgam of '60s cinematic excess and '30s crime drama. With a wigged-out production design and even some time-capsule pop tunes, the film follows a former wiseguy who's trying to go straight. But the new bosses just won't let him. This eventually puts him on the run, hiding out all over Japan. But this pop idol doesn't lie down easy, for no matter what the enemy dishes out he's always ready with fists blazing and a song on his lips. Yes, he's a nightclub singer, too. Director Suzuki has a quiet camera but a quirky reverence for the genre — that's a tough act when crooning to your girlfriend — but they sure look cool doing what they do. (Japanese with English subtitles) ★★★ DVD: $29.99, VHS: $29.99

Tokyo-Ga

(1985, 92 min, US/West Germany, Wim Wenders) Wenders' engrossing and entertaining "filmed dairy" of his 1983 trip to Tokyo is both a fascinating glimpse of the city and a personal metaphysical search for meaning. At the start of the trip,

Tokyo Story

Wenders aims to find the "pure" Japan that he knows and loves from the films of director Yasujiro Ozu. Instead of simplicity and order, however, Wenders becomes dazed by the kinetic energy of the city, as well as fascinated by the strange, and at times bizarre, lifestyles of the people. (Filmed in English) ★★★

Tokyo Olympiad

(1964, 170 min, Japan, Kon Ichikawa) This documentary of the 1964 Summer Olympics held in Japan makes for an extraordinary celebration of the human form. Utilizing over 160 cameramen, filming in Cinemascope and intercutting slow-motion and other special effects, Ichikawa captures the visual splendor of the Olympics to produce possibly the finest photographed film of athletic endeavor. Not interested in the glorification of man, as was Leni Riefenstahl's *Olympia*, Ichikawa instead focuses more on competition and the individual efforts of the athletes. This video, the rarely seen original director's cut, will enthrall both sports fans and non-fans alike. ★★★½ DVD Letterbox Criterion Collection: $39.99, VHS 2-tape set: $49.99

Tokyo Story

(1953, 135 min, Japan, Yasujiro Ozu) *Chishu Ryu, Chieko Higashiyama.* Ozu's quietly overpowering masterpiece is a deceptively simple tale about an elderly couple's visit to Tokyo and the less than enthusiastic reception they receive from their children. A master with the camera and with subtlety of statement, Ozu deftly and powerfully creates this vision of alienation in the modern world as the "new" Japan forced the traditional values out. A true masterpiece of world cinema. (Japanese with English subtitles) ★★★★ DVD Criterion Collection: $39.99

Tol'able David

(1921, 91 min, US, Henry King) *Richard Barthelmess, Ernest Torrence, Gladys Hulette.* Director King was raised in the backwoods of Virginia and returned there to shoot on real locations for this production. Barthelmess plays a young man — at first thought to be a coward — whose fate forces him to take on three of the foulest villains ever to be captured on film (they even kill his dog!). But it is the bucolic atmosphere that has made this the classic it is, preserved here with the love and care expected from a Kino release. King discusses the making of the film in a 16-minute interview shot on video just before his death. ★★★½ DVD: $29.99, VHS: $24.99

The Toll Gate

(1920, 73 min, US, Lambert Hillyer) *William S. Hart, Joseph Singleton, Anna Q. Nilsson.* Unfairly forgotten now, Hart was the Clint Eastwood of his day: stoic, silent, distant, with as much bad in him as good. Here he plays train robber Black Deering, betrayed by one of his own men, forced to flee into the unforgiving desert and into the arms of a forgiving widow. Tranferred from an original tinted print, the film exhibits some of its age in the last reel that will not affect the enjoyment of one of Hart's best films. ★★★ DVD: $24.99, VHS: $24.99

Tom and Huck

(1995, 93 min, US, Peter Hewitt) *Jonathan Taylor Thomas, Brad Renfro, Eric Schweig, Charles Rocket, Amy Wright.* A routine and almost lifeless adaptation of Mark Twain's "Tom Sawyer." Thomas plays Sawyer, a spunky, mischievous orphan being raised by his aunt. The story concentrates on his friendship with Huck Finn (Renfro) and their dilemma when they witness a murder and the wrong man is accused. The film is surprisingly tame, offers few misadventures, and has in Huck an angst-ridden 20th-century juvenile delinquent rather than a 19th-century youth bent on tomfoolery. ★★ DVD: $14.99, VHS: $14.99

Tom & Viv

(1994, 125 min, GB, Brian Gilbert) *Willem Dafoe, Miranda Richardson, Rosemary Harris, Tim Dutton.* Madness and passion are equally matched in this unsettling though beautifully filmed examination of the love affair, marriage and separation of writer T.S. Eliot and his wife Vivienne. Dafoe plays the American author who seems more at home in the reserved setting of the British upper crust. Richardson, in a mesmerizing, go-for-broke Oscar-nominated performance, is the aristocrat whose high-spiritedness settles the perfect tonic for the somber writer. They marry, and Eliot begins to achieve success in the field of poetry with his wife aiding him spiritually and editorially. However, as Eliot's star ascends, it soon becomes apparent that his wife is suffering from some sort of mental instability, which begins to threaten both their relationship and his career. As Viv's socially conscious but loving mother, Harris is excellent. ★★★ DVD: $19.99, VHS: $14.99

Tom, Dick and Harry

(1941, 86 min, US, Garson Kanin) *Ginger Rogers, George Murphy, Alan Marshall, Burgess Meredith.* Rogers sparkles in this delightful comedy with Ginger daydreaming about her three boyfriends, having to choose between them. ★★★

Tom Jones

(1963, 129 min, GB, Tony Richardson) *Albert Finney, Susannah York, Hugh Griffith, Joyce Redman, Edith Evans, Diane Cilento.* This Academy Award Winner for Best Picture and Director richly evokes the tenor of its times — both of the setting of the novel and of the era when it was filmed. Richardson uses every cinematic trick in the book — fast motion, jump cuts, rapid editing — to capture the joie de vivre of Henry Fielding's bawdy tale of a young rake's randy adventures in 18th-century England. Finney is brilliant in the lead role, and his seduction of Redman in the classic eating scene will make a gourmand out of the most abstemious. ★★★★ DVD: $14.99

tom thumb

(1958, 98 min, GB, George Pal) *Russ Tamblyn, Peter Sellers, Terry-Thomas.* Winning an Oscar for Best Special Effects, this musical based on the children's fairy tale proves true the adage that good things come in small packages. "Fun for the entire family" might be a worn epithet, but this movie certainly warrants its use. Kids will enjoy the animated performance of Tamblyn as the diminutive hero and Tom's toy friends, puppets brought to life by "Puppettoon" master Pal. Adults will particularly appreciate the antics of Terry-Thomas and Sellers, perfectly cast as greedy, bumbling antagonists. ★★★½ DVD: $24.99, VHS: $14.99

Tombstone

(1993, 132 min, US, George P. Cosmatos) *Kurt Russell, Val Kilmer, Michael Biehn, Jason Priestley, Bill Paxton, Billy Zane, Charlton Heston, Sam Elliott.* Slightly overlong and overly ambitious, *Tombstone* is an invigorating, extremely photogenic tale of legendary lawman Wyatt Earp's tenure in the shoot-'em-up town of Tombstone, Arizona. Russell is Wyatt, who has retired from peacekeeping and is ready to settle down. However, a notorious gang known as The Cowboys stands in his way. Of course, the film chronicles the famous gunfight at the O.K. Corral (an efficient and exciting sequence), and strives to explore Earp's personal life, as well. Though Russell firmly anchors the film, the acting honors go to Kilmer who gives an acerbic interpretation of the sickly Doc Holliday. ★★★ DVD Letterbox Basic Edition: $19.99, DVD Vista Series: $29.99, VHS: $9.99

Tommy

(1975, 110 min, GB, Ken Russell) *Ann-Margret, Oliver Reed, Roger Daltrey, Elton John, Tina Turner, Eric Clapton, Jack Nicholson, Paul Nicholas, Robert Powell.* The Who's rock opera stars Daltrey as the "deaf, dumb and blind boy" who becomes a pinball wizard and New Messiah. John is the dethroned champ, Clapton is the preacher and Turner is the electrifying acid queen. Ann-Margret received an Oscar nomination for her fiery portrayal of Tommy's mum. Directed by Russell with his usual flair for the bizarre. ★★★ DVD: $14.99

Tommy Boy

(1995, 96 min, US, Peter Segal) *Chris Farley, David Spade, Brian Dennehy, Bo Derek, Rob Lowe, Dan Aykroyd, Julie Warner. Tommy Boy,* about the moronic son of a multimillionaire, is unexpectedly funny. Farley stars as the title character, a recent college grad who returns home to work for his father's automotive company. When his father dies, Tommy must save the company from closing. *Tommy Boy* is peppered with lots of amusing physical schtick, and Farley and cohort Spade (as Tommy's acerbic assistant) make an effective comedy team. *Tommy Boy* may not be at the head of the class, but of all the "dumb" movies so far, it's one of the smartest. ★★½ DVD: $14.99, VHS: $9.99

Tomorrow

(1972, 103 min, US, Joseph Anthony) *Robert Duvall, Olga Bellin.* A startlingly good adaptation of William Faulkner's story, featuring Duvall in a tremendous performance as a workman who befriends and falls in love with a pregnant woman (Bellin) deserted by her husband and family. Horton Foote (*The Trip to Bountiful*) wrote the screenplay. ★★★ DVD: $29.99

Tomorrow Is Forever

(1946, 104 min, US, Irving Pichel) *Claudette Colbert, Orson Welles, George Brent, Natalie Wood.* A sumptuous, moving version of "Enoch Arden," featuring a great performance by Welles and a lovely portrayal by Colbert. Colbert plays a wife whose husband (Welles) dies at the end of WWI. At least that's what she thinks. She gives birth to his son, and later marries her boss. Twenty years later, her first husband, under a new identity, returns to America to work for her new husband. When he meets her and the son he never knew he had, he is faced with the dilemma of whether or not to reveal his identity to them. ★★★

Tomorrow Never Dies

(1997, 119 min, GB, Roger Spottiswoode) *Pierce Brosnan, Jonathan Pryce, Michelle Yeoh, Teri Hatcher, Judi Dench, Desmond Llewelyn.* Nonstop action sequences and campy, half-hearted one-liners are poor substitutes for the once excellent plotting and scripting of the earlier James Bond entries, but Brosnan makes a go of it. This time out, our hero must stop an egomaniacal media mogul named Carver — played with gusto by Pryce — who's out to start a war between Great Britain and China: to boost ratings! Yeoh is on hand as Bond's eventual ass-kicking sidekick. But the true stars of the film are, of course, the stuntmen — and that spectacular remote control BMW (the centerpiece of possibly the best scene in the entire film). (Sequel: *The World Is Not Enough*) ★★½ DVD: $19.99, VHS: $9.99

Tomorrow the World

(1944, 86 min, US, Leslie Fenton) *Fredric March, Betty Field, Agnes Moorehead, Skippy Homeier.* In this powerfully moving film adaptation of the award-winning Broadway play, a German youth, raised within the Nazi doctrine, is sent to live with his American uncle (March) during the war. His new family struggles with the boy's intolerance and trying to undo the Nazi influence. ★★★½ DVD: $24.99, VHS: $19.99

Tongues Untied

(1989, 56 min, US, Marlon Riggs) This highly acclaimed film combines poetry, personal testimony, rap and performance to describe the homophobia and racism that confronts gay African-Americans. A personal and at times angry documentary that is an impassioned cry to speak out about black gay lives, the film garnered surprising controversy when some PBS stations — disturbed by its subject matter — refused to broadcast it. Two of the more memorable lines state: "Black men loving black men is *the* revolutionary act"; and "If in America a black is the lowest of the low, what is a gay black?" ★★★ VHS: $29.99

Tombstone

Toni

(1935, 90 min, France, Jean Renoir) *Charles Blavette, Jenny Helia.* In an attempt at film realism, Renoir left the confines of the studio and soundstage and brought the action to the outdoors. His actors do not wear makeup, a more "natural" style of acting is used and Renoir places his camera at a distance in order for the characters and action to tell the story with the camera merely recording. The result is a wonderfully told tale of the loves and lives of four Italian immigrant miners who settle around Marseilles. (French with English subtitles) ★★★

Tonight and Every Night

(1945, 92 min, US, Victor Saville) *Rita Hayworth, Lee Bowman, Janet Blair.* Pleasant Hayworth musical about the wartime adventures — romantic and otherwise — of a group of showgirls working in London during the blitz. Rita romances RAF pilot Bowman, and must decide between love and duty when he is shipped abroad. ★★★

Tonio Kröger

(1964, 90 min, France/West Germany, Rolf Thiele) *Jean-Claude Brialy, Nadja Tiller, Gert Frobe.* Thomas Mann's autobiographical novella is faithfully brought to the screen in this dreamlike story of the problems encountered by a youth growing up in late 19th-century Germany. Born of a Prussian businessman and a fiery Italian woman, our hero struggles with whether he wants to belong to the bourgeois world or explore his artistic talents. This conflict between restraint and passion forces him to decide what world and lifestyle is best suited for him. (German with English subtitles) ★★

Too Beautiful for You

(1989, 91 min, France, Bertrand Blier) *Gérard Depardieu, Josiane Balasko, Carole Bouquet.* Depardieu stars as a wealthy businessman who has just about everything one could desire, including a dazzlingly beautiful wife (Bouquet). But when he meets his new secretary, Colette, a frumpy and slightly overweight middle-aged woman, and falls deeply and passionately in love with her, he finds his material values seriously imperiled. Director Blier has taken the basic premise of farce and turned it upside down; and while the film has a gentle comic flavor throughout, it is also a serious examination of the misplaced value given to beauty. Depardieu is excellent as always and Balasko is a treat as the broodingly seductive Colette. (French with English subtitles) ★★★ DVD Letterbox: $19.99, VHS: $19.99

Too Hot to Handle

(1938, 105 min, US, Jack Conway) *Clark Gable, Myrna Loy, Walter Pidgeon.* A fast-paced and extremely entertaining comedy with Gable in a particularly light mood as a newsreel journalist who courts aviatrix Loy from rival reporter Pidgeon. Gable and Loy, appearing together for the seventh time, are well matched in this alternately funny and action-flavored romp. Recommended, and a near-must for students of 1930s comedies. ★★½ VHS: $19.99

Too Late the Hero

(1969, 133 min, GB, Robert Aldrich) *Michael Caine, Cliff Robertson, Henry Fonda, Ian Bannen, Harry Andrews, Denholm Elliott, Ken Takakura.* Caine and Robertson are British and American officers in charge of a suicide mission to distract the Japanese on a small Pacific island. The two must come to grips with their cultural differences as they engage in a battle of wits with the local Japanese commander. ★★★ DVD: $14.99, VHS: $14.99

Too Many Girls

(1940, 85 min, US, George Abbott) *Lucille Ball, Eddie Bracken, Ann Miller, Desi Arnaz.* One of Ball's earliest starring roles, and the sassy redhead makes the most of it. A most engaging musical comedy, the story follows the romantic adventures of college students Lucy and Bracken, Miller and Arnaz (this is where they met). ★★★

Too Much Sun

(1990, 97 min, US, Robert Downey) *Eric Idle, Andrea Martin, Robert Downey, Jr., Ralph Macchio, Leo Rossi.* Two pampered children of a Beverly Hills millionaire learn they will lose their deceased father's $200 million fortune unless one of them produces an heir. The problem? Sonny (Idle) is gay and Bitsy (Martin) is a lesbian. The ensuing game of sexual musical chairs is further complicated by the arrival of a pair of two-bit hustlers (Downey, Macchio), who are willing to be adopted, for the right price. From the director of *Putney Swope*. ★★½

Too Outrageous

(1987, 110 min, Canada, Dick Benner) *Craig Russell, Holly McLaren.* Ten years after making the acclaimed, small-budget *Outrageous!*, director Benner and actor Russell teamed again for this not all-together successful sequel. Plump, wise-cracking hairdresser Robin (Russell), now a big hit as a female impersonator in New York, must still contend with his lack of a love life, hampered primarily by his friend and roommate Liza (McLaren) who still suffers from debilitating bouts of schizophrenia. A disappointing backstage memoir that is a bit stilted, oddly dated and not possessing the offbeat charms of the first film. ★★

Too Pretty to Be Honest

(1982, 95 min, France, Richard Balducci) *Jane Birkin, Bernadette Lafont.* Four very pretty girls who share an apartment on the French Riviera witness a bank robbery on a day trip to Nice. The next day, looking through a telescope, they see the man who might be the thief so, thinking that stealing from a thief is not really stealing, they plot an elaborate scheme to lift the money. (French with English subtitles) ★★½

Too Shy to Try

(1978, 89 min, France, Pierre Richard) *Pierre Richard, Aldo Maccione.* Richard directed and stars in this comedy about a bungling man who falls in love with a beautiful and sophisticated young woman. Unable to simply introduce himself to the young lady, our hero instead enrolls in a correspondence course in a valiant attempt to become the Casanova of his dreams. Don't expect Renoir, but fans of Richard (*Les Comperes, Tall Blond Man*) will be entertained in this romantic comedy. (French with English subtitles) ★★½

Too Young to Die

(1990, 100 min, US, Robert Markowitz) *Juliette Lewis, Brad Pitt, Michael Tucker, Alan Fudge, Emily Longstreth, Michael O'Keefe.* Pitt and Lewis pay a low-budget visit to *Natural Born Killers* territory with this made-for-TV movie. In The-Middle-of-Nowhere, Oklahoma, 14-year-old Amanda (Lewis) hits the road and is appropriated by Pitt, who delivers a dress rehearsal for his *Kalifornia* role. *Too Young to Die*'s somewhat plodding exposition is enhanced by competent performances, especially from Lewis as the tragic teen. Worth checking out if only to compare Lewis and Pitt with their more recent work. ★★½ VHS: $9.99

Tootsie

(1982, 110 min, US, Sydney Pollack) *Dustin Hoffman, Jessica Lange, Teri Garr, Dabney Coleman, Sydney Pollack, Bill Murray, Charles Durning.* Hoffman legitimizes transvestism in this glorious comedy and slyly stirring social criticism. Forced (?) to don women's garb to propel his acting career, Dustin becomes the queen of the daytime soaps and the thwarted victim of his attraction to a female costar (Academy Award winner Lange). The film features great dialogue and a sparkling supporting cast. ★★★★ DVD Letterbox: $19.99, VHS: $9.99

Top Gun

(1986, 94 min, US, Tony Scott) *Tom Cruise, Kelly McGillis, Val Kilmer, Anthony Edwards, Tom Skerritt, Meg Ryan, Tim Robbins, Michael Ironside, John Stockwell, Barry Tubb, Rick Rossovich, Whip Hubley, Adrian Pasdar.* Military jingoism, fine aerial photography, inane dramatics and young Cruise combined to make this one of the big box-office hits of the 1980s. Story follows hotshot Navy pilot Cruise and his attraction to instructor/astrophysicist (yeah, right) McGillis. ★★ DVD Letterbox: $19.99, DVD Letterbox Special Collector's Edition: 2-Disc Set: $19.99, VHS: $9.99, VHS Letterbox: $9.99

Top Hat

(1935, 99 min, US, Mark Sandrich) *Fred Astaire, Ginger Rogers, Edward Everet Horton, Helen Broderick, Eric Blore.* The quintessential Astaire-Rogers musical, *Top Hat* is a breathless combination of glorious music, marvelous dance routines, captivating and sometimes silly comedy, and a cast of characters anyone would want to invite to their next soirée. The film's contrivance of a plot centers on dancer Fred falling for model Ginger. But through a case of mistaken identity, she thinks he's married, and to a society friend she's about to meet. Horton is just perfect as Astaire's best friend. The score is one of their best, and includes "Cheek to Cheek," "Isn't This a Lovely Day to Be Caught in the Rain" and the title tune. ★★★★

Top Secret!

(1984, 90 min, US, David Zucker, Jerry Zucker, Jim Abrahams) *Val Kilmer, Lucy Gutteridge, Omar Sharif.* From the team that brought us *Airplane!* and *The Naked Gun* comes this funny spoof of the espionage-thriller genre. Kilmer stars as an Elvis-like pop star who travels to East Germany on a goodwill tour and gets wrapped up in the local intrigue. As in their other films, the ZAZ team throws up a relentless barrage of sight gags, pratfalls and one-liners, some of which miss their mark; but there are so many direct hits that the laughter never ceases. This is good, stupid, silly fun at its best. ★★★ DVD Letterbox: $14.99, VHS: $9.99

Topaz

(1969, 143 min, US, Alfred Hitchcock) *John Forsythe, Frederick Stafford, Philippe Noiret.* When American agent Forsythe and French counterpart Stafford uncover Russian infiltration in Cuba, a whirlwind chain of events whisks them around the globe and deep into high intrigue. Though the complex screenplay is occasionally baffling, Hitchcock sustains a tension throughout. ★★★ DVD: $29.99, VHS: $14.99

Topaze

(1933, 78 min, US, Harry D'Arrast) *John Barrymore, Myrna Loy.* Barrymore gives a sterling performance in this charming comedy based on Marcel Pagnol's play. Barrymore plays a naïve college professor who is unknowingly exploited by a shady businessman — or is he? ★★★

Topaze

(1933, 95 min, France, Louis Gasnier) *Louis Jouvet, Edwige Feuillere.* Based on the Marcel Pagnol play, this comedy of morals was a popular success on its initial release although Pagnol was disappointed with it and remade the film, directing it himself in 1936 and again in 1951. Interestingly, it is this version that has survived the test of time. Topaze (Jouvet), a naïve and scrupulously honest provincial schoolteacher, is unwittingly lured into a phony business scheme with a disreputable financier. About to take the fall, our hero soon realizes that doing the right thing is not always the wisest course and soon develops his own plot to not only swindle the swindler, but to have his mistress as well. (French with English subtitles) ★★★½ VHS: $59.99

Topkapi

(1964, 120 min, US, Jules Dassin) *Maximilian Schell, Melina Mercouri, Peter Ustinov, Robert Morley.* Dassin's often imitated gem of a movie about a gang of jewel thieves who plan an elaborate heist of the emerald encrusted dagger at the Topkapi Palace in Istanbul. Schell and Mercouri star, but it was Ustinov who grabbed the Oscar for Best Supporting Actor in his inspired portrayal of their lackey. ★★★★ DVD Letterbox: $19.99

El Topo

(1971, 124 min, Mexico, Alexandro Jodorowsky) *Alexandro Jodorowsky.* This religious allegory, which has taken on mythical cult proportions, is imbued with cryptic symbolism and graphically detailed violence. The story follows El Topo (Jodorowsky), who — with his seven-year-old son in tow — sets out on a bloody odyssey through an 1800s western frontier desert seeking revenge and religious fulfillment. Filled with Fellini-esque characters and biblical references, this eclectic "hippie western" seems a bit ridiculous today as compared to the early '70s when it was enthusiastically received; but through its powerful imagery and other-worldliness, *El Topo* still retains a strange power and beauty. ★★★

Topper

(1937, 184 min, US, Norman Z. McLeod) *Cary Grant, Constance Bennett, Roland Young, Billie Burke.* This delightful ghost comedy stars Grant and Bennett as the Kirbys, who are accidentally killed in a car crash and return as spirits to haunt the ordered life of their banker, Cosmo Topper. Young gives a remarkably funny performance as the harried Topper, and Burke is perfect as Topper's rather scatterbrained, but lovable wife. (Followed by 2 sequels) (DVD includes *Topper Returns*) ★★★½ DVD 2-film set: $19.99

Topper Returns

(1941, 88 min, US, Roy Del Ruth) *Roland Young, Joan Blondell, Billie Burke, Eddie Anderson.* More hilarity with Cosmo Topper and friends. Young repeats his role for a third time as the timid banker, who here befriends ghostly Blondell, helping her solve her own murder. The wonderful Burke also returns as Mrs. Topper. Though the original has more style, here the laughs are nonstop. (DVD includes *Topper*) ★★★½ DVD: $19.99

THE DISCERNING FILM LOVER'S GUIDE

Tora! Tora! Tora!

Topsy-Turvy

(1999, 160 min, GB, Mike Leigh) *Jim Broadbent, Allan Corduner, Ron Cook, Lesley Manville, Timothy Spall, Alison Steadman.* Leigh turns his sights from the ordinary lives of contemporary Brits and sets them towards those of two of England's most celebrated 19th-century composers, Gilbert & Sullivan. In this magical, captivating musical, Leigh explores the genesis behind the duo's most famous work, "The Mikado." Great sets and costumes underscore some marvelous musical sequences of the opera, and backstage politics haven't been this satisfying since *All about Eve.* An intelligent, elegant musical biography that's a joy to watch. And you don't have to know a stitch about opera to enjoy. ★★★★

Tora! Tora! Tora!

(1970, 143 min, US/Japan, Kinji Fukasuku, Richard Fleischer, Toshio Masuda) *Jason Robards, Joseph Cotten, Tatsuya Mihashi, Martin Balsam, James Whitmore.* This expensive war drama is an impeccably produced re-creation of the bombing of Pearl Harbor, and the events which led to the devastating action which thrust America into WWII. ★★★ DVD: $14.99, VHS: $9.99

Torch Song

(1953, 91 min, US, Charles Walters) *Joan Crawford, Michael Wilding, Marjorie Rambeau, Gig Young.* Music-filled melodrama about a domineering star (Crawford) who finds love and learns humility in the arms of a blind pianist (Wilding). Rambeau received an Oscar-nomination as Crawford's mother. ★★★

Torch Song Trilogy

(1988, 117 min, US, Paul Bogart) *Harvey Fierstein, Matthew Broderick, Anne Bancroft, Brian Kerwin, Karen Young, Charles Pierce, Eddie Castrodad, Ken Page.* Fierstein's breakthrough Tony Award-winning play (which ran almost four hours on the stage) about the life and loves of the most lovable drag queen in Brooklyn reaches the screen at half the running time but with most of the play's warm humor and acute insights intact.

Fierstein, in a partly autobiographical role, is both touching and hilarious as Arnold Beckoff, whose life is presented in three non-episodic acts which examine his relationships with his bisexual boyfriend (Kerwin), gay lover (Broderick), and mother (Bancroft). ★★★ DVD: $19.99

Torment

(1944, 105 min, Sweden, Alf Sjoberg) *Mai Zetterling, Stig Jarrel.* Bergman's first screenplay explores the themes recurrent throughout his film career: sexual conflict, moral dilemma and the vulnerable nature of love. This gritty drama follows the love triangle between a young college student, a sadistic teacher and the girl with whom both are involved. (Swedish with English subtitles) ★★★ VHS: $29.99

Torn Apart

(1989, 96 min, Israel, Jack Fisher) *Adrian Pasdar, Cecilia Peck.* The Romeo and Juliet story is given a new, Israeli slant in this well-intentioned story of a Jew who falls in love with an Arab. A young man, after spending six years in the United States, returns to Israel to enlist in the army and is soon reunited with his childhood friend, a lovely Arab woman. Their relationship sparks the reactions one would expect from their two families. A warm, humanist drama with convincing, heartfelt performances from the young leads. (Hebrew with English subtitles) ★★★

Torn Curtain

(1966, 128 min, US, Alfred Hitchcock) *Paul Newman, Julie Andrews, Lila Kedrova.* Renowned for a brutally protracted murder sequence, this tale of Cold War espionage features Newman as an atomic scientist charading as a defector in order to gain access to information on a valuable formula. An efficient thriller from Hitchcock. ★★★ DVD: $29.99, VHS: $14.99

Torrents of Spring

(1990, 102 min, France/GB/Italy, Jerzy Skolimowski) *Nastassja Kinski, Timothy Hutton.* Kinski rivals Rutger Hauer in starring in the greatest number of really bad foreign films but whose

charisma and sheer force of personality gives her fans the strength to wade through the seemingly interminable cinematic muck. This tepid costume drama of burning passions is adapted from Ivan Turgenev's novel. Kinski stars as a wealthy married temptress who playfully teases a young aristocrat (Hutton) torn between his love for two women. ★ DVD: $19.99

Torso

(1973, 92 min, Italy, Sergio Martino) *Suzy Kendall, Tina Aumont, Luc Merenda, John Richardson.* A series of grisly murders prompts a group of comely damsels to leave the city and take refuge in a secluded rural villa. Tthen, the murders continue at the new locale unabated. Unapologetically sleazy, the gory *Torso* is imaginatively directed, though not nearly as stylish as the best "giallos" (Italian thrillers) of the period. Filled with rampant nudity, sex and violence, this is definitely a product of its era; it's also a surprisingly entertaining and suspenseful (especially the last twenty minutes or so) shocker. ★★★ DVD: $29.99, VHS: $14.99

Tortilla Flat

(1942, 105 min, US, Victor Fleming) *Spencer Tracy, Frank Morgan, Hedy Lamarr, John Garfield, Akim Tamiroff.* Morgan's fearless portrayal of an eccentric dog lover highlights this moving screen adaptation of John Steinbeck's novel of life on the wrong side of the tracks. Tracy and Garfield are down-on-their-luck buddies who drift their way into a small California town and fall for the same woman (Lamarr at her best) while setting up a scam on Morgan. ★★★

The Torture Chamber of Baron Blood

(1972, 90 min, Italy, Mario Bava) *Joseph Cotten, Elke Sommer.* Intriguing set design and unusual lighting effects highlight this story of a young man who inadvertently brings back to life the vengeful corpse of his bloodthirsty, sadistic ancestor. (aka: *Baron Blood*) ★★

The Torture Chamber of Dr. Sadism

(1967, 90 min, West Germany, Harald Reinl) *Christopher Lee, Karin Dor.* Effective bit of Grand Guignol finds Lee dismembered for killing 12 virgins. But 40 years later, when his ever-faithful batman puts him back together, Chris is out to party with virgin #13. (aka: *Blood Demon* and *Castle of the Walking Dead*) ★★½ VHS: $19.99

Tosca's Kiss

(1985, 87 min, Switzerland, Daniel Schmid) The setting for this affectionate and moving documentary is Casa Verdi, a home for retired opera singers established by Guiseppi Verdi at the turn of the century. The focus is on the aging but still vibrant habitués who shamelessly preen, argue and perform for the viewer. (Italian with English subtitles) ★★★ VHS: $39.99

Total Eclipse

(1995, 112 min, France/GB, Agnieszka Holland) *David Thewlis, Leonardo DiCaprio, Romane Bohringer.* A laughably bad melodrama about the love affair of 19th-century poets Arthur Rimbaud and Verlaine. While delivering on the promise of an unblinking depiction of gay love, this fails in just about every other aspect. The story is set in France where 16-year-old Rimbaud (DiCaprio), teen rebel and poet, arrives in Paris to cooly make his mark on the world. His first order of business is to snag himself a sugar daddy — enter Verlaine (Thewlis), a 30ish disagreeable man who harbors the triple demons of greed, pretension and ambition. Sexual energy and narcissistic attraction fuel their ultimately tragic love-hate relationship. DiCaprio's portrayal is simply one of a sugar-cereal propelled, California teenager. ★ DVD: $24.99

Total Recall
(1990, 109 min, US, Paul Verhoeven) *Arnold Schwarzenegger, Sharon Stone, Rachel Ticotin, Ronny Cox, Michael Ironside.* The elements of this production are a clear recipe for success: Dutch helmer Verhoeven directing Arnold in a space sci-fi adventure based on a story by Phillip K. Dick (whose "Do Androids Dream of Electric Sheep?" inspired *Blade Runner*). The film's only flaw might be a few unpolished scenes and its more-than-too-much gratuitous violence. Beyond that, Verhoeven and Schwarzenegger romp through this high-speed, action-packed fugitive-on-the-run tale with a tongue-in-cheek and very playful glee. ★★★ DVD Special Edition: $14.99

Totally F***ed Up
(1994, 85 min, US, Gregg Araki) *James Duval, Roko Belic, Susan Behshid, Jenee Gill, Gilbert Luna, Craig Gilmore.* Araki's angry, entertaining and provocative "homomovie" follows the lives, loves and fucked-up misadventures of six teens (4 gays and 2 lesbians) whose friendship provide a '90s-style family unit. A successful combination of queer teen angst, homophobia, gay-bashing, AIDS and suicide. A witty, energetic and subversive drama. ★★★ VHS: $29.99

Toto the Hero (Toto le Heros)
(1991, 90 min, Belgium, Jaco Van Dormael) *Michel Bouquet, Jo De Backer.* Stylistically inventive and delightfully off-kilter, this bittersweet tale of the joys and traumas of childhood makes for a captivating and entertaining film. Thomas is a middle-class boy absorbed in a fantasy world of secret agents and flights of adventure. He is also convinced that he was switched at birth with Alfred, his rich neighbor's son. That idea, carried through to old age, becomes an obsession and obstacle to growth as Alfred becomes his lifelong nemesis — a

symbol of everything he is not. The film intercuts scenes from the boy's childhood with his life as a young man as well as the present, where Thomas, now an old man in a retirement home, decides to finally come to grips with his failures and lost dreams. A hard-edged comedy which captures the seemingly insignificant moments of childhood and their lasting, debilitating effect. (French with English subtitles) ★★★★

Touch
(1997, 97 min, US, Paul Schrader) *Bridget Fonda, Skeet Ulrich, Christopher Walken, Tom Arnold, Gina Gershon, Lolita Davidovich, Janeane Garofalo.* This unfocused adaptation of Elmore Leonard's novel is never sarcastic enough to be full-fledged satire, or serious enough to make much of an impact. While this offbeat film boasts a good ensemble, Schrader does not always know what to do with the story's strange characters. *Touch* seems to delight in poking fun at easy targets such as an airhead talk show hostess (Gershon), or an extremist religious group leader (Arnold). However, the film has considerably more trouble sustaining interest in its main character, Juvenal (Ulrich), a faith healer who is worshipped by just about everyone. *Touch* also suffers from choppy pacing and bad editing — as many scenes ring true as fall flat. ★★

The Touch
(1971, 112 min, Sweden, Ingmar Bergman) *Bibi Andersson, Max von Sydow, Elliott Gould.* Bergman's first English-language film certainly does not rank as one of the master's greatest works, but this sensitive and subtle story of a love triangle does have its moments. Andersson plays a "happily married" woman who, although settled and secure with doctor/husband von Sydow, is lured into an affair with volatile but magnetic archaeologist Gould. The human drama of the three, as they attempt to understand their actions and each other, makes this an interesting work. ★★½

A Touch of Class
(1972, 105 min, GB, Melvin Frank) *Glenda Jackson, Paul Sorvino, George Segal.* Jackson won her second Oscar as the vivacious Alessio, a Londoner in the "rag trade" who falls in love with an American businessman (Segal) who has a wife on the side. The dynamic chemistry between the two leads propels this witty, romantic and touching account of a brief love affair. ★★★½ DVD Letterbox: $19.99

Touch of Evil
(1958, 108 min, US, Orson Welles) *Charlton Heston, Orson Welles, Janet Leigh, Akim Tamiroff, Marlene Dietrich.* Cinema's legendary bad boy, Welles, directed and stars in this brooding, stylistic tour de force as a police inspector embroiled in a case on the Mexican border. A masterful exposé on moral decay, smothered in Gothic expressionism and tawdry urban landscapes. ★★★★ DVD: $14.99, VHS: $19.99

Tough Guys
(1986, 104 min, US, Jeff Kanew) *Burt Lancaster, Kirk Douglas, Dana Carvey, Charles Durning, Eli Wallach.* Lancaster and Douglas teamed a fifth time for this disappointing comedy which is not worthy of its two stars. The two screen legends play ex-cons, released after 30 years in prison, who find difficulty in adjusting to the 1980s lifestyle. ★★

Tough Guys Don't Dance
(1987, 110 min, US, Norman Mailer) *Ryan O'Neal, Isabella Rossellini, Wings Hauser, Lawrence Tierney.* Confusing murder mystery written and directed by Mailer (from his own novel) about a writer (O'Neal) accused of murder, forced to clear his name. A real curiosity, with director Mailer echoing the atmosphere of the film noir gems of long ago, but hampered by some cheesy dialogue and bizarre plot contrivances. ★★ DVD Letterbox: $19.99

Toute Une Nuit
(1982, 90 min, Belgium, Chantal Akerman) *Aurore Clement, Tcheky Karyo, Jan Decorte, Natalia Akerman.* Abandoning standard narrative plot, Akerman's own minimalist, avant-garde story of the follies of sex and love is set on one torrid summer night in Brussels. Told in a series of amorous fragments, the film follows the various mating rites of several couples as they meet, fall in love, eat, drink and then break up. An austere yet strangely riveting experimental melodrama that is certainly not for all audiences. (French with English subtitles) ★★★ VHS: $29.99

Tower of London
(1939, 93 min, US, Rowland V. Lee) *Basil Rathbone, Boris Karloff, Vincent Price.* Rathbone kills his way to the top as Richard III in this above-average historical thriller. Gleefully overacting, he leads a solid cast which also includes a young Price as a weakling Duke and Karloff as Richard's medieval "campaign organizer," the clubfooted executioner Mord. Playing out his crimes on a set of dolls made to represent his contemporaries in the royal court, Rathbone slowly gets bolder and bolder until his schemes are naturally undone in the end. (Remade in 1962 with Price taking the role of Richard) ★★★

The Towering Inferno
(1974, 165 min, US, John Guillermin) *Paul Newman, Steve McQueen, Faye Dunaway, William Holden, Richard Chamberlain, Robert Vaughn, Fred Astaire, Jennifer Jones.* A mammoth production can't hide the loose ends to this half-baked disaster epic. An all-star cast is featured to tell the story of a skyscraper's gala opening, and the crisis which follows when the building catches fire. Watch these smoked hams get roasted. The technical aspects of the film are very good, but it's especially mean-spirited. ★★½ DVD Letterbox: $9.99

Towers Open Fire
(1962, 35 min, US, Antony Balch) *William Burroughs.* Burroughs is featured in two shorts in this compilation of four art films from independent filmmaker Antony Balch. *Towers Open Fire* and *The Cut-Ups* attempt to make a cinematic equivalent to Burroughs' famous "cut and paste" style of writing. As Burroughs narrates, we watch a visual collage of his writing containing many of the author's key themes. Although trying at times (watching five minutes of voice-over intoning repeatedly "yes-no" is a good test), the films are of great interest to both experimental film lovers and Burroughs fans. ★★½ VHS: $29.99

Town & Country
(2001, 95 min, US, Peter Chelsom) *Warren Beatty, Diane Keaton, Garry Shandling, Goldie Hawn, Andie MacDowell, Jenna Elfman, Nastassja Kinski,*

Charlton Heston, Marian Seldes. In the vein of *Hudson Hawk* and *The Postman,* director Chelsom's sloppy, unfunny *Town & Country* joins the ranks of Hollywood's reigning big-budget mega-flop disasters. Beatty plays an aging architect enduring a midlife crisis; Keaton, Shandling and Hawn play his befuddled wife and friends, respectively. It's impossible to see what attracted such prestigious talent to this clumsy affair because the film's been so choppily edited that the plot never gains any comic momentum: punchlines are delivered without being properly set up; other jokes fall flat or are abandoned unfinished; and peripheral characters appear and disappear. It's a dreadful mess with one sole bright spot: Seldes' all-too-brief but deliciously vulgar turn as MacDowell's cranky, wheelchair-bound mother. ★½ DVD: $9.99, VHS: $9.99

The Town Is Quiet

(2000, 132 min, France, Robert Guediguian) *Ariane Ascaride, Jean-Pierre Darroussin, Gérard Meylan, Jacques Boudet.* Leisurely paced but ultimately rewarding, the politically charged *The Town Is Quiet* will appeal most to fans of John Sayles and Robert Altman, to whom Guediguian seems to owe somewhat of a debt. The intertwining lives of a handful of disparate characters in modern-day Marseilles form the basis of this ensemble drama — characters who may differ in class but who are all subject to the ennui of life's daily grind. Despite its slow pace, the film builds to a satisfying wrap-up, thanks especially to excellent performances and a confident use of music (can you remember the last time Joplin has been used this effectively?). Emotional, stirring if slightly overlong, *The Town Is Quiet* dissects a city and its inhabitants in personal, moving vignettes as it challenges our very notions of social behavior. (French with English subtitles) ★★★ DVD: $19.99, VHS: $29.99

A Town Like Alice

(1980, 301 min, Australia, David Stevens) *Bryan Brown, Helen Morse.* This mammoth drama of love and separation is taken from the best-selling novel by Neville Shute. The story is set against the brutal chaos of WWII. While in a Japanese POW camp in steamy Malaysia, an ever-cheerful Australian and an equally resilient English woman meet and fall in love. They are soon separated, but in the ensuing years meet again in the rugged outback of Australia. ★★★

The Toxic Avenger

(1985, 100 min, US, Michael Herz & Samuel Weil) Idiotic cult comedy, though not without a few laughs, about a goofy nerd who is pushed into toxic waste and comes out a super-human crime-fighter from New Jersey. Sick humor and effects abound. ★½ DVD: $24.99, VHS: $14.99

Toy Soldiers

(1991, 112 min, US, Daniel Petrie) *Sean Astin, Wil Wheaton, Keith Coogan, Louis Gossett, Jr., Denholm Elliott.* A group of young prep school students, led by rebellious Astin, band together to take back their school from gun-toting terrorists who are holding the rich kids for ransom. This is a surprisingly effective suspenser, with well-done action scenes and a young cast presenting believable and likable characters. ★★★ DVD Pan & Scan: $14.99, VHS: $9.99

Toy Story 2

Toy Story

(1995, 81 min, US, John Lasseter) *Voices of: Tom Hanks, Tim Allen, Don Rickles, Wallace Shawn, Jim Varney, Laurie Metcalf, R. Lee Ermey.* With the first all-computer-animated feature film, the folks at Disney have made more than just a technical marvel, *Toy Story* is an exhilarating combination of sight, sound and story which is as funny and entertaining as it is groundbreaking. Confirming every child's suspicions, *Toy Story* is set in a magical world where toys come to life — but only when humans aren't around. Six-year-old Andy's favorite toy is Woody, a pull-string talking cowboy. That is until a new toy arrives, a state-of-the-art astronaut named Buzz Lightyear, to rival Woody for Andy's affections. It's then a game of one-upmanship as the two toys engage in a series of captivating misadventures. This is one family film that delivers . . . to infinity and beyond. (Sequel: *Toy Story 2*) ★★★★ VHS: $22.99

Toy Story 2

(1999, 92 min, US, John Lasseter) *Voices of: Tom Hanks, Tim Allen, Jim Varney, Don Rickles, John Ratzenberger, Joan Cusack, Kelsey Grammer, Wallace Shawn, Wayne Knight, Annie Potts, R. Lee Ermey.* Displaying the same combination of superb animation and winning, funny story line as its predecessor, *Toy Story 2* is a worthy and entertaining sequel to the 1995 smash hit. When stolen by a toy collector who (shudder) keeps his toys in their original boxes, Woody finds his long-lost family (the rest of the original set), including Jessie and Stinky Pete. It's up to Buzz Lightyear and the gang to save Woody from a life packed in styrofoam. But does Woody really want to come back to Andy and friends? Another delightful comic adventure courtesy of Woody, Buzz and friends. ★★★½ DVD: $29.99, VHS: $22.99

Toys

(1992, 121 min, US, Barry Levinson) *Robin Williams, Michael Gambon, Joan Cusack, LL Cool J, Donald O'Connor.* Writer-director Levinson must have dropped acid one day and walked through F.A.O. Schwartz to come up with this colorful but mind-bogglingly leaden satire. Williams plays the son of a toy magnate who loses his inheritance of the company when his father passes away. Instead, the enterprise is given to his uncle, a nasty general (Gambon) who plans to produce war toys. Eventually, militaristic Gambon and innocent Williams have a showdown, and the destructive toys go ballistic. ★½ DVD: $14.99, VHS: $6.99

Toys in the Attic

(1963, 91 min, US, George Roy Hill) *Geraldine Page, Dean Martin, Wendy Hiller, Gene Tierney, Yvette Mimieux.* A good cast can't enliven this tedious Gothic drama based on Lillian Hellman's stage play. Martin plays the ne'er-do-well brother of spinsters Page and Hiller. With his young wife (Mimieux), he returns to his New Orleans home suspiciously boasting of new wealth. Their presence there paves the way to betrayal, recriminations, and long-hidden secrets exposed. Page and Hiller are effective, though even they can't overcome the film's contrivances. ★½

Traces of Red

(1992, 105 min, US, Andy Wolk) *James Belushi, Lorraine Bracco, Tony Goldwyn, William Russ.* An incredibly convoluted whodunit about a Palm Beach cop (Belushi) who becomes both hunter and hunted when his bedmates start turning up dead (murder or mercy — you decide). While the film offers credible performances and a decent mystery with a good deal of twists, there are ultimately no traces of logic to be found, and only traces of dread at the too-tricky-for-its-own-good surprise ending. ★½ VHS: $9.99

Track 29

(1988, 86 min, GB, Nicolas Roeg) *Gary Oldman, Theresa Russell, Christopher Lloyd, Sandra Bernhard, Colleen Camp, Seymour Cassel.* Roeg's playfully beguiling mystery stars Russell as a bored young woman trapped in a loveless and childless marriage with model train and S&M enthusiast Lloyd. The woman's life is changed when she is (possibly) visited by a young British stranger (Oldman) who claims that he is her abandoned-at-birth son. Is he a con man or prodigal son, a real person or only the figment of her rapidly deteriorating mind? Any fan of Roeg will know that the answer does not come simply in this visually exciting drama. ★★★ VHS: $14.99

Tracks

(1974, 90 min, US, Henry Jaglom) *Dennis Hopper, Dean Stockwell.* A Vietnam vet (Hopper) meets a wide array of characters while on a train. However, he is soon overtaken with war-induced paranoia. With a more traditional narrative than his other films, director Jaglom weaves a compelling and insightful tale — years before the subject matter became en vogue. ★★★ VHS: $7.99

Trading Hearts

(1987, 88 min, US, Neil Leifer) *Raul Julia, Beverly D'Angelo, Jenny Lewis.* Ineffective romantic romp about an over-the-hill baseball pitcher (Julia) and a minor league singer (D'Angelo) in 1957 Florida, complicated by a mischievous 11-year-old who thinks they should all live together. ★★ VHS: $14.99

Trading Places

(1983, 106 min, US, John Landis) *Eddie Murphy, Dan Aykroyd, Jamie Lee Curtis, Ralph Bellamy, Don Ameche, Denholm Elliott.* Aykroyd and Murphy are hilarious as a millionaire and street hustler, respectively, who trade places in this silly but vastly amusing comedy. The inspired casting is what raises this film above the usual "Saturday Night Live" alumni mode of filmmaking. Bellamy and Ameche are great as a pair of incredibly sleazy capitalist brothers. Elliott walks away with the film as an incredulous butler. And Curtis is the hooker with a heart of gold. ★★★½ DVD Letterbox: $14.99, VHS: $9.99

Traffic

(1971, 89 min, France, Jacques Tati) *Jacques Tati.* Tati stars as Monsieur Hulot, that charming and naïve fool, in this hilariously chaotic comedy. Armed with youthful enthusiasm, M. Hulot attempts to transport a car from France to Holland for an auto show, and the results are side-splitting. A satire on modern living, *Traffic* takes great pleasure in dissecting the absurdity of a situation where neurosis reigns behind the wheel. There is very little dialogue, and even though there are no subtitles, those who do not understand word one of French will be able to follow with ease this visually funny film. ★★★★ VHS: $19.99

Traffic

(2000, 147 min, US, Steven Soderbergh) *Michael Douglas, Benicio del Toro, Catherine Zeta-Jones, Don Cheadle, Dennis Quaid, Luis Guzman, Corey Spears, Erika Christensen, Miguel Ferrer, Amy Irving, Topher Grace, Benjamin Bratt, Albert*

Finney, James Brolin. Based on the BBC miniseries "Traffik," this explosive look at the internatonal drug trade is extraordinary filmmaking. Several story lines are skillfully woven together to examine the war on drugs — the complete arc from distribution to drug use to enforcement on both sides of the border. Among an outstanding ensemble: Douglas is the newly appointed drug czar fighting his own war at home; the exceptional, Oscar-winning Del Toro is a Mexican cop out to stop a cartel; Cheadle and Guzman are his American counterparts; Zeta-Jones is the wife of a drug dealer about to receive a quick lesson in business; and Christensen is Douglas' addicted daughter. Soderbergh brings an almost documentary-like feel to the movie, contrasting film stocks for different locales, and giving the film a tense, fly-on-the-wall perspective. It is masterful storytelling, with no moral indignation, no polemic at work. *Traffic* is set in an adult world, and is a mature and sobering wake-up call for not only parents and children, but our ineffectual government as well. Winner of 4 Academy Awards including Best Director. ★★★★ DVD Letterbox Criterion Collection: $39.99, DVD: $14.99, VHS: $9.99

Traffic in Souls

(1913, 88 min, US, George Loane Tucker) *Matt Moore, Jane Gail.* A docudrama decades before the coining of that dreadful term, *Traffic in Souls* dramatized some of the more sensational aspects of the 1910 Rockefeller White Slavery Report for New York City. As the gateway for America, N.Y.C. found itself the hub of a syndicate comprised of crooked judges, cops and criminals who kidnapped immigrating women into dens of prostitution. While some of the dramaturgy may be creaky, and the interior sets decidely *trompe l'oeil*, the location shooting gives *Traffic in Souls* the feeling of an bygone era tinged with a contemporary atmosphere. ★★★½ VHS: $29.99

The Tragedy of a Ridiculous Man

(1981, 116 min, Italy, Bernardo Bertolucci) *Ugo Tognazzi, Anouk Aimée.* This psychological parable on terrorism and the clash between capitalism and leftist politics in Italy is at best a muddled exercise that seems to purposefully confuse and distance its audience. Tognazzi is a self-made man and materialistic owner of a sprawling Parma cheese factory who witnesses his left-leaning son being forcibly thrown into a car and kidnapped. But was this a real abduction or was his son in collusion with his kid-

nappers? Not knowing for sure, he relunctantly raises the ransom, but is undecided whether he should help his son or use the money to prop up his failing business. An admirable but unsatisfying experience. (Italian with English subtitles) ★★ VHS: $59.99

The Tragedy of Carmen

(1983, 82 min, GB, Peter Brook) Brook gives a radical new look to Bizet's classic opera. Opting to emphasize the story over the spectacle, Brook has pared down the cast to seven, reduced the size of the orchestra and gone for a completely naturalistic look as filmed by cinematographer Sven Nykvist. For fans of Brook, this is a must; but the video's one flaw is that it lacks subtiling for the libretto. ★★★

The Trail of the Pink Panther

(1982, 97 min, GB, Blake Edwards) Shortly after Peter Sellers' death, Edwards slapped together this sorry excuse for a film out of old bits and pieces of yet unseen footage from earlier *Panther* films. These out-takes are strung together with a flimsy story line about a reporter who interviews anyone he can find who knew Clouseau. Not worth the film it's printed on. ★

The Train

(1965, 133 min, US, John Frankenheimer) *Burt Lancaster, Paul Scofield, Jeanne Moreau, Suzanne Flon, Michel Simon.* A solid, rousing thriller from director Frankenheimer. Set in 1944 Occupied France, the story follows the exploits of the French Resistance and trainman Lancaster who try to prevent the Nazis from shipping stolen art treasures to Germany via Burt's train. Scofield is the Nazi general assigned the task of guarding the confiscated art works. Like another actioner set almost entirely aboard a train, *The Taking of Pelham One Two Three*, from a simple plot line comes such high-powered suspense. ★★★½ DVD: $14.99

Training Day

(2001, 120 min, US, Antoine Fuqua) *Denzel Washington, Ethan Hawke, Scott Glenn, Cliff Curtis, Dr. Dre, Snoop Dogg, Tom Berenger, Harris Yulin, Macy Gray, Raymond J. Barry.* Denzel Washington has made a career in portraying likable or, at least, sympathetic characters, bringing to each some shred of human decency. To witness his mesmerizing, Oscar-winning performance in the intense *Training Day*, playing a rogue cop with no moral center, is to see a great actor at work. Washington plays Alonzo Harris, an undercover narcotics officer in Los Angeles, who takes rookie cop Jake Hoyt (a very effective Hawke) under his wing when Hoyt applies for Harris' elite group. In one day's time, Hoyt becomes involved in murder, drugs, conspiracy, police brutality and money laundering: It's a day Hoyt is not likely to forget. David Ayer's gritty screenplay may border on incredulous in a few scenes (especially a formulaic ending which belies the intelligence that came before it), but for the most part *Training Day* is an often hypnotic, hard-hitting, dark-edged thriller that goes for the gut. ★★★ DVD Letterbox: $14.99, VHS Includes bonus footage and alternate ending: $14.99

Trainspotting

(1996, 94 min, Scotland, Danny Boyle) *Ewan McGregor, Ewen Bremner, Jonny Lee Miller, Kevin McKidd, Robert Carlyle, Kelly MacDonald.* A swaggering, highly stylized and pulsating cinematic ride, *Trainspotting* is an in-your-face adaptation of Irvine Welch's novel and play about life among a merry band of heroin addicts living it up in the lower depths of Edinburgh. Refreshingly unrepen-

Erika Christensen and Topher Grace in Steven Soderbergh's *Traffic*

tent in tone, director Boyle puts a fun-filled spin on the world of skag as seen through the eyes of its narrator, Renton (McGregor). He's a wiry and likable antihero who takes up residence in a squalid squat with a group of fellow travellers. As much as it explores the drug subculture, *Trainspotting* is also a merciless social critique that ultimately eyes the pursuit of happiness through substance as the moral equal to that of material acquisition. Sheer excitement, it's punctuated nicely by a hip, drug-inspired rock soundtrack. ★★★★ DVD Letterbox 2-disc Director's Edition: $29.99

Trancers

(1985, 76 min, US, Charles Band) *Tim Thomerson, Helen Hunt.* Intriguing sci-fi adventure (with more than a nod to *The Terminator*) about a trooper from the year 2247 who is sent back to present-day Los Angeles to stop a mystic from murdering a future leader. (aka: *Future Cop*) ★★½ DVD: $9.99

Transmutations

(1986, 103 min, GB, George Pavlou) *Denholm Elliott, Miranda Richardson.* A sinister biochemist (Elliott) creates a subhuman species which dwells in the city's underground. Desperate for an antidote, the creatures seek out the only woman who can save them (Richardson). Penned but later disowned by horror maven Clive Barker. (aka: *Underground*) ★★ VHS: $79.99

The Transporter

(2002, 92 min, France/GB, Corey Yuen) *Jason Statham, Shu Qi, François Berleand, Matt Schulze, Ric Young.* In this unremarkable action vehicle, Statham plays an all-business, tough-as-nails transporter-for-hire, demonstrated in an exciting opening car chase. Of course, this amoral criminal must find his inner cuddly bear when his current package turns out to be a young woman (actually, he only joins her cause after the bad guys try to kill him, which kind of dampens the hero image). The film becomes less involving and slower as it goes, since there's no real story or characters to hold one's attention. As for the action, there's little of it, though an all-too-brief martial arts fight in an oil slick stands out. The whole project smacks of cowriter Luc Besson's cynical emptiness, but Statham's omnipresent charisma keeps it afloat. ★★ DVD Special Edition: $19.99, VHS: $12.99

Trapeze

(1956, 106 min, US, Carol Reed) *Burt Lancaster, Tony Curtis, Gina Lollabrigida, Katy Jurado.* Truly remarkable trapeze footage, and three very appealing lead performances make for a slick romantic drama set against the hurly-burly backdrop of a Parisian circus. Lancaster, in splendid physical condition and doing most of his own stunts, stars as a retired trapeze artist — the only man alive who can perform a triple somersault. He is sought after by Curtis to teach him that near-impossible trick. All is well between them until beautiful and conniving Lollabrigida enters the scene. *The Greatest Show on Earth* was never this good. ★★★

Trapped

(2002, 99 min, US, Luis Mandoki) *Charlize Theron, Stuart Townsend, Kevin Bacon, Courtney Love, Pruitt Taylor Vince, Dakota Fanning.* Theron plays the wife of a wealthy anesthesiologist who will do anything to ensure her daughter's safety when she's kidnapped. These hoary plot twists slowly grind *Trapped* through the typical, unimaginative middle-of-the-road thriller tropes until its

Ewan McGregor in *Trainspotting*

laughably bad climax. When it isn't crushingly dull, the film is rather unpleasant (this milks the situation of a cute little girl in jeopardy till it's dry). The sole redeeming feature is young Fanning, who is effective as the smart, resourceful but terrified kidnap victim. Nobody else bothers to try, and no one could really blame them. ★ DVD Letterbox: $14.99, VHS: $102.99

Trapped in Paradise

(1994, 111 min, US, George Gallo) *Nicolas Cage, Jon Lovitz, Dana Carvey, Madchen Amick, Donald Moffat.* Three bickering brothers hold up a bank on Christmas Eve in a Rockwell-like small town. Their problems begin when they can't get out of town and the townsfolk who they've just robbed kill them with kindness. Cage plays against type as the moral backbone of the trio, Lovitz is (surprise!) the acerbic one, and Carvey plays the slow-witted sibling with a penchant for kleptomania. The screenplay offers them numerous comic situations but rarely develops any of them, though the entire cast seems eager to please. ★★ DVD: $14.99, VHS: $9.99

Trash

(1970, 110 min, US, Paul Morrissey) *Holly Woodlawn, Joe Dallesandro, Jane Forth, Michael Sklar, Andrea Feldman.* Woodlawn is truly memorable as the trash-collecting lover of impotent drug fiend Dallesandro in this wonderfully realistic slice-of-life film about New York's druggies and counterculture denizens. In this, her screen debut, Holly's character preserves her dignity and moral righteousness despite poverty, squalor and a forced-to-masturbate-with-a-beer-bottle-because-my-boyfriend-can't-get-it-up life. It is her character, and not the cute but almost catatonic Joe, which works against the film's not-so-subtle antidrug message; an attitude which keeps with the director's moralistic and reactionary philosophy. ★★★

Trauma

(1993, 106 min, Italy, Dario Argento) *Christopher Rydell, Piper Laurie, Asia Argento.* A mysterious killer prowls the streets of Minneapolis. His trademark: he decapitates his victims with the Noose-O-Matic. Meanwhile, an illustrator, David (Rydell), meets Aura (A. Argento), a disturbed youth undergoing treatment for anorexia. When her parents, including her psychic mother (Laurie), fall victim to the "Headhunter Killer," Aura enlists David's help in finding their murderer. More heads roll before the

two lovers discover the true identity of the assassin. The film is alternately gaudy, energetic, deliberately unrealistic and forceful in its style. ★★½

Traveller

(1997, 101 min, US, Jack Green) *Bill Paxton, Mark Wahlberg, Julianna Margulies, James Gammon.* An offbeat, often compelling independent drama that greatly loses its way by story's end, *Traveller* is a shaggy character study about a group of con artists — or "travellers" — making their way across the back roads of rural America. Paxton is a seasoned though small-time hustler who takes his young, estranged cousin Wahlberg under his wing. The film introduces these modern gypsies as an American subculture who are fearful of outsiders but who cannot live without them. *Traveller* is at its best when concentrating on the scam — though nothing in the film nears the ingenuity or precision of *The Grifters*. However, a good cast brings conviction to their roles. the film's sloppy ending all but falls apart. ★★½ DVD: $14.99, VHS: $14.99

Travelling North

(1987, 98 min, Australia, Carl Schultz) *Leo McKern, Julia Blake.* Charming story of a retired civil engineer (McKern) who, suspecting that his days are numbered, takes off with his lady-love (Blake) for a life of peaceful contentment at a cottage by the lake. McKern is at his blustery best as the Mozart-loving foreman with a talent for hurting those who love him; the entire cast contributes to making this a minor gem. ★★★

Travels with My Aunt

(1972, 109 min, GB, George Cukor) *Maggie Smith, Alec McCowen, Louis Gossett, Jr., Robert Stephens, Cindy Williams.* Smith received an Academy Award nomination for her delightfully eccentric performance as Aunt Augusta in this giddy and incandescent screen version of Graham Greene's novel. After the death of her estranged sister, the high-living Augusta swoops in and whisks her very unwilling nephew Henry (McCowen), an affably stodgy banker, from his ordered existence and proceeds to introduce him to high adventure on the road. They set upon a worldwide quest to raise money for one of her former lovers who has been kidnapped, and misadventures compile. Smith's performance is pure enchantment, shading a likable and larger-than-life portrayal with whimsy, wit and wonder. ★★★½ VHS: $14.99

La Traviata

(1982, 110 min, Italy, Franco Zeffirelli) *Placido Domingo, Teresa Stratas.* Zeffirelli's lavish, powerful rendition of Verdi's opera stars Domingo and Stratas in emotionally charged performances as the doomed lovers. Not just for opera fans! (Italian with English subtitles) ★★★½ DVD: $24.99

Treasure Island

(1934, 105 min, US, Victor Fleming) *Jackie Cooper, Wallace Beery, Lionel Barrymore.* Flavorful adaptation of Robert Louis Stevenson's classic adventure yarn about pirates, hidden treasure, and the small boy involved with both. Cooper is the youngster who lives every small child's fantasy, and Beery is an appropriately flamboyant Long John Silver. ★★★

The Treasure of the Sierra Madre

(1948, 124 min, US, John Huston) *Humphrey Bogart, Walter Huston, Tim Holt.* A taut parable on human greed and corruptibility based on the novel by the mysterious B. Traven. Bogart gives a memorable performance as the edgy Fred C. Dobbs, whose moral bent is fractured by his discovery of gold. Holt and W. Huston (Academy Award for Best Supporting Actor) are his fellow prospectors, combating bandits, betrayal and the ill effects of the yellow dust. J. Huston won Best Director and Best Screenplay Oscars. ★★★★ DVD 2-disc Special Edition: $26.99

A Tree Grows in Brooklyn

(1945, 128 min, US, Elia Kazan) *Dorothy McGuire, James Dunn, Peggy Ann Garner, Joan Blondell.* An outstanding film version of Betty Smith's novel about the hardships facing an Irish family living in a turn-of-the-century Brooklyn tenement. McGuire is splendid as the mother, with an Oscar-winning performance by Dunn as her alcoholic husband. Garner won a special juvenile Oscar for her sensitive portrayal of a young girl looking to escape her environment, and Blondell gives one of her best performances as Garner's aunt. ★★★★ VHS: $6.99

The Tree of Wooden Clogs

(1978, 186 min, Italy, Ermanno Olmi) *Luigi Omaghi, Francesca Moriggi.* In this deceptively simple epic, Olmi brilliantly reconstructs the peasant life in the Lombardy region of Italy at the turn-of-the-century. The director, using a non-professional cast and filming in almost documentary-like fashion, quietly explores the lives of four peasant families told through the eyes of a young boy. Long and leisurely paced, with the story told in a mosaic of small incidents, the film is not for everybody; but for those with patience and an appreciative mind, this film will prove to be an absorbing work of art. (Italian with English subtitles) ★★★★ DVD: $24.99

Trees Lounge

(1996, 94 min, US, Steve Buscemi) *Steve Buscemi, Chloë Sevigny, Anthony LaPaglia, Eszter Balint, Carol Kane, Samuel L. Jackson, Seymour Cassel.* An impressive directorial debut for actor Buscemi, who has crafted a succulent little slice-of-life offering that is both perceptive and sweetly compassionate. Buscemi stars as Tommy, that guy from the neighborhood whose life seems perpetually on pause. The story chronicles the events of one summer in his life as he careens amid a Runyonesque cast of characters, each sharply if briefly brought into focus by an on-target ensemble. Buscemi also wrote the wry and poignant screenplay, which

The Treasure of the Sierra Madre

spritely delineates Tommy's less-than-beneficial role on those around him. Heavy material is delivered with a light hand, and an unerring recognition of the minute details that define and propel a person's life. ★★★½ DVD: $14.99

Tremors

(1990, 96 min, US, Ron Underwood) *Kevin Bacon, Fred Ward, Michael Gross, Reba McIntire.* Taking off where the 1950s "monster-on-the-rampage" films and the Roger Corman exploitation flicks left off, this fun and funny horror film has its tongue firmly planted in its cinematic cheek. Set in a lonely, dust-covered Western town, a small group of people are invaded by mysterious underground creatures who have more than a passing resemblance to the man-eating worms from *Dune*. Bacon and Ward are hilarious as two out-of-their-element handymen who must confront the shy platyhelminths as they murderously slither through the town. (Followed by 2 sequels and a TV series) ★★★ DVD Collector's Edition: $24.99, VHS: $9.99

Trespass

(1992, 95 min, US, Walter Hill) *Bill Paxton, Ice Cube, Ice T, William Sadler.* This urbanized retelling of the classic *Treasure of the Sierra Madre* marks a return to form for director Hill. Paxton and Sadler take the lead in this textbook "wrong place, wrong time" scenario about two "good ol' boy" firemen who go searching for buried treasure in an abandoned building just in time to witness a gangland hit by druglords Ice T and Ice Cube. Hill strikes just the right balance between well-drawn characterizations and gunplay galore to make this a welcome addition to the action genre. ★★★ DVD: $14.99, VHS: $9.99

The Trial

(1962, 119 min, France/Germany/Italy, Orson Welles) *Anthony Perkins, Jeanne Moreau, Orson Welles.* Franz Kafka's nightmarish novel of a man arrested for a crime that is never explained to him is brilliantly brought to the screen by Welles. Perkins is Josef K., a sensitive individual pursued by a repressive bureaucracy, obsessed by an undefined guilt and bewildered by the burden of living. Welles maintained complete artistic control of the production and the result is a difficult but unforgettable expressionistic mood piece. (Filmed in English) ★★★½ DVD: $29.99

The Trial

(1993, 120 min, GB, David Jones) *Jason Robards, Anthony Hopkins, Michael Kitchen, Kyle MacLachlan.* MacLachlan stars as the archetypal victim hero, Joseph K., in this austere but oddly engrossing adaptation of Franz Kafka's novel. Waking up on the morning of his birthday, K. finds himself under arrest for no stated reason and is slowly sucked into a byzantine and murky beauracracy. MacLachlan gives a sturdy interpretation of K., though he ill-advisedly attempts an English accent. Harold Pinter provides the screenplay, which while replete with his snappy dialogue, curiously fails to invoke any of Kafka's subversive humor. Filmed on location in Prague, the production is greatly enhanced by marvelous cinematography and art design. ★★★

Trial and Error

(1962, 78 min, GB, James Hill) *Peter Sellers, Richard Attenborough, Beryl Reid, David Lodge.* Sellers and Attenborough play barrister and client — and several other characters — in this droll British comedy which offers only a few rewarding moments. When a rather taciturn bird seed salesman (Attenborough) murders his ebullient wife (Reid) so he can spend more quality time with his beloved budgies, his incompetent, court-appointed lawyer (Sellers) sees one last chance to finally step from the shadows. What he sees in the harsh glare of the limelight leaves him unsettled and dissoluted. Too reverentially adapted from a minor stage play, *Trial and Error* remains as unassuming as its two protagonists. (GB title: *The Dock Brief*) ★★ VHS: $9.99

Trial and Error

(1997, 98 min, US, Jonathan Lynn) *Michael Richards, Jeff Daniels, Charlize Theron, Jessica Steen, Austin Pendleton, Rip Torn.* Playing straight man to Richards' lunatic, Daniels is a lawyer about to be married. His bachelor party is such a success, he's unable to go to court the next morning. Friend and actor Richards subs for him in court to ask for a continuance. But Richards is forced to continue the charade when the continuance is denied, and Daniels must coach Richards from the sidelines. Goofy and occasionally genuinely funny, *Trial and Error* benefits from Torn's presence as the defendant, though many scenes outside the courtroom lack the comic energy of the trial scenes. ★★½ DVD: $9.99, VHS: $4.99

Trial by Jury

(1994, 108 min, US, Heywood Gould) *Joanne Whalley-Kilmer, Armand Assante, William Hurt, Gabriel Byrne, Kathleen Quinlan.* Whalley-Kilmer plays a jurist who faces every jury member's nightmare: being physically coerced into finding the defendant innocent. But what's more of a nightmare is the silly scenario created by the writers as a responsible citizen faces criminals and the criminal system head-on. Sitting on the jury of a high-profile mobster (Assante), Whalley-Kilmer has her and her young son's life threatened by Assante's goons. As she grapples with the moral dilemma, nearly every man in sight falls in love with her. Though bordering on trashy fun, this could have been enjoyable had not Whalley-Kilmer given such a one-dimensional performance. ★★ DVD: $9.99, VHS: $6.99

The Trials of Oscar Wilde

(1960, 123 min, GB, Ken Hughes) *Peter Finch, Nigel Patrick, James Mason.* Finch as the vainglorious writer Oscar Wilde, who sued his lover's father, the Marquis of Queensbury, for libel. After losing the ill-considered suit, he was charged with sodomy and stood trial. An elaborate and intriguing courtroom drama. ★★★ VHS: $24.99

Les Tricheurs (The Cheats)

(1983, 95 min, France, Barbet Schroeder) *Jacques Dutronc, Bulle Ogier.* A slick drama about elegantly dressed gambling addicts on the island of Madera and their attempts at pulling off an elaborate swindle. Ogier is the "lucky" stranger who becomes an unwitting accomplice in Dutronc's scheme at the roulette wheel. (French with English subtitles) ★★★ DVD: $19.99, VHS: $19.99

trick

(1999, 90 min, US, Jim Fall) *Christian Campbell, John Paul Pitoc, Tori Spelling, Steve Hayes, Clinton Leupp (aka: Miss Coco Peru), Lorri Bagley, Kevin Chamberlin, Missi Pyle, Lacey Kohl.* The tables are turned on the typical gay film plot in this funny and romantic screwball comedy. Gabriel (Campbell), a cute, effervescent music composer, and Mark (Pitoc), a darkly handsome go-go boy, lock eyes and long to link loins but through a series of events just can't seem to ever be alone long enough to get it on. They spend the day enduring intrusions, visited by friends and separated by ex-lovers and future ex-lovers. In a cinematic gay world of cookie-cutter plots, *trick*'s seductive tale offers a fresh and exciting alternative, and one that speaks truths on love and relationships no matter what the sexual orientation. Spelling is quite memorable as Gabriel's bulldozing actress/singer-wannabe best friend. Her table-side rant is hilarious. ★★★ DVD: $24.99

Trick or Treat

(1986, 97 min, US, Charles Martin Smith) *Marc Price, Gene Simmons, Ozzy Osbourne.* Imaginative horror satire about a metalhead who plays an album backwards to evoke the spirit of a dead rock star. A headbanger's delight, which unfortunately derails about halfway through. ★★½

The Trigger Effect

(1996, 93 min, US, David Koepp) *Elisabeth Shue, Dermot Mulroney, Michael Rooker, Richard T. Jones, Kyle MacLachlan.* Koepp makes a satisfying directorial debut with this offbeat though uneven psychological thriller. With nods to *Miracle Mile* and "The Twilight Zone," the story focuses on man's baser instincts during time of crisis (here a power blackout) that ultimately pits neighbor against neighbor. Koepp begins the film beautifully, tracking the effect one person has on another, then that person on another and so on. The story then concentrates on a Los Angeles couple (MacLachlan, Shue) and their houseguest (Mulroney) as they begin to cope with an unexplained, city-wide blackout. Though Koepp's thesis of man reverting to his animal self is not new, he diffuses the obvious with inventive camerawork and a steady tension throughout the film. ★★½ DVD: $14.99, VHS: $14.99

Trilogy of Terror

(1975, 78 min, US, Dan Curtis) *Karen Black, Gregory Harrison.* Three eerie tales of the supernatural, with a smashing performance by Black. "The Zuni Fetish Doll," the African head-hunting doll from the climactic third episode, is a classic horror short. ★★★ VHS: $9.99

The Trio

(1998, 93 min, Germany, Hermine Huntgeburth) *Götz George, Christian Redl, Jeanette Hain, Felix Eitner, Angelika Bartsch, Uwe Rohde, Tana Schanzara.* Zobel (George), a fiftyish con man, works the streets with his longtime lover Karl (Redl) and his twentysomething daughter Lizzi (Hain). When Karl suddenly dies, the flim-flam/pickpocketing team is in need of a new member. That comes in the person of Rudolf (Eitner), a brash, sexy, wet-behind-the-ears thief. Lizzi falls in love with him and coaxes her distrustful dad into accepting him into their fold. But Dad eventually falls under Rudolf's seductive charms (and it becomes obvious Rudolf swings both ways). This infectious comedy delivers the goods in offering characters of varying sexual orientations and sex scenes. George is more than believable as the vain but aging Lothario and Eitner is disarmingly sexy as his playmate. (German with English subtitles) ★★★ DVD: $14.99, VHS: $9.99

The Trip to Bountiful

(1985, 106 min, US, Peter Masterson) *Geraldine Page, Rebecca DeMornay, John Heard, Carlin Glynn, Richard Bradford.* Page won a much-deserved (and overdue) Oscar for her lovely performance as an aging widow who literally runs away from her son's Houston apartment to return to the now-abandoned home of her youth. A fine, bittersweet comedy-drama impeccably performed by a first-rate cast. Screenplay by Horton Foote, based on his 1953 play. ★★★½

Triple Echo

(1980, 85 min, GB, Michael Apted) *Glenda Jackson, Oliver Reed, Brian Deacon.* Featuring understated acting and direction, this bizarre wartime drama stars Jackson as a woman living alone in a farmhouse. She meets a young soldier (Deacon) who, swayed by his attraction for her, impulsively deserts his unit and hides out in Jackson's house. When investigators begin snooping around, Deacon dresses in women's clothing and masquerades as Jackson's sister. The ruse works too well when burly sergeant Reed takes a fancy to "her." ★★½

The Triplets of Belleville

(2003, 80 min, Belgium, Sylvain Chomet) An inventive, totally original animated film, *The Triplets of Belleville* offers an astonishingly creative stream of consciousness ride from Vaudeville to the French countryside to the mob-infested slums of North America to the dreamlife of dogs. Almost completely wordless, this Academy Award nominee is unlike anything you've ever seen. The story has to do with a bicycle-obsessed orphan and his devoted grandmother, and the series of events that lead both of them to the path of the once-fashionable singing stars of yesteryear, The Triplets of Belleville. The jazzy animation is one-of-a-kind, no Pixar smoothness, here. The humor is charmingly offbeat, and the characters — especially the grandmother who would cross an ocean to rescue her grandson — are absolutely irresistible. A triumph of animation, comedy and invention. ★★★★ DVD Letterbox: $24.99

Tristana

(1970, 99 min, France/Italy/Spain, Luis Buñuel) *Fernando Rey, Catherine Deneuve, Franco Nero.* Little of Buñuel's overt surrealist style is evident in this intriguing black comedy of corrupt morals, religious bigotry and sexual abuse. Set in provincial Toledo in the 1920s, Rey plays Don Lupe, a vain, lascivious old man with strong socialist and anti-clerical thoughts who, on the death of a friend, becomes the guardian of the young and innocent Deneuve. Lupe soon seduces/rapes his ward, but neither possesses her heart nor ignites her passions. The girl eventually flees to the arms of a handsome painter (Nero), only to return a sick, emotionally cold woman intent on revenge. (Spanish with English subtitles) ★★½ VHS: $29.99

The Triplets of Belleville

Triumph of Love

(2002, 111 min, Clare Peploe) *Mira Sorvino, Fiona Shaw, Ben Kingsley, Jay Rodan, Ignazio Oliva, Rachael Stirling, Luis Molteni.* A fairy tale that is as good-natured as it is implausible, director/cowriter Peploe's *The Triumph of Love*, based on Pierre Marivaux's 18th-century play, concerns the fate of a royal throne and the lengths to which a conscientious usurper (Sorvino) will go to set things right. As in almost all fairy tales, there is some scheming done with the best of intentions — specifically, the princess must temporarily blur some gender lines in order to infiltrate the legitimate heir's inner sanctum. This gives way to a series of impersonations and comic antics that meander rather than crackle. But rather than poking holes in the plot, or snickering about its hackneyed conceit, it's likely the earnest performances and the amply handsome scenery will distract just long enough to overlook its shortcomings. ★★½ DVD Letterbox: $29.99, VHS: $12.99

Triumph of the Spirit

(1989, 120 min, US, Robert M. Young) *Willem Dafoe, Robert Loggia, Edward James Olmos.* Based on a true story, this intense, unrelenting drama recaptures the brutal years of a Greek boxer who, as a prisoner at Auschwitz, was forced to fight "to the death" — either his or his opponent's — to the amusement of his Nazi captors. Dafoe gives a powerful performance as the fighter who is sent to the death camp with his entire family — only to watch them die one by one. Filmed on location, the film is unflinchingly real in its depiction of daily existence. As Dafoe's endearing father, Loggia is outstanding; and Olmos is fine as a Gypsy kapo. ★★★ DVD Dual: $19.99

Triumph of the Will

(1936, 120 min, Germany, Leni Riefenstahl) German director Riefenstahl's infamous propaganda documentary about Hitler's 1934 Nazi Party Congress held in Nuremberg, which helped thrust the dictator to power. Although its aim is to glorify the Nazis, it is undeniably a powerful piece of filmmaking. (German with English subtitles) ★★★½ DVD: $34.99, VHS: $29.99

Trog

(1970, 91 min, GB, Freddie Francis) *Joan Crawford, Michael Gough.* Crawford's last film is a disastrous camp classic with Mommie Dearest herself as an anthropologist (!) who discovers a missing link. ★ VHS: $14.99

The Trojan War

(1997, 83 min, US, George Huang) *Will Friedle, Jennifer Love Hewitt, Marley Shelton, Lee Majors.* A sloppy, hodgepodge of *Some Kind of Wonderful* and *Adventures in Babysitting.* Brad, a Generic Cute Guy, is infatuated with Leah, the Generic Blonde. When she begins to coo for a little romance, Brad finds himself *sans* condom. He ventures out to the all-night drug store, only to encounter gangs, robberies, police, a salsa contest and other various obstacles. Clichéd, one-dimensional characters, pubescent wet-dream fantasies and a predictable happy ending are all punctuated by relentless alt-rock B sides and some quasi-hip dialogue. ★½ VHS: $79.99

The Trojan Women

(1972, 105 min, US/Greece, Michael Cacoyannis) *Katharine Hepburn, Irene Papas, Geneviève Bujold, Vanessa Redgrave, Patrick Magee.* Euripides' tragedy about the fall of Troy to Agamemnon's armies. Despite the somewhat listless production (Cacoyannis' work on the stage is far superior), the

outstanding cast delivers a group of superlative performances, making this an emotionally charged treatise on the horrors of war. ★★½

A Troll in Central Park

(1994, 76 min, US, Don Bluth) *Vocies of: Dom DeLuise, Cloris Leachman, Jonathan Pryce.* Bluth continues to create a great animated alternative to Disney and this film is much more than just another walk through the park. The story follows the adventures of Stanley, a sweet-natured troll with a green thumb who can grow anything, anywhere, until he meets an evil queen who does her best to stop him. With the help of two children who befriend him, he and they learn that "if you believe in yourself, you can do anything" — always a timely lesson. ★★★ DVD: $19.99, VHS: $9.99

Tron

(1982, 95 min, US, Steven Lisberger) *Jeff Bridges, David Warner, Bruce Boxleitner.* Excellent computer graphics highlight this intriguing though lethargic sci-fi thriller about a computer programmer who is zapped into a computer and forced to live out a video arcade game. ★★ DVD 20th Anniversary Collector's Edition: $19.99

Troop Beverly Hills

(1989, 105 min, US, Jeff Kanew) *Shelley Long, Craig T. Nelson, Betty Thomas.* Long takes her snooty "Cheers" persona and transplants it to a Beverly Hills wife and mother who takes her daughter's girl scout troop on an outing. This formulaic comedy does manage a few laughs, and is a pleasant entertainment. ★★½ DVD: $14.99, VHS: $9.99

Trouble Bound

(1992, 90 min, US, Jeffrey Reiner) *Michael Madsen, Patricia Arquette, Seymour Cassel.* Blood and Concrete director Reiner offers another serving of his specialized brand of slapstick black comedy in this entertaining road romance. Just out of jail, Harry Talbot wins a Lincoln Continental at a card game and heads to Las Vegas to start a new life. His luck soon changes when Kit, a philosophical Mafia princess on the run, gets into Harry's car and demands a quick getaway from her pursuing family — then they find a body in the trunk. Rubber burns and bullets fly. ★★★ DVD Pan & Scan: $14.99, VHS: $14.99

Trouble in Mind

(1986, 111 min, US, Alan Rudolph) *Keith Carradine, Kris Kristofferson, Geneviève Bujold, Divine, Joe Morton.* Rudolph weaves the themes of hope and despair, greed and jealousy, and lost and found love in this carefully spun noir drama. There's a fine supporting performance by Divine (playing a male character) as an underworld boss. Title sung by Marianne Faithfull. ★★★

Brad Pitt is the mighty Achilles in *Troy*

Trouble in Paradise

(1932, 82 min, US, Ernst Lubitsch) *Miriam Hopkins, Herbert Marshall, Kay Francis, Charlie Ruggles, Edward Everett Horton, C. Aubrey Smith.* Charming and funny from frame one, Lubitsch's classic comedy is a blissful marriage of great wit, a wonderful story and delightful storytelling — indeed, *Trouble in Paradise* is the result of a gifted director at the height of his ability. Marshall and Hopkins are enchanting as two thieves who fall in love. They plot to rob a beautiful perfume executive (Francis), but things become complicated when Marshall and Francis become romantically involved. Lubitsch displays an extraordinary air of sophistication as his grifters plot and ploy, creating a timeless comedy of whimsy, romance and guile. ★★★★ DVD Criterion Collection: $39.99

The Trouble with Angels

(1966, 112 min, US, Ida Lupino) *Rosalind Russell, Hayley Mills, June Harding, Mary Wickes, Binnie Barnes, Gypsy Rose Lee.* A joyous romp set in a Catholic girls' school, this nostalgic comedy stars Mills and Harding as two mischievous students constantly in trouble with the Sisters, and especially Mother Superior Russell. Lots of fun. (Sequel: *Where Angels Go, Trouble Follows*) ★★★ DVD: $24.99

The Trouble with Harry

(1956, 99 min, US, Alfred Hitchcock) *Shirley MacLaine, John Forsythe, Edmund Gwenn.* A mordant black comedy about a troublesome corpse that just won't stay buried. Hitchcock directed this offbeat gem with characteristically cheerful morbidity. ★★★ DVD: $29.99, VHS: $14.99

THE DISCERNING FILM LOVER'S GUIDE

Troy

(2004, 162 min, US, Wolfgang Petersen) *Brad Pitt, Eric Bana, Orlando Bloom, Diane Kruger, Brian Cox, Peter O'Toole, Sean Bean, Brendan Gleeson, Saffron Burrows.* Loosely adapting Homer's "The Iliad" (but eliminating the gods) for the big screen, director Petersen has crafted an epic that attempts to evoke memories of recent swordplay films such as *Gladiator* and even *The Lord of the Rings*. *Troy*, which isn't as successful as either film, does work on quite a few levels, and is entertaining throughout, but the occasional inferior dialogue and two romances lacking sparks very nearly sabotage this costly, handsome costumer. Set during the Trojan War circa 1200 BC, the story focuses on the Greek's greatest soldier Achilles (Pitt), who, of course, has been blessed by the gods. When Troy's two princes Hector (Bana) and Paris (Bloom) try to make peace with the Greeks after ten years of war, a possible truce is ruined when Paris falls in love with Helen (Kruger), Queen of Sparta, and she returns with Paris to Troy. The Greeks, led by Achilles, invade Troy, where numerous, impressive battle sequences take place. The cast is hit-or-miss: Bana and O'Toole (as King of Troy) are outstanding, each bringing an emotional depth the screenplay doesn't always supply; Bloom and Kruger are lackluster in poorly written roles; while Pitt, looking impossibly buff, seems to be in his own film giving a brooding, contemporary portrait of Achilles. The majority of the effects are excellent, and it is difficult to tell in most scenes whether effects are actually being used or not. In spite of a few serious flaws, *Troy* still manages through some great acting, major action scenes and compelling characters to offer a kind of excitement and spectacle to be savored. ★★★

True Believer

(1989, 103 min, US, Joseph Ruben) *James Woods, Robert Downey, Jr., Margaret Colin.* The spirit of the idealistic, free-spirited '60s meets the Reagan era in this suspenseful crime thriller. Woods, in a compelling performance, stars as a Greenwich Village defense lawyer, Eddie Dodd, whose once shining star has all but faded. When he is hired to defend a convicted murderer who may have been unjustly imprisoned, Dodd, grasping at a final chance for personal and moral redemption, attacks the case with the lost vigor of his youth. Downey is fine as the novice attorney who apprentices with Dodd. ★★★ DVD: $19.99, VHS: $9.99

True Colors

(1991, 111 min, US, Herbert Ross) *John Cusack, James Spader, Richard Widmark, Imogen Stubbs.* Solid performances by Cusack and Spader elevate this fairly intriguing though familiar political drama about friendship and betrayal. Cusack and Spader play college chums who are working their way up the political ranks in Washington D.C.: Cusack is an opportunistic senatorial aide, and Spader is an idealistic Justice attorney. When the former runs for Congress, each must pay a high cost for his ambition/principles. ★★½ DVD Letterbox: $14.99, VHS: $14.99

True Confessions

(1981, 119 min, US, Ulu Grosbard) *Robert De Niro, Robert Duvall, Charles Durning, Kenneth McMillan.* De Niro and Duvall give powerful performances in this gritty mystery set in 1930s Hollywood. The two acting greats are cast as brothers, one a priest and the other a police detective, who cross paths during a murder investigation. ★★★

True Crime

(1999, 127 min, US, Clint Eastwood) *Clint Eastwood, Isaiah Washington, James Woods, Denis Leary, Lisa Gay Hamilton, Diane Venora, Bernard Hill, Michael Jeter, Frances Fisher, Michael McKean.* The crusading reporter is alive and well and doing good once more in Eastwood's solid drama of redemption and justice. Clint plays Steve Everett, an ex-alcoholic investigative reporter who's just inherited an assignment to cover that evening's execution of a death-row inmate. Upon examining the facts, he soon suspects that the man, Frank Beachum (Washington), may be innocent. Like James Stewart's reporter in *Call Northside 777*, Everett is prepared to do what's needed to save an innocent man before it's too late. Director Eastwood maintains a tight grip on the action throughout, and as the final hour approaches, *True Crime* becomes downright suspenseful. Woods nearly steals the film with his sly turn as Everett's sardonic editor. ★★★ DVD: $14.99, VHS: $9.99, VHS Letterbox: $9.99

True Grit

(1969, 128 min, US, Henry Hathaway) *John Wayne, Kim Darby, Glenn Campbell.* Wayne won an Oscar for his colorful portrayal of Rooster Cogburn, an aging, one-eyed marshall who helps a teenage girl (Darby) track down her father's killer. A flavorful western adventure, the film is exciting, funny and atmospheric; and, in addition to offering a career role to its larger-than-life star, it's an affectionate tribute to a style of filmmaking director Hathaway and fellow compadres John Ford and Howard Hawks elevated to an art form. (Sequel: *Rooster Cogburn*) ★★★ DVD: $14.99, VHS: $9.99

True Identity

(1991, 93 min, US, Charles Lane) *Lenny Henry, Frank Langella, James Earl Jones, Melvin Van Peebles.* It's *Watermelon Man* for the '90s. Black British comedian Henry plays an unfortunate passenger on what appears to be a doomed airline flight. Thinking he's about to die, the mobster sitting next to him begins confessing a lifetime of crime. When the plane fails to crash, however, poor Lenny suddenly finds himself on the wrong end of the mob. He then goes "white" and the chase is on. It's an amusing premise which only delivers half the time, but it does showcase Henry to good advantage. ★★½

True Lies

(1994, 141 min, US, James Cameron) *Arnold Schwarzenegger, Jamie Lee Curtis, Tom Arnold, Bill Paxton, Tia Carrere, Charlton Heston, Art Malik.* After the disastrous *Last Action Hero*, Arnold Schwarzenegger reteams with his *T2* director for this totally overblown action/comedy that pays tribute to the James Bond films of yore (with a dash of family values thrown in for good measure). This time out, Arnold plays a secret agent who must save the world from a wimpy villain (Malik) with a nuclear warhead, and keep his in-the-dark wife (Curtis) from discovering his true identity. Though lacking any awe-inspiring special effects or a fleshed-out story line, the film features exceptional aerial stunt work and mega-hardware. ★★½ VHS: $9.99, VHS Letterbox: $14.99

True Love

(1989, 104 min, US, Nancy Savoca) *Annabella Sciorra, Ron Eldard, Aida Turturro.* The mating games and rituals of Italian-Americans in the Bronx are delightfully played out in this refreshing independent comedy-drama by newcomer Savoca. The story follows the final days leading up to the traditional wedding of Donna (Sciorra), a feisty and determined young lady, and Michael (Eldard), a likable but immature deli worker. This low-budget charmer is filled with wonderfully drawn characters and presents an all-too-real glimpse into the preparations, problems and doubts leading up to the fateful day. ★★★½ DVD Pan & Scan: $14.99

True Romance

(1993, 119 min, US, Tony Scott) *Christian Slater, Patricia Arquette, Gary Oldman, Dennis Hopper, Christopher Walken, Brad Pitt, Michael Rapaport, Val Kilmer, Bronson Pinchot, Saul Rubinek, James Gandolfini, Chris Penn, Tom Sizemore.* What seemed like an unlikely pairing of mucho-macho auteur Quentin Tarantino and British stylist-turned-Hollywood hack Scott has paid off in spades with a hip, bullet-strewn thriller that hits you so hard it makes you laugh. This high-energy Generation X road movie stars Slater as a trash culture-worshipping comic book salesman who meets happy hooker Arquette during a kung fu triple feature in Detroit. Taking inspiration from his imaginary "mentor" (the ghost of Elvis played by Kilmer), Slater decides to rescue his new love from her sexual servitude to a dreadlocked pimp (Oldman, in a marvelously over-the-top performance). After blowing him away, Slater accidentally picks up a suitcase full of cocaine. After a quickie marriage and a visit to the tattoo parlor, Slater and Arquette hightail it out of town in a purple Cadillac. Drawing from Sam Peckinpah, Hong Kong action flicks, David Lynch (on a good day), Sergio Leone and Jim Thompson novels, *True Romance* is a gritty, high-octane mishmash with a genuinely affecting romance between Slater and Arquette. ★★★★ DVD R-Rated: $19.99, DVD Unrated Director's Cut: $26.99, VHS Unrated: $9.99, VHS R-Rated: $9.99

True Stories

(1986, 111 min, US, David Byrne) *David Byrne, John Goodman, Swoosie Kurtz, Spalding Gray.* In this slightly surreal travelogue, Byrne takes us on a few typical days in the typical lives of the typical Texan town of Virgil whose citizens are really anything but typical, or are they? The film stands as an oddly amusing vision of the mundanity of real life. ★★½ DVD: $9.99, VHS: $14.99

True West

(1985, 110 min, US, Gary Sinise) *John Malkovich, Gary Sinise.* The explosive performances of Malkovich and Sinise highlight this fine play-on-film adaptation of Sam Shepard's off-Broadway hit about the volatile relationship between two brothers. It was this production which introduced Malkovich, as the menacing, slightly off-center thug, to a wide audience. Sinise, who plays Malkovich's educated, passive sibling, also directed the play's original run. ★★★½

La Truite (The Trout)

(1982, 105 min, France, Joseph Losey) *Isabelle Huppert, Jeanne Moreau, Jean-Pierre Cassel.* Huppert is coyly sinister in Losey's complex, funny and sensual melodrama about an innocent country girl who moves to Paris with her gay husband and vows to succeed in the business world with the aid of her feminine wiles. Cassel is a wealthy financier lured by Huppert's coquettish manner, much to the chagrin of his neglected wife (Moreau). (French with English subtitles) ★★★ DVD: $19.99

Truly, Madly, Deeply

(1991, 108 min, GB, Anthony Minghella) *Juliet Stevenson, Alan Rickman, Michael Maloney.* A highly entertaining romantic comedy with a supernatural twist. Stevenson excels as a young woman drowning in grief following the death of her lover (Rickman). When he returns from the grave to soothe her sorrows, however, he turns out to be more than she can handle — especially when he and a bunch of ghostly friends take up residence in her flat, hanging about all night watching videos. Both actors give outstanding performances and first-time writer-director Minghella imbues the film with a bittersweet mix of hilarity and melancholy. ★★★★ DVD Pan & Scan: $19.99

Truman Capote's A Christmas Memory

(1966, 51 min, US, Frank Perry) *Geraldine Page, Truman Capote, Donnie Melvin.* Beginning with his cousin's observation, "Oh my, it's fruitcake weather!," this Emmy Award-winning short film, produced for ABC Stage, is a sweetly nostalgic recollection of Truman Capote's youth in the rural South during the Depression. Page stars as his homespun "cousin" who takes care of the young Capote, with the story centering on their home life, the touching relationship between the two of them and her Christmas tradition of making over 30 fruitcakes as presents. A simple, quiet drama of love narrated by Mr. Capote himself. ★★★½ VHS: $19.99

The Truman Show

(1998, 103 min, US, Peter Weir) *Jim Carrey, Ed Harris, Laura Linney, Noah Emmerich, Natascha McElhone, Holland Taylor.* Giving a breakthrough performance, Carrey shines as Truman Burbank, a naïve, likable guy-next-door who — unbeknowst to him — is the star of a highly rated, hidden camera 24-hour TV show. Writer Andrew Niccol and director Weir have taken a most exploitable and inventive premise and created a brilliantly executed fable. When we first meet Truman Burbank, he's happy, married and, evidently, without a care in the world. But then a series of bizarre events unfold which begin to make Truman question his own sanity. It's only then does he realize that — for him — all the world's a soundstage. An often cynical comment on modern TV and commercialism, *The Truman Show* expertly walks that fine line between comedy and drama — it's thoroughly entertaining and often downright hypnotic. In support, Harris is especially good as Truman's "guardian angel," a corporate-minded artist whose bottom-line is ratings and who can't see the humanity which he's created. ★★★★ DVD Letterbox: $14.99, VHS: $9.99

Trust

(1990, 91 min, US, Hal Hartley) *Adrienne Shelley, Martin Donovan.* Hartley, the style-rich auteur of the MTV generation, scores with his brilliantly insightful second feature. Focusing again on young, angst-ridden suburban narcissists like those he introduced in *The Unbelievable Truth*, Hartley probes into seemingly shallow, mundane lives and comes up with funny, touching portraits of multi-dimensional charaters. Shelley plays a pregnant cheerleader, Donovan is a grenade-toting, burned-out computer whiz. Together they explore humanity, right on Long Island. ★★★½

The Truth about Cats and Dogs

(1996, 93 min, US, Michael Lehmann) *Janeane Garofalo, Uma Thurman, Ben Chaplin, Jamie Foxx.* When keeping a pet is a major life decision, what hope is there for relationships between humans? Garofalo is a pleasure as a talk radio show host who befriends her societal nemesis, a quintessential Beautiful Dumb Blonde (Thurman). Their initial stereotypes evolve into textured, believable personalities (due more to the performers than the script). A deliberate act of deception involving a too-good-to-be-true love interest (Chaplin) escalates into a slapstick comedy of errors and enjoys a resolution mostly found only in the movies. The script for this gender-switched "Cyrano de Bergerac" is wildly uneven, but it successfully depicts the everyday incivilities which define our public personas. ★★½ DVD: $9.99, VHS: $9.99

The Truth about Charlie

(2002, 104 min, US, Jonathan Demme) *Mark Wahlberg, Thandie Newton, Tim Robbins, Joong-Hoon Park, Ted Levine, Lisa Gay Hamilton, Charles Aznavour, Anna Karina.* For no apparent reason, director Demme has updated the nimbly comic Hitchcockian caper *Charade*. Newton steps into Audrey Hepburn's classy heels as a continental waif who returns to Paris to discover her new husband has been murdered. A trio of thugs wants dead hubby's stolen loot and they think she's got it. Wahlberg inherits the Cary Grant role as a shady smoothie who offers assistance but who might be just as crooked as the goons. Newton is appropriately bubbly and ditzy but Wahlberg is devoid of charm. Worse, he and Newton generate zero chemistry. Stylistically, Demme is paying tribute to the films of the French New Wave. However, combined with the film's maddeningly labyrinthine plot twists, the result is enough to pummel anyone into a dizzying stupor. Most unforgivably, the Parisian landscape is criminally underutilized. ★★ DVD Letterbox Double Feature includes the original *Charade*: $14.99, VHS: $9.99

Truth or Consequences, N.M.

(1997, 103 min, US, Kiefer Sutherland) *Vincent Gallo, Kiefer Sutherland, Mykelti Williamson, Kim Dickens, Kevin Pollak, Rod Steiger.* A taut thriller directed by actor Sutherland in his debut behind the camera, *Truth or Consequences, N.M.* is a violent, satisfying chase movie. Curtis (Sutherland) is the trigger happy ex-con fronting a gang of thieves intent on robbing a drug dealer and selling the stash to the mob. When the heist goes awry, and an undercover cop is killed, Curtis flees west with his partners. The film has some nifty plot twists and double crosses on the way to the title city where the final confrontation between the gang, the mob and the DEA takes place. Sutherland's crisp direction of this escalating crime spree is marred only slightly by some gratuitous bloodshed and unnecessary camera flourishes. ★★★ DVD: $14.99

Tsui Hark's Vampire Hunters

(2002, 90 min, Hong Kong, Wellson Chin) *Ken Chang, Michael Chow, Lam Suet.* Disappointing horror/action hybrid from ubiquitous Hong Kong producer Tsui Hark, this is certainly no *Mr. Vampire*, let alone another *Chinese Ghost Story*. The rather dull plot involving the titular group and their master fighting evil beasts in centuries-old China is hindered further by weak direction and editing which render the fight scenes nearly incomprehensible, and wholly uninvolving. *Vampire Hunters* does have some moments (there's an eerie vampire awakening scene at around the halfway mark), and the vampires have a nifty way of sucking the blood from their victims, but for the most part this is uninspired, unimaginative, and pandering to its target audience. For hard-core HK action enthusiasts only. (Cantonese with English subtitles) ★★ DVD Letterbox: $19.99, VHS Dubbed: $102.99

Tucker

(1988, 120 min, US, Francis Ford Coppola) *Jeff Bridges, Martin Landau, Dean Stockwell, Joan Allen, Christian Slater.* A wonderful piece of storytelling from director Coppola. Preston Tucker was the personification of the American Dream — a man who believed anyone's dream could come true. But his American Dream becomes the American Nightmare when he builds a futuristic luxury car all too well and is soon taken on by the big car manufacturers and crooked politicians, all afraid his design could set a new precedent in excellence and ruin their special interests. Based on a true story, Coppola has crafted a beautifully detailed period piece. ★★★½ DVD: $14.99, VHS: $14.99

Tuff Turf

(1985, 113 min, US, Fritz Kiersch) *James Spader, Kim Richards, Matt Clark, Robert Downey, Jr..* A very youthful Spader stars in this satisfying teen pic as a streetwise preppy who takes on an L.A. gang and falls for the gang leader's girlfriend (Richards). Not as formulaic as you'd expect, and Spader demonstrates the timing and intensity which would make him one of the movies' leading actors just a few years later. ★★½ DVD: $14.99, VHS: $9.99

Tumbleweeds

(1999, 100 min, US, Gavin O'Connor) *Janet McTeer, Kimberly J. Brown, Jay O. Sanders, Gavin O'Connor, Lois Smith.* McTeer's Oscar nomination is well-deserved for her portrayal of Mary Jo Walker, a woman who manages life with quick packing and long road trips in the middle of the night to parts unknown. Her one unassailable bond is with her daughter Ava (a solid performance from Brown). Putting their trust in fate and the mantra "a brand new day," they undertake another new school, another job search. Mary Jo, on the lookout for husband #5, is so busy deflecting the weirdos and picking yet again the wrong man, that she doesn't see the chance for happiness right in front of her. The film is about the coming-of-age of both mother and

The Truman Show

daughter, as Ava takes her first steps into adulthood and Mary Jo discovers the inner strength she's always had but never recognized. *Tumbleweeds* tells a familiar story without cliché or sentimentality; a story about loss and recovery, about learning when to leave and when to stay. ★★★½ DVD: $24.99, VHS: $19.99

The Tune

(1992, 80 min, US, Bill Plympton) Plympton's highly amusing and inventive short cartoons have long become a staple of animation festivals. His unique sense of humor and fantastical imagery are near breathtaking. By these standards, *The Tune*, Plympton's first feature cartoon, is a total disappointment. A struggling songwriter is magically transported to the land of Flooby Nooby where he receives an education in letting his artistic talents flow. Unfortunately, most of Plympton's ingenious comedy gets eaten up by unending song-and-dance routines which mostly fizzle. ★½ VHS: $9.99

Tune in Tomorrow

(1990, 105 min, US, Jon Amiel) *Keanu Reeves, Peter Falk, Barbara Hershey, Peter Gallagher.* This delightfully capricious and wildly imaginative comedy stars Falk as a famed radio script writer who is hired by a small station in New Orleans in the early 1950s. There he befriends adorable and painfully innocent 21-year-old Reeves, who has fallen in love with his thirtysomething, divorced aunt, Hershey. As they explore their forbidden passion, Falk surreptitiously manipulates their affair which, lo-and-behold, is echoed on his radio show. Based on a story by Peruvian author Mario Vargas Llosa, the film is filled with excursions into the absurd and surreal, especially when we are treated to stagings of the daily soap episodes. The honors go to Falk, whose quips about Albanian peasantry are sidesplitting. ★★★½ DVD Dual: $14.99

Tunes of Glory

(1960, 106 min, GB, Ronald Neame) *Alec Guinness, John Fraser, John Mills, Kay Walsh, Gordon Jackson, Dennis Price.* Guinness and Mills are outstanding in this memorable character study of two rival colonels: one careless, vicious renegade; the other a disciplined, well-mannered young officer who is slated to replace him. As the power is set to change hands at the Swiss Regiment, resentments and bitterness give rise to a violent confrontation and a shocking climax. ★★★★ DVD Letterbox Criterion Collection: $29.99, VHS: $29.99

The Tunnel of Love

(1958, 98 min, US, Gene Kelly) *Doris Day, Richard Widmark, Gia Scala, Gig Young.* Kelly made his directorial bow with this sly, relaxed comedy based on the Broadway hit. Day and Widmark play a married couple desperately trying to have a baby. Deciding to adopt, they encounter lots of red tape and counselor Scala. Through one of the many misunderstandings which provide much of the film's humor, Widmark thinks, in a drug and alcohol-induced moment, that he has fathered a baby — with Scala. It's all rather tame, but the screenplay's entendres still amuse. Young steals the show and gets the lion's share of the best lines. ★★★

Turbulence

(1997, 100 min, US, Robert Butler) *Lauren Holly, Brendan Gleeson, Ray Liotta, Ben Cross, Rachel Ticotin.* The airline industry is in for more trouble and bad public relations with this silly action flick. Holly is a stewardess (sorry. . . flight attendant) who puts on her best "Karen Black-*Airport '75*-I'm-gonna-save-this-plane" face when she goes up against a serial killer prisoner (Liotta) who takes control of their plane. He chases her, she chases him. He rants and raves. She cries and curses a lot. *Turbulence* dives out of control from the bombardment of cliché after cliché. ★½ DVD: $14.99, VHS: $9.99, VHS Letterbox: $9.99

Turkish Delight

(1974, 100 min, Netherlands, Paul Verhoeven) *Rutger Hauer, Monique Van De Ven.* Years before he burst into international stardom with the macabre and erotic *The 4th Man*, gifted Dutch filmmaker Verhoeven directed this acclaimed, sexually explicit drama. This is very much a film of its period, complete with jazz soundtrack, promiscuity, a hostile "establishment" and a "youth must be served" attitude. Hauer is at first little more than a callous lothario intent on bedding a maximum number of women until he falls in love. ★★★ DVD Letterbox: $29.99, VHS Letterbox: $14.99

The Turn of the Screw

(1992, 95 min, GB, Rusty Lemorande) *Patsy Kensit, Julian Sands, Stéphane Audran, Marianne Faithfull.* This eerie adaptation of the Henry James ghost story is brimming with Freudian imagery and atmosphere. Kensit stars as a prim governess who is hired by a truly whacked-out Sands (when is he anything else?) to tend to two small children living in a secluded English manor. Once there, of course, she is overcome by visions and other hauntings all of which seem to center around her repressed sexuality and a young boy. Faithfull plays the sole survivor of the ordeal who narrates the action. ★★½ VHS: $79.99

Turner & Hooch

(1989, 97 min, US, Roger Spottiswoode) *Tom Hanks, Mare Winningham, Craig T. Nelson.* Hanks plays an officious police detective whose investigation of a murder is slightly hampered when the sole witness is a slobbering and very ugly watchdog. While most of the humor is predictable, Hanks is always a pleasure to watch and the film is at least better than the similarly themed, dog-tired *K9*. ★★ DVD: $14.99, VHS: $9.99

The Turning Point

(1977, 119 min, US, Herbert Ross) *Shirley MacLaine, Anne Bancroft, Tom Skerritt, Mikhail Baryshnikov, Leslie Browne.* MacLaine and Bancroft give tour de force performances in this exquisite drama set in the world of ballet. Bancroft plays a star ballerina who is reunited with childhood friend MacLaine, now a housewife and dance teacher, when the latter's daughter comes to New York to study ballet. Baryshnikov also stars as a dancer who romances the young Browne. Skerritt gives a fine, understated performance as MacLaine's patient husband. The film features excellent ballet sequences, and can be enjoyed even by those not fond of the dance. ★★★

Turtle Diary

(1986, 97 min, GB, John Irvin) *Glenda Jackson, Ben Kingsley, Michael Gambon.* Esteemed British playwright Harold Pinter wrote the charming adaptation of this Russell Hoban ("Ridley Walker") novel. Kingsley and Jackson play a bookstore clerk and a children's writer, respectively, who conspire to set a pair of giant sea turtles loose from the London Zoo. What ensues is a gently metaphorical exploration of the meaning of liberation and rejuvenation. ★★★

The Tuskegee Airmen

(1995, 110 min, US, Robert Markowitz) *Cuba Gooding, Jr., Laurence Fishburne, Allen Payne, Andre Braugher, Malcolm-Jamal Warner, John Lithgow, Courtney Vance.* Recalling the story of the first American black pilots to serve in WWII, *The Tuskegee Airmen* is an inspiring story of courage and perseverance. Fishburne plays Hannibal Lee, a premed student from Iowa who is among the first cadets for pilot training. America has been at war for over a year, yet blacks were not allowed to fly planes. Lee and a small group of black enlistees must fight prejudice at home and overseas before being allowed to take on the Nazis. The ensemble is uniformly good, with Fishburne anchoring the film with a nuanced portrayal of determination and loyalty. A fitting tribute to the men of the 99th and 332nd squadrons. ★★★½ DVD: $14.99, VHS: $9.99

The Tuxedo

(2002, 95 min, US, Kevin Donovan) *Jackie Chan, Jennifer Love Hewitt, Jason Isaacs, Debi Mazar, Peter Stormare.* Playing his typical "Who, me?" Everyman character caught in incredible circumstances, Chan is his usual charming self. Unfortunately, his schlub cabbie character is paired with the decidedly charmless Love Hewitt. The two must stop a nefarious (and truly clichéd) Eurovillain from cornering the market on the world's water supply. The clueless Chan gets a boost from a high-tech tuxedo, which enables him to climb walls, sing and dance like James Brown, and fight like, well, Jackie Chan. Some occasional sparkle from Chan's fight scenes and Isaacs' witty James Bond riff can't really begin to compensate for the ludicrous screenplay and uninspired direction — not to mention the quality vacuum that is Love Hewitt. ★½ DVD Letterbox: $14.99, DVD Pan & Scan: $14.99, VHS: $9.99

Twelfth Night — Or What You Will

(1996, 134 min, GB, Trevor Nunn) *Imogen Stubbs, Helena Bonham Carter, Toby Stephens, Ben Kingsley, Nigel Hawthorne, Richard E. Grant.* Shakespeare's ribald tale of mistaken identity and transgendered hilarity is brought to the screen with verve and vigor. Stubbs is Viola, a young maiden who, shipwrecked and separated from her identical twin brother, takes on the appearance of a man (Cesario) in order to win favor in the court of Orsino (Stephens). Orsino, it turns out, is intent on winning the love of Olivia (Bonham Carter), and Cesario takes on the call of winning her over on behalf of the moody prince. But, of course, people's affections fail to land on their intended targets and before long all-out farce rules the day. Though occasionally dragged down by some sloppy filmmaking, Nunn delivers an uproarious and timely comic adventure — what pleasure the bawdy Bard can be! ★★★½ VHS: $19.99

12 Angry Men

(1957, 95 min, US, Sidney Lumet) *Henry Fonda, Lee J. Cobb, E.G. Marshall, Jack Klugman, Jack Warden, Ed Begley, Martin Balsam.* Fonda heads a magnificent cast in this brilliant adaptation of Reginald Rose's gripping jury room drama. Fonda plays a juror who, uncertain of the guilt of a youth on trial for killing his father, tries to dissuade the other 11 members who are about to cast votes of guilty. The story evaluates the responsibility of the judicial and jury system, and is a bristling exposé of racial and social intolerance. Notable not only for its superlative acting and direction (Lumet's film debut), but also for introducing a gallery of aspiring New York stage actors, some of whom would go on to great success in New York and Hollywood. (Remade in 1997) ★★★★ DVD: $14.99

The Twelve Chairs

(1970, 94 min, US, Mel Brooks) *Ron Moody, Frank Langella, Dom DeLuise.* Early Brooks always provides for solid comic entertainment, and this often-overlooked gem rates as one of his best. Moody, in a hilariously manic performance, plays a Russian aristocrat who sets out on a madcap search for a dining room chair containing a fortune in jewels hidden in its upholstery. Langella is a transient who helps with the quest, and DeLuise gives an uproarious, lunatic performance as Moody's rival for the jewels. ★★★½ VHS: $9.99

12 Monkeys

(1995, 130 min, US, Terry Gilliam) *Bruce Willis, Madeleine Stowe, Brad Pitt, Christopher Plummer, David Morse, Frank Gorshin.* A dark, multilayered sci-fi thriller inspired by the obscure French short *La Jetée.* Willis plays a prisoner in a futuristic underground society who is forced to go back in time to track down the mythic "Army of the 12 Monkeys" and study the germ warfare holocaust that wiped out most of humanity. Over-shooting the designated time period, he is thrown into an insane asylum where he must convince his shrink (Stowe) that he is not delusional (or *is* he?). Unlike most time travel stories, this hyper-intelligent screenplay devotes proper attention to the elements of tragedy, pathos and inevitability thereby distracting from the attendant conundrums and paradoxes inherent in the genre. A masterpiece of postapocalyptic grunge, *12 Monkeys* is replete with Gilliam's trademark set design of ductwork and steam vents. Pitt is exceptional as an off-the-wall asylum mate who's not as crazy as he seems. ★★★★

Twelve O'Clock High

(1949, 132 min, US, Henry King) *Gregory Peck, Dean Jagger, Hugh Marlowe, Gary Merrill.* Peck gives one of his finest performances in this stirring psychological WWII drama about the pressures facing pilots and the men sending them off to die. Peck plays the newly appointed commander whose inflexibility causes resentment among his men and leads to his own breakdown. A thoroughly involving war drama, unusual for its time in that the flag waving was reduced to a minimum, with more concern for personal relationships and psychological profile. Jagger, in his Oscar-winning role, stands out as the company clerk. ★★★½ DVD: $14.99, VHS: $9.99

Twentieth Century

(1934, 92 min, US, Howard Hawks) *Carole Lombard, John Barrymore, Walter Connelly, Roscoe Karns.* Hawks' lightning-quick, hilarious adaptation of the Hecht-MacArthur play was the first popular hit of the new "screwball comedy" genre, and those unfamiliar with this comic gem will be amazed at how relentlessly funny and inventive it is. Lombard and Barrymore have an ongoing, cross-country battle-of-the-sexes aboard a train en route to her Broadway opening. The two stars are phenomenal. Barrymore brings fiendish energy to the part of a down-on-his-luck, maniacal director, and Lombard combines dazzling wit with great beauty in her role as the pampered actress. ★★★★

Twenty Bucks

(1993, 91 min, US, Keva Rosenfeld) *Brendan Fraser, Christopher Lloyd, Linda Hunt, Steve Buscemi, Spalding Gray, Matt Frewer.* Based on a script that's been floating around Hollywood for over 50 years, *Twenty Bucks* has an interesting premise: Follow the life of a crisp twenty dollar bill as it passes from owner to owner, becoming limp, bloodied and torn in the process. Unfortunately, the people who come into contact with the bill, like delivery guy Fraser and homeless person/mystic Hunt, aren't as engaging as the original idea. ★★½

20 Dates

(1998, 92 min, US, Myles Berkowitz) *Myles Berkowitz, Tia Carrere.* Fledgling director Berkowitz has given himself 20 dates to find (and film) someone to love. Purposely skirting the line between documentary and scripted romantic comedy, he can only occasionally pull off the uncomfortable laughs he's aiming for. His biggest problem is casting himself as the romantic lead; he generates very little sympathy for his romantic foibles. Ultimately, the issues raised here regarding the documentary form make this much more successful as an experimental film than any sort of broad entertainment. ★★ VHS: $102.99

28 Days

(2000, 104 min, US, Betty Thomas) *Sandra Bullock, Viggo Mortensen, Dominic West, Diane Ladd, Elizabeth Perkins, Steve Buscemi, Marianne Jean-Baptiste, Alan Tudyk.* Against type, Bullock plays a fast-living substance abuser who is court ordered to spend 28 days in rehab. There she befriends a group of misfits and learns a little about herself. There's not much new in the addict-on-the-mends story line, and the small group that Bullock's Grace Cummings finds herself reluctantly becoming a part is straight from Central Casting. But if you can get beyond the misplaced sentimentality and tawdry laughs, there's an involving story of trying to get one's self on the right road at the heart of director Thomas' wayward film. Bullock can't quite compensate for the script's occasional lapses of judgment. ★★½ DVD: $14.99, VHS: $9.99

28 Days Later

(2003, 112 min, GB, Danny Boyle) *Cillian Murphy, Naomie Harris, Brendan Gleeson, Christopher Eccleston, Noah Huntley, Megan Burns.* A man awakes in his London hospital bed to discover that he is all alone . . . on the floor, in the building, on the street, in the city. With memories of *Day of the Triffids* dangling over the beginning of the intense, scary *28 Days Later*, writer Alex Garland and director Boyle ensure through atmospheric cinematography, lively editing and twists aplenty that this ain't your typical last-man-on-Earth zombie movie. A deadly virus, called "Rage," has decimated the world. Twenty-eight days after it was initially released on the population, our hero Jim (Murphy) leaves the hospital and wanders a deserted London — that is until he runs into fellow survivors and the monstrous infected. It then becomes a fight for their lives as this newly formed rag-tag group rallies to combat the invading hordes of zombies. At times explicitly gory, at times thought-provoking (Jim's constant search for a father figure is highly unexpected in such a genre piece), *28 Days Later* is certain to have you on edge from the first eerie shot to the exciting finale. ★★★½ DVD Letterbox: $19.99, DVD Pan & Scan: $19.99, VHS: $12.99

28 Up

(1985, 133 min, GB, Michael Apted) Originally made in four separate installments, Apted's fascinating documentary began with a series of interviews with English children at age seven. Over the years, he went back to follow up on their lives at ages 14, 21 and 28. The success and failure of these individuals to fulfill their dreams provide an informative and sometimes lamentable view of real life. ★★★

25th Hour

(2002, 134 min, US, Spike Lee) *Edward Norton, Philip Seymour Hoffman, Barry Pepper, Rosario Dawson, Anna Paquin, Brian Cox.* While Norton is top-billed in this Lee "joint," *25th Hour* works because of the talent of its ensemble cast and a director who cares about each member of that ensemble. The main story line involves Monty Brogan (Norton), a drug dealer whose refusal to quit while he's ahead lands him in custody. Given one last day before heading to the pen, Monty must tie up loose ends and come face-to-face with his bleak future. Lee has never been one to let only one story dominate, and he provides moments with each of his beloved actors that allow this intuitive drama to breathe outside of the fringes. New York City also gives a stellar performance in the first Hollywood film not to shy away from the realities of a post-9/11 perspective. Using images of Ground Zero and memorials of firefighters, Lee puts his characters into the real world to both face its challenges and heal all at once. ★★★½ DVD: $19.99, VHS: $9.99

25 Fireman's Street

(1973, 97 min, Hungary, István Szabó) *Lucyna Winnicka, Margit Makay, Károly Kovács, András*

Cillian Murphy wanders through a deserted London in *28 Days Later*

THE DISCERNING FILM LOVER'S GUIDE

Bálint. Set in the postwar era, this evocative and haunting film explores the dreams, memories and nightmares of a group of people living in an old house on the eve of its destruction. Through the course of the film, they recall a generation of happiness and tragedy as affected by the war. (Hungarian with English subtitles) ★★★½ VHS: $69.99

Twenty-Four Eyes

(1954, 158 min, Japan, Keisuke Kinoshita) *Hideko Takamine, Chishu Ryo.* The title of this beloved Japanese classic refers to the 24 eyes of the students of an elementary class on the remote island of Shodoshima. Set in the late 1920s, the students' calm and traditional way of life is changed when a shockingly modern young teacher from Tokyo arrives. The woman, who wears a suit like a man and rides a bike to work, is slowly accepted and eventually loved by her students. Both their bright futures and the new ideas of the teacher are shattered by the impending war as well as by a rising nationalism that stifles individual growth and transforms personal ambition into unflinching devotion to the state. (Japanese with English subtitles) ★★★

The 24 Hour Woman

(1999, 92 min, US, Nancy Savoca) *Rosie Perez, Marianne Jean-Baptiste, Patti LuPone, Karen Duffy.* Perez replicates the natural, unforced honesty of her performance in *Fearless* in *The 24 Hour Woman*, a frenetic reflection on the wonderful world of working motherhood. Director Savoca has structured the film with rhythms matching the pace of its inhabitants' lives. Perez is a producer of a live-broadcast A.M. TV show. Announcing her pregnancy before she has a chance to tell her family, it follows her pregnancy with as much accuracy as TV brings to most subjects it covers: not very much. As various experts parade across the screen, Perez and other parents do their best with the precipitous balancing act of earning a living and raising a family in the latter days of the 20th century. The film's penultimate scenes combine slapstick zaniness with modern-day terror, and leave us with the honest reality that there are no final resolutions, just eternal adjustment. ★★★ VHS: $105.99

24 Hours in London

(2000, 91 min, GB, Alexander Finbow) *Gary Olsen, Anjela Lauren Smith, Tony London, David Sonnethal.* Lowlife gangsters, trafficking in illegal human organ sales, experience a glitch in a major deal when a witness to a hit escapes into police protection. Almost shockingly clichéd in every respect — dialogue, situations, characters, shots — *24 Hours in London* desperately wants to be a down-and-dirty addition to the Tarantino/Guy Ritchie school of smart-alecky crime flicks. But despite its energy and fast pace, the film is just an empty, faux-nasty, unconvincing bit of posing. ★½ DVD: $9.99, VHS: $7.99

24 Nights

(1999, 97 min, US, Kieran Turner) *Kevin Isola, David Murtka, Stephen Mailer, Aida Turturro, Mary Louise Wilson, Mark Bateman.* A sweet if familiar romantic comedy of one person's search for love, *24 Nights* follows college dropout Jonathon (Isola), a young gay man whose childlike heart and string of broken affairs leaves him lonely but forever hopeful that he'll find true love. He writes to Santa for a special Christmas gift, and thinks it's been delivered early when he meets a new coworker. But things don't go exactly as Jonathon had planned. Through the help of friends and family, though, Jonathon

does finally receive his wish. Often funny and deceptively simple, this low-budget love story should charm in spite of some uneven pacing. ★★½ DVD: $19.99, VHS: $14.99

20 Million Miles to Earth

(1957, 82 min, Nathan Juran) *William Hopper, Joan Taylor.* Great special effects by Ray Harryhausen and an unusually good story highlight this sci-fi winner about a spacecraft's return from Venus and the deadly hitchhiker it inadvertently picks up and drops off for a sightseeing tour of Athens. Gotta love that alien! ★★★ DVD: $24.99

29th Street

(1991, 98 min, US, George Gallo) *Danny Aiello, Anthony LaPaglia, Lainie Kazan, Frank Pesce, Jr..* A slight though enjoyable depiction of the havoc and happiness that befalls an Italian-American family when they become winners of the New York State Lottery. Based on a true story, the film examines Frank Pesce, Jr.'s (LaPaglia) inexplicable dismay over the seemingly joyous news that he has become a multimillionaire. At times funny, the film draws its strength from the heart of the Pesce family where, although they are always fighting, true bonds of love prevail. ★★½ VHS: $19.99

Twenty-One

(1990, 92 min, GB, Don Boyd) *Patsy Kensit, Jack Shephard, Rufus Sewell.* Kensit seduces her way into the hearts of viewers in this hip examination of the excesses and maladies of coming-of-age in the '90s. The film is told largely through a series of flashbacks, with Kensit delivering a series of voice-over soliloquies on her budding philosophies and unique impressions of the crazy world around her. ★★½

21 Grams

(2003, 125 min, US, Alejandro González Iñárritu) *Sean Penn, Naomi Watts, Benicio del Toro, Charlotte Gainsbourg, Melissa Leo, Clea DuVall.* The lives of several groups of disparate strangers converge through a horrific accident and soul-numbing loss. Director Inarritu interweaves moments in time, traveling from past and present, character to character; arranging puzzle pieces into a meditative mosaic on human interconnectness, individual frailty and the crushing force of irre-

Edward Norton in Spike Lee's *25th Hour*

versible tragedy. Watts, Del Toro and Penn bring raw exposure to their characters' circumstances: the wife and mother who finds herself widowed and childless in an instant, one man whose attempts to construct a meaningful life are shattered in a single moment, and another man whose need for a donated organ makes him a reluctant benefactor of the profound grief of others. Inarritu's trademark multi-layered construction is at times distracting, but never to the point of diluting the film's powerful impact. A stark visual sense and compelling performances from the entire ensemble create a thoughtful contemplation on the mystery and transience of human existence, the ravages of tragic loss and the saving grace which can bless the human spirit in times of crisis. It's said the human body loses 21 grams at the moment of death. This film measures the full extent of that loss, the poisonous effects of personal devastation and the healing power of forgiveness and reconciliation. It does so by delivering a compelling portrait of ordinary human beings in extraordinary conditions. ★★★★ DVD: $26.99, VHS: $49.99

26 Bathrooms

(1985, 28 min, GB, Peter Greenaway) On a short break from feature filmmaking, director Greenaway made for British TV this delightfully wacky documentary that takes an entertaining peek into the bathrooms of Great Britain. Serious in a smirking cleverish way, Greenaway's unusual travelogue visits 26 different bathrooms in and around London - all of which seek to go beyond mere functionalism and celebrate the therapeutic pleasures of the bathing ritual. And keeping with his game-playing pastime, the film is broken up into alphabetical segments running from A to Z, i.e., A is for A Bathroom, D is for Dental Hygiene, F is for Fish. ★★★½ VHS: $19.99

20,000 Leagues under the Sea

(1916, 101 min, US, Stuart Paton) *Matt Moore, Jane Gail, Alan Holubar.* This early silent version of Jules Verne's classic adventure story was one of the first films to feature innovative special effects and underwater photography. The story follows the renegade Captain Nemo who discovers a sea monster from his submarine Nautilus. Newly remastered from an archive print. ★★★ DVD: $24.99, VHS: $24.99

647

20,000 Leagues under the Sea

(1954, 126 min, US, Richard Fleischer) *Kirk Douglas, James Mason, Peter Lorre, Paul Lukas.* Oscar-winning special effects highlight this exciting Disney film based on Jules Verne's story of ship-wrecked survivors becoming involved with the notorious Captain Nemo. ★★★½ DVD 2-disc Special Edition: $19.99, VHS: $14.99

Twice in a Lifetime

(1985, 117 min, US, Bud Yorkin) *Gene Hackman, Ann-Margret, Ellen Burstyn, Amy Madigan, Brian Dennehy.* Superior acting elevates this compelling family drama about a husband who leaves his wife and children for another woman. Hackman gives a virtuoso performance as the working-class family man starting life anew; and he gets terrific support. Intelligent screenplay by Colin Welland. ★★★½

Twilight

(1998, 96 min, US, Robert Benton) *Paul Newman, Susan Sarandon, Gene Hackman, James Garner, Stockard Channing, Reese Witherspoon, Giancarlo Esposito, Liev Schreiber.* In the twilight of his career, Newman demonstrates in this impassioned though intriguing noir mystery that charisma, talent and experience can often compensate for a convo-luted story, and that even in his early 70s, it's hard to take your eyes off those baby blues. Newman plays Harry Ross, a retired cop and private eye who is very nearly one of life's great losers. An alcoholic who's estranged from his family, relegated to ser-vants quarters and duties while staying with his movie star friends (Hackman, Sarandon), Harry finds himself smack in the middle of a dime novel mystery when a simple delivery job leads to a series of murders. Director Benton gives *Twilight* the look and feel of a 1940s noir, all dark and shadowy and mysterious. But style can't overcome a "B" story line and less-than-swift pacing. His cast, however, is marvelous. ★★½ DVD: $19.99, VHS: $14.99

The Twilight of the Golds

(1997, 90 min, US, Ross Marks) *Brendan Fraser, Jennifer Beals, Faye Dunaway, Garry Marshall, Jon Tenney, Rosie O'Donnell, Sean O'Bryan, Jack Klugman, John Schlesinger.* An absorbing "issue" drama, *The Twilight of the Golds* takes an intelligent approach to the story of a woman who learns her unborn child will be gay and contemplates abortion. The "problem" of being gay is sketchily addressed — it is even likened to a disease — but once view-ers get over this hurdle, the film is engrossing with-out descending into movie-of-the-week histrionics. As each member of the Gold family express their opinion about Suzanne's decision, they become torn apart by differences. While some of the scenes are a bit forced — especially those between Suzanne's gay brother (Fraser) and his lover — director Marks' film is compelling. Jonathan Tollins adapted his own play. ★★★ DVD: $14.99, VHS: $14.99

Twilight Zone: The Movie

(1983, 102 min, US, George Miller, Joe Dante, John Landis, Steven Spielberg) *Vic Morrow, John Lithgow, Scatman Crothers, Kathleen Quinlan, Kevin McCarthy.* Four episodes either based on teleplays from the classic TV series *Twilight Zone*, or close in theme and spirit. Though the most infa-mous of the four (directed by Landis) is the seg-ment starring Morrow — in which the actor and two children were killed — about a bigoted man who gets his comeuppance, the best is the finale, *Nightmare at 20,000 Feet* (directed by Miller) with

Lithgow outstanding as a frightened airline passen-ger (based on a TV episode starring William Shatner). Other episodes include Spielberg's *Kick the Can*, about a group of senior citizens who redis-cover their youth; and Dante's cartoon-like story of a young boy whose magical powers don't make him very popular. ★★½

Twin Dragons

(1992, 90 min, Hong Kong, Ringo Lam & Tsui Hark) *Jackie Chan, Maggie Cheung, Teddy Robin.* Too many cooks spoil this broth, which is tellingly labeled "A Film by Hong Kong Director's Guild." Bad dubbing and choppy editing don't help. At least Chan is fun as twins (one's a maestro; one's, well, Jackie Chan). A botched job for a gangster by Chan II, followed by a twin switcheroo, leads to many black-out-style gags and throwaway action sequences. Watch for one brilliant scene at least, set inside a car factory — that highlights what Chan does best. Famed directors John Woo and Kirk Wong helmed some scenes. ★★ DVD: $14.99, VHS: $9.99

Twin Falls Idaho

(1999, 110 min, US, Michael Polish) *Mark Polish, Michael Polish, Michele Hicks, Jon Greis, Garrett Morris, William Katt, Lesley Ann Warren.* Penny the hooker (Hicks) makes her way to her next appoint-ment at the seedy Imperial Hotel on Idaho Avenue. Her trick is, rather, *are* Francis (director Michael Polish) and Blake (Mark Polish), conjoined twins who share 3½ legs, two arms and their psyches. All three are outcasts, relegated to the Lynchian envi-rons of a faceless urban wasteland, at the mercy of the casual cruelty of the "normal." The film could have settled for mere shock value; instead, it is a remarkable meditation on loneliness and identity, told with unexpected sweetness and compassion. The moody and luminous cinematography is one element in this expression of a signature vision, laced with singular moments of profound tenderness in extraordinary circumstances. A haunting and lyri-cal film. ★★★½ DVD: $27.99, VHS: $21.99

Twin Peaks: Fire Walk with Me

(1992, 135 min, US, David Lynch) *Sheryl Lee, Chris Isaak, Madchen Amick, David Bowie, Dana Ashbrook, James Marshall, Grace Zabriskie, Kyle MacLachlan, Miguel Ferrer, David Lynch, Ray Wise, Eric DaRe, Peggy Lipton, Harry Dean Stanton, Kiefer Sutherland.* Very few contemporary filmmakers can ever be accused of originality and so it seems ironic that one of the most inventive of the lot, Lynch, is already giving way to self-tribute. Regardless of this, however, this necessary, quasi-Gothic mystery to the mythical hamlet of "Twin Peaks" recycles the insightful themes introduced in the series, scaling them up to near-operatic propor-tions to chronicle the events leading up to the mur-der of Laura Palmer. Lee reprises her role as the doomed nymphet. A fitting coda to the small-town saga and the successful effort of an innovator forced to walk the tightrope which spans the chasm between cinematic genius and televised mediocrity. ★★★ DVD Letterbox: $19.99, VHS: $14.99

Twin Town

(1997, 99 min, Wales, Kevin Allen) *Llyr Evans, Rhys Ifans, Dorien Thomas.* The glue-sniffing, dope-smok-ing Lewis brothers, known as "the twins" despite three years difference in age, barter prescription drugs from senior citizens and pilfer cars for ready cash. When a local pillar of society — a club owner with police in his pocket — refuses to compensate an injury on the job suffered by their construction work-er dad, the twins embark on a path of retribution that

veers from goofy prank to unexpected tragedy. The actors are unselfconscious and direct, uniformly engaging in their portrayals of lusts and obsessions and fragmented loyalties. Often compared to *Trainspotting*, *Twin Town* is similar in its blithe juxta-position of the remnants of Old World charm against the harsh realities of modern day vice. ★★★½

Twin Warriors

(1993, 93 min, Hong Kong, Yuen Woo-Ping) *Jet Li, Michelle Yeoh, Chin Siu-Ho.* In this over-the-top, entertaining martial arts film, the enduring Li plays Junbao, who with his childhood friend Tianbao grew up in the Shaolin Temple. When they are both expelled due to Tianbao's temper, they take different paths in the outside world: Tianbao turns his back on his friend and joins the military, Junbao learns Tai Chi. Eventually, they must con-front each other in a fight for honor. The fight choreography is first-rate, and the pace flows well. Fans of the old Saturday Night Kung Fu Theatre should enjoy this one. (aka: *The Tai Chi Master*) ★★★ DVD: $14.99, VHS: $9.99

Twins

(1988, 112 min, US, Ivan Reitman) *Danny DeVito, Arnold Schwarzenegger, Chloe Webb.* A one-joke comedy whose punchline wears thin soon after its telling. The appealing duo of Schwarzenegger and DeVito star as separated twin brothers (and scientif-ic experiments) who are reunited when the former leaves his island paradise in search of his roots. DeVito, who can get comic mileage from a phone book, rises above the nonsensical script and direc-tion. Yeah, it's funny Arnie and Danny are twins: for the first ten minutes. ★★ DVD: $14.99

Twins of Evil

(1971, 85 min, GB, John Hough) *Peter Cushing, Madeleine Collinson, Mary Collinson.* This sequel to *Vampire Lovers* and *Lust for a Vampire* continues the "Carmilla" story line, this time starring *Playboy*'s first twin playmates. Cushing returns as their puritanical adversary, appalled as much by their sexual proclivities as their dietary habits. ★★½

Twist and Shout

(1984, 105 min, Denmark, Bille August) *Lars Simonsen, Adam Tonsberg.* This harrowing, beauti-fully acted teenage rite-of-passage film from young Danish director August is a comedy-drama that explores a web of complex familial and romantic relationships surrounding four young friends. Never once sinking to the level of a typical American teenage coming-of-age film, *Twist and Shout* instead creates a kinetic excitement of youthful sexu-ality as director August proves himself wonderful-ly capable of portraying the agony and ecstasy of adolescent life. ★★★½ DVD Letterbox: $29.99

Twisted

(1997, 86 min, Australia, Christopher Robbin Collins & Samantha Lang) *Bryan Brown, Geoffrey Rush, Rachel Ward, Kimberly Davies.* A mixed bag, *Twisted* is an anthology of four super-natural tales that boast exactly one plot twist each. While no single episode of the quartet stands out, parts of the film are very atmospheric and the whole thing looks great. Yet there is little in way of sus-pense or creativity to heighten the drama. The four stories are linked by the theme of swapping identi-ties, but the characters are really only caricatures. The supernatural elements appear only superficially, and this will displease fans expecting a jolt or two. ★★ DVD: $24.99, VHS: $69.99

Twister

(1988, 93 min, US, Michael Almereyda) *Harry Dean Stanton, Crispin Glover, Dylan McDermott, Suzy Amis.* When the production wing of Vestron Pictures went under, *Twister* was unceremoniously released on video, bypassing theatrical release. Too bad, for it's an unqualified delight. This innovative comedy is set in a sprawling mansion in the middle of Kansas where Stanton is raising a family of lunatics. They include Amis as his daughter who has a tenuous grasp on reality; and Glover as his abundantly confused son. ★★★

Twister

(1996, 114 min, US, Jan De Bont) *Bill Paxton, Helen Hunt, Jami Gertz, Cary Elwes, Lois Smith, Philip Seymour Hoffman, Alan Ruck, Todd Field, Jeremy Davies.* A grand-slam if vacuous special effects extravaganza, *Twister* is a knockout when its F/X take center stage, but there's the matter of that story between the effects, and it's a whirlwind of mediocrity. The agreeable Hunt plays a scientist who chases tornadoes. Onto the scene comes her soon-to-be ex-husband (Paxton). He was once a tornado chaser but now he's a weatherman. The two get together and follow several tornadoes throughout the Midwest. But forget about the dialogue and story — the F/X are the real interest here, and each successive twister brings on more carnage and jaw-dropping effects culminating in a smash finale. ★★½ DVD: $14.99, VHS: $9.99, VHS Letterbox: $9.99

Two Daughters

(1962, 116 min, India, Satyajit Ray) *Ray's wonderful film is divided into two different stories but united in the theme of the first love. The first tale, "The Postmaster," is about a young girl's growing affection for her employer; the second, "The Conclusion," is a charming parable about a girl who is forced into a loveless marriage with a bland but successful man. Her frustrations grow until she leaves him in an effort to find real love. (Hindi with English subtitles) ★★★

2 Days in the Valley

(1996, 105 min, US, John Herzfeld) *James Spader, Danny Aiello, Glenne Headly, Teri Hatcher, Jeff Daniels, Eric Stoltz, Charlize Theron, Marsha Mason, Paul Mazursky.* Of the many post-Quentin Tarantino comedic, violent, multicharacter, noir criminal saga/thrillers, *2 Days in the Valley* is one of the most entertaining. Casting a cynical eye on a cold-blooded world and containing unpredictable twists that we've come to expect from good mysteries, the story begins as hired guns Aiello and Spader finalize a hit. Only Spader attempts to kill his partner and frame him for the murder. Barely escaping and on the run, Aiello hides out in the luxurious Valley home of a pompous art dealer. Meanwhile, Spader must return to the scene of the crime when his fee is locked away in the house, which is by now crawling with police — including Daniels and Stoltz. A zestful blend of Philip Marlowe glibness and contemporary inter-genre teasing. ★★★ DVD: $9.99

Two Deaths

(1996, 102 min, GB, Nicolas Roeg) *Michael Gambon, Sonia Braga, Patrick Malahide.* An intimate study of obsessional love related against the backdrop of the brutal absurdity of war evolves into an artfully constructed parable regarding the root causes of human self-destruction. Gambon plays a well-established, extremely comfortable surgeon hosting a sumptuous dinner party in an unspecified Eastern European city. Gambon's brilliant portrayal

of enigmatic moral ambivalence is stark counterpoint to Braga's earthy, sensual, intelligent and focused servant; his need to dominate and possess is forcefully confronted by her willful surrender. He relates their history to the assembled guests who, though horrified, in turn tell their own stories of loss and corruption. An intricate, involving and revelatory foray into the darkest components of the human psyche. ★★★

Two English Girls

(1971, 108 min, France, François Truffaut) *Jean-Pierre Léaud, Kika Markham.* A kindred companion to *Jules and Jim*, *Two English Girls* features Léaud as the pivotal figure alternately romancing two British sisters with sometimes tragic consequences. A lyrical rumination of passion's turbulent course. (French with English subtitles) ★★★ DVD: $19.99, VHS: $14.99

Two Evil Eyes

(1990, 121 min, US/Italy, Dario Argento & George Romero) *Harvey Keitel, Adrienne Barbeau, E.G. Marshall, Tom Savini, Kim Hunter.* Romero and Argento join forces in this Poe-meets-*Creepshow* horror anthology. Romero's clever adaptation of "The Case of M. Valdemar" stars Barbeau as a greedy wife whose hubby dies . . . or does he? Argento's turn is short on sense, but long on atmosphere. Keitel stars as a sadistic Weegee-style photographer who can't conceal his crimes from "The Black Cat." Music by Pino Donaggio. ★★

2 Fast 2 Furious

(2003, 103 min, US, John Singleton) *Paul Walker, Tyrese, Eva Mendes, Cole Hauser, James Remar.* Walker returns (sans Vin Diesel, alas) to nab some bad guys and tool around in snazzy cars. Unfortunately, director Singleton forgot to include the exciting action that made the first film such a pleasant surprise. In fact, this juvenile sequel is exactly what many assumed the first film would be. Here, we're "treated" to some rote driving that would put Starsky and Hutch to sleep, as well as some unconvincing (to be charitable) CGI work in lieu of stunt driving, that makes much of the film look like a lousy video game, and erases any sense of danger. A quick comparison to *Bullitt* or *The Road Warrior* proves there's no substitute for the real thing. This one's strictly for the kids . . . though even they're likely to be bored. ★ DVD Letterbox: $19.99, DVD Pan & Scan: $19.99, VHS: $9.99

Two for the Road

(1967, 111 min, GB, Stanley Donen) *Audrey Hepburn, Albert Finney, William Daniels, Eleanor Bron, Jacqueline Bisset.* Hepburn and Finney bring sophistication and spontaneity to their roles as a married couple looking back at the many paths they've traveled during a tumultuous 12-year marriage. Through a series of flashbacks, Frederic Raphael's fresh, innovative screenplay examines several crossroads in Hepburn's and Finney's lives, all while the couple are traveling on the road. *Two for the Road* is consistently charming, and is laced with a delightful sense of humor. In support, Daniels and Bron are near-perfect as "ugly American" tourists/traveling companions. ★★★½ VHS: $14.99

Two for the Seesaw

(1962, 119 min, US, Robert Wise) *Robert Mitchum, Shirley MacLaine.* A bittersweet romantic comedy based on William Gibson's acclaimed play. Mitchum plays a Midwest lawyer, about to divorce his wife of 12 years, who moves to New York City and becomes involved with "lovable crackpot waif"

MacLaine. Though on stage the story is a riveting character study, director Wise is unable to overcome the talkiness of a two-character play in his screen adaptation. But this is nonetheless an involving work, and Mitchum and MacLaine offer noteworthy performances. (The basis for the Broadway musical "SeeSaw") ★★★

Two Girls and a Guy

(1998, 84 min, US, James Toback) *Robert Downey, Jr., Heather Graham, Natasha Gregson Wagner.* While each awaits her boyfriend to return home, two women, Carla and Lou (Graham, Wagner), discover during small talk that they are seeing the same man. How these two united spirits band together and turn the tables on their two-timing beau forms the core of this caustic, clever and original sex comedy. Blake (Downey) is a self-absorbed actor who returns home to find his girlfriend Carla waiting for him. Unbeknownst to him, his other girlfriend Lou is also in waiting, and when they both confront him, the fireworks begin. But Toback's brand of fireworks is altogether raunchy, hilarious and rude. In Blake, the writer-director has found a near-perfect mouthpiece for ideas and sexual attitudes both men and women may think but would never say aloud. With a sprinkling of sexual sparring and maybe a little gratuitous nudity, *Two Girls and a Guy* is very much an adult entertainment — a social and sexual comedy you can actually bite your teeth into. ★★★½ DVD R-Rated: $9.99, VHS NC-17 version: $102.99, VHS R-Rated: $9.99

Two Girls and a Sailor

(1944, 125 min, US, Richard Thorpe) *June Allyson, Gloria DeHaven, Van Johnson, Lena Horne, Jimmy Durante.* Two singing-and-dancing sisters (Allyson, DeHaven) open up their dream canteen, with the help of a wily sailor (Johnson). A cute, bright musical entertainment typical of M-G-M's 1940s song-and-dance productions. ★★★ VHS: $19.99

200 Cigarettes

(1999, 99 min, US, Risa Bramon Garcia) *Ben Affleck, Janeane Garofalo, Casey Affleck, David Chappelle, Gaby Hoffmann, Kate Hudson, Courtney Love, Jay Mohr, Martha Plimpton, Christina Ricci, Paul Rudd, Elvis Costello.* A multistory film, *200 Cigarettes*, set on New Year's Eve 1981, has a stellar cast but also a mediocre-to-weak script. Some stories (Ricci's in particular) are snoozers, but the most clichéd and predictable one (Love and Rudd as best pals who you just *know* are going to end up together) is the most entertaining, due to the winning performances from the duo. There's little zip in the direction or dialogue, though the cast is most appealing. *200 Cigarettes* coasts on their collective charm. ★★ DVD: $19.99, VHS: $14.99

200 Motels

(1971, 98 min, US, Frank Zappa & Tony Palmer) *Frank Zappa, The Mothers of Invention, Ringo Starr, Theodore Bikel, Keith Moon.* Zappa and The Mothers of Invention are on the road in this incredibly bizarre "surrealistic documentary." ★★★

Two if by Sea

(1995, 95 min, US, Bill Bennett) *Denis Leary, Sandra Bullock, Stephen Dillane, Yaphet Kotto.* In this ordinary romantic comedy, Leary and Bullock are art thieves on the run from the law. Needing to hide out for several days, they find a mansion whose family is on vacation and play house. With the police and underworld associates on their trail, they bicker, befriend a friendless teen and attend fancy parties thrown by their handsome "neighbor." The two stars try to come off as the Tracy and Hepburn of the Bonnie and Clyde set, but the dialogue they are forced to recite is rarely funny or romantic, and their continual misadventures are very familiar. Cowriter Leary lost his bite with this one. ★★ DVD: $14.99, VHS: $9.99

The Two Jakes

(1990, 138 min, US, Jack Nicholson) *Jack Nicholson, Harvey Keitel, Meg Tilly, Ruben Blades, Eli Wallach.* Lacking the tension and chilling atmosphere of Roman Polanski's noirish classic *Chinatown*, this sequel directed by and starring Nicholson is fascinating and occasionally riveting. It's 1948, 11 years after the original. Private investigator Jake Gittes (Nicholson) is less ambitious, more portly, and content with mundane murder cases and rounds of golf. Problems arise when his client Jake Berman (Keitel) becomes involved in a murder. As the investigation ensues, Gittes finds himself face to face with his grisly past. Acting honors go to Keitel as Gittes' mysterious client. Nicholson demonstrates thoughtful competence as a director, but he sometimes bogs down in uninteresting side plots which lengthen the film. ★★★ DVD: $14.99, VHS: $19.99

Two-Lane Blacktop

(1971, 103 min, US, Monte Hellman) *Warren Oates, James Taylor, Laurie Bird, Dennis Wilson.* Ambitious, unique and one of the quintessential films of the '70s, this is the cross-country car race between GTO (Oates), the Driver (Taylor) and the Mechanic (Wilson). Filled with incredible music and startling cinematography, this remastered, letterboxed video is a must-have. Oates, who won a few acting awards for his performance, is outstanding; and, yes, this is probably the first time you saw a film character sing along with his car radio, which now has become a cliché. ★★★½ DVD Letterbox: $19.99

Two Moon Junction

(1988, 104 min, US, Zalman King) *Sherilyn Fenn, Martin Hewitt, Richard Tyson, Kristy McNichol.* A bored, blonde Fenn dumps her privileged life and vapid beau (Hewitt) and takes up with a rugged, muscle-bound carnival worker (Tyson). McNichol appears as a bisexual cowgirl in this cheesy T&A tale. ★★ DVD: $9.99

The Two Mrs. Carrolls

(1947, 99 min, US, Peter Godfrey) *Humphrey Bogart, Barbara Stanwyck, Alexis Smith.* Bogart is an artist who killed his first wife, but not until after using her as a model for his painting "Angel of Death." It's a few years later, and now he's married to Stanwyck. And now she's starting to show signs of illness. Smith is the beautiful socialite with whom he falls in love while plotting to kill the second Mrs. Carroll. This psychological thriller is heavy going for the most part, and it takes its good old time building to a rather exciting climax. ★★½

Two Mules for Sister Sara

(1970, 105 min, US, Don Siegel) *Clint Eastwood, Shirley MacLaine.* Eastwood and MacLaine make a good team in this entertaining comic western about

2001: A Space Odyssey

drifter Eastwood coming to the aid of nun MacLaine (who sure doesn't act very religious) in the Mexican desert. ★★★ DVD: $14.99

The Two of Us

(1967, 86 min, France, Claude Berri) *Michel Simon, Alain Cohen.* Simon stars as an old man whose fervent anti-Semitism is challenged when he develops a close relationship with a young Jewish boy in hiding during World War II. Their growing friendship and love makes this both a charming and moving film experience. ★★★

2000 Maniacs

(1964, 75 min, US, Hershell Gordon Lewis) *Tom Wood, Connie Mason, Jeffrey Allen, Ben Moore.* Lewis' "masterpiece." An unbelievably bloody carnage feast that will have its viewers glued to the screen despite their increasing repugnance. The story centers around a sleepy Southern town and its unusual way of celebrating the 100th anniversary of the Civil War: capture unsuspecting Northerners and proceed to do unspeakable acts on their person. Southern hospitality my ass. Filled with Confederate flags, gushing blood, and enough shock value to send John Waters into an orgasmic frenzy. (Camp rating ★★★★) ★ DVD: $24.99

2001: A Space Odyssey

(1968, 139 min, GB, Stanley Kubrick) *Keir Dullea, William Sylvester, Gary Lockwood.* Both a grand hypothesis on humankind's place in the universe and a pithy examination of our efforts to control our burgeoning technology before it controls us, Kubrick's milestone sci-fi epic is nothing less than brilliant. A visual masterpiece without equal, the film was years ahead of its time with regard to special effects and Kubrick established his mastery of choreographing music with image. (Sequel: *2010: The Year We Make Contact*) ★★★★ DVD: $19.99, VHS Pan & Scan: $14.99, VHS Letterbox: $14.99

2010: The Year We Make Contact

(1984, 116 min, US, Peter Hyams) *Roy Scheider, John Lithgow, Bob Balaban, Helen Mirren, Keir Dullea.* In this sequel to Kubrick's landmark *2001*, a new space expedition locates the wrecked

ship Discovery and learns the secret of its aborted mission. Though the special effects are commendable, the film doesn't share the original's narrative composition and intelligence — but then who'd actually expect it to? ★★ DVD: $14.99, VHS: $14.99

Two-Way Stretch

(1960, 87 min, GB, Robert Day) *Peter Sellers, Wildrid Hyde-White.* Sellers stars as a prisoner who leads his fellow inmates in a scheme to break out of jail, commit a robbery and then steal back to the safety of their cells. Sly fun. ★★★ DVD Letterbox: $19.99

Two Weeks Notice

(2002, 100 min, US, Marc Lawrence) *Sandra Bullock, Hugh Grant, Alicia Witt, Dana Ivey, Robert Klein, Heather Burns.* Having carved niches for themselves, Bullock and Grant have both proved to be reliable performers in breezy comedies. Bullock is the beautiful-but-she-doesn't-know-it klutzy charmer, and Grant the handsome-but-he-doesn't-know-it stammering charmer — both equipped with an arsenal of sassy one-liners, a mass of insecurities and an array of beguiling smiles. That's exactly what you get with *Two Weeks Notice*, an amiable, seen-it-before romantic comedy that benefits from the delectable first-time pairing of the two stars. Grant plays a real estate tycoon who can't seem to manage without his assistant/lawyer Bullock. When she gives notice, it takes a little time for them to know they were meant for each other. The two stars wring out whatever laughs are available in the formulaic script, using the talent and personality they've been nurturing for years. ★★½ DVD Letterbox: $19.99, DVD Pan & Scan: $19.99, VHS: $6.99

Two Women

(1960, 99 min, France/Italy, Vittorio De Sica) *Sophia Loren, Raf Vallone, Eleonora Brown, Jean-Paul Belmondo.* Loren won an Academy Award for her deeply moving, heart-wrenching portrayal of an Italian woman who, along with her daughter, is raped by soldiers during World War II. The affects of this brutalization on the woman and her relationship with her daughter are explored in this realistic and unforgettable film experience. (Italian with English subtitles) ★★★★ DVD: $9.99

U

U-571

(2000, 117 min, US, Jonathan Mostow) *Matthew McConaughey, Harvey Keitel, Bill Paxton, Jon Bon Jovi, Jake Weber, David Keith, T.C. Carson, Jack Noseworthy, Matthew Settle.* Exhibiting the same kind of tension which made his last feature *Breakdown* a white-knuckle journey, director Mostow journeys under the Atlantic to produce a taut, often thrilling WWII submarine actioner. McConaughey is a lieutenant on a U.S. sub whose crew have been sent on a secret mission: retrieve an Enigma code machine. The plan to overtake the disabled *U-571*, steal its decoder and sink the sub goes awry, and Tyler and his men must escape in the German sub with a Nazi destroyer on its heels. Loosely based on actual wartime incidents (the British actually pulled off a daring raid to retrieve the decoder), the story balances swift action scenes with wartime heroics by familiar but not clichéd characters. ★★★ DVD: $14.99, VHS Special Edition: $9.99

U.S. Marshals

(1998, 131 min, US, Stuart Baird) *Tommy Lee Jones, Wesley Snipes, Robert Downey, Jr., Joe Pantoliano, Kate Nelligan, Iréne Jacob.* Less a sequel to *The Fugitive* and more another chapter à la the James Bond films, *U.S. Marshals* brings back the crack government team, headed by Deputy Marshal Sam Gerard (Jones). It's involving, but we've been here before. Jones is still in good form as the no-nonsense Gerard, who is now after Mark Sheridan (Snipes), an escaped convict (via a well-staged airplane crash) who is wanted for a series of brutal, execution-style murders. Unlike Kimble, Sheridan's guilt is uncertain, which is supposed to add some mystery to the story but is ultimately distracting. Baird has staged some exciting chase scenes, and Jones and Snipes are formidable adversaries. ★★½ DVD Letterbox Special Edition: $14.99, VHS: $9.99, VHS Letterbox: $9.99

U-Turn

(1997, 125 min, US, Oliver Stone) *Sean Penn, Jennifer Lopez, Nick Nolte, Powers Boothe, Billy Bob Thornton, Joaquin Phoenix, Claire Danes, Jon Voight, Julie Hagerty, Liv Tyler.* With his most comic film to date, director Stone travels to the hot Arizona desert where a wrong turn and unfulfilled passions can lead to murder, or at least a damn entertaining time. Penn is Bobby, a motorist stranded in the dusty little town of Superior. Bobby's short stay while his car is fixed becomes an exercise in the bizarre. Blind men keep dead dogs, and a beautiful Native American woman (Lopez) and her sleazy white husband (Nolte) each want Bobby to murder the other. As Bobby tries to figure out allegiances and avoid the local sheriff (Boothe), his trip down the rabbit hole becomes increasingly strange and dangerous. Stone brings a vigorous energy to the film, and the humor, though dark and sarcastic, is focused and funny. A gritty, nasty, sexy, noirish, unpredictable ride. ★★★ DVD: $14.99, VHS: $9.99

L'Udienza

(1971, 120 min, Italy, Marco Ferreri) *Ugo Tognazzi, Claudia Cardinale, Michel Piccoli, Vittorio De Sica.* A provocative comedy of passion and alienation set against the intrigues of the modern Vatican. It follows a peculiar young man's quixotic attempts to obtain a private audience with the Pope, in order to share ideas which he is convinced can cure the ills of society. His attempts are constantly blocked by individuals who only pretend to be sympathetic to his cause. (Italian with English subtitles) ★★½

UFOria

(1980, 100 min, US, John Binder) *Cindy Williams, Harry Dean Stanton, Fred Ward.* This whacked-out comedy features a colorful assortment of oddball characters who are searching for fulfillment in a nowhere town at the edge of the Mojave Desert in a culture of revival tents and religious fanatics. Williams is a delightfully daffy, Bible-toting prophet who dreams of UFOs and a cosmic reenactment of Noah's Ark. ★★★

Ugetsu

(1953, 96 min, Japan, Kenji Mizoguchi) *Machiko Kyo, Masayuki Mori.* Two peasants leave their families; one to seek wealth in the city, the other to find fortune as a samurai warrior. An eerie and allegorical film on the suffering caused by greed. (Japanese with English subtitles) ★★★½ VHS: $24.99

The Ugly

(1998, 94 min, New Zealand, Scott Reynolds) *Paolo Rotondo, Rebecca Hobbs.* A scary movie if you consider musician Marilyn Manson frightening (the sequences with freakish dark-clothed and pale-skinned demons look just like him). Otherwise, you might think this wishful thriller about a controversial psychiatrist (Hobbs) taking on a mind-warping serial killer (Rotondo) in a series of uninteresting interviews to be hollow and unsuspenseful. ★½ DVD: $19.99

The Ugly American

(1963, 120 min, US, George Englund) *Marlon Brando, Eiji Okado.* Brando and Okada fought together in Sarkhan against the Japanese in WWII. More than a decade later, Brando returns to Sarkhan as its American ambassador; Okada is the leader of a popular underground nationalistic movement. This well-constructed political exposé, based on the book by William J. Lederer and Eugene Burdick, plays the personal friendship against the conflicting factions vying for power in the underdeveloped Southeast Asian country. Take care to follow the convolutions of intrigue — it all leads up to a chilling final shot. ★★★ DVD: $14.99, VHS: $19.99

UHF

(1989, 97 min, US, Jay Levey) *Weird Al Yankovic, Victoria Jackson, Kevin McCarthy.* The film debut of rock spoofer Yankovic is a genuinely funny and fast-paced take-off on TV, movies and Americana. "Weird Al" plays a daydreaming nobody who inadvertently gets control of a near-zero rated television station. Of course, he makes the station a huge success. But hilarious take-offs in the form of commercials and strange new shows (including a gun-toting Gandhi sequel, "Conan the Librarian" and "Wheel of Fish") help you forget the pedestrian plot and enjoy his special (if wicked) brand of comedy. ★★½ DVD Dual: $14.99

Ulee's Gold

(1997, 111 min, US, Victor Nunez) *Peter Fonda, Patricia Richardson, Jessica Biel, Christine Dunford, Tom Wood, Vanessa Zima.* Giving the performance of his career, Fonda excels in this beautifully detailed, subtle drama of a Florida beekeeper and his family. Looking very much like his dad, and bringing to the screen the same kind of idealism and sensitivity Henry cornered the market on, Peter plays Ulysses "Ulee" Jackson, a reticent widower raising his two granddaughters. When his estranged, jailed son asks him to help his wife, whose drug dependency has put her in harm's way, Ulee grudgingly agrees. Getting quite more than he bargained for, Ulee becomes an unwitting patriarch and hero as he redeems himself in the eyes of his family. Director Nunez has written a touching, involving story which is realized with a discerning eye; but more importantly, he has given Fonda a role rich in character and nuance. ★★★½ DVD: $14.99, VHS: $9.99

Ulysses

(1955, 104 min, US/Italy, Mario Camerini) *Kirk Douglas, Silvana Mangano, Anthony Quinn.* Douglas brings a degree of respectability to this favorful American-Italian coproduction about the adventures of the legendary Greek hero on his way home after the Trojan Wars, including encountering the cyclops and the sirens. ★★★

Will Estes, Jack Noseworthy, Matthew McConaughey and Jake Webber in *U-571*

Ulysses

(1967, 140 min, US/Ireland, Joseph Strick) *Milo O'Shea, Maurice Roeves.* Adapting James Joyce's massive novel to the screen was thought to be an impossible task, but Strick for the most part succeeds in filming the unfilmable with this tale of lust and longing. The story, photographed in a style of cinematic stream of consciousness, follows a 24-hour period in the life of young poet Stephen Daedalus as his odyssey takes him through the streets and brothels of Dublin. ★★½ DVD: $29.99

Ulysses' Gaze

(1996, 177 min, Greece, Theo Angelopoulos) *Harvey Keitel.* A mystical, visually stunning, soul-searching epic from the director of *Landscape in the Mist.* In one of his most impressive roles in an equally impressive career, Keitel stars as "A," a life-weary exiled Greek filmmaker who returns to his native country to attend a screening of his latest film. He soon becomes obsessed in finding the missing footage from a turn-of-the-century film, one which documents the Balkan area's people. His search turns into a cross-country odyssey, one that perilously takes him into the very soul of both the troubled Balkan region as well as himself. With beautiful imagery reminiscent of Andre Tarkovsky and the universal theme of man's longing for understanding and meaning, Angelopoulos' stimulating drama should stun even the most jaded viewer. (In English and Greek with English subtitles) ★★★½ DVD: $19.99, VHS: $29.99

Ulzana's Raid

(1972, 103 min, US, Robert Aldrich) *Burt Lancaster, Bruce Davison, Richard Jaeckel.* Top-notch western adventure with Lancaster as an experienced Indian scout helping new cavalry officer Davison in a counter-offensive against an Apache attack. Crisp direction from Aldrich separates this tale from other similarly themed westerns. ★★★

Umberto D

(1955, 89 min, Italy, Vittorio De Sica) *Carlo Battisti, Maria Pia Casilio.* De Sica's uncompromising masterpiece is a heartrending study of a lonely old man and his struggle to survive with dignity in post-war Italy. A haunting and well-crafted

film expertly told by the director. (Italian with English subtitles) ★★★★ DVD Criterion Collection: $29.99

The Umbrellas of Cherbourg

(1964, 91 min, France, Jacques Demy) *Catherine Deneuve, Nino Castelnuovo, Anne Vernon.* Beautifully restored version of Demy's classic, bittersweet musical of two young lovers (a luminous Deneuve and handsome Castelnuovo) separated by war. With its gorgeous pastel color scheme and attractive leads, *Umbrellas* apes the glamour of the Hollywood musical, but also undercuts this a bit with a gritty, working-class locale and everyday situations. All the dialogue is sung, and most of the music is low-key. There are no show-stopping, highly choreographed numbers; but what it lacks in bombast and spectacle it makes up for in emotional resonance. Demy perfectly captures the feel of first love, and the myriad obstacles thrown in the face of it. A thankfully rediscovered treasure about the losses — and gains — of growing up and moving on. Michel Legrand wrote the lovely score. (French with English subtitles) ★★★★ DVD: $24.99, VHS: $24.99

The Unapproachable

(1983, 92 min, West Germany, Krystof Zanussi) *Leslie Caron, Daniel Webb.* A former film star, living the life of a recluse, meets a handsome young man who, under his charming veneer, is actually a scheming and ruthless opportunist. A provocative thriller that explores their developing relationship and the shifting tides of power and sexual attraction. Caron's cooly passionate performance will captivate the viewer. A probing insight into the dangerous games which men and women all-too-often play. ★★★

The Unbearable Lightness of Being

(1988, 171 min, US, Philip Kaufman) *Daniel Day-Lewis, Juliette Binoche, Lena Olin, Derek De Lint, Erland Josephson, Stellan Skarsgård.* An erotic, witty and intelligent film adaptation of Milan Kundera's best-selling novel. Set against the backdrop of the Prague Spring of 1968, the story follows a young, womanizing Czech doctor who finds himself caught in the turmoil of the uprising despite his aversion to politics. Day-Lewis, Binoche and Olin all beautifully portray their characters' intertwined relationships against the powerfully evoked background of political upheaval and displacement. ★★★½

The Unbelievable Truth

(1990, 90 min, US, Hal Hartley) *Adrienne Shelley, Robert John Burke.* Director Hartley throws together vivid and quirky characters in a story of a high school cynic-turned-model (Shelley) living in a town disrupted by the return of an alleged murderer-turned-mechanic (Burke). Male territorialism, miscommunication and deals fuel the dialogue-driven plot of this offbeat winner. ★★★ DVD: $14.99, VHS Letterboxed: $9.99

Unbreakable

(2000, 107 min, US, M. Night Shyamalan) *Bruce Willis, Samuel L. Jackson, Robin Wright Penn, Spencer Treat Clark, Charlayne Woodard, Eamonn Walker.* Finding its inspiration from comic books, and even resembling a live-action comic at certain times, *Unbreakable* is director Shyamalan's follow-up to *The Sixth Sense.* Not wanting to tread the same ground but probably wanting to duplicate the "otherworldly" chills of his previous hit film, Shyamalan offers an eerie-looking enigma awash in uncertainties. Unfortunately, in doing so, he sets a trap for himself from which escape is difficult. Willis plays a college security officer who discovers (after a train wreck) that his body has the ability to heal itself instantly. Jackson is a comic book dealer who suffers from a rare bone disease. How these two come together — and why — is at the core of a slow-paced, muddled film that takes its time getting to what turns out to be an existential limbo. Though it shouldn't be compared to *Sense, Unbreakable* offers only a few thrills, ultimately failing on its own by not establishing either sufficient plot or character. ★★ DVD Vista Series: $19.99, VHS Exclusive Video Bonus Edition: $14.99

Uncle Buck

(1989, 99 min, US, John Hughes) *John Candy, Amy Madigan, Macaulay Culkin, Gaby Hoffman.* A pleasant and amusing comedy which offers Candy a chance to demonstrate a heretofore unseen paternal side to his mammoth personality. Big John stars as a black-sheep uncle who tests his limits (and the limits of those around him) when he baby-sits his two nieces and nephew for a few days. Some of this may be very predictable and formulaic territory for director Hughes, but it nevertheless works. ★★½ DVD: $14.99, VHS: $14.99

Uncle Sam

(1996, 91 min, US, William Lustig) *Bo Hopkins, Timothy Bottoms, Isaac Hayes, Robert Forster, P.J. Soles, William Smith.* A surprisingly enjoyable genre effort from scripter Larry Cohen and director Lustig, the team behind the *Maniac Cop* films. *Uncle Sam* follows a similar tack, but with a more interesting theme: Gulf War soldier and all-American jerk Sam is killed by friendly fire in the Middle East, but comes back from the dead to take revenge on all those he deems as un-American. His war-obsessed nephew, who idolizes Sam, begins to suspect the truth behind the rash of murders. *Uncle Sam* is more engrossing than scary, and less gimicky than you might think. ★★½ DVD Letterbox: $19.99

Uncommon Valor

(1983, 105 min, US, Ted Kotcheff) *Gene Hackman, Fred Ward, Patrick Swayze, Tim Thomerson, Reb Brown.* A father recruits his old Marine buddies to search for his son, missing in action in Laos for ten years. The screenplay and characters are action-adventure clichés, but the cast and competent direction from Kotcheff elevate it from its formulaic roots. ★★½ DVD: $14.99, VHS: $14.99

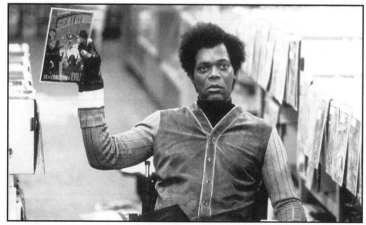

Samuel L. Jackson in *Unbreakable*

Under Capricorn

(1949, 117 min, GB, Alfred Hitchcock) *Ingrid Bergman, Joseph Cotten, Michael Wilding.* An unusual effort for Hitchcock — a period costume piece. Bergman is unhappily married to a respected but ruthless man. Cotten is superb as the vicious husband who drives her to alchoholism and the limits of her mental and physical endurance. Wilding costars as a visitor who wreaks havoc with Cotten. Not considered one of Hitch's classics, it's worth a look nonetheless for its marvelous acting and to see the director out of his usual milieu. ★★½ DVD: $19.99

Under Fire

(1983, 128 min, US, Roger Spottiswoode) *Nick Nolte, Joanna Cassidy, Gene Hackman, Jean-Louis Trintignant, Ed Harris.* The setting is Nicaragua during the overthrow of the Somoza regime by the Sandinistas. An American journalist (Cassidy) and a hotshot photographer (Nolte) find themselves caught in the cross fire of the revolution when Nolte uses a doctored photo to aid the rebel cause. A taut, engrossing drama about the moral and political issues of news reporting and the "objectivity" of the press. ★★★½ DVD Letterbox: $14.99

Under Heat

(1994, 92 min, US, Peter Reed) *Lee Grant, Robert Knepper, Eric Swanson.* Filmed in an "American Playhouse"-style fashion, this family drama centers on the summer visit of Dean (Swanson) to his rural New York family of brother Milo (Knepper) and his mother (Grant). Ostensibly, his return is to tell his family that he is HIV-positive, but troubles with his drug-addicted brother and his mother's cancer scare contribute in keeping his revelation a secret. The sappy approach and predictability undermine an otherwise worthy effort. ★★½

Under Milk Wood

(1973, 90 min, GB, Andrew Sinclair) *Richard Burton, Elizabeth Taylor, Peter O'Toole, Glynis Johns.* Set in lush and visually stunning Wales, this production of Dylan Thomas' classic play is performed with theatrical genius by its three leads. Thomas' glorious poetry sparkles in this tale of a day in the life of the mythical village of Llareggub. The film has been rightly accused of over-ambitiousness and, indeed, the sense of production does weigh some of the material down. But it still offers a sterling example of ensemble acting from three great thespians. ★★½

Under One Roof

(2002, 74 min, US, Todd Wilson) *Jay Wong, James Marks, Sandra Lee, James Quedado.* Often funny and nicely observed, *Under One Roof* is a heartfelt drama of one gay man's struggle for love that is hampered by sincere but unremarkable acting and a production that is unable to offset its low budget. Daniel (Wong) is a closeted Chinese-American gay man who lives with his mother and grandmother in San Francisco. He is out to his friends, but certainly not to his mother who is always trying to set him up with women. He keeps his life compartmentalized until handsome Robert (Marks) moves in downstairs. Inevitably, they end up in the sack and a tenuous relationship is formed. Their happiness is hampered by Daniel's wariness of a connection so close to home — for a Chinese boy brought up in a traditional family, being gay and proud is a huge step. ★★ DVD: $19.99, VHS: $9.99

Under Siege

(1992, 103 min, US, Andrew Davis) *Steven Seagal, Tommy Lee Jones, Gary Busey, Erika Eleniak.* Seagal reteams with his *Above the Law* director Davis to boldly go where Bruce Willis and Wesley Snipes have gone before: into the "one-man S.W.A.T. team" arena. In this "*Die Hard* on the high seas," Seagal has his most fulfilling effort, thanks mostly to Davis' slam-bang pacing. Seagal takes on the role of a military expert who just happens to be "moonlighting" as a ship's cook when high-tech pirates take over. Suspenseful action and over-the-top performances by Busey and Jones make this the Steven Seagal movie for people who don't like Steven Seagal. (Sequel: *Under Siege 2: Dark Territory*) ★★★ DVD: $19.99, VHS: $9.99

Under Siege 2: Dark Territory

(1995, 98 min, US, Geoff Murphy) *Steven Seagal, Eric Bogosian, Katherine Heigl, Morris Chestnut, Everett McGill.* Seagal is back as Casey Ryback, Navy SEAL-turned-cook, who must once again thwart a secret terrorist plot, kill all the bad guys, and save both a group of hostages and the world at large. This time he is pitted against an over-the-top Bogosian, a nutso weapons designer whiz who hijacks a moving train and a satellite, making the deadly services of the latter available to the highest international bidder. Mindless fun, though Seagal is still one of the most wooden actors lucky enough to be receiving a paycheck. ★★½ DVD: $19.99, VHS: $9.99

Under Suspicion

(1992, 100 min, GB, Simon Moore) *Liam Neeson, Laura San Giacomo.* The title of this old-fashioned murder mystery refers to the predicament of its two leads (Neeson, San Giacomo), who find themselves pointing fingers at each other over the murder of the latter's lover. Neeson stars as a sleazy private eye (circa 1959 England) whose livelihood of faking adulteries for divorce-seekers is cut short when one of his set-ups ends in murder — with him as a prime suspect. He immediately sets out to prove his innocence by pinning the blame on San Giacomo, who is the sole beneficiary of the murdered man. This innocent-man-wrongly-accused thriller sports a wild ending twist. ★★½ DVD: $19.99, VHS: $9.99

Under Suspicion

(2000, 110 min, US, Stephen Hopkins) *Gene Hackman, Morgan Freeman, Thomas Jane, Monica Bellucci.* One of those mishandled theatrical releases that deserves to find an audience on video, *Under Suspicion* is a compelling cat-and-mouse mystery that'll have you guessing right up until the end. Hackman portrays a prominent tax attorney in Puerto Rico who is being questioned by his friend, the police captain (Freeman). There was a brutal murder and rape of a young girl and Hackman is now the prime suspect. But did he do it? Flashbacks help provide insight into his possible guilt or innocence, and thankfully director Hopkins never allows this device to become either confusing or cloying. As would be expected, both Hackman and Freeman are first-rate. ★★★ DVD: $14.99, VHS: $9.99

Under the Cherry Moon

(1986, 98 min, US, Prince) *Prince, Jerome Benton, Kristin Scott Thomas, Francesca Annis.* Prince wrote, directed and stars in this universally trashed, amateurish tale of a tormented American gigolo working in the south of France. Filmed in black and white. ★

Under the Domim Tree

(1996, 102 min, Israel, Eli Cohen) *Kaipo Cohen, Juliano Mer, Gila Almagor, Riki Blich.* Based on the autobiography by Gila Almagor, *Under the Domim Tree* is the poignant and very compelling story of a group of orphaned Jewish teens, all survivors of the Holocaust, who come of age and battle very real demons while living in an Israeli youth settlement. On a melancholy note, the film begins slowly and sometimes confusingly as it introduces the children and adults, setting up the story with dispassion. But as the main characters are identified and the heart of the tale unfolds, *Under the Domim Tree* discovers its voice — and a haunting one at that. The story is touching without being depressing, and by the sheer courage demonstrated by those who shouldn't have to have their bravery tested, it's also inspirational. (Hebrew with English subtitles) ★★★ VHS: $19.99

Under the Earth (Debajo del Mundo)

(1986, 100 min, Poland/Spain, Beda Docampo Feijoo) *Victor Laplace.* This forceful drama celebrating the will of the human spirit recounts the story of a Jewish family's stubborn survival in the aftermath of the Nazi Occupation of wartime Poland. Forced to flee their stable life and live underground in subhuman conditions, the family endures two years of suffering yet remains together through their faith and a hope for a better future. (Spanish with English subtitles) ★★★

Under the Roofs of Paris

(1929, 95 min, France, René Clair) *Albert Prejean, Pola Illery.* The street life of Paris in the 1920s provides an exceptionally vivid backdrop to this lyrical love triangle of a street singer, his best friend, and the woman they both love. Note: This is a very early sound film, and the quality of sound is not up to par, but it is viewable. (French with English subtitles) ★★★ DVD Criterion Collection: $29.99, VHS: $19.99

Under the Sand

(2000, 90 min, France, François Ozon) *Charlotte Rampling, Bruno Cremer, Jacques Nolot, Alexandra Stewart.* Rampling is a revelation as a woman emotionally adrift after the disappearance of her husband in Ozon's stately, devastating character study. Marie and Jean are a happily married middle-aged couple who escape the city for their cottage retreat by the sea. One morning, Marie wakes up and finds Jean nowhere to be found. Did he drown? Is he lost? Did he leave her? With these questions swirling in her mind and heart, Marie is plunged into an emotional cauldron. Her friends and colleagues are all unable to pull Marie out of her inner turmoil as answers are difficult to come by and the truth is even more difficult to accept. It's almost a one-woman show as Rampling entrances not by what she says but how she thinks, reacts and feels. It's a superbly subtle performance. Ozon's leisurely pacing and obsession for getting into the soul of a fragile woman make this intense psychological drama a most satisfying experience. (French with English subtitles) ★★★½ DVD: $24.99, VHS: $19.99

Under the Sun

(1998, 115 min, Sweden, Colin Nutley) *Rolf Lassgard, Helena Bergstrom, Johan Widerberg.* Nominated for a Best Foreign Film Oscar, *Under the Sun* is a small-scale, though lush and affecting drama. Set in the 1956 Swedish countryside, the story basically a three character piece: lonely Olof, who's taking care of the family farm after his mother's death; his womanizing, America-obsessed

Diane Lane and Olivier Martinez in flagrante delicto in *Unfaithful*

friend Erik; and the sexy Ellen, who answers Olof's newspaper ad calling for a "young lady housekeeper." Both Olof and Ellen are keeping secrets from each other, which the increasingly manipulative Erik may use to his own advantage. Beautifully shot, simply told (though there is a wonderfully atmospheric dancehall sequence, making stylish use of an early rock 'n' roll ballad) and well-acted (especially by the luminous Bergstrom, real-life wife of director Nutley), *Under the Sun* is a tad overlong, but that takes nothing away from the compelling characters and involving dramatics which make this such a poignant experience. (Swedish with English subtitles) ★★★ DVD Subtitled: $29.99, VHS Subtitled: $49.99

Under the Sun of Satan

(1987, 98 min, France, Maurice Pialat) *Gérard Depardieu, Sandrine Bonnaire.* Pialat's stunning meditation on faith and the battle between good and evil won the Golden Palm for Best Picture at Cannes in 1987, but the controversial film was roundly booed upon that announcement. The story, told in an austere and direct style, is an adaptation of the Georges Bernanos 1926 novel about a tortured priest who feels unworthy of God's love until he encounters a pregnant teenager who has killed her lover. Depardieu is the village pastor who must battle Satan and Bonnaire is the wanton girl in this demanding, intense and provocative film. (French with English subtitles) ★★★ VHS: $29.99

Under the Volcano

(1984, 109 min, US, John Huston) *Jacqueline Bisset, Anthony Andrews, Albert Finney.* Huston's blistering adaptation of the Malcolm Lowry novel showcases a bravura performance by Finney as a former British consul in Mexico whose mental morass prompts a tragic descent into a private hell. Bisset is his estranged wife whose reappearance hastens the inevitable. ★★★½ VHS: $79.99

Undercover Blues

(1993, 95 min, US, Herbert Ross) *Kathleen Turner, Fiona Shaw, Stanley Tucci, Dennis Quaid, Larry Miller, Tom Arnold, Saul Rubinek.* Turner and Quaid play husband and wife espionage agents who know more about martial arts, explosives and the criminal mind than Bruce Lee, James Bond and Hannibal Lecter put together. Having taken time off to have a baby, the couple is lulled back into the realm of undercover when munitions are stolen by a Czechoslovakian sexpot. Nothing in this comedic caper seems genuine: the characters, dialogue and situations are all-too perfect and highly artificial. ★★½ DVD Dual: $14.99

Undercurrent

(1946, 116 min, US, Vincente Minnelli) *Katharine Hepburn, Robert Taylor, Robert Mitchum.* A familiar melodramatic thriller with Hepburn as a professor's daughter who marries an industrialist, only to suspect her new husband is evil. *Gaslight* and *Suspicion* did it better, though Hepburn turns in a good performance. ★★ VHS: $14.99

Underground

(1997, 167 min, France/Serbia, Emir Kusturica) *Miki Manojlovic, Lazar Ristovski, Mirjana Jokovic.* A surreal, subversive look at two men and the woman they love, *Underground* is both anarchic comedy and wartime tragedy. The story, about two Communist buddies who try desperately to survive the war in Yugoslavia, is secondary to the film's mesmerizing set pieces that depict an entire society living underground. Mixing dramatic scenes with newsreel footage, and throwing in an ode to filmmaking, Kusturica has made a demanding film, but one that makes a lyrical statement about life and love during wartime. (Serbo-Croatian with English subtitles) ★★★½ DVD Letterbox: $29.99, VHS: $29.99

The Underneath

(1995, 100 min, US, Steven Soderbergh) *Peter Gallagher, Elisabeth Shue, Shelley Duvall, Joe Don Baker.* An understated remake of the film noir classic *Criss-Cross* about a ne'er-do-well ex-con who returns home to "Smallville USA" and becomes involved with his old flame, her gangster boyfriend and an armored car robbery. Soderbergh's complex narrative (he coauthored the screenplay pseudonymously) relies on an impressive use of color tones to delineate time periods, thus giving the impression of layers being peeled away to reveal "the underneath" of his hauntingly etched characters. ★★★ DVD: $9.99, VHS: $19.99

Underworld

(2003, 120 min, US, Len Wiseman) *Kate Beckinsale, Scott Speedman, Shane Brolly, Michael Sheen, Bill Nighy.* A good horror premise — that of a war between a werewolf clan and a vampire clan — is squandered by lifeless direction and tired execution. Humorless and cliché-ridden, *Underworld* ponderously clomps through the motions as Goth-inspired vampires spout portentous dialogue and grunge-inspired werewolves (or "lycans" as the film calls them) snarl Theater 101-level ripostes in between morphing into unconvincing CGI creatures. The thin story is uninvolving, the action listless, the look of the film ripped off from *The Matrix, Batman*, etc — i.e., all the usual suspects. The unlikely casting of Beckinsale almost pays off; she looks great in shiny leather, and gives it her best, but is let down by crushingly dull storytelling. Not even trying to be scary, the film only offers Wiseman an excuse to trot out "cool" clotheshorses, then photograph them in "stylish" fight scenes. Not even fun as eye candy. ★½ DVD Letterbox: $28.99, DVD Pan & Scan: $28.99, DVD Unrated - 2 Disc Extended Edition: $34.99, VHS: $102.99

Underworld

(1997, 95 min, US, Roger Christian) *Denis Leary, Annabella Sciorra, Joe Mantegna, Traci Lords.* Leary does his best to make this Tarantino knockoff palatable, but to little avail. He plays Johnny Crown, an aging ex-con out to avenge his father's murder attempt. His other agenda is the rehabilitation of a childhood friend-turned-mobster (Mantegna at his most mannered and annoying). Artificial in the extreme, *Underworld* apes Tarantino to the point of embarrassment, with none of his style or wit. ★½

Underworld U.S.A.

(1961, 99 min, US, Samuel Fuller) *Cliff Robertson, Dolores Dorn, Beatrice Kay.* Fuller's unrelentingly gritty murder drama stars Robertson as a young man who, as a youngster, witnessed the brutal murder of his father at the hands of an organized crime syndicate. Vowing revenge, he becomes obsessed with righting his father's death by infiltrating the mob echelon and tracking down the killers. But his plans for revenge become complicated after he finds himself caught between the villainous mob and the FBI, who want him as an informer. ★★★

Unfaithful

(2002, 124 min, US, Adrian Lyne) *Richard Gere, Diane Lane, Olivier Martinez, Erik Per Sullivan, Chad Lowe.* Director Lyne (*Fatal Attraction*) is back exploring more marital missteps in this glossy, well-acted though superficial remake of Claude Chabrol's *An Unfaithful Wife.* Connie and Edward Sumner (Lane, Gere) seem to have the perfect life in Westchester County. He's a successful car exec and she's a happy wife and mother, and they live in luxury with their nine-year-old son. Why, then, did she begin an affair with the handsome Paul (Martinez), a charming bookseller she literally bumps into on the street? Other than because he's gorgeous and she can, the film never clearly explains Connie's motivations, which keeps this from being a truly satisfying tale of passion and betrayal. Lane is terrific, however, as the wayward wife, in search of something but not sure what. ★★½ DVD: $19.99, VHS: $12.99

Unfaithfully Yours

(1948, 105 min, US, Preston Sturges) *Rex Harrison, Linda Darnell, Rudy Vallee.* Through the bungling interference of his idiot brother-in-law Vallee, world-famous symphony conductor Harrison is led to believe that his adoring, doe-eyed wife Darnell is having an affair with his personal assistant. Contains classic sequences in which Harrison's revenge fantasies are brilliantly choreographed to various pieces of music he's conducting. Another nifty little number from Sturges. (Remade in 1984) ★★★½ VHS: $59.99

U

Unfaithfully Yours

(1984, 96 min, US, Howard Zieff) *Dudley Moore, Nastassja Kinski, Armand Assante, Albert Brooks.* Okay remake of the classic Preston Sturges comedy, with Moore reprising the Rex Harrison role as a conductor who believes his wife (Kinski) guilty of adultery, and fantasizes revenge and murder. Moore is rather good as the exasperated husband, and has a particularly funny scene inside a movie theatre. ★★½ VHS: $29.99

An Unfinished Piece
for the Player Piano

(1977, 105 min, USSR, Nikita Mikhalkov) *Alexander Kalyagin, Elena Solovel, Nikita Mikhalkov.* Mikhalkov adapts a Chekhov play which is set in a summer dacha and features an amazing array of ensemble acting. The passions, frustrations and failings of these members of the spoiled gentry provide the nucleus for this Russian *Rules of the Game*. A sumptuous, melancholy period piece. (Russian with English subtitles) ★★★½ VHS: $29.99

Unforgettable

(1996, 111 min, US, John Dahl) *Kim Cattrall, Linda Fiorentino, Peter Coyote, Ray Liotta, Christopher McDonald, David Paymer.* In this "A-budget," femme fatale-less thriller, Dahl concentrates on "hallucinatory cinema" such as *Jacob's Ladder* and *Don't Look Now*, rather than his accustomed '40s B-movie vocabulary. The results are mixed. Liotta stars as a forensics expert whose unending search for his wife's killer leads him to experiment on himself with a formula (developed by scientist Fiorentino) that enables him to experience the memories of murder victims — and in some cases, to actually see who murdered them. Dahl's visual stylization of Bill Geddie's screenplay focuses on the power of memory thereby adding an extra dimension to the story. ★★½ DVD Dual: $14.99

An Unforgettable Summer

(1994, 82 min, Romania, Lucian Pintilie) *Kristin Scott Thomas, Claudiu Bleont, Olga Tudorache, George Constantin.* Scott Thomas gives a haunting performance as the wife of a career officer (Bleont) posted in a remote and dangerous corner of eastern Romania during the mid-1920s, a land recently controlled by either Turk, Macedonian or Bulgarian forces. When the codified cruelties of her culture begin to poison her marriage, she is forced to choose between what she knows is right and what is best for her to believe in. Like his earlier work *The Oak*, director Pintilie has fashioned a tale with few "obvious" villains and even fewer clear answers. (English, Romanian, French and Bulgarian with English subtitles) ★★★

Unforgiven

(1992, 127 min, US, Clint Eastwood) *Clint Eastwood, Gene Hackman, Morgan Freeman, Richard Harris, Jaimz Woolvett, Saul Rubinek, Frances Fisher.* Eastwood's lyrical, craftsmanlike direction, a brilliantly structured screenplay by David Webb Peoples, a superlative ensemble cast and superior production values all contribute to make this Oscar-winning revisionist western a modern masterpiece. Eastwood stars as a retired gunfighter who answers the call when a group of prostitutes put a price on the head of a sadistic cowboy. As Clint makes his way, Hackman's tyrannical sheriff (Oscar winner Hackman) prepares for the expected onslaught of hired killers about to descend upon his small town. One of the many beauties of *Unforgiven* is director Eastwood's homage to the traditional western while at the same time expand-

ing the boundaries of the genre. Not since *Red River* has a film so successfully explored the complexities of moral ambiguity. The myth of the Old West is a bloody one and as Eastwood sees it, death is close up and not at all the stuff of lore. ★★★★ DVD Letterbox: $19.99, DVD 2-disc Special Edition: $26.99, VHS: $9.99, VHS Letterbox: $9.99

The Unforgiven

(1960, 125 min, US, John Huston) *Burt Lancaster, Audrey Hepburn, Lillian Gish, Audie Murphy.* Huston's unconventional western adventure concentrates more on racial tension between the white and Indian races than on the usual shoot-em-up hijinks. Set in 1850s Texas, the story concerns a ranching family who become at odds with both their neighbors and an Indian tribe when it is suspected that their adopted daughter is actually an Indian orphan. Gritty performances from the cast. ★★★

The Unholy

(1988, 100 min, US, Camilo Vila) *Ben Cross, Ned Beatty, William Russ, Hal Holbrook, Trevor Howard.* Cross plays a priest whose miraculous survival from a 20-story fall leads him to a New Orleans parish where demonic events have been occurring. Convoluted and not all that scary. ★½ VHS: $9.99

The Unholy Wife

(1957, 94 min, US, John Farrow) *Rod Steiger, Diana Dors, Tom Tryon.* With the help of her lover, an adulterous wife (Dors) plans to murder her husband (Steiger). But when the plan goes awry, the pair attempt to put him behind bars instead. A mediocre tale of jealousy and revenge. ★½

Unhook the Stars

(1996, 105 min, US, Nick Cassavetes) *Gena Rowlands, Marisa Tomei, Gérard Depardieu, Jake Lloyd, Moira Kelly.* Rowlands' marvelous performance is the centerpiece of this affecting, intuitive character study cowritten and directed by her (and John Cassavetes') son Nick. Rowlands is Mildred, a widow whose children have left home. Reluctant to face the future alone, Mildred's life takes an unusual turn when Monica (Tomei), her blowsy neighbor, asks Mildred to baby-sit. Thus begins a wonderful relationship between Mildred and six-year-old J.J., and a tentative one between her and Monica. Depardieu is a truck driver who knows what we know: Mildred and Gena are class acts all the way. ★★★ DVD: $14.99, VHS: $9.99

Union City

(1980, 87 min, US, Mark Reichert) *Deborah Harry, Everett McGill, Pat Benatar.* A jealous accountant with a lusty wife (Harry) kills a man who has been stealing his milk bottles. Murder and paranoia are set amongst the grit of an industrial city in this convoluted though moody noir tale. ★★½ DVD: $9.99, VHS: $9.99

Universal Soldier

(1992, 98 min, US, Roland Emmerich) *Jean-Claude Van Damme, Dolph Lundgren, Jerry Orbach.* It's 'Nam, 1969. Nice Cajun boy Van Damme is caught in a fight to the death with psycho sergeant Lundgren. Both die in the showdown only to reappear 25 years later when a group of sleazy Army scientists unveil a line of antiterrorist robots created from the bodies of dead U.S. soldiers. Of course, Dolph's naturally sadistic tendencies override his programming, renewing his old rivalry with honest Van Damme. Emmerich's testosterone-driven action film is short on any technical prowess, but it does qualify as dumb fun. (Followed by 2 sequels) ★★ DVD Letterbox: $14.99

Unlawful Entry

(1992, 111 min, US, Jonathan Kaplan) *Kurt Russell, Madeleine Stowe, Ray Liotta, Roger E. Mosley, Dick Miller.* Affluent L.A. couple Russell and Stowe have their home broken into. Into their lives enters friendly policeman Liotta. Thus begins yet another in the continuing long line of "from hell" psycho thrillers. This is nothing more than a first-draft throwaway which somehow bypassed rewrite and went straight to production. However, Liotta, as a menacing cop-on-the-beat, brings just the right amount of intoxicating villainy and demonic glee to his character. He almost makes it worthwhile. ★½ DVD: $14.99

Unmade Beds

(1997, 95 min, US, Nicholas Barker) *Aimee Copp, Michael De Stefano, Brenda Monte, Mikey Russo.* Mostly disturbing, at times amusing, but ultimately tiresome, *Unmade Beds* is a voyeuristic peek into the lives of four of New York City's legion of lonely hearts. Using a twist on documentary form, director Barker compiled hours of interviews with his four subjects and then wrote scripts for them to enact on camera — so we have real people playing themselves in a talking head interview format. Individually their stories are fascinating, repulsive, heartrending and perverse, but taken as a whole, their overall impact is downright depressing. Still, one can't help being drawn in by a kind morbid curiosity as Barker uncovers their lives and forces us to watch as if it were a train wreck. ★★ DVD: $19.99, VHS: $14.99

An Unmarried Woman

(1978, 124 min, US, Paul Mazursky) *Jill Clayburgh, Alan Bates, Cliff Gorman, Michael Murphy.* Clayburgh's sensational performance is the heart of director Mazursky's penetrating drama about a dutiful wife who learns to be self-reliant after her husband leaves her for another woman. Bates is Clayburgh's new and sensitive paramour. One of Mazursky's most accomplished and poignant films. ★★★½ VHS: $29.99

The Unnamable

(1988, 87 min, US, Jean-Paul Ouellette) *Charles King, Mark Stephenson.* A group of college students spend the night in a haunted house to dispel rumors that a horrible creature lives there. Guess what happens. Nothing new, and not all that proficient, but there are a few scares. Based on a story by H.P. Lovecraft. ★★ VHS: $14.99

Unnatural Pursuits

(1991, 143 min, GB, Christopher Morahan) *Alan Bates, Richard Wilson, Nigel Planer, Paul Zimat, Bob Balaban, Deborah Rush, John Mahoney.* Simon Gray's West End comedy dissecting the artistic process makes for a fast and gloriously funny adaptation. Bates is remarkable as disheveled, acerbic playwright Hamish Partt, a chain-smoking alcoholic whose obsession to rewrite his newest play takes him from London to Los Angeles to Dallas to New York all the while experiencing a mental breakdown. In a series of escalating hallucinations, Hamish is haunted by skateboarding street people when not breaking into musical production numbers. Gray's masterful script examines Hamish's deterioration as he has thrust upon him insecure stage directors, bombastic producers, flirtatious Southern belle reporters, self-centered actors and an ogling public. ★★★★ VHS: $19.99

The Unsinkable Molly Brown

(1964, 128 min, US, Charles Walters) *Debbie Reynolds, Harve Presnell, Ed Begley.* Reynolds has her best film role as mountain girl-cum-society darling and *Titanic* survivor Molly Brown in this splashy screen version of Meredith Willson's (*The Music Man*) Broadway musical. Songs include "I Ain't Down Yet" and "I'll Never Say No to You." ★★★ DVD: $19.99, VHS: $14.99

Unstrung Heroes

(1995, 93 min, US, Diane Keaton) *Andie MacDowell, John Turturro, Michael Richards, Maury Chaykin, Nathan Watt.* Young Steven Lidz (Watt) is not having a very good summer. His father (Turturro) is a narcissistic inventor who clings with almost religous zeal to the tenants of scientific inquiry. His mother (MacDowell) is slowly dying of cancer, though Steven hasn't been made privy to this fact. Finding it all too much to take, the 12-year-old Steven runs off to live with his two uncles (Richards, Chaykin), a pair of paranoid schizophrenic, socialist Jews who live in an apartment piled high with decades worth of newspapers and closets full of rubber balls. Tinged with melancholy and tempered with mirthful nostalgia, *Unstrung Heroes* provides many a warm-hearted moment. But ultimately the storytelling suffers at the hands of a script that, by trying to squeeze in too much, boils down to a series of loosely connected scenes that offer very little character development. ★★½ DVD: $9.99, VHS: $19.99

Untamed Heart

(1993, 102 min, US, Tony Bill) *Christian Slater, Marisa Tomei, Rosie Perez.* Slater gives a touching performance as a busboy whose childhood heart condition has left him emotionally and physically scarred. He's soon brought out of his silent shell by his love for a waitress (Tomei). They have a real chemistry — even if Slater is more alluring before he opens his mouth and begins to pour his guts out. Though its pacing is a little off (the beginning is slow and the ending unravels too quickly), *Untamed Heart* is a sweet, warm, there's-someone-out-there-for-everyone film that teeters quietly on the brink of being a real tearjerker. Special mention to Perez as Tomei's sidekick. ★★★ DVD: $14.99

Until the End of the World

(1991, 160 min, US, Wim Wenders) *William Hurt, Solveig Dommartin, Max von Sydow, Jeanne Moreau, Sam Neill.* Director Wenders takes the viewer on the ultimate 'round-the-world odyssey with this "futuristic" road movie (set in 1999) filled with lots of high-tech future shock images and gadgetry. Hurt is carrying a top secret device and on the run from industrial bounty hunters. He hooks up with Dommartin and together they lead their pursuers on a global chase. After 90 minutes of non-stop action, they wind up in the Australian Outback where the film slows to a more familiar Wenders crawl. As in his other films, Wenders portrays a world in which people are desperately seeking a sense of self-understanding while craving human contact — it's a world in which, despite the explosion in global communication technology, we are more alone than ever. ★★★ VHS: $19.99

Until They Sail

(1957, 95 min, US, Robert Wise) *Jean Simmons, Joan Fontaine, Paul Newman, Piper Laurie, Sandra Dee.* Based on James A. Michener's wartime novel, this military drama is vintage soap opera but it's not without its compelling moments. Simmons,

---

Fontaine, Laurie and Dee play sisters in WWII New Zealand. With the men of their village overseas, the town's women become romantic targets for the visiting American soldiers. Newman is one of them. Playwright Robert Anderson adapted the screenplay, which explores such adult themes as infidelity, wartime romance, and moral and sexual attitudes. ★★½ VHS: $19.99

The Untold Story

(1993, 95 min, Hong Kong, Herman Yau) *Anthony Wong, Danny Lee.* Based on a true incident, this grisly tale plays like *Silence of the Lambs* with a Chinatown twist. Wong stars as a restaurateur who becomes the prime suspect in a series of murders. The police department at first befriend him and sample his delicious complimentary pork buns, until they discover that they've found their missing persons — ground up within the filling of the buns! The remainder of the film shows their brutal attempts to make Wong confess to his crimes. Part police procedural and part serial killer horror film, *The Untold Story* is definitely meant for strong stomachs only, and will quite possibly change the way you look at dim sum. (Cantonese with English subtitles) ★★★½ DVD: $29.99, VHS: $79.99

The Untouchables

(1987, 119 min, US, Brian De Palma) *Kevin Costner, Robert De Niro, Sean Connery, Andy Garcia, Charles Martin Smith.* Director De Palma's crowning achievement is a rousing and grandly stylistic gangster movie set in crime-laden 1920s Chicago. Costner is Eliot Ness, an idealistic government agent who goes after mob kingpin Al Capone, getting a lot of help from the cop on the beat (Connery). De Niro plays Capone with over-the-top abandon, and Connery is amazing in his Oscar-winning portrayal. Garcia and Smith (both first-rate) are Ness' two other "untouchables." De Palma's train station sequence, a nod to the "The Odessa Steps" sequence in *Battleship Potemkin*, is a knockout. Written by David Mamet. ★★★★ DVD Letterbox: $19.99, DVD: $19.99, VHS: $9.99, VHS Letterbox: $9.99

Unzipped

(1995, 76 min, US, Douglas Keeve) *Isaac Mizrahi, Naomi Campbell, Cindy Crawford, Kate Moss, Linda Evangelista, Sandra Bernhard, Shalom Harlow, Eartha Kitt, Amber Valletta, Patricia Velasquez, Christy Turlington.* This delightfully playful documentary romp through the fashion world with designer Mizrahi is a surefire crowd pleaser due in large part to his irrepressible and engaging personality. The film's action centers around the swirl of creative energy Mizrahi and staff are pumping into preparing his fall '94 colllection. Amidst the chaos, Mizrahi lets loose a barrage of bitchy, yet not too vicious one-liners, social critiques and, of course, barbs at other designers. The film culminates with the Big Show in New York, which, in Mizrahi's case, is a brilliant piece of performance art. As raucous and raw as its subject, its at times annoyingly jagged camera work is saved only by masterful, zippy MTV-paced editing. ★★★ DVD: $19.99, VHS: $14.99

Up!

(1976, 80 min, US, Russ Meyer) Outrageously buxom women and dumb, muscular men laying their sexually aggressive prowess on the line. Narrated by a perpetually bouncing Kitten Natividad. Probably Russ' most explicit feature and definitely his most eccentric. ★★ DVD: $39.99, VHS: $69.99

Up at the Villa

(2000, 115 min, US/GB, Philip Haas) *Kristin Scott Thomas, Sean Penn, Anne Bancroft, Jeremy Davies, Derek Jacobi, James Fox.* W. Somerset Maugham's novella makes for a sumptuous romantic exercise of class conflict and romantic intrigue all set against the rising tide of Fascism in pre-WWII Italy. The luminous Scott Thomas is Mary, a widowed British expatriate living in Florence amid a small circle of wealthy friends. A proposal from an aging but well-placed politician sets in motion a weekend of soul-searching, parties and romantic indiscretions. This includes American playboy Rowley (Penn), who falls under the considerable charms of the reluctant fiancée. Director Haas' cast practically floats through this story of a sentried class abroad at the end of its days. Bancroft almost steals the movie as an American widow whose biting tongue and social status guarantees she's always holding court. ★★★½ VHS: $102.99

Up Close and Personal

(1996, 124 min, US, Jon Avnet) *Robert Redford, Michelle Pfeiffer, Kate Nelligan, Joe Mantegna, Stockard Channing, Glenn Plummer.* Loosely based on the life of Jessica Savitch by way of *A Star Is Born*, this polished if sometimes gawky romantic drama tracing the rise of a TV newscaster doesn't have as much to say about the news industry as it pretends to, but offers especially attractive performances from its two leads. Pfeiffer's aspiring newscaster comes under the tutelage of station manager Redford. She works her way up from weather girl to anchor as they fall in love and marry, experiencing the ups and downs inherent in a relationship marked by one spouse's sudden success. There are some good scenes that spotlight the business of news reporting, but the film also gives in to clichés and coincidences, neither of which suit the talents of its two stars. ★★½ DVD: $14.99, VHS: $9.99

Up in Arms

(1944, 106 min, US, Elliott Nugent) *Danny Kaye, Dana Andrews, Dinah Shore, Constance Dowling, Louis Calhern, Margaret Dumont.* In his feature film debut, Kaye wreaks havoc on an unsuspecting Army as a hypochondriac who gets drafted. Danny performs a few musical numbers, smuggles Dowling on board his South Pacific-bound ship, and manages to capture a few enemy soldiers. Shore plays a nurse who's sweet on him, and Andrews is Danny's bunkmate. Though it's slightly dated, Kaye's mugging and patter songs are genuinely entertaining, and there are plenty of laughs to go around. ★★½

Up in Smoke

(1978, 85 min, US, Lou Adler) *Cheech Marin, Tommy Chong.* This first (and best) film from that doped-up comic duo, Cheech & Chong, may be dated, but it still provides kilos of laughs. All we can say is that if there are still some of you out there who enjoy the occasional mind-bender, be grateful that this testament to the halcyon days of unbridled substance abuse is still available on video. ★★★ DVD: $14.99, VHS: $9.99

Up to a Certain Point

(1985, 70 min, Cuba, Tomás Gutiérrez Alea) *Oscar Alvarez, Mirta Ibarra.* Director Alea tackles several themes, including politics, male chauvinism and marital infidelity, to bring about the tale of a writer and his attempts at writing an anti-machismo film for his actress wife. Alvarez is the screenwriter Oscar, caught between his feelings of love and the direction of his project. Ibarra shines as Lina, the

---

independent and alluring dock worker who becomes the role model for his main character and the object of his affection. This film is well worth the effort not only for its interesting portrayal of somewhat modern-day Cuban life but also for its honesty in the portrayal of struggles which go beyond wage earnings. (Spanish with English subtitles) ★★★ VHS: $19.99

The Uprising

(1980, 96 min, Nicaragua, Peter Lilienthal) Filmed just months after the Sandinista revolution, this raw and impassioned drama recruited the real-life peasants and soldiers of the country to authentically re-create the atmosphere of a people and of a land thrust into turbulent revolt. The story, set in the university town of León, centers on a young man, a member of Somoza's National Guard who, with the help of his father, comes to be a supporter of the rebel Sandinistas. Kind of a fictionalized documentary, this simple and direct story celebrates the solidarity and heroics of these impoverished people. (Spanish with English subtitles) ★★★ VHS: $69.99

Uptown Saturday Night

(1974, 104 min, US, Sidney Poitier) *Bill Cosby, Sidney Poitier, Richard Pryor, Harry Belafonte, Flip Wilson, Roscoe Lee Browne.* Cosby wins $50,000 in the lottery. One problem though — his wallet was taken during a holdup. Cosby and Poitier must get through a maze filled with scheming gangsters, con men and women. A bit dated and not as good as its follow-up *Let's Do It Again*, but it certainly is fun. ★★½ DVD: $19.99

Uranus

(1991, 100 min, France, Claude Berri) *Gérard Depardieu, Michel Blanc, Jean-Pierre Marielle, Philippe Noiret.* This rather disappointing and convoluted drama is set in a small French village thrown into chaos immediately after WWII when the new government attempts to sort out who were the patriots and who were the collaborators. Depardieu steals the show as a drunken, brutish bully of a bartender with a newfound love of poetry who is falsely implicated as an informant. At the heart of the film is an interesting idea of a people torn apart and in near hysterics by their own actions, but the execution by director Berri is too slow and bland to create much involvement for the viewer. (French with English subtitles) ★★ VHS: $19.99

Urban Cowboy

(1980, 135 min, US, James Bridges) *John Travolta, Debra Winger, Scott Glenn.* Cowboy Travolta tries to lasso cowgirl Winger at Gilley's Bar in Texas in this involving romantic drama. The film which created the mechanical bull stir (for awhile). (The basis for a short-lived Broadway musical) ★★½ DVD Letterbox: $14.99, VHS: $9.99

Urban Legend

(1998, 99 min, US, Jamie Blanks) *Jared Leto, Alicia Witt, Rebecca Gayheart, Natasha Gregson Wagner, Loretta Devine.* A weak, cynical cash-in on the *Scream* craze. A hooked killer is offing folks at a university, utilizing scenarios of famous urban legends. The film opens with a botched rendition of the Scary Gas Station Attendant tale, then picks up a bit when old stalwart Robert "Freddie Krueger" Englund shows up. But it's all a rip-off of *Scream*'s post-modern, hip approach to its pop-culture savvy film characters. While the killer's a bit tougher to guess, this whole affair is ugly, pointless and rather cruel. (Sequel: *Urban Legends 2: Final Cut*) ★½ DVD: $19.99, VHS: $9.99

Urban Legends: Final Cut

(2000, 99 min, US, John Ottman) *Jennifer Morrison, Matthew Davis, Hart Bochner, Joseph Lawrence, Anthony Anderson, Loretta Devine.* This sequel to the surprise 1998 hit has only one returning character — Devine's Pam Grier-obsessed security guard — and a new crop of colorless teen victims. This time set at a fictitious film school, *Final Cut* begins rather promisingly, with a nice, creepy tone. Stock characters and cheesy dialogue notwithstanding, the first half of the film is slightly above-average slasher fare. Then the crap kicks in: killings become more arbitrary and ordinary, culminating with a risible wrap-up that rivals the original's climax in sheer stupidity. ★★ DVD: $19.99

Urbania

(1999, 103 min, US, Jon Shear) *Dan Futterman, Alan Cumming, Lothaire Bluteau, William Sage, Matt Keeslar, Barbara Sukowa.* An excitingly ambitious and original style of gay filmmaking is in evidence with *Urbania*, a feverish tale of one young man's search for sanity, retribution and love. In the urban jungle of nocturnal New York, Charlie (Futterman), traumatized by the violent gay bashing of his lover by a darkly sexy thug, has become a lost soul. With memories invading his mind, Charlie hits the streets, meeting a variety of strange storied characters. The intricately structured film builds to intensity as Charlie finds, befriends and is forced to decide the fate of the man he lusts and loathes. A taut, emotional and surreal story adapted from Daniel Reitz's play, "Urban Folk Tales." Futterman is mesmerizing as the vengeful gay man on a mission in this haunting *After Hours* for the queer set. ★★★½ DVD: $24.99

Urinal

(1991, 100 min, Canada, John Greyson) Less provocative and explicit than the title suggests, this low-budget Canadian production is a documentary-style talk fest centering on homosexual repression through the ages. The film's premise is that several prominently rumored gays, lesbians and bisexuals from the past (Yukio Mishima, Sergei Eisenstein, Frida Kahlo, Frances Loring, Langston Hughes and Florence Whyle) are mysteriously brought together in a Toronto apartment where they hold a series of discussions on the sociology of homosexuality and

how to counter gay repression. Despite its static and awkward dramatic pretensions, the film is an interesting and literate examination of gay and lesbian history as well as a call for action against discrimination. ★★½ VHS: $29.99

Used Cars

(1980, 111 min, US, Robert Zemeckis) *Kurt Russell, Jack Warden, Deborah Harmon.* It's the battle of the used car salesmen as Russell squares off against Warden in a no-holds-barred customer-getting contest. An uproarious and daffy comedy written by Bob Gale and director Zemeckis. ★★★ DVD: $14.99

Used People

(1992, 116 min, US, Beeban Kidron) *Shirley MacLaine, Marcello Mastroianni, Kathy Bates, Jessica Tandy, Marcia Gay Harden, Sylvia Sidney.* The comparisons of *Used People* to *Moonstruck* and *Fried Green Tomatoes* are inevitable. All share a sentimental bent without being too cute about it; members of near-dysfunctional families endear themselves to us and each other. It's the familiarity which makes this humorous and beguiling comedy-drama a welcome visitor. MacLaine plays a recently widowed Jewish wife and mother from Queens. On the day of her husband's funeral, she is asked on a date by determined Italian restaurateur Mastroianni. Against her better judgment, she agrees. What follows is a series of disastrous family get-togethers, culture clashes and romantic pursuits. The film is immeasurably aided by a good supporting cast. ★★★ VHS: $19.99

The Usual Suspects

(1995, 105 min, US, Bryan Singer) *Kevin Spacey, Benicio del Toro, Gabriel Byrne, Stephen Baldwin, Kevin Pollak, Chazz Palminteri, Pete Postlethwaite, Suzy Amis, Giancarlo Esposito, Paul Bartel.* This witty and ingenious noir thriller is a delicious up-and-down ride on a twisting plotline that involves a rag-tag assemblage of small-time hoods who, having met in a lineup, join forces and commit to performing *one* job together. Predictably, this leads to further involvement that ultimately begins to get out of hand. The group's reluctant leader, Dean Keaton (Byrne), is a former big-time grifter joined by a cou-

The Usual Suspects

ple of smaller hoodlums (Baldwin and Del Toro), a weapons expert (Pollak), and a talkative, crippled flunkie known as Verbal (Oscar winner Spacey). Opening with a grisly massacre on a lonesome San Pedro, California, pier, the film unfolds through flashback as the tale is told by Verbal, the lone survivor. To further thicken the already Byzantine plot is the lurking presence of a mythical underworld figure known as Keyser Söze, who may be the mastermind behind the massacre. Spacey walks away with the movie; his Verbal is a study in criminal paranoia accented by physical vulnerability. Director Singer and screenwriter Christopher McQuarrie (another Oscar winner) team to create a brilliant and timeless crime story that's an immediate classic of the genre. ★★★★ DVD Dual Special Edition: $19.99, VHS: $9.99

Utu

(1983, 124 min, New Zealand, Geoff Murphy) *Bruno Lawrence, Anzac Wallace, Kelly Johnson.* This violent and spectacularly photographed film crosses the boundaries of both art film and action flick. Set during the Maori uprising in rural 1870s New Zealand, the story focuses on a Maori ex-army sergeant whose family and village are wiped out during a raid and who becomes the radical and vengeful leader of a group of rebellious natives intent on eradicating the white settlers by any means possible. An exciting and bloody story of the fight for survival. ★★★ DVD: $29.99, VHS: $24.99

Utz

(1992, 95 min, Germany/GB/Italy, George Sluizer) *Armis Mueller-Stahl, Brenda Fricker, Peter Riegert, Paul Scofield.* From the director of the provocative *The Vanishing* comes this elegant, spare and quietly involving drama. Filmed in English, the story focuses on Baron von Utz (Mueller-Stahl), a wealthy Czechoslavakian collector of German porcelain figurines. Through a series of flashbacks, we learn of the roots of his lifelong obsession with his collection as well as his mysterious life. Riegert is an international antique broker who befriends him in the hope of obtaining the collection after his death and Fricker is his more-than-an-employee housekeeper. Beautiful locales in Prague provide an exotic backdrop to the gentle character study. ★★★ VHS: $19.99

Va Savoir

(2001, 154 min, France, Jacques Rivette) *Jeanne Balibar, Sergio Castellitto, Marianne Basler, Jacques Bonnaffé, Claude Berri.* To watch a Rivette film is to share his love of acting, his love of play and his love of love itself. The six central characters of *Va Savoir* begin rooted unhappily in their routines, and over the course of two-and-a-half hours find love both new and old and end up better for it. Interspersed are scenes of a Pirandello play, whose director and actress are drifting apart: She towards an old flame, he in pursuit of a lost Pirandello manuscript (and its lovely young keeper). The pairings twist about amiably, climaxing in whimsically drunken duel for the actress' affections. This is the flipside to his *L'Amour Fou*; the air stays light throughout, and nothing of too much

consequence happens. Unless you count l'amour. (French with English subtitles) ★★★½ DVD: $29.99, VHS Subtitled: $21.99

Vagabond

(1985, 105 min, France, Agnès Varda) *Sandrine Bonnaire, Macha Meril.* Bonnaire is mesmerizing in this hauntingly nihilistic account of an aimless young woman's final days. The beginning of the film finds the girl's frozen body in a ditch. Then told in flashback by the last people to have had contact with her, the film attempts to piece together the life and values of this complex teenager. A stunning film experience and one of the most important and powerful French films in recent memory. (French with English subtitles) ★★★★ DVD: $29.99, VHS: $29.99

Valdez Is Coming

(1971, 90 min, US, Edwin Sherin) *Burt Lancaster, Susan Clark, Richard Jordan, Hector Elizondo.* Lancaster gives a solid performance as Valdez, part-time lawman, part-time stagecoach shotgun, who is set up to kill a black man wrongly accused of murder. Realizing the mistake he has made, he attempts to accept responsibility for the dead man's pregnant Indian wife. This leads him on an odyssey through a barren, treacherous landscape populated by men without ethics or compassion. Good ensemble acting helps overcome a somewhat pedestrian treatment of an intriguing plot line which slowly unravels just who is guilty of what. Based on a novel by Elmore Leonard. ★★½ DVD Letterbox: $19.99

Valentina

(1983, 90 min, Spain, Antonio J. Betancor) *Anthony Quinn.* Adapted from Ramon J. Sender's celebrated novel, this deeply moving film, set in a small town in northern Spain, examines a pre-adolescent boy's passionate love for the lyrical Valentina and the efforts of their families to keep them apart. Quinn is featured as the boy's understanding teacher. (Spanish with English subtitles) ★★★

Valentine

(2001, 96 min, US, Jamie Blanks) *David Boreanaz, Denise Richards, Marley Shelton, Katherine Heigl.* A dorky young boy is humiliated at a middle school Valentine's Day dance, and ten years later, girls involved in the incident start turning up dead. For fans of '80s slasher fare, this by-the-numbers horror film is watchable for a while because it apes the formula so strictly. Soon, however, the poor acting, insulting caricatures and lack of suspense/scares wear on one's nostalgic glow. Catch seminal '80s holiday slasher *My Bloody Valentine* instead. ★½ DVD Letterbox: $14.99, VHS: $14.99

The Valley (Obscured by Clouds)

Valentino

(1977, 127 min, GB, Ken Russell) *Rudolf Nureyev, Leslie Caron, Michelle Phillips, Carol Kane, Seymour Cassel.* Russell creates some stunning visuals but comes up short in dramatic terms in this lurid exposé on the life of silent screen star Rudolph Valentino. Opening with the frenzied scene of his funeral, the film's flashbacks attempt to chart his rise to fame as well as uncover the man behind the image. As Valentino, Nureyev — who looks the part — is, unfortunately, wooden and uninspiring. Russell, who in the past has not side-stepped homosexual themes, curiously downplays the Latin Lover's gayness in favor of a man constantly trying to prove his masculinity. ★★

The Valley (Obscured by Clouds)

(1972, 106 min, France, Barbet Schroeder) *Bulle Ogier.* This legendary cult film is an aurally hypnotic and sensually seductive drama of the spiritual and sexual enlightenment of a group of Westerners who venture into the uncharted, mystic rainforest of New Guinea. With ravishing photography by Nestor Almendros, and a spacey soundtrack by Pink Floyd, the film follows a bored diplomat's wife (Ogier) whose search for the feathers of a near-extinct bird allows her to experience a transformation of spirit when she meets the indigenous Mapuga tribesmen and travels to a secret and strangely powerful "valley of the gods." (French with English subtitles) ★★★ DVD Letterbox Subtitled: $19.99

Valley Girl

(1983, 95 min, US, Martha Coolidge) *Nicolas Cage, Deborah Foreman, Frederic Forrest, Colleen Camp.* Like, can love last between a true Val (Foreman) and a punker from Hollywood (Cage)? It's, like, a war of the cliques in this amusing little film about California culture clashes. ★★½ DVD Special Edition: $14.99

Valley of the Dolls

(1967, 123 min, US, Mark Robson) *Patty Duke, Susan Hayward, Sharon Tate, Lee Grant, Martin Milner.* Trashy, melodramatic piece of camp heaven based on Jacqueline Susann's best-selling novel that takes us on a hell-bound highway of drugs, sex, drinks and infidelity and the rise and fall of starlets in the entertainment biz. The film, at times, drifts into cliché-ridden waters, but is nevertheless chock full of those absolutely absurd soap operaish elements which make this genre so much fun. ★★★ VHS: $14.99

Valmont

(1989, 137 min, France/GB, Milos Forman) *Colin Firth, Meg Tilly, Annette Bening, Henry Thomas, Fairuza Balk.* Opulent settings in exotic European locales and meticulously designed period costumes can't save this uninvolving drama, based on Choderlos de Laclos' 1782 novel "Les Liaisons Dangereuses." Sadly, director Forman misses the central idea behind the story of intrigue amidst the French aristocracy by not delving into the characters' icy hearts and as a result, the film is all spectacle and no soul. Stick to Stephen Frears' mesmerizing *Dangerous Liaisons*, made a year earlier, and based on the same story. ★ DVD Letterbox: $19.99

Vampire in Brooklyn

(1995, 95 min, US, Wes Craven) *Eddie Murphy, Angela Bassett, Allen Payne, Kadeem Hardison, Zakes Mokae.* Director Craven brings a seductive and eerie style to this shadowy vampire tale, but *Vampire in Brooklyn* ultimately succumbs to its unimaginative screenplay which is not nearly funny enough to be comedy or scary enough to be horror. Murphy is a vampire who comes to Brooklyn (in an impressively mounted opening) searching for a lost soul mate. He immediately finds her in the person of policewoman Bassett, and begins to court her while dining on Brooklyn's not-so-finest denizens. Though Bassett brings dimension to an underwritten role, neither star is serviced by a thoroughly flat and undeveloped story and dialogue. ★★ DVD Letterbox: $14.99, VHS: $9.99

Vampire Journals

(1997, 92 min, US, Ted Nicolaou) *Jonathan Morris, David Gunn, Kirsten Cere, Starr Andreeff.* A surprisingly enjoyable chiller, *The Vampire Journals* is a definite sleeper. Beginning rather abruptly, like some old-time serial chapter, the story details the efforts of a "good" master vampire while attempting to rid the world of an old, evil master vampire while attempting to repress his own vampiric nature. That's about it for story, but a terrific Gothic atmosphere is set early on and maintained throughout the entire film. Short on plot, long on mood, *Journal's* only real drawbacks are a ditsy heroine and an anticlimactic ending. ★★★ DVD: $24.99, VHS: $14.99

The Vampire Lovers

(1970, 88 min, GB, Roy Ward Baker) *Ingrid Pitt, Pippa Steele, Madeleine Smith, Peter Cushing.* Pitt sizzles as the sexy seductress Marcilla whose lust for blood is matched only by her lust for other beautiful maidens in this erotic adaptation of Sheridan Le Fanu's "Carmilla" from the house of Hammer. (DVD double feature with *Countess Dracula*) ★★★

Vampire's Kiss

(1989, 103 min, US, Robert Biermen) *Nicolas Cage, Jennifer Beals, Maria Conchita Alonso, Elizabeth Ashley.* If you thought Griffin Dunne had a bad night in Martin Scorsese's *After Hours*, wait till you get a load of New York's truly dark side. Cage stars as a literary agent who unwisely picks up beautiful Beals in a singles bar and, after a bite in the neck, becomes convinced that he's turning into a vampire. The film alternates between rip-roaring black comedy and mind-bendingly surrealistic fantasy. It is Cage's over-the-top performance which is at the heart of this sardonic work. ★★★ DVD Dual: $14.99

Les Vampires

(1915, 420 min, France, Louis Feuillade) *Edouard Mathé, Marcel Lévesque, Jean Ayme, Fernand Herrmann, Musidora.* Secret passage ways snake into your most private sanctums, poison gas wafts out of ventilation grates, trap doors drop you down into dark, dank dungeons — why, why, why? It's for the sheer joy of committing blackmail, extortion and murder! No one is safe from the criminal masterminds that make up *Les Vampires*. Led by the beautiful but deadly Irma Vep, this ruthless gang preys on the Parisian rich pre-WWI. What director Feuillade may have lacked in cinematic technique is more than made up for in audacity. Its very length — ten episodes, seven hours — is like uncomfortable slumber, a nightmare that keeps intruding the next day. *Les Vampires* still fascinates, still resonates. ★★★ DVD: $69.99, VHS: $99.99

Vampires: Los Muertos

(2002, 94 min, US, Tommy Lee Wallace) *Jon Bon Jovi, Cristián de la Fuente, Arly Jover, Darius McCrary, Natasha Gregson Wagner.* This corny sequel to *John Carpenter's Vampires* follows another band of Catholic Church-sponsored vampire hunters as they hunt a female vampire this time. That's about it for inventiveness in this uninvolving waste of time. It also doesn't help that the first film's engaging, un-PC nastiness is traded in for a tame, almost genteel tone. Director Wallace is a former protégé of Carpenter's, but displays none of his mentor's abilities in this tired outing. ★ DVD Dual: $19.99, VHS: $14.99

Vampyr

(1931, 83 min, France/Germany, Carl Dreyer) *Julian West, Sybille Schmitz.* Death and evil hover over everyone in Dreyer's psychological horror film. Dislocated shadows, eerie sounds and unexplained mysteries conspire to make *Vampyr* one of the screen's most visceral thrillers. (German with English subtitles) ★★★½ DVD: $24.99, VHS: $24.99

The Van

(1997, 105 min, Ireland, Stephen Frears) *Colm Meaney, Donal O'Kelly, Ger Ryan.* The third installment of Roddy Doyle's "Barrytown" trilogy (which includes *The Commitments*), *The Van* is a ramshackle character study about two unemployed Irishmen who set up a food cart that brings them closer together and almost tears them apart. Meaney is Larry, a bullying but tender-hearted man who goes along with his best friend Bimbo's (O'Kelly) plan to open a fish-and-chips van. The long-suffering Bimbo and the short-fused Larry have a wonderful camraderie, but they soon get on each other's nerves. Capitalizing on the fine performances from its two leads, Frears mines *The Van* for both humor and poignancy as it depicts the pressures of friends working together. Doyle's script captures the rough-edged world that produces these kinds of flawed but realistic characters. ★★★ VHS: $89.99

Van Gogh

(1992, 155 min, France, Maurice Pialat) *Jacques Dutronc, Alexandra London.* Unlike previous visions of the artist — Vincente Minnelli's *Lust for Life*, Robert Altman's *Vincent and Theo* or Paul Cox's documentary *Vincent* — this beautifully photographed look at Van Gogh's last days in Auvers-Sur-Oise eschews the standard portrait of a tortured soul. Instead we see a man who lusts after women, enjoys life's pleasures and who, in the end, may have taken his own life more out of remorse over his own sensitivities than his failure to gain acceptance. Dutronc won a César Award for Best Actor for his understated portrayal. (French with English subtitles) ★★★

Van Helsing

(2004, 132 min, US, Stephen Sommers) *Hugh Jackman, Kate Beckinsale, Richard Roxburgh, David Wenham, Shuler Hensley, Elena Anaya, Kevin J. O'Connor.* Monsters and bats and wolves, oh my. They're all here, but is Frankenstein and Dracula and Wolf Man. And that's part of the problem of this slick, over-produced, loud though at times strangely enjoyable vampire story that has bit off more than it can chew. Bram Stoker's Van Helsing is now a young, beefy superhero (played by the young, beefy Jackman) who works for the Vatican fighting the dark side. After tackling Dr. Jekyll, who looks suspiciously like The Hulk, Van Helsing travels to Transylvania. There he teams with Lara Croft-wannabe and vampire hunter Anna

Vagabond

(Beckinsale), and together they take on Dracula and his brides. Jackman and Beckinsale are both in rote mode, reciting lines with professionalism but adding nothing to characters who are given nothing substantial to recite. It is Roxburgh, however, as Dracula who has the most fun, and the actor creates a particuarly worthy heavy for the two to fight. Too bad the majority of the film doesn't have his panache. The CGI effects and makeup are terrific, but at this stage they oughta be. It's just that they bombard the viewer. If that's what you're looking for, then this is for you. *Van Helsing* is nonstop action. But it's also brainless and quite silly and lacks the verve that have made these monsters such great fun since the 1930s. ★★

Vanilla Sky

(2001, 130 min, US, Cameron Crowe) *Tom Cruise, Penélope Cruz, Cameron Diaz, Kurt Russell, Jason Lee, Noah Taylor, Timothy Spall, Tilda Swinton.* Jerry Maguire director Crowe and actor Cruise team again for this adaptation of Alejandro Amenábar's Spanish cult film *Open Your Eyes*. Despite some impressive visual flourishes and effectively eerie "Twilight Zone"-like renderings, *Vanilla Sky* fails to fully capture the hypnotic beauty of the original film, or set a solid foundation all its own. Cruise plays David Aames, a wealthy business scion who becomes caught in a nightmare after he casually drops his latest affair (Diaz, who makes the most of her few scenes) upon meeting the beautiful Sofia (a bland Cruz reprising her role from the original film). With fantasy and reality now blurred, David attempts to piece together the puzzle, and keep his new relationship with Sofia afloat. Unfortunately, many compelling scenes of David's numerous personal relationships are offset by pretentious and often confusing dramatics. As such, the film never takes flight as it could have. ★★½ DVD Letterbox: $14.99, VHS With Making-of Featurette: $9.99

Vanina Vanini

(1969, 125 min, Italy, Roberto Rossellini) *Sandra Milo, Laurent Terzieff.* Set in 1824, this opulent political and romantic drama is a complex neorealist-influenced film that deals with political and religious corruption, social inequality, guilt and betrayal. Young Pietro, a revolutionary soldier, is sent to Rome to kill a traitor to the cause. Needing to hide from the authorities, he finds refuge in the lavish home of an aristocrat where he falls in love with the man's beautiful daughter. The two travel back north but the social differences that keep them apart soon erupt into betrayal. (Italian with English subtitles) ★★★ VHS: $59.99

The Vanishing

(1988, 105 min, Netherlands, George Sluizer) *Barnard Pierre Donnadieu, Johanna Ter Steege.* This riveting psycho-thriller offers an unflinching look into the shadowy recesses of the human psyche. While on holiday in the south of France, a young Dutch couple stop for gas at a service station. While he fills the tank, she goes into a restaurant and mysteriously disappears without a trace. Unable to convince the police that foul play was involved, the man returns home, only to be haunted by her disappearance until he decides to retrace their steps, hoping to entrap the possible abductor/murderer. An unrelentingly taut account that eschews the easy depiction of violence for the much more menacing idea of psychological obsession and domination. (French and Dutch with English subtitles) (Sluizer made his own American remake in 1993) ★★★½ DVD Letterbox Criterion Collection: $29.99

The Vanishing

(1993, 110 min, US, George Sluizer) *Jeff Bridges, Kiefer Sutherland, Nancy Travis, Sandra Bullock, Park Overall, George Hearn.* If ever there was a film that screamed "see the original!" — this is it. Where the unique 1988 Dutch chiller was a tense, philosophical psycho-mystery, this remake is little more than a formulaic Hollywood spine-tingler. Sutherland stars as a young man whose life is shattered when his girlfriend (Bullock) inexplicably disappears at a road stop. He searches for her over the years until one day a slightly loony science professor (Bridges) shows up to shed some light on her fate. Director Sluizer, who also directed the original, has made a number of ill-advised changes including completely rewriting the ending which, in the first film, left the viewer with a stunned sense of helplessness. ★

Vanya on 42nd Street

(1994, 119 min, US, Louis Malle) *Wallace Shawn, Julianne Moore, Brooke Smith, Larry Pine, George Gaynes, Phoebe Brand, Andre Gregory, Madhur Jaffrey.* Gregory and Shawn assembled a group of actors on a pro-bono basis and spent four years rehearsing their bare-bones (no sets, no props, no nothin') production of David Mamet's adaptation of Chekhov's "Uncle Vanya." Entranced by their work, Malle set out to make a record and the result is invigorating. Filmed in the dilapidated New Amsterdam Theatre on 42nd Street in New York, *Vanya* is as close to true theatre on film as one will ever see. Mamet's script is 100% true to Chekhov and in the hands of stage director Gregory and his accomplished cast, this masterful examination of spiritual yearning in the face of brutal existential angst is brought vividly to life. ★★★★ DVD: $24.99

Variety

(1925, 75 min, Germany, E.A. Dupont) *Emil Jannings, Lya De Putti.* Classic silent melodrama with Jannings in fine form as an aging circus acrobat who falls in love with a beautiful young dancer, only to become involved in murder when a handsome young man shows affection for the girl. ★★★½

Variety

(1983, 97 min, US, Bette Gordon) *Sandy McLeod, Will Patton, Richard Davidson, Nan Goldin.* Christine (McLeod) works in the box office of a porno theatre in New York's (pre-Disney-fied) squalid Times Square district. Exposed to this thick aura of sexual promise and fantasy, she becomes obsessed — not with the films, but with the endless parade of men who come to consume them.

Eventually, she becomes fixated on one particular customer, and finds herself acting upon her own voyueristic urges. Gritty and complex, this is an often fascinating study of the chasm between sexual desire and its gratification. ★★★ VHS: $24.99

Variety Lights

(1952, 93 min, Italy, Alberto Lattuada & Federico Fellini) *Giulietta Masina, Carla Del Poggio.* Codirected by Fellini and Lattuada and starring their wives, *Variety Lights* explores the tawdry lifestyle of a traveling vaudeville troupe. When an ambitious young woman joins them, the group finds their lives shaken as the newcomer immediately begins an affair with the much older maestro. The blending of Lattuada's neorealist techniques with Fellini's budding imagination, as well as his interest in eccentric individuals, creates a world of alluring illusion beneath which lies the much sadder reality of everyday life. (Italian with English subtitles) ★★★ DVD: $29.99, VHS: $29.99

Varsity Blues

(1999, 104 min, US, Brian Robbins) *James Van Der Beek, Jon Voight, Paul Walker, Ron Lester, Scott Caan.* As conventionally formulaic as it is, *Varsity Blues* is still slickly enjoyable as any of those (good) '80s John Hughes comedies. Van Der Beek is Max, a Texas high school quarterback who becomes an overnight sensation when the first string QB is injured. Despite his ambivalence about his sudden stardom, he doesn't shun the spotlight. His control-freak coach (Voight), however, is constantly at odds with Max's "it's only a game" mentality. Even though the film has its stupid gags and minimal surprises, the acting is strong, and Max becomes a character who you really care about. ★★★ DVD: $14.99, VHS: $9.99

Vatel

(2000, 119 min, France/ GB, Roland Joffé) *Gérard Depardieu, Uma Thurman, Tim Roth, Timothy Spall, Julian Sands.* Depardieu plays the title character, a caterer hired by a destitute prince (Glover) to curry the favor of King Louis XIV (Sands). Cooking ensues, as does a requisite love triangle between Vatel, Louis and the ravishing Anne (Thurman). However, there's no passion here; all of the "sumptuous" elements are in place, but *Vatel* is a perfunctory period piece, with all the energy of a dusty dollhouse. This French film has an English-language script by Tom Stoppard, though Depardieu seems to be speaking his own Andre the Giant-inspired tongue. ★½ DVD: $19.99, VHS: $14.99

Vegas Vacation

(1997, 90 min, US, Stephen Kessler) *Chevy Chase, Beverly D'Angelo, Randy Quaid, Wallace Shawn, Wayne Newton.* Part of the appeal of the first *National Lampoon's Vacation* is its air of depravity and those wicked laughs. As the series grew into something of a franchise, little by little the humor that distinguished it dissipated, until all that's left is the feel-good family schtick at the heart of *Vegas Vacation*, the fourth in the series. The Griswolds venture to Las Vegas, where the entire family is seduced by its seediness and glamour. The supporting cast produces the few laughs the screenplay can muster, including Shawn as a smug card dealer, and Quaid, who once again saves the day as the family's ill-bred cousin, who can fry a steak like nobody's business. Newton's self-parody goes nowhere. ★★ DVD: $19.99, VHS: $14.99

The Velocity of Gary

(1998, 101 min, US, Dan Ireland) *Vincent D'Onofrio, Salma Hayek, Thomas Jane, Olivia d'Abo, Chad Lindberg.* An intriguing cast helps but can not save this personal urban drama filmed in the tradition of the Andy Warhol/Paul Morrissey collaborations, The story attempts to be a poignant yet hard-edged love fable set among the hustlers, trannies and homeless of New York City. It tells the tale of the strained love triangle between a charismatic bisexual, a male prostitute and a tempestuous Latina. Hayek stars as Mary Carmen, a hot-tempered beauty desperately in love with Valentino (D'Onofrio), a small-time porn actor with big time attitude. But things change when Gary (Jane), a sensitive rookie male prostitute also falls in love with the magnetic Valentino. Though the story is emotionally charged, the characters never feel real. Let them wallow in their fucked-up sexual situations! ★★ DVD: $19.99

Velvet Goldmine

(1998, 127 min, US/GB, Todd Haynes) *Ewan McGregor, Jonathan Rhys-Meyers, Toni Collette, Christian Bale, Eddie Izzard.* An emotionally cold but musically exciting and visually hallucinogenic story set in London's glitter rock world of the early 1970s. Unable to get the story or music rights to David Bowie's meteoric rise to rock stardom, Haynes instead offers a tale and soundtrack suspiciously similar to Bowie's Ziggy Stardust incarnation with a little bit of Iggy Pop thrown in as well. Rhys-Meyers is a sweet young man who transforms himself into glam rock superstar Brian Slade. He marries an intense American (Collette) but falls in love with fellow rocker Curt Wild (a wonderfully swaggering McGregor). At the height of his fame, he fakes his death. Now ten years later, a former fan/now reporter (Bale) sets out to uncover the truth and reasons for his self-destruction. What makes the film memorable are the loud fashions, some good acting, high-energy music and intensely druggy images. ★★★ DVD: $19.99

The Velvet Touch

(1948, 97 min, US, John Gage) *Rosalind Russell, Leo Genn, Claire Trevor, Sydney Greenstreet.* Russell gives a good performance in this nifty thriller as a famous stage actress who murders her producer and becomes involved in a cat-and-mouse game with the investigating police detective. ★★★

Vengeance Is Mine

(1979, 129 min, Japan, Shohei Imamura) *Ken Ogata.* This unrelenting probe of the criminal mind is powerfully brought to the screen by Imamura, director of the highly acclaimed *Ballad of Narayama* and long considered one of Japan's leading contemporary filmmakers. Structured in a documentary style, this exciting thriller casts Ogata as a killer on the run. He eludes the law's net and leads the police along a bloody path paved with fraud, violence and murder. An unusual and unforgettable portrait of a "man without a heart." (Japanese with English subtitles) ★★★½ VHS: $39.99

Venus Beauty Institute

(1999, 105 min, France, Tonie Marshall) *Nathalie Baye, Bulle Ogier, Samuel Le Bihan, Audrey Tautou, Jacques Bonnaffé.* Baye gives an endearing performance as Angèle, a woman about to enter middle age, guilty over the accidental injury inflicted on a loved one years ago, with a penchant for self-destructive behavior. Angèle's natural warmth and her tendency to help others, whether in her work as a beautician or her nurturing support of her friends, is in sharp contrast to the self-deprecating emptiness in her own life. Her denial of the possibility of love is so strong that she is flustered and confused by the sudden, unexpected appearance of a fervent offering of adoration. Baye's performance is well supported by the ensemble cast, who create a backdrop of distinct characters against which Angèle's explorations of the heart unfold. A gentle wit and wry humor inform director Marshall's episodic pacing, which flows seamlessly to replicate the hectic pace of modern daily life. An involving film that draws in the viewer with many moments of bemused recognition, deservedly a winner of 4 Césars, including Best Picture. (French with English subtitles) ★★★½ DVD: $14.99, VHS: $14.99

Venus in Furs

(1970, 90 min, GB, Jess Franco) *James Darren, Barbara McNair, Klaus Kinski.* A murky drama about a jazz musician who falls for a mysterious woman who is really a recently washed ashore corpse. In the end, she turns out to be the Angel of Death come to Earth to avenge a murder by twisting and contorting a psychopathic killer's already feeble mind. Confused yet? ★½

Vera Cruz

(1954, 94 min, US, Robert Aldrich) *Gary Cooper, Burt Lancaster, Denise Darcel, Cesar Romero, Ernest Borgnine, Charles Bronson.* Cooper and Lancaster are two adventurers involved in political intrigue in 1860s Mexico. A flavorful western. ★★★ DVD: $19.99

The Verdict

(1982, 129 min, US, Sidney Lumet) *Paul Newman, James Mason, Jack Warden, Charlotte Rampling, Milo O'Shea, Lindsay Crouse.* Newman gives an extraordinary performance as a down-on-his-luck lawyer given a last chance at self-redemption when he is hired in a medical malpractice case. A riveting courtroom drama and character study, with a superior supporting cast. ★★★½ DVD: $14.99, VHS: $6.99

Veronica Guerin

(2003, 98 min, US/Ireland, Joel Schumacher) *Cate Blanchett, Gerard McSorley, Ciaran Hinds, Brenda Fricker, Colin Farrell.* Regrettably superficial, *Veronica Guerin* — based on the real-life crusading Irish journalist — manages to be occasionally moving thanks to inherently interesting material and another terrific performance by Blanchett. As portrayed by Ms. Blanchett, Guerin is a tough, passionate writer determined to bring down the Dublin drug lords, in the face of death threats and physical violence. Despite her excellent turn, however, we still don't get a strong hold on what makes Veronica tick, and the brief running time, super-slick, TV-movie presentation, and uninspired wrap-up (which should have been quite emotional) render the whole film nearly disposable. The story was also told in the 2001 film *When the Sky Falls.* ★★ DVD Letterbox: $29.99, VHS: $102.99

Veronico Cruz

(1987, 106 min, Argentina/GB, Miguel Pereira) *Juan Jose Camero, Gonzalo Morales.* The bittersweet story about the relationship between a young boy and his schoolteacher is set against the debacle of the Malvinas/Falklands War. Perched high in the outback of the Argentinian highlands, a young boy is raised by his grandmother after his mother dies and his father abandons him. In this remote area, untouched by civilization, the boy, Veronico, grows up. His life, as well as that of the entire pueblo, is changed forever after the military junta invades their tranquil world and pits friend against friend in

James Stewart and Kim Novak in *Vertigo*

a relentless and senseless power struggle. A quietly moving drama of individuals caught up in the maelstrom of political zealousness. (Spanish with English subtitles) ★★★ VHS: $39.99

Veronika Voss

(1982, 104 min, Germany, Rainer Werner Fassbinder) *Rosel Zech, Hilmar Thate.* A stunning profile of a faded film star's descent into morphine addiction and emotional dependency is Fassbinder's eerie black-and-white tribute to *Sunset Boulevard.* A very un-Fassbinder-like cinematic tour de force with ceaseless camera movement and striking characterizations. The director's final film in his trilogy on the German condition during and immediately after WWII. (German with English subtitles) ★★★½ VHS Subtitled: $19.99

The Vertical Ray of the Sun

(2001, 112 min, France/Vietnam, Tran Anh Hung) *Tran Nu Yên-Kh, Nhu Quynh Nguyen, Le Khanh, Quang Hai Ngo. The Vertical Ray of the Sun,* a gorgeous film from the director of *The Scent of Green Papaya,* examines the lives of three sisters living in Hanoi. Set in present day, but having a timeless feel, this is one of the most stunningly beautiful films of recent years, with impeccable lighting, luscious colors and, of course, incredible scenery. The visuals are matched by the sound, with terrific music — from Lou Reed to traditional Vietnamese songs to orchestral — and omnipresent flora and fauna sounds, which add immeasurably to the dreamlike atmosphere. Thankfully, the drama isn't given short shrift, for, while not exactly plot driven, the film is never less than compelling, due as much to interesting characters and excellent performances as to the wonderful sound and vision. While the screen compositions may become a bit too precious at times, and the film ends very abruptly, these are tiny complaints, really, as the pleasures are so abundant. (Vietnamese with English subtitles) ★★★½ DVD: $29.99, VHS: $21.99

Vertigo

(1958, 120 min, US, Alfred Hitchcock) *James Stewart, Kim Novak, Barbara Bel Geddes.* Perhaps the most masterful achievement in a career strewn with classics, *Vertigo* is a multilayered summary of Hitchcock's prime obsessions: the fears of physical and psychological intimacy, emotional commitment

and mortality. Stewart is superb as the detective with a debilitating case of acrophobia, which costs him not only his job but also the woman he is desperately drawn to. Novak portrays the illusive heroine, a dreamlike incarnation of womanhood whose shifting identity unhinges Stewart's haunted hero. ★★★★ DVD Letterbox: $19.99

Very Bad Things

(1998, 100 min, US, Peter Berg) *Christian Slater, Jon Favreau, Cameron Diaz, Jeremy Piven, Daniel Stern, Jeanne Tripplehorn, Kobe Tai.* A black comedy which delivers on its dark, twisted premise but just isn't that funny, *Very Bad Things* marks the writing and directing debut of actor Berg. The film begins at breakneck pace, with groom-to-be Favreau and pals going to Vegas for a frolicking bachelor party. When a prostitute is accidentally killed, the five friends are faced with a decision: call the cops or bury the body in the desert. It's not difficult to figure out which one they choose. In no time, paranoia and guilt soon take their toll. Berg gives the film a visual verve, but as writer, he has failed to fully deliver. His tale is dark enough, but the gore and humor don't mesh. One dilutes the other. Meanspiritedness, absurd and funny can go hand-in-hand, but the film needs more irony, wit and substance to work as such. ★★½ DVD: $19.99, VHS: $14.99

A Very Brady Sequel

(1996, 89 min, US, Arlene Sanford) *Shelley Long, Gary Cole, Tim Matheson, Christopher Daniel Barnes, Christine Taylor, Jennifer Elise Cox, RuPaul, Rosie O'Donnell.* While some of the innovative satire of the first film may seem overly familiar the second time around, it should not stop anyone from enjoying this cutely funny and at times madcap spoof of the old TV sitcom. The plot revolves around the return of Carol's (Long) long-thought-dead husband (Matheson), who steals a valuable ancient horse statue (yes, the same one that was prominently displayed in the TV show). He then kidnaps the perky Mrs. Brady and takes her to Hawaii — with the loudly clothed, off-key, sing-songing Bradys in hot pursuit. Plenty of sexual innuendos, eye-poppingly loud (but groovy) threads and shamelessly mindless fun should divert both old TV fans and newcomers alike. ★★★ DVD: $14.99, VHS: $9.99

V

A Very Curious Girl

(1986, 105 min, France, Nelly Kaplan) *Bernadette Lafont, Georges Geret.* Kaplan's sexy comedy about a beautiful peasant girl who decides to sell sexual services to the men in the village. Soon, she has more power than she ever dreamed of and becomes involved in a series of hilarious events. (French with English subtitles) ★★½

A Very Natural Thing

(1973, 85 min, US, Christopher Larkin) *Robert Joel, Curt Gareth.* An important film in the history of American gay filmmaking, *A Very Natural Thing* is considered the first feature film on the gay experience made by an out-of-the-closet gay director to receive a commercial distribution. The simple but insightful story involves a 26-year-old gay man who leaves the priesthood and moves to New York City in the hopes of finding a meaningful relationship. Now a schoolteacher, he soon falls in love with a handsome young advertising executive. Though the film is rather sappy and tends to preach, it is nevertheless sensitively told and refreshingly romantic. ★★★ DVD: $29.99, VHS: $39.99

A Very Old Man with Enormous Wings

(1988, 90 min, Cuba, Fernando Birri) *Fernando Birri.* After a violent cyclone, a poor couple discover near their desolate farmhouse a mute winged man (played by director Birri). Not understanding him, they cage him in a chicken coop where the strange old man, with supernatural physical attributes, soon becomes the area's local attraction; drawing the curious, the derisive and the devout. A bizarre fable infused with magical realism, at times cruel images and comic confusion. (Spanish with English subtitles) ★★★ VHS Out of Print: $29.99

A Very Private Affair

(1962, 95 min, France/Italy, Louis Malle) *Brigitte Bardot, Marcello Mastroianni.* This early work by Malle is a steamy examination of the trials of movie stardom and features BB as a naive nymphet and newly found movie star who is constantly beset by fans, press and photographers. The underside of stardom is pointedly looked at in this romantic melodrama. ★★½

The Very Thought of You

(1999, 88 min, GB, Nick Hamm) *Monica Potter, Joseph Fiennes, Rufus Sewell, Tom Hollander, Ray Winstone.* Another daft romantic comedy about an American in Britain, this is an ultrathin piece of fluff made for Channel 4. Although usually their quality is considerably higher than this affair about three friends all falling for the same girl, director Hamm does employ a nice visual style at times. Potter (channelling Julia Roberts) is Martha, a young girl from Minneapolis who chucks everything and flies to London, meeting Daniel (Hollander), Frank (Sewell) and Laurence (Fiennes) along the way. Martha spends the entire film deciding which, if any, of these suitors is right for her. The film's lack of subtlety in every regard is easily its biggest flaw. ★★ DVD: $19.99, VHS: $9.99

Vibes

(1988, 99 min, US, Ken Kwapis) *Peter Falk, Jeff Goldblum, Cyndi Lauper.* A wacky comedy about two psychics (Goldblum, Lauper) who are thrown together in a quest for a lost South American treasure, being manipulated all the way by con man Falk. Lauper is appealing in her film debut in this totally silly but amiable romp. ★★½

Vice Versa

(1988, 100 min, US, Brian Gilbert) *Judge Reinhold, Fred Savage, Swoosie Kurtz.* Reinhold and Savage make this familiar body-switching comedy better than it really is thanks to their endearing performances. Though not as well conceived as *Big*, there's a lot to like in this tale about a department store manager and his young son exchanging identities. ★★½ DVD: $19.99

Victim

(1961, 100 min, GB, Basil Dearden) *Dirk Bogarde, Sylvia Syms, Dennis Price, Peter McEnery.* Long considered a landmark film for its complex and sophisticated treatment of homosexuality, this exceptional thriller stars Bogarde as a married, bisexual lawyer who risks his reputation by confronting a gang of blackmailers responsible for the death of his former lover. A thoughtful and compelling piece which was instrumental in breaking new ground. ★★★½ DVD: $19.99, VHS: $19.99

Victor/Victoria

(1982, 133 min, US/GB, Blake Edwards) *Julie Andrews, James Garner, Robert Preston, Lesley Ann Warren, Alex Karras, John Rhys-Davies, Graham Stark, Peter Arne, Norman Chancer.* This stylish, gender-bending, sexual/musical comedy stars Andrews as a female (Victoria) who passes as a gay male female impersonator (Victor). Preston offers a scintillating performance as her gay friend and mentor, Toddy. Garner is a Chicago gangster confusingly enchanted and attracted to Andrews, who thinks she is a man. Based on the 1933 German comedy, *Viktor und Viktoria*, Edwards' exuberant romp is full of snappy tunes and sophisticated hilarity. Warren gives a priceless performance as Garner's dumb-blonde mistress. ★★★★ DVD Letterbox: $19.99

Victor/Victoria

(1995, 146 min, US, Blake Edwards) *Julie Andrews, Tony Roberts, Michael Nouri, Rachel York.* A live performance of the Broadway show, based on the 1982 hit film, *Victor/Victoria* is a most entertaining adaptation. Andrews is in wonderful form as Victoria, an out-of-work singer whose life changes when she meets the flamboyant Toddy (Roberts). With his help, she becomes "Victor," an overnight sensation as a female impersonator in the nightclubs of Paris. Adapted and directed by Edwards, this stage version can't really compare with the classic original, but it's a delight and time well spent. ★★★ DVD: $19.99, VHS: $19.99

Victory

(1981, 110 min, US, John Huston) *Michael Caine, Sylvester Stallone, Pelé, Max von Sydow.* Standard WWII prison escape adventure is heightened by an exciting finale featuring a soccer game between Allied soldiers and their German captors. ★★ DVD: $9.99, VHS: $9.99

Videodrome

(1983, 90 min, Canada, David Cronenberg) *James Woods, Sonja Smits, Deborah Harry, Peter Dvorsky.* Woods' performance dominates this gritty horror tale from director Cronenberg. He plays the owner of a cable station whose programming choices begin to bring about horrifying hallucinations. Gory though spectacular special effects by Rick Baker. Not for all tastes. ★★★ DVD: $14.99, VHS: $9.99

La Vie Continue

(1982, 93 min, France, Moshe Mizrahi) *Annie Girardot, Jean-Pierre Cassel.* Girardot is marvelous as a sheltered middle-class woman who, when her husband suddenly dies, is forced to make adjustments in her life. Things brighten up when she finds herself in love again. Her budding new relationship is a joy to witness as it unfolds. (American remake: *Men Don't Leave*) (French with English subtitles) ★★★ VHS: $59.99

La Vie de Bohème

(1993, 100 min, France, Aki Kaurismäki) Anyone familiar with the works of Finnish director Kaurismäki (*Leningrad Cowboys Go America*) know that his films are low-key and the comedy is usually archly subtle — he's somewhat like a Finnish Jim Jarmusch. *La Vie de Bohème*, his first French production, proves to be no different. The story centers on the down-on-their-luck lives of three bedraggled men: Albanian painter Rodolfo, aspiring novelist Marcel, and Irish composer Schaunard. The resilient, likable trio find success, food and love always just out of their reach as they pursue their art regardless of the inevitable setbacks. There is humor in the tale but overall, the slow pacing, repetitive story line and somber look at life on the edge make this a must for Kaurismäki fans only. ★★ VHS: $19.99

Vietnam: Year of the Pig

(1968, 103 min, US, Emile de Antonio) This outstanding, Academy Award-nominated documentary offers a thought-provoking and riveting examination into America's involvement in the Vietnam War and Southeast Asia. ★★★½

View from the Top

(2003, 85 min, US, Bruno Barreto) *Gwyneth Paltrow, Christina Applegate, Mike Myers, Mark Ruffalo, Candice Bergen, Kelly Preston, Rob Lowe.* With such a high-profile cast, one's expectations for *View from the Top* would at least be slightly higher than a fourth installment of, say, *Sweet Home Alabama*. However, thanks to a formulaic script, few laughs and forced acting, that's exactly what you get. Paltrow plays a small-town girl following her dreams to become a world-class flight attendant. Also on board are a backstabbing friend, the on-again/off-again boyfriend and the gratuitous gay man thrown in for "spice." Paltrow walks through her character as if she is on drugs (which she must have been to accept this role in the first place). Even Myers in his role as the cross-eyed airline instructor is softened so much that he barely elicits a giggle. ★½ DVD: $29.99, VHS: $14.99

A View to a Kill

(1985, 131 min, GB, John Glen) *Roger Moore, Christopher Walken, Grace Jones.* One of the weakest of the Bond films is saddled with an anemic villain played by Walken who's simply not convincingly evil. Even Jones is unable to perk up the proceedings in this one. Moore is simply coasting as 007. (Sequel: *The Living Daylights*) ★★ VHS: $9.99

Vigil

(1984, 90 min, New Zealand, Vincent Ward) *Bill Kerr, Fiona Kay.* Told with strikingly stark visuals, this grim, atmospheric drama is set on a sheep farm in a desolate, darkly enchanted valley in New Zealand. The story is seen through the eyes of an 11-year-old girl, Toss. When her father dies accidentally, a mysterious stranger arrives and begins to help the family survive. Though helpful, Toss sees him as a predator; and one who must leave immediately. Director Ward spent five years making this bleak but mystical testimony to the beauty and immutability of nature and life. A startling directorial debut and a work of extraordinary beauty. ★★★½

THE DISCERNING FILM LOVER'S GUIDE

The Vikings

(1958, 114 min, US, Richard Fleischer) *Kirk Douglas, Tony Curtis, Janet Leigh, Ernest Borgnine.* Douglas and Curtis are Viking half brothers who set sail for the English coast in this fanciful, familiar tale of exploration and conquest. ★★½ DVD Letterbox: $14.99

Village of the Damned

(1960, 78 min, GB, Wolf Rilla) *George Sanders, Barbara Shelley.* Classic English horror and damned scary at that! This is a low-budget shocker about a group of strange, emotionless children who attempt to take over a small village by controlling the minds of the adults. An eerie chiller of the highest order. (Remade in 1995) ★★★½

Village of the Damned

(1995, 95 min, US, John Carpenter) *Christopher Reeve, Kirstie Alley, Michael Paré, Linda Kozlowski, Mark Hamill.* Based on the semiclassic 1960 chiller, this version features updated effects and splendid cinematography, but it is not really much different than the original in plot. The inhabitants of the coastal California town of Midwich suffer a strange sleeplike trance one day but emerge seemingly unharmed — until they discover all the townswomen are pregnant. A mass birth, facilitated by local doctor Reeve and federal epidemiologist Alley, results in a group of bizarre offspring who mature into eerie, super-intelligent adolescents. Carpenter is unable to ignite the story sufficiently, though the film is still moderately entertaining. ★★½ DVD: $14.99, VHS: $19.99

Vincent

(1987, 105 min, Australia, Paul Cox) This thoughtful and engrossing examination into the life and art of Vincent Van Gogh takes an unconventional approach in its efforts to reveal the artist's driving creative force. More of a filmed essay than biography, the movie attempts to piece together Van Gogh's final years by the reading of the many eloquent and insightful letters he wrote to his brother, Theo; while at the same time examining the artist's work — from his earliest line drawings to his last hallucinatory portraits and landscapes. More complex and abstract than the Kirk Douglas/Vincente Minnelli *Lust For Life* or Robert Altman's *Vincent and Theo*, Cox seems more interested in revealing the intellectual and articulate Van Gogh and not the simpler image of a tortured and mad painter. ★★★

Vincent & Theo

(1990, 138 min, US, Robert Altman) *Tim Roth, Paul Rhys.* With this most accomplished work, Altman sets his sights on the lives and the delicate relationship between artist Vincent Van Gogh and his brother, Theo. In a commanding performance, Roth plays the tortured genius, Vincent, who is irrevocably tied to his sibling; each in search of his own artistic identity and unable to break the confines of their bond. Rhys is equally as compelling as Theo. ★★★½

Vincent, François, Paul and the Others

(1974, 118 min, France, Claude Sautet) *Yves Montand, Gérard Depardieu, Stéphane Audran, Michel Piccoli.* An all-star cast highlights this elegant but dolorous drama of male mid-life crisis. Vincent, François and Paul are lifelong friends, all in their mid-fifties. The "others" are represented by a younger member of the group (Depardieu) along with their various wives and mistresses. The story

follows their weekly retreat to the country where underneath the jocular drinking and eating, difficult problems of love and life confront them all. A well-acted saga which explores the problems of bourgeois life from the male perspective. (French with English subtitles) ★★★

Violence at Noon

(1966, 99 min, Japan, Nagisa Oshima) *Saeda Kawaguchi, Akiko Koyama.* From Oshima, the director of *In the Realm of the Senses*, comes an equally disturbing and controversial examination of sensuality and passion. One of the founders of the Japanese New Wave, Oshima was strongly effected by Jean-Luc Godard, and Oshima's imagery and editing technique do not contradict this. Set in a rural Japanese commune, the story focuses on the unsettling relationship between a rapist/murderer, his wife and a woman he once raped. Protecting him from the police out of a perverted sense of loyalty, the women are strangely obedient to this man until a final confrontation. (Japanese with English subtitles) ★★★

Violent Cop

(1989, 103 min, Japan, Takeshi Kitano) *Takeshi Kitano, Maiko Kawakami, Makoto Ashikawa, Shirô Sano.* A molasses-paced action film, *Violent Cop* is even less satisfying than other films from the director because of a completely despicable, and, even more damaging, uninteresting lead character. Takeshi plays a cop who makes Dirty Harry look like a pussycat, beating or killing anyone who gets in his way of "justice." Too slow to be the guilty pleasure it might have been, and too ugly and superficial to be an affecting drama. (Japanese with English subtitles) ★★ DVD: $19.99, VHS: $19.99

The Violent Years

(1956, 57 min, US, William M. Morgan) *Jean Moorehead, Glenn Corbett.* Delinquent debutantes do drugs, rob gas stations, rape rich boys, and commit murder, mayhem and assorted pajama party violence. ★ DVD: $24.99, VHS: $7.99

Les Violons du Bal

(1974, 108 min, France, Michel Drach) *Jean-Louis Trintignant, Marie-José Nat.* Director Drach's remembrances of his Jewish childhood in Nazi-occupied France, as well as his attempts to get financing to make a film on the subject, are the two parallel stories in this affectionate personal drama. Using imaginative cross-cutting, Drach deftly weaves the two stories together into a perilous and deeply moving film. His son Michel charmingly plays the director as a young boy who, along with his lovely mother (played by Drach's real-life wife, Nat) and his two siblings, attempt to stay one step ahead of the Nazis and certain extradition to a labor camp. And while this heart-stopping drama unfolds, Drach — played by Trintignant — tries to interest people in the film project. (French with English subtitles) ★★★ VHS: $79.99

The Virgin Machine

(1988, 85 min, Germany, Monika Treut) *Ina Blum, Susie Bright.* This thought-provoking sexual odyssey tells the story of a young West German woman and her search for "romantic love." Frustrated by the emptiness and the emotional morass of her native

Hamburg, Dorothee decides to flee her home to search for her mother, who is living in San Francisco. Once arrived, however, her trek turns into a process of sexual discovery. Filmed in a steamy black and white, the film exudes a sensuality in which simple lust is transformed into glorious eroticism. While *The Virgin Machine* is clearly a feminist film about a woman's exploration of her own sexuality, its profound statement is one which applies to all. (In English and German with English subtitles) ★★★ DVD: $24.99, VHS: $29.99

The Virgin Queen

(1955, 92 min, US, Henry Koster) *Bette Davis, Richard Todd, Joan Collins.* Davis reprises her acclaimed role from 1939's *The Private Lives of Elizabeth and Essex* as Queen Elizabeth I, here coming in conflict with Walter Raleigh (well played by Todd). Davis, as usual, is commanding. ★★★ VHS: $19.99

The Virgin Soldiers

(1969, 96 min, GB, John Dexter) *Lynn Redgrave, Hywell Bennett, Nigel Davenport.* Beautiful cinematography enhances this little-known gem about the end of innocence (both sexually and otherwise) for a group of young British recruits going to battle in 1950s Singapore. A dewy-fresh Redgrave costars as the girl who escorts one of the boys (Bennet) into manhood. ★★★

The Virgin Spring

(1960, 88 min, Sweden, Ingmar Bergman) *Max von Sydow, Birgitta Valberg.* Based on a Swedish ballad, Bergman's quietly chilling morality play brilliantly captures the quality of ancient legends — their primitive passion, human sorrow, and abrupt beauty. Set in the Swedish countryside of the 14th century, it stars von Sydow as the tormented father whose daughter was raped and murdered after her sister invokes a pagan curse. In the spot of her death a magical spring bursts forth. (Swedish with English subtitles) ★★★★ VHS: $29.99

The Virgin Suicides

(2000, 97 min, US, Sofia Coppola) *Kirsten Dunst, Josh Hartnett, James Woods, Kathleen Turner, Danny DeVito, Scott Glenn, Michael Paré.* Sofia makes a most promising directorial debut with The

The Virgin Suicides

Virgin Suicides, a film of some power. The tale of the Lisbon family is a tragic one. The five Lisbon girls commit suicide, first Cecilia and then the rest. Our narrator is the grown voice of one of the five neighborhood boys whose lives have been marked forever by their fascination with the elusive and beautiful Lisbon girls. Being a fractured look at suburban repression, the dowdy design is as important as the smart adaptation of the Jeffrey Eugenides novel, for words and atmosphere are equally telling. The performances are understated and pitch perfect. Turner trades her sultry sex goddess for repressed matriarch, and Woods is moving as the clueless father. Among the teenagers, Dunst and Harnett are particularly affecting. ★★★ DVD: $14.99, VHS: $14.99

Virginia City

(1940, 121 min, US, Michael Curtiz) *Errol Flynn, Randolph Scott, Miriam Hopkins, Humphrey Bogart.* A follow-up to his successful *Dodge City*, Flynn is back in the saddle in this colorful Civil War western. There's intrigue and treachery at every turn as Union officer Flynn puts the stops on a Confederate gold shipment, and tangles with rebel officer Scott, spy Hopkins and Mexican outlaw Bogart. The cast comes off well, except for Bogie, looking ridiculous in his Ricardo Montalban mustache. ★★★ VHS: $19.99

Viridiana

(1961, 91 min, Spain, Luis Buñuel) *Fernando Rey, Silvia Pinal, Francesco Rabal.* Buñuel's controversial and brilliant surrealistic examination of good and evil is about a young novice and her loss of innocence at her rich uncle's estate. Contains the celebrated Last Supper scene. The film which caused Buñuel to be kicked out of Spain. (Spanish with English subtitles) ★★★★ VHS: $24.99

Virtual Sexuality

(1999, 92 min, GB, Nick Hurran) *Laura Fraser, Rupert Penry-Jones, Luke de Lacey, Kieran O'Brien.* A British teen sex comedy, *Virtual Sexuality* blends the genres of mismatched love and gender-bending with mixed results. Justine (Fraser) is a seventeen-year-old who lusts after Alex (O'Brien), the school jock. When her nerdy best friend Chas (de Lacey) takes her to a cyberspace fair, she creates her "perfect guy" (Penry-Jones) in a dating booth. However, things go haywire and Justine actually becomes the boy of her dreams. Suddenly, she/he has to grasp a new lifestyle and see things from a new perspective. The characters get into one improbably wacky situation after another in the name of frothy fun, but the "be yourself" message is clear. Much of the film is harmless; nevertheless, there is virtually nothing new here. ★★½ DVD: $24.99, VHS: $14.99

Virtuosity

(1995, 105 min, US, Brett Leonard) *Denzel Washington, Russell Crowe, Kelly Lynch, Stephen Spinella, William Forsythe, Louise Fletcher.* With more than a little in common with the far more entertaining *Demolition Man*, this mindless, slowly paced sci-fi adventure casts Washington as a former cop who's now behind bars and is the only one who can track down the nasty bad guy. The latter would be Crowe as a virtual reality villain who has come to life endowed with super powers and is killing everyone in sight. The film attempts to make a comment on violence and our appetite for it in our society, but *Virtuosity* gratuitously feeds that hunger with ridiculous plot developments, undefined characters and indiscriminate scenes of violence. ★ DVD: $19.99, VHS: $9.99

Virus

(1999, 99 min, US, John Bruno) *Jamie Lee Curtis, William Baldwin, Donald Sutherland, Joanna Pacula.* A terrible rip-off, *Virus* is pure sci-fi dreck. A tugboat crew happens upon a seemingly abandoned Russian research vessel and decide to claim it. But the investigation of the ship takes a turn for the clichéd as an alien force determines humans are a "virus," and must be destroyed. Unoriginal and visually dull, *Virus* at least has female characters that aren't cowering, bikini-clad bimbos, but in the end, it just doesn't matter. ★ DVD Letterbox DTS sound: $9.99, DVD: $9.99

A Virus Knows No Morals

(1986, 84 min, Rosa von Praunheim) Never one to tread softly on a controversial subject, von Praunheim tackles the issue of AIDS in this archaic black comedy. With several stories intercut throughout the film, von Praunheim's cast of weird characters includes a sex club owner who refuses to change his policies, claiming that, "I won't let them take away our freedom"; hysterical members of the press who are bent on making a story; and workers at a hospital where the deluge of AIDS patients causes them to become so bored and jaded that the night nurses roll dice to see which patient will die next. Gallows humor abounds as the director seeks to provoke, embarrass and enrage the audience into understanding the effects of the crisis. (German with English subtitles) ★★★ VHS: $39.99

Vision Quest

(1985, 107 min, US, Harold Becker) *Matthew Modine, Linda Fiorentino, Ronny Cox, Daphne Zuniga, Michael Schoeffling.* Modine and the fiery Fiorentino make an attractive twosome in this compelling drama about a high school wrestler going after the state championship. Madonna sings two songs. ★★★ DVD: $9.99

Visions of 8

(1972, 110 min, Various) The producer of this film had the intriguing idea to have eight different directors from around the world film various events of the 1972 Summer Olympics at Munich. Included in this menagerie of filmmakers are Kon Ichikawa, John Schlesinger, Milos Forman, Claude Lelouch and Mai Zetterling. The results are, as one would imagine, uneven. Although interesting, better examples of a filmmaker capturing the beauty and spectacle of this sporting event would be either Ichikawa's *Tokyo Olympiad* or Leni Riefenstahl's *Olympia*. ★★½

Visions of Light: The Art of Cinematography

(1993, 90 min, US, Arnold Glassman, Stuart Samuels, Todd McCarthy) Setting out to elevate cinematographers above their normal obscurity, this fascinating and entertaining documentary on the art behind making movies is a must-see for film connoisseurs. The film focuses on the works of 26 of the world's greatest all-time cinematographers and points to some of their finest contributions; examining several of moviedom's most famous shots and uncovering the various methods and mistakes which went into their creation. Film buffs will find the material so absorbing that they will be wishing for more at the end of the film's breezy 90 minutes. ★★★½ DVD: $24.99, VHS: $29.99

Les Visiteurs du Soir (The Devil's Envoys)

(1942, 110 min, France, Marcel Carné) *Arletty, Jules Berry.* This charming medieval fantasy scripted by Jacques Prévert is set in the 15th century and tells the story of two emissaries sent to earth by the Devil to corrupt two young lovers. Things don't work out too well for the bad guys as the male envoy falls in love with the young princess. It takes the Devil himself to intervene by turning the couple into stone; but, much to his dismay, their pure hearts continue to beat. Made during the German Occupation, this thinly veiled allegory — of Hitler as the Devil and France the lovers — surprisingly never had problems with the authorities. Sometimes a bit stilted and forced, this visually lush fairy tale is still a fine example of the Carné/Prévert style of poetic realism. (French with English subtitles) ★★★

The Visitors

(1996, 106 min, France, Jean-Marie Poiré) *Jean Reno, Christian Clavier, Valerie Lemercier.* The French take a lot of flack here in America for their questionable taste in comedy. *The Visitors*, a huge hit in France, will not help and the Jerry Lewis jokes. Reno is completely unappealing as a medieval knight who, along with his excruciating sidekick (cowriter Clavier, a twisted cross between Harpo Marx and Charles Manson), is transported to modern-day France by a senile wizard. The two wacky fishes-out-of-water bumble through France, insulting, threatening or assaulting everyone they meet; all the while destroying everything in their wake. There's a small amount of satire here, but like everything else in *The Visitors*, it's never developed. (French with English subtitles) ★½ DVD: $22.99, VHS: $19.99

Vital Signs

(1990, 103 min, US, Marisa Silver) *Jimmy Smits, Adrian Pasdar, Diane Lane, Norma Aleandro.* Routine medical drama about young med students and their professional and personal struggles. Aleandro brings a heartrending dignity to her dying cancer patient. ★★½

I Vitelloni (The Wastrels)

(1953, 109 min, Italy, Federico Fellini) *Franco Fabrizi, Alberto Sordi, Franco Interlenghi.* This neorealist masterpiece in an early work by Fellini, and more traditional in narrative, it doesn't hint to his future career in the cinema of the fantastic and surreal. Partly autobiographical, the story deals with the young, restless men of a small town on the Adriatic. Touching, powerful and graceful, the film is a refined social commentary on small-town mores and morals in postwar Italy. (Italian with English subtitles) ★★★★

Vito and the Others

(1992, 90 min, Italy, Antonio Capuano) Pubescent, angel-faced boys rove the streets of a decaying Naples terrorizing all with their petty crimes, drug dealing and prostitution in this lurid *Pixote*-influenced "exposé" on urban hopelessness. Twelve-year-old Vito, living with abusive relatives after his father wipes out his family in a murderous rampage, joins up with a band of future juvenile delinquents. Sent to prison after a busted drug deal, he slips further away when he is raped by fellow prisoners and returns to the streets a hardened hooligan, indifferent to emotion and love. Unlike *Pixote*, we never get to know much about young Vito nor are we shocked by his vicious antisocial behavior. It's too serious to be cheesy exploitation, too awkward to be effective drama. (Italian with English subtitles) ★★½ VHS: $59.99

Viva Zapata!

(1952, 113 min, US, Elia Kazan) *Marlon Brando, Anthony Quinn, Jean Peters, Joseph Wiseman.* Brando is exceptional as a Mexican peasant whose search for simple justice leads to rebellion and even-

V

tual triumph. Quinn won a Best Supporting Actor Oscar as Brando's brother. John Steinbeck wrote the script. ★★★½

Vive L'Amour

(1996, 119 min, Taiwan, Tsai Ming-Liang) *Yang Kuei-Mei, Lee Kang-Sheng, Chen Chao-Jung.* A remarkable film about passion and loneliness, *Vive L'Amour* eschews narrative convention by presenting its offbeat love story almost exclusively without dialogue. A young Taiwanese couple meet for anonymous sex in a vacant apartment. Unbeknowst to them, a sexually confused and suicidal young man is also living in the abandoned space. Writer-director Ming-Liang generates tremendous drama in a series of revealing episodes that examine the sensation of communication. As the camera eavesdrops on the daily routines of its unhappy characters, the film unfolds naturally — without music — using only the noise of everyday life as it builds inexoribly to a stunning conclusion. (Taiwanese with English subtitles) ★★★½ DVD: $14.99, VHS: $14.99

Vivre sa Vie

See: *My Life to Live*

Vixen

(1968, 70 min, US, Russ Meyer) *Erica Gavin.* A straightforward narrative of a bush pilot and his oversexed wife who live in the Canadian wilderness. It cost $76,000 to make and brought back over $7.5 million at the box office, bringing Meyer deserved recognition from major Hollywood studios. ★★★ DVD: $39.99

Voices of Sarafina!

(1988, 85 min, US, Nigel Noble) Interviews with cast members of the hit Broadway musical "Sarafina," with scenes from the show spliced with images of life in oppressive South African townships. A celebration of the courage and conviction of anti-Apartheid activists, set to the rhythm of Mbaganga street music (emulated on Paul Simon's "Graceland" album). ★★★ VHS: $29.99

Volcano

(1997, 102 min, US, Mick Jackson) *Tommy Lee Jones, Anne Heche, Don Cheadle, Gaby Hoffmann, Keith David.* Sporting his customary take-control but nice-guy gruffness, Jones plays a civil supervisor who's ready to rally the troops when L.A. is devastated by a volcano. Aided by geologist Heche, the two race against time in their attempt to outwit this force of nature and save the city. All the trappings of the disaster film are here, but *Volcano* has going for it an appealing ensemble, a quick pace, good effects and a story line which won't require you to smack your head (too often) in disbelief. Despite a heavy-handed racial angle and a terribly clichéd ending, *Volcano* is fun to watch as it speeds down Wilshire Boulevard and levels Los Angeles — any film which does that can't be all bad. ★★½ DVD Letterbox: $9.99, VHS: $9.99, VHS Letterbox: $19.99

Volere Volare

(1993, 92 min, Italy, Guido Manuli & Maurizio Nichetti) *Maurizio Nichetti, Angela Finocchiaro.* In this kinky cartoon comedy, Nichetti (*The Icicle Thief*) once again employs surreal film techniques to portray a very comical but human love story. A sexual fantasist for hire becomes enamored with Maurizio, a cartoon sound dubber who "brings his work home with him." The slapstick fun of the film adds spice to the witty writing and good performances. Unlike many American romances of today, *Volere Volare* is quirky without being smutty, and romantic without being schmaltzy. ★★★ VHS: $19.99

Volpone

(1939, 95 min, France, Maurice Tourneur) *Harry Bauer, Louis Jouvet.* Volpone (Bauer), a rich 16th-century Venetian merchant, pretends to be dying in order to observe how his "friends" react and jockey for his considerable inheritance and, in turn, take advantage of them. A droll satire on the ever-present human traits of power and greed. Based on the classic comedy by Ben Jonson. (French with English subtitles) ★★★

Volunteers

(1985, 106 min, US, Nicholas Meyer) *Tom Hanks, John Candy, Rita Wilson, Tim Thomerson.* Hanks and Candy breathe some life into this uneven comedy about a rich ne'er-do-well (Hanks) who travels to Thailand with a group of Peace Corps volunteers to escape his bookie. ★★ DVD: $9.99, VHS: $9.99

Von Ryan's Express

(1965, 117 min, US, Mark Robson) *Frank Sinatra, Trevor Howard, Edward Mulhare, James Brolin.* Sinatra lends authority to this exciting WWII adventure about a daring POW escape, led by American colonel Sinatra. Howard is a British general, at odds with the arrogant Yank. ★★★ DVD: $19.99, VHS: $14.99

Voyage en Ballon

(1959, 82 min, France, Albert Lamorisse) *Narrated by:, Jack Lemmon.* From the director of *The Red Balloon* comes this enchanting, multi-award-winning children's film. A young boy stows away in a gigantic balloon that his grandfather has built. Together, the two, captain and first mate, travel across France on a wonderful, humorous and suspenseful adventure. ★★★

Voyage in Italy

(1953, 94 min, Italy, Roberto Rossellini) *Ingrid Bergman, George Sanders.* This third Rossellini-Bergman collaboration (*Stromboli, Europa '51*) was panned by the critics and bombed at the box office on its initial release, but was revivified when the directors of the French New Wave hailed it as a masterpiece. Bergman and Sanders are a bored couple who travel to Italy to inspect a villa they have inherited. Against magnificent background settings (Mt. Vesuvius, Capri, the ruins of Pompeii), their faltering marriage finally breaks up; but through a "miracle," they are reunited. With little "action," this simple film is a romantically passionate story on the renewal of life and love. (aka: *Strangers*) (Filmed in English) ★★★ VHS: $59.99

Julie Delpy in *Voyager*

A Voyage Round My Father

(1983, 85 min, GB, Alvin Rakoff) *Laurence Olivier, Alan Bates, Jane Asher.* John Mortimer's splendid television adaptation of his own hit play. Semiautobiographical in nature, this often moving and sometimes funny reminiscence centers on the occasionally tumultuous relationship between an eccentric father (Olivier) and his son (Bates). ★★★ VHS: $19.99

Voyage Surprise

(1946, 108 min, France, Pierre Prévert) *Jean Bourgoin, Maurice Baquet.* This delightfully zany comedy by the Brothers Prévert (Jacques cowrote the story) tells of an old man's dream to arrange a mystery tour or "voyage surprise" on a ramshackle bus. The tourists are his family, elderly friends and various eccentrics who find themselves involved in a series of scary and comic adventures involving a wedding party, a brothel, anarchists, an evil Grand Duchess and the police. (French with English subtitles) ★★★½ VHS: $59.99

Voyage to the Bottom of the Sea

(1961, 106 min, US, Irwin Allen) *Raquel Welch, Walter Pidgeon, Joan Fontaine, Peter Lorre, Barbara Eden.* The crew of an atomic submarine desperately fights to save the Earth from impending destruction. Hokey fun. Look out for the giant squid! (The basis for a popular 1960s TV series) (DVD double feature with *Fantastic Voyage*) ★★½ DVD Double Feature: $14.99, VHS: $14.99

Voyager

(1991, 113 min, France/Germany, Volker Schlöndorff) *Sam Shepard, Julie Delpy, Dieter Kirchlechner, Traci Lind, Barbara Sukowa.* Exuding existential angst like there's no tomorrow, this ruminative drama of forbidden love spans six continents in this (by European standards) big-budget production. Shepard, in one of his best performances, is Walter Faber, a world-weary engineer who, because of a ruined love, retreats from the emotional world of life into the logical and predictable realm of his work. His emotional drifting ends when, after a series of improbable coincidences, he meets Sabeth, an alluring young lady (Delpy) half his age. Their affair takes them from Mexico's Yucatan Peninsula through Europe until his past catches up with him with disastrous results. An engaging story similar in filming and style to Wim Wenders' *Until the End of the World*. (Filmed in English) ★★★

Vukovar

(1994, 94 min, Yugoslavia, Boro Draskovic) *Mirjana Jokovic, Boris Isakovic.* A disturbing glimpse into the psyche of a war-ravaged nation, *Vukovar* uses its Romeo and Juliet tale (he's a Serb, she's a Croat) of star-crossed lovers to underscore the tragedy of the Yugoslavian conflict. Filmed in the all-but-destroyed city of Vukovar during the war in 1993, the film certainly has an authentic atmosphere to tell the story of a newly married couple whose happy union is disrupted by civil war. Having such a strong anti-war message, the film occasionally wanders into the heavy-handed arena, but its voice is articulate and director Draskovic's images are overwhelming. (Serbo-Croatian with English subtitles) ★★★½ VHS: $89.99

The Wackiest Ship in the Army

(1960, 99 min, US, Richard Murphy) *Jack Lemmon, Ricky Nelson, Chips Rafferty.* Lemmon stars as a WWII naval officer saddled with a crew of butterfingered land-lubbers while trying to carry off a perilous top secret mission in the South Pacific. An entertaining mixture of wacky comedy and wartime heroics. ★★★ VHS: $14.99

The Wacky World of Wills and Burke

(1985, 97 min, Australia, Bob Weis) This Monty Python-inspired spoof of the failed 1860 exploratory expedition in the Australian Outback is an outrageously satirical, lighthearted goofball of a movie. Burke, an elegantly dressed but slightly daft policeman, and the nerd astronomer Wills team up with 28 evil-smelling camels and an equally foul assortment of companions on a journey that leads them nowhere. It might be helpful for people unfamiliar with the historical event to watch the serious film *Burke and Wills* before renting this parody. ★★½

Wag the Dog

(1997, 105 min, US, Barry Levinson) *Dustin Hoffman, Robert De Niro, Anne Heche, Denis Leary, Willie Nelson, Woody Harrelson, Kirsten Dunst, Craig T. Nelson, William H. Macy.* What do you do when a sitting president on the verge of re-election finds himself rocked by a sex scandal? While State expeditions to foreign countries are always good diversions, nothing beats a war. And if there isn't enough time to fan a flare-up into a conflagration, you can just manufacture one. Who has the technology? Hollywood, of course. De Niro drolly underplays the spin doctor, a man with seemingly unlimited authority, who orchestrates the action while monitoring the pulse of public opinion. He signs on a frenetic film producer (a terrific Hoffman), who takes on the job with unbridled enthusiasm. The scenes depicting the manufacture of film at 11 will have you taping newscasts to replay them at slow speed, looking for glitches and evidence of blue screen. Director Levinson's execution of the wickedly funny and insightful script (cowritten by David Mamet) is flawless and unswerving. *Wag the Dog* is unflinching as it delivers frightening truths that can be addressed only in fiction in our brave new world at the end of the millennium. ★★★★ DVD: $19.99, VHS: $14.99

Walkabout

The Wages of Fear

(1953, 105 min, France, Henri-Georges Clouzot) *Yves Montand, Charles Vanel.* Four desperate men, all unscrupulous characters, are hired to transport several truckloads of nitroglycerin across the mountains and forests of South America in this compelling and suspenseful thriller. (American remake: *Sorcerer*) (French with English subtitles) ★★★★ DVD Criterion Collection: $29.99, VHS: $29.99

Wagner

(1983, 300 min, GB, Tony Palmer) *Richard Burton, Vanessa Redgrave, John Gielgud, Laurence Olivier, Joan Plowright, Arthur Lowe.* A huge international cast fails to help this glossy and uninspiring biography of the famed composer. Burton is only intermittently inspired as the lead. ★★

Wagonmaster

(1950, 85 min, US, John Ford) *Ben Johnson, Joanne Dru, Ward Bond.* Beautiful western locations highlight this Ford adventure about the perilous journey of a Morman wagon train heading west towards the Utah frontier. Johnson and Bond are two amblin' cowpokes who join the expedition. ★★★

Wagons East

(1994, 100 min, US, Peter Markle) *John Candy, John C. McGinley, Richard Lewis, Ellen Greene, Robert Picardo, Rodney A. Grant.* In his last film role, Candy plays a drunken wagonmaster who leads a group of unhappy settlers of the Old West on a journey back to a more civilized East. Unfunny to the point of embarrassment, the film goes to great lengths to set up its many *Blazing Saddles*-like jokes, but the punch lines fail to deliver. In a stereotypical portrayal, McGinley plays an effeminate bookseller. His final destination — with a handsome Indian brave in tow — proves to be one of the only real laughs in this otherwise amiable bomb. ★½ DVD: $9.99, VHS: $9.99

Wait until Dark

(1967, 108 min, US, Terence Young) *Audrey Hepburn, Alan Arkin, Richard Crenna, Efrem Zimbalist, Jr., Jack Weston.* This intense adaptation of Frederick Knott's stage thriller stars Hepburn as a recently blinded woman who is terrorized by drug traffickers when she innocently takes possession of a doll filled with heroin. The action takes place almost entirely in her apartment, which heightens the suspense and the feeling of helplessness — it's more effective than any slasher film could hope to be. Arkin is brilliant in the triple role as the head villain, and Crenna is a helpful detective. A pulse-pounding classic with an unforgettable finale. ★★★½ DVD: $19.99

Waiting

(2000, 80 min, US, Patrick Hasson) *Will Keenan, Keri Kenney, Hannah Dalton, Bill Robertson.* Attempting to capture a go-for-broke wackiness but coming up short, this indie comedy follows the crazy misadventures of a lovelorn waiter and his fellow employess at a South Philly Italian restaurant. Sean (Keenan) is slowly being driven insane both at home and on the job, a restaurant run by a cigar-chomping mafioso. Recently dumped by his girlfriend, Sean tries his luck at new romances. When he wakes up trapped in a locked leather mask, he realizes he's got to take charge of his life, or else. A film of caricature rather than character, *Waiting* has moments of comic cleverness, but can't totally overcome its low budget and droopy pacing. ★★ VHS: $9.99

Waiting for Guffman

(1997, 83 min, US, Christopher Guest) *Christopher Guest, Eugene Levy, Catherine O'Hara, Fred Willard, Parker Posey, Bob Balaban.* Proving the show must go on, *Waiting for Guffman* is an often hilarious though modest mockumentary from one of the talents behind the granddaddy of the genre, *This Is Spinal Tap*. Community theatre is the target, and for anyone who has ever been associated with their local playhouse, much of this will seem like nirvana. The characterizations and petty politics are on-target, the tacky production values are gloriously captured, and there's enough in-jokes to make any semi-insider feel particularly in the loop. But *Guffman* is also a bit slow between the laughs. When the comedy works, this sizzles (*My Dinner with Andre* action figures!); but Guest allows some scenes to drag with no upshot. Nevertheless, the laughs are plentiful and well observed. ★★★ DVD: $19.99

Waiting for the Light

(1990, 94 min, US, Christopher Monger) *Teri Garr, Shirley MacLaine, Vincent Schiavelli.* Garr is ready for major life changes when she inherits a diner in a small community. She packs up the kids and Aunt Zelda (MacLaine), a woman with a decidedly unique worldview, and heads out to a town about to be visited by an angel. Or so it seems. MacLaine gives another of her patented cantankerous, crotchety old lady performances, which is nonetheless endearing. A delightful cast revels in a serendipitous twist of fate in this quirky, charming film. ★★★ DVD Letterbox: $14.99

Waiting for the Moon

(1987, 87 min, US, Jill Godmilow) *Linda Hunt, Linda Bassett, Bruce McGill, Bernadette Lafont, Jacques Boudet, Andrew McCarthy.* The story of the tumultuous relationship between author Gertrude Stein and her lover/companion Alice B. Toklas. The film is minimalistic with long periods of dialogue between the women, in a style reminiscent of *My Dinner with Andre*. Upon its release, most critics disapproved of the film downplaying the women's lesbianism, opting instead for a more "matter of fact" attitude. ★★½ VHS: $29.99

Waiting to Exhale

(1995, 120 min, US, Forest Whitaker) *Whitney Houston, Angela Bassett, Loretta Devine, Lela Rochon, Gregory Hines, Wesley Snipes, Dennis Haysbert, Mykelti Williamson.* Probably a first for a Hollywood film, *Waiting to Exhale* centers of the relationships of four African-American women. The occasionally appealing though sometimes static film focuses less on the women's friendship (they have few scenes together) and more on their individual relationships with men, which produces a varying degree of success. Houston is the catalyst of the story, moving to Phoenix to start life anew and reuniting with her longtime friends. Her romantic scenes have all the snap of a Taster's Choice commercial, though she fares better when relating to her female costars. Bassett has an earthiness and tenderness missing from a lot of the other characters. ★★½ DVD: $14.99

Wake Island

(1942, 87 min, US, John Farrow) *Brian Donlevy, Robert Preston, Macdonald Carey, Albert Dekker, William Bendix.* One of the first films to show American involvment in WWII and one of the most stirring of war films made during that era, this tense, assured and exciting drama/actioner details the efforts of a group of Marines to defend the small Pacific island against the Japanese. Strong on both characterizations and fighting sequences, *Wake Island* was such a terrific morale booster it was shown to new recruits. A Best Picture nominee. ★★★½

Waking Life

(2001, 99 min, US, Richard Linklater) *Voices of:, Wiley Wiggins, Ethan Hawke, Julie Delpy, Adam Goldberg, Timothy Levitch, Steven Soderbergh, Richard Linklater.* Linklater's mesmeric rumination on the existential nature of dreams, life and death is a uniquely transporting cinematic trip. Live-action footage of real actors has been digitally tweaked, colored, shaded and contorted to create a fluid, animated universe that is eerily rooted in "reality" yet breezily defies the governing laws of physics. Wiggins wakes up to the weary realization that he's trapped inside an unending lucid dream. We follow him as he floats through the colorful, shape-shifting landscape and connects with a vaguely familiar assortment of closet nihilists, philosophers and anarchists, some of whom we've met before (Delpy and Hawke reprise their roles as the moonstruck lovers from *Before Sunrise*). Though the film's astonishing visual power is diminished on the home video screen, its lofty themes, combined with Linklater's unparalleled knack for capturing the raw angst of his generation, make *Waking Life* a truly groundbreaking achievement. ★★★★ DVD: $9.99, VHS: $9.99

Waking Ned Devine

(1998, 91 min, Ireland, Kirk Jones) *Ian Bannen, David Kelly, Fionnula Flanagan, Susan Lynch, James Nesbitt.* Though the studio tried to draw comparisons to *The Full Monty*, this wonderfully endearing comedy lacks that film's harder edge, but is just as pleasing in the laughs department. Still a charmer in his late 60s, Bannen is Jackie, a retiree living with his wife in the small Irish village Tulaigh Morh. Happy with a pint and the company of friends, Jackie's obsession is with the national lottery. When he reads in the paper that someone in his village has won, he sets out to find and ingratiate himself. But when it turns out that Ned Devine, the winner, has died of a heart attack, he devises a scheme — with the help of the entire town — to pass off his friend Michael (a wonderfully expressive Kelly) as the lucky ticket holder. With nary a mean bone in its aged body, *Waking Ned Devine* is a sweet, funny throwback to those British Ealing comedies. ★★★½ DVD: $14.99

Waking the Dead

(2000, 103 min, US, Keith Gordon) *Billy Crudup, Jennifer Connelly, Molly Parker, Janet McTeer, Paul Hipp, Hal Holbrook, Ed Harris.* An ambitious young lawyer — whose lifelong dream is to be president — is given the chance to run for the Senate. Unfortunately, during the election race, he keeps catching glimpses of his old girlfriend, who died 8 years earlier, and begins to emotionally unravel. Unusual film posits many interesting ideas and questions (ambition vs. ideals; can two politically dis-

parate people remain passionately in love; etc.) within an intriguing flashback- and forward-laden structure. Sadly, the two charismatic leads are saddled with some clichéd dialogue, spoken over an ill-chosen, cloying soundtrack. ★★ DVD: $19.99

Waking Up in Reno

(2002, 91 min, US, Jordan Brady) *Charlize Theron, Patrick Swayze, Natasha Richardson, Billy Bob Thornton, Penélope Cruz.* Two white-trash couples decide to drive to Reno for vacation, primarily to see a kick-ass monster truck show. En route, they discover and reveal some secrets about one another along the way. That alone should tip you off that this ain't gonna be a subtle, insightful satire. What is somewhat surprising is that this cast would agree to be in such a one-note, unfunny and truly stale marriage-on-the-rocks, sub-sitcom dud. While Swayze has one or two charming moments, and Thornton is always worth a look, the only one to emerge unscathed is Richardson, who brings a down-home sexiness and sweetness the rest of the film lacks. Unless you roar with laughter at the very mention of Jerry Springer, you'll find Reno a long haul. ★½ DVD: $19.99

Walk, Don't Run

(1966, 114 min, US, Charles Walters) *Cary Grant, Samantha Eggar, Jim Hutton.* Grant's last film is not the most fitting end to a brilliant comic career, but it is nevertheless a mostly enjoyable farce. In this remake of the classic *The More the Merrier*, Grant is an American businessman forced to share accomodations with Eggar and Hutton during the Tokyo Olympics. ★★½ DVD Dual: $24.99, VHS: $19.99

A Walk in the Clouds

(1995, 103 min, US, Alfonso Arau) *Keanu Reeves, Aitana Sanchez-Gijon, Anthony Quinn, Giancarlo Giannini, Angelica Aragon.* An alternately awkward and magical romantic drama, director Arau's first English-language film, set in the splendrous wine country of Napa Valley, basks in the mystical glow of lovers united. Unfortunately, these tender tales are surrounded by the clichés of a contrived beginning and a predictable, abrupt ending. Reeves is a WWII vet and orphan. Traveling by train, he meets a beautiful college student (Sanchez-Gijon) returning home and agrees to pose as her husband, since she's single and pregnant and certain to feel her father's wrath. Their relationship — like the film — becomes more satisfying once they arrive on the family's lush vineyards and fall in love. Reeves still seems uncomfortable with period pieces. ★★½ DVD: $14.99

A Walk on the Moon

(1999, 107 min, US, Tony Goldwyn) *Diane Lane, Liev Schreiber, Viggo Mortensen, Anna Paquin, Tovah Feldshuh.* Actor Goldwyn makes a remarkably assured directorial debut with this lovely, evocative and moving nostalgic romantic drama set in the last days of the '60s. With its dead-on re-creation of a Catskills vacation spot and familial relations, *A Walk on the Moon* uses the era's changing social attitudes as a backdrop for romantic exploration. Pearl (Lane) is a devoted wife and mother who feels defined only by those two jobs. Longing for more, she begins an affair with Walker (Mortensen), a hippie clothing salesman while on vacation. Though her husband Marty (Schreiber) is kind but inattentive, Pearl finds in Walker an outlet for dormant yearnings she had been unable to express. Pamela Gray's rich screenplay is humorous and intuitive; her full-blooded characters have been marvelously brought to life by a fine cast and sensitive direction. A small gem. ★★★½ DVD: $14.99, VHS: $9.99

Walk on the Wild Side

(1962, 114 min, US, Edward Dmytryk) *Laurence Harvey, Capucine, Barbara Stanwyck, Jane Fonda.* Inventive casting punctuates this tawdry tale of a good-natured Texan (Harvey) who travels to New Orleans to rescue his lost love (Capucine) from life in a brothel, run by a lascivious lesbian (Stanwyck). Fonda tags along in yet another "sexy bad girl" role. If ever a movie deserved the tag line "good trash," this is it. ★★½ DVD: $24.99

A Walk to Remember

(2002, 97 min, US, Adam Shankman) *Mandy Moore, Shane West, Peter Coyote, Daryl Hannah.* Love isn't such a many-splendored thing after the filmmakers of this cloying tear-jerker get finished with it. West plays an annoying big-man-on-high-school-campus who meets too-wholesome-to-be-true cutie-pie (and daughter of the local preacher) Moore, and slooow-ly they fall in love. Of course, this being based on a Nicholas Sparks novel, tragedy awaits one of them. In her first starring movie role, pop singing star Moore isn't all that bad (certainly more successful than Mariah or Britney). But the film is awash in gooey melodrama, relegating it to the level of an "Afterschool Special." ★★ DVD Letterbox: $26.99

Walkabout

(1971, 100 min, Australia, Nicolas Roeg) *Jenny Agutter, Lucien John, David Gulpilil.* Agutter is undeniably fetching as the budding young woman who, with her younger brother (John), is suddenly stranded in the wilderness. With a preternatural calm (and still clad in school uniforms), they venture into the Outback searching for civilization but find instead an aboriginal teen (Gulpilil) who's on his "walkabout" — an initiation ritual involving months of solo survival. With no common language, the threesome begin a trek that slowly breaks down their cultural barriers. Pieced together from chunks of loose narrative, and with a minimum of dialogue, *Walkabout* is at first very obtuse, but its attempt to blur the distinctions between the civilized and "primitive" worlds ultimately lacks subtlety; otherwise, maybe it would be seen as a classic. ★★★ DVD Criterion: $29.99, VHS: $29.99

Walker

(1987, 95 min, US, Alex Cox) *Ed Harris, Peter Boyle, Richard Masur, Marlee Matlin.* Harris plays a real-life soldier of fortune who declared himself president of Nicaragua in 1855 and ruled the country for two turbulent years. Cox's anarchic sense of humor permeates this piece, so as with most of his films, expect the unexpected. ★★

Walking and Talking

(1996, 83 min, US, Nicole Holofcener) *Anne Heche, Catherine Keener, Todd Field, Liev Schreiber, Kevin Corrigan.* A sympathetic approach and engaging portrayals elevate this regulation opus of twentysomethings struggling with faltering relationships and unfulfilling jobs. Somewhat episodic in structure, the film centers on two childhood friends (Heche, Keener) as one is about to marry and the other fears she is incapable of long-term commitment. Through many layers of miscommunications, hang-ups and obsessions, the film wanders the paths of each woman's personal growth as she attempts to bring order to a chaotic and often baffling world. The film's forgiving nature towards its characters' idiosyncracies encourages tolerance towards an uneven script and some awkward dialogue, ultimately resulting in an amusing and endearing examination of young adult life. ★★½ DVD Letterbox: $14.99, VHS: $9.99

W

The Wall

(1983, 117 min, Turkey, Yilmaz Guney) Guney, who directed the highly acclaimed film *Yol* from his prison cell, died of cancer soon after personally making his first and only film after his escape from Turkish prison. *The Wall* concerns the re-creation of the revolt in a children's prison in Ankara in 1976. The harsh living conditions suffered by the children as well as their eventual uprising are brutally depicted in this searing, honest and horrifying portrait of repression. A true political statement that tears at one's conscience. (Turkish with English subtitles) ★★★½ VHS: $69.99

Wall Street

(1987, 125 min, US, Oliver Stone) *Michael Douglas, Charlie Sheen, Martin Sheen, Daryl Hannah, Sean Young, James Spader.* Stone's riveting, but at times heavy-handed, morality tale stars Sheen as a young stock broker who falls under the spell of Wall Street's millions and loses sight of his humanity. Douglas was awarded an Oscar for his portrayal of a vicious, power hungry Ivan Boesky-like wheeler-dealer. Real-life dad Martin plays Charlie's proletariat father. ★★★ DVD: $14.99

Wallace & Gromit: A Close Shave

(1995, 30 min, GB, Nick Park) Gromit's knitting hobby is in trouble, as there's a wool shortage. Meanwhile, Wallace finds a bit of love at the wool shoppe in Wendoline, but is *her* dog a sheep rustler? It seems that way when a big-eyed lamb falls out of their truck and eats Wallace & Gromit out of house and home. The claymated man and dog have a good adventure, with some interesting inventions including a Knit-o-Matic machine, and a great chase featuring a ladder, two cars and a couple dozen sheep. It just misses that extra snap that "The Wrong Trousers" has, though it's good enough for Park's third Oscar for Best Animated Short. ★★★½

Wallace & Gromit: A Grand Day Out

(1992, 23 min, GB, Nick Park) Wallace is a homebody and budding inventor, with an unusually smart dog, Gromit, who spends his free time knitting. And, boy, do they both love cheese! In this, the first of three claymation Wallace & Gromit shorts from the British Aardman studios, they find that their icebox is cheeseless. Armed with a supply of crackers, they build a rocket and head to the largest supply of cheese in the universe. . .the moon! A charming adventure, though stylistically not quite up to the level of Park's later shorts. This is the only Wallace & Gromit film to *not* win an Oscar for Best Animated Short (it lost to Park's "Creature Comforts!") ★★★

Wallace & Gromit: The Wrong Trousers

(1993, 30 min, GB, Nick Park) Park's masterpiece, an endlessly inventive and breakneck adventure that happily merges such cinematic mainstays as the crime caper, the locomotive chase and the bad lodger. After a refreshing breakfast thanks to a complicated wake-up invention, Wallace finds that he's fresh out of money after building, for Gromit's birthday, a pair of robotic trousers for his walkies. He takes an evil penguin in as a tenant, who not only takes over Gromit's space, but plots the theft of a diamond in the city. Time for our silent canine hero to save the day! Tremendous rewatchable fun, for adults and kids alike, with a memorable, steely-eyed tuxedoed villain, and the most expressive clay animation you'll ever see. Winner of the Oscar for Best Animated Short. ★★★★

Walpurgis Night

(1938, 75 min, Sweden, Gustaf Edgren) *Ingrid Bergman, Victor Sjostrom.* Set during Walpurgis, the Swedish celebration of spring, this erotic comedy stars Victor Sjostrom as a conservative newspaperman with Bergman as his rebellious daughter. (Swedish with English subtitles) ★★★ VHS: $19.99

Waltz of the Toreadors

(1962, 105 min, GB, John Guillermin) *Peter Sellers, Margaret Leighton.* Sellers delivers a first-rate comic performance as a licentious army colonel in this wonderful rendition of Jean Anouilh's rollicking sexual farce. ★★★ DVD: $24.99, VHS: $14.99

The Wanderer (Le Gran Meaulnes)

(1987, 108 min, France, Jean-Gabriel Albicococo) *Brigitte Fossey, Jean Blaise.* An imaginative interpretation of Alain Fournier's classic novel, this visually exuberant fantasy tells the romantic story of a boy's first and true love. Set in a provincial town in turn-of-the-century France, young Augustin goes to a strange party one enchanted evening and meets the beautiful yet mysterious Yvonne (Fossey). When Yvonne disappears, our hero desperately tries to find her. A wild and remarkable re-creation of childhood memories and youthful innocence. (French with English subtitles) ★★★

The Wannsee Conference

(1984, 88 min, West Germany, Heinz Schirk) *Dietrich Mattausch, Gerd Brockmann.* A serious and startling re-creation of a meeting that occurred in a pleasant suburb on January 20, 1942. In attendance were such Nazi leaders as the Gestapo's Adolph Eichmann, Reinhard Heydrich of the Secret Police and 15 other state officials. Their mission: to decide upon and implement the so-called "final solution," sealing the fate of six million Jews. Based on the original secretary's notes, the film is presented in real time. Although concentration camps and executions were already a reality, this meeting marked the official beginning of the Third Reich's policy of mass murder and extermination. (German with English subtitles) ★★★ VHS: $19.99

Wanted Dead or Alive

(1986, 104 min, US, Gary Sherman) *Rutger Hauer, Gene Simmons, Robert Guillaume, William Russ.* Hauer has a lot of fun as a modern-day bounty hunter hired to catch, preferably alive, a terrorist (Simmons, of KISS). Definitely no more than your standard action-adventure film, but still entertaining. ★★ DVD Letterbox: $24.99, VHS: $14.99

The War

(1994, 126 min, US, Jon Avnet) *Elijah Wood, Kevin Costner, Mare Winningham, Lexi Randall.* As the youthful Stu, Wood is especially captivating in the strong ensemble cast that populates the small Mississippi town of Juliette. It's 1970. Stu's father, Stephen (Costner), has been an unsteady presence since his return from Vietnam, and his recent reentry into the family (Winningham and Randall as mother and daughter) coincides with increased hostilities with another family's children. With a few exceptions, the dialogue rings true as the father tries to impart to the son the lessons of war. While the film suffers a muddled point-of-view, it enjoys exceptional characterizations by each cast member. ★★★ DVD: $26.99, VHS: $7.49

War and Peace

(1968, 403 min, Russia, Sergei Bondarchuk) *Liudmila Savelyeva, Oleg Tabakov, Sergei Bondarchuk, Vyacheslav Tikhonov.* Reportedly the most expensive Russian film ever made, with final costs exceeding $100,000,000, this Academy Award-winning epic is a dazzling and monumental portrait of Russia during the Napoleonic Wars of 1805-1812. This definitive version of Tolstoy's classic novel follows four aristocratic families and the effects of Napoleon's onslaught of Europe and Russia on their lives. The spectacular battle sequences are considered the best ever filmed, with the director using over 120,000 soldiers. ★★★★ DVD Subtitled 3-Disc Set: $39.99, VHS Subtitled 3-Tape Set: $39.99, VHS Dubbed 3-Tape Set: $39.99

War and Peace

(1956, 208 min, US/Italy, King Vidor) *Audrey Hepburn, Henry Fonda, Mel Ferrer, Anita Ekberg, Vittorio Gassman, John Mills.* Hepburn and Fonda star in this technically superior but dramatically flat version of Tolstoy's epic novel. Well-staged battle sequences. ★★★ DVD: $14.99, VHS: $14.99

The War Game

(1966, 50 min, GB, Peter Watkins) Watkins' tremendously powerful "staged" documentary about the horrors of a nuclear attack on London made its mark well before the more commercial and less stunning "The Day After." Made for BBC-TV, the film never aired because its graphic re-creation of the burns and wounds suffered by the population were considered too controversial (read: antiwar). An extremely hard-hitting piece of quasi cinema verité. ★★★½ VHS: $29.99

The War of the Roses

(1989, 116 min, US, Danny DeVito) *Kathleen Turner, Michael Douglas, Danny DeVito.* In this wicked, hilarious black comedy, Douglas and Turner portray Oliver and Barbara Rose, a married couple whose once idyllic life — complete with two children, beautiful mansion and unlimited cash flow — has dissipated to a limb-breaking, psyche-smashing battle of the sexes. Sort of a demented '80s version of Tracy and Hepburn, Douglas and Turner — who always play well off each other — have rarely been funnier. ★★★½ DVD: $14.99, VHS: $14.99

The War of the Worlds

(1953, 85 min, US, Byron Haskin) *Gene Barry, Ann Robinson.* George Pal produced this classic sci-fi adventure based on the H.G. Wells novel about a Martian invasion of Earth, and the scientist (Barry) out to stop them. Highlighted by terrific Academy Award-winning special effects. ★★★½ DVD: $19.99, VHS: $9.99

War Requiem

(1989, 90 min, GB, Derek Jarman) Jarman teamed with producer Don Boyd to create this elaborate symphony of sight and sound. Using the same non-dialogue format as Boyd's *Aria* (which featured a segment by Jarman), they have brought cinematic life to Benjamin Britten's immensely powerful "War Requiem." Written for the opening of the new Coventry Cathedral (the original was destroyed in WWII), Britten's oratorio is punctuated by the haunting poetry of Wilfred Owen — who was killed just prior to Armistice Day in 1918 at the age of 27. This exceptionally stirring piece captures Britten's theme of innocence ruined by the ravages of war. ★★★

The War Room

(1993, 96 min, US, Chris Hegedus & D.A. Pennebaker) When filmmakers Pennebaker and Hegedus set out to document Bill Clinton's 1992 presidential campaign, they were hoping for unrestricted access to the candidate. Stonewalled by Clinton, they turned their attentions, instead, to his

W

two top campaign managers: ragin' Cajun chief strategist James Carville, and 31-year-old upstart communications director George Stephanopoulous. And so much the better. With a snappy and aggressive verité style, the film revels in the gritty and nonstop action of behind-the-scenes politics. Though certainly nonpartisan, it should still provide amusement no matter what your party affiliation. ★★★ DVD: $9.99

The War Zone

(1999, 99 min, GB, Tim Roth) *Ray Winstone, Freddie Cunliffe, Lara Belmont, Tilda Swinton.* Roth's directorial debut is a fully realized, gutwrenching exposé of a dirty family secret, delivered with lyrical brutality through superbly composed images and an economy of dialogue. The excellent cast imparts understated and well-crafted performances, revealing emotional depth in small, casual moments. The isolation of the windswept coastal region mirrors the family's insularity and detachment from the outside community. They go through the motions of an eerie hypernormalcy, strange silence permeating their shared space, until a chance glance through a window makes further denial impossible for one family member. Roth has artfully constructed a powerful and accomplished exploration of the deadening effect of an oft-told lie. ★★★½ DVD: $19.99, VHS Unrated: $14.99

Ward 6

(1976, 93 min, Yugoslavia, Lucian Pintilie) Yugoslavian theatre director Pintilie's adaptation of Anton Chekhov's powerful story paints the disturbing portrait of a Russian Empire in decline — moldering in moral rot. Set in a provincial town at the turn-of-the-century, a dedicated but troubled doctor oversees a grotesque, inhuman mental ward. Slowly numbed by the poverty and suffering, he finds solace with an inmate, the only one who seemingly comprehends the situation. A somber, claustrophobic work that uses a static camera and repetitive sounds (running water, banging machinery) to help us appreciate the suffocation of the people in this hopeless world. (Serbian with English subtitles) ★★★ VHS: $59.99

WarGames

(1983, 110 min, US, John Badham) *Ally Sheedy, Matthew Broderick, Dabney Coleman, John Wood.* A clever, entertaining computer-age adventure/thriller with Broderick as a high school hacker who taps into the Defense Department's computer and nearly starts World War III. ★★★ DVD: $14.99

Warlock

(1959, 122 min, US, Edward Dmytryk) *Henry Fonda, Richard Widmark, Anthony Quinn.* A lawman amd his sidekick (Fonda, Quinn) clean up a Western mining town; but another law enforcer, a reformed bandit (Widmark), challenges the pair to a final showdown. An efficient western with good action and nice characterizations. ★★★ VHS: $19.99

Warlock

(1988, 102 min, US, Steve Miner) *Julian Sands, Richard E. Grant, Lori Singer.* Sands plays the title character, an evil witch who escapes a fiery punishment in 17th-century Massachusetts by fleeing through time to present-day Los Angeles. Once there, he plans to restore "The Grand Grimoire" (the Satanic bible said to contain the lost name of God) and unleash the power to "unmake" the universe. Though the story line maintains some interest, this is no more than a grade-B supernatural thriller. (Followed by 2 sequels) ★★½ DVD: $14.99

Warm Nights on a Slow Moving Train

(1987, 91 min, Australia, Bob Ellis) *Wendy Hughes, Colin Friels.* "Catholic schoolteacher by day . . . high-class hooker by night." Yes, the concept does look like a typical exploitation flick, but appearances can deceive. For this Aussie import is a funny, erotic and wonderfully entertaining drama on the continual war between the sexes. Hughes stars as a quiet teacher who, on weekends, takes the night train from Melbourne to Sydney to visit her ailing brother. There she creates a new persona and becomes a classy hooker. Her cold approach to sex and relationships is challenged after she falls in love with one of her clients. Hughes' performance goes beyond the role of "the hooker with a broken heart" as she creates a memorable, believable and ultimately tragic character. ★★★

Warrior's Rest (Le Repos du Guerrier)

(1962, 98 min, France, Roger Vadim) *Brigitte Bardot.* Bardot stars as an innocent woman who, after saving the life of a man attempting suicide, finds herself becoming more deeply involved with him. Claiming her as the keeper of his soul, this mystery man soon moves in with her. Attracted by his charms and attention, Bardot falls in love and soon abandons her previous boyfriend and lifestyle. But the tables are turned as her love turns into a one-sided affair. A fine drama of obsessive love, power and commitment. (French with English subtitles) ★★★

The Warriors

(1979, 94 min, US, Walter Hill) *Michael Beck, James Remar, Deborah van Valkenburgh, David Patrick Kelly.* Controversial and violent teen pic about a New York City gang which is framed for the murder of a local hotshot and becomes hunted by all the other gangs in the city. ★★½ DVD: $19.99, VHS: $9.99

Wasabi

(2001, 94 min, France/Japan, Gerard Krawczyk) *Jean Reno, Michel Muller, Ryoko Hirosue, Carole Bouquet.* Reno plays a Parisian cop who is still mourning the fact that the love of his life — a beautiful Japanese woman — walked out on him 19 years before. When he receives word of her death, he travels to Japan, only to discover that her death was no accident and he has a 19-year-old daughter. Lapses in taste (particularly in the film's milking of Reno's violently abusive behavior for laughs), a clunky structure and an anemic, unsatisfying wrap-up peg this as the work of Luc Besson (who penned the script, such as it is). Hirosue is appealing as an extremely perky teenage girl, and contrasts amusingly with the always-laconic Reno, but the film offers little action, no threat, no suspense, and few laughs. Not as flavorful nor as spicy as its namesake, *Wasabi* is lightweight, breezy and unfulfilling. ★★ DVD: $19.99

The Wash

(1988, 93 min, US, Michael Toshiyuki Uno) *Mako, Nobu McCarthy.* Set in San Fransisco, this enormously appealing and overlooked gem revolves around a recently separated husband and wife who had met at a Japanese internment camp during WWII. Mako and McCarthy give two exceptional performances as the estranged couple, whose only contact with each other is when she sees him weekly to do his wash. The film's poignant, emotional center examines the wife's (McCarthy) personal conflict when she falls in love with another man, forcing her to confront the old-world values of her heritage and the ever-changing demands of a new way of life. ★★★½

The Wash

(2001, 94 min, US, D.J. Pooh) *Snoop Dogg, Dr. Dre, George Wallace, Angell Conwell, D.J. Pooh.* Stoner comedy fans alert: stock up on your recreational drug of choice before popping this one in your VCR. Despite DJ Pooh (who cowrote the original *Friday*) being behind the camera here, this *Car Wash* rip-off is pretty damned unfunny and, in the end, kind of depressing. Snoop and Dr. Dre play two stoners (Cheech and Chong they ain't) who land jobs at a car wash, and hijinks ensue. *The Wash* is barely a comedy, really; ninety percent of the gags can be seen in the trailer, and are basically comic relief to the half-assed drama of these two losers' daily lives. However, there is a decent soundtrack and plentiful booty on hand. ★½ DVD 2-disc set: $19.99, DVD Basic Edition: $14.99

Washington Square

(1997, 115 min, US, Agnieszka Holland) *Jennifer Jason Leigh, Ben Chaplin, Maggie Smith, Albert Finney.* Holland's adaptation of the Henry James novel (told before in 1949's *The Heiress*) is an at times uneven, but ultimately evocative and richly layered look at a young woman's struggle to break free of her overbearing father's repression. Leigh is Catherine Sloper, a socially inept young woman who dotes upon her father in a vain attempt to compensate for the fact that her mother died giving birth to her. This father-daughter tension becomes extreme when a young suitor, Morris Townsend (Chaplin), comes to call. They fall deeply in love, but Dr. Sloper withholds his consent believing Townsend to be a golddigger. It's a taut situation to be sure, but sadly *Washington Square* fails to fully capitalize and at times drags. Still, Leigh is magnificent, and Finney is positively stoic in his portrayal of a father who can't come to terms with the loss of his wife. ★★★ DVD: $9.99

The Wasp Woman

(1960, 66 min, US, Roger Corman) *Susan Cabot, Fred Eisley.* Corman's knock-off of the previous year's hit, *The Fly*, finds Susan Cabot using royal jelly to stay young forever. Instead it turns her into a killer queen bee. ★ VHS: $9.99

Watch It!

(1993, 102 min, US, Tom Flynn) *Peter Gallagher, John C. McGinley, Lili Taylor, Suzy Amis, Jon Tenney, Tom Sizemore. Watch It!* is a bitingly accurate comedy about the way men and women relate. A lot of credit has to go to writer-director Flynn for managing to merge bitter cynicism with sentimental (but not sickening) romance. Focusing on a group of "post-twentysomething" friends living in Chicago, *Watch It!* features Gallagher as a non-committing drifter who shows up one morning on the doorstep of his womanizing cousin Tenny. Spotlighting a few "male bonding" scenes, the film spends more time with its male characters than it does with the female ones. And it's a shame, because the characters played by Amis and Taylor are as engaging and complicated as any of the male characters. ★★★ VHS: $7.99

Watch on the Rhine

(1943, 114 min, US, Herman Shumlin) *Bette Davis, Paul Lukas, Lucile Watson, Geraldine Fitzgerald.* Lillian Hellman's cautionary drama about the rise of Nazism in the late 1930s gets a first-rate screen treatment. Lukas won an Oscar for his powerful portrayal of a German refugee, now living in Washington with his family, who is hunted by Nazi agents. Davis also stars as Lukas' wife, and Watson is very good as the "Everyperson" who chooses to ignore the coming catastrophe. ★★★½

The Watcher

(2000, 97 min, US, Joe Charbanic) *James Spader, Keanu Reeves, Marisa Tomei, Ernie Hudson, Chris Ellis.* Serial killer Reeves taunts a former nemesis — ex-FBI agent Spader — by sending him unidentified photos of young women and then giving him one full day to find and save them. Appallingly directed by Charbanic, the film has a fairly tense section where-in Spader and crew are desperately trying to find a soon-to-be victim. Otherwise, *The Watcher* is flat, uninvolving and clichéd. Reeves is just your typical crazy psycho, dancing to Rob Zombie and dropping evil one-liners. Spader looks annoyed to be here, and the ending just . . . ends. This isn't even amusing as bad cheese. ★ DVD: $14.99, VHS: $14.99

Watcher in the Woods

(1980, 84 min, US, John Hough) *Bette Davis, Carroll Baker, David MacCallum, Lynn-Holly Johnson.* Effective Disney-produced ghost story about an American family who move into Davis' British country estate, where the youngest girl is haunted by visions of Davis' long-lost daughter. (This is the edited version of the 108-minute theatri-cal release; however, the film was cut to tighten the rather confusing longer version, not because of cen-sorship or scares.) ★★½

Water

(1985, 95 min, GB, Dick Clement) *Michael Caine, Brenda Vaccaro, Valerie Perrine.* A congenial but generally inept comedy about a Caribbean British colony that is transformed by the discovery of a pure mineral water source within its tiny confines. What follows is a comedy of commercial and social exploitation with the local British governor (Caine) suddenly caught in a juggling match with greedy U.S. oil interests, an internal insurrection, and other assorted lunacies. ★★ VHS: $7.99

The Water Engine

(1992, 88 min, US, Steven Schachter) *Charles Durning, Patti LuPone, William H. Macy, John Mahoney, Joe Mantegna, Joanna Miles, Treat Williams.* A marvelous little film written by David Mamet that chronicles American corporate greed and the depths to which the money men will sink to protect their interests. Charles Lang (Macy) is an engineer in an auto factory. He has invented an inter-nal combustion engine fueled on water. After years developing the ideal non-polluting engine he tries to sell his invention only to find that the oil company's interests far outweigh any good the engine will do for society. ★★★ VHS: $49.99

The Waterboy

(1998, 89 min, US, Frank Coraci) *Adam Sandler, Kathy Bates, Henry Winkler, Fairuza Balk, Jerry Reed.* Having demonstrated a comic maturity in *The Wedding Singer*, it looked as if Sandler was definite-ly improving as a screen comedian. But with *The Waterboy*, an atrocious comedy of idiotic propor-tions, it's two giant steps backwards. He plays Bobby Boucher, a college football team's doofus waterboy, whose slow and slurred manner of speech could leave one with the impression that he's slight-ly retarded. Anyway, when head coach Winkler learns that waterboy can tackle anyone and every-one, the backwoods blunderer becomes the darling of the beer-guzzling, yahoo-cheering set. The jokes amount to Bobby tackling people and him talking like a bona fide moron. Oh, what wit. ★ DVD: $14.99, VHS: $9.99

The Waterdance

(1992, 106 min, US, Michael Steinberg & Neal Jimenez) *Eric Stoltz, Wesley Snipes, William Forsythe, Helen Hunt, Elizabeth Peña, Grace Zabriskie.* Superb work from an accomplished cast does justice to a well-balanced and finely crafted script from codirector Jimenez, based on his own experiences. Stoltz is a young writer who winds up in rehabilitation after becoming paralyzed in an acci-dent. Snipes and Forsythe are fellow paraplegics. Jimenez deftly avoids the potential heavy-handed-ness of his subject and instead tells his story with a wit and warmth which is unsentimental and uncom-promising and invites favorable comparison to Marlon Brando's first film vehicle, *The Men*. ★★★½ DVD Letterbox: $24.99

Waterfront

(1983, 287 min, Australia, Chris Thompson) *Greta Scacchi, Jack Thompson, Chris Haywood.* Fans of five-hour spectacles should enjoy this Australian *Last Exit to Brooklyn*. Set on the turbulent waterfront of Melbourne after WWII, the drama focuses on the bit-ter fight between striking dock workers, a right-wing prime minister, desperate Italians hired as "scabs" and the greedy owners intent on getting the shipyard humming again. The alluring Scacchi is an Italian immigrant reluctantly dragged into the labor battle and Thompson is a union leader who falls passion-ately in love with her. ★★★

Waterland

(1992, 95 min, GB, Stephen Gyllenhaal) *Jeremy Irons, Sinéad Cusack, Ethan Hawke, John Heard, Grant Warnock, Maggie Gyllenhaal.* Gyllenhaal's moody adaptation of the Graham Swift novel stars Irons as a high school history teacher whose past provides his jaded students with a somber lesson in history. Meanwhile, his present emulates the haunt-ing memories of his past. Cusack is superb as Irons' wife (a role she plays in real life) as is Hawke, whose disillusioned youth serves as the catalyst for Irons' looking into his past. At times confusing and often disjointed, this film is still a challenge worth taking. ★★★

Watermelon Man

(1970, 97 min, US, Melvin Van Peebles) *Godfrey Cambridge, Estelle Parsons.* Social comedy with a lot of bite about a bigoted white man who awakens one morning to discover that he has turned black. Cambridge's broad playing helps greatly in the enjoyment of this racial parable. ★★★

Watership Down

(1978, 93 min, Canada/GB, Martin Rosen) *Voices of:, John Hurt, Richard Briers, Ralph Richardson, Roy Kinnear, Zero Mostel.* A family of rabbits, their home field being torn apart by man's progress, go on a journey to find a new home. A beautifully animat-ed adaptation of Richard Adams' novel that doesn't pander to a kiddie audience. ★★★½ DVD: $19.99

Waterworld

(1995, 135 min, US, Kevin Reynolds) *Kevin Costner, Dennis Hopper, Jeanne Tripplehorn, Tina Majorino, Michael Jeter.* Half-fish, half-human mutant Costner (blatantly based on Mel Gibson's loner Mad Max) becomes involved in tribal warfare on a water-logged planet, the effects of the polar ice-caps melting. The set design and effects of *Waterworld* are impressive, but ultimately this is a formulaic, over-produced adventure film that is fun for awhile. Costing a stunning $175 million, the cause of much controversy, *Waterworld* can't help

but be weighed down by the weight of its own excess. ★★½ DVD Letterbox: $14.99, DVD DTS sound: ★★★ $14.99, VHS: $9.99, VHS Letterbox: $14.99

Waxwork

(1988, 97 min, US, Anthony Hickox) *Zach Galligan, David Warner, Deborah Foreman.* Inventive horror film with a most unusual premise: a group of teens (that's *not* the inventive part) spend a night at a mys-terious house of wax. Each visitor becomes part of the presentation by being hurled back in time and acting out the gruesome renderings. (Sequel: *Waxwork II: Lost in Time*) ★★★ VHS: $14.99

Waxworks

(1924, 83 min, Germany, Paul Leni) *Emil Jannings, Conrad Veidt, Werner Krauss, Wilhelm Dieterle.* This seldom seen masterpiece of German expressionism finds director Leni developing a visu-al style that he would take to Universal Studios where it would inspire the directors of *Dracula* and *Frankenstein*. A young writer (Dieterle) becomes the press agent of a carnival wax museum. When he begins to spin his tales about the statues of Haroun-al-Raschid, Ivan the Terrible and Jack the Ripper, he finds himself becoming entangled in his own tales. And all-star pre-war German cast plus innovative set design makes this one of the most eerie films of the silent era. ★★★★ DVD: $24.99, VHS: $24.99

Way Down East

(1920, 119 min, US, D.W. Griffith) *Lillian Gish, Richard Barthelmess, Lowell Sherman.* Classic silent melodrama, with Gish as the quintessential virtuous country girl seduced by the evil city slicker. Includes the famous scene with Gish trapped and washed away on an ice floe. ★★★★ DVD: $29.99, VHS: $24.99

The Way Home

(2002, 88 min, South Korea, Jeong-Hyang Lee) *Eul-Boon Kim, Seung-Ho Yoo, Kyung-Hoon Min.* A poignant, almost heartbreaking Korean drama about the fragile relationship between an estranged grand-son and grandmother. Sang-woo (Yoo), a bratty seven-year-old boy from the big city, is forced to live with his mute grandmother (Kim), a poor peasant, for several months. She has no plumbing, no wash-ing machine and lives miles from the nearest replacement batteries for his GameBoy. She is, how-ever, a sweet, selfless woman. At first, Sang-woo abuses this woman with insults and neglect, blind to her caring and affection. How Sang-woo eventually comes to depend and love his grandmother is at the heart of this story, deceptively simple and extremely moving. With no dialogue, Kim conveys a myriad of emotions through simple gestures and those haunt-ing eyes. (Korean with English subtitles) ★★★ DVD Subtitled: $19.99, VHS Subtitled: $72.99

The Way of the Gun

(2000, 119 min, US, Christopher McQuarrie) *Ryan Phillippe, Benicio del Toro, Juliette Lewis, Taye Diggs, James Caan.* Bristling with enough tes-terone-pumped moxie to incinerate the screen, this tense kidnapping thriller has the gritty edge of the best film noirs. Phillippe and del Toro are an unlike-ly duo of small-time punks who hatch a scheme to abduct a surrogate mother (Lewis) who's very-preg-nant with the child of a millionaire. By the time they realize the father is the local Mafioso, the boss' badass bodyguards and an ice-cool hit man (Caan) are already hunting them down. First-time director McQuarrie (screenwriter of *The Usual Suspects*) cer-tainly has a respect for the genre, but the stop-start nature of the film can be crippling. Thankfully, there's enough macho banter to keep things crackling, and there are plenty of showdowns and shootouts. ★★★ DVD: $9.99, VHS: $9.99, VHS Previously Viewed: $102.99

Way Out West

(1937, 66 min, US, James W. Horne) *Stan Laurel, Oliver Hardy.* One of Laurel & Hardy's funniest films, this classic western spoof has the boys delivering the deed of a gold mine to the wrong girl. ★★★½

The Way We Were

(1973, 118 min, US, Sydney Pollack) *Barbra Streisand, Robert Redford, Bradford Dillman, Viveca Lindfors, Murray Hamilton, James Woods.* Compelling romantic drama with Redford and Streisand meeting in college in the late 1930s and having an on-again, off-again affair over the next 15 years. Streisand plays a campus activist who is enamored by gorgeous WASP Redford, meeting years later when each has made a name for themselves. One of the first films to explore the Hollywood blacklist of the 1950s, though it is used merely as a subplot. ★★★ DVD: $19.99, VHS: $9.99

The Way West

(1967, 122 min, US, Andrew V. McLaglen) *Kirk Douglas, Robert Mitchum, Richard Widmark, Stubby Kaye, Sally Field.* A wagon train with an aging scout (Mitchum) and a ruthless U.S. Senator (Douglas) searches for the promised land of the Northwest Territories. ★★

Wayne's World

(1992, 95 min, US, Penelope Spheeris) *Mike Myers, Dana Carvey, Tia Carrere, Rob Lowe, Lara Flynn Boyle.* Meyers and Carvey bring their zany, head-banging brand of seriously adolescent humor from "S.N.L." to the big screen with way cool results. Wayne and Garth must fight to save their basement cable-TV show from the clutches of unscrupulous producer Lowe, and Wayne gets the hots for truly "babe-a-licious" Carrere. A post-punk Spheeris directed this hilarious ode to '90s teen culture. Destined to be a cultural signpost for decades to come — NOT! (Sequel: *Wayne's World 2*) ★★★ DVD Special Edition: $19.99, VHS: $9.99

Wayne's World 2

(1993, 94 min, US, Stephen Surjik) *Dana Carvey, Mike Myers, Tia Carrere, Christopher Walken, Kim Basinger, Ed O'Neill, Charlton Heston.* Wayne and Garth are back with this regurgitated yet nonetheless amusing sequel. Wayne takes on the task of organizing a massive outdoor rock concert, "Waynestock," in his home town of Aurora, Illinois. This sets the stage for a '70s-inspired amalgam of loosely tied together plot contrivances that for the most part offer winning one-liners, witticisms and spoofs. Twentysomethingers beware: Much of the film's humor seems aimed not at its target audience but Baby Boomers. ★★½ DVD Special Edition: $14.99, VHS: $9.99

We of the Never Never

(1983, 132 min, Australia, Igor Auzins) *Angela Punch McGregor, Arthur Digman.* Based on the true-life experience of popular Australian novelist Jeannie Gunn, this beautifully photographed, award-winning film focuses on the first white woman to live in the vast Outback of Australia's Northern Territory. With courage and determination she faces the many hardships of this barren land and the hostility of the men in the region, while acquiring a deep

compassion and respect for the Aborigines of the "never never," where one could ride all day and "never never" reach the horizon. ★★★

We the Living

(1942, 160 min, Italy, Goffredo Alessandrini) *Rossano Brazzi, Alida Valli, Fosci Giachetti.* The Russian Revolution is the fiery backdrop for this story of love's ability to endure the ravages of oppression. Based on the classic Ayn Rand novel, the film was made with great difficulty during Mussolini's reign in WWII Italy. With overtly antifascist themes, several of the film's key scenes were snipped for government screenings and then replaced for its world premiere at the 1942 Venice Film Festival. But the film was seized by authorities, and placed in a vault for decades until the late 1960s. Eventually, new prints were struck for this eloquent and deeply moving tale of love versus authority, and the film only in the early '90s received its first commercial screenings since World War II. (Italian with English subtitles) ★★★

We Think the World of You

(1988, 92 min, GB, Colin Gregg) *Alan Bates, Gary Oldman, Frances Barber.* This film version of J.R. Ackerley's best-selling 1961 novel about a love triangle between two men and a dog is not wholly successful and can be best described as an "interesting failure." Set in the rubble of post-WWII East-End London, the film stars Bates as the older, set-in-his-ways part-time lover of Oldman, a roughish charmer who divides his affections between his wife and child, and Bates. The situation is upset when Oldman is sent to prison for six months. The care and feeding of his beloved dog Evie, a charmer in her own right, is left to his mother. But Bates, desperate for a replacement love, begins to care for her and becomes obsessed with the dog; able to see in her qualities that his gaoled lover could never possess. Not your usual love story. ★★

We Were One Man

(1981, 105 min, France, Philippe Vallois) This touching, unusual love story chronicles the budding relationship between a wounded German soldier and the young French peasant who nurses him back to health. Excitable, dim-witted Guy's lonely existence is brightened when he comes upon Rolf in the forest. The two bask in playful, homoerotic exchanges until the war reenters their lives and tries to separate them. (French with English subtitles) ★★★ VHS: $49.99

We Were Soldiers

(2002, 138 min, US, Randall Wallace) *Mel Gibson, Madeleine Stowe, Greg Kinnear, Sam Elliott, Chris Klein, Keri Russell, Barry Pepper.* Braveheart collaborators Gibson and Wallace (who wrote that screenplay) reunite for this moving Vietnam War film that both examines the high cost of war and extols the heroism of soldiers on both sides of the battle. Based on the memoirs of Lt. Col. Hal Moore (stoically played by Gibson), the intense *We Were Soldiers* — like *Black Hawk Down* before it — looks at a single, lengthy battle and the inevitable, tragic loss that follows. It is 1965, and Moore and his men have arrived in Ia Drang, where American soliders immediately come under bloody attack from the North Vietnamese. Trying desperately to prevent a massacre, the men experience great loss and injury while trying to reconcile their presence there. *We Were Soldiers* follows the blueprint of the war film, and though the battle scenes are well staged, the film finds its strength in the small, intimate moments that occur on the battlefield and at home. ★★★ DVD Letterbox: $14.99, VHS: $9.99

We're No Angels

(1955, 106 min, US, Michael Curtiz) *Humphrey Bogart, Peter Ustinov, Aldo Ray, Joan Bennett, Basil Rathbone, Leo G. Carroll.* Engaging comic fluff with Bogey, Ustinov and Ray as Devil's Island escapees who are taken in by a French merchant family, who are unaware of their true identity. (Remade in 1989) ★★★ VHS: $14.99

We're No Angels

(1989, 108 min, US, Neil Jordan) *Robert De Niro, Sean Penn, Demi Moore, Hoyt Axton.* The idea of De Niro and Penn costarring in a remake of the 1955 Humphrey Bogart comedy *We're No Angels*, and having it written by David Mamet, must have looked great on paper. So what happened? This is a painfully unfunny comedy with De Niro and Penn as prison escapees who masquerade as priests to elude a search party. The film captures none of the spirit of playfulness which made the original so entertaining: this version is a heavy-handed misconception and strictly for fans of the two stars. ★ DVD Letterbox: $14.99, VHS: $14.99

Weapons of the Spirit

(1989, 90 min, US, Pierre Sauvage) This warm and gripping documentary traces an amazing event in World War II history that occurred in the small French village of Le Chambon. As Hitler plowed and pillaged his way through Europe, fleeing Jews began to arrive in the predominantly Protestant town, where they were undeniably and even enthusiastically given refuge. Although the Nazi threat was becoming increasingly more apparent, the brave and generous townspeople continued to offer not only food and shelter, but a complete acceptance of and genuine dedication to these 5,000 Jewish inhabitants. Director Sauvage, himself born in Le Chambon, celebrates the good will and delivers what is truly a labor of love. (English and French with English subtitles) ★★★½ VHS: $39.99

A Wedding

(1978, 125 min, US, Robert Altman) *Carol Burnett, Mia Farrow, Lillian Gish, Geraldine Chaplin, Lauren Hutton, Dennis Christopher, Paul Dooley, Viveca Lindfors, Pat McCormick.* Altman's enjoyable follow-up to *Nashville* utilizes the same multi-character collage which earmarked his classic film. Two very diverse families come together for a ritzy, upper-class wedding, revealing family skeletons and hidden passions, among other things. Burnett heads a very strong ensemble cast. ★★★ VHS: $29.99

The Wedding Banquet

(1993, 108 min, US/China/Taiwan, Ang Lee) *Winston Chao, Mitchell Lichtenstein, May Chin.* This wholesome gay comedy follows the family drama of Wai Tung (Chao), a transplanted Taiwanese gay man and now New York real estate entrepreneur who is constantly being nagged by his family about getting married. Living with his American boyfriend, Simon (Lichtenstein), Wai arranges a marriage-of-convenience with a wacky artist. The plan backfires, however, when his parents announce they are coming to New York to meet the bride! Frantically, the two lovers remove all vestiges of their relationship from the apartment, posing as landlord-tenant and bringing in the faux fiancée. All is well until the parents spearhead an elaborate wedding banquet that involves a night of gaudy excesses and some unwanted surprises. The delightful characters are the real attraction of this sexual and cultural comedy-of-errors which is both witty and perceptive. ★★★½ DVD: $14.99

The Wedding Gift

(1994, 87 min, GB, Richard Loncraine) *Jim Broadbent, Julie Walters, Sian Thomas.* An amiable comedy-drama based on the true story of one of the early sufferers of what has come to be known as "chronic fatigue syndrome." Because of a series of unexplainable ailments, Walters becomes dependent on husband Broadbent, who becomes her devoted caretaker. Eventually, he is smitten by a nearly blind novelist (Thomas), but he finds himself unable to cheat on his disabled wife. Walters, however, has another plan as she arranges for Thomas to take her place upon her death. Though this sounds like the basis for a bawdy comedy, *The Wedding Gift* is instead a slightly somber melodrama peppered with Broadbent's and Walter's witty repartee, which though pleasing to watch, is ultimately a letdown. ★★½ DVD: $19.99, VHS: $14.99

Wedding in Blood

(1973, 98 min, France, Claude Chabrol) *Stéphane Audran, Michel Piccoli.* The moral degeneration of the French middle class is familiar territory for Chabrol as he continues his favorite theme in this moody drama. Audrane and Piccoli are married to each other but both are unfaithful. Each one concocts a plan to murder the other in order to free themselves. Who will get it first? A nice mystery and psychological thriller. (French with English subtitles) ★★★½

Wedding in Galilee

(1988, 113 min, Israel, Michel Khleifi) *El Aleili, Nazih Akleh.* The son of Abu Adel, an elderly patriarch, is about to be married. His father wants him to have a traditional wedding ceremony lasting well into the night. But Abu Adel and his son are Palestinians living under a dusk-to-dawn curfew imposed by the Israeli military. In order to let his son have the wedding party, the father seeks the permission of the governor to suspend the curfew for the wedding night. The governor agrees, but only under the condition that he and his entourage be allowed to attend. So begins *Wedding in Galilee*, a timely and thought-provoking examination of Palestinian-Israeli tensions from the rarely heard Palestinian point of view. (Israeli and Arabic with English subtitles) ★★★ DVD Letterbox: $29.99, VHS: $24.99

Wedding in White

(1972, 103 min, Canada, William Fruet) *Carol Kane, Donald Pleasence.* One of the most important Canadian films of the 1970s, this gritty though sensitively handled drama is set in an impoverished village during WWII. It tells the unsettling story of a young girl who is raped by her brother's army buddy and then forced to marry a middle-aged bachelor to preserve the family honor. Kane is unforgettable as the young girl, and Pleasence is masterful as her unyielding father. ★★★½ DVD 30th Anniversary: $24.99, VHS 30th Anniversary: $19.99

The Wedding March

(1928, 117 min, US, Erich von Stroheim) *Erich Von Stroheim, Fay Wray, ZaSu Pitts.* The only film by von Stroheim where the villain is allowed to live — only because a sequel was never completed for him. Which is a shame because part two opens with the Wedding Night (Part two was completed by someone else and released overseas as *The Honeymoon*). It's another love triangle in old Vienna with von Stroheim himself playing the prince. ★★★½ VHS: $29.99

The Wedding Party

(1969, 92 min, US, Brian De Palma, Cynthia Munroe, Wilford Leach) *Charles Pfluger, Robert De Niro, Jill Clayburgh.* A groom-to-be meets his fiancée's extended family for the first time a few days before the wedding; claustrophobia and dread set in fast. Imaginative use of stop-action, fast and slow motion, non-sync sound and jump cuts enliven the screen debuts of Clayburgh as the bride-to-be and De Niro as a friend of the groom. Pfluger is engaging as the young man contemplating escape from his promise to marry. ★★ VHS: $14.99

The Wedding Planner

(2001, 104 min, US, Adam Shankman) *Jennifer Lopez, Matthew McConaughey, Bridgette Wilson-Sampras, Justin Chambers, Alex Rocco, Joanna Gleason, Charles Kimbrough, Fred Willard.* Mary Fiore (Lopez) is a woman who is in total control of her emotions, applying the same rigor to her nonexistent love life as she does to her successful career as a wedding planner. When she meets handsome doctor Steve Edison (McConaughey), she loosens the restraints just a bit — that is until she learns he's engaged and one of her clients. A cute premise, bearing no surprises but engaging nonetheless, emerges from Mary's predicament as both Mary and Steve set out to deny their feelings. That the outcome is never in doubt shouldn't come as a shock, for *The Wedding Planner* is the type of pleasant, formulaic romantic comedy that doesn't aim too high in its goals. ★★½ DVD: $14.99, VHS: $9.99

The Wedding Singer

(1998, 97 min, US, Frank Coraci) *Adam Sandler, Drew Barrymore, Christine Taylor, Steve Buscemi, Jon Lovitz, Alexis Arquette, Billy Idol.* Sandler matures on-screen right before your eyes with a controlled, funny performance in this often amusing though surprisingly sentimental romantic comedy. Sounding like a runner-up in a David Duchovny voice contest, Sandler plays a quick-witted, semi-talented wedding singer whose life takes a turn for the worse when he's dumped at the altar. Barrymore is a future bride who befriends him with the predictable consequences: they fall in love. Set in the mid-'80s, the film seems to name-drop a reference from that time period on cue about every ten minutes: some are funny, some are obvious. Barrymore is the real treasure here; she's absolutely beguiling. ★★½ DVD: $14.99

Weeds

(1987, 115 min, US, John Hancock) *Nick Nolte, William Forsythe, Rita Taggart, Joe Mantegna, Ernie Hudson, Anne Ramsey.* In this based-on-fact story, Nolte gives a stirring portrayal of a convict whose plays about life behind bars lead to his parole and his works being performed both off-Broadway and in prisons around the country. ★★★

Weekend

(1968, 103 min, France, Jean-Luc Godard) *Mirielle Darc, Jean Yanne, Jean-Pierre Léaud.* One of Godard's most successfully realized films, *Weekend* is a devastating attack on and an apocalyptic metaphor for the rapid collapse of Western capitalistic society. Beginning with a coherent plot (that soon goes astray), the story follows a bourgeois couple who travel by car from Paris to the country. The rural landscape they encounter soon becomes a nightmarish vision of chaos and destruction — with the road littered with traffic jams, burning cars, violence and death. A highlight of the film is the ten-minute tracking shot of the mammoth traffic jam that encapsulates all of the anarchy of a society in decay. (French with English subtitles) ★★★½ VHS: $19.99

Weekend at Bernie's

(1989, 97 min, US, Ted Kotcheff) *Andrew McCarthy, Jonathan Silverman, Terry Kiser.* *Weekend at Bernie's* is tasteless, sophomoric, and funny. McCarthy and Silverman are young corporate go-getters who get invited to the boss' palatial oceanfront home for the weekend — to be murdered. But the tables are turned, and it is Bernie who gets his. Only problem is, the boys think they're next, and to save themselves, they must make it look like Bernie is really alive. "Masterpiece Theatre" it's not. It's not even *The Trouble with Harry*. But it is for undemanding comedic tastes. (Sequel: *Weekend at Bernie's 2*) ★★½ DVD: $14.99, VHS: $9.99

Weekend at Bernie's 2

(1993, 89 min, US, Robert Klane) *Andrew McCarthy, Jonathan Silverman, Terry Kiser, Barry Bostwick.* An unfunny, even sillier follow-up to the 1989 surprise hit about the corpse that just won't stay dead. Kiser reprises his role as Bernie, who this time is reanimated by a Virgin Islands voodoo priestess who's after the money he embezzled before his demise. The humor is as macabre as in the first film, though it's really hard not to laugh at seeing Bernie dancing his way into the ocean with a harpoon through his head. ★½ DVD Dual: $19.99

Week-End at the Waldorf

(1945, 130 min, US, Robert Z. Leonard) *Ginger Rogers, Walter Pidgeon, Lana Turner, Van Johnson, Robert Benchley.* This updated version of *Grand Hotel* is a slick, surprisingly enjoyable comedy-drama. Set in New York at the Waldorf-Astoria directly at the end of WWII, the story follows the varied lives of those who have come to stay at the luxury hotel. Rogers is a famous actress who sort of wants to be alone. The ever-debonair Pidgeon is the war correspondent who keeps her from her solitude. This is basically played for laughs. More dramatic is the subplot between injured soldier Johnson and gold-digging stenographer Turner. Director Leonard nicely intercuts the numerous stories and elicits pleasant performances from the entire ensemble. ★★★ VHS: $19.99

The Weight of Water

(2000, 113 min, US, Kathryn Bigelow) *Catherine McCormack, Sean Penn, Elizabeth Hurley, Sarah Polley, Josh Lucas, Ciaran Hinds, Katrin Cartlidge.* Jean (McCormack), a photojournalist in an unhappy marriage, sails to the coast of New Hampshire to investigate the century-old double murder of two female Norwegian immigrants. Also on board are her has-been writer husband Thomas (Penn), his bland sailor brother Rich (Lucas), and Rich's gorgeous, scantily clad girlfriend Adaline (Hurley). Jealous tensions on the boat mount as Thomas lecherously ogles voluptuous Adaline while Jean gradually unravels the vexing mystery of the legendary killings. The film flashes back and forth from current day to 1873, but there's so much toggling between the two time lines that neither one ever gains any real momentum. The period sequences are exquisitely filmed, yet weighed down by a "Scarlet Letter"-like stodginess; a pointless storm-at-sea climax exists only to inject the modern-day finale with some much-needed adrenaline. A curious misfire. ★★½ DVD: $14.99

W

Weird Science

(1985, 94 min, US, John Hughes) *Anthony Michael Hall, Ilan Mitchell-Smith, Kelly LeBrock, Robert Downey, Jr., Bill Paxton.* A wasted comic fantasy about two high school boys (Hall, Mitchell-Smith) who create their "perfect" woman from a computer. LeBrock is the dream girl. ★ DVD Letterbox: $19.99, VHS: $9.99

Welcome Home, Roxy Carmichael

(1990, 97 min, US, Jim Abrahams) *Winona Ryder, Jeff Daniels.* A charming tale of an orphaned misfit who gets a new lease on life when she discovers that her mother may be a Hollywood star returning home for the first time in 15 years. Ryder's penchant for eccentric characterizations serves her well in her portrayal of Dinky Bossetti, a misanthropic teen whose only friends are the stray animals she keeps on a makeshift ark by the lake. Daniels is Denton Webb, the ex-lover who never got over losing Roxy. The overall warmth and sentimentality of the production make this an unqualified sleeper. ★★★ VHS: $14.99

Welcome to L.A.

(1977, 106 min, US, Alan Rudolph) *Keith Carradine, Sissy Spacek, Geraldine Chaplin, Harvey Keitel, Sally Kellerman, Lauren Hutton.* The rock music scene in Los Angeles gets the Rudolph treatment in this world of fragile egos, quickie love affairs and broken dreams. Produced by Robert Altman. ★★★

Welcome to Mooseport

(2004, 110 min, US, Donald Petrie) *Gene Hackman, Ray Romano, Marcia Gay Harden, Maura Tierney, Christine Baranski, Rip Torn, Fred Savage.* On paper, the idea of a former U.S. President becoming embroiled in small-town politics — by running against a hardware store owner for mayor with resulting wacky antics — is resplendent with comic possibilities. Unfortunately, someone forgot to tell screenwriter Tom Schulman. Giving this film more class than it deserves, Hackman is President Monroe "Eagle" Cole, whose retirement comes to an end when he's asked to run for mayor . . . only it's supposed to be unopposed and now down-to-earth Handy Harrison (Romano) is in the race, too. There's romantic subplots and the requisite "charming" locals to add to the political turmoil, but too few laughs are produced and a good cast is given very little to do. Romano is in "Ray" territory but still manages to be appealing, and Harden and Tierney are likable foils, but between the mushy music and forced shenanigans, it just doesn't come together. Too bad, this could have been good. ★½ DVD Widescreen: $27.99, DVD Pan & Scan: $27.99

Welcome to Sarajevo

(1997, 102 min, US, Michael Winterbottom) *Stephen Dillane, Woody Harrelson, Marisa Tomei, Kerry Fox, Emily Lloyd, Goran Visnjic, Emira Nusevic.* Director Winterbottom's astonishing film about life during wartime is heavy stuff, but *Welcome to Sarajevo* is distinguished by its focus on humanity. Henderson (Dillane), a jaded British news correspondent, is stunned by the atrocities and conditions that surround him in war-torn Bosnia. He and fellow journalists live in makeshift hotels, and booze it up nightly as the reports they file get buried in their country's telecasts. As Henderson befriends his new driver Risto (Visnjic), he investigates the real Sarajevo, and makes a risky decision to save the life of Emira (Nusevic), an orphan girl he meets one day. The film's tense centerpiece is the rescue of

Welcome to the Dollhouse

Emira, but Winterbottom also presents the fight to keep this illegally saved child in England where she can have a better life. The hard-hitting *Welcome to Sarajevo* is as powerful as it is poignant. ★★★½ DVD: $19.99, VHS: $9.99

Welcome to the Dollhouse

(1996, 87 min, US, Todd Solondz) *Heather Matarazzo, Brendan Sexton Jr., Daria Kalinina, Matthew Faber.* A rabid, blisteringly funny sneer at the hell of awkward adolescence, *Welcome to the Dollhouse* explores a wide range of topics from peer group terrorism, sexual identity crises, insufferable siblings, clueless parents, imprisonment in the educational system to the all-encompassing obsession of the first crush. Matarazzo is terrific as 11-year-old Dawn, who endures the unabashed cruelty of her fellow students and unrelenting criticism at home. Dawn approaches the daily cadence of ritual ostracism and humiliation with a weird solemnity — the unimpeachable martyrdom of the very young. This roiling emotional morass is brought into excruciatingly sharp focus when her brother's garage band gets a new lead singer — a suburban Adonis with a rep for nailing just about any available female. *Dollhouse* is touching, raucous, hilarious, cruel and insightful by turn. ★★★½ DVD: $27.99, VHS: $14.99

Welcome to Woop Woop

(1997, 90 min, Australia, Stephan Elliott) *Johnathon Schaech, Rod Taylor, Susie Porter, Dee Smart, Paul Mercurio, Rachel Griffiths.* Director Elliott's follow-up to his hilarious *The Adventures of Priscilla, Queen of the Desert* once again proves you can't make a cult film on purpose. This ramshackle comedy about Teddy (Schaech), a New York con man who inexplicably becomes a married prisoner in the Australian Outback, has lots of energy but no laughs. The town of Woop Woop rocks to the tunes of Rodgers and Hammerstein and makes dog food out of kangaroos and real dogs (ha-ha-ha). Teddy also learns that his father-in-law Daddy-O (Taylor) is the town leader who will shoot anyone who tries to escape. Although it starts out amusingly enough, once the film settles down in Woop Woop, it has nowhere to go. ★½

The Well

(1997, 102 min, Australia, Samantha Lang) *Pamela Rabe, Miranda Otto, Paul Chubb, Genevieve Lemon.* This refreshingly well-realized modern-day Gothic is conveyed with washed-out color, stark open landscapes, crowded interiors and intriguing characterizations. Katherine is the young girl brought in to an isolated farmhouse to do char work. She quickly becomes a lifeline to Hester, who lives there alone with her increasingly senile father. The freedom afforded by his death is soon compromised by dwindling income and Hester's increasing dependence on Katherine, a stranger who before long is her primary relationship. Katherine's progressive encroachment and Hester's emotional naiveté collide and rupture when a tragic accident exacerbates the building tensions in this dynamic. The underlying eerie elements that lurk just below the surface come to the fore when the two women conspire to cover up a crime. Effective, crisp direction guides this unsettling, atmospheric thriller to a satisfying resolution. ★★★½ DVD: $14.99, VHS: $14.99

The Welldigger's Daughter

(1941, 142 min, France, Marcel Pagnol) *Raimu, Fernandel, Josette Day.* The wonderful French character actor Raimu stars in this fabulous story of a simple French peasant whose humor and dignity is compromised by his daughter, who finds herself pregnant as her lover goes off to war. With this film, Pagnol continued his firm ability to take complex human predicaments and portray them for us in a rich, subtle manner. (French with English subtitles) ★★★

Wendigo

(2002, 92 min, US, Larry Fessenden) *Patricia Clarkson, Jake Weber, Erik Per Sullivan.* Indie horror auteur Fessenden strikes gold again (after *No Telling* and *Habit*) with this characteristically low-key, atmospheric mood piece. Weber and Clarkson (both excellent) play a well-to-do couple vacationing in a wintry, wooded small town with their young son. They cross paths with a hotheaded deer hunter, who can't seem to let an honest mistake go. Shaken a bit by the confrontation, the young boy takes solace in a myth — told to him by a mysterious Native American — of the wendigo, a half-man, half-deer vengeance spirit. Fessenden does wonders with his forest locale and some minimalist, pleasingly old-school special effects, and especially with Sullivan, who's just great as the smart, sensitive, wide-eyed boy. Those expecting hard-core, balls-to-the-wall terror will be let down; *Wendigo* is a slow, creepy, at times poetic horror flick that, like Fessenden's previous work, will stick with you long after the end credits roll. ★★★ DVD: $14.99, VHS: $102.99

Werewolf of London

(1935, 75 min, US, Stuart Walker) *Henry Hull, Warner Oland.* Hull plays the title creature in this early Universal horror film, made six years before Lon Chaney, Jr. immortalized himself as the more famous Wolfman. With no Gypsy lore and little of the moral anguish Chaney later portrayed, an English botanist is bitten by a werewolf on a specimen-collecting tour of Tibet. He returns to London only to realize the nature of his curse and recognizing his helplessness to stop the killing. The film lacks the scares of Chaney's version and, its protagonist is less interesting because he is not wracked by the hand-wringing guilt for which Chaney's Larry Talbot was famous. ★★ VHS: $14.99

W

West and Soda

(1965, 90 min, Italy, Bruno Bozzetto) Bozzetto's first full-length animated feature looks like a spaghetti western as done by Jay Ward. His clean lines and simple backgrounds perfectly mirror the moral and physical landscape inherent in these sorts of American melodramas. And it's funny, too. ★★★ VHS: $29.99

West Side Story

(1961, 152 min, US, Jerome Robbins & Robert Wise) *Natalie Wood, Richard Beymer, George Chakiris, Russ Tamblyn, Rita Moreno.* Whether referring to the stage or film version, this Leonard Bernstein-Stephen Sondheim musical is one of the all-time greats. Wood and Beymer are the star-crossed lovers in this updated "Romeo and Juliet" set against the backdrop of gang warfare in New York's Upper West Side. Tamblyn and Chakiris (Oscar winner) are the gang leaders, and Moreno (also an Oscar winner) is Chakiris' girlfriend. Expertly directed by Wise and Robbins (who also choreographed the classic dance numbers). Winner of 11 Academy Awards, including Best Picture. ★★★★ DVD Letterbox 2-disc Collector's Edition: $29.99, DVD Standard Edition: $14.99

Western Union

(1941, 94 min, US, Fritz Lang) *Robert Young, Randolph Scott, Dean Jagger.* Expansive western adventure with Young and Scott about the laying of the first transcontinental Western Union wire in the mid-1800s. ★★★ VHS: $39.99

The Westerner

(1940, 100 min, US, William Wyler) *Gary Cooper, Walter Brennan, Chill Wills, Forrest Tucker, Dana Andrews.* Solid western adventure with Cooper and Brennan whooping it up in the wild, wild West. Brennan won an Oscar (his third) as the infamous Judge Roy Bean, and he steals the show. ★★★½

Westfront 1918

(1930, 90 min, Germany, G.W. Pabst) *Gustav Diesl, Fritz Kampers.* Pabst's first sound film deals with trench warfare during the final days of World War I. Strongly antiwar, this intense drama deals with four ordinary German soldiers and the effects the war has on them. There is no glorification of battles won, but rather a meditation on the destructiveness, futility and horror of war. (German with English subtitles) ★★★

Westler: East of the Wall

(1985, 94 min, Germany, Wieland Speck) *Sigurd Rachman, Rancer Strecker.* A romantic and involving gay love story set before the fall of the East German Communist government and the crumbling of the Berlin Wall. The story follows the seemingly doomed love affair between a West Berliner and an East Berlin waiter. Having met during a visit to Alexanderplatz, the two young men soon fall in love, but discover that political forces beyond their control conspire to keep them apart. Shot clandestinely throughout East Germany, which gives the film a semidocumentary feel. (German wiith subtitles) ★★★

Westworld

(1973, 88 min, US, Michael Crichton) *Richard Benjamin, Yul Brynner, Dick Van Patten, James Brolin.* Crichton made his directorial debut with this highly original sci-fi thriller about a high-tech amusement park whose mechanical robots begin to rebel. Brolin and Benjamin are the tourists caught in the melee. Brynner is the gun-slinging robot ringleader. Lots of chills and much suspense. (Sequel: *Futureworld*) ★★★ DVD Letterbox: $19.99

Wetherby

(1985, 97 min, GB, David Hare) *Vanessa Redgrave, Judi Dench, Ian Holm, Joely Richardson.* Screenwriter-director Hare has fashioned a fascinating and thought-provoking film which tackles such uncomfortable themes as loneliness, loveless relationships and the death of innocence. Redgrave is a quiet Yorkshire schoolteacher who, after the violent suicide of a young man who entered her life, must search her past and present in order to arrive at some understanding of her priorities. ★★★½

Whale Rider

(2003, 101 min, New Zealand, Niki Caro) *Keisha Castle-Hughes, Rawiri Paratene, Vicky Haughton, Cliff Curtis.* On the surface, it's a simple tale about a girl who stands up for herself in the face of a sexist patriarchy, but through its mythology, cinematography and a remarkable turn by first-time actress Castle-Hughes, the often stunningly beautiful *Whale Rider* achieves a state of transcendence. Castle-Hughes plays Pai, the twin sister of the stillborn boy who was next in line to become chief of her Maori tribe. Though the lineage is steeped in legend and history, Pai's world is very modern; the wardrobe seems to be from Old Navy, the kids are more into goofing around than learning tradition, and her dad (Curtis), a widower from Pai's birth, has moved to Europe to be an artist. In danger of losing its identity, the tribe desperately needs a new leader, but Pai's grandfather (the imposing Paratene) is blind to the possibility that the very eager Pai could be the one. She eventually proves herself, of course, but not in any way that audiences could expect. From underwater whale footage to ruddy sunsets, the photography is lyrical — but it is Castle-Hughes' charming, understated performance that provides the true magic. ★★★½ DVD Special Edition: $19.99, VHS: $14.99

The Whales of August

(1987, 90 min, US, Lindsay Anderson) *Lillian Gish, Bette Davis, Ann Sothern, Vincent Price, Mary Steenburgen.* An eloquent rendition of David Berry's play about two aging sisters living out their final years together. Gish plays the tenderhearted and loving caretaker who patiently looks after sister Davis — who is blind, embittered and given to petulant outbursts. Both actresses play their parts exquisitely, each projecting a screen presence unscathed by the sands of time. In his first American production, Anderson leaves behind all the rampant political diatribe which are the hallmarks of his earlier works and concentrates on subtle human interaction — the result being a tender and heart-warming look at the delicate process of growing old. ★★★ DVD Dual: $14.99

What about Bob?

(1991, 99 min, US, Frank Oz) *Richard Dreyfuss, Bill Murray, Julie Hagerty, Charlie Korsmo.* Murray has his best role in years in this delightfully crazy comedy as a neurotic psychiatric patient who brings new meaning to the word hypochondria. Murray is passed around from doctor to doctor. His newest shrink is Dreyfuss, who after one session, goes with his family on vacation in New England leaving Murray on his own in New York. What's poor multiphobic Bob to do? Follow them, of course. Director Oz gets a lot of comic mileage from this absurd premise and the laughs are plentiful. ★★★ DVD: $9.99, VHS: $9.99

What Do You Say to a Naked Lady?

(1970, 90 min, US, Allen Funt) Director Funt, best known for the 1960s TV series "Candid Camera," takes that show's concept and expands upon it for the big screen. He secretly records the sometimes very funny reactions of various bystanders exposed to . . . women exposed. ★★★

What Dreams May Come

(1998, 114 min, US, Vincent Ward) *Robin Williams, Annabella Sciorra, Cuba Gooding, Jr., Max von Sydow, Rosalind Chao.* Guilty of not making the most of a fascinating premise, director Ward and adapter Ron Bass have opted for cerebral, New Age hocus pocus rather than whimsical or heartfelt fantasy in this tale of a husband whose love for his wife knows no bounds. Williams dies in a car crash,

West Side Story

leaving wife Sciorra to mourn his death. Eventually, he learns her grief prompted her to commit suicide; and therefore her soul is denied entry into Heaven. With the help of a couple angels (Gooding, von Sydow, Chao), he travels to Hell to rescue his wife. It's a harrowing journey, amazingly brought to life by spectacular art direction and effects. But the dramatics are lacking, and much of Williams' journey is slowly paced. *What Dreams May Come* is lovely to look at but it never fully captures the soul of eternal love. Based on Richard Matheson's novel. ★★½ DVD Special Edition: $14.99, VHS: $9.99

What Ever Happened to Baby Jane?

(1962, 132 min, US, Robert Aldrich) *Bette Davis, Joan Crawford, Victor Buono.* What more can be said about this camp favorite? Beyond the jet-black humor is a solid, well-made thriller. Davis, as an aging child star, chews the scenery in one of her most memorable screen performances. Crawford, as her crippled sister, is equally captivating. Sibling rivalry was never so wicked and never so much fun! (Remade in 1991) ★★★★ DVD: $19.99, VHS: $14.99

What Happened to Kerouac

(1986, 96 min, US, Lewis MacAdams & Richard Lerner) *Steve Allen, William Burroughs, Neal Cassady, Allen Ginsberg, Gregory Corso, Lawrence Ferlinghetti.* The enigmatic image of Beat novelist Jack Kerouac is put into focus in this engrossing documentary portrait of one of the most interesting American figures of the 1950s and early '60s. Once dubbed by *The New York Times* as a "Neanderthal with a typewriter," Kerouac's life and times are recounted through anecdotes from his friends and family. Included in the film are memorable appearances on Buckley's "Firing Line" and "The Steve Allen Show." A must for all Kerouac fans as well as those interested in the artist engulfed in the American culture. ★★★

What Happened Was . . .

(1994, 90 min, US, Tom Noonan) *Tom Noonan, Karen Sillas.* A first date takes a nightmarish turn in this meandering first film from actor Noonan. Michael (Noonan) and Jackie (Sillas) are coworkers in a law firm who develop an attraction for each other. Having dinner together, the two engage in the superficial banter of first dates, then progress deeper and deeper into darker, more personal territory as the evening wears on. Though the first half of the film works fairly well, its second-half "Twilight Zone" antics and macabre overtones unfortunately are wasted in this ambitious but unsuccessful experiment. ★★ VHS: $89.99

What Have I Done to Deserve This?

(1985, 100 min, Spain, Pedro Almodóvar) *Carmen Maura, Luis Hostalot, Chus Lampreave, Ryo Hiruma, Ángel de Andrés López, Gonzalo Suárez, Verónica Forqué.* Almodóvar's unbelievably funny, absurdist gem lept out of the post-Franco liberalization with the velocity of a cannonball. This twisted and surreal film focuses on a modern Spanish clan which bears more than a passing resemblance to the Addams family. Mom is a frustrated No-Doze addicted housewife who lives in a tiny high-rise with her miserable cab-driving husband (who once forged Hitler's diaries) and her two sons: a 14-year-old drug dealer and a precocious 12-year-old who casually seduces his friends' fathers and is finally sold to a gay dentist. Completing this thorny nest is their batty Grandma who longs to leave Madrid and, with her pet lizard, find a place in the country. Shall we call this "Fun for the whole family?" (Spanish with English subtitles) ★★★★ DVD: $24.99, VHS: $19.99

What Lies Beneath

(2000, 130 min, US, Robert Zemeckis) *Harrison Ford, Michelle Pfeiffer, Diana Scarwid, Joe Morton, James Remar.* Ford and Pfeiffer provide a lot of star power for this glossy, well-produced thriller, but not even celebrities of their order can overcome the film's underdeveloped screenplay. Pfeiffer plays a wife who becomes haunted by the spirit of an unknown young woman. Is she going crazy, and if not, did her husband (Ford) know her? A couple of good scenes provide a goose bump or two (including a tension-filled bathtub sequence), but the film suffers from a lethargic pace and who-cares plotting. A low-brow ghost story with a high-octane cast. ★★ DVD: $19.99, VHS: $9.99

What Planet Are You From?

(2000, 107 min, US, Mike Nichols) *Garry Shandling, Annette Bening, John Goodman, Greg Kinnear, Ben Kingsley, Linda Fiorentino.* Shandling is an alien sent to Earth to impregnate a woman — any woman — and return with child to his all-male home world. Enter Bening as an AA member leery of yet another bad relationship and, quicker than you can say "E.T. phone home," Shandling has forsaken his mission in favor of wooing and wedding her. Shandling's deadpan arrogance is put to somewhat effective use in this curiously tame comedy that starts out amusing, but loses much steam as the plot becomes bogged down in family values. ★★ DVD: $24.99, VHS: $9.99

What Price Glory?

(1952, 109 min, US, John Ford) *James Cagney, Dan Dailey, Corinne Calvet, William Demarest, Robert Wagner.* Remake of the classic silent comedy-drama based on Maxwell Anderson's play about the WWI exploits of two American soldiers who fall for the same woman while stationed in France. Victor McLaglen and Edmund Lowe had better success in the original as Capt. Flagg and Sgt. Quirt than Cagney and Dailey have here. ★★½ DVD: $14.99

What Price Hollywood?

(1932, 88 min, US, George Cukor) *Constance Bennett, Lowell Sherman, Neil Hamilton.* Adela Rogers St. John's story about an alcoholic director whose career goes down as the girl he made a star eclipses him. Needless to say this was remade several times as *A Star Is Born.* Bennett gives an strong performance in this suprisingly tough look at then-contemporary Hollywood. ★★★½

What Time Is It There?

(2001, 116 min, France/Taiwan, Tsai Ming-Liang) *Lee Kang-Sheng, Chen Shiang-chyi.* Director Tsai is a filmmaker oft spoken about in the same breath as Antonioni and Buster Keaton. What sounds like a strikingly disparate pairing is an apt description of the combination of urban isolation and deadpan comedy that marks his *What Time Is It There?* With the delicate touch of a silent movie director, Tsai crafts an elegiac story about loneliness, loss, love and synchronicity. A young watch vendor in the streets of Taipei sells his own watch to a young woman who is about to leave for Paris. The film shifts between the watch vendor, who begins setting Taipei clocks to Paris time in an attempt to connect with the woman, that same woman who now drifts lonely and disconnected in a foreign land, and the vendor's recently widowed mother whose behavior becomes increasingly erratic. Tsai's minimal use of dialogue and music and his extensive use of the long-take are quite refreshing. The viewer is given

ample time to digest the gorgeous cinematography and let the content of the character's lives stir our emotions rather than being told what and when to feel. (Mandarin, Taiwanese and French with English subtitles) ★★★½ DVD: $19.99

What Women Want

(2000, 126 min, US, Nancy Meyers) *Mel Gibson, Helen Hunt, Marisa Tomei, Mark Feuerstein, Alan Alda, Lauren Holly.* A gimmick movie whose gimmick actually works, this charming and funny romantic comedy features Gibson in his first romantic role. Mel plays a womanizing ad exec who — courtesy of a bathroom electrical mishap — develops the ability to hear women's thoughts. He first uses it to get an edge at work, but when he falls for his new boss (Hunt), he thinks he has the inside track to romantic success. Of course, a little soul-searching and a better understanding of the opposite sex follows. Wittier and not as offensive as you'd think a premise such as this would be, *What Women Want* benefits foremost from Gibson's natural, charismatic performance. The actor is up for any situation, tackling each indignity and triumph with good cheer. ★★★ DVD: $14.99, VHS Special Edition: $9.99

What's Cooking?

(2000, 109 min, US, Gurinder Chadha) *Mercedes Ruehl, Alfre Woodard, Joan Chen, Kyra Sedgwick, Julianna Marguiles, Lainie Kazan, Maury Chaykin, Dennis Haysbert, A. Martinez, Victor Rivers, Estelle Harris.* The story of four families celebrating Thanksgiving in melting-pot downtown Los Angeles forms the core of this appetizing comedy. Skillfully juggling its many stories, *What's Cooking* explores with both humor and heart the differences and common bonds shared by the culturally diverse characters. Ruehl heads a terrific ensemble as the matriarch of a Latino family, newly separated from her husband who has returned to find himself replaced by a younger man. Added to this mix are the joyful trials and tribulations of an African-American, Asian-American and Jewish family, who all come together by story's end. A charming slice of American urban life, this is a truer vision of American "family values." ★★★½ DVD Signature Selection: $19.99

What's Eating Gilbert Grape

(1993, 117 min, US, Lasse Hallström) *Johnny Depp, Leonardo DiCaprio, Juliette Lewis, Darlene Cates, Mary Steenburgen, Crispin Glover.* Living in a small Iowa town, Gilbert comes from a classic dysfunctional family: his 500-pound mother (Cates) won't move from the couch, and his younger brother (DiCaprio) is mentally retarded and constantly climbing the water tower. Into his bored life comes a pretty drifter (Lewis) who, as it turns out, has a profound effect on all the Grape family. Funny, touching and sweet, with a dash of gentleness to its drama, the film features first-rate performances by all, including a lovely turn by newcomer Cates. But it is Oscar nominee DiCaprio who walks away with the acting honors. ★★★ DVD: $14.99, VHS: $14.99

What's Love Got to Do with It?

(1993, 118 min, US, Brian Gibson) *Angela Bassett, Laurence Fishburne, Jenifer Lewis.* Bassett and Fishburne both received well-earned Oscar nominations for their roles as music greats Tina and Ike Turner in this intense musical biography. Infused with the same energy director Gibson brought to the story of another musical legend in *The Josephine Baker Story*, *What's Love* is a fascinating portrait of the professional and personal lives of the explosive couple. Based on Tina's autobiography, the story

What's Love Got to Do with It?

covers in varying detail Tina's childhood; her joining Ike's band and their marriage in the late 1950s: and her meteoric rise as a singer while at the same time experiencing heartbreak in her marriage. Bassett and Fishburne's performances display more soul and veracity than mere imitation, which is only one of the many strengths of the film. ★★★½ DVD: $14.99, VHS: $9.99

What's New, Pussycat?

(1965, 108 min, US, Clive Donner) *Peter O'Toole, Peter Sellers, Capucine, Romy Schneider, Paula Prentiss, Ursula Andress, Woody Allen).* Allen's first screenplay and first screen appearance is a comic free-for-all about a fashion editor (O'Toole) and his obsession with beautiful women. Sellers is hilarious as the psychiatrist who's even crazier than his patients. Tom Jones sings the title tune. ★★★

What's the Worst That Could Happen?

(2001, 98 min, US, Sam Weisman) *Martin Lawrence, Danny DeVito, John Leguizamo, Glenne Headly, Carmen Ejogo, Nora Dunn, Larry Miller, Richard Schiff, William Fichtner.* There are probably a few answers to the film's question: 1) Having to see it again 2) Having to see it a first time 3) Having to read about it. In all fairness, there's probably a good reason Lawrence and DeVito were drawn to this project. The premise isn't a bad one: A thief (Lawrence) has the ring his new girlfriend just gave to him stolen by his latest burglary victim (DeVito), and it's a game of one-upmanship to get it back. Unfortunately, screenwriter Matthew Chapman forgot the main ingredient: laughs. The characters try to be outrageous but have no comic footing, and as such the two stars are reduced to mugging, screaming and playing it over-the-top. ★½ DVD Special Edition: $14.99, VHS: $14.99

What's Up, Doc?

(1972, 94 min, US, Peter Bogdanovich) *Barbra Streisand, Ryan O'Neal, Madeline Kahn, Austin Pendleton, Kenneth Mars, Randy Quaid.* Bogdanovich's deliriously funny homage to screwball comedies, and *Bringing Up Baby* in particular. Streisand has rarely been funnier, and even the usually bland O'Neal is in good form, in this lunatic story of identical suitcases leading their owners on a merry chase throughout San Francisco. In her film debut as O'Neal's much-flustered fiancée, Kahn is priceless. ★★★½ DVD: $19.99, VHS: $9.99

What's Up, Tiger Lily?

(1966, 90 min, US, Woody Allen) A grade-B Japanese spy thriller, *Kagi No Kag*, is the ravaged victim of Allen's hilarious barbs as the search is on for the world's greatest egg salad recipe. Woody's dubbing the film in English with a steady stream of very funny one-liners extracts meaning from an otherwise innocuous yarn. Music by The Lovin' Spoonful. ★★★ DVD: $19.99

Whatever

(1998, 113 min, US, Susan Skoog) *Liza Weil, Chad Morgan, Katherine Rossetter, Frederic Forrest, Dan Montano.* A painfully hip '90s-era title marks an affecting, realistic coming-of-age drama set in the early '80s. Weil is extremely convincing as an alienated high schooler with a great talent for painting (guided by her supportive art teacher played with over-the-top zeal by Forrest), who is caught between her ne'er-do-well friends and her artistic dreams. While the inappropriate title suggest a sneering, pandering, clichéd slam at suburbia (and there is a dollop of that, unfortunately), *Whatever* is, for the most part, a tough but heartfelt portrait of a good but troubled kid going through universal growing pains. Nothing new here, but Skoog's sensitive script and direction, Weil's highly appealing performance, and a knockout soundtrack make this a winner. The ending is oddly moving and evocative. ★★★

Whatever Happened to Aunt Alice?

(1969, 101 min, US, Lee H. Katzin) *Geraldine Page, Ruth Gordon, Rosemary Forsyth, Robert Fuller, Mildred Dunnock.* In the tradition of *What Ever Happened to Baby Jane* comes this entertaining Gothic thriller from that film's producer about a wealthy widow (Page) whose housekeepers keep on disappearing. Gordon plays her newest domestic out to find out what's really happened to her predecessors. The pairing of Page and Gordon works extremely well, and the film even has some good chills to it. ★★★ DVD: $24.99

Whatever it Takes

(2000, 94 min, US, David Raynr) *Shane West, Marla Sokoloff, Jodi Lyn O'Keefe, James Franco, Richard Schiff.* A weak teen comedy, *Whatever It Takes* follows two guys who each like girls who don't like them. They strike a deal to . . . oh, forget it. It's the same stale stuff cribbed from *She's All That, Some Kind of Wonderful* and, yes, *Cyrano de Bergerac.* There's a tacky and desperate air to this mess. ★ DVD: $9.99, VHS: $9.99

The Wheeler Dealers

(1963, 100 min, US, Arthur Hiller) *James Garner, Lee Remick, Jim Backus, Phil Harris, Chill Wills, John Astin, Louis Nye.* Garner plays a Texas wheeler dealer who sets out to New York to rope in a couple deals and make a cool million. Remick is the first woman stock analyst on Wall Street who tries to lasso potential client Garner with some worthless stock. A lively if dated comedy ensues when these two players get together. The film tries to embrace a '60s feminist view, but ultimately only mocks it. With this in mind, however, there are genuine charming moments, due in large part to the gracious clowning of Garner, Remick and a seasoned supporting cast. ★★½

Wheels on Meals

(1984, 95 min, Hong Kong, Sammo Hung) *Jackie Chan, Yuen Biao, Sammo Hung, Benny "The Jet" Urquidez, Keith Vitali, Herb Edelman, Lola Forner.* The second of the three films prominently starring the three "king fu-teers" (the first was *Project A*, the last *Dragons Forever*), *Wheels on Meals* shows off Jackie and his two Peking Opera school brothers at the peak of their talent. Chan and Yuen run a fast food business in the busy streets of Barcelona. They both fall for a mysterious Spanish woman who is, unbeknownst to her, heir to a large fortune. When some evil-looking bad guys come after her, it's up to the fast-food pair to stop them. The plot is incidental to the outstanding comedy and action scenes, of which there are plenty. (Cantonese with English subtitles) ★★★ VHS Subtitled: $19.99

When a Man Loves a Woman

(1994, 126 min, US, Luis Mandoki) *Andy Garcia, Meg Ryan, Ellen Burstyn, Lauren Tom, Philip Seymour Hoffman.* The earnest, heartfelt performances of both Garcia and Ryan help elevate this familiar though touching drama of a husband and wife grappling with alcohol abuse. Michael and Alice Green are a couple as ordinary as their names. When Alice's frequent drinking binges become daily occurances, much to the terror of her husband and children, her ordinary life is reshaped by hospitalizations and AA meetings. Basically a three-act drama, the story divides its time examining Alice's alcohol excesses, her drying out, and finally the healing process, which proves as difficult for Michael as it is for Alice. ★★½ DVD: $9.99, VHS: $9.99

When a Stranger Calls

(1979, 97 min, US, Fred Walton) *Carol Kane, Charles Durning, Colleen Dewhurst, Rachel Roberts.* Suspenseful but ultimately unsatisfying tale of a killer who stalks a baby-sitter and her family, years after he murdered two of her charges. (Sequel: *When a Stranger Calls Back*) ★★ DVD Dual: $19.99

When Father Was Away on Business

(1985, 135 min, Yugoslavia, Emir Kusturica) *Moreno D'e Bartolli, Miki Manojlovic.* Focusing on one family's life in Communist Yugoslavia in the early 1950s, this tender, Fellini-esque drama unfolds with disarmingly gentle humor and perceptive political sentiments. The story takes the point of view of Malik, a six-year-old boy whose philandering father is exposed as an "anti-Tito/Stalin Communist" by his loose-lipped lover and his Communist Party brother-in-law. He is sent to prison and his absence is explained to Malik as a "business trip," but the boy soon discovers the truth and begins to understand the compromises and lies one must make to get by. A lusty, boisterous look at life in a society repressed but undetered by the political tyranny of the times. (Serbo-Croatian with English subtitles) ★★★½ VHS: $19.99

W

When Harry Met Sally . . .

(1989, 95 min, US, Rob Reiner) *Billy Crystal, Meg Ryan, Carrie Fisher, Bruno Kirby.* Crystal and Ryan sparkle in this enchanting comedy about the ups and downs of platonic friendship. Harry Burns (Crystal) and Sally Albright (Ryan) first meet through a rideshare in college, with Harry fetching a ride from Chicago to New York in Sally's car. Polar opposites, their relationship is doomed from the start. But over the years, things slowly warm up until eventually they are forced to confront their feelings about each other. Both actors shine and each have more than their share of truly hilarious scenes — not the least of which is Ryan's staged orgasm in a crowded New York delicatessen. Director Reiner has marched bravely into Woody Allen territory and handles the material deftly and crisply. ★★★½ DVD Special Edition: $14.99, VHS: $9.99

When I Close My Eyes

(1993, 94 min, Slovenia, Franci Flak) *Petra Govic, Mario Selih.* A chic and atmospheric thriller, *When I Close My Eyes* is a good-looking but obtuse story about obsession and revenge. When Ana (the ravishing Govac) is robbed by a handsome, leather-clad motorcyclist, she takes the opportunity to steal some money for herself. As the police investigate the crime, Ana becomes fascinated with the criminal and pursues him — romantically. Writer-director Flak needlessly complicates this simple, dangerous love story with a political subplot about the mysterious circumstances surrounding the death of Ana's father. The film's various intrigues are sometimes tough to follow, and the exposition does not always make perfect sense. Nevertheless, the gorgeous cast, the stylish Eastern European locations and the luminous cinematography compensate for the overall lack of sex and suspense. (Slovene with English subtitles) ★★½ DVD: $29.99, VHS: $79.99

When Night Is Falling

(1994, 94 min, Canada, Patricia Rozema) *Pascale Bussières, Rachael Crawford, Henry Czerny.* From the director of *I've Heard the Mermaids Singing* comes this refreshingly liberating tale of lesbian love. Camille (Bussières) is a Christian academician romantically involved with Martin (Czerny), a nice enough fellow teacher more interested in advancement than romance. Camille's repressed emotions and desire for true love come to the surface after she meets flamboyant circus performer Petra (Crawford). Despite being diametrical opposites, the two are attracted to each other. Its much appreciated romanticism and the casting of two attractive women aside, the film suffers from a symbolism-laden screenplay and a semi-catatonic lead actress (Bussières). However, the handling of the relationship is both exciting and hopeful. ★★★

When the Cat's Away

(1997, 91 min, France, Cédric Klapisch) *Garance Clavel, Zinedine Soualem, Olivier Py, Renée Le Calm.* If there is justice in the world, the video release of this zany cinematic frolic will include the film's French-language trailer that was shown in theatres here. In it, a rapid-fire voiceover introduces us to the wacky denizens of a Parisian neighborhood where a young woman has lost her cat all the while rattling off the film's tongue-twisting French title repeatedly. Rarely has a preview encapsulated a film's energy with such zest and hilarity. Klapisch's breezy yarn centers around Chloe (Clavel), an attractive, single, young woman who makes her living as an assistant on fashion shoots. Deciding to take a week's holiday by the sea, she leaves her kitty, Gris Gris, with a withered old neighborhood cat lady, Madame Renée (Le Calm). Upon her return, M. Renée makes it known that she's lost Gris Gris and a hunt begins throughout the entire arrondissement. The result is a whimsical, yet tender look at a modernizing Paris where construction sites abound and gentrification is all the rage. (French with English subtitles) ★★★

When the Party's Over

(1992, 114 min, US, Matthew Irmas) *Rae Dawn Chong, Fisher Stevens, Sandra Bullock, Brian McNamara.* Ostensibly a comedy-drama about the transition to adulthood, director Irmas' film seems aimed at (perhaps even made by) those who have not yet started the journey. In the ensemble tradition of such issue packed films as *St. Elmo's Fire*, this glossy film presents a house full of beautiful, successful young urban stereotypes trying to come to terms with adulthood and each other. The film is structured as a series of loosely connected flashbacks that lead up to a New Year's Eve crisis and the soul-searching powwow that follows. The relatively talented cast gives a feeble shot at trying to rise above the material. Young adulthood deserves a slightly less lamebrained rap. ★ DVD: $14.99

When the Whales Came

(1989, 100 min, GB, Clive Rees) *Paul Scofield, Helen Mirren, David Threlfall.* This somber story stars Scofield as a hermit who holds the secret of a mysterious island off the coast of England. Set just prior to the outbreak of WWI, the film chronicles his friendship with two young girls who break local taboo by befriending him. ★★ VHS: $14.99

When the Wind Blows

(1986, 80 min, GB, Jimmy T. Murakami) *John Mills, Peggy Ashcroft.* An unsettling and superior animated tale of a happily retired couple living out their golden years, until they must face living with the consequences of nuclear war. Music by David Bowie. ★★★

When We Were Kings

(1996, 105 min, US, Leon Gast) The 1974 "Rumble in the Jungle" between Muhammad Ali and reigning heavyweight champ George Foreman is the subject of this fascinating documentary, started in '74 during the media event in Zaire, but finished 22 years later by producer Taylor Hackford. The story of how underdog Ali managed to defeat the vastly favored Foreman is fascinating enough, but when added to the events which surrounded the fight — it was Don King's first major promotion and also featured musical acts James Brown and B.B. King — it becomes the stuff of legend. Its infectious good spirit and rousing portrait of a remarkable athlete and American hero make it well deserving of its Academy Award for Best Documentary. ★★★★ DVD Dual: $14.99

When Worlds Collide

(1951, 81 min, US, Rudolph Maté) *Richard Derr, Barbara Rush.* Good special effects highlight this sci-fi tale about the citizens of Earth preparing for the planet's destruction by an approaching meteor, and the rush to build a rocketship to send a group of selected survivors to another world. "And when worlds collide, said George Pal to his bride, I'm gonna give you a celluloid thrill." ★★★ DVD: $19.99, VHS: $14.99

Where Angels Fear to Tread

(1991, 113 min, GB, Charles Sturridge) *Helen Mirren, Judy Davis, Rupert Graves, Helena Bonham Carter.* This overlooked adaptation of E.M. Forster's novel is impressively produced, superbly acted and an extremely worthwhile effort. Mirren stars as Lilia Harriton, a wealthy widow who enrages her stodgy in-laws when she runs off to Italy and marries a swarthy young peasant, thereby threatening the family fortune. Lilia's brother and sister (Graves, Davis) are dispatched to Italy to try and talk some sense into the merry widow. All of the performances are first rate, but Davis steals the show with her truly over-the-top portrayal of the histrionic Harriet Harriton. The film sports a darker sense of humor and more tragic twists than the standard Forster fare, which makes it all-the-more entertaining and nearly as satisfying as *Howards End*. ★★★½ VHS: $19.99

Where Eagles Dare

(1968, 159 min, GB, Brian G. Hutton) *Richard Burton, Clint Eastwood, Mary Ure.* Released at the height of the Tet Offensive in 1968, this underrated WWII action adventure film did not make big waves at the box office. Seems people simply weren't hungry for more war images when they could be seen on TV every night. It's kind of a shame because this is a slam-bang cliff-hanger of a tale with Burton and Eastwood as two soldiers attempting to free an important officer from an escape-proof Nazi prison. Alistair MacLean adapted his own novel with great flair. ★★★½ DVD: $19.99, VHS: $14.99

Where Sleeping Dogs Lie

(1991, 92 min, US, Charles Finch) *Dylan McDermott, Sharon Stone, Tom Sizemore.* Whoever thought it prudent to awaken this "sleeping dog" no doubt wished to exercise his "basic instinct" for moneymaking by cashing in on the now-bankable talents of a pre-*Basic Instinct* Sharon Stone. But, despite her overwhelming presence on the display box, the icepick princess has less than 15 minutes of screen time as the agent (and sometimes lover) of a hapless screenwriter (McDermott) who passes off research work about a gruesome mass murder as fiction — only to have the real murderer show up on his doorstep. ★½

Where the Buffalo Roam

(1980, 100 min, US, Art Linson) *Bill Murray, Peter Boyle, Bruno Kirby.* Murray takes on the role — with middling results — of American "gonzo" journalist Hunter S. Thompson, whose passion for writing was equalled only by his love of drugs, alcohol and other vices. ★★ DVD: $24.99, VHS: $14.99

Where the Day Takes You

(1992, 107 min, US, Marc Rocco) *Dermot Mulroney, Ricki Lake, Will Smith, Sean Astin, Lara Flynn Boyle.* This film about the daily, sometimes tragic lives of teenage runaways coexisting in Los Angeles is determinedly somber — as are these kids' lives. And though the story covers little new ground of life on the street, the film possesses such grit and determination that it has an immediacy which cannot be ignored. Mulroney, trading his handsome looks for that of a scraggly druggie, gives a startling performance as the leader of a small clique living by their wits, sleeping under freeway off-ramps, and scrounging for change and food. A youthful cast is impressive. ★★½ DVD: $24.99

W

Where the Green Ants Dream

(1984, 100 min, Australia/Germany, Werner Herzog) *Bruce Spence, Wandjuk Marika, Norman Kaye.* Herzog juxtaposes the mystical primitivism of the Australian Aborigine against the expansionist threats of modern industry in this voyage into a world obsessed with conquest. Set against the arid flatlands of southern Australia, the film follows a large mining corporation's effort to extract uranium deposits from the Aborigines' sacred grounds, thereby destroying the landscape and shattering the slumber of the revered "green ants," whose interrupted dreaming would signify the death of the Aboriginal culture. A visually sumptuous work that contemplates the issues of cultural relations, imperialism and the wondrous mysteries of life itself. (In English) ★★★

Where the Heart Is

(1990, 107 min, US, John Boorman) *Dabney Coleman, Christopher Plummer, Crispin Glover, Joanna Cassidy.* An amiable and quirky comedy written by director Boorman and his daughter Telsche. Coleman stars as a wealthy businessman who decides to teach his three spoiled children a lesson in responsibility by forcing them out of the house and into a rundown tenement he owns. Though the story is unexceptional, the film is uplifted by winning performances all around; and by a collection of wonderful tromp l'oeil paintings. ★★½ DVD: $9.99

Where the Heart Is

(2000, 120 min, US, Matt Williams) *Natalie Portman, Ashley Judd, Stockard Channing, Sally Field, James Frain, Joan Cusack, Dylan Bruno, Keith David.* Portman plays Novalee, a young, pregnant trailer-park girl from Tennessee who is left behind by her no-account boyfriend. Finding refuge in a Wal-Mart, she hides and lives there by night until she delivers what the media calls "the Wal-Mart baby." Her brief notoriety introduces her to a series of quirky characters. There are too many "big" moments crammed together to produce any real dramatic flow, and the characters are of the "wear-their-emotions-on-their-sleeves" variety. Much of this will leave you with eyes rolling. ★★ DVD: $14.99, VHS: $6.99

Where the Hot Wind Blows

(1959, 125 min, France/Italy, Jules Dassin) *Melina Mercouri, Gina Lollobrigida, Yves Montand, Marcello Mastroianni.* Although this fiery Italian soap opera has an appealing all-star cast, there is little else in this tawdry melodrama to recommend. The story is about the decadence, from the peasants to the aristocracy, of a small town — sort of like an Italian *Peyton Place* (it's starting to sound better!). ★½

Where the Money Is

(2000, 89 min, US, Marek Kanievska) *Paul Newman, Linda Fiorentino, Dermot Mulroney.* Thanks to the winning performances of its two stars, this agreeable caper comedy is more enjoyable than it has any right to be. Looking impossibly sexy at age 70, Newman stars as a veteran bank robber who pretends to be a stroke victim in order to avoid a lifetime jail sentence. Fiorentino is equally effective as the nurse whose keen sense detects his scam and shortly thereafter convinces him to help her rob an armored truck. Blending the suspense of a heist film and the whimsy of a comedy, *Where the Money Is* allows one of our genuine movie icons to breathe easy in a setting in which he seems totally at home. ★★★ DVD: $26.99, VHS: $14.99

Where the River Runs Black

(1986, 101 min, US/Brazil, Christopher Cain) *Charles Durning, Peter Horton, Ajay Naidi, Conchata Ferrell.* A young boy born along the banks of the Amazon River is raised by dolphins when his mother is killed by gold prospectors. When he grows up, and encounters his mother's killers, he seeks revenge. Exquisite cinematography accentuates this compelling family film. ★★★

Where the Rivers Flow North

(1994, 104 min, US, Jay Craven) *Rip Torn, Tantoo Cardinal, Bill Raymond, Michael J. Fox, Treat Williams.* A poignant tale of an old logger who lives on a piece of land slated to be flooded for a new dam. Torn is a man possessed as he tries to beat the corporate world with his own schemes and pipe dreams. Cardinal plays his lover/companion with eloquence and conviction. Reminiscent in both style and story of *Wild River*, director Craven labored for many years on this labor of love. The beauty of the landscape reminds one of the lost innocence of America and the power of greed. ★★★½ DVD: $9.99

Where Were You When the Lights Went Out

(1968, 94 min, US, Hy Averback) *Doris Day, Robert Morse, Terry-Thomas, Steve Allen.* Day made quite a few entertaining sex comedies in the 1960s; unfortunately, this is not one of them. Averback, a successful TV sitcom director, shows little comic flair with this farce about the goings-on on the night of the New York City 1965 blackout. Doris plays a wife who thinks her husband is cheating on her. To make him jealous, she takes up with Morse . . . and gets caught in the blackout. ★½

Where's Picone

(1984, 122 min, Italy, Nanni Loy) *Giancarlo Giannini, Lina Sastri.* Giannini is hilarious as a sleazy con man who reluctantly becomes involved with the wife of a man who inexplicably disappears while in an ambulance going to the hospital. Alternating between a love story and slapstick comedy, the film has Giannini, as a two-bit hustler living on the wrong side of respectability, discovering that the esteemed missing man had a secret life that had strayed far from the norm. A bit silly at times, this genial comedy does pack some suspense and romance in exposing the corruption and duplicitousness of Italian society and bureaucracy. (Italian with English subtitles) ★★½ VHS: $29.99

Where's Poppa?

(1970, 82 min, US, Carl Reiner) *Ruth Gordon, Ron Liebman, Vincent Gardenia, George Segal.* Segal desperately tries to get rid of his senile mom (Gordon), who likes Froot Loops with Coke and has a penchant for biting his rear end. A savagely funny cult film that pokes fun at sex, muggings and motherhood. ★★★½ DVD Dual: $19.99

Which Way Is Up?

(1977, 94 min, US, Michael Schultz) *Richard Pryor, Lonette McKee, Margaret Avery.* Serio-comic look at life in central California's strife-torn farm community. Pryor plays three roles — a beleaguered worker, his cranky old father, and a hypocritical preacher. An American remake of Lina Wertmüller's *The Seduction of Mimi.* ★★½ DVD: $14.99

While the City Sleeps

(1956, 100 min, US, Fritz Lang) *Dana Andrews, Ida Lupino, Rhonda Fleming, George Sanders, Vincent Price, Howard Duff, Thomas Mitchell.* Another Lang opus on crime in the big city, this time counterplaying the search for a psychotic serial killer against a power struggle inside a huge media conglomerate. ★★★

While You Were Sleeping

(1995, 100 min, US, Jon Turtletaub) *Sandra Bullock, Bill Pullman, Peter Gallagher, Peter Boyle, Jack Warden, Glynis Johns.* Bullock and Pullman will bewitch many a heart in this beguiling romantic comedy, essentially a Cinderella tale except for the fact that it's Prince Charming who's asleep. Bullock is a lonely transit worker who saves the life of the handsome businessman (Gallagher) whom she admires from afar. As he lies in a coma, she is mistakenly identified as his fiancée, and then welcomed with open arms into his rather daffy family. All except Gallagher's brother, played with elfin charm by Pullman. Of course, they inevitably — but most endearingly — fall in love. Sure its a slight premise, but a most engaging cast, real chemistry between the two leads and a lively screenplay make this all-the-more entertaining. ★★★ DVD: $14.99, VHS: $9.99

Whipped

(2000, 85 min, US, Peter M. Cohen) *Amanda Peet, Brian Van Holt, Jonathan Abrahams, Zorie Barber, Judah Domke.* Whipped revolves around three repellent single men (and their equally repulsive married buddy), who spend most of their time in a diner sharing vulgar tales of their sexual exploits. Then one day, the three all tell of being in love, or is it like, with their latest hookup. Wouldn't you know it's the same woman (Peet), who turns the tables on them and their womanizing ways. Despite the allure of a three-Peet, the film's obnoxious bores are one-dimensional types, and the ceaseless dialogue is embarrassingly unfunny. ★ DVD: $29.99, VHS: $14.99

Whispers in the Dark

(1992, 103 min, US, Christopher Crowe) *Annabella Sciorra, Jamey Sheridan, Alan Alda, Jill Clayburgh, Anthony LaPaglia, John Leguizamo.* In this sexually candid shocker, Sciorra strikes just the right balance of naïveté and intellectual savvy as a lovelorn psychiatrist who comes to suspect that her new Prince Charming (Sheridan) may be a killer. Despite a major plot contrivance and a script so laden with psychobabble that Woody Allen may have penned it, the suspense makes this an involving murder mystery. ★★½ DVD Letterbox: $14.99, VHS: $19.99

The Whistle Blower

(1987, 104 min, GB, Simon Langton) *Michael Caine, Nigel Havers, John Gielgud, James Fox.* Compelling political drama reminiscent of *Missing* starring Caine as a father who investigates the death of his son, a translator for the British government who may have been murdered to cover up a security leak. Caine is masterful as the tormented father determined to uncover the truth behind his son's demise. ★★★ DVD Dual: $14.99

Whistle Down the Wind

(1962, 98 min, GB, Bryan Forbes) *Alan Bates, Hayley Mills, Bernard Lee.* This charming and extraordinary film is both a Christ parable and a poignant treatise on childhood innocence. Forbes, in a remarkable directorial debut, brings a deft and heartwarming touch to this story of an escaped criminal (Bates) who is found by three young children in their barn and is thought by them to be Christ. (The basis for a West End musical) ★★★½

W

Whistling in the Dark

(1941, 77 min, US, S. Sylvan Simon) *Red Skelton, Ann Rutherford, Conrad Veidt, Eve Arden.* Skelton lends his comic talents to this lightweight, mildly entertaining romp. He's a 1940s radio personality known as the Fox, a wily sleuth who always nails the bad guy. Veidt gives a pre-Branch Davidian interpretation of a loony cult leader who kidnaps Skelton and forces him to concoct the perfect murder. (Followed by 2 sequels) ★★½ VHS: $19.99

White

(1994, 93 min, France, Krzysztof Kieslowski) *Juliette Binoche, Julie Delpy, Zbigniew Zamachowski.* This, the second of Kieslowski's popular trilogy (the others being *Blue* and *Red*), is the weakest of the three, although still involving. This wry drama of obsession and revenge is played out within the symbolic battlefield of the new democratic Europe — rich Western Europe vs. the poor Eastern countries. The story centers on Karol (Zamachowski), a sweetly nerdish Polish hairdresser who travels to Paris and finds love in the arms of the beautiful Dominique (Delpy). Karol's inability to find a job and to speak the language results in impotency and a frustrated wife. A sexually wanting Dominique divorces him, an act that forces our enterprising hero to return home and plot an elaborate, far-fetched scheme of winning her back . . . on his terms. Uncomfortably misogynist with an unnecessary ending, the story lacks really likable characters but entertains nonetheless. (French and Polish with English subtitles) ★★½ DVD Subtitled: $19.99, VHS: $9.99

The White Balloon

(1995, 85 min, Iran, Jafar Panahi) *Aida Mohammadkhani, Mohsen Kalifi.* The White Balloon gives a quiet glimpse of a foreign land filled with familiar people, an important reminder that it is a government we hate — not a nation. The film has all the virtues of a Satyajit Ray work — most obviously *Pather Panchali* — in its simple tale of a little girl, both sweet and petulant, who loses then regains then loses again the money she has wheedled from her harried mother to buy a goldfish. If director Panahi had done no more than so perfectly captured the tenor and texture of a time, a town and a people, this film would be just as remarkable. (Farsi with English subtitles) ★★★★

The White Buffalo

(1977, 97 min, US, J. Lee Thompson) *Charles Bronson, Jack Weston, Kim Novack.* Unusual western parable with Bronson as Bill Hickok hunting the title bison, which represents the famous marksman's fear of death. ★★½

White Christmas

(1954, 120 min, US, Michael Curtiz) *Bing Crosby, Danny Kaye, Vera-Ellen, Rosemary Clooney, Dean Jagger, Mary Wickes.* Crosby and Kaye make the most of a tuneful Irving Berlin score in this popular holiday-themed musical. They play entertainers who come to the rescue of their old Army superior (Jagger). ★★★ DVD: $19.99, VHS: $9.99

The White Dawn

(1974, 109 min, US, Philip Kaufman) *Warren Oates, Timothy Bottoms, Louis Gossett, Jr..* A fascinating and original adventure tale about three turn-of-the-century whalers (Oates, Bottoms and Gossett) who are rescued by a tribe of Eskimos when their boat capsizes. A beautifully filmed fable. ★★★ DVD Letterbox Widescreen: $14.99

White Fang

(1991, 107 min, US, Randal Kleiser) *Ethan Hawke, Klaus Maria Brandauer, Seymour Cassel.* Based on the novel by Jack London, this rousing Disney adventure film is good entertainment for the entire family. The story follows the twin tales of a naive young man claiming his dead father's inheritance in the Klondike, and his befriending a wolf cub raised by the Indians. ★★★ DVD: $19.99, VHS: $9.99

White Heat

(1949, 114 min, US, Raoul Walsh) *James Cagney, Virginia Mayo, Edmond O'Brien, Margaret Wycherly.* Cagney's intense performance highlights this classic underworld drama about ruthless killer Cody Jarrett, he with the headaches and the mother fixation; and the cop determined to put him away. "Made it, Ma. Top of the world!" ★★★★ VHS: $14.99

White Hunter, Black Heart

(1990, 112 min, US, Clint Eastwood) *Clint Eastwood, Marisa Berenson, George Dzundza, Jeff Fahey, Timothy Spall.* This fictionalized account of film director John Huston's adventures while on the set of *The African Queen* is a challenging work for director Eastwood. And as an actor, he gives a bold performance with an uncanny impersonation of the mythic Huston, though it may take some getting used to "Dirty Harry" calling everyone "kid." The story follows Huston's obsession with shooting a giant elephant, and the effect it has on himself, his film crew and his guides. A film of epic scale presented in an intimate fashion, *White Hunter, Black Heart* is a picturesque excursion into the darker regions of man's soul. ★★★ DVD: $19.99

White Lie

(1991, 93 min, US, Bill Condon) *Gregory Hines, Annette O'Toole, Bill Nunn.* Hines gives a first-rate performance in this superior made-for-cable mystery. Hines plays a savvy New York City mayoral assistant who, upon receiving a picture of his father being lynched, returns to his Southern birthplace to uncover the truth behind the murder. One of the many interesting plot developments is having a black actor essay the role of the usually white Southern "redneck" sheriff (played with great relish by Nunn). ★★★½

White Man's Burden

(1995, 89 min, US, Desmond Nakano) *John Travolta, Harry Belafonte, Kelly Lynch, Margaret Avery, Sheryl Lee Ralph, Carrie Snodgress.* Taking the thought-provoking premise of the races switched on the economic and social levels, *White Man's Burden* is an intriguing idea which is only occasionally realized. In a world parallel to 1990s America except that whites are the minority and blacks are the ruling power, Travolta plays a hard-working family man who is fired after an misunderstanding. His attempt to extort money from his former boss (Belafonte) eventually leads to kidnapping him. The beginning of the film is particularly good in establishing this society, but once the "gimmick" has been set, and Travolta and Belafonte turn into the defiant ones, the story has trouble elaborating on its concept and a scenario of two men at odds with stereotypes rather than each other. ★★½ DVD: $9.99, VHS: $9.99

White Men Can't Jump

(1992, 115 min, US, Ron Shelton) *Wesley Snipes, Woody Harrelson, Rosie Perez, Tyra Ferrell, Kadeem Hardison.* Snipes is a street-smart Venice Beach basketball hustler. He's black. Harrelson is a bumpkin-looking basketball hustler. He's white. A most entertaining and hip comedy emerges when these two hoop con artists team up to sucker the denizens of Southern California's hard courts. It's a great sting: Snipes gets into a game and ultimately brings in rube Harrelson. Who could resist going one-on-one with the Great White Dork? In his first two films, Shelton proved himself to be a master of romantic repartee. Here, the snap and sizzle of a verbal rebound, the volley of masculine bombastics is what distinguishes Shelton's energized film. ★★★ DVD: $14.99, VHS: $9.99

White Mischief

(1988, 106 min, GB, Michael Radford) *Greta Scacchi, Charles Dance, Sarah Miles, Joss Ackland, Murray Head.* Lavishly entertaining and very sexy drama about English pleasure-seekers living in the "Happy Valley" in Kenya during WWII. Scacchi is both beautiful and ideally cast as a bored wife whose affair with an English lord (Dance) leads to murder. Miles and Head steal the show as cynical hedonists searching for the next party. Ackland gives a great performance as Scacchi's cuckold husband. ★★★

White Nights

(1957, 94 min, Italy, Luchino Visconti) *Marcello Mastroianni, Maria Schell, Jean Marais.* Based on a Fedor Dostoevsky short story and set within a misty, dreamlike seaside city, this sad love story was a great stylistic departure from Visconti's previous, neorealist features, *Senso* and *Ossessione*. Mastroianni stars as a young man, prowling the docks for a pick-up, who meets and fatefully falls in love with a mysterious, obsessive woman (Schell). In a series of brief walks, chases and attempted escapes, she reveals to him that she is waiting for her lover who, before going to sea, promised to return to her. While talking only of her long-gone lover (Marais), the two develop a relationship, but one destined to end in tragedy. (Italian with English subtitles) ★★★ VHS: $59.99

White Nights

(1985, 135 min, US, Taylor Hackford) *Gregory Hines, Mikhail Baryshnikov, Isabella Rossellini, Helen Mirren, Geraldine Page.* In probably the first musical political thriller, Baryshnikov stars as a Russian defector whose plane crash lands him back in the U.S.S.R. Hines is an American defector who befriends him. Though far more successful in its musical moments (which features terrific dancing by the two stars) than the convoluted political aspects, there's enough suspense and plot twists to keep most viewers involved. ★★½

White of the Eye

(1987, 110 min, US, Donald Cammell) *David Keith, Cathy Moriarty.* What on the surface appears to be just another psycho-on-the-loose thriller is actually a visually rich and offbeat sleeper, a suspense movie that cooly seduces you and then takes you in strange, unexpected directions. Some of director Cammell's hallucinatory imagery is reminiscent of his collaborations with Nicolas Roeg in the early '70s. A rare performance by the sublime Moriarty makes this an especially rewarding film. ★★★

White Oleander

(2002, 109 min, US, Peter Kosminsky) *Alison Lohman, Robin Wright Penn, Michelle Pfeiffer, Renée Zellweger, Patrick Fugit, Billy Connolly, Noah Wyle, Cole Hauser.* Mary Agnes Donoghue's sensitive adaptation of Janet Fitch's novel and an excellent ensemble combine to make *White Oleander* a moving, compelling story about a teen lost in the child welfare system that sidesteps the usual clichés.

Lohman, almost carrying the film on her young shoulders, plays Astrid, a beautiful and talented teen whose seemingly comfy suburban life in Los Angeles turns into a nightmare when her mother Ingrid is convicted of murder. Sent to a series of foster homes, Astrid's series of surrogate parents have no more credentials in raising children than Ingrid. It falls on Astrid to decipher the mixed signals at work against her, and to navigate on her own the difficult road to adulthood. Zellweger and Wright-Penn are both terrific as foster mothers each concealing personal agendas, and Pfeiffer is outstanding as Ingrid, so cold, calculating and fascinating it's difficult to take your eyes off her. ★★★ DVD Letterbox: $27.99, DVD Pan & Scan: $27.99, VHS: $6.99

White Palace

(1990, 104 min, US, Luis Mandoki) *Susan Sarandon, James Spader, Jason Alexander, Eileen Brennan, Kathy Bates, Steven Hill.* That age-old story of two unlikely people overcoming differences in age and background to find true love receives a fresh injection of star power in this touching romantic comedy. Sarandon and Spader star as, respectively, an earthy, 40-something burger joint queen and an uptight, late-20s Jewish yuppie. Though *White Palace* may be slightly sentimental and formulaic, Spader and Sarandon are as classically mismatched as any classically mismatched couple to come before them and both deliver sparkling performances: together they simply ooze sexuality. A real audience pleaser, with a few surprises and plenty of wit. ★★★

White River

(1999, 99 min, US, Arne Glimcher) *Bob Hoskins, Antonio Banderas, Ellen Barkin, Kim Dickens, Beau Bridges, Swoosie Kurtz, Randy Travis, Wes Bentley, Chad Lindberg.* Sort of a *We're No Angels* meets *O Brother, Where Art Thou?*, the quirky comic adventure *White River* is an often fun ride off the beaten track. Taking its time getting started, the film's array of eccentric characters soon win you over, even though the material isn't always up to the level of the fine cast. Hoskins plays Brother Edgar, a con man who finds it easier to peddle his wares under the protection of the cloth. Banderas is Morales, his sidekick newly and illegally arrived from Mexico. Together they travel across Arkansas selling "socks for God." They take a stranger turn than usual when they are kidnapped by the White River Kid, a mythic killer who just wants to meet his fiancée's hillbilly parents. Crooked singing sheriffs, blind madams and a dysfunctional Ma and Pa Kettle all cross their paths, making this offbeat comedy, if not totally successful, certainly original. ★★½ DVD Dual: $24.99, VHS: $14.99

The White Rose

(1982, 108 min, West Germany, Michael Verhoeven) *Lena Stoltze, Wulf Kessler.* This superb wartime thriller is based on the true story of a secret society of students who printed and distributed thousands of anti-Nazi leaflets under the Fuhrer's very nose, reporting the murder of 300,000 Jews and urging the citizenry to sabotage the war effort. Their ill-fated but extraordinary efforts are vividly brought to the screen by Verhoeven. (German with English subtitles) ★★★½

White Sands

(1992, 101 min, US, Roger Donaldson) *Willem Dafoe, Mickey Rourke, Mary Elizabeth Mastrantonio, Samuel L. Jackson.* An exciting quasi-political thriller with Dafoe as a small-town sheriff who finds a body with a suitcase full of cash and decides to investigate, much to the chagrin of drugs- and arms-runner Rourke. Mastrantonio is a whiny socialite who believes that crime does pay, and Jackson is the FBI agent on the case. ★★★ DVD: $14.99, VHS: $14.99

The White Sheik

(1951, 88 min, Italy, Federico Fellini) *Alberto Sordi, Giulietta Masina.* Fellini's first solo directorial effort is also his only full-fledged farce. Told with almost slapstick enthusiasm, the story follows the misadventures of a provincial couple honeymooning in Rome. The young wife wanders upon the filming of a low-brow picture and becomes infatuated with the "hero" — the White Sheik, a bungling and slightly effeminate Rudolph Valentino imitator. Passion drives her to mad pursuit of the actor while her baffled husband searches the Eternal City for his lost wife. (Italian with English subtitles) ★★★ DVD Criterion Collection: $29.99

White Squall

(1996, 127 min, US, Ridley Scott) *Jeff Bridges, Ryan Phillippe, John Savage, Scott Wolf, Jeremy Sisto, Zeljko Ivanek, Balthazar Getty, Caroline Goodall.* Though its story line is never really elevated above a "*Dead Poets Society* Go Boating" scenario, *White Squall* nevertheless manages to sustain interest thanks to some exceptional action scenes and the always reliable Bridges. Set during the early 1960s, the story centers on a group of high school teens summering on a "floating prep school" headed by Captain Jeff. The first half of the film essentially examines the varying relationships between the kids in very familiar fashion. However, the film's second half changes course when the titular storm, a sudden and violent torrent of water, engulfs and capsizes the ship and the crew members are left to fend for their lives. Director Scott handles the storm sequences with great assurance, but he's not as fortunate in creating totally believable dramatics between the young protagonists. ★★½ DVD: $9.99, VHS: $14.99

White Zombie

(1932, 73 min, US, Victor Halperin) *Bela Lugosi, Madge Bellamy.* Lugosi stars in this entertaining chiller as a warped magician who uses his powers to raise the dead and supply zombie laborers for a sinister plantation owner. ★★★ VHS: $19.99

Who Done It?

(1942, 75 min, US, Eric C. Kenton) *Bud Abbott, Lou Costello, Mary Wickes, William Bendix.* An uproarious Abbott and Costello romp, with Bud and Lou as a couple of soda jerks trying to break into radio who masquerade as private detectives after an on-the-air murder. DVD: $24.99 (DVD includes 7 other Abbott and Costello films) ★★★

Who Framed Roger Rabbit

(1988, 103 min, US, Robert Zemeckis) *Voices of:, Bob Hoskins, Christopher Lloyd, Joanna Cassidy, Stubby Kaye, Charles Fleischer, Kathleen Turner, Mae Questel.* Superb animation, almost every beloved cartoon character in our movie history and state-of-the-art special effects combine to produce one of the most glorious entertainments of the decade. Hoskins is a 1940s private detective hired to find out just who did frame Roger Rabbit, that successful, debonair and handsome animated cartoon hero. A toon-ful modern classic. ★★★★ DVD Dual Vista Series: $19.99, VHS Exclusive Video Bonus Edition: $14.99

The Who: The Kids Are Alright

(1979, 109 min, US, Jeff Stein) This frantically paced rockumentary paean to The Who will delight both their hard-core fans and those with a strong appreciation of good rock. Culled from interviews, concert footage and appearances on numerous TV variety shows (most notably "The Smothers Brothers"), the film offers a vivacious look at the group and their notorious hijinks, especially those of drummer Keith Moon, who proves to be beyond control. ★★★★ DVD Special Edition: $29.99, DVD Deluxe Edition: $22.99

Who Slew Auntie Roo

(1971, 90 min, US, Curtis Harrington) *Shelley Winters, Mark Lester, Ralph Richardson, Lionel Jeffries.* A kindly old widow's annual Christmas party for the local orphans takes a macabre, unexpected twist. A tame though spoofy foray into '70s Gothic horror. ★★½ DVD Letterbox Double Feature: $14.99, VHS: $69.99

Who'll Stop the Rain

(1978, 126 min, US, Karel Reisz) *Nick Nolte, Michael Moriarty, Tuesday Weld.* Nolte gives a riveting performance as an ex-Marine transporting heroin from Saigon to the U.S. during the Vietnam War, finding himself set up for a drug bust. ★★★ DVD Letterbox: $14.99

Who's Afraid of Virginia Woolf?

(1966, 129 min, US, Mike Nichols) *Richard Burton, Elizabeth Taylor, Sandy Dennis, George Segal.* Burton and Taylor deliver career best performances (Liz won an Oscar, Dick didn't) as a tortured college professor and his vitriolic wife in Edward Albee's scorching domestic drama. Segal and Dennis (at her mousiest) are the innocent young couple who spend a gut-wrenching, soul-baring evening with lush-ious Liz and down-and-out Dick. Brilliantly directed by Nichols. ★★★★ DVD: $19.99

Favorite Line: "I will hold your hand when it's dark and you're afraid of the boogeyman and I will tote your gin bottles out after midnight so no one can see but I will not light your cigarette. And that, as they say, is that." —*Richard Burton as George*

Who's Harry Crumb?

(1989, 98 min, US, Paul Flaherty) *John Candy, Jeffrey Jones, Annie Potts.* For the answer to the question posed by the title of this film, please choose one of the following: a) Who cares b) an imbecilic moron c) a bumbling private detective assigned to a kidnapping case: only because his boss is the kidnapper and the bad guy knows Crumb is too stupid to crack the case d) a character in a film which contains no wit and predictable sight gags e) all of the above. If you chose "e," you are correct. ★ DVD: $9.99, VHS: $9.99

Who's Singing Over There

(1985, 95 min, Yugoslavia, Slobodan Sijan) Gifted young director Sijan has created this comic, poignant antiwar satire set in Yugoslavia on the eve of the Nazi invasion. He contrasts the petty squabbles of the wild, provincial characters that have boarded a Belgrade-bound bus with our awareness of the catastrophic events that are about to occcur. (Serbo-Croatian with English subtitles) ★★★

Who's That Girl

(1987, 94 min, US, James Foley) *Madonna, Griffin Dunne, John Mills.* Madonna plays a spunky parolee out to clear her name who totally changes forever the mild existence of yuppie Dunne. An awkward attempt at screwball comedy. ★ VHS: $14.99

THE DISCERNING FILM LOVER'S GUIDE

Who's That Knocking at My Door?

(1968, 90 min, US, Martin Scorsese) *Harvey Keitel, Zina Bethune.* Scorsese's first feature film is a fascinating and highly charged drama that is essentially a primer for his breakthrough film, *Mean Streets.* Clearly autobiographical, the story features a muscular and baby-faced Keitel in the lead as a confused young man in New York's Little Italy obsessed with the moralistic trappings of Catholicism and indecisive about committing himself to a serious relationship with his girlfriend (Bethune). Scorsese's directorial talent and promise is much in evidence in this gritty and at times arty debut. ★★★ VHS: $19.99

Who's the Man

(1993, 90 min, US, Ted Demme) *Ed Lover, Doctor Dre, Denis Leary, Ice T., Queen Latifah.* Yo! MTV rap hosts Dre and Lover star as an inept pair of barbers who somehow become New York cops in this crazy hip-hop "Homeywood" laugher. The film focuses on the authority-questioning stars' mission to clean up their crumbling Harlem neighborhood and stop a nefarious real estate speculator's plan to gentrify the once-thriving area. Some witty urban humor highlights this otherwise silly comedy. ★★½ DVD: $19.99

Who's Who

(1978, 75 min, GB, Mike Leigh) *Bridget Kane, Simon Chandler, Adam Norton.* In one of his earliest films, director Leigh — who has proved to be a master at letting his camera "eavesdrop" on the mundane daily lives of England's working class — sets his sights on a group of London stock traders. Though slowly paced, the film elicits some hilarious skewerings of the British caste system as he focuses on these brokerage employees: One group of overprivileged, upper-class twits who hold a dinner party, the other middle-class Thatcherites whose loyalty to Crown and country borders on the surreal. ★★★ DVD: $29.99, VHS: $29.99

The Whole Nine Yards

(2000, 110 min, US, Jonathan Lynn) *Bruce Willis, Matthew Perry, Natasha Henstridge, Michael Clarke Duncan, Rosanna Arquette, Amanda Peet, Kevin Pollak.* Combining gangster shenanigans with pratfalls galore, *The Whole Nine Yards* is a dark comedy that ill-advisedly includes too many ingredients in the mix. Unfocused, often slowly paced and just not all that funny, the film wastes the promising premise of a guy-next-door, Oz (Perry), who learns his new neighbor is none other than the notorious Jimmy "The Tulip" Tudeski (Willis), a mob hit man turned informant. When Oz's wife convinces him to rat on Jimmy, he's thrust into an underworld Wonderland. Perry is amiable doing his nice-guy schtick, though Peet is the best here as a would-be assassin. Director Lynn seems to be missing a beat with much of the comedy, and far too many scenes lack snap. (Sequel: *The Whole Ten Yards*) ★★ DVD: $14.99, VHS: $9.99

The Whole Wide World

(1996, 111 min, US, Dan Ireland) *Vincent D'Onofrio, Renée Zellweger, Ann Wedgeworth, Harve Presnell.* Schoolteacher and aspiring writer Novalyne Price befriends an unusual, brusque pulp writer named Robert E. Howard (creator of the "Conan" series) in 1930s Texas. Based on Price's memoirs, *The Whole Wide World* follows their rocky relationship and the strains it withstands from his domineering mother, his adamant nonconformity and the simpleminded townsfolk's disapproval.

Ireland captures the atmosphere and pace of small-town Depression-era Americana beautifully, while D'Onofrio and Zellweger are both superb. Despite a rather uneven score and slight overlength, *The Whole Wide World* is an engaging, richly textured drama. ★★★ DVD Letterbox: $19.99

Whoopee!

(1930, 93 min, US, Thornton Freeland) *Eddie Cantor, Eleanor Hunt, Paul Gregory.* Cantor, re-creating his 1929 stage smash, is an absolute joy as a hypochondriac who heads West for his health and becomes involved in the locals' crazy shenanigans. Though some of the songs (those not sung by Cantor) are horribly out-of-date (fast-forward buttons will be pushed), the film does feature some interesting Busby Berkeley production numbers, as well as funny one-liners and, of course, the title tune. For those not familiar with Cantor, this is the place to start to become acquainted with the most popular comedian of his time, and one of the funniest (and unheralded) men in American film comedy. ★★★

Whore

(1991, 92 min, US/GB, Ken Russell) *Theresa Russell, Antonio Vargas.* The notorious Ken Russell, in a kind of follow-up to *Crimes of Passion*, takes a less-successful walk down those streets of despair, leaving behind his bag of psychedelic tricks. Sadly, what is intended as a searing insight into the world of prostitution completely misses the mark under Russell's histrionic mis-direction. Russell sleepwalks, er, streetwalks through this talky tale of a hooker on the run from her psychotic pimp. ★ VHS: $14.99

Whose Life Is It Anyway?

(1981, 118 min, US, John Badham) *Richard Dreyfuss, John Cassavetes, Christine Lahti, Kenneth McMillan, Bob Balaban.* First-rate screen version of Brian Clark's award-winning play starring Dreyfuss in a moving performance as an artist who, paralyzed from the neck down after an auto accident, petitions on the right to die. Though the subject matter sounds terribly depressing, the film is alive with a sardonic wit and features compelling performances from the supporting cast. ★★★ VHS: $79.99

Why Do Fools Fall in Love

(1998, 112 min, US, Gregory Nava) *Larenz Tate, Halle Berry, Viveca A. Fox, Lela Rochon, Little Richard.* An energetic courtroom drama/musical biography of Frankie Lymon, *Why Do Fools Fall in Love* tells the story of the 1950s doo-wop singer/songwriter from the perspective of his three widows, each of whom is fighting for his estate. Director Nava's film milks the story for all its sensationalism, emphasizing the cattiness of the spurned women. While *Fools* is enjoyable because it plays like a soap opera, it adresses some of its serious themes — racism, drug addiction, and the improprieties of music executives — too casually. Tate is magnetic as Lymon. ★★½ DVD: $9.99, VHS: $9.99

Why Does Herr R. Run Amok

(1970, 88 min, Germany, Rainer Werner Fassbinder) *Kurt Raab, Hanna Schygulla.* This devastating thriller on social conformity and the petit bourgeosie stars Raab as Herr R., a successful professional who inexplicably (yet in Fassbinder's thinking, inevitably) goes berserk and takes his own life; but not before killing his wife, a neighbor and his little son. A doomed, taut polemic of failed expectations and the banality of existence. (German with English subtitles) ★★★½

Why Shoot the Teacher?

(1976, 99 min, Canada, Silvio Narizzano) *Bud Cort, Samantha Eggar.* An amiable yet touching story of a dedicated schoolteacher (Cort) who faces the grim realities of life when he is hired to teach the children of an impoverished farming town in Alberta, Canada, during the Great Depression. Initially spurned by the adults, his icy reception soon changes to acceptance as he gradually adjusts to the difficult conditions and begins to understand his pupils and their way of life. An earnest and, at times, humorous film impressively directed. ★★★

Wicked City

(1992, 95 min, Hong Kong, Mak Tai Kit) *Tatsuya Nakadai.* The popular Japanese adult anime is given a hyperkinetic going-over in the inimitable Hong Kong style in this very entertaining live-action version. The sex and violence of the original have been significantly toned down and the story has been vastly altered as, this time around, we follow the adventures of two agents in the Anti-Reptoid Bureau, dedicated to hunting down and destroying renegade Reptoids. A forthcoming peace conference between the Reptoid leader (Nakadai) and a human delegation is threatened when treacherous elements in the Reptoid community plan a sabotage campaign. A wild and fun visual feast, the film sometimes sacrifices the cohesiveness of the plot in favor of a spectacular effect or action sequence. But what sequences they are. (In English and Mandarin with English subtitles) ★★★ VHS: $9.99

The Wicked Lady

(1945, 104 min, GB, Leslie Arliss) *James Mason, Margaret Lockwood, Michael Rennie.* This tame period melodrama stars Lockwood as an amoral, thrill-seeking aristocrat who teams up with highwayman Mason to embark on a life of crime. Released just after the end of WWII, the film caused a stir in its day on account of its bawdiness and perhaps the abundance of Ms. Lockwood's cleavage. (Remade in 1983) ★★½

The Wicked Lady

(1983, 98 min, GB, Michael Winner) *Faye Dunaway, Alan Bates, John Gielgud, Denholm Elliott.* Awkward remake of the 1945 programmer, this time with Dunaway camping it up as the British noblewoman by day and highway bandit by night. The film reflects the slipshod production usually associated with Cannon Films, and qualifies only as a guilty pleasure at best. ★½

Wicked Stepmother

(1988, 90 min, US, Larry Cohen) *Bette Davis, Barbara Carrera.* A witch (Davis) and her daughter (Carrera) make a living at marrying rich widowers, shrinking them to shoebox size, and absconding with their money. Davis, in her last film, withdrew from this dreadful project, and a double was used in many scenes. ★

The Wicker Man

(1973, 87 min, GB, Robin Hardy) *Christopher Lee, Britt Ekland, Edward Woodward.* A policeman visits a mysterious Scottish island to investigate the disappearance of a young girl. He discovers a pagan society, ruled by Lee, which has some surprises in store for him. The policeman gets a little heated up when he discovers the town's plans for a human sacrifice. A classic horror thriller in the Hammer tradition. ★★★ DVD Letterbox: $19.99, VHS Letterbox: $9.99, VHS Letterbox Collector's Edition: $14.99

Wide Awake

(1998, 100 min, US, M. Night Shyamalan) *Denis Leary, Dana Delany, Robert Loggia, Joseph Cross, Timothy Reifsnyder, Rosie O'Donnell.* Another story about a wise-beyond-his-years fifth grader, *Wide Awake* is an ambitious but ultimately unsuccessful look at a young boy's struggle with religious faith. Obviously, the film is a labor of love for writer-director Shyamalan, but the story about Johua Beal (Cross), and his quest to find God, lacks an appropriate epiphany. As Joshua grapples with losing his grandfather (Loggia), discovering the troubles other kids in his class are having, and finding his own place in life, his adventures are meant to be charming. They are not. Much of the drama is forced, and the hackneyed school situations have no depth. ★★ DVD: $19.99, VHS: $9.99

Wide Sargasso Sea

(1993, 100 min, Australia, John Duigan) *Karina Lombard, Nathaniel Parker, Rachel Ward, Michael York.* Sort of a prequel to Emily Brontë's "Jane Eyre," *Wide Sargasso Sea* reinterprets and updates the story and locates it on the steamy beaches of Jamaica. The story is told from the perspective of Rochester's (Parker) first wife, Antoinette (Lombard), a beautiful Creole woman whose family has a foreboding history. A tale of betrayal, love, madness and power, much of the subtext is ripped from the original novel turning the first half of this film adaptation into a semi-erotic mish-mash filled with shots of full frontal nudity, both male and female. Things pick up, however, in the second half when the story returns to its roots, focusing on the magical traditions of the island's people. ★★ DVD: $19.99, VHS: $19.99

Widow Coudorc

(1974, 92 min, France, Pierre Granier-Deferre) *Simone Signoret, Alain Delon.* Based on a novel by Georges Simenon, this excellent thriller features Signoret as a lonely widow who falls in love with a dangerous escaped convict. Similar in theme to the Catherine Deneuve drama, *Scene of the Crime*. (French with English subtitles) ★★★

The Widow of Saint-Pierre

(2000, 107 min, France, Patrice Leconte) *Juliette Binoche, Daniel Auteuil, Emir Kusturica, Philippe Magnan.* Stately composition and measured pacing inform director Leconte's treatment of actual events set in 1850 on the island of St. Pierre. Based on court records, the story recounts the aftermath of a childish prank by two drunks, resulting in murder. French justice of the time demands the guillotine, which must be transported to the remote fishing village. In the ensuing months, the townsfolk debate the intracacies and implications of capital punishment, a discussion made more complicated by the intended recipient, who shows true remorse and has become a fully integrated member of the community. Also brought to the fore is the unique character of the captain and his wife, whose developing relationship with the criminal underscores the couple's differences from the rest of the island community. The three principal players (Binoche, Auteuil, Kusturica) deliver deliberate and thoughtful performances, involving the viewer in each of their internal reflections as much as in the course of events. (French with English subtitles) ★★★½ DVD: $24.99

Widows' Peak

(1994, 101 min, GB, John Irvin) *Mia Farrow, Natasha Richardson, Joan Plowright, Jim Broadbent, Adrian Dunbar.* This lavish romp combines elements of Agatha Christie, *The Sting* and a little Merchant Ivory thrown in for extra measure. Plowright is the grand dame of a small 1920s Irish village beset by scandal when the personality clash between the town spinster (Farrow) and a free-spirited, newly arrived war widow (impeccably played by Richardson) gets out of hand. Plowright, the soul of decorum, takes it upon herself to keep the peace, and the results are humorously disastrous. Sparkling performances and bitchy dialogue help make *Widows' Peak* a delight. ★★★ VHS: $19.99

The Wife

(1996, 90 min, US, Tom Noonan) *Julie Hagerty, Tom Noonan, Wallace Shawn, Karen Young.* This claustrophobic little oddity stars Hagerty and Noonan as a couple of New Age therapists whose Sunday evening quiet is shattered when one of their patients (Shawn) and his ex-stripper wife (Young) unexpectedly show up at their door. As the evening progresses it becomes increasingly evident that the doctors need to heal themselves and, though she's no paragon of mental health, Young is the only one at the table being honest, however inappropriate. Nice camera work and editing make *The Wife* feel more zippy than it actually is, but the film can't quite rise above its "small" premise. ★★½ DVD: $14.99, VHS: $9.99

Wife vs. Secretary

(1936, 88 min, US, Clarence Brown) *Clark Gable, Myrna Loy, Jean Harlow, May Robson, James Stewart.* Another formulaic '30s love triangle, helped immensely by three very attractive leading performances. Gable stars as a successful publisher married to Loy. Harlow is his devoted secretary who becomes invaluable to him on a costly and time-consuming project, prompting the titular contest. ★★½ VHS: $19.99

Wifemistress

(1977, 110 min, Italy, Marco Vicario) *Marcello Mastroianni, Laura Antonelli.* Antonelli is a repressed, bedridden housewife until husband Mastroianni's clandestine affairs and flight from justice prod her into action. A spirited, erotic comedy-drama. ★★★

The Wild Angels

(1966, 124 min, US, Roger Corman) *Peter Fonda, Bruce Dern, Nancy Sinatra, Diane Ladd.* Fonda heads a group of fanatical motorcyclists bent on living their lives totally free of responsibility. This box-office hit started the '60s cycle film rage. ★★½ DVD: $14.99

Wild at Heart

(1990, 124 min, US, David Lynch) *Nicolas Cage, Laura Dern, Willem Dafoe, Diane Ladd, J.E. Freeman, Crispin Glover, Calvin Lockhart, Isabella Rossellini, Harry Dean Stanton, David Patrick Kelly, Sherilyn Fenn, John Lurie, Jack Nance, Pruitt Taylor Vince, Tracey Walter.* Lynch's dizzying, high-speed, high-energy love story follows the randy exploits of Sailor (Cage) and Lula, aka Peanut (Dern), as they wantonly cruise across the country. Cage and Dern deliver blistering performances as the loopy lovebirds. Oscar-nominee Ladd, Dern's real-life mom, is superb as her screen mom, a nightmarishly alcoholic and emotionally distressed witch who tries to derail the young lovers' romance. Dafoe steals the show with his portrayal of the ultimate "sleazoid," Bobby Peru. Filled with hilarious one-liners, some brutal violence and a lot of sweaty sex, *Wild at Heart* is an outrageous frolic that's "hotter than Georgia asphalt." ★★★

Wild Bill

(1995, 98 min, US, Walter Hill) *Jeff Bridges, Ellen Barkin, John Hurt, Diane Lane, Keith Carradine, David Arquette, Christina Applegate.* Hill's attempt to de-mythologize the legendary gunfighter and marshal is a superficial account of his last days, with a few interesting flashbacks thrown in for good measure. Bridges, though, is exceptional as the titular antihero, who comes to the town of Deadwood hoping to spend some quiet days. Several vengeance-seeking characters have also come to Deadwood, providing the film with numerous showdowns. Hill seems to be trying to attain the level of *The Man Who Shot Liberty Valance* in its deconstruction of a hero. He falls short of the mark. ★★ DVD: $19.99

The Wild Bunch

(1969, 144 min, US, Sam Peckinpah) *William Holden, Ernest Borgnine, Robert Ryan, Edmond O'Brien, Warren Oates.* Widely considered to be Peckinpah's best work, *The Wild Bunch* is a masterful piece of filmmaking, a mesmerizing treatment of contemporary American mythology utilizing to the fullest degree all aspects of the craft. The director incorporates exquisite cinematography, precision editing, arresting sound treatment and plot structure; each frame is composed with diligent care. In exploring personal rivalry within the human propensity to cling steadfastly to dying ways of life, and set within complex choreographies of violent action, Peckinpah moves from sweeping vistas to minute detail, restructuring time and place with balletic grace. This restored version runs 144 minutes, matching the European theatrical running time, an additional 10 minutes over the original U.S. running time. ★★★★ DVD: $14.99, VHS: $12.99

The Wild Duck

(1983, 96 min, Australia, Henri Safran) *Jeremy Irons, Liv Ullmann, Lucinda Jones.* An updated adaptation of Henrik Ibsen's play about the foibles of the Ekdal (Anglicized here to "Ackland") family. The production as a whole is uneven, but Irons' performance earns the viewers' attention. ★★

Wild Hearts Can't Be Broken

(1991, 89 min, US, Steve Miner) *Cliff Robertson, Gabrielle Amwar, Michael Schoeffling.* Anwar shines as Sonora, a teenaged orphan who follows her dream of becoming a horseback "diving girl" during the Depression. Robertson plays the traveling showman who gives her her big break. Although it's occasionally predictable and affected, this true story is inspiring and entertaining. ★★★ VHS: $9.99

Wild Horses

(1982, 88 min, New Zealand, Derek Morton) *Keith Aberdein, John Bach.* This exciting modern-day "western" is based on a true story about an enterprising city worker who captures and sells off the wild horses in Australia's national parks. His wrangling is soon confronted by a group of people who think that the horses are a nuisance and should be killed. A nail-biting climax ends this enjoyable feature. ★★★

Wild in the Streets

(1968, 97 min, US, Barry Shear) *Christopher Jones, Shelley Winters, Hal Holbrook, Millie Perkins, Richard Pryor.* A rock star gets the voting age lowered to 14, becomes President, and promptly has everyone over 30 carted off to internment camps. A '60s camp classic. ★★½

W

Wild Man Blues

(1998, 103 min, US, Barbara Kopple) After all sorts of creepy accusations, protracted legal battles and the breakup with Mia Farrow, Woody Allen has never been the same. How to show, then, that he's the same, old schlemiel we've known and loved for years? Commission this highly entertaining, revealing look into Allen's life, chronicling a 1996 European concert tour he took with his Dixieland band. Director Kopple was given all sorts of access to Allen, although he had say over final cut. Kopple captures Allen in some hilarious and often uncomfortable situations. Woody is the stressed, hypochondriacal, pampered American filmmaker, and his need for nurturing is obvious when we meet his elderly parents. Neither are impressed with their son's success. Dad shows more interest in the engraving of Woody's award, while Mom wishes he had chosen another profession. Oh, well. That's show biz. ★★★ DVD: $19.99

The Wild One

(1954, 79 min, US, Laslo Beneder) *Marlon Brando, Lee Marvin, Mary Murphy.* Brando dons his leather, mounts his bike and leads his roughneck motorcycle gang into a small, staid town, wreaking havoc with every sneer and mumble. A powerful performance well complemented by Marvin as an equally nasty hog rider. ★★★½ DVD: $19.99

Wild Orchid

(1990, 103 min, US, Zalman King) *Mickey Rourke, Carré Otis, Jacqueline Bisset.* A match made in smarm heaven: the movie's King of Kinks, Rourke, teams with King, who wrote *9½ Weeks* and then made his debut behind the camera with Sherilyn Fenn as a belle from hell in *Two Moon Junction.* There's little in the way of intelligence on display here and the sex has moved further south — to Rio. (Sequel: *Wild Orchid II: Two Shades of Blues*) ★ DVD Letterbox Contains both Unrated and R-Rated versions: $14.99

The Wild Party

(1975, 109 min, US, James Ivory) *James Coco, Royal Dano, David Dukes, Raquel Welch, Jennifer Lee, Perry King.* Veteran character actor Coco gives a poignant performance in a rare lead role as a fading silent comic. The wild Hollywood party is supposed to harken his comeback but ends in tragedy. This early Merchant Ivory production is loosely based on the Fatty Arbuckle scandal of the 1920s. ★★★ DVD: $14.99

Wild Reeds

(1994, 110 min, France, André Téchiné) *Gael Morel, Stéphane Rideau, Élodie Bouchez, Frédéric Gorny.* One of the most affecting depictions of gay first love ever committed to screen, this tender and knowing drama touchingly deals with friendship, coming out and teenage sexuality, all set against the political turmoil of the 1962 French/Algerian conflict. Set in a rural boarding school, the story revolves around the loves and friendships of three teenagers as well as an Algerian youth of 21. The central character is François (Morel), a handsome youth who falls for a fellow classmate, Serge (Rideau), a muscular student who in turn is attracted to Maite (Bouchez), Serge's best friend and a woman wise beyond her years. Entering this circle is Henri (Gorny), a troubled nationalist Algerian. A poignant drama that captures the universal esctasy, pain and loneliness of young love. Winner of 1995 César Awards for Best Picture, Screenplay, Actor and Female Discovery. (French with English subtitles) ★★★★ DVD: $19.99, VHS: $14.99

The Wild Ride

(1960, 90 min, US, Harvey Berman) *Jack Nicholson, Georgiana Carter.* A gang of roaring hot rodders get to race in the big time in this biker/bad girl/juvenile delinquent/rebel without a cause "gem." ★ VHS: $19.99

Wild Rovers

(1971, 138 min, US, Blake Edwards) *William Holden, Ryan O'Neal, Karl Malden, Lynn Carlin, Tom Skerritt, Rachel Roberts.* Released in a succession of box-office flops (*Darling Lili, The Carey Treatment*) by its director, this entertaining, light-hearted western drama got lost in the theatrical shuffle. It would be a shame to miss Holden's wonderful performance and the fine interplay between the film's characters in the story of two cowpokes who rob a bank and are chased through the countryside by a crazed posse. ★★★ VHS: $19.99

Wild Side

(1995, 96 min, US, Franklin Brauner) *Christopher Walken, Anne Heche, Steven Bauer, Joan Chen.* Though packaged in the guise of a standard soft-core action/thriller, everything that *Showgirls* tried but gloriously failed to be is in this *Wild Side.* Heche is Alex Lee, a banker by day and a high-class hooker by night. Both of her careers are sent in a tailspin after a $1,500 tryst with Bruno Buckingham (Walken), a bug-eyed, high-living businessman with criminal intentions. An elegant and gorgeous Chen is Virginia Chow, Bruno's wife who meets and immediately is attracted to the beautiful Alex. Before she realizes it, Alex is caught up in a plot to inject a computer virus into the national banking system, is a pawn of a sex-crazed FBI man, and in love (with Virginia) for the first time. Kinky! ★★★

Wild Strawberries

(1957, 93 min, Sweden, Ingmar Bergman) *Ingrid Thulin, Victor Sjostrom.* An elderly Stockholm professor (a brilliant Sjostrom) reviews the disappointments of his life while in the company of several boisterous youths. Effortlessly gliding through time, Bergman weaves a shimmering tapestry of memory and sensation. (Swedish with English subtitles) ★★★★ DVD Criterion Collection: $39.99, VHS: $29.99

Wild Things

(1998, 108 min, US, John McNaughton) *Kevin Bacon, Matt Dillon, Neve Campbell, Theresa Russell, Denise Richards, Daphne Rubin-Vega, Robert Wagner, Bill Murray.* Mix "Melrose Place" with *The Usual Suspects* and add some *Faster, Pussycat, Kill! Kill!* for good measure and you may get an idea of what delights this screwy "Florida noir" has to offer. Set primarily in an exclusive Everglades enclave, the film features Dillon as a popular high school counselor who's accused of rape. The supposed victim is the wealthy, spoiled daughter (Richards) of his former slut girlfriend (Russell). Dillon seeks help from a shyster lawyer (Murray), and, after some courtroom dramatics, finds himself off the hook — but not for long. With Stephen Peters' herky-jerky script, director McNaughton steers this sucker all over the genre map, careening from courtroom drama to carnal drama, to soap opera to satire and erotic thriller. Like the Everready Bunny, the plot complications keep going and going well into the final credits. Does it all make sense? Under close inspection, not really. But why complain? This is an "A" ticket ride in a "C" movie amusement park. (Sequel: *Wild Things 2*) ★★★ DVD Letterbox Unrated: $19.99

Wild Wild West

(1999, 107 min, US, Barry Sonnenfeld) *Will Smith, Kevin Kline, Kenneth Branagh, Salma Hayek, Ted Levine, M. Emmet Walsh.* Lightning doesn't strike twice for *Men in Black* director Sonnenfeld and star Smith with this bloated, big-screen version of the popular 1960s TV series. Everything that made *Men in Black* exciting and fun is missing here, from a sharply written screenplay full of funny lines and situations to taut direction to chemistry between the two leads. Smith is James West, secret agent par excellence in 1870s America. He's paired with master of disguise Artemus Gordon (Kline), and together they search for master criminal Dr. Arliss Loveless (Branagh). There's nothing wild about this west — only garish effects, silly exploits and boring repartee. ★ DVD Letterbox: $14.99, VHS: $9.99, VHS Letterbox: $9.99

Wildcats

(1986, 107 min, US, Michael Ritchie) *Goldie Hawn, James Keach, Swoosie Kurtz, Woody Harrelson, Wesley Snipes.* Hawn is the newly appointed football coach in a ghetto high school. There she comes in conflict with the macho head coach while slowly winning over the players. Goldie makes the best out of this harmless, clichéd comedy; and the film does produce a few laughs. ★★½ DVD Letterbox: $19.99, VHS: $9.99

Wilde

(1997, 117 min, GB, Brian Gilbert) *Stephen Fry, Jude Law, Vanessa Redgrave, Jennifer Ehle, Tom Wilkinson.* Fry makes for an uncannily realistic Oscar Wilde in this sumptuous biopic about the famed 19th-century Irish-born playwright. Director Gilbert's lavishly made film explores Wilde's unconventional lifestyle in Victorian England by tracing his life as family man who slowly succumbs to "the love that dare not speak its name" — one that ultimately leads to his trial and imprisonment. Much of *Wilde* is devoted to Oscar's strained love affair with Bosie (Law), the rich young man who casts a spell over him, and whose father (Wilkinson) wants to put an end to their relationship. While the scenes between Oscar and Bosie show how Wilde comes to accept who he is, episodes in his life depicting his trial, his love for his children, as well as his success as a literary figure flesh out this intimate portrait. ★★★ DVD Special Edition: $29.99

Wild Things

Wilder Napalm

(1993, 109 min, US, Glenn Gordon Caron) *Debra Winger, Arliss Howard, M. Emmet Walsh, Dennis Quaid, Jim Varney.* Reluctant telekinetic pyromaniac Wilder Foudroyant (Howard) matches his incendiary abilities with his equally conflagratory brother Wallace (Quaid) to keep the hand of his fetching pyromaniac wife Vida (Winger). Director Caron, creator of "Moonlighting," manages to retain the gleeful wackiness which permeated that TV show while allowing these accomplished performers sufficient latitude to uncover, layer by layer, telling moments of poignancy. An inventive, witty script and lively pacing contribute to this satisfactory examination of escalating sibling rivalry and lingering childhood guilt. ★★★ DVD: $24.99

Wildfire

(1992, 98 min, US, Zalman King) *Linda Fiorentino, Steven Bauer, Will Patton.* Erotic filmmaker King, long criticized for his excessively steamy forays into female sexuality (9½ Weeks, Wild Orchid), finally tones down his act and the result is this castrated drama about a happily married woman (Fiorentino) who must chose between the love of a good man (Patton) and the love of a gorgeous one (Bauer). Only in the sexual safety of the '90s could this be considered a dilemma. ★½ VHS: $79.99

Wildrose

(1984, 96 min, US, John Hanson) *Lisa Eichhorn, Tom Bower.* Eichhorn's perceptive and earnest performance elevates this compassionate drama about a divorced woman who takes a job at an iron works and meets hostility from her all-male coworkers. ★★★

Will Penny

(1968, 108 min, US, Tom Gries) *Charlton Heston, Joan Hackett, Donald Pleasence, Bruce Dern.* Heston gives one of his better performances in this exceptional western saga. Heston plays a weary, middle-aged cowboy who stays in a small town after being left in the desert for dead. He's then forced to fight the gang which left him there. Hackett is splendid as the pioneer woman who rescues him. ★★★½ DVD Letterbox: $14.99, VHS: $9.99

Will You Dance with Me?

(1959, 89 min, France, Michel Boisrons) *Brigitte Bardot, Henri Vidal.* A typical (for its time) but good, lighthearted crime mystery starring Bardot as a bewitching newlywed who becomes entangled in a web of blackmail and murder. (French with English subtitles) ★★½

Willard

(1971, 95 min, US, Daniel Mann) *Bruce Davison, Sandra Locke, Ernest Borgnine, Elsa Lanchester.* The story of a boy and his rat. This silly but effective horror tale stars Davison as a lonely young man who raises rats — who help him get revenge against those around him. (Remade in 2003) ★★½

Willard

(2003, 95 min, US, Glen Morgan) *Crispin Glover, Jackie Burroughs, R. Lee Ermey, Laura Elena Harring.* The always-eccentric Glover goes for the throat in this uneven remake of the '70s cult film. Willard is stuck in a crappy job with an emasculating boss (the perfectly cast Ermey) which he needs in order to take care of his dominating, ailing mother. This joyless existence is redeemed somewhat by the discovery of hundreds of trainable rats in his basement, which Willard plans to use to exact revenge and get his way. A mostly dour film, *Willard*

is still a must for Glover fans; who else could bring such passion to the command "Chew!" or elicit both chills and laughter from the desperate retort, "Start over?! I'm almost *done*!" when someone suggests he start a new life? The story is mildly interesting in fits and starts, and really doesn't improve much on the original, though the rats are cooler. Worth checking out is the Glover-directed video for his cover of Michael Jackson's "Ben"; it's a riot, and strikes the perfect tone that the movie often misses. ★★½ DVD Dual: $27.99, VHS: $8.99

William Shakespeare's A Midsummer Night's Dream

(1999, 115 min, US, Michael Hoffman) *Kevin Kline, Michelle Pfeiffer, David Strathairn, Rupert Everett, Calista Flockhart, Stanley Tucci, Christian Bale, Dominic West, Anna Friel, Roger Rees.* A sterling cast helps brings life to Shakespeare's splendiferous comedy, but director Hoffman's sporadic pacing and episodic delivery keeps this from being the magical carpet ride it should have been. Updating the tale to 19th-century Tuscany (this way all the characters can scurry here and there on bicycles), the story remains the same: these foolish mortals come in contact with the fairy world for a night of romantic escapades and misadventures. Hoffman gives the film a spectacular look — his attention to detail is remarkable. But his staging isn't fluid enough to fully capture the whimsy and discord of all these characters flailing about. But what a cast he has assembled. Not the definitive interpretation, but an able one. ★★★ DVD: $9.99, VHS: $9.99

William Shakespeare's Romeo + Juliet

(1996, 113 min, US/GB, Baz Luhrmann) *Leonardo DiCaprio, Claire Danes, John Leguizamo, Harold Perrineau, Paul Sorvino, Pete Postlethwaite, Diane Verona, Miriam Margolyes, Brian Dennehy.* Can Shakespeare appeal to the MTV crowd? The answer is a resounding "Aye!" in this delirious amalgam of styles, colors and kinetic camera movements. Using the original dialogue of the play (pared down for reasons of length), but reworking almost everything else about the scenario, Luhrmann and company have produced a work which is not only faithful to the original theme and feeling of the piece, but resonates particularly well for contemporary times. Set in a fictional Verona Beach, a neon-drenched cross between Miami and Los Angeles, the story of star-crossed lovers is set between rival business families, each with their own gun-toting gang members and peculiar dysfunctions. ★★★★ DVD Letterbox Special Edition: $14.99, VHS: $6.99

Willy Wonka and the Chocolate Factory

(1971, 98 min, US, Mel Stuart) *Gene Wilder, Jack Albertson.* A strange and delightful children's musical fantasy, with Wilder as an eccentric candy manufacturer who invites five contest-winning children to his mysterious factory. Songs includes "Candy Man." ★★★ DVD Letterbox: $19.99, DVD Pan & Scan: $19.99, VHS Includes the all-new documentary "Pure Imagination": $9.99

Wilson

(1944, 154 min, US, Henry King) *Alexander Knox, Charles Coburn, Geraldine Fitzgerald, Vincent Price.* Though acclaimed in its day, this reverent biography of America's 28th President has been long lost in the shadows of other 1940s bios. Nominated for Best Picture and winner of five Academy

Awards, this sincere and intelligent look at the life of Woodrow Wilson may suffer from over-glorification, but it is nevertheless a stirring examination of a political career. A history lesson told in cinematic chapters, the film traces Wilson's rise from Princeton University's president to New Jersey's governor to his two terms as commander-in-chief (elected in 1912 and 1916). Knox gives a solid portrayal of Wilson and he is given some inspiring speeches to recite. ★★★½ VHS: $19.99

Win a Date with Tad Hamilton

(2004, 96 min, US, Robert Luketic) *Kate Bosworth, Topher Grace, Josh Duhamel, Sean Hayes, Nathan Lane, Gary Cole, Ginnifer Goodwin.* A small-town girl (the winsome Bosworth) wins a date with her Hollywood heartthrob idol Tad Hamilton (Duhamel), much to the chagrin of her longtime platonic friend Pete (Grace). Worse for Pete, who is too afraid to show his amorous feelings, Tad seems to be falling for her. Sure, this kind of love triangle has been played to death, and sadly the script doesn't have the zippy dialogue that's de rigeur in romantic comedies. But there's a curious freshness to the proceedings, whether it's the remarkable innocence of the courtships, the complete avoidance of mean-spirited schenanigans, or the simple fact that Tad, who could easily be typed as an archvillain, is actually sweet and good-intentioned. This makes the inevitable return-to-the-small-town climax bittersweet, pitting the handsome Duhamel against the ample charms of Grace in a battle we'd rather not see either lose. Lane and Hayes are wasted in extended cameos as Tad's managers. ★★½ DVD Letterbox: $26.99, DVD Pan & Scan: $26.99, VHS: $22.99

Winchell

(1998, 108 min, US, Paul Mazursky) *Stanley Tucci, Glenne Headly, Christopher Plummer, Paul Giamatti.* Mazursky's direction replicates Winchell's own staccatto delivery, re-created brilliantly by Tucci in an Emmy Award-winning performance that is more channelled than acted. It could be said that Winchell laid the groundwork for the infotainment biz that dominates the airwaves today. He virtually created syndicated gossip, blurring the line between news and entertainment, between politics and performance. The film follows the arc of his career, from making a pitch for War Bonds after singing a tune on a vaudeville stage, to aligning with Joseph McCarthy in a twisted permutation of the patriotism of his youth. *Winchell* delivers the same frenetic entertainment as its subject matter. ★★★½ VHS: $9.99

Winchester '73

(1950, 92 min, US, Anthony Mann) *James Stewart, Millard Mitchell, Shelley Winters, Stephen McNally, Dan Duryea, Rock Hudson, Tony Curtis.* Superior western adventure with Stewart combing the wilderness for his one-of-a-kind rifle and his father's murderer. The film, which features exceptional cinematography, helped bring about the great revival of westerns in the 1950s. ★★★½ DVD: $14.99, VHS: $9.99

Wind

(1992, 123 min, US, Carroll Ballard) *Matthew Modine, Jennifer Grey, Cliff Robertson, Jack Thompson.* A stylishly produced, curiously enjoyable yet formulaic dramatic action story about a maverick sailor and his quest to win the America's Cup, sailing's most coveted prize. Modine and Grey star as the two halves of a boy-and-girl sailing team. She's

W

recently hung up her halyards, however, to pursue a career in aeronautics and he's just been offered to crew on an America's Cup yacht in Newport. Within the first 30 minutes of the film, Modine manages to lose not only his woman, but the Cup too. Can you guess where the script goes from there? Despite its complete predictability, *Wind* does manage to entertain thanks in large part to its remarkably filmed sailing sequences which amply convey the sheer exhilaration of sailing. ★★½ DVD: $24.99

The Wind

(1928, 88 min, US, Victor Sjostrom) *Lillian Gish, Lars Hanson, Montagu Love.* Sjostrom (forever identified as the old man in Ingmar Bergman's *Wild Strawberries*) was a renowned director in Sweden and made one of the greatest silent films over here. Gish gives her most riveting performance as a city-girl newlywed relocated to the desert. After she murders the man who rapes her, he comes back with the howling wind. Sjostrom makes us hear the unrelenting sand storm, the clatter of broken dishes and the footsteps on the wooden floors through brilliant editing and the use of close-ups. ★★★★

The Wind and the Lion

(1975, 120 min, US, John Milius) *Sean Connery, Candice Bergen, Brian Keith, John Huston.* Well-mounted but ultimately muddled adventure film loosely based on an actual event, with Connery as a Moroccan shiek who kidnaps an American widow (Bergen) and her children, setting off an international incident in which President Teddy Roosevelt (Keith) himself becomes involved. ★★½ DVD: $19.99, VHS: $19.99

Windhorse

(1998, 97 min, US/China, Paul Wagner) *Dadon, Jampa Kelsang, Richard Chang, Lu Yu, Taije Silverman.* Windhorses are small pieces of paper inscribed with prayers, which are scattered from the tops of Himalayan mountain passes as offerings to the gods. The film opens with two weary travelers coming upon a blanket of them as they cross from Tibet to Nepal. The story then turns back to the mid-1970s, when the brother and sister travelers were with their cousin, children at play, unwilling witnesses to the assassination of their grandfather at the hands of invading Chinese forces. These three each adapted to circumstances in strikingly different ways: one seeking pop stardom within the dominating Chinese culture, one wallowing in dissolution and self-destruction, and the third inviting great peril by becoming a Buddhist nun. Clandestinely shot by director Wagner, over one-third of the film's cast and crew credits read: "name withheld." A powerful and moving film. (In English and in Mandarin and Tibetan with English subtitles) ★★★½ VHS: $19.99

Windom's Way

(1957, 108 min, GB, Ronald Neame) *Peter Finch, Mary Ure.* Peter Finch stars in Neame's thoughtful tale about a British doctor working in a small Malayan village who tries to rally the locals against a Communist insurgency. ★★★

The Window

(1949, 73 min, US, Ted Tetzlaff) *Bobby Driscoll, Barbara Hale, Arthur Kennedy.* A taut, intriguing thriller about a small boy who witnesses a murder, though no one will believe his story. Driscoll is the youth. ★★★½

Window Shopping

(1986, 96 min, France, Chantal Akerman) *Delphine Seyrig, Charles Denner, Lio, Pascale Salkin.* Set within the friendly, artificial confines of Paris' "Toison d'Or" shopping mall, Akerman proves that she is not limited to producing serious, experimental studies with this delightfully witty, tongue-in-cheek musical that pays homage to Jacques Demy and M-G-M musicals. Actually nothing more than a stylish soap opera, the story follows Lili, the manager of a hair salon, and her various suitors. Plot twists abound, a chorus of shampoo girls break into song and love is always around the corner in this splashy, nonsensical lark that takes delight in its own frothiness while still retaining some insight into love in the modern age. (French with English subtitles) ★★★ VHS: $29.99

Window to Paris

(1993, 101 min, Russia, Yuri Mamin) *Agnes Soral, Sergui Dontsov, Victor Michailov.* This subversively hilarious albeit uneven Russian fantasy follows a music teacher and his new flatmates through a closet door that leads from their decaying St. Petersburg apartment to the opulent streets of Paris, where the stalls are filled with fresh produce and motorcycles litter the sidewalk. The intrepid band, exhausted from eking out a mean existence in a financially depleted Russia, fanatically embrace the opportunity to indulge in material excess. When they discover that the gateway stays open for only a certain period of time, they go for broke in their frenzy of acquisition, their physical experience of spatial refraction matched by the onset of Western ennui. Filmed with kinetic energy and a warm appreciation of human foibles. (Russian and French with English subtitles) ★★★

Windtalkers

(2002, 134 min, US, John Woo) *Nicolas Cage, Adam Beach, Christian Slater, Peter Stormare, Noah Emmerich, Mark Ruffalo, Frances O'Connor, Roger Willie, Brian Van Holt, Jason Isaacs.* Nothing says that just because *Saving Private Ryan* and *The Thin Red Line* ably portrayed the anguish of WWII, that no one can revisit the same era ever again. But one would hope that a filmmaker would bring a fresh perspective to the genre. *Windtalkers* examines the experiences of Navajo soldiers who worked as code talkers — surely their story had yet to be told in a Hollywood film. Unfortunately, it only serves as a gimmicky backdrop to a commonplace story of battle, and of one soldier's (and a whole one, at that) search for redemption. Cage plays Joe, a battle-scarred Marine who is assigned to look after Ben, a Native American radio operator whose Navajo language is used for code. Giving slight shrift to how the Native Americans adapt and endure, the focus is on Joe licking his battle wounds. Director Woo would seem a natural for the fight scenes, but the battles, though intense, are too obviously choreographed, ultimately lacking subtlety or honesty. Beach is quite good as the young, proud Navajo, though a few actors are unable to rise above some of the clichés. ★★ DVD Dual: $14.99, DVD 3-Disc Director's Edition: $29.99, VHS: $9.99

Wing Chun

(1994, 93 min, Hong Kong, Yuen Woo-Ping) *Michelle Yeoh, Donnie Yen, Cheng Pei Pei.* Serious kung fu unfortunately takes a back seat to comedy in this retelling of the story of Yim Wing Chun (Yeoh), a young girl who refined the southern Chinese fighting style eventually named after her. Returning to her village, Wing Chun saves a young widow from bandits after the woman is mistaken for Wing herself. When the widow is kidnapped by the bandits, Wing Chun must refine her martial arts skills in order to defeat the gang's leader. Yuen seems a bit unfocused, alternating between blistering kung fu sequences and some typically absurd Hong Kong comedic tomfoolery. It's an awkward pairing which — while entertaining and funny in places — doesn't work to the fullest effect. (Cantonese with English subtitles) ★★½

Wing Commander

(1999, 99 min, US, Chris Roberts) *Freddie Prinze, Jr., Saffron Burrows, Matthew Lillard, Tchéky Karyo, Jürgen Prochnow, David Warner.* After so many dreary films that have been adapted from video games, the creator of the Wing Commander games steps to the plate, directing one that makes the same old mistakes. The obligatory set-up involves an aged feline race called the Kilrathi who are out to take over the Earth. It's up to Prinze and pals to hop into their space fighters and shoot old-fashioned bullets and torpedoes at other ships. If that sounds uninventive, there's a heavy-handed subplot about space bigotry (Freddie is "part-Pilgrim"). ★ DVD: $9.99, VHS: $9.99

Winged Migration

(2003, 89 min, France, Jacques Perrin) Beautifully shot from planes, gliders and hot-air balloons, *Winged Migration* offers a fresh vision into the vastness of the bird world. The film jump-cuts between all manner of species, with the bird's migration cycle as its central theme — above storm systems, over continents, and over endless oceans with no rest until reaching shore. This is all managed with a bare minimum of narration, which lends itself to widescreen spectacle above and beyond the cut-and-dry nature segments one sees on the Discovery Channel. In the vein of *Anima Mundi* or *Baraka*, the film at once conveys a world of both colossal scope and minute detail; every shot is a richly colored, beautiful composition in which the subject's idiosyncrasies are brought to the fore, and in often humanizing ways. Perhaps the film's only flaw is its brief, albeit stoic, treatment of the perils faced by many birds on their journey — that of poachers, hunters and oil spills. Although these passages are less integrated and come off as feeble concessions to animal rights activism, they don't overshadow the sum total experience. True visual poetry with wide-ranging appeal. ★★★½ DVD: $26.99, VHS: $14.99

Wings

(1927, 139 min, US, William Wellman) *Gary Cooper, Clara Bow, Charles "Buddy" Rogers, Richard Arlen.* The first film to win the Oscar for Best Picture, this exciting silent war drama features good aerial effects to tell the story of two WWI pilots, and their love for the same girl. ★★★ VHS: $14.99

Wings of Desire

(1988, 130 min, West Germany, Wim Wenders) *Bruno Ganz, Solveig Dommartin, Otto Sander, Peter Falk.* A deeply moving and hauntingly beautiful affirmation of the human spirit. Sumptuously photographed in both black and white and color, the film reveals the world as seen by two angels (Ganz, Sander). As they hover over Berlin and listen to the lonely thoughts whispering through the minds of the disenfranchised and forgotten, we are mesmerized by their inherent compassion for humanity. Finally for Ganz's angel, this compassion turns to desire as he feels himself longing to experience the complexities of human emotions. Dommartin is stunning as

W

The Wings of the Dove

the trapeze artist whose beauty inspires Ganz to yearn for an earthbound existence. (Sequel: *Faraway, So Close*) (American remake: *City of Angels*) (German with English subtitles) ★★★★ DVD Letterbox Special Edition: $24.99

Wings of Fame

(1990, 109 min, GB, Otakar Votocek) *Peter O'Toole, Colin Firth.* They say that fame is fleeting, and in this invigorating drama starring O'Toole in the familiar role of a boozy Hollywood star), fame's disappearance holds more significance than just losing a good table at Spago's. When Valentin (O'Toole) is killed by what seems like a lunatic fan (Firth), who is then bumped off by a falling spotlight, both victims find themselves in a slightly puzzling hereafter. The island paradise, which at first seems like a green version of heaven, turns out to be inhabited only by those who are dead and famous. Resting somewhere in that amorphous gap between comedy and drama, this little "slice of life" (slice of death?) offers a devilishly ponderous glimpse into the great beyond. ★★★ VHS: $7.99

The Wings of the Dove

(1997, 101 min, GB, Iain Softley) *Alison Elliott, Helena Bonham Carter, Linus Roache, Charlotte Rampling, Elizabeth McGovern, Michael Gambon.* Set against the splendor of breathtaking Venice, love and romantic deceit blossom in the most unexpected ways in this beautifully realized, haunting version of Henry James' novel. Directed with delicate precision and unnerving melancholy by Softley, *The Wings of the Dove* soars as both a psychological study of conflicted emotions, and a love story gone awry. Bonham Carter is spellbinding as Kate Croy, an aristocrat who has been forbidden to see her lover Merton Densher (Roache), a handsome, working-class journalist. Their affair is put on hold until the arrival of Millie Theale (Elliott), a dying American heiress who is befriended by Kate and smitten with Merton. When they all take a trip to Venice, it is there Kate plots to bring her lover and best friend together. James has never been this satisfying on-screen, and Hossein Amini's smart, fluid screenplay, Softley's sensitivity, and a superb ensemble leave little doubt as to why. ★★★★ DVD: $19.99, VHS: $9.99

The Winslow Boy

(1999, 110 min, US, David Mamet) *Rebecca Pidgeon, Nigel Hawthorne, Jeremy Northam, Gemma Jones, Guy Edwards, Matthew Pidgeon.* This brilliantly nuanced adaptation of Terence Rattigan's 1946 play (and 1948 British film) finds writer-director Mamet setting aside his rough-hewn characters and rapid-fire profanities and settling down instead to a quiet costume drama that proves he is a writer beyond all previous conceptions of him. The story concerns the obsession that gripped the English in 1910 over a 13-year-old cadet at the Osborne Naval Academy who was accused of stealing a five-shilling postal order. The Winslow family, headed by a stoic but loving patriarch (Hawthorne) rallies around the young lad (Edwards) and demands that he be given a fair trial. His sister (R. Pidgeon), a suffragist, teams with their father and they beg the services of prominent opposition Member of Parliament Sir Robert Morton (Northam) to appeal their case before the government. Mamet interjects the story with wry humor and bubbling romantic tensions that cut through a veil of upper-crust reserve with a most satisfying élan. ★★★★ DVD: $27.99

The Winter Guest

(1998, 110 min, Scotland, Alan Rickman) *Phyllida Law, Emma Thompson, Sheila Reid, Sandra Voe, Arlene Cockburn.* Actor Rickman gets behind the lense to direct this tightly knit little adaptation of Sharman Macdonald's play. Set in a Scottish seaside hamlet where the winter's cold has frozen the sea solid, the action revolves around four separate tête-à-têtes: A couple of elderly women waiting for a bus and obsessing on death; a teenaged boy and girl who nervously flirt around the edges of their attraction; two young boys who skip school to spend time at the beach and muse about their impending adolescence; and a bereaved widow (Thompson) whose mother (real-life ma Law), is waging a campaign of relentless acerbity and tough love in an attempt to dislodge her from her icy grieving. Though claustrophobic and stagey, the film's cast never miss a beat, and Rickman keeps the flow of deep introspection moving steadily along. ★★★

Winter Kills

(1979, 97 min, US, William Richert) *Jeff Bridges, John Huston, Anthony Perkins, Richard Boone, Sterling Hayden, Elizabeth Taylor. Winter Kills* is a rare example of a film so wild, so utterly rambuncious and so bursting with invention that it defies description. Bridges is the sole innocent searching for clues to the decade-old assassination of his half-brother, a Kennedy-esque president. What he uncovers is a murky mass of conspiracies and the mammoth excessiveness of his tyrannical father (a hilariously obscene Huston). Don't miss this cynical swipe at the unravelling threads of the Stars and Stripes. ★★★ DVD Letterbox 2-disc set: $29.99

Winter Light

(1963, 80 min, Sweden, Ingmar Bergman) *Ingrid Thulin, Max von Sydow.* This chilling and powerful story of despair is the second of Bergman's trilogy (the others two being *The Silence* and *Through a Glass Darkly*) and for people who want to go over the edge in depression, a double feature with Bresson's *Diary of a Country Priest* should do it. The story concerns a disillusioned pastor who loses his vocation and watches as his congregation crumbles along with his faith. (Swedish with English subtitles) ★★★½ VHS: $29.99

Winter of Our Dreams

(1981, 90 min, Australia, John Duigan) *Judy Davis, Bryan Brown, Baz Luhrmann.* A decidedly different love story which traces the roots of identity, relationships and life on the edge. Brown stars as a former activist who meets Davis, a junkie hooker who becomes obsessively attached to him. Ms. Davis' incandescent performance is a tremendously moving portrait of misplaced desire and self-abuse. One of the finest films that came out of the Australian New Wave. ★★★½

Winter People

(1989, 110 min, US, Ted Kotcheff) *Kurt Russell, Kelly McGillis, Lloyd Bridges.* A widower (Russell) finds himself caught between two feuding families in the backwoods of the Carolina Mountains during the 1930s. Very little dramatic excitement. ★★ DVD: $14.99

Wired

(1989, 108 min, US, Larry Peerce) *Michael Chiklis, Ray Sharkey, J.T. Walsh.* Dreadful film version of Bob Woodward's novel about the life and death of comedian John Belushi. Chiklis may resemble Belushi, but he can't duplicate any of the comedian's classic bits, and Peerce's static direction and a dull screenplay certainly don't help. ★

Wisdom

(1987, 109 min, US, Emilio Estevez) *Emilio Estevez, Demi Moore, Tom Skerritt, Veronica Cartwright.* Estevez wasn't too wise when he wrote, directed and starred in this mangled social fable about an unemployed man who teams with a young woman (Moore) to become modern-day Robin Hoods. ★ VHS: $14.99

Wise Blood

(1979, 108 min, US, John Huston) *Brad Dourif, Daniel Shor, Harry Dean Stanton, Ned Beatty.* A zealous attack against authority and the follies of faith. A soldier (Dourif) returns to his Southern home town and wages a fanatical rebellion against the repressive values of his upbringing. Based on the Flannery O'Connor novel. ★★★½ VHS: $59.99

Wise Guys

(1986, 91 min, US, Brian De Palma) *Danny DeVito, Joe Piscipo, Ray Sharkey.* This annoying gangster spoof casts DeVito and Piscipo as low-level and bumbling hit men who pull a scam on their boss, only to be set up by him when their sting fails. ★★ VHS: $19.99

Wish You Were Here

(1987, 92 min, GB, David Leland) *Emily Lloyd, Tom Bell.* Lloyd gives a knockout performance in this poignant and well-aimed comedy-drama set in England in the early 1950s. Lloyd perfectly plays a sassy, sexually advanced teenager whose search for fulfillment and escape from her rigid father steers her

W

towards an ill-conceived affair with an older man, familial abandonment, and, ultimately, fervent independence. This could be — although it is not officially — the prequel to *Personal Services*, which was written by director Leland. ★★★½ DVD: $14.99

Wishmaster

(1997, 90 min, US, Robert Kurtzman) *Tammy Lauren, Andrew Divoff, Robert Englund, Tony Todd, Wendy Benson, Chris Lemmon.* *Wishmaster* has the look and feel of outtakes from cruddy flicks such as *The Horror Show* and *Deadtime Stories.* The nonsensical plot-like events have something to do with the Djinn (who resembles a cross between Spawn and Predator) granting the wishes of anyone who hinders his pursuit of the person who unleashed him from his statue. The acting is poor, the dialogue dopey, and the special effects underwhelming. (Followed by 2 sequels) ★ DVD: $14.99, VHS: $9.99

Witch Hunt

(1994, 101 min, US, Paul Schrader) *Dennis Hopper, Penelope Ann Miller, Eric Bogosian, Julian Sands.* Joseph Dougherty, writer of HBO's highly entertaining *Cast a Deadly Spell*, teams up with director Schrader for this whimsical sequel. Set in Hollywood in the 1940s where the art of witchcraft runs rampant, the story follows the adventures of private dick H. Phillip Lovecraft (Hopper), who is hired by a beautiful femme fatale (Ann Miller) to keep a watchful eye on her philandering husband. Great special effects spice up this comical, noir-esque feature, whose sets are designed to create a dreamlike Hollywood where almost anything could happen. ★★★ VHS: $9.99

Witchboard

(1986, 97 min, US, Kevin S. Tenney) *Tawny Kitaen, Kathleen Wilhoite, Rose Marie.* An evil spirit attempts to possess a young woman (Kitaen) who has been playing with a ouija board. An occasional fright but another in a long line of schlocky horror tales. ★★½

The Witches

(1990, 91 min, GB, Nicolas Roeg) *Anjelica Huston, Mai Zetterling, Jasen Fisher, Rowan Atkinson, Brenda Blethyn, Jane Horrocks.* Roeg's collaboration with Muppets creator Jim Henson on Roald Dahl's enchanting children's story is a smashing triumph — scary fun for the kids and thoroughly enjoyable for adults. During their vacation in Cornwall, nine-year-old Luke and his witch-wise grandmother come up against a coven of witches holding their annual meeting. Learning of the witches' fiendish plot to turn all of the children in England into mice — and despite being one of the first casualties — little Luke does battle to save his young peers. The majestically camp Huston costars as the evil and hideously ugly Grand High Witch. ★★★½ DVD: $9.99, VHS: $6.99

The Witches of Eastwick

(1987, 118 min, US, George Miller) *Jack Nicholson, Cher, Susan Sarandon, Michelle Pfeiffer, Veronica Cartwright.* An entertaining adult fantasy, loosely based on John Updike's novel. Cher, Pfeiffer and Sarandon play three dissimilar women who share a common problem: men. Together, they conjure up the "perfect" man, who arrives in the guise of Nicholson, truly a devilish rogue, who promptly proceeds to manipulate the ladies' lives. Cartwright — even with this powerhouse cast — steals the film as a snoopy society matron. ★★★ DVD: $14.99

With a Friend Like Harry . . .

(2001, 116 min, France, Dominik Moll) *Laurent Lucas, Sergi Lopéz, Mathilde Seigner, Sophie Guillemin.* Harry (Lopéz) is reserved, self-contained, decidedly controlled; he's going through the motions of a normal life as though there were a blueprint for that. At a roadside rest stop, he encounters old high school acquaintance Michel (Lucas), whose life has all the usual ordinary, messy inconveniences. Harry is traveling with a docile, yielding mistress; Michel's wife and female offspring are anything but docile. Harry remembers everything, but is not himself remembered. He relates details of Michel's school experiences while Michel struggles to place him. Yet Harry — calm, reasonable — smoothly insinuates himself into Michel's disordered life with covert amiability and disabling generosity. His overt concern for his newfound friends' well-being is a mask, a ploy of manipulation. He proselytizes his philosophy of life while providing an extreme solution to every condition he defines as a problem, precipitating a nightmare spiral of horrific events that unfold with Hitchcockian inevitability. *Harry* is a creepy delight, offering telling moments of chilling revelation that return to mind long after the film is over. Intelligently directed with authentic performances. (French with English subtitles) ★★★½ VHS Subtitled: $9.99, VHS Dubbed: $9.99

With Friends Like These

(1998, 105 min, US, Philip F. Messina) *Adam Arkin, Robert Costanzo, Beverly D'Angelo, David Strathairn, Elle Macpherson, Amy Madigan, Laura San Giacomo, Jon Tenney, Lauren Tom.* An ensemble comedy about four actors who are all best friends, and all out of work, *With Friends Like These* is a sitcom idea wrongly extended to feature length. Johnny (Costanzo) is told in confidence by talent agent (D'Angelo) that Martin Scorsese is looking to cast an unknown as Al Capone. Hoping to nail the role, Johnny asks his friend Armand (Strathairn) for help. What he doesn't know is that his buddies Steve (Arkin), and Dorian (Tenney) also want to audition for the part. Anger and betrayals mount up as the quartet of actors try (and fail) to keep secrets from each other, with the subtlty of machine gun fire. The four leads mug their way shamelessly through this unfunny comedy like raging bulls trying to out-act the other. ★★ VHS: $19.99

With Honors

(1994, 103 min, US, Alek Keshishian) *Joe Pesci, Brendan Fraser, Moira Kelly, Patrick Dempsey, Gore Vidal, Josh Hamilton.* As bland as cafeteria food, *With Honors* centers on the life of a determined-to-do-well Harvard student (Fraser) who loses his all-important term paper and must bargain with a feisty homeless man (Pesci) to get it back. Of course, Pesci is not simply a homeless man, but a homeless man with all the wisdom of the ages tucked neatly beneath his tattered jacket. He imparts this wisdom not only on Fraser but his three housemates, as well, in annoyingly large doses. Things get even worse when the roomies invite him to move in with them. ★½ DVD: $9.99, VHS: $9.99

Withnail and I

(1987, 105 min, GB, Bruce Robinson) *Richard E. Grant, Paul McGann, Richard Griffiths.* Two unemployed actors of disparate character, sharing a flat in 1969, go on holiday — subjecting themselves to each other's idiosyncrasies during the rigors of ill-planned travel. Nicely drawn character studies, and a sly commentary on the temperament of the times. ★★★ DVD Letterbox Criterion Collection: $29.99

Without a Clue

(1988, 106 min, GB, Thom Eberhardt) *Michael Caine, Ben Kingsley, Jeffrey Jones, Peter Cook.* A delightfully zany and often very funny takeoff on the Sherlock Holmes legend. What would have happend if Dr. Watson had been the real detective, and Holmes was nothing more than a third-rate actor hired to portray the famous sleuth? Caine and Kingsley, both in fine comic form, make the most of this novel premise which finds the famous duo on the case of the missing five-pound note plates stolen from the Royal Bank of England. 106 minutes of slightly silly, laugh-out-loud tomfoolery. ★★★ DVD: $14.99

Without a Trace

(1983, 119 min, US, Stanley R. Jaffe) *Kate Nelligan, Judd Hirsch, Stockard Channing.* Nelligan stars as a single mother whose young son leaves for school one morning and never returns. Hirsch is a sympathetic detective searching for the boy. Nelligan gives a good performance as the mother who never gives up hope. Though the film sometimes gives in to melodramatics, the where-how-why of the case is suspenseful. ★★½ VHS: $29.99

Without Anesthesia

(1982, 111 min, Poland, Andrzej Wajda) *Zbigniew Zapasiewicz, Ewa Dalkowska.* From the pen of director Wajda and coauthor Agnieszka Holland comes this jumpy, gritty Communist-era story of government control and the dissolution of a marriage. Zapasiewicz is convincing as a successful reporter and political analyst whose marriage falls apart, and he sets out to discover why. At the same time, he has fallen from grace with the powers that be. And making matters worse, his Kafka-esque downfall both personally and professionally is never explained. It seems to be accepted and everyone just goes with the flow of supression and inebriation. (Polish with English subtitles) ★★½ VHS: $29.99

Without Limits

(1998, 118 min, US, Robert Towne) *Billy Crudup, Donald Sutherland, Monica Potter.* The second feature film about legendary athlete Steve Prefontaine (the first being Steve James' 1997 *Prefontaine*) is a nice return to form for writer-director Towne (who tread similar ground with 1982's *Personal Best*). Crudup and Sutherland are superb as, respectively, "Pre" and his caring but no-nonsense track coach. The film wisely focuses on their compelling relationship. Towne also is able to gain insight into Pre's psyche and his personal relationships — something that the straightforward, informative and absorbing *Prefontaine* was unable to do sufficiently. And though the two films ultimately complement each other, *Without Limits* — with its nuanced performances and detailed characters, and demonstrating why Pre is considered a legend in his field — has the edge. ★★★ DVD: $9.99, VHS: $4.99

Without Love

(1945, 111 min, US, Harold S. Bucquet) *Katharine Hepburn, Spencer Tracy, Lucille Ball, Keenan Wynn.* Tracy is a scientist staying at widow Hepburn's boarding house in overcrowded, wartime Washington, D.C. For convenience's sake, the two marry and, of course, eventually fall in love. A charming romantic comedy with appealing performances by Kate and Spencer. ★★★ VHS: $14.99

Without Reservations

(1946, 101 min, US, Mervyn LeRoy) *Claudette Colbert, John Wayne, Don DeFore.* Pleasant comedy starring Colbert as a renowned Hollywood screenwriter, searching for an unknown to star in her next movie, who meets Marine flyer Wayne. (Wonder who gets the part?) Colbert is in good form, and Wayne — who didn't make many comedies — is actually quite funny. ★★★

Without You I'm Nothing

(1990, 90 min, US, John Boskovich) *Sandra Bernhard, Steve Antin, Cynthia Bailey, Lu Leonard, John Doe, Ken Foree.* The film version of Bernhard's audacious off-Broadway hit brims with libidinous wit and inventive characterizations. With unabashed artistic daring, Bernhard plunges into a melange of musical impersonations, poetry readings and monologues which put her on the cutting edge of standup comedy/performance art. Set in a sleepy little nightclub, Bernhard's act is played to a thinning and impassive-looking audience and culminates in a desperate and very revealing go-go dance to the tune of Prince's "Little Red Corvette." Sprinkled with moments of inspired comedic brilliance, *Without You . . .* establishes Bernhard as a hip, thoroughly campy urban (and urbane) satirist. ★★★½

Witness

(1985, 112 min, US, Peter Weir) *Harrison Ford, Kelly McGillis, Lukas Haas, Josef Sommer, Alexander Godunov, Danny Glover, Patti LuPone, Viggo Mortensen.* A gripping police thriller and extraordinary character study. In one of his most accomplished performances, Ford plays the odd man out on a force riddled with corruption who, in fleeing his pursuers, tumbles into the anachronistic Amish country. McGillis is very good as the Amish mother whose young son witnesses a murder. ★★★½ DVD Letterbox: $14.99, VHS: $9.99, VHS Letterbox: $9.99

The Witness

(1968, 108 min, Hungary, Pèter Bascó) After viewing this bitterly sarcastic satire of the chaotic and corrupt Communist government in Hungary, one is not only surprised that it was suppressed for 10 years, but that it was released at all during their reign. Set in 1949, the story revolves around Pelikan, a hapless party loyalist and a father of eight who is content with being a simple dike keeper. But after being caught by the authorities for illegally slaughtering a pig, he is immediately "rehabilitated" and promoted to jobs that he is totally unqualified for — from swimming pool manager, director of the Hungarian Orange Institute and even head of a socialist amusement park. A subversive little gem in the tradition of *1984* and *Brazil.* (Hungarian with English subtitles) ★★★ VHS: $59.99

Witness for the Prosecution

(1957, 106 min, US, Billy Wilder) *Charles Laughton, Marlene Dietrich, Tyrone Power, Elsa Lancaster, John Williams.* Based on the long-running Agatha Christie play, this proves to be an acting tour de force for all concerned. Dietrich is at her best as the wife of accused murderer Power. Laughton is brilliant as the defense attorney who agrees to take on the case, and Lancaster is his prohibitive nurse. To detail more of the plot would give it away. Suffice it to say that this is one whodunit that doesn't disappoint on any level. ★★★★ DVD Letterbox: $14.99

Wittgenstein

Witness to the Holocaust

(1987, 90 min, Israel, Lori Perlow) The 1961 trial of Adolf Eichmann, the SS Lieutenant-Colonel and Nazi expert of Jewish Affairs who headed the department that was responsible for the annihilation of European Jews is the subject in this penetrating documentary. Tried in Jerusalem and calling eyewitness accounts, Eichmann was found guilty of crimes against the Jewish people, crimes against humanity and of war crimes, and was executed in 1962. ★★★ VHS: $39.99

Wittgenstein

(1993, 75 min, GB, Derek Jarman) *Karl Johnson, Tilda Swinton.* Jarman's amusing, intellectual portrait of Austrian-born, British-educated philosopher Ludwig Wittgenstein is both a startling primer in low-budget filmmaking as well as a visually exuberant work. Considered one of the century's most influential philosophers, Wittgenstein's private and professional life is chronicled — from his prodigy childhood to his reluctant life as a professor at Cambridge. Jarman utilizes a pitch-black background, allowing the richly drawn, outrageously costumed characters and their witty, thought-provoking dialogue to take center stage. Johnson plays the eccentric philosopher, and Swinton is lavishly campy as Lady Ottoline. ★★★

The Wiz

(1978, 133 min, US, Sidney Lumet) *Diana Ross, Michael Jackson, Lena Horne, Richard Pryor, Mabel King, Ted Ross.* A modern updating of *The Wizard of Oz,* with Ross and Jackson heading an all-black cast. Based on the Tony Award-winning Broadway musical, we're invited to "ease on down the road" with Dorothy (Ross), whose Oz is downtown Manhattan. There are a couple of dazzling musical sequences, but Ross' lifeless portrayal fails to excite. King, singing "Don't You Bring Me No Bad News," and Ross, as the Cowardly Lion, steal the show ★★ DVD: $9.99, VHS: $9.99

The Wizard

(1989, 100 min, US, Todd Holland) *Fred Savage, Christian Slater, Beau Bridges.* Two brothers embark on a cross-country journey to attend a national video competition. A tedious road movie for kids which is as ill-conceived as it is trite. ★½

Wizard of Gore

(1970, 70 min, US, Hershell Gordon Lewis) *Ray Sager, Judy Cler, Wayne Ratay, Phil Laurenson.* Sager is Montag the Magician, a character whose monologues regarding man's fascination with the morbid seems to sum up director Lewis' own philosophies and motivations. With an incredible ending reminiscent of Buñuel. Has to be seen to be believed. ★ DVD: $24.99, VHS: $29.99

The Wizard of Loneliness

(1988, 111 min, US, Jenny Bowen) *Lukas Haas, Lea Thompson, John Randolph, Anne Pitoniak.* Young Haas (one of the most gifted child actors of the 1980s) is outstanding in this sensitive tale of a small boy who comes to live with his grandparents in New England during WWII. ★★½

The Wizard of Oz

(1925, 93 min, US, Larry Semon) *Larry Semon, Dorothy Dwan, Oliver Hardy.* A real treat for silent film fans or Oz fanatics. Now virtually forgotten, Semon was a popular comic in his day; here he plays the Scarecrow in an adaptation that owes more to Mack Sennett than L. Frank Baum. (Remade in 1939) ★★★ VHS: $24.99

The Wizard of Oz

(1939, 101 min, US, Victor Fleming) *Judy Garland, Frank Morgan, Ray Bolger, Jack Haley, Bert Lahr, Margaret Hamilton.* Follow the yellow brick road to the wonderful Wizard of Oz (a wiz of a wiz, if ever a wiz there was) and join Dorothy and all her friends in this immortal classic. Includes a behind-the-scenes documentary and footage of the cut musical sequence "Jitterbug." (Sequel: *Return to Oz*) (Remade as *The Wiz*) ★★★★ DVD: $19.99, VHS: $14.99

Wizards

(1977, 81 min, US, Ralph Bakshi) This sci-fi tale of a futuristic world mired in post-apocalyptic battles and neo-Hitlerian factions is imaginatively brought to the animated screen by Ralph Bakshi. ★★★ DVD: $14.99, VHS: $19.99

Wolf

(1994, 125 min, US, Mike Nichols) *Jack Nicholson, Michelle Pfeiffer, James Spader, Christopher Plummer, Kate Nelligan.* A mature tale of an underdog (Nicholson) who finally has his day when the bite of a wolf causes him to develop distinctly lupine properties. He soon rids himself of his cheating wife (Nelligan) and slimy best friend (Spader) and begins a steamy affair with an exquisitely icy "poor little rich girl" (Pfeiffer) just as a spate of gruesome killings befalls the city. Nicholson and Pfeiffer wear their roles like a pair of comfortable slippers, and Spader makes full use of his stock-in-trade creepiness. However, this is not the gorefest horror fans may be anticipating, and the dime-store special effects are bound to disappoint. ★★★ DVD: $14.99, VHS: $12.99

Wolf at the Door

(1987, 90 min, Denmark/France, Henning Carlsen) *Donald Sutherland, Jean Yanne, Max von Sydow.* Sutherland is Paul Gauguin, the French painter who rejected the art world and lifestyle of France at the height of his career to live simply and paint in Tahiti. After several years on the island, he visits Paris in 1893. The film is an in-depth study of the man as he spreads the word of Tahiti's beauty and raises money for his return. Sutherland's Gauguin is complex and contradictory. He is obnoxious, a bully, a misogynist, bombastic, loving to his dark-skinned favorites but cold and callous to his Scandinavian wife; but above all, a tortured and misunderstood artist. A superlative re-creation of the artist's character. (Filmed in English) ★★★

The Wolf Man

(1941, 70 min, US, George Waggner) *Lon Chaney, Jr., Claude Rains, Evelyn Ankers, Maria Ouspenskaya, Ralph Bellamy, Bela Lugosi.* Classic horror film with Chaney as the tormented Larry Talbot, man by day, but a wolf by night. More than just a damn good fright tale, *The Wolf Man* is very successful in presenting the moral conflict of a man confronted with his animal instincts. "Even the man who is pure in heart, and says his prayers by night/May become a wolf man when the wolfbane blooms, and the moon is full and bright." (Sequel: *Frankenstein Meets the Wolf Man*) ★★★½

Wolfen

(1981, 115 min, US, Michael Wadleigh) *Gregory Hines, Tom Noonan, Diane Venora, Edward James Olmos, Albert Finney.* When director Wadleigh, who hadn't done much since *Woodstock*, made this updated werewolf story, he concentrated on a stylish urban atmosphere of horror over the empty thrills of special effects. New York City detective Finney investigates a series of grisly and random murders being committed throughout the city. Hines is the eccentric coroner who helps him find out who and why. Though soon to be overused by others, Wadleigh brilliantly uses the recently developed stedi-cam to simulate the running wolves in a long, sinewy take. ★★★ DVD Letterbox: $19.99

A Woman at Her Window

(1977, 110 min, France, Pierre Granier-Deferre) *Romy Schneider, Philippe Noiret, Victor Lanoux.* Director Granier-Deferre collaborated with screenwriter Jorge Semprun (*Z*) to create this romantic drama set in the despotic era of Greece circa 1936. Schneider gives an outstanding performance as an aristocratic woman who pursues affairs with various noblemen while married to an Italian ambassador, who himself is involved in a series of affairs. Only when she harbors a political activist (Lanoux) and helps him escape does she becomes transformed, sacrificing wealth for true love. Told in a clever use of flashbacks, *A Woman at Her Window* is a convincing, engaging and well-made film. (French with English subtitles) ★★★ VHS: $29.99

A Woman at War

(1991, 115 min, GB, Edward Bennett) *Martha Plimpton, Eric Stoltz.* Based on the autobiography "Inside the Gestapo" by Helene Moszkiewicz, this moving story of individual courage takes place in Nazi-occupied Belgium. Plimpton gives a sturdy performance as Moszkiewicz who, upon the invasion of her country, joins the underground movement, changes her name, and infiltrates the Gestapo. Plimpton is commendable as the young Jewish woman who helps track down Jews by day and plays saboteur by night. This low-key film ably captures the dangerous tenor of the times, and manages to create a tension as to the heroine's fate even in the knowledge of the film's source. ★★★ VHS: $79.99

A Woman, Her Men and Her Futon

(1992, 90 min, US, Mussef Sibay) *Jennifer Rubin, Grant Show.* A low-keyed drama about the romantic exploits of a woman with two lovers too many. While not as provocative as its title implies, the film deserves kudos for its adult portrayal of a '90s woman who is sexual without being irresponsible. ★★ DVD: $9.99

A Woman in Flames

(1982, 106 min, West Germany, Robert van Ackeren) *Gudren Landgrebe, Robert Van Ackeren.* This volatile look at female sexuality, wish fulfillment and the obstacles hindering sexual equality became something of a *cause célèbre*. Its tone is peculiarly poised between social satire and razor-sharp melodrama. The plot reads like a supermarket tabloid, with a disgruntled bourgeois housewife who abandons her husband and studies to take up prostitution. ★★★

The Woman in Red

(1984, 87 min, US, Gene Wilder) *Gene Wilder, Gilda Radner, Charles Grodin, Joseph Bologna, Kelly LeBrock.* Occasionally amusing remake of the French romantic farce *Pardon Mon Affaire* with Wilder as a married man who falls for "the woman in red." ★★½ DVD Dual: $14.99

Woman in the Dunes

(1964, 123 min, Japan, Hiroshi Teshigahara) *Eiji Okada, Kuoko Kishida.* Kobo Abe's allegory of a man trapped with a strange woman in a sandpit is translated into a prize-winning work of art exploring the concepts of existence, freedom and eroticism. ★★★½ DVD: $29.99, VHS: $29.99

Woman in the Moon

(1929, 146 min, Germany, Fritz Lang) *Klaus Pohl, Willy Fritsch.* Lang's final silent film is a fascinating voyage of a group of people who are sent to the moon in search of gold, but find instead only greed and jealousy. The look of the rocket and other aspects of the science fiction film are amazing for the similarity to the real thing 40 years later. Not as accomplished as Lang's masterpiece, *Metropolis*, but nevertheless an enjoyable experience. ★★★

A Woman Is a Woman
(Une Femme est une Femme)

(1961, 84 min, France, Jean-Luc Godard) *Anna Karina, Jean-Claude Brialy, Jean-Paul Belmondo.* Godard's salute to the Hollywood musical is a giddy, improvisational romp up and down the boulevards of Paris. Karina stars as a bubbly, high-spirited striptease artist whose only desire is to have a child. Her boyfriend (Brialy), however, is preparing for an important bicycle race and doesn't wish to lose any "precious bodily fluids." So she turns to her lusting ex (Belmondo) who volunteers to do whatever he can. Godard infuses the proceedings with an uncharacteristic joyful humor making this by far his most lighthearted work. (French with English subtitles) ★★★ DVD Letterbox: $29.99

The Woman Next Door

(1981, 106 min, France, François Truffaut) *Gérard Depardieu, Fanny Ardant.* A dark, gripping melodrama with Depardieu and Ardant as a compulsive pair of ex-lovers, inadvertently reunited and driven to a tragic affair. (French with English subtitles) ★★★ DVD: $14.99, VHS: $14.99

A Woman of Affairs

(1928, 98 min, US, Clarence Brown) *Greta Garbo, John Gilbert, Douglas Fairbanks, Jr..* A compelling silent screen story starring a ravishing Garbo as an "unlucky-in-love" woman whose free-spirited lifestyle takes its toll. After losing the man of her dreams, she marries a man who shortly thereafter takes his own life. Then, Garbo embarks on a series of foreign affairs with globetrotting dignitaries. Finally, she is reunited with her true love years later, only to learn he is engaged to another woman. ★★★ VHS: $29.99

A Woman of Distinction

(1950, 85 min, US, Edward Buzzell) *Rosalind Russell, Ray Milland, Edmund Gwenn.* Campus hijinks '50s-style as professor Milland and college dean Russell are involved in a romantic scandal. The two stars are in good form and bring some spice to this pleasant comedy. ★★½

A Woman of Paris

(1921, 78 min, US, Charles Chaplin) *Adolphe Menjou, Edna Purviance.* Chaplin proved himself a master director in this, his only serious film in which he doesn't star (he only has a bit as a porter). An innocent country girl becomes an inamorata of a rich Parisian (Menjou, in the role that made him a star). Chaplin's tight narrative structure (rare in his own films) and the use of telling detail to delineate character and relationships was a revelation that inspired such directors as von Sternberg, von Stroheim, Lubitsch and others. ★★★½ VHS: $19.99

Woman of the Year

(1942, 112 min, US, George Stevens) *Katharine Hepburn, Spencer Tracy, Fay Bainter, Dan Tobin.* Tracy is a sports writer and Hepburn is a highly esteemed columnist in this top-notch battle-of-the-sexes comedy. The first pairing of Hepburn and Tracy, *Woman of the Year* displays the longtime screen duo's inimitable rapport. The great script was written by Ring Lardner, Jr. and Michael Kanin. (The basis for the Broadway musical) ★★★★ DVD: $19.99

Spencer Tracy and Katharine Hepburn match wits in *Woman of the Year*

Woman on Top

(2000, 91 min, US, Fina Torres) *Penélope Cruz, Murilo Benício, Harold Perrineau, Jr., Mark Feuerstein.* Light, easy on the palate but terribly insubstantial, the colorful *Woman on Top* attempts to mix the sensual culinary delights of *Like Water for Chocolate* with the fivolity of a Nora Ephron film. Needless to say, this could have used more time in the oven. The beautiful Cruz is a beguiling presence as Isabella, a Brazilian chef who discovers her handsome husband is cheating on her. She heads to San Francisco to reunite with her drag queen friend Monica (Perrineau), only to find fame and fortune as the host of a cooking show. Things heat up when Isabella's husband arrives to reconcile, only to find her producer also in romantic pursuit. Stretching the boundaries of magical illusion, the filmmakers seem content in trotting out romantic clichés and some questionable plot developments as Isabella casts her spell on one and all. ★★ DVD: $9.99, VHS: $6.99

Woman Times Seven

(1967, 99 min, US/Italy, Vittorio De Sica) *Shirley MacLaine, Vittorio Gassman, Michael Caine, Alan Arkin, Philippe Noiret, Peter Sellers, Anita Ekberg.* MacLaine mercilessly hams it up in this omnibus film which has her playing seven different, desirable women with seven different husbands and lovers in as many episodes. A light comic touch prevails throughout the film with some segments more successful than others. (Filmed in English) ★★½

A Woman under the Influence

(1974, 147 min, US, John Cassavetes) *Gena Rowlands, Peter Falk, Matthew Cassel.* The power of Cassavetes' films is that he strips away all the pretenses and protections we use to shield ourselves from our most frightening and shameful pain, and shoves our noses in it. Not too many actors can deliver that bare honesty; one of the few who does so without reservation is his wife Rowlands. She is mesmerizing as the working-class housewife who buckles under the strain of a limited existence, a brutish husband (Falk, in one of several strong collaborations with Caasavetes), insensitive relatives and an uncaring world. Rowlands is in turn heartbreaking, funny, delightful and frightening as a woman who is overwhelmed by a desperate inability to stay connected. ★★★½ DVD: $24.99, VHS: $14.99

A Woman without Love

(1951, 85 min, Mexico, Luis Buñuel) *Rosario Granados, Julio Villareal.* Director Buñuel's filmmaking career flourished during his self-imposed exile in Mexico, although most were simply potboilers for the domestic market, lacking in the director's trademark wry cinematic excesses. One of these, *A Woman without Love*, is a fiery soap opera about the barely supressed passions of hot-blooded Latins. A beautiful woman, locked in a loveless marriage with a middle-aged bourgeois, meets a handsome stranger. Their affair is short-lived but its memory is renewed 25 years later when her son receives an inheritance from a mysterious man. (Spanish with English subtitles) ★★½ VHS: $24.99

A Woman's Face

(1938, 104 min, Sweden, Gustaf Molander) *Ingrid Bergman.* Bergman plays against type in this dark melodrama about a disfigured woman who, disturbed by the happiness she will never know, blackmails illicit lovers. (Swedish with English subtitles) ★★½ VHS: $19.99

Robert Downey, Jr., Michael Douglas and Tobey Maguire in *Wonder Boys*

A Woman's Face

(1941, 105 min, US, George Cukor) *Joan Crawford, Melvyn Douglas, Conrad Veidt.* Crawford has a juicy role as an embittered, facially scarred woman whose personality changes when she undergoes plastic surgery. An interesting melodrama with many appealing moments. ★★★ VHS: $19.99

A Woman's Revenge

(1989, 133 min, France, Jacques Doillon) *Isabelle Huppert, Béatrice Dalle.* A puzzling love triangle gone sour proves to be the motivating force in this elegant, if long-winded drama of passion, seduction and female retribution. Dalle plays Suzi, a young beauty with a restless spirit who, a year after the death of her lover, meets up with his widow, Cecile (Huppert). Bitter at her husband's death and his unfaithfulness, Cecile seeks Suzi's companionship, but is her presence an offer of forgiveness and friendship or is there a darker, possibly treacherous motive? Freely adapted from Fyodor Dostoevsky's "The Eternal Husband," the film is a bit stage-bound and incessantly talky, but the soap opera-ish drama is filled with layers of revealing but conflicting revelations, accusations and intrigue. (French with English subtitles) ★★½ VHS: $59.99

A Woman's Tale

(1991, 93 min, Australia, Paul Cox) *Sheila Florance, Norman Kaye.* This delightful tale of aging is a life-affirming, realistic and often hilarious mini-masterpiece. Filmmaker Cox tailor-made this semiautobiographical story of a spirited modern woman of almost 80 years for acclaimed actress Florance. Her character, Martha, finding the world too cynical and heartless, refuses to accept society's constraints on her lifestyle and fights the establishment with compassion and humor. Her friends include her pets, a bed-ridden neighbor and even a local prostitute. Her sexuality is still important to her, and her frank talk is revealing, touching and hilarious. ★★★★

The Women

(1939, 133 min, US, George Cukor) *Norma Shearer, Joan Crawford, Rosalind Russell, Paulette Goddard, Joan Fontaine, Mary Boland, Marjorie Main, Lucile Watson, Butterfly McQueen.* Another in the long line of those great M-G-M all-star extravaganzas, this uproarious Cukor comedy (and cult favorite) more than lives up to its title: The cast is entirely female. Shearer heads the once-in-a-lifetime cast as Mary, a Manhattan socialite whose storybook existence is shattered when her husband leaves her for shopgirl Crawford. This puts Mary "on the road to Reno," where she meets a group of other divorce-bound women: worldly Boland, showgirl Goddard, and friends Fontaine and Russell (in a smashingly funny performance). Based on Claire Boothe's Broadway hit, this is about as funny as a film can get. (Remade as the 1956 musical *The Opposite Sex*) ★★★★ DVD: $19.99

Women from the Lake of Scented Souls

(1993, 106 min, China, Xie Fei) *Siqin Gaowa, Wu Yujuan.* History has a way of repeating itself, and so goes the plot as Xiang Ersao (Sigin), a determined and hard-working woman, is forced into marriage as a child to a sesame oil maker who knows nothing about business. Left to keep shop while her husband gets drunk with his friends, Ersao modernizes and increases business. While this adds to their position of power in the town, their epileptic son is too old to be single. Ersao decides to continue the cycle of arranged marriages by forcing a poorer family to promise their daughter to marry for payment of their debts. Bao Xianian's camera work is nowhere near as spectacular as some of the other films to come out of China recently, but there is a gritty realism to the film and good performances on par with the soap opera plot. (Mandarin with English subtitles) ★★½

Women in Love

(1970, 129 min, GB, Ken Russell) *Glenda Jackson, Jennie Linden, Oliver Reed, Alan Bates.* Russell's powerful rendition of the D.H. Lawrence classic centers on two Midlands sisters and the tempestuous relationships they form. Resolute Gudren (Jackson) becomes involved with the strong but boorish Gerald (Reed), while her romantically inclined sister Ursula (Linden) falls in love with the handsome but aloof Rupert (Bates). A masterful examination of sexual domination and repression, brilliantly portrayed by its cast — Jackson won an Oscar and international stardom for her gutsy, complex portrayal of Gudren. ★★★★ DVD: $19.99

Women on the Verge of a Nervous Breakdown

(1988, 88 min, Spain, Pedro Almodóvar) *Carmen Maura, Antonio Banderas, Julieta Serrano, Maria Barranco, Rossy De Palma.* Almodóvar's comic masterpiece is by far his most accessible film to date

W

and is largely responsible for familiarizing many American audiences with his unique talents. Based loosely on Jean Cocteau's "The Human Voice," the story follows Pepa — brilliantly portrayed by Maura — an actress whose life crumbles around her when she comes home one day to find her lover, Ivan, has left her. The ensuing hour-and-a-half turns into a hilarious comic romp as she tries to piece her life back together. Serrano is fabulous as Ivan's insane wife and Barranco is hysterical as Pepa's friend who is fleeing from Shiite terrorists. (Spanish with English subtitles) ★★★★ VHS Out of Print: $14.99

Wonder Boys

(2000, 112 min, US, Curtis Hanson) *Michael Douglas, Tobey Maguire, Frances McDormand, Robert Downey, Jr., Katie Holmes, Rip Torn, Richard Thomas, Philip Bosco.* One man's quest for personal redemption proves to be an unusually rewarding journey in the captivating dramatic comedy *Wonder Boys*, an intelligent, sardonic character study boasting a career performance by Douglas in the central role. Based on the novel by Michael Chabon, and brilliantly adapted by Steve Kloves, this wondrous mixture of satire and introspection takes place over the course of one weekend, but has all the wisdom and resource of a lifetime. Douglas is Professor Grady Tripp, whose life is in a bit of disarray. He hasn't finished a novel in seven years, his wife has just walked out on him, and the married woman with whom he's involved is pregnant. When his editor arrives expecting a finished work, it sets in motion a series of comic escapades that are ripe with the seeds of self-discovery. Douglas is a marvel as the disheveled Tripp, whose world-weariness and humor the actor wears like a glove. Douglas has never opened himself up to such an extent, and gives a mature, exciting performance. The ensemble cast is equally extraordinary. A dazzling entertainment. ★★★★ DVD: $14.99, VHS: $14.99

Wonder Man

(1945, 98 min, US, Bruce Humberstone) *Danny Kaye, Virginia Mayo, Vera-Ellen, S.Z. Sakall.* Kaye has a field day with this bright comic romp playing twins. When one brother, an outgoing and brash entertainer, is murdered, his ghost convinces his introverted sibling to impersonate him and find out who did the dastardly deed. Kaye has some wonderful bits, and is ably supported by a great supporting cast. ★★★

The Wonderful, Horrible Life of Leni Riefenstahl

(1993, 192 min, Germany, Ray Müller) It may never be possible to judge German director Leni Riefenstahl's cinematic accomplishments without regard to their historical context. Her 1932 film, *Blue Light*, in which she produced, directed and starred, captured Hitler's attention with its Wagnerian mysticism and haunting imagery. She was a trailblazer, one of the few women directors of the time. In this meticulously researched biography, replete with archival footage intercut with clips from her films, Riefenstahl maintains that she was politically ignorant and unaware of Hitler's ultimate intentions. Cantankerous and forceful at 90 years of age, she fervently denies references to close personal ties to Hitler and Goebbels; refutes speculation that she staged much of the spectacle in *Triumph of the Will*; and maintains that her interest was solely in the craft of filmmaking. This fascinating documentary allows her to speak freely, alternating between words and images. ★★★★ DVD: $29.99, VHS: $39.99

The Wonderful World of the Brothers Grimm

(1962, 129 min, US, George Pal & Henry Levin) *Laurence Harvey, Karl-Heinz Boehm, Claire Bloom, Terry-Thomas, Buddy Hackett.* Lavishly produced children's tale, featuring excerpts from brothers Jacob and Wilhelm Grimm's best-loved fairy tales, and taking a look at their lives. ★★★ VHS: $19.99

Wonderland

(1989, 103 min, GB, Philip Saville) *Emile Charles, Tony Forsyth, Robert Stephens, Robbie Coltrane.* This intriguing British thriller delves into an often overlooked subculture: gay youth. *Wonderland* is the story of the friendship between two gay teenagers from Liverpool who are forced to flee the city when they witness a gangland slaying at a local gay bar. Taking refuge at the home of a manipulative wealthy couple in Brighton, the boys' idyllic existence of freedom and safety is shattered when they meet the killers in a deadly confrontation. Both Charles as the dolphin-loving, soft-hearted Eddie and Forsyth as the street-wise, caring hustler Michael are excellent as the youths. (aka: *The Fruit Machine*) ★★★

Wonderland

(2000, 109 min, GB, Michael Winterbottom) *Ian Hart, Shirley Henderson, Kika Markham, Gina McKee, Molly Parker.* In this affecting drama, director Winterbottom apes the hand-held immediacy of Mike Leigh and John Cassavettes, but he manages to put a personal touch on the film, as well, to great success. The lives of three sisters and their parents are examined in intertwining stories, with emotions running the gamut from joy to depression, rage to quiet acceptance. A nice, if slightly overdone score complements the superb acting and camerawork to produce a richly involving film, culminating in a surprisingly satisfying (under the circumstances) ending. *Wonderland* is Winterbottom's best film to date, and despite its superficial resemblance to several recent British releases, is an original, heartfelt work. ★★★½ DVD: $24.99, VHS: $14.99

The Wood

(1999, 106 min, US, Rick Famuyiwa) *Taye Diggs, Omar Epps, Richard T. Jones, Sean Nelson, Malinda Williams.* A sweet and sometimes raunchy comedy by writer-director Famuyiwa, *The Wood* is two movies in one. In the contemporary story, Roland (Diggs) is getting cold feet on his wedding day. His two best friends Mike (Epps) and Slim (Jones) try to keep him focused, but, of course, chaos ensues. The other story involves the flashbacks to these three friends growing up in Englewood (the Wood). These scenes, set in the 1980s, form the better part of the film, especially in the sensitive moments in which young Mike (Nelson) tries to woo Alicia (Williams). While there are a few missteps (most notably a scene in which a convenience store is robbed), the bond between the trio of friends is solid. If viewers can overlook the many sophomoric moments, *The Wood* is pretty good. ★★★ DVD: $14.99, VHS: $9.99

The Wooden Gun

(1979, 91 min, Israel, Ilan Moshenson) Set in the tense atmosphere of 1950s Tel Aviv, this incisive film focuses on two rival groups of pre-teens whose behavior, motivated by their interpretations of the concepts of heroism, nationalism and friendship, raises hard questions. Portrayed are first-generation sabras (native-born Israelis), who are separated by a tremendous psychological gap from those who came to Israel from Europe, many of them Holocaust survivors. (Hebrew with English subtitles) ★★★ VHS: $79.99

The Wooden Man's Bride

(1995, 114 min, China, Huang Jianxin) *Chang Shih, Wang Lan, Ku Paoming, Wang Yumei.* Director Huang has created an entertaining, if fallacious, parable wherein repressive tradition is bested by noble peasant "outlaws." When the arranged marriage to an aristocrat comes undone by his untimely death, a beautiful innocent (Wang) is left with the prospect of an even more empty alliance: custom dictates she marry his proxy, a carved wooden effigy, and her scheming mother-in-law (Wang) is intent on upholding tradition. While *The Wooden Man's Bride* features the lush visual style of *Raise the Red Lantern* and *Shanghai Triad*, in its heart it is reactionary, its mind full of simplistic syllogisms. (Mandarin with English subtitles) ★★½ DVD: $24.99, VHS: $19.99

Woodstock

(1969, 225 min, US, Michael Wadleigh) It's been 35 years since the monumental rock festival which served as a gleaming triumph for the counterculture, and a fitting capsulization of the spirit of a decade. An unbelievable roster of performers includes Jimi Hendrix; The Who; Crosby, Stills, Nash and Young; and The Jefferson Airplane (bless their pointed little heads). This is the director's cut with 40 minutes of additional footage not in the theatrical release. (Sequel: *Woodstock '94*) ★★★½ DVD: $19.99, VHS Widescreen Director's Cut: $19.99

Working

(1982, 90 min, US, Kirk Browning & Stephen Schwartz) *Studs Terkel, Barry Bostwick, Rita Moreno, James Taylor, Eileen Brennan, Charles Durning, Barbara Hershey, Patti LaBelle, Scatman Crothers.* Based on the Broadway show, itself based on the Studs Terkel book, this folksy, consistently charming musical is a loving tribute to the working men and women across America. From a series of interviews with construction workers, waitresses, firemen, parking attendants, secretaries, truck drivers, cleaning women and even prostitutes, Terkel (who also narrates) explores the individual work ethic. These are balanced with jubilant songs that celebrate the workplace, the worker, and life itself. Score by Stephen Schwartz ("Pippin," "Godspell"). ★★★½ DVD: $24.99, VHS: $29.99

Working Girl

(1988, 113 min, US, Mike Nichols) *Melanie Griffith, Harrison Ford, Sigourney Weaver, Joan Cusack, Alec Baldwin, Philip Bosco, Kevin Spacey.* Griffith gives an enchanting performance in this "Cinderella" comedy set against the wheeling and dealing of Wall Street. Griffith plays a secretary who masquerades as her absentee boss (Weaver) when her employer steals a business idea from her. Part social satire, part love story, the film traces Griffith's successful business charade and her romance with a handsome associate (a restrained Ford). ★★★ DVD: $14.99

Working Girls

(1986, 90 min, US, Lizzie Borden) *Amanda Goodwin, Louise Smith.* In cinematic terms, the prostitute is usually portrayed either as a statuesque, high-priced call girl or as a drug-snorting, underaged, runaway streetwalker. *Working Girls*, on the other hand, is a wryly comical and non-judgmental tale about another, less melodramatic side of the "sex-for-sale" business. Feminist filmmaker Borden tells the story of a middle-class brothel nestled in a Manhattan high-rise. Essentially, the film is a day in the life of the shrewish madam and her "girls" as seen through the eyes of Molly, a young woman who, while ambivalent about her work, is nonetheless happy not to be working 9 to 5. ★★★ DVD: $24.99, VHS: $14.99

The World According to Garp

(1982, 136 min, US, George Roy Hill) *Robin Williams, Mary Beth Hurt, Glenn Close, John Lithgow, Hume Cronyn, Jessica Tandy, Amanda Plummer, Swoosie Kurtz, Jenny Wright.* Williams is the eponymous T.S. Garp in Hill's terrific adaptation of the wild and wooly John Irving best-seller. Close is marvelously funny as Garp's stringent celebrity mom, as is Lithgow as the transsexual, ex-Eagles tight end. ★★★½ DVD: $19.99, VHS: $9.99

A World Apart

(1988, 113 min, GB, Chris Menges) *Jodhi May, Barbara Hershey, Linda Mvusi, Jeroen Krabbé, Tim Roth.* Menges' emotionally charged look at Apartheid, political commitment and familial ties, as seen through the eyes of a 13-year-old white girl living in early 1960s South Africa. May gives a truly remarkable performance as the young girl who witnesses the gradual disintegration of her family when her mother, an anti-Apartheid activist, becomes a target of the South African government. Though the events are seen through the eyes of whites and not the real victims, the blacks themselves, it does not handicap the film; either in its excellence as a production or in the emergency of its issues. As the mother whose political conviction threatens personal well-being, Hershey is outstanding; and Mvusi is exceptional as the family's black maid. ★★★½

The World Is Not Enough

(1999, 128 min, GB, Michael Apted) *Pierce Brosnan, Sophie Marceau, Robert Carlyle, Denise Richards, Robbie Coltrane, Judi Dench, Desmond Llewelyn, John Cleese, Michael Kitchen.* Brosnan appears for the third time as super agent James Bond in this technically proficient though overly familiar espionage adventure. 007 goes up against a less formidable opponent in Carlyle's mangy terrorist, whose plans to manipulate world oil comes under attack by Bond and physicist Richards (oh, come on!) when James investigates the death of a Swiss banker. Dench plays a larger role as M, and this marks Llewelyn's last appearance as gadget-man Q. A speedboat chase down the Thames and an exciting ride through an oil pipeline highlight the action scenes, though this is just a wee bit too talky to rate as one of the better Bonds. (Sequel: *Die Another Day*) ★★½ VHS: $9.99

The World of Apu

(1959, 103 min, India, Satyajit Ray) *Soumitra Chatterjee, Sharmila Tagore.* This third segment of the famed Apu Trilogy is considered the masterpiece of the series. Apu unexpectedly marries the cousin of a friend and, after a brief idyllic marriage, is thrown into great despair when his young wife dies during childbirth. A long period of spiritual regeneration is consummated when Apu is reunited with his son five years later. The Apu Trilogy is considered one of the richest humanistic statements ever committed to film. (Bengali with English subtitles) ★★★★ DVD: $29.99, VHS: $19.99

The World of Henry Orient

(1964, 106 min, US, George Roy Hill) *Peter Sellers, Tippy Walker, Angela Lansbury, Tom Bosley, Paula Prentiss.* One of Sellers' most hilarious performances highlights this unsung comedy gem. He's a lady-killing, playboy concert pianist whose life is made miserable by the "adoration" of two pesky teenage girls. The girls' relationship and disparate social standings are at the base of this wonderful, poignant study of adolescence. ★★★½ DVD Dual: $19.99

A World of Strangers

(1962, 89 min, Denmark, Henning Carlsen) From Nobel Prize-winning author Nadine Gordimer comes this impassioned drama that exposes the hidden face of Apartheid. Shot in deep secrecy in South Africa because of its controversial political stance, the film focuses on an open-minded young Englishman, recently transferred to Johannesburg by a publishing company, who soon makes friends with both blacks and whites. But after witnessing the everyday brutality of the whites to the black Africans, he finds himself forced to take a stand. The film conveys eloquent insights into the harsh reality of an oppressive society based on racial separation and the conclusion that no one can remain neutral. ★★★ VHS: $59.99

The Worst Boy in Town

(1989, 60 min, Mexico, Enrique Gomez Vadillo) *Raul Buefil.* If this film received the exploitation treatment made famous by Roger Corman, the advertising angle might be something like, "Pepe — marauding macho thug by day ... coquettish transvestite whore by night!" Set in the slums of Mexico City, the film features Mexican TV star Buefil as the roughish Pepe, the leader of a gang of hunky thugs who spend their days playing pool, intimidating the neighbors and harassing young girls. But there is more to Pepe than his beefy body, tight pants and macho exterior . . . for, after the sun sets, he dons makeup, a wig and a sexy dress and visits the local transvestite bar, and in "her" new kittenish persona, looks for a good strong man who can give him a good . . . ! Not to be confused with great art, this entertaining melodrama is nonetheless fun. (Spanish with English subtitles) ★★½

Worth Winning

(1989, 103 min, US, Will MacKenzie) *Mark Harmon, Leslie Ann Warren, Madeleine Stowe, Maria Holvoe.* A handsome TV weatherman (Harmon) takes a bet challenging him to get engaged to three women in three months. Warren, Stowe and Holvoe are the prospective betrothed. Not very appealing, either comedically or story wise, but the cast does seem to be trying their best. ★★ VHS: $19.99

The Would-Be Gentleman

(1959, 111 min, France, Jean Meyer) The comic artistry of Jean-Baptiste Moliere is brought to the screen by Paris' renouned Comedie Francaise. Always eager to please his sovereign, Louis XIV, Moliere lambastes the rising bourgeoisie in this hilarious drawing room farce. The script bares its teeth on an idiotic member of the nouveau riche who bumbles and fumbles his way through a series of lessons as he vainly tries to educate himself to the level of the gentry. (French with English subtitles) ★★★

The Wounds (Rane)

(1998, 103 min, Srdjan Dragojevic) *Dusan Pekic, Milan Maric.* Two aimless sixteen-year-old pals in war-torn Serbia hook up with a local crime boss and eventually take over. They become locally famous after appearing on a popular TV show which spotlights criminals and "war heroes," and begin committing crimes specifically for the show's host. This obvious satire begins well and has some good moments, but soon gets less interesting (and more unpleasant and nihilistic) as it goes. *The Wounds* offers a peek or two into Serbia's hellish atmosphere in the early '90s, but by the end, the film resembles nothing so much as a typical, violent "hood" film with a foreign accent. (Serbo-Croatian with English subtitles) ★★ DVD: $29.99, VHS: $24.99

Woyzeck

(1979, 80 min, Germany, Werner Herzog) *Klaus Kinski, Eva Mattes.* Kinski gives a harrowing and unforgettable performance as a dim-witted but well-intentioned army private who is pushed over the edge of sanity by his common-law wife (Mattes) and a ruthless society. Herzog delivers a chilling and devastating parable of social repression and dormant rebellion. The film is adapted from scenes of a Georg Büchner play written in 1837, which was left unfinished after the death of the author at 23. (Remade in 1994) (German with English subtitles) ★★★ DVD: $29.99, VHS: $14.99

WR: Mysteries of the Organism

(1971, 86 min, Yugoslavia, Dusan Makavejev) *Milena Dravic, Jagoda Kaloper.* This strikingly original film by Makavejev, the bad boy of Yugoslavian cinema, is a clever, amusing and, at times, exasperating political satire which quite seriously proposes sex as an ideological imperative for liberation: a plea for Erotic Socialism. Using a montage method of filming, Makavejev examines the theories of sexologist Wilhelm Reich and juxtaposes documentary footage of Reich's disciples with two fictional stories — scenarios that propose a link between sexual energy and political liberation and repression with Stalinism. A breakthrough film which encapsulates the political and sexual revolution of its era. (Serbo-Croatian with English subtitles) ★★★½ VHS: $24.99

The Wraith

(1986, 92 min, US, Mike Marvin) *Charlie Sheen, Nick Cassavetes, Randy Quaid, Sherilyn Fenn.* Out-of-its-mind horror film about an out-of-this-world entity challenging a menacing Arizona hot rod gang to the death. ★

The Wreck of the Mary Deare

(1959, 100 min, US/GB, Michael Anderson) *Gary Cooper, Charlton Heston, Michael Redgrave, Alexander Knox, Richard Harris.* There's a good amount of suspense to this straightforward but nevertheless involving maritime adventure. Heston plays a salvager who happens upon a derelict ship, the Mary Deare. However, when he boards it, he discovers it is not abandoned: Captain Cooper is still on board. And he refuses to reveal the secret as to what actually happened. The film tries to maintain tension throughout as to whether Cooper is innocent or guilty of grounding the ship; it's much more successful as to why, not who. Good scenic design and special effects. ★★½

Wrestling Ernest Hemingway

(1993, 123 min, US, Randa Haines) *Richard Harris, Robert Duvall, Shirley MacLaine, Sandra Bullock.* The teaming of Harris and Duvall propels this somber but involving character study which is as alluring as it is tedious. Harris plays a 70-ish old salt who when not boasting of the titular bout is drunk in self-pity. Duvall is a Cuban ex-barber, whose life seems to revolve around the crush he has on a young waitress (Bullock). The story takes off when the two men befriend each other; predictably, each brings some sort of meaning to the other's life. There are some poignant moments, but the film is sabotaged by a humorless screenplay, which only accentuates the dreariness of these men's lives. Duvall, accent and all, is fascinating to watch. ★★½ VHS: $14.99

Written on the Wind

(1956, 99 min, US, Douglas Sirk) *Lauren Bacall, Rock Hudson, Robert Stack, Dorothy Malone.* Sirk's classic melodrama about the fall of an oil tycoon's family enjoyed a successful rerelease after a 20-year theatrical absence. Filmed in lurid color and acted in a heightened and exaggerated style, we watch the self-destructive antics of the Hadley children. The son (Stack) is a lush and his sister (Malone, in an Oscar-winning performance) is a nymphomaniac. Add "good girl" Bacall and Hudson and you get a continually enjoyable potboiler in the great 1950s Hollywood tradition. ★★★½ DVD Criterion Collection: $29.99

The Wrong Arm of the Law

(1962, 94 min, GB, Cliff Owen) *Peter Sellers, Lionel Jeffries, Nanette Newman, Bernard Cribbins.* Sellers excels in this comedy caper as Pearly Gates, a Cockney criminal mastermind whose recent scores are being hijacked by an Australian gang posing as cops. ★★★

The Wrong Box

(1966, 105 min, GB, Bryan Forbes) *Peter Sellers, Michael Caine, John Mills, Ralph Richardson, Peter Cook, Dudley Moore.* This beguiling farce is a sterling example of the great British comedies of the '60s. Based on a story coauthored by Robert Louis Stevenson, this merry romp concerns itself with an up-for-grabs inheritance and a migratory cadaver. The comedy is utter nonsense, a precursor to Monty Python, presented with superb precision and vigor by an all-star cast. ★★★½ VHS: $59.99

Wrong Is Right

(1982, 117 min, US, Richard Brooks) *Sean Connery, George Grizzard, Robert Conrad, Katharine Ross.* Fans of Connery should not miss this amusing, fast-paced story in which he plays a Scottish version of Geraldo Rivera: a superstar TV reporter whose deep involvement with his stories puts him in the middle of a violent U.S. government-hatched intrigue. The film's convoluted story, about our TV-dominated culture as well as a pre-Grenada lament on the impotency of America's strength, has some holes, but Connery is great in this breakneck action-comedy. ★★★ DVD: $24.99, VHS: $79.99

The Wrong Man

(1956, 105 min, US, Alfred Hitchcock) *Henry Fonda, Vera Miles, Anthony Quayle.* An unusual departure for Hitchcock, this semidocumentary focuses on a New York musician (Fonda) who is mistakenly arrested for a flurry of robberies. Based on a true story, this is a frightening glimpse at the rites of police and legal procedure and the ensuing dehumanization of imprisonment. Miles portrays the man's wife, broken by the shattering chain of misfortune. ★★★½

The Wrong Move

(1975, 103 min, West Germany, Wim Wenders) *Rudiger Vogler, Nastassja Kinski, Hanna Schygulla.* A young writer sets out from home to roam the country for adventure and inspiration. Along the way he meets an old singer and his mute companion, a juggler (14-year-old Kinski) and an actress

Kevin Costner (l.) and Gene Hackman in Lawrence Kasdan's *Wyatt Earp*

(Schygulla). They all join together in this stimulating journey through Germany. (German with English subtitles) ★★★

Wrong Turn

(2003, 95 min, US, Rob Schmidt) *Eliza Dushku, Jeremy Sisto, Desmond Harrington.* A group of nubiles are chased through the woods by a family of inbred cannibal hillbillies. This well-worn premise is ill-served here; while it's refreshing to see a modern horror film that is nearly free of self-reflexivity and dumb, safe jokes (there is one lamentable *Deliverance* reference, alas), *Wrong Turn* is still rather juvenile, silly and just not scary. Aside from one nifty shock, this is just a bunch of stupid kids running screaming through a forest for almost ninety minutes. Forget *Deliverance* and *Texas Chainsaw* comparisons; this can't hold a candle to nearly forgotten '80s cannibal-hillbilly cheesefests like *Final Terror* and *Just Before Dawn*. At least they had some kick to them. ★½ DVD Dual: $19.99

Wrongfully Accused

(1998, 85 min, US, Pat Proft) *Leslie Nielsen, Richard Crenna, Kelly Le Brock, Michael York, Sandra Bernhard.* Too little too late, *Wrongfully Accused* is a lightweight, amusing spoof which has some hilarious moments to offer but is sadly a reminder of better times of a comic genre which is slowly fizzling out. With *The Fugitive* as its main target, this genial parody has a spry Nielsen as Ryan Harrison, a concert violinist (that's funny in itself) who's framed for the murder of a tycoon (York). Found incredibly guilty, he escapes en route to prison thanks to a train accident (sound familiar?). They milk this for all it's worth. On the run (and trying to hide out in his yellow prison uniform in one of the film's best sight gags), Harrison is dogged by the persistent Lt. Fergus Falls (Crenna). As would be expected, Nielsen is game for almost any joke, and credit must go to this tireless actor for not only his good humor but his zeal as well. ★★½ DVD: $14.99, VHS: $9.99

Wuthering Heights

(1939, 103 min, US, William Wyler) *Laurence Olivier, Merle Oberon, Geraldine Fizgerald, David Niven.* Wyler's beautiful, haunting adaptation of the Emily Brontë novel of doomed love in pre-Victorian England. Olivier is the brooding Heathcliff and Oberon is his undying love Kathy. Have extra tissues on hand for this classic tearjerker. ★★★★

Wuthering Heights

(1953, 90 min, Mexico, Luis Buñuel) *Iraseme Dilian, Jorge Mistral, Lilia Prado, Ernesto Alonso.* Based on the Emily Brontë classic, Buñuel's Mexican potboiler is a steamy, characteristically sinister statement on obsessive love and lethal lust. Removed from the blustery Yorkshire shores to a dusty, sunbaked landscape, the film has an even greater sense of desperation. Alejandro (the film's Heathcliff) is a coiled serpent, dashing and deadly, who returns to his childhood home determined to reclaim the affections of his longtime love, Catalina. When she remains faithful to her husband, Alejandro spitefully marries her sister. Passions flair and defenses crumble in the final confrontation at Catalina's deathbed. (Spanish with English subtitles) ★★★

Wuthering Heights

(1970, 105 min, GB, Robert Fuest) *Timothy Dalton, Anna Calder-Marchall, Harry Andrews.* A well-made, atmospheric and romantic version of the Emily Brontë classic of doomed love in pre-Victorian England. Dalton makes a dashing Heathcliff. Of course, it doesn't compare to the 1939 Olivier-Oberon version, but what could? ★★★ DVD Dual: $14.99

Wuthering Heights

See: *Emily Brontë's Wuthering Heights*

Wyatt Earp

(1994, 190 min, US, Lawrence Kasdan) *Kevin Costner, Gene Hackman, Michael Madsen, Bill Pullman, Dennis Quaid, Isabella Rossellini, JoBeth Williams.* The curious real-life relationship between no-nonsense lawman Wyatt Earp (Costner) and tubercular cardshark Doc Holliday (Quaid) translates into an engrossing cinematic experience. Quaid's performance as the morally precarious, deathly ill and completely ironic Holliday is inspired and plays perfectly against Costner's dead-pan, straightlaced Earp. Unfortunately, the Earp/Holliday relationship takes up only a quarter of the film which devotes too much time to the admittedly picturesque vistas of the American West and to Costner's steely stares. A talented roster of actors deliver first-rate performances but none are able to sufficiently expand upon their less than delineated characters. ★★★ DVD Letterbox 2-disc Special Edition: $26.99, VHS: $8.99, VHS Letterbox Expanded Edition: $8.99

The X-Files: The Movie

(1998, 121 min, US, Rob Bowman) *David Duchovny, Gillian Anderson, Martin Landau, Blythe Danner, Armin Mueller-Stahl.* If you're not already conversant with the mythology of the popular sci-fi TV series, this film version nevertheless stands on its own as a marvelously crafted evocation of conspiracy theory and mistrust of government; simultaneously, it is a perfect keystone for the TV series. Events which transpired in prehistory are uncovered in present-day Texas, initiating a new phase of a cover-up of unimaginable proportions. A building with government offices is demolished in an apparent act of terrorism. The bodies of three firemen and a small boy are discovered; but did they die in the blast? Agents Mulder (Duchovny) and Scully (Anderson), part of an FBI team sent in by a warning phone call, barely escape the massive destruction. The swiftly paced story line unfolds without stinting on personal elements of characterization. ★★★ DVD Letterbox: $14.99, VHS: $9.99, VHS Letterbox: $24.99

X-Men

(2000, 104 min, US, Bryan Singer) *Patrick Stewart, Hugh Jackman, Ian McKellen, Halle Berry, Famke Janssen, Anna Paquin, Bruce Davison, James Marsden, Rebecca Romijn-Stamos.* Welcome to Mutant High! Or at least, that's what part of this action-packed comic book romp resembles. In this snappily produced live-action cartoon based on the Marvel Comics series, Stewart and McKellen are, respectively, Professor X and Magneto, arch enemies in the world of the Mutants. While Professor X runs a school for mutants where he trains these young evolutionary misfits, Magneto lurks in dark caves and plots to lay waste to the non-mutant world. Into the fray comes Paquin, a young woman who has no idea what's wrong with her (anyone she touches goes into a coma) and who has latched onto the irascible Wolverine (Jackman). Together, they find themselves at Professor X's private academy where the X-Men attempt to convert them to good. Will they join in time to stop Magneto's dastardly plot, or

will Magneto win their allegiance and put an end to the X-Men forever? It's all good, old-fashioned fun with the two titans of British acting (Stewart and McKellen) nicely paired off. (Sequel: *X2: X-Men United*) ★★★ DVD Letterbox X-Men 1.5 Collector's Edition: $26.99, VHS: $9.99

X2: X-Men United

(2003, 135 min, US, Bryan Singer) *Patrick Stewart, Hugh Jackman, Ian McKellen, Halle Berry, Famke Janssen, James Marsden, Rebecca Romijn-Stamos, Brian Cox, Alan Cumming, Bruce Davison, Anna Paquin.* With no fewer than fifteen major characters, the *X-Men* sequel *X2* is almost too much of a good thing. It features mutants who can stop time, walk through walls, freeze anything and manipulate fire, though the coolest creation is still Wolverine (Jackman), the sideburned manimal with knives for claws. A roller-coaster ride with great effects, this outing pits the mutant force against a mad scientist (Cox) who wants to kill all the mutants through mind control. It requires a unified effort on the part of the mutants, even relying on the evil Magneto (McKellen), whose jailbreak comes just in time. There aren't many individual showdowns like in the first film, but the action is nonstop and the film features terrific production design. A new addition, the teleporting Nightcrawler (Cumming), a German vampyr with some amusing issues regarding faith, is quite welcome. But it's still Jackman's show. *X2* is a feast for the eyes. ★★★ DVD Letterbox: $19.99, DVD Pan & Scan: $19.99, VHS: $22.99

Xanadu

(1980, 88 min, US, Robert Greenwald) *Olivia Newton-John, Gene Kelly, Michael Beck, Ren Woods, Sandahl Bergman, Matt Lattanzi.* A campy guilty pleasure, this quintessential 1980s "disco musical" was a box-office flop and despised by critics everywhere. True, the story of a muse (Newton-John) who comes to life to inspire a young artist (Beck) is loaded with sappy and sometimes silly plot developments, and director Greenwald, while possessing a talent for visuals, hasn't an idea about narrative. But for those willing to bask in its unpretentious and curiously effective fantasy elements and musical numbers, *Xanadu* is a disco-thumping, roller-boogeyin' lark. The good score helps. Kelly, in his final dramatic role (if you can call it dramatic), appears as sort of a wise sage who opens a dance hall and gets to perform a dance or two. ★★½ DVD: $14.99

Xica

(1976, 107 min, Brazil, Carlos Diegues) *Zeze Motta.* Diegues' exuberant historical comedy is based on the tale of a voluptuous black slave who single-handedly wrapped an 18th-century Brazilian village around her finger by conquering its wealthy diamond contractor with her sexual prowess. As she exploits her newfound powers, the townspeople become increasingly enraged at her extravagances and whimsical self-indulgence prompting them to call for a governmental investigator. Motta stars as the devil-may-care Xica, whose sexual bravado and powerful flamboyance captivates men and usurps their authority. The film sparkles with humor while touching on the subject of freedom, the spirit to survive and individual revolution. (Spanish with English subtitles) ★★★ VHS: $29.99

Xiu Xiu: The Sent Down Girl

(1999, 100 min, China, Joan Chen) *Lu Lu, Lopsang.* Director Chen is at this writing banned from her native China for her film, *Xiu Xiu: The Sent Down Girl*, which she filmed without government sanction in remote corners of the harshly beautiful countryside, smuggling the footage out of the country to avoid censorship. During China's Cultural Revolution, members of the professional and intellectual classes were removed from their urban homes and shipped to distant rural areas for political reeducation. Xiu Xiu is 15 years old when she is issued an army coat ten sizes too large for her and herded into military transport. Lost in a massive bureaucracy, subject to impersonal cruelty and casual malice, she is given arbitrary assignments by small men with too much power. The natural tendency to melodrama inherent in the story — which reflects millions of true stories — is ameliorated by the caliber of the performances, especially those of the two principle characters. A thoughtful and thought-provoking film. (Mandarin with English subtitles) ★★★

XX/XY

(2002, 91 min, US, Austin Chick) *Mark Ruffalo, Kathleen Robertson, Maya Stange, Petra Wright.* Talky, frustratingly uneven sexual drama about what happens after an aspiring filmmaker (Ruffalo, looking eerily like the love child of Freddy Mercury and Vincent D'Onofrio) convinces two college coed best friends (Robertson and Stange) to have a reckless threesome. Complications develop when he falls deeper for one but tries to maintain an uneasy relationship with the other. Ten years later, they reconnect and must confront all the unresolved sexual tension still tearing them apart. Earnest performances and an unconventional character dynamic help compensate for bland characters, some pedestrian plot twists and a pervasive sense that the script's view of progressive urban relationships isn't nearly as sharp as it the filmmakers think it is. ★★½ DVD: $14.99, VHS: $39.99

xXx

(2002, 124 min, US, Rob Cohen) *Vin Diesel, Asia Argento, Samuel L. Jackson, Marton Csokas, Danny Trejo.* Celebrated, uber-hyped Diesel plays the heir apparent to James Bond in this weak, smug, disappointing action film as an extreme sports star who is called upon by his government to become a secret agent. His skills come into play when he motorcycles, snowboards (outrunning an avalanche) and mumbles his way out of danger at every turn. This should have been good, stupid fun, despite (even because of) its truly idiotic premise. But *xXx* is strictly for 13-year-old boys — exemplified by Diesel's scolding of a bad-shot cop: "Quit thinking police, and

The X-Files: The Movie

Hugh Jackman is Wolverine in *X-Men*

start thinking Playstation." (The Care Bears movies had more respect for their intended audience.) Diesel and Cohen's previous collaboration, *The Fast and the Furious*, managed to entertain the 13-year-old in most of us by displaying macho guys, cool cars and hot chicks with a knowing wink and a boatload of energy. Sadly, *xXx* is slow, with action scenes that are rote and unimaginative, despite their ridiculous excesses. ★½ DVD Letterbox: $19.99, DVD Pan & Scan: $19.99, VHS: $14.99

Y Tu Mamá También

(2001, 105 min, Mexico, Alfonso Cuaron) *Maribel Verdú, Gael Garcia Bernal, Diego Luna, Carlos Remolina.* Tenoch and Julio, relatively well-off Mexico City teenagers and best friends, are living quite the carefree life with their girlfriends out of the country: smoking dope, mooching drinks at political functions, and masturbating the summer away. On a lark, they invite the beautiful, more mature Maribel on a road trip to a secret beach that doesn't exist; when she surprisingly accepts, they set off on a road trip that will allow her to experience a life free of her infidelitous husband, while the boys naturally take turns trying to get into her pants. It has all the trappings of a teen comedy (and comes complete with profane humor and a requisite semen shot), but this intimately insightful film shows much deeper, especially into the strains that sexuality places on friends who share everything. Bernal and Luna are so relaxed and uninhibited in their roles, that their bond becomes palpable. Cuarón paints a vivid portrait of Mexico: its volatile mix of military muscle, new development, and near-poverty affects our travellers at each step. This is a world rarely shown in America: not only the real Mexico, but the uncensored lives of teenagers and a twentysomething woman, each experiencing pain and comedy alike with compelling honesty. (Spanish with English subtitles) ★★★★ DVD Letterbox Uncut, unrated theatrical version: $14.99

Yaaba (Grandmother)

(1989, 90 min, Burkina Faso, Idrissa Ouedraogo) *Fatimata Sanga, Noufou Ouedraogo, Roukietou Barry.* Bila and Nopoko are young cousins in a small African village, whose residents eke out a rough living from an unforgiving land. Bila is a mischievous boy with a good heart, whose father is the town drunk; Nopoko, who has lost her mother, is caring

and joyful. They're bonded by mutual support and affection. The children befriend an old woman, Sana, who lives on the fringes of the village, ostracized as a witch. When Nopoko's life is endangered, Sana may be her only hope. The children who portray Bila and Nopoko deliver remarkable performances, authentic and natural and unselfconscious. While on the surface a small story covering a brief time, *Yaaba* touches on all the major themes of any human drama. Human nature is constant; charlatans and prejudices exist everywhere, and the same basic conflicts persist in all communities. A gentle story on the cycles of life and human perserverence. (Mooré with English subtitles) ★★★ VHS: $29.99

The Yakuza

(1974, 112 min, US, Sydney Pollack) *Robert Mitchum, Brian Keith, Richard Jordan.* An ex-cop (Mitchum) battles the Japanese mafia to rescue the kidnapped daughter of an old friend (Keith). Robert Towne and Paul Schrader cowrote the script. ★★½

Yanco

(1964, 90 min, Mexico, Servando Gonzales) *Ricardo Ancona.* A young boy in an Indian village thrives on music to escape the realities of his poverty-stricken surroundings, often running off to a secret hideout to play his homemade violin. One day, he meets an old man who is a master musician. The old man's violin becomes the instrument of their friendship as he teaches the child the wonders of music. Although in original Spanish language without subtitles, this beautifully-told tale conveys its story — whether you speak the language or not — through remarkably subtle yet overwhelming visual images. An affecting performance from Ancona as the young boy. ★★★

Yankee Doodle Dandy

(1942, 126 min, US, Michael Curtiz) *James Cagney, Joan Leslie, Walter Huston, Rosemary DeCamp, George Tobias, S.Z. Sakall.* Cagney won an Oscar for his classic performance as the legendary song-and-dance man George M. Cohan. It is ironic that Cagney, American movies' quintessential gangster, is best remembered and had his most popular role in this entertaining musical biography. Can anyone forget Cagney's immortal interpretation of the title tune? ★★★½ DVD 2-disc Special Edition: $26.99, VHS: $14.99

Yanks

(1979, 139 min, US, John Schlesinger) *Richard Gere, William Devane, Lisa Eichhorn, Vanessa Redgrave, Rachel Roberts.* An absorbing and literate WWII drama about American G.I.s stationed in England. Gere and Devane are but two of the "Yanks" who begin relationships with British women — Gere with young Eichhorn and Devane with married Redgrave. In support, Roberts gives a smashing performance as Eichhorn's inflexible mother. Fine direction from Schlesinger, who has a keen eye for the detail and atmosphere of the era. ★★★ VHS: $9.99

The Yards

(2000, 115 min, US, James Gray) *Mark Wahlberg, Joaquin Phoenix, Charlize Theron, Faye Dunaway, Ellen Burstyn, James Caan.* Director Gray creates an indelible portrait of rot in the Big Apple. Wahlberg plays a likable ex-con trying to go straight, doomed to be dragged back into a life on the other side of the law when he takes a job with his Uncle (Caan), an influential Transit Authority contractor. Phoenix is the childhood friend who's already made a name for

himself in the "company," and whose fits of sudden rage trigger a devastating chain of events. Gray has once again assembled a superb cast, but if the film misses greatness by "thissmuch" it's merely because the substantial weight of so many heavy-hitters makes the screenplay's rote emotional melodramatics seem all the more distracting. Still, the film's sweeping visual style is dreamily seductive and Gray's street-smart intensity could prompt one to compare him to Sidney Lumet as the new mastercraftsman of the New York crime story. ★★★ DVD: $14.99, VHS: $9.99

The Year My Voice Broke

(1987, 105 min, Australia, John Duigan) *Noah Taylor, Leone Carmen, Ben Mendelsohn.* A better look at puberty blues than Bruce Beresford's film of that title, and as affecting and lovingly crafted as Rob Reiner's *Stand by Me*, this tale of teenage troubles is set in an Australian backwater town in the early '60s. Childhood friends Freya and Danny, along with Freya's new hoodlum boyfriend Trevor, begin the difficult transition from childhood to adolescence as well as learn of the hidden secrets of the town's older generation. Non-stereotypical characterization, disarming humor and a bittersweet conclusion that avoids simple sentimentality save this overdone plot from being a cliché. ★★★

The Year of Living Dangerously

(1983, 115 min, Australia, Peter Weir) *Mel Gibson, Sigourney Weaver, Linda Hunt, Michael Murphy.* Gibson stars as a foreign correspondent whose attraction to a British attache (Weaver) pits his professional instincts against his personal allegiances. Weir directs with a discerning eye this torrid account of love and betrayal amidst Indonesia's 1965 military coup. Hunt won an Academy Award for her unforgettable performance as Gibson's male confidant. ★★★½ DVD Letterboxed: $19.99, VHS: $14.99

Year of the Comet

(1992, 89 min, US, Peter Yates) *Penelope Ann Miller, Timothy Daly, Ian Richardson, Louis Jordan, Art Malik.* The ever-perky Miller stars in this textbook romantic action/comedy about the downtrodden daughter of a wine dealer who reluctantly teams up with a dashing troubleshooter (Daly) to recover a stolen bottle of priceless wine. The good news is that this is acclaimed screenwriter William Goldman's first original script since *Butch Cassidy and the Sundance Kid*. The bad news is that it doesn't live up

Y Tu Mamá También

Yojimbo

to the standards of his earlier works, nor those of director Yates. Nevertheless, the film has a few enjoyable moments and will make a good date movie. ★★

Year of the Dragon

(1985, 125 min, US, Michael Cimino) *Mickey Rourke, John Lone.* Controversial police thriller with Rourke as a New York City police captain assigned to the Chinatown district to keep peace among the neighboring gangs. Once there, however, he comes in conflict with a local underworld boss (Lone). Oliver Stone wrote the screenplay which relies heavily on violence and police actioner clichés. ★★½ VHS: $14.99

Year of the Gun

(1991, 111 min, US, John Frankenheimer) *Andrew McCarthy, Sharon Stone, John Pankow, Valeria Golina.* After a slow start, lots of un-subtitled Italian and a less-than-compelling performance by McCarthy, this political thriller by Frankenheimer gets into gear, intensifies and delivers. Set in Rome during the late '70s, McCarthy plays a journalist writing a fictionalized account of a Red Brigade plot to kidnap Aldo Moro. Paranoia and violence quickly follow when the dangerously accurate manuscript is stolen. A good supporting cast includes Pankow as a mysterious professor, Stone as a mysterious photojournalist and Golina as McCarthy's mysterious girlfriend. ★★½ DVD: $19.99

A Year of the Quiet Sun

(1985, 106 min, Poland/West Germany, Krzysztof Zanussi) *Scott Wilson, Maja Komorowska.* Internationally renowned Polish filmmaker Zanussi directed this haunting and poignant love story set in a ravaged post-war Poland. An American soldier, sent to investigate war crimes, falls in love with a Polish widow. The film skillfully and sensitively captures their awkward attempts at communication, attempts that are at first hindered by the lack of a common language. A universal story about a love that is greater than the barriers of language and politics. (Polish with English subtitles) ★★★½ DVD Letterbox: $29.99

The Yearling

(1946, 134 min, US, Clarence Brown) *Gregory Peck, Jane Wyman, Claude Jarman, Jr., Chill Wills, Henry Travers, June Lockhart.* Classic screen ver-

sion of Marjorie Kinnan Rawling's Pulitzer Prize-winning novel about a small boy's love for a young deer. Peck and Wyman are fine as the child's parents, and Jarman gives a remarkable performance as the young boy. Beautifully photographed. (Remade in 1994) ★★★★ DVD: $12.99, VHS: $14.99

Yellow Earth

(1984, 89 min, China, Chen Kaige) *Xue Bai, Wang Xueqi.* An early film collaboration of two proponents of China's New Wave of cinema, Chen and Zhang Yimou, this film revolves around a young soldier sent out to gather folk songs which will be used by the Party to rouse the patriotism of the revolutionaries. Brother Gu, as the soldier is affectionately named, is treated with great respect at a wedding and is told to stay with a sheep-herding family in the hills. The young daughter, who is a fine singer, falls for the young soldier and decides to get out of her arranged marriage in order to join him in the city. This simple tale has the same sense of unfulfilled passion of other New Wave films, but the cinematography and performances save this from being one of the usual fare. (Mandarin with English subtitles) ★★★ VHS: $19.99

Yellow Submarine

(1968, 88 min, GB, George Dunning) *The Beatles.* Fantastic animated romp with the Fab Four fighting to save Pepperland from the Blue Meanies with the message that "All You Need is Love." Other Beatles' songs include "Nowhere Man," "Lucy in the Sky with Diamonds" and "When I'm Sixty-Four." Includes a previously unreleased animated performance of "Hey, Bulldog." ★★★½ DVD: $29.99, VHS: $19.99

Yentl

(1983, 134 min, US, Barbra Streisand) *Barbra Streisand, Mandy Patinkin, Nehemiah Persoff, Steven Hill, Amy Irving.* Streisand shines as both star and director in this underrated, likable musical based on a story by Isaac Bashevis Singer (*Enemies: A Love Story*). Set in turn-of-the-century Russia, Streisand plays a woman who disguises herself as a boy to gain admittance to a yeshiva, an all-male school for Talmudic study. Patinkin is a fellow student who befriends "Yentl, the Yeshiva Boy," and Irving nicely plays Patinkin's fiancée. The only complaint is why cast someone with the incredible vocal talents of Patinkin in a musical and not let him sing. ★★★

Yesterday, Today and Tomorrow

(1964, 119 min, Italy, Vittorio De Sica) *Sophia Loren, Marcello Mastroianni.* A tour de force for director De Sica as well as Loren and Mastroianni. This "battle-of-the-sexes" comedy is set in the framework of three episodes, each employing different stories, acting styles and locations (Rome, Milan and Naples). A delightful Academy Award-winning satire which features a striptease by Loren that still heats up the screen. ★★★★ VHS: $19.99

Yi Yi (A One and a Two)

(2000, 173 min, Taiwan, Edward Yang) *Wu Nienjen, Issey Ogata, Elaine Jin, Kelly Lee.* A mesmerizingly intimate epic that takes familial threads and expresses its emotions reservedly, despite the brash Americanization of the Taiwan it depicts. Director Yang has solid control of his drama, his eye similar to that of his 8-year-old character and namesake Yang-Yang (Chang). This inquisitive boy photographs the backs of people's heads, to show them what they can't see. That's an apt metaphor for the movie, which takes the time to explore how people come to make life's myriad of difficult decisions, and the matters of the heart that we take for granted. Yang-Yang's father, NJ (Nienjen), has just met his high school love (three decades later) and must balance his desires and his family. NJ's white-collar job is falling apart, his mother-in-law is in a coma, his older daughter is in a budding romance, and his brother-in-law has just undertaken a shotgun marriage. But those are the "what"s; *Yi Yi* is all about other questions: why do we make certain choices in our lives, how do we get there, and who does that ultimately make us? Absorbing, affecting, and surprisingly beautiful, *Yi Yi* is so moving precisely because it is so human. (In Taiwanese, Mandarin, Japanese and English with English subtitles) ★★★★ DVD: $24.99, VHS Pan & Scan: $19.99, VHS Letterbox: $19.99

Yiddle with a Fiddle (Yidl Mitn Fidl)

(1936, 92 min, Poland, Joseph Green) *Molly Picon.* This classic Yiddish musical-comedy stars Picon as a *shtetl* girl who, determined to discover a world closed off to her as a woman, disguises herself as a boy and joins up with a traveling band of musicians. Picon, luminous in the performance of her career, soon falls in love with one of her colleagues but, with delightfully humorous results, is forced to keep her identity hidden from him. Filled with Jewish songs, vaudeville skits and scenes of everyday life, this film provides a glimpse of Jewish life in Poland before it was tragically destroyed. The first international Yiddish hit, *Yiddle with a Fiddle* is considered by many to be the best Yiddish film of all time. (Yiddish with English subtitles) ★★★★ VHS: $79.99

Yojimbo

(1961, 110 min, Japan, Akira Kurosawa) *Toshiro Mifune, Eijiro Tono.* In the style of an American western, *Yojimbo* matches a cynical, wandering samurai against two merchant families battling for control of a country town. Kurosawa hilariously satirizes greed, linking it to paranoia, pomposity and cowardice. (Sequel: *Sanjuro*) (American remake: *Last Man Standing*) (Japanese with English subtitles) ★★★★ DVD: $29.99, VHS: $29.99

Yol

(1982, 111 min, Switzerland/Turkey, Serif Goren & Yilmaz Gurney) *Tarik Akan, Serif Sezer.* A devastating drama dealing with political, ethnic and cultural repression in contemporary Turkey. Secretly written and directed while still in prison, directors Goren and Gurney offer a harrowing vision as seen through the lives of five prisoners who are granted temporary furloughs to visit their families. (Turkish with English subtitles) ★★★½

You Are Not Alone

(1978, 90 min, Denmark, Ernst Johansen & Lasse Nielsen) Unique and lyrical, this tale explores the boundaries of friendship and love between two young boys in a private boarding school in Copenhagen. The headmaster's inability to cope with the pair's mounting sexuality leads to their rebellion. (Danish with English subtitles) ★★★ VHS: $29.99

You Can Count on Me

(2000, 111 min, US, Kenneth Lonergan) *Laura Linney, Mark Ruffalo, Matthew Broderick, Rory Culkin, Jon Tenney, Kenneth Lonergan.* A wonderful character study bolstered by two enchanting lead performances, writer-director Lonergan's comedy-drama is a blissfully adept study of a volatile brother-sister relationship. In a intuitive portrayal, Linney is captivating as Sammy, a single mother living in an upstate New York town who must cope with the arrival of her beloved but ne'er-do-well brother (an exceptional Ruffalo). Lonergan marvelously captures both the cadence of small-town America, and the expectations and disappointments that often define the relationship between siblings. Broderick plays her boss, with whom Sammy has an affair. ★★★½ DVD Letterbox: $14.99, VHS Special Edition: $14.99

You Can't Cheat an Honest Man

(1939, 76 min, US, George Marshall) *W.C. Fields, Edgar Bergen, Constance Moore, James Bush, Eddie "Rochester" Anderson.* A brisk comedy providing Fields a hilarious setting in which to flourish. As the entrepreneur of a traveling circus, Fields is adept at pulling up stakes and reaching the state line just before the law catches up with him. He also finds time to taunt children, shortchange his employees, and tangle with an assortment of wild animal and inanimate objects — particularly ventriloquist's dummy Charlie McCarthy. ★★★

You Can't Take It with You

(1938, 127 min, US, Frank Capra) *Jean Arthur, James Stewart, Lionel Barrymore, Edward Arnold, Spring Byington, Ann Miller.* Capra's zany and uproarious screen version of Kaufman and Hart's classic Broadway comedy. Arthur stars as the daughter of an outrageously eccentric family out to win over her boyfriend's (Stewart) conservative parents. Though there's a touch of Capra's trademark sentimentality, this doesn't detract from the total enjoyment of this Academy Award-winning Best Picture. Such an engaging ensemble. ★★★★ DVD: $29.99

You Only Live Once

(1937, 86 min, US, Fritz Lang) *Henry Fonda, Sylvia Sidney, Ward Bond, Margaret Hamilton.* Lang directed this powerful social drama with Fonda as a wrongly imprisoned ex-con who tries to go straight. Also with Sidney as his wife. Solid performances from the two leads. Based partly on the lives of Bonnie and Clyde. ★★★ DVD: $19.99

You Only Live Twice

(1967, 117 min, GB, Lewis Gilbert) *Sean Connery, Donald Pleasence, Lois Maxwell, Charles Gray.* SPECTRE steals both American and Soviet spacecrafts in an attempt to start WWIII. This James Bond adventure is the slightest of the Connery films, beset by plot holes and stiff supporting players; it only comes alive when Pleasence hits the screen as Blofeld. (Sequel: *On Her Majesty's Secret Service*) ★★

You So Crazy

(1994, 86 min, US, Thomas Schlamme) *Martin Lawrence.* Lawrence excels in this outrageous, untamed live concert performance where no stone is left unturned. Attacking everyone from Rodney King to Jeffrey Dahmer, this on-the-rise comic proves with no mercy that he is one of the funniest comedians to take the stage since Richard Pryor. Loud, rude and playfully offensive, this highly entertaining film is a must see for those in search of some trouser-wetting laughs. ★★★½ DVD: $14.99, VHS: $9.99

You Were Never Lovelier

(1942, 97 min, US, Willaim A. Seiter) *Fred Astaire, Rita Hayworth, Adolphe Menjou, Xavier Cugat, Larry Parks.* Astaire was never debonair-er and Hayworth never more breathtaking-er than in this charming tale of innocent seduction, well-intentioned meddling and haywire miscommunications. Astaire once commented that Hayworth was his favorite dancing partner. Watch this and see why. ★★★½ DVD: $24.99, VHS: $19.99

You'll Never Get Rich

(1941, 88 min, US, Sidney Lanfield) *Fred Astaire, Rita Hayworth, Robert Benchley.* Astaire and Hayworth make a most appealing team in this delightful musical comedy. Fred plays a Broadway hoofer and choreographer who gets drafted. He courts ravishing Rita and still manages to make the show go on. Cole Porter score includes "I Kissed My Baby Goodbye." ★★★ DVD: $19.99

You're a Big Boy Now

(1966, 96 min, US, Francis Ford Coppola) *Peter Kastner, Elizabeth Hartman, Geraldine Page, Rip Torn, Julie Harris, Karen Black.* A bit of a time warp, this outrageously entertaining coming-of-age comedy stars Kastner (for those old enough to remember, he was TV's "Ugliest Girl in Town") as a sheltered young man who leaves home and learns all about life, with help from dancer Hartman. Torn and Page are his parents — Page excels in what could be the most over-protective movie mom since Mrs. Bates. A real charmer. ★★★ VHS: $14.99

You've Got Mail

(1998, 119 min, US, Nora Ephron) *Tom Hanks, Meg Ryan, Greg Kinnear, Parker Posey, Jean Stapleton, Steve Zahn, Dave Chappelle.* Hanks and Ryan are reunited after *Sleepless in Seattle* (and actually have more than one scene together) in this genuinely sweet romantic comedy based on Ernst Lubitsch's charming 1940 comedy *The Shop Around the Corner* (itself based on the play "Parfumerie" by Miklos Laszlo). The story is basically the same but updated for '90s sensibilities: two antagonists are brought together and fall in love in spite of themselves. Though the original device was the personals in the newspaper, here the two become acquainted through e-mail. Ryan is the owner of a small, Upper West Side bookstore slowly going out of business. Hanks is the owner of a mega-bookstore which is contributing to its demise. How they come together makes for fetching comedy. ★★★ DVD: $19.99, VHS: $9.99

The Young Americans

(1993, 100 min, GB, Danny Cannon) *Harvey Keitel, Viggo Mortensen, Iain Glen.* Keitel is a DEA advisor brought into a drug war investigation in London who confronts the hit man (Mortensen) he has tracked for eight years. Director Cannon delivers a well-acted, well-mounted production with a finely crafted story line and succinctly drawn characters which lift the film above its potentially derivative subject matter. Keitel's portrayal is his most modulated in recent memory, and Glen is especially affecting as a young man inadvertently drawn into the center of the investigation. This moody actioner is surprisingly effective in engaging the viewer's attention and sympathies. ★★★ DVD: $14.99, VHS: $9.99

Young and Innocent

(1937, 82 min, GB, Alfred Hitchcock) *Nova Pilbeam, Derrick de Marney.* Plenty of Hitchcockian touches are to be found in this charming and chilling chase drama about a young man, falsely accused of murder, who, with the help of his girlfriend, pursues the real culprit: the man with the eye twitch! ★★★

Young Aphrodites

(1966, 87 min, Greece, Nikos Koundrouros) Filmed among the ruins of ancient Greece and using authentic shepherds and peasants, this exotic and sensual film presents the universal story of the physical longing and sexual attraction of two adolescents. This magnificently photographed film is a poetic ode to the beginning of adulthood and the loss of innocence. ★★★

Young at Heart

(1954, 117 min, US, Gordon Douglas) *Frank Sinatra, Doris Day, Gig Young, Ethel Barrymore.* Bright musical remake of *Four Daughters*, with Day as the daughter of a small-town musician who is courted by Sinatra. ★★★ DVD: $14.99

Young Catherine

(1991, 106 min, GB, Michael Anderson) *Vanessa Redgrave, Julia Ormond, Christopher Plummer.* Set in Russia of 1744, this period drama chronicles the power struggle between the Empress Elizabeth (Redgrave) and her daughter-in-law, Catherine (Ormond). Saddled with an impotent husband, Catherine bears a bastard child and attempts to have him installed on the throne. ★★★

Young Doctors in Love

(1982, 97 min, US, Garry Marshall) *Michael McKean, Sean Young, Dabney Coleman, Hector Elizondo.* A funny farce about life in a metropolitan hospital, in the tradition of *Airplane!* and *The Naked Gun.* Includes many a cameo from stars of TV soap operas. ★★★

Young Einstein

(1989, 90 min, Australia, Yahoo Serious) *Yahoo Serious, Odile Le Clezio.* Fans of *Bill and Ted's Excellent Adventure* might find humor in this minor comedy from Yahoo Serious. Once touted to be Australia's next great export, Serious directed, wrote and stars in this Albert Einstein spoof about the son of a Tazmanian farm family who knows inherently that he is destined for great things (i.e. splitting the atom to put bubbles in beer). Unfortunately, the film relies too heavily on Jeff Darling's vivid cinematography and fails to exploit the comedy of this potentially humorous premise. ★★ VHS: $14.99

XYZ

Young Frankenstein

(1974, 105 min, US, Mel Brooks) *Gene Wilder, Madeline Kahn, Teri Garr, Peter Boyle, Marty Feldman, Cloris Leachman, Howard Morris.* Brooks is at his best with this hilarious spoof of the *Frankenstein* films, hitting every comic mark with uncanny accuracy. Wilder stars as the soon-to-be demented doc, Dr. Frankenstein ("That's Frahnken*steen*), giving an inspired comic performance. Great in support are Feldman as Ygor ("That's Eye-gore"), the sardonic wit of the laboratory set, Kahn as the "Bride of Frankenstein," and Boyle as "the monster." Authentic sets from the 1930s films, astounding black-and-white cinematography, and an atmospheric score by John Morris contribute to the sheer delight of this comedy classic. ★★★★ DVD Special Edition: $14.99, VHS: $9.99

Young Guns

(1988, 107 min, US, Christopher Cain) *Emilio Estevez, Kiefer Sutherland, Charlie Sheen, Lou Diamond Phillips, Dermot Mulroney, Casey Siemaszko.* The Brat Pack on horses! Slick western adventure with the boys trying to tame the wild West, and get revenge for their mentor's murder. ★★½ DVD: $9.99, DVD Special Edition: $19.99

Young Guns 2

(1990, 105 min, US, Geoff Murphy) *Emilio Estevez, William Petersen, Kiefer Sutherland, Christian Slater, Lou Diamond Phillips, Alan Ruck, Balthazar Getty.* Annoying sequel to the 1988 hit finds Billy the Kid (Estevez) on the run from former friend-turned-bounty hunter Pat Garrett (Petersen). The cast is likable, but this one lacks the element of fun that made the first one watchable. ★½ DVD: $14.99, VHS: $9.99

The Young Lions

(1958, 167 min, US, Edward Dmytryk) *Marlon Brando, Montgomery Clift, Dean Martin, Hope Lange, Maximilian Schell.* A somewhat overlong but nevertheless mesmerizing WWII epic, based on Irwin Shaw's novel examining the volatile relationship between two American soldiers and a Nazi officer. Clift and Martin are the former; a rather restrained Brando is the German soldier undergoing a moral edification in light of his country's actions. ★★★ DVD: $19.99, VHS: $9.99

Young Man with a Horn

(1950, 112 min, US, Michael Curtiz) *Kirk Douglas, Lauren Bacall, Doris Day, Hoagy Carmichael.* The three leads are all quite good in this romantic drama about trumpeter Douglas trying to make it in the jazz world, and torn between Bacall and Day. Based on the life of Bix Beiderbecke. ★★★ VHS: $19.99

Young Master

(1980, 102 min, Hong Kong, Jackie Chan) *Jackie Chan, Yuen Biao, Wei Pai.* Made back when Jackie was beginning to exercise creative control over his own films, this amalgam of comedy and action shows him trying to make a movie firmly within the kung fu genre, while also developing his own unique comedic persona. Jackie is Ah Lung, a gifted kung fu student who is thrown out of his school in disgrace. Looking for his brother, who was also thrown out, he gets involved in a case of mistaken identity and is branded a fugitive. After clearing his name, he helps the authorities capture the real criminal. The story here is strictly by-the-numbers and the comedy touches are a bit forced, but the fighting scenes are all top-notch. The end fight scene, in particular, stands among the best that Jackie has done. (Cantonese with English subtitles) ★★★ DVD: $9.99, VHS: $19.99

The Young Philadelphians

(1959, 136 min, US, Vincent Sherman) *Paul Newman, Barbara Rush, Robert Vaughn, Alexis Smith, Brian Keith, Adam West.* Newman stars as a lawyer from the poor side of the tracks who works his way up the corporate and social ladders. Rush is the society woman he romances. Vaughn is quite good (he received an Oscar nomination) as Newman's old Army buddy. ★★★

The Young Poisoner's Handbook

(1996, 99 min, GB, Benjamin Ross) *Hugh O'Conor, Antony Sher, Ruth Sheen, Charlotte Coleman.* This very entertaining black comedy tells the true story of Graham Young, a young chemistry buff who becomes obsessed with some lethal concoctions and begins testing them, in a very scientifically sound manner, mind you, on other human beings. Motivated more by intellectual curiosity than hatred, he slowly poisons his mother and father in a series of carefully controlled experiments. That is, until he gets caught and sent to a psychiatric hospital. There he is taken under the wing of a doctor with a radical new method for treating psychotic misfits and Graham deludes both himself and his psychiatrist into believing that he is cured. The audience, however, knows better. The film revels in its dark comedy and its gleefully wicked re-creation/satire of England in the 1950s and '60s. ★★★

Young Sherlock Holmes

(1985, 108 min, US, Barry Levinson) *Nicholas Rowe, Alan Cox, Sophie Ward.* Steven Spielberg produced this stylish and very entertaining mystery adventure. Sherlock Holmes and Dr. Watson meet for the first time as schoolmates and investigate the apparent suicides of civic leaders. Terrific special effects include a stalking stained-glass window and pastries on parade. ★★★ DVD: $19.99, VHS: $14.99

Young Toerless

(1965, 90 min, Germany, Volker Schlöndorff) *Mathieu Carriere, Marian Seidowsky, Bernd Tischer, Jean Launay, Barbara Steele.* Schlöndorff's first film is an intense psychological thriller about a boy in a rural German boys' school who wants to report the torture of a fellow classmate, but encounters fear and intimidation. A chilling metaphor for the terror of living under Nazi rule. (German with English subtitles) ★★★½ VHS: $29.99

Young Winston

(1972, 157 min, GB, Richard Attenborough) *Simon Ward, Anne Bancroft, Robert Shaw, Ian Holm, John Mills.* Hold on to your horses. We're off on a two-and-a-half-hour essay on the youthful days of Winston Churchill. While hardly representative of Britain's finest hour, this is an interesting and entertaining account of the young Churchill's life — following him through a lonely childhood, battles in India, his exploits in the Boer Wars, and his first election to Parliament. The battle scenes are superb. ★★★

Youngblood

(1986, 109 min, US, Peter Markle) *Rob Lowe, Patrick Swayze, Cynthia Gibb, Ed Lauter, Fionnula Flanagan, Keanu Reeves.* Tedious sports drama with Lowe as a farmboy who joins a Canadian minor league hockey team, becoming involved with the coach's daughter. ★½ DVD: $14.99

Younger & Younger

(1994, 97 min, US, Percy Adlon) *Donald Sutherland, Lolita Davidovich, Brendan Fraser,*

Linda Hunt, Sally Kellerman, Julie Delpy. Whatever happened to Percy Adlon? After making a promising start in his native Germany, he came to the States and made the wonderful *Bagdad Cafe*. But after that came dreck and more dreck. This dreck concerns Jonathan Younger (Sutherland) and his storage company and all the quirky people that work there and visit and all the quirky things that happen in all the quirky places in and about the company. Now there's nothing wrong with quirky. But here the characters are just clichés, and they add nothing to an already pointless story. ★½ VHS: $14.99

Your Friends and Neighbors

(1998, 99 min, US, Neil LaBute) *Amy Brenneman, Aaron Eckhart, Ben Stiller, Catherine Keener, Nastassja Kinski, Jason Patric.* In a how-do-you-top-that second effort after his controversial debut film *In the Company of Men*, writer-director LaBute doesn't disappoint with this equally controversial, funny and penetrating look at a group of male friends and their affairs and camaraderie. Stiller is Jerry, a self-important professor whose routine bull sessions with Barry (Eckhart) and Cary (Patric) form the core of the film. But LaBute is much more interested in the dynamics of male-female relationships, and uses these get-togethers as a sounding board for his (characters?) most inner thoughts. Keener is excellent as Jerry's current fling, and her budding lesbian is the most interesting of these sexual provocateurs. Though Patric's steam-room tale of earlier sexual exploits is an unsettling and hypnotic scene which is certain to be the most talked about piece from the film. ★★★ DVD: $19.99, VHS: $9.99

Yours, Mine and Ours

(1968, 111 min, US, Melville Shavelson) *Henry Fonda, Lucille Ball, Van Johnson, Tim Matheson.* A theatrical "Brady Bunch," and not without some laughs. Fonda, widowed father of ten, marries widow Ball, mother of six. All hell breaks loose when they gather the kids and move in together. An old-fashioned, sentimental comedy. ★★½ DVD: $14.99

Z

(1969, 127 min, Algeria/France, Constantin Costa-Gavras) *Yves Montand, Irene Papas, Jean-Louis Trintignant, Charles Denner.* A swiftly moving political thriller on fascist corruption in the Greek government. Costa-Gavras has delivered an exciting, even riveting exposé of social ills and the abuses of power. Academy Award winner for Best Foreign Film. (French with English subtitles) ★★★★ DVD Masterworks Edition: $29.99, VHS: $14.99

Z.P.G.

(1972, 95 min, GB, Michael Campus) *Oliver Reed, Geraldine Chaplin.* This apocalyptic vision of overpopulation is set in the 21st century where reproduction is a crime punishable by death, gas masks are the hip new fashion accessory, and state-provided robot dolls are issued to couples who want to have children. Chaplin and Reed star as a couple who defy the government's stance of Zero Population Growth by having a real child in this grim but stylish pro-lifer's nightmare. ★★★ VHS: $14.99

Zabriskie Point

(1970, 110 min, US, Michelangelo Antonioni) *Mark Frechette, Daria Halprin, Rod Taylor, Harrison Ford.* A political and sociological time capsule that presents a disturbing view of 1960s America — a turbulent time of political unrest and student upheaval. This rambling study by Antonioni gets a bit bogged down in polemics and the result is a film less satisfying than *Blow-Up* in documenting the social ferment

XYZ

in a foreign country. Nonetheless, with sweeping photography set in Death Valley, a script cowritten by Sam Shepard, a cameo appearance by a young Ford and an explosive subject matter, the film is novel and compelling. (Filmed in English) ★★★

Zardoz

(1974, 105 min, GB, John Boorman) *Sean Connery, Charlotte Rampling.* Boorman's bizarre and overloaded science-fiction adventure is set in the year 2293 when the Eternals (a group of ageless intellectuals) live inside a dome and send orders to the Exterminator to kill the Brutals who inhabit the wasteland outside. Connery plays an Exterminator with a conscience who penetrates the secrets of the dome and enters a maze of mind-boggling imagery. Boorman's imagination runs wild like it never has. ★★½ DVD: $9.99, VHS: $19.99

Zatoichi

From the classic *The Life and Opinion of Masseur Ichi* springs a series of films chronicling the adventures of the blind swordsman in his travels through a rural Japan fraught with bandits, unscrupulous officials and waylaid innocents. Shintaro Katsu is engaging as the self-effacing massuese, whose sightlessness camoflages his unerring martial arts abilities. He drinks, he gambles and he kills only when necessary. He's a consistently entertaining character. First-rate production values, fine supporting casts and Katsu's endearing interpretation of his character make this series a guaranteed good time. (The inspiration for Rutger Hauer's action-adventure film *Blind Fury*.)

Zatoichi: The Tale of Zatoichi

(1962, 96 min, Japan, Kenji Misumi) *Shintaro Katsu.* The first entry in the *Zatoichi* series introduces Katsu as Zatoichi, a blind masseur in a small province who finds himself trapped in the middle of a war between rival Yakuza gangs. Aware of his remarkable reputation as a swordsman, one side tries to hire Zatoichi while the other side hires an equally reputable warrior to go up against him. Impressive martial arts choreography, involving characterizations and a well-crafted story set the bar for the rest of the series, which met the challenge with extraordinary consistency. (Japanese with English subtitles) ★★★½ DVD Subtitled: $19.99

Zatoichi: The Tale of Zatoichi Continues

(1962, 72 min, Japan, Kazuo Mori) *Shintaro Katsu, Tomisaburo Wakayama.* The feudal lord who has hired Zatoichi is mad — and Zatoichi's life is in peril when he discovers this fact, which would destroy the lord and his followers if it were made public. The Blind Masseur successfully defends himself against the crazed lord's samurais and hired Yakuza thugs, but then comes up against a nemesis from his past — an enigmatic, one-armed swordsman (played by Tomisaburo Wakayama, who is Katsu's real-life brother). Superbly executed martial arts, pristine black-and-white cinematography and an intriguing story line contribute to this superior entertainment. (Japanese with English subtitles) ★★★½ DVD Subtitled: $19.99

Zatoichi: New Tale of Zatoichi

(1963, 91 min, Japan, Tokuzo Tanaka) *Shintaro Katsu.* The Blind Masseur returns to his home prefecture to find that his former teacher, an impeccable swordsman, has hired himself out to a gang of unscrupulous, kidnapping thugs. He must also contend with his mentor's sister, whose offers of marriage put Zatoichi in an untenable position of a completely different sort. This is the first time an entry in the series was shot in color, adding another visual element to the already exemplary storytelling. (Japanese with English subtitles) ★★★ DVD Subtitled: $19.99

Zatoichi: The Fugitive

(1963, 86 min, Japan, Shintaro Katsu) The Blind Masseur's travels take him to the village of Shimonita, where he discovers that the resident band of criminals has put a price on his head. The bounty lures a skilled and vicious ronin, who nearly succeeds in slaying Ichi in their initial encounter. But Zatoichi's outrage isn't fully ignited until an innocent, defenseless local woman is slain without pity. His operatic slaughter of the gang is only prelude to the finale that pits his unconstrained rage against the samurai's audacious swordsmanship. (Japanese with English subtitles) ★★★ DVD Subtitled: $19.99

Zatoichi: On the Road

(1963, 87 min, Japan, Kimiyoshi Yasuda) *Shintaro Katsu.* Ichi and a companion travel to a village where the local warlord wants to hire the Blind Swordsman as his bodyguard. Under attack by a rival gang while in transit, the masseur negotiates his own safe passage, only to come across a dying man who has been trying to help an escaped servant girl get back to her family after a brutal rape by a lascivious feudal lord. Zatoichi agrees to take over the dying man's quest, fully realizing that he'll have to take on both feuding gangs to stay alive himself. An involving exploration of one honorable man caught between adherence to higher standards and the dictates of personal survival. (Japanese with English subtitles) ★★★ DVD Subtitled: $19.99

Zatoichi: Zatoichi's Flashing Sword

(1964, 82 min, Japan, Kazuo Ikehiro) *Shintaro Katsu.* Zatoichi is a houseguest of the peaceful Brunkiki boss Tsumugi when Tsumugi finds himself under attack from a rival yakuza boss, Yasuguro. Under the intricate demands of Japanese societal laws, Ichi's honorable host must ask him to leave. Yasuguro makes a bloody assault against the hapless boss while Ichi is out of the way, but the Blind Swordsman's sense of balance and retribution will not allow the execrable aggression to go unpunished. An exciting tale of quiet decency brutally disrupted by unbridled violence. (Japanese with English subtitles) ★★★ DVD Subtitled: $19.99

Zatoichi: Fight, Zatoichi, Fight

(1964, 87 min, Japan, Kenji Misumi) *Shintaro Katsu.* An ambush intended for Zatoichi results in the death of a helpless young woman, leaving her infant alone and defenseless. Ichi resolves to deliver the baby safely to his father — no mean trick, since his would-be assassins are in hot pursuit. That he is the sole protector of the small life in his care only strengthens the Blind Swordsman's determination to see the child to his father's arms; but just as a cruel twist of fate brought death to the baby's mother, so does the child's father become an enemy to Zatoichi, who must agains balance the moral dilemmas of self-preservation. (Japanese with English subtitles) ★★★ DVD Subtitled: $19.99

Zatoichi: Adventures of Zatoichi

(1964, 83 min, Japan, Kazuo Ikehiro) *Shintaro Katsu.* The hard-working merchants and laborers of a small, isolated village prepare tirelessly for the New Year celebration. But they find themselves under constant harassment from their corrupt overlords, who seem intent on setting new records in exploitation. Once again, Zatoichi's moral code of honor will not allow this abuse to go unanswered as he extracts justice with his unparalleled swordsmanship. (Japanese with English subtitles) ★★★ DVD Subtitled: $19.99

Zatoichi: Zatoichi's Revenge

(1965, 86 min, Japan, Kazuo Ikehiro) *Shintaro Katsu.* A dastardly plan to enslave young women and force them into prostitution results in the cold-blooded murder of the Blind Swordsman's venerable old master. Zatoichi responds with single-minded determination, and his fury knows no bounds until the women are liberated and his teacher's foul demise is avenged. This intense drama again demonstrates Ichi's ferocity when confronted by callous wrongdoing. (Japanese with English subtitles) ★★★ DVD Subtitled: $19.99

Zatoichi: Zatoichi and the Doomed Man

(1965, 77 min, Japan, Kazuo Ikehiro) *Shintaro Katsu.* Zatoichi's adventurous travels bring him into contact with a harmless, petty con man of exuberant wit and humor. The Blind Swordsman finds his fate entwined with that of an innocent man awaiting execution. The film fully utilizes both awe-inspiring martial artistry and the inventive, rambunctious slapstick that is a signature trademark of the series. (Japanese with English subtitles) ★★★ DVD Subtitled: $19.99

Zatoichi: Zatoichi and the Chess Expert

(1965, 87 min, Japan, Kenji Misumi) *Shintaro Katsu.* Zatoichi strikes up a friendship with a Samurai chess master on an undisclosed mission, becoming involved in a convoluted web of misplaced loyalties and deceit. (Japanese with English subtitles) ★★★ DVD: $19.99

Zatoichi: Zatoichi's Vengeance

(1966, 94 min, Japan, Kenji Misumi) *Shintaro Katsu.* Zatoichi comes upon a man waylaid by bandits. After killing the highwaymen, he hears the last request of the dying victim: To give a full purse to someone named Taichi. He finds the intended recipient, a small boy, in a village at the mercy of a brutal overlord. You can take it from there. (Japanese with English subtitles) ★★★ DVD: $19.99

Zatoichi: Zatoichi's Cane Sword

(1967, 93 min, Japan, Kenji Misumi) *Shintaro Katsu.* As Zatoichi undertakes to protect the village of Tonda from the vile exploitation of a gang of remorseless yakuza, he uncovers the history of his fabled cane sword; he also learns that the sword will not last forever, and in fact may fail while he still has need of it. Providing key information for the *Zatoichi* mythos, *Zatoichi's Cane Sword* also adeptly delivers the series' patented blend of sublimely orchestrated violence and sidesplitting slapstick. (Japanese with English subtitles) ★★★½ DVD: $19.99

Zatoichi Meets Yojimbo

(1970, 115 min, Japan, Kihachi Okamoto) *Toshiro Mifune, Shintaro Katsu.* Mifune re-creates his character Yojimbo from the Akira Kurosawa classic, here teaming with blind master swordsman Zatoichi (Katsu) to eliminate the gangsters who have taken over a small village and stolen and hid a fortune in gold belonging to the government. An action-filled and fun spoof of samurai films. (Japanese with English subtitles) ★★★½ DVD: $29.99, VHS: $29.99

Zazie dans le Metro

(1960, 88 min, France, Louis Malle) *Philippe Noiret, Catherine Demonget.* Nodding his appreciative head to the cinematic exuberance exhibited in Truffaut's *The 400 Blows* and Godard's *Breathless*, 28-year-old Malle joined the New Wave with this colorful, frenetic slapstick comedy. Zazie, foul-mouthed, precocious pre-teen brat, is

XYZ

Zebrahead

dropped off on her uncle's (Noiret) door by her philandering mother. In the next 36 hours, Zazie, accompanied by her befuddled uncle (a female impersonator), involves herself in a series of wild, mischievous antics as she embarks on her own personalized tour of Paris. Filled with cinematic tricks, jump-cuts and references to other films, this effervescent comedy, inspired by Raymond Queneau's novel, is not Malle's masterpiece but is unabashedly great anarchistic fun. (French with English subtitles) ★★★

Zebrahead

(1992, 100 min, US, Anthony Drazan) *Michael Rapaport, N'Bushe Wright, DeShonn Castle, Ray Sharkey, Helen Shaver.* First-time director Drazan's masterful debut transposes "Romeo and Juliet" onto the blighted 1990s urban landscape. Set in Detroit, the story centers around Jack, a gawky, wannabe homeboy who is amongst the few white kids in his high school. Trouble comes his way when he falls hard for his best friend's cousin Nikki, a savvy young black teen who has just moved from New York. While the story is not hard to predict, the easy-going performances of Rapaport and Wright as Zack and Nikki, along with Drazen's thoughtfully constructed script, make this an engaging and meaningful essay on race relations in the '90s. ★★★½ DVD Letterbox: $24.99

A Zed and Two Noughts

(1985, 115 min, GB, Peter Greenaway) *Andréa Ferréol, Brian Deacon, Eric Deacon, Frances Barber, Joss Ackland, Jim Davidson, Agnes Brulet, Guusje van Tilborgh, Gerard Thoolen, Ken Campbell, Wolf Kahler, Geoffrey Palmer, David Attenborough.* Another surrealist treat from Greenaway. Two ex-Siamese twins are made widowers by an auto accident and team up with the car's driver, who lost her leg in the wreck, to explore the processes of death and decay. Always one to shock his viewers, Greenaway follows their examinations with all of the visual fecundity that has become the hallmark of his filmmaking, right down to time-lapse images of decaying corpses of animals. The lush cinematography of Sacha Vierny may be lost on the small screen. ★★★ DVD: $14.99, VHS: $9.99

Zelig

(1983, 79 min, US, Woody Allen) *Woody Allen, Mia Farrow.* The sublime story of Leonard Zelig, the outstanding chameleon-man, whose ability to alter his appearance perplexed medical experts and captivated the public's imagination. Allen's hilarious pseudo-documentary tackles the perils of conformity and the rakishness of the media. ★★★★ DVD: $19.99

Zelly and Me

(1988, 87 min, US, Tina Rathborne) *Isabella Rossellini, Alexandra Johnes, Glynis Johns, David Lynch.* A neglected rich girl is befriended by her caring governess, much to the disdain of the youngster's mean-spirited grandmother. Heavy-handed and only occasionally moving, the film suffers from a slow pace and overly mannered dramatics. ★★

Zentropa

(1991, 107 min, Netherlands, Lars von Trier) *Udo Keir, Max von Sydow, Eddie Constantine, Barbara Sukowa.* This penetrating and mesmeric trip into the dark soul of Europe follows a young American pacifist of German descent who sojourns to post-WWII Deutschland in the belief that he can take part in the healing process of that devastated country. Once there, however, he finds himself snatched up in a nightmarish labyrinth of corruption and deceit involving American complicity in the reestablishment of the powerful industrialist families who had supplied the Nazis. Von Sydow's haunting narration sets the tone for the naïve Yankee's hypnotic entry into the bizarre purgatory of occupied Germany. Shooting mostly in shimmering black and white, von Trier uses spot coloring, scrims and other overtly theatrical devices to great effect. Combined with some excellent performances, these add to the film's harrowing sense of impending doom and alienation. (In English and German with English subtitles) ★★★½

Zero Effect

(1998, 116 min, US, Jake Kasdan) *Bill Pullman, Ben Stiller, Ryan O'Neal, Kim Dickens.* First-time director Kasdan (son of director Lawrence Kasdan) makes an impressive debut with this often exhilarating private eye comedy. The basic premise could launch a dozen paperbacks: Brilliant gumshoe has his greatest weakness (namely an inability to interact with people) tested in the toughest case of his career. While the story of a timber tycoon being blackmailed is solid but stale, the details make this film special. The environments we take for granted, such as a white-collar gym or a diner, are given such attention and character that they cease to be "locations." Even Stiller's sidekick has an important story of his own to tell, and it never seems like a subplot. As Daryl Zero, Pullman anchors the movie with his sociological nightmare of a P.I., always identifiable under his many smooth disguises. ★★★½ DVD: $19.99, VHS: $14.99

Zero for Conduct (Zéro de Conduite)

(1933, 44 min, France, Jean Vigo) Vigo's first fiction film was banned for anti-French sentiment and reissued in 1945 after the liberation. It is, in part, an autobiographical account of the director's boyhood days in boarding school and, in part, a rendering of childhood fantasy. Realistic, poetic and subversive. (French with English subtitles) ★★★★ VHS: $14.99

Zero Kelvin

(1995, 113 min, Norway, Hans Petter Moland) *Stellan Skarsgård, Bjorn Sundquist, Camilla Martens.* The lonely, frozen landscape of Greenland proves an appropriate backdrop to this tense, existential drama about alienation and emotional morass. Set in the early part of the 20th century, the story follows a Norwegian poet, Henrik (Eidsvold), and his trek to Greenland to join a fur-trapping expedition. With only Holm (Sundquist), a soft-spoken scientist, and Randbaek (Skarsgård), their brutish, vulgar foreman, as companions, Henrik finds himself less in conflict with nature and more at odds with his fellow man. Soon Henrik is thrust into physical peril in this icy, remote region where humanity can often be displaced. Director Moland's gradually accelerated pacing befits Henrik's internal struggle, eventually culminating into a brisk, suspenseful battle between the two men shaded by cold, unpredictable moral ambiguities. (Norwegian with English subtitles) ★★★ DVD: $29.99, VHS: $24.99

Zero Patience

(1993, 95 min, Canada, John Greyson) *Michael Callen.* From the director of the very serious *Urinal* comes this unexpectedly outrageous and satiric musical comedy about life in the age of AIDS. The story centers around "Patient Zero," Gaetan Dugas, a French-Canadian airline steward who was reported by health officials to be the man who brought AIDS to North America and helped rapidly spread it through promiscuous sexual activity. Gaetan returns from the dead to clear his name and solicits the help of 19th-century explorer (and now 20th-century AIDS researcher) Sir Richard Burton. Burton's development from a self-centered homophobe to an ACT-UP-styled queer is the centerpiece of this amazing story. The film also features several bizarre musical routines, inventively choreographed and sporting wittily queer lyrics. ★★★ VHS: $39.99

Zig Zag Story

(1983, 100 min, France, Patrick Schulmann) More enjoyable than one would expect, given its tacky video cover box and lack of any theatrical run in the United States, this imaginative *comédie érotique* follows the madcap adventures of a lovelorn color-blind painter, his fiesty girlfriend and his sleazy partner — a sex-obsessed photographer who takes great pleasure (and pride) in wallowing in his peculiar excesses. With many genuinely funny scenes and offering plenty of full frontal nudity (mostly female), this frantic comedy is a pleasant surprise. (French with English subtitles) ★★★ VHS: $59.99

ZigZag

(2002, 101 min, US, David S. Goyer) *Sam Jones III, John Leguizamo, Wesley Snipes, Oliver Platt, Natasha Lyonne, Elizabeth Peña.* From the writer of the film adaptations of the *Blade* series comes another adaptation, this time of a novel by Landon J. Napoleon that probes the sheer disparity of what parenthood means to different people. The title character, subtly rendered by newcomer Jones, is functionally autistic. In his life are an abusive father (Snipes, in a welcome dramatic turn), a mildly sadistic boss (Platt) to be protected from, and Singer (Leguizamo), his generous, terminally ill Big Brother. As the story unfolds, the desperate ZigZag is involved in some malfeasance and Singer makes it his life's work to extricate him from this entanglement because, well, he's got a good heart. A bit farfetched? Perhaps. But thanks in large part to the subdued, compellingly real performances by this ensemble, *ZigZag* manages to remind us that kind and generous spirits are out there in the world, and sometimes that's enough. ★★★ DVD: $24.99, VHS: $102.99

Zombie

(1979, 91 min, Italy, Lucio Fulci) *Ian McCulloch, Richard Johnson, Tisa Farrow.* In the wake of George Romero's *Dawn of the Dead* comes this graphic and quite disgusting zombie tale about a Caribbean Island with a living dead problem. ★ DVD Letterbox 2-disc set: $29.99

Zombie and the Ghost Train

(1991, 88 min, Finland, Mika Kaurismäki) The so-called "slacker" culture has got nothing on the Fins — if you think Austin is bleak, wait till you get a sight of Helsinki. The Zombie of the title is an alcoholic loser who happens to play a mean bass. The story centers on his escapades as he attempts to reconcile with his girlfriend and, possibly more importantly, join the Ghost Train (who look like Urge Overkill), the most famous band in town, although no one seems to have ever heard them play. Unfortunately, Zombie is aptly named for whenever an opportunity arises he's either too drunk or passed out somewhere. There's not much plot but plenty of beautiful imagery and insightful moments; sometimes producing a laugh, and sometimes a lump in the throat. (Finnish with English subtitles) ★★★ VHS: $14.99

Zoolander

(2001, 89 min, US, Ben Stiller) *Ben Stiller, Owen Wilson, Will Ferrell, Christine Taylor, Jon Voight, Milla Jovovich, Jerry Stiller.* There is something intangible about the fashion industry that is so inherently funny, that parodies seem doomed to fail. And when such great personalities in the industry exist (see: Isaac Mizrahi in the fun documentary *Unzipped*), why bother making one up? Stiller tries, starring as supermodel Derek Zoolander, in a film that might have played better as a five-minute skit on his old TV show. Derek has one look on the runway, a half-pout he dubs "blue steel" (which may be the only effective joke). The rest of the picture is a (het-erosexual!) love triangle between Derek, a reporter (Stiller's wife Taylor) and up-and-coming super-

model Hansel (Wilson); oh yes, there's also a plot to assassinate the prime minister of Malaysia — is that supposed to be funny? The biggest comic revelation is that models are idiots, while director Stiller uses more establishing shots than a '70s sitcom. Now, a film about Mr. Blackwell and his worst-dressed list? *That* would be funny . . . ★½ DVD Letterbox: $14.99, VHS: $9.99

Zooman

(1994, 95 min, US, Leon Ichaso) *Louis Gossett, Jr., Charles S. Dutton, Khalil Kain.* Sugar Hill director Ichaso delivers another tale of life in the streets of the inner city, clean and middle-class, but still full of violence and turmoil. Based on the play "Zooman and the Sign" by Charles Fuller, this very talky, unexciting but glossy adaptation is similar in story to *Boyz n the Hood* and *Crooklyn* — and though this family drama is occasionally insightful, there's very little that hasn't been seen before. Kain is very convincing in his portrayal of Zooman, the young hood who shoots the daughter of Gossett during a rampage. In order to find the killer, Gossett enlists the local media and riles up his neighbors to face a showdown with the young killer. The music evokes some of the rage that the family feels in their grief, but the narrative is not as developed as Fuller's excellent *A Soldier's Story.* ★★

Zoot Suit

(1982, 103 min, US, Luis Valdez) *Luis Valdez, Edward James Olmos, Tyne Daly.* Adapting his own play, Valdez's determinedly theatrical film is set in 1942 Los Angeles. Based on a real incident, the story follows a violent encounter between two Chicano gangs which results in murder, incarceration for the innocent as well as the guilty, and a bigoted justice system bent on throwing them all in prison. Narrating the proceedings and leading in wonderfully choreographed song and dance salsa is the cynical, serpentine Olmos. Unexpectedly timely in light of the recent L.A. police mugging, the film is an impassioned exposé on the prejudiced oppression of the American people and the failure of its lofty dream for the Mexican immigrants who attempt to assimilate. A serious but entertaining and lively musical. ★★★

Zorba the Greek

(1964, 146 min, US/Greece, Michael Cacoyannis) *Anthony Quinn, Alan Bates, Lila Kedrova.* An exceptionally accomplished screen version of the acclaimed Kazantzakis novel, with Quinn giving the performance of a lifetime as the title character. Set in Crete, the story follows the adventures of the fun-loving Zorba who takes a reserved Britisher (Bates) under his wing, teaching him his philosophy of life. Kedrova deservedly won an Oscar as Zorba's aging mistress. Features a terrific Mikis Theodorakis score. ★★★½ DVD Letterbox: $14.99, VHS: $19.99

Zorro, the Gay Blade

(1981, 93 min, US, Peter Medak) *George Hamilton, Lauren Hutton, Brenda Vaccaro.* After successfully spoofing the vampire movie in *Love at First Bite*, Hamilton sets his sights on the Zorro legend, with uneven results. Hamilton plays the twin sons of Zorro, one a swashbuckler, the other a gay bon vivant. Some laughs, and to its credit, not offensive. ★★½ DVD: $24.99, VHS: $9.99

Zouzou

(1934, 92 min, France, Marc Allégret) *Josephine Baker, Jean Gabin.* A semiautobiographical piece with Baker as a poor laundress who finds her way out of the gutter. Her first film, *Zouzou* is a little short on substantive plot, but Baker's presence nonetheless radiates and her musical numbers scintillate. (French with English subtitles) ★★½ VHS: $29.99

Zu: Warriors from the Magic Mountain

(1983, 98 min, Hong Kong, Tsui Hark) *Yuen Biao, Brigitte Lin, Sammo Hung, Damian Lau, Moon Lee, Norman Tsui, Meng Hoi.* Early in his career, Hark asked several American special effects technicians to come to Hong Kong and help him put together the kind of fantasy film that would blow audiences to the back of the theatre. The result was *Zu*, a tale rooted in Chinese mythology and legend, but boasting the most spectacular special effects (of the time), which allowed its heroes and villains to fly, shoot energy bolts from their hands or eyes, fight with colossal monsters and do anything that Tsui's fertile imagination could dream up. The plot concerns a young soldier's adventures in the mystical realm of the Zu Mountains, but it is mainly there to serve the astonishing visuals, putting its characters into the most surreal situations possible. Vibrant, colorful, funny, terrifying, romantic and ultimately moving, *Zu* is the classic Hong Kong fantasy film and has it all. (Cantonese with English subtitles) ★★★★

Zulu

(1964, 139 min, GB, Cy Endfield) *Michael Caine, Stanley Baker, Jack Hawkins, Patrick Magee.* An epic battle sequence highlights this exciting adventure about an undermanned British outpost in 1879 South Africa preparing to fend off an overwhelming tribe of Zulu warriors. (Prequel: *Zulu Dawn*) ★★★ DVD Letterbox: $14.99

Zulu Dawn

(1979, 121 min, US/Netherlands, Douglas Hickox) *Burt Lancaster, Peter O'Toole, Denholm Elliott.* A well-made war epic about England's bullheadedness in its handling of the Zulu nation — which led to Britain's worst ever military defeat at Isandhlwana in 1879. A prequel to the 1964 film *Zulu*, this film features excellent action sequences and outstanding location shooting. ★★★

Josephine Baker (l.) and Jean Gabin in *Zouzou*

INDEX: TLA FAVORITES

THE DISCERNING FILM LOVER'S GUIDE

Last Tango in Paris
The Last Temptation of
Christ
Late Chrysanthemums
Late for Dinner
Late Spring
Laura
Laurie Anderson: Home of
the Brave
Law of Desire
Lawrence of Arabia
Laws of Gravity
Leaving Las Vegas
Léolo
Lianna
Liebestraum
Life Is a Long Quiet River
Life Is Sweet
Like Water for Chocolate
The Lion in Winter
Liquid Sky
Little Buddha
Little Odessa
Living in Oblivion
Local Hero
Lone Star
The Lord of the Rings:
The Fellowship of the Ring
The Lord of the Rings:
The Two Towers
The Lord of the Rings:
The Return of the King
Lost in Translation
Luna Park
The Makioka Sisters
Malcolm
Man Bites Dog
Man Facing Southeast
The Manchurian
Candidate
Manhattan
Manon of the Spring
El Mariachi
Marquis
The Marriage of Maria
Braun
Masala
M.A.S.H.
Matador
Matewan
The Matrix
McCabe and Mrs. Miller
Mean Streets
Melvin and Howard
Memento
Men...
Menace II Society
Ménage
Metropolitan
Mi Vida Loca (My Crazy
Life)
Miami Blues
Michael Collins
A Midnight Clear
Miller's Crossing
Miracle Mile
Mistress
Modern Times
Mondo New York
Monster in a Box

Mother Night
Moulin Rouge
Mulholland Drive
Multiple Maniacs
My Brilliant Career
My Dinner with Andre
My Favorite Year
My Life as a Dog
My New Gun
My Own Private Idaho
Mystery Train
Naked
Naked Lunch
Naqoyqatsi
Nashville
The Nasty Girl
Network
Next Stop, Greenwich
Village
Night on Earth
The Nightmare Before
Christmas
1900
North by Northwest
Nostalghia
O Brother, Where Art Thou?
O Lucky Man!
The Official Story
Olivier, Olivier
On Top of the Whale
Once Were Warriors
The Opposite of Sex
Orphans
Othello
Out of Sight
Paperhouse
Parents
Paris Is Burning
Paris, Texas
Parting Glances
Passion Fish
Patti Rocks
Pecker
Pee-wee's Big Adventure
The People vs. Larry Flynt
The Phantom of the
Paradise
The Philadelphia Story
Pi
The Piano
Picnic at Hanging Rock
Pink Flamingos
The Player
Police Story
Polyester
Il Postino
Powaqqatsi
Pretty Baby
Primary Colors
Prizzi's Honor
The Producers
Proof
The Prophecy
Pulp Fiction
Pump Up the Volume
Punch-Drunk Love
The Purple Rose of Cairo
Putney Swope
Quest for Fire
Quills

Quiz Show
Radio Days
Raiders of the Lost Ark
Raise the Red Lantern
Raising Arizona
Ran
The Rapture
Rashomon
Red Sorghum
Repo Man
Requiem for a Dream
Reservoir Dogs
Resurrection
The Return of the Secaucus 7
Reversal of Fortune
Rhapsody in August
Richard III
River's Edge
The Road Warrior
The Rocky Horror Picture
Show
Roger & Me
Round Midnight
The Royal Tenenbaums
Ruby in Paradise
The Ruling Class
Run Lola Run
Rushmore
Safe
Le Samouraï
Santa Sangre
Scenes from the Class
Struggle in Beverly Hills
Seconds
The Secret Garden
Secret Honor
The Secret of Roan Inish
The Secret Rapture
Serial Mom
Seven Beauties
Seven Samurai
sex, lies and videotape
Shakespeare in Love
Shallow Grave
Shame
The Shape of Things
The Shawshank Redemption
She's Gotta Have It
She's So Lovely
Shock Treatment
Short Cuts
Siberiade
Sid & Nancy
Siesta
The Silence of the Lambs
Silverlake Life: The View
from Here
Singin' in the Rain
The Singing Detective
Six Degrees of Separation
Slacker
Slaughterhouse-Five
Sleeper
Sling Blade
Smile
Smiles of a Summer Night
Smithereens
Smoke
Smoke Signals
The Snapper

Something for Everyone
Something Wild
South Park: Bigger, Longer
& Uncut
The Spanish Prisoner
Spanking the Monkey
Speaking Parts
Spetters
Spike of Bensonhurst
Stalker
Star Wars
State and Main
Stop Making Sense
The Story of Adele H.
The Story of Qiu Ju
Stranger Than Paradise
Strangers in Good Company
The Station Agent
Strictly Ballroom
The Stunt Man
Sunset Boulevard
Sunshine State
Suture
The Sweet Hereafter
Sweetie
Swept Away
Swimming to Cambodia
Swoon
Tales of the City
Talk Radio
Talk to Her
Tampopo
The Tango Lesson
Tapeheads
Taxi Blues
Taxi Driver
Terminator
That Sinking Feeling
Thelma and Louise
The Thin Blue Line
The Thin Man
13 Conversations about
One Thing
32 Short Films about Glenn
Gould
This Is Spinal Tap
Tie Me Up! Tie Me Down!
Time Stands Still
The Tin Drum
Tin Men
To Die For
To Live
Tokyo Decadence
El Topo
Toto the Hero
Traffic
Trainspotting
The Treasure of the Sierra
Madre
Trees Lounge
Tremors
True Love
True Romance
Truman Capote's A
Christmas Memory
Trust
Tune in Tomorrow
The Twelve Chairs
12 Monkeys

Twin Peaks: Fire Walk with
Me
2 Days in the Valley
200 Motels
2001: A Space Odyssey
UFOria
The Umbrellas of Cherbourg
The Unbearable Lightness of
Being
Under Fire
Unforgiven
Until the End of the World
The Untouchables
Unzipped
The Usual Suspects
Vagabond
Vanya on 42nd Street
Victor/Victoria
Vincent & Theo
The Virgin Machine
The Virgin Spring
Visions of Light: The Art of
Cinematography
Voyager
Wallace & Gromit: A Close
Shave
Wallace & Gromit: A
Grand Day Out
Wallace & Gromit: The
Wrong Trousers
The Wash
The Wedding Banquet
Weekend
Welcome to L.A.
Welcome to the Dollhouse
What Have I Done to
Deserve This!
What's Eating Gilbert
Grape
Where the Green Ants
Dream
Where's Poppa?
Who's Afraid of Virginia
Woolf?
The Wild Bunch
Wild Reeds
William Shakespeare's
Romeo + Juliet
Wings of Desire
The Wings of the Dove
The Winslow Boy
Winter of Our Dreams
Without You I'm Nothing
A Woman in Flames
A Woman under the
Influence
The Women
Wonder Boys
The World According to
Garp
WR: Mysteries of the
Organism
Written on the Wind
X — The Unheard Music
Xica
Y Tu Mamá También
The Year of Living
Dangerously
Young Frankenstein
Zebrahead
Zelig
Zentropa

Index: Country of Origin

THE DISCERNING FILM LOVER'S GUIDE

The Fifth Monkey
Foreign Land
Four Days in September
Gabriela
Gilberto Gil: Kaya N'Gan
Daya
Happily Ever After
Her Summer Vacation
Hour of the Star
How Tasty Was My Little
Frenchman
I Love You
Kiss of the Spider Woman
Lady on the Bus
Love, Strange Love
Luzia
Madame Satã
The Man in the Box
The Naked Sun
O Amor Natural
Opera do Malandro
Orfeu
Pixote
Possible Loves
Princesa
Quilombo
Rachel Files: Assignment Rio
Raoni: The Fight for the
Amazon
Ritual of Death
Satanic Attraction
The Story of Fausta
Subway to the Stars
Terra em Transe
Tieta of Agreste
Vera
Where the River
Runs Black
Women in Fury
Xica

Burkina Faso
Tilaï
Yaaba (Grandmother)

Canada
Absolon
The Adjuster
Afterglow
All Around the Town
American Boyfriends
Anne of Avonlea
Anne of Green Gables
The Apprenticeship of Duddy
Kravitz
Ararat
Atlantic City
The Barbarian Invasions
The Bay Boy
Beautiful Dreamers
Beefcake
Behind the Veil: Nuns
Being at Home with Claude
Belly of the Beast
Better Than Chocolate
Black Christmas
Black Robe
Blind Trust
Boondock Saints
The Boys of St. Vincent
Broken Vows
The Brood
The Brotherhood III: Young
Demons
Bruiser

By Design
Calendar
Camilla
Careful
Century Hotel
The Changeling
Charms for the Easy Life
Chilly Dogs
Cirque du Soleil
The Claim
Clearcut
Crash
Crazy Moon
Cube
Dance Me Outside
Dancing in the Dark
Dead Ringers
Deadly Currents
Death Warrant
The Decline of the American
Empire
Desire
Dr. Bethune
Double Happiness
Dreamers of the Day
Elmore Leonard's Criminal
Records
The Escape
eXistenZ
Exotica
The Event
Family Viewing
The Fast Runner
Fire
The Five Senses
For the Moment
Forbidden Love: The
Unashamed Stories of
Lesbian
Fortune and Men's Eyes
The Fraternity
Ginger Snaps
Ginger Snaps II: Unleashed
Good Night Michelangelo
The Grey Fox
Grey Owl
The Gunrunner
The Hanging Garden
Haven't We Met Before?
The Haunting of Julia
Heartaches
Heaven on Earth
Heavy Metal
Highway 61
Highway of Heartache
Hiroshima
The Housekeeper
Hustler White
In the Land of the War
Canoes
In the Belly of the Dragon
Invasion
I've Heard the Mermaids
Singing
Jack Kerouac's Road
Jericho Mansions
Jesus of Montreal
Jesus' Son
Kids in the Hall: Brain
Candy
Kissed
Last Night
Leaving Metropolis
Leeches

Léolo
Liberty Stands Still
Life Classes
Lilies
Love and Human Remains
A Loving Father
Loyalties
Maelstrom
Mambo Italiano
Manufacturing Consent:
Noam Chomsky and the
Media
Map of the Human Heart
Marco Polo
Margaret's Museum
Maria Chapdelaine
Marquez – Tales Beyond
Solitude
Masala
Max
Meatballs
Men With Brooms
Mon Oncle Antoine
Murder by Decree
My American Cousin
My Life without Me
Next of Kin
Night Zoo
No Skin off My Ass
Northern Extremes
Outrageous!
The Outside Chance of
Maximilian Glick
A Paper Wedding
Paris, France
Paul Strand: Under the Dark
Cloth
The Perfect Son
Perfectly Normal
Posers
Pretend You Don't See Her
Prom Night
Punch
Rabid
The Reflecting Skin
The Rocketship Reel
Rude
Rub & Tug
Salut Victor!
The Savage Woman
Scanner Cop
Scanners 1, 2, 3
Scream of Stone
Seducing Maarya
See You Monday
Seizure
Set Me Free
The Sex of the Stars (Le Sexe
Des Étoiles)
Shivers
A Short Film Festival
The Silent Partner
Spacehunter: Adventures in
the Forbidden Zone
Speaking Parts
Spider
Stardom
The Statement
Straight from the Heart
Strangers in Good Company
Strangers in Good Company
Super 8½
The Sweet Hereafter
Sweet Movie

Tales from the Gimli Hospital
32 Short Films About Glenn
Gould
This Is My Father
Ticket to Heaven
To Catch a Killer
Two Brothers and Two Others
Urinal
Videodrome
Wasted
Watermelon's Baked and
Baking
Wedding in White
When Night Is Falling
Why Shoot the Teacher
Wisecracks
The Wrong Guy
Zero Patience

Chile
Johnny 100 Pesos
Sleeping Beauty

China
Autumn Moon
Big Shot's Funeral
The Blue Kite
Blush
China, My Sorrow
Combination Platter
The Day the Sun Turned
Cold
Dr. Bethune
Double Happiness
East Palace West Palace
The Emperor and the Assassin
The Emperor's Shadow
Ermo
Fall in Love with Versace
Farewell My Concubine
Fleeing by Night
Flowers of Shanghai
Frozen
Girl from Hunan
The Go-Masters
A Great Wall
Happy Times
Hard Boiled
The Honor of Dongfang Xu
Horse Thief
Ju Dou
The King of Masks
Life on a String
The Missing Gun
A Mongolian Tale
Moving the Mountain
Not One Less
Quitting
Raise the Red Lantern
Red Cherry
Red Firecracker, Green
Firecracker
Red Sorghum
The Reincarnation of Golden
Lotus
The Road Home
Shadow Magic
Shanghai Triad
Shower
So Close to Paradise
The Story of Qiu Ju
Suzhou River
Temptress Moon
To Live
Together

Unknown Pleasures
The Turandot Project
The Wedding Banquet
Windhorse
Women from the Lake of
Scented Souls
Women in Prison
The Wooden Man's Bride
Xiu Xiu: The Sent Down Girl
Yellow Earth

Columbia
Besame Mucho
El Immigrante Latino
Miracle in Rome
Los Niños Abandonados
Our Lady of the Assassins
Rodrigo D: No Future

Cuba
Bitter Sugar
Buena Vista Social Club
Butterflies on the Scaffold
(Mariposas en el
Andamio)
Cuba Feliz
Death of a Bureaucrat
Guantanamera!
I Am Cuba
The Last Supper
Letters from the Park
Life Is to Whistle
Memories of
Underdevelopment
Portrait of Teresa
Strawberry & Chocolate
Things I Left in Havana
Up to a Certain Point
Vampires in Havana
A Very Old Man with
Enormous Wings
Waiting List

Czech Republic
All My Loved Ones
Autumn Spring
Body Without Soul
Conspirators of Pleasure
Dark Blue World
Divided We Fall
Faust
Little Otik
Mandragora
Not Angels But Angels
Witches' Hammer

Czechoslovakia
Alice
The Boxer and Death
Closely Watched Trains
Ecstacy
The Elementary School
The Fireman's Ball
Jan Svankmajer: Alchemist of
the Surreal
Kolya
Larks on a String
The Last Butterfly
Loves of a Blonde
Scenes of the Surreal
The Shop on Main Street
Three Wishes for Cinderella
Valerie and Her Week of
Wonders
The White Dove

Denmark

All Things Fair
Babette's Feast
The Celebration
Creole Giselle
Dancer in the Dark
Day of Wrath
The Element of Crime
Emma's Shadow
Flickering Lights
Friends Forever
Gertrud
Hamsun
Heart of Light
Hip Hip Hurrah
Hunger
The Idiots
Italian for Beginners
The King Is Alive
The Kingdom
Kira's Reason: A Love Story
Ladies on the Rocks
Medea
Memories of a Marriage
Mifune
The Night Visitor
Nightwatch
Ordet
Pelle the Conqueror
Pretty Boy
Pusher
Rembrandt — 1669
The Silent Touch
Smilla's Sense of Snow
Twist and Shout
Wolf at the Door
A World of Strangers
You Are Not Alone

Dominican Republic

Neuba Yol

Egypt

Alexandria Again and
    Forever
Alexandria... Why?
Destiny (al Massir)
An Egyptian Story
Emigrant
The Other

Finland

Ambush
Ariel
Born American
Daddy and the Muscle
    Academy
Leningrad Cowboys Go
    America
The Man Without a Past
The Match Factory Girl
Zombie and the Ghost Train

France

À la Mode
À Nos Amours
À Nous la Liberté
The Accompanist
Act of Aggression
L'Addition
The Adventures of Felix
An Affair of Love
L'Age d'Or
Alias Betty
Alice and Martin

All the Mornings of the World
All Night Bodega
The Alley Cats
Alphaville
Amélie
Amen.
An Affair of Love (Une
    Liaison d'Amour)
And God Created Woman
And Hope to Die
And Now Ladies &
    Gentlemen
And Now My Love
The Anderson Platoon
Angele
L'Anne des Meduses
Aphrodite
L'Argent
Artemisia
As If It Were Yesterday
The Assassination of Trotsky
Asterix
L'Atalante
Au Revoir les Enfants
L'auberge Espagnole (The
    Spanish Apartment)
Autumn Tale
Bach and Broccoli
Bad Girls
Baise-Moi
The Baker's Wife
Le Bal
La Balance
Balzac: A Life of Passion
Band of Outsiders
Bandits
Barbarella
Barocco
The Bathers
The Battle of Austerlitz
Baxter
The Bear
Beatrice
Le Beau Marriage
Beau Pere
Le Beau Serge
Beaumarchais, the Scoundrel
Beauty and the Beast
Becoming Colette
Bed and Board
Beethoven
Beethoven's Nephew
Behind the Sun
Belle de Jour
La Belle Noiseuse
The Best Way
La Bete Humaine
Betty
Betty Blue
Between Heaven and Earth
Les Biches
The Big Blue
The Big Grab
    (Melodie en sous-sol)
Birgitt Haas Must
    Be Killed
Bitter Moon
Bizarre, Bizarre
Black Tights
Blood of a Poet
Blood of Beasts
    (Le Sang des Bêtes)
The Blood of Others
Blood Relatives

Blue
Blue Country
Blue Jeans
Bob le Flambeur
Bon Voyage &
    Aventure Malgache
Le Boucher
Boudu Saved
    from Drowning
La Boum
Boyfriends and Girlfriends
    (L'Ami de Mon Amie)
Breathless
The Bride Wore Black
Brief Crossing
Brotherhood of the Wolf
Buffet Froid
Cafe au Lait
La Cage aux Folles 1, 2, 3
Calle 54
Camille Claudel
Capitaine Conan
Carnage
Cartouche
Cat and Mouse
Celestial Clockwork
    (Mécanicas Célestes)
Celine and Julie
    Go Boating
La Cérémonie
César
César and Rosalie
Chanel Solitaire
Chaos
Charles et Lucie
Charlotte
Le Chat
The Château
A Chef in Love
Le Chèvre (The Goat)
Un Chien Andalou - Land
    without Bread
La Chienne
Children of Paradise (Les
    Enfants du Paradis)
Children of the Century
Chloë in the Afternoon
Chocolat
Choice of Arms
Les Chose de la Vie
    (The Things of Life)
Circle of Passion
Circus Angel
The City of Lost Children
Claire's Knee
Cleo from 5 to 7
    (Cleo de cinq a' sept)
The Clockmaker
Close to Leo
The Closet
Club de Femmes
Club Extinction
Cocktail Molotov
Un Coeur en Hiver
La Collectionneuse
Come Dance with Me (Voulez-
    vous danser avec moi?)
Les Comperes
Le Complot
Confidentially Yours
Contempt
Le Corbeau (The Raven)
Coup de Tête (Hothead)
Coup de Torchon

Cousin, Cousine
Le Crabe Tambour
The Crazy Ray/Entr'acte
Creezy
Crime and Punishment
The Crimes of M. Lange
The Crimson Rivers
Cross My Heart
Cyrano de Bergerac
Daddy Nostalgia
Dangerous Liaisons 1960
Danton
Day for Night
A Day in the Country
Dead Tired (Grosse Fatigue)
Deathwatch
Delicatessen
Delusions of Grandeur
Le Dernier Combat
    (The Last Battle)
Derrida
Les Destinées
Detective
Devil in the Flesh
    (Le Diable au Corps)
The Devil, Probably
Diabolically Yours
Diabolique (Les Diaboliques
    [The Fiends])
Diary of a Chambermaid
Diary of a Country Priest
Diary of a Mad Old Man
Diary of a Seducer
The Dinner Game
Dirty Dishes
Dirty Hands
The Discreet Charm of the
    Bourgeoisie
The Disenchanted (La
    Désenchantée)
Le Distrait
    (The Daydreamer)
Diva
Le Divorce
Dog Day (Canicule)
Don Giovanni
Don't Let Me Die on a
    Sunday
Donkey Skin
The Double Life of Veronique
Le Doulos
The Dreamlife of Angels
Dry Cleaning (Nettoyage à
    sec)
Duke of the Derby (Le
    Gentleman D'Epsom)
The Eagle Has Two Heads
    (L'Aigle à Deux Têtes)
The Earrings of
    Madame de...
East/West (Est/Ouest)
Edith and Marcel
8 Women
The Eighth Day
The Elegant Criminal
Elena and Her Men
The Elusive Corporal
Emmanuelle
Les Enfants Terribles
L'Enfer
Entre Nous
Esther Kahn
L'Etat Sauvage

L'Eté Meurtrier
    (One Deadly Summer)
The Eternal Return
Eyes without a Face
Fahrenheit 451
Fanny
Fantastic Planet
Le Femme Nikita
Femmes de Paris
    (Peek-a-boo)
Field of Honor
The Fifth Element
The Fire Within
    (Le Feu Follet)
Firelight
First Name: Carmen
The Flower of Evil
Forbidden Games
Four Adventures of Reinette
    and Mirabelle
The 400 Blows
Francois Truffaut: Stolen
    Portraits
Frantic
Franz
French Animation
French Can-Can
The French Detective
French Twist
The French Way
French Woman
Friday Night
Fruits of Passion
Full Moon in Paris
Full Speed (À Toute Vitesse)
The Game Is Over
Game of Seduction
A Gentle Woman (Une Femme
    Douce)
Germinal
Gervaise
Get Out Your Handkerchiefs
The Gift
The Gleaners and I
Godard/Truffaut Shorts
The Godson
Going Places
The Golden Boat
The Golden Bowl
The Good Old Naughty Days
Grain of Sand
Le Grand Chemin
Grand Illusion
La Grande Bouffe
The Green Room
The Gypsy
Hail Mary
The Hands of Orlac
Hanna K.
Happenstance
Happy New Year
    (La Bonne Annee)
Harem
Harrison's Flowers
Harvest
Hate
He Loves Me... He Loves Me
    Not
Head Against the Wall (La
    Tête Contre
    les Murs)
Head over Heels
    (A Coeur Joie!)
Heat of Desire (Plein sud)

THE DISCERNING FILM LOVER'S GUIDE

THE DISCERNING FILM LOVER'S GUIDE

And Now for Something
   Completely Different
And Now Ladies &
   Gentlemen
Angela's Ashes
The Angelic Conversation
Animal Farm
Another Country
Another Time,
   Another Place
Antonia and Jane
Apartment Zero
Aria
As You Like It
The Asphyx
The Assassination Bureau
The Assassination
   of Trotsky
Asylum
Autobiography of a Princess
The Avengers
An Awfully Big Adventure
B. Monkey
BackBeat
Bad Behavior
The Balcony
Ballad in Blue
Band of Brothers
Bandit Queen
Barnum
Barry Lyndon
Basil
Battle of Britain
The Bawdy Adventures
   of Tom Jones
Bean
Beat Girl
Beautiful People
Beautiful Thing
Becket
Bedazzled
Bedrooms and Hallways
Being Human
Bellman and True
The Belly of an Architect
Belly of the Beast
Bend It Like Beckham
Bent
Berserk
The Best of the Two Ronnies
Betrayal
Beyond Borders
Beyond the Fringe
Bhaji on the Beach
A Bigger Splash
Bilitis
Billy Budd
Billy Elliot
Billy Liar
Black Beauty
Black Narcissus
Blackmail
Blame It on the Bellboy
Bleak House
Bleak Moments
The Bliss of Mrs. Blossom
Blithe Spirit
Blow Dry
Blow-Up
Blue
Blue Ice
Blunt: The Fourth Man
The Borrowers
The Bostonians

The Boyfriend
Boyfriends
Brassed Off
Brazil
Breaking Glass
Breaking the Code
Breaking the Waves
Brides of Dracula
Brideshead Revisited
The Bridge on the
   River Kwai
A Bridge Too Far
Brief Encounter
Brighton Rock
Brimstone and Treacle
Britannia Hospital
Brother Sun, Sister Moon
Brothers Quay: Street of
   Crocodiles/The Cabinet of
   Jan Svankmajer
The Browning Version
   (1951, 1994)
The Buddha of Suburbia
Bugsy Malone
Bullet to Beijing
Bullshot
Burning Secret
Business as Usual
Buster
Butterfly Kiss
Butterfly Man
Butley
Caesar and Cleopatra
Calendar Girls
Cambridge Spies
Camelot
A Canterbury Tale
Captain Horatio Hornblower
The Captain's Paradise
The Captain's Table
Captives
Car Trouble
Caravaggio
Career Girls
Carlton-Browne of the F.O.
Carrington
Carry on Cleo
Carry on Cruising
Carry on Doctor
The Casebook of
   Sherlock Holmes
Casino Royale
Caught Looking/
   North of Vortex
The Cement Garden
The Chalk Garden
Chaplin
Chicken Run
Chariots of Fire
Chinese Boxes
Chocolat
A Chorus of Disapproval
Christabel
A Christmas Carol
City of Joy
Civilization
Clash of the Titans
The Class of Miss
   MacMichael
Clockwise
A Clockwork Orange
The Clouded Yellow
Clouds over Europe
Cold Comfort Farm

The Collection
The Collector
Comfort and Joy
The Comfort of Strangers
Coming Up Roses
The Company of Wolves
The Complete Beatles
Confidential Report
The Conqueror Worm
Consuming Passions
Contraband
The Cook, the Thief,
   His Wife & Her Lover
Copenhagen
Cousin Bette
Creature Comforts
The Creeping Flesh
Crimetime
Croupier
The Cruel Sea
Cry Freedom
Cry of the Banshee
Cry, the Beloved Country
The Crying Game
The Curse of Frankenstein
Curse of the Demon
Cyrano de Bergerac
Daddy Nostalgia
Damage
Damn the Defiant!
Dance with a Stranger
A Dangerous Man: Lawrence
   after Arabia
Dangerous Moonlight
Dante's Inferno
The Dark Angel
The Dark Crystal
Darling
Dark Journey
David Copperfield
The Dawning
A Day in the Death
   of Joe Egg
The Day of the Jackal
The Day of the Triffids
Dead of Night
Death and the Maiden
Death on the Nile
The Deceivers
December Flower
Deep Cover
Defence of the Realm
Demon Barber
   of Fleet Street
Desire
The Detective
   (Father Brown)
Devil Girl from Mars
The Devils
Die Another Day
Die! Die! My Darling!
Different for Girls
A Different Kind of Love
Dirty Pretty Things
Distant Voices, Still Lives
The Divorce of Lady X
The Doctor and the Devils
Dr. Faustus
Doctor in the House
Dr. Jekyll and Sister Hyde
Dr. No
Dr. Phibes Rises Again
Dr. Strangelove
Dr. Terror's House of Horrors

Dr. Who: Pyramids of Mars
Dr. Who and the Daleks
Doctor Zhivago
Dog Soldiers
The Dogs of War
A Doll's House
Don't Look Now
Dracula Has Risen
   from the Grave
Dracula: Prince of Darkness
The Draughtsman's Contract
Dreamchild
Dreaming of Joseph Lees
The Dresser
The Dressmaker
Drowning by Numbers
Drums
The Duellists
Duet for One
Dust Devil
The Eagle Has Landed
East Is East
Easy Riders, Raging Bulls
Easy Virtue
Eat the Rich
The Ebony Tower
Edge of Darkness
Edge of Sanity
Educating Rita
Edward II
Effi Briest
11 Harrowhouse
Elizabeth
The Elusive Pimpernel
Emily Brontë's Wuthering
   Heights
Emma
The Emperor's New Clothes
Empire State
Enchanted April
Encore
The Endless Game
Endless Night
Enemy at the Gates
The English Patient
An Englishman Abroad
The Englishman Who Went
   Up a Hill,
   But Came Down
   a Mountain
Enigma
The Entertainer
Entertaining Mr. Sloane
Erik the Viking
Esther Kahn
Field2
Eureka
Ever After
Evergreen
The Evil of Frankenstein
Evil Under the Sun
Excalibur
Experience Preferred...
   But Not Essential
Expresso Bongo
Eyes Wide Shut
Face
Fairy Tale: A True Story
The Fall of the Louse of Usher
The Fallen Idol
Family Life
   (Wednesday's Child)
Fanny Hill

Far from the
   Madding Crowd
The Far Pavillions
Farewell, My Lovely
The Favor, the Watch
   and the Very Big Fish
Fawlty Towers
The Fearless
   Vampire Killers
Feast of July
Fellow Traveler
ffolkes
Fiend without a Face
Fierce Creatures
The Fifth Monkey
Fire over England
First Love
First Men in the Moon
A Fish Called Wanda
For Your Eyes Only
Force 10 from Navarone
Foreign Body
A Foreign Field
Forever Young
The Forsyte Saga
Fortunes of War
The 49th Parallel
Four Days in July
The Four Feathers
The Four Musketeers
Four Weddings
   and a Funeral
1492: Conquest
   of Paradise
The Fourth Protocol
Frauds
French Lesson
The French Lieutenant's
   Woman
Frenzy
From Beyond the Grave
From Russia with Love
The Full Monty
Funeral in Berlin
Funny Bones
Gandhi
The Garden
The Gathering Storm
Georgy Girl
Get Carter
Get Real
Getting It Right
The Ghost Goes West
Ghost in the Noonday Sun
The Girl in a Swing
The Girl in the Picture
Girl with a Pearl Earring
Girl with Green Eyes
Girls on Top
Go Now
The Golden Voyage of Sinbad
GoldenEye
Goldfinger
The Good Father
A Good Man in Africa
The Good Thief
Goodbye, Mr. Chips
Gorgo
The Gorgon
Gothic
The Governess
Grave Indiscretion
Great Expectations
The Great Muppet Caper

THE DISCERNING FILM LOVER'S GUIDE

THE DISCERNING FILM LOVER'S GUIDE

Saint Clara
Sallah
Save the Lifeguard
Shoah
The Specialist
Take 2
They Were Ten
Time of Favor
Torn Apart
Trembling Before G-d
Under the Domim Tree
A Wall in Jerusalem
Wedding in Galilee
Witness to the Holocaust
Women
The Wooden Gun
Yana's Friends
Yossi & Jagger

Italy

Accattone!
Aclá
Acqua e Sapone
Aida
Alberto Express
All Screwed Up
Allegro Non Troppo
Allonsanfan
Alphaville
Amarcord
Amazon Jail
Amore
And the Ship Sails On
Andy Warhol's Dracula
Andy Warhol's Frankenstein
Arabian Nights
L'Avventura
The Bachelor
Le Bal
Basileus Quartet
The Battle of Austerlitz
Before the Revolution
Belle de Jour
Bellissima
Bellissimo
The Berlin Affair
Besieged
The Bicycle Thief
Il Bidone (The Swindlers)
Big Deal on
    Madonna Street
The Bird With the
    Crystal Plumage
Les Biches
Black Sunday
Blonde in Black Leather
Blood Feud
Blood and Roses
Blow-Up
The Boss Is Served
    (La Padrona e Servita)
Bread & Tulips
Brother Sun, Sister Moon
Bruno Bozzetto,
    Animator Pt. 1
Burn! (Queimada)
Cabiria
Cafe Express
Calle 54
Camille 2000
The Canterbury Tales
Carmen (Bizet's)
Caro Diario
The Cat O'Nine Tails

Cemetery Man
Children Are Watching Us (I
    Bambini Ci Guardano)
Christ Stopped at Eboli
The Church
Ciao, Professore!
Cinema Paradiso
City of Women
The Clowns
Club Extinction
The Conformist
Contempt
Conversation Piece
The Conviction
Corrupt
Count Dracula
Creepers
The Damned
Danger: Diabolik
Dark Eyes
Days
Death in Venice
The Decameron
Decameron #2 ...Le Altre
    Novelle del Boccaccio
Deep Red
Demons
Devil in the Flesh
Di Mamma Non
    Ce N'e una Sola
Diary of Forbidden Dreams
Dirty Hands
The Divine Nymph
Divorce — Italian Style
Doctor Butcher M.D.
La Dolce Vita
Don Giovanni
Double Face
Down and Dirty
The Easy Life
    (Il Sorpasso)
The Eclipse (L'Eclisse)
8½
1860
The Embalmer
The Emperor's New Clothes
Empty Canvas
Ernesto
Everybody's Fine
The Eyes, the Mouth
The Family
La Favorita
Fear
Fellini Satyricon
Fellini's Roma
Fiorile
A Fistful of Dollars
A Fistful of Dynamite
The Flavor of Corn
Flight of the Innocent
For a Few Dollars More
Forever Mary
Francesco
The Garden of the
    Finzi-Continis
General Della Rovere
The Genesis Children
Germany Year Zero
Germinal
Get Rita
Ginger and Fred
The Gold of Naples
The Golden Coach
Good Morning Babylon

The Good, the Bad and
    the Ugly
The Gospel According
    to St. Matthew
La Grande Bouffe
La Grande Bourgeoise (The
    Murri Affair)
La Grande Guerra
Il Grido (The Outcry)
The Grim Reaper
    (La Commare Secca)
Hatchet for a Honeymoon
The Hawks and
    the Sparrows
Head of the Family
Heaven
Henry IV
Hercules
His Secret Life
Honey
Husbands and Lovers
I Hate Blondes
The Icicle Thief
The Immortal Bachelor
In the Name of
    the Pope King
Indiscretion of an American
    Housewife
Inferno
The Inheritance
The Innocent
Intervista
Iris Blond
The Iron Crown
It Happened in the Park
Johnny Stecchino
A Joke of Destiny
Juliet of the Spirits
Kaos
The Key
The King's Whore
Lamerica
The Last Emperor
The Last Kiss
Last Tango in Paris
Laugh for Joy
Life Is Beautiful (1981,
    1998)
The Life of Leonardo Da
    Vinci
Lola
Love and Anarchy
Love in the City
Love Meetings
Lovers and Liars
Ludwig
Macaroni
Maléna
Malicious
Il Mare
Mamma Roma
Man with a Cross
Medea
Mediterraneo
Mille Bolle Blu
Miracle in Milan
Mondo Cane 1 & 2
The Monster
Muriel
Musica Proibita (Forbidden
    Music)
Mussolini and I
My House in Umbria
The Naked Sun

The Name of the Rose
Nana
Night Full of Rain
Night of the Shooting Stars
The Night Porter
Night Train to Venice
Nights of Cabiria
1900
1990 – The Bronx Warriors
Nostalghia
Notes for an
    African Orestes
La Notte
La Nuit de Varennes
Oedipus Rex
The Oldest Profession
Once Upon a Time
    in the West
Open City
Open Doors
Orchestra Rehearsal
The Organizer
Orlando
Ossessione
Otello
Padre Padrone
I Pagliacci
A Pain in the A–
Paisan
Pardon My Trunk
    (Buongiorno, Elefante!)
Partner
The Passenger
Passion d'Amore
The Passionate Thief
Phenomena
Pinocchio
Planet of the Vampires
Pool Hustlers
Porcile (Pigsty)
Portrait of a Woman, Nude
    (Nudo di Donna)
The Postman (Il Postino)
Princesa
Profumo di Donna
    (Scent of a Woman)
A Pure Formality
The Purple Taxi
Red Desert
The Red Tent
Respiro
Rocco and His Brothers
The Roof
Rorret
Sacco and Vanzetti
St. Michael Had a Rooster
Saló: 120 Days of Sodom
Santa Sangre
Scarlet Diva
La Scorta
Screw Loose
Secret Fantasy
The Secret Life of
    Sergei Eisenstein
Seduced and Abandoned
The Seduction of Mimi
Senso (Wanton Countess)
Sensual Man
Seven Beauties
Seven Deadly Sins
The Sheltering Sky
Shoeshine

Shoot Loud, Louder...
    I Don't Understand!
La Signora di Tutti
Simon Bolivar
The Sky is Falling
Sleepless
The Son's Room
Sotto Sotto
Spaghetti House
A Special Day
The Spider's Stratagem
The Star Maker
The Station
Stealing Beauty
The Story of Boys
    and Girls
The Story of the Dancing Frog
La Strada
Stromboli
Summer Night
Suspiria
Swept Away
Tales of Ordinary Madness
The Taming of the Shrew
The Tenth Victim
Teorema
Teresa Venerdi
La Terra Trema
This Man Must Die
Three Brothers
Tigers in Lipstick
Till Marriage Do Us Part
'Tis a Pity She's a Whore
To Forget Venice
Torrents of Spring
Torso
The Torture Chamber
    of Baron Blood
The Tragedy of a Ridiculous
    Man
Trauma
La Traviata
Tree of Wooden Clogs
Two Evil Eyes
Two Women
L'Udienza
Umberto D
Unsane
Utz
Vanina Vanini
Variety Lights
A Very Private Affair
I Vitelloni
Vito and the Others
Volere Volare
Voyage in Italy (Strangers)
War and Peace
Ways of Love (L'Amore)
We the Living
West and Soda
Where the Hot
    Wind Blows
Where's Picone?
White Nights
The White Sheik
Whoever Says the
    Truth Shall Die
Wifemistress
Wildflower
Woman Times Seven
Yesterday, Today
    and Tomorrow
Zombie

Ivory Coast

Black and White in Color
Faces of Women
Woubi Cheri

Jamaica

Bongo Man
Countryman
Dancehall Queen
The Harder They Come
Land of Look Behind
Life + Debt

Japan

Adrenaline Drive
Advancer Tina
The Affairs
After Life
An Actor's Revenge
Akira
Akira Kurosawa's Dreams
Akira Production Report
Angel Dust
Angel Sanctuary
Antarctica
Appleseed
An Autumn Afternoon
Audition
Baby Cart at the River Styx
Baby Cart to Hades
Baby Cart in Peril
Baby Cart in the Land of
 Demons
The Bad Sleep Well
The Ballad of Bering Strait
The Ballad of Narayama
Bastoni: Stick Handlers
Battle Angel
Bible Black
Bible Black: Second
 Sacrament
Black Lizard
Black Magic M-66
Black Rain
Blood – The Last Vampire
Blood Shadow
Boiling Point
Branded to Kill
Brother
The Burmese Harp
The Bushido Blade
Chaos
The City of Lost Souls
Cosplay Encyclopedia
Cruel Story of Youth
Cyber Ninja
Dangaio
Dark Water
De:vadasy
Dead or Alive
Demon Fighter Kocho
Dersu Uzala
Devil Hunter Yohko
Dirty Pair: Affair
 on Nolandia
Dirty Thoughts
Doctor Shameless
Dodes'ka-den
Dominion
Doomed Megalopolis — Part
 1, Haunted Megalopolis
Double Suicide
Drifting Weeds
 (Floating Weeds)

Drunken Angel
Early Summer
The Eel
Eight Clouds Rising
Eijanaika
Empire of Passion
Endurance
Enjo
Equinox Flower
Escaflowne: The Movie
Face of Another
The Family Game
Fires on the Plain
Fireworks (Hana-Bi)
Fist of the Northstar
Forest of Little Bear
The 47 Ronin,
 Parts 1 & 2
Freeze Me
Fruits of Passion
Fugitive Samurai
The Funeral
G-Saviour: The Movie
Gall Force — Eternal Story
Gall Force 2 — Destruction
The Gambling Samurai
Gate of Hell
Ghost in the Shell
Giant Robo — Episodes 1-4
Godzilla 2000
Godzilla, King of the
 Monsters
Godzilla vs. Biolante
Godzilla vs. the
 Sea Monster
Godzilla vs. the
 Smog Monster
Golden Demon
Gonza the Spearman
The Green Slime
Gunbuster
The Guyver,
 Episodes 1 & 2
Happiness of the Katakuris
Harakiri
Harmagedon
The Hidden Fortress
High and Low
Himatsuri
Hiroshima
The Human
 Condition, Part 1, 2, 3
I.K.U. (This Is Not Love.
 This Is Sex)
The Idiot
Ikiru
In the Realm of Passion
In the Realm of the Senses
Insect Woman
Irezumi
The Island
 (Hodaka No Shima)
Jungle De Ikou!
Kagemusha: The
 Shadow Warrior
Kai Doh Maru
Karen
Kikujiro
Kojiro
Kwaidan
Late Chrysanthemums
Late Spring
Laughing Target

Legend of 8 Samurai
Lensman
The Life and Opinion
 of Masseur Ichi
Life of Oharu
Lone Wolf and Cub Series
Love and Faith
Love Lessons
The Lower Depths
M.D. Geist
MacArthur's Children
Macross Two,
 Episodes 1 & 2
Maetel Legend
Mail Order Maiden 28
The Makioka Sisters
The Manster
Men Who Tread on
 the Tiger's Tail
Merry Christmas Mr
 Lawrence
Minbo: The Gentle Art
 of Japanese Extortion
Mishima: A Life in
 Four Chapters
The Mistress
Moon Child
Mother
Mothra
My Neighbor Totoro
My Sexual Harassment
The Mystery of Rampo
Nanami: First Love
9' O-Clock Woman
No Regrets for Our Youth
Nobody
Nomigi Pass
Odd Obsession
Okoge
One-Eyed Swordsman
Onibaba
Orguss, Episodes 1 & 2
Osaka Elegy
The Phoenix
Pistol Opera
The Pornographers
Princess Mononoke
Princess Yang Kwei Fei
Ran
Rashomon
The Razor – Sword of Justice
Record of a Tenement
 Gentleman
Red Beard
Red Lion
Return to Glory –
 Michelangelo Revealed
The Returner
Rhapsody in August
Rikisha-Man
Rikyu
Ringu 1 & 2
Robot Carnival
Rodan
Sabu
Saga of the Vagabonds
Samurai I , II, III
Samurai Banners
Samurai Reincarnation
Samurai Saga
Sandakan No. 8
Sanjuro
Sanshiro Sugata
Sansho the Baliff

The Sea Is Watching
Secret Desires
The Seven Samurai
Sex Demon Queen
Shall We Dance
Shogun Assassin
The Silk Road
Snow Country
Son of Godzilla
Spirited Away
Story of the Late
 Chrysanthemums
Stray Dog
Street of Shame
The Streetfighter
Suicide Club
Summer Vacation 1999
The Supergal
Sword of Doom
Sword of Fury I & II
Sword of Vengeance
Swords of Death
Tales of the Taira Clan (Shin
 Heike Monogatari)
Tampopo
A Taxing Woman
A Taxing Woman's Return
Tetsuo: The Iron Man
10 Tokyo Warriors
3x3 Eyes – Pts 1 & 2
Throne of Blood
Tokyo Decadence
Tokyo Drifter
Tokyo Godfathers
Tokyo Olympiad
Tokyo Story
Tora! Tora! Tora!
Twenty-Four Eyes
2LDK
Ugetsu
Urotsukidoji – Legend of the
 Overfiend
Urotsukidoji 2 – Legend of the
 Demon Womb
Vampire Hunter D: Bloodlust
Vengeance Is Mine
Versus
Very Private Lesson
Violence at Noon
Violent Cop
Visitor Q
War in Space
Wasabi
White Heaven in Hell
Woman in the Dunes
Yojimbo
Zatoichi – The Life and
 Opinion of Masseur Ichi
Zatoichi: Massuer Ichi and a
 Chest of Gold
Zatoichi Meets Yojimbo
Zatoichi: The Blind
 Swordsman and the Chess
 Expert
Zatoichi: The Blind
 Swordsman and
 the Fugitives
Zatoichi: The Blind
 Swordsman's Vengeance
Zeram

Korea

Attack the Gas Station!
Chunhyang

Desire
Doggy Poo
Herapurple: Devil Goddess
The Isle
Lies
Memento Mori (Whispering
 Corridors 2)
Poison
Reptilian
Shiri
Tell Me Something
301 302
The Way Home
Western Avenue
White Badge
Why Has Bodhi-Dharma Left
 for the East?
Wonsan Operation
Yongary, Monster from
 the Deep

Kyrgyzstan

Beshkempir: The Adopted Son

Luxembourg

Girl with a Pearl Earring
More
Tempo

Macedonia

Before the Rain

Martinique

Sugar Cane Alley

Mexico

All of Them Witches
 (Sobrenatural)
Amores Perros
Angel de Fuego
Between Pancho Villa and a
 Naked Woman (Entre
 Pancho Villa y una Mujer
 Desnuda)
Bloody Proof
El Bruto
Cabeza de Vaca
Cilantro y Perejil
Cronos
The Crime of Padre Amaro
The Criminal Life of
 Archibaldo de la Cruz
La Cucaracha
Danzón
Death in the Garden
Death on the Beach
Deep Crimson
Doña Barbara
Doña Herlinda
 and Her Son
Dreaming About You
Dust to Dust
El (This Strange Passion)
Enamorada (In Love)
Erendira
The Exterminating Angel
Fever Mounts in El Pao
Frida
From Dusk Till Dawn 3
The Great Madcap
 (El Gran Calavera)
Illusions Travel
 by Streetcar
The Last Call (Ultima
 Llamada)
Like Water for Chocolate

THE DISCERNING FILM LOVER'S GUIDE

INDEX: DIRECTORS

THE DISCERNING FILM LOVER'S GUIDE

THE DISCERNING FILM LOVER'S GUIDE

The Boat
The General
The Goat
The High Sign
The Love Nest
My Wife's Relations
The Navigator
Neighbors
One Week
Our Hospitality
The Saphead
Seven Chances
Sherlock, Jr.
Three Ages

Beeban Kidron

Antonia and Jane
Oranges Are Not the Only
Fruit
Shades of Fear
Swept from the Sea
To Wong Foo...Thanks for
Everything! Julie
Newmar
Used People

Krzysztof Kieslowski

Blue
Camera Buff
The Decalogue
The Double Life
of Veronique
No End
Red
White
(As writer)
Heaven

Takeshi "Beat" Kitano

Boiling Point
Brother
Fireworks (Hana-Bi)
Kids Return
Kikujiro
A Scene at the Sea
Sonatine
Violent Cop

Barbara Kopple

American Dream
Fallen Champ: The
Mike Tyson Story
Harlan County, U.S.A.
Wild Man Blues

Stanley Kramer

Bless the Beasts and
Children
The Defiant Ones
Guess Who's Coming
to Dinner
Inherit the Wind
It's a Mad, Mad,
Mad, Mad World
Judgment at Nuremberg
Not as a Stranger
Oklahoma Crude
On the Beach
The Pride and the Passion
The Runner Stumbles
R.P.M.

The Secret of Santa Vittoria
Ship of Fools

Stanley Kubrick

Barry Lyndon
A Clockwork Orange
Dr. Strangelove
Eyes Wide Shut
Full Metal Jacket
Killer's Kiss
The Killing
Lolita
Paths of Glory
The Shining
Spartacus
2001: A Space Odyssey

Akira Kurosawa

Akira Kurosawa's Dreams
The Bad Sleep Well
Dersu Uzala
Dodes'ka-den
Drunken Angel
The Hidden Fortress
High and Low
The Idiot
Ikiru
Kagemusha: The
Shadow Warrior
The Lower Depths
Madadayo
Men Who Tread on
the Tiger's Tail
No Regrets for Our Youth
One Wonderful Sunday
Ran
Rashomon
Red Beard
Rhapsody in August
Sanjuro
Sanshiro Sugata
Seven Samurai
Stray Dog
Throne of Blood
Yojimbo

Emir Kusturica

Arizona Dream
Black Cat White Cat
Do You Remember Dolly
Bell?
Time of the Gypsies
Underground
When Father Was Away on
Business

Neil LaBute

In the Company of Men
Nurse Betty
Possession
The Shape of Things
Your Friends and Neighbors

Ringo Lam

City on Fire
Full Contact
Maximum Risk
Replicant
The Suspect
Twin Dragons
The Victim

Fritz Lang

Beyond a Reasonable Doubt
The Big Heat

The Blue Gardenia
Clash By Night
Cloak and Dagger
Destiny
Fury
Hangmen Also Die
M
Metropolis
Ministry of Fear
Die Nibelungen
Rancho Notorious
The Return of Frank James
Scarlet Street
Siegfried
Spiders
Spies
Testament of Dr. Mabuse
The Thousand Eyes
of Dr. Mabuse
Western Union
While the City Sleeps
Woman in the Moon
You and Me
You Only Live Once

David Lean

Blithe Spirit
The Bridge on
the River Kwai
Brief Encounter
Doctor Zhivago
Great Expectations
Hobson's Choice
In Which We Serve
Lawrence of Arabia
Oliver Twist
A Passage to India
Ryan's Daughter
Summertime
This Happy Breed

Patrice Leconte

Felix and Lola
French Fried Vacation
Girl on the Bridge
The Hairdresser's Husband
Man on the Train
Monsieur Hire
Ridicule
The Widow of St. Pierre

Ang Lee

Crouching Tiger, Hidden
Dragon
Eat Drink Man Woman
The Hulk
The Ice Storm
Sense and Sensibility
Pushing Hands
Ride with the Devil
The Wedding Banquet

Spike Lee

Bamboozled
Clockers
Crooklyn
Do the Right Thing
4 Little Girls
Get on the Bus
Girl 6
He Got Game
Joe's Bed-Stuy Barbershop
Jungle Fever
Malcolm X

Mo' Better Blues
The Original Kings of
Comedy
School Daze
She's Gotta Have It
Summer of Sam
25th Hour

Mike Leigh

Abigail's Party
All or Nothing
Bleak Moments
Career Girls
Four Days in July
Grown Ups
Hard Labour
High Hopes
Home Sweet Home
Kiss of Death
Life Is Sweet
Meantime
Naked
Nuts in May
Secrets and Lies
Topsy-Turvy
Who's Who

Claude Lelouch

And Now My Love
L'Aventure c'est L'Aventure
Bandits
Bolero
La Bonne Année
Cat and Mouse
Edith and Marcel
Happy New Year
(La Bonne Année)
A Man and a Woman
A Man and a Woman:
20 Years Later
Les Misérables
Robert et Robert

Sergio Leone

A Fistful of Dollars
A Fistful of Dynamite
For a Few Dollars More
The Good, the Bad
and the Ugly
Once Upon a Time
in America
Once Upon a Time
in the West

Richard Lester

Butch and Sundance:
The Early Years
Cuba
The Four Musketeers
A Funny Thing
Happened on the
Way to the Forum
A Hard Day's Night
Help!
How I Won the War
Juggernaut
The Knack
The Mouse on the Moon
Petulia
Return of the Musketeers
The Ritz
Robin and Marian
Superman II

Superman III
The Three Musketeers

Barry Levinson

Avalon
Bandits
Bugsy
Diner
Disclosure
Envy
An Everlasting Piece
Good Morning, Vietnam
Jimmy Hollywood
Liberty Heights
The Natural
Rain Man
Sleepers
Sphere
Tin Men
Toys
Wag the Dog
Young Sherlock Holmes
(As writer)
...And Justice for All
Best Friends
High Anxiety
Inside Moves
Silent Movie
Unfaithfully Yours

Doug Liman

The Bourne Identity
Getting In
Go
Swingers

Richard Linklater

Before Sunrise
Before Sunset
Dazed and Confused
The Newton Boys
School of Rock
Slacker
SubUrbia
Tape
Waking Life

Ken Loach

Bread and Roses
Carla's Song
Family Life (Wednesday's
Child)
Hidden Agenda
Ladybird, Ladybird
Land and Freedom
My Name Is Joe
Navigators
Raining Stones
Riff Raff
Singing the Blues in Red
Sweet Sixteen

Richard Loncraine

Bellman and True
Brimstone and Treacle
Deep Cover
The Gathering Storm
The Haunting of Julia
The Missionary
My House in Umbria
Richard III
The Wedding Gift

THE DISCERNING FILM LOVER'S GUIDE

Joseph Losey
Accident
*The Assassination
of Trotsky*
Boom!
The Boy with Green Hair
The Criminal
A Doll's House
Don Giovanni
Eva
Galileo
The Go-Between
*The Gypsy & the
Gentleman*
Mr. Klein
Modesty Blaise
Roads to the South
*The Romantic
Englishwoman*
Secret Ceremony
The Servant
Steaming
Time without Pity
La Truite

Ernst Lubitsch
Angel
Bluebeard's Eighth Wife
Design for Living
Heaven Can Wait
The Merry Widow
Ninotchka
*The Shop Around
the Corner*
*The Student Prince at
Old Heidelberg*
That Uncertain Feeling
To Be or Not to Be
Trouble in Paradise

George Lucas
American Graffiti
*Star Wars - Episode I:
The Phantom Menace*
*Star Wars - Episode II:
Attack of the Clones*
*Star Wars - Episode IV:
A New Hope*
THX-1138
(As writer)
The Empire Strikes Back
Howard the Duck
*Indiana Jones and the Last
Crusade*
*Indiana Jones and the
Temple of Doom*
Radioland Murders
Raiders of the Lost Ark
Return of the Jedi
Willow

Baz Luhrmann
Moulin Rouge
Strictly Ballroom
*William Shakespeare's
Romeo + Juliet*

Sidney Lumet
The Anderson Tapes
Critical Care
Daniel
Deathtrap
Dog Day Afternoon

Equus
Fail-Safe
Family Business
The Fugitive Kind
Garbo Talks
Gloria
The Group
Guilty as Sin
The Iceman Cometh
*Just Tell Me What
You Want*
*Last of the Mobile Hot
Shots*
*Long Day's Journey
into Night*
Lovin' Molly
The Morning After
*Murder on the
Orient Express*
Network
Night Falls on Manhattan
The Pawnbroker
Power
Prince of the City
Q & A
Running on Empty
Serpico
Stage Struck
A Stranger Among Us
12 Angry Men
The Verdict
The Wiz

David Lynch
Blue Velvet
David Lynch's Hotel Room
Dune
The Elephant Man
Eraserhead
Lost Highway
Mulholland Drive
On the Air
The Straight Story
Twin Peaks
*Twin Peaks: Fire
Walk with Me*
Wild at Heart

Adrian Lyne
Fatal Attraction
Flashdance
Foxes
Indecent Proposal
Jacob's Ladder
Lolita
9½ Weeks
Unfaithful

Dusan Makavejev
The Coca-Cola Kid
Innocence Unprotected
*Love Affair: Or...
The Missing
Switchboard Operator*
Man Is Not a Bird
Montenegro
A Night of Love
Sweet Movie
*WR: Mysteries of
the Organism*

Terrence Malick
Badlands

Days of Heaven
The Thin Red Line

Louis Malle
Alamo Bay
Atlantic City
Au Revoir les Enfants
Calcutta
Crackers
Damage
Elevator to the Gallows
The Fire Within
Frantic
The Lovers
May Fools
Murmur of the Heart
My Dinner with Andre
Pretty Baby
Spirits of the Dead
Vanya on 42nd Street
A Very Private Affair
Viva Maria
Zazie dans le Métro

David Mamet
Heist
Homicide
House of Games
Oleanna
The Spanish Prisoner
Spartan
State and Main
Things Change
The Winslow Boy
(As writer)
About Last Night...
American Buffalo
The Edge
Glengarry Glen Ross
Hannibal
Hoffa
A Life in the Theater
*The Postman Always Rings
Twice*
Rising Sun
Ronin (uncredited)
The Untouchables
Vanya on 42nd Street
The Verdict
Wag the Dog
The Water Engine
We're No Angels

**Joseph L.
Mankiewicz**
All about Eve
The Barefoot Contessa
Cleopatra
Dragnet
Five Fingers
The Ghost and Mrs. Muir
Guys and Dolls
The Honey Pot
House of Strangers
Julius Caesar
A Letter to Three Wives
No Way Out
People Will Talk
Sleuth
Suddenly, Last Summer
There Was a Crooked Man
(As writer)
Diplomaniacs
Forsaking All Others

The Keys of the Kingdom
Manhattan Melodrama
Our Daily Bread

Anthony Mann
Bend of the River
Cimarron
Desperate
El Cid
The Far Country
*The Fall of the Roman
Empire*
The Glenn Miller Story
God's Little Acre
I Want to Live
The Man from Laramie
The Naked Spur
Railroaded!
Raw Deal
Strange Impersonation
Strategic Air Command
T-Men
The Tin Star
Thunder Bay
Winchester 73

Michael Mann
Ali
Collateral
Heat
The Insider
The Jericho Mile
The Keep
The Last of the Mohicans
Manhunter
Thief

Penny Marshall
Awakenings
Big
Jumpin' Jack Flash
A League of Their Own
The Preacher's Wife
Renaissance Man
Riding in Cars with Boys

Elaine May
The Heartbreak Kid
Ishtar
Mikey and Nicky
A New Leaf
(As writer)
The Birdcage
Heaven Can Wait
Primary Colors
Such Good Friends

Paul Mazursky
Alex in Wonderland
Blume in Love
*Bob & Carol &
Ted & Alice*
*Down and Out in
Beverly Hills*
Enemies: A Love Story
Faithful
Harry and Tonto
Moon over Parador
Moscow on the Hudson
*Next Stop, Greenwich
Village*
The Pickle
Scenes from a Mall
The Tempest

An Unmarried Woman
Willie and Phil
Winchell
(As writer)
I Love You Alice B. Toklas

Ross McElwee
Charleen/Backyard
Sherman's March
Six O'Clock News
Time Indefinite

John McNaughton
The Borrower
Girls in Prison
*Henry: Portrait of a Serial
Killer*
Lansky
Mad Dog and Glory
Normal Life
Sex, Drugs and Rock 'n' Roll
Wild Things

Jean-Pierre Melville
Bob le Flambeur
Le Cercle Rouge
Le Doulos
Les Enfants Terribles
Un Flic
The Godson
Leon Morin, Priest
Le Samouraï

Nicholas Meyer
Company Business
The Day After
The Deceivers
*Star Trek II:
The Wrath of Khan*
*Star Trek VI:
The
Undiscovered Country*
Time After Time
Volunteers

Russ Meyer
*Beneath the Valley of
the Ultravixens*
*Beyond the Valley of
the Dolls*
Blacksnake!
Cherry, Harry and Raquel
Common Law Cabin
Eve and the Handyman
Faster Pussycat! Kill! Kill!
*Finders Keepers,
Lovers Weepers*
*Good Morning...
and Goodbye*
The Immoral Mr. Teas
Lorna
Mondo Topless
Motor Psycho
Mudhoney
Supervixens
Up!
Vixen
*Wild Gals of the Naked
West!*

Nikita Mikhalkov
Anna
Burnt by the Sun
Close to Eden
Dark Eyes

Pier Paolo Pasolini

Accattone!
Arabian Nights
The Canterbury Tales
The Decameron
The Gospel According
*   to St. Matthew*
The Hawks and
*   the Sparrows*
Love Meetings
Mamma Roma
Medea
Notes for an
*   African Orestes*
Oedipus Rex
Porcile (Pigsty)
RoGoPaG
Saló: 120 Days of Sodom
Teorema

Alexander Payne

About Schmidt
Citizen Ruth
Election

Sam Peckinpah

The Ballad of
*   Cable Hogue*
Bring Me the Head
*   of Alfredo Garcia*
Cross of Iron
The Deadly Companions
The Getaway
Junior Bonner
The Killer Elite
Major Dundee
The Osterman Weekend
Pat Garrett and Billy
*   the Kid*
Ride the High Country
Straw Dogs
The Wild Bunch

Arthur Penn

Alice's Restaurant
Bonnie and Clyde
The Chase
Dead of Winter
Four Friends
Inside
The Left-Handed Gun
Little Big Man
The Miracle Worker
The Missouri Breaks
Night Moves
Penn & Teller Get Killed
Target

D.A. Pennebaker

Branford Marsalis: The
*   Music Tells You*
Company: Original
*   Cast Album*
Depeche Mode 101
Don't Look Back
Down from the Mountain
Monterey Pop
Moon over Broadway
Nine Hundred Nights: The
*   Story of Big Brother and*
*   the Holding Company*
*   with Janis Joplin*

The War Room
Ziggy Stardust

Wolfgang Petersen

Air Force One
Das Boot (The Boat)
Enemy Mine
In the Line of Fire
The Neverending Story
Outbreak
The Perfect Storm
Shattered
Troy

Maurice Pialat

À Nos Amours
LouLou
Police
Under the Sun of Satan
Van Gogh

Roman Polanski

Bitter Moon
Chinatown
Death and the Maiden
Diary of Forbidden Dreams
The Fearless
*   Vampire Killers*
Frantic
Knife in the Water
Macbeth
The Ninth Gate
The Pianist
Pirates
Repulsion
Rosemary's Baby
The Tenant
Tess

Sydney Pollack

Absence of Malice
Bobby Deerfield
The Electric Horseman
The Firm
Havana
Jeremiah Johnson
Out of Africa
Random Hearts
Sabrina
The Scalphunters
The Slender Thread
They Shoot Horses,
*   Don't They*
This Property
*   Is Condemned*
Three Days of the Condor
Tootsie
The Way We Were
The Yakuza

Sally Potter

The Man Who Cried
Orlando
The Tango Lesson

Michael Powell

Black Narcissus
A Canterbury Tale
Contraband
The Elusive Pimpernel
The 49th Parallel
I Know Where I'm Going
The Life and Death of
*   Colonel Blimp*

Peeping Tom
The Red Shoes
The Spy in Black
Stairway to Heaven
Tales of Hoffman
The Thief of Bagdad

Otto Preminger

Advise and Consent
Anatomy of a Murder
Bonjour Tristesse
The Cardinal
Carmen Jones
The Court-Martial
*   of Billy Mitchell*
Exodus
Forever Amber
The Human Factor
In Harm's Way
Laura
The Man with
*   the Golden Arm*
The Moon Is Blue
River of No Return
Saint Joan

Bob Rafelson

Black Widow
Blood & Wine
Five Easy Pieces
Head
The King of
*   Marvin Gardens*
Man Trouble
Mountains of the Moon
No Good Deed
The Postman Always Rings
*   Twice*
Stay Hungry

Sam Raimi

Army of Darkness
Crimewave
Darkman
The Evil Dead
Evil Dead II
For Love of the Game
The Gift
The Quick and the Dead
A Simple Plan
Spider-Man 1 & 2

Nicholas Ray

Born to Be Bad
55 Days at Peking
Flying Leathernecks
In a Lonely Place
Johnny Guitar
King of Kings
Knock on Any Door
Lightning over Water
On Dangerous Ground
Rebel without a Cause
They Live by Night

Satyajit Ray

Aparajito
Devi
Distant Thunder
The Home and the World
The Middleman (Jana
*   Aranya)*
Pather Panchali
The Stranger
Two Daughters

The World of Apu

Carol Reed

The Agony and the Ecstasy
The Fallen Idol
The Key
A Kid for Two Farthings
Kipps
Night Train to Munich
Odd Man Out
Oliver!
The Stars Look Down
The Third Man
Trapeze
The Unicorn

Carl Reiner

All of Me
Bert Rigby, You're a Fool
The Comic
Dead Men Don't
*   Wear Plaid*
Enter Laughing
Fatal Instinct
The Jerk
The Man with Two Brains
Oh, God!
The One and Only
Sibling Rivalry
Summer Rental
Summer School
That Old Feeling
Where's Poppa?

Rob Reiner

Alex & Emma
The American President
A Few Good Men
Ghosts of Mississippi
Misery
North
The Princess Bride
Stand by Me
The Story of Us
The Sure Thing
This Is Spinal Tap
When Harry Met Sally

Jean Renoir

La Bete Humaine
Boudu Saved from
*   Drowning*
La Chienne
The Crimes of M. Lange
A Day in the Country
Diary of a Chambermaid
Eléna and Her Men
The Elusive Corporal
French Can-Can
The Golden Coach
Grand Illusion
The Little Theatre
*   of Jean Renoir*
Madame Bovary
La Marseillaise
Picnic on the Grass
Renoir Shorts
The River
Rules of the Game
The Southerner
Toni

Alain Resnais

Hiroshima Mon Amour
Last Year at Marienbad

Mon Oncle D'Amerique
Muriel
Night and Fog
Providence
Same Old Song
Short 3: Authority
Stavisky

Tony Richardson

Blue Sky
The Border
The Charge of the Light
*   Brigade*
The Entertainer
Hamlet
The Hotel New Hampshire
Joseph Andrews
The Loneliness of the Long
*   Distance Runner*
Look Back in Anger
The Loved One
Mademoiselle
Ned Kelly
A Taste of Honey
Tom Jones

Guy Ritchie

Lock Stock & Two Smoking
*   Barrels*
Snatch
Swept Away

Martin Ritt

Back Roads
The Black Orchid
The Brotherhood
Casey's Shadow
Conrack
Cross Creek
The Front
The Great White Hope
Hombre
Hud
The Long Hot Summer
The Molly Maguires
Murphy's Romance
Norma Rae
Nuts
Paris Blues
Pete 'n' Tillie
Sounder
The Spy Who Came
*   in from the Cold*
Stanley and Iris

Jacques Rivette

La Belle Noiseuse
Celine and Julie Go
*   Boating*
Divertimento
Gang of Four
Joan the Maid
The Nun (La Religieuse)
Paris Belongs to Us
Secret Defense
Up/Down/Fragile
Va Savoir
Wuthering Heights

Yves Robert

My Father's Glory
My Mother's Castle
Pardon Mon Affaire
Pardon Mon Affaire, Too

INDEX: DIRECTORS

THE DISCERNING FILM LOVER'S GUIDE

INDEX: DIRECTORS

THE DISCERNING FILM LOVER'S GUIDE

INDEX: STARS

The In-Laws
Indian Summer
Jakob the Liar
The Jerky Boys
Joshua Then and Now
Last of the Red Hot Lovers
Little Murders
Mother Night
Picture Windows
Popi
The Rocketeer
The Russians Are Coming,
   the Russians Are Coming!
The Seven Percent Solution
Slums of Beverly Hills
Simon
13 Conversations about
   One Thing
Wait Until Dark
Woman Times Seven

David Arquette
The Alarmist
At Home with the Webbers
Beautiful Girls
Buffy The Vampire Slayer
Dead Man's Walk
Dream with the Fishes
Eight Legged Freaks
Fall Time
The Grey Zone
johns
Never Been Kissed
Never Die Alone
Pulp Fiction
Ravenous
Ready to Rumble
Roadracers
Scream 1, 2, 3
See Spot Run
3,000 Miles to Graceland
Where the Day Takes You
Wild Bill

Patricia Arquette
The Badge
Beyond Rangoon
Bringing Out the Dead
Ed Wood
Ethan Frome
Far North
Flirting with Disaster
Goodbye Lover
The Hi-Lo Country
Holes
Holy Matrimony
Human Nature
The Indian Runner
Infinity
Inside Monket Zetterland
Joseph Conrad's The Secret
   Agent
Little Nicky
Lost Highway
Nightmare on Elm Street 3
Nightwatch
Stigmata
Trouble Bound
True Romance
Wild Flower

Rosanna Arquette
After Hours
Amazon Women on the Moon

The Aviator
Baby, It's You
Big Bad Love
The Big Blue
Black Rainbow
Buffalo '66
Crash
Deceiver
Desperately Seeking Susan
8 Million Ways to Die
The Executioner's Song
The Flight of the Intruder
Gone Fishin'
Hope Floats
I'm Losing You
The Linguini Incident
New York Stories
Nowhere to Run
Pulp Fiction
Search and Destroy
Silverado
S.O.B.
Trading Favors
Things Behind the Sun
The Whole Nine Yards

Jean Arthur
Arizona
The Devil and Miss Jones
Easy Living
The Ex-Mrs. Bradford
A Foreign Affair
History Is Made at Night
A Lady Takes a Chance
Mr. Deeds Goes to Town
Mr. Smith Goes
   to Washington
The More the Merrier
Only Angels Have Wings
The Plainsman
Shane
The Talk of the Town
The Whole Town's Talking
You Can't Take It with You

Fred Astaire
The Band Wagon
The Barkleys of Broadway
The Belle of New York
Blue Skies
Broadway Melody of 1940
Carefree
Daddy Long Legs
A Damsel in Distress
Dancing Lady
Easter Parade
Finian's Rainbow
Flying Down to Rio
Follow the Fleet
Funny Face
The Gay Divorcee
Ghost Story
Holiday Inn
Let's Dance
On the Beach
The Purple Taxi
Roberta
Royal Wedding
Second Chorus
Shall We Dance
Silk Stockings
The Sky's the Limit
The Story of Vernon and
   Irene Castle

Swing Time
That's Entertainment, Pt. 2
Three Little Words
Top Hat
The Towering Inferno
Yolanda and the Thief
You Were Never Lovelier
You'll Never Get Rich
Ziegfeld Follies

Richard Attenborough
The Bliss of Mrs. Blossom
Brannigan
Brighton Rock
Doctor Dolittle
Elizabeth
The Flight of the Phoenix
The Great Escape
Hamlet
The Human Factor
I'm All Right, Jack
In Which We Serve
Joseph and the Amazing
   Technicolor Dreamcoat
Jurassic Park
The League of Gentlemen
Loot
The Lost World: Jurassic Park
The Magic Christian
Miracle on 34th Street
Only Two Can Play
Rosebud
The Sand Pebbles
Seance on a Wet Afternoon
Stairway to Heaven
Ten Little Indians
10 Rillington Place
Trial and Error

Stéphane Audran
Babette's Feast
Betty
Les Biches
The Black Bird
The Blood of Others
Blood Relatives
Les Bonnes Femmes
Le Boucher
Brideshead Revisited
La Cage aux Folles 3:
   The Wedding
Coup de Torchon
   (Clean Slate)
The Discreet Charm
   of the Bourgeoisie
La Rupture
Six in Paris
The Turn of the Screw
The Unfaithful Wife
Vincent, François, Paul
   and the Others
Wedding in Blood

Dan Aykroyd
Antz
The Blues Brothers
Blues Brothers 2000
Caddyshack II
Casper
Celtic Pride
Chaplin
Coneheads
The Couch Trip
Crossroads
The Curse of the Jade
   Scorpion

Diamonds
Doctor Detroit
Dragnet
Driving Miss Daisy
Dying to Get Rich!
Earth vs. the Spider
Evolution
Exit to Eden
Feeling Minnesota
50 First Dates
Getting Away with Murder
Ghostbusters 1 & 2
The Great Outdoors
Grosse Pointe Blank
The House of Mirth
Into the Night
It Came from Hollywood
Loose Cannons
Loser
My Fellow Americans
My Girl 1 & 2
My Stepmother Is an Alien
Neighbors
Nothing But Trouble
1941
North
Pearl Harbor
Sgt. Bilko
Sneakers
Spies Like Us
This Is My Life
Tommy Boy
Trading Places
Twilight Zone: The Movie

Lauren Bacall
Appointment with Death
The Big Sleep
Blood Alley
Dark Passage
Designing Woman
Diamonds
The Fan
A Foreign Field
Harper
How to Marry a Millionaire
Innocent Victim
Key Largo
The Mirror Has Two Faces
Misery
Mr. North
Murder on the Orient
   Express
My Fellow Americans
The Portrait
Ready to Wear
Sex and the Single Girl
The Shootist
To Have and Have Not
Woman's World
Written on the Wind
Young Man with a Horn

Kevin Bacon
The Air Up There
Apollo 13
Balto
The Big Picture
Criminal Law
Digging to China
Diner
End of the Line
Enormous Changes at
   the Last Minute
A Few Good Men
Flatliners

Footloose
Forty Deuce
Friday the 13th
He Said, She Said
Hollow Man
In the Cut
JFK
Murder in the First
My Dog Skip
Mystic River
National Lampoon's
   Animal House
Picture Perfect
Planes, Trains &
   Automobiles
Queens Logic
Quicksilver
The River Wild
She's Having a Baby
Sleepers
Stir of Echoes
Telling Lies in America
Trapped
Tremors
White Water Summer
Wild Things
(As director)
Losing Chase

Josephine Baker
The French Way
Princess Tam Tam
Zouzou

Alec Baldwin
Alice
Along Came Polly
Beetlejuice
Cats and Dogs
The Cooler
Dr. Seuss' The Cat in the
   Hat
Dress Gray
The Edge
Forever Lulu
The Getaway
Ghosts of Mississippi
Glengarry Glen Ross
Great Balls of Fire
Heaven's Prisoners
The Hunt for Red October
The Juror
Looking for Richard
Malice
Married to the Mob
The Marrying Man
Mercury Rising
Miami Blues
Outside Providence
Path to War
Pearl Harbor
Prelude to a Kiss
Second Nature
The Shadow
She's Having a Baby
State and Main
Talk Radio
Thomas and the Magic
   Railroad
Two Bits
Working Girl

Christian Bale
American Psycho
Captain Corelli's Mandolin
Empire of the Sun

THE DISCERNING FILM LOVER'S GUIDE

The Waterboy
White Palace

Warren Beatty
All Fall Down
Bonnie and Clyde
Bugsy
Bulworth
Dick Tracy
Dollars
The Fortune
Heaven Can Wait
Ishtar
Kaleidoscope
Lilith
Love Affair
Madonna: Truth or Dare
McCabe and Mrs. Miller
The Parallax View
Promise Her Anything
Reds
The Roman Spring of Mrs.
    Stone
Shampoo
Splendor in the Grass
Town and Country

Kate Beckinsale
Brokedown Palace
Cold Comfort Farm
Emma
The Golden Bowl
Haunted
The Last Days of Disco
Laurel Canyon
Pearl Harbor
Serendipity
Shooting Fish
Van Helsing
Underworld

Jean-Paul Belmondo
Borsalino
Breathless
Cartouche
Casino Royale
Le Doulos
High Heels
Is Paris Burning?
Just Another Pretty Face
Léon Morin, Priest
Le Magnifique
Les Miserables
Mississippi Mermaid
Moderato Cantabile
Pierrot le Fou
Un Singe en Hiver (Monkey
    in Winter)
Stavisky
The Swashbuckler
That Man from Rio
Two Women
A Woman Is a Woman
    (Une Femme Est
    une Femme)

John Belushi
The Blues Brothers
Continental Divide
Goin' South
National Lampoon's
    Animal House
Neighbors
1941
Old Boyfriends

Roberto Benigni
Down by Law
Life Is Beautiful
Johnny Stecchino
The Monster
Night on Earth
Pinocchio
Seeking Asylum
Son of the Pink Panther

Annette Bening
American Beauty
The American President
Bugsy
The Great Outdoors
The Grifters
Guilty by Suspicion
In Dreams
Love Affair
Mars Attacks!
Open Range
Postcards from the Edge
Regarding Henry
Richard III
The Siege
Valmont
What Planet Are You From?

Jack Benny
Broadway Melody of 1936
George Washington Slept Here
Guide for the Married Man
Hollywood Canteen
The Horn Blows at Midnight
It's a Mad, Mad, Mad,
    Mad World
It's in the Bag
The Meanest Man in the
    World
To Be or Not to Be

Ingrid Bergman
Adam Had Four Sons
Anastasia
Arch of Triumph
Autumn Sonata
The Bells of St. Mary's
Cactus Flower
Casablanca
The Count of Old Town
Dr. Jekyll and Mr. Hyde
Dollar
Eléna and Her Men
Fear
For Whom the Bell Tolls
Gaslight
Goodbye Again
Indiscreet
Inn of the Sixth Happiness
Intermezzo (1937 & 1939)
Joan of Arc
June Night
A Matter of Time
Murder on the Orient Express
Notorious
Only One Night
Spellbound
Stromboli
Swedenhielms
Under Capricorn
Voyage in Italy (Strangers)
A Walk in the Spring Rain
Walpurgis Night
A Woman Called Golda
A Woman's Face

Gael Garcia Bernal
Amores Perros
The Crime of Padre Amaro
Don't Tempt Me
Y Tu Mamá También

Sandra Bernhard
An Alan Smithe Film:
    Burn Hollywood Burn!
Dinner Rush
Heavy Petting
Hudson Hawk
Inside Monkey Zetterland
The King of Comedy
The Late Shift
Madonna: Truth or Dare
The Muppets Take
    Manhattan
Sesame Street Presents
    Follow That Bird
Somewhere in the City
Track 29
Unzipped
Without You I'm Nothing
Wrongfully Accused

Halle Berry
B.A.P.S.
Boomerang
Bulworth
Catwoman
Die Another Day
Executive Decision
Father Hood
The Flintstones
Girl 6
Gothika
Introducing Dorothy
    Dandridge
Jungle Fever
Monster's Ball
The Last Boy Scout
Losing Isaiah
The Program
Queen
Race the Sun
The Rich Man's Wife
Strictly Business
Swordfish
Why Do Fools Fall in Love
X-Men
X2: X-Men United

Juliette Binoche
Alice and Martin
Blue
Children of the Century
Chocolat
Code Unknown
A Couch in New York
Damage
Emily Brontë's Wuthering
    Heights
The English Patient
Hail Mary
The Horseman on the Roof
Jet Lag
The Lovers on the Bridge
Rendez-Vous
The Unbearable Lightness
    of Being
White
The Widow of St. Pierre

Jack Black
Bob Roberts
The Cable Guy
Cradle Will Rock
Dead Man Walking
Enemy of the State
Envy
High Fidelity
Ice Age
The Jackal
Jesus' Son
Mars Attacks!
Orange County
Saving Silverman
School of Rock
Shallow Hal
Waterworld

Karen Black
Airport 1975
Angel Blue
Auntie Lee's Meat Pies
Bound and Gagged: A
    Love Story
Burnt Offerings
Can She Bake a Cherry Pie?
Capricorn One
Chanel Solitaire
Come Back to the 5 &
    Dime, Jimmy Dean,
    Jimmy Dean
Conceiving Ada
Cries of Silence
Crimetime
The Day of the Locust
Easy Rider
Family Plot
Five Easy Pieces
The Great Gatsby
Homer and Eddie
House of 1,000 Corpses
In Praise of Older Women
Invaders from Mars
It's Alive III: Island
    of the Alive
Killing Heat
Mirror Mirror
Mr. Horn
Nashville
Overexposed
Portnoy's Complaint
Red Dirt
Rubin & Ed
Tales of the City
Trilogy of Terror
Who is Henry Jaglom
You're a Big Boy Now

Rubén Blades
All the Pretty Horses
Assassination Tango
Chinese Box
Color of Night
Cradle Will Rock
Crazy from the Heart
Critical Condition
Crossover Dreams
Dead Man Out
The Devil's Own
Disorganized Crime
Fatal Beauty
Homeboy
The Josephine Baker Story
The Lemon Sisters
Life with Mikey

The Milagro Beanfield War
A Million to Juan
Mo' Better Blues
Once Upon a Time in
    Mexico
One Man's War
Predator 2
The Super
The Two Jakes

Cate Blanchett
Bandits
Charlotte Gray
Elizabeth
The Gift
Heaven
An Ideal Husband
The Lord of the Rings: The
    Fellowship of the Ring
The Lord of the Rings:
    The Two Towers
The Lord of the Rings:
    The Return of the King
The Man Who Cried
The Missing
Oscar and Lucinda
Paradise Road
Pushing Tin
The Shipping News
The Talented Mr. Ripley
Veronica Guerin
The Wedding Party

Brenda Blethyn
Anne Frank
The Buddha of Suburbia
Daddy & Them
Little Voice
Lovely & Amazing
Music from Another Room
Pumpkin
A River Runs Through It
RKO 281
Saving Grace
Secrets & Lies
Sonny
The Wild Thornberrys
    Movie
The Witches

Dirk Bogarde
Accident
A Bridge Too Far
Daddy Nostalgia
Damn the Defiant!
The Damned
Darling
Death in Venice
Despair
Doctor in the House
The Fixer
I Could Go on Singing
Justine
May We Borrow Your
    Husband?
Modesty Blaise
Night Flight from Moscow
The Night Porter
Penny Princess
Permission to Kill
Providence
Quartet
The Servant
The Sleeping Tiger
Song without End
A Tale of Two Cities
Victim

Humphrey Bogart

Across the Pacific
Action in the North Atlantic
The African Queen
All Through the Night
The Amazing Dr. Clitterhouse
Angels with Dirty Faces
The Barefoot Contessa
Beat the Devil
The Big Sleep
Brother Orchid
Bullets or Ballots
Black Legion
The Caine Mutiny
Call It Murder
Casablanca
Chain Lightning
Conflict
Dark Passage
Dark Victory
Dead End
Dead Reckoning
Deadline USA
The Desperate Hours
The Enforcer
The Harder They Fall
High Sierra
In a Lonely Place
Key Largo
Kid Galahad
Knock on Any Door
The Left Hand of God
The Maltese Falcon
Marked Woman
The Oklahoma Kid
Passage to Marseille
The Petrified Forest
The Roaring Twenties
Sabrina
Sahara
Sirocco
Stand-In
Thank Your Lucky Stars
They Drive by Night
To Have and Have Not
The Treasure of the Sierra
    Madre
The Two Mrs. Carrolls
Virginia City
We're No Angels

Helena Bonham Carter

Big Fish
Fight Club
Francesco
Getting It Right
Hamlet
The Heart of Me
Howards End
Lady Jane
Live from Baghdad
Margaret's Museum
Mary Shelley's Frankenstein
Maurice
Merlin
A Merry War
Mighty Aphrodite
Novocaine
Planet of the Apes
Portraits Chinois
A Room with a View
Sweet Revenge
The Theory of Flight
Till Human Voices Wake
    Us

Twelfth Night
Where Angels Fear to Tread
The Wings of the Dove

David Bowie

Absolute Beginners
Basquiat
Christiane F.
The Fine Art of Separating
    People From Their Money
The Hunger
Into the Night
Just a Gigolo
Labyrinth
The Last Temptation of
    Christ
The Linguini Incident
The Man Who Fell to Earth
Merry Chrsitmas, Mr.
    Lawrence
Twin Peaks: Fire Walk with
    Me
Ziggy Stardust

Sonia Braga

Angel Eyes
The Burning Season
Doña Flor and Her Two
    Husbands
Empire
From Dusk Till Dawn 3
Gabriela
I Love You
Kiss of the Spider Woman
Lady on the Bus
The Milagro Beanfield War
Moon over Parador
The Rookie
Streets of Laredo
Tieta of Agreste
Two Deaths

Kenneth Branagh

Anne Frank Remembered
Celebrity
Dead Again
Fortunes of War
The Gingerbread Man
Hamlet
Henry V
Harry Potter and the
    Chamber of Secrets
High Season
How to Kill Your Neighbor's
    Dog
Look Back in Anger
Looking for Richard
Love's Labour's Lost
Mary Shelley's Frankenstein
A Month in the Country
Much Ado About Nothing
Othello
Peter's Friends
The Proposition
Rabbit-Proof Fence
The Road to El Dorado
Shackleton
Swing Kids
The Theory of Flight
Wild Wild West
(As director)
Dead Again
Hamlet
Henry V
Love's Labour's Lost
Mary Shelley's Frankenstein

A Midwinter's Tale
Much Ado About Nothing
Peter's Friends

Marlon Brando

Apocalypse Now
The Appaloosa
Bedtime Story
The Brave
Burn! (Queimada)
Candy
The Chase
Christopher Columbus: The
    Discovery
Desiree
Don Juan deMarco
A Dry White Season
The Formula
The Freshman
The Fugitive Kind
The Godfather
Guys and Dolls
The Island of Dr. Moreau
Julius Caesar
Last Tango in Paris
The Men
The Missouri Breaks
Morituri
Mutiny on the Bounty
The Night of the Following
    Day
The Nightcomers
On the Waterfront
One-Eyed Jacks
Reflections in a Golden Eye
Sayonara
The Score
A Streetcar Named Desire
Superman: The Movie
The Teahouse of the August
    Moon
The Ugly American
Viva Zapata!
The Wild One
The Young Lions
(As director)
One-Eyed Jacks

Jeff Bridges

Against All Odds
American Heart
Arlington Road
Bad Company
The Big Lebowski
Blown Away
The Contender
Cutter's Way
8 Million Ways to Die
The Fabulous Baker Boys
Fat City
Fearless
The Fisher King
Hearts of the West
Heaven's Gate
Jagged Edge
K-Pax
King Kong
Kiss Me Goodbye
The Last American Hero
The Last Picture Show
Masked and Anonymous
The Mirror Has Two Faces
The Morning After
The Muse
Nadine

Rancho Deluxe
Rapunzel
Seabiscuit
See You in the Morning
Simpatico
Starman
Stay Hungry
Texasville
Thunderbolt and Lightfoot
Tron
Tucker
The Vanishing
White Squall
Wild Bill
Winter Kills

Jim Broadbent

And Starring Pancho Villa
    as Himself
The Avengers
The Borrowers
Bridget Jones's Diary
Bullets Over Broadway
The Crying Game
Enchanted April
Gangs of New York
The Gathering Storm
The Good Father
Iris
Joseph Conrad's The Secret
    Agent
Life Is Sweet
Little Voice
Moulin Rouge
Nicholas Nickleby
Princess Caraboo
Richard III
Rough Magic
Smilla's Sense of Snow
Topsy-Turvy
The Wedding Gift
Widows' Peak

Matthew Broderick

Addicted to Love
Biloxi Blues
The Cable Guy
Election
Family Business
Ferris Bueller's Day Off
The Freshman
Glory
Godzilla
Good Boy!
Infinity
Inspector Gadget
Ladyhawke
A Life in the Theatre
The Lion King
Master Harold and the
    Boys
Max Dugan Returns
Mrs. Parker & the Vicious
    Circle
The Music Man
The Night We Never Met
1918
On Valentine's Day
Out on a Limb
The Road to Wellville
The Stepford Wives
The Thief and the Cobbler
Torch Song Trilogy
WarGames

You Can Count on Me
(As director)
Infinity

Adrien Brody

The Affair of the Necklace
Angels in the Outfield
Bread and Roses
Dummy
Harrison's Flowers
Jailbreakers
King of the Hill
The Last Time I Commited
    Suicide
Liberty Heights
Love the Hard Way
New York Stories
Oxygen
The Pianist
The Singing Detective
Six Ways to Sunday
Solo
Summer of Sam
Ten Benny
The Thin Red Line
The Undertaker's Wedding

Charles Bronson

Act of Vengeance
Apache
Assassination
Borderline
Breakheart Pass
Chato's Land
Death Wish 1 – 5
The Dirty Dozen
The Evil That Men Do
Family of Cops
4 for Texas
The Great Escape
Hard Times
House of Wax
The Indian Runner
Lola
The Magnificent Seven
Master of the World
The Mechanic
Miss Sadie Thompson
Mr. Majestyk
Once Upon a Time in the
    West
Red Sun
Rider on the Rain
The Sandpiper
Someone Behind the Door
Telefon
Ten to Midnight
This Property Is
    Condemned
Vera Cruz
The White Buffalo

Louise Brooks

Diary of a Lost Girl
Lulu in Berlin
Memories of Berlin: The
    Twilight of the Weimar
    Culture
Pandora's Box
Prix de Beauté
The Show Off

Pierce Brosnan

Around the World in 80
    Days
Dante's Peak
The Deceivers

THE DISCERNING FILM LOVER'S GUIDE

John Cleese
The Adventures of Pluto
  Nash
An American Tail – Fievel
  Goes West
And Now for Something
  Completely Different
The Bliss of Mrs. Blossom
Clockwise
Die Another Day
Erik the Viking
George of the Jungle
The Great Muppet Caper
Fawlty Towers
Fierce Creatures
A Fish Called Wanda
Harry Potter and the
  Sorcerer's Stone
Harry Potter and the
  Chamber of Secrets
How to Irritate People
Isn't She Great
Mary Shelley's Frankenstein
Monty Python and
  the Holy Grail
Monty Python's Life
  of Brian
Monty Python's
  Meaning of Life
The Out-of-Towners
Privates on Parade
Rat Race
Romance with a
  Double Bass
Rudyard Kipling's
  The Jungle Book
The Secret Policeman's Ball
The Secret Policeman's
  Other Ball
The Secret Policeman's
  Third Ball
Shrek 2
Silverado
Splitting Heirs
Time Bandits
Whoops Apocalypse
The World Is Not Enough
Yellowbeard

Montgomery Clift
From Here to Eternity
The Heiress
I Confess
Indiscretion of an American
  Wife
Judgment at Nuremberg
Lonelyhearts
The Misfits
A Place in the Sun
Raintree County
Red River
The Search
Suddenly, Last Summer
The Young Lions

George Clooney
Batman and Robin
Confessions of a Dangerous
  Mind
From Dusk Till Dawn
Intolerable Cruelty
O Brother, Where Art
  Thou?
Ocean's Eleven
One Fine Day

Out of Sight
The Peacemaker
The Perfect Storm
Solaris
South Park – Bigger,
  Longer & Uncut
Spy Kids 3-D
The Thin Red Line
Three Kings
Welcome to Collinwood
(As director)
Confessions of a Dangerous
  Mind

Glenn Close
Air Force One
Anne Frank Remembered
The Big Chill
Cookie's Fortune
Dangerous Liaisons
Le Divorce
The Elephant Man
Fatal Attraction
Hamlet
The House of the Spirits
Immediate Family
In the Gloaming
Jagged Edge
Light Years
Mary Reilly
Mars Attacks!
Maxie
Meeting Venus
The Natural
101 Dalmatians
102 Dalmatians
Orphan Train
The Paper
Paradise Road
Pinocchio
Reversal of Fortune
The Safety of Objects
Serving in Silence
Sarah, Plain and Tall
The Stepford Wives
The Stone Boy
Stones for Ibarra
Tarzan
Things You Can Tell Just
  by Looking at Her
The World According to
  Garp

Claudette Colbert
Bluebeard's Eighth Wife
Boom Town
Cleopatra
Drums along the Mohawk
The Egg and I
Guest Wife
I Cover the Waterfront
Imitation of Life
It Happened One Night
Let's Make It Legal
Midnight
The Palm Beach Story
The Sign of the Cross
Since You Went Away
So Proudly We Hail
Three Came Home
Tomorrow Is Forever
Without Reservations

Toni Collette
About a Boy
The Boys

Changing Lanes
Clockwatchers
Connie and Carla
Cosi
Dinner with Friends
The Efficiency Expert
8½ Women
Emma
The Hours
Japanese Story
Lilian's Story
Muriel's Wedding
The Pallbearer
Shaft
The Sixth Sense
Velvet Goldmine

Ronald Colman
Arrowsmith
Bulldog Drummond
A Double Life
If I Were King
Lost Horizon
The Prisoner of Zenda
Raffles
Random Harvest
A Tale of Two Cities
The Talk of the Town
The White Sister

Jennifer Connelly
A Beautiful Mind
Career Opportunities
Dark City
Far Harbor
Higher Learning
The Hot Spot
House of Sand and Fog
The Hulk
Inventing the Abbotts
Labyrinth
Mulholland Falls
Phenomena
Pollock
Requiem for a Dream
The Rocketeer
Some Girls
Waking the Dead

Sean Connery
The Anderson Tapes
Another Time, Another
  Place
The Avengers
A Bridge Too Far
Cuba
Darby O'Gill and the Little
  People
Diamonds Are Forever
Dragonheart
Dr. No
Entrapment
Family Business
Finding Forrester
A Fine Madness
First Knight
Five Days One Summer
From Russia with Love
Goldfinger
A Good Man in Africa
The Great Train Robbery
Highlander 1 & 2
The Hill
The Hunt for Red October
Indiana Jones and the Last
  Crusade

Just Cause
The League of Extraordinary
  Gentlemen
The Longest Day
The Man Who Would Be
  King
Marnie
Medicine Man
Meteor
The Molly Maguires
Murder on the Orient Express
The Name of the Rose
Never Say Never Again
Outland
Playing by Heart
The Presidio
The Red Tent
Rising Sun
Robin and Marian
Robin Hood: Prince of
  Thieves
The Rock
The Russia House
Sword of the Valiant
Thunderball
Time Bandits
The Untouchables
The Wind and the Lion
Wrong Is Right
You Only Live Twice
Zardoz

Tom Conti
American Dreamer
Beyond Therapy
Deep Cover
The Duellists
The Dumb Waiter
Gospel According to Vic
The Haunting of Julia
Merry Christmas Mr.
  Lawrence
Miracles
The Norman Conquests
The Princess and the Pea
Reuben, Reuben
Saving Grace
Shirley Valentine
Someone Else's America
Sub Down

Chris Cooper
Adaptation
American Beauty
The Bourne Identity
Boys
Breast Men
City of Hope
Great Expectations
Guilty by Suspicion
The Horse Whisperer
Lone Star
Matewan
Me, Myself & Irene
Money Train
October Sky
The Patriot
Return to Lonesome Dove
Seabiscuit
This Boy's Life
Thousand Pieces of Gold
A Time to Kill

Gary Cooper
The Adventures of
  Marco Polo

Along Came Jones
Ball of Fire
Beau Geste
Bluebeard's Eighth Wife
Casanova Brown
Cloak and Dagger
The Court-Martial of Billy
  Mitchell
The Cowboy and the Lady
Design for Living
A Farewell to Arms
For Whom the Bell Tolls
The Fountainhead
Friendly Persuasion
The General Died at Dawn
Good Sam
The Hanging Tree
High Noon
It
Lives of a Bengal Lancer
Love in the Afternoon
Meet John Doe
Mr. Deeds Goes to Town
Morocco
The Naked Edge
Northwest Mounted Police
The Plainsman
The Pride of the Yankees
The Real Glory
Sergeant York
They Came to Cordura
Vera Cruz
The Wedding Night
The Westerner
Wings
The Wreck of the
  Mary Deare

Kevin Costner
American Flyers
The Bodyguard
Bull Durham
Dances with Wolves
Dragonfly
Fandango
Field of Dreams
For Love of the Game
The Gunrunner
JFK
Madonna: Truth or Dare
Message in a Bottle
No Way Out
Open Range
A Perfect World
The Postman
Revenge
Robin Hood: Prince of
  Thieves
Silverado
Thirteen Days
3,000 Miles to Graceland
Tin Cup
The Untouchables
The War
Waterworld
Wyatt Earp
(As director)
Dances with Wolves
Open Range
The Postman

Tom Courtenay
Billy Liar
Doctor Zhivago
The Dresser
Happy New Year

THE DISCERNING FILM LOVER'S GUIDE

Frankenstein Created
  Woman
From Beyond the Grave
The Gorgon
Hamlet
Horror of Dracula
The Hound of the
  Baskervilles
The Legend of the Seven
  Golden Vampires
Madhouse
Moulin Rouge
The Mummy
The Naked Edge
The Satanic Rites of Dracula
She
The Skull
Star Wars
Tales from the Crypt
Time without Pity
Twins of Evil
The Vampire Lovers

Vincent D'Onofrio
Adventures in Babysitting
Being Human
The Blood of Heroes
Boys Life 2
The Cell
Chelsea Walls
The Dangerous Lives of
  Altar Boys
Dying Young
Ed Wood
Feeling Minnesota
Full Metal Jacket
Happy Accidents
Household Saints
Imaginary Crimes
Impostor
Men in Black
Mr. Wonderful
Mystic Pizza
The Newton Boys
The Player
The Salton Sea
Steal This Movie
Strange Days
Stuart Saves His Family
The 13th Floor
The Velocity of Gary
The Whole Wide World
The Winner

Willem Dafoe
Affliction
American Psycho
Animal Factory
Auto Focus
Basquiat
Body of Evidence
Born on the Fourth of July
Clear and Present Danger
Cry-Baby
The English Patient
eXistenZ
Far Away, So Close
Finding Nemo
Flight of the Intruder
The Hunger
The Last Temptation of
  Christ
Light Sleeper
The Loveless
Lulu on the Bridge

Mississippi Burning
New Rose Hotel
Off Limits
Pavilion of Women
Platoon
The Reckoning
Roadhouse 66
Shadow of the Vampire
Speed 2: Cruise Control
Spider-Man
Streets of Fire
To Live and Die in L.A.
Tom & Viv
Triumph of the Spirit
Victory
White Sands
Wild at Heart

Timothy Dalton
Agatha
American Outlaws
Beautician and the Beast
Brenda Starr
Chanel Solitaire
Cleopatra
Cromwell
The Doctor and the Devils
Flash Gordon
Hawks
Jane Eyre
The King's Whore
Licence to Kill
The Lion in Winter
The Living Daylights
Looney Tunes: Back in
  Action
Naked in New York
Permission to Kill
Possessed
The Rocketeer
Scarlett
Sextette
Wuthering Heights

Matt Damon
All the Pretty Horses
The Bourne Identity
The Bourne Supremacy
Chasing Amy
Courage Under Fire
Dogma
Finding Forrester
Geronimo
Gerry
Good Will Hunting
Jay & Silent Bob Strike
  Back
Jersey Girl
The Legend of Bagger
  Vance
Mystic Pizza
Ocean's Eleven
The Rainmaker
Rounders
Saving Private Ryan
School Ties
Spirit: Stallion of the
  Cimarron
Stuck on You
The Talented Mr. Ripley
Titan A.E.
(As writer)
Good Will Hunting

Claire Danes
Brokedown Palace
Home for the Holidays
The Hours
How to Make an American
  Quilt
I Love You, I Love You Not
Igby Goes Down
Les Misérables
Little Women
The Mod Squad
Polish Wedding
Princess Mononoke
The Rainmaker
Terminator 3: Rise of the
  Machines
To Gillian on Her 37th
  Birthday
U-Turn
William Shakespeare's
  Romeo + Juliet

Jeff Daniels
Arachnophobia
Blood Work
The Butcher's Wife
The Caine Mutiny Court-
  Martial
Chasing Sleep
Checking Out
Dumb and Dumber
Escanaba in da Moonlight
Fly Away Home
Gettysburg
Gods and Generals
The Grand Tour: Disaster
  in Time
Heartburn
The Hours
The House on Carroll Street
It's the Rage
Love Hurts
Marie
My Favorite Martian
101 Dalmatians
Pleasantville
The Purple Rose of Cairo
Radio Days
Redwood Curtain
Something Wild
Speed
Sweet Hearts Dance
Tanner '88
Terms of Endearment
Trial and Error
2 Days in the Valley
Welcome Home, Roxy
  Carmichael

Bette Davis
All about Eve
All This, and Heaven Too
The Anniversary
Another Man's Poison
As Summers Die
Beyond the Forest
The Bride Came C.O.D.
Burnt Offerings
The Cabin in the Cotton
The Catered Affair
The Corn Is Green
Dangerous
Dark Victory
Dead Ringer

Death on the Nile
Deception
Empty Canvas
The Great Lie
Hush...Hush, Sweet
  Charlotte
In This Our Life
Jezebel
John Paul Jones
Juarez
June Bride
The Letter
The Little Foxes
Madame Sin
The Man Who Came to
  Dinner
Marked Woman
Mr. Skeffington
The Nanny
Now Voyager
Of Human Bondage
The Old Maid
The Petrified Forest
Phone Call from a Stranger
Pocketful of Miracles
The Private Lives of
  Elizabeth and Essex
Return from Witch
  Mountain
Satan Met a Lady
The Star
A Stolen Life
Thank Your Lucky Stars
The Virgin Queen
Watch on the Rhine
Watcher in the Woods
The Whales of August
Whatever Happened to
  Baby Jane?
Wicked Stepmother

Geena Davis
The Accidental Tourist
Angie
Beetlejuice
Cutthroat Island
Earth Girls Are Easy
Fletch
The Fly
Hero
A League of Their Own
The Long Kiss Goodnight
Quick Change
Speechless
Stuart Little 1 & 2
Thelma and Louise
Tootsie

Judy Davis
Absolute Power
Alice
Barton Fink
Celebrity
Children of the Revolution
A Cooler Climate
Deconstructing Harry
Gaudi Afternoon
Georgia
Heatwave
High Tide
Husbands and Wives
Impromptu
Kangaroo
Life with Judy Garland: Me
  & My Shadows

My Brilliant Career
Naked Lunch
The New Age
On My Own
One Against the Wind
A Passage to India
The Reagans
The Ref
Serving in Silence
Where Angels Fear to Tread
Winter of Our Dreams
A Woman Called Golda

Ossie Davis
Bubba Ho-Tep
The Client
Death of a Prophet: The
  Last Days of Malcolm X
Dinosaur
Do the Right Thing
Dr. Dolittle
The Ernest Green Story
Get on the Bus
Gladiator
Grumpy Old Men
Harry and Son
The Hill
Hot Stuff
I'm Not Rappaport
Joe Versus the Volcano
Jungle Fever
King
A Man Called Adam
Mrs. Evers' Boys
Purlie Victorious
Roots: The Next Generation
The Scalphunters
School Daze
The Stand
Twelve Angry Men

Bruce Davison
Apt Pupil
At First Sight
The Baby-Sitter's Club
Brass Target
crazy/beautiful
The Crucible
The Cure
Dahmer
Far from Home
Grace of my Heart
High Crimes
It's My Party
The King Is Alive
Last Summer
The Lathe of Heaven
Longtime Companion
Love Life
Mame
Mother, Jugs & Speed
Mourning Becomes Electra
Paulie
Runaway Jury
Short Cuts
Short Eyes
Six Degrees of Separation
Spies Like Us
Summer Catch
The Strawberry Statement
The Summer of My German
  Soldier
Ulzana's Raid
Willard
X-Men
X2: X-Men United

INDEX: STARS

Foxes
Haunted Summer
I Am Sam
Jurassic Park I & III
Mask
Novocaine
October Sky
A Perfect World
Rambling Rose
Smooth Talk
Wild at Heart

Danny DeVito

Anything Else
Batman Returns
Big Fish
The Big Kahuna
Death to Smoochy
Drowning Mona
Get Shorty
Goin' South
Head Office
Heist
Hercules
Hoffa
Jack the Bear
The Jewel of the Nile
*John Grisham's The
  Rainmaker*
Junior
L.A. Confidential
Living Out Loud
Man on the Moon
Mars Attacks!
Matilda
The Mogul
*One Flew over the Cuckoo's
  Nest*
Other People's Money
Renaissance Man
Romancing the Stone
Ruthless People
Screwed
Terms of Endearment
*Throw Momma from the
  Train*
Tin Men
Twins
The War of the Roses
*What's the Worst That
  Could Happen?*
Wise Guys
(As director)
Hoffa
Matilda
*Throw Momma from the
  Train*
The War of the Roses

Cameron Diaz

Any Given Sunday
Being John Malkovich
Charlie's Angels 1 & 2
*Fear and Loathing in Las
  Vegas*
Feeling Minnesota
Gangs of New York
Head Above Water
Keys to Tulsa
The Last Supper
A Life Less Ordinary
The Mask
My Best Friend's Wedding
She's the One
Shrek 1 & 2
The Sweetest Thing

*There's Something about
  Mary*
*Things You Can Tell Just
  by Looking at Her*
Vanilla Sky
Very Bad Things

Leonardo DiCaprio

The Aviator
The Basketball Diaries
The Beach
Catch Me if You Can
Celebrity
Gangs of New York
The Man in the Iron Mask
Marvin's Room
The Quick and the Dead
This Boy's Life
Titanic
Total Eclipse
*What's Eating
  Gilbert Grape*
*William Shakespeare's
  Romeo + Juliet*

Marlene Dietrich

Angel
*Around the World in 80
  Days*
Blonde Venus
The Blue Angel
Destry Rides Again
The Devil Is a Woman
Dishonored
The Flame of New Orleans
Follow the Boys
A Foreign Affair
The Garden of Allah
Golden Earrings
Judgment at Nuremberg
Just a Gigolo
Kameradschaft
Kismet
Knight without Armour
The Lady Is Willing
Marlene
Morocco
No Highway in the Sky
Paris When It Sizzles
Pittsburgh
Rancho Notorious
The Scarlet Empress
Seven Sinners
Shanghai Express
The Song of Songs
The Spoilers
Stage Fright
Touch of Evil
Witness for the Prosecution

Taye Diggs

Basic
The Best Man
Brown Sugar
Chicago
Equilibrium
Go
House on Haunted Hill
*How Stella Got Her Groove
  Back*
Just a Kiss
Malibu's Most Wanted
New Best Friend
The Way of the Gun
The Wood

Matt Dillon

Albino Alligator
Beautiful Girls
The Big Town
Bloodhounds of Broadway
City of Ghosts
Deuces Wild
Drugstore Cowboy
The Flamingo Kid
Frankie Starlight
Golden Gate
Grace of my Heart
In & Out
Kansas
A Kiss Before Dying
Liar's Moon
Little Darlings
Mr. Wonderful
My Bodyguard
Native Son
One Night at McCool's
The Outsiders
Over the Edge
Rebel
Rumble Fish
The Saint of Fort Washington
Singles
Target
Tex
*There's Something about
  Mary*
To Die For
Wild Things
Women and Men 2

Divine

The Alternative Miss World
The Diane Linkletter Story
Divine Trash
Female Trouble
Hairspray
*I Wanna Be a Beauty
  Queen*
Lust in the Dust
Mondo Trasho
Multiple Maniacs
Out of the Dark
Pink Flamingos
Polyester
Trouble in Mind

Stephen Dorff

BackBeat
Blade
Blood and Wine
Cecil B. Demented
City of Industry
Deuces Wild
Earthly Possessions
Fear.com
The Gate
I Shot Andy Warhol
Innocent Lies
Judgment Night
The Power of One
Reckless
Rescue Me
S.F.W.

Illeana Douglas

*The Adventures of Pluto
  Nash*
Alive

Bella Mafia
Cape Fear
Dummy
Flypaper
Ghost World
Grace of my Heart
Happy, Texas
Message in a Bottle
New York Stories
The Next Best Thing
Picture Perfect
Pitch
Point of Origin
Search and Destroy
Stir of Echoes
To Die For
Weapons of Mass Distraction
Wedding Bell Blues

Kirk Douglas

Along the Great Divide
The Arrangement
The Bad and the Beautiful
The Big Sky
The Big Trees
The Brotherhood
Cast a Giant Shadow
Champion
The Devil's Disciple
Diamonds
Eddie Macon's Run
The Final Countdown
The Fury
Greedy
A Gunfight
Gunfight at the O.K. Corral
Home Movies
In Harm's Way
Is Paris Burning?
It Runs in the Family
A Letter to Three Wives
The List of Adrian Messenger
Lonely Are the Brave
Lust for Life
The Man from Snowy River
Once Is Not Enough
Oscar
Out of the Past
Paths of Glory
Posse
Saturn 3
Seven Days in May
Spartacus
*The Strange Love of
  Martha Ivers*
Strangers When We Meet
There Was a Crooked Man
Tough Guys
*20,000 Leagues Under the
  Sea*
Ulysses
The Vikings
The Way West
Young Man with a Horn

Michael Douglas

Adam at 6 A.M.
The American President
Basic Instinct
Black Rain
The China Syndrome
A Chorus Line
Coma
Disclosure

Don't Say a Word
Falling Down
Fatal Attraction
The Game
The Ghost and the Darkness
Hail, Hero!
The In-Laws
It Runs in the Family
The Jewel of the Nile
Napoleon and Samantha
One Night at McCool's
A Perfect Murder
Romancing the Stone
Shining Through
The Star Chamber
Traffic
Wall Street
The War of the Roses
Wonder Boys

Robert Downey, Jr.

Air America
Baby, It's You
Back to School
Black and White
Camp
Chances Are
Chaplin
Firstborn
Friends & Lovers
The Gingerbread Man
Gothika
Heart and Souls
Home for the Holidays
Hugo Pool
In Dreams
Johnny Be Good
The Last Party
Less Than Zero
Natural Born Killers
1969
One Night Stand
Only You
The Pick-Up Artist
Rented Lips
Restoration
Richard III
Short Cuts
The Singing Detective
Soapdish
Too Much Sun
True Believer
Tuff Turf
Two Girls and a Guy
U.S. Marshals
Weird Science
Wonder Boys

Richard Dreyfuss

Always
American Graffiti
The American President
Another Stakeout
*The Apprenticeship of
  Duddy Kravitz*
The Big Fix
The Buddy System
*Close Encounters of the
  Third Kind*
The Competition
The Crew
*Down and Out in Beverly
  Hills*

THE DISCERNING FILM LOVER'S GUIDE

Lillian Gish

The Battle of Elderbush
  Gulch
Birth of a Nation
Broken Blossoms
The Comedians
Duel in the Sun
The Great Chase
Intolerance
Judith of Bethulia
The Musketeers of Pig Alley
The Night of the Hunter
Orphans of the Storm
Portrait of Jennie
Sweet Liberty
The Unforgiven
Way Down East
A Wedding
The Whales of August
The White Sister
The Wind

Danny Glover

Angels in the Outfield
Antz
Bat 21
Beloved
Bopha!
Boesman and Lena
Buffalo Soldiers
The Color Purple
Dead Man Out
Escape from Alcatraz
Flight of the Intruder
Gone Fishin'
Grand Canyon
Iceman
Lethal Weapon 1, 2, 3, 4
Lonesome Dove
Mandela
Maverick
Operation Dumbo Drop
Places in the Heart
Predator 2
The Prince of Egypt
Pure Luck
A Rage in Harlem
The Rainmaker
A Raisin in the Sun
The Royal Tenenbaums
The Saint of Fort Washington
Silverado
Switchback
To Sleep with Anger
Witness

Whoopi Goldberg

The Associate
Bogus
Boys on the Side
Burglar
The Celluloid Closet
Clara's Heart
The Color Purple
Corrina, Corrina
The Deep End of the Ocean
Eddie
Fatal Beauty
Ghost
Ghosts of Mississippi
Girl, Interrupted
Homer and Eddie
How Stella Got Her Groove
  Back
Jumpin' Jack Flash

Kingdom Come
Leprechauns
The Lion King
The Little Rascals
Loaded Weapon 1
Made in America
Monkeybone
Moonlight and Valentino
Naked in New York
The Pagemaster
The Player
Rat Race
Sarafina!
Sister Act 1 & 2
Soapdish
Star Trek: Generations
The Telephone

Jeff Goldblum

The Adventures of
  Buckaroo Banzai
Annie Hall
Between the Lines
Beyond Suspicion
Beyond Therapy
The Big Chill
Death Wish
Deep Cover
Earth Girls Are Easy
The Favor, The Watch and
  the Very Big Fish
The Fly
The Great White Hype
Hideaway
Igby Goes Down
Independence Day
Into the Night
Invasion of the Body
  Snatchers
Jurassic Park
The Lost World: Jurassic
  Park
Mr. Frost
Nashville
Next Stop Greenwich
  Village
Nine Months
Powder
The Prince of Egypt
The Right Stuff
Silverado
The Tall Guy
Thank God It's Friday
Threshold
Transylvania 6-5000
Vibes

John Goodman

Always
Arachnophobia
The Babe
Barton Fink
The Big Easy
The Big Lebowski
Blues Brothers 2000
Born Yesterday
The Borrowers
Burglar
C.H.U.D.
Coyote Ugly
The Emperor's New Groove
Everybody's All-American
Fallen
The Flintstones
The Jack Bull

The Jungle Book 2
King Ralph
Masked and Anonymous
Monsters, Inc.
Matinee
Mother Night
O Brother, Where Art
  Thou?
One Night at McCool's
Punchline
Raising Arizona
Revenge of the Nerds
Sea of Love
Stella
Storytelling
The Survivors
True Stories
What Planet Are You From?

Gong Li

Chinese Box
The Emperor & the Assassin
Farewell My Concubine
Ju Dou
Raise the Red Lantern
Red Sorghum
Shanghai Triad
The Story of Qiu Ju
Temptress Moon
To Live

Cuba Gooding, Jr.

As Good As It Gets
Boat Trip
Boyz N the Hood
Chill Factor
Coming to America
Daybreak
A Few Good Men
The Fighting Temptations
Gladiator
Home on the Range
In the Shadows
Instinct
Jerry Maguire
Judgment Night
Lightning Jack
Losing Isaiah
Men of Honor
Outbreak
Pearl Harbor
Radio
Snow Dogs
Trading Favors
The Tuskegee Airmen
What Dreams May Come

Ruth Gordon

Abe Lincoln in Illinois
Action in the North
  Atlantic
Any Which Way You Can
The Big Bus
Dr. Ehrlich's Magic Bullet
Edge of Darkness
Every Which Way But
  Loose
Harold and Maude
Inside Daisy Clover
Maxie
My Bodyguard
Rosemary's Baby
The Trouble with Spies
Two Faced Woman
Whatever Happened to
  Aunt Alice?
Where's Poppa?

Heather Graham

Austin Powers: The Spy
  Who Shagged Me
The Ballad of Little Jo
Boogie Nights
Bowfinger
Committed
Diggstown
Don't Do It
Drugstore Cowboy
Entertaining Angels: The
  Dorothy Day Story
From Hell
Guilty as Charged
The Guru
I Love You to Death
Killing Me Softly
Lost in Space
Nowhere
Say It Isn't So
Scream 2
Shout
Sidewalks of New York
Six Degrees of Separation
Swingers
Two Girls and a Guy

Cary Grant

An Affair to Remember
Arsenic and Old Lace
The Awful Truth
The Bachelor and the
  Bobbysoxer
The Bishop's Wife
Blonde Venus
Bringing Up Baby
Charade
Destination Tokyo
The Eagle and the Hawk
Every Girl Should Be
  Married
Father Goose
The Grass Is Greener
Gunga Din
His Girl Friday
Holiday
Houseboat
The Howards of Virginia
I Was a Male War Bride
I'm No Angel
In Name Only
Indiscreet
Mr. Blandings Builds
  His Dream House
Mr. Lucky
Monkey Business
My Favorite Wife
Night and Day
None But the Lonely Heart
North by Northwest
Notorious
Once Upon a Honeymoon
Once Upon a Time
Only Angels Have Wings
Operation Petticoat
Penny Serenade
The Philadelphia Story
The Pride and the Passion
She Done Him Wrong
Suspicion
Sylvia Scarlett
The Talk of the Town
That Touch of Mink

To Catch a Thief
Topper
Walk, Don't Run

Hugh Grant

About a Boy
An Awfully Big Adventure
Bitter Moon
Bridget Jones's Diary
The Dawning
The Englishman Who Went
  Up a Hill, But Came
  Down a Mountain
Extreme Measures
Four Weddings and a
  Funeral
Impromptu
The Lair of the White
  Worm
Love Actually
Maurice
Mickey Blue Eyes
Night Train to Venice
Nine Months
Notting Hill
Our Sons
The Remains of the Day
Restoration
Rowing with the Wind
Sense and Sensibility
Sirens
Small Time Crooks
Two Weeks Notice

Seth Green

America's Sweethearts
Austin Powers 1, 2 & 3
Big Business
Can't Hardly Wait
Idle Hands
The Italian Job
Knockaround Guys
Notes from Underground
Party Monster
Radio Days
Rat Race
Scooby-Doo 2: Monsters
  Unleashed
Stonebrook

Pam Grier

Above the Law
The Adventures of Pluto
  Nash
The Arena
The Big Bird Cage
The Big Doll House
Bill & Ted's Bogus Journey
Black Mama, White Mama
Bones
Bucktown
Class of 1999
Coffy
Drum
Escape from L.A.
Fort Apache, The Bronx
Fortress 2 – Re-Entry
Foxy Brown
Friday Foster
Ghosts of Mars
Greased Lightning
Holy Smoke!
Jackie Brown
Jawbreaker
Mars Attacks!

INDEX: STARS

INDEX: STARS

INDEX: STARS

THE DISCERNING FILM LOVER'S GUIDE

THE DISCERNING FILM LOVER'S GUIDE

THE DISCERNING FILM LOVER'S GUIDE

INDEX: STARS

THE DISCERNING FILM LOVER'S GUIDE

INDEX: STARS

759

Robert Mitchum

Anzio
The Big Sleep
The Big Steal
Blood on the Moon
Cape Fear (1962 & 1991)
Crossfire
Dead Man
El Dorado
The Enemy Below
A Family For Joe
Farewell, My Lovely
Fire Down Below
Five Card Stud
The Grass Is Greener
Heaven Knows, Mr. Allison
Holiday Affair
Home from the Hill
The Last Tycoon
The List of Adrian Messenger
The Longest Day
Macao
Man with the Gun
Maria's Lovers
Midway
Mr. North
My Forbidden Past
The Night of the Hunter
Not as a Stranger
Out of the Past
Pursued
The Racket
River of No Return
Ryan's Daughter
Scrooged
Second Chance
Secret Ceremony
The Story of G.I. Joe
The Sundowners
That Championship Season
Thirty Seconds over Tokyo
Thunder Road
Track of the Cat
Two for the Seesaw
Undercurrent
The Way West
The Yakuza
Young Billy Young

Matthew Modine

And the Band Played On
Any Given Sunday
Baby, It's You
Birdy
The Blackout
The Browning Version
Bye Bye, Love
Cutthroat Island
Le Divorce
Equinox
Fluke
Full Metal Jacket
The Gamble
Gross Anatomy
The Hotel New Hampshire
In the Shadows
The Maker
Married to the Mob
Memphis Belle
Mrs. Soffel
One Last Score
Orphans
Pacific Heights
Private School

The Real Blonde
The Shipment
Short Cuts
Streamers
Vision Quest
Wind

Marilyn Monroe

All about Eve
As Young as You Feel
The Asphalt Jungle
Bus Stop
Clash by Night
Don't Bother to Knock
Gentlemen Prefer Blondes
How to Marry a Millionaire
Ladies of the Chorus
Let's Make It Legal
Let's Make Love
Love Happy
Love Nest
The Misfits
Monkey Business
Niagara
The Prince & the Showgirl
River of No Return
The Seven Year Itch
Some Like It Hot
There's No Business Like
    Show Business
We're Not Married

Demi Moore

About Last Night...
Beavis and Butt-Head do
    America
Blame It on Rio
The Butcher's Wife
Charlie's Angels: Full
    Throttle
Deconstructing Harry
Disclosure
A Few Good Men
G.I. Jane
Ghost
The Hunchback of Notre
    Dame
If These Walls Could Talk
Indecent Proposal
Mortal Thoughts
No Small Affair
Nothing But Trouble
Now and Then
One Crazy Summer
Parasite
Passion of Mind
St. Elmo's Fire
The Scarlet Letter
The Seventh Sign
Striptease
We're No Angels
Wisdom

Dudley Moore

Arthur 1 & 2
Bedazzled
Beyond the Fringe
Blame It on the Bellboy
Crazy People
The Disappearance of
    Kevin Johnson
Foul Play
The Hound of the
    Baskervilles

Like Father Like Son
The Mighty Kong
The Pickle
Romantic Comedy
Santa Claus: The Movie
10
Thirty Is a Dangerous Age,
    Cynthia
Unfaithfully Yours
The Wrong Box

Julianne Moore

Assassins
Benny & Joon
The Big Lebowski
Boogie Nights
Cast a Deadly Spell
Cookie's Fortune
The End of the Affair
Evolution
Far from Heaven
The Fugitive
The Hand that Rocks the
    Cradle
Hannibal
The Hours
An Ideal Husband
Laws of Attraction
The Lost World: Jurassic
    Park
Magnolia
A Map of the World
The Myth of Fingerprints
Nine Months
Psycho
Roommates
Safe
The Shipping News
Short Cuts
Surviving Picasso
Vanya on 42nd Street
World Traveler

Jeanne Moreau

Alberto Express
Alex in Wonderland
Balzac: A Life of Passion
The Bride Wore Black
Chimes at Midnight
Creezy
Dangerous Liaisons 1960
Diary of a Chambermaid
Elevator to the Gallows
Eva
Ever After
La Femme Nikita
The Fire Within
A Foreign Field
Frantic
Going Places
Grisbi
Heat of Desire
I Love You, I Love You Not
Jules and Jim
The Last Tycoon
Les Liaisons Dangereuses
The Little Theatre
    of Jean Renoir
The Lover
The Lovers
Lumiere
Mademoiselle
Map of the Human Heart
Mr. Klein
Moderato Cantabile

Monte Walsh
La Notte
The Old Lady Who
    Walked in the Sea
The Oldest Profession
Querelle
The Summer House
The Train
The Trial
La Truite (The Trout)
Until the End of the World
Viva Maria!
A Woman Is a Woman

David Morse

Bait
Contact
Crazy in Alabama
The Crossing Guard
Dancer in the Dark
Desperate Hours
Diary of a City Priest
Double Vision
Extreme Measures
The Getaway
The Good Son
The Green Mile
Hearts in Atlantis
The Indian Runner
The Langoliers
The Long Kiss Goodnight
Max Dugan Returns
The Negotiator
Proof of Life
The Rock
The Slaughter Rule
12 Monkeys

Viggo Mortensen

Albino Alligator
Boiling Point
Carlito's Way
The Crew
Crimson Tide
Daylight
Floundering
G.I. Jane
Hidalgo
The Indian Runner
The Lord of the Rings: The
    Fellowship of the Ring
The Lord of the Rings:
    The Two Towers
The Lord of the Rings:
    The Return of the King
A Perfect Murder
Prison
Portrait of a Lady
The Prophecy
Psycho
The Reflecting Skin
28 Days
A Walk on the Moon
The Young Americans

Armin Mueller-Stahl

Angry Harvest
Avalon
Colonel Redl
Forget Mozart
The Game
Holy Matrimony
The House of the Spirits
In the Presence of Mine
    Enemies

Inferno
Jakob the Liar
Jesus
Kafka
Lola
The Long Run
A Love in Germany
Mission to Mars
Music Box
Night on Earth
The Peacemaker
The Power of One
A Pyromaniac's Love Story
Shine
The Third Miracle
The Thirteenth Floor
Twelve Angry Men
Utz
The X-Files

Paul Muni

Angel on My Shoulder
Black Fury
Commandos Strike
    at Dawn
The Good Earth
I Am a Fugitive from
    a Chain Gang
Juarez
The Last Angry Man
The Life of Emile Zola
Scarface
A Song to Remember
The Story of Louis Pasteur

Eddie Murphy

The Adventures of Pluto
    Nash
Another 48 Hrs.
Best Defense
The Best of Eddie Murphy
Beverly Hills Cop 1, 2 & 3
Boomerang
Bowfinger
Coming to America
Daddy Day Care
Delirious
Distinguished Gentleman
Doctor Dolittle 1 & 2
Eddie Murphy: Raw
48 Hrs.
The Golden Child
Harlem Nights
The Haunted Mansion
Holy Man
I-Spy
Life
Metro
Mulan
The Nutty Professor 1 & 2
Shrek 1 & 2
Showtime
Trading Places
Vampire in Brooklyn
(As director)
Harlem Nights
(As writer)
Another 48 Hrs.
Beverly Hills Cop II
Eddie Murphy Raw
Harlem Nights
Vampire in Brooklyn

THE DISCERNING FILM LOVER'S GUIDE

Bill Murray

Caddyshack
Charlie's Angels
Cradle Will Rock
Ed Wood
Ghostbusters 1 & 2
Groundhog Day
Hamlet
Kingpin
Larger than Life
Little Shop of Horrors
Loose Shoes
Lost in Translation
Mad Dog and Glory
The Man who Knew Too
    Little
Meatballs
Osmosis Jones
Quick Change
The Razor's Edge
The Royal Tenenbaums
Rushmore
Scrooged
Space Jam
Stripes
Tootsie
What about Bob?
Where the Buffalo Roam
Wild Things
(As director)
Quick Change

Mike Myers

Austin Powers: International
    Man of Mystery
Austin Powers: The Spy
    Who Shagged Me
Austin Powers in
    Goldmember
Dr. Seuss' The Cat in the
    Hat
54
Pete's Meteor
Shrek 1 & 2
So I Married an Axe
    Murderer
View from the Top
Wayne's World 1 & 2
(As writer)
Austin Powers 1 & 2
Wayne's World 1 & 2

Liam Neeson

Before and After
The Big Man
Darkman
The Dead Pool
Deception
Ethan Frome
Excalibur
Gangs of New York
The Good Mother
Gun Shy
The Haunting
High Spirits
Husbands and Wives
K-19: The Widowmaker
Leap of Faith
Les Misérables
Love Actually
Michael Collins
The Mission
Nell
Next of Kin

The Phantom Menace
Rob Roy
Satisfaction
Schindler's List
Shining Through
Suspect
Under Suspicion

Sam Neill

Attack Force Z
Bicentennial Man
The Blood of Others
Children of the Revolution
Country Life
A Cry in the Dark
Dead Calm
Death in Brunswick
The Dish
Doctor Zhivago (2003)
Event Horizon
The Final Conflict
Forgotten Silver
The Good Wife
The Horse Whisperer
The Hunt for Red October
In the Mouth of Madness
Ivanhoe
Jurassic Park I & III
Memoirs of an Invisible Man
Merlin
Molokai: The Story of
    "Father Damien"
My Brilliant Career
One Against the Wind
The Piano
Plenty
Reilly: Ace of Spies
Restoration
Rudyard Kipling's
    The Jungle Book
Sirens
Sleeping Dogs
Snow White – A Tale of
    Terror
Until the End of the World
Victory

Paul Newman

Absence of Malice
Blaze
Buffalo Bill & the Indians
Butch Cassidy and the
    Sundance Kid
Cat on a Hot Tin Roof
The Color of Money
Cool Hand Luke
The Drowning Pool
Exodus
Fat Man and Little Boy
Fort Apache, The Bronx
From the Terrace
Harper
Harry and Son
Hombre
Hud
The Hudsucker Proxy
The Hustler
Lady L
The Left-Handed Gun
The Life and Times of
    Judge Roy Bean
The Long Hot Summer
The Mackintosh Man
Message in a Bottle
Mr. and Mrs. Bridge

Nobody's Fool
Paris Blues
Pocket Money
The Prize
Quintet
Road to Perdition
The Secret War of Harry
    Frigg
Silent Movie
The Silver Chalice
Slap Shot
Somebody Up There
    Likes Me
Sometimes a Great Notion
The Sting
Sweet Bird of Youth
Torn Curtain
The Towering Inferno
Twilight
Until They Sail
The Verdict
Where the Money Is
The Young Philadelphians
(As director)
The Effect of Gamma Rays
    on Man-in-the-Moon
    Marigolds
The Glass Menagerie
Harry and Son
Rachel, Rachel
The Shadow Box
Sometimes a Great Notion

Thandie Newton

Beloved
Besieged
Flirting
Gridlock'd
Jefferson in Paris
The Journey of August
    King
The Leading Man
Loaded
Mission: Impossible 2
Shade
The Truth about Charlie
The Young Americans

Jack Nicholson

About Schmidt
Anger Management
As Good As It Gets
Batman
Blood and Wine
The Border
Broadcast News
Carnal Knowledge
Chinatown
The Crossing Guard
Easy Rider
Ensign Pulver
The Evening Star
A Few Good Men
Five Easy Pieces
The Fortune
Goin' South
Head
Heartburn
Hell's Angels on Wheels
Hoffa
Ironweed
The King of Marvin Gardens
The Last Detail
The Last Tycoon
Little Shop of Horrors

Man Trouble
Mars Attacks!
The Missouri Breaks
On a Clear Day You Can
    See Forever
One Flew Over the Cuckoo's
    Nest
The Passenger
The Pledge
The Postman Always Rings
    Twice
Prizzi's Honor
Psych-Out
The Raven
Rebel Rousers
Reds
The Shining
The Shooting
Something's Gotta Give
Terms of Endearment
The Terror
Tommy
The Two Jakes
The Wild Ride
The Witches of Eastwick
Wolf
(As director)
Goin' South
The Two Jakes
(As writer)
Head
The Trip

Philippe Noiret

Birgitt Haas Must Be
    Killed
Cinema Paradiso
The Clockmaker
Coup de Torchon
Dead Tired (Grosse Fatigue)
The Family
Fort Saganne
La Grande Bouffe
The Holes (Les Gaspards)
I Don't Kiss (J'embrasse pas)
The Judge and the Assassin
Jupiter's Thigh
Justine
Life and Nothing But
Murphy's War
My New Partner
Next Summer
Night Flight from Moscow
The Night of the Generals
The Old Gun
The Postman (Il Postino)
The Purple Taxi
Revenge of the Musketeers
    (Daughter of D'Artagnan)
Three Brothers
Topaz
Uranus
La Vie de Château
A Woman at Her Window
Woman Times Seven
Zazie dans le Métro

Nick Nolte

Affliction
Afterglow
Another 48 Hrs.
Blue Chips
Breakfast of Champions
Cannery Row
Cape Fear

The Deep
Down and Out in Beverly
    Hills
Everybody Wins
Extreme Prejudice
Farewell to the King
48 Hrs.
The Golden Bowl
Grace Quigley
Heart Beat
The Hulk
I Love Trouble
I'll Do Anything
Jefferson in Paris
Lorenzo's Oil
Mother Night
Mulholland Falls
New York Stories
Nightwatch
North Dallas Forty
Northfork
Q & A
The Prince of Tides
Simpatico
Teachers
The Thin Red Line
Three Fugitives
Trixie
U-Turn
Under Fire
Weeds
Who'll Stop the Rain

Edward Norton

American History X
Death to Smoochy
Everyone Says I Love You
Fight Club
Frida
The Italian Job
Keeping the Faith
Out of the Past
The People vs. Larry Flynt
Primal Fear
Red Dragon
Rounders
The Score
25th Hour
(As director)
Keeping the Faith

Chris O'Donnell

The Bachelor
Batman Forever
Batman and Robin
Blue Sky
The Chamber
Circle of Friends
Cookie's Fortune
Fried Green Tomatoes
In Love and War
Mad Love
Men Don't Leave
Scent of a Woman
School Ties
The Three Musketeers
Vertical Limit

Rosie O'Donnell

Another Stakeout
Beautiful Girls
Exit to Eden
The Flintstones
Harriet the Spy
A League of Their Own

THE DISCERNING FILM LOVER'S GUIDE

THE DISCERNING FILM LOVER'S GUIDE

In God We Trust
Jo Jo Dancer, Your Life Is Calling
Lady Sings the Blues
Lost Highway
The Mack
Moving
The Muppet Movie
Richard Pryor – Here and Now
Richard Pryor – Live and Smokin
Richard Pryor Live on the Sunset Strip
See No Evil, Hear No Evil
Silver Streak
Some Kind of Hero
Stir Crazy
Superman III
The Toy
Uptown Saturday Night
Which Way Is Up?
Wholly Moses
Wild in the Streets
The Wiz
(As director)
Jo Jo Dancer, Your Life is Calling
Richard Pryor Here and Now
(As writer)
Blazing Saddles
Bustin' Loose
Jo Jo Dancer Your Life is Calling

Bill Pullman
The Accidental Tourist
Brain Dead
Bright Angel
Brokedown Palace
Casper
Crazy in Love
The End of Violence
The Favor
Igby Goes Down
Independence Day
Lake Placid
The Last Seduction
A League of Their Own
Liebestraum
Lost Highway
Lucky Numbers
Malice
Mr. Jones
Mr. Wrong
Newsies
Rocket Gilbraltor
Ruthless People
The Serpent and the Rainbow
Sibling Rivalry
Singles
Sleepless in Seattle
Sommersby
Spaceballs
Spy Games
29 Palms
While You Were Sleeping
Wyatt Earp
Zero Effect

Queen Latifah
The Bone Collector
Bringing Down the House
Brown Sugar

Chicago
The Country Bears
House Party 2
Living Out Loud
My Life
Set It Off
Sphere
Who's the Man

Dennis Quaid
The Alamo
All Night Long
Any Given Sunday
The Big Easy
Breaking Away
Come See the Paradise
The Day After Tomorrow
Dinner with Friends
D.O.A.
Dreamscape
Enemy Mine
Everybody's All-American
Far from Heaven
Flesh and Bone
Frequency
Great Balls of Fire
Innerspace
Jaws 3
The Long Riders
The Parent Trap
Playing by Heart
Postcards from the Edge
The Right Stuff
The Rookie
September 30, 1955
The Savior
Something to Talk About
Suspect
Switchback
Traffic
Undercover Blues
Wilder Napalm
Wyatt Earp

Randy Quaid
The Adventures of Pluto Nash
The Apprenticeship of Duddy Kravitz
Bloodhounds of Broadway
Bound for Glory
Bye Bye, Love
Caddyshack II
The Curse of the Starving Class
The Day the World Ended
Days of Thunder
Fool for Love
Foxes
Frankenstein
Freaked
Get on the Bus
Grind
Hard Rain
Heartbeeps
Home on the Range
Independence Day
Kingpin
Last Dance
The Last Detail
The Last Picture Show
Leprechauns
The Long Riders
Midnight Express

National Lampoon's Vacation
Brubaker
National Lampoon's Christmas Vacation
No Man's Land
Not Another Teen Movie
Of Mice and Men
The Paper
Quick Change
The Slugger's Wife
Streets of Laredo
Texasville
The Thin Blue Lie
Valentine's Day
Vegas Vacation
The Wild Life

Aidan Quinn
The Assignment
At Play in the Fields of the Lord
Avalon
Benny & Joon
Blink
Commandments
Crusoe
Desperately Seeking Susan
An Early Frost
Evelyn
The Handmaid's Tale
Haunted
In Dreams
Legends of the Fall
The Lemon Sisters
Looking for Richard
Mary Shelley's Frankenstein
Michael Collins
The Mission
Practical Magic
Reckless
Songcatcher
Stakeout
The Stars Fell on Henrietta
This Is My Father

Stephen Rea
Angie
Bad Behavior
The Butcher Boy
Citizen X
The Company of Wolves
Copenhagen
The Crying Game
Danny Boy
The Doctor and the Devils
The End of the Affair
Evelyn
Feardotcom
Four Days in July
A Further Gesture
Guinevere
In Dreams
Interview with the Vampire
Loose Connections
Michael Collins
The Musketeer
Princess Caraboo
Ready to Wear
Snow in August
This Is My Father
Trojan Eddie

Robert Redford
All the President's Men
Barefoot in the Park

A Bridge Too Far
Brubaker
Butch Cassidy and the Sundance Kid
The Candidate
The Chase
Downhill Racer
The Electric Horseman
The Great Gatsby
The Great Waldo Pepper
Havana
The Horse Whisperer
The Hot Rock
Indecent Proposal
Inside Daisy Clover
Jeremiah Johnson
The Last Castle
Legal Eagles
The Natural
Out of Africa
Sneakers
Spy Game
The Sting
Tell Them Willie Boy Is Here
This Property Is Condemned
Three Days of the Condor
Up Close and Personal
The Way We Were
(As director)
The Horse Whisperer
The Legend of Bagger Vance
The Milagro Beanfield War
Ordinary People
Quiz Show
A River Runs Through It

Vanessa Redgrave
Agatha
The Ballad of the Sad Cafe
Bella Mafia
Blow-Up
The Bostonians
Camelot
The Charge of the Light Brigade
Consuming Passions
Cradle Will Rock
Deep Impact
The Devils
The Gathering Storm
Girl, Interrupted
Good Boy!
The House of the Spirits
Howards End
If These Walls Could Talk 2
Isadora
Julia
Little Odessa
Looking for Richard
Lulu on the Bridge
A Man for All Seasons
Mary, Queen of Scots
Mission: Impossible
A Month by the Lake
Morgan!
Mother's Boys
Mrs. Dalloway
Murder on the Orient Express
Orpheus Descending
Playing for Time
The Pledge
Prick Up Your Ears
The Seven Percent Solution

Steaming
They Watch
The Trojan Women
Wagner
Wetherby
Wilde
Yanks
Young Catherine

Keanu Reeves
Babes in Toyland
Bill & Ted's Excellent Adventure
Bill & Ted's Bogus Journey
Bram Stoker's Dracula
Brotherhood of Justice
Chain Reaction
Devil's Advocate
Dream to Believe
Even Cowgirls Get the Blues
Feeling Minnesota
The Gift
Hardball
I Love You to Death
Johnny Mnemonic
The Last Time I Committed Suicide
Little Buddha
The Matrix
The Matrix Reloaded
The Matrix Revolutions
Much Ado about Nothing
My Own Private Idaho
Parenthood
Permanent Record
Point Break
The Prince of Pennsylvania
The Replacements
River's Edge
Something's Gotta Give
Speed
Sweet November
Tune in Tomorrow
A Walk in the Clouds
The Watcher

John C. Reilly
The Anniversary Party
Boogie Nights
Boys
Casualties of War
Chicago
For Love of the Game
Gangs of New York
The Good Girl
Hard Eight
The Hours
Magnolia
Never Been Kissed
Nightwatch
Out on a Limb
The Perfect Storm
The River Wild
The Settlement

Jean Reno
Beyond the Clouds
The Big Blue
The Crimson Rivers
Le Dernier Combat (The Last Battle)
La Femme Nikita
For Roseanna
French Kiss
Godzilla
Jet Lag

Tight Spot
The Whole Town's Talking
The Woman in the Window

Chris Rock

Bad Company
Beverly Hills Ninja
CB4
Doctor Dolittle
Dogma
Down to Earth
Head of State
Jay and Silent Bob Strike Back
Leathal Weapon 4
New Jack City
Nurse Betty
Osmosis Jones
Panther
Sgt. Bilko
(As writer)
CB4
Down to Earth

Sam Rockwell

Basquiat
Box of Moonlight
Celebrity
Charlie's Angels
Clownhouse
Confessions of a Dangerous Mind
Galaxy Quest
Glory Daze
The Green Mile
Heist
Jerry and Tom
Last Exit to Brooklyn
Lawn Dogs
Light Sleeper
Matchstick Men
Mercy
Safe Men
Welcome to Collinwood

Ginger Rogers

Bachelor Mother
The Barkleys of Broadway
Carefree
Cinderella
Fifth Avenue Girl
Flying Down to Rio
Follow the Fleet
Forever Female
42nd Street
The Gay Divorcee
Gold Diggers of 1933
Kitty Foyle
Lucky Partners
The Major and the Minor
Monkey Business
Once Upon a Honeymoon
The Primrose Path
Roberta
Roxie Hart
Shall We Dance
Stage Door
The Story of Vernon and Irene Castle
Swing Time
Tender Comrades
Tight Spot
Tom, Dick and Harry

Top Hat
Vivacious Lady
Week-End at the Waldorf
We're Not Married

Isabella Rossellini

Big Night
Blue Velvet
Cousins
Crime of the Century
Death Becomes Her
Empire
Fallen Angels
Fearless
The Funeral
Immortal Beloved
The Impostors
The Innocent
A Matter of Time
Merlin
Napoleon
The Odyssey
The Pickle
Roger Dodger
Siesta
The Sky is Falling
Tough Guys Don't Dance
White Nights
Wild at Heart
Wyatt Earp
Zelly and Me

Tim Roth

Bodies, Rest & Motion
Captives
The Cook, the Thief, His Wife & Her Lover
Deceiver
Everyone Says I Love You
Four Rooms
Gridlock'd
Heart of Darkness
The Hit
Hoodlum
Invincible
Jumpin' at the Boneyard
The Legend of 1900
Little Odessa
Lucky Numbers
Meantime
The Million Dollar Hotel
The Musketeer
No Way Home
Planet of the Apes
Pulp Fiction
Reservoir Dogs
Rob Roy
Rosencrantz and Guildenstern Are Dead
The Million Dollar Hotel
Vatel
Vincent and Theo
(As director)
The War Zone

Mickey Rourke

Angel Heart
Animal Factory
Another 9½ Weeks
Barfly
Body Heat
Buffalo '66
The Desperate Hours
Diner
Double Team
Eureka

Fall Time
Francesco
Get Carter
Harley Davidson and the Marlboro Man
Homeboy
John Grisham's The Rainmaker
Johnny Handsome
The Last Outlaw
Man on Fire
9½ Weeks
1941
Once Upon a Time in Mexico
Pope of Grennwich Village
A Prayer for the Dying
Rape and Marriage: The Rideout Case
Rumble Fish
Spun
White Sands
Wild Orchid
Year of the Dragon

Gena Rowlands

Another Woman
The Brink's Job
A Child Is Waiting
Crazy in Love
An Early Frost
Faces
Gloria
Hope Floats
Hysterical Blindness
I'm Almost Not Crazy
Light of Day
Lonely Are the Brave
Love Streams
The Mighty
The Neon Bible
Night on Earth
The Notebook

Once Around
Opening Night
Parallel Lives
Paulie
Playing by Heart
A Question of Love
Rapunzel
She's So Lovely
Something to Talk About
The Tempest
Tony Rome
Two-Minute Warning
Unhook the Stars
The Weekend
A Woman Under the Influence

Mercedes Ruehl

The Amati Girls
Another You
Crazy People
84 Charing Cross Road
The Fisher King
For Roseanna
Last Action Hero
Lost in Yonkers
Married to the Mob
The Minus Man
North Shore Fish
The Secret of My Success
Slaves of New York
What's Cooking?
Widows

Geoffrey Rush

The Banger Sisters
Children of the Revolution
Elizabeth
Finding Nemo
Frida
House on Haunted Hill
Intolerable Cruelty
Lantana
Les Misérables
A Little Bit of Soul
Mystery Men
Ned Kelly
Pirates of the Caribbean: The Curse of the Black Pearl
Quills
Shakespeare in Love
Shine
The Tailor of Panama
Twisted

Kurt Russell

Backdraft
The Barefoot Executive
The Best of Times
Big Trouble in Little China
Breakdown
Captain Ron
The Computer Wore Tennis Shoes
Dark Blue
Elvis – The Movie
Escape from L.A.
Escape from New York
Executive Decision
Follow Me Boys
The Fox and the Hound
The Mean Season
Miracle
Overboard
Silkwood
Soldier
Stargate
Superdad
Swing Shift
Tango and Cash
Tequila Sunrise
The Thing
Tombstone
3000 Miles to Graceland
Unlawful Entry
Used Cars
Winter People

Rosalind Russell

Auntie Mame
China Seas
The Citadel
Craig's Wife
Evelyn Prentice
Forsaking All Others
Gypsy
His Girl Friday
A Majority of One
Night Must Fall
Oh Dad, Poor Dad, Mama's Hung You in the Closet and I'm Feeling So Sad
Picnic
Reckless
Sister Kenny
They Met in Bombay
The Trouble with Angels
The Velvet Touch

A Woman of Distinction
The Women

Rene Russo

The Adventures of Rocky & Bullwinkle
Big Trouble
Buddy
Freejack
Get Shorty
In the Line of Fire
Lethal Weapon 3 & 4
One Good Cop
Outbreak
Ransom
Showtime
The Thomas Crown Affair
Tin Cup

Meg Ryan

Addicted to Love
Against the Ropes
Amityville 3: The Demon
Anastasia
Armed and Dangerous
City of Angels
Courage Under Fire
D.O.A.
The Doors
Flesh and Bone
French Kiss
Hanging Up
Hurlyburly
I.Q.
In the Cut
Innerspace
Joe Versus the Volcano
Kate & Leopold
Prelude to a Kiss
The Presidio
Proof of Life
Promised Land
Rich and Famous
Restoration
Sleepless in Seattle
Top Gun
When a Man Loves a Woman
When Harry Met Sally
You've Got Mail

Winona Ryder

The Age of Innocence
Alien: Resurrection
Autumn in New York
Beetlejuice
Bram Stoker's Dracula
Celebrity
The Crucible
Edward Scissorhands
Girl, Interrupted
Great Balls of Fire
Heathers
The House of the Spirits
How to Make an American Quilt
Little Women
Looking for Richard
Lost Souls
Lucas
Mr. Deeds
Night on Earth
1969
Reality Bites

Critical Condition
Demolition Man
Down in the Delta
Drop Zone
The Fan
Jungle Fever
King of New York
Liberty Stands Still
Major League
Money Train
Mo' Better Blues
Murder at 1600
New Jack City
One Night Stand
Passenger 57
Rising Sun
Streets of Gold
Sugar Hill
To Wong Foo...
U.S. Marshals
Undisputed
Waiting to Exhale
The Waterdance
White Men Can't Jump
Wildcats
ZigZag

Mira Sorvino
Amongst Friends
At First Sight
Barcelona
Beautiful Girls
Blue in the Face
Gods and Generals
The Great Gatsby
The Grey Zone
Lulu on the Bridge
Mighty Aphrodite
Mimic
The Replacement Killers
Romy and Michelle's High
  School Reunion
Summer of Sam
Sweet Nothing
Triumph of Love

Sissy Spacek
Affliction
Badlands
Blast from the Past
Carrie
Coal Miner's Daughter
Crimes of the Heart
The Good Ol Boys
The Grass Harp
Hard Promises
Heart Beat
In the Bedroom
JFK
Katherine
Last Call
The Long Walk Home
Marie
Missing
'Night, Mother
A Place for Annie
Prime Cut
A Private Matter
Raggedy Man
The River
The Straight Story
Streets of Laredo
Trading Mom
Tuck Everlasting
Violets Are Blue
Welcome to L.A.

Kevin Spacey
American Beauty
The Big Kahuna
A Bug's Life
Consenting Adults
Dad
Glengarry Glen Ross
Heartburn
Henry & June
Hurlyburly
Iron Will
K-Pax
L.A. Confidential
The Life of David Gale
Long Day's Journey
  into Night
Looking for Richard
Midnight in the Garden of
  Good and Evil
The Negotiator
Pay it Forward
Ordinary Decent Criminal
Outbreak
The Ref
Rocket Gilbraltor
See No Evil, Hear No Evil
Se7en
The Shipping News
A Show of Force
Swimming with Sharks
A Time to Kill
The Usual Suspects
Working Girl
(As director)
Albino Alligator

James Spader
Alien Hunter
Baby Boom
Bad Influence
Bob Roberts
Crash
Critical Care
Dream Lover
Endless Love
Jack's Back
Keys to Tulsa
Less Than Zero
Mannequin
The Music of Chance
Pretty in Pink
The Rachel Papers
Secretary
sex, lies, and videotape
Slow Burn
Stargate
The Stickup
Storyville
Supernova
True Colors
Tuff Turf
2 Days in the Valley
Wall Street
The Watcher
White Palace
Wolf

Sylvester Stallone
Antz
Assassins
Avenging Angelo
Cliffhanger
Cobra
Copland
Daylight
Death Race 2000

Demolition Man
Driven
Eye See You
F.I.S.T.
First Blood
Get Carter
Judge Dredd
Lock Up
The Lords of Flatbush
Nighthawks
Oscar
Over the Top
Paradise Alley
The Prisoner of Second
  Avenue
Rambo: First Blood Pt 2
Rambo III
Rhinestone
Rocky 1, 2, 3, 4, & 5
Shade
The Specialist
Spy Kids 3
Stop! or My Mom Will Shoot
Tango and Cash
Victory
(As director)
Paradise Alley
Rocky 2, 3, & 4
Staying Alive
(As writer)
Cliffhanger
Cobra
Driven
F.I.S.T.
The Lords of Flatbush
Over the Top
Paradise Alley
Rambo 1, 2, 3
Rhinestone
Rocky 1, 2, 3, 4, 5
Staying Alive

Terence Stamp
The Adventures of Priscilla,
  Queen of the Desert
Alien Nation
Billy Budd
Bliss
Bowfinger
The Collector
The Divine Nymph
Far from the Madding Crowd
Genuine Risk
The Haunted Mansion
The Hit
Kiss the Sky
Legal Eagles
The Limey
Love Walked In
Meetings with Remarkable
  Men
My Boss' Daughter
My Wife Is an Actress
The Real McCoy
Red Planet
The Sicilian
Star Wars: Episode I —
  The Phantom Menace
Superman I & II
Teorama
Wall Street
Young Guns

Barbara Stanwyck
Annie Oakley
Baby Face

Ball of Fire
The Bitter Tea
  of General Yen
Cattle Queen of Montana
Christmas in Connecticut
Clash by Night
Crime of Passion
Cry Wolf
Double Indemnity
East Side, West Side
Executive Suite
Golden Boy
Illicit
Ladies of Leisure
Ladies They Talk About
The Lady Eve
Lady of Burlesque
The Mad Miss Manton
The Maverick Queen
Meet John Doe
Night Nurse
The Night Walker
No Man of Her Own
The Purchase Price
Roustabout
Sorry, Wrong Number
Stella Dallas
The Strange Love of
  Martha Ivers
The Thorn Birds
Titanic
To Please a Lady
The Two Mrs. Carrolls
Union Pacific
Walk on the Wild Side

Mary Steenburgen
Back to the Future III
The Butcher's Wife
Casa de los Babys
Clifford
Cross Creek
Dead of Winter
Elf
End of the Line
Goin' South
The Grass Harp
Gulliver's Travels
Life as a House
Melvin and Howard
A Midsummer Night's
  Sex Comedy
Miss Firecracker
My Summer Story
Nixon
Nobody's Baby
One Magic Christmas
Parenthood
Philadelphia
Pontiac Moon
Powder
Ragtime
Romantic Comedy
Sunshine State
Time After Time
The Whales of August
What's Eating
  Gilbert Grape

Rod Steiger
Al Capone
American Gothic
The Amityville Horror
The Ballad of the Sad Cafe

Carpool
The Chosen
The Court-Martial of
  Billy Mitchell
Crazy in Alabama
Dirty Hands
Doctor Zhivago
End of Days
F.I.S.T.
A Fistful of Dynamite
Guilty as Charged
Henessey
The Hollywood Sign
The Hurricane
The Illustrated Man
In the Heat of the Night
Incognito
Innocence with Dirty
  Hands
The January Man
The Kindred
The Longest Day
The Loved One
Lucky Luciano
Men of Respect
Mars Attacks!
Modern Vampires
No Way to Treat a Lady
Oklahoma!
On the Waterfront
The Pawnbroker
Seven Thieves
The Specialist
Tales of the City
Truth or Consequences,
  N.M.
The Unholy Wife
Waterloo

James Stewart
After the Thin Man
Airport '77
An American Tail – Fievel
  Goes West
Anatomy of a Murder
Bandolero
Bell, Book and Candle
Bend of the River
The Big Sleep
Born to Dance
Broken Arrow
Call Northside 777
Cheyenne Autumn
The Cheyenne Social Club
Dear Brigitte
Destry Rides Again
The F.B.I. Story
The Far Country
The Flight of the Phoenix
The Glenn Miller Story
The Gorgeous Hussy
The Greatest Show on Earth
Harvey
How the West Was Won
It's a Wonderful Life
Made for Each Other
Magic Town
The Man From Laramie
The Man Who Knew
  Too Much
The Man Who
  Shot Liberty Valance
Mr. Hobbs Takes
  a Vacation

THE DISCERNING FILM LOVER'S GUIDE

Tilda Swinton

Adaptation.
Aria
The Beach
Blue
Caravaggio
Conceiving Ada
The Deep End
Edward II
Female Perversions
The Garden
The Last of England
Love Is the Devil
Orlando
The Statement
Teknolust
Vanilla Sky
War Requiem
The War Zone
Wittgenstein
Young Adam

Jessica Tandy

*batteries not included
Best Friends
The Birds
The Bostonians
Camilla
Cocoon
Cocoon: The Return
The Desert Fox
Driving Miss Daisy
Forever Amber
Foxfire
Fried Green Tomatoes
The Gin Game
Honky Tonk Freeway
The House on
   Carroll Street
Nobody's Fool
The Seventh Cross
Still of the Night
To Dance with the
   White Dog
Used People
The World According
   to Garp

Larenz Tate

Biker Boyz
Dead Presidents
The Inkwell
love jones
A Man Apart
Menace II Society
The Postman
Why Do Fools Fall in Love

Audrey Tautou

L'Auberge Espagnole
Amélie
Dirty Pretty Things
Happenstance
He Loves Me... He Loves
   Me Not
Les Marins perdus
Nowhere to Go But Up
The Spanish Apartment
Venus Beauty Institute

Elizabeth Taylor

Ash Wednesday
Beau Brummell
The Big Hangover
Boom!
Butterfield 8
Cat on a Hot Tin Roof

Cleopatra
The Comedians
Conspirator
A Date with Judy
Divorce His; Divorce Hers
Dr. Faustus
Elephant Walk
Father of the Bride
Father's Little Dividend
The Flintstones
Giant
Girl Who Had Everything
Ivanhoe
Jane Eyre
Julia Misbehaves
The Last Time I Saw Paris
A Little Night Music
Life with Father
A Little Night Music
Little Women
Love Is Better Than Ever
The Mirror Crack'd
National Velvet
A Place in the Sun
Raintree County
Reflections in a
   Golden Eye
The Sandpiper
Secret Ceremony
Suddenly, Last Summer
Sweet Bird of Youth
The Taming of the Shrew
Under Milk Wood
The V.I.P.s
Victory at Entebbe
Who's Afraid of Virginia
   Woolf?
Winter Kills
X, Y and Zee

Lili Taylor

The Addiction
All Revved Up
Anne Frank
Arizona Dream
Bright Angel
Casa de los Babys
Cold Fever
Dogfight
Gaudi Afternoon
Girls Town
The Haunting
High Fidelity
Household Saints
I Shot Andy Warhol
Live from Baghdad
Kicked in the Head
Killer: A Journal of Murder
Mrs. Parker & the Vicious
   Circle
Mystic Pizza
Pecker
Ransom
Ready to Wear
Rudy
Say Anything
Short Cuts
Watch It!
The Weather Underground

Noah Taylor

Almost Famous
Flirting
Lara Croft: Tomb Raider
Lara Croft Tomb Raider:
   The Cradle of Life
Max
One Crazy Night

Shine
Vanilla Sky
The Year My Voice Broke

Charlize Theron

The Astronaut's Wife
Celebrity
The Cider House Rules
Curse of the Jade Scorpion
Devil's Advocate
15 Minutes
The Italian Job
The Legend of Bagger
   Vance
Men of Honor
Mighty Joe Young
Monster
Reindeer Games
Sweet November
That Thing You Do!
Trapped
Trial and Error
Two Days in the Valley
Waking Up in Reno
The Yards

David Thewlis

American PerfeKt
Besieged
The Big Lebowski
Black Beauty
Dragonheart
Gangster No. 1
Harry Potter and the
   Prisoner of Azkaban
The Island of Dr. Moreau
James and the Giant Peach
Life is Sweet
The Miracle Maker
Naked
Prime Suspect 3
Restoration
Seven Years in Tibet
Timeline
Total Eclipse

Emma Thompson

Angels in America
Carrington
Dead Again
Fortunes of War
Harry Potter and the
   Prisoner of Azkaban
Henry V
Howards End
Impromptu
In the Name of the Father
Judas Kiss
Junior
Look Back in Anger
Love Actually
Much Ado About Nothing
Peter's Friends
Primary Colors
The Remains of the Day
Sense and Sensibility
The Tall Guy
Treasure Planet
The Winter Guest
Wit
(As writer)
Sense and Sensibility
Wit

Jack Thompson

Breaker Morant
Burke and Wills
Caddie
The Club

Deception
The Earthling
Excess Baggage
A Far Off Place
Flesh + Blood
Ground Zero
Jock Peterson
The Killing Beach
Last Dance
Mad Dog Morgan
Man from Snowy River
Merry Christmas, Mr.
   Lawrence
Midnight in the Garden of
   Good and Evil
Original Sin
South Pacific
Star Wars: Episode II –
   Attack of the Clones
The Sum of Us
Sunday Too Far Away
Waterfront
Wind
A Woman of Independent
   Means

Billy Bob Thornton

The Alamo
Armageddon
The Apostle
Bad Santa
The Badge
Bandits
Blood In Blood Out: Bound
   by Honor
Chopper Chicks in
   Zombietown
Dead Man
Homegrown
Indecent Proposal
Intolerable Cruelty
Levity
The Man Who Wasn't
   There
Monster's Ball
On Deadly Ground
One False Move
Primary Colors
Princess Mononoke
Pushing Tin
Red Rock West
A Simple Plan
Sling Blade
Tombstone
U-Turn
Waking Up in Reno
(As director)
All the Pretty Horses
Sling Blade
(As writer)
A Family Thing
The Gift
One False Move
Sling Blade

Uma Thurman

The Adventures of Baron
   Munchausen
The Avengers
Batman & Robin
Chelsea Walls
Dangerous Liaisons
Even Cowgirls Get the Blues
Final Analysis
Gattaca
The Golden Bowl
Henry & June
Hysterical Blindness

Jennifer 8
Johnny Be Good
Kill Bill: Vols. 1 & 2
Les Miserables
Mad Dog and Glory
A Month by the Lake
Pulp Fiction
Robin Hood
Sweet and Lowdown
Tape
The Truth About Cats &
   Dogs
Vatel
Where the Heart Is
Without Lying Down

Jennifer Tilly

American Strays
At Home with the Webbers
Bella Mafia
Bound
Bride of Chucky
Bullets Over Broadway
The Cat's Meow
The Crew
Dancing at the Blue Iguana
The Dress Code
Edie & Pen
Embrace of the Vampire
The Fabulous Baker Boys
Far From Home
Fast Sofa
The Getaway
The Haunted Mansion
Hide and Seek
High Spirits
Home on the Range
Hoods
House Arrest
Let it Ride
Liar, Liar
Made in America
Monsters, Inc.
Moving Violations
Music from Another Room
Relax... It's Just Sex!

Marisa Tomei

Anger Management
Chaplin
Equinox
The Flamingo Kid
Four Rooms
The Guru
Happy Accidents
In the Bedroom
Just a Kiss
King of the Jungle
My Cousin Vinny
My Own Country
Only You
Oscar
The Paper
The Perez Family
Slums of Beverly Hills
Someone Like You
Unhook the Stars
Untamed Heart
The Watcher
Welcome to Sarajevo
What Women Want
The Wild Thornberrys
   Movie

Lily Tomlin

All of Me
And the Band Played On
The Beverly Hillbillies

THE DISCERNING FILM LOVER'S GUIDE

Big Business
Blue in the Face
The Celluloid Closet
Flirting with Disaster
Get Bruce!
Getting Away with Murder
The Incredible Shrinking
    Woman
The Kid
Krippendorf's Tribe
The Late Show
Lily for President
Moment by Moment
Nashville
The Player
9 to 5
Orange County
The Search for Signs of
    Intelligent Life in the
    Universe
Shadows and Fog
Short Cuts
Tea with Mussolini

Spencer Tracy
Adam's Rib
Bad Day at Black Rock
Boom Town
Boys Town
Broken Lance
Captains Courageous
Cass Timberlane
Desk Set
The Devil at 4 O'Clock
Dr. Jekyll and Mr. Hyde
Edison the Man
Father of the Bride
Father's Little Dividend
Fury
Guess Who's Coming to
    Dinner
A Guy Named Joe
Inherit the Wind
It's a Mad, Mad, Mad,
    Mad World
Judgment at Nuremberg
Keeper of the Flame
The Last Hurrah
Libeled Lady
Mannequin
Men of Boys Town
The Mountain
Northwest Passage
The Old Man and the Sea
Pat and Mike
RiffRaff
San Francisco
Sea of Grass
The Seventh Cross
Stanley and Livingstone
State of the Union
Thirty Seconds over Tokyo
Tortilla Flat
Without Love
Woman of the Year

John Travolta
Basic
Battlefield Earth
Blow Out
Broken Arrow
Carrie
A Civil Action
The Devil's Rain
Domestic Disturbance
The Dumb Waiter
The Experts

Eyes of an Angel
Face/Off
The General's Daughter
Get Shorty
Grease
Look Who's Talking 1, 2,
    & 3
Lucky Numbers
Mad City
Michael
Perfect
Phenomenon
Primary Colors
Pulp Fiction
The Punisher
Saturday Night Fever
She's So Lovely
Swordfish
The Thin Red Line
Two of a Kind
Urban Cowboy
White Man's Burden

Stanley Tucci
The Alarmist
America's Sweethearts
Beethoven
Big Night
Big Trouble
Billy Bathgate
The Core
The Daytrippers
Deconstructing Harry
The 18th Angel
The Imposters
It Could Happen to You
Joe Gould's Secret
Jury Duty
Kiss of Death
A Life Less Ordinary
Maid in Manhattan
Men of Respect
Monkey Shines
Montana
The Pelican Brief
Prelude to a Kiss
The Public Eye
Road to Perdition
Undercover Blues
William Shakespeare's A
    Midsummer Night's
    Dream
Winchell
(As director)
Big Night
The Imposters
Joe Gould's Secret

Kathleen Turner
The Accidental Tourist
Baby Geniuses
Beautiful
Body Heat
A Breed Apart
Crimes of Passion
House of Cards
The Jewel of the Nile
Julia and Julia
The Man with Two Brains
Moonlight and Valentino
Naked in New York
Peggy Sue Got Married
Prince of Central Park
Prizzi's Honor
The Real Blonde
Romancing the Stone
Serial Mom

A Simple Wish
Switching Channels
Undercover Blues
V.I. Warshawski
The Virgin Suicides
The War of the Roses
Who Framed Roger Rabbit?

Lana Turner
Another Time, Another
    Place
Bachelor in Paradise
The Bad and the Beautiful
By Love Possessed
Cass Timberlane
Diane
Dr. Jekyll and Mr. Hyde
Green Dolphin Street
Homecoming
Honky Tonk
Imitation of Life
Johnny Eager
A Life of Her Own
Love Finds Andy Hardy
Madame X
Peyton Place
The Postman Always Rings
    Twice
The Sea Chase
Somewhere I'll Find You
The Three Musketeers
Who's Got the Action
Week-End at the Waldorf
Ziegfeld Girl

John Turturro
All Revved Up
Anger Management
Backtrack
Barton Fink
Being Human
The Big Lebowski
Box of Moonlight
Brain Donors
Clockers
Collateral Damage
The Color of Money
Company Man
Cradle Will Rock
Desperately Seeking Susan
Do the Right Thing
Fearless
Five Corners
Girl 6
Grace of my Heart
Gung Ho
Hannah and Her Sisters
He Got Game
Illuminata
Jungle Fever
The Luzhin Defence
Mac
Men of Respect
Miller's Crossing
Mr. Deeds
Mo' Better Blues
Monday Night Mayhem
Monkeybone
O Brother, Where Art Thou?
Off Beat
Quiz Show
Rounders
Search and Destroy
Secret Window
The Sicilian
The Source

State of Grace
13 Conversations about
    One Thing
To Live & Die in L.A.
Unstrung Heroes
(As director)
Mac
Illuminata

Liv Tyler
Armageddon
Can't Hardly Wait
Cookie's Fortune
Dr. T & the Women
Empire Records
Heavy
Inventing the Abbotts
Jersey Girl
The Lord of the Rings: The
    Fellowship of the Ring
The Lord of the Rings:
    The Two Towers
The Lord of the Rings:
    The Return of the King
One Night at McCool's
Onegin
Plunkett & Macleane
Silent Fall
Stealing Beauty
That Thing You Do!
U-Turn

Cicely Tyson
Always Outnumbered
    Always Outgunned
The Autobiography of Miss
    Jane Pittman
Bustin' Loose
The Comedians
Fried Green Tomatoes
The Heart Is a Lonely
    Hunter
Heat Wave
A Hero Ain't Nothin' But a
    Sandwich
Hoodlum
King
A Lesson Before Dying
A Man Called Adam
Oldest Living Confederate
    Widow Tells All
Riot in the Streets
The River Niger
Roots
Sounder
Wilma
A Woman Called Moses
Women of Brewster Place

Liv Ullmann
Autumn Sonata
The Bay Boy
A Bridge Too Far
Cries and Whispers
Dangerous Moves
The Emigrants
Forty Carats
Gaby, A True Story
Hour of the Wolf
Mindwalk
The New Land
The Night Visitor
The Ox
The Passion of Anna
Persona

Richard's Things
The Rose Garden
Scenes from a Marriage
The Serpent's Egg
Shame
The Wild Duck
Zandy's Bride
(As director)
Faithless
Private Confessions
Sofie

Mario Van Peebles
Ali
Blowback
The Cotton Club
Crazy Six
Delivery Boys
44 Minutes
Full Eclipse
Gang in Blue
Gunmen
Heartbreak Ridge
Highlander: The Final
    Dimension
Hot Shot
Identity Crisis
Jaws: The Revenge
Last Resort
Los Locos: Posse Rides Again
Love Kills
New Jack City
Panther
Posse
Riot in the Streets
Solo
Stag
Valentine's Day
(as director)
Baadasssss!
New Jack City
Panther
Posse

Vince Vaughn
The Cell
Clay Pigeons
A Cool Dry Place
Domestic Disturbance
The Locusts
The Lost World: Jurassic
    Park
Made
Old School
Psycho
Return to Paradise
South of Heaven, West of
    Hell
Starsky & Hutch
Swingers

Jon Voight
Ali
Anaconda
Boys Will Be Boys
Catch-22
The Champ
Coming Home
Conrack
A Decade under the
    Influence
Deliverance
Desert Bloom
A Dog of Flanders
Enemy of the State
Eternity

THE DISCERNING FILM LOVER'S GUIDE

Jane Eyre
Journey into Fear
The Lady from Shanghai
The Long Hot Summer
Macbeth
A Man for All Seasons
Man in the Shadow
The Man Who Saw
Tomorrow
Mr. Arkadin
Moby Dick
The Muppet Movie
Napoleon
Othello
Rikki-Tikki-Tavi
Someone to Love
Start the Revolution
without Me
The Stranger
Ten Days' Wonder
The Third Man
Three Cases of Murder
Tomorrow Is Forever
Touch of Evil
Transformers: The Movie
The Trial
Trouble in the Glen
The V.I.P.s
Voyage of the Damned
Waterloo
Who is Henry Jaglom

Mae West

Belle of the Nineties
Every Day's a Holiday
Go West, Young Man
Goin' to Town
I'm No Angel
Klondike Annie
My Little Chickadee
Myra Breckinridge
Night After Night
Sextette
She Done Him Wrong

Forest Whitaker

Article 99
Bank Robber
Battlefield Earth
Bird
Bloodsport
Blown Away
Body Snatchers
Consenting Adults
The Color of Money
Consenting Adults
Criminal Justice
The Crying Game
Deacons for Defense
Diary of a Hitman
Downtown
The Enemy Within
Fast Times at
Ridgemont High
The Feast of All Saints
4 Dogs Playing Poker
Ghost Dog: The Way of the
Samurai
Good Morning, Vietnam
Green Dragon
Jason's Lyric
Johnny Handsome
Last Light
Light It Up
Lush Life
Panic Room

Phenomenon
Phone Booth
Platoon
A Rage in Harlem
Smoke
Species
Stakeout
Vision Quest
(as director)
Hope Floats
Waiting to Exhale

Richard Widmark

Against All Odds
The Alamo
The Bedford Incident
Broken Lance
Cheyenne Autumn
Cold Sassy Tree
Coma
Don't Bother to Knock
A Gathering of Old Men
How the West Was Won
Judgment at Nuremberg
Kiss of Death
Madigan
Murder on the Orient Express
Night and the City
No Way Out
Panic in the Streets
Pickup on South Street
Road House
Rollercoaster
Saint Joan
The Street with No Name
The Swarm
To the Devil a Daughter
True Colors
The Tunnel of Love
Twilight's Last Gleaming
Warlock
The Way West

Dianne Wiest

The Associate
The Birdcage
Bright Lights, Big City
Bullets over Broadway
Cookie
Cops and Robbersons
Drunks
Edward Scissorhands
Falling in Love
Footloose
Hannah and Her Sisters
The Horse Whisperer
I Am Sam
I'm Dancing as Fast as I
Can
Independence Day
Little Man Tate
The Lost Boys
Parenthood
The Purple Rose of Cairo
Radio Days
The Scout
September
The Simple Life of Noah
Dearborn
The 10th Kingdom

Gene Wilder

Alice in Wonderland
Another You
Blazing Saddles
Bonnie and Clyde

Everything You Always
Wanted to Know About
Sex...
The Frisco Kid
Funny About Love
Hanky Panky
Haunted Honeymoon
The Little Prince
The Producers
Quackser Fortune Has a
Cousin in the Bronx
See No Evil, Hear No Evil
Silver Streak
Start the Revolution
without Me
Stir Crazy
Willy Wonka and the
Chocolate Factory
The Woman in Red
Young Frankenstein

Tom Wilkinson

Black Knight
Essex Boys
Eternal Sunshine of the
Spotless Mind
The Full Monty
The Gathering Storm
Girl with a Pearl Earring
The Governess
The Importance of Being
Earnest
In the Bedroom
Normal
Oscar and Lucinda
The Patriot
Priest
Prime Suspect 1
Ride with the Devil
Rush Hour
Shakespeare in Love
Sylvia
Wilde

Robin Williams

The Adventures of
Baron Munchausen
Aladdin
Aladdin and the King of
Thieves
Awakenings
Being Human
The Best of Times
Bicentennial Man
The Birdcage
Cadillac Man
Club Paradise
Dead Again
Dead Poets Society
Death to Smoochy
Deconstructing Harry
Father's Day
Ferngully
The Fisher King
Flubber
Get Bruce!
Good Morning, Vietnam
Good Will Hunting
Hamlet
Hook
Insomnia
Jack
Jakob the Liar
Joseph Conrad's The Secret
Agent
Jumanji
Moscow on the Hudson

Mrs. Doubtfire
Nine Months
One Hour Photo
Patch Adams
Popeye
Seize the Day
Shakes the Clown
The Survivors
The Tale of the Frog Prince
To Wong Foo...
Toys
What Dreams May Come
The World According
to Garp

Bruce Willis

Armageddon
Bandits
Beavis and Butt-Head do
America
Billy Bathgate
Blind Date
Bonfire of the Vanities
Breakfast of Champions
Color of Night
Death Becomes Her
Die Hard
Die Hard 2
Die Hard with
a Vengeance
The Fifth Element
Four Rooms
Hart's War
Hudson Hawk
In Country
The Jackal
The Kid
The Last Boy Scout
Last Man Standing
Loaded Weapon 1
Mercury Rising
Mortal Thoughts
Nobody's Fool
North
The Player
Pulp Fiction
Rugrats Go Wild
The Siege
The Sixth Sense
Striking Distance
Sunset
Tears of the Sun
That's Adequate
12 Monkeys
Unbreakable
The Whole Nine Yards
The Whole Ten Yards

Luke Wilson

Alex & Emma
Bad Seed
Best Men
Blue Streak
Bottle Rocket
Charlie's Angels
Dog Park
Home Fries
Legally Blonde
Legally Blonde 2: Red
White & Blonde
My Dog Skip
Old School
The Royal Tenenbaums
Rushmore
Scream 2
Soul Survivors
Telling Lies in America

Owen Wilson

Anaconda
Armageddon
Behind Enemy Lines
The Big Bounce
Bottle Rocket
Breakfast of Champions
The Cable Guy
The Haunting
I-Spy
Meet the Parents
The Minus Man
Permanent Midnight
The Royal Tenenbaums
Rushmore
Shanghai Knights
Shanghai Noon
Starsky & Hutch
Zoolander

Debra Winger

Betrayed
Big Bad Love
Black Widow
Cannery Row
A Dangerous Woman
Everybody Wins
Forget Paris
Leap of Faith
Legal Eagles
Mike's Murder
An Officer and
a Gentleman
Radio
Shadowlands
The Sheltering Sky
Terms of Endearment
Thank God It's Friday
Urban Cowboy
Wilder Napalm

Kate Winslet

Enigma
Eternal Sunshine of the
Spotless Mind
Faeries
Hamlet
Heavenly Creatures
Hideous Kinky
Holy Smoke!
Iris
Jude
A Kid in King Arthur's
Court
The Life of David Gale
Quills
Sense and Sensibility
Titanic

Shelley Winters

Alfie
The Balcony
Bloody Mama
Blume in Love
Buona Sera, Mrs. Campbell
Cleopatra Jones
The Delta Force
The Diary of Anne Frank
A Double Life
Elvis – The Movie
Enter Laughing
Executive Suite
Fanny Hill
The Great Gatsby
Greatest Story Ever Told
Harper

INDEX: THEMES

INDEX: THEMES

Road to Perdition
Ruby
Sniper
The Specialist
State of Siege
Suddenly
The Terminator
Terminator 2:
    Judgment Day
The Terrorist
The Times of Harvey Milk
Valentine's Day
When the Sky Falls
Winter Kills
Z

Astronauts
Apollo 13
Armageddon
The Astronaut's Wife
Capricorn One
Countdown
Deep Impact
First Man into Space
Marooned
Mission to Mars
Red Planet
The Right Stuff
Rocketman
SpaceCamp
Space Cowboys
2001: A Space Odyssey
2010

Atlantic City
Atlantic City
The King of Marvin
    Gardens
The Lemon Sisters
Owning Mahowny
Rounders
Snake Eyes
Suffering Bastards

Autobiographical
Adaptation
Almost Famous
Amarcord
Antwone Fisher
Au Revoir les Enfants
Barfly
A Bigger Splash
Biloxi Blues
Blaze
Born on the Fourth of July
A Brief History of Time
A Christmas Story
Diner
Distant Voices, Still Lives
Eleni
Girl, Interrupted
Heartburn
Henry & June
I Remember Mama
I'll Cry Tomorrow
I'm Dancing as
    Fast as I Can
It's My Party
Jo Jo Dancer, Your
    Life Is Calling
Julia

Long Day's Journey
    into Night
Lost in Yonkers
My Sister Eileen
My Summer Story
The Naked Civil Servant
Next Stop,
    Greenwich Village
Peppermint Soda
Places in the Heart
Poles Apart
Postcards from the Edge
Radio Days
A River Runs Through It
A Sense of Freedom
September 30, 1955
Thank You and
    Good Night
Things Behind the Sun
This Boy's Life
Tonio Kröger
A Voyage Round
    My Father
Who's That Knocking
    at My Door?
A Woman at War

Baseball
Amazing Grace and Chuck
Angels in the Outfield
    (1951 & 1994)
The Babe
The Babe Ruth Story
The Bad News Bears
Bang the Drum Slowly
The Bingo Long Traveling
    All-Stars & Motor Kings
Bull Durham
Cobb
Damn Yankees
Ed
Eight Men Out
The Fan
Fear Strikes Out
Field of Dreams
For Love of the Game
Hardball
It Happens Every Spring
The Jackie Robinson Story
A League of Their Own
The Life and Times of
    Hank Greenberg
Little Big League
Long Gone
Major League 1, 2, & 3
Mr. Baseball
The Natural
Pastime
The Pride of St. Louis
The Pride of the Yankees
The Rookie
The Sandlot
The Scout
61*
Stealing Home
The Stratton Story
Summer Catch
Take Me Out to
    the Ball Game
Talent for the Game
Trading Hearts
The Winning Team

Films that were the
Basis for Musicals
Anna and the King of Siam
    (The King and I)
Auntie Mame (Mame)
Cabiria (Sweet Charity)
A Christmas Carol (Scrooge)
Goodbye, Mr. Chips, 1939
    (Goodbye, Mr. Chips,
    1969)
I Am a Camera (Cabaret)
Little Shop of Horrors, 1960
    (Little Shop of Horrors,
    1986)
The Matchmaker
    (Hello, Dolly)
Oliver Twist (Oliver!)
The Philadelphia Story
    (High Society)
Purlie Victorious (Purlie)
Pygmalion (My Fair Lady)
The Shop Around the
    Corner (In the Good Old
    Summertime)
Smiles of a Summer Night
    (A Little Night Music)
A Star Is Born (1937)
    (A Star Is Born, 1954)
Viktor und Viktoria
    (Victor/Victoria)
The Wizard of Oz
    (The Wiz)
The Women
    (The Opposite Sex)

Basketball
Above the Rim
The Air Up There
BASEketball
The Basketball Diaries
Blue Chips
Celtic Pride
Eddie
Forget Paris
He Got Game
Hoop Dreams
Hoosiers
Juwanna Mann
Like Mike
Love & Basketball
"O"
The 6th Man
Space Jam
Sunset Park
Teen Wolf
That Championship Season
White Men Can't Jump

The Beatles
BackBeat
The Beatles Anthology
The Compleat Beatles
A Hard Day's Night
Help!
The Hours and Times
I Wanna Hold Your Hand
Let It Be
Magical Mystery Tour
Yellow Submarine

Berlin
Anita: Dances of Vice
Berlin Alexanderplatz
Berlin Express
Berlin: Symphony of a Great
    City
Beyond Silence

The Blue Hour
Cabaret
Far Away, So Close
Fatherland
Flirt
Funeral in Berlin
Germany Year Zero
Good Bye, Lenin!
Gotcha!
Grand Hotel
Hanussen
I Am a Camera
I Am My Own Woman
The Innocent
Invincible
Judgment in Berlin
The Luzhin Defence
M
Octopussy
One, Two, Three
The Promise
The Quiller Memorandum
The Search
The Serpent's Egg
The Spy Who Came in from
    the Cold
Torn Curtain
Taxi Zum Klo
Westler: East of the Wall
Wings of Desire

Blindness
Alligator Eyes
At First Sight
Blind Fury
Blind Light
Blink
Butterflies Are Free
Cactus
The Cat O'Nine Tails
City Lights
The Color of Paradise
Dancer in the Dark
The Day of the Triffids
The Enchanted Cottage
The Eye
It Happened in the Park
Jennifer 8
The Killer
Love! Valour! Compassion!
Magnificent Obsession
Marianela
The Miracle Worker
Night Is My Future
A Patch of Blue
Proof
Scent of a Woman
See No Evil, Hear No Evil
The Silence
The Spiral Staircase
Wait Until Dark
The Whales of August
The Zatoichi Series

Body Switching
All of Me
Big
Chances Are
Dream a Little Dream
18 Again
Face/Off
A Florida Enchantment
Fluke
Freaky Friday
Like Father, Like Son
Prelude to a Kiss
Something Special

Switch
Vice Versa

James Bond
Casino Royale
Diamonds Are Forever
Die Another Day
Dr. No
For Your Eyes Only
From Russia with Love
GoldenEye
Goldfinger
Licence to Kill
Live and Let Die
The Living Daylights
The Man with the
    Golden Gun
Moonraker
Never Say Never Again
Octopussy
On Her Majesty's
    Secret Service
The Spy Who Loved Me
Thunderball
Tomorrow Never Dies
A View to a Kill
The World Is Not Enough
You Only Live Twice

Boston
All the Rage
Altered States
The Boston Strangler
The Bostonians
Between the Lines
Blown Away
Bluehill Avenue
The Brink's Job
Celtic Pride
Coma
Far and Away
Good Will Hunting
Kicking and Screaming
Mystic River
Next Stop Wonderland
The Paper Chase
The Proposition
Southie
Squeeze
The Verdict
Vig

Boxing
Against the Ropes
Ali
Body and Soul
The Boxer
The Boxer and Death
Broken Noses
The Champ
Champion
Cock & Bull Story
Crossing the Line
Diggstown
Fat City
Gentleman Jim
Girlfight
Gladiator
Golden Boy
The Great White Hope
The Great White Hype
Hard Times
Here Comes Mr. Jordan
Homeboy
Joe and Max
The Kid from Brooklyn
Killer's Kiss

INDEX: THEMES

THE DISCERNING FILM LOVER'S GUIDE

Steel
Superman: The Movie
Superman II, III, IV
Tank Girl
The Shadow
Swamp Thing
Teenage Mutant
    Ninja Turtles I, II, III
Timecop
Unbreakable
X-Men
X2: X-Men United

Coming of Age

À la Mode
À Nos Amours
All over Me
Almost Famous
Amarcord
American Boyfriends
Among the Cinders
Angus
Anywhere but Here
The Bay Boy
Bend It Like Beckham
Bilitis
Blue Jeans
Bonjour Tristesse
La Boum
Breaking Away
Brighton Beach Memoirs
Camp
Cronica del Alba
The Dangerous Lives of
    Altar Boys
The Dawning
Desert Bloom
Dirty Dancing
Do You Remember Dolly
    Bell?
Edge of Seventeen
Ernesto
Fast Talking
First Love
Flirting
Forever Young
The 400 Blows
Fresh
Friends Forever
Get Real
The Getting of Wisdom
Ghost World
The Girl
Le Grand Chemin
Gregory's Girl
Hey Babu Riba
Holiday Hotel
The Horse Whisperer
Igby Goes Down
The Inkwell
King of the Hill
Kipperbang
Last Summer
Léolo
A Little Romance
The Mango Tree
Me without You
Mermaids
My American Cousin
My First Mister
My Life on Ice
Néa — The Young
    Emmanuelle
Nico & Dani
Norman Loves Rose

Old Enough
The Outside Chance of
    Maximilian Glick
Paradise
Peppermint Soda
Petit Con
Puberty Blues
Rain
Raising Victor Vargas
The Rascals
Real Women Have Curves
Red Kiss (Rouge Baiser)
Roger Dodger
The Royal Tenenbaums
Rushmore
Secondhand Lions
Simon Birch
The Slingshot
Slums of Beverly Hills
Smoke Signals
Smooth Talk
Son of the Shark
Spider-Man
Splendor in the Grass
Square Dance
Stand by Me
Sugar
Summer of '42
Telling Lies in America
Tendres Cousines
Thirteen
36 Fillette
Time Stands Still
Tumbleweeds
Twist and Shout
Valentina
The Wanderer (Le
    Gran Meaulnes)
The War
Whatever
White Squall
Wild Reeds
The Year My Voice Broke
You Are Not Alone
Young Aphrodites

Con Artists

Bedtime Story
Il Bidone (The Swindlers)
The Big Bounce
Cafe Express
Came a Hot Friday
Catch Me If You Can
Confidence
Curly Sue
Diggstown
Dirty Rotten Scoundrels
The Fortune Cookie
The Grifters
Heartbreakers
Honky Tonk
House of Games
The Impostors
The Lady Eve
Leap of Faith
The Man Who Be King
Matchstick Men
Maverick
Mo' Money
The Music Man
Nightmare Alley
Novocaine
Paper Moon
The Rainmaker
Skin Game

The Spanish Prisoner
The Squeeze
Stavisky
The Sting
The Sting II
Support Your Local
    Gunfighter
The Swindle
Sylvia Scarlett
Topaze
Vibes
Where's Picone?
White Men Can't Jump
White River

Concentration Camps

Anne Frank
Bent
The Boxer and Death
Christabel
Come See the Paradise
Forced March
Genghis Cohn
The Grey Zone
The Hiding Place
Holocaust
The Last Butterfly
The Last Days
Life Is Beautiful
Night and Fog
One Day in the Life of Ivan
    Denisovich
Playing for Time
Schindler's List
Seven Beauties
Shoah
Sophie's Choice
Sunshine
Train of Life
Triumph of the Spirit

Counterculture

Alice's Restaurant
Almost Famous
The Basketball Diaries
Basquiat
Between the Lines
Beyond the Valley of the
    Dolls
The Big Fix
Ciao! Manhattan
Desperately Seeking Susan
The Doors
Easy Rider
Even Cowgirls Get
    the Blues
Fear and Loathing in Las
    Vegas
Flashback
Get to Know Your Rabbit
Grass
Hair
Harold and Maude
Head
Hideous Kinky
I Love You, Alice B. Toklas
I Shot Andy Warhol
Joe
Jonah Who Will Be 25 in
    the Year 2000
Katherine
The Magic Christian
Masculin-Feminin
Medium Cool
More

Naked Lunch
Nico Icon
1969
Psych-Out
The Return of the
    Secaucus 7
Rude Awakening
Running on Empty
Scotland, PA
SLC Punk
Steal This Movie
Steelyard Blues
The Strawberry Statement
Timothy Leary's Dead
Trainspotting
Trash
The Trip
Up in Smoke
The Valley
    (Obscured by Clouds)
Weekend
Where the Buffalo Roam
Woodstock
Zabriskie Point

Courtroom

The Accused
Adam's Rib
The Advocate
Amistad
Anatomy of a Murder
...And Justice for All
The Bedroom Window
Beyond a Reasonable Doubt
Blind Faith
Chicago
A Civil Action
Class Action
Compulsion
Crime of the Century
Criminal Law
Deviant Obsession
The Devil and Daniel
    Webster
Evelyn
Fatal Vision
A Few Good Men
A Free Soul
From the Hip
Ghosts of Mississippi
Guilty as Sin
Hanna K.
High Crimes
I Want to Live
Illegally Yours
Inherit the Wind
Intolerable Cruelty
Jagged Edge
Judgment at Nuremberg
Judgment in Berlin
Jury Duty
Knock on Any Door
Legal Eagles
Legally Blonde
Liar Liar
The Life of Emil Zola
Love Among the Ruins
Madame X
Marked Woman
Midnight in the Garden of
    Good and Evil
Mr. Deeds Goes to Town
Murder
Music Box
My Cousin Vinny
Night Falls on Manhattan

Nuts
Open Doors
The Paradine Case
Philadelphia
A Place in the Sun
Presumed Innocent
Primal Fear
A Question of Love
Rampage
Reversal of Fortune
Roxie Hart
Rules of Engagement
Runaway Jury
Sacco and Vanzetti
Sergeant Rutledge
Sergeant Ryker
Sleepers
Snow Falling on Cedars
The Star Chamber
Suspect
A Time to Kill
To Kill a Mockingbird
Trian and Error
True Believer
Tucker
12 Angry Men
The Verdict
The Winslow Boy
Witness for the Prosecution

Deafness

Alpine Fire
Bangkok Dangerous
Beyond Silence
Children of a Lesser God
Copland
Hear No Evil
The Heart Is a Lonely
    Hunter
Johnny Belinda
The Miracle Worker
Mr. Holland's Opus
The Piano
See No Evil, Hear No Evil
Sound and Fury
Suspect
Tommy

The Depression

Angela's Ashes
Auntie Mame
Bonnie & Clyde
Boxcar Bertha
The Cider House Rules
Days of Heaven
The Education of Little Tree
Entertaining Angels: The
    Dorothy Day Story
The Grapes of Wrath
Honkytonk Man
Ironweed
The Journey of Natty Gann
Loser
Mame
O Brother, Where Art Thou?
Our Daily Bread
Paper Moon
Pennies from Heaven
Places in the Heart
The Purple Rose of Cairo
Road to Perdition
Seabiscuit
Sweet and Lowdown
Thieves Like Us
Two Bits
Rambling Rose

INDEX: THEMES

THE DISCERNING FILM LOVER'S GUIDE

Bellman and True
Big Fish
Blue Fin
Broken Lance
A Bronx Tale
Cafe Express
Character
City by the Sea
The Clockmaker
The Color of Paradise
Consiel de Famille
A Cool, Dry Place
Cry, The Beloved Country
Da
Dad
Domestic Disturbance
East of Eden
The Emerald Forest
Family Tree
Father
Field of Dreams
Frailty
Freedom Is Paradise
Frequency
Getting Even with Dad
Godsend
The Great Santini
He Got Game
Home from the Hill
The Horse
The House of the Seven
   Gables
I Never Sang for My Father
In the Name of the Pope King
In the Name of the Father
Indiana Jones and the Last
   Crusade
Islands in the Stream
John Q
Jungle 2 Jungle
Kaddish
Liar Liar
Life as a House
Life is Beautiful
Lone Star
The Lonely Man
Love Streams
Man of the House
Marvin and Tige
Memories of Me
My Baby's Daddy
Night Zoo
Nobody's Fool
Nothing in Common
October Sky
Padre Padrone
Parenthood
Pop & Me
Price of Glory
La Promesse
Quiz Show
Road to Perdition
Second Best
She's the One
Simple Men
Smoke
Spider
Success Is the Best Revenge
The Sum of Us
Sword of Vengeance
Target
This Is My Father
Time without Pity
To Paris with Love
Ulee's Gold

Vice Versa
A Voyage Round My Father
The War
The Whistle Blower
World and Time Enough

Film Noir

After Dark, My Sweet
Against All Odds
Alphaville
The American Soldier
Angel Heart Backfire
Behind Locked Doors
Beware, My Lovely
The Big Clock
The Big Combo
The Big Heat
The Big Sleep
The Big Squeeze
The Big Steal
Black Angel
Bleeding Vegas
Blood & Concrete
Blood & Wine
Blood Simple
The Blue Dahlia
The Blue Gardenia
Body Heat
Born to Kill
Bound
Brute Force
Cappuccino
Cast a Deadly Spell
Caught
China Moon
Chinatown
Choice of Arms
Cinema's Dark Side
   Collection
Clay Pigeons
Confidentially Yours
Cornered
Criss Cross
The Dark Corner
Dark Passage
Dead Reckoning
Deadline at Dawn
Delusion
Desperate
Detective
Detour
Devil in a Blue Dress
D.O.A.
Double Indemnity
Le Doulos
Fallen Angels
Farewell, My Lovely
Un Flic
Follow Me Quietly
Force of Evil
The Gangster
The Glass Key
Goodbye Lover
The Grifters
Gun Crazy
Gun Crazy
Hammett
Hangmen Also Die
Harper
He Walked by Night
Hit Me
The Hitch-Hiker
The Hot Spot
I Wake Up Screaming
In a Lonely Place

Johnny Apollo
Judas Kiss
Keys to Tulsa
Kill Me Again
The Killers
The Killers
Kiss Me Deadly
Kiss of Death
Kiss Tomorrow Goodbye
L.A. Confidential
The Lady in the Lake
The Last Seduction
The Last Way Out
Laura
Liebestraum
The Long Night
Love at Large
Love Is Colder Than Death
Love the Hard Way
Lured
Macao
The Maltese Falcon
The Man Who Wasn't
   There
Ministry of Fear
The Moon in the Gutter
Moonrise
The Most Terrible Time in
   My Life
Murder, My Sweet
Naked City
The Naked Kiss
Night and the City
The Night of the Hunter
No Good Deed
No Man of Her Own
Nocturne
Odds Against Tomorrow
On Dangerous Ground
Out of the Past
Palmetto
Panic in the Streets
Paris Express
Phantom Lady
Pickup on South Street
The Pitfall
Point Blank
Positive I.D.
The Postman Always Rings
   Twice
The Racket
Railroaded
Raw Deal
Red Rock West
Road House
Romeo Is Bleeding
The Salton Sea
Le Samouraï
Scarlet Street
Second Chance
The Set-Up
Shack Out on 101
Shock Corridor
The Singing Detective
Slamdance
The Strange Affair of Uncle
   Harry
Strange Impersonation
The Strange Love of
   Martha Ivers
Stranger on the Third Floor
Stray Dog
Sudden Fear
Suddenly
T-Men

The Tenant
They Live by Night
They Won't Believe Me
The Third Man
This Gun for Hire
This World, Then the
   Fireworks
Too Late For Tears
Touch of Evil
Trouble in Mind
Twilight
The Two Jakes
U-Turn
The Underneath
Underworld U.S.A.
The Usual Suspects
While the City Sleeps
Wild Things

Filmmaking

An Alan Smithee Film:
   Burn, Hollywood, Burn!
Alex in Wonderland
Almonds and Raisins
American Movie
America's Sweethearts
And Now My Love
The Bad and the Beautiful
The Barefoot Contessa
Barton Fink
Bellissima
Bellissimo
Beware a Holy Whore
The Big Picture
Big Shot's Funeral
Bombshell
Body Double
Bowfinger
Burden of Dreams
Cecil B. Demented
Chaplin
Ciao! Federico!
The Cigarette Girl
   of Mosselprom
The Comic
Committed
Contempt
Crimes and Misdemeanors
Dangerous Game
Day for Night
The Day of the Locust
Dead of Winter
Directed by Andrei
   Tarkovsky
Document of the Dead
duBEAT-E-O
Ed Wood
8½
The End of Violence
F/X
Fedora
The Fluffer
Forgotten Silver
Frances
Full-Tilt Boogie
George Stevens: A
   Filmmaker's Journey
Get Shorty
Gods and Monsters
Good Morning Babylon
The Hard Way
Hearts of Darkness: A
   Filmmaker's Apocalypse
Hearts of the West
Hollywood Ending

Hollywood Shuffle
Home Movies
I'm Almost Not Crazy
I Only Want You to Love
   Me
The Icicle Thief
In the Soup
Innocence Unprotected
Inside Hitchcock
Intervista
Irma Vep
Jacquot
Kisses in the Dark
The Last Movie
The Last Tycoon
Laugh for Joy
Lavender Limelight
Lightning over Water
Lisbon Story
Living in Oblivion
Loaded
Lost in La Mancha
Lulu in Berlin
The Making of Star
   Wars/The Empire Strikes
   Back
Man Bites Dog
A Man, a Woman
   and a Killer
A Man in Love
The Man in the Silk Hat
A Man Like Eva
Man of a Thousand Faces
Matinee
Michael Caine —
   Acting in Film
Mistress
Mulholland Drive
Mute Witness
My Life's in Turnaround
My Wife Is an Actress
Observations under
   the Volcano
One Night Stand
Passion
The Pickle
The Player
Postcards from the Edge
Pretty as a Picture: The Art
   of David Lynch
Real Life
RKO 281
S.O.B.
Search and Destroy
Shadow of the Vampire
The Shoot
Shoot or be Shot
Silent Movie
Simone
Singin' in the Rain
Six O'Clock News
A Slave of Love
Special Effects
Stand-In
The Star
A Star Is Born (1937, 1954)
The Star Maker
Stardust Memories
State and Main
The State of Things
Strangers Kiss
The Stunt Man
Success Is the Best Revenge
Sullivan's Travels
Sunset

THE DISCERNING FILM LOVER'S GUIDE

The Tall Guy
10 Rillington Place
The 39 Steps
Threads
To Sir, with Love
Tonight and Every Night
A Touch of Class
Trainspotting
Turtle Diary
28 Days Later
24 Hours in London
Victim
We Think the
    World of You
Werewolf of London
Who's Who
Wonderland
Yanks
Young Americans

Los Angeles
Against All Odds
American Gigolo
America's Sweethearts
An Alan Smithee Film:
    Burn Hollywood Burn
The Anniversary Party
Assault on Precinct 13
Bad Influence
Bar Girls
Barfly
Barton Fink
The Battle for L.A.
Beverly Hills Cop 1, 2, 3
Beyond Suspicion
Big Fat Liar
The Big Tease
Blade Runner
Blast from the Past
Blood In Blood Out: Bound
    by Honor
Blue Streak
Blue Thunder
Body Double
Boiling Point
The Boost
Border Radio
Bowfinger
Boys Life 2
The Boys Next Door
Boyz N the Hood
Brother
Buffy the Vampire Slayer
Bulworth
Calander Girl
Cast a Deadly Spell
The Charles
    Bukowski Tapes
The China Syndrome
Chinatown
Choose Me
Ciao! Manhattan
Clueless
Cobra
Color of Night
Colors
Confidence
The Couch Trip
Cover Me
D.O.A.
The Day of the Locust
Dead Again
Demolition Man
Desire and Hell
    at Sunset Motel

Die Hard
A Different Story
Double Dragon
Dragnet (1954)
Dragnet (1987)
duBEAT-E-O
Earthquake
Eating
Echo Park
Ed Wood
8 Million Ways to Die
Encino Man
Erin Brockovich
Escape from the
    Planet of the Apes
Escape from L.A.
Extreme Justice
Eye for and Eye
Falling Down
The Fast and the Furious
A Fine Mess
The First Power
44 Minutes
Foxes
Friday
Friend of the Family
Get Shorty
Go
Grand Canyon
Grief
Harper
Heat
Hollywood Homicide
The Hours
Hugo Pool
Hurlyburly
I Love You,
    Alice B. Toklas
I'll Do Anything
In a Lonely Place
An Inconvenient Woman
Inside Monkey Zetterland
Internal Affairs
Into the Night
It's My Party
Jack's Back
Jay and Silent Bob Strike
    Back
Jimmy Hollywood
Just the Two of Us
The Karate Kid
L.A. Story
The Lady in the Lake
The Last of the Finest
Laurel Canyon
Less Than Zero
Lethal Weapon 1, 2, 3, 4
Life Stinks
The Lonely Lady
The Long Goodbye
Lost Highway
Lovely & Amazing
Made
Magnolia
The Maltese Falcon
Man of a Thousand Faces
Memento
Menace II Society
Mi Vida Loca
    (My Crazy Life)
Miracle Mile
The Morning After
Mulholland Drive
Mulholland Falls
Multiplicity

The Muse
My Family (Mi Familia)
My Life
The Naked Gun
The New Age
The New Centurions
Night on Earth
1941
Norman, Is That You?
Once Bitten
The Onion Field
Out of Bounds
The Party
Perfect
The Player
Point Break
Postcards from the Edge
Predator 2
Pretty Woman
Pulp Fiction
Rebel without a Cause
Relentless
Reservoir Dogs
Rising Sun
The Rocketeer
The Rookie
Ruthless People
S.O.B.
Safe
The Salton Sea
Scenes from a Mall
Shampoo
Short Cuts
Showdown in Little Tokyo
Silverlake Life: The View
    from Here
Slaughter's Big Rip-Off
Species
Speed
Stand and Deliver
Stand-In
The Star
A Star Is Born (1937, 1954)
Stop! or My Mom
    Will Shoot
Strange Days
Sunset Boulevard
Swimming with Sharks
Swingers
Swordfish
Tales of Ordinary Madness
Talkin' Dirty After Dark
Tapeheads
10
The Terminator
Terminator 2:
    Judgment Day
Them!
To Live and Die in L.A.
Training Day
Trancers
The Trigger Effect
True Confessions
Tuff Turf
The Two Jakes
Volcano
Wag the Dog
Warlock
Welcome to L.A.
What Price Hollywood?
Whatever Happened
    to Baby Jane?
What's Cooking?
Where the Day Takes You
White Man's Burdon

Who Framed Roger Rabbit
The Wild Party
Witch Hunt
Wonderland
Zero Effect
Zoot Suit

Martial Arts
Above the Law
A Better Tomorrow,
    Pts. 1 & 2
The Big Brawl
Blind Fury
Bruce Lee: True Story
The Bushido Blade
The Chinatown Kid
Circle of Iron
Crouching Tiger, Hidden
    Dragon
Dragon Fist
Dragon: The Bruce Lee Story
The Duel
Enter the Dragon
Evil Cat
Fate of Lee Khan
Fist Power
Five Fingers of Death
Fugitive Samurai
The Glimmer Man
Gonza the Spearman
Half a Loaf of Kung Fu
The Honor of Dongfang Xu
The Hunted
Invincible
Jackie Chan's First Strike
Kai Doh Maru
Karate Cop
The Karate Kid
Kill Bill
The Killer
Kiss of the Dragon
Kojiro
The Last Dragon
Legend of 8 Samurai
The Life and Opinion
    of Masseur Ichi
Lucky Seven
Marked for Death
Master Killer
New Fists of Fury
Once a Thief
The One
One-Eyed Swordsman
Project A (Part 1 & 2)
Rage and Honor
Red Lion
Replicant
Return of the Dragon
Romeo Must Die
Rumble in the Bronx
Saga of the Vagabonds
Samurai I, II, & III
Samurai Reincarnation
Samurai Saga
Sanshiro Sugata
Seeding of a Ghost
Snake and Crane Arts of
    Shoalin
Supercop
Sword of Doom
Sword of Fury I & II
Swords of Death
3 Ninjas
Tube
Vampire Effect

Versus
Winners and Sinners
The Zatoichi Series

Mental Illness
Angel Baby
Another Woman
Asylum
Autumn Leaves
Awakenings
A Beautiful Mind
Benny & Joon
A Bill of Divorcement
The Butcher Boy
Captain Newman M.D.
The Caveman's Valentine
Clean, Shaven
Cosi
Crazy People
David and Lisa
Don Juan deMarco
Donnie Darko
The Dream Team
Elling
L'Enfer
Family Life
    (Wednesday's Child)
Fear Strikes Out
Girl, Interrupted
Harvey
Head Against the Wall
Henry IV
Hour of the Wolf
I Never Promised You a
    Rose Garden
Igby Goes Down
In the Mouth of Madness
Julien Donkey-Boy
King of Hearts
Kisses in the Dark
Lilith
The Madness of King
    George
Manic
Marvin's Room
Misery
Mr. Deeds goes to Town
Mr. Jones
Never Talk to Strangers
The Ninth Configuration
Nuts
One Flew Over the Cuckoo's
    Nest
The Other Sister
Outrageous
The Prince of Tides
Quills
Rain Man
Red Dragon
The Ruling Class
Shine
Shock Corridor
The Silence of the Lambs
The Sinful Nuns of Saint
    Valentine
Sling Blade
The Snake Pit
Spellbound
Spider
Stroszek
Sybil
They Might Be Giants
The Three Faces of Eve
Through a Glass Darkly
What About Bob?

*A Woman Under
  the Influence*

Mistaken Identity

As Young as You Feel
Beyond Suspicion
The Big Lebowski
Blame It on the Bellboy
Blue Streak
The Bride Wore Red
Casanova's Big Night
Christmas in Connecticut
Dave
Dead Tired
Desperately Seeking Susan
Double Take
Enemy of the State
Good Neighbor Sam
The Great Imposter
The Guardsman
Hail the Conquering Hero
Happy, Texas
Houseguest
Housesitter
I Married a Dead Man
I Married a Shadow
If Looks Could Kill
*In the Good Old
  Summertime*
The Inspector General
Johnny Stecchino
The Lady Eve
Lady by Choice
Lily in Love
The Love Letter
Maid in Manhattan
*The Man Who Knew Too
  Little*
*The Man With One Red
  Shoe*
Maybe... Maybe Not
Midnight
Minority Report
Mystery Date
Never Been Kissed
No Man of Her Own
North by Northwest
Nuns on the Run
Off Beat
Olivier, Olivier
Quality Street
*The Return of Martin
  Guerre*
Secret Admirer
Sommersby
Soul Man
*Start the Revolution without
  Me*
Suzhou River
Sylvia Scarlett
Taking Care of Business
Things Change
The 39 Steps
Top Hat
True Identity
*We're No Angels
  (1955, 1989)*
What's Up Doc
While You Were Sleeping
Yentl
*Yiddle with a Fiddle
  (Yidl Mitn Fidl)*

Mothers & Daughters

Antonia's Line
Anywhere but Here
Autumn Sonata
The Bad Seed
Bellissima
Carrie
Crooklyn
*Divine Secrets of the Ya-Ya
  Sisterhood*
Dolores Claiborne
Freaky Friday
*Glitter Goddess of
  Sunset Strip*
The Good Mother
Gypsy
Heartbreakers
Hideous Kinky
High Heels
High Tide
The Horse Whisperer
Hysterical Blindness
Imitation of Life
Ladies of the Chorus
Little Voice
Lovely & Amazing
Mermaids
Mildred Pierce
Mommie Dearest
Mommy
'Night, Mother
Not without My Daughter
One True Thing
Panic Room
Ponette
Postcards From the Edge
Real Women Have Curves
Secrets and Lies
Steel Magnolias
Stella
Stella Dallas
*Summer Wishes,
  Winter Dreams*
Terms of Endearment
Tumbleweeds
Two Women
White Oleander
The Winter Guest
A World Apart

Mothers & Sons

A.I. Artificial Intelligence
Alias Betty
*Alice Doesn't Live Here
  Anymore*
All Fall Down
Bloody Mamma
Bobbie's Girl
Bubble Boy
Dancer in the Dark
The Deep End
Frankie Starlight
Godsend
Heavy
The Hours
The Grifters
Igby Goes Down
Invisible Mom
The Krays
Little Man Tate
Maborosi
Madame X
*The Manchurian
  Candidate*

Men Don't Leave
Monster's Ball
Mother
New York Stories
*None But the
  Lonely Heart*
Oedipus Rex
Pickpocket
Psycho
Requiem for a Dream
Spanking the Monkey
Spider
*Stop! or My Mom
  Will Shoot*
A Stranger in Town
Suddenly, Last Summer
The Terence Davies Trilogy
*Throw Mama from
  the Train*
To Each His Own
To See Paris and Die
Torch Song Trilogy
Under Heat
Where's Poppa?
White Heat

Mountain Climbing

Cliffhanger
The Eiger Sanction
Fire on the Mountain
Five Days One Summer
Into Thin Air
K-2
Scream of Stone
Seven Years in Tibet
Touching the Void
Vertical Limit

Napolean

Anthony Adverse
The Battle of Austerlitz
*Bill & Ted's
  Excellent Adventure*
Conquest
Desiree
Juarez
Napolean
Quills
Time Bandits
War and Peace
Waterloo

Of **Native American** Interest

*Amazon: The Invisible
  People*
Big Eden
Billy Jack
Black Robe
Broken Arrow
Cabeza de Vaca
Cheyenne Autumn
Clearcut
The Comancheros
Dances with Wolves
The Dark Wind
Duel at Diablo
The Education of Little Tree
*Geronimo: An
  American Legend*
Grizzly Mountain
*I Heard the Owl Call my
  Name*
*In the Land of the War
  Canoes*

Incident at Oglala
Johnny Greyeyes
The Last of His Tribe
Little Big Man
A Man Called Horse
Pocahontas
Powwow Highway
Renegades
Return to Lonsome Dove
The Searchers
Shadow Hunter
Skins
Smoke Signals
*Tell Them Willie
  Boy Is Here*
Thunderheart
Tomahawk
The Unforgiven
War Party
Windtalkers
*World of Bill Moyers: The
  Faithkeeper*

Nazis

Above Suspicion
Aimee & Jaguar
All Through the Night
Apt Pupil
As If It Were Yesterday
The Assault
Bach in Auschwitz
Background to Danger
Bedknobs and Broomsticks
The Believer
Bent
Berlin Alexanderplatz
Berlin Express
The Blood of Others
The Boys from Brazil
Cabaret
Casablanca
Christabel
Come and See
Cornered
The Damned
David
The Desert Fox
Despair
Desperate Journey
The Dirty Dozen
Divided We Fall
Edge of Darkness
Enemy at the Gates
The Exiles
Eye of the Needle
Father
Fatherland
The 49th Parallel
Germany Year Zero
*Good Evening, Mr.
  Wallenberg*
The Harmonists
Hitler's Children
Hotel Terminus
The House on Carroll Street
The House on 92nd Street
In a Glass Cage
*Indiana Jones and the Last
  Crusade*
The Infiltrator
Inside the Third Reich
Invincible
Jakob the Liar
Judgment at Nuremberg
Julia

The Keep
The Last Five Days
A Man Escaped
*The Man who Captured
  Eichmann*
Marathon Man
Max
Mein Kampf
Mein Krieg
Morituri
Music Box
The Nazi Officer's Wife
Northern Pursuit
Notorious
The Odessa File
The Old Gun
Once Upon a Honeymoon
The Pedestrian
The Pianist
The Quiller Memorandum
Raiders of the Lost Ark
The Rocketeer
The Rose Garden
Salon Kitty
Schindler
Schindler's List
The Serpent's Egg
The Seventh Cross
Shining Through
The Sound of Music
Spitfire
The Stationmaster's Wife
The Stranger
Swing Kids
The Tenth Man
They Saved Hitler's Brain
13 Rue Madeleine
*To Be or Not To Be (1942,
  1983)*
Triumph of the Spirit
*Urotsukidoji 2: Legend of
  the Demon Womb*
Les Violons du Bal
The Wannsee Conference
Watch on the Rhine
The White Rose
A Woman at War
*The Wonderful, Horrible
  Life of Leni Riefenstahl*
The Young Lions

New York City

Across the Sea of Time
Addicted to Love
The Addiction
After Hours
The Age of Innocence
Alan and Naomi
Alice
*All the Vermeers in New
  York*
All Through the Night
Almost You
Alphabet City
Amateur
The Anderson Tapes
Angels in America
Angels over Broadway
Angels with Dirty Faces
Angie
Anna
Annie Hall
Anything Else
Arthur
The Associate

THE DISCERNING FILM LOVER'S GUIDE

Auntie Mame
Awakenings
Autumn in New York
Bad Lieutenant
Bananas
Barefoot in the Park
Basket Case
The Basketball Diaries
The Beast from
    20,000 Fathoms
Being John Malkovich
The Believers
Bell, Book and Candle
The Belle of New York
Bells Are Ringing
Big
Big Business
Bloodhounds of Broadway
Blue in the Face
Boiler Room
The Bone Collector
The Bonfire of the Vanities
The Boys in the Band
Breakfast at Tiffany's
Bright Lights, Big City
Brighton Beach Memoirs
Broadway Danny Rose
A Bronx Tale
The Brother from Another
    Planet
The Brothers McMullen
Bullets over Broadway
The Butcher's Wife
Can She Bake a Cherry Pie?
Carlito's Way
The Catered Affair
The Caveman's Valentine
Chain of Desire
Changing Face
Changing Lanes
Chelsea Walls
China Girl
A Chorus Line
The Chosen
C.H.U.D.
Ciao! Manhattan
City by the Sea
Clockers
Cocktail
Coming to America
Coogan's Bluff
Cops and Robbers
Corrupt
The Cotton Club
Cotton Comes to Harlem
Cradle Will Rock
Crimes and Misdemeanors
"Crocodile" Dundee I & II
Crooklyn
Crossfire
Crossing Delancey
Crossover Dreams
Cruel Intentions
Cruising
Dames
The Day After Tomorrow
Daybreak
Daylight
The Daytrippers
Dead End
Death Wish
Designing Woman
Desk Set
Desperate Characters
Desperately Seeking Susan

Diary of a Mad Housewife
Die Hard with a Vengeance
Dinner at Eight
Dinner Rush
Do the Right Thing
Docks of New York
Dog Day Afternoon
Don't Say a Word
Down to Earth
Down with Love
Drawing the Line: Keith
    Haring
The Dream Team
Dressed to Kill
duBEAT-E-O
Duplex
East Side, West Side
84 Charing Cross Road
End of Days
Enemies: A Love Story
Equinox
Escape from New York
Every Day's a Holiday
Exquisite Corpses
Eyes of Laura Mars
Eyewitness
F/X 1 & 2
Falling in Love
Fame
Family Business
The Fan
Fatal Attraction
15 Minutes
The Fifth Element
The First Deadly Sin
The Fisher King
Five Corners
Flesh
For Love or Money
The Foreigner
Forever Lulu
Fort Apache, The Bronx
Forty Carats
Frankenhooker
Frankie and Johnny
The French Connection
The Freshman
Fun Down There
Gangs of New York
Garbo Talks
Get Crazy
Ghost
Ghostbusters I & II
Girlfight
Gloria
God Told Me To
The Godfather I, II, & III
The Golden Boat
The Goodbye Girl
The Goodbye People
Goodfellas
A Great Day in Harlem
The Great Unpleasantness
Greetings
Gremlins 2: The New Batch
Guys and Dolls
Hair
Hamlet 2000
Hangin' with the Homeboys
Hannah and Her Sisters
The Hard Way
Hardcore
Hardcore #2 — The Films
    of R. Kern
Harlem Nights

Heavy Traffic
Hello, Dolly!
Hercules in New York
Hester Street
Hi, Mom!
Highlander
Hollywood Ending
Home Alone 2
The Hours
The House on 92nd Street
Household Saints
The Hudsucker Proxy
The Hustler
I Like It Like That
I Love You to Death
I Wanna Hold Your Hand
Igby Goes Down
I'm No Angel
El Immigrante Latino
In America
In the Soup
The Incident
The Indian in the
    Cupboard
Inferno
Interiors
It Could Happen to You
It Should Happen to You
Italianamerican/The Big
    Shave
Jacob's Ladder
James and the Giant Peach
The January Man
Jeffrey
The Jerky Boys
Joe
Joe Versus the Volcano
Joe's Bed-Stuy Barbershop
Joey Breaker
Juice
Jumpin' at the Boneyard
Jungle Fever
Just Another Girl on the
    I.R.T.
Just Like Weather
Kate & Leopold
Keeping the Faith
Kids
A King in New York
King Kong
The King of Comedy
King of New York
King of the Gypsies
Kiss of Death
Kissing Jessica Stein
Lady for a Day
Lady Sings the Blues
Last Action Hero
The Last Dragon
Last Exit to Brooklyn
Last of the Red Hot Lovers
Laws of Gravity
Legal Eagles
Lenny
Let's Do It Again
A Life of Her Own
Life with Mikey
Light Sleeper
The Linguini Incident
Liquid Sky
Little Murders
Little Nicky
Little Odessa
A Little Princess
Little Shop of Horrors

Live and Let Die
Living in Oblivion
Longtime Companion
Looking for Mr. Goodbar
Looking for Richard
Lost in Yonkers
Love at First Bite
Love with the Proper
    Stranger
Mac
Mad Dog and Glory
Maid in Manhattan
Mame
The Man in the Gray
    Flannel Suit
Manhattan
Manhattan Melodrama
Manhattan Murder Mystery
Mannequin
Marathon Man
Married to the Mob
Marty
The Matchmaker
Mean Streets
Men in Black I & II
Metropolitan
Midnight Cowboy
Mighty Aphrodite
Miracle on 34th Street
    (1947, 1994)
Miss Rose White
Mr. Deeds
Mixed Blood
Mo' Better Blues
Mobsters
Mondo New York
Money Train
Moonstruck
Morning Glory
Moscow on the Hudson
Mrs. Parker & the Vicious
    Circle
Mrs. Parkington
My Father Is Coming
My Favorite Year
My Man Godfrey
My Sister Eileen
Nadja
Naked City
Naked in New York
New Jack City
New Year's Day
New York, New York
New York Stories
News from Home
Next Stop, Greenwich
    Village
Night and the City
Night Falls on Manhattan
Night on Earth
The Night We Never Met
Nighthawks
No Way to Treat a Lady
Not for Publication
Nothing Sacred
The Odd Couple
Off Beat
Old Enough
On a Clear Day You Can
    See Forever
On the Town
Once Upon a Time in
    America
One Fine Day
One Good Cop

Only When I Laugh
The Out-of-Towners
Over the Brooklyn Bridge
Paid in Full
Panic Room
The Paper
Paradise Alley
Parting Glances
Party Monster
The Pawnbroker
Permanent Vacation
The Photographer
The Pickle
Pickup on South Street
Pieces of April
The Plot Against Harry
Pocketful of Miracles
Pollock
The Pope of Greenwich
    Village
Positive
Possessed
Postcards from America
The Pride of the Yankees
Prince of the City
The Prince of Tides
The Prisoner of Second
    Avenue
Prisoners of Inertia
Prizzi's Honor
The Producers
The Professional
Q & A
The Queen
Queens Logic
Quick Change
Quiz Show
Radio Days
A Rage in Harlem
Raging Bull
Ragtime
Ransom
Rear Window
Regarding Henry
Remo Williams
Report to the Commissioner
The Return of Superfly
Revolution: A Red Comedy
The Rose
Roseland
Rosemary's Baby
Sabrina (1995)
The Saint of Fort
    Washington
Saturday Night Fever
Scarlet Street
Scent of a Woman
Sea of Love
The Secret of My Success
Seize the Day
The Sentinel
Serendipity
Serpico
The Seventh Victim
The Shadow
She's Gotta Have It
She's The One
Sid and Nancy
Sidewalks of New York
Silence = Death
Single White Female
Six Degrees of Separation
The Sky's the Limit
Skyline
Slaves of New York

THE DISCERNING FILM LOVER'S GUIDE

Head of State
K Street
Kingfish: A Story of Huey
  P. Long
Kisses for My President
The Last Hurrah
The Last Party
The Last Supper
A Lion Is in the Streets
Louisiana Purchase
The Man from Mallorca
Mastergate
Medium Cool
Millhouse: A White Comedy
Mr. Smith Goes to
  Washington
Nixon
The Pelican Brief
The People vs. Larry Flynt
Power
Primary Colors
RFK
The Reagans
Running Mates
The Second Civil War
Secret Ballot
Secret Honor
The Seduction
  of Joe Tynan
The Senator Was Indiscreet
Seven Days in May
Sex and Justice
Speechless
State of the Union
Storyville
Sunrise at Campobello
Tanner '88, Vols. 1 — 3
Teddy Roosevelt: An
  American Lion
The Times of Harvey Milk
True Colors
The Uprising
Wag the Dog
Waking the Dead
The War Room
Wilson
Winter Kills

Political Thrillers

Absolute Power
All the President's Men
Armstrong
Betrayed
Beyond Rangoon
Blow Out
Clear and Present Danger
Conspiracy Theory
The Crying Game
Cuba
The Day of the Jackal
Defence of the Realm
Enemy of the State
The Enemy Within
Executive Action
Extreme Justice
The Fencing Master
Four Days in September
The Fourth Protocol
Ground Zero
Hidden Agenda
The Jackal
The Manchurian
  Candidate
Men with Guns
Murder at 1600

Nick of Time
No Way Out
On Dangerous Ground
Operation Cobra
The Package
The Parallax View
Patriot Games
The Peacemaker
Presumed Innocent
Seven Days in May
Shadow Conspiracy
Sleeping Dogs
Spirits of the Dead
State of Siege
Three Days of the Condor
Twilight's Last Gleaming
Under Fire
The Whistle Blower
Winter Kills
Z

Post-Apocalypse

A Boy and His Dog
Beneath the Planet
  of the Apes
The Blood of Heroes
Cafe Flesh
Circuitry Man
City Limits
Class of 1999
Def-Con 4
Delicatessen
Le Dernier Combat
  (The Last Battle)
The Element of Crime
Endgame
Executioners (Heroic Trio 2)
Glen and Randa
Hardware
Hell Comes to Frogtown
Mad Max
Mad Max Beyond
  Thunderdome
Miracle Mile
1990: The Bronx Warriors
Omega Man
On the Beach
Panic in Year Zero
Planet of the Apes
The Postman
Prayer of the Rollerboys
The Quiet Earth
The Road Warrior
Sexmission
Stalker

P.O.W.s

Andersonville
Another Time,
  Another Place
Bon Voyage &
  Aventure Malgache
Bridge on the River Kwai
The Brylcreem Boys
Come See the Paradise
The Deer Hunter
The Dunera Boys
The Elusive Corporal
Empire of the Sun
Grand Illusion
The Great Escape
The Highest Honor
The Human
  Condition, Part 3
In Love and War

King Rat
Merry Christmas
  Mr. Lawrence
Paradise Road
The Purple Heart
Rambo: First Blood Pt 2
Seven Years in Tibet
Stalag 17
Stalag Luft
Three Came Home
A Town Like Alice
Uncommon Valor
Victory
Von Ryan's Express

The President

Non-Fictional

Abe Lincoln in Illinois
  (Raymond Massey)
Abraham Lincoln
  (Walter Huston)
Amistad
  (Nigel Hawthorne)
Dick (Dan Hedaya)
Elvis Meets Nixon
  (Bob Gunton)
I.Q. (Keene Curtis)
Nixon (Anthony Hopkins)
Path to War
  (Michael Gambon)
Pearl Harbor (Jon Voight)
PT-109 (Cliff Robertson)
The Reagans (James Brolin)
Secret Honor
  (Philip Baker Hall)
Sunrise at Campobello
  (Ralph Bellamy)
Truman (Gary Sinise)
Wilson (Alexander Knox)

Priests

Absolution
The Agony and the Ecstacy
Angels with Dirty Faces
The Apostle
The Bells of St. Mary's
The Boys of St. Vincent
Boys Town
The Bishop's Wife
The Body
Broken Vows
Cousin Bobby
Crimes of Passion
Cry, the Beloved Country
The Dangerous Lives of
  Altar Boys
Diary of a City Priest
Diary of a Country Priest
Elmer Gantry
The End of the World
The Exorcist
Forbidden Fruit
The Fugitive
Going My Way
Heavens Above
I Confess
I Heard the Owl
  Call My Name
Jesus of Montreal
Judgment
Keeping the Faith
The Keys of the Kingdom
Leap of Faith
Leon Morin Priest
The Little Minister

A Man Called Peter
Mass Appeal
The Miracle of the Bells
Miss Sadie Thompson
The Mission
The Missionary
Molokai: The Story of
  "Father Damien"
Monsieur Vincent
Monsignor
The Name of the Rose
Nazarin
Night of the Iguana
On the Waterfront
The Preacher's Wife
Priest
The Proposition
A Question of Faith
The Reckoning
The Red and the Black
The Rosary Murders
The Runner Stumbles
El Sacerdote (The Priest)
San Francisco
Sanctuary
Saving Grace
The Shoes of the Fisherman
Signs
Sleepers
Stigmata
The Third Miracle
To Kill a Priest
True Confessions
Under the Sun of Satan
The Unholy
Wiseblood

Prisons

L'Addition
Against the Wall
Alien³
American History X
American Me
Angels with Dirty Faces
Animal Factory
L'Argent
Bad Boys
Beyond the Walls
The Big House
Birdman of Alcatraz
Blood In Blood Out: Bound
  by Honor
Borstal Boy
Boys of Cell Block Q
The Brig
Brubaker
Caged Heat
Captives
The Chamber
The Chase
Chattahoochee
Chicago
China, My Sorrow
Chopper
Conseil de Famille
Cool Hand Luke
Cube
Dead Heart
Dead Man Walking
Death Warrant
Deadlock
The Defiant Ones
Down by Law
Each Dawn I Die
Escape from Alcatraz

Escape from L.A.
Escape from New York
Das Experiment
Eye of Got
Fled
Flamingo Road
Forever Mary
Fortress
Fortune and Men's Eyes
Freedom Is Paradise
girlhood
Girls in Prison
The Green Mile
The Hard Word
The House of the Seven
  Gables
An Innocent Man
I Am a Fugitve from a
  Chain Gang
I Want to Live
In Hell
Inside
Interrogation
Johnny Handsome
Kiss of the Spider Woman
The Last Castle
Last Dance
Leo
Lessons at the
  End of Spring
Lock Up
Lockdown
The Longest Yard
Midnight Express
Mrs. Soffel
Murder in the First
No Escape
Papillon
Poison
Prison
Riot
Riot in Cell Block 11
Scum
A Sense of Freedom
The Shawshank Redemption
Short Eyes
Sullivan's Travels
Stir Crazy
Stranger Inside
Tango & Cash
There Was a Crooked Man
Two Way Stretch
Undisputed
The Visit
The Wall
Weeds
White Heat
White Oleander
Yol

Prostitution

American Gigolo
American Pimp
Amor Bandido
Angèle
Angel
Angels over Broadway
Baise-Moi
La Balance
The Balcony
The Ballad of Cable Hogue
The Banker
Belle de Jour
The Best Little Whorehouse
  in Texas

The Blue Hour
Boulevard
Butterfield 8
Chaos
The Cheyenne Social Club
Chicken Ranch
Cinderella Liberty
Confessions of a Blue Movie
  Star
Courtesans of Bombay
Crimes of Passion
Deceiver
Deuce Bigalow: Male Gigolo
Diary of a Lost Girl
Do You Remember
  Dolly Bell?
Doctor Detroit
Double Suicide
Elmer Gantry
Erendira
Fanny Hill
Flesh
Foreign Bodies
Freeway 2 – Confessions of
  a Trickbaby
Girl 6
The Gold of Naples
The Grim Reaper (La
  Commare Secca)
Half Moon Street
The Holy Land
I Love You
Insect Woman
Irma la Douce
The Isle
It Happened in the Park
johns
Keetje Tippel
  (Kathi's Passion)
The Killer Inside Me
Kitty and the Bagman
Klute
Last Exit to Brooklyn
Late Chysanthemums
Leaving Las Vegas
Love, Strange Love
Macho Dancer
Madame Hollywood
Madame Satā
Mamma Roma
The Man from Elysian
  Fields
Man of La Mancha
McCabe and Mrs. Miller
The Meatrack
Midnight Cowboy
Mighty Aphrodite
Milk Money
Mr. Smith Gets a Hustler
Moulin Rouge
My Own Private Idaho
Never on Sunday
Nights of Cabiria
Not Angels But Angels
The Oldest Profession
Osaka Elegy
The Owl and the Pussycat
Pandora's Box
Personal Services
Le Plaisir
Pretty Baby
Pretty Boy
Pretty Woman
The Primrose Path
Princesa

Queen Kelly
Rain
The Ripper
Risky Business
The Roman Spring of Mrs.
  Stone
Sansho the Baliff
Saved!
Some Came Running
Sonny
Spider
Star Maps
Stella Does Tricks
Story of Sin
Street Kid
Street of Shame
Street Smart
Sugar
Sweet Charity
This World, Then the
  Fireworks
Three Lives and only One
  Death
Trading Places
Tricks
The Velocity of Gary
Unforgiven
A Very Curious Girl
Vivre sa Vie
Walk on the Wild Side
Warm Nights on a Slow
  Moving Train
Whore
The Wicked Wicked West
Wild Orchid II: Two Shades
  of Blue
A Woman in Flames
Working Girls

Psychiatry
(see also Mental Illness)

Agnes of God
American PerfeKt
Analyze This
Analyze That
Antwone Fisher
Baton Rouge
The Believers
Beyond Therapy
Captain Newman, M.D.
Carefree
Color of Night
The Dark Mirror
Don Juan deMarco
Don't Say a Word
Don't Sleep Alone
Equus
Final Analysis
A Fine Madness
Gothika
K-Pax
Lantana
Murder in Mind
Nell
Pressure Point
Silent Fall
Spellbound
Still of the Night
Suddenly, Last Summer
Sybil
They Might Be Giants
Three Faces of Eve
Timothy Leary's Dead
What's New Pussycat

When Danger Follows you
  Home
Whispers in the Dark
The Wife
The Young Poisoner's
  Handbook

Religion
(see also Nuns; Priests; Jesus;
and Of Jewish Interest)

The Apostles
At Play in the Fields of the
  Lord
The Believer
Black Robe
The Body
Brother Sun, Sister Moon
The Cardinal
Carrie
A Cry in the Dark
The Dangerous Lives of
  Altar Boys
Demetrius and the
  Gladiators
The Devils
Devil's Playground
El (This Strange Passion)
Elmer Gantry
The Eyes of Tammy Faye
Francesco
The Godfather, Part III
Glory! Glory!
Gospel According to Vic
Hail, Mary
Heart of Tibet
Heaven Help Us
Hell House
I Was Possessed by God
Inherit the Wind
Jerusalem
Jesus of Montreal
Keeping the Faith
The Krishnamurti
  Collection
The Last Temptation
  of Christ
The Last Year
Latter Days
Leap of Faith
Left Behind
Little Buddha
The Mahabharata
Marjoe
The Milky Way
Miracle in Rome
Monsignor
The Omega Code
Ordet
Oscar and Lucinda
The Passion of the Christ
The Pope Must Die(t)
The Rapture
Resurrection
The Riddle of the Dead Sea
  Scrolls
Saved!
Seven Years in Tibet
The Sign of the Cross
Simon of the Desert
Sorceress
Susan and God
Thérèse
L'Udienza
Wide Awake
Witness

Road Movies

About Schmidt
The Adventures of Felix
Alice in the Cities
American PerfeKt
Ariel
Bail Jumper
Beavis and Butt-head Do
  America
Black Dog
Bound and Gagged:
  A Love Story
Boys on the Side
Breakdown
Candy Mountain
The Chase
Coupe de Ville
Detour
The Doom Generation
Easy Rider
Eurotrip
Fandango
Five Easy Pieces
Going Places
Goodbye Pork Pie
Gun Crazy
Harry and Tonto
Heartaches
Heaven's Burning
Highway 61
Invitation au Voyage
It Happened One Night
It's a Mad, Mad, Mad,
  Mad World
Joe Dirt
Kalifornia
Kings of the Road
Kiss or Kill
Leaving Normal
A Life Less Ordinary
Lisbon Story
The Living End
Loose Connections
Lost in America
Love Field
Mad Love
Me, Myself & Irene
Midnight Run
Niagara, Niagara
Outrageous Fortune
Paris, Texas
Planes, Trains and
  Automobiles
Powwow Highway
Rain Man
The Rain People
Rat Race
Rikky and Pete
Road Scholar
Road Trip
Rubin and Ed
Scarecrow
Sitting Ducks
Slate, Wyn and Me
Smoke Signals
Starlight Hotel
The Straight Story
Stranger Than Paradise
The Sugarland Express
Sullivan's Travels
The Sure Thing
Thelma and Louise

To Wong Foo, Thanks for
  Everything! Julie
  Newmar
Trading Favors
The Trip
Trouble Bound
True Romance
Until the End of the World
Voyager
Wild at Heart
The Wrong Move

Rome (Modern & Ancient)

Accattone
Androcles and the Lion
The Arena
Bellissima
Belly of an Architect
Ben Hur (1925, 1959)
Caesar and Cleopatra
Caligula
Cleopatra
Deep Red
Demetrius and
  the Gladiators
The Fall of the
  Roman Empire
Fellini Roma
Fellini Satyricon
A Funny Thing
  Happened on the
  Way to the Forum
Ginger and Fred
Gladiator
The Godfather, Part III
Hail Caesar
Hudson Hawk
Indiscretion of an American
  Wife
Julius Caesar
La Dolce Vita
Mille Bolle Blu
My Own Private Idaho
National Lampoon's
  European Vacation
Night on Earth
Quo Vadis
The Robe
Roman Holiday
Roman Scandals
The Roman Spring of Mrs.
  Stone
Saving Grace
The Sign of the Cross
Spartacus
A Special Day
Three Ages
The White Sheik
Year of the Gun
Yesterday, Today and
  Tomorrow

Royalty
(England)

Anne of the 1000 Days
Beckett
Cromwell
Elizabeth
Elizabeth R
Fire over England
Henry V (1944)
Henry V (1989)
John & Julie
King Ralph
Lady Jane

THE DISCERNING FILM LOVER'S GUIDE

THE DISCERNING FILM LOVER'S GUIDE

Stage-to-Screen: Comedies

About Last Night...
Advice from a Caterpillar
Ah, Wilderness!
Animal Crackers
Auntie Mame
Barefoot in the Park
Beyond Therapy
Biloxi Blues
Born Yesterday
The Boys in the Band
Brighton Beach Memoirs
Brilliant Lies
Bus Stop
Cactus Flower
La Cage aux Folles
California Suite
The Cemetery Club
Crimes of the Heart
Da
Desk Set
Don't Drink the Water
Double Wedding
Doubting Thomas
Educating Rita
Entertaining Mr. Sloane
Frankie and Johnny
The Front Page
George Washington
   Slept Here
The Gin Game
The Guardsman
The Haint
Happy Birthday, Gemini
Harvey
Heartbreak House
Holiday
I'm Not Rappaport
The Importance of
   Being Earnest
Jeffrey
Klondike Annie
Last of the Red Hot Lovers
Lily Tomlin:
   Appearing Nitely
Little Voice
Loot
Lost in Yonkers
Love! Valour! Compassion!
Mambo Mouth
The Man Who Came
   to Dinner
My Big Fat Greek Wedding
Noises Off!
Norman, Is That You?
The Odd Couple
On Golden Pond
Only When I Laugh
The Owl and the Pussycat
P.S. Your Cat is Dead
Period of Adjustment
The Philadelphia Story
Play It Again, Sam
Plaza Suite
Prelude to a Kiss
The Prince and
   the Showgirl
The Prisoner of
   Second Avenue
Private Lives
Psycho Beach Party
Purlie Victorious
The Rainmaker

The Ritz
Romantic Comedy
Rosencrantz and
   Guildenstern Are Dead
The Search for Signs of
   Intelligent Life in
   the Universe
She Done Him Wrong
Shirley Valentine
Six Degrees of Separation
The Solid Gold Cadillac
Stage Door
State of the Union
SubUrbia
The Sum of Us
A Thousand Clowns
Three Men on a Horse
Torch Song Trilogy
The Tunnel of Love
Twentieth Century
Two for the Seesaw
Without You I'm Nothing
The Women
You Can't Take It with You

Stage-to-Screen: Dramas

Agnes of God
Amadeus
Anastasia
Angels in America
Anna and the King of Siam
As Is
The Ballad of the Sad Cafe
Bent
Betrayal
Boesman & Lena
A Bronx Tale
The Browning Version
Buffalo Bill and the Indians
Cavalcade
Chelsea Walls
The Children's Hour
Command Decision
Copenhagen
The Corn Is Green
The Crucible
The Curse of the Starving
   Class
Dancing at Lughnasa
Dangerous Liaisons
Death and the Maiden
Deathtrap
Desire under the Elms
The Devil's Disciple
Disraeli
A Doll's House
Dracula
Dream Man
Driving Miss Daisy
Drunks
84 Charing Cross Road
The Elephant Man
The Emperor Jones
The Entertainer
Equus
Extremities
A Few Good Men
Fool for Love
Fortune and Men's Eyes
The Fugitive Kind
Gaslight
Glengarry Glen Ross
The Great White Hope
Hedda

The Homecoming
I Never Sang for My Father
I'm Not Rappaport
Inherit the Wind
K-2
The Laramie Project
Laughing Sinners
The Lion in Winter
The Little Foxes
Long Day's Journey into
   Night (1962, 1987)
Look Back in Anger
Love! Valour! Compassion!
Love and Human Remains
M. Butterfly
The M.O. of M.I.
The Madness of
   King George
The Magnificent Welles
A Majority of One
A Man for All Seasons
Marat/Sade
Marvin's Room
Mass Appeal
Master Harold and
   the Boys
The Miracle Worker
Mister Roberts
Moonlight and Valentino
'Night, Mother
The Night Larry Kramer
   Kissed Me
Night of the Iguana
One Flew Over the
   Cuckoo's Nest
Other People's Money
The Petrified Forest
The Piano Lesson
Picnic
Pygmalion
A Raisin in the Sun
Redwood Curtain
The Rose Tattoo
The Secret Rapture
The Shadow Box
Shadowlands
Six Degrees of Separation
Sleuth
A Soldier's Story
Stalag 17
Strange Interlude
Streamers
A Streetcar Named Desire
Suddenly, Last Summer
Summer and Smoke
Sweet Bird of Youth
Tape
Tea and Sympathy
That Championship Season
These Three
To Gillian on Her 37th
   Birthday
Toys in the Attic
12 Angry Men
Wait Until Dark
Watch on the Rhine
Who's Afraid of
   Virginia Woolf?
Whose Life Is It Anyway?
Wit
Witness for the Prosecution
Zooman

Stage-to-Screen: Musicals

Babes in Arms
Camelot
Can-Can
Chicago
Damn Yankees
DuBarry Was a Lady
Evita
The Fantasticks
Fiddler on the Roof
Finian's Rainbow
Flower Drum Song
Fosse
Funny Girl
A Funny Thing Happened
   on the Way to the Forum
Gentlemen Prefer Blondes
Grease
Guys and Dolls
Gypsy
Hair
Hello, Dolly!
How to Succeed in Business
   Without Really Trying
The King and I
Kiss Me Kate
Li'l Abner
A Little Night Music
Little Shop of Horrors
Mame
Man of La Mancha
The Music Man
My Fair Lady
Nuncrackers
Oklahoma!
Oliver!
On a Clear Day You Can See
   Forever
On the Town
One Night of Love
One Touch of Venus
Paint Your Wagon
Peter Pan
The Pirates of Penzance
The Rocky Horror
   Picture Show
1776
Show Boat
The Sound of Music
South Pacific
Stop the World I Want to Get
   Off
Sweet Charity
The Threepenny Opera
The Unsinkable
   Molly Brown
West Side Story
The Wiz

Street Kids

Accattone!
American Heart
Christiane F.
Dulces Navajas (Navajeros)
Finding Forrester
Girl Talk
Hurricane Streets
The Kid
Kids
Los Ninos Abandonados
Los Olvidados (The Young
   and the Damned)
Mandragora
Mondo

Pixote
Portrait of Jason
Rodrigo D: No Future
Salaam Bombay!
Speedway Junky
Street Kid
Streetwise
Where the Day Takes You
Who the Hell is Juliette?

Submarines

Action in the
   North Atlantic
The Atomic Submarine
Below
Blue Submarine No. 6
Das Boot
Crimson Tide
Destination Tokyo
Down Periscope
The Enemy Below
Home Front
The Hunley
The Hunt for Red October
Ice Station Zebra
K-19: The Widowmaker
On the Beach
Operation Petticoat
Run Silent, Run Deep
Silent Service
Steel Sharks
Sub Down
Submarines
20,000 Leagues
   Under the Sea
U-571
Up Periscope
Voyage to the Bottom
   of the Sea

Teenagers

Absolute Beginners
All the Real Girls
American Graffiti
Better Off Dead
Blue Car
The Breakfast Club
Bully
Burglar (1987)
Camp
Can't Hardly Wait
Clueless
The Craft
crazy/beautiful
Cruel Intentions
Cruel Story of Youth
Cry-Baby
The Dangerous Lives of
   Altar Boys
Dazed and Confused
Dirty Dancing
Disturbing Behavior
Doin' Time on Planet Earth
Due East
Dumb and Dumberer: When
   Harry Met Lloyd
Election
The Faculty
Fast Times at
   Ridgemont High
Ferris Bueller's Day Off
Flirting
Footloose
Ghost World
Gleaming the Cube

INDEX: THEMES

INDEX: THEMES

THE DISCERNING FILM LOVER'S GUIDE

INDEX: THEMES

APPENDIX A: TLA BESTS

Best Theatrical Films of 1990
1 *GoodFellas*
2 *The Grifters*
3 *The Cook, the Thief, His Wife and Her Lover*
4 *Sweetie*
5 *Dances with Wolves*
6 *Miller's Crossing*
7 *Last Exit to Brooklyn*
8 *Jesus of Montreal*
9 *Tune in Tomorrow*
10 *The Nasty Girl*

Best Director
1 **Martin Scorsese** (*GoodFellas*)
2 Stephen Frears (*The Grifters*)
3 Jane Campion (*Sweetie*)

Best Actor
1 **Jeremy Irons** (*Reversal of Fortune*)
2 Robert De Niro (*Awakenings*)
3 Gerard Depardieu (*Cyrano de Bergerac*)
   and Danny Glover (*To Sleep with Anger*)

Best Actress
1 **Anjelica Huston** (*The Grifters*)
2 Genevieve Lemon (*Sweetie*)
3 Helen Mirren (*The Cook, the Thief,*
   His Wife and Her Lover)

Best Supporting Actor
1 **Joe Pesci** (*GoodFellas*)
2 Bruce Davison (*Longtime Companion*)
3 John Turturro (*Miller's Crossing*)

Best Supporting Actress
1 **Jennifer Jason Leigh** (*Last Exit to Brooklyn*)
2 Whoopi Goldberg (*Ghost*)
3 Annette Bening (*The Grifters*)

Best Theatrical Films of 1991
1 *The Silence of the Lambs*
2 *Naked Lunch*
3 *My Own Private Idaho*
4 *Europa, Europa*
5 *JFK*
6 *Homicide*
7 *City of Hope*
8 *Thelma and Louise*
9 *Impromptu*
10 *Boyz N the Hood*

Best Director
1 **Jonathan Demme** (*The Silence of the Lambs*)
2 Agnieszka Holland (*Europa, Europa*)
3 David Cronenberg (*Naked Lunch*)

Best Actor
1 **Anthony Hopkins**
   (*The Silence of the Lambs*)
2 River Phoenix (*My Own Private Idaho*)
3 Robert De Niro (*Cape Fear*)

Best Actress
1 **Jodie Foster** (*The Silence of the Lambs*)
2 Judy Davis (*Impromptu*)
3 Susan Sarandon (*Thelma and Louise*)

Best Supporting Actor
1 **Laurence Fishburne** (*Boyz N the Hood*)
2 Michael Jeter (*The Fisher King*)
3 Robert Duvall (*Rambling Rose*)

Best Supporting Actress
1 **Mercedes Ruehl** (*The Fisher King*)
2 Juliette Lewis (*Cape Fear*)
3 Diane Ladd (*Rambling Rose*)

Best Theatrical Films of 1992
1 *The Player*
2 *The Crying Game*
3 *Howards End*
4 *Malcolm X*
5 *Reservoir Dogs*
6 *Delicatessen*
7 *Unforgiven*
8 *Aladdin*
9 *Bram Stoker's Dracula*
10 *Raise the Red Lantern*

Best Director
1 **Neil Jordan** (*The Crying Game*)
2 Robert Altman (*The Player*)
3 Tim Robbins (*Bob Roberts*)

Best Actor
1 **Denzel Washington** (*Malcolm X*)
2 Gary Oldman (*Bram Stoker's Dracula*)
3 Anthony Hopkins (*Howards End*)

Best Actress
1 **Emma Thompson** (*Howards End*)
2 Susan Sarandon (*Lorenzo's Oil*)
3 Miranda Richardson (*Enchanted April*)

Best Supporting Actor
1 **Gene Hackman** (*Unforgiven*)
2 Ned Beatty (*Hear My Song*)
3 Al Pacino (*Glengarry Glen Ross*)

Best Supporting Actress
1 **Judy Davis** (*Husbands and Wives*)
2 Vanessa Redgrave (*Howards End*)
3 Michelle Pfeiffer (*Batman Returns*)

Best Theatrical Films of 1993
1 *The Remains of the Day*
2 *Orlando*
   The Piano
4 *Schindler's List*
5 *Strictly Ballroom*
6 *Farewell My Concubine*
   Menace II Society
8 *Like Water for Chocolate*
9 *Much Ado About Nothing*
10 *The Fugitive*
   In the Name of the Father
   The Nightmare Before Christmas

Best Director
1 **James Ivory** (*The Remains of the Day*)
2 Steven Spielberg (*Schindler's List*)
3 Chen Kaige (*Farewell My Concubine*)

Best Actor
1 **Anthony Hopkins** (*The Remains of the Day*)
2 Daniel Day-Lewis (*In the Name of the Father*)
3 Jeff Bridges (*American Heart* and *Fearless*)

Best Actress
1 **Holly Hunter** (*The Piano*)
2 Emma Thompson (*The Remains of the Day*)

3 Stockard Channing (*Six Degrees of Separation*)

Best Supporting Actor
1 **Tommy Lee Jones** (*The Fugitive*)
2 Leonardo DiCaprio (*What's Eating Gilbert Grape*)
3 John Malkovich (*In the Line of Fire*)

Best Supporting Actress
1 **Anna Paquin** (*The Piano*)
2 Miriam Margolyes (*The Age of Innocence*)
3 Anjelica Huston (*Manhattan Murder Mystery*)
   and Gong Li (*Farewell My Concubine*)

Best Theatrical Films of 1994
1 *Pulp Fiction*
2 *Ed Wood*
3 *Quiz Show*
4 *Heavenly Creatures*
5 *The Last Seduction*
6 *Bullets over Broadway*
7 *To Live*
8 *Vanya on 42nd Street*
9 *The Hudsucker Proxy*
10 *The Shawshank Redemption*

Best Director
1 **Quentin Tarantino** (*Pulp Fiction*)
2 Robert Redford (*Quiz Show*)
3 Peter Jackson (*Heavenly Creatures*)

Best Actor
1 **John Travolta** (*Pulp Fiction*)
2 Ralph Fiennes (*Quiz Show*)
3 Paul Newman (*Nobody's Fool*)

Best Actress
1 **Linda Fiorentino** (*The Last Seduction*)
2 Jennifer Jason Leigh (*Mrs. Parker & the Vicious*
   Circle and *The Hudsucker Proxy*)
3 Jodie Foster (*Nell*)

Best Supporting Actor
1 **Martin Landau** (*Ed Wood*)
2 Samuel L. Jackson (*Pulp Fiction*)
3 Paul Scofield (*Quiz Show*)

Best Supporting Actress
1 **Dianne Wiest** (*Bullets over Broadway*)
2 Kirsten Dunst (*Interview with the Vampire*)
3 Uma Thurman (*Pulp Fiction*)

Best Theatrical Films of 1995
1 *The Usual Suspects*
2 *Leaving Las Vegas*
3 *Sense and Sensibility*
4 *Babe*
5 *Get Shorty*
6 *Apollo 13*
7 *Dead Man Walking*
8 *Nixon*
9 *Toy Story*
10 *The Postman*

Best Director
1 **Bryan Singer** (*The Usual Suspects*)
2 Mike Figgis (*Leaving Las Vegas*)
3 Chris Noonan (*Babe*)

THE DISCERNING FILM LOVER'S GUIDE

Best Actor
1 Nicolas Cage (*Leaving Las Vegas*)
2 Sean Penn (*Dead Man Walking*)
3 John Travolta (*Get Shorty*)

Best Actress
1 Elisabeth Shue (*Leaving Las Vegas*)
2 Susan Sarandon (*Dead Man Walking*)
3 Kathy Bates (*Dolores Claiborne*)

Best Supporting Actor
1 Kevin Spacey (*The Usual Suspects*)
2 Don Cheadle (*Devil in a Blue Dress*)
3 Brad Pitt (*12 Monkeys*)

Best Supporting Actress
1 Mira Sorvino (*Mighty Aphrodite*)
2 Joan Allen (*Nixon*)
3 Illeana Douglas (*To Die For*)

Best Theatrical Films of 1996
1 *Fargo*
2 *Lone Star*
3 *Secrets & Lies*
4 *Trainspotting*
5 *The English Patient*
6 *Welcome to the Dollhouse*
7 *Bound*
8 *Shine*
9 *Flirting with Disaster*
10 *William Shakespeare's Romeo + Juliet*

Best Director
1 Joel Coen (*Fargo*)
2 Mike Leigh (*Secrets & Lies*)
3 John Sayles (*Lone Star*)

Best Actor
1 Ralph Fiennes (*The English Patient*)
2 Chris Cooper (*Lone Star*)
3 Geoffrey Rush (*Shine*)

Best Actress
1 Frances McDormand (*Fargo*)
2 Brenda Blethyn (*Secrets & Lies*)
3 Emily Watson (*Breaking the Waves*)

Best Supporting Actor
1 William H. Macy (*Fargo*)
2 Cuba Gooding, Jr. (*Jerry Maguire*)
3 Derek Jacobi (*Hamlet*)

Best Supporting Actress
1 Courtney Love (*The People vs. Larry Flynt*)
2 Juliette Binoche (*The English Patient*)
3 Marianne-Jean Baptiste (*Secrets & Lies*)

Best Theatrical Films of 1997
1 *L.A. Confidential*
2 *Titanic*
3 *Boogie Nights*
4 *Good Will Hunting*
5 *Contact*
6 *The Sweet Hereafter*
7 *The Ice Storm*
8 *The Daytrippers*
9 *Wag the Dog*
10 *Chasing Amy*

Best Director
1 James Cameron (*Titanic*)
2 Curtis Hanson (*L.A. Confidential*)
3 Paul Thomas Anderson (*Boogie Nights*)

Best Actor
1 Jack Nicholson (*As Good As It Gets*)
2 Peter Fonda (*Ulee's Gold*)
3 Ian Holm (*The Sweet Hereafter*)

Best Actress
1 Jodie Foster (*Contact*)
2 Helena Bonham Carter
  (*The Wings of the Dove*)
3 Helen Hunt (*As Good As It Gets*)

Best Supporting Actor
1 Burt Reynolds (*Boogie Nights*)
2 Rupert Everett (*My Best Friend's Wedding*)
3 Robert Forster (*Jackie Brown*)

Best Supporting Actress
1 Julianne Moore (*Boogie Nights*)
2 Joan Cusack (*In & Out*)
3 Minnie Driver (*Good Will Hunting*)

Best Theatrical Films of 1998
1 *Saving Private Ryan*
2 *Bulworth*
3 *Out of Sight*
4 *Shakespeare in Love*
5 *Life Is Beautiful*
6 *The Truman Show*
7 *Happiness*
8 *Smoke Signals*
9 *The Opposite of Sex*
10 *Rushmore*

Best Director
1 Steven Spielberg (*Saving Private Ryan*)
2 Warren Beatty (*Bulworth*)
3 Peter Weir (*The Truman Show*)

Best Actor
1 Ian McKellen (*Gods and Monsters*)
2 Warren Beatty (*Bulworth*)
3 Nick Nolte (*Affliction*)

Best Actress
1 Cate Blanchett (*Elizabeth*)
2 Gwyneth Paltrow (*Shakespeare in Love*)
3 Jennifer Lopez (*Out of Sight*)

Best Supporting Actor
1 Billy Bob Thornton (*A Simple Plan*)
2 Bill Murray (*Rushmore*)
3 Al Freeman, Jr. (*Down in the Delta*)

Best Supporting Actress
1 Lisa Kudrow (*The Opposite of Sex*)
2 Joan Allen (*Pleasantville*)
3 Judi Dench (*Shakespeare in Love*)

Best Theatrical Films of 1999
1 *American Beauty*
2 *Magnolia*
3 *Being John Malkovich*
4 *The Insider*
5 *South Park: Bigger, Longer & Uncut*
6 *Run Lola Run*
7 *The Sixth Sense*
8 *Election*
9 *Boys Don't Cry*
10 *All about My Mother*

Best Director
1 Paul Thomas Anderson (*Magnolia*)
2 Sam Mendes (*American Beauty*)
3 M. Night Shyamalan (*The Sixth Sense*)

Best Actor
1 Kevin Spacey (*American Beauty*)
2 Russell Crowe (*The Insider*)
3 Richard Farnsworth (*The Straight Story*)

Best Actress
1 Hilary Swank (*Boys Don't Cry*)
2 Reese Witherspoon (*Election*)
3 Annette Bening (*American Beauty*) and
  Janet McTeer (*Tumbleweeds*)

Best Supporting Actor
1 Tom Cruise (*Magnolia*)
2 John Malkovich (*Being John Malkovich*)
3 Haley Joel Osment (*The Sixth Sense*)

Best Supporting Actress
1 Julianne Moore (*Magnolia*)
2 Cameron Diaz (*Being John Malkovich*)
3 Angelina Jolie (*Girl, Interrupted*)

Best Theatrical Films of 2000
1 *Crouching Tiger, Hidden Dragon*
2 *Traffic*
3 *Requiem for a Dream*
4 *Wonder Boys*
5 *Gladiator*
6 *Almost Famous*
7 *O Brother, Where Art Thou?*
8 *Billy Elliot*
9 *Before Night Falls*
10 *High Fidelity*

Best Director
1 Ang Lee
  (*Crouching Tiger, Hidden Dragon*)
2 Steven Soderbergh (*Traffic*)
3 Darren Aronofsky (*Requiem for a Dream*)

Best Actor
1 Michael Douglas (*Wonder Boys*)
2 Russell Crowe (*Gladiator*)
3 Javier Bardem (*Before Night Falls*)

Best Actress
1 Ellen Burstyn (*Requiem for a Dream*)
2 Laura Linney (*You Can Count on Me*)
3 Michelle Yeoh
  (*Crouching Tiger, Hidden Dragon*)

Best Supporting Actor
1 Benicio Del Toro (*Traffic*)
2 Willem Dafoe (*Shadow of the Vampire*)
3 Jeffrey Wright (*Shaft*)

Best Supporting Actress
1 Frances McDormand
  (*Almost Famous* and *Wonder Boys*)
2 Zhang Ziyi
  (*Crouching Tiger, Hidden Dragon*)
3 Marcia Gay Harden (*Pollock*)

Best Theatrical Films of 2001
1 *In the Bedroom*
2 *Amélie*
3 *The Lord of the Rings: Fellowship of the Ring*
4 *Moulin Rouge*
5 *Memento*
6 *Gosford Park*
7 *Amores Perros*
8 *Mulholland Drive*
9 *Hedwig and the Angry Inch*
10 *Shrek*

Best Director
1 Peter Jackson (*The Lord of the Rings*)
2 Todd Field (*In the Bedroom*)
3 Baz Luhrmann (*Moulin Rouge*)

Best Actor
1 Russell Crowe *(A Beautiful Mind)*
2 Tom Wilkinson *(In the Bedroom)*
3 Guy Pearce *(Memento)*

Best Actress
1 Sissy Spacek *(In the Bedroom)*
2 Tilda Swinton *(The Deep End)*
3 Naomi Watts *(Mulholland Drive)*

Best Supporting Actor
1 Ben Kingsley *(Sexy Beast)*
2 Ian McKellen *(The Lord of the Rings)*
3 Steve Buscemi *(Ghost World)*

Best Supporting Actress
1 Marisa Tomei *(In the Bedroom)*
2 Jennifer Connelly *(A Beautiful Mind)*
3 Maggie Smith *(Gosford Park)*

Best Theatrical Films of 2002
1 Y Tu Mamá También
2 Far from Heaven
3 The Lord of the Rings: The Two Towers
4 Gangs of New York
5 Adaptation.
6 The Pianist
7 Chicago
8 Igby Goes Down
9 Talk to Her
10 About Schmidt

Best Director
1 Martin Scorsese *(Gangs of New York)*
2 Todd Haynes *(Far from Heaven)*
3 Peter Jackson
   (The Lord of the Rings: Two Towers)

Best Actor
1 Daniel Day-Lewis *(Gangs of New York)*
2 Jack Nicholson *(About Schmidt)*
3 Nicolas Cage *(Adaptation.)*

Best Actress
1 Julianne Moore *(Far from Heaven)*
2 Nicole Kidman *(The Hours)*
3 Maggie Gyllenhaal *(Secretary)*

Best Supporting Actor
1 Dennis Quaid *(Far from Heaven)*
2 Chris Cooper *(Adaptation.)*
3 Alan Arkin
   (13 Conversations about One Thing)

Best Supporting Actress
1 Meryl Streep *(Adaptation.)*
2 Patricia Clarkson *(Far from Heaven)*
3 Kathy Bates *(About Schmidt)*

Best Theatrical Films of 2003
1 The Lord of the Rings: The Return of the King
2 Mystic River
3 Lost in Translation
4 Kill Bill: Vol. 1
5 American Splendor
6 21 Grams
7 Master and Commander
8 The Triplets of Belleville
9 City of God
10 The Station Agent

Special Mention: *Angels in America*

Best Director
1 Peter Jackson *(The Lord of the Rings: The Return of the King)*
2 Clint Eastwood *(Mystic River)*
3 Sofia Coppola *(Lost in Translation)*

Best Actor
1 Sean Penn *(Mystic River)*
2 Bill Murray *(Lost in Translation)*
3 Johnny Depp *(Pirates of the Caribbean)*

Best Actress
1 Charlize Theron *(Monster)*
2 Naomi Watts *(21 Grams)*
3 Scarlett Johansson *(Lost in Translation)*

Best Supporting Actor
1 Tim Robbins *(Mystic River)*
2 Alec Baldwin *(The Cooler)*
3 Benicio Del Toro *(21 Grams)*

Best Supporting Actress
1 Renee Zellweger *(Cold Mountain)*
2 Patricia Clarkson *(Pieces of April)*
3 Hope Davis *(American Splendor)*

APPENDIX B: AWARDS

1980

LOS ANGELES FILM CRITICS
Film: *Raging Bull*
Director: Roman Polanski *(Tess)*
Actor: Robert De Niro *(Raging Bull)*
Actress: Sissy Spacek *(Coal Miner's Daughter)*

NATIONAL BOARD OF REVIEW
Film: *Ordinary People*
Foreign Film: *The Tin Drum*
Director: Robert Redford *(Ordinary People)*
Actor: Robert De Niro *(Raging Bull)*
Actress: Sissy Spacek *(Coal Miner's Daughter)*

NATIONAL SOCIETY OF FILM CRITICS
Film: *Melvin and Howard*
Director: Martin Scorsese *(Ragin Bull)*
Actor: Peter O'Toole *(The Stunt Man)*
Actress: Sissy Spacek *(Coal Miner's Daughter)*

NEW YORK FILM CRITICS
Film: *Ordinary People*
Foreign Film: *Mon Oncle D'Amerique*
Director: Jonathan Demme *(Melvin and Howard)*
Actor: Robert De Niro *(Raging Bull)*
Actress: Sissy Spacek *(Coal Miner's Daughter)*

ACADEMY AWARDS
Film: *Ordinary People*
Foreign Film: *Moscow Does Not Believe in Tears*
Director: Robert Redford *(Ordinary People)*
Actor: Robert De Niro *(Raging Bull)*
Actress: Sissy Spacek *(Coal Miner's Daughter)*

1981

LOS ANGELES FILM CRITICS
Film: *Atlantic City*
Foreign Film: *Pixote*
Director: Warren Beatty *(Reds)*
Actor: Burt Lancaster *(Atlantic City)*
Actress: Meryl Streep
   (The French Lieutenant's Woman)

NATIONAL BOARD OF REVIEW
Film: *Red* and *Chariots of Fire*
Foreign Film: *Oblomov*
Director: Warren Beatty *(Reds)*
Actor: Henry Fonda *(On Golden Pond)*
Actress: Glenda Jackson *(Stevie)*

NATIONAL SOCIETY OF FILM CRITICS
Film: *Atlantic City*
Director: Louis Malle *(Atlantic City)*
Actor: Burt Lancaster *(Atlantic City)*
Actress: Marilla Pera *(Pixote)*

NEW YORK FILM CRITICS
Film: *Reds*
Foreign Film: *Pixote*
Director: Sidney Lumet *(Prince of the City)*
Actor: Burt Lancaster *(Atlantic City)*
Actress: Glenda Jackson *(Stevie)*

ACADEMY AWARDS
Film: *Chariots of Fire*
Foreign Film: *Mephisto*
Director: Warren Beatty *(Reds)*
Actor: Henry Fonda *(On Golden Pond)*
Actress: Katharine Hepburn *(On Golden Pond)*

1982

LOS ANGELES FILM CRITICS
Film: *E.T. The Extra-Terrestrial*
Foreign Film: *The Road Warrior*
Director: Steven Spielberg *(E.T.)*
Actor: Ben Kingsley *(Gandhi)*
Actress: Meryl Streep *(Sophie's Choice)*

NATIONAL BOARD OF REVIEW
Film: *Gandhi*
Foreign Film: *Mephisto*
Director: Sidney Lumet *(The Verdict)*
Actor: Ben Kingsley *(Gandhi)*
Actress: Meryl Streep *(Sophie's Choice)*

NATIONAL SOCIETY OF FILM CRITICS
Film: *Tootsie*
Director: Steven Spielberg *(E.T.)*
Actor: Dustin Hoffman *(Tootsie)*
Actress: Meryl Streep *(Sophie's Choice)*

NEW YORK FILM CRITICS
Film: *Gandhi*
Foreign Film: *Time Stands Still*
Director: Sydney Pollack *(Tootsie)*
Actor: Ben Kingsley *(Gandhi)*
Actress: Meryl Streep *(Sophie's Choice)*

ACADEMY AWARDS
Film: *Gandhi*
Foreign Film: *To Begin Again*

THE DISCERNING FILM LOVER'S GUIDE

Director: Richard Attenborough (*Gandhi*)
Actor: Ben Kingsley (*Gandhi*)
Actress: Meryl Streep (*Sophie's Choice*)

1983

LOS ANGELES FILM CRITICS

Film: *Terms of Endearment*
Foreign Film: *Fanny and Alexander*
Director: James L. Brooks
(*Terms of Endearment*)
Actor: Robert Duvall (*Tender Mercies*)
Actress: Shirley MacLaine
(*Terms of Endearment*)

NATIONAL BOARD OF REVIEW

Film: *Betrayal* and *Terms of Endearment*
Foreign Film: *Fanny and Alexander*
Director: James L. Brooks
(*Terms of Endearment*)
Actor: Tom Conti (*Merry Christmas Mr. Lawrence*
and *Reuben, Reuben*)
Actress: Shirley MacLaine
(*Terms of Endearment*)

NEW YORK FILM CRITICS

Film: *Terms of Endearment*
Foreign Film: *Fanny and Alexander*
Director: Ingmar Bergman
(*Fanny and Alexander*)
Actor: Robert Duvall (*Tender Mercies*)
Actress: Shirley MacLaine
(*Terms of Endearment*)

ACADEMY AWARDS

Film: *Terms of Endearment*
Foreign Film: *Fanny and Alexander*
Director: James L. Brooks
(*Terms of Endearment*)
Actor: Robert Duvall (*Tender Mercies*)
Actress: Shirley MacLaine
(*Terms of Endearment*)

1984

LOS ANGELES FILM CRITICS

Film: *Amadeus*
Foreign Film: *The Fourth Man*
Director: Milos Forman (*Amadeus*)
Actor: F. Murray Abraham (*Amadeus*) and
Albert Finney (*Under the Volcano*)
Actress: Kathleen Turner (*Crimes of Passion* and
Romancing the Stone)

NATIONAL BOARD OF REVIEW

Film: *A Passage to India*
Foreign Film: *Sunday in the Country*
Director: David Lean (*A Passage to India*)
Actor: Victor Banerjee (*A Passage to India*)
Actress: Peggy Ashcroft (*A Passage to India*)

NATIONAL SOCIETY OF FILM CRITICS

Film: *Stranger Than Paradise*
Director: Robert Bresson (*L'Argent*)
Actor: Steve Martin (*All of Me*)
Actress: Vanessa Redgrave (*The Bostonians*)

NEW YORK FILM CRITICS

Film: *A Passage to India*
Foreign Film: *Sunday in the Country*
Director: David Lean (*A Passage to India*)
Actor: Steve Martin (*All of Me*)
Actress: Peggy Ashcroft (*A Passage to India*)

ACADEMY AWARDS

Film: *Amadeus*
Foreign Film: *Dangerous Moves*
Director: Milos Forman (*Amadeus*)
Actor: F. Murray Abraham (*Amadeus*)
Actress: Sally Field (*Places in the Heart*)

1985

LOS ANGELES FILM CRITICS

Film: *Brazil*
Foreign Film: *The Official Story* and *Ran*
Director: Terry Gilliam (*Brazil*)
Actor: William Hurt (*Kiss of the Spider Woman*)
Actress: Meryl Streep (*Out of Africa*)

NATIONAL BOARD OF REVIEW

Film: *The Color Purple*
Foreign Film: *Ran*
Director: Akira Kurosawa (*Ran*)
Actor: William Hurt (*Kiss of the Spider Woman*)
and Raul Julia (*Kiss of the Spider Woman*)
Actress: Whoopi Goldberg (*The Color Purple*)

NATIONAL SOCIETY OF FILM CRITICS

Film: *Ran*
Director: John Huston (*Prizzi's Honor*)
Actor: Jack Nicholson (*Prizzi's Honor*)
Actress: Vanessa Redgrave (*Wetherby*)

NEW YORK FILM CRITICS

Film: *Prizzi's Honor*
Foeign Film: *Ran*
Director: John Huston (*Prizzi's Honor*)
Actor: Jack Nicholson (*Prizzi's Honor*)
Actress: Norma Aleandro (*The Official Story*)

ACADEMY AWARDS

Film: *Out of Africa*
Foreign Film: *The Official Story*
Director: Sydney Pollack (*Out of Africa*)
Actor: William Hurt (*Kiss of the Spider Woman*)
Actress: Geraldine Page (*The Trip to Bountiful*)

1986

LOS ANGELES FILM CRITICS

Film: *Hannah and Her Sisters*
Foreign Film: *Vagabond*
Director: David Lynch (*Blue Velvet*)
Actor: Bob Hoskins (*Mona Lisa*)
Actress: Sandrine Bonnaire (*Vagabond*)

NATIONAL BOARD OF REVIEW

Film: *A Room with a View*
Foreign Film: *Otello*
Director: Woody Allen
(*Hannah and Her Sisters*)
Actor: Paul Newman (*The Color of Money*)
Actress: Kathleen Turner
(*Peggy Sue Got Married*)

NATIONAL SOCIETY OF FILM CRITICS

Film: *Blue Velvet*
Director: David Lynch (*Blue Velvet*)
Actor: Bob Hoskins (*Mona Lisa*)
Actress: Chloe Webb (*Sid and Nancy*)

NEW YORK FILM CRITICS

Film: *Hannah and Her Sisters*
Foreign Film: *Decline of the American Empire*
Director: Woody Allen
(*Hannah and Her Sisters*)
Actor: Bob Hoskins (*Mona Lisa*)
Actress: Sissy Spacek (*Crimes of the Heart*)

ACADEMY AWARDS

Film: *Platoon*
Foreign Film: *The Assault*
Director: Oliver Stone (*Platoon*)
Actor: Paul Newman (*The Color of Money*)
Actress: Marlee Matlin
(*Children of a Lesser God*)

1987

LOS ANGELES FILM CRITICS

Film: *Hope and Glory*
Foreign Film: *Au Revoir les Enfants*
Director: John Boorman (*Hope and Glory*)
Actor: Steve Martin (*Roxanne*)
Actress: Holly Hunter (*Broadcast News*)

NATIONAL BOARD OF REVIEW

Film: *Empire of the Sun*
Foreign Film: *Jean de Florette/Manon of the Spring*
Director: Steven Spielberg (*Empire of the Sun*)
Actor: Michael Douglas (*Wall Street*)
Actress: Lillian Gish (*The Whales of August*) and
Holly Hunter (*Broadcast News*)

NATIONAL SOCIETY OF FILM CRITICS

Film: *The Dead*
Director: John Boorman (*Hope and Glory*)
Actor: Steve Martin (*Roxanne*)
Actress: Emily Lloyd (*Wish You Were Here*)

NEW YORK FILM CRITICS

Film: *Broadcast News*
Foreign Film: *My Life as a Dog*
Director: James L. Brooks (*Broadcast News*)
Actor: Jack Nicholson (*Ironweed* and
The Witches of Eastwick)
Actress: Holly Hunter (*Broadcast News*)

ACADEMY AWARDS

Film: *The Last Emperor*
Foreign Film: *Babette's Feast*
Director: Bernardo Bertolucci
(*The Last Emperor*)
Actor: Michael Douglas (*Wall Street*)
Actress: Cher (*Moonstruck*)

1988

LOS ANGELES FILM CRITICS

Film: *Little Dorrit*
Foreign Film: *Wings of Desire*
Director: David Cronenberg (*Dead Ringers*)
Actor: Tom Hanks (*Big*)
Actress: Genevieve Bujold (*Dead Ringers* and
The Moderns)

NATIONAL BOARD OF REVIEW

Film: *Mississippi Burning*
Foreign Film: *Women on the Verge
of a Nervous Breakdown*
Director: Alan Parker (*Mississippi Burning*)
Actor: Gene Hackman (*Mississippi Burning*)
Actress: Jodie Foster (*The Accused*)

NATIONAL SOCIETY OF FILM CRITICS

Film: *The Unbearable Lightness of Being*
Director: Philip Kaufman
(*The Unbearable Lightness of Being*)
Actor: Michael Keaton (*Beetlejuice* and
Clean and Sober)
Actress: Judy Davis (*High Tide*)

NEW YORK FILM CRITICS

Film: *The Accidental Tourist*
Foreign Film: *Women on the Verge of a Nervous
Breakdown*
Director: Chris Menges (*A World Apart*)
Actor: Jeremy Irons (*Dead Ringers*)
Actress: Meryl Streep (*A Cry in the Dark*)

ACADEMY AWARDS

Film: *Rain Man*
Foreign Film: *Pelle the Conqueror*
Director: Barry Levinson (*Rain Man*)
Actor: Dustin Hoffman (*Rain Man*)
Actress: Jodie Foster (*The Accused*)

1989

LOS ANGELES FILM CRITICS

Film: *Do the Right Thing*
Foreign Film: *Distant Voices, Still Lives* and *Story of Women*
Director: Spike Lee (*Do the Right Thing*)
Actor: Daniel Day-Lewis (*My Left Foot*)
Actress: Andie MacDowell
 (*sex, lies, and videotape*) and
 Michelle Pfeiffer
 (*The Fabulous Baker Boys*)

NATIONAL BOARD OF REVIEW

Film: *Driving Miss Daisy*
Foreign Film: *Story of Women*
Director: Kenneth Branagh (*Henry V*)
Actor: Morgan Freeman (*Driving Miss Daisy*)
Actress: Michelle Pfeiffer
 (*The Fabulous Baker Boys*)

NATIONAL SOCIETY OF FILM CRITICS

Film: *Drugstore Cowboy*
Director: Gus Van Sant (*Drugstore Cowboy*)
Actor: Daniel Day-Lewis (*My Left Foot*)
Actress: Michelle Pfeiffer
 (*The Fabulous Baker Boys*)

NEW YORK FILM CRITICS

Film: *My Left Foot*
Foreign Film: *Story of Women*
Director: Paul Mazursky
 (*Enemies, A Love Story*)
Actor: Daniel Day-Lewis (*My Left Foot*)
Actress: Michelle Pfeiffer
 (*The Fabulous Baker Boys*)

ACADEMY AWARDS

Film: *Driving Miss Daisy*
Foreign Film: *Cinema Paradiso*
Director: Oliver Stone
 (*Born on the Fourth of July*)
Actor: Daniel Day-Lewis (*My Left Foot*)
Actress: Jessica Tandy (*Driving Miss Daisy*)

1990

LOS ANGELES FILM CRITICS

Film: *GoodFellas*
Foreign Film: *Life and Nothing But*
Director: Martin Scorsese (*GoodFellas*)
Actor: Jeremy Irons (*Reversal of Fortune*)
Actress: Anjelica Huston (*The Grifters* and *The Witches*)

NATIONAL BOARD OF REVIEW

Film: *Dances with Wolves*
Foreign Film: *Cyrano de Bergerac*
Director: Kevin Costner (*Dances with Wolves*)
Actor: Robert De Niro (*Awakenings*) and
 Robin Williams (*Awakenings*)
Actress: Mia Farrow (*Alice*)

NATIONAL SOCIETY OF FILM CRITICS

Film: *GoodFellas*
Foreign Film: *Ariel*
Director: Martin Scorsese (*GoodFellas*)
Actor: Jeremy Irons (*Reversal of Fortune*)
Actress: Anjelica Huston (*The Grifters*)

NEW YORK FILM CRITICS

Film: *GoodFellas*
Foreign Film: *The Nasty Girl*

Director: Martin Scorsese (*GoodFellas*)
Actor: Robert De Niro (*Awakenings*) and
 (*GoodFellas*)
Actress: Joanne Woodward
 (*Mr. and Mrs. Bridge*)

ACADEMY AWARDS

Film: *Dances with Wolves*
Foreign Film: *Journey of Hope*
Director: Kevin Costner (*Dances with Wolves*)
Actor: Jeremy Irons (*Reversal of Fortune*)
Actress: Kathy Bates (*Misery*)

1991

LOS ANGELES FILM CRITICS

Film: *Bugsy*
Foreign Film: *La Belle Noiseuse*
Director: Barry Levinson (*Bugsy*)
Actor: Nick Nolte (*The Prince of Tides*)
Actress: Mercedes Ruehl (*The Fisher King*)

NATIONAL BOARD OF REVIEW

Film: *The Silence of the Lambs*
Foreign Film: *Europa, Europa*
Director: Jonathan Demme
 (*The Silence of the Lambs*)
Actor: Warren Beatty (*Bugsy*)
Actress: Geena Davis (*Thelma and Louise*) and
 Susan Sarandon (*Thelma and Lousie*)

NEW YORK FILM CRITICS

Film: *The Silence of the Lambs*
Foreign Film: *Europa, Europa*
Director: Jonathan Demme
 (*The Silence of the Lambs*)
Actor: Anthony Hopkins
 (*The Silence of the Lambs*)
Actress: Jodie Foster (*The Silence of the Lambs*)

ACADEMY AWARDS

Film: *The Silence of the Lambs*
Foreign Film: *Mediterraneo*
Director: Jonathan Demme
 (*The Silence of the Lambs*)
Actor: Anthony Hopkins
 (*The Silence of the Lambs*)
Actress: Jodie Foster (*The Silence of the Lambs*)

1992

LOS ANGELES FILM CRITICS

Film: *Unforgiven*
Foreign Film: *The Crying Game*
Director: Clint Eastwood (*Unforgiven*)
Actor: Clint Eastwood (*Unforgiven*)
Actress: Emma Thompson (*Howards End*)

NATIONAL BOARD OF REVIEW

Film: *Howards End*
Foreign Film: *Indochine*
Director: James Ivory (*Howards End*)
Actor: Jack Lemmon (*Glengarry Glen Ross*)
Actress: Emma Thompson (*Howards End*)

NATIONAL SOCIETY OF FILM CRITICS

Film: *Unforgiven*
Foreign Film: *Raise the Red Lantern*
Director: Clint Eastwood (*Unforgiven*)
Actor: Stephen Rea (*The Crying Game*)
Actress: Emma Thompson (*Howards End*)

NEW YORK FILM CRITICS

Film: *The Player*
Foreign Film: *Raise the Red Lantern*
Director: Robert Altman (*The Player*)
Actor: Denzel Washington (*Malcolm X*)
Actress: Emma Thompson (*Howards End*)

ACADEMY AWARDS

Film: *Unforgiven*
Foreign Film: *Indochine*
Director: Clint Eastwood (*Unforgiven*)
Actor: Al Pacino (*Scent of a Woman*)
Actress: Emma Thompson (*Howards End*)

1993

LOS ANGELES FILM CRITICS

Film: *Schindler's List*
Foreign Film: *Farewell My Concubine*
Director: Jane Campion (*The Piano*)
Actor: Anthony Hopkins (*The Remains of the Day*
 and *Shadowlands*)
Actress: Holly Hunter (*The Piano*)

NATIONAL BOARD OF REVIEW

Film: *Schindler's List*
Foreign Film: *Farewell My Concubine*
Director: Martin Scorsese (*The Age of Innocence*)
Actor: Anthony Hopkins (*The Remains of the Day*
 and *Shadowlands*)
Actress: Holly Hunter (*The Piano*)

NATIONAL SOCIETY OF FILM CRITICS

Film: *Schindler's List*
Foreign Film: *The Story of Qiu Ju*
Director: Steven Spielberg (*Schindler's List*)
Actor: David Thewlis (*Naked*)
Actress: Holly Hunter (*The Piano*)

NEW YORK FILM CRITICS

Film: *Schindler's List*
Foreign Film: *Farewell My Concubine*
Director: Jane Campion (*The Piano*)
Actor: David Thewlis (*Naked*)
Actress: Holly Hunter (*The Piano*)

ACADEMY AWARDS

Film: *Schindler's List*
Foreign Film: *Belle Epoque*
Director: Steven Spielberg (*Schindler's List*)
Actor: Tom Hanks (*Philadelphia*)
Actress: Holly Hunter (*The Piano*)

1994

LOS ANGELES FILM CRITICS

Film: *Pulp Fiction*
Foreign Film: *Red*
Director: Quentin Tarantino (*Pulp Fiction*)
Actor: John Travolta (*Pulp Fiction*)
Actress: Jessica Lange (*Blue Sky*)

NATIONAL BOARD OF REVIEW

Film: *Forrest Gump* and *Pulp Fiction*
Foreign Film: *Eat Drink Man Woman*
Director: Quentin Tarantino (*Pulp Fiction*)
Actor: Tom Hanks (*Forrest Gump*)
Actress: Miranda Richardson (*Tom & Viv*)

NATIONAL SOCIETY OF FILM CRITICS

Film: *Pulp Fiction*
Foreign Film: *Red*
Director: Quentin Tarantino (*Pulp Fiction*)
Actor: Paul Newman (*Nobody's Fool*)
Actress: Jennifer Jason Leigh (*Mrs. Parker & the
 Vicious Circle*)

NEW YORK FILM CRITICS

Film: *Quiz Show*
Foreign Film: *Red*
Director: Quentin Tarantino (*Pulp Fiction*)
Actor: Paul Newman (*Nobody's Fool*)
Actress: Linda Fiorentino (*The Last Seduction*)

THE DISCERNING FILM LOVER'S GUIDE

ACADEMY AWARDS
Film: *Forrest Gump*
Foreign Film: *Burnt by the Sun*
Director: Robert Zemeckis (*Forrest Gump*)
Actor: Tom Hanks (*Forrest Gump*)
Actress: Jessica Lange (*Blue Sky*)

1995

LOS ANGELES FILM CRITICS
Film: *Leaving Las Vegas*
Foreign Film: *Wild Reeds*
Director: Mike Figgis (*Leaving Las Vegas*)
Actor: Nicolas Cage (*Leaving Las Vegas*)
Actress: Elisabeth Shue (*Leaving Las Vegas*)

NATIONAL BOARD OF REVIEW
Film: *Sense and Sensibility*
Foreign Film: *Shanghai Triad*
Director: Ang Lee (*Sense and Sensibility*)
Actor: Nicolas Cage (*Leaving Las Vegas*)
Actress: Emma Thompson (*Carrington* and *Sense and Sensibility*)

NATIONAL SOCIETY OF FILM CRITICS
Film: *Babe*
Foreign Film: *Wild Reeds*
Director: Mike Figgis (*Leaving Las Vegas*)
Actor: Nicolas Cage (*Leaving Las Vegas*)
Actress: Elisabeth Shue (*Leaving Las Vegas*)

NEW YORK FILM CRITICS
Film: *Leaving Las Vegas*
Foreign Film: *Wild Reeds*
Director: Ang Lee (*Sense and Sensibility*)
Actor: Nicolas Cage (*Leaving Las Vegas*)
Actress: Jennifer Jason Leigh (*Georgia*)

ACADEMY AWARDS
Film: *Braveheart*
Foreign Film: *Antonia's Line*
Director: Mel Gibson (*Braveheart*)
Actor: Nicolas Cage (*Leaving Las Vegas*)
Actress: Susan Sarandon (*Dead Man Walking*)

1996

LOS ANGELES FILM CRITICS
Film: *Secrets and Lies*
Foreign Film: *La Ceremonie*
Director: Mike Leigh (*Secrets and Lies*)
Actor: Geoffrey Rush (*Shine*)
Actress: Brenda Blethyn (*Secrets and Lies*)

NATIONAL BOARD OF REVIEW
Film: *Shine*
Foreign Film: *Ridicule*
Director: Joel Coen (*Fargo*)
Actor: Tom Cruise (*Jerry Maguire*)
Actress: Frances McDormand (*Fargo*)

NATIONAL SOCIETY OF FILM CRITICS
Film: *Breaking the Waves*
Director: Lars von Trier (*Breaking the Waves*)
Actor: Eddie Murphy (*The Nutty Professor*)
Actress: Emily Watson (*Breaking the Waves*)

NEW YORK FILM CRITICS
Film: *Fargo*
Foreign Film: *The White Balloon*
Director: Lars von Trier (*Breaking the Waves*)
Actor: Geoffrey Rush (*Shine*)
Actress: Emily Watson (*Breaking the Waves*)

ACADEMY AWARDS
Film: *The English Patient*
Foreign Film: *Kolya*
Director: Anthony Minghella (*The English Patient*)
Actor: Geoffrey Rush (*Shine*)
Actress: Frances McDormand (*Fargo*)

1997

LOS ANGELES FILM CRITICS
Film: *L.A. Confidential*
Foreign Film: *La Promesse*
Director: Curtis Hanson (*L.A. Confidential*)
Actor: Robert Duvall (*The Apostle*)
Actress: Helena Bonham Carter
  (*The Wings of the Dove*)

NATIONAL BOARD OF REVIEW
Film: *L.A. Confidential*
Foreign Film: *Shall We Dance*
Director: Curtis Hanson (*L.A. Confidential*)
Actor: Jack Nicholson (*As Good as It Gets*)
Actress: Helena Bonham Carter
  (*The Wings of the Dove*)

NATIONAL SOCIETY OF FILM CRITICS
Film: *L.A. Confidential*
Foreign Film: *La Promesse*
Director: Curtis Hanson (*L.A. Confidential*)
Actor: Robert Duvall (*The Apostle*)
Actress: Julie Christie (*Afterglow*)

NEW YORK FILM CRITICS
Film: *L.A. Confidential*
Foreign Film: *Ponette*
Director: Curtis Hanson (*L.A. Confidential*)
Actor: Peter Fonda (*Ulee's Gold*)
Actress: Julie Christie (*Afterglow*)

ACADEMY AWARDS
Film: *Titanic*
Foreign Film: *Character*
Director: James Cameron (*Titanic*)
Actor: Jack Nicholson (*As Good as It Gets*)
Actress: Helen Hunt (*As Good as It Gets*)

1998

LOS ANGELES FILM CRITICS
Film: *Saving Private Ryan*
Foreign Film: *The Celebration*
Director: Steven Spielberg (*Saving Private Ryan*)
Actor: Ian McKellen (*Gods and Monsters*)
Actress: Fernanda Montenegro (*Central Station*)
  and Ally Sheedy (*High Art*)

NATIONAL BOARD OF REVIEW
Film: *Gods and Monsters*
Foreign Film: *Central Station*
Director: Shekhar Kapur (*Elizabeth*)
Actor: Ian McKellen (*Gods and Monsters*)
Actress: Fernanda Montenegro (*Central Station*)

NATIONAL SOCIETY OF FILM CRITICS
Film: *Out of Sight*
Foreign Film: *Taste of Cherry*
Director: Steven Soderbergh (*Out of Sight*)
Actor: Nick Nolte (*Affliction*)
Actress: Ally Sheedy (*High Art*)

NEW YORK FILM CRITICS
Film: *Saving Private Ryan*
Foreign Film: *The Celebration*
Director: Terrence Malick (*The Thin Red Line*)
Actor: Nick Nolte (*Affliction*)
Actress: Cameron Diaz
  (*There's Something about Mary*)

ACADEMY AWARDS
Film: *Shakespeare in Love*
Foreign Film: *Life Is Beautiful*
Director: Steven Spielberg (*Saving Private Ryan*)
Actor: Roberto Benigni (*Life Is Beautiful*)
Actress: Gwyneth Paltrow (*Shakespeare in Love*)

1999

LOS ANGELES FILM CRITICS
Film: *The Insider*
Foreign Film: *All about My Mother*
Director: Sam Mendes (*American Beauty*)
Actor: Russell Crowe (*The Insider*)
Actress: Hilary Swank (*Boys Don't Cry*)

NATIONAL BOARD OF REVIEW
Film: *American Beauty*
Foreign Film: *All about My Mother*
Director: Anthony Minghella
  (*The Talented Mr. Ripley*)
Actor: Russell Crowe (*The Insider*)
Actress: Janet McTeer (*Tumbleweeds*)

NATIONAL SOCIETY OF FILM CRITICS
Film: *Being John Malkovich* and *Topsy-Turvy*
Foreign Film: *Autumn Tale*
Director: Mike Leigh (*Topsy-Turvy*)
Actor: Russell Crowe (*The Insider*)
Actress: Reese Witherspoon (*Election*)

NEW YORK FILM CRITICS
Film: *Topsy-Turvy*
Foreign Film: *All about My Mother*
Director: Mike Leigh (*Topsy-Turvy*)
Actor: Richard Farnsworth
  (*The Straight Story*)
Actress: Hilary Swank (*Boys Don't Cry*)

ACADEMY AWARDS
Film: *American Beauty*
Foreign Film: *All about My Mother*
Director: Sam Mendes (*American Beauty*)
Actor: Kevin Spacey (*American Beauty*)
Actress: Hilary Swank (*Boys Don't Cry*)

2000

LOS ANGELES FILM CRITICS
Film: *Crouching Tiger, Hidden Dragon*
Foreign Film: *Yi Yi*
Director: Steven Soderbergh
  (*Erin Brockovich* and *Traffic*)
Actor: Michael Douglas (*Wonder Boys*)
Actress: Julia Roberts (*Erin Brockovich*)

NATIONAL BOARD OF REVIEW
Film: *Quills*
Foreign Film: *Crouching Tiger, Hidden Dragon*
Director: Steven Soderbergh
  (*Erin Brockovich* and *Traffic*)
Actor: Javier Bardem (*Before Night Falls*)
Actress: Julia Roberts (*Erin Brockovich*)

NATIONAL SOCIETY OF FILM CRITICS
Film: *Yi Yi*
Director: Steven Soderbergh (*Traffic*)
Actor: Javier Bardem (*Before Night Falls*)
Actress: Laura Linney
  (*You Can Count on Me*)

NEW YORK FILM CRITICS
Film: *Traffic*
Foreign Film: *Yi Yi*
Director: Steven Soderbergh
  (*Erin Brockovich* and *Traffic*)
Actor: Tom Hanks (*Cast Away*)
Actress: Laura Linney
  (*You Can Count on Me*)

ACADEMY AWARDS
Film: *Gladiator*
Foreign Film: *Crouching Tiger, Hidden Dragon*
Director: Steven Soderbergh (*Traffic*)
Actor: Russell Crowe (*Gladiator*)
Actress: Julia Roberts (*Erin Brockovich*)

2001

LOS ANGELES FILM CRITICS
Film: *In the Bedroom*
Foreign Film: *No Man's Land*
Director: David Lynch (*Mulholland Drive*)
Actor: Denzel Washington (*Training Day*)
Actress: Sissy Spacek (*In the Bedroom*)

NATIONAL BOARD OF REVIEW
Film: *Moulin Rouge*
Foreign Film: *Amores Perros*
Director: Todd Field (*In the Bedroom*)
Actor: Billy Bob Thornton (*Bandits, The Man Who Wasn't There* and *Monster's Ball*)
Actress: Halle Berry (*Monster's Ball*)

NATIONAL SOCIETY OF FILM CRITICS
Film: *Mulholland Drive*
Foreign Film: *In the Mood for Love*
Director: Robert Altman (*Gosford Park*)
Actor: Gene Hackman (*The Royal Tenenbaums*)
Actress: Naomi Watts (*Mulholland Drive*)

NEW YORK FILM CRITICS
Film: *Mulholland Drive*
Foreign Film: *In the Mood for Love*
Director: Robert Altman (*Godford Park*)
Actor: Tom Wilkinson (*In the Bedroom*)
Actress: Sissy Spacek (*In the Bedroom*)

ACADEMY AWARDS
Film: *A Beautiful Mind*
Foreign Film: *No Man's Land*
Director: Ron Howard (*A Beautiful Mind*)
Actor: Denzel Washington (*Training Day*)
Actress: Halle Berry (*Monster's Ball*)

2002

LOS ANGELES FILM CRITICS
Film: *About Schmidt*
Foreign Film: *Y Tu Mamá También*
Director: Pedro Almodóvar (*Talk to Her*)
Actor: Daniel Day-Lewis (*Gangs of New York*) and Jack Nicholson (*About Schmidt*)
Actress: Julianne Moore (*Far from Heaven* and *The Hours*)

NATIONAL BOARD OF REVIEW
Film: *The Hours*
Foreign Film: *Talk to Her*
Director: Phillip Noyce (*The Quiet American* and *Rabbit-Proof Fence*)
Actor: Campbell Scott (*Roger Dodger*)
Actress: Julianne Moore (*Far from Heaven*)

NATIONAL SOCIETY OF FILM CRITICS
Film: *The Pianist*
Foreign Film: *Y Tu Mamá También*
Director: Roman Polanski (*The Pianist*)
Actor: Adrien Brody (*The Pianist*)
Actress: Diane Lane (*Unfaithful*)

NEW YORK FILM CRITICS
Film: *Far from Heaven*
Foreign Film: *Y Tu Mamá También*
Director: Todd Haynes (*Far from Heaven*)
Actor: Daniel Day-Lewis (*Gangs of NY*)
Actress: Diane Lane (*Unfaithful*)

ACADEMY AWARDS
Film: *Chicago*
Foreign Film: *Nowhere in Africa*
Director: Roman Polanski (*The Pianist*)
Actor: Adrien Brody (*The Pianist*)
Actress: Nicole Kidman (*The Hours*)

2003

LOS ANGELES FILM CRITICS
Film: *American Splendor*
Foreign Film: *Man on a Train*
Director: Peter Jackson (*LOTR: Return of the King*)
Actor: Bill Murray (*Lost in Translation*)
Actress: Naomi Watts (*21 Grams*)

NATIONAL BOARD OF REVIEW
Film: *Mystic River*
Foreign Film: *The Barbarian Invasions*
Director: Edward Zwick (*The Last Samurai*)
Actor: Sean Penn (*Mystic River* and *21 Grams*)
Actress: Diane Keaton (*Something's Gotta Give*)

NATIONAL SOCIETY OF FILM CRITICS
Film: *American Splendor*
Foreign Film: *The Man without a Past*
Director: Clint Eastwood (*Mystic River*)
Actor: Bill Murray (*Lost in Translation*)
Actress: Charlize Theron (*Monster*)

NEW YORK FILM CRITICS
Film: *LOTR: Return on the King*
Foreign Film: *City of God*
Director: Sofia Coppola (*Lost in Translation*)
Actor: Bill Murray (*Lost in Translation*)
Actress: Hope Davis (*American Splendor* and *Secret Lives of Dentists*)

ACADEMY AWARDS
Film: *LOTR: Return of the King*
Foreign Film: *The Barbarian Invasions*
Director: Peter Jackson (*LOTR: Return of the King*)
Actor: Sean Penn (*Mystic River*)
Actress: Charlize Theron (*Monster*)

APPENDIX C: E.T.S. (ESTIMATED TICKET SALES)

TOP 10 STARS BY DECADE

TOP STARS OF 1930s
1 Clark Gable 613,400,000
2 Myrna Loy 441,600,000
3 Wallace Beery 392,800,000
4 Lionel Barrymore 383,300,000
5 Fredric March 351,800,000
6 Jean Harlow 347,500,000
7 William Powell 338,500,000
8 Mickey Rooney 331,700,000
9 Bette Davis 320,300,000
10 Jeanette MacDonald 314,500,000

TOP STARS OF 1940s
1 Bing Crosby 517,100,000
2 Bob Hope 461,300,000
3 Judy Garland 440,300,000
4 Gary Cooper 422,500,000
5 John Wayne 416,000,000
6 Spencer Tracy 403,500,000
7 Cary Grant 400,000,000
8 Ray Milland 375,800,000
9 Van Johnson 373,800,000
10 Mickey Rooney 372,000,000

TOP STARS OF 1950s
1 James Stewart 385,500,000
2 Jerry Lewis 365,900,000
3 Dean Martin 365,300,000
4 Frank Sinatra 339,200,000
5 Burt Lancaster 330,500,000
6 William Holden 330,000,000
7 John Wayne 316,000,000
8 Charlton Heston 292,000,000
9 Elizabeth Taylor 285,800,000
10 Deborah Kerr 272,500,000

TOP STARS OF 1960s
1 Julie Andrews 341,600,000
2 John Wayne 336,000,000
3 Richard Burton 264,600,000
4 Paul Newman 256,400,000
5 Sean Connery 253,600,000
6 Jack Lemmon 245,000,000
7 Natalie Wood 203,100,000
8 Dean Martin 202,500,000
9 Doris Day 201,800,000
10 Dick Van Dyke 199,800,000

TOP STARS OF 1970s
1 Robert Redford 265,100,000
2 Richard Dreyfuss 261,500,000
3 Burt Reynolds 241,100,000
4 Roy Scheider 223,800,000
5 Robert Shaw 210,200,000
6 Clint Eastwood 202,200,000
7 Gene Hackman 190,800,000
8 Marlon Brando 190,200,000

TOP STARS OF 1980s
1 Harrison Ford 415,200,000
2 Eddie Murphy 244,300,000
3 Dan Aykroyd 237,500,000
4 Bill Murray 230,000,000
5 Tom Cruise 177,300,000
6 Sylvester Stallone 176,500,000
7 Jack Nicholson 150,500,000
8 Richard Pryor 142,900,000
9 Clint Eastwood 137,800,000
10 Chevy Chase 136,000,000

9 Barbra Streisand 177,400,000
10 Madeline Kahn 175,100,000

TOP STARS OF 1990s
1 Tom Hanks 367,000,000
2 Robin Williams 342,500,000
3 Julia Roberts 262,600,000
4 Tommy Lee Jones 260,500,000
5 Bruce Willis 253,800,000
6 Harrison Ford 250,900,000
7 Jeff Goldblum 232,800,000
8 Jim Carrey 226,900,000
9 Arnold Schwarzenegger 224,100,000
10 Mel Gibson 222,200,000

TOP STARS OF ALL TIME (Estimated Ticket Sales)

1 Clark Gable 1,213,400,000	35 Elizabeth Taylor 573,200,000	69 Dustin Hoffman 437,100,000
2 John Wayne 1,147,600,000	36 Lionel Barrymore 572,900,000	70 Jean Arthur 436,300,000
3 Bing Crosby 1,068,900,000	37 Tom Hanks 561,800,000	71 Ronald Colman 435,500,000
4 James Stewart 1,003,400,000	38 Ginger Rogers 561,100,000	72 Julie Andrews 432,100,000
5 Cary Grant 945,500,000	39 Tyrone Power 559,500,000	73 Mel Gibson 425,600,000
6 Gary Cooper 930,200,000	40 Eddie Murphy 538,200,000	74 Gene Kelly 422,900,000
7 Spencer Tracy 917,500,000	41 Katharine Hepburn 534,600,000	75 Irene Dunne 422,500,000
8 Harrison Ford 861,300,000	42 Dorothy Lamour 527,600,000	76 Betty Grable 421,100,000
9 Mickey Rooney 833,800,000	43 Robert Redford 518,700,000	77 Leslie Howard 421,000,000
10 Gregory Peck 732,300,000	44 Lewis Stone 517,800,000	78 Anne Baxter 420,800,000
11 Bob Hope 719,900,000	45 Errol Flynn 517,300,000	79 Charles Boyer 410,300,000
12 Myrna Loy 717,000,000	46 Van Johnson 516,100,000	80 June Allyson 408,900,000
13 William Holden 687,900,000	47 Maureen O'Hara 511,900,000	81 Jeanette MacDonald 406,500,000
14 Humphrey Bogart 680,500,000	48 Robert Taylor 509,200,000	82 Joel McCrea 401,600,000
15 Bette Davis 679,700,000	49 Clint Eastwood 502,100,000	83 Charles Laughton 400,300,000
16 Frank Sinatra 679,600,000	50 Walter Pidgeon 498,700,000	84 John Travolta 399,500,000
17 Dean Martin 674,700,000	51 Ingrid Bergman 498,400,000	85 Shirley MacLaine 397,600,000
18 Olivia de Havilland 658,200,000	52 Lana Turner 496,600,000	86 Robert Young 395,800,000
19 Henry Fonda 657,400,000	53 Mary Astor 495,600,000	87 Tony Curtis 388,900,000
20 Paul Newman 655,800,000	54 Tom Cruise 488,700,000	88 Paulette Goddard 387,600,000
21 Burt Lancaster 644,600,000	55 Edward G. Robinson 484,200,000	89 John Barrymore 384,400,000
22 Fred MacMurray 644,300,000	56 Gene Hackman 480,800,000	90 Don Ameche 383,900,000
23 Barbara Stanwyck 637,000,000	57 Marlon Brando 479,500,000	91 Julia Roberts 377,800,000
24 Claudette Colbert 636,000,000	58 Jerry Lewis 474,600,000	92 Van Heflin 375,800,000
25 Judy Garland 629,900,000	59 David Niven 473,200,000	93 Dana Andrews 374,900,000
26 William Powell 624,800,000	60 Alan Ladd 472,100,000	94 Dick Powell 373,300,000
27 James Cagney 621,400,000	61 Susan Hayward 465,400,000	95 Claude Rains 372,800,000
28 Charlton Heston 615,000,000	62 Shirley Temple 463,500,000	96 Deborah Kerr 372,600,000
29 Ray Milland 608,500,000	63 Robert Mitchum 453,300,000	97 Burt Reynolds 370,800,000
30 Fred Astaire 607,200,000	64 Loretta Young 447,000,000	98 Richard Burton 366,800,000
31 Wallace Beery 599,600,000	65 Jack Lemmon 444,900,000	99 Richard Dreyfuss 365,800,000
32 Sean Connery 587,300,000	66 Robin Williams 442,900,000	100 Ava Gardner 364,300,000
33 Joan Crawford 584,300,000	67 Jack Nicholson 440,300,000	
34 Fredric March 575,100,000	68 Doris Day 439,500,000	

TOP 200 FILMS OF ALL TIME (Estimated Ticket Sales)

FILM (STUDIO, YEAR) .... Estimated Ticket Sales (as of May 2004)		
1 Gone with the Wind (MGM, 1939) 215,800,000	15 Star Wars – Episode I: The Phantom Menace (Fox, 1999) 91,000,000	30 West Side Story (UA, 1961) 74,000,000
2 Star Wars (Fox, 1977) 182,800,000	16 Raiders of the Lost Ark (Par, 1981) 89,600,000	31 Peter Pan (BV, 1953) 73,500,000
3 The Sound of Music (Fox, 1965) 167,000,000	17 Jurassic Park (U, 1995) 88,500,000	32 Grease (Par, 1978) 73,300,000
4 Snow White & Seven Dwarfs (BV, 1937)... 150,300,000	18 Pinocchio (BV, 1940) 86,100,000	33 The Jungle Book (BV, 1967) 73,000,000
5 E.T. The Extra-Terrestrial (U, 1982) 147,200,000	19 The Sting (U, 1973) 84,500,000	34 The Robe (Fox, 1953) 72,000,000
6 Jaws (U, 1975) 126,000,000	20 The Lion King (BV, 1994) 84,000,000	35 Butch Cassidy and the Sundance Kid (Fox, 1969) 72,000,000
7 Titanic (Par, 1997) 126,000,000	21 The Godfather (Par, 1972)..................... 82,300,000	36 Independence Day (Fox, 1996) 72,000,000
8 The Ten Commandments (Par, 1956) .. 120,000,000	22 Around the World in 80 Days (UA, 1956)....82,000,000	37 Beverly Hills Cop (Par, 1984) 71,500,000
9 Mary Poppins (BV, 1964) 109,500,000	23 Forrest Gump (Par, 1994) 78,500,000	38 Home Alone (Fox, 1990) 70,000,000
10 The Empire Strikes Back (Fox, 1980) 104,600,000	24 Cinderella (BV, 1950) 78,000,000	39 Ghostbusters (Col, 1984)..................... 68,000,000
11 Ben-Hur (MGM, 1959) 102,500,000	25 The Graduate (Emb, 1967) 77,600,000	40 The Best Years of Our Lives (RKO, 1946)....67,000,000
12 Return of the Jedi (Fox, 1983) 99,600,000	26 101 Dalmatians (BV, 1961) 76,500,000	41 Goldfinger (UA, 1964) 65,500,000
13 The Exorcist (WB, 1973) 93,500,000	27 Bambi (BV, 1942) 76,200,000	42 Airport (U, 1970) 65,000,000
14 Doctor Zhivago (MGM, 1965) 92,000,000	28 Lady and the Tramp (BV, 1955) 76,000,000	43 The Lord of the Rings: The Return of the King (NL, 2003) 64,500,000
	29 Spider-Man (Col, 2002) 75,000,000	

44 This Is the Army (WB, 1943) 64,000,000
45 Back to the Future (U, 1985) 64,000,000
46 Song of the South (BV, 1946) 63,300,000
47 Love Story (Par, 1970) 62,600,000
48 The Bells of St. Mary's (RKO, 1945) ... 62,500,000
49 The Greatest Show on Earth (Par, 1952) 62,000,000
50 The Passion of the Christ (New, 2004) ... 62,000,000
51 Thunderball (UA, 1965) 61,500,000
52 It's a Mad, Mad, Mad World (UA, 1963) 60,500,000
53 The Lord of the Rings:
   The Two Towers (NL, 2002) 60,500,000
54 Finding Nemo (BV, 2003) 60,500,000
55 King Kong (RKO, 1933) 60,000,000
56 Samson and Delilah (Par, 1950) 60,000,000
57 Saturday Night Fever (Par, 1977) 60,000,000
58 Tootsie (Col, 1982) 60,000,000
59 Harry Potter and the
   Sorcerer's Stone (WB, 2001) 60,000,000
60 Fantasia (BV, 1940) 59,500,000
61 The Towering Inferno (Fox, 1974) 59,500,000
62 Quo Vadis (MGM, 1951) 59,000,000
63 Bridge on the River Kwai (Col, 1957) ... 59,000,000
64 Batman (WB, 1989) 59,000,000
65 American Graffiti (U, 1973) 58,500,000
66 The Lord of the Rings: The Fellowship
   of the Ring (NL, 2001) 58,500,000
67 Sergeant York (WB, 1941) 58,000,000
68 Duel in the Sun (SRO, 1946) 58,000,000
69 From Here to Eternity (Col, 1953) 58,000,000
70 Superman (WB, 1978) 58,000,000
71 Aladdin (BV, 1992) 58,000,000
72 Blazing Saddles (WB, 1974) 57,500,000
73 Giant (WB, 1956) 56,500,000
74 The Sixth Sense (Hlywd, 1999) 56,500,000
75 Swiss Family Robinson (BV, 1960) 56,300,000
76 Star Wars – Episode II:
   Attack of Clones (Fox, 2002) 56,200,000
77 For Whom the Bell Tolls (Par, 1943) 56,000,000
78 One Flew over Cuckoo's Nest (UA, 1975) ... 56,000,000
79 Men in Black (Col, 1997) 56,000,000
80 White Christmas (Par, 1954) 55,500,000
81 Close Encounters (Col, 1977) 55,500,000
82 Twister (WB, 1996) 55,500,000
83 Smokey and the Bandit (U, 1977) 55,000,000
84 Toy Story 2 (BV, 1999) 55,000,000
85 Indiana Jones and the
   Temple of Doom (Par, 1984) 54,600,000
86 Shrek (Drm, 2001) 54,500,000
87 South Pacific (Magna, 1958) 54,000,000
88 The Poseidon Adventure (Fox, 1972) 54,000,000
89 Mrs. Doubtfire (Fox, 1993) 54,000,000
90 Pirates of the Caribbean (BV, 2003) 53,500,000
91 Cleopatra (Fox, 1963) 53,000,000
92 Rocky (UA, 1976) 53,000,000
93 The Big Parade (MGM, 1925) 52,500,000
94 The Shaggy Dog (BV, 1959) 52,500,000

95 The Lost World:
   Jurassic Park (U, 1997) 52,500,000
96 Animal House (U, 1978) 52,300,000
97 Mrs. Miniver (MGM, 1942) 52,000,000
98 Lawrence of Arabia (Col, 1962) 51,600,000
99 Ghost (Par, 1990) 51,500,000
100 The Longest Day (Fox, 1961) 51,000,000
101 Dr. Seuss' How the Grinch
   Stole Christmas (U, 2000) 51,000,000
102 Tom Jones (UA, 1963) 50,800,000
103 How the West Was Won (MGM, 1963) 50,500,000
104 Monsters, Inc. (BV, 2001) 50,500,000
105 Going My Way (Par, 1944) 50,000,000
106 The Rocky Horror
   Picture Show (Fox, 1975) 50,000,000
107 Toy Story (BV, 1995) 50,000,000
108 M*A*S*H (Fox, 1970) 49,800,000
109 20,000 Leagues
   Under the Sea (BV, 1954) 49,000,000
110 Terminator 2:
   Judgment Day (Tri, 1991) 48,500,000
111 Way Down East (UA, 1920) 48,000,000
112 The Jolson Story (Col, 1946) 48,000,000
113 The Matrix Reloaded (WB, 2003) 48,000,000
114 Gremlins (WB, 1984) 47,500,000
115 Boom Town (MGM, 1940) 47,000,000
116 Sleeping Beauty (BV, 1959) 47,000,000
117 The Parent Trap (BV, 1961) 47,000,000
118 "Crocodile" Dundee (Par, 1986) 47,000,000
119 Indiana Jones and the
   Last Crusade (Par, 1989) 46,700,000
120 Ben Hur (MGM, 1926) 46,500,000
121 Sayonara (WB, 1957) 46,500,000
122 The Love Bug (BV, 1969) 46,500,000
123 Harry Potter and the
   Chamber of Secrets (WB, 2002) 46,500,000
124 The Absent-Minded
   Professor (BV, 1961) 46,000,000
125 Every Which Way But Loose (WB, 1978) .. 46,000,000
126 Fiddler on the Roof (UA, 1971) 45,500,000
127 House of Wax (WB, 1953) 45,000,000
128 Shane (Par, 1953) 45,000,000
129 Funny Girl (Col, 1968) 45,000,000
130 9 to 5 (Fox, 1980) 45,000,000
131 Yankee Doodle Dandy (WB, 1942) 44,500,000
132 2001: A Space Odyssey (MGM, 1968) ... 44,500,000
133 Who Framed Roger Rabbit (BV, 1988) 44,500,000
134 The Fugitive (WB, 1993) 44,500,000
135 Batman Forever (WB, 1995) 44,500,000
136 Casablanca (WB, 1943) 44,400,000
137 What Price Glory (Fox, 1926) 44,000,000
138 Hell's Angels (RKO, 1930) 44,000,000
139 This Is Cinerama (CRC, 1952) 44,000,000
140 Peyton Place (Fox, 1957) 44,000,000
141 3 Men and a Baby (Touch, 1987) 44,000,000
142 Saving Private Ryan (Dream, 1998) 44,000,000
143 The Wizard of Oz (MGM, 1939) 43,800,000
144 Rambo: First Blood Pt 2 (Tri, 1985) 43,700,000
145 Young Frankenstein (Fox, 1974) 43,500,000
146 The Carpetbaggers (Par, 1964) 43,500,000

147 Guess Who's
   Coming to Dinner (Col, 1967) 43,500,000
148 On Golden Pond (U, 1981) 43,500,000
149 The 10 Commandments (Par, 1923) 43,000,000
150 Random Harvest (MGM, 1942) 43,000,000
151 Jaws 2 (U, 1978) 43,000,000
152 Kramer vs. Kramer (Col, 1979) 43,000,000
153 Dances with Wolves (Ori, 1990) 43,000,000
154 Home Alone 2 (Fox, 1992) 43,000,000
155 Cast Away (Fox, 2000) 43,000,000
156 An Officer & a Gentleman (Par, 1982) 42,800,000
157 The Covered Wagon (Par, 1923) 42,500,000
158 The Gold Rush (UA, 1925) 42,500,000
159 San Francisco (MGM, 1936) 42,500,000
160 The Caine Mutiny (Col, 1954) 42,500,000
161 Old Yeller (BV, 1957) 42,500,000
162 Beauty and the Beast (BV, 1991) 42,500,000
163 Meet Me in St. Louis (MGM, 1944) 42,000,000
164 Operation: Petticoat (U, 1959) 42,000,000
165 The Guns of Navarone (Col, 1961) 42,000,000
166 My Fair Lady (WB, 1964) 42,000,000
167 Superman 2 (WB, 1981) 42,000,000
168 Rain Man (MGM, 1988) 42,000,000
169 Pretty Woman (Touch, 1990) 42,000,000
170 The Singing Fool (WB, 1928) 41,500,000
171 Auntie Mame (WB, 1957) 41,500,000
172 Armageddon (Touch, 1998) 41,500,000
173 My Big Fat Greek
   Wedding (IFC, 2002) 41,500,000
174 David Copperfield (MGM, 1935) 41,000,000
175 Irma la Douce (UA, 1963) 41,000,000
176 Mission: Impossible (Par, 1996) 41,000,000
177 Austin Powers: The Spy
   Who Shagged Me (NL, 1999) 41,000,000
178 Bruce Almighty (U, 2003) 41,000,000
179 Stir Crazy (Col, 1980) 40,800,000
180 Fatal Attraction (Par, 1987) 40,700,000
181 Cat on a Hot Tin Roof (MGM, 1958) .. 40,500,000
182 Billy Jack (WB, 1971) 40,500,000
183 Rocky III (UA, 1982) 40,500,000
184 Liar Liar (U, 1997) 40,500,000
185 Rush Hour 2 (NL, 2001) 40,200,000
186 Apollo 13 (U, 1995) 40,100,000
187 Hearts of the West (Grif, 1918) 40,000,000
188 Four Horsemen
   of the Apocalypse (MGM, 1921) 40,000,000
189 Wings (Par, 1927) 40,000,000
190 The Egg and I (U, 1947) 40,000,000
191 Some Like It Hot (UA, 1959) 40,000,000
192 Psycho (Par/U, 1960) 40,000,000
193 Heaven Can Wait (Par, 1978) 40,000,000
194 Beverly Hills Cop 2 (Par, 1987) 40,000,000
195 Robin Hood:
   Prince of Thieves (WB, 1991) 40,000,000
196 Batman Returns (WB, 1992) 40,000,000
197 Mission: Impossible 2 (Par, 2000) 40,000,000
198 Signs (Touch, 2002) 39,300,000
199 Broadway Melody (MGM, 1929) 39,000,000
200 The Great Ziegfeld (MGM, 1936) 39,000,000